What Do Children Read Next?

A Reader's Guide to Fiction for Children

What Do Children Read Next?

A Reader's Guide to Fiction for Children

Candy Colborn

 **Gale Research Inc.**

DETROIT • WASHINGTON, D.C. • LONDON

Candy Colborn
Assistant Editor: Jeanne Teague

Gale Research Staff

Senior Editor: Linda Metzger
Coordinating Editor: Neil E. Walker
Associate Editors: Victoria Coughlin, Paula Cutcher-Jackson, Shelly Dickey
Assistant Editors: Julie Carnagie, Louise Gagne, Scott F. Heil, Monica Hubbard,
Prindle LaBarge, Michael Reade, Kurt Rosenkranz, Dana M. Shonta, Janine E. Wilcox

Production Director: Mary Beth Trimper
External Production Assistant: Shanna Philpott Heilveil
Art Director: Cynthia Baldwin
Graphic Designer: Mary Krzewinski
Cover Illustration: Terry Colon

Supervisor of Systems and Programming: Theresa Rocklin
Program Design: Daniel Bono

While every effort has been made to ensure the reliability of the information presented in this publication, Gale Research Inc. does not guarantee the accuracy of the data contained herein. Gale accepts no payment for listing; and inclusion in the publication of any organization, agency, institution, publication, service, or individual does not imply endorsement of the publisher. Errors brought to the attention of the publisher and verified to the satisfaction of the publisher will be corrected in future editions.

The paper used in this publication meets the minimum requirements of American National Standard for Information Sciences—Permanence Paper for Printed Library Materials, ANSI Z39.48-1984. ∞™

This book is printed on recycled paper that meets Environmental Protection Agency standards. ♻

ISBN 0-8103-8886-3

Printed in the United States of America

Published simultaneously in the United Kingdom
by Gale Research International Limited
(An affiliated company of Gale Research Inc.)

The trademark **ITP** is used under license.

10 9 8 7 6 5 4 3 2 1

Contents

Preface

What Do Children Read Next? is a readers advisory tool designed to match readers from Grades 1 through 8 with books that reflect their interests and concerns. It guides both reluctant and avid readers to new authors and titles for further reading. *What Do Children Read Next?* allows readers quick and easy access to specific information on both recent and classic juvenile titles. In addition, each entry provides alternate reading selections, giving children, parents, and librarians the answer to the frequently asked question "What do I read next?"

Highlights

• Compiled by Candy Colborn, a school librarian and well known expert on children's literature.

• Overview essay describes the history of children's literature and recent trends in the field.

• "Other book you might like," included in each entry, leads to the exploration of new authors or titles.

• Ten indexes help locate specific titles or offer suggestions for reading in favorite time periods or geographic locales, about special subjects or characters, or for a particular age level.

• All authors and titles listed in entries under "Other books by the author" and "Other books you might like" are indexed, allowing easy access to thousands of books recommended for further reading.

Details on 2000 titles...

What Do Children Read Next? contains entries for approximately 2000 books aimed at young readers. About half of these titles were published in the past five years; the remaining fifty percent are older titles which have stood the test of time and still remain accessible and relevant to today's young readers. Titles have been selected on the basis of their currency, appeal to readers, and literary merit.

What Do Children Read Next? was compiled by Candy Colborn, a media and computer specialist from Englewood, Colorado. An authority in children's literature, she has reviewed books for *School Library Journal* and *Teaching and Computers,* and has written articles and presented numerous workshops on computers in education.

The entries are listed alphabetically by author. Books by authors with more than one entry are then subarranged by title. The following information is provided where applicable:

- Author's name and real name if a pseudonym is used. Co-author, editor, and illustrator's names also given.

- Book title.

- Date and place of publication; name of publisher.

- Series name.

- Age Range: Indicates the grade levels for which the title is best suited.

- Subject(s): Up to three themes or topics covered in the story.

- Major character(s): Names of up to three featured characters and brief descriptions of them.

- Time Period(s): Tells when the story takes place.

- Locale(s): Tells where the story takes place.

- What the book is about: A brief plot summary.

- Where it's reviewed: Citations to reviews of the book, including the source of the review, date of the source, and page on which the review appears. Reviews are taken from general reviewing sources such as *Kirkus Reviews* and *Publishers Weekly*, as well as from sources which specialize in materials for younger readers, such as *School Library Journal* and *Horn Book*.

- Other books by the author: Titles and publication dates of other books the author has written, for those wanting to read more books by a particular writer.

- Other books you might like: Titles by other authors written on a similiar theme or in a similar style. A one sentence description of each of these titles whets the reader's appetite for additional titles.

Indexes Answer Reader's Questions...

The ten indexes in *What Do Children Read Next?* are the heart of the book. Used separately or in conjunction, they create many pathways to the featured titles, answering general questions or locating specific titles. For example:

"What are the best books for children?"
The AWARDS INDEX lists awards and citations given by experts in the field of children's literature. These titles are especially noteworthy.

"Do you know of any books set during the Civil War?"
The TIME PERIOD INDEX is a chronological listing of the time settings in which the main entries take place.

"Are there any books set in Africa?"
The GEOGRAPHIC INDEX lists titles by their locale, helping readers pinpoint an area in which they may have a particular interest.

"I like stories with a mystery in them. What do you suggest?"
The SUBJECT INDEX lists books by what they are about. Topics include such things as fiction genres (e.g. Fantasy, Ghost Stories, Mystery and Detective Stories), life and relationships (e.g. Family Life, Friendship, School), and subjects of concern to today's children (e.g. Dinosaurs, Ethnic Identity, Sports).

"Do you have any books with kids whose name is the same as mine?"
The CHARACTER NAME INDEX lists the characters named in the entries, helping readers who remember some information about a book, but not an author or title.

"Do you have any books with cats in them?"
The CHARACTER DESCRIPTION INDEX identifies the major characters by occupation (e.g. Astronaut, Doctor) or persona (e.g. Cat, Toy, Twin).

"Which books are good for third graders?"
The AGE LEVEL INDEX lists titles by grade levels for which they are best suited. The ability of individual readers may not necessarily reflect their actual age; the wide variety of age ranges allows the user to select titles for slower or more advanced readers.

"Which books have pictures by Tasha Tudor?"
The ILLUSTRATOR INDEX is an alphabetical listing of the illustrators of the main entry titles.

"What has Maurice Sendak written recently?"
The AUTHOR INDEX contains the names of all authors featured in the entries and those listed under "Other books you might like."

"Are there any books like A.A. Milne's *Winnie-the-Pooh*?"
The TITLE INDEX includes all main entry titles and all titles recommended under "Other books by the author" and "Other books you might like" in one alphabetical listing. By searching for a specific title, the reader can find out what other books are similar to a title they like.

The indexes can also be used to narrow down or broaden choices. A reader interested in stories set in England during World War II would consult the SUBJECT and GEOGRAPHIC indexes to see which titles appear in both. Someone interested in detective stories set during the 1930s could compare titles in the TIME PERIOD and CHARACTER DESCRIPTION indexes. And with the AUTHOR and TITLE indexes, which include all books listed under "Other books by the author" and "Other books you might like," it is easy to compile an extensive list of titles for further reading, not only with the titles recommended in a main entry, but also by seeing other titles to which the main entry or its recommended titles are similar.

Acknowledgements

Thanks to the staffs of the Denver Public Library and the Phoenix Public Library, where we spent many, many hours, and always found ready help when needed.

Thanks to Stan Massey, Pat Neel and the staff who maintain the NOTIS Information System for Cherry Creek Schools (Colorado), for not only maintaining a huge data base with fantastic searching capabilities, but for often keeping the system up when we know they would rather have gone home. Thanks to the Cherry Creek Media Specialists for the literally thousands of books they provided through interlibrary loan, in addition to their regular demanding work load. Especially at Ponderosa Elementary, we want to thank media specialist Carole Murray for her humor and cheerful encouragement when we lived in her library for days at a time. Thanks also to her aides, Fran Schneider and Cindy Wolff who processed the interlibrary loans and replaced all the books we pulled from Ponderosa's shelves.

PERC, the Professional Educator's Resource Center of Cherry Creek Schools, through its interlibrary loan system, located dozens of titles not available to us locally. Special thanks to Nancy Conklin who did the searching and sending.

Thanks to America Online for linking us with teachers and librarians across the country who were willing to "talk books" and stimulate ideas for connections and to Gayle Keresey who not only introduced me to America Online, but also was my first contact with Gale Research.

Thank you to Stacy Hudgens for hours at the computer looking up bibliographic references, and collecting books from the shelves at numerous libraries.

Finally, thanks to Jeanne Teague, my assistant editor, for her invaluable contributions, not only to the essential work of the book itself, but for her organizational prowess and her ability to see faster and better ways of doing things so that I was not buried in my own paperwork forever, and for helping me to keep plugging away when the numbers of entries remaining to finish seemed overwhelming.

--Candy Colborn

Suggestions Are Welcome

The editors welcome any comments and suggestions for enhancing and improving *What Do Children Read Next?* Please address correspondence to: Editor, *What Do Children Read Next?*, Gale Research Inc., 835 Penobscot Bldg., Detroit, Michigan 48226-4094; or call toll-free 1-800-347-4253.

Introduction

In my schooldays in Chicago in the late 40's and early 50's, there were no substitute teachers (I am a pre-boomer...the system was not yet geared up). When a teacher was absent, the principal came into the room, divided us into neat little groups, and assigned each group to another teacher who already had a full class. If you were lucky there was someone absent in that class and you might get a desk. More frequently you sat on the floor in the back of the room and worked on whatever you had brought with you to do.

I could not have survived without books. There were whole days with little to do but sit and read. I read the basal reader of whatever class I was in. If I could get my hands on a social studies book, I read that. If there had been a holiday or birthday, I read the newest Nancy Drew mystery my mother had bought me. I don't know how well it advanced our skills when our teacher was absent, but for me it cemented an already firmly built love affair with reading. I share with Judy Blume a love of the Betsy-Tacy books by Maud Hart Lovelace, and for years had a doll named Betsy in honor of that heroine. I read all the dog and horse stories I could find, remembering Walter Farley's "The Black," Marguerite Henry's "Misty," and Terhune's "Lad" as the best of all.

Our "library" was a locked room full of books in our K-8 school, opened one-half day a week by a traveling librarian that served many other schools. In the little time she had at our school, she knew me well enough to worry that by sixth grade I was not yet reading romance novels. I was still enchanted with horses. We compromised on *National Velvet*. Then I saw that there were other genres besides horse stories and promptly moved on to science fiction. I never did read romances. I hope Miss Heffernen doesn't still worry.

Once I began riding the bus alone, I discovered the public library and one librarian (only one) who would let me check out Heinlein, Clarke and Asimov, even though they were in the adult section where children were not allowed. I will always be grateful to that woman, though I never knew her name. I took the books home and read late into the night while my mother was working. My aunt who lived upstairs was in charge, and would knock on my bedroom window when my light was on too late. Then the flashlight came out and I read under the covers until I finished the book or fell asleep. It was tough keeping a fresh supply of batteries in those days. How much has children's literature changed since then?

I remember my own reading when I suggest books for kids and try not to limit them. If a book is too difficult, they will put it aside, and if their reading abilities surprise us, so much the better. This does not mean I am unaware of the children struggling with reading who need every step to be a small, successful one, but I trust teachers to let other staff know who those children are, so we care for them as well as for the confident and curious. "With books," says Natalie Babbitt, "your inner world has no walls." I'd like to introduce every child to that world, especially if their outer world is cruel and restricting.

Aiden Chambers describes introducing Sendak's *Where the Wild Things Are* and Garner's *The Owl Service* to his high school students in the same way — by reading them aloud. He describes his own and his students' reactions as "greedy astonishment" (Aidan Chambers, "The Difference of Literature: Writing Now for the Future of Young Readers," *Children's Literature in Education,* v. 24 , March 1993). "We are all capable," he reminds us, "of far more than those who want to manipulate us tell us we are."

When I coached an Odyssey of the Mind team of fifth graders, we took on *Moby Dick*. While it seems above most ten and eleven year olds, we managed it chapter by chapter, deciding page by page which events needed to be represented by their computer graphics and matching limericks.

We have certainly not changed our belief in the value of sharing books aloud. We continue to urge parents and caretakers to read aloud to children. "This simple, uncomplicated 15-minute-a-day exercise is not only one of the greatest intellectual (and emotional) gifts you can give a child; it is also the cheapest way to ensure the longevity of a culture" (Jim Trelease, *The New Read Aloud Handbook*). Corporate America sees such value in literate future employees, that they have actively supported reading with their dollars. Pizza Hut offers the "Book It" program, in which children are rewarded for their reading efforts with pizza coupons. In partnership with the International Reading Association, Sylvania launched "America's Official Reading Time" and offers schools and libraries a way to turn UPC labels into money for books.

The reasons kids read have not changed much. If they have the behavior modeled for them, they read first for *pleasure*. The adults around them enjoy it and share the love with them. These are the easy ones to satisfy, the ones who will read not only with the help of adults, but on their own as well. Reading is also *diversion*. We are painfully aware of the things from which our children need to escape. Today's children's books not only allow children to escape into fantasy, they offer ways to deal with reality by showing other kids who have to work through difficult issues. The validation of reading about someone surviving the situations they face can give children courage. Kids certainly read when they are *assigned* reading, and they read all day long in school in all different subjects. They read to pursue their own interests in dinosaurs, rockets, fashion, sports, horses, family problems, science. Those of us in the business of supplying them with books keep very busy meeting the diversity of interests, always knowing that we have constituents who prefer to have only one point of view prevail, not only in the classroom but in the resources the schools offer.

With current emphasis, controversial though it has become, on whole language, our selection of literature for children has become ever more critical as our budgets become smaller. I love seeing a novel being used as the framework for learning, and want to reassure those who fear that this approach abandons the teaching of reading *skills*. What better analogy to life? It is not all separated into neat subject areas. It comes at you all at once, and it makes sense to me to present it to children that way. Events are connected. Life is about making connections, with the world around us, with other people, and with the self inside.

In his introduction to *Once Upon a Time--Celebrating the Magic of Children's Books in Honor of the 20th Anniversary of Reading is Fundamental* (Putnam, 1986) Jim Trelease notes that when he asks children "why should we read?" they often respond "To find the answers." What are the questions? What kind of a person am I? Does the literature reflect the answers children have found, or does it lead them to new questions and new answers? As controversial as his titles, *We Are All in the Dumps with Jack and Guy* and *Fly Away Home* have become, Maurice Sendak is reflecting the plight of children who are targets of cruelty, abandonment, and homelessness. Our society's ills are not just reflected in novels for middle and older readers, but in the picture books for our youngest listeners as well. Sendak is reflecting the conditions that exist and calling attention to them. Certainly our children should be reading about these conditions. They are the ones who will carry on whatever efforts we have made toward solving them.

The children's book market has slowed its phenomenal growth and is leveling off, and the opening of new stores has reached a plateau (Diane E. Rocack, "Children's Bookstores: Applying the Brakes," *Publisher's Weekly*, Jan. 11, 1993). Libraries and bookstores are being more selective about the titles they carry. Will the controversial, the visionary, the untried, be neglected in favor of the proven sellers? Or will the classics be abandoned as racist, sexist, dated, class-conscious, and reflective of the culture that put the world in the mess we and our children have inherited?

Are things different now? We certainly still have dinosaurs, dogs and horses, war stories, sports stories and mysteries as front runners on kids lists. But some things have changed. Books about teen-age characters are showing up further and further down on the reading level scale. This is partly because of the need for high-interest, low-vocabulary books to entice reluctant or learning disabled readers, but I think another factor is that children are seeing, absorbing, and worrying about their lives as teenagers at earlier and earlier ages because it is such a topic of general conversation and certainly dominates the media, both documentary and drama. Will children's literature — indeed, will books in general — survive the onslaught of technology, of words racing through wires and fibers and flashing on screens? Aidan Chambers, in the article mentioned above, poses the question, and postulates that readers and writers must do for children's literature what actors, producers, writers and designers did for the theater when movies and radio began its demise and television threatened to finish it. Reinvent it! Concentrate on those things which make it unique. The same thing must happen, *is* happening, to books our children read. Maurice Sendak reinvented the picture book by allowing thoughts and feelings in that many assumed should not be there (*Where the Wild Things Are*). So did Ann Jonas (*Round Trip*), Graham Oakley (*Magical Changes*), Janet Ahlberg (*The Jolly Post-man*), Chris Van Allsburg (*Jumanji*, et. al.) and the whole world seems to be looking for Waldo, thanks to Martin Handford. Certainly judgements will differ as to which reinventions are good and lasting and which are deemed "gimmicks," but as we may argue the virtues of one invention or another, time and the children will be the true testers.

As I finished Chambers' article, I was enchanted with his description of what a book is, and how the connections between writer and reader, the space for the reaction and thought of the reader, is unique to the book. "Where children are concerned, therefore, the adults who are charged with the greater part of the responsibility of enabling children to become readers need to be clear about what they are doing and why. They can't afford to be confused or ignorant. Every child has only one chance: one chance to be three or four, or nine or ten, or fourteen or fifteen. If enabling adults get it wrong, a school leaver can't say, 'You didn't do too well at helping me. Why don't I go back to being three and start again, and you can have another try.'"

What a tremendous responsibility!

As one of the enabling adults, I continue to enjoy that responsibility and rejoice at the light shining in the eyes of any child or adult who is actively engaged in reading and responding to a good book.

Book Selection

What Do Children Read Next? is intended to be a tool, for both children and adults, to use in finding enjoyable books for readers, from newly independent beginning readers through eighth grade, based on what they already know they like. Thorough indexing also allows it to be used to find books many other ways, even if you don't start with a title in mind. Main entries for *WDCRN* were drawn from many different lists of children's books. We began with all the award winners we could find, from the Newberys to winners of local and regional competitions. We then worked from The Elementary School Library Collection, adding any Phase 1 titles that were not already on our list. (Although we used only the "Fiction" section, many of the books listed as fiction will be found in "Easy" sections in some libraries.) Titles were then drawn from Phases 2 and 3 of ESLC, Children's Catalog, School Library Journal's Best of the Year lists, and various specialized bibliographies, where needed to balance particular topics. While we believe we drew from "The Best" of children's literature, our most important criterion was finding books we believed children would enjoy.

The more prolific and popular authors, of course, represent multiple entries. When we listed other books by the same author, it became a challenge to decide which of an author's many other books should be included. If there were others on a similar topic, we included those. If the author's writing career spanned decades, we tried to include titles from various time periods. Occasionally, we included non-fiction titles by the same author, especially if related to the main entry in some way. Since we often worked surrounded by children in Ponderosa's media center, it was not hard to find the inspiration to think what might matter most to a six, eight, ten or twelve year old.

When fatigue set in, to keep the task from becoming mechanical, we kept children's faces in front of us — bright children who have been told by adults "those books are for older children," even though the adult may have had no idea of the child's abilities and mature world view. We thought of the children who are abused at home, hoping that some of the stories they found would give them courage and knowledge of a way out. Knowing how much middle graders love humor, we included plenty of it, especially those that combine humor with treatment of serious subjects that touch all children and families in crisis. We included those books that are on every list but few children seem to read, (most teachers and librarians have their favorite example). That doesn't mean there is not a reader somewhere who is a perfect match. We have not eschewed Nancy Drew, The Hardy Boys, or The Babysitters, nor have we avoided controversial or painful subjects. The goal was to entice children to read, to develop that critically important skill for success in this world, and have fun doing it. Finally, we added favorites of our own and of students through the years that may not have appeared on anyone else's list.

The Connections

Our first vision of five connecting books for each main entry was a stack of books dealing with the same topic, at exactly the same reading level, perhaps taking place in the same locale. If possible, they would contain the same number of pages, similar characters, and if we worked especially diligently, perhaps the same physical measurements. It would make such a neat stack. Once we started working, we quickly came back to reality, and the obvious complexity of good literature and the flexibility of inquiring minds. For example, Peggy Parish's *Good Hunting, Blue Sky*, is a humorous story about a young Native American boy who goes hunting with his new bow and arrow, and winds up being brought home by the quarry he intended for dinner. Following the Native American character seemed the most obvious connection, but another strong aspect of the book is the subject of hunting itself. Our connections include other Native American hunters (Oren Lyons, *Dog Story*), Davy Lane, a legendary North Carolina hunter, (Adele De Leeuw, *Uncle Davy Lane, Mighty Hunter*), a beautifully illustrated bear hunt (Lynd Ward, *The Biggest Bear*), a hunting dog story, (Lynn Sweat, *The Wonderful Hunting Dog*), and finally, humorous storytelling with strong conflicts around the morality of hunting (Roald Dahl, *The Magic Finger*). Every main entry, with the multiple themes and characterizations of good literature for any age, offered many possible directions. We hope readers will enjoy our particular choices.

Despite the focus on fiction, we found that a few non-fiction titles demanded inclusion. Some were award winners too good to leave out, and others were connections we couldn't resist. This is certainly not a book of poetry books, yet we could not resist suggesting e.e. cummings' *Hist Whist* to children who had just enjoyed Zilpha Keatley Snyder's *Witches of Worm*. After reading about some of the first views of human digestion in Epstein's biography of Dr. Beaumont, *The Man with a Hole in His Stomach* the non-fiction title *What Happens to a Hamburger* by Paul Showers, seemed a natural. We felt that readers of Amy Hest's *Maybe Next Year*, about the struggle of a ballet dancer to decide when she is ready for the next big step in her journey, should not miss Jill Krementz' *Very Young Dancer*. So sprinkled in among the fiction titles is a little biography, poetry and non-fiction from time to time.

Although the first consideration in choosing connections was matching the most obvious topics of the main entry: dogs, mystery stories, divorce, humorous stories, orphans, frontier and pioneer life...all the most common subject headings that came to mind, after the primary subject connection, many factors influenced our choice of connections. Often, instead of trying to keep books as alike as possible, we tried to show that the same human conditions exist in many cultures, and deliberately included books dealing with the same situation set in diverse locations. Other times, if a story took place in Wales, or New York City, or Australia or Eastern Europe, we kept to that location and included many different pictures of life in that particular place. We tried to put ourselves in the place of the child searching for the next good read, and imagined the many different aspects of a book that have appealed to readers.

Sometimes a particular trait of a main character led us to look for that same trait in other stories. Jack's perpetual feeling of inadequacy in Cresswell's *Ordinary Jack* led us to look for other protagonists who felt they were the least or the last. Jane Reid's love of and serious addiction to reading in Sefton's *In a Blue Velvet Dress* launched a search for more kids who found intense enjoyment, solace, or escape in reading. We found Science fiction matched nicely with contemporary fiction if the characters were struggling with the same issues. McIntyre's *Barbary*, a science fiction story about a girl who must adjust to a new home trying to smuggle her cat aboard a space station fits equally well with science fiction stories, cat stories, and stories of displaced children facing totally foreign environments.

Grade Level

One of the more difficult evaluations of a children's book is its reading level. Educators, parents, and librarians (especially catalogers!) have struggled with this one for decades. We have worked with Fry and Spache and Dolch and Degrees of Reading Power and many in between. In general, we accepted the grade level of whatever sources we were using, tempered by our own judgement as we looked at the books. In our research, however, we have found huge differences in grade level among the many review sources. Joe Lasker's *Tournament of Knights* is listed as grades one to three in *Bulletin of the Center for Children's Books* and as grades four to seven in *School Library Journal*. In many cases, it just depends on which aspect of the book becomes the focus in the mind of the reviewer, and we are as diverse in our reactions to literature, of course, as our students.

Though picture books were not part of our original plan, we found them on many lists of "favorite" and "best" fiction, and realized the wealth of wonderful literature they contain, at reading levels from wordless to beginner to adult, so we decided they should be included. In general, these books are mixed in with more traditional novels when the topic is appropriate and the reading level somewhere in the ballpark. When the reading level varies widely from the main entry, we have included the notation "related picture book." WDCRN does not claim to be a list of the best in picture books. Many, many excellent titles do not appear here just because they were not needed to connect with main entries. When a main entry is designated as "Grades 3 - 6," for example, the connections may lie anywhere in that range. Thinking of a child beginning third grade and a sixth grader on the verge of adolescence, not to mention different reading abilities among those children, there is obviously a great range in grades 3-6 alone. Suddenly our stacks of connections are beginning to look less and less like a matched set, and more like something that might have happened if Judi Barrett had written *Cloudy with a Chance of Children's Books*. We also kept in mind that whether or not a child enjoys and has success with a book depends at least as much on the child's motivation and interest in the topic as on his or her reading skill. Grade level indications are best served with a shaker of salt.

We hope that *WDCRN* will be a valuable and enjoyable resource for teachers and librarians, but we especially hope that its covers will soon be worn and faded from use by the children we envisioned as we wrote it.

READ ON!

--Candy Colborn, Jeanne Teague

A

Nina Ring Aamundsen

Two Short and One Long (Boston: Houghton Mifflin, 1990)

Age range: Grades 5-6

Subject(s): Prejudice; Friendship

Major character(s): Jonas, Child; Einar, Child

Time period(s): 1990s

Locale(s): Norway

What the book is about: Best friends, Jonas and Einar, two Norwegian boys, must come to terms with each other and their prejudices when a large family from Afghanistan moves into the neighborhood.

Where it's reviewed:
School Library Journal, October 1990, page 112
Publisher's Weekly, August 31, 1990, page 68

Awards the book has won:
Mildred L. Batchelder Award 1991

Other books you might like:
Margaret Balderson, *When Jays Fly to Barbmo*, 1968
   Teenaged Ingeborg faces tragedy during the German invasion of Norway.
Audree Distad, *Dakota Sons*, 1972
   Tad learns the true meaning of friendship when he begins to feel the town's prejudice against his new friend from the Indian school.
Barbara Girion, *Indian Summer*, 1990
   Joni has a difficult time on an Indian reservation, where her friends hold her responsible for the prejudice they encounter outside the reservation.
Sigurd Senje, *Escape!*, 1964
   A Norwegian boy and girl help the underground bring about the escape of a Russian prisoner from a German prison camp.
Doris Buchanan Smith, *Salted Lemons*, 1980
   Ten year old Darby Bannister moves from Washington DC to Atlanta during WWII, and is put down for being a "Yankee" and a "Jap-lover."

Barbara Mattes Abercrombie

Cat-Man's Daughter (New York: Harper and Row, 1981)

Age range: Grades 5-6

Subject(s): Divorce; Grandparents

Major character(s): Kate McAllister, Teenager; Riley McAllister, Grandparent

Time period(s): 1980s

Locale(s): New York, New York; California

What the book is about: Thirteen year old Kate feels like a pawn in her divorced parents' power game. She wants so much to have her parents together again that she and her grandmother, Riley, stage a fake kidnapping, hoping the parents' shared concern for Kate will bring them back together. She finally learns she must make her own way and accept her parents as they are.

Where it's reviewed:
Center for Children's Books Bulletin, December 1981, p 61
Horn Book, February 1982, page 49

Other books by the author:
Charlie Anderson, 1990 (picture book)
Run for Your Life, 1984

Other books you might like:
Carole S. Adler, *Tuna Fish Thanksgiving*, 1992
   13 year old Gilda's parents are divorcing and she is the only one interested in keeping the family together and looking out for her younger siblings.
Beverly Cleary, *Strider*, 1991
   In a series of diary entries, Leigh tells how he adjusts to his parents' divorce, acquires joint custody of a dog, and joins the track team.
Barbara Corcoran, *Hey, That's My Soul You're Stompin' On*, 1978
   While her parents discuss divorce, Rachel spends the summer with her grandparents and finds that everyone has problems, many more serious than hers.
Lois Duncan, *A Gift of Magic*, 1971
   A young girl gifted with extra sensory perception, adjusts to her parents' divorce.
Eloise Jarvis McGraw, *Hideaway*, 1983
   When his father forgets to come for him after his mother leaves on a wedding trip with her new husband, 12 year old Jeremy runs away.

Laurie Adams

Illustrator: Emily Arnold McCully

Alice and the Boa Constrictor (Boston: Houghton Mifflin, 1983)

Age range: Grades 3-5

Subject(s): Animals/Reptiles

Major character(s): Alice Whipple, Child; Sir Lancelot, Snake

Time period(s): 1980s

Locale(s): New York, New York (Manhattan)

What the book is about: Alice has a number of misadventures while trying to raise money to buy a pet bo a constrictor. Her family begins to appreciate Sir Lancelot when he captures a burglar. The outlandish predicaments in which Alice finds herself are fun and t he text includes a lot of information about boa constrictors.

Where it's reviewed:
Kirkus Reviews, March 1, 1983, page 245
School Library Journal, September 1983, page 114

Other books you might like:
Gabrielle Charbonnet, *Snakes Are Nothing to Sneeze At*, 1990
Although he's not furry and her best friend can't stand him, Annabel loves her new pet snake.
Ariane Dewey, *The Narrow Escapes of Davy Crockett*, 1990
Recounts the wild adventures of Davy Crockett, including his escape from a boa constrictor.
Kudrna C. Imbior, *To Bathe a Boa*, 1986
At bathtime, a youngster has to struggle to get his recalcitrant boa into the tub.
Peter Parnall, *Winter Barn*, 1986
An old barn shelters a wide variety of animals, including snakes, porcupines, cats and a skunk.
Janice May Udry, *Angie*, 1971
Whether she is greeting two creatures from outer space or eating stuffed boa constrictor for breakfast, Angie's life is never dull.

4

Richard Adams

Watership Down (New York: Macmillan, 1972)

Age range: Grades 6 and Up

Subject(s): Animals/Rabbits

Major character(s): Fiver, Rabbit, Psychic; Hazel, Rabbit; Bigwig, Rabbit

Time period(s): 1970s

Locale(s): Earth

What the book is about: A small band of rabbits begin to search for a safe haven to establish a new warren. Fiver has ESP, his brother Hazel is the leader. Bigwig is an impetuous fighter. Overshadowing all is the rabbit folk hero, El-ahrairah.

Where it's reviewed:
Horn Book, August 1974, page 365
Kirkus Reviews, January 15, 1974, page 67

Other books by the author:
Shardik, 1974

Other books you might like:
Alan Arkin, *The Clearing*, 1986

Bubber the lemming joins a group of forest animals in their quest for spiritual understanding and self-knowledge.
Brian Jacques, *Mattimeo*, 1990
The son of a warrior mouse learns to take up the sword and joins the rest of the animals resisting Slager the fox and his marauders.
Sterling E. Lanier, *The War for the Lot*, 1969
Urban rats invade a nearby wooded lot and the wood animals fight off the attack with the help of a boy.
Margaret Laurence, *Jason's Quest*, 1970
A young mole tries to discover the cause and cure for the strange sickness spreading over the city of Molanium.
Tamora Pierce, *Wild Magic: The Immortals*, 1992
Numair, Alanna, and Queen Thayet enlist the help of 13 year old Daine to battle the dreadful creatures that are attacking the kingdom of Tortall.

5

Carole S. Adler

Always and Forever Friends (New York: Clarion, 1988)

Age range: Grades 5-8

Subject(s): Friendship; Remarriage

Major character(s): Wendy, Preteen (6th grader); Honor, Preteen (6th Grader)

Time period(s): 1980s

Locale(s): United States

What the book is about: When her best friend Meg moves away, Wendy finds a sixth grade classmate and establishes a good relationship with Honor. Honor is bright, reserved and very mature compared to Wendy. In nurturing the friendship, Wendy realizes the same consideration must be given to family members as to good friends.

Where it's reviewed:
Booklist, April 1, 1988, page 1337
School Library Journal, Aapril 1988, page 98

Other books by the author:
Eddie's Blue-Winged Dragon, 1988
Good-Bye Pink Pig, 1985
The Cat That Was Left Behind, 1981
The Silver Coach, 1979

Other books you might like:
Joan W. Blos, *A Gathering of Days: A New England Girl's Journal, 1830-1832*, 1979
The journal of a 14 year old girl recording daily events in her small town, including her father's remarriage and the death of her friend.
Judith Caseley, *Starring Dorothy Kane*, 1992
Middle child Dorothy moves with her family to a new home and school, visits grandparents in Florida, and makes a new friend.
Carol Dines, *Best Friends Tell the Best Lies*, 1989
Fourteen year old Leah is loyal to her emotionally troubled friend, Tamara, while dealing with her mother's remarriage and her own interest in a boy.
Norma Fox Mazer, *Babyface*, 1990
Fourteen year old Toni is shaken when her father is seriously and unexpectedly ill and her life long friend, Julie, departs for California.
Marilyn Sachs, *Just Like a Friend*, 1989

Patti finds her relationships with family and friends changing as she comes to understand both herself and her mother better.

6

Carole S. Adler

The Cat That Was Left Behind (Boston: Houghton Mifflin, 1981)

Age range: Grades 4-6

Subject(s): Foster Homes; Adoption; Animals

Major character(s): Chad, Child; Polly Sorenic, Child, Adoptee

Time period(s): 1980s

Locale(s): Cape Cod, Massachusetts

What the book is about: Thirteen year old Chad is spending the summer with his new foster family at Cape Cod, but wants desperately to be reunited with his mother who lost custody of him when he was four years old. He adopts a stray cat and begins to trust the Sorenics, his foster family. When his mother writes that she is remarrying and does not want him, he lets go of the dream and considers joining the Sorenic family permanently.

Where it's reviewed:
Booklist, November 15, 1981, page 436
School Library Journal, November 1981, page 85

Other books by the author:
Always and Forever Friends, 1988
Goodbye Pink Pig, 1985
Fly Free, 1984
The Magic of the Glits, 1979

Other books you might like:
Eleanor Clymer, *Luke Was There*, 1973
    Luke is a counselor in a children's shelter and he comes through for Julius when he needs him the most.
Alison Morgan, *All Kinds of Prickles*, 1980
    Tragedy follows Paul to his foster home and when life seems the most hopeless, a kindly old man gives Paul some advice that helps him cope.
Joan Lowery Nixon, *A Family Apart*, 1987
    The six Kelly children leave their widowed mother behind to find better lives in the West as they board the 1856 Orphan Train bound for Kansas.
N.B. Norman, *Laughter in the Background*, 1980
    Twelve year old Marcie who has tolerated her mother's alcoholism for years decides she has had enough.
Hilma Wolitzer, *Toby Lived Here*, 1978
    When their mom has a nervous breakdown, Toby and her sister are cared for by loving foster parents.

7

Carole S. Adler

Good-Bye Pink Pig (New York: Putnam, 1985)

Age range: Grades 5-7

Subject(s): Grandparents; Imagination; Schools

Major character(s): Amanda, Child; Dale, Child; Pearly, Grandparent

Time period(s): Indeterminate

Locale(s): United States

What the book is about: Shy Amanda takes comfort in the make-believe world of her miniature pink pig, away from the elegant world of her mother and easy going life of her brother, until trouble enters her real and imaginary worlds and she learns to assert herself.

Where it's reviewed:
Center for Children's Books Bulletin, February, 1986, page 101
School Library Journal, December 1985, page 84
Booklist, December 15, 1985, page 622

Other books by the author:
Ghost Brother, 1990
Always and Forever Friends, 1988
Kiss the Clown, 1986
Fly Free, 1984

Other books you might like:
Achim Broger, *Little Harry*, 1979
    A small boy copes with the frustrating limitations of childhood by means of an active imagination which produces fanciful adventures.
Helen Cresswell, *The Winter of the Birds*, 1975
    A young English boy learns about true heroism, affection, and the power of imagination when his neighborhood is threatened by flocks of steel birds.
Eleanor Estes, *The Middle Moffat*, 1942
    Janey, the middle Moffat, has an imagination that leads her into many difficulties.
Ben Herman, *The Rhapsody in Blue of Mickey Klein*, 1981
    Wild flights of imagination tangle with the real life of a Jewish boy growing up in Dundalk, Maryland.
Susan Terris, *Pickle*, 1973
    Recently moved to San Francisco, a girl with a vivid imagination takes up the dare of the local children to visit the "witch" across the street.

8

Carole S. Adler

In Our House, Scott Is My Brother (New York: Macmillan, 1980)

Age range: Grades 5-6

Subject(s): Alcoholism; Brothers and Sisters; Stepfamilies

Major character(s): Jodi, Child; Donna, Step-Parent; Scott, Child

Time period(s): 1980s (1980)

Locale(s): Onondaga, New York

What the book is about: Since her mother's death, Jodi and her father have been very close. When he announces his remarriage, Jodi has trouble adjusting to a stepmother and new stepbrother, Scott. When Scott steals a valuable African necklace, and reveals that his mother has a drinking problem, Jodi has more than she can handle. True to Scott's prediction, he and his mother leave the relationship, but Jodi finds having a brother even for a little while has helped her learn and grow.

Where it's reviewed:
Center for Children's Books Bulletin, March 1980, p 125
School Library Journal, April 1980, page 119

Other books by the author:
Once in a While Hero, 1982
Some Other Summer, 1982
The Magic of the Glits, 1979
The Silver Coach, 1979

Other books you might like:
Betsy Byars, *The Summer of the Swans*, 1970
    A teenage girl gains new insight into herself and her family when her mentally retarded brother gets lost.
Barbara Corcoran, *A Horse Named Sky*, 1986
    Georgia and her mother move to Montana to get away from her alcoholic father, and Georgia pursues her dream of owning a horse.
N.B. Dorman, *Laughter in the Background*, 1980
    Twelve year old Marcie, who has tolerated her divorced mother's alcoholism for years, finally decides she can stand it no more.
Jackie French Koller, *If I Had One Wish*, 1991
    Alec wishes his little brother had never been born but when his wish comes true, his whole life changes.
Brenda Seabrooke, *Home Is Where They Take You In*, 1980
    As she comes to know a couple on a nearby ranch, a young girl sees her mother's alcoholism more clearly.

9

Carole S. Adler

The Magic of the Glits (New York: Macmillan, 1979)

Age range: Grades 5-6

Subject(s): Friendship

Major character(s): Jeremy, Child, Babysitter

Time period(s): 1970s

Locale(s): Cape Cod, Massachusetts

What the book is about: First Jeremy breaks his leg, then he has to take care of seven year old Lynette while his mother is busy with her painting. He builds sand castles for her and tells her stories about Glits, creatures who are neither human nor fairies. Jeremy's summer goes much better than he expected.

Where it's reviewed:
Horn Book, April 1979, page 187
Kirkus Reviews, February 1979, page 197

Awards the book has won:
Crabbery Award 1980

Other books by the author:
Mismatched Summer, 1991
Always and Forever Friends, 1988
Goodbye Pink Pig, 1985
Fly Free, 1984

Other books you might like:
Diana Gregory, *There's a Caterpillar in My Lemonade*, 1980
    Samantha's mother remarries and she refuses to believe anything good can come out of the changes in her life.
S.E. Hinton, *Tex*, 1979
    Their mother dead and abandoned by their father, Mace and Tex struggle to survive in a world whose harshness is tempered by thier love for each other.

Joan Phipson, *Fly Free*, 1979
    Two Australian boys face their own and each other's fears together, despite the clash of values.
Ruth Yaffe Radin, *Tac's Island*, 1986
    Tac and Steve become friends during the week Steve spends on Tac's home and island in Virginia.
Jan Slepian, *Getting on With It*, 1985
    Berry Brice and worrying about her parents' impending divorce, learns to accept change by getting involved with her grandmother's odd neighbors.

10

David A. Adler

Illustrator: Susanna Natti

Cam Jansen and the Mystery at the Monkey House
(New York: Viking, 1985)

Age range: Grades 2-4

Series: Cam Jansen

Subject(s): Animals/Monkeys; Mystery and Detective Stories

Major character(s): Jennifer ''Cam'' Jansen, Detective; Eric Shelton, Friend

Time period(s): 1980s

Locale(s): United States

What the book is about: In this, Cam's tenth adventure, she, Eric and Billy find that monkeys have disappeared from the zoo and are determined to solve the mystery.

Where it's reviewed:
Booklist, April 15, 1986, page 1214
School Library Journal, December 1985, page 64

Other books by the author:
Cam Jansen and the Carmine Prize, 1984
Cam Jansen and the Monster Movie, 1984
Cam Jansen and the Mystery of the Circus Clown, 1983
Cam Jansen and the Mystery of the Stolen Diamonds, 1980

Other books you might like:
Diana Hendry, *A Camel Called April*, 1991
    When the animals in Harry's dream settle in the park across the street, the gardener finds homes for them all, except the stubborn camel.
Nancy Winslow Parker, *Working Frog*, 1992
    Winston the bullfrog describes his life at the Reptile House at the Bronx Zoo.
Susan Pearson, *The 123 Zoo Mystery*, 1991
    Eagle-Eye Ernie and the Martian Club try to solve the mystery of who let all the classroom pets out of their cages.
Telma Robin, *At the Singapore Zoo*, 1991
    Ah Meng the orangutan and Wilma the elephant both live at the Singapore Zoo and have interesting experiences.
Piotr Wildon, *Escape From the Zoo!*, 1993
    A zoo keeper dreams that his animals escape and roam the streets. Or does he?

11

David A. Adler

Illustrator: Irene Travis

The Fourth Floor Twins and the Sand Castle Contest
(New York: Viking, 1988)

Age range: Grades 2-4

Subject(s): Mystery and Detective Stories

Major character(s): Donna Shelton, Twin; Diane Shelton, Twin; Gary, Twin

Time period(s): 1980s

Locale(s): United States

What the book is about: Donna and Diane enter the sand castle contest. The winners will get their picture in the paper and then Mrs. Rogers' dog disappears and the twins are hot on its trail.

Where it's reviewed:
Booklist, November 15, 1988, page 569
School Library Journal, January 1989, page 58

Other books by the author:
The Skyscraper Parade, 1987
The Silver Ghost Express, 1986
The Fish Switch Mystery, 1985
The Fortune Cookie Chase, 1985

Other books you might like:
Dana Brenford, *Tracks in the North Woods*, 1988
   While visiting Canada's North Woods, twins Peter and Jason, and their stepsister Kim, investigate the disappearance of an elderly woman hermit.
Lillian Hoban, *The Case of the Two Masked Robbers*, 1986
   Raccoon twins Arabella and Albert track down the robbers who stole Mrs. Turtle's eggs.
Marion M. Markham, *The Christmas Present Mystery*, 1984
   Twin sisters Mickey and Kate combine their skills to discover the explanation for a mysterious face that has appeared in a family photograph.
Marilyn Singer, *The Case of the Fixed Election*, 1989
   Twins David and Sam are up to their necks in trouble when they find themselves in the middle of the dirtiest election their school has ever seen.
Jamie Suzanne, *The Haunted House*, 1990
   Identical twins Elizabeth and Jessica think that the Mercandy house is haunted and that Nora Mercandy is a witch, until Elizabeth solves the mystery.

12

David A. Adler

Illustrator: Jean Jenkins

Jeffrey's Ghost and the Fifth Grade Dragon (New York: Holt, 1985)

Age range: Grades 3-5

Subject(s): Fantasy; Ghosts; Schools

Major character(s): Jeffrey Clark, Preteen, 5th Grader; Bradford, Spirit; Laura Lane, Friend

Time period(s): 1980s

Locale(s): United States

What the book is about: On the first day of school, Jeffrey Clark is already in a mess and gets sent to the principal's office for disturbing the class. He can't tell the principal it's all because of a 200 year old ghost named Bradford. Jeff and his friend, Laura, learn what school was like for Bradford (who died at age 10) and set out to find a bench buried 200 years before.

Where it's reviewed:
Booklist, February 15, 1986, page 864
School Library Journal, February 1986, page 79

Other books by the author:
Jeffrey's Ghost and the Ziffel Fair Mystery, 1987
Fourth Floor Twins and the Fish Snitch Mystery, 1985
Jeffrey's Ghost and the Leftover Baseball Team, 1984
Cam Jansen and the Mystery of the Dinosaur Bones, 1981

Other books you might like:
Frances Eagar, *Time Trouble*, 1976
   While staying at her convent school over Christmas, a young girl meets a mysterious young man she believes is a ghost from the sixteenth century.
Jeffrey Marlin, *Getting out the Ghost*, 1984
   The ghost who comes to life in a girl's body brings her some talents, but unpleasant aspects of the ghost's personality make havoc in her life.
Barbara A. Moe, *The Ghost Wore Knickers*, 1975
   New in school, Abby is chosen to go on a class camping trip and she hates it.
Megan Stine, *The Thundercats and the Ghost Warrior*, 1985
   The Thundercats must find the evil and wicked Grune the Destroyer and put him back in his tomb, but first must face enemy Mutants.
Martin Waddell, *Harriet and the Haunted School*, 1984
   When Harriet hides a circus horse in the closet at school, its nocturnal wanderings start a rumor that the building is haunted.

13

David A. Adler

Illustrator: Dick Gackenbach

My Dog and the Birthday Mystery (New York: Holiday, 1987)

Age range: Grades 1-2

Subject(s): Bicycles and Bicycling; Birthdays; Animals/Dogs

Major character(s): Jenny, Child; My Dog, Dog

Time period(s): 1980s

Locale(s): United States

What the book is about: Jenny and her dog, "My Dog", find themselves involved in a problem of a stolen bicycle which turns out to be a ruse to get her to a surprise birthday party.

Where it's reviewed:
Booklist, June 1, 1987, page 1527
Kirkus Reviews, March 15, 1987, page 473
Center for Children's Books Bulletin, May 1987, page 161

Other books by the author:
Benny Benny Baseball Nut, 1987
My Dog and the Green Sock Mystery, 1986
My Dog and the Knock Knock Mystery, 1985
Bunny Rabbit Rebus, 1983

Other books you might like:
Judy Delton, *A Birthday Bike for Brimhall*, 1985

Brimhall receives a bike for his birthday but is ashamed to admit he doesn't know how to ride it.

Crescent Dragonwagon, *Annie Flies the Birthday Bike*, 1993
Annie gets the bike of her dreams for her birthday but finds riding it is harder than she thought.

Errol Lloyd, *Sasha and the Bicycle Thieves*, 1988
When her new BMX is stolen, Sasha enlists the help of her friends in tracking down a ring of bicycle thieves.

Susan Beth Pfeffer, *Twin Surprises*, 1991
Relates Betsy's humorous efforts to keep a surprise birthday party for her twin sister a secret.

Jane Resh Thomas, *Wheels*, 1986
Elliott learns that winning isn't everything when he begins to race with the Big Wheel bike he got for his birthday.

14

Mary Adrain

Illustrator: Reisie Lonette

The Fireball Mystery (New York: Hastings, 1977)

Age range: Grades 3-5

Subject(s): Boats and Boating; Islands; UFOs

Major character(s): Tim Andrews, Child; Vicki Andrews, Child; Joey Baker, Neighbor

Time period(s): 1970s

Locale(s): United States

What the book is about: Tim and Vicki are living in a floating house and the boy next door likes to star gaze as much as they do. But, what are the eerie, many-colored lights floating across the water? Is the object on the island or from outer space?

Other books by the author:
The Mystery of the Dinosaur Graveyard, 1982
The Mystery of the Night Explorers, 1962

Other books you might like:
Margaret Goff Clark, *Barney and the UFO*, 1979
Barney is afraid to tell his foster parents that he has seen a UFO behind the house even when a hasty promise to a space boy leads him into trouble.

Milton Dank, *A UFO Has Landed*, 1983
When their biology teacher insists he saw a UFO and some aliens, the Galaxy Gang sets out to help him by gathering evidence to prove his story.

Gene DeWeese, *The Dandelion Caper*, 1986
Walter and Kathy are unprepared for the evil aliens they encounter in an abandoned house and the strange cat that comes to their rescue.

Dennis B. Fradin, *How I Saved the World*, 1986
After Shelley spots a UFO one summer night at a resort in northern Michigan, he becomes involved in a desperate effort to stop an alien invasion.

Shirley Parenteau, *Jelly and the Spaceboat*, 1981
Jelly and Rich find themselves headed down the Sacramento River on an unusual houseboat with a crew from outer space.

15

Janet Ahlberg

Jeremiah in the Dark Woods (New York: Viking Kestral, 1978)

Age range: Grades 1-3

Subject(s): Fantasy; Fairy Tale; Humor

Major character(s): Jeremiah Jones, Child

Time period(s): Indeterminate

Locale(s): Earth

What the book is about: With references to the three bears, seven dwarfs, five gorillas, a frog prince and sleeping beauties, the reader hears of Jeremiah who lives in the middle of the dark woods in his grandmother's house made of cake and sweet bread. Funny, happy ending and a good read aloud.

Where it's reviewed:
Booklist, May 1, 1978, page 1426
Kirkus, March 1, 1978, page 237
School Library Journal, May 1978, page 49

Other books by the author:
The Bear Nobody Wanted, 1992
The Jolly Postman, 1986
Funnybones, 1980
Each Peach Pear Plum, 1978

Other books you might like:
Anthea Bell, *The Strange Child*, 1984
A magical being comes into the unhappy lives of a brother and sister, leading them into a world of fantasy and adventure.

Jacob Grimm, *The Bear and the Kingbird*, 1979
When the bear insults the kingbird's chicks, a humorous battle ensues between the land animals and the flying creatures of the world.

Crockett Johnson, *Harold's Fairy Tale*, 1956
With his purple crayon Harold draws his way into an enchanted garden troubled by a giant witch.

Spencer Johnson, *The Value of Fantasy*, 1979
A brief biography of Hans Christian Andersen, which stresses the value of personal fantasies and imagination.

Donna Jo Napoli, *The Magic Circle*, 1993
A woman learns sorcery to become a healer, and is turned into a witch by spirits. She fights their power until her encounter with Hansel and Gretel.

16

Barbara Aiello

Illustrator: Loel Barr

It's Your Turn at Bat (Frederick, MD: 21st Century Books, 1988)

Age range: Grades 2-4

Subject(s): Cerebral Palsy; Physically Handicapped; Sports/Baseball

Major character(s): Mark Riley, 5th Grader, Handicapped (cerebral palsy); Brenda Dubrowski, Friend (classmate); Evvy Rothman, Teacher (aerobics instructor)

Time period(s): 1980s

Locale(s): Woodburn

What the book is about: While reluctantly doing research on sewing machines for a school report, Mark, a fifth grader with cerebral palsy, discovers that the money for his team's baseball jerseys for which he was responsible for is missing. He finds himself feeling more friendly toward sewing machines.

Where it's reviewed:
Booklist, March 15, 1989, page 1286
Kirkus Reviews, December 15, 1988, page 1807
School Library Journal, May 1989, page 102

Other books by the author:
Hometown Hero: Featuring Scott Whittaker, 1989
On with the Show, 1989
Friends for Life, 1988
Secrets Aren't (Always) for Keeps, 1988

Other books you might like:
Lisa Campbell Ernst, *Sam Johnson and the Blue Ribbon Quilt*, 1983
　　Sam discovers that he enjoys sewing various patches of cloth together but meets with scorn and ridicule when he asks to join his wife's quilting club.
Ellen Howard, *Circle of Giving*, 1984
　　Marguerite suddenly becomes shy, withdrawn, and ill at ease with other children until a girl with cerebral palsy moves in across the street.
Sherry Neuwirth Payne, *A Contest*, 1982
　　Even though Mike has cerebral palsy, he shows the children in his class that he can play to win when he gets the chance.
Harriette Robinet, *Jay and the Marigold*, 1976
　　A young boy born with cerebral palsy watches a flower grow in spite of its handicap. This shows him that he, too, can grow and blossom.
Joel Vecere, *A Story about Courage*, 1992
　　Jarrod, a new student who's confined to a wheelchair, tries out for the school basketball team.

| **17** |

Joan Aiken

Night Fall (New York: Holt, 1971)

Age range: Grades 4-6

Subject(s): Mystery and Detective Stories

Major character(s): Meg Frazer, Artist, Young Woman; George Barnard, Stock Broker; Toby Trevelyan, Businessman

Time period(s): 1960s

Locale(s): Penleggan, England

What the book is about: Haunted by a recurrent nightmare, Meg Frazer, a young English girl travels to Cornwall to trace the source of the dream. As a child, she had fallen down a cliffside, but has no memory of the event, only the nightmare. She is shocked to find that she was a witness to a murder, and is now in danger from the same person responsible for the murder years ago.

Where it's reviewed:
Horn Book, October 1971, page 487
Kirkus Reviews, May 1, 1971, page 508

Awards the book has won:
Edgar Allan Poe Award 1972

Other books by the author:
Last Slice of Rainbow, 1988
Black Hearts in Battersea, 1987
Up the Chimney Down and Other Stories, 1987
Midnight Is a Place, 1974

Other books you might like:
John Bellairs, *The Secret of the Underground Room*, 1990
　　When Father Higgins disappears, Johnny and Professor Childermass discover clues which lead them to England and a long-dead knight.
Dorothy Crayder, *The Riddles of Mermaid House*, 1977
　　Becky is a lonely newcomer who seeks solace in studying the marsh and is weary of people she meets there, one of whom may be setting fires in town.
Jane Louise Curry, *Ghost Lane*, 1979
　　Three children in an English village face danger as they track burglars.
Kathryn Lasky, *Double Trouble Squared*, 1991
　　In London, twins Liberty and July receive strange vibes from Arthur Conan Doyle's old house and discover a literary ghost.
Alison Prince, *Night Landings*, 1984
　　Harrie and Ian become convinced that smugglers are operating a landing strip near their English farm home.

| **18** |

Joan Aiken

Illustrator: Pat Marriott

The Wolves of Willoughby Chase (Garden City, NJ: Doubleday, 1962)

Age range: Grades 3-6

Subject(s): Animals/Wolves

Major character(s): Bonnie Willoughby-Green, Preteen; Sylvia Green, Cousin, Orphan; Mrs. Slighcarp, Governess

Time period(s): 1800s

Locale(s): England

What the book is about: A great English estate is surrounded by hungry wolves. Two girls are mistakenly left in the care of a wicked and scheming governess.

Where it's reviewed:
Publisher's Weekly, September 1968, page 63
Publisher's Weekly, May 22, 1981, page 77

Other books by the author:
The Stolen Lake, 1988
Dido and Pa, 1986
Nightbirds on Nantucket, 1969
Black Hearts in Battersea, 1964

Other books you might like:
Melvin Burgess, *The Cry of the Wolf*, 1990
　　A hunter determined to wipe out every wolf in England, almost succeeds but then finds himself the prey.
Clare Cooper, *Earthchange*, 1985
　　After a catastrophe turns Earth into a barren wilderness, young Rose looks for help and reaches a group of survivors trying to restore the Earth.
Jack London, *White Fang*, 1985
　　A dog-wolf of the northern wilderness eventually makes his peace with humans.

Elona Malterre, *The Last Wolf of Ireland*, 1990
A boy and girl attempt to save the last wolf in Ireland in the 1780s.
Whitley Strieber, *Wolf of Shadows*, 1985
A wolf and a woman form a mysterious bond in the aftermath of nuclear holocaust.

19

Vivien Alcock

Ghostly Companions (New York: Delacorte, 1987)

Age range: Grades 5-8

Subject(s): Ghosts; Short Stories

Time period(s): Indeterminate Past

Locale(s): England

What the book is about: A collection of ten short stories dealing with the supernatural, suspense and horror for strong upper grade readers. Also an excellent read aloud for the brave.

Where it's reviewed:
Booklist, June 15, 1987, page 1596
Horn Book, July 1987, page 460

Other books by the author:
The Monster Garden, 1988
The Mysterious Mr. Ross, 1987
The Cuckoo Sister, 1986
The Haunting of Cassie Palmer, 1982

Other books you might like:
Pam Conrad, *Stonewords: A Ghost Story*, 1990
Zoe discovers that her house is occupied by the ghost of an eleven year old girl who carries her back to the day of her death in 1870.
Mary Downing Hahn, *The Doll in the Garden*, 1989
Two girls find an antique doll in Miss Cooper's garden, then discover they can enter a ghostly turn-of-the-century world through a hole in the hedge.
Donn Kushner, *Uncle Jacob's Ghost Story*, 1986
Paul discovers the story of his great Uncle Jacob, who believed ghosts of two friends followed him from Poland to America.
J.B. Stamper, *More Tales for the Midnight Hour: Thirteen Stories*, 1987
Ghost and horror stories to read with all the lights on, or around the campfire at midnight if you have the courage.
Robert Westall, *The Haunting of Chas McGill and Other Stories*, 1983
A combination of horror and science fiction stories make this an exciting collection of tales.

20

Vivien Alcock

The Monster Garden (New York: Doubleday, 1988)

Age range: Grades 4-7

Subject(s): Genetic Engineering; Monsters; Science Fiction

Major character(s): Frances "Frankie" Stein, Scientist; Monnie, Monster; David, Child

Time period(s): 1980s

Locale(s): United States

What the book is about: Using a genetic agar stolen by her brother from their father's experiments in genetic engineering, Frankie creates a baby monster who begins to grow at an alarming rate. The problems of caring for and hiding the huge but gentle creature form the central theme of this novel, at once serious (as Frankie begins to understand her father) and humorous as Frankie and David try to keep Mannie's existence secret.

Where it's reviewed:
Horn Book, November/December, 1988, page 781
School Library Journal, October 1988, page 138

Other books by the author:
A Kind of Thief, 1991
The Mysterious Mr. Ross, 1987
The Cuckoo Sister, 1985
The Haunting of Cassie Palmer, 1980

Other books you might like:
Piers Anthony, *Balook*, 1990
A friendly prehistoric rhinoceros is genetically recreated in the near future.
Margaret C. Cooper, *Solution: Escape*, 1980
Thirteen year old Stefan discovers he is a clone who has been unknowingly taking part in an experiment and he decides he must escape.
Sylvia Engdahl, *The Doors of the Universe*, 1981
Scholar Noren finds he faces hostility as he tries to solve social problems, especially the taboo on genetic research.
Ellen MacGregor, *Miss Pickerell Takes the Bull by the Horns*, 1976
Miss Pickerell gets involved with cloned bulls, kidnappers and explaining responsibility to the governor and mayors.
Mary C. Ryan, *Me Two*, 1991
Thirteen year old Wilf accidentally clones himself when he messes up a science experiment, but the clone turns out to be a help to him.

21

Vivien Alcock

Travelers by Night (New York: Delacorte, 1985)

Age range: Grades 5-8

Subject(s): Animals/Elephants; Circus

Major character(s): Belle, Preteen; Charley, Entertainer (circus performer)

Time period(s): Indeterminate

Locale(s): Yald Forest, England

What the book is about: Twelve year old Belle, disfigured by a high wire accident, and her circus friend, Charley, decide to save an old performing elephant from the slaughterhouse.

Where it's reviewed:
Bulletin for the Center of Children's Books, October 1985, page 21
Horn Book, January/February 1986, page 54

Other books by the author:
A Kind of Thief, 1992
Ghostly Companions, 1987

Cuckoo Sister, 1985
The Haunting of Cassie Palmer, 1982

Other books you might like:
Carol Carrick, *The Elephant in the Dark*, 1988
 Through training an elephant, the first ever seen in early 1800s Massachusetts, orphan Will begins to feel important for the first time in his life.
Dean Harvey, *The Secret Elephant of Harlan Kooter*, 1992
 Harlan, a young resident of Pine View, Florida, tries to hide an escaped circus elephant.
Susan Saunders, *The Daring Rescue of Marlon the Swimming Pig*, 1987
 Two young boys get more than they bargained for when they try to save the swimming pig star of the local Aquarama from being sent to slaughter.
Barbara Smucker, *Incredible Jumbo: A Novel*, 1990
 In the 1870s, a young boy helps care for the huge African elephant at the London Zoo and accompanies him to America to be in P.T. Barnum's circus.
Robb White, *The Long Way Down: A Novel*, 1977
 A girl who wants to be a trapeze performer finds she has a lot to learn when she joins a circus.

| 22 |

Vivien Alcock

The Trial of Anna Cotman (New York: Delacorte, 1989)

Age range: Grades 5 and Up

Subject(s): Friendship; Clubs; Conduct of Life

Major character(s): Anna Cotman, Teenager; Lindy, Teenager

Time period(s): 1980s

Locale(s): United States

What the book is about: Anna is torn between wanting friends, even the bossy and demanding Lindy, and the ugly turn the secret society she belongs to has made. She speaks out against one of its members and is subjected to an inquisition.

Where it's reviewed:
Booklist, January 1, 1990, page 901
School Library Journal, February 1990, page 86

Other books by the author:
A Kind of Thief, 1991
Ghostly Companions, 1987
The Cuckoo Sister, 1985
The Haunting of Cassie Palmer, 1980

Other books you might like:
Miriam Cohen, *Laura Leonard's First Amendment*, 1990
 Laura finds she must determine her own beliefs in the face of community opposition to admitting a boy with AIDS to her school.
Ilene Cooper, *The Queen of the Sixth Grade*, 1988
 After helping her found a club, Robin accidentally gets on Veronica's wrong side and discovers how bossy and cruel she really is.
Liza Fosburgh, *Afternoon Magic*, 1989
 Thirteen year old Willy watches as Harold infiltrates his gang of latchkey children and leads them into dishonesty and vandalism.
Phyllis Reynolds Naylor, *All but Alice*, 1992

Alice decides the only way to stave off disasters is to be part of the crowd, no matter how boring and difficult.
Carol Beach York, *The Ten O'Clock Club*, 1970
 Only four girls are interested in becoming members of the Ten O'Clock Club, which is a success despite its low membership.

| 23 |

Louisa M. Alcott

Illustrator: Jessie Wilcox Smith

Little Women, or Meg, Jo, Beth and Amy (Boston: Little Brown, 1915)

Age range: Grades 5-8

Subject(s): Family Life; Civil War

Major character(s): Meg March, Teenager; Jo March, Teenager; Beth March, Teenager

Time period(s): 1860s

Locale(s): New England

What the book is about: The classic first juvenile novel of family life chronicles the joys and troubles of the four March sisters, as they work through their teen years and look forward to adulthood, surrounded by a warm, loving family. For the same audience as Laura Ingalls Wilder books. Don't forget it just because it's been around forever.

Where it's reviewed:
Kirkus Reviews, September 1, 1969, page 941
Publishers Weekly, September 2, 1968, page 29

Other books by the author:
Little Men, 1871
Hospital Sketches, 1863
Jo's Boys, 1886
Old Fashioned Girl, 1870

Other books you might like:
Norma Johnson, *Of Time and of Seasons*, 1975
 The Civil War is only one more complication in the life of Bridget's family in which everyone seems talented, except Bridget.
Lou Kassem, *Listen for Rachel*, 1986
 Moving to the mountains of Tennessee introduces Rachel to a possible calling as she learns about folk medicine from a local healer.
William McKay, *Young Indiana Jones and the Plantation Treasure*, 1990
 In 1913, fourteen year old Indiana Jones traces the route of the Underground Railway to help a young woman find her fortune, lost in the Civil War.
Carolyn Reeder, *Shades of Gray*, 1989
 After the Civil War, Will moves to the countryside with his aunt and the uncle he considers a traitor for not participating in the war.
Ann Rinaldi, *The Last Silk Dress*, 1988
 Susan finds a way to help the Confederate Army and uncovers a series of mysterious family secrets.

24

Sue Ann Alderson

Illustrator: Ann Blades

Ida and the Wool Smugglers (New York: McElderry Books, 1988)

Age range: Grades 1-3

Subject(s): Smuggling; Animals/Sheep

Major character(s): Ida, Child, Shepherd

Time period(s): Indeterminate Past

Locale(s): Canada

What the book is about: A young girl in a pioneering family in Canada proves she is old enough to accept responsibility when she saves a herd of sheep from smugglers.

Where it's reviewed:
Booklist, November 15, 1987, page 575
Kirkus Reviews, Janurary 5, 1988, page 119
School Library Journal, August 1988, page 77

Other books you might like:
Margaret Wise Brown, *Little Lost Lamb*, 1945
    A shepherd discovers that a lamb is missing and climbs the high mountain in the dark and cold to search for it.
Ivan Gantschev, *The Moon Lake*, 1981
    A shepherd follows a sheep to the secret lake that the moon bathes, but greedy townspeople soon learn that its banks are filled with silver and gold.
Roy Gerrard, *Rosie and the Rustlers*, 1989
    When Rosie and her wranglers visit the Cherokee, Greasy Ben and his gang steal her cattle. Rosie and her cowpunchers saddle up and round them up.
Dennis Haseley, *The Cave of Snores*, 1987
    A shepherd boy seeks help in the cave of snores when bad magic takes away his father's snores which protect the sheep and other shepherds.
Scott R. Sanders, *Warm as Wool*, 1992
    When Betsy's family move from Connecticutt to Ohio, she brings along a sockful of coins to buy sheep so that she can gather wool and make clothes.

25

Lloyd Alexander

The Black Cauldron (New York: Holt, 1965)

Age range: Grades 5 and Up

Series: Chronicles of Pyrdain

Subject(s): Fairy Tale; Fantasy

Major character(s): Taran, Farmer (Assistant pig-keeper); Prince Gwidion, Ruler

Time period(s): Indeterminate

Locale(s): Fictional Country

What the book is about: Taran embarks on a quest announced by Prince Gwydion to snatch the black cauldron from the hellish kingdom of Arawn, Lord of the Land of Death. Taran learns braggarts can become heroes and mighty kings can turn traitor.

Where it's reviewed:
Horn Book, June 1965, page 274

Library Journal, April 15, 1965, page 2016

Awards the book has won:
Newbery Honor

Other books by the author:
The Book of Three, 1964
The Castle of Llyr, 1966
Coll and His White Pig, 1965 (related picture book)

Other books you might like:
Richard Carylon, *The Dark Lord of Pengersick*, 1980
    Jago and Mabby enter the battle against the evil Lord of Pengersick.
Diana Wynne Jones, *The Power of Three*, 1976
    Three especially gifted children take part in a final confrontation between People of the Earth, the Sun, and the Moon.
Ursula Le Guin, *A Wizard of Earthsea*, 1968
    Sparrowhawk is rigorously trained by the Master wizard for the encounter with evil shadows.
John Masefield, *The Midnight Folk*, 1985
    Edward and his friends encounter witches, secret passages, and magic potions.
Anne McCaffrey, *Dragonsong*, 1976
    On Pern, where dragons and their riders fight the deadly thread, Menolly proves worthy of the Harperhall, even though females have never been harpers.

26

Lloyd Alexander

The Cat Who Wished to Be a Man (New York: Dutton, 1973)

Age range: Grades 3-5

Subject(s): Animals/Cats

Major character(s): Lionel, Cat; Magister Stephanus, Wizard; Pursewig, Political Figure (mayor)

Time period(s): 13th Century

Locale(s): England

What the book is about: Lionel, who lives with the wizard Magister Stephanus, wants to become human out of love for the innkeeper, Mistress Gillian. Medieval adventure of a country cat up against evil "city slickers."

Where it's reviewed:
Horn Book, October 1973, page 463
Library Journal, September 15, 1973, page 2647

Awards the book has won:
Boston Globe/Horn Book Award - Honor Book 1973

Other books by the author:
Town Cats and Other Tales, 1977
The Four Donkeys, 1972
The Marvelous Misadventures of Sebastian, 1971
Time Cat, 1963

Other books you might like:
Joan Davenport Carris, *Witch-Cat*, 1984
    A down-to-earth girl is made to see that she is a witch through the efforts of a magical cat.
Donald E. Caufield, *Never Steal a Magic Cat*, 1971
    Only the family dog and cat suspect that the beautiful silver-gray cat that has come to stay with them is a magical cat.
Wallace Cox, *The Tenth Life of Osiris Oaks*, 1972

A lonely boy tries to use his magic cat's mind reading abilities to help humanity.

Alice Duggan, *Violet's Finest Hour*, 1991
  Two young cats, Violet and Grim, use a magic flying cape to stop a gang of bank robbers.

Deborah Nourse Lattimore, *The Winged Cat: A tale of Ancient Egypt*, 1992
  In ancient Egypt, a servant girl and a High Priest must each find the right magic spell to open the twelve gates to the Nether World.

27

Lloyd Alexander

The First Two Lives of Lukas Kasha (New York: Dutton, 1978)

Age range: Grades 4-6

Subject(s): Space and Time; Fantasy

Major character(s): Lukas Kasha, Teenager, Apprentice

Time period(s): Indeterminate

Locale(s): Alternate Earth

What the book is about: After paying a silver penny to encourage a magician to perform in the town square, a carpenter's helper is conjured to a strange place where people call him the King of Abadan.

Where it's reviewed:
Horn Book, October 1978, page 513
School Library Journal, October 1978, page 141

Awards the book has won:
Crabbery Award 1979

Other books by the author:
Fortune-Tellers, 1992
Beggar Queen, 1984
The Black Cauldron, 1965
The Book of Three, 1964

Other books you might like:
Margaret Jean Anderson, *In the Circle of Time*, 1979
  Robert and his American friend, Jennifer, find a circle of stones which propel them into the 22nd century.
Gery Greer, *Max and Me and the Time Machine*, 1983
  Steve and Max travel back to the 13th century and find themselves preparing for a jousting tournament.
Eric Houghton, *Steps out of Time*, 1980
  Jonathan moves ahead in time and experiences events that will happen to his descendants in the future.
Myron Levoy, *The Magic Hat of Mortimer Wintergreen*, 1988
  Runaways Joshua and Amy meet up with the greatest magician on the American continent, in 1893, as they travel from South Dakota to New York City.
Anne Lindbergh, *The People in Pineapple Place*, 1982
  August stumbles across some interesting children who teach him to time travel through an alley called Pineapple Place.

28

Lloyd Alexander

The High King (New York: Holt, Rinehart & Winston, 1968)

Age range: Grades 5 and Up

Series: Chronicles of Prydain

Subject(s): Fairy Tale

Major character(s): Taran, Hero; Princess Eilonwy, Heroine, Royalty; Fflewddur Flam, Minstrel (Bard)

Time period(s): Indeterminate

Locale(s): Prydain, Fictional Country (Mythical land based on Welsh legend)

What the book is about: A young assistant pig-keeper becomes a hero in this final book of the Chronicles of Prydain. After a terrible winter march, Taran and a huge army arrive at Arawn's stronghold and Taran leads the quest to rescue Drnwyn, the sword that symbolizes the strength of the kingdom of Prydain.

Where it's reviewed:
Booklist, April 1968, page 920
Horn Book, April 1968, page 172
Kirkus, March 1, 1968, page 259

Awards the book has won:
Newbery Medal 1969

Other books by the author:
The Book of Three, 1964
The Castle of Llyr, 1966
The Black Cauldron, 1965
Taran Wanderer, 1967

Other books you might like:
Susan Cooper, *Over Sea, Under Stone*, 1965
  In this first book of The Dark is Rising series, three English children become part of the great battle between good and evil.
Madeleine L'Engle, *A Wrinkle in Time*, 1962
  First in a trilogy of books about the Murray children who travel through time by learning to "tesser."
Ursula Le Guin, *A Wizard of Earthsea*, 1968
  Sparrowhawk is trained by the Master wizard and comes face to face with evil shadows.
C.S. Lewis, *The Lion, the Witch, and the Wardrobe*, 1950
  Peter, Susan, Edmund and Luch discover the magic land of Narnia, meet a wicked witch and the mightly lion, Aslan.
J.R.R. Tolkien, *The Hobbit, or There and Back Again*,
  Home-loving hobbit Bilbo Baggins finds himself drawn into an adventure with a wizard, dwarves, and a fearsome dragon.

29

Lloyd Alexander

The Jedera Adventure (New York: Dutton, 1989)

Age range: Grades 5 and Up

Subject(s): Deserts; Adventure and Adventurers

Major character(s): Vesper Holly, Heroine; Professor Brinton "Brinnie" Garrett, Guardian; Maleesh, Magician

Time period(s): 1870s (1874)

Locale(s): Jedera, Fictional Country (in North Africa)

What the book is about: The further cliff-hanging adventures of Vesper Holly and Brinnie as they travel to a far off desert country. They intend to return a valuable book to an ancient library. After meeting the magician, Maleesh, and finding out about the political situation in the area, they manage to free enslaved inhabitants and save the day.

Where it's reviewed:
Horn Book, September 1989, page 624
Kirkus Reviews, April 1, 1989, page 543

Other books by the author:
The Drackenberg Adventure, 1988
The Eldorado Adventure, 1987
The Illyrian Adventure, 1986
The Foundling and Other Tales of Prydain, 1982

Other books you might like:
Judith Gorog, *Winning Scherazade*, 1991
   Having been released from her position as storyteller and doomed bride of the Sultan, Scheherazade is led into dangerous adventures in the desert.
Moses L. Howard, *The Ostrich Chase*, 1974
   Although the women are forbidden to participate in the hunt, a young Bushman girl determines to realize her dream of hunting an ostrich.
Madeleine L'Engle, *Many Waters*, 1986
   Sandy and Dennys are accidentally sent back to a strange Biblical time, in which mythical beasts live, and a man named Noah is preparing for a flood.
Ellen Kindt McKenzie, *A Bowl of Mischief*, 1992
   An abandoned child in the desert, found by a holy man, resists his teachings, but regret it years later when in a battle of wits whith a villain.
Pamela F. Service, *Vision Quest*, 1989
   Kate finds life dreary in her small Nevada desert town until contact with an Indian artifact sends her visions of a restless shaman from the past.

30

Lloyd Alexander

Illustrator: Ezra Jack Keats

The King's Fountain (New York: Dutton, 1971)

Age range: Grades 4-6

Subject(s): Kings, Queens, Rulers; Greed

Time period(s): Indeterminate Past

Locale(s): Fictional Country

What the book is about: In spite of the fact that it will deprive his subjects of water, a king decides to build himself a fancy fountain for his own pleasure. A wise man, a merchant and a strong man all try to dissuade him, but a poor man whose family will suffer tells the simple truth and the king hears him.

Where it's reviewed:
Booklist, September 1, 1971, page 55
Hornbook, August 1971, page 373
Kirkus Reviews, February 15, 1971, page 167

Other books by the author:
The Fortune Tellers, 1992
The Foundling and Other Tales of Pyrdain, 1982
Coll and His White Pig, 1965

Other books you might like:
Margaret Hodges, *The Golden Deer*, 1992

Buddha comes to the city of Benares in the form of a golden deer and persuades the King to stop killing all the deer in the area.
Eric A. Kimmel, *Three Sacks of Truth: A Story from France*, 1993
   With the aid of a perfect peach, a silver fife and his own resources, Petit Jean outwits a dishonest king and wins the hand of a princess.
Ellen Kindt McKenzie, *The King, the Princess and the Tinker*, 1992
   A good-hearted tinker and a curious young princess show a narrow minded king there are more important things in the world than his treasure.
Lynne Reid Banks, *The Adventures of King Midas*, 1992
   King Midas regrets his wish to turn all he touches to gold and must deal with a magician, a witch, and a dragon as he tries to undo the spell.
Julian F. Thompson, *Gypsyworld*, 1992
   Kidnapped and taken to a utopian Gypsy world a group of teenagers is tested to see how they cope in a place where Earth and its gifts are not abused.

31

Lloyd Alexander

The Marvelous Misadventures of Sebastian (New York: Dutton, 1970)

Age range: Grades 4-7

Subject(s): Adventure and Adventurers; Fantasy; Musicians

Major character(s): Sebastian, Musician (fiddler); Presto, Cat; Baron Pum-Hessel, Nobleman

Time period(s): Indeterminate Past

Locale(s): Hamelin-Loring, Germany

What the book is about: Fourth fiddler Sebastian meets many trials while crossing a Graustarkian kingdom to reach the arms of his princess.

Where it's reviewed:
Center for Children's Books Bulletin, February 1971, page 85
Hornbook, December 1970, page 628
New York Times Book Review, November 15, 1970, page 42

Awards the book has won:
National Book Award 1971

Other books by the author:
The High King, 1969
The Truthful Harp, 1967
The Castle of Llyr, 1966
The Black Cauldron, 1965

Other books you might like:
Anne McCaffrey, *Dragonsong*, 1976
   Forbidden by her father to indulge in music in any way, Menolly takes shelter with fire lizards, who along with her music, open a new life for her.
Robert Newton Peck, *King of Kazoo*, 1976
   A cowpuncher, a plumber, and a drummer set off to see the King of Kazoo in search of their hearts' desires: a purple cow, a sink to fix, and a drum.
Gloria Skurzynski, *What Happened in Hamelin?*, 1979

A novel of the Pied Piper legend told from the standpoint of a baker's assistant who dreams of freedom from his life and of a new life with the piper.

Laura Caroline Stevenson, *The Island and the Ring*, 1991
   After treachery destroys her kingdom, Tania discovers that it is her destiny to confront Ascanet, the ruthless lord enslaving the island of Elyssonne.

Patricia C. Wrede, *Dealing with Dragons*, 1990
   Bored with palace life, a princess goes off to live with a group of dragons and becomes involved with wizards who want to steal the dragons' kingdom.

| 32 |

Sue Alexander

Illustrator: Jeanette Winter

Witch, Goblin and Sometimes Ghost: Six Read Alone Stories (New York: Pantheon, 1976)

Age range: Grades 1-3

Subject(s): Friendship; Short Stories; Ghosts

Time period(s): Indeterminate

Locale(s): United States

What the book is about: Goblin has friends who will help him even when he is afraid, forgetful or crabby. Six stories tailored to beginning readers.

Where it's reviewed:
Booklist, December 15, 1976, page 613
Kirkus Reviews, October 15, 1976, page 1135
School Library Journal, February 1977, page 53

Other books by the author:
Who Goes out on Halloween?, 1990
Witch, Goblin and Ghost Are Back, 1985
Witch, Goblin and Ghost's Book of Things to Do, 1982
Witch, Goblin and Ghost in the Haunted Woods, 1981

Other books you might like:
Jim Davis, *Garfield's Ghost Stories*, 1992
   Five fun fables of phantoms and fearsome phenomenon.
Wilson Gage, *Mrs. Gaddy and the Ghost*, 1979
   Mrs. Gaddy finds a ghost in the kitchen can be good company.
Washington Irving, *The Legend of Sleepy Hollow*, 1991
   Beautiful illustrations accompany this retelling of Irving's classic tale of a headless horseman.
Alvin Schwartz, *Ghosts!*, 1991
   Presents seven easy to read ghost stories based on traditional folk tales and legends from various countries.
Betty Ren Wright, *The Ghost of Popcorn Hill*, 1993
   Martin and Peter acquire a mischievous new dog and two lonely ghosts.

| 33 |

Mabel Esther Allan

Illustrator: Charles Robinson

An Island in a Green Sea (New York: Atheneum, 1972)

Age range: Grades 4-6

Major character(s): Mairi, Preteen

Time period(s): 1970s

Locale(s): Scotland

What the book is about: Happy on the Outer Hebrides, eleven year old Mairi has no desire to leave when her family situation changes and takes her to new places.

Where it's reviewed:
Horn Book, October 1972, page 473
Kirkus Reviews, August 1, 1972, page 858

Awards the book has won:
Boston Globe/Horn Book Award - Honor Book 1973

Other books by the author:
Dream of Hunger Moss, 1983
The Mills Down Below, 1980
A Chill in the Lane, 1974
Wood Street Secret, 1970

Other books you might like:
Mary-Claire Helldorfer, *Almost Home*, 1987
   Vacationing at grandfather's home, Jesse meets an unusual girl and together they find things providing clues to understanding the past and present.
Belinda Hurmence, *The Nightwalker*, 1988
   Savannah wonders if her little brother, Poco, who sleepwalks, is setting the mysterious fires that are leveling the fishermen's shacks.
Clive King, *The Night the Water Came*, 1982
   A boy who survives a cyclone that destroys his island home near Bangladesh is mystified by the rescue workers, and only wants life to be as it was.
Eleanor Frances Lattimore, *Fair Boy*, 1958
   A girl visiting her great-aunt in South Carolina discovers the island, a summer home before a disastrous hurricane, is just as it was 60 years ago.
Judith St. George, *The Chinese Puzzle of Shag Island*, 1976
   A seemingly harmless trip to the family's ancestral home on a Maine Island turns dangerous for Kim.

| 34 |

Harry Allard

Miss Nelson Is Missing! (Boston: Houghton Mifflin, 1977)

Age range: Grades 2-3

Subject(s): Teachers; Humor; Schools

Time period(s): 1970s

Locale(s): United States

What the book is about: The kids in Room 207 take advantage of their teacher's good nature until she disappers and they are faced with a vile substitute. The mystery of what happened to Miss Nelson enlivens the story.

Where it's reviewed:
Horn Book, June 1977, page 296
School Library Journal, April 1977, page 52

Awards the book has won:
Edgar Allan Poe Award - Runner-up

Other books by the author:
Crash Helmet, 1977
Miss Nelson Has a Field Day, 1985
Miss Nelson Is Back, 1982
There's a Party at Mona's Tonight, 1981

Other books you might like:
Marc T. Brown, *Arthur's Teacher Trouble*, 1986
    Arthur and his friends complain when Mr. Rathburn works them too hard at school
James Howe, *Day the Teacher Went Bananas*, 1984
    Getting the location of the zoo and the school confused makes a very interesting situation for a new teacher.
Paula Kurzband Feder, *Where Does the Teacher Live?*, 1979
    Three classmates in an urban school become detectives to find out where their teacher lives.
John Burningham, *John Patrick Norman McHennessey: The Boy Who Was Always Late*, 1987
    John's teacher does not believe his wild stories of why he is always late.
Patricia Reilly Giff, *All About Stacy*, 1988
    Stacy decides what to put in her special "about me" box.

35

Bob Allison

The Kid Who Batted 1000 (New York: Doubleday, 1951)

Age range: Grades 5-6

Subject(s): Sports/Baseball; Humor

Major character(s): Popoff Pendergast, Manager (Sports) (baseball); Dave King, Teenager, Sports Figure (baseball player)

Time period(s): 1950s

Locale(s): United States

What the book is about: Popoff Pendergast is desperate for new players after several of his team members are injured or in a slump. He meets Dave King who wants to show Popoff his chickens and horses, but all Popoff can see is that Dave can hit anything that gets in range of his baseball bat.

Where it's reviewed:
Horn Book, December 1951, page 417
Kirkus Reviews, September 1, 1951, page 485

Other books you might like:
David Halecroft, *Championship Summer*, 1991
    Rivalry between the seventh and eight grade baseball players from Alden Junior High threatens their chance at state tournament.
Suzy Kline, *Orp Goes to the Hoop*, 1991
    All-star pitcher Orp goes out for basketball in seventh grade and finds his skills can transfer to another sport.
Gordon Korman, *The Zuchinni Warriors*, 1988
    Students at McDonald Hall find themselves with a football stadium and a gung-ho fried zucchini stick sponsor.
Mary Rodgers, *Summer Switch*, 1982
    Benjamin and his father suddenly switch roles. Ben is on his way to a conference with the head of Galaxy Films and dad is on his way to summer camp.
Alfred Slote, *Finding Buck McHenry*, 1981
    Jason believes that the school custodian is really Buck McHenry, a famous pitcher from the old Negro league.

36

E.M. Almedingen

Young Mark (New York: Farrar, 1968)

Age range: Grades 6 and Up

Major character(s): Mark Poltoratzky, Teenager, Traveller

Time period(s): 1740s

Locale(s): St. Petersburg, Russia

What the book is about: Mark leaves his home in the Ukraine to journey to St. Petersburg in the 1740s. He encounters peasants, merchants, pilgrims, priests and sorcerers. Sometimes the rescues from danger are more hair-raising than the adventures themselves. Slow starting but worth the effort for mature readers.

Where it's reviewed:
Horn Book, June 1968, page 327
Library Journal, March 15, 1968, page 1317

Awards the book has won:
Boston Globe/Horn Book Award - Honor Book 1968

Other books by the author:
Tomorrow Will Come, 1968
Little Katia, 1967

Other books you might like:
Marie Halun Bloch, *Displaced Person*, 1978
    A fourteen year old Ukranian refugee struggles to survive as a displaced person in Nazi Germany.
Vasil Bykau, *Pack of Wolves*, 1981
    When Levchuk visits a man he has not seen in thiry years, he discovers it is the same person he had saved from a pack of wolves as a baby.
Eric A. Kimmel, *Tartar's Sword*, 1974
    A Ukranian boy in 1623 joins the cossacks in hopes of freeing his people from Polish rule.
Gregory Maguire, *The Dream Stealer*, 1983
    Two children in a small Russian village set out to confront the Blood Prince, who appears in each generation to steal souls.
Elsa Posell, *Homecoming*, 1987
    The six Koshansky children and their mother struggle to survive in a small Ukranian town after the 1917 revolution.

37

Millys N. Altman

Racing in Her Blood (Philadelphia: Lippincott, 1980)

Age range: Grades 6-8

Subject(s): Sports/Auto Racing; Sex Roles

Major character(s): Jane Barton, Twin, Sports Figure (auto racer); John Barton, Parent; Jay Barton, Twin

Time period(s): 1970s

Locale(s): Pittsburgh, Pennsylvania

What the book is about: Jane Barton wants to race; this is her attempt to break into the male dominated world of auto racing. The tension in the pit, the excitement of the track, the thrill of taking the lead are all here as Jane proves that she can race—and win!

Where it's reviewed:
Best Sellers, August 1980, page 191

Center for Children's Books Bulletin, September 1980, page 1
School Library Journal, August 1980, page 73

Other books you might like:
Betty Baker, *The Great Desert Race*, 1980
   Driving a steam powered car, two women compete in the two day Great Mountain to Desert Race at the turn of the century.
Jane Duden, *Shirley Muldowny*, 1988
   Biography of the drag race driver who was the first woman to win the Winston World Championship and the Top Fuel Championship more than once.
James Hahn, *Janet Guthrie: Champion Racer*, 1979
   A biography of the first woman driver to qualify for the annual Indianapolis 500 mile auto race.
Ed Radlauer, *Motorcycle Winners*, 1981
   Nan is prepared to give up motorcycle racing forever until she gets some simple but sound advice from her aunt, a champion drag racer.
Alida M. Thacher, *Fastest Woman on Earth*, 1980
   Traces the death-defying career of Kitty O'Neil, a drag racer, stunt woman, and the holder of land speed records, who has been deaf since childhood.

`38`

Nikki Amdur

Illustrator: Ruth Sanderson

One of Us (New York: Dial, 1981)

Age range: Grades 4-6

Subject(s): Blind; Friendship; Moving, Household

Major character(s): Nora Pritchett, Writer; Walt Pritchett, Parent (Nora's father); Jerry Joralemon, Friend

Time period(s): Indeterminate

Locale(s): United States

What the book is about: When Nora moves to a new town, she learns that making friends takes more than waiting for someone to say hello. She outgrows her tendency to exaggerate while learning quite a bit from a boy who sees very clearly, even though he is blind.

Where it's reviewed:
Children's Book Review Service, March 1982, page 74
Center for Children's Books Bulletin, March 1982, page 121
Hornbook, February 1982, page 39

Other books you might like:
Mabel Esther Allan, *The View Beyond My Father*, 1977
   A fifteen year old discovers that it is her father as well as her blindness that binds her to a narrow world.
Deborah Kent, *Belonging: A Novel*, 1978
   Meg realizes that it's not her blindness that prevents her from joining the "in" crowd, but her own individuality.
Jackie French Koller, *The Last Voyage of the Misty Day*, 1992
   Having reluctantly moved after her father's death, Denise forges a healing friendship with a boat owner surrounded by considerable mystery.
Sharon Bell Mathis, *Listen for the Fig Tree*, 1974
   A black girl's first celebration of Kwanza gives her a sense of the past and strength to deal with her troubled mother and her own blindness.

Todd Strausser, *The Complete Computer Popularity Program*, 1984
   Tony feels he'll never have a social life because his father works for the unpopular nuclear power plant and his only friend is a recluse.

`39`

Mildred Ames

Nicky and the Joyous Noise (New York: Scribner's, 1980)

Age range: Grades 4-6

Subject(s): Music; Abandonment; Artists and Art

Major character(s): Nicky, Child, Musician; Ruby, Grandparent; Eduardo Estrada, Artist

Time period(s): 1980s

Locale(s): California

What the book is about: Eleven year old Nicky is sent to live with his maternal grandmother, whom he has never met. As he explores the neighborhood, he discovers Eduardo Estrada, a neighbor who has erected spires created from found objects. Meanwhile, Nicky has shown a talent for music and Ruby has arranged for him to take piano lessons. Intense relationships develop as Nicky helps Eduardo prove to the city that his structure is safe.

Where it's reviewed:
Kirkus Reviews, August 1, 1980, page 979
School Library Journal, August 1980, page 59

Other books by the author:
Cassandra-Jamie, 1985
Philo Potts, or, The Helping Hand Strikes Again, 1982
Anna to the Infinite Power, 1981
The Dancing Madness, 1980

Other books you might like:
Sandra Fenichel Asher, *Summer Begins*, 1980
   A girl finds her own strength, learns to assert herself, and begins to get along with her very preoccupied mother.
Corinne Gerson, *Son for a Day*, 1980
   Danny uses his charm and ingenuity and ends up with new friendships and a whole collection of substitute parents.
Judy Frank Mearian, *Someone Slightly Different*, 1980
   Marty gradually stops hoping for her long gone father's return as her grandmother teaches her that a loving family need not be a traditional one.
Pamela Sargent, *Watermusic*, 1986
   Playing the flute for a strange creature, discovered by an anthropologist, leads Laura into an adventure that challenges the imagination.
Alison Smith, *Billy Boone*, 1989
   Wanting more than anything to play the trumpet and loving a most unusual grandmother are all that it take to make life difficult for Billy Boone.

`40`

Mildred Ames

Philo Potts, or, The Helping Hand Strikes Again (New York: Macmillan, 1982)

Age range: Grades 4-6

Subject(s): Animals/Dogs; Humor; Mystery and Detective Stories

Major character(s): Philo Potts, Preteen (dognapper); Mopey, Dog; Cristabel, Preteen (dognapper)

Time period(s): 1980s

Locale(s): Los Angeles, California

What the book is about: To teach their neighbor a lesson Philo and Cristabel dognap Mopey, his neglected dog. When Mopey escapes and joins a band of wild strays, Philo and Cristabel have a lot more trouble on their hands than they bargained for.

Where it's reviewed:
Booklist, January 1, 1983, page 607
Center for Children's Books Bulletin, February 1983, page 101
School Library Journal, January 1983, page 69

Other books by the author:
Cassandra-Jamie, 1985
Anna to the Infinite Power, 1981
What Are Friends For?, 1978
Without Hats, Who Can Tell the Good Guys?, 1976

Other books you might like:
Barbara Brenner, *Mystery of the Disappearing Dogs*, 1982
  When their dog is kidnapped, twins Elena and Michael set out to solve the mystery of the dognapper.
Lois Duncan, *Hotel for Dogs*, 1971
  Liz and her brother wind up with nine stray dogs that need homes but must be kept a secret.
Margaret Poynter, *What's One More?*, 1985
  The author's story of her experiences as a pet rescuer, sharing her home with unwanted dogs, nursing ill dogs back to health and finding them homes.
Stephen Roos, *Love Me, Love My Werewolf*, 1991
  Bernie befriends a small stray dog who proves to be invaluable around the house and is a hit at the Pet Lovers Club Halloween party.
Carol Beach York, *Stray Dog*, 1981
  With the help of his brother, sister, and a friend, Frankie, a lonely eleven year old, cares for a stray dog until the unexpected happens.

41

Berthe Amoss

The Mockingbird Song (New York: Harper and Row, 1988)

Age range: Grades 5-6

Subject(s): Stepmothers; Old Age

Major character(s): Lindy, Child

Time period(s): 1980s

Locale(s): New Orleans, Louisiana

What the book is about: 11 year old Lindy moves next door with Miss Ellie when she is unable to accept a new stepmother. She hopes to make her father jealous, but when a new sister is born, she returns home and finds her place in the new family.

Where it's reviewed:
Booklist, April 1, 1988, page 1338
School Library Journal, May 1988, page 94

Awards the book has won:
Simon Award

Other books by the author:
The Chalk Cross, 1976
Secret Lives, 1979

Other books you might like:
Jan Mark, *Trouble Half-Way*, 1986
  Amy is put into close contact with her stepfather when her mother leaves to handle a family emergency.
Betty Bates, *Thatcher Payne-in-the-Neck*, 1985
  After Kib and Thatcher succeed in getting their widowed parents together, they find that being brother and sister is not as easy as they expected.
Andre Norton, *Red Hart Magic*, 1976
  Chris and Nan are having trouble in their blended family until they travel in time to the 17th century and learn to deal with their problems.
Doris Buchanan Smith, *The First Hard Times*, 1983
  12 year old Ancil, whose father was reported MIA in Vietnam, refuses to accept his mother's remarriage.
Zilpha Keatley Snyder, *The Headless Cupid*, 1971
  Difficulties occur in a new stepfamily, when Amanda, as a student of the occult, puts the other children through initiation rites.

42

Berthe Amoss

Secret Lives (New York: Dell, 1979)

Age range: Grades 5-8

Subject(s): Mystery and Detective Stories; Mothers and Daughters

Major character(s): Addie Agnew, Preteen

Time period(s): 1930s (1937)

Locale(s): New Orleans, Louisiana

What the book is about: Twelve year old Addie is living in New Orleans with her two aunts. Addie has been told that her mother died in a Honduran tidal wave seven years before. Addie discovers that her aunts are keeping the truth from her, and through some ingenious sleuthing, uncovers information about her dead mother's past.

Where it's reviewed:
Booklist, November 15, 1979, page 498
Kirkus Reviews, January 15, 1980, page 65
School Library Journal, November 1979, page 72

Other books by the author:
The Mockingbird Song, 1988
The Chalk Cross, 1976

Other books you might like:
R.E. Allen, *Ozzy on the Outside*, 1989
  Ozzy's mother's death affects him in many ways, but an unusual young woman he encounters while running away to New Orleans helps him face life again.
Jackie French Koller, *Nothing to Fear*, 1991

When his father moves away to find work and his mother becomes ill, Danny struggles to help his family during the Great Depression.

Gayle Pearson, *The Coming Home Cafe*, 1988
  Fearing that the Depression will never release its stranglehold on her family, Elizabeth leaves to ride the rails from town to town to look for work.

Pieter Van Raven, *A Time of Troubles*, 1990
  Having crossed the country with his father during the Depression, Roy encounters cruel exploitation by the Grower's Associaation.

Arvella Whitmore, *The Bread Winner*, 1990
  When both her parents are unable to find work during the great Depression, Sarah Ann saves the family by selling her prizewinning bread.

43

Margaret Jean Anderson

Illustrator: Charles Robinson

The Brain on Quartz Mountain (New York: Knopf, 1982)

Age range: Grades 3-5

Subject(s): Sports/Baseball; Scientific Experiments; Science Fiction

Major character(s): Dave Matheson, Preteen

Time period(s): 1980s

Locale(s): Woodgrove, Oregon

What the book is about: At the science research center where his dad is caretaker, Dave is roped into helping a peculiar professor with an experiment, "educating" a chicken brain being grown in a bottle. The job is dull until Dave realizes the brain is smart- very smart! Dave's role in Professor Botti's experiments on the chicken brain helps him compete for a trip to the World Series.

Where it's reviewed:
Booklist, February 1, 1983, page 722
Kirkus Reviews, July 1, 1982, page 733
School Library Journal, December 1982, page 62

Other books by the author:
The Ghost Inside the Monitor, 1990
The Journey of the Shadow Bairns, 1980
Searching for Shona, 1978
In the Circle of Time, 1970

Other books you might like:
Vivien Alcock, *The Monster Garden*, 1988
  Using a tissue sample she believes is from one of her father's experiments in genetic engineering, Frankie accidentally creates a monster of her own.

John Reynolds Gardiner, *The Strange Thing That Happened to Allen Brewster*, 1984
  Despite the disapproval of his parents and his formidable science teacher, Allen determines to do his science project on human photosynthesis.

Dean Hughes, *Nutty Knows All*, 1988
  Nutty Nutsell produces another memorable science fair project when his partner transfers photons of light to Nutty's brain, making his head glow.

John McNamara, *Revenge of the Nerd*, 1984

A genius with a reputation for being a nerd wreaks revenge on his tormentors using his latest science project.

Daniel Manus Pinkwater, *The Hoboken Chicken Emergency*, 1977
  Arthur goes to pick up the turkey for Thanksgiving dinner but comes back with a 260 pound chicken.

44

Margaret Jean Anderson

The Journey of the Shadow Bairns (New York: Knopf, 1980)

Age range: Grades 5-8

Subject(s): Brothers and Sisters; Orphans

Major character(s): Elspeth MacDonald, Orphan, Teenager; Robbie MacDonald, Orphan, Child

Time period(s): 1900s (1903)

Locale(s): At Sea; Canada

What the book is about: When her parents die suddenly leaving only a little money and one way passages from Liverpool, England, to Canada, thirteen year old Elspeth decides to take her four year old brother, Robbie, and make the journey themselves. She knows what their lives as orphans would be like in Scotland - slave-like labor for her and an orphanage for her brother. A journey into the unknown sounds better.

Where it's reviewed:
Hornbook, April 1981, page 187
Kirkus Reviews, January 15, 1981, page 74
School Library Journal, January 1981, page 56

Other books by the author:
The Druid's Gift, 1989
In the Circle of Time, 1979
Searching for Shona, 1978
To Nowhere and Back, 1975

Other books you might like:
Patricia Beatty, *That's One Ornery Orphan*, 1980
  Three unsuccessful adoption placements for a thirteen year old girl in 19th century Texas force her to face the placement she has tried hard to avoid.

Deborah Kestel, *Kidnapped*, 1992
  A sixteen year old orphan is kidnapped by his villainous uncle, later escapes, and becomes involved in the struggle of Scotland against English rule.

Janet Louise Lunn, *The Root Cellar*, 1985
  Twelve year old orphan, Rose, living with relatives on a Canadian farm, goes into the root cellar and befriends farm occupants who lived a century ago

L.M. Montgomery, *The Story Girl*, 1989
  A fourteen year old orphan spins irresistible tales for both young and old in the town of Carlisle on Prince Edward Island.

Joan Lowery Nixon, *The Specter*, 1982
  An orphan with Hodgkin's disease gets involved with her new hospital roommate, a nine year old girl who says her father's killer wants to kill her.

45

Mary Anderson

The Leipzig Vampire (New York: Dell, 1987)

Age range: Grades 5-7

Subject(s): Extrasensory Perception; Magicians; Twins

Major character(s): Amy Ferguson, Twin, Detective; Jamie Ferguson, Twin, Detective; Gustav Manheim, Scientist

Time period(s): 1980s

Locale(s): Monroe

What the book is about: Twins Amy and Jamie Ferguson have complementary abilities which serve them well as detectives. Jamie is brilliant and logical, while Amy is psychic and can see things others can't, though she hides this gift from everyone but Jamie. When she discovers she can communicate with the spirit of a Revolutionary War officer, things become exciting. When a German scientist comes to town to do research, Jamie and Amy decide to investigate him.

Where it's reviewed:
Booklist, March 1, 1988
School Library Journal, March 1988, page 186

Other books by the author:
The Curse of the Demon, 1989
The Hairy Beast in the Woods, 1989
Terror under the Tent, 1987
The Three Spirits of Vandermeer Manor, 1987

Other books you might like:
Richie Tankersley Cusick, *Vampire*, 1991
   The Dungeon of Horrors is Darcy's summer home. But the fun turns to terror when real bodies are found with the mark of the vampire on their throats.
Les Martin, *The Vampire*, 1989
   A young Englishman traveling on the Continent with the mysterious Lord Rutven comes to realize that his companion is an evil and murderous vampire.
Meredith Ann Pierce, *The Dark-Angel*, 1982
   The servant girl Aeriel must choose either to destroy her vampire master for his evil deeds or save him beccause of his beauty and potential greatness
Angela Sommer-Bodenburg, *My Friend, the Vampire*, 1986
   A horror story fan, Tony Noodleman's life becomes more thrilling than any book he's read when he befriends a couple of vampires named Rudolph and Anna
Tad Williams, *Child of an Ancient City*, 1992
   To entertain his dinner guests, Masrur, a Muslim soldier, tells of a vampire he met on an ill-fated trip through the Caucasas Mountains years before.

46

Mary Anderson

Step on a Crack (New York: Atheneum, 1978)

Age range: Grades 6-9

Subject(s): Child Abuse; Dreams and Nightmares

Major character(s): Sarah, Abuse Victim; Josie, Friend; Katrin, Relative (aunt)

Time period(s): 1970s

Locale(s): United States

What the book is about: Sarah and Josie set out to discover why Sarah has recurrent nightmares about killing her mother, then goes shoplifing. They also notice that when her mother's sister, Katrin, comes to visit, Sarah walks in her sleep.

Where it's reviewed:
Booklist, April 1, 1978, page 1247
Horn Book, June 1978, page 282

Other books by the author:
The Curse of the Demon, 1989
Catch Me, I'm Falling in Love, 1985
The Rise and Fall of a Teenage Wacko, 1980
Matilda's Masterpiece, 1978

Other books you might like:
Clare Bell, *Ratha and Thistle-Chaser*, 1990
   Newt, a crippled, solitary cat living with tusked creatures at the seashore, must face her terrifying past when Ratha's scout Thakur arrives.
Betsy Byars, *Cracker Jackson*, 1985
   After attempting to save his ex-babysitter from wife abuse, Cracker Jackson gains an adult insight into the sadness of failed heroics.
Jesse Harris, *Aidan's Fate*, 1992
   McKenzie's violent psychic visions expose a case of child abuse and spell doom for her boyfriend, Aidan.
Tormod Haugen, *The Night Birds*, 1982
   Jake struggles to come to grips with terrors real and imagined including his father's bouts of depression and his own nightmares.
Willo Davis Roberts, *Don't Hurt Laurie!*, 1977
   Laurie is physically abused by her mother; can she escape, and will anyone believe her story?

47

Jean F. Andrews

The Flying Fingers Club (Washington, DC: Gallaudet, 1988)

Age range: Grades 3-5

Subject(s): Deafness; Friendship; Learning Disabilities

Major character(s): Donald Dunbar, Child; Matt Morrissey, Handicapped (deaf); Susan Dunbar, Newspaper Carrier

Time period(s): 1980s

Locale(s): Kentucky

What the book is about: Nine year old Donald enters a new school and feels really lonely until he meets Matt, a deaf student, and his interpreter, on the bus the first day of school. They become friends and when Donald's sister, Susan, notices papers disappearing from her paper route, Donald, Matt, and Donald's friend Jackie, take on the mystery and the adventure begins.

Where it's reviewed:
Booklist, February 15, 1989, page 1007
Center for Children's Books Bulletin, February 1989, page 141
Small Press, June 1989, page 42

Other books by the author:
The Secret in the Dorm Attic, 1990

Other books you might like:
Sheila R. Cole, *Meaning Well*, 1974

A sixth grader learns the meaning of friendship too late to help a deaf classmate who desperately needs a friend.
Emily Hanlon, *The Swing*, 1979
   A deaf girl and a boy with family problems seek refuge at a swing which has come to have a special meaning for each of them.
Elisabeth MacIntyre, *The Purple Mouse*, 1975
   A girl with a hearing problem learns that her struggle to overcome her handicap has made her a stronger and happier person.
Elizabeth Rider Montgomery, *The Mystery of the Boy Next Door*, 1978
   Neighborhood children think the new boy is mean until he leads them on a mysterious puzzle-solving hunt. (Related picture book)
Penny Pollock, *Keeping It Secret*, 1982
   Sixth grader Wisconsin has difficulty adjusting to a new school in a new town where she is reluctant to admit that she wears a hearing aid.

48

Judie Angell

Dear Lola: Or, How to Build Your Own Family (Scarsdale, New York: Bradbury, 1980)

Age range: Grades 3-6

Subject(s): Orphans; Runaways

Major character(s): Arthur ''Lola'' Beniker, Teenager; Annie Beniker, Child

Time period(s): 1980s

Locale(s): United States

What the book is about: Six residents of St. Theresa's orphanage consider themselves a family and leave the orphanage rather than risk being split up. Arthur, 17, writes an advice column under the name Lola, so he can support the family wherever they go. When they settle in Sweet River, the children have trouble in school and townspeople get curious about Arthur's volume of mail. Their cover is blown, and as they move on, they learn to keep a lower profile.

Where it's reviewed:
Horn Book, February 1981, page 48
School Library Journal, January 1981, page 56

Other books by the author:
Don't Rent My Room, 1990
Home Is to Share.and Share.and Share, 1984
What's Best For You, 1981
In Summertime, It's Tuffy, 1977

Other books you might like:
Ann Sharpless Bond, *Adam and Noah and the Cops*, 1983
   Adam and Noah become involved with a stolen boat, drug smugglers, and a runaway horse.
Julia Cunningham, *Come to the Edge*, 1977
   After he is befriended by a sign painter, a confused runaway finds trust and a purpose for living.
Sid Fleischman, *The Midnight Horse*, 1990
   Touch enlists the help of a ghostly magician to stay out of the orphan house.
Alison Morgan, *Paul's Kite*, 1981

Ignored by his runaway mother, Paul amuses himself by visiting all the London place names on his Monopoly board, until a violent accident interferes.
Barbara Hobbs Withey, *The Serpent Ring*, 1988
   Eleven year old orphan Jenny Nash goes to Boston to live with a woman who is either a witch or a gypsy.

49

Judie Angell

In Summertime, It's Tuffy (Scarsdale, New York: Bradbury, 1977)

Age range: Grades 6 and Up

Subject(s): Camps and Camping

Major character(s): Tuffy, Preteen

Time period(s): 1970s

Locale(s): United States

What the book is about: Eleven year old Tuffy and her friends make a voodoo doll at summer camp and use it to put a spell on the head counselor.

Where it's reviewed:
Kirkus Reviews, May 1, 1977, page 485
School Library Journal, May 1977, page 58

Awards the book has won:
Ethical Culture School Book Award 1977

Other books by the author:
Home Is to Share.and Share.and Share, 1984
What's Best for You, 1981
Dear Lola: Or, How to Build Your Own Family, 1980
Secret Selves, 1979

Other books you might like:
Steven Kroll, *Breaking Camp*, 1985
   A high school junior at a summer camp for boys comes to realize some of the pranks are in fact vicious attacks on the ''weker'' boys.
Robert Lipsyte, *Summer Rules*, 1992
   A teenage boy has to deal with an unwanted summer camp job, his first love, and some crucial decisions.
Jahnna N. Malcolm, *Camp Clodhopper*, 1990
   Zan, Mary, Rocky and Gwen go to camp to become better ballerinas, only to find the teacher doesn't know ballet and their enemies are at a nearby camp.
Kate McMullan, *Great Advice From Lila Fenwick*, 1988
   Lila and her friend spend two weeks at a Boy Scout camp, where Lila's father is a camp doctor, having a wonderful time learning about boys and nature.
Joel L. Schwartz, *Upchuck Summer's Revenge*, 1990
   At camp, Richie tries to teach a group of ten year olds to play football, seeks avoid the bumbling Chuck, and plots revenge against obnoxious Jerry.

50

Judie Angell

Secret Selves (Scarsdale, NY: Bradbury, 1979)

Age range: Grades 6 and Up

Subject(s): Dating (Social Customs); Grandparents

Major character(s): Julie Ann Novick, Teenager; Rusty Parmette, Teenager

Time period(s): 1970s

Locale(s): United States

What the book is about: Julie calls Rusty, a boy she has a crush on and asks for "Wendell Farnum." She calls herself Barbara. Not wanting to be outdone by his brothers with girlfriends, Rusty goes along and pretends to be Wendell.

Where it's reviewed:
Center for Children's Books Bulletin, January 1980, page 86
Horn Book, February, 1980, page 52

Other books by the author:
Home Is to Share.and Share.and Share, 1984
Dear Lola: Or, How to Build Your Own Family, 1980
A Word From Our Sponsor: Or, My Friend Alfred, 1979
In Summertime, It's Tuffy, 1977

Other books you might like:
Bruce Clements, *Tom Loves Anna Loves Tom*, 1990
   From the first moment Tom sees Anna, he knows he loves her, although she is cautious at first, they develop a very special relationship.
Caroline B. Cooney, *The Girl Who Invented Romance*, 1988
   While waiting for her first big romance and observing the rocky love affairs of her parents and brother, Kelly invents a board game.
Lynn Hall, *Fair Maiden*, 1990
   Working at the Renaissance Fair, Jennifer finds her first love and an escape from the family problems at home.
Robert Lipsyte, *Summer Rules*, 1992
   A teenage boy has to deal with an unwanted camp job, his first love, and some critical decisions.
Susan Wojciechowski, *And the Other Gold*, 1987
   Patty becomes involved in many activities as she learns about the importance of friendship and the thrill of first love.

51

Judie Angell

A Word From Our Sponsor: Or, My Friend Alfred
(Scarsdale, New York: Bradbury, 1979)

Age range: Grades 4-6

Subject(s): Family Life; Humor

Major character(s): Alfred Caro, Scientist, Preteen (gifted child); Rudy, Friend; Gillian Tenser, Friend

Time period(s): 1970s

Locale(s): New York, New York (Manhattan)

What the book is about: When twelve year old Alfred tries to protect consumers from a drinking mug covered with a glaze containing dangerous amounts of lead, he discovers he must challenge his father's advertising agency. With his friends Rudy and Gillian, Alfred leads a consumer rebellion and takes his case to national television.

Where it's reviewed:
Children's Book Review Service, April 1979, page 86
Center for Children's Books Bulletin, April 1979, page 129
Kirkus Reviews, May 15, 1979, page 575

Awards the book has won:
Ethical Culture School Book Award 1979

Other books by the author:
Home Is to Share and Share and Share, 1984
Dear Lola: Or, How to Build Your Own Family, 1980
Secret Selves, 1979
Tina Gogo, 1978

Other books you might like:
Gordon R. Dickson, *Gremlins, Go Home!*, 1974
   Gremlins stranded on Earth centuries ago hit on a scheme to hitch a ride back to their own planet.
Susan Dudley Gold, *Toxic Waste*, 1990
   The causes and effects of chemical waste pollution, efforts to correct the problem, and how to get involved. (Non-fiction)
Clifford B. Hicks, *Alvin Fernald, Superweasel*, 1974
   Alvin's pollution project is geared to expose the biggest polluter in town, the owner of the chemical plant.
Caroline Stevermer, *River Rats*, 1992
   Twenty years after the holocaust called the Flash has destroyed civilization, orphans face danger as they steer a steamboat over toxic waters.
Judith Weber, *Lights, Camera, Cats!*, 1978
   A twelve year old girl auditions five cats for a TV commercial advertising a cat food brand that is her father's company's top rival.

52

Cora Annett

How the Witch Got Alf (New York: Watts, 1975)

Age range: Grades 3-4

Subject(s): Animals/Donkeys

Major character(s): Alf, Donkey

Time period(s): Indeterminate

Locale(s): Earth

What the book is about: Alf, the donkey, notices the attention the dog, cat and canary get from the Old Man and Old Woman. He tries to imitate them. He sings, tries to curl up in Old Woman's lap, and jumps on Old Man to lick his face. Discouraged at the responses he gets, Alf runs away and hides on the roof. The noise convinces the family a witch is about and the fun begins.

Where it's reviewed:
Booklist, April 15, 1975, page 864
School Library Journal, March 1975, page 84

Other books by the author:
When the Porcupine Moved In, 1971
Cora Annett's Homerhenry, 1970
The Dog Who Thought He Was a Boy, 1965

Other books you might like:
Andrew Davies, *Marmalade and Rufus*, 1983
   The adventures of a naughty girl and her talking donkey.
John Fante, *Bravo, Burro!*, 1970
   Manuel refuses to be parted from the burro he rescued from a cougar.
Wilma Pitchford Hays, *The Burro That Ran Away*, 1969
   A boy tracks down a runaway burro after it mysteriously escapes from the corral.
Scott O'Dell, *The Treasure of Topo-El-Bampo*, 1972
   Two burros sold to the slave-driving owners of a silver mine return to save the village from starvation.

Joanne Oppenheim, *The Donkey's Tale*, 1991
   Rhymed retelling of the fable about the man on his way to market who tries to take everyone's advice about what to do with his donkey.

53

William Arden

Alfred Hitchcock and the Three Investigators in the Secret of Shark Reef (New York: Random, 1979)

Age range: Grades 4-8

Subject(s): Hurricanes; Animals/Sharks

Major character(s): Pete Crenshaw, Detective; Bob Andrews, Detective; Jupiter Jones, Detective

Time period(s): 1970s

Locale(s): Rocky Beach, California

What the book is about: Pete, Bob and Jupiter, three young teens known as the Three Investigators, cope with an oil drilling rig, a hurricane, and frightening sharks.

Where it's reviewed:
Booklist, January 15, 1980, page 716
School Library Journal, February 1980, page 51

Other books by the author:
Mystery of Wreckers' Rock, 1986
Mystery of the Smashing Glass, 1984
Mystery of the Headless Shore, 1977
Secret of Phantom Lake, 1973

Other books you might like:
Robert Arthur, *Alfred Hitchcock and the Three Investigators in the Secret of Terror Castle*, 1964
   Peter, Bob and Jupiter are involved in a mystery in a castle with more fright than they bargained for.
Nancy Hale, *The Night of the Hurricane*, 1978
   A boy, his friends, and their parents discover many things about themselves and each other during a hurricane on the Massachusetts coast.
Marian Rumsey, *Carolina Hurricane*, 1977
   Lost on a crab boat in the middle of a South Carolina salt marsh, Morgan endures the full blast of a hurricane.
Andrew Salkey, *Hurricane*, 1979
   Joe and his sister face their first hurricane in Kingston, Jamaica, with a mixture of excitement and curiosity that gradually turns to fear.
Bryce Walton, *Hurricane Reef*, 1970
   A teen who has always wanted to be a marine scientist discovers in the Floria Keys the challenge of the profession he has chosen.

54

Edward Ardizzone

Ship's Cook Ginger (New York: Macmillan, 1978)

Age range: Grades 2-3

Subject(s): Sea Stories

Major character(s): Tim, Child; Ginger, Child

Time period(s): Indeterminate Past

Locale(s): At Sea

What the book is about: Tim and his friend, Ginger, are allowed to stay on board Captain McFee's ship when Tim's parents are called away. Tim handles the wheel in an emergency and Ginger pinch-hits as cook. Raspberry-sardine sandwiches are the order of the day.

Where it's reviewed:
Booklist, October 1, 1978, page 287
Kirkus Reviews, August 15, 1978, page 875

Other books by the author:
Tim to the Lighthouse, 1968
Diana and Her Rhinoceros, 1964
Peter the Wanderer, 1964
Johnny the Clockmaker, 1960

Other books you might like:
Jan Adkins, *Luther Tarbox*, 1977
   A lobsterman out in his boat in a heavy fog is approached by sailors, on varying sizes of boats and ships, seeking guidance into port.
Michael Foreman, *The Boy Who Sailed with Columbus*, 1991
   Leif, the ship's boy for Columbus, is captured by warring natives, marries an Indian woman and becomes a shaman.
Janet Greeson, *An American Army of Two*, 1992
   During the War of 1812 Rebecca and Abigail Bates save their town's ships from the British by simulating the approach of American troops.
Evelyn Wilde Mayerson, *The Cat Who Escaped from Steerage*, 1990
   Living in the steerage section of a steamship bound for America, Chanah tries to keep her newly found cat a secret.
Eve Titus, *Mr. Shaw's Shipshape Shoeshop*, 1970
   An old shoemaker who loved shoes and ships never dreamed he would one day be able to combine both loves by moving his Shipshape Shoeshop to a ship.

55

Alan Arkin

Illustrator: Joan Sandin

The Lemming Condition (New York: Harper, 1976)

Age range: Grades 4-7

Subject(s): Allegories; Behavior

Major character(s): Bubber, Lemming; The Crow, Crow

Time period(s): Indeterminate

Locale(s): Earth

What the book is about: Bubber opposes the mass suicide of his coampanions in this allegory which speaks to the lemming condition in all of us. He observes, after the desolation left by the rush to the sea, that the young lemmings are emerging, and that they are the future. Great for study of allegory and discussion of behavior patterns.

Where it's reviewed:
Booklist, April 15, 1976, page 1182
Hornbook, August 1976, page 394
Kirkus Reviews, April 1, 1976, page 389

Other books by the author:
The Clearing, 1986 (Sequel to "The Lemming Condition")

Other books you might like:
Eve Bunting, *Terrible Things: An Allegory of the Holocaust,* 1989
    The animals of the forest are carried away, one species after another, by the Terrible Things.
Larry Leonary, *Far Walker,* 1988
    Cast out by his fellow lemmings because he is so different, David embarks on a journey to find out why he was born and how he can be accepted.
Sidney B. Simon, *I am Loveable and Capable: A Modern Allegory on the Classical Putdown,* 1973
    The events of Randy's day demonstrate the human need to understand and care about others.
Jeanne Steig, *Consider the Lemming,* 1988
    Humorous poetry about lemmings and many other animals.
Kit Williams, *Book Without a Title,* 1984
    The reader may discover the real title of this allegory of seasons interwoven with the activities of a beekeeper, from clues hidden in the pages.

56

Laura Adams Armer, Author/Illustrator

Waterless Mountain (New York: Longmans, 1931)

Age range: Grades 4-6

Subject(s): Indians of North America

Major character(s): Younger Brother, Indian (Navajo); Baby Sister, Indian (Navajo); Elder Brother, Indian (Navajo)

Time period(s): 1920s

Locale(s): Arizona

What the book is about: Younger Brother, a Navajo Indian boy, learns about his own heritage and the beauty of nature, and is in training with his uncle for the office of Medicine Priest.

Where it's reviewed:
Books, September 6, 1931, page 6
New York Times, Octobet 18, 1931, page 19

Awards the book has won:
Newbery Medal 1932

Other books by the author:
In Navajo Land, 1962
Trader's Children, 1937

Other books you might like:
Grace Johnson Penney, *Moki,* 1960
    The story of a young Cheyenne girl who finds her own kind of courage in an unexpected way.
Margaret Kahn Garraway, *Old Hogan,* 1991
    Members of a Navajo family are excited about moving into a new home, but it saddens the hogan they are leaving behind. Related Picture Book
A.E. Cannon, *The Shadow Brothers,* 1990
    Marcus and his Navajo foster brother explore their different heritages.
George Arthur Bruce, *Some People Are Indians,* 1974
    Twelve stories reflecting the culture and conflicts of present day Navajo Indians.
Betty Biesterveld, *Six Days From Sunday,* 1973
    A Navajo boy faces the frightening prospect of going away to school.

57

William Armstrong

Illustrator: James Barkley

Sounder (New York: Harper & Row, 1969)

Age range: Grades 4-6

Subject(s): African Americans; Animals/Dogs; Poverty

Major character(s): Sounder, Dog

Time period(s): 1960s

Locale(s): Georgia

What the book is about: A young boy becomes the man of the family after his father is arrested for stealing food. The boy searches for his father who was sentenced to a chain gang and his dog, Sounder, who was shot during the arrest. In the search for his father, the boy meets a teacher and realizes his long time dream of learning to read.

Where it's reviewed:
Horn Book, December 1969, page 673
School Library Journal, December 1969, page 56

Awards the book has won:
Newbery Medal 1970

Other books by the author:
The Tale of Tawny and Dingo, 1979
The MacLeod Place, 1972
The Sour Land, 1971

Other books you might like:
Eloise Greenfield, *Talk about a Family,* 1978
    Genny counts on the return of her brother, Larry, to mend their parents' ailing marriage.
Joyce Hansen, *The Gift-Giver,* 1980
    10 year old Doris and her friend, Amir, help a friend become captain of the baseball team.
Betty Miles, *Sink or Swim,* 1986
    B.J., an 11 year old from New York City spends two weeks with the Roberts family in rural New Hampshire.
Langston Hughes, *Dream Keeper and Other Poems,* 1932
    Lyric poems reflecting a wide variety of the experience of Black Americans.

58

Frank Asch, Author/Illustrator

Pearl's Pirates (New York: Delacorte, 1987)

Age range: Grades 3-5

Subject(s): Adventure and Adventurers; Animals/Mice; Sailing

Major character(s): Pearl, Mouse; Wilbur, Mouse; Old Bill, Sailor

Time period(s): Indeterminate

Locale(s): At Sea

What the book is about: Pearl and Wilbur, two mice, get trapped in a crate and are headed for France on an ocean liner. If only they can launch the captain's model pirate ship they might get back to Jay who is in the hospital after a bicycle accident with a hit and run driver.

Where it's reviewed:
Booklist, June 1, 1978, page 1518

Center for Children's Books Bulletin, page 202
Kirkus Reviews, May 15, 1987, page 790

Other books by the author:
Journey to Terezor, 1989
Pearl's Surprise, 1984
Pearl's Promise, 1984
I Met a Pilgrim, 1972

Other books you might like:
Allan Baillie, *Adrift*, 1992
     While playing pirates with his little sister and her cat in an old crate on the beach, a young boy finds they are adrift at sea and he must save them.
Michael Bond, *Thursday Rides Again*, 1968
     The quiet country vacation of Thursday, the mouse, and his adopted family, is interrupted when they are kidnapped by a gang and taken to France.
John S. Goodall, *Jacko*, 1971
     After escaping his organ-grinder master, Jacko, a monkey, embarks on a perilous journey on a sailing ship.
Marietta D. Moskin, *Adam and the Wishing Charm*, 1977
     Caught up in the drama of ships and the sea, Adam must choose between his dream of being a sailor or returning to his responsibilities at home.
Doris Buchanan Smith, *Voyages: A Novel*, 1989
     While immobilized in a hospital bed, Janessa journeys into a world of dreamlike adventures with the gods of Norse legend.

59

Sandy Asher

Daughters of the Law (New York: Beaufort, 1980)

Age range: Grades 5-6

Subject(s): Jews; Mothers and Daughters; Identity

Major character(s): Denise Riley, Preteen; Ruthie Morgenstern, Preteen; Rabbi Davis, Religious

Time period(s): 1970s

Locale(s): United States

What the book is about: At twelve, Denise is idealistic and set on helping others. She gets more than she bargained for when she meets Ruthie. Ruthie's ambivalence about her upcoming Bat Mitzvah is only a reflection of the conflict in her family as a result of the Holocaust.

Where it's reviewed:
Center for Children's Books Bulletin, February 1981, p 106
School Library Journal, November 1980, page 81

Other books by the author:
Teddy Teabury's Fabulous Fact, 1985
Missing Pieces, 1984
Just Like Jenny, 1982
Summer Begins, 1980

Other books you might like:
Martha Derman, *The Friendstone*, 1981
     Eleven year old Sally's view of life expands when she becomes friends with a Jewish girl in the summer of 1929.
Marilyn Gould, *The Twelfth of June*, 1986
     Twelve year old Janis copes with her cerebral palsy and her changing feelings for her good friend, Barney, as he approaches his Bar Mitzvah.

Stephen Kaufman, *Does Anyone Here Know the Way to Thirteen?*, 1985
     Despite the trials and tribulations that fill the eight months preceding his dreaded Bar Mitzvah, Myron learns much about what it means to be Jewish.
Norma Klein, *Snapshots*, 1984
     The lives of Sean, preparing for his Bar Mitzvah, and his friend, Marc are disrupted when the boys' interest in photography gets them in trouble.
Gary Provost, *Good If It Goes*, 1984
     Twelve year old David, juggling demands of basketball competition and Bar Mitzvah, strives to please Kelly, his dream girl, as well as his family.

60

Sandy Asher

Illustrator: Cat B. Smith

Princess Bee and the Royal Goodnight Story
(Chicago: Whitman, 1990)

Age range: Grades 2-3

Subject(s): Princes and Princesses; Mothers and Daughters

Major character(s): Bee, Royalty (princess)

Time period(s): Indeterminate Past

Locale(s): Fictional Country

What the book is about: When her mother is gone, Princess Bee tests out the bedtime storytelling of the rest of the family. She ultimately must rely on herself and the memories of her mother to help her fall asleep.

Where it's reviewed:
Booklist, February 1, 1990, page 1084
School Library Journal, March 1990, page 184

Other books by the author:
Wild Words!, 1989
Teddy Teabury's Fabulous Fact, 1985

Other books you might like:
Lloyd Alexander, *The Town Cats*, 1977
     Eight stories of princesses, fiddlers, cobblers and kings.
Helme Heine, *Prince Bear*, 1989
     In the old days, any bear could become a prince and any princess could become a bear.
Tanith Lee, *Princess Hynchatti and Some Other Surprises*, 1973
     Twelve original fairy tales of young royals, wizards, fairy godmothers and dragons.
Marguerita Rudolph, *The Good Stepmother*, 1992
     Princess Elena persuades her father to let her choose the new queen.
Elizabeth Coatsworth, *The Snow Parlor*, 1971
     The snow parlor, the other side of the hill, the toymaker's housekeeper and the journey are all bedtime stories for the early reader.

61

Isaac Asimov

Fantastic Voyage (Boston: Houghton Mifflin, 1966)

Age range: Grades 6 and Up

Subject(s): Technothriller; Science Fiction

Major character(s): Alan Carter, Military Personnel (General); Donald Reid, Military Personnel (Colonel); Peter Lawrence Duval, Doctor

Time period(s): 1960s

Locale(s): United States

What the book is about: A team of five people enter a submarine and then are shrunk to microscopic size and injected into a man's carotid artery to try to save his life. They must fight giant antibodies and face all kinds of dangers to get to a blood clot and destroy it with a laser gun. The fate of the world depends on their mission.

Where it's reviewed:
Booklist, November 15, 1966, page 364
Hornbook, October 1966, page 587
Kirkus, January 15, 1966, page 86

Other books by the author:
All the Troubles of the World, 1989
Atlantis, 1987
Banquets of the Black Widowers, 1984
Dragon Tales, 1982

Other books you might like:
Janet Asimov, *Mind Transfer*, 1988
    Adam's experiences with mind transfer, a human space colony, and a robot world test the validity of humanity's growth through artificial intelligence.
Peter Dickinson, *Eva*, 1989
    After a terrible accident a girl wakes to discover she is in the body of a chimpanzee.
Pamela F. Service, *Stinker From Space*, 1988
    An agent of the Sylon Confederacy crashes on Earth and transfers his mind to the body of a skunk. He gets two children to help him find a way home.
Robert Silverberg, *Letters From Atlantis*, 1990
    While his body remains in a deep sleep, Roy transfers his mind into the body of a royal prince living in Atlantis 180 centuries ago.
H.G. Wells, *The Time Machine and the Invisible Man*, 1969
    Two classic themes of science fiction in stories from H.G. Wells, traveling in time and becoming invisible. An unabridged volume.

62

Janet Asimov

Norby, the Mixed-Up Robot (New York: Walker, 1984)

Age range: Grades 3-6

Subject(s): Computers; Robots; Science Fiction

Major character(s): Jefferson "Jeff" Wells, Teenager, Student (cadet); Norby, Robot; Ing The Ingrate, Villain

Time period(s): Indeterminate Future

Locale(s): Fictional Country (Manhattan International Territory)

What the book is about: When Jeff inadvertently taps into the master computer at the Space Academy, he sets off a series of chaotic mishaps that nearly get him expelled. Norby is a second hand robot with unusual abilities. Together they get

involved in the sinister plans of Ing the Ingrate, who intends to take over the Solar System.

Where it's reviewed:
Booklist, September 15, 1983, page 162
School Library Journal, December 1983, page 63

Other books by the author:
Norby Finds a Villain, 1987
Norby and the Queen's Necklace, 1986
Norby and the Invaders, 1985
Norby and the Lost Princess, 1985

Other books you might like:
John Bellairs, *The Eyes of the Killer Robot*, 1986
    Johnny Dixon is put in jeopardy when he and Professor Childermass try to find a robot made many years ago by an evil wizard.
Lillian Hoban, *The Laziest Robot in Zone One*, 1983
    Sol-1 helps all his friends with their work in the process of avoiding his own.
Alison Prince, *The Type One Super Robot*, 1986
    While spending the summer together, a boy and his uncle acquire a household robot with a mind of its own.
Alfred Slote, *The Trouble on Janus*, 1985
    Jack and his robot buddy, Danny One, set off for the planet Janus to rescue the young King Paul from his conniving uncle.
Marilyn Wilkes, *C.L.U.T.Z. and the Fizzion Formula*, 1985
    Rodney, his guardian robot, and his dog, are taken for industrial spies when they wander into a soda factory where a secret product is being made.

63

Janet Asimov

Illustrator: John Gampert

The Package in Hyperspace (New York: Walker, 1988)

Age range: Grades 4-7

Subject(s): Science Fiction; Space Travel

Major character(s): Ginnela "Ginn" Wayd, Preteen; Pete Wade, Child; Lof, Animal (pet Loffo), Alien

Time period(s): Indeterminate Future

Locale(s): Merkina, Planet—Imaginary; Outer Space

What the book is about: Grinnela and Pete find themselves trapped on a disabled spaceship and must figure out how to survive and how to get the ship out of hyperspace and return home.

Where it's reviewed:
Kirkus Reviews, September 1, 1988, page 1318
School Library Journal, November 1988, page 110

Other books by the author:
Norby and the Court Jester, 1991
Mind Transfer, 1988
Norby, the Mixed-Up Robot, 1983

Other books you might like:
Grace Chetwin, *Collidescope*, 1990
    When his spaceship crashes to earth, a highly advanced alien interferes with the lives of two teenagers living in different centuries.
Bruce Coville, *My Teacher Glows in the Dark*, 1991

When Peter discovers that his newest teacher glows in the dark, he's flying away from earth in a spaceship full of aliens and there's no one to help.

Louise Lawrence, *Moonwind*, 1986
A winner of a trip to earth's first lunar base falls in love with an E.T. who has been stranded on the moon for eons and wants to go home.

Alfred Slote, *C.O.L.A.R.: A Tale of Outer Space*, 1981
Stranded on an unknown planet when their spaceship runs out of fuel, the Jameson family must rely on their robot to save their lives.

Jane Werner Watson, *The Case of the Vanishing Spaceship*, 1982
Rick accompanies his father to Alaska to investigate mysterious electronic signals which may be coming from a UFO that has been seen in the area.

64

Co-Author: Richard Atwater, Florence Atwater

Illustrator: Robert Lawson

Mr. Popper's Penguins (Boston: Little, Brown and Company, 1938)

Age range: Grades 3-4

Subject(s): Animals/Birds

Major character(s): Mr. Popper, Maintenance Worker (house painter); Mrs. Popper, Housewife; Captain Cook, Penguin

Time period(s): 1930s

Locale(s): Stillwater

What the book is about: As a result of a letter to Admiral Drake, Mr. Popper receives a penguin whom he names Captain Cook. "Greta" comes to cheer up Captain Cook when he becomes lonely and soon, the Poppers have twelve penguins. They learn to perform and become world famous, but is fame the best thing for them?

Where it's reviewed:
Horn Book, December 1938, page 367

Awards the book has won:
Newbery Honor 1939
Lewis Carroll Shelf 1958

Other books you might like:
Mary Elise Monsell, *The Mysterious Cases of Mr. Pin*, 1989
Mr. Pin, a rockhopper penguin, leaves his home at the South Pole to be a detective in Chicago.

Mary Elise Monsell, *Mr. Pin: The Chocolate Files*, 1990
Mr. Pin, a rockhopper penguin and a detective in Chicago, investigates two cases involving chocolate.

Molly Cone, *Mishmash*, 1962
Pete's dog Mish walks into people's houses uninvited, jumps into cars for a free ride and sleeps in Pete's bed while Pete wakes up on the floor.

Scott Corbett, *The Hairy Horror Trick*, 1969
Two boys playing with a chemistry set mix a potion that puts hair on their own faces and makes the dog hairless.

Mary Q. Steele, *First of the Penguins*, 1973
Freaky things happen when George and Jim decide to find the first of all the penguins. More challenging reading.

65

Mary Jane Auch

Glass Slippers Give You Blisters (New York: Holiday House, 1989)

Age range: Grades 5-6

Subject(s): Theater; Grandparents

Major character(s): Kelly MacDonald, Preteen, Student (jr. high); Lisa, Preteen, Student (jr. high); Rebecca, Preteen, Student (jr. high)

Time period(s): 1980s

Locale(s): United States

What the book is about: Kelly hopes to get involved in junior high by being the star of the Cinderella play they are producing. Her daydreams do not always work out the way she would hope.

Where it's reviewed:
Horn Book, March/April 1989, page 207
School Library Journal, February 1989, page 80

Other books by the author:
Kidnapping Kevin Kowalski, 1990
Angel and Me and the Bayside Bombers, 1989
Mom Is Dating Weird Wayne, 1988
Cry Uncle, 1987

Other books you might like:
Mabel Esther Allan, *We Danced in Bloomsbury Square*, 1970
Twin sisters face a possible separation when they discover only one scholarship is available at the London ballet school where both want to study.

Nancy Baron, *Tuesday's Child*, 1984
Although Grace intends to become the first woman in baseball's big league, her mother insists she take ballet lessons instead.

Leona Harris, *Yvette*, 1970
Tiny Yvette, an eight year old chosen for the ballet class of the Paris Opera, worries about her size.

Pamela Jane, *Noelle of the Nutcracker*, 1986
At Christmas time, a beautiful ballerina doll who longs to dance is discovered in a toy store and coveted by two little girls, Ilyana and Mary Jane.

Cathy Ogren-Stefanec, *Sly, P.I.: The Case of the Missing Shoes*, 1989
When ballet star Lotta Oink's shoes disappear on opening night, self-made fox and old friend, Sly, P.I., solves the case.

66

Mary Jane Auch

Glass Slippers Give You Blisters (New York: Holiday House, 1989)

Age range: Grades 5-6

Subject(s): Grandparents; Theater; Artists and Art

Major character(s): Kelly, Child

Time period(s): 1980s

Locale(s): United States

What the book is about: Kelly sets her sights on starring in the play "Cinderella" at the beginning of junior high. A fast-paced story about daydreams which sometimes work out and sometimes do not.

Where it's reviewed:
Booklist, March 15, 1989
Horn Book, March 1989, page 207
School Library Journal, February 1989, page 80

Other books by the author:
Cry Uncle, 1987
Mom Is Dating Weird Wayne, 1988

Other books you might like:
Pamela F. Service, *When the Night Wind Howls*, 1987
    Sidonie gets mixed up with ghosts in the theater building and gets involved in a pact with the devil.
Noel Streatfeild, *Theatre Shoes*, 1945
    Holly, Sorrel, and Mark Forbes are enrolled in an acting academy in London by their actress grandmother while their father is a POW.
Marlene Fanta Shyer, *Adorable Sunday*, 1983
    13 year old Sunday auditions successfully for a job doing TV commercials, but finds the life of an actress is not all she expected.
E.L. Konigsburg, *Up from Jerico Tel*, 1986
    11 year olds Meanmarie and Malcolm encounter the deceased Tallulah Bankhead and are given the task of finding the actress's stolen necklace.
Bruce Hlibok, *Silent Dancer*, 1981
    Nancy, who is 10 yeards old and deaf, looks forward to ballet class and dreams of performing at Lincoln Center.

67

Mary Jane Auch

A Sudden Change of Family (New York: Holiday House, 1990)

Age range: Grades 4-6

Subject(s): Adoption; Family Life

Major character(s): Katy Jordan, Preteen; Linda Jordan, Parent (mother)

Time period(s): 1990s

Locale(s): Whitmarsh Point, Connecticut

What the book is about: Katy discovers that her mother, Linda, was adopted. Linda is more shocked than Katy. She sets out to find her birth parents. Katy is torn away from her grandmother and cousins and thrown into a whole new family situation.

Where it's reviewed:
Kirkus Reviews, November 1, 1990, page 1527
School Library Journal, December 1990, page 97

Other books by the author:
Mom Is Dating Weird Wayne, 1991
Seven Long Years Until College, 1991
Kidnapping Kevin Kowalski, 1990
Angel and Me and the Bayside Bombers, 1989

Other books you might like:
Elisabet McHugh, *Karen's Sister*, 1983
    Karen's mother adopts a second Korean child, and finds a husband with three children of his own.
Claudia Mills, *Boardwalk with Hotel*, 1985

Jessica wonders if her adoptive parents love her less than her brother and sister who were born later.
Marilyn Sachs, *What My Sister Remembered*, 1992
    While visiting her younger sister, Beth confronts painful memories of the death of her parents, and the adoption of the sisters by different families.
Elizabeth Scarboro, *Secret Language of the SB*, 1990
    Eleven year old Adam is not happy when he learns that his family is taking in a Taiwanese orphan until her adoptive family is ready for her.
Betty Ren Wright, *The Scariest Night*, 1991
    Erin finds herself extremely jealous of her adopted brother and turns to a medium for help.

68

Mary Jane Auch

The Witching of Ben Wagner (Boston: Houghton Mifflin, 1987)

Age range: Grades 3-6

Subject(s): Family Life; Moving, Household

Major character(s): Ben Wagner, Preteen; Susan Wagner, Child; Regina St. Clavi, Witch

Time period(s): 1980s

Locale(s): Lakeview, New York

What the book is about: The Wagners move to a small town on Lake Ontario where Mr. Wagner has purchased a barber shop. Twelve year old Ben has a disastrous first day at his new school, then he meets Regina, a girl he half believes is a witch. Strange things happen whenever she is around, and there are rumors that she comes from a family of witches.

Where it's reviewed:
School Library Journal, October 1987, page 124
Booklist, November 15, 1987, page 560
Kirkus Reviews, November 15, 1987, page 1623

Other books by the author:
Kidnapping Kevin Kowalski, 1990
Angel and Me and the Bayside Bombers, 1989
Glass Slippers Give You Blisters, 1989
Cry Uncle, 1987

Other books you might like:
Wilanne Schneider Belden, *Frankie!*, 1987
    The O'Riley family is far from normal, since it includes a wizard, a magician, and a witch. They are delighted when Mother's next baby is a griffin.
John Bellairs, *The Letter, the Witch and the Ring*, 1976
    A young girl takes a trip with a friend of the family only to get involved with a mysterious letter, a magic ring, and a powerful witch.
Monica Furlong, *Juniper*, 1991
    While apprenticed to the witch woman Juniper, a young girl struggles to save her family from the evil machinations of her power-hungry aunt Meroot.
Katharine Wilson Precek, *The Keepsake Chest*, 1992
    To ease the pain of having to leave her friends behind when she moves into the old farmhouse, Meg probes the historical background of an old chest.
Ann Warren Turner, *Rosemary's Witch*, 1991

After moving into an old house, Rosemary discovers that the nearby woods conceal a 150 year old witch, who once lived in the house.

69

Esther Averill, Author/Illustrator

Captains of the City Street: A Story of a Cat Club (New York: Harper, 1972)

Age range: Grades 3-5

Subject(s): Animals/Cats; Clubs; Identity

Major character(s): Sinbad, Cat, Vagrant; The Duke, Cat, Vagrant; Patchy Pete, Cat

Time period(s): 1970s

Locale(s): New York, New York

What the book is about: In spite of planning to remain independent, two young "tramp cats" are gradually drawn into the Cat Club, though they are skeptical about the clubs "rules and regulations." Something happens to change their minds, as they agree to become Captains of the City Streets for the rest of the cat club.

Where it's reviewed:
Booklist, April 15, 1973, page 809
Center for Children's Books Bulletin, July 1973, page 149
Hornbook, February 1973, page 47

Other books by the author:
The School for Cats, 1982
Jenny and the Cat Club, 1973
The Fire Cat, 1960
Jenny's Birthday Book, 1954

Other books you might like:
E.W. Hildick, *Manhattan Is Missing*, 1969
   A boy and his family sublet an apartment in New York on the condition that they take care of the owner's prized cat, but suddenly the cat disappears.
Auro Roseili, *The Cats' of the Eiffel Tower*, 1967
   How "le President" of France and his detective solve a problem that involves a "zillion" stray cats.
Sarah Sargent, *Edward Troy and the Witch Cat*, 1978
   Relates the experiences of Edward Troy the spring and summer he is nine years old.
Harriet May Savitz, *The Cats Nobody Wanted*, 1989
   The neighbors aren't very happy when Mrs. Beasley moves onto their street. They call her the cat lady because she takes stray cats.
George Selden, *Harry Cat's Pet Puppy*, 1974
   Harry Cat and Tucker Mouse try to find a permanent home for a young stray puppy they have befriended.

70

Avi

Illustrator: David Wiesner

Man From the Sky (New York: Knopf, 1980)

Age range: Grades 4-6

Subject(s): Robbers and Outlaws

Major character(s): Jamie Peters, Preteen; Ed Goddard, Thief; Gillian Lurie, Preteen

Time period(s): 1980s

Locale(s): Philadelphia, Pennsylvania

What the book is about: Eleven year old Jamie, is a dreamer who often sees knights and dragons in the clouds. One day, he spots a thief parachuting from an airplane. Ed Goddard had carefully planned his escape, but did not count on Jamie seeing him. A man in a business suit jumping out of an airplane with a large briefcase is an unusual sight.

Where it's reviewed:
Booklist, July 15, 1990, page 1678
School Library Journal, December 1980, page 72

Other books by the author:
Blue Heron, 1992
Something Upstairs: A Tale of Ghosts, 1988
Bright Shadow, 1985
Who Stole the Wizard of Oz?, 1981

Other books you might like:
Thomas J. Dygard, *Wilderness Peril*, 1985
   Two teenage boys camping in the Minnesota woods encounter a desperate airplane hijacker attempting to escape with three-quarters of a million dollars.
Kathryn Osebold Galbraith, *Something Suspicious*, 1985
   Lizzie and her best friend try to track down a bank robber called the Green Pillowcase Bandit and end up with more mysteries than they can handle.
Ruth Hallman, *Gimme Something, Mister!*, 1978
   With New Orleans alive with Mardi Gras revelers, a teenager becomes entangled in a plot that involves stolen jewels and voodoo.
Phyllis Reynolds Naylor, *The Mad Gasser of Bessledorf Street*, 1983
   Sam suspects the culprit who is gassing assembly line workers in the parachute factory lives in the hotel his family manages.
James Nichols, *Boundary Waters*, 1985
   Working for relatives at a camp among the lakes of northern Minnesota, Dave finds their search for loot from a hijacked plane drawing him into danger.

71

Avi

Romeo and Juliet - Together (and Alive!) at Last (New York: Orchard, 1987)

Age range: Grades 5-8

Subject(s): Schools; Plays; Humor

Major character(s): Pete Saltz, Teenager, 8th Grader; Anabell Stackpoole, Teenager, 8th Grader; Ed Sirow, Teenager, 8th Grader

Time period(s): 1980s

Locale(s): United States

What the book is about: The eighth grade's plan to get two reluctant "lovers" together by means of a classroom production of Shakespeare's play has some very unexpected results and a hilarious production.

Where it's reviewed:
Booklist, September 1, 1988, page 87
Center for Children's Books Bulletin, October 1987, page 21

Other books by the author:
Something Upstairs: A Tale of Ghosts, 1988
S.O.R. Losers, 1984
Shadrach's Crossing, 1983
Sometimes I Think I Hear My Name, 1982

Other books you might like:
Barbara Cohen, *The Long Way Home*, 1990
 Sally's relationship with an elderly bus driver who recites Shakespearian stories helps her cope with problems in her family.
Robin D. Jones, *No Shakespeare Allowed*, 1989
 The daughter of the town's annual Shakespeare festival director tries to convince her dad she doesn't want to become an actress.
Joan Lowery Nixon, *And Maggie Makes Three*, 1986
 Maggie joins the school drama club, wins a part in the school play and learns to deal with her maturing feelings.
Marilyn Singer, *The Case of the Sabotaged School Play*, 1984
 A boring school play becomes big news when sabotage is suspected.
Anne Terry White, *Will Shakespeare and the Globe Theater*, 1955
 A novel edition of the great author and his life and times.

72

Avi

Something Upstairs: A Tale of Ghosts (New York: Orchard, 1988)

Age range: Grades 5-6

Subject(s): Slavery; Space and Time; Ghosts

Major character(s): Kenny, Child

Time period(s): 1980s; 19th century

Locale(s): Providence, Rhode Island

What the book is about: The spirit of a young Black slave cannot rest until a contemporary boy is willing to travel to the 1800s to change the circumstances of his death.

Where it's reviewed:
Center for Children's Books Bulletin, September 1988, page 2
School Library Journal, October 1988, page 138

Other books by the author:
Blue Heron, 1991
Captain Grey, 1977
Devil's Race, 1984
Sometimes I Think I Hear My Name, 1982

Other books you might like:
Belinda Hurmence, *A Girl Called Boy*, 1982
 A young Black girl is suddenly transported to the days of slavery and struggles to escape.
Julius Lester, *This Strange New Feeling*, 1982
 Short stories, based on fact, interpreting the feelings of Blacks during slavery days. Advanced Readers
Lynne Gessner, *Navajo Slave*, 1976
 11-year-old Navajo Straight Arrow is captured by a Ute Warrior and sold to a spanish landholder as a slave.
Ann Warren Turner, *Nettie's Trip South*, 1987

Through the diary of a 10-year-old Northern girl readers see the ugly reality of slavery in 1859.
Paula Fox, *The Slave Dancer*, 1973
 13-year-old Jessie is kidnapped in New Orleans in 1840 and forced to play his fife aboard a slave ship.

73

Avi

Illustrator: Jeanette Adams

Sometimes I Think I Hear My Name (New York: Pantheon Books, 1982)

Age range: Grades 5-6

Subject(s): Divorce

Major character(s): Conrad Munay, Teenager; Nancy Sterling, Teenager

Time period(s): 1980s

Locale(s): St. Louis, Missouri; New York, New York

What the book is about: A teenage boy abandons his spring break trip to England to look for his divorced parents in New York City. He lives with his Uncle Carl and his Aunt Lu. He is stunned to find out that his parents really do not want to see him. He meets Nancy at a travel agency and visits her in New York. Her parents want to keep Nancy away from Conrad because they think he's a bad influence.

Where it's reviewed:
Children's Book Review Service, Spring 1982, page 115
School Library Journal, September 1982, page 133

Other books by the author:
Blue Heron, 1992
The Fighting Ground, 1984
Shadrach's Crossing, 1983
Who Stole the Wizard of Oz?, 1981

Other books you might like:
Nancy Bond, *The Best of Enemies*, 1978
 Expecting a lonely spring break, Charlotte becomes involved in her town's annual Patriot's Day Celebration.
Hadley Irwin, *The Original Freddie Ackerman*, 1992
 Trevor refuses to spend another summer with his extended family of divorced parents, stepparents and siblings, so he is sent to Maine to stay with two
Judy K. Morris, *The Crazies and Sam*, 1983
 A boy living with his divorced father in Washington, D.C. tries to come to terms with the complications of life.
Amos Oz, *Soumchi*, 1980
 A young boy in Jerusalem discovers his first love.
Phyllis A. Whitney, *The Mystery of the Crimson Ghost*, 1969
 Spending the summer in the country, a girl falls in love with a neighbor's horse, but her attempts to befriend the mare are thwarted.

74

Avi

Illustrator: Ruth E. Murray

The True Confessions of Charlotte Doyle (New York: Orchard, 1990)

Age range: Grades 5 and Up

Subject(s): Sea Stories; Adventure and Adventurers; Murder

Major character(s): Charlotte Doyle, Preteen, Sailor

Time period(s): 1800s (1802)

Locale(s): At Sea

What the book is about: Charlotte changes from a "proper" English girl to the swashbuckling mate of a mutinous crew sailing from England to Rhode Island in the early 1800s. Charlotte is accused of murder by the captain. Old fashioned adventure on the high seas.

Where it's reviewed:
Booklist, September 1, 1990, page 44
School Library Journal, September 1990, page 221

Other books by the author:
Blue Heron, 1992
Emily Upham's Revenge, 1992
Bright Shadow, 1985
Devil's Race, 1984

Other books you might like:
Diane Duane, *Deep Wizardry*, 1985
    During a summer vacation at the beach, thirteen year old wizard Nita and her friend, Kit, assist the whale wizard S'ree in combating an evil power.
Marguerite Murray, *Odin's Eye*, 1987
    Cicely's summer job at a seaside boarding house turns into a dangerous adventure as she stumbles across clues to an unsolved murder.
Richard Gavin Robinson, *Captain Sintar*, 1967
    Taken on board a ship when his rowboat capsizes, Tom is forced to sail with a sinister captain and his crew of blackguards.
Donald J. Sobol, *Great Sea Stories*, 1975
    A collection of adventures on the high seas, including "Evidence from a Shark," "Horror Ship," and "Ghost on the Quarterdeck."
Colin Thiele, *Blue Fin*, 1974
    Although his father thinks he is worthless, Steve finds their lives in is hands following a violent storm at sea.

B

75

Natalie Babbitt

The Devil's Storybook (New York: Farrar, Straus and Giroux, 1974)

Age range: Grades 3-5

Subject(s): Demons; Short Stories

Time period(s): Indeterminate Past

Locale(s): Earth

What the book is about: The devil is shown as a humorous, almost sympathetic character in these ten original stories. The devil loses almost as often as he wins. Easy reading but sophisticated content for middle graders, and an excellent read-aloud.

Where it's reviewed:
Booklist, September 1, 1974, page 37
Library Journal, October 15, 1974, page 2730

Other books by the author:
The Devil's Other Storybook, 1987
The Eyes of the Amaryllis, 1977
Goody Hall, 1971
Kneeknock Rise, 1970

Other books you might like:
Daniel Cohen, *Monsters You've Never Heard Of*, 1980
  Accounts of lesser known monsters including The Jersey Devil, Hairy Hands, Dover Demon, Spring Heeled Jack, and other phantom animals.
Collin McDonald, *Nightwaves: Scary Tales for After Dark*, 1990
  A collection of ghost and horror stories including a hunter from ancient Egypt and a woman who sells her husband's soul to the Devil.
Pamela F. Service, *When the Night Wind Howls*, 1987
  Ghosts appear at the community theatre thirteen year old Sidonie and her mother join.
Peter Silsbee, *The Temptation of Kate*, 1990
  A demon fights for the soul of a young girl troubled by her parents' divorce and by a recent move from New York City to the country.
Dorothy Van Woerkom, *Old Devil Is Waiting*, 1985
  Three stories involving devils of one sort or another. "The Clever Glassblower," "The Greedy Landlord," and "The Farmer's Wife."

76

Natalie Babbitt, Author/Illustrator

Goody Hall (New York: Farray, 1971)

Age range: Grades 4-6

Subject(s): Mystery and Detective Stories

Major character(s): Hercules Feltwright, Actor, Tutor; Mrs. Goody, Parent; Willet Goody, Child

Time period(s): 1890s

Locale(s): Goody Hall, England

What the book is about: Hercules is a bumbling actor who never gets his lines straight. He finally decides that the life of a tutor will better suit him and comes to the strange house called Goody Hall. There he stumbles over strange legends, disguises and clues that are as bizarre as the family history he at last unravels.

Where it's reviewed:
Booklist, July 15, 1971, page 954
Hornbook, August 1971, page 380
Kirkus Reviews, April 15, 1971, page 431

Other books by the author:
The Princess and Curdie, 1987
Herbert Rowbarge, 1982
The Eyes of the Amaryllis, 1977
Kneeknock Rise, 1970

Other books you might like:
Gillian Avery, *Maria Escapes*, 1992
  While living with her sole relative, an uncle in Oxford, Maria shares an odd tutor with the rowdy Smith brothers and has unusual countryside outings.
Eilis Dillon, *The Island of Ghosts*, 1989
  Before leaving the island of Inishglass for school in Galway, Dara and Bran visit their tutor who moved to a haunted island and plans to capture them.
Emily Moore, *Whose Side Are You On?*, 1988
  When Barbra's friend and sixth grade math tutor, T.J., disappears from school, she sets out to "rescue" him.
Diana Shaw, *Lessons in Fear: A Carter Colborn Mystery*, 1987
  When a despised biology teacher is found unconscious and other "accidents" continue to happen, teenage sleuth Carter Colborn suspects foul play.
John Rowe Townsend, *Downstream: A Novel*, 1987
  Alan, friendless and unhappy after moving to a small English village, falls in love with a twenty-three year old tutor whose presence causes problems.

77

Natalie Babbitt, Author/Illustrator

Knee-Knock Rise (New York: Farrar, Straus & Giroux, 1970)

Age range: Grades 3-5

Subject(s): Mountain Life; Mystery and Detective Stories

Major character(s): Egan, Child; Ada, Child; Uncle Ott

Time period(s): Indeterminate

Locale(s): Instep, Fictional City (Mythical town near the Mammoth Mountains)

What the book is about: Egan goes to visit relatives in the village of Instep at the foot of the Mammoth Mountains, home of the mysterious and terrifying Megrimum. On the last day of his visit, Egan climbs the dangerous mountain to confront the horrible monster.

Where it's reviewed:
Booklist, September 15, 1970, page 99
Horn Book, June 1970, page 295

Awards the book has won:
Newbery Honor 1971

Other books by the author:
Tuck Everlasting, 1975
The Search for Delicious, 1969
The Devil's Storybook
1974

Other books you might like:
Barbara Brenner, *The Mystery of the Plumed Serpent*, 1948
  Michael and Elena Garcia watch carefully when two strangers open a pet shop next door, and find themselves involved with a gold smuggling scheme.
Eleanor Clymer, *The Horse in the Attic*, 1983
  Exploring her new home, Caroline finds a painting of a filly named "Sprite." Good for both horse and mystery fans.
Vicki Berger Erwin, *Jamie and the Mystery Quilt*, 1987
  Jamie encounters adventures and finds gold when she interprets a map in the design of an old quilt.
Drew Stevenson, *The Case of the Wandering Werewolf*, 1987
  Raymond gets involved in finding out what the werewolf is doing in Lost Woods.

78

Natalie Babbitt

Illustrator: Natalie Babbitt

The Search for Delicious (New York: Farrar, 1969)

Age range: Grades 3-5

Subject(s): Fantasy

Major character(s): Vaungaylen "Gaylen", Child; DeCree, Political Figure (prime minister)

Time period(s): Indeterminate Past

Locale(s): Alternate Earth

What the book is about: Twelve year old Gaylen is dispatched by the King to take a poll of the kingdom to find the meaning of the word delicious. Unrest is growing in the Kingdom, and Gaylen keeps hearing rumors of a mysterious

mermaid named Ardis. As he continues his journey, Gaylen discovers the treachery behind the unrest.

Where it's reviewed:
Horn Book, August 1969, page 407
Kirkus Reviews, April 1, 1969, page 373

Other books by the author:
The Eyes of the Amaryllis, 1977
Tuck Everlasting, 1975
Goody Hall, 1971
Kneeknock Rise, 1970

Other books you might like:
Lloyd Alexander, *The Remarkable Journey of Prince Jen*, 1991
  Young Prince Jen embarks on a perilous quest bearing six unusual gifts.
Betty Baker, *Seven Spells to Farewell*, 1982
  On a long journey, a resourceful girl shares adventures and magic with a talking raven and a performing pig.
Lynne Reid Banks, *The Farthest Away Mountain*, 1991
  Dakin begins a journey to visit the farthest-away mountain, meet a gargoyle, and find a prince.
Mary Stewart, *Ludo and the Star Horse*, 1974
  A boy follows his horse on a journey through all the houses of the Zodiac.
Nancy Willard, *The Island of the Grass King*, 1979
  Anatole embarks on a fantastic journey to the island where the wild fennel grows.

79

Natalie Babbitt

Tuck Everlasting (New York: Farrar Straus and Giroux, 1975)

Age range: Grades 4-6

Subject(s): Fantasy; Kidnapping; Immortality

Major character(s): Winnie Foster, Child

Time period(s): 1880s

Locale(s): Treegap, Fictional Country

What the book is about: Winnie's adventures with the Tuck family involve a kidnapping, murder and a jailbreak. The Tuck family has found a spring with water that gives them life everlasting. After the adventures are over, Winnie has a life and death decision to make.

Where it's reviewed:
Kirkus Reviews, October 15, 1975, page 1181
Publisher's Weekly, October 5, 1975, page 87

Awards the book has won:
Christopher Award 1976

Other books by the author:
The Devil's Other Storybook, 1987
The Eyes of the Amaryllis, 1977
Goody Hall, 1971
Kneeknock Rise, 1970

Other books you might like:
Betty Baker, *Seven Spells to Farewell*, 1982
  On a long journey to find the Kingdom of Iskany and become a sorceress, a girl shares adventures and magic with a talking raven and a performing pup.
Otto Coontz, *Hornswoggle Magic*, 1981

Using seemingly magical methods, a "bag lady" helps two children save one's father's newsstand, threatened by a huge new vending machine.

Tamora Pierce, *Wild Magic: The Immortals*, 1992
Numair, Alanna and Queen Thayet enlist Daine's help in battling the dreadful Immortals that have begun to attack the Kingdom of Tortall.

Vivian Vande Velde, *A Hidden Magic*, 1985
Lost in a magic forest and separated from her prince, Jennifer seeks help from a kindly young sorcerer in a battle with an evil witch.

Holden Wetherbee, *The Wonder Ring*, 1978
When a poor and mistreated boy shows kindness to a beggar, the beggar gives him a magic ring.

| **80** |

Katharine Bacon

Pip and Emma (New York: Atheneum, 1986)

Age range: Grades 5-7

Subject(s): Brothers and Sisters; Grandparents

Major character(s): Pip, Preteen; Emma, Preteen; "Gee", Grandparent (Pip and Emma's grandmother)

Time period(s): 1980s

Locale(s): Doe's Crossing, Vermont

What the book is about: Pip faces meningitis and a thief of a friend during a summer in Vermont. The kids spend a terrifying night lost in the wood, go after a man illegally cutting trees on grandma's land and an encounter with escaped convicts. The summer affects brother and sister in different ways. Pip is resentful of their mother's year in Europe, while Emma loves the year on the farm.

Where it's reviewed:
Booklist, May 1, 1986, page 1307
Kirkus Reviews, March 1, 1986, page 387
School Library Journal, August 1986, page 89

Other books by the author:
Shadow and Light, 1987

Other books you might like:
Cora Cheney, *The Mystery of the Disappearing Cars*, 1964
Their scholarships are jeopardized when Windy and Sam are suspected of stealing a car which disappeared near the Vermont hotel where they work.

Barbara Dana, *Crazy Eights*, 1978
Sent to North Woods School in Vermont by a juvenile judge, fourteen year old Thelma struggles to define her identity and meaning in her life.

Dorothy Canfield Fisher, *Understood Betsy*, 1972
A small and timid girl discovers her own abilities and the world around her when she goes to live with relatives on a farm in Vermont.

John Ney, *Ox Goes North: More Trouble for the Kid at the Top*, 1973
Ox spends the summer at a Vermont camp where he becomes involved with rescuing his cabin mate from scheming grandparents.

Robert Newton Peck, *Kirk's Law*, 1981
A rugged life style in the Vermont woods with a feisty old hunter called Wishbone Kirk develops the character of a fifteen year old boy.

| **81** |

Martha Bacon

In the Company of Clowns (Boston: Little, Brown, 1973)

Age range: Grades 5-8

Subject(s): Orphans; Runaways

Major character(s): Gian-Piero, Orphan

Time period(s): 18th century

Locale(s): Venice, Italy

What the book is about: An orphan boy runs away from working in a convent kitchen to follow an actor who has tricked him. The boy sees a side of life he has never seen, and the Harlequin of the company convinces him that he can find his unknown father.

Where it's reviewed:
Horn Book, August 1973, page 376
Kirkus Reviews, April 1, 1973, page 382

Other books by the author:
The Third Road, 1971
Sophia Scrooby Preserved, 1968

Other books you might like:
Alan Collins, *Jacob's Ladder*, 1989
The world of brothers Jacob and Solly falls apart when they are orphaned and put in a Sydney children's home just as Hitler begins his rise to power.

Kathleen C. Phillips, *Katie McCrary and the Wiggins Crusade*, 1980
When orphaned Katie moves to a small town with her aunt and uncle in 1927, she befriends a family disliked by the entire town.

Cara Lockhart Smith, *Parchment House*, 1989
In a desolate orphanage in futuristic Britain, orphan Johnny Rattle pits his wits against the orphanage director, the cruel Reverend Slipper.

John Tomerlin, *The Sky Clowns*, 1973
A dedicated stunt flyer wants to help a failing air show.

Ursula Moray Williams, *Bogwoppit*, 1978
Samantha moves in with an unwelcoming aunt whose dilapidated house includes bogwoppits, rat-sized creatures with wings, fur, and blue eyes.

| **82** |

Enid Bagnold

National Velvet (New York: Morrow, 1935)

Age range: Grades 4-6

Subject(s): Animals/Horses

Major character(s): Velvet Brown, Equestrian (Teenager); Mi Taylor, Horse Trainer

Time period(s): Indeterminate Past

Locale(s): England

What the book is about: Velvet wins a piebald horse and dreams of riding in the Grand National, though she will have to disguise herself as a boy to enter. Mi Taylor helps get her to London, gets lodging and masquerades as a Russian-speaking boy jockey. Velvet wins the race and then is disqualified when it is discovered that she is a girl - but Velvet learns the best is yet to come.

Where it's reviewed:
Punch, July 19, 1978, page 109
Best Sellers, February 1, 1971, page 483

Other books by the author:
The Happy Foreigner, 1987
The Chalk Garden, 1956

Other books you might like:
Dorothy Callahan, *Julie Krone, a Winning Jockey*, 1990
Discusses the childhood, education, early riding career, major races, titles, views and personal life of jockey Julie Krone. (Biography)
Walter Farley, *The Black Stallion and the Girl*, 1971
Alec has a hard time persuading his partners to keep the girl he hires as a trainer and convincing them to let her race the Black Stallion.
Doris Gates, *Little Vic*, 1951
An undersized colt has the potential to be a winner, but it's only recognized by his stable boy who trains to be a jockey and chooses his favorite.
Will James, *Smoky the Cowhorse*, 1926
The experiences of a mouse-colored horse from his birth on the range to his eventual old age.
Barbara Willard, *The Miller's Boy*, 1976
In 15th century Sussex, a boy living with his grandfather dreams of having a friend his own age and a horse to take him away to live with his sister.

83

Carolyn Sherwin Bailey

Illustrator: Ruth Stiles Gannett

Miss Hickory (New York: Viking, 1946)

Age range: Grades 4-6

Subject(s): Dolls and Dollhouses

Major character(s): Miss Hickory, Toy (doll); T. Willard-Brown, Cat; Great-Granny Brown, Grandparent

Time period(s): 1940s

Locale(s): New Hampshire

What the book is about: An unwelcome guest forces Miss Hickory, who has apple twigs for a body and a hickory nut for a head, to look for a new home. Her many animal friends suggest different places, but her final home is a lovely surprise.

Where it's reviewed:
Booklist, November 1, 1946, page 74
Horn Book, November 1946, page 465
Library Journal, November 1, 1946, page 1544

Other books by the author:
Finnegan II (His Nine Lives), 1953
Favorite Stories for the Children's Hour, 1965 (Editor)

Other books you might like:
James Duffy, *Doll Hospital*, 1989
8-yr-old Alison runs a doll hospital where the ailments of the dolls reflect Alison's own long term illness.
Sheila Greenwald, *Secret Museum*, 1974
Jennifer and her friend, Lizzie, discover a doll house with a family of dolls who are alive.
Janet Louise Lunn, *Double Spell*, 1968

Twins Jane and Elizabeth find a doll in an antique shop which exerts a strange spell over them. (Challenging reading.)
Jean S. O'Connell, *The Dollhouse Caper*, 1975
The dollhouse family worries that the boys are going to discard them, and discover a burglary is being plotted.
Rachel Field, *Hitty: Her First Hundred Years*, 1957
A doll carved from mountain ash has many adventures, including a stint on a whaling ship.

84

Barbara Baker

Illustrator: Marsha Winborn

Digby and Kate (New York: Dutton, 1988)

Age range: Grades 1-3

Subject(s): Animals/Dogs; Friendship; Animals/Cats

Major character(s): Digby, Dog; Kate, Cat

Time period(s): 1980s

Locale(s): United States

What the book is about: In spite of many differences a dog and cat maintain a relationship that lasts through conflicts and changes, such as how to catch a mouse and what to fix for lunch.

Where it's reviewed:
Booklist, July 1988, page 1843
Kirkus Reviews, April 1, 1988, page 534
Publishers Weekly, March 11, 1988, page 103

Other books by the author:
Oh Emma, 1991
N-O Spells No, 1990
Digby and Kate Again, 1989
Third Grade Is Terrible, 1988

Other books you might like:
Lynley Dodd, *Hairy Maclary From Donaldson's Dairy*, 1992
A small black dog and his canine friends are terrorized by the local tomcat.
James Howe, *Rabbit-Cadabra*, 1993
When the animals in the Monroe household see a picture of Bunnicula the rabbit on a poster for a magician, they jump to an alarming conclusion.
Marcus Pfister, *Shaggy*, 1990
Although he is upset when a cat wants to move into his junkyard home, Shaggy comes to appreciate his new partner's presence.
Mark Saltzman, *The Adventures of Milo and Otis*, 1988
A young cat and dog discover the dangers and delights of the outside world when they wander away from the farm.
Jenny Wagner, *John Brown, Rose, and the Midnight Cat*, 1977
Rose's dog feels he can look after her without any help from a cat, but Rose has different ideas.

85

Betty Baker

Illustrator: Chuck Eckart

Dupper (New York: Greenwillow, 1976)

Age range: Grades 4-6

Subject(s): Animals; Artists and Art

Major character(s): Dupper, Prairie Dog

Time period(s): Indeterminate

Locale(s): United States

What the book is about: The other prairie dogs think Dupper is strange. But Dupper is an artist. He goes on a quest to find the Great Ants who can drive away the snake that threatens the prairie dog colony. He finds art much like his own while on his quest.

Where it's reviewed:
Center for Children's Books Bulletin, November 1976, page 381
Kirkus Reviews, June 15, 1976, page 684

Other books by the author:
The Spirit Is Willing, 1974
The Dunderhead War, 1967
Walk the World's Rim, 1965

Other books you might like:
Frank Asch, *Pearl's Promise*, 1984
  A mouse named Pearl sets out to save her brother from a pet store python.
Claude Clement, *The Voice of the Wood*, 1989
  A fairy tale that looks at the relationship between art and the artist.
Justin F. Denzel, *Boy of the Painted Cave*, 1988
  The story of a boy who longs to be a cave artist, set in Cro-Magnon times.
Dick Roughsey, *The Rainbow Serpent*, 1988
  An Australian aborigine's story, featuring a giant serpent that wriggled across the land carving out rivers and gorges.
Ann Warren Turner, *Time of the Bison*, 1989
  Scar Boy, of the Ice Age, wants to become a painter of caves.

86

Betty Baker

Seven Spells to Farewell (New York: Macmillan, 1982)

Age range: Grades 5-8

Subject(s): Fantasy; Voyages and Travels

Major character(s): Dru, Sorceress; Pitt, Raven; Humphrey, Pig

Time period(s): Indeterminate

Locale(s): Fictional Country

What the book is about: Dru, a young girl talented at making spells, but in need of training to learn to control her gift, joins a medicine show run by Dr. Blessing. On a long journey to find the kingdom of Iskany and become a sorceress, she shares adventures with a talking raven and a performing pig.

Where it's reviewed:
Center for Children's Books Bulletin, May 1982, page 162
School Library Journal, April 1982, page 65
Language Arts, November 1982, page 869

Other books by the author:
A Stanger and Afraid, 1972

And One Was a Wooden Indian, 1970
The Dunderhead War, 1967
Killer-of-Death, 1963

Other books you might like:
Barbara Ninde Byfield, *Andrew and the Alchemist*, 1977
  Andrew, an orphan, becomes apprenticed to an alchemist and begins a life of adventure.
Peter Dickinson, *Merlin Dreams*, 1988
  Nine stories of blood, magic and fabulous creatures, set in the dreams of the enchanted wizard, Merlin, as he lies imprisoned under a great stone.
Ethel Johnston Philips, *Tatterhood and Other Tales*, 1978
  A collection of traditional tales of magic and adventure from Norway, England, China and many other countries.
Lisa J. Smith, *The Night of the Solstice*, 1987
  Four children set out to rescue a sorceress held captive in a parallel world.
Jane Yolen, *The Magic Three of Solatia*, 1974
  The magic in the three silver buttons of the seawitch serves both Sianna of the Song and her son as they struggle against a ruthless wizard.

87

Betty Baker

The Spirit Is Willing (New York: Macmillan, 1974)

Age range: Grades 5-6

Subject(s): American West

Major character(s): Carrie, Teenager; Portia, Teenager

Time period(s): 1800s

Locale(s): Arizona

What the book is about: Carrie longs for excitement, Portia is dreamy. Carrie goes to see a mummy in the saloon.

Where it's reviewed:
Horn Book, August 1974, page 374
Kirkus Reviews, January 1, 1975, page 5

Other books by the author:
At the Center of the World, 1973
The Dunderhead War, 1967
Walk the World's Rim, 1965

Other books you might like:
Patricia Beatty, *How Many Miles to Sundown*, 1974
  In 1881, a tomboy, her brother and her pet longhorn accompany a young man searching for his father through the Southwest.
Rex Benedict, *Good Luck Arizona Man*, 1972
  A half-white Apache boy sets out to solve the mystery of his own origins and the hiding place of a gold treasure.
Edna Walker Chandler, *Almost Brothers*, 1971
  Part Sioux and part Arapahoe, Benji has a difficult time adjusting to life with the strange Indians and Chicanos in his new Arizona home.
Winifred Madison, *Maria Luisa*, 1971
  Her poor knowledge of English is only one of the handicaps experienced by a Spanish-speaking girl spending months with her relatives in California.
Don Schellie, *Me, Cholay and Co.: Apache Warriors*, 1973

With the help of a young Apache who becomes his best friend, a young man leads a small band of Apache children across fifty miles of Arizona desert.

88

Betty Baker

Walk the World's Rim (New York: Harper and Row, 1965)

Age range: Grades 5-6

Subject(s): Indians of North America

Major character(s): Chakoh, Child, Indian; Esteban, Slave

Time period(s): 16th century (1527)

Locale(s): Mexico; United States

What the book is about: An Indian boy, Chakoh, joins Cabeza de Vaca to "walk the world's rim," and bring horses back for the Cheyenne. As he begins to make friends with a black slave, Esteban, he changes many of the ideas he had about slaves. Chakoh returns to his tribe richer and wiser.

Where it's reviewed:
Horn Book, April 1965, page 174
Library Journal, March 15, 1965, page 1546

Other books by the author:
The Night Spider Case, 1984
The Great Desert Race, 1980
And One Was a Wooden Indian, 1970
The Dunderhead War, 1967

Other books you might like:
Clyde Robert Bulla, *Conquista*, 1978
    A tale of how the first Spanish horse escaped from his rider and was taken by a young Indian on a vision quest.
David Kherdian, *Bridger: The Story of a Mountain Man*, 1987
    Jim signs on for an expedition facing the elements, hunger and hostile Indians in 1822 to discover the source of the Missouri River.
Scott O'Dell, *Captive*, 1979
    Shipwrecked on a deserted island, Julian is forced to impersonate a lost Incan god and is caught in the violence of the Spanish invasion of Mexico.
Jeanne Williams, *Tame the Wild Stallion*, 1985
    In 1846, Joe is captured and held for a year by bandits. He learns that people are more important than rivalries and cultural differences.
G. Clifton Wisler, *Raid*, 1985
    Attempting to free his kid brother from raiding Comanches, Liege and his Black companion, Zeke, confront many obstacles on the Texas frontier.

89

Betty Baker

Illustrator: Sal Murdocca

Worthington Botts and the Steam Machine (New York: Macmillan, 1981)

Age range: Grades 1-3

Subject(s): Literacy; Robots; Inventions

Major character(s): Worthington Botts, Inventor

Time period(s): 1890s

Locale(s): United States

What the book is about: Worthington Botts wants a machine to do all of his chores so he can read. In the 1890s, he builds a steam powered robot to take care of all the things that interrupt his reading.

Where it's reviewed:
Booklist, July 15, 1981, page 1450
Kirkus Reviews, June 15, 1981, page 738
School Library Journal, September 1981, page 102

Other books by the author:
The Turkey Girl, 1983
Rat Is Dead and Ant Is Sad, 1981
All-by-Herself, 1980
Three Fools and a Horse, 1975

Other books you might like:
Isaac Asimov, *Robbie*, 1989
    When Gloria's mother deprives her of her beloved robot playmate, Robbie, Gloria is inconsolable.
Babette Cole, *The Trouble with Dad*, 1985
    Dad's fantastic robot creations cause the family to have incredible adventures.
Carolyn Sloan, *The Friendly Robot*, 1986
    A lonely robot prefers the company of a little boy to working in a factory.
Elizabeth Traynor, *My Best Friend Is a Robot*, 1991
    The adventures of a young child who spends more time with a robot buddy than with other children.
Martin Waddell, *Harriet and the Robot*, 1987
    Harriet, who brings trouble wherever she goes, gives her friend a doll - actually a large robot she has built herself and is unable to control.

90

Jeannie Baker, Author/Illustrator

Where the Forest Meets the Sea (New York: Greenwillow, 1988)

Age range: Grades 1-4

Subject(s): Conservation of Natural Resources

Time period(s): Indeterminate

Locale(s): Queensland, Australia

What the book is about: A young boy travels through the Great Barrier Reef and explores the rain forest in Australia. He imagines the aboriginal children who had played there over the centuries. He hopes the development of resorts in the area will not destroy the ancient beauty of the rainforest.

Where it's reviewed:
Horn Book, July/August 1988, page 475
School Library Journal, June/July 1988, page 83

Other books by the author:
Window, 1991
Home in the Sky, 1984
Grandfather, 1977

Other books you might like:
Jill Bailey, *Gorilla Rescue*, 1992

Emmanuel, an employee of the Rwandan National Park, saves several gorillas from poachers and goes on an expedition to count gorillas for a census.

Lisa Campbell Ernst, *Squirrel Park*, 1993
Stuart clashes with his father, a developer, over the design of a park that threatens an ancient oak tree where his squirrel friend, Chuck, lives.

Katharine Shelley Orr, *My Grandpa and the Sea*, 1990
Grandpa, a traditional fisherman, is forced from his livelihood because of increasingly efficient technology.

Mary Lyn Ray, *Pumpkins: A Story for a Field*, 1992
A man harvests and sells a bountiful crop of pumpkins so that he will be able to preserve the field from developers.

Nancy Luenn, *Song for the Ancient Forest*, 1993
Raven warns against the destruction of the ancient forests, but no one listens except a small child.

91

Glenn Balch

Illustrator: Ruth Sanderson

Buck, Wild (New York: Crowell, 1976)

Age range: Grades 5-6

Subject(s): Animals/Horses; American West

Major character(s): Buck, Horse

Time period(s): Indeterminate

Locale(s): Idaho

What the book is about: This is the story of a wild horse in a small band on the rugged Owyhee Range in Idaho. He constantly fights to keep his freedom. Even after capture by a ranch hand who loves him, he continues to fight.

Where it's reviewed:
Kirkus Reviews, October 1, 1976, page 1100
School Library Journal, November 1976, page 65

Other books by the author:
A Horse of Two Colors, 1969
Flaxy Mare, 1967
Runaways, 1963
Spotted Horse, 1961

Other books you might like:
Ann Nolan Clark, *Year Walk*, 1975
In 1910, a boy from the Spanish Basque country comes to Idaho to help his godfather herd sheep across the new frontier.

Justin F. Denzel, *Black Kettle: King of the Wild Horses*, 1974
A wild black stallion is protected from capture by an Indian youth.

Will James, *Smoky the Cowhorse*, 1927
The story of a cowpony from his wild colthood on the range through the events of his life.

Amy C. Laundrie, *Whinny of the Wild Horses*, 1990
Follows the adventures of a wild colt living on the Wyoming range from his birth to full-grown stallion.

Glen Rounds, *Wild Appaloosa*, 1983
A wild Appaloosa filly makes a young boy's dream come true.

92

Lorna Balian

The Sweet Touch (Nashville: Abingdon, 1976)

Age range: Grades 2-3

Subject(s): Food

Major character(s): Peggy, Child

Time period(s): 1970s

Locale(s): United States

What the book is about: Peggy's plastic ring conjures up a beginner genie. He can only grant one wish. After Peggy makes a wish, the genie doesn't know how to turn off the "Sweet Touch" and Peggy has a serious problem.

Where it's reviewed:
Kirkus Reviews, February 15, 1976, page 191
School Library Journal, September 1976, page 94

Other books by the author:
Amelia's Nine Lives, 1986
Garden for a Ground Hog, 1985
Humbug Rabbit, 1974
I Love You Mary Jane, 1967

Other books you might like:
Nathaniel Benchley, *The Magic Sled*, 1972
A boy's adventures begin when his magic sled grants his wish for snow.

Danita Ross Haller, *Not Just Any Ring*, 1982
Jessie's grandfather buys her a special silver ring, but she must depend on the magic in her heart and the strength of her hands in the desert.

Susan Jeschke, *Mia, Grandma and the Genie*, 1978
Mia comes to understand her grandmother's friendship with her household items, nature, and the ugly genie in the earthenware jar.

Arcadio Lobato, *Just One Wish*, 1989
A magic crystal ball, with the power of granting wishes, destroys the peace of a small village, and only the shepherd boy who found it can help.

Inga Moore, *The Sorcerer's Apprentice*, 1989
A sorcerer's young apprentice attempts to practice magic in his master's absence, with disastrous results.

93

Molly Bang, Author/Illustrator

The Buried Moon and Other Stories (New York: Scribner, 1977)

Age range: Grades 4-6

Subject(s): Magic; Folk Tales

Time period(s): Indeterminate

Locale(s): Earth

What the book is about: Five stories of magic; one is a blend of a Grimm fairy tale and a Japanese tale, two are from England, and the others from China and India.

Where it's reviewed:
New York Times Book Review, August 7, 1977, page 241
School Library Journal, February 1978, page 53

Other books by the author:
Delphine, 1988
The Paper Crane, 1985
Wiley and the Hairy Man, 1976
The Demons of Rajpur, 1973

Other books you might like:
Keith Baker, *The Magic Fan*, 1989
Despite his fellow villagers' laughter, Yoshi uses his skills to make a boat to catch the moon, a kite to reach the clouds, and a bridge.
Helen Cresswell, *Time Out*, 1990
Tweeny and her parents, servants in a London house in 1887, use a book of magic spells to travel forward 100 years to 1987 England.
David Day, *The Emperor's Panda*, 1986
Relates how the poor shepherd boy king became the emperor of all China with the help of the Master Panda, the most magical and wisest creature.
Paul Galdone, *The Table, the Donkey, and the Stick*, 1976
Three brothers who leave home because of a greedy goat, return to share with their father the magic rewards of their hard work.
Faith M. Towle, *The Magic Cooking Pot*, 1975
When the good man's magic ever-full pot of rice is stolen, the powerful goddess Durga gives him a pot full of demons as a means to solve the problem.

94

Antonia Barber

The Ghosts (New York: Farrar, Straus and Giroux, 1969)

Age range: Grades 4-6

Subject(s): Ghosts; Country Life; Gardens and Gardening

Major character(s): James, Preteen; Lucy, Preteen; Mr. Blunden, Employer

Time period(s): Indeterminate

Locale(s): Camden Town, England

What the book is about: Two youngsters meet ghosts from another time in the garden of the country estate where their mother is caretaker.

Where it's reviewed:
Booklist, January 1, 1970, page 563
Center for Children's Books Bulletin, February 1970, page 92
Kirkus, August 15, 1969, page 854

Other books you might like:
Margaret Hodges, *The High Riders*, 1980
Forced by his late arrival in England to live apart from the rest of his school crew team, Larry Dunlap gets involved with the locals and their ghosts
Louise Lawrence, *The Dram Road*, 1983
Ghosts on a historic rural road bring together a desperate young London punk running from a crime and a stubborn old man.
Christopher Leach, *Rosalinda*, 1978
A girl feels strangely compelled to reenact the life of a former resident of Warrender House.
Patricia A. McKillip, *The House on Parchment Street*, 1973
While staying with her cousin in England, a young girl helps him find a way of helping the troubled ghosts inhabiting the cellar of the house.

Robert Westall, *Ghost Abbey*, 1988
When her father's new job takes the family to an old English abbey, Maggie learns that both she and the building are haunted by ghosts from the past.

95

Antonia Barber

Illustrator: Nicola Bayley

The Mousehole Cat (New York: Macmillan, 1990)

Age range: Grades 4-6

Subject(s): Animals/Cats; Folk Tales

Time period(s): Indeterminate Past

Locale(s): Cornwall, England

What the book is about: Based on an old Cornish legend of Tom Bawcock, this is a tale of a town saved from starvation by a fisherman and his cat on Christmas Eve. Beautiful art work and beautiful language make this appealing to all ages.

Where it's reviewed:
Booklist, October 1, 1990, page 335
School Library Journal, October 1990, page 34

Other books by the author:
The Enchanter's Daughter, 1987
Satchelmouse and the Dinosaurs, 1987
The Ghosts, 1969

Other books you might like:
Paul Galdone, *King of the Cats: A Ghost Story*, 1980
As the gravedigger tells his wife a band of cats marched into the cemetery to mourn their dead king, their own cat listens with strange interest.
Helen Griffith, *Russian Blue*, 1973
Struggling to keep the valuable but injured cat he has grown to love, a ten year old's life becomes a mixture of deception and devotion.
James Herriot, *The Christmas Day Kitten*, 1986
True story of how an independent-minded stray cat gives a woman and her three Basset hounds a Christmas present.
Elizabeth Parsons, *The Upside-Down Cat*, 1981
A boy learns an important lesson about life when he discovers his cat, missing since the previous summer, living happily with an old fisherman.
Robert Westall, *Yaxley's Cat*, 1991
After Yaxley disappears, the inhabitants of an English village fear that his ugly old cat will uncover the secret they have been hiding.

96

Gary W. Barger

What Happened to Mr. Forester? (Boston: Houghton Mifflin, 1981)

Age range: Grades 6-8

Subject(s): Homosexuality/Lesbianism; Prejudice; Teachers

Major character(s): Louis Lamb, Preteen, 6th Grader; Jack Forster, Teacher; Aunt Zona, Guardian

Time period(s): 1950s (1958)

Locale(s): Kansas City, Missouri

What the book is about: Louis decides that sixth grade will be different. A new teacher takes an interest in him, coaches him in softball and helps him discover his real talent, writing. Louis questions the actions of those around him when Mr. Forster is accused of being a homosexual.

Where it's reviewed:
Booklist, January 1, 1982, page 595
Horn Book, February 1982, page 40

Other books by the author:
Life. Is. Not. Fair, 1984

Other books you might like:
Alice Childress, *Those Other People*, 1989
    Bigotry surfaces at Minitown High when a male teacher sexually assaults a fifteen year old girl and the only witnesses are a black boy and a teacher.
Bette Greene, *The Drowning of Stephen Jones*, 1991
    A group wants to ban all "anti-Christian" literature from the library and gay owners of an antique shop are persecuted.
A.M. Homes, *Jack*, 1989
    Jack's feelings about his father, who left him and his mother four years earlier, are further complicated when he finds out that his father is gay.
Marilyn Kaye, *Real Heroes*, 1993
    When his teacher tests HIV positive, Kevin is torn between loyalty to his father and his admiration for his favorite sixth grade teacher.
Ronald Koertge, *The Arizona Kid*, 1988
    Billy spends the summer with his gay uncle in Tucson and works at a racetrack where he falls in love with an outspoken horse exerciser named Cara.

97

Judi Barrett

Illustrator: Ron Barrett

Cloudy with a Chance of Meatballs (New York: Atheneum, 1978)

Age range: Grades 2-4

Subject(s): Food; Weather

Major character(s): Henry, Child; Grandpa, Grandparent; Mom, Parent

Time period(s): Indeterminate

Locale(s): Fictional Country

What the book is about: Grandpa tells Peter and his sister about the delicious life in the town of Chewandswallow where it rains soup and juice, snows mashed potatoes, and blows storms of hamburgers. The residents love the system, until the weather gets out of control and they are forced to flee.

Where it's reviewed:
Center for Children's Books Bulletin, February 1979, page 94
Kirkus Reviews, December 1, 1978, page 1303

Awards the book has won:
Buckeye (K-3 Honor) 1982
Colorado Children's Book Award 1980

Other books by the author:
I Hate to Go to Bed, 1977
Wind Thief, 1977

Peter's Pockets, 1974
Old MacDonald Had an Apartment House, 1969

Other books you might like:
Patricia Coombs, *Dorrie and the Weather Box*, 1966
    Dorrie, a little witch, wants to have a picnic but it's raining. She goes to her mother's room, mixes two spells together and creates a disaster.
Terrance Dicks, *Max's Amazing Summer*, 1991
    Max the talking cat must save the town from unusually hot weather and strange giant insects.
Dick Gackenbach, *Ida Fanfanny*, 1978
    Ida lives in a land of no weather until a salesman sells her four magical paintings.
Emily Hearn, *TV Kangaroo*, 1975
    Various animals react differently to the kangaroo's weather forecasts.
Mike Wilks, *The Weather Works*, 1983
    A vast and sprawling factory churns out weather in all its many forms.

98

James Barrie

Illustrator: Michael Hague

Peter Pan (New York: Scribners, 1991)

Age range: Grades 3-6

Subject(s): Fantasy

Major character(s): Wendy Darling, Child; John Darling, Child; Peter Darling, Child

Time period(s): Indeterminate

Locale(s): England; Never-Never-Land, Fictional Country

What the book is about: The classic tale of a boy who chose to never grow up. Wendy, John, and Michael join Peter in adventures in Never-Never-Land where they meet Captain Hook, the Indians, and the Pirates, and a clock-eating crocodile. Originally published in 1904.

Where it's reviewed:
Center for Children's Books Bulletin, March 1981, page 125
School Library Journal, December 1980, page 57

Other books by the author:
Peter and Wendy, 1911
The Little White Bird, 1902

Other books you might like:
Natalie Babbitt, *Tuck Everlasting*, 1987
    The Tuck family have a secret spring that prevents them from ever growing older.
Jane Louise Curry, *The Change-Child*, 1969
    In 16th century Wales, a girl's fair hair and lame foot make her suspect to her neighbors who fear she is a fairy child and capable of magic.
Mary Norton, *Are All the Giants Dead?*, 1975
    James tries to help Princess Dulcibel who is destined to marry a toad after her ball falls into the well.
Victor Osborne, *Moondream*, 1988
    When his cousin Katy is kidnapped by a Grabbly, Rupert enlists the help of flying pirates and a kindly badger to rescue her from Castle Dread.
Holden Wetherbee, *The Wonder Ring*, 1978

When a poor, mistreated boy show kindness to a beggar, he receives a magic ring.

99

Jennifer Bartoli

Illustrator: Joan Drescher

Nonna (New York: Harvey House, 1975)

Age range: Grades 1-3

Subject(s): Death; Grandparents

Time period(s): Indeterminate

Locale(s): United States

What the book is about: This is the story of a large Italian-American family. Every Saturday the whole family would gather at Grandmother's house. Her grandson tells of her death and how loved she was, and how much she is missed.

Where it's reviewed:
Booklist, June 15, 1975, page 1072
School Library Journal, September 1975, page 76

Other books by the author:
The Story of a Grateful Crane, 1977
Snow on Bear's Nose, 1976

Other books you might like:
Joanne E. Bernstein, *When People Die*, 1977
   This is one of the best books on death for primary school children. It discusses the cycle of life, buriel customs and religious beliefs.
Tomie De Paola, *Watch out for the Chicken Feet in Your Soup*, 1974
   Joey is a little embarrassed to take his friend, Eugene, to his old-fashioned grandmother's house for a visit.
Tony Johnson, *Pages of Music*, 1988
   In Sardinia, a shepherd fills the village with the joy of his music.
Steven Kroll, *Looking for Daniela*, 1988
   The story of a street performer who rescues a merchant's daughter, set in 19th century Italy.
Ilse Plume, *The Story of Befana*, 1981
   The Italian legend about the witch who delivers Christmas presents to the children.

100

Hosie Baskin

A Book of Dragons (New York: Knopf, 1985)

Age range: Grades 3-6

Subject(s): Dragons; Folk Tales

Time period(s): Indeterminate

Locale(s): Fictional Country

What the book is about: A collection of twenty dragons full of beauty and terror, taken from legends and myths, with approximately a half-page text for each creature. The stories are drawn from the Bible, Babylonia, China, medieval Europe, Greek mythology, Japan, Tolkien and the author's fantasy.

Where it's reviewed:
Hornbook, March/April 1986, page 189

School Library Journal, February 1986, page 62

Other books you might like:
Jane Launchbury, *Real Fairies and Other Tales*, 1986
   A collection of twelve fairy tales about princesses, dragons, fairies and magic by a variety of authors.
Gilles Ragache, *Myths and Legends of Dragons*, 1991
   Presents various myths and legends about dragons and discusses dragon lore from around the world.
Caroline Royds, *The Dragon, Giant and Monster Treasury*, 1988
   A collection of tales from various sources about the adventures of assorted giants, monsters and dragons.
Peter Sis, *Komodo!*, 1993
   A young boy who loves dragons goes with his parents to the Indonesian island of Komodo in hopes of seeing a real dragon. Includes factual information.
Stephanie S. Tolan, *Marcy Hooper and the Greatest Treasure in the World*, 1991
   Marcy, who can't seem to do anything right, has an adventure involving a dragon and treasure, which bolsters her self-esteem.

101

Lillian Bason

Illustrator: Margot Tomes

Those Foolish Molboes (New York: Coward, 1977)

Age range: Grades 2-4

Subject(s): Folk Tales

Time period(s): Indeterminate

Locale(s): Denmark

What the book is about: The people of Mols have been the objects of jokes for over two centuries. They are cheerfully stupid people. They bury a bell at sea and mark the spot with an "X" on a rowboat. They buy a small boat and wait for it to grow.

Where it's reviewed:
Horn Book, October 1977, page 529
School Library Journal, September 1977, page 100

Other books by the author:
Spiders, 1974
Castles and Mirrors and Cities of Sand, 1968

Other books you might like:
Jens Christian Bay, *Danish Fairy and Folk Tales*, 1899
   A collection of popular stories and fairy tales, translated from the Danish.
Jacob Grimm, *The Brave Little Tailor*, 1979
   Through cleverness, a young tailor, who kills seven flies with one blow, becomes a king.
Mary Cottam Hatch, *Thirteen Danish Tales*, 1947
   Based on Bay's translation, first published in America in 1899.
Virginia Haviland, *The Talking Pot*, 1990
   A retelling of a Danish tale in which a magical pot causes a poor family to triumph over a rich couple.
Helen Kronberg Olson, *Stupid Peter*, 1970
   Seven original fairy tales including "The Queen's Gift," "The Witch of the Forest," and "The Seven Lazy Sisters."

102

Betty Bates

It Must've Been the Fish Sticks (New York: Holiday, 1982)

Age range: Grades 5-6

Subject(s): Adoption; Identity

Major character(s): Brian, Teenager; Imogene, Parent

Time period(s): 1980s

Locale(s): Ohio

What the book is about: Thirteen year old Brian dreams of how things would be if he were with his mother instead of his adoptive mother, his father's second wife. He threatens to go find her on his own if his father won't help him. His father agrees, and Brian finds his mother, Imogene. She is in an abusive relationship and totally unable to care for him. After a near disaster, he decides to return home.

Where it's reviewed:
Booklist, June 15, 1982, page 1366
Center for Children's Books Bulletin, September 1982, page 2

Other books by the author:
That's What T.J. Says, 1982
Picking Up the Pieces, 1981
Love Is Like Peanuts, 1980
My Mom, the Money Nut, 1979

Other books you might like:
Pat Darby, *Visiting Miss Pierce*, 1986
    14 year old Barry, visiting an 83 year old woman in a nursing home and encouraging her to delve into her past, finds the project very meaningful.
Norma Klein, *What It's All About*, 1975
    The adoption of a Vietnamese orphan by 11 year old Bernadette's mother and stepfather is the beginning of a period of changing family relationships.
Anne Lindbergh, *Nobody's Orphan*, 1983
    Martha is convinced she's adopted, but thinks she wouldn't mind it so much if only her parents would let her have a dog.
Lila Perl, *Annabelle Starr, E.S.P.*, 1983
    Convinced she has ESP, Annabelle has second thoughts about her ''gift'' when she sees the fear a prediction causes in her adoptive brother.
Susan Sommer, *And I'm Stuck with Joseph*, 1984
    Sheila wants a baby sister, but her parents adopt a baby brother who is very difficult to love.

103

Betty Bates

My Mom, the Money Nut (New York: Holiday House, 1979)

Age range: Grades 5-7

Subject(s): Mothers and Daughters; Poverty; Singing

Major character(s): Fritzi Zimmer, Musician, Teenager; Mrs. Torcom, Musician; Hope, Teenager

Time period(s): 1970s

Locale(s): United States

What the book is about: Slowly, Fritzi understands why her mother stresses economic security as a goal, after visiting her grandfather. Fritzi only wants to sing, even if she can't make a living at it, and the tension between Fritzi and her mom keeps growing.

Where it's reviewed:
Booklist, March 1, 1979, page 1152
Center for Children's Books Bulletin, November 1979, page 41
School Library Journal, September 1979, page 128

Other books by the author:
Ask Me Tomorrow, 1987
It Must've Been the Fish Sticks, 1982
Ups and Downs of Jorie Jenkins, 1978
Bugs in Your Ears, 1977

Other books you might like:
Betsy Byars, *The Glory Girl*, 1983
    Anna, the one non-singing member of a gospel-singing family, feels left out, until the day the family bus is involved in an accident.
Mary S. Davidson, *A Superstar Called Sweetpea*, 1980
    Because her parents wish her to wait before pursuing a singing career, a high school junior begins a deception which affects all areas of her life.
Bette Greene, *Them That Glitter and Them That Don't*, 1983
    Though she has always been told the contrary, a Gypsy girl living in the south is convinced that she can use her singing talent to become someone.
Richard Peck, *Those Summer Girls I Never Met*, 1988
    Teens Drew and Steph reluctantly take a Baltic cruise with their heretofore unknown grandmother, a singing star of the 1940s.
Joyce Carol Thomas, *When the Nightingale Sings*, 1992
    Despite her foster mother's attempts to demean her, Marigold finds the song within her heart during a search for a gospel singer for a church choir.

104

Betty Bates

Illustrator: Jim Spence

Say Cheese (New York: Holiday, 1984)

Age range: Grades 3-5

Subject(s): Christmas; Family Life

Major character(s): Christy Hooper, Preteen, 5th Grader; Gilbert Trowbridge, Friend, 5th Grader

Time period(s): 1980s

Locale(s): United States

What the book is about: Because her dad is constantly singing at his work bench, Christy is able to identify an ''oldie'' and wins $100 in a radio contest. She wants to buy presents for all seven members of her family, but also wants a new dress which might help impress Gilbert Trowbridge, a boy in her fifth grade church school class. The decision she finally makes provides a memorable Christmas and shows that loving and caring are more important than just buying presents. (Also published as *Everybody Say Cheese*)

Where it's reviewed:
Booklist, November 15, 1984, page 440
Center for Children's Books Bulletin, December 1984, page 61

School Library Journal, January 1985, page 72

Other books by the author:
Hey There, Owlface, 1991
Ask Me Tomorrow, 1987
Call Me Friday the Thirteenth, 1983
Bugs in Your Ears, 1977

Other books you might like:
Charles Dickens, *A Christmas Carol: Being a Story of Christmas*, 1983
A miser learns the true meaning of Christmas when three ghostly visitors review his past and foretell his future.
Ruth Sawyer, *This Way to Christmas*, 1952
A lonely boy in snowy hill country at Christmas meets a fairy who introduces him to equally lonely neighbors who each tell a unique Christmas story.
Maxine Schur, *Samantha's Surprise: A Christmas Story*, 1986
The two weeks before Christmas are filled with activity as Samantha finishes her homemade presents and makes preparations for visiting relatives.
Janet Beeler Shaw, *Kirsten's Surprise: A Christmas Story*, 1986
Kirsten and her family celebrate their first Christmas in their new home on Uncle Olva's farm in mid-nineteenth-century Minnesota.
Theodore Taylor, *Maria, a Christmas Story*, 1992
Maria and her family are the first Mexican Americans to enter a float in the annual Christmas parade in San Lazaro, California.

105

Betty Bates

Thatcher Payne-in-the-Neck (New York: Holiday, 1985)

Age range: Grades 4-6

Subject(s): Remarriage; Stepfamilies; Friendship

Major character(s): Kib Slocum, Preteen; Thatcher Payne, Preteen

Time period(s): 1980s

Locale(s): Trout Lake, Illinois

What the book is about: Kib and Thatcher are long time friends who shared grief when Kib's mother and Thatcher's father were killed in the same plane crash. They bring their widowed parents together, but then begin to realize they made much better friends than siblings. Kib finds Thatcher a pain and to make matters worse, the adults are busy together all the time. It takes some work, but Kib and Thatcher adjust to having to share their parents and begin to build a new family.

Where it's reviewed:
Booklist, February 1, 1986, page 807
School Library Journal, December 1985, page 86

Other books by the author:
Great Male Conspiracy, 1986
Herbert and Hortense, 1984
That's What T.J. Says, 1982
Picking Up the Pieces, 1981

Other books you might like:
Bruce Brooks, *What Hearts*, 1992
After his parents divorce and his father remarries, Asa's sharp intellect and ability to forgive help him cope with all the changes in his new life.

Louise Fitzhugh, *Sport*, 1979
Eleven year old Sport lives happily with his absent minded father, but his ruthless and wealthy mother suddenly wants custody.
Anne Lindbergh, *Travel Far, Pay No Fare*, 1992
When Owen finds his cousin has a magic bookmark, he joins her in hopes of finding a way to prevent their parents' upcoming marriage.
Ann M. Martin, *Bummer Summer*, 1983
When Kammy has trouble accepting her new family after her father remarries, a summer at Camp Arrowhead helps her to put her life in perspective.
Ed McBain, *Me and Mr. Stenner*, 1976
When her mother remarries, an eleven year old learns she can love her stepfather and her real father at the same time.

106

Edith Battles

Witch in Room 6 (New York: Harper, 1987)

Age range: Grades 4-6

Subject(s): Schools; Witches and Witchcraft; Friendship

Major character(s): Cheryl Suzanne, Apprentice, Witch; Sean, Classmate

Time period(s): 1980s

Locale(s): United States

What the book is about: Cheryl Suzanne's family doesn't want her to associate with "regular" kids because she is an apprentice witch. All Sean wants is to be her friend.

Where it's reviewed:
Kirkus Reviews, June 1, 1987, page 854
School Library Journal, June 1987, page 92

Other books by the author:
Eddie Couldn't Find the Elephants, 1974
One to Teeter-Totter, 1973
Terrible Terrier, 1972
Terrible Trick or Treat, 1970

Other books you might like:
Monica Furlong, *Juniper*, 1991
While apprenticed to the witch woman Juniper, a young girl struggles to save her family from the evil of her power-hungry aunt, Meroot.
Ann M. Martin, *Karen's Little Witch*, 1991
Karen is afraid to go trick-or-treating with the neighbor's granddaughter, Druscilla, because she thinks Druscilla is a witch.
Phyllis Reynolds Naylor, *The Witch Returns*, 1992
Convinced that the woman who moved into the neighborhood is really the "dead" Mrs. Tuggle, Lynn and Mouse try to withstand her witchcraft.
Ann Rinaldi, *A Break with Charity: A Story about the Salem Witch Trials*, 1992
While waiting for a church meeting, Susanna English recalls the malice, fear and accusations of witchcraft that tore her village apart in 1692.
Stephanie S. Tolan, *The Witch of Maple Park*, 1993
Mackenzie is convinced that the mysterious older woman she sees around town is a witch and that she and her friend Casey must stop her.

| 107 |

Marion Dane Bauer

Foster Child (New York: Seabury, 1977)

Age range: Grades 5-6

Subject(s): Child Abuse; Foster Homes

Major character(s): Renny, Child, Runaway; Karen, Child, Runaway

Time period(s): 1970s

Locale(s): United States

What the book is about: Frightened by what might happen next, Renny takes Karen and runs away from a foster home when Mr. Beck caresses her. Her aunt has emptied out her house and placed Great-grandmother in a nursing home. They have to turn to Karen's mother for help.

Where it's reviewed:
Kirkus Reviews, May 1, 1977, page 485
School Library Journal, April 1977, page 74

Awards the book has won:
Golden Kite Fiction Honor Book 1977

Other books by the author:
A Dream of Queens and Castles, 1990
On My Honor, 1986
Like Mother, Like Daughter, 1985
Rain of Fire, 1983

Other books you might like:
Natalie Savage Carlson, *Ann Aurelia and Dorothy*, 1968
    Ann Aurelia must decide between her foster home and Dorothy's stable family and her own mother.
Patricia Hermes, *Heads, I Win*, 1988
    Bailey is foster-home smart. She always leaves before she can be dumped.
Jean Little, *Home From Far*, 1965
    After Jenny's twin was killed in an auto accident, her mother brings two foster children into their home, one a boy her same age.
Bel Mooney, *The Stove Haunting*, 1988
    An old cooking stove in an English country home transports Daniel back in time where he is a stove boy in a rector's house.
Hilma Wolitzer, *Toby Lived Here*, 1978
    Two sisters adjust in different ways to a foster home.

| 108 |

Marion Dane Bauer

On My Honor (New York: Clarion, 1986)

Age range: Grades 4-6

Subject(s): Promises; Death; Accidents

Major character(s): Joel, Child; Tony, Child

Time period(s): 1980s

Locale(s): United States

What the book is about: Joel's friend, Tony, is a headstrong show-off who will not listen to anyone's warnings. When Tony drowns in a place Joel promised never to go, Joel is terrified to tell what he knows.

Where it's reviewed:
Horn Book, May/June 1987, page 339
School Library Journal, November 1986, page 1986

Awards the book has won:
Newbery Honor

Other books by the author:
Like Mother, Like Daughter, 1985
Rain of Fire, 1983
Shelter From the Wind, 1976

Other books you might like:
Frank Etherington, *General*, 1983
    Students react when the General, a school crossing guard for generations of students, is fired.
Carolyn Polese, *Promise Not to Tell*, 1985
    A 12 year old girl is molested at a campground and learns the importance of letting her parents know what happened.
Mary Jane Auch, *Kidnapping Kevin Kowalski*, 1990
    When an accident disables Kevin, his best friends decide to kidnap him to free him from his over-protective mother.
Tatyana Bylinsky, *Before the Wildflowers Bloom*, 1989
    Carin and her family learn to cope after a tragic accident.
Betsy Byars, *The Glory Girl*, 1983
    Anna Glory and her family are involved in a terrible accident in the family bus.

| 109 |

Marion Dane Bauer

Shelter from the Wind (Boston: Houghton Mifflin, 1976)

Age range: Grades 5-8

Subject(s): Runaways

Major character(s): Stacy, Runaway; Ella, Recluse; Barbara, Step-Parent

Time period(s): 1970s

Locale(s): Cimarron City, Oklahoma

What the book is about: After her father remarries, Stacy runs away in search of her real mother, only to be befriended by an old woman who lives alone in the desert, and has a great deal to teach Stacy about life and love.

Where it's reviewed:
Horn Book, August 1976, page 394
School Library Journal, May 1976, page 56
Kirkus Reviews, April 1, 1976, page 389

Other books by the author:
Face to Face, 1991
A Dream of Queens and Castles, 1990
Like Mother, Like Daughter, 1985
Foster Child, 1977

Other books you might like:
Ellen H. Goins, *Big Diamond's Boy*, 1977
    Although he idolizes his father, Cotton realizes that Big Diamond doesn't always have his son's best interest at heart.
Lynn Hall, *Uphill All the Way*, 1984
    Callie longs to help a trouble-prone young man, but she finally comes to realize that some people cannot be changed.
Harold Keith, *Susy's Scoundrel*, 1976

An Amish girl in Oklahoma adopts two coyote pups, but their mother steals them back and their subsequent activities put them in deadly peril.

Anna Myers, *Red-Dirt Jessie*, 1992

Jessie, a girl living in the Oklahoma dust bowl during the Depression, tried to tame a wild dog and help her father recover from a nervous breakdown.

Joyce Carol Thomas, *Marked by Fire*, 1982

Abby, born in an Oklahoma cotton field in the wake of a tornado, learns the secrets of folk medicine from the healer Mother Barker, as she grows up.

110

Marion Dane Bauer

Illustrator: Alix Berenzy

Touch the Moon (New York: Ticknor, 1987)

Age range: Grades 3-5

Subject(s): Fantasy; Animals/Horses; Responsibility

Major character(s): Jennifer, Child; Moonseeker China, Horse

Time period(s): 1980s

Locale(s): United States

What the book is about: Angry over not getting a real horse, Jennifer throws away her toy horse gift and learns a lesson in responsibility, as the figurine becomes a real life palomino with the ability to talk back!

Where it's reviewed:
Booklist, September 15, 1987, page 144
Hornbook, September 1987, page 608
Kirkus, September 15, 1987, page 1388

Other books by the author:
Ghost Eye, 1992
Danger in the Endless Caves, 1988
The Kidnapped Falcon, 1988
On My Honor, 1986

Other books you might like:
Ida DeLage, *The Old Witch Goes to the Ball*, 1969
After she is mistaken for someone else at the Halloween Ball and consequently loses the prize for best costume, an angry old witch plans her revenge.
V.H. Drummond, *Phewtus the Squirrel*, 1987
A knitted squirrel has a chance to become real for a while and learns he vastly prefers life as a toy.
Lynn Hall, *The Secret Life of Dagmar Schultz*, 1988
Trapped in a dead Iowa community with no decent boys her age, Dagmar invents a fantasy boyfriend who gets her in terrible trouble.
Susan Saunders, *Back to Nature*, 1987
Jason's bossy pet rabbit Robot, who can secretly talk, stows away to accompany Jason on a camping trip, with chaotic and dangerous consequences.
Marjorie Weinman Sharmat, *Attila the Angry*, 1985
With the help of Angry Animals Anonymous, Attila the squirrel learns how to control his angry behavior.

111

Nina Bawden

Carrie's War (New York: Lippincott, 1973)

Age range: Grades 4-6

Subject(s): Mystery and Detective Stories

Major character(s): Carrie, Orphan; Nick, Orphan

Time period(s): 1940s

Locale(s): Druid's Bottom, Wales

What the book is about: Two children evacuated from London during the Blitz are sent to live in a small Welsh town. Their real happiness comes from visiting the farm of Mr. Evans' sister, where they meet another London orphan named Albert. Upset by a family feud, Carrie commits an act that will haunt her for years.

Where it's reviewed:
Horn Book, June 1973, page 2741
Kirkus Reviews, May 1, 1973, page 513

Other books by the author:
Henry, 1988
The Finding, 1985
Kept in the Dark, 1982
Devil by the Sea, 1976

Other books you might like:
Nina Bawden, *Three on the Run*, 1964
Held as a political prisoner in a London apartment, an African boy is helped to escape by two friends.
Beverly Haskell Lee, *The Secret of Van Rink's Cellar*, 1979
While searching for a ghost that haunts the house in which their mother is a maid, Sarah and Stephen become involved in the Revolutionary War effort.
Willo Davis Roberts, *Scared Stiff*, 1991
When their mother disappears, two brothers stay with an uncle who lives near an abandoned amusement park and begin a search which puts them in danger.
Mary Treadgold, *The Polly Harris*, 1970
While attending a London school to improve their grades, a brother and sister help their neighbors uncover a case of fraud.
Cynthia Voigt, *The Vandemark Mummy*, 1991
Phineas and Althea try to find out why a collection of Egyptian artifacts is the target of thieves.

112

Nina Bawden

Devil by the Sea (New York: Lippincott, 1976)

Age range: Grades 5-6

Subject(s): Family Life; Murder

Major character(s): Hilary, Child; Poppet, Child; Janet, Teenager

Time period(s): 1970s

Locale(s): United States

What the book is about: Hilary is nine when she and her brother see the strange old man go off with Poppet, who is later found murdered. When she tries to tell, she is punished for "lying." She is being watched and waited for.

Where it's reviewed:
Horn Book, August 1, 1976, page 847
Kirkus Reviews, August 1, 1976, page 847

Other books by the author:
Kept in the Dark, 1982
The Robbers, 1979
Rebel on a Rock, 1975
The Peppermint Pig, 1978

Other books you might like:
Patricia Beatty, *Wait for Me, Watch for Me, Eula Bee*, 1978
    With his father and brother away fighting the Civil War and much of his family killed in a Comanche raid, Lewellen tries to escape from the Indians.
Susan Dodson, *The Creep*, 1979
    After saving a young child from a molester, a teenage girl volunteers to help the police catch the man.
Kevin Henkes, *Words of Stone*, 1992
    Busy trying to deal with his emotions and fears concerning his dead mother, Blaze has his life changed when he meets Joselle.
E.L. Konigsburg, *Up From Jerico Tel*, 1986
    The spirit of a dead actress turns two children invisible and sends them out among a group of colorful street performers to solve a mystery.
Joan Lowery Nixon, *A Deadly Promise*, 1992
    Sarah risks her life to clear her murdered father's name and expose big-time criminal activity in the lawless mining town of Leadville, Colorado.

113

Nina Bawden

Illustrator: Joyce Powzyk

Henry (New York: Lothrop: 1988)

Age range: Grades 5-9

Subject(s): Animals/Squirrels; World War II

Major character(s): Henry, Squirrel

Time period(s): 1940s

Locale(s): England

What the book is about: Evacuated to the country from London during the bombings of World War II, a family tries to raise a baby squirrel, Henry, who has fallen from his nest. The story revolves around the reactions of the evacuated family to the squirrel - something lighter to think about than London under seige.

Where it's reviewed:
Booklist, April 15, 1988, page 1428
School Library Journal, April 1988, page 99
Center for Children's Books Bulletin, March 1988, page 130

Other books by the author:
Outside Child, 1989
The Robbers, 1979
Rebel on a Rock, 1978
Squib, 1971

Other books you might like:
Peggy Donaldson, *The Moon's on Fire*, 1980
    Having escaped from Nazi-occupied France, Janey, Tadek and Stefek are placed in the care of Janey's uncle whom they suspect of being an enemy spy.

Lois Lamplugh, *Falcon's Tor*, 1984
    After reading books about WWI, Aidan has thoughts of life in those horrifying days. Knocked unconcious in an accident, he wakes up in another time.
Jill Paton Walsh, *Fireweek*, 1969
    Two teenage runaways who refuse to be evacuated from London struggle to survive the blitz of 1940.
Alison Prince, *How's Business?*, 1987
    A young boy, sent to the country from London during WWII, comes into conflict with some local boys who find ways to test his courage.
Eileen Van Kirk, *A Promise to Keep*, 1990
    While spending the summer on a farm in the English countryside, Ellie falls in love with an Austrian refugee and faces a conflict of loyalties.

114

Nina Bawden

Kept in the Dark (New York: Lothrop, 1982)

Age range: Grades 5-8

Subject(s): Mystery and Detective Stories

Major character(s): Noel Jacobs, Child; Clara Jacobs, Child; Ambrose "Bosie" Jacobs, Child

Time period(s): 1980s

Locale(s): England

What the book is about: Three children visiting their grandparents encounter a wicked grandson/half-cousin. David is holding all of them prisoners while Noel and Clara and Bosie's father is in the hospital and their mother is with him. It is not safe to stay with David, but how can they escape?

Where it's reviewed:
Booklist, April 15, 1982, page 1093
Hornbook, June 1982, page 296
Kirkus Reviews, March 15, 1982, page 345

Other books by the author:
The Finding, 1985
Runaway Summer, 1969
The Witch's Daughter, 1966
Handful of Thieves, 1967

Other books you might like:
Dina Anastasio, *A Question of Time*, 1978
    Shortly after moving to a small town in Minnesota, a young girl's curiosity is aroused by four carved dolls resembling her great-grandfather's family.
Margaret Jean Anderson, *The Journey of the Shadow Bairns*, 1980
    When her parents die suddenly, a young, Scottish Girl decides she and her brother will fulfill the family plans to emigrate.
Eve Bunting, *Blackbird Singing*, 1980
    Marcus struggles to come to terms with himself, his parents' stormy relationship, and the huge flock of blackbirds that threatens their crops.
Betsy Byars, *Goodbye, Chicken Little*, 1979
    A boy discovers he doesn't have to feel personally responsible for his uncle's drowning.
Paula Fox, *How Many Miles to Babylon?*, 1967

James skips school to go to his secret place and is found by three teenage boys who force him to join their disappearing dog ring.

115

Nina Bawden

The Peppermint Pig (Philadelphia: Lippincott, 1975)

Age range: Grades 5-6

Subject(s): Animals/Pigs; Family Life

Major character(s): Poll Greengrass, Child; Theo Greengrass, Child; Johnnie, Pig

Time period(s): 1900s

Locale(s): London, England

What the book is about: After Poll and Theo's father flees to America, they move from their home in London to live with relatives in a Norfolk village where their mother works as a dressmaker. She buys the peppermint pig, the runt of the litter. He becomes a mischievous and beloved pet and the family that loves him provide humorous and exciting adventures.

Where it's reviewed:
Horn Book, June 1975, page 264
Kirkus Reviews, March 1, 1975, page 244

Other books by the author:
Henry, 1988
The Robbers, 1979
Rebel on a Rock, 1978
Devil by the Sea, 1976

Other books you might like:
Joan Davenport Carris, *Just a Little Ham*, 1989
   A family's pet pig delights them with her intelligence and personality, until her independence leads her to bad habits.
Adele Geras, *Apricots at Midnight: And Other Stories From a Patchwork Quilt*, 1977
   An elderly London dressmaker entertains a young relative with memories of the world of her youth.
Vicki Grove, *Goodbye, My Wishing Star*, 1988
   Jens, who adores the farm she has always lived on, is devastated when financial problems may force her family to sell and move to the city.
Robert Newton Peck, *A Day No Pigs Would Die*, 1972
   To a young Vermont farm boy, maturity comes early as he learns "doing what's got to be done," especially regarding his pet pig.
Virginia Vail, *All the Way Home*, 1987
   Val rescues Tiny and raises him as a pet. Val's city cousin is not happy about country life or the new pig.

116

Nina Bawden

The Robbers (New York: Lothrop, 1979)

Age range: Grades 4-6

Subject(s): Friendship; Crime and Criminals; Fathers and Sons

Major character(s): Philip Holbein, Child; Henry Holbein, Journalist; Darcy Jones, Streetperson

Time period(s): 1970s

Locale(s): London, England

What the book is about: When Philip visits his father and his new wife in London, he is surprised to learn the arrangement is to be permanent. He meets Darcy Jones, and learns the boy's desperate circumstances. When Darcy's older brother, Bing, is arrested for receiving stolen goods, Darcy tries to rob a wealthy neighbor and gets caught. A vivid portrayal of the harshness and double standards of poverty and wealth.

Where it's reviewed:
Horn Book, December 1979, page 661
School Library Journal, November 1979, page 73

Other books by the author:
Henry, 1988
The Finding, 1985
Kept in the Dark, 1982
Squib, 1971

Other books you might like:
Gibbs Davis, *Fishman and Charly*, 1983
   Eleven year old Tyler, known as Fishman, wants both to impress his stern father and save the gentle manatees he loves from the threat of poachers.
Barthe DeClements, *Monkey See, Monkey Do*, 1990
   Jerry's adored father seems unable to stay out of jail, making trouble for Jerry both at home and at school.
Brenda Guiberson, *Turtle People*, 1990
   Saddened by his father's absence and his mother's emotional distance, Richie retreats to a remote island and finds a great archeological mystery.
Doris Orgel, *Midnight Soup and a Witch's Hat*, 1987
   Looking forward to spending a whole week with her father in Oregon, Beck arrives to find she must share her father with Rosellen and her daughter.
Nancy Springer, *Red Wizard*, 1990
   Ryan is whisked from his world into a fantasy kingdom by an incompetent wizard, but the mistake helps him solve a problem with his own father.

117

Nina Bawden

Illustrator: Shirley Hughes

Squib (New York: Lothrop, 1971)

Age range: Grades 4-6

Subject(s): Child Abuse

Major character(s): Kate Pollack, Preteen; Robin, Friend; Henry Lincoln "Squib" Gladstone, Child

Time period(s): Indeterminate

Locale(s): England

What the book is about: Eleven year old Kate Pollack lost her brother years before when they were swept out to sea. Kate was rescued but Rupert was never found. Then she and her friends met a small boy named Squib at the park. He is a very strange child and about the age Rupert would have been. Why could Kate not stop thinking about Squib and why did he bring back such vivid memories of the tragedy when Rupert was lost? The trail leading to Squib's identity is an engrossing one.

Where it's reviewed:
Booklist, November 15, 1971, page 290
Hornbook, October 1971, page 482
Kirkus Reviews, July 15, 1971, page 738

Other books by the author:
Henry, 1988
The Peppermint Pig, 1975
Carrie's War, 1973
The House of Secrets, 1963

Other books you might like:
Allan Baillie, *Adrift*, 1983
    While playing pirates with his sister and her cat in an old crate he found on the beach, a boy suddenly discovers that they are adrift on the sea.
Louise Moeri, *The Girl Who Lived on the Ferris Wheel*, 1979
    Til realizes with increasing urgency that her divorced mother's violently abusive behavior is getting more and more out of control.
Rebecca Orr, *Gunner's Run*, 1980
    Gunner runs away from his abusive father, finds a friend in old Mr. Beltz, and begins to take a new pride in himself.
Gary Paulsen, *The Voyage of the Frog*, 1989
    When David goes out on his sailboat to scatter his recently deceased uncle's ashes to the wind, he is caught in a fierce storm.
Marilyn Sachs, *A December Tale*, 1976
    A foster child struggling to change her life is weakened by the bribes of an abusive mother, yet strengthened by conversations with Joan of Arc.

| 118 |

Byrd Baylor

Illustrator: Ronald Himler

Best Town in the World (New York: Scribner's, 1983)

Age range: Grades 3-4

Subject(s): City Life; Family Life

Major character(s): Father, Parent

Time period(s): Indeterminate Past

Locale(s): Texas

What the book is about: A father describes his childhood in the Texas town where he grew up. He remembers exploring caves, picking blackberries, and activities in the town. He remembers nights full of fireflies, stars, and music. The children listening wonder if they will ever find such a town.

Where it's reviewed:
Center for Children's Books Bulletin, April 1984, page 142
School Library Journal, March 1984, page 138

Other books by the author:
Hawk, I'm Your Brother, 1976
The Desert Is Theirs, 1975
When Clay Sings, 1972
Before You Came This Way, 1969

Other books you might like:
Frank Asch, *Dear Brother*, 1992
    Joey and Marvin stay up all night reading family letters they find in the attic.
Ann Jonas, *The Trek*, 1985

The city becomes a jungle, then a desert, as a child forges her way to school.
Ingrid Mennen, *Somewhere in Africa*, 1992
    Ashraf, a South African boy who lives in a big city, dreams of the African wild.
Mattie Lou O'Kelley, *Moving to Town*, 1991
    A rural family moves from their old farm to a house in the big city.
Mark Teague, *The Trouble with the Johnsons*, 1989
    Unhappy with their family's move to the city, Elmo and his cat visit their old house, but find that things are somehow not the same anymore.

| 119 |

Byrd Baylor

Illustrator: Peter Parnall

Hawk, I'm Your Brother (New York: Scribner, 1976)

Age range: Grades 3-5

Subject(s): Indians of North America; Animals/Birds

Major character(s): Rudy, Child

Time period(s): 1970s

Locale(s): United States

What the book is about: Rudy has always wanted to fly. Perhaps if he were brother to a hawk he might learn. He takes a young hawk from a cliff and keeps it on a string. The bird grows tame and Rudy grows in understanding.

Where it's reviewed:
Horn Book, October 1976, page 489
Kirkus Reviews, May 15, 1976, page 587

Awards the book has won:
Caldecott Honor Book 1977

Other books by the author:
The Other Way to Listen, 1978
The Way to Start a Day, 1978
They Put on Masks, 1974
Coyote Cry, 1972

Other books you might like:
Anne Eliot Crompton, *The Ice Trail*, 1980
    Two outcasts from an Indian tribe survive a hard winter.
Paul Goble, *Lone Bull's Horse Raid*, 1973
    Lone Bull's first battle, which allows him to stand before his people as a warrior.
Paul Pitts, *Racing the Sun*, 1988
    Brandon begins to understand his Navajo heritage after his grandfather comes to live with him.
Joyce Rockwood, *Groundhog's Horse*, 1978
    An eleven year old Cherokee decides to rescue his horse when it is stolen by the Cree.
Beatrice Siegal, *The Basket Maker and the Spinner*, 1987
    The fictionalized lives of a New England colonist named Mary Allen and a Wampanoag Indian woman named Yawata.

120

Martin Baynton, Author/Illustrator

Fifty Saves His Friend (New York: Crown, 1986)

Age range: Grades 1-2

Subject(s): Friendship; Animals/Rats

Major character(s): Fifty, Tractor; Norris, Rat

Time period(s): Indeterminate

Locale(s): United States

What the book is about: Norris, the rat and Fifty, the tractor, become good friends. Fifty pulls carts and logs all day but when someone is in danger, he goes to the rescue.

Where it's reviewed:
Booklist, June 15, 1986, page 1537
School Library Journal, May 1986, page 112

Other books by the author:
Why Do You Love Me?, 1988
Fifty and the Great Race, 1987
Fifty Gets the Picture, 1987
Fifty and the Fox, 1986

Other books you might like:
Virginia Lee Burton, *Katy and the Big Snow*, 1943
  Katy the tractor becomes the pride of the town when she plows a path for emergency workers to get out and help the town in a snowstorm.
Dahlov Ipcar, *One Horse Farm*, 1950
  Big Betty is the only horse on the farm and she works hard all year long at the different jobs on the farm until the day a tractor takes over.
Giyora Karmi, *'Night, Farm*, 1989
  A child at bedtime bids goodnight to the cornfield, tractor, chickens and other parts of the farm.
Elizabeth Laird, *The Day Sidney Ran Off*, 1990
  Duncan the tractor helps Stan the farmer look for a missing piglet.
Elizabeth Laird, *The Day the Ducks Went Skating*, 1991
  Stan's reliable farm tractor, Duncan, comes in handy when the ducks' pond freezes over and they cannot get to the water.

121

Nina Beachcroft

The Wishing People (New York: Dutton, 1982)

Age range: Grades 4-6

Subject(s): Fantasy; Magic; Wishes

Major character(s): Martha Grant, Preteen; Jonathan, Preteen

Time period(s): Indeterminate

Locale(s): Fictional Country

What the book is about: When Martha becomes the owner of an old weather house which forecasts weather, two wooden figures come to life because Martha wishes it so, and grant wishes to Martha and Jonathan. Their first wish is to be able to fly. They do, have a wonderful time, then realize that each wish lasts only a few hours. They make their next wishes very carefully, but have some very unexpected results.

Where it's reviewed:
Booklist, March 15, 1962, page 954
Kirkus, May 1, 1982, page 553
School Library Journal, December 1980, page 373

Other books by the author:
We'll Meet by Witchlight, 1973

Other books you might like:
Avi, *Bright Shadow*, 1985
  Having used four of the five wishes she can make for her hapless countrymen, Morwenna flees the kingdom to decide what to do with the last wish.
Ruth Chew, *The Wishing Tree*, 1980
  A bird and cat that talk and a special tree in a nearby park involve a brother and sister in some magical adventures.
Edward Eager, *Magic by the Lake*, 1985
  On vacation, four children find an entire lake full of magic, which they must tame and learn to handle in order to find the treasure that awaits them.
Diana Wynne Jones, *Castle in the Air*, 1990
  Abdullah, a carpet merchant and daydreamer, buys a magic carpet which changes his life, fulfills his dreams, and brings many dangerous adventures.
Pamela Stearns, *Into the Painted Bear Lair*, 1976
  Entering another world through a toy store, Gregory joins Sir Rosemary and a gourmet named Bear to experience princesses, spells, and hidden passages.

122

Patricia Beatty

Behave Yourself, Bethany Brant (New York: Morrow, 1986)

Age range: Grades 5-7

Subject(s): Family Life; Religion

Major character(s): Bethany Brant, Preteen (preacher's daughter)

Time period(s): 19th century

Locale(s): Texas

What the book is about: After the death of her mother, Bethany strives to adjust to a Texas town and her father's life as a circuit minister. Her curiosity leads to her being stranded on an escaped circus elephant in the middle of a lake. Hoping to build a church for her father, Bethany ends up in a saloon and a poker game, not expected behavior for a PK (preacher's kid).

Where it's reviewed:
Center for Children's Books Bulletin, October 1986, page 22
Horn Book, January/February 1987, page 54

Other books by the author:
Sarah and Me and the Lady From the Sea, 1989
Be Ever Hopeful, Hannalee, 1988
Something to Shout About, 1976
The Bad Bell of San Salvador, 1973

Other books you might like:
Barbara Corcoran, *Annie's Monster*, 1990
  Annie, from a small Maine town where her father is a minister, gets a new Irish wolfhound who soon causes Annie trouble due to his playful curiosity.
Ruth Nulton Moore, *Wilderness Journey*, 1979

Two boys travel across Pennsylvania in 1799 with a circuit preacher to find their mother whom they think is in Pittsburgh working and readying a home.

Phyllis Reynolds Naylor, *A String of Chances*, 1982
The daughter of a small town preacher not only discovers secrets which divide her family, but experiences her first uncertainties about her life.

Terry Pringle, *The Preacher's Boy: A Novel*, 1988
Relates the experiences of a young man growing up in a small Texas town in the shadow of his strict preacher father.

Betty Underwood, *The Forge and the Forest*, 1975
An orphaned French girl feels ambivalent about the iron-willed pastor who is her guardian, the growing abolition movement, and women's role in society

123

Patricia Beatty

Eben Tyne: Powdermonkey (New York: Morrow, 1990)

Age range: Grades 5 and Up

Subject(s): Civil War; Friendship

Major character(s): Eben Tyne, Teenager, Military Personnel (sailor, powdermonkey)

Time period(s): 1860s

Locale(s): Virginia

What the book is about: Eben Tyne has proved to be a cool headed sailor. He is selected to serve aboard the new Merrimac as it sails against the Yankee blockade off the Virginia coast. He becomes a powder monkey, the one who brings the gun powder up from the ship's hold. Vivid picture of the horrors of battle on the ironclad ships.

Where it's reviewed:
Booklist, October 1, 1990, page 325
School Library Journal, December 1990, page 98

Other books by the author:
Sarah and Me and the Lady From the Sea, 1989
Charley Skedaddle, 1987
Turn Homeward, Hannalee, 1984
Eight Mules From Monterey, 1982

Other books you might like:
Betsy Haynes, *The Ghost of the Gravestone Hearth*, 1977
While Charley is at the beach, the ghost of a sailor who died in 1712 persuades him to help dig for buried treasure.

Seymour Reit, *Ironclad!*, 1977
The historic battle between the Merrimac and the Monitor from the viewpoint of a young man serving aboard the Monitor.

Gloria Root Savoldi, *Tennessee Boy*, 1972
In 1865, two 13 year old boys, one black, one white, travel from the Tennessee mountains to Washington City.

Theodore Taylor, *The Odyssey of Ben O'Neal*, 1977
Ben and Teetoncey go to sea, she to escape a forced return to England and he to find his brother.

Colin Thiele, *Shadow Shark*, 1985
Two cousins join a group of fishermen in pursuit of a massive shark off southern Australia.

124

Patricia Beatty

Jayhawker (New York: Morrow, 1991)

Age range: Grades 5-8

Subject(s): Slavery; Underground Railroad

Major character(s): Lije Tully, Teenager, Spy

Time period(s): 1860s

Locale(s): Kansas

What the book is about: In the early years of the Civil War, teenage Kansas farm boy, Lije Tulley, becomes a Jayhawker, an abolitionist raider freeing slaves from the neighboring state of Missouri, and then goes undercover there as a spy.

Where it's reviewed:
Booklist, September 1, 1991, page 40
School Library Journal, January 1991, page 522

Other books by the author:
Who Comes with Cannons?, 1992
Melinda Takes a Hand, 1983
Lacy Makes a Match, 1979
I Want My Sunday, Stranger, 1977

Other books you might like:
Margaret Goff Clark, *Freedom Crossing*, 1980
After 4 years in the South, a 15 year old girl accepts slavery, and is horrified to learn her home in the North is part of the Underground Railroad.

Jean Fritz, *Brady*, 1960
A young Pennsylvania boy takes part in pre-Civil War anti-slavery activities.

Belinda Hurmence, *A Girl Called Boy*, 1982
A pampered young black girl on a family picnic is transported back to the days of slavery and must struggle to escape bondage.

Enid Meadowcroft, *By Secret Railway*, 1948
When David Morgan decides school is a waste of time in exciting Chicago in 1860, he meets Jim and winds up being involved in the Underground Railroad.

Barbara Smucker, *Runaway to Freedom*, 1977
Twelve year old Julilly and her crippled friend, Liza, run North toward freedom disguised as boys.

125

Patricia Beatty

Jonathan Down Under (New York: Morrow, 1982)

Age range: Grades 5-8

Subject(s): Miners and Mining

Major character(s): Jonathan Cole, Teenager

Time period(s): 1850s (1851)

Locale(s): Ballarat, Australia

What the book is about: Jonathan is involved in the Australian Gold Rush of 1851 after spending two years in California gold fields and in China with his father. They lead a meager existence, work to the point of exhaustion and are beset with financial and physical problems.

Where it's reviewed:
Center for Children's Books Bulletin, March 1983, page 121
Horn Book, February, 1983, page 50

Other books by the author:
Sarah and Me and the Lady From the Sea, 1989
Be Ever Hopeful, Hannalee, 1988
Charley Skedaddle, 1987
Something to Shout About, 1976

Other books you might like:
Annabel Johnson, *A Golden Touch*, 1963
   When a young teen travels to the west to join his father, he is disappointed that his dad is a poker dealer who has been thrown out of town.
Willard Manus, *The Mystery of the Flooded Mine*, 1969
   Bill Bryan helps in the search for gold in a flooded mine.
Maureen Pople, *A Nugget of Gold*, 1988
   Alternate chapters narrate intertwining stories of a teen girl in the 19th century Australian gold fields, and a modern teen.
Alison Smith, *A Trap of Gold*, 1985
   Margaret finds a mysterious, shadowy figure watching her as she searches for a lost gold nugget from an abandoned mine.
Nadia Wheatley, *My Place*, 1987
   The story of Australia's history as it might have been seen by children from 1788 to 1988.

126

Patricia Beatty

Red Rock over the River (New York: Morrow, 1973)

Age range: Grades 6 and Up

Subject(s): American West

Major character(s): Dorcas, Teenager

Time period(s): 1880s (1881)

Locale(s): Fort Yuma, Arizona

What the book is about: When a new girl arrives at Fort Yuma, Arizona, thirteen year old Dorcas finds herself involved in the escape of an outlaw from the prison across the river.

Where it's reviewed:
Horn Book, June 1973, page 268
Kirkus Reviews, December 15, 1972, page 1429

Awards the book has won:
Golden Kite Honor Book 1973

Other books by the author:
Behave Yourself, Bethany Brant, 1986
Jonathan Down Under, 1982
That's One Ornery Orphan, 1980
Lacy Makes a Match, 1979

Other books you might like:
Betty Baker, *The Spirit Is Willing*, 1974
   In an Arizona mining town in the 1880s, an encounter with "spiritism" gives a fourteen year old a new understanding of people.
Patricia Beatty, *How Many Miles to Sundown*, 1974
   In 1881, a tomboy, her brother, and her pet longhorn join a boy searching for his father through Texas and the New Mexico and Arizona territories.
Warwick Downing, *Kid Curry's Last Ride*, 1989

Spending the summer in the 1930s with his grandmother in Wyoming, Alex becomes involved with man who claims to be a member of Butch Cassidy's gang.
Isabelle Holland, *The Journey Home*, 1990
   Two orphan sisters in the late 1800s leave New York on the orphan train to seek a new home in the West.
Don Schellie, *Kidnapping Mr. Tubbs*, 1978
   Two teens sneak an elderly ex-cowboy out of his rest home for a visit to the ranch where he spent his life.

127

Delores Beckman

My Own Private Sky (New York: Dutton, 1980)

Age range: Grades 5-8

Subject(s): Babysitters; Physically Handicapped; Single Parent Families

Major character(s): Arthur Livingston Elliott, Preteen; Jennifer Wingford "Jenny" Kearns, Neighbor; David Ward "Pilgrim" Wingford, Parent, Aged Person

Time period(s): 1980s

Locale(s): Glenwood, California

What the book is about: Arthur and his mother move to California because of Arthur's allergies. When his mom goes to work, Arthur stays with a neighbor, Jenny Kearns, who is sixty, and Jenny's father who is eighty-five. Arthur expects it to be a terrible arrangement, but finds a surprisingly good friend in Jenny, who helps him overcome his fear of swimming as he helps her recover from an auto accident.

Where it's reviewed:
Booklist, May 1, 1980, page 1287
Center for Children's Books Bulletin, March 1980, page 75
Kirkus Reviews, July 15, 1980, page 909

Awards the book has won:
International Reading Association Children's Book Award 1981

Other books by the author:
Who Loves Sam Grant?, 1983

Other books you might like:
Marion Dane Bauer, *Face to Face*, 1991
   Picked on at school by bullies, Michael confronts his fears during a trip to Colorado to see his father who works as a white-water rafting guide.
Beverly Keller, *The Sea Watch: A Mystery*, 1981
   While aboard a luxury liner bound for Europe, a young boy who is plagued by allergies stumbles onto a mystery involving a wristwatch.
Susan E. Kirby, *Shadow Boy*, 1991
   After Arnie suffers a closed-head wound in a car accident, adjustment and recovery are difficult for him, his sister Cozy, and the whole family.
Jim Naughton, *My Brother Stealing Second*, 1989
   After his brother is killed in a car accident, Bobby tries to cope with the truth about his family, political corruption in town, and his own grief.
Jean Thesman, *When the Road Ends*, 1992
   Three foster children and an older woman recovering from an accident are abandoned by their slovenly caretaker and must try to survive on their own.

| 128 |

John Bellairs

Illustrator: Judith Gwyn Brown

The Treasure of Alpheus Winterborn (New York: Harcourt Brace, 1978)

Age range: Grades 5-7

Subject(s): Treasure; Horror; Family Problems

Major character(s): Alpheus Winterborn, Wealthy; Hugh Philpotts, Relative (nephew)

Time period(s): 1970s

Locale(s): Hoosac (Midwestern town)

What the book is about: A boy's family problems lead him to seek a buried treasure, supposedly hidden in the Hoosac Public Library. Anthony is led from one hair-raising experience to another, until he wonders if he will survive the search.

Where it's reviewed:
Booklist, March 1, 1978, page 1098
Kirkus Reviews, April 15, 1978, page 435
School Library Journal, May 1978, page 84

Awards the book has won:
New York Times Outstanding Books 1978

Other books by the author:
The Lamp from the Warlock's Tomb, 1988
The Dark Secret of Weatherend, 1984 (Sequel)
The Curse of the Blue Figurine, 1983
The House with a Clock in Its Walls, 1973

Other books you might like:
David Budbill, *Bones on Black Spruce Mountain*,
    Danny and Seth set out to explore Black Spruce Mountain, but the mountain appears to be haunted and their adventure gets out of hand.
Richard M. Koff, *Christopher*,
    Christopher knocks on the door of a haunted house, and meets the "Headmaster" who teaches him how to release the amazing powers of her mind.
Walter Macken, *Island of the Great Yellow Ox*, 1991
    A storm washes Conor, his brother, and two friends onto Ox Island where they become prisoners of Lady Agnes who wants to uncover the Druid Treasure.
Farley Mowat, *Lost in the Barrens*, 1962
    Jamie, new to Canada, and Awasin, son of a Cree Indian, explore the far northern wastelands, survive on their own, and discover a Viking treasure.
Barbara Brooks Wallace, *Peppermints in the Parlor*, 1980
    Sent to San Francisco to live with her aunt and uncle, newly orphaned Emily enters their once happy mansion only to find unimaginable horrors.

| 129 |

John Bellaris

The House with a Clock in Its Walls (New York: Dial, 1973)

Age range: Grades 4-6

Subject(s): Magic

Major character(s): Uncle Jonathan, Wizard; Lewis Barnavelt, Child, Ward; Mrs. Zimmerman, Witch

Time period(s): 1940s (1948)

Locale(s): New Zebedee, Michigan

What the book is about: Lewis is raised by his Uncle Jonathan after his parents are accidentally killed. He discovers that both his uncle and next door neighbor are into witchcraft. There is a magic clock in the house that is ticking its way to Doomsday.

Where it's reviewed:
Booklist, October 15, 1973, page 227
Kirkus Reviews, May 1, 1973, page 514

Awards the book has won:
Michigan Young Readers Award - Runnerup 1980

Other books by the author:
The Secret of the Underground Room, 1990
The Trolley to Yesterday, 1989
The Dark Secret of Weatherend, 1984
The Curse of the Blue Figurine, 1983

Other books you might like:
Vera Chapman, *Miranty and the Alchemist*, 1983
    While staying with Uncle Gervase, Miranty has many adventures as a result of her uncle's attempts to make gold.
Edward Eager, *Magic or Not?*, 1985
    Despite what the girl on the train said, James and Laura aren't really sure that the well by their new house is really magical.
Mark Jonathan Harris, *With a Wave of the Wand*, 1980
    Through her friendship with Mr. Tomaro, Marlee decides that magic is the only way to win back her father and reunite the family.
Judith Winship Hollands, *The Like Potion*, 1986
    Beverly is convinced that a love potion will make classmate Jason Baines hers forever.
Diana Wynne Jones, *The Magicians of Caprona*, 1980
    A story of rivalry and family feuds, with a strong dose of magic tossed in for good measure.

| 130 |

Natalie Maree Belting

Our Fathers Had Powerful Songs (New York: Dutton, 1974)

Age range: Grades 3-5

Subject(s): Indians of North America; Poetry

Locale(s): Canada; United States

What the book is about: Nine poems reflecting a reverence and closeness to nature and quiet joy in human dignity and the power of the gods. Nine different nations are represented.

Where it's reviewed:
Horn Book, August 1974, page 387
Kirkus Reviews, May 1, 1974, page 482

Other books by the author:
Whirlwind Is a Ghost Dancing, 1974
Summer's Coming In, 1970
The Stars Are Silver Reindeer, 1966
Calendar Moon, 1964

Other books you might like:
Tomie De Paola, *The Legend of the Indian Paintbrush*, 1988

Little Gopher follows his destiny of becoming an artist for his people.

Melinda Eldridge, *Salcott, the Indian Boy*, 1990
Salcott must prove his maturity and bravery by spearing a bear through the heart.

Paul Goble, *Beyond the Ridge*, 1989
At her death, an elderly Plains Indian woman experiences the afterlife believed in by her people.

Angela Shelf Medearis, *Dancing with the Indians*, 1991
While attending a Seminole Indian celebration, a black family watches and joins in several exciting dances.

Jane Yolen, *Encounter*, 1992
A Taino Indian boy recounts the landing of Columbus in 1492.

131

Nathaniel Benchley

Illustrator: Hilary Knight

Feldman Fieldmouse (New York: Harper, 1970)

Age range: Grades 2-4

Subject(s): Animals/Mice

Major character(s): Feldman Fieldmouse, Mouse

Time period(s): Indeterminate

Locale(s): United States

What the book is about: A boy who knows about mice rescues an orphaned mouse and takes care of him. The fieldmouse is visited by his uncle who teaches him to work and to take the risk of dancing in the moonlight.

Where it's reviewed:
Booklist, September 1, 1971, page 55
Kirkus Reviews, May 1, 1971, page 500
Hornbook, June 1971, page 285

Other books by the author:
The Several Tricks of Edgar Dolphin, 1970
A Ghost Named Fred, 1968
Oscar Otter, 1966
Red Fox and His Canoe, 1964

Other books you might like:
Franz Brandenberg, *Nice New Neighbors*, 1977
The Fieldmouse children find a way to make new friends when they move to a new house.

Eleanor Clymer, *A Search for Two Bad Mice*, 1982
When her younger sister threatens to ruin the family's trip to England because of their cat, Barbara finds a way to make the vacation a success.

Lilian Moore, *Don't Be Afraid, Amanda*, 1992
After her country penpal visits a town mouse in the city, she overcomes fear of the country to visit him among the pleasures and dangers of nature.

Ethel Pochocki, *The Attic Mice*, 1990
Recounts the adventures of a family of mice as they go shopping in the humans' kitchen, discover useful items in the attic, and celebrate Christmas.

Eve Titus, *Basil in Mexico*, 1976
Basil, mouse and master detective, seeking the truth behind the theft of the Mousa Lisa, must also solve the mystery of his companion's disappearance.

132

Nathaniel Benchley

Illustrator: Don Bolognese

George the Drummer Boy (New York: Harper, 1977)

Age range: Grades 2-3

Subject(s): Revolutionary War

Major character(s): George, Military Personnel

Time period(s): 1770s (1776)

Locale(s): Boston, Massachusetts, American Colonies

What the book is about: The American Revolution from a British drummer boy's point of view. What were the lights in the Old North Church? Ambushed by Minutemen at Lexington, George and his friends are drawn into the first battle.

Where it's reviewed:
Kirkus Reviews, March 15, 1977, page 283
School Library Journal, May 1977, page 76

Other books by the author:
Sweet Anarchy, 1979
Kilroy and the Gull, 1977
Beyond the Mists, 1975
Feldman Fieldmouse, 1971

Other books you might like:
Richard Berleth, *Samuel's Choice*, 1990
A slave in Brooklyn in 1776 faces a difficult choice when the fighting between the British and the colonists reaches his doorstep.

Patricia Edwards Clyne, *The Corduroy Road*, 1973
A young patriot's plan to escape from his Tory uncle are complicated by Redcoats swarming through the area and his discovery of an ill lieutenant.

Dorothy Hoobler, *The Sign Painter's Secret*, 1991
When the Redcoats occupy her house in Philadelphia, Annie MacDougal finds a way to help General Washington's troops at Valley Forge.

Susan Lee, *The Battle for Long Island and New York*, 1975
Unwilling to take sides, two brothers make up their minds when they become involved in the Battle of Long Island.

Ann Warren Turner, *Katie's Trunk*, 1992
Katie's family is not sympathetic to the rebel soldiers during the Revolution. She hides in her mother's wedding trunk when they invade her home.

133

Nathaniel Benchley

Illustrator: John Schoenherr

Kilroy and the Gull (New York: Harper, 1977)

Age range: Grades 3-5

Subject(s): Animals/Whales; Animals/Birds; Friendship

Major character(s): Kilroy, Whale; Morris, Seagull

Time period(s): 1970s

Locale(s): United States (Marineland)

What the book is about: Kilroy is captured and brought to a Marineland aquarium. He meets a hostile dolphin. He decides he can do all the tricks the dolphin can. But he can't communicate with the humans no matter how hard he tries. He finally teaches the humans some tricks.

Where it's reviewed:
Horn Book, June 1977, page 309
School Library Journal, October 1977, page 109

Other books by the author:
George the Drummer Boy, 1977
Sam the Minuteman, 1977
Necessary End, 1976
Snorri and the Strangers, 1976

Other books you might like:
J. Allan Bosworth, *A Wind Named Anne*, 1970
    In a New England town a boy makes friends with a killer whale that wanders into a bay and becomes its guardian.
Ann Coleridge, *Stranded*, 1987
    Tony joins a dangerous mission to roll several stranded whales back into the sea.
Abraham Rothberg, *The Boy and the Dolphin*, 1969
    A boy forms a close friendship with a dolphin with the aid of three secrets of the sea revealed to him by his fisherman father.
Elizabeth-Ann Sachs, *Kiss Me, Janie Tannenbaum*, 1992
    Janie gains a new perspective on boys when she and her boy-crazy best friend go on a whale watching expedition.
Theodore Taylor, *The Hostage*, 1987
    Jamie has second thoughts about harboring a killer whale that he and his father captured off the coast of Vancouver, British Columbia.

134

Nathaniel Benchley

Illustrator: Don Bolognese

Snorri and the Strangers (New York: Harper, 1976)

Age range: Grades 2-4

Subject(s): Vikings; Discovery and Exploration

Major character(s): Snorri Thorfinnsson, Viking

Time period(s): 11th century (1010)

Locale(s): North America

What the book is about: Snorri was born in America a thousand years ago. His people are Norweigians who travel to Iceland, Greenland, then south to the unknown continent. Based on historical fact.

Where it's reviewed:
Center for Children's Books Bulletin, February 1977, page 86
School Library Journal, December 1976, page 65

Other books by the author:
George the Drummer Boy, 1987
Sam the Minuteman, 1987
Demo and the Dolphin, 1981
Beyond the Mists, 1975

Other books you might like:
Giovanni Caselli, *A Viking Settler*, 1986
    Observes a young Viking boy who lives on a farm in Denmark around 900 AD, while his father sails on trading expeditions, until they move to England.
Frank Knight, *Olaf's Sword*, 1969

A young Viking boy receives his first sword but has no chance to use it until he joins a group sailing to newly discovered Vineland.
George DeLucenay Leon, *Explorers of the Americas before Columbus*, 1989
    Examines the voyages of Eric the Red, Leif Ericsson, the Norse settlements and ancient visitors to South and Latin America.
Robin May, *Canute and the Vikings*, 1984
    A short biography of the 11th century Danish King and Warrior which also discusses the history of the Vikings, their conquests, discoveries, culture,
Henry Treece, *Viking's Dawn*, 1956
    Thorkell and his crew sail and fight and die bravely aboard the Nameless searching for plunder and fortune. (Advanced readers.)

135

Anna Elizabeth Bennett

Illustrator: Helen Stone

Little Witch (New York: Lippincott, 1953)

Age range: Grades 3-5

Subject(s): Witches and Witchcraft; Schools

Major character(s): Minikin "Minx" Snickasnee, Witch, Child; Madame Snickasnee, Parent (Minx's mother), Witch; Mrs. Sputter, Parent (PTA President)

Time period(s): 1950s

Locale(s): Fictional Country

What the book is about: Minx, the little witch, does not like being a witch's child. Her mother has forbidden her to go to school, wash behind her ears or go to bed at night. Minx didn't like turning people into potted plants or cooking up horrid pots of Black Spell Brew. Minx really wanted to go to school!

Other books you might like:
Patricia Combs, *Dorrie and the Haunted Schoolhouse*, 1992
    Dorrie, the little witch, goes to school where she and Dither, a fellow student, cause chaos when they mix up some spells.
Frieda Hughes, *Getting Rid of Aunt Edna*, 1986
    Chronicles the adventures of Miranda, an apprentice witch, who lives with her two witch aunts and an assortment of unusual animals.
Gregory Maguire, *The Dream Stealer*, 1983
    A village of Russian peasants flee an evil wolf only to be saved by a little girl's dream and the knowledge of the witch, Baba Yaga.
Marian T. Place, *The Resident Witch*, 1970
    A lowly apprentice witch seeks a promotion in witchdom by becoming Resident Witch for a children's amusement park.
Janice May Udry, *Glenda*, 1969
    Glenda, the witch, decides she wants to be a school girl but fails to recognize her complete lack of success in the venture.

136

Jay Bennett
The Dangling Witness (New York: Delacorte, 1974)
Age range: Grades 5-8

Subject(s): Murder; Mystery and Detective Stories

Major character(s): Matthew Garth, Teenager; Julie Leonard, Teenager

Time period(s): 1970s

Locale(s): New York, New York (Brooklyn)

What the book is about: An eighteen year old boy who witnesses a murder decides to keep quiet after he is threatened by the killer, but finds his silence increasingly hard to bear. He is torn between what he knows is right and his instinct for survival. When he meets Julie, the sister of the murdered man, he thinks he has found help, but Julie is anything but helpful. Can Matt avoid the syndicate and control his own destiny?

Where it's reviewed:
New York Times Book Review, November 10, 1974, page 8
Publisher's Weekly, August 12, 1974, page 58

Awards the book has won:
Edgar Allan Poe Award 1975

Other books by the author:
Coverup: A Novel, 1991
The Haunted One, 1987
Shadows Offstage, 1974
Deathman, Do Not Follow Me, 1968

Other books you might like:
Barbara Corcoran, *The Person in the Potting Shed*, 1980
    On vacation with their mother and new stepfather in a plantation house near New Orleans, a boy and girl discover a murder and help track the killer.
Ben Mikaelsen, *Sparrow Hawk Red*, 1993
    Ricky, the Mexican-American son of a Drug Enforcement Agency man, tries to avenge his mother's murder.
Nancy Pitt, *Beyond the High White Wall*, 1986
    Witnessing the murder of a peasant outside her small town in the Russian Ukraine in 1903, Libby triggers a wave of hate against her family.
Willo Davis Roberts, *The View From the Cherry Tree*, 1975
    Rob admits having seen a murder, but no one believes him, except the murderer.

137

Jay Bennett

The Long Black Coat (New York: Delacorte, 1973)

Age range: Grades 6 and Up

Subject(s): Mystery and Detective Stories

Major character(s): Phil, Teenager

Time period(s): 1970s

Locale(s): United States

What the book is about: Seventeen year old Phil is terrorized by two of his dead brother's associates from Vietnam who demand from him a package he knows nothing about.

Where it's reviewed:
Kirkus Reviews, April 1, 1973, page 395
Library Journal, May 15, 1973, page 1702

Awards the book has won:
Edgar Allan Poe Award 1974

Other books by the author:
Sing Me a Death Song, 1990

The Birthday Murderer, 1977
The Killing Tree, 1972
The Deadly Gift, 1969

Other books you might like:
Dana Brookins, *Alone in Wolf Hollow*, 1978
    Two orphaned brothers are sent to live with an alcoholic uncle in the dark woods of Wolf Hollow and become deeply involved in a murder.
Harriet Graham, *The Chinese Puzzle*, 1987
    Two children, searching for their missing guardian, stumble into the dangers and evils of the opium trade in the London of the 1890s.
Eloise Jarvis McGraw, *The Money Room*, 1981
    Scott's grandfather always bragged about his Money Room. When desperate times come, the kids search for his treasure in order to save the family farm.
Carole Smith, *Who Burned the Hartley House?*, 1985
    When a house burns down shortly after Larry had entered it looking for a phone, he and his biker friends try to find out why.
Maia Wojciechowska, *Tuned Out*, 1968
    Jim keeps a journal as he waits for his brother to return from college. Instead of recording a fun-filled summer, Jim tells of Kevin's drug abuse.

138

Kathleen Benson

Illustrator: Emily Arnold McCully

Joseph on the Subway Train (Reading, Massachusettes: Addison-Wesley, 1981)

Age range: Grades 2-3

Subject(s): Trains; Missing Persons

Major character(s): Joseph, Child, 2nd Grader; Billy, Child; Fatso, Child

Time period(s): 1980s

Locale(s): New York, New York (Brooklyn)

What the book is about: When Joseph's second grade class takes a subway trip from Brooklyn, Joseph gets separated from his class and the crowds carry him along into the wrong train. He meets two boys who get him to play dangerous games on the moving train. He finally gets off the train and Transit Police help him get back to Brooklyn.

Where it's reviewed:
Kirkus Reviews, January 15, 1982, page 67
School Library Journal, March 1982, page 144

Other books you might like:
Jerome Brooks, *Make Me a Hero*, 1980
    Jake struggles with a sense of worthlessness in the face of a world crisis he can do nothing about as well as bullies and fake friends.
Pat Hutchins, *Follow That Bus!*, 1977
    Miss Beaver's third grade class goes from one adventure to another because she is terribly absent minded.
Pat Rhoads Mauser, *How I Found Myself at the Fair*, 1980
    A child goes to the state fair with her friend's family and gets lost. She panics before using her head to find her friend.
Richard Rosenblum, *My Block*, 1988

A grandfather remembers his Brooklyn city block fifty years ago, sharing what it was like before there were huge stores and bumper to bumper traffic.

Zilpha Keatley Snyder, *Come On Patsy*, 1982
Patsy is bossed around by an inconsiderate playmate who gets her into one mess after another until she learns to say "no!"

139

Polly Berrien Berends

Illustrator: James K. Washburn

The Case of the Elevator Duck (New York: Random House, 1973)

Age range: Grades 3-5

Subject(s): Housing; City Life; Animals/Birds

Major character(s): Gilbert, Child; Easter, Duck

Time period(s): 1970s

Locale(s): United States

What the book is about: When the housing project has a NO PETS rule, what can a detective do when he finds a duck in the elevator? Trying to find the owner is not as easy as it sounds. A funny tale of city life.

Where it's reviewed:
Booklist, January 15, 1974, page 538
Kirkus Reviews, October 5, 1973, page 1158

Other books by the author:
Ozma and the Wayward Wand, 1985
Ladybug and Dog and the Night Walk, 1980
Who's That in the Mirror?, 1968

Other books you might like:
Eve Bunting, *The Skate Patrol and the Mystery Writer*, 1982
Handwriting analysis and some fast roller-skating help Milton and James close in on the vandal who has been spray painting their apartment building.
Mary Blount Christian, *No Dogs Allowed, Jonathan!*, 1975
When Jonathan is finally successful in smuggling a huge sheep dog into his apartment building, he learns why dogs are against the rules.
Johanna Hurwitz, *Busybody Nora*, 1976
An inquisitive little girl lives with her parents and little brother, Teddy, in a large apartment building in New York.
Hanna Johansen, *The Duck and the Owl*, 1991
A duck and an owl contemplate starting a friendship, despite their differences in appearance and behavior.
Ursel Scheffler, *Rinaldo, the Sly Fox*, 1992
Rinaldo, the sly fox, tricks everyone but Bruno, the duck detective.

140

Stan Berenstain

Bears in the Night (New York: Random, 1971)

Age range: Grades 1-2

Subject(s): Animals/Bears; Bedtime

Major character(s): Brother, Bear; Sister, Bear

Time period(s): Indeterminate

Locale(s): United States

What the book is about: Bedtime should be a quiet, peaceful time, but Brother Bear and Sister Bear have other things in mind and go on a rampage. Seven bears sneak out of bed, through the window and across the dark countryside to investigate the source of a noise. Beginning Readers

Where it's reviewed:
Center for Children's Books Bulletin, April 1972, page 117
Kirkus Reviews, July 15, 1971, page 738
School Library Journal, February 1982, page 36

Other books by the author:
The Bears' Almanac, 1973
Old Hat, New Hat, 1970
Bears on Wheels, 1969
Inside, Outside, Upside Down, 1968

Other books you might like:
Lizi Boyd, *Sweet Dreams, Willy*, 1992
Not wanting to sleep at bedtime, Willy goes in search of others still awake, thus beginning adventures with birds, fish, the moon and stars.
Mary Lee Donovan, *Papa's Bedtime Story*, 1993
On a warm and rumbling night in June, a series of human and animal fathers tell bedtime stories to their children.
Kate Duke, *Aunt Isabel Tells a Good One*, 1992
Penelope and her Aunt Isabel make up an exciting bedtime story about the adventures of Prince Augustus and Lady Penelope.
Richard McGilvray, *Don't Climb Out the Window Tonight*, 1993
Flying ghosts and jogging giants are just two of the ten very good reasons a little girl makes up so she won't climb out of her window in the night.
Carly Simon, *Amy the Dancing Bear*, 1989
Mother Bear tries to persuade her young daughter Amy to stop dancing and go to bed, with unexpected results.

141

Terry Berger

Friends (New York: Messner, 1981)

Age range: Grades 2-3

Subject(s): Friendship

Major character(s): Simon, Child

Time period(s): 1980s

Locale(s): United States

What the book is about: Simon loves horses, movies, music, and being with his friends. This story introduces five of Simon's friends and tell what is special about each one's interests and abilities. Black and white photos compliment the text.

Where it's reviewed:
School Library Journal, November 1981, page 72

Other books by the author:
Ben's ABC Day, 1982
The Turtle's Picnic, 1982
Stepchild, 1980
Special Friends, 1979

Other books you might like:
Anne Eliot Crompton, *Rain Cloud Pony*, 1977
  Pat loves horses so much she dreams about them and reads about them constantly. Her dishonest neighbor teaches her to value more than material things.
Sheila Greenwald, *Here's Hermione*, 1991
  Rosy becomes the manager of her best friend's unusual rock band.
Nancy Springer, *They're All Named Wildfire*, 1989
  Jenny becomes unpopular when she befriends a black girl whose family moves into Jenny's duplex. She finds her new friend shares her love of horses.
Martin Waddell, *Harriet and the Haunted School*, 1985
  Harriet kidnaps a circus horse and hides it in a school closet where it is mistaken for the Slow Street Phantom.
Mildred Pitts Walter, *Ty's One Man Band*, 1980
  Ty's friends make fun of him when he tells them about his new, peg-legged friend who is coming to town, and will dance and make unusual music.

142

Margery Bernstein

Illustrator: Enid Warner Romanek

The First Morning: An African Myth (New York: Scribner, 1976)

Age range: Grades 2-3

Subject(s): Mythology; Africa

Major character(s): Spider, Spider; Fly, Fly; Mouse, Mouse

Time period(s): Indeterminate Past

Locale(s): Africa

What the book is about: The story of how light came to the world. A fly, a mouse, and a spider go to a land above the sky. The King makes them pass three tests. The box that is supposed to hold the light has a rooster inside instead.

Where it's reviewed:
Horn Book, April 1976, page 147
School Library Journal, March 1976, page 89

Other books by the author:
Summer Maker: An Ojibway Indian Myth, 1977
How the Sun Made a Promise and Kept It, 1974

Other books you might like:
Warren J. Halliburton, *Celebrations of African Heritage*, 1992
  Examines the different ways in which African heritage is celebrated, both in the US and Africa. (non-fiction)
Shannon K. Jacobs, *Song of the Giraffe*, 1991
  Inspired by a dream, Kisana braves a dangerous journey to find the fruit of the baobab tree and a long-lost spring to earn the respect of her tribe.
Eric A. Kimmel, *Anansi Goes Fishing*, 1992
  Anansi the spider plans to trick Turtle into catching a fish for his dinner. Explains the origin of the spider web.
Gerald McDermott, *Zomo the Rabbit*, 1992
  Zomo the Rabbit, an African trickster, sets out to gain wisdom.
Sheron Williams, *And in the Beginning*, 1992
  The story of how Mahtmi created the first man from the dark rich earth of Kilimanjaro.

143

Jeanne Betancourt

Puppy Love (New York: Avon, 1986)

Age range: Grades 4-6

Subject(s): Friendship; Remarriage

Major character(s): Aviva Granger, Teenager, 8th Grader; Josh Greene, Bully, Orphan; Bob Hanley, Teenager

Time period(s): 1980s

Locale(s): Burlington, Vermont

What the book is about: Aviva had been looking forward to eighth grade, hoping it would be a new start and her life would improve. But her mother is remarried and expecting a new baby, so there goes mom's attention. Her dad is in love and planning to marry "Miriam the Moron." The boy she has a crush on is going with another girl. Then why is she so concerned whether Josh Greene likes her or not?

Where it's reviewed:
Booklist, August 1986, page 1685
School Library Journal, December 1986, page 98

Other books by the author:
Valentine Blues: An Aviva Granger Story, 1990
Crazy Christmas, 1988
Turtle Time, 1985
The Rainbow Kid, 1983

Other books you might like:
Katharine Bacon, *Pip and Emma*, 1986
  Pip and his sister, Emma, find the summer spent with their grandmother in Vermont affecting them in different ways.
Marion Walker Doren, *Nell of Blue Harbor*, 1990
  Nell is forced to grow up quickly when she moves from a Vermont commune to the real world with parents not yet ready to accept their responsibilities.
Mary Towne, *Wanda the Worrywart*, 1989
  Wanda's worries become even greater than usual the summer vacation when her divorced stepgrandmother develops an interest in a prospective husband.
Robert Newton Peck, *Soup*, 1974
  The adventures and misadventures of two boys growing up in a small Vermont town, and finding more ways to get into trouble than you can imagine.
Mary Stolz, *Cider Days*, 1978
  A young girl's persistent overtures to a new neighbor result in friendship.

144

T. Ernesto Bethancourt

The Dog Days of Arthur Cane (New York: Holiday, 1976)

Age range: Grades 6-9

Subject(s): Animals/Dogs; Street Music and Musicians

Major character(s): Arthur Cane, Dog (Preteen); Tyree, Musician (street musician), Handicapped (blind)

Time period(s): 1970s

Locale(s): New York, New York (Greenwich Village)

What the book is about: Arthur, a schoolboy from Long Island, New York, discovers that he has been turned into a dog by a witch doctor. He makes his way to the Village, where he becomes a Seeing Eye dog for a blind street musician.

Other books by the author:
The Great Computer Dating Caper, 1984
Instruments of Darkness, 1979
Dr. Doom, Superstar, 1978
New York City, Too Far From Tampa Blues, 1975

Other books you might like:
Isabelle Holland, *The Unfrightened Dark:*, 1990
 When her beloved seeing-eye dog is kidnapped, Jocelyn, orphaned and blind, determines to solve the mystery surrounding his disappearance.
Elizabeth Levy, *The Shadow Nose*, 1983
 A young boy is the prime suspect when shadow paintings appear in his Greenwich Village neighborhood.
Colby Rodowsky, *Keeping Time*, 1983
 Drew, a member of a band of street performers, finds himself slipping back in time, where he acquires the strength to deal with his unusual lifestyle.
Sarah Sargent, *Jerry's Ghosts: The Mystery of the Blind Tower*, 1992
 Jerry discovers two ghostly children, trapped with their mad scientist uncle in the mansion that was their former home, and sets them free.
George Selden, *Irma and Jerry*, 1982
 The adventures of a cat and a dog living in New York City's Greenwich Village.

145

Audrey White Beyer

Dark Venture (New York: Knopf, 1968)

Age range: Grades 5-6

Subject(s): Slavery

Major character(s): Demba, Slave, Preteen; Adam Waite, Doctor

Time period(s): 1700s

Locale(s): Bristol, Rhode Island; Gambia

What the book is about: A 12 year old West African boy is captured by an alien tribe and sold into slavery. A young doctor in Bristol, Rhode Island, agrees to sail as ship's surgeon bound for the Ivory Coast to pick up "black gold." Their paths cross and the doctor buys Demba and brings him to America. A devasting look at the horror of slavery from several perspectives.

Where it's reviewed:
Horn Book, August 1968, page 426
Library Journal, September 15, 1968, page 3311

Awards the book has won:
Boston Globe/Horn Book Award - Honor Book 1968

Other books by the author:
Katherine Leslie, 1963
Sapphire Pendant, 1961

Other books you might like:
Dorothy Hoobler, *Next Stop, Freedom*, 1991
 Emily, a slave girl who longs to read, escapes with Harriet Tubman. (Easy Reading)
Ann Rinaldi, *Wolf by the Ears*, 1991

A slave of Thomas Jefferson, Harriet Hemings, has to decide between comfortable slavery and dangerous freedom.
Cynthia Voigt, *On Fortune's Wheel*, 1990
 14 year old Birle joins a young runaway nobleman and falls into slavery under a cruel prince.
Chelsea Quinn Yarbro, *Four Horses for Tishtry*, 1985
 Tishtry's wish to buy her family's freedom from slavery leads her to dangerous action.

146

Elizabeth T. Billington

Illustrator: Diane De Groat

Part-Time Boy (New York: Warne, 1980)

Age range: Grades 3-4

Subject(s): Friendship; Shyness

Major character(s): Jamie, Child; Mattie Swenson, Scientist

Time period(s): 1980s

Locale(s): United States

What the book is about: Jamie is the quiet, shy brother of two extroverted older brothers and his mother worries that he is alone too much. Then Jamie meets Mattie Swenson, a young woman who works at the Natural Science Center. They become friends and Jamie expands his interests to include learning about the wilderness. He returns to school still shy, but much more self-confident.

Where it's reviewed:
Horn Book, August 1980, page 404
School Library Journal, May 1980, page 65

Other books by the author:
The Move, 1984
Getting to Know Me: A Novel, 1982
The Randolph Caldecott Treasury, 1978

Other books you might like:
Robert Burch, *King Kong and Other Poets*, 1986
 A shy new girl makes a place for herself in her sixth grade class by writing poems.
Ilene Cooper, *Frances Takes a Chance*, 1991
 When her best friend moves away, shy fourth grader Frances McAllister must make new friends and in doing so, learns to stick up for herself.
Jean Marzollo, *The Best Friends' Club*, 1990
 A shy, Hispanic third grader visits her father in Texas and gains self-confidence that helps her make friends when she returns to school.
Georgess McHargue, *See You Later, Crocodile*, 1988
 When she befriends eccentric Aunt Aggie, shy 13 year old Johanna learns a great deal about the difficulties of old age and of maintaining friendship.

147

Ann Blades

Boy of Tache (Canada: Tundra, 1973)

Age range: Grades 3-6

Subject(s): Indians of North America; Grandparents

Major character(s): Charlie, Hunter, Indian

Time period(s): Indeterminate

Locale(s): British Columbia, Canada

What the book is about: Charlie, a boy of the Tache Indian Reserve in northern British Columbia, goes with his father to hunt beaver, and makes a daring trip to bring a doctor when his grandfather develops pneumonia. Included is a brief history of the Tache and a map of their homeground.

Where it's reviewed:
Library Journal, April 15, 1974

Other books by the author:
A Dog Came Too, 1993
Ida and the Wool Smugglers, 1987
A Candle for Christmas, 1986
Mary of Mile Eighteen, 1971

Other books you might like:
Dennis B. Fradin, *Hiawatha: Messenger of Peace*, 1992
    Recounts the life of the 15th century Iroquois Indian who brought five tribes together to form the long-lasting Iroquois Federation.
Paul Goble, *The Lost Children*, 1993
    Six neglected orphaned brothers decide to go to the Above World where they become the constellation of the "Lost Children" or Pleiades.
James A. Houston, *River Runners: A Tale of Hardship and Bravery*, 1992
    Two young boys, who have been sent into the Canadian interior to set up a fur-collecting station, are befriended by a Naskapi Indian family.
Howard A. Norman, *How Glooskup Outwits the Ice Giants*, 1989
    Tales featuring the mythical giant who roamed the coast of New England and Canada, created the Indian peoples and fought battles to protect them.
Susan Sharpe, *Spirit Quest*, 1991
    Vacationing on an Indian reservation, Aaron becomes friends with Robert, a young Quileute Indian who is preparing for his spirit quest.

148

Esther Silverstein Blanc

Illustrator: Tennessee Dixon

Berchick (Volcano, California: Volcano Press, 1971)

Age range: Grades 2-4

Subject(s): American West

Time period(s): 1910s

Locale(s): Wyoming

What the book is about: An orphaned colt becomes the pet of a Jewish family homesteading in Wyoming in the early 1900s. This gentle, loving story shows the difficult life of pioneer farmers. As a read aloud or independent reader, it will add another viewpoint of the settling of the West for young readers.

Other books you might like:
Catherine E. Chambers, *Frontier Farmer: Kansas Adventure*, 1984
    When Matt's father dies in 1881, he and his mother decide to stay on their Kansas homestead despite the perils of life on the frontier.

Joanna Cole, *It's Too Noisy!*, 1989
    Unable to stand his noisy and overcrowded home any longer, a farmer goes to the Wise Man for advice.
Mary Virginia Fox, *The Story of Women Who Shaped the West*, 1991
    Presents women who helped to shape the Western frontier in such diverse roles as schoolteacher, missionary, justice of the peace and homesteader.
A.I. Lake, *Women of the West*, 1990
    Describes the work of the early women homesteaders and presents brief biographies of several women prominent in Western history.
Michael McCurdy, *Hannah's Farm: The Seasons on an Early American Homestead*, 1988
    As the seasons roll by, all the members of Hannah's family engage in activities on their farm in the Berkshire Hills of Massachusetts.

149

Mary Blocksma

Illustrator: Sandra Cox Kalthoff

The Best Dressed Bear (Chicago: Children's Press, 1984)

Age range: Grades 1-2

Series: Just One More

Subject(s): Animals/Bears; Clothes

Time period(s): Indeterminate

Locale(s): Fictional Country

What the book is about: Controlled vocabulary story in which an overweight bear decides what to wear to a dance. "Socks" says the fox, "Get a shoe" says the kangaroo, a shirt and tie says the sheep. Children will love the fact that bear and his friends almost forget the most obvious, his pants! But he does leave the house a well-dressed bear.

Where it's reviewed:
Booklist, February 15, 1985, page 848
School Library Journal, August 1985, page 53

Other books by the author:
All My Toys Are on the Floor, 1986
Where's That Duck?, 1985
Rub-a-Dub-Dub: What's in the Tub?, 1984
Grandma Dragon's Birthday, 1983

Other books you might like:
Malorie Blackman, *A New Dress for Maya*, 1991
    Hoping for a new store dress, Maya disappointedly attends a party in adress her mothermade, but she is happily surprised by what the other girls wear.
Dennis Nolan, *Big Pig*, 1976
    Introduces big pig, fat bat, pudgie budgie, blimpy chimpy, thick chick, and other overweight members of the animal kingdom.
Christine Ross, *Lily and the Bears*, 1989
    Deciding to be big and brave rather than just a child, Lily spends her days in a bear suit but a mistake at the zoo causes her to regret her choice.
Shigeo Watanabe, *How Do I Put It On?*, 1984
    A bear demonstrates the right and wrong ways to put on a shirt, pants, cap and shoes.
Rosemary Wells, *Max's Dragon Shirt*, 1991

On a shopping trip to the department store, Max's determination to get a dragon shirt leads him away from his distracted sister and into trouble.

150

Joan W. Blos

A Gathering of Days: A New England Girl's Journal, 1830-1832 (New York: Charles Scribner's Sons, 1979)

Age range: Grades 3-5

Subject(s): Family Life

Major character(s): Catherine Hall, Teenager; Cassie Shipman, Teenager

Time period(s): 1830s

Locale(s): New Hampshire

What the book is about: A girl keeps a diary of an eventful two years in the 1830s. Catherine sees a shadowy figure that she thinks is a runaway slave. Her father brings home a new wife and her son. One of Catherine's best friends leaves school to work and another of Catherine's friends dies after a difficult illness.

Where it's reviewed:
Horn Book, August 1980, page 374
School Library Journal, November 1979, page 84

Awards the book has won:
Newbery Medal 1980
American Book Award 1980

Other books you might like:
Patricia MacLachlan, *Sarah, Plain and Tall*, 1985
   Sarah Wheaton comes from Maine to care for a motherless family.
Alice Dalgliesh, *Courage of Sarah Noble*, 1954
   Sarah journeys into the wilderness with her father to help him make a new home for their family.
William H. Hooks, *Pioneer Cat*, 1988
   9-year-old Kate travels the Oregon Trail with her family and tries to keep her cat, Snuggs, a secret.
Carla Stevens, *Trouble for Lucy*, 1979
   On the wagon train to Oregon, Lucy's fox terrier puppy causes all kinds of trouble.
Gloria Whelan, *Next Spring, an Oriole*, 1987
   10 year old Libby travels with her family from Virginia to Michigan.

151

Rhoda Blumberg

Commodore Perry in the Land of the Shogun (New York: Lothrop, 1985)

Age range: Grades 6 and Up

Subject(s): Biography

Major character(s): Matthew C. Perry, Military Personnel (Commodore), Historical Figure

Time period(s): 1850s

Locale(s): Yokohama, Japan

What the book is about: Details the 1854 opening of Japan to the United States and the deft hand of Commodore Matthew Perry in the negotiations. Appendices include President Fillmore's letter to the emperor, listings of presents exchanged, and more. (Non-Fiction)

Where it's reviewed:
Center for Children's Books Bulletin, July/August 1985, page 201
Horn Book, September/October 1985, page 576

Awards the book has won:
Newbery Honor 1986

Other books by the author:
First Time Travel Guide to the Bottom of the Sea, 1983
First Time Travel Guide to the Moon, 1980
Backyard Bestiary, 1979

Other books you might like:
James Clavell, *Shogun: A Novel of Japan*, 1975
   The adult novel of the history of the Shogun warriors.
Joseph Bryan Icenhower, *Perry and the Open Door to Japan*, 1973
   Discusses the role of Commodore Matthew Perry in the events from 1852-1854 which ended Japan's isolation.
Michael Macintyre, *The Shogun Inheritance*, 1981
   Japan and the legacy of the samurai, based on the BBC television series. (Non-Fiction)
Lensey Namioka, *The Coming of the Bear*, 1992
   Two unemployed Samurai are saved from drowning by the Ainus, a primitive people on a northern Japanese island.
Katherine Paterson, *The Master Puppeteer*, 1975
   A thirteen year old boy describes the poverty and discontent of 18th century Osaka and the world of puppeteers in which he lives.

152

Judy Blume

Are You There, God? It's Me, Margaret (Englewood Cliffs, NJ: Bradbury, 1970)

Age range: Grades 4-6

Subject(s): Adolescence; Religion

Major character(s): Margaret, Preteen

Time period(s): 1970s

Locale(s): New Jersey

What the book is about: Eleven year old Margaret is the daughter of a Jewish father and a Catholic mother. As she works at getting along in a new school, her personal project is to decide which religion, if any, to embrace herself, and she waits hopefully for the physical signs that she is growing up.

Where it's reviewed:
Booklist, January 15, 1971, page 418
Kirkus Reviews, October 1, 1970, page 1093
Center for Children's Books Bulletin, February 1971, page 87

Other books by the author:
Blubber, 1974
Deenie, 1973
Freckle Juice, 1971
Then Again, Maybe I Won't, 1971

Other books you might like:
Charlotte Herman, *What Happened to Heather Hopkowitz?*, 1981
   When Heather stays with family friends who are Orthodox Jews, it radically changes her feelings about her religion.
H.M. Hoover, *Only Child*, 1992
   Cody discovers that the Terran Corporation is destroying natives on the planet Patma, insect like inhabitants with their own language and religion.
Norma Howe, *God, the Universe, and Hot Fudge Sundaes*, 1984
   Troubled by her sister's death and her parents' separation, Alfie makes friends with Kurt, who helps her decide about religion, life and death.
Johanna Hurwitz, *Once I Was a Plum Tree*, 1980
   Increasingly aware of the difference between her family who are non-observant Jews and their Catholic neighbors, Gerry begins to explore her heritage.
Jean Little, *Kate*, 1971
   Product of a Jewish-Protestant marriage, Kate finds her dilemma over her religious leanings threatening her relationship with her best friend.

153

Judy Blume

Blubber (Scarsdale, New York: Bradbury, 1974)

Age range: Grades 4-6

Subject(s): Weight Control; Schools; Self-Perception

Major character(s): Linda, Preteen; Jill, Preteen; Wendy, Preteen

Time period(s): 1970s

Locale(s): United States

What the book is about: Linda is already an outsider when she gives a report on whales and talks about blubber. Wendy and her friends picked on Linda and started calling her "Blubber." Jill learns what it means to be an outcast when she defends Linda.

Where it's reviewed:
Kirkus Reviews, October 1, 1974, page 1059
Library Journal, November 15, 1974, page 3044

Other books by the author:
Superfudge, 1980
Deenie, 1973
Otherwise Known as Sheila the Great, 1972
Freckle Juice, 1971

Other books you might like:
Molly Cone, *Mishmash*, 1982
   When Mishmash the dog becomes overweight, Pete and Wanda try hypnosis and an exercise routine to get him slim again.
Robert Lipsyte, *One Fat Summer*, 1977
   An overweight fourteen year old boy experiences a turning point summer in which he learns to stand up for himself.
Lila Perl, *Fat Glenda Turns Fourteen*, 1991
   Glenda, after regaining lost weight, meets the very overweight Giselle, discovers plus-size modeling, and must retain her weight in order to model.
Marilyn Sachs, *The Fat Girl*, 1984

Jeff becomes obsessed with creating a new, beautiful person out of an unhappy fat girl, but when she begins to think independently, he loses control.
Mary Stolz, *The Bully of Barkham Street*, 1963
   A fat, eleven year old bully changes his attitude after playing the bugle at a school assembly, arguing with his older sister, and losing a fight.

154

Judy Blume

Fudge-a-Mania (New York: Dutton, 1990)

Age range: Grades 3-6

Subject(s): Vacations; Family Life; Humor

Major character(s): Peter "Pete" Hatcher, Preteen; Farley "Fudge" Hatcher, Child; Sheila Tubman, Preteen

Time period(s): 1990s

Locale(s): Maine

What the book is about: Pete describes a family vacation in Maine with the Tubmans, highlighted by the antics of his younger brother, Fudge, of *Tales of a Fourth Grade Nothing* and *Superfudge* fame.

Where it's reviewed:
Kirkus Reviews, September 15, 1990, page 1321
Publisher's Weekly, September 28, 1990, page 103

Awards the book has won:
Arizona Young Readers Award

Other books by the author:
Superfudge, 1980
Blubber, 1974
Deenie, 1973
Freckle Juice, 1971

Other books you might like:
Eleanor Clymer, *A Search for Two Bad Mice*, 1980
   When her younger sister threatens to ruin the family's trip to England because of their cat, Barbara finds a way to make the vacation a success.
Helen Cresswell, *Bagthorpes Haunted*, 1985
   While on vacation, the talented but strange Bagthorpe family tries to contact the ghosts of their supposedly haunted house.
Stephen Manes, *Hooples on the Highway*, 1978
   A seemingly simple auto trip to Philadelphia is fraught with adventures for the Hoople family.
Ann M. Martin, *Eleven Kids, One Summer*, 1991
   The adventures of a family with eleven children as they summer on the beach at Fire Island.
Stephanie S. Tolan, *The Great Skinner Getaway*, 1987
   Jennifer recounts the adventures of the Skinner family as they set off on a vacation across the US in a motor home.

155

Judy Blume

It's Not the End of the World (Scarsdale, New York: Bradbury, 1972)

Age range: Grades 4-6

Subject(s): Divorce

Major character(s): Amy, Child; Karen, Preteen; Jeff, Teenager

Time period(s): 1970s

Locale(s): United States

What the book is about: Six year old Amy cannot sleep at night because a divorce is in the works and she's afraid she'll wake up and find everyone gone. Her older brother and sister are not much help as they go through their own "growing up" problems as well as cope with the divorce.

Where it's reviewed:
Booklist, October 1, 1972, page 147
Hornbook, October 1972, page 466
Kirkus, April 15, 1972, page 476

Other books by the author:
Blubber, 1974
Deenie, 1973
Otherwise Known as Sheila the Great, 1972
Are You There, God? It's Me, Margaret, 1970

Other books you might like:
Anne Fine, *Alias Madame Doubtfire*, 1988
    Three children dread the day their mother figures out that their wonderful babysitter is really her ex-husband in disguise.
Stuart M. Glass, *A Divorce Dictionary*, 1980
    Alphabetically arranged definitions and discussions of a number of terms relating to divorce, from "abandonment" to "visitation rights," (Non-fiction)
Rebecca C. Jones, *Madeline and the Great (Old) Escape Artist*, 1983
    An unlikely friendship between an old lady and a girl with a recently diagnosed seizure disorder helps them both face the difficulties in their lives.
Jean Davies Okimoto, *My Mother Is Not Married to My Father*, 1979
    Cynthis and Sara learn their parents are divorcing and they will have to make many changes. A more light-hearted look at how divorce impacts children.
Denise Gosliner Orenstein, *When the Wind Blows Hard*, 1982
    After her parents' separation and her move to Klawock, Alaska, Shawn endures loneliness until she gains two new friends, Vesta and her grandmother.

| 156 |

Judy Blume

Just as Long as We're Together (New York: Orchard, 1987)

Age range: Grades 6 and Up

Subject(s): Friendship; Family Problems

Major character(s): Stephanie Hirsch, Preteen, 7th Grader; Rachel Robinson, Preteen

Time period(s): 1980s

Locale(s): Connecticut

What the book is about: Stephanie's relationship with her best friend, Rachel, changes during her first year in junior high. She tries to conceal a family problem and meets a new girl from California, Alison, and has a very special year in seventh grade.

Where it's reviewed:
Horn Book, January 1988, page 66
Junior Bookshelf, February 1988, page 40

Other books by the author:
Starring Sheila J. Freedman as Herself, 1977
It's Not the End of the World, 1972
Tales of a Fourth Grade Nothing, 1972
Then Again, Maybe I Won't, 1971

Other books you might like:
Tommy Hallowell, *Duel on the Diamond*, 1990
    Four junior high friends find their "war" with another clique of boys is costing their team a winning season.
Emily Hanlon, *The Swing*, 1979
    A deaf girl and a boy with family problems find refuge at a swing that has special meaning for both of them.
Susan Perkis Haven, *Is It Them or Is It Me?*, 1990
    Molly's first weeks in school provide her with unforgettable experiences, with new friends, teachers, and a crisis at home.
Norma Klein, *Robbie and the Leap Year Blues*, 1981
    Robbie tries to deal with a sudden deluge of girlfriends and the emotional problems of his parents.
Elsie McCutcheon, *Storm Bird*, 1987
    An English family has trouble with prejudice and other family problems.

| 157 |

Judy Blume

Illustrator: Amy Aitken

The One in the Middle Is the Green Kangaroo (New York: Bradbury, 1981)

Age range: Grades 2-4

Subject(s): Family Life; Plays; Schools

Major character(s): Freddy Dissel, Child, Actor; Mike Dissell, Child; Ellen Dissell, Child

Time period(s): 1980s

Locale(s): United States

What the book is about: Freddy knows being in the school play will give him the glory he deserves. He feels like the peanut butter in the sandwich between his older brother and little sister, and needs a chance to shine on his own.

Where it's reviewed:
Booklist, October 1, 1981, page 191
Kirkus Reviews, August 15, 1969, page 847
School Library Journal, October 1981, page 126

Other books by the author:
The Pain and the Great One, 1984
Super Fudge, 1980
Freckle Juice, 1971
Iggie's House, 1970

Other books you might like:
Patricia Reilly Giff, *The Almost Awful Play*, 1984
    Second grader Ronald Morgan inadvertently turns a failing class play into a success.
Arthur A. Levine, *Sheep Dreams*, 1993

Liza, a young sheep, is too shy to try out for her class play, but a crisis on opening night thrusts her into the spotlight.

Magdalen Nabb, *Josie Smith at School*, 1991
Spirited Josie has adventures and misadventures at school where she makes friends with a foreign student and takes part in the class play.

Marilyn Singer, *Twenty Ways to Lose Your Best Friend*, 1990
Emma loses her best friend when she votes for another girl to get the lead in the class play.

Elizabeth Winthrop, *Luke's Bully*, 1990
Skinny, shy third grader Luke cannot hide from Arthur, his personal bully, until it is time to pick roles for the school play.

158

Judy Blume

Superfudge (New York: Dutton, 1980)

Age range: Grades 2-4

Subject(s): Family Life; Humor; Brothers and Sisters

Major character(s): Peter, Child; Fudge, Child; Tootsie, Child

Time period(s): 1980s

Locale(s): Princeton, New Jersey

What the book is about: Peter is going into sixth grade, his younger brother, Fudge, is a royal pain and now there is a new baby. His parents decide they are going to move to Princeton, N.J. Peter copes with the new family in his own hilarious fashion.

Where it's reviewed:
Horn Book, October 1980, page 518
School Library Journal, August 1980, page 60

Awards the book has won:
California Young Reader Medal (Intermediate) 1983

Other books by the author:
Fudge-a-Mania, 1990
Tales of a Fourth Grade Nothing, 1972
Freckle Juice, 1971
Iggie's House, 1970

Other books you might like:
Larry Bograd, *Bernie Entertaining*, 1987
Ten year old Bernie's comic misadventures convince him that he will never be good at anything.

Lynn Hall, *The Secret Life of Dagmar Schultz*, 1988
Dagmar invents a fantasy boyfriend who proceeds to get her in trouble with her family and friends.

Beverly Keller, *Fowl Play, Desdemona*, 1989
Dez teams up with Sherman, an animal rights activist, to design posters for the school play with hilarious results.

Beverly Keller, *Rosebud, with Fangs*, 1985
Harry, the youngest of a family of five, is turned into a furry beast when his family is stranded in a scary forest.

Barbara Robinson, *My Brother Louis Measures Worms and Other Louis Stories*, 1988
Mary Elizabeth relates the humorous misadventures of her brother, Louis.

159

Judy Blume

Tiger Eyes (Scarsdale, New York: Bradbury, 1981)

Age range: Grades 5 and Up

Subject(s): Death

Major character(s): Gwendolyn Wexler, Parent; Davey Wexler, Teenager; Jason Wexler, Child

Time period(s): 1980s

Locale(s): Los Alamos, New Mexico

What the book is about: After her father dies during a holdup of his 7-11 store in Atlantic City, Davey and her family move to Los Alamos. Her aunt and uncle are overprotective and Davey has a hard time adjusting. Her friend, Wolf, brings Davey back to life.

Where it's reviewed:
Center for Children's Books Bulletin, September 1981, page 5
School Library Journal, November 1981, page 100

Awards the book has won:
California Young Reader Medal 1983

Other books by the author:
Starring Sally J. Friedman as Herself, 1980
It's Not the End of the World, 1972
Then Again, Maybe I Won't, 1971
Are You There, God? It's Me, Margaret, 1970

Other books you might like:
Cynthia DeFelice, *Devil's Bridge*, 1992
12 year old Ben must cope with the loss of his father, who died last year, and his mother's overprotectiveness when he enters the Striped Bass Derby.

Paula Fox, *A Place Apart*, 1981
After her father's death, Victoria and her mother move to a small town near Boston where she meets a wealthy boy who teaches her a valuable lesson.

Elizabeth Hathorn, *Thunderwith*, 1991
After she moves to the Australian outback following her mother's death, Laura's friendship with a strange and beautiful dog helps her adjust.

Charlotte MacLeod, *Cirak's Daughter*, 1982
An unexpected legacy from the father who deserted her as a baby starts Jenny on a dangerous search for answers about her father and her future.

Jacqueline Woodson, *Last Summer with Maizon*, 1990
Eleven year old Margaret tries to accept the inevitable changes that come one summer when her father dies and her best friend goes away to school.

160

N.M. Bodecker

Illustrator: Nina Winters

Carrot Holes and Frisbee Trees (New York: Atheneum, 1983)

Age range: Grades 3-4

Subject(s): Gardens and Gardening

Major character(s): William Plumtree, Gardener

Time period(s): Indeterminate

Locale(s): Tillbury Upper Village, Fictional City

What the book is about: The Plumtrees only want to have an enjoyable and productive garden, but their carrots get out of hand. They are hard to slice because they are so huge. They leave dangerous holes in the ground. The problem is solved when Plumtree offers to use his carrots to create post holes for a neighbor's new fence. He finds the world needs lots of holes dug, including one for a well, which takes the biggest carrot of all.

Where it's reviewed:
Booklist, November 1, 1983, page 404
Hornbook, February 1984, page 49
School Library Journal, January 1984, page 72

Other books by the author:
Mushroom Center Disaster, 1974
Miss Jaster's Garden, 1971
Magic or Not?, 1959

Other books you might like:
Jacqueline Balcells, *The Enchanted Raisin*, 1988
    Chilean children's tales include ''The Enchanted Raisin,'' ''The Buried Giant'' and ''The Princess and the Green Dwarf.''
Eleanor Frances Lattimore, *The Wonderful Glass House*, 1961
    When his aunt gives him a package of seeds, a boy becomes interested in flowers, has trouble with a goat in his garden, and visits a greenhouse.
Rosemary S. Nesbitt, *Colonel Meacham's Giant Cheese*, 1972
    A New York admirer of President Andrew Jackson presents him with a 1400 pound cheese.
Walter Wangerin, *Elisabeth and the Water Troll*, 1991
    A motherless girl rediscovers hope and love when a lonely, misunderstood water troll takes her down into his well.
Nicholas Wilde, *Sir Bertie and the Wyvern*, 1982
    Sir Bertie would rather garden than joust, but he accompanies his son on a quest when he needs a dragon to pose for the family coat of arms.

161

N.M. Bodecker, Author/Illustrator

Hurry, Hurry, Mary Dear! And Other Nonsense Poems (New York: Atheneum, 1976)

Age range: Grades 4-6

Subject(s): Humor; Poetry

Time period(s): Indeterminate

Locale(s): Denmark

What the book is about: Fun word play on adult idioms taken literally. Bodecker is a literary descendant of Lewis Carroll. Excellent for kids who think they hate poetry.

Where it's reviewed:
Horn Book, April 1977, page 181
School Library Journal, February 1977, page 61

Awards the book has won:
Christopher Award 1977

Other books by the author:
Carrot Holes and Frisbee Trees, 1983
A Person From Britain Whose Head Was the Shape of a Mitten, 1980

Miss Jaster's Garden, 1974
Mushroom Center Disaster, 1974

Other books you might like:
Lewis Carroll, *The Hunting of the Snark*, 1970
    A nonsense poem recounts the adventures of the Bellman and his crew and their challenges hunting a snark.
Kalli Dakos, *If You're Not Here, Please Raise Your Hand*, 1990
    An illustrated collection of poems about a variety of elementary school experiences.
Daniel Manus Pinkwater, *Attila the Pun*, 1981
    When the magic seer of Hoboken and the employees of the Magic Moscow summon the ghost of a famous person, they get a punster instead.
Carl Sandburg, *Rainbows Are Made: Poems*, 1982
    Seventy humorous and serious poems dealing with people, word play, everyday things, nature, night, and the sea.
Alvin Schwartz, *Witcracks*, 1973
    Traces the history and gives examples of shaggy-dog stories, and other jokes from American humor of the 19th and 20th centuries.

162

Cecil Bodker

The Leopard (New York: Atheneum, 1975)

Age range: Grades 4-6

Subject(s): Africa; Courage

Major character(s): Tibeso, Worker (cowherd)

Time period(s): Indeterminate Past

Locale(s): Ethiopia

What the book is about: An Ethiopian boy finds his life endangered when he discovers that a disguised blacksmith, not a leopard, is responsible for a great many missing cattle in the area.

Where it's reviewed:
Horn Book, April 1975, page 151
Kirkus Reviews, February 1, 1975, page 121

Awards the book has won:
Mildred L. Batchelder Award 1977

Other books by the author:
Silas and Ben-Godik, 1978
Silas and the Black Mare, 1978
Silas and the Runaway Coach, 1978

Other books you might like:
Laura Bannon, *Nemo Meets the Emperor*, 1957
    An Ethiopian boy has the job of watching the child of an American family and ends up presenting him to the Emperor.
Jean Bothwell, *African Herdboy*, 1970
    A young Masai herdboy's defense of his pet heifer from a lion precipitates a crisis within the tribe.
Sheila Gordon, *The Middle of Somewhere: A Story of South Africa*, 1990
    Rebecca and her family are threatened by forced removal to a bleak, distant development, to make room for a new suburb for white South Africans.
Moses L. Howard, *The Ostrich Chase*, 1974
    Although women are forbidden to participate in the hunt, a young Bushman girl is determined to realize her dream of hunting an ostrich.

163

Cecil Bodker

Silas and Ben-Godik (New York: Delacorte/Lawrence, 1978)

Age range: Grades 5-7

Subject(s): Adventure and Adventurers

Major character(s): Silas, Entertainer; Ben-Godik, Artisan (woodcarver)

Time period(s): Indeterminate Past

Locale(s): Denmark

What the book is about: Silas and the village boy take off on an adventure. They earn their own way, Silas as a performer and Ben-Godik as a woodcarver. They rescue a boy from the wicked Horse Crone, avoid silver ore thieves and catch a bear that has gotten loose.

Where it's reviewed:
Horn Book, February 1979, page 58
Kirkus Reviews, December 15, 1978, page 1356

Awards the book has won:
Boston Globe/Horn Book Award - Honor Book 1979

Other books by the author:
Silas and the Black Mare, 1978
Silas and the Runaway Coach, 1978
The Leopard, 1975

Other books you might like:
Erik Christian Haugaard, *The Untold Tale*, 1971
    In 17th century Denmark, a young orphan seeks his fortune during the wars with Sweden.
Niels Jensen, *Days of Courage: A Medieval Adventure*, 1973
    A boy and girl in Medieval Denmark journey through a land ravaged by the plague in search of a surviving relative.
Lois Lowry, *Number the Stars*, 1989
    The story of two friends and the depth of their friendship even when coping with the dangers of war-torn Denmark.
Bjarne B. Reuter, *Buster, the Sheikh of Hope Street*, 1991
    The misadventures of Buster, a highly imaginative Danish schoolboy, come to a climax when he must take over the lead role in the school play.
Victor Sharoff, *The Heart of the Wood*, 1971
    Forbidden by religious law to carve images, a young Jewish woodcarver faces a dilemma when the ruler of the city requests a bowl with carved figures.

164

Betty Boegehold

Illustrator: Cyndy Szekers

Pippa Pops Out: Four Read-Aloud/Read Alone Stories (New York: Knopf, 1979)

Age range: Grades 2-3

Subject(s): Animals/Mice

Major character(s): Pippa, Mouse; Weber, Duck; Ripple, Squirrel

Time period(s): Indeterminate

Locale(s): Fictional Country

What the book is about: Four stories about Pippa, an adventurous mouse. Pippa convinces her parents that she is big enough and old enough to play in the moonlight, learns to fly, and has a magic, wonderful surprise.

Where it's reviewed:
Booklist, June 15, 1929, page 1540
Kirkus, March 15, 1979, page 327
School Library Journal, May 1979, page 80

Other books by the author:
The Fight, 1991
Bear Underground, 1980
Hurray for Pippa, 1980
Three to Get Ready, 1965

Other books you might like:
Nathaniel Benchley, *Feldman Fieldmouse*, 1971
    A fieldmouse is visited by his uncle who teaches him to work and to take the risk of dancing in the moonlight.
Syd Hoff, *Baseball Mouse*, 1969
    Bernard is a field mouse - an infield mouse - who more than anything else wants to help the losing team win the pennant.
Adelaide Holl, *Moon Mouse*, 1969
    Determined to get to the moon, a baby field mouse climbs to the top of a large building and finds something that looks and tastes a lot like cheese.
Robert M. Quackenbush, *Sherrif Sally Gopher and the Haunted Dance Hall*, 1977
    Sherrif Sally Gopher solves the mystery of the haunted dance hall in time for a special performance by the famous dancer, Miss Annie Field Mouse.
Anne Rockwell, *A Bear, a Bobcat, and Three Ghosts*, 1977
    The traveling peddler Timothy Todd and his friends become involved in a moonlight chase with a bear, a bobcat, and three ghosts.

165

Godfried Bomans

Illustrator: Wouter Hoogendijk

The Wily Witch and All the Other Fairy Tales and Fables (Owings Mills, Maryland: Stemmer House, 1977)

Age range: Grades 4-6

Subject(s): Good and Evil; Witches and Witchcraft; Animals/Cats

Locale(s): Netherlands

What the book is about: The King disapproves of every one of Steppie's suitors until she finally dies unmarried. This is a full collection of tales by a popular Dutch author who has a deep sense of the ridiculous. Tales include kings and queens, wizards, spells, and other magic.

Where it's reviewed:
Booklist, July 15, 1977, page 1726
School Library Journal, September 1977, page 121

Other books you might like:
Edith Battles, *Witch in Room 6*, 1987
    Cheryl Suzanne is an eleven year old apprentice witch. Sean wants to be her friend to enjoy her witchly abilities and play well for various teams.
Katherine Mary Briggs, *Hobberdy Dick*, 1977

Hobberdy Dick is a hobgoblin who has guarded and governed Widford Manor in the Cotswolds for hundreds of years.

Joan Davenport Carris, *Witch-Cat*, 1984
 Rosetta is an experienced witch-cat commissioned to help Gwen realize her witch powers, a strange, frustrating and sometimes dangerous mission.

Frieda Hughes, *Getting Rid of Aunt Edna*, 1986
 Miranda is an apprentice witch who must figure out how to get visiting Aunt Edna (whose spells always misfire) to leave.

Zilpha Keatley Snyder, *The Witches of Worm*, 1972
 Jessica is forced to adopt a kitten she names Worm and decides it must be a witch-cat that makes her do terrible things and think awful thoughts.

166

Ann Sharpless Bond

Illustrator: Leonard Shortall

Saturdays in the City (Boston: Houghton, 1979)

Age range: Grades 3-5

Subject(s): City Life

Major character(s): Adam Tyler, Child, 4th Grader; Noah Carter, Child, 4th Grader; Miss Thomas, Teacher

Time period(s): 1970s

Locale(s): United States

What the book is about: Adam and Noah, a pair of enterprising fourth grade boys, spend adventurous times in the big city and amazing things always seem to happen to them. At the museum they find themselves inside a forest scene. They somehow get a free airplane trip to Washington, lunching with the pilot. They even, with no apparent effort, find themselves on a TV talk show, trying to explain their adventures.

Where it's reviewed:
Booklist, November 15, 1979, page 499
Center for Children's Books Bulletin, December 1979, page 36
Kirkus, October 15, 1979, page 1209

Other books by the author:
Adam and Noah and the Cops, 1983

Other books you might like:
Eth Clifford, *Never Hit a Ghost with a Baseball Bat*, 1993
 While exploring a trolley car museum, Mary Rose and her sister, JoBeth, encounter strange events that make them think the museum is haunted.

Hal George Evarts, *Jay-Jay and the Peking Monster*, 1978
 A southern California boy finds a box of bones that may be the remains of prehistoric Peking Man which have been missing from a museum since WWII.

E.L. Konigsburg, *From the Mixed-Up Files of Mrs. Basil E. Frankweiler*, 1967
 Having run away with her little brother to live in the Metropolitan Museum of Art, Claudia tries to preserve order. They experience a strange mystery.

Ethelyn M. Parkinson, *Higgins of the Railroad Museum*, 1970
 A teen and his dog, Higgins, spend the summer working at a railroad museum where they find plenty of action.

Niki Yektai, *The Secret Room*, 1992

When their family moves from a farm near Albany to New York City in 1903, Katharine and her brothers must adjust to life in proper society.

167

Michael Bond

Illustrator: Peggy Fortnum

A Bear Called Paddington (Boston: Houghton Mifflin, 1960)

Age range: Grades 2-4

Subject(s): Animals/Bears

Major character(s): Paddington, Bear

Time period(s): Indeterminate Past

Locale(s): London, England

What the book is about: A small bear from Peru is found in Paddington Station in London. When Mr. and Mrs. Brown take him into their home, their lives are changed forever. Paddington is a bear as adorable and mischievous as Winnie the Pooh.

Where it's reviewed:
Horn Book, February 1961, page 53
Library Journal, October 15, 1960

Other books by the author:
Paddington's Storybook, 1984
Paddington on Screen, 1982
Paddington on Top, 1980
Paddington Takes the Test, 1980

Other books you might like:
Hans DeBeer, *Little Polar Bear and the Brave Little Hare*, 1992
 Lars the polar bear teases his friend, Hugo the hare, for being afraid of everything, until the day they get lost in the snow.

Judy Delton, *A Birthday Bike for Brimhall*, 1985
 Brimhall receives a bike for his birthday but is ashamed to admit that he doesn't know how to ride it.

Terrance Dicks, *Enter T.R.*, 1985
 A young English boy receives a teddy bear from America who resembles Teddy Roosevelt and teaches him how to "walk softly but carry a big stick."

Sally Farrell Odgers, *Drummond: The Search for Sarah*, 1990
 A teddy bear, unexpectedly brought to life by Sarah and Nicholas, begins a search for his original owner, a Sarah from an earlier time.

Michael Pellowski, *Benny's Bad Day*, 1986
 Starting with his alarm clock going off too early, Benny Bear has a terrible, awful, bad day.

168

Michael Bond

Olga Carries On (New York: Hastings, 1977)

Age range: Grades 3-5

Subject(s): Animals

Major character(s): Olga da Polga, Guinea Pig

Time period(s): Indeterminate

Locale(s): England

What the book is about: How the French language started, the War of the Roses, and the English are all explained by this lively guinea pig. She is considerate of her three companions and is willing to share the glory when one of them gets depressed.

Where it's reviewed:
Booklist, November 15, 1977, page 5481
Junior Bookshelf, December 1976, page 319

Other books by the author:
Paddington's Storybook, 1984
The Complete Adventures of Olga da Polga, 1983
Paddington on Top, 1975
The Tales of Olga da Polga, 1973

Other books you might like:
Pat Hutchins, *Rats!*, 1989
    Sam's insistence on getting a pet rat eventually changes his family's entire daily routine and brings an exciting surprise.
Dick King-Smith, *Martin's Mice*, 1988
    A farm cat who doesn't want to catch mice keeps a family of them as pets.
Gunilla Brodde Norris, *The Friendship Hedge*, 1973
    Alice's determination to teach her best friend a lesson about the guinea pig that has come between them leads to a painful lesson for both girls.
Vivian Sathre, *JB Wigglebottom and the Parade of Pets*, 1993
    Because of his sister's allergies, JB doesn't have a pet to enter in the fourth grade class parade, and he has to deal with a bully.
Susanne Santoro Whayne, *Watch the House*, 1992
    Left alone for the day, the family pets venture outside and have a series of adventures that makes them appreciate their indoor life.

169

Nancy Bond

A String in the Harp (New York: Atheneum, 1976)

Age range: Grades 6 and Up

Subject(s): Space and Time; Legends

Major character(s): Becky Morgan, Child; Peter Morgan, Preteen; Jen Morgan, Teenager

Time period(s): 1970s

Locale(s): Amherst, Massachusetts; Wales

What the book is about: Three American children are unwillingly transplanted to Wales for one year. One of them finds an ancient harp tuning key that takes him back to the time of the great 6th century bard, Taliesin.

Where it's reviewed:
Booklist, April 1976, page 1108
School Library Journal, April 1976, page 84

Awards the book has won:
Boston Globe/Horn Book Award - Honor Book

Other books by the author:
A Place to Come Back To, 1985
The Voyage Begun, 1981
The Best of Enemies, 1978

Other books you might like:
Aidan Chambers, *Seal Secret*, 1981
    Stuck in an old cottage on the coast of Wales, William involves himself in the dangerous business of trying to rescue a seal.
Louise Lawrence, *Star Lord*, 1978
    After a mysterious ''something'' crashes on a mountain in Wales, Rhys finds and shelters an alien from a distant planet.
Elizabeth Levy, *Running out of Time*, 1980
    While running in the fog, practicing for a marathon, three friends are transported to ancient Rome and join in a slave revolt led by Spartacus.
Jenny Nimmo, *The Snow Spider*, 1986
    In this suspense-filled fantasy, ten year old Gwyn begins his search to see if he has inherited magical powers.
Jane Yolen, *The Devil's Arithmetic*, 1988
    While opening the door for Elijah during the Passover Seder, Hannah Stern is tranported to a 1942 Polish village and then a Nazi concentration camp.

170

Nancy Bond

The Voyage Begun (New York: Atheneum, 1981)

Age range: Grades 6 and Up

Subject(s): Ecology; Pollution

Major character(s): Paul Vickers, Teenager; Maggie Rudd, Activist (conservationist); Mickey Cafferty, Child

Time period(s): Indeterminate Future

Locale(s): Warren, Massachusetts

What the book is about: Living in the not-so-distant future, when the energy supply has been almost depleted, a teenage boy explores the deserted colonies near his father's Cape Cod research station, and begins to understand the long-term effects of recent climate and weather changes and environmental pollution on the land and the people.

Where it's reviewed:
Center for Children's Books Bulletin, November 1981, p 42
Horn Book, February 1982, page 50

Awards the book has won:
Boston Globe/Horn Book Award - Honor Book

Other books by the author:
A Place to Come Back To, 1984
Country of Broken Stone, 1980
The Best of Enemies, 1978
A String in the Harp, 1976

Other books you might like:
James Lincoln Collier, *When the Stars Begin to Fall*, 1986
    Angry that his entire family is considered to be poor trash, Harry defies his father and tries to prove a factory is polluting their community.
Betty Sue Cummings, *Let the River Be*, 1978
    A feisty woman and a retarded youth are brought together by their attempts to save a polluted river.
Clifford B. Hicks, *Alvin Fernald, Superweasel*, 1977
    Alvin's pollution project is geared to espose the biggest polluter in town, the owner of the chemical plant.
Ann M. Martin, *Dawn Saves the Planet*, 1992

Dawn thinks studying ecology is cool. She wants to start a recycling center at school, but she is so busy lecturing people that she doesn't have time.

Ian McMahan, *Lake Fear*, 1985

Ricky and his computer friend, ALEC, uncover a case of computer fraud, chemical pollution, and the illegal production of explosives.

171

Frank Bonham

The Friends of the Loony Lake Monster (New York: Dutton, 1972)

Age range: Grades 4-6

Subject(s): Conservation of Natural Resources; Dinosaurs

Major character(s): Gussie Grant, Child; Tex Fuller, Friend; Jane, Dinosaur

Time period(s): Indeterminate

Locale(s): Agate City, Oregon

What the book is about: Gussie's move from Los Angeles to Oregon opens a whole new world, but finding a baby dinosaur is not what she expects when she plays her French horn in the open air near her new ranch house. Gussie protects her pet dinosaur in this story that has a resourceful heroine and a lesson about conservation.

Where it's reviewed:
Booklist, March 15, 1973, page 711
Center for Children's Books Bulletin, January 1973, page 71
Kirkus Reviews, September 15, 1972, page 1097

Other books by the author:
The Forever Formula, 1979
A Dream of Ghosts, 1973
Chief, 1971
Cool Cat, 1971

Other books you might like:
Pam Conrad, *My Daniel*, 1989
Ellie and Stevie learn about a family legacy when their grandmother tells them stories of her brother's historical quest for dinosaur bones.
Bruce Coville, *The Dinosaur That Followed Me Home*, 1990
Stuart looks forward to another adventurous summer at Camp Haunted Hills, but he gets more than he bargained for.
Gerald Malcolm Durrell, *The Fantastic Dinosaur Adventure*, 1990
Three children travel back in time in their great uncle's time machine, intending to rescue baby dinosaurs from evil villains.
Jessica Hatchigan, *Dinosaurs Aren't Forever*, 1991
Molly and her friends find themselves in a race against time to save a big cement dinosaur from destruction.
Mordecai Richler, *Jacob Two-Two and the Dinosaur*, 1987
When Jacob's father brings him back a small lizard from Kenya, it grows to enormous proportions, and has to protect it from frightened grown-ups.

172

Frank Bonham

Illustrator: Alvin Smith

Mystery of the Fat Cat (New York: Dutton, 1968)

Age range: Grades 5-7

Series: Oak Street Boys Club

Subject(s): Animals/Cats; Mystery and Detective Stories

Major character(s): Buddy Williams, Preteen; Johnny "Little Pie" Pastelito, Preteen; Rich Smith, Preteen

Time period(s): 1960s

Locale(s): United States

What the book is about: Four Oak Street Boys Club members set out to prove foul play in the death of a cat. The boys just want to save their boys club from being torn down, but they find trouble instead.

Where it's reviewed:
Booklist, June 15, 1968, page 1183
Hornbook, August, 1968, page 426
Kirkus Reviews, April 1, 1968, page 402

Other books by the author:
The Forever Formula, 1979
Devilhorn, 1978
A Dream of Ghosts, 1973
Nitty Gritty, 1968

Other books you might like:
Carol Madden Adorjan, *Copy Cat Mystery*, 1990
Beth's summer was a bomb; first Paul backed out of their pet-sitting business, then the Goodalls moved away, then some creepy things start happening.
Ann M. Martin, *Mallory and the Ghost Cat*, 1992
While Mallory is baby-sitting, she finds a cat in the Craine's attic and names him Ghost Cat.
Mary Stolz, *The Bully of Barkham Street*, 1963
Martin was bigger and older than his classmates and didn't care about having friends, his family never listened to him, and his dog was taken away.
Robert Westall, *Yaxley's Cat*, 1991
After Yaxley disappears, the inhabitants of an English village fear that his ugly old coat will uncover the truth about the secret they are hiding.
Carol Beach York, *Dead Man's Cat*, 1972
Two children are sure that India, the cat, knows the location of her deceased master's stamp album worth $25,000.

173

Frank Bonham

The Rascals From Haskell's Gym (New York: Dutton, 1977)

Age range: Grades 5-7

Subject(s): Sports/Gymnastics

Major character(s): Sissy Benedict, Sports Figure (gymnast); Andrea Packwood, Sports Figure (gymnast); Bonnie Walker, Coach

Time period(s): 1970s

Locale(s): Meadowdale, California

What the book is about: Ever since Sissy quit Haskell's gym, unintentionally taking eighteen other gymnasts with her to the Butterflies Gymnastics club, the rivalry between the two clubs has been fierce. Sissy secretly calls the Rascals from Haskells the RATS from Haskells. They are always pulling sneaky tricks to keep the Butterflies from winning. Then the owner of Haskells puts economic pressure on the owner of the building where the Butterflies practice and Sissy and her father live. At the same time, her dad's money is stolen. Could the Rascals be responsbile?

Where it's reviewed:
Booklist, September 1, 1969, page 42
Center for Children's Books Bulletin, November 1969, page 38
Kirkus Reviews, May 1, 1969, page 513

Other books by the author:
Premonitions, 1984
Devilhorn, 1978
Chief, 1971
Cool Cat, 1971

Other books you might like:
Spring Hermann, *Flip City*, 1988
    Four girls whose family lives are very difficult compete in gymnastics for their gym, Flip City, the place they feel most at home.
Tim Kennemore, *The Fortunate Few*, 1981
    In a future society where young girls are raised as professional gymnasts, Jodie enjoys her status as the highest paid gymnast of her day.
Nancy Meltzoff, *A Sense of Balance*, 1978
    A promising fifteen year old gymnast begins to question the rigid structure of her life.
Sheri Cooper Sinykin, *Shrimpboat and Gym Bags*, 1990
    Bo copes with the pressure of moving, keeping his grades up so he can stay on the gymnastics team, and competing against a temperamental opponent.
Tricia Springstubb, *Eunice (the egg salad) Gottlieb*, 1988
    In the midst of assorted crises involving her siblings, Eunice struggles to master the vault for her school's upcoming gymnastics exhibition.

174

Crosby Bonsall

The Case of the Double Cross (New York: Harper and Row, 1980)

Age range: Grades 2-3

Subject(s): Wizards; Friendship; Sexism

Major character(s): Marigold, Child

Time period(s): 1980s

Locale(s): United States

What the book is about: Marigold and her friends want to belong to Wizard's private detective club but girls are not allowed. She does all kinds of things for the boys, from sharing her horse to saving them from a flood, all to no avail. Finally, she and her friends devise a scheme to trick the boys. Though the scheme is discovered, the boys and girls work out their differences and form a club together.

Where it's reviewed:
Kirkus Reviews, November 15, 1980, page 1463
School Library Journal, December 1980, page 71

Other books by the author:
Who's Afraid of the Dark?, 1980
The Goodbye Summer, 1979

Other books you might like:
Franz Brandenberg, *Leo and Emily's Big Ideas*, 1982
    Although each scheme seems to backfire, two friends have fun selling flags, scaring people and trying to build a shelter from the rain.
Malcolm Carrick, *Mr. Tod's Trap*, 1980
    Mr. Tod is a chauvinist fox who isn't nearly as tough or successful as he would have his family and friends believe.
Lucille Clifton, *My Friend Jacob*, 1980
    Sam is seven and Jacob is sixteen, and mentally retarded. The two teach each other many things and form a strong bond of friendship.
Tomie DePaola, *Olive Button Is a Sissy*, 1979
    Everyone thinks Oliver is a sissy because he enjoys a lot of things that people think only girls like. Oliver shows them!
Elizabeth Winthrop Mahoney, *Tough Eddie*, 1985
    Nellie blows Eddie's macho image by telling everyone that he has a secret doll house in his closet.

175

Crosby Bonsall

The Case of the Scaredy Cats (New York: Harper, 1971)

Age range: Grades 1-3

Subject(s): Clubs; Mystery and Detective Stories

Major character(s): Tubby, Child; Skinny, Child; Smitch, Child

Time period(s): Indeterminate

Locale(s): United States

What the book is about: What do you do when you find a bevy of girls in your secret clubhouse? Wizard, Tubby, Skinny and Smitch are convinced that boys are better than girls until they have to prove that *they* are not the scaredy cats.

Where it's reviewed:
Booklist, December 15, 1971, page 365
Center for Children's Books Bulletin, January 1972, page 71
Kirkus Reviews, November 1, 1971, page 1154

Other books by the author:
The Case of the Double Cross, 1980
The Case of the Dumb Bell, 1966
The Case of the Cat's Meow, 1965
The Case of the Hungry Stranger, 1963

Other books you might like:
Dale Fife, *Who Goes There, Lincoln?*, 1975
    Lincoln and his friends need a new clubhouse and investigate the possibilities of a building soon to be torn down.
Peggy Kahn, *The Handy Girls Can Fix It!*, 1984
    The Handy Girls, a group of girls who own a "fix it" shop, help two preschoolers build a clubhouse from a big carton.
Charles E. Martin, *For Rent*, 1986
    After renting their clubhouse to summer tourists, the children on an island find that being landlords is harder than they thought.

Stephen Mooser, *The Night of the Vampire Kitty*, 1991
Henry is practicing to be a ghost writer. He's got members of his club shivering. But soon even Henry starts to stutter with fright.

Harriet Ziefert, *The Small Potatoes and the Birthday Party*, 1985
The members of the Small Potatoes Club keep busy by making their clubhouse bigger and planning a surprise party for Molly's dog, Spot.

| 176 |

Crosby Bonsall

The Day I Had to Play with My Sister (New York: Harper, 1972)

Age range: Grades 1-2

Subject(s): Brothers and Sisters; Games

Time period(s): 1970s

Locale(s): United States

What the book is about: As hard as he tries, an older brother cannot seem to teach his little sister how to play hide-and-seek. A beginning reader.

Where it's reviewed:
Booklist, March 15, 1973, page 711
Kirkus Reviews, November 1, 1972, page 1237
Library Journal, May 15, 1973, page 1696

Other books by the author:
Who's Afraid of the Dark?, 1980
And I Mean It, Stanley, 1974
Mine's the Best, 1973
Piggle, 1973

Other books you might like:
Stan Berenstain, *The Berenstain Bears Get Stage Fright*, 1986
Sister Bear worries about her lines in the school play while Brother Bear has no fear. Guess who forgets lines during the performance?

Nancy White Carlson, *Heather Hiding*, 1990
Wishing she were taller and faster, like her big brother, Peter, Heather plays hide and seek with him and his friends.

Paul Fleischman, *Shadow Play: A Story*, 1990
While visiting the county fair, a brother and sister are enthralled by a shadow puppet show presentation of "Beauty and the Beast."

Ellen Javernick, *Where's Brooke?*, 1992
As a father looks all over for his young daughter, the reader can see her close by him all the time.

Paul Rogers, *Rain & Shine: Stories*, 1987
Seven episodes in the lives of Ned and his younger brother and sister, who play hide and seek, make spider pies and have an imaginary playmate.

| 177 |

Malcolm J. Bosse

The Cave Beyond Time (New York: Crowell, 1980)

Age range: Grades 5-6

Subject(s): Death; Orphans; Space and Time

Major character(s): Ben, Teenager, Time Traveller

Time period(s): 1980s

Locale(s): United States

What the book is about: After his father and brother are killed in a car wreck, fifteen year old Ben stays with his uncle who is leading an archeological dig in a cave in Arizona. Unable to move through his grief, Ben starts into the desert, is bitten by a rattler and finds himself thrown back in time. He joins mammoth hunters, then bison hunters, and finally a group of early farmers, and then returns to the present with a changed perspective.

Where it's reviewed:
Booklist, November 1980, page 402
School Library Journal, November 1980, page 83

Other books by the author:
Captives of Time, 1987
The Barracuda Gang, 1982
Ganesh, 1981
The 79 Squares, 1979

Other books you might like:
Honor Arundel, *The High House*, 1967
After the death of their parents, a young girl is separated from her brother and goes to live with an artistic aunt in Edinburgh.

Anthea Goddard, *The Aztec Skull*, 1977
After running away from the Children's Home, Jenny hides in the house of Diego Gama and becomes involved in the mystery of the Aztec skull.

Georgess McHargue, *The Turquoise Toad Mystery*, 1982
After Ben and his pet, join a group of archeologists looking for Indian artifacts in the Arizona desert, they help expose a ring of thieves.

Frances A. Miller, *The Truth Trap*, 1980
Following the death of their parents, Matthew and his dead sister run away to Los Angeles where he becomes the only suspect in a beating and murder.

Walter Dean Myers, *The Righteous Revenge of Artemis Bonner*, 1992
Fifteen year old Artemis journeys from New York City to Tombstone, Arizona in 1882 to avenge the murder of his uncle.

| 178 |

L.M. Boston

Illustrator: Peter Boston

The Sea Egg (New York: Harcourt, 1967)

Age range: Grades 3-5

Subject(s): Animals/Seals and Sea Lions; Legends; Sea Stories

Major character(s): Toby, Child; Joe, Child; Triton, Mythical Creature (merman)

Time period(s): Indeterminate

Locale(s): England

What the book is about: Two brothers buy an egg-shaped rock which hatches into a baby merman. Triton teaches them to swim well and become more comfortable in the sea. One moonlit night, Triton takes them to a magical beautiful sea cave and the boys realize the true beauty of the sea.

Where it's reviewed:
Booklist, June 1, 1967, page 1045
Hornbook, August 1967, page 460
Kirkus Reviews, April 15, 1967, page 498

Other books by the author:
The Fossil Snake, 1976
The Stones of Green Knowe, 1976
Treasure of Green Knowe, 1958
The Children of Green Knowe, 1955

Other books you might like:
Jane Yolen, *Neptune Rising: Songs and Tales of the Undersea Folk*, 1982
    A collection of stories and poems which feature merfolk.
Ethel Reader, *The Story of the Little Merman*, 1979
    Relates the varying adventures of the Little Merman in his underwater home and on land.
Ruth Park, *My Sister Sif*, 1986
    Riko manages to get her delicate older sister Sif and herself to their remote home, where an American scientist complicates Riko's life.
Mollie Hunter, *A Stranger Came Ashore: A Story of Suspense*, 1975
    Robbie becomes convinced that the stranger befriended by his family is one of the Selkie Folk and tries to get help against his magical power.
Sylvia Peck, *Seal Child*, 1989
    While entranced by the seals that swim off the shore of the Maine island where she visits during the holidays, Molly befriends an interesting girl.

179

L.M. Boston

Illustrator: Peter Boston

The Stones of Green Knowe (New York: Atheneum, 1976)

Age range: Grades 4-6

Subject(s): Space and Time; Magic

Major character(s): Roger d'Aulneaux, Child

Time period(s): 12th century

Locale(s): Green Knowe, England

What the book is about: Roger watches the building of his family's stone manor. He finds two ancient magic stones and finds he can travel in time to see all the other children who will live at Green Knowe.

Where it's reviewed:
Horn Book, December 1976, page 623
Kirkus Reviews, August 1, 1976, page 845

Other books by the author:
The Fossil Snake, 1976
The Guardians of the House, 1976
The Sea Egg, 1967
The Children of Green Knowe, 1955

Other books you might like:
Elisabeth Mace, *The Rushton Inheritance*, 1978

The young Rushtons find their daily life disrupted by a boy ghost from another time in search of a family secret.
Daniel Manus Pinkwater, *Borgel*, 1990
    Melvin recounts his extraordinary adventures in time and space with his 111-year-old sort of great-uncle Borgel.
Judith St. George, *The Mysterious Girl in the Garden*, 1981
    An American girl visiting Kew Gardens finds herself transported back to 1805 where she meets the future queen.
Russell Stannard, *The Time and Space of Uncle Albert*, 1989
    Gedanken's eccentric uncle sends her into outer space to help him conduct time-space experiments.
Geraldine Symons, *Crocuses Were Over, Hitler Was Dead*, 1977
    While visiting an old English manor, a young girl is befriended by one of its former inhabitants, a soldier killed during WWII.

180

Barbara Bottner

Dumb Old Casey Is a Fat Tree (New York: Harper and Row, 1979)

Age range: Grades 3-5

Subject(s): Ballet; Weight Control; Determination

Major character(s): Casey Stoner, Child, Dancer (ballet); Mrs. Bellanova, Teacher

Time period(s): 1970s

Locale(s): United States

What the book is about: Casey dreams of being a star ballerina, but is overweight and the least able dancer in her class. When she is cast as a tree in the recital, she is hurt and angry, and tells her friends her family will be on vacation and she cannot take part in the recital. After she stops feeling sorry for herself, she works hard and becomes "head tree" and receives many compliments.

Where it's reviewed:
*Kirkus Reviews - March 15, 1979, page 328
School Library Journal, April 1979, page 40

Other books by the author:
Mean Maxie, 1980
Big Boss! Little Boss!, 1979
Messy Myra, 1979

Other books you might like:
Jean Estoril, *Ballet for Drina*, 1957
    Will orphaned Drina be allowed to study ballet while her grandmother objects so much?
Patricia Reilly Giff, *Poopsie Pomerantz, Pick up Your Feet*, 1989
    Poopsie is determined to lose weight and become a world class ballerina.
Rumer Godden, *Thursday's Children*, 1987
    Doone Penny has an overwhelming desire to become a ballet dancer despite the ragging he gets from his macho brother.
Amy Hest, *Maybe Next Year*, 1982
    Kate is not sure she is ready, or really wants, to try out for the National Ballet Summer School.
Isabelle Holland, *Dinah and the Green Fat Kingdom*, 1978
    Dinah retreats to a fantasy world where "fat is beautiful" because of all the nagging she gets at home and at school.

| 181 |

Miriam Anne Bourne

Illustrator: Dick Gackenbach

What Is Papa Up To Now? (New York: Coward, 1977)

Age range: Grades 2-3

Subject(s): Inventions

Major character(s): Sally Franklin, Child; Benjamin Franklin, Inventor, Historical Figure

Time period(s): 18th century

Locale(s): United States

What the book is about: Sally describes Papa's excitement and pleasure at each discovery he makes while experimenting with electricity. They share an eager interest in science, which is explained for primary readers.

Where it's reviewed:
Kirkus Reviews, April 15, 1977, page 424
School Library Journal, October 1977, page 98

Other books by the author:
Nabby Adams' Diary, 1975
Second Car in Town, 1972
Tigers in the Woods, 1971
Raccoons Are for Loving, 1968

Other books you might like:
David A. Adler, *Eaton Stanley and the Mind Control Experiments*, 1985
  Two sixth grade boys try to control their teacher's mind but find the project gets out of hand very quickly.
Gery Greer, *Let Me Off This Spaceship!*, 1991
  When Tod and Billy are kidnapped by aliens, they try to make as much trouble on board ship as possible so the captain will return them to Earth.
Robert Lawson, *Ben and Me*, 1939
  The ''true story'' of Ben Franklin's genius, as told by his friend, the mouse, Amos.
Susan Beth Pfeffer, *Just Between Us*, 1980
  By taking part in her mother's experiment, Cass learns how to keep a secret, but then learns a secret that traps her between two friends.
Ann Shaffer, *The Camel Express*, 1989
  As part of an experiment in 1960, a camel fills in for a wounded pony on a Pony Express route.

| 182 |

Victoria Boutis

Illustrator: Gail Owens

Katy Did It (New York: Greenwillow, 1982)

Age range: Grades 2-4

Subject(s): Camps and Camping; Fathers and Daughters; Hiking

Major character(s): Katy Milonas, Child; Toby, Dog

Time period(s): Indeterminate

Locale(s): Adirondacks, New York

What the book is about: Katy hates camping, but when no one else is able to accompany her father on a special climb, she feels pleased to be asked to go along. The bad things happen: rain, dead animals, scary noises in the night, but Katy perseveres. When they reach their goal, a magnificent vista, her father's pride and her own sense of accomplishment are her rewards.

Where it's reviewed:
Center for Children's Books Bulletin, July 1982, page 202
School Library Journal, April 1982, page 66
Booklist, April 15, 1982, page 1093

Other books by the author:
Looking Out, 1988

Other books you might like:
Kathryn Lasky, *Jem's Island*, 1982
  Jem goes on his first overnight kayak trip with his father to an island in Penobscot Bay.
P.J. Petersen, *I Hate Camping*, 1991
  Dan thinks he is going to have a bad time when he is forced to go camping with his mother's boyfriend and his son, but the boys form a friendship.
Anne Rockwell, *The Night We Slept Outside*, 1983
  Camping for the first time on their deck, two brothers discover that the night is full of strange sights and sounds.
Allen Say, *The Lost Lake*, 1989
  A young boy and his father become close friends during a camping trip to the mountains.
Vera B. Williams, *Three Days on a River in a Red Canoe*, 1981
  Mother, Aunt Rosie and two children make a three day camping trip by canoe.

| 183 |

Selma Boyd

Illustrator: Carol Nicklaus

Footprints in the Refrigerator (New York: Watts, 1982)

Age range: Grades 1-2

Subject(s): Mystery and Detective Stories

Time period(s): 1980s

Locale(s): United States

What the book is about: Whose footprints appear mysteriously in the refrigerator? It is very difficult to pin point the perpetrator. Our heroine turns detective to solve the case.

Where it's reviewed:
Booklist, October 15, 1982, page 317
Children's Book Review Service, January 1983, page 44
School Library Journal, December 1982, page 82

Other books by the author:
I Met a Polar Bear, 1983
The How: Making the Best of a Mistake, 1981

Other books you might like:
Molly Cone, *Whose Footprints?*, 1990
  A mother and daughter discover and identify animal footprints in the snow on an intimate walk around their farm.
Judy Delton, *Brimhall Turns Detective*, 1983
  Huge footprints in the snow cause Brimhall the bear to try to identify and trap the ''monster.''
Ann Dodd, *Footprints and Shadows*, 1992
  Discusses where footprints and shadows go, as when footprints in the snow melt away or shadows are dispelled by light.
Kalil Gazi, *The Mystery of the Square Footprints*, 1980

While walking along the beach, five children find a set of strange, square footprints that lead them to a robot.
Babs Bell Hajdusiewicz, *Who Did This, Dainty Dinosaur?*, 1988
A little girl and her imaginary dinosaur companion search for the source of mysterious footprints.

184

Ray Bradbury

Illustrator: Joe Mugnaini

The Halloween Tree (New York: Knopf, 1982)

Age range: Grades 3-5

Subject(s): Fantasy; Halloween; Physics

Major character(s): Carapace Clavicle Moundshround, Spirit

Time period(s): Indeterminate

Locale(s): United States

What the book is about: Eight trick-or-treaters set out on Halloween, but they lose their leader, Pipkin. Carapace Clavicle Moundshround, climbing out from a leaf pile, offers to explain the origins of Halloween to them. He takes them on a broomstick-riding trip with a great ending.

Where it's reviewed:
Booklist, December 15, 1972, page 404
Kirkus Reviews, July 15, 1972, page 801
New York Times Book Review, October 29, 1972, page 8

Other books by the author:
Fever Dream, 1987
Dinosaur Tales, 1983
The April Witch, 1980
The Fog Horn, 1979

Other books you might like:
Avi, *No More Magic*, 1975
While searching for his bike that disappeared on Halloween, a boy and his friends become involved in adventure and magic.
Grace Chetwin, *On All Hallow's Eve*, 1984
Two sisters on their way home from a Halloween party step into another time period, where they engage the forces of good and evil.
Mary Norton, *Bedknobs and Broomsticks*, 1975
With the powers they acquire from a spinster who is studying to be a witch, three children go on a number of exciting and gruesome trips.
Russell Stannard, *The Time and Space of Uncle Albert*, 1989
Gedanken's eccentric uncle sends her into outer space in a spacecraft to help him conduct a series of experiments regarding the law of relativity.
Susan Whitcher, *Real Mummies Don't Bleed*, 1993
A collection of five scary stories, featuring the Egyptian underworld's intrusion into a Halloween costume contest and other strange goings on.

185

Irene Brady, Author/Illustrator

Doodlebug (Boston: Houghton Mifflin, 1977)

Age range: Grades 2-4

Subject(s): Animals/Horses

Major character(s): Jennifer Dickens, Teenager, Animal Lover; Doodlebug, Horse (pony)

Time period(s): 1970s

Locale(s): United States

What the book is about: Jennifer heals an injured pony. Doodlebug doesn't do much other than eat. He can't be ridden because his high-flying trot is a real bone-breaker. The only hope for him is to become a Hackney Pony and learn to pull a cart.

Where it's reviewed:
Booklist, October 1, 1977, page 284
Kirkus Reviews, August 15, 1977, page 849
School Library Journal, February 1978, page 54

Other books by the author:
Beaver Year, 1976
Owlet: The Great Horned Owl, 1974
A Mouse Named Mus, 1972

Other books you might like:
Ruth Carroll, *The Managing Hen and the Floppy Hound*, 1972
A young hound, considered worthless by the farm animals and Miss Lucy, proves himself by saving the life of a pet chicken.
Arthur Catherall, *Last Horse on the Sands*, 1973
A brother and sister risk their lives and that of an old cart horse while trying to rescue victims of a plane crash before the tide comes in.
Jane Belk Moncure, *Barbara's Pony, Buttercup*, 1977
Barbara and Buttercup are involved in a series of imaginary adventures.
Elise Primavera, *Basil and Maggie*, 1983
Maggie wants a show horse but gets Basil instead, and discovers this lumpy pony is something special.
Elizabeth Henning Sutton, *The Pony Champions*, 1992
Careless in her attempt to juggle her time between preparing for a pony competition and a tap dance recital, Meg allows her pony to become very sick.

186

Elizabeth Bram

Woodruff and the Clocks (New York: Dial, 1980)

Age range: Grades 1-2

Subject(s): Collectors and Collecting; Dreams and Nightmares

Major character(s): Woodruff, Child, Collector

Time period(s): Indeterminate

Locale(s): United States

What the book is about: The story of a boy who enjoys inventing adventures, collecting clocks and dreaming. Four easy to read stories about an unusual boy.

Where it's reviewed:
Booklist, April 15, 1980, page 1211
Kirkus Reviews, March 15, 1980, page 362
Publisher's Weekly, March 28, 1980, page 50

Other books by the author:
There Is Someone Standing on My Head, 1979
Saturday Morning Lasts Forever, 1978
The Man on the Unicycle and Other Stories, 1977
The Door in the Tree, 1976

Other books you might like:
Leon Steinmetz, *Clocks in the Woods,* 1979
    The forest animals realize that the sun is a more reliable clock than the clocks sold them by greedy porcupines.
Mary Stolz, *The Cuckoo Clock,* 1987
    Orphaned Erich's life as an unloved drudge begins to change when old Ula, the town's most skillful clockmaker, takes him on as his helper.
Anthony Taber, *The Boy Who Stopped Time,* 1993
    Julian stops the pendulum from swinging on the clock and has a marvelous adventure while the rest of the world is suspended in time.
Ann Tompert, *Sue Patch and the Crazy Clocks,* 1989
    The King of Tango appeals to Sue to fix his clocks because they are set at different times and he cannot function in the resulting chaos.
Sandra Ziegler, *All of Grandmother's Clocks,* 1977
    Billy learns to tell time from the many clocks in his grandparents' house.

| **187** |

Franz Brandenberg

Illustrator: Aliki

Leo and Emily (New York: Greenwillow, 1981)

Age range: Grades 1-2

Series: Greenwillow Read-Alone

Subject(s): Friendship; Magic; Neighbors and Neighborhoods

Major character(s): Leo, Child; Emily, Child

Time period(s): 1980s

Locale(s): United States

What the book is about: The friendship between two neighboring children, Leo and Emily, is the focus of this book. They get dressed in the dark, with humorous results, work out a trade, borrow toys and earn enough money to buy a rabbit for their magic show.

Where it's reviewed:
Booklist, April 15, 1981, page 1158
Center for Children's Books Bulletin, March 1981, page 126
Kirkus, April 1, 1981, page 429

Other books by the author:
Leo and Emily's Zoo, 1988
Leo and Emily and the Dragon, 1984
Leo and Emily's Big Ideas, 1982

Other books you might like:
Wayne Carley, *Mixed-Up Magic,* 1971
    An absent-minded witch tries to conjure up a dog for the dog show but can't remember the proper magic spell.
Patricia Coombs, *Dorrie and the Goblin,* 1972
    Dorrie rescues the Short High Sorcerer from a goblin spell and ensures the success of her mother's tea and magic show.
Marcel Marceau, *The Story of Bip,* 1976

Bip wants to be a magician who can show people the magic of their world.
James Marshall, *Fox on Stage,* 1993
    Fox makes a film for Grannie, takes part in a magic show, and puts on a play.
Mike Thaler, *Madge's Magic Show,* 1978
    Madge is a great magician and easily pulls several animals out of her hat, but not the one she wants.

| **188** |

Robbie Branscum

Illustrator: Deborah Howland

The Adventures of Johnny May (New York: Harper, 1984)

Age range: Grades 4-6

Subject(s): Grandparents; Mountain Life

Major character(s): Johnny May, Hunter; Gentle Tom, Mountain Man

Time period(s): 1940s

Locale(s): Arkansas

What the book is about: Johnny May is guilty of shooting a deer, even though it will feed the hill folk during the winter, and distressed because she thinks she saw Gentle Tom shoot a man.

Where it's reviewed:
Booklist, January 1, 1985, page 638
Hornbook, January 1985, page 49
School Library Journal, December 1984, page 88

Other books by the author:
Cameo Rose, 1989
The Girl, 1986
Cheater and Flitter Dick, 1983
The Murder of Hound Dog Bates, 1982

Other books you might like:
Clyde Robert Bulla, *White Bird,* 1990
    A lonely boy is found and reared by a hermit in the wilderness of the Tennessee mountains in the 1880s.
George Ella Lyon, *Borrowed Children,* 1988
    Amanda is given a holiday with her grandparents in Memphis where she finds her world beyond the drudgery of her Kentucky mountain family home.
Gary Paulsen, *Tracker,* 1984
    John must track a deer in the for his family's winter meat, and in doing so, finds himself drawn to the doe who leads him to hate his role as hunter.
Robert Newton Peck, *Banjo,* 1982
    While doing research for a school essay about a reclusive old mountain man, two boys fall into an abandoned mine shaft.
Carolyn Reeder, *Grandpa's Mountain,* 1991
    Carrie makes her annual summer visit to relatives in the mountains and watches her determined grandfather fight the government for his farm.

189

Robbie Branscum

The Murder of Hound Dog Bates (New York: Viking, 1982)

Age range: Grades 3-6

Subject(s): Mountain Life

Major character(s): Sassafras Bates, Teenager; Kelly O'Kelly, Police Officer

Time period(s): 1980s

Locale(s): Arkansas

What the book is about: Sassafras is sure that one of his aunts killed his favorite dog. He meets a Chicago policeman, O'Kelly, in the woods and invites him home for dinner to help solve the mystery.

Where it's reviewed:
Horn Book, December 1982, page 647
School Library Journal, December 1982, page 78

Awards the book has won:
Edgar Allan Poe Award 1983

Other books by the author:
The Girl, 1986
The Adventures of Johnny May, 1984
For Love of Jody, 1979
The Three Wars of Billy Joe Treat, 1975

Other books you might like:
Irene Hunt, *The Everlasting Hills*, 1985
    When a bitter mountain man cannot accept his son's mental retardation, the boy wanders into the woods and finds the father he never had.
Robert Newton Peck, *Banjo*, 1982
    Two boys fall into an abandoned mine shaft and only an old reclusive mountain man can save them.
Ellen Harvey Showell, *Our Mountain*, 1991
    Jimmy and Corey describe their family and home in the mountains of West Virginia.
Jesse Stuart, *Old Ben*, 1970
    Shan befriends a bull black snake, convincing his Kentucky mountain family to change their minds about snakes.
Jane Yolen, *Uncle Lemon's Spring*, 1981
    Uncle Lemon gets his spring in the middle of the driest summer on record and it brings him a lot of trouble.

190

Robbie Branscum

The Three Wars of Billy Joe Treat (New York: McGraw-Hill, 1975)

Age range: Grades 5-6

Subject(s): Farm Life

Major character(s): Billy Joe, Teenager

Time period(s): 1940s

Locale(s): Arkansas

What the book is about: When his brothers go off to war, Billy Joe takes on a larger share of the farm work. He insists that his Ma serve him more food and he refuses to eat until she

does. One of his other battles is with his teacher, Mr. Marshall, who turns out to be a spy.

Where it's reviewed:
Kirkus Reviews, January 15, 1976, page 78
School Library Journal, November 1975, page 71

Other books by the author:
Cameo Rose, 1989
The Girl, 1986
The Adventures of Johnny May, 1984
The Murder of Hound Dog Bates, 1982

Other books you might like:
Susan Clymer, *Four Month Friend*, 1990
    Staying with her uncle on his California farm, nine year old Dani feels unwelcome and unloved as she tries to save her pet goat from the butcher.
Berlie Doherty, *White Peak Farm*, 1984
    Teenage Jeannie copes with the triumphs and tragedies of her family as they face violent changes on their isolated Derbyshire farm.
Joan Lingard, *Between Two Worlds*, 1991
    A family of Latvian refugees encounters hard times in Canada and the three children must find jobs.
Phyllis Rossiter, *Moxie*, 1990
    Thirteen year old Drew helps his family hold on to their farm through the Dust Bowl of 1934.
Diana J. Wieler, *Last Chance Summer*, 1991
    A twelve year old runaway is given a last chance when he is sent to a farm with other "tough kids."

191

J.H. Brennan

Shiva: An Adventure of the Ice Age (New York: Lippincott, 1990)

Age range: Grades 5 and Up

Subject(s): Man, Prehistoric

Major character(s): Shiva, Prehistoric Human; Doban, Prehistoric Human

Time period(s): Indeterminate Past

Locale(s): Ancient Civilization

What the book is about: Shiva is attacked by a wolf and rescued by a naked, hairy boy who leaps on the wolf's back and kills it with his teeth. When he takes her back to her tribe, he is taken captive. Thag, Doban's father, prepares for war against Shiva's tribe. Only Shiva and Doban can prevent the confrontation.

Where it's reviewed:
School Library Journal, December 1990, page 100
Publisher's Weekly, October 12, 1990, page 65

Other books by the author:
Shiva Accused: An Adventure of the Ice Age, 1991
Barmy Jeffers and the Shrinking Potion, 1990
Dream of Destiny, 1980

Other books you might like:
Janet Asimov, *Norby and Yobo's Great Adventure*, 1989
    Jeff and his robot, Norby, accompany Admiral Yobo to prehistoric times to do research and the trip turns into a dangerous adventure.
William O. Steele, *The Magic Amulet*, 1979

A wounded young hunter must find a new group to join after he is left to die by his prehistoric family band.

Millstead Thomas, *Cave of Moving Shadows*,
A boy in Cro-Magnon times must choose between his training in sorcery and his desire to be a hunter.

Ann Turnbull, *Maroo of the Winter Caves*, 1984
Marov must take charge after her father is killed and lead her family to safety before winter comes.

Ann Warren Turner, *Time of the Bison*, 1987
Eleven year old Scar Boy discovers he has a gift for making pictures and becomes an apprentice to Painter of Caves.

| 192 |

Barbara Brenner

On the Frontier with Mr. Audubon (New York: Coward, 1977)

Age range: Grades 5 and Up

Subject(s): Frontier and Pioneer Life; Artists and Art

Major character(s): Joseph Mason, Teenager; John James Audubon, Historical Figure, Artist

Time period(s): 1820s

Locale(s): United States

What the book is about: Thirteen year old Joseph travels the Mississippi River, the swamps, forests and cities of the South with the famous naturalist Audubon. He tells the story of the great French artist who has gone from riches to rags in America.

Where it's reviewed:
Horn Book, June 1977, page 310
Kirkus Reviews, January 15, 1977, page 45

Other books by the author:
A Year in the Life of Rosie Bernard, 1983
The Mystery of the Plumed Serpent, 1981
Wagon Wheels, 1978
Little One Inch, 1977

Other books you might like:
Isaac Asimov, *It's Such a Beautiful Day*, 1985
In a future time, Richard Henshaw rediscovers the joys of the natural world.

Pam Conrad, *Prairie Songs*, 1985
This is a memorable portrayal of life on the Nebraska prairie, the struggle for survival and hardships on the frontier.

Jan Gleiter, *John James Audubon*, 1988
Determined to paint every bird in the U.S., Audubon sets off with a young assistant to travel down rivers and through forests.

Helen V. Griffith, *Georgia Music*, 1986
Working in the garden, listening to the birds and insects, a girl and her grandfather develop a strong bond which helps them through difficult times.

| 193 |

Barbara Brenner

Illustrator: Don Bolognese

Wagon Wheels (New York: Harper and Row, 1978)

Age range: Grades 2-4

Subject(s): Frontier and Pioneer Life; African Americans

Major character(s): Ed Muldie, Settler; Johnny Muldie, Child

Time period(s): 1870s

Locale(s): Nicodemus, Kansas

What the book is about: The story of a black family moving from Kentucky to Kansas after the Civil War. Based on a true story of famine, the kindness of Indians, and three boys who really lived.

Where it's reviewed:
New York Times Book Review, April 30, 1978, page 38
School Library Journal, September 1978, page 103

Other books by the author:
A Year in the Life of Rosie Bernard, 1983
On the Frontier with Mr. Audubon, 1977
Cunningham's Rooster, 1975
A Bird in the Family, 1962

Other books you might like:
Joan Anderson, *A Williamsburg Household*, 1988
Focus on events in the household of a white family and its black slaves in colonial Williamsburg in the 18th century.

Angela Shelf Medearis, *Picking Peas for a Penny*, 1990
A black girl describes the hard work and the rewards involved in growing up on a farm during the Depression of the 1930s.

Robert Henry Miller, *Reflections of a Black Cowboy*, 1991
Examines the contributions black cowboys have made to this country and to the legacy of the West, focusing on four individual cowboys. (non-fiction)

Ruth Pelz, *Black Heroes of the Wild West*, 1990
Biographical sketches of nine Afro-American pioneers.

Don Russell, *Cowboy on the Trail*, 1970
The adventures of Adam Bradford on a cattle drive from Texas to Kansas.

| 194 |

Harvey Brett

Immigrant Girl: Becky of Eldridge Street (New York: Holiday, 1987)

Age range: Grades 2-4

Subject(s): Emigration and Immigration; Jews

Major character(s): Becky Moscowitz, Immigrant; Max Moscowitz, Immigrant

Time period(s): 1910s (1910)

Locale(s): New York, New York

What the book is about: The life of Becky, an immigrant girl, and her family as they move to the Lower East Side of New York City from Russia. The nine of them squeeze into a three room apartment in a crowded and noisy neighborhood. Her grandmother teaches her Jewish traditions and practices as they struggle in their New World.

Other books by the author:
My Prairie Christmas, 1990
Cassie's Journey: Going West in the 1860's, 1988
My Prairie Year, 1986

Other books you might like:
Joanne E. Bernstein, *Dmitry: A Young Soviet Immigrant*, 1981
    An account of a Soviet Jewish boy and his parents who leave present-day Moscow and resettle in the United States.
Judith Caseley, *Apple Pie and Onions*, 1987
    Despite her embarrassment of her grandmother's public reminisces, Rebecca loves her and enjoys her stories about life in America after leaving Russia.
Barbara Cohen, *Molly's Pilgrim*, 1983
    When Molly's jewish mother dresses her Thanksgiving display doll in russian clothes, the teacher creates a discussion of the meaning of "pilgrim."
Patricia Polacco, *The Keeping Quilt*, 1988
    A homemade quilt ties together the lives of four generations of an immigrant Jewish family, remaining a symbol of their enduring faith and love.
Arthur Yorinks, *Oh, Brother*, 1989
    Milton and Morris, two orphaned immigrant brothers in New York, take jobs as trapeze artists, fruit peddlers, and tailors, and learn bitter lessons.

195

Jan Brett, Author/Illustrator

The Mitten: An Old Ukranian Folk Tale (New York: Putnam, 1989)

Age range: Grades 2-3

Subject(s): Folk Tales

Locale(s): Ukraine

What the book is about: Several animals sleep snugly in Nicki's lost mitten until the bear sneezes.

Where it's reviewed:
Booklist, September 15, 1989, page 172
Kirkus Reviews, August 15, 1989, page 1254

Other books by the author:
Goldilocks and the Three Bears, 1988
The First Dog, 1988
Annie and the Wild Animals, 1987

Other books you might like:
Steven Kellogg, *The Mystery of the Missing Red Mitten*, 1974
    Annie searches the neighborhood for her red mitten, the fifth she's lost this winter.
Jonathan London, *Froggy Gets Dressed*, 1992
    Froggy hops out into the snow for a winter frolic but is called back to get properly dressed.
Florence Slobodkin, *Too Many Mittens*, 1958
    The neighborhood knows twin boys have lost a red mitten, and soon, so many are returned to them, they start a service to return the surplus mittens.
James Stevenson, *Brrr!*, 1991
    When Maryann and Louie complain about the cold and snow, Grandpa tells them about the winter of 1908.
Alvin R. Tresselt, *The Mitten*, 1964
    An older version of the Ukrainian folktale, reprinted in 1989.

196

Patience Brewster, Author/Illustrator

Ellsworth and the Cats from Mars (New York: Houghton Mifflin/Clarion, 1981)

Age range: Grades 2-4

Subject(s): Space Exploration; Aliens; Animals/Cats

Major character(s): Ellsworth, Cat; Margaret, Cat, Alien (Martian)

Time period(s): Indeterminate Future

Locale(s): Outer Space

What the book is about: Ellsworth leads a normal cat life until he dreams about green Martian cats. At least he thinks it's all a dream until Margaret the Martian Cat visits him and takes him on an adventure in space.

Where it's reviewed:
Horn Book, June 1981, page 290
School Library Journal, April 1981, page 110

Other books by the author:
Rabbit Inn, 1991
Nobody, 1982

Other books you might like:
Amy Boesky, *Planet Was*, 1990
    Young Prince Hierre decides change is fun even though the royal policy on the Planet Was is never to change anything.
Chris L. Demarest, *The Lunatic Adventure of Kitman and Willy*, 1988
    Kitman and Willy's adventures take them into space, where they dislodge the moon and several stars from their places.
Tony Tallarico, *Look for Laura*, 1990
    Laura from the planet Maxx visits Earth. Look for her in the crowded places in this book.
Rosemary Wells, *Moss Pillows*, 1992
    Robert's visit to relatives is disasterous but a visit to the Bunny Planet cheers him up.
Jeanne Willis, *Earth Tigerlets as Explained by Professor Xargle*, 1990
    The alien, Professor Xargle, explains all about Earth Tigerlets, known on this planet as felines.

197

Sue Ellen Bridgers

All Together Now (New York: Knopf, 1979)

Age range: Grades 6 and Up

Subject(s): Mentally Handicapped; Grandparents

Major character(s): Casey Flanagan, Teenager; Dwayne Pickens, Handicapped (mentally retarded)

Time period(s): 1950s

Locale(s): United States

What the book is about: 12-year-old Casey is sent to live with her grandparents while her father is fighting the Korean War. She is not pleased with the arrangement but then meets Dwayne, a retarded man who is a boyhood friend of her father's. Casey fights for Dwayne's rights when his family wants him institutionalized.

Where it's reviewed:
Horn Book, April 1979, page 197
School Library Journal, May 1979, page 70

Awards the book has won:
Boston Globe/Horn Book Award 1979

Other books by the author:
Home Before Dark, 1976
Notes for Another Life, 1981
Permanent Connections, 1987
Sara Will, 1985

Other books you might like:
Peg Kehret, *Deadly Stranger*, 1987
   12-year-old Katie is adjusting to a new school and is terrified when her new friend is kidnapped.
Joycelyn Riley, *Only My Mouth Is Smiling*, 1982
   13-year-old Merle and her younger siblings move to a small town is Wisconsin where they must cope with their mother's erratic behavior.
Elfie Donnelly, *Offbeat Friends*, 1982
   Mari meets the strange Mrs. Panacek and tries to help when the old woman runs away from the mental hospital where she lives.
Sheila Greenwald, *Will the Real Gertrude Hollings Please Stand Up?*, 1983
   In spite of her learning disabilities, Gertrude finds she has something to teach Albert, her very successful cousin.
Irene Hunt, *The Everlasting Hills*, 1985
   When a mountain man rejects his mentally handicapped son, the boy wanders into the wilderness and finds a new father figure.

198

Sue Ellen Bridgers

Illustrator: Charles Robinson

Home Before Dark (New York: Knopf, 1977)

Age range: Grades 5-6

Subject(s): Migrant Labor; Stepmothers

Major character(s): James Earl, Parent; Stella Earl, Teenager

Time period(s): 1970s

Locale(s): United States

What the book is about: James inherits a tobacco farm from his younger brother, Newt. After years of following the crops, his family is finally able to settle down. After her mother dies, Stella must adjust to a new stepmother.

Where it's reviewed:
Horn Book, April 1977, page 165
School Library Journal, January 1977, page 99

Other books by the author:
Permanent Connections, 1987
Sara Will, 1985
Notes for Another Life, 1981
All Together Now, 1979

Other books you might like:
Eileen Dunlop, *Fox Farm*, 1978

Through caring for a stray fox cub, a boy realizes that he does have a home with his foster family, even thought his "real" family abandoned him.
Jane Gardam, *The Hollow Land*, 1981
   Young Harry Bateman spends the summer with his family year after year at Light Trees Farm in the Cumbrian fells country, until he feels it's his home.
Evelyn Sibley Lampman, *Go Up the Road*, 1972
   A Mexican-American and her family of migrant workers glimpse a more stable life and the possibility of sharing it.
Phyllis Rossiter, *Moxie*, 1990
   Drew, determined to help his family hold onto their farm during the Dust Bowl days of 1934, stubbornly tends his livestock and refuses to give up.
Nancy Covert Smith, *Josie's Handful of Quietness*, 1975
   Used to the hard life of her migrant family, Josie finally realizes her dream of a permanent home and school.

199

Katharine Mary Briggs

Kate Crackernuts (New York: Greenwillow, 1979)

Age range: Grades 6-8

Subject(s): Witches and Witchcraft

Major character(s): Katherine Lindsay, Child; Kate Maxwell, Child

Time period(s): 17th century

Locale(s): Scotland

What the book is about: Katharine Lindsay's father is the wealthy Laird. When he weds the mother of Kate Maxwell, Katherine's close, though secret, friend, the girls are delighted. But Kate is terrified to learn that her mother is a witch and terrible jealous of Katharine's status and beauty. The complexity of the story and the Scottish dialect makes this story derived from folklore difficult for some readers, but it is well worth the effort, especially for those interested in Scottish-English history.

Where it's reviewed:
Horn Book, June 1980, page 304
School Library Journal, May 1980, page 73

Other books by the author:
The Vanishing People, 1978
British Folktales, 1977
Hobberdy Dick, 1977
Folktales of England, 1965

Other books you might like:
Constance Fecher, *The Link Boys*, 1971
   In 17th century London, Tom learns the person responsible for his uncle's imprisonment is also the only person who can prevent his impending hanging.
William MacKellar, *The Witch of Glen Gowrie*, 1978
   A young Scottish boy doesn't believe in witches until he meets the old woman who lives in Glen Gowrie with her many animals.
Evelyn White Minshull, *The Dune Witch*, 1972
   Newly arrived in the Massachusetts colony, Priss is accused of being a witch due to her friendship with a strange girl that appears on the dunes.
Zilpha Keatley Snyder, *The Witches of Worm*, 1972
   A deeply disturbed girl believes that her strange behavior and destructive ways are due to bewitchment.

Ann Warren Turner, *Rosemary's Witch*, 1991
   After moving into an old house in a small New England town, Rosemary discovers that the nearby woods conceal a 150 year old witch.

200

Katherine Mary Briggs

Hobberdy Dick (New York: Greenwillow, 1977)

Age range: Grades 4-6

Subject(s): Witches and Witchcraft; Fairy Tale

Major character(s): Hobberdy Dick, Mythical Creature (hobgoblin)

Time period(s): Indeterminate Past

Locale(s): Widford Manor, England (Cotswold)

What the book is about: Hobberdy Dick is a hobgoblin who has "guarded and governed" Wildord Manor for centuries. When the last of the Cavalier family moves out, he decides to stay on. A Puritan townsman buys the Manor and the last heir becomes a gentlewoman for the new owner's wife.

Where it's reviewed:
Horn Book, June 1977, page 311
Kirkus Reviews, February 15, 1977, page 166

Other books by the author:
Kate Crackernuts, 1979

Other books you might like:
Anna Elizabeth Bennett, *Little Witch*, 1953
   Miniken Snickasse is the daughter of a witch who wants to be an ordinary child.
Patricia MacLachlan, *Tomorrow's Wizard*, 1982
   The Wizard and Murdoch are charged with fulfilling the most important wishes and curses made by the nearby villagers.
Phyllis Reynolds Naylor, *The Witch's Eye*, 1990
   Suspected witch-neighbor, Mrs. Tuggle, has died, but her glass eye has resurfaced, bringing new dangers and terrors to Lynn's family.
Mary Norton, *Bedknobs and Broomsticks*, 1957
   Two brothers and a sister receive a magic bed-knob which can grant their wish to be anywhere in the present or past.
Elizabeth George Speare, *The Witch of Blackbird Pond*, 1958
   Kit is an embarrassment to her Puritan relatives, and her sincere efforts to aid a reported witch soon bring her to trial as a witch herself.

201

Carol Ryrie Brink

Caddie Woodlawn (New York: Macmillan, 1935)

Age range: Grades 4-6

Subject(s): Frontier and Pioneer Life

Major character(s): Caddie Woodlawn, Child; Tom Woodlawn, Teenager; Warren Woodlawn, Child

Time period(s): 1860s

Locale(s): Wisconsin

What the book is about: The adventures of a tomboy living in Wisconsin in the 1860s are in turn exciting, humorous, and warm hearted. Caddie is a practical joker, and a daredevil, out of one scrape and into another, yet she has a warm enough heart to care about the people around her.

Where it's reviewed:
Booklist, June 3, 1935
Horn Book, May 1935, page 159j

Awards the book has won:
Newbery Medal 1936
Lewis Carroll Shelf 1959

Other books by the author:
Magical Melons, 1944
Winter Cottage, 1968
Louly, 1974
The Bad Times of Irma Baumlein, 1972

Other books you might like:
Elizabeth Enright, *Thimble Summer*, 1966
   Garnet finds a thimble in a dry creek bed and thinks the wonder summer she spends on a Wisconsin farm is just good luck.
Rachel Field, *Calico Bush*, 1966
   Maggie saves her family's lives by arranging a Maypole dance for attacking Indians.
Mary A. Hancock, *The Thundering Prairie*, 1969
   When two family members are injured before a land run in Oklahoma, the family's hopes are on 14-year-old Benjy and his mule.
Rose Wilder Lane, *Let the Hurricanes Roar*, 1985
   Originally published as Young Pioneers. The story of Molly and David and their child as they face the hardships of crossing the prairie.
Laura Ingalls Wilder, *Little House in the Big Woods*, 1953
   The first of the "Little House" series, this one tells of the small house in Wisconsin in 1870.

202

Bill Brittain

Illustrator: Charles Robinson

All the Money in the World (New York: Harper and Row, 1979)

Age range: Grades 2-4

Subject(s): Money; Fairies

Major character(s): Quentin Stowe, Child

Time period(s): Indeterminate

Locale(s): Earth

What the book is about: Quentin wishes he had more money than his father is able to give him. On his way home from a fishing trip, he catches a leprechaun and is granted three wishes. A funny look at the importance of money.

Where it's reviewed:
Kirkus Reviews, March 15, 1979, page 328
School Library Journal, March 1979, page 135

Other books by the author:
My Buddy, the King: A Novel, 1989
Dr. Dredd's Wagon of Wonders, 1987
Who Knew There'd be Ghosts?, 1985

The Devil's Donkey, 1981

Other books you might like:
Elizabeth Rose Bell, *Magic-Go-Round*, 1974
Money growing in the ground and exam answers in flour boxes are magic phenomena that Dorene and her boyfriend find useful, but should they use them?
Miriam Chaikin, *Yossi Asks the Angels for Help*, 1985
When he loses the Hannukah money he planned to use for presents for his sister and parents, Yossi prays for help.
Bernice Chardiet, *Martin and the Tooth Fairy*, 1991
Martin gets more from the tooth fairy than his friends at school, so he offers to put their teeth under his pillow, for a percentage!
Terrance Dicks, *TR Goes to School*, 1985
Jimmy's bear goes to school with him and helps him catch a bully and the thief who steals the lunch money.
James Marshall, *Yummers Too*, 1986
Emily tries to earn money to pay off debts created by her love of food, but her appetite keeps getting in the way.

203

Bill Brittain

Illustrator: Andrew Glass

The Devil's Donkey (New York: Harper, 1981)

Age range: Grades 3-6

Subject(s): Witches and Witchcraft

Major character(s): Dan'l, Child, Donkey; Old Magda, Witch

Time period(s): Indeterminate

Locale(s): Earth

What the book is about: A boy is turned into a donkey when he offends a witch. Only quick thinking, courage, and a bargain with the devil can set things right.

Where it's reviewed:
Childhood Education, September 1982, page 56
New York Times Book Review, September 26, 1982, page 39

Other books by the author:
Wings: A Novel, 1991
Professor Popkin's Prodigious Polish, 1990
Who Knew There'd Be Ghosts?, 1985
The Wish Giver: Three Tales of Coven Tree, 1983

Other books you might like:
Natalie Babbitt, *The Devil's Storybook*, 1974
Ten stories recount the Devil's exploits, successes and failures in Hell and in the world above.
Matt Christopher, *Devil Pony*, 1977
Stu comes to believe that his horse is in some way related to the Bancroft poltergeist.
William H. Hooks, *Mean Jake and the Devils*, 1981
Mean Jake has run-ins with Big Daddy Devil, Devil Junior, and Baby Deviline.
Collin McDonald, *Nightwaves: Scary Tales for After Dark*, 1990
A collection of horror stories featuring ghosts, spirits, and a mad killer.
William Sleator, *Blackbriar*, 1972
Trying to explain strange events, a boy discovers a group of English folk engaged in devil worship.

204

Bill Brittain

Illustrator: Andrew Glass

Dr. Dredd's Wagon of Wonders (New York: Harper, 1987)

Age range: Grades 3-5

Subject(s): Magic; Witches and Witchcraft; Devil

Major character(s): Dr. Dredd, Magician

Time period(s): Indeterminate Past

Locale(s): Coven Tree, New England

What the book is about: Coven Tree has been stricken by drought. Dr. Dredd arrives with his wagon full of ancient and mysterious things and Bufu, the Rainmaker. It's up to the New England teen age girls to deal with Dr. Dredd because no one else will. A suspenseful, witchy tale great for reading aloud.

Where it's reviewed:
Horn Book, September 1987, page 609
Kirkus Reviews, June 15, 1987, page 922

Other books by the author:
Who Knew There'd Be Ghosts, 1985
The Wish Giver: Three Tales of Coven Tree, 1983
The Devil's Donkey, 1981
All the Money in the World, 1979

Other books you might like:
John Bellaris, *The Mansion in the Mist*, 1992
Anthony and Miss Eells discover a chest that can transport them to another world and a maniacal group who is plotting the destruction of the Earth.
Diana Wynne Jones, *Stopping for a Spell*, 1993
Includes three stories: "Chair Person," "The Four Grannies," and "Who Got Rid of Angus Flint?"
Lynne Reid Banks, *The Adventures of King Midas*, 1992
King Midas regrets his wish to turn all he touches into gold, and must deal with a magician, a witch and a dragon as he tries to undo the magic spell.
Chris Van Allsburg, *The Widow's Broom*, 1992
A witch's worn out broom serves a widow well, until her neighbors decide the thing is wicked and dangerous.
Jane Yolen, *The Wizard of Washington Square*, 1969
David and Leilah are glad to meet the wizard who lives in the park until he accidentally turns David's dog into a statue and the statue is stolen.

205

Bill Brittain

Illustrator: Michele Chessare

Who Knew There'd Be Ghosts? (New York: Harper, 1985)

Age range: Grades 4-6

Subject(s): Ghosts; Mystery and Detective Stories

Major character(s): Essie Parnell, Spirit; Horace Parnell, Spirit; Tommy Donahue, Preteen

Time period(s): 1980s

Locale(s): Bramton

What the book is about: Three spunky youngsters join forces with two ghosts to save a historic mansion from being destroyed by a crooked antiques dealer.

Where it's reviewed:
Booklist, June 1, 1985, page 1392
Hornbook, July 1985, page 448
Kirkus Reviews, May 15, 1985, page J31

Other books by the author:
The Ghost From Beneath the Sea, 1992
The Wish Giver: Three Tales of Coven Tree, 1984
The Devil's Donkey, 1981
All the Money in the World, 1979

Other books you might like:
Pam Conrad, *Stonewords: A Ghost Story*, 1990
  Zoe house is haunted by the ghost of an eleven year old girl, who carries Zoe back to the day of her death in 1870, to try to alter that tragic event.
Sharon E. Heisel, *A Little Magic*, 1991
  Jessica and her cousin, Corky, a magic enthusiast, attempt to determine the truth behind the mysterious "ghosts" lurking in the neighborhood forest.
Liza Ketchum Murrow, *The Ghost of Lost Island*, 1991
  While helping her grandfather herd and shear his flock of sheep, Gabe encounters a mysterious woman who may be the ghost of a drowned milkmaid.
Sarah Sargent, *Jerry's Ghosts: The Mystery of the Blind Tower*, 1992
  Discovering two ghostly children, trapped with their mad scientist uncle, Jerry frees them from the 19th century mansion that was their former home.
Betty Ren Wright, *The Ghost of Popcorn Hill*, 1993
  Martin and Peter acquire a mischievous new dog and two lonely ghosts.

206

Bill Brittain

Illustrator: Andrew Glass

The Wish Giver: Three Tales of Coven Tree (New York: Harper and Row, 1983)

Age range: Grades 3-6

Subject(s): Wishes; Magic

Major character(s): Adam Fiske, Child; Thaddeus Blinn, Magician; Polly Kemp, Child

Locale(s): United States

What the book is about: Three people receive a white card with a red dot, guaranteed to make wishes come true. It does work, but not in the ways they had hoped. Polly wants attention, and she really gets it. Rowena gets a traveling salesman to "put down roots" but that doesn't work out too well. Adam wishes for water on his farm, and gets more than he bargained for.

Where it's reviewed:
Booklist, April 1, 1983, page 1028
Horn Book, June 1983, page 300
School Library Journal, April 1983, page 110

Awards the book has won:
Newbery Honor 1984

Other books by the author:
All the Money in the World, 1979
The Devil's Donkey, 1981
Who Knew There'd Be Ghosts?, 1985

Other books you might like:
Eugene Bradley Coco, *Wishing Well*, 1988
  A boy overhears an old man who is granted a simple wish and the boy tries his own, more elaborate plan.
Hazel Hutchins, *The Three and Many Wishes of Jason Reid*, 1988
  Jason makes a deal with the elf, Quicksilver, to allow his "third wish" to grant more wishes.
Edward Eager, *Seven-Day Magic*, 1962
  Abbie and her friends have many exciting adventures with a magic book, but it must be returned to the library at the end of seven days.
Edward Eager, *Half Magic*, 1954
  A family of children learns to wish carefully for twice what they want, because only half of each wish comes true.
Joan Aiken, *The Moon's Revenge*, 1987
  A boy makes a "deal" with spirits to achieve his dream of being a violinist, but he has no idea of the cost.

207

Betty Brock

Illustrator: Wallace Tripp

No Flying in the House (New York: Harper and Row, 1970)

Age range: Grades 3-5

Subject(s): Fantasy; Mystery and Detective Stories; Animals/Dogs

Major character(s): Annabel, Child; Gloria, Dog; Mrs. Vancourt, Householder

Time period(s): 1970s

Locale(s): United States

What the book is about: Gloria is a dog three inches high and three inches long and she talks. Her human is Annabel. Annabel and Gloria appear suddenly in Mrs. Vancourt's house and announce that they are going to live with her. Lots of secrets in this mystery-fantasy.

Where it's reviewed:
Kirkus Reviews, April 15, 1970, page 450
Library Journal, July 1970, page 2531

Other books by the author:
Shades, 1971

Other books you might like:
William Pene Du Bois, *Otto and the Magic Potatoes*, 1970
  The Baron is sure if he can study a dog two-and-a-half stories tall, he can improve the quality of his potatoes and roses.
Lynn Hall, *The Mystery of the Lost and Found Hound*, 1979
  A girl and her brother's efforts at tracing the owner of a lost beagle leads them to involvement with dog thieves.
Judith Whitelock McInerney, *Judge Benjamin*, 1985
  Judge Benjamin, a St. Bernard, solves a mystery while stranded with his family in an abandoned farmhouse during a blizzard.
Winslow Pels, *Miss Baba in the Doorknob of Destiny*, 1989

Miss Baba, a pedigree poodle and amateur detective, journeys to remote Mongolia to help a canine foundling discover the secret of her birthright.

Marilyn Singer, *Where There's a Will, There's a Wag*, 1986
Philip Barlowe, detective, and his dog, Sam Spayed, are hired to investigate the will of a woman who has left her fortune to a cat.

208

Dana Brookins

Alone in Wolf Hollow (Boston: Houghton/Clarion, 1978)

Age range: Grades 4-6

Subject(s): Orphans; Mystery and Detective Stories; Brothers

Major character(s): Bart, Orphan; Arnie, Child, Orphan; Uncle Charlie, Relative (uncle)

Time period(s): 1970s

Locale(s): United States

What the book is about: Orphaned Bart and Arnie are moved around the relatives until they end up with an uncle deep in the woods of Wolf Hollow. Uncle Charlie has a drinking problem and the two boys are left to solve the murder mystery they have become involved in.

Where it's reviewed:
Kirkus Reviews, June 15, 1978, page 636
School Library Journal, May 1978, page 84

Awards the book has won:
Edgar Allan Poe Award 1979

Other books by the author:
Who Killed Sack Annie, 1983

Other books you might like:
Malcolm J. Bosse, *The Cave Beyond Time*, 1980
After his father and brother are killed, Ben goes to stay with his uncle. Bitten by a rattlesnake, he suddenly finds himself transported back in time.
Vera Cleaver, *Trial Valley*, 1977
Mary Call is responsible for the younger children in her family. Her brother-in-law and the children find an abandoned child in the woods.
Barthe DeClements, *No Place for Me*, 1987
While Copper's mother is in treatment, she goes from one relative to another. Aunt Maggie, reputed to be a witch, brings her stability and comfort.
Sid Fleischman, *By the Great Horn Spoon*, 1963
Orphan Jack Flagg runs away from home and becomes involved in the Gold Rush of 1849 in California.

209

Bruce Brooks

Everywhere (New York: Harper, 1990)

Age range: Grades 5 and Up

Subject(s): Death; Grandparents

Time period(s): 1990s

Locale(s): United States

What the book is about: A boy meets a new friend, Dooley, who seems to save his grandfather with "soul-switching," a technique he learned from comic books. The boy must come to terms with how much he loves his grandfather. For mature readers.

Where it's reviewed:
Kirkus Reviews, April 1, 1990, page 1082
School Library Journal, September 1990, page 224

Other books by the author:
No Kidding, 1989
Midnight Hour Encores, 1986 (young adult)
The Moves Make the Man: A Novel, 1984

Other books you might like:
Betsy Byars, *The House of Wings*, 1972
Sammy's parents have deserted him and he is left with his grandfather in a deserted old house full of strange animals.
Peter Hartling, *Old John*, 1990
After Jacob and Laura's grandfather moves in, they come to know and love his independence and zest for life.
Dennis Haseley, *Shadows*, 1991
When Jamie is sent to live with relatives, his grandfather teaches himto make shadows on the wall. The "shadows" help save his grandfather's life.
Kristi Holl, *Just Like a Real Family*, 1983
When June's class visits a retirement home and kids are paired with an elderly friend, June's partner won't talk. But the relationship takes a turn.
Mollie Hunter, *The Mermaid Summer*, 1988
In this suspenseful folktale, two children learn how to outwit a vengeful mermaid.

210

Bruce Brooks

The Moves Make the Man: A Novel (New York: Harper & Row, 1984)

Age range: Grades 6 and Up

Subject(s): Sports/Basketball; Race Relations

Major character(s): Jerome, Teenager; Bix, Teenager

Time period(s): 1980s

Locale(s): North Carolina

What the book is about: Jerome is the only Black student in a newly integrated junior high. Bix becomes his best friend and Jerome teaches Bix to play basketball. A great story for anyone interested in sports and friendship.

Where it's reviewed:
Horn Book, March/April 1985, page 185
School Library Journal, December 1984, page 103

Awards the book has won:
Newbery Honor

Other books by the author:
Everywhere, 1990
Midnight Hour Encores, 1986
No Kidding, 1989

Other books you might like:
Karen Gardner, *The Case of the Basketball Joker and Other Mysteries*, 1990

Jack B. Quick and two friends set out to solve several mysteries.

Bruce Bassoff, *Supercharged: Or How a Good Kid becomes BAAAD and Saves His Basketball Team*, 1990
A boy inherits special power and lives out his fantasy of becoming a college basketball star.

C. Paul Jackson, *Beginner Under the Backboards*, 1974
Durant is gawky and awkward but over six-foot-four and struggles with developing his talent.

Suzy Kline, *Orp Goes to the Hoop*, 1991
A star baseball pitcher finds that many skills from his old sport can be transferred to basketball.

Alison Jackson, *Crane's Rebound*, 1991
Les has adventures as well as problems at summer basketball camp.

211

Jerome Brooks

Uncle Mike's Boy (New York: Harper, 1973)

Age range: Grades 5-6

Subject(s): Divorce; Alcoholism; Death

Major character(s): Pudge, Child; Mike, Relative (uncle)

Time period(s): 1970s

Locale(s): United States

What the book is about: Eleven year old Pudge is trying to adjust to his parents' divorce, his dad's drinking and mom's depression when his little sister is killed by a truck. Uncle Mike is the only one he can turn to. Uncle Mike is the perfect choice.

Where it's reviewed:
Kirkus Reviews, July 15, 1973, page 759
Library Journal, November 15, 1973, page 3448

Other books by the author:
Naked in Winter, 1990
The Testing of Charlie Hammelman, 1977

Other books you might like:
N.B. Dorman, *Laughter in the Background*, 1980
Marcie can't take her mother's alcoholism any longer.

Tormod Haugen, *The Night Birds*, 1982
Jake struggles with real and imagined terrors, including his father's bouts of depression and his own nightmares.

Natalie Honeycutt, *Ask Me Something Easy*, 1991
After her father leaves, Addie must cope with her angry, distant mother, perfect older sister and sensitive younger twins.

Yvette Moore, *Freedom Songs*, 1991
In the 60's, when Uncle Pete joins the Freedom Riders down South, Sheryl organizes a gospel concert in Brooklyn to help him.

Marc Talbert, *Double or Nothing*, 1990
Sam acquires from his beloved Uncle Frank both a knowledge of magic and wisdom to cope when he loses his uncle.

212

Walter R. Brooks

Illustrator: Kurt Wiese

Freddy the Detective (New York: Knopf, 1932)

Age range: Grades 3-6

Subject(s): Animals; Animals/Pigs; Mystery and Detective Stories

Major character(s): Freddy, Pig (Detective); Mr. Bean, Farmer; Jinx, Cat

Time period(s): Indeterminate Past

Locale(s): United States

What the book is about: Freddy, the pig, and all the farm animals who live with Mr. Bean decide to emulate Sherlock Holmes. Freddy's methods are funny, if not always successful as he tries to prove the innocence of Jinx, the cat, who has been accused by the thieving rat, Simon. Lots of snappy conversations among the animals make this fun to read.

Where it's reviewed:
Bookman, December 1932, page 847
New York Times, November 13, 1932, page 15

Other books by the author:
Freddy and the Men From Mars, 1987
Freddy Goes Camping, 1986
Freddy the Politician, 1986
The Collected Poems of Freddy the Pig, 1953

Other books you might like:
Arthur Conan Doyle, *The Return of Sherlock Holmes*, 1987
A baker's dozen of Holmes short stories for the middle reader.

William Kotzwinkle, *Trouble in Bugland: A Collection of Inspector Mantis Mysteries*, 1983
A quick-witted insect sleuth, Inspector Mantis, patterned after Sherlock Holmes, displays his brilliant powers of deduction in solving five mysteries.

James Marshall, *A Summer in the South*, 1977
A great detective, Eleanor Owl, is drawn into a mystery while vacationing at a beachside hotel.

Robert Newman, *The Case of the Somerville Secret*, 1981
Andrew and Sara help an inspector from Scotland Yard uncover the identity of a murderer and a monster associated with Lord Sommerville.

Mary Pope Osborne, *Spider Kane and the Mystery under the May-Apple*, 1992
With the help of a spider, a mother and a ladybug, a young butterfly tries to uncover a mystery involving a butterfly with whom he has fallen in love.

213

Fern G. Brown

Babysitter on Horseback (New York: Ballantine, 1988)

Age range: Grades 4-7

Subject(s): Babysitters; Animals/Horses; Mystery and Detective Stories

Major character(s): Melissa Mansfield, Teenager, Babysitter; Scott Robinson, Preteen; Roscoe Cannon, Neighbor

Time period(s): 1980s

Locale(s): Woodvale, Illinois

What the book is about: Melissa is pegged as irresponsible after leaving a stall door open, allowing her dad's beloved Arabian horse to get loose. Now she has lost Scott, the child she is babysitting for, when Scott goes to the barn to check on his horse and does not come back. Worse yet, a phone call comes from a kidnapper demanding $50,000 ransom. Of course, her father will not let Melissa join the posse searching for Scott, but her own investigations indicate the real kidnapper may be riding in the posse.

Where it's reviewed:
Booklist, February 15, 1989, page 1007
Publisher's Weekly, November 11, 1988, page 59
Voice of Youth Advocates, February 1989, page 283

Other books by the author:
Horses and Foals, 1986
Jockey—or Else!, 1978
You're Somebody Special on a Horse, 1977
Hard Luck Horse, 1975

Other books you might like:
Jesse Harris, *The Witness*, 1992
    McKenzie Gold gets entangled in a string of babysitter murders when her special psychic power allows her to see through the eyes of the killer.
Hawk Greenway, *The Trail North*, 1981
    Chronicles a sixteen year old boy's solo horseback journey from northern California up the Pacific Crest Trail to northern Washington.
Alison Cragin Herzig, *The Ten-Speed Babysitter*, 1987
    A babysitter's job is filled with surprises when his employer jets off to the Caribbean for the weekend and leaves him in charge of a toddler.
Stephen Schwandt, *The Last Goodie*, 1985
    Haunted by the unsolved abduction of his babysitter twelve years ago, Marty finds a clue and a new lead in the case and finds himself in danger.
Virginia Vail, *Horseback Summer*, 1990
    While spending the summer at a horse camp, Emily must fight to keep spoiled Caro Lescaux from taking the horse Emily loves.

214

Jeff Brown

Flat Stanley (New York: HarperCollins, 1964)

Age range: Grades 2-4

Subject(s): Humor

Time period(s): Indeterminate

Locale(s): Fictional Country

What the book is about: Stanley is flattened when he is hit by a falling bulletin board. There are some problems associated with being flat, but there is the fun of being able to squeeze into small spaces when you are only one inch deep, being sent through the mail to a friend's house, and catching an art thief while hanging on the wall at a museum. Stanley is happily returned to normal with a bicycle pump. Great read aloud.

Where it's reviewed:
Observer (London), January 10, 1971, page 23
Times Literary Supplement, June 6, 1968, page 582

Other books by the author:
A Lamp for the Lambchops, 1983

Other books you might like:
Marc T. Brown, *D.W. Thinks Big*, 1993

Even though her brother says she is too small to help with the wedding, D.W. proves she is just right when disaster strikes during the ceremony.
Oscar De Mejo, *La Bella Magellona and the Little Cavalier*, 1992
    Big-footed Magellona loves the little cavalier, who is so tiny that he goes for rides on her dog, but their love is doomed until they discover magic.
Florence Parry Heide, *Treehorn Times Three*, 1992
    A three-in-one volume containing three stories about the boy, Treehorn: "The Shrinking of Treehorn," "Treehorn's Treasure," and "Treehorn's Wish."
Rita Phillips Mitchell, *Hue Boy*, 1993
    Everyone in little Hue Boy's island village has suggestions on how to help him grow, but he learns to stand tall in a way all his own.
Susan Patron, *Five Bad Boys, Billy Que, and the Dustdobbin*, 1992
    The Dustdobbin under his bed shrinks Billy Que down to its own size to teach him what it is like to be small.

215

Jeff Brown

Illustrator: Lynn Wheeling

A Lamp for the Lambchops (New York: Harper, 1983)

Age range: Grades 2-5

Subject(s): Genies; Magic

Major character(s): Stanley Lambchop, Child; Prince Fawzi Haraz, Mythical Creature (genie); Arthur Lambchop, Child

Time period(s): Indeterminate

Locale(s): United States

What the book is about: A genie-in-training provides madcap adventures for the Lambchops. Prince Haraz is ready to grant any wish that is not cruel or evil or really nasty. As time goes by, the ever polite Lampchops wonder how to undo too much of a good thing.

Where it's reviewed:
School Library Journal, March 1984, page 156
New Yorker, December 5, 1983, page 206

Other books by the author:
Flat Stanley, 1964

Other books you might like:
William F. Buckley, *The Temptation of Wilfred Malachey*, 1985
    A poor boy in a rich school decides to become a "Robin Hood," which earns him good money, until he discovers a genie in the school's computer.
Ellen Conford, *Genie with the Light Blue Hair*, 1989
    Jean finds a genie in a lamp she receives for her birthday. She discovers that having her wishes come true isn't as great as she thought it would be.
Helen Cresswell, *Almost Good-Bye*, 1990
    While collecting things to sell for a school White Elephant sale, two friends are given a lamp with unexpected magic qualities.
Alice Low, *Genie and the Witch's Spells*, 1982

Genie has a hard time with her school work until she and Merlina, a witch who has trouble learning her spells, agree to a partnership.

Marianna Mayer, *Aladdin and the Enchanted Lamp*, 1985
Retells the adventures of Aladdin who, with the help of a genie, outwits outwits an evil sorcerer and wins the hand of a beautiful princess.

216

Marc T. Brown, Author/Illustrator

Arthur's Baby (Boston: Little Brown, 1987)

Age range: Grades 1-2

Subject(s): Family Life; Babies

Major character(s): Arthur, Child; D.W., Child; Kate, Child

Time period(s): Indeterminate

Locale(s): Fictional Country

What the book is about: Arthur gets all kinds of advice from friends and his sister, D.W., about coping with a new baby. When Kate comes home from the hospital, Arthur still feels uncomfortable but when he is able to stop her from crying, he begins to feel better.

Where it's reviewed:
Horn Book, November 1987, page 721
Kirkus Reviews, November 1, 1987, page 1571
Booklist, November 1, 1987, page 471

Other books by the author:
Arthur's April Fool, 1983
Arthur Goes to Camp, 1982
Arthur's Eyes, 1979
Arthur's Nose, 1976

Other books you might like:
Jennifer Barrett, *Kiki's New Sister*, 1992
    When Kiki suggests sending the baby back to the hospital, her parents suggest she spend a little more time with her before making a decision.
Nancy White Carlstrom, *Kiss Your Sister, Rose Marie!*, 1992
    Rose Marie is not at all sure she likes having to deal with her new sister, Baby Boo.
Dorian Haarhoff, *Desert December*, 1992
    A South African boy makes a long journey through the desert to join his parents in a mining village, reaching them on Christmas Day.
Hermann Moers, *Hugo's Baby Brother*, 1992
    Hugo, the young lion, although fully grown, resents sharing his mother's attention with his new baby brother.
Christine Ross, *Lily and the Present*, 1992
    Lily searches the stores for the perfect big, bright and beautiful present for her new baby brother.

217

Marc T. Brown

Illustrator: Laurence K Brown

The Bionic Bunny Show (Boston: Little Brown, 1984)

Age range: Grades 1-4

Subject(s): Animals/Rabbits; Television Programs

Major character(s): Wilbur Rabbit, Television Personality

Time period(s): 1980s

Locale(s): United States

What the book is about: Wilbur is the star of "The Bionic Bunny Show." He chases and catches some bank-robbing rats. When Wilbur goes home, he is a quiet, clumsy dad. The story shows the behind-the-scenes activities of TV production in a way accessible to younger children.

Where it's reviewed:
Center for Children's Books Bulletin, July/August 1984, page 201
School Library Journal, May 1984, page 62

Other books by the author:
DW Flips, 1987
Perfect Pigs, 1983
Spooky Riddles, 1983
Witches Four, 1980

Other books you might like:
Tomie De Paola, *The Knight and the Dragon*, 1980
    A cartoon picture show about an inexperienced knight and an inexperienced dragon who prepare to do battle.
Malka Drucker, *Series TV: How a TV Show Is Made*, 1983
    Describes how a TV show is made, from story idea through casting and filming to the airing of a finished show. (Nonfiction)
E.A. Hass, *Incognito Mosquito Takes to the Air*, 1986
    While on a TV talk show, the famous insect detective describes his adventures and solves a mystery on the air.
Kevin Henkes, *Return to Sender*, 1984
    Whitaker writes a letter to TV superhero, Frogman. His family stops laughing when he gets a reply.
Justine Korman, *Who Framed Roger Rabbit?*, 1988
    A rabbit and a detective solve a murder mystery, outwit the evil Judge Doom and rescue Toontown from annihilation.

218

Margaret Wise Brown, Author/Illustrator

Sneakers: Seven Stories about a Cat (Reading, Massachusetts: Addison Wesley, 1955)

Age range: Grades 2-4

Subject(s): Animals/Cats

Major character(s): Sneakers, Cat

Time period(s): Indeterminate

Locale(s): United States

What the book is about: With Sneakers, it is pounce, pounce, pounce all day long! When he isn't pouncing on peaches or brand new hats, he is just prowling around. He goes to the beach with the boy and his parents, and sleeps outside all night. Then he's off to the city and back to the country again, pouncing most of the way.

Where it's reviewed:
Hornbook, February 1980, page 79
Bookwatch, November 11, 1979, page 16
Publishers Weekly, September 10, 1979, page 75

Other books by the author:
Baby Animals, 1989
Four Fur Feet, 1961

Nibble, Nibble: Poems for Children, 1959
The Little Fur Tree, 1954

Other books you might like:
Janet Wyman Coleman, *Fast Eddie*, 1993
　　To the dismay of Puff the cat and Jones the squirrel, Fast
　　Eddie the raccoon takes on his human neighbors one final
　　time.
Iris Hiskey, *Cassandra Who?*, 1992
　　When Cassandra the cat is invited to a costume party by
　　someone she doesn't even know, the confusion begins.
Clare Turlay Newberry, *Marshmallow*, 1993
　　A cat who is used to being the center of attention learns to
　　share his home with a rabbit.
Katherine Potter, *My Mother the Cat*, 1993
　　When Jane gets her wish to have her mother switch places
　　with her cat, the resulting freedom to do anything she wants
　　turns out less than perfect.
Harriet Berg Schwartz, *Backstage with Clawdio*, 1993
　　Clawdio the theater cat describes how he keeps everything
　　running smoothly backstage during a production of "Peter
　　Pan."

219

Laurent De Brunhoff, Author/Illustrator

Babar and the Ghost: An Easy to Read Version (New
York: Random, 1986)

Age range: Grades 1-3

Subject(s): Castles; Animals/Elephants; Ghosts

Major character(s): Babar, Elephant; Celeste, Elephant

Time period(s): Indeterminate

Locale(s): Fictional Country

What the book is about: After a visit to Black Castle,
Babar, his wife Celeste, and their children, Pom, Flora and
Alexander, find a ghost named Baron Bardula has come home
with them.

Where it's reviewed:
Booklist, August 1986, page 1695

Other books by the author:
Isabelle's New Friend, 1989
Bonhomme and the Huge Beast, 1974
Anatole and His Donkey, 1963
The Story of Babar, 1933

Other books you might like:
Anna DiVito, *Elephants on Ice*, 1991
　　When a clumsy elephant named Dozer is challenged to an
　　ice skating contest by his schoolmate Otto, he wins in an
　　unexpected way.
Russell Hoban, *The Twenty Elephant Restaurant*, 1978
　　A man build a new table sturdy enough for an elephant to
　　dance on and works up to a restaurant with twenty dancing
　　elephants.
Arnold Lobel, *Uncle Elephant*, 1981
　　Uncle Elephant comes to the rescue when his nephew's
　　parents are lost at sea, and cares for him until they are found.
Tom Paxton, *Engelbert the Elephant*, 1990
　　An elephant's dancing skills and good manners surprise ev-
　　eryone at the royal ball, including the queen.
William Steig, *Doctor De Soto Goes to Africa*, 1992

Expert mouse dentist Doctor De Soto is called suddenly to
attend an elephant in Africa.

220

Bonnie Bryant

Horse Crazy (New York: Bantam, 1988)

Age range: Grades 4-6

Series: Saddle Club

Subject(s): Friendship; Animals/Horses

Major character(s): Carole Hanson, Preteen, Equestrian;
Stevie Lake, Preteen, Equestrian; Lisa Atwood, Teenager,
Equestrian

Time period(s): 1980s

Locale(s): United States

What the book is about: Three girls become friends at a
riding stable. Carole and Stevie are not sure about Lisa when
she shows up at Pine Hollow Stables in fancy riding gear and is
immediately chummy with the most stuck up girl they know. But
the three become good friends and take part in a scheme to
help Stevie make money so she won't miss out on a mountain
trail overnight trip.

Where it's reviewed:
Booklist, February 15, 1989, page 1007

Other books by the author:
Fox Hunt, 1992
Dude Ranch, 1989
Horse Sense, 1989
Horse Shy, 1988

Other books you might like:
Maggie Dana, *Racing for the Stars*, 1988
　　To earn money to buy her own horse, Kerry tries out for a
　　part in a film to be made at the Timber Ridge Riding Stables
　　where she lives.
Jean Slaughter Doty, *The Crumb*, 1976
　　A young girl and her pony become involved in the horse
　　show circuit when she gets a job helping out at a nearby
　　stable and riding school.
Isabelle Holland, *Toby the Splendid*, 1987
　　After disobeying her mother and buying a horse with her
　　babysitting money, Janet works for his upkeep but has no
　　money for riding lessons.
Ann Sheldon, *A Star in the Saddle*, 1989
　　Linda's horse, Amber, is used in a soap opera being shot
　　near her ranch. The show's star mistreats Linda and gets lost
　　in a forest fire with Amber.
Virginia Vail, *Surprise, Surprise!*, 1990
　　When her best friend Judy visits the riding camp where Emily
　　is spending the summer, Judy is a big hit with the other
　　campers and Emily feels jealous.

221

Emilie Buchwald

Illustrator: Barbara Flynn

***Gildaen: The Heroic Adventures of a Most Unusual
Rabbit*** (New York: Harcourt, 1973)

Age range: Grades 4-6

Subject(s): Fantasy; Animals/Rabbits

Major character(s): Gildaen, Rabbit; Grimald, Sorcerer; Evon, Child

Time period(s): Indeterminate Past

Locale(s): United States

What the book is about: Evon is a shape-changing boy with magical powers. He teams up with Gildaen to search for his true identity. They meet an outlaw, Hickory, who is loyal to the king who is being threatened by the evil Grimald. Gildaen returns home with many tales to tell.

Where it's reviewed:
Center for Children's Books Bulletin, July 1973, p 167
Kirkus Reviews, April 15, 1973, page 455

Other books by the author:
This Sporting Life, 1987 (poems about sports and games)
Floramel and Esteban, 1982

Other books you might like:
Richard Adams, *Watership Down*, 1972
    A group of rabbits searches for a place to live in peace - for those who like long stories (429 pages).
James Howe, *The Celery Stalks at Midnight*, 1983
    Chester the cat continues to try to prove that Bunnicula is a vampire rabbit.
Tamora Pierce, *Wild Magic: The Immortals*, 1992
    Thirteen year old Daine helps a mage, a knight, and a queen to battle immortal creatures attacking the kingdom.
Lynne Reid Banks, *The Indian in the Cupboard*, 1980
    A magic cupboard turns plastic toys into real life creatures.
Elvira Woodruff, *Back in Action*, 1991
    After finding the magic powder, Noah and Nate shrink to miniature and have exciting adventures.

222

David Budbill

Bones on Black Spruce Mountain (New York: Dial, 1978)

Age range: Grades 5 and Up

Subject(s): Friendship; Survival

Major character(s): Seth, Preteen, Camper (wilderness survivor); Daniel, Preteen, Camper (wilderness survivor)

Time period(s): 1970s

Locale(s): United States (Northeast Woods)

What the book is about: Daniel and Seth are hoping to find a legendary cave on their five day campout. Their struggle for survival deepens their friendship and mutual respect.

Where it's reviewed:
Horn Book, August 1978, page 392
School Library Journal, May 1978, page 64

Awards the book has won:
Dorothy Canfield Fisher Children's Book Award 1980

Other books by the author:
Snowshoe Trek to Otter River, 1976

Other books you might like:
Patricia Edwards Clyne, *Tunnels of Terror*, 1975

While searching for hidden treasure, five young people find themselves trapped in an underground cave by rising flood waters.
Evelyn Sibley Lampman, *Rattlesnake Cave*, 1974
    Spending four months in Montana, a friendless boy finds a new world opened to him when he makes friends with some local Indians.
Thomas Millstead, *Cave of the Moving Shadows*, 1979
    A twelve year old Cro-Magnon boy must choose between his training in sorcery and his desire to be a hunter.
Barbara A. Steiner, *Ghost Cave*, 1990
    Marc and two friends get lost in a cave inhabited by ghosts.
Bill Wallace, *Trapped in Death Cave*, 1984
    Gary and Brian discover both the buried treasure his grand-father died protecting, and the killer as well.

223

Clyde Robert Bulla

Illustrator: Ben Stahl

Almost a Hero (New York: Dutton, 1981)

Age range: Grades 4-5

Series: Skinny Books (Hi Interest, Low Vocabulary)

Subject(s): Dating (Social Customs); Orphans; Child Abuse

Major character(s): Chiefie, Abuse Victim, Orphan; Mr. Hatfield, Administrator (of orphanage); Maggic, Child, Orphan

Time period(s): 1930s

Locale(s): United States

What the book is about: Chiefie and Maggie are growing up in an orphanage during the Depression. The superintendent abuses Chiefie. After he grows up and joins the Navy, he returns to avenge his childhood.

Where it's reviewed:
Center for Children's Books Bulletin, March 1982, page 122
School Library Journal, February 1982, page 86

Other books by the author:
The Chalk Box Kid, 1987
The Cardboard Crown, 1984
Charlie's House, 1983
My Friend the Monster, 1980

Other books you might like:
Deborah Anderson, *Michael's Story*, 1986
    The case of a boy who was emotionally abused and what happened when he worked with a counselor.
Barbara S. Cole, *Don't Tell a Soul*, 1987
    Presents the point of view of both the abused child and the mother whose second husband is the abuser.
Rebecca Orr, *Gunner's Run*, 1980
    Gunner runs away from his abusive father, finds a friend in Mr. Beltz, and begins to take new pride in himself.
Marilyn Sachs, *A December Tale*, 1976
    A foster child struggling to change her unhappy life is hurt by an abusive foster mother, yet strengthened by imaginary contact with Joan of Arc.
Marya Smith, *Winter-Broken*, 1990
    Abused by an alcoholic father, Dawn finds friendship and love in a sympathetic farmer and his beautiful horse, Wildfire.

224

Clyde Robert Bulla

Illustrator: Thomas B. Allen

The Chalk Box Kid (New York: Random House, 1987)

Age range: Grades 2-4

Series: Stepping Stone Books

Subject(s): Artists and Art; Gardens and Gardening; Imagination

Major character(s): Gregory, Artist

Time period(s): 1980s

What the book is about: Gregory feels alone in a new house, new neighborhood and new school. Having no room for a garden, Gregory draws a garden on a blank wall. As the "chalk garden" grows, Gregory learns to give and earns the respect and friendship of others.

Where it's reviewed:
Booklist, December 1, 1987, page 628
School Library Journal, December 1987, page 71

Other books by the author:
The Beast of Lor, 1977
The Cardboard Crown, 1984
Shoeshine Girl, 1975

Other books you might like:
Geraldine Kaye, *Goodbye, Ruby Red*, 1974
　　Susie cuts a doll out of paper and it becomes very hard to get along with.
Leo Lionni, *Matthew's Dream*, 1991
　　A young mouse visits an art museum and decides to become a painter.
Mildred Pitts Walter, *Have a Happy*, 1989
　　Chris feels eclipsed because his birthday falls on Christmas and he takes solace in preparing a carving for Kwanzaa.
Ann Thwaite, *Rose in the River*, 1974
　　Rose goes on an outing with her family and has an adventure in the river.
Janet McNeill, *Magic Lollipop*, 1974
　　A little boy visits a witch's house and turns an ordinary lollipop into a magic one.

225

Clyde Robert Bulla

Illustrator: Joan Sandin

Daniel's Duck (New York: Harper, 1979)

Age range: Grades 2-4

Subject(s): Artists and Art

Major character(s): Jeff, Child (Woodcarver); Henry Pettigrew, Artisan (woodcarver)

Time period(s): Indeterminate

Locale(s): Tennessee

What the book is about: Jeff passionately wants to carve animals. When he tries, he gets his feelings hurt when people at the fair make fun of the wooden duck he has carved. As he runs to the river to throw the duck away, he meets Henry Pettigrew, a famous woodcarver, who convinces him that his work is good and he should keep carving.

Where it's reviewed:
Booklist, October 15, 1979, page 359
Hornbook, December 1979, page 659
Kirkus Reviews, November 1979, page 1259

Other books by the author:
Singing Sam, 1989
The Chalk Box Kid, 1987
Poor Boy, Rich Boy, 1982
Almost a Hero, 1981

Other books you might like:
Elizabeth Coatsworth, *The Cat Who Went to Heaven*, 1958
　　A little cat comes to the home of a poor Japanese artist and, by humility and devotion, brings him good fortune.
Demi, *The Artist and the Architect*, 1991
　　In ancient China, a jealous artist plots to eliminate the favorite architect of the emperor.
Elizabeth Haidle, *Elmer the Grump*, 1989
　　An unsociable, wood-carving elf changes his grumpy ways after rescuing an injured snail.
Diana Hendry, *The Rainbow Watchers*, 1989
　　Having just moved to the city, Hannah feels unsettled until she meets Eliza and Jenny and becomes a rainbow watcher for a local artist.
Ruth Yaffe Radin, *Carver*, 1990
　　Jon struggles to fit in at his new public school and hide his growing interest in woodcarving from his mom who still mourns the death of Jon's father.
John Halkin, *Fangs of the Werewolf*, 1987
　　A strange "wild dog" terrorizes Wales with brutal killings but an old wise woman knows a secret that eventually destroys the creature.
Louise Lawrence, *Star Lord*, 1978
　　A Welsh family is caught up in the struggle between the supernatural powers of a mountain and the technological powers of a star lord who crashes into
Elinor Lyon, *Green Grow the Rushes*, 1964
　　A girl from London, vacationing on the rugged Welsh coast with a snippy, spoiled companion, finds three adventurous friends whom she joins in a search
Ken Radford, *The Cellar*, 1989
　　From her first night in a old boarding house located in the hills of North Wales, a young girl is aware of mysterious ghostly presences and determines
Dixie Tenny, *Call the Darkness Down*, 1984
　　Morfa Owen, an American staying at a cottage in Wales while searching for traces of her Welsh grandparents, receives a series of mysterious messages b

226

Clyde Robert Bulla

Illustrator: Peter Burchard

Down the Mississippi (New York: Harper, 1954)

Age range: Grades 4-6

Subject(s): Rivers

Time period(s): Indeterminate

Locale(s): Mississippi River

What the book is about: A Minnesota farm boy gets a much desired chance to go down the Mississippi on a raft as the cook's helper. Instead of curing him of his wish to work on the river as his parents had hoped, it only strengthens his hope to become a riverman.

Where it's reviewed:
Booklist, June 15, 1954, page 424

Other books by the author:
The Cardboard Crown, 1984
The Beast of Lor, 1977
Marco Moonlight, 1976
Benito, 1961

Other books you might like:
Holling Clancy Holling, *Minn of the Mississippi*, 1979
  The adventures of a three-legged snapping turtle as she travels from the headwaters to the mouth of the Mississippi River.
F.N. Monjo, *Willie Jasper's Golden Eagle*, 1976
  An account of the famous 1870 steamboat race down the Mississippi between the Natchez and the Robert E. Lee, as told by a boy on board the Natchez.
A.L. Singer, *Davy Crockett and the King of the River*, 1991
  Davy and his trusted friend, Georgie Russell, are in for a wild ride down the mighty Mississippi in a race with Mike Fink, King of the River.
Mildred D. Taylor, *Mississippi Bridge*, 1990
  During a heavy rainstorm in rural Mississippi, a boy sees a bus driver order all black passengers off a crowded bus to make room for white passengers.
Gertrude Chandler Warner, *The Haunted Cabin Mystery*, 1991
  The Alden children travel on a Mississippi paddle-wheel steamer to visit an old family friend and investigate mysterious actions near the house.

227

Clyde Robert Bulla

Illustrator: Peter Burchard

Pocahontas and the Strangers (New York: Crowell, 1971)

Age range: Grades 3-5

Subject(s): Indians of North America; Biography

Major character(s): Pocahontas, Indian, Historical Figure; John Rolfe, Settler, Historical Figure; Captain John Smith, Settler, Historical Figure

Time period(s): 17th century

Locale(s): Jamestown, Virginia, American Colonies

What the book is about: An account of the life of Pocahontas woven about the few facts known from historical records.

Where it's reviewed:
Center for Children's Books Bulletin, July 1972, p 166
Horn Book, October 1971, page 474

Awards the book has won:
Christopher Award 1972

Other books by the author:
A Lion to Guard Us, 1981
Conquista, 1978
The Beast of Lor, 1977
Shoeshine Girl, 1975

Other books you might like:
Christian Feest, *The Powhatan Tribes*, 1990
  Explains the history, culture, and changing fortunes of the Powhatan Indians, the nation to which the famous Pocahontas belonged. (non-fiction)
Jean Fritz, *The Double Life of Pocahontas*, 1983
  A biography of the famous American Indian princess, emphasizing her life-long adulation of John Smith and the roles she played in two cultures.
Kate Jassem, *Pocahontas, Girl of Jamestown*, 1979
  A brief account of the life of the Indian princess who befriended Captain John Smith and the settlers of Jamestown.
Scott O'Dell, *The Serpent Never Sleeps: A Novel of Jamestown and Pocahontas*, 1987
  In the early 17th century, Serena travels to the new world, where she comes to know the hardships of colonial life, and the Princess Pocahontas.

228

Clyde Robert Bulla

Illustrator: Leigh Grant

Shoeshine Girl (New York: Crowell, 1975)

Age range: Grades 3-5

Subject(s): Friendship; Work

Major character(s): Sarah Ida, Child; Aunt Claudia, Relative; Al, Businessman (shoeshine man)

Time period(s): 1970s

Locale(s): United States

What the book is about: Sarah Ida stays with Aunt Claudia because she and her mom are not getting along. For pocket money, she gets a job shining shoes. When her employer, Al, gets hit by a car, Sarah Ida takes over the shoeshine stand.

Where it's reviewed:
Kirkus Reviews, October 15, 1975, page 11820

Other books by the author:
The Chalk Box Kid, 1987
The Cardboard Crown, 1984
Charlie's House, 1983
Almost a Hero, 1981

Other books you might like:
Carol Barkin, *Jobs for Kids*, 1990
  Offers tips to kids including listing your talents, finding a job, acting responsibly, handling disasters and setting prices. (non-fiction)
Tessa Duder, *Jellybean*, 1985
  Geraldine is tired of trying to fit into her busy mother's rehearsal schedule, but a new friend changes the situation.
Susan Beth Pfeffer, *Kid Power*, 1977
  Eleven year old Janie advertises to do odd jobs and is so successful she forms her own agency.
Jill Paton Walsh, *A Chance Child*, 1978
  Christopher searches for his half-brother, Creep, and keeps his personal log which describes the working conditions during the Industrial Revolution.
Gertrude Chandler Warner, *Benny Uncovers a Mystery*, 1976

Two brothers take summer jobs at a department store where strange events cast suspicion on them.

229

Anne Evelyn Bunting

The Empty Window (New York: Warne, 1980)

Age range: Grades 3-5

Subject(s): Death; Brothers and Sisters; Friendship

Major character(s): CG, Child; Sweeney, Child; Joe, Child, Invalid

Time period(s): 1980s

Locale(s): California

What the book is about: CG and his eight year old brother, Sweeney, have a close friend who is near death and want to give him a special present. They capture a parrot Joe loves watching but are afraid to see Joe themselves, fearing their own reaction to his condition. Joe's parents insist they present the gift themselves. Joe loves the bird, but asks the boys to release it so he can continue to watch it through the window. When Joe dies, the "empty window" takes on new meaning.

Where it's reviewed:
Kirkus Reviews, January 15, 1981, page 75
School Library Journal, February 1981, page 62

Other books by the author:
The Ghost Children, 1989
Is Anybody There?, 1988
The Happy Funeral, 1982
The Waiting Game, 1981

Other books you might like:
Eth Clifford, *The Remembering Box*, 1985
    Joshua spends each Friday night with his grandmother and her memories.
Patricia Reilly Giff, *The Gift of the Pirate Queen*, 1982
    Grace learns of another Grace O'Malley, whose courage as a 15th century pirate helps her find her own courage facing the death of her mom.
Susan McLean, *Pennies for the Piper*, 1984
    Bicks cares for her dying mother and shelters a badly abused little boy.
Doris Buchanan Smith, *A Taste of Blackberries*, 1973
    Accepting grief and guilt is the challenge for Jamie when his best friend suddenly dies from a bee sting.
Carol Beach York, *Remember Me When I am Dead*, 1980
    Odd notes from the past begin to appear in Jenny's notebook after the sister's mother dies.

230

Eve Bunting

Clancy's Coat (New York: Viking Kestrel, 1984)

Age range: Grades 1-3

Subject(s): Friendship

Major character(s): Clancy, Farmer; Tippitt, Tailor

Time period(s): Indeterminate

Locale(s): Ireland

What the book is about: Friendship, like a garden, can be revived with care and attention, as a farmer and a tailor prove. Bridget, Tippitt's cow, wrecks Clancy's garden. When Clancy brings Tippitt a coat to mend, they mend their friendship as well.

Where it's reviewed:
Horn Book, April 1984, page 181
School Library Journal, April 1984, page 99

Other books by the author:
Barney the Beard, 1975
The Big Cheese, 1977
High Tide for Labrador, 1975
Jane Martin, Dog Detective, 1984

Other books you might like:
Lauren A. Mills, *Rag Coat*, 1991
    Children tease Minna about her coat of scraps until she tells the story behind it.
Amy Hest, *The Purple Coat*, 1986
    Gabby begs her tailor grandfather to make her a purple coat for fall.
Jack Prelutsky, *The Terrible Tiger*, 1970
    A tiger eats the grocer, the baker, and the farmer, but regrets eating the tailor.
Elsa Maartman Beskow, *Pelle's New Suit*, 1962
    Pelle follows the process of the making of a new suit, and helps at each step.

231

Eve Bunting

The Ghost Children (New York: Clarion, 1989)

Age range: Grades 4-6

Subject(s): Orphans; Mystery and Detective Stories; Dolls and Dollhouses

Major character(s): Matt, Preteen, Orphan; Abby, Child, Orphan; Gerda, Relative (great-aunt), Guardian

Time period(s): 1980s

Locale(s): California

What the book is about: Orphaned twelve year old Matt and his younger sister are taken in by an aunt. Matt becomes involved with the life-sized dolls that belong to his aunt.

Where it's reviewed:
Booklist, April 1, 1989, page 1379
School Library Journal, March 1989, page 177

Other books by the author:
Is Anybody There?, 1988
Mother's Day Mice, 1986
The Happy Funeral, 1982
Empty Windows, 1980

Other books you might like:
Carolyn Sherwin Bailey, *Miss Hickory*, 1946
    Miss Hickory has many adventures after Great-granny Brown closes her New Hampshire home for the winter.
Carol Ryrie Brink, *The Bad Times of Irma Baumlein*, 1972
    Irma's bad times begin when she tells her classmates that she has the biggest doll in the world, and then has to prove it.
Rachel Field, *Hitty, Her First Hundred Years*, 1929
    Hitty, a doll of real character carved from a block of mountain ash, tells her life story of travel and adventure.

Rumer Godden, *The Doll's House*, 1962
  Adventures of a brave 100 year old Dutch farthing doll, her family, their Victorian dollhouse and the little English girls to whom they all belong.
William Sleator, *Among the Dolls*, 1975
  Vicky gets a dollhouse and projects conflicts with her family through her play with the dolls. The dolls do the same to get revenge on HER!

232

Eve Bunting

Illustrator: Amy Schwartz

Jane Martin, Dog Detective (New York: Harcourt, 1984)

Age range: Grades 2-3

Subject(s): Animals/Dogs; Mystery and Detective Stories

Major character(s): Jane Martin, Detective

Time period(s): Indeterminate

Locale(s): United States

What the book is about: For twenty-five cents a day, Jane Martin will solve your missing pet problem. She looks for clues, checks pawprints, tails suspects. Her first case is Tim Wilson, whose dog has been dognapped and the culprit is demanding $100 ransom. Jane solves the problem with her excellent deductive reasoning and returns the dog, Charlie, to Tim. With investigations and clues that young readers can follow, Jane will make lots of friends among newly independent readers.

Other books by the author:
Clancy's Coat, 1984
The Big Cheese, 1977
The Tongue of the Ocean, 1976
Barney the Beard, 1975

Other books you might like:
Herbert Best, *Desmond the Dog Detective: The Case of the Lone Stranger*, 1962
  A series of robberies, a mysterious lone stranger, and a big black sedan lead Desmond and his master, Gus, to investigate.
Dan Cohen, *The Case of the Missing Poodle*, 1979
  A poodle disappears from a dog show and sisters Ruthann and Polly help officer Greenwood find the dognapper.
Lynn Hall, *The Mystery of the Lost and Found Hound*, 1979
  A girl and her brother's efforts at tracing the owner of a lost beagle leads them to involvement with dog thieves.
Elizabeth Levy, *Something Queer Is Going On: A Mystery*, 1973
  The strange dognapping of Fletcher, the lazy Bassett hound, leads Jill and Gwen on a search that ends at a dog food commercial.
Marjorie Weinman Sharmat, *Nate the Great and the Sticky Case*, 1978
  Nate the Great and his dog Sludge try to track down Claude's missing Stegosaurus stamp.

233

Eve Bunting

Illustrator: Jan Brett

Mother's Day Mice (New York: Clarion, 1986)

Age range: Grades 2-3

Subject(s): Gifts; Animals/Mice; Holidays

Time period(s): 1980s

Locale(s): United States

What the book is about: Three mice leave the house early on Mother's Day to find perfect presents for Mother. The youngest wants to give her honeysuckle from the porch but cannot get to it safely. While searching, though, he learns a song, his perfect gift.

Where it's reviewed:
Center for Children's Books Bulletin, April 1986, page 143
Horn Book, May/June 1986, page 43

Other books by the author:
Fly Away Home, 1991
Scary, Scary Halloween, 1986
Clancy's Coat, 1984
The Man Who Could Call Down Owls, 1984

Other books you might like:
Barbara Cooney, *The Little Juggler*, 1961
  The French legend of the little juggler and his special Christmas Gift.
Muriel L. Feelings, *Zamani Goes to Market*, 1977
  Zamani's unselfishness is rewarded when he spends the first money he earns on a gift for his mother.
Kathryn Osebold Galbraith, *Laura Charlotte*, 1990
  A mom tells of her love for a toy elephant she was given as a child, a gift she has now passed on to her daughter.
Magdalen Nabb, *Josie Smith*, 1989
  The misadventures of a little girl as she shops for the perfect birthday gift for her mother, blackens a blackboard and cares for a lost cat.
Ann Tompert, *Little Otter Remembers*, 1977
  Little Otter selects a gift for his mom, searches for a pine cone and attends a coasting party with his relatives.

234

Eve Bunting

Illustrator: Diane De Groat

One More Flight (New York: Warne, 1976)

Age range: Grades 3-5

Subject(s): Runaways; Animals/Birds

Major character(s): Timmer, Teenager; Peter J. "Dobby" Dobson, Preteen; Miss Bee, Neighbor

Time period(s): 1970s

Locale(s): Glendon, California

What the book is about: Peter "Dobby" Dobson has run away from foster homes and the residential center over and over again. This time, he meets Timmer, an eighteen year old who cares for wounded birds. Dobby sees the care Timmer gives the birds and wishes someone would care that much for him. Though he would love to stay with Timmer, the center would never approve him as a foster parent. Dobby proves his bravery when Timmer needs medical care, and learns that, for birds and for people, freedom is not really freedom until you are ready for it.

Where it's reviewed:
Kirkus Reviews, March 15, 1976, page 321
School Library Journal, May 1976, page 57

Awards the book has won:
Golden Kite Award 1976

Other books by the author:
The Hideout, 1991
The Ghost Children, 1989
Is Anybody There?, 1988
Ghost's Hour, Spook's Hour, 1987

Other books you might like:
Eth Clifford, *Just Tell Me When We're Dead!*, 1983
    Two sisters and a runaway cousin for whom they are searching on an island find themselves in an unexpected adventure.
Ruth Hallman, *Breakaway*, 1981
    Kate and Rob, who has recently become deaf, run away to Georgia where Rob can learn to live independently without interference from his mother.
Walter Macken, *The Flight of the Doves*, 1992
    An English boy and his sister run away from their stepfather and set out to reach their grandmother in Northern Ireland.
Michael Morpurgo, *Mr. Nobody's Eyes*, 1989
    The adventures of a pair on the run: an escaped circus monkey and an ostracized English boy named Harry.
Gary Paulsen, *Tiltawhirl John*, 1977
    A runaway discovers that a carnival's razzle-dazzle doesn't shield it from the cruelties of life.

235

Eve Bunting

Our Sixth-Grade Sugar Babies (New York: Lippincott, 1990)

Age range: Grades 5-6

Subject(s): Schools

Major character(s): Vicki Charlip, Preteen; Harry Hogan, Preteen; Sam "Terrific Hunk - THUNK" Shub, Teenager

Time period(s): 1990s

Locale(s): California

What the book is about: Vicki and her best friend fear that their sixth grade project, carrying around a five pound bag of sugar to learn about parental responsibility, will make them look ridiculous in the eyes of the seventh grade boy they both love. When Vicki leaves her sugar baby with Mr. Ambrose, the elderly, senile man next door, and he loses track of it, her wrath drives him to try to find the "baby" and get lost himself. Vicki learns more responsibility than she counted on.

Where it's reviewed:
Booklist, October 15, 1990, page 441
School Library Journal, October 1990, page 113

Other books by the author:
The Wall, 1990
No Nap, 1989
A Sudden Silence, 1989
Sixth Grade Sleepover, 1987

Other books you might like:
Patricia Goehner Baehr, *Summer of the Dodo*, 1990

Tall, awkward, and inclined to act impulsively, Dodo Penny worries about 6th grade, but a summer teaching a real dodo to survive gives her confidence.
Norma Klein, *Confessions of an Only Child*, 1974
    Antonia goes through many emotional problems anticipating a baby in the family.
Katherine Marko, *Hang Out the Flag*, 1992
    In 1943, as she waits for her father to come home on leave, a girl in a small midwestern town tries to help the war effort by catching a German spy.
Colleen O'Shaughnessy McKenna, *The Truth about Sixth Grade*, 1991
    Collette finds herself unexpectedly popular when her fellow students find out she knows the world's most gorgeous teacher personally.
Kate McMullan, *The Great Eggspectations of Lila Fenwick*, 1991
    When faced with the challenges of sixth grade, Lila sees her "great ideas" backfire, but soon discovers good things can happen when least eggspected.

236

Eve Bunting

Our Sixth-Grade Sugar Babies (Philadelphia: Lippincott, 1990)

Age range: Grades 4-6

Subject(s): Babies; Honesty; Schools

Major character(s): Vicki, Preteen, 6th Grader; Ellie, Preteen, 6th Grader; Mrs. Oda, Teacher

Time period(s): 1990s

Locale(s): United States

What the book is about: Each member of a sixth grade class is entrusted with the welfare of a five pound sack of sugar. Questions of reliability, honesty and deception rise to the surface. Vicki is mostly worried about what a cute seventh grade boy will think about her carrying around a sack of sugar.

Where it's reviewed:
School Library Journal, December 1990, page 20
Center for Children's Books Bulletin, November 1990, page 55
Kirkus Reviews, November 1, 1990, page 1529

Other books by the author:
Coffin on a Case, 1992
The Hideout, 1991
The Ghost Children, 1989
Ghost of Summer, 1977

Other books you might like:
Hila Colman, *Confessions of a Storyteller*, 1981
    When she learns that her idolized music teacher is involved in a "mundane" relationship, Annie allows an accusation of improper conduct to stand.
John Donovan, *Remove Protective Coating a Little at a Time*, 1973
    Harry is more a pal than a son to his parents, but his friendship with Amelia fosters an honesty and directness that gives him courage to be himself.
Dean Hughes, *Honestly, Myron*, 1982

Myron takes his teacher's lesson on the importance of honesty very seriously and becomes absolutely honest at all times.

Catherine Frey Murphy, *Alice Dodd and the Spirit of Truth*, 1993

While spending the summer in a vacation cabin with her aunt and three year old cousin, a young girl finds herself involved in lies and deceptions.

Miriam Young, *Truth and Consequences*, 1975

A sixth grade girl amost ruins her relationship with her best friend until she learns to temper her honesty with a little tact.

237

Eve Bunting

Illustrator: Marie De John

The Robot Birthday (New York: Dutton, 1980)

Age range: Grades 1-3

Subject(s): Robots; Twins; Single Parent Families

Major character(s): Pam, Twin; Kerry, Twin; Mrs. Flitter, Babysitter

Time period(s): 1980s

Locale(s): United States

What the book is about: Mom, an electronics teacher, is late for the twins' birthday party and Pam and Kerry are surrounded by kids they don't know. They have just moved into a new house, and their mother invited the children of neighbors. When Mom does arrive, she brings a super-gift—a real working robot with remote controls. Not only is the robot a great toy, but it chases away bullies from the playground and acts as a warning when a bridge washes out. Woven into the story is the family's acceptance that Mom cannot replace their lost father, but is just fine being herself, with her own strengths and talents.

Where it's reviewed:
Center for Children's Books Bulletin, November 1980, page 48
Kirkus Reviews, July 1, 1980, page 835
School Library Journal, September 1980, page 56

Other books by the author:
Clancy's Coat, 1984
Blackbird Singing, 1980
The Cloverdale Switch, 1979
Barney the Beard, 1975

Other books you might like:
Isaac Asimov, *Norby and the Oldest Dragon*, 1990
Jeff Wells and his personal robot, Norby, find adventure when they travel to the planet Jamyn and attend the Grand Dragon's birthday party.
Betty Baker, *Worthington Botts and the Steam Machine*, 1981
In the 1890s, Worthington Botts builds a steam-powered robot to help him with his chores so he will have more time to read.
Joan Lowery Nixon, *Kidnapped on Astarr*, 1981
With a robot's help, two children search for a relative who has been kidnapped by the king on the planet Astarr and accused of making a secret weapon.
Scott Shirley, *Planet of the Robots*, 1982

A young space explorer, marooned on Planet Zare and surrounded by robots programmed to kill him, befriends the daughter of the planet's evil ruler.
Alfred Slote, *My Robot Buddy*, 1975
For his tenth birthday, Danny wants a robot so he'll have someone to play with.

238

Eve Bunting

Someone Is Hiding on Alcatraz Island (Boston: Houghton Mifflin, 1984)

Age range: Grades 6-9

Subject(s): Prisoners and Prisons; Gangs

Major character(s): Danny, Teenager

Time period(s): 1980s (1984)

Locale(s): San Francisco, California

What the book is about: When he gets in trouble with one of the toughest gangs in his San Francisco school, Danny flees to Alcatraz to escape them, but finds himself trapped with a Park Service employee in an old cell block by the gang. The gang members are frighteningly believable, the suspense is heavy and the setting is perfect for a thriller.

Where it's reviewed:
Horn Book, March/April 1985, page 177
School Library Journal, December 1984, page 100

Other books by the author:
Coffin on a Case, 1992
Will You Be My POSSLQ?, 1987
Face at the Edge of the World, 1985
The Haunting of Safekeep, 1985

Other books you might like:
Janet Green, *Us, Inside a Teenage Gang*, 1975
Fictionalized documentary in which six members of a teenage gang briefly lower their defenses to reveal a little about their personal lives.
S.E. Hinton, *That Was Then, This Is Now*, 1980
Mary and Bryon have been like brothers, but as their involvement with girls, gangs and drugs increases, their friendship seems to disintegrate.
Walter Dean Myers, *Scorpions*, 1988
After reluctantly taking on the leadership of a Harlem gang, Jamal finds that his enemies treat him with respect when he acquires a gun.
Richard Peck, *Secrets of a Shopping Mall*, 1979
Two eighth grade loners decide to take up residence in a department store: little do they know that thiers is not an original idea.
P.J. Petersen, *Nobody Else Can Walk It for You*, 1982
A group of young backpackers led by eighteen year old Laura must outwit three motorcyclists who terrorize them in a wilderness area.

239

Eve Bunting

Illustrator: Ronald Himler

The Wall (New York: Clarion, 1990)

Age range: Grades 2-4

Subject(s): Vietnam War; Monuments

Major character(s): Boy, Child; Father, Parent

Time period(s): 1990s

Locale(s): Washington, District of Columbia

What the book is about: A boy and his father locate the name of the boy's grandfather on the Vietnam War Memorial, a tribute to those who have lost their lives in war.

Where it's reviewed:
Booklist, April 1, 1990, page 1544
School Library Journal, May 1990, page 420

Other books by the author:
Fly Away Home, 1991
In the Haunted House, 1990
Happy Birthday Dear Duck, 1988
Ghost's Hour, Spook's Hour, 1987

Other books you might like:
Martin Auer, *The Blue Boy*, 1992
    When his parents die in a war, a boy from another planet rejects any form of kindness.
Lynn Hall, *The Mystery of the Caramel Cat*, 1981
    Willie's encounter with a feline ghost leads to strange dreams about events before the Civil War.
Jeanne M. Lee, *Ba-Nam*, 1987
    A young Vietnamese girl visiting her ancestors' graves finds the old gravekeeper frightening until a violent storm shows her the old woman's kindness.
Geraldine McCaughrean, *The Cherry Tree*, 1992
    After a war destroys their Japanese village and kills their father, Taichi and Yumiko find hope by caring for a cherry tree and watching it thrive.
Jane Yolen, *All Those Secrets of the World*, 1991
    When four year old Janie's father goes to war, Janie learns a secret of the world which helps her understand her father's long absence.

240

Eve Bunting

Illustrator: Donald Garrick

The Wednesday Surprise (New York: Clarion, 1989)

Age range: Grades 3-5

Subject(s): Grandparents; Literacy

Major character(s): Anna, Child, Tutor

Time period(s): 1980s

Locale(s): United States

What the book is about: On Wednesday nights when grandma stays with Anna, everyone thinks she is teaching Anna to read, when actually Anna is teaching grandma to read as a surprise for Dad's birthday. Donald Carrick's watercolors evoke the warmth of the family and the skill and joy of reading.

Where it's reviewed:
Horn Book, November 1989, page 756
Publisher's Weekly, October 12, 1990, page 66

Awards the book has won:
Jane Addams Children's Book Award 1990 Honor Book

Other books by the author:
In the Haunted House, 1990
A Sudden Silence, 1989
The Wall, 1989
The Man Who Could Call Down Owls, 1988

Other books you might like:
Jamie Gilson, *Do Bananas Chew Gum?*, 1980
    Sixth grader Matt can only read at a second grade level. He thinks he is dumb until he is convinced to cooperate with those who believe in him.
Edith Thacher Hurd, *I Dance in My Red Pajamas*, 1982
    Jenny visits with her grandparents and enjoys a wonderful, noisy day.
Natalie Kinsey-Warnock, *The Canada Geese Quilt*, 1989
    Worried that the new baby and her grandmother's illness will change things on the farm, Ariel combines her talents with grandmother's to make a quilt.
Mildred Pitts Walter, *Have a Happy*, 1989
    Chris's birthday falls on Christmas and is lost in the usual hub-bub of the holidays. He takes solace in the carvings he is preparing for Kwanzaa.
Laurence Yep, *Child of the Owl*, 1977
    Casey is far more American than Chinese. She lives with her grandmother in San Francisco's Chinatown for a while and learns of her rich heritage.

241

Robert Burch

Doodle and the Go-Cart (New York: Viking, 1972)

Age range: Grades 3-5

Subject(s): Farm Life

Major character(s): Doodle Rounds, Child; Glenn Carter, Child; Luke Stinson, Child

Time period(s): 1970s

Locale(s): Ripley, Georgia

What the book is about: Doodle's family's farm is not doing as well as it once did. Chicken prices have gone down and feed costs have gone up. Doodle's dream of owning a go-cart almost becomes a reality until he decides he cannot sacrifice his beloved mule, Addie, so Doodle keeps trying schemes to make money.

Where it's reviewed:
Horn Book, August 1972, page 368
Kirkus Reviews, April 15, 1972, page 476

Awards the book has won:
Georgia Children's Book Award 1974

Other books by the author:
King Kong and Other Poets, 1986
Ida Early Comes over the Mountain, 1980
Wilkin's Ghost, 1978

Other books you might like:
Betty Bates, *Hey There, Owlface*, 1991
    Brad forms a special relationship with the owls living in his family's barn, one that is threatened by a trigger-happy neighbor.
Susan Clymer, *Four Month Friend*, 1990
    Dani feels unwelcome and unloved as she tries to come up with a plan to save her pet goat, Tyler, from the butcher.

Shari Lewis, *How Kids Can Really Make Money*, 1979
 Interesting and practical ways for kids to make money. (Non-fiction)
Astrid Lindgren, *Emil's Pranks*, 1971
 Chaos seems to follow a Swedish boy everywhere he goes in the community.
Robert Newton Peck, *Trig*, 1977
 A young girl on a Vermont farm relates the events of the day her uncle bought her a genuine "Junior G-Man" machine gun.

242

Robert Burch

Ida Early Comes over the Mountain (New York: Viking, 1980)

Age range: Grades 4-6

Subject(s): Depression (Economic); Humor; Country Life

Major character(s): Randall Sutton, Child; Ida Early, Child-Care Giver (nanny)

Time period(s): 1930s

Locale(s): Georgia

What the book is about: Tough times in rural Georgia during the Depression take a lively turn when spirited Ida Early arrives to keep house for the Suttons. She makes everything fun, but kids at school make fun of her. And when Randall cannot bring himself to stand up for her, Ida shows her expertise extends to dealing with relationships as well as housekeeping.

Where it's reviewed:
Horn Book, December 1980, page 639
School Library Journal, October 1980, page 142

Awards the book has won:
Boston Globe/Horn Book Award - Honor Book

Other books by the author:
Christmas with Ida Early, 1983 (sequel to *Ida Early Comes over the Mountain.*)
King Kong and Other Poets, 1986

Other books you might like:
George Ella Lyon, *Borrowed Children*, 1988
 Amanda Perrit is saddled with adult responsibilities when her mother is ill, but a surprise trip to Memphis gives her a new perspective.
Constance C. Greene, *Dottie's Suitcase*, 1980
 Two motherless sisters, struggling to keep house for their father, see a robbery, find a suitcase of stolen money, and are faced with a moral dilemma.
Mary Stolz, *Ivy Larkin*, 1986
 The Depression forces the Larkin family to move to smaller and smaller apartments, while Ivy hates the private school she attends on scholarship.
Marian Potter, *A Chance Wild Apple*, 1982
 11 year old Maureen has a bit of good luck when she finds a special tree on her family's Missouri farm.
Lee Pennock Huntington, *Maybe a Miracle*, 1984
 11 year old Dorcas has a wonderful year even during the Depression, when she prays for a miracle to happen for her best friend.

243

Robert Burch

King Kong and Other Poets (New York: Viking Kestral, 1986)

Age range: Grades 4-7

Subject(s): Shyness; Poetry; Schools

Major character(s): Andy, 6th Grader; Marilyn, 6th Grader, Writer (poet)

Time period(s): 1980s

Locale(s): United States

What the book is about: Marilyn is a new girl in the sixth grade. She is very quiet, expressing her feelings through poetry. Andy gets to know her, and when her father, grieving over his wife's death, decides to return to California, she is sorely missed.

Where it's reviewed:
Booklist, November 15, 1986, page 506
Kirkus, October 1, 1986, page 1508

Other books by the author:
Isa Early Comes over the Mountain, 1980
Homefront Heroes, 1974
Queenie Peavy, 1966
Skinny, 1964

Other books you might like:
Patricia Goehner Baehr, *Faithfully, Tru*, 1984
 Tru, longing to be a poet, is torn between her mother's rigid values and the the talented but irresponsible father that she finally comes to meet.
Betsy Byars, *Beans on the Roof*, 1988
 As each of the five members of the Bean family tries to write a "roof" poem, they come to realize just how nice it is to be a Bean.
Beverley Dunlop, *The Poetry Girl*, 1983
 Growing up in New Zealand following WWII, Natalia uses poetry to escape from her problems at home and at school.
Nikki Grimes, *Growin'*, 1977
 Pump thinks her world has ended when her father, the only person who believed in her poetry, suddenly dies. That is, until she meets Jim Jim.
Gregory Maguire, *Lights on the Lake*, 1981
 Daniel lives with his parents in his grandmother's house in the mountains. He becomes involved with a grieving poet and a bird that reveals dreams.

244

Robert Burch

Queenie Peavy (New York: Viking, 1966)

Age range: Grades 4-6

Subject(s): Schools; Prisoners and Prisons; Country Life

Major character(s): Queenie Peavy, Child

Time period(s): 1960s

Locale(s): Georgia

What the book is about: Queenie thinks all her troubles will be over when her dad is released from prison. She is a problem child - chewing tobacco, talking back, throwing rocks and fighting. She pretends for a whole day that she has changed and finds that she likes being nice.

Where it's reviewed:
Horn Book, August 1966, page 433
Library Journal, June 15, 1966, page 3256

Awards the book has won:
Georgia Children's Book Award

Other books by the author:
D.J.'s Worst Enemy, 1965
Hut School and the Wartime Home-Front Heroes, 1974
Skinny, 1964
Simon and the Game of Chance, 1970

Other books you might like:
Vera Cleaver, *Delpha Green and Company*, 1972
    With the help of his daughter, a man who trained for the ministry while in prison, founds a church that revitalizes his community.
Patrick John Murphy, *Carlos Charles*, 1971
    A 12 year old paroled to a boat builder leads a promising life until his former prison companions appear.
Barthe DeClements, *Five-Finger Discount*, 1989
    10 year old Jerry has trouble in a new school when it is discovered that his father is in prison.
Evelyn Sibley Lampman, *Year of Small Shadow*, 1971
    While his father is in jail, an Indian boy works for the lawyer who got his father's sentence reduced to one year.
Betsy Byars, *The Not-Just-Anybody Family*, 1986
    Maggie and Vern cope with a brother in the hospital, a grandfather in jail, and a mother who travels with the rodeo.

245

Robert Burch

Skinny (New York: Viking, 1964)

Age range: Grades 4-6

Subject(s): African Americans; Orphans

Major character(s): Skinny, Orphan; Miss Bessie, Hotel Owner

Time period(s): 1960s

Locale(s): Georgia

What the book is about: Skinny is an illiterate orphan, son of a Georgia tenant farmer. He is taken in by Miss Bessie who owns a hotel. He helps run the hotel and becomes part of the small town. Sad ending.

Where it's reviewed:
Horn Book, June 1964, page 285
Library Journal, May 15, 1964, page 2215

Awards the book has won:
Georgia Children's Book Award 1969

Other books by the author:
Simon and the Game of Chance, 1970
Two That Were Tough, 1976
Tyler, Wilkin, and Skee, 1963
Wilkin's Ghost, 1978

Other books you might like:
Brenda Scott Wilkinson, *Ludell*, 1975
    Ludell is raised by her grandmother in Waycross, Georgia, and describes her town, school, and family.

Doris Buchanan Smith, *Dreams and Drummers*, 1978
    A young girl encounters difficulties growing up in a small Georgia town.
Mildred Teal, *Bird of Passage*, 1977
    A Great Blue Heron becomes a symbol of survival.
Janet Louise Lunn, *The Root Cellar*, 1981
    Rose ventures into her aunt's root cellar and meets people who lived on the farm a century ago.
Betty Levin, *Brother Moose*, 1990
    Two orphan girls, an Indian and his grandson make a perilous journey to Maine to search for a family.

246

Robert Burch

Illustrator: Lloyd Bloom

Wilkin's Ghost (New York: Viking, 1978)

Age range: Grades 5-6

Subject(s): Ghosts

Major character(s): Wilkin, Teenager; Alex Folsom, Wanderer

Time period(s): 1930s (1935)

Locale(s): Georgia

What the book is about: Wilkin is frightened by a "ghost" who turns out to be Alex Folsom. Alex is running away because he had been accused of being a thief. Wilkin tries to help Alex with a job and a place to stay. Alex wants him to hop a train and travel the country with him.

Where it's reviewed:
Horn Book, October 1978, page 514
Kirkus Reviews, November 1, 1978, page 1189

Other books by the author:
King Kong and Other Poets, 1986
Ida Early Comes over the Mountain, 1980
Two That Were Tough, 1978
Tyler, Wilkin, and Skee, 1963

Other books you might like:
Helen Cresswell, *The Night Watchman*, 1969
    Looking for something to fill his lonely days, a young boy meets two tramps who live in a world that hardly seems real.
Dirlie Herlihy, *Ludie's Song*, 1988
    In rural Georgia in the 1950s, a young white girl's secret friendship with a black family exposes them all to unforseen dangers.
Sarah Sargent, *Seeds of Change*, 1989
    Rachel discovers the beauties and dangers of a swamp when she travels to Georgia with her father who plans to convert the swamp into a theme park.
R. Conrad Stein, *Me and Dirty Arnie*, 1982
    Dan, a new-comer from Georgia, makes friends with Arnie, a street wise Chicago boy whose one ambition is to dig up dinosaur bones.
Mildred Teal, *Bird of Passage*, 1977
    The Great Blue Heron, living on the coastal marshes of Georgia and New England, become a symbol of survival for the characters of two short stories.

247

Nancy Ekholm Burkert

Valentine and Orson (New York: Farrar, 1989)

Age range: Grades 6 and Up

Subject(s): Middle Ages; Poetry

Major character(s): Alexander, Ruler (emperor); Pacolet, Storyteller (narrator); Bellisant, Royalty (princess)

Time period(s): 16th century (1555)

Locale(s): Flanders

What the book is about: Twin brothers are separated at birth. One is raised as a knight, and the other as a wild animal in the forest. When they meet, they become friends and try to discover the circumstances causing their separation. Though the narrator speaks in 1555, the story takes places much earlier. The form is a folk play in iambic pentameter couplets. For students interested in poetry, the Middle Ages, and/or beautiful art work.

Where it's reviewed:
Booklist, September 1, 1989, page 71
Kirkus Reviews, September 15, 1989, page 1400
Publisher's Weekly, August 11, 1989, page 454

Awards the book has won:
Boston Globe/Horn Book Award - Honor Book

Other books you might like:
Daniel Curley, *Billy Beg and the Bull*, 1978
  In Ireland in the days of the heroes, the son of a king and his bull set out to find a new life away from the boy's stepmother.
Elizabeth Gray, *Adam of the Road*, 1942
  Eleven year old Adam travels the roads of 13th century England searching for his missing father, a minstrel, and his stolen red spaniel, Nick.
Katherine Marcuse, *The Devil's Workshop*, 1979
  A twelve year old boy becomes apprenticed to Johann Gutenberg who is believed by the townspeople to be a devil.
Gloria Skurzynski, *The Minstrel in the Tower*, 1988
  In the year 1195, Roger and his sister, Alice, travel the French countryside in search of their ailing mother's estranged brother, a wealthy baron.
Robert Westall, *The Cats of Seroster*, 1984
  In Medieval France, huge powerful cats and a magic dagger help Cam, a young English jack-of-all-trades, through some unusual and dangerous adventures.

248

Frances Hodgson Burnett

Illustrator: Margot Tomes

Sara Crewe (New York: Scholastic, 1986)

Age range: Grades 4-6

Subject(s): Schools/Boarding Schools; Orphans

Major character(s): Sara Crewe, Orphan

Time period(s): Indeterminate Past

Locale(s): England

What the book is about: Sara was raised in India. Her father has sends her to a boarding school in England. His death affects the way Sara is treated at school. A long popular, melodramatic story expanded further in *A Little Princess*.

Where it's reviewed:
Children's Literature in Education, Winter 1988, page 199

Other books by the author:
The Secret Garden, 1949
That Lass O' Lowrie's, 1889
Little Lord Fauntleroy, 1886
A Little Princess, 1905

Other books you might like:
Natalie Savage Carlson, *Luvvy and the Girls*, 1971
  Luvvy is delighted that she is old enough to accompany her half-sister to boarding school.
Ellen Conford, *Dear Mom, Get Me Out of Here!*, 1992
  Trapped in a terrible boarding school, Paul joins his classmates in attempting to uncover the shocking past of their headmaster, Mr. Pickles.
Penelope Farmer, *Charlotte Sometimes*, 1969
  When she awakens on her second day at boarding school, a young firl finds she has moved in time to 1918.
Jody Sorenson, *The Secret Letters of Mama Cat*, 1988
  Meredith deals with moving to Texas, the departure of her sister to a boarding school for the deaf, and the death of her grandmother.
Elvira Woodruff, *The Secret Funeral of Slim Jim the Snake*, 1993
  Ten year old Nick lives above the funeral home run by his strict uncle but dreams of becoming a truck driver like his dead father.

249

Frances Hodgson Burnett

The Secret Garden (Philadelphia: Lippincott, 1911, 1938)

Age range: Grades 3-6

Subject(s): Orphans; Physically Handicapped; Gardens and Gardening

Major character(s): Mary Lennox; Colin Craven, Orphan, Handicapped

Time period(s): 1900s

Locale(s): Yorkshire, England

What the book is about: When her parents die of cholera, Mary is sent to live with Archibald Craven, an uncle who owns Misselthwaite Manor. The old manor has many secrets and Mary is not allowed in the locked rooms. After hearing crying, she discovers a child, Colin, who has been hidden away. She, Colin and Dickon enter a garden that has been locked for years. Both the garden and the children respond to care and begin to bloom again.

Where it's reviewed:
Booklist, October 1911, page 76
Bookman, October 1911, page 183

Other books by the author:
Little Lord Fauntleroy, 1886
Sara Crewe, 1986

Other books you might like:
Jeannette Eyerly, *The Seeing Summer*, 1981

10 year old Carey is shocked to learn her new neighbor, Jenny is blind. Jenny is kidnapped and Carey attempts to rescue her.

Marguerite DeAngeli, *The Door in the Wall*, 1949

10 year old Robin is unable to walk and has trouble adjusting to a new life until the monks at the medieval monastary of Marks show him a new skill.

Philippa Pearce, *Tom's Midnight Garden*, 1958

Tom discovers that when the clock strikes 13, a garden appears that does not exist the rest of the time.

| 250 |

Sheila Burnford

The Incredible Journey (Boston: Little Brown, 1961)

Age range: Grades 6-8

Subject(s): Wilderness; Animals; Survival

Major character(s): Bodger, Dog; Tao, Cat; Luath, Dog

Time period(s): Indeterminate Past

Locale(s): Ontario, Canada

What the book is about: A Labrador Retriever, a Terrier, and a Siamese cat journey two hundred fifty miles through the Canadian wilderness to return home. Together they battle starvation, exposure, a bobcat and a bear, and resist the human beings who would detain them.

Where it's reviewed:
Atlantic Provinces Book Review, November 1983, page 2
Books & Bookmen, August 1969, page 38
Top of the News, Winter 1978, page 189

Other books by the author:
Bel Ria, 1979
Mr. Noah and the Second Flood, 1973

Other books you might like:
Vivien Alcock, *Travelers by Night*, 1983
Two children kidnap an old elephant and begin a dangerous journey to a safari park to find the elephant a home and save it from the slaughterhouse.
Jim Kjelgaard, *Snow Dog*, 1948
A dog born in the wilderness and left to fend for himself after his mother and brothers are killed is won over by the trapper deserted by his mother.
Jack London, *White Fang*, 1985
The adventures of a northern wilderness dog who is part wolf, and who eventually makes his peace with humans.
Honore Morrow, *On to Oregon!*, 1954
Based on the true story of seven children traveling by covered wagon 2000 miles from Missouri to Oregon in the mid 19th century.
Kenneth Thomasma, *Naya Nuki, Shoshoni Girl Who Ran*, 1983
After being taken prisoner by an enemy tribe, Naya Nuki escapes and makes a 1000 mile journey through the wilderness in search of her own people.

| 251 |

Hester Burton

Illustrator: Victor G. Ambrus

Beyond the Weir Bridge (New York: Crowell, 1969)

Age range: Grades 5 and Up

Subject(s): Plague

Major character(s): Richard, Teenager; Richends, Teenager; Thomas, Teenager

Time period(s): 17th century

Locale(s): England

What the book is about: Three young people in 17th century England maintain their close relationship despite their political and religious differences, the tragedy of the Great Plague, and the two boys' rivalry for a girl's love.

Where it's reviewed:
Horn Book, December 1970, page 622
Library Journal, July 1971, page 2368

Other books by the author:
Riders of the Storm, 1973
Henchmans at Home, 1972
In Spite of All Terror, 1969
Castors Away!, 1963

Other books you might like:
Joan Aiken, *The Cuckoo Tree*, 1971
Dido Twite is caught up in the plots against 18th century Stuarts in England.
Eloise Jarvis McGraw, *Master Cornhill*, 1973
Victim of both the Great Plague and the Great Fire of London, a homeless, peniless youth must decide what direction his life should take.
Scott O'Dell, *The Hawk That Dare Not Hunt by Day*, 1975
Amid political turmoil and threats of Plague, Tom Barton risks helping William Tyndale publish and smuggle into England the Bible he has translated.
Jill Paton Walsh, *A Parcel of Patterns*, 1983
Villagers of Eyam battle the Plague by cutting themselves off and sixteen year old Mall is separated from the boy she hopes to marry.
Jean Ure, *Plague*, 1991
Three teenagers attempt to survive on their own when a devastating plague sweeps London.

| 252 |

Leo Buscaglia

Illustrator: Carol Newsom

A Memory for Tino (New York: Morrow, 1988)

Age range: Grades 4-6

Subject(s): Friendship

Major character(s): Tino, Child; Mrs. Gladys Sunday, Neighbor; Samuel, Friend

Time period(s): 1980s

Locale(s): United States

What the book is about: A little boy wonders what it is like to have a "memory," and his new friendship with the elderly Mrs. Sunday results in a beautiful one. The lady they all said was a vampire turns out to be a kind and gentle person.

Where it's reviewed:
Booklist, April 1, 1988, page 1339
Kirkus Reviews, April 1, 1988, page 535

School Library Journal, May 1988, page 95

Other books by the author:
Seven Stories of Christmas Love, 1987
Bus Nine to Paradise, 1986
Loving Each Other, 1984
The Fall of Freddy the Leaf, 1982

Other books you might like:
John Branfield, *The Fox in Winter*, 1982
    A teen makes friends with a Cornishman who, after his wife's death, stays alone in the house they had shared, only needing someone to talk with.
Adele Geras, *Apricots at Midnight: And Other Stories From a Patchwork Quilt*, 1977
    A dressmaker entertains a young relative with memories of the world of her youth with scraps from elegant dresses that she has sewn into a quilt.
Libby Gleeson, *Eleanor, Elizabeth*, 1990
    Having left the town and the friends of her childhood, an Australian girl finds the land and the house of her grandmother to be an alien place.
Ben Shecter, *Grandma Remembers*, 1989
    A boy and his grandmother take a final tour of the house she is leaving and relive memories of the wonderful times experienced there.
Theresa Tomlinson, *Summer Witches*, 1989
    Two friends convert an old air-raid shelter into a den and help an old woman overcome her painful memories of WWII.

253

Beverly Butler

My Sister's Keeper (New York: Dodd Mead, 1980)

Age range: Grades 4-6

Subject(s): Fires; Survival

Major character(s): Mary James, Child, Settler

Time period(s): 1870s (1871)

Locale(s): Peshtigo, Wisconsin

What the book is about: In 1871, Mary joined her sister deep in the woods of Peshtigo, Wisconsin where the hardships of childbirth, forest fires and long, slow recuperation deepen the family bond.

Where it's reviewed:
Kirkus Reviews, March 15, 1980, page 370
School Library Journal, April 1980, page 120

Awards the book has won:
Golden Archer Award 1983

Other books by the author:
Maggie by My Side, 1987

Other books you might like:
Anne Lindbergh, *Worry Week*, 1985
    Spending a week alone at their Maine beach cottage shows three sisters that freedom carries a lot of responsibility.
Louise Moeri, *Downwind*, 1984
    The Dearborn family seeks refuge in the hills during a time of panic following a nuclear meltdown at a nearby atomic plant.
Maureen Crane Wartski, *The Lake Is on Fire*, 1981

Recovering from an accident that killed his best friend and left him blinded, Ricky is alone in a mountain cabin when lightning starts a forest fire.
Robb White, *Firestorm*, 1979
    A forest ranger catches a boy he suspects started the fire that threatens to destroy them both.
Elizabeth Wild, *Along Came a Black Bird*, 1988
    Two strays enter the lives of the Berry family; an injured crow and a boy who steals. Both need lots of love and understanding from these sisters.

254

Oliver Butterworth

Illustrator: Louis Darling

The Enormous Egg (Boston: Little, Brown, 1956)

Age range: Grades 3-5

Subject(s): Dinosaurs; Fantasy; Humor

Major character(s): Nate Twitchell, Preteen

Time period(s): 1950s

Locale(s): Freedom, New Hampshire

What the book is about: Nate is amazed when one of the hens lays a three-and-a-half pound egg. Even the size does not prepare him for the nature of the occupant - a Triceratops. Nate's responses to the critter are classic humor. A funny story that has stood the test of time.

Where it's reviewed:
Booklist, March 15, 1956, page 298
Library Journal, April 15, 1956, page 1042

Other books by the author:
The Narrow Passage, 1973
The Trouble with Jenny's Ear, 1960

Other books you might like:
Wayne Anderson, *Dragon*, 1992
    After hatching from an egg that fell into the sea, a creature resembling a fish, an insect, a bird and a snake, sets out to find its own kind.
Jacqueline A. Ball, *Sneeze-O-Saurus*, 1990
    Sara finds that her brother gets all the attention because he is ill. She fakes being sick so she will be noticed, too. Then she really gets the flu.
Rose Estes, *The Children of the Dragon*, 1985
    In the mythical kingdom of Gallardia, the Dragonlord's three children must fight to save themselves and the one remaining egg of the guardian dragon.
William Mayne, *Antar and the Eagles*, 1990
    Abducted and raised by eagles, a young boy is sent on a mission to rescue a lost egg, and in the process, save the race of eagles.
Tor Seidler, *The Tar Pit*, 1987
    Edward has only one real friend, a loving, brave dinosaur, with whom he finds adventure at a pond full of dark, oily goo and daydreams.

255

Betsy Byars

Illustrator: Robert Grossman

The 18th Emergency (New York: Viking, 1973)

Age range: Grades 4-6

Subject(s): City Life; Bullies

Major character(s): Mouse, Child; Ezzy, Child; Marv Hammerman, Bully

Time period(s): 1970s

Locale(s): United States

What the book is about: Ezzy has survival plans for major emergencies, like tarantulas and octupi and lions in the jungle, but none for IBLB (imminent beating by large boy). "Mouse" tries to avoid the bully and get adult sympathy, but he finally has to face Hammerman on his own.

Where it's reviewed:
Horn Book, August 1973, page 376
Kirkus Reviews, April 1, 1973, page 382

Awards the book has won:
Dorothy Canfield Fisher Children's Book Award 1975

Other books by the author:
The Cartoonist, 1978
The TV Kid, 1978
After the Goat Man, 1977
The Pinballs, 1977

Other books you might like:
Anna Grossnickle Hines, *Tell Me Your Best Thing*, 1991
    Eight year old Sophie joins a club formed by the class bully and finds herself being hurt by her best friend.
Constance Hiser, *Ghosts in Fourth Grade*, 1991
    James and his friends create a haunted house to scare Mean Mitchell, the class bully.
Gordon Korman, *Radio Fifth Grade*, 1989
    Disaster results when the "Venice Menace" bullies his classmates into letting him on the school's radio program, "Kidsview."
Susan Rowan Masters, *The Secret Life of Hubie Hartzel*, 1990
    Eleven year old Hubie copes with a sick cat, a crush on a teacher, the loss of his best friend and the threat of the class bully.
Elizabeth Winthrop, *Luke's Bully*, 1990
    Skinny, shy Luke cannot hide from the bully, Arthur, until it is time to pick roles for the school play.

256

Betsy Byars

Illustrator: Ruth Sanderson

The Animal, the Vegetable, and John D. Jones (New York: Delacorte, 1982)

Age range: Grades 4-6

Subject(s): Brothers and Sisters; Single Parent Families

Major character(s): Clara, Child, Vacationer; Deenie, Child, Vacationer; John D. Jones, Child, Vacationer

Time period(s): 1980s

Locale(s): United States

What the book is about: Two sisters are looking forward to a vacation with their divorced father and are upset that they will be sharing a beach house with a friend of their father's and her son, John D. Jones. In the sniping that ensues, John nicknames Clara "Animal," and Deenie "Vegetable." When Clara is apparently lost at sea, the families begin to work together and all are relieved when Clara is found safe.

Where it's reviewed:
Center for Children's Books Bulletin, June 1982, page 183
Horn Book, June 1982, page 284

Awards the book has won:
Crabbery Award 1983

Other books by the author:
The Two-Thousand Pound Goldfish, 1982
The Cybil War, 1981
Night Swimmers, 1980
Good-Bye Chicken Little, 1979

Other books you might like:
Patricia Calvert, *The Stone Pony*, 1982
    After her sister dies, JoBeth tries to bury her feelings of guilt by absorbing herself in the study of a stone pony from Persia at the local museum.
Alison Jackson, *My Brother the Star*, 1990
    Competing for attention with his adorable little brother who stars in TV commercials, Les tries out for a coveted spot on the county basketball team.
Jerry Spinelli, *Who Put That Hair in My Toothbrush?*, 1984
    The rivalry between Megin and Greg intensifies when she ruins his science project and he retaliates by throwing her hockey stick into the pond.
Erika Tamar, *It Happened at Cecilia's*, 1989
    Andy's life with his father is threatened when his father falls in love, their restaurant is a hit and the Mafia wants a cut of their profits.
Mary Phraner Warren, *The Haunted Kitchen*, 1976
    Three children move to Oregon to live with their recently divorced father and discover that their house seems to be haunted.

257

Betsy Byars

Illustrator: Melodye Rosales

Beans on the Roof (New York: Delacorte, 1988)

Age range: Grades 3-5

Subject(s): Family Life; Poetry

Major character(s): Anna Bean, Preteen; George Bean, Child; Jenny Bean, Child

Time period(s): 1980s

Locale(s): United States

What the book is about: George is not allowed to play up on the roof because his sister, Anna, is up there writing a roof poem. Eventually the whole family comes up with "roof poems" except George. He feels terrible about himself until he comes up with a two line "roof poem" and feels part of the family again. A warm family story for early or reluctant readers.

Where it's reviewed:
Center for Children's Books Bulletin, November 1988, page 66
Horn Book, January/February 1989, page 63

Other books by the author:
Bingo Brown, Gypsy Lover, 1990
The Cybil War, 1981
The Cartoonist, 1978
After the Goat Man, 1974

Other books you might like:
Roald Dahl, *The Twits*, 1980
   Two terrible old people enjoy playing nasty tricks on others
   but a family of monkeys outwits them.
Lois Lowry, *Switcharound*, 1985
   13 year old JP and 11 year old Caroline spend the summer
   with their father and his "new" family against their will, so
   they plan to get revenge.
Barbara Park, *The Kid in the Red Jacket*, 1987
   Among other adjustments involved in moving, ten year old
   Howard has to live on a street named Chester Pewe.
Louis Phillips, *How Do You Lift a Walrus with One Hand?*,
1988
   Funny answers to questions about many topics: family life,
   travel, science, and others.
Louis Sacher, *Marvin Redpost: Kidnapped at Birth?*, 1992
   No one can convince Marvin that he is a birth member of the
   family because he is the only one with red hair.

258

Betsy Byars

Illustrator: Jacqueline Rogers

The Blossoms and the Green Phantom (New York:
Delacorte, 1987)

Age range: Grades 4-6

Subject(s): Family Life; Inventions

Major character(s): Junior Blossom, Child; Pop, Grandparent; Mud, Dog

Time period(s): 1980s

Locale(s): United States

What the book is about: Junior tries to gain the recognition
of his family by launching an airship made of helium-filled
garbage bags. A Blossom promise can never be broken and
the family has promised to insure the success of his newest
invention.

Where it's reviewed:
Horn Book, March/April 1987, page 207
School Library Journal, May 1987, page 96

Other books by the author:
Coast to Coast, 1992
The Blossoms Meet the Vulture Lady, 1986
The Not-Just-Anybody Family, 1986
Cracker Jackson, 1985

Other books you might like:
Dorothy Haas, *Burton's Zoom Zoom Va-Room Machine*, 1990
   Evil Professor Savvy tries to steal Burton's newest invention, a
   rocket-powered skateboard.
Thomas McKean, *The Secret of the Seven Willows*, 1991
   To prevent the selling of their ancestral home, Martha and
   Tad use the power of a magical ring to travel back in time.
Jenny Pausacker, *Fast Forward*, 1991
   Kieran finds he can speed up time or travel in the past with
   his grandmother's Anti-Boredom machine.

Elaine L. Schulte, *Zack and the Magic Factory*, 1976
   Zack becomes involved with thieves who are trying to steal
   his aunt's latest invention.
Jay Williams, *Danny Dunn and the Smallifying Machine*, 1969
   Danny and the Professor are in danger when the Professor's
   new invention is accidentally switched on.

259

Betsy Byars

Burning Questions of Bingo Brown (New York: Viking
Kestrel, 1988)

Age range: Grades 5-6

Subject(s): Schools; Adolescence

Major character(s): Bingo Brown, Child

Time period(s): 1980s

Locale(s): United States

What the book is about: Along with the expected concerns of a 12-year-old boy, Bingo also deals with the talk of
suicide by his favorite teacher. A good mixture of humor and
hard subjects.

Where it's reviewed:
Booklist, April 15, 1988, page 1426
School Library Journal, May 1988, page 95

Awards the book has won:
Arizona Young Readers Award

Other books by the author:
Bingo Brown's Guide to Romance, 1992
Bingo Brown, Gypsy Lover, 1990
Bingo Brown and the Language of Love, 1989
Beans on the Roof, 1988
After the Goat Man, 1974

Other books you might like:
George Ella Lyon, *Red Rover, Red Rover*, 1989
   When everyone in Sumi's life is gone or unavailable, she
   finds herself facing adolescence alone.
Sandra McCuaig, *Blindfold*, 1990
   Benji and his blind older brother Joel share a special bond
   until their suicide leaves a friend with grief and guild. (Mature readers)
Susan Richards Shreve, *Family Secrets*, 1979
   8-year-old Sammy copes with death, divorce, suicide, cheating and terminal illness.
Kin Platt, *Chloris and the Freaks*, 1975
   Adjusting to her father's suicide and mother's remarriage
   leads a young girl to astrology.

260

Betsy Byars

Illustrator: Richard Cuffari

The Cartoonist (New York: Viking, 1978)

Age range: Grades 4-6

Subject(s): Family Life; Privacy

Major character(s): Alfie, Preteen

Time period(s): 1970s

Locale(s): United States

What the book is about: Alfie has a space in the attic of his home so private that it can only be reached by ladder and a trap door. He has a place to escape his mom's nagging and his grandfather's stories. His passion is drawing cartoons of "Super Caterpillar."

Where it's reviewed:
Booklist, May 15, 1978, page 1490
Center for Children's Book Bulletin, September 1978, page 4
Hornbook, June 1978, page 274

Other books by the author:
The Not-Just-Anybody Family, 1986
The Pinballs, 1977
The House of Wings, 1972
The Midnight Fox, 1968

Other books you might like:
Coleen E. Booth, *Going Live*, 1992
  A young TV performer finds her private life in conflict with her career.
Hope Campbell, *Mystery at Fire Island*, 1978
  While spending the summer on Fire Island, a promising young cartoonist and her brother observe the mysterious activities of their neighbor.
Johanna Hurwitz, *Nora and Mrs. Mind-Your-Own Business*, 1977
  Because Nora and her brother live in an apartment, personal privacy, making friends, and finding places to play are sometimes problems.
Enid Richemont, *The Time Tree*, 1989
  Rachel and Joanna experience a summer when past and present overlap when a girl dressed in an old fashioned dress appears at their secret place.
Allen Say, *The Luk-Keepers Apprentice*, 1974
  A fourteen year old boy lives on his own in Tokyo and becomes apprenticed to a famous Japanese cartoonist.

261

Betsy Byars

Illustrator: Guy Byars

The Computer Nut (New York: Viking, 1984)

Age range: Grades 3-5

Subject(s): Computers; Aliens; Science Fiction

Major character(s): Kate, Child, Computer Expert; BB-9, Alien

Time period(s): 1980s

Locale(s): United States

What the book is about: Kate spends lots of time communicating with others by way of her computer and a phone line. She acquires an online secret admirer who appears human in form, but is an alien and plans to visit Earth soon. The alien comes for a visit, but it does not go well because he cannot understand Earth humor.

Where it's reviewed:
Center for Children's Books Bulletin, January 1985, page 81
Horn Book, November/December 1984, page 756

Other books by the author:
The Seven Treasure Hunts, 1991

Wanted—Mud Blossom, 1991
Beans on the Roof, 1988
The TV Kid, 1976

Other books you might like:
Nicholas Fisk, *Trillions*, 1971
  When strange geometric objects appear in the sky, a thirteen year old boy tries to communicate with them before they are attacked from earth.
Keo Felker Lazarus, *The Gizmo from Outer Space*, 1970
  Two boys discover a device that allows them to communicate with beings from another planet.
Stuart Paltrowitz, *The Science Fiction Computer Storybook*, 1983
  Twenty science fiction stories to read and program in BASIC on a home computer.
E.T. Randall, *Cosmic Kidnappers*, 1985
  Drawn into a computer and out again into an alien spaceship, the reader must make the choices to get safely home to Earth.
George Zebrowski, *The Star Will Speak*, 1985
  It is the 21st century and Earth has just received the first communication from a life form in another solar system. Lissa helps try to decode it.

262

Betsy Byars

Illustrator: Gail Owens

The Cybil War (New York: Viking, 1981)

Age range: Grades 4-6

Subject(s): Friendship

Major character(s): Simon, Preteen, 5th Grader; Cybil Ackerman, Preteen; Tony Angotti, Preteen

Time period(s): 1980s

Locale(s): United States

What the book is about: Fifth grader Simon has loved Cybil since second grade. Tony, Simon's friend, begins to show an interest in Cybil, too. Simon and his mother are slowly working through the pains of divorce, and Simon becomes increasingly irritated with Tony's lying and boasting. A story of growing up.

Where it's reviewed:
Center for Children's Books Bulletin, July/August 1981, page 209
Horn Book, June 1981, page 300

Awards the book has won:
Sequoyah Children's Book Award 1984

Other books by the author:
Bingo Brown and the Language of Love, 1989
Cracker Jackson, 1985
The Cartoonist, 1978
The Summer of the Swans, 1970

Other books you might like:
Robert Thomas Allen, *Violin*, 1976
  Chris throws away a violin he can't play and he and his friend, Danny, see an old man pick it up and make beautiful music. The three become friends.
Elisabeth Dyjak, *I Should Have Listened to Moon*, 1990

A girl must come to terms with growing up when her best friend develops an interest in makeup and boys and her forgetful grandmother moves in.

Adrienne Jones, *Long Time Passing: A Novel*, 1990
In the turbulence of the late 60s, while his father is serving as a Marine officer in Vietnam, Jonas falls in love with a free-spirited flower child.

Janice Jones, *Secrets of a Summer Spy*, 1990
Ronnie belongs to a trio of friends that seems to be falling apart, but she finds solace with an elderly friend who is a retired pianist.

Marsha Qualey, *Everybody's Daughter*, 1991
Unable to decide between two boys, Beamer is forced to examine how growing up in a commune has shaped her personality.

263

Betsy Byars

The Glory Girl (New York: Viking, 1983)

Age range: Grades 5-7

Subject(s): Family Life; Singing; Accidents

Major character(s): Anna Glory, Preteen; Newt, Relative (uncle)

Time period(s): 1980s

Locale(s): United States

What the book is about: Anna is the only one in her family who does not sing in the family gospel group. She further sets herself apart by her relationship with Newt, an uncle recently paroled from prison. When some tough guys run the Glory bus off the road, it's Newt who rescues them. Excellent character development of an unusual family.

Where it's reviewed:
Horn Book, October 1983, page 569
School Library Journal, November 1983, page 88

Other books by the author:
Cracker Jackson, 1985
The Animal, the Vegetable, and John D. Jones, 1982
The Cybil War, 1981
After the Goat Man, 1974

Other books you might like:
Francesca Lia Block, *Cherokee Bat and the Goat Guys*, 1992
With their parents away, four young people form a rock band that becomes wildly popular, bringing them more "freedom" than they know how to handle.

Susi L. Fowler, *Fog*, 1992
A visitation by deep fog traps a family in their house and causes them to rediscover their love of making music.

Suzanne Newton, *I Will Call It Georgie's Blues*, 1983
Because the minister's children have difficulty conforming to the roles their father pushes upon them, Neal feels he must hide his interest in jazz.

Katherine Paterson, *Come Sing, Jimmy Jo*, 1985
When his family becomes a successful country music group, Jimmy feels left out until he becomes the singer and his life is changed drastically.

Erika Tamar, *Blues for Silk Garcia*, 1983
Linda, who resembles her father and has his gift for music, pursues the truth about her long absent father and her own interest in the guitar.

264

Betsy Byars

Illustrator: Ann Grifalconi

The Midnight Fox (New York: Viking, 1968)

Age range: Grades 4-6

Subject(s): Farm Life; Animals/Foxes

Major character(s): Tony, Child; Millie, Farmer (Tony's aunt); Petie Burkis, Friend

Time period(s): 1960s

Locale(s): United States

What the book is about: When Tony is told he will spend two months on a farm with his aunt and uncle he is not delighted. He hates animals and they hate him back, or so he thinks until a black fox becomes the focus of his life.

Where it's reviewed:
Booklist, September 1, 1983, page 95
Hornbook, February 1964, page 51
Kirkus Reviews, October 1, 1968, page 1111

Other books by the author:
Wanted.Mud Blossom, 1991
Night Swimmers, 1980
Goodbye, Chicken Little, 1979
Trouble River, 1969

Other books you might like:
Betty Bates, *Hey There, Owlface*, 1991
Nine year old Brad forms a special relationship with the owls roosting in his family's barn, one that is threatened by a trigger-happy neighbor.

Eileen Dunlop, *Fox Farm*, 1978
Through caring for a stray fox cub, an abandoned ten year old gradually accepts the fact that he does have a place in his foster family.

Michael W. Fox, *Vixie, the Story of a Little Fox*, 1973
Follows the adventures of a red fox from the time she is left on her own until she mates, produces a litter, and teaches them to be independent.

Joyce McDonald, *Mail-Order Kid*, 1988
When ten year old Flip orders a fox through the mail, his attempts to tame it help him to better understand his newly adopted brother from Korea.

Jane Resh Thomas, *Fox in a Trap*, 1987
Daniel help his Uncle Peter trap the foxes that have been plaguing the family farm, until finding a severed fox paw makes him question their efforts.

265

Betsy Byars

Illustrator: Troy Howell

Night Swimmers (New York: Delacorte, 1980)

Age range: Grades 5-6

Subject(s): Single Parent Families; Brothers and Sisters

Major character(s): Retta Anderson, Child; Roy Anderson, Child; Shorty Anderson, Singer

Time period(s): 1980s

Locale(s): United States

What the book is about: Retta cares for her two brothers while their dad pursues his career as a country-western singer. She prides herself on finding interesting things for them to do, including sneaking into a private swimming pool for night swims. When they are discovered, near-tragedy results.

Where it's reviewed:
Horn Book, June 1980, page 293
School Library Journal, April 1980, page 105

Awards the book has won:
Boston Globe/Horn Book Award - Honor Book - 1980

Other books by the author:
The House of Wings, 1972
The-Not-Just-Anybody Family, 1986
The Midnight Fox, 1968
The Pinballs, 1977

Other books you might like:
Patricia Beatty, *That's One Ornery Orphan*, 1980
    Hallie is "picked" by three different families and has lots of trouble until she finds a home with the family she has been avoiding all the time.
Margaret Greaves, *Cat's Magic*, 1981
    Louise Higgs is sent to live with an aunt where she discovers a magic cat.
Mary Riskind, *Wild Cat Summer*, 1985
    By caring for two cats, Vicki learns that you cannot change animals to suit yourself.
Barbara Brooks Wallace, *Peppermints in the Parlor*, 1980
    When Emily goes to San Francisco in the 1890s, she becomes a detective to regain her inheritance and expose fraud.

266

Betsy Byars

The Pinballs (New York: Harper, 1977)

Age range: Grades 5-6

Subject(s): Foster Homes; Friendship

Major character(s): Carlie, Teenager, Abuse Victim; Harvey, Teenager, Handicapped; Thomas, Child

Time period(s): 1970s

Locale(s): United States

What the book is about: Pinballs are people who get sent somewhere to be out of the way. They have no choices in their lives. Carlie has been abused by her stepfather, Harvey is in a wheelchair because his father ran over him. Carlie and Thomas J. help each other to find they have friends and they have choices.

Where it's reviewed:
Kirkus Reviews, January 1, 1977, page 3
School Library Journal, March 1977, page 143

Awards the book has won:
California Young Reader Medal 1980

Other books by the author:
Good-bye Chicken Little, 1979
The Cartoonist, 1978
After the Goat Man, 1977
The TV Kid, 1976

Other books you might like:
Mildred Ames, *Without Hats, Who Can Tell the Good Guys?*, 1976
    A young boy is convinced he will never get used to his foster family and dreams his father will return for him.
Kristi Holl, *No Strings Attached*, 1988
    June finds sharing a house with her mother and foster grandfather requires lots of difficult adjustments.
Joan Lowery Nixon, *Caught in the Act*, 1988
    Eleven year old Michael is sent to a foster home in Missouri with a mean owner, a bullying son, and dangerous secrets.
Katherine Paterson, *The Great Gilly Hopkins*, 1978
    An eleven year old foster child tries to cope with her own sadness and fear and pushes away anyone who offers friendship.
Gail Radley, *The Golden Days*, 1991
    Convinced his new foster parents do not want him, eleven year old Cory runs away with an old lady from a nearby nursing home.

267

Betsy Byars

Illustrator: Ted Coconis

The Summer of the Swans (New York: Viking Press, 1970)

Age range: Grades 5-6

Subject(s): Adolescence; Mentally Handicapped

Major character(s): Sarah Godfrey, Child; Charlie Godfrey, Child; Joe Malley, Child

Time period(s): 1970s

Locale(s): United States

What the book is about: Sara is feeling unhappy with herself and her life when she takes Charlie, her mentally retarded brother to see the swans. When Charlie wanders away from home and gets lost, Sara learns a great deal about herself as she searches for him.

Where it's reviewed:
Booklist, June 15, 1970, page 1276
Horn Book, February 1971, page 54

Awards the book has won:
Newbery Medal 1971

Other books by the author:
The Animal, the Vegetable, and John D. Jones, 1982
After the Goat Man, 1974
The Glory Girl, 1977

Other books you might like:
Robbie Branscum, *For Love of Jody*, 1979
    Frankie struggles with her mother's favoring her retarded child, Jody.
Gene Kemp, *The Turbulent Term of Tyke Tiler*, 1977
    Tyke Tyler and metally handicapped Danny Price specialize in getting into scrapes and creating turmoil in their school
Sylvia Cassedy, *M.E. and Morton*, 1987
    M.E. (Mary Ellen) and a strange new neighbor, Polly, work to understand M.E.'s retarded brother, Morton.
Jan Slepian, *Alfred Summer*, 1980

Four friends, Lester, who suffers from cerebral palsy, Alfred, a retarded boy, Myron and Claire have adventures in Brooklyn of the 1930s.

268

Betsy Byars

Illustrator: Richard Cuffari

The Winged Colt of Casa Mia (New York: Hearst, 1973)

Age range: Grades 4-6

Subject(s): Fantasy; Aunts and Uncles

Major character(s): Charles Cutter, Preteen; Coot Collins, Stuntman, Rancher

Time period(s): 1960s

Locale(s): Marfa, Texas

What the book is about: A young boy visits the Texas ranch of his uncle who had been a movie stuntman. Charles wants his uncle to be a hero, the superman he had seen in the movies. Uncle Coot just wants to be seen as a regular person. Mrs. Minney says the mare she bought from Uncle Coot has given birth to a winged colt!

Where it's reviewed:
Center for Children's Books Bulletin, March 1974, page 107
Hornbook, February 1974, page 47
Kirkus Reviews, October 1, 1973, page 1094

Other books by the author:
Wanted.Mud Blossom, 1991
The 2,000 Pound Goldfish, 1982
The 18th Emergency, 1981
After the Goat Man, 1974

Other books you might like:
Mary Blount Christian, *Growin' Pains*, 1985
   Ginny Ruth feels stifled in her small, dying Texas town, despite her special relationship with physically impaired Mr. Billy.
Terry Deary, *The Custard Kid*, 1980
   The Custard Kid, who wants only to be a Hollywood stuntman, finds himself accidentally pursuing an outlaw career instead.
Ardath Mayhar, *Carrots and Miggle*, 1986
   When Carrot's distant relative, Emigha, moves from a scholarly English home to the Ramsden Ranch in Texas, everyone has to make adjustments.
Carolyn Meyer, *The Luck of Texas McCoy*, 1984
   In order to keep the ranch left to her by her grandfather, Texas sells some acreage to a movie company as a location for western films.
Willo Davis Roberts, *Jo and the Bandit*, 1992
   En route to stay with her uncle in the late 1960s, Jo experiences a stagecoach robbery and becomes involved with a reluctant young outlaw.

269

Barbara Ninde Byfield

Illustrator: Deane Hollinger

Andrew and the Alchemist (New York: Doubleday, 1977)

Age range: Grades 4-6

Subject(s): Alchemy; Magic

Major character(s): Andrew, Orphan, Apprentice; P.C. Delver, Sorcerer; Mrs. Strawspinner, Clerk (shopkeeper)

Time period(s): Indeterminate Past

Locale(s): Fictional Country

What the book is about: Eleven year old Andrew has just become orphaned when he is found by Delver, who makes him an apprentice in magic. Mrs. Strawspinner and her daughter, Sassie, have a shop above Delver's cellar. Sassie and Andrew have to rescue Delver when even his sorcery cannot save him.

Where it's reviewed:
Horn Book, June 1977, page 312
Kirkus Reviews, December 1, 1976, page 1264

Other books by the author:
The Haunted Tower, 1976
The Haunted Ghost, 1973

Other books you might like:
Joseph Bato, *The Sorcerer*, 1976
   Ao'h, a tribal outcast, becomes an apprentice to a sorcerer and discovers he possesses unusual power over the beasts and the elements.
Anna Kirwan-Vogel, *The Jewel of Life*, 1991
   Duffy, young apprentice to an alchemist, finds within himself a natural magic that opens doorways into other worlds but endangers their households.
Marianna Mayer, *The Sorcerer's Apprentice*, 1989
   A Greek fable about an apprentice who practices magic in his master's absence.
Tom McGowen, *The Magical Fellowship*, 1991
   In 3000 B.C. Lithin, an apprentice magician, and his father set out to unite the warring races of wizards, humans, Little People and dragons.
Robert Newman, *The Testing of Tertius*, 1973
   With Merlin subdued by an evil spell, his apprentice tries to break the spell and save Britain.

270

Tatyana Bylinsky

Before the Wildflowers Bloom (New York: Crown, 1989)

Age range: Grades 3-5

Subject(s): Miners and Mining; Italian Americans; Death

Major character(s): Carmela "Carm", Immigrant

Time period(s): 1910s (1916)

Locale(s): Hastings, Colorado

What the book is about: Carmela recalls her childhood in a small Colorado mining town about the time of World War I. Her family lived in a company owned town, and faced the tragedy of a mine explosion.

Where it's reviewed:
Horn Book, March/April 1989, page 208
School Library Journal, February 1989, page 66

Other books you might like:

Jenny Davis, *Good-Bye and Keep Cold*, 1987
  Edda's mother is courted by the man responsible for her young father's death in a mine accident in a small Kentucky town.
Page Edwards, *Scarface Joe*, 1984
  Joe spends a summer in Colorado where his relationship with a girl of another social class gives him both a physical and emotional scar.
Beatrice S. Smith, *The Road to Galveston*, 1973
  In the late 1880s, a young boy travels from Colorado to Texas to find the father he has never seen.
Laurence Swinburne, *Detli*, 1970
  Recounts the troubles of Eastern European immigrants in dealing with the hostilities of America when the group settles in a Pennsylvanos mining town.
Val Valentine, *The Great Durango and Silverton Train Robbery*, 1984
  This account of a famous Colorado train robbery gives a vivid picture of life in early days of the West.

C

271

Eileen Cade-Edwards

Squirrel in My Teacup! (Boston: Houghton Mifflin, 1981)

Age range: Grades 4-6

Subject(s): Animals/Squirrels

Major character(s): Russell, Child; Forest, Squirrel

Time period(s): Indeterminate

Locale(s): Canada

What the book is about: Russell buys a tiny, bedraggled squirrel from the class bully. His three brothers, mom and dad and Russell are really challenged by the task of feeding and raising Forest. They realize Forest will only be happy back in the wild.

Where it's reviewed:
Canadian Children's Literature, #33, 1984, page 57

Other books you might like:
Nina Bawden, *Henry*, 1988
  Evacuated to the English countryside during WWII, a fatherless family tries to raise a baby squirrel that has also lost its home.
Dorothy Chlad, *Animals Can Be Special Friends*, 1985
  Some of the rules for taking care of pets and treating animals at the zoo and in the wild. (Non-fiction)
Dan Elish, *The Great Squirrel Uprising*, 1992
  Aided by Sally, a ten year old human, Scruff the squirrel leads squirrels and birds in a blockade of New York's Central Park in protest of the litter.
Glen Rounds, *The Snake Tree*, 1966
  The author describes the wildlife he has seen around his home in rural North Carolina.
Ernest Shepard, *Betsy and Joe*, 1966
  Portrays the rare and humorously affectionate relationship between a tramp and a squirrel.

272

Mary Calhoun

Illustrator: Erick Ingraham

Cross-Country Cat (New York: Morrow, 1979)

Age range: Grades 2-3

Subject(s): Animals/Cats

Major character(s): Henry, Cat

Time period(s): 1970s

Locale(s): United States

What the book is about: When he becomes lost in the mountains, a cat with the unusual ability of walking on two legs finds his way home on cross-country skiis.

Where it's reviewed:
Horn Book, August 1979, page 404
Kirkus Reviews, May 1, 1979, page 512

Awards the book has won:
Little Archer Award 1980
Colorado Children's Book Award 1981

Other books by the author:
Jack the Wise and the Cornish Cuckoos, 1979
The Battle of Reuben Robin and Kite Uncle John, 1973
Camels Are Meaner Than Mules, 1971
Goblin Under the Stairs, 1968

Other books you might like:
Jeanne Dixon, *Lady Cat Lost*, 1981
  The cats hold the family together after Kenneth's dad leaves. Oona, his sister, stops being selfish when Kenneth's cat is lost and they search for it.
Dorothy Haas, *Poppy and the Outdoors Cat*, 1981
  Poppy Flower longs for a pet and she manages to get an outdoor and an indoor cat in this warm, fuzzy story.
Miska Miles, *Jenny's Cat*, 1979
  Jenny succeeds in keeping Patches, and makes a good friend along the way.
Elizabeth Parsons, *The Upside-Down Cat*, 1981
  A cat loved by a boy and an old man creates a friendship between the two built of respect and understanding.
Bill Wallace, *A Dog Called Kitty*, 1980
  Ricky has good sense and a good heart, and he overcomes his fear of dogs when a stray wins his loyalty and affection.

273

Mary Calhoun

Illustrator: Simms Taback

Euphonia and the Flood (New York: Parents, 1976)

Age range: Grades 1-3

Subject(s): Floods

Major character(s): Euphonia, Rescuer; Briskly, Broom; Fatly, Pig

Time period(s): Indeterminate

Locale(s): Fictional Country

What the book is about: Euphonia is a no-nonsense lady whose motto is, "If a thing is worth doing, it's worth doing well." When a creek floods, Euphonia, Briskly and Fatly go about rescuing animals whether they want to be rescued or not.

Where it's reviewed:
Kirkus Reviews, August 1, 1976, page 841
School Library Journal, November 1976, page 43
Booklist, October 15, 1976, page 321

Other books by the author:
The Night the Monster Came, 1982
Medicine Show, 1976
Old Man Whickutt's Donkey, 1975
Ownself, 1975

Other books you might like:
Wende Devlin, *Hang On, Hester!*, 1980
    Hester courageously hangs on to her house when it is swept downriver during a flood.
Russell E. Erickson, *Warton and Morton*, 1976
    Two brother toads on a camping trip are separated during a flash flood and before reuniting have much more adventure than they bargained for.
Blair Lent, *Molasses Flood*, 1992
    One January day a molasses tank in front of Charley's house explodes and the molasses carries his house from the Boston waterfront through the town.
Michael Morpurgo, *Jo-Jo the Melon Donkey*, 1987
    A mistreated donkey in Renaissance Venice gains self-respect when he becomes a hero during a devastating flood.
Chris Van Allsburg, *Ben's Dream*, 1982
    On a rainy day, Ben has a dream in which he and his house float by the monuments of the world, all half submerged in flood water.

274

Mary Calhoun

Katie John and Heathcliff (New York: Harper and Row, 1980)

Age range: Grades 4-6

Subject(s): Dating (Social Customs); Schools

Major character(s): Katie John Tucker, 7th Grader; Jason, Preteen; Edwin, Preteen

Time period(s): 1980s

Locale(s): United States

What the book is about: The summer before seventh grade, Katie John reads *Wuthering Heights* and becomes obsessed with the romantic hero, Heathcliff. When school starts, the former boy-hater looks for a "Heathcliff" and becomes involved in school activities. She tries to interest Jason but finds that the quieter Edwin is really more her type.

Where it's reviewed:
Kirkus Reviews, October 15, 1980, page 1357
School Library Journal, November 1980, page 70

Other books by the author:
Cross-Country Cat, 1980
Snow Cat, 1980
The Witch Who Lost Her Shadow, 1979
Katie John, 1960

Other books you might like:
Scott Corbett, *Steady, Freddy*, 1970
    When she finds a frog in her purse after visiting the zoo, a girl decides she'll keep him, even thought the boy next door wants to return him.
Alison Jackson, *Crane's Rebound*, 1991
    Les must cope with loneliness, peer pressure, boy-girl problems and a talented but obnoxious roommate.
Ronald Kidd, *Sammy Carducci's Guide to Women*, 1991
    A short sixth grader gets pointers from his older brother on handling women, and tries them out on his classmates.
Tunie Munson, *A Fistful of Sun*, 1974
    Newly moved to the country a lonely city girl finds solace in a barn loft where an equally lonely boy raises pigeons.
Elizabeth-Ann Sachs, *Where Are You, Cow Patty?*, 1984
    When Courtney and Harold begin dating, Janie feels left out, but then has a chance to watch a calf being born.

275

Mary Calhoun

Illustrator: Leslie Morrill

The Night the Monster Came (New York: Morrow, 1982)

Age range: Grades 3-5

Subject(s): Animals/Bears; Monsters; Courage

Major character(s): Andy Reilly, Child

Time period(s): 1980s

Locale(s): United States

What the book is about: When he is left at home alone, nine year old Andy is sure he sees Bigfoot's footprints in the snow. He phones his mother, who comes right home, but dogs nosing in the garbage have destroyed any tracks. Alone again, he hears a noise and sees a flash of fur. This time, he realizes the monster is a bear, and is able to trap the bear in the garage by the time his father, a deputy sherrif, comes home.

Where it's reviewed:
Booklist, October 1, 1982, page 201
School Library Journal, August 1982, page 94

Other books by the author:
Horse Comes First, 1974
Camels Are Meaner than Mules, 1971
High Wind for Kansas, 1965
Katie John, 1960

Other books you might like:
Mary Blount Christian, *Sebastian and the Baffling Bigfoot*, 1990
    Sebastian the dog and his detective master search for Bigfoot and other suspects when a guest is attacked by something "big and hairy" at the inn.
Hal George Evarts, *Bigfoot*, 1973
    Hired as a guide for an eccentric professor doing research on the legendary Bigfoot in Idaho, Dingo conducts his own investigation.
Helen Kronberg Olson, *The Secret of Spirit Mountain*, 1980
    Tom is terrified when he is sent to live with his grandfather, an Indian who reportedly is hiding something awful on Spirit Mountain.
Marian T. Place, *Nobody Meets Bigfoot*, 1976

A young boy accompanies his adventurous grandmother on an expedition searching for Bigfoot in the Northwest woods.
Drew Stevenson, *The Case of the Horrible Swamp Monster*, 1984
When the sixth grade decides to film a monster movie as a class project, the camera reveals something unexpected.

276

Ruth Calif

The Over-the-Hill Ghost (Gretna, Louisiana: Pelican, 1988)

Age range: Grades 3-5

Subject(s): Ghosts; Mystery and Detective Stories

Major character(s): Jamie Boyd, Preteen; Sylvester ''Scooter'' Johnson, Friend; Elmer, Spirit

Time period(s): 1980s

Locale(s): United States

What the book is about: Jamie finds nothing to do in the country until he meets Elmer, an over the hill ghost who can't return until he completes a mission. An old couple who lived in his house were murdered leaving a buried treasure on their land. Jamie and Elmer set out to find the treasure and solve the mystery.

Where it's reviewed:
Booklist, July 1988, page 1832
School Library Journal, December 1988, page 102

Other books you might like:
Betsy Haynes, *The Ghost of Gravestone Hearth*, 1977
Charley's summer at the beach promises to be uneventful until the ghost of a sailor who died in 1712 persuades him to help dig for buried treasure.
Nancy K. Robinson, *The Ghost of Whispering Rock*, 1992
While spending the summer at her family's cabin in the woods, Amy copes with the visit of bored and spoiled Erika by inventing a story about a ghost.
Elizabeth Silverthorne, *The Ghost of Padre Island*, 1975
Mysterious occurrences during a vacation spent in search for a lost Indian site lead a family of four to treasure and the identity of a ghost.
G.C. Skipper, *The Ghosts at Manor House*, 1978
While doing research for their term paper, two youngsters find it difficult to ignore rumors about the ghosts at the site of a colonial ironworks.
Elizabeth Van Steenwyk, *The Ghost in the Gym*, 1983
Toby, the first girl member of the cross-country track team, then finds herself involved in discovering whether the ghost in the gym is real or not.

277

Larry Callen

Illustrator: Marvin Friedman

Pinch (Boston: Little, Brown, 1976)

Age range: Grades 4-6

Subject(s): Country Life; Animals/Pigs

Major character(s): Pinch Grimball, Preteen; Tony Garmouche, Businessman (storekeeper); Homer, Pig

Time period(s): Indeterminate Past

Locale(s): Four Corners, Louisiana

What the book is about: Training hunting pigs in rural Louisiana is the theme of this funny story of a boy and his pig, Homer. Pinch becomes the owner of Homer through some fairly slick dealing in this humorous story of country life.

Where it's reviewed:
Booklist, May 1, 1976, page 1260
Hornbook, August 1976, page 394
Kirkus, February 1, 1976, page 134

Other books by the author:
Contrary Imaginations, 1991
If the World Ends, 1983
The Muskrat War, 1980
The Deadly Mandrake, 1978

Other books you might like:
Susan Fleming, *The Pig at 37 Pinecrest Drive*, 1981
His mother's latest ''educational experience'' gives Terry the fame he thought he wanted, a quick lesson in politics, and firsthand knowledge of pigs.
Clifford B. Hicks, *Alvin's Swap Shop*, 1976
While running a swap shop, a group of youngsters become involved in the mystery of a sunken ship.
Jill Rose Klevin, *The Turtle Street Trading Company*, 1982
The Turtles of Turtle Street plot a way to earn enough money to go to Disneyland by forming a trading company, which becomes an enormous success.
Eloise Jarvis McGraw, *The Seventeenth Swap*, 1986
Having no money, a thirteen year old begins a series of swaps to get the child for whom he babysits a pair of cowboy boots.
Alfred Slote, *The Trading Game*, 1990
During a summer of baseball card trading, Andy makes discoveries about his father, his grandfather, who played professional baseball, and himself.

278

Larry Callen

Illustrator: Marvin Friedman

Sorrow's Song (Boston: Little, Brown, 1979)

Age range: Grades 4-6

Subject(s): Animals/Birds; Mutism

Major character(s): Pinch, Child; Sorrow Nix, Child, Handicapped (mute)

Time period(s): 1970s

Locale(s): Four Corners (southern town); United States

What the book is about: Pinch's best friend, Sorrow, is a mute girl who develops an attachment to a wounded crane she has cared for. Pinch and Sorrow encounter John Barrow, who wants to sell the crane to the Zoo Man. In a desperate move, Pinch and Sorrow steal the crane, but Barrow recovers it. The next morning, having been troubled by Sorrow's emotion, Barrow sets it free.

Where it's reviewed:
Horn Book, August 1979, page 411

Kirkus Reviews, July 15, 1979, page 792

Other books by the author:
Who Kidnapped the Sherrif?, 1985
If the World Ends, 1983
The Muskrat War, 1980
Pinch, 1975

Other books you might like:
Julia Cunningham, *Far in the Day*, 1972
    A mute boy finds an outlet for his talents as a mime in an obscure circus.
Isabel Langis Cusack, *Mr. Wheatfield's Loft*, 1979
    Developing an interest in homing pigeons leads to a change in Ellis' life. He has been mute since he witnessed his father's death.
Helen Griffith, *The Mysterious Appearance of Agnes*, 1975
    A small child mysteriously appears in a remote 16th century German village, grows into an emotionally disturbed mute and is accused of witchcraft.
Keith Robertson, *In Search of a Sandhill Crane*, 1973
    Dismayed at the prospect of a summer in the Michigan wilderness, a young boy becomes increasingly fascinated by nature.
Susan Richards Shreve, *Lucy Forever and Miss Rosetree, Shrinks*, 1987
    Two 6th grade girls, one the daughter of a psychiatrist, come upon a small mute child from an orphanage and become determined to help her talk.

279

Patricia Calvert

The Hour of the Wolf (New York: Collier Macmillan, 1983)

Age range: Grades 5-8

Subject(s): Sports/Dog Sled Racing; Suicide

Major character(s): Jake, Preteen, Sports Figure (musher)

Time period(s): 1980s

Locale(s): Alaska

What the book is about: Following his suicide attempt, Jake sees himself as a loser. Then he enters the 1000 mile Iditarod International Dog Sled Race from Anchorage to Nome. He proves he has the courage to finish in memory of his Athabascan Indian friend who dies.

Where it's reviewed:
Booklist, January 1, 1984, page 678
Horn Book, February 1984, page 59

Other books by the author:
When Morning Comes, 1989
Hadder MacColl, 1985
The Money Creek Mare, 1981
The Snowbird, 1980

Other books you might like:
Mary Blount Christian, *Singin' Somebody Else's Song*, 1988
    Tormented by the memory of his best friend's suicide, Gideon struggles to fulfill their shared dream of breaking into the country music industry.
Stella Pevsner, *How Could You Do It, Diane?*, 1989
    As Bethany struggles to find the reasons why her sister committed suicide, her parents try to repress the memory.
Ann Rabinowitz, *Bethie*, 1989

Growing up in New York City during WWII, Beth's friendship with Grace is strained as Grace grows despondent following her parents' divorce.
Joyce Sweeney, *Right Behind the Rain*, 1987
    Carla watches with growing concern as her adored and talented older brother begins to crack under the pressure of always having to be perfect.
Maureen Crane Wartski, *My Name Is Nobody*, 1988
    A desperate teenager on the brink of suicide is rescued by a retired policeman who gives the boy a home and an appreciation for life.

280

Ann Cameron

Illustrator: Thomas B. Allen

The Most Beautiful Place in the World (New York: Knopf, 1988)

Age range: Grades 3-6

Subject(s): Grandparents

Major character(s): Juan, Child

Locale(s): Guatemala

What the book is about: A young boy in a small Central American town struggles to make his way in the world when his mother deserts him. In spite of his difficult life, he teaches himself to read and discovers that "the most beautiful place" is anywhere where someone loves you.

Where it's reviewed:
Booklist, January 1, 1989, page 784
School Library Journal, January 1989, page 62

Awards the book has won:
Charlie May Simon Children's Book Award

Other books by the author:
Julian, Dream Doctor, 1990
Julian's Glorious Summer, 1987
Julian, Secret Agent, 1988
The Stories Julian Tells, 1981

Other books you might like:
Louise Moeri, *The Forty-Third War*, 1989
    12-year-old Uno is drafted into the army in a Central American country fighting for freedom.
Charlotte Orr Gantz, *Boy with Three Names*, 1973
    A fatherless Guaymi Indian decides to seek his future in the white culture.
David Nelson Blair, *Fear the Condor*, 1992
    10-year-old Bartolina experiences great changes in the way of life of her Aymara Indian people.
Elizabeth Bowne, *Cocha*, 1990
    A brave Uru Indian boy ventures beyond his floating island to discover the world outside.

281

Ann Cameron

Illustrator: Ann Strugnell

The Stories Julian Tells (New York: Pantheon, 1981)

Age range: Grades 2-4

Subject(s): African Americans; Brothers

Major character(s): Julian, Child; Huey, Child

Time period(s): 1980s

Locale(s): United States

What the book is about: In these five stories about his middle class Black family, Julian relates stories about frogs wearing shoes and moving the sun. Julian always manages to trick his younger brother, Huey, and come out on top.

Where it's reviewed:
Center for Children's Books Bulletin, January 1982, page 83
School Library Journal, October 1981, page 140

Other books by the author:
The Most Beautiful Place in the World, 1988
Julian's Glorious Summer, 1987
More Stories Julian Tells, 1986
Harry the Monster, 1980

Other books you might like:
Andrew Bronin, *Gus and Buster Work Things Out*, 1975
    Four short stories featuring two brothers, who, in spite of occasional conflicts, are still good friends.
Karama Fufuka, *My Daddy Is a Cool Dude*, 1975
    A black child's view of the holidays, family life, and the neighborhood.
Sharon Bell Mathis, *Sidewalk Story*, 1971
    When her best friend's family is evicted from their apartment, a black girl decides to do something about the situation.
Dindga McCannon, *Peaches*, 1974
    A young black girl growing up in Harlem tells about her life with her family and her ambitions to be an artist.
Rosemary Wells, *Don't Spill It Again, James*, 1977
    Three stories about James and his sometimes bossy, sometimes tender, older brother.

☐ **282**

Eleanor Cameron

Beyond Silence (New York: Dutton, 1980)

Age range: Grades 5-8

Subject(s): Death; Fantasy

Major character(s): Andy Cames, Teenager; Alexander Cames, Parent

Time period(s): 1980s

Locale(s): Cames, Scotland

What the book is about: Andy begins to have strange experiences when he and his father go to Scotland and the castle where his father spent his youth. The trip was supposed to help Andy forget his brother's death and help him get on with his life. Staying in the ancestral castle only plunges Andy deeper into the past, literally, when he meets one of his ancestors.

Where it's reviewed:
Booklist, October 1, 1980, page 207
Hornbook, December 1980, page 646
Kirkus Reviews, January 15, 1981, page 78

Other books by the author:
Julia and the Hand of God, 1977

The Court of the Stone Children, 1973
A Room Made of Windows, 1971
A Spell Is Cast, 1964

Other books you might like:
Susan Cooper, *The Boggart*, 1993
    After visiting the castle in Scotland which her family has inherited, Emily finds that she has accidentally brought back a creature called a Boggart.
Dorothy Gilman, *The Maze in the Heart of the Castle*, 1983
    Consumed with grief after the deaths of his parents, Colin accepts the challenge of the maze of Rheembeck Castle and unravels the maze in himself.
William MacKellar, *Kenny and the Highland Ghost*, 1980
    A boy staying in an ancient Scottish castle with his family befriends and tries to help the cowardly ghost who lives there.
William MacKellar, *Mystery of Mordach Castle*, 1970
    Young Duncan MacDonald and Alan Campbell carry on their clans' ancient feud until the night they find themselves together in haunted Mordach Castle.
Victor Osborne, *Moondream*, 1989
    When his cousin Katy is kidnapped at night, Rupert enlists the aid of flying pirates and a badger to rescue her from the wizard in Castle Dread.

☐ **283**

Eleanor Cameron

The Court of the Stone Children (New York: Dutton, 1973)

Age range: Grades 4-6

Subject(s): Space and Time; Mystery and Detective Stories; Museums

Major character(s): Nina Harmsworth, Child; Dominique de Lombre, Time Traveller

Time period(s): 1970s; 1800s

Locale(s): San Francisco, California; France

What the book is about: In this time fantasy/mystery story, Nina, unhappy and lonely in San Francisco, discovers a French museum and becomes fascinated by its contents. She meets Domi, a girl from Napoleon's France, who wants Nina to help her prove that her father was not a traitor. Great detective work, and Nina's passionate involvement in Domi's quest make this an exciting and satisfying story. Children who feel "different" from their peers will love meeting Nina.

Where it's reviewed:
Kirkus Reviews, October 15, 1973, page 1159
New York Times Book Review, November 4, 1973, page 28

Awards the book has won:
National Book Award

Other books by the author:
Beyond Silence, 1980
A Room Made of Windows, 1982
That Julia Redfern, 1982
To the Green Mountains, 1975

Other books you might like:
E.L. Konigsburg, *From the Mixed-Up Files of Mrs. Basil E. Frankweiler*, 1967

Claudia and her brother Jamie run away and take up residence in the Metropolitan Museum of Art in New York. Soon they're embroiled in a mystery.

Mansfield Kirby, *The Secret of Thut-Mouse ****or Basil Beaudesert's Revenge*, 1985
Two clever mice plot revenge on the museum cat in this fast moving tale set among the Egyptian artifacts.

Nancy Bond, *A String in the Harp*, 1976
During a visit to Wales, the Morgan children find a strange key that takes them back to the time of the great Welsh bard, Taliesin.

Zilpha Keatley Snyder, *The Egypt Game*, 1976
April and Melanie set up an Egyptian temple in an old junk yard and become involved in a murder.

284

Eleanor Cameron

Illustrator: Gail Owens

Julia and the Hand of God (New York: Dutton, 1977)

Age range: Grades 4-6

Subject(s): Authorship; Brothers and Sisters

Major character(s): Julia Redfern, Preteen; Greg Redfern, Child

Time period(s): 1970s

Locale(s): Berkeley, California

What the book is about: Greg and Julia and their mother live with their critically ill Gramma. Gramma likes Greg but picks on Julia all the time. A series of crises in the family leads Julia to see her family in a different light and reaffirms her ambition to be a writer. The story is told against the backdrop of the fire that swept through Berkeley. Sequel: A Room Made of Windows

Where it's reviewed:
Kirkus Reviews, November 15, 1977, page 1196
School Library Journal, November 1977, page 53

Other books by the author:
The Private Worlds of Julia Redfern, 1988
Julia's Magic, 1984
That Julia Redfern, 1982
Beyond Silence, 1980

Other books you might like:
Judith Clarke, *Riffraff*, 1992
An eccentric writer brings about a friendship between two unusual nine year olds, rowdy, forceful Sophia and shy, artistic Sam.

Louise Fitzhugh, *Harriet the Spy*, 1964
11 year old Harriet keeps a secret notebook filled with observations (not always complimentary) about her classmates. Then her classmates find it.

Liza Fosburgh, *Mrs. Abercorn and the Bunce Boys*, 1986
Crusty Mrs. Abercorn, a retired writer of mysteries, takes two brothers under her wing and teaches them a lesson in trust and friendship.

Sheila Greenwald, *Write On, Rosy!*, 1988
When Rosy realizes she does not have a life-long ambition like her best friend does, she decides to become an investigative reporter.

Marilyn Sachs, *A Summer's Lease*, 1979

A teenage girl's driving ambition to be a writer prevents her from forming normal friendships. A favorite teacher tries to help.

285

Eleanor Cameron

Illustrator: Trina S. Hyman

A Room Made of Windows (Boston: Little Brown, 1971)

Age range: Grades 5-6

Subject(s): Authorship; Family Life

Major character(s): Julia Redfern, Child; Mrs. Moore, Recluse; Adie Kellerman, Child

Time period(s): 1970s

Locale(s): San Francisco, California

What the book is about: Julie lives with her widowed mother across the bay from San Francisco with an assortment of neighbors, all with their own problems. Her best friend lives with an alcoholic father and Julie helps Adie cope when her brother runs away. Julia intends to be a writer and her observations help develop well rounded characters. (Sequel to *Julia and the Hand of God*.)

Where it's reviewed:
Horn Book, June 1971, page 290
Library Journal, May 15, 1971, page 1780

Awards the book has won:
Boston Globe/Horn Book Award 1971

Other books by the author:
Julia and the Hand of God, 1977
That Julia Redfern, 1982
The Court of the Stone Children, 1973
To the Green Mountains, 1975

Other books you might like:
Mary Jane Auch, *Cry Uncle*, 1987
11 year old Davey has a close relationship with an elderly man taken in by his family. Davey is concerned when the man seems to become a child again.

Betsy Byars, *The Blossoms and the Green Phantom*, 1987
Junior's latest invention

Constance C. Greene, *Your Old Pal, Al*, 1979
Al(exandra)'s life is complicated by her father and his new wife, and a new friend, Polly.

Johanna Hurwitz, *The Law of Gravity*, 1978
When her best friends are gone during vacation, Margot takes on the task of getting her mother to go downstairs.

Jean Heyn, *Tessie C. Price*, 1979
After their mother is killed in an accident, the children persuade their father to buy an old boat and use it as a home.

286

Silver Donald Cameron

Illustrator: Alan Daniel

The Baitchopper (Toronto, Canada: Lorimer, 1982)

Age range: Grades 5-6

Subject(s): Fishing; Labor Conditions

Major character(s): Andrew Gurney, Teenager

Time period(s): Indeterminate Past

Locale(s): Nova Scotia, Canada

What the book is about: Andrew's father and other fishermen are involved in a strike at the fish packing company. Andrew and his friends are as divided as their fathers. Andrew and his friend are set adrift in a stormy sea and they battle to save the fishing boat.

Where it's reviewed:
Books in Canada, December 1982, page 12
Quill and Quire, February 1983, page 38

Other books by the author:
Schooner, 1984

Other books you might like:
Jean Craighead George, *Shark Beneath the Reef*, 1989
    On the Island of Coronado, a young Mexican fisherman comes of age as he becomes aware of the politics, corruption and changes around him.
Marguerite Murray, *Like Seabirds Flying Home*, 1988
    Shelley's dying father brings her family to the Nova Scotia fishing village where he was born.
Gary Paulsen, *The Voyage of the Frog*, 1989
    When David goes out on his boat to scatter his recently deceased uncle's ashes, he is caught in a fierce storm and must survive many days on his own.
Colin Thiele, *Blue Fin*, 1974
    Although his father has always considered him incompetent, Steve suddenly finds their lives in his hands following a violent storm at sea.
Budge Wilson, *The Leaving, and Other Stories*, 1992
    A collection of short stories which show a variety of experiences and feelings of growing up in Nova Scotia.

| 287 |

Barbara Campbell

A Girl Called Bob and a Horse Called Yoki (New York: Dial, 1982)

Age range: Grades 4-6

Subject(s): African Americans; Animals/Horses; World War II

Major character(s): Barbara "Bob", Preteen; Yoki, Horse

Time period(s): 1940s

Locale(s): St. Louis, Missouri

What the book is about: Barbara, nicknamed Bob, is the heroine of this tale of a family in St. Louis during WWII. Her best friends are Yoki, the milk cart horse and Chuckie. When Chuckie and Bob find out that Yoki is headed for the glue factory, they get into a very involved scheme which leaves Bob very confused about right and wrong. Alternate title, *Taking Care of Yoki*

Where it's reviewed:
Booklist, August 1982, page 1521
Hornbook, August 1982, page 398
School Library Journal, April 1982, page 67

Other books you might like:
Avi, *Who Was That Masked Man, Anyway?*, 1992

In the early 1940s, when everyone is thinking about WWII, Frankie gets in trouble because of his preoccupation with his favorite radio programs.
Edward Frascino, *Eddie Spaghetti on the Homefront*, 1983
    Eddie does as much as a boy can for the war effort during WWII.
Marian Potter, *Blatherskite*, 1980
    A talkative ten year old living in rural Missouri in the 1930s becomes the heroine of her family and community by putting her busy tongue to good use.
Joyce Rockwood, *Groundhog's Horse*, 1978
    A Cherokee sets off on a one-day raid of a Creek village to rescue his "unusual" horse.
Joyce Carol Thomas, *The Golden Pasture*, 1986
    The exquisite horse Carl Lee finds on his grandfather's farm one summer helps him to understand his difficult father better.

| 288 |

Truman Capote

Christmas Memory (New York: Random, 1956)

Age range: Grades 4 and Up

Subject(s): Christmas; Aunts and Uncles

Major character(s): Truman Capote, Child, Historical Figure; Sook Faulk, Cousin

Time period(s): Indeterminate Past

Locale(s): Alabama

What the book is about: Autobiographical story about the author's Christmas as a youngster, showing the tender relationship between himself and an aged aunt. Good for read aloud to primaries, fun for middle graders to read on their own. Newly illustrated version available (Random, 1989).

Where it's reviewed:
Best Sellers, December 1, 1966, page 322
Harper, December 1966, page 132

Other books you might like:
Sharon Phillips Denslow, *Riding with Aunt Lucy*, 1991
    On drives with his friend Leonard's great-aunt, Walter never knows what the trio will discover.
Georgia Guback, *The Carolers*, 1992
    A group of carolers goes from house to house as they share the beauty of Christmas.
Betty Hager, *Old Jake and the Pirate's Treasure*, 1980
    Four Alabama children look for pirate treasure using a map belonging to an old Cajun fisherman.
Nancy Ruth Patterson, *The Christmas Cup*, 1989
    Megan and her grandmother turn a worthless old cup to good use by saving money in it to buy a gift for a special person at Christmastime.
Christine Barker Widman, *The Lemon Drop Jar*, 1992
    A little girl makes a winter visit to her great-aunt, who brings out her lemon drop jar to brighten the gray day, stimulating family memories.

289

Dale Bick Carlson

Call Me Amanda (New York: Dutton, 1981)

Age range: Grades 4-6

Subject(s): Friendship; Self-Perception; Schools

Major character(s): Amanda Gordon, Preteen, 6th Grader; Dana Gordon, Writer, Parent; Sally, Friend

Time period(s): 1980s

Locale(s): Longtree, New Jersey

What the book is about: Amanda has several problems, among them her reclusive nine year old brother, David, dissatisfaction with her looks and a best friend fixated on clothes and boys. When there is a series of threats, Amanda is fearful she will be accused. When things start disappearing from her school and neighborhood, Amanda spends the last months before leaving sixth grade trying to find the thief, and fearing she is an amnesiac and is herself the thief.

Where it's reviewed:
Children's Book Review Service, February 1982, page 65
Publisher's Weekly, July 10, 1981, page 91
School Library Journal, December 1981, page 61

Other books by the author:
The Mystery of the Galaxy Games, 1984
Charlie the Hero, 1983
The Plant People, 1977
A Wild Heart, 1977

Other books you might like:
Judy Blume, *It's Not the End of the World*, 1972
    When her parents divorce, a sixth grader struggles to understand that sometimes people are unable to live together.
Christine Nostlinger, *Marrying Off Mother*, 1978
    In order to escape her grandmother's household, Sue arranges a ski vacation designed to make her mother marry a man who despises the entire family.
Jean Davies Okimoto, *Norman Schnurman, Average Person*, 1982
    A sixth grader who doesn't like sports wishes he could find something to do that would make his dad, a former football college star, proud of him.
Penny Pollock, *Keeping It Secret*, 1982
    Wisconsin, also known as Mary Lou, has difficulty adjusting to a new school in a new town where she is reluctant to admit she wears a hearing aid.
Linda R. Weltner, *Beginning to Feel the Magic*, 1981
    A sixth grader experiences emotional highs and lows during a year filled with a class play, a sudden illness, a baby sister and a boyfriend.

290

Lori M. Carlson

Illustrator: Jose Ortega

Where Angels Glide at Dawn (New York: Lippincott, 1990)

Age range: Grades 3-6

Subject(s): Short Stories

Time period(s): Indeterminate

Locale(s): South America

What the book is about: A collection of Latin American stories, translated into English. Rabbits, out-of-work clowns, governesses with secret lives, grandmothers with scary tales fill these stories including surprise endings and unusual twists. Life and mysteries of the other America.

Where it's reviewed:
Booklist, December 15, 1990, page 819
School Library Journal, December 1990, page 100

Other books you might like:
David Nelson Blair, *Fear the Condor*, 1992
    Bartolina sees changes in her people's way of life when her father and other Aymara Indians are sent to fight in the Bolivian war against Paraguay.
Ann Cameron, *The Most Beautiful Place in the World*, 1988
    Growing up in a Central American town, Juan discovers the value of hard work, the joy of learning and the location of a beautiful place.
Ann Nolan Clark, *The Secret of the Andes*, 1952
    Interwoven into the story of a young llama herder is the history of the conquerors and the value of continuing ancient Incan traditions.
Deborah Nourse Lattimore, *Why There Is No Arguing in Heaven: A Mayan Myth*, 1989
    The first Creator God of the Mayas challenges the Moon Goddess and Lizard House to create a being to worship him.
Susan Hand Shetterly, *The Dwarf-Wizard of Uxmal*, 1990
    With the magical help of a woman who hatched him from an egg, tiny Tol proves himself greater than the ruler of the city Uxmal and becomes its leader.

291

Natalie Savage Carlson

Illustrator: John Kaufmann

The Empty Schoolhouse (New York: Harper and Row, 1965)

Age range: Grades 3-5

Subject(s): African Americans

Major character(s): Emma, Servant (maid); Lullah, Child

Time period(s): 1960s

Locale(s): Louisiana

What the book is about: Lullah goes to the parochial school with the white children. Her friendship with OraLee has its ups and downs. There are ominous strangers at the motel where her older sister, Emma, works.

Where it's reviewed:
Booklist, September 15, 1965, page 92
Kirkus Reviews, August 1, 1965, page 751

Other books by the author:
The Ghost in the Lagoon, 1984
A Grandmother for the Orphelines, 1980
The Family Under the Bridge, 1958
The Talking Cat and Other Stories of French Canada, 1952

Other books you might like:
Robert Coles, *Saving Face*, 1972
    A school incident with racial overtones creates problems within a white policeman's family.

Carol Fenner, *Randall's Wall*, 1991
  Artistically talented but struggling with poverty, Randall builds a defensive wall to protect himself from the pain of human relationships.
May Justus, *New Boy in School*, 1963
  When his family moves from Louisiana to Tennessee, Lennie discovers he is the only black person in his classroom.
Ann Waldron, *The Integration of Mary-Larkin Thornhill*, 1975
  School brings many changes to the life of a southern girl as she enters junior high.
Sandra Weiner, *It's Wings That Make Birds Fly*, 1968
  The experiences and feelings of a black boy and his friends in New York City.

| 292 |

Natalie Savage Carlson

Illustrator: Garth Williams

Family Under the Bridge (New York: Holt & Rinehart, 1958)

Age range: Grades 3-5

Subject(s): Family Life; Poverty

Major character(s): Armand, Streetperson

Time period(s): 1950s

Locale(s): Paris, France

What the book is about: Armand, the tramp, lives under one of the Seine's bridges in Paris. He has everything he needs. He knows where to get free food and how to avoid the responsibility of children, whom he calls "little starlings." When three children and their proud but impoverished mother take up residence under the bridge, his life, and his attitudes change dramatically.

Where it's reviewed:
Booklist, October 15, 1958, page 104
Horn Book, December 1958, page 468

Awards the book has won:
Newbery Honor

Other books by the author:
Alphonse, That Bearded One, 1954
Ann Aurelia and Dorothy, 1968
Befana's Gift, 1969
Carnival in Paris, 1962

Other books you might like:
Julia Cunningham, *The Silent Voice*, 1981
  The story of Auguste, an orphan mute, and Phillipe, a bully who terrorizes him and almost destroys his chance to work with a great teacher.
Betsy Byars, *After the Goat Man*, 1974
  Figgy and his grandfather have to move from their home in the country when their land is taken for a highway.
Kathryn Kilby Borland, *Good-By to Stony Crick*, 1974
  A family is forced by fire and poverty to leave their Appalachian home.
Belinda Hurmence, *Tough Tiffany*, 1980
  11 year old Tiffany, youngest member of a poor North Carolina family, begins the journey to adulthood.
Pat Hutchins, *The Mona Lisa Mystery*, 1981
  A class takes a school trip to Paris and lands right in the middle of a mystery.

| 293 |

Natalie Savage Carlson

Illustrator: Andrew Glass

The Ghost in the Lagoon (New York: Lothrop, 1984)

Age range: Grades 2-4

Subject(s): Treasure; Ghosts; Swamps

Major character(s): Timmy Hawkins, Child; Mr. Hawkins, Parent (Timmy's father); Mrs. Hawkins, Parent (Timmy's mother)

Time period(s): Indeterminate

Locale(s): South

What the book is about: One year, when the corn crop is poor and the Hawkins family is hungry, Timmy and his father go fishing at the lagoon to put food on the table. They flee from a ghost in the swamp while they are searching for food, but as the family grows hungrier, Timmy gets brave enough to challenge the creature and scares him away. Even better than fish, Timmy comes up with the treasure the ghost was guarding.

Where it's reviewed:
Booklist, February 15, 1985, page 842
Center for Children's Books Bulletin, April 85, page 143
School Library Journal, February 1985, page 71

Other books by the author:
Surprise in the Mountains, 1983
King of the Cats and Other Tales, 1980
Jaky or Dodo?, 1978
The Empty Schoolhouse, 1965

Other books you might like:
Robert Bright, *Georgie and the Buried Treasure*, 1979
  Georgie the ghost tries to discourage his neighbor from digging for buried treasure.
Dudley Bromley, *North to Oak Island*, 1977
  Robbed of all his money and desperate to get to the New World, Will becomes a stowaway on a pirate ship captained by a woman.
Mary Blount Christian, *Swamp Monsters*, 1983
  A duo of young swamp monsters who are convinced that children are make-believe find themselves in school with real children and a substitute teacher.
Caroline B. Cooney, *Safe as the Grave*, 1979
  A young girl inadvertently discovers clues leading to a long lost treasure.
Mercer Mayer, *Liza Lou and the Yeller Belly Swamp*, 1976
  With her quick thinking, Liza Lou manages to outwit all the haunts, gobblygooks, witches and devils in the Yeller Belly Swamp.

| 294 |

Natalie Savage Carlson

Illustrator: Garth Williams

The Happy Orpheline (New York: Harper, 1957)

Age range: Grades 3-5

Subject(s): Orphans

Major character(s): Brigitte, Orphan

Time period(s): Indeterminate Past

Locale(s): France

What the book is about: Brigitte, happy in a French orphanage, tries to avoid being adopted. When the girls visit a dog cemetary, Brititte gets left behind and has an adventure with a woman whose husband is a pretender to the French throne.

Where it's reviewed:
Publisher's Weekly, July 14, 1969, page 177

Other books by the author:
A Grandmother for the Orphelines, 1980
Ann Aurelia and Dorothy, 1968
The Orphelines in the Enchanted Castle, 1964

Other books you might like:
Mindy Bingham, *Minou*, 1987
    A cat abandoned in the streets of Paris, discovers self reliance by working as a mouser at the Notre Dame Cathedral.
Julia Cunningham, *Flight of the Sparrow*, 1980
    After stealing a valuable painting for the band of street urchines who have adopted her, a ten year old orphan must flee Paris.
Jeffrey Eger, *The Statue in the Harbor: A Story of Two Apprentices*, 1985
    Ten year old Philippe becomes apprenticed as a coppersmith to his father in the Parisian foundry where the Statue of Liberty is being constructed.
George Mendoza, *Lost Pony*, 1976
    Text and photos unfold the wanderings of an orphan boy on the streets of Paris as he dreams of owning a horse.
K.M. Peyton, *Going Home*, 1982
    In France, two English children run away from their temporary guardians and set off for their home and mother who's recovering from a breakdown.

295

Carol Carrick

Illustrator: Donald Carrick

The Elephant in the Dark (New York: Clarion, 1988)

Age range: Grades 5-6

Subject(s): Animals/Elephants; Orphans

Major character(s): Will, Orphan; Toong Talong, Elephant

Time period(s): 1810s (1810)

Locale(s): Massachusetts

What the book is about: Based on an actual incident, this story tells of the relationship developed between an orphan boy, Will, and the first elephant ever seen in Massachusetts. Toong Talong was left left by a traveling show and Will becomes his keeper, and gains confidence in himself as well.

Where it's reviewed:
Kirkus, October 1, 1988, page 1465
Booklist, November 15, 1988, page 572
School Library Journal, December 1988, page 103

Other books by the author:
The Empty Squirrel, 1981
Some Friend, 1979

Other books you might like:
Arthur Catherall, *The Big Tusker*, 1970

A Thai boy is faced with the dilemma of subduing his elephant maddened with pain and rescuing his uncle trapped in a cave-in.
Gillian Cross, *Great Elephant Chase*, 1992
    In 1881, Tad helps a girl get a mighty Indian elephant to friends in Nebraska while being pursued by two unscrupulous villains.
Dean Harvey, *The Great Elephant of Harlan Kooter*, 1992
    Harlan, a young resident of Pine View, Florida, tries to hide an escaped circus elephant.
Willis Lindquist, *Haji of the Elephants*, 1976
    Haji's greatest wish is realized when he is given an elephant to ride, but then he is threatened by both animals and humans.
Wilson Rawls, *Summer of the Monkeys*, 1976
    In the late 1800s, an Ozark mountain boy spends the summer trying to recapture monkeys escaped from a traveling circus.

296

Carol Carrick

Illustrator: Donald Carrick

Some Friend (Boston: Houghton Mifflin, 1979)

Age range: Grades 4-6

Subject(s): Friendship; Self-Respect

Major character(s): Mike, Child; Robb, Child; Kenny, Child

Time period(s): 1970s

Locale(s): United States

What the book is about: 10 year olds Mike and Robb have been friends since kindergarten, but have had quarrels all along, usually because Robb insists on getting his own way. He gets Mike into one project after another, always taking profits for himself and blaming someone else when projects fizzle. As Mike deals with Robb's lack of caring, he learns as much about himself and his own values as he does about Robb.

Where it's reviewed:
Booklist, December 15, 1979, page 609
School Library Journal, December 1979, page 81

Other books by the author:
The Elephant in the Dark, 1988
What a Wimp, 1983
The Crocodiles Still Wait, 1980
Octopus, 1978

Other books you might like:
Deborah Davis, *The Secret of the Seal*, 1989
    10 year old Kyo, an Eskimo boy, faces a difficult choice between friendship for a seal and loyalty to his family.
Norma Fox Mazer, *Mrs. Fish, Ape, and Me, the Dump Queen*, 1980
    A friendless girl, teased because her uncle manages the town dump, finds a friend in Mrs. Fish, the school custodian.
Betty Miles, *Maudie and Me and the Dirty Book*, 1980
    11 year old Kate's life becomes quite extraordinary when she become involved with Maudie Schmidt and an interschool reading project.
Robert Newton Peck, *Soup's Drum*, 1980

Rob totes Soup's huge drum through the 4th of July parade before he realizes Soup hasn't carried his share, but Rob gets even.

Mary Francis Shura, *The Josie Gambit*, 1986
Chess-loving Greg isn't looking forward to visiting his grandmother for six months, but an outgoing family involves him in some lifelike chess moves.

297

Carol Carrick

Illustrator: Donald Carrick

Stay Away From Simon! (New York: Clarion, 1985)

Age range: Grades 2-4

Subject(s): Mentally Handicapped

Major character(s): Simon, Teenager, Handicapped (mentally retarded); Lucy, Teenager; Josiah, Child

Time period(s): 1830s

Locale(s): Martha's Vineyard, Massachusetts

What the book is about: A girl gradually learns to accept a retarded teenager after he rescues her and her brother during a blizzard. Lucy reflects the prejudice of the village toward Simon—she both fears and ridicules him. After Simon guides her and Josiah home, Lucy begins to see Simon as he is, isolated, lonely, and well meaning.

Where it's reviewed:
Center for Children's Books Bulletin, November 1985, page 43
School Library Journal, April 1985, page 85

Other books by the author:
Alladin and the Wonderful Lamp, 1989
The Elephant in the Dark, 1988
What a Wimp, 1983
Some Friend, 1979

Other books you might like:
Anne Norris Baldwin, *A Little Time*, 1978
A ten year old girl learns to understand her younger brother who has Down's Syndrome.
Patricia Hermes, *Who Will Take Care of Me?*, 1983
Twelve year old Mark fears the death of his grandmother will separate him from his retarded younger brother, so he takes the boy and runs away.
Karen Hesse, *Wish on a Unicorn*, 1991
Maggie feels burdened by her seven year old sister until a crisis shows how special Hannie really is.
Hazel Krantz, *For Love of Jeremy*, 1990
Wendy and her mother move to Florida to enroll Wendy's Down's Syndrome brother in a dolphin therapy program.
Gene Smith, *The Hayburners*, 1974
A wealthy family is influenced by a retarded man hired for the summer.

298

Donald Carrick, Author/Illustrator

Harald and the Great Stag (New York: Clarion, 1988)

Age range: Grades 2-3

Subject(s): Middle Ages; Hunting

Major character(s): Harald, Child

Time period(s): 14th century

Locale(s): England

What the book is about: Harald's world is full of courage, mystery and reward. He devises a clever scheme to protect the animals from the baron and his royal guests who are hunting the great stag.

Where it's reviewed:
Booklist, March 15, 1988, page 1253
Horn Book, July/August 1988, page 477
School Library Journal, April 1988, page 78

Other books by the author:
Deer in the Pasture, 1976
Harald and the Giant Knight, 1982
Morgan and the Artist, 1985
Tree, 1971

Other books you might like:
Ute Krause, *Nora and the Great Bear*, 1989
Nora dreams of hunting the great bear, until she gets lost in the forest and the bear seems to help her.
Brian Wildsmith, *Hunter and His Dog*, 1979
A dog trained to retrieve birds finds that he is too kind-hearted for the job.
Ross E. Hutchins, *Tonka, the Cave Boy*, 1973
A boy living 8000 years ago goes hunting, survives the death of his father and tames a wolf cub.
Lynn Sweat, *The Wonderful Hunting Dog*, 1973
A dog owner solves the problem when her dog is not fast enough to catch rabbits.
Miska Miles, *Hoagie's Rifle-Gun*, 1970
Hunting for food becomes difficult for an Appalachian family when the game has a name.

299

Malcolm Carrick, Author/Illustrator

The Wise Men of Gotham (New York: Viking, 1975)

Age range: Grades 4-6

Subject(s): Humor

Time period(s): Indeterminate

Locale(s): Gotham, Fictional Country

What the book is about: The silly Gotham people love spring, so they capture a cuckoo to try to capture spring. When a huge eel eats all the fish in the net, they throw him into a river to drown. The blacksmith burns down his forge to get rid of the wasps. Obviously Gotham could use some wisdom.

Where it's reviewed:
Center for Children's Books Bulletin, September 1975, page 4
Kirkus Reviews, March 1, 1975, page 234
School Library Journal, September 1975, page 99

Other books by the author:
Some Friend, 1979
I Can Squash Elephants, 1978
Mr. Pedagogue's Sneeze, 1975
Splodges, 1975

Other books you might like:
John Ciardi, *The Hopeful Trout and Other Limericks*, 1989
  A collection of limericks about such characters as the Elephant Boy, the fast fiddler from Middletown, and the silly old skinflint named Quince.
Mordicai Gerstein, *Tales of Pan*, 1986
  A collection of tales about the Greek god pan and his relatives and some of the grand and silly things they did.
Nancy Jewell, *Two Silly Trolls*, 1992
  Nip and Tuck, two troll brothers, share silly experiences, including building a house without a roof and getting lost on the way to their own picnic.
Steve Sanfield, *The Feather Merchants and Other Tales of the Fools of Chelm*, 1991
  Thirteen traditional Eastern European Jewish tales of the town of Chelm and its silly citizens.
Alvin Schwartz, *All of Our Noses Are Here, and Other Noodle Tales*, 1985
  A collection of five stories about a family of silly people, based on noodle folklore from America, Japan, Korea and the Arabian Nights.

300

Joan Davenport Carris

Illustrator: Doug Cushman

Aunt Morbelia and the Screaming Skulls (Boston: Little Brown, 1990)

Age range: Grades 4-6

Subject(s): Old Age; Learning Disabilities

Major character(s): Todd, Preteen; Morbelia, Relative (great aunt), Aged Person

Time period(s): 1990s

Locale(s): United States

What the book is about: Todd expects the worst when Aunt Morbelia moves in with his family with her fascination with superstition and the supernatural. As it turns out, Aunt Morbelia's talents as a teacher and organizer help Todd to cope with his dyslexia and overcome the hurdles it presents with good humor.

Where it's reviewed:
Kirkus Reviews, October 1, 1990, page 1392
School Library Journal, August 1990, page 145

Other books by the author:
Just a Little Ham, 1989
Hedgehogs in the Closet, 1988
Witch-Cat, 1984
When the Boys Ran the House, 1982

Other books you might like:
Jeanne Betancourt, *My Name Is Brain Brian*, 1993
  Although he is helped by his new teacher after being diagnosed as dyslexic, Brian has problems with school and people he thought were his friends.
Barthe DeClements, *6th Grade Can Really Kill You*, 1985
  Helen fears her lack of improvement in reading may leave her stuck in sixth grade forever, until a teacher recognizes her problem.
Joyce Hansen, *Yellow Bird and Me*, 1986

Doris becomes friends with Yellow Bird as she helps him with his studies and his part in the school play, and discovers that he is dyslexic.
Kevin Henkes, *The Zebra Wall*, 1988
  When Adine's mother has a new baby, eccentric Aunt Irene comes to stay and shares Adine's bedroom, an event which requires a great deal of adjustment.
Betty Ren Wright, *A Ghost in the House*, 1991
  Strange things happen when Sarah is alone in the house with Great-Aunt Margaret, who appears to be the victim of a ghost.

301

Joan Davenport Carris

Illustrator: Carol Newsom

Hedgehogs in the Closet (New York: Lippincott, 1988)

Age range: Grades 5-6

Subject(s): Moving, Household; Schools

Major character(s): Nick Howard, Preteen; Marty Howard, Teenager; Diggery Holmes, Preteen

Time period(s): 1980s

Locale(s): Baggsley-on-Thames, England

What the book is about: Eleven year old Nick is not looking forward to moving to England for two years with his family. He protests loudly, then agrees to hang on through the fall until New Year's. By then he has met Diggery and Akbar, he has discovered Rugby, and has his own pet, Spike, the hedgehog hidden in his closet. Nick begins to enjoy England and turns out to be a great ambassador for the US. Learning Britticisms along with the Howard family is lots of fun.

Where it's reviewed:
Booklist, February 1, 1988, page 9310

Awards the book has won:
Charlie May Simon Children's Book Award Nominee

Other books by the author:
Aunt Morbelia and the Screaming Skulls, 1990
Just a Little Ham, 1989
Pets, Vets, and Marty Howard, 1984
When the Boys Ran the House, 1982

Other books you might like:
Nina Bawden, *The House of Secrets*, 1963
  The Mallory children find a secret passage into the mysterious old house next door, which leads them to excitement and trouble.
John Bellaris, *The Secret of the Underground Room*, 1990
  When Father Higgins disappears, Johnny and Professor Childermass follow clues to England and a long-dead knight.
Morris Gleitzman, *Two Weeks with the Queen*, 1991
  Sent to live with relatives in England, when his younger brother develops a rare form of cancer, Colin tries to see the queen and help find a cure.
Edith Nesbit, *The Railway Children*, 1992
  When their father is sent to prison, three London children move to the country where they keep busy preventing accidents on the nearby railway.
Jane Trahey, *The Clovis Caper*, 1990

Clovis was the biggest, bounciest dog Martin had ever seen, and when the family moved to England, it seemed they would not be able to take Clovis.

302

Joan Davenport Carris

Illustrator: Carol Newsom

Pets, Vets, and Marty Howard (New York: Lippincott, 1984)

Age range: Grades 5-7

Subject(s): Animals; Humor; Veterinarians

Major character(s): Marty Howard, Preteen; Justice "Jut" Howard, Teenager; Dr. Cameron, Veterinarian

Time period(s): 1980s

Locale(s): United States

What the book is about: Marty Howard takes a job in Dr. Cameron's vet clinic after school. He is thrilled to breathe life into a puppy delivered by cesarean section, but depressed by all the animals who are abused or abandoned. Plenty of humor among the lively Howard family and the wild activities at the clinic. A vivid picture of veterinary science in a good story.

Where it's reviewed:
Booklist, December 15, 1984, page 586
Center for Children's Books Bulletin, November 1984, page 42
School Library Journal, November 1984, page 122

Other books by the author:
A Ghost of a Chance, 1992
Aunt Morbella and the Screaming Skulls, 1990
Just a Little Ham, 1989
When the Boys Ran the House, 1982

Other books you might like:
Gene DeWeese, *Whatever Became of Aunt Margaret?*, 1990
  David and Julie discover an amazing secret about Aunt Margaret when they try to help her protect an animal lover from being "podified" by aliens.
James Howe, *Morgan's Zoo*, 1984
  When the Chelsea Park Zoo is about to close, the desolate animal keeper is helped by a TV newscaster and the the animals themselves in keeping it open
Marcia Polese, *Frankie and the Fawn*, 1974
  An injured fawn has the good fortune to be found by two youngsters whose mother is a vet.
Eugene Pool, *The Captain of Battery Park*, 1978
  A preteen girl and a veterinarian, who wears a black tricorn and a gold earring, nurse an injured tern they find in New York's Battery Park.
Judith Bernie Stromman, *Champ Hobarth*, 1993
  Marty, a failure in a family of achievers, finds something to fight for in a stray dog and the homeless pets at the local animal shelter.

303

Joan Davenport Carris

Illustrator: Carol Newsom

When the Boys Ran the House (New York: Lippincott, 1982)

Age range: Grades 3-5

Subject(s): Responsibility; Family Life

Major character(s): Justin "Jut" Howard, Preteen; Marty Howard, Child; Nurse Amazon Brown, Coach

Time period(s): 1980s

Locale(s): United States

What the book is about: Three brothers take on house-keeping and baby-sitting responsibilities when their mother is ill and dad is in Europe on business. A nurse turns out to be a basketball star and coaches Jut to help him make the basketball team. The expected hilarious mistakes occur—strange food, dead mice hidden in the wall, and lost kids. They are all glad when dad returns, but they have all learned a great deal in his absence.

Where it's reviewed:
Kirkus Reviews, September 15, 1982, page 1056
School Library Journal, February 1983, page 74

Other books by the author:
Aunt Morbelia and the Screaming Skulls, 1990
Rusty Timmon's First Million, 1985
Pets, Vets, and Marty Howard, 1984
The Revolt of 10X, 1980

Other books you might like:
Suzanne Butler, *The Chalet at Saint-Marc*, 1968
  Four kids trapped in a Swiss chalet by avalanches face the responsibility of making a mature decision when a neighbor becomes seriously ill.
Arthur Catherall, *Red Sea Rescue*, 1969
  Following an unexpected sandstorm, a young Arab and his sister must accept the responsibility of tending the lighthouse and the life of their father,
Stella Pevsner, *Sister of the Quints*, 1987
  Natalie's life undergoes chaotic changes when her step-mother has quints and their roomy Chicago home becomes a huge nursery.
Linda L. Strauss, *The Alexandra Ingredient*, 1988
  Just when she is trying to prove herself to her parents, Alexandra has to face all kinds of problems.
Ellen Weiss, *The Tiny Parents*, 1989
  Shrinking to the size of two and a half inches when one of their experiments goes haywire causes all kinds of problems for Mr. and Mrs. Bicker.

304

Joan Davenport Carris

Illustrator: Beth Peck

Witch-Cat (New York: Lippincott, 1984)

Age range: Grades 4-6

Subject(s): Fantasy; Witches and Witchcraft; Animals/Cats

Major character(s): Gwen, Child; Rosetta, Cat

Time period(s): 1980s

Locale(s): Ohio

What the book is about: An experienced witch-cat, Rosetta, finds her mission to be frustrating. Rosetta is supposed to help Gwen, a typically skeptical modern day child, realize her witchpowers. Gwen eventually realizes that the best power she has, is the power of love and friendship.

Where it's reviewed:
Booklist, May 1, 1984, page 1236
School Library Journal, September 1984, page 114

Other books by the author:
Hedgehogs in the Closet, 1988
Rusty Timmon's First Million, 1985
Pets, Vets, and Marty Howard, 1984
When the Boys Ran the House, 1982

Other books you might like:
Ruth Chew, *The Witch and the Ring*, 1989
   A sister and brother find a ring that brings a special cat, a witch, and a series of adventures into their lives.
Barbara Corcoran, *Which Witch Is Which*, 1983
   After a series of catnappings, twins follow a frightening old woman to an abandoned house where they find both the cats and danger.
Camilla Fegan, *Late for Hallowe'en*, 1966
   When a witch and a black cat come to live in her garden, a little girl has many adventures in magic.
Sarah Sargent, *Edward Troy and the Witch Cat*, 1978
   Tells the story of Edward Troy the spring and summer he is nine years old.
Zilpha Keatley Snyder, *The Witches of Worm*, 1972
   A lonely preteen is convinced that the cat she finds is possessed by a witch and is responsible for her own strange behavior.

305

Lewis Carroll (Pseudonym of Charles Lutwidge Dodgson)

Illustrator: Anthony Brown

Alice's Adventures in Wonderland (New York: Random, 1988)

Age range: Grades 4-8

Subject(s): Fantasy

Major character(s): Alice, Child

Time period(s): Indeterminate Past

Locale(s): England; Wonderland, Fictional Country

What the book is about: Anthony Brown's detailed, colorful illustrations make this a good choice among the many editions available of this classic, originally published in 1865. His quirky details not only support Carroll's text but sometimes extend past it. Readers and reviewers devoted to the established illustrations of Sir John Tenniel may not care for the change, but the present generation of children will love it.

Where it's reviewed:
Horn Book, March/April 1989, page 208
School Library Journal, November 1988, page 110

Other books by the author:
The Crocodile, 1988
Jabberwocky, 1985
Poems of Lewis Carroll, 1974
The Hunting of the Snark, 1876

Other books you might like:
T.A. Barron, *The Ancient One*, 1992

While helping her Great Aunt Melanie protect an Oregon forest, Kate goes back in time and faces the evil Gashra who also wants to destroy the forest.
Alan Garner, *Elidor*, 1965
   While exploring a church that is being razed in a Manchester slum, four children are drawn into another world where they must fight an evil power.
Josepha Sherman, *Child of Faerie, Child of Earth*, 1992
   Percinet, who is half-human, loves the mortal daughter of a medieval count, and leaves his world to defend her against her cruel stepmother sorceress.
Elizabeth Winthrop, *The Battle for the Castle*, 1993
   William uses a magic token to return through a toy castle in his attic to the medieval land of Sir Simon, menaced by hungry rats on a skeleton ship.
Jane Yolen, *Wizards's Hall*, 1991
   A young apprentice wizard saves the wizards' training hall by trusting and believing in himself.

306

Anne Carter

Illustrator: John Butler

Molly in Danger (New York: Crown, 1987)

Age range: Grades 1-2

Subject(s): Floods; Animals

Major character(s): Molly, Mole

Time period(s): Indeterminate

Locale(s): United States

What the book is about: Ousted by a flood, Molly the Mole must find a new place to live.

Where it's reviewed:
Booklist, July 1987, page 1676
School Library Journal, September 1987, page 161
Parents Magazine, November 1987, page 94

Other books by the author:
Fisherwoman, 1991
12 Dancing Princesses, 1989
Scurry's Treasure, 1987
Ruff Leaves Home, 1986

Other books you might like:
Mary Calhoun, *Euphonia and the Flood*, 1976
   Curious to see where the flood is going, an old woman packs her broom and pig into her boat and sets out to follow it.
Virginia Gross, *The Day It Rained Forever*, 1991
   Christina Berwind and her family live in Johnstown. When the rains come, the dam holding Lake Conemaugh bursts releasing a horrible flood on the town.
Shirley Rousseau Murphy, *Tattie's River Journey*, 1983
   When Tattie's house floats away on a flooded river, she takes in several animals and people and has a wonderful ride.
Lydia Pender, *The Useless Donkeys*, 1980
   The Quigley children love their two donkeys but Mr. Quigley threatens to get rid of them because they are useless until the flood.
Chris Van Allsburg, *Ben's Dreams*, 1982

On a terrifically rainy day, Ben has a dream in which he and his house float by the monuments of the world, half submerged in flood water.

307

Sylvia Cassedy

Behind the Attic Wall (New York: Crowell, 1983)

Age range: Grades 5-6

Subject(s): Orphans; Ghosts; Fantasy

Major character(s): Maggie, Orphan; Harriet, Relative (great-aunt); Lillian, Relative (great-aunt)

Time period(s): 1980s

Locale(s): United States

What the book is about: Maggie learns to care and return love from two mysterious dolls who live behind the attic wall. Friendless and alone in her aunts' gloomy old house, Maggie discovers Miss Christabel and Timothy John living a strange, secret life.

Where it's reviewed:
Horn Book, February 1984, page 49
School Library Journal, October 1983, page 156

Other books by the author:
Lucie Babbidge's House, 1989
M.E. and Morton, 1987
Pierino and the Bell, 1966

Other books you might like:
James Duffy, *Doll Hospital*, 1989
   Invalid Alison sets up a hospital for dolls and eventually goes to the hospital herself hoping for a permanent cure.
Catherine Dexter, *The Oracle Doll*, 1985
   Three youngsters become the guardians of a talking doll that is actually the reincarnated Oracle of Delphi.
Marjorie Stover, *When the Dolls Woke*, 1985
   Dolls come awake to help their new owner find a treasure hidden in their dollhouse.
Betty Ren Wright, *The Dollhouse Murders*, 1983
   A dollhouse becomes, for Amy and her retarded sister, a clue to the solution of grisly murders.
Richard Kennedy, *Amy's Eyes*, 1985
   A girl's only memento of her father, a sea-captain doll, comes to life and leads her onto the high seas.

308

Sylvia Cassedy

Lucie Babbidge's House (New York: Crowell/HarperCollins, 1989)

Age range: Grades 5-8

Subject(s): Dolls and Dollhouses; Emotional Problems; Orphans

Major character(s): Lucie Babbidge, Orphan; Delia, Friend (pen pal)

Time period(s): Indeterminate Past

Locale(s): United States

What the book is about: Having found a dollhouse full of dolls in the orphanage where she leads an unhappy existence, Lucie creates a secret life for herself in which she is part of a loving family. Her powers of imagination find a connection between the dolls and the family of her English pen pal, Delia. A powerful story of life in another spiritual plane.

Where it's reviewed:
Horn Book, November/December 1989, page 768
School Library Journal, September 1989, page 272

Other books by the author:
The Best Cat Suit of All, 1991
M.E. and Morton, 1987
Behind the Attic Wall, 1984
Birds, Frogs and Moonlight, 1967

Other books you might like:
John Bellairs, *The Spell of the Sorcerer's Skull*, 1984
   Johnny Dixon takes a tiny skull from a haunted dollhouse, releasing forces that capture Professor Childermass and lead Johnny to a deserted island.
Betty Levin, *Landfall*, 1979
   When Liddy visits her pen pal on an island off the Scottish coast, she becomes involved in events that reveal the truth of the islanders' seal legends
Colby Rodowsky, *P.S. Write Soon: A Novel*, 1978
   A physically handicapped girl uses her letters to a pen pal as an outlet for daydreams about her family and herself.
Marjorie Stover, *Midnight in the Dollhouse*, 1990
   A family of dolls helps their young owner, who has been left lame by an accident, find a clue to hidden treasure.
Betty Ren Wright, *The Dollhouse Murders*, 1983
   A ghostly dollhouse and moving dolls help Amy and her retarded sister solve the mystery surrounding grisly murders that took place long ago.

309

Patrick Skene Catling

Illustrator: Margot Apple

The Chocolate Touch (New York: Morrow, 1952)

Age range: Grades 3-5

Subject(s): Food; Greed

Major character(s): John Midas, Child; Mary Midas, Child; Susan Buttercup, Friend

Time period(s): Indeterminate

Locale(s): United States

What the book is about: It all started when John found the funny old coin. The man in the candy store was more than happy to trade a box of chocolate for it. John loved chocolate more than anything, at least he thought so at the beginning of this story.

Where it's reviewed:
Booklist, July 1, 1979, paege 1579
Children's Book Review Service, May 1979, page 97
School Library Journal, September 1979, page 131

Other books by the author:
John Midas in the Dreamtime, 1986

Other books you might like:
Dick King-Smith, *The Queen's Nose*, 1983

Harmony, who loves animals but isn't allowed to keep a pet, is given a magic coin and seven wishes.

Daniel Manus Pinkwater, *Fat Men from Space*, 1977
Through his radio tooth, William learns of an invasion by spacemen who are taking the earth's supply of junk food.

Lynne Reid Banks, *The Adventures of King Midas*, 1992
Midas regrets his wish to turn all he touches into gold and must deal with a magician, a witch, and a dragon as he tries to undo the magic spell.

Neal Shusterman, *The Eyes of Kid Midas*, 1992
Kevin is entranced when he finds a pair of sunglasses that turn his desires into reality, but then things start to get out of control.

Robert Kimmel Smith, *Chocolate Fever*, 1972
Henry loves chocolate more than anything in the world. He is so ashamed when he comes down with the first case of Chocolate Fever that he runs away.

310

Rebecca Caudill

Illustrator: William Pene Du Bois

A Certain Small Shepherd (New York: Holt, Rinehart and Winston, 1965)

Age range: Grades 2-4

Subject(s): Christmas; Schools; Plays

Major character(s): Jamie, Child, Handicapped (mute); Saro, Child (Jamie's sister); Honey, Child (Jamie's sister)

Time period(s): 1960s

Locale(s): Hurricane Gap, Appalachians

What the book is about: Jamie is bitterly unhappy because he cannot sing with his schoolmates in the Christmas pageant. However, when an understanding teacher assigns him the coveted role of the shepherd and he learns the significance of the Biblical shepherds, he is overjoyed. His pleasure is shattered, however, because on Christmas Eve a terrible blizzard cancels the pageant. His shepherd's robe and crook lie useless until, unexpectedly, Jamie's iminaginative and loving nature finds a very special use for them.

Where it's reviewed:
Booklist, December 1, 1965, page 360
Kirkus Reviews, Octobesr 15, 1965, page 1077
School Library Journal, December 1978, page 32

Other books by the author:
Saturday Cousins, 1989
Contrary Jenkins, 1969
Pocket Full of Cricket, 1964
The Best Loved Doll, 1962

Other books you might like:
Jean Anderson, *Pioneer Children of Appalachia*, 1986
Text and photos from a living history village in West Virginia recreate the pioneer life of young people in Appalachia in the early 19th century.

Clyde Robert Bulla, *White Bird*, 1990
A lonely boy is found and reared by a hermit in the wilderness of the Tennessee mountains in the 1880s.

Jo Carson, *Stories I Ain't Told Nobody Yet: Selection From the People Pieces*, 1989

A collection of first person poems taken from the actual authors in the rural Appalachian region.

Berniece T. Hiser, *The Adventure of Charlie and his Wheat-Straw Hat*, 1986
Poverty in Charlie's Appalachian home during the Civil War keep him from buying a straw hat for school, so he and his grandmother make it themselves.

Cynthia Rylant, *When I Was Young in the Mountains*, 1982
Reminiscences of the pleasure of life in the mountains as a child.

311

Rebecca Caudill

Susan Cornish (New York: Viking, 1955)

Age range: Grades 6 and Up

Subject(s): Farm Life; Teachers

Major character(s): Susan Cornish, Teenager

Time period(s): 1950s

Locale(s): United States

What the book is about: At 18, Susan decides to teach in a run-down southern school, and she brings new life to the school and the community. She teaches for three years among the impoverished sharecropper communities.

Where it's reviewed:
Booklist, July 1, 1955, page 452
Horn Book, August 1955, page 266

Awards the book has won:
Nancy Bloch Memorial Award

Other books by the author:
Far Off Land, 1964
House of the Fifers, 1954
My Appalachia, 1966
Schoolhouse in the Woods, 1949

Other books you might like:
Leigh Dean, *Rufus Gideon Grant*, 1970
Rufus views his family's sharecropper existence in light of his dreams to be a zoologist.

William Armstrong, *Sounder*, 1969
When a sharecropper father is jailed for stealing food, his son must grow up and learn to survive.

Crystal Thrasher, *Between Dark and Daylight*, 1979
12 year old Seely faces the Depression and the threat of violence.

Mildred D. Taylor, *Song of the Trees*, 1975
A black family struggles to save their forest during the Depression.

312

Donald E. Caufield

Illustrator: Jan Palmer

Never Steal a Magic Cat (Garden City, New Jersey: Doubleday, 1971)

Age range: Grades 3-4

Subject(s): Animals/Cats; Magic

Major character(s): Pandora, Cat; Dandylion, Dog; Maurice, Cat

Time period(s): Indeterminate Past

Locale(s): Fictional Country

What the book is about: Before her death, an old woman entrusts the fabled bracelet of Morendor to her cat, Pandora. Pandora finds a new home, but only the family cat and dog suspect that the beautiful silver grey cat that comes to stay with them has magical powers.

Where it's reviewed:
Kirkus Reviews, May 1, 1971, page 500
Library Journal, July 1971, page 1193
Publisher's Weekly, May 10, 1971, page 42

Awards the book has won:
Dorothy Canfield Fisher Children's Book Award 1973

Other books you might like:
Lloyd Alexander, *The Cat Who Wished to Be a Man*, 1973
    When he begins dealing with humanity, Lionel the cat begins to understand why his wizard master was reluctant to change him into a man.
Natalie Savage Carlson, *Spooky Night*, 1982
    A witch's black cat who wishes to become a family pet must perform one last bit of magic before he can be free.
Ruth Chew, *The Witch and the Ring*, 1989
    A sister and brother find a ring that brings a special cat, a witch, and a series of adventures into their lives.
Camilla Fegan, *Late for Hallowe'en*, 1966
    When a witch and a black cat come to live in her garden, a little girl has many adventures in magic.
Catherine Hiller, *Abracatabby*, 1981
    No one believes Adam when the boy tells them that his cat possesses unusual and extraordinary powers.

| 313 |

Winifred Cawley

Illustrator: Fermin Rocker

Gran at Coalgate (New York: Holt, 1975)

Age range: Grades 6 and Up

Subject(s): Grandparents

Major character(s): Jinnie Friend, Child; Gran, Grandparent

Time period(s): 1920s

Locale(s): Coalgate, England (Northumberland)

What the book is about: Jinnie is sent to her grandmother's to rest, after she becomes ill from worrying about an exam. The backdrop is the miners' General Strike in northern England in the 1920s. Gran is the complete opposite of Jinnie's conservative, strict father. She allows Jinnie to do all sorts of things her dad would never allow.

Where it's reviewed:
Horn Book, April 1976, page 160
School Library Journal, December 1975, page 57

Other books by the author:
Feast of the Serpent, 1969

Other books you might like:
Catherine Cookson, *Mrs. Flanagan's Trumpet*, 1980

In 1890, on the east coast of England, Eddie finds himself allied with his prickly and reputedly deaf grandmother in the struggle to free his sister.
Susan Gates, *The Burnhope Wheel*, 1989
    After finding photos of miners and a gigantic water wheel, both involving the abandoned lead mines nearby, Ellen begins to dream of events long ago.
Penelope Lively, *The Driftway*, 1972
    Traveling an ancient country road while running to his grandmother, a boy glimpses events in the road's past that help him cope with his own present.
Maureen Pople, *The Other Side of the Family*, 1986
    Staying with her Australian grandmother, away from war torn England, Katherine discovers an unexpected character and revelations about her family.
Noel Streatfeild, *Theatre Shoes, or Other People's Shoes*, 1945
    When their father is captured during the war, three children come to London to live with their grandmother, and join their cousins in school.

| 314 |

Miriam Chaikin

Illustrator: Yossi Abolfia

Aviva's Piano (New York: Ticknor, 1986)

Age range: Grades 2-4

Subject(s): Communal Living; Jews; Music

Major character(s): Aviva, Child, Musician (pianist)

Time period(s): 1980s

Locale(s): Kfar Giladi, Israel (near Lebanon)

What the book is about: Aviva has been waiting for her beloved piano since her family moved. The long awaited piano will not fit through the door of the family's home in Israel until a rocket grazes the roof and leaves a big hole.

Where it's reviewed:
Booklist, May 15, 1986, page 1392
Kirkus Reviews, March 15, 1986, page 474
School Library Journal, August 1986, page 80

Other books by the author:
Feathers in the Wind, 1989
Esther, 1987
Yossi Tries to Help God, 1987
How Yossi Beat the Evil Urge, 1983

Other books you might like:
Molly Cone, *The House in the Trees: A Story of Israel*, 1968
    As a young American boy in modern Israel searches for materials to build a tree house, he learns about the life and customs of the Jewish people.
Paul J. Deegan, *The Kibbutz: Life on an Israeli Commune*, 1971
    After discussing briefly the history of Israel and the philosophy of the kibbutz, describes the way of life on a modern kibbutz. (Non-Fiction)
Michelle Edwards, *Chicken Man*,
    Each time Chicken Man was moved into a new job on the kibbutz, someone else wants to take that job instead, and the chickens suffer as a consequence.
Mira Meir, *Alina: A Russian Girl Comes to Israel*, 1982

A young girl who has recently come to Isreal from Russia with her family misses her old home and feels out of place in her new country.

Allegra Taylor, *A Kibbutz in Israel*, 1987

Describes the life of an Israeli boy who lives with his family on a kibbutz.

315

Miriam Chaikin

Illustrator: Richard Egielski

I Should Worry, I Should Care (New York: Harper and Row, 1979)

Age range: Grades 4-6

Subject(s): Friendship; Jews; Family Life

Major character(s): Molly, Child; Celia, Child

Time period(s): 1940s

Locale(s): New York, New York (Brooklyn, Manhattan)

What the book is about: Molly, the oldest of four children, resists the family's move from a small apartment in Manhattan to a larger first floor apartment in Brooklyn, even though it's a nicer place. The action shifts from Molly's effort to understand new friends to the family's concern over the plight of Jews in Europe at the beginning of WWII.

Where it's reviewed:
Horn Book, August 1979, page 411
Kirkus Reviews, May 1, 1979, page 517

Other books by the author:
Feathers in the Wind, 1989
Friends Forever, 1988
Getting Even, 1982
Finders Weepers, 1980

Other books you might like:
Mort Gerberg, *The All-Jewish Cartoon Collection*, 1986
Cartoons, strictly kosher, with a glossary in the back - in case you need it.
Charlotte Herman, *The House on Walenska Street*, 1990
Eight year old Leah, her two younger sisters and widowed mother live in a small Russian town in 1913.
Robert Lehrman, *The Store That Mama Built*, 1992
In 1917, twelve year old Birdie and her siblings help their recently widowed mother run a store.
Shari Lewis, *One-Minute Jewish Stories*, 1989
Twenty stories from various aspects of Jewish life, all suitable for reading in one minute.
Susan Beth Pfeffer, *Turning Thirteen*, 1988
As she prepares for her Bat Mitzvah, Becky undergoes a change in her thinking that jeopardizes both faith and friendship.

316

Stephen Chance

Septimus and the Danedyke Mystery (Nashville, Tennessee: Nelson, 1973)

Age range: Grades 5-8

Subject(s): Robbers and Outlaws

Major character(s): Rev. Septimus Treloar, Detective, Religious

Time period(s): Indeterminate

Locale(s): England

What the book is about: What could thieves possibly want to steal from a church? The thieves in this story capture Septimus and his two young assistants and hold them on a boat. Their escape and capture of the criminals and the blackmail of their leader make for exciting reading.

Where it's reviewed:
Booklist, January 1, 1974, page 483
Kirkus Reviews, September 1, 1973, page 972
Center for Children's Books Bulletin, April 1974, page 125

Other books by the author:
The Stone of Offering, 1977

Other books you might like:
John Bellaris, *The Curse of the Blue Figurine*, 1983
Johnny Dixon is plunged into a terrifying mystery when he removes a blue figurine from a church.
Robin F. Brancato, *Blinded by the Light*, 1978
A college freshman infiltrates the Light of the World Church in search of her missing brother.
Walter Dean Myers, *The Hidden Shrine*, 1985
Chris and Ken find themselves pursuing a band of thieves through the back alleys and waterways of Hong Kong.
Eleanora E. Tate, *The Secret of Gumbo Grove*, 1987
While helping restore the cemetery of the old Baptist Church, Raison solves the mystery surrounding the founding of her home town.
Nicholas Wilde, *Death Knell*, 1990
Tim and Jamie investigate the unsolved murder of old Mr. Jefford who was found with a smashed skull in the church crypt.

317

Carol Chapman

Illustrator: Kelly Oechsli

Herbie's Troubles (New York: Dutton, 1981)

Age range: Grades 1-2

Subject(s): Bullies; Schools

Major character(s): Herbie, 1st Grader; Jimmy Joe, Bully, 1st Grader

Time period(s): 1980s

Locale(s): United States

What the book is about: Six year old Herbie loves school until a new kid, Jimmy Joe turns out to be a bully. His friends suggest telling Jimmy Joe to stop, sharing a treat with him, and punching him in the nose, but none of these ideas works. Herbie figures out how to handle Jimmy Joe all by himself.

Where it's reviewed:
Children's Book Review Service, June 1981, page 93
Kirkus Reviews, June 15, 1981, page 734

Awards the book has won:
California Young Reader Medal 1985

Other books by the author:
The Tale of Meshka the Kvetch, 1980

Ig Lives in a Cave, 1979
Barney Bipple's Magic Dandelions, 1977

Other books you might like:
Larry Dane Brimner, *Cory Colman, Grade 2*, 1990
   Cory's birthday party is ruined by the class bully who turns out not to be so bad in the end.
Joanna Cole, *Bully Trouble*, 1989
   Arlo and Robbie work out a red-hot scheme for discouraging the neighborhood bully.
Doug Cushman, *Camp Big Paw*, 1990
   Cyril and his cabin mates Ben and Obie run into trouble with the camp bully at Camp Big Paw.
Lisa Passen, *Fat, Fat Rose Marie*, 1991
   A little girl must stand up to the class bully who keeps picking on her overweight friend.
Scott Taylor, *Dinosaur James*, 1990
   People doubt the value of James' dinosaur obsession until it helps him deal with the playground bully.

318

Carol Chapman

Illustrator: Bruce Begen

Ig Lives in a Cave (New York: Dutton, 1979)

Age range: Grades 1-3

Subject(s): Cave Dwellers; Parent and Child; Man, Prehistoric

Major character(s): Ig, Prehistoric Human

Time period(s): Indeterminate Past

Locale(s): Earth

What the book is about: Even though the young boy in this story lives in prehistoric times, he faces many of the same problems youngsters face today.

Where it's reviewed:
School Library Journal, May 1979, page 80
Kirkus Reviews, March 1, 1979, page 261
Center for Children's Books Bulletin, September 1979, page 4

Other books by the author:
Herbie's Troubles, 1981
The Tale of Meshka the Kvetch, 1980
Barney Bipple's Magic Dandelions, 1977

Other books you might like:
Jan Brett, *The First Dog*, 1988
   Kip the Cave Boy and Paleowolf each face hunger and danger on a journey long ago. When they learn to help one another, Paleowolf becomes the first dog
Cathy East Dubowski, *Cave Boy*, 1988
   A cave boy gives his grumpy chief something previously unseen for his birthday, and makes him smile.
Dennis B. Fradin, *Beyond the Mountain, Beyond the Forest*, 1978
   In the face of the unrelenting cold, a young cave boy decides to go beyond the forest and find a warmer place for his people to live.
Ross E. Hutchins, *Tonka, the Cave Boy*, 1973
   Recounts the adventures of a boy living 8,000 years ago in an Alabama cave as he hunts, copes with the death of his father, and tames a wolf cub.
Ann Warren Turner, *Time of the Bison*, 1987

Scar Boy, one of a group of primitive cave dwellers, discovers that he has a gift for drawing and becomes an apprentice to The Painter of Caves.

319

Gabrielle Charbonnet

Illustrator: Abby Carter

Snakes Are Nothing to Sneeze At (New York: Holt, 1990)

Age range: Grades 2-4

Subject(s): Animals/Reptiles; Allergies

Major character(s): Annabel, Child; Wilfred, Snake; Charlotte, Child

Time period(s): 1990s

Locale(s): United States

What the book is about: Annabel's father is allergic to any animal with fur, feathers, or hair. Annabel desperately wants a pet. Wilfred seems to be the answer. Wilfred is a grass snake who is quite friendly and doesn't seem to mind wearing a pink satin ribbon. Charlotte isn't so sure about snakes.

Where it's reviewed:
Booklist, August 1990, page 2170
Kirkus Reviews, June 15, 1990, page 871

Other books by the author:
Boodil My Dog, 1992
Else Marie and Her Seven Little Daffodils, 1991

Other books you might like:
Laurie Adams, *Alice and the Boa Constrictor*, 1983
   After learning in science class that boa constrictors make wonderful pets, Alice saves her money until she has enough to buy Sir Lancelot.
Eth Clifford, *Harvey's Horrible Snake Disaster*, 1984
   Whenever Harvey's cousin Nora comes to visit, trouble is bound to follow.
Robert J. Leydenfrost, *The Snake That Sneezed*, 1970
   Recounts how Harold, the snake, gained fame and fortune.
Trinka Hakes Noble, *The Day Jimmy's Boa Ate the Wash*, 1980
   Jimmy's boa constrictor wreaks havoc on the class trip to a farm.
Glen Rounds, *Mr. Yowder and the Train Robbers*, 1981
   Mr. Yowder outwits a gang of robbers with the help of some friendly rattlesnakes.

320

Suzy McKee Charnas

The Bronze King (Boston: Houghton Mifflin, 1985)

Age range: Grades 5-7

Subject(s): Fantasy; Witches and Witchcraft; Science Fiction

Major character(s): Tina Valentine Marsh, Hero; Paavo, Musician; Joel, Friend (Paaro's assistant)

Time period(s): Indeterminate

Locale(s): New York, New York (Manhattan)

What the book is about: What is going on? Tina doesn't know until she meets a strange old street fiddler named Paavo. What he explains to Tina sends her on a fantastic quest. Only Paavo and his young friend, Joel, can help her, as Tina begins a battle to save the world from unearthly evil power.

Where it's reviewed:
Kirkus Reviews, October 1, 1985, page 1087
Publisher's Weekly, October 25, 1985, page 66
School Library Journal, November 1985, page 94

Other books by the author:
The Golden Thread, 1989
The Silver Glove, 1988
The Vampire Tapestry, 1980

Other books you might like:
Grace Chetwin, *Collidescope*, 1990
    When his spaceship crashes to Earth, an alien interferes with the lives of two teens living on the island of Manhattan during different centuries.
Tom McGowen, *The Magical Fellowship*, 1991
    In an effort to save the earth from being destroyed by creatures from beyond the sky, Lithim and his father set out to unite the warring races.
Shirley Rousseau Murphy, *Medallion of the Black Hound*, 1989
    The power of the medallion brings David into a world called Meryn where he must join in the battle of good against evil.
Anthony Simmons, *The Optimists of Nine Elms*, 1975
    A brother and sister befriend an old street musician and his dog, and discover that there can be magic in life.
Sherwood Smith, *Wren's Quest*, 1993
    While Wren and Prince Conor set off to uncover the secret of her parentage, a sinister wizard creates havoc back home in Cantimoor.

321

Mary Chase

Illustrator: Don Bolognese

The Wicked Pigeon Ladies in the Garden (New York: Knopf, 1968)

Age range: Grades 4-6

Subject(s): Fantasy; Ghosts; Elves

Major character(s): Maureen Swanson, Preteen; Delbert Moody, Neighbor; Leaper, Mythical Creature (leprechaun)

Time period(s): 1960s

Locale(s): United States

What the book is about: Maureen Swanson is known as the terror of the neighborhood, but once she gets into the Old Messerman Place, she finds a group of strange sisters who are more of a terror than she was. There is a leprechaun in the garden who warns her about the seven sisters, and seven portraits in the upstairs hall which seems to be arranged differently every time she looks at them. Maureen had more than met her match.

Where it's reviewed:
Center for Children's Books Bulletin, February 1969, page 90
Hornbook, February 1969, page 52
Kirkus Reviews, October 15, 1968, page 1162

Other books by the author:
Harvey, 1971
Wicked Wicked Ladies in the Haunted House, 1968
Mrs. McThing: A Play, 1952

Other books you might like:
Antonia Barber, *The Ghosts*, 1969
    A brother and sister meet two strange children in the garden of their new home with whom they travel to another century.
Kathleen Green, *Leprechaun Tales*, 1968
    Eleven original stories about the fairy folk of Ireland-leprechauns, banshees, the Pooka, and others.
Dick King-Smith, *Paddy's Pot of Gold*, 1990
    Brigid enjoys making friends with Paddy the leprechaun and wonders if he has a pot of gold.
Brian Patten, *Mr. Moon's Last Case*, 1975
    Mr. Moon searches for a figure that he saw jump from a bridge. While some say it was a small child or man, he believes it was a leprechaun.
Riley K. Smith, *Manachar and Munachar: Two Celtic Tales*, 1977
    Two Celtic tales about a gnome who tries to find a gad and his friend who makes a deal with a leprechaun.

322

Janet Chenery

Illustrator: Ben Shecter

The Toad Hunt (New York: Harper, 1967)

Age range: Grades 1-3

Series: I-Can-Read

Subject(s): Animals; Animals/Frogs and Toads

Major character(s): Teddy, Child; Peter, Child

Time period(s): Indeterminate

Locale(s): United States

What the book is about: Teddy and Peter find lots of animals while hunting for a toad. Turtles, a salamander, polliwogs and frogs.then at the end of their search, they find something brown and bumpy.

Where it's reviewed:
Booklist, July 15, 1967, page 1192
Hornbook, August 1967, page 458
Kirkus Reviews, May 1, 1967, page 559

Other books by the author:
Pickles and Jake, 1975
Wolfie, 1969
Golden Book of Lost Worlds, 1963

Other books you might like:
Crosby Bonsall, *Mine's the Best*, 1973
    Two small boasters carry on a hilarious argument as to who has the better balloon.
Russell E. Erickson, *A Toad for Tuesday*, 1974
    A toad captured by an owl on Thursday, saves him to eat until Tuesday, the owl's birthday, but the five days in between lead him to change his plans.
Sandi Barrett Ruch, *Junkyard Dog*, 1990
    Follows the exciting adventures of Toad and mean old Slobber, the junkyard dog, as they form an unlikely friendship and find a place to call home.
Susan Schade, *Toad on the Road*, 1992

A free-wheeling Toad takes his friend Cat and other animal friends on a spirited road trip.
Clyde Watson, *Mister Toad*, 1992
Mr. Toad loves his house inside a stone wall, until it is invaded by unwanted visitors.

| 323 |

Charles Chestnutt

Illustrator: John Ross

Conjure Tales (New York: Dutton, 1973)

Age range: Grades 5-8

Subject(s): African Americans; Occult; Slavery

Time period(s): Indeterminate Past

Locale(s): United States

What the book is about: A collection of stories originally published in 1899. Full of humor, action and drama, they clearly reveal the cruel injustices of slavery as they reflect the lives of the people who survived it.

Where it's reviewed:
Book World, November 11, 1973, page 2C
Kirkus Reviews, September 15, 1973, page 1035

Other books you might like:
Patricia Beatty, *Jayhawker*, 1991
During the Civil War, Kansan farm boy Lije Tulley becomes a Jayhawker, an abolitionist raider freeing slaves from Missouri, and then an undercover spy
James Berry, *Ajeemah and His Son*, 1992
A father and his son are each affected differently by their experiences as slaves in Jamaica in the early 19th century.
Kate Connell, *Tales From the Underground Railroad*, 1993
Describes the efforts of the vast, secretive network of sympathetic people who helped blacks escape slavery in the South.
Stuart A. Kallen, *Days of Slavery*, 1990
A history of Blacks in America from 1619-1863.
Mary E. Lyons, *Letters From a Slave Girl*, 1992
A fictionalized version of the life of Harriet Jacobs, in the form of letters that she might have written prior to her escape from slavery in 1842.

| 324 |

Grace Chetwin

Gom on Windy Mountain (New York: Lothrop, 1986)

Age range: Grades 4-7

Series: From Tales of Gom in the Legends of Ulm

Subject(s): Fantasy; Gold; Wizards

Major character(s): Stig, Parent, Worker (woodcutter); Gom, Wizard, Telepath; Dismas Skellar, Villain

Time period(s): Indeterminate Past

Locale(s): Fictional Country

What the book is about: Gom, son of Stig, a woodcutter, knows the language of animals and is one with nature. His telepathic powers give rise to whispers of wizardry. Gom searches for both his heritage and his destiny and a cache of gold on Windy Mountain.

Where it's reviewed:
Horn Book, November/December 1986, page 743
School Library Journal, May 1986, page 89

Other books by the author:
Friends in Time, 1992
The Crystal Stair, 1988
Out of the Dark World, 1985
On All Hallow's Eve, 1984

Other books you might like:
Ben Bova, *The Dueling Machine*, 1969
The Dueling Machine helps keep peace throughout the universe until a terrestrial power devises a telepathic means of controlling the machine.
H.M. Hoover, *Children of Morrow*, 1985
After an unfortunate murder, two telepathic children, members of a primitive civilization, are led to escape by a friendly, unseen voice.
Peg Kehret, *Sisters, Long Ago*, 1990
When Willow Page nearly drowns, she envisions scenes from a past life which lead to an exploration of mental telepathy.
Jim Slater, *The Boy Who Saved Earth*, 1979
The telepathic powers and super intelligence of a boy from a friendly alien planet are instrumental in saving Earth from invasion by evil aliens.
Joan D. Vinge, *Psion*, 1982
A delinquent who has spent his life lying and stealing becomes involved in a research project which unleashes his extraordinary telepathic powers.

| 325 |

Ruth Chew, Author/Illustrator

Do-it-Yourself Magic (New York: Scholastic, 1987)

Age range: Grades 3-5

Subject(s): Burglary; Fantasy; Magic

Major character(s): Scott Walker, Child; Rachel Walker, Child

Time period(s): 1980s

Locale(s): New York, New York

What the book is about: Rachel and Scott can make objects grow larger or smaller, and with their magic hammer, zap a burglar down to size. Held captive in the toothbrush glass, Chester, the burglar, has to get used to being so tiny.

Where it's reviewed:
Booklist, Feburary 1, 1988, page 932
Kirkus Reviews, December15, 1987, page 1731
School Library Journal, March 1988, page 188

Other books by the author:
Mostly Magic, 1982
The Would-Be-Witch, 1977

Other books you might like:
Roald Dahl, *Esio Trot*, 1992
Shy Mr. Hoppy devises a plan to win the heart of his true love by teaching her a spell to make her tortoise shell grow bigger.
Gene DeWeese, *The Adventures of a Two-Minute Werewolf*, 1983

Walt, discovering in himself a tendency to turn into a werewolf, puts his talent to constructive use.

Michael Pellowski, *Magic Broom*, 1986

Brenda Bunny adopts a magic broom on the condition it hide its magic from her parents, but when a robber enters their home the magic needed.

Todd Strasser, *Home Alone: A Novelization*, 1990

Kevin regrets his wish to live alone when his parents forget him when they leave for a trip to Paris and he must protect his home from burglars.

Elvira Woodruff, *Back in Action*, 1991

After finding the magic powder again, Noah and his friend, Nate, shrink to the size of Noah's miniature toy men and have an exciting adventure.

326

Alice Childress

A Hero Ain't Nothin' but a Sandwich (New York: Coward, 1973)

Age range: Grades 6-9

Subject(s): Drugs

Major character(s): Benjie, Teenager; Butler Craig, Step-Parent

Time period(s): 1970s

Locale(s): United States

What the book is about: Everyone says Benjie is a junkie. He insists he can quit the stuff whenever he wants. The story is told by Benjie, his mom, grandmother, stepfather, and school principal. Butler Craig turns out to be the real hero.

Where it's reviewed:
Kirkus Reviews, August 1, 1973, page 818
Library Journal, October 15, 1973, page 3153

Other books by the author:
Those Other People, 1989
Like One of the Family, 1986
Rainbow Jordan, 1981
When the Rattlesnake Sounds: A Play, 1975

Other books you might like:
Rose Blue, *Nikki 108*, 1973

When her brother dies of a heroin overdoes, Nikki decides to try to avoid the sordidness and hopelessness in the lives of her brother's friends.

Matt Christopher, *Tackle Without a Team*, 1989

Unjustly dismissed from the football team for drug possession, Scott must clear himself by finding out who planted the marijuana in his duffel bag.

Felice Holman, *Secret City, U.S.A.*, 1990

Against all odds, Benno and his friends in the ghetto turn an abandoned house into a shelter for the homeless.

Donna Walsh Inglehart, *Breaking the Ring*, 1991

Three girls, spending a summer with their grandparents on the St. Lawrence River, find cocaine on an island and become suspected of drug dealing.

William Sleator, *Run*, 1973

Three teens, thrown together by chance in an isolated house, become increasingly aware of a threat lurking in the darkness outside.

327

Alice Childress

Illustrator: Charles Lilly

When the Rattlesnake Sounds: A Play (New York: Coward, 1975)

Age range: Grades 5-9

Subject(s): African Americans; Slavery; Biography

Major character(s): Harriet Tubman, Activist (abolitionist), Historical Figure; Celia, Activist (abolitionist), Worker (laundress); Lennie, Activist (abolitionist), Worker (laundress)

Time period(s): 19th century

Locale(s): New Jersey

What the book is about: Based on the summer when Harriet Tubman worked as a laundress at a resort hotel. The two girls who worked with Harriet vowed to put their pay towards the antislavery cause. Harriet encourages them with her struggle for freedom.

Where it's reviewed:
Horn Book, June 1976, page 301
Kirkus Reviews, December 1, 1975, page 1340

Other books by the author:
Those Other People, 1989
Like One of the Family, 1986
Rainbow Jordan, 1981
A Hero Ain't Nothin' but a Sandwich, 1975

Other books you might like:
Marlene Targ Brill, *Allen Jay and the Underground Railroad*, 1993

Recounts how Allen Jay, a Quaker boy living in Ohio in the 1840s, helped a fleeing slave escape his master and make it to freedom.

Helen Pierce Jacob, *The Diary of Strawbridge Place*, 1978

A family of Quakers operating a station on the Underground Railroad spirits slaves from Ashtabula, Ohio, across Lake Erie to freedom.

Jane Kristof, *Steal Away Home*, 1969

Two slave boys run away from their South Carolina plantation in an attempt to reach their freed father five hundred miles to the north.

Marcia M. Matthews, *The Freedom Star*, 1971

When his parents have to make a sudden escape without him, a young slave is left to follow the Underground Railroad to Canada alone.

Faith Ringgold, *Aunt Harriet's Underground Railroad in the Sky*, 1992

With Harriet Tubman as guide, Cassie retraces the steps of escaping slaves on the Underground Railroad in order to reunite with her younger brother.

328

Kay Chorao

Ups and Downs with Oink and Pearl (New York: Harper, 1986)

Age range: Grades 1-3

Subject(s): Brothers and Sisters; Animals/Pigs

Major character(s): Oink, Pig; Pearl, Pig

Time period(s): Indeterminate

Locale(s): United States

What the book is about: Oink and Pearl share their adventures. They include a "super-fizz" soda; a cranky, elderly pig suspected of eating piglets; and a lesson in how to share.

Where it's reviewed:
Booklist, March 15, 1986, page 1089
Kirkus Reviews, May 15, 1986, page 791
School Library Journal, May 1986, page 112

Other books by the author:
The Good-Bye Book, 1992
Dracula's Cat, 1990
Cathedral Mouse, 1988

Other books you might like:
Mary Hofstrand, *By the Sea*, 1984
   A young pig relates how his daily routine changes when his parents take him to the seashore.
William H. Hooks, *The Three Little Pigs and the Fox*, 1989
   In the Appalachian version of the classic tale, Hamlet, the youngest pig, rescues her two greedy brothers from the "mean, tricky old drooly-mouth fox"
Miska Miles, *This Little Pig*, 1980
   The runt of a litter of pigs enjoys being the leader of her brothers and sisters, even if it only lasts a short while.
Abigail Pizer, *Penelope Pig*, 1989
   Tired of living in a sty and wallowing around in the mud, a young pig tries to move into the Potters' farmhouse.
Jean Van Leeuwen, *Oliver and Amanda's Halloween*, 1992
   Olive and Amanda Pig's Halloween activities include making their costumes, getting a pumpkin for a jack-o-lantern and going trick-or-treating.

329

Arthur Bowie Chrisman

Illustrator: Else Hasselriis

Shen of the Sea (New York: Dutton, 1925)

Age range: Grades 3-5

Subject(s): Folk Tales

Major character(s): Ah Mee, Child

Time period(s): Indeterminate Past

Locale(s): China

What the book is about: Sixteen Chinese folk tales explore China's culture from why chopsticks are used to how wisdom is attained. Readers will learn about the practical philosophy of Chinese existence.

Where it's reviewed:
Booklist, January 1926, page 167
Bookman, December 1925, page 460
Saturday Review, November 7, 1925, page 275

Awards the book has won:
Newbery Medal 1926

Other books you might like:
Marilee Heyer, *Weaving a Dream: A Chinese Folktale*, 1986
   An old brocade weaver loses herself in a painting she finds in the marketplace.
Margaret Greaves, *Once There Were No Pandas*, 1985

In the forests of China, a small girl's sacrifice for a friendly white bear brings about the appearance of the first pandas.
Rosalind C. Wang, *Fourth Question*, 1991
   A young man, Yee-Lee, goes on a journey to the Wise Man to discover the reason for his poverty.
Doreen Rappaport, *Journey of Meng*, 1991
   A woman searches for her husband who has been forced into slavery.
Elizabeth Lewis, *Young Fu of the Upper Yangtze*, 1960
   Young Fu moves to a big city and buys an alarm clock. He must pay the $5 debt or bring great shame on his family.

330

Eileen Christelow, Author/Illustrator

Henry and the Red Stripes (New York: Clarion, 1982)

Age range: Grades 2-3

Subject(s): Animals/Rabbits

Time period(s): Indeterminate

Locale(s): United States

What the book is about: A small, brown rabbit finds a very good reason for not painting red stripes on his fur.

Where it's reviewed:
Kirkus Reviews, August 15, 1982, page 934
School Library Journal, September 1982, page 106

Awards the book has won:
Little Archer Award 1983

Other books by the author:
Gertrude the Bulldog Detective, 1992
Five Little Monkeys Sitting in a Tree, 1991
The Completed Hickory Dickory Dock, 1990
Five Little Monkeys Jumping on the Bed, 1989

Other books you might like:
Tilde Michels, *Rabbit Spring*, 1988
   As newborn rabbits and hares grow up as neighbors, the rabbit's father notes how different they are.
Inga Moore, *Oh, Little Jack*, 1992
   Little Jack is too small to do what the rest of his family can do, until his grandfather comes up with a surprise.
Susan Pearson, *Molly Moves Out*, 1979
   Molly is so upset by the things her brothers and sisters do, she finally moves into a house of her own.
Beatrix Potter, *The Tale of Peter Rabbit*, 1902
   Peter disobeys his mom when he goes into Mr. McGregor's garden.
Margery Williams, *The Velveteen Rabbit*, 1922
   A stuffed rabbit becomes a boy's best friend and learns what it means to be real, and to be loved.

331

Mary Blount Christian

Illustrator: Irene Trivas

The Doggone Mystery (Chicago: Whitman, 1980)

Age range: Grades 2-3

Subject(s): Animals/Dogs; Mystery and Detective Stories

Major character(s): Clara Brown, Child; Jason Brown, Child; Ruffles, Dog

Time period(s): 1980s

Locale(s): United States

What the book is about: Three children and an uncoordinated dog track down the mastermind behind a rash of household robberies, all done while families were on vacation. The children systematically eliminate newspapers piling up, lights left off, and mail pile up as possible tip offs to the thief. When they discover what each house had in common, they and the police find the thief.

Where it's reviewed:
School Library Journal, December 1980, page 71

Awards the book has won:
Edgar Allan Poe Award - Runner-up

Other books by the author:
April Fool, 1982
Two Ton Secret, 1981
The Devil Take You, Barnabas Beane, 1980
The Lucky Man, 1979

Other books you might like:
Polly Berrien Berends, The Case of the Elevator Duck, 1973
  Gilbert finds a lost duck in the elevator of his apartment building and must do some secret detective work to find its owner.
Eth Clifford, The Dastardly Murder of Dirty Pete, 1981
  Traveling across country with their father, Mary Rose and Jo-Beth stumble upon a fake ghost town that once was an old movie set.
E.W. Hildick, The Case of the Purloined Parrot, 1990
  The McGurk organization, four boys and two girls, foil the cat rustlers who've been kidnapping pets.
Joan M. Lexau, The Rooftop Mystery, 1968
  Sam and Albert are helping Sam's family move to a new home within walking distance. Sam finds any distance too long if he can be seen carrying a doll.
Robert M. Quackenbush, Express Train to Trouble, 1981
  When troublesome George Ruddy Duck disappears on the express train to Cairo, Miss Mallard applies her detective genius to find out what happened.

332

Mary Blount Christian

Illustrator: Jane Dyer

Penrod's Pants (New York: Macmillan, 1986)

Age range: Grades 1-3

Subject(s): Animals/Bears

Major character(s): Penrod, Porcupine; Griswold, Bear

Time period(s): Indeterminate

Locale(s): United States

What the book is about: Penrod the Porcupine and Griswold the Bear share five adventures in this beginning reader.

Where it's reviewed:
Booklist, April 15, 1986, page 1229
School Library Journal, May 1986, page 112

Center for Children's Books Bulletin, May 1986, page 162

Other books by the author:
Penrod Again, 1987
The Toady and Dr. Miracle, 1985
April Fool, 1982
The Lucky Man, 1979

Other books you might like:
Cora Annett, When the Porcupine Moved In, 1971
  A rabbit schemes to get a porcupine out of his house when living together strains their friendship.
Sid Fleischman, Here Comes McBroom, 1992
  A collection of three new stories about the farmer who'd rather sit on a porcupine than tell a lie.
Terry Webb Harshman, Porcupine's Pajama Party, 1988
  Porcupine bakes cookies, watches a monster move and gets scared in the dark when his two best friends sleep over.
Phil Mendez, Kissyfur and the Birthday Hugs, 1986
  The animals in Paddlecab County are a little hesitant about giving Stickey the porcupine what he wants for his birthday, a hug.
Janwillem Van De Wetering, Hugh Pine and Something Else, 1989
  Hugh Pine, a porcupine, takes his first vacation when he accompanies Mr. McTosh to Brooklyn, New York.

333

Mary Blount Christian

Illustrator: Lisa McCue

Sebastian (Super Sleuth) and the Bone to Pick Mystery (New York: Macmillan, 1983)

Age range: Grades 3-5

Series: Sebastian (Super Sleuth)

Subject(s): Archeology; Mystery and Detective Stories

Major character(s): Sebastian, Dog (English sheepdog), Detective; John Quincy Jones, Detective; Lady Sharon, Dog

Time period(s): Indeterminate

Locale(s): England

What the book is about: Sebastian, an English sheepdog, and his roommate, John Q. Jones, investigate a mystery involving woolly mammoth bones at the Bosworthington Museum. They wind up at a fossil dig in this fun installment of the Sebastian series.

Where it's reviewed:
Booklist, January 1, 1984, page 678
Center for Children's Books Bulletin, February 1984, page 104
Kirkus Reviews, September 1, 1984, page J157

Other books by the author:
Sebastian (Super Sleuth) and the Santa Claus Caper, 1984
Sebastian (Super Sleuth) and the Secret of the Skewered Skier, 1984
Sebastin (Super Sleuth) and the Crumby Yummies Caper, 1983
Sebastian (Super Sleuth) and the Hair of the Dog Mystery, 1982

Other books you might like:

David A. Adler, *Cam Jansen and the Mystery of the Dinosaur Bones*, 1981
   When she notices some bones missing from a dinosaur skeleton in the museum, a young girl with a photographic memory tries to learn who did it and why.

M.V. Carey, *The Three Investigators in the Mystery of the Wandering Cave Man*, 1982
   Three young sleuths investigate the disappearance of a caveman's bones from a museum and uncover skulduggery at the science foundation.

Rose Estes, *The Three Investigators in the Case of the Dancing Dinosaur*, 1985
   The three investigators have been asked to save a precious fossil, but they must rescue their client as well.

Georgess McHargue, *Funny Bananas*, 1975
   Ben's efforts to catch the vandal plaguing the natural history museum are complicated by a ''witch'' and a strange animal haunting the museum.

Carolyn Smith, *The Mystery of the Missing Dinosaur Bone*, 1981
   Jeannie, Jim and David help their friend Professor Dooley find a dinosaur bone missing from the museum.

| 334 |

Sally Christie

Illustrator: Peter Kavanagh

Mean and Mighty Me (New York: Dutton, 1991)

Age range: Grades 2-3

Subject(s): Bullies; Canoeing; Grandparents

Time period(s): Indeterminate

Locale(s): England

What the book is about: The unnamed hero of this story finally is allowed to take his grandfather's canoe out on the river - by himself! The canoe is harder to paddle than he imagined, some big kids make fun of him, and then an old ugly dead fish comes floating by. How can a smelly fish solve a bully problem?

Where it's reviewed:
Hornbook Guide, Fall 1991, page 255
School Library Journal, November 1991, page 90

Other books you might like:

Nathaniel Benchley, *Red Fox and His Canoe*, 1964
   A young Indian boy receives a larger canoe along with some unseen complications.

Beatrix Potter, *The Tale of Mr. Jeremy Fisher*, 1983
   A frog fishing from his lily pad boat doesn't catch any fish, but one catches him.

Anne Rockwell, *Out to Sea*, 1980
   A brother and sister are inadvertently swept out to sea while playing in an old row boat they have found on the beach.

Allen Say, *The Feast of Lanterns*, 1976
   Two young brothers living in a fishing village on a small Japanese island steal their uncle's boat to visit the mainland for the first time.

A.C. Stewart, *The Boat in the Reeds*, 1960
   A nine year old boy finds an old boat and keeps it a secret until he meets a mysterious man who seems to know all about boats and how to repair them.

| 335 |

John Christopher

When the Tripods Came (New York: Dutton, 1988)

Age range: Grades 4-8

Subject(s): Science Fiction

Major character(s): Laurie, Teenager; Andy, Teenager

Time period(s): Indeterminate Future

Locale(s): England

What the book is about: This prequel to the Tripod trilogy will entice young science fiction readers as well as provide satisfaction to those who have already read the trilogy. We see the original invasion of the sixty foot high metal creatures and their frighteningly plausible take over of the Earth. Some humans, Laurie among them, try to escape the tyrannical mental and physical slavery of the Tripods. Lots of drama and suspense in this exciting battle against an alien invasion.

Where it's reviewed:
Horn Book, September/October 1988, page 625
School Library Journal, August 1988, page 92

Other books by the author:
The Guardians, 1970
The Pool of Fire, 1969
The City of Gold and Lead, 1968
The White Mountains, 1967

Other books you might like:

Jeremy Burnham, *Children of the Stones*, 1977
   A British astrophysicist and his son unlock the secret of the Stone Circle constructed at Milbury about 3000 B.C.

Michael De Larrabeiti, *The Borribles*, 1976
   In a future London, a war erupts between the Borribles, a gang of creatures who formerly were children, and their arch enemies, the Rumbles.

Peter Dickinson, *The Devil's Children*, 1986
   After the mysterious Changes begin, twelve year old Nicola finds herself wandering alone in an England where everyone suddenly hates machines.

Dennis B. Fradin, *How I Saved the World*, 1986
   After thirteen year old Shelly spots a UFO one summer night at a northern Michigan resort, he becomes involved in an effort to stop an alien invasion.

Jim Slater, *The Boy Who Saved Earth*, 1979
   The telepathic powers and super intelligence of a fourteen year old boy from a friendly alien planet help save Earth from invasion by evil aliens.

| 336 |

John Christopher

The White Mountains (New York: Macmillan, 1967)

Age range: Grades 5-7

Subject(s): Science Fiction

Time period(s): Indeterminate Future

Locale(s): Winchester, England

What the book is about: Their flight through a strange world of one hundred years in the future will remind some readers of Huck Finn on the Mississippi. Three boys live in a time of the Tripods, where the rite of passage is called ''capping," during which a cap placed on a person's head allows the Tripods to control them. Did the Tripods come from another planet, or are they rebellious human-made machines?

Where it's reviewed:
Booklist, July 1, 1967, page 1144
Hornbook, June 1967, page 351
Kirkus Reviews, February 1, 1967, page 136

Other books by the author:
Dragon Dance, 1986
Beyond the Burning Lands, 1971
The Pool of Fire, 1968
The City of Gold and Lead, 1967

Other books you might like:
Gary L. Blackwood, *Beyond the Door*, 1991
    A high school science student enters a paralled universe and must answer the question "is a macchine worth more than the people it serves?"
H.M. Hoover, *Only Child*, 1992
    Cody discovers that the Terran Corporation, in colonizing the planet Patma, is illegally destroying the intelligent native inhabitants.
Louise Lawrence, *Andra*, 1991
    In a repressive underground society of the future, teenage Andra yearns for freedom and launches a massive youth rebellion against the system.
Lois Lowry, *The Giver*, 1993
    Given his lifetime assignment at the ceremony of Twelve, Jonas becomes the receiver of memories, and discovers the terrible truth about his society.
Caroline Stevermer, *River Rats*, 1992
    Tomcat and a group orphans face danger when crossing the toxic waters of the Mississippi, about twenty years after the holocaust known as "The Flash."

337

Matt Christopher

Illustrator: Harvey Kidder

Catch That Pass! (Boston: Little, Brown, 1969)

Age range: Grades 3-5

Subject(s): Sports/Football

Major character(s): Jim Nardi, Sports Figure (football); Bucky Hayes, Sports Figure (football); Doug Nardi, Coach

Time period(s): 1960s

Locale(s): United States

What the book is about: The Cadets and Vulcans meet on the football field. Jim has trouble holding on to the pass. His life is complicated by the fact that the coach is also his football star older brother. He has a lot to work through before the season is over.

Where it's reviewed:
Kirkus Reviews, August 1, 1969, page 775
Library Journal, December 15, 1969, page 4619
Teacher, October 1974, page 109

Other books by the author:
Touchdown for Tommy, 1985
Football Fugitive, 1976
Counterfeit Tackle, 1965
Crackerjack Halfback, 1962

Other books you might like:
Paul Baczewski, *Just for Kicks*, 1990
    Brandon doesn't suspect the difficulties in store for him as manager of the varsity football team when his sister joins and becomes the star punter.
Thomas J. Dygard, *Forward Pass*, 1989
    To improve his struggling football team's chances of winning, Coach Gardner brings in a new wide receiver, Jill Winston.
David Halecroft, *Breaking Loose*, 1990
    Star football player Matt Greene is pressured by his all-pro father, which may cost the Panthers their perfect record.
Tommy Hallowell, *Last Chance Quarterback*, 1990
    Sam tries to build his football team's confidence in his abilities as quarterback and finally gets a chance to prove himself at the end of the season.
Gloria D. Miklowitz, *Anything to Win*, 1989
    To increase his chances of winning a college scholarship, a high school quarterback risks his health by taking anabolic steroids to gain weight.

338

Matt Christopher

Illustrator: Daniel Vasconcellos

The Dog That Pitched a No-Hitter (Boston: Little Brown, 1988)

Age range: Grades 2-4

Subject(s): Sports/Baseball; Animals/Dogs; Extrasensory Perception

Major character(s): Mike, Sports Figure; Harry, Dog; Mr. Wilson, Coach

Time period(s): 1980s

Locale(s): United States

What the book is about: Mike's telepathic dog, Harry, is able to send him secret signals about opposing players on the baseball field, but Mike's weak arm requires them to find another plan to save the game.

Where it's reviewed:
Booklist, May 15, 1988, page 1606
School Library Journal, August 1988, page 79
Publisher's Weekly, April 8, 1988, page 94

Other books by the author:
Skateboard Tough, 1991
The Hit-Away Kid, 1988
The Spy on Third Base, 1988
Shortstop From Tokyo, 1970

Other books you might like:
Wayne Carley, *Percy the Parrot Strikes Out*, 1971
    The White Sox and the Jets have trouble at the game with their mascots - a noisy parrot and a large dog.
Syd Hoff, *Baseball Mouse*, 1969
    Bernard was a field mouse - an infield mouse - who more than anything else wanted to help the losing team win the pennant.
Constance Hiser, *Dog on Third Base*, 1991
    James and the gang are busy with spring baseball practice until James's dog, Tog, whom they use for third base, disappears.

Ellen Leroe, *Ghost Dog*, 1993
Artie gets help from his new pet Ghost dog, and invisible pug, after someone steals the valuable baseball card his grandfather gave him.
Ann McGovern, *Scram, Kid!*, 1974
In his frustration at being left out of the baseball game, a young boy imagines some strange and funny things.

339

Matt Christopher

Illustrator: Harvey Kidder

Shortstop From Tokyo (Boston: Little Brown, 1970)

Age range: Grades 3-5

Subject(s): Sports/Baseball; Japanese Americans

Major character(s): Stogie Crane, Preteen; Hideko "Sam" Suzuki, Preteen; Bob Dirkus, Coach

Time period(s): 1960s

Locale(s): Westport, New York

What the book is about: Stogie wants to play shortstop for the Mohawks, but a new boy from Japan gets the position. Stogie tries not to become resentful but he can't help it, and when Sam's glove is found ruined in Stogie's yard, it looks as though they will never be friends.

Where it's reviewed:
Center for Children's Books Bulletin, July 1970, page 173
Kirkus Reviews, April 15, 1970, page 451
Library Journal, May 15, 1970, page 1963

Other books by the author:
The Fox Steals Home, 1978
No Arm in Left Field, 1974
The Kid Who Only Hit Homers, 1972
The Year Mom Won the Pennant, 1968

Other books you might like:
Mel Cebulash, *Ruth Marini of the Dodgers*, 1983
Ruth is the star of her high school team and the Los Angeles Dodgers think she may be good enough to become pro baseball's first female player.
Barbara Cohen, *Benny*, 1977
A German refugee's unhappiness affords Benny Rifkind a chance to show his family that he has concerns other than baseball and the 1939 World's Fair.
Donald Honig, *Johnny Lee*, 1971
A black teen who leaves Harlem to play professional baseball in the South encounters racial attitudes that he has never experienced before.
Robert Lipsyte, *Jock and Jill: A Novel*, 1982
Jack Rider, aspiring baseball star, meets Jillian, a girl who makes him reevaluate all his priorities.
Alfred Slote, *Stranger on the Ball Club*, 1970
Trying hard to adjust to a new town, Tim wants to return the expensive baseball glove he found before the real owner accuses him of stealing it.

340

Matt Christopher

Illustrator: Larry Johnson

Soccer Halfback (Boston: Little Brown, 1978)

Age range: Grades 4-6

Subject(s): Family Life; Sports/Soccer

Major character(s): Jarvis "Jabber" Morris, Sports Figure (soccer player); Mose Borman, Sports Figure (soccer player); Ray Pike, Coach

Time period(s): 1970s

Locale(s): Birch Valley, New York

What the book is about: Jabber Morris, in love with soccer, faces pressure from his mother, brother and uncle to switch his sport to football. Pete even tries to guilt trip Jabber, telling him their football star father, if he were alive, would want Jabber to play football. A good family story with lots of on-the-field action for soccer fans.

Where it's reviewed:
School Library Journal, September 1978, page 132

Other books by the author:
Undercover Tailback, 1992
Skateboard Tough, 1991
The Hit-Away Kid, 1988
Jackrabbit Goalie, 1978

Other books you might like:
David Halecroft, *Breaking Loose*, 1992
Star football player, Matt Greene, is pressured by his all-pro father, which may cost the Panthers their perfect record.
Tommy Hallowell, *Shot From Midfield*, 1991
Justin finally gets to prove his athletic abilities when he goes to summer soccer camp for three weeks.
Marion Renick, *Sam Discovers Soccer*, 1975
A broken arm means that Sam can't play baseball for the summer, but it doesn't mean that he can't play soccer.
Ivy Ruckman, *This Is Your Captain Speaking*, 1987
Overshadowed by his athletic older brother, Tom skips soccer practice to visit a nursing home where he befriends a retired sea captain.
Brenda Seabrooke, *Jerry on the Line*, 1990
Jerry, latchkey kid and aspiring soccer star, starts an unusual friendship with a younger latchkey kid when she calls his phone number by mistake.

341

Kornei Chukovsky

The Silver Crest: My Russian Boyhood (New York: Holt, 1976)

Age range: Grades 6 and Up

Subject(s): Authorship; Outcasts

Major character(s): Kornei Chukovsky, Outcast, Bastard Son; Timosha Makarov, Child; Mr. Burgmeister, Principal

Time period(s): 1890s (1893)

Locale(s): Odessa, Russia

What the book is about: Son of an unwed mother, eleven year old Kornei is forced to leave school for being "undesirable." He tries to stay in school and keep his friends. Everything he feels when he loses the silver school crest from his cap is universal. Kornei becomes a homeless painter, and is scorned by most "respectable" people, but grows up to be a very distinguished storyteller, historian, and man of letters.

Where it's reviewed:
Horn Book, August 1976, page 414
School Library Journal, April 1976, page 84

Other books by the author:
Bonjour Poussin, 1982
Good Morning Chick, 1980
Ookie Spooky, 1979
From Two to Five, 1968

Other books you might like:
Judie Angell, *One-Way to Ansonia*, 1985
    At the turn of the century, Rose immigrates from Russia to America and finds life filled with employment, marriage, motherhood and self-determination.
Michelle Kavanaugh, *Emerald Explosion*, 1988
    Disbelieving the official report of his mother's death, Patrick travels to the Soviet Union. He learns about Russia, his mother, and himself.
Robert Lehrman, *The Store That Mama Built*, 1992
    In 1917, Birdie and her siblings, children of Russian immigrants, help their widowed mother run the family store, hoping to succeed in America.
Efraim Sevela, *We Were Not like Other People*, 1989
    Separated from his family when the Germans invaded Russia during WWII, a boy learns to fend for himself and earn a living wherever he can.
Eileen Bluestone Sherman, *Independence Avenue*, 1990
    Elias arrives alone in Kansas City in 1907, finds employment and friends, but also receives bad news about his family back in Russia.

342

Patricia Clapp

I'm Deborah Sampson: A Soldier in the War of the Revolution (New York: Lothrop, 1977)

Age range: Grades 5 and Up

Subject(s): Biography; Revolutionary War; Women Soldiers

Major character(s): Deborah Sampson, Military Personnel (soldier), Historical Figure

Time period(s): 1770s

Locale(s): American Colonies

What the book is about: Deborah Sampson disguises herself and serves as Robert Shurtlieff in the Continental Army. Deborah tells the story of her childhood, the death of the young soldier she was to marry, and some of the hardships she faces during her time of service in the army.

Where it's reviewed:
Horn Book, August 1977, page 437
Kirkus Reviews, March 15, 1977, page 284

Other books by the author:
Tamarack Tree, 1986
Witches' Children, 1982
Jane-Emily, 1969
Constance: A Story of Early Plymouth, 1968

Other books you might like:
James Lincoln Collier, *My Brother Sam Is Dead*, 1974

Recounts the tragedy that strikes the Meeker family during the Revolution, when one son joins the rebels and the rest of the family try to be neutral.
Harold Felton, *Deborah Sampson, Soldier of the Revolution*, 1976
    A slightly easier version of Deborah Sampson's story, focusing on her bravery and the admiration she gained from fellow soldiers.
Ann McGovern, *The Secret Soldier*, 1975
    A biography of Deborah Sampson for early readers.
Ruth Nulton Moore, *Distant Thunder*, 1991
    Staying in a Moravian community of Bethlehem, Pennsylvania when the Revolution breaks out, Kate and her friends show kindness in the midst of war.
Elvira Woodruff, *George Washington's Socks*, 1991
    10 year old Matt and four friends are transported back to the time of George Washington and the Revolution, and experience the horrors of war.

343

Patricia Clapp

Jane-Emily (New York: Lothrop, Lee and Shepard, 1969)

Age range: Grades 5-7

Subject(s): Supernatural; Ghosts

Major character(s): Louisa Armory, Relative (aunt); Jane, Child; Emily Canfield, Spirit

Time period(s): 1910s (1912)

Locale(s): Massachusetts

What the book is about: After seeing the image of a dead girl in a crystal ball, Jane becomes possessed by the ghost of Mrs. Canfield's daughter, Emily.

Where it's reviewed:
Booklist, July 1, 1969, page 1224
Center for Children's Books Bulletin, July 1969, page 172
Hornbook, October 1969, page 538

Other books by the author:
Tamarack Tree, 1986
I'm Deborah Sampson: A Soldier in the War of the Revolution, 1977
King of the Dollhouse, 1974

Other books you might like:
Mary Downing Hahn, *Wait Till Helen Comes*, 1986
    Molly and Michael dislike their spooky stepsister Heather, but realiz e they must try to save her when she's about to follow a ghost to her doom.
Reby Edmond MacDonald, *The Ghosts of Austwick Manor*, 1982
    Hillary and Heather find themselves entering the 16th century as a direct result of their older brother Don's inheritance.
Ellen Harvey Showell, *The Ghost of Tillie Jean Cassaway*, 1978
    Willy and his sister follow different trails as they pursue the ghost of a young girl who died in their Appalachian community.
Betty Ren Wright, *The Pike River Phantom*, 1988
    Rachel and Charlie become linked with the ghost of a fierce old lady who is eerily involved in the SunBonnet Queen Contest which Rachel dreams about.
Thelma Hatch Wyss, *A Stranger Here*, 1993

While spending the summer in Idaho taking care of her sick aunt, Jada meets a spirit from the past and tries to discover the reason for his return.

344

Ann Nolan Clark

Illustrator: Jean Charlot

The Secret of the Andes (New York: Viking, 1952)

Age range: Grades 5 and Up

Subject(s): Indians of South America

Major character(s): Cusi, Indian (Inca); Chuto, Indian (Inca)

Time period(s): 1950s

Locale(s): Cuzco, Peru

What the book is about: The old Indian Chuto teaches young Cusi the ways of the Incas and the skills of shepherding llamas. Cusi still wants to know more and leaves home until he discovers the secret of his destiny and the source of true contentment.

Where it's reviewed:
Horn Book, June 1952, page 174
Library Journal, May 1, 1952, page 799

Awards the book has won:
Newbery Medal 1953

Other books by the author:
All This Wild Land, 1976
Hoofprints on the Wind, 1972
In My Mother's House, 1941
To Stand Against the Wind, 1978

Other books you might like:
Ellen M. Dolan, *The Coming of the Sun: An Inca Indian Legend*, 1987
   This picture book presents the legend that explains how the city of Cuzco was founded.
Gillian Cross, *Born of the Sun*, 1983
   Paula and her father journey to find a lost Incan city Challenging reading.
Ronald Syme, *Francisco Pizarro, Finder of Peru*, 1963
   A biography of the Spanish soldier who conquered the Inca Empire of Peru.

345

Joan Clark

Wild Man of the Woods (New York: Viking, 1986)

Age range: Grades 4-7

Subject(s): Bullies; Indians of North America

Major character(s): Stephen, Preteen; Louie Barrows, Cousin; Old Angus, Artisan (carver)

Time period(s): Indeterminate

Locale(s): Rocky Mountains, Canada

What the book is about: Stephen spends a summer vacation in the Canadian Rockies where, when fighting with his cousin against two neighborhood boys, he dons a mask made by a mysterious Indian mask carver, and seems possessed by hatred and violence.

Where it's reviewed:
Booklist, September 1, 1986, page 59
Quill & Quire, December 1985, page 30
School Library Journal, September 1986, page 132

Other books you might like:
Jeanne Betancourt, *More than Meets the Eye*, 1990
   Elizabeth's romantic interest in an Asian American student angers a prejudiced bully named Brad.
Elisa Bialk, *Tizz in the Canadian Rockies*, 1968
   A girl takes her horse along on the family vacation in the new camper to the Canadian Rockies.
Julia Cunningham, *Wolf Roland*, 1983
   After losing his donkey to a wolf, a man is roused to such sorrow and anger that he challenges the beast to take the donkey's place and pull the cart.
Jan Hudson, *Sweetgrass*, 1989
   Living on the western Canadian prairie in the 19th century, Sweetgrass, a Blackfoot teen, saves her family from a smallpox epidemic.
Jenny Nimmo, *The Chestnut Soldier*, 1989
   To purge the anger from an ancient Welsh demon god and to soothe a moody troubled soldier, Gwyn Griffiths draws on the strength of his namesake.

346

Mavis Thorpe Clark

The Sky Is Free (New York: Macmillan, 1976)

Age range: Grades 6 and Up

Subject(s): Orphans; Runaways

Major character(s): Sam, Runaway; Tony, Orphan; Bob Kelly, Miner

Time period(s): 1970s

Locale(s): Opal Town, Australia

What the book is about: Tony and Sam travel across country together. Each is running to find himself. Tony is an orphan searching for his past, and Sam is fleeing a comfortable suburban home and family. With no money, equipment, food or friends, they rob a store and soon find themselves in trouble. They are given a probationary term working for an opal mine. They both gain insights into themselves, freedom and responsibility.

Where it's reviewed:
Kirkus Reviews, July 15, 1976, page 798
School Library Journal, November 1976, page 67

Other books by the author:
The Hundred Islands, 1976
If the Earth Falls In, 1976
Spark of Opal, 1973

Other books you might like:
Judie Angell, *Dear Lola: Or, How to Build Your Own Family*, 1980
   Six orphans, ages five to eighteen, run away from an orphanage and establish a successful household.
Walter Macken, *The Flight of the Doves*, 1968

A twelve year old English boy and his seven year old sister run away from their abusive stepfather and set out to reach their grandmother.

Michael Morpurgo, *Mr. Nobody's Eyes*, 1989
An escaped circus monkey and an outcast English boy named Harry make an unusual pair of runaways.

Judith Bernie Strommen, *Grady the Great*, 1990
11 year old Grady, plannning to run away to join his best friend in California, finds his secret endangered by his new "friend" next door.

Pieter Van Raven, *Pickle and Price*, 1990
Tired of living with an abusive father and an unloving mother who supervise a rural prison farm, 13 year old Pickle and his friend travel the country.

347

Joan Clarke

Early Rising (Philadelphia: Lippincott, 1976)

Age range: Grades 5 and Up

Subject(s): Family Life

Major character(s): Erica, Teenager; Beatrice, Young Woman (Erica's sister)

Time period(s): 1880s

Locale(s): England

What the book is about: Erica and her brothers are being raised by her widowed minister father. Beatrice comes home to help with the younger children. Erica is so eager for a mother substitute, she can't see Beatty as she really is.

Where it's reviewed:
Kirkus Reviews, August 15, 1976, page 906
School Library Journal, October 1976, page 105

Other books you might like:
Joan Aiken, *The Cuckoo Tree*, 1988
As a result of an accident, a young girl is faced with foiling a Hanoverian plot to put St. Paul's cathedral on rollers and roll it into the Thames.

Susan Cooper, *The Dark Is Rising*, 1977
Will discovers he is the last of the Old Ones, destined to face the final battle between good and evil.

Alan Garner, *The Aimer Gate*, 1978
Robert learns that his secret place has another secret the day his soldier uncle comes home to help with the corn harvest.

Nigel Gray, *The Deserter*, 1977
Four English children form a close friendship with a young deserter from the British army and help him escape from the authorities.

Patricia Miles, *A Disturbing Influence*, 1979
Andrew is drawn into a mystery involving a rock festival, counterfeit money, a runaway neighbor and a deserted farmhouse.

348

Pauline Clarke

Illustrator: Cecil Leslie

Torolov the Fatherless (Salem, New Hampshire: Faber, 1978)

Age range: Grades 5 and Up

Subject(s): Vikings; Orphans

Major character(s): Torolov, Orphan

Time period(s): 10th century

Locale(s): England

What the book is about: During the reign of Ethelred the Unready, a Viking orphan is stranded when his ship leaves while he is ashore without permission. He is rasied by a loving, elderly earl. The earl dies fighting the Vikings at the Battle of Maldron. Torolov's loyalties are no longer divided.

Where it's reviewed:
Center for Children's Books Bulletin, April 1979, p 132

Other books by the author:
The Two Faces of Silenius, 1972
The Return of the Twelves, 1962

Other books you might like:
J.S. Andrews, *The Green Hill of Nendrum*, 1970
A boy is transported back in time to a 10th century monastery threatened by a Viking raid.

Peter Burchard, *Stranded, A Story of New York in 1875*, 1967
Recounts the fortunes of an abandoned Scottish youth in the fourth Ward slums of lower Manhattan when political gangs ruled the city.

Kevin Crossley-Holland, *The Sea Stranger*, 1973
A young Saxon boy longs to be like the gentle stranger who lands a small boat near his home on the Essex coast in 653.

Malcolm C. Jensen, *Lief Erikson, the Lucky*, 1979
Describes Leif Erikson's boyhood in Iceland, his father's voyage to Greenland, and his own voyage to North America circa 1000 A.D. (Biography)

Eloise Jarvis McGraw, *The Striped Ships*, 1991
Juliana, a Saxon girl, loses her home and family when the Normans conquer England in 1066, and seeks to order her life by working on a tapestry.

349

Beverly Cleary

Beezus and Ramona (New York: Morrow, 1955)

Age range: Grades 3-4

Subject(s): Schools; Sisters

Major character(s): Beatrice "Beezus" Quimby, Child; Ramona Quimby, Child; Henry Huggins, Child

Time period(s): 1950s

Locale(s): United States

What the book is about: Beezus' biggest problem is her little sister, Ramona. Beezus is very patient most of the time, but eventually she becomes so exasperated that she decides that she does not like Ramona at all. Beezus knows sisters are supposed to love each other all the time, like Mother and Aunt Beatrice, but with a sister like Ramona, it seemes impossible.

Where it's reviewed:
Junior Bookshelf, February 1979, pages 28
Times Educational Supplement, December 1, 1978, page 24
Times Educational Supplement, May 15, 1981, page 29

Other books by the author:
Muggie Maggie, 1991

Ramona and Her Father, 1977
Ellen Tebbits, 1951
Henry Huggins, 1950

Other books you might like:
Oliver Butterworth, *The Enormous Egg*, 1956
Nate's hen laid an egg so big that he had to help her turn it every few hours until "Uncle Beazley" hatched. Great family or classroom read-aloud.
Liza Ketchum Murrow, *Allergic to My Family*, 1992
Living with five brothers and sister, a pet skunk and two nutty parents, Rosie sometimes feels that her family is too busy to appreciate her.
Phyllis Reynolds Naylor, *The Boys Start the War*, 1993
Disgusted that a family with three girls moves into the house across the river, Wally and his three brothers declare a practical joke war on the them.
Keith Robertson, *Henry Reed's Big Show*, 1970
Henry had meant to merely launch his career as a producer, but before summer was over, he had organized a rock music festival and a wild west rodeo.
Thomas Rockwell, *How to Eat Fried Worms*, 1973
Two boys set out to prove that worms can make a delicious meal, and think of creative ways to serve them.

350

Beverly Cleary

Illustrator: Paul O. Zelinsky

Dear Mr. Henshaw (New York: Morrow, 1983)

Age range: Grades 4-6

Subject(s): Authorship; Parent and Child

Major character(s): Leigh Botts, Child; Boyd Henshaw, Writer

Time period(s): 1980s

Locale(s): United States

What the book is about: Through letters written to his favorite author, Leigh finds the spirit and courage to deal with his problems. Who is stealing from his lunch box? Can Leigh become an author in his own right? Does Leigh's father really love him, even though he left?

Where it's reviewed:
Horn Book, October 1983, page 570
School Library Journal, September 1983, page 120

Other books by the author:
Strider, 1991
Girl from Yamhill: A Memoir, 1988 (Biography)
Lucky Chuck, 1984
Ralph S. Mouse, 1982

Other books you might like:
Jean Fiedler, *Year the World Was out of Step with Jancy Fried*, 1981
A 12 year old Jewish girl exchanges letters with her Austrian cousin during Hitler's rise to power.
Barbara Ware Holmes, *Charlotte the Starlet*, 1988
Charlotte writes a novel that gains her many admirers but almost costs her her best friend.
Janice Marriott, *Letters to Lesley*, 1991
12 year old Henry plots to marry off his mother to the father of his new pen pal.

Colby Rodowsky, *P.S. Write Soon: A Novel*, 1978
A physically handicapped girl shares her daydreams with a pen pal.
Zilpha Keatley Snyder, *Libby on Wednesday*, 1990
Unhappy in an accelerated 8th grade program, Libby makes new friends in a writing workshop.

351

Beverly Cleary

Illustrator: Louis Darling

Ellen Tebbits (New York: Morrow, 1951)

Age range: Grades 3-5

Subject(s): Schools; Family Life

Major character(s): Ellen Tebbits, Child; Austine Allen, Child; Otis Spofford, Child

Time period(s): 1950s

Locale(s): Oregon

What the book is about: Ellen has boasted that she can ride horses, until she proves she can't. She's a "substitute rat" in the school version of "The Pied Piper" and gets hopelessly tangled up with a maypole dance. A fun book for middle readers.

Where it's reviewed:
Book World, June 10, 1979, page E2
Catholic Library World, April 1981, page 389
Teacher, May 1978, page 106

Other books by the author:
Jean and Johnny, 1959
Beezus and Ramona, 1955
Henry and Beezus, 1952
Henry Huggins, 1950

Other books you might like:
Ilene Cooper, *Frances Dances*, 1991
As she takes ballet lessons and participates in a school play, a timid fourth grader confronts her fears and learns a lesson about friendship.
Deirdre Corey, *Yours 'til the Meatball Bounces*, 1990
Stevie's friends, Laura and Meg, want to be in the school play but Stevie can't dance or act.
Betsy Haynes, *The Bragging War*, 1989
When snooty Laura begins bragging about her big slumber party and invites everyone but the Fabulous Five, Beth decides to launch a counter campaign.
Magdalen Nabb, *Josie Smith at School*, 1990
Spirited Josie has adventures and misadventures at school, where she befriends a foreign student and takes part in the class play.
Bjarne B. Reuter, *Buster the Sheikh of Hope Street*, 1991
Buster, a highly imaginative Danish schoolboy, must take over the lead role in the school play on the night of the performance.

352

Beverly Cleary

Illustrator: Louis Darling

The Mouse and the Motorcycle (New York: Morrow, 1965)

Age range: Grades 3-5

Subject(s): Animals/Mice; Hotels, Motels

Major character(s): Ralph, Mouse; Keith, Child, Vacationer

Time period(s): 1960s

Locale(s): United States

What the book is about: Ralph lives in Room 215 of the old, dilapidated Mountain View Inn. Keith and his parents stay at the motel for a few days. A small toy motorcycle is Keith's prize possession but turns out to be just the right size for Ralph. Then the mouse's adventures begin.

Where it's reviewed:
Horn Book, December 1965, page 628
Library Journal, December 15, 1965, page 5510

Awards the book has won:
Young Reader's Choice Award 1968

Other books by the author:
Girl from Yamhill: A Memoir, 1988 (Biography)
Lucky Chuck, 1984
Ralph S. Mouse, 1982
Runaway Ralph, 1977

Other books you might like:
Roger W. Drury, *The Champion of Merrimack County*, 1976
    O'Crispin is a mouse on a bicycle who races around the rim of an antique bathtub and causes all manner of trouble for his family.
Brian Jacques, *Mariel of Redwall*, 1992
    The mousemaid Mariel achieves victory at sea for the animals of Redwall Abbey, fighting the savage pirate rat, the wild warlord of rodent corsairs.
Dick King-Smith, *Martin's Mice*, 1988
    A cat who doesn't want to catch mice keeps a family of them as pets in the barn. When he is given away to a lady in town, he gets a new point of view.
Robert Kraus, *The Hoodwinking of Mrs. Elmo*, 1987
    Besides working as servants for a wealthy elephant, a mouse couple protect her from an evil cousin who plots to steal her fortune.
William Steig, *Abel's Island*, 1976
    Castaway on an uninhabited island, Abel, a very civilized mouse, finds that he has what it takes to survive and return home.

353

Beverly Cleary

Illustrator: Paul O. Zelinsky

Ralph S. Mouse (New York: Morrow, 1982)

Age range: Grades 3-5

Subject(s): Animals/Mice

Major character(s): Ralph Smart, Mouse; Ryan Bramble, Child

Time period(s): 1980s

Locale(s): Cucaracha, California

What the book is about: Ralph S. still lives at the Mountain View Inn. In order to save his friend Matt's job, Ralph convinces Ryan to take him to live at the Irwin J. Sneed Elementary School.

Where it's reviewed:
Center for Children's Books Bulletin, September 1982, page 5
Horn Book, December 1982, page 648

Awards the book has won:
Golden Kite Award 1982

Other books by the author:
Ramona Quimby, Age 8, 1981
The Mouse and the Motorcycle, 1965
Emily's Runaway Imagination, 1961
Henry and Beezus, 1952

Other books you might like:
Robert Kraus, *The Hoodwinking of Mrs. Elmo*, 1987
    Besides working as servants, a mouse couple protects Mrs. Elmo, an elephant, from her evil cousin.
Mary DeBall Kwitz, *The Bell Tolls at Mousehaven Manor*, 1991
    Count Von Flittermouse, a body-changing vampire bat, kidnaps Violet Mae Mouse in hopes of gaining fluid from the Fountain of Youth.
Lilian Moore, *Don't Be Afraid, Amanda*, 1992
    Amanda overcomes her fear of the country in order to visit her pen pal, Adam.
George Selden, *Harry Kitten and Tucker Mouse*, 1986
    A hungry mouse and a lonely kitten become friends and seek adventure and fortune together in the streets and subways of New York City.
Eve Titus, *Anatole and the Pied Piper*, 1979
    Anatole, the mouse, is called upon to be a hero when an ambitious musician concocts a scheme involving twenty-four school mice at a picnic.

354

Beverly Cleary

Illustrator: Alan Tiegreen

Ramona and Her Father (New York: Morrow, 1977)

Age range: Grades 3-6

Subject(s): Family Life; Fathers and Daughters

Major character(s): Ramona Quimby, Child, 2nd Grader; Beatrice "Beezus" Quimby, Child

Time period(s): 1970s

Locale(s): United States

What the book is about: The family routine is upset during Ramona's year in second grade, when her father unexpectedly loses his job. Even though family finances and relationships are strained, life goes on with plenty of love and laughs.

Where it's reviewed:
Kirkus Reviews, July 15, 1977, page 727
School Library Journal, November 1977, page 54

Awards the book has won:
Boston Globe/Horn Book Award - Honor Book 1978
Garden State Children's Book Award 1980

Other books by the author:
Dear Mr. Henshaw, 1983
Ramona the Brave, 1975
Ellen Tebbits, 1951

Henry Huggins, 1950

Other books you might like:
Carolyn Haywood, *Betsy and Billy*, 1941
  Betsy, Billy and their friends enjoy and learn from the many activities in the second grade.
Suzy Kline, *Song Lee in Room 2B*, 1993
  Spring becomes a memorable time for Miss Mackles' second grade classroom due to the antics of Horrible Harry and the special insights of shy Song Lee.
Lila Perl, *Tybee Trimble's Hard Times*, 1984
  A fourth grader whose father is unemployed sets out to earn the price of a ticket to the circus.
Peter Roop, *Ahyoka and the Talking Leaves*, 1992
  Ahyoka helps her father, Sequoyah, in his quest to create a system of writing for his people.
Molly Mia Stewart, *Elizabeth's Super-Selling Lemonade*, 1990
  Elizabeth and Jessica sell lemonade to make money to help their second grade class buy a wedding present for their teacher, but there is a problem.

355

Beverly Cleary

Illustrator: Alan Tiegreen

Ramona Quimby, Age 8 (New York: Morrow, 1981)

Age range: Grades 3-5

Subject(s): Family Life

Major character(s): Ramona Quimby, Child

Time period(s): 1980s

Locale(s): United States

What the book is about: Ramona's mom works full time and her dad has gone back to college. She is in a new school, with new friends and a new teacher. She has to put up with a spoiled four year old every afternoon. Triumphs and major disasters.

Where it's reviewed:
Horn Book, October 1981, page 533
School Library Journal, August 1981, page 54

Other books by the author:
Muggie Maggie, 1990
Ramona Forever, 1984
Ralph S. Mouse, 1982
Ramona the Pest, 1968

Other books you might like:
Judy Delton, *Kitty From the Start*, 1987
  Kitty moves to a new neighborhood and faces the task of making friends in her new third grade class.
Jane Flory, *Miss Plunkett to the Rescue*, 1983
  A former third grade teacher comes out of retirement to become a spy and risks her life to save her country.
Candice Ransom, *Ladies and Jellybeans*, 1991
  As Wendy starts third grade she worries about writing in cursive, the Cold War, and her father's new job.
Dian Curtis Regan, *The Class with the Summer Birthdays*, 1991
  Because all of Brittany's third grade classmates have birthdays between May and August, the class never gets to celebrate birthdays at school.
Karen Lynn Williams, *Baseball and Butterflies*, 1990

Daniel finds his summer butterfly project threatened by his little brother and his best friend.

356

Beverly Cleary

Illustrator: Paul O. Zelinsky

Strider (New York: Morrow, 1991)

Age range: Grades 4-9

Subject(s): Divorce; Animals/Dogs; Authorship

Major character(s): Leigh Botts, Teenager, Writer; Strider, Dog

Time period(s): 1980s

Locale(s): United States

What the book is about: In this sequel to *Dear Mr. Henshaw*, fourteen year old Leigh Botts is still working through his feelings about his parents' divorce when an abandoned dog named Strider comes into his life. Leigh has longed for a dog forever, and he and his friend, Barry, work out a joint custody arrangement. Leigh moves into mid-adolescence, finds a place on the track team with his peers, and begins to accept his parents' divorce.

Where it's reviewed:
Booklist, July 1991, page 2041
Horn Book, September/October 1991, page 595

Other books by the author:
Dear Mr. Henshaw, 1983
Mitch and Amy, 1967
Sister of the Bride, 1963
Fifteen, 1956

Other books you might like:
Carole S. Adler, *Shelter on Blue Barns Road*, 1981
  Trying to escape her troubled family, thirteen year old Betsy hides a Doberman Pinscher, who is to be destroyed because of his vicious reputation.
William F. Hallstead, *Tundra*, 1984
  Separated from his fifteen year old owner, who already has problems with her divorced mother, a Siberian Husky experiences life-threatening hardships.
Cordelia Jones, *A Cat Called Camouflage*, 1971
  A cat named Camouflage helps Ruth face her parents' divorce and life in a new town.
Barbara Wersba, *Wonderful Me: A Novel*, 1989
  Heidi, a lonely child of divorced parents and a serious dog lover, falls for a young man, but realizes she needs to establish her own indepence first.
Joan Winslow, *Romance Is a Riot*, 1983
  Ann has problems with parents who are separating, a persistent ex-boyfriend, an unsympathetic best friend, and even her dog.

357

Vera Cleaver

Illustrator: Ellen Raskin

Ellen Grae (Philadelphia: Lippincott, 1967)

Age range: Grades 3-6

Subject(s): Friendship; Imagination; Secrets

Major character(s): Ellen Grae, Preteen; Ira, Recluse; Rosemary, Preteen

Time period(s): Indeterminate

Locale(s): Thicket

What the book is about: Ellen Grae is an eleven year old with a rich imagination and in general, an "attitude." She knows great stories but most grown ups and some kids think they only happen in her head. She is the only one in town who can get Ira, a recluse with a pet goat named Missouri, to talk. She believes something awful happened in the swamp years ago and must struggle with what she knows, her affection for Ira, and her sense of right and wrong.

Where it's reviewed:
Kirkus Reviews, March 15, 1967, page 339
Library Journal, September 15, 1967, page 3184
Publisher's Weekly, April 10, 1967, page 80

Other books by the author:
Belle Pruitt, 1988
Hazel Rye, 1983
Dust of the Earth, 1975
Grover, 1970

Other books you might like:
Avi, Who Was That Masked Man, Anyway?, 1992
During World War II, sixth grader Frankie Wattleson gets in trouble at home and at school because of his preoccupation with his favorite radio shows.
Gilbert B. Cross, Mystery at Loon Lake, 1986
When three friends explore an old, man-made tunnel in the cliff beyond the swamp, they disturb someone who then attempts to murder them.
Sigrid Heuck, The Hideout, 1988
Rebecca, a German orphan during WWII, meets a boy hiding out in a nearby cornfield and they create their own imaginary fantasy world.
Kathleen Leverich, Hilary and the Troublemakers, 1992
A homework-eating owl, an angry piggy bank, several talking sheep, and some snow people help Hilary to make the right decisions at home and at school.
Bjarne B. Reuter, Buster, the Sheikh of Hope Street, 1991
The adventures of Buster, an imaginative Danish schoolboy, come to a climax when he takes over the lead role in the school play on performance night.

358

Vera Cleaver

Hazel Rye (New York: Lippincott, 1983)

Age range: Grades 5-7

Subject(s): Fathers and Daughters

Major character(s): Hazel Rye, Preteen, Landlord; Millard Rye, Parent (Farmer), Farmer

Time period(s): Indeterminate

Locale(s): Florida

What the book is about: A strong father-daughter conflict dominates this story of eleven year old Hazel Rye who is smart, enterprising, creative all the things her father does not expect a girl to be. When a family arrives at their citrus farm with no

place to stay, Hazel rents them a small place located in an orange grove her father had given to her. Good realistic dialogue and vivid Florida Ridge setting.

Where it's reviewed:
Horn Book, June 1983, page 301
School Library Journal, September 1983, page 120

Other books by the author:
Belle Pruitt, 1988
Dust of the Earth, 1975
Delpha Green and Company, 1972
Grover, 1970

Other books you might like:
Elizabeth Feuer, Paper Doll, 1990
Leslie's poignant struggle for independence makes this a touching and dynamic portrayal of the complex relationship between a woman and her father.
R. Rozanne Knudsen, You Are the Rain, 1974
A camping trip into the Florida Everglades becomes a dangerous adventure for two incompatible girls who get separated from their group.
Lois Lenski, Strawberry Girl, 1973
Set in a little know backwoods region of Florida, this Newbery winner tells the story of the feud between the Slaters and the Boyers.
Theresa Nelson, The 25iracle, 1986
Motherless Elvira looks for a mother and instead finds the father she hardly knew she had.
Ann Waldron, The Luckie Star, 1977
A preteen is not looking forward to summer with the family in Florida, but a sunken treasure makes the whole thing worthwhile.

359

Vera Cleaver

Illustrator: Eric Nones

Sugar Blue (New York: Lothrop, 1984)

Age range: Grades 5-7

Subject(s): Aunts and Uncles; Family Life

Major character(s): Ella, Child; Amy "Sugar Blue" Blue, Relative (aunt), Preteen

Time period(s): Indeterminate

Locale(s): United States

What the book is about: The arrival of a four year old niece changes many family relationships and attitudes. Aunt Ella, eleven years old, finds her relationship with her little niece changing her view of herself and life in general.

Where it's reviewed:
Hornbook, August 1984, page 464
Kirkus Reviews, May 1, 1984, page J37
School Library Journal, May 1984, page 77

Other books by the author:
Kissimmee Kid, 1991
I Would Rather Be a Turnip, 1981
The Mock Revolt, 1981
Where the Lilies Bloom, 1969

Other books you might like:
Avi, Emily Upham's Revenge, 1978

During the summer of 1875, a girl is sent to live with her wealthy uncle and becomes involved in a very suspicious bank robbery.
Patricia Clapp, *Jane-Emily*, 1969
While spending the summer in an old house, a girl and her niece become aware of the presence of a spirit who seems determined to harm them.
Kevin Henkes, *The Zebra Wall*, 1988
Aunt Irene comes to help the eccentric and loving Vorlob family prepare themselves for a new baby.
Barbara Holland, *Creepy-Mouse Coming to Get You*, 1985
A young boy finds that it is up to him to shield his sister and baby nephew from her quick-tempered husband, recently released from prison.
Norma Johnston, *The Sanctuary Tree*, 1977
Tish faces the death of her grandfather, parting from her sweetheart, and the birth of a niece.

| 360 |

Vera Cleaver, Author/Illustrator

Co-Author: Bill Cleaver

Where the Lilies Bloom (Philadelphia: Lippincott, 1969)

Age range: Grades 5 and Up

Subject(s): Brothers and Sisters; Mountain Life; Orphans

Major character(s): Mary Call Luther, Teenager

Time period(s): 1960s

Locale(s): United States

What the book is about: When her sharecropper father dies, 14 year old Mary and her 10 year old brother secretly bury him so they can keep their home. Mary becomes head of the family and cares for her brother and retarded sister. She sells medicinal plants to keep the family afloat and fends off the landlord who wants to marry her.

Where it's reviewed:
Horn Book, October 1969, page 540
Library Journal, December 15, 1969, page 4602

Awards the book has won:
Boston Globe/Horn Book Award - Honor Book 1970

Other books by the author:
Belle Pruitt, 1988
Dust of the Earth, 1975
Delpha Green and Company, 1972
Grover, 1970

Other books you might like:
Dianne Case, *Love, David*, 1991
Anna watches as her brother involves himself in illegal activities to escape the poverty of his life in South Africa.
Patricia Hermes, *Mama, Let's Dance*, 1991
Three abandoned youngsters keep their situation a secret so authorities will not split them up and send them to separate foster homes.
Hadley Irwin, *The Original Freddie Ackerman*, 1992
Freddie refuses to spend another summer with his extended family, and goes to Maine to visit two eccentric aunts and gets involved in a mystery.
Willo Davis Roberts, *To Grandmother's House We Go*, 1990

To avoid foster home care, three children run away to a grandmother they have never seen, where they find a cold reception and a terrible secret.
Cynthia Voigt, *Dicey's Song*, 1982
The four abandoned Tillerman children find a home with their grandmother.

| 361 |

Eth Clifford

Illustrator: George Hughes

Help! I'm a Prisoner in the Library (Boston: Houghton Mifflin, 1979)

Age range: Grades 3-5

Subject(s): Weather; Libraries

Major character(s): Mary Rose Onetree, Child; JoBeth Onetree, Child; Harry Onetree, Parent (father)

Time period(s): 1970s

Locale(s): Indianapolis, Indiana

What the book is about: Because their dad, who is called "last minute Harry," runs out of gas, Mary Rose and JoBeth run into the library just at closing time to use the bathroom. Not knowing they are there, Miss Finton, the librarian, locks up and leaves and the girls are stuck in the library for the night. Hilarious and a little scary.

Where it's reviewed:
Booklist, November 15, 1979, page 500
Kirkus Reviews, December 15, 1979, page 1429
School Library Journal, November 1979, page 63

Other books by the author:
Scared Silly, 1988
Just Tell Me When We're Dead!, 1983
The Strange Reincarnation of Hendrik Verloom, 1982
The Dastardly Murder of Dirty Pete, 1981

Other books you might like:
E.J. Bird, *The Blizzard of 1896*, 1990
Uncle Tim tells in his own words, amazing things that happened during the powerful snow storm in the West in 1896.
John R. Erickson, *Lost in the Blinded Blizzard*, 1991
While battling a blizzard to get cough syrup for Baby Mollie, Hank the Cowdog performs several other heoric deeds along the way.
Susan Fleming, *Trapped on the Golden Flyer*, 1978
During a blizzard, the train Paul is taking west becomes frozen to the tracks and the passengers are drawn together in a fight for survival.
Priscilla Homola, *The Willow Whistle*, 1983
Though only eleven, Annie knows she loves Conrad. Papa is furious until a raging South Dakota blizzard helps him see Conrad in a new light.
Carla Stevens, *Anna, Grandpa and the Big Storm*, 1981
Anna's grandfather is bored with city life until he and Anna are stranded on the 3rd Avenue El during the blizzard of 1888.

362

Eth Clifford

The Killer Swan (Boston: Houghton Mifflin, 1980)

Age range: Grades 5-6

Subject(s): Suicide; Stepfamilies

Major character(s): Lex Mebbin, Teenager; Stella Mebbin, Parent; Steve Mebin, Step-Parent

Time period(s): 1980s

Locale(s): United States

What the book is about: Recovering from his father's suicide, and adjusting to a new stepfather has kept Lee off balance. After the family moves to the country, two swans settle in their pond. The male is sightless in one eye, and when provoked, extremely aggressive. The struggle to keep one of the cygnets, named Survivor, safe, and protect others from the murderous cob, breaks down the barriers between Lee and his stepfather.

Where it's reviewed:
Center for Children's Books Bulletin, March 1981, page 129
School Library Journal, November 1980, page 84

Other books by the author:
Just Tell Me When We're Dead!, 1983
The Rocking Chair Rebellion, 1978
The Curse of the Moonraker: A Tale of Survival, 1977
Burning Star, 1974

Other books you might like:
Mary Calhoun, *Julie's Tree*, 1988
    After the death of her mother, Julie leaves her grandmother's home to join her father in a new town.
Dean Hughes, *Switching Tracks*, 1982
    After his father's death, Mark Austin becomes withdrawn and depressed. Only he and his mother know the death was not an accident.
Sandra McCuaig, *Blindfold*, 1990
    Benji and his blind older brother, Joel, share a special bond until they commit suicide, which devastates their friend, Sally.
Lygia Bojunga Nunes, *My Friend, the Painter*, 1991
    A young boy becomes friends with the artist in the apartment upstairs and tries to understand when his friend commits suicide.
Kin Platt, *Chloris and the Freaks*, 1975
    Adjusting to her father's suicide and mother's remarriage leads a young girl to study astrology.

363

Eth Clifford

Illustrator: Mary Beth Owens

The Man Who Sang in the Dark (Boston: Houghton Mifflin, 1987)

Age range: Grades 3-6

Subject(s): Blind; Depression (Economic); Family Life

Major character(s): Leah, Preteen

Time period(s): 1920s (1929)

Locale(s): Philadelphia, Pennsylvania

What the book is about: Leah, her brother and widowed mother support themselves by running a boarding house in Philadelphia during the Depression. The story revolves around their interactions with the various boarders. A sub-plot involves the possibility of letting Leah's brother go to live with a wealthy family who can provide more for him than his mother can. Pat, happy ending.

Where it's reviewed:
Horn Book, November/December 1987, page 736
School Library Journal, October 1987, page 124

Other books by the author:
I Never Wanted to Be Famous, 1986
The Remembering Box, 1985
The Rocking Chair Rebellion, 1978
The Wild One, 1974

Other books you might like:
Meg Ashley, *The Secret of the Old House*, 1982
    When Beth and her mother inherit an old house, they decide to renovate it and take in boarders, unaware that two people don't want them there.
Barbara Corcoran, *The Sky Is Falling*, 1988
    In Boston during the early days of the Great Depression, Annah's affluent life style comes to an abrupt end when she is sent to live on an island.
Edith S. McCall, *Better than a Brother*, 1988
    The adventures of a young girl growing up at the turn of the century in Wisconsin, where her family runs a boarding house for ice cutters.
Ken Radford, *The Cellar*, 1989
    From her first night in an old boarding house, a young girl is aware of mysterious ghostly presences and determined to find an explanation.
Arvella Whitmore, *The Bread Winner*, 1990
    When both her parents are unable to find work and pay the bills during the Great Depression, resourceful Sarah sells her bread to make money.

364

Eth Clifford

Illustrator: Donna Diamond

The Remembering Box (Boston: Houghton Mifflin, 1985)

Age range: Grades 3-6

Subject(s): Jews; Grandparents; Death

Major character(s): Joshua Beck, Child; Grandma Golding, Grandparent

Time period(s): 1940s (1942)

Locale(s): United States

What the book is about: Joshua's weekly visits to his beloved grandmother on the Jewish Sabbath give him an understanding of love, family, and tradition, which help him accept her death. A warm portrayal of a traditional Jewish family.

Where it's reviewed:
Horn Book, March/April 1986, page 200
School Library Journal, December 1985, page 87

Other books by the author:
I Hate Your Guts, Ben Brooster, 1989
Harvey's Horrible Snake Disaster, 1984

Just Tell Me When We're Dead!, 1983
Help! I'm a Prisoner in the Library, 1979

Other books you might like:
Barbara Cohen, *The Christmas Revolution*, 1988
   Emily is forced to think about her Jewish heritage when the new boy at school, an Orthodox Jew, refuses to participate in the school Christmas party.
Mel Glenn, *Squeeze Play: A Baseball Story*, 1989
   With the support of the gentle Mr. Janowicz, Jeremy speaks out against his bullying teacher and his mandatory after-school baseball games.
Ilse Koehn, *Mischling, 2nd Degree*, 1977
   The memoirs of a German girl who became a leader among the Hitler youth while her family kept from her the secret of her partial Jewish heritage.
Kathryn Lasky, *The Night Journey*, 1981
   Rache ignores her parents wishes and persuades her great grandmother to tell the story of her escape from Czarist Russia.
Susan Terris, *Whirling Rainbows*, 1974
   A thirteen year old adopted Jewish girl of American Indian heritage seeks to find her real self at summer camp.

365

Lucille Clifton

Illustrator: Ann Grifalconi

Everett Anderson's Friend (New York: Holt, 1976)

Age range: Grades 1-2

Subject(s): African Americans; Friendship; Poetry

Major character(s): Everett Anderson, Child; Maria, Child; Kirk, Child

Time period(s): 1970s

Locale(s): United States

What the book is about: Having eargerly anticipated the new neighbors, a boy is disappointed to get a whole family of girls.

Where it's reviewed:
Booklist, September 1, 1976, page 34
Hornbook, October 1976, page 515
Kirkus Reviews, April 15, 1976, page 462

Other books by the author:
Amifika, 1977
All Us Come Across the Water, 1973
The Boy Who Didn't Believe in Spring, 1973
Don't You Remember?, 1973

Other books you might like:
Michael Bedard, *Emily*, 1992
   When a mother and child visit their reclusive neighbor, Emily (Dickinson) who stays in her house writing all day, there is a special exchange of gifts
Arthur Dorros, *Abuela*, 1991
   While riding on a bus with her grandmother, a little girl imagines that they are carried up into the sky and fly over New York City.
Ann M. Martin, *Rachel Parker, Kindergarten Show-Off*, 1992
   Five year old Olivia's new neighbor Rachel is in her class, and they must overcome feelings of jealousy and competition before they can become friends

Patricia Polacco, *Mrs. Katz and Tush*, 1992
   A long lasting friendship develops between Larnel, a young Afro-American, and Mrs. Katz, a lonely Jewish widow.
Faith Ringgold, *Dinner at Aunt Connie's House*, 1993
   While having dinner at Aunt Connie's, Melody meets her new adopted cousin and twelve Afro-American women who leave their portraits and join the dinner

---

366

Lucille Clifton

Illustrator: Dale Payton

The Lucky Stone (New York: Delacorte, 1979)

Age range: Grades 2-3

Subject(s): African Americans; Grandparents

Major character(s): Tee, Child

Time period(s): 1970s

Locale(s): United States

What the book is about: Tee loves listening to her great-grandmother tell tales of her "lucky stone" and the generations it has seen. When her great-grandmother falls ill, Tee is not allowed in the hospital but sneaks in anyway. Great-grandmother tells her where to find the stone, and it begins to be lucky for her.

Where it's reviewed:
Horn Book, April 1980, page 171
School Library Jouranl, March 1980, page 119

Other books by the author:
The Times They Used to Be, 1974
All Us Come Across the Water, 1973
Amifika, 1973
Don't You Remember?, 1973

Other books you might like:
Barbara Cohen, *213 Valentines*, 1991
   Wade has trouble adjusting when he is transferred to a special class for the gifted.
Patricia Polacco, *Mrs. Katz and Tush*, 1992
   A friendship developes between a young Afro-American and Mrs. Katz, a lonely Jewish widow.
Faith Ringgold, *Tar Beach*, 1991
   A young girl dreams of flying above her Harlem home, claiming all she sees for herself and her family.
Alice Walker, *Finding the Green Stone*, 1991
   After saying unkind things to family and friends, Johnny loses both his green stone and his interest in life.
Mildred Pitts Walter, *Two and Too Much*, 1990
   7 year old Brandon's attempt to take care of his 2 year old sister Gina results in one disaster after another.

367

Lucille Clifton

Illustrator: Susan Jeschke

The Times They Used to Be (New York: Holt, 1974)

Age range: Grades 5-6

Subject(s): African Americans; Civil Rights; Prejudice

Major character(s): Mama, Preteen; Tassie, Preteen

Time period(s): 1940s (1948)

Locale(s): United States

What the book is about: A young black girl relates the adventures of the summer her Uncle Sunny died and her best friend broke in sin because she wasn't saved.

Where it's reviewed:
Kirkus Reviews, June 1, 1974, page 580
Library Journal, September 15, 1974, page 2262

Other books by the author:
An Ordinary Woman, 1974
Don't You Remember?, 1973
Good, Says Jerome, 1973
The Boy Who Didn't Believe in Spring, 1973

Other books you might like:
John F. Grabowski, *Jackie Robinson*, 1991
    A biography of the black athlete who broke the color barrier in major league baseball when he joined the Brooklyn Dodgers in 1947.
Lorenz B. Graham, *North Town*, 1965
    The Williams family leaves the South for the North in search of opportunity, but David finds his new world confusing and unpredictable.
Francine Haskins, *I Remember "121"*, 1991
    The author describes her life from age three to nine, and celebrates growing up in a traditional African-American community in Washington, D.C.
Jill Krementz, *Sweet Pea: A Black Girl Growing up in the Rural South*, 1969
    Text and photographs describe the family, home, school, and amusements of a ten year old black girl living in the rural South.
Norman L. Macht, *Satchel Paige*, 1991
    Surveys the life of the first baseball player in the Negro Leagues to be inducted into the Baseball Hall of Fame.

368

Shirley Climo

Illustrator: Eileen McKeating

Gopher, Tanker, and the Admiral (New York: Crowell, 1984)

Age range: Grades 4-6

Subject(s): Burglary; Money; Old Age

Major character(s): Christopher "Gopher" Spratt, Preteen; Randy Segal, Friend; Admiral Clark, Neighbor

Time period(s): 1980s

Locale(s): California

What the book is about: Eleven year old Gopher doesn't get along too well with his neighbor, the Admiral, until he becomes a hero. It's pretty funny business as Gopher, Tanker and the Admiral become involved in one complication after another, trying to solve the neighborhood burglaries.

Where it's reviewed:
Booklist, June 1, 1984, page 1396
Center for Children's Books Bulletin, September 1984, page 2
School Library Journal, May 1984, page 101

Other books by the author:
T.J.'s Ghost, 1989
A Month of Seven Days, 1987
The Cobweb Christmas, 1982
Piskies, Spriggans, and Other Magical Beings, 1980

Other books you might like:
Sarah Ellis, *Next-Door Neighbors*, 1989
    Her family's move to a new town in Canada leaves shy, Peggy feeling lonely and uncomfortable, until she befriends the unconventional George.
Phyllis Green, *Mildred Murphy, How Does Your Garden Grow?*, 1977
    Her loneliness disappears when Mildred befriends a secretive woman living in a condemned garage.
Diane Johnston Hamm, *Second Family*, 1992
    A lonely senior citizen, shares his Seattle home with a recently divorced mother and her son, Rodney, who is having problems adjusting to the move.
Jill Paton Walsh, *Gaffer Sampson's Luck*, 1984
    James's difficulty in adjusting to a new school and life is further complicated by the request of an elderly neighbor to find his lucky piece.
Gail Rock, *A Dream for Addie*, 1975
    Despite their age difference, Addie discovers she has something in common with the actress who is otherwise friendless in her old hometown.

369

Eleanor Clymer

The Get-Away Car (New York: Dutton, 1978)

Age range: Grades 3-6

Subject(s): Runaways; Grandparents

Major character(s): Maggie, Preteen, Runaway

Time period(s): 1970s

Locale(s): United States

What the book is about: A young girl's grandmother has a knack for helping people with their problems while solving her own at the same time. When Aunt Rhubarb tries to send Grandma to a nursing home, Maggie and Grandma decide to run away and there are others who want to run away with them.

Where it's reviewed:
Center for Children's Books Bulletin, February 1979, page 97
Kirkus Reviews, September 15, 1978, page 1016

Awards the book has won:
Sequoyah Children's Book Award 1981

Other books by the author:
My Mother Is the Smartest Woman in the World, 1984
Horatio Solves a Mystery, 1980
A Search for Bad Mice, 1980
Leave Horatio Alone, 1974

Other books you might like:
Lucille Clifton, *The Lucky Stone*, 1979
    This series of stories is tied together by a lucky stone and the love between a great grandmother and her great granddaughter.
Hadley Irwin, *What about Grandma?*, 1982

Rhys realizes that "part of me would die with Grandma but part of her would live in me," as she deepens her understanding of mothers and daughters.

Judy Frank Mearian, *Someone Slightly Different*, 1980
Mary Martha's grandmother teachers her that a loving family need not be a traditional one as Marty grows in self-confidence and understanding.

Robert Somerlott, *Blaze*, 1981
Runaway David finds that his grandfather and his dog are all starved for affection and they help each other create a loving home together.

Elizabeth Winthrop, *Marathon Miranda*, 1979
Miranda refuses to allow her asthma to limit her as she confronts and overcomes her fear of failure.

370

Eleanor Clymer

Illustrator: Ted Lewin

The Horse in the Attic (New York: Bradbury, 1983)

Age range: Grades 4-6

Subject(s): Animals/Horses; Moving, Household; Artists and Art

Major character(s): Caroline Keating, Preteen; Betsy Brownell, Friend; Ssprite, Horse

Time period(s): 1980s

Locale(s): New York, New York; Bridgeton

What the book is about: A father shares his love of art and horses with his daughter, Caroline. The family vacations in a village where Caroline takes horseback riding lessons. When they return to the city, they are miserable and miss the rural life. The buy a house and return to Bridgeton, and Caroline looks forward to reliving the previous summer. However, she finds that owning a horse and caring for it full time is a much different matter than just taking lessons. When she finds a painting of a horse in the attic, she and her father attempt to trace the history of the horse and find the artist.

Where it's reviewed:
Booklist, January 15, 1984, page 747
Center for Children's Books Bulletin, December 1983, page 64
Hornbook, October 1983, page 571

Other books by the author:
My Mother Is the Smartest Woman in the World, 1984
Santiago's Silver Mine, 1973
Big Pile of Dirt, 1968
Chipmunk in the Forest, 1965

Other books you might like:
Sophy Burnham, *Buccaneer*, 1977
A young girl defies her father and risks her life in pursuit of her dream to ride a great bay thoroughbred.

Barbara Campbell, *A Girl Called Bob and a Horse Called Yoki*, 1982
In St. Louis during WWII, Bob makes secret plans to save the life of an old horse that pulls the milk delivery wagon.

Sheila Dolan, *The Wishing Bottle*, 1979
Nora never gives up hope for a pony to fill the barn behind her family's home despite the voices of reason that tell her wishing won't make things so.

William Harry Harding, *Alvin's Famous No-Horse*, 1992
With encouragement from his teacher and help from his classmates, Alvin struggles with his efforts to draw a horse for the school art exhibit.

Louise Moeri, *A Horse for X Y Z*, 1977
When a twelve year old girl seizes a chance to ride a spirited horse, her ride becomes more than she expected.

371

Eleanor Clymer

Illustrator: Diane De Groat

Luke Was There (New York: Holt, 1973)

Age range: Grades 4-6

Subject(s): Foster Homes; Runaways

Major character(s): Julius, Child; Luke, Social Worker

Time period(s): 1970s

Locale(s): United States

What the book is about: Julius is afraid of being abandoned. Both his dad and step dad had left home, his mom was hospitalized and he and his brother went to a children's home. When his social worker, Luke, leaves his job, Julius runs away.

Where it's reviewed:
Horn Book, April 1974, page 147
Kirkus Reviews, December 1, 1973, page 1309

Other books by the author:
Leave Horatio Alone, 1974
Take Tarts as Tarts Is Passing, 1974
Chipmunk in the Forest, 1973
Santiago's Silver Mine, 1973

Other books you might like:
R.E. Allen, *Ozzy on the Outside*, 1989
Ozzy's mother's death affects him in many ways, but an unusual young woman he encounters while running away to New Orleans helps him face life again.

Barbara Corcoran, *The Hideaway*, 1987
Running away from a Massachusetts reform school, Tom, aided by his sister, hides from the police until he can clear himself of a drunk driving charge.

Dean Hughes, *Family Picture*, 1989
Feeling unwanted, an eleven year old orphan runs away from his foster home and lives on the streets until he finds a new type of family at a hotel.

Theresa Nelson, *The Beggar's Ride*, 1992
Twelve year old Clare flees an unhappy home life and tries to survive on the streets of Atlantic City with a small gang of homeless kids.

Ruth Thomas, *The Runaways*, 1987
Finding a lot of money and being threatened by their parents for not turning it in, Julia and Nathan flee London for Brighton and the open countryside

372

Eleanor Clymer

My Brother Stevie (New York: Holt, 1967)

Age range: Grades 3-5

Subject(s): Orphans; Teacher-Student Relationships

Major character(s): Annie Jenner, Preteen; Stevie Jenner, Preteen; Miss Stover, Teacher

Time period(s): 1960s

Locale(s): United States

What the book is about: Stevie and Annie live with their grandmother who reluctantly took them in. Annie is relieved when Stevie gets a new teacher who can help her trouble-making little brother.

Where it's reviewed:
Booklist May 1, 1967, page 944
Hornbook, June 1967, page 346
Kirkus Reviews, March 1, 1967, page 268

Other books by the author:
The Big Pile of Dirt, 1968
Horatio, 1968
Chipmunk in the Forest, 1965
The Latchkey Club, 1949

Other books you might like:
Malorie Blackman, *Girl Wonder and the Terrific Twins*, 1991
    The plans that Maxine, the Girl Wonder, and her younger brothers, the Terrific Twins, come up with usually mean trouble for their mother.
Julia Cunningham, *Flight of the Sparrow*, 1980
    After stealing a valuable painting for the band of street urchins who have adopted her, a ten year old orphan must flee Paris.
Ellen Matthews, *The Trouble with Leslie*, 1979
    Despite being in charge of his three year old sister and the house while his mother goes to college, Eric finds the summer isn't wasted.
Jill Paton Walsh, *Matthew and the Sea Singer*, 1993
    Birdy rescues Matthew from his orphan master and discovers he has a voice of priceless beauty that eventually causes his mysterious disappearance.
Marilyn Sachs, *Underdog*, 1985
    Lonely, confused and in need of love in her new life with an aunt and uncle in San Francisco, a twelve year old orphan searches for her lost dog.

373

Belle Coates

Mak (Boston: Houghton Mifflin, 1981)

Age range: Grades 6 and Up

Subject(s): Indians of North America; Orphans; Fear

Major character(s): Makosica "Mike" Mallory, Teenager; Pop Williams, Foster Parent; Chuck Eagle, Scientist (paleontologist)

Time period(s): 1980s

Locale(s): Minnesota

What the book is about: Mak, an orphan who is one-quarter Indian, wants to stay in Montana to search for his "wasic," symbol of personal power. When he finds it, and it turns out to be a fossil, he is torn between his "Indianess" and the prospect of archaeological crews coming, which would benefit the Indians economically. His struggle provides the reader with many insights into the Native Americans' struggle to retain their culture.

Where it's reviewed:
School Library Journal, November 1981, page 102

Other books by the author:
Sign of the Open Hand, 1962
That Colt Fireplug, 1958
Little Maverick Cow, 1957
Barn Cat, 1955

Other books you might like:
Thomas A. Dyer, *The Whipman Is Watching*, 1979
    The struggles of Angie and Cultus, two Native Americans, to find a place in white society without surrendering their own values.
Jamake Highwater, *I Wear the Morning Star*, 1986
    Sitko, growing up in a hostile white world that does not respect his Native American heritage, finds refuge in painting pictures.
Scott O'Dell, *Thunder Rolling in the Mountains*, 1992
    A young Nez Perce girl relates how her people were driven off their land by the U.S. Army.
Pamela F. Service, *Vision Quest*, 1989
    Contact with an Indian artifact sends Kate visions of a restless shaman, and drags her and her friend, Jimmy, to the Nevada of long ago.
Kenneth Thomasma, *Pathki Nana, Kootenai Girl*, 1991
    The story of a Kootenai girl in Montana and her solitary adventure in the mountains to seek her guardian spirit.

374

Elizabeth Coatsworth

Illustrator: Lynd Ward

The Cat Who Went to Heaven (New York: Macmillan, 1930)

Age range: Grades 5-6

Subject(s): Animals/Cats

Major character(s): Good Fortune, Cat

Time period(s): Indeterminate

Locale(s): Japan

What the book is about: An unnamed housekeeper brings a cat into the household of her master, a starving artist. The artist names her Good Fortune and soon the artist is commissioned to paint the death of Buddha to hang in the temple. Good Fortune watches as he includes all the animals in the painting but excludes the cat, which legend says rebelled against the Lord Buddha and is excluded from heaven. As an act of love, the artist paints Good Fortune into the picture. The priest is furious and promises to burn the painting the next day. The artist wakes to shouts and cries the next day, and finds that a miracle has saved the painting and made him famous.

Where it's reviewed:
Children and Their Literature, 1969, page 284
Reading with Children, 1940, page 104

Awards the book has won:
Newbery Medal 1931

Other books by the author:
Jock's Island, 1963

The Sod House, 1954
Daisy, 1973

Other books you might like:
Allen Say, *The Feast of Lanterns*, 1976
    Bozu and Kozo, who live on a Japanese island, steal their uncle's boat and row to the mainland.
Yoshiko Uchida, *Two Foolish Cats*, 1987
    Two quarreling cats seek advice from an old monkey. Easy reading, gr. 2-4.
Hanasaka Jijii, *Old Man Who Made the Trees Bloom*, 1985
    A white dog, Shiro, gives his master the power to make the trees bloom early.
Lloyd Alexander, *Town Cats and Other Tales*, 1977
    Eight tales in which a cat is always the main character. Broad interest, challenging reading.

375

Elizabeth Coatsworth

Illustrator: Krystyna Turska

Marra's World (New York: Greenwillow, 1975)

Age range: Grades 3-5

Subject(s): Islands; Animals/Seals and Sea Lions

Major character(s): Marra, Child; Alison Dunbar, Child; Nerea, Parent (mother)

Time period(s): 1970s

Locale(s): Maine

What the book is about: Marra lives with her dad and an angry grandmother. She is lonely, dreamy, and a slow learner, ridiculed by her classmates. When a new girl comes to the school, Marra's world changes. She and Alison explore the island together, and the Dunbars treat Marra like their own daughter. A boat trip in the fog reveals to Marra who her mother was, and why the family refuses to talk about her.

Where it's reviewed:
Kirkus Reviews, October 1, 1975, page 1129
Publisher's Weekly, August 4, 1975, page 56

Other books by the author:
The Werefox, 1975
All-of-a-Sudden Susan, 1974
The Cat and the Captain, 1974
The Cat Who Went to Heaven, 1958

Other books you might like:
Alec Lea, *To Sunset and Beyond*, 1970
    Recounts the reactions of all those affected when a young boy becomes lost in the fog on a English moor.
Anne Lindbergh, *The Worry Week*, 1985
    Left alone for a week in the family's summer house on a Maine island, Allegra and her two sisters scrounge for food and search for buried treasure.
Colleen O'Shaughnessy McKenna, *Murphy's Island*, 1990
    Collette has to go with her large, often trying family to a small island and start sixth grade as the new kid in school.
Sylvia Peck, *Seal Child*, 1989
    While entranced by the seals that swim off the shore of the Maine island she visits on holidays, Molly befriends an interesting girl.
Ron Roy, *Nightmare Island*, 1981

On their first solo camping trip to Little Island off the coast of Maine, Harley and his brother are engulfed by a fire that starts on an oil slick.

376

Catherine C. Coblentz

Illustrator: Janice Holland

The Blue Cat of Castle Town (New York: McKay, 1949)

Age range: Grades 3-5

Subject(s): Animals/Cats; American Colonies; Fantasy

Major character(s): Thomas Dake, Carpenter; Ebenezer Southmayd, Artisan (pewterer)

Time period(s): Indeterminate Past

Locale(s): Castleton, Vermont, American Colonies

What the book is about: A wandering cat changes the course of a town's early history. Castle Town is a town of yesterday, a town not built to seem like yesterday, a town not restored, but kept in the Bright Enchantment. The Blue Cat's destiny is to find a friendly hearth and inspire its owner with the beauty and wisdom of the river's song.

Other books you might like:
Marguerite Henry, *Justin Morgan Had a Horse*, 1954
    An work horse raised in Vermont and known as "Little Bub" becomes the sire of a famous American breed and takes the name of his owner, Justin Morgan.
Stewart Hall Holbrook, *America's Ethan Allen*, 1949
    A biography of the patriot and soldier who led the Green Mountain Boys in the capture of Fort Ticonderoga from the British in 1775.
Robert Newton Peck, *Hang for Treason*, 1976
    A Vermont youth becomes involved with Ethan Allen and the Green Mountain Boys despite his father's Tory leanings in the early days of the Revolution.
Seymour Reit, *Guns for General Washington*, 1990
    Frustrated with life Washington's army, Will Knox takes charge of moving 183 cannons from Fort Ticonderoga to Boston in the dead of winter.
Susan Fromberg Schaeffer, *The Dragons of North Chittendon*, 1986
    Follows the adventures of Arthur, a young dragon living in Vermont, as he grows up, marries, becomes leader of his tribe, and deals with humans.

377

Eleanor Coerr, Author/Illustrator

Illustrator: Deborah Kogan Ray

Chang's Paper Pony (New York: Harper, 1988)

Age range: Grades 1-2

Series: I Can Read Book

Subject(s): Chinese Americans; Miners and Mining; Animals/Horses

Major character(s): Chang, Child; Big Pete, Miner

Time period(s): 1850s

Locale(s): San Francisco, California

What the book is about: In San Francisco during the 1850s gold rush, Chang, son of Chinese immigrants, wants a pony but cannot afford one until his friend, Big Pete, finds a solution.

Where it's reviewed:
Kirkus Reviews, June 1, 1988, page 825
Booklist, July 1988, page 1843
Publishers Weekly, June 24, 1988, page 112

Other books by the author:
Mieko and the Fifth Treasure, 1993
The Josephina Story Quilt, 1986
The Bell Ringer and the Pirates, 1983
The Big Balloon Race, 1981

Other books you might like:
Crosby Bonsall, *The Case of the Hungry Stranger*, 1992
    Wizard and his friends are clueless when they are sent on the trail of a blueberry pie thief. (I Can Read Book)
Doug Cushman, *Aunt Eater's Mystery Vacation*, 1992
    A mystery loving anteater has a chance to solve several mysteries during her vacation at the Hotel Bathwater. (I Can Read Book)
Edith Thacher Hurd, *Johnny Lion's Bad Day*, 1970
    Johnny has a bad cold and the medicine he took as well as the dreams he had were terrible. (I Can Read Book)
Anola Pickett, *Old Enough for Magic*, 1989
    Peter's sister doesn't think he is old enough to own a magic set, but when she turns herself into a frog, it is Peter who figures how to get her back.
Paul Yee, *Tales From Gold Mountain: Stories of the Chinese in the new World*, 1989
    Eight stories reflecting the optimism of the Chinese who overcame prejusice and adversity to build a unique place for themselves in North America.

378

Eleanor Coerr

Illustrator: Ronald Himler

Sadako and the Thousand Paper Cranes (New York: Putnam, 1977)

Age range: Grades 3-5

Subject(s): Nuclear Warfare; Cancer

Major character(s): Sadako Sasaki, Child

Time period(s): 1950s

Locale(s): Hiroshima, Japan

What the book is about: Once a wonderful runner, Sadako develops leukemia at age eleven, af aftereffect of the bombing of Hiroshima. Legend says that she will get well if she makes 1000 paper cranes, but she only lives long enough to make 644. After her death, her classmates make the rest of the cranes.

Where it's reviewed:
Horn Book, August 1977, page 438
Kirkus Reviews, March 5, 1977, page 284
Booklist, May 1, 1977, page 1348

Other books by the author:
Chang's Paper Pony, 1988
The Big Balloon Race, 1981
Jane Goodall, 1977

Biography of a Kangaroo, 1976

Other books you might like:
Molly Bang, *The Paper Crane*, 1985
    A mysterious man enters a restaurant and pays for his dinner with a paper crane that magically comes alive and dances.
Karl Bruckner, *The Day of the Bomb*, 1962
    The effects of war on Japan and the world are seen through the experiences of one family that survives the bombing of Hiroshima.
Gary Soto, *Pacific Crossing*, 1992
    Lincoln Mendoza spends a summer with a host family in Japan, encountering new experiences and making new friends.
Hiroyuki Takahashi, *The Foxes of Chironupp Island*, 1976
    The old couple who visits the island every summer befriends a tiny fox cub. All their lives change when war comes to Japan.
Bill Wallace, *The Christmas Spurs*, 1990
    A small private miracle one Christmas helps Nick accept the fate of his younger brother, Jimmy, who is dying of leukemia.

379

Barbara Cohen

213 Valentines (New York: Holt/Redfeather, 1991)

Age range: Grades 3-4

Subject(s): Gifted Children; African Americans; Holidays

Major character(s): Wade Thompson, Child (gifted)

Time period(s): 1990s

Locale(s): United States

What the book is about: Wade is not thrilled with the idea of leaving Woodlawn School to attend a school for gifted children. Dink, a nerd from Woodlawn is going too. Wade is not pleased, but at least there will be two new black kids instead of one. When he has trouble adjusting, he plans to send himself 213 valentines signed by celebrities.

Where it's reviewed:
Booklist, September 1, 1991, page 52
Kirkus Reviews, August 1, 1991, page 1008

Other books by the author:
The Long Way Home, 1990
First Fast, 1987
Molly's Pilgrim, 1983
The Carp in the Bathtub, 1972

Other books you might like:
Charlotte Herman, *Max Malone, Superstar*, 1992
    Max loses a part in a commercial and decides his job will be to manage the career of his friend, Austin.
Marilyn Levinson, *Fourth-Grade Four*, 1989
    Fourth grader Alex refuses to wear his eyeglasses anywhere but home.
Stephen Manes, *Monstra vs. Irving*, 1989
    Irving plans to scare his sister with a magic potion, but when she drinks it, she becomes a monster.
Ellen Kindt McKenzie, *Stargone John*, 1990
    Six year old John has a terrible school experience until a blind, retired teacher reaches out to him.
Dian Curtis Regan, *The Class with the Summer Birthdays*, 1991

Brittany's third grade class never gets to celebrate birthdays because they were all born in the summer.

380

Barbara Cohen

Benny (New York: Lothrop, 1977)

Age range: Grades 4-6

Subject(s): Jews

Major character(s): Benny Rifkind, Child; Arnulf, Refugee

Time period(s): 1930s (1939)

Locale(s): New Jersey

What the book is about: Benny loves to play baseball and wants to go to the World's Fair, but he has to take care of the family store while his mother recovers from surgery. Benny shows compassion for the German refugee, Arnulf, who nobody wants.

Where it's reviewed:
Kirkus Reviews, April 1, 1977, page 350
School Library Journal, September 1977, page 124

Other books by the author:
The Secret Grove, 1985
Yussel's Prayer, 1981
The Carp in the Bathtub, 1977
Bitter Herbs and Honey, 1976

Other books you might like:
Barbara Cohen, *The Christmas Revolution*, 1987
   Emily is forced to think about her Jewish heritage when the new boy, an Orthodox Jew, refuses to take part in school Christmas celebrations.
Charlotte Herman, *The Difference of Ari Stein*, 1976
   After he moves to Brooklyn, Ari decides he can meet new and different friends while keeping his personal beliefs.
Pamela Melnikoff, *Plots and Players*, 1988
   Robin, Philip and Frances are exiled Portuguese Jews secretly practicing their faith in intolerant 16th century London.
Eileen Bluestone Sherman, *Independence Avenue*, 1990
   Elias, a 14 year old Russian immigrant, arrives alone in Kansas City in 1907 and must find new family and friends while worrying about those at home.
Jane Yolen, *The Devil's Arithmetic*, 1988
   Hannah resents the traditions of her Jewish heritage until time travel places her in the middle of a small Jewish village in Nazi occupied Poland.

381

Barbara Cohen

Illustrator: Joan Helpern

The Carp in the Bathtub (New York: Lothrop, 1972)

Age range: Grades 3-4

Subject(s): Family Life; Jews; Holidays

Major character(s): Leah, Child; Harvey, Child; Joe, Fish

Time period(s): 1940s

Locale(s): Flatbush, New York

What the book is about: Two Jewish children decide that the carp in the bathtub should be rescued before it becomes Passover gefilte fish.

Where it's reviewed:
Booklist, November 1, 1972, page 242
Center for Children's Books Bulletin, December 1972, page 54
Kirkus Reviews, July 15, 1972, page 801

Other books by the author:
213 Valentines, 1991
First Fast, 1987
Gooseberries to Oranges, 1982
Benny, 1977

Other books you might like:
Cynthia Jameson, *The Clay Pot Boy*, 1973
   Wanting a son, the old man and woman make a clay pot boy who comes to life and begins eating everything in sight.
Deborah Miller, *Only Nine Chairs*, 1982
   Speculates in rhyme how to handle nineteen guests at a Seder dinner when there are only nine chairs.
F.N. Monjo, *The Secret of Sachem's Tree*, 1972
   The Wadsworth children abandon plans for Halloween mischief to help prevent the King's representative from taking away Connecticut Colony's charter.
Allen Say, *Once Under the Cherry Blossom Tree*, 1974
   A cherry tree growing from the top of the wicked landlord's head is the beginning of his misfortunes and a better life for the villagers.
Marjorie Weinman Sharmat, *Morris Brookside, a Dog*, 1973
   Mr. and Mrs. Brookside worry about Morris and the dog's choice of friends.

382

Barbara Cohen

Illustrator: Michael J. Derany

Molly's Pilgrim (New York: Lothrop, 1983)

Age range: Grades 2-4

Subject(s): Jews; Holidays; Schools

Major character(s): Molly, Child, Immigrant; Miss Stickley, Teacher

Time period(s): 1890s

Locale(s): Winter Hill

What the book is about: The other girls make fun of Molly and she wants to return to Russia. Molly thinks she will never belong, until the day she brings Mama's Pilgrim doll to school for the class Thanksgiving project. The children think it doesn't fit at all, but Miss Stickley explains that it is exactly the meaning of pilgrim.

Where it's reviewed:
Booklist, October 1, 1983, page 261
Children's Book Review Service, October 1983, page 15
Center for Children's Books Bulletin, February 1984, page 104

Other books by the author:
Yussel's Prayer, 1983
King of the Seventh Grade, 1982
Thank You, Jackie Robinson, 1974
The Carp in the Bathtub, 1972

Other books you might like:
Roslyn Bresnick-Perry, *Leaving for America*, 1992
The author recalls her early days in a small Jewish town in western Russia and the last days before she and her mother join her father in the U.S.
Brett Harvey, *Growing Up on Eldridge Street*, 1987
Becky, whose Jewish family has emigrated from Russia to avoid persecution, finds growing up in New York City in 1910 a vivid and exciting experience.
Arthur A. Levine, *All the Lights in the Night*, 1991
Moses and his little brother, Benjamin, find a way to celebrate Hanukkah during their dangerous emigration to Palestine.
Maira Meir, *Aline: A Russian Girl Comes to Israel*, 1982
A young girl who has recently come to Israel from Russia with her family misses her old home and feels out of place in her new country.
Maxine Schur, *Schnook the Peddler*, 1985
A young boy in turn of the century Russia finds that looks are often deceiving after he steals then tries to return a dreidel to the peddler, Schnook.

383

Barbara Cohen

Illustrator: Diane De Groat

The Orphan Game (New York: Lothrop, 1988)

Age range: Grades 4-6

Subject(s): Cousins; Summer

Major character(s): Sally Berg, Twin; Emily Berg, Twin; Miranda, Child (Sally and Emily's cousin)

Time period(s): 1980s

Locale(s): Long Beach Island, New Jersey

What the book is about: Twins Sally and Emily must put up with stuck-up cousin Miranda during a summer at the Jersey shore. In fact, this may be the worst summer of Sally's life. A lot of disasters can happen in a month.

Where it's reviewed:
Booklist, June 15, 1988, page 1733
Kirkus Reviews, May 1, 1988, page 690
School Library Journal, August 1988, page 92

Other books by the author:
The Christmas Revolution, 1987
People Like Us, 1987
Molly's Pilgrim, 1986
King of the Seventh Grade, 1982

Other books you might like:
Avi, *A Place Called Ugly*, 1981
At the end of the summer, Owen refuses to leave the house which has been his family's summer home for ten years, and is scheduled for demolition.
Mary Haynes, *Catch the Sea*, 1989
While her artist father is away trying to arrange an exhibit, Lily stays at the beach cottage and discovers her own artistic talents.
Shirley Hughes, *Here Comes Charlie Moon*, 1980
Charlie Moon spends the summer at the beach with his aunt, who owns a novelty shop and his cousin Ariadne, who is not his favorite person.

Karin N. Mango, *Just for the Summer*, 1990
Working as a lifeguard at a New Hampshire beach, Jenny finds herself falling in love with a reclusive boy tormented by the death of his father.
Ann M. Martin, *Eleven Kids, One Summer*, 1991
Adventures of a family with eleven children during the summer on the beach at Fire Island.

384

Barbara Cohen

Illustrator: Richard Cuffari

Thank You, Jackie Robinson (New York: Lothrop, 1974)

Age range: Grades 4-6

Subject(s): Sports/Baseball; Friendship

Major character(s): Sam, Child; Davy, Cook

Time period(s): 1950s

Locale(s): New York, New York (Brooklyn)

What the book is about: Sam loves baseball, but has never been to a real game until sixty year old Davy takes him to Ebbet's Field to see the Brooklyn Dodgers. They talk about race relations and the problems they have when they travel to different ball parks.

Where it's reviewed:
Center for Children's Books Bulletin, September 1974, page 31
Kirkus Reviews, April 15, 1974, page 423

Other books by the author:
The Secret Grove, 1985
Molly's Pilgrim, 1983
Yussel's Prayer, 1981
The Carp in the Bathtub, 1972

Other books you might like:
Kay Brown, *Willy's Summer Dream*, 1989
Willy, slow in school and the object of neighborhood ridicule, develops self-confidence while being tutored by an older girl.
Vaunda Micheaux Nelson, *Mayfield Crossing*, 1993
Black students from the closed Mayfield Crossing school encounter prejudice for the first time at their new schools. Only baseball unites everyone.
Deborah Savage, *A Stranger Calls Me Home*, 1992
Paul, Simon, and Fiona, three teens living in New Zealand, become involved in a complex friendship as they search for the truth of their related pasts
Richard Scott, *Jackie Robinson*, 1987
Traces the life of the athlete who broke the color barrier in major league baseball when he joined the Brooklyn Dodgers in 1947.
Mildred D. Taylor, *Mississippi Bridge*, 1990
During a heavy rainstorm in 1930s rural Mississippi, a white boy sees a bus driver throw all the blacks off a bus to make room for white riders.

385

Miriam Cohen

Illustrator: Lillian Hoban

When Will I Read? (New York: Greenwillow, 1977)

Age range: Grades 1-2

Subject(s): Literacy; Schools

Major character(s): Jim, Child

Time period(s): 1970s

Locale(s): United States

What the book is about: Jim, a first grader, impatient to begin reading, doesn't realize there is more to reading than just books, but he works at learning to read and shares his joy when he is successful.

Where it's reviewed:
Center for Children's Books Bulletin, November 1977, page 44
Kirkus Reviews, August 15, 1977, page 845
School Library Journal, November 1977, page 44

Other books by the author:
It's George, 1988
Liar, Liar, Pants on Fire!, 1985
Jim's Dog Muffins, 1984
Jim Meets the Thing, 1981

Other books you might like:
Lorraine Aseltine, *First Grade Can Wait*, 1988
  Luke does not feel ready to move on from kindergarten to first grade. He is relieved when his parents and teacher decide he can stay in kindergarten.
Lillian Hoban, *Arthur's Prize Reader*, 1978
  Although Arthur loses the Super Chimp Club contest, his pupil, his sister Violet, wins the first grade reading competition and a prize for them both.
Dorothy Fay Richards, *Thomas James the Second and Friends*, 1977
  A first grader anticipates meeting new friends in books when he starts school and learns to read.
Muriel Stanek, *My Mom Can't Read*, 1986
  When Tina asks her mom for help with reading, she discovers her mother can't read. A concerned teacher helps them to find tutors to learn together.
Patty Wolcott, *Where Did that Naughty Little Hamster Go?*, 1974
  A group of first graders search the classroom for their missing hamster.

⌐386¬

Peter Zachary Cohen

Illustrator: Alan Moyler

Foal Creek (New York: Atheneum, 1972)

Age range: Grades 5-8

Subject(s): Camps and Camping; Fishing; Drugs

Major character(s): Gil Aravon, Teenager; Frank Aravon, Student

Time period(s): 1970s

Locale(s): United States

What the book is about: Two brothers go on a fishing trip. One goes to fish, the other to collect $25,000 worth of marijuana he has harvested and hidden. The county sheriff has the barn staked out, and on the night of a violent storm, many paths cross and many people are changed.

Where it's reviewed:
Horn Book, April 1973, page 141
Kirkus Reviews, August 1, 1972, page 864

Awards the book has won:
Friends of American Writers Juvenile Book Merit Award 1973

Other books by the author:
Deadly Game at Stony Creek, 1978
Bee, 1975
Bull in the Forest, 1969
Muskie Hook, 1969

Other books you might like:
Gary L. Blackwood, *Wild Timothy*, 1986
  Timothy reluctantly goes camping with his father, and when he becomes lost, discovers he can survive on his own.
Ken Brynildsen, *School's Out*, 1982
  Four friends have an eventful summer, including a gang encounter, construction in their beloved woods, and an eventful fishing trip.
Matt Christopher, *Tackle Without a Team*, 1989
  Unjustly dismissed from the football team for drug possession, Scott must clear himself by finding out who planted marijuana in his gym bag.
Thomas J. Dygard, *Wilderness Peril*, 1985
  Two teenage boys camping in the Minnesota woods encounter a desperate airplane hijacker attempting to escape with $750,000.
Gary Paulsen, *Canyons*, 1990
  Finding a skull on a camping trip in the canyons outside El Paso, Texas, Brennan becomes involved with the fate of a young Apache Indian.

⌐387¬

Joanna Cole

Illustrator: Dirk Zimmer

Bony-legs (New York: Four Winds, 1983)

Age range: Grades 2-4

Subject(s): Halloween; Folk Tales; Witches and Witchcraft

Major character(s): Sasha, Child; Bony-Legs, Witch

Time period(s): Indeterminate

Locale(s): Union of Soviet Socialist Republics

What the book is about: Sasha's aunt sends her on an errand to borrow a needle and thread. The errand becomes an adventure when Sasha is confronted by a hungry witch. Her only defense is a magical mirror and comb, which she earned through her kindness. Based on a Baba Yaga tale from Afanas'ev's *Russian Fairy Tales*.

Where it's reviewed:
Horn Book, February 1984, page 47
School Library Journal, December 1983, page 79

Other books by the author:
Don't Tell the Whole World, 1990
Mixed-Up Magic, 1987
Scary Book, 1991
Secret Box, 1971

Other books you might like:
Jane Werner Watson, *Which Is the Witch*, 1979
   Jenny dresses as a witch for Halloween but is terrified when a real witch switches places with her.
Ida DeLage, *Old Witch's Party*, 1976
   An old witch invites children to a "real" Halloween party.
Patricia Coombs, *Dorrie and the Halloween Plot*, 1976
   Dorrie foils the plan of Halloween demons and is rewarded by flying lessons.
Miriam Young, *Witch Mobile*, 1969
   Four little witches are a toy shop mobile during the day but all that changes at night.
Carolyn Haywood, *Halloween Treats*, 1981
   A collection of short stories for Halloween: for reading aloud and independent readers.

388

Joanna Cole

Illustrator: Donald Carrick

Doctor Change (New York: Morrow, 1986)

Age range: Grades 2-4

Subject(s): Fantasy

Major character(s): Tom, Apprentice, Hero; Kate, Child; Doctor Change, Wizard (Shape)

Time period(s): 1900s

Locale(s): Earth

What the book is about: Young Tom discovers that Doctor Change can turn himself into a variety of objects. He learns the man's secret and confronts the evil wizard. With the help of Kate, a girl he has helped before, Tom fools Doctor Change out of a fortune.

Where it's reviewed:
Center for Children's Books Bulletin, October 1986, page 46
School Library Journal, October 1986, page 158

Other books by the author:
Don't Tell the Whole World!, 1990
Ready, Set, Read! A Beginning Reader's Treasury, 1990
The Magic School Bus: Inside the Earth, 1987
Secret Box, 1971

Other books you might like:
Brian Ball, *The Quest for Queenie*, 1988
   Harry and Jill are chosen by a talking sword to rescue a damsel from the Bad Wizard, but the damsel is Harry's spaniel who doesn't want to be rescued.
Elizabeth Starr Hill, *Ever-After Island*, 1977
   Two children accompany their father to a remote island which they discover to be inhabited by elves, mermaids, a wizard, and other magical creatures.
Maxine Kumin, *The Wizard's Tears*, 1975
   The new wizard tries to solve all the town's problems but carelessness with his own magic tears creates a tragedy instead.
Victor Osborne, *Moondream*, 1988
   When his cousin Katy is kidnapped by a Grabbly, Rupert enlists the help of flying pirates and a badger to rescue her from the wizard in Castle Dread.
Jane Yolen, *Wizard's Hall*, 1991

A young apprentice wizard saves the wizard's training hall by trusting and believing in himself.

389

Joanna Cole

The Magic School Bus, Lost in the Solar System (New York: Scholastic, 1990)

Age range: Grades 2-6

Subject(s): Astronomy; Space Exploration

Major character(s): Ms. Frizzle, Teacher

Time period(s): 1990s

Locale(s): Outer Space

What the book is about: Ms. Frizzle and her class blast-off in their famous school bus. They share a zany exploration of space and learn a lesson in astronomy and the wonders of the universe. Non-fiction but just as much fun as good fiction.

Where it's reviewed:
Book World, October 14, 1990, page 10
School Library Journal, August 1990, page 136

Other books by the author:
The Magic School Bus: Inside the Human Body, 1989
The Magic School Bus: Inside the Earth, 1987
The Magic School Bus at the Water Works, 1986

Other books you might like:
Bruce Coville, *Space Brat*, 1992
   The piece of eggshell that got stuck behind his ear the day he was hatched made Blork cry, but baby Splatoons aren't supposed to cry.
Maureen George, *The Neighbor From Outer Space*, 1992
   Katie, Chrissy, Maddie and Brian accidentally discover that their neighbor, Mr. Dugan, is an alien from outer space.
Gery Green, *Let Me Off This Spaceship!*, 1991
   Tod and Billy are captured by alien creatures. They make as much trouble as possible to convince the spaceship captain take them back to Earth.
Marjorie Weinman Sharmat, *School Bus Cat*, 1990
   When Charlie finds a wet cat hiding under her seat in the school bus, she and Max decide to find it a home.
Nick Sullivan, *The Seventh Princess*, 1983
   When her school bus becomes a princess's carriage, Jennifer finds herself in a land where she is Princess Miranda, the next victim of an evil Duke.

390

Joanna Cole

Illustrator: Marylin Hafner

The Missing Tooth (New York: Random, 1989)

Age range: Grades 1-2

Subject(s): Friendship

Major character(s): Arlo, Child; Robby, Child

Time period(s): 1980s

Locale(s): United States

What the book is about: Best friends Arlo and Robby are almost identical in what they wear, what they like, and even where they have teeth missing, but when Robby insists on betting who is going to lose the next tooth, their friendship is endangered.

Where it's reviewed:
Booklist, March 1, 1989, page 1198
School Library Journal, May 1989, page 82

Other books by the author:
Big Goof and Little Goof, 1989
Mixed-Up Magic, 1987
Norma Jean, Jumping Bean, 1987
Aren't You Forgetting Something, Fiona?, 1983

Other books you might like:
Tom Birdseye, *Airmail to the Moon*, 1988
　　When the tooth that she was saving for the tooth fairy disappears, Ora Mae sets out to find the thief and send him "airmail to the Moon."
Carol Carrick, *Norman Fools the Tooth Fairy*,
　　When Norman fools the tooth fairy by slipping her a fake tooth, he is surprised by a visit from the tooth monster.
Bernice Chardiet, *Martin and the Tooth Fairy*, 1991
　　When Martin receives more money from the Tooth Fairy than his friends, he offers to put their teeth under his pillow for a percentage of the profits.
Steven Kroll, *Loose Tooth*, 1984
　　Jealous when his brother's loose tooth gets him all the attention, Flapper decides to steal the tooth before the Tooth Fairy can come.
Robin Pulver, *The Holiday Handwriting School*, 1991
　　With Mrs. Holiday's help, the Easter Bunny, Santa Claus and the Tooth Fairy learn to improve the notes they leave children after their visits.

| 391 |

Sheila R. Cole

Illustrator: Paul Raynor

Meaning Well (New York: Watts, 1974)

Age range: Grades 5 and Up

Subject(s): Friendship; Alcoholism; Deafness

Major character(s): Susan, Preteen; Mrs. Winter, Teacher

Time period(s): 1970s

Locale(s): North Valley, California

What the book is about: A sixth grader learns the meaning of friendship too late to help a classmate who desperately needs a friend. Lisa learns a painful lesson; just to mean well means nothing, it's the doing that counts.

Where it's reviewed:
Center for Children's Books Bulletin, September 1974, p 3
Kirkus Reviews, February 1, 1974, page 109

Awards the book has won:
Golden Kite Honor Book 1974

Other books you might like:
Barthe DeClements, *No Place for Me*, 1987
　　Copper goes from one relative to another while her mom is in rehab, drying out.
N.B. Dorman, *Laughter in the Background*, 1980

Marcie decides she can't take her mom's drinking any more, after years of putting up with it.
Nancy Smiler Levinson, *Annie's World*, 1990
　　Annie, who has been nearly deaf since she was seven, must leave her school and be mainstreamed into a public high school.
Susan Richards Shreve, *The Gift of the Girl Who Couldn't Hear*, 1991
　　Two friends, one of whom is deaf, help each other when tryouts are held for the school production of "Annie."
Anne Snyder, *First Step*, 1975
　　A high school girl comes to understand her mother's problem and how to control its effect on her life.

| 392 |

James Lincoln Collier

My Brother Sam Is Dead (New York: Four Winds, 1974)

Age range: Grades 5-8

Subject(s): Brothers; Revolutionary War

Major character(s): Tim Meeker, Teenager; Sam Meeker, Teenager

Time period(s): 1770s (1775)

Locale(s): Redding, Connecticut, American Colonies

What the book is about: General Putnam executes Tim's brother, Sam, as a cattle thief. The charge is untrue. Tim is more concerned about his family's problems during wartime than which side is right or wrong.

Where it's reviewed:
Booklist, October 15, 1974, page 241
Kirkus Reviews, September 1, 1974, page 948

Awards the book has won:
Newbery Honor 1975
Jane Addams Children's Book Award, Honor Book 1975

Other books by the author:
Planet out of the Past, 1982
Winter Hero, 1978
The Bloody Country, 1976
Rich and Famous, 1975

Other books you might like:
John Beatty, *Who Comes to King's Mountain*, 1975
　　Explores the divided loyalties of Scottish southerners during the American Revolution.
Deborah H. DeFord, *An Enemy Among Them*, 1987
　　A young Hessian soldier questions his loyalty to his king after fighting with the British in America during the Revolutionary War.
Dorothea Jensen, *The Riddle of Penncroft Farm*, 1989
　　Lars Olafson moves to a farm near Valley Forge and meets the ghost of an 18th century ancestor who tells of his life during the American Revolution.
Ruth Nulton Moore, *Distant Thunder*, 1991
　　In the Moravian community of Bethlehem, Pennsylvania during the American Revolution, Kate and friends show how a peaceful people can help in wartime.
Seymour Reit, *Guns for General Washington*, 1990
　　Under siege in George Washington's army, Will Knox and his brother, Colonel Henry Knox, try moving cannon from Fort Ticonderoga to Boston in winter.

393

James Lincoln Collier

Planet out of the Past (New York: Macmillan, 1983)

Age range: Grades 5-8

Subject(s): Fantasy; Man, Prehistoric; Science Fiction

Major character(s): Char, Researcher (assistant); Weddy Jones, Explorer; Nuell Joher, Explorer

Time period(s): Indeterminate

Locale(s): Pleiste, Planet—Imaginary

What the book is about: Young people search for hominids on another planet similar to Earth, and experience all the dangers of prehistoric times on Earth - mastodons, jaguars and even primitive inhabitants.

Where it's reviewed:
Booklist, February 1, 1984, page 812
Kirkus Reviews, November 1, 1983, page J201
School Library Journal, January 1984, page 73

Other books by the author:
Give Dad My Best, 1976
Rich and Famous, 1975
My Brother Sam Is Dead, 1974
The Teddy Bear Habit, 1967

Other books you might like:
Piers Anthony, Balook, 1990
    A friendly prehistoric rhinoceros is genetically recreated in the near future.
Peter Dickinson, A Bone from a Dry Sea, 1992
    In two parallel stories, a member of a tribe advances the lot of her people, and a girl is present on a dig in Africa when fossil remains are found.
Monica Hughes, The Guardian of Isis, 1982
    Settlers on the planet Isis, under an absolute ruler, have lost all the technology of their ancestors and revert back to a primitive society.
Madeleine L'Engle, A Swiftly Tilting Planet, 1978
    The youngest of the Murry children must travel through time and space in a battle against an evil dictator who would destroy the entire universe.
Thomas Millstead, Cave of the Moving Shadows, 1979
    A boy living in Cro-Magnon times must choose between his training in sorcery and his desire to be a hunter.

394

Carlo Collodi (Pseudonym of Carlo Lorenzini)

The Adventures of Pinocchio (New York: Macmillan, 1925)

Age range: Grades 4-6

Subject(s): Adventure and Adventurers; Fantasy

Major character(s): Mastro "Cherry" Antonio, Carpenter; Geppetto Polendina, Artisan (woodcarver); Pinocchio, Toy (puppet)

Time period(s): Indeterminate Past

Locale(s): Europe

What the book is about: A classic fantasy, originally published in Italy in 1883. A woodcarver makes a puppet from a piece of talking wood. The puppet, Pinocchio, an walk and

talk like a real boy, but he repeatedly lies and disobeys his "father", which gets him into no end of trouble. Eventually he saves his father's like and is rewarded by a guardian fairy who turns him into a real boy. This original story is *not* the tidy, sentimentalized version on the 1940 Walt Disney film.

Where it's reviewed:
Booklist, February 15, 1984, page 856
Center for Children's Books Bulletin, February 1984, page 105
Publisher's Weekly, December 9, 1983, page 50

Other books you might like:
Carol Carrick, The Empty Squirrel, 1981
    In three episodes Paul catches a fish for dinner, makes a puppet from an abandoned stuffed animal, and brings home a turtle for a pet.
Elizabeth Cleaver, Petrouchka, 1979
    The story of the ballet, based on a Russian folk tale, in which a puppet with a soul tries to win the love of a ballerina during a Shrovetide fair.
Linda Gondosch, The Monsters of Marble Avenue, 1988
    One mishap after another dogs Luke's attempt to put on a puppet show.
Kathryn Lasky, Puppeteer, 1985
    Text and photos follow Paul Vincent Davis, a professional hand puppeteer, as he mounts a production of Aladdin and His Wonderful Lamp.
Katherine Paterson, The Master Puppeteer, 1975
    A boy describes the poverty and discontent of 18th century Osaka and the world of puppeteers in which he lives.

395

Hila Colman

Nobody Has to Be a Kid Forever (New York: Crown, 1976)

Age range: Grades 4-6

Subject(s): Family Life; Abandonment

Major character(s): Sarah Grinell, Teenager; Millie, Teen-ager

Time period(s): 1970s

Locale(s): United States (New England)

What the book is about: Sarah is celebrating her thirteenth birthday, but it is anything but happy. Her mother has left the family, and Sarah feels unloved and unwanted. She is angry at her father for being so complacent and hopeless. She has so many problems, she is sure she isn't a kid anymore.

Where it's reviewed:
Kirkus Reviews, February 1, 1976, page 138
School Library Journal, April 1976, page 72

Awards the book has won:
Garden State Children's Book Award 1979

Other books by the author:
Rich and Famous Like My Mom, 1988
The Amazing Miss Laura, 1976
Diary of a Frantic Kid Sister, 1973

Other books you might like:
Betsy Byars, The Two-Thousand Pound Goldfish, 1987
    Abandoned by a mother who is hiding from the FBI, Warren escapes into horror movies.

Graham Salisbury, *Blue Skin of the Sea*, 1992
  Growing up in Hawaii, Sonny tries to come to terms with his feelings for his fisherman father and the sea that dominates his life.
Doris Buchanan Smith, *Dreams and Drummers*, 1978
  Growing up is not so easy for a girl in a small Georgia town.
Julie Thayer, *The Lamb Who Went to Paris*, 1980
  Abandoned by its mother at birth, a lamb is rescued by three children and taken to live in their Paris apartment.
Jean Thesman, *The Rain Catchers*, 1991
  Growing up in a house full of women, Grayling learns to deal with death, love and the unanswered questions raised by her widowed mother's abandonment.

396

Hila Colman

The Secret Life of Harold the Birdwatcher (New York: Crowell, 1978)

Age range: Grades 3-4

Subject(s): Conduct of Life; Hero

Major character(s): Harold, Child

Time period(s): 1970s

Locale(s): United States

What the book is about: Nine year old Harold watches birds and longs to be a hero. Unfortunately, Harold is the one who has to be rescued from the river on a class field trip. He does protect the ducks from a hunter and becomes friends with the boy who rescued him.

Where it's reviewed:
Kirkus Reviews, April 1, 1978, page 372
School Library Journal, September 1978, page 132

Other books by the author:
Rich and Famous Like My Mom, 1988
Tell Me No Lies, 1978
Sometimes I Don't Love My Mother, 1977

Other books you might like:
Matt Christopher, *The Hit-Away Kid*, 1988
  Barry McGee, hit-away batter for the Mudders, likes to win so much he tends to bend the rules.
Esther Hautzig, *Riches*, 1992
  After following the advice of the wisest rabbi in the area, a rich storekeeper discovers that giving of himself is better than merely giving money.
Florence Parry Heide, *Fables You Shouldn't Pay Any Attention To*, 1978
  Short stories highlighting carelessness, greed, lying, selfishness and other questionable qualities.
David Pownall, *The Bunch From Bananas*, 1980
  Crime and catastrophe are thwarted in the town of Santa Margarita del Banana by young Bernard who has taken up crime fighting and heroism as hobbies.
L.B. Taylor, *Rescue! True Stories of Heroism*, 1978
  Stories of the teens who were awarded the Carnegie Hero Fund Commission medal of honor for their heroic efforts at saving lives.

397

Padraic Colum

Illustrator: Willy Pogany

The Golden Fleece and the Heroes Who Lived Before Achilles (New York: Macmillan, 1921)

Age range: Grades 6 and Up

Subject(s): Mythology

Major character(s): Jason, Hero

Time period(s): Indeterminate Past

Locale(s): Greece

What the book is about: An unusual book of Greek myths. Rather than short stories, Colum's book is a continuous narrative. Using Jason and his quest as the central theme, he weaves in all the Greek tales outside of Homer with the gift of a rare storyteller.

Where it's reviewed:
Dial, November 1921, page 612
Literary Review, November 12, 1921, page 163

Awards the book has won:
Newbery Honor

Other books by the author:
Castle Conquer, 1923
Children of Odin, 1948
Creatures, 1927
Girl Who Sat By the Ashes, 1968

Other books you might like:
James Riordan, *Illustrated Treasury of Myths and Legends*, 1991
  Twenty-five tales of courage, daring, and romance.
Mary Pope Osborne, *Favorite Greek Myths*, 1989
  Twelve tales from Greek mythology.
Leonard Everett Fisher, *Olympians: Great Gods and Goddesses of Ancient Greece*, 1984
  Stories of the Greek myths with portraits of the Olympians.
Ghislaine Vautier, *Shining Stars: Greek Legends of the Zodiac*, 1981
  Retelling of the Greek myths associated with the constellations.
Ingri D' Aulaire, *Norse Gods and Giants*, 1967
  Tells of the nine worlds of Odin and mythic stories of companions.

398

Molly Cone

Illustrator: Robert MacLean

The Amazing Memory of Harvey Bean (Boston: Houghton Mifflin, 1980)

Age range: Grades 3-6

Subject(s): Family Life; Memory; Recycling (Waste)

Major character(s): Harvey Bean, Preteen; Alex Katz, Scavenger; Dottie Katz, Spouse

Time period(s): Indeterminate

Locale(s): United States

What the book is about: Harvey's memory is very poor, but he is unlikely to forget the summer he spends with Mr. and

Mrs. Katz. Mr. Katz can't stand to see anything go to waste, including a boy like Harvey.

Where it's reviewed:
Hornbook, August 1980, page 404
Kirkus Reviews, July 1, 1980, page 836
School Library Journal, August 1980, page 62

Other books by the author:
Dance around the Fire, 1974
Number Four, 1972
Annie, Annie, 1969
Mishmash, 1962

Other books you might like:
Paula Danziger, *Earth to Matthew*, 1991
    Matthew Martin finds himself on the threshold of becoming a teenager in suburban America and experiencing conflicts regarding his future.
Betty Levin, *The Trouble with Gramary*, 1988
    Merkka's longing for a conventional existence is threatened by the art projects of her grandmother, whose metal collection offends residents in town.
Ann M. Martin, *Dawn Saves the Planet*, 1992
    Dawn thinks studying ecology is cool. She wants to start a recycling center, but she is so busy lecturing people that she doesn't have the time.
Claudia Mills, *Dinah for President*, 1992
    Dinah, in her first year of middle school, struggles to grow up and discovers the value of recycling and of friendship with the elderly.
Susan Saunders, *The New Stephanie*, 1991
    Stephanie tries to prove just how caring she can be even if it means helping her mother clean and volunteering at the local recycling center.

399

Molly Cone

Mishmash (Boston: Houghton Mifflin, 1962)

Age range: Grades 4-6

Subject(s): Animals/Dogs; Humor

Major character(s): John "Pete" Peters, Preteen; Mishmash, Dog; Wanda Sparling, Neighbor

Time period(s): 1960s

Locale(s): Tacoma, Washington

What the book is about: When Pete's parents say he can get a dog, he can hardly believe his wish is finally coming true. He brings home a huge, black, friendly mutt named Mishmash - who turns out to be not quite the pet he expected. Mishmash walks into neighbor's houses uninvited, leaps into sports cars hoping for a ride, and sleeps in Pete's bed with his head on the pillow. And the troubles have just begun for this loveable, wacky dog who thinks he is a human.

Where it's reviewed:
Grade Teacher, October 1971, page 96

Other books by the author:
Mishmash and the Robot, 1981
The Amazing Memory of Harvey Bean, 1980
Annie, Annie, 1969
Mishmash and the Substitute Teacher, 1963

Other books you might like:
Betsy Byars, *Wanted.Mud Blossom*, 1991
    Convinced that Mud is responsible for the disappearance of the school hamster over the weekend, Junior Blossom wants to try the dog for his crime.
Eve Feldman, *Dog Crazy*, 1992
    Relates Sara's humorous attempts to get a dog.
Charles A. Perkins, *Wilderness Friend*, 1966
    Because his gentle St. Bernard, Molly, cannot stay out of trouble in town, a young boy eventually offers his loyal companion to the Mounties.
Janice Lee Smith, *It's Not Easy Being George*, 1989
    More episodes in the life of Adam Joshua, as he shares problems with his dog, George, and experiences a pet show and an all-night library sleepover.
Barbara Wersba, *You'll Never Guess the End*, 1992
    While experiencing a minor nervous breakdown, Joel tries to cope with his brother's sudden fame, a devoted dog, and a kidnapping.

400

Ellen Conford

Anything for a Friend (Boston: Little, Brown, 1979)

Age range: Grades 4-6

Subject(s): Moving, Household; Friendship

Major character(s): Wallis Green, Preteen; Stafford "Stuffy" Sternwood, Preteen

Time period(s): 1970s

Locale(s): New York, New York

What the book is about: Wallis is sure the family's move to New York City will be just another in a long line of hateful places with no friends. Adding to her difficulties, her home was once the site of a murder. Though it does make her a center of interest, Stuffy exploits it by holding a seance and charging admission. Wallis does make friends, and is better prepared when the next move takes them to California.

Where it's reviewed:
Kirkus Reviews, May 1, 1979, page 518
School Library Journal, September 1979, page 132

Other books by the author:
If This Is Love, I'll Take Spaghetti, 1983
Lenny Kendall, Smart Aleck, 1983
Hail, Hail, Camp Timberwood, 1978
The Luck of Pokey Bloom, 1975

Other books you might like:
Nikki Amdur, *One of Us*, 1981
    When Nora moves to a new town, she learns that making friends takes more than waiting for someone else to say hello.
Barbara Hood Burgess, *Oren Bell*, 1991
    Oren and his twin, Latonya, come to terms with the condemned house next door which they believe is haunted.
Mary Haynes, *The Great Pretenders*, 1990
    Molly has gotten off to a bad start by insulting the mayor's daughter in her new town.
Stephen Roos, *My Favorite Ghost*, 1988
    The legend of a ghost on the island inspires money-hungry Derek to dupe his friends into paying admission to a haunted house.

Margaret Sutton, *The Haunted Attic*, 1976
When Judy and her family move into a haunted house, she is determined to solve the mystery of the ghost in the attic.

401

Ellen Conford

Illustrator: Gail Rockwell

Dreams of Victory (Boston: Little Brown, 1973)

Age range: Grades 4-6

Subject(s): Dreams and Nightmares; Humor; Imagination

Major character(s): Victory "Vic" Benneker, Preteen; Janey, Friend; Mark Vogel, Friend

Time period(s): 1970s

Locale(s): Oakdale

What the book is about: When her day dreams continually conflict with reality, Victory becomes convinced of her inferiority. She wants to be an actress, beauty queen, figure skater and astronaut. Fortunately, a class essay in imagination gives her a new perspective.

Where it's reviewed:
Booklist, May 15, 1973, page 904
Hornbook, August 1973, page 378
Kirkus Reviews, February 15, 1973, page 186

Other books by the author:
Jenny Archer, Author, 1989
Lenny Kendall, Smart Aleck, 1983
Anything for a Friend, 1979
Hail, Hail, Camp Timberwood, 1978

Other books you might like:
Dale Bick Carlson, *Charlie the Hero*, 1983
A sixth grade boy with a burning desire to be a hero finds a body in a field and hopes it will make his dream come true.
Barthe DeClements, *The 4th Grade Wizards*, 1988
After her mother dies, Marianne becomes a daydreamer and begins to fall behind in her schoolwork.
William Pene Du Bois, *The Alligator Case*, 1965
When a circus and three visitors come to town, a detective, known to most people as a young daydreaming boy, meets his first challenge.
Marjorie Lewis, *Wrongway Applebaum*, 1984
Always a little slow and awkward, Applebaum dreams of being on the fifth grade baseball team and impressing everyone with his spectacular playing.
Susan Trott, *The Sea Serpent of Horse*, 1973
When Livvie's friend, Horse, takes off on a nightmare ride to the depts of the sea, the world of reality and delirium blend into a terrifying fantasy.

402

Ellen Conford

Illustrator: Arvis Stewart

Felicia the Critic (Boston: Little Brown, 1973)

Age range: Grades 5-7

Subject(s): Honesty; Interpersonal Relations

Major character(s): Felicia, Child

Time period(s): 1970s

Locale(s): United States

What the book is about: Felicia writes lists of suggestions for a policeman, her aunt the writer, and her cousin's wedding. Some of her ideas work, but they are perceived as criticism and they all embarrass her family. Felicia's attitude makes it difficult for her to make friends.

Where it's reviewed:
Kirkus Reviews, November 1, 1973, page 1199
Horn Book, December 1973, page 591

Other books by the author:
Hail, Hail, Camp Timberwood, 1978
Just the Thing for Geraldine, 1974
Dreams of Victory, 1973
Why Can't I Be William?, 1973

Other books you might like:
Barbara Hall, *Fool's Hill*, 1992
Libby's efforts to figure out who she is are influenced by her relationships with family and friends in the small town where she lives.
Leah Jerome, *No Hitter*, 1991
Breezy's achievement in pitching the first no-hitter in league history causes problems when she doesn't give her team any credit for her success.
Catherine Frey Murphy, *Alice Dodd and the Spirit of Truth*, 1993
While spending the summer in a vacation cabin with her aunt and three year old cousin, a young girl finds herself involved in lies and deceptions.
Phyllis Reynolds Naylor, *All but Alice*, 1992
Alice decides that the only way to stave off personal and social disaters is to be part of the "in crowd," no matter how boring and difficult.
Louis Sacher, *The Boy Who Lost His Face*, 1989
David learns to regret pandering to others for the sake of popularity after he receives a curse from a woman whom he and his friends attacked.

403

Ellen Conford

Illustrator: Gail Owens

Hail, Hail, Camp Timberwood (Boston: Little, Brown, 1978)

Age range: Grades 5-6

Subject(s): Camps and Camping

Major character(s): Melanie, Child

Time period(s): 1980s

Locale(s): United States

What the book is about: Melanie is an only child. She learns about relating with other kids during her two month stay at camp. She also learns that sometimes she has to stand up for herself.

Where it's reviewed:
Center for Children's Books Bulletin, September 1979, page 97
Kirkus Reviews, December 1, 1978, page 1306

Awards the book has won:
California Young Reader Medal 1982

Other books by the author:
The Revenge of the Incredible Dr. Rancid and His Youthful Assistant, Jeffrey, 1987
Anything for a Friend, 1979
The Luck of Pokey Bloom, 1975
Dreams of Victory, 1973

Other books you might like:
Paula Danziger, *There's a Bat in Bunk Five,* 1982
  Marcy is a young camp counselor; each person she works with helps her come out of herself and turn her sensitivity out instead of in.
Harriet Gilbert, *Running Away,* 1979
  Jane lives apart from her large family at boarding school. She longs for her parents' love, but comes to realize she must make a life for herself.
Elizabeth Levy, *Come Out Smiling,* 1981
  Believable dialogue and skillful characterization mark this story about Jenny, a senior at Camp Secajawea, who is stuggling with her identity.
Jane O'Connor, *Yours Till Niagara Falls, Abby,* 1979
  On her own for the first time at summer camp, Abby must cope with separation from her home, harassment by bunkmates and her own lack of confidence.
Robert Kimmel Smith, *Jelly Belly,* 1981
  Until Ned is ready to lose weight, even sending him to weight loss camp doesn't solve his eating problem.

404

Ellen Conford

Jenny Archer to the Rescue (Boston: Little Brown, 1990)

Age range: Grades 2-4

Subject(s): Humor

Major character(s): Jenny Archer, Child, Heroine

Time period(s): 1990s

Locale(s): United States

What the book is about: With the help of her parents and a first aid kit, Jenny is ready to be a heroine. She invents a game called "Accident" and practices bandaging with disasterous results. First aid and fun fill this story for independent readers.

Where it's reviewed:
Kirkus Reviews, December 15, 1990, page 1736
School Library Journal, December 1990, page 74

Other books by the author:
If This Is Love, I'll Take Spaghetti, 1983
Seven Days to a Brand New Me, 1981
Anything for a Friend, 1979

Other books you might like:
Petronella Breinburg, *Doctor Shawn,* 1975
  A little boy and his sister play at being doctor and nurse.
Sid Fleischman, *McBroom's Almanac,* 1984
  Entries include farm-tips, how-to's, McProverbs, nature lore, cartoons, and McBroom's calendar of important dates.
Charles Keller, *What's Up Doc?,* 1984
  A collection of jokes about doctors and dentists.
Judy Pedersen, *The Tiny Patient,* 1989

A young girl and her grandmother find a sparrow with a broken wing and nurse it back to health.
P.K. Roche, *Webster and Arnold and the Giant Box,* 1980
  Webster and Arnold find a huge box and pretend it is all sorts of different things.

405

Ellen Conford

Illustrator: Walter Gaffney-Kessell

Lenny Kendall, Smart Aleck (Boston: Little, Brown, 1983)

Age range: Grades 5-6

Subject(s): Schools

Major character(s): Lenny, Preteen; Artie, Preteen

Time period(s): 1940s (1946)

Locale(s): United States

What the book is about: Lenny is an eleven year old budding comedian. He is as touching as he is funny in this novel of the early postwar middle class. Lenny practices his craft in front of the bathroom mirror, on the roof of his apartment building, anywhere he can to achieve his goal of becoming a stand-up comic. But with an enemy like Mousie, he wonders if he'll have any future at all.

Where it's reviewed:
Horn Book, August 1983, page 442
School Library Journal, May 1983, page 70

Other books by the author:
A Case for Jenny Archer, 1988
If This Is Love, I'll Take Spaghetti, 1983
Anything for a Friend, 1979
And This Is Laura, 1977

Other books you might like:
Sheila Greenwald, *The Mariah Delany Lending Library Disaster,* 1977
  When local libraries begin to shorten hours for lack of funding, Mariah sets up her own library using her parents' books.
Douglas Arthur Hill, *Penelope's Pendant,* 1990
  Penny finds a slightly damaged pendant on the beach and discovers that it gives her the power to move herself and other objects through space.
Dean Hughes, *Nutty, the Movie Star,* 1991
  Nutty, hoping to improve his image with his fellow fifth graders, finds his popularity unexpectedly boosted when he gets a small part in a movie.
Stephen Roos, *My Horrible Secret,* 1983
  With the prospect of Camp Hit-a-Homer looming before him, Warren, whose older brother is a super athlete, resorts to desperate measures to avoid it.
Susan Terris, *Octopus Pie,* 1983
  Kris relates the events in her household when her father brings home a live octopus.

406

Ellen Conford

Illustrator: Bernice Lowenstein

The Luck of Pokey Bloom (New York: Simon and Schuster, 1975)

Age range: Grades 4-6

Subject(s): Contests

Major character(s): Charlotte "Pokey" Bloom, Child; Gordon "Gordie" Bloom, Teenager (Pokey's brother); George Fisher, Neighbor

Time period(s): 1970s

Locale(s): United States

What the book is about: The warm, sunny family story about a young girl who has a compulsive interest in contests, and her brother, who is undergoing the pangs of first love. Pokey has entered a Redimix Cake Mix contest, hoping to win $10,000.

Where it's reviewed:
Hornbook, August 1975, page 380
Kirkus Reviews, April 15, 1979, page 453
School Library Journal, September 1975, page 100

Other books by the author:
You Never Can Tell, 1984
To All My Fans with Love, From Sylvia, 1983
And This Is Laura, 1977
Dreams of Victory, 1973

Other books you might like:
Rebecca Busselle, *Bathing Ugly*, 1988
    Chosen to compete in the camp's bathing ugly contest, overweight Betsy causes the campers to rethink the imporatnace of outward appearance.
Gloria Houston, *Littlejim*, 1990
    Littlejim, a boy living in a rural community in the early 1900s hopes to win a newspaper essay contest and thus gain the respect of his stern father.
Suzy Kline, *Orp and the Chop Suey Burgers*, 1990
    Orville enters a cooking contest, which he has high hopes of winning with his recipe for chop suey burgers.
Patti Sherlock, *Four of a Kind*, 1991
    Andy lives with Grandpa and dreams of driving his two draft horses, Maggie and Tom, in a pulling contest.
Barbara A. Steiner, *Dolby and the Woof-Off*, 1991
    Bo teaches his dog Dolby some unusual tricks in an attempt to win the Woof-Off contest.

| **407** |

Ellen Conford

Illustrator: Charles Carroll

Me and the Terrible Two (Boston: Little Brown, 1974)

Age range: Grades 4-6

Subject(s): Friendship; Neighbors and Neighborhoods; Twins

Major character(s): Dorrie Kimball, Preteen; Haskell Conger, Twin; Conrad Conger, Twin

Time period(s): 1970s

Locale(s): New York

What the book is about: Dorrie's best friend, Marlene, moves to Australia and Haskell and Conrad move into Marlene's house. They tease Dorrie, make noise early in the morning and send threatening mail to her dog, Sherman. Can she survive the "Terrible Two" long enough to find their "good side?"

Where it's reviewed:
Booklist, July 15, 1974, page 1251
Hornbook, August 1974, page 375
Kirkus Reviews, April 1, 1974, page 363

Other books by the author:
If This Is Love, I'll Take Spaghetti, 1983
Anything for a Friend, 1979
Hail, Hail, Camp Timberwood, 1978
Dreams of Victory, 1973

Other books you might like:
Eth Clifford, *The Dastardly Murder of Dirty Pete*, 1981
    While traveling to the west coast, two sisters and their father have quite an adventure when they get lost and find a ghost town.
Jamie Gilson, *Hello, My Name is Scrambled Eggs*, 1985
    When his folks host a Vietnamese family that has come to settle in their town, Harvey enjoys Americanizing twelve year old Tuan.
Andre Norton, *Star Ka'at*, 1976
    Two intriguing stray cats communicate with Jim and Elly Mae convincing them that the cats are aliens from another planet.
Stella Pevsner, *Me, My Goat, and My Sister's Wedding*, 1985
    Doug and his friends keep their pet goat a secret, but before long, sightings of the high-spirited animal occur at very inappropriate places.
Linda Joy Singleton, *Almost Twins*, 1991
    Frankie feels left out of the twins' activities until she meets a girl at the beach who looks just like her.

| **408** |

Marita Conlon-McKenna

Illustrator: Donald Teskey

Under the Hawthorne Tree (New York: Holiday House, 1990)

Age range: Grades 4-6

Subject(s): Famine Victims

Major character(s): Eily O'Driscoll, Child; Michael O'Driscoll, Child; Peggy O'Driscoll, Child

Time period(s): 1840s

Locale(s): Ireland

What the book is about: When the potato famine hits Ireland, the O'Driscolls are doomed. Father goes off to find work, Mother goes off to find father, and Eily is left with Michael, 9, and Peggy, 7. When their parents fail to return, the children are rounded up to be taken to the workhouse, but they escape and face hunger, thirst, and disease in a dangerous journey to find their elderly aunts in a distant city.

Where it's reviewed:
Center for Children's Books Bulletin, December 1990, page 81
School Library Journal, December 1991, page 100

Other books you might like:
Elizabeth Coatsworth, *The Wanderers*, 1972
    Father Ambrosius, an orphan, an outcast and the dog, Seuman, wander through Ireland.

Daniel Curley, *Billy Beg and the Bull*, 1978
  The son of a king and his bull set out to find a new life in Ireland in the days of great heroes.
Leonard Everett Fisher, *Across the Sea From Galway*, 1975
  In 1849, following the potato famine, three Irish children are sent on an ill-fated journey to Boston.
Elona Malterre, *The Last Wolf of Ireland*, 1990
  A boy and girl living in Ireland in the 1780s attempt to save the last wolf left in the country.
Joan Lowery Nixon, *The Gift*, 1983
  Brian, visiting his Irish relatives, tries to prove that his great-grandfather's tales of leprechauns are true.

409

Pam Conrad

My Daniel (New York: Harper and Row, 1989)

Age range: Grades 5-6

Subject(s): Brothers and Sisters; Frontier and Pioneer Life

Major character(s): Daniel, Teenager, Archaeologist; Julia, Grandparent (grandmother)

Time period(s): 1980s

Locale(s): Nebraska; New York

What the book is about: While visiting her grandchildren in New York, Julia takes them to the Museum of Natural History. She tells them the story of her brother, life on the Nebraska plains, and the dinosaur bone wars of the 19th century.

Where it's reviewed:
Kirkus Reviews, May 1, 1989, page 688
School Library Journal, April 1989, page 117

Awards the book has won:
Arizona Young Readers Award

Other books by the author:
The Tub People, 1989
Staying Nine, 1988
Taking the Ferry Home, 1988
Holding Me Here, 1988

Other books you might like:
Betsy Byars, *Trouble River*, 1969
  Dewey Martin and his grandmother must make their way down the Trouble River on a home-made raft to escape hostile Indians.
Bruce Clements, *I Tell a Lie Every So Often*, 1974
  In 1848, Henry's lies to his brother, Clayton, start them off on a search for their cousin Hanna who had been taken by the Indians in 1833.
Sid Fleischman, *Mr. Mysterious and Company*, 1962
  In the 1880s, a traveling magic show plays the frontier towns westward to California.
Weyman B. Jones, *Edge of Two Worlds*, 1968
  The story of a young Missouri boy and an old Cherokee Indian who face a long and difficult journey across the plains together.
Ivy Ruckman, *Night of the Twisters*, 1984
  Dan, his baby brother and his best friend, Arthur, survive a night in Grand Island, Nebraska when the town is hit by seven tornadoes.

410

Pam Conrad

Illustrator: Darryl S Zudek

Prairie Songs (New York: Harper and Row, 1985)

Age range: Grades 5-6

Subject(s): Frontier and Pioneer Life

Major character(s): Louisa, Child; Dr. Berryman, Doctor

Time period(s): 19th century

Locale(s): Nebraska

What the book is about: Louisa's life in a loving pioneer family on the Nebraska prairie is altered by the arrival of a new doctor and his beautiful, tragically frail wife.

Where it's reviewed:
Center for Children's Books Bulletin, September 1985, page 4
Horn Book, January/February 1986, page 57

Awards the book has won:
Boston Globe/Horn Book Award - Honor Book

Other books by the author:
Prairie Visions, 1991
Stonewords: A Ghost Story, 1990
My Daniel, 1989
Holding Me Here, 1986

Other books you might like:
Cynthia DeFelice, *Weasel*, 1990
  In the frontier wilderness of 1839, 11 year old Nathan runs afoul of the renegade killer known as Weasel and makes a discovery about revenge.
Paul Fleischman, *The Borning Room*, 1991
  At the end of her life, Georgina remembers what it was like growing up on the Ohio frontier.
Laurie Lawlor, *Addie's Dakota Winter*, 1989
  In her new pioneer home, 10 year old Addie finds an unlikely friend and learns about courage.
Robert McClung, *Hugh Glass, Mountain Man*, 1990
  A fictionalized biography of an Old West hero, Hugh Glass, fur trapper.
Walt Morey, *Year of the Black Pony*, 1976
  A boy in the Oregon country in the early 1900s experiences the death of his father, his mother's remarriage, and the attainment of a dream.

411

Pam Conrad

Stonewords: A Ghost Story (New York: Harper & Row, 1990)

Age range: Grades 5-9

Subject(s): Ghosts; Supernatural; Time Travel

Major character(s): Zoe, Preteen; Zoe Louise, Spirit

Time period(s): 1990s; Indeterminate Past

Locale(s): Earth

What the book is about: When Zoe comes to live with her grandparents as a very young child, she easily accepts the presence of "Zoe Louise," a very vivid, ghostly presence, and indeed, they are good friends throughout most of Zoe's childhood. Zoe Louise finally reveals that she was killed in a fire at age eleven, and Zoe travels in time to try and help Zoe Louise escape the fire and live a full life. A ghost story that is very convincing and very scary. Great read aloud.

Where it's reviewed:
Booklist, March 1, 1990, page 1338
Horn Book, September/October 1990, page 600

Other books by the author:
My Daniel, 1989
Taking the Ferry Home, 1988
Holding Me Here, 1986
Prairie Songs, 1985

Other books you might like:
Antonia Barber, *The Ghosts*, 1969
A brother and sister meet two strange children in the garden of their new home with whom they return to another century.
Margaret Buffie, *The Haunting of Frances Rain*, 1987
Lizzie digs up a pair of old glasses and finds out she can see ghosts from the past when she wears them.
Penelope Lively, *Uninvited Ghosts and Other Stories*, 1984
Short fantasy stories featuring a cast of monsters and beasts, griffins and ghosts.
Hilary H. Milton, *Escape From High Doom*, 1984
The reader visits Noose City, a Texas ghost town famous for its ghosts which reappear each year on the anniversaries of their deaths.
Stephen Ryan, *The Gitter, the Googer and the Ghost*, 1983
Best friends and ghost hunters, known as Gitter and Googer, think they have a chance to find a real ghost when Gitter's family inherits an old house.

412

Joyce Cool

The Kidnapping of Courtney Van Allen and What's-Her-Name (New York: Knopf, 1981)

Age range: Grades 5-7

Subject(s): Kidnapping

Major character(s): Jan Travis, Child, Captive (kidnap victim); Courtney Van Allen, Child, Captive (kidnap victim)

Time period(s): 1980s

Locale(s): New York, New York

What the book is about: Wealthy Courtney and middle class Jan get involved in a kidnapping plot. Jan is kidnapped along with her world-famous wealthy friend, and the kidnappers demand something other than money. The girls match wits with a governess who hates children and a ninety-eight year old silent screen star with purple hair. The girls survive the ordeal and become both heroes and friends.

Where it's reviewed:
Booklist, October 15, 1981, page 298
Center for Children's Books Bulletin, October 1981, page 26
Kirkus Reviews, November 15, 1981, page 1407

Other books you might like:
Peter Dickinson, *The Seventh Raven*, 1981
In a bungled attempt to kidnap an ambassador's son, four revolutionaries make hostages of a hundred children rehearsing an opera.
R. Parker McVey, *Mystery at the Ball Game*, 1985

The reader overhears a conversation about a plot to kidnap a millionaire's son, and makes decisions which determine the outcome of the story.
Richard Parker, *Four Desperate Days*, 1974
Terrorist guerillas kidnap three children instead of one. Then begins the wait to see if government officials will meet the terrorists' demands.
Sherwood Smith, *Wren's Quest*, 1993
While Wren and Prince Connor set off to uncover her parentage, a sinister wizard creates havoc back home in Cantimoor.
Bruce Stone, *Half Nelson, Full Nelson*, 1985
When his parents separate, Nelson and his friend Heidi concoct a plan to kidnap Nelson's little sister and bring his family back together.

413

Olivia Coolidge

Illustrator: Milton Johnson

Come by Here (Boston: Houghton Mifflin, 1970)

Age range: Grades 5-6

Subject(s): African Americans; Death

Major character(s): Minty Lou Payson, Child; Big Lou Payson, Parent

Time period(s): 1900s

Locale(s): Baltimore, Maryland

What the book is about: In the early 1900s in Baltimore, a middle class black child has a difficult struggle regaining the comfortable life she knew before her parents were killed. As she is passed from relative to relative, she gradually comes to life again, and fights to regain the life her mother had dreamed for her.

Where it's reviewed:
Booklist, April 1, 1971, page 659
Horn Book, February 1971, page 49

Other books by the author:
Tales of the Crusades, 1970
Marathon Looks on the Sea, 1967
King of Men, 1966
Egyptian Adventures, 1954

Other books you might like:
Barbara Hood Burgess, *Oren Bell*, 1991
Twelve year old Oren and his twin sister, Latonya, are afraid of a condemned house next door which they believe is haunted
Michael Capizzi, *Getting It All Together*, 1972
A fourteen year old, adjusting to his father's death, finds his life further complicated by new family problems.
Hugh Barnett Cave, *Conquering Kilmarnie*, 1989
As Peter and his father mourn the deaths of Peter's mother and brother, the arrival of a young black boy changes their lives dramatically.
Harriette Robinet, *Children of the Fire*, 1991
A young black girl named Hallelujah lives through the great Chicago fire with courage and resourcefulness.
Johnniece Marshall Wilson, *Robin on His Own*, 1990
A black boy whose family is in crisis tries to cope with the death of his mother.

414

Patricia Coombs, Author/Illustrator

Dorrie and the Pin Witch (New York: Lothrop, 1989)

Age range: Grades 1-2

Subject(s): Witches and Witchcraft; Halloween

Major character(s): Dorrie, Heroine, Child; Pin Witch, Witch

Time period(s): Indeterminate

Locale(s): United States

What the book is about: Dorrie suspects that the evil Pin Witch is responsible for the witches' angry behavior on the day of the Witches' Ball.

Where it's reviewed:
Booklist, April 15, 1989, page 1465
Center for Children's Books Bulletin, April 1989, page 191
School Library Journal, April 1989, page 78

Other books by the author:
Dorrie and the Dreamland Monsters, 1982
Dorrie and the Screebit Ghost, 1979
The Magic Pot, 1977
Dorrie and the Haunted House, 1970

Other books you might like:
Lorna Balian, *Humbug Potion: An A-B-Cipher*, 1984
   A homely witch is delighted to find a secret recipe for beauty but it is written in a code that the reader must help her decipher.
Norman Bridwell, *The Witch Goes to School*, 1992
   A normal day at school becomes special when the Witch comes for a visit and uses her magic.
Mirko Gabler, *The Alphabet Soup*, 1992
   When he follows the witch twins Gurgla and Blog home from school, Zack almost becomes the final ingredient in alphabet soup.
Margaret Hillert, *The Witch Who Went for a Walk*, 1982
   While taking a walk on Halloween night, a witch and her cat are frightened by three children in costume.
Erica Silverman, *Big Pumpkin*, 1992
   A witch trying to pick up a big pumpkin on Halloween discovers the value of cooperation when she gets help from a series of monsters.

415

Barbara Cooney

Hattie and the Wild Waves (New York: Viking, 1990)

Age range: Grades 2-3

Subject(s): Beaches; Artists and Art

Major character(s): Hattie, Child, Wealthy

Time period(s): 1900s

Locale(s): New York, New York (Brooklyn)

What the book is about: Hattie's father builds houses so they can afford vacations to Coney Island and Long Island. Hattie wishes on the waves. She decides she'll become a painter. This is a picture of old-fashioned life in a wealthy German household at the turn of the century.

Where it's reviewed:
Kirkus Reviews, October 1, 1990, page 1392
School Library Journal, December 1990, page 75

Other books by the author:
Emily, 1992
Island Boy, 1990
Little Brother and Little Sister, 1982
The Little Juggler, 1961

Other books you might like:
Eric Carle, *Draw Me a Star*, 1992
   An artist's drawing of a star begins the creation of an entire universe.
Natalie Kinsey-Warnock, *The Canada Geese Quilt*, 1989
   Ariel combines her artistic talent with her grandmother's knowledge to make a very special quilt.
Thomas Locker, *The Young Artist*, 1989
   A talented young artist struggles with his sense of integrity as he paints the king's courtiers.
Max Velthuijs, *Crocodile's Masterpiece*, 1991
   Crocodile is inspired to even greater heights by Elephant's enthusiasm for his paintings.
Diane Wolkstein, *Little Mouse's Painting*, 1992
   Little Mouse creates a painting which looks like three different things to three different friends.

416

Otto Coontz

Mystery Madness (Boston: Houghton Mifflin, 1982)

Age range: Grades 5-7

Subject(s): Mystery and Detective Stories; Dishonesty

Major character(s): Murray Boyd, Preteen; Blanche Boyd, Preteen; Maria, Worker (housekeeper)

Time period(s): 1980s

Locale(s): Boston, Massachusetts

What the book is about: Murray wrongly believes his sister committed a crime when he heard the shot, the high-pitched cry and Blanche begging Maria to forgive her over the phone. Now the housekeeper is missing and there's a dark stain on the floor where the rug had been.

Where it's reviewed:
Booklist, April 1, 1983, page 1042
Kirkus Reviews, April 15, 1982, page 489
School Library Journal, May 1982, page 83

Other books by the author:
Isle of the Shapeshifters, 1983
The Night Walkers, 1982
Hornswoggle Magic, 1981

Other books you might like:
Nicole Christopher, *Where the Cavern Ends*, 1970
   When his sister is kidnapped on their Bermuda vacation, Mark realizes his family is at the mercy of criminals who have planned this far in advance.
John Durham, *Me and Arch and the Pest*, 1970
   Two boys acquire a German Shepherd whose disappearance involves them in a crime.
Mary James, *The Shuteyes*, 1993

A boy is carried off by a giant one-eyed parrot to the planet Alert, where sleeping is a crime, and those who do sleep are called "shuteyes."

Browning Norton, *Johnny/Bingo*, 1971

As the only witnesses to a bank robbery, two boys are held hostage with the threat that they will die if they attempt to escape.

Curt Schleier, *You'd Better Not Tell*, 1979

A young boy, living in a neighborhood where police are the enemy, must make a decision regarding evidence that his best friend's brother is a mugger.

417

Susan Cooper

Illustrator: Alan E. Cober

The Dark Is Rising (New York: Atheneum, 1973)

Age range: Grades 5-7

Subject(s): Fantasy; Good and Evil

Major character(s): Will Stanton, Preteen

Time period(s): Indeterminate

Locale(s): Wales

What the book is about: On his eleventh birthday, Will Stanton discovers that he is one of the "Old Ones," those who have special powers and a primary role in the battle of good and evil. The power of the Dark is on the rise. During the twelve days of Christmas Will must learn to use his gifts to defeat the forces of evil and save his sister.

Where it's reviewed:
Horn Book, June 1973, page 286
Kirkus Reviews, March 15, 1973, page 315

Awards the book has won:
Newbery Honor 1974

Other books by the author:
The Boggart, 1993
Silver on the Tree, 1977
The Grey King, 1975
Greenwitch, 1974

Other books you might like:
Richard Carlyon, *The Dark Lord of Pergersick*, 1980

Mabby and Jago determine to defeat the Lord of Pergersick, an evil sorcerer who has filled the lives of the people of the area with misery and terror.

Grace Chetwin, *On All Hallow's Eve*, 1984

Two sisters coming home from a Halloween party step into another time, where the forces of good and evil involve them in a life or death adventure.

John Dowd, *Ring of Tall Trees*, 1992

Dylan and his friends call on ancient rituals and Rave the Trickster to help stop loggers from clearing an old growth forest near Dylan's farm.

J. Allison James, *Runa*, 1993

Runa's carefree summer on a Swedish island changes as she is caught up in the rites of her Viking ancestors and the will of ancient Norse gods.

Jacklyn O'Hanlon, *The Door*, 1978

A girl passes through the mysterious door of the Master Gatherer and finds herself in the center of a struggle between good and evil.

418

Susan Cooper

Greenwitch (New York: Atheneum, 1974)

Age range: Grades 5-6

Series: The Dark Is Rising Sequence

Subject(s): Good and Evil; Fantasy

Major character(s): Will Stanton, Preteen; Jane Drew, Friend

Time period(s): Indeterminate Past

Locale(s): Cornwall, England

What the book is about: The three Drew children visit a Cornish village where their uncle, Merry, and Will Stanton are part of the struggle between good and evil. The Greenwitch is constructed each year by the villages, but they don't know she comes to life.

Where it's reviewed:
Horn Book, August 1974, page 375
Kirkus Reviews, May 15, 1974, page 533

Other books by the author:
Silver on the Tree, 1977
The Grey King, 1975
The Dark Is Rising, 1973
Over Sea, Under Stone, 1966

Other books you might like:
Mabel Esther Allan, *A Chill in the Lane*, 1974

While vacationing in Cornwall with her family, an adopted girl finds herself strangely and frighteningly involved with the past.

Shirley Climo, *Piskies, Spriggans, and Other Magical Beings*, 1981

Retells nine tales about the mortals and magical beings who reside in Cornwall.

Christopher Leach, *The Great Book Raid*, 1979

An assortment of heroic literary figures assembles to help Jim and his mother keep their coastal property in Cornwall away from a land developer.

Jill Paton Walsh, *A Parcel of Patterns*, 1983

Mall Percival tells how the plague came to her Derbyshire village of Eyam in the year 1665.

David Wiseman, *Jeremy Visick*, 1981

Twelve year old Matthew is drawn almost against his will to help a boy his own age who was lost in a mining disaster a century before.

419

Susan Cooper

Illustrator: Michael Heslop

The Grey King (New York: Atheneum, 1975)

Age range: Grades 5 and Up

Series: The Dark Is Rising

Subject(s): Fantasy; Good and Evil

Major character(s): Will Stanton, Immortal; Bran Davies, Friend (Albino)

Time period(s): 1970s

Locale(s): Wales

What the book is about: Will moves to his uncle's farm in Wales to regain his health after a bout with hepatitis. With the help of the albino, Bran, and the dog, Cafall, Will battles the Grey King, an enemy from the Dark. This story has interesting ties to the Legend of King Arthur.

Where it's reviewed:
Horn Book, October 1975, page 461
School Library Journal, October 1975, page 104

Awards the book has won:
Newbery Medal 1976

Other books by the author:
Over Sea, Under Stone, 1966 (First in The Dark Is Rising Series)
Greenwitch, 1974
The Dark Is Rising, 1981
Silver on the Tree, 1977

Other books you might like:
Gwyn Thomas, *Tales from the Mabinogion*, 1984
    Tales of the Celtic gods - superhuman deeds taken from ancient manuscripts illustrated with full page drawings.
Nancy Bond, *A String in the Harp*, 1976
    Peter is taken back in time and relives the life story of the great Welsh bard, Taliesin.
Jenny Nimmo, *The Snow Spider*, 1986
    10 year old Gwyn begins a quest to see if he has inherited magical powers.

420

Susan Cooper

Illustrator: Ashley Bryan

Jethro and the Jumbie (New York: Atheneum, 1979)

Age range: Grades 2-3

Subject(s): Anger; Brothers and Sisters

Major character(s): Jethro, Child; Thomas; Timothy Dawson, Friend

Time period(s): Indeterminate

Locale(s): Caribbean

What the book is about: Jethro's brother, Thomas, promised to take him fishing when he was eight. Now that Jethro is almost there, Thomas says he is still too small to go. Jethro stomps off in anger. On the trail, he meets a jumbie, a ghostly creature with fearsome powers. Jethro's refusal to believe in jumbies saps the creature's strength until Jethro offers him a deal. Jethro believes, and the jumbie makes Thomas keep his promise to Jethro.

Where it's reviewed:
Booklist, December 15, 1979, page 610
Hornbook, February 1980, page 51
Kirkus Reviews, February 1, 1980, page 120

Other books by the author:
The Boggart, 1993
Matthew's Dragon, 1991
Selkie Girl, 1986
The Silver Cow: A Welsh Tale, 1983

Other books you might like:
Arnold Adoff, *Flamboyan*, 1988

One afternoon, Flamboyan, a girl named after the tree with red blossoms the same color as her hair, dreamily flies over her Caribbean island home.
Kitty Binger, *Mary Guy*, 1993
    Mary Guy finds a way to make the governor of a tiny Caribbean island repeal his laws prohibiting fun.
Jimmy Buffet, *The Jolly Man*, 1988
    Relates the adventures of a fisherman who finds a magic guitar floating in the Caribbean Sea.
Nancy White Carlson, *Baby-O*, 1992
    Three generations of a West Indian family gather together on a jitney that takes them and their wares to the local market.
Pat McKissack, *A Million Fish, More or Less*, 1992
    A boy learns that the truth is often stretched on the Bayou Clapateaux and gets to tell his own version of a bayou tale when he goes fishing.

421

Susan Cooper

Illustrator: Margery Gill

Over Sea, Under Stone (New York: Harcourt, 1965)

Age range: Grades 4-6

Series: The "Dark is Rising" Sequence

Subject(s): Fantasy; Supernatural; Time Travel

Major character(s): Barney Drew, Child, Vacationer; Simon Drew, Child, Vacationer; Jane Drew, Child, Vacationer

Time period(s): Indeterminate Past

Locale(s): Cornwall, England

What the book is about: Three children on a holiday in Cornwall find an ancient manuscript which sends them on a dangerous quest for a grail that would reveal the true story of King Arthur. This is the first in the Dark Is Rising sequence. High fantasy in the Dark versus Light tradition.

Where it's reviewed:
Booklist, September 15, 1966, page 118
Hornbook, August 1966, page 434
Kirkus Reviews, March 15, 1966, page 301

Other books by the author:
Silver on the Tree, 1977
The Grey King, 1975
Greenwitch, 1974
The Dark is Rising, 1973

Other books you might like:
Mabel Esther Allan, *A Chill in the Lane*, 1974
    While vacationing in Cornwall with her family, a sixteen year old adopted girl finds herself strangely and frighteningly involved with the past.
Penelope Lively, *The Wild Hunt of the Ghost Hounds*, 1986
    The revival of an ancient dance in an English village stirs up legendary unseen spirits which terrify a girl and her friend.
Carolyn F. Logan, *The Power of the Rellard*, 1986
    Lucy finds herself and other siblings in the midst of a power struggle with agents of an ancient evil.
Rosemary Wells, *Through the Hidden Door*, 1987
    Two boys stumble upon the remains of an ancient underground civilization.
David Wiseman, *Jeremy Visick*, 1981

Matthew is drawn against his will to help a boy his own age who was lost in a mining disaster a century before.

422

Susan Cooper

Illustrator: Warwick Hutton

The Silver Cow: A Welsh Tale (New York: Atheneum, 1983)

Age range: Grades 3-5

Subject(s): Magic; Folk Tales

Major character(s): Huw, Musician; Gwilym, Parent (Huw's father)

Time period(s): Indeterminate Past

Locale(s): Wales

What the book is about: In return for his harp playing, the magic people of the lake have sent young Huw a silver cow. The cow and her descendents give such rich milk that Huw's father, Gwilym, beomes wealthy. But Gwilym is greedy and refuses to let Huw go to school. When Gwilym arranges to have the aging cow slaughtered, the magic people call all silver cows back to the lake, and each one becomes a shining white water lily in the Welsh mountain lakes.

Where it's reviewed:
Horn Book, June 1983, page 287
School Library Journal, April 1983, page 99

Other books by the author:
The Dark Is Rising, 1981
Silver on the Tree, 1977
The Grey King, 1975
Over Sea, Under Stone, 1966

Other books you might like:
Nancy Bond, *A String in the Harp*, 1976
  An unwilling American transplanted to Wales for a year finds an ancient harp tuning key that takes him back to the 6th century. (Older readers)
Olwen Bowen Davies, *Tales From the Mabinogion*, 1969
  Fifteen episodes from the Mabinogion, a collection of medieval Welsh tales.
Jenny Nimmo, *Orchard of the Crescent Moon*, 1991
  Nia. the middle girl in a large Welsh family, discovers her own artistic talent as she uncovers the dark secret shared by two families.
Ellen Pugh, *More Tales From the Welsh Hills*, 1971
  Ten beautiful stories of folklore, includes a guide to pronunciation of the Welsh names and words.
Paul Yee, *Roses Sing on New Snow*, 1991
  Maylin, a cook in her family's restaurant, finally receives the recognition she deserves when a governor from China visits New World Chinatown.

423

Scott Corbett

Illustrator: Troy Howell

The Donkey Planet (New York: Dutton, 1979)

Age range: Grades 4-6

Subject(s): Animals/Donkeys; Science Fiction

Major character(s): Jason Scully, Detective; Frank Barnes, Scientist, Detective; Gru, Police Officer (chief)

Time period(s): Indeterminate Future

Locale(s): Vanaris, Planet—Imaginary (the donkey planet)

What the book is about: Jason and Frank, adult detectives, are sent by thought projection to Vanaris, a planet in another solar system nine light years away to exchange metal samples. The Vanarians exist in a police state, and donkeys are the only means of transportation. When they arrive, Frank has become a donkey, and Jason is a Vanarian boy. Only their quick wits and help from a Valerian girl named Zil keep them from falling into the clutches of the evil Gru, and get them safely back to Earth.

Where it's reviewed:
Children's Book Review Service, April 1979, page 1200
Center for Children's Books Bulletin, November 1979, page 44
Kirkus Reviews, July 15, 1979, page 792

Other books by the author:
The Deadly Hoax, 1981
Diamonds Are More Trouble, 1969
Cop's Kid, 1968
Cutlass Island, 1962

Other books you might like:
Andrew Davies, *Marmalade and Rufus*, 1983
  The adventures of a very bad little girl and her similarly behaved, talking donkey.
John Fante, *Bravo, Burro!*, 1970
  Despite his father's objections, Manuel refuses to be parted from the burro he rescued from a fight with a cougar.
Scott O'Dell, *The Treasure of Topo-El-Bampo*, 1972
  Two burros sold to the slave-driving owners of a silver mine eventually return to save their village from starvation.
Janice Lee Smith, *Serious Science*, 1993
  Devastated when his little sister and his dog, George, demolish his science project, Adam becomes inventive in coming up with a replacement.
Geoffrey T. Williams, *Adventures Beyond the Solar System*, 1988
  Planetron, the transformer robot turned spacecraft, speeds Will on an exciting journey into the far reaches of our galaxy.

424

Scott Corbett

The Hockey Girls (New York: Dutton, 1976)

Age range: Grades 4-6

Subject(s): Sports/Hockey

Major character(s): Irma, Teenager; Miss Tingley, Coach

Time period(s): 1970s

Locale(s): United States

What the book is about: There is a new compulsory sports program for girls at Wagstaff High which throws the freshman girls into a fury, until they get involved in the program. The coach is elderly English teacher Miss Tingley. Two rivals learn to cooperate for the good of the team.

Where it's reviewed:
Kirkus Reviews, March 15, 1976, page 321
School Library Journal, May 1976, page 80

Other books by the author:
The Black Mask Trick, 1976
Captain Butcher's Body, 1976
The Case of the Burgled Blessing Box, 1976
The Boy Who Walked on Air, 1975

Other books you might like:
Sharon Brain, *My Mother Made Me!*, 1978
  The mothers of four girls decide to turn them into hockey players.
Matt Christopher, *The Hockey Machine*, 1986
  Abducted by a "fan" and forced to become a member of a professional junior hockey team, Steve Crandall must play not only to win, but also to survive.
Lois I. Fisher, *Sarah Dunes, Weird Person*, 1981
  It takes a lot before Sarah, a thirteen year old goalie, discovers she isn't as weird as she thought.
David Halecroft, *Power Play*, 1990
  Seventh grader Derrick Larson is good enough to play on the eighth grade hockey team, but if he does, he will leave his friends behind.
Donald Honig, *Fury on Skates*, 1974
  A young hockey star questions the violence of the game and his own enjoyment of it.

425

Scott Corbett

Illustrator: Paul Galdone

Home Run Trick (Boston: Little Brown, 1973)

Age range: Grades 4-6

Subject(s): Sports/Baseball

Major character(s): Kerby Maxwell, Child; Fenton Claypool, Child; Alfred J. Carmody, Landlord

Time period(s): 1970s

Locale(s): United States

What the book is about: The Panthers are excited when Mr. Fowler wants them to play an exhibition game for Taylorville Sporting Goods. The trouble starts when they find out that the Taylorville "Toms" are not the Tomcats but the Tomboys. They try to make a loss look convincing so they don't have to play the girls' team.

Where it's reviewed:
Horn Book, June 1973, page 270
Kirkus Reviews, March 1, 1973, page 254

Awards the book has won:
Golden Archer Award 1978
Mark Twain Award 1976

Other books by the author:
The Deadly Hoax, 1981
The Hockey Girls, 1976
Here Lies the Body, 1974
The Lemonade Trick, 1960

Other books you might like:
Mel Glenn, *Squeeze Play: A Baseball Story*, 1989

Jeremy finds the company of elderly Mr. J a relief after the pressures of school and a rigid baseball coach.
Robie H. Harris, *Rosie's Double Dare*, 1980
  Rosie wants to fill the vacancy on her brother's baseball team, but first she has to get through the double dare the boys insist on.
Jonah Kalb, *The Goof That Won the Pennant*, 1976
  Coach Venuti has to turn around a team convinced that they are born losers. Based on a true story.
Marjorie Lewis, *Wrongway Applebaum*, 1984
  Stanley is the class klutz who joins the baseball team coached by his baseball-crazy grandmother.

426

Scott Corbett

Illustrator: Jon McIntosh

The Mysterious Zetabet (Boston: Little, Brown, 1979)

Age range: Grades 2-4

Subject(s): Letters

Major character(s): Zachary Zwicker, Student; Zyzmund the Zeventh, Ruler

Time period(s): Indeterminate

Locale(s): Zyxland, Fictional Country; Auburn, Alabama

What the book is about: Zachary Zwicker enters a land with a topsy-turvy alphabet. In order to find his way back out of Zyxland, Zachary must meet the challenge of the Zetabet.

Where it's reviewed:
Center for Children's Books Bulletin, September 1979, page 4
Kirkus Reviews, May 15, 1979, page 576
School Library Journal, September 1979, page 107

Other books by the author:
The Foolish Dinosaur Fiasco, 1978
The Black Mask Trick, 1976
The Great Custard Pie Panic, 1974
Dr. Merlin's Magic Shop, 1973

Other books you might like:
Gilbert Adair, *Alice through the Needle's Eye*, 1984
  Alice travels through the eye of a needle and meets many unusual creatures including the letters of the alphabet.
Arthur Geisert, *Pigs From A to Z*, 1986
  Seven piglets cavort through a landscape of hidden letters as they build a tree house.
Jody Linscott, *Once upon A to Z : An Alphabet Odyssey*, 1991
  In an alliterative text, the amazing appetite of Andy leads him to meet Daisy the Delivery Girl with whom he forms the wonderful musical group.
Jeanne Modesitt, *The Story of Z*, 1990
  Tired of being the last in line and feeling unappreciated, Z walks off the alphabet and decides to start her own.
Leslie Tryon, *Albert's Alphabet*, 1991
  Clever Albert uses all the supplies in his workshop to build an alphabet for the school playground.

427

Scott Corbett

Illustrator: Geff Gerlach

The Red Room Riddle (Boston: Little Brown, 1972)

Age range: Grades 3-5

Subject(s): Ghosts

Major character(s): Bruce Crowell, Preteen; Bill Slocum, Preteen (Bully); Jamie Bly, Maintenance Worker (caretaker)

Time period(s): 1920s

Locale(s): United States

What the book is about: The scary story of two boys in a haunted house in the 1920s on Mount Alban, the wealthiest part of town. Virgil had said something awful happened on Beardsley Drive. Bruce and Bill check it out Halloween night.

Where it's reviewed:
Hornbook, June 1972, page 267
Kirkus Reviews, April 1, 1972, page 399
Library Journal, May 15, 1972, page 1928

Other books by the author:
The Trouble with Diamonds, 1985
The Mystery Man, 1970
Cop's Kid, 1968
The Mailbox Trick, 1961

Other books you might like:
Lynn Cullen, *The Backyard Ghost*, 1993
  Eleanor's desperate attempts to become popular at her new school are complicated by the discovery that her back yard is haunted by a Civil War Ghost.
Carolyn Haywood, *Halloween Treats*, 1981
  Short Halloween stories to read aloud near the holiday, or for indedpendent reading.
Constance Hiser, *Ghosts in Fourth Grade*, 1991
  James and his friends turn the old Hathaway house into a haunted house to scare Mean Mitchell, the class bully, on Halloween night.
Robert Newton Peck, *Higbee's Halloween*, 1990
  Life in quiet Clod Corners changes for Higbee and Quincy when they decide to make the nasty Striker kids the target of a grand Halloween prank.
Nancy K. Robinson, *The Ghost of Whispering Rock*, 1992
  While spending the summer at her family's cabin, Amy copes with the visit of the bored and spoiled Erika by inventing a story about a local ghost.

| 428 |

Barbara Corcoran

Child of the Morning (New York: Atheneum, 1982)

Age range: Grades 5-6

Subject(s): Epilepsy; Friendship; Fear

Major character(s): Susan Bishop, Child (epileptic)

Time period(s): 1980s

Locale(s): Maine

What the book is about: After being hit in the head with a vollyball, Susan begins to have "little spells" which the doctor dismisses as headaches. Susan gets involved with a summer theatre, first as a helper, later as a performer. When she suffers a blackout during a performance, the attending doctor asks her how long she has had epilepsy and Susan is shocked. With proper treatment, her seizures come under control and she is optimistic about her future.

Where it's reviewed:
Booklist, April 1, 1982, page 1014
Center for Children's Books Bulletin, June 1982, p 184

Other books by the author:
The Private War of Lillian Adams, 1989
The Sky Is Falling, 1988
A Horse Named Sky, 1986
The Person in the Potting Shed, 1980

Other books you might like:
Mary Jane Auch, *Glass Slippers Give You Blisters*, 1989
  Kelly discovers her artistic identity, with the help of her grandmother, by helping design a production of her junior high's drama club.
Marilyn Gould, *Golden Daffodils*, 1982
  Wishing for a miracle to make her normal, a girl with cerebral palsy transfers from a special school to a regular classroom.
Ellen Howard, *Edith Herself*, 1987
  Edith goes to live with her older sister and her dour husband in their stern Christian farming household, and the adjustment aggravates her epilepsy.
Rebecca C. Jones, *Madeline and the Great (Old) Escape Artist*, 1983
  An unlikely friendship develops between an old lady and a girl with a recently diagnosed seizure disorder.
Susan Terris, *Stage Brat*, 1980
  Linnett learns a lot about herself and the theatre when she is chosen to play Peter Pan in a repertory production.

| 429 |

Barbara Corcoran

The Clown (New York: Atheneum, 1975)

Age range: Grades 5-6

Subject(s): Orphans; Refugees

Major character(s): Liza, Orphan; Grigol, Entertainer (clown)

Time period(s): 1970s

Locale(s): Moscow, Union of Soviet Socialist Republics

What the book is about: Liza is the orphaned daughter of an American diplomat. She is living in Moscow with her aunt and uncle. She helps smuggle a Russian clown, who is being chased by the KGB, out of the country for political reasons.

Where it's reviewed:
Horn Book, October 1975, page 461
Kirkus Reviews, July 1, 1975, page 717

Other books by the author:
The Private War of Lillian Adams, 1989
Hey, That's My Soul You're Stompin' On, 1978
Meet Me at Tamerlane's Tomb, 1975
A Dance to Still Music, 1974

Other books you might like:
Vasil Bykau, *Pack of Wolves*, 1981
  A group of disabled Russian partisans makes its way to a medical unit while being pursued by traitorous partisans, German soldiers, and vicious dogs.
Hugh Barnett Cave, *The Voyage*, 1988

His father's jail sentence leaves 11 year old Vinnie and his mother in dire straits. When his father escapes, Vinnie must choose between his parents.

James Lincoln Collier, *Jump Ship to Freedom*, 1981
In 1787, a 14 year old slave, anxious to buy freedom for himself and his mother, escapes from his dishonest master and tries to find help.

Yoko Kawashima Watkins, *So Far From the Bamboo Grove*, 1986
A fictionalized autobiography in which eleven year old Yoko escapes from Korea to Japan with her mother and sister at the end of WWII.

Vladimir Zheleznikov, *Scarecrow*, 1990
12 year old Lena comes to live with her eccentric grandfather in a small Russian town and finds herself mocked and persecuted by a gang.

430

Barbara Corcoran

I Am the Universe (New York: Atheneum, 1986)

Age range: Grades 5-8

Subject(s): Illness; Family Problems

Major character(s): Kit, Teenager, Care Giver; Daniel, Genius (Kit's little brother), 3rd Grader

Time period(s): 1980s

Locale(s): United States

What the book is about: Kit's mother is operated on for a brain tumor, and the task of holding the family together falls on Kit. Her older brother starts dating and becomes a stranger. Daniel, her younger brother, a certifiable genius, is flunking third grade, and her younger sister needs more and more attention.

Where it's reviewed:
Center for Children's Books Bulletin, December 1986, page 64
School Library Journal, October 1986, page 171

Other books by the author:
Annie's Monster, 1990
August, Die She Must, 1984
Child of the Morning, 1982
All the Summer Voices, 1973

Other books you might like:
Frank Bonham, *The Forever Formula*, 1979
A seventeen year old wonders if he has a brain tumor or is suffering from hallucinations. The truth is startling, incredible, and dangerous.

Chris Crutcher, *The Crazy Horse Electric Game*, 1987
Willie is a star athlete. An accident leaves him crippled and unable to speak clearly. He can't imagine facing the people who once saw him as strong.

John Gunther, *Death Be Not Proud*, 1965
A father's account of his teenage son's courageous fight for life during the fifteen months he was dying of a brain tumor.

Kathryn Lance, *Going to See Grassy Ella*, 1993
Hoping to be cured of cancer, a twelve year old and her sister go to a faith healer in New York where they become pawns in a gangster battle.

Jean Little, *Mama's Going to Buy You a Mockingbird*, 1984

Jeremy and Sarah learn to cope with their grief and completely changed lives during their father's battle with cancer.

431

Barbara Corcoran

Mystery on Ice (New York: Atheneum, 1985)

Age range: Grades 5-8

Subject(s): Mystery and Detective Stories

Major character(s): Kim, Preteen; Stella, Preteen; Galen Smith, Preteen

Time period(s): 1980s

Locale(s): New Hampshire

What the book is about: Kim and Stella are excited about a winter trip to Camp Allegro. There will be skiing and skating, ice boating and good friends. Things are less pleasant, however, when a mysterious visitor arrives, wild men make threats against the girls in the camp, and Galen, the pest, disappears.

Where it's reviewed:
Booklist, April 15, 1985, page 1190
Center for Children's Books Bulletin, March 1985, page 122
School Library Journal, May 1985, page 109

Other books by the author:
Family Secrets, 1992
Annie's Monster, 1990
August, Die She Must, 1984
All the Summer Voices, 1973

Other books you might like:
John Durham, *Me and Arch and the Pest*, 1970
Two boys acquire a German shepherd whose disappearance involves them in a crime.

Constance C. Greene, *Isabelle Shows Her Stuff*, 1984
Eight year old Guy tries to change his good image with the help of Isabelle the Itch. They both learn what being a tough guy really means.

Carli Laklan, *Ski Bum*, 1973
A young man on a pleasure trip becomes caught up in a drama at Big Snow ski resort when he joins the Ski Patrol.

Elizabeth Levy, *Cold as Ice*, 1988
Working at a New York City sports arena during a pre-olympic skating exhibition, Kelly meets two male skaters threatened by mysterious accidents.

Gary Paulsen, *Dunc and Amos and the Red Tattoos*, 1993
Dunc and Amos, at camp for two weeks, overhear a threat against the director and discover that camp funds have been stolen.

432

Barbara Corcoran

Illustrator: Richard L. Shell

Sasha, My Friend (New York: Atheneum, 1969)

Age range: Grades 5-8

Subject(s): Country Life; Animals/Wolves

Major character(s): Hallie Winthrop, Teenager; Birdie Penney, Neighbor, Handicapped

Time period(s): 1960s

Locale(s): Beaver Creek, Montana

What the book is about: Hallie's mother is dead and her father needs to leave Los Angeles for his health. Hallie and her dad go to Montana, where he lived as a boy. Her school is by correspondence and she is very lonely. Aside from one neighbor, her only company is Sasha, a wolf she raised from a pup. But wolves are dangerous on a Montana ranch.

Where it's reviewed:
Booklist, February 1, 1970, page 667
Hornbook, October 1969, page 540
Kirkus Reviews, August 1, 1969, page 783

Other books by the author:
Annie's Monster, 1990
I Am the Universe, 1986
Child of the Morning, 1982
Rising Damp, 1980

Other books you might like:
Joan Davenport Carris, *Stolen Bones: A Novel*,
    While spending the summer with his paleontologist mother at a dig in Montana, Alec tries to solve a mystery surrounding some missing fossils.
Mel Ellis, *Flight of the White Wolf*, 1970
    A boy and his pet wolf flee before a state wide hunt to locate and destroy the animal.
Jean Craighead George, *Julie of the Wolves*, 1972
    Running away from home and a forced marriage, an Eskimo girl becomes lost on the North Slope of Alaska and survives by becoming part of a wolf pack.
Evelyn Sibley Lampman, *Rattlesnake Cave*, 1974
    While spending time with relatives in Montana, a friendless boy finds a new world open to him when he makes friends with local Indians.
Ann Turnbull, *The Wolf King*, 1975
    A young Bronze Age boy sets out to kill the wolf king, a mysterious figure who controls a wolf pack that has been raiding the local villages.

433

Alan Coren

Illustrator: John Astrop

Arthur the Kid (Boston: Little Brown, 1978)

Age range: Grades 4-6

Subject(s): Robbers and Outlaws

Major character(s): Arthur William Foskett, Detective, Child

Time period(s): Indeterminate

Locale(s): United States

What the book is about: This is a spoof of a western desperado tale. A gang of three are miserable failures at every crime they attempt. Ten year old Arthur answers their ad for a boss, and they think he's Billy the Kid.

Where it's reviewed:
Kirkus Reviews, June 1, 1978, page 594
School Library Journal, September 1978, page 133

Other books by the author:
Buffalo Arthur, 1978
Golfing for Cats, 1978

The Lone Arthur, 1978
The Peanut Papers, 1978

Other books you might like:
Avi, *Emily Upham's Revenge: A Massachusetts Tale*, 1978
    During the summer of 1875, a girl is sent to live with her wealthy uncle and becomes involved in a very suspicious bank robbery.
John R. Erickson, *The Original Adventures of Hank the Cowdog*, 1988
    Hank the Cowdog, Head of Ranch Security, is framed for something that was not his fault at all.
Sid Fleischman, *Me and the Man on the Moon-Eyed Horse*, 1977
    Young Clint's ingenious scheme foils a villainous train wrecker's attempt to rob the circus train.
Jack Prelutsky, *The New Kid on the Block: Poems*, 1984
    Humorous poems about strange creatures and people, including some very strange cowboys.
Glen Rounds, *Mr. Yowder and the Giant Bull Snake*, 1978
    A sign painter and a giant bull snake cause a commotion when they replace Buffalo Bill as official buffalo hunters for the United States Army.

434

June Counsel

Illustrator: Jill Bennett

A Dragon in Class Four

Age range: Grades 3-5

Subject(s): Dragons; Fantasy

Major character(s): Sam, Child; Scales, Dragon

Time period(s): Indeterminate

Locale(s): England

What the book is about: A group of British children and a dragon work through various projects.

Where it's reviewed:
Center for Children's Books Bulletin, October 1984, page 21
School Library Journal, December 1984, page 79

Other books by the author:
But Martin!, 1984

Other books you might like:
Gillian Bradshaw, *The Land of Gold*, 1992
    After the murder of her parents, a Nubian princess is helped to her rightful place on the throne by two friendly Egyptians and the dragon Hathor.
Brenda Seabrooke, *The Dragon That Ate Summer*, 1992
    While recuperating from a skateboard accident, Alastair finds an unusual new pet in Mr. Hobson's petunia garden.
Betsy Sterman, *Backyard Dragon*, 1993
    With the help of three friends, a young boy and his grandfather help a 15th century Welsh dragon find its way home.
Brad Strickland, *Dragon's Plunder*, 1992
    Having been kidnapped by former pirates, Jamie agrees to help their leader, a living corpse, find the dragon of Windrose Island.
Laurence Yep, *Dragon War*, 1992
    The dragon princess and her companions fight a war against the Boneless King in order to rescue their friend and restore the dragons' underwater home.

435

Harold Courlander

Illustrator: Monica Vachula

Cow-Tail Switch and Other West Africa Stories (New York: Holt, 1947)

Age range: Grades 5-6

Subject(s): Africa; Folk Tales

Locale(s): Africa

What the book is about: 17 stories, mostly from the Ashanti country, show origins of folk sayings and customs, and animal trickery and ingenuity. Powerful parables and vivid images make this a delight for all ages and an excellent read-aloud.

Where it's reviewed:
Booklist, March 1, 1947, page 209
Horn Book, March 1947, page 113

Awards the book has won:
Newbery Medal 1948

Other books by the author:
Fire on the Mountain, 1950
Hat Shaking Dance, 1957
Ride with the Sun, 1955
Uncle Bouqui of Haiti, 1942

Other books you might like:
Lynn Joseph, *Wave in Her Pocket*, 1991
   On the island of Trinidad, Tantie tells six stories, some of them from West Africa.
Joanna Troughton, *How Stories Came into the World*, 1989
   When lightning strikes a mouse's door, he reveals the secret of how stories escaped into the world.
Kathleen Arnott, *Dragons, Ogres, and Scary Things*, 1974
   Tale about a magic drum with the power to make animals dance, and a story about a child-stealing ogre.
Nick Greaves, *When Hippo Was Hairy and Other Tales From Africa*, 1988
   Folk tales stressing the value of African wildlife and folklore.
Ashley Bryan, *Dancing Granny*, 1977
   Spider Ananse, gets his granny started dancing so he can raid her gar den but his plan backfires.

436

Helen Coutant

Illustrator: Vo-Dinh

First Snow (New York: Knopf, 1974)

Age range: Grades 3-4

Subject(s): Family Life; Death; Vietnamese

Major character(s): Lien, Child

Time period(s): 1970s

Locale(s): United States (New England)

What the book is about: Lien does not understand the words "grandmother is dying." She searches for an answer in the newly fallen snow. Seeing the snow change to water, and the gray skies clear to sunshine, Lien begins to understand the cycles of life and death.

Where it's reviewed:
Kirkus Reviews, November 1974, page 1150
Library Journal, November 15, 1974, page 3035

Awards the book has won:
Christopher Award 1975

Other books by the author:
The Gift, 1983

Other books you might like:
Ann Nolan Clark, *To Stand Against the Wind*, 1978
   A young refugee recalls life in his Vietnamese village before and during the war.
Paige Dixon, *Promises to Keep*, 1974
   An insecure boy is sure he will be subjected to ridicule from the town when his orphaned Vietnamese cousin comes to live with his family.
Mary Holmes, *Dust of Life*, 1992
   Anh welcomes her cousing Lan to California and tries to help her deal with her terrible past.
Jeanne M. Lee, *Ba-Nam*, 1987
   A young Vietnamese girl visiting the graves of her ancestors finds the old gravekeeper frightening until a storm reveals the old woman's kindness.
Jayne Pettit, *My Name Is San Ho*, 1992
   A twelve year old boy adjusts to life in the US with his mother and American Marine stepfather.

437

Bruce Coville

The Ghost Wore Gray (New York: Bantam, 1988)

Age range: Grades 4-6

Subject(s): Ghosts; Mystery and Detective Stories

Major character(s): Nina Tanleven, Preteen, 6th Grader; Chris Gurley, Friend, 6th Grader

Time period(s): 1980s

Locale(s): Syracuse, New York

What the book is about: Sixth graders unravel a hundred year old mystery at a country inn. Nina convinces her father, an architect, to take her and her best friend, Chris, along to stay at an old inn they're restoring. They are not surprised to see a faded photo of a handsome confederate soldier, but they are more than a little shocked when the ghost of the soldier shows up for dinner that night.

Where it's reviewed:
Booklist, September 15, 1988, page 168
School Library Journal, September 1988, page 183

Other books by the author:
The Dinosaur That Followed Me Home, 1990
How I Survived My Summer Vacation, 1988
The Ghost in the Third Row, 1987
Amulet of Doom, 1985

Other books you might like:
Elaine Marie Alphin, *The Ghost Cadet*, 1991
   Twelve year old Benjy, in Virginia visiting his grandmother, meets the ghost of a cadet killed in the Civil War and helps him recover a gold watch.
Lynn Hall, *The Mystery of the Caramel Cat*, 1981

Willie's encounter with a feline ghost outside a deserted mansion leads to a strange dream about events which occurred prior to the Civil War.

William Heuman, *Buffalo Soldier*, 1969
An ex-Confederate soldier goes West where he meets and becomes friends with Trooper Joel Tibbs, the son of a former slave.

John Shults Lawson, *The Spring Rider*, 1968
A brother and sister become involved with the ghost of a Union soldier who, each spring, reenacts an old Civil War battle with his regiment.

Marilyn Redmond, *Henry Hamilton, Graduate Ghost*, 1982
Henry Hamilton, a Civil War ghost newly graduated from Spiritual Specter University, mistakenly haunts a modern suburban home with a large family.

438

Bruce Coville

Illustrator: Katherine Coville

The Monster's Ring (New York: Pantheon, 1982)

Age range: Grades 4-6

Subject(s): Halloween; Magic; Monsters

Major character(s): Russell Crannaker, Monster, Preteen; Eddie, Bully; Missy Freebaker, Friend

Time period(s): 1980s

Locale(s): Kennituck Falls

What the book is about: Russell, a timid boy eager to frighten Eddie, the bully of Boardman Road Elementary School, finds a ring that turns him into a monster. Russell and his family and the whole town have the most uproarious Halloween ever, and Russell discovers that getting into magic is a lot easier than getting out of it. Suspenseful and funny, a great combination.

Where it's reviewed:
Children's Book Review Service, October 1982, page 17
New York Times Book Review, October 31, 1982, page 27
School Library Journal, February 1983, page 75

Other books by the author:
Goblins in the Castle, 1992
The Ghost in the Big Brass Bed, 1991
The Ghost Wore Gray, 1988
The Unicorn Treasury, 1988

Other books you might like:
Ruth Chew, *The Witch and the Ring*, 1989
A sister and brother find a ring that brings a special cat, a witch, and a series of adventures into their lives.
Constance Hiser, *Ghosts in Fourth Grade*, 1991
James and his friends turn the old Hathaway House into a haunted house to scare Mean Mitchell, the class bully, on Halloween night.
Dave Ross, *How to Prevent Monster Attacks*, 1986
A humorous guide to monsters, with suggestions on avoiding them and defending yourself against them if attacked.
Simon Seymour, *Einstein Anderson Sees through the Invisible Man*, 1983
The sixth grade science sleuth solves ten more puzzling cases, one involving an allergic monster and another an invisible man.
Drew Stevenson, *The Case of the Wandering Werewolf*, 1987

Raymond Almond, the Often Nervous, and J. Huntley English, Monster Hunter, try to track down the wolflike beast haunting Lost Woods

---

439

M.F. Craig

The Mystery at Peacock Place (New York: Scholastic, 1986)

Age range: Grades 5-6

Subject(s): Mystery and Detective Stories

Major character(s): Hobie Morgan, Preteen; Shadow, Dog

Time period(s): Indeterminate

Locale(s): United States

What the book is about: Hobie gets involved in trying to find an old woman, when his dog, Shadow, chases a rabbit on to old Mrs. Peacock's property. What he sees inside the Peacock mansion terrifies him, but he feels he must investigate. His friend, Ben, is too busy to help, so Hobie takes off on his own.

Where it's reviewed:
Booklist, September 15, 1986, page 136
School Library Journal, October 1986, page 172

Other books you might like:
M.S. Craig, *The Mystery at Wolf River*, 1989
Kate and her best friend, Bugs, solve a mystery involving a drowning dog and a mansion.
Stephen Mooser, *Secret in the Old Mansion*, 1988
Horace and Mildred hire the young professionals at Treasure Hounds to find out where Aunt Henrietta stashed her fortune before died.
Bonnie Pryor, *The Twenty-Four-Hour Lipstick Mystery*, 1989
To earn money for charm school, eleven year old Cassie works for the owner of a spooky mansion and uncovers a mystery surrounding a secret room.
Peter Silsbee, *Love Among the Hiccups*, 1989
Palmer, a tour guide in the Thousand Islands, finds his romantic misadventures complicated by the strangers fighting over a decaying mansion.
Wilma Yeo, *The Girl in the Window*, 1988
Kiley's friend is kidnapped. No one admits that she's back, but Kiley has just seen her at the window of the Alcott mansion or was that a ghost?

440

Dorothy Crayder

Illustrator: Velma Ilsley

She and the Dubious Three (New York: Atheneum, 1974)

Age range: Grades 5-7

Subject(s): Heroine; Kidnapping; Trains

Major character(s): Maggie, Child

Time period(s): 1970s

Locale(s): Venice, Italy

What the book is about: Maggie becomes suspicious while travelling on a train that the baby across the aisle does not belong to the couple he's with. He must have been kidnapped! A reluctant traveler from Iowa, Maggie becomes quite the heroine.

Where it's reviewed:
Booklist, September 1, 1974, page 391
Publisher's Weekly, July 22, 1974, page 70

Other books by the author:
The Joker and the Swan, 1981
The Riddles of Mermaid House, 1977
She, the Adventuress, 1973

Other books you might like:
Lynn Hall, *Too Near the Sun*, 1970
    A boy living in Icaria, Iowa, in 1875 finds himself in growing conflict with the socialistic principles of his community.
Cynthia King, *Sailing Home*, 1982
    After two years with a hippie family, Paul returns to finish school and sail again with the girl friend whose father's false accusations made him run.
Lee Kingman, *The Peter Pan Ring*, 1970
    A girl discovers why people drop out of society when she becomes part of a Boston hippie colony.
Suzanne Newton, *C/O Arnold's Corners*, 1974
    A twelve year old girl upsets her family and her small southern community when she befriends a "hippie", a young mother, and a black classmate.
Louise Dickinson Rich, *Summer at High Kingdom*, 1975
    The members of a hippie commune established on a nearby farm have a marked effect on the attitudes of a young Maine boy and his family.

441

Helen Cresswell

The Beachcombers (New York: Macmillan, 1972)

Age range: Grades 5-8

Subject(s): Fantasy

Major character(s): Ned Kerne, Tourist; Fiony Dallaker, Scavenger (Beachcomber); Jack Pickering, Friend

Time period(s): 1970s

Locale(s): England

What the book is about: A missing treasure, a boy held by a group of thieves, and a family of beachcombers are elements combined in this suspenseful adventure. Ned finds himself caught in the struggle between a family of beachcombers and a family of scavengers who are watching for treasure to come in on the high tide. Ned realizes that if the Scavengers find the treasure first, the Beachcombers will be destroyed. The reader, like Ned, must choose between two conflicting worlds.

Where it's reviewed:
Booklist, March 1, 1973, page 646
Hornbook, February 1973, page 52
Center for Children's Books Bulletin, January 1973, page 74

Other books by the author:
Moondial, 1987
Dear Shrink, 1982
The Bongleweed, 1973
The Night Watchman, 1969

Other books you might like:
Sarita Kendall, *The Bell Reef*, 1990

Anxious to sunken treasure, two teenagers enlist the help of a trained dolphin and determine to carry out their hunt despite ghost stories.
Walter Macken, *Island of the Great Yellow Ox*, 1991
    A storm washes Conor, his little brother and two friends upon Ox Island where they become prisoners of the eccentric lady in search of a treasure.
Todd Strausser, *Beyond the Reef*, 1989
    Chris and his parents move from New York to Key West, but the thrill fades when Dad's obsession with finding sunken treaure angers many residents.
Bill Wallace, *Danger in Quicksand Swamp*, 1989
    Ben and Jake battle alligators, quicksand, and a murderer when they search for buried treasure on an island in a swamp.
Robert Westall, *Stormsearch*, 1992
    Tim's discovery of a model ship on an English beach leads him to an unsolved mystery involving an heiress, a drunkard, and a fanatic miser.

442

Helen Cresswell

The Bongleweed (New York: Macmillan, 1973)

Age range: Grades 4-6

Subject(s): Gardens and Gardening

Major character(s): Becky Finch, Preteen; Jason, Child; Mr. Harper, Scientist

Time period(s): Indeterminate

Locale(s): England (Pew Gardens)

What the book is about: Becky is the daughter of the head gardener of Pew Gardens, headed by Mr. Harper. Jason, the Harper's house guest, helps Becky protect the bongleweed. A wildly growing plant, it grows two feet two days after planting. Becky's dad joins the cause.

Where it's reviewed:
Kirkus Reviews, October 15, 1973, page 1159
Library Journal, October 15, 1973, page 3143

Other books by the author:
The Bower Birds, 1973
Lizzie Dripping, 1973
Up the Pier, 1973
The Beachcombers, 1972

Other books you might like:
Catherine Dexter, *Gertie's Green Thumb*, 1983
    Gertie, lover of plants and animals, finds a working wishbone in the park and turns her family's home into a magical House of Nature.
Sonia Levitin, *Jason and the Money Tree*, 1974
    When Jason plants a money tree, he finds himself in conflict with the law and nature.
Nancy McArthur, *The Escape of the Plant That Ate Dirty Socks*, 1992
    The sock-eating plants are on the move, and heading right for trouble.
Andre Norton, *Star Ka'ats and the Plant People*, 1979
    Follows the adventures of two children and a super race of cats as they rescue a group of plant people.
Judith St. George, *The Mysterious Girl in the Garden*, 1981

Visiting Kew Gardens, an American girl is transported back to Kew Palace in 1805 where she meets Princess Charlotte Augusta, future Queen of England.

443

Helen Cresswell

Dear Shrink (New York: Macmillan, 1982)

Age range: Grades 5-8

Subject(s): Foster Homes; Orphans

Major character(s): Oliver Saxon, Teenager; William Saxon, Teenager; Lucy Saxon, Child

Time period(s): 1980s

Locale(s): England

What the book is about: Oliver's story of four miserable months in the lives of the Saxons is tense and frightening at times. Their parents are on a six month expedition to the Amazon. Ollie, William, and seven year old Lucy suddenly discover what it is like to be without an adult to take anything but official notice of them.

Where it's reviewed:
Booklist, September 15, 1982, page 112
Center for Children's Books Bulletin, October 1982, page 23
Hornbook, February 1983, page 51

Other books by the author:
Absolute Zero, 1978
A Game of Catch, 1977
Ordinary Jack, 1977
The Winter of the Birds, 1976

Other books you might like:
Joan Aiken, *Go Saddle the Sea*, 1977
    In 1821, an orphaned boy runs away from his unhappy home in Spain to England where he tries to find his father's family.
Nina Bawden, *The Finding*, 1985
    When an unexpected inheritance threatens to change his life with his adopted family in London, an eleven year old foundling runs away from home.
Frances Hodgson Burnett, *A Little Princess*, 1990
    Sara Crewe, a pupil at Miss Minchin's London school, is left in poverty when her father dies, but is later rescued by a mysterious benefactor.
Leon Garfield, *Young Nick and Jubilee*, 1989
    A meeting with a pickpocket and a pupil from a charity school sets events in motion that change the lives of an orphaned brother and sister.
Noel Streatfeild, *Thursday's Child*, 1970
    Proud of her unusual history, a nameless orphan faces with spirit, the unbearable conditions of an early 20th century English orphanage.

444

Helen Cresswell

Illustrator: Ati Forberg

A Game of Catch (New York: Macmillan, 1977)

Age range: Grades 3-5

Subject(s): Space and Time

Major character(s): Kate, Child; Hugh, Child

Time period(s): 1970s

Locale(s): England

What the book is about: Just before they leave for Canada, Kate and Hugh have an adventure in a deserted museum. Kate is sure she hears laughter. Nobody else can see the two children from an 18th century painting.

Where it's reviewed:
Horn Book, June 1977, page 312
Kirkus Reviews, January 1, 1977, page 4

Other books by the author:
The Secret World of Polly Flint, 1982
Ordinary Jack, 1977
Two Hoots and the King, 1977
The Bongleweed, 1976

Other books you might like:
Vivien Alcock, *The Sylvia Game*, 1982
    During a seaside trip with her artist father, Emily meets a gypsy's son and a young heir, who notice her resemblance to a girl in a Renoir painting.
Molly Bang, *Tye May and the Magic Brush*, 1981
    In a dream a poor orphan is given a brush that brings to life everything she paints.
Patrick Skene Catling, *John Midas in the Dreamtime*, 1986
    At the site of sacred cave painting in the Australian outback, John Midas slips back thousands of years and finds himself among an aboriginal tribe.
Andre Norton, *Wraiths of Time*, 1976
    Sent through space and time into the ancient Nubian Kingdom of Mero e, a museum expert must help preserve African civilization from evil people.
Robert Westall, *The Watch House*, 1977
    One summer on the north English coast, a girl's presence in a nearby museum with relics of shipwrecks and rescues releases a powerful and evil ghost.

445

Helen Cresswell

Moondial (New York: Macmillan, 1987)

Age range: Grades 5-7

Subject(s): Child Abuse; Ghosts; Space and Time

Major character(s): Minty Kane, Witch; Mary, Relative (aunt)

Time period(s): 1870s (1871)

Locale(s): England

What the book is about: Minty Kane, a modern girl who is a witch, is left with her Aunt Mary after her mother is in an accident. Minty's concern for her mother pushes her to develop her sixth sense to the point where she can time travel using the garden sundial. She travels back in time to save Tom and Sarah, two abused children who are trapped in 1871.

Where it's reviewed:
Horn Book, January/February 1988, page 68
School Library Journal, November 1987, page 104

Other books by the author:
The Secret World of Polly Flint, 1984
Dear Shrink, 1982
My Aunt Polly, 1979
Absolute Zero, 1978

Other books you might like:
Chris Crutcher, *Chinese Handcuffs*, 1989
　Troubled by his older brother's violent suicide, Dillon gets involved in his friend Jennifer's awful secret about what her stepfather is doing to her
Jesse Harris, *Aidan's Fate*, 1992
　McKenzie's violent psychic visions expose a case of child abuse and spell doom for her boyfriend, Aidan.
Marilyn Reynolds, *Telling*, 1989
　After being sexually abused by the father of the children she is babysitting, Cassie must find the strength and wisdom to deal with the problem.
Willo Davis Roberts, *Don't Hurt Laurie!*, 1977
　Laurie is physically abused by her mother; can she escape, and will anyone believe her story?
Doris Buchanan Smith, *Tough Chauncey*, 1974
　Abused by his grandfather and neglected by his mother, a "tough" teen sees running away as the only solution until a friend gives him an alternative.

446

Helen Cresswell

Ordinary Jack (New York: Macmillan, 1977)

Age range: Grades 5-6

Series: Bagthorpe Saga

Subject(s): Family Life; Humor

Major character(s): Jack Bagthorpe, Preteen; Parker Bagthorpe, Relative (uncle); Daisy Bagthorpe, Cousin

Time period(s): 1970s

Locale(s): England

What the book is about: The entire Bagthorpe family is nutty, except for Jack, whose behavior approaches normal. His brothers and sisters and parents are all very talented, with "many strings to their bows," while Jack is very ordinary. His uncle Parker who lives nearby with a free spirited wife and daughter who paints on walls and starts fires, decides to help Jack prove that his gift is prophetic visions. Great satire for language lovers.

Where it's reviewed:
Kirkus Reviews, October 1, 1977, page 1048
Publisher's Weekly, October 31, 1977, page 59

Other books by the author:
Absolute Zero, 1978
Bagthorpes Unlimited, 1978
A Game of Catch, 1977
The Bongleweed, 1976

Other books you might like:
Roald Dahl, *The Twits*, 1980
　The misadventures of two terribly old people who enjoy playing nasty tricks and are finally outwitted by a family of monkeys.
C.G. Draper, *A Holiday Year*, 1988

Ned celebrates each holiday throughout the year in a memorable fashion.
Elizabeth Starr Hill, *Fangs Aren't Everything*, 1985
　Victim of an ancient family curse that turns him into a wolfman when the moon is full, a young man tries to hide that fact from his friends.
Beverly Keller, *Desdemona Moves On*, 1992
　Chronicles the comic mishaps of Desdemona and her family after they move into a luxurious new house.
Jerry Smith, *Pretzel and Pop's Closetful of Stories*, 1991
　Pop tells Pretzel humorous stories about various family members.

447

Linda Crew

Children of the River (New York: Delacorte, 1989)

Age range: Grades 5 and Up

Subject(s): Asian Americans

Major character(s): Sundara Sovann, Teenager; Jonathan McKinnon, Teenager; Ravy Souvann, Child

Time period(s): 1970s (1979)

Locale(s): Oregon

What the book is about: Having fled Cambodia four years earlier to escape the Khmer Rouge army, Sundara is torn between remaining faithful to her own people and enjoying life as a "regular" American. Her family expects to choose a husband for her, but she has met Jonathan and prefers her own choice.

Where it's reviewed:
Kirkus Reviews, January 15, 1989, page 121
School Library Journal, March 1989, page 198

Awards the book has won:
Golden Kite Award 1989 (Honor Award)

Other books by the author:
Ordinary Miracles, 1993
Nekomah Creek, 1991
Someday I'll Laugh about This, 1990

Other books you might like:
Cora Cheney, *The Treasures of Lin Li-ti*, 1969
　During the evacuation of refugees from China in the late 1940s, an 11 year old boy becomes separated from his family and must make his own way.
Wolfgang Ecke, *Flight Toward Home*, 1970
　Recounts a young boy's attempts during and after WWII to escape from East Germany to his grandmother in West Germany.
Joan Lingard, *Between Two Worlds*, 1991
　Arriving in Canada after WWII, a family of Latvian refugees faces illness and financial hardship.
William McGuire, *Southeast Asians*, 1991
　Describes how refugees from Vietnam, Cambodia, and Laos struggled to build new lives in America and preserve their national heritage. (non-fiction)
Ilse-Margret Vogel, *Tikhon*, 1984
　A Russian soldier without ID, in post-WWI Germany, becomes a unique and much-loved companion to a young girl when her parents hide him.

448

Gilbert B. Cross

Terror Train! (New York: Macmillan, 1987)

Age range: Grades 4-6

Subject(s): Mystery and Detective Stories; Trains

Major character(s): Jeff Glover, Preteen; Vo Nguyen, Adoptee (Jeff's brother); Mrs. Larkin, Writer

Time period(s): 1980s

Locale(s): Chicago, Illinois

What the book is about: Jeff and his adopted brother, Nguyen, are traveling from Chicago to Portland, Oregon, by train. When a fellow passenger dies suddenly, they join forces with an elderly mystery writer to investigate and find the guilty party.

Where it's reviewed:
Booklist, MKay 1, 1987, page 1365
School Library Journal, August 1987, page 81

Other books by the author:
A Witch Across Time, 1990
Mystery at Moon Lake, 1986
A Hanging at Tyburn, 1983

Other books you might like:
Allan Baillie, *Little Brother*, 1992
  In Cambodia after the Vietnam War, Vithy overcomes social upheaval, a hostile jungle, and his inability to trust, in order to rescue his older brother
Bess Clayton, *Tracks*, 1986
  Two restless brothers, Monroe and Blue, learn about life and people while following the railroad tracks in the Southwest during the Depression.
Alan Cohen, *Railroad Arthur*, 1977
  Ten year old Arthur must not only solve a series of train robberies, but must clear his own name of suspicion.
Jamie Gilson, *Hello, My Name Is Scrambled Eggs*, 1985
  When his folks host a Vietnamese family that has come to settle in their town, Harvey enjoys Americanizing twelve year old Tuan.
A.C. Stewart, *The Quarry Line Mystery*, 1973
  Through an afternoon's misadventure riding trains, a young English boy stumbles on a mystery involving a disappearing freight train.

449

Gillian Cross

On the Edge (New York: Holiday, 1984)

Age range: Grades 5-6

Subject(s): Kidnapping; Mystery and Detective Stories; Terrorism

Major character(s): Tug, Teenager; Jinny, Teenager

Time period(s): 1980s

Locale(s): United States

What the book is about: Two young people discover unknown strengths inside themselves when one is kidnapped and the other tries to save him. Terrorists have taken Tug, the son of a reporter. Jinny becomes suspicious of the house next door and takes action.

Where it's reviewed:
Horn Book, July 1985, page 453
School Library Journal, August 1985, page 73

Awards the book has won:
Edgar Allan Poe Award - Runner-up

Other books by the author:
Wolf, 1991
A Map of Nowhere, 1988
Roscoe's Leap, 1987
Born of the Sun, 1983

Other books you might like:
Browning Norton, *Johnny/Bingo*, 1971
  As the only witnesses to a bank robbery, two boys are held hostage with the threat that their families will die if they try to escape.
Richard Parker, *Three by Mistake*, 1974
  Through unforeseen circumstances, terrorists kidnap three children instead of one, and wait out the government officials' response to their demands.
Susan Lowry Rardin, *Captives in a Foreign Land*, 1984
  Six young American children whose parents are diplomats, are smuggled to an Arab land while their captors demand an end to all war.
Adrienne Richard, *The Accomplice: A Novel*, 1973
  Benjy joins his archeologist father in Israel, hoping to get to know him better, and becomes involved in a terrororist plot.
Geoffrey Trease, *The Baron's Hostage*, 1975
  The lives of a boy, laying claim to a barony, and a girl, whose marriage has been arranged, become entwined during the 13th century Baron's War.

450

Gillian Cross

Wolf (New York: Holiday, 1991)

Age range: Grades 6-8

Subject(s): Communal Living; Mothers and Daughters; Animals/Wolves

Major character(s): Casey, Teenager; Goldie, Parent (Casey's mother); Robert, Teenager (Lyall's Son)

Time period(s): 1990s

Locale(s): England

What the book is about: Casey usually lives with her grandmother, Nan, but occasionally Grandma goes through spells and tells Casey to go stay with her mother for awhile. This time the search takes Casey to a run-down shack her mother is sharing with a new boyfriend, Lyall, and his teenage son, Robert. Casey reluctantly joins their project, a multi-media extravaganza about wolves, but still wonders why Nan sent her away and who the strange visitor was before she left. A fast plot with a breathless and startling ending.

Where it's reviewed:
Booklist, January 15, 1991, page 1052
Horn Book, May/June, 1991, page 336

Other books by the author:
Chartbreaker, 1986
On the Edge, 1986
Born of the Sun, 1983
The Iron Way, 1979

Other books you might like:
Bettie Waddell Cannon, *Begin the World Again*, 1991
  Feeling trapped in the farm commune where she lives, fifteen year old Lake can't hide from the problems of the farm and her parents.
Marsha Qualey, *Everybody's Daughter*, 1991
  Beamer is forced to examine how growing up in a commune in the north woods of Minnesota has shaped her personality.
Louise Dickinson Rich, *Summer at High Kingdom*, 1975
  The members of a hippie commune established on a nearby farm have a marked effect on the attitudes of a young Maine farm boy and his family.
Harriet Sirof, *The Real World: A Novel*, 1985
  A fifteen year old who lives with her ardent feminist mother begins to learn how others live when she first visits her father, a successful architect.
Marion Dane Walker, *Nell of Blue Harbor*, 1990
  Eleven year old Nell has to grow up quickly when she moves from a Vermont commune to the real world with parents not ready to accept responsibilities.

451

Vera G. Cumberlege

Illustrator: Charles Mikolaycak

Shipwreck (Chicago: Follett, 1974)

Age range: Grades 3-5

Subject(s): Boats and Boating; Shipwrecks; Rescue Work

Major character(s): Jim, Child

Time period(s): Indeterminate

Locale(s): England

What the book is about: Anxious for the day when he can row out with the lifeboat crew, Jim is unhappy that the old boat is to be replaced with a powered one until he witnesses a shipwreck during a storm.

Where it's reviewed:
Booklist, September 15, 1974, page 98
School Library Journal, March 1975, page 94
Center for Children's Books Bulletin, February 1975, page 92

Other books you might like:
Pam Conrad, *The Lost Sailor*, 1992
  A sailor famed for his seamanship and luck is shipwrecked on a tiny island, where his darkest hours give rise to rescue and a new life.
Philippe Dupasquier, *Jack at Sea*, 1986
  Life aboard a British warship brings Jack into contact with a naval battle, press gangs, floggings, and shipwreck, until he makes his way home.
Sue L. Hamilton, *Royal Mail Steamship Titanic*, 1988
  A ship officer's account of the *Titanic*'s last hours. A fictional account based on factual data.
Kathryn Long Humphrey, *Shipwrecks: Terror and Treasure*, 1991
  Examines the discovery and exploration of the shipwrecks of the *Mary Rose*, *Concepcion*, and *Titanic*.
Ann McGovern, *Nicholas Bentley Stoningpot III*, 1982
  A bored little rich boy is shipwrecked on a remote island where he is happier than he has ever been before.

452

Julia Cunningham

Illustrator: James Spanfeller

Dorp Dead (New York: Pantheon, 1965)

Age range: Grades 4-6

Subject(s): Gifted Children; Orphans

Major character(s): Gilly Ground, Orphan, Preteen; Mr. Kobalt, Carpenter; Mash, Dog

Time period(s): Indeterminate

Locale(s): Fictional Country

What the book is about: A very bright boy, who has learned in a year in an orphanage how to withdraw himself completely, is apprenticed to a ladder maker into whose timed routine he fits very well, until he realizes the threat to his own existence. He escapes from the deranged Kobalt with the help of his dog, Mash, ans sets out to make a life of his own.

Where it's reviewed:
Center for Children's Books Bulletin, October 1965, page 30
School Library Journal, December 1978, page 32
Library Journal, April 15, 1965, page 2018

Other books by the author:
Come to the Edge, 1977
Dear Rat, 1977
Far in the Day, 1972
Burnish Me Bright, 1970

Other books you might like:
Robert Burch, *Skinny*, 1964
  An orphan temporarily working at Miss Bessie's hotel hopes arrangements can be made for him to stay there instead of being sent to an orphan's home.
Matt Christopher, *Touchdown for Tommy*, 1959
  A young boy worries about making the football team and convincing his foster parents to adopt him.
Doris Gates, *Sensible Kate*, 1943
  Orphaned Kate longs to be pretty. When she goes to live with her new foster parents, she meets an artist couple who recognize her real qualities.
Astrid Lindgren, *Rasmus and the Vagabond*, 1960
  After running away from the orphanage to find a home and parents, a boy finds himself with a tramp father, a mother, a kitten and a home of his own.
Eleanor Spence, *The Switherby Pilgrims*, 1967
  A young English lady moves her ten orphan charges to Australia where they carve out a new life for themselves in the severe Australian bush.

453

Julia Cunningham

Flight of the Sparrow (New York: Pantheon, 1980)

Age range: Grades 5-6

Subject(s): Good and Evil; Stealing

Major character(s): Little Cigarette, Orphan; Eel, Villain; Mago, Hero

Time period(s): Indeterminate

Locale(s): Paris, France

What the book is about: Little Cigarette agrees to steal a painting from an artist who trusts her. Filled with self-contempt for what she has done, she flees Paris and takes a long journey. Cigarette is involved in the ancient struggle between good and evil.

Where it's reviewed:
Center for Children's Books Bulletin, December 1980, page 68
School Library Journal, October 1980, page 144
Kirkus Reviews, January 1, 1981, page 7

Awards the book has won:
Boston Globe/Horn Book Award - Honor Book 1981

Other books by the author:
The Silent Voice, 1981
Come to the Edge, 1977
Burnish Me Bright, 1970
Dorp Dead, 1965

Other books you might like:
Jennifer Armstrong, *Steal Away*, 1992
    In 1855, two teen girls, one white and one black, run away from a southern farm and make the difficult journey north to freedom.
Paul Berna, *A Truckload of Rice*, 1968
    A young boy used a goldfish to track down the thief who tries to steal the money that is to send a truckload of rice to starving Chandrapur.
Milton Dank, *The Dangerous Game*, 1977
    Love of Paris and France prompts a sixteen year old to join the resistance movement shortly after the Nazi invasion of 1940.
Monica Hughes, *Sandwriter*, 1985
    Traveling to the island of Roshan to meet the young man that his aunt wantsw her to marry, Princess Anita becomes involved in a deadly power struggle.
Patricia Wrightson, *The Ice Is Coming*, 1977
    Ruthless, ancient forces of fire and ice engage in a titanic struggle with the oldest Nargun and his people.

| 454 |

Julia Cunningham

Illustrator: Peter Sis

Oaf (New York: Knopf, 1985)

Age range: Grades 3-5

Subject(s): Fantasy; Magic

Major character(s): Oaf, Child

Time period(s): Indeterminate

Locale(s): Fictional Country

What the book is about: A small boy named Oaf receives three gifts from his aunt - a phrase, a magic red leather cap, and a promise of treasure. When he turns eight, Oaf is sent to seek his fortune with a band of talking animals. He tries to rescue five dwarves and a danging fox from their cruel master.

Where it's reviewed:
Booklist, March 1, 1986, page 1016
Children's Book Review Service, April 1986, page 99
Center for Children's Books Bulletin, April 1986, page 144

Other books by the author:
Wolf Roland, 1983
Come to the Edge, 1977
Burnish Me Bright, 1970
Dorp Dead, 1965

Other books you might like:
Camilla Fegan, *Late for Hallowe'en*, 1966
    When a witch and a black cat come to live in her garden, a little girl has many adventures in magic.
Alf Proysen, *Mrs. Pepperpot in the Magic Wood*, 1968
    Seven adventures of the woman who, at the most inconvenient times, shrinks to the size of a pepperpot.
Dorothy Lewis Robertson, *Fairy Tales from Viet Nam*, 1968
    Eight tales sent by letter from a Saigon war refugee to his foster mother in the United States.
Jack Sendak, *Martze*, 1968
    A boy who believes he can do magic travels, brings unhappiness to those who do not wish their lives changed, but helps a girl who needs a friend.
Anne Sinclair Williams, *Secret of the Round Tower*, 1968
    With a little magic a medieval family's white "foal" becomes a unique unicorn, but rather than turn him over to the king, they set him free.

| 455 |

Julia Cunningham

Tuppenny (New York: Dutton, 1978)

Age range: Grades 4-6

Subject(s): Conformity; Murder; Mystery and Detective Stories

Major character(s): Tuppenny, Wanderer; Jessica Standing, Child; John Mason, Murderer

Time period(s): Indeterminate

Locale(s): England

What the book is about: Tuppenny seems to need nothing and do nothing, yet she affects everyone whose life she touches. She meets the Standings and reminds the boy, Victor, of his sister Jessica who has been gone for a year. She works for a couple who sent their daughter away. Finally, she encounters the evil that haunts the local church and has destroyed the minister's child.

Where it's reviewed:
Booklist, October 15, 1978, page 371
Hornbook, December 1978, page 639
School Library Journal, November 1978, page 72

Other books by the author:
Oaf, 1986
The Silent Voice, 1981
The Treasure Is the Rose, 1973
Far in the Day, 1972

Other books you might like:
M.S. Craig, *The Seven Stone*, 1972
    Maggie learns many things when she befriends the strange new girl in her class.
William Faulkner, *The Wishing Tree*, 1964
    A strange boy leads a birthday-girl and her companions on a hunt for the wishing tree which brings them many surprising and magical adventures.

Stephen Mooser, *Orphan Jeb at the Massacree*, 1984
Twelve year old Jeb sets out alone for Nevada in 1860 in search of his prospector father, only to find he is in jail to be hanged for murder.

Jean Davies Okimoto, *Who Did It, Jenny Lake?*, 1983
On vacation in Hawaii, Jennifer and Freddie, classmates and friends, take time out from having fun to investigate the murder of an elderly friend.

Ellen Harvey Showell, *Cecelia and the Blue Mountain Boy*, 1983
Enroute to the Chester Music Festival, a boy hears about the young girl who changed Chester from a gloomy town to one of dancing and music.

456

Ann Curry

The Book of Brendan (New York: Holiday 1990)

Age range: Grades 5-7

Subject(s): Arthurian Legend; Knights and Knighthood; Good and Evil

Major character(s): Eric, Child; Myrddin, Magician; Father Brendan, Religious

Time period(s): 8th century (725)

Locale(s): Holybury Abbey, England

What the book is about: Young Eric lives at Holybury Abbey and assists Father Brendan who is writing a book about healing remedies. When Myrddin, an evil magician, appears at the Abbey, Eric and a visitor foil his plan to seize power, relying on magical beasts and the help of Arthur, Guinevere, and Merlin, summoned from sleep on the Isle of Truth.

Where it's reviewed:
Booklist, March 15, 1991, page 1445
Voice of Youth Advocates, October 1990, page 226

Other books you might like:
Sir Thomas Malory, *King Arthur and His Knights of the Round Table*, 1950
Classic tale of the adventures of King Arthur and his knights and kingdom.

William McCay, *Young Indiana Jones and the Ghostly Riders*, 1991
In 1913, young Indiana Jones finds an ancient silver ring that may have belonged to King Arthur and travels back in time to solve a crisis.

Pamela F. Service, *Winter of Magic's Return*, 1985
Convinced that a new age of magic is about to begin in the wake of a nuclear holocaust, a young Merlin and two friends try to bring back King Arthur.

T.H. White, *The Sword in the Stone*, 1939
Adaptation of the Arthurian adventures for young readers.

Jane Yolen, *The Dragon's Boy*, 1990
Young Arthur meets a dragon and comes to accept him as friend and mentor.

457

Jane Louise Curry

The Big Smith Snatch (New York: Margaret K. McElderry, 1989)

Age range: Grades 4-6

Subject(s): Burglary; Old Age; Moving, Household

Major character(s): Belinda Rainbow "Boo" Smith, Preteen; Cisco Smith, Child; Poppy Smith, Child

Time period(s): 1980s

Locale(s): Los Angeles, California; Pittsburgh, Pennsylvania

What the book is about: When their pregnant mother gets sick on the eve of their move from California to Pennsylvania, the four younger Smith children find themselves in the custody of the city, in foster care with the Dickery family, leaving their twelve year old sister, Boo, with the help of eccentric old Auntie Moss, to somehow trace their whereabouts and get the family back together again, before the kids are turned into burglars by the Dickerys.

Where it's reviewed:
Bookwatch, December 1989, page 7
Horn Book Guide, July 1989, page 86

Other books by the author:
Little Little Sister, 1989
Back in the Before Time, 1987
Me, Myself and I, 1987
The Lotus Cup, 1986

Other books you might like:
James Lincoln Collier, *My Crooked Family*, 1991
Living in a seedy part of a big city in 1910, thirteen year old Roger falls in with criminals and learns an unpleasant secret about his father.

Gene DeWeese, *The Adventures of a Two-Minute Werewolf*, 1983
Fourteen year old Walt, learning that he can turn into a werewolf, puts his talent to constructive use in thwarting the activities of a burglary gang.

Rosa Guy, *New Guys around the Block*, 1983
Harlem teen Imamu Jones, repainting his alcoholic mother's apartment, suspects one of his friends of burglaries and other crimes.

Lila Perl, *Dumb Like Me, Olivia Potts*, 1976
Ten year old Olivia prefers not living up to the academic performances of her brother and sister, until she tries to solve some local burglaries.

Todd Strasser, *Home Alone: A Novelization*, 1990
The parents of seven year old Kevin McCallister accidently forget him when they leave for a trip to Paris, and he must protect his home from burglars.

458

Jane Louise Curry

The Watchers (New York: Atheneum, 1975)

Age range: Grades 5-6

Subject(s): Stepfamilies

Major character(s): Ray, Teenager

Time period(s): 1970s

Locale(s): Twillys' Green, West Virginia

What the book is about: Ray comes to Twillys' Green to get away from his stepmother. Something is not quite as usual with his relatives. The family, like their ancestors, fight as guardians of a sacred site.

Where it's reviewed:
Kirkus Reviews, September 1, 1975, page 998
School Library Journal, November 1975, page 73
Booklist, November 15, 1975, page 451

Other books by the author:
Back in the Before Time, 1987
Parsley, Sage, Rosemary and Time, 1975
The Lost Farm, 1974
The Daybreakers, 1970

Other books you might like:
John Christopher, *The Guardians,* 1970
  In the divided England of the distant future, an orphan boy leaves the packed urban center known as the Conurb, hoping for a simpler country life.
Catherine Dexter, *The Oracle Doll,* 1985
  When they become the guardians of a talking doll that is the reincarnated Oracle of Delphi, three youngsters learn how difficult their task will be.
John Forrester, *The Secret of the Round Beast,* 1986
  While the rebel Ryland is imprisoned on the moon by the Overone Guardians, his teenage children and their allies fight on Old Earth against the Gorid.
Tony Shearer, *The Praying Flute: Song of the Earth Mother,* 1991
  Little Girl travels to the realm of the Earth Guardians and is given a praying flute which sings of harmony with the Earth.
David Wiseman, *Blodwen and the Guardians,* 1983
  Blodwen and her family, because of a threat to their village, become allied with the Guardians of the tombs of long-dead chieftains, who fear humans.

| 459 |

Philip Curtis

Illustrator: Tony Ross

Invasion of the Comet People (New York: Knopf, 1983)

Age range: Grades 4-7

Subject(s): Aliens; Science Fiction

Major character(s): Simon "Spikey" Jackson, Preteen; Jason Taylor, Alien; Mr. Browser, Teacher

Time period(s): Indeterminate

Locale(s): England

What the book is about: Spiky discovers that his new friend, Jason, and his parents are an outer-space family from Halley's Comet and that their plans pose grave danger to the Earth.

Where it's reviewed:
Booklist, April 15, 1983, page 1093
Children's Book Review Service, April 1983, page 92
School Library Journal, April 1983, page 112

Other books by the author:
Invasion From Below the Earth, 1980
Invasion of the Brain Sharpeners, 1979

Other books you might like:
Milton Dank, *A UFO Had Landed,* 1983
  When their biology teacher is in danger of being fired because he insists that he saw a UFO and aliens, the Galaxy Gang set out to help Mr. Dawson.
Gene DeWeese, *What Ever Became of Aunt Margaret?,* 1990
  David and Julie discover an amazing secret about Aunt Margaret when they help her protect an elderly animal lover from being "podified" by aliens.
Gery Greer, *Jason and the Aliens Down the Street,* 1991
  Jason meets Cooper Vor and Lootna, aliens from space now living on Earth, and travels with them to a planet to recover a stolen energy crystal.
Andre Norton, *The Day of the Ness,* 1975
  Hal traces a frantic SOS to a group of friendly space aliens help captive inside a mountain by the evil Ness who plans to take over the world.
Roberta Wiegand, *The Year of the Comet,* 1984
  Sarah finds much to enjoy in her family's life, despite fears that the appearance of Halley's Comet may signal the end of the world.

| 460 |

Isabel Langis Cusack

Illustrator: Carol Nicklaus

Ivan the Great (New York: Crowell, 1978)

Age range: Grades 2-4

Subject(s): Honesty

Major character(s): Robby, Child; Ivan, Parrot

Time period(s): 1970s

Locale(s): United States

What the book is about: Robby has always been an honest, polite child. Only he can hear Ivan speak. Ivan is conceited and tells a lot of fibs and funny stories.

Where it's reviewed:
Center for Children's Books Bulletin, January 1979, page 76
School Library Journal, March 1979, page 138

Other books by the author:
Mr. Wheatfield's Loft, 1979

Other books you might like:
David A. Adler, *The Fourth Floor Twins and the Disappearing Parrot Trick,* 1986
  Two sets of twins launch a wild chase when the "disappearing parrot" in their school talent show really disappears.
Bonnie Bishop, *No One Noticed Ralph,* 1979
  An independent parrot flies out into the world to meet people, but no one notices him until he spots a fire and saves the day.
Eve Bunting, *The Empty Window,* 1980
  With his younger brother's help, C.G. captures a wild parrot for his friend who is dying.
Eric Deleon, *Pitch and Hasty Check It Out,* 1988
  Two boys investigating a mysterious voice coming from a pinball machine become involved with a parrot-smuggling ring.
Anico Surany, *Lora, Lorita,* 1969

A Colombian boy persists in trying to teach his "stupid" parrot to talk, only to find that success means he must dispose of the bird.

461

Doug Cushman

Uncle Foster's Hat Tree (New York: Dutton, 1988)

Age range: Grades 1-2

Subject(s): Storytelling

Major character(s): Merle, Mouse

Time period(s): Indeterminate

Locale(s): United States

What the book is about: Merle the Mouse enjoys a feast of stories due to Uncle Foster's hats and after the stories, he gets to try on the hats.

Where it's reviewed:
Booklist, December 1, 1988, page 656
School Library Journal, December 1988, page 84

Other books by the author:
Aunt Eater's Mystery Vacation, 1992
Aunt Eater Loves a Mystery, 1987
The Missing Mystery, 1987
Giants, 1980

Other books you might like:
Joan W. Blos, *Martin's Hats*, 1984
   A variety of hats afford Martin many adventures.
Irina Hale, *How I Found a Friend*, 1992
   Teddy bears and hats provide the opening for a friendship between two young children.
Ralph Leemis, *Mister Momboo's Hat*, 1991
   An elephant's hat takes off on adventures of its own.
Dr. Seuss, *The 500 Hats of Bartholomew Cubbins*, 1965
   Each time Bartholomew Cubbins attempts to obey the King's order to take off his hat, he finds there is another one on his head.
Nancy Van Laan, *This Is the Hat: A Story in Rhyme*, 1992
   Cumulative verses follow an old man's hat as it becomes a home for a spider, mouse, and other creatures before returning to it rightful owner.

462

Margery Cuyler

The Trouble with Soap (New York: Dutton, 1982)

Age range: Grades 5-6

Subject(s): Friendship; Humor; Peer Pressure

Major character(s): Laurie Endersby, Teenager; Lucinda "Soap" Sokoloff, Teenager

Time period(s): 1980s

Locale(s): United States

What the book is about: When Laurie and "Soap" put Saran Wrap over the boys' toilet at school, they are suspended for two weeks, and both wind up being sent to a private girls' school. When Soap refuses to make new friends, and persists in getting into trouble, Laurie is torn between her friendship and her desire to make new friends and fit in. Lots of good humor as the girls test their friendship.

Where it's reviewed:
Horn Book, april 1982, page 162
Kirkus Reviews, April 1, 1982, page 417

Other books by the author:
Daisy's Crazy Thanksgiving, 1990
Shadow's Baby, 1989
Weird Wolf, 1989
Freckles and Willie, 1986

Other books you might like:
Natalie Savage Carlson, *Lurvy and the Girls*, 1971
   Lurvy is delighted that she is finally old enough to accompany her older sisters to boarding school.
Ilene Cooper, *The Queen of the Sixth Grade*, 1988
   After helping Veronica start the Awesome Kennedy Girls, Robin accidentally gets on her wrong side and finds out how bossy and cruel Veronica is.
Thomas J. Dygard, *Rebound Caper*, 1983
   Gary, known for his pranks, creates a sensation when he switches from the boy's to the girl's basketball team.
Astrid Lindgren, *Emil's Pranks*, 1971
   Chaos follows this Swedish farm boy everywhere he goes.
Robert Newton Peck, *Mr. Little*, 1979
   Disappointed that the celebrated Miss K will not be their teacher, Finley and Stanley pull pranks on the new teacher in their small town.

D

463

Roald Dahl

Illustrator: Quentin Blake

The BFG (New York: Farrar, Straus and Giroux, 1982)

Age range: Grades 3-6

Subject(s): Giants

Major character(s): Sophie, Orphan; Big Friendly Giant, Mythical Creature (giant)

Time period(s): Indeterminate

Locale(s): Giantland, Fictional Country

What the book is about: Sophie is save by the BFG and finds herself in a strange environment. The nine giants in Giantland eat children, unlike BFG. BFG is friendly because he had no mother and no one else to teach him to be a proper giant.

Where it's reviewed:
Center for Children's Books Bulletin, January 1983, page 86
School Library Journal, December 1982, page 48

Other books by the author:
Going Solo, 1986
Giraffe and the Pelly and Me, 1985
The Witches, 1983
The Magic Finger, 1966

Other books you might like:
Stephen Krensky, The Perils of Putney, 1978
  When the disappearance of the world's only Fair Damsel upsets the balance of peace, a giant with no experience as a hero agrees to search for her.
Ruth Shannon Odor, Learning about Giants, 1981
  The characteristics of real and imaginary giants and famous stories about giants from the Bible, mythology, folklore and literature.
Scott R. Sanders, Bad Man Ballad, 1986
  Eli Jackson and a lawyer in early 19th century Ohio set out to find a murderer who might be a "Bigfoot."
Jonathan Swift, Gulliver's Travels, 1726
  On two voyages, an Englishman becomes shipwrecked in a land where people are six inches high and stranded in a land of giants.
Kathy Kennedy Tapp, Moth-Kin Magic, 1983
  Members of the Mothkin family, people less than an inch tall, must escape or die when they are captured by giants and imprisoned in glass bottles.

464

Roald Dahl

Illustrator: Joseph Schindelman

Charlie and the Chocolate Factory (New York: Knopf, 1964)

Age range: Grades 4-6

Subject(s): Food; Fantasy; Espionage

Major character(s): Verucca Salt, Child (brat); Charlie Bucket, Hero

Time period(s): Indeterminate

Locale(s): Fictional Country

What the book is about: Charlie and four of his less than wonderful friends tour an extraordinary chocolate factory. They all meet with disaster except for Charlie.

Where it's reviewed:
Center for Children's Books Bulletin, April 1965, page 115
School Library Journal, October 1976, page 105

Awards the book has won:
New England Round Table of Children's Librarians 1972
Surrey School 1975

Other books by the author:
Charlie and the Great Glass Elevator, 1972
Fantastic Mr. Fox, 1970
The Magic Finger, 1966
James and the Giant Peach, 1961

Other books you might like:
Patrick Skene Catling, The Chocolate Touch, 1952
  A boy acquires a magical gift that turns everything his lips touch into chocolate.
Dan Elish, The Worldwide Dessert Contest, 1988
  John enters his apple pancake against sly Sylvester's double-chocolate-fudge-raspberry-coconut-lime swirl in the worldwide dessert contest.
Florence Parry Heide, Banana Blitz, 1983
  Jonah thinks his problems will be over if he can win the prize offered by the American Banana Institute for watching its commercials.
Amalie Sharfman, Papa's Secret Chocolate Dessert, 1972
  To everyone's surprise, Jean-Pierre saves the day when his father, a great chef, is too ill to cook.
Marilyn Singer, A Nose for Trouble, 1985
  Canine detective Samantha Spayed helps her master investigate industrial espionage at La Maison de Beaute.

465

Roald Dahl

Illustrator: Jill Bennett

Danny, the Champion of the World (New York: Knopf, 1975)

Age range: Grades 4-6

Subject(s): Fathers and Sons; Hunting

Major character(s): Danny, Child; Mr. Hazell, Businessman (brewery owner)

Time period(s): 1970s

Locale(s): England

What the book is about: Motherless Danny and his story-telling father live in an old gypsy caravan behind a filling station. Their relationship is a good one, and dad helps as Danny tries to save the birds of the woods before Mr. Hazell's shooting party.

Where it's reviewed:
Horn Book, April 1876, page 153
School Library Journal, November 1975, page 74

Awards the book has won:
California Young Reader Medal 1979

Other books by the author:
Matilda, 1988
The Witches, 1983
The Magic Finger, 1966
James and the Giant Peach, 1961

Other books you might like:
Mary Blount Christian, *Linc*, 1991
　　Linc can do nothing to please his father, a former high school football hero, until he agrees to go on a deer-hunting expedition.
Peter Zachary Cohen, *Deadly Game at Stony Creek*, 1978
　　A pack of wild killer dogs is hunted down by two teenage boys.
Ross E. Hutchins, *Tonka, the Cave Boy*, 1973
　　The adventures of a boy living 8,000 years ago in an Alabama cave as he goes hunting, copes with the death of his father, and tames a wolf cub.
Miska Miles, *Hoagie's Rifle-Gun*, 1970
　　Hunting animals for food is a necessity for Hoagie's poor Appalachian family, but it becomes difficult when game has a name.
Ester Wier, *The Hunting Trail*, 1974
　　Traces the first three and a half years of a coyote's life as he struggles against the dangers posed by man and nature.

466

Roald Dahl

Illustrator: Michel Simeon

James and the Giant Peach (New York: Knopf, 1961)

Age range: Grades 3-5

Subject(s): Magic; Orphans

Major character(s): James Henry Trotter, Orphan; Aunt Sponge, Relative (aunt); Aunt Spiker, Relative (aunt)

Time period(s): Indeterminate

Locale(s): England

What the book is about: James is sent to live with his two mean aunts after his parents are eaten by a rhinocerous in London. One day, James meets an old man in a strange dark-green suit who gives him a bag of magic. Then the fun begins.

Where it's reviewed:
Book World, November 12, 1978, page E2
Christian Science Monitor, December 4, 1978, page B19
Saturday Review, January 13, 1973, page 65

Other books by the author:
Charlie and the Great Glass Elevator, 1975
Fantastic Mr. Fox, 1970
The Magic Finger, 1966
Charlie and the Chocolate Factory, 1964

Other books you might like:
Mary Anderson, *The Terrible Thing in the Bath*, 1989
　　Cassie and Barney are cousins who detest each other. They are thrown together for a year when an eccentric aunt takes them to England.
Molly Bang, *Tye May and the Magic Brush*, 1981
　　In a dream a poor orphan is given a brush that brings to life everything she paints.
Barbara Ninde Byfield, *Andrew and the Alchemist*, 1977
　　Andrew, an orphan, becomes apprenticed to an alchemist and begins a life of danger and adventure.
Marianna Mayer, *Aladdin and the Enchanted Lamp*, 1985
　　Retells the adventures of Aladdin who, with the help of a genie from a magic lamp, outwits an evil sorcerer and wins the hand of a beautiful princess.
Anthony Simmons, *The Optimists of Nine Elms*, 1974
　　A brother and sister befriend an old street musician and his dog and discover that there can be magic in life.

467

Roald Dahl

Illustrator: William Pene Du Bois

The Magic Finger (New York: Harper Collins, 1966)

Age range: Grades 3-5

Subject(s): Hunting; Magic; Wildlife Conservation

Major character(s): The Girl, Child; Mrs. Winter, Teacher; Philip Gregg, Neighbor

Time period(s): Indeterminate

Locale(s): Fictional Country

What the book is about: When her teacher, Mrs. Winter, calls her a stupid little girl, the unnamed eight year old girl points a finger at her and she grows whiskers and a bushy tail. The child vows never to use her "magic finger" again. But when her neighbors, Mr. and Mrs. Gregg and their sons, Philip and William, continue to shoot and kill animals, she cannot resist using her powers again. The Greggs turn into a family of birds.

Where it's reviewed:
Booklist, October 15, 1966, page 264
Hornbook, December 1966, page 709
Kirkus Reviews, August 15, 1966, page 830

Other books by the author:
Dirty Beasts, 1983

The BFG, 1982
Fantastic Mr. Fox, 1970
James and the Giant Peach, 1961

Other books you might like:
Adele De Leeuw, *Uncle Davy Lane, Mighty Hunter*, 1970
Five tales about the exploits of the mightiest hunter in North Carolina.
Peggy Parish, *Good Hunting, Blue Sky*, 1989
Blue Sky, a young Indian boy, goes hunting to bring food home, only to have the food bring him home instead.
Bill Peet, *The Gnats of Knotty Pine*, 1975
The smallest creatures of Knotty Pine Forest avert the horrors of the hunting season in a very "sportsgnatlike" way.
Lynd Ward, *The Biggest Bear*, 1952
Johnny goes hunting for a bearskin to hang on his family's barn and returns with a small bundle of trouble.
Laurence Yep, *The Curse of the Squirrel*, 1987
Hunting little animals ceases to be a sport on Farmer Johnson's farm after a giant squirrel curses his best hunting dog.

468

Roald Dahl

Illustrator: Quentin Blake

Matilda (New York: Viking-Kestral, 1988)

Age range: Grades 3-6

Subject(s): Schools; Humor; Magic

Major character(s): Matilda, Genius; Miss Honey, Teacher; Trunchbull, Principal (headmistress)

Time period(s): Indeterminate Past

Locale(s): England

What the book is about: Neglected by her parents, genius Matilda turns to Mrs. Phelps, her librarian, and Miss Honey, her teacher. She avenges her teacher by ridding the school of mean headmistress Trunchbull.

Where it's reviewed:
Kirkus Reviews, August 15, 1988, page 1237
School Library Journal, October 1988, page 143

Awards the book has won:
Arizona Young Readers Award

Other books by the author:
Danny, the Champion of the World, 1975
James and the Giant Peach, 1961
The Magic Finger, 1966

Other books you might like:
Sheila Greenwald, *Alvin Webster's Sure Fire Plan for Success (and How It Failed)*, 1987
Gifted fifth grader Alvin Webster finds out he does not know all the answers when it comes to tutoring and accepting a new brother.
Susan Beth Pfeffer, *Dear Dad, Love Laurie*, 1989
Laurie's letters to her divorced father tell about her sixth grade year and her efforts to enter the gifted/talented program.
Joyce Sweeney, *Face the Dragon*, 1990
14-year-old Eric skips ninth grade and enters an accelerated high school program. Challenging Reading.
Mary Robinson, *The Amazing Volvano and the Mystery of the Hooded Rat*, 1988

Maria's pet rat, an integral part of her magic act, is kidnapped.
Willo Davis Roberts, *The Magic Book*, 1986
Alex and his friends decide to try to cast a spell on the school bully.

469

Roald Dahl

Illustrator: Quentin Blake

The Witches (New York: Farrar, 1983)

Age range: Grades 3-6

Subject(s): Death; Witches and Witchcraft; Grandparents

Time period(s): Indeterminate

Locale(s): England

What the book is about: A boy and his grandmama save English children from being turned into mice by witches. Mourning the death of his parents, and fearing the death of the over eighty year old grandmother, when he is turned into a mouse permanently, he is also granted a shorter life span and less chance of separation from his deeply-loved, cigar-smoking grandmother.

Where it's reviewed:
Horn Book, April 1984, page 194
School Library Journal, January 1984, page 74

Other books by the author:
Esio Trot, 1990
Boy Tales of Childhood, 1984
Dirty Beasts, 1983
The BFG, 1982

Other books you might like:
Katharine Bacon, *Shadow and Light*, 1987
Emma, looking forward to summer on her grandmother's Vermont farm, learns that she is fatally ill and wants Emma's help in her remaining months.
Nina Beachcroft, *Well Met by Witchlight*, 1972
From the little lady they meet when she drops out of a tree in the woods, three children learn that there are good and bad witches.
Ruth Chew, *The Would-Be Witch*, 1976
Two children are convinced that the owner of a nearby antique shop is a witch.
Peter Dickinson, *Heartsease*, 1969
In a future England when anyone knowledgeable about machines is punished as a witch, four children dare to aid in the escape of a "witch" left to die.
Stephen Krensky, *The Witching Hour*, 1981
The Wynd family pits its forces against a group of witches with a ghastly plan to turn the town's children into monsters.

470

Tessa Dahl

Illustrator: Korky Paul

Gwenda and the Animals (New York: Viking, 1990)

Age range: Grades 2-4

Subject(s): Zoos; Animals

Major character(s): Gwenda, Child, Animal Lover

Time period(s): 1990s

Locale(s): United States

What the book is about: Gwenda watches her relatives tease and make fun of the animals at the zoo. She feels terrible about it. She sneaks back into the zoo and hides til closing time. She talks with the caged animals about what they have to put up with.

Where it's reviewed:
Kirkus Reviews, September 1, 1990, page 1248
School Library Journal, December 1990, page 75

Other books by the author:
Babies, Babies, Babies, 1990
School Can Wait, 1990
The Same but Different, 1989

Other books you might like:
David A. Adler, *Cam Jansen and the Mystery at the Monkey House*, 1985
    Cam uses her photographic memory to solve a monkey smuggling mystery at the city zoo.
Phyllis Barker, *Legs: The Story of a Giraffe*, 1991
    A young giraffe growing up in Kenya is captured and transported to a zoo.
Franz Brandenberg, *Leo and Emily's Zoo*, 1990
    Two children decide to open their own zoo and charge admission, and their families turn disaster into success.
Nancy Winslow Parker, *Working Frog*, 1992
    Winston describes his life at the Reptile House of the Bronx Zoo.
Wendy Pfeffer, *Popcorn Park Zoo*, 1992
    A zoo in New Jersey rescues and cares for animals that are sick, old, abused, or about to be destroyed.

471

Tessa Dahl

Illustrator: Korky Paul

School Can Wait (New York: Viking, 1991)

Age range: Grades 3-5

Subject(s): Christmas; Humor; Santa Claus

Major character(s): Jack, Child

Time period(s): 1990s

Locale(s): United States

What the book is about: Jack discovers Blitzen in his backyard and he and his parents fly the lost reindeer back to the North Pole. The trip turns out to be the beginning of a long series of tasks, one funnier than the next. Jack will not be home in time for school.

Where it's reviewed:
Booklist, January 15, 1992, page 940
Times Educational Supplement, December 7, 1990, page 31

Other books by the author:
Babies, Babies, Babies, 1991
Gwenda and the Animals, 1990
The Same but Different, 1989

Other books you might like:
L. Frank Baum, *The Life and Adventures of Santa Claus*, 1983

Describes the life of Santa Claus from birth through old age and into immortality. Well illustrated by Cowles Clark.
Shirley Hughes, *Another Helping of Chips*, 1986
    Four funny stories of Chips and his friend, Jessie, two in comic strip format, two in a combination of text and comics.
Gary Paulsen, *A Christmas Sonata*, 1992
    When a little boy spends Christmas with his dying cousin, they discover that Santa Claus really does exist.
Robert Newton Peck, *Soup on Ice*, 1985
    Rob and Soup create an incredible appearance by Santa Claus and his sleigh in their small Vermont town.
Margret Rettich, *The Silver Touch*, 1978
    Twenty-three stories of humorous incidents that can really happen during the Christmas holidays.

472

Alice Dalgliesh

Illustrator: Helen Sewell

Bears on Hemlock Mountain (New York: Atheneum, 1952)

Age range: Grades 1-3

Subject(s): Animals/Bears; Frontier and Pioneer Life

Major character(s): Jonathan, Child

Time period(s): 19th century

Locale(s): Pennsylvania

What the book is about: What happens to 8 year old Jonathan when he is sent to borrow an iron kettle from his aunt who lives "over the mountain?" Recommended read aloud for youngest readers.

Where it's reviewed:
Booklist, September 1, 1952, page 19
Horn Book, April 1952, page 99

Awards the book has won:
Newbery Honor

Other books by the author:
Adam and the Golden Cock, 1959
Enchanted Book, 1947
Gulliver Joins the Army, 1942
Little Angel, 1943

Other books you might like:
Mordecai Gerstein, *Anytime Mapleson and the Hungry Bears*, 1990
    Anytime meets bears in the woods and invites them home for pancakes.
James A. Houston, *Long Claws: An Arctic Adventure*, 1981
    An Eskimo brother and sister encounter hungry bears while bringing a caribou home to their hungry family.
Sally Farrell Odgers, *Drummond: The Search for Sarah*, 1990
    A teddy bear brought to life searches for his original owner.
Hannah Muschq, *Two Little Bears*, 1986
    Two young bears explore their environment and learn survival skills.
John Fort, *June the Tiger*, 1975
    When old Mrs. Pickney's house is attacked by a bear, her dog takes revenge on the culprit.

473

Alice Dalgliesh

Illustrator: Leonard Weisgard

Courage of Sarah Noble (New York: Scribner, 1954)

Age range: Grades 3-5

Subject(s): Frontier and Pioneer Life; Indians of North America

Major character(s): Sarah Noble, Child; John Noble, Parent

Time period(s): 1700s (1702)

Locale(s): New Milford, Connecticut

What the book is about: This is a pioneer adventure for new readers, the story of the founding of New Milford, Connecticut. Sarah moves to the wilderness with her father at the beginning of the 1700s, and learns that bravery in the face of fear is the greatest courage of all.

Where it's reviewed:
Horn Book, August 1954, page 246

Awards the book has won:
Newbery Honor

Other books by the author:
Blue Teapot, 1937
Davenports and Cherry Pie, 1949
Enchanted Book, 1947
Thanksgiving Story, 1954 (related picture book)

Other books you might like:
Gloria Whelan, *Next Spring, an Oriole*, 1987
  When 10 yaer old Libby travels by covered wagon, she helps an Indian girl with measles, and they learn to depend on each other.
Carla Stevens, *Trouble for Lucy*, 1979
  Lucy's puppy causes trouble on the wagon train to Oregon in 1843.
Cynthia DeFelice, *Weasel*, 1990
  11 year old Nathan runs afoul of a renegade killer while alone in the frontier wilderness in 1839.
Joan Anderson, *Joshua's Westward Journal*, 1987
  Josh and his family travel to Illinois in 1836.
Jane Flory, *The Great Bamboozelement*, 1982
  The Dowells trade their Pennsylvania farm for a floating emporium and set off down the Monongahela River.

474

Mischa Damjan

Illustrator: Dusan Kallay

December's Travels (New York: Dial, 1986)

Age range: Grades 2-3

Subject(s): Christmas; Fantasy; Seasons

Major character(s): December, Child; March, Child; October, Child

Time period(s): Indeterminate

Locale(s): Fictional Country

What the book is about: December is a solitary boy given a magic gift by the North Wind. He can visit other boys, March, June and October. The journey shows him March's swirling storms, June's sunny days and October's bountiful orchards and sweet smelling hay. The experience changes him so that even when he stays only in December, he appreciates the world and his friends much more.

Where it's reviewed:
Booklist, September 15, 1986, page 127
Booklist, September 15, 1986, page 138
Publisher's Weekly, July 25, 1986, page 186

Other books by the author:
The False Flamingoes, 1968
The Magic Paintbrush, 1967
The Wolf and the Kid, 1967
Mau, King of the Cats, 1961

Other books you might like:
Tedd Arnold, *Mother Goose's Words of Wit and Wisdom: A Book of Months*, 1990
  A collection of Mother Goose rhymes centered around the months of the year.
Nancy White Carlstrom, *How Do You Say It Today, Jesse Bear?*, 1992
  Rhymed text and illustration describe Jesse Bear's activities from January to December.
Mordicai Gerstein, *The Story of May*, 1993
  The month of May travels to meet her father, December, and meets all of her relatives, the other months of the year, along the way.
Clare Walker Leslie, *Nature All Year Long*, 1991
  Describes the different plants, animals, and landscapes that can be seen outdoors each month of the year.
Elizabeth Slote, *Nelly's Garden*, 1991
  Little Nelly Dragon enjoys the different flowers each month in her garden.

475

Barbara Dana

Illustrator: Eileen Christelow

Zucchini (New York: Harper, 1982)

Age range: Grades 3-5

Subject(s): Friendship; Shyness

Major character(s): Zucchini, Ferret

Time period(s): 1980s

Locale(s): New York, New York (the Bronx)

What the book is about: Zucchini is convinced that there is more to life than the Bronx Zoo. He decides to head for his real home on the prairie. He gets caught in a drain and is taken to the ASPCA where he forms a friendship with a very shy boy.

Where it's reviewed:
Kirkus Reviews, October 1, 1982, page 1105
School Library Journal, October 1982, page 150

Awards the book has won:
Land of Enchantment Children's Book Award 1986

Other books by the author:
Young Joan, 1991
Necessary Parties, 1986

Other books you might like:
Mary Jane Auch, *Kidnapping Kevin Kowalski*, 1990

When an accident partially paralyzes Kevin and his mother becomes overprotective, Ryan and Mooch decide the only way to liberate him is to kidnap him.

Clyde Robert Bulla, *The Cardboard Crown*, 1984
A strange girl arrives at Adam's farmhouse, wearing a golden crown and a shimmering dress. She says she is a lost princess and asks for shelter.

Russell E. Erickson, *A Toad for Tuesday*, 1974
Warton, the toad, sets out on skiis to visit his aunt. He is captured by an owl who threatens to eat him.

Alane Ferguson, *Cricket and the Crackerbox Kid*, 1990
Cricket thinks she has a friend in Dominic, until they quarrel over ownership of a dog and their classroom becomes a courtroom to decide who's right.

Patricia Foley, *John and the Fiddler*, 1990
John befriends Sam MacLoegaire, an old violin maker who teaches him the beauty of music and friendship.

476

Paula Danziger

Can You Sue Your Parents for Malpractice? (New York: Delacorte, 1979)

Age range: Grades 6-8

Subject(s): Family Life; Individuality; Sisters

Major character(s): Lauren Allen, Teenager; Zack Davids, Teenager; Linda Allen, Entertainer (comedian)

Time period(s): 1970s

Locale(s): United States

What the book is about: Confused about her life at home and at school, Lauren learns the importance of being her own person. She meets Zack when they both take a course in "Law for Children and Young People." He's a younger boy and she has to stand up to the kids who call her a "cradle robber" for going out with him.

Where it's reviewed:
Booklist, May 1, 1979, page 1361
Kirkus Reviews, June 1, 1979, page 641
School Library Journal, April 1979, page 67

Other books by the author:
It's an Aardvark-Eat-Turtle World, 1985
The Divorce Express, 1982
The Pistachio Prescription, 1978
The Cat Ate My Gymsuit, 1974

Other books you might like:
Vera Cleaver, *The Whys and Wherefores of Littabelle Lee*, 1973
When adversity makes Littabelle sole support of her two grandparents, her desperate situation teaches her about law, human nature, and her future.

Sonia Levitin, *Jason and the Money Tree*, 1974
When Jason plants a money tree, he finds himself in conflict with both the law and nature.

Jeffrey Marlin, *Appeal to the Heart*, 1985
Serving as Chief Justice in a mock court for her law course, Sandrine finds her decision affected by her involvement with both student lawyers.

Leonie Ossowski, *Star Without a Sky*, 1985

In the last days of World War II, five young Germans discover a Jewish boy hiding in a cellar and are torn over whether to turn him in or not.

Arvella Whitmore, *You're a Real Hero, Amanda*, 1985
Devote to her pet rooster, Amanda determines to fight the law forbidding chickens in town and runs into a series of unexpected problems.

477

Paula Danziger

The Cat Ate My Gymsuit (New York: Delacorte, 1974)

Age range: Grades 5 and Up

Subject(s): Teachers; Child Abuse

Major character(s): Marcy Lewis, Teenager, Abuse Victim; Barbara Finney, Teacher

Time period(s): 1970s

Locale(s): New Jersey

What the book is about: Marcy has a bully for a father and a bright, sympathetic English teacher. When Ms. Finney gets fired, Marcy and her friends protest, and get suspended from school. Her dad is against "bleeding heart radicals."

Where it's reviewed:
Kirkus Reviews, November 15, 1974, page 1206
Library Journal, November 15, 1974, page 3052

Other books by the author:
Remember Me to Harold Square, 1987
The Divorce Express, 1982
The Pistachio Prescription, 1978

Other books you might like:
Betsy Byars, *Cracker Jackson*, 1985
After trying to save his ex-babysitter from wife abuse, Cracker Jackson gains adult insight into the sadness of failed heroics.

Matt Christopher, *Takedown*, 1990
As he is helped by an assistant referee for a wrestling match with the neighborhood bully, Sean begins to wonder if the coach is his long-lost father.

Harry Mazer, *The War on Villa Street*, 1978
A boy comes to terms with his relationship with his drunken and abusive father, the menace of a local bully and his gang, and his love for running.

Isabella Taves, *Not Bad for a Girl*, 1972
An eleven year old playing little league baseball experiences hatred and abuse from adults whose traditional thinking reserves baseball for boys.

Linda Woolverton, *Running Before the Wind*, 1987
Kelly finds running an outlet for her feelings of love and hate for her abusive father, especially when his sudden death brings both relief and guilt.

478

Paula Danziger

The Divorce Express (New York: Delacorte, 1982)

Age range: Grades 5-6

Subject(s): Friendship; Divorce

Major character(s): Phoebe, Teenager; Rosie, Teenager

Time period(s): 1980s

Locale(s): Woodstock, New York; New York, New York (Manhatten)

What the book is about: Phoebe's parents are divorced and she spends half the week with each and gets terribly confused. The arrangement changes so she spends weekends with her mother and rides the "divorce express" to New York City. When her mother begins dating a man she can't stand, Phoebe takes it very hard. As she and her mom communicate more, and mom gets serious about the father of Phoebe's best friend, Rosie, Phoebe begins to calm down and look at her own life, independent of her parents.

Where it's reviewed:
Horn Book, October 1982, page 516
School Library Journal, October 1982, page 158

Other books by the author:
Remember Me to Harold Square, 1987
There's a Bat in Bunk Five, 1982
Nothing's Fair in Fifth Grade, 1981
The Pistachio Prescription, 1978

Other books you might like:
Lois I. Fisher, *Rachel Vellars, How Could You?*, 1984
    Cory changes schools after her parents divorce and she moves in with her father.
Susan Perkis Haven, *Maybe I'll Move to the Lost and Found*, 1988
    Gilly tries to assert herself as she copes with her parents' divorce, friendship problems, and a lack of self-confidence.
Mavis Jukes, *Getting Even*, 1988
    Maggie gets conflicting advice from her crazy friend, Iris, and both of her parents, who are still at war after two years of divorce.
Denise Gosliner Orenstein, *When the Wind Blows Hard*, 1982
    After her parents' separation and a subsequent move to Klawock, Alaska, Shawn endures lonliness until she meets Vesta and her grandfather.
Robert Kimmel Smith, *The Squeaky Wheel*, 1990
    Moving to a new neighborhood after his parents' divorce, Mark has trouble with new friends and his dad's absence.

479

Paula Danziger

Make Like a Tree and Leave (New York: Delacorte, 1990)

Age range: Grades 5-6

Subject(s): Family Life; Schools

Major character(s): Matthew Martin, Preteen, 6th Grader; Brian Bruno, Preteen; Vanessa Singer, Preteen

Time period(s): 1990s

Locale(s): United States

What the book is about: Sixth grader Matthew gets into trouble at home and at school, like the time he wrapped a friend in a total body cast trying to study mummies. He spars with his older sister, but when May Nichols, a visitor to school who makes great chocolate chip cookies, breaks her hip, Matthew and the kids pitch in to help her.

Where it's reviewed:
Booklist, August 1990, page 2176
School Library Journal, October 1990, page 114

Other books by the author:
This Place Has No Atmosphere, 1988
Can You Sue Your Parents for Malpractice?, 1987
Remember Me to Harold Square, 1987

Other books you might like:
Larry Bograd, *Bernie Entertaining*, 1987
    His comic misadventures at school and home do not seem very funny to Bernie.
Judith Clarke, *Al Capsella and the Watchdogs*, 1991
    Whether goofing off with his friends or avoiding an over-eager girlfriend, Al suffers from constant surveillance by a horde of watchdog parents.
Nancy Hayashi, *The Fantastic Stay-Home-From-School Day*, 1992
    Leona and Eddie plan a fantastic day at home that backfires when Eddie gets sent to school and they each go from one disaster to another.
Beverly Keller, *Fowl Play, Desdemona*, 1989
    Dez and Sherman team up to design posters for the school play with humorous results.
Louis Sachar, *There's a Boy in the Girls' Bathroom*, 1987
    A loveable misfit learns to believe in himself when he gets to know the new school counselor.

480

Paula Danziger

Remember Me to Harold Square (New York: Delacorte, 1987)

Age range: Grades 4-6

Subject(s): Friendship

Major character(s): Kendra, Teenager; Frank, Teenager; O.K., Child

Time period(s): 1980s

Locale(s): New York, New York

What the book is about: Kendra and Frank explore New York City with Kendra's little brother, O.K. This is a fun book that sometimes turns serious as they experience the sights, tastes, and sounds of New York.

Where it's reviewed:
Horn Book, January 1988, page 63
School Library Journal, November 1987, page 114

Other books by the author:
The Divorce Express, 1987
This Place Has No Atmosphere, 1986
The Pistachio Prescription, 1978

Other books you might like:
Barbara Douglass, *Skateboard Scramble*, 1979
    Jody is the new kid in town and she has something to prove to everyone, and to herself.
Marjorie Franco, *So Who Hasn't Got Problems?*, 1979
    This is a fast paced story of an eventful summer in the life of a young teenage girl and her friends.
Jan Greenberg, *The Iceberg and Its Shadow*, 1980
    Anabeth finds that the excitement of being popular is less satisfying than real friendship.

Emily Hanlon, *The Swing*, 1979
Beth and Danny develop a bond out of their love of animals and their need for the consolation of the swing.
Frederick J. Lipp, *Some Lose Their Way*, 1980
Vanessa and David find their way past the misconceptions they have about each other to form an enduring, nurturing friendship.

481

Paula Danziger

There's a Bat in Bunk Five (New York: Delacorte, 1980)

Age range: Grades 5-6

Subject(s): Camps and Camping; Responsibility

Major character(s): Marcy, Teenager, Counselor (camp); Ted, Teenager, Counselor (camp); Ginger, Child, Camper

Time period(s): 1980s

Locale(s): New York

What the book is about: Humorous, first person narrative of Marcy, a camp counselor-in-training. Marcy falls in love with Ted, another counselor, and meets Ginger, a very negative, troubled camper. Marcy begins to lose some of her self-absorption and has a wonderful, memorable summer.

Where it's reviewed:
Center for Children's Books Bulletin, December 1980, page 68
School Library Journal, January 1981, page 68

Awards the book has won:
Crabbery Award 1982

Other books you might like:
Brock Cole, *The Goats*, 1987
A boy and girl are stripped and left on Goat Island as part of an annual prank played on campers that don't fit in.
Ellen Conford, *Hail, Hail, Camp Timberwood*, 1978
Melanie, an only child, spends two months at camp. She learns how to relate to other kids and how to stand up for herself.
Jamie Gilson, *4B Goes Wild*, 1983
Two fourth grade classes go on a three day camping trip.
Annabel Johnson, *The Grizzly*, 1964
Eleven year old David is on a camping trip with his divorced father when his dad is injured by a grizzly and their pickup truck is disabled.
Marilyn Sachs, *A Summer's Lease*, 1979
Gloria changes during a summer in which Mrs. Horn invites her and her rival, Jerry, to the Horn summer home to help take care of a group of younger ch

482

Rosamond Dauer

Illustrator: Byron Barton

Bullfrog Grows Up (New York: Dell, 1976)

Age range: Grades 1-3

Subject(s): Animals/Frogs and Toads; Animals/Mice

Major character(s): Bullfrog, Frog

Time period(s): Indeterminate

Locale(s): United States

What the book is about: Two mice bring home a tadpole for a pet. Soon he grows up to be a pillow-fighting, card-playing, hamburger-eating bullfrog, who is much bigger than anyone in the mouse family. Though he is happy with his adopted family, Bullfrog finally agrees that the time has come for him to leave and find a spacious pond for himself.

Where it's reviewed:
Booklist, February 15, 1976, page 859
Hornbook, June 1976, page 284
Kirkus Reviews, March 15, 1976, page 318

Other books by the author:
The 300 Pound Cat, 1981
Bullfrog and Gertrude Go Camping, 1980
Bullfrog Builds a House, 1977
Mrs. Piggery Snout, 1977

Other books you might like:
Judy Brook, *Tim Mouse Goes Down the Stream*, 1969
When Willy Frog is captured by fierce river rats, Tim Mouse sets sail on his little raft to the rescue.
Peter Holeinone, *The Story of the Hare and the Tortoise and Other Tales*, 1990
23 fairy tales including "The Fox and the Stork", "The Wolf and the Crane" and "The Vain Crow."
Leo Lionni, *Fish Is Fish*, 1970
When his friend, the tadpole, becomes a frog and leaves the pond to explore the world, the little fish decides that maybe he can also leave.
John Steptoe, *The Story of Jumping Mouse*, 1984
The gifts of Magic Frog and his own hopeful and unselfish spirit bring Jumping Mouse finally to the Far-Off Land where no mouse goes hungry.
Marjorie Flack, *Tim Tadpole and the Great Bullfrog*, 1934
Traces Tim Tadpole's growth to a big frog who is at last able to go sit in the sun with his friends.

483

James Daugherty, Author/Illustrator

Daniel Boone (New York: Viking, 1939)

Age range: Grades 3-5

Subject(s): Frontier and Pioneer Life

Major character(s): Daniel Boone, Frontiersman, Historical Figure

Time period(s): 18th century

Locale(s): Pennsylvania; North Carolina

What the book is about: This is the biography of Daniel Boone, American pioneer. It reaches back to the freedom, stillness, and danger of untrod forests beyond the borders of settlements. Lonely trappers, Indians in ambush, and settlers, fill the book.

Where it's reviewed:
Booklist, December 15, 1939, page 155
Horn Book, September 1939, page 293
Library Journal, November 1, 1939, page 839

Awards the book has won:
Newbery Medal 1940

Other books by the author:
Landing of the Pilgrims, 1950
Marcus and Narcissa Whitman, 1953
Of Courage Undaunted, 1951
Poor Richard, 1941

Other books you might like:
Laurie Lawlor, *Daniel Boone*, 1988
   Biography of Daniel Boone for advanced students interested in historical background as well as adventure.
Carol Greene, *Daniel Boone: Man of the Forest*, 1990
   A biography of Daniel Boone for early readers. A "Rookie Biography."
Jim Hargrove, *Daniel Boone: Pioneer Trailblazer*, 1985
   Traces the life of Daniel Boone from his youth in Pennsylvania, to his explorations of Virginia, the Carolinas, Kentucky and Missouri.
Susan Baker, *Explorers of North America*, 1990
   Includes descriptions of Columbus, the Pilgrims and Daniel Boone.
Olive R. Cook, *Trails to Pussey*, 1986
   Nathan journeys to find his father who disappeared on a trek during the settlement of Missouri in the 1830s.

| 484 |

Ashok Davar, Author/Illustrator

The Wheel of King Asoka (Chicago: Follett, 1977)

Age range: Grades 2-3

Subject(s): Peace; War

Major character(s): King Asoka, Ruler (king); King Bindusara, Ruler (king)

Time period(s): 1st century

Locale(s): India

What the book is about: Two thousand years ago, King Asoka ruled India. One day after a fierce battle, he was so struck with the grief and suffering of war, he sent messages of peace to neighboring countries and began to rule his empire with love and justice.

Where it's reviewed:
Booklist, October 1, 1977, page 286
School Library Journal, January 1978, page 77

Awards the book has won:
Christopher Award 1978

Other books you might like:
Ann Axworthy, *Anni's India Diary*, 1992
   A ten year old's diary entries chronicle the magical sights and sounds she and her family encounter as they explore India.
Ruskin Bond, *The Cherry Tree*, 1991
   A little girl plants a cherry seed and cares for the tree, a special symbol of life and hope.
Aleph Kamal, *The Bird Who Was an Elephant*, 1990
   A bird visits a colorful village in India, seeing a spice shop, a sacred cow, a snake charmer and a palmist.
Rudyard Kipling, *The Jungle Book*, 1991
   The adventures of Mowgli, a boy raised by wolves and the wild animals of the Indian jungle.
William Papas, *Taresh the Tea Planter*, 1968

The "naughtiest" boy in an Indian village becomes a responsible tea planter.

| 485 |

Andrew Davies

Conrad's War (New York: Crown, 1980)

Age range: Grades 4-6

Subject(s): Space and Time; World War II

Major character(s): Conrad Pike, Preteen, Time Traveller

Time period(s): 1980; 1940s

Locale(s): Germany

What the book is about: Conrad's parents can't understand his love for war and guns. Conrad decides to build a tank. He assembles bicycle wheels, cardboard and wood with such intensity that a time change takes place and he finds himself at the controls of a real tank, participating in WWII.

Where it's reviewed:
Horn Book, April 1980, page 171
Kirkus Reviews, March 15, 1980, page 364
School Library Journal, April 1980, page 107

Awards the book has won:
Boston Globe/Horn Book Award 1980
Guardian Award for Children's Fiction

Other books by the author:
Marmalade and Rufus, 1980

Other books you might like:
Avi, *Who Was That Masked Man, Anyway?*, 1992
   While everyone else in the early 1940s is worried about WWII, Frankie gets in trouble because of his preoccupation with his favorite radio programs.
Barbara Corcoran, *The Private War of Lillian Adams*, 1989
   During WWI, most of Lillian's time is spent looking for spies and aiding the war effort.
Dale Fife, *North of Danger*, 1978
   Twelve year old Arne makes a dangerous trip over glaciers and through blizzard conditions to warn his father about the Nazi occupation.
Michelle Magorian, *Back Home*, 1984
   Twelve year old Rusty returns to England after spending five years during WWII in the United States.
Harry Mazer, *The Last Mission*, 1979
   A fifteen year old enlists in the US Air Force using his brother's birth certificate and takes part in twenty-four missions before he is shot down.

| 486 |

Burke Davis

Runaway Balloon: The Last Flight of Confederate Air Force One (New York: Coward, 1976)

Age range: Grades 3-5

Subject(s): Civil War; Balloons

Major character(s): General Joe Johnson, Military Personnel (soldier); Lieutenant John Randolph Bryan, Military Personnel

Time period(s): 1860s (1862)

Locale(s): Richmond, Virginia

What the book is about: The story of the brief and near disasterous history of the balloon created by the Confederate Army to spy on Union troops, based on a true incident of the Civil War. The General asks Confederate women to donate silk for a balloon. A young Lieutenant Bryan flies the patchwork balloon very well, the first time. The second flight leaves him naked in a runaway balloon.

Where it's reviewed:
Kirkus Reviews, June 1, 1976, page 635
School Library Journal, October 1976, page 106

Other books by the author:
Mr. Lincoln's Whiskers, 1978
Black Heroes of the American Revolution, 1976
Biography of a King Snake, 1975
The Billy Mitchell Story, 1969

Other books you might like:
Paul Fleischman, *Bull Run*, 1993
    Northerners, Southerners, generals, couriers, dreaming boys and worried sisters describe the first battle of of the Civil War.
Patricia Lee Gauch, *Thunder at Gettysburg*, 1975
    Fourteen year old Tillie becomes involved in the tragic battle of July 1-3, 1863.
Lynn Hall, *The Mystery of the Caramel Cat*, 1981
    Willie's encounter with a feline ghost outside a deserted mansion leads to a strange dream about events just before the Civil War.
Betty Ren Wright, *The Red Badge of Courage*, 1981
    During his service in the Civil War, a young Union soldier deals with his conflicting emotions about war.

487

Deborah Davis

Illustrator: Judy Labrasca

The Secret of the Seal (New York: Crown, 1989)

Age range: Grades 3-4

Subject(s): Animals/Seals and Sea Lions; Eskimos; Indians of North America

Major character(s): Kyo, Preteen, Hunter; Kudlah, Parent; Annawee, Parent

Time period(s): Indeterminate

Locale(s): Alaska (Aleutian Islands)

What the book is about: The story of Kyo who lives in a remote Arctic settlement and befriends a seal. One day, he takes his harpoon out onto the frozen bay, hoping to kill his first seal. When he meets his quarry, however, and sees his trusting face, Kyo knows he has met a friend.

Where it's reviewed:
Booklist, June 15, 1989, page 1820
School Library Journal, November 1989, page 105

Other books you might like:
Raymond Creekmore, *Lokoshi Learns to Hunt Seals*, 1946
    Lokoshi, an Eskimo boy, goes on a seal hunt with his Papa.
Arnold A. Griese, *At the Mouth of the Luckiest River*, 1973

An Athabascan Indian boy confronts his tribe's medicine man in an effort to prevent trouble with the Eskimos.
James A. Houston, *Wolf Run: A Caribou Eskimo Tale*, 1971
    When the caribou herds fail to return in the spring, famine becomes so acute that a young Eskimo boy sets out alone in search of food.
Peggy Parish, *Ootah's Lucky Day*, 1970
    Although everyone thinks Ootah too young to hunt, he brings home a walrus when the rest of the hunters return empty handed.
Carter Wilson, *On Firm Ice*, 1969
    A series of tales about the life of a Netsilik Eskimo family during the long winter of northern Canada.

488

N.J. Dawood

Illustrator: Ed Young

Tales From the Arabian Nights (New York: Doubleday, 1978)

Age range: Grades 5-6

Subject(s): Fairy Tale

Major character(s): Scheherazade, Storyteller

Time period(s): 14th century

Locale(s): Middle East

What the book is about: This 1978 edition includes a few stories never before included in children's editions of the classic story of Scheherazade. Based on three versions of the original Arabic, most tales end with a promise about the next adventure.

Where it's reviewed:
Center for Children's Books Bulletin, January 1979, page 78
School Library Journal, January 1979, page 52

Other books by the author:
Aladdin and Other Tales from the Arabian Nights, 1989

Other books you might like:
Barbara Cohen, *Seven Daughters & Seven Sons*, 1982
    A retelling of an Arabic tale in which a woman disguises herself as a man and opens up a shop in order to help her impoverished family.
Marguerite Henry, *Gaudenzia, Pride of the Palio*, 1960
    A story, based on real events, about a boy and a half-Arabian mare who enter the Palio, an annual race in Siena, Italy.
Jean Russell Larson, *The Glass Mountain and Other Arabian Tales*, 1971
    Seven traditional tales from the Middle East include "Ali and the Griffin," "Zeki the Witless," and "King Ping."
George Selden, *The Genie of Sutton Place*, 1973
    A young boy recounts the events of the summer when he had the services of an Arabian genie at his disposal.
Robert Louis Stevenson, *New Arabian Nights*, 1915
    Stories from the Arabian Nights tales, including "The Rajah's Diamond," "A Lodging for the Night," and "Providence and the Guitar."

| 489 |

Alexandra Day

Frank and Ernest (New York: Scholastic, 1988)

Age range: Grades 2-4

Subject(s): Restaurants

Major character(s): Frank, Bear; Ernest, Elephant

Time period(s): Indeterminate

Locale(s): United States

What the book is about: Frank and Ernest take care of a small business when owners are away. They are hired by Mrs. Miller to run her diner, but they had no idea they had to learn a whole new language to handle the job. A four-page glossary of diner jargon is a wonderful resource for word play with kids.

Where it's reviewed:
Center for Children's Books Bulletin, September 1988, page 5
School Library Journal, August 1988, page 80

Other books by the author:
Carl's Masquerade, 1992
River Parade, 1992
Frank and Ernest Play Ball, 1990
Carla Goes Shopping, 1989

Other books you might like:
Eileen Christelow, *The Robbery at the Diamond Dog Diner*, 1986
   Lola Dog doesn't wear her diamonds to the diner when she hears there are jewel theives in town, but Glenda Feathers has a BIG MOUTH!
Russell Hoban, *The Twenty Elephant Restaurant*, 1978
   A man builds a table sturdy enough for an elephant to dance on and works up to a restaurant with twenty dancing elephants.
Maryann Kovalski, *Pizza for Breakfast*, 1991
   Frank and Zelda learn the folly of making wishes when they ask for more customers at their pizza place.
Daniel Manus Pinkwater, *Blue Moose*, 1975
   A man who runs a restaurant on the edge of the woods meets a talking blue moose who becomes the new head waiter.
Lisl Weil, *Gertie and Gus*, 1977
   The ambitious wife of a bear who loves to fish changes their comfortable home life by pushing her husband into bigger and bigger business endeavors.

| 490 |

Marguerite De Angeli, Author/Illustrator

The Door in the Wall (New York: Doubleday, 1949)

Age range: Grades 4-6

Subject(s): Physically Handicapped; Historical

Major character(s): Robin de Bureford, Handicapped; Brother Luke, Religious

Time period(s): 13th century

Locale(s): London, England; Lindsay, England

What the book is about: Robin, the lame son of a noble family in 13th century England is sent away from his home to escape the plague. He learns wood carving and the minstrel life and proves his courage in the face of battle.

Where it's reviewed:
Children and Their Literature, 1969, page 325

Awards the book has won:
Newbery Medal 1950

Other books by the author:
Bright April, 1946
Black Fox of Lorne, 1956
Copper-Toed Boots, 1938
Skippack School, 1939

Other books you might like:
Elizabeth Marie Pope, *Perilous Gard*, 1974
   As punishment, Kate is sent to be kept at the Perilous Gard, a mysterious castle in a remote part of England.
Gloria Skurzynski, *The Minstrel in the Tower*, 1988
   When they attempt to find their mother's brother, Roger and Alice are kidnapped and made captives in a tower and held for ransom.
Rosemary Sutcliff, *Brother Dusty-Feet*, 1952
   11-year-old Hugh runs away and joins a troupe of players in Elizabethan England.
Clyde Robert Bulla, *The Beast of Lor*, 1977
   A story of a runaway elephant befriended by a runaway boy in medieval Britain.
David Macaulay, *Castle*, 1977
   Detailed drawings tell the story of the building and defense of a castle in 13th century Wales. Non-fiction.

| 491 |

Marguerite De Angeli

Fiddlestrings (Garden City, NY: Doubleday, 1974)

Age range: Grades 3-5

Subject(s): Family Life; Sports/Baseball; Music

Major character(s): Dailey De Angeli, Child, Musician (violinist)

Time period(s): 1910s

Locale(s): Atlantic City, New Jersey

What the book is about: Dai is torn between playing the violin and playing baseball. He visits his aunt in Philadelphia, where he can have a better music education. Fun blend of pranks, baseball, music and a loving family.

Where it's reviewed:
Kirkus Reviews, February 15, 1974
Library Journal, April 15, 1974, page 1218

Other books by the author:
The Lion in the Box, 1975
The Door in the Wall, 1974
Empty Barn, 1966
Henner's Lydia, 1936

Other books you might like:
Matt Christopher, *Challenge at Second Base*, 1992
   When Stan is tempted to quit baseball after a few setbacks, he receives a mysterious note telling him to stick it out.
Kathryn Cristaldi, *Baseball Ballerina*, 1992
   A baseball-loving girl worries that the ballet class she takes will ruin her reputation with the other members of the baseball team.
Dean Hughes, *All Together Now*, 1991

The Dodgers make their way to the regional championship, up against the toughest team in California.

Lensey Namioka, *Yang the Youngest and His Terrible Ear*, 1992

Recently arrived in Seattle from China, musically untalented Yingtao is faced with a violin concert when he would rather be playing baseball.

Alfred Slote, *Make-Believe Ball Player*, 1989

Although he's not very good at baseball, ten year old Henry uses his imagination to become a better baseball player.

492

Marguerite De Angeli

The Lion in the Box (Garden City, NY: Doubleday, 1975)

Age range: Grades 3-5

Subject(s): Christmas

Major character(s): Lili Scher, Child; Anna Scher, Housekeeper; Betty Scher, Child

Time period(s): 1900s (1910)

Locale(s): New York, New York

What the book is about: Five children are in Anna Scher's family. She works as a cleaning lady in Madison Avenue buildings. The older girls do the housework at home while Mama is away and look after the younger children. What little they have, they share with the neighbors. A huge box arrives for Christmas from Mrs. Stix. Based on a true story.

Where it's reviewed:
Kirkus Reviews, October 1, 1975, page 1129
School Library Journal, October 1975, page 81

Other books by the author:
Fiddlestrings, 1974
Turkey for Christmas, 1965
The Door in the Wall, 1949
Bright April, 1946

Other books you might like:
Wayne Carley, *Charley the Mouse Finds Christmas*, 1972
On Christmas Eve a mouse is lonesome in his empty department store.
Tom T. Hall, *Christmas in the Old House*, 1989
Bobby and Brenda learn a lesson about forgiveness and the Christmas spirit when they sneak into an abandoned house and decorate the tree they find.
James Howe, *The Fright Before Christmas*, 1988
Harold the dog and Chester the cat try to figure out why Howie the puppy dreads the arrival of Santa Claus.
Nancy Ruth Patterson, *The Christmas Cup*, 1989
Eight year old Megan and her grandmother turn a worthless old cup to good use by saving money in it to buy a gift for a special person at Christmas.
Paul Theroux, *A Christmas Card*, 1978
Lost in a New England snowstorm, a family is sheltered by a mysterious old man who disappears the next morning, leaving behind a magical gift.

493

Meindert De Jong

Illustrator: Maurice Sendak

Along Came a Dog (New York: Harper & Row, 1958)

Age range: Grades 3-5

Subject(s): Animals/Birds; Animals/Dogs

Time period(s): 1950s

Locale(s): United States

What the book is about: The friendship of a timid, lonely dog and a little red hen who loses her toes in a frost. The farmer drives the dog away and he keeps coming back to protect the hen from a preying hawk and hopefully gain a home for himself.

Where it's reviewed:
Booklist, May 15, 1958, page 540
Horn Book, June 1958, page 196
Kirkus Reviews, February 15, 1958, page 134

Awards the book has won:
Newbery Honor

Other books by the author:
Big Goose and Little White Duck, 1963
The Easter Cat, 1971
Good Luck, Duck, 1950
Last Little Cat, 1961

Other books you might like:
Stephen Manes, *Some of the Adventures of Rhode Island Red*, 1990
Rhode Island Red leaves his home among the chickens and becomes a hero.
Dick King-Smith, *The Fox Busters*, 1978
A community of chickens preyed on by hungry foxes is saved by the birth of three wonder chicks.
Claudia Mills, *At the Back of the Woods*, 1982
Clarisse admires her best friend, Emily, who isn't afraid of anything.
Jill Tomlinson, *Hilda the Hen Who Wouldn't Give Up*, 1980
Despite the objections of her keeper, Hilda decides to raise a family of chicks.
Clem Philbrook, *Ollie, the Backward Forward*, 1971
The Bulldogs' teamwork suffers when their mascot dog is arrested for killing chickens.

494

Meindert De Jong

Illustrator: Maurice Sendak

The House of Sixty Fathers (New York: Harper & Row, 1956)

Age range: Grades 5-6

Subject(s): World War II; Courage

Major character(s): Tien Pao, Child (Chinese), Refugee; Glory-of-the-Republic, Pig

Time period(s): 1940s

Locale(s): China

What the book is about: Tien Pao is separated from his family and ends up in Japanese controlled territory, from which his family has just escaped. Accompanied only by his pet pig, he must make a dangerous journey in search of his family. Along the way, he encounters Chinese guerrillas and Japanese soldiers, and is able to help an American airman.

Where it's reviewed:
Booklist, December 1, 1956, page 180
Horn Book, December 1956, page 448

Awards the book has won:
Newbery Honor

Other books by the author:
Far Out the Long Canal, 1964
Horse Came Running, 1970
Puppy Summmer, 1966
Shadrach, 1953

Other books you might like:
Emily Cheney Neville, *The China Year*, 1991
　　Henrietta Rich spends a year in China when her father accepts a teaching position in Beijing.
Michael Morpurgo, *King of the Cloud Forests*, 1987
　　Ashley must choose between a village of violence and tests of courage.
Kathy Lynn Emerson, *Julia's Mending*, 1987
　　In 1887, Julia's parents have gone to China and Julia goes to a farm in upstate New York and breaks her leg.
David Day, *Emperor's Panda*, 1986
　　A poor young shepherd boy becomes emperor of all China.

495

Meindert De Jong

Illustrator: Maurice Sendak

Shadrach (New York: Harper and Row, 1953)

Age range: Grades 4-6

Subject(s): Animals/Rabbits; Animals

Major character(s): Davie, Child

Time period(s): 1950s

Locale(s): Netherlands

What the book is about: Davie's grandfather promises him a real live rabbit. Davie learns the joy and anxiety of having a life to protect. This is a story of changing family relationships as Davie grows up.

Awards the book has won:
Newbery Honor

Other books by the author:
Far Out the Long Canal, 1964
Hurry Home, Candy, 1953
Journey From Peppermint Street, 1968
The Singing Hill, 1962

Other books you might like:
Gertie Evenhuis, *What about Me?*, 1974
　　A young boy searches for a way to help the resistance movement in Amsterdam during the German occupation.
Jay Williams, *Youngest Captain*, 1972
　　A Dutch boy fulfills his greatest longing to steer his family's boat.
Susan E. Kirby, *Culligan Man Can*, 1988
　　Eli finds friendship with his neighbor, Mr. Murphy, and his rabbits.

Deborah Howe, *Bunnicula: A Rabbit Tale of Mystery*, 1979
　　Chester the cat tries to warn his human family that their baby bunny may be a vampire.

496

Anne De Roo

Scrub Fire (New York: Atheneum, 1980)

Age range: Grades 5-6

Subject(s): Courage; Fear; Survival

Major character(s): Michelle Seton, Teenager; Jason Seton, Child; Andrew Seton, Preteen

Time period(s): 1980s

Locale(s): New Zealand

What the book is about: A teenage girl, Michelle, and her two younger brothers are camping with their aunt and uncle in the bush country of New Zealand when a campfire blazes out of control and the kids are separated from the adults. They survive a near-drowning, Jason becomes very ill, and Michelle and Andrew struggle on to get help. The story is enhanced by vivid descriptions of survival techniques.

Where it's reviewed:
Center for Children's Books Bulletin, January 1981, page 91
School Library Journal, November 1980, page 72

Other books you might like:
Jack Bennett, *The Voyage of the Lucky Dragon*, 1981
　　Centering on young Quan, who never loses hope, this is a memorable, unsentimental account of a courageous search for freedom.
Lynn Hall, *Half the Battle*, 1982
　　Two brothers, one of whom is blind, learn to put themselves in each other's shoes for the first time during a two day horseback ride.
James A. Houston, *River Runners: A Tale of Hardship and Bravery*, 1979
　　Two boys survive in the harsh but beautiful country of northern Canada during the fur-trading days of the 19th century.
Judith Kinter, *Cross-Country Caper*, 1980
　　Scott makes a courageous choice to lose a cross-country race in order to expose a drug ring.
Pauline Coggeshall Smith, *Brush Fire!*,
　　Asked to house-sit, Johnny shows courage and quick thinking when facing a motorcycle gang and a brush fire, leading him to rethink his future plans.

497

Barthe DeClements

Five-Finger Discount (New York: Delacorte, 1989)

Age range: Grades 4-6

Subject(s): Honesty; Fathers and Sons; Bullies

Major character(s): Jerry Johnson, Child

Time period(s): 1980s

Locale(s): United States

What the book is about: After Jerry's father goes to jail, he and his mom move to a new neighborhood. Grace, the girl next door, helps him look at his values from a new point of view. He deals with a blackmailing bully and his own stealing.

Where it's reviewed:
Booklist, May 1, 1989, page 1547
School Library Journal, April 1989, page 101

Other books by the author:
Double Trouble, 1987
I Never Asked You to Understand, 1986
No Place for Me, 1987
Sixth Grade Can Really Kill You, 1985

Other books you might like:
Johanna Hurwitz, *The Cold and Hot Winter*, 1988
    Derek and Rory are delighted with a visitor until they begin to discover things missing. Sequel to *Hot and Cold Summer*.
Barbara Ware Holmes, *Charlotte Cheetham, Master of Disaster*, 1985
    A 5th grader who keeps telling lies tells the most outlandish lie of all.
Hila Colman, *Confession of a Storyteller*, 1981
    Annie fails to stand up for a teacher who is accused of improper conduct.
Marion Dane Bauer, *Face to Face*, 1991
    Michael takes a trip to Colorado to see his father and is able to confront his fear of bullies.
Anna Grossnickle Hines, *Tell Me Your Best Thing*, 1991
    8-year-old Sophie joins a club formed by the class bully and is hurt by her best friend.

498

Barthe DeClements

Fourth Grade Wizards (New York: Viking Kestrel, 1988)

Age range: Grades 4-6

Subject(s): Death; Grief

Major character(s): Marianne, Child; Jack, Child

Time period(s): 1980s

Locale(s): United States

What the book is about: Marianne's mother is killed in a plane crash. Encouraged by her teacher and her friend, Jack, she works through her abandonment and loneliness. A modern day fairy tale in which all her dreams come true.

Where it's reviewed:
Kirkus Reviews, September 1, 1988, page 1321
School Library Journal, October 1988, page 143

Other books by the author:
Five-Finger Discount, 1989
No Place for Me, 1987
Nothing's Fair in Fifth Grade, 1987
Sixth Grade Can Really Kill You, 1985

Other books you might like:
Eve Bunting, *Happy Funeral*, 1982
    The Chinese-American funeral customs help Laura and her family accept the death of a beloved family member.
Norma Klein, *Confessions of an Only Child*, 1974
    8 year old Antonia has mixed feelings about a new sibling, but when the baby is born prematurely and dies, she feels the grief.
Susan Mclean, *Pennies for the Piper*, 1981

10 year old Bix cares for her dying mother and an abused little boy.
Patricia Hermes, *Mama Let's Dance*, 1991
    Abandoned by their mother after the death of their father, three youngsters try to keep the situation secret so they won't be split up.
Judy Carole Rhodes, *The King Boy*, 1991
    Benjy shares many special times with his grandfather but it is not until after the old man's death that a family secret is revealed.

499

Barthe DeClements

No Place for Me (New York: Viking, 1987)

Age range: Grades 5-7

Subject(s): Alcoholism; Aunts and Uncles; Witches and Witchcraft

Major character(s): Copper Jones, Preteen; Maggie "Margo" Jones, Witch (Cooper's aunt); Mrs. Thompson, Teacher

Time period(s): 1980s

Locale(s): Everett, Washington

What the book is about: Copper Jones is shuttled back and forth between relatives while her mother is drying out in a rehab center. She lives with an aunt and uncle for awhile, but her aunt Dorothy fears her bad influence on her own girls and Copper feels totally unwanted. When she is sent to live with her aunt Maggie who is a witch, she finds someone who really cares and a school where students are actually nice to the new kid.

Other books by the author:
Wake Me at Midnight, 1991
Monkey See, Monkey Do, 1990
Five-Finger Discount, 1989
Double Trouble, 1987

Other books you might like:
Peggy King Anderson, *Safe at Home!*, 1992
    As his mother tries to hide her drinking problem, Tony spends more time taking care of the house and his sister and less time playing baseball.
Cynthia D. Grant, *Shadow Man*, 1992
    Charming but reckless Gabe, drunk as usual, smashes his truck into a tree and dies, sending waves of shock and grief through his small town.
Jan Marino, *The Day That Elvis Came to Town*, 1991
    Wanda feels betrayed when her parents' glamorous boarder doesn't introduce her to Elvis Presley, and it takes a near tragedy to reunite them.
Bill Wallace, *Never Say Quit*, 1993
    Angry when they are excluded from the soccer team, Justine and other school misfits form their own team with a coach who drinks heavily.
Jacqueline Woodson, *The Dear One*, 1991
    Feni has to adjust when the pregnant young daughter of an old friend of her mother's comes to stay with them.

Barthe DeClements

Nothing's Fair in Fifth Grade (New York: Viking, 1981)

Age range: Grades 4-6

Subject(s): Weight Control; Friendship; Schools

Major character(s): Jennifer, Preteen; Elsie, Preteen, Tutor

Time period(s): 1980s

Locale(s): United States

What the book is about: Jennifer narrates the story of a new girl in her class, overweight class outcast, Elsie. When Elsie is caught stealing, and is having trouble in math, Elsie is hired to tutor Jennifer and is able to pay back what she stole. Jennifer learns that Elsie's home life offers little love, and the girls become friends.

Where it's reviewed:
Kirkus Reviews, September 1, 1981, page 1082
School Library Journal, April 1981, page 125

Awards the book has won:
California Young Reader Medal 1986

Other books by the author:
Fourth Grade Wizards, 1988
No Place for Me, 1987
Sixth Grade Can Really Kill You, 1985
Seventeen and In Between, 1984

Other books you might like:
Carol Lea Benjamin, *Nobody's Baby Now*, 1984
    Olivia has to care for her invalid grandmother after school and she's extremely unhappy about being overweight.
Marilyn Gould, *Golden Daffodils*, 1982
    Wishing for a miracle to make her perfect and normal, a fifth grader transfers from a special school to a regular classroom.
Ann Pilling, *The Big Pink*, 1987
    Angela, overweight and self-conscious, struggles to gain acceptance at a girls' boarding school.
Marilyn Sachs, *The Fat Girl*, 1984
    Jeff becomes obsessed with creating a beautiful new person out of an unhappy fat girl, and his ambition backfires on him.
Sheri Cooper Sinykin, *The Next Thing to Strangers*, 1991
    While visiting their grandparents at a trailer park in Arizona, a diabetic boy and an overweight girl learn a lot about self-acceptance.

Cynthia DeFelice

Illustrator: Leah P. Preiss

The Strange Night Writing of Jessamine Colter (New York: Macmillan, 1988)

Age range: Grades 4-6

Subject(s): Extrasensory Perception; Science Fiction

Major character(s): Jessamine Colter, Widow(er), Artist; Calamine "Callie" Williams, Apprentice; Jacob Carpenter, Restauranteur

Time period(s): Indeterminate

Locale(s): United States

What the book is about: Jessie, an elderly calligrapher who writes announcements and notices of birth, marriage and death for the townfolk, discovers that she has the ability to predict the future in her writings.

Where it's reviewed:
School Library Journal, November 1988, page 124
Booklist, October 1, 1988, page 264
Kirkus Reviews, July 15, 1988, page 1058

Other books by the author:
Devil's Bridge, 1992
Weasel, 1990
The Dancing Skeleton, 1989

Other books you might like:
Patricia Beatty, *Behave Yourself, Bethany Brant*, 1986
    A preacher's daughter with a penchant for getting into trouble has an eventful year and a half as all the predictions of a fortune teller come true.
Nina Beachcroft, *The Wishing People*, 1980
    When Martha becomes the owner of a house which forecasts weather, its two married inhabitants magically grant ten wishes to her and her friend.
Pat Kibbe, *The Hocus-Pocus Dilemma*, 1979
    Convinced that she has psychic powers, a ten year old girl makes predictions for the members of her large family that seem to come true.
James Duncan Lawrence, *ESP McGee and the Haunted Mansion*, 1983
    Convinced that something spooky is going to happen at the old Frome mansion, Edward "ESP" and his friend, Matt, decide to test ESP in the mansion.
Lila Perl, *Annabelle Starr, E.S.P.*, 1983
    Convinced that she has ESP, Annabelle has second thoughts about her "gift" when she sees the prediction causes in her adoptive brother.

Cynthia DeFelice

Weasel (New York: Macmillan, 1990)

Age range: Grades 4-6

Subject(s): Frontier and Pioneer Life; Revenge

Major character(s): Weasel, Villain; Nathan Fowler, Preteen; Molly Fowler, Child

Time period(s): 1830s (1839)

Locale(s): Ohio

What the book is about: Weasel is a terrible villain who commits horrible atrocities in the frontier wilderness. When Nathan's family is victimized, he swears vengence and makes a surprising discovery about the concept of revenge. A story of moral choices.

Where it's reviewed:
Booklist, May 15, 1990, page 1795
School Library Journal, May 1990, page 104

Other books by the author:
The Dancing Skeleton, 1989

Other books you might like:
Sherry Garland, *Best Horse on the Force*, 1991

When Brandon and Wayne try to take revenge on a mounted policeman, their joke backfires on their favorite horse.

Ellen Howard, *Chickenhouse House*, 1991
   Alena and her family move to new farmland on the prairie but must live in a chickenhouse because there is no time to build a house before winter.

Laurie Lawlor, *Addie's Dakota Winter*, 1989
   Ten year old Addie finds an unlikely friend and, stranded alone during a blizzard, learns about courage.

Evelyn White Minshull, *The Cornhusk Doll*, 1987
   Caught and injured in a bear trap, an Indian and his daughter stay with a pioneer family where hatred finally gives way to friendship.

George Shannon, *The Gang and Mrs. Higgins*, 1981
   When the Anderson Gang raids the pioneer trading post in Kansas, Mrs. Higgins uses their bad habits to save the gold.

503

Daniel Defoe

Illustrator: E. Boyd Smith

The Life and Strange and Surprising Adventures of Robinson Crusoe (Boston: Houghton Mifflin, 1909)

Age range: Grades 6 and Up

Subject(s): Islands; Shipwrecks; Survival

Major character(s): Robinson Crusoe, Castaway; Friday, Servant

Time period(s): 17th century (1659-1696)

Locale(s): Caribbean (an island in the Caribbean)

What the book is about: Captured by pirates in London, Crusoe is taken as a prisoner to the Moorish port of Sallee and sails to Brazil aboard a Portugese ship. Shipwrecked in the Caribbean he struggles for survival on a deserted island for thirty-five years with a fellow castaway, a cannibal named "Friday" by Crusoe. Orginally published in 1719.

Where it's reviewed:
Times Literary Supplement, March 17, 1966, page 224

Other books by the author:
The Journal of the Plague Year, 1722
Moll Flanders, 1722

Other books you might like:
Brock Cole, *The Goats*, 1987
   Stripped and marooned on a small island by their fellow campers, a boy and girl slowly form a deep friendship and decide to run away without a trace.

Eth Clifford, *The Curse of the Moonraker: A Tale of Survival*, 1977
   The survivors of a strange shipwreck in the Auckland Islands fight for survival under seemingly hopeless conditions.

Betty Levin, *Put on My Crown*, 1985
   Cast ashore on a bleak island, survivors of a shipwreck find the islanders' treatment of them kind, yet strange and a little frightening.

Scott O'Dell, *Island of the Blue Dolphins*, 1990
   Left alone on for eighteen years on an island off the coast of California, a young Indian girl survives and also finds some happiness in her solitude.

Theodore Taylor, *Teetoncey*, 1974

Ben rescues an English girl from a shipwreck off the Outer Banks of North Carolina. She joins his family but never speaks. First novel of a trilogy.

504

Bruce Degen

The Little Witch and the Riddle (New York: Harper, 1980)

Age range: Grades 1-3

Series: I Can Read Book

Subject(s): Magic; Witches and Witchcraft

Major character(s): Lily, Witch; Otto, Mythical Creature (ogre)

Time period(s): Indeterminate

Locale(s): Fictional Country

What the book is about: A little witch and her friend, Otto Ogre, must find the answers to a riddle before they can open the book of magic secrets that Lily has gotten from her grandmother.

Where it's reviewed:
Booklist, April 15, 1980, page 1211
Kirkus Reviews, March 15, 1980, page 362
School Library Journal, May 1980, page 81

Other books by the author:
Jamberry, 1992
Jesse Bear, What Will You Wear?, 1986
The Josephina Story Quilt, 1986
Commander Toad in Space, 1980

Other books you might like:
Betty Boegehold, *Chipper's Choices*, 1981
   Chipper the chipmunk devises stories, poems, and riddles to help her and her friends through the long winter nights.

Arthur Crowley, *The Wagon Man*, 1981
   The Wagon Man, who lures children away from their homes, is challenged by one of the boys to a riddle game on which the fate of all children rests.

Lillian Nordlicht, *The Alligator with the Lean Mean Smile*, 1985
   Small Hippo and Big Rhino face a hungry alligator who engages them in a riddle-solving battle of wits.

Beatrix Potter, *The Tale of Squirrel Nutkin*, 1987
   Squirrel Nutkin would rather ask an old owl riddles than gather nuts with the other squirrels.

Lisl Weil, *The Riddle Monster*, 1980
   A horrible monster who eats anyone unable to answer its riddles is given its just reward by a thoughtful prince.

505

Meindert DeJong

Hurry Home, Candy (New York: Harper and Row, 1953)

Age range: Grades 4-6

Subject(s): Animals/Dogs; Family Life

Major character(s): Candy, Dog

Time period(s): 1950s

Locale(s): United States

What the book is about: The story of a lonely little lost dog who survives several terrifying adventures and is finally taken home after months of searching by his loving family.

Where it's reviewed:
Horn Book, December 1953, page 456
Library Journal, January 1, 1954, page 72

Awards the book has won:
Newbery Honor

Other books by the author:
Along Came a Dog, 1958
A Horse Came Running, 1970
Puppy Summer, 1966
Shadrach, 1953

Other books you might like:
James Duffy, *Cleaver and Company*, 1991
    13 year old Sarah is kept busy working in her family's diner and taking care of their dog, Cleaver.
Betsy Byars, *Wanted.Mud Blossom*, 1991
    Junior Blossom is convinced that the dog, Mud, should be tried for the disappearance of the school hamster.
Helen Griffith, *Rafa's Dog*, 1983
    When tragedy strikes a family, a child finds consolation in a relationship with a stray dog.
Patricia Lee Gauch, *Kate Alone*, 1980
    When Kate's dog bites a friend of the family, Kate has a difficult decision to make.
Nan Hayden Agle, *Tarr of Belway Smith*, 1969
    A labrador retriever decides to teach his family a lesson by running away from home.

506

Meindert DeJong

Illustrator: Maurice Sendak

The Singing Hill (New York: Harper, 1962)

Age range: Grades 3-5

Subject(s): Animals/Horses

Major character(s): Raymond "Ray", Child; Martin, Relative (brother)

Time period(s): 1950s

Locale(s): United States

What the book is about: A small boy gains self-confidence through his love for an old horse. Ray discovers and passionately befriends an old abandoned horse in a nearby hilltop pasture. When his friend is threatened, the boy is able to rise from the lonliness of his childhood to the courage of love.

Awards the book has won:
Hans Christian Andersen Award 1962
Newbery Medal 1962

Other books by the author:
A Horse Came Running, 1970
Journey From Peppermint Street, 1968
Far Out the Long Canal, 1964
The House of Sixty Fathers, 1956

Other books you might like:
Linda Gruenberg, *Hummer*, 1990

When a man agrees to let Hummer train his Arabian horse for a horse show, it is the one bright spot in her life with a mentally ill mother.
Dorothy Nafus Morrison, *Somebody's Horse*, 1986
    Jenny's good care transforms a pathetic, sick and abandoned horse into a splendid jumper, but there remains the question of who the real owner is.
Robert Newton Peck, *The Horse Hunters*, 1988
    In 1932 in Florida, Ladd finds himself traveling alone more than 100 miles to bring back wild horses for the rodeo and for breeding.
Dona Schenker, *Throw a Hungry Loop*, 1990
    A boy with a talent for throwing loops and who lives on a ranch with his father and grandfather yearns for a roping house.
Nancy Springer, *Not on a White Horse*, 1988
    When Rhiannon sees an Arabian gelding in the woods near her home, her life finds a focus as she learns to deal with family problems.

507

Meindert DeJong

The Wheel on the School (New York: Harper and Row, 1954)

Age range: Grades 4-6

Subject(s): Animals/Birds

Major character(s): Lina, Child; Jella, Child

Time period(s): 1950s

Locale(s): Shora, Netherlands

What the book is about: The school children of a Dutch village attempt to lure storks into nesting in their village. Soon everyone in the village is helping them. They learn about themselves and others as they search for wheels to put on the steep roofs of Shora for the storks.

Where it's reviewed:
Booklist, November 15, 1954, page 137
Horn Book, December 1954, page 431

Awards the book has won:
Newbery Medal 1955

Other books by the author:
The House of Sixty Fathers, 1956
Hurry Home, Candy, 1953
Shadrach, 1953
The Singing Hill, 1962

Other books you might like:
Hilda Van Stockum, *The Winged Watchman*, 1962
    10 year old Joris and his brother, Dirk Jan, live for a chance to help the patriots of the Dutch Underground during World War II.
Carole S. Adler, *Fly Free*, 1984
    Shari seeks refuge from her abusive mother by watching birds in the woods and mountains near her home.
Margaret Wise Brown, *Wheel on the Chimney*, 1954
    This Caldecott honor picture book tells a story of storks returning to Hungary where farmers tie wheels to their chimneys to support the birds' nests.
Mary Mapes Dodge, *Hans Brinker*, 1945

Although he has only homemade wooden skates, Hans dreams of entering the grand race and winning silver skates.

508

M.C. Delaney

Illustrator: Lisa McCue

Henry's Special Delivery (New York: Dutton, 1984)

Age range: Grades 3-6

Subject(s): Fantasy; Humor; Animals/Bears

Major character(s): Henry Barrett Whitfield, Preteen; Homer, Panda; Heather Callahan, Girlfriend

Time period(s): 1980s

Locale(s): United States

What the book is about: Henry gets much more than he bargained for when he sends for the panda offered on the back of a cereal box. Homer is a wisecracking, comfort-loving collector of tacky postcards. Henry was hoping to get the attention of elusive, panda-crazed Heather. They all end up involved with Martian honeymooners and sea faring burglars among other things.

Where it's reviewed:
Bookliset, July 1984, page 1547
Center for Children's Books Bulletin, July, 1984, page 202
School Library Journal, October 1984, page 156

Other books by the author:
The Marigold Monster, 1983

Other books you might like:
Helen Cresswell, The Piemakers, 1980
　A "grand contest" gives the pie-making Roller family of Danby Dale a chance to reclaim the family honor after their pie for the king has failed.
David Day, The Emperor's Panda, 1986
　Relates how the poor young shepherd king became the emperor of all China with the help of the Master Panda.
Miriam Schlein, The Year of the Panda, 1990
　A Chinese boy rescues a starving baby panda and learns why they are endangered and what the government is doing to save them.
Vera B. Williams, Stringbean's Trip to the Shining Sea, 1988
　Stringbean describes his trip to the West Coast in a series of postcards.
William Wise, The Terrible Trumpet, 1966
　Disappointed when his prize in a cereal contest is a trumpet instead of the puppy he wanted, a boy tries to play the instrument anyway.

509

Eric Deleon

Pitch and Hasty Check It Out (New York: Watts, 1988)

Age range: Grades 3-5

Subject(s): Mystery and Detective Stories; Games; Smuggling

Major character(s): Pitch, Preteen, Detective—Amateur; Hasty, Preteen, Detective—Amateur

Time period(s): 1980s

Locale(s): United States

What the book is about: Pitch hears a mysterious voice coming from a pinball machine at the mall. He and his friend, Hasty, wind up in a ventilator shaft trying to track down the voice that keeps saying, "Something wrong, something wrong." When they track the voice, they find it belongs to a parrot and they find themselves smack in the middle of a parrot smuggling ring.

Where it's reviewed:
Booklist, October 1, 1988, page 264
Kirkus Reviews, July 1, 1988, page 970

Other books you might like:
Steve Bradley, The Candy Man, 1977
　When Peg first meets a fellow traveler to New York, she has no idea he is about to involve her in a deadly game of smuggling.
Stephen Manes, That Game From Outer Space: The First Strange Thing That Happened to Oscar Noodleman, 1983
　Oscar becomes obsessed with the new video machine in Hughie's pizza parlor and finds himself involved in an adventure with aliens from outer space.
Kenneth Oppel, Colin's Fantastic Video Adventure, 1985
　Colin discovers that the spaceships in his favorite video game are actually controlled by tiny men, who promise to help him in an upcoming contest.
Kathy Pelta, The Parrot Man Mystery, 1989
　While operating a pet-sitting business, Margaret Drusilla and her friends, Wil and Denise, uncover a parrot smuggling operation in Malibu, California.
Alison Prince, Night Landings, 1984
　Harrie and her brother Ian become convinced that smugglers are operating from the airfield near their English farm home.

510

Judy Delton

Angel's Mother's Wedding (Boston: Houghton Mifflin, 1987)

Age range: Grades 3-6

Subject(s): Remarriage; Family Life; Weddings

Major character(s): Angel, Child

Time period(s): 1980s

Locale(s): United States

What the book is about: Angel's mother is getting married. In addition to all the feelings Angel has about this, she feels her mother is not preparing properly for the wedding so she takes over.

Where it's reviewed:
Booklist, October 1, 1987, page 318
Horn Book, September 1987, page 610

Other books by the author:
Kitty from the Start, 1987
Angel's Mother's Boyfriend, 1986
My Grandpa's in a Nursing Home, 1986
I'll Never Love Anything Ever Again, 1985

Other books you might like:
Larry Bograd, *The Fourth-Grade Dinosaur Club*, 1989
  Billy feels everything is going wrong, from a remarriage at home to bullies at school and prejudice against Juan, his best friend at school.
Barbara Corcoran, *A Dance to Still Music*, 1974
  Deafened by an illness, Margaret runs away, fearing that her mother's remarriage means she will be sent to boarding school.
Elisabet McHugh, *Karen's Sister*, 1983
  Karen's mother adopts a second Korean child and finds a husband with three children of his own.
Barbara Park, *My Mother Got Married and Other Disasters*, 1989
  Twelve year old Charles experiences many problems in adjusting to a new stepfamily.
Jayne Pettit, *My Name Is San Ho*, 1992
  A Vietnamese boy tries to adjust to his new life in the U.S. with his mother and American Marine stepfather.

511

Judy Delton

Illustrator: Alan Tiegreen

Cookies and Crutches (New York: Dell, 1988)

Age range: Grades 1-2

Series: Pee Wee Scouts #1

Subject(s): Accidents; Cooks and Cookery; Scouting

Major character(s): Molly Duff, Child; Mrs. Peters, Leader (Pee Wee Scouts); Mary Beth Kelly, Child

Time period(s): 1980s

Locale(s): United States

What the book is about: The Pee Wee Scouts are excited. This week they are going to bake cookies and earn their baking badge. Next week is a big skating party. The cookies at the meeting are delicious, but when Molly and Mary Beth take the recipe home, their limited skills at reading directions result in disaster. When they go skating, Molly sprains her ankle and cannot earn the skating badge. But she winds up with a "Good Patient" badge which makes her feel special indeed.

Where it's reviewed:
Booklist, June 1, 1988, page 1681
Publisher's Weekly, June 10, 1988, page 79
School Library Journal, June 1984, page 87

Other books by the author:
Bad, Bad Bunnies, 1990
No Time for Christmas, 1988
Brimhall Turns Detective, 1983
Duck Goes Fishing, 1983

Other books you might like:
Ellen Conford, *What's Cooking, Jenny Archer?*, 1989
  Follows the comic mishaps of Jenny Archer as she goes into the business of preparing lunches for friends at school.
Suzy Kline, *Orp and the Chop Suey Burgers*, 1990
  Eleven year old Orville enters a cooking contest which he has high hopes of winning with his recipe for chop suey burgers.
Jean Rossbach, *Bernie, the Beagle Who Liked German Cooking*, 1991

The adventures of Bernie, a beagle whose talent for German cooking helps him succeed in life.
Kathy Kennedy Tapp, *Den 4 Meets the Jinx*, 1988
  Adam never suspects the his bratty sister may be the only person who can keep his Cub Scout den from dissolving.
Mike Thaler, *Pack 109*, 1988
  Five rodents make up Pack 109 and this is the story of their adventures.

512

Judy Delton

My Mom Hates Me in January (Morton Grove, Illinois: Albert Whitman, 1977)

Age range: Grades 2-4

Subject(s): Mothers and Sons; Winter

Time period(s): 1970s

Locale(s): United States

What the book is about: A little boy finds it is the winter blues and not his behavior that makes his mother impatient in January, and she makes it clear to him that he is loved in spite of her moods.

Where it's reviewed:
Center for Children's Books Bulletin, November 1977, page 44
School Library Journal, February 1978, page 46

Awards the book has won:
North Dakota Children's Choice Award 1980

Other books by the author:
Brimhall Comes to Stay, 1978
Penny-Wise, Fun-Foolish, 1977
Three Friends Find Spring, 1977
Two Is Company, 1976

Other books you might like:
Mary Holmes, *Dust of Life*, 1992
  Anh welcomes her cousin Lan from Vietnam and tries to help her come to terms with her traumatic past.
Kiyonori Kaizuki, *A Calf Is Born*, 1990
  Describes the birth of a calf on a cold winter's night and his first day of life as he learns to stand, goes out doors, and nuzzles up to his mother.
Selma Lagerlof, *The Changeling*, 1992
  A farmer's wife becomes the foster mother of a troll's child and her kind treatment of the changeling secures the return of her own son.
Lissa Rovetch, *Trigwater Did It*, 1989
  Arnie's invisible friend gets him into all sorts of trouble until Arnie decides to make him behave.
Barrie Wade, *Little Monster*, 1990
  Mandy, who is usually well-behaved, tries acting like her brother, showing her mom there is a little monster in everyone.

513

Judy Delton

Illustrator: Anne S. O'Brien

The Mystery of the Haunted Cabin (Boston: Houghton Mifflin, 1986)

Age range: Grades 3-5

Subject(s): Ghosts; Mystery and Detective Stories; Vacations

Major character(s): Barry Harrison, Child; Robin Harrison, Preteen; Spencer, Friend

Time period(s): 1940s

Locale(s): Horseshoe Lake, Minnesota

What the book is about: After a night in a cabin in the Minnesota woods, Robin, Barry and Spencer try to find out more about the prior owner and the identity of the voice they heard warning them to leave.

Where it's reviewed:
Booklist, October 15, 1986, page 347
Kirkus Reviews, July 15, page 1123
School Library Journal, January 1987, page 72

Other books by the author:
Camp Ghost-Away, 1988
Back Yard Angel, 1983
Lee Henry's Best Friend, 1980
Kitty in the Middle, 1979

Other books you might like:
Robert Bright, *Georgie and the Noisy Ghost*, 1971
  Fortunately for the Whittakers and the noisy ghost in the beach cottage they rent, their personal quiet ghost, Georgie, comes along on vacation.
Eth Clifford, *Never Hit a Ghost with a Baseball Bat*, 1993
  While exploring a trolley car museum, Mary Rose and Jo Beth encounter voices from nowhere.
Liza Ketchum Murrow, *The Ghost of Lost Island*, 1991
  While shepherding his grandfather's flock on an island off the coast of Maine, Gabe encounters the ghost of a drowned milkmaid.
Ben Schecter, *The Whistling Whirligig*, 1974
  While spending Christmas vacation with his history teacher, a lonely boy makes friends with the ghost of a runaway slave.
Catherine Sefton, *In a Blue Velvet Dress*, 1973
  With the help of a ghost in a blue velvet dress, bookworm Jane survives the disaster of finding herself on vacation without a single book.

514

Justin F. Denzel

Illustrator: Taylor Oughton

Snowfoot: White Reindeer of the Arctic (Champaign, IL: Garrard, 1976)

Age range: Grades 3-5

Subject(s): Animals/Deer

Major character(s): Taku Bokar, Preteen; Mangus Bokar, Parent

Time period(s): Indeterminate

Locale(s): Arctic (Lapland)

What the book is about: A Lapp boy assumes the responsibility for raising a wounded white fawn. The fawn grows to be a large reindeer, capable of assuming the responsibility of being hitched to the lead sled.

Where it's reviewed:
School Library Journal, February 1977, page 60

Other books by the author:
Hunt for the Last Cat, 1991
Boy of the Painted Cave, 1988
Black Kettle: King of the Wild Horses, 1974
Champion of Liberty: Henry Knox, 1969

Other books you might like:
Beverly Brodsky, *Sedna: An Eskimo Myth*, 1975
  Sedna, mother of all sea animals, tells the story of her life and helps the starving Inuit.
James A. Houston, *Long Claws: An Arctic Adventure*, 1981
  An Eskimo brother and sister make a perilous trek across the storm-swept tundra to bring back a frozen caribou to their hungry family.
Lee Kingman, *The Secret Journey of the Silver Reindeer*, 1968
  A Lapp boy undertakes a secret journey to his ancestral burial ground, proving he has the courage and inherited right to be head of the family.
Ingrid Pelletier, *Daughter of Lapland*, 1970
  A girl is apprehensive about returning to live in Lapland where her father died on the annual expedition to the coast.
Seymour Reit, *Race Against Death*, 1976
  A dog sled relay makes a life and death race against time through an Alaskan blizzard with a supply of serum needed to stop a diptheria epidemic.

515

Jo Dereske

Glom Gloom (New York: Atheneum, 1985)

Age range: Grades 5-7

Subject(s): Fantasy

Major character(s): Raymond Fibbey, Adventurer; Wicker Bugle, Aged Person; Merrily Cumbers, Adventurer

Time period(s): Indeterminate

Locale(s): Waterpushin, Fictional Country

What the book is about: Raymond fights to save the Bulkings, a peace-loving people, from the evil Weeuns. No one remembers the old rhyme about the Garter Gates until Raymond and friends discover the danger that lies behind them.

Where it's reviewed:
Children's Book Review Service, Winter 1986, page 64

Other books by the author:
Lone Sentinel, 1989

Other books you might like:
Philip Curtis, *Invasion From Below the Earth*, 1980
  A strange creature called a Burrower contacts a young boy to warn him about the threat humans pose to the creature's subterranean kingdom.
Dennis B. Fradin, *How I Saved the World*, 1986
  After Shelley spots a UFO at a rundown resort in northern Michigan, he becomes involved in a desperate effort to stop an alien invasion.
Alan Garner, *Elidor*, 1965

While exploring a church that is being razed in a Manchester slum, four children are drawn into another world where they must combat an evil power.

Daniel Manus Pinkwater, *Lizard Music*, 1976
When left to take care of himself, a young boy becomes involved with a community of intelligent lizards who tell him of an invasion from outer space.

Jim Slater, *The Boy Who Saved Earth*, 1979
The telepathic powers and super intelligence of a boy from a friendly alien planet are instrumental in saving earth from invasion by evil aliens.

516

Gene DeWeese

The Dandelion Caper (New York: Putnam, 1986)

Age range: Grades 5-7

Subject(s): Animals/Cats; Science Fiction

Major character(s): Calvin Willeford, Preteen, Traveller (space traveller); Kathy Entsminger, Preteen, Traveller (space traveller); Dandelion, Spy, Alien

Time period(s): Indeterminate Future

Locale(s): East Gradwohl, Earth

What the book is about: Calvin and Kathy have often rescued "tourists" from outer space. When they discover the presence of aliens in their hometown, they help Dandelion, a top agent in an alien law enforcement group, search for a gang of evil aliens.

Where it's reviewed:
Center for Children's Books Bulletin, March 1987, page 124
School Library Journal, November 1986, page 88

Other books by the author:
The Calvin Nullifier, 1987
Black Suits From Outer Space, 1985
Nightmare Universe, 1985
The Adventures of a Two-Minute Werewolf, 1983

Other books you might like:
Victor Appleton, *Ark Two*, 1982
Tom Swift travels to the planet Aquilla in pursuit of an ecological system, SeaGlobe, stolen from the space colony New America.
G.R. Crosher, *The Awakening Water*, 1977
Thirteen year old Watford Nine John breaks out of the strict regime imposed after the devastation of 1997.
H.M. Hoover, *Away Is a Strange Place to Be*, 1990
Abby is kidnapped in the year 2349 to serve as slave labor on an artificial world under construction.
Pamela Sargent, *Alien Child*, 1988
A girl who is isolated and kept company only by a furry guardian realizes she is the last human being left on Earth.
Jeff Sutton, *Alien from the Stars*, 1970
The sole survivor of a wreck in space eludes the many earth agents who are chasing him.

517

Catherine Dexter

Mazemaker (New York: Morrow, 1989)

Age range: Grades 5-7

Subject(s): Time Travel; Space and Time; Mazes

Major character(s): Winnie, Preteen (12 years old), Time Traveller

Time period(s): 1980s (1989); 1880s (1889)

Locale(s): Earth

What the book is about: In this convincing time shift fantasy, twelve year old Winnie is hurled back in time and marooned on a 19th century estate until she can solve a maze and return to the present. The time shift is very believable and readers are drawn into the plot.

Where it's reviewed:
Center for Children's Books Bulletin, April 1989, page 192
School Library Journal, May 1989, page 103

Other books by the author:
The Gilded Cat, 1992
The Oracle Doll, 1985
Gertie's Green Thumb, 1983

Other books you might like:
Carol Gaskin, *The Master of Mazes*, 1985
As a dweller in the Forgotten Forest, the reader makes his or her own decisions which determine the course of the story.
Gary Paulsen, *Culpepper's Cannon*, 1992
Dunc Culpepper and his friend, Amos, go back in time to 1862 while researching the Civil War cannon in the town square.
Gillian Rubinstein, *Skymaze*, 1989
A group of children explore a video-game maze that suddenly becomes dangerously real and forces them to face their own problems as well as the maze.
Elvira Woodruff, *The Disappearing Bike Shop*, 1992
Fifth graders Freckles and Tyler meet an unusual bicycle salesman and inventor who turns out to be Leonardo da Vinci traveling through time.

518

Catherine Dexter

The Oracle Doll (New York: Macmillan, 1985)

Age range: Grades 5-8

Subject(s): Dolls and Dollhouses; Mythology

Major character(s): Rose Wilson, Preteen; Lucy Wilson, Child; James Leon Handry, Preteen

Time period(s): 1980s

Locale(s): United States

What the book is about: Rose, Lucy, and Jamie become the guardians of a talking doll who speaks much more than the children ever expected. It begins when Mrs. Wilson, Lucy and Rose are almost run down by a car and it is actually Gabby, the doll, who yells "Watch Out" and saves their lives. Rose and Lucy, along with neighbor James, discover Gabby is actually a reincarnation of the Oracle of Delphi. Gabby's predictions grow more mysterious and frightening as the children struggle to find the rightful owner.

Where it's reviewed:
Booklist, November 1, 1985, page 403

Other books by the author:
The Gilded Cat, 1992
Mazemaker, 1989
Gertie's Green Thumb, 1983

Other books you might like:
Harold Courlander, *The Son of the Leopard*, 1974
    A young boy is cast out from his village and wanders performing many heroic deeds, until the fulfillment of a prophecy helps him find his identity.
Kate McMullan, *Under the Mummy's Spell*, 1992
    When Peter kisses a mummy mask on a dare, he finds that he has fulfilled an age-old prophecy and must contend with an ancient Egyptian sorceress.
Edward Packard, *Olympus: What Is the Secret of the Oracle?*, 1988
    As an Earth Inspector, the reader travels back in time to Greece in 400 BC to search out the Oracle of Delphi and discover the secret of her powers.
Richard L. Purtill, *Enchantment at Delphi*, 1986
    Fascinated by the ruins at Delphi, a young girl manages to slip into the site when it is deserted and finds herself involved in a strange adventure.
Penina Keen Spinka, *Mother's Blessing*, 1992
    Around the year 1000 a Chumash Indian girl follows the call of her spirit guide and seeks to fulfill a prophesy that she will lead her people.

519

Peter Dickinson

Annerton Pit (Boston: Little Brown, 1977)

Age range: Grades 6-8

Subject(s): Blind; Ghosts

Major character(s): Jake Bertold, Handicapped (blind), Teenager; Martin Bertold, Teenager (Jake's brother)

Time period(s): Indeterminate Past

Locale(s): England

What the book is about: Blind, thirteen year old Jake helps free his grandfather and brother from revolutionaries. Death and fear haunt the blackness of the maze with a shape Jake must confront in a deep, whispering tunnel and in his own mind.

Where it's reviewed:
Booklist, January 15, 1978, page 810
Hornbook, April 1978, page 150
Kirkus Reviews, August 1, 1977, page 788

Other books by the author:
The Devil's Children, 1986
The Blue Hawk, 1976
The Gift, 1974
The Dancing Bear, 1973

Other books you might like:
Joan Aiken, *The Shadow Guests*, 1980
    A boy arrives at his cousin's home in England unprepared for the supernatural furor his presence unleashes.
Jane Louise Curry, *Ghost Lane*, 1979
    Three children in an English village face danger as they try to track down the criminals responsible for burglaries in a strange, old house.

Catherine Dexter, *Mazemaker*, 1989
    Playing in a maze, Winnie is hurled back in time and marooned on a 19th century estate until she can solve the maze and return to the present.
William Mayne, *It*, 1977
    A young English girl encounters a disturbing restless spirit which she doesn't understand, but knows she can put to rest.
Patricia A. McKillip, *The House on Parchment Street*, 1973
    While staying with her cousin in England, a girl helps him find a way of helping the troubled ghosts inhabiting the cellar of the house.

520

Peter Dickinson

A Box of Nothing (New York: Delacorte, 1985)

Age range: Grades 5-8

Subject(s): Fantasy

Major character(s): James, Preteen; Burra, Alien (Sentient Rubbish Pile)

Time period(s): 1980s

Locale(s): United States

What the book is about: James is trapped in a weirdly changed garbage dump inhabited by patrols of armed giant rats, huge seagulls and an intelligent pile of rubbish named Burra. James' box of Nothing becomes his key to escape to his parallel existence in the "real" world.

Where it's reviewed:
Horn Book, September/October 1988, page 630
School Library Journal, June/July 1988, page 103

Other books by the author:
Eva, 1989
The Devil's Children, 1986
Heartsease, 1986
The Blue Hawk, 1976

Other books you might like:
Christopher Carpenter, *The Twilight Realm*, 1985
    Five young people addicted to a fantasy role-playing game are transformed into characters with remarkable powers and sent into a parallel world.
Cathy Livoni, *Elements of Time*, 1983
    Sael, a young man with violent emotions and bizarre visions, experiences a terrifyingly vivid premonition of the destruction of his world.
Lisa J. Smith, *The Night of the Solstice*, 1987
    Four children set out to rescue a sorceress held captive in a parallel world.
Caroline Stevermer, *River Rats*, 1992
    Nearly 20 years after the holocaust has destroyed civilization, Tomcat and a group of other orphans face danger as they steer a boat on toxic waters.
Roger Zelazny, *A Dark Traveling*, 1987
    When a scientist learns that aliens in a parallel world are waging a secret war against the Earth, he disappears and his children set out to find him.

521

Peter Dickinson

Eva (New York: Delacorte, 1989)

Age range: Grades 5-8

Subject(s): Scientific Experiments; Science Fiction; Transplants

Major character(s): Eva, Experimental Subject

Time period(s): Indeterminate Future

Locale(s): Earth

What the book is about: The planet is severely overpopulated, the wilderness has completely disappeared, and Eva, the daughter of a zoologist, has been in a terrible car accident. Her neuron memory is transplanted into the body of a dead female chimp, yet she retains her human intelligence and instincts. She wakes up immobilized, and realizes that her mother is not telling her the whole story of what happened to her.

Where it's reviewed:
Booklist, January 15, 1990, pge 994
Locus, May 1989, page 46
Five Owls, May 1990, page 92

Other books by the author:
Emma Tupper's Diary, 1988
City of Gold, 1980
Annerton Pit, 1977
Chance Luck Destiny, 1975

Other books you might like:
John Christopher, *Empty World*, 1977
    When a deadly virus kills off most of the world's population, a teenaged boy tries to survive in seemingly empty England.
Mary Haynes, *Raider's Sky*, 1987
    After a chemical accident kills off most of the world's population, Pokey finds a new life with a group of elderly people living in Virginia.
Norma Klein, *A Honey of a Chimp*, 1980
    Relates the escapades of a chimpanzee who moves in with a human family in New York City.
Sandy Landsman, *Castaways on Chimp Island*, 1987
    Four laboratory chimps, participants in an experiment to learn sign language, are placed on a jungle island to return to nature.
Ron Roy, *The Chimpanzee Kid*, 1985
    An animal rights activist, Harold finds a friend in the new boy in class who agrees to help him in his plan to free a caged lab chimp.

522

Peter Dickinson

The Gift (Boston: Little, Brown, 1974)

Age range: Grades 5 and Up

Subject(s): Extrasensory Perception

Major character(s): Davy Price, Preteen, Psychic; Ian Price, Teenager; Penny Price, Teenager

Time period(s): 1970s

Locale(s): Wales

What the book is about: Only Davy's grandmother and sister know he has inherited the gift of mind reading, and Grandmother has warned that using the gift brings bad luck. Davy is startled to receive a stranger's viscious and psychotic thoughts. His own father is involved in a plot that leads to danger, confrontation and death.

Where it's reviewed:
Horn Book, October 1974, page 141
Kirkus Reviews, May 15, 1974, page 540

Other books by the author:
The Seventh Raven, 1981
The Fires of Autumn, 1974
The Poison Oracle, 1974
The Dancing Bear, 1973

Other books you might like:
Joseph Claro, *I Can Predict the Future*, 1972
    A junior high boy comes to regret his gift of predicting the future when his peers start treating him like a freak.
Lois Duncan, *A Gift of Magic*, 1971
    Nancy's gift of ESP brings her fame, but also more problems than even she could have predicted.
Beatrice Gormley, *The Ghastly Glasses*, 1985
    Andrea discovers her new glasses give her mental control over family and friends, but her attempts to "improve" them are disastrous.
Virginia Hamilton, *Dustland*, 1989
    Four children, all with extraordinary mental powers, go far into the future to a region called Dustland. (sequel to *Justice and Her Brothers*)
Richard Peck, *Blossom Culp and the Sleep of Death*, 1986
    Blossom, who has "second sight", helps an Egyptian princess regain her tomb and saves a suffragette school teacher from losing her job in 1914.

523

Peter Dickinson

Illustrator: Alan Lee

Merlin Dreams (New York: Delacorte, 1988)

Age range: Grades 4-6

Subject(s): Fantasy; Magic

Major character(s): Merlin, Magician; Scipiod, Monster; Sir Tremalin, Knight

Time period(s): Indeterminate Past

Locale(s): Fictional Country

What the book is about: Nine tales from the mind of a dreaming Merlin about a rusty knight, a basilisk who turns his master into stone, a reading hermit, and a knight who can hunt as a dog. Unicorns, knights, dragons and damsels abound for the "Dungeon and Dragons" crowd.

Where it's reviewed:
Booklist, February 1, 1989, page 938
Horn Book, March/April 1989, page 210

Other books by the author:
The Devil's Children, 1986
Heartease, 1986
The Weathermonger, 1986
Giant Cold, 1983

Other books you might like:
Susan Cooper, *Over Sea, Under Stone*, 1965
Three children on find an ancient manuscript which sends them on a quest for a grail that will reveal the true story of King Arthur.
Douglas Arthur Hill, *Blade of the Poisoner*, 1987
Jarral and three friends with strong psychic talents fight the evil of Prince Mephtik the Poisoner who serves the Demon-Driver.
John Dendall, *Under Dragon's Wing*, 1984
Prince Treon must find a way, with the help of a magical dragon ring and an ancient sorcery book, to rid the country of the evil Crimson Wizard.
Pamela F. Service, *Winter of Magic's Return*, 1985
Believing a new age of magic is about to begin after the nuclear holoccaust, a young resurrected Merlin and two friends bring King Arther back.
J.R.R. Tolkien, *The Hobbit, or, There and Back Again*, 1938
The adventures of well-to-do hobbit, Bilbo Baggins, who lives happily in his comfortable home until a wandering wizard named Gandalf grants his wish.

524

Lucy Diggs

Illustrator: Emily Arnold McCully

Selene Goes Home (New York: Atheneum, 1989)

Age range: Grades 2-4

Subject(s): Animals/Cats; Moving, Household

Major character(s): Selene, Cat

Time period(s): Indeterminate

Locale(s): United States

What the book is about: Feline Selene is shocked to discover her owner is moving to a houseboat, and she decides to return to her former home. She befriends a seagull who flies her to her old house. The new occupants include a large dog and Selene determines to return to Margaret. She befriends a calico stray and brings her along.

Where it's reviewed:
Booklist, June 1, 1989, page 1721
Horn Book, May/June 1989, page 87

Other books by the author:
Moon in the Water, 1988
Everyday Friends, 1986

Other books you might like:
Sylvia Cassedy, *The Best Cat Suit of All*, 1991
When Mike has a cold and can't go out in his cat suit on Halloween, no on can cheer him up, until his last visitor, who has the best cat suit of all.
Marjorie Flack, *The Story about Ping*, 1961
A little duck finds adventure on the Yangtze River when he is too late to board his master's houseboat one evening.
Miska Miles, *Jenny's Cat*, 1979
Lonely in their new town, Jenny is delighted when a stray cat comes to their house, but her mother is not.
Shirley Parenteau, *Jelly and the Spaceboat*, 1981
Jelly and Rich find themselves headed down the Sacramento River on an unusual houseboat with a crew from outer space.

Jo Ann Stover, *The Binnes and the Dogs and Cats From Everywhere*, 1971
Moving the furniture outside is only one of the ways the Binnies try to cope with all the dogs and cats that descend on them.

525

Fred D'Ignazio

Illustrator: Larry Pearson

Chip Mitchell: The Case of the Robot Warriors (New York: Lodestar Books, 1984)

Age range: Grades 5-7

Subject(s): Computers; Literature; Mystery and Detective Stories

Major character(s): Chip Mitchell, Computer Expert; Kate Marconi, Computer Expert

Time period(s): 1980s

Locale(s): Pine Hill, North Carolina

What the book is about: The reader is asked to supply the answers to eight mysteries which are solved by young computer whiz Chip Mitchell and his partner, Kate Marconi.

Where it's reviewed:
Booklist, March 1, 1984, page 966

Other books by the author:
Chip Mitchell: Case of the Chocolate Covered Bugs, 1985
Chip Mitchell: Case of the Stolen Computer Brains, 1983
Working Robots, 1982
Katie and the Computer, 1979

Other books you might like:
Milton Dank, *The Computer Game Murder*, 1985
When Larry receives a message on his computer screen that his playing partner is in trouble, a long and dangerous investigation begins.
Paula Danziger, *Not for a Billion Gazillion Dollars*, 1992
Matthew, trying desperately to buy a coveted computer program, learns the importance of money and eventually starts his own business.
Dean Marney, *The Computer That Ate My Brother*, 1985
Harry is alarmed when his computer takes on a life of his own and zaps his obnoxious older brother.
E.T. Randall, *Cosmic Kidnappers*, 1985
Drawn into a computer and out again into an alien spaceship far away from home, the reader must figure out a way to get back to Earth.
Seymour Simon, *Chip Rogers, Computer Whiz*, 1984
A computer whiz uses his computer and his friend to track down a gem robber. Readers are encouraged to use their own computers to solve the mystery.

526

Barbara Dillon, Author/Illustrator

Mrs. Tooey and the Terrible Toxic Tar (New York: Harper, 1988)

Age range: Grades 3-5

Subject(s): Babysitters; Magic; Witches and Witchcraft

Major character(s): Craig Saunders, Preteen; Margo Saunders, Preteen; Alice Tooey, Babysitter, Witch

Time period(s): 1980s

Locale(s): Summerton

What the book is about: Craig and Margo Saunders seem to be the only kids left in Summerton - all their friends have taken off for spring break. Even their parents are taking a trip. When the last minute babysitter roars up in a red Camaro and charges breathlessly into the house with her knapsack, the kids begin to get the idea the week may be unusual. Not only is Mrs. Tooey a witch, but her sister, Velma, is also a witch who plans to destroy the town with the Terrible Toxic Tar.

Other books by the author:
My Stepfather Shrank!, 1992
A Mom by Magic, 1990
Mr. Chill, 1985
The Good-Guy Cake, 1980

Other books you might like:
Terrance Dicks, *A Spell for My Sister*, 1991
    Mike MacMagic, youngest in a family of witches, suspects his sister's boyfriend when family heirlooms disappear and his sister's behavior changes.
Lynn Hall, *Dagmar Schultz and the Powers of Darkness*, 1989
    Edgar, Iowa's only warlock, agrees to use his powers to make James fall in love with Dagmar if she can convince Aunt Gretchen to date Edgar.
Jayne Harvey, *Great-Uncle Dracula*, 1992
    Emily finds it hard enough adjusting to a new town, Transylvania USA, populated by vampires, witches and the like, without the bullying of a classmate
Steve Senn, *The Sand Witch*, 1987
    On vacation at the beach, Frick and Jenny help a witch from outer space search for giant candy-eating crabs.
Betsy Sterman, *Too Much Magic*, 1986
    Two brothers have a grand time wishing for all sorts of things with the help of a magic cube the younger brother finds on the playground.

527

Paige Dixon

Illustrator: Grambs Miller

Summer of the White Goat (New York: Atheneum, 1977)

Age range: Grades 5-7

Subject(s): Animals/Goats; Mountain Life

Major character(s): Gordon Mohlen, Student—High School

Time period(s): 1970s

Locale(s): Rocky Mountains

What the book is about: High school senior Gordon Mohlen spends a summer in Glacier National Park observing the mountain goats that live on the high slopes. Living in a small chalet, he climbs the mountain each day to observe and explore. He watches the goats cope with avalanches, hawks, mountain lions and storms. A beautifully written story for all lovers of nature.

Where it's reviewed:
Booklist, September 15, 1977, page 192

Kirkus Reviews, March 1, 1977, page 223
School Library Journal, November 1977, page 55

Other books by the author:
The Search for Charlie, 1976
May I Cross Your Golden River, 1975
Silver Wolf, 1973
Lion on the Mountain, 1972

Other books you might like:
Jeffrey Carroll, *Climbing to the Sun*, 1977
    An Indian boy's cocern for a wild mountain goat leads him into encounters which reveal to him much more about life.
Ben Mikaelsen, *Rescue Josh McGuire*, 1991
    Josh and a bear cub destined for laboratory testing run away to the mountains of Montana, and must fight for their lives in a sudden snowstorm.
Pamela Powell, *The Turtle Watchers*, 1992
    Three sisters on a Caribbean Island band together to protect a nest of leatherback turtle eggs from poachers and natural enemies.
Theodore Taylor, *The Weirdo*, 1991
    Chip Clewt fights to save the black bears in the Powhaten National Wildlife Reserve, North Carolina.
Kenneth Thomasma, *Pathki Nana, Kootenai Girl*, 1991
    The story of a Kootenai girl living in northwestern Montana, and the adventures she has while seeking her guardian spirit in the mountains.

528

Nanabah Chee Dodge

Illustrator: Jeffrey Lunge

Morning Arrow (New York: Lothrop, 1975)

Age range: Grades 4-6

Subject(s): Indians of North America

Major character(s): Morning Star, Indian (Navajo)

Time period(s): 1970s

Locale(s): Monument Valley, Utah

What the book is about: A ten year old Navajo boy wants to buy a shawl for his elderly grandmother. When he trades his best ram for the shawl, the ram escapes and returns to the boy. The story introduces many Navajo phrases and traditions.

Where it's reviewed:
Kirkus Reviews, March 15, 1975, page 306
School Library Journal, September 1975, page 79

Other books you might like:
Hubert Evans, *Son of the Salmon People*, 1981
    Hal returns to his home in British Columbia to find that a strange white man is bullying his people, deforesting the slopes and ruining the river.
Lynne Gessner, *Malcolm Yucca Seed*, 1977
    A young Indian boy plots and schemes for the "real" Navajo name he longs for.
Lynne Gessner, *Navajo Slave*, 1976
    When the white soldiers attack his village, Straight Arrow is captured by Utes and sold into slavery on the ranch of a Spanish landholder.
Miska Miles, *Annie and the Old One*, 1971
    A Navajo girl unravels each day's weaving to protect her grandmother from death.

Paul Pitts, *Racing the Sun*, 1988
  A Navajo boy is torn between the suburban life he has always known and the heritage his father and grandfather share with him.

529

Elfie Donnelly

So Long, Grandpa (New York: Crown, 1981)

Age range: Grades 4-6

Subject(s): Death; Cancer; Grandparents

Major character(s): Micky Nidetzky, Child; Linda Nidetzky, Child; Grandpa Nidetzky, Grandparent (grandfather)

Time period(s): 1980s

Locale(s): Austria

What the book is about: Ten year old Micky is very close to his grandfather and does not really comprehend when he is told Grandpa has cancer. The family plans a vacation to the Canary Islands, and Grandpa, though ill, goes along. Micky and Grandpa discuss death and dying, funeral customs, and whether or not there is an afterlife. When Grandpa dies, Micky's father shows him a letter Grandpa left urging Micky not to be sad, and to care for the old man's "treasures."

Where it's reviewed:
Kirkus Reviews, August 1, 1981, page 934
School Library Journal, May 1981, page 63

Other books by the author:
Tina into Two Won't Go, 1983
Offbeat Friends, 1982

Other books you might like:
Jan Greenberg, *A Season In-Between*, 1979
  Carrie's life at the exclusive academy she attends is made more painful when she discovers that her father is dying of cancer.
Madeleine L'Engle, *A Ring of Endless Light*, 1980
  Vicky and her family are spending the summer with her beloved grandfather who is dying of leukemia.
Jean Little, *Mama's Going to Buy You a Mockingbird*, 1985
  Dealing with the uncertainties of his father's illness which proves to be terminal cancer, Jeremy finds himself riding an emotional roller coaster.
Jane Resh Thomas, *Saying Goodbye to Grandma*, 1988
  Traveling with her parents to her grandmother's funeral, Suzie grieves with them and remembers special times.
Mary Stolz, *By the Highway Home*, 1971
  Catty's life is one big disaster. Her brother is killed, her father loses his job, the family home burns down and she can't live with her sister.

530

Judy Donnelly

Illustrator: Keith Kohler

The Titanic: Lost.and Found (New York: Random, 1987)

Age range: Grades 2-4

Subject(s): Shipwrecks

Time period(s): 1910s (1912); 1980s (1985)

Locale(s): *R.M.S. Titanic*, At Sea

What the book is about: An account of the sinking and the rediscovery of the *Titanic* written for early readers. The book tells the story of how the ship set sail and capsized, and has a chapter on the location of the hull in 1985. Content makes this good for reluctant readers as well.

Where it's reviewed:
Center for Children's Books Bulletin, June 1987, page 182
School Library Journal, June 7, 1987, page 80

Other books by the author:
All Around the World, 1991
Moonwalk, 1989
Tut's Mummy: Lost.and Found, 1988
True-Life Treasure Hunts, 1984

Other books you might like:
Sue L. Hamilton, *Royal Mail Steamship Titanic*, 1988
  A ship's officer's account based on factual data.
Evelyn Wilde Mayerson, *The Cat Who Escaped From Steerage*, 1990
  Living in the steerage section of a steamship bound for America, Chanah tries to keep her newly found cat a secret.
Gloria Rand, *Salty Sails North*, 1990
  Salty the dog and his master Zach sail north to Alaska, encountering other ships, a storm, wild animals on the shore, and an iceberg.
Nancy Shaw, *Sheep on a Ship*, 1989
  Sheep on a deep-sea voyage run into trouble when it storms and are glad to come paddling into port.
Hans Wilhelm, *Pirates Ahoy!*, 1987
  Bored farm animals turn different vehicles into pirate ships to create excitement.

531

Marion Walker Doren

Borrowed Summer (New York: Harper, 1986)

Age range: Grades 4-6

Subject(s): Old Age; Nursing Homes; Grandparents

Major character(s): Gram, Grandparent (great-grandmother), Patient; Jan, Preteen; Carl, Patient

Time period(s): 1980s

Locale(s): United States

What the book is about: Gram, Jan's great-grandmother, is in a nursing home after falling and breaking her hip and no longer seems like the same person. Jan fears she is deteriorating, so she and her friends set out to rescue Gram and her friend, Carl, from the home. They furnish an abandoned house, hoping to keep Gram and Carl hidden.

Where it's reviewed:
Center for Children's Books Bulletin, February 2, 1987, page 104
School Library Journal, December 1986, page 101

Other books by the author:
Nell of Blue Harbor, 1990

Other books you might like:
Judie Angell, *Dear Lola: Or, How to Build Your Own Family*, 1981

Six parentless kids ranging in age from five to eighteen, run away from the orphanage, and, as a family, establish a household miles away.

Vera Cleaver, *Trial Valley*, 1977
  The three Luther children, who have raised themselves since their father died, find an abandoned boy near their house in the Great Smoky Mountains.

Anne Fine, *The Granny Project*, 1983
  Four British children try to keep their grandmother out of a nursing home.

Peni R. Griffin, *Hobkin*, 1992
  Two sisters run away from their abusive stepfather and settle in an abandoned house in West Texas, only to find that they are not alone.

Felice Holman, *Secret City, U.S.A.*, 1990
  Against all odds, Benno and his friends in the ghetto turn an abandoned house into a shelter for the homeless.

532

Jean Slaughter Doty

Illustrator: Ted Lewin

Can I Get There by Candlelight? (New York: Macmillan, 1980)

Age range: Grades 5-7

Subject(s): Animals/Horses; Space and Time

Major character(s): Gail Simmons, Equestrian (preteen), Time Traveller; Hilary Blake, Equestrian, Time Traveller; Candlelight, Horse

Time period(s): 1980s; 19th century

Locale(s): United States

What the book is about: A girl magically enters the world of the 19th century. Gail and her horse, Candlelight, wander onto the grounds of a large estate called Babylon and meet Hilary, a girl Gail's age, who loves riding as much as Gail does. Together, they spend an enchanted summer.

Where it's reviewed:
Booklist, March 1, 1980, page 980
Hornbook, August 1980, page 405
Kirkus Reviews, March 15, 1980, page 364

Other books by the author:
If Wishes Were Horses, 1984
Dark Horse, 1983
Winter Pony, 1975
Summer Pony, 1973

Other books you might like:
Elaine Marie Alphin, *The Ghost Cadet*, 1991
  In Virginia visiting an unknown grandmother, Benjy meets the ghost of a Virginia Military Institute cadet who was killed in the Battle of New Market.
Matt Christopher, *Return of the Headless Horseman*, 1982
  Two boys on a fishing trip are startled by a headless horseman, believed to be the ghost of a 19th century horse thief.
Margaret Goff Clark, *Mystery Horse*, 1972
  The peace of the Tuscarora reservation is shattered when rumors of a ghost horse sighting begin.
Lynn Cullen, *The Backyard Ghost*, 1993

Eleanor's attempts to break into the popular crowd at her new school are complicated by her discovery that her yard is haunted by a Civil War ghost.

Patricia Cecil Hass, *Swampfire*, 1973
  Three youngsters camping in the Great Dismal Swamp decide to catch the ghost horse running loose in the swamp.

533

Jean Slaughter Doty

The Crumb (New York: Greenwillow, 1976)

Age range: Grades 5-6

Subject(s): Animals/Horses; Mystery and Detective Stories

Major character(s): Jan Ashford, Businessman (stable owner); Alex, Horse Trainer; Cindy, Teenager

Time period(s): 1970s

Locale(s): United States

What the book is about: Cindy trades part-time work at Ashford Stables for the boarding of her horse, Crumb. She doesn't trust Alex, who has a strange way of treating his prize horse. Which horse did he use a hypodermic needle on?

Where it's reviewed:
Horn Book, August 1976, page 395
Kirkus Reviews, March 15, 1976, page 321

Other books by the author:
Yesterday's Horses, 1985
Dark Horse, 1983
Winter Pony, 1975

Other books you might like:
Claire Burch, *High Stakes*, 1992
  Lucy and Liz help solve a mystery at the race track in Saratoga Springs.
Michael Hardcastle, *Kickback*, 1989
  Ros is determined to restore her reputation and find out what happened to the stable's prize horse that disappeared under her care.
Isabelle Holland, *Perdita*, 1984
  A girl suffering from amnesia takes a job on a horse farm where she finds she rides well, yet is haunted by an elusive fear.
K.M. Peyton, *Poor Badger*, 1990
  Having become devoted to a pony who is being mistreated by his owner, Ros decides to steal him in the night and hide him in a place of safety.
Elizabeth Van Steenwyk, *Quarter Horse Winner*, 1980
  As she tries to get a place on the Midtown Stables gymkhana team, Holly becomes more sensitive to the needs of other people and of her horse.

534

Jean Slaughter Doty

Illustrator: Dorothy H. Chhuy

Dark Horse (New York: Morrow, 1983)

Age range: Grades 4-6

Subject(s): Animals/Horses; Horsemanship

Major character(s): Abby, Preteen; Sandpiper, Horse

Time period(s): 1980s

Locale(s): United States

What the book is about: Abby discovers that a new horse at High Hickory Stable, where she volunteers, is a fine jumper. Sandpiper suddenly becomes violent and Abby intervenes after the decision has been made to kill the horse. She risks riding Sandy to prove he will cooperate as long as he isn't in the show ring. There is more information about jumping competition here than in most horse stories.

Where it's reviewed:
Horn Book, August 1983, page 442
School Library Journal, September 1983, page 122

Other books by the author:
Yesterday's Horses, 1985
If Wishes Were Horses, 1984
Winter Pony, 1975
Summer Pony, 1974

Other books you might like:
Marylois Dunn, *The Absolutely Perfect Horse*, 1989
    Annie buys an ailing pony to keep him from being destroyed.
Helen Griffith, *Blackface Stallion*, 1980
    The story of a wild stallion set in northern Mexico.
Jessie Haas, *Keeping Barney*, 1982
    Sarah decides to accept the responsibility of boarding a horse.
Lynn Hall, *Megan's Mare*, 1983
    Megan feels a close psychic bond with her new horse, Berry.
Elizabeth Levy, *The Case of the Counterfeit Racehorse*, 1980
    A mystery involving the switching of two look-alike horses.

535

Crescent Dragonwagon

Illustrator: Leslie Morrill

I Hate My Sister Maggie (New York: Macmillan, 1989)

Age range: Grades 2-4

Subject(s): Babies; Brothers and Sisters

Major character(s): Harry, Child; Maggie, Child (Harry's sister)

Time period(s): Indeterminate

Locale(s): United States

What the book is about: Harry is fed up with his bratty little sister, Maggie. He is convinced that he hates her until his mother tells him a secret that puts everything in a totally different perspective.

Where it's reviewed:
Booklist, April 1, 1989, page 1382

Other books by the author:
Diana, Maybe, 1987
Always, Always, 1984
I Hate My Brother Harry, 1983
If You Call My Name, 1981

Other books you might like:
Judy Blume, *The Pain and the Great One*, 1974

A six year old (The Pain) and his eight year old sister (The Great One) see each other as troublemakers and the best-loved in the family.
Veronika Martenova Charles, *The Crane Girl*, 1992
    Jealous of the new baby, Yoshiko goes to live among the cranes whose magic transforms her into one of their young for a while.
Jonathan Franklin, *Don't Wake the Baby*, 1991
    Despite warnings not to disturb the sleeping baby, Marvin creep's into the baby's room and conjures up a world of noisy and colorful adventures.
Mordecai Gerstein, *The Gigantic Baby*, 1991
    The more a baby cries, the more she grows, until her brother thinks of a way to reverse the process.
Morse Hamilton, *Big Sisters Are Bad Witches*, 1981
    The sibling rivalry of two sisters improves when a third child on the way promises to turn little sister into big sister.

536

Crescent Dragonwagon

Illustrator: Peter Elwell

Margaret Ziegler Is Horse Crazy (New York: Macmillan, 1988)

Age range: Grades 2-4

Subject(s): Family Life; Animals/Horses

Major character(s): Margaret Ziegler, Child, Animal Lover (loves horses); Rodney Ziegler, Relative (brother to Margaret)

Time period(s): 1980s

Locale(s): United States

What the book is about: Although Margaret has never been on a horse, she draws them, reads about them, dreams and talks about them. She knows that when she goes to Country Life Riding Day Camp, she will have a wonderful way with horses and be an expert rider. The reality is that, last in the alphabet, Margaret gets the last horse who is old and cranky and promptly steps on her foot before she ever mounts. Sent home to care for her injury, she never wants to go back until a very loving family encourages her to try again.

Where it's reviewed:
Center for Children's Books Bulletin, July 1988, page 226
School Library Journal, June 1988, page 90

Other books by the author:
Home Place, 1990
Winter Holding Spring, 1990
Dear Miss Moshki, 1986
Strawberry Dress Escape, 1975

Other books you might like:
Berlie Doherty, *Snowy*, 1993
    When other children bring their pets to school, Rachel feels left out because she can't bring in the horse that pulls the barge on which she lives.
William Harry Harding, *Alvin's Famous No-Horse*, 1992
    With encouragement from his teacher and help from his classmates, Alvin struggles with his efforts to draw a horse for the third grade art exhibit.
Ursula Le Guin, *A Ride on the Red Mare's Back*, 1992

With the aid of her magic wooden horse, a brave girl travels to the High House in the mountains to rescue her kidnapped brother from the trolls.

Jacqueline Briggs Martin, *The Finest Horse in Town*, 1992
Long ago, two sisters in Maine owned a remarkable gray horse named Prince, who became a legend in their family.

David M. McPhail, *Annie and Company*, 1991
When her father tells her that the world is full of things that need fixing, young Annie, with her cat and horse, sets out to fix them.

537

Joan Drescher, Author/Illustrator

My Mother's Getting Married (New York: Dutton, 1986)

Age range: Grades 2-4

Subject(s): Remarriage; Stepfathers

Major character(s): Katy, Child; Ben, Step-Parent; Miss Tuck, Teacher

Time period(s): Indeterminate

Locale(s): United States

What the book is about: Katy is not looking forward to the change that her mother's marriage will bring. Ben is kind of nice, but he takes up too much of her mother's time.

Where it's reviewed:
Booklist, May 1, 1986, page 1309
Center for Children's Books Bulletin, April 1986, page 145
School Library Journal, May 1986, page 72

Other books by the author:
Your Doctor, My Doctor, 1987
Max and Rufus, 1982
The Marvelous Mess, 1980
Your Family, My Family, 1980

Other books you might like:
Lucille Clifton, *Everett Anderson's 1 2 3*, 1977
As a boy's mother considers remarriage, he considers the numbers one, two and three. Sometimes they're lonely, crowded, or just right.

Kathryn Ewing, *Things Won't Be the Same*, 1980
Upset by her mother's coming remarriage, Marcy is upset further when she learns she'll be staying with her father whom she hardly remembers.

Ezra Jack Keats, *Louie's Search*, 1980
Louie goes out looking for a new father and instead he finds a music box which he is accused of stealing. Or is that all he finds?

Judith Vigna, *Daddy's New Baby*, 1982
A near disaster helps a child of divorced parents soften her feelings toward her father's new baby.

Betty Ren Wright, *My New Mom and Me*, 1981
After her widowed father remarries, a young girl's cat helps her make a few important discoveries about herself.

538

Roger W. Drury

Illustrator: Fritz Wegner

The Champion of Merrimack County (Boston: Little Brown, 1976)

Age range: Grades 4-6

Subject(s): Animals/Mice; Bicycles and Bicycling; Humor

Major character(s): Janet Berryfield, Child; O'Crispin, Mouse

Time period(s): 1970s

Locale(s): United States

What the book is about: Janet and her mother can hardly believe what they find in Mr. Berryfield's treasured bathtub - a mouse on a bicycle, racing around the rim! O'Crispin skids on a piece of soap and dislocates his tail, leaving a horrible scratch on the tub. Then the fun begins.

Where it's reviewed:
Kirkus Reviews, October 1, 1976, page 1092
School Library Journal, January 1977, page 90

Awards the book has won:
Christopher Award 1977

Other books by the author:
The Finches' Fabulous Furnace, 1971

Other books you might like:
Nathaniel Benchley, *Feldman Fieldmouse*, 1971
Uncle Feldman teaches Fendall to leave his cage and become independent in spite of the dangers.

Beverly Cleary, *The Mouse and the Motorcycle*, 1965
Ralph, the mouse, receives a toy motorcycle that is just his size.

W.J. Corbett, *Song of Pentecost*, 1983
Forced to move, the mice of Pentecost farm are aware that dangers await them from the snake, the owl, and the fox.

Rumer Godden, *Mousewife*, 1982
The mousewife thinks there must be something else to life beyond housekeeping.

Brian Jacques, *Redwall*, 1986
The animals of Redwall Abbey, forced to do battle with the evil rat Cluny and his band of thugs, find a hero in young Matthias.

539

William Pene Du Bois, Author/Illustrator

Gentleman Bear (New York: Farrar, Straus and Giroux, 1985)

Age range: Grades 3-5

Subject(s): Toys

Major character(s): Sir Billy Browne-Browne, Child; Sir Peter Browne-Browne, Parent; Bayard, Toy (teddey bear)

Time period(s): 20th century (1913-1985r)

Locale(s): London, England

What the book is about: Billy Browne-Browne and Bayard, his beloved bear, live in London. Whenever Billy gets new clothes, Bayard gets a matching outfit. In the course of their adventures, Billy and Bayard get involved in an athletic contest at the Berlin Olympics and a Coronation Day kidnapping. When Billy is sixty-eight and Bayard sixty-four, they are still inseparable.

Where it's reviewed:
Booklist, March 15, 1986, page 1080
Center for Children's Books Bulletin, April 1986, page 99
School Library Journal, April 1986

Other books by the author:
Call Me Bandicoot, 1970
The Three Policemen, 1960
The Giant, 1954
The Great Geppy, 1940

Other books you might like:
Judith Clarke, *Teddy B. Zoot*, 1990
    A kindhearted teddy bear journeys to his owner's elementary school in the middle of the night to retrieve a math assignment.
Barbara Dillon, *The Teddy Bear Tree*, 1982
    From the buried glass eye of an ancient teddy bought at a rummage sale grows a strange tree that bears surprising fruit.
Deborah Howe, *Teddy Bear's Scrapbook*, 1980
    One rainy afternoon, Teddy Bear decides to bring out his scrapbook which contains photographs and clippings from his long and illustrious past.
A.A. Milne, *The Pooh Story Book*, 1965
    Three adventures of Christopher Robin and his friends - a house is built for Eeyore, Piglet is surrounded by water and Pooh invents a new game.
Sally Farrell Odgers, *Drummond: The Search for Sarah*, 1990
    A teddy bear, unexpectedly brought to life by Sarah and Nicholas, begins a search for his original owner, a Sarah from earlier times.

540

William Pene Du Bois, Author/Illustrator

Twenty-One Balloons (New York: Viking, 1947)

Age range: Grades 4-6

Subject(s): Balloons; Voyages and Travels

Major character(s): Professor William Waterman Sherman, Teacher

Time period(s): 1880s (1883)

Locale(s): San Francisco, California; Krakatoa, Indonesia

What the book is about: Professor Sherman sets out to cross the Pacific Ocean in a balloon. When his balloon crashes, he finds himself on the island of Krakatoa. He discovers a secret the islanders have kept hidden.

Where it's reviewed:
Booklist, March 15, 1947, page 296
Horn Book, March 1947, page 214

Awards the book has won:
Newbery Medal 1948

Other books by the author:
Call Me Bandicoot, 1970
Gentleman Bear, 1985
The Giant, 1988
The Great Geppy, 1940

Other books you might like:
Myron Levoy, *The Magic Hat of Mortimer Wintergreen*, 1988
    In 1893, 13 year old Joshua and his sister, Amy, travel to New York City with the help of an unpredictable magic hat.

F.N. Monjo, *Prisoners of the Scrambling Dragon*, 1980
    A 13 year old describes his first voyage aboard a Yankee trading vessel bound for China.
Dorothy Crayder, *She, the Adventuress*, 1973
    Maggie spends ten days on a ship travelling from the US to Italy.
Jonathan Gathorne-Hardy, *The Airship Ladyship Adventure*, 1977
    Accidentally taking off in her father's airship, Jane has incredible adventures.
Aaron Percefull, *Balloons, Zepplins, and Dirigibles*, 1983
    A history of the building and use of non-rigid airships from the 1780s on. (Non-fiction)

541

Diane Duane

So You Want to Be a Wizard (New York: Delacorte, 1983)

Age range: Grades 5-8

Subject(s): Fantasy; Magic; Bullies

Major character(s): Kit, Preteen; Nita, Teenager (13-years-old); Fred, Mole

Time period(s): 1980s

Locale(s): New York, New York (Manhattan)

What the book is about: Thirteen year old Nita, tormented by a gang of bullies because she won't fight back, finds the help she needs in a library book on wizardry. Then Nita and her friends embark on a journey to retrieve the Book of Night with Moon, which the evil starshuffler has hidden. A classic battle between good and evil.

Where it's reviewed:
Horn Book, December 1983, page 716
School Library Journal, January 1984, page 74

Other books by the author:
High Wizardry, 1990
Spock's World, 1989
Deep Wizardry, 1985
My Enemy, My Ally, 1984

Other books you might like:
Wilanne Schneider Belden, *Frankie!*, 1987
    The O'Riley family is expecting a baby. It turns out to be a griffin which fits well in a family which already includes a some unusual characters.
John Bellairs, *The Eyes of the Killer Robot*, 1986
    Thirteen year old Johnny Dixon is put in jeopardy when he and Professor Childermass try to find a robot made long ago by an evil wizard.
Suzy McKee Charnas, *The Silver Glove*, 1988
    A New York City teen teams up with her sorceress grandmother to protect her mother from her new boyfriend, an evil wizard.
Carol Gaskin, *The War of the Wizards*, 1985
    The reader becomes an apprentice to the wizard Caladrius and makes plot choices which determine the outcome of the war of the wizards.
Robin McKinley, *The Hero and the Crown*, 1984
    Aerin, with the help of the Blue Sword and the wizard, Luthe, wins her birthright in this high fantasy adventure.

542

Tessa Duder

Jellybean (New York: Viking Kestral, 1986)

Age range: Grades 5-6

Subject(s): Single Parent Families; Orchestra; Mothers and Daughters

Major character(s): Geraldine, Preteen

Time period(s): 1980s

Locale(s): New Zealand

What the book is about: The only child of a single mother, Geraldine is tired of having to fit into her mother's busy orchestra schedule, and the endless rounds of sitters and loneliness. Things begin to change when she discovers a new friend and realizing that she has choices and ambitions of her own, decides she wants to become a conductor.

Where it's reviewed:
Center for Children's Books Bulletin, November 1986, page 47
School Library Journal, January 1987, page 73

Other books by the author:
Alex in Rome, 1992
Journey to Olympia, 1992
In Lane 3, Alex Archer, 1989

Other books you might like:
Nancy J. Hopper, *Hang On, Harvey!*, 1983
    Flute player Harvey finds being in the middle school orchestra is more complicated than he had imagined.
Ronald Kidd, *Sizzle and Splat*, 1983
    Two high school members of a youth orchestra investigate the sabotage of a benefit concert and the kidnapping of the orchestra association president.
Cynthia Rylant, *A Kindness*, 1988
    Having spent fifteen years happily alone with his mother, Chip finds his world threatened when she becomes pregnant.
Pamela F. Service, *When the Night Wind Howls*, 1987
    Sidonie and her mother join lead actor Sid to uncover the evil behind strange apparitions in the community theater.
Diantha Warfel, *The Violin Case Case*, 1978
    Bax's aspirations to join a symphony orchestra involve him with a beautiful old violin which is desired by dangerous and elusive strangers.

543

Betsy Duffey

Illustrator: Leslie Morrill

A Boy in the Doghouse (New York: Simon and Schuster, 1991)

Age range: Grades 2-3

Subject(s): Animals/Dogs

Major character(s): George, Child; Lucky, Dog

Time period(s): 1990s

Locale(s): United States

What the book is about: George is in trouble because he has not taught his dog, Lucky, proper manners. Lucky, mean-while, is trying to train George to scratch him behind the ears and feed him ham. With the help of a book from the vet, they work things out. Readers will enjoy the shift in point of view from George to Lucky and back again.

Where it's reviewed:
School Library Journal, September 1991, page 232

Other books by the author:
Puppy Love, 1992
Gadget War, 1991
The Math Whiz, 1990

Other books you might like:
Prudence Andrew, *Dog!*, 1973
    A ten year old boy who is forbidden to have a dog finds a stray and hides him in an abandoned car.
Cora Annett, *The Dog Who Thought He Was a Boy*, 1965
    The Popperson family searches for a way to make Ralph understand that he is a dog.
Byrd Baylor, *Amigo*, 1963
    Desperately wanting a pet to love, a boy decides to tame a prairie dog who has already decided to tame the boy for his own pet.
Lynn Hall, *Troublemaker*, 1974
    Violence, loneliness and hardship are the only companions of a thirteen year old boy until he finds a mangy brown dog named Buster.
Susan Saunders, *Tyrone Goes to School*, 1992
    When a boy takes his dog to obedience school, he finds out something about his own learning ability.

544

Betsy Duffey

The Math Whiz (New York: Viking, 1990)

Age range: Grades 2-4

Subject(s): Schools

Major character(s): Marty, Child

Time period(s): 1990s

Locale(s): United States

What the book is about: Marty is great at Math. When he starts third grade at a new school, he finds he is terrible at PE and is always the last one picked for teams. He faces his limitations head on and tries to solve the problem.

Where it's reviewed:
Booklist, September 15, 1990, page 160
Kirkus Reviews, August 15, 1990, page 1167

Other books by the author:
Gadget War, 1991

Other books you might like:
Beverly Cleary, *Muggie Maggie*, 1990
    Third grader Maggie resists learning cursive until she discovers the world that opens up to those who can read and write it.
Natalie Honeycutt, *The All New Jonah Twist*, 1986
    Jonah's efforts to survive third grade are made more difficult by the new boy in class who may be his best friend or may beat him up.
Laurie Lawlor, *How to Survive Third Grade*, 1988
    Ernest has a difficult time in third grade until he finds a friend and experiences success.

Phyllis Reynolds Naylor, *One of the Third Grade Thonkers*, 1988
  8 year old Jimmy is determined to keep his wimpy younger cousin out ou his special club for rough, tough, terrible boys.
Alix Kates Shulman, *Bosley on the Number Line*, 1970
  On the night before his tenth birthday, a boy is transported to a land beyond the Milky Way where his adventures involve New Math.

545

James Duffy

Missing (New York: Scribner's, 1988)

Age range: Grades 4-6

Subject(s): Kidnapping; Missing Persons

Major character(s): Kate Prescott, Child; Sandy Prescott, Child; Agatha Bates, Police Officer

Time period(s): 1980s

Locale(s): Wingate, New Hampshire

What the book is about: Kate, a ten year old with a history of running away, is kidnapped by a lonely, confused man who wants a little girl of his own. When the police are stumped, a retired police officer is able to help.

Where it's reviewed:
Reading Teacher, October 1989, page 62
School Library Journal, March 1988, page 188

Other books by the author:
Cleaver and Company, 1991
The Christmas Gang: A May Gray Mystery, 1989
Doll Hospital, 1989

Other books you might like:
Eve Bunting, *The Hideout*, 1991
  Andy hides out in a hotel and stages his own kidnapping.
Larry Callen, *Who Kidnapped the Sherrif?*, 1985
  Pat and Violet get involved in wild events one summer in the town of Tickfaw.
Catherine Cookson, *Go Tell It to Mrs. Golightly*, 1977
  A blind girl who is sent to stay with her grandfather stumbles upon a kidnapping in their small town.
Harry Mazer, *Someone's Mother Is Missing*, 1990
  Lisa and her cousin, Sam, search for Lisa's emotionally disturbed mother who has disappeared from her home.
Kin Platt, *The Ghost of Hellsfire Street*, 1980
  Steve is the only witness to a kidnapping and sorts through the clues in his Long Island town.

546

James Duffy

Illustrator: Barbara McClintock

The Revolt of the Teddy Bears: A May Gray Mystery (New York: Crown, 1985)

Age range: Grades 3-5

Subject(s): Animals/Dogs; Toys

Major character(s): May Gray, Dog (poodle); Pierre Noir, Police Officer (chief inspector); Victor Gray, Dog

Time period(s): Indeterminate

Locale(s): Paris, France

What the book is about: Teddy Bears attack Paris, forcing the distinguished poodle detective, May Gray, out of retirement to solve the case. The Terrible Teddies riot in the street, smack mail carriers, bounce up and down on taxis, and otherwise wreak havoc.

Where it's reviewed:
Reading Teacher, October 1985, page 98

Other books by the author:
Uncle Shamus, 1992
Cleaver Company, 1991
Man in the River, 1990
The Christmas Gang: A May Gray Mystery, 1989

Other books you might like:
Nathaniel Benchley, *Snip*, 1981
  The routine life of a tired old beagle named Duncan is upset by a mischievous young poodle named Snip.
Judith Clarke, *Teddy B. Zoot*, 1990
  A kindhearted teddy bear journeys to his owner's elementary school in the middle of the night to retrieve her math assignment.
Barbara Dillon, *What's Happened to Harry?*, 1982
  Harry becomes entangled with a witch on Halloween night and is transformed into a poodle.
Maggie Glen, *Ruby to the Rescue*, 1992
  Ruby the teddy bear is taken to school by her owner and carries out a plan to save two unwanted teddies in the playhouse there.
Linda Gondosch, *Brutus, the Wonder Poodle*, 1990
  When Ryan's parents give him a toy poodle puppy, Ryan is disappointed that the dog is not bigger, but quickly learns that Brutus is the best dog ever.

547

Jane Duncan

Illustrator: Mairi Hedderwick

Brave Janet Reachfar (Boston: Houghton Mifflin, 1975)

Age range: Grades 4-6

Subject(s): Animals/Sheep; Weather

Major character(s): Janet Reachfar, Preteen; "Herself", Grandparent

Time period(s): Indeterminate

Locale(s): Highlands, Scotland

What the book is about: Scottish farm life is depicted through the adventures of young Janet and her relationship with her tyrannical grandmother. During a sudden snowstorm, Janet ventures out onto a forbidden hill to rescue a lost sheep only to wind up in need of rescue herself.

Where it's reviewed:
Booklist, July 15, 1975, page 1190
Kirkus Reviews, May 15, 1975, page 561
School Library Journal, September 1975, page 79

Other books by the author:
Janet Reachfar and Chickabird, 1978

Other books you might like:
Mollie Hunter, *The Haunted Mountain*, 1972
  After angering the fairy creature of the Highlands, a stubborn Scot is thirteen years bringing an end to their terrible revenge against him.
Alec Lea, *Temba Dawn*, 1974
  A Scottish boy accepts responsibility for raising a calf from birth, a task which helps him adjust to the eventual loss of the family's dairy farm.
Iris Macfarlane, *The Mouth of the Night*, 1973
  A selection of stories first published in Tales of the West Highlands. "The Sea Maiden," "The Sporran Full of Gold" and many more.
William MacKellar, *A Dog Called Porridge*, 1985
  Strange things happen to Davie and his beloved but unusual uncle after a strange-looking dog becomes part of their lives in the Scottish Highlands.
Joan Tate, *Wild Boy*, 1973
  A Yorkshire boy often dreams of living alone on the moors until he meets a strange boy who is doing just that.

548

Lois Duncan

Illustrator: Arvis Stewart

A Gift of Magic (Boston: Little, Brown, 1971)

Age range: Grades 5-8

Subject(s): Divorce; Extrasensory Perception

Major character(s): Nancy Garrett, Psychic; Kirby Garrett, Dancer; Elizabeth Garrett, Parent (Nancy and Kirby's mother)

Time period(s): 1970s

Locale(s): Palmelo, Florida

What the book is about: In the prologue, we see the Garrett children's grandmother leaving gifts to her grandchildren. Kirby gets the gift of dance, Brendon, music and her voice fades as she tells about the third gift. Nancy's special gift is ESP, a power she does not understand and does not know how to control. When she wishes her sister, Kirby, would not go away to study dance, Kirby falls and breaks her leg. Coping with her parents' divorce and discovering how to use her gift in positive ways show Nancy's depth of character. A good family story.

Where it's reviewed:
Booklist, November 15, 1971, page 291
Hornbook, April 1972, page 152
Kirkus Reviews, September 1, 1971, page 944

Other books by the author:
Birthday Moon, 1989
Don't Look Behind You, 1989
Daughters of Eve, 1979
Summer of Fear, 1977

Other books you might like:
Charles L. Grant, *Fire Mask*, 1991
  Cliff's premonitions and dreams about a mysterious fire lead him and his friends into a fatal confrontation with perpetrators of a terrifying evil.
Jesse Harris, *The Obsession*, 1993

McKenzie Gold's friendship with Sharon Roderick, the new girl in town, turns deadly when Sharon starts to abuse McKenzie's psychic powers.
James Duncan Lawrence, *ESP McGee and the Haunted Mansion*, 1983
  Convinced something spooky is going to happen at the old Frome mansion, Edward "ESP" McGee and his best friend test McGee's ESP to explore the house.
Lila Perl, *Annabelle Starr, E.S.P.*, 1983
  Convinced she has ESP, Annabelle has second thoughts about her "gift" when she sees the fear a prediction causes in her adoptive brother.
Pamela F. Service, *Being of Two Minds*, 1991
  Connie's ability to share "mental visits" with the prince of Thulgaria proves useful when he's mysteriously kidnapped.

549

Lois Duncan

Illustrator: Leonard Shortall

Hotel for Dogs (Boston: Houghton Mifflin, 1971)

Age range: Grades 4-6

Subject(s): Animals/Dogs; Friendship; Schools

Major character(s): Bruce Walker, Preteen, Animal Lover; Liz Walker, Preteen, Animal Lover; Alice Collins, Relative (aunt)

Time period(s): 1970s

Locale(s): Elmwood, New Jersey

What the book is about: When the Walkers move from New Mexico to New Jersey, Liz is unhappy that they cannot take their dachshund, Bebe, with them. Their Aunt Alice is allergic to dogs. But they are drawn to dogs and they accumulate so many strays that they set up a hotel for them in an abandoned house.

Where it's reviewed:
Kirkus Reviews, March 1, 1971, page 235
Library Journal, May 15, 1971, page 1802

Other books by the author:
Locked in Time, 1985
From Spring to Spring, 1982
Down a Dark Hall, 1974
A Gift of Magic, 1971

Other books you might like:
Prudence Andrew, *Dog!*, 1973
  A boy who is forbidden to have a dog finds a stray and hides him in an abandoned car.
Meindert De Jong, *Along Came a Dog*, 1958
  A stray dog earns a home for himself by protecting a little red hen and her chicks from a preying hawk.
Margaret Poynter, *What's One More?*, 1985
  The story of a pet rescuer that shares her home with stray dogs, nursing injured dogs back to health and finding them homes with caring owners.
Barbara Brooks Wallace, *The Farewell Kid*, 1990
  Heidi decides against college after high school and devotes herself to stray dogs instead. When she meets a photographer, her life changes.
Carol Beach York, *Stray Dog*, 1981

With the help of his brother, sister, and friend, Frankie, a lonely eleven year old cares for a stray dog until the unexpected happens.

550

Lois Duncan

Summer of Fear (Boston: Little, Brown, 1976)

Age range: Grades 6 and Up

Subject(s): Witches and Witchcraft

Major character(s): Rachel Bryant, Teenager; Julia, Teenager; Mike Gallagher, Teenager

Time period(s): 1970s

Locale(s): New Mexico

What the book is about: Cousin Julia's parents are killed in an auto accident and she comes to live with Rachel and her family. Everyone seems to be enchanted with Julia except Rachel and her dog. Rachel notices Julia's odd behavior, strange possessions and attitudes, and becomes convinced that Julia is a witch who must be stopped. Julia is a wedge between Rachel and those she loves.

Where it's reviewed:
Kirkus Reviews, June 15, 1976, page 691
School Library Journal, December 1976, page 69

Awards the book has won:
Dorothy Canfield Fisher Children's Book Award 1978

Other books by the author:
The Third Eye, 1984
Killing Mr. Griffin, 1978
Down a Dark Hall, 1976
Ransom, 1966

Other books you might like:
Mary Anderson, *The Terrible Thing in the Bottle*, 1989
　　Cassie and Barney are thrown together when an eccentric aunt takes them to England and they meet Vicky, who makes them think she's cast a spell.
L.M. Boston, *An Enemy at Green Knowe*, 1964
　　The inhabitants of Green Knowe become involved with black magic when a modern day witch attempts to find books of witchcraft hidden in the house.
Lynne Gessner, *To See a Witch*, 1978
　　A 12 year old pre-Columbian Indian boy considered childish by his tribe finds acceptance as a man when his cousin is accused of being a witch.
Mary Downing Hahn, *The Time of the Witch*, 1982
　　Laura tells an old woman of her wish that her parents were back together again without realizing that she is speaking to a real witch.
Phyllis Reynolds Naylor, *The Witch Herself*, 1978
　　As more people fall under Mrs. Tuggle's spells, Lynn and Mouse grow more desperate in their efforts to find a way to stop the old woman's evil.

551

Eileen Dunlop

Illustrator: Peter Farmer

Elizabeth, Elizabeth (New York: Holt, 1977)

Age range: Grades 5-6

Subject(s): Space and Time

Major character(s): Elizabeth, Time Traveller

Time period(s): 1970s; 1700s

Locale(s): Scotland

What the book is about: At first Elizabeth is fascinated to find a mirror that takes her back into the 18th century and in to the body of another Elizabeth. Eventually, however, she discovers that in taking on this historical identity, she is losing her own.

Where it's reviewed:
Horn Book, June 1977, page 314
School Library Journal, May 1977, page 67

Other books by the author:
Finn's Island, 1992
The Valley of Deer, 1989
The House on Mayferry Street, 1976

Other books you might like:
Margaret Jean Anderson, *The Druid's Gift*, 1989
　　A girl, living in the time of the Druids on a tiny and remote island, is able to travel forward in time to shape the history of her island home.
Frances Hendry, *Quest for a Kelpie*, 1986
　　In the days before the Scottish uprising in 1745, a young girl dreams of riding a wild horse.
Mollie Hunter, *The Kelpie's Pearls*, 1964
　　An old woman of the Scottish Highlands makes friends with a kelpie, sees the Loch Ness monster, and practices some of her grandmother's magic.
William MacKellar, *A Dog Called Porridge*, 1985
　　Strange things begin to happen to Davie and his uncle when a strange-looking dog becomes part of their lives in the Scottish Highlands.
A.C. Stewart, *Silas and Con*, 1977
　　An abandoned boy sets out through the wilds of northwest Scotland to seek a new life for himself with only a stray as a companion.

552

Gerald Durrel

The Talking Parcel (Philadelphia: Lippincott, 1974)

Age range: Grades 4-7

Subject(s): Fantasy; Magic

Major character(s): Penelope, Child; Peter, Child; Simon, Child

Time period(s): Indeterminate

Locale(s): Athens, Greece; Mythologia, Fictional Country

What the book is about: Three children journey to Mythologia to recover stolen books of magic. Mythologia is ruled by H.H. Junketberry, an absent minded magician. Fire-breathing cockatrices are trying to enslave all the other animals there.

Where it's reviewed:
Kirkus Reviews, April 15, 1975, page 453
School Library Journal, May 1975, page 54

Other books by the author:
Zoo in My Luggage, 1975
The Donkey Rustlers, 1968
Whispering Land, 1961
My Family and Other Animals, 1957

Other books you might like:
Edward Eager, The Time Garden, 1958
  Four cousins spending a summer in a house by the sea, discover a magic thyme garden from which they embark on a number of adventures in Thyme.
Edward Packard, Olympus: What Is the Secret of the Oracle?, 1988
  As an Earth Inspector, the reader travels back in time to Greece in 400 B.C. to search out the Oracle of Delphi and discover the secret of her powers.
Richard L. Purtill, Enchantment at Delphi, 1986
  Fascinated by the temple ruins at Delphi, a young girl manages to slip into the deserted site and finds herself involved in strange adventures.
Willo Davis Roberts, The Magic Book, 1986
  When Alex and his friends try the spells in an old book, things don't happen quite as they expected, but they try a spell on the school bully.
William Wise, Monster Myths of Ancient Greece, 1981
  Briefly recounts six Greek myths featuring hideous monsters who were eventually slain by courageous heroes.

| 553 |

Sandra Dutton

Illustrator: Matthew Clark

The Magic of Myrna C. Waxweather (New York: Atheneum, 1987)

Age range: Grades 3-5

Subject(s): Behavior; Fairies; Schools

Major character(s): Bertha Zuchelli, Preteen, 5th Grader; Myrna C. Waxweather, Spirit (fairy godmother), Entertainer (Vaudeville star); Miss Van Crockett, Principal

Time period(s): 1980s

Locale(s): Watson

What the book is about: Bertha is disliked by other fifth graders because she is considered a model pupil and teacher's pet. On top of that, the principal puts Bertha in charge of the clean plate club, another step toward instant unpopularity. Then a strange apparition appears in her room, claiming to be her fairy godmother, Myrna C. Waxweather. On Myrna's advice, Bertha launches into a campaign of unorthodox behavior

Where it's reviewed:
Booklist, August 1987, page 1745
Kirkus Reviews, March 1, 1987, page 372
School Library Journal, April 1987, page 93

Other books by the author:
Tales of Belva Jean Copenhagen, 1989
The Cinnamon Hen's Autumn Day, 1988

Other books you might like:
T. Ernesto Bethancourt, The Tomorrow Connection, 1984

Two musicians, stranded in 1906, seek Harry Houdini's help, travel the vaudeville circuit, and arrive in San Francisco in time for the big earthquake.
Burton Cohen, Nelson Makes a Face, 1978
  A fairy godmother attempts to reform a mischievous little boy by freezing three expression on his face.
Beatrice Gormley, Fifth Grade Magic, 1982
  When she doesn't get a part in the fifth grade play, Gretchen desperately conjures up a well-meaning but not very efficient fairy godmother.
Dang Manh Kha, In the Land of Small Dragon, 1979
  In the Land of Small Dragon, a dutiful daughter, mistreated by her stepmother, is rewarded by her fairy godmother.
Charlotte Pomerantz, The Downtown Fairy Godmother, 1983
  Olivia wishes for a fairy godmother and gets a Fairy Godmother Grade C, still in training and limited in powers, who takes her around New York City.

| 554 |

Thomas A. Dyer

The Whipman Is Watching (Boston: Houghton Mifflin, 1979)

Age range: Grades 5-8

Subject(s): Indians of North America; Prejudice

Major character(s): Marta, Dancer; Cultus, Teenager (Marta's brother), Indian (native American); Angie, Cousin, Indian (native American)

Time period(s): 1970s

Locale(s): Red Salmon, Oregon (Indian Reservation)

What the book is about: Children living on an American Indian reservation try to retain their identity in an all-white school. Angie and her teen cousin, Cultus, must learn to face the problems brought on by their growing frustrations as they are caught between the world of the reservation and the world outside.

Where it's reviewed:
Booklist, January 15, 1980, page 717
Kirkus Reviews, February 1, 1980
School Library Journal, November 1979, page 75

Other books by the author:
Way of His Own, 1981

Other books you might like:
James A. Houston, Drifting Snow: An Arctic Legend, 1992
  Having been taken from her Arctic home when a tiny child, a teenager returns to look for her parents and learn once again about the Eskimo culture.
Jan Hudson, Dawn Rider, 1990
  Kit Fox's sixteenth year is filled with preparation for an important buffalo run, her sister's upcoming marriage, and skirmishes with their enemy.
Evelyn Sibley Lampman, Cayuse Courage, 1970
  Ashamed to return to his people after his arm is amputated, a young Cayuse Indian remains among white settlers in Oregon.
Phyllis Root, The Listening Silence, 1992
  A young Indian girl triumphs over her fears and proves herself worthy to be the mystical healer of her village.
Penina Keen Spinka, Mother's Blessing, 1992

An intelligent girl, rejected by her father, follows the call of her spirit guide and seeks to fulfill a prophesy that she will lead her people.

555

Thomas J. Dygard

Quarterback Walk-On (New York: Morrow, 1982)

Age range: Grades 5-8

Subject(s): Sports/Football

Major character(s): Denny Westbrooke, Sports Figure (football player); Scott "Earthquake" Morrison, Sports Figure (football player); Wally Polk, Coach

Time period(s): 1980s

Locale(s): Texas

What the book is about: Denny Westbrooke wants to be a football coach, so he goes to Sutton State, a college with an excellent team, so he can learn as much as possible. Happy being a fourth string quarterback, he has no illusions about being a starter, much less a star. When injuries and a suspension sideline all the other quarterbacks, Denny finds himself a terrified starting quarterback. The "big game" is an exciting one which will keep sports fans turning pages until the last point is scored.

Where it's reviewed:
Booklist, February 15, 1982, page 754

Christian Science Monitor, October 8, 1982, page B12
School Library Journal, May 1982, page 86

Other books by the author:
Forward Pass, 1989
Halfback Tough, 1986
Rebound Caper, 1983
Running Scared, 1977

Other books you might like:
Delores Beckman, Who Loves Sam Grant?, 1983
  Samantha's life is complicated by her on-and-off relationship with her school's quarterback, and by the parrot, El Loro, a rival school's mascot.
William Campbell Gault, Quarterback Gamble, 1970
  No one believed Jug had the makings of a professional football player except the coach of the Chicago Miners who gambled with Jug.
William L. Heath, Most Valuable Player, 1973
  For four years Pete has looked forward to receiving the most valuable player award in football. Then a phenomenal new player joins the team.
Gloria D. Miklowitz, Anything to Win, 1989
  To increase his chances of winning a college scholarship, a talented high school quarterback risks his health by taking anabolic steroids.
Mike Neigoff, Goal to Go, 1970
  Andy, a sophomore quarterback on the second team, believes that since the coach is continually challenging him, he wants him out of the game.

E

556

Edward Eager

Illustrator: N.M. Bodecker

Seven-Day Magic (New York: Harcourt, 1962)

Age range: Grades 5-6

Subject(s): Adventure and Adventurers; Magic

Major character(s): Fredericka, Child; Abbie, Child (Fredericka's sister); Barnaby, Inventor

Time period(s): 1950s

Locale(s): Butterfield, Connecticut

What the book is about: Just after Fredericka wished on the book for an adventure with wizards and witches, the green-eyed dragon flew over, low enough to scoop her up and disappear with her in a puff of purple smoke. The Seven-Day book of magic caused an awful lot of trouble. The children must learn the book's rules and tame its magic.

Other books by the author:
The Time Garden, 1985
The Well-Wishers, 1985
Magic or Not?, 1984
Half Magic, 1954

Other books you might like:
Gillian Bradshaw, *The Land of Gold*, 1992
    After the murder of her parents, a Nubian princess is helped to her rightful place on the throne by two friendly Egyptians and the dragon, Hathor.
Sherryl Jordan, *The Wednesday Wizard*, 1991
    Trying to warn his absent master of dragon danger, Weasel makes a slight miscalculation in magic spell and finds himself beamed into the future.
Donn Kushner, *A Book of Dragon*, 1987
    Nonesuch, the last in a line of dragons, uses his unique ability to change in size to survive for six centuries.
Betsy Sterman, *Backyard Dragon*, 1993
    With the help of three friends, a young boy and his grandfather help a fifteenth-centruy Welsh dragon find its way home.
Patricia C. Wrede, *Searching for Dragons*, 1991
    With the aid of King Mandanbar, princess Cimorene rescues the dragon Kazul and saves the Enchanted Forest from a band of wicked wizards.

557

P.D. Eastman, Author/Illustrator

Are You My Mother? (New York: Random, 1960)

Age range: Grades 1-2

Time period(s): Indeterminate

Locale(s): United States

What the book is about: A bird falls from the nest and looks for its mother, encountering many different animals in its search.

Where it's reviewed:
School Library Journal, May 1979, page 38
Saturday Review, December 9, 1972, page 76
School Librarian, December 1982, page 324

Other books by the author:
Flap Your Wings, 1969
Best Nest, 1968
Fish Out of Water, 1961
Go Dog Go, 1961

Other books you might like:
Michael Berenstain, *Peat Moss and Ivy and the Birthday Present*, 1986
    In preparing an extra special birthday present for their mother, two young chipmunks find adventure in an owl's nest.
Anne Braff Brodzinsky, *The Mulberry Bird: Story of an Adoption*, 1986
    Facing insurmountable problems, a young bird mother makes an adoption plan for her much loved baby, giving him a stable home and two loving parents.
Janell Cannon, *Stellaluna*, 1993
    After she falls headfirst into a bird's nest, a baby bat is raised like a bird until she is reunited with her mother.
Keiko Kasza, *A Mother for Choco*, 1992
    A lonely little bird named Choco goes in search of a mother.
Hope Ryden, *The Raggedy Red Squirrel*, 1992
    Describes the habits of a mother red squirrel as she makes a nest and cares for two babies until they can care for themselves.

558

Wolfgang Ecke
Illustrator: Rolf Rettich

The Castle of the Red Gorillas (Englewood Cliffs, NJ: Prentice, 1983)

Age range: Grades 5-8

Subject(s): Literature; Mystery and Detective Stories

Time period(s): Indeterminate

Locale(s): United States; Europe

What the book is about: A collection of nineteen mysteries set in Europe and the United States with solutions to be provided by the reader based on clues in the text. Includes a section with solutions, explanations and indications of degree of difficulty for each story.

Where it's reviewed:
Booklist, September 1, 1983, page 83
School Library Journal, September 1983, page 132
Voice of Youth Advocates, December 1983, page 278

Other books by the author:
The Midnight Chess Game, 1983
The Bank Holdup, 1982
The Invisible Witness, 1980
The Face at the Window, 1979

Other books you might like:
Lucinda Landon, *Meg Mackintosh and the Mystery at the Medieval Castle*, 1989
    Meg and her classmates are witnesses to the theft of a chalice at a medieval castle. The reader is challenged to solve the mystery before Meg does.
Louis Phillips, *263 Brainbusters: Just How Smart Are You, Anyway?*, 1985
    A collection of mathematical and verbal barin-teasing questions interspersed with "brain vacation" jokes.
George Shannon, *More Stories to Solve: Fifteen Folktales From around the World*, 1990
    Fifteen brief folktales in which there is a mystery or problem that the reader is invited to solve before the resolution is presented.
Murray Shaw, *The Adventures of the Dancing Men*, 1993
    Two adventures of Sherlock Holmes with a section identifying the clues in the story and explaining Holmes' reasoning in solving the mysteries.
Falcon Travis, *Super Sleuth: Mini Mysteries for You to Solve*, 1985
    Describes 43 crime puzzles, which the reader tries to solve with the aid of clues, codes, alibis and other evidence.

559

Allan W. Eckert

Illustrator: John Schoenherr

Incident at Hawk's Hill (Boston: Little Brown, 1971)

Age range: Grades 6 and Up

Subject(s): Wilderness; Survival; Animals/Badgers

Major character(s): Ben MacDonald, Child

Time period(s): 1870s

Locale(s): United States

What the book is about: Six year old Ben disappears in the prairie grass around his home. A very small boy, he is adopted by a badger and lives in her den. Within two months he becomes a wild boy.

Where it's reviewed:
Booklist, July 15, 1971, page 1826
Kirkus Reviews, March 1, 1971, page 252

Awards the book has won:
Newbery Honor

Other books by the author:
Dark Green Tunnel, 1984
The Conquerors, 1971
In Search of a Whale, 1970
Wilderness Empire, 1969

Other books you might like:
William Bell, *Crabbe's Journey*, 1986
    Feeling misunderstood, Crabbe runs away to live in the woods where he meets a mysterious woman. She teaches him about outdoor survival and more.
Molly Burkett, *The Year of the Badger*, 1972
    A young English boy recounts his family's experiences with a badger they've raised from a sick baby.
Mel Ellis, *Caribou Crossing*, 1971
    Two boys' dream of a fishing lodge in the Canadian wilderness comes true but at the expense of the natural wonders they wanted to share.
Marilyn Halvorson, *Hold On, Geronimo*, 1987
    Having lost the use of his right hand and gotten into a private war with his cousin, Lance doesn't think things can get worse.
Jim Kjelgaard, *Wild Trek*, 1963
    A trapper and his dog travel into the Caribou Mountains to rescue a naturalist and a pilot, whose plane has crashed.

560

Walter D. Edmonds

Illustrator: Paul Lantz

The Matchlock Gun (New York: Dodd, Mead, 1941)

Age range: Grades 2-4

Subject(s): French and Indian War

Major character(s): Edward Van Alstyne, Child; Trudy Van Alstyne, Child; Gertrude Van Alstyne, Parent

Time period(s): 1750s

Locale(s): New York

What the book is about: A 10 year old boy in Colonial New York is fascinated by the old-fashioned gun hanging on the wall. Edward later has the opportunity to fire it when Indians threaten him, his mother, and baby sister.

Where it's reviewed:
Horn Book, November 1941, page 448

Awards the book has won:
Newbery Medal 1942
Lewis Carroll Shelf 1960

Other books by the author:
Bert Breen's Barn, 1975

Other books you might like:
Arnold Lobel, *On the Day Peter Stuyvesant Sailed into Town*, 1971

In 1647, Peter Stuyvesant made the Dutch families of New Amsterdam clean up their town. Non-fiction, told in rhyme

Alice Dalgliesh, *The Courage of Sarah Noble*, 1954
  Sarah accompanies her father into the wilderness to help build a home for the family.

William H. Hooks, *Pioneer Cat*, 1988
  9 year old Kate tries to keep her cat, Snuggs, a secret from the rest of the wagon train.

561

Amy Ehrlich

Illustrator: Steven Kellogg

Leo, Zack and Emmie (New York: Dial, 1981)

Age range: Grades 1-2

Subject(s): Friendship

Major character(s): Emmie Williams, Child; Leo, Child; Zack, Child

Time period(s): 1980s

Locale(s): New York, New York

What the book is about: The story of three friends written for beginning readers. Emmie is a great tomboy, and poor Zack feels left out at recess. The three of them learn that no matter what, the friendship among the three of them will prevail.

Where it's reviewed:
Booklist, February 15, 1982, page 760
Hornbook, February 1982, page 39
Kirkus Reviews, January 1, 1982, page 5

Other books by the author:
Leo, Zack and Emmie Together Again, 1987
Thumbelina, 1979
The Everyday Train, 1978
Zeek Silver Moon, 1972

Other books you might like:
Sue Alexander, *More Witch, Goblin and Ghost Stories*, 1978
  The further adventures of three friends who go on a picnic, learn about honesty, and discover a remedy for insomnia.
Robert Fremlin, *Three Friends*, 1975
  Three friends, Pig, Cat and Squirrel, discuss Pig's problems, hold a circus, and buy a new suit.
Edward Marshall, *Fox and His Friends*, 1982
  In three separate episodes, Fox wants to play with his friends, but duty in one form or another always interferes.
Stephen Mooser, *The Case of the Slippery Sharks*, 1988
  Three friends involved in searching for treasure become involved in searching for stolen goods.
Hazel Hutchins Wilson, *The Three and Many Wishes of Jason Reid*, 1988
  Eleven year old Jason is granted three wishes which land him and his friends in some hilarious scrapes.

562

Phyllis Rose Eisenberg

Illustrator: Susan Jeschke

A Mitzvah Is Something Special (New York: Harper, 1978)

Age range: Grades 2-4

Subject(s): Grandparents

Major character(s): Lisa, Child; Esther, Grandparent; Dorrie, Grandparent

Time period(s): 1970s

Locale(s): United States

What the book is about: Lisa brings her two very different grandmothers together. Grandma Esther loves to cook and bake, and Grandma Dorrie hates cooking but loves to play her flute and tell stories, and they both love Lisa very much. They both explain to Lisa that a "mitzvah" is a special, very BIG blessing. Lisa lovingly arranges a mitzvah for her two grandmothers.

Where it's reviewed:
Booklist, October 1, 1978, page 291
Kirkus Reviews, November 1, 1978, page 1184
School Library Journal, October 1978, page 132

Other books by the author:
You're My Nikki, 1992
Don't Tell Me a Ghost Story, 1982

Other books you might like:
Rose Blue, *The Thirteenth Year: a Bar Mitzvah Story*, 1977
  As his Bar Mitzvah approaches, a young boy has mixed emotions about its meaning and how it will affect him.
Eth Clifford, *The Remembering Box*, 1985
  Nine year old Joshua's visits to his grandmother on the Jewish sabbathteach him about love, family, and tradition which helps him accept her death.
Emily Arnold McCully, *Grandmas at Bat*, 1993
  Pip's two grandmothers, who cannot agree on anything, take over coaching her baseball team and create chaos.
Bert Metter, *Bar Mitzvah, Bat Mitzvah*, 1984
  Describes Jewish ceremonies of Bar and Bat Mitzvah. Discusses their hitory and their effect on the lives of those who have experienced them.
Philip Sendak, *In Grandpa's House*, 1985
  A talking bird, a friendly giant, and other fantastic creatures help David find his missing grandfather and learn lessons every Jewish boy should know

---

563

Dan Elish

Illustrator: John Stadler

Jason and the Baseball Bear (New York: Orchard, 1990)

Age range: Grades 3-6

Subject(s): Sports/Baseball; Animals

Major character(s): Jason Munson, Preteen, Sports Figure (Little Leaguer); Whitney, Bear (polar bear)

Time period(s): 1990s

Locale(s): United States

What the book is about: Jason is able to communicate with animals, most importantly Whitney, a polar bear who is, in truth, responsible for Jason's incredible batting average. The city zoo also includes a literature spouting gnu who gives the inspiring speech before the "big game" making reference to the Gettysburg Address (Jason is translating, of course). A must for Little Leaguers.

Where it's reviewed:
Booklist, April 1, 1990, page 1548
Horn Book, September/October 1990, page 600

Other books by the author:
The Great Squirrel Uprising, 1992
The Worldwide Dessert Contest, 1988

Other books you might like:
Matt Christopher, *Return of the Home Run Kid*, 1992
  Sylvester Coddmyer III is having a dismal baseball season until he take advice from a mysterious ex-player named Checko and plays more aggressively.
Michael W. Fox, *Dr. Fox's Fables: Lessons From Nature*, 1980
  Twenty-two fables explore relationships between animals and between animals and humans.
Daphne Doward Hogstrom, *One Silver Second: A Fable for All Ages*, 1972
  As each animal finds a voice that fits its personality, it forgets the common voice that once allowed animals to talk and live together peacefully.
Alfred Slote, *Jake*, 1971
  After searching for and trying a number of coaches for his Little League team, Jake finds a musician who helps win games in a spectacular manner.
John Weston, *The Boy Who Sang the Birds*, 1976
  During a fierce winter marked by strange bird behavior, an older boy, living alone, takes in a child who seems to be able to talk to animals.

564

Dan Elish

Illustrator: John Steven Gurney

The Worldwide Dessert Contest (New York: Orchard, 1988)

Age range: Grades 4-7

Subject(s): Contests; Food

Major character(s): John Applefeller, Cook (chef); Sylvester S. Sweet, Villain; Josiah Benson, Maintenance Worker (janitor)

Time period(s): 1980s

Locale(s): Appleton

What the book is about: Gentle John Applefeller enters his trampoline size apple pancake against sly Sylvester Sweet's double-chocolate-fudge-raspberry-coconut-lime swirl in the Worldwide Dessert Contest. Sylvester Sweet *always* wins the contest, but this year, Stanley, John's assistant, listens to Josiah Benson, the contest janitor, who knows something about why Sylvester Sweet always wins.

Where it's reviewed:
Booklist, June 15, 1988, page 1735
Kirkus, May 15, 1988, page 760
School Library Journal, May 1988, page 96

Other books by the author:
The Great Squirrel Uprising, 1992
Jason and the Baseball Bear, 1990

Other books you might like:
Roald Dahl, *Charlie and the Chocolate Factory*, 1964
  Each of five children who discover an entry ticket into Mr. Willie Wonka's strange chocolate factory takes advantage of the situation in their own way
Suzy Kline, *Orp and the Chop Suey Burgers*, 1990
  Orville enters a cooking contest, which he has high hopes of winning with his recipe for chop suey burgers.
Mary Nash, *Mrs. Coverlet's Magicians*, 1961
  While the housekeeper is away participating in a baking contest, Toad Persever resorts to his magic kit to get rid of the babysitter, Miss Penalty.
Daniel Manus Pinkwater, *Slaves of Spiegel: A Magic Moscow Story*, 1982
  Steve Nickelson, assistant Norman Bleistift, and the Magic Moscow restaurant are sent through space to an intergalactic junk food cooking contest.
Amalie Sharfman, *Papa's Secret Chocolate Dessert*, 1972
  To everyone's surprise, Jean-Pierre saves the day when his father, a famous chef, is too ill to cook.

565

Shan Ellentuck, Author/Illustrator

Yankel the Fool (Garden City, NY: Doubleday, 1973)

Age range: Grades 4-6

Subject(s): Clergy; Jews

Major character(s): Yankel, Outcast (village fool), Criminal

Time period(s): Indeterminate

Locale(s): Earth

What the book is about: Yankel is dismissed as the village fool by the townspeople. In desperation, he has turned to a life of crime. A wonderworking rabbi comes to town and convinces everyone that Yankel is an unrecognized scholar and sage.

Where it's reviewed:
Booklist, June 15, 1973, page 988
Kirkus Reviews, May 1, 1973, page 517

Other books by the author:
My Brother Bernard, 1968
Upside Down Man, 1965

Other books you might like:
Syd Lieberman, *Joseph the Tailor and Other Jewish Tales*, 1988
  A collection of folk and Biblical tales for middle graders.
Anne E. Neimark, *One Man's Valor*, 1986
  The story of a German Jew who became a great rabbi and national spiritual leader and fought courageously against the Nazi persecution.
Isaac Bashevis Singer, *The Golem*, 1982
  A clay giant miraculously brought to life by a saintly rabbi saves a Jewish banker who has been falsely accused in the Prague of Emperor Rudolf II.
Carol Snyder, *Ike and Mama and the Seven Surprises*, 1985
  Ike's mother promises that he'll have seven surprises in the month before his Bar Mitzvah, even though nothing is going very well so far.
Margot Zemach, *It Could Always Be Worse*, 1976
  Unable to stand his overcrowded and noisy home any longer, a poor man goes to the rabbi for advice.

566

Scott Eller

Short Season (New York: Scholastic, 1985)

Age range: Grades 5-7

Subject(s): Sports/Baseball; Brothers

Major character(s): Brad Harris, Sports Figure (baseball player); Dean Harris, Sports Figure (baseball player); Lisa Harris, Child

Time period(s): 1980s (1981)

Locale(s): Adrian, Michigan

What the book is about: Brad and Dean Harris, brothers eleven months apart, are a great combination in Little League. Brad is hitting over .500 and Dean covers Brad's weak right field with his own strong center. But Dean suddenly quit the team and won't tell Brad why. He disappears for hours at a time, and Brad worries that Dean might be into drugs or other serious trouble. We see the whole family work through various problems, as the brothers' relationship matures. Includes lots of descriptions of the baseball games for the serious player or fan.

Where it's reviewed:
Booklist, August 1985, page 1663
School Library Journal, October 1985, page 171

Other books by the author:
First Base, First Place, 1993
21st Century Fox, 1989

Other books you might like:
Curtis Kent Bishop, *Little League Victory*, 1967
    A boy with exceptional athletic ability and a problem temper finds his place on a Little League team through the sympathetic insight of a good coach.
Matt Christopher, *Tackle Without a Team*, 1989
    After being dismissed from the football team for drug possession, Scott learns the only way to clear himself is to find out who planted the marijuana.
William E. Coles, *Funnybone: A Novel*, 1992
    When Christine's brother disappears, the word "drugs" is whispered in connection with him. She finds blaming others easier than blaming her brother.
Marilyn Levinson, *And Don't Bring Jeremy*, 1985
    New in the neighborhood and eager to be part of the crowd, Adam finds it difficult to deal with the needs of his brother suffering from a disability.
Robert E. Swindells, *Follow a Shadow*, 1990
    Headed for trouble with drugs and alcohol, a boy who longs to escape his world discovers a mysterious portrait of a man much like himself.

567

Leona Ellerby

King Tut's Game Board (Minneapolis: Lerner, 1980)

Age range: Grades 6 and Up

Subject(s): Atlantis

Major character(s): Justin Sanders, Teenager; Nathan Alistant, Teenager

Time period(s): 1980s

Locale(s): Egypt

What the book is about: With a mysterious friend he meets while vacationing in Egypt, Justin makes astonishing discoveries about two ancient civilizations. The pair make their way to the Valley of the Kings and the remote Temple of Abu Simbel.

Where it's reviewed:
Children's Book Review Service, April 1980, page 87
School Library Journal, August 1980, page 76

Awards the book has won:
Ethical Culture School Book Award 1980

Other books you might like:
Erick Berry, *Honey of the Nile*, 1963
    Intrigue flourishes in the court of Ankhesenpanton and Tutankhamun as opposing religious groups vie for the leadership of ancient Egypt.
Dorothy Sharp Carter, *His Majesty, Queen Hatshepsut*, 1987
    A fictionalized account of the life of Hatshepsut, a queen in ancient Egypt who declared herself King and ruled as such for more than twenty years.
Collin McDonald, *Nightwaves: Scary Tales for After Dark*, 1990
    A collection of horror stories featuring a spirit hunter from ancient Egypt.
Jenny Nimmo, *The Chestnut Soldier*, 1991
    To purge the anger from an ancient Welsh god, Gwyn Griffiths draws on the strength of his namesake and ancestor in magic, Gwydion Gwyn.
Cynthia Voigt, *The Vandemark Mummy*, 1991
    When their father is made responsible for a collection of ancient Egyptian artifacts, Phineas and his sister, Althea, try to find the thieves threaten

568

Mel Ellis

Flight of the White Wolf (New York: Holt, 1970)

Age range: Grades 5 and Up

Subject(s): Animals/Wolves

Major character(s): Russ, Teenager; Gray, Wolf

Time period(s): 1970s

Locale(s): United States

What the book is about: Russ and his escaped "pet" wolf run away from the people who want to kill Gray. This story deals with prejudice and ignorance about the ways of wolves. A powerful, gripping story.

Where it's reviewed:
Kirkus Reviews, May 1, 1970, page 505
Library Journal, May 15, 1970, page 1911

Awards the book has won:
Dorothy Canfield Fisher Children's Book Award 1972

Other books by the author:
The Wild Runners, 1976
Ironhead, 1970
When Lightning Strikes, 1970
Wild Goose, Brother Goose, 1970

Other books you might like:
Joan Aiken, *The Wolves of Willoughby Chase*, 1963

Two children are sent to a country estate where they have to tackle a mean governess, survive a pack of wolves and restore the estate to its owners.

Jean Craighead George, *Julie of the Wolves*, 1972
Fleeing an unwanted marriage, Julie becomes lost in the arctic wilderness and is saved by a pack of wolves who accept her, and whom she comes to love.

James A. Houston, *Frozen Fire*, 1977
An Eskimo boy and his classmate go in search of Matthew's lost father. They face a seventy-five mile trek homeward in whirling snow and bitter cold.

James Lippincott, *Wilderness Champion*, 1944
On his way to his ranger cabin in the Alberta mountains, Johnny loses his favorite pup, Reddy, who becomes the running mate of an old black wolf.

Jack London, *The Call of the Wild*, 1903
After being stolen from his home, Buck is used as a sled dog in the Klondike. Despite many struggles, he soon becomes the leader of a pack of wolves.

569

Sarah Ellis

A Family Project (New York: McElderry, 1988)

Age range: Grades 6-8

Subject(s): Death; Family Life; Grief

Major character(s): Jessica, Preteen; Lucie, Child

Time period(s): 1980s

Locale(s): United States

What the book is about: Eleven year old Jessica does a school project in preparation for a new baby sister. When baby Lucie is a victim of crib death, the family is shattered. A new, stronger family bond is created in dealing with the loss. A tender story of a family dealing with grief.

Where it's reviewed:
Horn Book, May/June 1988, page 350
School Library Journal, March 1988, page 188

Other books by the author:
Pick-Up Sticks, 1992
Next-Door Neighbors, 1990

Other books you might like:
Vera Cleaver, *Belle Pruitt*, 1988
When her baby brother dies suddenly of pneumonia, Belle is devastated.

Lynn Hall, *The Soul of the Silver Dog*, 1992
Feeling rejected by her family after her younger sister's death, Cory adopts a blind show dog and trains him for agility competition.

Buzz King, *Silicon Songs*, 1990
Max, a computer whiz with no conventional family, tries to concentrate his life on electronic networks while his beloved Uncle Pete lies dying.

Gloria McLendon, *My Brother Joey Died*, 1982
A child goes through the difficult process of adjusting to the sudden illness and death of a brother.

Colby Rodowsky, *Fitchett's Folly*, 1987
Sarey resents a new family member, Faith, whom she blames for her father's death, which occured when he saved Faith from a shipwreck.

570

Sarah Ellis

Next-Door Neighbors (New York: Macmillan, 1990)

Age range: Grades 4-6

Subject(s): Shyness; Friendship

Major character(s): Peggy Davies, Preteen; Sing, Gardener; George Slobodkin, Preteen

Time period(s): 1950s (1957)

Locale(s): Canada

What the book is about: A painfully shy minister's daughter encounters prejudice, arrogance and short-sightedness in an elderly neighbor. She learns to look outward instead of focusing on her own insecurities. She explores the meaning of friendship and convictions.

Where it's reviewed:
Booklist, March 1, 1990, page 1340
School Library Journal, March 1990, page 217

Other books by the author:
A Family Project, 1988

Other books you might like:
Margaret Jean Anderson, *The Journey of the Shadow Bairns*, 1980
A young Scottish girl and her four year old brother pursue family plans to relocate to Canada even after their parents die suddenly.

Betty Baker, *The Night Spider Case*, 1984
In the 1890s in New York City, Lambert reluctantly teams up with a neighbor to investigate an empty house.

Mary Alice Downie, *Honor Bound*, 1971
Members of a Loyalist family become separated when they flee Philadelphia for Canada following the Revolutionary War.

Jean Little, *From Anna*, 1972
When the family moves from Germany to Canada, a nine year old girl discovers the reason for her awkwardness.

Mary Francis Shura, *The Josie Gambit*, 1986
Greg is apprehensive about spending six months with his grandmother, but a relationship with a troubled girl shows him what real friendship can be.

571

M.J. Engh

Illustrator: Leslie Bowman

The House in the Snow (New York: Watts, 1987)

Age range: Grades 4-6

Subject(s): Adventure and Adventurers; Haunted Houses

Major character(s): Benjamin, Orphan

Time period(s): 1980s

Locale(s): United States

What the book is about: Orphan Benjamin lands in a house of robbers who have cloaks that make them invisible. With the help of a group of friends, Benjamin plans to take over the house and outwit the robbers.

Where it's reviewed:
Center for Children's Books Bulletin, September 1987, page 6

Kirkus Reviews, July 1, 1987, page 990
School Library Journal, September 1987, page 179

Other books by the author:
Wheel of the Winds, 1988
Arslan, 1987

Other books you might like:
Susan Cooper, *The Boggart*, 1993
  After returning home from Scotland, Emily finds that she has accidentally brought back a boggart, an invisible and mischievous spirit.
Robert Cormier, *Fade*, 1988
  Paul, son of French Canadian immigrants, inherits the ability to become invisible, but this power soon leads to death, destruction, and no escape.
Anne Lindbergh, *The People in Pineapple Place*, 1982
  August adjusts to his new home in Washington, D.C., with the help of the children of Pineapple Place, a street and people invisible to all but him.
Dorothy Nafus Morrison, *Vanishing Act*, 1989
  Jo finds a strange device that makes objects vanish, but doesn't realize how dangerous it is until she accidentally turns herself invisible.
Andre Norton, *House of Shadows*, 1984
  Mike and Susan feel a sense of urgency and terror as they try to protect their brother who is threatened by an invisible and powerful force.

572

Elizabeth Enright

Illustrator: Jane Dyer

Gone-Away Lake (New York: Harcourt, Brace, 1957)

Age range: Grades 5-6

Subject(s): Family Life; Vacations

Major character(s): Portia, Child; Foster, Child; Julian, Child

Time period(s): 1950s

Locale(s): United States

What the book is about: Portia, Foster and Julian discover a swamp that had once been a lake with houses where the summer people lived. Life becomes happy from that moment on, for the rest of the summer.

Where it's reviewed:
Booklist, May 15, 1957, page 481
Horn Book, June 1957, page 224

Awards the book has won:
Newbery Honor

Other books by the author:
Four-Story Mistake, 1942
Return to Gone-Away, 1961
Saturdays, 1941
Sea Is All Around, 1940

Other books you might like:
Donna Walsh Englehart, *Breaking the Ring*, 1991
  Three girls spend their summer vacation at their grandparents' house and discover cocaine hidden on an island.
Jerry Spinelli, *Dump Days*, 1988

J.D. Kidd and his best friend resolve to have the perfect summer vacation.
LouAnn Gaeddert, *Your Former Friend, Matthew*, 1984
  Gail is devastated when her best friend ignores her after a vacation in the country.
Barbara Rinkoff, *A Guy Can Be Wrong*, 1970
  Carlos does not appreciate being sent to stay with a family in the suburbs for two weeks.
Ruth Loomis, *Valley of the Hawk*, 1969
  Summer vacation on her aunt and uncle's ranch is miserable for a young girl until she makes friends with an Indian girl.

573

Elizabeth Enright, Author/Illustrator

The Saturdays (New York: Holt Rinehart, 1941)

Age range: Grades 5-7

Subject(s): Family Life; Single Parent Families

Major character(s): Cuffy, Housekeeper, Child-Care Giver; Mona Melendy, Teenager; Miranda "Randy" Melendy, Child

Time period(s): 1940s

Locale(s): New York

What the book is about: The four Melendys live with their widowed father, a writer, and their housekeeper, Cuffy, in an old brownstone. Tired of wasting their Saturdays, they pool their resources for at least one good spree.

Where it's reviewed:
Hornbook, August 1984, page 499

Other books by the author:
Gone-Away Lake, 1957
Spiderweb for Two, 1951
Then There Were Five, 1944
The 4-Story Mistake, 1942

Other books you might like:
Barbara Corcoran, *Family Secrets*, 1992
  After her family moves to the town where her father grew up, Tracy discovers she is adopted, and gets new insights into what constitutes a family.
Sarah Ellis, *Next-Door Neighbors*, 1989
  Her family's move to a new town leaves Peggy feeling lonely, until she befriends the unconventional George and her neighbor's Chinese servant.
Anne Fine, *The Book of the Banshee: A Novel*, 1992
  Will feels his younger sister, suddenly transformed into a teenage banshee, is responsible for turning the family home into a veritable war zone.
Phyllis Reynolds Naylor, *Alice in April*, 1993
  Alice discovers that turning thirteen will make her the Woman of the House at home, so she starts a campaign to get more appreciation.
Ethel Footman Smothers, *Down in the Piney Woods*, 1992
  The joys and frustration of family life are portrayed through the eyes of Annie Rye, the daughter of a black sharecropper.

574

Elizabeth Enright, Author/Illustrator

Thimble Summer (New York: Rinehart, 1938)

Age range: Grades 4-6

Subject(s): Farm Life

Major character(s): Garnet Linden, Child; Eric Swanstrom, Orphan; Citronella Hauser, Child

Time period(s): 1930s

Locale(s): Esau's Valley, Wisconsin

What the book is about: After finding a silver thimble, a young girl's summer becomes magically filled with excitement. Her family opens their home to an orphan and Garnet enters her pig in competition at the fair.

Where it's reviewed:
Christian Science Monitor, August 25, 1938, page 6
New York Times Book Review, August 21, 1938, page 10

Awards the book has won:
Newbery Medal 1939

Other books by the author:
Four-Story Mistake, 1942
Gone Away Lake, 1957
Return to Gone-Away, 1961
Saturdays, 1941

Other books you might like:
Anne Pellowski, *Betsy's Up and Down Year*, 1983
  Betsy struggles with sibling rivalry, rattlesnakes, and the death of her grandfather on her family's Wisconsin farm.
Anne Pellowski, *Willow Wind Farm: Betsy's Story*, 1981
  The adventures of seven year old Betsy and her Wisconsin farm family.
Natalie Kinsey-Warnock, *The Night the Bells Rang*, 1991
  A Vermont farm boy helps with chores and sees young men go to war during the last year of WWI.
Carole S. Adler, *A Tribe for Lexi*, 1991
  12-year-old Lexi finds that only her withdrawn cousin, Jeb, offers friendship when she visits a relative's farm in upper New York state.
Gary Paulsen, *The Foxman*, 1977

575

Sam Epstein

Illustrator: Joseph Scrofani

Dr. Beaumont and the Man with the Hole in His Stomach (New York: Coward, 1978)

Age range: Grades 4-7

Subject(s): Medicine; Doctors

Major character(s): William Beaumont, Doctor; Alexis St. Martin, Patient

Time period(s): 1810s

Locale(s): Canada

What the book is about: Beaumont, an army doctor, is asked to treat nineteen year old Alexis St. Martin who has been accidentally shot in the stomach. Although the hole in his stomach never healed, St. Martin lived to be 83. Beaumont used him for years to study digestion. This is a fascinating biography for anyone interested in medicine and/or ethics, and has excellent descriptions of the workings of digestion.

Where it's reviewed:
Science Books and Films, March 1979, page 232

Social Education, August 1979, page 299

Other books by the author:
She Never Looked Back, 1980
Secret in a Sealed Bottle, 1979
Hurricane Guest, 1964
The Andrews Raid, 1956

Other books you might like:
Carol Greene, *Elizabeth Blackwell, First Woman Doctor*, 1991
  Biography of the first woman doctor in the United States who worked in both the United States and England to open medicine to women.
Lynn Groh, *Walter Reed, Pioneer in Medicine*, 1971
  A biography of the army doctor who is best known for his discover of the way in which Yellow Fever is spread.
Stephanie McPherson, *The Worker's Detective: A Story about Dr. Alice Hamilton*, 1992
  The biography of a social worker and doctor whose work brought attention to the health risks associated with certain jobs.
Paul Showers, *What Happens to a Hamburger*, 1985
  This science book explains how food is used to make energy, strong bone, and solid muscles as they pass through the digestive system.
Judith St. George, *Dear Dr. Bell—Your Friend, Helen Keller*, 1992
  Follows the parallel lives of Helen Keller and Alexander Graham Bell who continued to support and encourage each other after their first meeting.

576

Eleanor Estes, Author/Illustrator

Ginger Pye (New York: Harcourt, Brace and Company, 1951)

Age range: Grades 3-5

Subject(s): Animals/Dogs; Family Life

Major character(s): Jared "Jerry" Pye, Child; Rachel Pye, Child; Ginger Pye, Dog

Time period(s): 20th century

Locale(s): Cranbury, New York

What the book is about: Ginger, the dog of the Pye family, is stolen on Thanksgiving Day. The children are convinced that he has been abducted by a stranger in a yellow hat. After months of searching, Ginger is found the following May by the most unlikely hero.

Where it's reviewed:
Horn Book, May 1951, Page 182
New York Times Book Review, April 22, 1951, Page 30

Awards the book has won:
Newbery Medal 1952

Other books by the author:
The Hundred Dresses, 1944
The Moffats, 1941
Pinky Pye, 1958 (Sequel to *Ginger Pye*.)

Other books you might like:
Molly Cone, *Mishmash*, 1962
  Pete's dog, Mishmash, is constantly in trouble because he thinks he's "people."

Beverly Cleary, *Henry and Beezus*, 1952
  Henry and his dog, Ribsy, try to earn enough money for a bicycle.
Charlotte Towner Graeber, *Fudge*, 1987
  10 year old Chad promises to care for the new puppy, Fudge, all by himself.
Jean Little, *Lost and Found*, 1986
  Luch and Jan search for the owners of a lost puppy.
Tim Schoch, *Flash Fry, Private Eye*, 1986
  11 year old Flash Fry and his canine detective land a haunted house while trying to settle a feud.

577

Eleanor Estes

Illustrator: Jacqueline Ayer

The Lost Umbrella of Kim Chu (New York: Atheneum, 1978)

Age range: Grades 3-4

Subject(s): Chinese Americans

Major character(s): Kim Chu, Child; Mae Lee, Child

Time period(s): 1970s

Locale(s): New York, New York

What the book is about: Nine year old Kim Chu borrows her father's umbrella, not knowing it has a secret compartment in the handle. The umbrella disappears while she is at the library. She and her friend, Mae Lee, follow the culprit to Staten Island.

Where it's reviewed:
Center for Children's Books Bulletin, March 1979, page 113
Horn Book, February 1979, page 60

Other books by the author:
Pinky Pye, 1958
Ginger Pye, 1951
Rufus M., 1943
The Moffats, 1941

Other books you might like:
Angela Banner, *Around the World with Ant and Bee*, 1981
  Bee's hunt for his lost umbrella takes Ant and Bee on a trip around the world.
Daniel Manus Pinkwater, *Roger's Umbrella*, 1981
  Roger's umbrella becomes increasingly more wild and uncontrollable until he meets three old ladies who teach him how to talk to it.
Uri Shulevitz, *The Strange and Exciting Adventures of Jeremiah Hush.*, 1986
  Quiet, serious Jeremiah Hush, a monkey who lives alone, becomes involved in adventures at the Shake'n'Roll Dancin Hole in a search for an umbrella.
Ann Tompert, *Three Foolish Tales*, 1979
  Raccoon and Skunk attempt to trick fox out of his umbrella by telling tales of foolish animals, but Fox proves who is really foolish.
Taro Yashima, *Umbrella*, 1958
  Momo eagerly waits for a rainy day so she can use the red boots and umbrella she received for her birthday.

578

Eleanor Estes

Illustrator: Louis Slobodkin

Rufus M. (New York: Harcourt Brace, 1943)

Age range: Grades 3-6

Subject(s): Sports/Baseball; Family Life

Major character(s): Rufus Moffat, Child; Miss Wells, Teacher

Time period(s): 1940s

Locale(s): Cranberry, New England

What the book is about: Rufus is a self-reliant individual, inventive and independent as he tries to help the family out with his beans, the money he found in the ice, and his uncanny southpaw skill at baseball during World War II on the home front.

Where it's reviewed:
Times Literary Supplement, December 5, 1975, page 1460

Awards the book has won:
Newbery Honor 1944

Other books by the author:
The Curious Adventure of Jimmy McGee, 1987
The Lost Umbrella of Kim Chu, 1978
Ginger Pye, 1951
The Hundred Dresses, 1944

Other books you might like:
Avi, *Who Was That Masked Man, Anyway?*, 1992
  In the early forties when everyone else is worried about WWII, Frankie Wattleson gets in trouble because of his preoccupation with his radio programs.
Robert Burch, *Homefront Heroes*, 1974
  Describes the impact of WWII on a sixth grade class in Georgia. Originally published as *Hut School and the Wartime Home-Front Heroes*.
Judy Glassman, *The Morning Glory War*, 1990
  Jeannie, a fifth grades during WWII, supports the war effort at home and writes to a soldier overseas while enduring the dislike of her harsh teacher.
Katherine Marko, *Hang Out the Flag*, 1992
  In 1943, as she waits for her father to come home on leave, a girl in a midwestern town tries to help the war effort by looking for German spies.
Gary Paulsen, *The Cookcamp*, 1991
  During WWII, a little boy is sent to live with his grandma, a cook in a camp for workers building a road through the wilderness.

579

Eleanor Estes

Illustrator: Edward Ardizzone

The Witch Family (New York: Harcourt, 1960)

Age range: Grades 3-6

Subject(s): Witches and Witchcraft

Major character(s): Amy, Child; Clarissa, Child; Malachi, Bee

Time period(s): 1950s

Locale(s): Washington, District of Columbia

What the book is about: Amy and Clarissa love to draw pictures of witches. They banish Old Witch to the glass hill. Old Witch tries to be good, but never quite succeeds. Malachi, the magic bumblebee, guards the girls from Old Witch and her doings.

Where it's reviewed:
Growing Point, September 1975, page 2689

Other books by the author:
The Curious Adventures of Jimmy McGee, 1987
Ginger Pye, 1951
The Hundred Dresses, 1944
The Moffats, 1941

Other books you might like:
Phyllis Reid Fenner, *Princesses and Peasant Boys*, 1944
  Eighteen fairy tales including The Princess on the Glass Hill and The Sleeping Beauty in the Wood
Donna Jo Napoli, *The Magic Circle*, 1993
  After learning sorcery to become a healer, a woman is turned into a witch by evil spirits and fights their power until she meets Hansel and Gretl.
George Sand, *The Mysterious Tale of Gentle Jack and Lord Bumblebee*, 1988
  Adopted by the evil Lord Bumblebee, Jack refuses to be as wicked as the Lord and his followers and escapes to an island where only goodness is known.
Angela Sommer-Bodenburg, *The Vampire Moves In*, 1985
  Banished by his family for making friends with a human, a little vampire comes to his only friend and lives in the basement of his apartment.
Jane Yolen, *The Mermaid's Three Wisdoms*, 1978
  A mermaid who cannot speak is banished from her undersea home and sent to live as a human where she is found by a girl with a hearing impairment.

580

Jonathan Etra

Illustrator: Steve Bjorkman

Aliens for Breakfast (New York: Random, 1988)

Age range: Grades 3-5

Subject(s): Aliens; Science Fiction

Major character(s): Richard Bickerstaff, Preteen; Aric, Alien, Space Explorer; Dorf, Alien

Time period(s): 1980s

Locale(s): United States

What the book is about: Richard is eating Alien Crisp cereal when a creature climbs up the side of his bowl. Aric claims he is on a mission to wipe out cosmic troublemakers called "Dranes" and needs Richard's help in a race against time. One of the alien Denebians is masquerading as a student in Richard's class.

Where it's reviewed:
Booklist, January 15, 1989, page 870
Center for Children's Books Bulletin, December 1988, page 96

Other books by the author:
Aliens for Lunch, 1991

Other books you might like:
Bruce Coville, *My Teacher Is an Alien*, 1989
  Susan Simmons can tell that her new substitute teacher is strange, but when she catches him peeling off his face, she realizes just how strange he is.
Ken Follett, *The Power Twins*, 1990
  Uncle Grigorian, who turns out to be an alien, takes the Price Twins to the capital of the Galactic Empire.
Gery Greer, *Jason and the Aliens Down the Street*, 1991
  Jason meets Cooper Vor and Lootna, aliens who now live on Earth, and travels with them to retrieve a stolen energy crystal from a distant planet.
Andre Norton, *Star Ka'at*, 1976
  Two stray cats communicate with Jim and Elly Mae, convincing them that the cats are aliens from another planet.
G. Clifton Wisler, *The Mind Trap*, 1990
  Scott's identity as a telepathic alien from another planet may be exposed when he's imprisoned in a research institute for psychic children.

581

Margery Evernden

Illustrator: Cindy Wheeler

The Kite Song (New York: Lothrop, 1984)

Age range: Grades 6-7

Subject(s): Emotional Problems; Family Problems; Friendship

Major character(s): Jamie Hovanec, Child (disturbed); Ron Hovanec, Veteran (Vietnam); Clem Hovanec, Cousin

Time period(s): 1980s

Locale(s): Rivertson, Pennsylvania

What the book is about: Jamie has endured enough in eleven years to keep him shut up in his silence forever. When his mother is found dead, a Christmas card in a drawer gives the name of his half-brother, Ron, who refuses to let Jamie be put in a children's home and agrees to care for Jamie himself. With the help of a special education teacher, he begins to come to terms with the things that have made it difficult for him to speak and love: the teasings and beatings at school, an alcoholic father at home and the loss of his mother.

Where it's reviewed:
School Library Journal, October 1984, page 166

Other books by the author:
Of Swords and Sorcerers, 1993
The Dream Keeper, 1985

Other books you might like:
Karen Ackerman, *The Broken Boy*, 1991
  Solly recounts his friendship with a mentally disturbed boy.
Mary Downing Hahn, *The Wind Blows Backward*, 1993
  Although they share many things in common, a shy girl's attraction to a popular classmate is tempered by her fear of his moody, self-destructive side.
Susan Beth Pfeffer, *Family of Strangers*, 1992
  Abby chronicles her growing desperation in a family whose members are devoid of love, bent on self-destruction and one who always seemed perfect.
Marilyn Sachs, *What My Sister Remembered*, 1992

While visiting her sister, Beth confronts painful memories of the sudden death of her parents and the adoption of the sisters by different families.

Erika Tamar, *The Truth about Kim O'Hara*, 1992
Andy is often baffled by his girlfriend Kim's apparent coolness and rigidity until her tragic past is revealed.

582

Kathryn Ewing

Things Won't Be the Same (New York: Harcourt Brace Jovanovich, 1980)

Age range: Grades 3-5

Subject(s): Stepfamilies; Remarriage

Major character(s): Marcy, Child

Time period(s): 1980s

Locale(s): San Francisco, California

What the book is about: Marcy visits her father while her mother is honeymooning with her new husband, Bill, She gets to know her dad and enjoys the relaxed life-style and takes in interest in stamp collecting while helping in her dad's shop. When she returns to Pennsylvania and has to adjust not only to Bill, but his ten year old daughter, Carole Anne, she thinks she would rather live with her father. A realistic and sensitive portrayal.

Where it's reviewed:
Center for Children's Books Bulletin, March 1981, p 131
School Library Journal, January 1981, page 59

Other books by the author:
A Private Matter, 1975

Other books you might like:
Louise Fitzhugh, *Sport*, 1979
Eleven year old Sport lives happily with his absentminded father until his mother suddenly wants custody of him.
Kevin Henkes, *Two under Par*, 1987
When his mother's new marriage takes them into a new household, Wedge struggles with his feelings of dislike for his stepfather.
Mary Reeves Mahoney, *The Hurry-Up Summer*, 1987
Twelve year old Letty resents her father's new girlfriend and tries to grow up in a hurry to keep him from remarrying.
Jean Davies Okimoto, *It's Just Too Much*, 1980
When her mother remarries, twelve year old Cynthia faces new stepbrothers and junior high at the same time.
Bonnie Pryor, *Rats, Spiders and Love*, 1986
Samantha schemes to prevent her mother's remarriage.

F

583

Margery Facklam

Trouble with Mothers (New York: Clarion, 1989)

Age range: Grades 5-6

Subject(s): Censorship; Mothers and Sons

Major character(s): Luke Troy, Teenager; Maggie Troy, Child; Martha Troy, Writer, Teacher

Time period(s): 1980s

Locale(s): United States

What the book is about: What is a boy to do when his teacher-mother's historical novel, *The Passionate Pirate*, is given as an example of "pornography" that should be banned from schools and libraries? Matters worsen when Luke gets the assignment to interview Major Madison, a crusader who is out to censor the book.

Where it's reviewed:
Booklist, March 1, 1989, page 1190
School Library Journal, May 1989, page 104

Other books by the author:
Do Not Disturb, 1989
Partners for Life, 1989
Spare Parts for People, 1988

Other books you might like:
Nat Hentoff, *The Day They Came to Arrest the Book*, 1982
    Students and faculty become embroiled in a censorship case over Huckleberry Finn.
William Jay Jacobs, *Mother, Aunt Susan and Me*, 1979
    Harriot highlights the efforts of her mother and her mother's friend (Susan B. Anthony) in the early fight for the rights of women.
Janice Marriott, *Letters to Lesley*, 1991
    Henry plots to solve all of his problems by marrying off his eccentric mother.
Betty Miles, *Maudie and Me and the Dirty Book*, 1980
    Kate's ordinary life in a small Massachusetts town heats up when she becomes involved in an inter-school reading project.
Lisa Orr, *Censorship: Opposing Viewpoints*, 1990
    Censorship, freedom of speech, critical thinking skill activities and a list of organizations to contact. (Non-ficton)

584

Norma Farber

Illustrator: Tomi De Paola

Six Impossible Things Before Breakfast (Reading, MA: Addison-Wesley, 1977)

Age range: Grades 2-4

Subject(s): Fantasy; Wishes

Major character(s): Mrs. Molly Manning, Householder

Time period(s): 1970s

Locale(s): New York

What the book is about: A forgotten batch of dough rises to the sky; a woman blows bubbles that never break but fill her house; riding a unicorn; a lady who leaves her shopping bag on the bus; a royal father with a drooping daugher all fill out this folk-like tale.

Where it's reviewed:
Center for Children's Books Bulletin, April 1977, page 123
Hornbook, June 1977, page 307
School Library Journal, April 1977, page 66

Other books by the author:
Return of the Shadows, 1992
All Those Mothers at the Manger, 1985
How to Ride a Tiger, 1983
As I Was Crossing Boston Common, 1975

Other books you might like:
Cynthia Birrer, *The Lady and the Unicorn*, 1987
    A princess wandering on an estate discovers that she is the only one with the ability to see a lonely unicorn and break the spell enchanting it.
Carol Chapman, *Barney Bipple's Magic Dandelion*, 1977
    Barney Bipple doesn't heed Miss Merkle's suggestion concerning complicated wishes until it is almost too late.
Bruce Coville, *Sarah's Unicorn*, 1985
    Although she tries to keep her friendship with Oakhorn a secret, Sarah's wicked aunt finds out and is determined to rob the unicorn of his magic.
Margaret Hillert, *A Friend for Dear Dragon*, 1985
    A boy and his pet dragon make friends with their new neighbors, a girl and her unicorn.
Janet Lorimer, *The Biggest Bubble in the World*, 1982
    Harvey and Jeremy blow a hugh sticky bubble that bounces through town picking up everything in its path.

585

Carol J. Farley

Illustrator: Tom Newsom

The Case of the Vanishing Villain (New York: Avon, 1986)

Age range: Grades 5-6

Subject(s): Mystery and Detective Stories; Sisters; Gifted Children

Major character(s): Felice Jennifer "Flee Jay" Saylor, Detective; Clarice Saylor, Child (gifted); Norris Rawlings, Convict

Time period(s): 1980s

Locale(s): Michigan

What the book is about: Twelve year old Flee Jay is disgusted because her ten year old sister, Clarice, gets all the credit for solving a mystery when they are trapped aboard a ferry on Lake Michigan with an escaped convict, so she details the whole story from her point of view. An exciting mystery with a very vivid portrayal of living with a younger sister who is so bright and beautiful that it is hard to find a spot outside her shadow.

Where it's reviewed:
School Library Journal, November 1986, page 88

Other books by the author:
The Case of the Lost Lookalike, 1988
Mystery of the Melted Diamonds, 1986
Mystery in the Ravine, 1976
Mystery of the Fog Man, 1966

Other books you might like:
Franklin W. Dixon, *The Secret of Wildcat Swamp*, 1969
  An archeological expedition in the West turns into a desperate attempt to capture robbers and an escaped convict. A Hardy Boys Mystery.
Dayton O. Hyde, *Island of the Loons*, 1984
  During the year he is held prisoner on an uninhabited island, a boy watches his captor change from a desperate criminal to a gentler man.
Hope Dahle Jordan, *Danger at Loud Lake*, 1974
  A girl spending her seventeenth summer at a lake deepens her relationship with a retarded cousin and becomes involved with an escaped convict.
C.L.G. Martin, *Day of Darkness, Day of Light*, 1989
  Daniel helps to save his town of Menominee, Michigan, from a devastating fire that swept through the western Great Lakes states on October 7, 1871.
Gloria Whelan, *The Secret Keeper*, 1990
  Sixteen year old Ali comes face to face with murder and kidnapping during what promised to be a pleasant summer on Lake Michgan.

586

Carol J. Farley

Illustrator: Lynn Sweat

The Garden Is Doing Fine (New York: Atheneum, 1975)

Age range: Grades 4-6

Subject(s): Family Life; Death

Major character(s): Corrie Sheldon, Babysitter; Lewie, Babysitter; Joseph Sheldon, Parent

Time period(s): 1940s (1945)

Locale(s): Pointer, Michigan

What the book is about: Corrie refuses to believe that her father is dying until she realizes that no matter what happens, a part of him will always live in her. She struggles with her resentment, guilt and regrets.

Where it's reviewed:
Horn Book, October 1975, page 462
School Library Journal, September 1975, page 118

Awards the book has won:
Golden Kite Award 1975

Other books by the author:
Mystery of the Melted Diamonds, 1986
Twilight Waves, 1981
Ms. Isabel Cornell, Herself, 1980
Loosen Your Ears, 1977

Other books you might like:
Tatyana Bylinsky, *Before the Wildflowers Bloom*, 1989
  Carm and her family learn to cope after the death of Papa in a tragic coal mine accident.
Vera Cleaver, *Belle Pruitt*, 1988
  When her adored baby brother dies of pneumonia, Belle is left to cope with the devastating effects on her family.
Barbara Frisbie Juneau, *Sad but OK: My Daddy Died Today*, 1988
  Through the eyes of her nine year old daughter, the author shares the events in her family when her husband was faced with terminal brain cancer.
Karin Lorentzen, *Lanky Longlegs*, 1982
  Di must face, along with her parents, the knowledge that her small brother will not live much longer.
Mary Pope Osborne, *Run, Run as Fast as You Can*, 1982
  Hallie worries about popularity and faces an unexpected tragedy when her family moves to Virginia.

587

Walter Farley

Illustrator: Keith Ward

The Black Stallion (New York: Random, 1941)

Age range: Grades 4-7

Subject(s): Animals/Horses; Horse Racing; Shipwrecks

Major character(s): Alec Ramsey, Child; Henry Dailey, Horse Trainer

Time period(s): 1940s

Locale(s): New York; At Sea

What the book is about: Homeward bound from India aboard the Steamer Drake, Alec is bored until he discovers a wild black stallion aboard. Slowly, one sugar cube at a time, Alec tries to befriend the Black, and when they are shipwrecked, he and the still very wild stallion survive together. Alec finally returns home with the Black and with the help of Henry Daily, prepares the Black to race.

Where it's reviewed:
Growing Point, November 1978, page 3406

Times Educational Supplement, July 11, 1980, page 28
Teacher, May 1978, page 109

Other books by the author:
The Young Black Stallion, 1989
The Black Stallion Legend, 1983
Man O' War, 1962
The Island Stallion, 1948

Other books you might like:
Joan Aiken, *Bridle the Wind,* 1983
    After being interupted by a shipwreck, amnesia, and a stay
    in a French monastery, Felix's journey to Spain continues in
    the company of a boy he saved.
Eth Clifford, *The Curse of the Moonraker: A Tale of Survival,*
1977
    The survivors of a strange whipwreck in the Auckland Islands
    fight for survival under seemingly hopeless conditions.
Daniel Defoe, *Robinson Crusoe,* 1983
    In the 1600s, an Englishman becomes the sole survivor of a
    shipwreck and lives for nearly thirty years on a deserted
    island.
Helen Griffith, *Blackface Stallion,* 1980
    Follows the life of a wild horse living in the desert of northern
    Mexico as he grows from a foal to a magnificent stallion with
    a herd of his own.
Betty Levin, *Put on My Crown,* 1985
    Cast ashore on a bleak island, survivors of a shipwreck find
    the islanders' treatment of them kind, yet strange and a little
    frightening.

588

Walter Farley

Black Stallion Mystery (New York: Random, 1957)

Age range: Grades 4-7

Subject(s): Animals/Horses; Mystery and Detective Stories

Major character(s): Alec Ramsey, Teenager, Equestrian;
Henry Dailey, Horse Trainer

Time period(s): 1950s

Locale(s): United States

What the book is about: After ''The Black'' wins the Brooklyn Handicap Race, Alec and Henry try to solve the mystery of
three yearlings from Spain who have the same confirmation as
The Black. Alec encounters an old friend, Tabari, who seeks
revenge on the horse who killed her father. Reviews of this
volume in the 50s were quite critical of the pacing and melodrama, but fans of Alec and the stallion will not care.

Where it's reviewed:
Kirkus Reviews, July 15, 1957, page 487
Christian Science Monitor, November 7, 1957, page 13

Other books by the author:
The Black Stallion Legend, 1983
The Black Stallion Challenged, 1964
The Black Stallion and Flame, 1960
The Horse-Tamer, 1958

Other books you might like:
Claire Birch, *High Stakes,* 1992
    Lucy and Liz help solve a mystery at the racetrack in Sara-
    toga Springs.
Ann Sharpless Bond, *Adam and Noah and the Cops,* 1983

Adam and Noah become involved with a runaway horse,
drug smugglers, and a woman about to give birth on top of a
twenty story building.
Margaret Goff Clark, *Mystery Horse,* 1972
    The peaceful Indian reservation is shattered by the sighting
    of a ghost horse just after a real horse is stolen.
Lynn Hall, *The Mystery of Pony Hollow,* 1992
    While exploring the family's new farm, Sarah stumbles upon
    a skeleton and a supernatural mystery, involving the ponies
    who lived there before.
Michael Hardcastle, *Kickback,* 1989
    Ros is determined to restore her reputation and find out what
    happened to the prize horse that disappeared while under
    her care.

589

Walter Farley

Illustrator: James Schucker

Little Black, a Pony (New York: Random, 1961)

Age range: Grades 1-3

Subject(s): Animals/Horses

Major character(s): Little Black, Horse; Big Red, Horse

Time period(s): Indeterminate

Locale(s): United States

What the book is about: The story of a boy and a pony,
both anxious to grow up. As hard as he tries, Little Black cannot
do everything that Big Red does.

Other books by the author:
Great Dane Thor, 1966
The Horse-Tamer, 1958
Blood Bay Colt, 1950
The Black Stallion, 1951

Other books you might like:
C.W. Anderson, *Blaze and the Mountain Lion,* 1993
    While riding through open country near his family's ranch
    house, Billy and his pony, Blaze, come across a dangerous
    mountain lion.
Eleanor Coerr, *Chang's Paper Pony,* 1988
    During the 1850s gold rush, Chang, the son of Chinese
    immigrants, wants a pony but cannot afford one until his
    friend, Big Pete, finds a solution.
Lynn Hall, *Mrs. Portree's Pony,* 1986
    Addie, a foster child, seeks comfort in the company of a
    pony and begins an enriching relationship with his owner
    who has lost her own daughter.
K.M. Peyton, *Poor Badger,* 1990
    Having become devoted to a pony who is being mistreated
    Ros decides to steal him in the night and hide him in a safe
    place.
Ann Shaffer, *The Camel Express,* 1989
    As part of an experiment in 1860, a camel fills in for a
    wounded pony on a Pony Express route.

590

Susan Clement Farrar

Illustrator: Ruth Sanderson

Samantha on Stage (New York: Dial, 1979)

Age range: Grades 3-6

Subject(s): Ballet; Friendship; Jealousy

Major character(s): Samantha, Preteen, Dancer

Time period(s): 1970s

Locale(s): Australia

What the book is about: Samantha has always been the best in her ballet class. When she sees the new Russian girl dance, she begins to wonder who will get the lead in the Nutcracker ballet, and it affects her attempts to make friends with the new girl.

Where it's reviewed:
Center for Children's Books Bulletin, September 1979, page 6
School Library Journal, April 1979, page 54

Awards the book has won:
West Australian Young Readers Book Award 1983

Other books you might like:
Mirian Cohen, *Born to Dance Samba*, 1984
  A girl who has spent her life wishing to be chosen Carnival Queen must cope with the jealousy incurred by a new girl who is her only competitor.
Carolyn Keene, *The Scarlet Slipper Mystery*, 1974
  Nancy Drew comes to the aid of the owners of a dancing school when they receive death threats.
Florence McNeil, *Miss Page and Me*, 1982
  Anxious to prove that she can dance, Jane is devastated when the new gym teacher won't let her dance in the school play.
Louis Sacher, *Johnny's in the Basement*, 1990
  Johnny's parents decide that he is old enough for dancing lessons and too old to collect bottle caps anymore.
Ellen Switzer, *The Nutcracker: A Story and a Ballet*, 1985
  Describes the Tchaikovsky ballet, the Hoffman story on which it was based, with photographs and interviews with members of the New York City Ballet.

591

Paula Kurzband Feder

Illustrator: Lillian Hoban

Where Does the Teacher Live? (New York: Dutton, 1979)

Age range: Grades 1-2

Subject(s): Teachers; Schools

Major character(s): Alba, Child; Nancy, Child; Mrs. Greengrass, Teacher

Time period(s): 1970s

Locale(s): United States

What the book is about: Nancy, Willie and Alba try to find out where their teacher lives. They hide behind a bush after school and sure enough, she comes out, so they decide she must not live at school. They think she gets on a bus, but she actually walked behind it. The next day, she takes a cab, then rides in a friend's car. The day the find where she really lives is the best day of all, because they get to ride in an ice cream truck with Mrs. Greengrass and her uncle.

Where it's reviewed:
Booklist, May 15, 1979, page 1445

Center for Children's Books Bulletin, September 1979, page 6
Kirkus, March 1, 1979, page 261

Other books by the author:
Did You Lose the Car Again?, 1991

Other books you might like:
Eve Bunting, *Our Teacher's Having a Baby*, 1992
  During first grade teacher Mrs. Neal's pregnancy, her class writes letters to the baby, thinks up possible names, and designs a baby room.
Andrew Clements, *Billy and the Bad Teacher*, 1992
  Billy lists the things he dislikes about his teacher, but when he thinks about what his new teacher should be like, he makes an interesting discovery.
Miriam Cohen, *See You in Second Grade!*, 1989
  At a year-end beach picnic, Anna Maria, Jim, and the others know they will miss first grade and their teacher, but still look forward to second grade.
Patricia Reilly Giff, *Purple Climbing Days*, 1985
  With the help of the meanest substitute teacher in the whole school, Richard "Beast" Best learns a lesson about fear.
Bernice Myers, *It Happens to Everyone*, 1990
  Michael and his mother, a teacher, nervously prepare for the first day of school.

592

Carol Fenner

Randall's Wall (New York: Macmillan, 1991)

Age range: Grades 5-8

Subject(s): Gifted Children; Socially Handicapped; Artists and Art

Major character(s): Randall Lord, Preteen; Jane, Classmate

Time period(s): 1990s

Locale(s): United States

What the book is about: The rest of the fifth grade won't have anything to do with Randall Lord. He seems different, he smells, he has even had head lice. A classmate, Jean, takes him home for a bath and a meal. His father is abusive, his mother terrified, the family has no bathtub or running water. When Randall's artistic abilities are discovered, he finds a path out of hell and the upbeat ending is cheering, if not entirely believable.

Where it's reviewed:
Booklist, April 1, 1991, page 1567
Horn Book, July/August, 1991, page 455

Other books by the author:
Summer of Horses, 1989
The Skates of Uncle Richard, 1978
Gorilla Gorilla, 1973
Christmas Tree on the Mountain, 1966

Other books you might like:
Carole S. Adler, *Fly Free*, 1984
  Shari, abused at home by a mother who resents her, is befriended by a neighbor who shares her love of birds and the outdoors.
Robbie Branscum, *The Girl*, 1986
  Left with her four brothers and sisters in the care of a cruel grandmother who resents their existence, an 11 year old girl struggles for survival.

Kaye Gibbons, *Ellen Foster*, 1987
  Having suffered abuse and misfortune for much of her life, a young child searches for a better life and finally gets a break in a loving home.
Michelle Magorian, *Good Night, Mr. Tom*, 1981
  A battered child learns to embrace life when he is adopted by an old man in the English countryside during WWII.
Doris Buchanan Smith, *Tough Chauncey*, 1974
  Abused by his grandfather and neglected by his mother, a teen sees running away as the only solution until a friend offers an alternative.

593

Carol Fenner

Illustrator: Carol Forberg

The Skates of Uncle Richard (New York: Random House, 1978)

Age range: Grades 3-4

Subject(s): African Americans; Sports/Ice Skating

Major character(s): Marsha, Child; Richard, Relative (uncle)

Time period(s): 1970s

Locale(s): United States

What the book is about: When she was six years old, Marsha first saw skaters on television. Now nine, she has seen her first black skater and longs for her own skates. She gets Uncle Richard's old hockey skates for Christmas. They are ugly, but they show that Uncle Richard really understands her dream.

Where it's reviewed:
Horn Book, April 1979, page 191
Kirkus Reviews, January 15, 1979, page 65

Other books by the author:
Randall's Wall, 1991
A Summer of Horses, 1989
Ice Skates!, 1978
Tigers in the Cellar, 1963

Other books you might like:
Jim Arnosky, *Mouse Writing*, 1983
  A pair of skating mice trace out the letters of the cursive alphabet on the ice.
Louise Betts, *Hans Brinker*, 1988
  A short version of the famous tale of a Dutch boy and girl who work to find a doctor for their father and win a skating competition.
Leonard Kessler, *Old Turtle's Winter Games*, 1983
  A group of animals organize winter games and compete in such events as sled races, skating, skiing and ice hockey.
Ann M. Martin, *Karen's Roller Skates*, 1988
  When Karen falls down on her new roller skates, she breaks her wrist. Will she be able to find someone famous to sign her cast?
L.E. Wolfe, *The Case of the Screaming Skates and Other Mysteries*, 1991
  Jack B. Quick and his detective squad investigate the sabotage of a skating rink and other sports related mysteries.

594

Edward Fenton

Phantom of Walkaway Hill (Garden City, New York: Doubleday, 1961)

Age range: Grades 4-6

Subject(s): Mystery and Detective Stories; Animals/Dogs; Family Life

Major character(s): James Gregory Smith Jr., Child; Amanda Little, Writer (poet)

Time period(s): 1960s

Locale(s): Walkaway Hill, New York

What the book is about: James receives a letter from his friends, Amanda and Obie, telling him about a mystery to be solved. They travel to join James, and spend time enjoying the snow in the country, play games about the Abominable Snowman, and have lots of fun in the process of solving the mystery. They are very surprised when they learn the true identity of the "phantom."

Where it's reviewed:
Booklist, April 15, 1961, page 526
Horn Book, August 1961, page 343

Other books by the author:
Aleko's Island, 1948
Fierce John, 1959
Penny Candy, 1970
Refugee Summer, 1982

Other books you might like:
David Wood, *Phantom Killer of the Flying M*, 1971
  David and his sister search southwestern Colorado for a mysterious phantom that is killing livestock.
Betty Ren Wright, *The Pike River Phantom*, 1988
  Rachel and Charlie become linked with a mad ghost.
Alexandra Whitaker, *Dream Sister*, 1986
  Ann is troubled by a recurring dream in which a phantom sister tries to communicate with her.
Donna Hill, *Eerie Animals*, 1983
  Seven stories of strange creatures, including a mind-reading dog, a supernatural squirrel, and a ghostly cat.
Freeman H. Hubbard, *Train That Never Came Back*, 1952
  Eight railroad stories, all including strange or mysterious happenings.

595

Alane Ferguson

Cricket and the Crackerbox Kid (New York: Bradbury, 1990)

Age range: Grades 5-6

Subject(s): Animals/Dogs; Schools; Friendship

Major character(s): Cricket, Child; Dominic, Child

Time period(s): 1990s

Locale(s): United States

What the book is about: Rich-kid Cricket thinks she has found a friend in Dominic, who lives in low-income housing called crackerboxes, until they quarrel over the ownership of a dog. Their school classroom becomes the court room to decide the matter.

Where it's reviewed:
Booklist, March 15, 1990, page 1445
School Library Journal, March 1990, page 217

Other books by the author:
The Practical Joke War, 1991
Show Me the Evidence, 1989

Other books you might like:
Joan Davenport Carris, *The Greatest Idea Ever*, 1990
   Gus's ideas get him into trouble as he tries to train his new dog and battle his enemy, Nanny Vincent.
Sandi Barrett Ruch, *Junkyard Dog*, 1990
   Follows the exciting adventures of Toad and mean old Slobber, the junkyard dog, as they form a friendship and try to find a home.
Louis Sacher, *Dogs Don't Tell Jokes*, 1991
   Gary, ''the Goon,'' tries to change his clowning image and make new friends at school.
Janice Lee Smith, *It's Not Easy Being George*, 1989
   Zany episodes in the life of Adam Joshua and his ''ordinary'' dog, George.
Judie Wolkoff, *In a Pig's Eye*, 1986
   Best friends Maisie and Glenda fight and make up through everything from a dog show to editing their own newspaper.

596

Rachel Field

Calico Bush (New York: Macmillan, 1931)

Age range: Grades 5-7

Subject(s): Frontier and Pioneer Life

Major character(s): Marguerite ''Maggie'' Ledoux, Servant; Dolly Sargent, Wealthy

Time period(s): 1740s (1743)

Locale(s): Maine

What the book is about: The story of a young French girl ''bound out'' in service in pioneer America. Calico Bush is the name given to the low-growing sheep laurel with its deep pink blossoms. Marguerite adapts to her new life as the calico bush did to its rugged terrain, growing hardy, resourceful, and beautiful.

Where it's reviewed:
Booklist, November 1, 1966, page 328
Hornbook, December 1966, page 716
Library Journal, November 15, 1966, page 577

Awards the book has won:
Newbery Honor 1931

Other books by the author:
Poems, 1957
Prayer for a Child, 1944
Hitty: Her First Hundred Years, 1930

Other books you might like:
Clyde Robert Bulla, *Charlie's House*, 1983
   A poor, friendless English boy, shipped to America as an indentured servant, runs away from his cruel master and dreams of building his own house.
Deborah H. De Ford, *An Enemy Among Them*, 1987
   Spending time with a German American family after the Revolutionary War causes a Hessian soldier to question his loyalty to his king.

Paul Fleischman, *Saturnalia*, 1990
   In 1680s Boston William, a Narraganset Indian, is productive as a printer's apprentice, but is anxious to make a connection with his Indian heritage.
Jan O'Donnell Klaveness, *The Griffin Legacy*, 1983
   Amy becomes involved with Lucy Griffin's spirit and begins a quest for silver stolen from the church by Lucy's lover during the American Revolution.
Ruth Nelson Moore, *Distant Thunder*, 1991
   When the American Revolution breaks out, Kate and her friends demonstrate how peaceful people can help alleviate the suffering brought on by war.

597

Rachel Field

Illustrator: Dorothy P. Lathrop

Hitty: Her First Hundred Years (New York: Macmillan, 1929)

Age range: Grades 3-6

Subject(s): Dolls and Dollhouses

Major character(s): Hitty, Toy (doll); Phoebe Preble, Child; Clarissa Pryce, Child

Time period(s): 19th century

Locale(s): Maine; Bombay, India; Philadelphia, Pennsylvania

What the book is about: Hitty was carved from mountain ash wood over a hundred years ago. She travels from Maine to the South Seas and India before returning to America. She lives through many experiences on land and sea with charm and a sturdy spirit.

Where it's reviewed:
Booklist, December 29, page 125
Saturday Review of Literature, November 16, 1929, page 392

Awards the book has won:
Newbery Medal 1930

Other books by the author:
American Folk and Fairy Tales, 1929
Pocket Handkerchief Park, 1929

Other books you might like:
Jane Gardam, *Through the Dolls' House Door*, 1987
   Two dolls amuse themselves by telling stories about their exciting pasts.
Sylvia Cassedy, *Lucie Babbidge's House*, 1989
   Orphan Lucie creates a secret life for herself with a dollhouse full of dolls.
Catherine Dexter, *The Oracle Doll*, 1988
   Three youngsters become the guardians of a talking doll that is actually the reincarnated Oracle of Delphi.
Marjorie Stover, *When the Dolls Woke*, 1985
   Long neglected dolls come awake and help their new owner find a treasure hidden in their dollhouse.
Carolyn Sherwin Bailey, *Miss Hickory*, 1946
   A country doll made of an applewood twig with a hickory nut for a head has many adventures.

| 598 |

Julia Fields

Illustrator: Jerry Pinkney

The Green Lion of Zion Street (New York: Macmillan, 1988)

Age range: Grades 2-3

Subject(s): School Buses; Monuments

Time period(s): 1980s

Locale(s): United States

What the book is about: A group of children waiting for the school bus on a cold, foggy morning imagine that the stone lion statue in a nearby park has come alive and is about to attack them. The older children tease and scare the younger kids.

Where it's reviewed:
Horn Book, July/August 1988, page 478
School Library Journal, May 1988, page 96

Other books you might like:
Kay Chorao, *Cathedral Mouse*, 1988
  Little Mouse is befriended by a stone carver at a cathedral.
Donald Crews, *School Bus*, 1984
  Follows the progress of school buses as they take children to school and bring them home again.
Sharon Phillips Denslow, *Bus Riders*, 1993
  When their regular bus driver gets sick, Warren, Louise and the other bus riders must endure a string of substitute drivers.
Ursula Le Guin, *Fire and Stone*, 1989
  When the dragon comes swooping down with its tongue of flickering fire, only Min and Podo have the foresight to feed it what it seems to want.
Cara Reichel, *A Stone Promise*, 1991
  A young stonecutter vows to create a magnificent statue for an poor village whose inhabitants can no longer see beauty in anything around them.

| 599 |

Dale Fife

Destination Unknown (New York: Dutton, 1981)

Age range: Grades 5-8

Subject(s): Sea Stories; World War II

Major character(s): Jon, Preteen

Time period(s): 1940s

Locale(s): Atlantic Ocean

What the book is about: During WWII, Jon stows away on a Norweigian fishing ship that is crossing the Atlantic, and shares the harrowing adventures of the other occupants as they head for North America.

Where it's reviewed:
Booklist, February 1, 1982, page 706
Hornbook, February 1982, page 41
School Library Journal, November 1981, page 90

Other books by the author:
The Sesame Seed Snatchers, 1983
North of Danger, 1978
Ride the Crooked Wind, 1973

What's New Lincoln?, 1970

Other books you might like:
Richard Humble, *U-Boats*, 1990
  A brief history of German submarine warfare during WWII and the measures taken by the Allies to combat the U-Boats.
Ruth Kluger, *The Secret Ship*, 1978
  The author relates the tremendous obstacles involved in secretly and illegally transporting European Jews by sea to Palestine to escape the nazis.
Ruthanne Lum McCunn, *Sole Survivor*, 1985
  Biography of Lim Poon, the sole survivor of a disaster at sea during World War II in the Atlantic.
Bernhard Rogge, *The German Raider* **Atlantis**, 1956
  Captain Rogge's own story of his two years' voyage on the *Atlantis* during WWII.
Eva-Lis Wuorio, *To Fight in Silence*, 1973
  During the Nazi occupation of Denmark, a young Norwegian joins with his Danish cousins in a secret plan to keep Jews out of the concentration camps.

| 600 |

Dale Fife

Illustrator: Joan Drescher

Follow That Ghost! (New York: Dutton, 1979)

Age range: Grades 2-4

Subject(s): Ghosts; Mystery and Detective Stories

Major character(s): Chuck, Detective, Child; Jason, Detective, Child; Glory, Client, Child

Time period(s): 1980s

Locale(s): United States

What the book is about: Chuck and Jason, hired by their neighbor, Glory, to solve the case of a ghost that is bothering her, take the case with payment promised in fudge. After many days of sleuthing and collecting all the clues, they discover that a tapping, troublesome ghost has a very common explanation.

Where it's reviewed:
Center for Children's Books Bulletin, April 1980, page 150
Kirkus Reviews, February 15, 1980, page 215
School Library Journal, March 1980, page 120

Other books by the author:
The Sesame Seed Snatchers, 1983
Destination Unknown, 1981
North of Danger, 1978
Ride the Crooked Wind, 1973

Other books you might like:
Constance Hiser, *Ghosts in Fourth Grade*, 1991
  James and his friends turn the old Hathaway house into a haunted house to scare Mean Mitchell, the class bully, on Halloween night.
Jennifer Jordan, *Ghosts and Witches*, 1991
  Spooky the Teapot Ghost, Sizzle the Grumpy Dragon, Silly Tilly Witch and Bigwig's Bedtime.
Grace Maccarone, *The Ghost on the Hill*, 1990
  Joey, a third grader, goes on a class trip to state forest where he secretly searches for the Great Spirit of the Wannatuck tribe.
John Rae, *The Third Twin: A Ghost Story*, 1980

Shamus and his twin brother become involved with a host of unhappy ghosts during the night the boys spend locked in Westminster Abbey.

Nancy K. Robinson, *The Ghost of Whispering Rock*, 1992
While spending the summer at her family's cabin in the woods, Amy copes with the visit of the bored and spoiled Erika by inventing a ghost story.

601

Dale Fife

Who's in Charge of Lincoln? (New York: Coward-McCann, 1965)

Age range: Grades 2-3

Subject(s): African Americans

Major character(s): Lincoln Farmer, Child

Time period(s): 1960s

Locale(s): New York

What the book is about: Eight year old Lincoln is asked by a stranger to carry his "lunch" to the subway corner. When he discovers the bag contains money, he takes the train to Washington where his older sister can help him decide what to do with it. Lincoln is able to return home before he is missed.

Where it's reviewed:
Center for Children's Books Bulletin, July/August 1965, page 160
Kirkus Reviews, April 15, 1965, page 433

Other books by the author:
The Empty Lot, 1991
Destination Unknown, 1981
Follow That Ghost!, 1979
The Fish in the Castle, 1965

Other books you might like:
Denise Burden-Patmon, *Imani's Gift at Kwanzaa*, 1992
An Afro-American girl learns the real meaning of Kwanzaa.
Vivian Church, *Colors Around Me*, 1971
Explains the meaning of the words "Black," "Negro," and "Afro-American," and describes the varied hues a Black child can be.
Margo Humphrey, *The River That Gave Gifts*, 1987
Four children each make their own special gift to give the beloved elderly women of the town.
Mildred Pitts Walter, *Two and Too Much*, 1990
Seven year old Brandon's attempt to take care of his two year old sister Gina results in one disaster after another.
Catherine Stock, *Secret Valentine*, 1991
A child makes valentines for her family and then adds a special name to her list. She receives a secret valentine in return.

602

Charles J. Finger, Author/Illustrator

Tales from Silver Lands (Garden City, NY: Doubleday, 1924)

Age range: Grades 6 and Up

Subject(s): Folk Tales

Time period(s): Indeterminate Past

Locale(s): South America

What the book is about: 19 legendary tales from the South American Indians. The stories are about jungle animals, fairies, giants, earth people, witches, mirrors and star maidens.

Where it's reviewed:
Booklist, December 24, 1924,
Saturday Review of Literature, December 13, 1924, page 380

Awards the book has won:
Newbery Medal 1925

Other books by the author:
Bushrangers, 1924
Courageous Companions, 1929
Highwaymen, 1924
In Lawless Lands, 1924

Other books you might like:
Flora, *Feathers like a Rainbow*, 1989
Drab birds in the Amazon Forest all decide to steal colors from the hummingbird.
Sigmund A. Levine, *Indian Corn and Other Gifts*, 1974
Facts, myths, legends and superstitions about corn.
Elsie Spicer Eells, *Tales From the Amazon*, 1958
Tales and legends from the Indians of Brazil and other South American countries.
Joanna Troughton, *How the Birds Changed Their Feathers*, 1986
Turning into a great water snake when he puts some colorful beads around his neck, a young boy terrorizes the Indinas until he is killed by the birds.

603

Winifred Finlay

Danger at Black Dyke (New York: Phillips, 1968)

Age range: Grades 6 and Up

Subject(s): Mystery and Detective Stories

Major character(s): Geordie Bickerton, Preteen; Tim Charlton, Preteen; Hart "Bud" Riley, Fugitive

Time period(s): 1960s

Locale(s): Northumberland, England

What the book is about: Using their knowledge of Hadrian's wall in Northumberland, three youngsters hide a mysterious man whom they later discover was a potential pawn for an unsuccessful Latin American revolution. Their efforts to help the young American frustrate the plans of the strangers and lead them into both hilarity and danger.

Where it's reviewed:
Horn Book, April 1969, page 177
Library Journal, February 15, 1969, page 883

Awards the book has won:
Edgar Allan Poe Award 1970

Other books you might like:
John Bellaris, *The Secret of the Underground Room*, 1990
When Father Higgins disappears, Johnny and Professor Childermass discover clues which lead them to England and a long-dead knight.
Jane Louise Curry, *Ghost Lane*, 1979

Three children in an English village face danger as they track down burglers in a strange old house.

Barbara Constance Freeman, *The Other Face*, 1975
  In the long line of distinctive Dovewood faces, another face occasionally appears. Betony has that other face and unlocks its mystery.

Gail Hamilton, *A Candle to the Devil*, 1975
  The quiet seaport town in Cornwall seems peaceful until a painting is stolen and Daphne senses hate and fear all around her.

Philip Turner, *The Grange at High Force*, 1967
  3 English boys and a retired admiral rescue an eccentric old neighbor from a blizzard and solve the mystery of a long-missing Norman church statue.

| 604 |

Ann Finlayson

Illustrator: W.T. Mars

Greenhorn on the Frontier (New York: Warne, 1974)

Age range: Grades 5-8

Subject(s): Frontier and Pioneer Life

Major character(s): Harry Warrilow, Settler; Sukey Warrilow, Settler; John Penn, Settler

Time period(s): 1760s

Locale(s): Pennsylvania, American Colonies

What the book is about: Just before the American Revolution, an English brother and sister walk through the forests of Pennsylvania to the land that Harry has bought from John Penn. In Pittsburgh, they meet McBain, who falls in love with Sukey. The land struggle between Virginia and Pennsylvania is a little-studied part of our Revolutionary history.

Where it's reviewed:
Center for Children's Books Bulletin, October 1974
Kirkus Reviews, June 1, 1974, page 587

Other books by the author:
Silver Bullet, 1978
House Cat, 1974
Rebecca's War, 1972
Redcoat in Boston, 1971

Other books you might like:
Patricia Beatty, *Me, California Perkins*, 1968
  Apalled by conditions in the silvermining town, problems occur between Mr. and Mrs. Perkins, until their daughter's needs reconcile them.
Ann Nolan Clark, *All This Wild Land*, 1976
  Arriving in Minnesota in the late 1800s, with plans to homestead, a Finnish family is faced with the problems of starting a new life.
James Lincoln Collier, *The Bloody Country*, 1976
  In the mid-18th century, a family moves from Connecticut to Pennsylvania and becomes involved in the property conflict between the two states.
Stig Ericson, *Dan Henry in the Wild West*, 1976
  A young Swede who arrives in Minnesota hoping to homestead yields to the call of the West and sets out to seek his fortune.
Jane Flory, *The Golden Venture*, 1976

Determined to accompany her father to the California gold fields, a young girl stows away in a westward bound wagon.

| 605 |

Dorothy Canfield Fisher

Understood Betsy (New York: Hearst Corporation, 1917)

Age range: Grades 5-6

Subject(s): Country Life; Orphans

Major character(s): Elizabeth Ann ''Betsy'', Orphan

Time period(s): 1900s (1906)

Locale(s): Vermont

What the book is about: Elizabeth Ann is sent to Vermont to live with distant relatives. There are lots of new experiences in store for her and suddenly, she realizes she has become a healthier, happier girl with a new name and a new pleasure in being alive.

Where it's reviewed:
Booklist, May 15, 1972, page 823
Hornbook, October 1979, page 558
Publisher's Weekly, January 17, 1972, page 59

Other books by the author:
Twenty Grand Short Stories, 1967
Paul Revere and the Minute Men, 1950

Other books you might like:
Katharine Bacon, *Shadow and Light*, 1987
  Emma is devastated to learn that her grandmother is terminally ill and wants Emma to help her live her last month in peace and dignity.
Barbara Dana, *Crazy Eights*, 1978
  Sent to North Woods School in Vermont by a juvenile court judge, fourteen year old Thelma struggles to define her identity and meaning in life.
Marilyn Cram Donahue, *Straight Along a Crooked Road*, 1985
  As her family travels from Vermont to California in the early 1850s, Luanna learns to accept life for what it brings, no matter where.
Marion Walker Doren, *Nell of Blue Harbor*, 1990
  Nell is forced to grow up quickly when she moves from a Vermont commune to the real world with parents not yet ready to accept responsibility.
Robert Newton Peck, *Kirk's Law*, 1981
  A rugged life style in the Vermont woods with a feisty old hunter called Wishbone Kirk develops the character of a fifteen year old boy.

| 606 |

Leonard Everett Fisher, Author/Illustrator

The Warlock of Westfall (Garden City, NY: Doubleday, 1974)

Age range: Grades 5-6

Subject(s): Witches and Witchcraft

Major character(s): Samuel Swift, Eccentric; John Hayward, Preteen; Richard Spencer, Preteen

Time period(s): 1700s

Locale(s): Westfall, Massachusetts

What the book is about: A group of boys accuse an old man of witchcraft when they discover he has invented an imaginary family to keep himself company and he is hanged by the villagers. The same hysteria brings about the abandonment of the village. A dramatic tale of witch hunting in colonial America.

Where it's reviewed:
Horn Book, June 1974, page 282
Kirkus Reviews, February 1, 1974, page 110

Other books by the author:
Cyclops, 1991
The Alamo, 1987
Across the Sea from Galway, 1975
The Death of the Evening Star: The Diary of a Young New England Whaler, 1972

Other books you might like:
Claude Clayton, *The Stratford Devil*, 1984
   A fictionalized account of the struggles of a Puritan settlement and events leading to the historical hanging of the Stratford Devil.
Gilbert B. Cross, *A Witch Across Time*, 1990
   Spending the summer on Martha's Vineyard, Hannah encounters the ghost of a woman falsely executed as a witch in 1692 and seeks to clear her name.
Eileen Dunlop, *The Valley of Deer*, 1989
   Finding an old family Bible in her house leads Anne on a quest to solve the mystery surrounding the death of a Scottish woman accused of witchcraft.
Monica Furlong, *Juniper*, 1991
   While apprentice to a witch, Juniper struggles to save her family from her power-hungry aunt Meroot. Prequel to *Wise Child*.
Ann Rinaldi, *A Break with Charity: A Story about the Salem Witch Trials*, 1992
   In 1706, Susanna English recalls the malice, fear, and accusations of witchcraft that tore her village apart in 1692.

607

John D. Fitzgerald

The Great Brain Reforms (New York: Dial, 1973)

Age range: Grades 4-6

Subject(s): Family Life

Major character(s): John D. Fitzgerald, Preteen; Tom Fitzgerald, Teenager; Sweyn Fitzgerald, Teenager

Time period(s): 1890s (1898)

Locale(s): Adenville, Utah

What the book is about: During summer vacation, JD arrives at a means of reforming his older brother, Tom, The Great Brain, and ending his career as a swindler.

Where it's reviewed:
Horn Book, June 1973, page 271
Kirkus Reviews, April 15, 1973, page 456

Awards the book has won:
Young Reader's Choice Award 1976

Other books by the author:
The Great Brain Does It Again, 1975
Brave Buffalo Fighter, 1973
The Great Brain at the Academy, 1972
The Great Brain, 1967

Other books you might like:
Ida Chittum, *The Hermit Boy*, 1972
   During their summer vacation in the Ozarks, two girls befriend a mysterious boy who lives alone in the woods.
Wilson Gage, *Mike's Toads*, 1970
   A 6th grader volunteers his brother's services once too often without consulting him, and ends up having to spend summer vacation caring for a toad.
Beverly Keller, *Rosebud, with Fangs*, 1985
   When a family of five is stranded in the woods, Henry is turned into a furry beast, but a madman wants to use him to control the world.
Barbara Robinson, *My Brother Louis Measures Worms and Other Louis Stories*, 1988
   Mary Elizabeth relates the misadventures of Louis and the other members of her unpredictable, very odd family.
Stephen Wunderli, *The Blue Between the Clouds*, 1992
   Two Moons, a Navajo boy living in Utah in 1939 in the home of his schoolmate, Matt, helps Matt pursue his dream of flying.

608

Louise Fitzhugh, Author/Illustrator

Harriet the Spy (New York: Harper, 1964)

Age range: Grades 4-6

Subject(s): Authorship; School Life

Major character(s): Harriet Welsch, Child; Ole Golly, Nurse

Time period(s): 1960s

Locale(s): United States

What the book is about: Encouraged by Ole Golly, Harriet tries to "find out" about everything she can. She keeps a secret notebook which her school friends pounce on and read. Harriet then has to deal with the fallout from her friends who read what she really thinks about them.

Where it's reviewed:
Horn Book, February 1965, page 74
Library Journal, November 15, 1964, page 4638

Awards the book has won:
Sequoyah Children's Book Award 1967

Other books by the author:
The Long Secret, 1965
Nobody's Family Is Going to Change, 1974
Sport, 1979

Other books you might like:
Lois Lowry, *Anastasia at This Address*, 1991
   13-year-old Anastasia answers a personals ad with an exaggerated description, never expecting the unknown man to show up at a friend's wedding.
Ellen Conford, *Jenny Archer, Author*, 1989
   Jenny gets carried away when writing her autobiography for a school assignment. (Easy reading)
Barbara Ware Holmes, *Charlotte the Starlet*, 1988

Charlotte turns her great imagination, which has often gotten her into trouble, to writing a book.

Ruth White, *Sweet Creek Holler*, 1988
As she grows, Ginny gains a sense of community and learns how gossip can destroy lives in her Appalachian Mountain town.

Marjorie Weinman Sharmat, *Getting Something on Maggie Marmelstein*, 1971
Thad Smith does not get along with Maggie, but when he "gets something" on her, he does not use it.

| 609 |

Louise Fitzhugh

Nobody's Family Is Going to Change (New York: Farrar Straus and Giroux, 1974)

Age range: Grades 5-8

Subject(s): African Americans; Parent and Child; Dancing

Major character(s): Emma, Preteen

Time period(s): 1970s

Locale(s): United States

What the book is about: There is considerable misunderstanding within a middle-class black family, and also much humor and warmth. Determination to become a lawyer, and her brother's dreams to become a dancer help Emma realize that children have to take the initiative since parents rarely change.

Where it's reviewed:
Booklist, February 1, 1975, page 570
Kirkus Reviews, December 1, 1974, page 1252
School Library Journal, January 1975, page 53

Other books by the author:
Sport, 1979
I Am Five, 1978
The Long Secret, 1965
Harriet the Spy, 1964

Other books you might like:
Coleen E. Booth, *Going Live*, 1992
A young TV performer finds her private life in conflict with her career.

Elizabeth Starr Hill, *Broadway Chances*, 1992
Fitzi, finally settled into a normal life after years of street performances with her parents, gets a chance to star in a Broadway musical.

Lois Lowry, *Anastasia's Chosen Career*, 1987
Anastasia acquires poise, self-confidence, a friend and advice on becoming a bookstore owner when she commutes to Boston to take a modeling course.

Mary Spelman, *First Serve*, 1976
Relates the events of a summer during which a talented teen tennis play must make a commitment not only to her tennis career, but to herself.

Luke Wallin, *Ceremony of the Panther*, 1987
John, a Miccosukee Indian, is torn between a shiftless life in the Everglades and his father's ambitions for him to carry on the shaman tradition.

| 610 |

Louise Fitzhugh

Sport (New York: Delacorte, 1979)

Age range: Grades 4-6

Subject(s): Family Problems; Divorce; Child Custody

Major character(s): Sport, Preteen

Time period(s): 1970s

Locale(s): United States

What the book is about: Eleven year old Sport lives happily with his absent-minded father. Suddenly his wealthy and ruthless mother wants custody of him.

Where it's reviewed:
Kirkus Reviews, July 15, 1979, page 793
School Library Journal, May 1979, page 61

Awards the book has won:
Crabbery Award 1980

Other books by the author:
Bang Bang You're Dead Teacher, 1979
Nobody's Family Is Going to Change, 1974
The Long Secret, 1965
Harriet the Spy, 1964

Other books you might like:
Matt Christopher, *The Fox Steals Home*, 1978
Bobby learns that his father, who has been coaching him in base running, intends to move away.

Gary Paulsen, *Hatchet*, 1987
Brian spends fifty-four days in the wilderness with only the hatchet his mother has given him; he learns he can even survive his parents' divorce.

Lois Ruby, *Pig-Out Inn*, 1987
Davi gets caught in the middle of a custody battle for her brother.

Robert Kimmel Smith, *The Squeaky Wheel*, 1990
Mark adjusts to a new neighborhood, new friends and his father's absence.

Marc Talbert, *Pillow of Clouds*, 1991
Chester must decide who will get custody of him, and he is burdened with guilty feelings about the parent he will leave behind.

| 611 |

Paul Fleischman

Illustrator: Marcia Sewall

The Birthday Tree (New York: Harper, 1979)

Age range: Grades 3-4

Subject(s): Trees; Fantasy

Major character(s): Jack, Child

Time period(s): Indeterminate

Locale(s): United States

What the book is about: An apple tree mirrors the experiences of a couple's son, Jack. They both grow tall together. When the boy is sad, the tree's branches hang heavy. When Jack is cold, the leaves shiver. When Jack goes to sea, the tree reflects his fortunes and misfortunes.

Where it's reviewed:
Booklist, June 15, 1979, page 1535
Kirkus, May 15r, 1979, page 573
School Library Journal, September 1979, page 110

Other books by the author:
Time Train, 1991
Shadow Play: A Story, 1990
Rondo in C, 1988
Finzel the Farsighted, 1983

Other books you might like:
Gladys Yessayan Cretan, *Sunday for Sona*, 1973
An Armenian-American girl growing up in San Francisco in the 1930s has trouble convincing her family that she wants to be a sailor.
Marjorie Lewis, *Ernie and the Mile Long Muffler*, 1982
Inspired by the beautiful sweater his sailor uncle has knitted, Ernie decides to knit the world's longest muffler and gets his 4th grade class to help
Mira Lobe, *The Grandma in the Apple Tree*, 1970
An Austrian boy is sad that he has no grandmother until he discovers one sitting in his apple tree.
Margaret Mahy, *Sailor Jack and the Twenty Orphans*, 1970
Sailor Jack goes to work for pirates in order to raise enough money to adopt twenty orphans.
Ruth Wallace-Brodeur, *The Godmother Tree*, 1992
When Laura moves with her family to another farm, she slowly begins to build connections to the place, her family, and to herself.

612

Paul Fleischman

The Borning Room (New York: Harper, 1991)

Age range: Grades 5-9

Subject(s): Frontier and Pioneer Life; Birth

Major character(s): Georgina Lott, Narrator; Clement Bock, Teacher; Titus Lott, Teenager

Time period(s): 19th century (1851-1918)

Locale(s): Ohio

What the book is about: Georgina remembers how most of her life's turnings have taken place in the borning room next to the kitchen, where she herself was born in 1851. Fleischman shows Georgina hiding a runaway slave, who ultimately helps with a difficult birth for Georgina's mother, the death of her grandfather, attended by preaches urging repentance, the death of her mother when a new doctor uses chloroform during childbirth, the illness of two brothers, and an awareness of dawning love for the teacher, Mr. Bock. The spring after they are married, Georgina takes her place in the borning room and gives birth.

Where it's reviewed:
Booklist, October 1, 1991, page 328
Kirkus Reviews, August 1, 1991, page 1009

Other books by the author:
Saturnalia, 1990
Shadow Play: A Story, 1990
The Half-a-Moon Inn, 1980
The Birthday Tree, 1979

Other books you might like:
Cynthia DeFelice, *The Strange Night Writing of Jessamine Colter*, 1988
Jessie, an elderly calligrapher who writes announcements and notices of birth, marriage and death for the townsfolk, is able to predict the future.
Libby Gleeson, *Eleanor, Elizabeth*, 1990
Having left the town and friends of her childhood, a 12 year old Australian girl finds the land and house of her grandmother to be an alien place.
Elizabeth Laird, *Loving Ben*, 1989
Anna's teen years bring maturity and fulfillment as she experiences the birth and death of a loved and loving hydrocephalic brother.
Katharine Wilson Precek, *The Keepsake Chest*, 1992
To ease the pain of leaving friends when she moves to an Ohio farmhouse, 13 year old Meg probes the historical background of an old chest she finds.
Eleanor Spence, *The Devil Hole*, 1976
The birth of an autistic child drastically changes the lives of the once happy members of an Australian family.

613

Paul Fleischman

Illustrator: Marcia Sewall

Finzel the Farsighted (New York: Dutton, 1983)

Age range: Grades 3-5

Subject(s): Folk Tales

Major character(s): Finxel, Psychic (fortune teller), Handicapped (nearly blind)

Time period(s): Indeterminate Past

Locale(s): Plov, Yugoslavia (Slavic village)

What the book is about: Finzel the fortune teller is so near blindness that he becomes easy prey. Finzel can see into the past or future by "reading" the produce grown by an individual. The problem is that he is very nearsighted and sometimes mixes up the produce and gives the prediction to the wrong people. He also gives the villain an idea for robbing Finzel, taking advantage of his nearsightedness. A fast paced, lighthearted folktale.

Where it's reviewed:
Center for Children's Books Bulletin, January 1984, page 86
School Library Journal, December 1983, page 65

Other books by the author:
Townsend's Warbler, 1992
Time Train, 1991
Saturnalia, 1990
The Path of the Pale Horse, 1983

Other books you might like:
Malcolm Carrick, *Happy Jack*, 1979
Happy Jack bumbles his way into a fortune and a wife in spite of his stupidity.
Gudrun Helgadottir, *Flumbra*, 1985
When the dim-witted giantess Flumbra falls in love, her escapades upset all of Iceland.
Beverly Keller, *A Small, Elderly Dragon*, 1984

When the kingdom is overtaken by a sorcerer, Princess Dorma, nearsighted and awkward, helps an elderly dragon find the power to save the villagers.

Samuel Marshak, *The Month-Brothers*, 1983
A young girl outwits her stepmother and stepsister with the help of the Month Brothers who use their magic to help her do almost impossible tasks.

Seymour Reit, *Benvenuto and the Carnival*, 1976
A fortune teller sees danger ahead for Benvenuto the dragon after he is captured and placed in a carnvial.

614

Paul Fleischman

Illustrator: Andrew Glass

Graven Images (New York: Harper and Row, 1982)

Age range: Grades 5-8

Subject(s): Mystery and Detective Stories; Suspense

Time period(s): Indeterminate

Locale(s): Earth

What the book is about: Three tales, each focusing on a "chiseled figure." One is a figurehead from a ship on which all had perished. The statue holds whispered secrets. The second is about an awkward apprentice and the third is the story of a sculptor with a ghost for a patron.

Where it's reviewed:
Horn Book, December 1982, page 656
School Library Journal, September 1982, page 137

Awards the book has won:
Newbery Honor 1983

Other books by the author:
The Borning Room, 1991
Rear View Mirror, 1986
Coming-and-Going Men, 1985
The Path of the Pale Horse, 1983

Other books you might like:
Vivien Alcock, *The Stonewalkers*, 1981
A garden statue of Belladonna, brought to life by a flash of lightning, gathers a stone army from gardens and churches as two girls watch.

Michael James Bradley, *The Shaping Room*, 1978
Seeking an escape from his sister, the neighborhood bully, and himself, Stephen learns the shaping of dreams from his sculptor professor.

Joan Clark, *Wild Man of the Woods*, 1985
Stephen visits his cousing Louie in the Rockies and meets Angus, a mysterious Indian mask carver.

Emily Hanlon, *The Wing and the Flame*, 1980
As a friendship develops between two boys, one of them inspires a reclusive sculptor to work for the first time since his family was killed.

Jackie Vivelo, *A Trick of the Light*, 1987
Nine short ghost stories to read as the light fades at dusk, including "A Game of Statues."

615

Paul Fleischman

Illustrator: Kathy Jacobi

The Half-a-Moon Inn (New York: Harper, 1980)

Age range: Grades 4-5

Subject(s): Kidnapping; Mutism; Physically Handicapped

Major character(s): Aaron, Handicapped (mute); Miss Grackle, Innkeeper

Time period(s): Indeterminate

Locale(s): United States

What the book is about: Aaron sets out to search for his mother in a snowstorm. Unable to speak, he is brutalized by an evil innkeeper. A haunting tale, with an ingenious and happy ending.

Where it's reviewed:
Horn Book, June 1980, page 294
School Library Journal, October 1980, page 145

Awards the book has won:
Golden Kite Honor Book 1980

Other books by the author:
The Borning Room, 1991
Coming-and-Going Men, 1985
Graven Images, 1982
The Birthday Tree, 1979

Other books you might like:
Julia Cunningham, *The Silent Voice*, 1981
A street urchin who cannot speak is befriended by a famous Parisian mime. They change each other's lives.

Isabel Langis Cusack, *Mr. Wheatfield's Loft*, 1979
An interest in homing pigeons leads to a signficant change in the life of Ellis Hampton who has been mute since he witnessed his father's death.

Lila Hopkins, *Eating Crow*, 1988
To befriend Zeke, a mute boy, Croaker must swallow his pride, after which a bully's terrifying attack on Zeke's pet crow tests their friendship.

Glen Rounds, *Blind Outlaw*, 1980
A blind outlaw horse is tamed by a boy who cannot speak.

Kenneth Thomasma, *Soun Tetoken: Nez Perce Boy*, 1984
Although mute since his parents' death, a young Nez Perce boy has a happy life until war with the whites in 1877 changes his life forever.

616

Paul Fleischman

Illustrator: Eric Beddows

Joyful Noise: Poems for Two Voices (New York: Harper & Row, 1988)

Age range: Grades 3 and Up

Subject(s): Animals/Insects; Poetry

Time period(s): Indeterminate

What the book is about: Poetry about bugs of all kinds. From lovelorn moths yearning for light bulbs to grasshoppers to butterflies, each is personified by habits and habitats. Best read by two people.

Where it's reviewed:
Booklist, February 15, 1988, page 1000
Kirkus Reviews, December 15, 1987, page 1732
School Library Journal, February 1988, page 79

Awards the book has won:
Newbery Medal 1989

Other books by the author:
The Birthday Tree, 1979
I Am Phoenix, 1986
Rondo in C, 1988
Shadow Play: A Story, 1990

Other books you might like:
Eileen Fisher, *When It Comes to Bugs*, 1986
   Illustrated poems about all kinds of bugs.
William Roscoe, *Butterfly's Ball and the Grasshopper's Feast*, 1967
   Poetry about insects.
Kiyoshi Soya, *House of Leaves*, 1987
   A sudden rain sends a little girl under cover where she is joined by a multitude of insects.
Katy Hall, *Buggy Riddles*, 1986
   Insect riddles for young jokers.
Stephen Manes, *Chocolate-Covered Ants*, 1990
   Max and his little brother, Adam, make a bet about eating chocolate covered ants.

617

Paul Fleischman

The Path of the Pale Horse (New York: Harper and Row, 1983)

Age range: Grades 5 and Up

Subject(s): Yellow Fever

Major character(s): Asclepius "Lep" Nye, Apprentice; Apollo Nye, Artisan (silversmith); Ussiah Botkin, Benefactor

Time period(s): 1790s (1793)

Locale(s): Philadelphia, Pennsylvania

What the book is about: Lep, an apprentice to a doctor, goes to help his master take care of yellow fever victims in Philadelphia during the epidemic of 1793. As soon as they enter the ghostly city, master and apprentice become separated and Lep's adventure really begins.

Where it's reviewed:
Booklist, April 1, 1983, page 1032
School Library Journal, September 1983, page 133

Awards the book has won:
Golden Kite Honor Book 1983

Other books by the author:
Townsend's Warbler, 1992
The Borning Room, 1991
Saturnalia, 1990
Graven Images, 1982

Other books you might like:
Lloyd Alexander, *The Philadelphia Adventure*, 1990
   In 1876, Dr. Helvitius' evil schemes plunge Verper Holly and her friends into danger in the wild Pennsylvania countryside.
Catherine Cookson, *Blue Baccy*, 1972

In 1851, a wheelwright's apprentice delivers a message for his master, only to find himself in the middle of a dangerous smuggling operation.
Mary Alice Downie, *Honor Bound*, 1971
   Members of a Loyalist family become separated when they flee Philadelphia for Canada following the Revolutionary War.
Scott O'Dell, *The 290*, 1976
   A shipyard apprentice finds high adventure aboard the SS Alabama, a confederate ship which sails the Atlantic destroying Union vessels.
Ludek Pesek, *The Earth Is Near*, 1973
   A doctor accompanying the first expedition to Mars describes the journey and the mental and physical challenges that face the astronauts.

618

Sid Fleischman

Illustrator: William Harmuth

The Bloodhound Gang and the Case of the Secret Message (New York: Random, 1981)

Age range: Grades 3-4

Series: The Bloodhound Gang

Subject(s): Mystery and Detective Stories; Smuggling

Major character(s): Vikki, Teenager, Detective; Ricardo, Teenager, Detective; Zach, Preteen, Detective

Time period(s): 1980s

Locale(s): United States

What the book is about: A trio of young detectives known as the Bloodhound Gang, uses deductive reasoning to solve baffling crimes. In this story, they witness a purse snatch and what looks like a kidnapping, and find the purse containing a secret message that everyone in town seems to be after. When "Mr. Big" shows up to collect the purse and the kids have already returned it to its owner (keeping the mysterious scrap of paper) the kids are terrified as Mr. Big and his thugs tear the apartment to pieces, and find themselves deeply involved in a smuggling ring. Fast action and snappy dialogue in this series based on the Bloodhound Gang created on TV's 3-2-1 Contact show.

Where it's reviewed:
Booklist, December 15, 1981, page 553
Kirkus Reviews, October 1, 1981, page 1235
School Library Journal, December 1981, page 81

Other books by the author:
The Case of the 264 Pound Burglar, 1982
The Case of the Cackling Ghost, 1981
The Case of the Flying Clock, 1981
The Case of the Princess Tomorrow, 1981

Other books you might like:
Eric Deleon, *Pitch and Hasty Check It Out*, 1988
   Two boys investigating a mysterious voice coming from a pinball machine become involved with a parrot smuggling ring.
David Pownall, *The Bunch From Bananas*, 1980
   Crime and catastrophe are thwarted in the town of Santa Margarita del Banana by young Bernard who has taken up crime fighting and heroism as hobbies.

Robert M. Quackenbush, *Bicycle to Treachery: A Miss Mallard Mystery*, 1985

While on a bicycle trip across Holland, Miss Mallard runs into danger when she unwittingly uncovers a smuggling operation.

Francene Sabin, *Secret of the Haunted House*, 1982

The Maple Street Six club visit a haunted house and find a mysterious message.

Marjorie Weinman Sharmat, *Nate the Great and the Musical Note*, 1990

When Rosamond turns a phone message from Pip's mother into a music lesson with secret meaning, Nate the Great steps in.

| 619 |

Sid Fleischman

By the Great Horn Spoon (New York: Random, 1963)

Age range: Grades 4-7

Subject(s): Miners and Mining; Orphans; Humor

Major character(s): Jack Flagg, Orphan, Adventurer; Praiseworthy, Worker (butler); Joshua Swain, Sea Captain

Time period(s): 1840s (1849)

Locale(s): California

What the book is about: Orphan Jack Flagg and the butler, Praiseworthy, stow away aboard the sailing ship Lady Wilma, bound from Boston to San Francisco around the Horn. Jack has left his sisters, Constance and Sarah, in Boston with their Aunt Arabella while he tries to make their fortune in the gold fields of California. Both aboard ship and in California, Jack and Praiseworthy have wild adventures and meet colorful characters. Paperback version is called Bullwhip Griffin.

Where it's reviewed:
Language Arts, October 1982, page 759
New Statesman, May 28, 1965, page 848
Observer, April 18, 1965, page 26

Other books by the author:
The Midnight Horse, 1990
Humbug Mountain, 1978
Chancy and the Grand Rascal, 1966
The Ghost in the Noonday Sun, 1978

Other books you might like:
Jane Flory, *The Golden Venture*, 1976
A girl stows away in a wagon headed for the Californaia gold fields, and finds herself in an adventure requiring all her wits and emotional resources.
May Yonge McNeer, *The California Gold Rush*, 1950
Traces the history of the gold rush in California including anecdotes about legendary characters and fabulous "strikes" of the mining camps.
Alfred Reynolds, *The Adventures of Rattlesnake Ralph*, 1973
A young man finds adventure and lasting friendship with a rattlesnake named George in the gold fields of California.
Susan Terris, *Tucker and the Horse Thief*, 1979
An abused and neglected girl, posing as a boy, finds both warmth and uneasiness in a friendship with a boy who doesn't suspect she is a girl.
Laurence Yep, *Mountain Light*, 1985

After losing his home in a rebellion against the Manchus in China, Squeaky, travels to America to seek his fortune in the Californian gold fields.

| 620 |

Sid Fleischman

Illustrator: Peter Sis

The Ghost in the Noonday Sun (New York: Greenwillow, 1965)

Age range: Grades 5-6

Subject(s): Treasure; Pirates; Ghosts

Major character(s): Oliver Finch, Child; Captain Scratch, Pirate; Aunt Katy, Innkeeper

Time period(s): 1800s

Locale(s): Nantucket, Massachusetts

What the book is about: Twelve year old Oliver tries to escape from pirates who take him to an island to find the ghost and treasure of Gentleman Jack. This is a tale of treachery, intrigue and suspense.

Where it's reviewed:
Booklist, September 1, 1965, page 54
Hornbook, October 1965, page 490
Kirkus Reviews, March 1, 1965, page 245

Other books by the author:
The Scarebird, 1988
The Whipping Boy, 1987
Humbug Mountain, 1978
Chancy and the Grandy Rascal, 1966

Other books you might like:
Scott Corbett, *Captain Butcher's Body*, 1976
Two boys confront the ghost of a long-dead pirate on an island off the coast of New England.
Betty Hager, *Old Jake and the Pirate's Treasure*, 1980
Four Alabama children look for pirate treasure using a map belonging to an old Cajun fisherman.
Sarita Kendall, *The Bell Reef*, 1990
Two teens and a trained dolphin attempt to recover a sunken treasur despite ghost stories and mysterious underwater noises surrounding the Reef.
Parker Rossman, *Pirate Slave*, 1977
A twelve year old boy captured by Muslim pirates is forced into a life of piracy and slave trading.
Leonard Wibberley, *The Crime of Martin Coverly*, 1980
After being visited by a man in 18th century clothing who resembles his uncle, Nick finds himself aboard his uncle's pirate ship in the 1720s.

| 621 |

Sid Fleischman

Illustrator: Eric Von Schmidt

The Ghost on Saturday Night (Boston: Little, Brown, 1974)

Age range: Grades 3-5

Subject(s): Ghosts; American West

Major character(s): Opie, Child; Etta, Professor, Relative (Opie's great-aunt); Professor Pepper, Occultist (ghost rider)

Time period(s): 19th century

Locale(s): Golden Hill, California

What the book is about: The big, ugle stranger gives Opie a ticket. It said "ADMIT TWO." Admit two to what? What kind of show could it be? Opie goes, and it turned out to be the scariest night of his life in this Wild West adventure.

Where it's reviewed:
Booklist, July 15, 1974, page 1252
Kirkus Reviews, May 15, 1974, page 535
Center for Children's Books Bulletin, December 1974, page 61

Other books by the author:
The Case of the Cackling Ghost, 1981
Jingo Django, 1971
Longbeard the Wizard, 1970
Chancy and the Grand Rascal, 1966

Other books you might like:
L.E. Blair, *The Ghost of Eagle Mountain*, 1990
  The school ski trip becomes a journey into Allison's Native American heritage when she and her friends begin to live the legend of Eagle Mountain.
Caron Lee Cohen, *Bronco Dogs*, 1991
  Bank robbers Sixgun Gus and Cannonball Clyde get into the worst trouble ever and become ghosts, but remain good friends.
John R. Erickson, *Hank the Cowdog: The Case of the Halloween Ghost*, 1989
  Hank the cowdog has a scary adventure when he and his cowardly companion, Drover, find themselves in a strange and spooky place on Halloween night.
Bruce Roberts, *Ghosts of the Wild West*, 1976
  A collection of short stories about ghosts in the West, including "Wild Bill Hickock and the Ghost Gunman" and "The Ghost of Cripple Creek."
Alice Durland Ryniker, *Eagle Feather*, 1980
  Charlie Little Otter, a Crow Indian boy in the Pryor Mountains, dreams of the "time before now" and finds himself in a dark and mysterious adventure.

622

Sid Fleischman

Illustrator: Eric Von Schmidt

Humbug Mountain (Boston: Little, Brown, 1978)

Age range: Grades 4-6

Subject(s): Humor; American West

Major character(s): Wiley, Child; Glorietta, Child; Shagnasty, Outlaw

Time period(s): Indeterminate Past

Locale(s): West (Dakota Territory)

What the book is about: Wiley and Glorietta are children of an itinerant printer and newspaper publisher on the Missouri River. They foil villains and route nasty varmints as they make a home for themselves in a beached boat on the banks of the river. They discover a petrified man, rescue their grandfather and outwit the outlaws Shagnasty and the Fool Killer.

Where it's reviewed:
Center for Children's Books Bulletin, March 1979, p 113
Horn Book, December 1978, page 640

Awards the book has won:
Boston Globe/Horn Book Award - Fiction Honor 1979
National Book Award Finalist 1979

Other books by the author:
The Whipping Boy, 1986
Kate's Secret Riddle Book, 1979
The Ghost on Saturday Night, 1974
Chancy and the Grand Rascal, 1966

Other books you might like:
Patricia Beatty, *By Crumbs, It's Mine!*, 1976
  While stranded in the Arizona territory in the 1880s, a thirteen year old girl finds herself the owner of a traveling hotel.
John R. Erickson, *Hank the Cowdog and Let Sleeping Dogs Lie*, 1989
  Hank the Cowdog, Head of Ranch Security, pursues an elusive chicken murderer.
Stephen Manes, *The Great Gerbil Roundup*, 1988
  To put the town of Gerbil, Pennsylvania on the map, the citizens open the 1st National Drive-Thru Museum of American Sightseeing and Clean Rest Rooms.
Robert Newton Peck, *Soup's Hoop*, 1990
  Soup's crazy plan to help his town's basketball team to victory includes constructing a musical instrument called a spitzentootie.
Stephen Roos, *Twelve-Year-Old Vows Revenge!*, 1990
  Two student newspaper reporters spend the summer trying to get even with each other, and in the process, abuse the right of a free press.

623

Sid Fleischman

Illustrator: Jos. A. Smith

Jim Ugly (New York: Greenwillow, 1992)

Age range: Grades 3-5

Subject(s): Animals/Dogs; Mystery and Detective Stories

Major character(s): Jake Bannock, Child; Sam Bannock, Actor, Parent

Time period(s): 1890s

Locale(s): Blowfly, Nevada

What the book is about: After attending his father's funeral, Jake tries to deal with his dad's part timber wolf "one man dog," whom he calls Jim Ugly. Neighbors think him a sheep killer and want him shot. Jake decides to run away with the dog, and eventually uncovers a mystery involving stolen diamonds and a dead man who isn't dead. An entertaining and fast-paced adventure.

Other books by the author:
The Midnight Horse, 1990
McBroom's Almanac, 1984
Me and the Man on the Moon-Eyed Horse, 1977
Jingo Django, 1971

Other books you might like:
Mary Francis Shura, *The Mystery at Wolf River*, 1989

Kate and Bugs solve a mystery involving a drowning dog and a mansion. Meanwhile, Kate decides her little brother is not so pesky after all.

John R. Erickson, *Every Dog Has His Day*, 1989
   Hank the cowdog gets into more and more trouble before he is able to find a happy solution to his problems.

James Howe, *Return to Howliday Inn*, 1992
   The Monroe family pets are again boarded at Chateau Bow-Wow, where some spooky goings on serve as a distraction from the kennel's poor food.

Lynn Hall, *The Tormentors*, 1990
   When his German Shepherd vanishes, Sox sets out to find the the thief and discovers a ring of dangerous dog trainers who kidnap animals for profit.

Colin West, *Monty, the Dog Who Wears Glasses*, 1990
   The adventures of Monty, the dog who wears glasses to remind himself to stay out of trouble.

624

Sid Fleischman

Illustrator: Walter Lorraine

McBroom the Rainmaker (New York: Grosset, 1973)

Age range: Grades 2-4

Subject(s): Humor; Weather

Major character(s): Josh McBroom, Farmer; Melissa McBroom, Parent; Will McBroom, Child

Time period(s): Indeterminate

Locale(s): United States

What the book is about: Plagued by giant mosquitos and a drought so bad that the cows give powdered milk, McBroom brings the rain with a great plan. He chases a rain cloud and plants Instant Giant Onions in a wagonbed. The mosquitos attack the onions and help make it rain.

Where it's reviewed:
Center for Children's Books Bulletin, April 1974, page 128
Library Journal, March 15, 1974, page 880

Other books by the author:
Humbug Mountain, 1978
McBroom and the Beanstalk, 1978
McBroom Tells a Lie, 1976
The Wooden Cat Man, 1973

Other books you might like:
Ned Delaney, *Cosmic Chickens*, 1988
   Three chickens from outer space help Hank save his farm from the greedy Mr. Sneezle.

Virginia Hamilton, *Drylongso*, 1992
   As a great wall of dust moves across their drought-stricken farm, a family's distress is relieved by a young man who literally blows into their lives.

Johanna Hurwitz, *The Adventures of Ali Baba Bernstein*, 1985
   Eight year old David is convinced that his life will be more adventurous when he changes his name to Ali Baba.

Robert Pierce, *The Day of the Wind, Rain, and Snow*, 1978
   Extremes in the weather cause suspense and excitement for several children in this collection of three stories.

Eleanor Schick, *Rainy Sunday*, 1980
   A young girl enjoys some unexpected pleasures on a rainy day.

625

Sid Fleischman

Illustrator: Peter Sis

The Whipping Boy (New York: Greenwillow, 1986)

Age range: Grades 4-6

Subject(s): Robbers and Outlaws; Princes and Princesses; Adventure and Adventurers

Major character(s): Prince Horace "Brat", Royalty; Jemmy, Servant; Hold-Your-Nose Billy, Outlaw

Time period(s): Indeterminate

Locale(s): Fictional Country

What the book is about: Prince Brat is bored with royal life and he and his whipping boy, Jemmy, escape from the palace. They are soon detained by Hold-Your-Nose Billy and his sidekick, Cutwater, who plan to hold the prince for ransom (though they are confused as to who the prince really is). The boys escape with the help of Betsy and her trained bear, Petunia. When they finally return to the castle, the prince is a changed boy.

Where it's reviewed:
Booklist, May 1, 1986, Page 1018
Horn Book, May/June 1986, Page 325

Awards the book has won:
Newbery Medal 1987

Other books by the author:
The Ghost in the Noonday Sun, 1965
Humbug Mountain, 1978
Me and the Man on the Moon-Eyed Horse, 1977

Other books you might like:
Howard Pyle, *King Story*, 1973
   A soldier returning from the wars befriends an elderly man and wins a beautiful princess.

Diane Wolkstein, *Red Lion*, 1977
   A young prince who is afraid to fight a red lion runs away but finds he must deal with his own fear.

Louise Moeri, *Journey to the Treasure*, 1986
   Victoria and Trevor follow Victoria's grandfather in a search for a gold statue taken by robbers.

Natalie Babbitt, *The Search for Delicious*, 1969
   The Prime Minister's son, Gaylen, finds the kingdom in turmoil when he is sent to find out what people consider "delicious."

Mark Twain, *The Prince and the Pauper*, 1882
   A prince and a boy off the street look so much alike they are able to change places and live each other's lives.

626

Alice Mulcahey Fleming

Welcome to Grossville (New York: Scribner, 1985)

Age range: Grades 4-6

Subject(s): Divorce; Friendship; Moving, Household

Major character(s): Michael Bailey, Preteen; Jenny Bailey, Child

Time period(s): 1980s

Locale(s): Humboldt

What the book is about: The summer after his parents divorce and he has to move to a less affluent neighborhood, Michael copes with learning the true meaning of friendship and finding new values in his rapidly changing life.

Where it's reviewed:
Booklist, April 1, 1985, page 1119
Center for Children's Books Bulletin, May 1985, page 164
School Library Journal, May 1985, page 88

Other books by the author:
The King of Prussia and a Peanut Butter Sandwich, 1988
Something for Nothing, 1978
America Is Not All Traffic Lights: Poems of the Midwest, 1976

Other books you might like:
Patricia Hermes, *Kevin Corbett Eats Flies*, 1986
    Kevin is finally living in a town where he feels happy. Alone with his father since his mother's death, Kevin is afraid of moving again.
Barbara Park, *The Kid in the Red Jacket*, 1987
    Moving across country is not Howard's idea of a good time. He is surprised that his new neighbor, Molly Vera, actually likes him.
Joanne Rocklin, *Jace the Ace*, 1990
    Dreams of glory and an overactive imagination cause Jason, newly arrived in L.A., to suspect innocent people of crimes and to lie.to his classmates.
Jan Slepian, *Getting on with It*, 1985
    Sent to stay with his grandmother, Berry's worries about his parents' divorce are diluted by his interest in the curious house next door.
Alfred Slote, *Moving In*, 1988
    Moving for the third time since his mother's death, Robby finds he is faced with adjusting to a new school and preventing his father's remarriage.

627

Ian Fleming

Chitty-Chitty-Bang-Bang (New York: Random House, 1964)

Age range: Grades 5 and Up

Subject(s): Fantasy; Automobiles

Major character(s): Commander Caractacus Pott, Parent; Jeremy Pott, Child; Jemima Pott, Child

Time period(s): 1960s

Locale(s): England

What the book is about: Chitty Chitty Bang Bang is a magical car. Commander Pott rescues the racing car from the junk heap. After two sneezes and two explosions, the car starts and names itself in the process. Chitty Chitty Bang Bang flies, floats, and has a talent for getting the Pott family out of trouble.

Where it's reviewed:
Horn Book, April 1965, page 167
Library Journal, November 15, 1964, page 4646

Other books you might like:
Betty Baker, *The Great Desert Race*, 1980
    Driving a steam-powered car, two young women compete in the two day Great Mountain to Desert Race at the turn of the century.
Brian Ball, *The Quest for Queenie*, 1988

Harry and Jill are chosen by a magic talking sword to rescue a damsel from the Bad Wizard in Mandragora.
John Bibee, *The Magic Bicycle*, 1983
    John finds a rusty old bicycle in the dump which magically lives up to its name, the Spirit Flyer.
Holden Wetherbee, *The Wonder Ring*, 1978
    When a poor and mistreated boy shows kindness to a beggar, the beggar thanks him by giving him a magic ring.
Jane Yolen, *Wizard's Hall*, 1991
    A young apprentice wizard saves the wizard's training hall by trusting and believing in himself.

628

James Flora, Author/Illustrator

Grandpa's Ghost Stories (New York: Atheneum, 1978)

Age range: Grades 2-3

Subject(s): Ghosts; Grandparents

Time period(s): Indeterminate

Locale(s): United States

What the book is about: A wishbone in his pocket is the reminder to the unnamed narrator of all the stories he hears while sitting on grandpa's lap during a ferocious thunderstorm. Grandpa tells of skeletons, witches, spiders, ghosts, and werewolves and how he narrowly escaped from each dangerous situation. Lavishly illustrated with pictures showing great, scary deatils that seem to march across the pages with a life of their own.

Where it's reviewed:
Booklist, September 15, 1978, page 216
Hornbook, October 1978, page 510
Kirkus Reviews, October 1, 1978, page 1066

Other books by the author:
The Great Green Turkey Creek Monster, 1976
Stewed Goose, 1973
Pishtosh Bullwash Wimple, 1972
Joking Man, 1968

Other books you might like:
Charles Dickens, *A Christmas Carol: Being a Ghost Story of Christmas*, 1986
    An abridged version of this classic ghost story with all the characters depicted as animals.
Phyllis Rose Eisenberg, *Don't Tell Me a Ghost Story*, 1982
    An older brother tells a scary ghost story to his younger brother, only to have the tables turned on him.
Jim Kraft, *Scary Tales*, 1990
    Five scary stories in which Garfield encounters a monster, a ghost, and even a computer gone haywire.
Edward Marshall, *Four on the Shore*, 1985
    Hoping to scare away Spider's little brother Willy, Lolly, Spider and Sam each tell a spooky story, but then Willy has a story of his own to tell.
Megan Stine, *Mysterious Max*, 1988
    Jeffrey loves to tell a good story, but it actually turns out that his new best friend is a mischief-loving ghost from the 1950s named Max.

629

James Flora, Author/Illustrator

The Great Green Turkey Creek Monster (New York: Atheneum, 1976)

Age range: Grades 2-4

Subject(s): Halloween

Major character(s): Mr. Bogwater, Clerk (storekeeper); Argie Bargle, Hero

Time period(s): Indeterminate

Locale(s): Turkey Creek

What the book is about: A Great Green Hooligan vine has been sent by mistake with a shipment of seeds. It keeps growing and growing for six days straight. Only Argie Bargle can get the vine back into the seed it started from before it destroys the town.

Where it's reviewed:
Horn Book, December 1976, page 621
Kirkus Reviews, July 1, 1976, page 725

Awards the book has won:
Colorado Children's Book Award 1979

Other books by the author:
Grandpa's Ghost Stories, 1978
The Day the Cow Sneezed, 1975

Other books you might like:
Ray Bradbury, *The Halloween Tree*, 1972
　　A group of children and a spirit go back through time to discover the beginnings of Halloween.
Constance Hiser, *Ghosts in Fourth Grade*, 1991
　　James and his friends turn the old Hathaway House into a haunted house to scare Mean Mitchell, the class bully.
Mona Kerby, *38 Weeks Till Summer Vacation*, 1989
　　Nora Jean and her friends are kept busy with a snake in the girls' room, a scary Halloween fun house, and a pizza party in the library.
Robert Newton Peck, *Higbee's Halloween*, 1990
　　Clod's Corner is not quite the same after the very nasty Striker kids move in and Higbee decides to pull a Halloween prank on them.
Mary Stolz, *The Scarecrows and Their Child*, 1987
　　While looking for employment, two scarecrows become separated from their cat child, finding each other on Halloween.

630

Jane Flory

Illustrator: Blanche Sims

Miss Plunkett to the Rescue (Boston: Houghton Mifflin, 1983)

Age range: Grades 3-6

Subject(s): Mystery and Detective Stories; Spies

Major character(s): Augusta Plunkett, Spy; Frederick J. Ponsonby, Spy (Inspector General); Dirty Digby, Spy

Time period(s): 1980s

Locale(s): Fictional Country (Nether Dilchwood)

What the book is about: When Inspector General Ponsonby of Pugwell's Bureau of International Prying and Spy-ing drops in on Miss Plunkett, we know something is up for sure. A top secret document has vanished. It is the plans for the great Dandy Doodle Noodle Machine, the thing on which the economy of Nether Dilchwood depends, as noodles are their main export. It is up to Miss Plunkett to make sure the document does not fall into the hands of Dirty Digby. Fast action in this melodrama for kids.

Where it's reviewed:
Center for Children's Books Bulletin, September 1983, page 6
Kirkus Reviews, March 1, 1983, page 246
School Library Journal, April 1979, page 42

Other books by the author:
The Great Bamboozlement, 1982
It Was a Pretty Good Year, 1977
The Golden Venture, 1976
One-Hundred and Eight Bells, 1963

Other books you might like:
Bill Brittain, *My Buddy, the King: A Novel*, 1989
　　When King Tokab of Kokobway is saved from choking on a frankfurter by Tim Quilt, they become fast friends and together outwit a plot to kill the king.
Margaret Mahy, *The Terrible Topsy-Turvy, Tissy-Tossy Tangle*, 1986
　　The famous spy, Iris La Bonga, sets out to steal an inventor's mysterious potion.
Diane Redfield Massie, *Chameleon the Spy and The Case of the Vanishing Jewels*, 1984
　　Chameleon the Spy outwits a phony prince and princess who have robbed Beantown residents of their jewels.
Michael McBrier, *Oliver and the Amazing Spy*, 1988
　　Oliver enlists the help of his friend's pet ferret to pull a prank on a blackmailing buddy.
Jane Yolen, *Commander Toad and the Intergalactic Spy*, 1986
　　Commander Toad and the crew of Star Warts are asked to rout out Tip Toad, Space Fleet's greatest and most elusive spy.

631

Louise Munro Foley

Illustrator: John Heinly

Tackle-22 (New York: Delacorte, 1978)

Age range: Grades 2-4

Subject(s): Brothers and Sisters; Sports/Football

Major character(s): Lenny, Sports Figure, Child; Chub, Sports Figure, Child; Herbie, Child

Time period(s): Indeterminate

Locale(s): United States

What the book is about: When Steve gets the mumps, the Wildcats are without a quarterback for Saturday's game. They are about to cancel when they run into the opposing team, the Spacemen, who goad them into promising to play. Chub's younger brother volunteers, and he turns out to be a successful player even though he only knows three rules.

Where it's reviewed:
Children's Book Review Service, February 1979, page 64
Center for Children's Books Bulletin, April 1979, page 135
School Library Journal, March 1979, page 121

Other books by the author:
The Sinister Studios of KESP-TV, 1983
Somebody Stole Second, 1972
Job for Joey, 1970
Sammy's Sister, 1970

Other books you might like:
Matt Christopher, *The Great Quarterback Switch*, 1984
Michael, confined to a wheelchair after an accident, uses mental telepathy to communicate football plays to his quarterback twin, Tom.
Dorothy Joan Harris, *The School Mouse and the Hamster*, 1979
When his friend, Toby, gets the mumps, Jonathan finds that after school blackboard duty isn't much fun until he meets a mouse with interesting ideas.
Eleanore Hartson, *Maxie's Mystery Files: The Stalled Mall and Other Crazy Cases*, 1987
Four mini-mysteries in which strange events such as a football team falling asleep in a huddle and snow in the science lab are investigated by Maxie.
John Ibbitson, *The Wimp and the Jock*, 1986
Ridiculously poor at sports, Randy horrifies himself and his friends when he answers a bully's taunts by saying he'll try out for the football team.
Bonnie-Alise Leggat, *Punt, Pass & Point!*, 1992
When Amy, the only girl and star player on her school's football team, breaks her arm, her parents insist that she give up football and take up ballet

---

632

Timothy Foote

Illustrator: Normand Chartier

The Great Ringtail Garbage Caper (New York: Houghton, 1980)

Age range: Grades 4-6

Subject(s): Animals; Ecology

Major character(s): Nip Jordan, Maintenance Worker (garbage collector); Tuck Taylor, Maintenance Worker (garbage collector)

Time period(s): 1980s

Locale(s): Cambridge, Massachusetts

What the book is about: The raccoons revolt when garbage collection at a summer resort becomes too efficient. The younger raccoons have never eaten "natural food," they miss Smuckers jam and Cocoa Puffs, Pringles and Bumble Bee tuna cans. Those smart college kids have gone too far and they must be stopped!

Where it's reviewed:
Publisher's Weekly, April 11, 1980, page 78
School Library Journal, May 1980, page 66

Other books by the author:
World of Bruegel, 1968

Other books you might like:
Janet Wyman Coleman, *Fast Eddie*, 1993
To the dismay of Puff the cat and Jones the squirrel, Fast Eddie the raccoon takes on his human neighbors one final time.
Lillian Hoban, *Here Come Raccoons!*, 1977

Twins Albert and Arabella save their fellow raccoons from the wrath of the skunks and possums when a conflict develops over opening garbage cans.
Robert Franklin Leslie, *Ringo, the Robber Raccoon: The True Story of a Northwoods Rogue*, 1984
An account of the close friendship the author developed with a wild raccoon while searching for Sasquatch in the British Columbia wilderness.
H.M. Menino, *Pandora, a Raccoon's Journey*, 1985
Follows the adventures of a young raccoon as she wanders from her den, is adopted by a farm girl, and travels around with a carnival.
Sterling North, *Rascal*, 1963
The author recalls his carefree life in a small midwestern town at the close of WWI, and his adventures with his pet raccoon, Rascal.

633

Esther Forbes

Illustrator: Lynd Ward

Johnny Tremain

Age range: Grades 4-6

Subject(s): Revolutionary War

Major character(s): Johnny Tremain, Apprentice (Silversmith); Mrs. Latham, Parent; Dusty Miller, Child

Time period(s): 1770s (1793)

Locale(s): Boston, Massachusetts

What the book is about: A 13-year-old boy living in Boston is caught up in the events leading to the Revolutionary War. After injuring his hand, Johnny gives up his plans to become a silversmith, and becomes a messenger for the Sons of Liberty. He witnesses the Boston Tea Party and the Battle of Lexington.

Awards the book has won:
Newbery Medal 1944

Other books you might like:
Patricia Edwards Clyne, *The Corduroy Road*, 1973
Young Tib Wade helps a wounded colonial lieutenant return to his platoon with vital information.
Patricia Lee Gauch, *This Time, Tempe Wick?*, 1974
When ten thousand soldiers camp on Tempe's farm in the 1780s and then mutiny, the results are both exciting and humorous.
Bryna Stevens, *Deborah Sampson Goes to War*, 1984
Deborah Sampson disguises herself as a man to join her countrymen in fighting the British. Biography
James Lincoln Collier, *My Brother Sam Is Dead*, 1974
Tim Meeker is left to help at home while his older brother, Sam, leaves to join the Continental Army.
Scott O'Dell, *Sarah Bishop*, 1980
Sarah flees the brutality of the Revolutionary War only to be charged with witchcraft because of her unusual behavior.

634

Liza Fosburgh

Illustrator: Catherine Stock

Bella Arabella (New York: Macmillan, 1985)

Age range: Grades 4-5

Subject(s): Schools/Boarding Schools; Animals/Cats; Remarriage

Major character(s): Arabella Fitzgerald, Preteen; Miranda, Cat

Time period(s): 1920s

Locale(s): New York

What the book is about: Arabella gets her wish when she wants to become a cat to escape her unhappy life and then wishes she were a little girl again. Arabella thinks she can avoid being sent to boarding school by her mother's fourth husband, but she finds her new life filled with unknown terrors.

Where it's reviewed:
Booklist, January 15, 1986, page 756
Center for Children's Books Bulletin, March 1986, page 127
School Library Journal, March 1986, page 162

Other books by the author:
The Wrong Way Home, 1990
Summer Lion, 1987
Mrs. Abercorn and the Bunce Boys, 1986

Other books you might like:
Larry Bograd, *The Fourth-Grade Dinosaur Club*, 1989
    Billy feels that everything in his life is wrong, from his hectic homelife to the bullies at school and his spoiled friendship with his best friend.
Barbara Corcoran, *A Dance to Still Music*, 1974
    Deafened by an illness, Margaret runs away in fear that her mother's remarriage may mean she'll go to a boarding school for the deaf.
Elisabet McHugh, *Beethoven's Cat*, 1988
    After a cat named Ludwig discovers from a book that he resemble Ludwig van Beethoven's cat, he suspects he carries the spirit of the dead composer.
Berniece Rabe, *Tall Enough to Own the World*, 1989
    Unable to read, Joey is often in trouble at school for his rebellious behavior until a series of circumstances help him conquer his problems.
Phyllis Anderson Wood, *A Five-Color Buick and a Blue-Eyed Cat*, 1975
    Two friends team up and use an olf five color Buick to pick up and deliver pet shipments during the summer.

635

Michael W. Fox

Illustrator: Charles Frace

The Wolf (New York: Coward, 1973)

Age range: Grades 2-4

Subject(s): Animals/Wolves

Time period(s): Indeterminate

Locale(s): United States

What the book is about: This story traces the lives of five wolf cubs and their relationship to their family, the pack, humans, and the environment.

Where it's reviewed:
Horn Book, August 1973, page 392

Kirkus Reviews, January 15, 1973, page 62

Awards the book has won:
Christopher Award 1974

Other books by the author:
What Is Your Cat Saying?, 1982
What Is Your Dog Saying?, 1976
Ramu and Chennai: Brothers of the Wild, 1975
Vixie, the Story of a Little Fox, 1973

Other books you might like:
Melvin Burgess, *The Cry of the Wolf*, 1990
    A hunter determined to wipe out every wolf in England almost succeeds, but then finds himself the prey.
Margery Cuyler, *Weird Wolf*, 1989
    When Harry Walpole discovers he is a werewolf, his attempts to break the curse are unsuccessful until he is aided by his pushy friend, Abby.
Sid Fleischman, *Jim Ugly*, 1992
    The adventures of twelve year old Jake and Jim Ugly, his father's mongrel/wolf dog as they travel through the Old West.
Gregory Maguire, *The Dream Stealer*, 1983
    A village of Russian peasants rebuild their homes on a train to flee an evil wolf, and are saved by a little girl's dream and knowledge of a witch.
Whitley Strieber, *Wolf of Shadows*, 1985
    After a nuclear holocaust, a wolf and a human woman form a mysterious bond that brings each close to the spirits of the shattered earth.

636

Paula Fox

Illustrator: Paul Giovanopoulos

How Many Miles to Babylon? (New York: D. White, 1967)

Age range: Grades 4-5

Subject(s): Gangs; African Americans

Major character(s): James Douglas, Child; Grace, Relative (aunt)

Time period(s): 1960s

Locale(s): New York, New York (Brooklyn)

What the book is about: Ten year old James skips school to go to his secret place, a deserted house, where he is found by three teenage boys, Gino, Stick, and Blue, who force him to join their dognapping ring as a finder.

Where it's reviewed:
Booklist, May 1, 1973, page 837
Center for Children's Books Bulletin, December 1967, page 59
Hornbook, October 1967, page 593

Other books by the author:
Monkey Island, 1991
The Moonlight Man, 1986
One-Eyed Cat, 1984
The King's Falcon, 1969

Other books you might like:
Frank Bonham, *The Golden Bees of Tulami*, 1974

Trying not to give in to Turk Ransom's pressure to join a gang, Cool Hankins finds unexpected support from an African stranger on a strange adventure.

Miriam Cohen, *Robert and Dawn Marie 4 Ever*, 1986
A boy in Brooklyn who grew up in the foster care system learns respect and love with a parochial school girl and the eccentric couple who take him in.

Kay Brown, *Willy's Summer Dream*, 1989
Willy, slow in school and ridiculed in his Brooklyn neighborhood, gains confidence from the tutoring of an older girl and other summer experiences.

Eth Clifford, *Will Somebody Please Marry My Sister?*, 1992
In 1920s Brooklyn, Abel and friend Hilda try to find a husband for Abel's doctor sister to marry.

Rosa Guy, *The Ups and Downs of Carl Davis III*, 1989
Carl Davis III writes of his unhappiness as well as his gradual change of heart on being sent to a small southern town to live with his grandmother.

637

Paula Fox

Illustrator: Ingrid Fetz

Maurice's Room (New York: Collier, 1966)

Age range: Grades 2-4

Subject(s): Collectors and Collecting; Humor

Major character(s): Maurice, Child; Jacob, Friend

Time period(s): Indeterminate

Locale(s): United States

What the book is about: An eight year old campaigns to protect his bedroom full of junk. He and Jacob consider these treasures and are determined to protect them from adult attempts to distract them from their goal.

Where it's reviewed:
Booklist, November 15, 1966, page 376
Hornbook, October 1966, page 561
Kirkus Reviews, February 1, 1966, page 109

Other books by the author:
Lily and the Lost Boy, 1987
Blowfish Live in the Sea, 1970
Dear Prosper, 1968
How Many Miles to Babylon?, 1967

Other books you might like:
Judith Gorog, *In a Messy, Messy Room*, 1990
A collection of scary stories with humorous or unexpected endings.

Jon Madian, *Beautiful Junk: A Story of the Watts Tower*, 1968
A young boy learns how an old man came to build three towers out of "beautiful junk" in the Watts section of Los Angeles.

Sandi Barrett Ruch, *Junkyard Dog*, 1990
Follows the exciting adventures of Toad and mean old Slobber, the junkyard dog, as they form an unlikely friendship and find a place to call home.

Susan Russo, *Joe's Junk*, 1982
Joe's parents insist on a garage sale to dispose of the junk Joe has collected when his room begins to smell and he has a hard time finding things.

Ann Tompert, *It May Come in Handy Someday*, 1975

An old couple leads a peaceful life in their little cottage until the day the old man brings home his first load of junk.

638

Paula Fox

Monkey Island (New York: Watts/Orchard, 1991)

Age range: Grades 5 and Up

Subject(s): Homeless

Major character(s): Clay Garrity, Preteen, Runaway; Buddy, Teenager, Runaway; Calvin, Teacher, Streetperson

Time period(s): 1990s

Locale(s): New York, New York

What the book is about: Eleven year old Clay is on his own in New York City. His father has lost his job and disappeared and his mother leaves one day and doesn't return. After five days, Clay, frightened of the authorities, runs away and lives on the street. He finds friends, Calvin and buddy, who share the park with him. A vivid picture of the homeless.

Where it's reviewed:
Booklist, September 1, 1991, page 51

Other books by the author:
The Moonlight Man, 1986
One-Eyed Cat, 1984
The Slave Dancer, 1973

Other books you might like:
Barbara Aiello, *Hometown Hero: Featuring Scott Whittaker*, 1989
Fifth grader Scott reveals in his diary how he copes with his asthma and about his encounter with a homeless person in the library.

Jean Craighead George, *The Missing 'Gator of Gumbo Limbo: An Ecological Mystery*, 1992
Sixth grader Liza, one of five people living in an unspoiled forest in southern Florida, searches for a missing alligator.

Felice Holman, *Slake's Limbo*, 1974
Thirteen year old Aremis Slake, hounded by his fears and misfortunes, flees into New York's subway tunnels. He thinks he may live there permanently.

Jill Pinkwater, *Tails of the Bronx: A Tale of the Bronx*, 1991
In their search for a group of missing cats, a group of children in the Bronx encounters the problems of homelessness firsthand.

Stephanie S. Tolan, *Sophie and the Sidewalk Man*, 1992
Sophie is torn between her desire to buy a beautiful toy hedgehog and her compassion for a hungry street person.

639

Paula Fox

Illustrator: Irene Trivas

One-Eyed Cat (Scarsdale, New York: Bradbury, 1984)

Age range: Grades 5 and Up

Subject(s): Clergy; Guns and Gun Control

Major character(s): Ned Wallis, Child

Time period(s): 1930s (1935)

Locale(s): New York

What the book is about: 11 year old Ned Wallis shoots a stray cat with his new air rifle and is devastated with guilt because he has been trying to be the perfect person his minister father wants him to be. Ned is eventually able to take responsibility for the incident.

Where it's reviewed:
Center for Children's Books Bulletin, October 1984, page 24
Horn Book, January/February 1985, page 57

Awards the book has won:
Newbery Honor

Other books by the author:
Blowfish Live in the Sea, 1970
How Many Miles to Babylon?, 1967
Lily and the Lost Boy, 1987
Servant's Tale, 1984

Other books you might like:
Pat Ross, *Gloria and the Super Soaper*, 1982
   Gloria loves her collection of toy guns, but more than anything she would like to catch a real robber.
Rose Blue, *The Preacher's Kid*, 1975
   When her minister father supports a school busing issue, Linda finds herself questioning her own values.
Bill Wallace, *Totally Disgusting*, 1991
   The cat Mewkiss proves to be strong and brave in a crisis.
Bill Wallace, *Snot Stew*, 1989
   Brother and sister cats are taken in by a family and learn to get along with humans.
Jan Slepian, *The Broccoli Tapes*, 1989
   Sara sends taped reports back to her sixth grade class, including news of adoption of a wild cat, a new friendship, and the death of her grandmother.

640

Paula Fox

Illustrator: Saul Lambert

Portrait of Ivan (New Jersey: Bradbury, 1969)

Age range: Grades 5-7

Subject(s): Fathers and Sons; Russian Americans

Major character(s): Ivan, Preteen; Matt Mustazza, Artist; Miss Manderby, Model

Time period(s): 1960s

Locale(s): Florida

What the book is about: Ivan's world expands while his portrait is painted. His mother was Russian. She had left Russia in a sled pulled across the snow by horses. After the sled crossed the border, she had gone on to Warsaw. Now, a stranger poses as his mother in the portrait his father has commissioned of Ivan.

Where it's reviewed:
Booklist, Febraury 1, 1970, page 670
Center for Children's Books Bulletin, February 1970, page 96
Hornbook, April 1970, page 159

Other books by the author:
The Village by the Sea, 1988
Lily and the Lost Boy, 1987
A Place Apart, 1980

The Stone-Faced Boy, 1968

Other books you might like:
Grigorii Baklanov, *Forever Nineteen*, 1989
   The experiences of a nineteen year old Soviet lieutenant on the front during World War II as he defends his Russian homeland from the Nazis.
Nancy Pitt, *Behind the High White Wall*, 1986
   Witnessing a murder in the Ukraine in 1903, Libby triggers a wave of hate against her Jewish family, making them consider emigrating to America.
Jerry Segal, *The Place Where Nobody Stopped*, 1991
   A Jewish man plants himself in a lonely Russian baker's house and establishes a family while waiting for permission to go to America.
Neal Shusterman, *Dissidents*, 1989
   Derek, son of the recently deceased American ambassador to the Soviet Union, decides to smuggle a Russian dissident's daughter out of Moscow.
Vladimir Zheleznikov, *Scarecrow*, 1990
   Lena comes to live with her grandfather in a small Russian town and finds herself persecuted by a gang of her classmates at her new school.

641

Paula Fox

Illustrator: Keith Eros

The Slave Dancer (New York: Bradbury, 1973)

Age range: Grades 6 and Up

Subject(s): Slavery; Kidnapping

Major character(s): Jessie Bollier, Captive, Musician; Ras, Slave; Benjamin Stout, Sailor

Time period(s): 1840s

Locale(s): New Orleans, Louisiana

What the book is about: Jessie is kidnapped and taken aboard a slave ship to play his fife while the slaves are forced to exercise. When the ship is destroyed in a storm, Jessie and a young black boy must try to survive together.

Where it's reviewed:
Booklist, January 1, 1974, page 484
Horn Book, December 1973, page 596

Awards the book has won:
Newbery Medal 1974

Other books by the author:
How Many Miles to Babylon?, 1967
One-Eyed Cat, 1984
Lily and the Lost Boy, 1987
The Village by the Sea, 1988
Monkey Island, 1991

Other books you might like:
James Lincoln Collier, *Jump Ship to Freedom*,
   Daniel's owner sends him to sea to keep him from buying his mother and father's freedom.
Ann Warren Turner, *Nettie's Trip South*, 1987
   A 10 year old northern girl experiences the ugliness of slavery just before the Civil War.
Peg Kehret, *Deadly Stranger*, 1987
   Katie's "first day" friend in her new school is kidnapped and Katie is involved in a hit and run accident.

Milton Meltzer, *All Times, All People*, 1980
  This history of slavery in all parts of the world tells how slaves lived in many different cultures. (Non-fiction)

642

Paula Fox

Illustrator: Donald A. Mackay

The Stone-Faced Boy (Scarsdale, New York: Bradbury, 1968)

Age range: Grades 4-6

Subject(s): Family Life; Brothers and Sisters

Major character(s): Mr. Oliver, Health Care Professional (optometrist); Rachel Oliver, Teenager; Gus Oliver, Preteen

Time period(s): 1960s

Locale(s): United States

What the book is about: Only his strange great aunt seems to understand the thoughts of a boy who has spent his life concealing his emotions on an eerie, snowy night after rescuing a dog that dislikes him, at four in the morning in a raging snowstorm. Gus is stuck in the middle of a large family, and staying in a cramped room full of nightmares until the visit of the mysterious Aunt Hattie is over.

Where it's reviewed:
Booklist, January 15, 1969, page 546
Hornbook, February 1969, page 53
School Library Journal, December 1978, page 33

Other books by the author:
Amzat and His Brothers, 1993
Blowfish Live in the Sea, 1970
How Many Miles to Babylon?, 1967
The King's Falcon, 1969

Other books you might like:
Hetty Burlingame Beatty, *Blitz*, 1961
  A fire horse is displaced by motorized trucks, sold to a cruel peddler, rescued from a horsemeat factory, and becomes a hero in a snowstorm.
Carol J. Farley, *Mystery of the Melted Diamonds*, 1986
  Kipper and his cousin Larry get caught in a Kansas snowstorm and become involved in the search for stolen diamonds.
Roderic Jeffries, *Trapped*, 1972
  Hampered by darkness and a snowstorm, the river patrol tries to locate two boys before the tide seeps them off the mudflats where they are trapped.
Harry Mazer, *Snow Bound*, 1973
  Two teenagers caught in a snowstorm face a fight for survival in a desolate area.
Elizabeth Van Steenwyk, *Terror on the Rebound*, 1983
  After their van is wrecked during a snowstorm, the members of a girls' basketball team take refuge in an isolated house holding unimagined secrets.

643

Paula Fox

The Village by the Sea (New York: Orchard, 1988)

Age range: Grades 4-6

Subject(s): Aunts and Uncles; Beaches

Major character(s): Emma, Child; Bea, Relative (aunt); Bertie, Child

Time period(s): 1980s

Locale(s): Peconic Bay

What the book is about: When her father has open-heart surgery, ten year old Emma is sent to stay with her quarrelsome aunt and rather strange uncle. Emma experiences jealousy and the power of love and forgiveness. Emma and Bertie build a village of things that have washed up on the beach.

Where it's reviewed:
Center for Children's Books Bulletin, July/August 1988, page 227
Horn Book, September/October 1988, page 625

Other books by the author:
Monkey Island, 1991
The Slave Dancer, 1988
Lily and the Lost Boy, 1987
How Many Miles to Babylon?, 1967

Other books you might like:
David A. Adler, *The Fourth Floor Twins and the Sand Castle Contest*, 1988
  After winning a sand castle contest, two sets of twins solve a mystery. (Easy Reading)
Margaret Joyce Baker, *The Sand Bird*, 1973
  At a jumble sale, three children buy an unusual sand-filled glass swan that makes wishes come true.
Jo Dereske, *My Cousin, the Poodle*, 1991
  While staying with their eccentric aunt and uncle, Barbara and Tommy find their visit dominated by the poodle, Terry Berry.
Graham Salisbury, *Blue Skin of the Sea*, 1992
  Sonny tries to come to terms with his feelings for his father and the sea that dominates their lives.
Marilyn Singer, *It Can't Hurt Forever*, 1978
  Eleven year old Ellie describes her experiences during twelve days of hospitalization for heart surgery.

644

Russell Freedman

Lincoln: A Photobiography (New York: Clarion, 1987)

Age range: Grades 6 and Up

Subject(s): Biography; Presidents

Major character(s): Abraham Lincoln, Historical Figure, Political Figure

Time period(s): 19th century

Locale(s): New Salem, Illinois

What the book is about: Contrasting Lincoln's legends and the facts, his childhood, self-education, early business and entry into politics are highlighted here. The second half of the book covers his presidency and assassination.

Where it's reviewed:
Booklist, December 15, 1987, page 705
School Library Journal, December 1987, page 93

Awards the book has won:
Newbery Medal 1988

Other books by the author:
Franklin Delano Roosevelt, 1990
Buffalo Hunt, 1988
Indian Chiefs, 1987
Cowboys of the Wild West, 1985

Other books you might like:
LaVere Anderson, *Abe Lincoln and the River Robbers,* 1971
　Recounts the adventures of a nineteen year old Abe Lincoln
　and his friend, Allen Gentry, on a flatboat journey down the
　Ohio and Mississippi Rivers.
Brent K. Ashabranner, *A Memorial for Mr. Lincoln,* 1992
　Describes Lincoln's role in American history and describes
　the planning and building of the monument dedicated to him
　in 1922.
Janet Halliday Ervin, *More than Halfway There,* 1970
　Although his father has told him that book learning is foolish
　for a woodsman, Albert plans to change his mind after he
　meets Abraham Lincoln.
Jim Hargrove, *Abraham Lincoln: 16th President,* 1988
　Traces the life of the frontier clerk, storekeeper, lawyer,
　politicain, and Civil War president.
William Jay Jacobs, *Lincoln,* 1991
　Describes the life and achievements of the Civil War presi-
　dent.

645

Barbara Constance Freeman

A Haunting Air (New York: Dutton, 1977)

Age range: Grades 5-6

Subject(s): Ghosts; Fantasy

Major character(s): Melissa, Preteen; Hanny, Spirit (ghost)

Time period(s): 1970s

Locale(s): Bellwood, England

What the book is about: A child of the past proves to be
the sad little ghost who sings the haunting air heard by Melissa
and her neighbor. Henry was the illegitimate child of a servant
who had longed for a baby to love. Good blend of reality and
fantasy.

Where it's reviewed:
Horn Book, April 1978, page 163
Kirkus Reviews, December 1, 1977, page 1270

Other books by the author:
A Pocket of Silence, 1978
The Summer Travellers, 1978
The Other Face, 1977

Other books you might like:
Carole S. Adler, *Footsteps on the Stairs,* 1982
　Dodie and Anne pursue two ghosts that are haunting their
　summer house.
Joan Aiken, *The Shadow Guests,* 1980
　Ghosts appear to Cosmo Autry to seek his help in breaking
　the power of a curse.
Sylvia Cassedy, *Behind the Attic Wall,* 1983
　Maggie, a difficult girl, is contacted by ghosts in the large
　house where two great-aunts live.
Daniel Cohen, *The Restless Dead,* 1987

Eleven ghost stories from around the world.
E.W. Hildick, *The Ghost Squad Breaks Through,* 1984
　Ghosts and the ghost squad work together to prevent a
　crime.

646

Berniece Freschet

Illustrator: Gina Freschet

Bernard Sees the World (New York: Scribner, 1976)

Age range: Grades 1-3

Subject(s): Animals/Mice; Voyages and Travels

Major character(s): Bernard, Mouse, Traveller

Time period(s): 1970s

Locale(s): Boston, Massachusetts

What the book is about: Bernard loves to read about far
away places. He decides to travel by skateboard, bike, a
rowing shell, ship, and a rocket to the moon. He comes home in
time for Christmas.

Where it's reviewed:
Kirkus Reviews, August 1, 1976, page 842
School Library Journal, October 1976, page 97

Other books by the author:
Bernard of Scotland Yard, 1978
The Happy Dromedary, 1977
Grizzly Bear, 1976
Lizard Lying in the Sun, 1975

Other books you might like:
Elizabeth Bram, *Woodruff and the Clocks,* 1980
　The story of a boy who loves inventing adventures.
Raymond James, *The Time Machine,* 1993
　A scientist invents a time machine and travels far into the
　future, where he discovers the Eloi and the underground
　Morlocks.
Roxie Munro, *The Inside-Outside Book of Paris,* 1992
　A look at the Eiffel Tower, Arch of Triumph, the Metro
　subway and a puppet theater in Paris.
Jon Scieszka, *The Good, the Bad, and the Goofy,* 1992
　The Time Warp Trio find themselves in the Wild West of
　yesteryear, rubbing elbows with cowboys and Indians.
Vera B. Williams, *Stringbean's Trip to the Shining Sea,* 1988
　A journey from Kansas to the West Coast, with Stringbean
　sending postcards along the way.

647

Ina R. Friedman

Illustrator: Allen Say

How My Parents Learned to Eat (Boston: Houghton Mifflin, 1984)

Age range: Grades 1-3

Subject(s): Japanese Americans

Time period(s): Indeterminate

Locale(s): Yokohama, Japan

What the book is about: A small girl describes how her American sailor father and Japanese mother learned to adapt to each other's style of eating during their courtship. "That's why," the story ends, "at our house, some days we eat with chopsticks and some days we eat with knives and forks."

Where it's reviewed:
Center for Children's Books Bulletin, January 1985, page 83
Horn Book, January/February 1985, page 44

Awards the book has won:
Christopher Award

Other books you might like:
Geraldine McCaughrean, *The Cherry Tree*, 1992
  Tai-Chi and Yumiko find new hope nursing a cherry tree after their father's death.
Allen Say, *Tree of Cranes*, 1991
  A Japanese boy learns of Christmas when his mother decorates a tree with paper cranes.
Helene Clare Pittman, *Gift of the Willows*, 1988
  A willow tree symbolizes the desire of a Japanese potter and his wife to overcome obstacles.
Marilyn Hirsh, *How the World Got Its Color*, 1972
  A Japanese girl borrows her father's paints to help the gods finish the colorless world.
Taro Yashima, *Seashore Story*, 1967
  An old Japanese story about a fisherman who rode on a turtle's back to a place under the sea.

648

Babbis Friis-Baastad

Don't Take Teddy (New York: Scribners, 1967)

Age range: Grades 5-7

Subject(s): Mentally Handicapped

Major character(s): Mikkel Grabseth, Teenager, Runaway; Teddy Grabseth, Teenager, Handicapped (mentally retarded)

Time period(s): 1960s

Locale(s): Norway

What the book is about: Mikkel's fifteen year old brother, Teddy, is mentally retarded. His neighbors say he should be locked away. When Teddy accidentally hurts someone, Mikkel runs away, taking Teddy with him into the mountains of Norway.

Where it's reviewed:
Library Journal, May 15, 1967, page 2020
Saturday Review, April 22, 1967, page 100

Awards the book has won:
Mildred L. Batchelder Award 1969

Other books by the author:
Kristy's Courage, 1965

Other books you might like:
Louise Albert, *But I'm Ready to Go*, 1976
  A slightly retarded fifteen year old girl tries to become a singer in order to win approval from her family and friends.
Emily Hanlon, *It's Too Late for Sorry*, 1978
  Fifteen year old Kenny's involvement with the mentally retarded youth on his block brings out the best and worst in him.
Eleanor Means Hull, *Alice with the Golden Hair*, 1981

An 18 year old mentally retarded girl has problems adjusting to her job in a nursing home, but soon finds friendship and a feeling of self worth.
David Melton, *A Boy Called Hopeless*, 1986
  Mary Jane describes her family's reaction when they discover that her younger brother is brain injured.
Robert Newton Peck, *Clunie*, 1979
  A teenage boy risks his own popularity to give friendship and support to a retarded girl who is harrassed by her classmates.

649

Jean Fritz

Illustrator: Margot Tomes

And Then What Happened, Paul Revere? (New York: Coward McCann, 1973)

Age range: Grades 3-5

Subject(s): Revolutionary War

Major character(s): Paul Revere, Patriot, Historical Figure

Time period(s): 1770s

Locale(s): Boston, Massachusetts, American Colonies

What the book is about: Paul Revere loved people and excitement. The description of his ride is funny, fast-paced, and historically accurate. The book includes description of his life and some American friends and enemies.

Where it's reviewed:
Book World, November 11, 1973, page 3C
Kirkus Reviews, October 1, 1973, page 1100

Awards the book has won:
Boston Globe/Horn Book Award - Honor Book 1974

Other books by the author:
Bully for You, Teddy Roosevelt, 1991
Can't You Make Them Behave, King George?, 1977
What's the Big Idea, Ben Franklin?, 1976
Where Was Patrick Henry on the 29th of May?, 1975

Other books you might like:
Leonard Everett Fisher, *Two If by Sea*, 1970
  Recounts the events on the eve of April 18, 1775, when Paul Revere made his historic ride to warn the colonists of the approaching British.
Esther Forbes, *America's Paul Revere*, 1991
  A biography of the patriot of the Revolution who had many trades, including silver work, copper work, casting of bells, engraving and dentistry.
Marc Kornblatt, *Paul Revere and the Boston Tea Party*, 1987
  As a time traveler, you can follow Paul Revere and discover who was responsible for the Boston Tea Party.
Robert Lawson, *Mr. Revere and I*, 1981
  The life of the Revere family and the doings of the Sons of Liberty as told from the point of view of Paul Revere's horse.
Martin Lee, *Paul Revere*, 1987
  A biography of the Revolutionary War patriot who was also a renowned silversmith.

650

Jean Fritz

Illustrator: Ed Young

The Double Life of Pocahontas (New York: Putnam, 1983)

Age range: Grades 4-6

Subject(s): Biography; American Colonies

Major character(s): Pocahontas, Indian, Historical Figure; Powhatan, Indian, Historical Figure; Captain John Smith, Settler, Historical Figure

Time period(s): 17th century (1607-1622)

Locale(s): Jamestown, Virginia, American Colonies

What the book is about: This is the story of the divided loyalties of an Indian woman in the 1600s. She is held hostage by the settlers, converts to Christianity, and experiences great conflict between her two cultures.

Where it's reviewed:
Center for Children's Books Bulletin, January 1984, page 86
Horn Book, December 1983, page 724

Awards the book has won:
Boston Globe/Horn Book Award - Non-Fiction 1984

Other books by the author:
Shh! We're Writing the Constitution, 1987
Homesick: My Own Story, 1982
The Good Giants and the Bad Pukwidgies, 1982
Where Do You Think You're Going, Christopher Columbus?, 1980

Other books you might like:
Elizabeth Campbell, *Jamestown: The Beginning*, 1974
    Describes the founding of Jamestown, the first permanent English settlement in North America. (Non-fiction)
Carol Greene, *Pocahontas: Daughter of a Chief*, 1988
    A brief biography of the American Indian princess who befriended John Smith, protected him from her father, and helped the Jamestown colonists.
Mary Holmes, *Two Chimneys*, 1992
    In 1628, after six years on her family's Virginia tobacco plantation, Katherine doesn't want to go after learning of her betrothal to an English heir.
Florence Jackson, *Blacks in America, 1791-1863*, 1971
    Traces black history in America, from their landing at Jamestown to the framing of the constitution. Includes contributions of some famous black men.
Scott O'Dell, *The Serpent Never Sleeps: A Novel of Jamestown and Pocahontas*, 1987
    In the early 1700s, Serena Lynn, determined to be with her longtime love, travels to America, learns of colonial hardships, and meets Pocahontas.

651

Jean Fritz

Illustrator: Lynd Ward

Early Thunder (New York: Coward-McCann, 1967)

Age range: Grades 5-8

Subject(s): Revolutionary War

Major character(s): Daniel West, Teenager

Time period(s): 1770s (1775)

Locale(s): Salem, Massachusetts

What the book is about: Although he is a dedicated Tory, Daniel hates the growing violence of the Whig-Tory conflict which splits Salem and its people. He despises the Liberty Boys creeping up to Tory porches with buckets of garbage. Daniel's struggle to find his place and a stand he can take proudly is resolved in a true event that nearly starts the American Revolution.

Where it's reviewed:
Booklist, December 1, 1967, page 446
Center for Children's Books Bulletin, February 1968, page 93
Kirkus Reviews, October 1, 1967, page 1218

Other books by the author:
The Double Life of Pocahontas, 1983
Magic to Burn, 1964
Brady, 1960
The Cabin Faced West, 1958

Other books you might like:
Deborah H. DeFord, *An Enemy Among Them*, 1987
    A young Hessian soldier questions his loyalty to his king after fighting with the British in America during the Revolutionary War.
Esther Forbes, *Johnny Tremain*, 1943
    After injuring his hand, a silversmith's apprentice in Boston becomes a messenger for the Sons of Liberty in the days before the American Revolution.
Dorothea Jensen, *The Riddle of Penncroft Farm*, 1989
    Lars Olafson moves to a farm near Valley Forge and meets the ghost of an 18th century ancestor, who tells of his life during the American Revolution.
Ruth Nulton Moore, *Distant Thunder*, 1991
    In the Moravian community of Bethlehem, Pennsylvania during the American Revolution, Kate and friends show how a peaceful people can ease war's woes.
Seymour Reit, *Guns for General Washington*, 1990
    Under seige in George Washington's army, Will Knox and his brother Colonel Henry Knox try to move 183 cannon from Fort Ticonderoga to Boston in winter

652

Jean Fritz

Illustrator: Margot Tomes

Homesick: My Own Story (New York: Putnam, 1982)

Age range: Grades 4-6

Subject(s): Religion

Major character(s): Jean, Child; Lin Nai Nai, Governess; Andrea, Friend

Time period(s): 1920s

Locale(s): Hankow, China

What the book is about: A fictionalized autobiography of Jean Fritz growing up in China. Her father is the director of the YMCA in Hankow. She loves the city and the Yangtze River, but feels homesick away from her family in Pennsylvania.

Where it's reviewed:
Center for Children's Books Bulletin, July/August 1982, page 206

Horn Book, December 1982, page 649

Awards the book has won:
Newbery Honor 1983

Other books by the author:
Make Way for Sam Houston, 1986
The Double Life of Pocahontas, 1983
Early Thunder, 1967
The Cabin Faced West, 1958

Other books you might like:
Margaret Scrogin Chang, *In the Eye of War*, 1990
During the final days of Japanese occupation, Shao-Shao celebrtes his birthday, observes holidays with his family and befriends a traitor's daughter.
Betty Vander Els, *Leaving Point*, 1987
Home from boarding school for Christmas, Ruth and her brothers find that Communist Revolution has changed Ruth's friendship with a young Chinese girl.
Kathy Lynn Emerson, *Julia's Mending*, 1987
When her parents have gone to China without her, Julia is sent to New York where she breaks her leg and heals her anger.
Michael Morpungo, *King of the Cloud Forests*, 1987
After being rescued in Tibet by a tribe who believe he is a god, Ashley must choose between returning to his village or stay with the tribe.
Emily Cheney Neville, *The China Year*, 1991
Henrietta Rich, a New York City teenager, spends a year in China when her father accepts a teaching position in Beijing.

653

Margaret Walden Froehlich

Hide Crawford Quick (Boston: Houghton Mifflin, 1983)

Age range: Grades 5-8

Subject(s): Babies; Physically Handicapped

Major character(s): Gracie Prayther, Preteen; Crawford Prayther, Child; Olive Moore, Child-Care Giver (Nanny)

Time period(s): 1940s (1942)

Locale(s): Erie, Pennsylvania

What the book is about: On Thanksgiving Day, Gracie's baby brother is born. With four girls already, everyone wanted a boy. Why isn't he being named for Daddy? The family finds itself sharing the burden of a terrible secret when baby Crawford comes home.

Where it's reviewed:
Booklist, May 15, 1983, page 1215
Hornbook, April 1983, page 165
School Library Journal, August 1983, page 76

Other books by the author:
Reasons to Stay, 1986

Other books you might like:
Dennis Covington, *Lizard*, 1991
Sent by his guardian to live at a school for retarded boys, Lizard escapes with the help of an actor who gives him a role in his acting company.
Lois Metzger, *Barry's Sister*, 1992
Ellen's hatred for her brother Barry, who has cerebral palsey, changes to an obsessive love, and she must find a proper balance for her life.
Carolyn Meyer, *Killing the Kudu*, 1990
Suffocating from his mother's overprotectiveness, Alex, a paraplegic, finds freedom and his first love with the cousin who crippled him years ago.
Linda Lee Ratto, *Coping with a Physically Challenged Brother or Sister*, 1992
Young people talk about how they feel as siblings of the physically challenged. (Non-Fiction)
Nancy Springer, *Colt*, 1991
A boy with a crippling disease learns, through horseback riding, to overcome his own anxieties and to help others in dealing with their problems.

G

Dick Gackenbach

Hattie Be Quiet, Hattie Be Good (New York: Harper, 1977)

Age range: Grades 1-3

Subject(s): Behavior; Animals/Rabbits

Major character(s): Hattie, Child

Time period(s): 1920s

Locale(s): United States

What the book is about: Two stories about Hattie for beginning readers. In the first, Hattie tries to be quiet for a whole hour. In the second, she shows her caring friendship by visiting a friend who is sick.

Where it's reviewed:
Booklist, May 15, 1977, page 1420
Kirkus Reviews, February 1, 1977, page 90
School Library Journal, May 1977, page 75

Other books by the author:
Hurray for Hattie Rabbit, 1986
More From Hound and Bear, 1979
Hound and Bear, 1976

Other books you might like:
Jeffrey Allen, *Bonzini! The Tattooed Man*, 1976
  The children in a quiet Texas town have their lives brightened by a tattooed man from a circus.
Beverly Keller, *When Mother Got the Flu*, 1984
  A young boy tries to be very quiet and good while his mother has the flu, but the situation gets out of hand.
Jan Mark, *Fun*, 1987
  James has his own quiet ideas about having fun, often incompatible with the somewhat frantic efforts of his devoted parents to show him a good time.
Marjorie Weinman Sharmat, *Hooray for Father's Day*, 1987
  Father Mule's two children spend Father's Day showering him with gifts that leave him exhausted, when the gift he really needs is peace and quiet.
Tobi Tobias, *Quiet or Noisy? That's a Good Question!*, 1977
  Simple text and illustrations introduce a variety of things and situations considered quiet or noisy.

Age range: Grades 4-6

Subject(s): Animals/Dogs; Depression; Grandparents

Major character(s): Bruce Hardy, Preteen; Gramps, Grandparent

Time period(s): 1980s

Locale(s): United States

What the book is about: Bruce is dismayed to find his grandfather in a severe depression when he arrives to spend the summer. Before summer is over and Bruce is ready to leave, they re-establish their close bond and Bruce hopes a new dog will keep Gramps from being lonely.

Where it's reviewed:
Booklist, April 15, 1989, page 1466
School Library Journal, May 1989, page 104

Other books by the author:
Daffodils in the Snow, 1984
Your Former Friend, Matthew, 1984
The Kid with the Red Suspenders, 1983
Just Like Sisters, 1981

Other books you might like:
Achim Broger, *The Day Chubby Became Charles*, 1990
  Afraid that her grandmother might be dying, Julia discovers a new friend with whom she can talk about her fears.
Patricia Hermes, *Who Will Take Care of Me?*, 1983
  Terrified that the death of the grandmother who was their guardian will separate them, Mark decides to run away with his retarded younger brother.
Norma Johnston, *Return to Morocco*, 1988
  Shortly after she and her grandmother arrive in Morocco, Tori finds herself faced with sudden death and a secret from her grandmother's past.
Jody Sorenson, *The Secret Letters of Mama Cat*, 1988
  Meredith has to deal with moving to Texas, the departure of her sister to a boarding school for the deaf, and the death of her grandmother.
Ivan Southall, *The Mysterious World of Marcus Leadbeater*, 1990
  Trying to cope with the death of his beloved grandfather, Marc goes to visit his grandmother, only to find her mysteriously missing.

LouAnn Gaeddert

A Summer Like Turnips (New York: Holt, 1989)

Wanda Gag, Author/Illustrator

ABC Bunny (New York: Coward-McCann, 1933)

Age range: Grades 2-3

Subject(s): Animals/Rabbits

Time period(s): Indeterminate

Locale(s): United States

What the book is about: An alphabet book which tells, in verse and pictures, the story of a little rabbit's adventures in storm and sunshine.

Where it's reviewed:
Booklist, November 1933, page 150
Saturday Review of Literature, November 18, 1933, page 279

Awards the book has won:
Newbery Honor

Other books by the author:
Funny Thing, 1929
Millions of Cats, 1928
Snippy and Snappy, 1931

Other books you might like:
Beatrix Potter, *The Tale of Peter Rabbit*, 1987
   The disobedient rabbit ignores his mother's directions and goes to Mr. McGregor's garden.
David A. Adler, *Bunny Rabbit Rebus*, 1983
   Mother rabbit is forced into trading to get food for little rabbit.
Adrienne Adams, *Easter Egg Artists*, 1976
   Orson decides to try many different styles of painting in his family's Easter egg painting business.
Marc T. Brown, *The Bionic Bunny Show*, 1984
   The Bionic Bunny is an ordinary family rabbit who becomes a hero on TV through the costume and special effects.
Judy Delton, *Hired Help for Rabbit*, 1988
   Overworked rabbit hires a squirrel who can't cook as a cook, and a hedgehog who can't clean as a clean up helper.

657

Wanda Gag, Author/Illustrator

Millions of Cats (New York: Coward-McCann, 1928)

Age range: Grades 2-3

Subject(s): Animals/Cats

Time period(s): Indeterminate

Locale(s): United States

What the book is about: An old man goes out to get one cat for his wife and brings home millions and millions of cats.

Where it's reviewed:
Booklist, November 1928, page 74
Saturday Review of Literature, September 22, 1928, page 149

Awards the book has won:
Newbery Honor

Other books by the author:
ABC Bunny, 1933
Funny Thing, 1929
Snippy and Snappy, 1931

Other books you might like:
Lorna Balian, *Amelia's Nine Lives*, 1986

When Nora's cat, Amelia, disappears, friends, one by one, give Nora replacement black cats.
Patricia Reilly Giff, *Powder Puff Puzzle*, 1987
   Dawn Bosco and her cohorts search for Dawn's escaped cat, Powder Puff.
Clare Turlay Newberry, *April's Kittens*, 1940
   Three new kittens are too many for a small apartment.
George Selden, *Harry Kitten and Tucker Mouse*, 1086
   A mouse and a kitten become friends in this prequel to *A Cricket in Times Square*.

658

Wilson Gage

Illustrator: Marylin Hafner

The Crow and Mrs. Gaddy (New York: Greenwillow, 1984)

Age range: Grades 1-3

Subject(s): Animals/Birds; Humor

Major character(s): Mrs. Gaddy, Housewife

Time period(s): Indeterminate

Locale(s): United States

What the book is about: Dirty tricks are the order of the day whe a crow and Mrs. Gaddy try to outdo each other. The crow eats the seeds Mrs. Gaddy has planted. She gets back at him by planting small white stones which he eats. He then takes all the clothespins from her washline and so it goes, until they realize there is more fun to life than tricks, and get their lives on track, more or less.

Where it's reviewed:
Horn Book, June 1984, page 325
School Library Journal, May 1984, page 96

Other books by the author:
Mrs. Gaddy and the Fast-Growing Vine, 1985
Cully Cully and the Bear, 1983
Down in the Boondocks, 1977
Mike's Toads, 1970

Other books you might like:
Jana Dillon, *Jeb Scarecrow's Pumpkin Patch*, 1992
   Jeb Scarecrow comes up with a wonderful plan to scare the crows away from his pumpkin patch.
Jack Gantos, *Willy's Raiders*, 1980
   Willy's Raiders, who always play fair, prove the good guys always win when they go for the championship against the Weasels, who play dirty tricks.
Sarah Hayes, *The Crumbling Castle*, 1992
   Hoping to enjoy a quiet life working spells in his new castle, Zeb the wizard finds his peace broken by Jason the crow and other zany occupants.
Elizabeth Baldwin Hazelton, *Sammy, the Crow Who Remembered*, 1969
   The true story of a crow who returned to the family he had known, loved, and played with when he was a very young bird.
Betty Jean Lifton, *Joji and the Dragon*, 1957
   With the help of his friends, a kind scarecrow is able to prove he is scarier than Toho the Terrible.

659

Wilson Gage

Illustrator: Glen Rounds

Down in the Boondocks (New York: Greenwillow, 1977)

Age range: Grades 2-4

Subject(s): Farm Life; Poetry

Time period(s): Indeterminate

Locale(s): United States

What the book is about: Easy text tells the story of a near-deaf farmer who is impervious to noise and a robber who isn't. The farmer thinks life is peaceful and quiet, the robber thinks it is incredibly noisy and spooky.

Where it's reviewed:
Booklist, October 15, 1977, page 382
Hornbook, February 1978, page 41
Kirkus Reviews, August 15, 1977, page 848

Other books by the author:
Mrs. Gaddy and the Fast-Growing Vine, 1985
The Crow and Mrs. Gaddy, 1984
Cully Cully and the Bear, 1983
Squash Pie, 1976

Other books you might like:
Peter Chirsten Asbjornsen, *The Man Who Kept House*, 1992
　　Convinced that his work in the fields is harder than his wife's work at home, a farmer trades places with his wife for a day.
Patricia Demuth, *The Ornery Morning*, 1991
　　Farmer Bill wakes up late one morning to find that all of his animals, from the rooster to the cat, refuse to do any work.
Gerda Mantinband, *The Blabbermouths*, 1992
　　Although he swears not to reveal the source of his new-found wealth, a farmer tells his wife and then a neighbor, and soon the news is all over town.
W. Nikola-Lisa, *Storm*, 1993
　　A farmer and family watch as a thunderstorm sweeps into the valley, surrounds them, and then rushes off again.
Mary Riskind, *Apple Is My Sign*, 1981
　　A ten year old boy returns to his parents' apple farm for the holidays after his first term at a school for the deaf in Philadelphia.

660

Ernest J. Gaines

Illustrator: Don Bolognese

A Long Day in November (New York: Dial, 1971)

Age range: Grades 5-8

Subject(s): African Americans; Family Problems; Religion

Major character(s): Sonny, Child; Eddie, Parent

Time period(s): 1940s

Locale(s): United States (Sugarcane plantation)

What the book is about: The events of a day as seen through the eyes of a young black boy on a southern sugarcane plantation in the 1940s. On this day his parents argue, separate, and then are reconciled with the help and advice of Madame Toussaint, a woman knowledgeable in the ways of voodoo.

Where it's reviewed:
Booklist, May 1, 1973, page 838
Center for Children's Books Bulletin, February 1972, page 91
Hornbook, April 1972, page 153

Other books by the author:
A Gathering of Old Men, 1983
In My Father's House, 1978
The Autobiography of Miss Jane Pittman, 1971
Bloodline, 1968

Other books you might like:
Berthe Amoss, *The Chalk Cross*, 1976
　　A young girl in 19th century New Orleans struggles between her growing familiarity with voodoo and the precepts of the church.
Judith Illsley Gleason, *Santeria, Bronx*, 1975
　　An African exhibit at the museum draws Raymond deeper into a mystical and powerful religion based on the beliefs of the Yoruba people of Africa.
Virginia Hamilton, *M.C. Higgins, the Great*, 1974
　　As strip mining creeps closer to his house in the Ohio hills, M.C. is torn between trying to get his family away and fighting for the home they love.
Mildred D. Taylor, *The Road to Memphis*, 1992
　　In 1941, a black youth, sadistically teased by two white boys in rural Mississippi, severly injures one of them and tries to flee the state.
Mary Alexander Walker, *To Catch a Zombi*, 1979
　　In 1784, a young black boy leaves the Louisiana swamps where his family lives and goes to New Orleans where he gains knowledge to improve his life.

661

Kathryn Osebold Galbraith

Illustrator: Floyd Cooper

Laura Charlotte (New York: Philomel, 1990)

Age range: Grades 2-3

Subject(s): Toys; Gifts

Major character(s): Laura Charlotte, Child

Time period(s): 1990s

Locale(s): United States

What the book is about: A little girl begs her mom to tell her the story, again, of her gray flannel elephant. The favorite toy was made by her grandmother and given to her mother and then passed on to her. A strong story of intergenerational love.

Where it's reviewed:
Booklist, February 1, 1990, page 1091
School Library Journal, April 1990, page 90

Other books by the author:
Look Snow, 1992
Roommates, 1990
Something Suspicious, 1987
Waiting for Jennifer, 1987

Other books you might like:
Jane Hissey, *Old Bear*, 1986
　　A group of toy animals tries various ways of rescuing Old Bear from the attic.
Helen Kay, *The First Teddy Bear*, 1985

The first Teddy Bear came to be because President Theodore Roosevelt refused to shoot a little bear during a hunt.

Judith Kerr, *Mog and Bunny*, 1988

The family threatens to throw away their cat's favorite toy until they discover the extent of Mog's love and loyalty toward Bunny.

Emily Arnold McCully, *The Christmas Gift*, 1988

When a little mouse's favorite Christmas gift is broken, Grandpa consoles her with a toy train from his own childhood.

David M. McPhail, *Those Terrible Toy-Breakers*, 1980

Walter and Bernie set a trap for the lion, tiger and elephant who break Walter's toys that are left outside overnight.

662

Kathryn Osebold Galbraith

Something Suspicious (New York: Atheneum, 1985)

Age range: Grades 4-6

Subject(s): Mystery and Detective Stories; Robbers and Outlaws

Major character(s): Lizzie, Preteen; Ivy, Preteen

Time period(s): 1980s

Locale(s): United States

What the book is about: Lizzie and her friend, Ivy, are on the trail of the bank robber known as the Green Pillowcase Bandit, and end up with more mysteries than they can handle.

Where it's reviewed:
Booklist, October 1, 1985, page 258

Other books by the author:
Roommates and Rachel, 1991
Roommates, 1990
Come Spring, 1979

Other books you might like:
Avi, *Emily Upham's Revenge: A Massachusetts Adventure*, 1992

During the summer of 1875, a girl sent to live with her wealthy uncle in Massachusetts and becomes involved in a very suspicious bank robbery.

Sid Fleischman, *The Whipping Boy*, 1986

A bratty prince and his whipping boy have many adventures when they accidentally trade identities after becoming involved with dangerous outlaws.

Les Martin, *Oliver Twist*, 1990

A simplified retelling of the adventures of an orphan boy who lives in a 19th century English workhouse until he joins a gang of thieves.

Willo Davis Roberts, *Jo and the Bandit*, 1992

While traveling to her uncle's in the late 1860s, Jo experiences a stagecoach robbery and becomes involved with a reluctant young outlaw.

Harvey Watson, *Bob War and Poke*, 1991

Hired as a chauffeur and cook, two back country brothers have many adventures until discovering their employers are bank robbers and thieves.

663

Ruth Stiles Gannett, Author/Illustrator

My Father's Dragon (New York: Random House, 1948)

Age range: Grades 3-5

Subject(s): Dragons; Fantasy

Major character(s): Elmer Elevator, Child

Time period(s): Indeterminate

Locale(s): Fictional City

What the book is about: Elmer befriends an old alley cat and in return learns the story of a captive baby dragon on Wild Island. He sails to Tangerina, meets up with various wild animals and rescues the dragon.

Where it's reviewed:
Horn Book, July 1948, page 266
Kirkus Reviews, April 15, 1948, page 194

Awards the book has won:
Newbery Honor

Other books by the author:
Katie and the Sad Noise, 1961
Dragons of Blueland, 1951
Elmer and the Dragon, 1950

Other books you might like:
L.M. Boston, *The Sea Egg*, 1967

Toby and Joe buy a wonderful egg-shaped stone. When they put it in a tide-pool, a playmate hatches out of the egg and leads them into adventure.

Bruce Coville, *The Monster's Ring*, 1982

Russell is sick of being bullied by Eddie, so he buys a ring which promises to change him into a dragon.

Rumer Godden, *The Dragon of Og*, 1981

Angus Og and his wife, Matilda, inherit Tundergarth Castle. One day she discovers that the River of Milk is home to a beautiful dragon.

Shirley Rousseau Murphy, *Valentine for a Dragon*, 1984

In love with the silvery dragon, a shey demon tries to express his love with gifts, all destroyed by the dragon because she doesn't understand.

Laurence Yep, *Dragon of the Lost Sea*, 1982

A royal Chinese dragon, outlawed by her clan for taking a magic pearl joins forces with a human to find an enchantress, hoping to free her sea.

664

Ann O'Neal Garcia

Spirit on the Wall (New York: Holiday, 1982)

Age range: Grades 5-8

Subject(s): Cave Dwellers; Physically Handicapped; Grandparents

Major character(s): Mat-Maw, Prehistoric Human

Time period(s): Indeterminate Past

Locale(s): Earth

What the book is about: The fiercely independent Mat-Maw, who lives in the inner depths of the cave, defies all clan customs in order to permit her crippled granddaughter to develop her artistic gifts.

Where it's reviewed:
Booklist, June 1, 1982, page 1312
School Library Journal, March 1982, page 147

Other books you might like:
J.H. Brennan, *Shiva Accused: An Adventure of the Ice Age*, 1991
    As the Star Jamboree approaches, another tribe falsely accuse the Shingu girl, Shiva, of murdering the Hag, the leader of all the tribal witch women.
Oliver Butterworth, *The Narrow Passage*, 1973
    Two boys on an expedition in southern France decide to protect the prehistoric cave they discover from desecration and public scrutiny.
Anne Eliot Crompton, *The Sorcerer*, 1971
    After being injured by a bear, a prehistoric youth discovers he has the power to capture on cave walls the shapes and spirits of various animals.
Justin F. Denzel, *Hunt for the Last Cat*, 1991
    Thorn feels conflicting loyalties when members of his clan blame his friend, Fonn, a girl from a rival clan, for the marauding actions of a tiger.
Thomas Millstead, *Cave of the Moving Shadows*, 1979
    A twelve year old boy living in Cro-Magnon times must choose between his training in sorcery and his desire to be a hunter.

665

Jane Gardam
Illustrator: Peggy Fortnum

A Few Fair Days (New York: Greenwillow, 1971)

Age range: Grades 4-6

Subject(s): Aunts and Uncles

Major character(s): Lucy, Child; Kitty, Relative (aunt); Jake, Child

Time period(s): 1930s

Locale(s): Yorkshire, England

What the book is about: Nine everyday episodes in a child's life in pre-WWII Yorkshire. The arrival of a mysterious stranger, an abandoned house, summers at grandmother's farm, a little brother and a great assortment of aunts complement Lucy herself, who ranges from melancholy to wildly funny. Charming and funny description of a nearly extinct way of life.

Where it's reviewed:
Booklist, October 15, 1972, page 201
Center for Children's Books Bulletin, May 1973, page 137
Kirkus Reviews, July 1, 1972, page 724

Other books by the author:
Through the Dolls' House Door, 1987
The Hollow Land, 1981
Bilgewater, 1977
The Summer After the Funeral, 1973

Other books you might like:
Frances Hodgson Burnett, *The Secret Garden*, 1911
    Mary comes to live in a lonely house on the Yorkshire moors and discovers an invalid cousin and the mysteries of a locked garden.
Adele Geras, *Apricots at Midnight: And Other Stories From a Patchwork Quilt*, 1977

An elderly dressmaker entertains a relative with memories of her youth, evoked by scraps of elegant dresses that she has sewn into a quilt.
Beth Hilgartner, *A Murder for Her Majesty*, 1986
    Horrified at having witnessed her father's murder and scared that the killers are agents of Queen Elizabeth I, Alice hides in the Yorkshire cathedral.
Anthony Horowitz, *The Devil's Door-Bell*, 1983
    Martin's new life with a foster mother on a Yorkshire farm quickly becomes a nightmare where evil and unbelievable happenings seem to threaten him.
Kate Douglas Wiggin, *Rebecca of Sunnybrook Farm*, 1903
    Horrified at the thought of caring for talkative, Rebecca, her spinster aunts nevertheless spend seven difficult years raising their niece.

666

Jane Gardam

Through the Dolls' House Door (New York: Greenwillow, 1966)

Age range: Grades 4-6

Subject(s): Dolls and Dollhouses; Fantasy

Major character(s): Claire, Child; Mary, Child; Miss Bossy, Toy (doll)

Time period(s): Indeterminate

Locale(s): Wales; England

What the book is about: Two girls lose interest in playing with their dollhouse after moving from London to Wales but the dolls in the house amuse themselves by telling stories about their exciting pasts.

Other books by the author:
A Few Fair Days, 1987
Bilgewater, 1976
The Summer After the Funeral, 1973
A Long Way From Verona, 1971

Other books you might like:
Roger S. Baum, *Dorothy of Oz*, 1989
    With the aid of Lion, Scarecrow, the Tin Man, and Tugg, Dorothy battles Jester, who is using a magic wand to turn the citizens of Oz into china dolls.
Susan Cooper, *The Grey King*, 1986
    Will Stanton, visiting in Wales, is swept into a desperate quest to find the golden harp and to awaken the ancient Sleepers.
Mary Dawson, *Tecwyn: The Last of the Welsh Dragons*, 1967
    The last of the fire breathing dragons hatches in Pennyben, Wales, placing a serious drain on the town's coal supply.
Ann Halam, *The Daymaker*, 1987
    Endowed with mystical powers, young Zanne takes a journey in search of the mysterious "daymaker" in order to become a full-fledged covenor.
Janet Louise Lunn, *Twin Spell*, 1969
    Attracted to an antique doll, twins buy the toy and soon find themselves haunted by powerful memories of ancestral twins who had also owned the dolls.

667

John Reynolds Gardiner

Illustrator: Cat B. Smith

General Butterfingers (Boston: Houghton Mifflin, 1986)

Age range: Grades 4-6

Subject(s): Old Age; Veterans

Major character(s): Walter, Preteen

Time period(s): 1980s (1986)

Locale(s): United States

What the book is about: Walter outwits the nasty nephew who wants to evict a trio of elderly veterans of WWII. Walter gets to work and makes a plan to keep the elderly men safe.

Where it's reviewed:
Booklist, January 15, 1987, page 781
Center for Children's Books Bulletin, February 1987, page 106
School Library Journal, January 1987, page 74

Other books by the author:
The Strange Thing That Happened to Allen Brewster, 1984
Top Secret, 1984
Stone Fox, 1980

Other books you might like:
Nina Bawden, *Humbug*, 1992
    When Cora is sent to stay next door with Aunt Sunday, she is tormented by Aunt Sunday's daughter, but finds an ally in Aunt Sunday's elderly mother.
Anne Eliot Crompton, *The Snow Pony*, 1991
    After moving to Massachusttes, Jannie finds it hard to make friends and takes a job with Mr. Flower, a hermit, helping him train and groom a pony.
Elisabeth Dyjak, *I Should Have Listened to Moon*, 1990
    A girl comes to terms with growing up and growing old when her best friend becomes interested in boys, and her grandmother moves in to share her room.
David M. Schwartz, *Supergrandpa*, 1991
    A grandfather, barred from entering the 1000 mile Tour of Sweden because of his age, unofficially joins the bicycle race and emerges victorious.
Mary Stolz, *Stealing Home*, 1992
    Thomas and his grandfather find life in their small house in Florida changed when Great-aunt Linzy comes to stay.

668

John Reynolds Gardiner

Illustrator: Marcia Sewall

Stone Fox (New York: Crowell/HarperCollins, 1980)

Age range: Grades 3-5

Subject(s): Sports/Dog Sled Racing; Grandparents

Major character(s): Willy, Child; Searchlight, Dog (sled dog); Stone Fox, Sports Figure (dog sled racer), Indian

Time period(s): Indeterminate

Locale(s): Jackson, Wyoming

What the book is about: When grandpa seems to be losing the will to live, little Willy is determined to save the potato farm for him. Willy hopes to pay back the taxes on his grandfather's farm with the purse from a sled dog race he enters. Willy hopes seeing the farm safe again will give Grandpa the desire to live again. Stone Fox, an Indian dog sled racer, is Willy's stiffest competition, and it turns out that Stone Fox is the one who saves him. A story no child or adult should miss.

Where it's reviewed:
Horn Book, June 1980, page 294
Kirkus Reviews, May 1, 1980, page 584

Other books by the author:
General Butterfingers, 1986
The Strange Thing That Happened to Allen Brewster, 1984
Top Secret, 1984

Other books you might like:
Ellen M. Dolan, *Susan Butcher and the Iditarod Trail*, 1993
    Describes the annual dog sled race from Anchorage to Nome, Alaska, and the life of the first person to win it for three consecutive years.
Daniel Manus Pinkwater, *Aunt Lulu*, 1991
    Tired of working as a librarian in Alaska, Aunt Lulu takes her sled and her fourteen huskies and moves to Parsippany, New Jersey.
Seymour Reit, *Race Against Death*, 1976
    In the winter of 1925, a dog sled relay races against time in an Alaskan blizzard with a supply of serum needed to stop a diphtheria epidemic in Nome.
Patricia Seibert, *Mush! Across Alaska in the Longest Sled Dog Race*, 1992
    Describes the annual Iditarod Sled Dog Race in Alaska and the sled dogs who compete in it.
Natalie Standiford, *The Bravest Dog Ever*, 1989
    Recounts the life of Balto, the sled dog who saved Nome in 1925.

669

James B. Garfield

Follow My Leader (New York: Viking, 1957)

Age range: Grades 4-6

Subject(s): Accidents; Blind; Animals/Dogs

Major character(s): Jimmy Carter, Preteen; Mike Adams, Preteen; Chuck Wilson, Preteen

Time period(s): 1950s

Locale(s): United States

What the book is about: After a neighborhood baseball game, Art Davis finds a firecracker. As they argue about whether or not to light it, Mike Adams grabs it and strikes a match. As it starts to sputter, he panics and accidentally throws it toward Jimmy. It explodes in Jimmy's face and blinds him. The story tells how Jimmy copes with the tragedy, learns to use a guide dog, and how the boys involved work at repairing the damage done to their friendships.

Other books you might like:
Mary Blount Christian, *Mystery at Camp Triumph*, 1986
    Recently blinded in an auto accident, Angie begins to cope with her handicap when she investigates the sabotaging of the summer camp she is attending.
Dennis Covington, *Lizard*, 1991

Lizard, a bright, deformed youngster, escapes from a Louisiana school for retarded boys with the aid of an actor who enrolls him in his company play.

James Duffy, *Uncle Shamus*, 1992
Ten year old Akers and his friend Marleena meet a blind, black ex-convict who moves to their Oklahoma shanty town and they help him with a secret plan

Jaap ter Haar, *The World of Ben Lighthart*, 1977
Blinded by an accident, a young boy decides he won't let his handicap keep him from his friends and family.

Nicholas Wilde, *Into the Dark*, 1987
A lonely boy's new friend has a frightening secret.

670

Leon Garfield

Footsteps (New York: Delacorte, 1980)

Age range: Grades 5 and Up

Major character(s): William Jones, Child; Alfred Diamond, Businessman

Time period(s): 18th century

Locale(s): London, England

What the book is about: William's father tells him that he had stolen from his business partner just before he dies. William travels to London, hoping to set things right, and travels from childhood to maturity.

Where it's reviewed:
Center for Children's Books Bulletin, September 1980, page 8
Horn Book, October 1980, page 525

Other books by the author:
Young Nick and Jubilee, 1989
The Empty Sleeve, 1988
The Night of the Comet, 1979
Apprentices, 1978
Black Jack, 1969

Other books you might like:
Ann Cheetham, *The Pit*, 1990
Oliver, a contemporary London boy, finds himself thrown back in time to the middle of a plague epidemic.

Philip Pullman, *Spring-Heeled Jack*, 1991
Three children escape from a London orphanage and are reunited with their father with the help of the legendary Spring-Heeled Jack.

Noel Streatfeild, *When the Sirens Wailed*, 1976
Three young evacuees from war-torn London try to return to their home when their country host dies suddenly.

671

Leon Garfield

Smith (New York: Pantheon, 1967)

Age range: Grades 6 and Up

Subject(s): Murder; Crime and Criminals

Major character(s): Smith, Thief (Pickpocket); Mr. Mansfield, Judge (Magistrate)

Time period(s): 18th century

Locale(s): London, England (Newgate Prison)

What the book is about: 12 year old Smith witnesses the murder of a visiting squire whose pocket he has just picked, then must use all his wits to escape the murderess, who realizes that Smith has the document she wants.

Where it's reviewed:
Horn Book, December 1967, page 758
Library Journal, November 15, 1967, page 4250

Awards the book has won:
Boston Globe/Horn Book Award 1968

Other books by the author:
The Ghost Downstairs, 1972
Mister Corbett's Ghost, 1969
The Night of the Comet, 1979
Young Nick and Jubilee, 1989

Other books you might like:
Tom McGowen, *The Magician's Apprentice*, 1987
A young pickpocket becomes apprenticed to a magician and together they search for lost knowledge.

Florence Parry Heide, *Mystery at MacAdoo Zoo*, 1973
Three children track down a pickpocket loose in the zoo.

Philip Pullman, *Spring-Heeled Jack*, 1991
Three children escape from a London orphanage and try to find their father.

Ann Cheetham, *The Pit*, 1990
A modern boy finds himself thrown back in time to mid-seventeenth century, plague-ridden London.

Ann Schlee, *Ask Me No Questions*, 1976
Laura is sent to the country from London to escape the cholera in 1848.

672

Leon Garfield

Illustrator: Ted Lewin

Young Nick and Jubilee (New York: Delacorte, 1989)

Age range: Grades 5-7

Subject(s): Brothers and Sisters; Robbers and Outlaws; Orphans

Major character(s): Nick, Preteen; Jubilee, Child

Time period(s): 18th century

Locale(s): London, England

What the book is about: Orphaned siblings Nick, 10, and Jubilee, 9, live in 18th century London. They make an arrangement with a Mr. Owen, a thief and pickpocket and are accepted as students at a charity school, while Owen poses as their father. The details of Cockney London bring the story alive and readers will love the resourceful children and fast pace of the story.

Where it's reviewed:
Booklist, August 1989, page 1975
Horn Book, October/November 1989, page 619

Other books by the author:
The Empty Sleeve, 1988
Mr. Corbett's Ghost, 1982
The Ghost Downstairs, 1972
Jack Holborn, 1965

Other books you might like:
Christopher Leach, *Free, Alone and Going*, 1972

A London schoolboy decides to cut loose from his old existence and seek adventures in far off places.

Alison Morgan, *Paul's Kite*, 1981

Virtually ignored by his runaway mother, Paul amuses himself by visiting all the London place names on his Monopoly board until an accident occurs.

Walter G. Oleksy, *If I'm Lost, How Come I Found You?*, 1977

A restless orphan, recently escaped from an orphanage, holes up with bank robbers and appears on TV as a hero.

Enid Richemont, *The Magic Skateboard*, 1993

On his way home from a school in London just before Christmas, Danny meets a strange looking woman who transforms his skateboard into a flying carpet.

Mary Stolz, *Bartholomew Fair*, 1990

Six people attend London's Bartholomew Fair and come away with unforgettable experiences.

673

Alan Garner

The Owl Service (New York: Walck, 1967)

Age range: Grades 6-9

Subject(s): Fantasy

Major character(s): Alison, Teenager; Roger Bradley, Teenager (Alison's step-brother); Gwyn, Teenager (housekeeper's son)

Time period(s): 1960s

Locale(s): Aber, Wales

What the book is about: An unusual pattern in a dinner service unleashes an evil spell as three teens are drawn into the power of a tragic legend.

Where it's reviewed:
Kirkus Reviews, September 15, 1968, page 1058
Publishers Weekly, September 30, 1968, page 61

Awards the book has won:
Carnegie Medal 1967

Other books by the author:
Elidor, 1981
The Lad of the Gad, 1980
The Aimer Gate, 1978
Granny Reardun, 1977

Other books you might like:
John Halkin, *Fangs of the Werewolf*, 1987

A strange "wild dog" terrorizes Wales with brutal killings but an old wise woman knows a secret that eventually destroys the creature.

Louise Lawrence, *Star Lord*, 1978

A Welsh family is caught up in a struggle between the supernatural powers of a mountain and the technological powers of a starlord who crashes into it

Elinor Lyon, *Green Grow the Rushes*, 1964

A girl from London vacationing on the Welsh coast joins three adventurous friends in a search for the cliffborne track of an old Roman road.

Ken Radford, *The Cellar*, 1989

A young girl in an old boarding house in the hills of North Wales is aware of mysterious ghostly presences and searches for an explanation.

Dixie Tenny, *Call the Darkness Down*, 1984

Morfa, an American in Wales searching for traces of her grandparents, receives mysterious messages before realizing that someone is trying to kill her

674

Sheila Garrigue

All the Children Were Sent Away (Scarsdale, NY: Bradbury, 1976)

Age range: Grades 3-5

Subject(s): World War II; Refugees

Major character(s): Sara, Refugee; Lady Drume, Guardian

Time period(s): 1940s

Locale(s): Vancouver, British Columbia, Canada

What the book is about: Along with other English children during WWII, Sara is put aboard the HMS Duke of Perth. Lady Drume does not want eight year old Sara to be friends with the cockney children, Maggie and Ernie, but they help her fight the lonliness and pain.

Where it's reviewed:
Kirkus Reviews, May 1, 1976, page 534
School Library Journal, May 1976, page 59

Other books by the author:
The Eternal Spring of Mr. Ito, 1985
Between Friends, 1978

Other books you might like:
Claire Hutchet Bishop, *Twenty and Ten*, 1984

A nun and twenty French children hide ten young Jewish refugees from the Nazis.

Dale Fife, *North of Danger*, 1978

A boy's adventures in Norway during WWII.

Bill Gillham, *Home Before Long*, 1984

Two British children leave London and Dorset during the air raids of WWII.

Judith Kerr, *When Hitler Stole Pink Rabbit*, 1972

This is an exciting story of a German-Jewish family and their escape from Nazi Germany.

Ian Serraillier, *The Silver Sword*, 1959

A WWII story of Polish children who are separated from their parents, and finally reunited.

675

Doris Gates

Illustrator: Paul Lantz

Blue Willow (New York: Viking, 1940)

Age range: Grades 5-6

Subject(s): Migrant Labor

Major character(s): Janey, Preteen

Time period(s): 1940s

Locale(s): California

What the book is about: Janey's most cherished hope is to find a home and a mantelpiece for her Blue Willow plate. She hopes that the valley her family has come to, which so resembles the pattern on her treasured plate, will be their permanent home.

Where it's reviewed:
Grade Teacher, January 1971, page 112

Awards the book has won:
Newbery Honor 1941

Other books by the author:
A Filly for Melinda, 1984
A Morgan for Melinda, 1982
The Elderberry Bush, 1968
Little Vic, 1968

Other books you might like:
Linda Climo, *Chester's Barn*, 1986
    This is a story about a winter's day in a barn on Prince Edward Island.
Emily Crofford, *A Matter of Pride*, 1981
    Meg's father is a tenant farmer on an Arkansas cotton plantation; her mother is afraid of the canal, the snakes, and other dangers in their lives.
Elizabeth Enright, *Thimble Summer*, 1966
    Garnet thinks that most of the happiness and good luck of her summer on a Wisconsin farm comes from her finding of a thimble in the dry creek bed.
Phyllis Reynolds Naylor, *Night Cry*, 1984
    Ellen has to fend for herself on a Mississippi farm, and she fears caring for the horse that threw and killed her brother.
Kate Seredy, *Good Master*, 1961
    Kate, a headstrong tomboy from Budapest, learns gentle ways when she goes to live with her uncle in the country.

676

Doris Gates

A Morgan for Melinda (New York: Viking, 1980)

Age range: Grades 5-6

Subject(s): Death; Animals/Horses; Guilt

Major character(s): Melinda Ross, Child; Cal Ross, Parent; Muriel "Missy" Zinn, Aged Person (wise woman)

Time period(s): 1980s

Locale(s): United States

What the book is about: Ten year old Melinda wants her father to be proud of her and tries to ride the horse he buys for her even though she is terrified of him. Melinda feels the horse was really meant for her brother, who died of leukemia. She still feels guilty that she is living and he is not. When Muriel, a woman in her seventies, comes to take riding lessons, she not only helps Melinda overcome her fear of riding, but also helps her work through her guilt about her brother.

Where it's reviewed:
Kirkus Reviews, May 15, 1980, page 644
School Library Journal, February 1980, page 54

Other books by the author:
A Filly for Melinda, 1984
A Fair Wind for Troy, 1978
The Warrior Goddess Athena, 1972
Blue Willow, 1940

Other books you might like:
Jean Slaughter Doty, *Dark Horse*, 1983

Abby realizes the new horse at High Hickory is an excellent jumper.
Jessie Haas, *Keeping Barney*, 1982
    Sarah decides to accept the responsibility of boarding a horse.
June Andrea Hanson, *Summer of the Stallion*, 1979
    Janey's relationship with her grandfather is the center of this beautiful love story.
Dorothy Nafus Morrison, *Somebody's Horse*, 1986
    Jenny's joy at finding a horse is dampened by the sight of the neglected, uncared-for animal.
Mary Ann Whitley, *A Circle of Light*, 1983
    A young man rides his horse in a desperate attempt to aid his embattled tribesman.

677

Jonathan Gathorne-Hardy

Illustrator: Glo Coalson

Operation Peeg (Philadelphia: Lippincott, 1972)

Age range: Grades 4-6

Subject(s): Adventure and Adventurers

Major character(s): Jane Charrington, Preteen; Jemima Garing, Friend; Mrs. Deal, Housekeeper

Time period(s): 1970s

Locale(s): Scotland (Peeg School)

What the book is about: Jarred loose from the ocean floor by a tremendous explosion, the island occupied by Jane and Jemima and Mrs. Deal (while the rest of the school is on an outing from which the girls were excluded because of a food fight) floats out to sea under the command of two British sailors who think WWII is still in progress.

Where it's reviewed:
Center for Children's Book Bulletin, January 1975, page 77
Hornbook, April 1975, page 147
Kirkus Reviews, October 1, 1974, page 1060

Other books by the author:
Jane's Adventures in and out of the Book, 1981
The Airship Ladyship Adventure, 1977

Other books you might like:
Joan Aiken, *Winterthing: A Play for Children*, 1972
    Four children and their aunt come to live in a cottage on an island off the Scottish coast said to be inhabited by the spirit of winter.
Nina Bawden, *The Witch's Daughter*, 1991
    On a Scottish island, a friendship develops between Perdita, a blind girl and her brother, who look for orchids, explore caves and meet jewel thieves.
Eileen Dunlop, *Finn's Island*, 1991
    A boy's opportunity to visit a remote Scottish island helps him mend his relationship with his "failure" father and look to the future.
Betty Levin, *Landfall*, 1979
    When Liddy visits her friend on an island off the Scottish coast, she becomes involved in events that reveal the truth of the legends about seals.
Ian Strachan, *The Flawed Glass*, 1989

A girl's life on a remote Scottish island is made difficult by a physical handicap, until an American businessman buys the island.

678

William Campbell Gault

Showboat in the Backcourt (New York: Dutton, 1976)

Age range: Grades 6-9

Subject(s): Sports/Basketball; Friendship; Race Relations

Major character(s): John Fitzgerald "Jay" King, Sports Figure; Paul Salvatore, Sports Figure

Time period(s): 1970s

Locale(s): Boston, Massachusetts

What the book is about: Jay King and Paul Salvatore start playing basketball together in high school. They stick together on the basketball court. When they enter college, the pros seem further away than ever. They do not make varsity in their first year. Lots of court action descriptions as the young men work their way to the pros.

Where it's reviewed:
Kirkus Reviews, May 1, 1976, page 534
School Library Journal, May 1976, page 80

Other books by the author:
Super Bowl Bound, 1980
The Sunday Cycles, 1979
Thin Ice, 1978
The Big Stick, 1975

Other books you might like:
Dean Hughes, *Point Guard*, 1992
    Jackie Willis hopes to convince the coach of the basketball team in Angel Park that she can play as well as the boys.
Elizabeth Levy, *The Tryouts*, 1979
    A group of eighth-graders take matters into their own hands when one of their friends fails to make the new co-ed basketball team.
Walter Dean Myers, *The Outside Shot*, 1984
    Playing basketball for a small midwest college, a Harlem boy works with a child needing physical therapy and experiences corruption in college sports.
Robert Newton Peck, *Soup's Hoop*, 1990
    Soup's crazy plan to help his town's basketball team win includes a musical instrument called a spitzentootle and trapping the evil Janice Riker.
Megan Stine, *Long Shot*, 1990
    The Three Investigators become involved in tracking down a basketball scandal when Pete receives a corrupt offer from a local college.

679

Barbara Gehrts

Don't Say a Word (New York: McElderry, 1986)

Age range: Grades 6-9

Subject(s): World War II

Major character(s): Anna Singelmann, Teenager

Time period(s): 1940s

Locale(s): Berlin, Germany

What the book is about: Living in Berlin during WWII, Anna finds herself and her family growing more and more aware of the dangerous direction in which her country is moving as her friends start to die.

Where it's reviewed:
Booklist, October 1, 1986, page 217
Kirkus, October 1, 1986, page 1516
Publisher's Weekly, September 26, 1986, page 87

Other books you might like:
Frank Baer, *Max's Gang*, 1983
    Five German children make a dangerous trip home from Czechoslovakia in 1945, in the desperate hope of being reunited with their Berlin families.
T. Degens, *The Visit*, 1982
    At a family gathering in Berlin years after WWII, Kate relives some of the events in the diary of a dead aunt who was once a member of Hitler Youth.
Sigrid Heuck, *The Hideout*, 1988
    Rebecca, living in an German orphanage during WWII, meets a boy hiding out in a nearby cornfield, where they create their own imaginary fantasy world.
Joan Lingard, *Tug of War*, 1989
    The twins Astra and Hugo Petersons and their family flee Latvia ahead of the Russian army in 1944 and become homeless refugees in Germany.
Carol Matas, *Daniel's Story*, 1993
    Daniel, whose family suffers as the Nazis rise to power in Germany, describes his imprisonment in a concentration camp and his eventual liberation.

680

Mark Geller

My Life in the Seventh Grade (New York: Harper and Row, 1986)

Age range: Grades 5-7

Subject(s): Friendship; Schools

Major character(s): Marvin Berman, 7th Grader

Time period(s): 1980s

Locale(s): United States

What the book is about: Reviews of this journey through seventh grade vary widely from "a well written, and perceptive story of one boy's hazardous journey through seventh grade" (VOYA) to "aspects of its content make it both inappropriate for its intended audience and offensive in general." (SLJ) Issues are stereotyping, anti-Catholic bias and a non-observant Jew railing against established Jewish institutions. Still it is in phase one of the Elementary School Library Collection so readers should have good access and be able to decide for themselves.

Where it's reviewed:
Center for Children's Books Bulletin, July/August 1986, page 207
School Library Journal, May 1986, page 91
Voice of Youth Advocates, August 1986, page 142

Other books by the author:
Who's on First?, 1992
The Strange Case of the Reluctant Partners, 1990
Raymond, 1988

What I Heard, 1987

Other books you might like:
Constance C. Greene, *A Girl Called Al*, 1969
   A girl, her friend, Al, and the assistant superintendent of an apartment building form a mutually needed friendship, with the usual joys and sorrows.
Elizabeth B. Keeton, *Second-Best Friend*, 1985
   Having lost all her clothes in a cyclone, Vanessa borrows a dress from a friendless girl, not knowing the dress is stolen.
Megan McDonald, *The Bridge to Nowhere*, 1993
   Hallie is adjusting to friendship with an exciting older boy when her father, an out of work bridge builder, becomes a stranger in his own home.
Phyllis Reynolds Naylor, *Alice in April*, 1993
   While trying to survive seventh grade, Alice discovers that turning thirteen will make her the Woman of the House at home.
Lee Wardlaw, *The Seventh Grade Weirdo*, 1992
   You don't have to do much to be dubbed a weirdo when your name is Christopher Robin and you're the older brother of a genius named Winnie.

681

Mark Geller

Raymond (New York: Harper, 1988)

Age range: Grades 5-7

Subject(s): Alcoholism; Child Abuse

Major character(s): Raymond Cole, Runaway; Mrs. Washington, Nurse; Miss Green, Social Worker

Time period(s): 1980s

Locale(s): Gary, Indiana

What the book is about: Raymond is smart, tough and scared. His teachers and friends don't know about what he has to endure at home. The situation becomes so desperate that he feels he has no other choice than to run away in order to salvage his life.

Where it's reviewed:
Booklist, September 1, 1988, page 76
Kirkus Reviews, July 15, 1988, page 1060
School Library Journal, September 1988, page 198

Other books by the author:
Who's on First?, 1992
The Strange Case of the Reluctant Partners, 1990
What I Heard, 1987
My Life in the Seventh Grade, 1986

Other books you might like:
Marilyn Halvorson, *Cowboys Don't Cry*, 1984
   Suffering from his mother's death and the alcoholism and estrangement of his father, Shane hopes things will be better when they go live on a farm.
Jane Claypool Miner, *A Day at a Time: Dealing with an Alcoholic*, 1982
   When her father seems unable to stop drinking, Ellen decides to attend an Alateen meeting to help her cope with his alcoholism.
Helen K. Passey, *Speak to the Rain*, 1989

After his mother's death, Janna's father starts to drink heavily and her younger sister is possessed by the spirits of a tribe of drowned Indians.
Stephen Roos, *You'll Miss Me When I'm Gone*, 1988
   Convinced that he is a rotten kid and disgusted that his father is still taking advantage of his mother, Marcus turns to alcohol.
Marcia Wood, *The Search for Jim McGwynn*, 1989
   Jamie, who has an alcoholic father, spends the summer searching for the true identity of the local but elusive detective novel author.

682

Jean Craighead George

Illustrator: John Schoenherr

Julie of the Wolves (New York: Harper and Row, 1972)

Age range: Grades 5-6

Subject(s): Eskimos; Animals/Wolves; Courage

Time period(s): 1970s

Locale(s): Alaska

What the book is about: When she is forced into a marriage long before she is ready, Julie runs away from her Alaskan home and is able to survive in the wilderness by learning to communicate with a pack of wolves. More difficult than survival is deciding where she belongs. Is she Miyax, daughter of Kaupgen, or Julie Edwards who belongs in an entirely different culture?

Where it's reviewed:
Kirkus, November 15, 1972, page 1312
New York Times Book Review, January 21, 1973, page 8
School Library Journal, January 1973, page 75

Awards the book has won:
Newbery Medal 1973

Other books by the author:
My Side of the Mountain, 1959
The Talking Earth, 1983
Wounded Wolf, 1978
On the Far Side of the Mountain, 1990

Other books you might like:
Rutherford George Montgomery, *Iceblink*, 1969
   Exiled from his Alaskan village, Metek voyages through the Bering Sea and Aleutian Islands and joins a Russian voyage on a seal hunt.
Arnold A. Griese, *The Way of Our People*, 1975
   Kano's coming of age and killing a moose bring him no joy because his heart is filled with fear of hunting alone.
Jean Rogers, *Goodbye, My Island*, 1983
   Esther knows this will be the last winter she spends on an island in the Bering Strait and looks carefully at the life and culture of the Eskimoes.
Helen Caswell, *Shadows From the Singing House*, 1968
   This collection of Eskimo stories explains why the world is as it is, and why people behave as they do.

683

Jean Craighead George, Author/Illustrator

My Side of the Mountain (New York: Dutton, 1959)

Age range: Grades 4-6

Subject(s): Survival; Nature; Outdoor Life

Major character(s): Sam Gribley, Child

Time period(s): 1950s

Locale(s): Catskills, New York

What the book is about: A New York boy conducts a successful winter experiment in self-sufficient living in a remote area of the Catskills.

Where it's reviewed:
Booklist, December 1959, page 72
Horn Book, October, 1959, page 389

Awards the book has won:
Newbery Honor

Other books by the author:
Julie of the Wolves, 1972
On the Far Side of the Mountain, 1990
The Talking Earth, 1983
Wounded Wolf, 1978

Other books you might like:
Isaac Asimov, *It's Such a Beautiful Day*, 1985
    When a "transporter door" fails to function, Richard rediscovers the joys of the natural world.
Helen V. Griffith, *Georgia Music*, 1986
    Working in a garden, a girl and her grandfather form a bond with nature and each other. A picture book format with appeal to older readers.
Gary Paulsen, *Island*, 1988
    15 year old Wil finds an island where he can commune with nature and finds time for keeping a journal and art work.
Donald J. Sobol, *Encyclopedia Brown's Book of the Wacky Outdoors*, 1987
    A series of stories about outdoor adventures, full of wit and humor, based on true incidents.
Mary W. Sullivan, *Earthquake 2099*, 1982
    When an earthquake separates Philip from his parents, only Vita's knowledge of surviving in the wild saves them.

684

Jean Craighead George

River Rats, Inc. (New York: Dutton, 1979)

Age range: Grades 4-7

Subject(s): Feral Children; Survival

Major character(s): Joe Zero, Teenager; Crobar Flood, Teenager, Friend

Time period(s): 1970s

Locale(s): Arizona (Grand Canyon, Colorado River)

What the book is about: A run down the Colorado River turns into a story of survival. Traveling illegally at night on the Colorado River with a mysterious cargo, two boys are shipwrecked and must depend for survival on their own ingenuity and a wild boy they find living along the river.

Where it's reviewed:
Booklist, March 15, 1979, page 1156
Hornbook, April 1979, page 193
Kirkus Reviews, July 1, 1979, page 740

Other books by the author:
The Cry of the Crow, 1980
Hook a Fish, Catch a Mountain, 1975
Julie of the Wolves, 1972
Coyote in Manhattan, 1968

Other books you might like:
John R. Burger, *Children of the Wild*, 1978
    A collection of true stories and legends about children who were raised by animals.
Paul Samuel Jacobs, *Born into the Light*, 1988
    When some "feral children" are found in a New England town during the 1930s, only young Roger suspects they are not earthly creatures.
William Mayne, *Antar and the Eagles*, 1990
    Abducted and raised by eagles, a young boy is sent on a mission to rescue a lost egg and, in the process, save the race of eagles.
Joan D. Vinge, *Tarzan, King of the Apes*, 1983
    An infant, left alone in the African jungle after the deaths of his parents, is adopted by an ape and brought up without ever seeing another human.
Jane Yolen, *Children of the Wolf: A Novel*, 1984
    In 1920 in India two children that have been raised by wolves are discovered and brought to an orphanage to be taught human behavior again.

685

Jean Craighead George

The Talking Earth (New York: Harper and Row, 1983)

Age range: Grades 6-9

Subject(s): Ecology; Swamps; Indians of North America

Major character(s): Billie Wind, Teenager, Indian (Seminole)

Time period(s): 1980s

Locale(s): Florida (Everglades)

What the book is about: A young Seminole, Billie Wind, lives with her tribe, but has been to the Kennedy Space Center School and has some very modern ideas. Questioning the teaching of her ancestors, she is advised to go into the Everglades to see if the animals and land can speak to her. She ventures alone to listen, and finds that the land and animals do talk, and their messages cry out to us to save the earth.

Where it's reviewed:
Center for Children's Books Bulletin, December 1983, page 67
School Library Journal, December 1983, page 74

Other books by the author:
The Shark Beneath the Reef, 1989
Julie of the Wolves, 1972
Who Really Killed Cock Robin?, 1971
My Side of the Mountain, 1959

Other books you might like:
Walter Farley, *The Black Stallion's Ghost*, 1969

Alec's life is changed after he spends a night lost in the Everglades with a Frenchman who is helping him search for the runaway black stallion.

James Ralph Johnson, *Everglades Adventure*, 1970
While on a survival test in the Everglades, two boys become the foster parents of a panther cub.

Kathleen Kudlinski, *Night Bird: A Story of the Seminole Indians*, 1993
Night Bird, whose clan of Seminole Indians is fighting to preserve its way of life, must decide whether to seek land and a future in distant Oklahoma.

Beatrice Levin, *John Hawk: White Man, Black Man, Indian Chief*, 1988
Runaway slave John White travels with Osceola to a settlement, where he becomes involved in the struggle of the Seminole to protect their land.

Luke Wallin, *Ceremony of the Panther*, 1987
John, a Miccosukee Indian, is torn between a shiftless life in the Everglades and his father's ambition for him to carry on the shaman tradition.

686

Jean Craighead George

Who Really Killed Cock Robin? (New York: Dutton, 1971)

Age range: Grades 5-7

Subject(s): Ecology; Environmental Problems; Mystery and Detective Stories

Major character(s): Tony Isidora, Activist (environmentalist), 8th Grader; Mary Ann Lambert, Activist (environmentalist), 8th Grader

Time period(s): 1970s

Locale(s): Saddleboro

What the book is about: Eighth grader Tony Isidora follows a trail of environmental clues to try to figure out what ecological imbalances might have caused the death of the town's best known robin. Tony and his friend, Mary Ann, track down the killer and the reader follows a mystery that deals with the complexity of modern environmental pollution.

Where it's reviewed:
Booklist, December 15, 1971, page 366
Center for Children's Books Bulletin, January 1972, page 74
Kirkus Reviews, September 1, 1971, page 945

Other books by the author:
Hook a Fish, Catch a Mountain, 1975
Julie of the Wolves, 1972
Coyote in Manhattan, 1968
Gull #737, 1964

Other books you might like:
Ruth Park, *My Sister Sif*, 1986
Riko manages to get her delicate older sister, Sif, and herself to their remote home, where a scientist complicates Riko's life.

Alison Cragin Herzig, *Shadows on the Pond*, 1985
Dangerous intruders threaten to destroy the secluded beaver pond which is Jill's only refuge from her many problems.

Nancy Bond, *The Voyage Begun*, 1981

Living in the not so distant future when the energy supply has been almost depleted, a boy explores and understands environmental polution.

Betty Sue Cummings, *Let a River Be*, 1978
A feisty woman and a retarded youth are brought together by their attempts to save a polluted river.

Harriett Mandelay Luger, *Chasing Trouble*, 1976
A tough city kid is sent to live in the country where she reluctantly finds herself caring about the land, ecology, and a pocket gopher.

687

Corinne Gerson

Illustrator: Velma Ilsley

Son for a Day (New York: Atheneum, 1980)

Age range: Grades 3-6

Subject(s): Single Parent Families; Friendship; Resourcefulness

Major character(s): Danny, Child; Aunt Dorothy, Guardian

Time period(s): 1980s

Locale(s): New York, New York (the Bronx)

What the book is about: Danny is often left alone while his aunt is at work and he designs a plan of action to have friends and fun. He goes to the zoo and gets to know "zoodaddies" who are there with their sons. He often gets invited to lunch and dinner, and develops a great list of names and phone numbers of new friends. When he joins a boy and his news commentator mother, his story is told on the evening news. Danny is sure he is in big trouble, but gets positive support and encouragement, and is ready when his mother returns.

Where it's reviewed:
Center for Children's Books Bulletin, September 1980, page 9
School Library Journal, May 1980, page 67
Christopher Award, 1981

Other books by the author:
Tread Softly, 1979

Other books you might like:
Karen Ackerman, *The Leaves in October*, 1991
Nine year old Livvy struggles to understand when her father loses his job and takes her and her brother to live in a shelter for the homeless.

Tom Birdseye, *Tucker*, 1990
Tucker is happy living with his divorced father until his sister moves back in and claims their mother wants them to become one family again.

Beverly Keller, *No Beasts! No Children!*, 1983
Desdemona, her father, the twins, and three dogs learn to cope with a strict housekeeper, a heartless landlord, and an odd aunt.

Norma Klein, *Robbie and the Leap Year Blues*, 1981
Eleven year old Robbie tries to cope with a sudden deluge of girl friends and the emotional problems of his divorced parents.

Judy K. Morris, *The Crazies and Sam*, 1983
A boy living with his divorced father tries to come to terms with the contradictions of life, love, and responsibility.

688

Mary-Joan Gerson

Illustrator: Eliza Moon

Omoteji's Baby Brother (New York: Walck, 1974)

Age range: Grades 2-3

Subject(s): Family Life; Africa

Major character(s): Omoteji, Child

Time period(s): Indeterminate

Locale(s): Nigeria

What the book is about: Omoteji tries to be helpful when his mother has a new baby. His peers tease him about helping the women and each of the adult members of his family spurn his attempt to help. He has a wonderful idea, a present for the newborn.

Where it's reviewed:
Kirkus Reviews, June 15, 1974, page 630
Library Journal, September 15, 1974, page 2245

Other books by the author:
When the Sky Is Far Away, 1974

Other books you might like:
Verna Aardema, *Tales From the Story Hat*, 1960
    A short collection of stories and folktales from Africa.
Dorian Haarhoff, *Desert December*, 1991
    A South African boy journeys through the desert to join his parents in a mining village and to see his new baby sister.
Rachel Isadora, *At the Crossroads*, 1991
    South African children gather to welcome home their fathers who have been away working in the mines.
Lynn Joseph, *A Wave in Her Pocket*, 1991
    Tantie tells the children six stories, some from West Africa, some from Trinidad, and some from her own imagaination.
David Lee Miller, *Baby*, 1985
    Two Americans discover a brontosaurus family in the African jungle and try to protect it from evil men who are after it.

689

David Getz

Thin Air (New York: Holt, 1990)

Age range: Grades 5-7

Subject(s): Asthma; Mainstreaming in Education

Major character(s): Jacob Katz, Teenager (Asthmatic); Isaac Katz, Teenager (Jacob's brother); Cynthia, Teenager (classmate)

Time period(s): 1980s

Locale(s): New York, New York (Manhattan)

What the book is about: Jacob is anxious to start sixth grade. Though his parents would prefer to enroll him in a special school for chronically ill children because his asthma causes him to miss classes so often, Jacob is determined to go to a regular school and be a regular kid, even though he suffers daily attacks. Jacob is a likeable hero, and readers develop a sensitivity to chronic illness because of coming to know Jacob, not as a result of preachy writing. Jacob's parents come to realize that he has the same need to assert his independence as any teenager and the family is strengthened.

Where it's reviewed:
Booklist, October 5, 1990, page 442
School Library Journal, January 1991, page 90

Other books by the author:
Almost Famous, 1992

Other books you might like:
Paula Danziger, *The Pistachio Prescription*, 1978
    Reacting to her family's constant quarreling, Cassie has frequent asthma attacks.
Gunilla Brodde Norris, *The Top Step*, 1970
    A youngster who has been told he will outgrow his asthma attacks waits anxiously for that to happen.
Ann Rabinowitz, *Knight on Horseback*, 1987
    After picking up a small wooden knight on horseback, Eddy finds himself pursued through England by a mysterious time traveler.
Jean Thesman, *Appointment with a Stranger*, 1989
    Very self-conscious about her asthma attacks, Keller finds solace in the company of an attractive but mysterious boy at a remote pond.
Elizabeth Winthrop, *Marathon Miranda*, 1979
    Miranda feels left out of everything until she meets a jogger training for a Marathon. Despite her fear of an asthma attack, Miranda begins to run.

690

Faye Gibbons

King Shoes and Clown Pockets (New York: Morrow, 1989)

Age range: Grades 5-6

Subject(s): Friendship

Time period(s): 1980s

Locale(s): Alabama

What the book is about: Raymond has just moved to Alabama. His dad has a new job, but everything else is the same, including hand-me-down clothes and ugly brown shoes. Then, he meets Bruce Mannis, the son of a local junk dealer, who shows him how to be independent and proud, no matter what you wear. In this rich rural setting, they becomes friends and help each other through difficulties.

Where it's reviewed:
Booklist, January 1, 1990, page 913
Kirkus Reviews, October 15, 1989, page 1529

Other books by the author:
Mighty Close to Heaven, 1985
Some Glad Morning, 1982

Other books you might like:
Thomas J. Dygard, *Wilderness Peril*, 1985
    Two boys camping in the Minnesota woods encounter a desperate hijacker attempting to escape with three quarters of a million dollars.
Nancy Garden, *What Happened in Marston*, 1971
    A middle class white boy and a black boy from the slums have trouble sorting out their friendship when a race war breaks out in their neighborhood.
Mildred D. Taylor, *The Road to Memphis*, 1990

Teased by two white boys in 1940s rural Mississippi, a black youth severely injures one of the boys and enlists help in fleeing the state.

Ann Waldron, *Scaredy Cat*, 1978
Jane, a child of the Depression years in Alabama, lives in fear of being kidnapped.

Rosemary Wells, *Through the Hidden Door*, 1987
Two boys stumble on the remains of an ancient underground civilization.

691

Davis Gibbs

Fishman and Charly (Boston: Houghton Mifflin, 1983)

Age range: Grades 6-8

Subject(s): Animals; Single Parent Families

Major character(s): Tyler "Fishman" Hawkins, Preteen, Animal Lover; Charlene "Charly" Hawkins, Relative (Tyler's sister); Colonel Hawkins, Parent

Time period(s): 1980s

Locale(s): Echo Bay, Florida

What the book is about: A lonely boy finds an animal friend in a manatee named Pie. Eleven year old Tyler Hawkins, know as Fishman to his sister, Charly, faces the double challenge of impressing his stern father and saving the gentle manatee he loves from the poachers who are slaughtering them.

Other books by the author:
Christy's Magic Glove, 1992
Major-League Melissa, 1991
Swann Song, 1982
Maud Flies Solo, 1981

Other books you might like:
Jean Craighead George, *The Talking Earth*, 1983
Billie ventures out alone into the Everglades to test the legends of her Indian ancestors and learns the importance of listening to the earth.

Helen V. Griffith, *Foxy*, 1984
Camping in the Florida Keys with his parents, Jeff finds an abandoned, mistreated dog that he desperately wants for his own.

Kathryn Lasky, *Shadows in the Water*, 1992
The Starbuck twins use their telepathic powers and the aid of some dolphins to help their father catch a gang dumping toxic waste in the Florida Keys.

Robert Newton Peck, *Arly*, 1989
Although Arly seems bound to follow in his father's footsteps as a field worker in Jailtown, his ideas change when a schoolteacher comes to town.

Bryce Walton, *Hurricane Reef*, 1970
A teen who has always wanted to be a marine scientist discovers in the Florida Keys the challenges of the profession he has chosen.

692

Patricia Reilly Giff

Illustrator: Blanche Sims

The Beast in Ms. Rooney's Room (New York: Dell, 1984)

Age range: Grades 2-3

Series: Kids of Polk Street School

Subject(s): Schools

Major character(s): Richard "Beast" Best, Child, 2nd Grader; Emily Arrow, Child, 2nd Grader; Mrs. Paris, Teacher

Time period(s): 1980s

Locale(s): United States

What the book is about: Richard Best is nicknamed "Beast" by his second grade class, and his adventures and frustrations begin this Polk Street series with lively characters and hilarious messes.

Where it's reviewed:
Los Angeles Times Book Review, September 16, 1984, page 5
Publisher's Weekly, August 31, 1984, page 437
School Library Journal, December 1984, page 80

Other books by the author:
All about Stacy, 1989
In the Dinosaur's Paw, 1985
The Candy Corn Contest, 1984
December Secrets, 1984

Other books you might like:
Florence Parry Heide, *The Problem with Pulcifer*, 1982
Pulcifer's preference for books is considered a grave problem by the television addicted world around him.

Suzy Kline, *Herbie Jones and the Dark Attic*, 1992
Herbie's friend, Ray, and some classmates in his fourth grade reading group help him adjust when he moves into a new bedroom in the attic.

Rita Marshall, *I Hate to Read*, 1992
As a boy who hates to read unwillingly looks at a book, the characters come alive and interest him so much that he starts turning pages about them.

Gary Paulsen, *Nightjohn*, 1993
Sarny's brutal life as a slave becomes even more dangerous when a newly arrived slave offers to teach her how to read.

Berniece Rabe, *Tall Enough to Own the World*, 1989
Unable to read, Joey is often in trouble at school for his rebellious behavior until a teacher, a neighbor, a cat and his new stepfather help him.

693

Patricia Reilly Giff

Illustrator: Leslie Morrill

Fourth Grade Celebrity (New York: Delacorte, 1979)

Age range: Grades 4-5

Subject(s): Friendship; School Life; Brothers and Sisters

Major character(s): Casey Valentine, Preteen (4th grader), Writer; Walter Moles, Preteen (4th grader)

Time period(s): 1970s

Locale(s): United States

What the book is about: Casey is tired of living in the shadow of her older sister and decides to be president of her fourth grade class. Her best friend, Walter, agrees to help her if she will take over for him with a pen pal his mother has insisted he correspond with. Casey does become president, although not exactly by election, and she begins a school newspaper. Lively humor and fast paced action make this a favorite.

Where it's reviewed:
Christian Science Monitor, October 15, 1979, page B4
School Library Journal, October 1979, page 150

Other books by the author:
The Gift of the Pirate Queen, 1982
The Winter Worm Business, 1981
The Girl Who Knew It All, 1979

Other books you might like:
Cynthia Blair, *Chocolate Is My Middle Name*, 1992
Carla and the Bubble Gum Gang put all of their detective skills to work when Carla's older sister, Kelly, is accused of stealing.
Paula Danziger, *Everyone Else's Parents Said Yes*, 1989
Matthew cannot resist the temptation to play practical jokes on his older sister and the girls in his class, which invites them to play a joke on him.
Natalie Honeycutt, *Ask Me Something Easy*, 1991
Addie must cope with the absence of her father, her hostile, disturbed mother, perfect older sister and sensitive younger twins.
Barbara M. Joosse, *Anna, the One and Only*, 1988
Third grader Anna Skoggen struggles to express herself and finally finds a way to be true to herself and still be friends with her older sister.
Anne Pellowski, *Betsy's Up and Down Year*, 1983
Betsy struggles with sibling rivalry, an encounter with a rattlesnake, a birthday party and coping with the death of her grandfather.

694

Patricia Reilly Giff

Illustrator: Anthony Kramer

Have You Seen Hyacinth Macaw? (1981)

Age range: Grades 4-6

Subject(s): City Life; Mystery and Detective Stories

Major character(s): A. Roberta "Abby" Jones, Detective; Potsie, Friend

Time period(s): 1980s

Locale(s): New York, New York

What the book is about: Abby Jones, a would-be detective, misunderstands clues and thinks her brother is a thief. Abby investigates by squeezing through windows, sneaking on subways and even sneaking into an apartment in the middle of the night. She and her friend, Potsie, also work on mysteries involving a mysterious new neighbor, a missing person and a theft.

Where it's reviewed:
Booklist, March 15, 1981, page 1027
Kirkus Reviews, September 1, 1981, page 1083
School Library Journal, May 1981, page 84

Other books by the author:
All About Stacy, 1988
B-E-S-T Friends, 1988
Tootsie Tanner, Why Don't You Talk?, 1987
Loretta P. Sweeney, Where Are You?, 1984

Other books you might like:
Maureen George, *The Neighbor From Outer Space*, 1992
When Katie, Chrissy, Maddie and Brian learn that their neighbor, Mrs. Dugan, is an alien from outer space, their quiet summer suddenly becomes crazy.
Patricia Reilly Giff, *Matthew Jackson Meets the Wall*, 1990
Matthew's life is made difficult by his family's move from New York toOhio, the disappearance of their cat, and a tough neighborhood boy.
Constance Hiser, *Scoop Snoops*, 1993
When their neighbor is robbed on Halloween night, a group of fourth grade reporters decide to try to find the thief.
Phyllis Reynolds Naylor, *The Witch's Eye*, 1990
Though suspected witch-neighbor Mrs. Tuggle has died, her glass eye resurfaces, bringing new dangers and terrors.
Jane Breskin Zalben, *The Fortuneteller in 5B*, 1991
The unexpected arrival of a flamboyant new neighbor teaches Alexandria that the loss of a loved one is a universal experience.

695

Patricia Reilly Giff

Illustrator: Leslie Morrill

Left-Handed Shortstop (New York: Delacorte, 1980)

Age range: Grades 4-6

Subject(s): Sports/Baseball; Ecology

Major character(s): Walter Moles, Activist (Environmentalist); Casey Valentine, Friend; Gunther "Goony" Reed, Sports Figure

Time period(s): 1980s

Locale(s): High Flats

What the book is about: Walter would rather devote his time to ecology than baseball. There hasn't been a left-handed shortstop since Willie Keeler in 1892! Goony won't let Walter admit he can't play ball. Somehow, he's got to learn how to be a great shortstop in a hurry or find a way to weasel out of the game.

Where it's reviewed:
Booklist, September 15, 1980, page 114
Kirkus, February 1, 1981, page 141
School Library Journal, December 1980, page 74

Other books by the author:
Diana, 20th Century Princess, 1991
The War Began at Supper, 1991
Tootsie Tanner, Why Don't You Talk?, 1987
Mother Teresa, Sister to the Poor, 1986

Other books you might like:
Alison Cragin Herzig, *The Boonsville Bombers*, 1991
Anxious to play on her brother's team, Emma learns to field well, but still can't join because other team members own the bat and make the rules.
Johanna Hurwitz, *Baseball Fever*, 1981
Ezra's dad doesn't understand baseball at all, so how can he understand his son?
Alfred Slote, *Make-Believe Ball Player*, 1989
Using his imagination to create heroic images of himself as a great athlete, Henry, a real klutz in sports, does become a hero.

Richard Aldrich Summers, *Ball-Shy Pitcher*, 1970
Boys with varied ethnic backgrounds and personal problems forget differences as they strive for a common goal in the Little League.
Karen Lynn Williams, *Baseball and Butterflies*, 1990
Daniel's younger brother is a pain because he seems to do everything better than Daniel. Daniel would rather catch butterflies than play baseball.

696

Patricia Reilly Giff

Illustrator: Leslie Morrill

Poopsie Pomerantz, Pick up Your Feet (New York: Delacorte, 1989)

Age range: Grades 4-6

Subject(s): Ballet; Dancing; Weight Control

Major character(s): Poopsie Pomerantz, Dancer; Tracy Matson, Friend

Time period(s): 1980s

Locale(s): Gypsy Wild

What the book is about: Poopsie's plans for self-improvement include losing enough weight to fit into a medium size bathing suit and becoming a prima ballerina. But her best friend, Tracy, makes fun of her lessons and terrifies her with her tales of kidnappers on the loose.

Where it's reviewed:
Booklist, March 1, 1989, page 1191
Hornbook, May 1989, page 390
School Library Journal, June 1989, page 104

Other books by the author:
Garbage Juice for Breakfast, 1989
In the Dinosaur's Paw, 1985
The Gift of the Pirate Queen, 1982
Have You Seen Hyacinth Mccaw?, 1981

Other books you might like:
Carol Lea Benjamin, *Nobody's Baby Now*, 1984
Olivia, unhappy because she is overweight and because she must care for her invalid grandmother after school, comes to terms with both problems.
Vicki Grove, *The Fastest Friend in the West*, 1990
When her best friend dumps her to be with the popular kids, overweight Lori shares an unusual but brief friendship with a homeless girl.
Isabelle Holland, *The House in the Woods*, 1991
Feeling overweight, unattractive, and unloved by her adoptive father, Bridget learns to put aside her escapist fantasies and live in the real world.
Robert Lipsyte, *One Fat Summer*, 1977
An overweight fourteen year old boy experiences a turning point summer in which he learns to stand up for himself.
Lila Perl, *Fat Glenda Turns Fourteen*, 1991
Glenda, extremely unhappy after regaining the pounds she worked hard to lose, meets overweight Giselle and discovers the world of plus-size modeling.

697

Patricia Reilly Giff

Illustrator: Blanche Sims

Purple Climbing Days (New York: Delacorte, 1985)

Age range: Grades 2-3

Series: Kids of Polk Street School

Subject(s): Schools

Major character(s): Richard "Beast" Best, Child; Matthew Jackson, Child; Mrs. Miller, Teacher (substitute)

Time period(s): 1980s

Locale(s): United States

What the book is about: Richard "Beast" Best loses courage in the face of the climbing rope in gym class. Mrs. "Miller the Killer," the meanest substitute teacher in the whole school, finds out about his secret. What will she do to him?

Where it's reviewed:
Booklist, August 1985, page 1671
School Library Journal, November 1985, page 70

Other books by the author:
Sunny Side Up, 1986
Lazy Lions, Lucky Lambs, 1985
Say Cheese, 1985
Snaggle Doodles, 1985

Other books you might like:
Mary Blount Christian, *Swamp Monsters*, 1983
A duo of young swamp monsters who are convinced that children are make-believe find themselves in school with real children and a substitute teacher.
Terrance Dicks, *Teacher's Pet*, 1990
David's clumsy and loveable dog, Goliath, helps him out of trouble with a seemingly mean math teacher and saves the teacher's job at the same time.
Jamie Gilson, *Thirteen Ways to Sink a Sub*, 1982
The boys and girls in the fourth grade devise a contest to "sink" their substitute teacher by making her cry.
Ann Lawlor, *The Substitute*, 1977
Before the regular teacher returns to her class, substitute Mrs. O'Mallyho pulls a baby grand piano from her bag and charms the children into dancing.
Peggy Parish, *Teach Us, Amelia Bedelia*, 1977
The very literal minded Amelia Bedelia becomes a substitute teacher for a day.

698

Patricia Reilly Giff

Illustrator: Leslie Morrill

Rat Teeth (New York: Delacorte, 1984)

Age range: Grades 4-6

Subject(s): Sports/Baseball; Divorce

Major character(s): Radcliffe "Cliffie" Sampson, Preteen; Amy Warren, Neighbor (Pest)

Time period(s): 1980s

Locale(s): New York, New York (Queens)

What the book is about: The kids call Cliffie "Rat Teeth" because his two front teeth stick out a mile and he can't get braces until his father builds his practice with more patients. But Cliffie is tough, because acting tough keeps him from crying.

Where it's reviewed:
Booklist, July 1984, page 1548
Center for Children's Books Bulletin, September 1984, page 5
School Library Journal, May 1984, page 79

Other books by the author:
Have You Seen Hyacinth McCaw?, 1981
The Winter Worm Business, 1981
Left-Handed Shortstop, 1980
The Girl Who Knew It All, 1979

Other books you might like:
Thomas J. Dygard, *Halfback Tough*, 1986
New at Graham High, Joe joins the football team and begins to change his tough guy outlook as he becomes absorbed by the game and gains new friends.
Ruth Hallman, *Tough Is Not Enough*, 1981
Kurt, a streetwise teen used to taking care of himself, forms a friendship with Laura Mae, a mountain girl whose father is a drunkard and a thief.
Harriett Mandelay Luger, *Chasing Trouble*, 1976
To keep her out of trouble, a city kid is sent to live in the country where she finds herself caring about the land, ecology and a pocket gopher.
Phyllis Reynolds Naylor, *One of the Third Grade Thonkers*, 1988
Ashamed of his cousin, Jimmy is determined to keep him out of his special club for tough boys, until an accident shows the true meaning of courage.
Robert Kimmel Smith, *Mostly Michael*, 1987
Michael's diary reflects his eleventh year, as he copes with braces, troublesome relatives, a little sister, the school play, and a spelling bee.

699

Theo E. Gilchrist

Illustrator: Glen Rounds

Halfway Up the Mountain (Philadelphia: Lippincott, 1978)

Age range: Grades 2-3

Subject(s): Cooks and Cookery; Robbers and Outlaws

Major character(s): Bloodcoe, Thief

Time period(s): 19th century

Locale(s): United States

What the book is about: An old man and a half-blind old woman drive off a bandit using the old woman's method of cooking beef.

Where it's reviewed:
Booklist, July 15, 1978, page 1738
Kirkus Reviews, October 1, 1978, page 1070
School Library Journal, December 1978, page 64

Other books you might like:
Caron Lee Cohen, *Bronco Dogs*, 1991
Bank robbers Sixgun Gus and Cannonball Clyde get into the worst trouble ever and become ghosts, but remain best friends.
Terry Deary, *The Custard Kid*, 1980

The Custard Kid, who wants only to be a Hollywood stuntman, finds himself accidentally pursuing an outlaw career instead.
Jean Rossbach, *Bernie, the Beagle Who Liked German Cooking*, 1991
The adventures of Bernie, a beagle whose talent for German cooking helps him succeed in life.
Tomi Ungerer, *The Three Robbers*, 1991
Three robbers terrify the countryside until they are subdued by the charm of a little girl named Tiffany.
Marcia K. Vaughan, *Wombat Stew*, 1984
A dingo intent on making wombat stew receives cooking suggestions from the other animals, unaware that they are protecting their fellow creature.

700

Mel Gilden

Harry Newberry and the Raiders of the Red Drink (New York: Holt, 1987)

Age range: Grades 4-7

Subject(s): Humor; Mothers and Sons

Major character(s): Harry Newberry, Preteen; Tuatara, Hero

Time period(s): 1980s

Locale(s): Yupitz, Fictional Country

What the book is about: Harry Newberry is crazy about comic books and especially those about the superhero, Tuatara. As he keeps trying to interest his mom in the comic books, his investigations lead him to believe she is actually the famed superhero. Harry is on the trail of the evil Bonnie Android to thwart her plans for the Slingshot of Doom. High humor and outrageous action for those who will be reading Douglas Adams' *Hitchhikers Guide to the Galaxy* in a couple of years.

Other books by the author:
Monster Mashers, 1989
Outer Space and All That Junk, 1989
Things That Go Bark in the Park, 1989
The Return of Captain Conquer, 1986

Other books you might like:
Babette Cole, *Supermoo!*, 1992
A bovine superhero crusades against the evil spreaders of filth and pollution.
Ellen Conford, *Lenny Kendell, Smart Aleck*, 1983
Lenny wants to become the world's greatest stand-up comic, but with an enemy like Mousie he wonders if he'll have any future at all.
Lois Duncan, *Wonder Kid Meets the Evil Lunch Snatcher*, 1988
Terrorized by an evil bully at his new school, Brian devises, with the help of a fellow comic book fan, a plan involving a new super hero.
Robert Lipsyte, *The Chemo Kid*, 1992
When the drugs he takes for chemotherapy transform Fred from wimp to superhero, he and his friends plot to rid the town of hazardous toxic waste.
William McCay, *Funny Business*, 1989
The Three Investigators track a costumed thief at a comic book convention.

701

Bill Gillham

Illustrator: Francis Mosley

The Rich Kid (London: Deutsch, 1985)

Age range: Grades 4-6

Subject(s): Kidnapping

Major character(s): Jo, Captive (kidnap victim); Christos Andreas, Captive (kidnap victim)

Time period(s): 1980s

Locale(s): England

What the book is about: Jo, son of a village mechanic, and Christos, the millionaire's boy, are kidnapped. Though they come from completely different worlds, their need to plan an escape brings them together. Jo is released and is able to ehlp in the rescue of Christos. Though Jo identifies the man responsible, no one believes him and only when he is able to tell authorities how many times the kidnapper's car went under and overpass by noticing the static on the car radio, are they able to trace the route and rescue Christos.

Where it's reviewed:
Center for Children's Books Bulletin, October 1985, page 26
School Library Journal, February 1986, page 85

Other books you might like:
Larry Callen, *Who Kidnapped the Sherrif?*, 1985
    Pat O'Leary and his friend, Violet, get involved in the sherrif's kidnapping and other wild events.
Catherine Cookson, *Mrs. Flanagan's Trumpet*, 1976
    Staying with his grandparents, Eddie finds himself allied with his grandmother in a struggle to free his sister and the housemaid from white slavers.
Barbara Holland, *Prisoners at the Kitchen Table*, 1979
    Two friends, one usually the leader and the other the follower, find their roles reversed when they must plot to escape from kidnappers.
Joan Phipson, *The Cats*, 1976
    Two kidnapped brothers in Australia save their abductors from destruction by a tribe of feral cats they have cruelly abused.
Catherine Woolley, *Libby Shadows a Lady*, 1974
    A mystery set in New York City where a girl inadvertently breaks up a kidnapping ring supplying babies for adoption.

702

Jamie Gilson

Do Bananas Chew Gum? (New York: Lothrop, 1980)

Age range: Grades 4-6

Subject(s): Babysitters; Learning Disabilities

Major character(s): Sam Mott, Child; Mrs. Huggins, Teacher

Time period(s): 1980s

Locale(s): Illinois

What the book is about: Sam Mott is in sixth grade, but can only read at a second grade level and is convinced that he is stupid. His parents think his difficulty stems from frequent moves. When he gets a baby-sitting job, he has trouble because he can't read instructions. An unlikely friendship devel-ops between Sam and Alicia, the brightest student in the class, who needs to learn to stop telling people she is smart, just as Sam needs to stop saying he is dumb.

Where it's reviewed:
Center for Children's Books Bulletin, March 1981, p 133
School Library Journal, August 1980, page 64

Awards the book has won:
Carl Sandburg Award 1981

Other books by the author:
Itchy Richard, 1991
Hobie Hanson, Greatest Hero of the Mall, 1989
Double Dog Dare, 1988
Hobie Hanson, You're Weird, 1987

Other books you might like:
Jeanne Gehret, *Learning Disabilities and the Don't Give Up Kid*, 1990
    Alex, a child with dyslexia, learns about his problem and what can be done to solve it. (Related picture book)
Sheila Greenwald, *Will the Real Gertrude Hollings Please Stand Up?*, 1983
    An eleven year old child with a learning disability spends several weeks with an overachieving cousin.
Marilyn Levinson, *And Don't Bring Jeremy*, 1985
    Sixth grader Adam finds it difficult to come to terms with the needs of his older brother who suffers from a learning disability.
Joanne Rocklin, *Discovering Martha*, 1991
    Martha begins to learn the guitar and believes it possesses magic.
Mary Waldorf, *Jake McGee and His Feet*, 1980
    Jake takes an important step toward dealing with his reading disability on the day he runs away from school.

703

Jamie Gilson

Illustrator: John Wallner

Harvey, the Beer Can King (New York: Lothrop, 1978)

Age range: Grades 4-6

Subject(s): Collectors and Collecting

Major character(s): Harvey William Trumble, 6th Grader, Collector; Quint Calkins, 6th Grader, Magician; Suzanna Brooks, 6th Grader, Collector

Time period(s): 1970s (1978)

Locale(s): Pittsfield

What the book is about: When the local newspaper announces a contest for sixth grade "Superkid," both Harvey with his beer can collection and Quint with his magic act, think they can win. As competition heats up, Quint and Harvey's friendship seems to be in jeopardy. The relationships and families are realistic, and the ending is not pat, but very satisfying.

Where it's reviewed:
Booklist, May 1, 1978, page 1430
Center for Children's Books Bulletin, November 1978, page 43
Kirkus Reviews, May 1, 1978, page 497

Awards the book has won:
Juvenile Book Merit Award 1978

Other books by the author:
Thirteen Ways to Sink a Sub, 1982
Can't Catch Me, I'm the Gingerbread Man, 1981
Do Bananas Chew Gum?, 1981
Dial Leroi Rupert, DJ, 1979

Other books you might like:
Ellen Conford, *Can Do, Jenny Archer*, 1991
　　Attempting to win a can-collecting contest, the winner of
　　which will direct a class movie, Jenny risks losing her best
　　friend.
Norma Howe, *Shoot for the Moon*, 1992
　　The trip to Italy she wins in a yo-yo contest gives Gina a new
　　perspective on relationships, responsibility, and herself.
Stephen Krensky, *A Big Day for Scepters*, 1977
　　Calander, a collector of magic, finds himself involved in
　　more than he bargained for when he goes on a quest for a
　　mysterious scepter.
Barbara Park, *Almost Starring Skinnybones*, 1988
　　Alex is convinced that he will be a star and impress his
　　teammates when, as the winner of a cat food essay contest,
　　he is asked to make a commercial.
Barbara A. Steiner, *Dolby and the Woof-Off*, 1991
　　Bo teaches his dog Dolby some unusual tricks in an attempt
　　to win the Woof-Off contest.

704

Jamie Gilson

Itchy Richard (New York: Clarion, 1991)

Age range: Grades 2-3

Subject(s): Schools

Major character(s): Richard, Child; Ben, Child; Mrs.
Zookey, Teacher

Time period(s): 1990s

Locale(s): United States

What the book is about: Richard feels left out because he
does not have a yo-yo. But when it is discovered that someone
in his class has head lice, the yo-yo doesn't seem quite as
important.

Where it's reviewed:
Booklist, September 15, 1991, page 150

Other books by the author:
Double Dog Dare, 1988
4B Goes Wild, 1983
13 Ways to Sink a Sub, 1982

Other books you might like:
Suzy Kline, *Horrible Harry in Room 2B*, 1988
　　Doug finds that being Harry's best friend can get him into
　　some horrible situations.
Joanne Oppenheim, *Mrs. Peloki's Substitute*, 1987
　　Mrs. Peloki has a bad time with some difficult second grad-
　　ers.
Amy Schwartz, *Begin at the Beginning*, 1983
　　Sara gets stuck when she must paint a picture for the second
　　grade art show.
Molly Mia Stewart, *Elizabeth's Super-Selling Lemonade*, 1990

Elizabeth and Jessica sell lemonade to buy a wedding pres-
ent for their teacher, but Jessica spends all the money.
Marie Tenaille, *The Day the Dragon Came to School*, 1988
　　Daniel the dragon spends a day in second grade.

705

Jamie Gilson

Illustrator: Linda Strauss Edwards

Thirteen Ways to Sink a Sub (New York: Lothrop, 1982)

Age range: Grades 3-5

Subject(s): Teachers; School Life

Major character(s): Hobie Hanson, Child; Svetlana
Ivanovich, Teacher; Nick Rossi, Child

Time period(s): 1980s

Locale(s): Stockton, Illinois

What the book is about: When their regular teacher, Mr.
Star, is away, the students in 4B try every trick they can think of
to "sink the sub," Ms. Ivanovich, with hilarious results.

Where it's reviewed:
Booklist, October 1, 1982, page 244

Awards the book has won:
Sequoyah Children's Book Award 1985

Other books by the author:
Itchy Richard, 1991
Sticks and Stones and Skeleton Bones, 1991
Do Bananas Chew Gum?, 1982
Can't Catch Me, I'm the Gingerbread Man, 1981

Other books you might like:
Nancy Hayashi, *The Fantastic Stay-Home-From-School Day*,
1992
　　A day-at-home scheme for Leona and Eddie backfires when
　　Eddie gets sent to school and goes from disaster to disaster.
Janet Johnson, *Ellie Brader Hates Mr. G.*, 1991
　　Ellie's substitute teacher, Mr. Garrett, seems mean and un-
　　fair, until his handling of several class crises changes Ellie's
　　feelings toward him.
Mary Robinson, *The Amazing Valvano and the Mystery of the
Hooded Rat*, 1988
　　Maria is excited about her plans to perform a magic act at
　　school until her pet rat, an important part of the act, is
　　kidnapped.
Marilyn Singer, *The Case of the Fixed Election*, 1989
　　Dave and Sam Bean find themselves mixed-up in the dirtiest
　　election the school has ever seen.
Barbara Brooks Wallace, *Miss Switch to the Rescue*, 1981
　　When Rupert's friend, Amelia, is kidnapped, Miss Switch the
　　witch returns disguised as a substitute teacher to help rescue
　　her.

706

Fred Gipson

Illustrator: Ronald Himler

Curly and the Wild Boar (New York: Harper & Row,
1979)

Age range: Grades 4-6

Subject(s): Country Life; American West

Major character(s): Curly Wagoner, Preteen; Catfish Waggoner, Parent (Curly's father)

Time period(s): 19th century

Locale(s): Mason County, Texas

What the book is about: Curly's encounter with a wild boar produces a rip snorting adventure. He repeatedly puts himself in danger in his determination to kill the creature that has destroyed his prize watermelon.

Where it's reviewed:
Center for Children's Books Bulletin, September 1979, page 8
Kirkus Reviews, April 1, 1979, page 388
School Library Journal, May 1979, page 35

Other books by the author:
Little Arliss, 1978
Savage Sam, 1962
Old Yeller, 1956
Recollection Creek, 1955

Other books you might like:
Patricia Beatty, *Billy Bedamned, Long Gone By*, 1977
   Uncle Rudd tells tall tales about his life with the cowboys, Indians and Confederates in Texas.
Larry Callen, *Pinch*, 1975
   A boy growing up in a country town becomes involved with a pig he trains to hunt and a mean, crafty gentleman who teaches him the art of trickery.
Arthur Catherall, *Kalu and the Wild Boar*, 1973
   A boy of India tangles courageously with a tiger and a wild boar to save his father's crops.
Wynelle Catlin, *Old Wattles*, 1975
   A Texas farm girl is continually frustrated by the elusive turkey hen whose eggs she is supposed to find.
Edna Walker Chandler, *Popcorn Patch*, 1969
   A boy tries to grow a popcorn and watermelon crop to earn money for the new saddle he wants so badly.

707

Fred Gipson

Old Yeller (New York: Harper and Row, 1956)

Age range: Grades 4-6

Subject(s): Animals/Dogs; Frontier and Pioneer Life

Major character(s): Travis, Teenager; Old Yeller, Dog

Time period(s): 1950s

Locale(s): Texas

What the book is about: Travis lives with his mother and father and little brother in a log cabin in the Texas hill country. Travis is left in charge of the family and farm when his father goes on a 600 mile cattle drive to Abilene. His dog, Old Yeller, fights thieving raccoons, bulls, grizzly bears and wolves to help protect the family.

Where it's reviewed:
Horn Book, October 1956, page 371
Kirkus Reviews, May 1, 1956, page 320

Other books by the author:
Curly and the Wild Bear, 1979
Little Arliss, 1978

Savage Sam, 1962
Cowhand, 1953 (non-fiction)

Other books you might like:
Mildred Ames, *Philo Potts, or, The Helping Hand Strikes Again*, 1982
   Philo and Cristabel kidnap a neighbor's neglected dog but run into trouble when the dog makes friends with a pack of unruly strays.
John E. Baur, *Dogs on the Frontier*, 1964
   Non-fiction accounts of the part played by dogs in the settling of the American West.
Helen Griffith, *Foxy*, 1984
   Camping in the Florida Keys with his parents, Jeff finds an abandoned, mistreated dog that he wants to keep for his own.
Karin Lorentzen, *Lanky Longlegs*, 1982
   Nine year old Di is busy taking care of a litter of pups and at the same time dealing with her brother's impending death.
Bill Wallace, *Red Dog*, 1987
   Twelve year old Adam finds his courage tested when he is left in charge of his home in the mountains of Wyoming in the 1860s.

708

Barbara Girion

Like Everybody Else (New York: Scribners, 1980)

Age range: Grades 5-6

Subject(s): Jews; Friendship; School Life

Major character(s): Samantha "Sam" Gold, Preteen; Sue Ellen, Child; Eileen Gold, Writer

Time period(s): 1980s

Locale(s): United States

What the book is about: Samantha, who wants to be like everyone else, worries about fitting in because her home is not always neat and her mom is not a traditional homemaker, but a writer of children's books. When her mother tries her hand at writing for adults, the result is a sexually explicit novel which embarrasses Sam terribly. As Sam prepares for her Bat Mitzvah, she deals with many truths that help her mother see her own career in a new light.

Where it's reviewed:
Kirkus Reviews, January 15, 1981, page 75
School Library Journal, February 1981, page 65

Other books by the author:
Indian Summer, 1990
Very Brief Season, 1984
Misty and Me, 1979
A Tangle of Roots, 1979

Other books you might like:
Chaya M. Burnstein, *Rifka Bangs the Teakettle*, 1970
   Life in 1904 Czarist Russia is difficult for a Jewish girl who wants to understand the attitudes of her neighbors and go to school with her brothers.
Jean Fiedler, *The Year the World Was out of Step with Jancy Fried*, 1981
   A 12 year old Jewish girl is caught in a whirlwind that includes a boy, a school play, and letters from an Austrian cousin as Hitler rises to power.

Gloria Goldreich, *Season of Discovery*, 1976
   A young Jewish girl, in the year of her Bat Mitzvah, gains an understanding of herself and her people's past.
Bert Metter, *Bar Mitzvah, Bat Mitzvah*, 1984
   This non-fiction work describes coming-of-age ceremonies and discusses both their history and their effects on the lives of those who experience them.
Susan Beth Pfeffer, *Turning Thirteen*, 1988
   Although initially afraid she'll lose her best friend unless they prepare for their Bat Mitzvahs together, Becky undergoes a change in her thinking.

709

Libby Gleeson

I Am Susannah (New York: Holiday, 1989)

Age range: Grades 5-7

Subject(s): Mystery and Detective Stories; Friendship

Major character(s): Susannah, Preteen; Kim, Preteen; Blue Lady, Neighbor

Time period(s): Indeterminate

Locale(s): Australia

What the book is about: When Kim moves away, Susie is bereft and daunted at the prospect of facing life without her sidekick. Her response is a bitter, self-imposed isolation. She spies on "The Blue Lady" who has moved into Kim's old home. At first, she hates her, until Susie realizes that they have something in common.

Where it's reviewed:
Booklist, May 15, 1989, page 1648
Hornbook, September 1989, page 628
Kirkus Reviews, February 1, 1989, page 209

Other books by the author:
Eleanor, Elizabeth, 1990

Other books you might like:
Ellen Conford, *Me and the Terrible Two*, 1974
   No one, Dorrie vows, can take the place of her best friend who has moved to Australia, so when twin boys move in next door, the war is on.
Carol Drinkwater, *The Haunted School*, 1985
   Fanny, a teacher, must contend with rumors of ghosts and the townspeople's suspicions before opening a proper school in colonial Australia.
Elizabeth Hathorn, *Thunderwith*, 1991
   After moving to Australia following her mother's death, Laura's friendship with a dog helps her adjust to an unfamiliar father and stepfamily.
Maureen Pople, *A Nugget of Gold*, 1988
   Two stories, one of a 19th century girl in the Australian goldfields; the other of a present day girl who finds a link with the past in a gold nugget.
Colin Thiele, *The Shadow on the Hills*, 1977
   A young boy is caught in a dilemma when his friend, an old hermit, is accused of burning down their small Australian farming community.

710

Mel Glidden

The Planetoid of Amazement (New York: HarperCollins, 1991)

Age range: Grades 5-6

Subject(s): Science Fiction; Humor

Major character(s): Rodney Congruent, Teenager; Grubber Young, Alien; Drum, Alien

Time period(s): 1990s (1991)

Locale(s): Earth; Outer Space

What the book is about: Rodney Congruent opens an envelope addressed to his father and embarks on his very first solo adventure. He meets Grubber Young and Drum, alien treasure hunters looking for the Legendary Treasure Planet, which they think is Earth. Together they travel to the Planetoid of Amazement and match wits with the dread Slignathi.

Other books by the author:
The Return of Captain Conquer, 1986
Harry Newberry and the Raiders of the Red Drink, 1989

Other books you might like:
Daniel Manus Pinkwater, *Alan Mendelsohn, the Boy from Mars*, 1979
   Alan and Leonard buy the Klugarsh Mind Control System and have wild adventures through space and time.
William Sleator, *Strange Attractors*, 1990
   Two men, a scientist and his alter ego, pursue Max, who is in possession of a time machine.
Frank Asch, *Journey to Terezor*, 1989
   Matt and his parents are transported to a mysterious planet ruled by robots.
Margaret Mahy, *Aliens in the Family*, 1986
   Jake Raven protects his stepsister and stepbrother from an alien and flees from a creature who can alter time.

711

Molly Gloss

Outside the Gates (New York: Atheneum, 1986)

Age range: Grades 5-7

Subject(s): Fantasy; Outcasts

Major character(s): Vren, Animal Lover; Rusche, Worker

Time period(s): Indeterminate Past

Locale(s): Earth

What the book is about: Vren, who communicates with animals and old Rusche, who can control the weather, are banished beyond the High Gates. The outcasts are afraid to trust others like themselves. Scorned as children, living in separate solitude in the Great Forest, Vren and Rusche find a new, gentle existence until a spellbinder misusing his power upsets their lives again.

Where it's reviewed:
Center for Children's Books Bulletin, October 1986, page 26
Horn Book, March/April, 1987, page 209

Other books you might like:
Nina Beachcroft, *The Wishing People*, 1980

When Martha becomes the owner of an old weather house which forecasts weather, its two married inhabitants magically grant ten wishes to her.

Bill Brittain, *Wings: A Novel*, 1991
 When twelve year old Ian grows an unsightly pair of wings he becomes an embarrassment to his politically ambitious father and must look for help.

Alfred Reynolds, *Kiteman of Karanga*, 1985
 Karl, banished from his home for cowardice, uses his kitewing glider to fly across the desert to look for a new life.

Pamela Stearns, *Into the Painted Bear Lair*, 1976
 Entering another world through a toy store, Gregory joins Sir Rosemary and a Bear on a journey involving princesses, magic spells and hidden passages.

James Thurber, *The Wonderful O*, 1985
 Relates what happened when an evil sea captain banished the letter ''O'' from the island, Ooroo.

712

Paul Goble, Author/Illustrator

The Friendly Wolf (Scarsdale, NY: Bradbury, 1975)

Age range: Grades 2-3

Subject(s): Indians of North America

Major character(s): Little Cloud, Indian; Bright Eyes, Indian

Time period(s): Indeterminate

Locale(s): United States

What the book is about: While berry-picking, Little Cloud and his sister wander away from the tribe and get lost. They find shelter in a wolf's den. The wolf helps them find their way home, and the tribe forms a friendship with the wolves.

Where it's reviewed:
Junior Bookshelf, February 1975, page 38
School Library Journal, February 1976, page 381

Other books by the author:
Dream Wolf, 1990
Beyond the Ridge, 1989
The Girl Who Loved Wild Horses, 1978
Lone Bull's Horse Raid, 1973

Other books you might like:
Betty Boegehold, *A Horse Called Starfire*, 1990
 A young Indian boy proudly brings home a golden mare who ran free when the Spanish explorer who owned her died.
Jamake Highwater, *Moonsong Lullaby*, 1981
 A gentle night poem involving animals, plants, and Native American culture.
Jay Leech, *Bright Fawn and Me*, 1979
 A Cheyenne girl takes care of her sister at a tribal fair set in the 19th century.
Evelyn White Minshull, *The Cornhusk Doll*, 1987
 Mary gives her most treasured possession to an Indian girl to prove her friendship in this pioneer story.
Bettys Waterton, *A Salmon for Simon*, 1987
 A small Canadian Indian has a great adventure with a live salmon.

713

Paul Goble

Her Seven Brothers (New York: Bradbury, 1988)

Age range: Grades 2-4

Subject(s): Indians of North America; Folk Tales

Major character(s): Maiden, Maiden, Indian

Time period(s): Indeterminate Past

Locale(s): United States

What the book is about: A Native American legend from the Cheyenne, about how the Big Dipper was created. A young maiden and her seven brothers escaped the Chief of the Buffalo Nation by traveling to safety on the Star Prairie.

Where it's reviewed:
Center for Children's Books Bulletin, April 1988, page 156
Horn Book, July/August 1988, page 506

Other books by the author:
Dream Wolf, 1990
Beyond the Ridge, 1989
Buffalo Woman, 1984
Friendly Wolf, 1974

Other books you might like:
Terri Cohlene, *Quillworker: A Cheyenne Legend*, 1990
 Legends tell the origins of the stars, and the history and culture of the Cheyenne Indians.
Stefan Czernecki, *Pancho's Pinata*, 1992
 On Christmas Eve, Pancho rescues a star from a cactus and receives the gift of happiness.
Wilhelm Grimm, *The Falling Stars*, 1985
 A poor child who is generous to others receives a reward from the heavens.
Montzalee Miller, *My Grandmother's Cookie Jar*, 1987
 The cookies from grandmother's Indian head jar are always accompanied by stories of Indian heritage and pride.
Jean Guard Monroe, *They Dance in the Sky*, 1987
 A collection of legends about the stars from various North American Indian cultures. (Older readers)

714

Rumer Godden

Illustrator: Ann Strugnell

Mr. McFadden's Hallowe'en (New York: Viking, 1975)

Age range: Grades 4-6

Subject(s): Halloween

Major character(s): Selina, Child; Mr. McFadden, Aged Person (grouch)

Time period(s): Indeterminate

Locale(s): Scotland

What the book is about: McFadden is a crusty old man nobody likes. He has land he refuses to sell to the village for a park. When he is injured, Selina and her family are the only ones to help him. The family is made outcast by the villagers for helping McFadden.

Where it's reviewed:
Horn Book, October 1975, page 452
Kirkus Reviews, August 1, 1975, page 848

Other books by the author:
The Rocking Horse Secret, 1978
The Peacock Spring, 1976
Candy Floss and Impunity Jane, 1975
Little Plum, 1975

Other books you might like:
Ray Bradbury, *The Halloween Tree*, 1972
    Boys visit a deserted house and find some rather strange vegetation in this story by the science fiction great.
Virginia Hamilton, *Willie Bea and the Time the Martians Landed*, 1983
    A story built around the halloween night on which Orson Welles made his famous invasion from Mars broadcast, "The War of the Worlds."
Sheila Hayes, *Speaking of Snapdragons*, 1982
    Heather feels left out and lonely until she meets an old man named Duffy.
Jeffrey Keller, *Tramp Steamer and the Silver Bullet*, 1984
    A Halloween caper involving two best friends turns into a baffling puzzle that involves an abandoned house.
Victoria Whitehead, *The Chimney Witches*, 1987
    On Halloween Eve, Ellen gets caught up in the activities of the witches who live in the chimney.

715

Rumer Godden

Illustrator: Juliet Stanwell Smith

The Rocking Horse Secret (New York: Viking, 1978)

Age range: Grades 4-6

Subject(s): Mystery and Detective Stories

Major character(s): Tabitha "Tibby" Winters, Child; Jed, Handyman

Time period(s): Indeterminate Past

Locale(s): Pomeroy Place, England

What the book is about: Tibby solves many problems when she finds a will hidden in a rocking horse. Terrible changes occur in the house where Tibby's mother works, but although Tibby knows something that may make all the difference, she doesn't feel she can divulge the secret.

Where it's reviewed:
Booklist, July 7, 1978, 1678
Kirkus Reviews, April 1, 1978, page 374
School Library Journal, September 1978, page 136

Other books by the author:
Listen to the Nightingale, 1992
Kindle of Kittens, 1979
Little Plum, 1963
Impunity Jane, 1954

Other books you might like:
Nina Bawden, *The Finding*, 1985
    When an unexpected inheritance threatens to change his life with his adopted family in London, an eleven year old foundling runs away from home.
John Bellairs, *The Mummy, the Will, and the Crypt*, 1983
    Johnny and Professor Childermass look for the hidden will left by an eccentric cereal tycoon who wished to make life difficult for his heirs.
Patricia Elmore, *Susannah and the Blue House Mystery*, 1980

After the death of the kindly old man, a girl and her friends piece together elusive clues in hopes of finding a treaure he has left to them.
Dick King-Smith, *Harry's Mad*, 1984
    Harry's legacy from his great-uncle, a talking parrot, proves to be a much more exciting gift than he ever imagined.
Charlotte MacLeod, *Cirak's Daughter*, 1982
    A legacy from the father who deserted her starts Jenny on a search for answers to questions concerning her father, his death, and her future.

716

M.B. Goffstein

Two Piano Tuners (New York: Farrar, 1970)

Age range: Grades 3-4

Subject(s): Musicians

Major character(s): Debbie Wemstock, Child; Reuben Weinstock, Worker (piano tuner); Isaac Lipman, Musician

Time period(s): Indeterminate

Locale(s): United States

What the book is about: Debbie wants to become a piano tuner like her grandfather. She loves to go with him when he works. But Grandpa wants her to become a concert pianist. When Grandpa sends her to Mrs. Perlman with a request to delay the tuning of her piano, Debbie begins to tune it herself. With the help of concert pianist Isaac Lipman, Grandpa realizes that it is the best thing to let Debbie follow her own heart.

Where it's reviewed:
Booklist, September 15, 1970, page 106
Center for Children's Books Bulletin, October 1970, page 25
Kirkus Reviews, April 15, 1970, page 499

Other books by the author:
A House, A Home, 1989
Our Prairie Home: A Picture Album, 1988
Family Scrapbook, 1978
Goldie, the Dollmaker, 1969

Other books you might like:
Melinda Green, *Rachel's Recital*, 1979
    Rachel, who dislikes piano lessons so much she won't practice, faces her first recital unprepared.
Ronald Kidd, *Rapunzel, Sort Of*, 1992
    Danny's determination to get a mysterious piano player to join his band leads to an act of heroism.
Phyllis Reynolds Naylor, *Josie's Troubles*, 1992
    Josie and Sarah break one of the legs of Sarah's mother's piano bench, and must take a series of odd jobs to raise the money to repair it.
Donna Rupert, *The Dragon's Path*, 1979
    Forgetting the warning not to stray off the forest path, Alexander follows a sound of music to a village where everyone seems continually happy.
Laura Storms, *Careers with an Orchestra*, 1983
    Describes fifteen different career possibilities with a professional orchestra, including piano tuner.

717

Ellen H. Goins

Big Diamond's Boy (Nashville: Nelson, 1977)

Age range: Grades 5-6

Subject(s): Depression (Economic)

Major character(s): Albert Harvey, Gambler; Albert "Cotton" Harvey, Child

Time period(s): 1930s

Locale(s): United States (Rural South)

What the book is about: Albert "Big Diamond" Harvey is a shiftless gambler who refuses to let his intimidated wife work. He think education for his son, "Cotton" is a waste of time, since "Big Diamond" is teaching him the art of gambling. Mother defiantly goes to work and Big Diamond goes off to make a fortune.

Where it's reviewed:
Kirkus Reviews, May 1, 1977, page 486
School Library Journal, March 1977, page 151

Other books by the author:
Long Winter's Sleep, 1978 (Non-fiction)
Treasures of the Nest, 1978 (Non-fiction)
David's Pockets, 1972

Other books you might like:
Vera Cleaver, *The Mock Revolt*, 1971
    During the Great Depression, Ussy tries to avoid becoming part of the establishment and gains an understanding of his wish to revolt.
Eth Clifford, *The Man Who Sang in the Dark*, 1987
    A story of the way the inhabitants of a bleak Philadelphia apartment building become "family" during the Great Depression.
Irene Hunt, *No Promises in the Wind*, 1981
    During the Great Depression, Josh is forced to make his own way in life.
Marian Potter, *A Chance Wild Apple*, 1982
    A Depression era story of a young girl on a Missouri farm.
Crystal Thrasher, *End of a Dark Road*, 1982
    The story of a family's survival in Indiana during the Depression. Sequel to *A Taste of Darkness*.

718

Barbara Diamond Goldin

Illustrator: Erika Weihs

Cakes and Miracles (New York: Viking, 1991)

Age range: Grades 1-3

Subject(s): Blind; Jews; Holidays

Major character(s): Hershel, Handicapped (blind), Baker; Basha, Parent (Hershel's mother), Baker

Time period(s): 1890s

Locale(s): Europe

What the book is about: Blind Hershel and his widowed mother help support themselves by baking hamantashen to sell at Purim. Hershel's job is to haul wood and water for the baking and shape the cookies into marvelous designs from the pictures he has in his head. One day an angel appears to Hershel and tells him to create what he sees in his mind. He makes figurines from clay which sell very well and give him ideas for a possible career. Includes recipe for hamantashen.

Where it's reviewed:
Booklist, January 15, 1991, page 1062
Horn Book, July/August 1991, page 447

Other books by the author:
The Magician's Visit, 1993
Fire!, 1992
The World's Birthday: A Rosh Hoshanah Story, 1990
Just Enough Is Plenty, 1988

Other books you might like:
Miriam Chaikin, *Make Noise, Make Merry*, 1983
    Retells the story and meaning of Purim, the symbols and how the feast is celebrated. (Non-fiction)
Barbara Cohen, *Here Come the Purim Players*, 1984
    All the Jews in the Prague ghetto watch a troupe of local players renact the story of Queen Esther.
Molly Cone, *Purim*, 1967
    The story and customs of the gayest of Jewish holidays which celebrates how Queen Esther saved her people from the wicked Haman.
Yuri Suhl, *The Purim Goat*, 1980
    Hoping to earn some money so his pet goat won't be sold to pay a debt, a poor Jewish boy teaches the animal to dance.
Jane Breskin Zalben, *Goldie's Purim*, 1991
    Although Goldie is scared at first, she overcomes her stage fright to play Queen Esther in the synagogue's celebration of Purim.

719

Kelly Goldman

Illustrator: Don Maden

Sherlick Hound and the Valentine Mystery (Niles, Illinois: Whitman, 1989)

Age range: Grades 3-4

Subject(s): Animals/Dogs; Mystery and Detective Stories

Major character(s): Princess Penelope Poodle, Dog; Sherlick Hound, Detective; Sir Archibald Airedale, Dog

Time period(s): Indeterminate

Locale(s): Dogtown, Fictional Country

What the book is about: The "Dog-Honest Detective" uses logic and deductive reasoning to find out who stole Princess Penelope Poodle's ruby-studded collar. He doggedly checks out all of Dogtown's high society including Scoop Schnauzer, Gloria Vanderdog, etc. Difficult vocabulary and cute puns make this harder to read than the forty page beginning reader look indicates.

Where it's reviewed:
Booklist, April 15, 1989, page 1466
School Library Journal, June 1989, page 88

Other books you might like:
Nathaniel Benchley, *Snip*, 1981
    The routine life of a tired old beagle named Duncan is upset by a mischievous young poodle named Snip.
Barbara Dillon, *What Happened to Harry?*, 1982
    Harry becomes entangled with a witch on Halloween night and is transformed into a poodle.

James Duffy, *The Revolt of the Teddy Bears: A May Gray Mystery*, 1985
   Teddy bears are running amok in Paris and Chief Inspector May Gray, a poodle, is determined to find out why.
Linda Gondosch, *Brutus, the Wonder Poodle*, 1990
   When Ryan's parents give him a toy poodle puppy, Ryan is disappointed that the dog is not bigger, but quickly learns that Brutus is the best dog ever.
Margaret Bloy Graham, *Benjy and His Friend Fifi*, 1988
   Lovable mutt Benjy accompanies his shy, nervous poodle friend Fifi to her first dog show, where chaotic adventures ensue.

720

Linda Gondosch

Illustrator: Patricia H Lincoln

The Best Bet Gazette (New York: Lodestar/Dutton, 1989)

Age range: Grades 4-6

Subject(s): Newspapers; Journalism

Major character(s): Judy Oliver, Preteen, Journalist

Time period(s): 1950s (1954)

Locale(s): United States

What the book is about: In the summer of 1954, competition with two rival girls in producing a neighborhood newspaper and her experience in dealing with a friend's case of polio, help ten year old Judy Oliver develop an understanding of how a newspaper ought to be written.

Where it's reviewed:
Library Talk, May 1990, page 24
School Library Journal, November 1989, page 108

Other books by the author:
Brutus, the Wonder Poodle, 1990
The Monsters of Marble Avenue, 1988
Who Needs a Bratty Brother?, 1985
Who's Afraid of Haggerty House?, 1987

Other books you might like:
Norma Fox Mazer, *Bright Days, Stupid Nights*, 1992
   During a summer internship on a newspaper, Vicki develops a love-hate relationship with Chris and writes a sensational story.
Lisa Norby, *Star Reporter*, 1989
   Karen describes the antics of classmates in the school newspaper. (Fifth Grade S.T.A.R.S. #5)
Stephen Roos, *Twelve Year Old Vows Revenge!*, 1990
   Two student newspaper reporters spend the summer trying to get even with each other, and in the process, abuse the right of a free press.
Marjorie Weinman Sharmat, *Mysteriously Yours, Maggie Marmelstein*, 1982
   Named the mystery columnist for the school newspaper, Maggie revels in the power she can exert.
Catherine Woolley, *Cathy Leonard Calling*, 1961
   Ten year old Cathy enjoys being society reporter for the local paper but finds it leaves little time for homework or family.

721

Gloria Gonzalez

The Glad Man (New York: Knopf, 1975)

Age range: Grades 4-6

Subject(s): Sports/Baseball; Homeless

Major character(s): Melissa, Child; Glad Man, Streetperson

Time period(s): 1970s

Locale(s): United States

What the book is about: Melissa wants to play for the St. Louis Cardinals, but she'll settle for making the school team. She and her younger brother find the old flower seller, the Glad Man, living in a bus by the dump. They decide to rescue him when the city tries to take away his home.

Where it's reviewed:
Kirkus Reviews, September 15, 1975, page 1066
School Library Journal, October 1975, page 98

Other books by the author:
Gaucho, 1977

Other books you might like:
Nancy Baron, *Tuesday's Child*, 1984
   Grace wants to play baseball but her mother wants her to follow a ballet career.
Scott Eller, *Short Season*, 1985
   Dean quits the baseball team, leaving Brad feeling alone until he learns to make friends without his brother.
Patricia Reilly Giff, *Left-Handed Shortstop*, 1980
   Walter tries everything possible not to play baseball.
E.L. Konigsburg, *About the B'nai Bagels*, 1969
   Mark's mother is the manager of the Little League team he is on, and his older brother is the coach. Lots of baseball and high humor.
Stephen Roos, *My Horrible Secret*, 1983
   Warren's big problem is that he can't play baseball.

722

Shirley Gordon

Illustrator: Charles Robinson

The Boy Who Wanted a Family (New York: Harper and Row, 1980)

Age range: Grades 2-4

Subject(s): Foster Homes; Adoption

Major character(s): Michael, Child, Adoptee; Miss Finch, Social Worker; Miss Graham, Parent (adoptive), Writer

Time period(s): 1980s

Locale(s): United States

What the book is about: After a succession of foster homes, seven year old Michael longs to be adopted. After two unsuccessful placements, and hope and encouragement from Miss Finch, his social worker, he is placed with Miss Graham. She is unlike any other adult Michael has lived with. She isn't married, keeps her Christmas tree up all year, and writes books for a living. After a trial year, the adoption papers are signed and a new family is formed.

Where it's reviewed:
Kirkus Reviews, May 1, 1980, page 584
School Library Journal, April 1980, page 93
Booklist, June 1, 1980, page 1424

Other books by the author:
Crystal's Christmas Carol, 1989
Me and the Bad Guys, 1980
Grandma Zoo, 1978
Green Hornet Lunchbox, 1970

Other books you might like:
Roslyn Banish, *A Family Forever*, 1992
    Jennifer describes her adoption by a family after four years of living as a foster child with many different families.
Jeannette Franklin Caines, *Abby*, 1973
    Pre-schooler Abby enjoys her special place in the family as the adopted child.
Natalie Savage Carlson, *The Happy Orpheline*, 1957
    Brigitte, happy in a French orphanage, tries to avoid being adopted.
Holly Keller, *Horace*, 1991
    Horace, an adopted child, realizes that being part of a family depends on how you feel and not how you look.
Joyce McDonald, *Mail-Order Kid*, 1988
    Flip has his world turned upside down when his parents adopt Todd from Korea.
Roberta Silman, *Somebody Else's Child*, 1976
    As a result of his friendship with his school bus driver, Peter gains a greater understanding of what it means to be adopted.

723

Beatrice Gormley

Illustrator: Emily Arnold McCully

Best Friend Insurance (New York: Dutton, 1983)

Age range: Grades 5-7

Subject(s): Friendship; Cloning; Mothers and Daughters

Major character(s): Maureen Harrity, Preteen; Tracey Argos, Friend; Mr. Costue, Insurance Agent

Time period(s): 1970s

Locale(s): United States

What the book is about: Just when Maureen feels she has been demoted to second-best friend status by her former best friend, Tracey, a rather unusual insurance agent turns up, guaranteeing replacement of lost friends within twenty-four hours. There is something strangely familiar about the new friend who shows up.

Where it's reviewed:
Booklist, February 1, 1984, page 813
Center for Children's Books Bulletin, October 1983, page 16
School Library Journal, February 1984, page 70

Other books by the author:
The Ghastly Glasses, 1985
Fifth Grade Magic, 1982
Mail-Order Wings, 1981

Other books you might like:
Carole S. Adler, *Always and Forever Friends*, 1988

Searching for a friend to replace Meg, who has moved, Wendy establishes a friendship with Honor, and learns about family relationships along the way.
Ellen Conford, *Anything for a Friend*, 1979
    Wallis feels very put upon. Not only does she have a weird first name, but her family has moved so much it is hard to make friends.
Constance C. Greene, *Ask Anybody*, 1983
    Schuyler and her friends Rowena and Betty aren't sure what to make of Nell. She wears green nail polish, knowslove spells, and can drive a truck.
Lila Perl, *Marleen, the Horror Queen*, 1985
    Mom is a bodybuilder, and Marleen has discovered new interests, Alex and Duncan. Life's normal, until Marleen learns that revenge isn't always sweet.
Mary C. Ryan, *Me Two*, 1991
    Cloning himself accidentally, Wilf discovers the advantages and disadvantages of being two people.

724

Judith Gorog

No Swimming in Dark Pond and Other Chilling Tales
(New York: Philomel, 1987)

Age range: Grades 5-8

Subject(s): Horror; Short Stories

Time period(s): Indeterminate

Locale(s): United States

What the book is about: Scary stories for the campfire: Too short to develop real suspense or tension, these stories will work as one at a time read-alouds. Some of the thirteen horror stories are based on folktales, others are original, each written in a slightly different style as if by different authors. For fans of the macabre.

Where it's reviewed:
Center for Children's Books Bulletin, July/August 1987, page 207
School Library Journal, March 1987, page 158

Other books by the author:
On Meeting Witches at Wells, 1991
Winning Scheherazade, 1991
Three Dreams and a Nightmare, and Other Tales of the Dark, 1988
A Taste for Quiet and Other Disquieting Tales, 1982

Other books you might like:
Vivien Alcock, *Ghostly Companions*, 1987
    Ten stories of strange and supernatural events set in England.
E.L. Flood, *The Fly*, 1991
    A scientist finds himself slowly turning into a fly after an experiment goes wrong.
Rita Golden Gelman, *Vampires and Other Creatures of the Night*, 1991
    Includes "out of the night" creatures, vampires, werewolves and other personal and terrifying monsters.
Collin McDonald, *Nightwaves: Scary Tales for After Dark*, 1990
    Horror stories featuring a spirit hunter from Egypt, ghosts at a dam, a woman who sells her husband's soul to the devil and a killer in the woods.
George Mendoza, *Hairticklers*, 1989

Thirteen scary stories featuring the dreaded Gumberoo, the crafty cougarfish, a whole houseful of good luck spiders, and some very naughty people.

725

Deborah Gould

Illustrator: Cheryl Harness

Grandpa's Slide Show (New York: Lothrop, 1987)

Age range: Grades 2-4

Subject(s): Death; Grandparents

Major character(s): Sam, Child; Douglas, Child; Grandpa, Grandparent

Time period(s): 1980s

Locale(s): United States

What the book is about: Whenever they visit Grandpa and Grandma, Sam and Douglas always watch a slide show and it is a very special time with Grandpa as he shares family memories. After Grandpa dies, the children experience the gathering of family and friends, the funeral, and finally, watch another slide show to remember and say goodbye to Grandpa.

Where it's reviewed:
Children's Book Review Service, January 1988, page 47
Language Arts, February 1988, page 192
Tribune Books (Chicago), February 7, 1988, page 6

Other books by the author:
Camping in the Temple of the Sun, 1992
Aaron's Shirt, 1989
Terry's Creature, 1989
Brendan's Best-Timed Birthday, 1988

Other books you might like:
Eve Bunting, *The Happy Funeral*, 1982
   A little Chinese American girl pays tribute to her grandfather as she assists in the preparations for his funeral.
Carol Carrick, *The Foundling*, 1977
   Memories of his dog, killed in an accident, cause Christopher to resist his parents' efforts to adopt a puppy.
Janice Cohn, *I Had a Friend Named Peter*, 1987
   When Betsy learns about the death of a friend, her parents and kindergarten teacher answer questions about dying, funerals, and the burial process.
Paul Rogers, *From Me to You*, 1987
   A grandmother shares her memories of three generations with a young granddaughter and presents her with a precious gift.
Ben Shecter, *Grandma Remembers*, 1989
   A boy and his grandmother take a final tour of the house she is leaving and relive memories of the wonderful times experienced there.

726

Marilyn Gould

Golden Daffodils (Reading, Massachusetts: Addison-Wesley, 1982)

Age range: Grades 4-6

Subject(s): Cerebral Palsy; Epilepsy; School Life

Major character(s): Janis Ward, Child (Handicapped); Barney Fuchs, Child

Time period(s): 1980s

Locale(s): United States

What the book is about: Janis, who has cerebral palsy and epilepsy, is mainstreamed for the first time in fifth grade, and sometimes even her technique of imagining golden daffodils is not enough to cheer her through many difficulties. She must deal with kids who try to help too much, as well as those who taunt and tease. A story of a girl with determination and grit.

Where it's reviewed:
Booklist, March 15, 1983, page 969
School Library Journal, April 1983, page 114

Other books you might like:
Barbara Corcoran, *Child of the Morning*, 1982
   Susan struggles as her epilepsy interferes with her desire to excel in the theater.
Patricia Hermes, *What If They Knew?*, 1980
   A young girl with epilepsy tries to keep her condition a secret from her classmates.
Alison Cragin Herzig, *A Season of Secrets*, 1982
   Brooke's parents are determined to keep secret the fact that her brother, Benji, has epilepsy.
Jan Slepian, *Alfred Summer*, 1980
   Four friends, all outcasts, two because of disabilities and two because of personalities, find strength in each other.
Helen Young, *What Difference Does It Make, Danny?*, 1980
   A young boy with epilepsy proves his abilities as an athlete.

727

Fran Grace

Branigan's Dog: A Novel (Scarsdale, New York: Bradbury, 1981)

Age range: Grades 5 and Up

Subject(s): Fires; Stepfamilies; Death (of a Pet)

Major character(s): Casey Branigan, Teenager; D-Dog, Dog; Rush, Step-Parent

Time period(s): 1980s

Locale(s): California

What the book is about: Casey is an angry, frustrated boy who lives in an Old West fantasy world and can only communicate through his dog. He cannot get along with his stepfather, Rush, or Rush's daughter, Melanie. When Casey's dog dies, Casey retreats even further and finally gets help after setting fire to his house. Includes brief sexual encounters and profanity, and presents a realistic picture of the recovery of a profoundly troubled boy.

Where it's reviewed:
Center for Children's Books Bulletin, March 1982, page 128
School Library Journal, January 1982, page 87

Other books by the author:
Very Private Performance, 1983

Other books you might like:
Karen Ackerman, *The Broken Boy*, 1991

Solly recounts his friendship with a mentally disturbed boy.
Bruce Brooks, *The Moves Make the Man: A Novel*, 1984
A black boy and an emotionally troubled white boy in North Carolina form a precarious friendship.
Willo Davis Roberts, *To Grandmother's House We Go*, 1990
Three children run off to their grandmother's house, where they find a cold reception and a terrible secret.
Eileen Thompson, *The Golden Coyote*, 1971
Snubbed by his tribe and desolate over his grandfather's death, a young Pueblo Indian runs away with his pet coyote pup.
John Rowe Townsend, *Rob's Place*, 1987
Lonely and unhappy, Rob finds a refuge on a "South Sea" island in the local park.

728

Charlotte Towner Graeber

Illustrator: Cheryl Harness

Fudge (New York: Lothrop, 1987)

Age range: Grades 3-6

Subject(s): Animals/Dogs; Responsibility

Major character(s): Chad, Child; Fudge, Dog

Time period(s): 1980s

Locale(s): United States

What the book is about: Chad's parents agree to let him take the puppy, Fudge, on a trial basis if he takes care of her. His mom is expecting twins and she needs rest. The family remains flexible even during crisis.

Where it's reviewed:
Center for Children's Books Bulletin, July 1987, page 207
School Library Journal, August 1987, page 83

Other books by the author:
The Thing in Kats' Attic, 1984
Mustard, 1982
Grey Cloud, 1979

Other books you might like:
Sheila Burnford, *The Incredible Journey*, 1961
A half-blind English bull terrier, a rambunctious yellow Labrador Retriever and a spunky Siamese cat travel 250 miles across the Canadian wilderness.
Barbara Corcoran, *Annie's Monster*, 1990
Annie's monster is an Irish wolfhound named Flanagan, whose size and exuberance have frightened people in the New England town where they live.
Diana Wynne Jones, *Dogsbody*, 1988
Sirius, falsely accused in the heavens of losing the Zoi, is sentenced to earth as a pup to find the sacred object, which has fallen as a meteorite.
June Jordan, *Kimako's Story*, 1981
Kimako lives in New York City and enjoys exploring the world around her, especially when she becomes a "sitter" for a neighbor's Airedale for a week.
Wilson Rawls, *Where the Red Fern Grows*, 1961
A boy growing up in the Ozarks achieves his heart's desire in the ownership of two redbone hounds.

729

Charlotte Towner Graeber

Illustrator: Lloyd Bloom

Grey Cloud (New York: Four Winds, 1979)

Age range: Grades 4-6

Subject(s): Friendship; Animals/Birds

Major character(s): Tom, Preteen; Orville Breen, Animal Lover (pigeon keeper); Grey Cloud, Pigeon

Time period(s): 1970s

Locale(s): United States

What the book is about: Tom is unhappy in the new rural environment dictated by his father's poor health and the need for a quiet lifestyle. His life begins to take on meaning when he meets Orville, who raises racing pigeons. Conflicts with self and classmates make for lots of action in this otherwise quietly told tale.

Where it's reviewed:
Kirkus Reviews, February 15, 1980, page 216
School Library Journal, January 1980, page 70

Other books by the author:
Fudge, 1987
The Thing in Kat's Attic, 1984
Mustard, 1982

Other books you might like:
Betsy Byars, *The House of Wings*, 1972
Sammy learns to respect and love his grandfather as they care for an injured crane together.
Jean Craighead George, *The Cry of the Crow*, 1980
Mandy finds a helpless baby crow in the woods and tames it.
Dan Gopal Mukerji, *Gay-Neck: The Story of a Pigeon*, 1968
The story of a boy from India and his brave carrier pigeon during WWI.
Tunie Munson, *A Fistful of Sun*, 1974
Newly moved to the country, a lonely girl finds solace in a barn loft where an equally lonely boy raises pigeons.
Walter Wangerin, *Potter, Come Fly to the First of the Earth*, 1985
Potter cannot accept the death of his friend until an oriole appears at his window and takes him on a journey of understanding.

730

Charlotte Towner Graeber

Illustrator: Emily Arnold McCully

The Thing in Kat's Attic (New York: Dutton, 1984)

Age range: Grades 3-5

Subject(s): Mothers and Daughters; Self-Reliance; Single Parent Families

Major character(s): Kit, Child; Holly, Child; Putter, Dog

Time period(s): 1980s

Locale(s): New Albany, New York

What the book is about: Kat worries about the noise in the attic, but Mom is determined to get to the bottom of the problem. Mom sets mousetraps in the attic, but they don't work, except to snap Putter, the family dog, in the nose. She rejects electronic traps as too expensive and does not want poison in her house. Finally, determined to solve the problem in spite of there no longer being a "man in the house" she finds a piece of loose siding which had let animals into the attic, and they were NOT mice.

Where it's reviewed:
Booklist, January 1, 1985, page 641
Children's Book Review Service, February 1985, page 71
Center for Children's Books Bulletin, March 1985, page 126

Other books by the author:
Fudge, 1987
The Somebody Kid, 1985
Mustard, 1982
Grey Cloud, 1979

Other books you might like:
Corinne Gerson, *Son for a Day*, 1980
  With his mother on the West Coast and his aunt working nights and weekends, Danny becomes a helper for single parent families.
Corrine Gerson, *How I Put My Mother Through College*, 1981
  When Jess's newly divorced mother decides to go back to college, Jess, in a reversal of roles, listens to her ideas and advises her on her problems.
Norma Klein, *Mom, the Wolf Man and Me*, 1972
  An eleven year old girl describes her life and relationship with her mother who has never married.
Elisabet McHugh, *Raising a Mother Isn't Easy*, 1983
  An eleven year old Korean orphan adopted by a single woman decides that her mother should have a husband.
Doris Orgel, *My War with Mrs. Galloway*, 1985
  Rebecca, whose divorced mother is a doctor, has an on-going war with her babysitter, Mrs. Galloway, until one day the two reach an unexpected truce.

731

Ada Graham

Jacob and Owl (New York: Coward, McCann and Geoghegan)

Age range: Grades 3-4

Subject(s): Divorce; Friendship; Single Parent Families

Major character(s): Jacob, Preteen

Time period(s): 1980s

Locale(s): United States

What the book is about: Eleven year old Jacob is solitary and does not make friends easily. A move to a small town after a divorce does not make things easier. He finds a wounded owl in the woods and cares for it, then is devastated when it must be returned to the wild. Jacob gradually makes friends working at a wildlife sanctuary.

Where it's reviewed:
Horn Book, April 1982, page 163
School Library Journal, March 1982, page 147

Other books by the author:
Coyote Song, 1979
Falcon Flight, 1979
Whale Watch, 1979
Wildlife Rescue, 1970

Other books you might like:
Karen Ackerman, *The Leaves in October*, 1991
  Livvy tries to understand after her mother leaves and her father loses his job and takes the family to live in a homeless shelter.
Tom Birdseye, *Tucker*, 1990
  Tucker likes living alone with his divorced father, until his sister moves in with them and claims that their mother wants them all together again.
Mary Calhoun, *Julie's Tree*, 1988
  After the death of her mother, Julie joins her father in a new town and tries to save a tree threatened by a new parking lot.
Maxine B. Rosenberg, *Living with a Single Parent*, 1992
  Seventeen children describe life in a single parent home. (Non-fiction)
Mary Tannen, *Huntley Nutley and the Missing Link*, 1983
  Huntley finds an australopithecene in a ravine during the winter and brings him home. His confused father, an eminent scientist, thinks it's a maid.

732

Kenneth Grahame

The Reluctant Dragon (New York: Holiday House, 1938)

Age range: Grades 3-5

Subject(s): Animals/Sheep; Middle Ages

Major character(s): St. George, Knight

Time period(s): Indeterminate Past

Locale(s): England

What the book is about: Everyone knows that when a dragon shows up, a knight must be sent to kill it. How to arrange a combat without anyone getting mortally hurt is the challenge.

Where it's reviewed:
New York Times Book Review, November 13, 1983, page 41
School Library Journal, November 1983, page 77

Other books by the author:
The Wind in the Willows, 1908

Other books you might like:
Byrd Baylor, *Coyote Cry*, 1972
  When a coyote steals one of his collie's pups to raise, a shepherd boy learns that wild creatures must follow their own instincts.
Arcadio Lobato, *Just One Wish*, 1989
  A magic crystal ball that can grant wishes destroys the peace of a small village, and only the shepherd boy who originally found it can save the day.
Mercer Mayer, *Whinnie the Lovesick Dragon*, 1986
  Whinnie the dragon falls in love with Alfred the knight, but she has trouble convincing him to accept her as a suitable romantic companion.
Zilpha Keatley Snyder, *The Changing Maze*, 1985
  A shepherd boy braves the evil magic of a wizard's maze to save his pet lamb.
Piero Ventura, *The Painter's Trick*, 1977
  A hungry traveling painter tricks five monks who envision themselves as St. George slaying the dragon.

733

Kenneth Grahame

Illustrator: Ernest H. Shepard

The Wind in the Willows (New York: Scribners, 1908)

Age range: Grades 4-8

Subject(s): Adventure and Adventurers; Fantasy

Major character(s): Toad, Toad; Rat, Rat; Mole, Mole

Time period(s): Indeterminate

Locale(s): England

What the book is about: Toad, Rat, Mole and Badger have adventures along the river bank, take to the open road and their cart gets overturned by a passing motorcar. They eventually return to reclaim Toad Hall from weasels, ferrets and stoats who have taken over during their absence. The classic story is always wonderful for reading aloud. There are many edition to choose from.

Where it's reviewed:
Center for Children's Books Bulletin, July/August 1983, page 209
School Library Journal, September 1983, page 122

Other books by the author:
The Reluctant Dragon, 1938

Other books you might like:
Peter Hunter Blair, *The Coming of Pout*, 1969
    A brother and sister meet a mysterious creature who asks them to join his search for a way to break the spell cast upon him.
C.S. Lewis, *Boxen: The Imaginary World of the Young C.S. Lewis*, 1985
    Maps, histories, sketches and stories created by C.S. Lewis as a child to describe his private fantasy world known as Animal-Land or Boxen.
Tom McGowen, *Odyssey From River Bend*, 1975
    Some of the animals of River Bend risk the dangers of a journey to the Haunted Land in search of the secret to the magic of the Long Ago Ones.
Brian Jacques, *Mossflower*, 1988
    Martin the warrior mouse and Gonff the mousethief set out to find the missing ruler of Mossflower.
J.R.R. Tolkien, *The Hobbit, or There and Back Again*, 1966
    Bilbo Baggins finds himself involved with wizard, dwarfs and dragons in a mad journey to wrest from Smagu the dragon his hoard of forgotten gold.

734

Robert Graves

Illustrator: Maurice Sendak

The Big Green Book (New York: Crowell-Collier, 1962)

Age range: Grades 2-3

Subject(s): Aunts and Uncles; Magic

Major character(s): Jack, Child

Time period(s): Indeterminate ("Long Ago")

Locale(s): United States

What the book is about: A little boy finds a big green book in the attic and learns many handy magic spells that he uses with surprising results. First, he turns himself into an old man, then makes himself disappear. Then he turns his grouchy old aunt and uncle into happy, likeable people. He gambles with them using magic and wins $100,000. Jack is the child triumphing against kindly but restrictive adults. In the end, he uses his magic to study efficiently and stays at the top of his class.

Where it's reviewed:
Junior Bookshelf, October 1979, page 272
New Statesman, May 19, 1978, page 682
Observer (London), July 23, 1978, page 21

Other books by the author:
An Ancient Castle, 1981

Other books you might like:
Polly Berrien Berends, *Ozma and the Wayward Wand*, 1985
    While Dorothy is visiting Oz, the royal gardener's son takes Queen Ozma's wand without asking and endangers Emerald City with uncontrollable spells.
Sarah Hayes, *The Crumbling Castle*, 1992
    Hoping to enjoy a quiet life working spells in his new castle, Zeb the wizard finds his peace broken by Jason the crow and other zany occupants.
Jack Kent, *The Wizard of Wallaby Wallow*, 1971
    A mouse helps a wizard discover what's lacking in his magic spells.
Ross Martin Madsen, *Perrywinkle and the Book of Magic Spells*, 1986
    A seven year old boy, with the help of his talking crow, learns to be a wizard like his father.
Joan Lowery Nixon, *Magnolia's Mixed-Up Magic*, 1983
    Magnolia Possum and her grandmother experiment with spells from an old magic book unaware that the instructions on how to undo them are missing.

735

Elizabeth Gray

Illustrator: Robert Lawson

Adam of the Road (New York: Viking, 1942)

Age range: Grades 5-6

Subject(s): Musicians; Animals/Dogs

Major character(s): Adam, Child; Nick, Dog; Roger, Minstrel

Time period(s): 13th century (1294)

Locale(s): England

What the book is about: A traveling minstrel, his son, and their dog, travel in England in 1294. The dog is stolen and Adam becomes separated from his father. Adam searches for his father and his dog for many months before they are reunited.

Where it's reviewed:
Booklist, May 1, 1942, page 334

Awards the book has won:
Newbery Medal 1943
Spring Book Festival (Middle Honor) 1942

Other books you might like:
E.L. Kongisburg, *A Proud Taste for Scarlet and Miniver*, 1973

As they wait for Henry II to be admitted to Heaven, members of the court tell the story of Eleanor of Aquitaine.

Alison Uttley, *Traveller in Time*, 1939
　　Penelope goes back in time and is involved in a plot to free Mary, Queen of Scots.

Elizabeth Marie Pope, *Perilous Gard*, 1974
　　Sent to a mysterious castle as punishment, Kate is in involved in a weird series of events.

Rosemary Sutcliff, *Flame-Colored Taffeta*, 1986
　　12-yr-old Damaris rescues a wounded man and becomes involved with spying and smuggling.

Marguerite DeAngeli, *The Door in the Wall*, 1949
　　10 year old Robin is struck lame and is taken to St. Mark's hospice to escape the plague in London.

736

Genevieve Gray

Illustrator: Greta Matus

Ghost Story (New York: Lothrop, 1975)

Age range: Grades 3-5

Subject(s): Ghosts

Major character(s): Papa, Spirit (ghost); Mama, Spirit (ghost)

Time period(s): 1970s

Locale(s): United States

What the book is about: The ghost family in a derelict mansion is annoyed when their home is invaded by junkies. Then they are invaded by graduate students studying ESP. The junkies think it's a stakeout and take off, but the graduate students can't be scared away.

Where it's reviewed:
Kirkus Reviews, February 1, 1975, page 1224
School Library Journal, April 1975, page 52

Other books by the author:
Varnell Roberts, Super Pigeon, 1975
Send Wendell, 1974
Sore Loser, 1974

Other books you might like:
Sid Fleischman, *The Ghost on Saturday Night*, 1974
　　When Opie earns two tickets to a ghost-raising show, he has no idea they are front row seats at a bank robbery.

Sam McBratney, *The Ghosts of Hungryhouse Lane*, 1988
　　This funny story tells of three ghosts who are evicted from their usual resting place when the unruly Sweet family arrives on the scene.

Jim O'Connor, *Ghost in Tent 19*, 1988
　　Danny and his friends from tent 19 put together clues from dreams and treasure maps to piece together a mystery at camp.

Stephen Roos, *My Favorite Ghost*, 1988
　　Derek comes up with a plan to make money by convincing kids there is a ghost in the Coffin mansion.

Betty Ren Wright, *Christina's Ghost*, 1985
　　Ghosts lead ten year old Christina to investigate a thirty year old murder in the spooky Victorian house she is sharing with grouchy Uncle Ralph.

737

Genevieve Gray

Illustrator: Ann Grifalconi

How Far, Felipe? (New York: Harper and Row, 1978)

Age range: Grades 1-3

Subject(s): Mexican Americans; Animals/Donkeys

Major character(s): Felipe, Child; Filomena, Donkey

Time period(s): 1770s (1775)

Locale(s): California

What the book is about: Uncle Carlos and Aunt Maria join Colonel Anza's caravan of families leaving Mexico to farm rich lands in California. Their six children, nephew Felipe, and Felipe's donkey, Filomena, join the caravan, and though they worry about the donkey, Filomena survives to be a great help on the farm.

Where it's reviewed:
Catholic Library World, February 1979, page 312
Language Arts, January 1979, page 49

Other books by the author:
Ghost Story, 1975
Send Wendell, 1974
Casey's Camper, 1973
A Kite for Bennie, 1972

Other books you might like:
Andrew Davies, *Marmalade and Rufus*, 1983
　　The adventures of a spirited little girl and her talking donkey.

Wende Devlin, *Cranberry Summer*, 1992
　　Maggie and Mr. Whiskers are able to provide a home for a lost donkey.

Albert Lamorisse, *Bim, the Little Donkey*, 1973
　　The Caliph's spoiled and friendless son readjusts his values when he becomes involved with a poor boy and his donkey.

Michael Morpurgo, *Jo-Jo the Melon Donkey*, 1987
　　A mistreated donkey in Renaissance Venice gains selfrespect after becoming a hero during a devastating flood.

Joanne Oppenheim, *The Donkey's Tale*, 1991
　　A rhymed retelling of the fable about the poor man and his son who try to take the advice of everyone they meet while traveling with their donkey.

738

Nigel Gray

Illustrator: Ted Lewin

The Deserter (New York: Harper, 1977)

Age range: Grades 4-6

Subject(s): Friendship

Major character(s): Andy, Preteen; Christine "Chris", Preteen; Dave, Military Personnel

Time period(s): Indeterminate Past

Locale(s): England

What the book is about: Four English children find an army deserter hiding in an abandoned house and help him escape the police. There is something different about Dave.

You can talk to him about hard things, like being scared and lonely.

Where it's reviewed:
Booklist, January 1, 1978, page 747
Kirkus Reviews, October 1, 1977, page 1049
School Library Journal, October 1977, page 111

Other books you might like:
Patricia Beatty, *Charley Skedaddle*, 1987
   In the Civil War, a twelve year old Boy from New York City joins the Union Army, deserts during a battle in Virginia, and meets a hostile old woman.
Linda Crew, *Children of the River*, 1989
   Having fled Cambodia to escape the Khmer Rouge, Sundara is torn between faithfulness to her people and being a "regular" girl in an Oregon high school
Mary Downing Hahn, *Stepping on the Cracks*, 1991
   In 1944, while her brother is fighting overseas, Marga helps the school bully, Gordy, when she finds him hiding his own brother, an army deserter.
Lois Lamplugh, *Falcon's Tor*, 1984
   Reading about WWI, Aidan becomes obsessed with life in those horrible days. Knocked out in a mysterious accident, he wakes in a strange place and time
Theodore Taylor, *The Children's War*, 1971
   When the Japanese invade the isolated Alaskan home of a twelve year old boy and take all the men prisoner, he helps an Army spy get information.

739

Patsey Gray

Barefoot a Thousand Miles (New York: Walker, 1984)

Age range: Grades 6-8

Subject(s): Animals/Dogs; Indians of North America

Major character(s): Jim, Teenager; Quick, Dog

Time period(s): 1980s

Locale(s): Arizona; California

What the book is about: Jim, a young Apache boy, sets out to retrieve his pet dog, taken from the reservation. Another boy had given Jim's dog, Quick, to a tourist out of malice and Jim is determined to get his dog back. The loyalty between boy and dog is well drawn.

Where it's reviewed:
Center for Children's Books Bulletin, May 1984, page 165
School Library Journal, May 1984, page 88

Other books by the author:
J.R.R. Tolkien's The Hobbit, 1968 (drama)
The Littlest Angel: A Christmas Play in One Act, 1964 (drama)
Locoi the Bronc, 1961
Horse in Her Heart, 1960

Other books you might like:
Thomas Baird, *Finding Fever*, 1982
   Two very dissimiliar teenage boys become unwilling allies in a hunt for the operators of a statewide dognapping ring.
Rex Benedict, *Good Luck Arizona Man*, 1972
   A half-white Apache boy sets out to solve the mystery of his own heritage and the hiding place of a gold treasure.
E.J. Bird, *The Rainmakers*, 1993

An Anasazi boy shares his adventures with his pet bear and best friend the summer he is eleven.
Isabelle Holland, *The Unfrightened Dark*, 1990
   When her beloved seeing-eye dog is kidnapped, Joycelyn, orphaned and blind since the age of twelve, determines to solve the mystery.
Don Schellie, *Me, Cholay and Co.: Apache Warriors*, 1973
   With the help of a Apache who becomes his best friend, a boy leads a small band of Apache children across fifty miles of Arizona desert.

740

Margaret Greaves

Cat's Magic (New York: Harper, 1981)

Age range: Grades 5-8

Subject(s): Animals/Cats; Orphans; Space and Time

Major character(s): Louise Genevieve Higgs, Orphan; Harriet, Relative (aunt); Charlie Parkinson, Neighbor

Time period(s): 1980s; 1860s

Locale(s): England

What the book is about: Louise saves a kitten from drowning and is rewarded with the ability to travel in time. During several trips to Victorian England, she meets and rescues two of her ancestors. Intriguing mix of gothic mystery and time travel.

Where it's reviewed:
Booklist, March 15, 1981, page 1028
Kirkus Reviews, May 15, 1981, page 633
School Library Jouranl, April 1981, page 127

Other books by the author:
A Net to Catch the Wind, 1979
The Great Bell of Peking, 1975
King Solomon and the Hoopoes, 1975
Stone of Terror, 1974

Other books you might like:
Lloyd Alexander, *Time Cat*, 1963
   Jason and his magic cat Gareth travel through time to visit countries all over the world during different periods of history.
Joan Davenport Carris, *Witch-Cat*, 1984
   A down-to-earth girl is made to see that she is a witch through the efforts of a magical cat.
Ruth Chew, *The Witch and the Ring*, 1989
   A sister and brother find a ring that brings a special cat, a witch, and a series of adventures into their lives.
Catherine Dexter, *The Gilded Cat*, 1992
   Maggie buys a mummified cat at a yard sale and is drawn into a frightening world of ancient Egyptian magic.
Diana Wynne Jones, *Charmed Life*, 1977
   Gwendolen and her brother find the Chrestomancie Castle family's magic powers difficult to counter with the powers of the Coven Street witches.

741

Margaret Greaves
Illustrator: Stephen Gammell

A Net to Catch the Wind (New York: Harper, 1979)

Age range: Grades 2-4

Subject(s): Unicorns; Fantasy; Princes and Princesses

Major character(s): Magus, Wizard; Mirabelle, Royalty (princess); Starlight, Mythical Creature (unicorn)

Time period(s): Indeterminate Past

Locale(s): Europe

What the book is about: A king uses his daughter to trap a unicorn. But the princess shows her father the importance of freedom and love when he tries to capture the silver colt that is dear to her.

Where it's reviewed:
Kirkus Reviews, April 15, 1979, page 451
School Library Journal, September 1979, page 110

Other books by the author:
The Naming, 1992
Tattercoats, 1990
The Rainbow Sun, 1975
Stone of Terror, 1974

Other books you might like:
Cynthia Birrer, *The Lady and the Unicorn*, 1987
    A princess wandering on her uncle's estate discovers that she is the only one with able to see a lonely unicorn and break the spell enchanting it.
Bruce Coville, *The Unicorn Treasury*, 1988
    A collection of stories, poems, and unicorn lore about this mythical creature.
Suzanne Lord, *Return of the Unicorn: A Story and Activity Book*, 1990
    The evil Duke of Malefort has put Dragon under a spell and it's up to Beldin the unicorn to save Dragon and the castle. Includes mazes and puzzles.
Marianna Mayer, *The Unicorn and the Lake*, 1990
    When a serpent poisons the lake where all the animals drink, only the unicorn has the power to save them.
Otfried Preussler, *The Tale of the Unicorn*, 1989
    Three brothers set out to hunt for the unicorn whose horn is made of ivory and whose hooves are pure gold.

742

Phyllis Green

Illustrator: Joel Schick

Bagdad Ate It (New York: Watts, 1980)

Age range: Grades 1-2

Subject(s): Animals/Dogs

Major character(s): Bagdad

Time period(s): 1980s

Locale(s): United States

What the book is about: A dieting puppy gets into trouble eating things he shouldn't.

Where it's reviewed:
Booklist, January 15, 1981, page 705
School Library Journal, December 1980, page 68

Awards the book has won:
California Young Reader Medal (Primary) 1984

Other books by the author:
Chucky Bellman Was So Bad, 1991
Eating Ice Cream with a Werewolf, 1983
It's Me, Christy, 1977
Ice River, 1975

Other books you might like:
Betsy Duffey, *Puppy Love*, 1992
    Evie and Megan start the Pet Patrol to solve animal problems and they soon have their hands full taking care of an army of homeless puppies.
Alison Cragin Herzig, *The Big Deal*, 1992
    Sam's parents agree to let him have a puppy if he will take care of it, but as the puppy grows into a large dog, Sam isn't sure he keep his promise.
Brian Mangas, *Follow That Puppy!*, 1991
    Grandpa gets more than he bargained for when he tries to take a frisky puppy for a walk.
Jan M. Robinson, *The December Dog*, 1969
    After running away from a cruel master, a dog finds she must seek the company of humans again when her puppy is hurt.
Barbara Williams, *Gary and the Very Terrible Monster*, 1973
    The trouble-causing monster that only Gary can see disappears when he gets a real puppy.

743

Phyllis Green

Illustrator: Patti Stren

Eating Ice Cream with a Werewolf (New York: Harper and Row, 1983)

Age range: Grades 3-6

Subject(s): Babysitters; Magic; Witches and Witchcraft

Major character(s): Brad Gowan, Preteen; Nancy Gowan, Child; Phoebe Hadley, Babysitter

Time period(s): 1980s

Locale(s): United States

What the book is about: Phoebe Hadley has a new found interest in witchcraft, so when she arrives to babysit for Brad and his sister while their parents vacation in Bermuda, strange things are bound to happen. Each time Phoebe casts a spell it "sort of" comes true, just close enough to keep everyone guessing. Not a heavy plot, but lots of fun, action and humor.

Where it's reviewed:
Horn Book, June 1983, page 302
School Library Journal, August 1983, page 65

Other books by the author:
Mildred Murphy, How Does Your Garden Grow?, 1977
Wild Violets, 1977
Ice River, 1975
Nantucket Summer, 1974

Other books you might like:
Brenda Guiberson, *Instant Soup*, 1991
    Darlene's plans to spend her winter break at the mall are scrapped when Mom gives Darlene the job of babysitting her four year old cousin.
Mavis Jukes, *Wild Iris Bloom*, 1992
    Twelve year old Iris is angry at being left with a babysitter and gives her the slip, but learns a dangerous and disturbing lesson in the process.

Colleen O'Shaughnessy McKenna, *Mother Murphy*, 1992
    When Mrs. Murphy has to get off her feet because she's expecting a baby, Collette takes over with surprising results.
Doris Orgel, *My War with Mrs. Galloway*, 1985
    Rebecca has an ongoing war with her babysitter until one day the two reach an unexpected truce.
Stephanie S. Tolan, *The Witch of Maple Park*, 1992
    Casey's friend MacKenzie is convinced that the old woman they see around town is a witch and they must do something about her.

| 744 |

Phyllis Green

Illustrator: John Wallner

Gloomy Louis (Chicago: Whitman, 1980)

Age range: Grades 3-4

Subject(s): Sports/Baseball; Moving, Household; Self-Respect

Major character(s): Louie Bix, Child

Time period(s): 1980s

Locale(s): Detroit, Michigan

What the book is about: Louis is glum about his family's move from Detroit to Phoenix, and it affects everything, including his performance on the baseball field. When he hears his parents talking about someone who has a "loser" attitude, he thinks they are talking about him, but they are not. A heroic rescue gives Louie a new confidence in himself and helps him form a more positive attitude.

Where it's reviewed:
Children's Book Review Service, January 1981, page 34
School Library Journal, March 1981, page 144

Other books by the author:
Eating Ice Cream with a Werewolf, 1983
Mildred Murphy, How Does Your Garden Grow?, 1977
Wild Violets, 1977
Ice River, 1975

Other books you might like:
Matt Christopher, *Return of the Home Run Kid*, 1992
    Sylvester Coddmyer III is having a dismal baseball season until he takes advice from an ex-ballplayer named Cheeko.
Dan Elish, *Jason and the Baseball Bear*, 1990
    Jason is the only one who can talk with animals, thereby improving his teams' chances of winning the championship with the help of Whitney.
Mary Haynes, *The Great Pretenders*, 1990
    In her new town, Molly starts off by insulting the mayor's daughter, but with her baseball prowess and two friends, she hopes to redeem herself soon.
P.J. Petersen, *The Fireplug Is First Base*, 1990
    A small baseball player surprises his bigger teammates when he finally gets his chance at bat.
Alfred Slote, *The Trading Game*, 1990
    Andy discovers a lot about his father, his grandfather who played professional baseball, and himself.

| 745 |

Jan Greenberg

The Iceberg and Its Shadow (New York: Farrar, Straus and Giroux, 1980)

Age range: Grades 5-6

Subject(s): Friendship; Peer Pressure

Major character(s): Anabeth, Preteen, 6th Grader; Rachel, Preteen, 6th Grader; Mindy, Preteen, 6th Grader

Time period(s): 1980s

Locale(s): United States

What the book is about: The friendship between sixth graders Anabeth and Rachel has been firm since kindergarten, but is upset by the arrival of Mindy who quickly becomes a class leader. In this fast paced, humorous story, Anabeth learns what it is like to be ostracized, and how valuable true friendship is.

Where it's reviewed:
Center for Children's Books Bulletin, April 1981, p 151
School Library Journal, January 1981, page 60

Other books by the author:
Just the Two of Us, 1988
No Dragons to Slay, 1983
Pig-Out Blues, 1982
A Season In-Between, 1979

Other books you might like:
Sheila Greenwald, *Here's Hermione*, 1991
    Rosy becomes the manager of her best friend's unusual rock band.
Nancy Hayashi, *The Fantastic Stay-Home-From-School Day*, 1992
    Best friends Leona and Eddie plan a fantastic day at home that backfires.
Gordon Korman, *Macdonald Hall Goes Hollywood*, 1991
    Bruno and Boots become friends with the star of a film crew shooting on location at Macdonald Hall.
Susan Beth Pfeffer, *Darcy Downstairs*, 1990
    Darcy's cousin April moves into the upstairs apartment and they become inseparable.
Doris Buchanan Smith, *The Pennywhistle Tree*, 1991
    A rift develops between Jonathan and his best friends when a new boy moves into the neighborhood.

| 746 |

Bette Greene

Illustrator: Charles Lilly

Philip Hall Likes Me, I Reckon Maybe (New York: Dial, 1974)

Age range: Grades 5-6

Subject(s): Friendship; African Americans

Major character(s): Beth Lambert, Preteen; Philip Hall, Preteen

Time period(s): 1970s

Locale(s): Arkansas

What the book is about: Philip is the cutest, smartest boy in Beth's class. She starts to wonder if he outdoes her in everything because she lets him. This story is filled with funny, lively adventures with a fresh look at friendship.

Where it's reviewed:
Kirkus Reviews, October 15, 1974, page 1102
Publisher's Weekly, August 12, 1974, page 74

Awards the book has won:
Newbery Honor

Other books by the author:
The Drowning of Stephan Jones, 1991 (for Young Adults)
Get On Out of Here, Philip Hall, 1981
Summer of My German Soldier, 1973

Other books you might like:
William Armstrong, *Sounder*, 1969
   The share cropper steals a ham and some sausage to feed his hungry family. A tale of the courage of a boy, his father, and their dog.
Robbie Branscum, *The Adventures of Johnny May*, 1984
   Johnny May shoots a deer to bring to her hungry grandparents for Christmas, and confronts a much admired friend when she sees him shoot another man.
Barbara Campbell, *A Girl Called Bob and a Horse Called Yoki*, 1982
   When Bob discovers that Yoki the milk cart horse is going to the glue factory, he gets involved in a caper where he can't tell right from wrong.
Emily Crofford, *A Matter of Pride*, 1981
   Meg's father is a tenant farmer on an Arkansas cotton plantation, her mother has to face many fears.
Joyce Carol Thomas, *The Golden Pasture*, 1986
   The portrayal of the life style of Black horse ranchers in Oklahoma adds special insight as the reader sees Carol work with the stallion, Cloudy.

747

Carol Greene

Illustrator: Gene Sharp

Hi, Clouds (Chicago: Childrens, 1983)

Age range: Grades 1-2

Series: Rookie Reader

Subject(s): Weather

Time period(s): Indeterminate

Locale(s): United States

What the book is about: A beginning reader in which two unnamed children see many objects in the clouds, as they watch them become fat and thin, white and gray, then turn into dogs, sheep, dragons and castles.

Where it's reviewed:
Booklist, August 1983, page 1470
Shool Library Journal, November 1983, page 63

Other books by the author:
The Golden Locket, 1992
Ice Is.Whee!, 1983
Shine, Sun, 1983
Hinny Winny Bunco, 1982

Other books you might like:
Joni Mitchell, *Both Sides Now*, 1992

An illustrated version of her song, in which clouds, love, and life itself appear differently from various persepctives.
Nicholas van Pallandt, *The Butterfly Night of Old Brown Bear*, 1991
   Determined to capture a beautiful moth for his collection, Old Brown Bear finds himself following the elusive creature into the clouds.
Dalia Hardof Renberg, *Hello, Clouds*, 1985
   A child imagines familiar shapes and exciting adventures in the clouds passing overhead.
Peter Spier, *Dreams*, 1986
   Two children watch cloud formations and interpret them for themselves.
Jasper Tomkins, *Nimby*, 1982
   A playful cloud finally meets a friend with whom he can be himself.

748

Constance C. Greene

Illustrator: Donna Diamond

Beat the Turtle Drum (New York: Viking, 1976)

Age range: Grades 4-6

Subject(s): Brothers and Sisters; Death; Animals/Horses

Major character(s): Kate, Preteen; Joss, Child

Time period(s): 1970s

Locale(s): United States

What the book is about: This is Kate's story about Joss, her younger sister. Everyone loves Joss, she is loving and a great friend. Her dream for a pony comes true on her eleventh birthday. Kate and Joss climb a tree for a picnic and Joss falls and breaks her neck. Kate lives through the tremendous loss and grief.

Where it's reviewed:
Horn Book, December 1976, page 6241
Kirkus Reviews, August 1, 1976, page 845

Other books by the author:
Dotty's Suitcase, 1980
I and Sproggy, 1978
I Know You, Al, 1975
The Ears of Louis, 1974

Other books you might like:
Vera Cleaver, *Grover*, 1970
   After his mother's suicide and his father's resultant breakdown, Grover must face the hard realities of death and trouble.
Scott Corbett, *Grave Doubts*, 1982
   Les and Wally look for clues to the sudden death of an eccentric millionaire in the last crossword puzzle the old man worked on.
Virginia Lee, *The Magic Moth*, 1972
   A family's adjustment to the death of Maryanne, one of five children, seen through the eyes of her brother.
Jean Little, *Home From Far*, 1965
   After Jenny's twin brother is killed in a car accident, her mother brings two foster children into their home, one a boy her own age.
Wylly Folk St. John, *The Ghost Next Door*, 1971

A family accepts the reality of a beloved member's death in this unusual story.

| 749 |

Constance C. Greene

Illustrator: Nola Langner

The Ears of Louis (New York: Viking, 1974)

Age range: Grades 3-5

Subject(s): Teasing; Prejudice

Major character(s): Louis, Child; Matthew, Child; Mrs. Beeble, Neighbor

Time period(s): 1970s

Locale(s): United States

What the book is about: Louis is a small boy with big ears, and he wants to play football. The boys at school tease him and call him "Sugar Bowl" until they find out he is a buddy of the older football players. He plays poker with his next door neighbor, Mrs. Beeble. His friend Matthey actually likes his ears.

Where it's reviewed:
Kirkus Reviews, November 1, 1974, page 1151
Publisher's Weekly, November 11, 1974, page 49

Other books by the author:
Isabelle and Little Orphan Frannie, 1988
Isabelle Shows Her Stuff, 1984
Getting Nowhere, 1977
Isabelle the Itch, 1973

Other books you might like:
Nan Hayden Agle, *Maple Street*, 1970
    Margaret's best friend moved away from Maple Street because she said the neighborhood was going downhill, but Margaret thought differently.
Robert Burch, *D.J.'s Worst Enemy*, 1965
    When the mischievous teasing and fibbing that make D.J. his own worst enemy bring serious injury to his brother and sister, D.J. must make a choice.
Molly Cone, *Number Four*, 1972
    A young Indian tries to understand the meaning of his heritage and his place in the world as he faces the prejudices of the white townspeople.
LouAnn Gaeddert, *The Kid with the Red Suspenders*, 1983
    When some of his schoolmates tease him unmercifully about being "Mommy's Little Lamb," Hamilton sets out to prove he can be tough.
Isabelle Holland, *Green Andrew Green*, 1984
    When Andrew Green actually turns green and suffers teasing and ostracization, he learns that power does not breed popularity: one must give love.

| 750 |

Constance C. Greene

Illustrator: Byron Barton

A Girl Called Al (New York: Viking, 1969)

Age range: Grades 5-7

Subject(s): City Life; Friendship

Major character(s): Alexandra "Al", Teenager; Mr. Richards, Worker (apartment superintendent)

Time period(s): 1960s

Locale(s): New York

What the book is about: A seventh grade girl, her slightly overweight girlfriend Al, and the assistant superintendent of their apartment building form a mutually needed friendship with the usual, and a few unusual, joys and sorrows.

Where it's reviewed:
Booklist, July 15, 1969, page 1274
Hornbook, August 1969, page 411
Kirkus Reviews, April 15, 1969, page 441

Other books by the author:
Isabelle and Little Orphan Frannie, 1988
Just Plain Al, 1986
Al(exandra) the Great, 1982
Double Dare O'Toole, 1981

Other books you might like:
L.E. Blair, *The Ghost of Eagle Mountain*, 1990
    A ski trip becomes a journey into Allison's Native American heritage when she and her friends begin to live the legend of Eagle Mountain.
Mark Geller, *The Strange Case of the Reluctant Partners*, 1990
    Thomas is dismayed by a seventh grade English assignment requiring him and the intelligent and unusual Elaine to write biographies of each other.
Elizabeth B. Keeton, *Second-Best Friend*, 1985
    Having lost all her clothes in a cyclone, Vanessa borrows a dress from a friendless girl to wear to a dance, not knowing the borrowed is stolen.
Kathilyn Solomon Proboz, *The Girls Strike Back: The Making of the Pink Parrots*, 1990
    A group of girls, led by Amy Breeze Hawk, form their own all-girl baseball team in protest of the discriminatory practices of the local baseball team.
Todd Strasser, *The Complete Computer Popularity Program*, 1984
    Since his father works for the unpopular nuclear plant and his only friend Paul is a social recluse, Tony worries that he'll never have a social life.

| 751 |

Constance C. Greene

Illustrator: Emily Arnold McCully

I and Sproggy (New York: Viking, 1978)

Age range: Grades 4-6

Subject(s): Brothers and Sisters; Stepfamilies

Major character(s): Adam, Preteen; Sproggy, Preteen

Time period(s): 1970s

Locale(s): New York, New York

What the book is about: Eleven year old Adam is not delighted when his English stepsister, Sproggy, comes to visit. He discusses the situation with the philosophic handyman in their apartment house who gives him some good advice. Many things work to change his mind and he eventually comes to like her and takes advantage of an unexpected invitation to take Sproggy to a party at Gracie Mansion, the Mayor's house.

Where it's reviewed:
Booklist, September 1, 1987, page 48
Hornbook, October 1978, page 516
Kirkus Reviews, September 1, 1978, page 950

Other books by the author:
Al's Blind Date, 1989
Isabelle and Little Orphan Frannie, 1988
Isabelle Shows Her Stuff, 1984
Beat the Turtle Drum, 1976

Other books you might like:
Mary Jane Auch, *Out of Step*, 1992
  After his father remarries, Jeremy feels that there is no place for him in a family which includes a stepsister his age who is a superb athlete.
Eileen Dunlop, *The Maze Stone*, 1982
  Fanny and her stepsister are drawn into strange events around their Scottish home which seem related to the disappearance of a young man in 1914.
Elizabeth Hathorn, *Thunderwith*, 1991
  Moving to the Australian outback after her mother's death, Laura befriends a strange and beautiful dog who helps her adjust to her new life.
Ellen Leroe, *The Peanut Butter Poltergeist*, 1987
  Eleven year old M.J. seeks revenge on her stepsister by faking a poltergeist in their summer cottage, only to face a seemingly real poltergeist.
Barbara Park, *My Mother Got Married and Other Disasters*, 1989
  Charles experiences many difficulties in adjusting to a new stepfather, stepsister and stepbrother.

752

Constance C. Greene

Illustrator: Emily Arnold McCully

Isabelle the Itch (New York: Dell, 1973)

Age range: Grades 4-6

Subject(s): Friendship; Newspapers; Sex Roles

Major character(s): Isabelle "Izzy", Newspaper Carrier; Herbie, Classmate; Mary Eliza, Friend

Time period(s): 1970s

Locale(s): United States

What the book is about: Isabelle longs to have her brother's paper route. Finally, for one week, she gets her chance. That's when she meets Mrs. Stern. With the help of Mrs. Stern and the new girl in her class, Isabelle learns she can move mountains if she can only channel her energy.

Where it's reviewed:
Booklist, July 15, 1979, page 1634
Center for Children's Books Bulletin, February 1974, page 95
Kirkus Reviews, October 1, 1973, page 1095

Other books by the author:
Just Plain Al, 1986
Isabelle Shows Her Stuff, 1984
Double Dare O'Toole, 1981
I and Sproggy, 1978

Other books you might like:
Beverly Cleary, *Henry and the Paper Route*, 1957

One of Cleary's favorite heroes, Henry Huggins, provides laughs for readers as he copes with everyday home and school, and takes on a paper route.
Helen Cresswell, *Absolute Zero*, 1978
  The members of the talented and eccentric Bagthorpe family channel their energy into slogan writing.
Beverly Keller, *The Sea Watch: A Mystery*, 1981
  While aboard a luxury line bound for Europe, a young boy who is plagued by allergies stumbles onto a mystery involving a wristwatch.
Betty Miles, *The Real Me*, 1974
  A girl tells about her efforts to end sex discrimination in choosing classes at school and her fight to have a paper route.
Mary Francis Shura, *The Riddle of Raven's Gulch*, 1975
  Bart decides to investigate the reason why the ravine along his paper route is considered haunted.

753

Constance C. Greene

Your Old Pal, Al (New York: Viking, 1979)

Age range: Grades 5-8

Subject(s): Jealousy; Remarriage

Major character(s): Alexandra "Al", Preteen

Time period(s): 1970s

Locale(s): United States

What the book is about: Al has decided that it's time for something "memorable" to happen to her. Her father is newly married and she meets an interesting boy, Brian, at the wedding. She has to struggle with her new family, as well as the jealousy of her best friend.

Where it's reviewed:
Kirkus Reviews, October 1, 1979, page 1145
Publisher's Weekly, October 29, 1979, page 82
School Library Journal, October 1979, page 150

Other books by the author:
Isabelle Shows Her Stuff, 1984
Al(exandra) the Great, 1982
I Know You, Al, 1975
A Girl Called Al, 1969

Other books you might like:
Linda Cline, *Weakfoot*, 1975
  A boy living near the Okefenokee Swamp in the early 20th century befriends a fugitive, slays a panther, and becomes involved in his first romance.
Caroline B. Cooney, *The Girl Who Invented Romance*, 1988
  While waiting for her first big romance and observing the rocky love affairs of her parents and brother, Kelly develops a board game called Romance.
Phyllis Reynolds Naylor, *Alice in Rapture, Sort Of*, 1989
  Alison discovers love is about the most mixed-up thing that can happen to you when she has her first boyfriend the summer before seventh grade.
Peter D. Sieruta, *Heartbeats and Other Stories*, 1989
  Includes nine short stories covering such themes as sibling rivalry, friendship, a room of one's own, madness, first love and lost love.
Alfred Slote, *Love and Tennis*, 1979

A tennis player's experiences in the world of competive sports help him come to terms with his parents' divorce, his first romance and his ambition.

754

Eloise Greenfield

Illustrator: George Ford

Alesia (New York: Philomel, 1981)

Age range: Grades 5 and Up

Subject(s): Physically Handicapped

Major character(s): Alesia Revis, Teenager, Handicapped; Lisa Hall, Teenager

Time period(s): 1980s

Locale(s): United States

What the book is about: Alesia was disabled in an auto accident when she was nine years old. This story is her diary and tells how she, now seventeen, deals with her multiple handicaps. An insightful and inspiring story.

Where it's reviewed:
Center for Children's Books Bulletin, January 1982, page 85
School Library Journal, March 1982, page 157

Other books by the author:
Nathaniel Talking, 1988
Grandmama's Joy, 1980
Talk about a Family, 1978
Sister, 1974

Other books you might like:
Connie Baron, *The Physically Disabled*, 1988
    Discusses various causes of disabilities. (Non-fiction)
Mary Blount Christian, *Mystery at Camp Triumph*, 1986
    Recently blinded in an accident, Angie comes to terms with her handicap as she tries to find the saboteur at the summer camp for disabled children.
Matt Christopher, *The Great Quarterback Switch*, 1984
    Michael, confined to a wheelchair after an accident, uses telepathy to communicate football plays to his quarterback twin, Tom.
Hilary H. Milton, *Emergency! 10-33 on Channel 11!*, 1977
    A distress call sent over a CB radio brings a rescue party to a camper that has overturned on a lonely road.
Jean Thesman, *When the Road Ends*, 1992
    Three foster children and a woman recovering from a serious accident are abandoned by their caretaker and must survive on their own.

755

Eloise Greenfield

Illustrator: Jan S. Gilchrist

Nathaniel Talking (New York: Black Butterfly, 1988)

Age range: Grades 3-6

Subject(s): African Americans; Poetry

Major character(s): Nathaniel B. Free, Child, Writer (poet)

Time period(s): 1980s

Locale(s): United States

What the book is about: Nathaniel is a spunky nine year old poet who raps and rhymes about his world - what he knows, the loss of his mother, making friends, school, grandma's "bones," Daddy singing the blues. Included are instructions for creating twelve-bar blues poems.

Where it's reviewed:
Kirkus Reviews, June 15, 1989, page 916
School Library Journal, August 1989, page 146

Awards the book has won:
Coretta Scott King Award 1991

Other books by the author:
Night on Neighborhood Street, 1991
Grandpa's Face, 1988
Under the Sunday Tree, 1988
Africa Dream, 1987

Other books you might like:
Nikki Giovanni, *Spin a Soft Black Song*, 1971
    Thirty-five poems record the feelings of Black children.
June Jordan, *The Voice of the Children*, 1970
    Twenty Black and Puerto Rican children write their poetic impressions of growing up in the ghettos of America.
Leslie Jones Little, *Children of Long Ago*, 1988
    Poems reflecting earlier, simpler days with grandmothers who read aloud and children who walk barefoot and pick blackberries for their dolls.
Pat McKissack, *The Dark-Thirty: Southern Tales of the Supernatural*, 1992
    A collection of ghost stories with African-American themes, designed to be told during the "dark-thirty," the half hour before sunset.
Cornelius Van Wright, *Make a Joyful Sound*, 1991
    A collection of poems for children by Afro-American poets.

756

Eloise Greenfield

Illustrator: Moneta Barnett

Sister (New York: Crowell, 1974)

Age range: Grades 4-5

Subject(s): African Americans; Death; Family Life

Major character(s): Doretha, Teenager; Alberta, Teenager

Time period(s): 1970s

Locale(s): United States

What the book is about: Thirteen year old Doretha is African-American and confused by her mixed feelings about herself. She has always idolized her older sister, Alberta. She starts to see that she really doesn't want to be like Alberta at all. After her father dies, she begins to withdraw from her sister and mother.

Where it's reviewed:
Horn Book, October 1974, page 136
Kirkus Reviews, May 15, 1974, page 535

Other books by the author:
Koya DeLaney and the Good Girl Blues, 1992
Alesia, 1981
She Come Bringing Me That Little Baby Girl, 1974
Rosa Parks, 1973

Other books you might like:
Natalie Savage Carlson, *The Empty Schoolhouse*, 1965
  Older sister Emma tells a story about Lullah and her attendance, with white children, of the parochial school.
Harvey Hanson, *Game Time*, 1975
  A thirteen year old African-American boy living in Chicago tries to come to terms with what he is and what other people want him to be.
Mary Stolz, *Go Fish*, 1991
  After spending the day fishing in the Gulf of Mexico with Grandfather, Thomas has a quiet evening on the porch hearing about his African heritage.
Eleanora E. Tate, *Front Porch Stories at the One Room School*, 1992
  Margie and her younger cousin forget their boredom when her father entertains them with stories about people and events in their small town's past.
Mildred D. Taylor, *The Friendship and the Gold Cadillac: Two Stories*, 1989
  Two stories about racial relations that reveal how much progress has been made in the battle for civil rights.

757

Sheila Greenwald

Give Us a Great Big Smile, Rosy Cole (Boston: Houghton Mifflin, 1981)

Age range: Grades 3-4

Subject(s): Friendship; Problem Solving; Humor

Major character(s): Rosy Cole, Child

Time period(s): 1980s

Locale(s): United States

What the book is about: Ten year old Rosy feels pressure to excel at the violin because her uncle plans to do a book about her, as he has about each of her older sisters when they were ten. Unfortunately, she is not very good at the violin, and she devises an ingenious scheme to get herself out of the situation. Fast paced and humorous.

Where it's reviewed:
Horn Book, August 1981, page 421
Kirkus Reviews, July 1, 1981, page 800

Other books by the author:
Blissful Joy and the SATs, 1982
The Mariah Delany Lending Library Disaster, 1981
It All Began with Jane Eyre or, The Secret Life Fanny Dillman, 1980
All the Way to Wit's End, 1979

Other books you might like:
Kitty Barne, *Barbie*, 1969
  Barbie's dream to play the violin seems hopeless in her small English town until Simon comes up with a plan.
Marguerite De Angeli, *Fiddlestrings*, 1974
  Dai decides the hours he has to spend practicing the violin are worth it, even though at times he has his doubts.
Patricia Foley, *John and the Fiddler*, 1990
  A young boy befriends an old violin maker who teaches him the beauty of music and friendship.
Norah Lofts, *Rupert Hatton's Story*, 1973

In 18th century England, a boy's passion for the violin, despite his father's opposition, causes a disaster which results in a totally new life.
Lensey Namioka, *Yang the Youngest and his Terrible Ear*, 1992
  Recently arrived in Seattle from China, musically untalented Yingtao is faced with giving a violin performance to attract new students for his father.

758

Sheila Greenwald

It All Began with Jane Eyre, or the Secret Life of Franny Dillman (Boston: Little, Brown, 1980)

Age range: Grades 4-5

Subject(s): Imagination; Literacy

Major character(s): Franny Dillman, Preteen (bibliophile); Wilson Dillman, Teenager (Teenager)

Time period(s): 1980s

Locale(s): New York, New York (the Bronx)

What the book is about: Avid reading and a vivid imagination get Franny Dillman into hot water when she turns from the classics to modern teen novels. Franny uncovers an appalling affair, and finds herself caught in a whirlwind of intrigue and suspicion.

Where it's reviewed:
Booklist, May 1, 1980, page 1291
Center for Children's Books Bulletin, September 1980, page 10
Hornbook, August 1980, page 407

Other books by the author:
Here's Hermione, 1991
Rosy's Romance, 1989
All the Way to Wit's End, 1979
The Atrocious Two, 1978

Other books you might like:
Nancy Hayashi, *Cosmic Cousin*, 1988
  During trips to the public library, Eunice seeks to learn the identity of Cosmic Cousin, who like her loves science fiction and is leaving her notes.
Florence Parry Heide, *The Problem with Pulcifer*, 1982
  Pulcifer's parents, teacher, principal, and even the librarian are distressed. He does not want to watch television. He wants to read.
Suzy Kline, *Herbie Jones*, 1985
  Herbie, while in the third grade, finds bones in the bathroom, wanders away from his class on a field trip, and moves up to a higher reading group.
Anne Lindbergh, *Travel Far, Pay No Fare*, 1992
  When Owen finds that his cousin has a magic bookmark, they enter different stories in hopes of preventing their parents' upcoming marriage.
Hilary McKay, *The Exiles*, 1992
  The four Conroy sisters spend a wild summer at the seaside with Big Grandma, who tries to substitute fresh air and hard work for their reading habits.

759

Sheila Greenwald

Mariah Delany's Author-of-the-Month Club (Boston: Little Brown, 1990)

Age range: Grades 4-6

Subject(s): Authorship; Humor

Major character(s): Mariah Delany, Preteen; Leah Coopersmith, Friend; T.M. Obermeyer, Writer

Time period(s): 1980s

Locale(s): New York

What the book is about: When Mariah Delany sees how excited her classmates are to meet a popular author, she is off on her next scheme, certain it is the most brilliant idea yet. She makes plans to invite authors to come and sign books and tell those private "how I did it" stories to her friends. Just as the plan gets off the ground, disaster strikes and Mariah finds herself in hot water.

Where it's reviewed:
Booklist, November 15, 1990, page 626
Booklist, December 1, 1990, page 742
Hornbook Guide, July 1990, page 77

Other books by the author:
It All Began with Jane Eyre; or The Secret Life of Fanny Dillman, 1990
Rosy Cole's Great American Guilt Club, 1985
The Atrocious Two, 1978
The Mariah Delany Lending Library Disaster, 1977

Other books you might like:
Betsy Byars, *The Moon and I*, 1991
   While describing her humorous adventures with a blacksnake, Betsy Byars recounts her childhood anecdotes and explains how she writes a book.
Helen McCann, *What Do We Do Now, George?*, 1991
   George's plans to raise money for his school and keep a percentage for himself create chaos and get him in trouble with friends and the authorities.
Daniel Manus Pinkwater, *Author's Day*, 1993
   In this comedy of errors, a famous author visits an elementary school.
Philip Ridley, *Dakota of the White Flats*, 1991
   In searching for a woman's jewel-encrusted turtle, Dakota and Treacle tangle with a recluse author and almost become a midnight menu for mutant eels.
Louis Sacher, *Wayside School Is Falling Down*, 1989
   More humorous episodes from the classroom on the thirteenth floor at Wayside School.

760

Sheila Greenwald, Author/Illustrator

The Secret in Miranda's Closet (Boston: Houghton Mifflin, 1989)

Age range: Grades 3-5

Subject(s): Dolls and Dollhouses; Mothers and Daughters; Sex Roles

Major character(s): Miranda Alexis Perry, Preteen; Towney Ordway, Neighbor; Olivia Perry, Parent, Feminist

Time period(s): 1980s

Locale(s): United States

What the book is about: Miranda's mother, Olivia, often leaves her with neighbors for the weekend. Olivia has been very careful to bring Miranda up without emphasis on traditional sex roles. Olivia is an ardent feminist and Miranda's experience with dolls is very limited. When Miranda finds a beautiful doll and lovely wardrobe for her in an attic trunk, she is thrilled. Knowing her mom's feelings, she keeps the doll a secret until another child spills the beans. Then its time for Miranda to develop her own values, guided by but independent of, her mother.

Other books by the author:
Alvin Webster's Surefire Plan for Success (and How it Failed), 1987
Blissful Joy and the SAT's, 1982
Give Us a Great Big Smile, Rosy Cole, 1981
All the Way to Wit's End, 1979

Other books you might like:
Daniel Curley, *Ann's Spring*, 1977
   Because Earth Mother is busy with tornadoes and hailstorms, her daughter has to use her own powers to start spring.
Hadley Irwin, *The Lilith Summer*, 1979
   A girl relates her experiences during the summer she spends as a companion to a seventy-seven year old woman.
Joseph McNair, *Commander Coatrack Returns*, 1989
   When Lisa's brother starts becoming more independent, and she finds herself disagreeing with a feminist friend, she plays make believe with a boy.
Harriet Sirof, *The Real World: A Novel*, 1985
   A teen who lives with her mother, an ardent feminist, in a woman's commune, discovers how others live when she visits her father, an architect.
Luke Wallin, *Ceremony of the Panther*, 1987
   A young Miccosukee Indian is torn between the shiftless life in the Everglades and his father's ambitions for him to carry on the shaman traditon.

761

Gery Greer

Max and Me and the Time Machine (San Diego: Harcourt, Brace, Jovanovich, 1983)

Age range: Grades 5 and Up

Subject(s): Space and Time; Knights and Knighthood; Middle Ages

Major character(s): Max, Child; Steve, Child; Sir Bevis, Knight

Time period(s): 13th century

Locale(s): England

What the book is about: Mayhem occurs when a time machine takes Steve, as a knight, and Max, as his horse, back to the Middle Ages. Steve becomes Sir Robert Marshall, the Green Falcon. For three days Steve and Max joust with an evil knight, win a lovely lady, and nearly get themselves killed.

Where it's reviewed:
Center for Children's Books Bulletin, October 1983, page 28
School Library Journal, May 1983, page 71

Other books by the author:
Let Me Off This Spaceship!, 1991
Max and Me and the Wild West, 1988

Other books you might like:
Gene Kemp, *Jason Bodger and the Priory Ghost*, 1985
When Jason visits an ancient priory, he meets a girl who lived eight centuries before.
E.W. Hildick, *The Case of the Dragon in Distress*, 1991
McGurk members are transported back to the 12th century and encounter an evil princess.
Eric P. Kelly, *Trumpeter of Krakow*, 1966
A Polish family in the Middle Ages guards a great secret treasure.
Elizabeth Winthrop, *The Castle in the Attic*, 1985
A gift of a toy castle involves William in adventure, magic, and a personal quest.
Tamora Pierce, *Alanna: The First Adventure*, 1983
11 year old Alanna, determined to be a knight, disguises herself as a boy to become a royal page.

762

Gery Greer

This Island Isn't Big Enough for the Four of Us! (New York: Crowell, 1987)

Age range: Grades 4-6

Subject(s): Camps and Camping

Major character(s): Peter, Child; Scott, Child

Time period(s): 1980s

Locale(s): United States

What the book is about: A good book for reluctant readers. Peter and Scott plan a camping trip to a deserted island only to find two girls and an adult chaperone already there ahead of them. They team up with a recluse who lives in a treehouse and the fun begins.

Where it's reviewed:
Center for Children's Books Bulletin, September 1987, page 8
School Library Journal, August 1987, page 83

Other books by the author:
Jason and the Aliens Down the Street, 1991
Let Me Off This Spaceship!, 1991
Max and Me and the Wild West, 1988
Max and Me and the Time Machine, 1983

Other books you might like:
Jamie Gilson, *4B Goes Wild*, 1983
Fourth graders on a three-day camping trip with their teachers experience frights and delights.
Margaret Goff, *Death at Their Heels*, 1975
When his older stepbrother takes him on a camping trip to Algonquin Park in Canada, Denny is unaware they are fleeing from a murderer.
Gary Paulsen, *Canyons*, 1990
Finding a skull on a trip to the canyons outside El Paso, Brennan becomes involved in the fate of a young Apache Indian who lived in the 1800s.
P.J. Petersen, *I Hate Camping*, 1991
Dan expects a terrible time camping with his mother's boyfriend and Mike's son, Raymond, but a surprising friendship results.

Ron Roy, *Nightmare Island*, 1981
On their first camping trip to Little Island, Harley and his younger brother are engulfed by fire.

763

Diana Gregory

There's a Caterpillar in My Lemonade (Reading, MA: Addison-Wesley, 1980)

Age range: Grades 4-6

Subject(s): Remarriage; Sports/Swimming

Major character(s): Samantha, Preteen, Sports Figure (swimmer); Cathy, Preteen

Time period(s): 1980s

Locale(s): United States

What the book is about: Sam is unhappy at the prospect of her mother's remarriage. She joins the swim team with her best friend, Cathy, to avoid contact with Mr. Hooten, her prospective stepfather. As it turns out, the swimming forms a bond, since Mr. Hooten used to swim competitively and is able to help Sam cope when her error disqualifies her relay team.

Where it's reviewed:
School Library Journal, January 1981, page 61

Other books by the author:
The Fog Burns Off by Eleven O'Clock, 1981
I'm Boo.That's Who, 1979

Other books you might like:
Judith Gorog, *No Swimming in Dark Pond and Other Chilling Tales*, 1987
Stories including "No Swimming in Dark Pond," "How I Kill My Stepmothers," "Tim the Alien," "Family Vacation," and other short horror stories.
Mary Downing Hahn, *The Spanish Kidnapping Disaster*, 1991
New stepsisters are forced to accompany their parents on their honeymoon and bragging gets them kidnapped with their little brother.
Sandra Love, *Melissa's Medley*, 1978
A young teen deals with the pressures, rivalries, sacrifices and rewards of competitive swimming.
David Masterson, *Get Out of My Face!*, 1991
Kate's adjustment to her new stepbrother is made even more difficult when they have to help each other survive in the wilderness.
Jean Rogers, *Raymond's Best Summer*, 1990
Raymond's boring summer becomes exciting when he learns how to swim and helps the police catch a gang of thieves.

764

Kristiana Gregory

Jenny of the Tetons (San Diego: Harcourt Brace, 1989)

Age range: Grades 6 and Up

Subject(s): Frontier and Pioneer Life; Indians of North America

Major character(s): Carrie Hill, Teenager, Orphan; Beaver Dick, Trapper

Time period(s): 1800s

Locale(s): Idaho

What the book is about: Orphaned by an Indian raid while traveling West with a wagon train, fifteen year old Carrie is befriended by an English trapper and taken to live with his Indian wife and their six children.

Where it's reviewed:
Center for Children's Books Bulletin, March 1989, page 170
Kirkus Reviews, May 15, 1989, page 763

Awards the book has won:
Golden Kite Award 1989

Other books by the author:
Earthquake at Dawn, 1992
The Legend of Jimmy Spoon, 1990

Other books you might like:
Joan W. Blos, *Brothers of the Heart*, 1987
    Shem spends six months in the Michigan wilderness alone with a dying Indian woman who helps him survive and face the difficulty of being handicapped.
Betsy Byars, *Trouble River*, 1969
    When he builds a raft, a boy never dreams it will be the only means of escape for him and his grandmother when hostile Indians threaten their cabin.
Eleanor B. Heady, *Sagesmoke: Tales of the Shoshoni-Bannock Indians*, 1973
    Twenty folk tales explaining the creation of the world, pine nuts, Indian music and other traditions.
G. Clifton Wisler, *Winter of the Wolf*, 1981
    Fourteen year old TJ saves the life of a Comanche boy during an Indian raid and they subsequently hunt a large silver wolf purported to be the devil.
G. Clifton Wisler, *The Wolf's Tooth*, 1987
    When Elias moves to an Indian reservation on the Texas frontier, where his father will be a teacher, he shares adventures with a Tonkawa Indian boy.

765

Arnold A. Griese

Illustrator: Glo Coalson

At the Mouth of the Luckiest River (New York: Crowell, 1973)

Age range: Grades 4-6

Subject(s): Indians of North America

Major character(s): Tatlek, Child, Handicapped (crippled)

Time period(s): 1870s

Locale(s): Alaska, North America

What the book is about: Tatlek is a crippled, fatherless Athabascan Indian boy who uses sled dogs to help him hunt. The medicine man tries to convince him that using sled dogs, which he learned from the Eskimos, will make the spirits angry. The medicine man says the Eskimos are coming to kill the tribe. Can Tatlek prevent a war caused by a lie?

Where it's reviewed:
Kirkus Reviews, June 1, 1973, page 599
Library Journal, September 15, 1973, page 2650

Other books by the author:
The Wind Is Not a River, 1978
The Way of Our People, 1975

Other books you might like:
Betty Baker, *The Big Push*, 1972
    Describes the disruption of a Hopi tribe when the children are forced to go to school and learn the ways of the white culture.
Eleanor Coerr, *The Bell Ringer and the Pirates*, 1983
    An Indian boy rings the Mission bells to warn of danger and signal safety when pirates attack.
Peggy Parish, *Good Hunting, Blue Sky*, 1988
    Blue Sky, a young Indian boy, goes hunting to bring food home, only to have the food bring him home instead.
Peter Roop, *Ahyoka and the Talking Leaves*, 1992
    Ahyoka helps her father, Sequoyah, in his quest to create a system of writing for his people.
Virginia Driving Hawk Sneve, *The Chichi Hoohoo Bogeyman*, 1975
    When a strange creature appears on the South Dakota prairie, Mary Jo and her two Native American cousins battle the Sioux River to reach safety.

766

Arnold A. Griese

Illustrator: Haru Wells

The Way of Our People (New York: Harper, 1975)

Age range: Grades 4-6

Subject(s): Hunting; Indians of North America

Major character(s): Kano, Hunter, Indian; Napak, Hunter, Indian

Time period(s): 1830s (1838)

Locale(s): Anvik, Alaska

What the book is about: The story of an adolescent boy's growth to maturity in an accurate picture of life within the Alaska Anvik community. Kano must overcome his fear of the "devil animals" (bears) the Nakani, who may take the form of a man or woman, and becoming lost in the dark forest.

Where it's reviewed:
Center for Children's Books Bulletin, February 1976, page 97
Kirkus Reviews, September 15, 1975, page 1066
School Library Journal, November 1975, page 77

Other books by the author:
The Wind Is Not a River, 1978
At the Mouth of the Luckiest River, 1973

Other books you might like:
Betty Biesterveld, *Six Days From Sunday*, 1973
    In his last days before the frightening prospect of going away to school, a Navaho boy's adventure help him appreciate the old ways of his ancestors.
Eve Bunting, *A Gift for Lonny*, 1973
    The whale in the lagoon not only leaves Lonny a gift but enables him to overcome a gnawing fear.
Aylette Jenness, *In Two Worlds: A Yup'ik Eskimo Family*, 1989
    Text and photographs document the life of a Yup'ik Eskimo family, residents of a small Alaskan town on the coast of the Bering Sea.
Frances Lackey Paul, *Kahtahah*, 1976
    Draws on the experiences of a real person to recreate the life of a Tlingit Indian girl of 19th century Alaska.
Phyllis Root, *The Listening Silence*, 1992

A young Indian girl triumphs over her fears and proves herself worthy to be the mystical healer of her village.

767

Arnold A. Griese

Illustrator: Glo Coalson

The Wind Is Not a River (New York: Crowell, 1978)

Age range: Grades 4-6

Subject(s): Eskimos; World War II

Major character(s): Sasan, Child, Eskimo; Sidak, Child, Eskimo; Taro, Military Personnel

Time period(s): 1940s (1942)

Locale(s): Attu Village, Alaska

What the book is about: The Japanese take over Attu Village during WWII and only Sasan and her brother Sidak escape. Their father is away and both their mother and grandmother are dead. They find a wounded enemy soldier, Taro, and learn about trust and loyalty. Sasan remembers her grandmother's words: "Troubles are like the wind, they do not go on forever. The wind is not a river." Based on an actual event.

Where it's reviewed:
Kirkus Reviews, January 1, 1979, page 5
School Library Journal, December 1978, page 52
Booklist, December 15, 1978, page 685

Other books by the author:
The Way of Our People, 1975
At the Mouth of the Luckiest River, 1973

Other books you might like:
Judy Glassman, *The Morning Glory War*, 1990
   Jeannie, a fifth grader during WWII, supports the war effort at home and writes to a soldier overseas while enduring the dislike of a harsh teacher.
Chester G. Osborne, *The Memory String*, 1984
   Darath and his sister spend a winter on the Siberian peninsula learning to heal, to use the moon sticks and remembering stories of the memory string.
Harry W. Paige, *The Summer War*, 1983
   While at summer camp in the Adirondacks, Ely's discovery of a buried skeleton uncovers the hatred that swirled around German-Americans during WWII.
Jean Rogers, *Goodbye, My Island*, 1983
   Twelve year old Esther Atoolik tells of the last winter her people spent on King Island, Alaska, in the early 1960s.
Judith St. George, *In the Shadow of the Bear*, 1983
   Annie's week in Alaska at her father's company's camp stretches her mental and physical limits as she must deal with hostile Russians and survival.

768

Ann Grifalconi, Author/Illustrator

The Village of Round and Square Houses (Boston: Little, Brown, 1986)

Age range: Grades 1-3

Subject(s): Africa; Grandparents; Folk Tales

Major character(s): Grandmother, Storyteller

Time period(s): Indeterminate Past

Locale(s): Cameroons, Africa

What the book is about: Why the women live in round houses and the men in square ones in a West African village. When Naka Mountain erupted, all of the village was swept away, except for one round and one square house. Each survivor must have a time to be together and a time to be apart.

Where it's reviewed:
Horn Book, January/February 1987, page 44
School Library Journal, August 1986, page 82

Other books by the author:
Flyaway Girl, 1992
Osa's Pride, 1989
Darkness and the Butterfly, 1987
City Rhythms, 1965

Other books you might like:
Kathleen Arnott, *Spiders, Crabs, and Creepy Crawlers*, 1978
   Two Nigerian stories explain why flamingos stand on one leg and why spiders are often found under stones.
Dorian Haarhoff, *Desert December*, 1991
   An African boy makes a long journey through the desert to join his parents, reaching them on Christmas Day and seeing his new baby sister.
Virginia Kroll, *Masai and I*, 1992
   Linda, a little girl who lives in the city, learns about East Africa and the Masai and imagines what her life might be like if she were Masai.
Tololwa Marti Mollel, *A Promise to the Sun*, 1992
   An African story explaining why bats only come out of their caves at night.
Mildred Pitts Walter, *Brother to the Wind*, 1985
   With the help of Good Snake, a young African boy gets his dearest wish.

769

Helen Griffith

Illustrator: Victor G. Ambrus

Just a Dog (New York: Holiday, 1975)

Age range: Grades 5-6

Subject(s): Animals/Dogs

Time period(s): Indeterminate

Locale(s): Spain

What the book is about: A mutt's story, set in Spain, told from the pup's point of view. She is loved by a boy whose parents won't let him keep her. She becomes a stray and learns a great deal about people. She is finally rescued by a family that has known and fed her.

Where it's reviewed:
Kirkus Reviews, April 15, 1975, page 453
School Library Journal, September 1975, page 103

Other books by the author:
The Mysterious Appearance of Agnes, 1975
Witch Fear, 1975

Other books you might like:
Walt Morey, *Scrub Dog of Alaska*, 1971
   A pup, abandoned because of his small size, turns out to be a winner.

Farley Mowat, *The Dog Who Wouldn't Be*, 1957
  The humorous story of Mutt, a dog of character and personality, and his boy.
Theodore Taylor, *The Trouble with Tuck*, 1981
  The story of a golden Labrador Retriever who becomes blind.
Albert Payson Terhune, *Lad: A Dog*, 1959
  One of the best loved dog stories of all time.
Elizabeth Van Steenwyk, *Three Dog Winter*, 1987
  A story of dog racing, Scott and his Malamute, Kaylah.

770

Helen V. Griffith

Illustrator: Joseph Low

Alex and the Cat (New York: Greenwillow, 1982)

Age range: Grades 1-3

Subject(s): Animals; Animals/Dogs

Major character(s): Alex, Dog

Time period(s): 1980s

Locale(s): United States

What the book is about: Alex, a dog, tries to be everything but a dog. He wants to be treated like a cat, live like a wolf, and tries to restore a baby robin to its nest like a bird. Finally he settles for just being himself.

Where it's reviewed:
Booklist, March 15, 1982, page 965
Hornbook, June 1982, page 284
Kirkus Reviews, March 1, 1982, page 273

Other books by the author:
Caitlin's Doll, 1990
Georgia Music, 1986
Alex Remembers, 1983
Mine Will, Said John, 1980

Other books you might like:
Barbara Baker, *Digby and Kate Again*, 1989
  Digby the Dog and Kate the Cat share four adventures: Hunting, bicycling, letter writing and raking the leaves.
Joan Drescher, *Max and Rufus*, 1982
  A dog, Rufus, and his boy, Max, agree to change places for a while.
Rose Impey, *Desperate for a Dog*, 1988
  Two sisters desperate to get a dog meet with their father's refusal until the family is asked to take care of a sick neighbor's dog for a few weeks.
Liesel Moak Skorpen, *His Mother's Dog*, 1978
  A young boy is disappointed when his puppy follows his mother everywhere, but the situation changes with the advent of a new baby.
Lane Smith, *The Big Pets*, 1991
  A little girl explores the mysterious dream world where small children play with their pets which range from cats and dogs to snakes and crickets.

771

Helen V. Griffith

Foxy (New York: Greenwillow, 1984)

Age range: Grades 4-6

Subject(s): Animals/Dogs

Major character(s): Jeff, Child; Amber, Neighbor

Time period(s): 1980s

Locale(s): Florida

What the book is about: While camping in the Florida Keys, Jeff finds an abandoned, mistreated dog that he desperately wants for his own. Trust begins to grow between both timid personalites. When Jeff believes the dog is dead, Amber, a classmate, knows it isn't true and Jeff finds he has another friend.

Where it's reviewed:
Center for Children's Books Bulletin, June 1984, page 186
School Library Journal, May 1984, page 80

Other books by the author:
Caitlin's Doll, 1990
The Dog at the Window, 1984
Rafa's Dog, 1983
Grip: A Dog Story, 1978

Other books you might like:
Bianca Bradbury, *Dogs and More Dogs*, 1968
  A young boy takes in one abandoned dog and he and his friends are moved to start an animal shelter.
John W. Chambers, *Finder*, 1981
  Jenny finds an abandoned dog in a mysterious house on Fire Island.
Beverly Cleary, *Strider*, 1991
  In a series of diary entries, Leigh tells how he acquires an abandoned dog, among other things.
R.A. Montgomery, *The Haunted House*, 1981
  A "Plot-Your-Own" story featuring a dog that disappears into an abandoned (and perhaps haunted) house.
Prudence Andrew, *Dog!*, 1973
  A ten year old boy who is not allowed to have a dog at home, finds a stray and hides him in an abandoned car.

772

Helen V. Griffith

Illustrator: James Stevenson

Georgia Music (New York: Greenwillow, 1986)

Age range: Grades 2-3

Subject(s): Grandparents; Music; Nature

Time period(s): Indeterminate

Locale(s): Georgia; Baltimore, Maryland

What the book is about: This is the story of a young girl who spends a wonderful long summer with her grandfather in Georgia. They tend a garden and in the evenings Grandpa plays the harmonica and teaches the girl to sing songs. When he gets too sick to live alone, he comes to live with the family in Baltimore. He misses the "Georgia Music" of birds, crickets and grasshoppers until the girl brings out the harmonica and begins to imitate the "Georgia Music" they both love.

Where it's reviewed:
Center for Children's Books Bulletin, December 1986, page 67
Horn Book, November/December 1986, page 733

Awards the book has won:
Boston Globe/Horn Book Award - Honor Book

Other books by the author:
Caitlin's Doll, 1990
Emily and the Enchanted Frog, 1989
Grandaddy's Place, 1987
Alex and the Cat, 1982

Other books you might like:
Kate Aver, *Joey's Way*, 1992
   During each of the four seasons, five year old Joey shows that she has her own special way of doing things.
Kevin Henkes, *Grandpa and Bo*, 1986
   Young Bo spends the summer with his grandfather in the country and has a wonderful time.
Lyn Littlefield Hoopes, *Mommy, Daddy and Me*, 1988
   A little boy and his parents sail over to visit Grandfather on a sunny day.
Poupa Montaufier, *One Summer at Grandmother's House*, 1985
   A reminiscence about a French girl and her family spending a typical summer with her grandmother in Alsace.
Diane Palmisciano, *Garden Partners*, 1989
   A child and her grandmother plant seeds, care for their garden all summer, and share their harvest with friends and family.

773

Helen V. Griffith

Illustrator: James Stevenson

Grandaddy's Place (New York: Greenwillow, 1987)

Age range: Grades 1-3

Subject(s): Farm Life; Grandparents

Major character(s): Janetta, Child

Time period(s): Indeterminate

Locale(s): United States

What the book is about: At first Janetta does not like her grandfather, his farm, or his animals, because they all seem strange to her. With warmth and humor, we see Janetta adjust and get to know her "grandaddy." Tall tales humor abounds in this story of two generations.

Where it's reviewed:
Horn Book, November/December 1987, page 723
School Library Journal, October 1987, page 112

Other books by the author:
Grandaddy and Janetta, 1993
Mine Will, Said John, 1992
Emily and the Enchanted Frog, 1989
Alex and the Cat, 1982

Other books you might like:
Jan Andrews, *The Auction*, 1990
   Todd and his grandfather prepare for the sale of the farm and its contents by telling stories and making scarecrows.
Hope Norman Coulter, *Uncle Chuck's Truck*, 1993
   When Uncle Chuck's truck gets stuck in the mud while he is taking food to the cows on his farm, the cows come to the rescue.
Verde Cross, *Great-Grandma Tells of Threshing Day*, 1992

A little girl and her brother help out on a threshing day in the early 1900s.
Virginia Hamilton, *Drylongso*, 1992
   As a great wall of dust moves across their drought-stricken farm, a family's distress is relieved by a young man who literally blows into their lives.
Carolyn Otto, *That Sky, That Rain*, 1990
   As a storm approaches, a young girl and her grandfather take the farm animals into the shelter of the barn and watch the rain begin.

774

Maria Gripe

Illustrator: Harold Gripe

The Glassblower's Children (New York: Delacorte, 1973)

Age range: Grades 4-6

Subject(s): Fairy Tale; Fantasy; Kidnapping

Major character(s): Klas, Child (kidnap victim); Klara, Child (kidnap victim); Albert, Artisan (glassblower)

Time period(s): Indeterminate

Locale(s): Noda Diseberga, Sweden

What the book is about: The glassblower has seen ominous signs that his children are in danger, and he seeks help from a good witch. She is the sister of the evil governess who bullies the children after they are stolen by a rich Lord who is trying to please his unhappy Lady. They are imprisoned in a mansion surrounded by the River of Forgotten Memories, with only their reflections for company. A classic story of good and evil.

Where it's reviewed:
Kirkus Reviews, May 1, 1973, page 515
Library Journal, July 1973, page 2194

Other books by the author:
Elvis and His Friends, 1976
Elvis and His Secret, 1976
In the Time of the Bells, 1976
Julia's House, 1975

Other books you might like:
Caroline Baxter, *The Stolen Telesm*, 1975
   Two children are drawn into a battle with the evil forces of Darkness after they find a winged horse and an ancient stone.
Grace Chetwin, *On All Hallow's Eve*, 1984
   Two sisters on their way home from a party step into another time period where the forces of good and evil draw them into a life or death adventure.
Susan Cooper, *Over Sea, Under Stone*, 1965
   Three children on a holiday in Cornwall find an ancient manuscript which sends them on a dangerous quest for the Holy Grail.
Carolyn Keene, *The Phantom of Venice*, 1985
   Nancy Drew travels to Venice to investigate the kidnapping of a famous glassblower and the disappearance of an artist.
John Masefield, *The Box of Delights*, 1984
   Kay becomes involved in a fantastic adventure when he becomes the guardian of the mysterious box of delights.

775

Judith Groch

Play the Bach, Dear! (Garden City: Doubleday, 1978)

Age range: Grades 4-6

Subject(s): Musicians

Major character(s): Hilary, Preteen; Miss Orpheo, Teacher (piano teacher)

Time period(s): 1970s

Locale(s): United States

What the book is about: Eleven year old Hilary takes piano lessons, plays terribly and dreads her upcoming recital. Miss Orpheo scolds, insists on more practice and urges Hilary to relax. Much to Hilary's surprise, she comes to the rescue at the recital.

Where it's reviewed:
Childhood Education, January 1979, page 168

Other books you might like:
Nat Hentoff, *Does This School Have Capital Punishment?*, 1981
  Sam's history project about a legendary jazz musician and a dispute with a trouble-making classmate enliven his first year at Burr Academy.
William Sleator, *Fingers*, 1983
  Sam likes his mother's bizarre scheme to revitalize his younger brother's flagging career as a piano prodigy, and agrees to help.
Erika Tamar, *Blues for Silk Garcia*, 1983
  Linda, who resembles her father and has his gift for music, pursues the truth about her long-absent parent, now that he has died.
Jean Ure, *See You Thursday*, 1981
  Marianne finds an unexpected friend in her mother's new lodger, Abe, a young piano teacher who has been blind since birth.
Betty Ren Wright, *The Midnight Mystery*, 1989
  Rosie discovers that having nine fingers can be an assett as she faces the challenges of an upcoming piano recital and the absence of her father.

776

Morton Grosser

Illustrator: David K. Stone

The Snake Horn (New York: Atheneum, 1973)

Age range: Grades 5-6

Subject(s): Space and Time; Music

Major character(s): Danny, Preteen

Time period(s): 17th Century; 1970s

Locale(s): United States

What the book is about: One of his father's friends gives Danny a tartoeld, an old musical instrument made in the form of a snake. When Danny plays it, the original owner, from the 17th century, appears in his room. Danny's dad is a loving jazz musician who learns a lot from the time traveler.

Where it's reviewed:
Booklist, September 1, 1973, page 50

Kirkus Reviews, February 1, 1973, page 114

Other books by the author:
The Fabulous Fifty, 1990

Other books you might like:
Berthe Amoss, *The Chalk Cross*, 1976
  A young girl living in 19th century New Orleans struggles between her growing familiarity with voodoo and the precepts of the church.
T. Ernesto Bethancourt, *Tune in Yesterday*, 1978
  Two teenage boys with a passion for jazz and big band music accidentally find a way to go back in time and wind up in 1942.
L.M. Boston, *The Children of Green Knowe*, 1955
  Tolly comes to live with his great-grandmother at an ancient house and becomes friends with three children who lived there in the 17th century.
Colby Rodowsky, *Keeping Time*, 1983
  Drew travels to 16th century England where he acquires the strength to deal with his unusual life style.
Cynthia Voigt, *Building Blocks*, 1984
  In a trip back in time, Brann meets his father as a ten year old and learns for the first time to love and understand him.

777

Vicki Grove

Goodbye, My Wishing Star (New York: Putnam, 1988)

Age range: Grades 5-6

Subject(s): Poverty; Farm Life; Family Life

Major character(s): Jens Tucker, Child

Time period(s): 1980s

Locale(s): United States

What the book is about: A very real look at the farm crisis from a child's point of view. Through her contact with two abandoned children, Jens learns to appreciate her close family as they struggle with growing poverty.

Where it's reviewed:
Bulletin for the Center of Children's Books, September 1988, page 9
School Library Journal, August 1988, page 94

Other books by the author:
The Fastest Friends in the West, 1990

Other books you might like:
Patricia Willis, *Place to Claim as Home*, 1991
  13 year old Henry helps Miss Morrison on her farm in 1943 and discovers that her gruffness conceals a secret from her past.
Berlie Doherty, *White Peak Farm*, 1984
  Jeannie faces violent changes on the Derbyshire farm where she lives.
Ellen Howard, *Sister*, 1990
  Alena and her family face the hardships of growing up on a farm in the late 1800s.
Jane Resh Thomas, *The Princess in the Pigpen*, 1989
  Elizabeth travels from Elizabethan England to a farm in modern Iowa but no one believes her story of where she has come from.
Joan Lowery Nixon, *A Place to Belong*, 1989

On a Missouri farm in 1856, Danny plots to get his foster father to send for and marry his mother.

778

Elizabeth Guilfoile

Illustrator: Mary Stevens

Nobody Listens to Andrew (Chicago: Follett, 1957)

Age range: Grades 1-3

Subject(s): Family Life

Major character(s): Andrew, Child; Ruthy, Child; Bobby, Child

Time period(s): 1950s

Locale(s): United States

What the book is about: Andrew tries to tell the adults around him that there is a bear in his bed. But nobody listens to him until he becomes very assertive and they realize that he really does have something important to say.

Where it's reviewed:
Catholic Library World, April 1981, page 389

Other books by the author:
Valentine's Day, 1965
Have You Seen My Brother?, 1962

Other books you might like:
Stephen Cosgrove, Gabby, 1984
    After alienating nearly everyone she knows, talkative Gabby finally learns that it is also important to listen.
Rick Fitzgerald, Helen and the Great Quiet, 1989
    Helen is disturbed by what she perceives as a great quiet in the world, until she her family in listening to all the soft, gentle sounds around her.
Suzanne Gruber, The Monster under My Bed, 1985
    At bedtime, a little bear finds that there is a logical explanation for those monster noises coming from beneath his bed.
Roger Hargreaves, Little Miss Chatterbox, 1985
    Little Miss Chatterbox loses a series of job because of her tendency to talk on and on when she should be listening to her customers' requests.
Barbara J. Neasi, Listen to Me, 1986
    Whenever Mom and Dad are too busy to talk and to listen, Grandma saves the day, helping out and being a good listener.

779

Nancy Gurney

The King, the Mice, and the Cheese (New York: Random, 1965)

Age range: Grades 1-2

Series: Beginner Books

Subject(s): Kings, Queens, Rulers

Time period(s): Indeterminate

Locale(s): Fictional Country

What the book is about: The king calls on wise men to stop the mice from eating his cheese. They try bringing in cats, who chase the mice, but eat all the meat and fish they can find and irritate the king as much as the mice. So on with the dogs, lions, and elephants. Of course, the mice are brought back to chase the elephants away, and the king makes a deal to share his cheese with them and they become friends.

Where it's reviewed:
Center for Children's Books Bulletin, February 1966, page 98
Christian Science Monitor, November 4, 1965, page B2
Kirkus Reviews, July 15, 1965, page 676

Other books by the author:
Impossible Dogs and Troublesome Cats, 1970

Other books you might like:
Christian Garrison, Flim and Flam & the Big Cheese, 1976
    Flim, the slender, patient brother, decides to teach Flam, his fat, greedy brother, a lesson about selfishness.
Adelaide Holl, Moon Mouse, 1969
    Trying to reach the moon, a baby field mouse climbs a large building and finds a big, round, yellow object tasting very much like cheese.
Jack Kent, Socks for Supper, 1978
    When a poor couple exchanges socks for cheese and milk, they receive more than expected.
Eve Titus, Anatole, 1990
    A French mouse decides to earn an honest living by tasing the cheese in a cheese factory and leaving notes about its quality.
Jean Van Leeuwen, The Great Cheese Conspiracy, 1969
    Tired of gangster movies and a steady diet of candy wrappers, three theatre mice try to rob a cheese shop.

780

Rosa Guy

Illustrator: Caroline Binch

Paris, Pee Wee, and Big Dog (New York: Delacorte, 1985)

Age range: Grades 3-5

Subject(s): African Americans

Major character(s): Paris, Preteen; Pee Wee, Preteen; Big Dog, Preteen

Time period(s): 1980s

Locale(s): New York, New York

What the book is about: Paris is supposed to be cleaning his family's new apartment in New York City, but when his friends from the old neighborhood show up, they are off on great adventures. They get mixed up with a gang, and Big Dog's mouth gets them in trouble with the police. Paris wonders if he can get back to the apartment before his mother realizes he has skipped out.

Where it's reviewed:
Booklist, December 1985, page 572
Hornbook, January 1986, page 58
Center for Children's Books Bulletin, November 1985, page 47

Other books by the author:
Caribbean Carnival, 1992
The Music of Summer, 1992
Billy the Great, 1991
The Ups and Downs of Carl Davis III, 1989

Other books you might like:

Jaqueline Turner Banks, *Project Wheels*, 1993

While raising money to buy her classmate Wayne a motorized wheelchair, eleven year old Angela's relationships with her four friends begin to change.

Eloise Greenfield, *Koya DeLaney and the Good Girl Blues*, 1992

Koya DeLaney, an eleven year old African-American girl, has trouble expressing anger, until her cousin, a popular male singer, comes to town.

Angela Johnson, *Toning the Sweep: A Novel*, 1993

On a visit to her grandmother Ola, who is dying of cancer in her house in the desert, Emmie hears many stories about the past and her family history.

Walter Dean Myers, *Mop, Moondance, and the Nagasaki Knights*, 1992

After T.J. and his younger brother are adopted, they try to win a baseball tournament in their New Jersey home town and help a homeless teammate.

Erika Tamar, *It Happened at Cecilia's*, 1989

Andy's life changes when his father falls in love, their manhattan restaurant is discovered and the Mafia come for a cut of the increasing business.

H

Dorothy Haas

Illustrator: Cathy Bobak

Burton's Zoom Zoom Va-Room Machine (New York: Bradbury, 1990)

Age range: Grades 4-6

Subject(s): Sports/Skateboarding; Inventions

Major character(s): Burton Bell Whitney Knockwurst, Child; Edisonia Knockwurst, Child; Newton Knockwurst, Child

Time period(s): 1990s

Locale(s): United States

What the book is about: Burton is the oldest of an eccentric family. His dad is a composer, his mom works in a think tank, Edisonia is inventing a harp-flute and little Newton has a photographic memory. Burton has invented a dog-washing machine, a toasterpowered orange juicer, and a bed-maker. Now he is working on a rocket-powered skateboard.

Where it's reviewed:
Booklist, September 15, 1990, page 160
Kirkus Reviews, August 1990, page 1085

Other books by the author:
Burton and the Giggle Machine, 1992
The Friendship Test, 1990
The Haunted House, 1988
Not Starring Jilly!, 1989

Other books you might like:
Jerome Beatty, *Bob Fulton's Terrific Time Machine*, 1982
    A young boy's invention is able to transport him in time, but can he get home again?
Betsy Byars, *The Blossoms and the Green Phantom*, 1987
    Junior tries desperately to make a success of his secret invention.
Patricia Reilly Giff, *Snaggle Doodles*, 1985
    Emily tries to get along with bossy Linda in their group studying inventions. (Easy reading).
Jenny Pausacker, *Fast Found*, 1989
    12 year old Kieran can speed up time or travel in the past with his grandmother's Anti-Boredom machine.
Jay Williams, *Danny Dunn and the Universal Glue*, 1977
    Danny Dunn goes fishing to try out a new invention and winds up saving a dam.

Dorothy Haas

Illustrator: Jeffrey Lindberg

The Haunted House (New York: Scholastic, 1988)

Age range: Grades 3-5

Series: Peanut Butter and Jelly

Subject(s): Birthdays; Haunted Houses

Major character(s): Jillian "Jilly" Matthews, Preteen; Polly "Peanut" Matthews, Preteen; Jennifer Partimkin, Friend

Time period(s): 1980s

Locale(s): United States

What the book is about: For a unique birthday party, Jilly and Peanut create a haunted house in the basement and invite their class to visit. A few extra, mysterious guests appear and along with super costumes and tricks and treats, make the party one of the spookiest ever.

Where it's reviewed:
Booklist, April 15, 1989, page 1475
Emerging Librarian, May 1989, page 51
School Library Journal, March 1989, page 177

Other books by the author:
The Friendship Test, 1990
To Catch a Crook, 1988
The Secret Life of Dilly McBean, 1986
The Bears Upstairs, 1978

Other books you might like:
Linda Gondosch, *The Witches of Hopper Street*, 1986
    Three girls, not invited to a classmate's Halloween party, decide to sabotage the event by becoming real witches and casting some spells.
Ann M. Martin, *Karen's Little Witch*, 1991
    Karen is afraid to go trick-or-treating with her neighbor's granddaughter, Druscilla, whom Karen fears is a witch.
Annabelle Prager, *The Spooky Halloween Party*, 1989
    Albert doesn't recognize anyone at Nicky's Halloween party, even when they take off their masks.
Stephen Roos, *Love Me, Love My Werewolf*, 1991
    Bernie befriends a small, stray dog who proves to be invaluable around the house and is a hit at the Pet Lover's Club Halloween party.
Susan Saunders, *Haunted Halloween Party*, 1986
    A spooky Halloween adventure where the reader's choices determine the outcome.

783

Dorothy Haas

Illustrator: Jeffrey Lindberg

New Friends (New York: Scholastic, 1988)

Age range: Grades 3-5

Series: Peanut Butter and Jelly

Subject(s): Friendship; Moving, Household

Major character(s): Polly ''Peanut'' Butterman, Child; Jillian ''Jilly'' Matthews, Preteen; Ceci, Preteen

Time period(s): 1980s

Locale(s): Minneapolis, Minnesota; Evanston, Illinois

What the book is about: While moving from Minneapolis, Polly and her family find a stray puppy at a picnic area. He becomes ''Nibbsie.'' At their new home, Polly meets Jillian and finds that they are as different from each other as two girls could be. Can the two possibly become friends?

Where it's reviewed:
Booklist, February 15, 1989, page 1008

Other books by the author:
Burton and the Giggle Machine, 1992
The Friendship Test, 1990
The Haunted House, 1988
Peanut and Jilly Forever, 1988

Other books you might like:
Barbara Corcoran, Family Secrets, 1992
    After moving with her family to the town, Tracy discovers that she is adopted, a surprise that brings her new insight into what constitutes a family.
Beverly Keller, Desdemona Moves On, 1992
    Chronicles the comic mishaps of twelve year old Desdemona and her family after they move into a luxurious new house.
A.M. Monson, The Deer Stand, 1992
    When her family moves into the wilds and Bits has trouble making new friends at school, she spends her time trying to tame a deer near her home.
George Selden, Harry Cat's Pet Puppy, 1974
    Harry Cat and Tucker Mouse try to find a permanent home for a young stray puppy they have befriended.
Jane Resh Thomas, Courage at Indian Deep, 1984
    Forced to move to northern Minnesota from a comfortable life in Minneapolis, a family finds the need to make some big adjustments.

784

Dorothy Haas

Illustrator: Margot Apple

Poppy and the Outdoor Cat (Niles, Illinois: Whitman, 1981)

Age range: Grades 3-4

Subject(s): Animals/Cats

Major character(s): Poppy Flowers, Child, Animal Lover; Tink Becker, Friend

Time period(s): 1970s

Locale(s): United States

What the book is about: Mrs. Flowers can't allow her daughter to bring her cat indoors because their house is to small for a pet in addition to their large family. Poppy Flower trains her newly-found cat to be an ''outdoor cat.''

Where it's reviewed:
Booklist, March 15, 1981, page 1028
Center for Children's Books Bulletin, June 1981, page 193
School Library Journal, May 1981, page 64

Other books by the author:
Not Starring Jilly!, 1989
The Secret Life of Dilly McBean, 1986
Tink in a Tangle, 1984
The Bears Upstairs, 1981

Other books you might like:
Janet Wyman Coleman, Fast Eddie, 1993
    To the dismay of Puff the cat and Jones the squirrel, Fast Eddie the raccoon takes on his human neighbors one final time.
Janet Taylor Lisle, The Dancing Cats of Applesap, 1984
    A shy ten year old gets together with one hundred remarkable cats to bring notoriety to Applesap, and to save their beloved Rigg's Drug Store.
Miska Miles, Jenny's Cat, 1979
    Rather than give up her pet cat, Jenny decides to run away and take the cat with her.
Phyllis Reynolds Naylor, The Grand Escape, 1993
    After years of being strictly house cats, Marco and Polo escape into the dangerous outside world and are sent on three challenging adventures.
Elizabeth Parsons, The Upside-Down Cat, 1981
    A cat becomes separated from her owners before they leave their Maine summer home.

785

Mary Downing Hahn

Daphne's Book (New York: Clarion, 1983)

Age range: Grades 5 and Up

Subject(s): Child Abuse; Friendship

Major character(s): Jessica, Writer; Daphne, Artist, Abuse Victim

Time period(s): 1980s

Locale(s): United States

What the book is about: When Jessica is paired with the class outcast for a project, she comes to like and respect Daphne and realizes that the girl is not safe at home, but she denies the friendship to her classmates. An honest portrayal of a friendship in the face of peer pressure.

Where it's reviewed:
Center for Children's Books Bulletin, January 1984, page 87
School Library Journal, October 1983, page 168

Other books by the author:
Dead Man in Indian Creek, 1990
Following the Mystery Man, 1988
Sara Summer, 1981
The Spanish Kidnapping Disaster, 1991

Other books you might like:
Rachel Vail, Wonder, 1991

12 year old Jessica enters junior high and finds herself ignored and friendless.

Patricia Hermes, *I Hate Being Gifted*, 1990
  KT's friendships are threatened when she is selected for the gifted/talented program at her school.

Ilene Cooper, *The Queen of the Sixth Grade*, 1988
  After helping her friend found a secret club, Robin finds what kind of person Veronica really is.

Joyce Hansen, *Yellow Bird and Me*, 1986
  Doris helps a friend with his studies and discovers that he has dyslexia.

Susan Beth Pfeffer, *Truth or Dare*, 1984
  When her two best friends go to another school, 11 year old Cathy tries to replace them with the "perfect" Jessica.

786

Mary Downing Hahn

December Stillness (New York: Clarion, 1988)

Age range: Grades 5-6

Subject(s): Vietnam War; Veterans

Major character(s): Kelly, Child; Mr. Weems, Veteran (Vietnam)

Time period(s): 1980s

Locale(s): United States

What the book is about: A homeless man is killed in a traffic accident after being banned from the library. Kelly's father comes to terms with his own war memories at the Vietnam War Memorial. Kelly looks at difficult social issues.

Where it's reviewed:
Center for Children's Books Bulletin, September 1988, page 9
Horn Book, November/December 1988, page 786
School Library Journal, October 1988, page 161

Other books by the author:
Daphne's Book, 1983
Dead Man in Indian Creek, 1990
The Doll in the Garden, 1989
Following the Mystery Man, 1988

Other books you might like:
Katherine Paterson, *Park's Quest*, 1988
  11-year-old Park is searching for information about his father who died in Vietnam and meets a Vietnamese-American girl named Thanh.
Candy Dawson Boyd, *Charlie Pippin*, 1987
  11-year-old Charlie wants to find out everything she can about the Vietnam War which killed not only her father but all his dreams.
Doris Buchanan Smith, *The First Hard Times*, 1983
  Ancil, devoted to the memory of her MIA father, has difficulty accepting a new stepfather.
Ann Nolan Clark, *To Stand Against the Wind*, 1978
  A young refugee in the United States ponders his life in a Vietnamese village.
Carol J. Farley, *Sergeant Finney's Family*, 1969
  The Finneys have to adjust to a new town, school, and friends when their dad is assigned to Vietnam.

787

Mary Downing Hahn

The Doll in the Garden (New York: Clarion, 1989)

Age range: Grades 4-6

Subject(s): Space and Time; Ghosts

Major character(s): Ashley, Child; Kristi Child

Time period(s): 1980s

Locale(s): United States

What the book is about: After Ashley and Kristi find an antique doll buried in old Miss Cooper's garden, they discover that they can enter a ghostly turn-of-the-century world by going through a hole in the hedge.

Where it's reviewed:
Center for Children's Books Bulletin, March 1990, p 171
Kirkus Reviews, April 1, 1989, page 546

Other books by the author:
Stepping on the Cracks, 1991
Dead Man in Indian Creek, 1990
Following the Mystery Man, 1989
December Stillness, 1988

Other books you might like:
Kathryn Lasky, *Double Trouble Squared*, 1991
  Twelve year old telepathic twins, Liberty and July, receive strange emanations from a place once lived in by Arthur Conan Doyle.
Reby Edmond MacDonald, *The Ghosts of Austwick Manor*, 1982
  Hillary and Heather find themselves entering the 16th century to save Don from an ancient curse.
Pat McKissack, *The Dark-Thirty: Southern Tales of the Supernatural*, 1992
  A collection of ghost stories with African-American themes designed to be told in the last half-hour before sunset.
Barbara A. Steiner, *Ghost Cave*, 1990
  While hunting for an Indian burial site, Marc and two friends get lost in a haunted cave.
Nicholas Wilde, *Into the Dark*, 1987
  A lonely boy's new friend has a frightening secret.

788

Mary Downing Hahn

Following the Mystery Man (New York: Clarion, 1988)

Age range: Grades 5-7

Subject(s): Boarding Houses; Fathers and Daughters

Major character(s): Madigan, Preteen, 6th Grader; Clint James, Boarder

Time period(s): Indeterminate

Locale(s): United States

What the book is about: Sixth grader Madigan is certain that her grandmother's new boarder is none other than her missing father. By the time she lets herself recognize the signs that he is a thief, she's followed him too far. She finds a gun hidden in his room and the tension mounts. Sometimes quiet and sad, the characters are well drawn and readers will easily identify with Madigan.

Where it's reviewed:
Horn Book, July/August, 1988, page 493
School Library Journal, April 1988, page 100

Other books by the author:
Dead Man in Indian Creek, 1990
The Doll in the Garden, 1989
Jellyfish Season, 1985
Sara Summer, 1979

Other books you might like:
Sandy Asher, *Missing Pieces*, 1984
    Heather experiences many changes, but it is the tragic death of her father that enables her to change her relationship with her mother.
Elizabeth Gray, *Adam of the Road*, 1987
    The adventures of Adam as he travels the open roads of England searching for his missing father, a minstrel, and his stolen red spaniel, Nick.
Joan Lowery Nixon, *High Trail to Danger*, 1991
    Sarah travels from Chicago to Colorado, to locate her missing father, but she finds that the mention of his name brings an attempt on her life.
P.J. Petersen, *The Freshman Detective Blues*, 1987
    Eddie and Jack find a skeleton weighted down in the lake and Jack thinks it just might be his father who has been missing for nine years.
Meg Wolton, *The Dream Book*, 1986
    When Claudia meets tough Danger Roth, the two girls start sharing strange dreams in which Claudia's missing father sends her cryptic messages.

789

Mary Downing Hahn

Stepping on the Cracks (New York: Clarion, 1991)

Age range: Grades 5-6

Subject(s): World War II; Bullies; Child Abuse

Major character(s): Margaret Baker, Child; Elizabeth Crawford, Child

Time period(s): 1940s (1944-45)

Locale(s): College Hill, Maryland

What the book is about: Margaret and Elizabeth begin sixth grade during WWII. As they try to cope with Gordy Smith, the worst bully in class, they find themselves coping with losses from the war, as well as a situation of terror and abuse in their own class. An excellent portrayal of both traditional patriotism and anti-war sentiments.

Where it's reviewed:
Booklist, October 15, 1991, page 436
Horn Book, November 1991, page 736

Other books by the author:
December Stillness, 1988
The Doll in the Garden, 1989
Tallahassee Higgins, 1987
The Time of the Witch, 1982

Other books you might like:
Carol Carrick, *What a Wimp*, 1983
    Barney copes with a post-divorce family and a bully named Lenny.
Robin F. Brancato, *Don't Sit Under the Apple Tree*, 1975

In the summer of 1945, Ellis learns how to find her place in a group of friends and begins to understand the world outside her Pennsylvania home.
Janet Hickman, *The Stones*, 1976
    The misguided patriotism of a group of boys during WWII leads to an almost devastating tragedy.
Linda Woolverton, *Running Before the Wind*, 1987
    12-year-old Kelly finds relief from the fear and frustration of an abusive father by running early in the morning and late at night.
Michelle Magorian, *Good-night Mr. Tom*, 1982
    Twists and turns characterize this story of an abused evacuee from London during WWII.

790

Mary Downing Hahn

Tallahassee Higgins (New York: Clarion, 1987)

Age range: Grades 5-7

Subject(s): Vietnam War; Family Problems; Aunts and Uncles

Major character(s): Tally Higgins, Preteen; Dave, Relative (uncle); Thelma, Relative (aunt)

Time period(s): 1980s

Locale(s): United States

What the book is about: Talley's father was killed in the Vietnam War; now her mother has taken off on the back of a motorcycle bound for Hollywood where her boyfriend "knows people" in the film industry. Talley is sent to live with her Uncle Dave and Aunt Thelma. This is a sad, humorous, believable and readable book about growing up.

Where it's reviewed:
Booklist, March 1, 1987, page 1012
Kirkus Reviews, February 1, 1987, page 219
School Library Journal, June 1987, page 96

Other books by the author:
Stepping on the Cracks, 1991
December Stillness, 1988
Wait Till Helen Comes, 1986
Daphne's Book, 1983

Other books you might like:
Candy Dawson Boyd, *Charlie Pippin*, 1987
    Charlie hopes to understand her father by finding out everything she can about the Vietnam War, the war that let him survive but killed his dream.
Morse Hamilton, *Effie's House*, 1990
    A teenage girl with a terrible secret runs away from home, seeking counsel from the father she will not believe was killed in Vietnam.
Shannon Kennedy, *Daddy, Please Tell Me What's Wrong*, 1988
    Jenny tries to understand the strange behavior of her father, a Vietnam War veteran.
Katherine Paterson, *Park's Quest*, 1988
    Park makes some startling discoveries when he travels to his granfather's farm in Virginia to learn about his father who died in the Vietnam War.
Judie Wolkoff, *A Stranger in the Family*, 1980
    Deeply disturbed by his Vietnam experiences, Marcie's father drinks heavily and terrorizes his family.

791

Mary Downing Hahn

Wait Till Helen Comes (New York: Ticknor, 1986)

Age range: Grades 4-6

Subject(s): Ghosts; Stepfamilies

Major character(s): Molly, Child; Michael, Child; Heather, Child

Time period(s): Indeterminate

Locale(s): United States

What the book is about: Things go from bad to worse for Molly and Michael and their stepsister, Heather, when Heather becomes involved in a frightening relationship with the ghost of a dead child.

Where it's reviewed:
Horn Book, November/December 1986, page 744
School Library Journal, October 1986, page 176

Other books by the author:
Dead Man in Indian Creek, 1990
The Doll in the Garden, 1989
Daphne's Book, 1983
Sara's Summer, 1979

Other books you might like:
Eve Bunting, *The Haunting of SafeKeep*, 1985
    Sara, abandoned by her mother as a child, takes a summer caretaker job at a Victorian restoration site and meets an abandoned child and two ghosts.
Catherine Sefton, *The Haunting of Ellen*, 1974
    A teenage girl living on the coast of Northern Ireland begins to be haunted by a ghost who seems to be asking for help.
R.L. Stine, *Cheerleaders: The Third Evil*, 1992
    Corky is tormented night after night by dreams of her dead sister, Bobbi. What terrifying message is Bobbi trying to tell her?
David Storr Unwin, *The Girl in the Grove*, 1974
    Jon wants to be friends with Paul but he tries to prevent her from becoming acquainted with the strange girl she meets in the woods.
Robert Westall, *The Stones of Muncaster Cathedral*, 1993
    After Joe Clarke begins work on a spire of Muncaster's medieval cathedral, terrible things occur because of an evil force associated with a gargoyle.

792

Lynn Hall

Danza! (New York: Scribner's, 1981)

Age range: Grades 4-6

Subject(s): Animals/Horses; Grandparents

Major character(s): Paulo, Preteen

Time period(s): 1940s

Locale(s): Puerto Rico; United States

What the book is about: Eleven year old Paulo is present at the birth of a Paso Fino colt who is named Danza. An American, Major Kessler, later becomes interested in the horse and Paulo and Danza go to the States with him. Difficult family relationships and details about an unusual breed of horse make this more than just another "horse story."

Where it's reviewed:
Kirkus Reviews, November 15, 1981, page 1408
School Library Journal, November 1981, page 92

Other books by the author:
The Ghost of the Great River Inn, 1981
The Horse Trader, 1981
The Leaving, 1980
Mystery of the Plum Park Pony, 1980

Other books you might like:
Walter Farley, *The Young Black Stallion*, 1989
    The early life of the black stallion in the mountains of Arabia before he was captured and brought to the West.
Sherry Garland, *Best Horse on the Force*, 1991
    Brandon and Wayne try to take revenge on a mounted policeman and their joke backfires on their favorite horse, Skyjacker.
Anna Sewell, *Black Beauty*, 1990
    A horse of 19th century England tells his life story.
Nancy Springer, *Colt*, 1991
    A young boy with a crippling disease learns, through a horseback riding program, to reach out to help others.
Jean Thompson, *Ghost Horse of the Palisades*, 1986
    Molly's life with her widowed father is made exciting by the reappearance of a white stallion no one has been able to catch.

793

Lynn Hall

Illustrator: Ray Cruz

In Trouble Again, Zelda Hammersmith (San Diego: Harcourt, Brace, 1987)

Age range: Grades 4-6

Subject(s): Schools

Major character(s): Zelda Hammersmith, Preteen, 4th Grader

Time period(s): 1980s

Locale(s): United States

What the book is about: These are five episodes in the life of zany fourth grader Zelda Hammersmith, in which she deals with a bad report card, a boy who doesn't want to be her boyfriend, and other tribulations.

Where it's reviewed:
Center for Children's Books Bulletin, March 1988, page 137
Horn Book, May 1988, page 351

Other books by the author:
Fair Maiden, 1990
Here Comes Zelda Claus and Other Holiday Disasters, 1989
The Secret Life of Dagmar Schultz, 1988
Ride a Dark Horse, 1987

Other books you might like:
Joan Davenport Carris, *The Greatest Idea Ever*, 1990
    Fourth grade is turmoil for Gus whose ideas get him in trouble as he tries to train his dog, organize an art show and battle his enemy, Nanny Vincent.
Ilene Cooper, *Frances Dances*, 1991
    As she takes ballet lessons and acts in a school play, a timid fourth grader confronts her fears and learns a lesson about friendship.

Patricia Reilly Giff, *Fourth Grade Celebrity*, 1979
  Cassandra Eleanor Valentine searches for a way to become a celebrity at school.
Elizabeth Levy, *Keep Ms. Sugarman in the Fourth Grade*, 1992
  Jackie, who has always had trouble in school begins to improve with her new teacher, and is crushed when Ms. Sugarman is promoted to principle.
Elvira Woodruff, *Awfully Short for the Fourth Grade*, 1989
  Nine year old Noah disrupts school when his wish comes true. He becomes small and his miniature toy men come to life.

794

Lynn Hall

Murder at the Spaniel Show (New York: Scribner, 1988)

Age range: Grades 4-6

Subject(s): Blind; Animals/Dogs; Mystery and Detective Stories

Major character(s): Tabitha "Tabby", Teenager; Turner Quinn, Animal Trainer (kennel owner); Nancy Polaski, Animal Trainer (kennel manager)

Time period(s): 1980s

Locale(s): Katonah, New York

What the book is about: Tabitha (stuck with the nickname Tabby, which makes her feel like people are calling a cat) takes a job at Quintessence Kennel to learn about the care and training of show dogs. She loves the work, but finds herself in the middle of a mystery that threatens her life.

Where it's reviewed:
Booklist, December 1, 1988, page 640
Center for Children's Books Bulletin, November 1988, page 73
Kirkus Reviews, November 15, 1988, page 1674

Other books by the author:
The Soul of the Silver Dog, 1992
Windsong, 1992
Danger Dog, 1986
The Mystery of the Schoolhouse Dog, 1979

Other books you might like:
Natalie Savage Carlson, *Jaky or Dodo?*, 1978
  A Parisian mongrel successfully leads a double life until both of his "owners" enter him in the same dog show.
Betty Cavanna, *You Can't Take Twenty Dogs on a Date*, 1977
  When Jo is forced to give up her plans for college, she opens a boarding kennel for dogs.
Jim Kjelgaard, *Irish Red*, 1951
  Called runt, misfit, and troublemaker, Big Red's son Mike escapes from a training kennel to join the two men he loves in their forest retreat.
Barbara A. Steiner, *Dolby and the Woof-Off*, 1991
  Bo teaches his dog Dolby some unusual tricks in an attempt to win the Woof-Off contest.
Judie Wolkoff, *In a Pig's Eye*, 1986
  Best friends, Maisie and Blenda, fight and make up as all best friends do, through everything from a dog show competition to editing their own paper.

795

Lynn Hall

The Solitary (New York: Scribner, 1986)

Age range: Grades 6 and Up

Subject(s): Self-Reliance; Family Problems; Animals/Rabbits

Major character(s): Jane Cahill, Teenager; Iva Oliphant, Store Owner; Beau Smith, Neighbor

Time period(s): 1980s

Locale(s): Prosper, Arkansas (The Ozarks)

What the book is about: Five year old Jane was left with an aunt and uncle by her abused mother who had just killed her father. Now, at seventeen, Jane is ready to leave their household, which harbors so much hostility toward her, and be on her own. She returns to the house where she grew up, faces down the demons of memory, raises rabbits, and learns to care about herself. A friend remembers a quote which expresses the theme: "Loneliness is poverty of self. Solitude is richness of self."

Where it's reviewed:
Center for Children's Books Bulletin, December 1986, page 68
School Library Journal, January 1987, page 82

Awards the book has won:
Golden Kite Honor Book 1986

Other books by the author:
The Soul of the Silver Dog, 1992
Windsong, 1992
Halsey's Pride, 1990
Danza!, 1981

Other books you might like:
Cynthia D. Grant, *Kumquat May, I'll Always Love You*, 1986
  Abandoned by her mother, Livvy decides she is smart and self-reliant enough to live by herself if she can only keep her situation a secret.
Katherine Paterson, *Lyddie*, 1991
  Lyddie, a poor farm girl, is determined to gain her independence by becoming a factory worker in Massachusetts in the 1840s.
Gary Paulsen, *The River*, 1991
  Because of his success surviving alone in the wilderness for 54 days, Brian is asked to undergo a similar experience to help psychologists.
Susan Richards Shreve, *The Masquerade*, 1980
  When their father is jailed for embezzlement and their mother suffers a nervous breakdown, four young people try to cope with the circumstances.
Neal Shusterman, *What Daddy Did: A Novel*, 1991
  A fourteen year old boy living with his grandparents learns his father is to be released from prison after killing his mother and he is apprehensive.

796

Lynn Hall

Illustrator: Sandy Rabinowitz

The Something Special Horse (New York: Scribner's, 1985)

Age range: Grades 5-8

Subject(s): Fathers and Sons; Animals/Horses

Major character(s): Chris Eklund, Musician, Equestrian; Junior Ecklund, Teenager (Chris' brother)

Time period(s): 1980s

Locale(s): Bellefont, Missouri

What the book is about: Chris hates the fact that his father is a "kill buyer." He bids at auctions for horses no one else wants and sells them for meat. When a new mare, Lucy, comes in with a mysterious combination of letters and numbers branded on her neck, Chris runs away with her to save her from the meat market and determines to find the owner. If he can survive the grueling ten hour ride to Greencrest Farms, he may be successful.

Where it's reviewed:
School Library Journal, August 1986, page 37
Booklist, March 15, 1985, page 1058
School Library Journal, May 1985, page 109

Other books by the author:
Danza!, 1981
Dragon's Delight, 1981
Dragon Defiant, 1977
Flash, Dog of Old Egypt, 1973

Other books you might like:
Joanna Campbell, *The Wild Mustang*, 1989
    Tracy and her brother Colin rescue an injured black mustang which leads to problems as her father seems to hate all horses.
Marguerite Henry, *San Domingo, the Medicine Hat Stallion*, 1972
    In pre Civil-War Wyoming, a teen's life is complicated when his strangely hostile father trades the boy's beloved horse to the Pony Express.
Dorothy Nafus Morrison, *Somebody's Horse*, 1986
    Jenny is happy to be visiting relatives but is saddened by the sight of a very neglected horse.
Joyce Carol Thomas, *The Golden Pasture*, 1986
    The exquisite horse twelve year old Carl Lee finds on his grandfather's farm one summer helps him to understand his difficult father better.
Jean Thompson, *Ghost Horse of the Palisades*, 1986
    Molly's quiet life on the ranch with her widowed father is enlivened by the reappearance of a mysterious white stallion no one has ever captured.

797

William F. Hallstead

Tundra (New York: Crown, 1984)

Age range: Grades 5-9

Subject(s): Animals/Dogs; Divorce

Major character(s): Jamie Harwood, Teenager; Tundra, Dog; Marjorie Harwood, Parent (Jamie's mother)

Time period(s): 1980s

Locale(s): United States

What the book is about: Jamie already has her hands full, dealing with her divorced mother. When her Siberian Husky, Tundra, strays from home, Jamie is distraught. Tundra has

---

perilous adventures before returning to his mistress. He is hit by a car, shot at and dognapped. For all dog lovers.

Where it's reviewed:
Booklist, January 15, 1985, page 718
School Library Journal, February 1985, page 75

Other books by the author:
The Launching of Linda Bell, 1981
The Man Downstairs, 1979

Other books you might like:
Judie Angell, *A Home Is to Share.and Share.and Share*, 1984
    When the Muchmore children start taking in stray animals, their parents are at first good humored, but when the town shelter closes, business booms.
Helen Griffith, *Rafa's Dog*, 1983
    A Spanish child who befriends a stray dog finds that relationship helpful when tragedy strikes his family.
Emily Cheney Neville, *Garden of Broken Glass*, 1975
    An unsatisfactory relationship with his siblings and his alcoholic mother leads a young boy to find solace with neighborhood friends and a stray dog.
Alice Putnam, *Westering*, 1990
    Traveling with his family in a wagon train from Missouri to Oregon in 1850, Jason finds a stray dog that proves useful during the dangerous journey.
Barbara Wersba, *The Farewell Kid*, 1990
    Heidi decides against college to devote herself to stray dogs instead, but the appearance of photographer Harvey Beaumont adds another dimension.

798

Carol Hamilton

Illustrator: Jeremy Guitar

The Dawn Seekers (Niles, Illinois: Whitman, 1987)

Age range: Grades 4-6

Subject(s): Animals; Deserts

Major character(s): Quentin Carmichael, Rat; Harry, Centipede; Jeroboam, Jerboa

Time period(s): Indeterminate

Locale(s): Fictional Country (Desert)

What the book is about: When it is time for Quentin, a nocturnal kangaroo rat, to leave his mother and establish a home of his own, he meets Jeroboam who introduces him to the daylight world, and helps him build his home. Together they establish what they call the "Rodent School of Learning and Adventure." As they travel the desert together, they have many adventures, and it is Jeroboam who gives his life to save Quentin when he is attacked by a sidewinder rattlesnake.

Where it's reviewed:
Booklist, May 15, 1987, page 1446
Kirkus Reviews, January 1, 1987, page 56
School Library Journal, March 1987, page 160

Other books you might like:
Pat Hutchins, *Rats!*, 1989
    Sam's insistence on getting a pet rat eventually changes his family's entire daily routine and brings an exciting surprise.
Annabel Johnson, *I Am Leaper*, 1990

Leaper, a kangaroo rat who can talk with humans, and a boy named Julian defeat a "monster" who has been terrorizing the desert where she lives.

Mary DeBall Kwitz, *Shadow over Mousehaven Manor*, 1989
Minabell Mouse's animal friends come to her rescue when the Prairie Pirates, a gang of vicious rats, threaten to take over her ancestral home.

Sterling E. Lanier, *The War for the Lot*, 1969
When they lose their home to urban renewal, the city rats decide to invade a nearby wooded lot.

Joan Balfour Payne, *The Piebald Princess*, 1954
A lazy and imperious cat saves the water rats from a flood, loses her regal disguise, and is content to remain with the bog folk as a cook's cat.

799

Virginia Hamilton

Arilla Sun Down (New York: Greenwillow, 1976)

Age range: Grades 6 and Up

Subject(s): Interracial Marriage; African Americans; Indians of North America

Major character(s): Arilla Adams, Preteen, 7th Grader; Jack Sun Run, Teenager; Sun Adams, Parent

Time period(s): 1970s

Locale(s): Cliffville, Midwest

What the book is about: Seventh grader Arilla's mother is a black dancer and her father is part Black and part Native American. While Arilla identifies strongly with her mother, her brother identifies with his Indian heritage. An excellent story about teenage life in general, and the interracial family in particular.

Where it's reviewed:
Book World, April 8, 1979, page L2

Other books by the author:
The All Jahdu Storybook, 1991
Cousins, 1990
The House of Dies Drear, 1978
Justice and Her Brothers, 1978

Other books you might like:
Edna Walker Chandler, *Indian Paintbrush*, 1975
Maria Lopez, part Indian and part Mexican, has difficulty finding her own identity on the Sioux reservation where she lives.

Mark Mathabane, *Love in Black and White*, 1992
The triumph of love over prejudice and taboo; interracial marriages. (Non-fiction)

Margaret Sacks, *Beyond Safe Boundaries*, 1989
Elizabeth comes of age in 1960s South Africa as her older sister joins a secret group to oppose apartheid.

Alan Schroeder, *Josephine Baker*, 1991
Biography of the black American entertainer who achieved fame in Paris in the 1920s and was awarded the French Legion of Honor for her work in WWII.

Mildred D. Taylor, *Let the Circle Be Unbroken*, 1981
Four black children in rural Mississippi during the Depression experience bigotry and hard times, but learn from their parents pride and self-respect.

800

Virginia Hamilton

The Bells of Christmas (San Diego: Harcourt, Brace, 1989)

Age range: Grades 4-6

Subject(s): Christmas; Family Life

Major character(s): Jason, Child

Time period(s): 1890s (1890)

Locale(s): Ohio

What the book is about: Twelve year old Jason describes the wonderful Christmas of 1890 that he and his family celebrated in Springfield, Ohio.

Where it's reviewed:
Kirkus Reviews, October 1, 1989, page 1474
School Library Journal, October 1989, page 42

Other books by the author:
Anthony Burns: The Defeat and Triumph of a Fugitive Slave, 1988
In the Beginning, 1988
The People Could Fly, 1985
House of Dies Drear, 1968

Other books you might like:
Mildred Ames, *Grandpa Jake and the Grand Christmas*, 1990
Lizzie's family is suffering hard times during the Depression until Grandpa Jake appears.

Betty Bates, *Say Cheese*, 1984
When Christy wins $100 in a radio contest, she is torn between buying something for the whole family or something for herself.

Rosalie Maggio, *The Music Box Christmas*, 1990
Despite recent troubles, Nick is determined to find a way for the family to have a happy Christmas celebration.

June Lewis Shore, *What's the Matter with Wakefield?*, 1974
"Borrowing" the class money to buy himself a fishing rod brings Wakefield grief when he is unable to pay it back.

Nola Thacker, *Till's Christmas*, 1991
Eleven year old Till, a modern day Scrooge, thinks her family's Christmas customs are hokey until she catches the Christmas spirit.

801

Virginia Hamilton

Cousins (New York: Philomel, 1990)

Age range: Grades 5 and Up

Subject(s): Death; Cousins

Major character(s): Cammy, Teenager; Gram Tut, Grandparent; Patty Ann, Cousin

Time period(s): 1990s

Locale(s): United States

What the book is about: Patty Ann is near-perfect and sometimes patronizing. She drowns while saving the life of another cousin. Cammy feels everything intensely. Only with Gram Tut's wisdom and the return of her father can Cammy work through her grief and loss, and accept the reality that someday, Gram will die too.

Where it's reviewed:
Booklist, October 1, 1990, page 330
Kirkus Reviews, August 1, 1990, page 1085

Other books by the author:
The Bells of Christmas, 1990
The Dark Way, 1990
Justice and Her Brothers, 1989
The People Could Fly, 1985

Other books you might like:
Betsy Byars, *A Blossom Promise*, 1987
　After a big flood in Alderson County, the Blossom family copes with the aftermath in their own unique style.
Vera Cleaver, *Belle Pruitt*, 1988
　When her baby brother dies of pneumonia, 11 year old Belle is left to cope with the effects on her family.
Marilyn Halvorson, *Cowboys Don't Cry*, 1984
　After his mother's death and his father's alcoholism, Shane hope a move to Alberta will turn things around.
Marya Smith, *Across the Creek*, 1989
　Rye's friendship with a mysterious girl across the creek helps him to cope with the death of his mother.
Paul Zindel, *A Begonia for Miss Applebaum*, 1989
　Discovering that their beloved former teacher is terminally ill, Henry and Zelda join her in confronting death with courage.

802

Virginia Hamilton

Illustrator: Eros Keith

The House of Dies Drear (New York: Macmillan, 1968)

Age range: Grades 4-7

Subject(s): African Americans; Mystery and Detective Stories

Major character(s): Thomas Small, Teenager; Pluto, Maintenance Worker

Time period(s): 1960s

Locale(s): Ohio

What the book is about: Thirteen year old Thomas comes with his family to Ohio because his father is to teach college history in the town where Dies Drear had once operated a station on the Underground Railway. They move into his long abandoned house and their neighbors try to scare them away from finding lost treasure.

Where it's reviewed:
Horn Book, October 1968, page 563
Library Journal, October 15, 1968, page 4731

Awards the book has won:
Edgar Allan Poe Award

Other books by the author:
Drylongso, 1992
Cousins, 1990
The Mystery of Drear House, 1987 (Sequel to "House of Dies Drear")
Junius Over Far, 1985

Other books you might like:
Helen Pierce Jacob, *The Diary of Strawbridge Place*, 1978
　A family of Quakers operates a station on the Underground Railroad and spirits slaves from Ashtabula, Ohio, across Lake Erie to freedom.

Betty Miles, *I Would If I Could*, 1982
　During 1930, a girl spends the summer visiting her grandmother in rural Ohio.
F.N. Monjo, *The Drinking Gourd*, 1970
　A New England white boy helps a African-American family escape slavery on the Underground Railroad.
Ellen Raskin, *The Westing Game*, 1978
　A convoluted and fascinating mystery that involves a group of people deciphering a will to see who inherits a fortune.
R. Conrad Stein, *The Story of the Underground Railroad*, 1981
　A simple history of an engrossing aspect of the struggle against slavery. (Non-fiction)

803

Virginia Hamilton

Illustrator: Barry Moser

In the Beginning: Creation Stories from Around the World (New York: Harcourt, 1988)

Age range: Grades 5-7

Subject(s): Creation; Mythology

Time period(s): Indeterminate Past

Locale(s): Earth

What the book is about: An illustrated collection of twenty-five myths from various parts of the world, explaining the creation of the world.

Where it's reviewed:
Booklist, September 15, 1988, page 160
Kirkus Reviews, September 15, 1988, page 1403

Awards the book has won:
Newbery Honor

Other books by the author:
The All Jahdu Storybook, 1991
Cousins, 1990
Dark Way Stories from the Spirit World, 1990
The People Could Fly, 1985

Other books you might like:
Padraic Colum, *The Golden Fleece and the Heroes Who Lived Before Achilles*, 1921
　Describes the cycle of myths about the Argonauts and the quest for the Golden Fleece and tales of the creation of Heaven and Earth.
Paul Goble, *The Great Race of Birds and Animals*, 1985
　A retelling of the Cheyenne and Sioux myth about the Great Race, a contest to settle whether humans or buffalo should be the guardians of Creation.
Ted Hughes, *Tales of the Early World*, 1988
　Creation stories including, "How Sparrow Saved the Birds," "The Guardian," "The Making of Parrot," and "The Shawl of the Beauty of the World."
Frederick Laing, *Tales From Scandinavia*, 1979
　A collection of Scandinavian myths which explain the creation of gods, giants and people.
Richard Lewis, *All of You Was Singing*, 1991
　A lyrical account of the earth's creation and the advent of music.

804

Virginia Hamilton

Justice and Her Brothers (New York: Harcourt, 1978)

Age range: Grades 6-8

Subject(s): African Americans; Brothers and Sisters; Fantasy

Major character(s): Justice "Ticey" Douglas, Preteen; Thomas Douglas, Twin; Lee Douglas, Twin

Time period(s): Indeterminate

Locale(s): United States

What the book is about: Three children, Justice Douglas and her identical older twin brothers, Thomas and Lee, find themselves in a strange relationship because they all have gifts of supersensory powers. Their adventures read like science fiction, or is this just another way to look at reality? Followed by *Dustland* and *The Gathering*.

Where it's reviewed:
Booklist, October 1, 1978, page 294
Hornbook, October 1978, page 517
Kirkus Reviews, November 15, 1978, page 1253

Other books by the author:
A Little Love, 1984
The Magical Adventures of Pretty Pearl, 1983
Dustland, 1980
The Gathering, 1980

Other books you might like:
Charles L. Grant, *Fire Mask*, 1991
    Cliff's premonitions and dreams about a mysterious fire lead him and his friends into a fatal confrontation with perpetrators of a terrifying evil.
Jesse Harris, *The Obsession*, 1993
    McKenzie Gold's friendship with Sharon Roderick, the new girl in town, turns deadly when Sharon starts to abuse McKenzie's psychic powers.
Kathryn Lasky, *Shadows in the Water*, 1992
    The Starbuck Twins use their telepathic powers and the aid of some dolphins help their father catch a gang dumping toxic waste in the Florida Keys.
Madeleine L'Engle, *Many Waters*, 1986
    The Murry twins are accidentally sent back to a Biblical period, in which mythical beasts roam the desert and a man named Noah is building a boat.
Janet Louise Lunn, *Twin Spell*, 1969
    Strangely attracted to an antique doll, twins buy the toy and soon find themselves haunted by powerful memories of twins who were owners of the doll.

805

Virginia Hamilton

Illustrator: Jerry Pinkney

The Planet of Junior Brown (New York: Macmillan, 1971)

Age range: Grades 5 and Up

Subject(s): Friendship; African Americans

Major character(s): Junior Brown, Teenager (musician); Buddy Clark, Teenager (streetperson)

Time period(s): 1970s

Locale(s): United States

What the book is about: The "planet" is a ten planet solar system build by the school janitor. Junior is a 300 pound musical prodigy with an overprotective mother. Buddy is a homeless classmate who lives by his wits. Together, they hide out in a secret cellar room at school.

Where it's reviewed:
Library Journal, October 15, 1971, page 3474
Saturday Review of Literature, November 13, 1971, page 61

Awards the book has won:
Newbery Honor

Other books by the author:
The All Jahdu Storybook, 1991
Cousins, 1990
M.C. Higgins, the Great, 1974
Zeely, 1967

Other books you might like:
Bruce Brooks, *The Moves Make the Man: A Novel*, 1984
    A Black boy and an emotionally troubled white boy in North Carolina form a precarious friendship.
Robert Lipsyte, *The Contender*, 1967
    A Harlen high school drop-out decides boxing isn't the life he wants and he makes other choices.
Kay Smith, *Skeeter*, 1989
    Two young boys befriend an old Black man who is a legendary hunter.
Eleanora E. Tate, *Just an Overnight Guest*, 1980
    When a disruptive and neglected four year old moves in with her family, Margie has trouble adjusting.
Mildred Pitts Walter, *Mariah Keeps Cool*, 1990
    Twelve year old Mariah plans a great summer but her sister Lynn ruins her plans.

806

Virginia Hamilton

Sweet Whispers, Brother Rush (New York: Philomel, 1982)

Age range: Grades 5-8

Subject(s): African Americans; Ghosts; Mentally Handicapped

Major character(s): Tree, Teenager; Dab, Handicapped (retarded); Brother Rush, Spirit

Time period(s): 1980s

Locale(s): United States

What the book is about: Tree's mom is a practical nurse who is gone most of the time. Tree becomes Dab's caretaker. He has a rare disease called porphyria. Through flashbacks with Brother Rush, a ghost, she comes to understand what happened to Dab.

Where it's reviewed:
Center for Children's Books Bulletin, July/August 1982, page 207
Horn Book, October 1982, page 505

Awards the book has won:
Boston Globe/Horn Book Award 1983
Newbery Honor 1983

Other books by the author:
The All Jahdu Storybook, 1991
Cousins, 1990
The Magical Adventures of Pretty Pearl, 1983
Arilla Sun Down, 1976

Other books you might like:
Mildred Ames, *Conjuring Summer In*, 1986
Bernadette experiments with psychic forces in her unhappiness over the family's move to California, but finds unexpected and dangerous consequences.
Clayton Bess, *Story for a Black Night*, 1982
An African father tells his son about the disaster that followed the night a baby with smallpox was abandoned in his family's house.
Eloise Greenfield, *Childtimes*, 1979
Childhood memories of three generations of black women who grew up between the 1880s and 1950s.
Donn Kushner, *Uncle Jacob's Ghost Story*, 1986
Paul discovers the story of his Great Uncle Jacob who believed that the ghosts of two friends followed him from Poland to America.
Sharon Bell Mathis, *Listen for the Fig Tree*, 1974
A black teen's first celebration of Kwanza gives her a sense of the past and strength to deal with her troubled mother and her own blindness.

807

Virginia Hamilton

Illustrator: Symeon Shimin

Zeely (New York: Macmillan, 1967)

Age range: Grades 4-7

Subject(s): African Americans

Major character(s): Elizabeth "Geeder" Perry, Child; Zeely Tabor, Neighbor

Time period(s): 1960s

Locale(s): United States

What the book is about: Geeder and her little brother spend the summer on their uncle's farm. She is fascinated by six-and-a-half foot tall Zeely, the daughter of a neighbor farmer. When Geeder finds a picture of a Watusi queen who looks like Zeely, she tells everyone she is really a queen.

Where it's reviewed:
Horn Book, April 1967, page 205
Library Journal, May 15, 1967, page 2028

Awards the book has won:
Nancy Bloch Memorial Award 1967

Other books by the author:
The All Jadhu Storybook, 1991
Cousins, 1990
The People Could Fly, 1985
M.C. Higgins, the Great, 1974

Other books you might like:
Georgene Faulkner, *Melindy's Happy Summer*, 1949
A young black girl from Boston spends part of her summer on a farm in Maine.
Ernest J. Gaines, *A Long Day in November*, 1971
A young black boy on a cane plantation remembers the day his parents separated and were reconciled.

Joan Kane Nichols, *All but the Right Folks*, 1985
A young black boy discovers the mother he never knew was white and spends an unforgetable summer with his white grandmother in New York City.
Joyce Carol Thomas, *The Golden Pasture*, 1986
12 year old Carol Lee develops a friendship with a beautiful horse on his grandfather's farm, and comes to understand his difficult father better.
Johnniece Marshall Wilson, *Robin on His Own*, 1990
A black boy whose family is in transition comes to terms with the death of his mother.

808

Dennis Hamley

Illustrator: Meg Rutherford

Hare's Choice (New York: Delacorte, 1988)

Age range: Grades 5 and Up

Subject(s): Death; Animals/Rabbits; Schools

Time period(s): Indeterminate

Locale(s): England

What the book is about: A dead hare is immortalized when a group of schoolchildren make up a story about her. Since she is a "book" rabbit, she has the choice of ordinary animal heaven or the literary heaven where she will meet Peter Rabbit, Fiver, Wilbur, etc. Readers must draw their own conclusions about which choice she will make.

Where it's reviewed:
Center for Children's Books Bulletin, May 1990, page 214
School Library Journal, May 1990, page 106

Other books by the author:
Tigger and Friends, 1988

Other books you might like:
Bruce Brooks, *Everywhere*, 1990
Afraid his grandfather will die after suffering a heart attack, a boy agrees to join Dooley in performing a mysterious ritual called soul switching.
Elizabeth Coatsworth, *The Cat Who Went to Heaven*, 1958
A little cat comes to the home of a poor Japanese artist and, by humility and devotion, brings him good fortune.
Emily Rhoads Johnson, *A House Full of Strangers*, 1992
Flora finds solace in the woods near her home following the death of her grandmother and the arrival of a large, noisy family of relatives.
Eleanora E. Tate, *Front Porch Stories at the One Room School*, 1992
Margie and her cousin forget their boredom when Margie's father entertains them with stories about people and events in their small town's past.
Margot Zemach, *Jake and Honeybunch Go To Heaven*, 1982
The exuberance of a man and his mule newly arrived in heaven causes so much furor that God gives them one last chance before He throws them out.

809

Diane Johnston Hamm

Bunkhouse Journal (New York: Scribner's, 1990)

Age range: Grades 5 and Up

Subject(s): Ranch Life; Fathers and Sons; Diaries

Major character(s): Sandy Mannix, Teenager, Runaway

Time period(s): 1910s (1910)

Locale(s): Wyoming

What the book is about: Sandy has run away from Denver and an alcoholic father to live on his cousin's ranch in Wyoming. He has to deal with his father's neglect, his brother's rejection of their father, and his mother's death years before.

Where it's reviewed:
Horn Book, November 1990, page 748
School Library Journal, December 1990, page 102

Other books you might like:
Marion Dane Bauer, *Face to Face*, 1991
  Thirteen year old Michael sets out to see his father, a rafting guide in Colorado, whom he has not seen in eight years.
Barthe DeClements, *Monkey See, Monkey Do*, 1990
  Jerry's home and school life are both marred by the fact that his father cannot seem to stay out of jail.
Jenny Nimmo, *The Snow Spider*, 1986
  On his tenth birthday, Gwyn discovers he has magical powers that help him heal his relationship with his father.
Graham Salisbury, *Blue Skin of the Sea*, 1992
  Sonny tries to come to terms with his feelings for his fisherman father and the vast sea which dominates his life.
Robert Kimmel Smith, *Mostly Michael*, 1987
  The diary of eleven year old Michael, as he copes with the ups and downs of family life.

810

Sibyl Hancock

Illustrator: Erick Ingraham

Old Blue (New York: Putnam, 1980)

Age range: Grades 1-3

Subject(s): American West

Major character(s): Davy, Child; Old Blue, Bull

Time period(s): 1870s (1878)

Locale(s): Texas; Kansas

What the book is about: An easy reader telling about a boy's first trail drive and the lead steer, Old Blue. Old Blue likes to sleep around the campfire, and with the cowboys, leads the rest of the cattle on the trail drive. Old Blue led cattle from Texas to Kansas for eight years, lived to be twenty years old, and his horns are now on display in a museum in Canyon, Texas.

Where it's reviewed:
Booklist, January 15, 1981, page 705
School Library Journal, December 1980, page 65
School Library Journal, February 1982, page 37

Other books by the author:
Esteban and the Ghost, 1983
Freaky Francie, 1979
The Blazing Hills, 1975
The Grizzly Bear, 1974

Other books you might like:
Catherine E. Chambers, *Texas Roundup : Life on the Range*, 1984

A boy learns a great deal about life on the range when he is at last allowed to accompany the ranch hands on the spring roundup.
Alvin G. Davis, *A Day in the Life of a Cowboy*, 1991
  Describes the activities and ditues of a Texas cowboy on the first day of the spring roundup.
James McCague, *When Cowboys Rode the Chisholm Trail*, 1969
  Reveals the excitement and danger of a cowpuncher's life by following a cattle drive on the Chisholm Trail in 1870.
Neil Morris, *Longhorn on the Move*, 1989
  Presents the adventures of a young cowboy during a cattle drive from Texas to the north.
Robert M. Quackenbush, *Texas Trail to Calamity: A Miss Mallard Mystery*, 1986
  When her horse runs away with her across the desert, Miss Mallard, the famous ducktective, finds herself at a forbidding ranch.

811

Emily Hanlon

The Swing (Scarsdale: Bradbury, 1979)

Age range: Grades 5-7

Subject(s): Deafness; Honesty; Stepfamilies

Major character(s): Beth Hampton, Preteen; Danny Grady, Teenager

Time period(s): 1970s

Locale(s): Chester Falls

What the book is about: Beth and Danny both find solace in the swing that hangs from an old oak between their houses. Beth is deaf and Danny is forced into his stepfather's business, slaughtering cows, which he detests. Climbing a mountain without permission, Beth encounters a mother bear and cub, and the hunting of the bears forces a wedge between Beth and Danny.

Where it's reviewed:
Horn Book, August 1979, page 414
Kirkus Reviews, July 15, 1979, page 797

Other books by the author:
Love Is No Excuse, 1982
Circle Home, 1981
The Wing and the Flame, 1980
It's Too Late for Sorry, 1978

Other books you might like:
Elizabeth De Trevino, *Nacar, the White Deer*, 1963
  Lalo, a mute herder, nurses a sickly white deer until the inevitable parting causes a crisis.
Wayne Dodd, *A Time of Hunting*, 1975
  A teenager's values and perceptions change during the Depression days in Oklahoma, especially regarding hunting, his only way of earning money.
Veronica Robinson, *David in Silence*, 1965
  A deaf boy encounters varying reactions when he first shares the usual activities of children who can hear.
Susan Richards Shreve, *The Gift of the Girl Who Couldn't Hear*, 1991
  Two friends, one of whom is deaf, help each other when tryouts are held for a seventh grade production of "Annie."
Virginia Frances Voight, *Red Blade and the Black Bear*, 1973

An Indian boy befriends an orphaned cub, the bond between them grows stronger as each saves the other's life.

What the book is about: Obi escapes from slavery during the Civil War, joins a black Union regiment, and soon becomes involved in the fighting at Fort Pillow, Tennessee. The historical setting and detail do not overwhelm the story, which shows Obi as a thoughtful young man concerned with both freedom and loyalty. Each chapter begins with quotes from various sources which shed light on the historical situation.

Where it's reviewed:
Center for Children's Books Bulletin, July/August 1986, page 209
School Library Journal, August 1986, page 100

Other books by the author:
Out From This Place, 1988
Yellow Bird and Me, 1986
Home Boy, 1982
The Gift-Giver, 1980

Other books you might like:
Jean Fritz, *Brady*, 1960
   A young Pennsylvania boy takes part in the pre-Civil War anti-slavery activities.
Betsy Haynes, *Slave Girl*, 1973
   Relates the trials of a young slave girl at the beginning of the Civil War.
Belinda Hurmence, *Tancy*, 1984
   At the end of the Civil War, a young house slave on a small plantation searches for her mother who was mysteriously sold when Tancy was a baby.
Milton Meltzer, *Underground Man*, 1972
   A courageous young white man aids slaves escaping from Kentucky in pre-Civil War days.
Margaret Walker, *Jubilee*, 1966
   The fortunes of a mulatto girl, as a slave during the Civil War and then as a woman freed by the Emancipation Proclamation.

812

Joyce Hansen

The Gift-Giver (Boston: Houghton Mifflin, 1980)

Age range: Grades 4-6

Subject(s): Responsibility; African Americans; Foster Homes

Major character(s): Doris, Preteen, 5th Grader; Sherman, Preteen; Amir, Preteen

Time period(s): 1980s

Locale(s): New York, New York

What the book is about: Doris and her fifth grade friends like playing together, but Doris' parents keep her home to avoid the drug scene. She occasionally defies her parents and goes anyway, and we see her friendship develop with Sherman and Amir, both of whom live in foster homes. Doris proves her reliability when both her parents must work and she cares for the apartment and her younger brother, Gerald.

Where it's reviewed:
Center for Children's Books Bulletin, January 1981, p 94
Horn Book, December 1980, page 641

Other books by the author:
Out From This Place, 1988
Which Way Freedom?, 1986
Yellow Bird and Me, 1986
Home Boy, 1982

Other books you might like:
Victoria Boutis, *Cooking Out*, 1988
   Happy to be part of the "in" crowd, Ellen's growing awareness of her parents' social concerns forces her to make a choice about what really matters.
Jessie Haas, *Keeping Barney*, 1982
   Actually having a horse and taking care of it turns out to be more than Sarah bargained for.
Judy K. Morris, *The Crazies and Sam*, 1983
   A boy living in Washington, D.C. tries to come to terms with some of the contradictions in life.
Neal Shusterman, *The Shadow Club*, 1988
   A group of friends form a club of "second bests" and play tricks on each other's rivals.
Linda L. Strauss, *The Alexandra Ingredient*, 1988
   Alexandra is trying hard to convince her parents that she is mature and responsible and she is faced with all kinds of challenges.

813

Joyce Hansen

Which Way Freedom? (New York: Walker, 1986)

Age range: Grades 6-9

Subject(s): Civil War; Slavery

Major character(s): Obi, Slave

Time period(s): 1860s

Locale(s): Tennessee

814

Ron Hansen

Illustrator: Margot Tomes

The Shadowmaker (New York: Harper, 1987)

Age range: Grades 3-5

Subject(s): Fantasy; Wizards

Major character(s): Shadowmaker, Wizard; Drizzle, Orphan; Soot, Orphan

Time period(s): Indeterminate Past

Locale(s): Fictional Country

What the book is about: Drizzle and her brother, Soot, save the day when they outwit Shadowmaker, who is selling the wrong shadows to everyone.

Where it's reviewed:
Horn Book, September/October 1987, page 605
School Library Journal, August 1987, page 83

Other books you might like:
Amy Aitken, *Ruby the Red Knight*, 1983
   Ruby, imagining she is a Knight of the Round Table, tries to solve the mystery of the disappearing realm and faces a giant, a dragon, and a wizard.
Elizabeth Starr Hill, *Ever-After Island*, 1977

Two children accompany their scientist father on a trip to a remote island where they discover elves, mermaids, a wizard and other magical creatures.

Maxine Kumin, *The Wizard's Tears*, 1975
The new wizard tries to solve all the town's problems, but carelessness with his own magic tears creates a tragedy instead.

Susan Saunders, *Dorothy and the Magic Belt*, 1985
Dorothy, the Tin Woodman, the Scarecrow, and Jack Pumpkinhead, travel across Oz in search of the young wizard who stole Princess Ozma's magic belt.

Nancy Springer, *Red Wizard*, 1990
Ryan is taken into a fantasy world by an bumbling wizard, where he may avert a crisis with a rebel warlock and solve a problem with his own father.

815

June Andrea Hanson

Illustrator: Gloria Singer

Summer of the Stallion (New York: Macmillan, 1979)

Age range: Grades 6-8

Subject(s): Grandparents; Animals/Horses

Major character(s): Janey Anderson, Preteen; Grandpa Anderson, Grandparent

Time period(s): 1970s

Locale(s): Forsyth, Montana

What the book is about: Janey's father and grandfather have a hard time with each other. A stallion changes everything. Wild and beautiful, powerful and aggressive, the horse is a troublemaker and Grandpa wants him off the place. Janey takes an important first step towards maturity and independence when she takes a hand in the situation.

Where it's reviewed:
Booklist, April 15, 1979, page 1295
Kirkus Reviews, 1979, page 636
School Library Journal, March 1979, page 139

Other books by the author:
Winter of the Owl, 1980

Other books you might like:
Patricia Beatty, *Something to Shout About*, 1976
The women of a Montana mining town disrupt life when they try to raise money for a new school.

Barbara Corcoran, *A Row of Tigers*, 1969
A Montana tomboy struggling to adjust to her father's death makes friends with a hunchback who has spent many years trying to accept his misfortune.

Robert Scott McKinnon, *Moose, Bruce and the Goose*, 1969
An abandoned greyhound puppy and a wounded Canada goose form a partnership that becomes famous throughout Montana.

Sam Savitt, *Wild Horse Running*, 1973
A Montana boy is torn by his desire to keep an injured mustang and his conviction that wild horses should be protected in their natural state.

Ann Warren Turner, *Third Girl From the Left*, 1986
Sarah leaves Maine for the harsh Montana environment as a mail-order bride, and is soon left a widow with a 2000-acre ranch to run.

816

Mark Jonathan Harris

Come the Morning (New York: Bradbury, 1989)

Age range: Grades 5-8

Subject(s): Homeless; Family Problems

Major character(s): Ben Gibson, Streetperson, Teenager

Time period(s): 1980s

Locale(s): El Paso, Texas; Los Angeles, California

What the book is about: After leaving his home in El Paso for Los Angeles, hoping to find his father, Ben, along with his mother and siblings, winds up on the streets. Mrs. Gibson has a letter from her husband, but the return address is a false lead, and the family's meager funds will allow them only a room in a skid-row flat hotel. When their remaining cash is stolen, the entire family is out on the streets.

Where it's reviewed:
Horn Book, September/October 1989, page 629
School Library Journal, March 1989, page 198

Other books by the author:
Solay, 1993
Confessions of a Prime Time Kid, 1985
The Last Run, 1981
With a Wave of the Wand, 1980

Other books you might like:
Karen Ackerman, *The Leaves in October*, 1991
After her mother leaves them, nine year old Livvy struggles to understand why she and her father and brother are living in a shelter for the homeless.

Eth Clifford, *Never Hit a Ghost with a Baseball Bat*, 1993
While exploring a trolley car museum, eleven year old Mary Rose and her sister, Jo-Beth, encounter strange voices and other weird events.

Hila Colman, *Rich and Famous Like My Mom*, 1988
Cass ventures into the streets to escape her overprotective home, and encounters a way of life she never imagined.

James Howe, *Dew Drop Dead: A Sebastian Barth Mystery*, 1990
While starting a homeless shelter at the church, Sebastian and his friends, Corrie and David, solve a mystery involving a dead man found in an inn.

Ellen Switzer, *Anyplace But Here: Young, Alone and Homeless*, 1992
Examines the problems that lead young people to live on the streets. Also provides information on how to get help. (nonfiction)

817

Mark Jonathan Harris

With a Wave of the Wand (New York: Lothrop, 1980)

Age range: Grades 4-6

Subject(s): Magic; Divorce

Major character(s): Marlee, Preteen, 5th Grader; Jeremy, Child; Mr. Tomaro, Magician

Time period(s): 1940s

Locale(s): Venice, California

What the book is about: When her parents separate, Marlee, a fifth grader, resents the move to a quaint old house in Venice, California. She even manages not to like Mr. Tomaro, a magician who lives next door, and continues to hope for her parents' reconciliation. Gradually, Mr. Tomaro interests Marlee not only in magic, but in ways to make friends and deal with reality.

Where it's reviewed:
Kirkus Reviews, March 15, 1980, page 3651
School Library Journal, March 1980, page 132

Other books by the author:
Confessions of a Prime Time Kid, 1985
The Last Run, 1981

Other books you might like:
Alice Mulcahey Fleming, *Welcome to Grossville*, 1985
    The summer after his parents' divorce, Michael learns the true meaning of friendship and new values in his changing life.
Johanna Hurwitz, *DeDe Takes Charge!*, 1984
    A year after her father has left for good, DeDe helps her mother cope with the realities of life after divorce.
Jean Davies Okimoto, *My Mother Is Not Married to My Father*, 1979
    Cynthia and her little sister try to adjust to their parents' separation and divorce.
Lois Ruby, *Pig-Out Inn*, 1987
    Spending the summer helping her mom run a truckstop diner, Dovi becomes involved in a custody battle over her brother.
Robert Kimmel Smith, *The Squeaky Wheel*, 1990
    Mark has trouble adjusting to a new neighborhood, new friends, and his father's absence.

| 818 |

Terry Webb Harshman

Illustrator: Doug Cushman

Porcupine's Pajama Party (New York: Harper, 1988)

Age range: Grades 1-3

Series: I Can Read Book

Subject(s): Fear; Monsters

Major character(s): Otter, Baker; Porcupine, Spirit

Time period(s): Indeterminate

Locale(s): Fictional Country

What the book is about: Porcupine, Otter and Owl have fun at a pajama party, watch a scary movie, "Monster Bat," and then cannot sleep.

Where it's reviewed:
Booklist, July 1988, page 1843
Kirkus June 15, 1988, page 898
School Library Journal, October 1988, page 121

Other books you might like:
David A. Adler, *Cam Jansen and the Mystery of the Monster Movie*, 1984
    A fifth grader uses her photographic memory, her mother, and her friend, Eric, to find a missing reel of a monster film they go to see.
Eve Feldman, *Animals Don't Wear Pajamas*, 1992

Describes what sixteen different animals do at bedtime, including the elephant, sea otter, and parrotfish.
Charlotte Herman, *On the Way to the Movies*, 1980
    Simon is sure his little brother is too young to go to the monster movie with him, but on the way to the movies he begins to wonder.
Amy Hest, *Pajama Party*, 1992
    Casey, Jenny and Kate have a pajama party complete with sleeping bags, chocolate chip cookies and scary stories.
Susan Pearson, *The Spooky Sleepover*, 1991
    Two weeks before Halloween Ernie invites three friends for her first sleepover, complete with a feast, games, and ghost stories.

| 819 |

Carole Hart

Illustrator: Edward Frascino

Delilah (New York: Harper, 1973)

Age range: Grades 3-4

Subject(s): Family Life; Sports/Basketball

Major character(s): Delilah, Child

Time period(s): 1970s

Locale(s): United States

What the book is about: Ten year old Delilah loves playing basketball with the garbageman, drumming, and singing with a band in the park. Both of her parents work and take turns with the housework. She has many adventures and loving parents, though Delilah cries when they fight. High humor and adventure.

Where it's reviewed:
Center for Children's Books Bulletin, April 1974, page 130
Kirkus Reviews, October 1, 1973, page 1096

Other books by the author:
Now or Never, 1991 (Older readers)

Other books you might like:
Christel Kleitsch, *Cousin Markie and Other Disasters*, 1992
    Ben doesn't get along with his younger cousin and is sure his visit will ruin his own chances to get a skateboard.
Lois Lowry, *Attaboy, Sam!*, 1992
    Sam is able to help his sister with the poem she is writing for their mother's birthday but his efforts to create a special perfume are disastrous.
Sharon Bell Mathis, *The Hundred Penny Box*, 1975
    Michael's love for his great-great-aunt leads him to intercede with his mother, who wants to toss out all her old things.
William Taylor, *Knitwits*, 1992
    Nine year old Kenny's life becomes chaotic when he gets himself into a bet that he can knit something for the baby his mother is expecting.
Martin Waddell, *Little Obie and the Flood*, 1991
    Through hardships and good times, Little Obie, Grandad, Effie and newly adopted Marty grow to be a real family.

| 820 |

Peter Hartling

Crutches (New York: Lothrop, 1988)

Age range: Grades 6 and Up

Subject(s): Friendship

Major character(s): Thomas, Child; Crutches, Veteran; Bronka, Rescuer

Time period(s): 1940s

Locale(s): Vienna, Austria; Germany

What the book is about: Separated from his mother at a train station, Thomas is befriended by a one-legged vet who helps Thomas survive, protecting him, and shepherding him out of Austria and into Germany.

Where it's reviewed:
Horn Book, November/December 1988, page 787
School Library Journal, November 1988, page 111

Awards the book has won:
Mildred L. Batchelder Award 1989

Other books by the author:
Old John, 1990
Oma, 1977

Other books you might like:
Doris Orgel, *Devil in Vienna*, 1978
    A Jewish girl and the daughter of a Nazi struggle to maintain their friendship in 1938.
Christine Nostlinger, *Fly Away Home*, 1975
    A young girl recalls what life was like in Vienna toward the end of WWII.
Jane Louise Curry, *Ice Ghosts Mystery*, 1972
    The three Bird children become involved in a literally earth-shaking plot when they fly to Austria in search of the missing Mr. Bird.
Ursula Moray Williams, *Boy in a Barn*, 1970
    A boy stranded in an Austria village takes refuge in the same barn in which his father hid just 20 years earlier.

821

Peter Hartling

Old John (New York: Lothrop, 1990)

Age range: Grades 4-7

Subject(s): Old Age; Grandparents

Major character(s): Old John, Grandparent; Laura Schirmers, Preteen; Jacob Schirmers, Child

Time period(s): 1990s

Locale(s): Stuttgart, Germany

What the book is about: John may be old, but he won't be forgotten. He turns his family completely upside down when he moves in with them. It takes a lot of doing, but he finally wins his entire family over in this very funny book.

Where it's reviewed:
Booklist, May 15, 1990, page 1800
School Library Journal, July 1990, page 76

Other books by the author:
Crutches, 1988
Oma, 1977

Other books you might like:
Berthe Amoss, *The Mockingbird Song*, 1988

Unable to get along with a new stepmother, eleven year old Lindy goes to live with the elderly lady next door.
LouAnn Gaeddert, *A Summer Like Turnips*, 1989
    While spending his summer at his grandfather's retirement village, Bruce helps gramps recover from the death of his wife.
Kristi Holl, *No Strings Attached*, 1988
    June has trouble adjusting to life with her foster grandfather, but loves him as part of the family.
Gary Paulsen, *The Haymeadow*, 1992
    Fourteen year old John comes of age and gains self reliance the summer he spends in the Wyoming mountains.
Mary C. Ryan, *The Voice from Mendelsohn's Maple*, 1990
    Penny's expectations of a boring summer are changed when she meets an elderly, practically naked, woman in a tree and becomes mixed up in a mystery.

822

Peter Hartling

Illustrator: Jutta Ash

Oma (New York: Harper, 1977)

Age range: Grades 3-5

Subject(s): Grandparents; Old Age

Major character(s): Kalle, Child, Orphan; Oma, Grandparent, Guardian

Time period(s): 1970s

Locale(s): Munich, Germany

What the book is about: The story of an elderly German woman and her small, orphaned grandson. The two cope with the differences and conflicts brought on by poverty as well as the changes in the lifestyle of each of them.

Where it's reviewed:
Kirkus Reviews, November 15, 1977, page 1197
School Library Journal, September 1977, page 129

Awards the book has won:
German Children's Book Prize 1976

Other books by the author:
Old John, 1990
Crutches, 1988

Other books you might like:
Elisabeth Dyjak, *I Should Have Listened to Moon*, 1990
    A twelve year old girl must come to terms with growing up when her forgetful grandmother moves in to share her room.
Marion Walker Doren, *Borrowed Summer*, 1986
    Upset that her great-grandmother and a friend are dying of neglect in a grim nursing home, Jan and her Sunshine Club concoct a plan to get them out.
Marj Gurasich, *Letters to Oma*, 1989
    After her family moves from Germany to Texas, Tina writes letters to her grandmother telling of the struggle to preserve their German heritage.
Emily Rhoads Johnson, *A House Full of Strangers*, 1992
    Flora finds solace in the woods following the death of her grandmother and the arrival of a large, noisy family of relatives.
Mary Stolz, *Stealing Home*, 1992

Though they still listen to baseball and go fishing, Thomas and his grandfather find life in Florida changes when Great-Aunt Linz comes to stay.

823

Dennis Haseley

Illustrator: Leslie Bowman

Shadows (New York: Farrar, Straus and Giroux, 1991)

Age range: Grades 3-5

Subject(s): Family Problems; Country Life

Major character(s): Jamie, Child

Time period(s): 1990s

Locale(s): West Virginia

What the book is about: Jamie's lonely life with his aunt and uncle in rural West Virginia changes when Grandpa comes to visit and teaches him to make shadow pictures. The shadow theme exists at both the real and symbolic levels, and Jamie comes to understand his parents as people, not just shadows in his past. A family story, adventure and mystery, fast paced and short, perfect for reluctant readers.

Where it's reviewed:
Booklist, July 1991, page 2045
Horn Book, July/August 1991, page 456

Other books by the author:
The Thieves' Market, 1991
The Cave of Snores, 1987
The Soap Bandit, 1984
The Old Banjo, 1983

Other books you might like:
Marcia Brown, *Shadow*, 1982
   Free verse evoking the eerie, shifting images of the beliefs and ghosts of the past brought to life wherever there is light, fire and a storyteller.
Blaise Cendrars, *Shadow*, 1982
   Translations of poetry from France and Africa with themes of shades and shadows.
Michael Ende, *Ophelia's Shadow Theater*, 1989
   Elderly Miss Ophelia, the prompter in a failed theater, collects unattached shadows and teaches them to perform the great comedies and tragedies.
Virginia Hamilton, *Jahdu*, 1980
   When his shadow steals his magic dust, Jahdu must try to recover it.
Marilyn Sachs, *Underdog*, 1985
   Lonely, confused, and in need of love in her new life with an aunt and uncle in San Francisco, an orphan searches for her long lost dog.

824

Jon Francis Hassler

Jemmy (New York: Atheneum, 1980)

Age range: Grades 6 and Up

Subject(s): Indians of North America; Alcoholism; Artists and Art

Major character(s): Jemmy Stott, Teenager; Otis Chapman, Artist; Marty, Child

Time period(s): 1980s

Locale(s): Minnesota

What the book is about: Jemmy, a half Chippewa, half white girl, drops out of high school to care for house and siblings and her alcoholic father. After withdrawing from school, she is caught in a storm and takes refuge in a barn. She meets Otis Chapman, an artist who takes an interest in Jemmy and her family, eventually helping both Jemmy and her father plot new directions for their lives.

Where it's reviewed:
Center for Children's Books Bulletin, October 1980, page 33
School Library Journal, August 1980, page 76

Other books by the author:
Four Miles to Pinecone, 1977

Other books you might like:
Annabel Johnson, *Gamebuster*, 1990
   A high school senior discovers a body in the trunk of his car and becomes involved in a fight against dispossessing the Navajos of their lands.
Sally M. Keehn, *I Am Regina*, 1991
   Ten year old Regina is kidnapped by Indians in western Pennsylvania and struggles to hold on to memories of her earlier life as she grows up.
Penina Keen Spinka, *White Hare's Horses*, 1991
   In 16th century California, a young Chumash Indian must save her people from Aztec invaders.
Chap Reaver, *A Little Bit Dead*, 1992
   In 1876, after interfering with an attempted lynching, Reece finds his own life in danger.
Susan Sharpe, *Spirit Quest*, 1991
   Eleven year old Aaron becomes friends with Robert, a young Quileute Indian who is preparing for his Spirit Quest.

825

Elizabeth Hathorn

Illustrator: Julie Vivas

The Tram to Bondi Beach (New York: Kane/Miller, 1989)

Age range: Grades 1-3

Subject(s): Trains

Major character(s): Keiran, Child (paperboy)

Time period(s): 1930s

Locale(s): Sydney, Australia

What the book is about: In 1930 Sydney, Keiran begs his father to allow him to sell newspapers on the Tram, which passes their home on the way to Bondi Beach. When Keiran jumps off the moving tram one night, his father restricts his sales to the sidewalk, but Keiran has already seen his dream. He wants to be the driver of the tram.

Where it's reviewed:
Booklist, June 1, 1989, page 1723
Horn Book, July/August 1989, page 474

Other books by the author:
Thunderwith, 1991
Freya's Fantastic Surprise, 1989

Other books you might like:
Graeme Base, *My Grandma Lived in Gooligulch*, 1990
   Grandma, who lives with a large collection of animals in her small Australian town, takes a disastrous trip to the seaside.
Nan Bodsworth, *A Nice Walk in the Jungle*, 1989
   Tim repeatedly tries to warn his teacher on the class nature walk in the jungle that they are being followed by a hungry boa constrictor.
Mike Dumbleton, *Dial-a-Croc*, 1991
   Vanessa makes a lot of money when she captures a crocodile in the Australian outback and gets him to work for her until the crocodile becomes homesick
Michael F. Page, *The Great Bullocky Race*, 1984
   Two well know competitive Australian bullockies, accompanied by their more peaceable children, try to prove their superiority in a cattle driving race
Helen Smith, *Kenju's Forest*, 1989
   Kenju's neighbors laugh at him for planting and tending his cedar forest, but the trees bring joy to several generations of children.

826

Wilhelm Hauff

Illustrator: Monika Laimgruber

The Adventures of Little Mouk (New York: Macmillan, 1975)

Age range: Grades 4-5

Subject(s): Magic; Dwarves

Major character(s): Mouk, Dwarf

Time period(s): Indeterminate

Locale(s): Turkey

What the book is about: Mouk is a dwarf who goes into the world to seek his fortune. A dog helps him find a magic stick and magical shoes. A messenger of the king thinks Mouk has stolen the treasure he had found with his magical stick and Mouk takes revenge on the king.

Where it's reviewed:
Horn Book, June 1975, page 257
School Library Journal, April 1975, page 53

Other books by the author:
Cold Stone Heart, 1965

Other books you might like:
Paul Biegel, *The King of the Copper Mountains*, 1969
   In order to keep the old king's heart beating until the magic potion arrives, each animal tells a story so interesting the king longs for another.
Godfried Bomans, *The Wily Witch and All the Other Fairy Tales and Fables*, 1977
   Collected tales of kings and queens, wizards and witches, spells and other magic.
Mark Jonathan Harris, *With a Wave of the Wand*, 1980
   Marlee tries to bring her parents back together with the help of magic.
Tom McGowen, *The Magician's Apprentice*, 1987
   A young pickpocket becomes apprenticed to a magician who opens a whole new world, not only of magic and healing, but of kindness and adventure.
Richard Parker, *Spell Seven*, 1971

Life becomes unpredictable and dangerous when Caroline discovers that the wand she bought for her brother's conjurer set really does work magic.

827

Erik Christian Haugaard

The Boy and the Samurai (Boston: Houghton Mifflin, 1991)

Age range: Grades 6-9

Subject(s): Buddhism; Samurai

Major character(s): Saru, Orphan

Time period(s): 16th century

Locale(s): Japan

What the book is about: Saru is a homeless, ragged orphan adrift in a poverty-stricken city. Scavenging for food and fighting for survival, Saru learns to face danger with cunning and self-reliance. A poor Buddhist priest shelters him in his temple. When a young Samurai comes, sorrowing for his wife, only Saru can help in her rescue from the evil provincial warlord. Excellent for units on Japanese history.

Where it's reviewed:
Horn Book, May/June 1991, page 336
School Library Journal, April 1991, page 119

Other books by the author:
Princess Horrid, 1990
Prince Boghole, 1987
Samurai's Tale, 1984
Leif the Unlucky, 1982

Other books you might like:
Carella Alden, *Sunrise Island*, 1971
   Explains the origins of the tea ceremony, the costumes and equipment of the Samurai, the gardens, scrolls, wood blocks and other art forms of Japan.
Emily Crofford, *Born in the Year of Courage*, 1991
   In 1841, rescued by an American whaling ship after being shipwrecked, Manjiro decides to live in America and work towards opening US-Japan trade.
Lensey Namioka, *Island of Ogres*, 1989
   An unemployed Samurai reluctantly helps solve a mystery and prevent the overthrow of a young ruler on an island in medieval Japan.
Katherine Paterson, *Of Nightingales That Weep*, 1974
   The vain young daughter of a Samurai finds her comfortable life ripped apart when opposing warrior clans begin a struggle for control of Japan.
Phyllis A. Whitney, *Secret of the Samurai Sword*, 1958
   When Celia and her brother visit Japan, Celia discovers the ghost of an ancient Samurai wandering about in the dark.

828

Erik Christian Haugaard

Little Fishes (Boston: Houghton Mifflin, 1967)

Age range: Grades 6-8

Subject(s): World War II

Major character(s): Guido, Child, Orphan

Time period(s): 1940s

Locale(s): Naples, Italy

What the book is about: 12 year old Guido is able to keep himself and two other war orphans alive and hopeful for the future in occupied Italy during WWII. They make their way to Casino and the Allied lines.

Where it's reviewed:
Horn Book, June 1967, page 352
Library Journal, May 15, 1967, page 2028

Awards the book has won:
Boston Globe/Horn Book Award 1967

Other books by the author:
The Boy and the Samurai, 1991
Prince Boghole, 1987
The Untold Tale, 1971
Orphans of the Wind, 1966

Other books you might like:
Leonard Everett Fisher, *Letters From Italy*, 1977
   An Italian family immigrates to the US, and a son returns to Italy during WWII.
Mary Downing Hahn, *Stepping on the Cracks*, 1991
   Margaret gets an unusual perspective on war when she finds the town bully is hiding his brother, an army deserter.
Sigrid Heuck, *The Hideout*, 1988
   An orphan in Germany during WWII hides out with a boy in a cornfield where they create their own fantasy world.
Joan Lingard, *Tug of War*, 1990
   Twins Astra and Hugo flee Latvia before the advancing Russian armies arrive in 1944 and find themselves refugees in Germany.
Zilpha Keatley Snyder, *The Famous Stanley Kidnappping Case*, 1979
   Kidnappers in Italy get more than they bargained for when their American captives tell them how to run a kidnapping.

829

Tormod Haugen

The Night Birds (New York: Delacorte, 1982)

Age range: Grades 4-6

Subject(s): Child Abuse; Emotional Problems

Major character(s): Jake Hansen, Child; Erik Hansen, Parent (Mentally Ill Person); Linda Hansen, Parent

Time period(s): 1980s

Locale(s): Norway

What the book is about: When Jake's father tries teaching junior high and has a nervous breakdown, Jake is not ready for the changes in his dad. Mood swings and disappearances become commonplace. Sometimes everything is wonderful, other times he hardly knows this is the same person he knew as his father. Jake begins to deal with his father's bouts of depression and his own nightmares. Friendship and family love help Jake separate imaginary fears from real ones.

Where it's reviewed:
Kirkus Reviews, September 1, 1982, page 998
School Library Journal, September 1982, page 108

Awards the book has won:
Norwegian Children's Book Prize

Other books you might like:
Karen Ackerman, *The Broken Boy*, 1991
   Solly recounts his friendship with a mentally disturbed boy.
Natalie Honeycutt, *Ask Me Something Easy*, 1991
   After her father leaves the family, Addie must cope with her hostile, distant mother, perfect older sister, and sensitive younger twins.
Louise Dickinson Rich, *Three of a Kind*, 1970
   An eleven year old orphan helps an emotionally disturbed four year old boy to heal and get well.
Susan Terris, *The Drowning Boy*, 1972
   A twelve year old boy who feels he is considered an idiot at home finds self-confidence helping a schizophrenic six year old staying with a neighbor.
Linda R. Weltner, *Beginning to Feel the Magic*, 1981
   A sixth grader experiences highs and lows during a year filled with a class play, illness, a baby sister and a boyfriend.

830

Esther Hautzig

The Endless Steppe: Growing Up in Siberia (New York: Crowell, 1968)

Age range: Grades 5-7

Subject(s): World War II

Major character(s): Esther Rudomin, Child, Refugee

Time period(s): 1940s

Locale(s): Vilna, Poland

What the book is about: Autobiography of Polish Jews of wealth and prestige torn from their home in Vilna and sent by cattle car to the Siberian frontier. They spend five years in exile in impossible conditions where just obtaining food and shelter become the goals of life. The positive side is that Esther discovers Russian literature. (Autobiography)

Where it's reviewed:
Horn Book, June 1968, page 311
Kirkus Reviews, March 15, 1968, page 343

Awards the book has won:
Boston Globe/Horn Book Award - Honor Book 1968
Jane Addams Children's Book Award 1969

Other books by the author:
A Gift for Mama, 1981
Case Against the Wind, 1975

Other books you might like:
Iurii Iosifovich Korinets, *There, Far Beyond the River*, 1973
   A teenage boy recounts the events of the journey with his uncle to the north of Russia.
Evgenii Samoilovich Ryss, *Search Behind the Lines*, 1974
   Two children face the perils of the German occupation of Russia during WWII.
Efraim Sevela, *We Were Not Like Other People*, 1989
   Separated from his family when the Germans invade Russia during WWII, a boy learns to fend for himself and earn a living whenever and however he can.
Yuri Suhl, *On the Other Side of the Gate*, 1975
   The story of a Jewish couple confined to a ghetto during the Nazi occupation of Poland during WWII.
Alki Zei, *The Sound of Dragon's Feet*, 1979

Time spent with her tutor opens Sasha's eyes to more of life in turn-of-the-century Russia than her sheltered life had allowed her to experience.

831

Esther Hautzig

Illustrator: Donna Diamond

A Gift for Mama (New York: Viking, 1981)

Age range: Grades 3-5

Subject(s): Holidays; Family Life; Gifts

Major character(s): Sara Domin, Child; Grandmother Hanna, Grandparent; Aunt Margola, Relative (aunt)

Time period(s): 1940s

Locale(s): Vilma, Poland

What the book is about: With Mother's Day coming soon, Sara wants to buy something special, even though her mother insists the best gifts are handmade. Sara works to mend clothes for her friends and earns the money to buy slippers to match her mother's satin robe. Mother is at first, not enthusiastic about a "store bought" gift, but when she learns how hard Sara worked, she truly appreciates the gift.

Where it's reviewed:
Center for Children's Books Bulletin, September 1981, page 10
Horn Book, August 1981, page 423

Other books by the author:
Case Against the Wind, 1975
The Endless Steppe: Growing Up in Siberia, 1968

Other books you might like:
Ann Cameron, *Julian, Dream Doctor*, 1990
    Julian and Huey try to find the perfect birthday gift for their dad.
Suzy Kline, *Herbie Jones and the Class Gift*, 1987
    Annabelle trusts Herbie and Raymond with the job of picking up the class's gift to their teacher.
Elizabeth Levy, *The Case of the Mind Reading Mommies*, 1989
    A young detective and her partner solve a case involving disappearing presents, a talking doorknob, and a magical Mother's Day show.
Walter O'Meara, *The Sioux Are Coming*, 1971
    A Chippewa family flees from the Sioux and the son has to test his resourcefulness.
Harriette Robinet, *Children of the Fire*, 1991
    A young black girl lives through the great Chicago fire with courage and resourcefulness.

832

Juanita Havill

Illustrator: Emily Arnold McCully

It Always Happens to Leona (New York: Crown, 1989)

Age range: Grades 3-5

Subject(s): Brothers and Sisters; Family Relations

Major character(s): Leona, Runaway; Roscoe, Sports Figure (motorcycle racer)

Time period(s): 1980s

Locale(s): Chicago, Illinois

What the book is about: Leona is in the middle - between cuddly brother Albert and perfect sister Victoria. She is feeling left out and decides to run away with Uncle Rosco, a motorcycle racer.

Where it's reviewed:
Booklist, July 1989, page 1903
Kirkus Reviews, June 1, 1989, page 837
School Library Journal, August 1989, page 140

Other books by the author:
The Magic Fort, 1991
Jamaica Tag Along, 1989
Leroy and the Clock, 1988
Jamaica's Find, 1986

Other books you might like:
Marion Dane Bauer, *Shelter from the Wind*, 1976
    After her father remarries, Stacy runs away in search of her real mother, only to be befriended by a wizened old woman who lives alone in the desert.
Matt Christopher, *Dirt Bike Racer*, 1979
    Ron Baker finds a minibike while scuba diving and, with the help of a former motorcycle rider and racer, restores the bike and enters competition.
Hila Colman, *That's the Way It Is, Amigo*, 1975
    Running from problems at home, David goes to Mexico where a boy from a poor Indian village teaches him something about pride and responsibility.
Eleanor Frances Lattimore, *Proudfoot's Way*, 1978
    Left alone at their farm with a housekeeper she dislikes while her father starts a new medical practice in a neighboring state, Phoebe runs away.
Ed Radlauer, *Motorcycle Winners*, 1982
    Nan is prepared to give up motorcycle racing forever until she gets some simple but sound advice from her aunt, a champion drag racer.

833

Geoffrey Hayes

The Alligator and His Uncle Tooth: A Novel of the Sea (New York: Harper, 1977)

Age range: Grades 3-5

Subject(s): Animals/Alligators; Sea Stories; Aunts and Uncles

Major character(s): Corduroy, Alligator; Uncle Tooth, Sea Captain (Alligator); Auntie Heck, Store Owner

Time period(s): Indeterminate

Locale(s): Fictional Country

What the book is about: Corduroy, an alligator, is fascinated by the sea yarns his old Uncle Tooth tells him; how he outwitted a huge sea lizard with the help of oranges, or how the rats that sailed his ship caused his downfall.

Where it's reviewed:
Booklist, May 15, 1977, page 1420
Hornbook, August 1977, page 441

Kirkus Reviews, April 1, 1977, page 350

Other books by the author:
Hocus and Pocus at the Circus, 1983
Muffie Mouse and the Busy Birthday, 1978
When the Wind Blew, 1977
Bear by Himself, 1976

Other books you might like:
Rosalie K. Fry, *Mungo*, 1972
   A youngster's loneliness comes to an end when he discovers a prehistoric sea monster off the Scottish coast.
Thacher Hurd, *Mama Don't Allow*, 1984
   Miles and his Swamp Band have the time of their lives playing at the Alligator Ball, until they discover the menu includes Swamp Band soup.
Jean Wilson Kennedy, *The Nunga Punga and the Booch*, 1975
   Tranquil life on the shores of the Arabian Sea is disrupted by a hungry tiger.
Rudyard Kipling, *Just So Stories*, 1987
   A dozen stories by the author of children's classics about whales and camels, leopards and armadillos, crabs and butterflies.
Arnold Lobel, *Uncle Elephant*, 1981
   Uncle Elephant comes to the rescue when his nephew's parents are lost at sea and cares for him until they are found again.

834

Geoffrey Hayes

The Secret of Foghorn Island (New York: Random, 1988)

Age range: Grades 2-3

Series: Step into Reading: Step 3 Book

Subject(s): Islands; Mystery and Detective Stories; Shipwrecks

Major character(s): Otto, Detective, Dragon; Tooth, Detective, Dragon; Sid, Rat

Time period(s): Indeterminate

Locale(s): Foghorn Island, Fictional Country

What the book is about: Otto and Uncle Tooth, detectives, investigate four shipwrecks on Foghorn Island, which brings them in touch with the dangerous Sid Rat.

Where it's reviewed:
Booklist, October 1, 1988, page 330

Other books by the author:
The Treasure of the Lost Lagoon, 1991
The Mystery of the Pirate Ghost, 1985
Patrick Comes to Puttyville and Other Stories, 1978
The Alligator and His Uncle Tooth: A Novel of the Sea, 1977

Other books you might like:
Susan Cooper, *Matthew's Dragon*, 1991
   The dragon in Matthew's book comes to life and takes him for an amazing ride.
Vera G. Cumberlege, *Shipwreck*, 1974
   Jim is unhappy that the old boat is to be replaced by a powered one until he witnesses a shipwreck.
David Rounds, *Cannonball River Tales*, 1992

Tall tales about Tom Terry, whose home by the banks of the Cannonball River is populated by several unusual characters.
Elizabeth Slote, *Nelly's Grannies*, 1993
   Nelly and Mike Dragon visit one grandmother in the country and the other grandmother in the city.
Rosemary Sutcliffe, *The Minstrel and the Dragon Pup*, 1993
   When a minstrel's dragon pup is stolen by a wicked showman, the minstrel's songs suffer.

835

Sarah Hayes

Illustrator: Helen Craig

Mary, Mary (New York: Macmillan, 1990)

Age range: Grades 2-3

Subject(s): Giants; Courage

Major character(s): Mary, Child

Time period(s): Indeterminate

Locale(s): England

What the book is about: Mary refuses to be afraid of the giant who lives on the hill above her town. She helps the giant clean up his looks and his house. He invites the townspeople to his house to play.

Where it's reviewed:
Kirkus Reviews, September 1, 1990, page 1251
School Library Journal, December 1990, page 78

Other books by the author:
The Crumbling Castle, 1992
Robin Hood, 1989
Gruesome Giants, 1986
This Is the Bear, 1986

Other books you might like:
Bruce Coville, *The Foolish Giant*, 1978
   A not very bright but friendly giant named Harry has some exciting adventures.
Helgadottir Gudrun, *Flumbra*, 1985
   When the dim-witted Flumbra falls in love, her escapades upset all of Iceland.
Howard A. Norman, *How Glooskup Outwits the Ice Giants*, 1989
   Six tales about the mythical giant who roamed the coast of New England and Canada, created the Native American peoples and fought battles to protect t
Jon Scieszka, *Knights of the Kitchen Table*, 1991
   The magic book Joe got from his uncle transports him to the time of knights, dragons, and giants.
Pete Seeger, *Abiyoyo*, 1986
   Banished from town as a mischiefmaker, a boy and his dad are welcomed back when they find a way to make the giant threatening the town disappear.

836

Sheila Hayes

Speaking of Snapdragons (New York: Lodestar, 1982)

Age range: Grades 4-6

Subject(s): Friendship; Gardens and Gardening; Old Age

Major character(s): Heather Mallory, Preteen; Marshall Benedict, Neighbor; Thomas Worthington Duffy, Aged Person

Time period(s): 1980s

Locale(s): Oakfield, Ohio

What the book is about: Duffy has the most beautiful garden Heather has ever seen. He not only understands flowers, but understands Heather. The old man who lives up the hill becomes very important to her.

Where it's reviewed:
Booklist, February 1, 1983, page 724
Center for Children's Books Bulletin, February 1983, page 109
School Library Journal, November 1982, page 85

Other books by the author:
You've Been Away All Summer, 1986
Me and My Mona Lisa Smile, 1981
The Carousel Horse, 1978
Gift Horse, 1978

Other books you might like:
Eth Clifford, *The Rocking Chair Rebellion*, 1978
    A teenager chronicles her involvement with the residents of Maple Ridge Home for the Aged and their revolution.
Salley Kelley, *Summer Growing Time*, 1971
    June and her grandmother live in their own world, absorbed in gardening, until racial unrest in the town intrudes on their lives.
Katharine Wilson Precek, *The Keepsake Chest*, 1992
    To ease the pain of having to leave her friends behind when she moves into an old farmhouse, Meg probes the historical background of an old chest.
Gail Rock, *A Dream for Addie*, 1975
    Despite their age difference, Addie discovers she has something in common with the actress who is otherwise friendless in her old home town.
Alison Smith, *Reserved for Mark Anthony Crowder*, 1978
    A sixth-grader who believes everyone including his family thinks him odd, spends his summer tending the family garden and cultivating his self-esteem.

837

Sheila Hayes

You've Been Away All Summer (New York: Dutton, 1986)

Age range: Grades 5-7

Subject(s): Friendship

Major character(s): Fran, Preteen; Sarah, Preteen; Marcia, Preteen

Time period(s): 1980s

Locale(s): New York, New York (Manhattan)

What the book is about: Fran finds that her best friend, Sarah, has made a new friend, and Fran detests Marcia, feeling that she has stolen Sarah from her.

Where it's reviewed:
Horn Book, May/June 1986, page 331
School Library Journal, September 1986, page 135

Other books by the author:
No Autographs Please, 1984
Speaking of Snapdragons, 1982
Me and My Mona Lisa Smile, 1981
The Carousel Horse, 1978

Other books you might like:
Melissa Brennan, *Could This Be Love?*, 1991
    Casey has fallen in love with her best friend, Peter, and is trying to get him to notice her in a romantic way.
Ilene Cooper, *Frances and Friends*, 1991
    Frances is crushed when a new girl threatens to come between her and Polly, until she realizes that best friends don't have to do everything together.
Vicki Grove, *The Fastest Friend in the West*, 1990
    When her best friend dumps her to be with the popular kids, overweight Lori shares an unusual but brief friendship with a homeless girl.
Nancy Lamb, *The Breat Mosquito, Bull and Coffin Caper*, 1992
    Hoping to never forget his best friend, Jimmy, who is moving away, Zander pledges to undergo three difficult and scary ordeals with him.
Judith Bernie Strommen, *Grady the Great*, 1990
    Grady, planning to run away to join his best friend in California, finds his secret endangered by Burgess, the pest who moves in next door.

838

Carolyn Haywood, Author/Illustrator

Eddie's Valuable Property (New York: Morrow, 1975)

Age range: Grades 2-4

Subject(s): Family Life; Possessions; Moving, Household

Major character(s): Eddie, Child; Jimmie, Child

Time period(s): 1970s

Locale(s): United States

What the book is about: Eddie collects junk, but his dad insists he must get rid of it because they are moving. He has a garage sale and gets a dog. At his new house, Eddie and Jimmie become best friends. They start a club and help another boy become more likable.

Where it's reviewed:
Kirkus Reviews, March 15, 1975, page 307
School Library Journal, May 1975, page 55

Other books by the author:
Eddie's Friend Boodles, 1991
Halloween Treats, 1981
Eddie and Gardenia, 1951
Betsy and Billy, 1941

Other books you might like:
Paula Fox, *Maurice's Room*, 1966
    8 year old Maurice's struggle to protect his bedroom full of treasured "junk" from his parents undergoes a transformation when the family moves.
Mel Gilden, *Outer Space, and All That Junk*, 1989
    A boy works for his uncle one summer only to discover him collecting junk in the belief that he is helping aliens return to their home in outer space.
Patricia Tracy Lowe, *The Runt*, 1984

Nine year old Angus moves with his family from a coastal town to a farm and learns how to care for animals, and the consequences of irresponsibility.

Bonnie Pryor, *Horses in the Garage*, 1992
 Samantha finds a way to cope with her stepfather, new home and school, when she makes friends with unconventional Jasmine and learns to ride a horse.

Maggie Twohill, *Bigmouth*, 1986
 A well-meaning young girl, who talks more than she listens, garbles a message from her father's boss, leading the family to think they are moving.

839

Barbara Shook Hazen

Illustrator: Charles Robinson

Amelia's Flying Machine (Garden City, NY: Doubleday, 1977)

Age range: Grades 2-4

Subject(s): Biography; Airplanes

Major character(s): Amelia Earhart, Child, Historical Figure; Jimmy, Child

Time period(s): 1910s

Locale(s): Kansas

What the book is about: Amelia wants to earn a trip to the Chicago World's Fair. At home in Kansas with her sister and cousins at grandmother's house, Amelia is bored. She decides to build her own roller coaster, even though Jimmy teases her. Based on the childhood of Amelia Earhart.

Where it's reviewed:
Kirkus Reviews, August 15, 1977, page 851
School Library Journal, November 1977, page 48

Other books by the author:
What's Mine Is Mine, 1986
The Ups and Downs of Marvin, 1977
The Gorilla Did It, 1976
Why Couldn't I Be an Only Kid Like You?, 1975

Other books you might like:
Betsy Byars, *Coast to Coast*, 1992
 Birch encourages her grandfather to fulfill his dream of flying his Piper Cub from South Carolina to California, then tells him she is coming along.

Charles Hammer, *Wrong-Way Ragsdale*, 1987
 Emmett and his sister take off in their father's Taylorcraft, make a forced landing in the mountains, and try to survive in the wilderness.

Patricia Lauber, *Lost Star*, 1988
 Traces the life of Amelia Earhart, the first female pilot to fly across the Atlantic, who disappeared over the Pacific in 1937. (Biography)

Hilary H. Milton, *Blind Flight*, 1980
 Flying with her uncle, Debbie, who has been blind for about a year, must suddenly take control of the plane when her uncle passes out.

John Tomerlin, *The Sky Clowns*, 1973
 A dedicated stunt flyer wants to help a failing air show.

840

Barbara Shook Hazen

Illustrator: Nancy Kincade

Even If I Did Something Awful (New York: Atheneum, 1981)

Age range: Grades 1-2

Subject(s): Parent and Child; Love

Time period(s): 1980s

Locale(s): United States

What the book is about: A mother declares she will always love her child, even if she gets orange crayon on the carpet (though she would have to clean it up) or gave the baby away (but mom would bring it back). Mom admits she might get angry, but will not stop loving her child.

Where it's reviewed:
Kirkus Reviews, October 15, 1981, page 1292
School Library Journal, November 1981, page 76

Awards the book has won:
Christopher Award 1982

Other books by the author:
Fang, 1987
If It Weren't for Benjamin, 1981
Step on It, Andrew, 1981
The Gorilla Did It, 1974

Other books you might like:
Anthony Brown, *Changes*, 1990
 Waiting at home for his parents', a boy ponders his father's remarks, "Things are going to change around here," and imagines all kinds of changes.

Holly Keller, *Horace*, 1991
 Horace, an adopted child, realizes that being part of a family depends on how you feel, not how you look.

Ann Warren Turner, *Through Moon and Stars and Night Skies*, 1990
 A boy who came from far away to be adopted remembers how unfamiliar and frightening his new home was, before he accepted the love to be found there.

Judith Viorst, *The Good-Bye Book*, 1992
 A child, on the verge of being left behind by parents who are going out for the evening, comes up with a variety of excuses.

Harriet Ziefert, *Later, Rover*, 1991
 Everyone in Andy's family has an excuse for not playing him, except the dog, but Rover tires Andy to the point he has to make excuses to the dog.

841

Betsy Hearne

Illustrator: Ronald Himler

Eli's Ghost (New York: McElderry, 1987)

Age range: Grades 5-7

Subject(s): Ghosts; Swamps; Mothers and Sons

Major character(s): Eli Wilson, Preteen

Time period(s): 1980s

Locale(s): South (small town)

What the book is about: Eli learns that his mother is not dead, but has fled to the swamp, and he goes in search of her. When he nearly drowns in a whirlpool, his ghost is freed from his body and boy and ghost coexist. Eli's friends, Lily and Tater, find him reunited with his mother in her home in the swamp. Eli's ghost is able to get into all the mischief Eli never dreamt of. Humor and fast pace make this an above average ghost story.

Where it's reviewed:
Horn book, October 1987, page 612
School Library Journal, April 1, 1987, page 94

Other books by the author:
Home, 1979
South Star, 1977

Other books you might like:
Bill Brittain, *The Ghost From Beneath the Sea*, 1992
When a stranger threatens to turn an old mansion into an amusement park, three youngsters join forces with a trio of ghosts to outwit the plan.
Lynn Cullen, *The Backyard Ghost*, 1993
Eleanor's attempts to break into the popular crowd at her school are complicated by the discovery that her backyard is haunted by a Civil War ghost.
Dean Hughes, *Nutty's Ghost*, 1993
Nat's not sure he wants to be an actor when he deals with an overzealous director, jealous friends, and an apparition that doesn't want the film made.
Jan Slepian, *Back to Before*, 1993
Eleven year old cousins Linny and Hilary find themselves transported back to their old Brooklyn neighborhood to a time just before Linny's mother died
Thelma Hatch Wyss, *A Stranger Here*, 1993
While spending the summer in Idaho taking care of her sick aunt, Jada Sinclair meets a spirit from the past and tries to discover the reason for his r

---

842

Bessie Holland Heck

Cave-in at Mason's Mine (New York: Scribner's, 1980)

Age range: Grades 2-3

Subject(s): Courage; Family Life

Major character(s): Joey Johnson, Child

Time period(s): 1980s

Locale(s): Rocky Mountains

What the book is about: On vacation with his parents in the Rocky Mountains, Joey, age nine, is exploring a cave with his father when a cave-in traps his father and Joey must go for help. He gets back to their cabin, but his mother has gone for groceries. Joey flags down a car, his father is rescued and will recover, and Joey is a hero.

Where it's reviewed:
Booklist, March 1, 1981, page 963
School Library Journal, May 1981, page 64

Other books by the author:
Golden Arrow, 1981

Other books you might like:
Lionel Bender, *Cave*, 1989

A geological explanation of the reasons and ways caves are formed with a discussion of their uses throughout history. (Non-fiction)
Dale Fife, *North of Danger*, 1978
Arne undertakes a two-hundred mile trip on skis to warn his father of a German invasion of their town in Norway.
Kathleen Kudlinski, *Hero over Here*, 1990
A young boy must look after his sick mother and sister while his father and brother fight in WWI.
Toby Talbot, *The Rescue*, 1973
Jacques' father brings home a lamb to slaughter for a feast and Jacques tries to save it.
Ann Warren Turner, *Time of the Bison*, 1987
Scar Boy, a cave dweller, discovers that he has a gift for making pictures and becomes an apprentice to the Painter of Caves.

843

Florence Parry Heide

Banana Blitz (New York: Holiday House, 1983)

Age range: Grades 3-5

Subject(s): Food; Schools/Boarding Schools; Contests

Major character(s): Jonah Krock, Student; Lewis "Goober" Trane, Student

Time period(s): 1980s

Locale(s): United States

What the book is about: Fairlee School students have refrigerators and TV's in their rooms. Candy bar addict Jonah, arriving at school, thinks his problems will be over if he can just win the prize offered by the American Banana Institute for watching its commercials. But his roommate turns out to be the boy he's been avoiding all summer.

Where it's reviewed:
Kirkus Reviews, June 1, 1983, page 619
School Library Journal, August 1983, page 66

Awards the book has won:
Crabbery Honor 1984

Other books by the author:
Tales for the Perfect Child, 1985
Banana Twist, 1978
Growing Anyway Up, 1976
The Key, 1971

Other books you might like:
Penelope Farmer, *Charlotte Sometimes*, 1969
When she awakens on her second day at boarding school, a young girl finds she has gone back in time to 1918.
John D. Fitzgerald, *The Great Brain at the Academy*, 1972
Tom faces the challenge of life at a strict Catholic boarding school, which he spices up with daring exploits and money making schemes.
Liza Fosburgh, *Bella Arabella*, 1985
Spoiled ten year old Arabella thinks that she can avoid being sent to boarding school by becoming a cat.
Constance Hiser, *No Bean Sprouts, Please!*, 1989
Fourth grader James is resigned to his mother's healthy but boring lunches until he gets a very unusual lunchbox for his birthday.
Jean Van Leeuwen, *Benjy and the Power of Zingies*, 1982

Benjy, tired of being small for his age, decides to build his body by eating the breakfast cereal of sports stars.

844

Florence Parry Heide

Growing Anyway Up (Philadelphia: Lippincott, 1976)

Age range: Grades 5-6

Subject(s): Behavior; Adolescence

Major character(s): Florence Stirkel, Preteen; Nina, Relative (aunt)

Time period(s): 1970s (1976)

Locale(s): Pennsylvania

What the book is about: Florence moves with her mother to be near her Aunt Nina. She hates the private school she is sent to, and the man who marries her mother. Aunt Nina helps her face a problem she has repressed for years, and grow in self-confidence and out of her strange behavior.

Where it's reviewed:
Horn Book, June 1976, page 288
Kirkus Reviews, May 1, 1976, page 535

Awards the book has won:
Golden Kite Honor Book 1976

Other books by the author:
Body in the Brillstone Garage, 1980
Mystery of the Bewitched Bookmobile, 1975
When the Sad One Comes to Stay, 1975
The Hidden Box Mystery, 1973

Other books you might like:
Jim Arter, *Gruel and Unusual Punishment*, 1991
   Undaunted by his second stint in seventh grade, Arnold continues to specialize in annoying and anti-social behavior until a teacher he calls Apeface t
Dee Jacobs, *Laura's Gift*, 1980
   13 year old twin sisters try to cope with strict regulations at the school they attend and with the crippling disease which strikes one of them.
Mary Stolz, *Ivy Larkin*, 1986
   In New York City during the Depression, Ivy has to cope with feeling out of place at her elegant private school and with her father's losing his job.
Stephanie S. Tolan, *A Time to Fly Free*, 1983
   Josh, who finds private school unbearable, joins forces with an elderly man in tending injured birds.
Budge Wilson, *Thirteen Never Changes*, 1989
   When Lorinda inherits grandmother's diaries, she finds she's not alone in how she sometimes feels; she learns about another side of her grandmother.

845

Florence Parry Heide

Illustrator: Seymour Fleishman

Mystery of the Bewitched Bookmobile (Chicago: Whitman, 1975)

Age range: Grades 4-6

Subject(s): Mystery and Detective Stories

Major character(s): Terri Firestone, Librarian; Cindy Temple, Child; Olga Ratchett, Spy

Time period(s): 1970s

Locale(s): United States

What the book is about: Why would anyone break into a bookmobile and not take anything? Cindy and her friends in the Spotlight Club investigate.

Where it's reviewed:
Center for Children's Books Bulletin, February 1975, page 94
Library Journal, December 15, 1974, page 3277

Awards the book has won:
Golden Archer Award 1976

Other books by the author:
Banana Twist, 1978
The Shrinking of Treehorn, 1975
When the Sad One Comes to Stay, 1975
Mystery of the Melting Snowman, 1974

Other books you might like:
Joan Aiken, *Mortimer's Cross*, 1983
   The adventures of Arabel and her rave, Mortimer, in the library, a disappearing taxi, and a portrait on glass.
Wilma Pitchford Hays, *The Ghost at Penniman House*, 1979
   When she sees someone with a dog near the old haunted house, a young girl is convinced he's the ghost of a long dead relative.
Elizabeth Levy, *Something Queer at the Library: A Mystery*, 1977
   Gwen and Jill's discovery of mutilated library books has something to do with the dog show in which they have entered their dog.
Thomas F. Pursell, *Mr. Kruger's Treasure*, 1977
   The quick thinking of the Adams children saves an old man's most treasured possession from burglars.
Gertrude Chandler Warner, *The Deserted Library Mystery*, 1991
   At an old library, the Alden children discover a boy who needs their help and a stranger who is after a valuable object they find in the library.

846

Florence Parry Heide

Illustrator: Edward Gorey

Treehorn's Treasure (New York: Holiday, 1981)

Age range: Grades 2-4

Subject(s): Money; Family Life; Communication

Major character(s): Treehorn, Child

Time period(s): 1980s

Locale(s): United States

What the book is about: Treehorn has a money tree in his back yard. It blooms dollar bills, but the grown-ups never notice a thing. Treehorn is able to stockpile gum and comics before the magic is undone.

Where it's reviewed:
Horn Book, February 1982, page 42
School Library Journal, November 1981, page 76

Other books by the author:
Growing Anyway Up, 1976
The Shrinking of Treehorn, 1971
Tales for the Perfect Child, 1985
Treehorn's Wish, 1984

Other books you might like:
Loreen Leedy, *Monster Money Book*, 1992
  Members of the Monster Club discuss what to do with the $54 in their teasury.
Barbara Ann Porte, *Fat Fanny, Beanpole Bertha and the Boys*, 1991
  Berta and Fanny teach Fanny's triplet brothers to tap dance to raise money to look for Berth'a lost father.
Vera B. Williams, *Music, Music for Everyone*, 1984
  Rosa and her band play in the street to earn money while Rosa's grandmother is sick.
Mary Francis Shura, *Jefferson*, 1984
  Neighbohood children work at earning money to give Jefferson a birthday party.
Graham Oakley, *Church Mice in Action*, 1982
  The Church Mice enter Samson in a cat show to win money to fix the church roof.

847

Joan Heilbroner

This Is the House Where Jack Lives (New York: Harper, 1962)

Age range: Grades 1-2

Series: I Can Read Book

Subject(s): Apartments; Poetry

Major character(s): Jack, Child

Time period(s): Indeterminate

Locale(s): Fictional Country

What the book is about: The House is involved in a series of amusing events in this story that closely resemble the classic "The House That Jack Built."

Where it's reviewed:
School Library Journal, February 1982, page 37

Other books by the author:
Tom the TV Cat, 1984
Meet George Washington, 1964
Robert, the Rose Horse, 1962
The Happy Birthday Present, 1961

Other books you might like:
Tedd Arnold, *No Jumping on the Bed!*, 1987
  Walter lives near the top floor of a tall apartment building, where one night his habit of jumping on his bed leads to a tumultous fall.
Johanna Hurwitz, *Busybody Nora*, 1976
  Relates the adventures of an inquisitive girl who lives in a large apartment building in New York with her parents and little brother, Teddy.
Ezra Jack Keats, *Apt. 3*, 1971
  On a rainy day, two brothers try to discover who is playing the harmonica they hear in their apartment building.
Nancy Durrell McKenna, *A Family in Hong Kong*, 1987
  Describes the life of ten year old Tse Yik Ming who lives in an apartment building in Hong Kong.

Pat Ross, *M & M and the Halloween Monster*, 1991
  While getting ready for Halloween, Mandy and Mimi observe creepy things in their apartment building and conclude that a monster is lurking.

848

Hans-Eric Hellberg

Illustrator: Joan Sandin

Grandpa's Maria (New York: Morrow, 1974)

Age range: Grades 3-4

Subject(s): Grandparents; Family Life

Major character(s): Maria, Child; Grandpa, Grandparent

Time period(s): 1970s

Locale(s): Sweden

What the book is about: Seven year old Maria finds it hard to understand why her mom has to go to a rest home, but she feels safe as long as Grandpa is near. Her father, divorced from her mother, has a second family. Even though she is uncomfortable with them, she accepts the situation.

Where it's reviewed:
Kirkus Reviews, October 15, 1974
Library Journal, November 15, 1974, page 3046

Other books by the author:
Ben's Lucky Hat, 1965

Other books you might like:
Nan Gilbert, *The Strange New World Across the Street*, 1979
  Robbie has trouble re-establishing a relationship with his estranged father and coping with his new environment when he leaves his grandparents' home.
JoAnn Bren Guernsey, *Journey to Almost There*, 1985
  To prevent her grandfather from going to a nursing home, Alison drives him from Minnesota to Massachusetts where her estranged artist father lives.
Norma Klein, *Older Men*, 1987
  When her mother is hospitalized for a nervous breakdown, Elise must radically alter her perceptions of both of her parents.
Gail Radley, *The Golden Days*, 1991
  Cory is convinced that his new foster parents don't really want him, so he decides to run away with an old lady from the nearby nursing home.
Don Schellie, *Kidnapping Mr. Tubbs*, 1978
  Two teens sneak an elderly ex-cowboy out of his rest home for a visit to the ranch where he spent his life.

849

Doris Wild Helmering

Illustrator: Heidi Palmer

I Have Two Families (Nashville: Abingdon, 1981)

Age range: Grades 1-2

Subject(s): Divorce

Major character(s): Patty, child; Michael, Child

Time period(s): 1980s

Locale(s): United States

What the book is about: Eight year old Patty and her younger brother, Michael, are understandably anxious when their parents announce they are getting a divorce. The parents are supportive and the children spend time with each one. An optimistic and reassuring narrative for younger children.

Where it's reviewed:
Booklist, March 15, 1981, page 1028
School Library Journal, September 1981, page 108

Other books by the author:
We're Going to Have a Baby, 1978

Other books you might like:
C.B. Christiansen, *My Mother's House, My Father's House*, 1989
   A child describes having two different houses in which to live, and what it is like to travel back and forth between them.
Paul Z. Hogan, *Will Dad Ever Move Back Home?*, 1991
   When a child is bitterly unhappy over her parents' divorce, she and her family discover that talking about it to each other can help a lot.
Emily Moore, *Something to Count On*, 1991
   Ten year old Lorraine's behavior problems at school are aggravated by her family situation and eased by an understanding new teacher.
Trudy Osman, *Where Has Daddy Gone?*, 1989
   A boy experiences the anger and sorrow involved in seeing his parents get divorced, but realizes they still love him.
Barbara Park, *Don't Make Me Smile*, 1981
   A young boy has trouble adjusting to his parents' divorce.

850

Diana Hendry

Illustrator: Elsie Lennox

A Camel Called April (New York: Lothrop, 1991)

Age range: Grades 2-3

Subject(s): Animals/Camels; Dreams and Nightmares

Major character(s): Harold "Harry" Yorick, Child; April, Camel

Time period(s): Indeterminate

Locale(s): Vagary Park, England

What the book is about: Six year old Harry has always had strange dreams, but after he has chicken pox, his dreams get stranger. He dreams of a lion, and when he wakes up, a lion has stranded four adults on the jungle gym in Vagary Park. The animals from Harry's dreams are taken care of one by one, but when he dreams up a camel named April, April likes the life in Harry's dreams and Vagary Park and decides to stay. Local officials see the possibilities and make April the Camel-in-Residence and sell rides on her.

Where it's reviewed:
School Librarian, August 1990, page 108
School Librarian, August 1991, page 1286

Other books by the author:
Christmas on Exeter Street, 1989
The Rainbow Watchers, 1989

Other books you might like:
Page McBrier, *Secret of the Missing Camel*, 1987

Oliver's pet care service faces its greatest challenge when he is asked to watch a camel being kept illegally in a fenced-in back yard and it escapes
Bill Peet, *Pamela Camel*, 1984
   A tired and dejected circus camel finds long sought after recognition along a railroad track.
Ann Shaffer, *The Camel Express*, 1989
   As part of an experiment in 1860, a camel fills in for a wounded pony on a Pony Express route.
Robert E. Swindells, *The Very Special Baby*, 1977
   A camel born with three humps helps three wise men carry gifts to a newborn king.
Rosemary Wells, *Abdul*, 1975
   An old mother camel's new baby, Abdul, is a strange looking creature that causes all sorts of problems.

851

Kevin Henkes, Author/Illustrator

Margaret and Taylor (New York: Greenwillow, 1983)

Age range: Grades 2-3

Subject(s): Brothers and Sisters

Major character(s): Margaret Tippet, Child; Taylor Tippet, Child

Time period(s): 1980s

Locale(s): United States

What the book is about: Whether it's a matter of balloons or a birthday present for Grandfather, Margaret knows how to get the better of her little brother, Taylor.

Where it's reviewed:
Center for Children's Books Bulletin, March 1984, page 127
Kirkus Reviews, September 1, 1983, page J162
School Library Journal, February 1984, page 72

Other books by the author:
Two under Par, 1987
Return to Sender, 1984
Clean Enough, 1982
All Alone, 1981

Other books you might like:
Franz Brandenberg, *Aunt Nina and Her Nephews and Nieces*, 1983
   Going to visit Aunt Nina to celebrate Fluffy's birthday is better than anything else, but best of all is the brand new litter of kittens.
Beatrice Schenk DeRegniers, *Snow Party*, 1959
   A lonely farm wife in Dakota longs for a party. A blizzard strands all kinds of people and soon the farmhouse is bursting with music and dancing.
Steven Kellogg, *Much Bigger than Martin*, 1976
   Henry hates being Martin's little brother, and always being the butt of all the jokes when the big boys are around.
Patricia Larkin, *Oh, Brother!*, 1987
   Aaron is the oldest, but Benji seems to get all of the fun and attention while Aaron is stuck with all the responsibility.
David M. McPhail, *Party*, 1990
   While his father sleeps, a boy and his stuffed animals, who come to life, have a party in this warm, fuzzy story.

852

Kevin Henkes

The Zebra Wall (New York: Greenwillow, 1988)

Age range: Grades 4-6

Subject(s): Family Life; Brothers and Sisters

Major character(s): Adine Vorlob, Preteen; Bernice Vorlob, Child; Carla Vorlob, Child

Time period(s): 1980s

Locale(s): United States

What the book is about: Adine and her sisters await the sixth child in their family. Of course the five girls expect it will be another. All of a sudden, Mother announces this baby's name will begin with a Z instead of an F (to follow Adine, Bernice, Carla, Dot and Effie) This one will be named Zachary!

Where it's reviewed:
Center for Children's Books Bulletin, April 1988, page 159
School Library Journal, April 1988, page 100

Other books by the author:
Words of Stone, 1992
Jessica, 1989
Chester's Way, 1988
Bailey Goes Camping, 1985

Other books you might like:
Betsy Byars, *Bingo Brown, Gypsy Lover*, 1990
   A sixth grade boy deals with the prospect of a new baby brother and a long-distance love relationship.
Sheila Greenwald, *Alvin Webster's Sure Plan for Success (and How It Failed)*, 1987
   Gifted 5th grader Alvin Webster, accustomed to being the best at everything, has to adjust when he finds out a new baby brother is on the way.
Pat Kibbe, *The Hocus-Pocus Dilemma*, 1979
   Convinced she has psychic powers, a ten year old girl makes predictions for the members of her large family which seem to come true.
Joanne Rocklin, *Dear Baby*, 1988
   During the months of her mother's pregnancy, Farla writes a series of letters to the unborn baby describing her feelings toward family members.
Susan Sommer, *And I'm Stuck with Joseph*, 1984
   Sheila wants a baby sister, but her parents adopt a baby brother who is very difficult to love.

853

Marguerite Henry

Illustrator: Wesley Dennis

Justin Morgan Had a Horse (New York: Rand McNally, 1954)

Age range: Grades 4-6

Subject(s): American Colonies; Animals/Horses

Major character(s): Joel Goss, Student; Justin Morgan, Teacher; Little Bub, Horse

Time period(s): 1780s

Locale(s): Randolph, Vermont, American Colonies

What the book is about: The forefather of American Morgan horses, Little Bub starts life as a small colt used to pay a debt. With Joel's love, Little Bub grows to be a magnificent horse in this endearing horse tale.

Other books by the author:
Mustang: Wild Spirit of the West, 1966
Black Gold, 1957
Brighty of the Grand Canyon, 1953
King of the Wind, 1948

Other books you might like:
Marilyn Cram Donahue, *Straight Along a Crooked Road*, 1985
   As her family travels from Vermont to settle in California, in the early 1850s, Luanna learns to accept life for what it is, no matter where.
Dorothy Canfield Fisher, *Understood Betsy*, 1972
   A small and timid girl discovers her own abilities and the world around her when she goes to live with relatives on a farm in Vermont.
Katherine Paterson, *Lyddie*, 1991
   Poor Vermont farm girl Lyddie Worthen is determined to gain her independence by becoming a factory worker in Lowell, Massachusetts in the 1840s.
Robert Newton Peck, *Hang for Treason*, 1976
   A Vermont youth helps Ethan Allen and the Green Mountain Boys despite his father's Tory leanings in the early days of the Revolutionary War.
Manly Wade Wellman, *Brave Horse: The Story of Janus*, 1968
   An 18th century horse brought from England to Virginia who recovered from lameness to win one more race and began the American Quarterhorse breed.

854

Marguerite Henry

Illustrator: Wesley Dennis

King of the Wind (Chicago: Rand McNally, 1948)

Age range: Grades 4-6

Subject(s): Animals/Horses; Mutism

Time period(s): 18th century

Locale(s): Windsor, Ontario, Canada; Meknes, Morocco; Versailles, France

What the book is about: A mute stableboy saves the life of a foal who is the ancestor of Man O War. He becomes the foal's caretaker and best friend. Though intended as a gift for the boy king, Louis XV of France, Agba's foal and the other horses are thin and weak from their journey and are rejected. Boy and horse travel through Morocco and France and finally find a safe harbor in England.

Where it's reviewed:
Horn Book, November 1948, page 463
New York Times Book Review, November 14, 1948, page 3

Awards the book has won:
Newbery Medal 1949

Other books by the author:
San Domingo, the Medicine Hat Stallion, 1972
Justin Morgan Had a Horse, 1954
Misty of Chincoteague, 1974

Other books you might like:
Glen Rounds, *Blind Outlaw*, 1980
   An "outlaw horse" is brought in with the animal round up and only a nameless mute boy can tame him.
Jean Thompson, *Ghost Horse of the Palisades*, 1986
   Molly's father is obsessed with the wild stallion known as Ghost, who has stolen his mare.
Clyde Robert Bulla, *Conquista*, 1978
   A young Indian alone on the great plains waits for a sign from the gods when he sees a horse escaped from the Spanish, the first any Indian has seen.

| **855** |

Marguerite Henry

Illustrator: Wesley Dennis

Misty of Chincoteague (New York: Macmillan, 1947)

Age range: Grades 4-6

Subject(s): Animals/Horses

Major character(s): Paul Beebe, Child; Maureen Beebe, Child; Grandma Beebe, Grandparent

Time period(s): 1940s

Locale(s): Chincoteague Island, Virginia

What the book is about: The legend is that the wild ponies of Assateague are descended from a boatload of Spanish horses shipwrecked three hundred years ago. A Virginia brother and sister take part in the annual pony drive and capture a special wild pony and her foal.

Where it's reviewed:
Horn Book, January 1948, page 38
Kirkus Reviews, October 15, 1947, page 581

Awards the book has won:
Newbery Honor

Other books by the author:
Misty's Twilight, 1992
Sea Star, Orphan of Chincoteague, 1970
Stormy, Misty's Foal, 1963
Gaudenzia, Pride of the Palio, 1960

Other books you might like:
Barbara Corcoran, *A Horse Named Sky*, 1986
   Georgia's one goal, when she moves to Montana, is to own a horse, a dream that remains remote until a neighbor promises to sell her a wild mustang.
Walter Farley, *The Black Stallion Legend*, 1983
   The black stallion helps save an Indian tribe during a time of disaster, thereby fulfilling an ancient prophecy.
Mary Holmes, *Thunder Foot*, 1992
   In 1730, Running Dog finds a horse, an animal unknown to the Cheyenne, and brings it back to his tribe.
Dorothy Nafus Morrison, *Somebody's Horse*, 1986
   When Jenny's care transforms a pathetic horse into an incredible jumper, there remains the question of who is the owner of the horse.
Michael Slade, *The Horses of Central Park*, 1992
   Wendell and Judith help the horses who pull the carriages in Central Park to have one glorious night of freedom.

| **856** |

Marguerite Henry

Illustrator: Robert Lougheed

San Domingo, the Medicine Hat Stallion (New York: Rand McNally, 1972)

Age range: Grades 4-7

Subject(s): Animals/Horses; American West

Major character(s): Peter Lundy, Horse Trainer; San Domingo, Horse; Jethro Lundy, Parent (Peter's father)

Time period(s): 19th century (1850-1860)

Locale(s): Nebraska

What the book is about: Peter Lundy has a talent for treating and training animals. When he is twelve, he is given a foal with the head markings of a medicine hat, which the Indians consider sacred. Peter names him San Domingo, trains him until he has a beautiful, powerful two year old. His father, who loves a bargain, trades San Domingo for a thoroughbred and Peter is shattered. Peter leaves home and joins the Pony Express and he happily meets San Domingo again.

Where it's reviewed:
Social Education, October 1980, page 481

Other books by the author:
Cinnabar the One O'Clock Fox, 1980
Black Gold, 1957
Brighty of the Grand Canyon, 1953
Benjamin West and His Cat Grimalkin, 1947

Other books you might like:
Patricia Calvert, *The Money Creek Mare*, 1981
   Sharing her father's dream of having a champion horse farm, Ella Rae secretly takes his crippled red mare to mate with a famous stallion.
Walter Farley, *The Horse-Tamer*, 1958
   An 18th century carriage maker turns professional horse tamer and deals with many vicious or badly trained horses, and one unscrupulous showman.
Lynn Hall, *The Horse Trader*, 1981
   A fatherless teenage girl's special friendship with Harley, the local horse trader and con man, begins to change after she buys one of his horses.
Amy C. Laundrie, *Whinny of the Wild Horses*, 1990
   Follows the adventures of a wild colt living on the Wyoming range from his birth to the time when he is a full grown stallion.
Bill Wallace, *Red Dog*, 1987
   Living with his family in the rugged mountains, Adam finds his courage put to the test when he is left in charge of the household.

| **857** |

Nat Hentoff

Jazz Country (New York: Harper, 1965)

Age range: Grades 6 and Up

Subject(s): Race Relations; Music

Major character(s): Tom Curtis, 12th Grader, Musician

Time period(s): 1960s

Locale(s): United States

What the book is about: Tom Curtis, a high school senior, struggles to make a place for himself in professional jazz. The reader shares his passion for music and his efforts to become part of the Black experience.

Where it's reviewed:
Horn Book, October 1965, page 517
Library Journal, May 15, 1965, page 2418

Awards the book has won:
Nancy Bloch Memorial Award 1965

Other books by the author:
The Day They Came to Arrest the Book, 1982
Does This School Have Capital Punishment?, 1981
This School Is Driving Me Crazy, 1976
Jazz Makers, 1957 (non-fiction)

Other books you might like:
T. Ernesto Bethancourt, *Tune in Yesterday*, 1978
  Two teenage boys with a passion for jazz and big band music accidentally find a way to go back in time to 1942.
Gillian Cross, *Chartbreaker*, 1986
  Young Janis joins a rock group to escape her depressed mother and her hostile boyfriend.
Carolyn Keene, *Deadly Intent*, 1986, 198
  Nancy Drew tries to find a missing rock star who disappeared just after calling Nancy with "someting important to tell her."
Suzanne Newton, *I Will Call It Georgie's Blues*, 1983
  Because his father is a minister, Neal feels he must hide his passion for jazz.
Erika Tomar, *Blues for Silk Garcia*, 1983
  15 year old Linda resembles her father and has his gift for music, and must deal with his death.

858

Nat Hentoff

This School is Driving Me Crazy (New York: Delacorte, 1975)

Age range: Grades 5 and Up

Subject(s): School Life; Fathers and Sons

Major character(s): Sam Davidson, 6th Grader; Mr. Kozodoy, Teacher; Mr. Davidson, Teacher (headmaster)

Time period(s): 1970s

Locale(s): United States

What the book is about: Sam's dad is headmaster of the boys' school Sam attend. Sam is always up to something, but he is falsely accused by a thief. The real bullies are discovered and the attitudes of the teachers are exposed.

Where it's reviewed:
Kirkus Reviews, November 15, 1975, page 1296
School Library Journal, February 1976, page 53

Awards the book has won:
Golden Archer Award 1980

Other books by the author:
Boston Boy, 1986
The Day They Came to Arrest the Book, 1982
Does This School Have Capital Punishment?, 1981

Other books you might like:
Ellen Conford, *You Can Never Tell*, 1984

Kate is disappointed when the soap opera star attending her school is not as exciting as his screen counterpart.
Betsy Haynes, *The Fabulous Five in Trouble*, 1990
  A group of five friends seem to be growing apart after starting junior high school
Alice Low, *Genie and the Witch's Spells*, 1982
  Genie has a hard time with her schoolwork until she and Merlina, a witch who has trouble learning her spells, begin a partnership and help each other.
Helen McCann, *What Do We Do Now, George?*, 1989
  George's plans to raise money for his school and keep a percentage for himself create chaos and get him in trouble with friends and the authorities.
Richard Shaw, *Shape Up, Burke*, 1976
  Pat and his father, a former policeman, don't agree on very many things and Pat is to be sent to a military school to "shape up."

859

Dirlie Herlihy

Ludie's Song (New York: Dial, 1988)

Age range: Grades 6-8

Subject(s): Friendship; Race Relations; Kidnapping

Major character(s): Martha, Teenager; Ludie, Teenager, Abuse Victim

Time period(s): 1950s

Locale(s): Georgia

What the book is about: We see the prejudice and racial hatred of the 1950s South in this story of thirteen year old Martha who visits her aunt and uncle in Georgia. Martha develops a friendship with Ludie, a black girl who has been sexually abused and almost burned to death. Martha gets to know Ludie's brother, Chili, and she and Chili are kidnapped. Chili is beaten and Martha is called a nigger lover. Not subtle, this gives a vivid picture of the kinds of abuses which finally ignited the Civil Rights Movement.

Where it's reviewed:
Horn Book, November/December, 1988, page 788
School Library Journal, September 1988, page 198

Other books you might like:
Gary W. Barger, *Life. Is. Not. Fair.*, 1984
  Louis and his aunt are startled and upset when a black family moves next door to their Kansas City home in 1958.
Beth Bland Engel, *Big Words*, 1982
  Sandy befriends a black man she finds hiding on her father's property after he has been accused of murdering a white woman in their Georgia town.
Virginia Hamilton, *A White Romance*, 1987
  Tally befriends a white girl who shares her passion for running and becomes involved with a drug dealer.
Margaret Sacks, *Beyond Safe Boundaries*, 1989
  Elizabeth comes of age in 1960s South Africa as her older sister joins a secret group opposed to the country's racial policies.
Mildred D. Taylor, *The Road to Memphis*, 1992
  A black youth, sadistically teased by two white boys in Mississippi, severely injures one of them and enlists help in trying to flee the state.

860

Charlotte Herman

Our Snowman Had Olive Eyes (New York: Dutton, 1977)

Age range: Grades 5-7

Subject(s): Grandparents

Major character(s): Sheila, Child; Rita, Friend; Bubbie, Grandparent

Time period(s): 1970s

Locale(s): United States

What the book is about: Before Bubbie, her grandmother, came to live with Sheila and her family, Sheila's friend, Rita, warned her it would be terrible sharing her room, having two women bossing her around all day, and all kinds of trouble. But Bubbie is not at all like that. Sheila enjoys her attention, watching her make her favorite cookies without a recipe, and helping her make a snowman with just the right eyes.

Where it's reviewed:
Booklist, January 1, 1978, page 747
Hornbook, April 1978, page 166
Kirkus, December 1, 1977, page 1266

Other books by the author:
A Summer on Thirteenth Street, 1991
Millie Cooper, Take a Chance, 1988
What Happened to Heather Hopkowitz?, 1981
The Difference of Ari Stein, 1976

Other books you might like:
Jeanne Betancourt, *Home Sweet Home*, 1988
  Tracy's family moves from New York City to Grandmother Tilly's farm. Anya, a new russian exchange student, becomes one of her few friends.
Martha Derman, *The Friendstone*, 1981
  Sally's view of life expands when she befriends a Jewish girl in the summer of 1929, while in the Catskills with her beloved great-grandmother.
Amy Hest, *Maybe Next Year*, 1982
  Kate, who lives with her grandmother on Manhattan's Upper West Side, must resolve the conflict between her ballet and her home life.
Suzanne Newton, *A Place Between*, 1986
  Arden must move from her beloved home town to an unwelcoming city and adjust to living with her widowed grandmother.
Mildred Pitts Walter, *Trouble's Child*, 1985
  Martha longs to leave her Louisiana island home for high school where she hopes to broaden her life and hopefully the lives of the other islanders.

861

Charlotte Herman

What Happened to Heather Hopkowitz? (New York: Dutton, 1981)

Age range: Grades 5-6

Subject(s): Jews; Religion; Secrets

Major character(s): Heather Hopkowitz, Teenager; Shani Greenwald, Teenager

Time period(s): 1980s

Locale(s): United States

What the book is about: Heather's parents, who are non-observant Jews, go on a month-long cruise, and Heather stays with the Greenwalds who are Orthodox. Heather enjoys the power of their faith and begins to develop her own. When her parents return, they are shocked at the change in Heather's attitudes and the family works through the problems and comes to appreciate Heather's faith.

Where it's reviewed:
Booklist, November 1, 1981, page 388
School Library Journal, December 1981, page 64

Other books by the author:
Max Malone and the Great Cereal Rip-Off, 1990
On the Way to the Movies, 1981
My Mother Didn't Kiss Me Goodnight, 1980
Our Snowman Had Olive Eyes, 1977

Other books you might like:
Chester Aaron, *Gideon*, 1982
  After losing family and friends, Gideon must bury religion and identity to survive the Warsaw Ghetto and Treblinka concentration camp in WWII.
Barbara Barrie, *Lone Star*, 1990
  Moving from Chicago to Corpus Christi, Texas, in 1944, a young Jewish girl copes with a new lifestyle which alienates her orthodox grandfather.
Johanna Hurwitz, *Once I Was a Plum Tree*, 1980
  Gerry knows she is Jewish, but when she meets Edgar, she becomes really interested in learning about her heritage.
Howard Muggamin, *The Jewish Americans*, 1988
  Discusses the history, culture and religion of the Jews, factors encouraging their emigration, and their acceptance in North America. (Non-fiction)
White Deer of Autumn, *Ceremony - In the Circle of Life*, 1983
  Little Turtle, a Native American boy who grew up in the city without knowing his heritage, is visited by a Spirit, who introduces him to his culture.

862

Patricia Hermes

Illustrator: Carol Newsom

Heads, I Win (San Diego: Harcourt Brace, 1988)

Age range: Grades 4-6

Subject(s): Politics; Foster Homes; Schools

Major character(s): Bailey Wharton, Preteen; Kevin Corbett, Preteen

Time period(s): 1980s

Locale(s): United States

What the book is about: In this sequel to *Kevin Corbett Eats Flies*, Bailey runs for class president, hoping that popularity will secure her place in her current foster home.

Where it's reviewed:
Booklit, June 15, 1988, page 1737
Kirkus Reviews, May 15, 1988, page 761
School Library Journal, August 1988, page 95

Other books by the author:
Mama, Let's Dance, 1991

I Hate Being Gifted, 1990
Kevin Corbett Eats Flies, 1986
Friends Are Like That, 1984

Other books you might like:
Johanna Hurwitz, *Class President*, 1990
   Julio hides his own leadership ambitions to help another candidate win the nomination for class president.
Claudia Mills, *Dinah for President*, 1992
   In her first year of middle school, Dinah struggles to become a big fish, while discovering the value of recycling and friendship with the elderly.
Judy K. Morris, *The Kid Who Ran for Principal*, 1990
   A shy sixth grader learns how to assert herself when she is encouraged to run for interim principal of her school.
Barbara Park, *Rosie Swanson: Fourth Grade Geek for President*, 1991
   Average, unpopular Rosie runs for class president against two of the most popular kids in the class.
Lila Perl, *Don't Ask Miranda*, 1979
   When Miranda is asked to cheat to help her candidate win the school election, she must make some painful choices.

863

Patricia Hermes

I Hate Being Gifted (New York: Putnam, 1990)

Age range: Grades 4-6

Subject(s): Gifted Children; Friendship

Major character(s): KT, Preteen; Melinda, Preteen; Chrissy, Preteen

Time period(s): 1990s

Locale(s): United States

What the book is about: KT has been selected for the Learning Enrichment Activity Program. She is no longer in homeroom with her best friends. She watches as Erica takes her place in her old circle of friends. LEAP isn't nearly as bad as she imagined, but losing her friends is very painful.

Where it's reviewed:
Kirkus Reviews, December 1, 1990, page 1672
School Library Journal, December 1990, page 103

Other books by the author:
Mama, Let's Dance, 1991
Heads, I Win, 1988
A Place for Jeremy, 1987
What If They Knew?, 1980

Other books you might like:
Roald Dahl, *Matilda*, 1988
   Matilda's imaginative wickedness allows her to visit revenge on unloving parents, defeat the headmistress and return Miss Honey where she belongs.
Mary Downing Hahn, *Daphne's Book*, 1983
   Jessica and Daphne work on a book for a school contest. Jessica becomes aware of conditions in Daphne's home that threaten her health and safety.
Paul Kropp, *Moonkid and Liberty*, 1990
   Libby and Ian live with their non-conformist father. They are starting at a new school when their mother wants them to move with her to California.
Phyllis Reynolds Naylor, *The Agony of Alice*, 1985

Motherless Alice wants a gorgeous role model who does everything right. When she is placed in homely Mrs. Plotkin's class she is greatly disappointed.
Susan Richards Shreve, *The Flunking of Joshua T. Bates*, 1984
Sometimes children are held back in school even if they are smart.

864

Patricia Hermes

Nobody's Fault (New York: Harcourt Brace Jovanovich, 1981)

Age range: Grades 4-6

Subject(s): Death; Guilt

Major character(s): Emily Taylor, Child; Matthew "Monse" Taylor, Child

Time period(s): 1980s

Locale(s): United States

What the book is about: Emily and Matthew (Monse, short for monster) are typical siblings, both loving and competitive. Emily is hunting for a dead snake to frighten Monse when he falls off the riding mower, is run over, and bleeds to death. Emily feels deep guilt and needs help to come to terms with it.

Where it's reviewed:
School Library Journal, December 1981, page 64

Other books by the author:
I Hate Being Gifted, 1990
Be Still My Heart, 1989
A Time to Listen, 1987
What If They Knew?, 1980

Other books you might like:
Betsy Byars, *A Blossom Promise*, 1987
   In the aftermath of a big flood, the Blossom family copes in rare style.
Richard Kennedy, *Come Again in the Spring*, 1976
   An old man tries to outsmart death with the help of the birds who come to his cabin.
Richard Peck, *Close Enough to Touch*, 1981
   A boy trying to recover from the loss of his girlfriend meets an unusual girl. (Mature Readers)
Marc Talbert, *Dead Birds Singing*, 1985
   After his mother is killed and his sister badly injured in a car accident, Matt faces life with a new family and a deep sense of anger.
Paul Zindel, *A Begonia for Miss Applebaum*, 1989
   Discovering that a former teacher is terminally ill, Henry and Zelda join her on excursions and help her confront death with quiet courage.

865

Patricia Hermes

What If They Knew? (New York: Harcourt, 1980)

Age range: Grades 4-5

Subject(s): Epilepsy; Friendship

Major character(s): Jeremy, Child; Libby, Child; Mimi, Child

Time period(s): 1980s

Locale(s): New York, New York (Brooklyn)

What the book is about: A ten year old girl, staying with her grandparents for the summer, is appalled to discover that her parents won't be returning as planned. She must start in a new school and somehow hide the fact that she is epileptic.

Where it's reviewed:
Reading Teacher, January 1981, page 486
Times Educational Supplement, June 5, 1981, page 38

Awards the book has won:
Crabbery Award 1981

Other books by the author:
Mama, Let's Dance, 1991
Be Still My Heart, 1989
A Time to Listen, 1987
Nobody's Fault, 1981

Other books you might like:
Ann R. Blakeslee, *After the Fortune Cookies*, 1989
    Allison fights to protect her grandfather from the schemes of other family members and seeks the courage to stand up to her spiteful cousin, Caroline.
Sheila Cragg, *Run Patty Run*, 1980
    The story of a very special long-distance runner who lights the way for others. (Biography)
Tom McGowen, *Epilepsy*, 1989
    Discusses the causes of epilepsy, diagnosis and treatment, and what to do if someone is having a seizure. (Non-fiction)
Deborah M. Moss, *Lee, the Rabbit with Epilepsy*, 1989
    Lee is diagnosed with epilepsy but learns that with medicine her seizures can be controlled. (Related picture book)
Zoa Sherburne, *Why Have the Birds Stopped Singing?*, 1974
    During a seizure, epileptic Katie travels to a time when epilepsy is misunderstood and is mistaken for her epileptic great great great grandmother.

866

Patricia Hermes

You Shouldn't Have to Say Goodbye (San Diego: Harcourt Brace Jovanovich, 1982)

Age range: Grades 5-8

Subject(s): Cancer; Death; Mothers and Daughters

Major character(s): Sarah Morrow, Teenager

Time period(s): 1980s

Locale(s): United States

What the book is about: Sarah learns that her mother is dying of cancer, and experiences rage and denial. Her mother tries to face reality and tell Sarah the things she will need to know to take care of herself, but Sarah does not want to hear. After her mother's death, Sarah reads the journal her mother kept for her. An authentic portrayal of grief.

Where it's reviewed:
Kirkus Reviews, November 1, 1982, page 1192
School Library Journal, February 1983, page 76

Other books by the author:
Mama, Let's Dance, 1991
Heads, I Win, 1988
Who Will Take Care of Me?, 1983

Nobody's Fault, 1982

Other books you might like:
Dean Hughes, *Switching Tracks*, 1982
    A lonely ninth grader, struggling with a sense of responsibility for his father's suicide, learns that his new friend has cancer.
Robert Lipsyte, *The Chemo Kid*, 1992
    Fred is amazed when the drugs he takes as part of chemotherapy change him into a superhero.
Peggy Mann, *There Are Two Kinds of Terrible*, 1977
    Rob's mom goes to the hospital for tests and never comes back.
Lois Ruby, *Miriam's Well*, 1993
    When Miriam develops bone cancer, a battle follows over whether or not she should be treated.
Hans Stolp, *The Golden Bird*, 1990
    The visits of a phoenix-like golden bird are a great comfort to ten year old Daniel who is dying of cancer.

867

James Herriot

Illustrator: Peter Barrett

Only One Woof (New York: St. Martin's, 1985)

Age range: Grades 2-3

Subject(s): Animals/Dogs; Animals/Sheep; Farm Life

Major character(s): Gyp, Dog (sheep dog); Sweep, Dog; Mr. Wilkin, Farmer

Time period(s): 1930s

Locale(s): Yorkshire, England

What the book is about: Sweep is taken by a sheep farmer and become an excellent sheepdog. Gyp stays at Mr. Wilkin's farm and never barks, until one day at the sheepdog trials, when he sees his brother, Sweep, again.

Where it's reviewed:
Horn Book, March/April 1986, page 192
School Library Journal, January 1986, page 57

Other books by the author:
Smudge, 1991
Blossom Comes Home, 1988
Bonny's Big Day, 1987
Moses the Kitten, 1985

Other books you might like:
Frances Hodgson Burnett, *The Secret Garden*, 1910
    Mary comes to live in a lonely house on the Yorkshire moors and discovers an invalid cousin and the mysteries of a locked garden.
Lynn Hall, *Megan's Mare*, 1983
    Megan, daughter of a Yorkshire horse trainer, helps the beautiful problem mare, Berry, overcome her fear of wooden bridges.
Edith Thacher Hurd, *The Black Dog Who Went into the Woods*, 1980
    A family has to cope with the death of their beloved pet dog.
Joan Tate, *Wild Boy*, 1973
    A Yorkshire boy often dreams of living alone on the moors until he meets a strange boy doing just that.

868

Kathleen Hersom

The Half-Child (New York: Simon and Schuster, 1989)

Age range: Grades 5-7

Subject(s): Sisters; Superstition

Major character(s): Lucy Emerson, Preteen; Sarah Emerson, Child, Handicapped

Time period(s): 17th century

Locale(s): Yorkshire, England

What the book is about: In 17th century Yorkshire, Lucy cares for her younger sister, Sarah, who villagers think is a changeling, a fairy child substituted by the fairies for a human child. One day, another baby is born to the Emerson family and Sarah mysteriously disappears. Have the fairies finally reclaimed her?

Where it's reviewed:
School Library Journal, November 1991, page 117

Awards the book has won:
Pick of the Year - English Schoolchildren

Other books by the author:
The Copycat, 1989

Other books you might like:
Beth Hilgartner, *A Murder for Her Majesty*, 1986
    Having witnessed her father's murder, eleven year old Alice Tuckfield takes refuge in a boys' choir school connected to the great cathedral in York.
Jan Slepian, *Risk n' Roses*, 1990
    Skip prizes friends so much, she allows her friend, Jean, to act spitefully toward her retarded sister.
Alexandra Whitaker, *Dream Sister*, 1986
    Dreams of a strange, ghostly sister disturb ten year old Ann, a bright sensitive child with a pesky younger sister.
David Wiseman, *Blodwen and the Guardians*, 1983
    The tiny Guardians enlist the help of a human girl, Blodwen, to stop construction which threatens to destroy their home.
Patricia Wrightson, *A Little Fear*, 1983
    Mrs. Tucker seeks sanctuary in an old cottage but a stubborn gnome resents her and her dog and promises to make trouble.

869

Alison Cragin Herzig

The Ten-Speed Babysitter (New York: Dutton, 1987)

Age range: Grades 5-7

Subject(s): Babysitters; Hurricanes

Major character(s): Tony Patterson, Babysitter, Teenager; Maisie DuBois, Employer; Duncan DuBois, Child

Time period(s): 1980s

Locale(s): West Hazardsville, Connecticut

What the book is about: Tony takes his bicycle with him when he goes to West Hazardsville, Connecticut to babysit for Maisie DuBois' son, Duncan. A snap of a babysitting job proves quite a test for Tony when he has to cope by himself for the weekend; things being stolen, strange phone calls late at night. Then when Tony goes with a new friend, Tremaine, to the beach, Duncan disappears. They discover him in a rookery, surrounded by nesting, hostile birds, and bring him back to safety. Just about the time Mrs. DuBois is due home, a hurricane hits, delays her and knocks out the phone. A robbery while Tony and Duncan are in the house is the final straw. Tony may never babysit again!

Where it's reviewed:
Booklist, October 1, 1987, page 319
Kirkus Reviews, September 15, 1987, page 1393
School Library Journal, September 1987, page 179

Other books by the author:
The Big Deal, 1992
The Boonsville Bombers, 1991
Sam and the Moon Queen, 1990
Oh, Boy, Babies, 1980

Other books you might like:
Nancy Hale, *The Night of the Hurricane*, 1978
    A young boy, his friends, and their parents discover many things about themselves and each other during a hurricane on the Massachusetts coast.
Marian Rumsey, *Carolina Hurricane*, 1977
    Lost in a crab boat in the middle of the South Carolina salt marsh, Morgan endures the full brunt of the hurricane.
Andrew Salkey, *Hurricane*, 1979
    Joe and his sister face their first hurricane in Kingston, Jamaica with a mixture of excitement and curiosity that gradually turns to fear.
James Stevenson, *Here Come's Herb's Hurricane!*, 1973
    Herb, the rabbit, organizes a hurricane alarm system for the animals which seems a terrific idea until something unexpected happens.
Charlene Joy Talbot, *The Great Rat Island Adventure*, 1977
    A young boy accompanies his preoccupied ornithologist father on a summer expedition and encounters a hurricane.

870

Lilo Hess

The Good Luck Dog (New York: Scribner, 1985)

Age range: Grades 2-4

Subject(s): Animals/Dogs; Deafness

Major character(s): Heather, Handicapped (deaf); Rahloo, Dog

Time period(s): 1980s

Locale(s): United States

What the book is about: A terrier is dognapped and intended for lab experiments, but ends up in training as a companion for a deaf girl.

Where it's reviewed:
Center for Children's Books Bulletin, June 1985, page 186
School Library Journal, August 1985, page 65

Other books by the author:
That Snake in the Grass, 1987
Secrets in the Meadow, 1986
Diary of a Rabbit, 1982
A Dog by Your Side, 1977

Other books you might like:
Patricia Curtis, *Cindy, Hearing Ear Dog*, 1981

Describes the training of young dogs, selected from pounds and humane shelters, to help deaf owners by alerting them to sounds they cannot hear.

Phyllis Raybin Emert, *Hearing Ear Dogs*, 1985

Discusses the history, training, uses and breeds of dogs who work with the deaf, and lists hearing dog programs in the United States.

Stephen Golder, *Buffy's Orange Leash*, 1988

Describes Buffy's selection and training as a hearing ear dog, and tells how he helps his deaf owners.

Mary Ellen Siegel, *More than a Friend: Dogs with a Purpose*, 1984

Describes some of the jobs for which dogs have been trained and their work as hunters, shepherds, guides for the handicapped, guards, and more.

Linda Yeatman, *Buttons:The Dog Who Was More Than a Friend*, 1985

Being separated from his human family, a mother and son who are both deaf, a puppy becomes a hearing ear dog and later is reunited with his owners.

871

Amy Hest

Illustrator: Jacqueline Rogers

Getting Rid of Krista (New York: Morrow, 1988)

Age range: Grades 3-5

Subject(s): Animals/Dogs; Family Life

Major character(s): Gillian "Gillie", Child; Hank, Friend

Time period(s): 1980s

Locale(s): United States

What the book is about: Her older sister is too perfect to believe, so Gillian, nine, and her friend plan to get her "discovered" and sent to Broadway.

Where it's reviewed:
Booklist, March 1, 1988, page 1181
Center for Children's Books Bulletin, May 1988, page 179
Hornbook, July 1988, page 494

Other books by the author:
Pajama Party, 1992
Love You, Soldier, 1991
Pete and Lily, 1986
Maybe Next Year, 1982

Other books you might like:
Stan Berenstain, *The Berenstain Bears and the Nerdy Nephew*, 1993

Brother and Sister don't realize the problems they will face when they agree to help Professor Actual Factual's super-smart nephew fit in at school.

Marsha Wilson Chall, *Mattie*, 1992

Mattie's adventures include selling her brother, finding the perfect Valentine's Day gift for an obnoxious classmate, and cutting her brother's hair.

Linda Glaser, *Keep Your Socks on, Albert!*, 1992

Adventures of a young brother and sister who enjoy each other but can't resist teasing.

Debi Gliori, *My Little Brother*, 1992

When it appears that magic spells, vanishing cremes, and other schemes to rid her of her brother have finally worked, a sister has second thoughts.

Constance Hiser, *Sixth-Grade Star*, 1992

Getting a part in the school play doesn't keep Jill from being jealous of the attention her sister gets from her participation in beauty pageants.

872

Amy Hest

Love You, Soldier (New York: Four Winds, 1991)

Age range: Grades 3-4

Subject(s): Jews; World War II

Major character(s): Katie, Child; Mrs. Leitstein, Neighbor; Louise, Friend (pregnant)

Time period(s): 1940s

Locale(s): New York, New York

What the book is about: Seven year old Katie longs for her soldier father to come home, but of course life goes on as she and her mother wait. A pregnant friend moves in with them and Katie is a hero for helping Louise get to the hospital. When the bad news comes that Katie's father has been killed, the family's love sustains them.

Where it's reviewed:
Children's Book Review Service, October 1991, page 19
Horn Book, September 1991, page 591

Other books by the author:
Go-Between, 1992
Pajama Party, 1992
Ring and the Window Seat, 1990
Getting Rid of Krista, 1988

Other books you might like:
Miriam Chaikin, *Lower! Higher! You're a Liar!*, 1984

Molly, the daughter of Palestinian parents, organizes a club to boycott the neighborhood bully in Brooklyn during WWII.

Riki Levinson, *Dinnie Abbie Sister-R-R!*, 1987

Growing up in Brooklyn means dancing in the rain, baking with her aunt, and helping her brother through a serious illness.

Sonia Livitin, *Silver Days*, 1989

A prosperous immigrant family lives in New York City until Papa decides to move to California during WWII.

Yuri Suhl, *The Purim Goat*, 1980

Hoping to earn some money so his pet goat won't be sold to pay a debt, a poor Jewish boy teaches the animal to dance.

Terry W. Treseder, *Hear O Israel: A Story of the Warsaw Ghetto*, 1990

A Jewish boy describes life in the Warsaw Ghetto and his family's removal to Treblinka.

873

Amy Hest

Maybe Next Year (New York: Clarion, 1982)

Age range: Grades 4-6

Subject(s): Ballet; Jews

Major character(s): Kate Newman, Preteen, Dancer; Peter Robinson, Teenager, Dancer

Time period(s): 1980s

Locale(s): New York, New York

What the book is about: Kate and her friend Peter are excited about auditions for the National Ballet Summer School. Meanwhile, Nana, Kate's guardian, takes in a roomer who starts a cookie business. When Kate decides she is not ready for the audition, her teacher and friends are disappointed but support her decision.

Where it's reviewed:
Center for Children's Books Bulletin, February 1983, page 109
Horn Book, December 1982, page 649

Other books by the author:
Pajama Party, 1992
Best Ever Goodbye Party, 1989
Midnight Eaters, 1989
Getting Rid of Krista, 1988

Other books you might like:
Karen Strickler Dean, *Between Dances*, 1982
   Maggie Adams is torn between her career as a ballet dancer and her pending marriage.
James David Landis, *The Sisters Impossible*, 1979
   Lily's beginning ballet classes draw her unexpectedly closer to her haughty older sister, already an advanced dancer.
Jahnna N. Malcolm, *The Terrible Tryouts*, 1989
   Five girls have to take ballet lessons and don't like the idea.
Nancy Robison, *Ballet Magic*, 1982
   Stacey is the tallest girl in her class but is still able to excel at ballet.
Jean Ure, *You Win Some, You Lose Some*, 1984
   Jamie's decision to leave school and become a ballet dancer brings him problems but strengthens his character.

874

Amy Hest

The Ring and the Window Seat (New York: Scholastic, 1990)

Age range: Grades 2-3

Subject(s): Virtues

Major character(s): Annie, Child; Stella, Relative (aunt)

Time period(s): 1940s

Locale(s): United States

What the book is about: Annie visits Aunt Stella on her birthday. A storm ruins her party, but it does bring an unexpected guest. Although she has been saving for a ring, Stella decides to give her bundle of nickles to a carpenter who is trying to rescue a little girl from a war-torn country.

Where it's reviewed:
Kirkus Reviews, December 1, 1990, page 1673
School Library Journal, December 1990, page 79

Other books by the author:
Fancy Aunt Jess, 1990
Travel Tips From Harry, 1990
The Purple Coat, 1986
The Crack of Dawn Walkers, 1984

Other books you might like:
Mary Blount Christian, *The Devil Take You, Barnabas Beane!*, 1980
   When he sees the devil's hoofprints in the snow around his house, a selfish man quickly changes his ways.
Heather Forest, *The Baker's Dozen: A Colonial American Tale*, 1988
   A greedy baker who offends a mysterious old woman suffers misfortune in his business, until he discovers what happens when generosity replaces greed.
Beatrice Gormley, *Ellie's Birthstone Ring*, 1992
   As she plans her seventh birthday party, Ellie must decide whether or not to invite an older girl who lives nearby.
Angela McAllister, *The King Who Sneezed*, 1988
   Mean and stingy King Parsimonious does not care about the comfort of his subjects, until he tries to find out why his castle is so cold.
Eleanor Schick, *Rainy Sunday*, 1981
   A young girl enjoys some unexpected pleasures on a rainy day.

875

Janet Hickman

Illustrator: Richard Cuffari

The Stones (New York: Macmillan, 1976)

Age range: Grades 4-6

Subject(s): Prejudice; World War II

Major character(s): Jack, Vagrant; Garrett, Child

Time period(s): 1940s

Locale(s): United States (Midwestern Town)

What the book is about: When Garrett and his friends discover that the old man they have been teasing is a German-American named Adolph Schilling, they torment him even more. When they steal cans from his storage shed, a dog is accidentally killed. Garrett learns about prejudice when Jack saves his little sister's life.

Where it's reviewed:
Kirkus Reviews, July 15, 1976, page 794
School Library Journal, October 1976, page 107

Other books by the author:
Thunder Pup, 1981
Zoar Blue, 1978

Other books you might like:
Matt Christopher, *The Basket Counts*, 1991
   Long practice improves Mel's value as a basketball player, but how does he surmount the prejudice of a teammate?
Matt Christopher, *No Arm in Left Field*, 1974
   A poor throwing arm and prejudice from one white boy keep a black junior high student from enjoying his position on the baseball team.
William Crane, *Encore*, 1983
   Darlene and Sheryle help their band teacher overcome the principal's prejudice against him and their band.
June Andrea Hanson, *Winter of the Owl*, 1980
   Thirteen year old Janey learns some important lessons about friendship, prejudice, and the nature of independence.
John R. Tunis, *Keystone Kids*, 1990

When two brothers join the Dodgers, one becomes the manager faced with the task of uniting a team rife with prejudice against the Jewish rookie.

876

Janet Hickman

Thunder Pup (New York: Macmillan, 1981)

Age range: Grades 3-5

Subject(s): Animals/Dogs; Friendship; Moving, Household

Major character(s): Linnie McKay, Child; Darla Champion, Child; Harry, Dog

Time period(s): 1950s

Locale(s): Midwest

What the book is about: Linnie wants a dog for her tenth birthday more than anything else. Shortly before her birthday, Darla, the daughter of an Army buddy, comes to stay with Linnie. Unfortunately, Darla hates the country and hates (and fears) dogs. Linnie's own fear is thunderstorms, and she and Darla, in helping each other, find they have more in common than they thought. A special treat for dog lovers.

Where it's reviewed:
Center for Children's Books Bulletin, December 1981, page 69
School Library Journal, November 1981, page 92

Other books by the author:
Zoar Blue, 1978
The Stones, 1976

Other books you might like:
Patricia Lee Gauch, Kate Alone, 1980
　　Kate must decide what to do with her vicious dog.
Helen Griffith, The Dog at the Window, 1984
　　Alison's dream of owning a dog is fulfilled when she meets fierce and lonely Wolf, a German Shepherd.
Lynn Hall, The Mystery of the Schoolhouse Dog, 1979
　　Is the white dog in the abandoned schoolhouse real or a ghost dog?
Lilo Hess, The Good Luck Dog, 1985
　　A terrier is kidnapped and intended for laboratory experiments, but she ends up in training as a companion for a deaf girl.
Walt Morey, The Lemon Meringue Dog, 1980
　　A narcotics squad dog must prove his worth.

877

Clifford B. Hicks

Illustrator: Eileen Christelow

Alvin Fernald, Master of a Thousand Disguises (New York: Holt, 1986)

Age range: Grades 3-6

Subject(s): Treasure; Mystery and Detective Stories

Major character(s): Alvin Fernald, Preteen; Shori, Friend; Daphne, Child

Time period(s): 1980s

Locale(s): Riverton

What the book is about: Alvin and his friend, Shori, and sister, Daphne the Pest thwart the criminals who stole a widow's inheritance. They uncover hidden treasure, a long forgotten love affair, and a secret cave in their home town.

Where it's reviewed:
Booklist, May 15, 1986, page 1396
School Library Journal, May 1986, page 92

Other books by the author:
Alvin Fernald, TV Anchorman, 1980
Alvin's Swap Shop, 1976
Alvin's Secret Code, 1963
The Marvelous Inventions of Alvin Fernald, 1960

Other books you might like:
John W. Chambers, Footlight Summer, 1983
　　A girl working at a theater can't understand her mother's aversion to theater until she finds out the truth about the father she thought was dead.
Barbara Corcoran, Child of the Morning, 1982
　　A girl who has recently learned she has epilepsy joins a summer theater group and aspires to be an actress, but fears having a seizure onstage.
Constance C. Greene, Star Shine, 1985
　　When their mother joins a theater group, Jenny and Mary learn to take care of themselves until a movie company comes to town and Jenny lands a part.
Mary Pope Osborne, Best Wishes, Joe Brady, 1984
　　Sunny Dickens is happy with her life in Summerville, North Carolina, until she falls for a famous soap-opera star named Joe Brady who's come to town.
Joyce Sweeney, Right Behind the Rain, 1987
　　Carla watches with growing concern as her adored and extremely talented brother begins to crack under the pressure of always having to be perfect.

878

Jamake Highwater

Illustrator: Fritz Scholder

Anpao: An American Indian Odyssey (New York: Lippincott, 1977)

Age range: Grades 6 and Up

Subject(s): Indians of North America; Folk Tales

Major character(s): Anpao, Indian, Child

Time period(s): Indeterminate Past

Locale(s): United States

What the book is about: Traditional tales taken from North American Indian tribes woven into one story that relates the adventures of one boy as he grows to manhood.

Where it's reviewed:
Kirkus Reviews, October 1, 1977, page 1053
School Library Journal, October 1977, page 124

Awards the book has won:
Boston Globe/Horn Book Award - Honor Book 1978
Newbery Honor 1978

Other books by the author:
I Wear the Morning Star, 1986
The Ceremony of Innocence, 1985
Eyes of Darkness: A Novel, 1985

Song from the Earth, 1976

Other books you might like:

James A. Houston, *Drifting Snow: An Artic Legend,* 1992
Having been taken away from her Arctic home as a child, a teen returns to look for her parents and learn once again of her Eskimo culture.

Scott O'Dell, *Thunder Rolling in the Mountains,* 1992
A Nez Perce girl relates how her people were driven off their land by the US Army and forced to retreat north until their surrender.

Chap Reaver, *A Little Bit Dead,* 1992
After interfering with the attempted lynching of a Yahi Indian, Shanti, Reece finds his life in danger as he becomes involved with Shanti's people.

Penina Keen Spinka, *White Hare's Horses,* 1971
In 16th century California, a young Chumash Indian must find the courage to save her people from Aztec invaders with their frightening horses.

Kenneth Thomasma, *Kunu: Escape on the Missouri,* 1989
Following the removal of his people from Minnesota to South Dakota, a Winnebago boy embarks on a journey to return to his grandfather in his homeland.

879

E.W. Hildick

Illustrator: Lisl Weil

The Case of the Condemned Cat (New York: Macmillan, 1978)

Age range: Grades 4-6

Subject(s): Animals/Cats; Mystery and Detective Stories

Major character(s): Jack McGurk, Detective; Wanda Grieg, Detective; Willie Sandowsky, Detective

Time period(s): 1970s

Locale(s): United States

What the book is about: Match wits with Jack McGurk and his partners who are hired by Ray Williams to find out who (or what) killed one of the Overshaw's prize doves. It is Ray's cat, Whiskers, who is accused and he wants the McGurk organization to clear the cat's name.

Where it's reviewed:
Handbook, April 1976, page 155
Kirkus, October 15, 1975, page 1184
School Library Journal, December 1975, page 66

Other books by the author:
The Case of the Bashful Bank Robber, 1981
The Case of the Phantom Frog, 1979
The Case of the Invisible Dog, 1977
The Case of the Nervous Newsboy, 1976

Other books you might like:
Frank Bonham, *Mystery of the Fat Cat,* 1968
Four friends, whose club closes for lack of money, try to find an old tomcat whose inheritance is meant for the club but is being misused by others.

Blanche Boshinski, *Aha and the Jewel of Mystery,* 1968
A haughty royal cat and a slave boy escape Egypt hoping to discover the boy's identity and the meaning of the jewel on the cat's collar.

Barbara Corcoran, *Which Witch Is Which?,* 1983

A series of catnappings, including their own cat, lead twins to a scary old woman and an abandoned house where they find both the cats and danger.

Florence Parry Heide, *The Mystery of the Silver Tag,* 1972
When a missing valuable cat turns up in a neighbor's house, three friends conclude that the man is a thief and set out to rescue the animal.

Jean Lewis, *Kathi and Hash San - The Case of Measles,* 1972
With the help of her wise Japanese cat and detective skills, Kathi exonerates the cat next door from a crime he did not commit.

880

E.W. Hildick

Illustrator: Jan Palmer

Manhattan Is Missing (New York: Doubleday, 1969)

Age range: Grades 4-6

Subject(s): Animals/Cats

Major character(s): Peter Clarke, Preteen; Benjie Clarke, Child; Hugh, Friend

Time period(s): 1960s

Locale(s): New York, New York

What the book is about: Manhattan, a prized Siamese cat, is kidnapped and the culprits demand $200 ransom for Manhattan's safe return. Peter, his brother Benjie, and their pal Hugh search New York for the missing feline in this lively mystery.

Where it's reviewed:
Hornbook, June 1969, page 306
Kirkus Reviews, January 15, 1969, page 54
School Library Journal, February 1978, page 35

Other books by the author:
Case of the Desperate Drummer, 1993
The Ghost Squad Flies Concorde, 1985
The Great Rabbit Rip-Off, 1976
The Doughnut Dropout, 1972

Other books you might like:
Marion Dane Bauer, *Ghost Eye,* 1992
Purrloom Popcorn, a beautiful cat with one blue eye and one gold eye, receives his first real love from a lonely girl and an array of ghost cats.

Barbara M. Joosse, *Anna and the Cat Lady,* 1992
When Anna rescues a stray kitten, it leads her into friendship with Mrs. Sarafiny, an eccentric old woman with many cats and a strange conviction.

Janet Taylor Lisle, *The Dancing Cats of Applesap,* 1984
A shy ten year old gets together with one hundred remarkable cats to bring notoriety to Applesap, and to save their beloved Jigg's Drug Store.

Phyllis Reynolds Naylor, *The Grand Escape,* 1993
After years of being house cats, Marco and Polo escape into the dangerous outside world and are sent on three challenging adventures.

Linda Stewart, *Sam the Cat Detective,* 1993
Sam the cat detective takes on the case of a pretty young cat who comes into his office and purrs out her unhappy story.

Beth Hilgartner

A Murder for Her Majesty (Boston: Houghton Mifflin, 1986)

Age range: Grades 5-8

Subject(s): Cathedrals; Mystery and Detective Stories

Major character(s): Alice Tuckfield, Noblewoman

Time period(s): 16th century

Locale(s): York, England

What the book is about: Alice disguises herself as a boy and hides among the choirboys at Yorkshire Cathedral to escape her father's murderers. She witnessed the murder and fears the killers are agents of Queen Elizabeth I. In addition to a tense murder mystery, the descriptions of daily life in the Elizabethan era are vivid and detailed. A book to bring mystery lovers to embrace historical fiction.

Where it's reviewed:
Center for Children's Books Bulletin, September 1986, page 9
School Library Journal, October 1986, page 176
Publishers Weekly, September 26, 1986, page 83

Other books by the author:
The Feast of the Trickster, 1991
Colors in the Dreamweaver's Loom, 1989
Great Gorilla Grins, 1979
A Necklace of Fallen Stars, 1979

Other books you might like:
Gillian Bradshaw, *The Land of Gold*, 1992
    After the murder of her parents, a Nubian princess is helped to her rightful place on the throne by two friendly Egyptians and the dragon, Hathor.
Willo Davis Roberts, *The View From the Cherry Tree*, 1975
    Rob admits having seen a murder, but no one believes him except the murderer.
Joan Lowery Nixon, *Caught in the Act*, 1988
    Eleven year old Michael Patrick Kelly from New York City is sent to a foster home in Missouri with many secrets, one of which may be murder.
Nancy Pitt, *Beyond the High White Wall*, 1986
    Witnessing the murder of a peasant outside her small town in the Russian Ukraine prompts Libby and her family to consider emigrating to America.
Jane Resh Thomas, *The Princess in the Pigpen*, 1989
    Elizabeth, a duke's daughter sick with fever, travels through time from Elizabethan England to a farm town in modern Iowa.

Elizabeth Starr Hill

The Street Dancers (New York: Viking/Penguin, 1991)

Age range: Grades 5-8

Subject(s): Acting; Theater

Major character(s): Fitzi, Child, Entertainer

Time period(s): Indeterminate

Locale(s): New York, New York

What the book is about: Fitzi and her parents are part-time actors, part-time street performers in New York City, and Fitzi has begun to hate it. She is tutored by her parents at home, but more than anything else she wants to go to public school. A warm family story with a vivid portrait of the theatrical life.

Where it's reviewed:
Booklist, June 15, 1991, page 1966
School Library Journal, June 1991, page 106

Other books by the author:
Broadway Chances, 1992
When Christmas Comes, 1989
Bells, 1970
Evan's Corner, 1967

Other books you might like:
T. Ernesto Bethancourt, *New York City, Too Far From Tampa Blues*, 1975
    Newly arrived from Florida with his family, a young Spanish-American boy tells of his experiences living in Brooklyn.
Jack Durish, *Dream Pirate*, 1981
    When Rick quits his job to manage a promising rock group, he doesn't anticipate the numerous problems, including music pirates, that await him.
E.L. Konigsburg, *Up From Jerico Tel*, 1986
    The spirit of a dead actress turns two children invisible and sends them out among a group of street performers to search for a missing necklace.
John M. Langataff, *Shimmy Shimmy Coke-ca-bop!*, 1973
    A collection of city children's street games and rhymes with photographs, text, and in some cases, music.
Colby Rodowsky, *Keeping Time*, 1983
    Drew, a member of a band of street performers in Baltimore, finds himself slipping back in time to 16th century England.

Kirkpatrick Hill

Toughboy and Sister (New York: McElderry, 1990)

Age range: Grades 4-6

Subject(s): Brothers and Sisters; Survival

Major character(s): Toughboy, Preteen, Indian; Sister, Child, Indian; Natasha, Neighbor

Time period(s): Indeterminate Past

Locale(s): Alaska

What the book is about: Ten year old Toughboy and Sister are left at a remote fishing cabine when their father goes into the village to drink. He dies in a drunken stupor. These two Athabascan Indian children must fend for themselves. Good survival story, a little easier to read than Gary Paulsen.

Where it's reviewed:
Booklist, September 15, 1990, page 160
Horn Book, March/April 1991, page 198

Other books you might like:
Allan Baillie, *Adrift*, 1992
    While playing pirates with his little sister and her cat in an old crate he finds on the beach, a young boy suddenly discovers they are adrift.
Charles Hammer, *Wrong-Way Ragsdale*, 1987
    In a moment of anger, Emmett and his sister, Essie, take their father's airplane, make a forced landing, and have to survive in a mountain wilderness.
Jean Rogers, *The Secret Moose*, 1985

A young boy living in Alaska develops an interest in moose and their habits after he sees a moose in his backyard and decides to follow it.

Marian Rumsey, *Danger on Shadow Mountain*, 1970
A twelve year old boy struggles to rescue his kidnapped brother in the Alaskan wilderness.

Cecily Stern, *A Different Kind of Gold*, 1981
A young girl in the Alaskan wilderness helps her family save the land from developers.

884

Anna Grossnickle Hines

Illustrator: Gail Owens

Cassie Bowen Takes Witch Lessons (New York: Dutton, 1985)

Age range: Grades 3-5

Subject(s): Conduct of Life; Friendship; Schools

Major character(s): Cassie Bowen, Child; Agatha Gifford, Child; Brenda Bolter, Child

Time period(s): 1980s

Locale(s): United States

What the book is about: Cassie is disgusted when she finds she has to work with Agatha Gifford, an unpopular new girl, on a school project. When Agatha suggests they work at her house after school, Cassie is horrified. Everyone says the house Agatha lives in is haunted and Agatha's grandmother is a witch. When Cassie overcomes her fears and gets to know Agatha, she finds out about more important things than witchcraft.

Where it's reviewed:
Booklist, Febraury 1, 1986, page 810
Children's Book Review Service, January 1986, page 55
Center for Children's Books Bulletin, February 1986, page 110

Other books by the author:
Bethany for Real, 1985
Come to the Meadow, 1984
Maybe a Band-Aid Will Help, 1984
Taste the Raindrops, 1983

Other books you might like:
Molly Albright, *Fright Night*, 1989
Missy accepts a challenge from Stephanie to spend Halloween night with her dog in a haunted house.
Linda Gondosch, *Who's Afraid of Haggerty House?*, 1987
Kelly's attempt to sell Christmas cards to the lady in the haunted house begins a mutually enjoyable friendship for them both.
Mary-Claire Helldorfer, *Spook House*, 1989
Will thinks he is going to dislike the boy and girl who move in next door, until the threy get together to turn an old mansion into a haunted house.
Peggy Parish, *Haunted House*, 1971
Three children are uneasy when they learn their parents have bought a reputedly haunted house.
Patricia Windsor, *Two Weirdos and a Ghost*, 1991
Best friends Martha and Teddy do their best to help Martha's new neighbors who are afraid to stay in their house because they think it is haunted.

885

Constance Hiser

Illustrator: Carolyn Ewing

No Bean Sprouts, Please! (New York: Holiday, 1989)

Age range: Grades 2-4

Subject(s): Magic; Schools; Food

Major character(s): James, Child; Mean Mitchell, Child; Tag, Dog

Time period(s): 1980s

Locale(s): United States

What the book is about: James' mother packs very healthy lunches which James hates: bean sprouts, soybean sandwiches, unsweetened yogurt. No one will trade lunch items with James. Then for his ninth birthday, he gets a very special lunchbox from his Uncle Wesley. Everything put in the lunch box turns into something wonderful; candy bars, hot cheeseburgers, french fries, cookies. When the lunch box disappears, James blames Mean Michael, but when he and his friends follow a trail of cookie crumbs to find the thief, they get a big surprise.

Where it's reviewed:
Booklist, December 1, 1989, page 743
School Library Journal, November 1989, page 83

Other books by the author:
Critter Sitters, 1992
Sixth Grade Star, 1992
Dog on Third Base, 1991
Ghosts in Fourth Grade, 1991

Other books you might like:
Ellen Conford, *What's Cooking, Jenny Archer?*, 1989
Jenny goes into the business of making lunches for her friends at school.
Dorothy J. Daniel, *Pasta, Pies and Magic Potions*, 1988
Stories, poems and books about food.
William Pene Du Bois, *Porko Von Popbutton*, 1969
A 274 pound thirteen year old boy whose sole passion is food is sent to a boarding school where he is miserable until he winds up on the hockey team.
Florence Parry Heide, *Banana Blitz*, 1983
TV and candy bar addict Jonah thinks his problems will be over if he can just win the prize offered by the American Banana Institute.
Daniel Manus Pinkwater, *Slaves of Spiegel: A Magic Moscow Story*, 1982
Steve, Norman, and the Magic Moscow restaurant are transported through space to compete in an intergalactic junk food cooking contest.

886

Bruce Hlibok

Silent Dancer (New York: Messner, 1981)

Age range: Grades 3-5

Subject(s): Deafness; Ballet

Major character(s): Nancy, Child, Handicapped (deaf); Ms. Baylis, Teacher

Time period(s): 1980s

Locale(s): New York

What the book is about: Ten year old Nancy loves Fridays because she takes her ballet class on that day. Nancy is deaf, and the story describes her special classes as well as the special sound system used in ballet class for hearing impaired students. Excellent photographs.

Where it's reviewed:
Booklist, March 15, 1982
School Library Journal, April 1982, page 70

Other books you might like:
Lorraine Aseltine, *I'm Deaf and It's Okay*, 1986
    A young boy describes the frustrations caused by his hearing loss and the encouragement he gets from a deaf teenager.
Ken Kesey, *The Sea Lion: A Story of the Sea Cliff People*, 1991
    Taunted for his small size and bad leg, Eemook proves his worth by saving his tribe from an evil and powerful spirit that visits one stormy night.
James David Landis, *The Sisters Impossible*, 1979
    Two talented sisters vie for a coveted position in a ballet production.
Gary Paulsen, *The Monument*, 1991
    Rocky is self-conscious about her leg braces until her life is changed by the artist who comes to her small Kansas town to design a war memorial.
Gloria Whelan, *Hannah*, 1991
    Hannah doesn't go to school because she is blind, until a new teacher comes to board at her house.

887

Julia Hoban

Illustrator: Lillian Hoban

Quick Chick (New York: Dutton, 1989)

Age range: Grades 2-3

Subject(s): Animals/Birds; Farm Life; Independence

Major character(s): Jenny Hen, Chicken; Alice, Pig; Mabel, Goat

Time period(s): Indeterminate

Locale(s): United States

What the book is about: Although he seems much slower than the other chicks, Jenny Hen's youngest chick finally earns his name, Quick Chick, when the cat arrives

Where it's reviewed:
Kirkus Reviews, March 1, 1989, page 377
School Library Journal, July 1989, page 66

Other books by the author:
Buzby, 1990
Amy Loves the Rain, 1989
Amy Loves the Snow, 1989
Amy Loves the Sun, 1988

Other books you might like:
Martin Bax, *Edmond Went Far Away*, 1989
    Edmond bids good-bye to all the animals on the farm and goes exploring to the "far away" land just over the hill.
Reeve Lindbergh, *The Day the Goose Got Loose*, 1990
    The day the goose gets loose, havoc reigns at the farm as all the animals react.
Mercer Mayer, *Appelard and Liverwurst*, 1978

Aided by a wayward rhinoceros, Appelard and his motley farm animals finally have a successful harvest.
Drew Nelson, *Wild Voices*, 1991
    Relates a winter story of two farm dogs and each of five wild animals: a fox, a lynx, a horse, a wolf and a puma.
Nadine Bernard Westcott, *Skip to My Lou*, 1989
    When a young boy is left in charge of the farm for a day, chaos erupts as the animals take over the house. Includes the music to "Skip to my Lou."

888

Lillian Hoban, Author/Illustrator

Arthur's Honey Bear (New York: Harper, 1974)

Age range: Grades 1-3

Series: I Can Read Book

Subject(s): Toys

Major character(s): Arthur, Chimpanzee; Violet, Chimpanzee (Arthur's sister)

Time period(s): Indeterminate

Locale(s): Fictional Country

What the book is about: Arthur decides to give away all his old toys, except his bear, but his sister convinces him to give away Honey Bear as well.

Where it's reviewed:
Center for Children's Books Bulletin, September 1974, page 9
Hornbook, August 1974, page 371
Kirkus Reviews, May 15, 1974, page 533

Other books by the author:
Arthur's Loose Tooth, 1985
Arthur's Funny Money, 1981
Arthur's Prize Reader, 1978
Arthur's Pen Pal, 1976

Other books you might like:
Maggie Glen, *Ruby to the Rescue*, 1992
    Ruby the teddy bear is taken to school by her owner and carries out a plan to save two unwanted teddies in the playhouse there.
Jane Hissey, *Old Bear*, 1986
    A group of toy animals try various ways of rescuing Old Bear from the attic.
Ginnie Hoffman, *Who Wants an Old Teddy Bear?*, 1978
    Andy at first rejects the teddy bear he is given for a present, but through a strange turnabout he learns to love it.
Joan Phillips, *Lucky Bear*, 1986
    A teddy bear's luck saves him from one calamity after another and eventually finds him a home.
Ellen Stoll Walsh, *Theodore All Grown Up*, 1981
    Theodore considers himself quite grown up until he starts giving away his old toys.

889

Lillian Hoban

I Met a Traveller (New York: Harper, 1977)

Age range: Grades 5-7

Subject(s): Divorce; Jews; Single Parent Families

Major character(s): Josie Hayden, Immigrant, Preteen; Mira Yanovitch, Immigrant; Catherine Aleson, Preteen

Time period(s): 1970s

Locale(s): Israel

What the book is about: When her parents are divorced, eleven year old Josie leaves Connecticut with her mother and goes to live in Israel. In addition to adjusting to a whole new country and culture, Josie must cope with a new school, not entirely welcoming, her mother's unconventional love life, and her own deep homesickness. Mira, an old woman recently arrived from Russia, becomes her best friend.

Where it's reviewed:
Booklist, September 1, 1977, page 41
Kirkus Reviews, October 1, 1977, page 1049
School Library Journal, November 1977, page 57

Other books by the author:
Ready-Set Robot!, 1982
New Neighbors for Nora, 1979
The Easter Cat, 1971

Other books you might like:
Sonia Levitin, *The Return*, 1987
    Desta and her Falasha family, Jews suffering from discrimination in Ethiopia, finally flee the country and attempt the dangerous journey to Israel.
Thelma Nurenberg, *The Time of Anger*, 1975
    The slowly developing friendship between the young people of a kibbutz and a nearby Arab village is threatened by the outbreak of the Six-Day War.
Israel M. Wiesler, *Methuselah's Gang*, 1980
    A group of children befriend an old man with a very long beard and together they have many adventures in which the beard plays an important part.
Lynne Reid Banks, *One More River*, 1992
    Lesley is upset when her parents abandon their comfortable life in Canada for a kibbutz in Israel prior to the 1967 war.
Amos Oz, *Soumchi*, 1980
    A young boy in modern day Jerusalem trades away one possession after another, only to find something much more wonderful.

890

Lillian Hoban, Author/Illustrator

Ready, Set, Robot (New York: Harper, 1982)

Age range: Grades 1-3

Series: I Can Read Book

Subject(s): Robots

Major character(s): Sol-1, Robot; Big Rover, Dog

Time period(s): Indeterminate Future

Locale(s): Outer Space

What the book is about: A robot, Sol-1, competes in a space race. When robots from all over Zone One gather to race in the Digi-Maze, a power pack mix-up almost causes disaster for Sol-1.

Where it's reviewed:
Center for Children's Books Bulletin, June 1982, page 189
Kirkus Reviews, March 1, 1982, page 274
School Library Journal, May 1982, page 81

Other books by the author:
The Laziest Robot in Zone One, 1983
Arthur's Pen Pal, 1976
The Big Hello, 1976
Arthur's Honey Bear, 1974

Other books you might like:
Isaac Asimov, *Robbie*, 1989
    When Gloria's mother deprives her of her beloved robot playmate Robbie, Gloria is inconsolable and goes into a serious decline.
Debie Cotton, *Messy Marcy MacIntyre*, 1990
    Marcy's messiness makes her a one-girl disaster area at school, until she reveals a talent that makes her worth knowing.
Judith Gorog, *In a Messy, Messy Room*, 1990
    A collection of scary stories with humorous or unexpected endings.
Robert Newton Peck, *Little Soup's Bunny*, 1993
    Easter is on the way and Soup and Rob are ready. They have a baby rabbit named Bucky who loves to eat carrots, and they are dyeing Easter eggs.
Beatrix Potter, *The Tale of Mrs. Tittlemouse*, 1987
    The story of a little mouse's funny house, the visitors she has there, and how she finally rids herself of the untidy, messy ones.

891

Russell Hoban

Illustrator: Garth Williams

Bedtime for Frances (New York: Harper, 1960)

Age range: Grades 1-2

Subject(s): Animals/Badgers; Bedtime

Major character(s): Frances, Badger

Time period(s): Indeterminate

Locale(s): Fictional Country

What the book is about: Frances tries everything she can think of to keep from going to bed on time. She has trouble going to sleep because of frightening sounds and objects that may be going to get her.

Where it's reviewed:
Booklist, September 1, 1983, page 93
New York Times Book Review, November 13, 1977, page 40
School Library Journal, March 1980, page 105

Other books by the author:
Bargain for Frances, 1970
Best Friends for Frances, 1969
Tom and the Two Handles, 1965
Bread and Jam for Frances, 1964

Other books you might like:
Margaret Burdick, *Bobby Otter and the Blue Boat*, 1986
    Bobby Otter, one of the inhabitants of Maple Forest, tries to find something valuable enough to trade for the blue boat in Mr. Badger's store.
Paul Cox, *The Case of the Botched Book*, 1992
    When Badgibberish sends Archibald a book recounting Archibald's success in solving the case of the prankish cockatoos, Archibald finds a new mystery.
Nancy White Carlstrom, *No Nap for Benjamin Badger*, 1991

When Ben refuses to nap, Mother Badger tells him rhymes about all the animals that take naps until they both fall asleep.

Elizabeth MacDonald, *Mr. Badger's Birthday Pie*, 1989
When a thieving fox steals the pie Miss Poppy has baked for Mr. Badger's birthday, all the animals give chase.

Erica Silverman, *Warm in Winter*, 1989
A cozy visit with friend rabbit, featuring a soft flannel nightie and hot carrot soup, convinces a skeptical Badger that you can be warm in winter.

892

Russell Hoban

Illustrator: Lillian Hoban

The Mouse and His Child (New York: HarperCollins, 1967)

Age range: Grades 4-6

Subject(s): Animals/Mice; Christmas; Toys

Major character(s): Father, Mouse; Son, Mouse; Mannie, Rat

Time period(s): 1950s

Locale(s): England

What the book is about: A tin father and son dance under a Christmas tree until they break the ancient clockwork rules and are themselves broken. Rescued from a trash can and repaired by a tramp, they set out on a perilous odyssey to follow a child's dream of a family and a place of their own.

Where it's reviewed:
Booklist, January 15, 1968, page 593
Center for Children's Books Bulletin, May 1968, page 143
Kirkus, September 15, 1967, page 1134

Other books by the author:
Tom and the Two Handles, 1965
A Babysitter for Frances, 1964
Bread and Jam for Frances, 1964
The Sorely Trying Day, 1964

Other books you might like:
Anna Braune, *The Wonderful Toys*, 1990
Seven toys who have enjoyed a peaceful existence in an attic trunk are threatened when the owners of the house decide to clean out the attic.

Jane Hissey, *Old Bear Tales*, 1988
Adventures of the playroom toys as they have parties, enjoy the seasons and go on holiday.

James Howe, *Babes in Toyland*, 1986
The classic story, based on the 1903 operetta, of how Jane and Alan are chased by their evil uncle Barnaby who wants to kill them for their fortune.

Elizabeth A. Lynn, *The Silver Horse*, 1984
Susannah follows her brother and his beautiful silver horse to the Land of Lost Toys, where she finds herself in the middle of a fantastic adventure.

A.A. Milne, *The House at Pooh Corner*, 1928
Ten adventures of Pooh, Eeyore, Tigger, Piglet, Owl and other friends of Christopher Robin.

893

Cyril Walter Hodges

Plain Lane Christmas (New York: Coward, 1978)

Age range: Grades 3-4

Subject(s): City Life; Christmas

Major character(s): Philip Goodall, Child; Sue Goodall, Child; Penny Pettifer, Child

Time period(s): Indeterminate Past

Locale(s): England

What the book is about: Plain Lane is a small, quaint street stuck between a busy modern business district and a major highway. It has small shops that the residents live above. In order to save Plain Lane from demolition, the children organize a massive Christmas celebration including a children's bazaar which is a huge success. After a wonderful Chinese New Year festival takes place, Plain Lane is so popular, it is no longer threatened with destruction.

Where it's reviewed:
Center for Children's Books Bulletin, December 1978, page 631
Kirkus Reviews, December 15, 1978, page 1357

Other books by the author:
Playhouse Tales, 1975

Other books you might like:
Valentine Davies, *Miracle on 34th Street*, 1985
The lives of three people are changed by an old man who insists he is Santa Claus.

Diana Hendry, *Christmas on Exeter Street*, 1989
Christmas brings relatives, friends, and strangers to the house on Exeter Street where the celebration becomes a crowded but festive occasion.

Trinka Hakes Noble, *Apple Tree Christmas*, 1984
In 1881, when their apple tree is felled by a storm just before Christmas, a farm girl and her family discover the tree was important to the family.

Francene Sabin, *The Great Santa Claus Mystery*, 1982
While on a Christmas shopping trip, the Maple Street Six become involved in a frantic search for a sneaky Santa.

Carly Simon, *The Boy of the Bells*, 1990
A young boy, with a little advice from Santa Claus, performs a miracle on Christmas day, restoring joy to his little sister's heart.

894

Margaret Hodges

Illustrator: Richard Cuffari

The Freewheeling of Joshua Cobb (New York: Farrar, 1974)

Age range: Grades 3-5

Subject(s): Camps and Camping; Bicycles and Bicycling

Major character(s): Joshua Cobb, Preteen, Camper; Crane, Preteen, Camper; Dusty, Teenager, Camper

Time period(s): 1970s

Locale(s): United States (New England)

What the book is about: Josh goes on a bicycle camping trip with his former camp counselor, Dusty, and a group of friends. Crane is the younger sister of the girl Josh has a crush on. He gets to see the ocean for the first time, camp out, and even appreciate unusual Crane.

Where it's reviewed:
Horn Book, October 1974, page 137
Library Journal, September 15, 1974, page 2270

Other books by the author:
Hauntings: Ghosts and Ghouls From Around the World, 1991
Baldur and the Mistletoe, 1974
Persephone and the Springtime, 1974
The Fire Bringer: A Paiute Legend, 1973

Other books you might like:
Avi, *No More Magic*, 1975
   While searching for his bicycle that disappeared on Halloween, a boy and his two friends become involved in a magic adventure.
Michael McBrier, *Getting Oliver's Goat*, 1988
   Oliver's new job, taking care of an unpredictable goat, jeopardizes his chances of winning the big bicycle race.
Betty Miles, *I Would If I Could*, 1982
   After the bicycle she's been longing for is a disappointment, a young girl spends the summer at her grandmother's and learns a valuable lesson.
Johnniece Marshall Wilson, *Oh, Brother!*, 1988
   Alex's older brother bullies him, taking his bicycle and his money, until Alex discovers a way to stand up for himself.
Elvira Woodruff, *The Disappearing Bike Shop*, 1992
   Fifth graders Freckle and Tyler meet an unusual bicycle salesman and inventor who turns out to be Leonardo da Vinci, traveling through time.

895

Syd Hoff, Author/Illustrator

Mrs. Brice's Mice (New York: Harper, 1988)

Age range: Grades 1-2

Series: Early I Can Read Book

Subject(s): Individuality; Animals/Mice

Time period(s): Indeterminate

Locale(s): Fictional Country

What the book is about: Mrs. Brice has twenty-five mice, but one stands out from all the others. The twenty-four do everything together. Whenever Mrs. Brice plays the piano and sings, twenty-four mice dance around her - one very small mouse dances on her hand. In fact, the small mouse does everything differently. When there is trouble, who else comes to the rescue?

Where it's reviewed:
Booklist, December 1, 1988, page 656
School Library Journal, April 1989, page 83

Other books by the author:
Amy's Dinosaur, 1974
Baseball Mouse, 1969
Stanley, 1962
Albert the Albatross, 1961

Other books you might like:
Eugene Fern, *Pepito's Story*, 1991

Pepito's use of his gift for dancing to bring the Mayor's daughter back to health demonstrates that what makes him "different" makes him special.
Libba Moore Gray, *Miss Tizzy*, 1993
   The eccentric Miss Tizzy, a beloved friend to all the children in her neighborhood, needs their help in remaining happy when she is sick in bed.
Marissa Moore, *But Not Kate*, 1992
   Kate compares herself to other kids in school and fears there is nothing special about her, until she becomes the magician's helper at an assembly.
Teddy Slater, *The Wrong-Way Rabbit*, 1993
   Tibbar, the backward bunny, does everything the opposite from what's expected, walking backwards and going up the down stairs.
Chyng Feng Sun, *Square Beak*, 1993
   Square Beak, famous for the beautiful and unusual eggs she lays, abandons an egg-laying contest and returns to the life she loves.

896

E.T.A. Hoffman

Illustrator: Maurice Sendak

The Nutcracker (New York: Crown, 1984)

Age range: Grades 3-8

Subject(s): Ballet; Fables

Major character(s): Marie, Child

Time period(s): Indeterminate

Locale(s): Land of Sweets, Fictional Country

What the book is about: This translation of Hoffman's classic stems from the costume and set designs for the Pacific Northwest Ballet's 1981 production. For reading aloud, paging through to enjoy the illustrations, middle grade independent readers, comparisons with other editions of the tale - a beautiful book to use in any of a hundred ways.

Where it's reviewed:
Horn Book, January/February 1985, page 53
School Library Journal, November 1984, page 125

Other books you might like:
S.T. Aksakov, *The Scarlet Flower*, 1989
   A young woman's love transforms a monster into a handsome prince in this retelling of a classic Russian folktale, a version of "Beauty and the Beast."
Fred H. Crump, *Beauty and the Beast*, 1992
   A retelling of the traditional fairy tale in which a beautiful maid releases a handsome prince from the spell which has made him an ugly beast.
David Cutts, *Adventures of Tom Thumb*, 1988
   Relates a tiny boy's adventures in a cow's mouth, a fish's belly, on the back of a mouse, and at King Arthur's table.
Mary Lewis Wang, *The Lion and the Mouse*, 1986
   An easy to read retelling of the well-known fable in which a little mouse saves the life of the king of beasts.
Hans Wilhelm, *Tales From the Land under my Table*, 1983
   Tales of a greedy giant and a clever stranger, a grouchy king and a mouse jester, a war between cabbages and cucumbers, and a bird wanting more color.

897

Nonny Hogrogian, Author/Illustrator

The Contest (New York: Greenwillow, 1976)

Age range: Grades 3-5

Subject(s): Robbers and Outlaws; Folk Tales

Major character(s): Ehleezah, Fiance(e)

Time period(s): Indeterminate

Locale(s): Armenia

What the book is about: The same girl, Ehleezah, is engaged to two different robbers. They decide to find out which is the most clever. They end up realizing they are both too good for the faithless girl and go into business together.

Where it's reviewed:
Horn Book, December 1976, page 618
School Library Journal, November 1976, page 48

Awards the book has won:
Caldecott Honor Book

Other books by the author:
The Cat Who Loved to Sing, 1988
The Glass Mountain, 1985
The Dog Writes on the Window with His Nose, 1977
Handmade Secret Hiding Places, 1975

Other books you might like:
M.J. Engh, *The House in the Snow*, 1987
　Nine boys outwit the invisible robbers who have inhabited the house in the snow for generations.
Kathryn Osebold Galbraith, *Something Suspicious*, 1985
　Lizzie and her best friend track down the Green Pillowcase Bandit and more mysteries than they can handle.
Suzy Kline, *Herbie Jones and Hamburger Head*, 1989
　Herbie and Ray stop a robbery at the local bank, then try to find a good home for the robber's dog.
Pat Ross, *Gloria and the Super Soaper*, 1982
　Gloria loves her collection of toy guns, but more than anything she wants to capture a real robber.

898

Kristi Holl

Just Like a Real Family (New York: Macmillan, 1983)

Age range: Grades 4-6

Subject(s): Grandparents; Old Age

Major character(s): June Finch, Preteen; Franklin Cooper, Aged Person

Time period(s): 1980s

Locale(s): United States

What the book is about: June Finch gets involved in a class project to adopt grandparents from a retirement home. When she is paired with sour old Franklin Cooper, she's disappointed to find him bitter, bad-tempered, thorny and wanting nothing to do with her. But June does not give up easily.

Where it's reviewed:
Booklist, April 15, 1983, page 1094
Kirkus Reviews, May 1, 1983, page 523
School Library Journal, May 1983, page 72

Other books by the author:
No Strings Attached, 1988

Other books you might like:
Margaret E. Bechard, *My Sister, My Science Report*, 1990
　Tess feels stuck with the class nerd for a partner in a science project. But they become good friends as they study an unlikely subject, Tess' sister.
Sheila Greenwald, *Rosy Cole Discovers America!*, 1992
　Disappointed in the poor immigrant ancestors she discovers during a class project to research family roots, Rosy cooks up a clan of royal relatives.
Diane Johnston Hamm, *Second Family*, 1992
　Mr. Torkleson, a lonely senior citizen, shares his home with a recently divorced mother and her son, who is having problems adjusting to the move.
Betsy Haynes, *Melanie's Identity*, 1990
　While working on a genealogy project of family living class, Melanie uncovers a shocking secret about her past.
Norma Fox Mazer, *A Figure of Speech*, 1973
　The very special relationship between Jenny and her grandfather leads to tragedy when Jenny's parents want to place him in a home for senior citizens.

899

Isabelle Holland

Alan and the Animal Kingdom (Philadelphia: Lippincott, 1977)

Age range: Grades 5-6

Subject(s): Secrets; Animals; Orphans

Major character(s): Alan, Orphan; Aunt Jessie, Guardian; Dr. Harris, Veterinarian

Time period(s): 1970s

Locale(s): New York, New York

What the book is about: Alan's great-aunt dies, unidentified, in a hospital. He is afraid he'll lose his beloved pets, so he decides to keep her death a secret. Dr. Harris stops drinking to win Alan's respect, and tries to help him keep his secret.

Where it's reviewed:
Horn Book, June 1977, page 314
School Library Journal, March 1977, page 145

Other books by the author:
The Journey Home, 1990
Dinah and the Green Fat Kingdom, 1978
The Man Without a Face, 1977
Of Love and Death and Other Journeys, 1975

Other books you might like:
T.A. Barron, *Heartlight*, 1990
　Kate and her grandfather use one of his inventions to travel faster than the speed of light on a mission to save the sun from a premature death.
Barbara Griffiths, *Frankenstein's Hamster*, 1992
　A collection of ten stories featuring a schoolboy with a talent for taxidermy, the highwayman of death, and other disturbing characters.
Virginia Hamilton, *Cousins*, 1990
　Concerned that her grandmother may die, Cammy is unprepared for the death of another family member.
Emily Rhoads Johnson, *A House Full of Strangers*, 1992

Flora finds solace in the woods following the death of her grandmother and the arrival of many noisy relatives.
Gary Paulsen, *A Christmas Sonata*, 1992
When a boy spends Christmas with his dying cousin, they discover that Santa really does exist.

900

Isabelle Holland

The Journey Home (New York: Scholastic, 1990)

Age range: Grades 4-6

Subject(s): Orphans; Sisters; American West

Major character(s): Maggie Lavin, Child; Annie Lavin, Child; Priscille Russell, Foster Parent

Time period(s): 19th century

Locale(s): New York, New York; Kansas

What the book is about: After their mother dies, Maggie and Annie leave New York City on one of the orphan trains that delivered thousands of tenement youngsters to adoptive homes during the second half of the 19th century. On the Kansas prairie, they learn to deal with hard work and the hostility of some towards Irish Roman Catholics.

Where it's reviewed:
Kirkus Reviews, September 15, 1990, page 1324
School Library Journal, December 1990, page 103

Other books by the author:
The Unfrightened Dark, 1990
God, Mrs. Muskrat, and Aunt Dot, 1983
Journey for Three, 1974
Amanda's Choice, 1970

Other books you might like:
Ruth M. Arthur, *On the Wasteland*, 1975
A young orphan discovers a dream world which allows her to escape from reality, but her attachment to the fantasy almost ends in disaster.
Joan Lowery Nixon, *A Family Apart*, 1987
Six siblings are sent by the Children's Aid Society of New York to live with farm families in Missouri in 1860. (First of the ''Orphan Train Quartet''.)
Walter G. Olesky, *Quacky and the Crazy Curve Ball*, 1981
A twelve year old orphan proves his resourcefulness by making a basketball team and trapping the ''Hungry Burglar.''
Margaret Storey, *The Family Tree*, 1973
Kate, an orphan, goes to stay with a cousin and discovers that she is part of a wonderful family.
Noel Streatfeild, *Thursday's Child*, 1970
A nameless orphan faces the unbearable conditions of an early 20th century English orphanage.

901

Isabelle Holland

Now Is Not Too Late (New York: Lothrop, 1980)

Age range: Grades 5-6

Subject(s): Alcoholism; Child Abuse; Dreams and Nightmares

Major character(s): Kathy Barrett, Preteen; Marianne, Preteen; Elizabeth, Artist

Time period(s): 1980s

Locale(s): Maine

What the book is about: Cathy loves spending the summer with her grandmother and this summer she becomes curious about a woman named Elizabeth, who is called the Wicked Witch. Cathy begins to model for Elizabeth who illustrates children's books. One day, Cathy and a friend see Elizabeth going into a church and overhear her confess at an AA meeting that she verbally abused her daughter. Memories flood back and Cathy realizes that Elizabeth is her mother.

Where it's reviewed:
Center for Children's Books Bulletin, March 1980, p 135
Horn Book, June 1980, page 296

Other books by the author:
Empty House, 1983
Dinah and the Green Fat Kingdom, 1978
Amanda's Choice, 1970
Cecily, 1967

Other books you might like:
Katherine Leiner, *Something's Wrong in My House*, 1988
8 young people describe life in families with alcoholics, the effects on the other family members, and the help they have found. (Non-fiction)
Cynthia Scales, *Potato Chips for Breakfast*, 1986
A woman describes her teenage years as the daughter of two alcoholic parents.
Brenda Seabrooke, *Home Is Where They Take You In*, 1980
As she becomes closer to a couple living on a nearby ranch, a girl realizes there is nothing left between herself and her alcoholic mother.
Marya Smith, *Winter-Broken*, 1990
Abused by her alcoholic father, Dawn finds friendship and love in a sympathetic farmer and his beautiful horse, Wildfire.
Shelley Stoehr, *Crosses*, 1991
Unhappy at home, Nancy and Katie adopt punk lifestyles and find relief in cutting themselves, until Nancy is forced to confront her problems.

902

Marion Holland, Author/Illustrator

A Big Ball of String (New York: Random, 1958)

Age range: Grades 1-2

Subject(s): Imagination; Poetry

Time period(s): 1950s

Locale(s): United States

What the book is about: A child dreams of what he would do with a ball of string and finds many creative ways to use it.

Other books by the author:
Teddy's Camp Out, 1963
Tree for Teddy, 1957

Other books you might like:
Steven Kroll, *The Magic Rocket*, 1992
Felix's dog, Atom, is abducted by a flying saucer and Felix must rescue him by following in a magic rocket.

Richard McGilvray, *Don't Climb Out the Window Tonight*, 1993
Flying ghosts and jogging giants are just two of the reasons a girl makes up so she won't climb out of her window in the middle of the night.

Kin Platt, *Darwin and the Great Beasts*, 1992
During a visit to the LaBrea Tar Pits, Darwin imagines what it would be like to live in prehistoric times and try to outwit huge beasts.

Patricia Polacco, *Appelemando's Dreams*, 1991
Villagers are convinced that Appelmando won't amount to much because he always dreams. But in time his dreams change the village and villagers.

Michael Elsohn Ross, *Become a Bird and Fly*, 1992
Using his imagination, Nicky changes into a bird and takes flight.

903

Holling Clancy Holling, Author/Illustrator

Minn of the Mississipppi (Boston: Houghton Mifflin, 1951)

Age range: Grades 4-6

Subject(s): Animals/Turtles

Major character(s): Minn, Turtle

Time period(s): Indeterminate

Locale(s): Mississippi River

What the book is about: The adventure of a three-legged snapping turtle as she travels from the headwaters to the mouth of the Mississippi River. Shows the life cycle of the turtle and the geography, history, ecology and climate of the Mississippi River. In adition to full page, full color illustrations, the margins are filled with notes, diagrams, maps of the journey and explanations. Wonderful for all ages from browsing to serious nature study.

Awards the book has won:
Newbery Honor 1952

Other books by the author:
Pagoo, 1957
Seabird, 1948
Tree in the Trail, 1947
Paddle-to-the-Sea, 1941

Other books you might like:
Carol Carrick, *The Empty Squirrel*, 1981
In three episodes Paul catches a fish for dinner, makes a puppet from a stuffed animal left outside, and brings home a turtle for a pet.

Betty Sue Cummings, *Turtle*, 1981
The pet turtle of an elderly Florida woman wanders away, spends a year in the world, and finally returns to its owner, larger and the worse for wear.

Karen Greenfield, *Sister Yessa's Story*, 1992
Sister Yessa tells about a Great Turtle who carried all animals of the world on his back and dropped them in the place they wanted to live.

Pamela Powell, *The Turtle Watchers*, 1992
Esther, Philomena and Amelia, sisters on a Caribbean island, band together to protect a nest of leatherback turtle eggs.

Robert M. Quackenbush, *Calling Doctor Quack*, 1978

Dr. Quack treats the complaints of the pond community residents, all of which can be traced to the strange behavior of Mr. Snapping Turtle.

904

Holling Clancy Holling

Paddle-to-the-Sea (Boston: Houghton Mifflin, 1941)

Age range: Grades 3-5

Subject(s): Voyages and Travels; Indians of North America

Major character(s): Paddle-to-the-Sea, Toy (wooden carving), Indian (wooden carving)

Time period(s): 1910s

Locale(s): Lake Nipigon, Ontario, Canada; Great Lakes

What the book is about: A wooden carving of an Indian in a conoe, made by an Indian boy, makes a journey form Lake Superior all the way to the Atlantic Ocean. A copper plate is attached to it along the way and messages are added by each person who finds the carving, then sends it on its way again. Years later, the boy, now a guide, discovers the fate of his carving. Nice introduction to the geography of the Great Lakes waterway.

Where it's reviewed:
Hornbook, October 1983, page 551

Awards the book has won:
Caldecott Honor Book 1942
Lewis Carroll Shelf 1962

Other books by the author:
Pagoo, 1957
Minn of the Mississippi, 1951
Seabird, 1948
Tree in the Trail, 1942

Other books you might like:
Nathaniel Benchley, *Red Fox and His Canoe*, 1964
A young Indian boy receives a large canoe along with some unforseen complications.

Lorenz B. Graham, *Song of the Boat*, 1975
A small African boy helps his father locate the right tree to make a new canoe to replace the one broken by an alligator.

Dorris Heffron, *A Nice Fire and Some Moonpennies*, 1971
Determined to try as many new experiences as she can, a Canadian-Indian girl hitchhikes to Toronto with her dog.

Jan Hudson, *Sweetgrass*, 1984
On the western Canadian prairie in the 1900s, Sweetgrass, a fifteen year old Blackfoot Indian girl, saves her family from a smallpox epidemic.

Vera B. Williams, *Three Days on a River in a Red Canoe*, 1981
Mother, Aunt Rosie and two children make a three-day camping trip by canoe.

905

Holling Clancy Holling, Author/Illustrator

Seabird (Boston: Houghton Mifflin, 1948)

Age range: Grades 4-6

Subject(s): Sea Stories; Sailing

Major character(s): Ezra Brown, Sailor

Time period(s): 1830s

Locale(s): At Sea

What the book is about: Ezra Brown carves an ivory gull in 1832 when he was a boy. The carving brings good luck to him and his sea-faring descendents as they travel aboard ship to all parts of the world.

Awards the book has won:
Commonwealth Club of California 1948
Newbery Honor 1949

Other books by the author:
Minn of the Mississippi, 1951
Pagoo, 1948
Tree in the Trail, 1942
Paddle-to-the-Sea, 1941

Other books you might like:
Donald Silver, *The Baitchopper*, 1982
   Andrew becomes involved in the strike which his father and other fishermen start to gain better wages from the fish packing company.
Harold Cole, *A Few Thoughts on Trout*, 1986
   A young boy shows two outsiders some of the best spots to catch brook trout and later is devastated when their greed ruins the brooks.
Bill Freeman, *First Spring on the Grand Banks*, 1978
   John and Meg return to Newfoundland with their friend, Canso, only to find that his father has died and his boat is being claimed by a greedy merchant
Arthur Ransome, *We Didn't Mean to Go to Sea*, 1983
   The four Swallows find themselves adrift in the North Sea when a storm blows up while they are aboard the cutter ''Goblin'' and its captain is ashore.
Colby Rodowski, *Fitchett's Folly*, 1987
   When Papa's involvement with a shipwreck saves a girl's life but costs him his own, Sarey is determined to find a new home for the girl.

906

Felice Holman

Illustrator: Ben Shecter

The Escape of the Giant Hogstalk (New York: Scribner, 1974)

Age range: Grades 3-6

Subject(s): Plague; Gardens and Gardening

Major character(s): Anthony, Vacationer; Lawrence, Vacationer

Time period(s): 1970s

Locale(s): England

What the book is about: Anthony and Lawrence find a giant hogstalk while on vacation. They give the seeds to the staff at Kew Gardens. the hogstalk grows until it bursts the roof of the greenhouse. Scattering its seeds, it starts a plague of severe rashes.

Where it's reviewed:
Horn Book, June 1974, page 283
Kirkus Reviews, April 1, 1974, page 363

Other books by the author:
Secret City, U.S.A., 1990
The Drac, 1975
Slake's Limbo, 1974
I Hear You Smiling, 1973

Other books you might like:
Catherine Dexter, *Gertie's Green Thumb*, 1988
   Gertie finds a magical wishbone in the park and turns her home into a magical House of Nature.
Terrance Dicks, *Max's Amazing Summer*, 1991
   Max, a talking cat, must save the town from giant insects when a greedy member of the garden club starts making a new kind of fertilizer.
William Kotzwinkle, *The Ants Who Took Away Time*, 1978
   Giant ants steal the Great Timepiece and cause time to stand still around the world.
Nancy McArthur, *The Escape of the Plant That Ate Dirty Socks*, 1992
   The sock-eating plants are on the move.and heading right for trouble!
Judith St. George, *The Mysterious Girl in the Garden*, 1981
   During daily visits to Kew Gardens an American girl finds herself transported back to Kew Palace in 1805, where she meets the future queen of England.

907

Felice Holman

Secret City, U.S.A. (New York: Scribner, 1990)

Age range: Grades 6-9

Subject(s): Homeless; Poverty; Gangs

Major character(s): Benno, Teenager

Time period(s): 1980s

Locale(s): United States

What the book is about: We see urban poverty and violence through the eyes of Benno and his friends, living in squalid tenements and in the streets. A house that somehow survived razing exists, covered by rubble and debris, the boys move in and make it a home, and envision the transformation that could occur if many others did the same. Benno grows in leadership when the boys must confront a violent gang, and in dealing with city authorities. Though some reviewers criticize the fairy tale ending, the picture of survival in urban ''wilderness'' is nonetheless vivid.

Where it's reviewed:
Booklist, May 1, 1990, page 1704
School Library Journal, April 1990, page 140

Other books by the author:
The Wild Children, 1983
The Drac, 1975
Slake's Limbo, 1974
The Future of Hooper Toote, 1972

Other books you might like:
Eve Bunting, *The Haunting of Kildoran Abbey*, 1978
   Caught in a severe famine, eight hungry, homeless youngsters join forces to steal food from the rich.
Paula Fox, *Monkey Island*, 1991

Forced to live on the streets of New York City after his mother disappears from their hotel room, Clay is befriended by two men who help him survive.

Mark Jonathan Harris, *Come the Morning*, 1989
Ben and his family find themselves living among the poor and homeless when they leave El Paso for Los Angeles to look for Ben's father.

Joan Lingard, *Tug of War*, 1989
Fourteen year old twins and their family flee Latvia in 1944 and find themselves homeless refugees in war-torn Germany.

Barbara Wersba, *Just Be Gorgeous: A Novel*, 1988
Feeling unattractive and misunderstood by her parents, a teen realizes she is special through her friendship with a homeless street performer.

908

Felice Holman

Slake's Limbo (New York: Scribner, 1974)

Age range: Grades 5-6

Subject(s): Trains; Poverty

Major character(s): Aremis Slake, Teenager, Streetperson

Time period(s): 1970s

Locale(s): New York, New York

What the book is about: Running from bullies, thirteen year old Aremis Slake jumps to the track bed in the subway. That's where he finds his hideout. A mistake in construction has created a chamber underneath the Commodore Hotel. Aremis stays there, surviving by reselling discarded newspapers and getting odd sweep up jobs, for four months. Illness and near disaster bring him to the surface. A jolting account of poverty and loneliness.

Where it's reviewed:
Kirkus Reviews, November 1, 1974, page 1160
Library Journal, November 15, 1974, page 3046

Other books by the author:
Secret City, U.S.A., 1991
At the Top of My Voice and Other Poems, 1970
Blackmail Machine, 1968
The Cricket Winter, 1967

Other books you might like:
Otto Coontz, *Hornswoggle Magic*, 1981
Using seemingly magical methods, a strange "bag lady" helps two children save one's father's newsstand threatened by a huge new vending machine.

Sheila Greenwald, *Blissful Joy and the SATs*, 1982
Bliss's life moves along as she is carefully planned until she is befriended on the subway by a strange dog.

Eloise Jarvis McGraw, *Master Cornhill*, 1973
Victim of both the Great Plague and the Great Fire of London, a homeless, penniless youth must decide what direction his life should take.

Neal Shusterman, *Speeding Bullet*, 1991
Nick becomes famous after rescuing a little girl from a speeding subway train, and he looks for other people to rescue.

Nancy Willard, *The Firebrat*, 1988

Riding on the New York subway, Molly and Sean exit into the Crystal Empire and join a giant tortoise on a mission to save the Empire.

909

Efner Tudor Holmes

Illustrator: Tasha Tudor

Amy's Goose (New York: Harper, 1977)

Age range: Grades 2-4

Subject(s): Farm Life; Animals/Birds

Major character(s): Amy, Child

Time period(s): Indeterminate

Locale(s): New England

What the book is about: Amy nurses a wild goose back to health after rescuing it from the jaws of a hungry fox. In the spring, she must learn to let it go free instead of keeping it a prisoner on the farm.

Where it's reviewed:
Booklist, January 1, 1978, page 747
Language Arts, May 1978, page 617
School Library Journal, February 1978, page 48

Other books by the author:
Carrie's Gift, 1978
The Christmas Cat, 1976

Other books you might like:
Betty Bates, *Hey There, Owlface*, 1991
Brad forms a special relationship with the owls roosting in his family's barn, one that is threatened by a trigger-happy neighbor.

Eve Bunting, *Goose Dinner*, 1981
A family realizes how much they love their cantankerous pet goose when it is wounded in a fight with a raccoon.

Betsy Day, *Stefan & Olga*, 1991
A disastrous harvest forces Stefan to sell his beloved goose, Olga, but a practical application of his musical talent saves the day.

Reeve Lindbergh, *The Day the Goose Got Loose*, 1990
The day the goose gets loose, havoc reigns at the farm as all the animals react.

David M. McPhail, *Farm Boy's Year*, 1992
Diary entries and illustrations evoke a boy's life on a New England farm in the 1800s.

910

Natalie Honeycutt

Josie's Beau (New York: Watts, 1987)

Age range: Grades 5-7

Subject(s): Dating (Social Customs); Summer

Major character(s): Josie, Preteen; Beau, Preteen

Time period(s): 1980s

Locale(s): United States

What the book is about: Josie's summer is busy as she tries to help her friend, Beau, buy the skateboard of his dreams and they both have trouble with a bully.

Where it's reviewed:
Center for Children's Books Bulletin, December 1987, page 66
School Library Journal, December 1987, page 86

Other books by the author:
Juliet Fisher and the Foolproof Plan, 1992
Ask Me Something Easy, 1991
The All New Jonah Twist, 1986
Invisible Lissa, 1985

Other books you might like:
Matt Christopher, *Skateboard Tough*, 1991
　　When Brett's skateboarding improves after using a skateboard mysteriously unearthed in his front yard, his friends start wondering if it is haunted.
Barbara Douglass, *Skateboard Scramble*, 1978
　　Jody is uneasy about the skateboarding competition her father wants her to enter because she would be competing against her best friend.
Gary Paulsen, *Dune Get Tweaked*, 1992
　　Dunc and Amos are hot on the trail of a stolen skateboard!
Brenda Seabrooke, *The Dragon That Ate Summer*, 1992
　　While recuperating from a skateboard accident, Alastair finds an unusual new pet in Mr. Hobson's petunia garden.
Mary Stolz, *The Explorer of Barkham Street*, 1985
　　Reformed bully Martin thinks about adventures as an explorer and a sports star, until real life becomes as exciting as his daydreams.

911

Elizabeth Honness

Illustrator: Paul Frame

Mystery of the Maya Jade (Philadelphia: Lippincott, 1971)

Age range: Grades 5-7

Subject(s): Indians of Central America; Mystery and Detective Stories

Major character(s): Toby Burns, Teenager; Pam Bacon, Teenager

Locale(s): Guatemala

What the book is about: Toby and Pam meet on top of a Mayan pyramid in the jungles of Guatemala. Once they are safely down from the dizzying heights, they become friends, glimpse two men running away after the theft of a rare jade figurine from the Tikal museum, and wind up involved in a fascinating tour of Guatemala to solve the mystery of the stolen figurine.

Where it's reviewed:
Kirkus Reviews, January 15, 1971, page 51
Library Journal, May 15, 1971, page 1820
Publisher's Weekly, June 7, 1971, page 56

Other books by the author:
The Etruscans: An Unsolved Mystery, 1972
Mystery of the Pirate's Ghost, 1966
Mystery of the Secret Message, 1961
Mystery at the Doll Hospital, 1955

Other books you might like:
Omar S. Castaneda, *Among the Volcanoes*, 1991
　　Isabel, a Mayan girl in contemporary Guatemala, must care for her sick mother and continue her search for her own identity in a changing world.
Franklin W. Dixon, *The Clue in the Embers*, 1972
　　In solving the mystery of two missing medallions, the Hardy Boys wind up in a desolate area of Guatemala at the mercy of dangerous thugs.
Betty Jean Lifton, *Jaguar, My Twin*, 1976
　　Shun, a descendant of the Mayas, becomes ill when his twin soul, a young jaguar, is released from the supernatural corral.
Scott O'Dell, *The Amethyst Ring*, 1983
　　Seminarian Julian Escobar, worshipped by the Mayans as the god Lord Kukulcan, sees the fall of the native civilizations with the coming of the Spanish
Leon Ware, *The Jade Monkey Mystery*, 1969
　　With his father on a business trip in the Far East, a fifteen year old boy is sought by a secret pirate clan for his knowledge of a jade fragment.

912

William H. Hooks

Illustrator: Brian Pinkney

The Ballad of Belle Dorcas (New York: Knopf, 1990)

Age range: Grades 4-6

Subject(s): Slavery; African Americans; Magic

Major character(s): Belle Dorcas, Young Woman; Joshua, Slave; Granny Lizard, Witch (conjure woman)

Time period(s): 19th century

Locale(s): Wilmington, North Carolina

What the book is about: Belle Dorcas is a "free-issue" woman, the offspring of a white master and a black slave. Though her mother hopes she will marry a free-issue black man, Belle falls in love with Joshua, a slave. When a cruel, new master tries to separate them, Belle goes to a "conjure woman" and buys a spell to keep Joshua from being sold. Little does she know that keeping Joshua on the plantation will have devastating results.

Where it's reviewed:
Kirkus Reviews, August 1, 1990, page 1087
School Library Journal, October 1990, page 116

Other books by the author:
Little Poss and the Terrible Houns, 1992
A Dozen Dizzy Dogs, 1990
The Gruff Brothers, 1990
Mr. Bubble Gum, 1989

Other books you might like:
Richard A. Boning, *Escape!*, 1975
　　Relates the daring escape by train of a slave couple from Georgia to Philadelphia in 1848.
Dorothy Hoobler, *Next Stop, Freedom*, 1991
　　Emily, a slave girl who longs to read, escapes with the help of Harriet Tubman.
Anna Catherine Josephs, *Mountain Boy*, 1985

14 year old Thomas Zachary helps a group of escaped Union prisoners elude Confederate soldiers in the mountains of North Carolina.

Steve Sanfield, *The Adventures of High John the Conquerer*, 1989

A collection of sixteen tales about High John the Conquerer, the traditional trickster hero of blacks during and immediately after the Civil War.

Ann Warren Turner, *Nettie's Trip South*, 1987

A 10 year old northern girl visits Richmond, Virginia, and witnesses a slave auction.

913

William H. Hooks

Circle of Fire (New York: Atheneum, 1982)

Age range: Grades 5-8

Subject(s): African Americans; Gypsies; Racism

Major character(s): Harrison Hawkins, Preteen; Kitty Fisher, Preteen; Scrap Fisher, Preteen

Time period(s): 1930s (1936)

Locale(s): North Carolina

What the book is about: Three friends, one white and two black children, try to thwart an attack on some Irish gypsies by the Ku Klux Klan. Harrison begins to think his father may be involved in the Klan plot. He has serious thinking to do and decisions to make.

Where it's reviewed:
Center for Children's Books Bulletin, October 1982, page 27
Horn Book, October 1982, page 517

Other books by the author:
A Flight of Dazzle Angels, 1988
Mean Jake and the Devils, 1981
The Mystery on Bleeker Street, 1980
The 17 Gerbils of Class 4A, 1976

Other books you might like:
Fred J. Cook, *The Ku Klux Klan: America's Recurring Nightmare*, 1980
Explores the pattern of racial bigotry, religious intolerance, violence, and exploitation by the Klan since its founding in the post-Civil War era.
Helen Cresswell, *The Secret World of Polly Flint*, 1982
Polly Flint, a girl who sees things other people cannot, finds herself involved with the "time gypsies" of Grimstone who are trapped in time.
Beth Bland Engel, *Big Words*, 1982
Twelve year old Sandy befriends a young black man she finds hiding on her father's property in Georgia in the mid-sixties.
Bette Greene, *Them That Glitter and Them That Don't*, 1983
A young gypsy girl living in the rural south is convinced she can use her singing talent to become someone special.
Phyllis Reynolds Naylor, *Footprints at the Window*, 1981
Dan searches for the gypsies he once knew in New York and is led into calamity involving the Black Death.

914

H.M. Hoover

Orvis (New York: Viking Kestral, 1987)

Age range: Grades 5-8

Subject(s): Robots; Science Fiction

Major character(s): Orvis, Robot; Toby, Survivor; Thaddeus, Survivor

Time period(s): Indeterminate Future

Locale(s): Earth

What the book is about: In this exploration of the impact of future technology on humanity, Toby and Thaddeus are living in an inhospitable wilderness, with only the obsolete robot, Orvis, for help in their efforts to survive and escape the wilderness.

Where it's reviewed:
Horn Book, September 10, 1987, page 617
School Library Journal, June/July 1987, page 96

Other books by the author:
Away Is a Strange Place to Be, 1990
Another Heaven, Another Earth, 1981
The Lost Star, 1979
Delikon, 1977

Other books you might like:
Janet Asimov, *Mind Transfer*, 1988
Adam Durant's experiences with mind transfer and his adventures with humans and robots test the validity of human growth with artificial intelligence.
John Bellaris, *The Eyes of the Killer Robot*, 1986
Johnny Dixon is put in jeopardy when he and Professor Childermass try to find a robot made many years ago by an evil wizard.
Ellen Leroe, *Robot Raiders*, 1987
Bixby Wyler battles against all odds to reconstruct his girl humanoid for NASA's Mars Landing Project.
Scott R. Sanders, *The Engineer of Beasts*, 1988
Mooch alienates authorities of her floating domed city by helping build realistic robot animals and by seeking out the wild animals left outside.
Alfred Slote, *Omega Station*, 1986
Jack Jameson and his robot twin, Danny One, must save the universe from a mad scientist.

915

Lee Bennett Hopkins

Mama (New York: Knopf, 1977)

Age range: Grades 3-5

Subject(s): Mothers and Sons; Stealing; Single Parent Families

Major character(s): Mama, Thief

Time period(s): 1970s

Locale(s): United States

What the book is about: Mama prefers plastic flowers to real ones, and scorns African violets because they are "foreign" flowers. Raising two boys, who are never named, she does what she can to make sure they have everything they need. When she works for a butcher, she steals steak, she steals clothes from a department store. The oldest boy knows she does what she does out of love, but it causes him great pain.

Where it's reviewed:
Kirkus Reviews, April 1, 1977, page 351
School Library Journal, October 1977, page 114

Other books by the author:
Beat the Drum, Independence Day Has Come, 1977
A Haunting We Will Go, 1977
Thread One to a Star, 1976
On Our Way, 1974

Other books you might like:
Larry Bograd, *Poor Gertie*, 1986
  Puzzled by her father's departure and wishing her mother didn't have to worry so much about money, Gertie loses herself in her drawings.
Beverly Keller, *No Beasts! No Children!*, 1983
  After her mother goes away to find herself, Desdemona, her father, the twins and the three dogs learn to cope with many strict and heartless people.
Lois Lowry, *The 100th Thing about Caroline*, 1983
  When their mother dates a man who has been told to "eliminate the children" by the first of May, Caroline and her brother fear they will be victims.
Elisabet McHugh, *Raising a Mother Isn't Easy*, 1983
  An eleven year old Korean orphan, adopted by a single woman, decides her mother should have a husband.
Alison Smith, *Help! There's a Cat Washing in Here!*, 1981
  Henry takes charge of the family for two weeks to allow his mother uninterrupted time to work on her art portfolio.

916

Nancy J. Hopper

Ape Ears and Beaky (New York: Dutton, 1984)

Age range: Grades 4-8

Subject(s): Anger; Sports/Baseball; Mystery and Detective Stories

Major character(s): Scott, Teenager; Beaky, Teenager

Time period(s): 1980s

Locale(s): United States

What the book is about: The thread running through this mystery story is Scott's effort to learn to control his temper. It has gotten him thrown off one baseball team and caused his humiliation on yeat another. Scott becomes involved with the "enemy," Beaky, in an effort to catch professional thieves who have been robbing condominiums.

Where it's reviewed:
Horn Book, January/February 1985, page 54
School Library Journal, December 1984, page 99

Other books by the author:
The Queen of Put-Downs, 1991
The Truth or Dare Trap, 1985
The Seven and One-Half Sins of Stacey Kendall, 1982
Secrets, 1979

Other books you might like:
Madeleine Edmondson, *Anna Witch*, 1982
  A little witch makes a discovery about life without mother after a loss of temper clashes with a loss of patience.

Trish Kennedy, *Baseball Card Crazy*, 1993
  While staying with his grandparents on their farm, Oliver searches diligently for the long-lost baseball card collection his father had as a boy.
Mike Neigoff, *Ski Run*, 1972
  During a ski vacation, Rick learns that he has to control his temper if he is to control his skis and get along with people.
Walter G. Oleksy, *Quacky and the Crazy Curve Ball*, 1981
  When faced with two challenges, making a baseball team for thirteen year olds and trapping the "Hungry Burgler," an orphan proves his resourcefulness.
Robert H. Wells, *Five-Yard Fuller of the N.Y. Gnats*, 1967
  A young man from the country, already famous for his football prowess, rescues a professional baseball team from the cellar of the league.

917

James A. Houston, Author/Illustrator

Frozen Fire (New York: Atheneum, 1977)

Age range: Grades 5-6

Subject(s): Survival; Eskimos

Major character(s): Kayak, Eskimo; Matthew "Mattoosie" Morgan, Preteen

Time period(s): 1960s

Locale(s): Frobisher Bay, Northwest Territories, Canada

What the book is about: Matthew's father is a prospector. When he disappears after filing an incorrect flight plan to throw off other prospectors, Matthew and his friend Kayak take a snowmobile and go to rescue him. The gas tank leaks and they face a seventy-five mile homeward journey through incredible hardships. The friendship of the boys and the picture of the Eskimo in transition make this a great story, based on true events.

Where it's reviewed:
Kirkus Reviews, November 15, 1977, page 1197
School Library Journal, November 1977, page 57

Other books by the author:
Drifting Snow: An Arctic Legend, 1992
The Falcon Bow, 1986
Ice Swords: An Undersea Adventure, 1985
Black Diamonds, 1982

Other books you might like:
Midas Dekkers, *Arctic Adventure*, 1987
  Two Dutch brothers risk their lives in an attempt to stop the crew of a whaling boat from harpooning a Greenland whale.
Nancy Leunn, *Arctic Unicorn*, 1986
  Living in a remote Eskimo village, Kala finds her life disrupted by the arrival of a young hunter and by her discovery of her own special powers.
Harry Mazer, *Snow Bound*, 1973
  Two teenagers caught in a snowstorm face a fight for survival in a desolate area.
Marian Rumsey, *Danger on Shadow Mountain*, 1970
  A boy struggles to rescue his kidnapped brother in the Alaskan wilderness.
Caroline Tapley, *John Come Down the Backstay*, 1974

A young sailor tells of his experiences on the sailing ship Fox during two years spent searching for an exploring party lost twelve years before.

918

Elizabeth Howard

Illustrator: Michael W. Kaluta

Mystery of the Metro (New York: Random, 1987)

Age range: Grades 6-9

Series: My Name Is Paris

Subject(s): Mystery and Detective Stories

Major character(s): Paris MacKenzie, Detective, Teenager; Madame Meduse, Villain

Time period(s): 1900s

Locale(s): Paris, France

What the book is about: A fast paced mystery set in turn of the century Paris, featuring Paris MacKenzie, a sixteen year old from Chicago with a vivacious personality and a passion for Sherlock Holmes. When she visits her namesake city, she finds her uncle has died mysteriously and vows to bring his killer to justice. She finds herself in a deadly game with a formidable opponent, the hypnotic Madame Meduse.

Where it's reviewed:
School Library Journal, October 1987, page 139

Other books by the author:
Mystery of the Deadly Diamond, 1987
Mystery of the Magician, 1987
A Scent of Murder, 1987

Other books you might like:
Thea Brown, *The Secret Cross of Lorraine*, 1981
    While visiting friends in France, Twyla tries to find the elusive owner of the lost Cross of Lorraine.
Eleanor Cameron, *The Court of the Stone Children*, 1973
    Aided by the journal of a young woman who lived in 19th century France, Nina solves a murder mystery dormant since the time of Napoleon.
Betty Cavanna, *Stamp Twice for Murder*, 1981
    Mysterious events occur when a sixteen year old American girl and her family come to France to claim their legacy of an abandoned country cottage.
Gaston Leroux, *The Phantom of the Opera*, 1911
    A viscount seeks to unravel the mystery of the Paris Opera House and rescue the woman he loves from the threat of the Phantom of the Opera.
Joan Lowery Nixon, *A Candidate for Murder*, 1991
    Cary finds her life in danger when she uncovers a plot to sabotage her father's political campaign for governor of Texas.

919

Ellen Howard

Circle of Giving (New York: Atheneum, 1984)

Age range: Grades 4-6

Subject(s): Physically Handicapped

Major character(s): Marguerite, Child; Francie, Handicapped (cerebral palsy)

Time period(s): 1920s

Locale(s): Los Angeles, California

What the book is about: Marguerite has trouble making friends in her new Los Angeles neighborhood. When a new family arrives, she makes friends with Francie, a victim of cerebral palsy. Descriptions of Francie's affliction would not be acceptable today. Such words as "cripple" and "hopeless" and a stereotyped martyr mother mark this as set in the 1920s.

Where it's reviewed:
Center for Children's Books Bulletin, April 1984, page 149
School Library Journal, August 1984, page 74

Other books by the author:
Chickenhouse House, 1991
Edith Herself, 1987
Her Own Story, 1988
Sister, 1990

Other books you might like:
Carole S. Adler, *Eddie's Blue-Winged Dragon*, 1988
    Eddie becomes the owner of a brass dragon which helps him in his struggle with cerebral palsy.
Barbara Aiello, *It's Your Turn at Bat*, 1988
    Mark, a 5th grader with cerebral palsy, discovers that the money for his team's baseball jerseys, for which he is responsible, is missing.
Ivan Southall, *Let the Balloon Go*, 1968
    A 12-year-old handicapped by cerebral palsy and desperate for independence does what he has been expressly forbidden to do.
Sherry Newirth, *A Contest*, 1982
    Mike shows the children in his class that his cerebral palsy does not keep him from playing when he is given a chance. Related Picture Book.

920

Ellen Howard

Illustrator: Ronald Himler

Edith Herself (New York: Atheneum, 1987)

Age range: Grades 4-6

Subject(s): Epilepsy; Farm Life; Orphans

Major character(s): Edith, Child, Orphan

Time period(s): 1890s

Locale(s): United States

What the book is about: In the late 19th century, orphaned Edith faces a new life with her sister's family. She has epilepsy, and the strain of adjusting to the stern Christian farming household seems to aggravate her condition. Edith comes to terms with her life and with the reactions of people who don't understand her illness.

Where it's reviewed:
Kirkus Reviews, January 1, 1987, page 57
School Library Journal, April 1987, page 96

Other books by the author:
Chickenhouse House, 1991
Sister, 1990

Her Own Song, 1988
Gillyflower, 1986

Other books you might like:
Barbara Aiello, *Trick or Treat or Trouble*, 1989
    Just as his friends misunderstand his epilepsy, Brian's misconceptions about a funeral home are cleared up on Halloween night.
Barbara Girion, *A Handful of Stars*, 1981
    Julie, suddenly stricken with epilepsy, must learn to live with her condition as doctors try to help her with medication.
Lynn Hall, *Halsey's Pride*, 1990
    March, an epileptic, comes to live with her dog-breeder father, and learns about love, truth, and gains the courage to cope with difficulties.
Patricia Hermes, *What If They Knew?*, 1980
    A ten year old must start in a new school and somehow hide the fact that she is an epileptic.
Rebecca C. Jones, *Madeline and the Great (Old) Escape Artist*, 1983
    An unlikely friendship between an old lady and a sixth grade girl with a recently diagnosed seizure disorder, helps them both face their problems.

921

Ellen Howard

Her Own Song (New York: Atheneum, 1988)

Age range: Grades 3-6

Subject(s): Chinese Americans; Prejudice; Adoption

Major character(s): Mellie, Child; Geem-Wah, Worker (Chinese launderer)

Time period(s): 1900s

Locale(s): Seattle, Washington

What the book is about: Mellie was sold as an infant to a Chinese family. Taken away by the authorities and given to her white adoptive parents, Mellie now searches for her real parents with the help of Geem-Wah. Based on a true story.

Where it's reviewed:
Center of Children's Books Bulletin, November 1988, page 75
Horn Book, November/December 1988, page 783

Other books by the author:
Chickenhouse House, 1991
Edith Herself, 1987
Sister, 1990
When Daylight Comes, 1985

Other books you might like:
Theodore Taylor, *Tuck Triumphant*, 1991
    Helen and her blind dog Friar Tuck face challenges when they realize the Korean boy they have adopted is deaf.
Joyce McDonald, *Mail-Order Kid*, 1988
    Ten-year-old Flip orders a fox through the mail and he copes with understanding both it and his newly adopted Korean brother.
Walter Dean Myers, *Me, Mop and the Moondance Kid*, 1988
    Adopted brothers T.J. and Moondance keep in touch with their friend still in the orphanage and try to wreak revenge on baseball rivals.
Linda Walvoord Girard, *Adoption Is for Always*, 1986

Parents of an adopted child make her adoption day a family holiday. Related picture book.
Claudia Mills, *Boardwalk with Hotel*, 1985
    Jessica discovers she was adopted because her parents thought they couldn't have children and wonders if they love her less than siblings born later.

922

Ellen Howard

Sister (New York: Atheneum, 1990)

Age range: Grades 5 and Up

Subject(s): Farm Life; Family Life

Major character(s): Alena Osterman, Teenager; Johnny Malcolm, Teacher

Time period(s): 1880s (1886)

Locale(s): Illinois

What the book is about: Alena wants to stay in school and her teacher thinks she may be able to get a scholarship to go further in her education. When her mother's baby is born, Alena is the only one to help with the delivery. The birth scene is one of the most powerful ones in the book. Her hopes for schooling are dashed when her mother dips into a deep depression following the death of the newborn and Alena must take care of the family.

Where it's reviewed:
Booklist, November 1, 1990, page 522
School Library Journal, November 1990, page 140

Other books by the author:
The Cellar, 1992
Edith Herself, 1987
Gillyflower, 1986
Her Own Song, 1986

Other books you might like:
Kathy Lynn Emerson, *Julia's Mending*, 1987
    When her missionary parents go to China without her, snobbish Julia is sent to upstate New York where she breaks her leg and heals her angers.
Kate Seredy, *The Singing Tree*, 1967
    Life changes drastically for a Hungarian family when WWI upsets their peaceful contented life and the children are left in charge of the farm.
Susan Sharpe, *Chicken Bucks*, 1992
    When hard times force Mark to change his 4-H project from raising a calf to selling eggs, he finds the experience both challenging and rewarding.
Ruth Wallace-Brodeur, *The Godmother Tree*, 1988
    When ten year old Laura moves with her family to yet another new farm, Laura slowly begins to build connections to the place, her family, and herself.
Andrea Wyman, *Red Sky at Morning*, 1991
    In 1909, Callie finds she must grow up quickly when death and other hardships leave her alone on the family farm with her ailing grandfather.

923

Deborah Howe

Illustrator: Alan Daniel

Bunnicula: A Rabbit Tale of Mystery (New York: Atheneum, 1979)

Age range: Grades 3-6

Subject(s): Animals/Rabbits; Vampires

Major character(s): Harold Monroe, Dog; Chester, Cat; Bunnicula, Rabbit

Time period(s): 1970s

Locale(s): United States

What the book is about: Although laughed at by Harold the dog, Chester the cat tries to warn his human family that their foundling baby bunny must be a vampire.

Where it's reviewed:
Kirkus Reviews, July 1, 1979, page 741
School Library Journal, May 1979, page 81

Awards the book has won:
Dorothy Canfield Fisher Children's Book Award 1981

Other books by the author:
Return to Howliday Inn, 1992
Nighty-Nightmare, 1987
The Celery Stalks at Midnight, 1983
Howliday Inn, 1982

Other books you might like:
Mary DeBall Kwitz, *The Bell Tolls at Mousehaven Manor*, 1991
  Count Von Flittermouse, a body-changing vampire bat, kidnaps Violet Mae Mouse in hopes of gaining a bottle of fluid from the fountain of youth.
Elizabeth Levy, *Dracula Is a Pain in the Neck*, 1983
  Robert fears that his plastic Dracula doll is responsible for strange goings-on at camp.
Angela Sommer-Bodenburg, *My Friend, the Vampire*, 1984
  Tony's life becomes one thrill after another when he befriends vampires Rudolph and Anna.
Angela Sommer-Bodenburg, *The Vampire Moves In*, 1982
  Banished by his friends and family for making friends with a human, a little vampire moves into the basement of Tony's apartment building.
Jane Yolen, *Vampires: A Collection of Original Stories*, 1991
  Thirteen original vampire stories by a variety of authors.

924

Fanny Howe

Race of the Radical (New York: Viking, 1985)

Age range: Grades 5-8

Subject(s): Bicycles and Bicycling; Sports

Major character(s): Alex Porter, Sports Figure; Robinson Porter, Child; Rosie Porter, Child

Time period(s): 1980s

Locale(s): Meridian, California

What the book is about: Alex, an expert racer on a lighter-than-air bicycle, the Radical, fights to save his bike from irresponsible race promoters. Explore the world of bicycle motocross, from the local tracks to the nationals, where Alex joins the tough competition to win a place with the professionals.

Where it's reviewed:
Booklist, November 15, 1985, page 493
Center for Children's Books Bulletin, October 1985, page 29

Other books by the author:
Radio City, 1984
Blue Hills, 1981
White Slave, 1980

Other books you might like:
Matt Christopher, *Dirt Bike Racer*, 1979
  Ron Baker finds a minibike while scuba diving, and with the help of a former motorcycle rider and racer, restores the bike and enters competition.
William Campbell Gault, *The Sunday Cycles*, 1979
  Two cousins graduate from a little "Sunday fun" to dirt tracks, desert racing, and motocross.
Paul Kropp, *Dirt Bike*, 1982
  A cyclist, with the help of a former member of Alcoholics Anonymous, learns to control his drinking and restores a sense of purpose in his life.
Margaret Nettles Ogan, *Acuna Brutes*, 1973
  A college senior determines to master the powerful Spanish Acuna motorcycles and participate in the motocross races through Death Valley and Baja.
Ed Radlauer, *Motorcycle Winners*, 1982
  Nan is prepared to give up motorcycle racing forever until she gets some simple but sound advice from her aunt, a champion drag racer.

925

James Howe

Dew Drop Dead: A Sebastian Barth Mystery (New York: Atheneum, 1990)

Age range: Grades 5-6

Series: A Sebastian Barth Mystery

Subject(s): Mystery and Detective Stories; Homeless

Major character(s): David Lepinsky, Preteen; Corrie Wingate, Preteen; Sebastian Barth, Detective

Time period(s): 1990s

Locale(s): Pembroke

What the book is about: While setting up a homeless shelter at the church, Sebastian and his friends, Corrie and David, solve the mystery of a dead man found in an abandoned inn.

Where it's reviewed:
Horn Book, January 1990, page 159
School Library Journal, April 1990, page 120

Other books by the author:
The Celery Stalks at Midnight, 1990
Hot Fudge, 1990
The Fright Before Christmas, 1989
Pinky and Rex, 1989

Other books you might like:
Alison Cragin Herzig, *Sam and the Moon Queen*, 1990
  Sympathetic to a homeless girl's plight, Sam tries to find food for her and medical attention for her dog.

Felice Holman, *Secret City, U.S.A.*, 1990
  Against all odds, Benno and his friends convert an abandoned building into a shelter for the homeless.
Dean Hughes, *Family Pose*, 1989
  Feeling unwanted, an orphan runs away from his foster home and lives on the streets until he finds a new type of family at a hotel.
Jill Pinkwater, *Tails of the Bronx: A Tale of the Bronx*, 1991
  In their search for a group of missing cats, children in the Bronx encounter the problems of the homeless first hand.
Susan Wojciechowski, *Patty Dillman of Hot Dog Fame*, 1989
  Patty becomes involved in working at a shelter where she finds a new friend far more sensitive than the football player she lost her heart to.

926

Janni Howker

Isaac Campion (New York: Greenwillow, 1986)

Age range: Grades 6 and Up

Subject(s): Death; Animals/Horses

Major character(s): Dan Campion, Teenager; Isaac Campion, Child

Time period(s): 1900s (1901)

Locale(s): United States

What the book is about: Dan dies at age 18, when he slips and impales himself on a railing. Isaac is twelve years at the time. Eighty-three years later, Isaac tells the story of how his world changed following Dan's death and his saddened adulthood.

Where it's reviewed:
Kirkus Reviews, April 15, 1987, page 639
School Library Journal, June 1987, page 107

Awards the book has won:
Boston Globe/Horn Book Award - Honor Book 1987

Other books by the author:
The Nature of the Beast, 1986
Badger on the Barge, 1985

Other books you might like:
Johanna Hurwitz, *The Rabbi's Girls*, 1982
  Moving to a new town, the birth of a sister and the death of her father, make 1923 a difficult year for eleven year old Carrie Levin.
Valerie A. Lutters, *The Haunting of Julie Unger*, 1977
  The vivid memory of her dead father threatens to isolate a twelve year old girl from the rest of her family and push her to the brink of madness.
Susan McLean, *Pennies for the Piper*, 1981
  A ten year old, known for her emotional strength, takes it upon herself to provide her mother with a proper funeral.
Mary Pope Osborne, *Run, Run as Fast as You Can*, 1982
  Eleven year old Hallie Pines worries about popularity and faces an unexpected tragedy when her family moves to Virginia.
Bill Wallace, *Trapped in Death Cave*, 1984
  Gary is convinced that his grandfather did not die a natural death, and he and his friend, Brian, set out to find his grandfather's killer.

927

John Hoyland

Illustrator: Richard Vicary

The Ivy Garland (London: Allison and Busky, 1983)

Age range: Grades 4-6

Subject(s): Ghosts

Major character(s): Jamie Andrews, Child; Linda Froggatt, Preteen; Diane Andrews, Preteen

Time period(s): 1970s

Locale(s): Wickendale, England (Derbyshire Peak District)

What the book is about: A strange boy appears in the mist wearing clothes from sseveral centuries past and an ivy garland around his neck. Spellbinding suspense follows in this English story of an age-old curse threatening a young girl.

Where it's reviewed:
Center for Children's Books Bulletin, July 1983, page 211
School Library Journal, March 1984, page 160

Other books you might like:
Mollie Hunter, *The Mermaid Summer*, 1988
  Jon and Anna try to discover the secret way to undo a mermaid's curse on their grandfather.
Siny R. Iterson, *The Curse of Laguna Grande*, 1973
  A young boy in a remote area of Colombia tries to discover the circumstances surrounding his father's abduction many years before.
Reby Edmond MacDonald, *The Ghosts of Austwick Manor*, 1982
  Hillary and Heather find themselves in the 16th century as the result of their brother's inheritance. Can they save him from an ancient curse?
Robert Newman, *Grettir the Strong*, 1968
  Grettir's inability to avoid a fight keeps him in continual trouble, and ultimately the curse of one he killed causes his death.
Andre Norton, *House of Shadows*, 1984
  Mike and Susan feel a mounting sense of urgency and terror as they try to protect their younger brother who is threatened by an ancient family curse.

928

Charlotte S. Huck

Illustrator: Anita Lobel

Princess Furball (New York: Greenwillow, 1989)

Age range: Grades 2-3

Subject(s): Princes and Princesses

Major character(s): Furball, Royalty (princess)

Time period(s): Indeterminate Past

Locale(s): England

What the book is about: A princess runs away from home when her father, the king, insists she marry an ogre. In charge of her own destiny, she wraps herself in a thousand furs, takes some small treasures, and finds her own life partner, a king in a distant land.

Where it's reviewed:
Center for Children's Books Bulletin, October 1989, page 779

School Library Journal, September 1989, page 240

Other books you might like:
Babette Cole, *Princess Smartypants*, 1986
  Not wishing to marry any of her royal suitors, Princess Smartypants devises difficult tasks at which they all fail, until Prince Swashbuckle appears.
Jane Langton, *The Hedgehog Boy*, 1985
  A princess is forced to marry a hedgehog boy and is astounded when remorse over a thoughtless act of hers transforms him into a handsome young man.
Ellen Kindt McKenzie, *The King, the Princess and the Tinker*, 1992
  A good-hearted tinker and a curious young princess show a narrow-minded king that there are more important things in the world than treasure.
Anne Sibley O'Brien, *The Princess and the Beggar*, 1992
  A sad princess finds happiness after marrying a beggar in this Korean folktale.
Sally Scott, *The Magic Horse*, 1985
  In order to marry the princess he loves, a Persian prince must outwit an evil magician and use a magic horse to his advantage.

929

Jan Hudson

Dawn Rider (New York: Philomel, 1990)

Age range: Grades 5 and Up

Subject(s): Indians of North America

Major character(s): Kit Fox, Indian; Found Arrow, Indian

Time period(s): 1750s (1750)

Locale(s): United States

What the book is about: Kit Fox is a sixteen year old Blackfoot Indian in 1750. She is drawn to the first wild horse the men of her village have captured. Her friend, Found Arrow, helps her keep her unapproved riding secret. She rides to the Cree camp in search of guns needed for an imminent enemy attack.

Where it's reviewed:
Center for Children's Books Bulletin, February 1991, page 143
Kirkus Reviews, December 1, 1990, page 1673

Other books by the author:
Sweetgrass, 1990

Other books you might like:
Paul Goble, *The Girl Who Loved Wild Horses*, 1978
  After becoming lost in a storm, a young Indian girl joins and lives with a herd of wild horses until finally, she becomes one herself.
Evelyn Sibley Lampman, *White Captives*, 1975
  The story of Live Oatman's five years of slavery among the Apache and Mohave indians, first recorded in 1857.
Betty Levin, *Brother Moose*, 1990
  Orphans Nell and Louisa, on their way to foster homes in rural Canada, find they will have to spend the winter with a runaway Indian and his grandson.
Scott O'Dell, *Streams to the River, River to the Sea*, 1986
  The story of the Shoshone girl who served as an interpreter and guide for the Lewis and Clark expedition, Sacajawea.

Kenneth Thomasma, *Om-Kas-Toe of the Blackfeet*, 1986
  Born into a Blackfeet family in the early 1700's, young Om plays a large role in bringing the first elk dog to the tribe.

930

Dean Hughes

Family Pose (New York:Atheneum, 1989)

Age range: Grades 5 and Up

Subject(s): Runaways; Orphans; Homeless

Major character(s): David, Runaway; Paul, Hotel Worker (bellboy)

Time period(s): 1980s

Locale(s): United States

What the book is about: A hotel's night shift crew becomes family for David. All loners in their own right, the bellboy sneaks him into a room and feeds him and the desk clerk, telephone operator and cocktail waitress unite to offer David the love and respect he needs.

Where it's reviewed:
Booklist, April 1, 1989, page 1384
School Library Journal, April 1989, page 102

Other books by the author:
Total Soccer, 1992
All Together Now, 1991
Family Picture, 1990
Line Drive, 1990

Other books you might like:
William Bell, *Crabbe's Journey*, 1986
  A Canadian teenager runs off to live in the woods where a mysterious woman teaches him survival skills.
Brock Cole, *The Goats*, 1987
  Stripped and marooned on a small island by fellow campers, a boy and girl run away and disappear without a trace.
Barbara Corcoran, *Don't Slam the Door When You Go*, 1972
  Three girls run away from their home in Florida to try to find a home in a Montana ghost town.
Peni R. Griffin, *Hobkin*, 1992
  Two sisters run away from an abusive stepfather and settle in an abandoned house, only to find they are not alone there.
Gayle Pearson, *The Coming Home Cafe*, 1988
  In the summer of 1933, Elizabeth leaves home to ride the rails looking for work.

931

Dean Hughes

Honestly, Myron (New York: Atheneum, 1982)

Age range: Grades 3-5

Subject(s): Honesty; Conduct of Life

Major character(s): Myron Singleton, Preteen; Lustre Bright, Preteen

Time period(s): 1980s

Locale(s): United States

What the book is about: Fifth grader Myron Singleton believes in telling the truth, often to a fault. He causes a near-riot at home when his parents discover (thanks to Myron) that they have been keeping secrets from each other. Myron gets into politics when he makes comments about an upcoming bond issue, and the media goes nuts. A humorous springboard for a discussion of honesty.

Where it's reviewed:
Kirkus Reviews, April 15, 1982, page 489
School Library Journal, August 1982, page 117

Other books by the author:
Making the Team, 1990
Family Pose, 1989
Theo Zephyr, 1987
Jelly's Circus, 1986

Other books you might like:
Patricia Reilly Giff, *Meet the Lincoln Lions Band*, 1992
    Chrissie wants to be in the marching band, but lying about her ability messes things up.
Laura Hawkins, *Figment, Your Dog, Speaking*, 1991
    A talking dog with a knack for changing people's lives helps Marcella deal with her tendency to tell wild stories to get attention.
Lois Lowry, *Your Move, JP!*, 1990
    Lovestruck JP finds himself trying to impress his new interest but his life becomes very complicated when a simple lie gets out of control.
Ann M. Martin, *Karen's Pen Pal*, 1992
    Karen thinks having a pen pal in New York City is very cool, but when her pal Maxie turns out to be a big braggart, Karen starts to make up stories.
P.J. Petersen, *Liars*, 1992
    In the remote town of Alder Creek, California, Sam and friends become involved in strange eventse because of his new power to detect a person's lies.

932

Dean Hughes

Nutty and the Case of the Ski-Slope Spy (New York: Atheneum, 1985)

Age range: Grades 4-6

Series: Nutty Nutsell

Subject(s): Mystery and Detective Stories; Sports/Skiing; Spies

Major character(s): William Bilks, Preteen; Nutty Nutsell, Detective, Preteen; Bilbo, Preteen

Time period(s): 1980s

Locale(s): Utah

What the book is about: Student council president Nutty Nutsell takes his show on the road this time as he organizes a student ski trip. After finding mysterious plans in their hotel bathroom, they discover they are stolen computer documents. The person who left the plans wants them back and will use the code name Russian Roulette. Before the mystery is solved, the boys are involved in wild ski chases, an escape from a locked hotel room, and all kinds of threats, so that their lives are in serious danger.

Where it's reviewed:
School Library Journal, January 1986, page 68

Other books by the author:
Family Picture, 1989
Theo Zephyr, 1987
Nutty and the Case of the Mastermind Thief, 1985
Nutty for President, 1981

Other books you might like:
Lisa Eisenberg, *Mystery at Snowshoe Mountain Lodge*, 1987
    A rash of pranks and mysterious accidents at an old ski lodge is investigated by teenage sleuths who finally discover the surprising culprit.
Susan Schaumbert Gordon, *Skiing for the Prize*, 1992
    The High-Fives join the Downhillers Ski Club until Ron Porter and his bullyboy raiders threaten to drive them off the slopes.
Carli Laklan, *Ski Bum*, 1973
    A young man on a pleasure trip becomes caught up in a dream at Big Snow ski resort when he joins the Ski Patrol.
Christine Nostlinger, *Marrying Off Mother*, 1978
    In order to escape her grandmother's restrictive household, Sue arranges a vacation designed to make her mother marry a man who despises the family.
Olive M. Price, *The Dog That Watched the Mountain*, 1967
    The story of a Swiss youth's perseverance to gain loyalty, love, and obedience from a sober, unaffectionate dog selected to help him in ski class.

933

Dean Hughes

Theo Zephyr (New York: Atheneum, 1987)

Age range: Grades 4-6

Subject(s): Imagination; Jealousy

Major character(s): Brad Hill, Child; Gil Brimhall, Child; Mrs. Hardy, Teacher

Time period(s): 1980s

Locale(s): Grandview, Utah

What the book is about: Theo Zephyr is Brad's imaginary friend and ally in his struggle with Gil, the athletic and math whiz. One day Theo shows up in the flesh and daydreams start coming true. Only Brad knows that Theo is not "real."

Where it's reviewed:
Center for Children's Books Bulletin, July/August 1987, page 210
School Library Journal, October 1987, page 126

Other books by the author:
Family Pose, 1989
Nutty, the Movie Star, 1989
Millie Willenheimer and the Chestnut Corporation, 1983
Switching Tracks, 1982

Other books you might like:
Lynn Hall, *Dagmar Schultz and the Green-Eyed Monster*, 1991
    Jealous of a pretty and popular new student, thirteen year old Dagmar decides to get even with humorous results.
Pamela Jane, *Just Plain Penny*, 1990
    Imaginative Penelope learns to distinguish between real and invented drama when she spends the summer in her "boring" little town writing a play.
Bjarne B. Reuter, *Buster, the Sheikh of Hope Street*, 1991

Buster, a very imaginative schoolboy, must draw on all his imagination to take over the lead in the school play at the very last minute.

John Rowe Townsend, *Rob's Place*, 1987
  With many family disappointments going on, Rob invents a fantastic imaginary refuge on a "South Sea" island in the local park.

Betty Ren Wright, *The Scariest Night*, 1991
  When her family spends the summer in Milwaukee so her brother can attend piano school, Erin finds herself jealous and turns to a medium for help.

934

Monica Hughes

Sandwriter (New York: Holt, 1988)

Age range: Grades 5-8

Subject(s): Fantasy; Princes and Princesses

Major character(s): Antia, Royalty (princess); Jodril, Royalty (prince); Eskoril, Tutor

Time period(s): Indeterminate

Locale(s): Kamalant, Fictional Country (Roshan Desert)

What the book is about: A pampered princess visits the land of the prince she will marry some day and comes to understand another culture. A little romance, a little magic, and a happy ending.

Where it's reviewed:
Center for Children's Books Bulletin, March 1988, page 138
School Library Journal, March 1988, page 214

Other books by the author:
The Isis Pedlar, 1984
The Guardian of Isis, 1982
The Keeper of the Isis Light, 1982
Beyond the Dark River, 1981

Other books you might like:
Carolyn F. Logan, *The Power of the Rellard*, 1986
  Lucy, repeating the fourth grade for medical reasons, finds herself and her siblings in the midst of a power struggle with agents of an ancient evil.
George MacDonald, *The Princess and Curdie*, 1987
  Aided by a fairy queen who provides monstrous but gentle assistants, a miner's son helps the king and princess save their kingdom from their enemies.
Lensey Namioka, *White Serpent Castle*, 1976
  During the struggle for a warlord's territory, two unemployed samurai attempt to secure power for the rightful heir.
Sherwood Smith, *Wren to the Rescue*, 1990
  With the help of a prince and an apprentice wizard, Wren strives to rescue her best friend, a princess named Tess, from the fortress of a wicked king.
Laura Caroline Stevenson, *The Island and the Ring*, 1991
  After treachery destroys her kingdom, Princess Tania discovers that she must confront Ascanet, the ruthless lord enslaving the island of Elyssone.

935

Ted Hughes

Illustrator: Dirk Zimmer

The Iron Giant: A Story in Five Nights (New York: HarperCollins, 1988)

Age range: Grades 3-5

Subject(s): Giants; Monsters; Recycling (Waste)

Major character(s): Hogarth, Child; Iron, Mythical Creature (giant)

Time period(s): Indeterminate

Locale(s): Australia

What the book is about: The Iron Giant has a huge hunger for metal. Hogarth found a neat way to clean up scrap metal and trash, by feeding the Giant. When a huge Space-Bat-Angel-Dragon landed in Australia, the Iron Giant became the Earth's champion.

Where it's reviewed:
Book World, March 13, 1988, page 12
Center for Children's Book Bulletin, June 1988, page 208

Other books by the author:
Tales of the Early World, 1991
The River, 1983
The Tiger's Bones and Other Plays for Children, 1974
How the Whale Became, 1963

Other books you might like:
Franz Brandenberg, *What Can You Make of It?*, 1977
  A family of field mice finally find a way to use their collection of rubbish
Bruce Coville, *The Foolish Giant*, 1978
  The adventures of a not very bright but friendly giant named Harry.
Loreen Leedy, *The Great Trash Bash*, 1991
  The animal citizens of Beaston discover better ways to recycle and control their trash.
Pete Seeger, *Abiyoyo*, 1986
  Banished from the town for making mischief, a boy and his father are welcomed back when they find a way to make the dreaded giant Abiyoyo disappear.
Steve Senn, *The Sand Witch*, 1987
  On vacation at the beach, Frick and Jenny help a witch from outer space search for a giant candy-eating crab.

936

Ted Hughes

Illustrator: Andrew Davidson

Tales of the Early World (New York: Farrar, 1988)

Age range: Grades 5 and Up

Subject(s): Creation; Animals

Time period(s): Indeterminate Past

Locale(s): Earth

What the book is about: Ten original creation stories with a lyrical beauty that include a shiver of the dark. The stories play with Genesis, Native American myth, Blake's "Tyger! Tyger!" and Kipling's "Just So Stories." One story includes God's creation of the horse to be woman's playmate.

Where it's reviewed:
Center for Children's Books Bulletin, June 1991, page 240
School Library Journal, May 1991, page 93

Other books by the author:
The Iron Giant: A Story in Five Nights, 1988
Under the North Star, 1981 (Poetry)
The Tiger's Bones and Other Plays for Children, 1974
How the Whale Became, 1963

Other books you might like:
Ronald Leonard Bacon, *Maori Legends*, 1984
    Creation stories from the Maori people.
Rosemary Border, *Nuka's Tale*, 1981
    Nuka's grandmother tells him how light first came to the world and how the land first rose up from the sea. An Eskimo legend.
Kenneth McLeish, *In the Beginning*, 1984
    Creation myths from around the world.
G.M. Mullett, *Spider Woman Stories: Legends of the Hopi Indians*, 1979
    Hopi Indian legends of the creation and the adventures of the hero Tiyo and Twin War Gods.

937

Irene Hunt

Across Five Aprils (Chicago: Follett, 1964)

Age range: Grades 5 and Up

Subject(s): Civil War

Major character(s): Jethro Creighton, Child; Ellen Creighton, Parent; Shadrach Yale, Teacher

Time period(s): 1860s (1861-1865)

Locale(s): Illinois

What the book is about: Beginning in April of 1861 the realities of the Civil War come to a farm in Illinois as brothers fight on opposite sides. Nine year old Jethro assumes the position of man of the family while wondering if his brothers will return.

Where it's reviewed:
Horn Book, June 1964, page 291
Library Journal, April 15, 1964, page 1871

Awards the book has won:
Newbery Honor

Other books by the author:
The Everlasting Hills, 1985
The Lottery Rose: A Novel, 1976
No Promises in the Wind, 1970
Up a Road Slowly, 1966

Other books you might like:
Elaine Marie Alphin, *The Great Cadet*, 1991
    12 year old Benjy meets the ghost of a Virginia Military Institute cadet who was killed in battle in 1864 and helps him recover a treasured watch.
Patricia Lee Gauch, *Thunder at Gettysburg*, 1975
    Fourteen year old Tillie becomes involved in the tragic Battle of Gettysburg.
Milton Meltzer, *Underground Man*, 1990
    A courageous young white man aids slaves escaping from Kentucky in pre-Civil War days.
Laura Jan Shore, *The Sacred Moon Tree*, 1986

Twelve year old Phoebe disguises herself as a boy and travels with her friend, Jotham, behind enemy lines during the Civil War.
G. Clifton Wisler, *Red Cap*, 1991
    A young Yankee drummer boy displays great courage when he's captured and sent to Andersonville prison.

938

Evan Hunter

Me and Mr. Stenner (New York: Lippincott, 1976)

Age range: Grades 5 and Up

Subject(s): Stepfamilies

Major character(s): Abby, Preteen; Mr. Stenner, Step-Parent

Time period(s): 1970s

Locale(s): United States

What the book is about: Mr. Stenner moved in when Abby's parents separated and he becomes her stepfather. Abby loves her father and resents Stenner's efforts to be friendly. While in Europe on vacation, she realizes that she has actually come to love her new stepfather, without loving her father any less.

Where it's reviewed:
Kirkus Reviews, July 15, 1976, page 795
School Library Journal, October 1976, page 117

Other books by the author:
Love, Dad, 1981
The Chisholms, 1976

Other books you might like:
Mary Jane Auch, *Seven Long Years Until College*, 1991
    When her stepfather restricts her actions, and her best friend prepares to move to Cleveland, Natalie takes drastic steps to avoid change in her life.
Mary Haynes, *Wordchanger*, 1983
    Twelve year old William finds his stepfather has created a machine capable of changing the printed word and fears that his intentions are sinister.
S.E. Hinton, *Taming the Star Runner*, 1988
    Sent to live with his uncle after a violent confrontation with his stepfather, Travis finds life in a small Oklahoma town confining.
Jan Mark, *Trouble Half-Way*, 1985
    Driving through England with her new stepfather, Amy gains a new view of herself, her stepfather, and the country through which she is travelling.
Christine McDonnell, *Count Me In*, 1986
    Katie has a difficult time adjusting to her new family situation, especially after her mother and new stepfather announce they are expecting a baby.

939

Mollie Hunter

The Mermaid Summer (New York: Harper and Row, 1988)

Age range: Grades 4-6

Subject(s): Mermaids; Magic

Major character(s): Eric Anderson, Grandparent; Anna Anderson, Child; Jon Anderson, Child

Time period(s): 1980s

Locale(s): Scotland

What the book is about: Eric Anderson leaves his Scottish fishing village after his boat is dashed to pieces on the rocks, but he sends wonderful gifts back to his grandchildren. Meanwhile, Anna faces down a tempermental mermaid to save her fishing village and to bring her grandfather home.

Where it's reviewed:
Horn Book, January/February 1989, page 70
School Library Journal, June/July 1988, page 105

Other books by the author:
A Furl of Fairy Wind, 1977
The Wicked One, 1977
The Kelpie's Pearls, 1976
The Haunted Mountain, 1972

Other books you might like:
Thomas G. Aylesworth, *The Story Dragons and Other Monsters*, 1980
    Discusses the dragon, kraken, basilisk, mermaid and harpy.
Susan Clymer, *The Glass Mermaid*, 1986
    Becca can hardly believe her eyes. There under the tree on Christmas Eve are two tiny people who are stealing her favorite ornament, a glass mermaid.
Eileen Dunlop, *Clementina*, 1985
    Daisy's Scottish vacation is being ruined by a relationship with the strange girl, Clementina, until she is linked to another Clementina from the past
Joanna Russ, *Kittatinny: A Tale of Magic*, 1978
    A woman warrior, a sleeping beauty, a baby satyr, and a mermaid encourage a young girl into accepting free womanhood.
Jane Yolen, *The Mermaid's Three Wisdoms*, 1978
    A mermaid who cannot speak is banished from her undersea home and sent to live on land as a human where she is found by a girl with a hearing problem.

940

Mollie Hunter

A Sound of Chariots (New York: Harper & Row, 1972)

Age range: Grades 6-9

Subject(s): Authorship; Poetry; Religion

Major character(s): Bridie McShane, Child; Aileen McShane, Preteen; Mrs. Wallace, Neighbor

Time period(s): 1940s (post-WWII)

Locale(s): Scotland

What the book is about: A young girl growing up in Scotland after WWII tries to come to terms with her grief over her father's death and her increasing sense of the passage of time. Bridie explores her place in the family, trying to be strong, not cry, and continue with her duties when her father dies. Her struggle with her religious beliefs, growing up in a community of the Brethren, who sharply divide the congregation into Saints and Sinners, will feel familiar to adolescents beginning their own journeys.

Other books by the author:
Cat, Herself, 1985
Hold On to Love, 1983
A Stranger Came Ashore: A Story of Suspense, 1975
The Haunted Mountain, 1972

Other books you might like:
Lucy Cullyford Babbitt, *Where the Truth Lies: A Novel*, 1993
    Three young people from countries with different religions set out to end the war that has been caused by these disparate beliefs.
T. Ernesto Bethancourt, *Nightmare Town*, 1979
    The residents of Celestial, Arizona, and the object of their strange religion, are unlike anyone or anything a sixteen year old has ever encountered.
Judy Blume, *Are You There, God? It's Me, Margaret*, 1970
    Faced with the difficulties of growing up a choosing a religion, a twelve year old girl talks over her problems with her own private God.
Terry Dunnahoo, *Who Cares about Espie Sanchez?*, 1975
    Unwanted by her mother, Espie is offered a new home, one in which both religion and police work play too big a part for her liking.
Anita Heyman, *Exit From Home*, 1977
    A Jewish youth training to be a rabbi in oppressive turn of the century Russia is exposed to worldly ideas which change his attitude toward religion.

941

Mollie Hunter

A Stranger Came Ashore: A Story of Suspense (New York: Harper and Row, 1975)

Age range: Grades 6 and Up

Subject(s): Magic

Major character(s): Finn Larson, Tailor; Rob, Child

Time period(s): Indeterminate Past

Locale(s): Scotland

What the book is about: Is Finn Larson really the only survivor of a shipwreck? Or is he really a "seal man" come to steal Robbie's sister away? The folklore of the Selkies and the customs of the islands are woven into this struggle between good and evil, as Robbie tries to get help against magical powers from the wizard.

Where it's reviewed:
Horn Book, December 1975, page 592
School Library Journal, September 1975, page 105

Awards the book has won:
Boston Globe/Horn Book Award - Honor Book

Other books by the author:
The Mermaid Summer, 1988
The Three Day Enchantment, 1985
The Wicked One, 1977

Other books you might like:
Charlotte Koplinka, *The Silkies: A Novel of the Shetlands*, 1978
    The winter Karin loses her hearing and her father disappears at sea, the mystery of the origins of her mother, a beautiful and unusual woman, unfolds.
Andrew Lang, *The Chronicles of Pantouflia*, 1981

Two original fairy tales, by the renowned collector of folklore, in which Prince Prigio and Prince Ricardo struggle against the forces of evil.

Caroline Moorhead, *Legends of Britain*, 1968
Fifteen legends from England, Scotland and Wales, including ten about King Arthur and the Knights of the Round Table.

William Neville Scott, *Many Kinds of Magic*, 1990
An assortment of folktales with themes of magic and enchantment from Australia, Ireland and Japan.

Duncan Williamson, *Fireside Tales of the Traveller Children: Twelve Scottish Tales*, 1983
Twelve tales including "Mary and the Seal," "The Goat That Told Lies," and the "The Night of Peace."

942

Thacher Hurd

The Pea Patch Jig (New York: Crown, 1986)

Age range: Grades 1-3

Subject(s): Animals/Mice; Gardens and Gardening

Major character(s): Clem, Farmer; Baby, Mouse

Time period(s): Indeterminate

Locale(s): United States (Farmer Clem's garden)

What the book is about: Baby Mouse goes from one adventure to another. She chases a fox away with a pea and becomes a hero. Dressed in a diaper and red bow, she romps through beautiful pictures.

Where it's reviewed:
Center for Children's Books Bulletin, October 1986, page 28
Horn Book, November/December 1986, page 735

Other books by the author:
Little Mouse's Birthday, 1992
Little Mouse's Big Valentine, 1990
Blackberry Ramble, 1989
Axle the Freeway Cat, 1981

Other books you might like:
Gail Herman, *Fievel's Big Showdown*, 1992
Fievel uses a clever trick to rescue his sister and their friends from a big cat, thus proving he is not a fraidy mouse.

Leo Lionni, *Matthew's Dream*, 1991
A visit to an art museum inspires a young mouse to become a painter.

Bill Martin, Jr., *Barn Dance!*, 1986
Scarecrow waits until dark and then calls all the animals together for a dance until the sun comes up.

Eve Titus, *Anatole over Paris*, 1991
A giant kite lifts Anatole and his family into the sky over Paris, and only his ingenuity can bring them safely home again.

Ellen Stoll Walsh, *Mouse Paint*, 1989
Three white mice discover jars of red, blue and yellow paint and explore the world of color.

943

Ruth Hurlimann, Author/Illustrator

The Cat and Mouse Who Shared a House (New York: D. White, 1971)

Age range: Grades 1-2

Subject(s): Fairy Tale; Folk Tales; Animals/Mice

Time period(s): Indeterminate

Locale(s): United States

What the book is about: A town mouse and a country mouse decide to marry but can't agree on where they should live.

Where it's reviewed:
Horn Book, June 1974, page 277
Kirkus Reviews, January 15, 1974, page 51

Awards the book has won:
Mildred L. Batchelder Award 1976

Other books by the author:
The Proud White Cat, 1977
The Mouse with the Daisy Hat, 1971

Other books you might like:
Frank Asch, *Here Comes the Cat!*, 1989
A mouse rides a bicycle, boat, plane and fish in order to elude the cat. Text in English and Russian.

Marcia Brown, *Once a Mouse*, 1989
As it changes from mouse, to cat, to dog, to tiger, a hermit's pet also becomes increasingly vain.

Heather Buchanan, *George and Matilda Mouse and the Floating School*, 1990
After a scary encounter with a cat, a class of mice finds a safer location for its school.

Gail Herman, *Fievel's Big Showdown*, 1992
Fievel uses a clever trick to rescue his sister and their friends from a big cat.

Graham Oakley, *The Church Mouse*, 1972
A lonely mouse living in a church with only a friendly, sleepy cat for company, devises a plan to get all the mice in town to move in with him.

944

Belinda Hurmence

The Nightwalker (New York: Clarion, 1988)

Age range: Grades 5-7

Subject(s): Dreams and Nightmares

Major character(s): Savannah "Savvy", Child; Pocosin, Child

Time period(s): 1980s

Locale(s): Shackleford Bank, North Carolina

What the book is about: Local fishermen's shacks are burned in response to environmentalists' proposal to make a National Seashore out of traditional fishing grounds. Savvy fears her little brother is possessed by the nightwalking arsonist of local Indian legends.

Where it's reviewed:
Center of Children's Books Bulletin, October 1988, page 41
Horn Book, January/February 1989, page 70

Awards the book has won:
Simon Award

Other books by the author:
A Girl Called Boy, 1982
Before Freedom, 1989

My Folks Don't Want to Talk to Me About Slavery, 1984
Tough Tiffany, 1980

Other books you might like:
Willo Davis Roberts, *Pet-Sitting Peril*, 1983
  A boy who does odd jobs in an apartment house becomes involved with a gang of arsonists.
Carol Russell Law, *The Case of the Weird Street Firebug*, 1980
  Stephanie searches for an arsonist she believes is setting fires in the neighborhood.
Dorothy Crader, *The Riddles of Mermaid House*, 1977
  Trying to find a quiet place to study, Becky encounters people she thinks may be responsible for fires in the town.
Leonard Todd, *Best Kept Secret of the War*, 1984
  Ten-year-old Cam Reed fights important battles at home while his dad is in Europe fighting the Germans in 1944.
Theodore Taylor, *Teetoncey*, 1874
  11-year-old Ben rescues an English girl from a ship wreck off North Carolina's Outer Banks, but she cannot speak. First of a Trilogy.

945

Belinda Hurmence

Tough Tiffany (New York: Doubleday, 1980)

Age range: Grades 5-7

Subject(s): African Americans; Poverty; Grandparents

Major character(s): Tiffany Cox, Preteen; Dawn Cox, Single Parent; Granny Turner, Grandparent

Time period(s): 1980s

Locale(s): North Carolina

What the book is about: Tiffany, youngest of six, is delighted when four bunk beds are delivered to her house, especially when they are all in one stack and she gets the top one. Mother bought the beds even though she could not afford them, and Tiffany is later able to help pay for them when Granny gives her a check for all her help. When Tiffany finds her sister in labor, she summons a police car and gets her sister to the hospital. Tiffany is a great heroine.

Where it's reviewed:
Center for Children's Books Bulletin, March 1980, page 135
Horn Book, June 1980, page 297

Other books by the author:
Before Freedom, 1989
The Nightwalker, 1988
My Folks Don't Want Me to Talk about Slavery, 1984
A Girl Called Boy, 1982

Other books you might like:
Kathryn Kilby Borland, *Good-By to Stony Crick*, 1975
  When Jeremy's family is forced by fire and poverty to leave their Appalachian home, he finds Chicago overwhelming.
Rosa Guy, *Edith Jackson*, 1978
  A black teen tries to keep her family together but sees her world collapse as her younger sisters reject her inept mothering.
Joan Kane Nichols, *All but the Right Folks*, 1985
  A young black boy finds out that his mother was white and he spends the summer with his grandmother in New York City.
Virginia Sorensen, *Around the Corner*, 1971

A black boy's mother forbids him to associate with the "poor white squatters," but when she goes into labor a number of misunderstandings are righted.
Adrien Stoutenburg, *Where to Now, Blue?*, 1978
  Blueberry tries to run away from her poor home with a six year old tag along from the orphanage.

946

Johanna Hurwitz

Illustrator: John Wallner

Aldo Peanut Butter (New York: Morrow, 1990)

Age range: Grades 3-5

Subject(s): Family Life; Animals/Dogs

Major character(s): Aldo, Child

Time period(s): 1990s

Locale(s): United States

What the book is about: Aldo receives five dogs for his eleventh birthday. He is only allowed to keep two of them, and calls them Peanut and Butter. When their parents have to leave for two weeks, Aldo and his sisters are left to cope with each other and the two puppies.

Where it's reviewed:
Booklist, September 1, 1990, page 51
Kirkus Reviews, July 15, 1990, page 1003

Other books by the author:
Class Clown, 1987
The Adventures of Ali Baba Bernstein, 1985
Aldo Ice Cream, 1981
Aldo Applesauce, 1979

Other books you might like:
Beverly Cleary, *Henry Huggins*, 1950
  When Henry adopts a dog, Ribsy, fun follows them everywhere.
Carolyn Haywood, *Eddie's Friend Boodles*, 1991
  A visit to the circus inspires Boodles to experiment with clown make-up and try to teach his dog, Poochie, to do tricks.
Judith Whitelock McInerney, *Judge Benjamin: The Superdog Gift*, 1986
  Judge Benjamin, a St. Bernard, and his mate take care of their human family with humorous results.
Daniel Manus Pinkwater, *The Magic Moscow*, 1980
  Relates the adventures of Edward, grandson of a famous TV dog, and his owner, Stever, who manages a Hoboken ice cream stand.
Barbara A. Steiner, *Oliver Dibbs to the Rescue*, 1985
  Ollie embarks on a series of moneymaking ventures, beginning with painting his dog with tiger stripes.

947

Johanna Hurwitz

Illustrator: Diane De Groat

Aldo Peanut Butter (New York: Morrow, 1990)

Age range: Grades 4-6

Subject(s): Animals/Dogs; Family Life

Major character(s): Aldo, Preteen; Peanut, Dog; Butter, Dog

Time period(s): 1980s

Locale(s): United States

What the book is about: Peanut and Butter, the two dogs Aldo gets for his eleventh birthday, create chaos inside the house while his parents are out of town, and get accused of tearing up the neighbor's lawn.

Where it's reviewed:
Booklist, September 1, 1990, page 51
Kirkus Reviews, July 15, 1990, page 1003

Other books by the author:
Hurray for Ali Baba Bernstein, 1989
Russell and Elisa, 1989
Class Clown, 1987
Yellow Blue Jay, 1986

Other books you might like:
Beverly Cleary, *Henry Huggins*, 1950
  When Henry adopts Ribsy, a dog of no particular breed, humorous adventures follow.
Eve Feldman, *Dog Crazy*, 1992
  The story of Sara's persistent and humorous efforts to get a dog of her own.
Gen LeRoy, *Taxi Cat and Huey*, 1992
  A bassett hound's peaceful life with a human couple is changed when a rambunctious and adventurous cat joins the family.
Judith Whitelock McInerney, *Judge Benjamin: The Superdog Rescue*, 1984
  Great Gramps almost regrets his decision when, after a bad fall, he allows Judge Benjamin and the O'Rileys to move in and run things on his farm.
Janice Lee Smith, *It's Not Easy Being George*, 1989
  Adam Joshua shares problems with his dog George and lives through school events such as a pet show and an all-night sleepover in the library.

948

Johanna Hurwitz

Illustrator: Ray Cruz

Baseball Fever (New York: Morrow, 1981)

Age range: Grades 3-6

Subject(s): Sports/Baseball

Major character(s): Ezra Feldman, Sports Figure, Child; Harris Feldman, Child, Student; Dr. Feldman, Doctor, Parent

Time period(s): 1970s

Locale(s): Flushing, New York

What the book is about: Ezra has a big problem with his dad. Mr. Feldman doesn't understand baseball, having grown up in Europe, and he doesn't understand Exra's passion for the game. How can Ezra come up a winner if he and his dad are on opposite teams?

Where it's reviewed:
Booklist, January 1, 1982, page 597
Hornbook, December 1981, page 664
Kirkus, January 15, 1982, page 68

Other books by the author:
Roz and Ozzie, 1992
School's Out, 1991
Class President, 1990
Russell and Elisa, 1989

Other books you might like:
Patricia Reilly Giff, *Left-Handed Shortstop*, 1980
  There's no way Walter can be the star Goony keeps saying he is. A left-handed shortstop is almost unheard of.
Jeffrey Kelly, *The Basement Baseball Club*, 1987
  On a losing streak since a new player joined their rival baseball team, the McCarthy Roaders hope that the street's newcomer will give them a boost.
E.L. Konigsburg, *About the B'nai Bagels*, 1969
  Mark tells about his troubles in general, especially on the Little League baseball team managed by his mother and coached by his big brother.
Michael A. Kusugak, *Baseball Bats for Christmas*, 1990
  Set in the Arctic Circle. A supply plane brings Christmas trees to the Eskimos that eventually end up as baseball bats.
Alfred Slote, *Hang Tough, Paul Mather*, 1973
  Paul, who is great as a pitcher and loves it, discovers he has leukemia and is hospitalized, but he sneaks out and plays for the team.

949

Johanna Hurwitz

Illustrator: Susan Jeschke

Busybody Nora (New York: Morrow, 1976)

Age range: Grades 2-3

Subject(s): Apartments; City Life; Neighbors and Neighborhoods

Major character(s): Nora, Child; Henry, Worker (doorman); Mrs. Wurmbrand, Widow(er), Neighbor

Time period(s): 1970s

Locale(s): New York, New York

What the book is about: Relates the adventures of an inquisitive little girl who lives in a large apartment building in New York City with her parents and little brother, Teddy. Nora wants to have a party for all two hundred residents in her building. Stone Soup seemed like a good place to start, and when Mrs. Wurmbrand's daughter comes to visit, what better place for a party?

Where it's reviewed:
Booklist, March 15, 1976, page 1046
Hornbook, June 1976, page 284
Kirkus Reviews, February 15, 1976, page 200

Other books by the author:
Russell and Elisa, 1989
Rip-Roaring Russell, 1983
New Neighbors for Nora, 1979
Nora and Mrs. Mind-Your-Own Business, 1977

Other books you might like:
Bill Apablasa, *Rhymin' Simon and the Mystery of the Fat Cat*, 1991
  Rhymin' Simon, a detective who loves to make rhymes, helps out when his neighbor's cat disappears
Franz Brandenberg, *Nice New Neighbors*, 1977

The Fieldmouse children find a way to make new friends when they move to a new house.

Terrance Dicks, *Goliath and the Buried Treasure*, 1984
  Canine Goliath's fondness for digging holes gets him into big trouble with the neighbors but also transforms him into the most unlikely hero in town.

Ida Lutrell, *The Bear Next Door*, 1991
  Three episodes in the developing friendship of Vic Bear and Arlo Gopher demonstrate how they are good neighbors.

Harriet May Savitz, *The Cats Nobody Wanted*, 1989
  Frankie's neighbors aren't very happy when Mrs. Beasley moves onto their street and call her the cat lady because she takes in stray cats.

| 950 |

Johanna Hurwitz

Illustrator: Sheila Hamanaka

Class Clown (New York: Morrow, 1987)

Age range: Grades 2-4

Subject(s): Schools; Behavior

Major character(s): Lucas Cott, Child, 3rd Grader

Time period(s): 1980s

Locale(s): United States

What the book is about: Lucas has so much energy, he drives everyone around him nuts! Third grade is his center ring. He finds it very difficult to turn over a new leaf when he decides to become a perfect student.

Where it's reviewed:
Kirkus Reviews, May 1, 1987, page 720
School Library Journal, August 1987, page 86

Other books by the author:
"E" is for Elisa, 1991
Class President, 1990
School's Out, 1990
Yellow Blue Jay, 1986

Other books you might like:
Barbara Baker, *Third Grade Is Terrible*, 1989
  Liza is sure that being moved away from her best friend and into the class with the strictest teacher in the school will make for a terrible year.

Bruce Coville, *The Monster's Ring*, 1982
  Russell is tired of being bullied by Eddie, so he buys a ring which will turn him into a monster.

Suzy Kline, *Herbie Jones and the Class Gift*, 1987
  Herbie and Raymond earn money toward a class gift for their teacher, then an accident forces them to come up with a replacement for the broken gift.

Barbara Park, *Maxie, Rosie, and Earl - Partners in Grime*, 1990
  When their disciplinary meetings with the principal are postponed, three students skip school with humorous results.

Susan Richards Shreve, *The Flunking of Joshua T. Bates*, 1984
  Joshua is devastated when he finds he must repeat the third grade.

| 951 |

Johanna Hurwitz

Illustrator: Carolyn Ewing

The Cold and Hot Winter (New York: Morrow, 1988)

Age range: Grades 4-6

Subject(s): Honesty; Friendship

Major character(s): Derek Curry, Preteen, 5th Grader; Rory Dunn, Preteen, 5th Grader; Bolivia Raab, Preteen

Time period(s): 1980s

Locale(s): Woodside, New Jersey

What the book is about: Fifth grader Derek and his best friend, Rory, are delighted when their neighbor's niece, Bolivia, comes to town for a visit. She is unlike any girl they have ever known and they enjoyed her last visit immensely. However, a lot of missing objects make Derek begin to doubt someone's honesty.

Where it's reviewed:
Center for Children's Books Bulletin, November 1988, page 75

Other books by the author:
Aldo Peanut Butter, 1990
Hurray for Ali Baba Bernstein, 1989
Class Clown, 1987
The Hot and Cold Summer, 1984

Other books you might like:
Carol Fenner, *Randall's Wall*, 1991
  A talented boy has built a wall of defense to protect himself from the pain of relationships-a wall which crumbles when a classmate interferes.

Jamie Gilson, *Sticks and Stones and Skeleton Bones*, 1991
  Hobie, whose class is meeting in a shopping mall due to a flood at school, has a fight with his best friend that gets worse as the day goes on.

Ivy Ruckman, *Melba the Brain*, 1979
  A young genius' experiment with spliced energies acquaint her with a strange cat and hurtle her light years beyond Earth to a planet ruled by animals.

Bill Wallace, *The Biggest Klutz in Fifth Grade*, 1992
  Tired of being taunted for his clumsiness, Pat makes a bet that he can get through the summer and start school without any broken bones or stiches.

Miriam Young, *Truth or Consequences*, 1975
  A sixth grade girl amost ruins her relationship with her best friend until she learns to temper her honesty with a little tact.

| 952 |

Johanna Hurwitz

Illustrator: Diane De Groat

Hurricane Elaine (New York: Morrow, 1986)

Age range: Grades 3-5

Subject(s): Family Life; Animals/Dogs

Major character(s): Elaine Sossi, Teenager; Aldo Sossi, Preteen; Karen Sossi, Child

Time period(s): 1980s

Locale(s): United States

What the book is about: Elaine, at fifteen, and the eldest of the Sossi children, can blame most of her typical teenage troubles on her impulsiveness. Her brother, Aldo, loses his cat to an automobile and ends up with five puppies for his birthday. A portrait of one kind of many "typical" American families.

Where it's reviewed:
Center for Children's Books Bulletin, December 1986, page 69
School Library Journal, November 1986, page 89

Other books by the author:
Class President, 1990
Tough-Luck Karen, 1982
Aldo Applesauce, 1981
Aldo Ice Cream, 1981

Other books you might like:
Lisa Eisenberg, *Lexie on Her Own*, 1992
 It takes all Lexie's resources to get through a bad case of holiday depression.
Liza Ketchum Murrow, *Allergic to My Family*, 1992
 Rosie feels that her family - two unusual parents, six siblings and a pet skunk, have no time for her.
Louis Sacher, *Johnny's in the Basement*, 1981
 Johnny's love is collecting bottle caps, but when he turns eleven, his parents insist that the bottle caps are out and dancing classes are in.
Ethel Smothers, *Down in the Piney Woods*, 1992
 Annie Rye, ten year old daughter of a sharecropper, shares the joys and frustrations of family life.
Nancy Hope Wilson, *Bringing Nettie Back*, 1992
 Friends Clara and Nettie have very different families, but it enriches their friendship.

953

Johanna Hurwitz

Illustrator: Ingrid Fetz

The Law of Gravity (New York: Morrow, 1978)

Age range: Grades 3-5

Subject(s): Mothers and Daughters

Major character(s): Esther, Preteen; Joseph "Bernie" Bernazzoli, Preteen

Time period(s): 1970s

Locale(s): New York, New York

What the book is about: Everything that goes up, must come down, except for Margot's mother. She stays four flights up in their apartment and gardens on the roof and has not been down in the nine years the Greens have lived there. Margot hopes to get her mom to come down by the end of the summer. After much frustration, and scaring the wits out of her mother by not coming home one night, Margot realizes that love and trust are more important than her idea of how her mother should behave.

Where it's reviewed:
Booklist, July 15, 1979, page 1635
Childhood Education, January 1979, page 168

Other books by the author:
Class President, 1990
Hurray for Ali Baba Bernstein, 1989

Aldo Applesauce, 1979
New Neighbors for Nora, 1979

Other books you might like:
Constance C. Greene, *Star Shine*, 1985
 Jenny and Mary must learn to care for themselves when their stage-struck mother joins a summer theater group.
Susan Hill, *The Glass Angels*, 1991
 Tilly looks forward to spending Christmas with her mother until illness and an accident threaten to destroy her plans.
Elisabet McHugh, *Raising a Mother Isn't Easy*, 1983
 An eleven year old Korean orphan adopted by a single woman decides that her mother should have a husband.
Colleen O'Shaughnessy McKenna, *Fourth Grade Is a Jinx*, 1989
 When Collette sees her own mother take over the job of teaching her fourth grade class, it is almost more embarrassment than she can cope with.
Sheila Schwartz, *Like Mother, Like Me*, 1978
 A girl witnesses her mother's difficult and sometimes humorous change to an independent person after her father abandons the family.

954

Johanna Hurwitz

Illustrator: Ingrid Fetz

Once I Was a Plum Tree (New York: Morrow, 1980)

Age range: Grades 4-6

Subject(s): Jews; Prejudice; Religion

Major character(s): Gerry Flam, Child; Edgar Wulf, Child

Time period(s): 1940s

Locale(s): United States

What the book is about: Gerry Flam's two best friends are Catholic, and though she is Jewish, she is not quite sure what that means. When she meets Edgar, the son of her piano teacher, and learns that he and his family fled Germany just before WWII, she becomes interested in learning about her own heritage.

Where it's reviewed:
Center for Children's Books Bulletin, June 1980, page 192
School Library Journal, February 1980, page 57

Other books by the author:
The Cold and Hot Winter, 1988
Class Clown, 1987
The Adventures of Ali Baba Bernstein, 1985
Aldo Applesauce, 1979

Other books you might like:
Mary Baylis-White, *Sheltering Rebecca*, 1991
 In the days before WWII, Sally becomes friends with a young Jewish refugee from Germany.
Eve Feldman, *Seymour, the Formerly Fearful*, 1990
 Seymour Goldfarb learns to overcome some of his fears when his Israeli cousin comes to America for the summer.
Karen Hesse, *Letters From Rifka*, 1992
 In letters to her cousin, a Jewish girl chronicles her family's flight from Russia in 1919.
Jerry Segal, *The Place Where Nobody Stopped*, 1991

A Jewish man plants himself in a lonely Russian baker's house and establishes a family while waiting for permission to emigrate to America.
Sholem Aleichem, *Around the Table: "Family Stories of Sholom Aleichem"*, 1991
The retellings of five stories of families observing the rituals and traditions of Jewish holidays.

955

Johanna Hurwitz

Illustrator: Lillian Hoban

Rip-Roaring Russell (New York: Morrow, 1983)

Age range: Grades 2-3

Subject(s): Housing; Schools/Preschool

Major character(s): Russell, Child

Time period(s): 1980s

Locale(s): United States

What the book is about: The exploits of a self-willed four year old. Russell attends nursery school, envies his baby sister and plays with neighborhood children. This book shows great adult-child relationships.

Where it's reviewed:
Bulletin for the Center of Children's Books, January 1984, page 89
Horn Book, December 1983, page 710

Other books by the author:
Super Duper Teddy, 1991
The Hot and Cold Summer, 1984
New Neighbors for Nora, 1979
Busybody Nora, 1976

Other books you might like:
Carol Madden Adorjan, *The Electric Man*, 1981
Alanna is lonely when she moves to an apartment in the big city until the "electric man" enlarges her view of life.
Tony Bradman, *Dilly and the Horror Movie*, 1987
A mischievious young dinosaur goes to nursery school for the first time, gets a scare from a horror movie and has other adventures.
Elizabeth Starr Hill, *Evan's Corner*, 1991
Needing a place to call his own, Evan is thrilled when his mother indicates that their crowded apartment has eight corners, one for each family member
Julie Thayer, *The Lamb Who Went to Paris*, 1980
Abandoned by its mother at birth, a lamb is rescued by three children and taken to live in their Paris apartment.
Sylvie Wickstrom, *Turkey on the Loose*, 1990
A turkey gets loose in an apartment house and creates havoc.

956

Johanna Hurwitz

Illustrator: Lillian Hoban

Russell Sprouts (New York: Morrow, 1987)

Age range: Grades 1-2

Subject(s): Schools; Growing Up

Major character(s): Russell Michaels, Child; Teddy, Child; Elisa Michaels, Child

Time period(s): 1980s

Locale(s): New York, New York

What the book is about: Six year old Russell is now in the first grade, where he encounters report cards, a school Halloween party, and science class. He learns some new words that jolt his parents, and gets lost in a movie theatre.

Where it's reviewed:
Horn Book, September/October 1987, page 605
School Library Journal, September 1987, page 164

Other books by the author:
Bunk Mates, 1986
Russell Rides Again, 1986
Rip Roarin' Russell, 1984
Baseball Fever, 1981

Other books you might like:
Beverly Cleary, *Ramona the Brave*, 1975
Six year old Ramona needs help coping with an unsympathetic first grade teacher.
Miriam Cohen, *See You in Second Grade!*, 1989
At the end of the year picnic, the children in first grade realize they will miss their teacher, but are very ready for second grade.
Steven Kroll, *Annabelle's Un-Birthday*, 1991
Annabelle tells a fib about her birthday on the first day in second grade and must face the consequences.
Muriel Stanek, *My Mom Can't Read*, 1986
First grader Tina asks her mother for help reading and discovers they must learn together.
Karen Lynn Williams, *First Grade King*, 1992
Joey King learns to read, makes friends, and has his first encounter with a bully.

957

Johanna Hurwitz

Illustrator: Susan Jeschke

Superduper Teddy (New York: Morrow, 1980)

Age range: Grades 2-3

Subject(s): Brothers and Sisters; City Life; Shyness

Major character(s): Teddy, Child, Kindergartener; Nora, Child

Time period(s): 1980s

Locale(s): United States

What the book is about: Six chapters tell stories about five year old Teddy. He is very shy and hates the idea of going to a birthday party. He listens to Grandpa's modern version of Cinderella, gets his first job, finds an acceptable pet for the family, and brings his whole kindergarten class home for milk and cookies.

Where it's reviewed:
Childhood Education, May 1981, page 300
School Library Journal, December 1980, page 53

Other books by the author:
Roz and Ozzie, 1992
Russell and Elisa, 1989

All About Aldo, 1981
Baseball Fever, 1981

Other books you might like:
Beverly Cleary, *Beezus and Ramona*, 1955
    Beezus knows she should love her sister, but four year old Ramona seems impossible to live with.
Ilene Cooper, *Frances Four-Eyes*, 1991
    A shy fourth grader becomes more assertive as she dances the lead role at a recital and starts to wear her new glasses.
Judy Delton, *Back Yard Angel*, 1983
    Although ten year old Angel loves her little brother, Rags, the constant responsibility of caring for him can get very tiresome.
Shirley Hughes, *The Big Alfie and Annie Rose Storybook*, 1988
    Presents the experiences of nursery school student Alfie and his younger sister, Annie Rose.
Linda Lehmann, *Better than a Princess*, 1978
    A seven year old girl is joined on a long trip from Germany to America by a brother and sister she didn't know existed.

958

Johanna Hurwitz

Illustrator: Diane De Groat

Tough-Luck Karen (New York: Beech Tree Books, 1982)

Age range: Grades 4-6

Subject(s): Moving, Household; Schools

Major character(s): Karen Sossi, Preteen, Babysitter; Aldo Sossi, Child; Elaine Sossi, Child

Time period(s): 1980s

Locale(s): Woodside, New Jersey

What the book is about: Aldo and Elaine adjust just fine to their new town, but Karen has nothing but tough luck making friends and staying on top of her schoolwork. She's a whiz in the kitchen, but that's no help with math or English or science. Just when she's finally landed a steady babysitting job, her mother grounds her until her grades pick up.

Where it's reviewed:
Booklist, October 1, 1982, page 246
Hornbook, October 1982, page 517
Kirkus, August 1, 1982, page 868

Other books by the author:
Bunkmates, 1987
Class Clown, 1987
The Rabbi's Girls, 1982
The Law of Gravity, 1978

Other books you might like:
Jennie Abbott, *The Boy Who Remembered Everything*, 1988
    When a group of friends known as the Super Squad begin babysitting for a six year old with a fantastic memory, he improves all of their lives.
Phyllis Green, *Nantucket Summer*, 1974
    A.D. takes a summer babysitting job on Nantucket Island and finds it better than she expected despite her employer's mental problems and a ghost.
Ann M. Martin, *The Ghost at Dawn's House*, 1988

The members of the babysitters club split their time between babysitting and investigating the spooky noises behind Dawn's bedroom wall.
Martha Tolles, *Katie's Babysitting Job*, 1985
    When several pieces of valuable jewelry disappear during Katie's first babysitting job, she must discover the explanation to clear her own name.
Suzanne Weyn, *True Blue*, 1991
    Sam risks her babysitting job at the Palm Pavilion Hotel and her friendship with Chris and Liza by befriending worldly but competitive Trisha Royce.

959

Pat Hutchins

Illustrator: Laurence Hutchins

The Curse of the Egyptian Mummy (New York: Greenwillow, 1983)

Age range: Grades 5-7

Subject(s): Scouting; Mystery and Detective Stories

Major character(s): Akela, Leader; Skip, Assistant; Miss Hylyard, Businesswoman (camp owner)

Time period(s): 1980s

Locale(s): Hampstead, England

What the book is about: A group of English Cub Scouts happen upon a frightening mystery. An unidentified body, the victim of a deadly snake bite, has been found in the village to which they are going. Is the curse of an Egyptian mummy at work?

Where it's reviewed:
Booklist, March 1, 1984, page 967
Kirkus Reviews, November 1, 1983, page J192
School Library Journal, December 1983, page 82

Other books by the author:
The Mona Lisa Mystery, 1981
The House That Sailed Away, 1975
The Wind Blew, 1974
Rosie's Walk, 1968

Other books you might like:
E.W. Hildick, *The Case of the Muttering Mummy*, 1986
    The McGurk Organization goes to work to find out why an exert on ancient Egyptian artifacts is interested in Joey's purchase of a small golden cat.
Kate McMullan, *Under the Mummy's Spell*, 1992
    When Peter kisses a mummy mask on a dare, he finds that he has fulfilled an age-old prophecy and must contend with an ancient Egyptian sorceress.
Joan Lowery Nixon, *The House on Hackman's Hill*, 1985
    Jeff and Debbie come to the house on Hackman's Hill to look for a stolen Egyptian mummy that old Mr. Karsten has told them about.
Kathy Kennedy Tapp, *Den 4 Meets the Jinx*, 1988
    Adam never suspects that his bratty sister may be the only one who can save his Cub Scout den from dissolving.
Cynthia Voigt, *The Vandemark Mummy*, 1991
    When their father is responsible for a collection of Egyptian artifacts, Phineas and his sister try to find out why it is the target of thieves.

960

Pat Hutchins

Illustrator: Laurence Hutchins

Follow That Bus! (New York: Knopf, 1977)

Age range: Grades 2-4

Subject(s): Robbers and Outlaws; Schools; Mystery and Detective Stories

Major character(s): Miss Beaver, Teacher; Morgan, Student; Mr. Coatsworth, Driver (bus driver)

Time period(s): 1970s

Locale(s): London, England

What the book is about: A school picnic becomes a cops-and-robbers chase involving two holdup men who find that a group of second graders visiting a farm are more than they bargained for.

Where it's reviewed:
Booklist, June 1, 1977, page 1498
Hornbook, August 1977, page 442
Kirkus Reviews, April 1, 1977, page 351

Other books by the author:
Rats!, 1989
The Mona Lisa Mystery, 1981
The Best Train Set Ever, 1978
The House That Sailed Away, 1975

Other books you might like:
Beatrice Curtis Brown, *Jonathan Bing*, 1968
    Episodes from the life of eccentric Jonathan Bing who comforts goldfish and reads stories so he can reuse the letters to make up new stories.
Arlene Dubanevich, *Pig William*, 1990
    Always a dawdler, Pig William misses his ride to the school picnic but in a sudden turn of events the picnic comes to him.
Suzy Kline, *Herbie Jones*, 1985
    Herbie's experiences in the third grade include finding bones in the boys' bathroom, and wandering away from his class on their field trip.
Peggy Parish, *Be Ready at Eight*, 1979
    Absent-minded Miss Molly tries to remember why she tied a string around her finger, and why all her friends plan to see her at eight.
William Taylor, *Agnes the Sheep*, 1990
    An eccentric old lady leaves her large and nasty sheep, Agnes, to Belinda and Joe, setting off a wild and woolly sheep chase.

961

Pat Hutchins, Author/Illustrator

The Very Worst Monster (New York: Greenwillow, 1985)

Age range: Grades 1-3

Subject(s): Monsters; Brothers and Sisters

Major character(s): Billy Monster, Monster; Hazel Monster, Monster

Time period(s): 1980s

Locale(s): United States

What the book is about: Everyone expects the baby, Billy, to grow up to be the Very Worst Monster. Hazel tries to get everyone's attention away from Billy, with very monstrous behavior.

Where it's reviewed:
Horn Book, May 1985, page 304
Kirkus Reviews, March 1, 1985, page 16

Other books by the author:
Silly Billy, 1992
Tidy Titch, 1991
What Game Shall We Play?, 1990
Where's the Baby?, 1988

Other books you might like:
Robert L. Crowe, *Clyde Monster*, 1976
    One night Clyde Monster refuses to go to bed because he is afraid that people are hiding and will try to scare him.
Tony Johnson, *Four Scary Stories*, 1978
    Exciting tales from the monster's point of view.
Jack Prelutsky, *The Baby Uggs Are Hatching!*, 1982
    Strange critters hatch along the sidewalk like flowers sprout in a garden.
Tony Ross, *I'm Coming to Get You*, 1984
    Will Tommy be destroyed by the monster? Surprise!
Daisy Wallace, *Monster Poems*, 1976
    A collection of poems about monsters.

962

Dayton O. Hyde

Island of the Loons (New York: Atheneum, 1984)

Age range: Grades 6-8

Subject(s): Kidnapping; Survival

Major character(s): Jimmy, Captive (kidnap victim); Riggs, Convict (escaped)

Time period(s): 1980s

Locale(s): Michigan (island in Lake Superior); United States

What the book is about: Jimmy is kidnapped by an escaped convict and kept prisoner on a deserted island for a year. During this time he sees his captor, Riggs, change from a desperate criminal to a gentler person who is really interested in the wildlife and lore of the island. Some suspense as Jimmy tries to escape, but the real adventure here is the growth of the characters.

Where it's reviewed:
Center for Children's Books Bulletin, February 1985, page 108
School Library Journal, November 1984, page 132

Other books by the author:
Don Coyote, 1986
The Major, the Poacher and the Wonderful One Trout River, 1985
Strange Companion: A Story of Survival, 1975
Cranes in My Corral, 1971

Other books you might like:
Mel Ellis, *An Eagle to the Wind*, 1978
    In the forests along Lake Superior in 1893, a teenage boy watches the activities of a pair of eagles that symbolize his own passage to adulthood.
Carol J. Farley, *The Case of the Vanishing Villain*, 1986

Two sisters, trapped on a ship in Lake Michigan with an escaped convict, try to discover his whereabouts and bring him to justice.

Willo Davis Roberts, *Megan's Island*, 1988
   Megan's mother takes her and her younger brother to the lake cottage a week before school ends; then they find mysterious strangers following them.

Ouida Sebestyen, *The Girl in the Box*, 1988
   Kidnapped and left in an underground room, Jackie tries to contact the outside world by writing messages and sending them through a slit in the door.

Gloria Whelan, *The Secret Keeper*, 1990
   Ali comes face to face with murder and kidnapping during what promised to be a pleasant summer on Lake Michigan.

I

963

Rose Impey

No-Name Dog (New York: Dutton, 1990)

Age range: Grades 2-3

Subject(s): Animals/Dogs

Major character(s): Dusty, Dog

Time period(s): 1990s

Locale(s): United States

What the book is about: Two sisters pick a puppy and the problems begin. The puppy is an escape artist, chews everything she can find and scares the animals and people in the neighborhood. Everyone in the family votes on a name for her, but the puppy chooses her own name. (Sequel to *Desperate for a Dog*)

Where it's reviewed:
Booklist, July 1990, page 2091
Kirkus Reviews, June 1, 1990, page 799

Other books by the author:
The Ankle Grabber, 1989
Desperate for a Dog, 1989
A Letter to Santa Claus, 1989
Scare Yourself to Sleep, 1988

Other books you might like:
Terrance Dicks, *Goliath's Birthday*, 1992
  Despite his good intentions, Goliath the dog's behavior jeopardizes the plans for his birthday party.
Betsy Duffey, *A Boy in the Doghouse*, 1991
  George is faced with the task of training his new puppy, Lucky.
Lynn Hall, *Barry, the Bravest St. Bernard*, 1992
  Relates the feats of Barry, the best dog ever at the St. Bernard Monastery.
Steven Kroll, *Andrew Wants a Dog*, 1992
  When his dad refuses to let him have a dog, Andrew decides to become one, with the help of a very realistic costume from a magic shop.
Sharon Salisbury O'Toole, *Brave Dog Blizzard*, 1992
  Blizzard the sheepdog fights hard to protect the flock while his fam ily is away at the county fair.

964

Washington Irving

The Legend of Sleepy Hollow (New York: Baker, 1923)

Age range: Grades 3 and Up

Subject(s): Ghosts; Folk Tales; Supernatural

Major character(s): Ichabod Crane, Teacher; Brom Bones, Bully

Time period(s): 18th century

Locale(s): Tarry Town, New York, American Colonies

What the book is about: A superstitious schoolmaster, in love with a wealthy farmer's daughter, has a terrifying encounter with the Galloping Hessian of the Hollow. This is a wonderful Halloween tale about Ichabod Crane and the ghost of a headless horseman.

Where it's reviewed:
Library Journal, April 15, 1966, page 2210
New York Times Book Review, May 8, 1966, page 40

Other books by the author:
Washington Irving's Tales of the Supernatural, 1982
Castles in Spain: From the Alhambra, 1971
The Bold Dragoon, 1930
Rip Van Winkle, 1848

Other books you might like:
Mary Anderson, *The Rise and Fall of a Teenage Wacko*, 1980
  Laura, who feels like the family misfit, returns early from the family vacation in the Catskill Mountains and has her own adventures in New York City.
Nancy Bond, *Another Shore*, 1988
  Lyn, working in a reconstructed colonial village in Nova Scotia, suddenly finds herself back in 1744, when the French people are at war with England.
Gardell Dano Christensen, *Colonial New York*, 1969
  Traces New York State history from its discovery by Henry Hudson in 1609 to the inauguration of George Washington 180 years later. (Non-fiction)
Sonia Levitin, *Roanoke: A Novel of the Lost Colony*, 1973
  An English youth and an Indian girl are caught up in the events leading the the mysterious disappearance of the colony at Roanoke, Virginia.
Elizabeth George Speare, *The Witch of Blackbird Pond*, 1958
  In 1687, Kit Tyler moves from the Caribbean to Connecticut Colony. Her friendship with a strange old woman leads to her trial for witchcraft.

965

Washington Irving

Rip Van Winkle (1848)

Age range: Grades 3 and Up

Subject(s): American Colonies

Major character(s): Rip Van Winkle, Spouse (henpecked); Wolf, Dog; Dame Van Winkle, Spouse

Time period(s): 18th century

Locale(s): Kaatskill Mountains, New York

What the book is about: A story of early Dutch settlers along the Hudson River. Rip is a man tormented by his wife who greatly disapproved of his laziness. His only solace is to steal away to the woods with his dog, Wolf. On one of these strolls Rip encounters rather strange gentlemen, joins them in a keg, and wakes up to a different world indeed.

Where it's reviewed:
Booklist, February 1, 1967, page 586
Library Journal, January 15, 1967, page 350
Publisher's Weekly, November 20, 1967, page 56

Other books by the author:
Tales of the Supernatural, 1982
Castles in Spain: From the Alhambra, 1971
The Bold Dragoon, 1930
The Legend of Sleepy Hollow, 1928

Other books you might like:
Ann Curry, *The Book of Brendan*, 1989
    Father Brendan from Holybury Abbey and his young friends battle the evil magician Myrddin with the aid of Arthur, Guinevere, Merlin, and magic beasts.
Paul Samuel Jacobs, *Sleepers, Wake*, 1991
    Dody, a space pioneer of the future, wakes long before anyone else during his ship's journey and grows old while his family continues to sleep.
Dorothy Hults, *New Amsterdam Days and Ways*, 1963
    The history of the Dutch settlers of New York. (Non-fiction)
Robert Silverberg, *Letters From Atlantis*, 1990
    While his body remains in deep sleep, Roy transfers his mind into the mind of a royal prince living in Atlantis 180 centuries ago.

966

Hadley Irwin

Bring to a Boil and Separate (New York: Atheneum, 1980)

Age range: Grades 5-8

Subject(s): Divorce; Friendship

Major character(s): Kathryn "Katie" Warner, Teenager (thirteen year old); Martha "Marti" Walker, Friend

Time period(s): 1980s

Locale(s): Dawson, Yukon Territory, Canada

What the book is about: Katie's world begins falling apart during her thirteenth summer when her parents, both veterinarians, decide to get a divorce. She and her brother, Dinty, face the loss of the life they are used to and try to cope with change.

Where it's reviewed:
Booklist, April 1, 1980, page 1128
Center for Children's Books Bulletin, July 1980, page 215
Kirkus Reviews, April 1, 1980, page 440

Other books by the author:
Can't Hear You Listening, 1990
Kim/Kimi, 1987
Moon and Me, 1981
The Lilith Summer, 1979

Other books you might like:
Anne Alexander, *The Live a Lie*, 1975
    Hurt by her parents' divorce and living with her father, Jennifer changes her name and tells people that her mother is dead.
Judy Blume, *It's Not the End of the World*, 1972
    When her parents divorce, a sixth grader struggles to understand that sometimes people are unable to live together.
Dorothy Hamilton, *Mindy*, 1973
    Mindy strives to understand her position in her parents' lives after their divorce and to adjust to the loneliness of a new way of life.
Norma Klein, *Taking Sides*, 1974
    Twelve year old Nell adjusts to life with her father and five year old brother after her parents' divorce.
Harry Mazer, *Guy Lenny*, 1971
    A boy feels like a ping pong ball when his father decides to remarry and plans to send him to live with his mother whom he hasn't seen in seven years.

J

967

Brian Jacques

Illustrator: Gary Chalk

Redwall (New York: Philomel, 1986)

Age range: Grades 5-9

Subject(s): Animals/Mice; Fantasy; Good and Evil

Major character(s): Matthias Mouse, Hero, Mouse; Constance, Badger; Warbeak, Sparrow

Time period(s): Indeterminate Past

Locale(s): Fictional Country

What the book is about: The evil rat, Cluny, and his band of terrorists threaten the peaceful life at medieval Redwall Abbey. The hero of the story is the mouse, Matthias, who is convinced he can save the Abbey if he can only find the sword of Martin the Warrior. Constant action takes the form of individual treachery as well as battle after battle as this tale of Good vs Evil unfolds. A cross between *Watership Down* and *King Arthur*.

Where it's reviewed:
Horn Book, January/February 1988, page 71
School Library Journal, August 1987, page 96

Other books by the author:
Mariel of Redwall, 1992
Seven Strange and Ghostly Tales, 1991
Mattimeo, 1990
Mossflower, 1988

Other books you might like:
E.M. Almedingen, *A Candle at Dusk*, 1969
   An eighth century Frankish boy obtains his father's skeptical permission to live for a time at the neighboring abbey in order to learn to read.
Eve Bunting, *The Haunting of Kildoran Abbey*, 1978
   Caught in the grip of severe famine, eight hungry, homeless children join forces to steal food from the rich and feed the poor.
Ann Curry, *The Book of Brenden*, 1989
   When the evil magician Myrddin appears, Father Brenden and his young friends must rely on magical beasts to stop him.
Bernice Grohskopf, *Blood and Roses*, 1979
   Upset by his mother's plans to remarry, Robinson meets the ghost of William Caxton and helps find a manuscript in Westminster Abbey for centuries.
John Rae, *The Third Twin: A Ghost Story*, 1980

Shamus and his twin brother become involved with a host of unhappy ghosts during the night they spend locked in Westminster Abbey.

968

Mary James

Shoebag (New York: Scholastic, 1990)

Age range: Grades 4-6

Subject(s): Animals/Insects

Major character(s): Stuart Bagg, Cockroach; Eunice Biddle, Child; Tuffy Buck, Bully

Time period(s): 1990s

Locale(s): Boston, Massachusetts

What the book is about: A young cockroach is transmuted into a boy. Even though he realizes that there are some advantages to being human, mostly he just feels revulsion at the change, but he is able to change the lives of those around him before he returns to life as a cockroach.

Where it's reviewed:
Horn Book, January 1990, page 255
School Library Journal, June 1990, page 124

Other books you might like:
E.A. Hass, *Incognito Mosquito Takes to the Air*, 1986
   The famous insect detective describes his adventures outwitting bad guys and solves a mystery while on a TV talk show.
Annabel Johnson, *I Am Leaper*, 1990
   Leaper, a kangaroo rat who can communicate with humans, gets Julian to help defeat a "monster" in the desert where she lives.
William MacKellar, *The Witch of Glen Gowrie*, 1978
   A young Scottish boy doesn't believe in witches until he meets an old woman with many animals.
Jose Maria Sanchez-Silva, *Ladis and the Ant*, 1969
   An eight year old boy meets an ant whose bite makes him small enough to go exploring the world of insects.
Hazel Hutchins Wilson, *Herbert's Stilts*, 1972
   A boy has strange experiences involving animals just like those he carved on his stilts.

969

Tove Jansson

Finn Family Moomintroll (New York: Avon, 1948)

Age range: Grades 4-6

Subject(s): Fantasy

Major character(s): Moomintroll, Mythical Creature (troll); Sniff, Mythical Creature (troll); Snufkin, Mythical Creature (troll)

Time period(s): Indeterminate

Locale(s): Moomin Valley, Finland

What the book is about: On the first day of spring, three trolls find a Hobgoblin's hat. The Moomin family then have a very busy summer, filled with discovery and adventure with a Hemulen, a Snork Maiden and a Hobgoblin searching for the King's Ruby.

Where it's reviewed:
National Observer, February 7, 1966, page 23
New York Review of Books, December 9, 1965, page 38

Other books by the author:
Moominsummer Madness, 1991
Tales From Moominvalley, 1963
Comet in Moominland, 1959
Moominland Midwinter, 1958

Other books you might like:
William L. Heath, *The Earthquake Man*, 1980
    When a troll gives the O'Grady family a lot of misery, a peculiar man appears and vows to rid the family of the pest.
Stephen Krensky, *A Troll in Passing*, 1980
    Morgan comes to realize that he is not like the other trolls and after several unusual adventures, leaves the troll caves for a new life outside.
Selma Lagerlof, *The Changeling*, 1989
    A farmer's wife becomes the foster mother of a troll's child and her humane treatment of the changeling eventually secures the return of her own son.
Irmelin Sandman Lilius, *The Goldmaker's House*, 1980
    A tiny Finnish town buzzes with speculation about Turiam the alchemist, but only his housekeeper and maid-servant know the true nature of his work.
Walter Wangerin, *Elisabeth and the Water Troll*, 1991
    A motherless girl rediscovers hope and love when a lonely misunderstood water troll takes her down into his well.

970

Randall Jarrell

Animal Family (New York: Pantheon Books, 1965)

Age range: Grades 1-5

Subject(s): Animals; Fantasy; Survival

Time period(s): Indeterminate

Locale(s): Fictional Country

What the book is about: A man, a woman and a boy are wrecked on an uninhabited coast. As years pass, the boy becomes a man and his parents grow old and die. One by one, the man forms a new family, including a mermaid, a bear and a lynx. Fantasy with a touch of mystery.

Where it's reviewed:
Booklist, January 15, 1966, page 487
Center for Children's Books Bulletin, February 1966, page 100
Hornbook, February 1966, page 45

Awards the book has won:
Newbery Honor 1966

Other books by the author:
The Lost World, 1965
The Bat-Poet, 1964
The Gingerbread Rabbit, 1964
The Woman at the Washington Zoo, 1961

Other books you might like:
Gus Cazzola, *To Touch the Deer*, 1981
    Convinced that his mother is dead and unable to face life with his new stepfather, Robert runs off and learns the basic principles of survival.
Michael French, *Pursuit: A Novel*, 1982
    After a boy falls to his death on a hiking trip, his brother is pursued through the wilderness by the man he believes responsible.
David Mathieson, *Trial by Wilderness*, 1985
    A girl survives a plane crash off the coast of British Columbia, and then faces survival in the wilderness.
Robert Newton Peck, *Jo Silver*, 1985
    Kenny's hike through the Adirondacks in search of a writer becomes a fight for survival as he realizes he is not alone in the hostile wilderness.
Elizabeth George Speare, *The Sign of the Beaver*, 1983
    Left alone to guard the family's wilderness home, a boy is hard pressed to survive until local Indians save his life and share their skills.

971

Randall Jarrell

Illustrator: Maurice Sendak

The Bat-Poet (New York: Collier, 1964)

Age range: Grades 3-5

Subject(s): Animals; Poetry

Major character(s): Bat, Bat

Time period(s): Indeterminate

Locale(s): Earth

What the book is about: A bat who can't sleep days makes up poems about the woodland creatures he now perceives for the first time. The other bats think he's a bit of an oddball. When you are a poet, you need someone to listen to you. Maybe the other animals would like to hear his poems about them.

Where it's reviewed:
Hornbook, August 1981, page 453
Junior Bookshelf, June 1978, page 141
New York Times Book Review, April 3, 1977, page 52

Other books by the author:
Fly by Night, 1976

Other books you might like:
Janell Cannon, *Stellaluna*, 1993

After she falls headfirst into a bird's nest, a baby bat is raised like a bird until she is reunited with her mother.

Leo Leonni, *Frederick*, 1963
Frederick, the mouse poet, stores up something special for the long, cold winter.

Tololwa Marti Mollel, *A Promise to the Sun*, 1992
An African legend explaining why bats come out at night.

Angela Royston, *Night-Time Animals*, 1992
Text and photographs describe some animals that are active at night, such as foxes, bats, owls and fieldmice. (Non-fiction)

Eve Titus, *Why the Wind God Wept*, 1972
Many try but only the poet is able to discover why the Wind God is unhappy in his temple. A Mexican Indian legend.

972

Gail Jarrow

If Phyllis Were Here (Boston: Houghton Mifflin, 1987)

Age range: Grades 4-6

Subject(s): Self-Reliance; Mothers and Daughters; Working Mothers

Major character(s): Libby Pruitt, Preteen; Phyllis, Grandparent; Candace Stewart, Preteen

Time period(s): 1980s

Locale(s): Boston, Massachusetts

What the book is about: When Phyllis, the grandmother who has always taken care of her, moves to Florida, eleven year old Libby finds it difficult to adjust to the changes in her life. Her parents are both very busy and she keenly feels the loss of Phyllis. The pain, growth, love and humor as the family reknits itself are vivid and moving.

Where it's reviewed:
Kirkus Reviews, August 15, 1987, page 1241
School Library Journal, September 1987, page 180

Other books you might like:
Vera Cleaver, *Moon Lake Angel: A Novel*, 1987
Kitty Dale, whose mother does not want to deal with a child, spends the summer with Aunt Petal and eventually learns to accept her mother's weakness.

Lael Littke, *Blue Skye*, 1990
Skye, who has been on the road with her mother most of her life, finds what a stable home is like when she moves in with her grandfather.

Joan Phipson, *Bianca*, 1988
Hubert and his sister Emily find Bianca wandering the countryside with amnesia after a scene with her mother. They take her home to their own family.

Jean Van Leeuwen, *Dear Mom, You're Ruining My Life*, 1989
Samantha's eleventh year includes losing her last baby teeth, towering over every boy in dance school, and being mortified by everything her mom does.

Elizabeth Van Steenwyk, *Barrel Horse Racer*, 1977
Wendy's ambition to become Barrel Horse Race champion conflicts with her mother's desire that she model her life after a globe-trotting aunt.

973

Niels Jensen

Days of Courage; A Medieval Adventure (New York: Harcourt, 1973)

Age range: Grades 5 and Up

Major character(s): Uncle Nicholas, Religious; Hanna, Orphan; Luke, Child

Time period(s): 14th century

Locale(s): Denmark

What the book is about: Two children meet after they have both survived the plague. Hanna has no family, Luke has an uncle in a distant village. He urges her to travel with him to find Uncle Nicholas and a new life.

Where it's reviewed:
Library Journal, November 15, 1973, page 3466

Awards the book has won:
Danish Children's Book Prize 1972

Other books by the author:
When the Land Lay Waste, 1973

Other books you might like:
Paula Fox, *The King's Falcon*, 1969
With the help of a falcon, an ineffectual medieval king trades the troubled, boring life of royalty for the freedom of a falconer.

Consuelo Joerns, *The Midnight Castle*, 1983
A family of mice makes itself at home in a toy castle only to find that the medieval inhabitants become real at the stroke of midnight.

Francoise Lebrun, *The Days of Charlemagne*, 1985
Gerald, a nine year old pursuing his studies in a monastery, takes part in a grand reception for the visiting Emperor Charlemagne.

Neil Morris, *Secret of the Forest*, 1983
When they lose their mother's falcon during a hunt, a brother and sister search for it in the forest.

Diana Stewart, *The Hunchback of Notre Dame*, 1981
Retells in simple language the tale of the hunchbacked bellringer of medieval Notre Dame, Quasimodo, whose love for Esmerelda had a tragic ending.

974

Annabel Johnson

Illustrator: Gilbert Riswold

The Grizzly (New York: Harper & Row, 1964)

Age range: Grades 5-7

Subject(s): Animals/Bears; Camps and Camping; Parent and Child

Major character(s): David, Preteen, Camper; Mark, Parent, Camper (sportsman); Jeanne, Parent

Time period(s): 1960s

Locale(s): Trapper's Creek

What the book is about: A young boy and his estranged father find themselves united for the first time on a camping trip, by facing the sinister threat of a grizzly bear. David is forced to take charge when the bear injures his father. He finds resources in himself that he never dreamed he had.

Other books by the author:
Gamebuster, 1990
The Danger Quotient, 1984
An Alien Music, 1982
Count Me Gone, 1968

Other books you might like:
Margaret Elizabeth Bell, *The Peril Strait*, 1971
Unlike his father and brother, Mike can't hunt animals with a gun but accidentally learns that he can hunt them more effectively with a camera.
Gary L. Blackwood, *Wild Timothy*, 1986
Timothy, more interested in reading, joins his father on a camping trip and, when he becomes lost in the woods, learns that he can survive on his own.
Mary Blount Christian, *Linc*, 1991
Linc, a sensitive, artistic teenager, can do nothing to please his father, a former high school football hero, until Linc joins him on a hunting trip.
Paige Dixon, *Lion on the Mountain*, 1972
When his father says they are taking a paying guest on their hunting trip, a young boy fears the guest wants to kill and not photograph animals.
Nan Gilbert, *The Strange New World Across the Street*, 1979
When he leaves his grandparents' home to live with his widowed father, Robbie has difficulty with his estranged parent and his new environment.

975

Crockett Johnson, Author/Illustrator

Harold and the Purple Crayon (New York: Harper, 1955)

Age range: Grades 1-2

Subject(s): Artists and Art; Fantasy

Major character(s): Harold, Child, Artist

Time period(s): Indeterminate

Locale(s): United States

What the book is about: A little boy draws all of the things necessary for him to go for a walk in the moonlight with his purple crayon. Harold has adventures across the sea, up a mountain and through the air, and he begins to wonder if he'll ever get back home.

Where it's reviewed:
Publisher's Weekly, May 22, 1981, page 77
Reading Teacher, January 1978, page 426
Times Literary Supplement, December 8, 1972, page 498

Other books by the author:
Harold's ABC, 1963
A Picture for Harold's Room, 1960
Harold's Circus, 1957
Harold's Trip to the Sky, 1957

Other books you might like:
Lee Ames, *Make 25 Crayon Drawings of the Circus*, 1980
Step by step instructions for making 25 crayon drawings of circus subjects.
Anthea Bell, *The Strange Child*, 1984

A magical being comes into the unhappy lives of a brother and sister, leading them into a world of fantasy and adventure.
John S. Goodall, *The Midnight Adventures of Kelly, Dot and Esmeralda*, 1972
A koala bear, a doll, and a mouse encounter adventure and danger when they climb into a picture on the wall of the nursery.
Margaret Hillert, *Happy Easter, Dear Dragon*, 1981
A boy and his pet dragon celebrate Easter by enjoying the spring flowers and baby animals and coloring eggs.
James Mayhew, *Katie's Picture Show*, 1989
While visiting the museum with her grandmother, Katie has a fantastic adventure going into and becoming part of the pictures she has seen.

976

Laura Jean Johnson

Where Is Freddy? (New York: Harper, 1986)

Age range: Grades 1-2

Series: I Can Read Book

Subject(s): Animals/Mice; Mystery and Detective Stories

Major character(s): Tweedy, Mouse, Detective; Rollo, Sidekick

Time period(s): Indeterminate

Locale(s): Fictional Country

What the book is about: Why are coat hangers, a laundry basket and the cook's Swiss chocolate missing? Who are the two shadows on the lawn? Mrs. Twombly's grandson, Freddy, has disappeared and mouse detective Tweedy is called in to conduct a search.

Other books by the author:
Rollo and Tweedy and the Ghost at Dougal Castle, 1992
Ottie and the Star, 1979

Other books you might like:
Russell Hoban, *The Marzipan Pig*, 1986
The marzipan pig, eaten by a mouse, starts a chain of events leading to another mouse who in her turn discovers another marzipan pig to eat.
Emily Perl Kingsley, *An American Tail*, 1986
In 1885, the Mousekewitz family leaves Russia. Separated during the voyage, Fievel searches for his family and has many adventures in New York City.
Doris Orgel, *Godfather Cat and Mousie*, 1986
A cat and a mouse live together in harmony until it is revealed that a hungry cat can't be trusted.
George Selden, *Harry Kitten and Tucker Mouse*, 1986
A hungry mouse and a lonely kitten become friends and seek adventure and fortune together in the streets and subways of New York City.
Eve Titus, *Anatole and the Thirty Thieves*, 1969
Anatole the mouse returns from vacation to find he is sorely needed to help solve the mystery of the Great Cheese Robbery.

977

Tony Johnston

Illustrator: Lloyd Bloom

Yonder (New York: Dial, 1988)

Age range: Grades 2-4

Subject(s): Country Life; Family Life; Seasons

Time period(s): Indeterminate

Locale(s): United States

What the book is about: This picture book shows three generations in a rural setting, beginning with a farmer and his bride. They begin their life together by planting a tree, and celebrate each birth with a new "tree of life." A portrayal of rural American life in an earlier, simpler time. Repetition and rhythm make this a good read aloud.

Where it's reviewed:
Horn Book, July/August 1988, page 480
School Library Journal, May 1988, page 85
Publishers Weekly, February 12, 1988, page 84

Other books by the author:
Lorenzo, the Naughty Parrot, 1992
I'm Gonna Tell Mama I Want an Iguana, 1990
The Quiet Story, 1986
Five Little Foxes and the Snow, 1977

Other books you might like:
Kate Aver, *Joey's Way*, 1992
    During each of the four seasons, while enjoying the beauty of nature with her family, Joey shows that she has her own special way of doing things.
Lucille Clifton, *Everett Anderson's Year*, 1974
    A poem which tells about seven year old Everett's activities month to month.
Kevin Hawkes, *His Royal Buckliness*, 1992
    Carried off to a frozen land by the giants to be their king, Lord Buckliness misses the delight of summer and spring.
Sachiko Komoto, *Chessie the Long Island Squirrel*, 1992
    Follows Chessie the squirrel through the four seasons and from infancy to motherhood.
Golden Macdonald, *The Little Island*, 1974
    The passing of the seasons and the activities of the animals as they change are shown on a small island.

978

Diana Wynne Jones

Archer's Goon (New York: Greenwillow, 1984)

Age range: Grades 5-8

Subject(s): Fantasy; Wizards; Brothers and Sisters

Major character(s): Howard Sykes, Teenager; Anthea "Awful" Sykes, Child

Time period(s): Indeterminate Past

Locale(s): England

What the book is about: Howard and Awful are surprized to find the "Goon" sitting in their kitchen. He has come to collect the 2,000 words their father owes him. Howard learns some startling information about his family, including the fact that he is adopted, and his father is connected with the seven wizards that run the town.

Where it's reviewed:
Horn Book, April 1984, page 202
School Library Journal, March 1984, page 160

Awards the book has won:
Boston Globe/Horn Book Award - Honor Book 1984

Other books by the author:
Eight Days of Luke, 1988
The Lives of Christopher Chant, 1988
Fire and Hemlock, 1984
Warlock at the Wheel and Other Stories, 1984

Other books you might like:
John Bellaris, *The Revenge of the Wizard's Ghost*, 1985
    Thirteen year old Johnny Dixon's life is threatened by an evil spirit possessing him. His friends and an elderly professor try to help.
Diane Duane, *High Wizardry*, 1990
    When her younger sister uses the family computer with its special wizard software to travel to worlds light years away, Nita has to find her.
Ellen Miles, *Wizards and Warriors*, 1990
    Matthew joins Kuros, a knight, on a quest to vanquish a wizard with terrifying powers. (Based on the game by Acclaim.)
Laurence Yep, *Dragon Cauldron*, 1991
    A dragon named Shimmer, a monkey wizard, a reformed witch and two humans go on a quest to mend the magic cauldron needed to repair the dragon's home.
Mary Frances Zambreno, *A Plague of Sorcerers*, 1991
    When a magic plague begins to take its toll of the Wizards in the Empire, wizard apprentice Jermyn and his skunk, Delia, try to combat the magic.

979

Diana Wynne Jones

Castle in the Air (New York: Greenwillow, 1990)

Age range: Grades 6-8

Subject(s): Fantasy; Adventure and Adventurers; Magic

Major character(s): Abdullah, Merchant; Flower-in-the-Night, Royalty (princess)

Time period(s): Indeterminate Past

Locale(s): Fictional Country

What the book is about: Constantly misunderstood, first imprisoned and then captured by a desert bandit, Abdullah wriggles out of danger after danger with the help of a weary, but loyal, magic carpet, a genie, and a panther. This is "Arabian Nights" with a twist.

Where it's reviewed:
Horn Book, March/April 1991, page 206
School Library Journal, April 1991, page 141

Other books by the author:
Howl's Moving Castle, 1987
Archer's Goon, 1984
Cart and Cwidder, 1975
Dogsbody, 1975

Other books you might like:
John Bellairs, *The Lamp from the Warlock's Tomb*, 1988
    Anthony Monday and Miss Eells recover a magic lamp stolen from a warlock's tomb.

Ellen Conford, *Genie with the Light Blue Hair*, 1989
Jean receives a lamp for her birthday and discovers a wish granting genie, but finds having wishes come true has its own downside.

Andrew Lang, *Arabian Nights*, 1951
Twenty of the traditional tales told by Scheherazade in an attempt to save her life.

George Selden, *The Genie of Sutton Place*, 1973
A young boy has a genie at his beck-and-call for the entire summer.

Joanne Webster, *The Love Genie*, 1978
Fourteen year old Jennie finds that having her own genie does not make life as simple as she thought it would.

980

Diana Wynne Jones

Charmed Life (New York: Greenwillow, 1978)

Age range: Grades 5-6

Subject(s): Magic; Orphans; Witches and Witchcraft

Major character(s): Eric "Cat" Chant, Child; Gwendolyn Chant, Child; Mrs. Sharp, Guardian

Time period(s): Indeterminate Past

Locale(s): England

What the book is about: For every historic event, there are alternative outcomes, so different worlds exist at the same time. In the Chant children's world, witches and warlocks are accepted, and younsters with talent are taught witchcraft. The orphans are taken in by a wealthy enchanter and talented Gwen is given witch's lessons. Gwen is so gifted that she attracts the attention of the Chrestomanci, and she and Cat are inprisoned in his castle.

Where it's reviewed:
America, December 9, 1978, page 442
Guardian Weekly, January 1, 1979, page 15

Other books by the author:
Castle in the Air, 1990
The Power of Three, 1979
Who Got Rid of Angus Flint?, 1979
The Ogre Downstairs, 1975

Other books you might like:
Suzy McKee Charnas, *The Golden Thread*, 1989
Bosanka, an alien from another world, wants Valentine to use her magical powers to help Bosanka return home.

Patricia Clapp, *Witches' Children*, 1982
In 1692, when young girls of Salem suddenly find themselves subject to fits of screaming and strange visions, some believe they've seen the devil.

Kate Gilmore, *Enter Three Witches*, 1990
Bren fears having the girl of his dreams meet his family of witches, until his family attends a school play and he finds a meeting has taken place.

Judith Gorog, *On Meeting Witches at Wells*, 1991
A collection of short stories about witches told for middle readers.

Stephen Krensky, *The Witching Hour*, 1981
The Wynd family pits its forces against a group of witches with a ghastly plan to turn the town's children into monsters.

981

Diana Wynne Jones

Dogsbody (New York: Greenwillow, 1977)

Age range: Grades 6 and Up

Subject(s): Animals/Dogs; Fantasy; Mystery and Detective Stories

Major character(s): Kathleen, Child; Robin, Child; Sirius, Dog

Time period(s): Indeterminate

Locale(s): Heaven; Earth

What the book is about: Sirius the dog star, is banished to earth (having been tried and found guilty of a murder he did not commit) as a puppy, with a mission to search for the lost Zoi, the murder weapon of the stars. Sirius discovers that humans have power, and though Kathleen loves him, she cannot protect him from the "someone" who will stop at nothing, even destroying the Earth, to keep Sirius from finding the Zoi. Non stop action in a unique, witty and engaging fantasy for all ages.

Where it's reviewed:
Booklist, May 15, 1977, page 1421
Hornbook, June 1977, page 319
Kirkus Reviews, February 1, 1977, page 95

Other books by the author:
Castle in the Air, 1991
Howl's Moving Castle, 1986
Archer's Goon, 1984
Charmed Life, 1977

Other books you might like:
Roy A. Gallant, *The Constellations: How They Came to Be*, 1991
A guide to identifying constellations with an explanation of the mythology surrounding them.

McClure Jones, *Cast Down the Stars*, 1978
When the villagers are threatened by barbarian tribe, Glory finds she needs more than scientific knowledge to help the those she loves most.

Louise Lawrence, *The Power of Stars: A Story of Suspense*, 1972
A girl possessed by a strange force which is energized by starlight must be stopped from her destructive acts.

Richard Moeschl, *Exploring the Sky*, 1989
One hundred astronomy projects, with information on related mythology, history, culture and peoples.

Vivian Laubach Thompson, *Hawaiian Myths of Earth, Sea and Sky*, 1966
Presents twelve Hawaiian myths which explain how the earth and stars came to be.

982

Diana Wynne Jones

Howl's Moving Castle (New York: Greenwillow, 1986)

Age range: Grades 5-8

Subject(s): Fantasy; Witches and Witchcraft; Wizards

Major character(s): Sophie, Worker (hat shop apprentice); Howl, Wizard; Witch of the Waste, Witch

Time period(s): Indeterminate

Locale(s): Market Chipping, Fictional Country

What the book is about: Eldest of three sisters in a land where it is considered to be a misfortune, Sophie is resigned to her fate as a hat shop apprentice until a witch turns her into an old woman. She seeks refuge in the castle of the wizard Howl, who is frantically trying to escape the curse the witch has put on him.

Where it's reviewed:
Booklist, June 1, 1986, page 1455
Hornbook, May 1986, page 331
Kirkus Reviews, June 1, 1986, page 868
School Library Journal, August 1986, page 101

Awards the book has won:
Boston Globe/Horn Book Honor 1986

Other books by the author:
The Homeward Bounders, 1981
Cart and Cwidder, 1977
Charmed Life, 1977
Eight Days of Luke, 1975

Other books you might like:
John Bellairs, *The Dark Secret of Weatherend*, 1984
  Anthony and his friend Miss Eells, the librarian, try to stop an evil wizard from turning the world into an icy wasteland.
Suzy McKee Charnas, *The Silver Glove*, 1988
  A teen teams up with her sorceress grandmother to protect her mother from her new boyfriend, an evil wizard bent on stealing people's souls.
Alan Garner, *The Weirdstone of Brisingamen: A Tale of Alderley*, 1963
  The ghastly creatures that plague Susan and Colin are a mystery until Susan discovers that the stone in her barcelet is the magical Firefrost.
Ursula Le Guin, *A Wizard of Earthsea*, 1968
  A boy grows to manhood while attempting to subdue the evil he unleashed on the world as an apprentice to the Master Wizard.
Elizabeth Winthrop, *The Battle for the Castle*, 1993
  William uses the magic token to return through the toy castle in his attic, to the land of Sir Simon, which is now menaced by a skeleton ship.

983

Rebecca C. Jones

The Believers (New York: Arcade, 1989)

Age range: Grades 5-8

Subject(s): Cults; Foster Homes; Religion

Major character(s): Tibby, Adoptee; Veronica, Journalist; Evelyn, Relative (aunt), Child-Care Giver

Time period(s): 1980s

Locale(s): United States

What the book is about: Tibby rarely sees her adoptive mother, Veronica, a glamorous TV reporter, and has become adept at sneaking around Aunt Evelyn, who cares for Tibby while Veronica is out of town. Tibby is supposed to stay away from "The Believers," a fundamentalist sect that meets in a nearby barn, but she is drawn by a budding friendship with Verl. A crisis forces her to make a difficult choice.

Where it's reviewed:
Center for Children's Books Bulletin, September 1989, page 8
School Library Journal, November 1989, page 110

Other books by the author:
Germy Blew the Bugle, 1990
Germy Blew It—Again!, 1988
Germy Blew It, 1987
Angie and Me, 1981

Other books you might like:
T. Ernesto Bethancourt, *Instruments of Darkness*, 1979
  Members of a religious cult headed by a powerful Rumanian mystic become involved in strange events.
Franklin W. Dixon, *Cult of Crime*, 1987
  The Hardy Boys try to free their friend, Holly, from a murderous mountain cult and the lunatic Rajah.
Constance Leonard, *Aground*, 1984
  Tracy James leaves her contented life in Florida and becomes involved in a mind controlling cult in Maine.
Jill Pinkwater, *The Disappearance of Sister Perfect*, 1987
  Sherelee Holmes (who claims relation to the famous Sherlock) goes undercover into the compounds of a dangerous cult.
Stephanie S. Tolan, *Good Courage*, 1988
  As his mother searches for her own personal truth, Ty is dragged from one commune to another, and the latest one, the Kingdom, is intolerable.

984

Terry Jones

Illustrator: Michael Foreman

Nicobobinus (New York: P. Bedrick, 1986)

Age range: Grades 5-7

Subject(s): Dragons; Middle Ages

Major character(s): Nicobobinus, Child; Rosie, Child

Time period(s): Indeterminate Past (Middle Ages)

Locale(s): Fictional Country (Land of the Dragons)

What the book is about: Nicobobinus and his friend, Rosie, go to the land of the Dragons to seek a cure for his golden foot. They meet up with pirates, murderous monks, moving mountains and a ship that can cook!

Where it's reviewed:
Booklist, July 1986, page 1613
School Library Journal, August 1986, page 94
Publisher's Weekly, April 25, 1986, page 83

Other books by the author:
The Saga of Erik the Viking, 1983
Fairy Tales, 1981

Other books you might like:
Rose Estes, *The Children of the Dragon*, 1985
  In the mythical kingdom of Gallardia, the Dragonlord's three children must fight to save themselves and the one remaining egg of the guardian dragon.
Susan Fletcher, *Dragon's Milk*, 1989
  An outsider adopted by an Elythian family as a baby possesses the power to understand dragons and uses the power to save her younger sister.
Shirley Rousseau Murphy, *The Ivory Lyre*, 1987

With the help of four dragons, dragonbards Tebriel and Kiri are instrumental in inciting an uprising against the Dark and in finding a magical lyre.

Brad Strickland, *Dragon's Plunder*, 1992
Kidnapped by former pirates because of his ability to whistle up the wind, Jamie agrees to help their leader find the dragon of Windrose Island.

Patricia C. Wrede, *Calling on Dragons*, 1993
Queen Cimorene turns to her friends for help when troublesome wizards make their way back into the Enchanted Forest and begin to soak up its magic.

985

Toeckey Jones

Go Well, Stay Well (New York: Harper and Row, 1980)

Age range: Grades 5-7

Subject(s): Apartheid; Race Relations

Major character(s): Candice "Candy", Teenager; Rebecca "Becky" Mpala, Teenager; Dirk, Teenager

Time period(s): 1970s (1976)

Locale(s): Johannesburg, South Africa; Soweto, South Africa

What the book is about: A white girl in South Africa meets a black girl her own age, and a friendship begins in spite of social pressures. The two fifteen year olds challenge their country's apartheid system as they try to overcome the deep-rooted prejudices in themselves.

Where it's reviewed:
Booklist, May 1, 1980, page 1268
Hornbook, June 1980, page 307
Kirkus Reviews, May 15, 1980, page 650

Other books by the author:
Skindeep, 1986

Other books you might like:
Dianne Case, *Love, David*, 1991
Anna watches as her brother upsets the family by involving himself in illegal activities to escape from the poverty of his home life in South Africa.

Sheila Gordon, *The Middle of Somewhere: A Story of South Africa*, 1990
Rebecca and her family, living in a South African village, are threatened with forced removal to a bleak development, to make room for white suburbs.

Beverly Naidoo, *Journey to Jo'burg*, 1986
Naledi and her brother travel to the city to find their mother because their sister is dying.

Margaret Sacks, *Beyond Safe Boundaries*, 1989
Elizabeth comes of age in 1960s South Africa as her older sister joins a secret group opposed to the country's racial policies.

Norman Silver, *No Tigers in Africa: A Novel*, 1990
Newly arrived in England from South Africa, a fifteen year old's family deteriorates, as the effects of having lived under apartheid take their toll.

986

Marykate Jordan

Illustrator: Judith Friedman

Losing Uncle Tim (Chicago: Whitman, 1989)

Age range: Grades 1-3

Subject(s): AIDS (Disease); Death; Aunts and Uncles

Major character(s): Daniel, Child; Tim, Relative (uncle)

Time period(s): 1980s

Locale(s): United States

What the book is about: Daniel loves his Uncle Tim, who loves to make tents from quilts and play checkers with him. When he notices that Tim tires easily and sees Tim's health declining, he asks his parents what is wrong, and they explain to him that Uncle Tim has AIDS. After he understands, Daniel becomes Tim's most faithful visitor and after his death, Daniel inherits several treasures from his uncle's antique shop.

Where it's reviewed:
Horn Book, January/February 1990, page 52
School Library Journal, January 1990, page 84

Other books you might like:
Barbara Aiello, *Friends for Life*, 1988
When the members of a video club find out their club sponsor has AIDS, they have a variety of reactions before learning more about the disease.

Leone Castell Anderson, *It's O.K. to Cry*, 1979
Two brothers must deal with the death of a favorite uncle.

Jo Carson, *You Hold Me and I'll Hold You*, 1992
When a great-aunt dies, a young child finds comfort in being held, and in holding, too.

Nancy Jewell, *Time for Uncle Joe*, 1980
The changing seasons trigger a little girl's loving memories of her late uncle.

Gary Paulsen, *A Christmas Sonata*, 1992
When a little boy spends Christmas with his dying cousin, they discover that Santa really does exist.

987

William Joyce, Author/Illustrator

George Shrinks (New York: Harper, 1985)

Age range: Grades 1-2

Major character(s): George, Child

Time period(s): 1970s

Locale(s): United States

What the book is about: While taking care of a cat and his own baby brother, George becomes the size of a mouse. He has an adventure in a toy plane, the cat attacks, and only his parents coming home in time can save him.

Where it's reviewed:
Horn Book, November/December 1985, page 729
School Library Journal, October 1985, page 156

Other books by the author:
Bently and Egg, 1992
Nicholas Cricket, 1991
A Day with Wilbur Robinson, 1990
Humphrey's Bear, 1987

Other books you might like:
Marcia Brown, *Once upon a Mouse: A Fable Cut in Wood*, 1961
   A hermit changes a mouse into bigger and bigger animals.
Kay Chorao, *Lemon Moon*, 1983
   The animals on a little boy's quilt come to life at night.
Ann Jonas, *The Quilt*, 1984
   The patches on a little girl's quilt are places she can visit.
Chris Van Allsburg, *Ben's Dream*, 1982
   Ben falls asleep and visits all the places he was studying about for his social studies test.
Mercy Yates, *The Story of Tom Thumb*, 1973
   A tiny boy is swallowed in turn by a cow, a fish, and a giant, and finally ends up at King Arthur's court.

988

Mavis Jukes

Illustrator: Lloyd Bloom

Like Jake and Me (New York: Knopf, 1984)

Age range: Grades 3-4

Subject(s): Fathers and Sons; Stepfamilies; Animals/Insects

Major character(s): Alex, Child; Jake, Step-Parent

Time period(s): 1980s

Locale(s): United States

What the book is about: Alex feels that he does not have much in common with his stepfather until he becomes concerned about a spider and her young just as Jake is caring for his pregnant wife.

Where it's reviewed:
Bulletin for the Center of Children's Books, February 1985, page 109
Horn Book, March/April 1985, page 179

Awards the book has won:
Newbery Honor

Other books by the author:
Blackberries in the Dark, 1985
Getting Even, 1988
No One Is Going to Nashville, 1984

Other books you might like:
Mary Downing Hahn, *The Spanish Kidnapping Disaster*, 1991
   Stepsisters Amy and Felix are kidnapped when Felix boasts about the family's wealth to a stranger.
Barbara Aiello, *Business Is Looking Up*, 1988
   A visually impaired 11-year-old sets up a greeting card service for stepfamilies.
Alfred Slote, *A Friend Like That*, 1988
   11-year-old Robbie is taking drastic steps to keep his father from developing a new love interest.
A.C. Stewart, *Silas and Con*, 1977
   A 10-year-old boy, abandoned by his mother and abusive stepfather, seeks a new life with only his dog as a companion.
Scott Corbett, *Take a Number*, 1974
   When a 7th grader's fondly remembered stepfather comes back into his life, he seems a different and dangerous person.

989

Mavis Jukes

Illustrator: Lloyd Bloom

No One Is Going to Nashville (New York: Knopf, 1983)

Age range: Grades 2-4

Subject(s): Stepmothers; Animals/Dogs

Major character(s): Sonia, Child; Max, Dog

Time period(s): 1980s

Locale(s): Tennessee

What the book is about: A stray dog creates a tug-of-war of feelings among a weekend family - father, stepmother and child. Sonia's mom says no dogs are allowed in their apartment building. Her dad says "no dog" too. Sonia's stepmother is the one who eventually changes her mind.

Where it's reviewed:
Horn Book, February 1984, page 54
School Library Journal, November 1983, page 78

Other books by the author:
Getting Even, 1988
Like Jake and Me, 1984
Blackberries in the Dark, 1982

Other books you might like:
Carol Lea Benjamin, *The Wicked Stepdog*, 1982
   When her father remarries, ten year old Louise has to adjust to a stepmother and a slobbering golden retriever.
Mary Blount Christian, *No Dogs Allowed, Jonathan!*, 1975
   When Jonathan smuggles a sheep dog into his apartment, he finally understands why dogs are not allowed.
Helen V. Griffith, *Alex and the Cat*, 1982
   Three stories about Alex who wants to be treated like the family cat, or live like a wolf, or put a baby robin back in its nest.
Steven Kroll, *Is Milton Missing?*, 1975
   Richard searches for his dog in the apartment next door.
Cynthia Rylant, *Henry and Mudge and the Happy Cat*, 1990
   Henry's family takes in a ugly stray cat and watches the bond it forms with their dog, Mudge.

990

Norton Juster

Illustrator: Jules Feiffer

The Phantom Tollbooth (New York: Random, 1961)

Age range: Grades 4-8

Subject(s): Fantasy; Humor

Major character(s): Milo, Preteen; Tock, Dog (watchdog); Alec Bings, Friend

Time period(s): Indeterminate

Locale(s): Fictional Country

What the book is about: Milo is chronically bored. Neither words nor numbers can charm him. One day he finds a surprise package in his room labeled, "To Milo, Who Has Plenty of Time." It contains a tollbooth through which Milo passes into a strange land of Dictionopolis and Digitopolis, lands of words and numbers constantly at war.

Where it's reviewed:

New York Times Book Review, November 7, 1971, page 47
New York Times Book Review, February 13, 1972, page 12

Other books by the author:

Otter Nonsense, 1982
Alberic the Wise, 1965

Other books you might like:

Carole S. Adler, *Help, Pink Pig!*, 1990
Moving to Los Angeles with her mother, a lonely girl escapes boredom and a neighborhood bully by entering a fantasy world with her magical toy pig.

Gery Greer, *Max and Me and the Wild West*, 1988
Steve and his friend, Max, take their time machine to an old Wild West boom town where they chase Gentleman John Hooten, Rhyming Robber of the Rockies

Jenny Pausacker, *Fast Forward*, 1989
With his grandmother's new invention, the Anti-Boredom Machine, Kieran can speed up time or travel into the past, but this soon creates more problems.

Vivian Vande Velde, *A Well-Timed Enchantment*, 1990
A girl and her cat disappear back in time to retrieve a lost watch.

Elvira Woodruff, *The Disappearing Bike Shop*, 1992
Freckle and Tyler meet an unusual bicycle salesman and inventor who turns out to be Leonardo da Vinci, traveling through time.

K

991

Jonah Kalb

Illustrator: Sandy Kossin

The Goof That Won the Pennant (Boston: Houghton Mifflin, 1976)

Age range: Grades 3-5

Subject(s): Sports/Baseball; Humor

Major character(s): Venuti, Coach

Time period(s): 1970s

Locale(s): United States

What the book is about: The Blazers are a bad, losing baseball team. Coach Venuti believes that if the team can develop some confidence, they can win, and once they find out that winning is more fun than losing, things will turn around. The coach does turn them around, in a goof that is actual baseball history.

Where it's reviewed:
Booklist, February 1, 1977, page 834
Kirkus Reviews, October 15, 1976, page 1137

Other books by the author:
The Easy Hockey Book, 1977
The Easy Baseball Book, 1976
The Kids' Candidate, 1975
How to Play Baseball Better than You Did Last Year, 1974

Other books you might like:
Scott Corbett, *The Baseball Trick*, 1965
  A potion from Kirby's chemistry set designed to combat the ringers on the opposing baseball team yields surprising results for Kerby and his friends.
Johanna Hurwitz, *Baseball Fever*, 1981
  Ten year old Ezra tries to convince his scholarly father that his baseball fever is not wasting his mind.
Beman Lord, *Bats and Balls*, 1962
  After Bob's finger is hurt by an inside pitch, he has trouble getting back into the game even when the injury has healed.
Peggy Parish, *Play Ball, Amelia Bedelia*, 1972
  Amelia Bedelia, who knows very little about baseball, stands in for a sick player during a game.
Gary Paulsen, *Hitting, Pitching, and Running, Maybe*, 1976
  A humorous commentary on different aspects of baseball using photographs of professional players.

992

Ellen Kandoian, Author/Illustrator

Maybe She Forgot (New York: Dutton, 1990)

Age range: Grades 1-2

Subject(s): Mothers and Daughters; Fear

Major character(s): Jessie, Child, Dancer

Time period(s): 1990s

Locale(s): United States

What the book is about: Jessie waits for her mother to pick her up from her first dance class. Her phone call home goes unanswered and tears fill Jessie's eyes. She doesn't know what obstacles her mom faces and Jessie fears that she has been forgotten.

Where it's reviewed:
Booklist, October 1, 1990, page 339
Kirkus Reviews, August 15, 1990, page 1177

Other books by the author:
Molly's Seasons, 1992
Rainy Day Rhymes, 1992
Is Anybody Up?, 1989
Under the Sun, 1987

Other books you might like:
Sally Hobart Alexander, *Sarah's Surprise*, 1990
  Fearful Sarah comes to the rescue when her mother hurts her ankle while hFiking on the beach.
James Howe, *Pinky and Rex Go to Camp*, 1992
  Although his best friend, Rex, is excited about going to camp, Pinky is afraid of leaving home.
Patricia Polacco, *Thunder Cake*, 1990
  Grandma finds a way to dispel her grandchild's fear of thunderstorms.
Ann Tompert, *Will You Come Back for Me?*, 1988
  Suki is worried about being left in day care for the first time until her mother reassures her that she loves her and will always return for her.
Martin Waddell, *Let's Go Home, Little Bear*, 1993
  When Little Bear is frightened by the noises he hears while walking in the snowy woods, his friend, Big Bear, reassures him.

993

Bess Kaplan

The Empty Chair (New York: Harper, 1978)

Age range: Grades 5-7

Subject(s): Death; Stepmothers; Holidays, Jewish

Major character(s): Rebecca ''Becky'' Devine, Writer, Preteen; Saul Devine, Child; Johnny Felange, Bully

Time period(s): 1930s

Locale(s): Winnipeg, Manitoba, Canada

What the book is about: Beth is dismayed when her Aunts Sadie and Leah help plan her father's remarriage and expect her to accept a new stepmother while still grieving for her mother who died in childbirth. Becky is an engaging heroine who gives a thoughtful and detailed portrait of a family adjusting to grief and change. Includes glossary of Yiddish words.

Where it's reviewed:
Booklist, May 1, 1978, page 1432
Kirkus Reviews, June 1, 1978, page 599
School Library Journal, May 1978, page 68

Other books you might like:
Riki Levinson, *Boys Here, Girls There*, 1993
    The year that Jennie starts school brings many changes to her loving Jewish family, including father's loss of his job and the birth of a new baby.
Sonia Levitin, *The Golem and the Dragon Girl*, 1993
    Jewish Jonathon and Chinese-American Laurel gradually become friends, but they must deal with ancestral spirits and changing family relationships.
Vicky Shiefman, *Goodbye to the Trees*, 1993
    Despite the excitement and confusion of her new life in America, Fagel can't forget the family she left behind in Russia.
Sholem Aleichem, *Around the Table: "Family Stories of Sholom Aleichem"*, 1991
    Depicts five families observing the rituals and traditions of Jewish holidays together.
Sydney Taylor, *A Papa Like Everyone Else*, 1966
    Two Jewish girls and their mother, living on a farm in post-WWI Czechoslovak Republic, wait for father to send money so they can join him in America.

994

Jean Karl

Beloved Benjamin Is Waiting (New York: Dutton, 1978)

Age range: Grades 4-6

Subject(s): Cemeteries; Monuments

Major character(s): Lucinda, Child; Benjamin, Spirit

Time period(s): 1970s

Locale(s): United States

What the book is about: Lucinda's parents fight all the time, so it's better to be out of the house. She finds an abandoned caretaker's house in a nearby cemetary. She finds a glowing statue with the words ''Beloved Benjamin.born 1882.Aged 7'' carved on it. Benjamin is somehow present in the statue, and she and Benjamin begin an interesting relationship.

Where it's reviewed:
Childhood Education, February 1979, page 223
Language Arts, April 1979, page 441

Other books by the author:
The Search for the Ten-Winged Dragon, 1990
Strange Tomorrow, 1985
But We Are Not of Earth, 1981
The Turning Place, 1979

Other books you might like:
Vivien Alcock, *The Stonewalkers*, 1981
    A garden statue of Belladonna is brought to life by a flash of lightning and gathers a stone army from gardens and churches as Poppy and Emma watch.
Eve Bunting, *The Haunting of Safekeep*, 1985
    Eighteen year old Sara takes a summer job as a caretaker at a Victorian restoration site and encounters a foundling and two ghosts.
Paul Fleischman, *Graven Images*, 1982
    Three of Fleischman's best stories: ''The Binnacle Boy,'' ''Saint Crispin's Follower,'' and ''The Man of Influence.''
Phyllis Reynolds Naylor, *Bernie and the Bessledorf Ghost*, 1990
    Bernie tries to solve the mystery of a troubled young ghost who wanders the halls at night in the hotel where Bernie lives.
Philippa Pearce, *The Way to Sattin Shore*, 1983
    When a tombstone with her father's name suddenly disappears from the graveyard, Kate witnesses the unraveling of a mystery surrounding his death.

995

Jean Karl

But We Are Not of Earth (New York: Dutton, 1981)

Age range: Grades 5-8

Subject(s): Science Fiction; Space Travel

Major character(s): Romula ''Rom'' Linders, Preteen; Bitsy Halab, Friend; Waver Wistrow, Friend

Time period(s): Indeterminate Future

Locale(s): Planet—Imaginary (Meniscus F)

What the book is about: When Rom and her friends hear about the special space exploration program, they are determined to be part of it. It seems like the only way out of the dull life on Meniscus F. They don't count on finding Ariel, the beautiful Earth-like planet, and there is something on Ariel more dangerous than they could have imagined.

Where it's reviewed:
Booklist, June 1, 1981, page 1299
Hornbook, June 1981, page 309
Kirkus Reviews, July 15, 1981, page 872

Other books by the author:
Strange Tomorrow, 1985
Beloved Benjamin Is Waiting, 1978
The Turning Place, 1976

Other books you might like:
Victor Appleton, *Ark Two*, 1982
    Tom Swift and his crew travel to the planet Aquilla to recover SeaGlobe, an ecological system stolen from the space colony New America.
Keith Deutsch, *Space Travel in Fact and Fiction*, 1980

Covers the past and future of space travel, including UFO's, science fiction films, plans for space labs and the technology of space travel.

Sandy Landsman, *The Gadget Factor*, 1984
Two college freshmen create the ultimate computer game, but complications arise when their formulas for time travel also work in the real world.

Madeleine L'Engle, *A Swiftly Tilting Planet*, 1978
The youngest of the Murry children must travel through time and space in a battle against an evil dictator who would destroy the entire universe.

Pamela F. Service, *All's Faire*, 1993
Kevin meets a gypsy girl while touring with his parents in medieval shows and they travel back to real medieval times.

996

Kathleen Karr

It Ain't Always Easy (New York: Farrar, Straus, Giroux, 1990)

Age range: Grades 5 and Up

Subject(s): Orphans; Emigration and Immigration

Major character(s): Jack McConnell, Orphan; Mandy, Runaway, Abuse Victim (Eight-years-old)

Time period(s): 1880s (1882)

Locale(s): New York, New York

What the book is about: Children of the immigrant poor were expendable in the 1880s. Mandy is an eight year old runaway who needs Jack's protection to survive. They miss the orphan train to Nebraska. Jack rescues Mandy from an abusive family. They face child labor, mill work, gangs and the Children's Aid Society.

Where it's reviewed:
Kirkus Reviews, October 1, 1990, page 1325
Publisher's Weekly, September 28, 1990, page 103

Other books by the author:
Gideon and the Mummy Professor, 1993
Oh, Those Harper Girls! or, Young and Dangerous, 1992

Other books you might like:
Ruth M. Arthur, *On the Wasteland*, 1975
A young orphan discovers a dream world which allows her to escape the unpleasant realities of everyday life in the orphanage.

Rumer Godden, *Listen to the Nightingale*, 1992
When she wins a scholarship to a ballet school, Lottie is torn between her lifelong dream to be a dancer and her love for a puppy.

Walter G. Olesky, *If I'm Lost, How Come I Found You?*, 1977
A restless, runaway orphan holes up with bank robbers and appears on TV as a hero.

Norah A. Perez, *Breaker*, 1988
After his father's death, fourteen year old Pat is forced to go to work in the coal mines.

Pamela Sykes, *Mirror of Danger*, 1974
An orphan comes to live with distant cousins and suddenly finds herself getting glimpses into the past.

997

Erich Kastner

Little Man (New York: Knopf, 1966)

Age range: Grades 4-6

Subject(s): Circus; Fairy Tale

Major character(s): Maxie Pichelsteiner, Orphan; Hokus Von Pokus, Magician

Time period(s): 1930s

Locale(s): Germany

What the book is about: Maxie Pichelsteiner, an orphan two inches tall, lives with his guardian, Hokus Von Pokus, a circus magician. Sleeping in a match box, Maxie dreams of becoming a performer—and of growing to eight feet tall.

Where it's reviewed:
Library Journal, December 1966, page 6192
New York Times Book Review, November 6, 1966, page 40

Awards the book has won:
Mildred L. Batchelder Award 1968

Other books by the author:
Little Man and the Big Thief, 1969
Puss in Boots, 1957
Simpletons, 1957
Emil and the Detectives, 1930

Other books you might like:
Hans Christian Andersen, *Thumbelina*, 1865
A tiny girl is stolen by an ugly toad and eventually makes her way to happiness in a warm southern land.

Elizabeth Enright, *Zeee*, 1965
A tiny fairy who hates people finds a special someone and a safe place to live.

Richard Jesse Watson, *Tom Thumb*, 1989
A boy no bigger than his father's thumb has many adventures and becomes the smallest knight of the Round Table.

Oscar Wilde, *Selfish Giant*, 1984
A selfish giant opens his garden to children and is rewarded by a friendship with a tiny child.

998

Keiko Kasza, Author/Illustrator

The Wolf's Chicken Stew (New York: Putnam, 1987)

Age range: Grades 2-3

Subject(s): Animals/Wolves; Animals/Birds

Major character(s): Uncle Wolf, Wolf

Time period(s): Indeterminate

Locale(s): Earth

What the book is about: A wolf plans to fatten a chicken for his stew. Instead, he becomes "Uncle Wolf" to one hundred baby chicks.

Where it's reviewed:
Center for Children's Books Bulletin, May 1987, page 170
School Library Journal, August 1987, page 70

Other books by the author:
A Mother for Choco, 1992
When the Elephant Walks, 1990
Pigs' Picnic, 1988

Other books you might like:
Marcia Brown, *Stone Soup: An Old Tale*, 1957
    The traditional folktale of the hen, the wolf, and stone soup.
Paul Galdone, *The Three Little Pigs*, 1970
    The traditional story of the pigs finally outsmarting the wolf.
Tony Ross, *Stone Soup*, 1987
    A wolf plans to eat a hen, but she "outfoxes" him by making stone soup for him.
Tony Ross, *The Three Pigs*, 1983
    Three pigs move from a city apartment to three houses in the country.
Marjorie Weinman Sharmat, *Walter the Wolf*, 1975
    Walter loves to play violin and not bite. A fox convinces him to go into the biting business.

999

Bobbi Katz

The Manifesto and Me - Meg (New York: Watts, 1974)

Age range: Grades 4-6

Subject(s): Women's Rights

Major character(s): Meg, Preteen; Abigail Witherspoon, Feminist

Time period(s): 1970s

Locale(s): United States

What the book is about: Meg starts a conscious-raising group. The girls get arrested for "burning without a permit," burning TAFFY TEEN dolls. Elderly Abby is the heroine who insists on going to jail for the girls.

Where it's reviewed:
Kirkus Reviews, August 1, 1974, page 804
Library Journal, November 15, 1974, page 3047

Other books you might like:
Lois Duncan, *Daughters of Eve*, 1979
    A teacher uses the guise of feminist philosophy to manipulate the lives of a group of girls, with chilling results.
Norma Klein, *The Cheerleader*, 1985
    Evan and Karin cause quite a stir when they form a cheerleading squad for the girls' softball team.
R. Rozanne Knudsen, *Zanballer*, 1972
    Zan Hagen, whose principal opposes her "unladylike" activities, leads her dance class on to the athletic field to form a girls' football team.
Suzanne Fisher Staples, *Shabanu, Daughter of the Wind*, 1989
    Shabanu, daughter of a Pakistani nomad, is pledged in marriage to a wealthy older man whose money will help her family, but she has some misgivings.
Sue Stops, *Dulcie Dando, Soccer Star*, 1992
    Dulcie, a talented soccer player, proves that girls are just as capable as boys when she is given a chance to play on the school team.

1000

Geraldine Kaye

Illustrator: Jennifer Northway

Comfort Herself (London: Deutsch, 1985)

Age range: Grades 4-7

Subject(s): Interracial Marriage

Major character(s): Comfort, Preteen

Time period(s): 1980s

Locale(s): United States

What the book is about: AFter Comfort's mother is killed by a bus, she searches out her blood relatives. Her grandparents in Penfold take Comfort in until her father sends for her from Ghana. After a short stay, she travels up country to her grandmother's village. Comfort is able to assimilate both of her races within herself and choose to settle in England, the country in which she feels she has the most opportunity.

Where it's reviewed:
Center for Children's Books Bulletin, September 1985, page 11
School Library Journal, October 1985, page 174

Other books by the author:
Cathy's Best Day, 1985
Day After Yesterday, 1981
Goodbye, Ruby Red, 1976
Joanna All Alone, 1974

Other books you might like:
Arnold Adoff, *All the Colors of the Race*, 1982
    A collection of poems written from the point of view of a child with a black mother and a white father.
Adrienne Jones, *So, Nothing Is Forever*, 1974
    The children of an interracial marriage struggle to keep together after the sudden death of their parents.
Maxine B. Rosenberg, *Living in Two Worlds*, 1986
    A photo essay about the special world of bi-racial children.
Jacqueline Roy, *Soul Daddy*, 1992
    Life for Hannah, Rosie and their white mother changes when their black rock star father and his daughter, move into their suburban London home.
Dori Sanders, *Clover: A Novel*, 1990
    Within hours of marrying a white woman, a little girl's father dies leaving her and her new mother to adjust to their new home in South Carolina.

1001

Marilyn Kaye

Daphne (San Diego: Harcourt, 1987)

Age range: Grades 5-7

Subject(s): Identity; Schools; Sisters

Major character(s): Daphne, Preteen, 7th Grader; Lydia, Teenager (Daphne's sister); Cassie, Teenager (Daphne's sister)

Time period(s): 1980s

Locale(s): United States

What the book is about: Taking advice from her sisters about entering junior high is not making matters easier for Daphne. Lydia wants her to be a leader, work on the school paper, and run for office. Her social sister, Cassie, wants to make sure she gets in with the "right crowd" and join the pep club. After trying for a time to please everyone, Daphne realizes that she must be herself and find her own way.

Where it's reviewed:
Booklist, July 1987, page 1680
Kirkus Reviews, April 15, 1987, page 640
School Library Journal, June 1987, page 97

Other books by the author:
Atonement of Mindy Wise, 1991
Cassie, 1987
Lydia, 1987
Phoebe, 1987

Other books you might like:
Linda Hirsch, *You're Going Out There a Kid, but You're Coming Back a Star*, 1982
  Margaret is convinced that the real stuff of life—boys, love, popularity—is quickly passing her by and she must take steps to correct the situation.
Lois Lowry, *A Summer to Die*, 1977
  Meg envys her sister's beauty and popularity. Her feelings make it difficult to cope with Molly's strange illness and eventual death.
Robert Newton Peck, *Clunie*, 1979
  A teenage boy risks his own popularity to give friendship and support to a retarded girl who is harassed by her classmates.
Susan Terris, *Two P's in a Pod*, 1977
  The new girl decides to make Pru a leader in their sixth grade class. Pru enjoys her new popularity until she learns the importance of being herself.
Barbara Brooks Wallace, *The Secret Summer of L.E.B.*, 1974
  Lizabeth risks her popularity with the other sixth graders by becoming friends with the class outcast.

1002

Luqman Keele

Java Jack (New York: Crowell, 1980)

Age range: Grades 4-8

Subject(s): Anthropology; Space and Time

Major character(s): Jack Robinson, Teenager; Amy, Relative (aunt)

Time period(s): 1970s

Locale(s): Neosho, Missouri; Maggasang, Indonesia

What the book is about: The story of a mystical journey to Indonesia by a boy searching for his parents. Jack makes his way from Missouri to Tokyo, Hong Kong, Bangkok and Jakarta when he hears, on the news, that his parents are missing and presumed dead.

Where it's reviewed:
Hornbook, June 1980, page 297
Kirkus, May 1, 1980, page 584
School Library Journal, May 1980, page 68

Other books you might like:
Janet Asimov, *Norby Finds a Villain*, 1987
  Jeff and his robot, Norby, travel backwards and forwards in time and find themselves prisoners on an alien planet in another universe.
Alison Farthing, *The Mystical Beast*, 1976
  Lavinia loses the ancient power for which she is responsible and persuades two kids to help her recapture it in the strange world of the Other Side.

Elaine Masters, *Ali and the Ghost Tiger*, 1970
  No matter what he is doing, Ali is obsessed by the thought of the ghost tiger and the fever it brings.
Jon Scieszka, *Your Mother Was a Neanderthal*, 1993
  The Time Warp Trio have an adventure in prehistoric times, where cave art is a form of graffiti and "rock" music takes on a whole new meaning.
Alfred Slote, *Omega Station*, 1983
  Jack Jameson and his robot twin, Danny One, must save the universe from a mad scientist.

1003

Peg Kehret

Nightmare Mountain (New York: Dutton, 1989)

Age range: Grades 5-6

Subject(s): Mystery and Detective Stories; Ranch Life

Major character(s): Molly Neuman, Child; Glendon Baldwin, Preteen; Karen Baldwin, Relative (aunt)

Time period(s): 1980s

Locale(s): Washington

What the book is about: Twelve year old Molly's visit to her aunt and uncle's llama ranch leads her into danger and suspense. Within days of Molly's arrival, Aunt Karen is desperately ill. Cousin Glendon somehow thinks it's Molly's fault. Then when a valuable llama disappears, Molly and Glendon run into danger when they pursue the thief.

Where it's reviewed:
Booklist, September 15, 1989, page 184
School Library Journal, October 1989, page 120

Other books by the author:
Terror at the Zoo, 1992
Cages, 1991
Deadly Stranger, 1987

Other books you might like:
Ellen Alexander, *Llama and the Great Flood*, 1989
  In this Peruvian myth about the great flood, a llama warns his master of the coming destruction and suggests taking refuge in the Andes.
William Arden, *The Three Investigators in the Mystery of the Moaning Cave*, 1965
  Vacationing on a California ranch, three boys decide to investigate strange wails that come from a mysterious cave where a famous outlaw disappeared.
Ann Nolan Clark, *The Secret of the Andes*, 1952
  An Indian boy who tends llamas in a hidden valley in Peru learns the traditions and secrets of his Inca ancestors.
Joan Lowery Nixon, *A Candidate for Murder*, 1991
  Cary finds her life in danger when she uncovers a plot to sabotage her father's political campaign for governor of Texas.
Zilpha Keatley Snyder, *And the Condors Danced*, 1987
  Carly turns eleven in 1907, and life is filled with playing detective, watching condors, and observing a fierce feud.

1004

Harold Keith

Rifles for Watie (New York: Thomas Y. Crowell, 1957)

Age range: Grades 6 and Up

Subject(s): Civil War

Major character(s): Jeff Bussey, Teenager, Military Personnel (soldier); Stand Watie, Military Personnel (General, Confederate Army)

Time period(s): 1860s

Locale(s): Kansas

What the book is about: 16-year-old Jeff joins the Union Army during the Civil War. He's later forced to join the Confederate Army. After befriending several Confederate families, he recognizes the merits of both Union and Confederate ideas.

Where it's reviewed:
Booklist, November 15, 1957, page 172
Horn Book, December 1957, page 500
Kirkus Reviews, August 15, 1957, page 586

Awards the book has won:
Newbery Medal 1958

Other books by the author:
Boys' Life of Will Rogers, 1937
The Obstinate Land, 1977
Pair of Captains, 1951
Susy's Scoundrel, 1974

Other books you might like:
G. Clifton Wisler, Red Cap, 1991
  A young Yankee drummer boy is captured and sent to Andersonville Prison.
Janet Hickman, Zoar Blue, 1978
  Two young members of a pacifist community in Ohio are caught up in the turbulence of the Civil War.
Laura Jan Shore, The Sacred Moon Tree, 1986
  12 year old Phoebe disguises herself as a boy in order to rescue a friend from behind enemy lines during the Civil War.
Patricia Beatty, Turn Homeward, Hannalee, 1984
  12 year old Hannalee leaves home with a promise to return to her mother when the Civil War ends.
Ann Schlee, Strangers, 1972
  During the Civil War, a girl living on a remote island becomes involved with a strange boy fleeing the Roundheads.

1005

Victor Kelleher

The Red King (New York: Dial, 1990)

Age range: Grades 5-8

Subject(s): Fantasy; Good and Evil

Major character(s): Petie, Magician; Timkin, Acrobat; Red King, Villain

Time period(s): Indeterminate Past

Locale(s): Fictional Country

What the book is about: Aided only by a trained bear and a monkey, Petie and Timkin challenge the power of the evil Red King who rules the Forest Lands by spreading the red fever to

those who refuse to pay him tribute. A true "quest" story focusing on the battle between good and evil.

Where it's reviewed:
Center for Children's Books Bulletin, July/August, 1990, page 269
School Library Journal, July 1990, page 89

Other books by the author:
Rescue!, 1992
Brother Night, 1991

Other books you might like:
Paul R. Fisher, The Princess and the Thorn, 1980
  Mole finds himself drawn into a battle between good and evil in which all the powers of the world gather around him and the lost Great Sword.
Tanith Lee, Black Unicorn, 1991
  Sixteen year old Tanaquil reconstructs a unicorn which lures her away to find a city by the sea and the way to a perfect world.
Andre Norton, Quag Keep, 1978
  Seven strangers, each wearing a similar bracelet, meet and become pawns in the struggle between good and evil.
Pamela F. Service, Weirdos of the Universe, Unite!, 1992
  Mandy and Own accidentally summon up five mythological beings who need their aid in defending the Earth from space invaders.
Laurence Yep, Dragon War, 1992
  The dragon princess, Shimmer, and her friends, fight a war against the evil Boneless King to rescue their friend, Thorn.

1006

Beverly Keller

Illustrator: Diane Paterson

Fiona's Bee (New York: Coward, 1975)

Age range: Grades 1-2

Subject(s): Animals/Bees; Friendship

Major character(s): Fiona, Child

Time period(s): 1970s

Locale(s): United States

What the book is about: Fiona, a lonely child, rescues a drowning bee who climbs up her hand to her shoulder. She takes a walk to the park hoping the bee will fly away. All of her friends think the bee is a pet and they all want to walk Fiona home. She suddenly has lots of new friends.

Where it's reviewed:
Kirkus Reviews, October 1, 1975, page 1128

Other books by the author:
Only Fiona, 1988
The Bee Sneeze, 1982
Fiona's Flea, 1981
The Beetle Bush, 1976

Other books you might like:
Angela Banner, Around the World with Aunt and Bee, 1981
  Bee's hunt for his lost umbrella takes Ant and Bee on a trip around the world.
Adelaide Holl, Small Bear's Busy Day, 1977
  Small Bear has fun and adventure as he deals with honey bees, a capsized raft, and a monster jack-o-lantern.

Norma Q. Hare, *Who Is Root Beer?*, 1977
Four insects, Bee, Ant, Bug and Butterfly, find an empty root beer can and in the search for its owner, become friends.

Margaret Knox, *Betsey's Bee Tree*, 1980
Returning from her very first day of gathering pollen and nectar in the field, Betsey finds bandit bees trying to steal her colony's honey.

Arnold Lobel, *The Rose in My Garden*, 1984
A variety of flowers grows near the hollyhocks that give shade to the bee that sleeps on the only rose in a garden.

| 1007 |

Beverly Keller

No Beasts! No Children! (New York: Lothrop, 1983)

Age range: Grades 4-6

Subject(s): Humor; Housing; Single Parent Families

Major character(s): Desdemona Blank, Preteen; Mr. Troup, Neighbor; Mrs. Farisee, Housekeeper

Time period(s): 1980s

Locale(s): United States

What the book is about: A father and three children, Desdemona and twins Antony and Aida, and three dogs cope when a mother takes off. They learn to adjust to a strict housekeeper, an unpleasant landlord and an odd aunt.

Where it's reviewed:
Booklist, September 1, 1983, page 87
Kirkus Reviews, February 1, 1983, page 121
School Library Journal, May 1983, page 32

Other books by the author:
Fowl Play, Desdemona, 1989
Only Fiona, 1988
Desdemona, Twelve Going on Desperate, 1986
Rosebud, with Fangs, 1985

Other books you might like:
Amy Hest, *Pete and Lily*, 1986
When Pete's widowed mother starts dating Lily's divorced father, the two girls decide they need to control the situation.

Gordon Korman, *Losing Joe's Place*, 1990
Jason and his two friends move into Jason's brother's apartment and manage to wreak havoc in it during one funny and memorable summer.

Astrid Lindgren, *The Children on Troublemaker Street*, 1964
Jonas, Maria, and Lotta Nyman have a year of roughhouse adventures and prove that, while they are around, anything can happen.

Barbara Williams, *The Crazy Gang Next Door*, 1990
When a gang of wild children, claiming to be midgets, take over next door while the owner is away, Kim must figure out how to get rid of them.

Maia Wojciechowska, *Hey, What's Wrong with This One?*, 1969
Three brothers have everything they want except a mother and after the latest housekeeper leaves, they decide to help their father find a new wife.

| 1008 |

Steven Kellogg

Pinkerton, Behave! (New York: Dial, 1979)

Age range: Grades 2-3

Subject(s): Animals/Dogs

Major character(s): Pinkerton, Dog

Time period(s): Indeterminate

Locale(s): United States

What the book is about: Pinkerton cannot seem to behave, so he is enrolled in obedience school. He flunks every test and disrupts the entire class. But a robbery proves that Pinkerton's way of doing things works just fine.

Where it's reviewed:
Horn Book, February 1980, page 46
Kirkus Reviews, February 15, 1980, page 211

Awards the book has won:
Little Archer Award 1982

Other books by the author:
There Was an Old Woman, 1979
Much Bigger than Martin, 1976
Island of the Skog, 1973
The Mystery Beast of Ostergeest, 1971

Other books you might like:
Norman Bridwell, *Clifford, the Small Red Puppy*, 1985
Clifford begins life as a very small red puppy, but once he starts growing into a very large red dog, there seems to be no limit to his size.

John Hamberger, *The Lazy Dog*, 1971
A dog chases a runaway beach ball across the countryside.

June Jordan, *Kimako's Story*, 1981
A little girl describes her life in the city and her outdoor adventures with the dog she is taking care of for a friend.

Nancy Winslow Parker, *Poofy Loves Company*, 1980
Sally is overwhelmed by a large, overly friendly dog when she and her mother visit a friend.

Chris Van Allsburg, *The Garden of Abdul Gasazi*, 1979
When the dog he is caring for runs away from Alan into the garden of the retired dog-hating magician, a spell seems to be cast over the contrary dog.

| 1009 |

Eric P. Kelly

Illustrator: Janina Domanska

Trumpeter of Krakow (New York: Macmillan, 1928)

Age range: Grades 4-6

Subject(s): Middle Ages

Major character(s): Joseph, Teenager

Time period(s): 15th century

Locale(s): Krakow, Poland

What the book is about: A 15-year-old boy in 15th century Poland is involved in the mystery and intrigue surrounding a precious jewel. Joseph occasionally takes his father's place as trumpeter and has the opportunity to send a warning through the trumpet's tune that saves the famous magic crystal from the Cossacks of Tarnov.

Where it's reviewed:
Booklist, December 1928, page 128
Outlook, July 3, 1929, page 390

Awards the book has won:
Newbery Medal 1929

Other books by the author:
Treaure Mountain, 1937
Amazing Journey of David Ingram, 1949
From Star to Star, 1944
Golden Star of Halich, 1931

Other books you might like:
Uri Orlev, *Island on Bird Street*, 1983
  A Jewish boy is alone in the Warsaw Ghetto during World War II and must learn the tricks of survival.
Yuri Suhl, *On the Other Side of the Gate*, 1975
  Experiences of a young Jewish couple in German occupied Poland.
E.W. Hildick, *The Case of the Dragon in Distress*, 1991
  A group of friends is transported back to the 12th century where they encounter an evil princess who tries to hold them captive.
Gene Kemp, *Jason Bodger and the Priory Ghost*, 1985
  When Jason visits an ancient priory, he meets a girl who lived 8 centuries before.
Gery Greer, *Max and Me and the Time Machine*, 1983
  Steve and Max travel in a time machine to the year 1250 where they land in the middle of a jousting match.

1010

Jeffrey Kelly

Tramp Steamer and the Silver Bullet (Boston: Houghton Mifflin, 1984)

Age range: Grades 5-7

Subject(s): Schools/Boarding Schools; Humor; Mystery and Detective Stories

Major character(s): Stearns Obadian "Tramp" Steamer, Child; Ginger Steamer, Child (Tramp's sister); Steven "Silver Bullet" Branch, Child

Time period(s): 1980s

Locale(s): Elyria, New York

What the book is about: A Halloween caper involving two best friends turns into a baffling puzzle that involves an abandoned old house. They do odd jobs for two crazy old ladies who live in a spooky house filled with spaghetti-eating plants. Then Sally moves into town.

Where it's reviewed:
Booklist, March 1, 1985, page 984
School Library Journal, December 1984, page 99

Other books by the author:
The Basement Baseball Club, 1987

Other books you might like:
David Carkeet, *Quiver River*, 1991
  The summer is full of promise for Ricky and Nate when they are hired to work at a lake resort in the Sierras.
Ellen Conford, *Dear Mom, Get Me Out of Here!*, 1992
  Trapped in a dreadful boarding school, Paul joins his classmates in an attempt to uncover the shocking past of their headmaster, Mr. Pickles.

Roald Dahl, *Matilda*, 1989
  Matilda applies her untapped mental abilities to rid the school of the evil, child-hating headmistress, Miss Trunchbull.
John D. Fitzgerald, *The Great Brain at the Academy*, 1972
  In Mormon Utah, the Great Brain faces the challenge of life at a Catholic boarding school with his daring exploits and money making schemes.
Gordon Korman, *The Twinkie Squad*, 1992
  Chaos spreads when Douglas, an eccentric sixth grader, joins the Twinkie Squad, a special group for problem students.

1011

Gene Kemp

Illustrator: Chantel Fouracre

The Well (New York: Faber, 1984)

Age range: Grades 4-7

Subject(s): Family Life

Major character(s): Annie Sutton, Preteen; Tom Sutton, Preteen

Time period(s): 1930s

Locale(s): England

What the book is about: Episodes in the growing-up years of Anne Sutton in pre- WWII England. Each episode is separate, but the family portraits are consistent and link the vignettes squabbles between Annie and Tom, which Annie's longing for a kitten and other siblings. A warm family picture that will appeal as independent reading or as a read aloud.

Where it's reviewed:
Horn Book, March/April 1985, page 179
School Library Journal, March 1985, page 168

Other books by the author:
Gowie Corby Plays Chicken, 1979
The Turbulent Term of Tyke Tiler, 1977

Other books you might like:
Dick Cate, *Old Dog, New Tricks*, 1978
  Billy's dad doubts he can learn a new trade after years in an English coal mine, just as he doubts the family dog can ever be properly trained.
Judith Kerr, *When Hitler Stole Pink Rabbit*, 1971
  The adventures of a nine year old Jewish girl and her family in the early 1930s, as they travel from Germany to England.
William Mayne, *Gideon Ahoy!*, 1989
  Eva's chaotic but cheerful family life in a small town changes when Gideon her brain-damaged, deaf brother gets a job on the local canal boat.
Alison Morgan, *Paul's Kite*, 1982
  Virtually ignored by his runaway mother, Paul amuses himself by visiting all the London place names on his Monopoly board until an accident occurs.
Barbara Willard, *The Iron Lily*, 1973
  Orphaned by the Plague and disowned by her "brother's" widow who claims she is not true kin, Lilias begins an attempt to discover her birth parents.

1012

Carol Kendall

Illustrator: Erik Blegvad

Gammage Cup (New York: Harcourt, Brace and World, 1959)

Age range: Grades 5-6

Subject(s): Fantasy

Major character(s): Fooley, Balloonist; Gummy, Writer; Curley Green, Artist (Painter)

Time period(s): Indeterminate (Year of the Gammage 880)

Locale(s): Fictional Country

What the book is about: The Minnipins live lives of isolation and conformity, censoring and exiling any among them who show initiative and creativity. When their ancient enemies, The Hairless Ones, threaten them, it is the exiles who save the day.

Where it's reviewed:
Booklist, December 15, 1959, page 248
Library Journal, February 15, 1960, page 845

Other books you might like:
Margery Sharp, *The Rescuers*, 1959
  Miss Bianca, founder of the Mouse Prisoners Aid Society, masterminds the rescue of a mouse poet from a dungeon.
Mary Norton, *The Borrowers*, 1953
  Tiny people who live hidden in a house are responsible for the disappearance of those things that people "lose."
J.R.R. Tolkien, *The Hobbit, or There and Back Again*, 1937
  Home-loving Hobbit Bilbo Baggins has fantastic adventures on his way to becoming an "expert treasure hunter."
W.J. Corbett, *Song of Pentecost*, 1983
  The mice of Pentecost Farm are forced to move and fear facing the snake, the owl and the fox.
Randall Jarrell, *Animal Family*, 1965
  A family with a hunter, a mermaid, a bear, a lynx and a boy live in a house near the sea.

1013

Thomas Keneally

Illustrator: Stephen Ryan

Ned Kelly and the City of the Bees (Boston: Godine, 1981)

Age range: Grades 5-7

Subject(s): Animals/Bees; Fantasy

Major character(s): Ned Kelly, Student; Nancy Clancy, Preteen; Apis, Worker, Bee

Time period(s): Indeterminate

Locale(s): Australia

What the book is about: With a drop of magic, Ned is made small enough to spend the summer in a beehive. He is enchanted with his new friends, and with them he shares a summer of adventure.

Where it's reviewed:
Hornbook, October 1981, page 535
Kirkus, September 15, 1981, page 1160
School Library Journal, November 1981, page 93

Other books you might like:
Robert Lawson, *The Fabulous Flight*, 1984
  Peter becomes so small he takes a trip by way of a pet seagull.
William Mayne, *Salt River Times*, 1980
  Twenty-one interlocking stories about the lives of the poeple in a small community along Australia's Salt River.
Joan Lowery Nixon, *The Other Side of Dark*, 1986
  Stacy awakens from a four year coma ready to identify, locate and prosecute the young man who murdered her mother and wounded her.
Clem Philbrook, *Ollie's Team Plays Biddy Baseball*, 1970
  Learning from bees studied in school, Ollie becomes a drone instead of a worker, only to discover that drones don't win games for their baseball team.
Seymour Simon, *Einstein Anderson, Science Sleuth*, 1980
  Adam "Einstein" Anderson uses his knowledge of science to discover the cause of a shrinking table, uncover a UFO hoax, win a bet with Pat the Brat.

1014

Richard Kennedy

Illustrator: Marcia Sewall

Richard Kennedy: Collected Stories (New York: Harper & Row, 1987)

Age range: Grades 4-7

Subject(s): Short Stories

Time period(s): Indeterminate

Locale(s): Fictional Country

What the book is about: Depth of characterization mark these fourteen diverse stories. Romance, fantasy, allegory, serious moral tales and parables are all here, each with its own memorable characters. These are wonderful read aloud, and will be devoured by short story lovers who read well enough to enjoy Kennedy's rich use of language.

Where it's reviewed:
Horn Book, May-June 1988, page 358
School Library Journal, November 1987, page 105

Other books by the author:
Delta Baby and Two Sea Songs, 1979
The Lost Kingdom of Karnica, 1979
The Mouse God, 1979
The Rise and Fall of Ben Gizzard, 1978

Other books you might like:
Joan Aiken, *The Green Flash, and Other Tales of Horror, Suspense, and Fantasy*, 1971
  Aiken at her scary best with many different kinds of haunting tales.
Judith Gorog, *Three Dreams and a Nightmare, and Other Tales of the Dark*, 1988
  Sixteen short stories of fantasy, the supernatural and the macabre.
Diana Wynne Jones, *Warlock at the Wheel and Other Stories*, 1984
  "Warlock at the Wheel," "The Plague of Peacocks," "The Fluffy Pink Toadstool," and others.
C.S. Lewis, *Boxen: The Imaginary World of the Young C.S. Lewis*, 1985

Maps, histories, sketches and stories created by C.S. Lewis as a child to describe his private fantasy world, known as Animal-Land or Boxen.

George MacDonald, *The Wise Woman and Other Stories*, 1980

"The Wise Woman, or The Lost Princess," "Little Daylight," "Cross Purposes," and "The Castle, a Parable."

1015

Richard Kennedy

Illustrator: Marcia Sewall

Song of the Horse (New York: Dutton, 1981)

Age range: Grades 4-5

Subject(s): Animals/Horses; Poetry

Major character(s): Spirit, Horse

Time period(s): Indeterminate

Locale(s): United States

What the book is about: A prose poem about a girl and her love for her horse, highlighted with dramatic black and white full page illustrations. The girl describes her feelings, and the sensations of grooming and riding her horse. For lovers of language and horses.

Where it's reviewed:
Booklist, January 15, 1982, page 649
Hornbook, April 1982, page 157
School Library Journal, March 1982, page 136

Other books by the author:
Delta Baby and Two Sea Songs, 1979
The Rise and Fall of Ben Gizzard, 1978
Oliver Hyde's Dishcloth Concert, 1977
Come Again in the Spring, 1976

Other books you might like:
Joanna Campbell, *A Horse of Her Own*, 1988
   A story about Penny's summer and the love of a horse.
Patricia Sayer Fusco, *Marina & Ruby: Training a Filly with Love*, 1977
   Pictures and text record a girl's raising her horse to maturity. Includes information on training and health care.
Patricia Hubbell, *A Grass Green Gallop: Poems*, 1990
   A collection of poems celebrating the beauty, motion and sounds of horses, from newborn foals, to thoroughbreds, to old cart horses.
Marianna Mayer, *The Black Horse*, 1984
   A poor Irish prince wins the love of the Princess of the Mountains after helping her to escape the wicked Sea King with the aid of a mysterious horse.
Sean O'Huigin, *The Ghost Horse of the Mountains*, 1991
   In this narrative poem, a storm overwhelms the Royal Canadian Mounties, scattering their horses in all directions.

1016

X.J. Kennedy

Illustrator: Michele-Chessare

The Owlstone Crown (New York: Atheneum, 1983)

Age range: Grades 5-8

Subject(s): Child Abuse; Fantasy; Orphans

Major character(s): Timothy Tibbs, Twin, Orphan; Verity Tibbs, Twin, Orphan; Lewis O. Ladybug, Detective

Time period(s): Indeterminate

Locale(s): Alternate Earth

What the book is about: Two orphans, cruelly treated by the Brimbels, escape to another world. Timothy and Verity are caught up in a struggle against a despicable tyrant and his wicked ally.

Where it's reviewed:
Booklist, March 1, 1984, page 992
Kirkus Reviews, November 1, 1983, page 78
School Library Journal, January 1984, page 78

Other books by the author:
The Beasts of Bethlehem, 1992
Knock at a Star, 1982
The Phantom Ice Cream Man, 1979
One Winter Night in August, 1975

Other books you might like:
John Bellaris, *The Mansion in the Mist*, 1992
   While spending the summer in an old house on a desolate island, Anthony and Miss Eells discover a chest that can transport them to another world.
Alexander Key, *The Magic Meadow*, 1975
   As five crippled children imagine themselves in another beautiful world, one of them finds he can help the rest escape to a strange new place.
Ruth Nichols, *The Marrow of the World*, 1972
   Philip and Linda, attempting to explore an ancient castle beneath the lake, become involved in another world.
Jacklyn O'Hanlon, *The Door*, 1978
   A girl passes through the mysterious door of the Master Gatherer and finds herself in the center of a struggle between Good and Evil.
Ramon Royal Ross, *Harper and Moon*, 1993
   Harper has always liked Moon, but their friendship is tested when Harper makes a discovery about his older friend when Moon joins the army in 1953.

1017

M.E. Kerr

Little Little (New York: Harper, 1981)

Age range: Grades 5 and Up

Subject(s): Minorities; Dwarves

Major character(s): Sydney Cinnamon, Dwarf, Teenager; Little Little La Belle, Dwarf, Teenager; Knox Lionel, Dwarf, Religious (Preacher)

Time period(s): Indeterminate

Locale(s): Earth

What the book is about: This story of relationships among three dwarves, explores the treatment of those who are different from the majority. Partly a love story, this book raises the reader's awareness of minorities.

Where it's reviewed:
Center for Children's Books Bulletin, April 1981, page 153
Horn Book, June 1981, page 309

Awards the book has won:
Golden Kite Award 1981

Other books by the author:
I Stay Near You, 1985
Gentlehands, 1978
I'll Love You When You Are More Like Me, 1977
Love Is a Missing Person, 1975

Other books you might like:
Audree Distad, *Dakota Sons*, 1972
  Tad learns the meaning of friendship when he feels the town's prejudice against his new friend.
Charlotte Herman, *The Difference of Ari Stein*, 1976
  After moving to Brooklyn, Ari decides he can meet new and different friends while keeping true to his own beliefs.
Barbara Murphy, *Home Free*, 1970
  During a summer in South Carolina, a boy from New York and his black friend learn first hand about the violence of prejudice.
Mildred D. Taylor, *Roll of Thunder, Hear My Cry*, 1976
  A black family in the 1930s American South is faced with prejudice and discrimination which the children cannot understand.
Yoshiko Uchida, *A Jar of Dreams*, 1981
  A young girl grows up in a Japanese-American family during the 1930s in California amid great prejudice.

1018

Illustrator: Leonard Kessler

Old Turtle's Soccer Team (New York: Greenwillow, 1988)

Age range: Grades 1-2

Subject(s): Sports/Soccer; Animals/Turtles

Major character(s): Old Turtle, Coach, Turtle; Big Raccoon, Sports Figure (soccer player), Raccoon

Locale(s): United States

What the book is about: Old Turtle's team gets in shape to face the Big Raccoon Rockets. They kick, dribble, run and pass. They practice and practice. Together, under Old Turtle's guidance, the animals learn how to play soccer and learn the meaning of good sportsmanship.

Where it's reviewed:
School Library Journal, October 1988, page 123
Booklist, December 1, 1988, page 656
Center for Children's Books Bulletin, October 1988, page 42

Other books by the author:
The Sweeneys From 9D, 1985
Old Turtle's Baseball Stories, 1982
Pig's New Hat, 1981
Here Comes the Strikeout, 1965

Other books you might like:
Harry Allard, *Miss Nelson Has a Field Day*, 1985
  The notorious Miss Swamp reappears at the Smedley School, this time to shape up the football team and help them win at least one game.
Peter Catalanotto, *Dylan's Day Out*, 1989
  Dylan, a dalmation, escapes from home and becomes involved in a soccer game between the penguins and the skunks.
Alexandra Day, *Frank and Ernest Play Ball*, 1990

An elephant and a bear take over the management of a baseball team for one night and learn about cooperation, responsibility and baseball.
Sue Stops, *Dulcie Dando, Soccer Star*, 1992
  Dulcie, a talented soccer player, proves that girls can play as well as boys when given a chance.
Amanda Vesey, *Hector's New Sneakers*, 1993
  All Hector wants for his birthday is a pair of sneakers like everyone else, with go-fast stripes, black and blue trim, and soccer ball logo.on the sid

---

1019

Dayal Kaur Khalsa

How Pizza Came to Queens (New York: Potter: Tundra Books, 1989)

Age range: Grades 1-2

Subject(s): Italian Americans; Emigration and Immigration

Major character(s): Mrs. Pelligrino, Immigrant

Time period(s): 1950s (1950)

Locale(s): New York, New York (Queens)

What the book is about: When Mrs. Pelligrino visits relatives in New York, all they know of Italian language and cuisine is "spaghetti, macaroni and lasagna." Even though she speaks little English, the children try to cheer her up by finding the ingredients she needs to make pizza for them for the very first time.

Where it's reviewed:
Booklist, April 1, 1989, page 1386
School Library Journal, May 1989, page 86

Other books by the author:
Cowboy Dreams, 1990
Julian, 1989
I Want a Dog, 1987
Tales of a Gambling Grandma, 1986

Other books you might like:
Bill Basso, *The Top of the Pizzas*, 1977
  An ugly pizza maker loses his job because of his looks but finally finds work making pizzas on the roof of an old skyscraper.
Michelle Dionetti, *Coal Mine Peaches*, 1991
  Beginning with her grandfather's boyhood in Italy, a young girl describes his arrival in U.S. and his experiences in the Italian-American community.
Maryann Kovalski, *Pizza for Breakfast*, 1991
  Frank and Zelda learn the folly of making wishes when they ask for more customers at their pizza restaurant.
Lisa Passen, *Uncle's New Suit: A Sort of True Story*, 1992
  When Uncle Carmen gets a new job, a close-knit Italian family celebrates by taking him shopping for a new suit.
Harriet Langsam Sobol, *Cosmo's Restaurant*, 1978
  Follows a family through a typical day's activities running their small Italian restaurant in New York City.

1020

Dayal Kaur Khalsa, Author/Illustrator

Tales of a Gambling Grandmother (New York: Potter, 1986)

Age range: Grades 2-4

Subject(s): Gambling; Grandparents; Emigration and Immigration

Time period(s): 1980s

Locale(s): United States

What the book is about: A picture of the warm relationship of a Russian immigrant and her granddaughter. Grandma tells her grandaughter of her training by a card shark, which she put to good use earning money for the family. Excellent portrait of a strong, independent, loving woman.

Where it's reviewed:
Center for Children's Books Bulletin, November 1986, page 52
School Library Journal, October 1986, page 162

Other books by the author:
Cowboy Dreams, 1990
How Pizza Came to Queens, 1989
My Family Vacation, 1988
I Want a Dog, 1987

Other books you might like:
Brett Harvey, *Immigrant Girl: Becky of Eldridge Street*, 1987
    Becky, whose family has emigrated from Russia to avoid being persecuted as Jews, finds growing up in New York City a vivid and exciting experiment.
Stephen Mooser, *The Hitchhiking Vampire*, 1989
    En route to join their mother, Jamie and her brother pick up a hitchhiker and soon find themselves helping to place a $12,000 bet in Las Vegas.
Marietta D. Moskin, *Waiting for Mama*, 1975
    A Russian immigrant family living in New York in the early 1900s prepares for the long awaited arrival of their mother and baby sister.
George Panetta, *The Shoeshine Boys*, 1971
    When his father loses his job to automation, Tony decides to help support the family by becoming a shoeshine boy.
Pat Ross, *Hannah's Fancy Notions*, 1988
    When Hannah sets out to make something for her sister who works to support the family, she doesn't suspect the far-reaching consequences of her gift.

1021

David Kherdian

Illustrator: Paul Geiger

The Mystery of the Diamond in the Wood (New York: Knopf, 1983)

Age range: Grades 5-7

Subject(s): Robbers and Outlaws; Hermits; Mystery and Detective Stories

Major character(s): Sam Svoboda, Preteen; Howie Baker, Preteen; Trapper Jack, Recluse

Time period(s): 1940s (1943)

Locale(s): LaSalle, Wisconsin

What the book is about: Two boys find a stash of diamond rings in a hollow tree in Taylor's Woods. Laughed at by the police, they decide to capture the thief themselves.

Where it's reviewed:
Booklist, October 1, 1983, page 297
Center for Children's Books Bullein, January 1984, page 90
School Library Journal, December 1983, apge 83

Other books by the author:
Juna's Journey, 1993
Beyond Two Rivers, 1981
It Started with Old Man Bean, 1980
The Road From Home: The Story of an Armenian Girl, 1979

Other books you might like:
Ida Chittum, *The Hermit Boy*, 1972
    During their summer vacation in the Ozarks, two girls befriend a mysterious boy who lives alone in the woods.
Nancy Garden, *The Door Between*, 1987
    Melissa's father plans a housing development in woods considered sacred by a mysterious hermit. She must find a way to pacify the angry hermit.
Virginia Masterman-Smith, *The Great Egyptian Heist*, 1982
    Angel Wilson and her two friends find a cache of diamonds in an Egyptian coffin.
Margaret Sutton, *The Spirit of Fog Island*, 1976
    The receipt of a confusing message, signed "Your Husband," sends Judy off to an Indian reservation in northern Wisconsin.
Carolyn Keene, *The Message in the Hollow Oak*, 1972
    Nancy tackles a mystery professional detectives have failed to solve, finding a valuable centuries-old message in a hollow oak tree in Illinois.

1022

David Kherdian

The Road From Home: The Story of an Armenian Girl (New York: Greenwillow, 1979)

Age range: Grades 5 and Up

Subject(s): Biography

Major character(s): Vernon Dumehjian, Refugee (Armenian); Yeghsa Dumehjian, Refugee (Armenian), Child; Apkar Dumehjian, Refugee (Armenian), Child

Time period(s): 20th century

Locale(s): Turkey

What the book is about: Vernon moves from family to orphanage to refugee camp. The love of her father, grandmother and aunt sustain her. They survive fires, bombs, disease and starvation fleeing from Turkey to Syria and eventually coming to the US.

Where it's reviewed:
Horn Book, June 1979, page 318
Kirkus Reviews, June 1, 1979, page 644

Awards the book has won:
Boston Globe/Horn Book Award - Non-Fiction 1979

Other books by the author:
A Song for Uncle Harry, 1989
The Mystery of the Diamond in the Wood, 1983
Beyond Two Rivers, 1981
I Sing the Song of Myself, 1978

Other books you might like:
Arra S. Avakian, *The Armenians in America*, 1977
 Discusses the history of the Armenian people and the contributions made by Armenian immigrants and their descendents to U.S. history and culture.
Kerop Bedoukian, *Some of Us Survived*, 1978
 The story of an Armenian boy and his survival of the Armenian massacres in Turkey.
Gaye Hicyilmaz, *Against the Storm*, 1992
 Mehmet moves from his Turkish village with flowers everywhere to a shantytown in the city of Ankara and finds almost unbearable misery.
Norma Johnston, *The Delphic Choice*, 1989
 Visiting relatives in Turkey, Meredith is involved in efforts to free her uncle, a hostage negotiator for a peace mission, who is now a hostage, too.
Barbara K. Walker, *A Treasury of Turkish Folktales*, 1988
 Thirty-four Turkish folktales about jinns and giants, padishahs and peasants, and beloved heroes such a Keloglan, the bald boy.

1023

Diana Kidd

Illustrator: Lucy Montgomery

Onion Tears (New York: Orchard, 1991)

Age range: Grades 3-5

Subject(s): Foster Homes; Vietnamese; Grief

Major character(s): Nam-Huong, Child; Chu Minh, Cook; Auntie, Relative (aunt)

Time period(s): 1980s

Locale(s): Australia

What the book is about: A story of the resilience of the human spirit. A young Vietnamese girl tries to adjust to her new life in Australia where she lives with a kind Vietnamese woman after the loss of her family. Children at school tease her at first because she is different, but when they do try to make friends, Nam is too sad and lonely to notice. She gradually comes out of her shell and learns, with help, to deal with her grief and enjoy her friends.

Where it's reviewed:
Horn Book, May/June 1991, page 330
School Library Journal, June 1991, page 108

Other books you might like:
Jack Bennett, *The Voyage of the Lucky Dragon*, 1981
 A young Vietnamese boy and his family travel to Indonesia, Singapore, and finally Australia to find safety.
Tricia Brown, *Lee Ann: The Story of a Vietnamese-American Girl*, 1991
 A young Vietnamese-American girl describes her life at school and at home, and the family's celebration of Tet, the Vietnamese New Year.
Ann M. Martin, *Yours Truly, Shirley*, 1988
 Shirley, a fourth grader with dyslexia, feels inferior to her gifted older brother and newly adopted Vietnamese sister.
Lynette Dyer Vuong, *The Brocaded Slipper*, 1992
 Five Vietnamese fairy tales including "Little Finger of the Watermelon Patch," and "The Lampstand Princess."
Gloria Whelan, *Goodbye, Vietnam*, 1992

Thirteen year old Mai and her family embark on a dangerous sea voyage from Vietnam to Hong Kong to escape the brutal Vietnamese government.

1024

Christi Killien

Rusty Fertlanger, Lady's Man (Boston: Houghton Mifflin, 1988)

Age range: Grades 5-7

Subject(s): Artists and Art; Sexism; Sports/Wrestling

Major character(s): Rusty Ferlanger, Artist (cartoonist), Teenager; Carlin, Friend; Sue Hines, Sports Figure (wrestler)

Time period(s): 1980s

Locale(s): Seattle, Washington

What the book is about: Rusty, an unathletic daydreaming artist who is only on his high school's wrestling team because he needs the physical education credit, faces the ultimate "humiliation" when he is scheduled to wrestle a girl in a public match.

Where it's reviewed:
Booklist, May 15, 1988, page 1610
Hornbook, September 1988, page 633
School Library Journal, March 1988, page 192

Other books by the author:
The Daffodils, 1992
Fickle Fever, 1988
All of the Above, 1987
Putting on an Act, 1986

Other books you might like:
Matt Christopher, *Takedown*, 1990
 As he is helped by a referee to prepare for a wrestling match with a bully, Sean begins to wonder if his mentor could be his long lost father.
Scott Corbett, *The Hockey Girls*, 1976
 The new compulsory sports program throws the freshman girls at Wagstaff High into a fury, until they get involved.
Brent Filson, *The Puma*, 1979
 After he is thrown off the team, Sonny seeks to regain his position as star wrestler, and to close the distance between his father and himself.
Jerry Spinelli, *There's a Girl in my Hammerlock*, 1991
 Maisie joins her school's formerly all male wrestling team despite opposition from other students, her best friend, and her own teammates.
William Jon Watkins, *A Fair Advantage*, 1975
 A hospitalized high school wrestler reconstructs moments from his wrestling past to find why he has been injured.

1025

Eric A. Kimmel

Illustrator: Glen Rounds

Charlie Drives the Stage (New York: Holiday, 1989)

Age range: Grades 2-4

Subject(s): Sex Roles; American West

Major character(s): Roscoe McCorkle, Political Figure (senator); Charlie Drummond, Teenager, Driver (stagecoach driver)

Time period(s): 19th century

What the book is about: In the old West, Senator McCorkle announces on Tuesday that he must be in Washington by Friday. Charles has to drive him to the train station in La Grande, past avalanches in the pass, road agents on the road and Indians on the warpath. On top of all this, the river is rising and the bridge is out.

Where it's reviewed:
Publisher's Weekly, May 12, 1989, page 292
School Library Journal, June 1989, page 89

Other books by the author:
Anansi Goes Fishing, 1992
Boots and His Brothers, 1992
Four Gallant Sisters, 1992
Baba Yaga: A Russian Folktale, 1991

Other books you might like:
Jan Gletier, Annie Oakley, 1985
 The life of the frontier woman who was famous for her skills as a sharpshooter which she demonstrated in Buffalo Bill's Wild West Show.
A.I. Lake, The Pony Express, 1990
 Describes the history of the Pony Express and the daring riders who risked their lives to deliver the mail.
A.I. Lake, Women of the West, 1990
 Describes the work of the early woman homesteaders and presents brief biographies of several women prominent in Western history.
Angela Shelf Medearis, The Zebra-Riding Cowboy: A Folk Song From the Old West, 1992
 In this western folk song, an educated fellow mistaken for a greenhorn proves his cowboy ability by riding a wild horse.
Robert M. Quackenbush, She'll be Coming' 'Round the Mountain, 1973
 An illustrated interpretation of the familiar song done in the form of a Wild West show which could be performed.

1026

Eric A. Kimmel

Illustrator: Trina S. Hyman

Hershel and the Hanukkah Goblins (New York: Holiday House, 1989)

Age range: Grades 3-4

Subject(s): Holidays; Demons; Jews

Major character(s): Hershel, Child

Time period(s): 1980s

Locale(s): United States

What the book is about: Hershel agrees to spend all eight nights of Hanukkah in a haunted synagogue to rid the village of goblins. He deals with seven of the goblins rather easily. On the eighth night he has to deal with the King of Goblins.

Where it's reviewed:
Horn Book, January 1990, page 52
New York Times Book Review, December 17, 1989, page 29

Other books by the author:
The Chanukkah Guest, 1990
I Took My Frog to the Library, 1990
Charlie Drives the Stage, 1989
Anansi and the Moss-Covered Rock, 1988

Other books you might like:
Malka Drucker, Grandma's Latkes, 1992
 Grandma explains the meaning of Hanukkah while showing Molly how to cook latkes for the holiday.
Bobbi Katz, A Family Hanukkah, 1992
 Rachel and Jonathan join their aunts, uncles and cousins at their grandparents' house for a traditional Hanukkah celebration.
Sandy Lanton, Daddy's Chair, 1991
 When Michael's father dies, the family sits shiva, observing the Jewish week of mourning, and remembers the good things about him.
Shulamith Oppenheim, The Lily Cupboard, 1992
 Miriam, a young Jewish girl, is forced to leave her parents and hide with strangers during the German occupation of Holland.
Gloria Pushker, Toby Belfer Never Had a Christmas Tree, 1991
 Toby's is the only Jewish family in a small Louisiana town, so she gives a party for her friends to explain Hanukkah customs.

1027

Clive King

Me and My Million (New York: Kestral, 1976)

Age range: Grades 6-9

Subject(s): Crime and Criminals

Major character(s): Ringo, Preteen; Elvis, Teenager

Time period(s): 1970s

Locale(s): London, England

What the book is about: Ringo's brother, Elvis, asks him to do a small job, a cinch, really. Take a laundry bag and leave it at the end of the #41 bus route. Suddenly Ringo finds himself in possession of a stolen painting worth a million pounds. Lost, broke, and unable to read even simple signs, scared witless by Angel Jim, Ringo's troubles are just beginning.

Where it's reviewed:
Kirkus Reviews, November 1, 1979, page 1267
School Library Journal, October 1979, page 151

Awards the book has won:
Guardian Award Runner Up 1976
Boston Globe/Horn Book Award - Honor Book 1980

Other books by the author:
Ninny's Boat, 1980
The Devil's Cut, 1979
The Night the Water Came, 1973
The Town That Went South, 1959

Other books you might like:
Charles Dickens, Charles Dickens' Oliver Twist, 1968
 An adaptation of Dicken's story of the orphan forced to practice thievery and live a life of crime in 19th century London.
Ivan Kusan, The Mystery of the Stolen Painting, 1975

Two Yugoslav boys visiting Paris become involved with the theft of the Mona Lisa.

Louise Lawrence, *The Dram Road*, 1983
Ghosts on a historic rural road bring together a desperate young London punk running from a crime and a stubborn old man.

Sir Compton Mackenzie, *The Stairs That Kept Going Down*, 1973
In the London house his family occupies, a ten year old boy discovers a secret, seemingly endless, staircase that leads him to the scene of a crime.

Robert Newman, *The Case of the Vanishing Corpse*, 1980
When Andrew returns to London from boarding school, he becomes embroiled in several mysteries.

1028

Clive King

The Night the Water Came (New York: Harper, 1982)

Age range: Grades 5-7

Subject(s): Weather; Rescue Work

Major character(s): Apu, Survivor; Ahmed, Relative (uncle)

Time period(s): 1980s

Locale(s): Kukuri Mukuri Char, Bangladesh (an island off the coast of Bangladesh)

What the book is about: Apu is eleven years old when a cyclone destroys his island home, leaving him the only one alive. He is well able to survive, for he has always taken care of himself and fresh water and roots to eat are still abundant. When a helicopter spots him and strange soldiers "rescue" him, the resulting journey is even more terrifying to Apu than the cyclone was.

Where it's reviewed:
Booklist, July 1982, page 1445
Hornbook, June 1982, page 288
Kirkus, April 1, 1982, page 418

Other books by the author:
Ninny's Boat, 1981
The Town That Went South, 1959
Hamid of Aleppo, 1958

Other books you might like:
Allan Baillie, *Little Brother*, 1992
In Cambodia after the war, Vithy learns to overcome social upheaval, a hostile jungle and his inability to trust in order to rescue his older brother.

Arthur Catherall, *Jungle Rescue*, 1968
Following a series of mishaps, a bridge-repairing crew abandons camp, leaving a young Hindu boy to rescue the injured engineer from the deadly jungle.

Ruth Hallman, *Rescue Chopper*, 1980
Eleven episodes, featuring a Coast Guard search and rescue team which, despite internal rivalry, manages to effect dangerous helicopter rescues.

Lensey Namioka, *The Coming of the Bear*, 1992
Two unemployed Samurai are saved from drowning by the Ainus, a primitive people on a northern Japanese island.

Walter G. Oleksy, *Nature Gone Wild*, 1982
Describes notable tornado, cyclone, flood, hurricane, fire and volcano disasters of recent times. (Non-fiction)

1029

Dick King-Smith

Illustrator: Lynette Hemmant

Ace, the Very Important Pig (New York: Crown, 1990)

Age range: Grades 3-5

Subject(s): Animals/Pigs

Major character(s): Ace, Pig

Time period(s): 1990s

Locale(s): United States

What the book is about: An intelligent, loveable pig becomes a VIP when he gains nationwide fame. He is helped by a clever house cat and hindered by a Corgi with an attitude. Ace remains happy with his simple existence.

Where it's reviewed:
Horn Book, September 1990, page 602
School Library Journal, December 1990, page 23

Other books by the author:
Pretty Polly, 1992
Sophia's Snail, 1989
The Fox Busters, 1988
Babe: The Gallant Pig, 1985

Other books you might like:
Nina Bawden, *The Peppermint Pig*, 1975
Polly finds it hard to cope with changes in the family until she acquires a special pet pig.

Michael Bond, *Olga Takes Charge*, 1982
Olga, a guinea pig, attempts to save the Sawdust family from the effects of drought and takes up jogging.

John Jiler, *Wild Berry Moon*, 1982
A pig escapes into the forest to give birth and plots with a snake to save her piglets from the farmer.

Mary Stolz, *Quentin Corn*, 1985
Realizing his fate is to be spareribs, a pig disguises himself as a boy, runs away, and gets a job.

Will Watkins, *Sid Seal, Houseman*, 1989
A young pig in a wealthy family finds his life changed when a seal comes to work in his home.

1030

Dick King-Smith

Illustrator: Mary Rayner

Babe: The Gallant Pig (New York: Crown, 1983)

Age range: Grades 5-6

Subject(s): Animals/Pigs; Farm Life

Major character(s): Hogget, Farmer; Babe, Pig

Time period(s): 1980s

Locale(s): United States

What the book is about: A pig destined for eventual butchering arrives at the farmyard, is adopted by an old sheep dog, Fly, and discovers a special secret to success. He becomes a sheep-herding pig and saves the herd from rustlers.

Where it's reviewed:
Horn Book, July 1985, page 449
School Library Journal, August 1985, page 66

Other books by the author:
Paddy's Pot of Gold, 1992
Martin's Mice, 1989
The Mouse Butcher, 1982
Pigs Might Fly: A Novel, 1982

Other books you might like:
Mary Blount Christian, *Goody Sherman's Pig*, 1991
  Goody Sherman begins a legal battle over her pig that ends up dividing the legislative department of the colony into two independent branches.
Caroline Fairless, *Hambone*, 1980
  Jeremy's memorial to Hambone, his pet pig, is a big success because of the love given to it.
Zibby Oneal, *The Improbable Adventures of Marvelous O'Hara Soapstone*, 1972
  The Soapstone family finds it very difficult to cope with their pig when she falls in love with the cement dolphin in the park pond.
Cathy Stefanec-Ogren, *Sly, P.I.: The Case of the Missing Shoes*, 1989
  When ballet star Lotta Oink's toe shoes disappear on opening night, self-made fox and old friend, Sly, P.I., solves the case.
E.B. White, *Charlotte's Web*, 1952
  Classic story of Wilbur, the pig, and Charlotte, the spider, who saved him from becoming bacon and pork chops.

1031

Dick King-Smith

Illustrator: Jon Miller

The Fox Busters (New York: Delacorte, 1978)

Age range: Grades 4-6

Subject(s): Animals/Birds; Animals/Foxes

Time period(s): Indeterminate

Locale(s): Fictional Country (Foxearth Farm)

What the book is about: While four foxes plan and train for the ultimate chicken raid at Foxearth Farm, the "fox busters," (three chicks who have fully developed flight feathers and unusual ariel abilities) condition themselves to end forever the plague of foxes on the farm. A Chaunticleerian sage with a feminist twist.

Where it's reviewed:
Junior Bookshelf, December 1978, page 301
School Librarian, March 1979, page 39
Times Literary Supplement, July 7, 1978, page 770

Other books by the author:
Ace, the Very Important Pig, 1990
Harry's Mad, 1987
The Elephant's Child, 1985
Pigs Might Fly: A Novel, 1982

Other books you might like:
Margaret Jean Anderson, *The Brain on Quartz Mountain*, 1982
  Dave's role in Professor Botti's experiment on a chicken's brain helps him compete for a trip to the World Series.
Stephen Manes, *Some of the Adventures of Rhode Island Red*, 1990

A diminutive red-haired man no bigger than a hen's egg, leaves his home and travels, becoming a legendary figure through his many heroic exploits.
Daniel Manus Pinkwater, *The Hoboken Chicken Emergency*, 1977
  Arthur goes to pick up the turkey for Thanksgiving but comes back with a 260 pound chicken.
Angela Sommer-Bodenburg, *The Vampire on the Farm*, 1985
  Tony and his friend, Rudolph, the vampire, get into trouble when the farmer's wife discovers that someone has been sucking all the chickens' eggs dry.
Jill Tomlinson, *Hilda the Hen Who Wouldn't Give Up*, 1980
  Despite the objection of her keeper, a small, brown speckled hen decides to raise a family of chicks.

1032

Dick King-Smith

Illustrator: Jill Bennett

Harry's Mad (New York: Crown, 1987)

Age range: Grades 4-6

Subject(s): Humor; Animals/Birds

Major character(s): Harry Holdsworth, Preteen; Madison, Parrot

Time period(s): 1980s

Locale(s): London, England

What the book is about: Ten year old Harry receives a gift from an American uncle who is a linguistics professor - a parrot who can chat just like a human being, plays checkers with Harry, helps Dad with crossword puzzles, and even has new recipes for Mom. All goes well, and hilariously, until Madison is parrot-napped and Dad purchases a lame, lisping replacement. The pace is quick and the action fun. Read this aloud if you can lisp well.

Where it's reviewed:
Horn Book, July/August, 1987, page 463
School Library Journal, May 1987, page 101

Other books by the author:
Pretty Polly, 1992
The Fox Busters, 1988
Babe: The Gallant Pig, 1983

Other books you might like:
Larry Callen, *Who Kidnapped the Sheriff?*, 1985
  Pat O'Leary and his friend, Violet, get involved in the sheriff's kidnapping and other wild events one summer in the town of Tickfaw.
Peni R. Griffin, *The Treasure Bird*, 1992
  With clues from a talking parrot, Jessy and her stepbrother, Matt discover the whereabouts hidden treasure in Uncle Matthew's old house in Texas.
Victor Osborne, *Moondream*, 1988
  When his cousin, Katy, is kidnapped by a Grabbly, Rupert enlists the aid of flying pirates and a kindly badger to rescue her from Castle Dread.
Mary Robinson, *The Amazing Valvano and the Mystery of the Hooded Rat*, 1988
  Maria is excited about her plans to perform a magic act in the school talent show until her rat, part of the show, is kidnapped.

Phyllis Anderson Wood, *A Five-Color Buick and a Blue-Eyed Cat*, 1975

Fainting canaries, an x-rated parrot, and a neurotic cat become part of the job when two friends use an old Buick to pick up and deliver pets.

1033

Dick King-Smith

Illustrator: Mary Rayner

Pigs Might Fly: A Novel (New York: Viking, 1982)

Age range: Grades 3-6

Subject(s): Farm Life; Physically Handicapped; Animals/Pigs

Major character(s): Daggie Dogfoot, Pig; Mrs. Barleylove, Pig (Daggie's mother); Felicity, Duck

Time period(s): Indeterminate

Locale(s): England

What the book is about: In Gloustershire, the runt of a litter of pigs is called a "dag," so Mrs. Barleylove's runt with puppy-like feet is called Daggie Dogfoot. The Pigman plans to remove him from the litter but is distracted by rats, and Daggie not only survives, but makes his way back to his mother and thrives. When Felicity the duck tries to teach Daggie to fly, he plunges instead into the water and learns that he can swim. That ability is destined to make him a hero.

Where it's reviewed:
Booklist, June 15, 1982, page 1368
Kirkus Reviews, April 1, 1982, page 605
School Library Journal, August 1982, page 99

Other books by the author:
Lady Daisy, 1993
Ace, the Very Important Pig, 1990
The Fox Busters, 1988
Babe: The Gallant Pig, 1985

Other books you might like:
John Jiler, *Wild Berry Moon*, 1982
A pig escapes into the forest to give birth, and with the help of a snake, saves her piglets from the fate the farmer had planned.
Zibby O'Neal, *The Improbable Adventures of Marvelous O'Hara Soapstone*, 1972
The Soapstone family finds it difficult to cope when their pig falls in love with a cement dolphin in the lily pond.
Mary Stolz, *Quentin Corn*, 1985
Realizing his fate is to become spareribs, a pig disguises himself as a boy, runs away, gets a job and becomes friends with a little girl.
Will Watkins, *Sid Seal, Houseman*, 1989
Waltham de Swine, a young pig in a rather wealthy family, finds his life enriched by a seal who comes to work in his home.
E.B. White, *Charlotte's Web*, 1952
Wilbur the pig is desolate when he realizes his likely fate, but he is both cheered and saved by a loving spider named Charlotte.

1034

Lee Kingman

The Luck of the Miss L. (Boston: Houghton Mifflin, 1986)

Age range: Grades 5-7

Subject(s): Boats and Boating; Sports; Self-Confidence

Major character(s): Alec, Preteen, Sports Figure (rower); Stomper, Preteen, Sports Figure (rower)

Time period(s): 1980s

Locale(s): United States (small seacoast town)

What the book is about: Alec faces obstacles at every turn as he practices rowing for the Junior Rower's Race. After a near drowning, he faces a crisis of confidence and the warm three generation extended family support he receives enables him to keep going and keep training for the race. Readers who compete in any sport will sympathize with Alec's desire to beat his rival, Stomper.

Where it's reviewed:
Center for Children's Books Bulletin, September 1986, page 11
School Library Journal, August 1986, page 94

Other books by the author:
Head over Wheels, 1978
Break a Leg Betsy, Maybe, 1976
Peter Pan Bag, 1970
Year of the Raccoon, 1966

Other books you might like:
Betsy Byars, *Goodbye, Chicken Little*, 1979
A boy discovers that he doesn't have to feel personally responsible for his uncle's drowning.
Arthur Catherall, *Kidnapped by Accident*, 1969
While rowing to their Baltic Island home, a fourteen year old boy and his sister collide with a yacht and begin a hectic three day adventure.
M.S. Craig, *The Mystery at Wolf River*, 1989
Kate and her best friend, Bugs, solve a mystery involving a drowning dog and a mansion.
R. Rozanne Knudson, *Rinehart Shouts*, 1987
A timid boy spends his summer bird watching, writing to friend, and competing with his grandmother and chauffeur in a Washington, D.C. boat race.
William R. Koehler, *A Dog Called Lucky Tide*, 1988
With the help of a big dog he has rescued from drowning, sixteen year old Tim attempts to clear logs from his family land.

1035

Natalie Kinsey-Warnock

Illustrator: Leslie Bowman

The Canada Geese Quilt (New York: Cobblehill Books/ Dutton, 1989)

Age range: Grades 3-6

Subject(s): Farm Life; Quilts; Grandparents

Major character(s): Ariel, Preteen

Time period(s): 1940s

Locale(s): Miles Hill, Vermont

What the book is about: Worried that the coming of a new baby and her grandmother's serious illness will change the warm, familiar life on her family's Vermont farm, ten year old Ariel combines her artistic talent with her grandmother's knowledge to make a very special quilt. Ariel's relationship with her grandmother and the effect of grandmother's illness on Ariel are finely drawn.

Where it's reviewed:
Booklist, October 1, 1989, page 352
Kirkus Reviews, August 1, 1989, page 1159

Other books by the author:
Wilderness Cat, 1992
The Night the Bells Rang, 1991
Wild Horses of Sweetbriar, 1990

Other books you might like:
Kathy Lynn Emerson, *Julia's Mending*, 1987
   In 1887, Julia is sent to a farm in upstate New York where she breaks her leg. While it mends she learns to love and heal her anger.
Kristi Holl, *Just Like a Real Family*, 1983
   June's foster grandfather is an old crab who doesn't like children in general, and June in particular.
Ellen Howard, *Sister*, 1990
   Alena, the oldest in a large family, longs for an education but the realities of caring for the family add burdensome responsibilities.
Gary Paulsen, *The Foxman*, 1977
   A town boy sent to live on a remote wilderness farm forms a friendship with an elderly, disfigured man who teaches him many things.
Susan Sharpe, *Chicken Bucks*, 1992
   When hard times force Mark to change his 4-H project, he finds the experience both challenging and rewarding.

1036

Natalie Kinsey-Warnock

Illustrator: Ted Rand

The Wild Horses of Sweetbriar (New York: Dutton, 1990)

Age range: Grades 2-3

Subject(s): Animals/Horses; Islands

Time period(s): 1900s (1903)

Locale(s): Nantucket, Massachusetts (Sweetbriar Island)

What the book is about: A Coast Guard family share a lonely island with a band of wild horses. The horses and family alike enjoy the summer and fall, and struggle to survive the harsh winter with determination and hope.

Where it's reviewed:
Booklist, November 1, 1990, page 528
School Library Journal, December 1990, page 82

Other books by the author:
Wilderness Cat, 1992
The Night the Bells Rang, 1991
The Canada Geese Quilt, 1989

Other books you might like:
Walter Farley, *The Black Stallion*, 1986
   Young Alec Ramsay is shipwrecked on a desert island with a horse destined to play an important part in his life.

Donna Grosvenor, *The Wild Ponies of Assateague Island*, 1975
   Text and photos describe the lives of the wild ponies of Assateague, including the annual pony penning on nearby Chincoteague Island.
Ann Burnett Malcolmson, *Captain Ichabod Paddock, Whaler of Nantucket*, 1970
   Bewitched by a mermaid, Captain Ichabod forgets his vow not to return home before killing Crooked Jaw, the whale he has pursued for ten years.
Charles E. Martin, *Island Winter*, 1984
   Staying behind on the island after the summer people have left, Heather wonders what there will be to do.
Brinton Turkle, *Rachel and Obadiah*, 1978
   Both Rachel and Obadiah want to earn some money by carrying the news of the next ship's arrival to Nantucket.

1037

Jim Kjelgaard

Big Red (New York: Holiday, 1945)

Age range: Grades 5-9

Subject(s): Animals/Dogs; Outdoor Life

Major character(s): Danny, Trapper; Big Red, Dog (Irish Setter); Robert Fraley, Rancher

Time period(s): 1940s

Locale(s): United States (Wintapi Wilderness, 300 miles from New York City)

What the book is about: There is no way Danny can afford to buy the champion Irish Setter from Mr. Haggin, but Haggin sees the love the boy has for the dog and entrusts the dog's care to Danny. Boy and dog roam the Wintapi wilderness, feud with the huge bear, Old Majesty, and battle a wolverine in the high peaks of the wilderness. Danny also learns how to show Champion Sylvester's Boy (Red's real name) and how to care for him on the show circuit.

Where it's reviewed:
Growing Point, November 1980, page 3775
Kliatt, Winter 1977, page 5

Other books by the author:
Wild Trek, 1981
Coyote Song, 1969
Boomerang Hunter, 1960
Buckskin Bridge, 1947

Other books you might like:
Kristiana Gregory, *Jenny of the Tetons*, 1989
   Orphaned by an Indian raid while traveling West with a wagon train, Carrie is befriended by the English trapper, Beaver Dick.
Judith St. George, *In the Shadow of the Bear*, 1983
   Annie's week in Alaska at her father's company's camp stretches her mental and physical limits as she must deal with hostile Russians.
Bill Wallace, *Red Dog*, 1987
   Living with his family in the rugged, often dangerous, mountains, Adam finds his courage put to the test when he is left in charge of the household.
Robert McClung, *Hugh Glass, Mountain Man*, 1990

A fictionalized biography of the legendary hero of the Old West, who as a fur trapper in 1823, survived an attack by a grizzly bear.

Alice Putnam, *Westering*, 1990
Traveling with his family in a wagon train from Missouri to Oregon in 1850, Jason finds a stray dog that proves useful during the dangerous journey.

1038

Monica Klein

Illustrator: Nola Langner

The Backyard Basketball Superstar (New York: Knopf, 1981)

Age range: Grades 1-3

Subject(s): Sports/Basketball; Brothers and Sisters

Major character(s): Jeremy, Child, Sports Figure (basketball player)

Time period(s): 1980s

Locale(s): United States

What the book is about: Jeremy is upset when his sister tries out for his basketball team. Even though he wants to select the best player, he wishes it hadn't turned out to be his sister.

Where it's reviewed:
Booklist, December 15, 1981, page 553
Center for Children's Books Bulletin, November 1981, page 48
Kirkus Reviews, November 1, 1981, page 1343

Other books you might like:
Debbie Dadey, *Leprechauns Don't Play Basketball*, 1992
There's a mystery going on between the new basketball coach and the third-grade teacher, Mrs. Jeepers.
Dean Marney, *Dirty Socks Don't Win Games*, 1992
Brent and his friends are persuaded to play basketball against a girls' team which has a real coach, a real offense, and a pizza place as a sponser.
Elizabeth Van Steenwyk, *Terror on the Rebound*, 1983
After their van is wrecked during a snowstorm, the members of a girls's basketball team take refuge in an isolated house that holds many secrets.
Joel Vecere, *A Story about Courage*, 1992
Jarrod, a new student who's confined to a wheelchair, tries out for the school basketball team.
Charlotte Zolotow, *William's Doll*, 1972
William's father gives him a basketball and a train but these do not make him want a doll less.

1039

Norma Klein

Illustrator: Richard Cuffari

Confessions of an Only Child (New York: Pantheon, 1974)

Age range: Grades 4-7

Subject(s): Family Problems; Death

Major character(s): Antonia "Toe", Child

Time period(s): 1970s

Locale(s): United States

What the book is about: The idea that mom is expecting a baby is less than thrilling to eight year old Antonia. When her brother is born prematurely and dies, she is surprised at her own sense of loss. Another brother is born the next year and Toe and her classmates have a great discussion about birth.

Where it's reviewed:
Center for Children's Books Bulletin, June 1974, p 159
Kirkus Reviews, February 1, 1974, page 110

Other books by the author:
Give Me One Good Reason, 1974
Naomi in the Middle, 1974
It's Not What You Expect, 1973
Mom, the Wolf Man and Me, 1972

Other books you might like:
Chas Carner, *Tawny*, 1978
Trey, adjusting to the death of his twin brother, adopts and cares for an injured dove.
Patricia Hermes, *Nobody's Fault*, 1981
Emily likes to play baseball and tease her brother, but her happy life is interrupted when her brother has a fatal accident.
Elizabeth Laird, *Loving Ben*, 1989
Anna's teen years bring maturity as she experiences the birth and death of a loving hydrocephalic brother and works with a child with Down's syndrome.
Gloria McLendon, *My Brother Joey Died*, 1982
A child goes through the difficult process of adjusting to the sudden illness and death of a brother.
Ann Rinaldi, *Term Paper*, 1980
Nick's teacher-brother assigns her a term paper on the topic of death in their family, in hopes that she will release supressed emotion about it.

1040

Robin Klein

Illustrator: Noela Young

Enemies (New York: Dutton, 1989)

Age range: Grades 3-5

Subject(s): Friendship

Major character(s): Mary-Anna Clutterworth, Child; Sandra Sutton, Child

Time period(s): 1980s

Locale(s): Australia

What the book is about: Mary-Anna and Sandra are bitter enemies until they have to spend an afternoon in town together and get lost. Both of them have an amazing ability for hateful remarks, but they are able to move from enmity to friendship.

Where it's reviewed:
Horn Book, July/August 1989, page 483
School Library Journal, September 1989, page 252

Other books by the author:
Penny Pollard's Passport, 1990
Come Back to Show You I Could Fly, 1989
Laurie Loved Me Best, 1988
Ratbags and Rascals: Funny Stories, 1984

Other books you might like:
Kathleen Benson, *Joseph on the Subway Train*, 1981
  Eight year old Joseph gets separated from his class on a trip from Brooklyn to Manhattan by subway.
Crosby Bonsall, *The Goodbye Summer*, 1979
  Allie hates endings and goodbyes until her friend, Ms. Lenya, helps her learn some things can never be lost.
Lynn Hall, *Mrs. Portree's Pony*, 1986
  Addie seeks comfort in the company of a beautiful pony, and begins a solid relationship with the pony's owner, who has lost her own daughter.
Kathleen Leverich, *Best Enemies*, 1989
  After Felicity trades her nasty tricks for friendship, Priscilla decides she'd rather have Felicity as an enemy.
Judie Wolkoff, *In a Pig's Eye*, 1986
  Fourth graders and best friends Maisie and Glenda fight and make up as best friends are likely to do.

1041

Jill Ross Klevin

Illustrator: Linda Strauss Edwards

The Turtle Street Trading Company (New York: Delacorte, 1982)

Age range: Grades 4-7

Subject(s): Clubs; Money

Major character(s): Mikey McGrath, Preteen; Morgan J. Pierpont III, Preteen; Priscilla Jane "PJ" Alberoy, Preteen

Time period(s): 1980s

Locale(s): United States

What the book is about: The secret Turtle Club has only four members: twelve year old Morgan, the founder, Mikey, Priscilla Jane (PJ) and Fergy Weintraub. Sanford, Morgan's younger brother, is the mascot. Since you must live on Turtle Street to join, no one else is eligible, even though their neat T-shirts interest other kids in joining. The club wants to do great things, and it's Fergy and Morgan who come up with a fantastic fund raising scheme involving recycling toys, and the Turtles are off and running with their kids' Flea Market.

Where it's reviewed:
Booklist, November 1, 1982, page 371
Center for Children's Books Bulletin, September 1982, page 13
Kirkus Reviews, October 15, 1982, page 1154

Other books by the author:
Miss Perfect, 1984
Far From H.O.M.E., 1982
Turtles Together Forever!, 1982
The Best of Friends, 1981

Other books you might like:
Shirley Climo, *Gopher, Tanker, and the Admiral*, 1984
  A boy and his dog accept a summer job as companions to an old man, only to become involved in solving some neighborhood burglaries.
John D. Fitzgerald, *The Great Brain at the Academy*, 1972
  The Great Brain faces the challenge of life at a strict Catholic boarding school with daring exploits and money-making schemes.
Kathy S. Kyte, *The Kids' Complete Guide to Money*, 1984

A guide to making one's money supply last longer through sensible spending, bartering, borrowing, sharing and swapping. (Non-fiction)
Stephen Roos, *The Cottontail Caper*, 1992
  Rabbit owner Erin is outraged because she was hoping her rabbit would be chosen to lead the Easter Parade held by the Pet Lovers Club.
Susan Saunders, *Rent-a-Star*, 1989
  A club of girls hire themselves out for odd jobs to earn money to fix up their clubhouse, which is in danger of being torn down by land developers.

1042

Eric Knight

Illustrator: Marguerite Kirmse

Lassie Come Home (New York: Holt, Rinehart and Winston, 1940)

Age range: Grades 4-6

Subject(s): Animals/Dogs

Major character(s): Joe Carraclough, Child; Lassie, Dog; Sam Carraclough, Parent

Time period(s): 1940s

Locale(s): Greenall Bridge, England

What the book is about: When the family is forced to go on welfare, Lassie is sold to a wealthy man and taken to Scotland. Lassie keeps her loyalty to her boy in England, escapes from the kennels in Scotland and returns to her true master, over 400 miles away.

Where it's reviewed:
Horn Book, September 1940, page 345
Library Journal, July 1940, page 596

Awards the book has won:
Young Reader's Choice Award 1943

Other books you might like:
Sheila Burnford, *The Incredible Journey*, 1961
  Two dogs and a cat befriend each other and struggle to find their way home over 200 miles of wilderness.
Meindert De Jong, *Hurry Home, Candy*, 1953
  A distraught family spends months searching for their missing dog and almost gives up hope.
Suzy Kline, *Herbie Jones and Hamburger Head*, 1989
  After Herbie and Ray foil a robbery attempt at the local bank, they try to find a good home for the robber's dog.
Phyllis Reynolds Naylor, *Shiloh*, 1991
  Marty finds a lost beagle and tries to hide it from its real owner, a mean-spirited man who mistreats his animals.
Bill Wallace, *Red Dog*, 1987
  Twelve year old Adam lives with his family in the rugged Wyoming mountains in the 1860s and is left in charge during his stepfather's absence.

1043

R. Rozanne Knudson

Rinehart Lifts (New York: Farrar, Straus, Giroux, 1980)

Age range: Grades 4-6

Subject(s): Sports; Friendship

Major character(s): Arthur Rinehart, Preteen; Zan Hagen, Friend

Time period(s): 1970s

Locale(s): Arlington, Virginia

What the book is about: Rinehart is as uncoordinated as a person can be. The stars of the school teams actually pay him not to play. He'd rather cheer for his friend, Zan, but she wants him to get into a sport, any sport! Is weight lifting the answer?

Where it's reviewed:
Booklist, September 1, 1980, page 45
Kirkus Reviews, September 15, 1980, page 1232
School Library Journal, May 1980, page 88

Other books by the author:
Julie Brown Racing with the World, 1988
Martina Navratilova Tennis Power, 1986
Babe Didrikson Athlete of the Century, 1985
Zan Hagen's Marathon, 1984

Other books you might like:
Michael H. Dessent, *Baseball Becky*, 1982
    When uncoordinated Becky joins a softball team she learns a great deal about competition.
Caary Paul Jackson, *Beginner under the Backboards*, 1974
    Nearly 6'5", a skinny and uncoordinated fourteen year old joins the basketball beginner's squad and finds that he has unsuspected talent.
Marilyn Kaye, *Lydia*, 1987
    Lydia forms an alternative school newspaper and campaigns in favor of permitting girls to try out for the football team.
Alfred Slote, *The Biggest Victory*, 1972
    The only thing Randy enjoys about baseball is having it over with so he can go fishing, but his father insists that he participate on the school team.
Doris Buchanan Smith, *Kick a Stone Home*, 1974
    A shy teen, who finds comfort with sports, comes to understand herself, her divorced parents and other people around her.

1044

Jackie French Koller

Illustrator: Carol Newsom

Impy for Always (Boston: Little Brown, 1989)

Age range: Grades 2-4

Subject(s): Cousins; Family Life; Friendship

Major character(s): Imogene "Impy", Child; Christina "Teeny", Preteen (Impy's cousin)

Time period(s): 1980s

Locale(s): United States

What the book is about: Eight year old Imogene (Impy) eagerly awaits the visit of her twelve year old cousin Chistina (Teeny) whom she hasn't seen for two years. Teeny isn't into dolls anymore and hates getting wet. Impy is unwilling to accept Teeny's new interest in boys, until Teeny is able to talk her into a more understanding mood.

Where it's reviewed:
Booklist, June 15, 1989, page 1823
School Library Journal, September 1989, page 229

Other books by the author:
Fish Fry Tonight, 1992
Mole and Shrew Step Out, 1992
If I Had One Wish, 1991
The Dragonling, 1990

Other books you might like:
LouAnn Gaeddert, *Just Like Sisters*, 1981
    Carrie hopes she and her cousin will become just like sisters during Kate's stay, brought about by her parents' separation.
Rumer Godden, *Great Grandfather's House*, 1993
    7 year old Keiko, a careless and spoiled Japanese girl, spends three months in the country with relatives, and gradually become easier to live with.
Len Hilts, *Timmy O'Dowd and the Big Ditch*, 1988
    In the late 1800s, young Timmy O'Dowd and his city cousin must forget their quarrels and work together when the Erie Canal is damanged by storms.
Rose Impey, *Scare Yourself to Sleep*, 1988
    Two cousins spending the night in a tent in the dark backyard with a little help from brother Simon.
Shirley Rousseau Murphy, *The Song of the Christmas Mouse*, 1990
    Rick's efforts at capturing a beautiful wild mouse for a pet seems constantly threatened by his cousin who has come for a visit.

1045

E.L. Konigsburg, Author/Illustrator

From the Mixed-Up Files of Mrs. Basil E. Frankweiler (New York: Atheneum, 1967)

Age range: Grades 4-6

Subject(s): Artists and Art; Runaways; Brothers and Sisters

Major character(s): Claudia, Preteen, Runaway; Jamie, Child, Runaway; Mrs. Basil E. Frankweiler, Wealthy (statue owner), Widow(er)

Time period(s): 1960s

Locale(s): New York, New York

What the book is about: A sister and brother run away from home and spend a week hiding in New York's Metropolitan Museum of Art. Claudia and Jamie must learn how to survive being on their own without being caught. While at the museum, they also help unravel a mystery surrounding a statue.

Where it's reviewed:
Horn Book, October 1967, page 595
New York Times Book Review, November 5, 1967, page 44
School Library Journal, October 1967, page 175

Other books by the author:
Father's Arcane Daughter, 1976
About the B'nai Bagels, 1969
Jennifer, Hecate, MacBeth, William McKinley and Me, Elizabeth, 1967

Other books you might like:
Bianca Bradley, *Boy on the Run*, 1975

Nick runs away from his mother and tries to survive on a rugged Massachusetts island.

Brock Cole, *The Goats*, 1987
   Marooned on a small island by fellow campers, a boy and girl who are both outcasts become friends and decide to run away.

Barbara Corcoran, *Don't Slam the Door When You Go*, 1972
   Three girls run away from their homes in Florida to live in a Montana ghost town.

Dean Hughes, *Family Picture*, 1990
   Feeling unwanted, an 11 year old orphan runs away from his foster home and lives on the streets.

Marilyn Sachs, *At the Sound of the Beep*, 1990
   A brother and sister run away from home and take up residence in Golden Gate Park.

E.L. Konigsburg, Author/Illustrator

Jennifer, Hecate, Macbeth, William McKinley and Me, Elizabeth (New York: Atheneum, 1967)

Age range: Grades 3-5

Subject(s): Friendship; African Americans; Witches and Witchcraft

Major character(s): Elizabeth, 5th Grader; Jennifer, Witch, 5th Grader

Time period(s): 1960s

Locale(s): New York, New York

What the book is about: Two 10 year old girls become friends in fifth grade. Jennifer is the only black child in her class, and Elizabeth is her only friend. Jennifer offers lessons in "witchcraft," her only defense against mean people.

Where it's reviewed:
Horn Book, April 1967, page 206
Library Journal, May 15, 1967, page 2022

Awards the book has won:
Newbery Honor

Other books by the author:
Journey to an 800 Number, 1982
Father's Arcane Daughter, 1976
A Proud Taste for Scarlet and Miniver, 1973
From the Mixed-Up Files of Mrs. Basil E. Frankweiler, 1967

Other books you might like:
John Bellaris, *The Letter, the Witch, and the Ring*, 1976
   A young girl gets involved with a mysterious letter, a magic ring and a powerful witch.
Jane Louise Curry, *Parsley, Sage, Rosemary and Time*, 1975
   10 year old Rosemary picks a sprig of "time" and finds herself in the 18th century.
Barthe DeClements, *No Place for Me*, 1987
   Copper Jones is sent to live with her Aunt Maggie who is a practicing witch.
Phyllis Reynolds Naylor, *The Witch Returns*, 1992
   Lynn and Mouse try to understand an old woman who moved into the neighborhood even though they fear she is a witch.

E.L. Konigsburg

Journey to an 800 Number (New York: Atheneum. 1982)

Age range: Grades 5-8

Subject(s): Animals/Camels; Remarriage

Major character(s): Rainbow Maximilian Stubbs, Preteen; Sarah Stubbs, Parent; Woody Stubbs, Parent, Entertainer

Time period(s): 1980s

Locale(s): Smilax, Texas

What the book is about: A father decides to take his newborn son outside blindfolded and name the child for the first thing he sees. It turns out to be a rainbow, so the boy is called Rainbow, shortened to Bo. Many years later, when his mother remarries and goes off on a honeymoon, Maximilian, who now prefers to be called Max, visits with his show biz father and his trained camel, Ahmed. Max learns about love, loyalty, appearances, and pretense from the unusual characters he meets when he lives with his dad. Thought provoking with lots of humor.

Where it's reviewed:
Booklist, May 1, 1982, page 1161
Hornbook, June 1982, page 289
Kirkus Reviews, March 1, 1982, page 275

Other books by the author:
Up From Jerico Tel, 1986
Throwing Shadows, 1979
The Second Mrs. Giaconda, 1975
A Proud Taste for Scarlet and Miniver, 1973

Other books you might like:
Carol Lea Benjamin, *The Wicked Stepdog*, 1982
   When her father remarries, Louise has to deal with an unwanted stepmother and her golden retriever, and finally learns what it means to share and love
Mary Calhoun, *Camels Are Meaner than Mules*, 1971
   A fictionalized account of the US Army's efforts to utilize camels in the Southwest Territory in 1857.
Kevin Henkes, *Two under Par*, 1987
   His mother's new marriage to a miniature golf course owner causes Wedge to struggle with feelings of resentment and dislike for his stepfather.
Robert Scott McKinnon, *To Yellowstone, a Journey Home*, 1975
   With the help of a highway patrolman, an old bull elk, his mate, and a camel calf stray from a circus, try to reach Yellowstone before hunting season.
Alfred Slote, *A Friend Like That*, 1988
   When Robbie tries to stop his widowed father from developing a new love interest, his friend, Beth, has to help him come to terms with the situation.

E.L. Konigsburg

Up From Jerico Tel (New York: Atheneum, 1986)

Age range: Grades 4-6

Subject(s): Actors and Actresses; Mystery and Detective Stories; Supernatural

Major character(s): Jeanmarie Troxell, Preteen; Malcolm Soo, Preteen; Tallulah Bankhead, Spirit, Actress

Time period(s): 1970s

Locale(s): Long Island, New York

What the book is about: Jeanmarie and Malcolm are both loners who feel invisible. They become friends over the burial of a dead blue jay. Digging in the earth mound they call Jerico Tel, they are whisked underground by the red-headed ghost of Tallulah who needs their help recovering her lost diamond.

Where it's reviewed:
Horn Book, May/June 1986, page 327
School Library Journal, May 1986, page 93

Other books by the author:
Journey to an 800 Number, 1982
Throwing Shadows, 1979
Father's Arcane Daughter, 1976
From the Mixed-Up Files of Mrs. Basil E. Frankweiler, 1967

Other books you might like:
Laurie Adams, *Alice Whipple in Wonderland*, 1989
　　Alice wants to be the lead in the play *Alice's Adventures in Wonderland*, being put on by Miss Barton's School for Girls.
Hope Campbell, *Looking for Hamlet: A Haunting at Deep Lake*, 1987
　　On vacation in an old Adirondack hotel, a young actress uncovers a mystery of the death of a girl who was to play Ophelia in a 1943 Hamlet production.
James Howe, *Stage Fright: A Sebastian Barth Mystery*, 1986
　　Young Sebastian Barth investigates the tangle of warnings and ominous accidents surrounding a famous actress visiting his home town.
Robert Newman, *The Case of the Murdered Players*, 1985
　　The similiarity in the deaths of two London actresses to three others killed ten years before make Andrew and Inspector Wyatt fear for Andrew's mother
Pamela F. Service, *Then the Night Wind Howls*, 1987
　　Sidonie, when joining a community theater in her new Indiana hometown, investigates ghosts and learns of something sad and evil which she tries to fix

---

| 1049 |

Leonie Kooiker

Illustrator: Carl Hollander

The Magic Stone (New York: Morrow, 1978)

Age range: Grades 3-5

Subject(s): Fantasy; Witches and Witchcraft

Major character(s): Chris, Child

Time period(s): Indeterminate

Locale(s): Netherlands

What the book is about: The Fine Thread Association members are ordinary citizens: a grandmother, a deaf cafe owner, a doctor, a truck driver. Or are they? Chris finds a powerful magic stone and doesn't want to work any evil magic with it, even when he discovers its power.

Where it's reviewed:
Horn Book, August 1978, page 396
Kirkus Reviews, June 1, 1978, page 595

Other books by the author:
Legacy of Magic, 1981

Other books you might like:
Terrance Dicks, *A Spell for My Sister*, 1991
　　Mike, the youngest in a family of witches, wizards and magicians, suspects his sister's new boyfriends of foul play when family heirlooms disappear.
Kate Gilmore, *Enter Three Witches*, 1990
　　Bren is fearful of having the girl of his dreams meet his family of witches, but after a school play, he realizes a meeting has already taken place.
Judith Gorog, *On Meeting Witches at Wells*, 1991
　　A collection of dark stories told in a scheherazade fashion for middle readers.
Patricia Miles, *The Gods in Winter*, 1978
　　Adam wonders if their new housekeeper has supernatural powers that have brought about a cold winter in England.
Walter Dean Myers, *Mojo and the Russians*, 1977
　　Drusilla threatens Dean with magical vengeance if he keeps trying to trap the Russians who are visiting Willie.

| 1050 |

Yuri Korinetz

Illustrator: George Armstrong

There, Far Beyond the River (Chicago: O'Hara, 1973)

Age range: Grades 5-6

Major character(s): Petya, Relative (uncle), Activist; Misha, Child

Time period(s): 1960s

Locale(s): Union of Soviet Socialist Republics

What the book is about: Thirteen year old Misha and Uncle Petya go off on a long trip to northern Russia. There is a great deal of action and adventure along the way. Uncle Petya has a boisterous reunion with an old friend from the days when they were young political activists.

Where it's reviewed:
Kirkus Reviews, November 1, 1973, page 1212
Times Literary Supplement, September 28, 1973, page 1113

Awards the book has won:
Russian Children's Book of the Year
German Children's Book Prize, Runner-up 1972

Other books you might like:
E.M. Almedingen, *The Crimson Oak*, 1981
　　Peter, a Russian peasant boy in 1739, crosses paths with the exiled Princess Elizabeth and realizes that his fate is linked to hers.
Kathryn Lasky, *The Night Journey*, 1981
　　Rach ignores her parents' wishes and gets her great-grandmother to relate the story of her escape from czarist Russia.
Gregory Maguire, *The Dream Stealer*, 1983
　　A village of Russian peasants flee an evil wolf, only to be saved by a little girl's dream and the knowledge of the witch, Baba Yaga.
Jerry Segal, *The Place Where Nobody Stopped*, 1991
　　A Jewish man plants himself in a lonely Russian baker's house and establishes a family while waiting for permission to go to America.
Vladimir Zheleznikov, *Scarecrow*, 1990

Twelve year old Lena comes to live with her eccentric grandfather in a small Russian town and finds herself persecuted at school.

1051

Gordon Korman

No Coins, Please (New York: Scholastic, 1984)

Age range: Grades 3-5

Subject(s): Business Enterprises; Humor

Major character(s): Rob, Counselor (camp); Dennis, Counselor (camp); Artie, Preteen, Camper

Time period(s): 1980s

Locale(s): United States

What the book is about: Taking six eleven year olds on a cross country camping trip is more than Rob and Dennis hand bargained for. Artie manages to make over $100,000 through various outrageous schemes.

Where it's reviewed:
Center for Children's Books Bulletin, November 1985, page 50

Other books by the author:
The Zucchini Warriors, 1988
I Want to Go Home, 1983

Other books you might like:
Lloyd Alexander, *The Fortune-Tellers*, 1992
    A carpenter in the West African country of Cameroon goes to a fortune teller and finds the predictions of his future coming true in an unusual way.
Joanne Rocklin, *Sonia Begonia*, 1986
    Sonia is determined to be a business woman and follow in her parents' and brother's footsteps.
Pat Ross, *Hannah's Fancy Notions*, 1988
    When Hannah makes something special for her sister who works to support the family, she doesn't suspect the far-reaching consequences of her gift.
Susan Sussman, *Casey the Nomad*, 1985
    Casey is fascinated by nomads, but he is upset to learn that his own father will be traveling across the country for two years on business.
Leon Ware, *The Jade Monkey Mystery*, 1969
    While accompanying his father on a business trip to the Far East, a teen becomes of great interest to a secret pirate clan.

1052

Gordon Korman

The Zucchini Warriors (New York: Scholastic, 1988)

Age range: Grades 4-6

Subject(s): Sports/Football; Humor

Major character(s): Bruno, Student; Boots, Student

Time period(s): 1980s

Locale(s): Ontario, Canada

What the book is about: Roommates Bruno and Boots find obstacles in their way as they try to lead the Zucchini warriors

to a victorious football season and earn a new recreation center for their boarding school, McDonald Hall.

Where it's reviewed:
Booklist, January 1, 1989, page 791
School Library Journal, September 1988, page 184

Other books by the author:
Losing Joe's Place, 1990
Don't Care High, 1985
No Coins, Please, 1984
Beware the Fish, 1980

Other books you might like:
Ellen Conford, *Dear Mom, Get Me Out of Here!*, 1992
    Trapped in a dreadful boarding school, Paul joins his classmates in attempting to uncover the shocking past of their headmaster, Mr. Pickles.
William Robert Cox, *Home Court Is Where You Find It*, 1980
    A basketball star from a broken home who has been expelled from three schools in California enters an eastern boarding school that has a losing team.
John D. Fitzgerald, *The Great Brain at the Academy*, 1972
    The Great Brain responds to the challenge of life at a strict Catholicboarding school with daring exploits and moneymaking schemes.
Florence Parry Heide, *Banana Blitz*, 1983
    TV and candy addict Jonah, new to Fairlee School, hopes to solve his problems by winning the prize for watching the American Banana Institute ads.
Isabelle Holland, *The Man Without a Face*, 1972
    A fatherless teen forms an unusual relationship with a man living near his summer home who helps him prepare for his entrance exams to boarding school

1053

Irina Korschunov

Illustrator: Reinhard Michl

Small Fur (New York: Harper & Row, 1984)

Age range: Grades 2-3

Subject(s): Elves; Friendship

Major character(s): Small Fur, Mythical Creature (elf)

Time period(s): Indeterminate

Locale(s): Fictional Country

What the book is about: After losing his best friend, Brown Fur, Small Fur is very sad because he must play alone. then one day, a magic gate appears and the boring woods are suddenly full of wonders for Small Fur. He meets a green-haired Nock and experiences the thrill of flying. He meets Curly fur, and again has a best friend to share playing ball, hiding from fog witches and counting the stars in the sky.

Other books by the author:
Small Fur Is Getting Bigger, 1990
Adam Draws Himself a Dragon, 1986
Foundling Fox, 1984
A Night in Distant Motion, 1983

Other books you might like:
Laura Alden, *Learning about Fairies*, 1982
    Describes the appearance and behavior of fairies, also known as imps, hobgoblins, elves, pixies, leprechauns, sprites, and brownies.

Roger Duvoisin, *The Three Sneezes and Other Swiss Tales*, 1941

Thirty-seven folk tales from the French and German areas of Switzerland.

Betsy James, *The Red Cloak*, 1989

In this free retelling of an old Scottish ballad, Jan's friend Tam has disappeared. Jan helps rescue him from elves with the help of a red cloak.

Morgan Matthews, *Squeaky Shoes*, 1986

When a shoemaking elf discovers no one will buy his shoes because they squeak, he decides to make quiet shoes called "sneakers."

Barbara Brooks Wallace, *The Barrel in the Basement*, 1985

Pudding, the youngest of the three Furkins living in a barrel in the basement, proves a shy Furkin is capable of a great deed.

1054

Jeanie Kortum

Illustrator: Duguld Stermer

Ghost Vision (New York: Pantheon, 1983)

Age range: Grades 5-8

Subject(s): Eskimos

Major character(s): Panipaq, Preteen; Peter, Parent; Avataq, Cousin

Time period(s): 1970s

Locale(s): Siorapaluk, Greenland (polar ice cap)

What the book is about: A Greenland Eskimo realizes that his son has special mystical powers. Panipaq is troubled by a feeling of being different, by visions he doesn't understand and by a growing lack of respect for old traditions on the part of his contemporaries

Where it's reviewed:
Booklist, February 1, 1984, page 814
Center for Children's Books Bulletin, February 1984, page 110
School Library Journal, January 1984, page 78

Other books you might like:
J.H. Brennan, *Shiva's Challenge: An Adventure of the Ice Age*, 1992

Shiva submits to an ordeal in the frozen wasteland north of her tribe's camp, to test her potential for becoming shaman for the Shingu people.

Ann Halam, *The Daymaker*, 1987

Endowed with mystical powers, young Zanne takes a journey in search of the mysterious "daymaker" in order to become a full-fledged covenor.

Nancy Luenn, *Arctic Unicorn*, 1986

Kala finds life in her Eskimo village disrupte by a hunter who has lived among white people and the discovery that she has "shaman" powers.

Susan Price, *Ghost Song*, 1992

When a magical shaman visits a trapper and tries to claim his son Ambrosi, the father resists, while Ambrosi learns the secrets of his true identity.

Luke Wallin, *Ceremony of the Panther*, 1987

Raincrow, a young Indian, is torn between the shiftless life in the Everglades and his father's ambitions for him to carry on the shaman traditions.

1055

William Kotzwinkle

Illustrator: Joe Servello

Trouble in Bugland: A Collection of Inspector Mantis Mysteries (Boston: Godine, 1983)

Age range: Grades 5-8

Subject(s): Mystery and Detective Stories; Animals/Insects

Major character(s): Channing Booklouse, Teacher, Insect; Inspector Mantis, Detective, Insect (praying mantis); Adrian C. Gallgnat, Criminal, Insect

Time period(s): Indeterminate Past

Locale(s): England

What the book is about: An all-insect cast in a take-off on Sherlock Holmes mysteries. Whether or not readers are fans of the original, they will enjoy this spoof with an ingenious cast of insects as they tackle five mysteries. Because of the deductive reasoning used to solve crimes, serious mystery fans will not be disappointed.

Where it's reviewed:
Horn Book, April 1984, page 196
School Library Journal, February 1984, page 74

Other books by the author:
Exile, 1987
Dream of Dark Harbor, 1979
The Nap Master, 1979
Leopard's Tooth, 1976

Other books you might like:
Doug Cushman, *Aunt Eater's Mystery Vacation*, 1992

A mystery-loving anteater has a chance to solve several mysteries during her vacation at the Hotel Bathwater.

E.A. Hass, *Incognito Mosquito, Private Insective*, 1982

The mosquito detective tells of his adventures with such famous insects as Mickey Mantis, F. Flea Bailey, and the Warden of Sting Sting prison.

Rudyard Kipling, *Just So Stories for Little Children*, 1902

Twelve stories about animals, insects and other subjects.

Mary Pope Osborne, *Spider Kane and the Mystery under the May-Apple*, 1992

Helped by a spider, a moth, and two ladybug friends, a young butterfly tries to solve a mystery involving a gossamer-winged butterfly that he loves.

Eve Titus, *Basil in Mexico*, 1976

Basil mouse, the master detective, seeks the truth behind the theft of the Mousa Lisa and also tries to solve his companion's disappearance.

1056

Stephen Krensky

Illustrator: Susanna Natti

Lionel at Large (New York: Dial, 1986)

Age range: Grades 1-2

Series: Easy-to-Read Book

Subject(s): Family Life

Major character(s): Lionel, Child; Louise, Child (Lionel's sister)

Time period(s): Indeterminate

Locale(s): United States

What the book is about: Louise's snake is loose in her brother Lionel's room and he hates snakes. Lionel also copes with going to the doctor and getting a shot, sleeping over at a friends's house, and eating his veggies in order to get dessert.

Where it's reviewed:
Booklist, May 15, 1986, pge 1404
Kirkus Reviews, April 15, 1986, page 639
School Library Journal, May 1986, pge 113

Other books by the author:
Lionel and Louise, 1992
Lionel in the Spring, 1990
Lionel in the Fall, 1987
The Lion Upstairs, 1983

Other books you might like:
Harry Allard, *The Cactus Flower Bakery*, 1991
    A nearsighted armadillo meets an ostracized snake in the desert and, not knowing what kind of animal she is, helps her open a bakery.
Mary Crockett, *Snake in the Camp*, 1975
    Toby's fake snake upsets everyone at camp.
Joan De Hamel, *Hemi's Pet*, 1985
    Hemi decides to enter his three year old sister in the school pet show because, after all, she's alive and I love her and I look after her.
Fred Rogers, *Going to the Doctor*, 1986
    Describes what a child can expect to see and do on a visit to the doctor's office.
Mavis Smith, *A Snake Mistake*, 1991
    After Farmer Henry used light bulbs as fake eggs to fool his hens into laying more eggs, Jake the Snake makes a big mistake.

1057

Joseph Krumgold

Illustrator: Jean Charlot

.and Now Miguel (New York: Crowell, 1953)

Age range: Grades 4-6

Subject(s): Animals/Sheep; Brothers

Major character(s): Miguel Chavez, Child

Time period(s): 1950s

Locale(s): Taos, New Mexico

What the book is about: 12-year-old Miguel works very hard to be allowed to join the men when they take their sheep to summer pastures. A wonderful look into the rich cultural heritage of Hispanic shepherds and a boy growing to manhood.

Where it's reviewed:
Horn Book, December 1953, page 456
Kirkus Reviews, August 1, 1953, page 42

Awards the book has won:
Newbery Medal 1954

Other books by the author:
Onion John, 1959

Other books you might like:
David Macaulay, *BAAA*, 1985
    Sheep take over the world when the last person has left the Earth. Satire for mature readers.
Joan Price, *Truth Is a Bright Star*, 1982
    A 12-year-old Hopi boy develops a friendship with a trapper who bought him from Spanish soldiers in 1832.
Tony Hillerman, *The Boy Who Made a Dragonfly*, 1972
    Zuni myth in which children gain the wisdom to lead their people.
Ann Nolan Clark, *Year Walk*, 1975
    A Spanish boy comes to Idaho to help his godfather herd sheep across the Northwest frontier.
Patricia Beatty, *The Bad Bell of San Salvador*, 1973
    A young Comanche refuses to accept the ways of his Mexican captors but wins their respect and admiration.

1058

Joseph Krumgold

Illustrator: Symeon Shimin

Onion John (New York: Crowell, 1959)

Age range: Grades 5-6

Subject(s): Emigration and Immigration; Parent and Child

Major character(s): Andy Rusch, Child; Onion John, Immigrant, Aged Person (eccentric)

Time period(s): 1950s

Locale(s): Serenity, New Jersey

What the book is about: The members of the Rotary Club in a small town attempt to transform an eccentric old man's way of life. 12-year-old Andy is the only one who seems to understand Onion John's language and his philosophy of life and he forms a strong friendship with the old man.

Where it's reviewed:
Booklist, November 15, 1959, page 191
Horn Book, December 1959, page 482

Awards the book has won:
Newbery Medal 1960

Other books by the author:
.And Now Miguel, 1953

Other books you might like:
Yoshiko Uchida, *Samurai of Gold Hill*, 1972
    Koichi and his Samurai father emigrate to Gold Hill, California, in 1869.
Charlene Joy Talbot, *An Orphan for Nebraska*, 1979
    Kevin journeys to the US from Ireland in 1872 and finds a home with a Nebraska newspaper editor.
Nancy Pitt, *Beyond the High White Wall*, 1986
    When 13 year old Libby witnesses a murder in the family cornfield, the family is determined to emigrate to the United States.
Barbara Smucker, *Days of Terror*, 1979
    An account of forces emigration of Russian Mennonites to western Canada.

1059

Harry Kullman

The Battle Horse (Scarsdale, New York: Bradbury, 1981)

Age range: Grades 5 and Up

Subject(s): Social Classes

Major character(s): Buffalo Bill, Businessman; Roland, Student; Kossan, Child

Time period(s): 1930s

Locale(s): Stockholm, Sweden

What the book is about: Told through the eyes of a young, poor boy, this story explores the tension between the "haves" and the "have nots." The plot revolves around a backyard knightly joust.

Where it's reviewed:
Horn Book, October 1981, page 543
School Library Journal, May 1981, page 74

Awards the book has won:
Mildred L. Batchelder Award 1982

Other books you might like:
Richard Church, The White Doe, 1968
    The friendship of two boys of different social classes is threatened by an insensitive, class-conscious boy who moves into their neighborhood.
William Golding, Lord of the Flies, 1954
    Classic story of school boys stranded on an island who establish their own social classes.
Erik Christian Haugaard, The Untold Tale, 1971
    In 17th century Denmark, a young orphan seeks his fortune during the wars with Sweden.
E.W. Hildick, The Case of the Dragon in Distress, 1991
    The McGurk Organization is transported back in time to the 12th century where they encounter an evil princess who tries to hold them captive.
Robert Newman, The Testing of Tertius, 1973
    Merlin is subdued by an evil spell. Tertius, his apprentice, tries to break the spell and save Britain.

1060

Maxine Kumin

The Wizard's Tears (New York: McGraw-Hill, 1975)

Age range: Grades 2-4

Subject(s): Wizards; Fantasy

Major character(s): Macadoo, Farmer

Time period(s): Indeterminate Past

Locale(s): Fictional Country

What the book is about: The old Wizard of Drocknock has lost his touch. A boy wizard is able to end the drought, cure the chicken pox and find the lost cows. Wizard tears are needed to break the drought, but the young wizard goes overboard, peels an onion and begins to abuse his magic. Unfortunately, all the townspeople are turned to frogs. The old wizard tells him the solution is right under his nose.

Where it's reviewed:
Kirkus Reviews, August 15, 1975, page 911
School Library Journal, November 1975, page 64

Other books by the author:
Joey and the Birthday Present, 1971
When Grandmother Was Young, 1969
A Winter Friend, 1961
Archibald, the Traveling Poodle, 1960

Other books you might like:
Brian Ball, The Quest for Queenie, 1988
    Harry and Jill are chosen by a magic talking sword to rescue a damsel from the bad wizard in Mandragora.
Ida DeLage, The Old Witch Gets a Surprise, 1981
    The old witch and the wizard fly off to adventure on a great dragon balloon until the balloon falls during a storm.
Sarah Hayes, The Crumbling Castle, 1992
    Zeb the Wizard wants to work his spells in peace in his new castle, but Jason the crow and the castle's other occupants leave him no peace.
Michael Pellowski, Mixed-Up Magic, 1989
    Waldo the Wizard discovers some wacky changes in his powers after his clumsy assistant drops the wizard's magic wand.
Carol Beach York, The Secret House, 1992
    Miss Plum tells a scary story about a wicked wizard to the girls at the orphanage, but two girls notice a house nearby is like the one in the story.

1061

William Kurelek

A Northern Nativity: Christmas Dreams of a Prairie Boy (Montreal: Tundra Books, 1976)

Age range: Grades 3-6

Subject(s): Christmas; Dreams and Nightmares

Major character(s): William, Preteen

Time period(s): 1930s

Locale(s): Manitoba, Canada

What the book is about: A series of dreams come true to a Canadian boy. Twenty paintings are accompanied by stories of many "Holy Families." A fisherman is turned away at a wharf, three radiant figures are housed in a gas station because the motel is full, and an Indian family waits at a trapper's door.

Where it's reviewed:
Kirkus Reveiws, November 15, 1976, page 1225
School Library Journal, October 1976, page 87

Other books by the author:
They Sought a New World, 1985
Lumberjack, 1976
A Prairie Boy's Summer, 1975
A Prairie Boy's Winter, 1973

Other books you might like:
Susan Hill, The Glass Angels, 1991
    Tilly looks forward to spending Christmas with her mother in their small attic apartment until illness and an accident threaten their plans.
Maxinne Rhea Leighton, An Ellis Island Christmas, 1992
    Having left Poland and braved ocean storms to join her father in America, Krysia arrives at Ellis Island on Christmas Eve.
Gary Paulsen, A Christmas Sonata, 1992

When a little boy spends Christmas with his dying cousin, they discover that Santa really does exist.

Patricia Pendergraft, *As Far as Mill Springs*, 1991
Tired of being bounced from one foster home to another, Robert and his friend embark on a journey to find his mother and spend Christmas with her.

Michael J. Rosen, *Elijah's Angel: A Story for Chanukah and Christmas*, 1992
A woodcarver gives an angel to a Jewish friend, who struggles with accepting the Christmas gift until he finds friendship is the same in any religion.

1062

Mary DeBall Kwitz

Illustrator: Lisa C. Ernst

Gumshoe Goose, Private Eye (New York: Dial, 1988)

Age range: Grades 1-2

Series: Dial Easy-to-Read

Subject(s): Animals/Birds; Mystery and Detective Stories

Major character(s): Ellery "Gumshoe" Goose, Detective; Inspector Goose, Detective, Parent (Gumshoe's father); Fat Fox, Villain

Time period(s): Indeterminate

Locale(s): United States

What the book is about: Gumshoe Goose and his father, Inspector Goose, go to the rescue of the kidnapped Baby Chick-Chick. Who could have left the note saying, "leave chocolate cake under the oak tree tonight or else Baby Chick-Chick will be in a sandwich tomorrow." A case of fowl play and lots of giggles for beginning readers.

Where it's reviewed:
Booklist, December 1, 1988, page 656
School Library Journal, December 1988, page 88

Other books by the author:
Little Chick's Friend Duckling, 1992
Little Chick's Breakfast, 1983
Little Chick's Big Day, 1981
Mouse at Home, 1966

Other books you might like:
Roger Duvoisin, *Petunia's Christmas*, 1990
A goose, to save a handsome gander who is being fattened for Christmas, disguises herself, begs, and makes and sells Christmas decorations.

Don Freeman, *Will's Quill*, 1975
A goose named Willoughby visits London, meets a friendly actor-playwright named Shakespeare, and helps make literary history.

Joanna Galdone, *Gertrude, the Goose who Forgot*, 1975
While searching for her missing house key, a forgetful goose finds her party regalia instead.

Bill Peet, *Cock-a-Doodle Dudley*, 1990
Dudley the rooster's ability to make the sun rise with his crowing is questioned by a spiteful goose, whose malice almost destroys the rooster.

Marjorie Weinman Sharmat, *Griselda's New Year*, 1989
Griselda Goose attempts to carry out her New Year's resolutions, but her good deeds backfire.

L

1063

Albert Lamorisse

The Red Balloon (Garden City, New York: Doubleday, 1956)

Age range: Grades 2-4

Subject(s): Balloons; Bullies

Major character(s): Pascal, Child

Time period(s): 1950s

Locale(s): Paris, France

What the book is about: Pascal, a young boy, finds a red balloon with a mind of its own floating across the skies of Paris. Pascal runs into all sorts of difficulties including rules against balloons on the streetcars, strict school regulations and bullies who deflate the balloon by throwing stones at it. Suddenly, all the balloons of Paris collect around the boy and lift him to the sky on a wonderful, heart warming trip. Always popular in combination with the film/video on which it is based.

Where it's reviewed:
Christian Science Monitor, September 18, 1978, page B14
Kliatt, Winter 1979, page 11
Reading Teacher, April 1982, page 789

Other books you might like:
Alan Baker, *Benjamin's Balloon*, 1990
  Benjamin blows up a balloon and begins a travel adventure that causes him a certain amount of worry.
Karen M. Glennon, *Miss Eva and the Red Balloon*, 1990
  Miss Eva, an old-fashioned schoolmarm, leads a routine life until one of her students gives her a magic balloon.
Nigel Gray, *A Balloon for Grandad*, 1988
  Unhappy when he loses his silver and red balloon, Sam is comforted by imagining it on its way to visit his grandfather in Egypt.
Phyllis Reynolds Naylor, *The Boy with the Helium Head*, 1982
  A young boy has unusual experiences after leaving the doctor's office with a balloon full of medicine and a head full of helium.
Alan Wade, *I'm Flying*, 1990
  A little boy floats away on his balloon across mountains, plains, cities and the sea, until he lands on a desert island.

1064

Evelyn Sibley Lampman

Rattlesnake Cave (New York: Atheneum, 1974)

Age range: Grades 4-6

Subject(s): Indians of North America

Major character(s): Jamie, Preteen; Aunt Nora, Relative; White Fang, Indian

Time period(s): 1970s

Locale(s): Montana

What the book is about: Jamie wants to learn to ride and learn all he can about Native American culture. White Fang does not warm up easily towards a white boy, but his grandson and Jamie become friends. Together, they restore a sacred medicine bag to its proper burial site.

Where it's reviewed:
Center for Children's Books Bulletin, September 1974, p 12
Kirkus Reviews, March 15, 1974, page 300

Other books by the author:
Squaw Man's Son, 1978 (for advanced readers)
Bargain Bride, 1977
White Captives, 1975
Once upon the Little Big Horn, 1971

Other books you might like:
Belle Coates, *Mak*, 1981
  An orphan of mixed heritage struggles to preserve Indian ways while working with white men on his reservation in the Montana badlands.
Paige Dixon, *The Search for Charlie*, 1976
  Accompanied by an Indian friend, a girl pursues her young brother's kidnapper through the forests of Montana.
Jack Farris, *Me and Gallagher*, 1982
  A young man looks back on the formation, in 1863, of the Montana vigilante movements and the part he played in the bloody events that followed.
Adrienne Richard, *Pistol*, 1969
  Chronicles a boy's progressive isolation from his family as he grows up in Montana during the Depression.
Kenneth Thomasma, *Pathki Nana, Kootenai Girl*, 1991
  A story of an Indian girl living in the beautiful Flathead Lake area of northwest Montana before non-Indian people arrived, and her vision quest.

1065

James David Landis

The Sisters Impossible (New York: Bantam, 1979)

Age range: Grades 5-7

Subject(s): Ballet; Sisters

Major character(s): Lily Leonard, Dancer; Saundra Leonard, Dancer; Meredith Meredith, Dancer

Time period(s): 1970s

Locale(s): New York, New York

What the book is about: Lily's father buys her ballet shoes and insists she take ballet lessons though Lily resists because she doesn't want to compete with Saundra, her older sister. But Lily's beginning classes unexpectedly bring her closer to her haughty older sister, already an advanced dancer. Perhaps Lily can even keep Saundra from falling to pieces during an important audition.

Where it's reviewed:
Book World, May 11, 1980, page 18
Kirkus Reviews, October 1, 1979, page 1145
School Library Journal, October 1979, page 151

Other books by the author:
Looks Aren't Everything, 1990
The Band Never Dances, 1989
Joey and the Girls, 1987
Daddy's Girl, 1984

Other books you might like:
Karen Strickler Dean, *Maggie Adams, Dancer*, 1980
 A young girl is determined to succeed as a ballet dancer despite the ambivalent attitudes of her parents and her boyfriend.
Louise Fitzhugh, *Nobody's Family Is Going to Change*, 1974
 Family disagreements over her brother's efforts to become a dancer and her desire to be a lawyer show Emma that the children must initiate change.
Merrill Joan Gerber, *Also Known as Daszia! The Belly Dancer!*, 1987
 Pressured to lose weight in an exercise class, a sixteen year old girl instead joins a belly dancing class, finding independence and self confidence.
Claudia Mills, *The Secret Carousel*, 1983
 When her older sister goes to New York to be a ballet dancer, ten year old Lindy becomes bored by her life with her grandparents in a small Iowa town.
Jean Ure, *You Win Some, You Lose Some*, 1984
 Jamie's decision to leave school and become a ballet dancer brings him problems but strengthens his character.

1066

Lucinda Landon, Author/Illustrator

Meg Mackintosh and the Mystery at the Medieval Castle (Boston: Little Brown, 1989)

Age range: Grades 2-4

Series: Solve It Yourself Mystery

Subject(s): Castles; Mystery and Detective Stories

Major character(s): Meg Mackintosh, Detective

Time period(s): 1980s

Locale(s): England

What the book is about: While Meg and her class visit a castle, they become eye-witnesses to the theft of a priceless silver chalice. The reader is asked to solve the mystery before Meg does, from clues presented in the text and illustrations.

Where it's reviewed:
Booklist, June 15, 1989, paege 1824
School Library Journal, November 1989, pge 87

Other books by the author:
Meg Mackintosh and the Mystery in the Locked Library, 1993
Meg Mackintosh and the Mystery at Camp Creepy, 1990
Meg Mackintosh and the Case of the Missing Babe Ruth Baseball, 1989
Meg Mackintosh and the Case of the Curious Whale Watch, 1987

Other books you might like:
David Macauley, *Black and White*, 1990
 Four brief "stories" about parents, trains, and cows, or is it really all one story?
George Shannon, *More Stories to Solve: Fifteen Folktales From around the World*, 1991
 Fifteen brief folktales in which there is a mystery or a problem that the reader is invited to solve before the resolution is presented.
Murray Shaw, *The Adventure of the Abbey Grange: The Boscombe Valley Mystery*, 1991
 Presents two Sherlock Holmes adventures, each accompanied by a section identifying the clues mentioned and explaining how each mystery was solved.
Donald J. Sobol, *Encyclopedia Brown and the Case of the Disgusting Sneakers*, 1990
 America's Sherlock Holmes in sneakers continues his war on crime in ten more cases, the solutions to which are found in the back of the book.
Tony Tallarico, *Search for Susie*, 1990
 Search for Susie at the Big Fun Amusement Park on the carousel, the ferris wheel, at the fun house, in the ice cream shop and on the roller coaster.

1067

Sandy Landsman

Castaways on Chimp Island (New York: Atheneum, 1986)

Age range: Grades 5-8

Subject(s): Animals/Monkeys; Animals, Treatment of; Survival

Major character(s): Danny, Chimpanzee; Nibbles, Chimpanzee; Tarzan, Chimpanzee

Time period(s): 1980s

Locale(s): United States

What the book is about: Danny, the lab chimp, gets sent to Chimp Island with the others whom scientists have labeled "unteachable." Used to TV, hamburgers and comfortable beds, Nibbles and Danny complain. Tarzan is ostracized because he can't communicate with a computer. Roger rallies them to survival while hatching a plot to get back to civilization.

Where it's reviewed:
Center for Children's Books Bulletin, May 1986, page 171
School Library Journal, August 1986, page 94

Other books by the author:
The Gadget Factor, 1984

Other books you might like:
Anna Coates, *Dog Magic*, 1991

Matt gets a surprise when his dog, Toby, speaks to him. Toby wants Matt to rescue his newborn puppies from a woman who has taken them to a laboratory.

Peter Dickinson, *Eva*, 1988
    After a terrible accident, a young girl wakes up to discover that she has been given the body of a chimpanzee.

John Donovan, *Family: A Novel*, 1976
    A chimp has spent his life taking part in tests in human labs. When a new experiment comes along that scares him, he escapes with three other chimps.

Norma Klein, *A Honey of a Chimp*, 1980
    Relates the escapades of a chimpanzee who moves in with a human family in New York City.

Ron Roy, *The Chimpanzee Kid*, 1985
    Harold is interested in animal rights and finds a friend in a new boy in class who agrees to help him in his plan to free a caged laboratory chimp.

1068

Carolyn Lane

Ghost Island (Boston: Houghton Mifflin, 1985)

Age range: Grades 4-6

Subject(s): Camps and Camping; Ghosts

Major character(s): Sally, Camper; Emmy, Camper

Time period(s): 1980s

Locale(s): United States

What the book is about: Four girls set out to spy on the boys' camp across the alke and end up marooned on Ghost Island instead, where Sally becomes convinced that its name is for real.

Where it's reviewed:
Booklist, August 1985, page 1667
Children's Book Review Service, August 1985, page 132
School Library Journal, September 1985, page 134

Other books by the author:
Echoes in an Empty Room, 1980
Princess, 1979
The Winnemah Spirit, 1975
The Voices of Greenwillow Pond, 1972

Other books you might like:
Scott Corbett, *Captain Butcher's Body*, 1976
    Two boys confront the ghost of a long dead pirate on an island off the coast of New England.
Sid Fleischman, *The Ghost in the Noonday Sun*, 1986
    Twelve year old Oliver tries to escape from pirates who take him to an island to find the ghost and treasure of Gentleman Jack.
Jan O'Donnell Klaveness, *Ghost Island*, 1985
    When Delia returns to the lake where her family had vacationed, she finds things greatly changed from the happy times of her childhood.
Stephen Roos, *My Favorite Ghost*, 1988
    The legend of a ghost inspires money-hungry Derek to dupe his friends into paying admission to a supposedly haunted house.
Elizabeth Silverthorne, *The Ghost of Padre Island*, 1975
    Mysterious occurrences during a vacation spent in search for a lost Indian site lead a family of four to treasure and the identity of a ghost.

1069

Jane Langton

The Fledgling (New York: Harper and Row, 1980)

Age range: Grades 4-6

Subject(s): Animals/Birds; Fantasy

Major character(s): Georgie Dorian, Child; Frederick Hall, Step-Parent; Alexandra Dorian Hall, Parent

Time period(s): 1980s

Locale(s): Concord, Massachusetts

What the book is about: After eight year old Georgie discovers that she can jump from the porch and float to the rooftop, learning to fly in the company of an aging, graceful Canada Goose is simply the next logical step. But the compulsive Madeleine Prawn and a gun-toting citizen threaten the night fliers' lives.

Where it's reviewed:
Center for Children's Books Bulletin, July/August 1980, page 218
Horn Book, August 1980, page 408

Awards the book has won:
Newbery Honor

Other books by the author:
Fragile Flag, 1984
The Astonishing Stereoscope, 1971
Swing in the Summerhouse, 1967
Diamond in the Window, 1962

Other books you might like:
Paul S. Bernsen, *The Goose That Went to Hollywood*, 1976
    A young goose who breaks her wing during her first southern migration becomes the center of a legal controversy.
Betty Brock, *No Flying in the House*, 1970
    In this mystery/fantasy, Annabel and a 3 1/2" talking dog named Gloria announce that they have come to live with the wealthy Mrs. Vancourt.
Betsy Byars, *Coast to Coast*, 1992
    Birch encourages her grandfather to fulfill his dream of flying his old Piper Cub to California, and then tells him she is coming along.
Margaret Goff, *Barney in Space*, 1981
    Barney is transported to the moon where Rokell, a dangerous Gark from the planet Ornam, awaits him.

1070

Joe Lasker, Author/Illustrator

He's My Brother (Chicago: Whitman, 1974)

Age range: Grades 2-4

Subject(s): Schools; Mentally Handicapped

Major character(s): Jamie, Child

Time period(s): 1970s

Locale(s): United States

What the book is about: It is difficult for slow learners, knowing they can't keep up with their peers. Teasing and irritation just makes it all worse. Jamie's older brother makes it clear that Jamie is loved and respected by his family. Achieving what most call "success" is not all there is to life.

Where it's reviewed:
Center for Children's Books Bulletin, June 1974, page 159
Library Journal, September 15, 1974, page 2250

Other books by the author:
Tournament of Knights, 1986
Lentil Soup, 1977
The Strange Voyage of Neptune's Car, 1977
Tales of a Seadog Family, 1974

Other books you might like:
Alan Brightman, *Like Me*, 1976
A youngster looks at his mentally handicapped friends and points out that every human being is worth the same, but some people go slower than others.
Carol Carrick, *Stay Away From Simon!*, 1985
Lucy and her younger brother examine their feelings about a mentally handicapped boy they both fear when he follows them home one snowy day.
Linda Kneeland, *Cookie*, 1989
When four year old Molly with Down's Syndrome learns to talk with her hands, she is better able to ask for what she wants.
Lucia B. Smith, *A Special Kind of Sister*, 1979
A young girl describes her relationship with her brain damaged sister.
Betty Ren Wright, *My Sister Is Different*, 1981
Carlo struggles with positive and negative feelings about his mentally handicapped sister.

1071

Joe Lasker, Author/Illustrator

A Tournament of Knights (New York: Crowell, 1986)

Age range: Grades 2-5

Subject(s): Knights and Knighthood

Major character(s): Lord Justin, Nobleman, Knight; Sir Rolf, Knight

Time period(s): Indeterminate Past (medieval times)

Locale(s): England

What the book is about: Picture book showing all the pageantry and color of a medieval tournament. A young lord must defend his father against an experienced knight, but the details in the illustrations are stronger than the story. A special useful feature is a glossary and labeled illustration of a mounted knight and all his equipment.

Where it's reviewed:
Horn Book, March/April, 1987, page 204
School Library Journal, November 1986, page 91

Other books by the author:
The Great Alexander the Great, 1983
The Do-Something Day, 1982
Merry Ever After: The Story of Two Medieval Weddings, 1976
He's My Brother, 1973

Other books you might like:
Barbara Shook Hazen, *The Knight Who Was Afraid of the Dark*, 1989
When the castle bully discovers bold Sir Fred is secretly terrified of the dark, he tries to stir up trouble between the knight and Lady Wendylyn.
Margaret Hodges, *Don Quixote and Sancho Panza*, 1992

An abridged version of an eccentric country gentleman who tilts at windmills, sets wrongs to right, and dreams dreams.
Ali Mitgutsch, *A Knight's Book*, 1991
Young Wolflieb relates the medieval adventures of his poor but brave master, Sir Frank von Fidelstein.
Mary Pope Osborne, *The Knight at Dawn*, 1993
Jack and his sister use the magic treehouse to travel back to the Middle Ages where they explore a castle and are helped by a mysterious knight.
Gregg Reyes, *Once There Was a Knight, and You Can Be One Too!*, 1987
Two children playing knights have adventures as they defeat an ogre and become King and Queen. Includes directions for making story and play props.

1072

Kathryn Lasky

Illustrator: Ronald Himler

Jem's Island (New York: Macmillan, 1982)

Age range: Grades 3-5

Subject(s): Camps and Camping; Fathers and Sons; Sports/Kayaking

Major character(s): Jem, Camper

Time period(s): 1980s

Locale(s): Penobscot Bay, Maine

What the book is about: Jem and his father set out on his first overnight camping trip via kayak to an island in Penobscot Bay.

Where it's reviewed:
Booklist, November 15, 1982, page 446
Hornbook, February 1983, page 45
School Library Journal, February 1983, page 78

Other books by the author:
I Have an Aunt on Marlborough Street, 1992
Fourth of July Bear, 1991
Dinosaur Dig, 1990
Sugaring Time, 1983

Other books you might like:
Elizabeth Gillette Baker, *Tammy Camps in the Rocky Mountains*, 1970
During a Rocky Mountain camping trip, Tammy's enthusiastic picture taking becomes frustrating for her father and brother and dangerous for her.
Jeannie Baker, *Where the Forest Meets the Sea*, 1987
On a camping trip with his father, a boy thinks about the history of the plant and animal life around him and wonders about their future.
Victoria Boutis, *Katy Did It*, 1982
Katy doesn't enjoy hiking or camping, but something makes her decide to join her father on a three-day hike in the Adirondacks.
Ruth Hallman, *Tough Is Not Enough*, 1981
On a camping trip, Kurt, a streetwise teenager forms an alliance with Laura Mae, a mountain girl whose father is a drunkard and a thief.
Otto Penzler, *Danger! White Water*, 1976

Text and photographs explore the challenge of white water canoeing and kayaking, the equipment involved, and the skills needed. (Non-fiction)

1073

Kathryn Lasky

Illustrator: Catherine Stock

Sea Swan (New York: Macmillan, 1988)

Age range: Grades 2-4

Subject(s): Old Age; Grandparents; Sports/Swimming

Major character(s): Elzibah Swan, Grandparent; Claire, Child; Jeremy, Child

Time period(s): 1980s

Locale(s): Boston, Massachusetts

What the book is about: At the age of seventy-five, Elzibah Swan decides to take up swimming, a pasttime which enriches her life. She even gets a wetsuit so she can swim in the winter, and moves to be near the sea. The book includes many letters she writes to her young grandchildren telling them about her new interest.

Where it's reviewed:
Booklist, September 15, 1988, page 161
Kirkus Reviews, August 1, 1988, page 1152
School Library Journal, December 1988, page 25

Other books by the author:
Surtsey, the Newest Place on Earth, 1991
Dinosaur Dig, 1990
Double Trouble Squared, 1991
Dollmaker, 1981

Other books you might like:
Glenn Halak, *A Grandmother's Story*, 1992
    An old woman performs a timely rescue of her fisherman grandson after a storm.
Amy Hest, *The Go-Between*, 1992
    Lexi gets more than she bargained for when she acts as a go between for her grandmother and Mr. Singer across the street.
E.L. Konigsburg, *Amy Elizabeth Explores Bloomingdales*, 1992
    The many sights of New York City provide lots of distractions for Amy and her grandmother as they try to make a trip to Bloomingdales.
Jay O'Callahan, *Tulips*, 1992
    Famous for his pranks, Pierre has never dared to play a trick on his Grand Ma Mere, but one day he does dare.
Mark Shasha, *Night of the Moonjellies*, 1992
    Seven year old Mark helps his grandmother and other family members run their seaside hot dog stand and then has a surprise at the end of the day.

1074

Kathryn Lasky

Illustrator: Christopher G Knight

Sugaring Time (New York: Macmillan, 1983)

Age range: Grades 3-5

Subject(s): Outdoor Life; Farm Life

Major character(s): Jonathon Lacey, Child

Time period(s): Indeterminate

Locale(s): Vermont

What the book is about: The family makes maple syrup. They break the trail to the maple grove, tap the trees, wait for a cold spell, then gather the sap to boil.

Where it's reviewed:
Horn Book, June 1983, page 323
School Library Journal, May 1983, page 73

Awards the book has won:
Newbery Honor 1984

Other books by the author:
Dinosaur Dig, 1990
Puppeteer, 1985
A Baby for Max, 1984
The Weaver's Gift, 1980

Other books you might like:
Diane L. Burns, *Sugaring Season: Making Maple Syrup*, 1990
    Describes, in text and photographs, the making of maple syrup from tapping the tree and collecting the sap to cooking and packaging.
Elizabeth Gemming, *Maple Harvest: The Story of Maple Sugaring*, 1976
    Traces the history of maple sugaring and describes the traditional and modern methods of making maple syrup and sugar.
Gail Gibbons, *The Missing Maple Syrup Sap Mystery*, 1979
    Mr. and Mrs. Mapleworth try to find out who is stealing the maple sap they are gathering to make maple syrup.
Bruce Hiscock, *The Big Tree*, 1991
    Follows the development of a maple tree from its growth from a seed during the American Revolution to its maturity in the late twentieth century.
Edward Jam, *The Year of Fire*, 1993
    While they boil down sap from their maple trees to make syrup, a Canadian grandfather tells his granddaughter of the worst fire he has ever known.

1075

Jean Lee Latham

Illustrator: John O. Cosgrove

Carry On, Mr. Bowditch (Boston: Houghton Mifflin, 1955)

Age range: Grades 3-6

Subject(s): Ships; Biography

Major character(s): Nathaniel Bowditch, Sailor (navigator), Historical Figure

Time period(s): 18th century

Locale(s): Salem, Massachusetts

What the book is about: 12 year old Nathaniel is indentured to serve on a clipper ship. He studies the stars, teaches himself navigation, and writes *The American Practical Navigator* which is still used today.

Where it's reviewed:
Booklist, October 15, 1955, page 82
Horn Book, October 1955, page 368

Awards the book has won:
Newbery Medal 1956

Other books by the author:
Elizabeth Blackwell, 1975
Far Voyager, 1970
Man of the Monitor, 1962
Medals for Morse, 1955

Other books you might like:
Alison Smith, *Come Away Home*, 1991
  A sea monster is blown off course and becomes trapped in a Scottish loch.
Elizabeth Borten de Trevino, *El Guero: A True Adventure Story*, 1989
  El Guero and his family are sent into exile and travel by sea to Acapulco and Baja California.
Ivy Ruckman, *This Is Your Captain Speaking*, 1987
  Tom visits a nursing home where he develops a friendship with a retired sea captain.
Dale Fife, *Destination Unknown*, 1981
  A 12 year old boy stows away on a Norwegian fishing boat during World War II.
John J. Loeper, *Golden Dragon*, 1978
  A young boy's journey by clipper ship from New York, around Cape Horn, to San Francisco in 1850.

1076

Anne Laurin

Illustrator: Charles Mikolaycak

Perfect Crane (New York: Harper, 1982)

Age range: Grades 2-4

Subject(s): Animals/Birds; Fantasy; Magicians

Major character(s): Gami, Magician; Old Miki, Farmer

Time period(s): Indeterminate Past

Locale(s): Japan

What the book is about: Blessed with great magic, Gami is nevertheless very lonely, for he assumes no one but magicians are interested in magic, so he seldom speaks to the townspeople. One dark night, he discovers he can breathe life into the animals and flowers he folds from paper. He creates a crane from the finest rice paper and it becomes a living, breathing bird which becomes his closest companion and attracts many people to Gami. When migration time comes, the bird must leave, but the friends remain and Gami uses his magic to comfort and heal many friends. The crane always returns to Gami in the proper season.

Where it's reviewed:
Booklist, April 1, 1981, page 1105
Kirkus Reviews, May 1, 1981, page 568
School Library Journal, April 1981, page 114

Other books by the author:
Little Things, 1978

Other books you might like:
Keith Baker, *The Magic Fan*, 1989
  Despite the laughter of others, Yoshi builds a boat to catch the moon, a kite to reach the clouds, and a bridge that mimics the rainbow.
Eve Bunting, *Magic and the Night River*, 1978

A Japanese boy and his grandfather fish successfully with their cormorants because they have treated the birds with kindness.
Ryerson Johnson, *Kenji and the Magic Geese*, 1992
  One of the geese in the picture on Kenji's wall flies off to join the wild geese in the sky and then returns to the picture with interesting results.
Tony Johnston, *The Badger and the Magic Fan*, 1990
  Stealing a young goblin's magic fan, a badger makes a fortune after using the fan to make a rich girl's nose grow.
David McKee, *The Magician and the Sorcerer*, 1974
  With the help of his sister, a witch, a bird and a wise man, a magician confronts an evil sorcerer who tries to gain favor with the king.

1077

Carol Russell Law

Illustrator: Bill Morrison

The Case of the Weird Street Firebug (New York: Knopf, 1980)

Age range: Grades 3-5

Subject(s): Arson; Mystery and Detective Stories

Major character(s): Stephanie, Child

Time period(s): Indeterminate

Locale(s): United States

What the book is about: While taking a course from the Dangerfield Detective School, Steffi, Mutt and Jeff track down the origin of several mysterious fires and the arsonist Steffi believes is setting fires in her neighborhood.

Where it's reviewed:
Booklist, October 1, 1980, page 254
Catholic Library World, April 1981, page 403
Schoool Library Journal, December 1980, page 73

Other books you might like:
Terrance Dicks, *The Baker Street Irregulars in the Case of the Cimema Swindle*, 1980
  The Irregulars investigate a theater fire which appears to be arson.
Carol J. Farley, *The Mystery of the Fiery Message*, 1983
  Cousins Kip and Larry investigate the rash of mysterious fires in their community.
Maurice Gee, *The Fire-Raiser*, 1986
  In 1915 Kitty Wix and her friends try to stop the arsonist who is terryfying their small New Zealand town.
Belinda Hurmence, *The Nightwalker*, 1988
  Savannah wonders if her brother, Poco, who sleepwalks, is setting the fires that are leveling the fishermen's shacks near their island home.
Willo Davis Roberts, *The Pet-Sitting Peril*, 1990
  A boy who does odd jobs in an apartment house becomes involved with arsonists employed by the owner who plans to destroy it to collect the insurance.

1078

Felicia Law

Illustrator: Judy Brook

Darwin and the Voyage of the Beagle (United Kingdom: Deutsch, 1985)

Age range: Grades 4-6

Subject(s): Discovery and Exploration; Biography

Major character(s): Charles Darwin, Scientist, Historical Figure; Captain Fitzroy, Sea Captain; Ben Sweet, Servant (cabin boy)

Time period(s): 1830s

Locale(s): *HMS Beagle*, At Sea

What the book is about: The fictionalized account of the *Beagle* sailing on a five year voyage, beginning in 1831, to chart coastlines and waters. Charles Darwin is aboard and studies plants, animals, fossils and rocks, and relates his knowledge to cabin boy Ben Sweet, along with commentary on social issues. A combination of adventure and biography for anyone interested in Darwin's work.

Where it's reviewed:
Booklist, August 1985, page 1667
School Library Journal, November 1985, page 87

Other books you might like:
Sam Epstein, *Mister Peale's Mammoth*, 1977
    Enthralled by natural history, a famous painter establishes a museum in his home and organizes a scientific expedition to dig up a mammoth skeleton.
Steve Parker, *Charles Darwin and Evolution*, 1992
    Traces Darwin's life from his early years, through his expedition aboard the *HMS Beagle* and the development of his theory of evolution.
Kin Platt, *Darwin and the Great Beasts*, 1992
    During a visit to the La Brea Tar Pits, a boy imagines what it would be like to live in prehistoric times and try to outwit huge beasts.
Renee Skelton, *Charles Darwin and the Theory of Natural Selection*, 1987
    A biography of Darwin and the development of his theory of evolution by natural selection.
Betsy Warren, *Wilderness Walkers: Naturalists in Early Texas*, 1987
    Brief biographies of twelve naturalists who studied the plants and animals of early 19th century Texas.

1079

Laurie Lawlor

Illustrator: Gioia Fiammenghi

Second Grade Dog (Niles, Illinois: Whitman, 1990)

Age range: Grades 1-3

Subject(s): Animals/Dogs; Schools

Major character(s): Bones, Dog

Time period(s): 1990s

Locale(s): United States

What the book is about: Bones is so bored home alone all day that he dons shorts, shirt, sneakers, and backpack, practices walking on his hind legs, then reports for second grade. He and the students have a very adventurous day.

Where it's reviewed:
Center for Children's Books Bulletin, March 1990, page 168

School Library Journal, June 1990, page 103

Other books by the author:
Addie's Dakota Winter, 1989
Daniel Boone, 1989
How to Survive Third Grade, 1988
Addie Across the Prairie, 1986

Other books you might like:
Jeffrey Allen, *The Secret Life of Mr. Weird*, 1982
    Sally and Sydney find the dog they call Mr. Weird to be a poor pet, even though he has some unique talents.
Linda Gondosch, *Brutus, the Wonder Poodle*, 1990
    Ryan tries to train his poodle, Brutus, to live up to his name.
Yasuko Kimura, *Fergus and the Sea Monster*, 1976
    Fergus doesn't know what to do with the funny blue monster who is growing bigger and bigger and following him everywhere.
Marilyn Singer, *Chester, the Out-of-Work Dog*, 1992
    Chester's attempts to find a herding job after his humans move into town prove disastrous until he meets a group of lost children.
David Updike, *Seven Times Eight*, 1990
    Truman wakes up in the morning to find he is in the body of his dog, Max, and Max is in him!

1080

James Duncan Lawrence

Illustrator: Leonard Kessler

Binky Brothers, Detectives (New York: Harper, 1968)

Age range: Grades 1-2

Subject(s): Brothers; Mystery and Detective Stories

Major character(s): Dinky Binky, Detective; Pinky Binky, Detective

Time period(s): Indeterminate

Locale(s): United States

What the book is about: When Dinky, the younger of the Binky Brothers, solves the case of the missing catcher's mitt, he become a full partner with his brother, Pinky, in their detective agency.

Where it's reviewed:
Booklist, July 15, 1968, page 1286
Center for Children's Books Bulletin, June 1968, page 161
Kirkus Reviews, April 1, 1968, page 390

Other books by the author:
Binky Brothers and the Fearless Four, 1970

Other books you might like:
Stan Berenstain, *The Berenstain Bears and the Missing Honey*, 1987
    Sister Bear, Brother Bear, Cousin Fred, and his hound, Snuff, search for the thief who stole Papa Bear's blackberry honey.
Eleanore Hartson, *Maxie's Mystery Files: The Stalled Mall and Other Crazy Cases*, 1987
    Four mini-mysteries in which inexplicable events occur are investigated by Maxie and her younger brother.
Thomas F. Pursell, *The Prize Tomatoes Mystery*, 1977
    Peg and her brother search for the destroyer of the prize tomatoes she planned to enter in a gardening contest at the county fair.
Adrian Robert, *Secret of the Haunted Chimney*, 1985

Brian and his brother try to discover the source of the mysterious sounds coming from their chimney.

Jan Wahl, *The Screeching Door: or, What Happened at the Elephant Hotel*, 1975

While vacationing in Atlantic City, a brother and sister meet a ghost in the Elephant Hotel.

1081

Louise Lawrence

Star Lord (New York: Harper and Row, 1978)

Age range: Grades 5-7

Subject(s): Science Fiction; Supernatural

Time period(s): 1970s

Locale(s): Wales

What the book is about: A Welsh family is caught up in the struggle between the supernatural powers of a mountain and the technological powers of a star lord who crashes into it.

Where it's reviewed:
Center for Children's Books Bulletin, December 1978, page 65
Kirkus Reviews, December 1, 1978, page 1310
School Library Journal, October 1978, page 156

Other books by the author:
Andra, 1991
Moonwind, 1987
Children of the Dust, 1985
The Dram Road, 1983

Other books you might like:
Judy Allen, *The Spring on the Mountain*, 1973
While vacationing in the country, three English children become drawn by a curious legend about a nearby mountain and embark on a strange adventure.
Nancy Bond, *A String in the Harp*, 1976
One of three american children in Wales for a year finds an old harp-tuning key that takes him back to the time of the 6th century bard, Taliesen.
John Halkin, *Fangs of the Werewolf*, 1987
A strange "wild dog" terrorizes Wales with brutal killings, but an old wise woman knows a secret that eventually destroys the creature.
Jenny Nimmo, *Orchard of the Crescent Moon*, 1991
Nia, from a large Welsh family, finds her own special artistic talent as she learns the dark secret shared by the Llewelyn and Griffiths families.
Ken Radford, *The Cellar*, 1989
While in an old boarding house in the hills of North Wales, a young girl is aware of ghostly presences and tries to find a reason for the haunting.

1082

John Shults Lawson

Spring Rider (New York: Crowell, 1968)

Age range: Grades 6-8

Subject(s): Ghosts; Civil War

Major character(s): Jacob, Child; Gray, Relative (sister); Hannibal, Spirit, Military Personnel (union soldier)

Time period(s): 1860s; 1960s

Locale(s): Virginia

What the book is about: From the dust of an old Civil War battlefield, Union and Confederate troops rise each spring to continue battle. Hannibal falls in love with Gray and must choose between saving her, or taking her with him in death.

Where it's reviewed:
Horn Book, October 1968, page 564
Library Journal, December 15, 1968, page 4732

Awards the book has won:
Boston Globe/Horn Book Award 1968

Other books you might like:
Elaine Marie Alphin, *The Ghost Cadet*, 1991
Benjy meets the ghost of a Virginia Military Institute cadet who was killed in the Battle of New Market in 1864.
Jean Hague, *The Whispering House*, 1970
Three orphans realize they must prove that their great-great-grandfather did not betray the Union during the Civil War.
Janet Hickman, *Zoar Blue*, 1978
Two members of a German pacifist group are caught up in the turmoil of the American Civil War.
Ann Rinaldi, *The Last Silk Dress*, 1988
During the Civil War, Susan finds a way to help the Confederate Army and uncovers a series of mysterious family secrets.
Gloria Root Savoldi, *Tennessee Boy*, 1972
In 1865, two boys discover much about themselves and the war as they travel together to Washington City.

1083

Robert Lawson

Ben and Me (Boston: Little Brown, 1939)

Age range: Grades 3-5

Subject(s): Biography; Fantasy; Animals/Mice

Major character(s): Amos, Mouse; Benjamin Franklin, Historical Figure, Inventor

Time period(s): 18th century

Locale(s): Boston, Massachusetts, American Colonies; Philadelphia, Pennsylvania, American Colonies

What the book is about: Amos has written a biography of his good friend, Ben Franklin. Acutally, Amos explains that he is responsible for many of the great Franklin's accomplishments, experiments and discoveries.

Where it's reviewed:
Booklist, February 15, 1980, page 840

Awards the book has won:
Lewis Carroll Shelf 1961

Other books by the author:
Ferdinand, 1978
Captain Kidd's Cat, 1956
Edward, Hoppy and Me, 1952
The Fabulous Flight, 1949

Other books you might like:
Nathaniel Benchley, *George the Drummer Boy*, 1977

A view of the incidents at Lexington and Concord, which were the start of the American Revolution, as seen from the eyes of George, a drummer boy.

Peter Burchard, *Whaleboat Ride*, 1977

A sixteen year old boy guides a flotilla of American whaleboats across Long Island Sound to raid British-occupied Sag Harbor.

Jean Fritz, *What's the Big Idea, Ben Franklin?*, 1982

A brief biography of the 18th century printer, inventor, and statesman who played an influential role in the early history of the United States.

Elizabeth Rider Montgomery, *Ben Franklin's Philadelphia*, 1967

Descriptions of life in Philadelphia in 1787, the time of the Constutitional Convention covering customs, travel, dress, the market and fire fighting.

Augusta Stevenson, *Ben Franklin, Boy Printer*, 1962

The boyhood of the printer, inventor, and statesman whose patriotism helped the thirteen colonies to attain independence.

1084

Robert Lawson, Author/Illustrator

Rabbit Hill (New York: Viking, 1944)

Age range: Grades 3-6

Subject(s): Animals/Rabbits; Fantasy

Time period(s): Indeterminate

Locale(s): Connecticut

What the book is about: The wild animals living on Rabbit Hill learn that "new folks" are moving into the house that has been empty so long. The animals soon learn the people are kind and are willing to share their garden with the animals.

Where it's reviewed:
Booklist, October 15, 1944, page 62
Children and Books, 1972, page 230
Horn Book, November 1944, page 47

Awards the book has won:
Newbery Medal 1945

Other books by the author:
Ben and Me, 1939
Captain Kidd's Cat, 1956
Mr. Revere and I, 1953
Robert Lawson, Illustrator, 1972

Other books you might like:
Richard Adams, *Watership Down*, 1972
The adventures of a group of rabbits looking for a safe place to establish a new warren.
Kenneth Grahame, *The Wind in the Willows*, 1908
The adventures of Toad, Mole, Rat and Badger, who live along a river. (Many editions)
Joel Chandler Harris, *Complete Tales of Uncle Remus*, 1955
Illustrated edition of the classic tales of Uncle Remus.
Tilde Michels, *Rabbit Spring*, 1988
As newborn rabbits and hares develop, the reader gets a sense of the difference.
Beatrix Potter, *Complete Adventures of Peter Rabbit*, 1982
Four stories telling all the adventures of Peter Rabbit and his cousin, Benjamin Bunny.

1085

Ursula Le Guin

Illustrator: Gail Garraty

The Tombs of Atuan (New York: Atheneum, 1971)

Age range: Grades 5 and Up

Subject(s): Fantasy

Major character(s): Arha "Tenar", Religious (priestess); Ged, Wizard

Time period(s): Indeterminate Past

Locale(s): Alternate Earth

What the book is about: Arha is five when she is consecrated High Priestess and renamed Tenar. Her life is then spent in the barren Place of the Tombs of Atuan. Ged is searching for the powerful Ring of Erreth-Akbe. Tenar must choose between good and evil.

Where it's reviewed:
Horn Book, October 1971, page 490
Library Journal, September 15, 1971, page 2930

Awards the book has won:
Newbery Honor

Other books by the author:
Very Far Away From Anywhere Else, 1976
The Farthest Shore, 1972
A Wizard of Earthsea, 1968

Other books you might like:
Grace Chetwin, *On All Hallow's Eve*, 1984
Two sisters step into another time period where the forces of good and evil involve them in a life-or-death adventure.
Elizabeth A. Lynn, *The Silver Horse*, 1984
Eleven year old Susannah follows her brother to the Land of Lost Toys and a fantastic adventure.
Shirley Rousseau Murphy, *Medallion of the Black Hound*, 1989
David is brought into a world called Meryn where he joins in the battle of good and evil.
Andre Norton, *Here Abide Monsters*, 1973
Two teenagers are transported back to the time of Arthur where they are in the middle of an exciting battle.
Vivian Vande Velde, *A Hidden Magic*, 1985
Lost in a magic forest and separated from her prince, Princess Jennifer seeks help from a kindly young sorcerer in battling an evil witch.

1086

Ursula Le Guin

Illustrator: Ruth Robbins

A Wizard of Earthsea (Berkeley: Parnassus, 1968)

Age range: Grades 5 and Up

Subject(s): Fantasy; Magic; Wizards

Major character(s): Sparrowhawk, Apprentice, Wizard; Vetch, Teenager

Time period(s): Indeterminate Past

Locale(s): Alternate Earth

What the book is about: A boy grows to manhood while attempting to subdue the evil he unleashed on the world as an apprentice to the Master Wizard.

Where it's reviewed:
Center for Children's Books Bulletin, May 1969, page 144
Horn Book, February 1969, page 59

Awards the book has won:
Boston Globe/Horn Book Award 1969

Other books by the author:
Fire and Stone, 1989
Catwings, 1988
Leese Webster, 1979
The Tombs of Atuan, 1971

Other books you might like:
Carol Gaskin, *The War of the Wizards*, 1985
  The reader, as apprentice Caladrius, becomes involved in the war of the wizards. Reader's choices determine the development of the plot.
Diana Wynne Jones, *Archer's Goon*, 1984
  Thirteen year old Howard learns that he is adopted and that his father is connected with the seven wizards who run the town.
Ellen Miles, *Wizards and Warriors*, 1990
  Matthew joins Kuros, a valiant knight, on a quest to vanquish a wizard with terrifying powers.
Jane Yolen, *Wizard's Hall*, 1991
  A young apprentice wizard saves the wizard's training hall by trusting and believing in himself.
Mary Frances Zambreno, *A Plague of Sorcerers*, 1991
  When a plague begins to take its toll on the wizards in the empire, Jermyn, an apprentice wizard and Delia, his skunk familiar, must stop it.

1087

Michael Leach

Don't Call Me Orphan (Philadelphia: Westminster Press, 1979)

Age range: Grades 5-6

Subject(s): Orphans; Abandonment

Major character(s): Kenny, Teenager; Father McCabe, Religious (priest); Joey Sands, Child

Time period(s): 1970s

Locale(s): United States

What the book is about: Thirteen year old Kenny has been in the Bethlehem Home for boys for four years. His parents are unable to care for him, but Father McCabe assures him he is not an orphan, for he has many people to care for him. Kenny learns to make friends, gets involved with the swim team, and learns to depend on himself.

Where it's reviewed:
Children's Book Review Service, July 1979, page 128
School Library Journal, March 1979, page 141

Other books you might like:
Vera Cleaver, *Where the Lilies Bloom*, 1969
  Mary has promised her dying father she'll care for the children and keep them out of the county charity home.
Dorothy Canfield Fisher, *Understood Betsy*, 1917

In 1906, Elizabeth Ann moves from the city to Vermont where she learns how to understand others and be understood.
Dorothy Haas, *The Secret Life of Dilly McBean*, 1986
  Dilly has special powers that his new friends, his guardians and a friendly scientist help him learn to control.
Alexander Key, *Escape to Witch Mountain*, 1968
  Tia and Tony know they are special, and they are hunting for a special home full of magic and music.
Noel Streatfeild, *Circus Shoes*, 1985
  When their aunt dies, Peter and Santa run away to join Uncle Gus, learning what you do counts more than who you are, when you fill circus shoes.

1088

Virginia Lee

Illustrator: Richard Cuffari

The Magic Moth (Boston: Houghton Mifflin, 1972)

Age range: Grades 4-6

Subject(s): Death; Grief

Major character(s): Maryanne Foss, Preteen; Mark Oliver "Mark-O" Foss, Child

Time period(s): Indeterminate

Locale(s): United States

What the book is about: This story explores the impact the middle child's death has on her family. Mark-O's thoughts, actions, his feelings of wonder, anger, and his questions, uncertainties and confusion about death are very believeable and helpful for children who have lost a sibling.

Where it's reviewed:
Booklist, July 1, 1972, page 942
Center for Children's Books Bulletin, April 1972, page 125
Kirkus Reviews, February 15, 1972, page 193

Other books you might like:
Vera Cleaver, *Belle Pruitt*, 1988
  When her adored baby brother suddenly dies of pneumonia, eleven year old Belle is left to cope with the devastating effects on her family.
Janni Howker, *Isaac Campion*, 1986
  After the death of his brother, Isaac's relationship with his father grows worse as his father's obsession with hatred poisons their family's life.
Elizabeth Laird, *Loving Ben*, 1989
  Anna's teen years brings fulfillment as she experiences the birth and death of a hydrocephalic brother and works with a child with Down's Syndrome.
Jan Marino, *Eighty-Eight Steps to September*, 1989
  A little girl's happy preschool life changes when she learns her brother isn't going to come home from the hospital.
Steven Tiger, *Heart Disease*, 1986
  Describes how the heart and circulatory system work and discusses heart defects, heart attacks and other heart malfunctions. (Non-fiction)

1089

Madeleine L'Engle

Meet the Austins (New York: Vanguard, 1961)

Age range: Grades 5-7

Subject(s): Doctors; Family Life; Orphans

Major character(s): Vicky Austin, Preteen; Maggy Hamilton, Orphan; John Austin, Teenager

Time period(s): 1960s

Locale(s): United States

What the book is about: The story of a country doctor's family told by the twelve year old daughter, and their reaction to having Maggy, a "spoiled orphan," come to live with them, and the loss of a beloved uncle in a plane crash. At first, Vicky thinks their family will never be happy again. But Maggy adjusts and we see the warmth of the Austin family, which is happily continued in other stories.

Where it's reviewed:
Book World, April 12, 1981, page 12
School Library Journal, February 1984, page 31
Times Literary Supplement, May 19, 1966, page 433

Other books by the author:
An Acceptable Time, 1989
A Circle of Quiet, 1972
The Arm of the Starfish, 1965
Camilla, 1965

Other books you might like:
Julie Andrews, *Mandy*, 1971
   Lonely for a place of her own, a ten year old orphan creates a secret home in a deserted cottage.
Dean Hughes, *Family Picture*, 1989
   Feeling unwanted, an eleven year old orphan runs away from his foster home and lives on the streets until he finds a new type of family at a hotel.
Joan Lowery Nixon, *A Place to Belong*, 1989
   Having traveled with his young sister from New York to a foster home in Missouri, Danny plots to get his foster father to marry his mother.
Louise Dickinson Rich, *Sally*, 1970
   An eleven year old orphan girl living in a foster home in Maine helps draw out an emotionally disturbed four year old boy.
Theodore Taylor, *Walking Up a Rainbow*, 1986
   An orphan and her elderly guardian, accompanied by a tough drover and his crew try to raise money and save the girls home from a debt collector.

1090

Madeleine L'Engle

A Ring of Endless Light (New York: Farrar, 1980)

Age range: Grades 5 and Up

Subject(s): Animals/Dolphins; Death

Major character(s): Vicky Austin, Teenager; Adam, Scientist (marine biologist)

Time period(s): 1980s

Locale(s): United States

What the book is about: Vicky's beloved grandfather has terminal cancer. She learns that coming to terms with death is an affirmation of life. Every character is linked to a recent death of a loved one. She finds comfort with the pod of dolphins with whom she has been doing research.

Where it's reviewed:
Center for Children's Books Bulletin, September 1980, page 14
Horn Book, August 1980, page 414

Other books by the author:
AN Acceptable Time, 1989
Many Waters, 1986
Ladder of Angels, 1979
Dragons in the Waters, 1976

Other books you might like:
Barbara Cohen, *The Long Way Home*, 1990
   Sally's relationship with a bus driver who recites Shakespeare storieshelps her to cope with her mother's cancer and her separation from her twin.
Carson Davidson, *Fast-Talking Dolphin*, 1978
   When Eric finds a talking dolphin in a trout pond, he uses all his knowledge and skill to save its life.
Morris Gleitzman, *Two Weeks with the Queen*, 1991
   Sent to England to live with relatives when his brother is diagno sed with cancer, Colin tries to visit the Queen to help find a cure.
Christopher Lucas, *Tiki and the Dolphins*, 1974
   A Tahitian boy helps a young, friendly dolphin and a troubled French painter with their problems.
Scott O'Dell, *Zia*, 1976
   A young Indian girl is caught between the traditional world of her mother and the present world of the Mission.

1091

Lois Lenski, Author/Illustrator

Strawberry Girl (Philadelphia: Lippincott, 1945)

Age range: Grades 4-6

Subject(s): Farm Life

Major character(s): Birdie Boyer, Child

Time period(s): 20th century

Locale(s): Florida

What the book is about: After moving to the Florida backwoods to be small crop farmers, a family encounters many difficulties. Birdie's determination helps the family endure the strawberry crop failure and the troublesome neighbors.

Where it's reviewed:
Booklist, September 1945, page 22
Library Journal, September 15, 1945, page 822
Kirkus Reviews, June 1, 1945, page 252

Awards the book has won:
Newbery Medal 1946

Other books by the author:
Bayou Suzette, 1943
Blue Ridge Billy, 1946
Judy's Journey, 1947
Puritan Adventure, 1944

Other books you might like:

Vera Cleaver, *Kissimmee Kid*, 1981
  12 year old Evelyn goes to stay with relatives on a Florida ranch and discovers her brother-in-law is a cattle rustler.
Marjorie Kinnan Rawlings, *The Yearling*, 1938
  Jody comes to terms with the harsh life of the Florida backwoods a century ago.
Hazel Krantz, *For Love of Jeremy*, 1990
  Wendy and her mother move to Key West, Florida, to enroll Wendy's brother in a dolphin therapy program.
Mary Stolz, *Land's End*, 1973
  12 year old Joshua finds his life changed by a new family that moves to an abandoned house near his home in the Florida Keys.
Doris Gates, *Blue Willow*, 1940
  A young girl in a migrant family cherishes the hope of someday having a home in which to display her blue willow plate.

1092

Ellen Leroe

Illustrator: Jacqueline Rogers

The Peanut Butter Poltergeist (New York: Dutton, 1987)

Age range: Grades 4-6

Subject(s): Ghosts; Stepfamilies

Major character(s): M.J., Preteen

Time period(s): 1980s

Locale(s): United States

What the book is about: M.J. plays a trick on his obnoxious new stepsister in a haunted house, only to find she has turned the tables on him.

Where it's reviewed:

Booklist, January 15, 1988, page 864
Center for Children's Books Bulletin, December 1987, page 69
School Library Journal, January 1988, page 75

Other books by the author:

Leap Frog Friday, 1992
Have a Heart, Cupid Delaney, 1986
The Plot Against the Pom-Pom Queen, 1985
Confessions of a Teenage TV Addict, 1983

Other books you might like:

Penelope Lively, *The Ghost of Thomas Kempe*, 1973
  The ghost of a 17th century sorcerer emerges as a poltergeist and attempts to make young James his apprentice.
Marilyn Singer, *Ghost Host*, 1988
  Football star Bart wishes to rid his house of a poltergeist while keeping the friendly ghosts also haunting it, who agree to help him win a game.
Gloria Skurzynski, *The Poltergeist of Jason Morey*, 1975
  When their orphaned cousin comes to live with them, the Kessler family learns that he has brought a poltergeist with him.
Patricia Windsor, *Home Is Where Your Feet Are Standing*, 1975
  Convinced that the mysterious and troublesome events in the family cottage are due to his "poltergeist disease," Colin takes matters in his own hands.
W.J.M. Wippersberg, *Bad Times for Ghosts*, 1986

Young Max Poltergeist and his ghost family fall on hard times as they come to realize that humans are no longer afraid of ghosts.

1093

Gen LeRoy

Emma's Dilemma (New York: Harper and Row, 1975)

Age range: Grades 4-6

Subject(s): Grandparents; Allergies; Animals/Dogs

Major character(s): Emma, Teenager; Herbie, Child; Lucy, Child

Time period(s): 1970s

Locale(s): New York, New York

What the book is about: Emma loves her dog, Pearl, and she also loves her grandmother. Unfortunately, Grandmother is allergic to dogs. Six year old Herbie, the neighbor Emma baby-sits, is her greatest comfort.

Where it's reviewed:

Horn Book, October 1975, page 464
Kirkus Reviews, July 1, 1975, page 712

Other books by the author:

Lucky Stiff, 1981
Cold Feet, 1979
Hotheads, 1977
Bridget, 1973

Other books you might like:

Berthe Amoss, *The Mockingbird Song*, 1988
  Unable to get along with her new stepmother, Lindy goes to live with the elderly lady next door, returning only after the birth of a baby sister.
Berlie Doherty, *Granny was a Buffer Girl*, 1986
  The night before Jess goes to France for a year, her parents and grandparents gather to celebrate and share stories of their lives.
Helen Griffith, *Running Wild*, 1977
  A young boy living with his grandparents faces a dilemma when his dog has a second litter of puppies that his grandparents cannot let him keep.
Evelyn Slaatten, *In the Captain's Shoes*, 1978
  An orphaned boy goes to live with his unusual grandfather, subsequently sharing many adventures and learning the meaning of friendship.
Carol Snyder, *The Great Condominium Rebellion*, 1981
  Stacy and Marc visit their newly retired grandparents in their Florida condominium where the restrictive rules stir them to rebel.

1094

Theo LeSieg

Illustrator: Roy McKie

Ten Apples Up on Top (New York: Random, 1961)

Age range: Grades 1-2

Subject(s): Animals; Mathematics

Time period(s): Indeterminate

Locale(s): Fictional Country

What the book is about: In this nonsense story for beginning readers, a lion, a dog and a tiger try to pile apples on their heads with hilarious results.

Other books by the author:
The Tooth Book, 1981
The Eye Book, 1968
Come Over to My House, 1966
I Wish That I Had Duck Feet, 1965

Other books you might like:
Kathryn Cave, *Out for the Count: A Counting Adventure,* 1992
   When he can't sleep, Tom begins to count sheep who go to sleep on his bedroom floor except for one that leads him into many numerical adventures.
Denise Fleming, *Count!,* 1992
   The antics of lively and colorful animals present the numbers one to ten, twenty, thirty, forty and fifty.
Carol Partridge Ochs, *When I'm Alone,* 1993
   A little girl tries to explain that it was an assortment of animals, from ten aardvarks to one kitten, that made the mess for which she is blamed.
Teri Sloat, *From One to One Hundred,* 1991
   Illustrations of people and animals introduce the numbers one through ten and then, counting by tens, move on up to one hundred.
Eve Spencer, *Animal Babies 1,2,3,* 1990
   Numbers from one to ten are illustrated with different baby animals and information is provided about their traits and habits.

| 1095 |

Kathleen Leverich

Illustrator: Susan Condie Lamb

Best Enemies (New York: Greenwillow, 1989)

Age range: Grades 2-3

Subject(s): Friendship; Schools

Major character(s): Felicity, Child; Priscilla, Child

Time period(s): 1980s

Locale(s): United States

What the book is about: On her first day at school, Priscilla meets Felicity, who turns out to be a serious manipulator. After Felicity trades her nasty tricks for friendship, Priscilla decides she'd rather have her as an enemy.

Where it's reviewed:
Booklist, April 15, 1989, page 1468
Booklist, June 15, 1991, page 1965

Other books by the author:
Hilary and the Troublemakers, 1992
Best Enemies Again, 1991
Hungry Fox and the Foxy Duck, 1978

Other books you might like:
Ilene Cooper, *Frances Dances,* 1991
   As she takes ballet lessons and participates in a school play, a shy fourth grader confronts her fears and learns a lesson about friendship.
Elizabeth Hathorn, *Freya's Fantastic Surprise,* 1988

Jealous of Miriam's big surprise, Freya invents one surprise after another for the school paper, until her mother supplies her with a real surprise.
Suzy Kline, *Horrible Harry and the Green Slime,* 1989
   Harry and Doug are on a secret mission to celebrate "Charlotte's Web," learn how to make green slime, and put on a skit warning about smoking.
Jean Marzollo, *The Best Friends' Club,* 1990
   A shy third grader visits her father in Texas and gains self-confidence that helps her make friends when she returns to school.
Enid Richemont, *The Time Tree,* 1989
   Rachel and Joanna find themselves where past and present worlds merge and a mysterious girl in old-fashioned clohtes appears at their secret place.

| 1096 |

Betty Levin

Brother Moose (New York: Greenwillow, 1990)

Age range: Grades 6-9

Subject(s): Indians of North America; Frontier and Pioneer Life; Orphans

Major character(s): Nell, Orphan; Louisa, Orphan; Joe, Grandparent, Indian

Time period(s): 1890s

Locale(s): Maine; Canada

What the book is about: Two homeless children are taken in charge by Joe, a Native American, and his grandson, Peter. Together they travel from Canada to Maine and face the natural dangers of the wilderness so that Nell can reach a foster mother who, she hopes, will also take Louisa in. During the trip, Joe relates Glooskeb myths which encourage them in their struggle for survival. Shows the strength of love and caring in the face of prejudice.

Where it's reviewed:
Center for Children's Books Bulletin, May 1990, page 219
School Library Journal, July 1990, page 77

Other books by the author:
The Trouble with Gramary, 1988
The Ice Bear, 1986
Put on My Crown, 1985
A Binding Spell, 1984

Other books you might like:
Gillian Avery, *Maria Escapes,* 1992
   Maria lives with her uncle in Oxford, shares an eccentric tutor with the Smith brothers and enjoys unusual adventures in the English countryside.
Avi, *Punch with Judy,* 1993
   An outcast boy, orphaned by the Civil War, is taken in by the owner of a traveling medicine show and years later confirms the man's faith in him.
Robin Moore, *The Bread Sister of Sinking Creek,* 1990
   Fourteen year old Maggie Callahan, who has a special talent for making bread, struggles to survive on the Pennsylvania frontier in the late 1700s.
Ramon Royal Ross, *Harper and Moon,* 1993
   Harper has always liked Moon, an abused, orphaned older boy, but their friendship is tested by a discovery Harper makes when Moon joins the Army.

Charlene Joy Talbot, *An Orphan for Nebraska*, 1979
Orphaned on the journey to America in 1872, a young Irish boy finally makes his way to Nebraska where he goes to work for a newspaper editor.

1097

Betty Levin

The Ice Bear (New York: Greenwillow, 1986)

Age range: Grades 5-8

Subject(s): Adventure and Adventurers; Freedom

Major character(s): Wat, Baker (baker's helper); Kaila, Handicapped (mute)

Time period(s): Indeterminate Past

Locale(s): Thyrne, Fictional Country

What the book is about: Wat, a baker's helper, finds himself a hero when he helps the kidnapped bear cub of the King to flee. Kaila, a mute girl, hopes to return with the bear to her distant homeland, the Land of the White Falcons. Both become pawns in the power struggle which rages in the Kingdom of Thyrne.

Where it's reviewed:
Horn Book, January/February 1987, page 56
School Library Journal, October 1986, page 192

Other books by the author:
Mercy's Mill, 1992
Put on My Crown, 1985
The Keeping Room, 1981
The Beast on the Brink, 1980

Other books you might like:
T.A. Baron, *The Ancient One*, 1992
While helping her aunt protect a redwood forest from loggers, Kate goes back five centuries and faces the Gashra, who wants to destroy the forest.
Monica Hughes, *The Promise*, 1992
A promise made by her parents before she was born sends princess Rania to Roshan to learn about the wind and rain from a woman known as Sandwriter.
Tanith Lee, *Black Unicorn*, 1991
With her talent for mending things, Tanaquil brings to life a unicorn which helps her find the way to a perfect world.
Hugh Lofting, *Gub-Gub's Book*, 1992
On a succession of evenings, the animals settle into Dr. Doolittle's kitchen to hear Gub-Gub, the pig, read parts of his book on food.
Josepha Sherman, *Child of Faerie, Child of Earth*, 1992
Percinet, half-human son of a queen of Faerie, falls in love with a mortal and leaves his realm of magic to defend her against a sorceress.

1098

Betty Levin

The Trouble with Gramary (New York: Greenwillow, 1988)

Age range: Grades 5-8

Subject(s): Grandparents; Recycling (Waste); Sculptors

Major character(s): Merkka, Preteen

Time period(s): 1980s

Locale(s): Maine

What the book is about: Merkka just wants to fit in - a difficult task when her grandmother is creating sculptures from scrapmetal, and irritating other citizens of their small Maine village, who consider them eyesores. As conflict within the family and throughout the village grows, Merkka learns to formulate her own values and throws her hand in to help Gramary.

Where it's reviewed:
Horn Book, May/June, 1988, page 353
School Library Journal, April 1988, page 102

Other books by the author:
Brother Moose, 1990
The Ice Bear, 1986
A Binding Spell, 1984
The Beast on the Brink, 1980

Other books you might like:
David A. Adler, *The Fourth Floor Twins and the Skyscraper Parade*, 1987
When a famous sculpture is stolen from the museum, two sets of twins team up to track down the thief.
Michael James Bradley, *The Shaping Room*, 1978
Seeking an escape from his dominating sister, the neighborhood bully, and himself, Stephen learns the shaping of dreams from his sculpture professor.
Windfred Madison, *Max's Wonderful Delicatessen*, 1972
A would-be sculptor leaves home and sets up a studio in San Francisco's dock area.
Claudia Mills, *Dinah for President*, 1992
Dinah Seabrook struggles to become a big fish in middle school and discovers both recycling and friendship with the elderly.
Cara Reichel, *A Stone Promise*, 1991
A stonecutter vows to create a statue for an impoverished village whose people can see nothing beautiful around them. (Related picture book)

1099

Edna S. Levine

Illustrator: Gloria Kamen

Lisa and Her Soundless World (New York: Human Sciences Press, 1974)

Age range: Grades 3-5

Subject(s): Deafness

Major character(s): Lisa, Child, Handicapped (deaf)

Time period(s): 1970s

Locale(s): United States

What the book is about: Eight year old Lisa is finally diagnosed with deafness after her parents realize that something is wrong. The book makes clear why deaf children have difficulty learning to speak, why they feel angry and unloved, and that halting speech is not due to a lack of intelligence.

Where it's reviewed:
Center for Children's Books Bulletin, October 1974, p 31
Library Journal, September 15, 1974, page 2250

Other books you might like:
Jean F. Andrews, *The Secret in the Dorm Attic*, 1990
 While visiting Matt at a school for the deaf, Donald discovers something strange going on in the attic of the dorm, and becomes involved in a theft.
Barbara Corcoran, *A Dance to Still Music*, 1974
 Deafened by an illness, Margaret refuses to accept her condition and runs away, fearing her mother's remarriage will make her life worse.
Joy Cowley, *The Silent One*, 1981
 A deaf-mute boy who has tamed a huge white turtle becomes the target of supersitious people in his small village.
Penny Pollock, *Keeping It Secret*, 1982
 Wisconsin (Mary Lou) has difficulty adjusting to a new school in a new town, where she is reluctant to admit she wears a hearing aid.
Jody Sorenson, *The Secret Letters of Mama Cat*, 1988
 Meredith deals with several crises; moving to Texas, the departure of her sister to a boarding school for the deaf, and the death of her grandmother.

1100

Nancy Smiler Levinson

Illustrator: Carolyn Croll

Clara and the Bookwagon (New York: Harper, 1988)

Age range: Grades 2-3

Subject(s): Frontier and Pioneer Life; Literacy

Major character(s): Clara, Child

Time period(s): Indeterminate Past

Locale(s): United States

What the book is about: A true story about a young girl who wants to read despite her father's objections. Clara lives a rough life on the family farm. Her dream is fulfilled when a horse-drawn bookwagon visits with the county's first traveling library.

Where it's reviewed:
Booklist, April 1, 1988, page 1355
Kirkus Reviews, April 1, 1988, page 541
School Library Journal, May 1988, page 102

Other books by the author:
Snowshoe Thompson, 1992
Annie's World, 1990
I Lift My Lamp, 1986
Make a Wish, 1983

Other books you might like:
James J. Rawls, *Dame Shirley and the Gold Rush*, 1993
 Relates how a series of letters, writen by a woman known as Dame Shirley were instrumental in inciting the California Gold Rush.
Scott R. Sanders, *Here Comes the Mystery Man*, 1993
 The Goodwin family's pioneer home is visited by the traveling peddler, who brings wondrous things and amazing tales from far away.
Janet Beeler Shaw, *Kirsten Saves the Day: A Summer Story*, 1988
 Kirsten is proud and excited when she finds a bee tree full of honey, but makes the mistake of trying to harvest the honey herself.

Ann Warren Turner, *Grass Songs*, 1993
 A collection of seventeen poems describing the experience of traveling West during the 1800s, as seen through the eyes of pioneer women.
Martin Waddell, *Little Obie and the Flood*, 1991
 Through hardships and good times, Little Obie, Grandad, Effie, and newly adopted Marty grow to become a real family.

1101

Nancy Smiler Levinson

Illustrator: Joan Sandin

Snowshoe Thompson (New York: HarperCollins, 1992)

Age range: Grades 1-2

Series: I Can Read Book

Subject(s): Frontier and Pioneer Life; Mountain Life

Major character(s): John Thompson, Postal Worker (letter carrier); Danny O'Riley, Child

Time period(s): 19th century

Locale(s): Sierra Nevada Mountains, California

What the book is about: Danny is disappointed when heavy snows cut off the mail. He has just written his dad a letter and hopes to hear from him. John Thompson skis ninety miles through a snowstorm to deliver the mail. Based on a true story.

Where it's reviewed:
Booklist, December 1, 1991, page 710
Horn Book, January/February 1992, page 66

Other books by the author:
Annie's World, 1990
Christopher Columbus, Voyager to the Unknown, 1990
Clara and the Bookwagon, 1988
I Lift up My Lamp, 1986

Other books you might like:
Joan Anderson, *Joshua's Westward Journal*, 1987
 In 1836, Joshua and his family travel as pioneers into Illinois where they survive disastrous hardships to establish a prosperous farm of their own.
Betty Brandt, *Special Delivery*, 1988
 A history of the postal service describing ways mail has been sent over the years. (Non-fiction)
Adrian Henri, *The Postman's Palace*, 1990
 A French postman turns his house into a palace that he saw in a dream, adding to it daily over a period of thirty-three years. Based on a real story.
Samuel Marshak, *Hail to Mail*, 1990
 A certified letter follows its intended recipient all over the world as the postal service attempts to catch up to him.
Alice Putnam, *Westering*, 1990
 Traveling with his family in a wagon train from Missouri to Oregon in 1850, Jason finds a stray dog that proves useful during the dangerous journey.

1102

Riki Levinson

Illustrator: Helen Cogancherry

Dinnie Abbie Sister-R-R! (Scarsdale, New York: Bradbury, 1987)

Age range: Grades 2-4

Subject(s): Jews; Brothers and Sisters

Major character(s): Jennie, Child; Abbie, Child; Dinnie, Child

Time period(s): 1930s

Locale(s): New York, New York (Brooklyn)

What the book is about: A novel of Jennie, growing up in Brooklyn in a Jewish family, and her two brothers who are "full of beans." Abbie is stricken with a paralyzing illness and his recovery is slow and difficult for "sister" to understand.

Where it's reviewed:
Booklist, April 15, 1987, page 1292
Hornbook, July 1987, page 459
Kirkus, March 15, 1987, page 474

Other books by the author:
Our Home Is the Sea, 1988
I Go with My Family to Grandma's, 1987
Watch the Stars Come Out, 1985

Other books you might like:
Miriam Chaikin, *I Should Worry, I Should Care*, 1979
    A young Jewish girl and her family adjust to a new neighborhood and new friends at a time when radio is telling of Hitler's rise to power in Europe.
Linda Gondosch, *The Best Bet Gazette*, 1989
    In the summer of 1954, competition with two rival neighborhood girls and a friend's case of polio teach Judy how a newspaper should be written.
Dick King-Smith, *Sophie's Tom*, 1991
    Befriending a stray cat helps a very determined child adjust to school, learn about friends, and pursue her dreams.
Robert Lehrman, *The Store That Mama Built*, 1992
    In 1917, Birdie and her siblings, the children of Jewish immigrants from Russia, help their recently widowed mother run the family store.
Kathy Kennedy Tapp, *Den 4 Meets the Jinx*, 1988
    Adam's bratty five year old sister, Jessie, ruins everything he tries to do with his Cub Scout den. He never suspects she may be the den's only savior

---

1103

Sonia Levitin

Illustrator: Charles Robinson

Journey to America (New York: Atheneum, 1970)

Age range: Grades 5 and Up

Subject(s): Jews; Refugees; World War II

Major character(s): Platt, Refugee

Time period(s): 1940s

Locale(s): Europe

What the book is about: A Jewish family, Mr. Platt, his wife and two daughters, flee Berlin in Nazi Germany in 1938. They endure many separations and hardships. Mr. Platt goes to America, and mother and daughters seek refuge in Switzerland until Mr. Platt can send for them.

Where it's reviewed:
Center for Children's Books Bulletin, February 1971, page 95
Hornbook, April 1970, page 162
Kirkus Reviews, March 1, 1970, page 243

Other books by the author:
Annie's Promise, 1993
Silver Days, 1989 (Sequel to *Journey to America*)
Incident at Loring Groves, 1988
The Mark of Conte, 1976

Other books you might like:
Olga Levy Drucker, *Kindertransport*, 1992
    The author describes the circumstances in Germany after Hitler came to power, evacuating Jewish children to England.
Margery Evernden, *The Dream Keeper*, 1985
    Her parents' impending separation leads a gifted musician to discover the story of her greatgrandmother's immigration to America from Poland.
Anne K. Rose, *Refugee*, 1977
    Traces a twelve year old Jewish girl's flight from Belgium prior to Hitler's invasion and her life in New York until she is eighteen at war's end.
Aranka Siegal, *Grace in the Wilderness: After the Liberation, 1945-1948*, 1985
    Liberated from a German concentration camp at the end of World War II but haunted by the memory of her ordeal, Piri starts a strange new life.
Erika Tamar, *Good-bye Glamour Girl*, 1984
    When Liesl, a Jewish refugee from Nazi-occupied Vienna, arrives in New York, she is determined to leave her European heritage behind.

1104

Myron Levoy

Alan and Naomi (New York: Harper and Row, 1977)

Age range: Grades 5 and Up

Subject(s): Mental Illness; World War II

Major character(s): Alan Silverman, Teenager, Sports Figure (stickball player); Naomi, Teenager, Neighbor

Time period(s): 1940s

Locale(s): New York, New York

What the book is about: Alan only excels at stickball. It is the only thing that "proves" he is not a sissy to the neighborhood boys. His mother insists that he visit the "crazy" French girl who lives in the building. He learns that Naomi is not only Jewish, like him, but she witnessed the brutal death of her father and barely escaped with her own life in Nazi-occupied France. Alan decides to comply with his mother's wishes, and a very special friendship is formed.

Where it's reviewed:
Horn Book, December 1977, page 664
School Library Journal, November 1977, page 59

Awards the book has won:
Boston Globe/Horn Book Award - Honor Book

Other books by the author:
The Magic Hat of Mortimer Wintergreen, 1988
Pictures of Adam, 1986
The Witch of Fourth Street and Other Stories, 1972

Other books you might like:

Barbara Cohen, *King of the Seventh Grade*, 1982
  Abram's secure world becomes unstable when his mother reveals she is not Jewish, therefore, there will be no Bar Mitzvah.
Bess Kaplan, *The Empty Chair*, 1978
  Beth is dismayed when her Jewish relatives help plan her father's remarriage.
Gary Provost, *David and Max*, 1988
  David spends a summer at the beach with his grandfather, a survivor of the Holocaust, and learns about strength and the ability to overcome grief.
Philip Sendak, *In Grandpa's House*, 1985
  Translated from the Yiddish, these are stories of an Eastern European Jewish immigrant and the family he created in America.
Sydney Taylor, *All-of-a-Kind Family*, 1980
  Warm and moving stories of Jewish family life in New York City.

| 1105 |

Myron Levoy

Illustrator: Gabriel Lisowski

The Witch of Fourth Street and Other Stories (New York: Harper, 1972)

Age range: Grades 4-7

Subject(s): Short Stories; Poverty

Time period(s): 20th century

Locale(s): New York, New York

What the book is about: Eight different stories about growing up poor on the lower east side of New York City in the early twentieth century. Some of the best stories are "Keplik, the Match Man," "Andreas and the Magic Bells," and "The Hanukkah Santa Claus."

Where it's reviewed:
Kirkus Reviews, February 1, 1972, page 136
Library Journal, May 15, 1972, page 1915
Publisher's Weekly, April 1, 1972, page 72

Other books by the author:
The Magic Hat of Mortimer Wintergreen, 1988
Picture of Adam, 1986
The Hanukkah of Great-Uncle Otto, 1984
Alan and Naomi, 1977

Other books you might like:
Robert Maiorano, *Worlds Apart: The Autobiography of a Dancer From Brooklyn*, 1980
  A soloist with the New York City Ballet recounts his rise from poverty and the tough streets of Brooklyn to success in the world of dance.
Isaac Metzker, *A Bintel Brief*, 1971
  The book consists of sixty years of letters from the lower east side of New York City to the newspaper, *The Jewish Daily Forward*.
Ben Sonder, *The Tenement Writer: An Immigrant's Story*, 1993
  Follows a young Jewish immigrant from Poland as she struggles to build a new life in America and fulfill her dreams of becoming a writer.
Sydney Taylor, *More All-of-a-Kind Family*, 1954

The story of five young Jewish girls growing up in New York's lower east side before the first world war.
Bernard Wolf, *Firehouse*, 1983
  Describes the work of fire fighters who operate out of a fire station on New York's lower east side, a neighborhood plagued by arson in recent years.

| 1106 |

Elizabeth Levy

Illustrator: Ellen Eagle

The Case of the Mind Reading Mommies (New York: Simon and Schuster, 1989)

Age range: Grades 3-5

Subject(s): Magic; Magicians; Mystery and Detective Stories

Major character(s): Kate, Preteen, Detective—Amateur; Max, Preteen, Detective—Amateur

Time period(s): 1980s

Locale(s): United States

What the book is about: Kate and Max, detective partners, find themselves in the middles of puzzling mishaps involving mothers. Presents disappear and a doorknob talks. They plan a magic show that they hope will end with great presents for parents. Instructions for several magic tricks are included.

Where it's reviewed:
Booklist, May 1, 1989, page 1550
School Library Journal, June 1989, page 106

Other books by the author:
Dracula Is a Pain in the Neck, 1983
The Shadow Nose, 1983
Frankenstein Moved in on the Fourth Floor, 1979

Other books you might like:
Avi, *No More Magic*, 1975
  While searching for his bicycle that disappeared on Halloween, a young boy and his two friends become involved in a magic adventure.
John Bellairs, *The Chessmen of Doom*, 1991
  Johnny, Fergie and Professor Childermass encounter a madman bent on destroying the world when they must spend the summer at a desolate estate.
Elizabeth Levy, *The Case of the Dummy with the Cold Eyes*, 1991
  When a young detective and her partner add a ventriloquist's dummy to their magic act, they find themselves involved in a complicated mystery.
James Marshall, *Fox on Stage*, 1993
  Fox makes a film for Grannie, takes part in a magic show, and puts on a play.
Catherine Siracusa, *The Giant Zucchini*, 1993
  Edgar Mouse and Robert Squirrel grow a zucchini for the county fair, not knowing that it has magic powers when they sing to it.

| 1107 |

Elizabeth Levy

Illustrator: Mordicai Derstein

Dracula Is a Pain in the Neck (New York: Harper, 1983)

Age range: Grades 3-4

Subject(s): Camps and Camping; Toys; Vampires

Major character(s): Robert, Child; Sam, Preteen

Time period(s): 1980s

Locale(s): United States

What the book is about: Robert feels that his plastic Dracula doll is responsible for the spooky doings at his sleep-away camp. He inisisted on taking it, along with his security blanket, even though his older brother, Sam, warned him it would cause trouble, and Sam's prediction was right on!

Where it's reviewed:
Booklist, June 1, 1983, page 1277
Center for Children's Books Bulletin, May 1983, page 170
Kirkus Reviews, January 15, 1983, page 63

Other books by the author:
Keep Ms. Sugarman in the Fourth Grade, 1992
Mister Big Time, 1981
Frankenstein Moved in on the Fourth Floor, 1979
Nice Little Girls, 1974

Other books you might like:
Jayne Harvey, *Great-Uncle Dracula*, 1992
    Emily Normal must adjust to a new town, Transylvania, U.S.A., populated by vampires, witches and the like, and to a bullying classmate.
Mary Hoffman, *Dracula's Daughter*, 1989
    A family raises the baby found on their doorstep even though she develops sharp and pointed teeth, until Dracula comes to claim her as his own.
James Duncan Lawrence, *ESP McGee and the Haunted Mansion*, 1983
    Convinced that something spooky is going to happen at the old Frome mansion, ESP McGee and his best friend, Matt, explore the supposedly empty house.
Vina Lyles, *The Spooky Hand Mystery*, 1973
    When a spooky hand causes things to disappear at a summer fair, three children turn detective.
Stephanie Spinner, *Dracula*, 1982
    Having deduced the double identity of Count Dracula, a wealthy Transylvanian nobleman, a small band of people vow to rid the world of the evil vampire

---

1108

Elizabeth Levy

Illustrator: Blanche Sims

Running out of Magic with Houdini (New York: Knopf, 1981)

Age range: Grades 3-5

Subject(s): Fantasy; Magic; Time Travel

Major character(s): Nina, Preteen; Francie, Sports Figure

Time period(s): 1910s (1912)

Locale(s): New York, New York

What the book is about: Three youngsters travel through time to the days of Harry Houdini. When he is threatened by con artists whose sham he has exposed, the three children save his life.

Where it's reviewed:
Booklist, November 1, 1981, page 390
School Library Journal, December 1981, page 86
Children's Book Review Service, Winter 82, page 58

Other books by the author:
Boys in the Gym, 1990
Captain of the Team, 1989
The Case of the Wild River Ride, 1981
Running out of Time, 1980

Other books you might like:
Thea Beckman, *Crusade in Jeans*, 1975
    A young boy who volunteers to travel through time to the Middle Ages arrives during the Children's Crusade and is caught in its momentum.
Marc Brandel, *The Mine of Lost Days*, 1974
    On a visit to Ireland, Henry falls into a haunted copper mine, and discovers that he and his new friends can travel into the past.
Sherryl Jordan, *The Wednesday Wizard*, 1991
    Trying to warn his absent master, the wizard, of dragon danger, an apprentice finds himself traveling in time.
Robert C. Lee, *Timequake*, 1982
    After an earthquake briefly disrupts their canoe trip, Randy and Morgan travel into the future where the country has lapsed into medieval society.
E.W. Hildick, *The Case of the Weeping Witch*, 1992
    While working on a school project, the members of the McGurk organization travel back to 1692 and find themselves accused of witchcraft.

1109

Elizabeth Levy

Illustrator: Mordicai Gerstein

Something Queer at the Library: A Mystery (New York: Dell, 1977)

Age range: Grades 2-4

Subject(s): Dog Shows; Libraries; Vandalism

Major character(s): Jill, Child; Gwen, Child

Time period(s): 1970s

Locale(s): United States

What the book is about: Jill and Gwen try to track doen the person who is defacing books in the library. Their discovery of some mutilated books strangely links up with a dog show in which they have entered their dog.

Where it's reviewed:
Booklist, November 1, 1977, page 478
Kirkus Reviews, August 15, 1977, page 847
Scholl Library Journal, December 1977, pages 61

Other books by the author:
Something Queer at the Ball Park, 1984
Something Queer at the Haunted School, 1982
Something Queer at the Lemonade Stand, 1982
Something Queer on Vacation, 1980

Other books you might like:
Judith Casely, *Sophie and Sammy's Library Sleepover*, 1993
    A loving and sensitive book-loving little girl teaches her brother to enjoy books.
Carol J. Farley, *The Case of the Lost Lookalike*, 1988

While spending part of the summer at Magic Lake, Flee and her sister become involved with a hermit, vandalism, and a mystery about a kidnapped child.

Lucinda Landon, *Meg Mackintosh and the Mystery in the Locked Library*, 1993
Meg investigates the theft of a rare book from a locked library. The reader is challenged to solve the mystery before Meg.

Gary Paulsen, *Amos Gets Famous*, 1993
Amos and Dunc stumble upon a burglary ring when they decipher a code they find in a library book.

Thomas Rockwell, *The Thief*, 1977
Tim doesn't understand his playmate who vandalizes an old man's shack and is suspected of theft.

1110

C.S. Lewis

Illustrator: Pauline Baynes

The Lion, the Witch, and the Wardrobe (New York: Macmillan, 1950)

Age range: Grades 3-6

Series: Chronicles of Narnia

Subject(s): Good and Evil; Fantasy

Major character(s): Peter, Child; Susan, Child; Aslan, Lion

Time period(s): Indeterminate

Locale(s): England; Narnia, Fictional Country

What the book is about: Four English children, spending a holiday in an old estate, find their way to the land of Narnia. They have many strange adventures, become kings and queens, meet the royal lion, Aslan, and become involved in the battle between good and evil.

Where it's reviewed:
Kirkus Reviews, September 1, 1950, page 515
Saturday Review of Literature, December 9, 1950, page 42

Awards the book has won:
Lewis Carroll Shelf 1962

Other books by the author:
Horse and His Boy, 1954
Prince Caspian, 1951
Silver Chair, 1953
Voyage of the Dawn Treader, 1952

Other books you might like:
Betsy Hearne, *Home*, 1979
Megan and Randall's search for the lost king, Brendan, takes them to a strange land inhabited by lion-like men.

Shirley Rousseau Murphy, *Medallion of the Black Hound*, 1989
David is cast into a world called Meryn, where he joins in the battle of good and evil.

Andre Norton, *Here Abide Monsters*, 1973
Two teenagers are transported to the Avalon of King Arthur's time where they become embroiled in a battle of good and evil.

Jacklyn O'Hanlon, *The Door*, 1978
An 11 year old girl passes through the mysterious door of the Master Gatherer.

1111

Elizabeth Lewis

Illustrator: Ed Young

Young Fu of the Upper Yangtze (Philadelphia: Winston, 1932)

Age range: Grades 5-6

Subject(s): Apprentices

Major character(s): Young Fu, Child

Time period(s): 1930s

Locale(s): Chungking, China

What the book is about: A fatherless boy living in China during the Revolution learns that not all people can be trusted, but kindness can be rewarded. Young Fu encounters badits, fire and flood among his adventures.

Where it's reviewed:
Booklist, May 1932, page 394
Books, July 17, 1932, page 5

Awards the book has won:
Newbery Medal 1933
Lewis Carroll Shelf 1960

Other books by the author:
Homing, Girl of New China, 1933

Other books you might like:
Jean Fritz, *Homesick: My Own Story*, 1982
Jean Fritz recounts her childhood in Hankow, China, during the 1920s.

Meindert De Jong, *The House of Sixty Fathers*, 1956
Tien Pao struggles to find his family after being separated from them during the Japanese invasion of China.

Laurence Yep, *Serpent's Children*, 1984
Gallant returns to his village to find his wife dead and his children barely alive.

Catherine Edwards Sadler, *Heaven's Reward: Fairy Tales from China*, 1985
Six fairy tales span two thousand years of Chinese history.

Ellen Howard, *Her Own Song*, 1988
Sold as an infant to a Chinese family, then taken away by authorities and given to white adoptive parents, Mellie now searches for her real parents.

1112

Marjorie Lewis

Illustrator: Margot Apple

Wrongway Applebaum (New York: Putnam, 1984)

Age range: Grades 3-5

Subject(s): Sports/Baseball; Grandparents; Schools

Major character(s): Stanley Applebaum, Sports Figure; Sophie, Grandparent, Coach

Time period(s): 1980s

Locale(s): United States

What the book is about: Always a little slow and awkward, Applebaum dreams of being on the baseball team and impressing everyone with his spectacular playing. He finds a sponsor for the team and a coach (both his grandmother).

Some of the kids aren't too sure about being sponsored by a knitting shop and coached by an old lady.

Where it's reviewed:
School Library Journal, January 1986, page 31
Booklist, March 15, 1985, page 1060
Center for Children's Books Bulletin, February 1985, page 111

Other books by the author:
The Boy Who Would Be a Hero, 1982
Ernie and the Mile Long Muffler, 1982

Other books you might like:
Charlotte Herman, *Our Snowman Had Olive Eyes*, 1977
    Sheila develops a special relationship with her grandmother, Bubbie, when she comes to live with the family.
Alfred Slote, *Jake*, 1971
    Uncle Lenny is only interested in music, now. How can Jake convince him to coach his Little League team?
Alison Smith, *Billy Boone*, 1989
    Billy fights for her right to take trumpet lessons and spend time with her unorthodox grandmother, even though her parents object to both.
Robert Kimmel Smith, *Bobby Baseball*, 1989
    Because he believes himself to be a super player and has some luck against weaker teams, Bobby mutinies against his coach (who is also his father).
Paul Robert Walker, *The Slugger's Club*, 1993
    When baseball equipment starts disappearing from BJ's Little League team, he and his friends form the Slugger's Club to investigate the crime.

1113

Rob Lewis, Author/Illustrator

The White Bicycle (New York: Farrar, Straus and Giroux, 1988)

Age range: Grades 2-3

Subject(s): Bicycles and Bicycling

Time period(s): Indeterminate

Locale(s): United States

What the book is about: When a boy gives up his rusty, dirty bike to the junk heap, the bike is recovered over and over again by people who need it and use it until it finally ends up where it belongs.

Where it's reviewed:
Booklist, Ocetober 15, 1988, page 411
School Library Journal, March 1989, page 164

Other books by the author:
Tidy Up Trevor, 1993
Henrietta's First Winter, 1990
Friska, the Sheep That Was Too Small, 1987
Hello Mr. Scarecrow, 1987

Other books you might like:
Eve Bunting, *Summer Wheels*, 1992
    The Bicycle Man fixes up old bicycles and offers both his friendship and the use of the bikes to the neighborhood kids.
Michael Crowley, *Shack and Back*, 1993
    Crater insults T-Ball and causes her to quit the Spurwink Gang, just when they need her riding talent to win a bike race.

Judy Delton, *A Birthday Bike for Brimhall*, 1985
    Brimhall receives a bicycle for his birthday but is ashamed to admit that he doesn't know how to ride it.
Crescent Dragonwagon, *Annie Flies the Birthday Bike*, 1993
    Annie gets the bicycle of her dreams for her birthday, but finds riding it is harder than she thought.
James Marshall, *Fox on the Job*, 1988
    Fox tries to earn money for a new bicycle in several different jobs.

1114

Thomas P. Lewis

Illustrator: Beth Weiner Woldin

Call for Mr. Sniff (New York: Harper, 1981)

Age range: Grades 1-2

Subject(s): Animals/Dogs; Mystery and Detective Stories

Major character(s): Mr. Sniff, Dog (hound)

Time period(s): Indeterminate

Locale(s): Fictional Country

What the book is about: A hound becomes a super sleuth and is lured to a birthday party in his honor by a mystery.

Where it's reviewed:
Booklist, March 15, 1981, page 1037
Kirkus Reviews, April 15, 1981, page 502
School Library Journal, May 1981, page 83

Other books by the author:
Frida's Office Day, 1989
The Blue Rocket Fun Show, 1986
Mr. Sniff and the Motel Mystery, 1984
Clipper Ship, 1978

Other books you might like:
David A. Adler, *My Dog and the Birthday Mystery*, 1987
    With the help of her dog, Jenny spends her birthday investigating a bicycle theft and wondering why no one seems to remember it is her special day.
Norman Bidwell, *Count on Clifford*, 1985
    Activities at a birthday party for Clifford, the big red dog, provides opportunities for counting balloons, presents, and other objects.
Nicholas Heller, *Happy Birthday, Moe Dog*, 1988
    All the letters that spell Happy Birthday help Moe Dog enjoy his birthday.
Eve Rice, *Benny Bakes a Cake*, 1981
    When the dog eats Benny's birthday cake, Daddy comes to the rescue.
Harriet Ziefert, *The Small Potatoes and the Birthday Party*, 1985
    The members of the Small Potatoes Club keep busy by making their clubhouse bigger and planning a surprise party for Molly's dog, Spot.

1115

Joan M. Lexau

Illustrator: Marylin Hafner

The Dog Food Caper (New York: Dial, 1985)

Age range: Grades 1-3

Subject(s): Animals/Dogs; Mystery and Detective Stories

Major character(s): Willy Nilly, Child; Mr. Spring, Neighbor; Miss Happ, Witch

Time period(s): Indeterminate

Locale(s): United States

What the book is about: Willy is accused when Mr. Spring finds dog food all over the house, and Willy is the dog sitter. Willy asks Miss Happ, a witch, to help solve the mystery and clear him.

Where it's reviewed:
Booklist, March 15, 1985, page 1062
Hornbook, May 1985, page 308
Kirkus Reviews, March 1, 1985, page J10

Other books by the author:
I Hate Red Rover, 1979
The Rooftop Mystery, 1968

Other books you might like:
Alexandra Day, *Carl's Masquerade*, 1992
 Carl, a large dog, and the baby in his charge fit right in when they follow Mom and Dad to a PTA masquerade party.
Alison Cragin Herzig, *The Big Deal*, 1992
 Sam's parents agree to let him have a puppy if he will take care of it, but the puppy grows out of Sam'a ability to keep his promise.
Dick King-Smith, *The Invisible Dog*, 1993
 Events conspire to turn Jane's imaginary harlequin Great Dane into a real dog.
Steven Kroll, *Andrew Wants a Dog*, 1992
 When his father refuses to let him have a dog, Andrew decides to become one, with the help of a very realistic dog costume from a magic shop.
Betty Ren Wright, *The Ghost of Popcorn Hill*, 1993
 Martin and Peter acquire a mischievous new dog and two lonely ghosts.

1116

Joan M. Lexau

I Hate Red Rover (New York: Dutton, 1979)

Age range: Grades 2-3

Subject(s): Games; Grandparents

Major character(s): Jill, Child

Time period(s): 1970s

Locale(s): United States

What the book is about: Seven year old Jill hates playing Red Rover. She can't hold tight and can't break through opposing lines because she is so small. Jill's relationship with her grandfather is the stable force in her life, and he helps her cope with learning to get along at school.

Where it's reviewed:
Center for Children's Books Bulletin, October 1979, page 31
School Library Journal, September 1979, page 116

Other books by the author:
The Spider Makes a Web, 1979
Striped Ice Cream Web, 1978

Other books you might like:
Sue Alexander, *Lila on the Landing*, 1987
 Lila is a clumsy girl who always gets left out of games, but eventually her quiet games attract the others, especially Alan.
James Flora, *Grandpa's Ghost Stories*, 1978
 During a terrible lightning storm a little boy sits on grandpa's lap and listens to scary stories.
Helen V. Griffith, *Grandaddy's Place*, 1987
 Janetta loves her grandaddy and his home in the country.
Deborah Hartley, *Up North in Winter*, 1986
 In 1911, Grandpa has to walk six miles from work, across a frozen lake. On his way he finds a dying fox. The two save each other's lives.
Chris Van Allsburg, *Jumanji*, 1981
 Two children happen upon a board game that comes to life as they play it.

1117

Joan M. Lexau

Illustrator: John Wilson

Striped Ice Cream (New York: Harper, 1968)

Age range: Grades 3-6

Subject(s): African Americans; Single Parent Families

Major character(s): Becky, Child

Time period(s): 1960s

Locale(s): United States

What the book is about: The conquest of poverty is realistically portrayed in this warmly told story about a fatherless black family as they work together. A seven year old girl is resigned to the fact that her mother cannot afford anything special for her birthday, but she doesn't understand why her sisters and brother seem to turn against her, until the big day arrives.

Where it's reviewed:
Center for Children's Books Bulletin, September 1968, page 11
Publisher's Weekly, April 29, 1968, page 78
School Library Journal, December 1978, page 33

Other books by the author:
The Dog Food Caper, 1985
The Poison Ivy Case, 1983
I Hate Red Rover, 1979
The Rooftop Mystery, 1968

Other books you might like:
Dianne Case, *Love, David*, 1991
 Anna watches as her older brother upsets the family by involving himself in illegal activities to escape the poverty of his home life in South Africa.
Hila Colman, *Rachel's Legacy*, 1978
 After her mother dies, Ellie Levine learns she left an unexecuted will, which could relieve the poverty of Ellie and her father during the Depression.
Judy Delton, *Kitty in the Summer*, 1980
 Kitty's summer in the country is filled with new experiences, from "purchasing" a pagan baby to exposure to real poverty.
John Fante, *1933 Was a Bad Year*, 1985

In a small, poverty-ridden town in 1933, under pressure from his father to go into the family business, Dominic Molise longs to fulfill his own dreams

Margaret Walden Froehlich, *Reasons to Stay*, 1986
  After her mother's death, twelve year old Babe learns some hard truths about her mother's life that shake her confidence and sense of self worth.

1118

Betty Jean Lifton

Illustrator: Ann Leggett

Jaguar, My Twin (New York: Atheneum, 1976)

Age range: Grades 4-6

Subject(s): Indians of North America

Major character(s): Shun, Indian

Time period(s): Indeterminate Past

Locale(s): Mexico

What the book is about: The Zinacanter Indians remain distinct within Mexico, following their own gods and rituals. Shun dreams of his twin spirit, the jaguar, who lives with the gods. When Shun is stricken down by an evil shaman, his recovery and the jaguar are closely tied.

Where it's reviewed:
Horn Book, December 1976, page 625
School Library Journal, October 1976, page 108

Other books by the author:
I'm Still Me, 1981
Cock and the Ghost Cat, 1965
Joji and the Dragon, 1957

Other books you might like:
Toni De Gerez, *My Song Is a Piece of Jade*, 1984
  An anthology of fragments of poems originally composed in the Nahuatl language in honor of the gods of ancient Mexico.
Burdetta Johnson, *Little Dickens, Jaguar Cub*, 1970
  Chronicles the relationship between a jaguar cub and a man hunting Indian ruins in the swamps of Mexico's west coast.
Joan Price, *Truth Is a Bright Star*, 1982
  Understanding and friendship develop between a Hopi Indian boy and the fur trapper who buys him from Spanish soldiers in 1832.
Eve Titus, *Why the Wind God Wept*, 1972
  Many try, but only the poet is able to discover why the wind god is unhappy in his temple.
B. Traven, *The Creation of the Sun and Moon*, 1968
  A retelling of an ancient Mexican Indian legend about how the sun and moon were created from bits of stars gathered by two brave warriors.

1119

Anne Lindbergh

Illustrator: Kinuko Craft

Bailey's Window (New York: Harcourt, 1984)

Age range: Grades 3-6

Subject(s): Fantasy; Space and Time

Major character(s): Bailey Bond, Time Traveller; Anna, Cousin; Ingrid, Friend

Time period(s): 1980s

Locale(s): United States

What the book is about: When their grumpy cousin, Baily Bond, accidentally creates a window to anywhere with his painting, Anna and Carl and their friend, Ingrid, are in for a magical summer of visiting faraway places.

Where it's reviewed:
Booklist, May 1, 1984, page 1250
Center for Children's Books Bulletin, July 1984, page 208
School Library Journal, May 1984, page 82

Other books by the author:
The Shadow on the Dial, 1987
The Hunky-Dory Diary, 1986
The People in Pineapple Place, 1982
Osprey Island, 1974

Other books you might like:
Grace Chetwin, *On All Hallow's Eve*, 1984
  Two sisters on their way home from a party step into another time period, where the forces of good and evil involve them in a life or death adventure.
Virginia Hamilton, *Dustland*, 1980
  Four children, all possessing extraordinary mental powers, are projected far into the future to a bleak region called Dustland.
Sherryl Jordan, *The Wednesday Wizard*, 1991
  Trying to warn his absent master of dragon danger, Weasel makes a slight miscalculation in a magic spell and finds himself beamed into the future.
Madeleine L'Engle, *An Acceptable Time*, 1989
  Polly O'Keefe goes to spend a quiet visit with her grandparents. She meets several unusual people who lead her on a trip back through time.
Elizabeth Winthrop, *The Battle for the Castle*, 1993
  William uses the magic token to return through the toy castle in his attic, to a medieval land, which is now menaced by a skeleton ship.

1120

Anne Lindbergh

The People in Pineapple Place (San Diego: Harcourt, Brace Jovanovich, 1982)

Age range: Grades 3-6

Subject(s): Space and Time

Major character(s): August Brown, Child; April Anderson, Time Traveller; Mike O'Malley, Time Traveller

Time period(s): 1980s

Locale(s): Washington, District of Columbia

What the book is about: After a divorce, 10-year-old August has moved to Washington, D.C. with his mother. He has no friends and is stuck with a baby-sitter who spends all day on the phone. He discovers April and the people of Pineapple Place, a town which moves through space and time. He has great adventures and gradually his mother comes to understand about his "invisible" friends.

Where it's reviewed:
Booklist, September 15, 1982, page 116
School Library Journal, October 1982, page 153

Other books by the author:
The Prisoner of Pineapple Place, 1988
The Shadow on the Dial, 1987
The Worry Week, 1985

Other books you might like:
Mary Downing Hahn, *The Doll in the Garden*, 1989
    After Ashley and Kristi find an antique doll, they discover they can enter a ghostly turn-of-the-century world by going through a hole in the hedge.
Helen Cresswell, *Moondial*, 1987
    While staying with her mother's godmother, Minty finds herself drawn to a mysterious sundial which takes her back in time.
Patrick Skene Catling, *John Midas in the Dreamtime*, 1987
    While visiting the site of a cave painting in Australia, John slips back thousands of years and finds himself among a prehistoric Aboriginal tribe.
Zilpha Keatley Snyder, *The Truth about Stone Hollow*, 1974
    The new boy at school introduces Amy to the secrets of Stone Hollow where the circles of time converge.
Edward Eager, *Knight's Castle*, 1989
    Four children find a magic way to go back into the time of Ivanhoe and Robin Hood.

| 1121 |

Anne Lindbergh

Illustrator: Kathryn Hewitt

The Worry Week (New York: Harcourt, 1985)

Age range: Grades 5-7

Subject(s): Sisters

Major character(s): Allegra "Legs" Sloane, Preteen; Alice Sloane, Teenager; Edith "Minnow" Sloane, Child

Time period(s): 1980s

Locale(s): North Haven Island, Maine

What the book is about: Left alone with her sisters for a week in Maine, eleven year old "Legs" spends most of her time tending to and worrying about her siblings. What she hoped would be a week of great freedom turns out to be lack of money, scary noises at night, rashes, stomach aches and starving. Eating mussels and mushrooms might be freedom, but it isn't much fun.

Where it's reviewed:
Booklist, June 1, 1985, page 1402
Publisher's Weekly, March 22, 1985, page 60
School Library Journal, August 1985, page 67

Other books by the author:
Travel Far, Pay No Fare, 1992
The Prisoner of Pineapple Place, 1988
Bailey's Window, 1984
Nobody's Orphan, 1983

Other books you might like:
Peni R. Griffin, *The Treasure Bird*, 1992
    With clues from a talking parrot, Jessy and her stepbrother discover the whereabouts of a hidden treasure in Uncle Matthew's old house in Texas.

Welwyn Wilton Katz, *Whalesinger*, 1990
    A scientific field trip brings together two teenagers, an emotionally isolated boy and a girl who shares a bond with two gray whales in the area.
Jackie French Koller, *The Last Voyage of the Misty Day*, 1992
    Having reluctantly moved to Maine after her father's death, Denise forges a healing friendship with a boat owner surrounded by considerable mystery.
Walter Dean Myers, *The Righteous Revenge of Artemis Bonner*, 1992
    Fifteen year old Artemis journeys from New York City to Tombstone, Arizona, in 1882, to avenge the murder of his uncle.
Robert Louis Stevenson, *Treasure Island*, 1883
    While going through the possessions of a deceased guest, the mistress of the inn and her son find a treasure map that leads to a pirate's fortune.

| 1122 |

Gunnel Linde

Illustrator: Otto S. Svend

Trust in the Unexpected (New York: Macmillan, 1984)

Age range: Grades 3-5

Subject(s): Anger; Guilt

Major character(s): Katie, Child; Joey, Child

Time period(s): 1980s

Locale(s): Sweden

What the book is about: Katie throws her brother's bicycle into the river, and then must deal with the consequences. Ashamed and guilty, she tries various ways to either recover or replace the bike.

Where it's reviewed:
Horn Book, January/February 1985, page 54
School Library Journal, April 1985, page 88

Other books by the author:
The Invisible League and the Royal Guest, 1970
The White Stone, 1966

Other books you might like:
Paula Fox, *One-Eyed Cat*, 1984
    A boy shoots a stray cat with his new air rifle, subsequently suffers from guilt, and eventually assumes responsibility for it.
Astrid Lindgren, *Emil in the Soup Tureen*, 1970
    The adventures of prankster Emil, who strands his little sister atop a flagpole, disappears from a locked woodshed, and gets his head stuck in a bowl.
Ulf Nilsson, *If You Didn't Have Me*, 1987
    Living with farm relatives in Southern Sweden while his parents build a new town home, a young boy finds inner strength and unexpected entertainment.
Joan Sandin, *The Long Way Westward*, 1989
    The experiences of two young brothers and their immigrant Swedish family, from their New York arrival through the trip to their new Minnesota home.
Janet Beeler Shaw, *Meet Kirsten, An American Girl*, 1986
    Kirsten and her family experience many hardships as they travel from Sweden to the Minnesota frontier in 1854.

1123

Astrid Lindgren

Illustrator: Ilon Wikland

The Ghost of Skinny Jack (New York: Viking, 1988)

Age range: Grades 1-4

Subject(s): Brothers and Sisters; Ghosts

Major character(s): Skinny Jack, Handyman (farmhand)

Time period(s): Indeterminate Past (medieval times)

Locale(s): England

What the book is about: Two children listen to their grandmother tell the story of Skinny Jack, a farmh and who played a trick on a church organist who Jack despised. The trick backfi red and Jack's blood turned to ice. One hundred years later a brave young woman carried the frozen ghost to the organist's grave where Jack begged forgiveness . After hearing the story, the children start home through the woods, but as tw ilight approaches they sense the ghost's presence. Great suspense with eerie il lustrations.

Where it's reviewed:
Booklist, January 1, 1989, page 791
Center for Children's Books Bulletin, November 1988, page 78

Other books by the author:
Ronia, the Robber's Daughter, 1983
Of Course Polly Can Do Almost Anything, 1977
Springtime in Noisy Village, 1966
The Tomten, 1961

Other books you might like:
Daniel Cohen, *The Ghosts of War*, 1990
  Recounts stories of ghosts connected with war, from haunted battlefields to soldiers' premonitions of death.
Phyllis Rose Eisenberg, *Don't Tell Me a Ghost Story*, 1982
  An older brother tells a scary story to his younger brothers, only to have the tables turned on him.
Margaret Mahy, *A Tall Story and Other Tales*, 1991
  Tall tales, stories of witches and ghosts for scary sharing.
Sam McBratney, *The Ghosts of Hungryhouse Lane*, 1988
  The three mischievious Sweet children discover that their new house is home to three eccentric ghosts who want only to be left alone.
Betty Ren Wright, *Ghosts Beneath Our Feet*, 1984
  While in a ghost town, Katie's relationship with a rebellious stepbrother improves as they find out why there are literally ghosts beneath their feet.

1124

Astrid Lindgren

Illustrator: Louis S. Glanzman

Pippi Longstocking (New York: Viking, 1950)

Age range: Grades 3-6

Subject(s): Humor; Orphans

Major character(s): Pippi Longstocking, Orphan; Tommy Settergren, Neighbor; Annika Settergren, Neighbor

Time period(s): 1950s

Locale(s): Villa Villekulla, Sweden

What the book is about: Escapades of a little girl who lives with a horse and a monkey, with no parents, at the edge of a Swedish village. Pippi goes in search of her lost father, a sea captain, and has exciting adventures and great silliness with her friends Tommy and Annika.

Where it's reviewed:
Observer (London), November 7, 1976, page 23
Reading Teacher, March 1981, page 635
Reading Teacher, April 1982, page 793

Other books by the author:
The Brothers Lionheart, 1975
Emil in the Soup Tureen, 1970
The Children on Troublemaker Street, 1964
The Children of Noisy Village, 1962

Other books you might like:
Sid Fleischman, *Jingo Django*, 1971
  An orphan boy resolves to follow a treasure map he finds inscribed on a whale's tooth.
Maria Gripe, *Hugo and Josephine*, 1969
  Everything changes for the minister's small daughter when she meets and becomes friends with an unusual little boy.
Harry Kullman, *The Battle Horse*, 1981
  The children on a Stockholm street engage in a modern day jousting tournament in which the rich are knights and the poor are the horses who bear them.
Mary Tannen, *The Lost Legend of Finn*, 1982
  Determined to find out the truth about their father, Bran and Fiona use their uncle's magic book and go back in time to 9th century Ireland.
Marie Louise Wallin, *Tangles*, 1980
  A Swedish girl relates the deeply felt joys and sorrows of her relationship with her horse and her best friend.

1125

Astrid Lindgren

Illustrator: J.K. Lambert

Ronia, the Robber's Daughter (New York: Viking, 1983)

Age range: Grades 3-5

Subject(s): Robbers and Outlaws

Major character(s): Ronia, Child; Matt, Thief

Time period(s): Indeterminate

Locale(s): Norway

What the book is about: Ronia, who lives with her father and his band of robbers in a castle in the woods, causes trouble when she befriends the son of a rival chieftain.

Where it's reviewed:
Horn Book, June 1983, page 304
Kirkus Reviews, April 15, 1983, page 459

Awards the book has won:
Mildred L. Batchelder Award 1984

Other books by the author:
Mardie, 1979
The Brothers Lionheart, 1975
Emil in the Soup Tureen, 1970
Mischievous Meg, 1962

Other books you might like:
Avi, *Man From the Sky*, 1980

A man parachutes from an airplane with a large amount of money, only to be seen by a boy who has a reputation for seeing things in the clouds.

M.J. Engh, *The House in the Snow*, 1987
Nine boys outwit the invisible robbers who have inhabited the house in the snow for generations, by using the robbers' own cloak of invisibility.

Sid Fleischman, *The Whipping Boy*, 1989
A bratty prince and his whipping boy trade places after becoming involved with dangerous outlaws.

Kathryn Osebold Galbraith, *Something Suspicious*, 1985
Lizzie and her friend track down a bank robber called the Green Pillowcase Bandit and end up with more mysteries than they can handle.

Robin D. Jones, *No Shakespeare Allowed*, 1989
As the daughter of a director of the town's Shakespeare festival, Portia fears she can never escape the theatre.

1126

Jennie D. Lindquist

Illustrator: Garth Williams

The Golden Name Day (New York: Harper, 1955)

Age range: Grades 3-5

Subject(s): Grandparents; Swedish Americans

Major character(s): Nancy, Child

Time period(s): Indeterminate

Locale(s): Minnesota

What the book is about: Nancy longs to celebrate her own name day when she spends a summer with her Swedish-American grandparents

Other books by the author:
The Little Silver House, 1986

Other books you might like:
Allyson McGill, *The Swedish Americans*, 1988
Discusses the history, culture and religion of the Swedes. (Non-fiction)

Poupa Montaufier, *One Summer at Grandmother's House*, 1985
Separate stories describe a memorable grandmother and her house in Alsace.

Gayle Pearson, *The Coming Home Cafe*, 1988
Fearing the Depression will hold her family helpless forever, Elizabeth leaves to ride the rails from town to town looking for work.

Joan Sandin, *The Long Way Westward*, 1989
Relates the experiences of two young brothers and their family, immigrants from Sweden, as they journey to their new home in Minnesota.

Janet Beeler Shaw, *Happy Birthday, Kirsten!*, 1987
On a Minnesota farm in the mid-1800s, the hard working members of the Larson family find time to celebrate Kirsten's tenth birthday.

1127

Esther Linfield

The Lion of the Kalahari (New York: Greenwillow, 1976)

Age range: Grades 5 and Up

Subject(s): Africa

Major character(s): Skankwan, Chieftain (African bushman), Teenager

Time period(s): 1970s

Locale(s): South Africa

What the book is about: Eight year old Skankwan was left alone in the desert when his father was murdered. He had already learned hunting and survival skills. He lives for the day he can avenge his father. At sixteen, he becomes the Lion of the Kalahari, a tribal leader.

Where it's reviewed:
Kirkus Reviews, September 1, 1976, page 973

Other books you might like:
Jean Bothwell, *African Herdboy*, 1970
A young Masai herdboy's defense of his pet heifer from a lion precipitates a crisis within the tribe.

Dianne Case, *Love, David*, 1991
Anna watches as her older brother upsets the family by involving himself in illegal activities to escape the poverty of his home in South Africa.

Betty Dinneen, *Make Way for the Ark*, 1977
The completion of the Kariba Dam in Central Africa disrupts the lives of the Batonga people and endangers the lives of thousands of animals.

Beverly Naidoo, *Journey to Jo'burg*, 1985
Naledi and her younger brother make a journey of over three hundred kilometers to find their mother in Johannesburg, South Africa.

Jenny Seed, *Vengence of the Zulu King*, 1970
An account of a Zulu boy who might have explored with Henry Flynn, a white hero of the Zulus.

1128

Janet Taylor Lisle

Afternoon of the Elves (New York: Orchard, 1989)

Age range: Grades 5-8

Subject(s): Elves; Friendship; Mental Illness

Major character(s): Hilary, Child; Sara Kate Connolly, Preteen; Jane Webster, Preteen

Time period(s): 1980s

Locale(s): United States

What the book is about: Nine year old Hilary has a happy home, lots of friends, and everything she wants. Eleven year old Sara Kate is an outcast, thin, poorly dressed, failing in school, living in a run-down house with a weedy yard. Sara Kate has an elf village and the two girls become friends. Was Sara Kate's father really a criminal? Why did no one ever see her mother? The urge to find out finally leads Hilary past the elf houses to the bleak and secretive threshold of Kate's own.

Where it's reviewed:
Booklist, August 1989, page 1979
Hornbook, September 1989, page 622
Kirkus Reviews, August 1, 1989, page 1161

Awards the book has won:
Newbery Honor 1990

Other books by the author:
The Lampfish of Twill, 1991
The Great Dimpole Oak, 1987
Sirens and Spies, 1985
The Dancing Cats of Applesap, 1984

Other books you might like:
Bill Brittain, *Wings: A Novel*, 1991
    When Ian grows a pair of wings, he embarrasses his politically ambitios father and must look for help from class outcast Anita and her mother.
Elizabeth Starr Hill, *Ever-After Island*, 1977
    Two children accompany their scientist father on an expedition to a remote island inhabited by elves, mermaids, a wizard and other magical creatures.
Barbara M. Joosse, *Anna and the Cat Lady*, 1992
    When Anna rescues a stray kitten, she becomes friends with Mrs. Sarafiny, and strange old woman with many cats and a fear that Martians are after her.
Richard Peck, *Through a Brief Darkness*, 1973
    Forced to decide if her father was a criminal, Karen must rely on her own instincts and judgement as her situation becomes increasingly terrifying.
Barbara Brooks Wallace, *The Secret Summer of L.E.B.*, 1974
    Lizabeth risks her popularity with the other sixth graders by becoming friends with the class outcast.

1129

Janet Taylor Lisle

Illustrator: Joelle Shefts

The Dancing Cats of Applesap (Scarsdale, New York: Bradbury, 1984)

Age range: Grades 4-6

Subject(s): Animals/Cats

Major character(s): Melba Morris, Preteen; Mr. Jiggs, Store Owner; Miss Toonie, Clerk

Time period(s): 1980s

Locale(s): Applesap, New York

What the book is about: When both the town of Applesap in general and Jiggs Pharmacy in particular are going downhill, Melba discovers that the cats at Jiggs Drugstore have a special talent for dancing, and she takes advantage of it to not only save Jiggs Drug Store and put Applesap on the map, but into the *Guiness Book of World Records* as well.

Where it's reviewed:
Children's Book Review Service, August 1984, page 152
Center for Children's Books Bulletin, July 1984, page 208
School Library Journal, October 1984, page 159

Other books by the author:
The Lampfish of Twill, 1991
Afternoon of the Elves, 1989
The Great Dimpole Oak, 1987
Sirens and Spies, 1985

Other books you might like:
Marion Dane Bauer, *Ghost Eye*, 1992
    Purrloom Popcorn, a beautiful cat with one blue eye and one gold eye, receives his first real love from a lonely girl and an array of ghost cats.
Janet Wyman Coleman, *Fast Eddie*, 1993

To the dismay of Puff the cat and Jones the squirrel, Fast Eddie the raccoon takes on his human neighbors one final time.
Barbara M. Joosse, *Anna and the Cat Lady*, 1992
    When Anna rescues a stray kitten, it leads her into friendship with an eccentric old woman with many cats and a paranoid conviction.
Phyllis Reynolds Naylor, *The Grand Escape*, 1993
    After years of being house cats, Marco and Polo escape into the dangerous outside world and are sent on three challenging adventures.
Linda Stewart, *Sam the Cat Detective*, 1993
    Sam the cat detective takes on the case of a pretty yong cat who comes into his office and purrs out her unhappy story.

1130

Janet Taylor Lisle

Illustrator: Stephen Gammell

The Great Dimpole Oak (New York: Orchard, 1987)

Age range: Grades 4-7

Subject(s): Trees

Time period(s): Indeterminate

Locale(s): Dimpole, Earth

What the book is about: The Great Dimpole Oak is hundreds of feet tall and, tens of feet thick, with roots as thick as fire hoses coiled around its base. The tree is the answer to the many wishes of the townspeople, including two boys seeking revenge against a bully, an old man hoping for a birthday party, shy lovers, and a swami from Bombay.

Where it's reviewed:
Horn Book, January/February 1988, page 64
School Library Journal, December 1987, page 86

Other books by the author:
The Lampfish of Twill, 1991
Afternoon of the Elves, 1989
Sirens and Spies, 1986
The Dancing Cats of Applesap, 1984

Other books you might like:
Mary Marsy Buff, *The Big Tree*, 1946
    A giant five-thousand-year-old Sequoia, called Wa-No-Na by the Indians, tells its life story.
Nellie Burchardt, *What Are We Going to Do, Michael?*, 1973
    When urban renewal threatens a large magnolia tree in their block, the neighborhood residents combine forces to save it.
Mary Calhoun, *Julie's Tree*, 1988
    After her mother's death, Julie joins her father in a new town where she makes new friends and tries to save a tree threatened by a new parking lot.
Paula Danziger, *Make Like a Tree and Leave*, 1990
    Matthew gets into trouble at home and at school, spars with his older sister, and helps save an elderly friend's property from a developer.
Louanne Norris, *An Oak Tree Dies and a Journey Begins*, 1979
    A big, old oak tree on a riverbank is felled by weather and age and, after life on the ground, in the river, and at sea, becomes beach driftwood.

1131

Ada B. Litchfield

Illustrator: Sonia O. Lisker

Captain Hook, That's Me (New York: Walker, 1982)

Age range: Grades 2-3

Subject(s): Moving, Household; Physically Handicapped

Major character(s): Judy Johnson, Handicapped (3rd Grader); Bunny Johnson, Child; Miss Morris, Teacher

Time period(s): 1980s

Locale(s): United States

What the book is about: Judy, a third grader who can run and skate and do lots of things well, is afraid the children in her new school will feel sorry for her because she has a steel hook instead of a left hand. A very caring teacher eases the transition with a special surprise for Judy.

Where it's reviewed:
Children's Book Review Service, August 1982, page 135

Awards the book has won:
Crabbery Honor

Other books by the author:
Making Room for Uncle Joe, 1984
Words in Our Hands, 1980
A Cane in Her Hand, 1977
A Button in Her Ear, 1976

Other books you might like:
Nan Holcomb, *Patrick and Emma Lou*, 1989
  Despite his excitement over walking with a new walker, three year old Patrick finds it isn't easy and needs lot of encouragement from his friend.
James Hurst, *The Scarlet Ibis*, 1988
  Ashamed of his younger brother's physical handicaps, an older brother teaches him how to walk and pushes him to attempt more strenuous activities.
Kathleen Muldoon, *Princess Pooh*, 1989
  Jealous of her invalid sister's royal treatment, Patty Jean tries out the wheelchair and discovers life in a wheelchair is no fun at all.
Harriette Robinet, *Ride the Red Cycle*, 1980
  Jerome, crippled since the age of two, struggles to realize his dream of riding a cycle.
Linda Yeatman, *Perkins: The Cat Who Was More than a Friend*, 1987
  Although David is blind, he knows his cat, Perkins, better than anyone. When David realizes his cat was switched with another cat, no one belives him.

1132

Jean Little

Illustrator: Laura Fernandez

Different Dragons (New York: Viking, 1987)

Age range: Grades 3-6

Subject(s): Fear; Animals/Dogs

Major character(s): Ben, Child; Rosa, Relative (aunt); Gulliver Gallivant, Dog

Time period(s): 1980s

Locale(s): United States

What the book is about: Ben, who seems to be afraid of everything is especially afraid of his aunt's dog. He learns that everyone has fears of some kind to face. When he goes to visit Aunt Rosa's for his first weekend away from home, he has to face her Labrador Retriever. When a thunderstorm shows the dog to be more marshmallow than furious threat, Ben and the dog become fast friends.

Where it's reviewed:
Center for Children's Books Bulletin, July/August 1987, page 214
School Library Journal, June/July 1987, page 98

Other books by the author:
Lost and Found, 1985
From Anna, 1972
Kate, 1971
Home From Far, 1965

Other books you might like:
Lawrence Balter, *Linda Saves the Day: Understanding Fear*, 1989
  Linda's mother patiently helps her overcome her intense fear of dogs so Linda can go to a party given by a friend who has a dog.
Barbara Shook Hazen, *Alone at Home*, 1992
  Amy experiences some scary moments when she finally gets the chance to babysit herself.
Kevin Henkes, *Words of Stone*, 1992
  Busy trying to deal with his fears and feelings about his dead mother, Blaze has his life changed when he meets boisterous and irresistible Joselle.
Johanna Hurwitz, *The Up and Down Spring*, 1993
  While vacationing at Bolivia's house in New York, Rory tries to hide his fear of flying after Bolivia suggests a trip in her uncle's airplane.
Suzy Kline, *Herbie Jones and the Dark Attic*, 1992
  Herbie's friend, Ray, and some classmates in his fourth grade reading group help him adjust when he moves into a new bedroom in the attic.

1133

Jean Little

Illustrator: Joan Sandin

From Anna (New York: Harper, 1972)

Age range: Grades 4-6

Subject(s): Physically Handicapped

Major character(s): Anna, Child

Time period(s): 1930s

Locale(s): Canada

What the book is about: Fleeing the growing Nazi menace, Anna's family emigrates to Canada. Anna sees the move as a disaster. She fears her new teachers and language because she cannot learn to read. Things turn around for her when she finally gets glasses and a supportive teacher and classmates.

Where it's reviewed:
Booklist, December 15, 1972, page 405
Center for Children's Books Bulletin, January 1973, page 78

Other books by the author:
Stars Come Out Within, 1990
Lost and Found, 1985
Listen for the Singing, 1977
Stand in the Wind, 1975

Other books you might like:
Joy Cowley, *The Silent One*, 1981
    A deaf-mute boy who has tamed a huge white turtle becomes the target of superstitious people in his small village.
Gary Paulsen, *The Monument*, 1991
    Rocky, self-conscious about the braces on her legs, has her life changed by an artist who comes to her small Kansas town to design a war memorial.
Nancy Springer, *Colt*, 1991
    A young handicapped boy learns to help himself and others through a horseback riding program.
Marjorie Stover, *Midnight in the Dollhouse*, 1990
    A family of dolls help their lame owner find a clue to hidden treasure.
Nicholas Wilde, *Into the Dark*, 1987
    A lonely boy's new friend has a frightening secret.

1134

Jean Little

Illustrator: Joan Sandin

Look through My Window (New York: Harper, 1970)

Age range: Grades 4-6

Subject(s): Family Life; Tuberculosis

Major character(s): Emily Ann Blair, Preteen; Kate Bloomfield; Roger Sutherland, Relative (uncle)

Time period(s): 1970s

Locale(s): Riverside, Ontario, Canada

What the book is about: Emily can't believe her family is going to move into a huge eighteen room house and her wild cousins are moving in with them. Going from being an "only child" to part of a very large family can be very rewarding, if sometimes exasperating!

Where it's reviewed:
Booklist, September 15, 1970, page 108
Center for Children's Books Bulletin, January 1971, page 76
Hornbook, December 1970, page 620

Other books by the author:
Hey World, Here I Am!, 1989
Different Dragons, 1986
Stand in the Wind, 1975
Kate, 1971

Other books you might like:
Eleanor Cameron, *A Spell Is Cast*, 1964
    During her visit to Tarnhelm, a huge old house on the California coast, Cory Winterslow discovers the secret of her past.
Susan Cooper, *The Boggart*, 1993
    After visiting Scotland and returning home to Canada, Emily finds that she has brought back a boggart, an invisible and practical joking spirit.
T. Degens, *On the Third Ward*, 1990
    A group of children in a tuberculosis ward deal with life, death, and plans to escape while listening to stories about the "Empress of China."

Sarah Ellis, *Next-Door Neighbors*, 1989
    The move to a new town leaves Peggy feeling lonely and uncomfortable until she befriends George and the Chinese servant of her neighbor, Mrs. Manning.
Nancy Hope Wilson, *Bringing Nettie Back*, 1992
    Clara's life is enriched by her friendship with Nettie, whose family is different from her own, but then a serious brain condition threatens Nettie.

1135

Jean Little

Mama's Going to Buy You a Mockingbird (New York: Viking Kestrel, 1984)

Age range: Grades 5-8

Subject(s): Cancer; Death; Family Problems

Major character(s): Jeremy, Child; Sarah, Child

Time period(s): 1980s

Locale(s): United States

What the book is about: Young Jeremy and Sarah learn to cope with their grief and drastically changed lifestyle during their father's battle with cancer, which forces their mother to sell their house and return to school full time.

Where it's reviewed:
Children's Book Review Service, August 1985, page 132
Center for Children's Books Bulletin, June 1985, page 189
School Library Journal, October 1985, page 174

Other books by the author:
Look through My Window, 1970
One to Grow On, 1969
Home From Far, 1965
Mine for Keeps, 1962

Other books you might like:
Alden R. Carter, *Sheila's Dying*, 1987
    Just as high school junior Jerry Kincaid is considering breaking up with his girlfriend, he discovers that she has a terminal case of cancer.
C.B. Christiansen, *A Small Pleasure*, 1989
    Wray Jean overloads on scholastic and extracurricular activities in order to find her identity and ease the pain of her father's death from cancer.
Cynthia D. Grant, *Phoenix Rising, or, How to Survive Your Life*, 1989
    Helen's death from cancer shatters the lives of her family, especially sister Jessie who tries to cope with her pain by reading Helen's diary.
Buzz King, *Silicon Songs*, 1990
    Max, a computer wizard with no conventional family, tries to concentrate his life on electronic networks while his uncle lies dying of brain cancer.
Barbara Garland Polikoff, *Life's a Funny Proposition, Horatio*, 1992
    As Horatio tries to adjust to the death of his father from lung cancer, O.P., Horatio's grandfather, mourns the loss of his dog, Mollie.

1136

Penelope Lively

Illustrator: Ann Dalton

Boy Without a Name (Berkeley: Parnassus, 1975)

Age range: Grades 4-6

Subject(s): Orphans

Major character(s): Thomas Mason, Child, Apprentice; John, Artisan (stonemason); Eliza, Parent

Time period(s): 17th century (1630s)

Locale(s): Swinfield, England

What the book is about: After his apprenticeship ends with the death of his master, a boy returns to his birthplace because he has nowhere else to go. Named Thomas by the poorhouse overseer, he askes to be apprenticed to the stonemason of the beautiful church in the village. He has a gift for working with stone, so he adds "Mason" to his name when he carves it on the church wall. He has found a place to belong.

Where it's reviewed:
Kirkus Reviews, November 1, 1975, page 1229
Observer, July 20, 1975, page 23

Other books by the author:
The Whispering Knights, 1976
The House in Norham Gardens, 1974 (for advanced readers)
The Driftway, 1973
The Ghost of Thomas Kempe, 1973

Other books you might like:
Vera Cleaver, *Trial Valley*, 1977
    The three Luther children, who have raised themselves since their father died, find an abandoned boy near their house in the Great Smoky Mountains.
Rumer Godden, *Listen to the Nightingale*, 1992
    When she wins a scholarship to a famous ballet school, orphan Lottie is torn between her lifetime dream and her love for a puppy.
Les Martin, *Oliver Twist*, 1990
    A simplified retelling of the adventures of an orphan boy who lives in the squalor of a nineteenth-century English workhouse.
Jerry Spinelli, *Maniac Magee*, 1990
    Jeffrey "Maniac" Magee's exploits become legendary as he accomplishes feats of cleverness and athletic prowess and changes many lives.
Mary Stolz, *The Cuckoo Clock*, 1987
    Orphaned Erich's life as an unloved drudge begins to change when old Ula, the town's most skillful clockmaker, takes him on as a helper.

1137

Penelope Lively

Illustrator: Anthony Maitland

The Ghost of Thomas Kempe (New York: Dutton, 1973)

Age range: Grades 4-6

Subject(s): Ghosts

Major character(s): James Harrison, Preteen

Time period(s): 1970s

Locale(s): England

What the book is about: When the Harrisons move into an old house, strange things begin to happen. Messages and notes written in Old English begin to appear, signed by long dead Thomas Kempe. James is accused of everything the ghost actually does.

Where it's reviewed:
Kirkus Reviews, August 15, 1973, page 883
Publisher's Weekly, October 8, 1973, page 97

Awards the book has won:
Carnegie Medal

Other books by the author:
Fanny's Sister, 1980
A Stitch in Time, 1976
The Whispering Knights, 1976
The Driftway, 1973

Other books you might like:
Joan Aiken, *Return to Harken House*, 1988
    Julia spends the summer with her father and finds that he only cares about her stepmother, who is unaware of the voices that haunt Julia every night.
Scott Corbett, *Captain Butcher's Body*, 1976
    Two boys confront the ghost of a long-dead pirate on an island off the coast of New England.
Kathryn Lasky, *Double Trouble Squared*, 1991
    In London with their family, telepathic twins receive strange emanations from an early residence of Arthur Conan Doyle and discover a literary ghost.
Patricia A. McKillip, *The House on Parchment Street*, 1973
    While staying with her cousin in England, a young girl helps him find a way of helping the troubled ghosts inhabiting the cellar of the house.
Robert Westall, *Ghost Abbey*, 1988
    When her father's new job takes the entire family to an old Abbey in England, Maggie discovers that both she and the building are haunted by ghosts.

1138

Penelope Lively

A Stitch in Time (New York: Dutton, 1976)

Age range: Grades 4-6

Subject(s): Space and Time

Major character(s): Maria, Preteen

Time period(s): 1970s

Locale(s): England

What the book is about: Maria cannot convince her busy parents that she is hearing noises from the past. She finds an unfinished sampler made by a child who lived in the house a century ago, and suspects a tragedy. Maria makes friends with one of the children in the large, lively family next door.

Where it's reviewed:
Kirkus Reviews, November 1, 1976, page 1169
Times Literary Supplement, July 16, 1976, page 885

Other books by the author:
Boy Without a Name, 1976
The House in Norham Gardens, 1974
The Driftway, 1973

The Ghost of Thomas Kempe, 1973

Other books you might like:
Margaret Jean Anderson, *The Druid's Gift*, 1989
Given the gift of seeing the future, a girl is able to travel forward in time and experience some of the events which are to come.
Sally Farrell Odgers, *Drummond: The Search for Sarah*, 1990
A teddy bear, brought to life by Sarah and Nicholas, begins a search for his original owner, a Sarah from an earlier time.
Daniel Manus Pinkwater, *Borgel*, 1990
Melvin recounts his adventures in time and space with his 111 year old sort-of-Great-Uncle Borgel.
Ruth Williams, *The Silver Tree*, 1992
Micki must go back in time to stop a wish she has made from coming true, and destroying her family.
Elizabeth Winthrop, *The Battle for the Castle*, 1993
William uses the magic token to return to the medieval land of Sir Simon, which is menaced by a skeleton ship bearing a plague of rats.

1139

Arnold Lobel, Author/Illustrator

Frog and Toad All Year (New York: Harper, 1976)

Age range: Grades 1-2

Series: An I Can Read Book

Subject(s): Animals/Frogs and Toads; Friendship

Major character(s): Frog, Frog; Toad, Toad

Time period(s): Indeterminate

Locale(s): United States

What the book is about: Frog and Toad, two good friends, share experiences in each season of the year, including sledding, telling stories, sharing ice cream and raking leaves.

Where it's reviewed:
Horn Book, December 1976, page 621
Kirkus Reviews, June 15, 1976, page 683

Awards the book has won:
Christopher Award 1977

Other books by the author:
Ming Lo Moves the Mountain, 1982
Fables, 1980
Frog and Toad Are Friends, 1970
Giant John, 1964

Other books you might like:
David Lee Harrison, *The Case of Og, the Missing Frog*, 1972
After searching all over town for his missing frog, a boy realizes his pet has just been lonley.
Elinor Lander Horwitz, *The Strange Story of the Frog Who Became a Prince*, 1971
The handsome frog is very happy being a frog and is not at all pleased when a witch turns him into a prince.
Ellen Leroe, *Leap Frog Friday*, 1992
Oliver has a big problem when he uses his new magic rocks and changes his brother into a frog.
Mary Jane Roth, *His Majesty, the Frog*, 1971
A girl thinks her frog might turn into a prince but a boy her age just views it as an addition to his collection.
Mike Thaler, *In the Middle of the Puddle*, 1988

A frog and a turtle watch the rain turn their puddle into an ocean before the sun returns things to normal.

1140

Arnold Lobel, Author/Illustrator

Frog and Toad Together (New York: Harper and Row, 1971)

Age range: Grades 1-2

Subject(s): Animals/Frogs and Toads; Animals/Frogs and Toads; Gardens and Gardening

Major character(s): Toad, Toad; Frog, Frog

Time period(s): Indeterminate

Locale(s): Fictional Country

What the book is about: Toad gets so lost when he loses his list of things to do, he ends up going to bed. Frog reads poetry and plays music to his seedlings to help them grow. Lighthearted reading for early readers.

Where it's reviewed:
Horn Book, June 1972, page 264
Library Journal, May 15, 1972, page 1926

Awards the book has won:
Newbery Honor 1973
Children's Book Showcase 1973

Other books by the author:
The Devil and Mother Crump, 1987
Fables, 1980
Frog and Toad Are Friends, 1970
Giant John, 1964

Other books you might like:
Paul Adshead, *The Chicken That Could Swim*, 1989
Great confusion reigns in the garden when Silky the chicken hatches a duck egg and the new duckling wants to join his brothers and sister in the pond.
Marjorie Flack, *Tim Tadpole and the Great Bullfrog*, 1934
The reader follows Tim Tadpole's growth to a big frog who is at last able to go sit in the sun with his friends.
Shari Lewis, *One-Minute Animal Stories*, 1986
A collection of twenty familiar and not-so-familiar one minute stories involving animals.
Mike Thaler, *The Yellow Brick Toad*, 1978
Jokes, riddles, cartoons and funny stories concerning frogs and toads.
Richard Scarry, *More Adventures of Tinker and Tanker*, 1963
The adventures of a rabbit and a hippo with their animal friends and enemies.

1141

Arnold Lobel, Author/Illustrator

Owl at Home (New York: Harper, 1975)

Age range: Grades 1-2

Series: I Can Read Book

Subject(s): Animals/Birds; Winter

Major character(s): Owl, Owl

Time period(s): Indeterminate

Locale(s): United States

What the book is about: Owl shows that not all owls are wise. He lets the winter in the door to warm itself up, is terrified by two bumps in his bed (his feet) and runs up and down stairs trying to be in both places at once.

Where it's reviewed:
Kirkus Reviews, September 15, 1975, page 1064
Publisher's Weekly, October 27, 1975, page 53

Other books by the author:
Ming Lo Moves the Mountain, 1982
Days with Frog and Toad, 1979
Frog and Toad All Year, 1976
The Man Who Took the Indoors Out, 1974

Other books you might like:
Mary Carey, *The Owl Who Loved Sunshine*, 1977
    Young Leander trains to be a proper owl until he discovers sunshine and a new way of life.
Ronald Himler, *Little Owl, Keeper of the Trees*, 1974
    Little Owl makes a new friend, learns to fly, and celebrates his birthday.
Lyn Littlefield Hoopes, *My Own Home*, 1991
    One foggy day, a lost little owl finds out what home is when he realizes he is already there.
Pat Hutchins, *Good Night, Owl*, 1972
    Because all the other animals' noises keep him from sleeping, Owl watches for a chance to take his revenge.
Hanna Johansen, *The Duck and the Owl*, 1991
    A duck and an owl comtemplate starting a friendship, despite their differences in appearance and behavior.

1142

Arnold Lobel

Illustrator: Arnold Lobel

Uncle Elephant (New York: Harper, 1981)

Age range: Grades 1-3

Subject(s): Animals/Elephants; Aunts and Uncles

Major character(s): Uncle Elephant, Elephant

Time period(s): Indeterminate

Locale(s): Earth

What the book is about: Uncle Elephant takes wonderful care of his nephew, whose parents are lost at sea. Uncle Elephant cares for him until his parents are rescued. Uncle Elephant is full of stories, tricks, and songs especially written for young elephants.

Where it's reviewed:
Horn Book, December 1981, page 662
School Library Journal, December 1981, page 74

Other books by the author:
Turnaround Wind, 1988
The Rose in My Garden, 1984
The Man Who Took the Indoors Out, 1974
Lucille, 1964

Other books you might like:
Graeme Base, *The Eleventh Hour*, 1988
    The reader is invited to solve the mystery when an elephant's eleventh birthday dinner is stolen on the eleventh hour of the eleventh day.

Laurent de Brunhoff, *Babar's Battle*, 1992
    Discord between the elephants and the rhinos threatens war, but King Babar has a plan to keep the peace.
Alexandra Day, *Frank and Ernest Play Ball*, 1990
    An elephant and a bear take over the management of a baseball team.
Rudyard Kipling, *The Elephant's Child*, 1989
    Rudyard Kipling's tale of how the elephant's "satiable curiosity" resulted in elephant's having long trunks.
William Steig, *Doctor De Soto Goes to Africa*, 1992
    Expert mouse dentist Doctor De Soto is called to Africa to work on the sore tooth of a desperate elephant.

1143

Thomas Locker, Author/Illustrator

Family Farm (New York: Dial, 1988)

Age range: Grades 2-4

Subject(s): Family Life; Farm Life

Major character(s): Mike, Child; Sarah, Child

Time period(s): 1980s

Locale(s): Warren

What the book is about: A farm family nearly loses their home until they hit on the idea of growing and selling pumpkins and flowers to supplement their corn and milk sales. Beautifully illustrated.

Where it's reviewed:
Center for Children's Books Bulletin, May 1988, page 183
Kirkus Reviews, February 1, 1988, page 202
School Library Journal, April 1988, page 82

Other books by the author:
The Boy Who Held Back the Sea, 1987
Sailing with the Wind, 1986
The Mare on the Hill, 1985
Where the River Begins, 1984

Other books you might like:
Tony Johnston, *Yonder*, 1988
    As the plum tree changes in the passing seasons, so do the lives of a three-generation farm family.
Dick King-Smith, *Cuckoobush Farm*, 1988
    Hazel loves all the newborns on the farm in spring, and is delighted to learn she will have a baby brother or sister by Christmas.
Nancy Smiler Levinson, *Clara and the Bookwagon*, 1988
    Clara's dream of enriching her life on the family farm is fulfilled when a horse-drawn bookwagon visits with the country's first traveling library.
Katherine Paterson, *The Smallest Cow in the World*, 1991
    Though Rosie is the meanest cow in the herd, Marvin is inconsolable when she is sold and he and his family move to another dairy farm.
David L. Weitzman, *Thrashin' Time: Harvest Days in the Dakotas*, 1991
    A young boy describes his life on the family farm in North Dakota in 1912, particularly the arrival of a new steam powered threshing machine.

1144

Hugh Lofting

The Voyages of Dr. Doolittle (New York: Lippincott, 1922)

Age range: Grades 4-6

Subject(s): Fantasy; Animals

Major character(s): Dr. Doolittle, Veterinarian; Tommy Stubbins, Child; Long Arrow, Naturalist

Time period(s): Indeterminate Past

Locale(s): Spidermonkey Island, England

What the book is about: 10-year-old Tommy Stubbins becomes an assistant to Dr. Doolittle, the man who can talk to animals. The doctor and Tommy spend two years traveling around the world, encountering many unusual people and adventures along the way.

Where it's reviewed:
Nation, New York, December 6, 1922, page 620

Awards the book has won:
Newbery Medal 1923

Other books by the author:
Dr. Doolittle's Puddleby Adventures, 1952
Dr. Doolittle's Return, 1933
Story of Dr. Doolittle, 1988
Twilight of Magic, 1967

Other books you might like:
Brian Jacques, *Mariel of Redwall*, 1992
  The housemaid Mariel achieves victory at sea for the animals of Redwall Abbey, fighting the savage pirate rat. Sequel to *Mattimeo*, 1990.
Hugh Gardner, *Tales from the Marble Mountain*, 1949
  Adventures of four animal friends - Bear, Ostrich, Owl and Goat - as they seek their fortune.
Georgess McHargue, *Stoneflight*, 1975
  Jamie uses her power to put life into the stone animals that decorate New York buildings.
Joan Balfour Payne, *The Piebald Princess*, 1954
  A lazy, imperious cat claims to be a real Siamese princess.

1145

Carolyn F. Logan

The Power of the Rellard (London: Angus and Robertson, 1987)

Age range: Grades 6-9

Subject(s): Fantasy; Good and Evil; Physically Handicapped

Major character(s): Lucy, Child; Georgie, Preteen; Shelley, Teenager

Time period(s): Indeterminate

Locale(s): England

What the book is about: After a long illness, which leaves the youngest permanently handicapped, three children are given a toy theater. They begin to act out games and weave an elaborate fantasy and Lucy comes to believe she has magic powers. She is convinced she holds the power of the Rellard, a force the children invented as part of the family. George and Shelley begin to believe her and are drawn into a terrifying battle of wits and magic, and their whole family and home hang in the balance.

Where it's reviewed:
Booklist, August 1987, page 1749
Kirkus Reviews, February 15, 1988, page 281
School Library Journal, November 1987, page 105

Other books you might like:
James Clavell, *James Clavell's Thrump-o-Moto: A Fantasy*, 1986
  When a tiny wizard whisks Patricia and her crutches from her home, she encounters his family, an evil ghoul, and a magic cure for her handicap.
Paul R. Fisher, *The Princess and the Thorn*, 1980
  Mole finds himself drawn into a battle between good and evil in which all the powers of the world seem to gather around him and the lost Great Sword.
Alan Garner, *The Weirdstone of Brisingamen: A Tale of Alderley*, 1960
  A girl and her brother are catapulted into a battle between good and evil for possession of a magic stone of great power that is in her braclet.
Pat O'Shea, *The Hounds of the Morrigan*, 1985
  When a ten year old boy finds an old book of magic in a bookshop in Ireland, the forces of good and evil gather to do battle over it.
Joan D. Vinge, *Willow: Based on the Motion Picture*, 1988
  In a magical land, a poor farmer is entrusted with the care of an infant who is destined to become a good and wise queen.

1146

Robert Lopshire

Put Me in the Zoo (New York: Beginner Books, 1960)

Age range: Grades 1-2

Subject(s): Circus; Zoos

Time period(s): Indeterminate

Locale(s): United States

What the book is about: A very talented and unique "dog" knows he is different from other dogs and thinks he belongs in the zoo, but finds that his talents make him better suited to performing in the circus.

Other books by the author:
I Am Better Than You!, 1968
I Want to Be Somebody New!, 1986

Other books you might like:
Tomie De Paola, *Jingle, the Christmas Clown*, 1992
  Staying behind when their circus moves on, a clown and a troupe of baby animals put on a special Christmas show for a village too poor to celebrate.
Lois Ehlert, *Circus*, 1992
  Leaping lizards, marching snakes, a bear on the high wire, and others perform in an unusual circus.
Sandy Nightingale, *Pink Pigs Aplenty*, 1992
  Just how many pink pigs are there in the piggies circus and what are those pastel porcine performers doing?
Bill Peet, *Encore for Eleanor*, 1981
  Eleanor the Elephant, a retired circus star, finds a new career as the resident artist in the city zoo.
James Stevenson, *The Flying Acorns*, 1993

Three squirrels looking for excitement in their lives pull together an acrobatics act for the circus that is coming to their part of the forest.

1147

Athena V. Lord

Illustrator: Jean Jenkins

Today's Special: Z.A.P and Zoe (New York: Macmillan, 1984)

Age range: Grades 4-6

Subject(s): Depression (Economic); Greek Americans

Major character(s): Zach, Preteen; Zoe, Child

Time period(s): 1930s (1939)

Locale(s): New York (upstate New York)

What the book is about: Innocence abounds in the fast-moving episodes of Zach and Zoe, Greek-American children growing up in a small town in upstate New York during the Great Depression.

Where it's reviewed:
Horn Book, January/February 1985, page 54
School Library Journal, January 1985, page 77

Other books by the author:
Luck of Z.A.P. and Zoe, 1987
A Spirit to Ride the Whirlwind, 1981
Pilot for Spaceship Earth, 1978

Other books you might like:
Mildred Ames, *Grandpa Jake and the Grand Christmas*, 1990
   Lizzie's family is suffering hard times during the Depression until long-lost Grandpa Jake appears on their doorstep and generates some needed changes
Eileen Charbonneau, *The Ghosts of Stony Clove*, 1988
   A forbidding and possibly haunted old estate affects the fortunes of two young people for whom life is difficult in their upstate New York small town.
Paula Fox, *Lily and the Lost Boy*, 1987
   Lily grows closer to her older brother Paul during a spring on the Greek island of Thasos, until an unpredictable American boy disrupts their lives.
Arvella Whitmore, *The Bread Winner*, 1990
   When both her parents are unable to find work and pay the bills during the Depression, Sarah Ann saves the family by selling her homemade bread.
Phyllis S. Yingling, *My Best Friend Elena Pappas*, 1986
   A child learns about the Greek American culture when she becomes friends with Elena Pappas and shares family experiences.

1148

Bette Bao Lord

Illustrator: Marc Simont

In the Year of the Boar and Jackie Robinson (New York: Harper, 1984)

Age range: Grades 4-6

Subject(s): Chinese Americans; Moving, Household; Schools

Major character(s): Shirley Temple Wong, Child, Immigrant

Time period(s): 1940s (1947)

Locale(s): New York, New York (Brooklyn)

What the book is about: Shirley Temple Wong keeps a monthly journal of her first year in America, 1947. She adjusts to her new country, new language, and culture in Brooklyn, New York. Her hero is the baseball great, Jackie Robinson, who broke some barriers of his own.

Where it's reviewed:
Center for Children's Books Bulletin, October 1984, page 30
School Library Journal, December 1984, page 84

Other books you might like:
Heidi Chang, *Elaine, Mary Lewis, and the Frogs*, 1988
   Elaine feels lost in her new, small town Iowa home, until she shares a science project involving frogs.
Eleanor Estes, *Lost Umbrella of Kim Chu*, 1978
   9 year old Kim Chu leaves her father's umbrella in the library and launches a search to recover it.
Lensey Namioka, *Yang the Youngest and His Terrible Ear*, 1992
   Yingtao is pressured to give a violin recital to attract new students for his father, but he would rather be playing baseball.
Paul Yee, *Tales From Gold Mountain: Stories of the Chinese in the New World*, 1989
   Eight stories of Chinese families making a place for themselves in North America.
Laurence Yep, *The Star Fisher*, 1991
   Joan Lee and her family move from Ohio to West Virginia in the 1920s.

1149

Lois Lowry

All About Sam (Boston: Houghton Mifflin, 1988)

Age range: Grades 3-5

Subject(s): Brothers and Sisters; Family Life

Major character(s): Sam Krupnik, Child (Anastasia's Little Brother)

Time period(s): 1980s

Locale(s): United States

What the book is about: From birth through nursery school, we follow the adventures of Anastasia Krupnik's little brother. Sam is a hero in the Ramona class. Recommended Read-Aloud.

Where it's reviewed:
Center of Children's Books Bulletin, October 1988, page 46
Horn Book, January/February 1989, page 72

Awards the book has won:
Simon Award

Other books by the author:
Us and Uncle Fraud, 1984
One Hundredth Thing About Caroline, 1983

Other books you might like:
Beverly Cleary, *Ramona the Pest*, 1968

Ramona's overzealous good intentions and incredible curiosity result in her becoming a kindergarten drop out.
Ann Cameron, *The Stories Julian Tells*, 1981
Julian delights in tricking Huey, his gullible younger brother.
Sue Alexander, *Nadia the Willful*, 1983
When her favorite brother, Hamed, disappears in the desert, Nadia refuses to give him up for dead.
Judy Blume, *The One in the Middle Is the Green Kangaroo*, 1981
Freddie gets a great boost in self-esteem from successfully performing in a school play.
Joyce McDonald, *Mail-Order Kid*, 1988
10-year-old Flip Doty tries to adjust to a newly adopted brother who does embarrassing things in public.

1150

Lois Lowry

Anastasia Krupnik (Boston: Houghton Mifflin, 1979)

Age range: Grades 5-6

Subject(s): Family Life; Authorship

Major character(s): Anastasia Krupnik, Child

Time period(s): 1970s

Locale(s): United States

What the book is about: Anastasia discovers writing, in her tenth year of life. She deals with birth, death, rejection and ridicule, and especially jealousy. Anastasia loves to writing poetry, Wordsworth, and a sixth grade boy. She has a wild temper that brings a lot of problems. Then, she realizes that her mom is about to have a baby.

Where it's reviewed:
Center for Children's Books Bulletin, January 1980, page 99
Horn Book, December 1979, page 663

Other books by the author:
Anastasia at This Address, 1991
Anastasia Again!, 1988
Anastasia at Your Service, 1982
Autumn Street, 1980

Other books you might like:
Marion Dane Bauer, *A Dream of Queens and Castles*, 1990
In England with her mother for a year, Diana meets an eccentric old man and shares his frustrations.
Sarah Ellis, *Next-Door Neighbors*, 1990
A move to a new town leaves Peggy shy and uncomfortable until she befriends the unconventional George.
Polly Horvath, *No More Cornflakes*, 1990
Hortense worries that her family is falling apart, but gradually discovers that change is not always bad.
Joan Lowery Nixon, *And Maggie Makes Three*, 1986
Twelve year old Maggie joins a drama club, begins to make friends, and learns to deal with having an unusual family life.
Elizabeth Wild, *Along Came a Black Bird*, 1988
Three sisters and their pet crow befriend a lonely boy from a neighboring farm and discover some of the harsher realities of life.

1151

Lois Lowry

Anastasia, Ask Your Analyst (Boston: Houghton Mifflin, 1984)

Age range: Grades 4-6

Subject(s): Brothers and Sisters; Family Life

Major character(s): Anastasia Krupnik, Teenager

Time period(s): 1980s

Locale(s): United States

What the book is about: Coping with being 13 leads Anastasia to believe she needs therapy. When her father refuses, she buys a bust of Sigmund Freud and talks to it, sometimes answering her own questions.

Where it's reviewed:
Center for Children's Books Bulletin, May 1984, page 169
Horn Book, June 1984, page 330

Other books by the author:
Anastasia Again!, 1982
Anastasia at Your Service, 1983
Anastasia Krupnik, 1980
The 100th Thing about Caroline, 1983

Other books you might like:
Juanita Havill, *It Always Happens to Leona*, 1989
Leona decides to run away from her family with Uncle Rosco, a bicycle racer.
Bianca Bradbury, *Those Traver Kids*, 1972
Their mother's remarriage to a brutal man poses threats to the four Traver children.
Constance C. Greene, *Al(exandra) the Great*, 1982
Al must sacrifice a summer visit to her father to take care of her sick mother in New York City.
Barbara A. Steiner, *Tessa*, 1988
Tessa must choose between living in the city with her mother and staying with her father in the Arkansas woods.
Mavis Jukes, *Getting Even*, 1988
10-year-old Maggie gets conflicting advice about how to deal with an obnoxious classmate.

1152

Lois Lowry

Autumn Street (Boston: Houghton Mifflin, 1980)

Age range: Grades 5-6

Subject(s): Death; War

Major character(s): Elizabeth, Child; Tatie, Housekeeper; Charles, Child

Time period(s): 1940s

Locale(s): Pennsylvania

What the book is about: Elizabeth stays with her grandparents when her soldier father goes to war. She and Charles become great friends. When horror and tragedy strike home, Liz learns about love from Charles' grandmother.

Where it's reviewed:
Center for Children's Books Bulletin, November 1980, page 57
Horn Book, August 1980, page 409

Other books by the author:
Number the Stars, 1989
Switcharound, 1985
Anastasia Krupnik, 1979
Find a Stranger, Say Goodbye, 1978

Other books you might like:
Mary Baylis-White, *Sheltering Rebecca*, 1991
    In the days before the Second World War, Sally becomes friends with Rebecca, a young Jewish refugee from Germany.
Robert Cormier, *Other Bells for Us to Ring*, 1990
    Darcy feels isolated in her French-Canadian neighborhood during WWII until she meets a new friend.
Charlotte Herman, *A Summer on Thirteenth Street*, 1991
    Shirley and her buddy, Morton, are affected in many ways by WWII.
Jack Lasenby, *The Mangrove Summer*, 1988
    With rumors that the Japanese are to invade New Zealand, George's family moves into the bush country to survive.
Carol Matas, *Lisa's War*, 1987
    Lisa and other teenage Jews become involved in the underground resistance movement in Denmark.

1153

Lois Lowry

Number the Stars (Boston: Houghton Mifflin, 1989)

Age range: Grades 4-6

Subject(s): World War II; Friendship; Jews

Major character(s): Annemarie Johansen, Preteen; Ellen Rosen, Preteen; Kirsti Johansen, Child

Time period(s): 1940s (1943)

Locale(s): Copenhagen, Denmark

What the book is about: In 1943, during the German occupation of Denmark, ten year old Annemarie learns how to be brave and courageous when she helps shelter her Jewish friend, Ellen, from the Nazis. A finely drawn portrait of the Danish resistance as well as the bravery of two young girls.

Where it's reviewed:
Booklist, March 1, 1989, page 1194
School Library Journal, March 1989, page 177

Awards the book has won:
Jane Addams Children's Book Award, Honor Book

Other books by the author:
Your Move, 1990
Rabble Starkey, 1987
Switcharound, 1985
Autumn Street, 1980

Other books you might like:
Jane Whitbread Levin, *Star of Danger*, 1966
    A fourteen year old German Jew escapes Nazi persecution by fleeing to Denmark, but lives with the knowledge he is still not out of danger.
Carol Matas, *Lisa's War*, 1987
    During the Nazi occupation of Denmark, Lisa and other teenage Jews become involved in an underground resistance movement and eventually must flee.
Ida Vos, *Hide and Seek*, 1991

A young Jewish girl living in Holland tells of her experiences during the Nazi occupation, her years in hiding, and the after shock.
Irving Werstein, *That Denmark Might Live: The Saga of the Danish Resistance in World War Two*, 1967
    Describes the Danish resistance movement including rescue and evacuation of Danish Jews, sabotage, shortwave communication, illegal press and more.
Eva-Lis Wuorio, *To Fight in Silence*, 1973
    During the Nazi occupation of Denmark, a young Norweigian joins with his Danish cousins in the secret plan to prevent the deportation of Jews.

1154

Lois Lowry

Rabble Starkey (New York: Houghton Mifflin, 1987)

Age range: Grades 5-6

Subject(s): Friendship; Mental Illness; Mothers and Daughters

Major character(s): Parable "Rabble" Starkey, Child; Sweet Hosanna Starkey, Parent; Veronica Bigelow, Child

Time period(s): 1980s

Locale(s): United States

What the book is about: Rabble and her mother Sweet Hosanna move into the Bigelow's house to take care of the children after Mrs. Bigelow's hospitalization for mentall illness. Veronica is Rabble's best friend. When Mrs. Bigelow recovers, Rabble must prepare for a change, as her own mom goes to college to become a teacher.

Where it's reviewed:
Center for Children's Books Bulletin, March 1987, page 130
Horn Book, July/August 1987, page 463

Awards the book has won:
Boston Globe/Horn Book Award

Other books by the author:
Your Move, J.P.!, 1990
Number the Stars, 1989
Anastasia's Chosen Career, 1987
A Summer to Die, 1977

Other books you might like:
Vera Cleaver, *Moon Lake Angel: A Novel*, 1987
    Kitty Dale, whose mother does not want to deal with a child, spends the summer with Aunt Petal and eventually learns to accept her mother's weakness.
Susan Fletcher, *The Stuttgart Nanny Mafia*, 1991
    In an effort to gain more time alone with her mother, Aurora schemes to get rid of Tanja, a nineteen year old au pair from Germany.
Rebecca C. Jones, *The Believers*, 1989
    Unhappy with her mother's frequent absences from home, Tibby finds solace in a religious sect, until a crisis forces her to make a difficult choice.
Lael Littke, *Blue Skye*, 1990
    Eleven year old Skye, who has spent most of her life on the road with her mother, finally discovers what it is like to have a real home and family.
Mary Riskind, *Follow That Mom!*, 1986

Eleven year old Maxine creates as much mischief as possible to convince her mother to quit the Girl Scouts.

1155

Lois Lowry

Illustrator: Jenni Oliver

A Summer to Die (Boston: Houghton Mifflin, 1977)

Age range: Grades 5-7

Subject(s): Brothers and Sisters; Death; Individuality

Major character(s): Margaret "Meg" Chalmers, Teenager; Molly Chalmers, Teenager; Will "Loony Willy" Banks, Neighbor

Time period(s): 1970s

Locale(s): Macwahoc Valley, Maine

What the book is about: Meg envies her sister's beauty and popularity. Her feelings don't make it any easier for her to cope with Molly's strange illness and eventual death.

Where it's reviewed:
Hornbook, August 1977, page 451
Kirkus Reviews, May 1, 1977, page 493
School Library Journal, May 1977, page 36

Other books by the author:
Switcharound, 1985
Us and Uncle Fraud, 1984
The 100th Thing about Caroline, 1983
Taking Care of Terrific, 1983

Other books you might like:
Hila Colman, The Family Trap, 1982
    With her father dead and her mother in a mental institution, Becky petitions the juvenile court to become an emancipated minor.
James D. Forman, The Big Bang, 1989
    As the lone survivor of a car accident that killed his older brother and seven friends, Chris tries to sort his feelings of guilt, grief and anger.
R.L. Stine, Cheerleaders: The Third Evil, 1992
    Corky is tormented night after night by dreams of her dead sister, Bobbi, and the fear that she is in danger herself.
Marc Talbert, Dead Birds Singing, 1985
    After his mother is killed and his sister is badly injured in a car accident, Matt faces life with a new family and a deep feeling of anger.
Phyllis Anderson Wood, Get a Little Lost, Tia, 1978
    With his father dead and mother working, a teenage boy is given the responsibility of looking after his sister, a task that proves exasperating.

1156

Lois Lowry

Us and Uncle Fraud (Boston: Houghton Mifflin, 1984)

Age range: Grades 4-6

Subject(s): Aunts and Uncles; Floods; Stealing

Major character(s): Claude, Relative (uncle); Louise, Child; Marcus, Child

Time period(s): 1980s

Locale(s): United States

What the book is about: Two children become disillusioned with their Uncle Claude. They at first see him as a fun and exciting visitor, but he leaves them abruptly with an empty promise and evidence that he might be a thief.

Where it's reviewed:
Booklist, September 15, 1984, page 130
Publisher's Weekly, July 27, 1984, page 143

Other books by the author:
Number the Stars, 1989
Rabble Starkey, 1987
Switcharound, 1985
Taking Care of Terrific, 1983

Other books you might like:
Clive Barker, The Thief of Always: A Fable, 1992
    After a mysterious stranger promises to end his boredom with a trip to the magical Holiday House, Harvey learns that his fun has a high price.
Faye Gibbons, Mighty Close to Heaven, 1985
    Dave runs away from his grandparents' and through the Georgia mountains to join his wandering father, finding both disappointment and understanding.
Alexander Key, Escape to Witch Mountain, 1968
    When a mysterious man claiming to be their uncle acquires custody, Tia and Tony run away to keep him from evily enslaving their unusual powers.
James Munves, The Treasure of Diogenes Sampuez, 1979
    After his father's death, Diogenes, his sister, and a friend travel over the Colombian mountains seeking help from a brother against a greedy uncle.
Adrienne Richard, Wings, 1974
    Her relationship with Radyar, the dashing, sensitive astrologer brings both joy and disappointment to a small girl in southern California after WWI.

1157

Janet Louise Lunn

The Root Cellar (New York: Scribner's, 1983)

Age range: Grades 5 and Up

Subject(s): Space and Time; Orphans

Major character(s): Rose Larkin, Orphan, Time Traveller; Susan Anderson, Teenager; Will Morrissay, Military Personnel (soldier)

Time period(s): 1860s (1865)

Locale(s): Canada

What the book is about: 12 year old orphan, Rose, is sent to live with unknown relatives on a farm in Canada. Rose matures, learning sensitivity and love when she travels through the root cellar to 1865. She makes friends for the very first time. The physical surroundings and conditions during the Civil War are vividly protrayed.

Where it's reviewed:
Horn Book, October 1983, page 575
School Library Journal, September 1983, page 124

Other books by the author:
Shadow in Hawthorn Bay, 1986

Twin Spell, 1969

Other books you might like:
Dean Hughes, *Family Pose*, 1989
  An 11 year old orphan runs away from his foster home and finds a new family.
Marilyn Sachs, *Underdog*, 1985
  Living with her aunt and uncle in San Francisco, a 12 year old orphan searches for her long-lost dog.
Cara Lockhart Smith, *Parchment House*, 1989
  In an orphanage set in future Britain, Johnny Rattle matches wits with a cruel orphanage director.
Pamela Sykes, *Mirror of Danger*, 1974
  An orphan who comes to live with distant cousins gets a glimpse into the past.
Barbara Hobbs Withey, *The Serpent Ring*, 1988
  11 year old Jenny goes to live with Kesha Kropas, a strange woman who is either a witch or a Gypsy.

1158

Ida Luttrell

Illustrator: Doug Cushman

Tillie and Mert (New York: Harper, 1985)

Age range: Grades 1-3

Subject(s): Animals

Major character(s): Tillie, Skunk; Mert, Mouse

Time period(s): Indeterminate

Locale(s): Fictional Country

What the book is about: Tillie the skunk and Mert the mouse are best friends and they do everything together, from buying bargains at Weasel's garage sale to telling fortunes and opening their own grocery store.

Where it's reviewed:
Center for Children's Books Bulletin, January 1986, page 90
Publihser's Weekly, December 13, 1985, page 53
School Library Journal, December 1985, page 102

Other books by the author:
Milo's Toothache, 1992
The Bear Next Door, 1991
Mattie and the Chicken Thief, 1988
Lonesome Lester, 1984

Other books you might like:
Nancy White Carlstrom, *Fish and Flamingo*, 1993
  Two unlikely friends, Fish and Flamingo, spend time together, help each other out, and tell stories about their different lives.
Keiko Kasza, *The Rat and the Tiger*, 1993
  In his friendship with Rat, Tiger takes advantage and plays the bully because of his greater size, but one day Rat stands up for his rights.
Robin Michal Koontz, *Chicago and the Cat*, 1993
  A pushy cat takes over the home of Chicago the Rabbit, but then the two become friends.
Jerry Newman, *Green Earrings and a Felt Hat*, 1993
  Two best friends have a disagreement. After returning each other's borrowed possessions, they discover that it is their friendship they miss the most.
John Schindel, *I'll Meet You Halfway*, 1993

After not seeing one another for a long time, two friends each bring a special gift when they set out to meet for a reunion.

1159

George Ella Lyon

Borrowed Children (New York: Orchard Books, 1988)

Age range: Grades 5-6

Subject(s): Family Life; Mountain Life

Major character(s): Amanda "Mandy", Preteen

Time period(s): 1930s

Locale(s): Kentucky

What the book is about: Mandy uncovers her mother's past and her family's present situation. A family's history and their dreams, travels, and the love that binds them, is told in this story of the Depression era.

Where it's reviewed:
Horn Book, May/June 1988, page 354
School Library Journal, March 1988, page 197

Other books by the author:
Who Came Down That Road?, 1992
Cecil's Story, 1991
Outside Inn, 1991
Come a Tide, 1990

Other books you might like:
Robert Burch, *Ida Early Comes over the Mountains*, 1980
  Tough times in rural Georgia during the Depression take a lively turn when Ida Early comes to keep house for the Suttons.
Pat Edwards, *Nelda*, 1987
  Nelda and her family know hard times during the Depression, but when Nelda becomes friends with the elderly Miss Mattie May, things begin to look up.
Maureen Pople, *The Other Side of the Family*, 1986
  Sent from England to an Australian grandmother during the bombing of London, Katherine makes startling discoveries about her family.
Carolyn Reeder, *Grandpa's Mountain*, 1991
  Eleven year old Carrie visits her relatives in the Blue Ridge Mountains during the Depression ande watches her Grandfather fight to keep his land.
Arvella Whitmore, *The Bread Winner*, 1990
  Sarah Ann saves her family from the poorhouse by selling her prizewinning homemade bread.

1160

George Ella Lyon

Illustrator: Stephen Gammell

Come a Tide (New York: Orchard, 1990)

Age range: Grades 2-3

Subject(s): Floods; Country Life

Time period(s): 1990s

Locale(s): United States

What the book is about: A girl provides a lighthearted account of the spring floods at her rural home.

Where it's reviewed:
Booklist, February 1, 1990, page 1092
School Library Journal, June 1990, page 104
Publishers Weekly, January 12, 1990, page 60

Other books by the author:
Who Came Down That Road?, 1992
Cecil's Story, 1991
Outside Inn, 1991
Father Time and the Day Boxes, 1985

Other books you might like:
Mary Calhoun, *Euphonia and the Flood*, 1976
Curious to see where the flood is going, an old woman packs her broom and pig into her boat and sets out to follow it.
Genevieve Gray, *Has Anyone Seen Buddy Bascom?*, 1977
Twelve year old Buddy Bascom and Ryan survive the Big Thompson flood, but Ryan's father and brother are killed.
Ron Hirschi, *Harvest Song*, 1991
A little girl and her grandmother share the activities of a country life.
Lydia Pender, *The Useless Donkeys*, 1980
The Quigley children love their two donkeys but Mr. Quigley threatens to get rid of them.
Chris Van Allsburg, *Ben's Dream*, 1982
Ben has a dream in which he and his house float by the monuments of the world, half submerged in flood water.

M

1161

David Macaulay

BAAA (Boston: Houghton Mifflin, 1985)

Age range: Grades 5-7

Subject(s): Allegories; Animals/Sheep

Time period(s): Indeterminate

Locale(s): Earth

What the book is about: A sophisticated fantasy about a world inhabited by humanistic sheep after the last human is gone from the earth. The sheep try to create a perfect world, but make the same choices for greed and corruption that humans made.

Where it's reviewed:
Center for Children's Books Bulletin, September 1985, page 13
School Library Journal, October 1985, page 183

Other books by the author:
Black and White, 1990
Why the Chicken Crossed the Road, 1987
Motel of the Mysteries, 1979
Castle, 1977

Other books you might like:
Eve Bunting, Terrible Things: An Allegory of the Holocaust, 1989
　　In a reaction to the Holocaust, the author tells of animals being carried away one, not knowing if they'd stick together, they could end the tragedy.
Ursula Le Guin, Fish Soup, 1992
　　When the Thinking Man and the Writing Woman of Maho discuss having a child, children appear, shaped by their expectations of what a child should be.
John Rowe Townsend, Forest of the Night, 1975
　　An allegorical interpretation of William Blake's poem, "The Tyger."
Gerda Wagener, Leo the Lion, 1991
　　An allegory about Leo the Lion who searches for someone who will show him love and affection.
Kit Williams, Book Without a Title, 1984
　　The reader may discover the real title of this allegory of seasons interwoven with the activities of a beekeeper, from clues hidden in the pages.

1162

David Macaulay

Why the Chicken Crossed the Road (Boston: Houghton Mifflin, 1987)

Age range: Grades 2-4

Subject(s): Robbers and Outlaws; Humor; Animals/Birds

Major character(s): Desperate Dan, Thief

Time period(s): Indeterminate

Locale(s): Fictional Country

What the book is about: A chain of events is started when a chicken startles some cows who stampede over a bridge, which collapses onto a train, thus allowing Desperate Dan, the robber, to escape from custody. A really funny book.

Where it's reviewed:
Horn Book, January/February 1988, page 55
School Library Journal, December 1987, page 86

Other books by the author:
Black and White, 1990
BAAA, 1985

Other books you might like:
Constance C. Greene, Odds on Oliver, 1993
　　Oliver's attempts to be a hero result in such humorous disasters as going up a tree to rescue a cat and getting stuck himself.
Margaret Mahy, Bubble Trouble and Other Poems and Stories, 1991
　　A collection of funny stories and poems from New Zealand with a baby flying in a bubble, a love struck crocodile, and a grandmother tired of winter.
Peggy Parish, Amelia Bedelia, 1963
　　A literal-minded housekeeper causes a ruckus in the household when she attempts to make sense of some instructions.
Louis Sacher, Marvin Redpost: Kidnapped at Birth?, 1992
　　Red-haired Marvin is convinced that the reason he looks different from the rest of his family is that he is really the lost Prince of Shampoon.
Carol Beach York, Pudmuddles, 1993
　　After their marriage, Mr. and Mrs. Pudmuddle move into their backwards home where they soon discover there is no basement and the roof has blown off.

1163

David Macauley

Black and White (Boston: Houghton Mifflin, 1990)

Age range: Grades 2-4

Subject(s): Games/Literary

What the book is about: This is a book with hidden corners; a secret garden of a book that may become a children's puzzle classic. A strong game element invites reader involvement. The stories overlap with a lot of fun.

Where it's reviewed:
Horn Book, September/October 1990, page 593
School Library Journal, June 1990, page 104

Other books by the author:
Why the Chicken Crossed the Road, 1987
BAAA, 1985

Other books you might like:
Kelli C. Foster, *Bub and Chub*, 1992
    Invites the reader to guess where bear and lion cubs Bub and Chub are while they are making a hubbub as they scrub.
Taro Gomi, *Bus Stops*, 1988
    A bus follows its daily route, discharging and taking on passengers. The reader is prompted to find objects or people in the different pictures.
Elizabeth Rider Montgomery, *The Mystery of the Boy Next Door*, 1978
    Neighborhood children think the new boy is mean until he leads them on a mysterious puzzle solving hunt.
George Shannon, *More Stories to Solve: Fifteen Folktales From around the World*, 1991
    Fifteen brief folktales in which there is a mystery or problem that the reader is invited to solve before the solution is presented.
Tony Tallarico, *Detect Donald*, 1990
    Find Donald and other amusing things as he travels to ancient Rome, colonial America, prehistory, the Middle Ages, Napoleon's France, and the future.

1164

Betty MacDonald

Illustrator: Hilary Knight

Hello, Mrs. Piggle-Wiggle (New York: Harper, 1950)

Age range: Grades 3-5

Subject(s): Behavior; Humor; Short Stories

Major character(s): Jordan Carmody, Parent; Melody Foxglove, Child; Philip Carmody, Child

Time period(s): Indeterminate

Locale(s): Fictional Country

What the book is about: When ten year old Philip Carmody becomes such a show off that it disrupts his school and home life as well, his teacher suggests to Mrs. Carmody that she call Mrs. Piggle-Wiggle, who seems to have a cure for anything that ails children, all left to her by Mr. Piggle-Wiggle in a magic trunk. Show offs, crybabies, whisperers, bullies and slowpokes are all fair game for the magical cures. Every parent wants her phone number.

Where it's reviewed:
Teacher, January 1977, page 134

Other books by the author:
Mrs. Piggle-Wiggle, 1957
Mrs. Piggle-Wiggle's Magic, 1957
Onions in the Stew, 1955
Mrs. Piggle-Wiggle's Farm, 1954

Other books you might like:
Joan Davenport Carris, *Just a Little Ham*, 1989
    A family's pet pig delights them with her personality, until she acquires such bad habits that they are afraid they've created a monster.
Mel Gilden, *Monster Mashers*, 1989
    Danny and his monster pals are thrilled when their old friend Zelda Bella turns up as the star of the new TV show, "Mother Scary's Matinee."
Ann M. Martin, *Karen's Prize*, 1990
    Karen wins spelling contest after contest and thinks it is great while her friends think she is a show off.
Nancy K. Robinson, *Veronica, the Show-Off*, 1982
    Although lonely and desperately in need of friends, Veronica overwhelms her new classmates with her outrageous behavior in a bid for attention.
George Shannon, *The Gang and Mrs. Higgins*, 1981
    When the Anderson gang raids the pioneer trading post in Kansas, Mrs. Wiggins uses their bad habits to save the gold.

1165

George MacDonald

Illustrator: Charles Mozley

At the Back of the North Wind (New York: Watts, 1963)

Age range: Grades 5-8

Subject(s): Fairy Tale; Fantasy

Major character(s): Diamond, Child; Mr. Coleman, Neighbor; North Wind, Spirit

Time period(s): Indeterminate Past

Locale(s): Scotland

What the book is about: A boy named Diamond (after his father's favorite horse) has a conversation with the North Wind which blows into his hayloft bedroom. Personified as a beautiful woman, North Wind convinces Diamond to come with her to see the world. Riding "at the back," Diamond feels none of the chill of the wind but sees the sights as she flies through the sky, always returning Diamond safely to his home. Philosophical and descriptive, the story will charm good readers who love fantasy. (Facsimile of 1919 printing)

Where it's reviewed:
AB Bookman's Weekly, November 13, 1978, page 2953
Reprint Bulletin-Book Reviews, March 30, 1978, page 33
Spectator, December 5, 1970, page R19

Other books by the author:
The Day Boy and Night Girl, 1988
The Gray Wolf, 1980
The Light Princess, 1978
The Golden Key, 1967

Other books you might like:
Jean Craighead George, *The Talking Earth*, 1983

Billie goes out alone into the Everglades to test the legends of her Indian ancestors and learns the importance of listening to the Earth's message.

Jane Langton, *The Fledgling*, 1980
Georgie's fondest hope, to be able to fly, is fleetingly fulfilled when she is befriended by a Canada goose.

Patricia A. McKillip, *Harpist in the Wind*, 1979
The Prince of Hed solves the puzzle of his future when he learns to harp the wind and understands his own relationship with another harpist.

Deborah Moulton, *The First Battle of Morn*, 1988
Torin is in the center of the struggle for his planet, Morn, where the rulers want him for their "mind child" and the rebels want him as their hero.

Patricia Wrightson, *Journey Behind the Wind*, 1981
Once again, Wirrun, the young Australian Aborigine is called to free his land from an alien red-eyed thing whose master steals men's spirits.

1166

Reby Edmond MacDonald

The Ghosts of Austwick Manor (New York: Atheneum, 1982)

Age range: Grades 5-8

Subject(s): Dolls and Dollhouses; Fantasy; Mystery and Detective Stories

Major character(s): Hillary MacDonald, Preteen; Heather MacDonald, Child; Donald MacDonald, Teenager

Time period(s): 1980s

Locale(s): Scotland

What the book is about: Hillary and Heather are upset when their older brother, Donald, receives an inheritance. It includes a dollhouse (a replica of the family manor in England) and four sets of dolls. They are warned that they must leave them untouched. The girls ignore the warning and find they can travel in time, and try to save Donald from the results of an ancient curse.

Where it's reviewed:
Horn Book, August 1982, page 406
School Library Journal, May 1982, page 85

Awards the book has won:
Crabbery Honor 1982

Other books by the author:
Guest House, Very Exclusive, 1982
Fiddlers in the Forest, 1938

Other books you might like:
Margaret Jean Anderson, *The Druid's Gift*, 1989
Given the gift of seeing the future, a girl living at the time of the Druids travels forward in time and experiences events tied to her own history.

John Bellaris, *The Trolley to Yesterday*, 1989
Johnny and Professor Childermass discover a trolley which takes them back to Constantinople in 1453 as the Turks are invading the Byzantine Empire.

David Gifaldi, *Gregory, Maw and the Mean One*, 1992
The Mean One threatens a small western town. A young boy and the crow that raised him take the meany back in time to discover the source of his rage.

Thomas McKean, *The Secret of the Seven Willows*, 1991
To prevent the selling of their ancestral home, Martha and Tad use the power of a magical ring which makes it possible to travel back in time.

Ellen Weiss, *The Poof Point*, 1992
When Norton and Marigold Bicker's time machine malfunctions, their children try to save them as they mentally become younger and younger.

1167

Ellen MacGregor

Illustrator: Charles Geer

Miss Pickerell and the Blue Whales (New York: McGraw-Hill, 1983)

Age range: Grades 3-5

Subject(s): Ecology; Science Fiction; Animals/Whales

Major character(s): Miss Lavinia Pickerell, Traveller (Space)

Time period(s): Indeterminate

Locale(s): Fictional Country (Square Toe County); Outer Space

What the book is about: While traveling on the space shuttle, Miss Pickerell discovers that it is hauling a spy satellite programmed to spread nuclear reactor fragments. Can she figure out a way to stop the disaster?

Where it's reviewed:
Booklist, July 1983, page 1403
School Library Journal, October 1983, page 160

Other books by the author:
Miss Pickerell and the SuperTanker, 1978
Miss Pickerell and the Weather Satellite, 1971
Miss Pickerell Goes to the Arctic, 1954
Miss Pickerell Goes Undersea, 1953

Other books you might like:
Ann Coleridge, *Stranded*, 1987
Tony joins in a dangerous mission to roll several stranded whales back into the sea.

Jean Craighead George, *Hook a Fish, Catch a Mountain*, 1975
After catching a vanishing species of fish, Spinner and her cousin Alligator do some ecological detecting to determine where the fish came from.

Ruth Park, *My Sister Sif*, 1986
Riko manages to get her delicate older sister and herself to their remote home, where an American scientist complicates Riko's life.

Nancy Robison, *Space Hijack!*, 1979
When a passenger hijacks their Moon shuttle, Mark and Ted use the difference in gravity to escape from the space people that the hijacker controls.

Theodore Taylor, *The Hostage*, 1987
Jamie has second thoughts about harboring a killer whale that his father and he captured, and plan to sell to a sea amusement park.

1168

Walter Macken

The Flight of the Doves (New York: Macmillan, 1968)

Age range: Grades 5-7

Subject(s): Brothers and Sisters; Orphans; Runaways

Major character(s): Finn Dove, Preteen; Derval Dove, Child

Time period(s): Indeterminate Past

Locale(s): Ireland

What the book is about: Two children, a twelve year old English boy and his seven year old sister run away from a cruel stepfather in England to find their grandmother's home in western Ireland, despite the publicity about their flight and a police search for them.

Where it's reviewed:
Booklist, April 15, 1968, page 997
Center for Children's Books Bulletin, April 1968, page 131
Kirkus Reviews, February 15, 1968, page 183

Other books by the author:
Island of the Great Yellow Ox, 1966
The Green Hills and Other Stories, 1956
Rain on the Wind, 1951

Other books you might like:
Terrence Blacker, *Homebird*, 1993
    Nicky Morrison runs away from boarding school and problems at home to the tough life on the streets of London.
Marita Conlon-McKenna, *Wildflower Girl*, 1992
    In the mid 19th century, Peggy O'Driscoll sets out alone from Ireland for America, hoping to make a better life for herself.
Leonard Everett Fisher, *Across the Sea from Galway*, 1975
    In 1849, following the potato famine, an Irish boy and his brother and sister are sent by their parents on an ill-fated journey to Boston.
Michael Morpurgo, *Mr. Nobody's Eyes*, 1990
    Follows the adventures of an extraordinary pair on the run: an escaped circus monkey and an ostracized young English boy named Harry.
Hilda Van Stockum, *Penengro*, 1972
    Unhappy living with the people who had taken him from a Dublin orphanage, a young boy runs away and joins a group of gypsies.

1169

Patricia MacLachlan

Illustrator: Lloyd Bloom

Arthur, for the Very First Time (New York: Harper, 1980)

Age range: Grades 4-6

Subject(s): Animals/Pigs

Major character(s): Arthur, Preteen; Great Aunt Elda, Guardian; Great Uncle Wrisby, Guardian

Time period(s): 1980s

Locale(s): United States

What the book is about: Arthur's relatives are very offbeat. They climb trees and speak French to their pet chickens. The pig, Bernadette, becomes Arthur's favorite. The transfor-

mation of this problem child is made complete by his friend, Moira.

Where it's reviewed:
Center for Children's Books Bulletin, September 1980, p 15
School Library Journal, October 1980, page 149

Awards the book has won:
Golden Kite Fiction Award 1980

Other books by the author:
Journey, 1991
Sarah, Plain and Tall, 1988
Cassie Binegar, 1982
Through Grandpa's Eyes, 1980

Other books you might like:
Nina Bawden, *The Peppermint Pig*, 1975
    Polly finds it difficult to adjust to the sudden change in the family fortunes when she gets a special pet.
Carol J. Farley, *Loosen Your Ears*, 1977
    Josh reminisces about his boyhood on the farm and his many interesting relatives.
Hila Feil, *The Windmill Summer*, 1972
    Tired of being nagged by her relatives, a girl goes to live by herself in her great-grandfather's windmill.
Virginia McCall, *Adassa and Her Hen*, 1971
    Except for a chance meeting with the Prime Minister, a Jamaican girls' pet chicken would have been sold at market.
Phyllis Reynolds Naylor, *Beetles, Lightly Toasted*, 1987
    Andy competes with his know-it-all cousin with some unusual food sources, testing them on friends and family.

1170

Patricia MacLachlan

Sarah, Plain and Tall (New York: Harper, 1985)

Age range: Grades 3-6

Subject(s): Frontier and Pioneer Life; Stepmothers

Major character(s): Caleb Whiting, Child; Anna Whiting, Child; Sarah Wheaton, Mail Order Bride, Step-Parent

Time period(s): 1800s

Locale(s): Kansas

What the book is about: A pioneer sends for a wife and mother for his children. His mail order bride-to-be is Sarah, from Maine. She charms the children with her stories of the sea, and they help her learn to love the prairie. A beautiful story of the formation of a family.

Where it's reviewed:
Horn Book, September/October 1985, page 557
School Library Journal, May 1985, page 92

Awards the book has won:
Newbery Medal 1986

Other books by the author:
Unclaimed Treasures, 1984
Seven Kisses in a Row, 1983
Cassie Binegar, 1982
Arthur, for the Very First Time, 1980

Other books you might like:
Carol Ryrie Brink, *Caddie Woodlawn*, 1973
    The classic, well-loved story of one year of life (1864) on a pioneer farm in Wisconsin.

Sid Fleischman, *Chancy and the Grand Rascal*, 1966
  A young boy sets out to find his brothers and sisters, separated by the death of their parents during the Civil War.
Marguerite Henry, *San Domingo, the Medicine Hat Stallion*, 1972
  Peter comes to the Nebraska territory in the mid-1800s, his first love is an Indian pony he grows up with, and it serves with him in the Pony Express.
Ann Warren Turner, *Grasshopper Summer*, 1989
  In 1874, Sam and his family move from Kentucky to the southern Dakota Territory, where harsh conditions and a horde of grasshoppers threaten.
Laura Ingalls Wilder, *Little House in the Big Woods*, 1953
  A log cabin in the woods of Wisconsin, far from any town, is the home of Laura, her family, and Pa, a great teller of stories and singer of songs.

1171

Patricia Maclachlan

Illustrator: Maria Pia Marrella

Seven Kisses in a Row (New York: Harper and Row, 1983)

Age range: Grades 2-4

Subject(s): Aunts and Uncles; Family Life

Major character(s): Emma, Child; Evelyn, Relative (aunt); Elliot, Relative (uncle)

Time period(s): 1980s

Locale(s): United States

What the book is about: Change from regular family routine is difficult for Emma when her aunt and uncle take care of her while her parents are at a convention. Emma learns to accept people as they are in this amusing and comfortable story.

Where it's reviewed:
Horn Book, June 1983, page 305
School Library Journal, April 1983, page 115

Other books by the author:
Journey, 1991
Sarah, Plain and Tall, 1985
Tomorrow's Wizard, 1982
Through Grandpa's Eyes, 1980

Other books you might like:
June Counsel, *But Martin!*, 1984
  The extra terrestrial who comes to school with the children helps them to learn tolerance for people's different cultures and colors.
Michelle Edwards, *A Baker's Portrait*, 1991
  Michelin paints portraits that do not flatter her sitters, but she learns an enduring lesson when she must paint her kindly aunt and uncle.
Isabelle Holland, *God, Mrs. Muskrat, and Aunt Dot*, 1983
  In a letter to God, recently orphaned Rebecca explains her loneliness living with her aunt and uncle and how helpful her imaginary friend has been.
Barbara Ann Porte, *Harry Gets an Uncle*, 1991
  Harry is worried about being the ring bearer at his Aunt Rose's wedding, after his friend Dorcas tells him what went wrong at another wedding.

Valerie Tripp, *Changes for Samantha: A Winter Story*, 1992
  When she learns Nellie and her sisters have been sent to an orphanage, Samantha, now living with her aunt and uncle in New York City, tries to help.

1172

Patricia Maclachlan

Illustrator: Kathy Jacobi

Tomorrow's Wizard (New York: HarperCollins, 1982)

Age range: Grades 4-6

Subject(s): Magic; Short Stories; Wishes

Major character(s): Tomorrow's Wizard, Wizard; Murdoch, Apprentice

Time period(s): Indeterminate Past

Locale(s): Fictional Country

What the book is about: Maclachlan's insight into human nature shines through these six stories in the fairy tale style. Tomorrow's Wizard's job is to grant wishes and implement curses, which he does with wisdom and humor. A feast for short story lovers.

Where it's reviewed:
Hornbook, June 1982, page 290
School Library Journal, April 1982, page 72
Christian Science Monitor, May 14, 1982, page B9

Other books by the author:
Sarah, Plain and Tall, 1985
Unclaimed Treasures, 1984
Seven Kisses in a Row, 1983
Cassie Binegar, 1982

Other books you might like:
Isaac Asimov, *Magical Wishes*, 1986
  A large collection of stories by several authors about wishes and magic fulfillment.
Bill Brittain, *The Wish Giver: Three Tales of Coven Tree*, 1983
  When a strange little man comes to the church social promising he can give people exactly what they ask for, three young believers each make a wish.
Jeff Brown, *A Lamp for the Lambchops*, 1983
  A genie-in-training provides madcap adventures for the Lambchops until they realize it is best to unwish their wishes.
Maeve Henry, *A Gift for a Gift*, 1992
  Fran meets a mysterious man who holds the power to fulfill all of her wishes.
Dick King-Smith, *The Queen's Nose*, 1983
  Harmony, who loves animals but isn't allowed to keep a pet, is given a magic coin with seven wishes.

1173

Patricia MacLachlan

Unclaimed Treasures (New York: Harper & Row, 1984)

Age range: Grades 5-6

Subject(s): Family Life; Individuality

Major character(s): Willa, Child

Time period(s): 1980s

Locale(s): United States

What the book is about: Willa wants to feel important and imagines herself in love with the father of her friend, Horace. She interacts with many delightful and weird characters and finally realizes that her true love is Horace himself.

Where it's reviewed:
Center of Children's Books Bulletin, April 1984, page 151
Horn Book, August 1984, page 467

Awards the book has won:
Boston Globe/Horn Book Award - Honor Book 1984

Other books by the author:
Arthur, for the Very First Time, 1980
Cassie Binegar, 1982
Journey, 1991
Tomorrow's Wizard, 1982

Other books you might like:
Eve Merriam, *Fighting Words*, 1992
    Two friends, envious of each other, meet for a shouting fight.
Emily Moore, *Whose Side Are You On?*, 1988
    When Barbara's friend and math tutor disappears from school, she decides to rescue him.
Bonnie Pryor, *Vinegar Pancakes and Vanishing Cream*, 1987
    Martin tries to find his own strengths amid siblings who are athletic, smart, or cute.
Jane Sutton, *Me and the Weirdos*, 1981
    10-year-old Cindy is often embarrassed by her "weird" parents but comes to accept their uniqueness.
Patti Stren, *There's a Rainbow in My Closet*, 1979
    Emma learns from her grandmother why its good to be different.

1174

Winifred Madison

Call Me Danica (New York: Four Winds, 1977)

Age range: Grades 5-6

Subject(s): Emigration and Immigration

Major character(s): Danica, Preteen

Time period(s): 1970s

Locale(s): Vancouver, British Columbia, Canada

What the book is about: Danica's family joins relatives in Canada after her father dies in Croatia (Yugoslavia). Living in a crowded basement with little money, no friends, and an accent that makes her obviously a foreigner, Danica has a difficult time adjusting. She dreams of becoming a doctor.

Where it's reviewed:
Kirkus Reviews, March 1, 1977, page 229
School Library Journal, November 1977, page 59

Other books you might like:
Carol Ann Bales, *Tales of the Elders*, 1977
    Memories of twelve people who immigrated to America during the period of the Great Migration between 1900 and 1930.(non-fiction)
Clara Ingram Judson, *They Came From Dalmatia*, 1945
    Petar and his family emigrate from Yugoslavia to Mississippi where he works in a shrimp factory, learns English and finds a treasure.
Vladimir Kavcic, *The Golden Bird*, 1969

Eighteen tales from Slovenia tell of clever and magical animals, beautiful princesses, brave princes, ogres and demons.
Josip Kriskovic, *Milan and His Runaway Uncle*, 1970
    When his uncle suddenly leaves their home, a young Yugoslav boy discovers many things about family relationships.
Peggy Mann, *A Present for Yanya*, 1975
    In Yugoslavia not long after WWII, Yanya dreams of owning a doll she sees in a market window, knowing her family can never afford to buy it.

1175

Winifred Madison

Maria Luisa (Philadelphia: Lippincott, 1971)

Age range: Grades 5-6

Subject(s): Prejudice; Mexican Americans

Major character(s): Maria Luisa, Child, Immigrant (Mexican); Juan, Child, Immigrant (Mexican); Miss Stein, Teacher

Time period(s): 1970s

Locale(s): San Francisco, California

What the book is about: While their mother recuperates from tuberculosis, Maria Luisa and her little brother, Juan, go live with relatives in San Francisco. They face many challenges and prejudices, including White/Mexican, English versus non-English speaking, and city versus country. When a teacher forms a special group for kids having trouble with English, Maria begins to do better and makes a special friend.

Where it's reviewed:
Booklist, December 1, 1971, page 334
Kirkus Reviews, September 1, 1971, page 955

Other books by the author:
Homecoming Queen, 1983
Sing about Us, 1982
Dance with Me, 1981
Growing Up in a Hurry, 1973

Other books you might like:
T. Ernesto Bethancourt, *The Me Inside of Me: A Novel*, 1985
    When Afredo Flores suddenly becomes a very wealthy orphan, he discovers that having money creates many new problems.
Carol Dines, *Best Friends Tell the Best Lies*, 1989
    Leah's loyalty and devotion to her troubled friend, Tamara, focuses her conflicting emotions about her own attachment to a young Mexican American.
Terry Dunnahoo, *Who Needs Espie Sanchez*, 1977
    Espie Sanchez's curiosity is aroused by a young wealthy girl who befriends her after both are involved in a tragic traffic accident.
Gary Soto, *Baseball in April and Other Stories*, 1990
    A collection of eleven short stories focusing on the everyday adventures of Hispanic young people in Fresno, California.
Theodore Taylor, *The Maldonado Miracle*, 1973
    A twelve year old Mexican boy crosses the border illegally to join his father in California and witnesses a miracle.

1176

Ross Martin Madsen

Illustrator: Dirk Zimmer

Perrywinkle and the Book of Magic Spells (New York: Dial, 1986)

Age range: Grades 1-3

Subject(s): Wizards

Major character(s): Perrywinkle, Apprentice, Wizard

Time period(s): Indeterminate Past

Locale(s): Fictional Country

What the book is about: Learning to be a wizard can have its dangers, and Perrywinkle manages to encounter all kinds of them as he goes on with his wizard training with the help of his talking crow.

Where it's reviewed:
Booklist, April 15, 1986, page 1229
Kirkus Reviews, April 15, 1986, page 639
School Library Journal, May 1986, page 113

Other books you might like:
Barbara Brenner, *The Color Wizard*, 1989
  Rhymed text and illustrations relate how Wizard Gray changed his very gray world with color.
Patricia Coombs, *Dorrie and the Amazing Magic Elixir*, 1974
  Left in charge of an elixer that will make one spell-proof, Dorrie, the little witch, foils the Green Wizards attempt to steal it.
Ron Hansen, *The Shadowmaker*, 1987
  A cunning little girl named Drizzle rescues her town from the bedlam created by the mysterious Shadowmaker, a wizard who makes new shadows for people.
Michael Pellowski, *Mixed-Up Magic*, 1989
  Waldo the Wizard discovers some wacky changes in his powers after his clumsy assistant drops Waldo's magic wand.
Audrey Wood, *Elbert's Bad Word*, 1988
  After shocking the elegant garden party by using a bad word, Elbert learns some acceptable substitutes from a helpful wizard.

1177

Michelle Magorian

Good Night, Mr. Tom (New York: Harper and Row, 1981)

Age range: Grades 5-9

Subject(s): Child Abuse; Artists and Art; World War II

Major character(s): William Beech, Child, Abuse Victim; Thomas Oakley, Widow(er)

Time period(s): 1940s

Locale(s): Little Weirwold, England

What the book is about: Eight year old Will is sent away from London during the war. His mother has included a belt and a note that Will is a very bad boy and must be watched constantly. Thomas Oakley, who has agreed to care for Will, discovers bruises and sores all over the disturbed boy. When Will returns to his mother and she again abuses him, Thomas rescues him and eventually begins adoption proceedings.

Where it's reviewed:
Booklist, April 15, 1982, page 1087
Center for Children's Books Bulletin, March 1982, page 134
School Library Journal, April 1982, page 73

Other books by the author:
Not a Swan, 1992
Who's Going to Take Care of Me?, 1990
Back Home, 1984

Other books you might like:
Barbara S. Cole, *Don't Tell a Soul*, 1987
  Presents two points of view about sexual abuse, that of the child and that of the mother whose second husband is the abuser.
Charlotte Culin, *Cases of Glass, Flowers of Time*, 1979
  Fourteen year old Claire, a victim of child abuse, gradually finds love in the world with the help of two unlikely friends.
Hadley Irwin, *Abby, My Love*, 1985
  In love since junior high, Abby finally shares with Chip the secret she has kept so long, that her father sexually abuses her.
Jesse Harris, *Aidan's Fate*, 1992
  McKenzie's violent psychic visions expose a case of child abuse and spell doom for her boyfriend, Aidan.
Marilyn Reynolds, *Telling*, 1989
  After being sexually abused by the father of the child she is babysitting, Cassie faces the situation and finds the strength to deal with it.

1178

Gregory Maguire

The Lightning Time (New York: Farrar, Straus and Giroux, 1978)

Age range: Grades 5-7

Subject(s): Conservation of Natural Resources; Grandparents

Major character(s): Daniel Rider, Preteen

Time period(s): 1970s

Locale(s): New York

What the book is about: After the illness of his mother, twelve year old David moves to his grandmother's home in northern New York State. He finds more strength in himself than he knew he had when he helps his grandmother resist land developers who wish to purchase her property in the Adirondack Mountains and build a resort.

Where it's reviewed:
Booklist, July 1, 1978, page 1680
Hornbook, October 1978, page 517
Kirkus Reviews, July 15, 1978, page 750

Other books by the author:
I Feel Like the Morning Star, 1989
The Dream Stealer, 1983
Lights on the Lake, 1981

Other books you might like:
Helene Conway, *The End Is the Beginning*, 1972
  After his father's death, an Irish boy assumes responsibility for protecting the family estate, including a grant to a piece of land in Maryland.

Jean Craighead George, *The Missing 'Gator of Gumbo Limbo: An Ecological Mystery*, 1992
　　Liza, one of five homeless people living in an forest in southern Florida, searches for a missing alligator destined for official investigation.
Don Moser, *A Heart to the Hawks*, 1975
　　Mike's passion for natural history causes him to fight a land developer's destruction of his woodland haven with persuasion and then with violence.
Marian Potter, *Mark Makes His Move*, 1986
　　Mark tries to find a solution for two problems: how to protect himself from a bully and now save Mrs. McSeiggen's property from land developers.
Cecily Stern, *A Different Kind of Gold*, 1981
　　A young girl in the Alaskan wilderness helps save the land from developers.

1179

Margaret Mahy

Illustrator: Wendy Smith

The Blood and Thunder Adventure on Hurricane Peak (New York: McElderry, 1989)

Age range: Grades 5-8

Subject(s): Humor; Magic; Schools

Major character(s): Sir Quincey Judd-Sprocket, Industrialist; Belladonna Doppler, Inventor; Mrs. Thoroughgood, Teacher

Time period(s): Indeterminate

Locale(s): Hookywalker, Fictional Country

What the book is about: The name of the school sets the tone of this rollicking mystery/magic tale—The Unexpected School on Hurricane Peak. The students line up against Sir Quincey and his gang to solve several mysteries and have great and humorous good times in the process. Great read aloud.

Where it's reviewed:
Booklist, October 15, 1989, page 460
Kirkus Reviews, August 1, 1989, page 1162
School Library Journal, October 1989, page 120

Other books by the author:
Dangerous Spaces, 1991
The Door in the Air and Other Stories, 1991
Aliens in the Family, 1986
The Haunting, 1982

Other books you might like:
Bill Brittain, *The Fantastic Freshman*, 1988
　　Miraculous luck from a magic charm grants Stanley his deepest desire, to be a VIP in his high school.
Douglas Arthur Hill, *Penelope's Pendant*, 1990
　　Penny finds a slightly damaged pendant on the beach and discovers it gives her the power to move herself and other objects through space.
Betty MacDonald, *Hello, Mrs. Piggle Wiggle*, 1957
　　A woman with a magic way of curing children's bad habits tries her hand with a bully, a whisperer, a slowpoke, a show-off and a crybaby.
Mary Nash, *Mrs. Coverlet's Magicians*, 1961

While the housekeeper is away participating in a baking contest, Todd Persever resorts to his magic kit to get rid of the babysitter, Miss Penalty.
Ivan Southall, *Head in the Clouds*, 1972
　　An accident-prone boy decides to work some magic spells to punish friends who have forgotten him while he is recovering from his latest mishap.

1180

Margaret Mahy

Dangerous Spaces (New York: Viking, 1991)

Age range: Grades 5-9

Subject(s): Ghosts

Major character(s): Anthea, Orphan; Flora, Cousin

Time period(s): 1980s

Locale(s): Viridian, New Zealand

What the book is about: Anthea moves into her uncle's large, noisy family, (which includes the ghost of her grandfather), because of her parents' untimely death. In her grief and discomfort, Anthea is ready for the wide open spaces of Viridian, a land created by her great-uncle, who also needed "space."

Where it's reviewed:
Center for Children's Books Bulletin, May 1991, page 222
Horn Book, May/June 1991, page 121

Other books by the author:
The Door in the Air and Other Stories, 1991
Garden Party, 1987
Aliens in the Family, 1986
The Haunting, 1983

Other books you might like:
Maurice Gee, *The Fire-Raiser*, 1986
　　In 1915, Kitty Wix and her friends try to stop the arsonist who is terrifying their small New Zealand town.
Marie M. Keesing, *Hidden Valleys and Unknown Shores*, 1978
　　Two youngsters describe their adventures in an isolated New Zealand valley where their father runs a general store.
Jack Lasenby, *The Mangrove Summer*, 1988
　　With rumors that the Japanese are to invade New Zealand, George's family moves into the bush country to survive during World War II.
William Mayne, *Low Tide*, 1992
　　A tidal wave begins an adventure for three New Zealand children.
Gillian Leigh Tarlton, *The Two Worlds of Coral Harper*, 1983
　　After her mother drowns, Coral leaves her father's bayside New Zealand home for her mother's family in Auckland where she refines her musical talent.

1181

Margaret Mahy

Illustrator: Jonathan Allen

The Great White Man-Eating Shark (New York: Dial, 1990)

Age range: Grades 2-4

Subject(s): Greed; Animals/Sharks

Major character(s): Norvin, Child

Time period(s): 1990s

Locale(s): United States

What the book is about: Norvin pretends to be a shark to scare off other swimmers and have the cove to himself. Unfortunately a boy in a shark costume attracts the attention of a real shark who has romantic designs on him. *Jaws* and *The Boy Who Cried Wolf* mixed in an amusing story.

Where it's reviewed:
Booklist, February 15, 1990, page 1168
Horn Book, March 1990, page 193

Other books by the author:
Underrunners, 1992
The Blood and Thunder Adventure on Hurricane Peak, 1989
The Man Whose Mother Was a Pirate, 1986
The Boy with Two Shadows, 1971

Other books you might like:
Heather Forest, *The Baker's Dozen: A Colonial American Tale*, 1988
    A greedy baker who offends a mysterious old woman suffers a misfortune in his business until he discovers what happens when generosity replaces greed.
Jack Gantos, *Greedy Greeny*, 1979
    A little monster, having disobeyed his mother by eating the watermelon intended for the family's dessert suffers for his greed in a dream.
Mirra Ginsburg, *Two Greedy Bears*, 1976
    A clever fox teaches two bears a lesson about greed.
Simon Henwood, *A Piece of Luck*, 1989
    A man who finds a piece of luck dreams up the perfect place for his treasure.
Frank Remkiewicz, *Greedy Anna*, 1992
    Anna is going through a phase where she wants everything for herself, except the lima beans.

1182

Margaret Mahy

The Haunting (New York: Atheneum, 1982)

Age range: Grades 5 and Up

Subject(s): Supernatural; Extrasensory Perception

Major character(s): Barney Palmer, Child

Time period(s): 1940s

Locale(s): United States

What the book is about: Supernatural story of the haunting of an 8 year old and his strange family. Barney is terrified by the repetition of images and messages that proclaim "Barney is Dead." Barney had a great-uncle who was a magician with ESP and the ability to evoke illusions. Great-uncle Cole's brother's name was also Barney.

Where it's reviewed:
Center for Children's Books Bulletin, October 1982, page 31
School Library Journal, August 1982, page 119

Other books by the author:
Dangerous Spaces, 1991

Memory, 1987
The Tricksters, 1986
Dragon of an Ordinary Family, 1969

Other books you might like:
Eileen Dunlop, *The House on the Hill*, 1987
    Children visiting their great-aunt Jane uncover a 50 year old mystery.
Nancy Garden, *The Door Between*, 1987
    Nancy must travel to the "Otherworld" to pacify the hermit to be safe from supernatural wild dogs. Sequel to Watersmeet.
Nancy Garden, *Fours Crossing*, 1981
    13 year old Melissa goes to live with her grandmother in a small New Hampshire town where winter never ends.
Susan Gates, *The Burnhope Wheel*, 1989
    15 year old Ellen is disturbed by dreams and is tempted to reenact a century old tragedy.
E.L. Konigsburg, *Up From Jerico Tel*, 1986
    The spirit of a dead actress makes two children invisible and then sends them to search for a missing necklace.

1183

Margaret Mahy

Underrunners (New York: Viking, 1992)

Age range: Grades 5 and Up

Subject(s): Kidnapping; Orphans; Mystery and Detective Stories

Major character(s): Tristram "Tris" Catt, Preteen; Winola, Orphan; Selsey Firebone, Spy

Time period(s): 1990s

Locale(s): Gideon Bay, New Zealand

What the book is about: Tris Catt and Selsey Firebone, the secret agent that dwells within Tris, know the network of tunnels called the underrunners, that are a special place of refuge from his disturbed family. He shares them with no one until he meets Winola, who has impressively tunneled her way out of the Children's Home. For Tris, finding Winola is a rare gift, for she accepts Selsey matter-of-factly, and joins in Tris and Selsey's imaginative adventures. They need each other when a mysterious stranger invades the underrunners.

Where it's reviewed:
Booklist, February 1, 1992, page 1028
School Library Journal, March 1992, page 238

Other books by the author:
Dangerous Spaces, 1991
The Door in the Air and Other Stories, 1991
The Blood and Thunder Adventure on Hurricane Peak, 1989
The Haunting, 1982

Other books you might like:
Nina Bawden, *The Finding*, 1985
    When an unexpected inheritance threatens to change his life with his adopted family in London, an eleven year old foundling runs away from home.
Tracy Friedman, *The Orphan and the Doll*, 1988
    Amanda, an orphan, receives a mysterious note from her grandmother, and Henriette, a beautiful French china doll, is the only one who can help her.
Vonda N. McIntyre, *Barbary*, 1988

Orphaned Barbary finds a new home on a space station but has to try to smuggle her cat, Mickey, in along with her.

Joseph McNair, *Commander Coatrack Returns*, 1989
When things at home and with friends seem to be falling apart for Lisa, she begins a game of make-believe with a new boy at school.

Noel Streatfeild, *Thursday's Child*, 1970
Proud of her unusual history, a nameless orphan faces the unbearable conditions of an early 20th century English orphanage.

1184

Beverly Major

Illustrator: Erick Ingraham

Porcupine Stew (New York: Morrow, 1982)

Age range: Grades 2-5

Subject(s): Animals; Fantasy

Major character(s): Thomas, Child; True Blue, Cat

Time period(s): Indeterminate

Locale(s): United States

What the book is about: Thomas follows the Dream and finds out exactly how porcupines throw their quills. He goes to the Perpetuannual Porcupine Parade and Picnic, the event of his lifetime. He sees Sir Rex the St. Bernard honored as the Dog Who Has Been Most Help to the Procupines. He has a whole new appreciation for porcupine stew!

Where it's reviewed:
Booklist, February 1, 1983, page 724
Kirkus Reviews, September 15, 1982, page 1057
School Library Journal, November 1982, page 70

Other books by the author:
The Magic Pizza, 1978

Other books you might like:
Diane Gess, *Sunshine Porcupine*, 1979
The evil and energy-eating Ugli-Unks plan to eat all the energy in Eggwood, but Procupine engages the help of the sun as an alternate power source.

Fern Powell, *The Porcupine and the Tiger*, 1969
All the animals are unhappy when Tiger kills Lion in combat and proclaims himself king, but none dare challenge his claim except Procupine.

Leon Steinmetz, *Pip Stories*, 1980
In four separate adventures, an energetic porcupine tries to fly, reach the moon, become famous, and find the sun.

Patti Stren, *Hug Me*, 1977
A porcupine wants a friend to hug more than anything else in the world.

Lynd Ward, *Nic of the Woods*, 1965
A dog learns about skunks, porcupines, and bears when his master takes him to Canada for a summer in the woods.

1185

Kevin Major

Hold Fast (New York: Dell, 1978)

Age range: Grades 5-7

Subject(s): Orphans; Runaways

Major character(s): Ken, Teenager

Time period(s): 1970s

Locale(s): Canada

What the book is about: After his parents are killed in an auto accident, fourteen year old Ken's younger brother is sent to live with elderly relatives, but Ken is sent to another town to live with an aunt and uncle. His life changes so much, and his uncle's discipline is so harsh, Ken enlists his cousin to help his runaway attempt.

Where it's reviewed:
Booklist, July 1, 1980, page 1609
Hornbook, February 1984, page 99
Kirkus Reviews, May 15, 1980, page 651

Awards the book has won:
Canadian Library Award
Canada Council (Author) 1978

Other books by the author:
Blood Red Ochre, 1990
Dear Bruce Springsteen: A Novel, 1987
Far From Shore, 1980

Other books you might like:
William Bell, *Crabbe's Journey*, 1986
Feeling misunderstood at home and at school, a teen runs off to live in the woods where he meets a woman who teaches him to take charge of his life.

Barbara Corcoran, *Stay Tuned*, 1991
En route to a relative's house, Stevie meets three young people with no place to live and takes a detour with them into a new life.

Peni R. Griffin, *Hobkin*, 1992
Two sisters run away from their abusive stepfather and settle in an abandoned house in West Texas, only to find that they are not alone.

Marilyn Harris, *The Runaway's Diary*, 1971
A diary of a young girl's experiences during the three months she spends in Canada after running away from her troubled home.

Gail Radley, *The Golden Days*, 1991
Convinced he is unwanted in his new foster home, Cory runs away with his new friend, an old lady from the nearby nursing home.

1186

G. Majors

Who Would Want to Kill Hallie Panky's Cat? (New York: Hastings, 1981)

Age range: Grades 4-6

Subject(s): Animals/Cats; Mystery and Detective Stories

Major character(s): Hallie Panky, Preteen

Time period(s): 1980s

Locale(s): United States

What the book is about: Someone threatens the life of Hallie's cat and she sets out to find out who it is.

Where it's reviewed:
Booklist, November 15, 1981, page 440

School Library Journal, December 1981, page 82

Other books you might like:
William Arden, *The Secret of the Crooked Cat*, 1970
Because they are present when a mysterious man steals a prize at the carnival, the Three Investigators are off on another mystery adventure.
John T. Foster, *Marcos and That Curious Cat*, 1970
Marcos has just four days to solve the mystery of Shady Hall with the assistance of two helpers and a large black cat.
Florence Parry Heide, *The Mystery of the Silver Tag*, 1972
When a missing cat shows up in their odd neighbor's house, three friends conclude the man is a thief and set out to rescue the cat.
E.W. Hildick, *A Cat Called Amnesia*, 1976
The four Bleeker children try desperately to solve the mystery of Amnesia, a very special cat.
Carol Beach York, *Dead Man's Cat*, 1972
Two children are convinced that India, the cat, knows the location of her dead owner's stamp album worth $25,000.

1187

Stephen Manes

Illustrator: Tom Huffman

Be a Perfect Person in Just Three Days (New York: Clarion, 1982)

Age range: Grades 3-5

Subject(s): Behavior; Humor

Major character(s): Milo Crinkley, Child; Elissa Crinkley, Preteen; Dr. K. Pinkerton Silverfish, Writer

Time period(s): 1980s

Locale(s): United States

What the book is about: Milo, tired of problems with his sister, parents, and classmates, finds a book which promises to make him perfect in just three days if he will follow instructions exactly. From wearing a stalk of broccoli around his neck to refusing to eat for a whole day, Milo does many strange things and in the end, learns a very interesting lesson.

Where it's reviewed:
Booklist, July 1, 1982, page 1446
Publisher's Weekly, April 23, 1982, page 93

Awards the book has won:
Crabbery Honor 1983

Other books by the author:
Make Four Million Dollars by Next Thursday!, 1991
That Game From Outer Space: The First Strange Thing That Happened to Oscar, 1983
I'll Live, 1982
Socko!, 1982

Other books you might like:
Larry Bograd, *Bernie Entertaining*, 1987
Ten year old Bernie's comic misadventures at home and at school don't seem very funny to him.
Miriam Chaikin, *Feathers in the Wind*, 1989
Yossi learns the rabbi's lesson about not speaking in an evil tongue firsthand when he tries to repair the damage done by a joke gone sour.
Margaret Mahy, *Bubble Trouble and Other Poems and Stories*, 1991

A collection of humorous poems and stories featuring a baby flying in a bubble and other strange doings.
Dianne Snyder, *George and the Dragon Word*, 1991
When George turns great-aunt Agatha into a dragon by shouting an ugly magic word, the twosome visits Wordsworth to get the word to reverse the spell.
Kerstin Sundh, *Augusta Can Do Anything!*, 1973
The Professor arrives in Oppelunda with his computer, Augusta, who is so lifelike she has grown arms and legs.

1188

Stephen Manes

Chocolate-Covered Ants (New York: Scholastic, 1990)

Age range: Grades 3-5

Subject(s): Animals/Insects; Gambling; Brothers

Major character(s): Adam, Child; Max, Child

Time period(s): 1990s

Locale(s): United States

What the book is about: Adam gets an ant farm for his birthday. Max tells Adam that people eat chocolate covered ants and makes a bet with his little brother. Mom calls off the bet, but Adam gets the last laugh.

Where it's reviewed:
Booklist, September 1, 1990, page 51
School Library Journal, December 1990, page 105

Other books by the author:
Make Four Million Dollars by Next Thursday!, 1991
Some of the Adventures of Rhode Island Red, 1990
Monstra vs. Irving, 1989
Be a Perfect Person in Just Three Days, 1982

Other books you might like:
Florence Parry Heide, *Banana Blitz*, 1983
TV and candy bar addict Jonah thinks his problems will be over if he can win a prize from the American Banana Institute for watching its commercials.
Constance Hiser, *No Bean Sprouts, Please!*, 1989
James is resigned to his mother's healthy but boring lunches until he gets a very unusual lunchbox for his birthday.
Phyllis Reynolds Naylor, *Beetles, Lightly Toasted*, 1987
Andy competes with his know-it-all cousin by creating some very unusual recipes and trying them out on his friends.
Thomas Rockwell, *How to Eat Fried Worms*, 1973
Two boys set out to prove that worms can be served and consumed many different ways.
Nancy Willard, *The High Rise Glorious Skittle Skat Roarious Sky Pie Angel Food Cake*, 1990
As she is preparing a special cake for her mother's birthday, a girl is surprised by three angels who have dropped in for a taste.

1189

Stephen Manes

Illustrator: William Joyce

Some of the Adventures of Rhode Island Red (New York: Lippincott, 1990)

Age range: Grades 4-6

Subject(s): Fantasy

Major character(s): Rhode Island Red "Little Man"

Time period(s): Indeterminate

Locale(s): United States

What the book is about: Though born of human parents, but appearing somehow under Old Rhody, the hen, Rhode Island Red is no bigger than a hen's egg. He travels throughout Rhode Island and has wild and wacky adventures. This tall tale begs to be read aloud.

Where it's reviewed:
Booklist, June 15, 1994
School Library Journal, July 1990, page 77

Other books by the author:
Comedy High, 1992
Chocolate-Covered Ants, 1990
Monstra vs. Irving, 1989
Chicken Trek, 1987

Other books you might like:
Patricia Beatty, *Billy Bedamned, Long Gone By*, 1977
    Two youngsters meet their Uncle Rudd who tells them tall tales about his life with the cowboys, Indians and Confederates.
Sid Fleischman, *Jim Bridger's Alarm Clock*, 1978
    Three tall tales about Jim Bridger and several of his unbelievable discoveries of the West.
Brian Gleeson, *Pecos Bill*, 1988
    Presents tall tales about one of America's favorite heroes from Texas.
Glen Rounds, *The Morning the Sun Refused to Shine*, 1984
    When the sun doesn't rise one morning, the King of Sweden contacts Paul Bunyan and asks him to find the cause of the catastrophe.
Alvin Schwartz, *Whoppers: Tall Tales and Other Lies*, 1975
    A collection of tall tales involving animals, the weather, narrow escapes and many other topics.

1190

Peggy Mann

There Are Two Kinds of Terrible (New York: Doubleday, 1977)

Age range: Grades 5 and Up

Subject(s): Death; Mothers and Sons

Major character(s): Rob, Teenager

Time period(s): 1970s

Locale(s): United States

What the book is about: Summer begins with a broken arm for Rob, then things go from bad to worse. His mother goes to the hospital for tests, and never comes back. An only child, Rob goes through the loss and grief when his mother dies of cancer. A gradual growth and change happen for Rob and his dad.

Where it's reviewed:
Kirkus Reviews, June 15, 1977, page 626
School Library Journal, January 1977, page 94

Other books by the author:
The Drop In, 1979
The Man Who Bought Himself, 1975
My Dad Lives in a Downtown Hotel, 1973
The Story of the Flower Boxes, 1966

Other books you might like:
Martha Brooks, *Two Moons in August*, 1991
    Kieran, a new boy visiting her small town for the summer helps Sidonie and her family come together again following the death of Sidonie's mother.
Edward Fenton, *The Morning of the Gods*, 1987
    Depressed over the death of her mother, Carla makes a visit to her mother's aunt and uncle in Greece where she finds comfort and joy with the family.
Patricia Hermes, *You Shouldn't Have to Say Goodbye*, 1982
    Sara's mother is facing terminal cancer and Sara cannot accept her mother's efforts to help her prepare for the loss.
Deborah Moulton, *Summer Girl*, 1992
    Because her mother is dying, Tommy is sent to live with her father, and she gradually understands him and the death of the woman they both love.
Marya Smith, *Across the Creek*, 1989
    Rye's friendship with a mysterious girl across the creek helps him to cope with the death of his mother.

1191

Fran Manushkin

Illustrator: Dirk Zimmer

Buster Loves Buttons (New York: Harper, 1985)

Age range: Grades 1-3

Subject(s): Collectors and Collecting

Major character(s): Buster, Child; Kippy, Child

Time period(s): 1980s

Locale(s): United States

What the book is about: Buster's zeal for collecting buttons reaches manic proportions. After buying all the buttons he can, Buster begins stealing them off people's clothes until Kippy and her dog decide to stop him.

Where it's reviewed:
Center for Children's Books Bulletin, September 1985, page 14
School Library Journal, May 1985, page 107

Other books by the author:
Be Brave Baby Rabbit, 1990
Hocus and Pocus at the Circus, 1983
The Tickle Tree, 1982
The Perfect Christmas Picture, 1980

Other books you might like:
Helen Cresswell, *Almost Good-Bye*, 1990
    While collecting things to sell for a school White Elephant Sale, two friends are given a lamp with unexpected magic qualities.
Trish Kennedy, *Baseball Card Crazy*, 1993
    While staying on his grandparents' farm, Oliver searches diligently for the long-lost baseball card collection his father amassed as a boy.
Shari Lewis, *Things Kids Collect*, 1980

Suggests activities for collectors interested in more than twenty-five different collectibles such as rocks, keys, buttons, menus, etc. (Non-fiction)

Diane Redfield Massie, *Lobster Moths*, 1985
The professor and his cat are avid collectors of lobster moths until the lobster moth takes things in hand and turns them both into lobster moths.

Nicolas van Pallandt, *The Butterfly Night of Old Brown Bear*, 1990
Determined to capture a beautiful moth for his collection, Old Brown Bear finds himself following the elusive creature into the clouds.

| 1192 |

Richard J. Margolis

Illustrator: Robert Lopshire

Wish Again, Big Bear (New York: Collier, 1972)

Age range: Grades 1-3

Subject(s): Animals/Bears; Wishes

Major character(s): Big Bear, Bear

Time period(s): Indeterminate

Locale(s): Earth

What the book is about: A variation on the story of the granting of three wishes, featuring a bear and a fish. The crafty fish Big Bear catches avoids being eaten by granting his captor three wishes.

Where it's reviewed:
Kirkus, February 15, 1972, page 192
Christian Science Monitor, May 4, 1972, page B2
Library Journal, May 15, 1972, page 1926

Other books by the author:
Secrets of a Small Brother, 1984
Big Bear, Spare That Tree, 1980
Big Bear to the Rescue, 1975
Homer and the Ghosts, 1972

Other books you might like:
Valerie Scho Carey, *The Devil and Mother Crump*, 1987
The Devil meets his match in a feisty old baker woman who tricks him into granting her three very strange wishes.
Hazel Hutchins, *The Three and Many Wishes of Jason Reid*, 1985
Eleven year old Jason is granted three wishes which land him and his friends in some amazing scrapes.
Arcadio Lobato, *Just One Wish*, 1989
A crystal ball that can grant wishes destroys the tranquility of a small village and only the shepherd boy who found it can save the day.
Eric Metaxas, *The Fisherman and His Wife*, 1990
A new edition of the classic tale of the fisherman's greedy wife who is never satisfied with the wishes granted her by an enchanted fish.
Bernadette Watts, *St. Francis and the Proud Crow*, 1987
After St. Francis grants his wish for a golden cage, Crow realizes the folly of envy and the value of freedom and love.

| 1193 |

Jan Marino

The Day That Elvis Came to Town (Boston: Little Brown, 1991)

Age range: Grades 6-8

Subject(s): African Americans; Alcoholism; Racism

Major character(s): Wanda Sue Dohr, Waiter/Waitress, Housekeeper; Mercedes Washington, Musician (jazz singer); April May, Boarder

Time period(s): 1960s (1964)

Locale(s): Harmony, Georgia

What the book is about: Wanda is very resentful that she must not only give up her room in her parents' boarding house to make room for a new boarder, but also function as a waitress and housekeeper. When the new boarder, a talented and warm hearted jazz singer, Mercedes Washington, makes a fuss over Wanda and claims to know Wanda's hero, Elvis Presley, personally, the relationship and Wanda's attitudes begin to change. Mercedes leaves Wanda's life, but not before Wanda gets to go to a real Elvis concert.

Where it's reviewed:
Center for Children's Books Bulletin, February 1991, page 147
School Library Journal, January 1991, page 114

Other books by the author:
Like Some Kind of Hero, 1992
88 Steps to September, 1989

Other books you might like:
Rosa Guy, *New Guys around the Block*, 1983
Harlem teen Imamu Jones, hopes to help his mother overcome alcoholism, while suspecting one of his friends may be guilty of a series of burglaries.
John Holladay, *Where's Elvis?*, 1992
The reader follows Elvis Presley as he travels and must try to find him in the illustrations of the crowded places he visits.
Robert Kimmel Smith, *The War With Grandpa*, 1984
Pete declares wholesale war when he has to give up his room because Grandpa moves in.
Bill Wallace, *Never Say Quit*, 1993
Excluded from the soccer team, several school misfits form their own team headed by a coach who drinks heavily, but who gives them a special gift.
Jacqueline Woodson, *The Dear One*, 1991
Twelve year old Feni has to adjust when the pregnant young daughter of an old friend of her mother's comes to stay with them.

| 1194 |

Marion M. Markham

Illustrator: Emily Arnold McCully

The Halloween Candy Mystery (Boston: Houghton Mifflin, 1982)

Age range: Grades 2-4

Subject(s): Halloween; Twins

Major character(s): Mickey Dixon, Twin; Kate Dixon, Twin

Time period(s): 1980s

Locale(s): United States

What the book is about: The Dixon Twins, Mickey and Kate, and their brother use their powers of deduction and scientific expertise to catch a burglar on Halloween night.

Where it's reviewed:
Booklist, October 1, 1982, page 247
School Library Journal, December 1982, page 82
Children's Book Review Service, January 1983, page 46

Other books by the author:
The Valentine's Day Mystery, 1992
The April Fool's Day Mystery, 1991
The Thanksgiving Day Parade Mystery, 1986
The Christmas Present Mystery, 1984

Other books you might like:
Wende Devlin, *Cranberry Halloween*, 1990
    On Halloween night, the people of Cranberryport almost lose the money they have raised to build a new dock.
Constance Hiser, *Scoop Snoops*, 1993
    When their neighbor is robbed on Halloween night, a group of fourth grade reporters decide to try to find the thief.
Elizabeth Levy, *Something Queer at the Haunted School*, 1982
    Two amateur detectives investigate a haunting of their school that starts around Halloween.
Marjorie Weinman Sharmat, *Nate the Great and the Halloween Hunt*, 1989
    Nate and his dog, Sludge, try to solve a case on Halloween night and find themselves locked in a haunted house.
Judith St. George, *The Halloween Pumpkin Smasher*, 1978
    Mary Grace and her imaginary friend, Nellie, plan to find out who has been smashing all of the jack-o-lanterns the week before Halloween.

1195

Dean Marney

Just Good Friends (New York: Harper, 1982)

Age range: Grades 5-8

Subject(s): Friendship; Sex Roles; Schools

Major character(s): Boyd, Teenager, 7th Grader; Marica, Teenager, 7th Grader; Louella "Lou", Teenager, 7th Grader

Time period(s): 1980s

Locale(s): Pine Springs, California

What the book is about: Three pals stick together through the ups and downs of seventh grade. Suddenly, Boyd realizes he's falling in love with one of his best friends. This story explores the impact of changing sex roles from a young man's point of view.

Where it's reviewed:
Booklist, July 1982, page 1446
School Library Journal, November 1982, page 88

Other books by the author:
Dirty Socks Don't Win Games, 1992
You, Me and Gracie Makes Three, 1989
The Trouble with Jake's Double, 1988
The Computer That Ate My Brother, 1985

Other books you might like:
James D. Forman, *Becca's Story*, 1992

A Civil War romance concerning a Michigan girl and the two soldiers trying to get her attention.
Kate Gilmore, *Remembrance of the Sun*, 1986
    Jill falls in love with an Iranian rebel just at the time when the Shah's repressive treatment of his people is making violent revolution inevitable.
Amos Oz, *Soumchi*, 1980
    A young boy in modern-day Jerusalem trades away one possession after another only to find something more wonderful in life - his first love.
David Rees, *Silence*, 1981
    A teenage boy goes to London looking for a runaway girl he loves, and finds himself in new and puzzling relationships.
Margaret Shaw, *A Wider Tomorrow*, 1990
    Bobby asks her grandmother's advice about her future, and learns of her life as a suffragette, an ambulance driver and as a young girl in love.

1196

Edward Marshall

Illustrator: James Marshall

Four on the Shore (New York: Dial, 1985)

Age range: Grades 1-2

Subject(s): Storytelling

Major character(s): Willy, Child, Storyteller

Time period(s): Indeterminate

Locale(s): United States

What the book is about: Three friends try to get rid of little Willie by telling scary stories, but he tells the scariest of all. The older children claim Willie's story didn't scare them at all, but they quickly decline when he offers to tell another one. For beginning readers.

Where it's reviewed:
Horn Book, May/June 1985, page 309
School Library Journal, May 1985, page 107

Other books by the author:
Fox and His Friends, 1982
Three by the Sea, 1981
Space Case, 1980
Troll Country, 1980

Other books you might like:
Kay Chorao, *Ralph and the Queen's Bathtub*, 1974
    Ralph runs away from his family to a tall scary house where he is sure a giant witch lives, peeks in the window, and has the adventure of his life.
Phyllis Rose Eisenberg, *Don't Tell Me a Ghost Story*, 1982
    An older brother tells a scary ghost story to his younger brother, only to have the tables turned on him.
Astrid Lindgren, *The Ghost of Skinny Jack*, 1987
    After visiting their grandmother and hearing a ghost story, a brother and sister take a scary walk through the woods.
Mercer Mayer, *You're the Scaredy Cat*, 1974
    A scary story followed by strange noises drives the campers inside during their night in the backyard.
Carol Beach York, *The Secret House*, 1992
    Miss Plum tells a scary story to the girls at the orphanage, but only Phoebe and Tatty see the nearby house that seems like the one in the story.

1197

Edward Marshall

Illustrator: James Marshall

Space Case (New York: Dial, 1980)

Age range: Grades 2-3

Subject(s): Halloween; Science Fiction

Major character(s): The Thing, Alien

Time period(s): 1980s

Locale(s): United States

What the book is about: A neon yellow, robot-like creature from space lands on Earth on Halloween. He spends the night with a friendly child, is mistaken for a science project at school, and promises to return for Christmas.

Where it's reviewed:
Center for Children's Books Bulletin, March 1981, p 136
Horn Book, October 1981, page 509

Awards the book has won:
California Young Reader Medal 1986

Other books by the author:
Four on the Shore, 1985
Fox All Week, 1984
Three by the Sea, 1981
Troll Country, 1980

Other books you might like:
Sylvia Cassedy, The Best Cat Suit of All, 1991
    Mike has a cold and is not allowed to go trick-ortreating, but a special visitor in the best cat suit of all cheers him up.
Terrance Dicks, T.R.'s Halloween, 1985
    Jimmy and his talking Teddy Roosevelt bear go trick-ortreating and help an old woman who is being robbed.
Patricia Polacco, Picnic at Mudsock Meadow, 1992
    William hopes to impress Hester by winning a competition at the Halloween picnic.
Pat Ross, M & M and the Halloween Monster, 1991
    Mandy and Mimi conclude that a monster is lurking in the basement of their apartment building.
Mary Stolz, The Scarecrows and Their Child, 1987
    While looking for work, two scarecrows become separated from their cat child, finding each other again on Halloween.

1198

James Marshall, Author/Illustrator

Fox on the Job (New York: Dial, 1988)

Age range: Grades 1-2

Subject(s): Bicycles and Bicycling; Employment

Major character(s): The Fox, Fox; Louise, Fox (The Fox's sister); Carmen, Frog

Time period(s): Indeterminate

Locale(s): United States

What the book is about: Fox hates to work, but when his mother tells him he must earn his own money for a new bicycles, he rises to the occasion and gets the job done.

Where it's reviewed:
Booklist, April 1, 1988, page 1355
Kirkus Reviews, April 1, 1988, page 542

School Library Journal, June 1988, page 93

Other books by the author:
Fox on Stage, 1993
The Cut-Ups Cut Loose, 1987
Three up a Tree, 1986
The Stupids Step Out, 1974

Other books you might like:
Eileen Christelow, Glenda Feathers Casts a Spell, 1990
    Glenda's inablility to keep her spells straight involves her in a bank robbery and a chase to catch the crooks.
Roger Hargreaves, Little Miss Chatterbox, 1985
    Little Miss Chatterbox loses a series of jobs because of her tendency to talk on and on. Eventually, though, she finds the right job for her.
Melanie Martin, Morris, the Millionaire Mouse, 1989
    Overjoyed when he wins the million dollar raffle, Morris Mouse decides to quit his job and buy everything he's ever wanted.
Michael McBrier, Getting Oliver's Goat, 1989
    Oliver's new job, taking care of an unpredictable goat, jeopardizes his chances of winning the big bicycle race.
Brad Sneed, Luckey Russell, 1992
    A kitten named Russell wants to have an important job to do on the farm.

1199

James Marshall

George and Martha Back in Town (Boston: Houghton Mifflin, 1984)

Age range: Grades 1-2

Subject(s): Friendship; Animals/Hippos

Major character(s): George, Hippopotamus; Martha, Hippopotamus

Time period(s): Indeterminate

Locale(s): Earth

What the book is about: Five stories of George and Martha as they chase jumping beans, high dive, play practical jokes and learn to follow the rules. Just one of many books about George and Martha.

Where it's reviewed:
Horn Book, June 1984, page 320
Kirkus Reviews, May 1, 1984, page 132

Other books by the author:
Round and Round, 1988
Rapscallion Jones, 1983
Taking Care of Carruthers, 1983
Rise and Shine, 1976

Other books you might like:
Iris Hiskey, Hannah the Hippo's No Mud Day, 1991
    Hannah finds she cannot stay clean even on the day Aunt Lil is coming to visit.
Lillian Nordlicht, The Alligator with the Lean Mean Smile, 1985
    Small Hippo and Big Rhino face a hungry alligator who engatges them in a riddle-solving battle of wits.
James Stevenson, Oh No, It's Waylon's Birthday!, 1989
    Three short stories featuring Waylon the Elephant celebrating his 249th birthday, Gardner the Hippo looking for a quiet place to sleep, and others.

Jane Sutton, *What Should Hippo Wear?*, 1979
For the jungle dance, Bertha invents an eyecatching outfit only to discover that her date, Fred, invited her for her plain, everyday self.

Mike Thaler, *Hippo Lemonade*, 1986
Hippo and his friends share a variety of adventures including making a wish, selling lemonade and telling a scary story.

1200

Ann M. Martin

Ten Kids, No Pets (New York: Scholastic, 1988)

Age range: Grades 4-6

Subject(s): Family Life; Humor; Moving, Household

Major character(s): Dagwood "Woody" Rosso, Preteen; Faustine Rosso, Child; Abbie Rosso, Preteen

Time period(s): Indeterminate

Locale(s): New Jersey

What the book is about: The ten Rosso children, spaced a year apart and named alphabetically (Abbie, Bainbridge, Calandra, Dagwood, etc.) find their life rambunctious and exciting when their family leaves New York City for a big old farmhouse and new friends. Now that they are in the country, the ten children begin to lobby for a pet. They head for the pound to adopt a dog, but wind up with a kitten they found in a ditch on the way.

Where it's reviewed:
Booklist, June 15, 1988, page 1739
Kirkus Reviews, April 1, 1988, page 542
School Library Journal, May 1988, page 98

Other books by the author:
Karen's Baby, 1992
Just a Summer Romance, 1987
Inside Out, 1984
Bummer Summer, 1983

Other books you might like:
Ellen Conford, *Dreams of Victory*, 1973
When her daydreams continually conflict with reality, Victory becomes convinced of her inferiority until a class essay gives her a new perspective.

Beverly Keller, *Desdemona Moves On*, 1992
Chronicles the comic mishaps of Desdemona and her family after they move into a luxurious new house.

Colleen O'Shaughnessy McKenna, *Murphy's Island*, 1990
Collette Murphy has to go with her large, often trying family to a small island and start sixth grade as the new girl in school.

Barbara Park, *The Kid in the Red Jacket*, 1987
Howard moves with his family to a distant state, lives on a street named Chester Pewe, adjusts to a new school, and is shadowed by a neighborhood girl

Bonnie Pryor, *Poison Ivy and Eyebrow Wigs*, 1993
Martin has a busy year as he tries to find his own identity both at school and in his large and busy family.

1201

Ann M. Martin

With You and Without You (New York: Holiday, 1986)

Age range: Grades 6-9

Subject(s): Death; Family Life; Fathers

Major character(s): Lisa, Preteen

Time period(s): 1980s

Locale(s): United States

What the book is about: Twelve year old Lisa learns that her father has heart disease. In the story, we see Lisa and her family deal with the illness, death, and grieving process. There are numerous sub-plots, and Martin's portrayal of the guilt and confusion that plague adolescents is right on target.

Where it's reviewed:
Center for Children's Books Bulletin, May 1986, page 174
School Library Journal, August 1986, page 104

Other books by the author:
Claudia and the Genius of Elm Street, 1991
California Girls, 1990
Inside Out, 1984
Bummer Summer, 1983

Other books you might like:
Barbara M. Joosse, *Pieces of the Picture*, 1989
Emily moves from Chicago to rural Wisconsin after her father's death. She struggles to understand her mother and deal with her own mixed feelings.

Jackie French Koller, *The Last Voyage of the Misty Day*, 1992
Denise moves to Maine after her father's death in Manhattan, and forges a healing relationship with a boat owner surrounded by considerable mystery.

Charlotte MacLeod, *Cirak's Daughter*, 1982
An unexpected legacy from the father who deserted her starts Jenny on a dangerous search for answers concerning her father, his death, and her future.

Robert Pierik, *Rookfleas in the Cellar*, 1979
His father's death makes twelve year old Danny the "man of the house" which has both advantages and problems for Danny.

Laura Caroline Stevenson, *Happily Ever After*, 1990
When her father dies, Rebecca is sent to live with the mother she thought had abandoned her, and learns new truths about her family.

1202

Ann M. Martin

Yours Truly, Shirley (New York: Holiday House, 1988)

Age range: Grades 4-6

Subject(s): Learning Disabilities; Adoption; Brothers and Sisters

Major character(s): Shirley Basini, Preteen, Handicapped (dyslexic); Joe Basini, Student—College; Jackie Basini, Child

Time period(s): 1980s

Locale(s): United States

What the book is about: Shirley is a fourth grader coping with dyslexia. Her older brother is a brilliant college student and her new sister is a whiz kid, skipping from first to advanced third grade. Shirley feels dumb and hates school.

Where it's reviewed:
Kirkus Reviews, October 1, 1988, page 1473
Publisher's Weekly, September 30, 1988, page 69

Other books by the author:
Slam Book, 1987
Me and Katie the Pest, 1985
Stage Fright, 1984
Bummer Summer, 1983

Other books you might like:
Barthe De Clements, *6th Grade Can Really Kill You*, 1985
   Helen feels that her lack of reading skills may keep her in sixth grade forever, until a special teacher gives her the help she needs.
Patricia Reilly Giff, *The Girl Who Knew It All*, 1979
   Always in trouble, Tracy discovers most of her problems stem from the fact that she doesn't read well.
Joyce Hansen, *Yellow Bird and Me*, 1986
   Doris becomes friends with Yellow Bird as she helps him with studies and discovers he has dyslexia.
Natalie Honeycutt, *The Best-Laid Plans of Jonah Twist*, 1988
   Jonah worries about a school report he must do with a bossy partner and about his kitten eating his brother's hamster.
Tim Kennemore, *Wall of Words*, 1982
   Kim tries to cope with the absence of her beloved father and her sister's terror of school.

| 1203 |

Bill Martin, Jr.

The Ghost-Eye Tree (New York: Holt Rinehart, 1985)

Age range: Grades 1-2

Subject(s): Fear; Brothers and Sisters; Ghosts

Major character(s): Mr. Cowlander, Milkman; Ellie, Child

Time period(s): 1980s

Locale(s): United States

What the book is about: A mother asks her son and daughter to go to Mrs. Cowlander's barn to get some fresh milk. The barn is across town, down a deserted country road, past a haunted oak tree, and the children have a very scary journey.

Where it's reviewed:
Book World, November 10, 1985, page 19
Publishers Weekly, September 6, 1985, page 66

Other books by the author:
Happy Hippopotami, 1991
Polar Bear, Polar Bear, What Do You Hear?, 1991
Chicka Chicka Boom Boom, 1989
The Magic Pumpkin, 1989

Other books you might like:
Eve Bunting, *Scary, Scary Halloween*, 1986
   A family of cats watches the parade of strange creatures on Halloween.
Natalie Savage Carlson, *Spooky and the Ghost Cat*, 1985
   Spooky meets a strange white cat that is under the spell of a witch.
Emily Herman, *Hubnuckles*, 1985

Hubnuckles is a ghostly figure that appears only on Halloween.
Anne Rockwell, *Thump, Thump, Thump*, 1981
   The Thing has lost his hairy toe and the old woman has found it.
Brinton Turkle, *Do Not Open*, 1981
   When Miss Moody opens a bottle marked "Do Not Open," a monster appears and she must use her wits to vanquish it.

| 1204 |

Bill Martin, Jr.

Illustrator: Ted Rand

Knots on a Counting Rope (New York: Holt, 1987)

Age range: Grades 2-4

Subject(s): Grandparents; Blind

Major character(s): Boy-Strength-of-Blue-Horses, Indian

Time period(s): 1980s

Locale(s): United States

What the book is about: The special bond between a blind Indian boy and his grandfather is shown as Boy-Strength-of-Blue-Horses listens to his grandfather reminisce about the boy's birth, his first horse, and an exciting horse race.

Where it's reviewed:
Kirkus Reviews, August 15, 1987, page 1243
School Library Journal, December 1987, page 38

Other books by the author:
Barn Dance!, 1987
Here Are My Hands, 1987
The Ghost-Eye Tree, 1985

Other books you might like:
Barbara Diamond Goldin, *Cakes and Miracles*, 1991
   Blind Hershel finds he has special gifts he can use to help his mother during the Jewish holiday of Purim.
Ellen Kindt McKenzie, *Stargone John*, 1990
   John, withdrawn and having difficulty in school, is befriended by a blind, retired teacher who shares the world of reading and writing with him.
Philip Newth, *Roly Goes Exploring: A Book for Blind and Sighted Children*, 1977
   Roly explores geometric shapes. Text and pictures are accessible to both blind and sighted children.
Gloria Whelan, *Hannah*, 1991
   Hannah, a blind girl in the late 19th century, doesn't go to school until a new teacher comes to board at their house.
David Wisniewski, *Elfwyn's Saga*, 1990
   Elfwyn finds a way to erase the curse cast on her family.

| 1205 |

Toshi Maruki, Author/Illustrator

Hiroshima No Pika (New York: Lothrop, 1982)

Age range: Grades 4-6

Subject(s): Nuclear Warfare; World War II

Major character(s): Mii, Child

Time period(s): 1940s (1945)

Locale(s): Hiroshima, Japan

What the book is about: A retelling of a mother's account of what happened to her family during the Flash that destroyed Hiroshima, August 6, 1945. Though in picture book format, this is a graphic and powerful portrayal of the suffering and devastation wrought by the atomic bomb. It is written with the fervent hope that "The Flash" will never happen again. Though listed some places as a grade 2-4 book, adults should read this together with younger children and be prepared to help them with questions and feelings afterward.

Where it's reviewed:
Center for Children's Books Bulletin, October 1982, page 31
Horn Book, October 1982, page 531

Awards the book has won:
Mildred L. Batchelder Award 1981
Ehon Nippon Prize (Most excellent picture book of Japan)

Other books by the author:
The Hiroshima Murals, 1985 (Adult book)

Other books you might like:
Eleanor Coerr, *Sadako and the Thousand Paper Cranes*, 1977
   Hospitalized with leukemia, a child in Hiroshima races to fold 1000 paper cranes because of an old legend which said this would cure sickness.
Christobel Mattingly, *The Miracle Tree*, 1985
   Separated by the explosion of the atomic bomb, a husband, wife and mother are eventually reunited.
Martin McPhillips, *Hiroshima*, 1985
   Traces the development of the atomic bomb and how the decision was made to drop it on Hiroshima. (non-fiction)
Junko Morimoto, *My Hiroshima*, 1987
   The author recalls her happy childhood in Hiroshima abrupty halted on August 6, 1945, when her known world was hideiously destoyed by the atomic bomb.
Keiji Nakazawa, *Barefoot Gen: The Day After*, 1988
   A cartoon format telling the story of the bombing of Hiro-shima.

1206

Jean Marzollo

The Green Ghost of Appleville (New York: Scholastic, 1989)

Age range: Grades 2-3

Series: 39 Kids on the Block

Subject(s): Ghosts; Friendship

Major character(s): Mary Kate, Child; Jane, Child; Fizz, Child

Time period(s): 1980s

Locale(s): United States

What the book is about: Mary Kate and her friend, Jane, are teased by Fizz, who tells them a Green Ghost haunts a house near the cemetery. When a new boy, Rusty, and his grandmother move into the house, he and Mary Kate invite all the kids to the "haunted house."

Where it's reviewed:
Booklist, March 15, 1990, page 1471

Other books by the author:
The Best Friends' Club, 1990

Chicken Pox Strikes Again, 1990
Best Present Ever, 1989

Other books you might like:
Alvin Schwartz, *Scary Stories 3: More Tales to Chill Your Bones*, 1991
   Both traditional and modern stories of ghosts, haunts, and monsters.
Janice Lee Smith, *There's a Ghost in the Coatroom*, 1991
   The children in Mrs. D's class discover a ghost while pre-paring a Christmas feast.
Juliet Snape, *I'm Not Frightened of Ghosts*, 1987
   Lizzie faces mysterious happenings in a haunted house, not really believing a ghost is the real explanation.
Craig Strete, *Big Thunder Magic*, 1990
   Thunderspirit, a very small and timid ghost, rescues his friend, Nanabee the sheep, from the zoo.
Stephen Wyllie, *Ghost Train: A Spooky Hologram Book*, 1992
   Three ghosts looking for homes settle into the "ghost train" ride at an amusement park.

1207

Jean Marzollo

Illustrator: Blanche Sims

Soccer Sam (New York: Random, 1987)

Age range: Grades 1-2

Subject(s): Sports/Soccer; Mexicans

Major character(s): Marco, Child; Sam, Child

Time period(s): 1980s

Locale(s): United States

What the book is about: Marco, from Mexico, spends a year with his friend Sam in the United States and the boys organize a soccer team. Marco teaches Sam and all the second graders to play soccer.

Where it's reviewed:
Booklist, August 1987, page 1754
School Library Journal, September 1987, page 167

Other books by the author:
Jed and the Space Bandits, 1987
Red Sun Girl, 1983
Jed's Junior Space Patrol, 1982
Robin of Bray, 1982

Other books you might like:
Mary Jane Auch, *Angel and Me and the Bayside Bombers*, 1989
   Having been kicked off the third grade soccer team, Brian challenges them to a match against his own team, which he and his cousin, Angel, organize.
Colin McNaughton, *Soccer Crazy*, 1981
   Clumsy substitute player Bruno is determined to save the day for his soccer team.
Margaret Park, *Harvey and Rosie and Ralph*, 1992
   A magic spell turns Harvey's dog, Rosie, into a girl just long enough to help pull his soccer team out of its slump.
Sue Stops, *Dulcie Dando, Soccer Star*, 1992
   Dulcie, a talented soccer player, proves that girls are just as capable as boys when she's given the chance to play on the school team.
Erika Tamar, *Soccer Mania*, 1993

Pete and his friends, who enjoy playing pick-up soccer, get registered as an official team and discover the negative aspects of competition.

1208

John Masefield

Illustrator: Faith Jaques

The Box of Delights (New York: Macmillan, 1984)

Age range: Grades 5-7

Subject(s): Fantasy; Animals/Wolves

Major character(s): Kay Harker, Hero; Abner Brown, Magician; Peter Jones, Friend

Time period(s): 1920s

Locale(s): Seekings, England

What the book is about: Abridged version of the story of a boy pitted against the forces of evil, involved in a fantastic adventure. Kay finds himself guardian of the mysterious Box of Delights.

Where it's reviewed:
Horn Book, January/February 1985, page 78
School Library Journal, February 1985, page 78

Other books by the author:
Grace Before Plowing, 1966
The Midnight Folk, 1957

Other books you might like:
Melvin Burgess, The Cry of the Wolf, 1990
    A hunter determined to wipe out every wolf in England almost succeeds, but then finds himself the prey.
Elizabeth Goudge, The Little White Horse, 1946
    Maria Merryweather, her governess, and dog arrive at her ancestral home in an enchanted village in England where bliss is marked by a dark shadow.
Peter Hunter Blair, The Coming of Pout, 1969
    While in England, a brother and sister meet a mysterious creature who can telescope time and asks them help break the spell cast upon him.
Welwyn Wilton Katz, The Third Magic, n 1988
    Adolescent Morgan Lefevre is mistaken for one of her ancestors while visiting England, summoned to the world of Nwm and caught between two Magics.
Victor Kelleher, The Red King, 1989
    A magician and an acrobat challenge the power of the evil King who rules the Forest Lands by spreading the red fever to those who don't pay tribute.

1209

Pat Rhoads Mauser

Illustrator: Gail Owens

A Bundle of Sticks (New York: Atheneum, 1982)

Age range: Grades 4-6

Subject(s): Bullies; Martial Arts

Major character(s): Ben, Preteen, Martial Arts Expert

Time period(s): 1980s

Locale(s): United States

What the book is about: Ben is victimized by the class bully. When he tries to fight back, he gets quite a beating. His parents enroll him in a martial arts class. Ben surprises himself by winning a purple belt. The bully is in for a surprise too!

Where it's reviewed:
Horn Book, August 1982, page 407
School Library Journal, May 1982, page 86

Awards the book has won:
Dorothy Canfield Fisher Children's Book Award 1982

Other books by the author:
Patti's Pet Gorilla, 1987
Rip-Off, 1985
How I Found Myself at the Fair, 1980

Other books you might like:
Carol Carrick, What a Wimp, 1983
    Lenny keeps calling Barney a wimp at his new school. Finally, Barney decides to tackle the problem on his own.
Aidan Chambers, Present Takers, 1983
    Bullied beyond talking by Melanie Prosser, Lucy and her friends at school band together in support of each other in a non-aggressive resistance pact.
Ellen Conford, The Revenge of the Incredible Dr. Rancid and His Youthful Assistant Jeffrey, 1980
    Jeffrey fantasizes about standing up to class bully, Dewey Belasco. When he gets his chance, he fights back and becomes a superhero to his classmates.
Lois Duncan, Wonder Kid Meets the Evil Lunch Snatcher, 1988
    Brian, his sister, and two friends create a superhero who turns the tables on Brian and his gang of bullies.
Marian Potter, Mark Makes His Move, 1986
    Daily bullied by the Skinner brothers, Mark escapes into a fantasy world until he realizes that won't solve his problem.

1210

Marianna Mayer

Illustrator: Michael Hague

The Unicorn and the Lake (New York: Dial, 1982)

Age range: Grades 2-4

Subject(s): Unicorns; Animals/Reptiles

Major character(s): Unicorn, Hero; Serpent, Villain

Time period(s): Indeterminate Past

Locale(s): Fictional Country

What the book is about: This is the story of how the unicorn saved the other animals living near a lake from death, drought, and destruction when a serpent poisons the drinking water. Only by courage can they be freed from fear.

Where it's reviewed:
New York Times Book Review, January 9, 1983, page 32
School Library Journal, November 1982, page 71

Awards the book has won:
Colorado Children's Book Award 1984

Other books by the author:
The Golden Swan, 1990
Noble-Hearted Kate, 1990
Unicorn Alphabet, 1989

Me and My Flying Machine, 1971

Other books you might like:
Gale Cooper, *Unicorn Moon*, 1984
  A princess searches for the meaning of true love in order to break the spell over a young man she sees constantly in her dreams.
Susan Cooper, *The Silver Cow: A Welsh Tale*, 1983
  A young Welsh boy is rewarded for his beautiful harp playing with a silver cow, the gift of the magic people of the lake.
Nancy Luenn, *Unicorn Crossing*, 1987
  Jenny hopes to fulfill her desire to see a real unicorn on her vacation when she helps Mrs. Donovan pick roses one misty morning.
Louise Moeri, *The Unicorn and the Plow*, 1982
  A poor starving farmer is persuaded by his two oxen to wait one more day before he sells one and kills the other for food.
Jane Yolen, *The Transfigured Hart*, 1975
  A boy and girl become convinced that the white deer they discover in the woods is a unicorn.

1211

Mercer Mayer, Author/Illustrator

Liza Lou and the Yeller Belly Swamp (New York: Parents, 1976)

Age range: Grades 1-3

Subject(s): Monsters; Swamps

Major character(s): Liza Lou, Child; Swamp Haunt, Monster; Jane, Relative (aunt)

Time period(s): Indeterminate

Locale(s): United States (Swampland)

What the book is about: With her quick thinking, in the tradition of Br'er Rabbit, Liza Lou manages to outwit all the haunts, gobblygooks, witches and devils in the Yeller Belly Swamp. Mercer Mayer's great pictures and lots of chants and excitement make this great for storytelling/read aloud.

Where it's reviewed:
Kirkus Reviews, April 15, 1976, page 351
School Library Journal, November 1976, page 50

Awards the book has won:
California Young Reader Medal (Primary) 1983

Other books by the author:
Just a Daydream, 1989
The Great Cat Chase, 1974
What Do You Do with a Kangaroo?, 1973

Other books you might like:
Mary Blount Christian, *Go West, Swamp Monsters!*, 1985
  Four young swamp monsters put on cowboy clothes and go in search of the wild, wild West.
Henrik Drescher, *Simon's Book*, 1983
  Simon flees from a friendly monster with the aid of some drawing pens and a bottle of ink.
Ruthanna Long, *The Great Monster Contest*, 1977
  The beasts of the Horrendous Swamp reveal their true nature when they gather to choose a champion monster.
Pat Ross, *M & M and the Halloween Monster*, 1991
  Getting ready for Halloween, Mandy and Mimi observe creepy things and conclude that a monster is lurking in the basement of their apartment building.

Meyer Seltzer, *Hide-and-Go-Shriek Monster Riddles*, 1990
  More than one hundred funny riddles about vampires, ghouls, ghosts, werewolves and other monsters.

1212

Ardath Mayhar

Medicine Walk (New York: Atheneum, 1985)

Age range: Grades 5-7

Subject(s): Deserts; Survival

Major character(s): Burr, Survivor

Time period(s): 1980s

Locale(s): United States

What the book is about: When Burr's father has a heart attack and dies while flying them in a small plane, Burr must survive on his own, because they strayed from their filed flight plan to see the petrified forest. Burr uses knowledge gained from an Apache foreman on the family ranch back home. These memories and the appearance of a cougar which Burr adopts as his totem, keep him going.

Where it's reviewed:
Booklist, December 15, 1985, page 629
School Library Journal, February 1986, page 87
Center for Children's Books Bulletin, February 1986, page 115

Other books by the author:
A Place of Silver Silence, 1988
Carrots and Miggle, 1986
Exile on Vlahil, 1984
Lords of the Triple Moon, 1983

Other books you might like:
Daniel Defoe, *Robinson Crusoe*, 1978
  The classic desert island survival story of Robinson Crusoe's thirty years of survival told in comic strip form.
Franklin W. Dixon, *The Hardy Boys' Handbook: Seven Stories of Survival*, 1980
  All seven of these Hardy Boys stories involve Joe and Frank in survival situations in water, desert and jungle.
Gloria Skurzynski, *Lost in the Devil's Desert*, 1982
  Eleven year old Kevin finds himself alone and lost in the Utah desert with only his wits to help him survive.
Willy Whitefeather, *Willy Whitefeather's Outdoor Survival Handbook for Kids*, 1990
  Advice for young people on how to survive if lost or stranded in the woods or desert. (Non-fiction)
Gurney Williams, *True Escape and Survival Stories*, 1977
  Presents accounts of seven instances of escape and survival, and includes a section of tips for the reader.

1213

William Mayne

Drift (New York: Delacorte, 1986)

Age range: Grades 5-8

Subject(s): Indians of North America; Survival

Major character(s): Rafe Considine, Teenager; Tawena, Indian

Time period(s): Indeterminate Past

Locale(s): North America

What the book is about: A white boy and an Indian girl are trapped on an ice floe with a bear in an adventure set in the North American wilderness. They are rescued by two Indian women. The survival lore of the Indians and their understanding of nature are an important part of this suspenseful story.

Where it's reviewed:
Center for Children's Books Bulletin, June 1986, page 4426
School Library Journal, August 1986, page 104

Other books by the author:
Low Tide, 1992
Antar and the Eagles, 1990
Gideon, Ahoy!, 1989
A Game of Dark, 1971

Other books you might like:
James J. Alison, *Sing for a Gentle Rain*, 1990
A boy's search for an explanation to a dream leads him to an Anasazi cliff village, where a young Indian girl needs his help to save her people.
Anne Merrick Epstein, *Good Stones*, 1977
An agin ex-con who lives as a hermit joins with an orphan and together make a life for themselves surviving the elements and the rejection of society.
Gary Paulsen, *Dunc Breaks the Record*, 1992
Dunc and Amos crash in the wilderness while hang gliding, but things go from bad to worse when they are captured by a wild man!
Mildred Teal, *Bird of Passage*, 1972
The Great Blue Heron living on the coastal marshes of Georgia and New England becomes a symbol of survival for the characters of two short stories.
Jean Thesman, *When the Road Ends*, 1992
Spending a summer in the country, three foster children and a woman recoving from an accident are left by the caretaker and must survive on their own.

| 1214 |

Harry Mazer

Cave under the City (New York: Harper and Row, 1986)

Age range: Grades 5-8

Subject(s): Brothers; Survival

Major character(s): Tolly, Preteen; Bubber, Child

Time period(s): 1930s

Locale(s): New York, New York (The Bronx)

What the book is about: When their father leaves New York to look for work, and their mother is hospitalized with tuberculosis, twelve year old Tolly and his brother take to the streets rather than go to the children's shelter. Even though they are two homeless boys, Tolley's alternating protectiveness and exasperation with Bubber are typical of siblings in more normal circumstances.

Where it's reviewed:
Center for Children's Books Bulletin, January 1987, page 93
Horn Book, March/April 1987, page 211

Other books by the author:
The Island Keeper, 1981

The Last Mission, 1979
The Dollar Man, 1974
Guy Lenny, 1971

Other books you might like:
Judith Berck, *No Place to Be: Voices of Homeless Children*, 1992
Details the grave situation facing homeless children and their parents who live in shelters and welfare hotels. (Non-Fiction)
Vera Cleaver, *Trial Valley*, 1977
The three Luther children, who have raised themselves since their father died, find an abandoned boy near their home in the Great Smoky Mountains.
Paula Fox, *Monkey Island*, 1991
Forced to live on the streets of New York City after his mother disappears, eleven year old Clay is befriended by two men who help him survive.
Virginia Hamilton, *The Planet of Junior Brown*, 1986
A leader in New York's underground world of homeless children, Buddy Clark is responsible for protecting an overweight, emotionally disturbed friend.
Felice Holman, *The Wild Children*, 1983
Left alone after his family is arrested during the Bolshevik Revolution, Alex falls in with a gang of other desperate, homeless children.

| 1215 |

Harry Mazer

The Last Mission (New York: Delacorte, 1979)

Age range: Grades 6-9

Subject(s): Jews; Prisoners and Prisons; World War II

Major character(s): Jack Raab, Teenager (prisoner of war), Military Personnel (aerial gunner); Chuckie, Military Personnel; Gary Martin, Pilot

Time period(s): 1940s (1944)

Locale(s): New York, New York; Europe

What the book is about: A fifteen year old Jewish New Yorker enlists in the Air Force using his older brother's birth certificate. After twenty-four bombing missions on which he is the gunner, he is shot down over Czechoslovakia. He is the only member of the crew to survive and becomes a prisoner of war. He escapes during the German front's collapse. Non-stop action for WWII and adventure fans.

Where it's reviewed:
School Library Journal, November 1979, page 91
Kirkus Reviews, January 1, 1980, page 10
Hornbook, February 1980, page 63

Other books by the author:
Bright Days, Stupid Nights, 1992
Cave under the City, 1986
The Island Keeper, 1981
Guy Lenny, 1971

Other books you might like:
Milton Dank, *Khaki Wings*, 1980
Edward applies to the Royal Flying Corps to train as a pilot and soon finds himself in the thick of the bitter and disillusioning WWI.
Richard Alexander Hough, *Flight to Victory*, 1985

Sixteen year old Will leaves his home, school and youth behind to become a pilot during WWI.

Irina Korschunov, *A Night in Distant Motion*, 1983
When Regine, a Nazi supporter, falls in love with a Polish prisoner, she notices for the first time the injustices and horrors going on around her.

Earle Rice, *Tiger, Lion, Hawk*, 1979
An American Flying Tiger and Japan's most famous fighter pilot agree to meet in battle over China during WWII.

Sigurd Senje, *Escape!*, 1964
A Norwegian boy and girl help the underground bring about the escape of a Russian prisoner from a German prison during the WWII occupation of Norway.

1216

Harry Mazer

Snow Bound (New York: Delacorte, 1973)

Age range: Grades 5-9

Subject(s): Survival; Runaways

Major character(s): Tony Laporte, Runaway; Cindy Reichert, Hitchhiker

Time period(s): 1970s

Locale(s): New York

What the book is about: In this survival story, Tony and Cindy spend eleven days snow bound together. Tony is a more than slightly spoiled teen. When his parents actually say no when he asks to keep a stray dog, he takes revenge by running away in his mother's car, picks up a hitchhiker and drives into a snowstorm with no driver's license and no common sense. Trying to impress the aloof girl he picked up, he drives wildly and wrecks the car in a remote area of New York state. He and Cindy, bickering and waiting for a rescue that never comes, finally realize they will have to cooperate to get out of this mess together.

Where it's reviewed:
Booklist, September 15, 1973, page 123
Kirkus Reviews, April, 1, 1973, page 384
Library Journal, July 1973, page 2202

Other books by the author:
City Light, 1988
Cave under the City, 1986
The Last Mission, 1979
The Dollar Man, 1974

Other books you might like:
R.M. Ballantine, *The Coral Island*, 1977
Three boys, shipwrecked on a desert island, create an idyllic society despite typhoons, wild hogs and pirates, who kidnap one of the boys.

Eth Clifford, *The Curse of the Moonraker: A Tale of Survival*, 1977
The survivors of a strange shipwreck in the Auckland Islands fight for survival under seemingly hopeless conditions.

Dwight William Jensen, *There Will Be a Road*, 1978
Two young men spend the winter in the mountains cutting trees for posts, living in a dugout, and ultimately fighting for their lives in a blizzard.

James Ralph Johnson, *Wild Venture*, 1961

Accepting a challenge, two boys, equipped with only hunting knives, prove their ingenuity by spending a week in the wild.

Hilary H. Milton, *The Brats and Mr. Jack*, 1980
A brother and sister run away from their orphanage and are befriended by an unusual old "bum" with a secretive lifestyle.

1217

Norma Fox Mazer

After the Rain (New York: Morrow, 1987)

Age range: Grades 5 and Up

Subject(s): Grandparents; Death

Major character(s): Rachel, Teenager; Izzy, Grandparent (grandfather)

Time period(s): 1980s

Locale(s): United States

What the book is about: Rachel's grandfather, Izzy, is seen realisticly as taciturn and graceless, even after his death. Rachel has made a special effort to get to know him better and feels his loss deeply. A story of family love and young adulthood.

Where it's reviewed:
Horn Book, September/October 1987, page 619
School Library Journal, May 1987, page 116

Awards the book has won:
Newbery Honor

Other books by the author:
C, My Name Is Cal, 1990
B, My Name Is Bunny, 1987
Three Sisters, 1986
Downtown, 1984

Other books you might like:
Ann Blades, *Boy of Tache*, 1984
Charlie makes a daring trip to bring a doctor when his grandfather develops pneumonia.

Betsy Byars, *The House of Wings*, 1972
Abandoned by his parents at grandfather's, Sammy is lovingly won over by caring for a wounded crane with his grandfather.

Bessie Holland Heck, *Golden Arrow*, 1981
Randy wants a motorcycle more than anything and he is willing to work on his grandfather's farm to earn enough money.

Kristi Holl, *Just Like a Real Family*, 1983
June can't get her foster grandfather to talk to her until her final success with him helps her solve other problems, just like a real family.

Joan Tate, *Luke's Garden and Gramp: Two Novels*, 1981
Luke's Garden tells the story of Luke whose innocent becomes the target of violence. Gramp tells of the love between Simon and his grandfather.

1218

Norma Fox Mazer

The Solid Gold Kid (New York: Delacorte, 1977)

Age range: Grades 5-8

Subject(s): Kidnapping

Major character(s): Derek Chapman, Captive

Time period(s): 1970s

Locale(s): United States

What the book is about: Derek Chapman hitches a ride and later realizes he has unwittingly assisted in what he has anticipated and dreaded - his own kidnapping. Four other adolescents are also kidnapped and each reacts differently to their harrowing situations.

Where it's reviewed:
Booklist, June 1, 1977, page 1499
Kirkus Reviews, April 1, 1977, page 360
School Library Journal, November 1975, page 93

Other books by the author:
After the Rain, 1987
B, My Name Is Bunny, 1987
Taking Terri Mueller, 1983
A Figure of Speech, 1973

Other books you might like:
Caroline B. Cooney, *The Face on the Milk Carton*, 1990
  A photograph of a missing girl on a milk carton leads Janie on a search for her real identity.
Willo Davis Roberts, *Babysitting Is a Dangerous Job*, 1985
  Darcy tries to cope with three bratty children and a kidnapping puts all of them in the hands of three dangerous villains.
Jean Thesman, *Rachel Chance*, 1992
  When Rachel's brother is taken by a traveling revivalists, she sets out with her grandma, a hired hand and a neighbor in an attempt to get him back.
Barbara Wersba, *You'll Never Guess the End*, 1992
  In the middle of a small nervous breakdown, Joel tries to cope with the complications caused by a famous brother and the kidnapping of a friend.
Gloria Whelan, *The Secret Keeper*, 1990
  Sixteen year old Ali comes face to face with murder and kidnapping during what he hoped would be a pleasant summer on Lake Michigan.

| **1219** |

Norma Fox Mazer

Taking Terri Mueller (New York: Morrow, 1983)

Age range: Grades 6-8

Subject(s): Kidnapping; Divorce

Major character(s): Terri Mueller, Teenager; Phil Mueller, Parent

Time period(s): 1980s

Locale(s): United States

What the book is about: Fourteen year old Terri remembers only life with her father, but then she discovers that he kidnapped her from her mother after a divorce and her mother is still alive.

Where it's reviewed:
Booklist, December 1, 1981, page 500
Voice of Youth Advocates, April 1982, page 36

Awards the book has won:
Edgar Allan Poe Award

Other books by the author:
D, My Name Is Danita, 1991
Babyface, 1990
When We First Met, 1982
Mrs. Fish, Ape, and Me, the Dump Queen, 1981

Other books you might like:
Carole S. Adler, *If You Need Me*, 1988
  Dora is increasingly worried as tension grows between her father and stepmother.
Catherine Cookson, *Mrs. Flanagan's Trumpet*, 1976
  Eddie finds himself allied with his unpleasant grandmother in the struggle to free his sister and the household maid from white slavers.
Richard Parker, *Three by Mistake*, 1974
  Terrorist guerrillas kidnap three children instead of one.
Joan Phipson, *The Cats*, 1976
  Two kidnapped brothers in Australia save their abductors from destruction by a tribe of feral cats that they have cruelly abused.
Catherine Woolley, *Libby Shadows a Lady*, 1974
  A girl in New York City inadvertently breaks up a kidnapping ring supplying babies for adoption.

| **1220** |

Geraldine McCaughrean

A Pack of Lies (New York: Oxford University Press, 1988)

Age range: Grades 5-7

Subject(s): Short Stories; Storytelling

Major character(s): Ailsa, Child; MCC Berkshire, Wanderer

Time period(s): 1980s

Locale(s): United States

What the book is about: A young man, MCC Berkshire, wanders into an antique store where Ailsa and her mother barely make a living. Each of the twelve stories involves making a sale to an unconvinced customer. Exaggerated stereotypes and outrageous parody fill the stories with comedy, mystery and adventure.

Where it's reviewed:
Booklist, June 1, 1989, page 1718
School Library Journal, May 1989, page 126
Kirkus Reviews, June 1, 1989, page 839

Awards the book has won:
Carnegie Medal
Guardian Award for Children's Fiction

Other books by the author:
Greek Myths, 1992
El Cid, 1989
A Little Lower than the Angels, 1987
The Canterbury Tales, 1984

Other books you might like:
Barbara Griffiths, *Frankenstein's Hamster*, 1992
  Ten scary stories featuring a schoolboy with a talent for taxidermy, the highwayman of death, and other disturbing characters.
Paul Jennings, *Unmentionable!: More Amazing Stories*, 1993

A collection of short stories about the scary, the supernatural and the unusual.

Pat McKissack, *Dark-Thirty: Southern Tales of the Supernatural*, 1992

A collection of ghost stories with African-American themes designed to be told in the evening when ghosts seem most real.

Gary Soto, *Local News*, 1993

A collection of thirteen short stories about the everyday lives of Mexican-American young people in California's central valley.

Oscar Wilde, *Stories for Children*, 1991

"The Selfish Giant,"" The Nightingale and the Rose," "Devoted Friend," "The Happy Prince," "The Remarkable Rocket" and "Young King."

1221

Robert McClung

Hugh Glass, Mountain Man (New York: Morrow, 1990)

Age range: Grades 6-9

Subject(s): Survival; American West

Major character(s): Hugh Glass, Trapper, Mountain Man; Jim Bridger, Mountain Man

Time period(s): 1820s (1823)

Locale(s): Rocky Mountains

What the book is about: Jim Bridger and John Fitzgerald abandon Hugh Glass and take his rifle after Glass is mauled by a grizzly. Glass has to fight Indians, the elements, and most of all, get control of himself. He means to take revenge on Bridger and Fitzgerald. Vivid and powerful, with details of the mountain country, and for those who like painstaking details, the blow by blow of Glass's injuries. Shows how revenge and forgiveness can affect events. Based on two years of Glass's life, written as fiction because of varying accounts make accurate biography impossible.

Where it's reviewed:
Booklist, November 1, 1990, page 518
Kirkus Reviews, September 15, 1990, page 1327

Other books by the author:
Shag, 1991
Major, 1988
Rajpur, 1982
Little Burma, 1958

Other books you might like:
John Logan Allen, *Jebediah Smith and the Mountain Men*, 1991

Chronicles the exploits of the mountain men who opened many trails and passages through the American West in the early 19th century.

Lawrence Cortesi, *Jim Beckwourth, Explorer-Patriot of the Rockies*, 1971

A biography of the Negro blacksmith from St. Louis who became a trapper, mountain man, adopted Crow chief and guerilla fighter in the Mexican War.

Joseph N. Heard, *The Black Frontiersmen*, 1969

Traces the adventures of ten Blacks who participated in the struggle between Indians and settlers during the development of the American frontier.

Walt Morey, *Canyon Winter*, 1972

Stranded for 6 months in the Rocky Mountains following a plane crash, a teen is taken in by an old hermit who teaches him the ways of the wilderness.

Marian Rumsey, *Danger on Shadow Mountain*, 1970

A twelve year old boy struggles to rescue his kidnapped brother in the Alaskan wilderness.

1222

Emily Arnold McCully, Author/Illustrator

The Grandma Mix-Up (New York: Harper, 1988)

Age range: Grades 1-3

Subject(s): Babysitters; Grandparents

Major character(s): Pip, Child

Time period(s): 1980s

Locale(s): United States

What the book is about: Two very different grandmothers arrive to babysit and young Pip doesn't know how to handle the situation and keep them both happy.

Where it's reviewed:
Booklist, December 1, 1988, page 656
School Library Journal, March 1989, page 166

Other books by the author:
Grandmas at Bat, 1993
Grandmas at the Lake, 1990
Zaza's Big Break, 1989
The Christmas Gift, 1988

Other books you might like:
Eve Bunting, *The Wednesday Surprise*, 1991

On Wednesday nights when Grandma stays with Anna, everyone thinks she is teaching Anna to read. What a surprise!

Nancy L. Carlson, *A Visit to Grandma's*, 1991

When Tina and her parents go spend Thanksgiving with grandma in Florida, they are shocked to find that she is different than when she lived on a farm.

Janette Sebring Lowrey, *Six Silver Spoons*, 1971

A Boston brother and sister travel to their grandmother's house on the eve of the battle at Concord.

Susan Roth, *Another Christmas*, 1992

The year after Grandpa's death, Ben's family spends Christmas in Puerto Rico, where Grandma keeps the holiday familiar but a little bit different.

Jan Wahl, *Who Will Believe Tim Kitten?*, 1978

Tim Kitten has his great-grandmother's talent for telling tales, but no one will believe his stories.

1223

Collin McDonald

Nightwaves: Scary Tales for After Dark (New York: Cobblehill, 1990)

Age range: Grades 5-9

Subject(s): Magic; Supernatural; Short Stories

Time period(s): Indeterminate

Locale(s): Earth

What the book is about: A collection of short stories about supernatural happenings. A radio that tells tomorrow's news today, a music teacher who sells the souls of her orphan students to keep her youth, a spell that turns a normal dog into a monster, and a woman who sees the ghost of a childhood friend are just a few of the eight eerie stories in this collection with twists and turns of plot to keep the pages turning. A good source for storytellers.

Where it's reviewed:
Booklist, October 1, 1991, page 125
School Library Journal, December 1990, page 104

Other books you might like:
James Berry, *The Future-Telling Lady and Other Stories*, 1993
 Children's stories of magic and ghosts from the West Indies.
Paul Jennings, *Unmentionable! More Amazing Stories*, 1993
 A collection of nine stories about the scary, supernatural or the unusual including an ice maiden with a deadly kiss, and a magic harmonica and more.
Myron Levoy, *The Witch of Fourth Street and Other Stories*, 1972
 Eight stories of witches, electric trains, magic bells, an fish angel, and the Hannukah Santa Claus from New York City.
Philippa Pearce, *The Shadow Cage*, 1977
 Ten stories of the supernatural and scary.
Jane Yolen, *The Faery Flag*, 1989
 A collection of stories and poems on various fairy tale, ghostly and supernatural themes.

1224

Joyce McDonald

Mail-Order Kid (New York: Putnam, 1988)

Age range: Grades 3-6

Subject(s): Adoption; Brothers; Animals/Foxes

Major character(s): Philip "Flip" Doty, Preteen; Todd Doty, Orphan, Adoptee; Vickie, Fox

Time period(s): 1980s

Locale(s): New Jersey

What the book is about: An only child all his ten years, Flip is trying to adjust to his newly adopted brother, Todd, from Korea. When Flip orders a fox through the mail, his experiences in trying to tame it help him to understand Todd better.

Where it's reviewed:
Booklist, June 1, 1988, page 1676
Center for Children's Books Bulletin, June 1988, page 211
School Library Journal, May 1988, page 98

Other books by the author:
Homebody, 1991

Other books you might like:
Mary Jane Auch, *Pick of the Litter*, 1988
 When her mother becomes pregnant after years of trying, an eleven year old adopted child realizes that being an only child had its advantages.
Elisabet McHugh, *Karen's Sister*, 1983
 Karen, an adopted Korean orphan, is joined by a foster sister.
Marilyn Sachs, *What My Sister Remembered*, 1992

While visiting her sister, Beth confronts memories of her parents' sudden death and the subsequent adoption of the sisters by different families.
Doris Buchanan Smith, *Moonshadow of Cherry Mountain*, 1982
 A mountain family with adopted children and a dog must learn to deal with their new neighbors who bring some "modern" changes to their mountain home.
Theresa Tomlinson, *Riding the Waves*, 1993
 In an English seaside town, Matt befriends an elderly woman who helps him fulfill his dream of surfing and learns to accept his having been adopted.

1225

Lila McGinnis

The 24-Hour Genie (New York: Holt, 1990)

Age range: Grades 3-4

Subject(s): Extrasensory Perception; Magic

Major character(s): Andrew, Child; Jo, Mythical Creature (genie); Uncle Donald, Relative (uncle)

Time period(s): 1990s

Locale(s): United States

What the book is about: Andrew found Jo, a genie, in a shoe-polish bottle left by his uncle. His math answers and a new bike disappear twenty-four hours later. Jo's magic only lasts that long, and he can't do the same magic twice.

Where it's reviewed:
Horn Book Guide, January 1990, page 246
School Library Journal, December 1990, page 104

Other books by the author:
Auras and Other Rainbow Secrets, 1984

Other books you might like:
Hazel Hutchins, *The Three and Many Wishes of Jason Reid*, 1988
 Jason is granted three wishes which land him and his friends in some amazing predicaments.
Amy Lawson, *Star Baby*, 1992
 Allie wishes on a falling star for a baby sister and receives a star baby instead.
Lila Perl, *Annabelle Starr, E.S.P.*, 1983
 Annabelle has second thoughts about her gift when she sees the fear it produces in her adopted sister.
Colby Rodowsky, *Evy-Ivy-Over*, 1978
 Mary Rose October, better known as Slug, goes to live with her grandmother who has ESP.
Tobi Tobias, *Jane, Wishing*, 1977
 Janes wishes for better looks, talent, a friend, a kitten, and a room of her own - but decides to be happy anyway.

1226

Lila McGinnis

Illustrator: Amy Rowen

The Ghost Upstairs (New York: Hastings House, 1982)

Age range: Grades 4-6

Subject(s): Ghosts; Humor

Major character(s): Otis White, Spirit; Albert Shook, Preteen; Sally Shook, Teenager

Time period(s): 1980s

Locale(s): United States

What the book is about: Albert has trouble explaining his sudden neatness and better grades but who would believe him if he revealed that an eleven year old ghost who can't stand a mess has moved into his room? The ghost is Otis White who moved into the Shook's house when his own house was torn down. Otis keeps Albert, and everyone else, hopping!

Where it's reviewed:
Booklist, October 15, 1982, page 314
School Library Journal, September 1983, page 124
Children's Book Review Service, December 1982, page 37

Other books by the author:
The 24-Hour Genie, 1990
Auras and Other Rainbow Secrets, 1984

Other books you might like:
Patricia Coombs, *Dorrie and the Witch's Imp*, 1975
 The wicked Gloris conjures up a double for Dorrie, but the double arouses suspicion with its unnatural neatness and courtesy.
Paula Hendrich, *Who Says So?*, 1972
 A girl loses her best friend, an imaginary creature, at the end of a fun-filled summer but gains a new flesh and blood friend who seems very familiar.
Sorche Nic Leodhas, *Gaelic Ghosts*, 1963
 Ten humorous ghost stories from Scottish folklore.
Megan Stine, *Max Onstage*, 1989
 Max, the ghost, has never appeared to anybody but Jeffrey, but lately Jeffrey's friend, Kenny, is starting to believe Max might be real after all.
Betty Ren Wright, *The Ghost of Ernie P.*, 1990
 After an accident kills Ernie and cuts short his Top Secret Plan, his friend Jeff is haunted by Ernie's ghost and pushed toward carrying out the plan.

1227

Tom McGowen

Odyssey From River Bend (Boston: Little, Brown, 1975)

Age range: Grades 4-6

Subject(s): Science Fiction; Animals

Major character(s): Kipp, Badger

Time period(s): Indeterminate Future

Locale(s): Fictional Country

What the book is about: Humans have died out on the planet because they abandoned science and could no longer cope with drought and disease. Only animals remain. Kipp has a thirst for knowledge and goes off seeking a hidden treasury. The city is inhabited by chimpanzees.

Where it's reviewed:
Kirkus Reviews, May 1, 1975, page 513
School Library Journal, September 1975, page 107

Other books by the author:
Loneliness of the Long Distance Runner, 1992

Other books you might like:
Piers Anthony, *Balook*, 1990
 A friendly pre-historic rhino is genetically recreated in the near future.
Gene DeWeese, *The Dandelion Caper*, 1986
 Having rescued many stranded tourists from outer space, Walter and Kathy are unprepared for the evil aliens they encounter in an abandoned house.
Peter Dickinson, *The Devil's Children*, 1986
 After the mysterious Changes begin, Nicole finds herself abandoned and wandering in England where everyone has developed a hatred of machines.
Mirra Ginsburg, *Alice*, 1977
 Six stories about a five year old living in the 21st century and her adventures with interplanetary visitors and strange animals.
Jane Yolen, *The Robot and Rebecca and the Missing Owser*, 1981
 Rebecca and her mechanical companion investigate the mysterious disappearance of two rare, dog-like animals known as owsers.

1228

Eloise Jarvis McGraw

Illustrator: Jim Arnosky

Joel and the Great Merlini (New York: Pantheon, 1979)

Age range: Grades 3-4

Subject(s): Magic; Magicians

Major character(s): Joel Penny, Magician; Sammy Penny, Child; Merlini the Great, Magician

Time period(s): 1970s

Locale(s): United States

What the book is about: Joel has loved magic since he was four. Just as he abandons "gimmick" tricks and learns real sleight of hand magic, he makes a fervent wish that he could do real magic. His wish brings a magician named Merlini, who allows him to do real magic. But for all the flash, Joel finds the kind of magic he makes himself is much more satisfying.

Where it's reviewed:
Center for Children's Books Bulletin, April 1980, page 156
School Library Journal, February 1980, page 58
School Library Journal, March 1981, page 109

Other books by the author:
A Tangled Web, 1993
The 17th Swap, 1986

Other books you might like:
Marjorie N. Allen, *Farley, Are You for Real?*, 1976
 A young boy knows that genies don't exist until Farley changes his mind by granting him three wishes.
Marion Dane Bauer, *Touch the Moon*, 1987
 When the china horse Jennifer receives for her birthday is magically transformed into a real horse, they share an evening of fantastic adventures.
Patricia Coombs, *The Magician and McTree*, 1984
 By mistake, an old, old magician causes his cat McTree to talk and thus begins a series of exciting adventures for the feline.
Michael Palin, *The Mirrorstone*, 1986

A schoolboy is snatched into another world by the scientist Salaman, who forces him to brave underwater terrors in a quest for the Mirrorstone.

Jack Sendak, *Martze*, 1968

A boy who believes he can do magic travels only brings unhappiness to those who do not wish their lives changed, but helps a girl who needs a friend.

1229

Eloise Jarvis McGraw

The Money Room (New York: Atheneum, 1981)

Age range: Grades 5-7

Subject(s): Treasure; Mystery and Detective Stories

Major character(s): Scott "Scotty" Holloway, Teenager; Melinda "Lindy" Holloway, Child; Dorrit L. Suggs, Villain

Time period(s): Indeterminate

Locale(s): Dover, Oregon

What the book is about: Scott and his sister set out to find great-grandfather's Money Room on his farm in Oregon, but soon realize that someone else is searching as well, and may be a danger to them.

Where it's reviewed:
Booklist, September 15, 1981, page 110
Center for Children's Books Bulletin, March 1982, page 134
Kirkus, November 1, 1981, page 1345

Other books by the author:
The Golden Goblet, 1986
Master Cornhill, 1973
Greensleeves, 1968
Moccasin Trail, 1952

Other books you might like:
Avi, *Windcatcher*, 1991
Learning to sail during a visit to his grandmother at the Connecticutt shore, Tony hears of sunken treasure and follows a couple on a strange search.
Welwyn Wilton Katz, *Whalesinger*, 1990
A field trip on the California coast, near possible sunken treasure, brings together two teens, an withdrawn boy and a girl interested in two whales.
Willo Davis Roberts, *More Minder Curses*, 1980
When the Minder Curse involves Danny with the old Caspitorian house, he learns its haunted secret, finds lost treasure, and foils an evil scheme.
Todd Strasser, *Beyond the Reef*, 1989
Chris and his parents move from New York to Key West where Dad's obsession with sunken treasure angers some locals and threatens to split the family.
Bill Wallace, *Danger in Quicksand Swamp*, 1989
Ben and Jake battle alligators, quicksand, and a murderer when they search for buried treasure on an island in a swamp.

1230

Eloise Jarvis McGraw

Really Weird Summer (New York: Atheneum, 1977)

Age range: Grades 5 and Up

Subject(s): Space and Time

Major character(s): Nels, Preteen

Time period(s): 1970s

Locale(s): Oregon

What the book is about: Four children in Oregon spend the summer of their parents' divorce with a little known great aunt and uncle. Nels finds a secret passageway to a part of the building that no longer exists, and meets a strange boy whose family is trapped in a leftover pocket of time.

Where it's reviewed:
Horn Book, October 1977, page 532
Kirkus Reviews, April 15, 1977, page 427

Awards the book has won:
Edgar Allan Poe Award 1978

Other books by the author:
Striped Ships, 1991
Mara, Daughter of the Nile, 1953
Moccasin Trail, 1952
Crown Fire, 1951

Other books you might like:
Lois I. Fisher, *Rachel Vellars, How Could You?*, 1984
Cory changes schools when she goes to live with her father after her parents' divorce, and has some adjustments to make in choosing and holding friend
Brenda Guiberson, *Turtle People*, 1990
Depressed by his father's absence and his mother's withdrawal, Richie retreats to a remote island near his home and finds an archeological mystery.
Monte Killingsworth, *Eli's Songs*, 1991
Shipped off to relatives in Oregon while his father is touring with his rock band, Eli comes to love the magnificent trees of a nearby forest.
Peg Kehret, *Nightmare Mountain*, 1989
Molly's visit to her aunt and uncle's ranch leads her into unexpected danger and suspense.
Doris Orgel, *Midnight Soup and a Witch's Hat*, 1987
Having anticipated a whole week with her dad in Oregon, Becky finds she has to share him with his friend Rosellen and her bratty six year old.

1231

Eloise Jarvis McGraw

The Trouble with Jacob (New York: McElderry, 1988)

Age range: Grades 5-8

Subject(s): Ghosts; Twins

Major character(s): Jacob, Spirit; Andy Peterson, Twin; Kat Peterson, Twin

Time period(s): 1980s

Locale(s): Harper's Mill, Oregon (Cascade foothills)

What the book is about: Andy and Kat, unhappy at spending the summer in Oregon, meet frail Jacob, a strange boy who is hard to find, hard to talk to, and yet strangely compelling.

Where it's reviewed:
Booklist, April 15, 1988, page 1425
Kirkus Reviews, March 1, 1988, page 365
School Library Journal, April 1988, page 102

Other books by the author:
The Money Room, 1981
The Golden Goblet, 1961
Mara, Daughter of the Nile, 1953

Other books you might like:
T.A. Barron, *The Ancient One*, 1992
    While helping aunt Melanie protect a redwood forest from loggers, Kate goes back in time to face an evil creature bent on destroying the same forest.
Mary Downing Hahn, *Wait Till Helen Comes*, 1986
    Molly and Michael dislike their spooky stepsister Heather, but know they must try to save her when she seems ready to follow a ghost child to her doom
Barbara Hood Burgess, *Oren Bell*, 1991
    Oren and his twin, Latonya, deal with the condemned house next door which they believe to be haunted and the cause of the tragedies in their lives.
Kathryn Lasky, *Double Trouble Squared*, 1991
    Telepathic twins Liberty and July receive strange emanations from an early residence of Arthur Conan Doyle and discover a literary ghost.
Janet Louise Lunn, *Twin Spell*, 1969
    Strangely attracted to an antique doll, 12-year-old twins buy it and find themselves haunted by tragic memories of the doll's previous owners.

1232

Leslie McGuire, Author/Illustrator

This Farm is a Mess (New York: Parents, 1981)

Age range: Grades 1-3

Subject(s): Cleanliness; Animals; Farm Life

Major character(s): Farmer Wook, Farmer

Time period(s): Indeterminate

Locale(s): United States

What the book is about: Farmer Wood has too much to do and his farm is a mess—the truck won't start, t he chickens are roosting in the dining room because their coop has no roof, cat s are running loose in the kitchen, and the cows have moved into the living roo m until the barn is cleaned. The farmer goes to the city on vacation and in his absence the animals put things to rights. However, they discover that they can not do everything and when the farmer returns they all work together to keep up the farm.

Where it's reviewed:
Booklist, November 15, 1981, page 446
Kirkus Reviews, October 15, 1981, page 1295
School Library Journal, December 1981, page 76

Other books by the author:
Fred in Charge, 1991
Baby Night Owl, 1989
Jane Goodall's Animal World: Lions, 1989
Miss Mopp's Lucky Day, 1981

Other books you might like:
Jane Burton, *Animals Keeping Clean*, 1989
    Photos and text show how animals use water, dust, tongues, claws and beaks to keep themselves clean. (Non-fiction)
Stephen Caitlin, *You Dirty Dog*, 1988

    While Dan the dog takes a nap, his animal friends give him a bath.
Aileen Fisher, *Clean as a Whistle*, 1969
    Not wanting to take baths, three children get lost in the woods where they meet a deaf lady who shows them that many animals are cleaner than them.
Robert Kraus, *Buggy Bear Cleans Up*, 1989
    Buggy Bear, who never bathes or washes his clothes, alienates the other animals at school until he falls in love and decides to clean up his act.
Diane Paterson, *Soap and Suds*, 1984
    A woman hangs her clean clothes on the line to dry, but they don't stay clean long, thanks to her many pets and her little boy.

1233

Georgess McHargue

The Turquoise Toad Mystery (New York: Delacorte, 1982)

Age range: Grades 4-6

Subject(s): Archeology; Mystery and Detective Stories

Major character(s): Ben Pollock, Preteen; Dave Frito, Coatimundi; Bryant Cosette, Archaeologist

Time period(s): 1980s

Locale(s): Arizona (desert country)

What the book is about: Twelve year old Ben Pollack joins a family friend on her archaeological expedit ion to the Arizona desert. He and his pet coatimundi, Frito, have more adventur es than they had anticipated, including scorpions in their tent and a gang of t hieves who attack the dig in search of legendary treasure.

Where it's reviewed:
Booklist, May 1, 1982, page 1162
Kirkus Reviews, April 15, 1982, page 490
Publishers Weekly, March 26, 1982, page 74

Other books by the author:
See You Later, Crocodile, 1988
The Talking Table Mystery, 1977
Funny Bananas, 1975
The Wonderful Wings of Harold Harrabescu, 1971

Other books you might like:
Dana Brenford, *The Guardian of the Hopewell Treasure*, 1988
    Accompanying their parents on an archeological dig three sibling investigators discover that someone does not want the area disturbed.
Walter Farley, *The Island Stallion*, 1976
    A boy and his archeologist friend spend two weeks on a desolate Caribbean island where they discover many unusual objects.
Carl R. Green, *The Mole People*, 1985
    A team of archeologists digging in the Middle East discovers an underground civilization of Mole People.
Pamela F. Service, *The Reluctant God*, 1990
    As his brother prepares to mount the throne of Egypt, Prince Ameni is sealed in a secret tomb, to be found years later by an archeologist's daughter.
Megan Stine, *The Mummy's Curse*, 1992

a young Indiana Jones meets Lawrence of Arabia and encounters a mystery involving a mummy's curse and a murdered guard at an archaeological dig.

1234

Elisabet McHugh

Illustrator: Anita Riggio

Beethovan's Cat (New York: Atheneum, 1988)

Age range: Grades 3-6

Subject(s): Animals/Cats

Major character(s): Ludwig "Wiggie", Cat; Josh, Cat

Time period(s): 1980s

Locale(s): United States

What the book is about: Wiggie comes to believe that he must be a descendant of Ludwig von Beethovan's remarkable cat. Josh, the other cat in the Carter family and Winston, their bulldog, are no help at all as Wiggie goes through haunted times. Even the vet thinks he needs a shrink.

Where it's reviewed:
Booklist, March 15, 1988, page 1265
Kirkus Reviews, April 1, 1988, page 541
School Library Journal, April 1988, page 103

Other books by the author:
Wiggie Wins the West, 1989
Karen and Vicki, 1984
Karen's Sister, 1983
Raising a Mother Isn't Easy, 1983

Other books you might like:
Barbara Dana, *Rutgers and the Water Snouts*, 1969
  A bulldog is happy when he discovers a strange object he names water-snout. When he becomes sad that it disappears, his friends help him look for it.
Julia First, *Move Over, Beethoven*, 1978
  Aware of her talent, a seventh grader thinks she wants to be a concert pianist, but isn't sure she wants to spend all her time practicing.
Peg Kehret, *Sisters, Long Ago*, 1990
  When Willow Paige nearly drowns, she envisions scenes from a past life which lead to an exploration of reincarnation and mental telepathy.
William Sleator, *Fingers*, 1983
  Sam agrees to compose "new works" by a long dead composer and present them to his brother, whose career as a piano prodigy is faltering.
Jane Yolen, *The Stone Silenus*, 1984
  A year after her poet father has been found dead, a strange faun-boy appears to Melissa, seeming to be the reincarnation of her father's spirit.

1235

Judith Whitelock McInerney

Illustrator: Leslie Morrill

Judge Benjamin, Superdog (New York: Holiday, 1982)

Age range: Grades 4-6

Subject(s): Animals/Dogs; Grandparents

Major character(s): Judge Benjamin, Dog (St. Bernard); Seth O'Riley, Preteen; Kathleen O'Riley, Child

Time period(s): 1980s

Locale(s): Decatur, Illinois

What the book is about: The humorous adventures of a St. Bernard who lives with the O'Riley family. Judge Benjamin, the Superdog, narrates this happy tale of Mr. and Mrs. O'Riley, Seth, Kathleen and Ann Elizabeth, and the messes they get into. When Grandma and her new boyfriend, Henry, come for a visit, things get really wild.

Where it's reviewed:
Booklist, June 1, 1982, page 1315
Booklist, July 1983, page 1403
School Library Journal, August 1982, page 118

Other books by the author:
Judge Benjamin: The Superdog Gift, 1986
Judge Benjamin: The Superdog Surprise, 1985
Judge Benjamin: The Superdog Rescue, 1984
Judge Benjamin: The Superdog Secret, 1983

Other books you might like:
Anna Coates, *Dog Magic*, 1991
  Matt gets a surprise when his dog, Toby, speaks to him. Toby needs Matt's help to rescue his puppies from a woman who has taken them to a laboratory.
Charles A. Perkins, *Wilderness Friend*, 1966
  Because his St. Bernard, Molly, cannot stay out of trouble in town, a boy offers his companion to the Royal Canadian Mounted Police as a patrol dog.
David Harry Walker, *Big Ben*, 1969
  As a result of an automobile accident, two children acquire a St. Bernard pup that creates increasing trouble in proportion to his increasing size.
Barbara Willard, *A Dog and a Half*, 1971
  Not wanting a dog around, Jill's father gives her an impossibly small sum of money with which to buy one, but Jill finds a St. Bernard for free.
Barbara Williams, *Mitzi and the Elephants*, 1985
  Mitzi becomes friends with the elephant keeper at the zoo from whom she hopes to learn how to train big animals so she can get a St. Bernard puppy.

1236

Colleen O'Shaughnessy McKenna

Too Many Murphys (New York: Scholastic, 1988)

Age range: Grades 3-5

Subject(s): Family Life; Brothers and Sisters

Major character(s): Collette Murphy, Child, 3rd Grader; Jeff Murphy, Child; Laura Murphy, Child

Time period(s): 1980s

Locale(s): United States

What the book is about: Third grader Collette loves her brothers and sister, but sometimes the noisy pests can be too much. She wonders what it would be like to be an only child and finds a surprising answer when her wish comes true for a day.

Where it's reviewed:
Kirkus Reviews, September 1, 1988, page 1325

Publisher's Weekly, August 26, 1988, page 90

Other books by the author:
Mother Murphy, 1992
The Truth about Sixth Grade, 1991
Murphy's Island, 1990
Fifth Grade: Here Comes Trouble, 1989

Other books you might like:
Mary Jane Auch, *Pick of the Litter*, 1988
    An eleven year old adopted child realizes that being an only child has its advantages when her mother becomes pregnant after years of sterility.
Patricia Clapp, *King of the Dollhouse*, 1974
    A miniature royal family moves into the dollhouse of an only child and keeps her company the summer her mother is writing a story for children.
Tessa Duder, *Jellybean*, 1985
    The only child of a single mother, Geraldine is tired of having to fit into her mother's busy schedule, but things change when she meets a new friend.
Norma Klein, *Confessions of an Only Child*, 1974
    Between the time her brother is born prematurely and dies, and the time the next baby is born, Antonia gradually adjusts to not being the only child.
Marilyn Sachs, *Dorrie's Book*, 1975
    An only child relates the problems she experiences when her mother has triplets.

1237

Ellen Kindt McKenzie

Illustrator: William Low

Stargone John (New York: Holt, 1990)

Age range: Grades 4-6

Subject(s): Blind; Emotional Problems; Teachers

Major character(s): Liza Bain, Child; John Bain, Child (emotionally disturbed)

Time period(s): 1890s

Locale(s): Midwest

What the book is about: John, a shy and introverted first grader, has trouble in school because he is often "star gone," what we would today call "lost in space," and frequently gets whacked by the teacher for not paying attention. His sister, nine year old Liza, is the only one who can consistently get through to him, and he tells her about his special imaginary friend. Finally, an adult, a retired, blind teacher, is able to accept what makes John special and help him to make use of his abilities. An introspective story especially good for sharing adult to child.

Where it's reviewed:
Booklist, November 15, 1990, page 658
School Library Journal, December 1990, page 105

Other books by the author:
A Bowl of Mischief, 1992
The King, the Princess and the Tinker, 1992

Other books you might like:
Barbara Aiello, *Secrets Aren't (Always) for Keeps*, 1988
    After hiding her learning problems from her Australian pen pal, Jennifer becomes very apprehensive when her friend comes to visit.

Jeanne Gehret, *Learning Disabilities and the Don't Give Up Kid*, 1990
    Alex, a child with dyslexia, learns about his and other learning problems and what is done to solve them.
Lynn Hall, *The Mystery of the Schoolhouse Dog*, 1979
    During the renovation of an old one-room schoolhouse, a lonely little boy finds a mysterious dog that helps him cope with his lonliness.
Gordon Korman, *The Twinkie Squad*, 1992
    Chaos spreads when Douglas, an eccentric sixth grader, joins the special counseling group for problem students.
Glendon Fred Swarthout, *Whales to See The*, 1975
    A group of children with learning disabilities have problems coping with the many social pressures they face everyday.

1238

Robin McKinley

Beauty: A Retelling of the Story of Beauty and the Beast (New York: HarperCollins, 1978)

Age range: Grades 5-8

Subject(s): Fairy Tale

Major character(s): Beauty, Heroine; Beast, Royalty (prince)

Time period(s): Indeterminate Past

Locale(s): France

What the book is about: Kind Beauty grows to love the Beast at whose castle she is compelled to stay and through her love, releases him from the spell which had turned him from a handsome prince into an ugly beast. A good version for reading aloud in middle grades, or for gifted readers.

Where it's reviewed:
Booklist, October 15, 1982, page 353
Center for Children's Books Bulletin, December 1978, page 67
Kirkus Reviews, December 1, 1978, page 1307

Other books by the author:
The Outlaws of Sherwood, 1988
The Hero and the Crown, 1984
The Blue Sword, 1982
The Door in the Hedge, 1981

Other books you might like:
Felice Holman, *The Drac*, 1975
    Five tales including "The Invisible Demon," "The Carpenter's Crop," "The Terror or Nerluc," "The Lady of the Moor," and "The Flying Serpent."
Ruth Manning-Sanders, *Jonnikin and the Flying Basket: French Folk and Fairy Tales*, 1969
    Seventeen fairy tales from France.
Sir Arthur Thomas Quiller-Couch, *The Sleeping Beauty and Other Fairy Tales From the Old French*, 1978
    A collection of classic French tales, including "The Sleeping Beauty," "Cinderella," and "Beauty and the Beast."
Sherwood Smith, *Wren to the Rescue*, 1990
    With the help of a prince and an apprentice wizard, Wren strives to rescue her best friend, a princess named Tess, from the fortress of a wicked king.
Nancy Willard, *Beauty and the Beast*, 1992

A kind and beautiful woman, through her great capacity to love, releases a handsome young man from the spell which made him into an ugly beast.

Robin McKinley

The Blue Sword (New York: Greenwillow, 1982)

Age range: Grades 5-8

Subject(s): Fantasy

Major character(s): Harry Crew, Warrior

Time period(s): Indeterminate Past

Locale(s): Damar, Fictional Country

What the book is about: First in a series, *The Blue Sword* tells the story of Harry Crewe, an independent young woman drawn to the mountain home of the Hillfolk across the desert. Corlath, the king of the Hillfolk, has Harry kidnapped and she eventually comes to love her life with the Hillfolk, rises to a position of respect, becomes guardian of the Blue Sword, and is a lead warrior in a battle against the Northerners. A strong female character in a story with great pace and action.

Where it's reviewed:
Booklist, October 1, 1982, page 198
Center for Children's Books Bulletin, February 1983, page 112
School Library Journal, January 1983, page 86

Awards the book has won:
Newbery Honor 1983

Other books by the author:
The Light Princess, 1988
The Outlaws of Sherwood, 1988
The Hero and the Crown, 1985
Tales From the Jungle Book, 1985

Other books you might like:
Bernard Euslin, *Heraclea: A Legend of Warrior Women*, 1978
  Retells the daring exploits of Heraclea, a gigantic young woman who in later Greek myths became the male hero, Heracles.
Beth Hilgartner, *The Feast of the Trickster*, 1991
  Companions from another planet visit Earth to bring Alexandra Scarsdale, a young woman earlier woven into their world, back to their true home.
Monica Hughes, *The Promise*, 1992
  A promise made by her parents before she was born sends Princess Raina to Roshan to learn of the wind and rain from the woman known as Sandwriter.
Ardath Mayhar, *Soul-Singer of Tyrnos*, 1981
  Yeleve, a young woman who can sing the image of a soul onto the wall behind her, discovers that a powerful evil is overcoming her country.
Meredith Ann Pierce, *The Woman Who Loved Reindeer*, 1985
  When a strange golden baby is brought to her, a girl is unaware that this unusual child will help fulfill her destiny as leader of her people.

Robin McKinley

The Door in the Hedge (New York: Greenwillow, 1981)

Age range: Grades 4-6

Subject(s): Fantasy; Fairy Tale

Time period(s): Indeterminate Past

Locale(s): Fictional Country

What the book is about: Lyric retelling of older tales, plus two new, folk-style tales from this great weaver of fantasy. Stories include *Door in the Hedge*, *Princess and the Frog*, *Golden Hind*, and *Twelve Dancing Princesses*. Good for reading aloud or as inspiration for creative writing.

Where it's reviewed:
Booklist, February 15, 1981, page 810
Hornbook, August 1981, page 433
Kirkus Reviews, July 15, 1981, page 876

Other books by the author:
The Outlaws of Sherwood, 1988
The Hero and the Crown, 1984
The Blue Sword, 1982
Beauty: A Retelling of the Story of Beauty and the Beast, 1978

Other books you might like:
Val Biro, *Hungarian Folk-Tales*, 1978
  Adaptations from the works of Emil Kolozsuari Grandpierre and Gyula Illyes.
Gwyn Jones, *Scandinavian Legends and Folk Tales*, 1956
  A large collection of Northern European stories for reading aloud or enjoying alone.
Ursual Le Guin, *A Ride on the Red Mare's Back*, 1992
  With the aid of her magic wooden horse, a brave girl travels to the High House in the mountains to rescue her kidnapped brother from the trolls.
David Vozar, *Yo, Hungry Wolf!: A Nursery Rap*, 1993
  A retelling in rap verse of *The Three Little Pigs*, *Little Red Riding Hood*, and *The Boy Who Cried Wolf*.
Lynette Dyer Vuong, *The Brocaded Slipper*, 1992
  A collection of Vietnamese fairy tales.

Robin McKinley

The Hero and the Crown (New York: Greenwillow, 1984)

Age range: Grades 6 and Up

Subject(s): Fantasy; Dragons

Major character(s): Aerin, Royalty (Princess); Luther, Healer; King Arlbeth, Ruler

Time period(s): Indeterminate Past

Locale(s): Fictional Country

What the book is about: The daughter of a "witch-woman" tries to win people's trust. After studying her mother's recipes, Aerin sets out to gain the Hero's Crown. On the way, she fights dragons, meets a wizard, and battles an evil mage. A blending of sword and sorcery, romance and adventure.

Where it's reviewed:
Booklist, October 1, 1984, page 211
New York Time Book Review, January 27, 1985, page 29
School Library Journal, October 1984, page 169

Awards the book has won:
Newbery Medal 1985

Other books by the author:
A Blue Sword, 1982
Black Beauty, 1986
The Door in the Hedge, 1981

Other books you might like:
Patricia C. Wrede, *Searching for Dragons*, 1991
  Princess Cimorene rescues the dragon Kazul and saves the forest from wicked wizards.
Patricia C. Wrede, *Dealing with Dragons*, 1990
  A princess bored with traditional life fights against disreputable wizards.
Tanith Lee, *Princess Hynchatti and Some Other Surprises*, 1972
  Twelve fairy tales about princes and princesses with surprising action.
Beverly Keller, *A Small, Elderly Dragon*, 1984
  Young Princess Dorma helps a small, elderly dragon save nearby villagers.

1242

Robin McKinley

The Outlaws of Sherwood (New York: Greenwillow, 1988)

Age range: Grades 5-8

Subject(s): Legends

Major character(s): Robin Hood, Hero, Outlaw; Maid Marion, Noblewoman

Time period(s): 12th century (1100s)

Locale(s): Sherwood Forest, England

What the book is about: By killing a man, Robin determines his own fate and must dwell in the forest with his band. Marion's love for him brings about a show-down with the sherrif and praise from the king. In this retelling, Robin is cautious, careful, and has less skill as an archer than Maid Marion. McKinley helps the reader take a fresh look at an old legend. King Richard offering Marion the office of Sherrif of Notingham may shake up historians, but most readers will enjoy the altered perspective.

Where it's reviewed:
HornBook, March/April 1989, page 218
School Library Journal, January 1989, page 94

Other books by the author:
Deerskin, 1993
The Hero and the Crown, 1984
The Blue Sword, 1982
The Door in the Hedge, 1981

Other books you might like:
Sarah Hayes, *Robin Hood*, 1989
  Retells the adventures of Robin Hood and his band in Sherwood Forest as they right wrongs and fight injustice.
Bernard Miles, *Robin Hood, His Life and Legend*, 1979
  Chronicles the life and adventures of Robin Hood who lived with his band of followers in Sherwood Forest, dedicated to fight against tyranny.
Howard Pyle, *The Merry Adventures of Robin Hood*, 1968

Recounts the legend of Robin Hood, who plundered the King's purse and poached his deer and whose generosity endeared him to the poor.
Marilyn Singer, *Lizzie Silver of Sherwood Forest*, 1986
  Inspired by her latest obsession (Robin Hood) Lizzie begins to scheme to follow Tessa into music school.
Eugenia Stone, *Robin Hood's Arrow*, 1948
  An account of Dan of the Mill and his adventures with Robin Hood and the merry men of Sherwood Forest.

1243

Pat McKissack

Illustrator: Brian Pinkney

Dark-30: Southern Tales of the Supernatural (New York: Knopf, 1992)

Age range: Grades 5-9

Subject(s): African Americans; Ghosts; Supernatural

Time period(s): Indeterminate Past

Locale(s): United States

What the book is about: A collection of ghost stories with African American themes designed to be told during the Dark Thirty- the half hour before sunset, when ghosts seem all too believable.

Where it's reviewed:
Publisher's Weekly, September 7, 1992, page 96

Awards the book has won:
Newbery Honor 1993

Other books by the author:
A Million Fish, More or Less, 1992
Mirandy and Brother Wind, 1988
Who Is Coming?, 1986
Country Mouse and City Mouse, 1985

Other books you might like:
Judith Gorog, *On Meeting Witches at Wells*, 1991
  A collection of dark short stories told in a Sheherazade fashion for middle readers.
Virginia Hamilton, *Sweet Whispers, Brother Rush*, 1982
  Tree, resentful her working mother leaves her in charge of a retarded brother, begins to view things differnetly after encountering her uncle's ghost.
Virginia Hamilton, *Willie Bea and the Time the Martians Landed*, 1983
  In October of 1938, a black family is caught up in the fear generated by the Orson Welles "Martians Have Landed" broadcast.
Eleanora E. Tate, *Front Porch Stories at the One Room School*, 1992
  Margie and her cousin forget their boredom when Margie's fater entertains them with stories about people and events in their Missouri town's past.
Joyce Carol Thomas, *Journey*, 1988
  Meggie spearheads an investigation into the disappearances and murders of young people in her town, discovering a plot to rob others of their youth.

1244

Pat McKissack

Illustrator: Rachel Isadora

Flossie and the Fox (New York: Dial, 1986)

Age range: Grades 2-3

Subject(s): African Americans; Animals/Foxes; Folk Tales

Major character(s): Flossie Finley, Child

Time period(s): Indeterminate

Locale(s): United States

What the book is about: Flossie has to deliver a basket of eggs to Miz Vida. She takes a shortcut and meets a fox notorious for stealing eggs. She makes him prove himself by comparing him to other animals before she will even consider being frightened of him.

Where it's reviewed:
Horn Book, January/February 1987, page 48
School Library Journal, October 1986, page 164

Other books by the author:
Constance Stumbles, 1988
Monkey Monkey's Trick, 1988
Messy Bessy, 1987
Mirandy and Brother Wind, 1983

Other books you might like:
Molly Bang, *Wiley and the Hairy Man*, 1976
    Wiley and his mother must outwit the Hairy Man.
Linda Haywood, *All Stuck Up*, 1990
    Brer Fox makes a tar baby in order to catch Brer Rabbit.
James Marshall, *Fox on Stage*, 1993
    Fox makes a film for Grannie, takes part in a magic show, and puts on a play.
Ursel Scheffler, *Rinaldo, the Sly Fox*, 1992
    Rinaldo tricks everyone but Bruno, the duck detective.
Ellen Stoll Walsh, *You Silly Goose*, 1992
    A silly goose mistakes a mouse for a fox until the real fox arrives and sets her straight.

1245

Pat McKissack

A Long Hard Journey: The Story of the Pullman Porter (New York: Walker, 1989)

Age range: Grades 6 and Up

Subject(s): Trains

Major character(s): George Mortimer Pullman, Inventor, Historical Figure; Stanley Buder, Historian; Nathaniel Hall, Railroad Worker

Time period(s): 1850s

Locale(s): United States

What the book is about: A chronicle of the first black-controlled union, made up of Pullman Porters, who after years of unfair labor practices, staged a battle against a corporate giant, resulting in a "David and Goliath" ending. Part of the Walker's American History Series for young people. Includes index and bibliography.

Where it's reviewed:
Booklist, September 15, 1989, page 187

Kirkus Reviews, October 15, 1989, page 1532

Awards the book has won:
Jane Addams Children's Book Award 1990
Coretta Scott King Award 1991

Other books by the author:
Jesse Jackson: A Biography, 1989
Frederick Douglass: The Black Lion, 1987
Mary McLeod Bethune: A Great American Educator, 1985
Martin Luther King, Jr., 1984

Other books you might like:
Mary Collins Dunne, *Reach Out, Ricardo*, 1971
    The life of a Mexican-American becomes increasingly complicated when his father joins the grape worker's strike.
Sally Hankey, *A. Phillip Randolph*, 1989
    A biography of the civil rights activist who organized the Brotherhood of Sleeping Car Porters.
Hadley Irwin, *I Be Somebody*, 1984
    A young black boy in the early 1900s hears his community talk about moving to Canada to escape the prejudices and problems they face in the US.
Marilyn Sachs, *Call Me Ruth*, 1982
    The daughter of a Russian immigrant family, newly arrived in Manhattan in 1908, has conflicting feelings about her mother's radical union involvement.
Sarah E. Wright, *A. Phillip Randolph: Integration of the Workplace*, 1990
    A biography of the organizer of the Brotherhood of Sleeping Car Porters, the Pullman porter's union.

1246

Pat McKissack

Illustrator: Jerry Pinkney

Mirandy and Brother Wind (New York: Knopf, 1988)

Age range: Grades 2-3

Subject(s): African Americans; Dancing; Weather

Major character(s): Mirandy, Child; Ezel, Child; Miss Poinsettia, Magician

Time period(s): 1900s (1906)

Locale(s): South

What the book is about: Mirandy is sure that she'll win the cake walk if she can catch Brother Wind for her partner. When she finally catches him, she ends up wishing for her boyfriend, Ezel, to overcome his clumsiness.

Where it's reviewed:
Booklist, January 1, 1989, page 792
School Library Journal, February 1989, page 74

Awards the book has won:
Simon Award

Other books by the author:
Nettie Jo's Friends, 1989
Constance Stumbles, 1988
Flossie and the Fox, 1986
King Midas and His Gold, 1986

Other books you might like:
Donald Crews, *Shortcut*, 1992
    Children taking a shortcut by walking along a railroad track find excitement and danger when a train approaches.

Angela Shelf Medearis, *Dancing with the Indians*, 1991
While attending a Seminole Indian celebration, a black family watches and joins in several exciting dances.

Denise Lewis Patrick, *Red Dancing Shoes*, 1993
Delighted with her shiny new red shoes, a little girl dances through town to show them off to everyone she knows.

Patricia Polacco, *Chicken Sunday*, 1992
To thank Eula for her wonderful Sunday chicken dinners, three children sell decorated eggs and buy her a beautiful Easter hat.

Alan Schroeder, *Ragtime Tumpie*, 1989
Tumpie, Josephine Baker as a child, longs to find the opportunity to dance amid the poverty and vivacious street life of St. Louis in the early 1900s.

1247

Ian McMahan

Lake Fear (New York: Macmillan, 1985)

Age range: Grades 5-7

Series: Microkid Mystery

Subject(s): Computers; Mystery and Detective Stories

Major character(s): Ricky Foster, Detective; ALEC, Artificial Intelligence; James Stanley, Doctor

Time period(s): 1980s

Locale(s): Cascade, Washington

What the book is about: Ricky and "ALEC" (Access Linkage to Electronic Computer), who is a disembodied personality in a computer, team up to solve the mystery of a strange rash afflicting people at Lake Fear. As they investigate the source of the strange disease, Ricky and ALEC uncover a case of computer fraud, chemical pollution, and the illegal production of explosives.

Where it's reviewed:
Center for Children's Books Bulletin, November 1985, page 52
School Library Journal, October 1985, page 175

Other books by the author:
Footwork, 1986
The Lost Forest, 1985
The Fox's Lair, 1983

Other books you might like:
Barbara Bartholomew, *The Great Gradepoint Mystery*, 1983
The grades of Ricky and his friends inexplicably drop. They suspect someone may be tampering with the school computer.

Matt Christopher, *Superchaged Infield*, 1985
Penny Farrell, captain and third baseman of the Hawks softball team, tries to uncover the reason for the strange behavior of two teammates.

Milton Dank, *The Computer Game Murder*, 1985
When Larry receives a message on his computer screen during a game, indicating his partner is in trouble, a dangerous investigation begins.

Fred D'Ignazio, *Chip Mitchell: The Case of the Chocolate Covered Bugs*, 1985
The reader is asked to supply the answer to two more cases which are solved by young computer whiz, Chip Mitchell.

Dora Pantell, *Miss Pickerell and the War of the Computers*, 1984
As supermarket prices begin to rise mysteriously, Miss Pickerell finds herself caught in the middle of a war of computers.

1248

Colin McNaughton, Author/Illustrator

Jolly Roger and the Pirates of Abdul, the Skinhead (New York: Simon and Schuster, 1988)

Age range: Grades 3-5

Subject(s): Pirates

Major character(s): Roger, Preteen; Cookee, Cook, Parent

Time period(s): Indeterminate Past

Locale(s): Earth

What the book is about: Roger's father was lost at sea. Unhappy with his shrewish mother who expects him to do chores, Roger joins a pirate band, and when they hear his tale of woe, they attack Roger's mother. They are no match for her and wind up doing the chores themselves. Cookee turns out to be - ta dum - Roger's long lost father. A bit too pat, perhaps, but lots of fun.

Where it's reviewed:
Booklist, February 1, 1989, page 940
School Library Journal, March 1989, page 166

Other books by the author:
Crazy Bear: Four Stories in One Big Book, 1983
If Dinosaurs Were Cats and Dogs, 1981
Anton B. Stanton, 1979
The Rat Race, 1978

Other books you might like:
Tony Bradman, *Peril at the Pirate School*, 1990
The pirate children are sent away to a pirate school, but are in danger when they realize the "teachers" are trying to find their parents treasures.

Tony Bradman, *Revenge at Ryan's Reef*, 1991
While visiting Granny, the Bluebeard pirate family discovers a plot to steal a treasure chest intended for the retired pirates' home.

William H. Hooks, *Lo-Jack and the Pirates*, 1991
When Jack is kidnapped by a band of greedy pirates, he persists in misunderstanding all of the captain's orders.

Lisa Norby, *Treasure Island*, 1990
Based on the Robert Louis Stevenson classic, an inkeeper's son finds a treasure map that leads him to pirate's fortune. (Step-Up Classics)

Jane Yolen, *Commander Toad and the Space Pirates*, 1987
When Commander Salamander and his band of pirates capture the "Star Warts" spaceship, Commander Toad is forced to hop the plank.

1249

Janet McNeill

We Three Kings (Boston: Little, Brown, 1974)

Age range: Grades 4-6

Subject(s): Accidents; Christmas

Major character(s): Dan Agnew, Child; Roger, Bully

Time period(s): 1970s

Locale(s): England

What the book is about: Dan's father is severely depressed about an accident that hospitalized a child. Dan suspects that his bully cousin, Roger, was the real cause of the bicycle accident. A gang of delinquents nearly ruin the Nativity play, and Don and Roger have to work together.

Where it's reviewed:
Kirkus Reviews, September 15, 1974, page 1008
Library Journal, October 15, 1974, page 2721

Other books by the author:
Wait for It, 1979
Ever After, 1975
The Prisoner in the Park, 1971
Goodbye, Dove Square, 1969

Other books you might like:
Avi, *No More Magic*, 1975
  While searching for his bike that disappeared on Halloween, a boy and his friends become involved in a magic adventure.
Becky Thomas Lindberg, *Speak Up, Chelsea Martin!*, 1991
  Chelsea deals with a bully, has a fight with her best friend, and learns to speak up for herself.
Francine Pascal, *The Hand-Me-Down Kid*, 1980
  When a thief steals her sister's bike, which she borrowed without asking permission, Ari learns a lot about dealing with people.
Faythe Dyrud Thureen, *Jenna's Big Jump*, 1993
  Jenna tries to stand up to the fourth grade bully and plans an act of daring and bravery to prove herself to her mother.
Johnniece Marshall Wilson, *Oh, Brother!*, 1988
  Alex's older brother bullies him, taking his bike and his money, until Alex discovers a way to stand up for himself.

1250

David M. McPhail

Pig Pig and the Magic Photo Album (New York: Dutton, 1986)

Age range: Grades 1-3

Subject(s): Animals/Pigs

Major character(s): Pig Pig, Pig

Time period(s): Indeterminate

Locale(s): Fictional Country

What the book is about: Pig Pig looks through a photo album and "falls" into several pictures until he finds one of his own living room.

Where it's reviewed:
Horn Book, July 1986, page 443
School Library Journal, May 1986, page 81

Other books by the author:
Annie and Company, 1991
Adam's Smile, 1987
A Big Fat Enormous Lie, 1978
The Bear's Toothache, 1972

Other books you might like:
Felicia Bond, *Poinsettia and her Family*, 1981
  Poinsettia realizes she loves and misses her family when they leave her home while looking for a bigger house.
Nancy L. Carlson, *Louanne Pig in Making the Team*, 1985
  Louanne tries out for cheerleading and Archie Cat tries out for the football team.
Mary Rayner, *Mrs. Pig Gets Cross*, 1986
  In each of seven stories, the Pig family show how much fun they have together.
Mitchell Shamat, *The Seven Sloppy Days of Phineas Pig*, 1983
  Phineas, a very neat pig, visits his cousin in order to learn how to be sloppy and become popular at school.
Martha Weston, *Peony's Rainbow*, 1981
  The adventures of Peony Pig who wants a rainbow of her very own and what she does when she gets one.

1251

Florence Crannel Means

Knock at the Door, Emmy (Boston: Houghton Mifflin, 1956)

Age range: Grades 6-9

Subject(s): Migrant Labor

Major character(s): Emmy Lou Lane, Teenager

Time period(s): 1950s

Locale(s): United States

What the book is about: Emmy grew up traveling the country with her family of migrant workers. She hungered for an education. This story tells of her struggle out of poverty and ignorance and of the people who helped her have faith in herself.

Where it's reviewed:
Booklist, July 1, 1956, page 466
Library Journal, July 1956, page 1722

Awards the book has won:
Nancy Bloch Memorial Award 1956

Other books by the author:
Alicia, 1953
A Candle in the Mist, 1931
Ranch and Ring, 1932

Other books you might like:
Earl Hamner, *Spencer's Mountain*, 1961
  Novel on which the popular TV series, "The Waltons," was based.
Celia Strang, *Foster Mary*, 1979
  Mary's dreams for her foster children include a warm house and regular meals.
Nancy Covert Smith, *Josie's Handful of Questions*, 1975
  After the hard life of her migrant family, Josie finally has a permanent home and school.
Theodore Taylor, *The Maldonado Miracle*, 1973
  A 12-year-old Mexican boy crosses the border illegally to join his father in California and is witness to a miracle.
Evelyn Sibley Lampman, *Go Up the Road*, 1972
  A 12-year-old Mexican-American and her family of migrant workers look toward a more stable way of life.

1252

Florence Crannel Means

The Moved Outers (Boston: Houghton Mifflin, 1945)

Age range: Grades 5-8

Subject(s): Japanese Americans; World War II

Major character(s): Sumiko "Sue" Ohara, Teenager; Kimio "Kim" Ohara, Teenager

Time period(s): 1940s (1941)

Locale(s): Denver, Colorado; California

What the book is about: Overnight, Sue and her family become targets of a nation's racial anxieties and misguided patriotism. The Ohara family is uprooted and moved into detainment camps, where they live under demoralizing conditions for the duration of the war.

Awards the book has won:
Newbery Honor 1945

Other books by the author:
Carver's George, 1991
Our Cup Is Broken, 1969
A Candle in the Mist, 1959
Shuttered Windows, 1938

Other books you might like:
Daniel S. Davis, *Behind Barbed Wire: The Imprisonment of Japanese Americans during World War II,* 1982
    Discusses the imprisonment of Japanese Americans in camps during WWII, their way of life there, and their assimilation back into society after the war
Deborah Gesensway, *Beyond Words: Images From America's Concentration Camps,* 1987
    A picture of life in American relocation camps during World War II.
Marcia Savin, *The Moon Bridge,* 1992
    The friendship of Mitzi Fujimoto and Ruthie Fox changes when World War II begins and Mitzi and her family are forced to go into an internment camp.
Shizuye Takashima, *A Child in Prison Camp,* 1971
    A Japanese-Canadian girl recounts the experiences of the three years she and her family spent in a Canadian internment camp during World War II.
Yoshiko Uchida, *The Invisible Thread,* 1991
    Yoshiko Uchido describes growing up in Berkeley, California and her family's internment in a Nevada camp during World War II.

1253

Judy Frank Mearian

Two Ways about It (New York: Dial, 1979)

Age range: Grades 5-8

Subject(s): Cancer; Cousins

Major character(s): Annie, Preteen; Lou, Preteen

Time period(s): 1970s

Locale(s): United States

What the book is about: Eleven year old Annie decides that having her older cousin Lou spend summers with her has a lot of hidden rewards and their relationship undergoes subtle changes during a family crisis.

Where it's reviewed:
Booklist, December 15, 1979, page 613
Center for Children's Books Bulletin, January 1980, page 100
Kirkus Reviews, January 15, 1980, page 67

Other books by the author:
Someone Slightly Different, 1980

Other books you might like:
Alden R. Carter, *Shelia's Dying,* 1987
    Just as Jerry Kincaid is considering breaking up with his girlfriend, he discovers that she has a terminal case of cancer.
Cynthia D. Grant, *Phoenix Rising, or, How to Survive Your Life,* 1989
    Helen's death from cancer shatters the lives of her family, especially her sister Jessie who copes with her feelings by reading Helen's diary.
Angela Johnson, *Toning the Sweep: A Novel,* 1993
    While vising her grandmother, who is dying of cancer, Emmie hears many stories about her family history and begins to understand her relatives better.
Robert Lipsyte, *The Chemo Kid,* 1992
    When chemotheraphy drugs transform him from a wimp into a superhero, Fred and his friends plot to rid the town's water supply of toxic waste.
Ann M. Martin, *Jessi's Wish,* 1991
    Jessi makes a special wish for a little girl with cancer.

1254

Cornelia Meigs

Invincible Louisa (Boston, Little Brown, 1933)

Age range: Grades 4-7

Subject(s): Biography

Major character(s): Louisa May Alcott, Historical Figure, Writer

Time period(s): 19th century

Locale(s): Germantown, Pennsylvania; Boston, Massachusetts; Concord, Massachusetts

What the book is about: Biography of Louisa May Alcott and her family tells of the courage that Louisa needed in order to overcome the many hardships the family faced. Louisa became the person the entire family could depend on for emotional and material support.

Where it's reviewed:
Booklist, July 1933, page 345

Awards the book has won:
Newbery Medal 1963

Other books by the author:
Swift Rivers, 1932
Jane Addams, 1970
Scarlet Oak, 1938
Trade Wind, 1927

Other books you might like:
Neil Cohen, *Jackie Joyner-Kersee,* 1992
    Biography of the Olympic gold medalist and world champion in both long jump and heptathlon.
Jeri Ferris, *Native American Doctor,* 1991
    Biography of Susan La Flesche Picotte, first Native American woman to graduate from medical school.

Patricia Reilly Giff, *Diana, 20th Century Princess*, 1991
  Biography of Diana, Princess of Wales.
Rose Blue, *Diane Sawyer: Super Newswoman*, 1990
  Biography of Diane Sawyer, first female correspondent on TV's "60 Minutes."
Lillie Patterson, *Oprah Winfrey: Talk Show Host and Actress*, 1990
  Traces Oprah from humble beginnings in Mississippi to national fame.

1255

Judith Mellecker

Illustrator: Robert Andrew Parker

The Fox and the Kingfisher (New York: Knopf, 1990)

Age range: Grades 2-3

Subject(s): Death; Remarriage; Fantasy

Major character(s): Daisy Reynolds, Child; Desmond Reynolds, Child

Time period(s): 1900s

Locale(s): England

What the book is about: When Daisy and Desmond's father decides to remarry, they complain to a magical stable boy. He turns them into a fox and a kingfisher and their adventures make them long for home. The story deals with the acceptance of death and the possibility of becoming close to a new mother.

Where it's reviewed:
Center for Children's Books Bulletin, December 1990, page 941
School Library Journal, December 1990, page 84

Other books by the author:
Randolph's Dream, 1990

Other books you might like:
Fred J. Fisher, *A Punkin in the Frost*, 1992
  Eddie journeys to a cemetery to say goodbye to his best friend who was killed in an accident.
Rosalie Maggio, *The Music Box Christmas*, 1990
  Despite his grandmother's recent death and his mean father's return, Nick is determined to have a real Christmas with his family.
Barbara Garland Polikoff, *Life's a Funny Proposition, Horatio*, 1992
  As Horatio tries to adjust to the death of his father, his grandfather mourns the loss of his dog, Mollie.
Judy Carole Rhodes, *The King Boy*, 1991
  Benjy's childhood in Arkansas is enriched by times he spends with his grandfather. After his death Benjy learns the old family secret.
Betty Ren Wright, *A Ghost in the House*, 1991
  Strange things happen when Sarah is alone in the house with great-aunt Margaret, who seems to be the victim of a vengeful ghost.

1256

Judith Mellecker

Illustrator: Robert Andrew Parker

Randolph's Dream (New York: Knopf, 1991)

Age range: Grades 2-3

Subject(s): Dreams and Nightmares; Fathers and Sons; World War II

Time period(s): 1940s (1940)

Locale(s): England

What the book is about: In the summer of 1940, a young English boy dreams he saves his father's life. The family has been separated by the war. The historical setting will not interfere with children relating to the tense emotions and the opening of one heart to another. A poignant description of life in wartime Britain.

Where it's reviewed:
Booklist, February 1, 1991, page 1128
School Library Journal, May 1991, page 81

Other books by the author:
The Fox and the Kingfisher, 1990

Other books you might like:
Dick Cate, *Old Dog, New Tricks*, 1981
  Billy's dad doubts he can learn a new trade after years spent in an English coal mine, just as he doubts the family dog can ever be properly trained.
Kathleen Krull, *Alex Fitzgerald's Cure for Nightmares*, 1990
  When Alex moves to California to live with her father for a year, she is plagued by nightmares and fears her new friends will discover her secret.
Joan Tate, *Wild Boy*, 1973
  A Yorkshire boy often dreams of living alone on the moors until he meets a strange boy who is doing just that.
Theresa Tomlinson, *Summer Witches*, 1989
  Two friends convert an old air-raid shelter into a den and help an old woman to overcome painful memories of WWII.
Harve Zemach, *Awake and Dreaming*, 1970
  A young man is haunted by nightmares until a witch gives him a magic formula for untroubled sleep

1257

Louise Meriwether

Illustrator: David Brown

Don't Ride the Bus on Monday: The Rosa Parks Story (Englewood Cliffs, New Jersey: Prentice Hall, 1973)

Age range: Grades 3-5

Subject(s): Biography; African Americans; Civil Rights Movement

Major character(s): Rosa Parks, Activist, Historical Figure

Time period(s): 20th century

Locale(s): Montgomery, Alabama

What the book is about: This is a much fuller account of Rosa Parks than just her part in the Montgomery bus boycott. She exemplifies the quiet courage of many Black citizens, and the experience of discrimination that Black children have suffered.

Where it's reviewed:
Booklist, June 1, 1973, page 949
Kirkus Reviews, December 15, 1972, page 1430

Other books by the author:
The Heart Man: Dr. Daniel Hale Williams, 1973
The Freedom Ship of Robert Small, 1971

Other books you might like:
Teresa Noel Celsi, *Rosa Parks and the Montgomery Bus Boycott*, 1991
  A brief biography of the woman in Montgomery, whose experiences with segregation led to her role in the Civil Rights Movement.
Mark Davies, *Malcolm X: Another Side of the Movement*, 1990
  A biography of the Afro-American who led a movement to unite Black people throughout the world.
Brian Feinberg, *Nelson Mandela*, 1992
  A biography of the Black South African leader, focusing on his struggle to overthrow the tyrannies of apartheid.
Rosa Parks, *Rosa Parks: My Story*, 1992
  Rosa Parks own story of her struggle in the Civil Rights Movement and the Montgomery bus boycott. (for older readers)
Diane Sansevere-Dreher, *Stephen Biko*, 1991
  Biography of Stephen Biko, orator and writer, who challenged the South African government and its system of apartheid.

1258

Jean Merrill

Illustrator: Frances Gruse Scott

Maria's House (New York: Atheneum, 1974)

Age range: Grades 3-5

Subject(s): Poverty; Artists and Art; Housing

Major character(s): Maria, Child; Miss Lindstrom, Teacher

Time period(s): 1970s

Locale(s): United States

What the book is about: Maria loves art lessons at the museum, until she has to draw a picture of her house. She is ashamed that she is poor and lives in a tenement. Her mother helps her accept who she is and where she lives.

Where it's reviewed:
Kirkus Reviews, July 15, 1974, page 743
Library Journal, November 15, 1974, page 3048

Other books by the author:
The Girl Who Loved Caterpillars, 1992
The Bumper Sticker Book, 1974
The Toothpaste Millionaire, 1974
The Pushcart War, 1973

Other books you might like:
Julia Cunningham, *The Treasure Is the Rose*, 1973
  Though Ariane lives in poverty, her castle is invaded by three strangers determined to find a treasure.
Howard Fast, *The Magic Door*, 1979
  When he has just the right feeling, Tony can open the door in his New York City tenement backyard and step through to the past.
Sally Fisher, *The Tale of the Shining Princess*, 1980
  A beautiful moon princess who is sent to Earth for punishment temporarily becomes the daughter of a poor bamboo cutter and his wife.

Louis Sacher, *Marvin Redpost: Why Pick on Me?*, 1993
  A small incident during recess threatens to turn nine year old Marvin into the outcast of his third grade class.
Yuri Suhl, *The Purim Goat*, 1980
  Hoping to earn some money so his pet goat won't be sold to pay a debt, a poor Jewish boy teaches the animal to dance.

1259

Jean Merrill

Illustrator: Jan Palmer

The Toothpaste Millionaire (Boston: Houghton Mifflin, 1972)

Age range: Grades 3-5

Subject(s): Employment; Money

Major character(s): Rufus Mayflower, Child; James, Child; Kate, Preteen

Time period(s): 1970s

Locale(s): Cleveland, Ohio

What the book is about: A young girl describes how her school friend made over a million dollars by creating and marketing a cheaper and better toothpaste.

Where it's reviewed:
Horn Book, October 1974, page 137
Kirkus Reveiws, May 1, 1974, page 480

Awards the book has won:
Dorothy Canfield Fisher Children's Book Award 1976
Sequoyah Children's Book Award 1977

Other books by the author:
Please Don't Eat My Cabin, 1972
The Black Sheep, 1969
The Pushcart War, 1964
The Superlative Horse, 1961

Other books you might like:
Barbara Aiello, *Business Is Looking Up*, 1988
  A visually impaired eleven year old sets up a greeting card service for step families, and realizes there is more to business than just making money.
Charlotte Herman, *Max Malone Makes a Million*, 1991
  Max and Gordy are frustrated with attempts to get rich, while a neighbor, Austin, makes money at every turn.
Rebecca C. Jones, *Germy Blew It—Again!*, 1988
  In order to pay off a school debt, Germy goes into the gerbil breeding business.
Stephen Manes, *Make Four Million Dollars by Next Thursday!*, 1991
  Can an ordinary kid become a multimillionaire in one short week? Jason Nozzle thinks he can.
Stephen Roos, *My Favorite Ghost*, 1988
  The legend of a ghost on the island inspires money hungry Derek to dupe his friends into paying admission to a supposedly haunted house.

1260

Susan Meyers

Illustrator: Gioia Fiammenghi

P.J. Clover, Private Eye: The Case of the Missing Mouse (New York: Dutton, 1985)

Age range: Grades 4-6

Series: P.J. Clover, Private Eye

Subject(s): Mystery and Detective Stories

Major character(s): Pamela Jean "P.J." Clover, Detective; Butch Bigelow, Preteen; Stacy Jones, Preteen

Time period(s): 1980s

Locale(s): Mill Creek, California

What the book is about: P.J. and her friend, Stacy, are on the case of a stolen Mickey Mouse bank - a collector's item worth over $1000. P.J.'s career is on the line, for she has vowed that if she can't catch the thief, she'll give up detective work forever.

Where it's reviewed:
Booklist, November 1, 1985, page 412
School Library Journal, May 1985, page 110

Other books by the author:
P.J. Clover, Private Eye: The Case of the Halloween Hoot, 1990
P.J. Clover, Private Eye: The Case of the Borrowed Baby, 1988
P.J. Clover, Private Eye: The Case of the Stolen Laundry, 1981
Melissa Finds a Mystery, 1966

Other books you might like:
Margaret Goff Clark, *The Latchkey Mystery,* 1985
   Eleven year old Minda forms a group to watch for a burglar who is breaking into houses in their neighborhood.
Eth Clifford, *Scared Silly,* 1988
   Mary Rose constantly quarrels with her sister, Beth, but they work together when a visit to a magic museum involves them in a complex mystery.
Eileen Dunlop, *The House on Mayferry Street,* 1976
   An invalid teenage girl and her eleven year old brother uncover secrets of past generations who lived in their family's house in Edinburgh.
Lois Lowry, *The 100th Thing about Caroline,* 1983
   When their mother starts to date the mystery man on the fifth floor, Caroline and her brother fear they will become the target of his crimes.
Willo Davis Roberts, *What Could Go Wrong?,* 1989
   During a trip between Seattle and San Francisco, Gracie and her cousins, Charlie and Eddie, get involved with some sinister characters and situations.

1261

Tilde Michels

Illustrator: Kathi Bhend

Rabbit Spring (New York: Harcourt, 1988)

Age range: Grades 2-4

Subject(s): Animals/Rabbits

Major character(s): Silla, Rabbit, Parent; Rahm, Rabbit, Parent; Polko, Rabbit, Cousin

Time period(s): Indeterminate

Locale(s): United States

What the book is about: It is spring and Rahm, a wild rabbit, and his mate await their first litter. They become the proud parents of seven baby rabbits. They teach the babies, and the reader, how rabbits live, what they need to be healthy and safe, and how they relate to other animals.

Where it's reviewed:
Booklist, April 1, 1988, page 1352
Hornbook, July 1988, page 491
School Library Journal, September 1988, page 184

Other books by the author:
What a Beautiful Day!, 1992
At the Frog Pond, 1989
Come Here, Little Hedgehog, 1988
Who's That Knocking at My Door?, 1986

Other books you might like:
Kate Banks, *The Bunnysitters,* 1991
   Hoping to make enough money so they can finish building a derby car, two boys offer to take care of a neighbor's rabbit.
Jan Feder, *The Life of a Rabbit,* 1982
   The life of a wild rabbit and his family, followed by text and illustrations presenting the physical characteristics and behavior of rabbits.
Robert Newton Peck, *Little Soup's Bunny,* 1993
   Easter is on the way and Soup and Rob are ready. They have a baby rabbit named Bucky who loves to eat carrots, and they are dyeing Easter eggs.
Alvin R. Tresselt, *The Rabbit Story,* 1989
   A young rabbit is caught by a farmer and kept in a pen by his little boy, and finally escapes to return to the free life of the other wild rabbits.
Jan Wahl, *The Rabbit Club,* 1990
   During the summer at his grandparents' farm, Fritz stumbles across some unusual rabbits.

1262

Betty Miles

Just the Beginning (New York: Knopf, 1976)

Age range: Grades 4-7

Subject(s): Family Life

Major character(s): Catherine "Cathy" Myers, Teenager; Julia Myers, Teenager (Cathy's older sister); Clara Myers, Parent (Cathy and Julia's mother)

Time period(s): 1970s

Locale(s): Camden Woods

What the book is about: Being relatively poor in an upper class neighborhood causes problems for thirteen year old Cathy. While all her friends' mothers have a cleaning woman, Cathy's mother is a cleaning woman. Then on top of that, Cathy gets suspended from school.

Where it's reviewed:
Booklist, May 15, 1976, page 1338
Hornbook, August 1976, page 399
Kirkus Reviews, March 15, 1976, page 323

Other books by the author:
Maudie and Me and the Dirty Book, 1980
The Trouble with Thirteen, 1979
A Day of Autumn, 1967
Having a Friend, 1959

Other books you might like:
Vivien Alcock, *A Kind of Thief,* 1991

When her father is suddenly arrested and put into prison, Elinor finds that she has to face many unpleasant truths about him and their way of life.

Sarah Ellis, *Pick-Up Sticks*, 1992
Thirteen year old Polly's rebellion against her unmarried, fiercely independent mother comes to a head when they must find a new apartment.

Sherry Garland, *The Silent Storm*, 1993
Alyssa has not spoken since seeing her parents die in a hurricane. Now, another storm threatens the home she and her grandfather share.

Ray Prather, *Fish and Bones*, 1992
Bones, intent on collecting the reward for finding a bank robber, discovers some of the ugly secrets hidden in his small Florida town.

Rachel Vail, *Do-Over*, 1992
Whitman has to deal with the anger he feels toward his father when his parents separate, his own interest in girls, and acting in his first play.

1263

Betty Miles

The Real Me (New York: Knopf, 1974)

Age range: Grades 4-6

Subject(s): Family Life; Women's Rights

Major character(s): Barbara Fisher, Preteen; Richard Fisher, Teenager; Marion Fisher, Journalist

Time period(s): 1970s

Locale(s): Fair Park, New York

What the book is about: Barbara finds out what women's rights mean when she is forbidden, by company policy, to take over her brother's paper route. When she is not allowed to sign upo for tennis at school, because it is offered for boys only, she decides to take action. Her parents and brother back her up. A story that is not only about rights, but about family love and support.

Where it's reviewed:
Booklist, September 1, 1974, page 45
Kirkus Reviews, October 1, 1974, page 1061

Other books by the author:
The Secret Life of the Underwear Champ, 1981
Maudie and Me and the Dirty Book, 1980
The Trouble with Thirteen, 1979
Looking On, 1978

Other books you might like:
Patricia Beatty, *Hail Columbia*, 1970
Louisa recounts how the visit of her suffragette aunt changed the lives of the family and the whole town.

Tessa Duder, *Jellybean*, 1985
The only child of a single mother, Geraldine is tired of having to fit into her mother's busy orchestra schedule, but soon things begin to change.

Patricia Foote, *Girls Can be Anything They Want*, 1980
Brief biographies of fifteen women who successfully pursued careers in fields at one time considered to be primarily the domain of men.

Rhea Beth Ross, *Bet's On, Lizzie Bingman!*, 1988

Fourteen year old Lizzie decides to prove her independence in 1914 after hearing her brother's speech encouraging men to shelter and protect women.

Judith St. George, *The Girl with Spunk*, 1975
When Josie loses her job due to gossip, she realizes that the women's rights convention could help her start a new life.

1264

Miska Miles

Illustrator: Peter Parnall

Annie and the Old One (Boston: Atlantic-Little, 1971)

Age range: Grades 3-5

Subject(s): Indians of North America; Death; Grandparents

Major character(s): Annie, Child, Indian

Time period(s): 1970s

Locale(s): Arizona

What the book is about: A Navajo girl unravels a day's weaving on a rug, whose completion, she believes, will mean the death of her grandmother.

Where it's reviewed:
Horn Book, August 1971, page 376
Kirkus Reviews, June 15, 1971, page 641

Awards the book has won:
Christopher Award 1972

Other books by the author:
Beaver Moon, 1978
Aaron's Door, 1977
Eddie's Bear, 1970
Fox and the Fire, 1966

Other books you might like:
Eleanor Clymer, *The Spider, the Cave and the Pottery Bowl*, 1971
Kate and her brother find the clay that grandmother uses to teach her how to make bowls as old as time in designs unique to the Hopi.

Lynne Gessner, *Malcolm Yucca Seed*, 1977
Malcolm longs for a "real" Navajo name, like his older brothers, but knows he has to earn it.

Paul Goble, *Beyond the Ridge*, 1989
As her family mourns and prepares her body for the spirit world, an old Plains Indian woman's spirit moves towards the afterlife.

Scott O'Dell, *Sing Down the Moon*, 1970
In the spring of 1864, white soldiers burned the village of Bright Morning's Navajo people and forced their migration along the "Trail of Tears."

Paul Pitts, *Racing the Sun*, 1988
Brandon has only known life in the suburbs when he is faced with conflict as he learns of his Navajo heritage from his father and grandfather.

1265

Patricia Miles

The Gods in Winter (New York: Dutton, 1978)

Age range: Grades 5-6

Major character(s): Adam Bramble, Child; Mrs. Korngold, Housekeeper

Time period(s): Indeterminate

Locale(s): England

What the book is about: The Brambles have moved to a new home in the English countryside. Adam begins to think the housekeeper has supernatural powers and is somehow responsible for the cold, cold winter.

Where it's reviewed:
Horn Book, October 1978, page 518
Kirkus Reviews, July 15, 1978, page 750

Other books by the author:
A Disturbing Influence, 1979

Other books you might like:
Nancy Bond, *Country of Broken Stone*, 1980
  From the moment they arrive at the isolated old stone house in the north of England, Penelope has a sense of foreboding.
Helen Cresswell, *Time Out*, 1990
  Tweeny and her parents, servants in a London house in 1887, use a book of magic spells to travel forward in time 100 years to 1987 England.
Geraldine Symons, *Crocuses Were Over, Hitler Was Dead*, 1977
  While visiting an old English manor, a young girl is befriended by one of its former inhabitants, a soldier killed during WWII.
Geoffrey Trease, *A Flight of Angels*, 1988
  Sheila and her friends solve a four hundred year old mystery while exploring the caves under Nottingham for a class project.
Robert Westall, *The Devil on the Road*, 1978
  Seeking shelter from a sudden rainstorm in an old barn, a motorcyclist finds himself back in a 17th century England troubled by witch hunts.

1266

Claudia Mills

After Fifth Grade, the World (New York: Macmillan, 1989)

Age range: Grades 4-6

Subject(s): Schools; Teachers

Major character(s): Heide Patricia Ahlenslagen, Child; Mrs. Richardson, Teacher; Lynette Lambert, Child

Time period(s): 1980s

Locale(s): United States

What the book is about: A ten year old earthshaker must learn to understand her own limitations and to cooperate with others. She battles Mrs. Richardson for harassing her best friend, Lynette. Heidi tries to shape up everyone she knows.

Where it's reviewed:
Booklist, July 1989, page 1906
School Library Journal, April 1989, page 103

Other books by the author:
Hannah on Her Way, 1991
Dynamite Dinah, 1990
Cally's Enterprise, 1988
The Secret Carousel, 1987

Other books you might like:
Paula Danziger, *The Cat Ate My Gymsuit*, 1974
  When a favorite teacher is fired, a junior high student has the courage to fight for reinstatement.
Sheila Solomon Klass, *Kool Ada*, 1991
  Ada moves from coal mining country to the slums of Chicago, gets a new teacher, and learns to stand up for herself.
Colleen O'Shaughnessy McKenna, *Merry Christmas, Miss McConnell!*, 1990
  A fifth grader with problems at home and a tough teacher expects a terrible Christmas, but it turns out to be one of the best.
Robert Newton Peck, *Arly*, 1989
  Arly Poole seems destined to be a field worker like his father, but things change when a school teacher comes to town.
Cheryl Zach, *Benny and the No Good Teacher*, 1992
  Fourth grade starts badly for Benny. He is separated from his best friend and he has a strict new teacher.

1267

Claudia Mills

At the Back of the Woods (New York: Four Winds, 1982)

Age range: Grades 4-6

Subject(s): Courage; Mental Illness; Superstition

Major character(s): Clarisse, Child, Handicapped (mentally retarded); Mrs. Spinelli, Neighbor; Emily, Child

Time period(s): 1940s

Locale(s): United States

What the book is about: Ten year old Clarisse and her friends find the difference between unthinking bravery and real courage as they deal with mental illness, taunting classmates, and mental retardation and accidents. A short book that deals effectively with many issues.

Where it's reviewed:
Booklist, July 1982, page 1447
Publisher's Weekly, May 14, 1982, page 216

Other books by the author:
Dynamite Dinah, 1990
After Fifth Grade, the World, 1989
Cally's Enterprise, 1988
Boardwalk with Hotel, 1985

Other books you might like:
Patricia Hermes, *Who Will Take Care of Me?*, 1983
  Twelve year old Mark decides to run away with his retarded younger brother so they will not be separated after the death of their guardian grandmother
Barbara M. Joosse, *Anna and the Cat Lady*, 1992
  When nine year old Anna rescues a stray kitten, it leads her into a relationship with an elderly woman.
Daniel Keyes, *Flowers for Algernon*, 1988
  Mentally retarded Charlie Gordon participates in an experiment which turns him into a genius, temporarily. (Creative's Classic Short Stories)
Joseph McNair, *Commander Coatrack Returns*, 1989
  When Lisa's retarded five year old brother starts becoming more independent from her, she begins a game of make-believe with a boy at school.
Jane Claypool Miner, *She's My Sister*, 1982

Mary Lou's secret of having a retarded sister threatens to be revealed and ruin her carefully constructed social life.

1268

Claudia Mills

Dynamite Dinah (New York: Macmillan, 1990)

Age range: Grades 5-6

Subject(s): Behavior; Friendship; School Life

Major character(s): Dinah Seabrooke, Child; Suzanne Kelly, Child; Benjamin Seabrooke, Child

Time period(s): 1990s

Locale(s): Riverdale

What the book is about: Dinah is an unstoppable crowd-pleaser who loves all the attention she can get. When baby brother Ben comes along and Dinah's best friend, Suzanne, wins the role of Becky in the school production of *Tom Sawyer*, their friendship is put to the test.

Where it's reviewed:
Booklist, March 15, 1990, page 1453
School Library Journal, July 1990, page 77

Other books by the author:
After Fifth Grade, the World, 1989
Cally's Enterprise, 1988
The One And Only Cynthia Jane Thornton, 1986
Boardwalk with Hotel, 1985

Other books you might like:
Carole S. Adler, *One Sister Too Many*, 1989
  With the family coping with the constant crying of three month old Meredith, only Case notices the baby sitter is behaving very oddly.
Betsy Byars, *Bingo Brown, Gypsy Lover*, 1990
  A sixth grade boy deals with the prospect of a new baby brother and a long distance girlfriend.
Judy Delton, *Angel's Mother's Baby*, 1992
  Twelve year old Angel thinks she and her brother Rags have the perfect family until she finds out her mother is going to have a baby.
Sarah Ellis, *A Family Project*, 1986
  Eleven year old Jessica and her family eagerly prepare for the changes a new baby will bring to their lives.
Ethel Footman Smothers, *Down in the Piney Woods*, 1992
  The joys and frustrations of family life are portrayed through the eyes of Annie Rye, the ten year old daughter of a black sharecropper.

1269

Claudia Mills

The One and Only Cynthia Jane Thornton (New York: Macmillan, 1986)

Age range: Grades 4-6

Subject(s): Individuality; Schools; Sisters

Major character(s): Cynthia Jane Thornton, Preteen, 5th Grader; Lucy Thornton, Child (gifted), 5th Grader

Time period(s): 1980s

Locale(s): Northridge, New England

What the book is about: When her look-alike younger sister, Lucy, gets promoted into her fifth grade class, Cynthia feels that she must fight to retain her own individuality and self-esteem.

Where it's reviewed:
Publisher's Weekly, August 22, 1986, page 99

Other books by the author:
Boardwalk with Hotel, 1985
All the Living, 1983
The Secret Carousel, 1983
Luisa's American Dream, 1981

Other books you might like:
Mildred Ames, *Is There Life on a Plastic Planet?*, 1975
  Feeling unhappy, a young girl welcomes the opportunity of having a look-alike life-sized doll take her place at home and at school.
Claire Hutchet Bishop, *The Five Chinese Brothers*, 1938
  Five brothers who look alike outwit the executioner by using their extraordinary individual qualities.
Carol J. Farley, *The Case of the Lost Lookalike*, 1988
  While spending the summer at Magic Lake, Flee and her bright younger sister become involved with a hermit and a case of vandalism.
Patricia Reilly Giff, *The Winter Worm Business*, 1981
  When his look-alike cousin moves to town, acts like an idiot in school, and takes away his friend, fifth grader Leroy is sure his life is ruined.
Carol Beach York, *The Look-Alike Girl*, 1980
  Two teenage girls promote the friendship between a lonely wealthy widow and and eight year old who resembles the woman's dead daughter.

1270

A.A. Milne

The House at Pooh Corner (New York: Dutton, 1956)

Age range: Grades 1-6

Subject(s): Toys; Animals/Bears

Major character(s): Christopher Robin, Child; Winnie-the-Pooh, Toy, Bear; Eeyore, Toy, Donkey

Time period(s): Indeterminate Past

Locale(s): England

What the book is about: The continuation of Winnie the Pooh, Christopher Robin and friends from "Winnie-the-Pooh." A house is built for Eeyore, Tigger is unbounced, Pooh invents a new game, and finally they go to Galleons Lap, a secret circle of trees in the enchanted forest. Originally published in 1928.

Where it's reviewed:
Book World, November 8, 1970, page 3
Instructor, April 1970, page 144
Publisher's Weekly, August 24, 1970, page 64

Other books by the author:
When We Were Very Young, 1924
The Little Engine That Could, 1960
The World of Pooh, 1957
Winnie-the-Pooh, 1926

Other books you might like:
Margery Williams Bianco, *The Velveteen Rabbit*, 1922
  By the time the velveteen rabbit is dirty, worn out, and about to be burned, he has almost given up hope of ever finding the magic called Real.
Terrance Dicks, *Sally Ann and the School Show*, 1992
  Sally Ann and the other dolls help Mrs. Foster raise enough money to keep the day care center open.
Akiko Hayashi, *Aki and the Fox*, 1991
  Aki and her toy fox Kon make an adventurous journey to Grandma's house so that she can mend Kon's arm.
Michael Ratnett, *Jenny's Bear*, 1991
  Jenny loves all of the hundreds of toy bears that she owns, but what she wants most of all in the world is to meet a real live bear.
Elvira Woodruff, *Back in Action*, 1991
  After finding the magic powder again, Noah and his friend Nate shrink to the size of Noah's miniature toy men and have an exciting adventure.

1271

A.A. Milne

Winnie-the-Pooh (New York: Dutton, 1926)

Age range: Grades 2-6

Subject(s): Animals/Bears; Toys; Fantasy

Major character(s): Christopher Robin, Child; Winnie-the-Pooh, Toy, Bear; Eeyore, Toy, Donkey

Time period(s): Indeterminate Past

Locale(s): England

What the book is about: Christopher Robin and Pooh are the main characters in this classic story. Well known friends Kanga and Roo, Eeyore the donkey, and Piglet share adventures with Christopher Robin and Pooh. Read aloud as soon as children will listen, and they'll read it again themselves later. A part of our literary heritage no child or adult should miss.

Where it's reviewed:
Booklist, January 15, 1975, page 508
Kirkus Reviews, November 15, 1971, page 1213
School Library Journal, March 1975, page 88

Other books by the author:
Eeyore Has a Birthday, 1990
Christopher Robin Book of Verse, 1967
The World of Pooh, 1957
The House at Pooh Corner, 1928

Other books you might like:
Barbara Dillon, *Who Needs a Bear?*, 1981
  A teddy bear, a doll, and a stuffed monkey leave their secure but dull attic, seeking new homes.
Peter Goodspeed, *A Rhinoceros Wakes Me up in the Morning*, 1982
  A zoo of stuffed animals helps a small boy through his daily activities.
Margaret Hillert, *The Purple Pussycat*, 1981
  A stuffed pussycat comes to life at night and sets out to explore the world.
James Howe, *Pinky and Rex*, 1990
  Rex and her friend, Pinky, who each own many stuffed animals, find visiting the museum and its gift shop complicated by Pinky's little sister, Amanda.

Bill Watterson, *Calvin and Hobbes*, 1987
  A collection of comic strips following the adventures of Calvin and his stuffed tiger, Hobbes.

1272

Else Holmelund Minarik

Illustrator: Maurice Sendak

Little Bear (New York: Harper, 1957)

Age range: Grades 1-2

Subject(s): Animals/Bears; Mothers

Major character(s): Little Bear, Bear; Mother Bear, Bear

Time period(s): Indeterminate

Locale(s): United States

What the book is about: The adventures of Mother Bear and Little Bear, in the cold, to the moon, making birthday soup and wishes. An engaging story for beginning readers.

Where it's reviewed:
New Catholic World, March 1973, page 89
New York Times Book Review, April 23, 1978, page 43
Teacher, October 1978, page 170

Other books by the author:
A Kiss for Little Bear, 1968
Little Bear's Visit, 1961
Little Bear's Friend, 1960
No Fighting! No Biting!, 1958

Other books you might like:
Frank Asch, *Moondance*, 1993
  Bear fulfills his dreams of dancing with the moon.
Kathy Caple, *Fox and Bear*, 1992
  Fox and Bear, mismatched friends, find that they can get along with each other very well despite their differences.
Doug Cushman, *Possum Stew*, 1990
  Possum tricks Gator and Bear, but they get back at him when they tell him they are going to make possum stew.
Tony Johnston, *Little Bear Sleeping*, 1991
  In this story told in verse, a yawning bear tries to convince his mother that it isn't time for be.
John Schoenherr, *Bear*, 1991
  Searching for his mother, a young bear finds his own independence.

1273

Louise Moeri

Downwind (New York: Dutton, 1984)

Age range: Grades 5-7

Subject(s): Accidents; Survival

Major character(s): Ephraim, Preteen

Time period(s): 1980s

Locale(s): California

What the book is about: When a threatened melt-down at an emergency power plant threatens the valley, Ephraim, his two younger siblings and mom and dad try to escape the valley in their car and trailer with very little preparation. The mood of panic and the way the family interacts under pressure are the crux of the story, as they face a situation potentially more dangerous than the radiation leak.

Where it's reviewed:
Horn Book, April 1984, page 197
School Library Journal, September 1984, page 120

Other books by the author:
The Forty-Third War, 1989
Journey to the Treasure, 1986
First the Egg, 1982
The Girl Who Lived on the Ferris Wheel, 1979

Other books you might like:
Anne Fine, *My War with Goggle-Eyes*, 1989
    Kitty doesn't like her mother's boyfriend, especially his views on the anit-nuclear issue, until events prompt her to find him a place in the family.
Martyn N. Godfrey, *The Last War*, 1986
    As one of the lucky ones who survived a nuclear bomb, Brad believes that someday all will be well again until he meets Angel.
Annabel Johnson, *Finders, Keepers*, 1981
    A boy and his sister flee from Denver following a catastrophic explosion at a nearby nuclear power plant, hoping to survive in the mountains.
Robert E. Rubenstein, *When Sirens Scream*, 1981
    A boy tries to arrive at a decision - to side with his father or the townspeople over the safety of a nuclear power plant after an accident.
Robert E. Swindells, *A Serpent's Tooth*, 1988
    A workman falls ill on the site of a proposed nuclear waste dump, which Lucy's second sight reveals is a buriel site for victims of the Black Death.

1274

Nicolasa Mohr

Illustrator: Ray Cruz

Felita (New York: Dial, 1979)

Age range: Grades 4-6

Subject(s): Puerto Rican Americans

Major character(s): Felita, Child; Abuelita, Grandparent (grandmother)

Time period(s): 1980s

Locale(s): New York, New York

What the book is about: A Puerto Rican family moves to an area where Spanish is not spoken. Only Felita's grandmother realizes how much Felita will miss her old neighborhood, and Gigi, her best friend.

Where it's reviewed:
Booklist, December 1, 1979, page 559
Hornbook, February 1980, page 56
Kirkus Reviews, February 1, 1980, page 127

Other books by the author:
All for the Better, 1993 (Non-Fiction)
Going Home, 1986
El Bronx Remembered, 1975
Nilda: A Novel, 1973

Other books you might like:
T. Ernesto Bethancourt, *New York City, Too Far From Tampa Blues*, 1975
    A Spanish American boy from Florida tells of his experiences in Brooklyn and his friendship with an Italian boy who shares his love of music.
Caroline Crane, *Don't Look at Me That Way*, 1970
    A Puerto Rican girl's hopes of leaving the squalor she lives in are dashed when her mother dies leaving her responsbile for five brothers and sisters.
Gloria Gonzalez, *Gaucho*, 1977
    A Puerto Rican boy in New York is torn by conflicting desires; return to his native land or appreciate the opportunity available in his new one.
Bob Teague, *Adam in Blunderland*, 1971
    Blaming adults for society's evils, three children wish themselves to a land populated by kids, only to find it plagued by the same evils.
Piri Thomas, *Stories from El Barrio*, 1978
    Stories of Spanish Americans in New York City.

1275

F.N. Monjo

Grand Papa and Ellen Aroon (New York: Holt, 1974)

Age range: Grades 2-4

Subject(s): Biography; Presidents

Major character(s): Ellen Aroon, Child, Historical Figure; Thomas Jefferson, Grandparent, Historical Figure

Time period(s): 1800s

Locale(s): United States

What the book is about: Ellen Aroon is a favorite grandchild of Thomas Jefferson. Told from a child's point of view, the story offers information about what Jefferson was like, what he thought about people, and all the things that kept him so busy.

Where it's reviewed:
Publisher's Weekly, October 21, 1974, page 51

Other books by the author:
The One Bad Thing about Father, 1987
King George's Head Was Made of Lead, 1974
Me and Willie and Pa, 1973
Poor Richard in France, 1973

Other books you might like:
Miriam Anne Bourne, *Patsy Jefferson's Diary*, 1976
    A fictionalized diary of "Patsy" Jefferson records the highlights of her life with "Papa," Thomas Jefferson.
Leonard Everett Fisher, *Monticello*, 1988
    Describes the planning and construction of Thomas Jefferson's dream home.
Carol Greene, *Thomas Jefferson: Author, Inventor, President*, 1991
    Describes the life of Thomas Jefferson, who was an accomplished statesman and inventor.
Helen Albee Monsell, *Thomas Jefferson: Third President of the United States*, 1939
    The story of the childhood of Thomas Jefferson. (Childhood of Famous Americans Series)
Robert M. Quackenbush, *Who Let Muddy Boots into the White House?*, 1986

A biography of Andrew Jackson from his backwoods beginnings to his days as a war hero and finally, president.

1276

F.N. Monjo

Illustrator: Richard Cuffari

Zenas and the Shaving Mill (New York: Coward, 1976)

Age range: Grades 3-5

Subject(s): Quakers; Revolutionary War

Major character(s): Zenas, Teenager, Pacifist

Time period(s): 1770s

Locale(s): Nantucket, Massachusetts, American Colonies

What the book is about: Seventeen year old Zenas is a Quaker during the Revolutionary War. He sails back to Nantucket from the mainland, and describes the life of the Quakers. They are caught between patriots, Tories and the British because they refuse to fight for anyone.

Where it's reviewed:
Horn Book, October 1976, page 508
Kirkus Reviews, April 1, 1976, page 398

Other books by the author:
Prisoners of the Scrambling Dragon, 1980
A Namesake for Nathan, 1977
Letters to Horseface, 1975
Me and Willie and Pa, 1973

Other books you might like:
Clyde Robert Bulla, *Charlie's House*, 1983
  Charlie Brig is shipped, as an indentured servant, from England to Colonial America.
Esther Forbes, *Johnny Tremain*, 1943
  The story of a young silversmith's apprentice who plays an important part in the Revolution.
Patricia Lee Gauch, *Aaron and the Green Mountain Boys*, 1987
  An historical novel, set in American Revolutionary times.
Scott O'Dell, *Sarah Bishop*, 1980
  A first-person narrative of a girl who lived through the American Revolution and its toll of suffering and misery.
G. Clifton Wisler, *This New Land*, 1987
  Richard and his family begin a new life in Plymouth in 1620.

1277

Mary Elise Monsell

Illustrator: Eileen Christelow

The Mysterious Cases of Mr. Pin (New York: Atheneum, 1989)

Age range: Grades 2-4

Subject(s): Mystery and Detective Stories; Animals/Birds

Major character(s): Mr. Pin, Penguin

Time period(s): Indeterminate

Locale(s): Chicago, Illinois

What the book is about: Mr. Pin is a rockhopper penguin and he has come to Chicago from the South Pole to be a detective.

Where it's reviewed:
Booklist, May 15, 1989, page 1652
Kirkus Reviews, April 15, 1989, page 627
School Library Journal, June 1989, page 91

Other books by the author:
Toohy and Wood, 1992
Crackle Creek, 1990
Armadillo, 1991
Mr. Pin: The Chocolate Files, 1990

Other books you might like:
Lisa Eisenberg, *Man in the Cage*, 1981
  Ann, a pet store employee, becomes involved in a robbery case when she finds a corpse in an animal cage and a poodle missing.
Lynn Hall, *The Mystery of Pony Hollow*, 1992
  On her family's new farm, Sarah stumbles upon a skeleton and a supernatural mystery involving the ponies who lived there forty years ago.
Georgess McHargue, *Funny Bananas*, 1975
  Ben's efforts to catch the vandal plaguing the natural history museum are complicated by a "witch" and a strange animal who are haunting the museum.
Virginia Vail, *Petnapped!*, 1990
  Valentine Taylor, the daughter of a veterinarian, investigates reports of missing pets.
Evelyn Witter, *The Mystery of Animal Haven*, 1979
  Roger's knowledge of animals becomes particularly useful when he is kidnapped.

1278

L.M. Montgomery

Anne of Green Gables (New York: Grosset and Dunlap, 1908)

Age range: Grades 5-9

Subject(s): Friendship

Major character(s): Anne Shirley, Orphan; Gilbert Blythe, Preteen

Time period(s): 1890s

Locale(s): Prince Edward Island, Canada

What the book is about: Readers who meet Anne in this book will have a friend to read about for many volumes, not to mention film adaptations. Anne, an orphan, is taken in by a middle-aged brother and sister (who were expecting a boy to help with heavy chores). Anne's personality and mischief-making lightens their lives. This book shows Anne in school, at home, and feuding with Gilbert Blythe.

Where it's reviewed:
Bookwatch, September 19, 1976, page H4
School Library Journal, September 1980, page 43

Other books by the author:
Anne of Ingleside, 1939
Anne's House of Dreams, 1917
Anne of the Island, 1915
Anne of Windy Poplars, 1936

Other books you might like:

Dawna Lisa Buchanan, *The Falcon's Wing*, 1992
  After her mother's death, Bryn tries to make a new life when her father moves them to her aunt's home, where her cousin with Down's Syndrome lives.

Evelyn Sibley Lampman, *The Bandit of Mok Hill*, 1969
  An orphan joins a show as a vocalist. When he gets to California, he plans to meet his bandit friend. However, he discovers his friend kills.

Janet Louise Lunn, *The Root Cellar*, 1985
  Rose, sent to live with relatives on a farm, ventures into the cellar and finds herself making friends with people who lived there centuries ago.

Martha Bennett Stiles, *Kate of Still Waters*, 1990
  A young girl chronicles the joys and problems of her family's life on their farm in central Kentucky.

Diana Walker, *The Hundred Thousand Dollar Farm*, 1977
  The lives of a close-knit farm family are disrupted by the arrival of a young loner and an offer of a small fortune for their farm.

1279

Bel Mooney

The Stove Haunting (Boston: Houghton, 1988)

Age range: Grades 5-7

Subject(s): Fantasy; Time Travel; Labor and Labor Classes

Major character(s): Daniel, Time Traveller, Servant

Time period(s): 1980s; 1830s (1835)

Locale(s): England

What the book is about: An old cooking stove in an English country house transports Daniel back in time where he is stove boy in a rector's house. As a kitchen servant, he becomes involved in the local farm workers' dangerous plan to form a union.

Where it's reviewed:

Center for Children's Books Bulletin, May 1988, page 185
School Library Journal, May 1988, page 99

Other books you might like:

Bruce Coville, *The Dinosaur That Followed Me Home*, 1990
  Stuart looks forward to Camp Haunted Hills each summer, but this year, camp includes a trip for Stuart and his friends to the time of the dinosaurs.

Peni R. Griffin, *A Dig in Time*, 1991
  Twelve year old Nan and her younger brother travel back through time by way of artifacts they found in their own back yard.

Thomas McKean, *The Secret of the Seven Willows*, 1991
  In danger of losing their ancestral home, Martha and Tad use the power of a magic ring to travel back to the past in order to change the future.

Jon Scieszka, *The Good, the Bad, and the Goofy*, 1992
  The Time Warp Trio find themselves in the Wild West of the old days, surrounded by cowboys and Indians.

William Sleator, *The Green Futures of Tycho*, 1991
  Eleven year old Tycho finds an egg shaped object and uses it to travel in time, then struggles with the future he sees for himself and his family.

1280

Emily Moore

Just My Luck (New York: Dutton, 1983)

Age range: Grades 4-6

Subject(s): African Americans; Animals/Dogs; Ethics

Major character(s): Olivia, Preteen

Time period(s): 1980s

Locale(s): United States

What the book is about: Olivia desperately wants a dog, and her only hope for earning the money for one is to solve a dognapping and collect the reward. Olivia and Jeffrey set out to find Mrs. Dingle's lost dog. When they solve the mystery, the dognapper proves to be an elderly friend. Should Olivia report him and collect a reward, or pretend the dog came home on its own, protect her friend, and give up hope of a new puppy for herself?

Where it's reviewed:

Horn Book, February 1983, page 47
School Library Journal, January 1983, page 77
Booklist, March 1, 1983, page 908

Other books by the author:

Whose Side Are You On?, 1988
Something to Count On, 1980

Other books you might like:

Matt Christopher, *The Hit-Away Kid*, 1988
  Barry McGee enjoys winning so much that he has a tendency to bend the rules. Then the dirty tactics of another pitcher gives him a new perspective.

Shirley Climo, *Gopher, Tanker, and the Admiral*, 1984
  When other money-making efforts fail, a boy and his dog accept a summer job as companions to an old man, and become involved in solving burglaries.

Paula Fox, *How Many Miles to Babylon?*, 1980
  James skips school to go to his secret place, a deserted house, where he is found by three teenage boys who force him to join a dognapping ring.

Dean Hughes, *Millie Willenheimer and the Chestnut Corporation*, 1983
  When her father cuts off her allowance, Millie uses her ingenuity to corner the market on chestnuts before she is forced to question her own ethics.

Barbara Willard, *A Dog and a Half*, 1971
  Not wanting a dog around, Jill's father gives her an impossibly small amount of money with which to buy one, but Jill finds a St. Bernard for free.

1281

Lilian Moore

Illustrator: Sharon Wooding

I'll Meet You at the Cucumbers (New York: Atheneum, 1988)

Age range: Grades 2-5

Subject(s): Animals/Mice; Friendship

Major character(s): Adam Mouse, Writer (poet), Mouse; Junius Mouse, Mouse; Amanda Mouse, Mouse

Time period(s): Indeterminate Past

Locale(s): United States

What the book is about: Adam wants to meet his pen pal, Amanda. They decide to meet at the Farmer's Market. Junius and Adam travel to the big city where Adam despairs when his dear friend admits he might like to stay in the city.

Where it's reviewed:
Horn Book, July/August 1988, page 492
School Library Journal, December 1988, page 26

Other books by the author:
Adam Mouse's Book of Poems, 1992
Riddle Walk, 1971
Everything Happens to Stuey, 1960
The Snake That Went to School, 1957

Other books you might like:
Barbara Brenner, *Too Many Mice*, 1992
    When Nita and her mother use a bunch of cats to get rid of the mice in their house, it is the beginning of an overabundance of animals.
Randall Jarrell, *The Bat-Poet*, 1964
    A young bat, unappreciated by his fellow bats, becomes aware of the beauty around him and creates poetry to celebrate what he sees.
Dick King-Smith, *Martin's Mice*, 1988
    A farm cat who doesn't want to catch mice keeps a family of them as pets in the barn.
Shirley Rousseau Murphy, *The Song of the Christmas Mouse*, 1990
    Rick tries to capture a beautiful wild mouse but a visiting younger cousin is always in the way.
Ethel Pochocki, *The Attic Mice*, 1990
    A family of mice go shopping in the human's kitchen, explore the attic, and get ready for Christmas.

`1282`

Stephen Mooser

Illustrator: Tomie De Paola

Funnyman and the Penny Dodo (New York: Watts, 1984)

Age range: Grades 2-3

Series: Funnyman

Subject(s): Humor; Mystery and Detective Stories

Major character(s): Funnyman, Detective

Time period(s): Indeterminate

Locale(s): Europe

What the book is about: Funnyman, a detective who can't stop making jokes and puns, takes his strange sense of humor with him on the case of a stolen stamp - the Penny Dodo, the rarest stamp at the Royal Stamp Show.

Other books by the author:
The Fright-Face Contest, 1989
Funnyman Meets the Monster From Outer Space, 1987
Funnyman's First Case, 1981
Ghost with the Halloween Hiccups, 1977

Other books you might like:
Ann Cameron, *Julian Secret Agent*, 1988

When Julian, his little brother Huey, and their friend Gloria decide to be "crime busters" they find themselves in one adventure after another.
Ellen Conford, *A Case for Jenny Archer*, 1988
    After reading three mysteries in a row, Jenny becomes convinced that the neighbors across the street are up to no good and decides to investigate.
Daniel Manus Pinkwater, *The Muffin Fiend*, 1986
    Wolfgang Amadeus Mozart helps Inspector LeChat catch the thief who is stealing all the muffins of Europe.
Nicki Street, *The Joker*, 1981
    As a joke, Mike pretends he understands the conversation of four Russian men on a bus, but it's not funny when two of them pursue him firing guns.
Bernard Wiseman, *Barber Bear*, 1987
    Presents the adventures of Barber Bear in puns and illustrations.

`1283`

Stephen Mooser

Illustrator: George Ulrich

My Halloween Boyfriend (New York: Dell, 1989)

Age range: Grades 2-4

Series: Creepy Creatures Club Adventures

Subject(s): Halloween; Monsters

Major character(s): Jody Grimes, Child; Henry Potter, Child; Rosa Dorado, Child

Time period(s): 1980s

Locale(s): United States

What the book is about: The Creepy Creatures Club members know a TV crew is coming to film a monster story in their classroom. Jody is so excited at the chance to be discovered on TV that she won't work on her book report. Her research for the TV role turns out to be just what is needed for an excellent book report.

Other books by the author:
The Man Who Ate a Car, 1991
That's So Funny I Forgot to Laugh, 1990
Monster Holiday, 1989
Monsters in the Outfield, 1989

Other books you might like:
Miriam Cohen, *The Real Skin Rubber Monster Mask*, 1990
    Jim isn't sure what he wants to be for Halloween, but he knows he wants it to be scary.
Rose Impey, *Scare Yourself to Sleep*, 1988
    Two cousins spending the night in a tent in the dark back yard succeed in scaring each other, with a little help from brother Simon.
Drew Stevenson, *The Case of the Horrible Swamp Monster*, 1984
    When the sixth grade decides to film a monster movie as a class project, the camera reveals something unexpected.
Daisy Wallace, *Monster Poems*, 1976
    Seventeen poems about different kinds of monsters.
Walter Wangerin, *Thistle*, 1983
    Plain Thistle can only cry as one by one her family is eaten by the monster, but her gentle bargain with a witch saves them all.

1284

Walt Morey

Canyon Winter (New York: Dutton, 1972)

Age range: Grades 5-7

Subject(s): Conservation of Natural Resources; Mountain Life

Major character(s): Peter Grayson, Teenager; Omar Pickett, Recluse

Time period(s): 1970s

Locale(s): Rocky Mountains

What the book is about: When 15 year olf Peter Grayson's plane crashes in the Rockies, the pilot is kil led and Peter must survive on his own. Just when he is ready to give up hope, h e finds the cabin of Omar Pickett, a "canyon rat" who lives with wild animals. Peter gains more than survival from Omar and his animal friends.

Where it's reviewed:
Booklist, February 1, 1973, page 530
Kirkus Reviews, November 1, 1972, page 1246
Library Journal, January 15, 1973, page 262

Other books by the author:
Gloomy Gus, 1970
Angry Waters, 1969
Home Is the North, 1967
Gentle Ben, 1965

Other books you might like:
Thomas Baird, *Walk out a Brother*, 1983
 After his father dies, sixteen year old Don runs away from his hated older brother and crosses paths with a murderer in the Rocky Mountains.
Annabel Johnson, *Finders, Keepers*, 1981
 A boy and his rebellious sister flee Denver following a catastrophic explosion at a nearby power plant, hoping to survive in the mountains.
Ben Mikaelsen, *Rescue Josh McGuire*, 1991
 When Josh runs away to the mountains with an orphaned bear cub destined for laboratory testing, they must fight for their lives in a sudden snowstorm.
Robert Newton Peck, *Jo Silver*, 1985
 Kenny's hike through the Adirondacks in search of a writer becomes a fight for survival as he realizes he is not alone in the hostile wilderness.
P.J. Petersen, *Going for the Big One*, 1986
 Left penniless while their father is looking for work in Alaska, three youngsters start out on what becomes a dangerous trek over the mountains.

1285

Walt Morey

Illustrator: John Schoenherr

Gentle Ben (New York: Dutton, 1965)

Age range: Grades 4-6

Subject(s): Animals/Bears

Major character(s): Mark Anderson, Preteen; Gentle Ben, Bear

Time period(s): 1960s

Locale(s): Alaska

What the book is about: This story traces the friendship between a boy and a bear in the rugged Alaskan territory. Mark is lonely after his brother, Jamie, dies. Ben is a huge brown bear whose owner keeps him chained. Only Mark's parents are able to save Ben when the townspeople become determined to destroy him.

Where it's reviewed:
Booklist, January 1, 1966, page 452
Center for Children's Books Bulletin, April 1966, page 134
Kirkus Reviews, August 1, 1965, page 751

Awards the book has won:
Sequoyah Children's Book Award 1968
ALA Notable Book

Other books by the author:
The Lemon Meringue Dog, 1980
Operation Blue Bear, 1975
Angry Waters, 1969
Kavik the Wolf Dog, 1968

Other books you might like:
Patricia Calvert, *The Hour of the Wolf*, 1983
 Following his suicide attempt, a loner is sent to Alaska where he subsequently enters the Iditarod Trail Race from Anchorage to Nome.
Jean Craighead George, *Water Sky*, 1987
 A boy who goes to Barrow, Alaska, to live with friends of his father for awhile, learns the importance of whaling to the Eskimo culture.
Jack London, *The Call of the Wild*, 1987
 An unusual dog, part St. Bernard, part Scotch shepherd, is forcibly taken to Alaska where he eventually becomes the leader of a wolf pack.
P.J. Petersen, *Going for the Big One*, 1986
 Three children begin a dangerous trek to a small town to wait for their father after their stepmother leaves them penniless.
Judith St. George, *In the Shadow of the Bear*, 1983
 Annie stretches her mental and physical limits dealing with hostile Russians and survival in the wilderness during a week in Alaska.

1286

Walt Morey

Illustrator: Peter Parnall

Kavik the Wolf Dog (New York: Dutton, 1968)

Age range: Grades 5-6

Subject(s): Animals/Dogs; Animals/Wolves

Major character(s): Andy Evans, Child, Animal Lover; Mr. Hunter, Wealthy (dog owner); Kavik, Dog (champion sled dog)

Time period(s): 1960s

Locale(s): Alaska

What the book is about: Raised to be a champion sled dog, Kavik was sold to Mr. Hunter. Rescued by Andy after a plane crash and nursed back to health, Kavik never forgets Andy and struggles to return to him after being reclaimed by Mr. Hunter.

Where it's reviewed:
Horn Book, October 1968, page 565
Library Journal, September 15, 1968, page 332

Awards the book has won:
Dorothy Canfield Fisher Children's Book Award 1968

Other books by the author:
Canyon Winter, 1972
Scrub Dog of Alaska, 1971
Angry Waters, 1969
Gentle Ben, 1966

Other books you might like:
Jean Craighead George, *Water Sky*, 1987
　　A boy goes to Barrow, Alaska, and learns the importance of whaling to the Eskimo culture.
Evelyn C. Nevin, *Extraordinary Adventures of Chee Chee McNerney*, 1971
　　A 14 year old girl travels to the Alaskan goldfields with two strange companions.
Scott O'Dell, *Black Star, Bright Dawn*, 1988
　　Bright Dawn faces the challenge of the Iditarod race when her father is injured.
Scott O'Dell, *Carlota*, 1977
　　A young girl takes part in the battle of San Pasqual during the last days of the war between the Californians and the Americans.
Seymour Reit, *Race Against Death*, 1976
　　A sled dog relay carries diphtheria serum to stop an epidemic in Nome in 1925.

1287

Walt Morey

Runaway Stallion (New York: Dutton, 1973)

Age range: Grades 4-6

Subject(s): Animals/Horses

Major character(s): Jeff Hunter, Child

Time period(s): 1970s

Locale(s): United States

What the book is about: Jeff Hunter solves personal problems through rescuing a race horse. Jeff is usually considered a "clodhopper" by youngsters in the ranching community where he lives, but his reputation changes after he conquers his own fears in a search for a magnificent red stallion.

Where it's reviewed:
Booklist, January 15, 1974, page 544
Kirkus Reviews, June 15, 1973, page 643
Library Journal, October 15, 1973, page 3149

Other books by the author:
Gloomy Gus, 1989
Sandy and the Rock Star, 1979
Year of the Black Pony, 1976
Scrub Dog of Alaska, 1971

Other books you might like:
Carol Fenner, *A Summer of Horses*, 1989
　　Ten year old Faith struggles to overcome her fear of horses and her feelings of jealousy toward her talented older sister.
Doris Gates, *A Morgan for Melinda*, 1980
　　Even though Melinda fears riding, her father buys her a horse, and it is only through friendship with an elderly writer that she overcomes her fear.
Lynn Hall, *Danza!*, 1981

While in the United States with one of his grandfather's Paso Fino stallions, a Puerto Rican teen discovers his true feelings about horses.
Isabelle Holland, *Perdita*, 1984
　　A girl suffering from amnesia takes a job on a horse farm where she finds she rides well but is haunted by an elusive fear.
Michael Morpurgo, *War Horse*, 1982
　　Joey, the horse, relates his experiences growing up on an English farm, his survival as a calvary horse in WWI, and his reunion with his master.

1288

Walt Morey

Illustrator: Fredrika Spillman

Year of the Black Pony (New York: Dutton, 1976)

Age range: Grades 5-6

Subject(s): Frontier and Pioneer Life; Stepfamilies; Animals/Horses

Major character(s): Chris, Child; Frank Chase, Step-Parent

Time period(s): 1900s (1900)

Locale(s): Oregon

What the book is about: Chris falls in love with a wild beautiful pony in a neighbor's herd. He never expects his stepfather to buy him. Frank Chase loves Chris and his sister, but their mother has only married him to provide for her children.

Where it's reviewed:
Horn Book, August 1976, page 399
School Library Journal, April 1976, page 77

Other books by the author:
Operation Blue Bear, 1976
Canyon Winter, 1972
Angry Waters, 1969
Kavik the Wolf Dog, 1968

Other books you might like:
Elisa Bialk, *Wild Horse Island*, 1951
　　Jim's father is the new manager of a pedigree horse ranch. During the winter, a wild horse returns and Jim hopes to tame her.
S.E. Hinton, *Taming the Star Runner*, 1988
　　Sent to live with his uncle after a confrontation with his stepfather, Travis finds small town life confining until he meets a horse trainer.
David Masterton, *Get Out of My Face!*, 1991
　　Kate's adjustment to her obnoxious stepbrother is made more difficult when they have to help each other survive on a dangerous wilderness journey.
Bonnie Pryor, *Horses in the Garage*, 1992
　　Samantha finds a way to cope with her new stepfather, new home and school, when she makes friends with Jasmine and learns to ride a horse.
Sam Savitt, *Wild Horse Running*, 1973
　　A boy finds an injured mustang and is torn by his desire to keep him and his conviction that wild horses should be protected in their natural state.

1289

Alison Morgan

Illustrator: Joan Sandin

A Boy Called Fish (New York: Harper and Row, 1973)

Age range: Grades 4-6

Major character(s): Jimmy, Child; Fish, Child; Floss, Dog

Time period(s): 1970s

Locale(s): England

What the book is about: Jimmy tells the story of a lonely, strange boy named Fish. Only finding a dog brings love to Fish. When Floss is accused of killing sheep, Fish's dad decides to kill her. Fish runs off to hide in the hills.

Where it's reviewed:
Horn Book, October 1973, page 467
Kirkus Reviews, March 1, 1973, page 255

Other books by the author:
Paul's Kite, 1982
All Kinds of Prickles, 1980
At Willie Tucker's Place, 1975

Other books you might like:
Charlotte Baker, *Cockleburr Quarters*, 1972
 A young boy grows as an individual through his efforts to keep a half-blind mother dog and her eight puppies alive.
Barbara Corcoran, *Annie's Monster*, 1990
 Thirteen year old Annie finds herself in trouble when she tries to deal with the playful curiosity of a large dog.
William MacKellar, *The Ghost of Grannock Moor*, 1973
 Davie rejects the German Shepherd he is given to replace his Collie, but feels responsible when the dog runs away and is suspected of killing sheep.
Walt Morey, *Scrub Dog of Alaska*, 1971
 After a sled dog is raised by a young boy, the dog's cruel owner demands his return.
Mary Francis Shura, *Mister Wolf and Me*, 1979
 Thirteen year old Miles desperately tries to prove his German Shepherd has not been killing a farmer's sheep.

1290

Michael Morpurgo

Mr. Nobody's Eyes (New York: Viking, 1990)

Age range: Grades 5-9

Subject(s): Animals/Monkeys; Runaways

Major character(s): Harry, Preteen; Ocky, Chimpanzee

Time period(s): 1940s

Locale(s): England

What the book is about: Young Harry is unhappy at school and at home. When a trained chimp, Ocky, escapes from a circus, Harry runs away to try to rescue him. His travels are exciting and dangerous, and the post WWII setting is vivid.

Where it's reviewed:
Booklist, May 1, 1990, page 1708
Hornbook Guide, January 1990, page 243
Kirkus Reviews, February 1, 1990, page 182

Other books by the author:
Waiting for Anya, 1991
King of the Cloud Forests, 1988
Twist of Gold, 1987
Why the Whales Came, 1985

Other books you might like:
Vivien Alcock, *Travelers by Night*, 1983
 Two children kidnap an elephant and begin a dangerous journey to a safari park to find the elephant a home and save it from the slaughterhouse.
Eth Clifford, *Harvey's Marvelous Monkey Mystery*, 1987
 Harvey finds himself embroiled in a mystery when a monkey appears at his bedroom window in the middle of the night.
Peter Dickinson, *Eva*, 1988
 After a terrible accident, a young girl wakes up to discover that she has been given the body of a chimpanzee.
Sandy Landsman, *Castaways on Chimp Island*, 1986
 Four laboratory chimps, participants in an experiment to learn sign language, are placed on a jungle island to return to nature.
Wilson Rawls, *Summer of the Monkeys*, 1976
 In the late 1800s, an Ozark Mountain boy spends the summer trying to recapture some monkeys and a clever chimp that escaped from the circus.

1291

Michael Morpurgo

Waiting for Anya (New York: Viking, 1991)

Age range: Grades 5-8

Subject(s): World War II; Jews

Major character(s): Jo, Shepherd; Benjamin, Refugee; Anya, Refugee

Time period(s): 1940s

Locale(s): Lescun, France

What the book is about: In occupied France during WWII, Jo, a young shepherd, discovers that Benjamin is hiding Jewish children and smuggling them over the border into Spain. Benjamin is waiting for his daughter, Anya, who was separated from him when they were fleeing Nazi fire in Paris. Jo gets to know one of the German soldiers and realizes that he longs for peace as much as she does. Anya finally does appear, tempering the tragedy of the loss of Benjamin and Leah at Auschwitz.

Where it's reviewed:
Booklist, May 15, 1991, page 1792
Horn Book, July/August 1991, page 458

Other books by the author:
Twist of Gold, 1993
Mr. Nobody's Eyes, 1990
King of the Cloud Forests, 1988
War Horse, 1983

Other books you might like:
Claire Hutchet Bishop, *Twenty and Ten*, 1952
 During WWII, children fleeing Nazi-occupied France find refuge in a Catholic school.
Eilis Dillon, *Children of Bach*, 1992
 A Hungarian Jewish family of talented musicians escapes Nazi persecution during WWII.

Myron Levoy, *Alan and Naomi*, 1977
In New York of the 1940s, a boy tries to befriend a girl traumatized by Nazi brutality in France.
Hans Peter Richter, *Friedrich*, 1970
A young German boy recounts the fate of his best friend, a Jew, during the Nazi regime.
Renee Roth-Hano, *Touch Wood: A Girlhood in Occupied France*, 1988
Renee, a young Jewish girl, and her family flee their home in Alsace and live a precarious existence in Paris until they escape to a convent.

| **1292** |

John Morressy

Illustrator: Stan Skardinski

The Humans of Ziax II (New York: Walker, 1974)

Age range: Grades 2-4

Subject(s): Aliens; Science Fiction

Major character(s): Toren Mallixxan, Settler; Commander Mallixxan, Parent, Military Personnel

Time period(s): Indeterminate

Locale(s): Ziax II, Planet—Imaginary

What the book is about: Toren is surprised to find himself being held prisoner on planet Ziax II by a friendly group of furry, nature-loving space aliens. They manage to subdue the vicious "sork" in the gampal forest while returning Toren to his fellow Earthmen.

Where it's reviewed:
Booklist, November 15, 1974, page 345
Center for Children's Books Bulletin, April 1975, page 135
Library Journal, December 15, 1974, page 3269

Other books by the author:
A Voice for Princess, 1986
The Drought on Ziax II, 1978
Blackboard Davalier, 1966

Other books you might like:
Lynn Haney, *The Last Starfighter Storybook*, 1984
After breaking the record of scoring over one million on a video game, Alex is recruited by beings from the planet Rylos to fight in a war.
Leo P. Kelley, *King of the Stars*, 1979
Don, Steve, and Ellen are moved ahead in space by the alien Holgo and find themselves locked in fierce battle with King Yorro's silver soldiers.
Joan Lowery Nixon, *Kidnapped on Astarr*, 1981
With a robot's help, two children search for a relative who has been kidnapped by a king on the planet Astarr and accused of making secret weapons.
Dyan Sheldon, *Harry the Explorer*, 1991
Chicken's cat Harry, who is actually an alien from the planet Arcana, takes her on an adventure that gets her into all kinds of trouble.
Jeanne Willis, *Earth Tigerlets as Explained by Professor Xargle*, 1991
The alien Professor Xargle explains all about Earth Tigerlets, known on this planet as felines.

| **1293** |

Jane Morton

I Am Rubber, You are Glue (New York: Beaufort Books, 1981)

Age range: Grades 3-5

Subject(s): Sports/Baseball

Major character(s): Bentley "Bart" Barton, Child, Sports Figure (baseball player); Mr. Simms, Coach, Sports Figure (baseball player); Randy Simms, Child

Time period(s): 1980s

Locale(s): United States

What the book is about: Bart wants desperately to pitch for his Little League team, but that spot always seems to go to the coach's son, Randy. As Bart tries to cope with his father's new political campaign, he always seems to be doing stupid things in public and begins to withdraw. When he sees a robbery in progress, tosses the keys from the getaway car and calls police, he becomes a hero and things begin to turn around for him.

Where it's reviewed:
Booklist, December 15, 1981, page 550
School Library Journal, December 1981, page 67

Other books by the author:
No Place for Cal, 1989
Running Scared, 1979

Other books you might like:
Matt Christopher, *The Fox Steals Home*, 1978
Bobby is upset when he learns that his divorced father, who has been coaching him in base running, intends to move away.
Eleanor Clymer, *My Mother Is the Smartest Woman in the World*, 1982
Kathleen decides that her mother is so good at problem solving that she should run for mayor.
Dan Elish, *Jason and the Baseball Bear*, 1990
Jason is the only team member who can talk with animals and he improves his team's chances with the help of a polar bear named Whitney.
Marilyn Singer, *The Case of the Fixed Election*, 1989
Twins are up to their necks in trouble in the dirtiest election their school has ever seen.
Richard Aldrich Summers, *Ball-Shy Pitcher*, 1970
Boys with varied ethnic backgrounds and personal problems forget differences as they strive for a common goal in Little League.

| **1294** |

Arlene Mosel

Illustrator: Blair Lent

The Funny Little Woman (New York: Dutton, 1972)

Age range: Grades 1-3

Subject(s): Folk Tales

Major character(s): Funny Little Woman, Heroine; Oni, Monster

Time period(s): Indeterminate

Locale(s): Japan

What the book is about: The laughing woman loves making rice dumplings. One rolls away and she chases after it and is captured by the dreadful oni, terrible underground demons.

Where it's reviewed:
Horn Book, December 1972, page 587
Library Journal, December 15, 1972, page 4068

Awards the book has won:
Little Archer Award 1976

Other books by the author:
Tikki Tikki Tembo, 1968

Other books you might like:
Barbara Brenner, *Little One Inch*, 1977
    Although he is only an inch tall, Issun Boshi cleverly defeats several demons.
William H. Hooks, *Peach Boy*, 1992
    Found floating on the river inside a peach by an old couple, Momotaro grows up and fights the demons who have terrorized the village for years.
Jean Merrill, *The Girl Who Loved Caterpillars*, 1992
    From 12th century Japan, this is the story of Izumi who resists social and family pressure as she befriends caterpillars and other creatures.
Patricia Montgomery Newton, *The Five Sparrows*, 1982
    When a kindly old woman is richly rewarded for nursing a sparrow back to health, a greedy neighbor attempts to emulate her and brings trouble.
Sumiko Yagawa, *The Crane Wife*, 1981
    After Yohei tends a wounded crane, a beautiful woman begs to become his wife and weaves an exquisite silken fabric three times on her loom.

1295

Marietta D. Moskin

Illustrator: Richard Lebenson

Waiting for Mama (New York: Coward, 1975)

Age range: Grades 3-5

Subject(s): Emigration and Immigration; Jews

Major character(s): Becky, Child

Time period(s): 1900s (1900)

Locale(s): New York, New York

What the book is about: A Russian Jewish immigrant family, at the turn-of-the-century, comes to America to escape the Czarist persecutions. Mama has to stay behind because the baby was ill. For two years, Papa, Becky, and his brother and sister work and save to bring Mama to America.

Where it's reviewed:
Kirkus Reviews, April 15, 1975, page 456
School Library Journal, September 1975, page 108

Other books by the author:
Dream Lake, 1981
In Search of God, 1979
Lysbet and the Fire Kittens, 1975

Other books you might like:
Chaya M. Burnstein, *Rifka Bangs the Teakettle*, 1970
    In 1904 Czarist Russia, a Jewish girl tries to understand the attitudes of her Gentile neighbors and go to school with her brothers.

James I. Clark, *Russia Under the Czars*, 1989
    The history of czarist Russia from the foundation of the Russian state at Kiev in the mid-800s to the beginning of the Romanov rule. (non-fiction)
Sheila Greenwald, *Rosy Cole Discovers America!*, 1992
    Disappointed in the poor European ancestors she discovers during a class project to research family roots, Rosy cooks up a clan of royal relatives.
Kathryn Lasky, *The Night Journey*, 1981
    Rache ignores her parents' wishes and persuades her great-grandmother to relate her story of escape from czarist Russia.
Nancy Smiler Levinson, *I Lift up My Lamp*, 1986
    A biography of Emma Lazarus, activist for humane causes, friend to immigrants and author of the words inscribed on the Statue of Liberty.

1296

Farley Mowat

The Dog Who Wouldn't Be (Boston: Little Brown, 1957)

Age range: Grades 4-7

Subject(s): Animals/Dogs

Major character(s): Farley, Preteen; Mutt, Dog

Time period(s): 1920s (1929)

Locale(s): Saskatoon, Saskatchewan, Canada

What the book is about: The humorous story of Mutt, a dog of character and personality, and his boy, Farley. Mutt climbs trees and ladders, wears goggles as he rides in the car and has a genius for hunting; A marvelous dog for a boy growing up on the Canadian frontier.

Where it's reviewed:
Book World, March 8, 1981, page 12
School Library Journal, September 1980, page 43
Voices of Youth Advocates, June 1981, page 51

Other books by the author:
The Curse of the Viking Grave, 1966
Never Cry Wolf, 1963
Owls in the Family, 1962
Ordeal by Ice, 1961

Other books you might like:
Mildred Ames, *Philo Potts, or, The Helping Hand Strikes Again*, 1982
    Philo and his friend kidnap a neglected dog, hoping to make his owner appreciate him, but plans go awry when the dog becomes friends with some strays.
Roy Chapman Andrews, *Quest in the Desert*, 1950
    A scientific expedition to explore the Gobi Desert faces many challenges, but survives with the help of the leader's dog and a Mongolain ruler.
Charlotte Baker, *Cockleburr Quarters*, 1972
    A black boy grows as an individual through his efforts to keep a half-blind mother dog and her eight puppies alive.
Bianca Bradbury, *Dogs and More Dogs*, 1968
    When a boy takes in an abandoned mongrel and finally prevails upon his family to keep the dog, he and his friends start an Amimal Welfare Club.
Barbara Brenner, *Mystery of the Disappearing Dogs*, 1982

The Garcia twins become detectives in pursuit of dognappers, fearing that their dog, Perro, has become the victim of Operation Hot Dog.

`1297`

Dan Gopal Mukerji

Illustrator: Boris Artzbasheff

Gay-Neck: The Story of a Pigeon (New York: Dutton, 1927)

Age range: Grades 4-6

Subject(s): Animals/Birds

Time period(s): 1940s

Locale(s): India

What the book is about: Gay Neck is trained to be a carrier pigeon in India. The first part of the book follows him from hatching through training as a carrier pigeon. In the second part, he experiences quiet times in the wilderness and the chaos of war.

Where it's reviewed:
Growing Point, January 1970, page 1464
The Outlook, October 5, 1927, page 156
Saturday Review of Literature, October 15, 1927, page 215

Awards the book has won:
Newbery Medal 1928

Other books by the author:
Chief of the Herd, 1929
Ghond, the Hunter, 1928
Hindu Fables, 1929
Son of Mother India Answers, 1928

Other books you might like:
Charlotte Towner Graeber, *Gery Cloud*, 1979
   Tom is lonely in the country and makes friends with Orville who raises racing pigeons.
George Selden, *Chester Cricket's Pigeon Ride*, 1981
   Chester Cricket meets a pigeon named Lulu who takes him on a ride to get a nighttime aerial view of life.
Franklin W. Dixon, *Hooded Hawk Mystery*, 1985
   When their peregrine falcon brings down a homing pigeon carrying rubies, the Hardy boys find themselves involved with kidnappers.
John Shearer, *Billy Jo Jive and the Case of the Missing Pigeons*, 1978
   Young detectives search the streets for a pigeon thief.

`1298`

Jill Murphy

Worlds Apart (New York: Putnam, 1989)

Age range: Grades 4-6

Subject(s): Mothers and Daughters; Fathers and Daughters

Major character(s): Susan, Preteen

Time period(s): 1980s

Locale(s): London, England

What the book is about: Though happy living with her mother in London, Susan is consumed by curiosity about the identity of her father and goes on a quest to look for him.

Where it's reviewed:
Center for Children's Books Bulletin, March 1989, page 177
School Library Journal, March 1989, page 178

Other books by the author:
Jeffrey Strangeways, 1992
Bad Spell for the Worst Witch, 1982
The Worst Witch Strikes Again, 1980
Peace at Last, 1980

Other books you might like:
Eve Bunting, *The Hideout*, 1991
   Feeling unloved by his mother and a stepfather, Andy stages his own kidnapping in order to obtain money to pay for a trip to England to see his dad.
Hila Colman, *Tell Me No Lies*, 1978
   After finding out the truth about her absent father, a twelve year old girl learns about the difficult choices people must sometimes make.
Philip Pullman, *Spring-Heeled Jack*, 1989
   Three children escape from an orphanage and after a series of misadventures are reunited with their father through the efforts of Spring-Heeled Jack.
Jacqueline Roy, *Soul Daddy*, 1992
   Life for Hannah, her twin sister Rosie, and their white mother changes when her black, rock star father and his daughter move into their home.
Erika Tamar, *Blues for Silk Garcia*, 1983
   Linda, who resembles her father and has his gift for music, pursues the truth about her long-absent parent now that he has died.

`1299`

Jill Murphy, Author/Illustrator

The Worst Witch (New York: Avon, 1974)

Age range: Grades 3-5

Subject(s): Witches and Witchcraft; Schools

Major character(s): Mildred Hubble, Witch; Maud, Witch; Miss Hardbroom, Teacher

Time period(s): Indeterminate

Locale(s): Fictional Country

What the book is about: Mildred's first year at Miss Cackle's Academy for Witches is a disaster. There was one witch whose bootlaces always trailed on the floor, whose kitten was grey instead of black and who was afraid of the dark. She always crashed her broom into the dustbin during flying practice and was always in trouble.

Where it's reviewed:
Center for Children's Books Bulletin, October 1980, page 38
School Library Journal, September 1980, page 62
Publisher's Weekly, June 13, 1980, page 73

Other books by the author:
Worlds Apart, 1988
All in One Piece, 1987
Five Minutes Peace, 1986
The Worst Witch Strikes Again, 1980

Other books you might like:
Sheila Greenwald, *Write On, Rosy!*, 1988
    When Rosy realizes she does not have a life long ambition, she decides to become a reporter and investigates the headmistress with unexpected results.
Alice Low, *Genie and the Witch's Spells*, 1981
    Genie has a hard time with her school work until she and Merlina, a witch who has trouble learning her spells, enter into a partnership.
Liz Matthews, *Teeny Witch Goes to School*, 1991
    Teeny Witch does not want to leave her aunts and spend the day in school, but after the first day of school she finds it to be a place of fun.
Jane O'Connor, *Lulu Goes to Witch School*, 1987
    Lulu starts witch school and meets a classmate who is best at everything.
Janice May Udry, *Glenda*, 1969
    Glenda, the witch, decides she wants to be a school girl but fails to recognize her complete lack of success at the venture.

1300

Shirley Rousseau Murphy

Illustrator: Donna Diamond

The Song of the Christmas Mouse (New York: HarperCollins, 1990)

Age range: Grades 3-5

Subject(s): Animals/Mice; Christmas; Cousins

Major character(s): Rick, Child; Hattie Lou, Cousin; Claire, Relative (Aunt)

Time period(s): Indeterminate

Locale(s): United States

What the book is about: Rick is excited about the possibilities of catching a beautifully colored wild mouse which his mother calls "silver parfait ripple." As the Christmas season arrives, Rick's younger cousin comes to visit and makes a shambles of Ricks plans and almost ruins his holiday. The children and understanding parents are fully developed characters, making this a choice for independent readers and an excellent read-aloud.

Where it's reviewed:
Kirkus, August 15, 1990, page 1171
School Library Journal, October 1990, page 38
Publisher's Weekly, September 28, 1990, page 102

Other books by the author:
The Flight of the Fox, 1978
The Pig Who Could Conjure the Wind, 1978
Poor Jenny, Bright as a Penny, 1974
Elmo Doolan and the Search for the Golden Mouse, 1970

Other books you might like:
Susan Hill, *The Glass Angels*, 1991
    Tilly looks forward to spending Christmas with her mother in their small attic apartment, until illness and an accident threaten her plans.
Colleen O'Shaughnessy McKenna, *Merry Christmas, Miss Mc-Connell!*, 1990
    A girl with a tough new teacher and problems at home expects a terrible Christmas, only to have it turn out to be one of the best.

Nancy Ruth Patterson, *The Christmas Cup*, 1989
    Megan and her grandmother turn a worthless old cup to good use by saving money in it to buy a gift for a special person at Christmas.
Janice Lee Smith, *There's a Ghost in the Coatroom*, 1991
    While planning a medieval Christmas feast for their parents, Adam Joshua and the other children in Mrs. D's class, discover a ghost in the coatroom.
Nola Thacker, *Till's Christmas*, 1991
    Till, a modern-day Scrooge, thinks her family's Christmas customs are hokey until she catches the Christmas spirit.

1301

Bernice Myers, Author/Illustrator

Sidney Rella and the Glass Sneaker (New York: Macmillan, 1985)

Age range: Grades 2-4

Subject(s): Humor; Fairies; Sports/Football

Major character(s): Sidney Rella, Child

Time period(s): Indeterminate

Locale(s): Fictional Country

What the book is about: Sidney dreams of being a football hero but he has to stay home and clean house while his older brothers go to football practice. One day he meets his fairy godmother in the garden. A football field replaces the castle and Sidney wears glass sneakers in this Cinderella spoof.

Where it's reviewed:
Center for Children's Books Bulletin, April 1986, page 155
School Library Journal, March 1986, page 150
Children's Book Review Service, December 1985, page 41

Other books by the author:
Flying Shoes, 1992
Millionth Egg, 1991
Crybaby, 1990
Apple War, 1973

Other books you might like:
Bruce Bassoff, *Supercharged: Or How a Good Kid Becomes BAAAD and Saves His Basketball Team*, 1990
    A teen sports enthusiast inherits a special power and lives out his fantasy of being a college basketball star.
William J. Brooke, *A Telling of the Tales*, 1990
    Contemporary retellings of five classics: Cinderella, Sleeping Beauty, Paul Bunyan, John Henry, and Jack and the Beanstalk.
Shirley Climo, *The Egyptian Cinderella*, 1989
    In this version of Cinderella set in Egypt in the 6th century BC, Rhodopes, a slave girl, is eventually chosen by the Pharoah to be his queen.
Gail B. Graham, *The Beggar in the Blanket and Other Vietnamese Tales*, 1970
    Eight Vietnamese folktales include an Oriental Cinderella, and a legend explaining why crows seems to vanish from Vietnam during the month of Ngau.
William Mayne, *A Year and a Day*, 1976
    Two girls find a strange boy in the woods who doesn't seem to speak, eat or sleep.

1302

Walter Dean Myers

Adventure in Granada (New York: Puffin, 1985)

Age range: Grades 5-8

Subject(s): Adventure and Adventurers; Mystery and Detective Stories

Major character(s): Ken, Teenager, Detective; Chris, Teenager, Detective

Time period(s): 1980s

Locale(s): Spain

What the book is about: Teenagers Ken and Chris accompany their anthropologist mother to Granada where they befriend a boy accused of stealing an old cross.

Where it's reviewed:
Booklist, April 15, 1986, page 1226
School Library Journal, April 1986, page 91

Other books by the author:
Fallen Angels, 1988
Crystal, 1987
The Hidden Shrine, 1985
Hoops, 1981

Other books you might like:
Lisa Eisenberg, *Mystery at Snowshoe Mountain Lodge*, 1987
    A rash of pranks and mysterious accidents at an old ski lodge is investigated by teenage sleuths who are shocked when they discover the true culprit.
Elizabeth Howard, *Mystery of the Metro*, 1987
    A Chicago teen with a fondness for Sherlock Holmes travels to Paris, arrives to visit her uncle only to find him dead, and investigates on her own.
Elizabeth Levy, *The Dani Trap*, 1984
    Dani volunteers to work in a police investigation of illegal liquor sales to teens, and is framed as an accomplice in a liquor store holdup.
Ruth Nulton Moore, *Ghost Town Mystery*, 1987
    Accompanying their father to a ghost town in Nevada, twins Sara and Sam discover peculiar nocturnal activities and clues to a hidden treasure of gold.
Jo Stewart, *Run From Danger*, 1981
    While on a trip through Spain, Meg inadvertently becomes the owner of an antique necklace that someone else desperately wants.

1303

Walter Dean Myers

Mojo and the Russians (New York: Viking, 1977)

Age range: Grades 5-6

Subject(s): Occult

Major character(s): Dean, Preteen; Kwami, Preteen; Drusilla, Witch

Time period(s): 1970s

Locale(s): New York, New York

What the book is about: Seven kids growing up on the upper west side of New York, become suspicious of the Russian men who visit their friend, Willie. They plan to trap the men.

Drusilla, Willie's woman, has convinced them she will wreak Mojo (occult) vengence on Dean.

Where it's reviewed:
Kirkus Reviews, October 15, 1977, page 1098
School Library Journal, November 1977, page 74

Other books by the author:
Brainstorm, 1977
Fast Sam, Cool Clyde and Stuff, 1977
Social Welfare, 1977

Other books you might like:
Frieda Hughes, *Getting Rid of Aunt Edna*, 1986
    Miranda lives with her Aunt Agatha, a witch, and their home is invaded by inept Aunt Edna, who can't get her spells right!
Leonie Kooiker, *The Magic Stone*, 1978
    Chris finds a magic stone, but he is reluctant to use it when he discovers its power.
Zilpha Keatley Snyder, *The Headless Cupid*, 1971
    Amanda, a student of the occult, upsets her new family with strange initiation rites and rituals.
Robert E. Swindells, *The Moonpath and Other Tales of the Bizarre*, 1983
    Five stories of the occult and mysterious happenings.
Victoria Whitehead, *The Chimney Witches*, 1987
    Ellen gets caught up in the activities of the witches who live in the chimney.

1304

Walter Dean Myers

Somewhere in the Darkness (New York: Scholastic, 1992)

Age range: Grades 6-8

Subject(s): African Americans; Fathers and Sons; Prisoners and Prisons

Major character(s): Jimmy Little, Teenager; Cephus "Crab" Little, Parent, Criminal (escaped convict)

Time period(s): 1980s

Locale(s): New York, New York; Chicago, Illinois; Arkansas

What the book is about: Jimmy accompanies his father, Crab, who has recently escaped from prison, on a trip that turns out to be a time of often painful discovery for both of them. Crab knows this may be his last chance to show Jimmy who he really is.

Where it's reviewed:
Booklist, February 1, 1992, page 1028
Hornbook, May 1992, page 344
Kirkus Reviews, May 15, 1992, page 673
Voice of Youth Advocates, June 1992, page 98

Awards the book has won:
Boston Globe/Horn Book Award - Honor Book 1992
Coretta Scott King Award 1993

Other books by the author:
Fallen Angels, 1988
Scorpions, 1988
Motown and Didi, 1984
The Legend of Tarik, 1981
It Ain't All for Nothin', 1978
Fast Sam, Cool Clyde and Stuff, 1975

Other books you might like:
Vivien Alcock, *A Kind of Thief*, 1991
   When her father is suddenly arrested and put in prison, Elinor finds that she has to face many unpleasant truths about him and their way of life.
Barthe DeClements, *Breaking Out*, 1991
   As Jerry enters junior high, he continues to adjust to the fact that his father is in prison for theft.
Ann Gabhart, *Discovery at Coyote Point*, 1989
   Ance solves the mystery of his father's disappearance six years earlier while staying with his grandparents in the mountains.
David Gifaldi, *One Thing for Sure*, 1986
   Dylan can't bring himself to forgive his father who is serving time in an Oregon prison for illegally cutting timber.
Dayton O. Hyde, *Island of the Loons*, 1984
   Held prisoner by an escaped convict on an uninhabited island, a young boy watches his captor change from a hardened criminal to a gentle man.

1305

Walter Dean Myers

The Young Landlords (New York: Puffin/Penguin, 1979)

Age range: Grades 5-7

Subject(s): Friendship; City Life; Housing

Major character(s): Paul, Teenager

Time period(s): 1970s

Locale(s): New York, New York

What the book is about: Paul and his friends are working hard to gather evidence to exonerate a buddy who was falsely accused of theft. At the same time, they and their Action Group almost accidentally acquire a run-down tenement building with a most unusual assortment of tenants. A fast paced, funny portrait of Harlem.

Where it's reviewed:
Booklist, December 1, 1979
Hornbook, October 1979, page 535
Kirkus Reviews, January 15, 1980, page 70

Awards the book has won:
Coretta Scott King Award 1980

Other books by the author:
The Mouse Rap, 1990
Fallen Angels, 1988
Scorpions, 1988
Motown and Didi, 1984

Other books you might like:
Alice Childress, *A Hero Ain't Nothin' but a Sandwich*, 1973
   The life of a thirteen year old Harlem teen on his way to becoming a heroin addict is seen from his viewpoint and those of several people around him.
Rosa Guy, *New Guys around the Block*, 1983

Harlem teen Imamu Jones begins to suspect one of his friends may be guilty of a series of burglaries and other crimes.
Robert Lipsyte, *The Contender*, 1967
   A Harlem high school dropout escapes from a gang of punks into a boxing gym where he learns that being a contender is hard and discouraging work.
Dindga McCannon, *Wilhemina Jones, Future Star*, 1980
   A young black girl growing up in Harlem in the mid 1960s dreams of pursuing an art career and leaving the oppressive atmosphere of her home.
Brenda Scott Wilkinson, *Ludell's New York Time*, 1980
   Ludell moves from Georgia to New York City during the spring of her senior year and struggles to adjust to life in Harlem.

1306

Mildred Myrick

Illustrator: Arnold Lobel

The Secret Three (1963)

Age range: Grades 1-3

Subject(s): Clubs; Lighthouses

Major character(s): Tom, Child; Billy, Child; Mark, Child

Time period(s): 1960s

Locale(s): United States

What the book is about: A boy on an island lighthouse exchanges messages with two boys on the mainland using a bottle to carry messages with the tide.

Where it's reviewed:
Library Journal, October 15, 1973, page 3163
New York Times Book Review, December 19, 1982, page 27

Other books by the author:
Ants Are Fun, 1968

Other books you might like:
Edward Ardizonne, *Tim to the Lighthouse*, 1968
   One stormy night the lighthouse is dark, so Tim awakens Captain McFee and they row out to see what has happened to the keeper and the light.
Robert Kraske, *The Twelve Million Dollar Note*, 1977
   A collection of true stories about notes found in bottles that were put into the ocean.
Barbara Rinkoff, *The Case of the Stolen Code Book*, 1971
   When not asked to join the Secret Agents Club, the new boy sets out to prove he would be a worthy member.
Francene Sabin, *Secret of the Haunted House*, 1982
   The Maple Street Six club visit a haunted house and find a mysterious message.
Hildegarde Hoyt Smith, *The Little Red Lighthouse and the Great Gray Bridge*, 1942
   A little lighthouse on the Hudson River regains its pride when it finds out that it is still useful and has an important job to do.

N

1307

Magdalen Nabb

Illustrator: Pirkko Vainio

Josie Smith (New York: McElderry Books, 1989)

Age range: Grades 2-4

Subject(s): Animals/Cats

Major character(s): Josie Smith, Child

Time period(s): 1980s

Locale(s): England

What the book is about: Josie is as engaging a heroine as Beverly Cleary's Ramona, in her less boisterous way. The energetic English schoolgirl tries to earn money for her mum's birthday and smuggle a forbidden cat, which the family cannot afford, to her bedroom. Children will identify with her knack for getting into trouble. A good chapter book for newly independent readers.

Where it's reviewed:
Booklist, April 1, 1990, page 1558
Horn Book, January/February 1990, page 59

Other books by the author:
Josie Smith and Eileen, 1992
Josie Smith at School, 1991

Other books you might like:
Terrance Dicks, *Teacher's Pet*, 1990
    David's clumsy and lovable dog Goliath helps him get out of trouble with a seemingly mean math teacher and saves the teacher's job at the same time.
Gery Greer, *Let Me Off This Spaceship!*, 1991
    When Tod and Billy are kidnapped by aliens, they try to make as much trouble as possible on the ship so that the captain will take them back to Earth.
Elizabeth Levy, *Keep Ms. Sugarman in the Fourth Grade*, 1992
    Under Ms. Sugarman's guidance, Jackie develops more self-confidence, but is crush when she gets promoted to principal in the middle of the year.
Jeffrey Moss, *Bob and Jack: A Boy and His Yak*, 1992
    Jack and his pet yak become inseparable friends, playing together, protecting each other, and occasionally running into trouble.
Dyan Sheldon, *Harry the Explorer*, 1991
    Chicken's cat Harry, who is actually an alien from the planet Arcana, takes her on an adventure that gets her into all kinds of trouble.

1308

John Nagenda

Illustrator: Charles Lilly

Mukasa (New York: Macmillan, 1973)

Age range: Grades 4-6

Subject(s): Africa; School Life

Major character(s): Mukasa, Child

Time period(s): 1970s

Locale(s): Uganda

What the book is about: Mukasa is an only child with a very protective mother. She talks his father into sending Mukasa to school. He falls in love with learning. Although his ancestors have always been goat herders, the young Ugandan's mother is determined that her son get an education.

Where it's reviewed:
Horn Book, August 1973, page 380
Kirkus Reviews, December 15, 1972, page 1429

Other books you might like:
Lilian Gould, *Jeremy and the Gorillas*, 1977
    After fleeing his home during a Mau Mau uprising, a young boy is accepted by a troop of gorillas living in southwest Uganda.
Alice Lightner Hopf, *Biography of a Rhino*, 1972
    Moved to a national park in Uganda to protect her species, a young white rhino becomes a pet of the rangers and tourists.
Shannon K. Jacobs, *Song of the Giraffe*, 1991
    Seeking respect from her tribe and inspired by a dream, Kisana braves a dangerous journey to find the fruit of the baobab tree and a long-lost spring.
Naomi Mitchison, *The Family at Ditlabeng*, 1970
    During a long drought in Botswana, when money for school is scarce, a girl discovers her skill for making pottery.
Parker Rossman, *Pirate Slave*, 1977
    A twelve year old boy captured by Muslim pirates is forced into a life of piracy and slave trading.

1309

Beverly Naidoo

Illustrator: Eric Velasquez

Chain of Fire (New York: HarperCollins, 1989)

Age range: Grades 5-9

Subject(s): Apartheid

Major character(s): Naledi, Teenager; Taolo, Teenager

Time period(s): 1980s

Locale(s): Bophelong, South Africa

What the book is about: When the authorities in South Africa decide Naledi's village is to be destroyed and the villages relocated, many of the students join a resistance movement. The story, a sort of docudrama, vividly portrays the forced removal of millions of blacks to worthless barren lands labeled "homelands."

Where it's reviewed:
Booklist, March 15, 1990, page 1430
School Library Journal, May 1990, page 108

Other books by the author:
Journey to Jo'Burg, 1987

Other books you might like:
Dianne Case, *Love, David*, 1991
    Anna watches as her brother upsets the family by involving himself in illegal activities to escape from the poverty of his home life in South Africa.
Sheila Gordon, *The Middle of Somewhere: A Story of South Africa*, 1990
    Rebecca and her family, living in a South African village, are threatened with eviction to a distant development to make room for a new white suburb.
Margaret Sacks, *Beyond Safe Boundaries*, 1989
    Elizabeth comes of age in 1960s South Africa as her older sister joins a secret group opposed to the country's racial policies.
Norman Silver, *No Tigers in Africa: A Novel*, 1990
    Arriving in England from South Africa, a teen's family deteriorates as the effects of apartheid life takes a toll on all aspects of their lives.
Michael Williams, *Crocodile Burning*, 1992
    Seraki hopes to earn enough money to get his brother out of prison by joing a musical which espresses rage at conditions in his South African town.

1310

Phyllis Reynolds Naylor

The Agony of Alice (New York: Atheneum, 1985)

Age range: Grades 4-6

Subject(s): Self-Perception; Schools; Teacher-Student Relationships

Major character(s): Alice McKinley, Preteen, 6th Grader; Miss Cole, Teacher; Mrs. Plotkin, Teacher

Time period(s): 1980s

Locale(s): Silver Springs, Maryland

What the book is about: Alice is in the midst of trying to survive sixth grade without making a total idiot of herself. When her teacher turns out to be the overweight, not-very-cool Mrs. Plotkin, she is sure her chances of becoming a sophisticated teenager are doomed. However, she discovers that what is inside people is more important than the outer package. Fast paced and full of the humor and frustration that almost-teens will easily identify with.

Where it's reviewed:
Book World, May 11, 1986, page 17
Children's Book Review Service, March 1986, page 92
School Library Journal, January 1986, page 70

Other books by the author:
Alice in Rapture, Sort Of, 1989
Bodies in the Besseldorf Hotel, 1986
The Solomon System, 1983
Eddie, Incorporated, 1980

Other books you might like:
Mildred Ames, *Cassandra-Jamie*, 1985
    Once she decides to arrange her father's marriage to the English teacher she adores, Jamie begins to discover people are not always as they seem to be
Marion Dane Bauer, *Like Mother, Like Daughter*, 1985
    Leslie has trouble relating to her mother and turns to her new journalism advisor at school, until a crisis puts a different perspective on things.
Lynn Hall, *The Giver*, 1987
    A growing attachment between Mary McNeal and her homeroom teacher tests her character and proves her maturity.
Stanley Kiesel, *Skinny Malinky Leads the War for Kindness*, 1984
    Skinny Malinky attempts to foil Mr. Foreclosure's dastardly plan and the kids and the teachers continue their war but with different tactics.
Colleen O'Shaughnessy McKenna, *Fourth Grade Is a Jinx*, 1989
    When fourth grader Collette sees her own mother take over the job of teaching her class, life becomes more chaotic and embarrassing than she can stand

---

1311

Phyllis Reynolds Naylor

Alice in Rapture, Sort Of (New York: Collier, 1989)

Age range: Grades 6-8

Subject(s): Sex Roles; Single Parent Families; Family Life

Major character(s): Alice, 7th Grader; Patrick, 7th Grader

Time period(s): 1980s

Locale(s): United States

What the book is about: Alice works at growing up in the summer between sixth and seventh grades. She is so taken with her first crush that her dad labels it "the summer of the first boyfriend." Alice often misses her dead mother, but learns that following her own interests usually takes her in the right direction. Sequel to *Agony of Alice*.

Where it's reviewed:
Booklist, March 1, 1989, page 1194
Horn Book, May/June, 1989, page 372

Other books by the author:
Bernie and the Besseldorf Ghost, 1990
The Agony of Alice, 1985
The Dark of the Tunnel, 1985
All Because I'm Older, 1981

Other books you might like:
Adele Geras, *The Tower Rose*, 1990

Living in a secluded girls' school where her foster mother is headmistress, Megan falls in love with the man her foster mother has chosen for herself.

Lynn Hall, *Fair Maiden*, 1990
Working at the Renaissance Fair, Jennifer finds her first love and an escape from family problems at home.

Robert Lipsyte, *Summer Rules*, 1992
A teenage boy has to deal with an unwanted summer camp job, his first love, and some crucial decisions.

Nava Semel, *Becoming Gershona*, 1990
Living in Tel-Aviv in 1958, Gershona experiences first love, learns a family secret, and crosses the line between childhood and adulthood.

Susan Wojciechowski, *And the Other Gold*, 1987
Dreading starting back to school, Patty becomes involved in many activities as she learns the importance of friendship and the thrill of first love.

| 1312 |

Phyllis Reynolds Naylor

Illustrator: Leslie Morrill

All Because I'm Older (New York: Atheneum, 1981)

Age range: Grades 2-3

Subject(s): Brothers and Sisters; Family Life; Humor

Major character(s): Peter, Child; John, Child; Stephanie, Child

Time period(s): 1980s

Locale(s): United States

What the book is about: No matter how well he behaves, eight year old John seems to get blamed when it is five year old Peter who causes all the trouble. John narrates this tale of a day at home and a shopping trip with dad, during which Peter gets him in trouble over their little sister, Stephanie, the grocery store, and everyplace else.

Where it's reviewed:
Children's Book Review Service, August 1981, page 124
Center for Children's Books Bulletin, October 1981, page 34
Kirkus Reviews, July 15, 1981, page 873

Other books by the author:
Josie's Troubles, 1992
The Boy with the Helium Head, 1982
How Lazy Can You Get?, 1979
Jennifer Jean, the Cross-Eyed Queen, 1967

Other books you might like:
Ronda Armitage, *Harry Hates Shopping!*, 1992
Mother Koala must get the upper hand when her two children Harry and Matilda quarrel during a shopping trip.
Linda Glaser, *Keep Your Socks On, Albert!*, 1992
Adventures of a young brother and sister who enjoy each other but can't resist teasing.
Robie H. Harris, *Rosie's Razzle Dazzle Deal*, 1982
Rosie constantly falls into trouble, but her brother always gets the blame.
Ellen Howard, *The Cellar*, 1992
When she is teased about not being big enough to do any important jobs on the farm, Faith proves that she is brave enough to go into the dark cellar.

Barbara Park, *Junie B. Jones and a Little Monkey Business*, 1993
Junie thinks that her new baby brother is really a monkey, and her report of this news creates excitement and trouble in her kindergarten class.

| 1313 |

Phyllis Reynolds Naylor

Beetles, Lightly Toasted (New York: Atheneum, 1987)

Age range: Grades 5-6

Subject(s): Animals/Insects; Cousins; Contests

Major character(s): Andy Moller, Child

Time period(s): 1980s

Locale(s): United States

What the book is about: In order to win a prize of $50 in an essay contest, fifth grader Andy Moller decides to create recipes using insects as the main ingredient. He tests his recipes on unsuspecting family and friends.

Where it's reviewed:
Kirkus Reviews, July 1, 1987, page 999
School Library Journal, October 1987, page 128

Other books by the author:
Bernie and the Besseldorf Ghost, 1990
The Year of the Gopher, 1987
The Keeper, 1986
Eddie, Incorporated, 1980

Other books you might like:
Deborah Gangloff, *Albert and Victoria*, 1989
Two best friends enjoy life in the walls of the Empire State Building until Victoria decides not to hibernate for the winter.
E.A. Hass, *Incognito Mosquito, Private Insective*, 1982
The mosquito detective tells of his adventures with Mickey Mantis, F. Flea Bailey, and the Warden of Sting Sting Prison.
E.A. Hass, *Incognito Mosquito Takes to the Air*, 1986
On a TV talk show, the famous insect detective solves a mystery on the air.
Stephen Manes, *Chocolate-Covered Ants*, 1990
Max and his little brother make a bet about eating chocolate covered ants.
Thomas Rockwell, *How to Eat Fried Worms*, 1973
Two boys set out to prove that worms can make a delicious meal.

| 1314 |

Phyllis Reynolds Naylor

Illustrator: Blanche Sims

Eddie, Incorporated (New York: Atheneum, 1980)

Age range: Grades 4-6

Subject(s): Employment; Success; Babysitters

Major character(s): Eddie Anselmino, Child, Babysitter; Mr. Clemmons, Inventor

Time period(s): 1980s

Locale(s): United States

What the book is about: Twelve year old Eddie lives in a family where everyone works and takes part in business, and he tries one thing after another to establish a business of his own. He finally hits on the idea of a baby-sitting agency and his business takes off with humor and hard work.

Where it's reviewed:
Horn Book, June 1980, page 302
Kirkus Reviews, July 1, 1980, page 838

Other books by the author:
Faces in the Water, 1981
Footprints at the Window, 1981
Shadows on the Wall, 1980
How Lazy Can You Get?, 1979

Other books you might like:
Paula Danziger, *Not for a Billion Gazillion Dollars*, 1992
　　Matthew needs money to buy a coveted computer program, and he learns the importance of money in his own business.
Brenda Guiberson, *Instant Soup*, 1991
　　Darlene would rather be at the mall during winter break, instead she has to baby-sit her four year old cousin.
Jay Litvin, *How to Be a Super Sitter*, 1991
　　Advice on getting jobs, keeping business going, and safe handling of babies and children.
Keith Robertson, *Henry Reed's Think Tank*, 1986
　　Henry and Midge become consultants for Grover's Corner and end up with a lot of trouble!
Jean Van Leeuwen, *Benjy in Business*, 1983
　　Benjy tries several schemes to earn money for a baseball glove.

1315

Phyllis Reynolds Naylor

Maudie in the Middle (New York: Atheneum, 1988)

Age range: Grades 5-6

Subject(s): Family Life

Major character(s): Maudie Simms, Child; Miss Richardson, Teacher

Time period(s): 1910s

Locale(s): Iowa

What the book is about: Maudie, the middle of seven children, finds it hard to get the attention of her family. When a crisis hits the family, she has a chance to be seen in a really positive light.

Where it's reviewed:
Kirkus Reviews, March 1, 1988, page 367
School Library Journal, May 1988, page 100

Other books by the author:
Alice in Rapture, Sort Of, 1989
The Agony of Alice, 1985
The Solomon System, 1983

Other books you might like:
Dina Anastasio, *A Question of Time*, 1978
　　A young girl's curiosity is aroused by four carved dolls resembling her great grandfather's family.
Heidi Chang, *Elaine, Mary Lewis, and the Frogs*, 1988
　　Chinese-American Elaine Chow feels like an outcast in a small Iowa town until she shares a science project and makes a new friend.

Lynn Hall, *Dagmar Schultz and the Green-Eyed Monster*, 1991
　　Jealous of a popular new student, Dagmar decides to get even, with humorous results.
Bonnie Pryor, *Vinegar Pancakes and Vanishing Cream*, 1987
　　Martin tries to find his place in a family of talented siblings.
Frances Wosmek, *Brown Bird Singing*, 1986
　　A Chippewa Indian girl is raised by a white family in a small Minnesota town.

1316

Phyllis Reynolds Naylor

Night Cry (New York: Atheneum, 1984)

Age range: Grades 5-6

Subject(s): Farm Life; Kidnapping

Major character(s): Ellen, Teenager

Time period(s): 1980s

Locale(s): Mississippi

What the book is about: Ellen is in charge of the Mississippi farm while her father travels. She is frightened of caring for the horse who threw and killed her brother, and she is uncomfortable with an elderly neighbor and the strangers her father hired to work the farm. When Ellen discovers that the strangers are kidnappers, she sets out to rescue their victim.

Where it's reviewed:
Horn Book, June 1984, page 331
School Library Journal, April 1984, page 126

Awards the book has won:
Edgar Allan Poe Award 1985

Other books by the author:
Alice in Rapture, Sort Of, 1989
Bodies in the Besseldorf Hotel, 1986
The Agony of Alice, 1985
The Solomon System, 1983

Other books you might like:
James Duffy, *Missing*, 1988
　　A ten year old who often runs away is kidnapped by a lonely and confused man who wants a child of his own.
Jeannette Eyerly, *The Seeing Summer*, 1981
　　Carey has just learned to adjust to a blind playmate when the blind child is kidnapped and Carey takes on the job of locating her.
Barbara Holland, *Prisoners at the Kitchen Table*, 1979
　　Two friends must make maximum use of their differing abilities to escape from kidnappers.
Kin Platt, *The Ghost of Hellsfire Street*, 1980
　　Steve, the only witness to a "maybe" kidnapping, collects clues to solve the mystery in his Long Island town.
Zilpha Keatley Snyder, *The Famous Stanley Kidnapping Case*, 1979
　　Kidnapped children advise their captors on running a better kidnapping and proper nutrition for children.

1317

Phyllis Reynolds Naylor

Illustrator: Walter Gaffney-Kessell

One of the Third Grade Thonkers (New York: Atheneum, 1988)

Age range: Grades 3-4

Subject(s): Accidents; Clubs; Courage

Major character(s): Jimmy Novak, Child; David, Cousin

Time period(s): 1980s

Locale(s): United States

What the book is about: Jimmy and his third grade pals form an elite macho club and plan to spend the summer creating a clubhouse in an old garage, but it takes a wreck on the Mississippi for them to learn what bravery is really about. When Jim's cousin David arrives, he is immediately branded as a scaredy cat. Both the boys are anxious about ailing parents and they learn to derive strength from each other.

Where it's reviewed:
Booklist, October 1, 1988, page 324
Book World (Washington Post), August 14, 1988, page 10
Kirkus Reviews, July 15, 1988, page 1062

Other books by the author:
Maudie in the Middle, 1988
Beetles, Lightly Toasted, 1986
The Agony of Alice, 1985
Eddie, Incorporated, 1980

Other books you might like:
Mary Jane Auch, *Angel and Me and the Bayside Bombers*, 1990
    Having been kicked off the third grade soccer team, Brian challenges them to a match against his own team, which he and his cousin, Angel, organize.
William Harry Harding, *Alvin's Famous No-Horse*, 1992
    With encouragement from a teacher and help from his classmates, Alvin struggles with his efforts to draw a horse for the third grade art show.
Dean Hughes, *Making the Team*, 1990
    Third grade rookies who make the Little League baseball team are not immediately accepted by the older players.
Grace Maccarone, *The Return of the Third Grade Ghosthunters*, 1989
    Something is haunting the third grade's class trip and its up to the third grade ghosthunters to find out what it is.
Candice Ransom, *Ladies and Jellybeans*, 1991
    As Wendy starts third grade in the late 1950s, she worries about cursive writing, show and tell, the Cold War and her father's new job.

1318

Phyllis Reynolds Naylor

Shiloh (New York: Atheneum, 1991)

Age range: Grades 3-6

Subject(s): Animals, Treatment of; Animals/Dogs

Major character(s): Marty Preston, Preteen; Shiloh, Dog (Beagle); Judd Travers, Hunter

Time period(s): 1990s

Locale(s): Friendly, West Virginia

What the book is about: Eleven year old Marty finds a young Beagle near the Shiloh schoolhouse and discovers the

dog's owner mistreats him, as well as all his other animals. Marty tries to hide the dog, even though he knows it does not belong to him. In addition to being a wonderful "dog story," this novel shows the reader Marty's struggle to figure out the "right thing" to do, and his responsibility to demand justice.

Where it's reviewed:
Kirkus Reviews, September 1, 1991, page 1163
School Library Journal, September 1991, page 258
Publishers Weekly, July 12, 1991, page 66

Awards the book has won:
Newbery Medal 1992

Other books by the author:
The Boys Start the War, 1993
Beetles, Lightly Toasted, 1987
The Agony of Alice, 1985
The Dark of the Tunnel, 1985

Other books you might like:
Bianca Bradbury, *Dogs and More Dogs*, 1968
    When a young boy takes in an abandoned mongrel, and finally prevails upon his family to keep the dog to save it from being put to sleep or mistreated,
Lynn Hall, *The Mystery of the Lost and Found Hound*, 1979
    A girl and her brother's efforts at tracing the owner of a lost Beagle leads them to involvement with dog thieves.
Syd Hoff, *The Man Who Loved Animals*, 1982
    A biography of the founder of the American Society for the Prevention of Cruelty to Animals
Edith Thacher Hurd, *The Black Dog Who Went into the Woods*, 1980
    A family has to deal with the grief surrounding the loss of their beloved pet dog.
Maurice Sendak, *Higglety, Pigglety Pop! or There Must Be More to Life*, 1967
    A Sealyham terrier has everything a dog could want at home, but leaves in search of adventure.

1319

Phyllis Reynolds Naylor

Illustrator: Joe Burleson

Witch Weed (New York: Delacorte, 1991)

Age range: Grades 4-6

Subject(s): Supernatural; Witches and Witchcraft

Major character(s): Lynn Morley, Preteen; Marjorie Beasley, Preteen; Mrs. Tuggle, Witch

Time period(s): 1990s

Locale(s): Indiana

What the book is about: A series of mysterious events and the strange behavior of a group of their schoolmates convinces Lynn and her best friend, Mouse, that the destructive power of a witch recently killed in a fire is still very much alive.

Where it's reviewed:
Booklist, September 15, 1991, page 152
Kirkus Reviews, August 1, 1991, page 1014
Publisher's Weekly, June 21, 1991, page 65

Other books by the author:
The Witch Returns, 1992
The Witch Herself, 1978

Witch's Sister, 1975

Other books you might like:
John Bellairs, *The Vengence of the Witch-Finder*, 1993
 While visiting a distant cousin in the English countryside, Lewis accidentally unleashes demonic forces and summons the ghost of an evil wizard.
Peter Dickinson, *Heartsease*, 1986
 At a future time when anyone knowledgeable about machines is punished as a witch, four children aid in the escape of a ''witch'' left for dead.
Monica Furlong, *Juniper*, 1991
 While apprenticed to the witch woman, Juniper, a young girl struggles to save her family from the evil machinations of her power-hungry aunt Meroot.
Kate Gilmore, *Enter Three Witches*, 1990
 Bren is fearful of having the girl of his dreams meet his family of witches, but realizes that a meeting has already taken place.
Jane Little, *Sneaker Hill*, 1967
 Aunt Miranda, studying for her certificate in witchcraft, manages to stir up a troublesome brew.

1320

Phyllis Reynolds Naylor

Illustrator: Gail Owens

Witch's Sister (New York: Atheneum, 1975)

Age range: Grades 4-6

Subject(s): Witches and Witchcraft

Major character(s): Judith Morley, Preteen; Mrs. Tuggle, Neighbor (mentor); Lynn Morley, Teenager

Time period(s): 1970s

Locale(s): Cowden's Creek, Indiana

What the book is about: Lynn is convinced that her older sister, Judith, is becoming a witch. The strange, elderly neighbor is teaching Judith about the occult, Lynn is just sure! She must rescue Judith from Mrs. Tuggle's grasp before it is too late.

Where it's reviewed:
Booklist, April 1, 1975, page 818
Hornbook, August 1975, page 383
Kirkus, February 1, 1975, page 122

Other books by the author:
Alice in April, 1993
The Witch Returns, 1992
The Witch Herself, 1978
Witch Water, 1977

Other books you might like:
Eileen Dunlop, *The Valley of Deer*, 1989
 Finding an old family Bible in her house leads Anne on a quest to solve the mystery surrounding the death in 1726 of a woman accused of witchcraft.
Diana Wynne Jones, *Witch Week*, 1982
 When a teacher at a boarding school finds a note accusing someone in his class of witchcraft, magical things happen and an Inquisitor is summoned.
Lee Kingman, *Escape From the Evil Prophecy*, 1973
 A brother and sister in 11th century Iceland try to escape the prophecy of a sorceress.
Evelyn White Minshull, *The Dune Witch*, 1972

Newly arrived in the Massachusetts colony, Priss is accused of witchcraft due to her friendship with a strange girl who appears on the dunes.
Carol Beach York, *I Will Make You Disappear*, 1974
 Two young girls spending a vacation with their family in a gloomy house begin to play at witchcraft.

1321

Theresa Nelson

And One for All (New York: Orchard, 1989)

Age range: Grades 6-10

Subject(s): Friendship; Vietnam War

Major character(s): Geraldine, Preteen; Sam, Activist

Time period(s): 1960s

Locale(s): New York (upstate New York)

What the book is about: Geraldine's older brother, Wing, enlists in the Marines, while his best friend, Sam, is an anti-war activist. When Wing is killed at Khe Sanh, Geraldine goes to Washington to confront and blame Sam, who is in the middle of a protest march. Well drawn characters highlight the effect of the Vietnam War on family and friends.

Where it's reviewed:
Booklist, March 15, 1989, page 1302
Horn Book, March/April 1989, page 218

Other books by the author:
The Beggar's Ride, 1992
Devil Storm, 1987
The 25Miralce, 1986

Other books you might like:
Sherry Garland, *Song of the Buffalo Boy*, 1992
 determined to avoid an arrangede marriage, Loi runs away with the boy she loves and in hopes of going to the US to find her American father.
Morse Hamilton, *Effie's House*, 1990
 A girl with a terrible secret runs away from home seeking counsel from the father she will not believe was killed in Vietnam.
Sollace Hotze, *Acquainted with the Night*, 1992
 Molly and her cousin become very close, during the summer, as she helps him deal with his father's suicide and his experiences in the Vietnam War.
Adrienne Jones, *Long Time Passing: A Novel*, 1990
 While his father is serving in Vietnam, Joans falls in love with a flower child and begins to question his own attitude towards the Vietnam War.
Marc Talbert, *The Purple Heart*, 1992
 When his wounded father comes home from Vietnam, Luke finds it difficult adjusting to the emotionally shaken man who's unlike the hero of his dreams.

1322

Theresa Nelson

The Twenty-Five Cent Miracle (New York: Bradbury, 1986)

Age range: Grades 5-7

Subject(s): Fathers and Daughters

Major character(s): Elvira Trumbull, Preteen; Henry "Hank" Trumbull, Parent (Elvira's father)

Time period(s): 1980s

Locale(s): Calder, Texas

What the book is about: Hank Trumbull, raising his eleven year old daughter Elvira alone, thinks his sister, Darla, could do a better job. He would know what to do with a boy, but quiet, thoughtful Elvira perplexes him. Elvira wants to stay with her dad, so she hatches a plan to introduce him to Miss Ivy, the librarian, who has two sons who need a father. Wise and warm-hearted story.

Where it's reviewed:
Booklist, April 15, 1986, page 1226
Children's Book Review Service, Spring 1986, page 136
Center for Children's Books Bulletin, June 1986, page 192

Other books by the author:
The Beggar's Ride, 1992
And One for All, 1989
Devil Storm, 1987

Other books you might like:
Carole S. Adler, *If You Need Me*, 1988
    Lyn is increasingly worried as tension grows between her stepmother and her father and begins to be attracted to her friend's mother.
Mary Blount Christian, *Growin' Pains*, 1985
    Ginny Ruth feels stifled in her small, dying Texas town, despite her special relationship with physically impaired Mr. Billy.
Amy Hest, *Pete and Lily*, 1986
    When Pete's widowed mother starts dating Lily's divorced father, the two girls decide they need to control the situation.
Mary Reeves Mahoney, *The Hurry-Up Summer*, 1987
    Living with her widowed father in their small town, Letty resents his new girlfriend and tries to grow up in a hurry to stop him from remarrying.
Willo Davis Roberts, *Jo and the Bandit*, 1992
    En route to stay with her uncle in Texas in the late 1860s, Jo experiences a stagecoach robbery and becomes involved with a reluctant young outlaw.

| 1323 |

Edith Nesbit

Five Children and It (New York: Dell, 1957)

Age range: Grades 4-6

Subject(s): Fairy Tale; Fantasy; Magic

Major character(s): Anthea "Panther", Child; Cyril, Child; Jane, Child

Time period(s): Indeterminate Past

Locale(s): Camden Town, England

What the book is about: Five children discover a furry creature with the ability to grant wishes when they are playing in a gravel pit. They are led into magical adventures. They hope to dig a hole to Australia to see if the people walk upside down.

Where it's reviewed:
Atlantic Monthly, December 1969, page 151

New York Review of Books, October 25, 1984, page 19

Other books by the author:
Book of Dragons, 1986
The House of Arden, 1986
The Phoenix and the Carpet, 1986
The Story of the Amulet, 1986

Other books you might like:
Katharine Mary Briggs, *Hobberdy Dick*, 1955
    A hobgoblin is charged with the protection of an unloving Puritan family who come to live at an English manor in 1652.
Mary Calhoun, *Ownself*, 1975
    A girl tries to resolve the increasing conflict between her own predilection for magic and fairies and her father's strict Methodism.
James Clavell, *James Clavell's Thrump-o-Moto: A Fantasy*, 1986
    When a wizard whisks Patricia and her crutches from her home, she encounters his family, an evil ghoul, and the hope of magic cure for her handicap.
M.S. Craig, *Happles and Cinnamunger*, 1981
    When the Taggart family's housekeeper wins a trip around the world, her replacement brings a troop of fairies into the house.
Kathleen Thompson, *Out of the Bug Jar*, 1981
    Tom Jenkins relates how he caught a tooth fairy in his bug jar two years earlier and Marvin's reluctance to be released from captivity.

| 1324 |

Edith Nesbit

The Railway Children (New York: Puffin/Penguin, 1988)

Age range: Grades 3-7

Subject(s): Brothers and Sisters; Prisoners and Prisons; Trains

Major character(s): Roberta, Preteen; Peter, Preteen; Phyllis, Child

Time period(s): Indeterminate Past

Locale(s): London, England

What the book is about: Bobbie, Peter, and Phyllis try to solve the mystery of their father's disappearance. Mother only tells them something has happened and Father will be away, and she will be spending a lot of time away from home. The railroad plays a large part in their life as they go about figuring out what happened. They make friends with Perks the Porter and the stationmaster. An old fashioned story, originally published in 1906, still popular with middle readers.

Other books by the author:
The Phoenix and the Carpet, 1904
Story of the Treasure Seekers, 1899
Five Children and It, 1905

Other books you might like:
Vivien Alcock, *A Kind of Thief*, 1991
    When her father is arrested and put in prison, Elinor finds that she has to face many unpleasant truths about their way of life.
Lyll Becerre de Jenkins, *The Honorable Prison*, 1988
    Because of the stand of her journalist father against the military ruler of their Latin American country, Marta and family become government prisoners.

Walter Dean Myers, *Somewhere in the Darkness*, 1992
A teenage boy accompanies his father, who has recently escaped from prison, on a trip that turns out to be a painful time of discovery for them both.
Ethelyn M. Parkinson, *Higgins of the Railroad Museum*, 1970
A teen and his dog, Higgins, spend the summer working at a railroad museum where they find plenty of action.
Alida E. Young, *Land of the Iron Dragon*, 1978
A Chinese boy is left without a family in the United States and joins the crews building the transcontinental railroad in the 1860s.

1325

John Neufeld

Illustrator: Loren Dunlap

Edgar Allan (New York: S.G. Phillips, 1968)

Age range: Grades 4-6

Subject(s): Prejudice; Adoption; African Americans

Major character(s): Edgar Allan, Child, Adoptee; Reverend Fickett, Religious; Mary Nell Fickett, Teenager

Time period(s): 1960s

Locale(s): California

What the book is about: A white minister and his family adopt a three year old black boy and the all-white California community where they live reacts very negatively. A cross is burned on their lawn, the minister is threatened with the loss of his church, and Mary Nell, the Fickett's teenage daughter threatens to leave home.

Where it's reviewed:
Horn Book, April 1969, page 172
Library Journal, December 15, 1968, page 4725

Other books by the author:
Sharelle, 1983
For All the Wrong Reasons, 1973
Lisa, Bright and Dark, 1969

Other books you might like:
Julia First, *I, Rebekah, Take You, the Lawrences*, 1981
Even after she has been adopted, twelve year old Rebekah wonders if she wouldn't be better off back at the orphanage with her friends.
Miska Miles, *Aaron's Door*, 1977
Unable to adjust to the idea of being adopted, Aaron locks his door against the world.
Mary Jane Miller, *Me and My Name*, 1990
Erin faces decisions about adoption by her stepfather and a game of truth or dare at a slumber party.
Walter Dean Myers, *Mop, Moondance, and the Nagasaki Knights*, 1992
After TJ and his brother are adopted, they face an international baseball tournament and try to help a homeless teammate.
Gunilla Brodde Norris, *The Good Morrow*, 1969
A black girl is convinced that the loud, aggressive girl who shadows her at camp is a racist.

1326

Emily Cheney Neville

The 17th Street Gang (New York: Harper, 1966)

Age range: Grades 5-7

Subject(s): Friendship

Major character(s): Clement Charles ''CC'' Vanderpane, Preteen; Louise DeWitt, Preteen; Hollis Rourke, Preteen

Time period(s): 1960s

Locale(s): New York, New York

What the book is about: A group of preteens hang out together in their 17th Street neighborhood, and decide what to do about Hollis, the ''new kid on the block,'' who is not their type. Led by Clement Charles ''CC'' Vanderpane, the gang makes a plan to take care of Hollis. But tragedy strikes, and nothing goes according to plan when Hollis and Minnow fall through a manhole.

Where it's reviewed:
Booklist, November 1, 1966, page 326
Hornbook, October 1966, page 570
Kirkus Reviews, September 15, 1966, page 977

Other books by the author:
The China Year, 1991
Garden of Broken Glass, 1975
Traveler From a Small Kingdom, 1968
It's Like This, Cat, 1963

Other books you might like:
Beth Cruise, *Class Trip Chaos*, 1992
Excitement and romance abound when the Bayside High gang arrives in New York City for their senior class trip.
Ann M. Martin, *Jessi and the Jewel Thieves*, 1993
Jessi can't wait to get to New York City to see her friend Quint dance in his first big ballet.
Anne Mazer, *Moose Street*, 1992
Lena Rosen, the only Jewish child on Moose Street, sees life as an insider and as an outsider.
Sylvia Peck, *Kelsey's Raven*, 1992
Kelsey's secure life is changed when she finds a raven in her chimney, her friendship with her best friend fractures and her mother falls in love.
Barbara Wersba, *Just Be Gorgeous: A Novel*, 1988
Feeling misunderstood by her parents, a teen realizes she is someone special through her friendship with a homeless street performer.

1327

Clare Turlay Newberry, Author/Illustrator

Marshmallow (New York: Harper, 1942)

Age range: Grades 2-4

Subject(s): Animals/Cats; Friendship; Animals/Rabbits

Major character(s): Oliver, Cat; Marshmallow, Rabbit; Miss Tilly, Animal Lover

Time period(s): Indeterminate

Locale(s): United States

What the book is about: A cat who is used to being the center of attention learns to share his home with a rabbit. One day when Miss Tilly is gone, Oliver opens the door separating him from the rabbit and discovers it is pleasant to have someone to play and nap with.

Awards the book has won:
Caldecott Honor Book 1943

Other books by the author:
Ice Cream for Two, 1953
April's Kittens, 1940
Barkis, 1938
Mittens, 1936

Other books you might like:
Robin Michal Koontz, *Chicago and the Cat*, 1993
A pushy cat takes over the home of Chicago, the rabbit, but then the two become friends.
John E. McCormack, *Rabbit Travels*, 1984
A very fast rabbit and a very slow hare, the best of friends, ride in a sailwagon, put up only so long with a know-it-all frog, and build a riverboat.
Susan Pearson, *Molly Moves Out*, 1979
Molly is so upset by the things her brothers and sisters do, she finally moves into a house of her own.
Erica Silverman, *Warm in Winter*, 1989
A cozy visit with her friend, Rabbit, a soft flannel nightie and hot carrot soup convinces a skeptical Badger that you really can be warm in winter.

1328

Robert Newman

The Case of the Baker Street Irregular: A Sherlock Holmes Story (New York: Atheneum, 1984)

Age range: Grades 4-6

Subject(s): Kidnapping; Mystery and Detective Stories

Major character(s): Andrew Craigie, Orphan; Herbert Dennison, Guardian; Screamer, Streetperson

Time period(s): 19th century

Locale(s): London, England

What the book is about: After losing his parents, Andrew is now in the care of the mysterious Mr. Dennison, who brings Andrew to London with very little explanation. When Mr. Dennison is kidnapped, Andrew is very alone, and to make it worse, the cab driver last seen with Mr. Dennison is now following Andrew. Andrew meets Screamer, a street urchin connected with the Baker Street Irregulars, and Andrew gets to meet the great Sherlock Holmes. Holmes is able to find out what happened to Mr. Dennison, as well as provide Andrew with other information even more important to him.

Where it's reviewed:
Hornbook, August 1978, page 397
Kirkus Reviews, February 15, 1978, page 184
School Library Journal, May 1978, page 85

Other books by the author:
The Case of the Frightened Friend, 1984
The Case of the Threatened King, 1982
The Case of the Somerville Secret, 1981
The Case of the Vanishing Corpse, 1980

Other books you might like:
Jennifer Austin, *Ticket to Danger*, 1990

When Cassie arrives at the airport in London, she discovers that Alexandra has been kidnapped, and even Scotland Yard has no clue where she is.
Eve Bunting, *Coffin on a Case*, 1992
Henry Coffin, son of a private investigator, helps a high school girl in her dangerous attempts to find her kidnapped mother.
Dorothy Crayder, *She and the Dubious Three*, 1974
Maggie discovers that adventure can lead to near disaster as well as to opportunity.
Carolyn Keene, *Mystery of Crocodile Island*, 1978
A detective's attempts to uncover a group of poachers on Crocodile Island involves her with kidnapping, reptiles, enemy boats and a sinsister racket.
Thomas McKean, *Moroccan Mystery*, 1986
Three children visiting Morocco become involved in dangerous adventures with a ring of kidnappers.

1329

Robert Newman

The Case of the Murdered Players (New York: Atheneum, 1985)

Age range: Grades 3-7

Subject(s): Mystery and Detective Stories

Major character(s): Andrew Tillett, Preteen; Peter Wyatt, Police Officer (Scotland Yard); Verna Tillett, Actress, Parent (Andrew's Mother)

Time period(s): 1890s

Locale(s): London, England

What the book is about: Two young people help a Scotland Yard inspector solve a mystery involving a murdered actress. Andrew Tillett gets a call from his friend, Inspector Wyatt at Scotland Yard. Two actresses have been murdered in the same way as three unsolved murders from ten years before, and Andrew's mother, the actress Verna Tillett, is clearly in danger. Can Andrew and his friend, Sara, and Scotland Yard, find the murderer before another victim is claimed?

Where it's reviewed:
Booklist, September 1, 1985, page 67
School Library Journal, October 1985, page 185

Other books by the author:
The Case of the Frightened Friend, 1984
The Case of the Etruscan Treasure, 1983
Night Spell, 1977
The Boy Who Could Fly, 1967

Other books you might like:
Hope Campbell, *Looking for Hamlet: A Haunting at Deep Lake*, 1987
While vacationing in the Adirondacks, a young actress uncovers a mystery surrounding the death of a girl who was to play Ophelia in Hamlet.
James Howe, *Stage Fright: A Sebastian Barth Mystery*, 1986
Young Sebastian Barth investigates the tangle of warnings and ominous accidents surrounding a famous actress visiting his home town.
Carolyn Keene, *The Mysterious Image*, 1984
Nancy Drew searches for a kidnapped actress and to clear one of her father's clients, a photographer, accused of stealing ideas for his images.

E.L. Konigsburg, *Up From Jerico Tel*, 1986
The spirit of actress Tallulah Bankhead turns two children invisible and sends them out to search for a missing necklace.
Alfred Slote, *The Clone Catcher*, 1982
In the 21st century, Arthur Dunn is summoned to track down a runaway clone urgently needed to provide organ transplants for her parent, an actress.

1330

Suzanne Newton

An End to Perfect (New York: Viking, 1984)

Age range: Grades 6-8

Subject(s): Child Abuse; Friendship

Major character(s): Arden Gifford, Preteen; Hill Gifford, Teenager; Dorothy JoAnna "DorJo" Huggins, Friend

Time period(s): 1970s

Locale(s): Haverlee, North Carolina; Grierson, North Carolina

What the book is about: Arden's seemingly perfect life changes when her older brother, Hill, decides to leave home and her best friend has increasingly serious family problems.

Where it's reviewed:
Booklist, December 1, 1984, page 527
Hornbook, January 1985, page 61
Kirkus Reviews, November 1, 1984, page J97

Other books by the author:
Where Are You When I Need You?, 1991
A Place Between, 1986
I Will Call It Georgie's Blues, 1983
C/O Arnold's Corners, 1974

Other books you might like:
Bruce Brooks, *The Moves Make the Man: A Novel*, 1984
A black boy and an emotionally troubled white boy in North Carolina form a precarious friendship.
Kristi Holl, *Perfect or Not, Here I Come*, 1986
Life may not be fair, but Tara, seeking justice, finds out how to make the best of things.
Gloria Houston, *Littlejim*, 1990
Littlejim, a bookish boy living in a rural North Carolina community hopes to win a newspaper essay contest and thus the respect of his stern father.
Belinda Hurmence, *Tough Tiffany*, 1980
Tiffany, youngest member of a poor family in rural North Carolina, takes her first steps toward adulthood.
Mary Pope Osborne, *Best Wishes, Joe Brady*, 1984
Sunny Dickens is happy with her life in Summerville, North Carolina, until she falls for a famous soap-opera star named Joe Brady who's come to town.

1331

Jenny Nimmo

The Snow Spider (New York: Dutton, 1987)

Age range: Grades 4-7

Subject(s): Brothers and Sisters; Magic

Major character(s): Gwyn, Magician, Child (10 years old); Eirlyo, Spirit; Bethan, Child (Gwyn's missing sister)

Time period(s): Indeterminate Past

Locale(s): Wales

What the book is about: Gwyn discovers he has magical powers, and he is determined to use them to find out what happened to his sister and try to heal the breach that has existed between him and his father ever since Bethan's disappearance. A silvery spider's web holds images for him: a pale silvery girl who seems to be the reincarnation of his sister.

Where it's reviewed:
Horn Book, September/October 1987, page 613
School Library Journal, August 1987, page 87

Other books by the author:
Emlyn's Moon, 1987
Orchard of the Crescent Moon, 1987

Other books you might like:
Jane Louise Curry, *The Magical Cupboard*, 1976
Felicity's existence in a horrible 18th century orphanage is changed when the owner, greedy Parson Grout, steals what he believes is a magic cupboard.
Dick King-Smith, *The Queen's Nose*, 1983
Ten year old Harmony loves animals but is not allowed to keep a pet. When she is given a magic coin with seven wishes, what will she choose?
Andre Norton, *Dragon Magic*, 1972
Four boys of various ethnic origins find a puzzle whose magic power takes each of them back to an important time in their own ethnic history.
Ellen Pugh, *More Tales From the Welsh Hills*, 1971
Stories of magic and mystery taken from Welsh folklore.
Jane Yolen, *The Stone Silenus*, 1984
A year after her father was found dead in a swimming pool, a strange faun-boy appears to Melissa, and seems to possess part of her father's spirit.

1332

Joan Lowery Nixon

Danger in Dinosaur Valley (New York: Putnam, 1978)

Age range: Grades 2-3

Subject(s): Dinosaurs; Sports/Baseball

Major character(s): Diplodocus, Dinosaur; Tyrannosaurus Rex, Dinosaur

Time period(s): Indeterminate Past

Locale(s): Earth

What the book is about: Dip and his family have to outwit Tyrannosaurus Rex. In order to fight the terrible carnivores, they have to learn from time travelers, a new skill. Dip and his parents practice pitching rocks held in their mouths, just like the Giants.

Where it's reviewed:
Kirkus Reviews, April 15, 1978, page 435
School Library Journal, May 1978, page 81

Other books by the author:
Bigfoot Makes a Movie, 1979
The New Year's Mystery, 1979
The Son Who Came Home Again, 1977

Other books you might like:
Scott Corbett, *The Foolish Dinosaur Fiasco*, 1978
　　Nick and his dog go down Dr. Merlin's magic tunnel and find themselves dealing with dinosaurs.
Gerald Malcolm Durrell, *The Fantastic Dinosaur Adventure*, 1989
　　Three children travel back through time in their great-uncle's time machine, intending to rescue baby dinosaurs from evil villains.
David Lee Miller, *Baby*, 1985
　　Two Americans discover a brontosaurus family in the African jungle and try to protect it from evil men who are after the unusual find.
Kin Platt, *Darwin and the Great Beasts*, 1992
　　Visiting LaBrea Tar Pits, a boy named Darwin imagines life among the dinosaurs, sabertooth tigers and other huge beasts.
Hudson Talbott, *We're Back: A Dinosaur Story*, 1987
　　Creatures from prehistoric times travel to the 20th century and create excitement at the Museum of Natural History in New York.

1333

Joan Lowery Nixon

A Family Apart (New York: Bantam, 1987)

Age range: Grades 5-6

Series: Orphan Train Quartet

Subject(s): Foster Homes; Underground Railroad

Major character(s): Frances Kelly, Child; Petey Kelly, Child

Time period(s): 1850s (1856)

Locale(s): Kansas

What the book is about: The six Kelly children board the Orphan Train in 1856 leaving their widowed mother behind in New York City. Frances, the eldest, masquerades as a boy to be able to stay with Petey as they are adopted by a family in the Kansas Territory.

Where it's reviewed:
Booklist, September 15, 1987, page 151
Publisher's Weekly, October 9, 1987, page 89

Other books by the author:
A Place to Belong, 1989 (Orphan Train Quartet)
Caught in the Act, 1988 (Orphan Train Quartet)
In the Face of Danger, 1988 (Orphan Train Quartet)

Other books you might like:
Judie Angell, *Dear Lola: Or, How to Build Your Own Family*, 1980
　　A group of children from an orphanage survive on their own, with the help of the oldest who supports them by writing an advice column for a newspaper.
Judie Angell, *Home Is to Share.and Share.and Share*, 1984
　　The capacity of the Munchmore kids to care for stray animals is pushed to the limits when a local animal shelter closes.
Lynn Hall, *Mrs. Portree's Pony*, 1986
　　Thirteen year old Addie thinks a pony is the answer to the lack of security and love in her lonely life.
Katherine Paterson, *The Great Gilly Hopkins*, 1978

Eleven year old Gilly has been from one foster home to another when Maime loves her enough to break through her anger.
Celia Strang, *Foster Mary*, 1979
　　Mary and Alonzo, migrant apple pickers, struggle to make a permanent home for themselves and their four foster children.

1334

Joan Lowery Nixon

Illustrator: Andrew Glass

The Gift (New York: Macmillan, 1983)

Age range: Grades 4-6

Subject(s): Grandparents; Elves

Major character(s): Brian, Child

Time period(s): Indeterminate Past

Locale(s): Ireland

What the book is about: Brian's Irish great-grandfather tells him stories of leprechauns, pookas and banshees, while Brian is visiting the family farm. Brian doesn't know whether to believe the tales or not. The old man obviously does, but the rest of the family says they're nonsense. Then one night, Brian sees the magical creatures for himself.

Where it's reviewed:
Booklist, April 1, 1983, page 1036
Kirkus Reviews, May 1, 1983, page 524
School Library Journal, May 1983, page 74

Other books by the author:
A Family Apart, 1987
The House on Hackman's Hill, 1986
Maggie, Too, 1985
A Deadly Game of Magic, 1983

Other books you might like:
Daniel Curley, *Billy Beg and the Bull*, 1978
　　In Ireland in the days of the heroes, the son of a king and his bull set out to find a new life away from the boy's stepmother.
Kathleen Green, *Leprechaun Tales*, 1968
　　Eleven stories about Ireland's leprechauns, banshees, the Pooka and others, including one about a tailor who made a jacket out of magic cloth.
Dick King-Smith, *Paddy's Pot of Gold*, 1990
　　Brigid enjoys making friends with Paddy the leprechaun and wonders if he has a pot of gold.
Clair Warner Livesay, *At the Butt End of the Rainbow*, 1970
　　Twelve tales based on Irish folk traditions and characters including fairies, leprechauns, and legendary heroes.
Elizabeth Shub, *Seeing Is Believing*, 1979
　　Two stories about Tom and the piskies, The Leprechaun's Trick and Pisky Mischief.

1335

Joan Lowery Nixon

Haunted Island (New York: Scholastic, 1987)

Age range: Grades 5-7

Subject(s): Ghosts; Islands

Major character(s): Chris Holt, Teenager; Amy Holt, Preteen; Elizabeth Holt, Parent

Time period(s): 1980s

Locale(s): Mississippi River

What the book is about: Chris and Amy's aunt Jenny has purchased the Island View Inn, and the island in the Mississippi River for which it is named, thinking the lovely island will attract guests to the inn. When a local carpenter tells her that the island is owned by the ghosts Joshua and Shadow, Chris and Amy are on their way to solving a two hundred year old mystery and fighting for their lives.

Where it's reviewed:
Booklist, March 15, 1987, page 1132
Kliatt, Spring 1987, page 24
School Library Journal, May 1987, page 102

Other books by the author:
Caught in the Act, 1988
And Maggie Makes Three, 1986
Casey and the Great Idea, 1980
Adventures of the Red Tape Gang, 1974

Other books you might like:
John Bellairs, *The Spell of the Sorcerer's Skull*, 1984
    When Johnny takes a tiny skull from a haunted dollhouse, demonic forces are released, capturing Professor Childermass and leading Johnny on a chase.
Eilis Dillon, *The Island of Ghosts*, 1989
    Before leaving for school in Galway, Dara and Bran visit their tutor who has moved to a haunted island and has plans to keep the boys there forever.
Sid Fleischman, *The Midnight Horse*, 1990
    Touch enlists the help of the Great Chaffalo, a ghostly magician, to thwart his great-uncle's plans to put Touch into the orphan house.
Stephen Roos, *My Favorite Ghost*, 1988
    The legend of a ghost on the island inspires money-hungry Derek to dupe his friends into paying admission to a supposedly haunted house.
Catherine Sefton, *In a Blue Velvet Dress*, 1973
    With the help of a ghost in a blue velvet dress, bookworm Jane survives the disaster of finding herself on vacation without a single book.

1336

Joan Lowery Nixon

High Trail to Danger (New York: Bantam, 1991)

Age range: Grades 4-6

Subject(s): Mystery and Detective Stories; American West

Major character(s): Sarah Lindley, Teenager

Time period(s): 1970s

Locale(s): Chicago, Illinois; Leadville, Colorado

What the book is about: After her mother's death, Sarah Lindley leaves Chicago for the wild west of the 1970s to find her father. She copes with mystery and murder in Leadville, Colorado, and learns what it means to take care of herself in a lawless town.

Where it's reviewed:
Kirkus Reviews, June 5, 1991, page 791

School Library Journal, July 1, 1991, page 88

Other books by the author:
A Deadly Promise, 1992 (Sequel to High Trail to Danger)
A Candidate for Murder, 1991
Whispers From the Dead, 1989
A Deadly Game of Magic, 1983

Other books you might like:
Patricia Beatty, *Melinda Takes a Hand*, 1983
    Thirteen year old Melinda is stranded in the Colorado town of Goldendale in the year 1893.
Tatyana Bylinsky, *Before the Wildflowers Bloom*, 1989
    Carm and her family lose Papa in an accident and must learn to cope with life in a coal mining town in Colorado.
Bruce Clements, *The Face of Abraham Candle*, 1969
    Abraham Candle joins two men to search for Indian artifacts in Mesa Verde in 1893.
Val Valentine, *The Great Durango and Silverton Train Robbery*, 1984
    Novelette in the "dime novel" tradition of times in the wild west of outlaws and train robbers.
David Wood, *Phantom Killer of the Flying M*, 1971
    David and his sister search southwestern Colorado for the mysterious animal that is killing the rancher's livestock.

1337

Joan Lowery Nixon

The House on Hackman's Hill (New York: Scholastic, 1986)

Age range: Grades 4-6

Subject(s): Haunted Houses; Mummies

Major character(s): Jeff, Child; Debbie, Child (Jeff's cousin); Mr. Karsten, Neighbor

Time period(s): 1980s

Locale(s): United States

What the book is about: Jeff and Debbie decide to investigate the old haunted house and find themselves trapped overnight in a blizzard with a mummy that lives.

Where it's reviewed:
Booklist, June 15, 1986, page 1543

Other books by the author:
A Candidate for Murder, 1991
The Gift, 1983
The Seance, 1980
The Kidnapping of Christina Lattimore, 1979

Other books you might like:
Rick Brightfield, *The Gruesome Guests*, 1990
    Four scary stories involving a spooky lighthouse, a phantom mask, a haunted house and a mysterious photograph.
Linda Gondosch, *Who's Afraid of Haggety House?*, 1987
    Kelly's attempt to sell Christmas cards to the lady in the haunted house begins a mutually enjoyable friendship.
Peggy Parish, *Haunted House*, 1971
    Three children are uneasy when they learn their parents have bought a supposedly haunted house.
Judith St. George, *Haunted*, 1980
    Alex, is haunted by a force leading him to discover and one trying to kill him when he is hired to house-sit the scene of a murder-suicide.

Cynthia Voigt, *The Vandemark Mummy*, 1991
Phineas and Althea try to find out why a collection of ancient Egyptian artifacts, that their father is responsible for, is the target of thieves.

| 1338 |

Joan Lowery Nixon

The Kidnapping of Christina Lattimore (New York: Harcourt, 1979)

Age range: Grades 5 and Up

Subject(s): Kidnapping

Major character(s): Christina Lattimore, Teenager, Captive; Cristabel Lattimore, Grandparent, Wealthy

Time period(s): 1970s

Locale(s): Houston, Texas

What the book is about: A teenage girl is kidnapped, but when freed, is accused of masterminding the scheme to extort money from her wealthy grandmother.

Where it's reviewed:
Horn Book, August 1979, page 423
School Library Journal, September 1979, page 160

Awards the book has won:
Edgar Allan Poe Award 1980

Other books by the author:
A Family Apart, 1987
Maggie, Too, 1985
A Deadly Game of Magic, 1983
The Gift, 1983

Other books you might like:
Lois Duncan, *The Third Eye*, 1984
Worried by her psychic powers, Karen overcomes her fears and helps the police locate missing children.
Peni R. Griffin, *A Dig in Time*, 1991
Spending the summer with their grandmother, Nan and her younger brother find objects in the yard and discover how to use them to travel back in time.
Norma Johnson, *The Potter's Wheel*, 1988
Laura learns many family secrets while attending her wealthy grandmother's birthday celebration in a Pennsylvania village.
Kathleen Kilgore, *The Ghost-Maker*, 1984
Because Lee suspects that his wealthy grandmother is being victimized by a spiritualist, he gets a job as an assistant to a friendly psychic.
Mary Francis Shura, *The Sunday Doll*, 1988
Emmy finds herself sheltered again from the family's problems when she is hastily sent away to Aunt Harriett's for the summer.

| 1339 |

Joan Lowery Nixon

Maggie Forevermore (New York: Harcourt, 1987)

Age range: Grades 5-7

Subject(s): Grandparents; Movie Industry; Remarriage

Major character(s): Maggie Ledoux, Teenager (daughter of a movie producer); Kiki, Step-Parent

Time period(s): 1980s

Locale(s): Malibu, California

What the book is about: When her movie producer father calls from California to invite her for Christmas, Maggie is less than thrilled. She decides to make the best of it all, and before long she begins to realize she has a real friend in her dad's new wife. They join forces to help an aspiring young actress rid herself of an unscrupulous agent.

Where it's reviewed:
Center for Children's Books Bulletin, April 1987, page 152
School Library Journal, March 1987, page 164

Other books by the author:
Encore, 1990
Caught in the Act, 1988
And Maggie Makes Three, 1986
Maggie, Too, 1985

Other books you might like:
Mary Jane Auch, *Out of Step*, 1992
After his father remarries, 12 year old Jeremy begins to feel there is no place for him in the new family.
Candy Dawson Boyd, *Chevrolet Saturdays*, 1993
When he enters fifth grade after his mother's remarriage, Joey has trouble adjusting to his new teacher and new stepfather.
Scott Corbett, *Take a Number*, 1974
When a seventh grader's handsome, charming and happily remembered stepfather comes back into her life, he seems a different and dangerous person.
Barbara Dillon, *My Stepfather Shrank!*, 1992
9 year old Mallory discovers that her new stepfather has been shrunk accidentally and tries to return him to normal size before her mother gets home.
J.P. Reading, *The Summer of Sassy Jo*, 1989
Thirteen year old Sara Jo copes with her conflicting emotions as she spends the summer with her mother, who abandoned her as a child.

| 1340 |

Joan Lowery Nixon

Illustrator: Linda Bucholtz-Ross

Magnolia's Mixed-Up Magic (New York: Putnam, 1983)

Age range: Grades 1-2

Subject(s): Animals; Magic

Major character(s): Magnolia Possum, Opossum; Grandma Possum, Opossum, Grandparent

Time period(s): Indeterminate

Locale(s): Earth

What the book is about: When Magnolia Possum's grandmother buys a dusty old magic book from Mrs. Fox's store, Magnolia points at Bernard Beaver and he disappears. Unfortunately, the last few pages of the book are missing. How will Magnolia ever make Bernard reappear?

Where it's reviewed:
Center for Children's Books Bulletin, September 1983, page 14

Kirkus Reviews, June 1, 1983, page 618

Awards the book has won:
Crabbery Award 1984

Other books by the author:
Maggie, Too, 1985
A Deadly Game of Magic, 1983
The Gift, 1983
The Specter, 1982

Other books you might like:
Ellen Conford, *Impossible, Possum*, 1971
　If his sister hadn't played a mean trick on him, a young possum might never have learned to hang by his tail.
Judy Delton, *Brimhall Turns to Magic*, 1979
　Brimhall learns enough magic to make a rabbit appear in a hat, but not enough to make him vanish.
Mem Fox, *Possum Magic*, 1983
　When Grandma Poss's magic turns Hush invisible, the two possums make a tour of Australia to find the food that will make her visible again.
Joan Phillips, *Gretchen and the Lost Carousel*, 1982
　Gretchen and her friends help a group of carousel horses looking for their missing carousel after a day magically spent in the forest as real horses.
Donald Wayne, *The Adventures of Little White Possum*, 1970
　While trying to hitch a ride to the persimmon tree for a snack, the lost possum discovers there is no tail like a possum's tail.

1341

Andre Norton

Illustrator: Judith Gwyn Brown

Lavender-Green Magic (New York: Crowell, 1974)

Age range: Grades 4-7

Subject(s): African Americans; Space and Time; Witches and Witchcraft

Major character(s): Holly Wade, Preteen; Judy Wade, Twin; Crockett "Crock" Wade, Twin

Time period(s): 1970s; 1770s

Locale(s): Sussex, Massachusetts

What the book is about: When their father is MIA in Vietnam, the Wade children move in with their grandparents so their mother can return to her work as a nurse. Holly is horrified. Not only has her whole world collapsed, but her grandparents live in a junkyard! But when she and her twin brother and sister, Crockett and Judy, begin to explore their new home, they find a secret house which transports them to Colonial America and a feud between two powerful witches.

Other books by the author:
House of Shadows, 1984
Red Hart Magic, 1976

Other books you might like:
Avi, *Something Upstairs: A Tale of Ghosts*, 1988
　Kenny discovers that his new house is haunted by the spirit of a black slave boy who asks Kenny to come back in time and help prevent his murder.
Lou Kassem, *A Haunting in Williamsburg*, 1990
　Staying in a house once owned by her ancestors, Jayne meets an old family ghost who is haunted by a terrible wrong and wants Jayne to help her.

Marilynne K. Roach, *Encounters with the Invisible World*, 1977
　Ten tales of ghosts, witches and the devil himself in New England.
Elizabeth George Speare, *The Witch of Blackbird Pond*, 1958
　In 1687, Kit Tyler moves from the Caribbean to Connecticut Colony. Her friendship with a strange old woman leads to her trial for witchcraft.
David B. Weems, *Son of an Earl, Sold for a Slave*, 1993
　After being kidnapped and sold as a bond servant, James struggles with his identity and his loyalty to his loyalty to the Revolutionary cause.

1342

Andre Norton

Ride the Green Dragon (New York: Atheneum, 1985)

Age range: Grades 5-7

Subject(s): Crime and Criminals; Mystery and Detective Stories

Major character(s): Tracy Wayne, Preteen; Jared Wayne, Preteen; Pooky, Dog

Time period(s): 1980s

Locale(s): New Jersey

What the book is about: The Wayne family moves into the Vargen place, the former quarters of a circus company, designed like a castle. Very strange things happen to Tracy and Jared as they begin to unravel a series of mysteries that involves several generations.

Where it's reviewed:
Center for Children's Books Bulletin, February 1986, page 115

Other books by the author:
Red Hart Magic, 1976
Android at Arms, 1971
The Beast Master, 1959
At Swords' Points, 1954

Other books you might like:
Mildred Ames, *Conjuring Summer In*, 1986
　Bernadette plays with psychic forces and black magic in her sadness over the family's move to California, but murders and a threat on her life ensue.
Richard M. Koff, *Christopher*, 1981
　Christopher enters a supposedly haunted house on a dare where he meets a mysterious man who teaches him to use mental powers he never knew existed.
Joan Lowery Nixon, *The Haunted House on Honeycutt Street*, 1991
　While preparing for a circus, neighbors see flashing lights from the Blair's empty house.
Berniece Rabe, *Naomi*, 1975
　During the 1930s, a Missouri farm girl is told by a fortune teller that she will die before she is fourteen.
Jane Breskin Zalben, *The Fortuneteller in 5B*, 1991
　The unexpected arrival of a flamboyant new neighbor teaches Alexandria that the loss of a loved one is a universal experience.

1343

Mary Norton

Illustrator: Eric Blegvad

Bedknob and Broomsticks (New York: Harcourt Brace Jovanovich, 1957)

Age range: Grades 4-6

Subject(s): Fantasy; Witches and Witchcraft; Witches and Witchcraft

Major character(s): Charles Wilson, Child; Carey Wilson, Child; Paul Wilson, Child

Time period(s): Indeterminate Past

Locale(s): England

What the book is about: The Wilson children meet an elderly woman who is studying to become a witch. They go on magical trips with her that are both exciting and dangerous. *Magic Bed-Knob* and *Bonfires and Broomsticks* are contained in this one volume.

Where it's reviewed:
Instructor, May 1975, page 107
Times Educational Supplement, May 2, 1980, page 24

Other books by the author:
Are All the Giants Dead?, 1975
Poor Stainless: A New Story about the Borrowers, 1971
The Borrowers Afield, 1970
The Borrowers, 1952

Other books you might like:
Clive Barker, *The Thief of Always: A Fable*, 1992
    After a mysterious stranger promises to end his boredom with a trip to the magical Holiday House, Harvey learns that his fun has a high price.
Claudia Paley, *Benjamin the True*, 1969
    The witch that Benjamin finds in a neighbor's cellar is neither good nor bad, just powerful. But when her power is not enough Benjamin must help her.
Mary Jo Stephens, *Witch of the Cumberlands*, 1974
    After the prophesied arrival of three children on Devil's Mountain, a gentle old woman thought to be a witch solves the old mystery of a mine disaster
Kathleen Thomas, *Goats Are Better than Worms*, 1984
    When Jake the goat wins a balloon ride in a drawing, Ellen accompanies her on what turns out to be a magical trip to a fantastic island.
Ann Warren Turner, *Rosemary's Witch*, 1991
    Moving into an old house in a small New England town, Rosemary learns that the woods hide an old witch who once lived in the house and wants it back.

1344

Mary Norton

Illustrator: Beth Krush

The Borrowers (New York: Harcourt, Brace, Jovanovich, 1952)

Age range: Grades 4-6

Subject(s): Fantasy

Major character(s): Pod Clock, Mythical Creature; Homily Clock, Mythical Creature; Arrietty Clock, Mythical Creature

Time period(s): Indeterminate

Locale(s): England

What the book is about: A family of very small people live in a quiet country home. They are called the Clock family because the entrance to their tiny "apartment" is under the grandfather clock in the hall. They survive by "borrowing" things from their host family. A lost spool of thread becomes a clothes line, a matchbox, a bed. Arrietty puts the family in danger when she meets a boy who has come to the country to regain his health. Now a human knows about their existence. First of a series.

Where it's reviewed:
Booklist, September 1, 1983, page 96
New Statesman, November 14, 1980, page 20
New York Times Book Review, February 13, 1972, page 12

Awards the book has won:
Carnegie Medal 1952

Other books by the author:
The Borrowers Avenged, 1986
The Borrowers Afield, 1970
The Borrowers Aloft, 1961
The Borrowers Afloat, 1955

Other books you might like:
Elizabeth Goudge, *The Little White Horse*, 1946
    In 1842, newly orphaned Meria Merryweather, her governess, and dog arrive at her ancestral home in an enchanted village in England.
Peter Hunter Blair, *The Coming of Pout*, 1969
    A brother and sister meet a mysterious creature who can telescope time. He asks them to join his search for a way to break the spell cast upon him.
Carol Kendall, *The Whisper of Glocken*, 1965
    Following a flood, a group of little people begin a quest to restore an ancient treasure and make the valley of the Watercress safe again.
Joan Lowery Nixon, *The Gift*, 1983
    Grandfather has told Brian Irish folktales about the wee people, but he's not sure he should believe them until the night he sees them for himself.
Emily Rodda, *Finders Keepers*, 1990
    While playing a computer game, Patrick is transported to a parallel world and asked to play a game in which he must find three lost items to win.

1345

Mary Norton

Illustrator: Beth Krush

Poor Stainless: A New Story about the Borrowers (New York: Harcourt, 1966)

Age range: Grades 3-5

Subject(s): Fantasy

Major character(s): Homily, Parent (Arrietty's mother); Arrietty, Child; Stainless, Child

Time period(s): Indeterminate

Locale(s): Fictional Country

What the book is about: A short story about the Borrowers, very small people who live in hidden places and are responsible for many of the small things big people are always losing. In this story, Arrietty urges her mother, Homily, to tell a story about a time when her cousin, Stainless, was lost, and all the Borrowers had to search for him. Though this postdates the longer Borrowers books, its brevity makes it a good introduction to the series.

Where it's reviewed:
Booklist, July 1, 1971, page 908
Center for Children's Books Bulletin, September 1971, page 13
Hornbook, June 1971, page 289

Other books by the author:
The Borrowers Avenged, 1982
Are All the Giants Dead?, 1975
The Borrowers Aloft, 1959
The Borrowers Afield, 1955

Other books you might like:
Susan Clymer, *The Glass Mermaid*, 1986
    Becca can't believe her eyes when she spots two tiny people under the Christmas tree, and they are stealing her favorite ornament, a glass mermaid.
John Peterson, *The Littles to the Rescue*, 1981
    A family of tiny people experiences a crisis when a baby is born during a snowstorm.
Jonathan Swift, *Gulliver's Travels*, 1983
    On two voyages, an Englishman becomes shipwrecked in a land where people are six inches high, and stranded in a land of giants.
Kathy Kennedy Tapp, *Moth-Kin Magic*, 1983
    Several members of a Mothkin family, tiny people less than an inch tall, must escape or die when they are captured by giants and imprisoned.
Boris Zhitkov, *How I Hunted the Little Fellows*, 1979
    Fascinated by the life-like miniature of a steamer on his grandmother's shelf, a young boy becomes convinced that there are little people inside.

1346

Christine Nostlinger

Illustrator: Carol Nicklaus

Konrad (New York: Watts, 1977)

Age range: Grades 4-6

Subject(s): Fantasy

Major character(s): Konrad, Android, Child; Mrs. Bartolotti, Guardian (eccentric)

Time period(s): 1970s

Locale(s): Austria

What the book is about: Konrad is a factory made, perfect seven year old. He is delivered by mistake to scatterbrained Mrs. Bartolotti. Konrad is too perfect for much popularity. He always does his homework and is perfectly polite and never challenges authority. Mrs. Bartolotti has to reprogram Konrad to be a scamp when the factory tries to reclaim him.

Where it's reviewed:
Horn Book, December 1977, page 665
School Library Journal, November 1977, page 60

Awards the book has won:
Mildred L. Batchelder Award 1979

Other books by the author:
Marrying Off Mother, 1982
Luke and Angela, 1979
Girl Missing, 1976
Fly Away Home, 1975

Other books you might like:
Isaac Asimov, *Robbie*, 1989
    Gloria's mother takes away her beloved robot playmate, Robbie, and Gloria falls apart.
Ray Bradbury, *The Complete Poems of R. Bradbury*, 1982
    Includes the haunted computer, the android pope, robot mice and robot men in a robot town, and more.
Mel Gilden, *Harry Newberry and the Raiders of the Red Drink*, 1989
    Comic fan Harry becomes convinced his mother is the superhero Tuatara, especially when he helps her fight the evil Bonnie Android.
Florence Parry Heide, *Tales for the Perfect Child*, 1985
    Vignettes of children whose less than desirable behavior is masked in insidious but acceptable ways.
Andre Norton, *Android at Arms*, 1971
    Awaking from a mind-frozen state, Andas Kastor must discover if he is the rightful human Emperor of Inyanga or an evil android double.

O

1347

Robert C. O'Brien

Illustrator: Zena Bernstein

Mrs. Frisby and the Rats of NIMH (New York: Atheneum, 1971)

Age range: Grades 4-6

Subject(s): Animals/Mice; Animals/Rats; Courage

Major character(s): Timothy Mouse, Mouse; Mrs. Frisby, Mouse, Parent (Timothy's mother); Nicodemus, Rat

Time period(s): 1970s

Locale(s): United States

What the book is about: A group of rats given human intelligence through experiments at the National Institute of Mental Health (NIMH) escapes from the laboratory to establish their own community. Mrs. Frisby, a mouse, seeks help from the rats when one of her children becomes ill. While at their community, she learns of her husband's courageous part in "The Plan."

Where it's reviewed:
Center for Children's Books Bulletin, October 1971, page 29
Horn Book, August 1971, page 385

Awards the book has won:
Newbery Medal 1972

Other books by the author:
The Silver Crown, 1968
Z for Zachariah, 1988

Other books you might like:
Jane Leslie Conly, *Racso and the Rats of NIMH*, 1986
    The original Rats of NIMH and their descendants try to thwart the destruction of their home in Thorne Valley.
Nathaniel Benchley, *Feldman Fieldmouse*, 1971
    Fendall Mouse lives a comfortable life, but a visit from his uncle challenges him to leave the cage and strike out on his own.
W.J. Corbett, *Song of Pentecost*, 1983
    The mice of Pentecost farm are forced to move and face the dangers of the outside world.
Roger W. Drury, *The Champion of Merrimack County*, 1976
    A bicycle-riding mouse causes hilarity at the Berryfield home.
Robert Lawson, *Ben and Me*, 1939
    The story of the mouse, Amos, who was a personal friend of Benjamin Franklin and was responsible for most of Ben's inventions.

1348

Robert C. O'Brien

Z for Zachariah (New York: Atheneum, 1974)

Age range: Grades 5-6

Subject(s): Science Fiction

Major character(s): Ann Burden, Child; John Loomis, Engineer

Time period(s): Indeterminate Future

Locale(s): United States

What the book is about: Ann survives a nuclear holocaust in a hidden valley in the US. John is an engineer and has a ruthless desire to exploit his surroundings. They struggle for survival together. Ann learned her alphabet in Sunday School, and she assumes that Z for Zachariah means the last man.

Where it's reviewed:
Horn Book, June 1975, page 276
Library Journal, April 1, 1975, page 694

Awards the book has won:
Edgar Allan Poe Award 1976
Jane Addams Children's Book Award, Honor Book 1976

Other books by the author:
Mrs. Frisby and the Rats of NIMH, 1971
The Silver Crown, 1968

Other books you might like:
Victor Appleton, *Crater of Mystery*, 1983
    Tom Swift and his crew are instrumental in delivering the planet Verita from a nuclear holocaust.
James D. Dorman, *Doomsday Plus 12*, 1984
    In the year 2000, twelve years after the world nuclear holocaust, a group of Oregon teens combats the militarists and assures the peace of the future.
Gregory Maguire, *I Feel Like the Morning Sun*, 1989
    Three teens in a post-holocaust survival colony find that their shelter has become a prison and decide to break out.
Pamela F. Service, *Winter of Magic's Return*, 1985
    Convinced that a new age of magic is about to begin in the wake of the nuclear holocaust, a young resurrected Merlin and two friends set out to bring
Whitley Strieber, *Wolf of Shadows*, 1985
    In the aftermath of a nuclear holocaust, a wolf and a woman form a mysterious bond that brings each close to the spirits of the shattered earth.

1349

Jean S. O'Connell

Illustrator: Erik Blegvad

The Dollhouse Caper (New York: Crowell, 1976)

Age range: Grades 3-5

Subject(s): Dolls and Dollhouses; Robbers and Outlaws; Fantasy

Major character(s): Todd, Toy (Doll)

Time period(s): 1970s

Locale(s): United States

What the book is about: A family of dolls comes to life when no people are around. They are almost caught by burglars. The family is concerned that the three brothers who own them may get rid of them. At the same time, they try to leave clues for their humans about the imminent robbery.

Where it's reviewed:
Kirkus Reviews, January 15, 1976, page 63
School Library Journal, April 1976, page 63

Other books you might like:
Catherine Dexter, *The Oracle Doll*, 1985
    Three youngsters are guardians of a talking doll that is the reincarnated Oracle of Delphi.
Helen V. Griffith, *Caitlin's Holiday*, 1990
    When her new doll comes alive, Caitlin's delight turns to frustration as the doll displays a nasty temperament.
Pamela Stearns, *The Mechanical Doll*, 1979
    A court musician breaks the mechanical doll that replaced him as the king's favorite, and then the doll must restore the musician's life.
Marjorie Stover, *Midnight in the Dollhouse*, 1990
    A family of dolls helps the hanicapped young owner find a clue to hidden treasure.
Betty Ren Wright, *The Dollhouse Murders*, 1983
    A dollhouse filled with ghostly light and dolls that change places leads Amy and her sister to solve a grisly murder that happened years before.

1350

Jane O'Connor

Illustrator: Emily Arnold McCully

Lulu and the Witch Baby (New York: Harper, 1986)

Age range: Grades 1-3

Subject(s): Sisters; Witches and Witchcraft

Major character(s): Lulu, Witch

Time period(s): Indeterminate

Locale(s): Fictional Country

What the book is about: A serious case of sibling rivalry upsets a family of witches. Lulu begins to change her mind about her pesky baby sister when she thinks that one of her spells has made the baby disappear.

Where it's reviewed:
Booklist, October 1, 1986, page 277
Kirkus Reviews, July 15, 1986, paege 1122

Other books by the author:
Sir Small and the Dragon Fly, 1988

Lulu Goes to Witch School, 1987
The Teeny Tiny Woman, 1986
Dandee Diamond Mystery, 1982

Other books you might like:
Othello Bach, *Lilly, Willy, and the Mail-Order Witch*, 1983
    When Lilly sends for the Mail-Order Witch to perform magic on her messy room, her brother Willy has his doubts.
Nancy White Carlstrom, *Kiss Your Sister, Rose Marie!*, 1992
    Rose Marie is not at all sure she likes having to deal with her new sister, Baby Boo.
Barbara Dillon, *Mrs. Tooey and the Terrible Toxic Tar*, 1988
    Margo and Craig's new babysitter, Mrs. Tooey, turns out to be a witch, who enlists them in fighting her evil sister Velma's plot to destroy Summerton.
Morse Hamilton, *Big Sisters Are Bad Witches*, 1981
    The sibling rivalry of two sisters lessens when a third child on the way promises to turn little sister into big sister.
Fran Manushkin, *Hocus and Pocus at the Circus*, 1983
    A young witch tries in vain to teach her little sister how to spook a Halloween circus.

1351

Jane O'Connor

Illustrator: Margot Apple

Yours Till Niagara Falls, Abby (New York: Hastings, 1979)

Age range: Grades 3-5

Subject(s): Camps and Camping; Friendship

Major character(s): Abby, Child, Camper; Roberta, Child, Camper

Time period(s): 1970s

Locale(s): United States

What the book is about: Abby's experience at summer camp is her first time away from home, and she hates it. Her best friend, Merle, broke an ankle and went home, so Abby feels very alone. Older campers harass her, she gets poison ivy, and loses a picnic lunch by forgetting to lock the food chest. When a new camper, Roberta, arrives and seems even more of a misfit, Abby helps her to fit in and finds camp actually enjoyable.

Where it's reviewed:
Kirkus Reviews, December 1, 1979, page 1376
School Library Journal, December 1979, page 88

Awards the book has won:
Golden Sower Award 1982

Other books by the author:
Super Cluck, 1991
Molly the Brave and Me, 1990
Lulu and the Witch Baby, 1986
Just Good Friends, 1983

Other books you might like:
Tommy Hallowell, *Shot From Midfield*, 1991
    Justin finally proves himself when he goes to summer soccer camp for three weeks.
Alison Jackson, *Crane's Rebound*, 1991
    Les must cope with lonliness, peer pressure, boy-girl problems, and a talented but obnoxious roommate at basketball camp.

Colleen O'Shaughnessy McKenna, *Eenie, Meanie, Murphy, NO!*, 1990

Collette tries desperately to retrieve her secret diary, which has been stolen and read aloud at camp.

Sheri Cooper Sinykin, *The Buddy Trap*, 1991

At a camp dominated by war games, Cam endures his cruel tentmates and tries to keep his love for the flute a secret.

Jean Van Leeuwen, *The Great Summer Camp Catastrophe*, 1992

Three mice are accidentally shipped from a department store to a summer camp in Vermont.

1352

Scott O'Dell

Black Star, Bright Dawn (Boston: Houghton Mifflin, 1988)

Age range: Grades 5-8

Subject(s): Eskimos; Sports/Dog Sled Racing

Major character(s): Bright Dawn, Teenager, Sports Figure (musher); Black Star, Dog

Time period(s): 1980s

Locale(s): Alaska

What the book is about: Bright Dawn takes over for her injured father in the Iditarod Sled Dog Race from Anchorage to Nome. She faces not only the competition but the dangers of the race itself. She proves herself a resourceful heroine in this fast paced survival tale, which shows not only the race, but the conflict of Eskimo and white cultures.

Where it's reviewed:
Center for Children's Books Bulletin, June 1988, page 213
School Library Journal, May 1988, page 110

Other books by the author:
Thunder Rolling in the Mountains, 1992
My Name Is Not Angelica, 1989
Castle in the Sea, 1983
Carlota, 1977

Other books you might like:
Patricia Calvert, *The Hour of the Wolf*, 1983

Following his suicide attempt, a loner and a loser is sent to Alaska, where he enters the 1,000 mile Iditarod race in memory of his dead indian friend.

John Reynolds Gardiner, *Stone Fox*, 1980

Little Willie hopes to pay the back taxes on his grandfather's farm with the purse from a sled dog race he enters.

Daniel Manus Pinkwater, *The Magic Moscow*, 1980

Relates the adventures of Edward, grandson of a famous TV sled dog, with his owner, Steve, who manages a Hoboken ice cream stand.

Seymour Reit, *Race Against Death*, 1976

In the winter of 1925, a dog sled relay makes a race against time through an Alaskan blizzard with a supply of serum needed to stop an epidemic.

Charles M. Schulz, *What a Nightmare, Charlie Brown*, 1978

Snoopy dreams about the rough life of a sled dog in the frozen north.

1353

Scott O'Dell

Island of the Blue Dolphins (Boston: Houghton Mifflin, 1960)

Age range: Grades 4-6

Subject(s): Survival; Indians of North America

Major character(s): Karana, Indian

Time period(s): Indeterminate Past

Locale(s): San Nicolas Island, California

What the book is about: An Indian girl spends eighteen years alone on the Island of the Blue Dolphins. Karana learns about nature and herself as she struggles to survive. She both tames wild animals to combat her loneliness and battles animals for her life.

Where it's reviewed:
Booklist, April 1960, page 489
New York Times Book Review, March 27, 1960, page 40

Awards the book has won:
Newbery Medal 1961

Other books by the author:
The Black Pearl, 1967
Carlota, 1977
Sing Down the Moon, 1970
Zia, 1976

Other books you might like:
Louise Moeri, *Downwind*, 1984

12-year-old Ephraim and his family find themselves threatened after fleeing home to escape a radiation leak.

Kenneth Thomasma, *Kunu: Escape on the Missouri*, 1989

A Winnebago Indian boy embarks on a dangerous journey to return to his dying grandfather.

David Masterson, *Get Out of My Face!*, 1991

Kate and her obnoxious step-brother must survive a dangerous wilderness journey.

Jean Craighead George, *On the Far Side of the Mountain*, 1990

Sam's peaceful existence in his wilderness home is disrupted when his sister runs away.

Charles Hammer, *Wrong-Way Ragsdale*, 1987

13-year-old Emmett and his little sister make a forced landing and try to survive in the wilderness.

1354

Scott O'Dell

Sarah Bishop (Boston: Houghton Mifflin, 1980)

Age range: Grades 5-8

Subject(s): Revolutionary War

Major character(s): Sarah Bishop, Refugee, Recluse; James Bishop, Parent (Tory)

Time period(s): 1770s

Locale(s): Long Island, New York, American Colonies

What the book is about: Sarah is befriended by a young Quaker and an Indian couple when she flees the brutality of the Revolutionary War. She has lost both her brother and father and fled Long Island. She lives off the land and becomes a recluse. When her unusual behavior results in charges of witchcraft, the Quaker defends her.

Where it's reviewed:
Booklist, May 1, 1980, page 1297
Hornbook, April 1980, page 174
Kirkus, June 1, 1980, page 717

Other books by the author:
Captive, 1979
Zia, 1976
Sing Down the Moon, 1970
Island of the Blue Dolphins, 1960

Other books you might like:
Patricia Beatty, *Who Comes with Cannons?*, 1992
    In 1861, Truth, an Indiana Quaker girl staying with relatives running a station of the Underground Railroad, has her world changed by the Civil War.
Barbara Chamberlain, *Ride the West Wind*, 1979
    Nathan and his family join a group of of other Quakers sailing to America, but the voyage is plagued by suspicion, sickness and superstition.
Helen Pierce Jacob, *The Diary of Strawbridge Place*, 1978
    A family of Quakers operating a station on the Underground Railroad spirits slaves from Ashtabula, Ohio, across Lake Erie to freedom.
Norma Johnston, *The Delphic Choice*, 1989
    Visiting Turkish relatives, Meredith tries to free her uncle, a Quaker hostage negotiator, who is taken hostage by an Islamic terrorist group.
Elizabeth Gray Vining, *The Taken Girl*, 1972
    An orphan girl taken on as a helper in a Quaker household including John Greenleaf Whittier gets involved in the anti-slavery movement in Philadelphia

---

1355

Scott O'Dell

Sing Down the Moon (Boston: Houghton Mifflin, 1970)

Age range: Grades 4-6

Subject(s): Indians of North America

Major character(s): Bright Morning, Indian; Kit Carson, Frontiersman, Historical Figure

Time period(s): 1860s

Locale(s): Canyon de Chelly, Arizona

What the book is about: Bright Morning is kidnapped and enslaved by the Spaniards until she is rescued by her husband-to-be. White soldiers force them out of their ancestral home and drive them on a four hundred mile march to Fort Sumner.

Where it's reviewed:
Horn Book, December 1970, page 623
Library Journal, November 15, 1970, page 4046

Awards the book has won:
Newbery Honor

Other books by the author:
Thunder Rolling in the Mountains, 1992
My Name Is Not Angelica, 1989
Black Star, Bright Dawn, 1988
Island of the Blue Dolphins, 1960

Other books you might like:
Lynne Gessner, *Navajo Slave*, 1976
    Straight Arrow is taken captive and sold into slavery to a Spanish landowner, but he never stops trying to escape and return to his home.
Robin Moore, *Maggie Among the Seneca*, 1990
    Maggie journeys across the Pennsylvania frontier and is taken captive by a band of Seneca warriors.
Paul Pitts, *Racing the Sun*, 1988
    Twelve year old Brandon Rogers faces conflict between his suburban life and the Navajo heritage he has learned from his grandfather.
Chap Reaver, *A Little Bit Dead*, 1992
    In 1876, after interfering with the attempted lynching of a young Yahi Indian, Reece finds his own life in danger.
Barbara Williams, *The Secret Name*, 1972
    A nine year old girl recounts the chages in her family's life after a young Navajo girl comes to stay with them.

1356

Kelly Oechsli, Author/Illustrator

Mice at Bat (New York: Harper, 1986)

Age range: Grades 1-2

Subject(s): Sports/Baseball; Animals/Mice

Major character(s): Big Jax, Rat, Sports Figure (baseball player)

Time period(s): Indeterminate

What the book is about: Two rival baseball teams prepare for the big game. When the human baseball game is over, two teams of mice take over the ballpark to play their own championship game.

Where it's reviewed:
Kirkus Reviews, May 15, 1986, page 792
Publisher's Weekly, May 30, 1986, page 63
School Library Journal, May 1986, page 113

Other books by the author:
Boober Fraggle's Celery Souffle, 1984
Home Sweet Home, 1983
The Dog Who Insisted He Wasn't, 1976
A House for Little Red, 1970

Other books you might like:
Matt Christopher, *The Dog That Pitched a No-Hitter*, 1988
    Mike's telepathic dog, Harry, can send him signals about the opposing baseball players, but Mike's weak pitching arm requires another gamesaving plan.
Ned Delaney, *Two Strikes, Four Eyes*, 1976
    Afraid that his teammates will tease him, Toby refuses to wear his glasses until he realizes that playing well is more important.
Chris Economos, *The New Kid*, 1989
    A chimpanzee substitutes for a sick baseball player.
Syd Hoff, *Baseball Mouse*, 1969
    Bernard is a field mouse, an infield mouse, who more than anything wants to help the losing team win the pennant.
Leonard Kessler, *The Worst Team Ever*, 1985
    Old Turtle and Melvin Moose help the worst baseball team in the swamp win the final game of the season.

| 1357 |

Uriel Ofek

Illustrator: Lloyd Bloom

Smoke Over Golan (New York: Harper and Row, 1979)

Age range: Grades 5-6

Subject(s): Israel-Arab War; Friendship; War

Major character(s): Eitan Avivi, Child; Saleem, Child

Time period(s): 1970s (1973)

Locale(s): Israel

What the book is about: Five year old Eitan's family moves to a farm in the Golan Heights and Eitan becomes friends with Saleem, a young Syrian boy who has crossed the border into Israel chasing a lost donkey. A vivid portrayal of the effects of war on family and friendship.

Where it's reviewed:
Horn Book, October 1979, page 536
School Library Journal, October 1979, page 153

Other books by the author:
My Shalom, My Peace: Paintings and Poems by Jewish and Arab Children, 1975

Other books you might like:
Mary Baylis-White, *Sheltering Rebecca*, 1991
    In the days before the Second World War, twelve year old Sally becomes friends with Rebecca, a young Jewish refugee from Germany.
Tamar Bergman, *The Boy From Over There*, 1989
    Avramik, a young Holocaust survivor, has trouble adjusting to life on a kibbutz in the days before the first Arab-Israeli war.
Adrienne Richard, *The Accomplice: A Novel*, 1973
    Hoping to get better acquainted with his archaeologist father, Benjy joins him on a dig in Israel and becomes involved in an Arab terrorist plot.
Theresa Tomlinson, *Summer Witches*, 1989
    Two friends convert an old air raid shelter into a den to help an old woman overcome her painful memories of World War Two.
Ilse-Margret Vogel, *Tikhon*, 1984
    A Russian soldier trapped in post-World War I Germany, becomes a valued companion to young Inge when her parents shelter him in their basement.

| 1358 |

Walter G. Oleksy

Quacky and the Crazy Curve Ball (New York: McGraw Hill, 1981)

Age range: Grades 5-7

Subject(s): Sports/Baseball; Mystery and Detective Stories; Orphans

Major character(s): Quacky, Orphan, Preteen

Time period(s): 1980s

Locale(s): United States

What the book is about: When faced with two challenges, the "Hungry Burglar" and making the baseball team, Quacky proves resourcefulness.

Where it's reviewed:
Booklist, July 15, 1981, page 1449
Children's Book Review Service, April 1981, page 78
School Library Journal, May 1981, page 86

Other books by the author:
Bug Scanner and the Computer Mystery, 1983
The Pirates of Deadman's Cay, 1982
If I'm Lost, How Come I Found You?, 1977
Laugh, Clown, Cry, 1976

Other books you might like:
Matt Christopher, *Pressure Play*, 1993
    Travis, less obsessed with baseball than his fellow team members, tries to balance his playing with his hobby of horror videos.
John R. Cooper, *The Mystery at the Ball Park*, 1952
    The mystery that suddenly surrounds their baseball park doesn't deter Mel Martin and his teammates from pursuing a Big Six Championship.
Monica Hughes, *Hunter in the Dark*, 1982
    A teenage boy goes on a secret hunting trip alone in an effort to come to terms with his leukemia and to test his strength in battling the elements.
Harriette Robinet, *Children of the Fire*, 1991
    A young black girl named Hallelujah lives through the great Chicago fire with courage and resourcefulness.
Hilary H. Milton, *Tornado!*, 1983
    Stranded on the road by a flood and tornadoes, his mother wounded and sister in desperate need of medical help, Paul exhibits heroism.

| 1359 |

Stephen Ryan Oliver

Illustrator: Cherie R. Wyman

The Gitter, the Googer and the Ghost (Minneapolis: Carolrhoda, 1983)

Age range: Grades 3-5

Subject(s): Ghosts

Major character(s): Gitter, Paranormal Investigator (ghost hunter); Googer, Paranormal Investigator (ghost hunter)

Time period(s): Indeterminate

Locale(s): Maine

What the book is about: Best friends and ghost hunters, Gitter and Googer, think they have a chance to find a real ghost when Gitter's family inherits an old, spooky house in Maine.

Where it's reviewed:
Booklist, January 1, 1984, page 683
Children's Book Review Service, November 1983, page 28
School Library Journal, February 1984, page 76

Other books you might like:
James Cowan, *Trouble at Moosehead Lake*, 1993
    Five stories of emergency rescues by Davey Mountain and Matt Rich, trained to react in emergency situations.
Donn Fendler, *Lost on a Mountain in Maine*, 1992
    A twelve year old describes his nine day struggle to survive after being separated from his companions in the mountains of Maine in 1939.
Nancy Garden, *My Sister, the Vampire*, 1992

A beautiful summer turns deadly for Sarah, Tim and Jenny as they discover the horrifying truth about the strange new owners of Spool Island.

Lee Bennett Hopkins, *A-Haunting We Will Go: Ghostly Stories and Poems*, 1977
A collection of more than a dozen ghosts, ghoulies and unexplained happenings.

Liza Ketchum Murrow, *The Ghost of Lost Island*, 1991
While helping his grandfather herd and shear his flock of sheep on a small island, Gabe encounters a woman who may be the ghost of a drowned milkmaid.

1360

Zibby Oneal

In Summer Light (New York: Viking, 1985)

Age range: Grades 5 and Up

Subject(s): Artists and Art; Identity; Family Life

Major character(s): Ian Jackson, Student; Marcus Brewer, Artist

Time period(s): 1980s

Locale(s): Massachusetts

What the book is about: Kate's father is a famous painter. He dismisses her efforts at art and she is not looking forward to spending the summer in his overpowering presence. When Ian arrives to catalog her dad's paintings, she responds to his kindness and perception and grows to understand how to be an artist's daughter and still maintain her own identity.

Where it's reviewed:
Horn book, November/December 1985, page 742
School Library Journal, October 1985, page 186

Awards the book has won:
Boston Globe/Horn Book Award 1986

Other books by the author:
A Long Way to Go, 1990
Maude and Walter, 1985
A Formal Feeling, 1983
The Language of Goldfish, 1981

Other books you might like:
M.B. Goffstein, *Daisy Summerfield's Style*, 1975
An aspiring young artist learns the difference between creating art and putting on airs.

JoAnn Bren Guernsey, *Journey to Almost There*, 1985
To prevent her grandfather's going to a nursing home, Alison drives him from Minnesota to Massachusetts where her estranged artist father lives.

Mary Haynes, *Catch the Sea*, 1989
While her artist father is away, thirteen year old Lily stays alone, and discovers her own inner resources and artistic talent.

Marguerite Henry, *Benjamin West and His Cat Grimalkin*, 1947
A young Quaker boy discovers and develops his talent as an artist.

Mary Stolz, *Pangur Ban*, 1988
Cormac, wanting to pursue artistic work, leaves his family family in 9th century Ireland and goes on to create an illuminated manuscript.

1361

Shulamith Oppenheim

Illustrator: Lillian Hoban

The Selchie's Seed (Scarsdale, New York: Bradbury, 1975)

Age range: Grades 4-6

Subject(s): Folk Tales

Major character(s): Edward Sinclare, Fisherman; Ursilla Sinclare, Spouse; Marian Sinclare, Preteen

Time period(s): Indeterminate Past

Locale(s): Scotland

What the book is about: Selchies are the seal-people of Scottish legends. Edward and Ursilla are fisher folk. Their daughter, Marian, is bewitched by a white whale. Marian goes eagerly to her love, wearing a magic sealskin belt that has transformed her into a mermaid.

Where it's reviewed:
Center for Children's Books Bulletin, April 1976, page 129
Kirkus Reviews, November 15, 1975, page 1287

Other books by the author:
The Lily Cupboard, 1992
Appleblossom, 1991
Waiting for Noah, 1990

Other books you might like:
Rumer Godden, *Mr. McFadden's Hallowe'en*, 1975
A young girl and her pony befriend a dour farmer on the Scottish border.

Mollie Hunter, *The Haunted Mountain*, 1972
After angering the fairy creatures of the Highlands, a stubborn Scot spends thirteen years bringing an end to their revenge against him.

Mollie Hunter, *The Kelpie's Pearls*, 1964
An old woman of the Scottish Highlands makes friends with a kelpie, sees the Loch Ness monster, and practices some of her grandmother's witchcraft.

Alison Smith, *Come Away Home*, 1991
Angus, a young sea monster, is blown off course and becomes trapped in a Scottish loch.

A.C. Stewart, *Ossian House*, 1974
An eleven year old city dweller inherits his grandfather's estate in Scotland where he must deal with hostile cousins.

1362

Doris Orgel

A Certain Magic (New York: Dial, 1975)

Age range: Grades 4-6

Subject(s): World War II; Refugees

Major character(s): Jenny, Preteen; Aunt Trudl, Refugee

Time period(s): 1970s

Locale(s): England

What the book is about: Jenny finds the diary of her Aunt Trudl, a refugee from Austria during WWII. Trudl had been convinced that her emerald ring had evil, magical powers so she had hidden it. Jenny tracks down the emerald ring and returns it to her aunt with a confession about prying.

Where it's reviewed:
Horn Book, August 1976, page 400
School Library Journal, May 1976, page 62

Other books by the author:
Nobodies and Somebodies, 1991
Whiskers, Once and Always, 1986
The Child From Far Away, 1971
In a Forgotten Place, 1967

Other books you might like:
John Bellaris, *The Letter, the Witch, and the Ring*, 1976
 A young girl takes a trip with a friend of the family only to get involved with a mysterious letter, a magic ring, and a powerful witch.
T. Degans, *The Visit*, 1982
 At a family gathering in Berlin, years after WWII, Kate relives some of the events described in the diary of a dead aunt.
Ruth Minsky Sender, *To Life*, 1988
 A Holocaust survivor recounts her liberation from a Nazi concentration camp, her search for surviving family, and immigrating to America.
Steve Senn, *A Circle in the Sea*, 1981
 Through the powers of a ring, a thirteen year old girl with problems enters an undersea world where she becomes a dolphin and aids the whales.
Mary Q. Steele, *Wish, Come True*, 1979
 A ring that belonged to their great grandfather has more magical powers than Megan and her brother realize.

1363

Doris Orgel

Devil in Vienna (New York: Dial, 1978)

Age range: Grades 4-6

Subject(s): World War II; Jews

Major character(s): Inge Dornenwald, Teenager, Friend; Lieselotte Vesseley, Teenager, Friend

Time period(s): 1930s (1938)

Locale(s): Vienna, Austria

What the book is about: A Jewish girl and the daughter of a Nazi have been best friends since they started school, but in 1938 the two teens find their close relationship difficult to maintain.

Where it's reviewed:
Horn Book, February 1979, page 70
School Library Journal, November 1978, page 66

Awards the book has won:
Golden Kite Fiction Honor Book 1978

Other books by the author:
Merry Merry FIBruary, 1977
Little John, 1972
A Certain Magic, 1971
In a Forgotten Place, 1967

Other books you might like:
Edith Baer, *A Frost in the Night*, 1980
 Young Eva Bentheim tells the story of her childhood in Thalstadt, Germany, from 1932 to the election of Hitler as Prime Minister.
Sonia Levitin, *Journey to America*, 1987

As hostilities in Germany increase, Mr. Platt goes to America and Mrs. Platt and the Platt daughters go to Switzerland until Mr. Platt sends for them.
Marietta D. Moskin, *I Am Rosemarie*, 1987
 The Nazi occupation of Holland means less and less freedom for Rosemarie and her parents until they are sent to a concentration camp by the Gestapo.
Renee Roth-Hano, *Touch Wood: A Girlhood in Occupied France*, 1988
 Fleeing Alsace in 1940, the Roth family experiences the horrors and losses of war as they seek refuge in occupied Paris.
Joseph Ziemian, *The Cigarette Sellers of Three Crosses Square*, 1975
 After surviving the Warsaw Ghetto, a group of Jewish children go on living in Warsaw and earn their living by selling cigarettes in the city.

1364

Uri Orlev

The Island on Bird Street (Boston: Houghton Mifflin, 1983)

Age range: Grades 5-6

Subject(s): Holocaust; Jews; World War II

Major character(s): Alex, Preteen; Boruch, Manager; Bolek, Government Official (Polish liason)

Time period(s): 1940s

Locale(s): Warsaw, Poland

What the book is about: Eleven year old Alex lives in a hideout in the almost deserted Warsaw ghetto. Everyday he lowers a rope ladder he has made to hunt for food and firewood. Although he must wonder daily if he will be discovered, his strength and optimism and the hope for his father's return keep him going.

Where it's reviewed:
Horn Book, April 1984, page 197
Kirkus Reviews, March 1, 1984, page 16

Awards the book has won:
Mildred L. Batchelder Award 1984
Mordechai Bernstein Award (Israel) 1981

Other books by the author:
Man From the Other Side, 1991

Other books you might like:
Tamar Bergman, *The Boy from Over There*, 1988
 Two children in Israel, Avramik, a Holocaust survivor, and Rina, a sabra, struggle with rivalry and loss.
Marietta D. Moskin, *I Am Rosemarie*, 1987
 Rosemarie Brenner and her family face the horror of the concentration camp.
Hans Peter Richter, *Friedrich*, 1970
 As Hitler grows in power, Friedrich struggles to maintain his friendship with a gentile boy.
David Rubinowicz, *Diary of David Rubinowicz*, 1982
 David is twelve years old during the German occupation of Poland in 1940 and writes of his experiences during the Holocaust.

1365

Uri Orlev

The Man From the Other Side (Boston: Houghton Mifflin, 1991)

Age range: Grades 6-9

Subject(s): Jews; Anti-Semitism; Holocaust

Major character(s): Marek, Teenager; Jozek, Refugee

Time period(s): 1940s (1943)

Locale(s): Warsaw, Poland

What the book is about: This fictional account is based on a true story of a Polish boy living in Nazi-occupied Warsaw. The memoir follows fourteen year old Marek through some harrowing experiences. His Catholic mother informs Marek that his father was a Jew who was killed in prison because he was a Communist. The boy has extremely negative feelings about Jews. When he helps Jozek, a Polish Jew hidden from Nazi's and Anti-Semitic Poles, he begins a series of events that ultimately results in Jozek's violent death at the hands of the Nazis and Marek's narrow escape.

Where it's reviewed:
Booklist, June 15, 1991, page 1951
School Library Journal, September 1991, page 283

Other books by the author:
Island on Bird Street, 1985

Other books you might like:
Tamar Bergman, *Along the Tracks*, 1991
    A young Jewish boy is driven from his home by the German invasion. He undergoes many hardships before enjoying a normal homelife again.
Christa Laird, *Shadow of the Wall*, 1990
    Living in the Warsaw Ghetto, Misha is befriended by the director of the orphanage and finds a purpose to life when he joins a resistance organization.
Michael Mark, *Toba at the Hands of a Thief*, 1985
    Presents eleven episodes from the life of a Polish teenager as she prepares to leave her family for a new life in America during the early 1900s.
Terry W. Treseder, *Hear, O Israel: A Story of the Warsaw Ghetto*, 1990
    A Jewish boy describes life in the Warsaw Ghetto and his family's ultimate transference to and decimation in the camp of Treblinka.
Jane Yolen, *The Devil's Arithmetic*, 1988
    Hannah resents the traditions of her Jewish heritage until time travel places her in the middle of a small Jewish town in Nazi-occupied Poland.

1366

Edward Ormondroyd

Castaways on Long Ago (Berkeley, CA: Parnassus, 1973)

Age range: Grades 4-6

Subject(s): Supernatural

Major character(s): Linda Waite, Child, Vacationer; Dudley Waite, Child, Vacationer; Richard Waite, Child, Vacationer

Time period(s): 1970s

Locale(s): United States

What the book is about: Three children are spending a vacation on a farm while their parents attend a conference. They become caught up in the mystery of the boy on Long Ago Island. He is clearly trying to get them to visit him, but they have been forbidden to go to the island. How can they get there? How did the boy get there? When they get to the island, they find not a boy but a ghost.

Where it's reviewed:
Center for Children's Books Bulletin, February 1974, page 99
Horn Book, april 1974, page 150

Other books by the author:
All in Good Time, 1975
Theodore, 1966
Time at the Top, 1963
David and the Phoenix, 1957

Other books you might like:
Bill Brittain, *Dr. Dredd's Wagon of Wonders*, 1987
    The drought-stricken town of Coven Tree makes a deal for the services of Bufu, the Rainmaker.
Lois Duncan, *Down a Dark Hall*, 1974
    A boarding school with only four students turns out to be a cover for very strange mental/artistic experiments.
Nancy Garden, *The Door Between*, 1987
    Melissa realizes she must find and pacify a mysterious hermit to save a village from attacks by seemingly supernatual wild dogs.
Susan Gates, *The Burnhope Wheel*, 1989
    Ellen is obsessed with dreams and mental images tempting her to re-enact a tragedy from a century ago.
Patricia Wrightson, *Balyet*, 1989
    Jo falls under the spell of a secret thing in the Australian hills - a girl endlessly alive.

1367

Edward Ormondroyd

Time at the Top (New York: Bantam, 1963)

Age range: Grades 5-9

Subject(s): Fantasy; Science Fiction; Time Travel

Major character(s): Susan Shaw, Time Traveller; Mrs. Clutchett, Neighbor; Victoria, Teenager

Time period(s): 1960s (1960); 1880s (1881)

Locale(s): United States

What the book is about: Still appealing after thirty years, this is the story of Susan, who innocently takes an elevator which goes to the seventh floor in a six story building. She steps out of the elevator into 1881 America and has adventures that change the course of history.

Where it's reviewed:
Growing Point, May 1976, page 2880
Junior Bookshelf, June 1976, page 166
Times Literary Supplement, April 2, 1976, page 392

Other books by the author:
All in Good Time, 1975
Castaways on Long Ago, 1973
David and the Phoenix, 1957

Other books you might like:
John Bellairs, *The Ghost in the Mirror*, 1993
  Rose Rita Pottinger and Mrs. Zimmerman are transported back to 1828 to save the Weiss family from being destroyed by a wicked wizard.
Marie D. Goodwin, *Where Towers Pierce the Sky*, 1989
  An apprentice astrologer who travels to war-torn France in 1429 takes Lizzie with him where she becomes a double-agent protecting Joan of Arc.
E.W. Hildick, *The Case of the Weeping Witch*, 1992
  While working on a school project, the members of the McGurk Organization travel back to 1692 and find themselves involved in charges of witchcraft.
Richard Peck, *Voices After Midnight*, 1989
  Chad and Luke uncover a mystery involving the former tenants of the rented house their family lives in when the two brothers travel back to 1888.
Vivian Vande Velde, *A Well-Timed Enchantment*, 1990
  A girl and her cat disappear back in time to retrieve a lost watch.

| 1368 |

Mary Pope Osborne

Last One Home (New York: Dial, 1986)

Age range: Grades 5-7

Subject(s): Brothers and Sisters; Remarriage; Divorce

Major character(s): Bailey, Preteen

Time period(s): 1980s

Locale(s): United States

What the book is about: Twelve year old Bailey struggles with her feelings of loneliness after her parents' divorce when her father plans to remarry and her brother prepares to leave for military service.

Where it's reviewed:
Center for Children's Books Bulletin, June 1986, page 192
School Library Journal, May 1986, page 108

Other books by the author:
American Tall Tales, 1991
Best Wishes, Joe Brady, 1984
Love Always, Blue, 1984
Run, Run as Fast as You Can, 1982

Other books you might like:
C.S. Adler, *Tuna Fish Thanksgiving*, 1992
  Gilda's parents are getting divorced and she seems to be the only one interested in keeping the family together and caring for her brother and sister.
Robbie Branscum, *The Saving of P.S.*, 1977
  A twelve year old Arkansas girl rejects the idea of her preacher father's remarriage, and sets about destroying it.
Bruce Brooks, *What Hearts*, 1992
  After his mother remarries, Asa's sharp intellect and capacity for forgiveness help him deal with the inabilities of his new world.
A.M. Monson, *The Secret of Sanctuary Island*, 1991
  While still becoming accustomed to his father's remarriage, thirteen year old Todd and a friend set out to prove they observed a burglary that no one
Kyoko Mori, *Shizuko's Daughter*, 1993

After her mother's suicide when she is twelve, Yuki spends years living with her distant father and resentful new wife.

| 1369 |

Mary Pope Osborne

Illustrator: DyAnne DiSalvo-Ryan

Mo to the Rescue (New York: Dial, 1985)

Age range: Grades 1-3

Subject(s): Animals; Friendship; Sheriffs

Major character(s): Mo, Lawman (sheriff), Beaver

Time period(s): Indeterminate

Locale(s): Fictional Country

What the book is about: Four tales about sheriff Mo, the beaver, and his hilarious ways of helping the members of his community.

Where it's reviewed:
Booklist, October 15, 1985, page 342

Other books by the author:
The Knight at Dawn, 1993
Dinosaurs Before Dark, 1992
Mo and His Friends, 1989
Beauty and the Beast, 1987

Other books you might like:
Nancy L. Carlson, *Take Time to Relax*, 1991
  Tina the beaver and her family constantly rush off in different directions, until a storm keeps them snowbound at home.
Helme Heine, *The Pearl*, 1985
  Beaver thinks he has found a treasure, but a bad dream about what greed might do to his friends makes him think twice about it.
John Himmelman, *The Day-Off Machine*, 1990
  Graham's new invention combines with a big snowfall to force his busy beaver family to take a day off from their chores.
Amy MacDonald, *Little Beaver and the Echo*, 1990
  While trying to make friends with the voice across the pond, which is his own echo, a lonely little beaver meets some real friends along the way.
Karen Wagner, *Silly Fred*, 1989
  Silly Fred Pig decides to be more serious, like a beaver, only to discover that his life is not much fun without somersaults and songs.

| 1370 |

Pat O'Shea

The Hounds of the Morrigan (New York: Holiday, 1986)

Age range: Grades 5-9

Subject(s): Fantasy; Mythology

Major character(s): Pidge, Child; Brigit, Child; Dagda, Spirit

Time period(s): Indeterminate Past

Locale(s): Galway, Ireland

What the book is about: When ten year old Pidge finds an old book of magic in a bookshop in Ireland, the forces of good and evil gather to do battle over it. Pidge and Brigit are drawn into a battle of Irish spirits. Dagda protects them on their quest to destroy the evil serpent confined by St. Patrick. The Morrigan is a triple goddess of battle, evil, and sorrow. Great high fantasy for voracious readers. (469 pages)

Where it's reviewed:
Booklist, April 1, 1986, page 1144
School Library Journal, March 1986, page 78

Other books by the author:
Finn Mac Cool and the Small Men of Deeds, 1987

Other books you might like:
Grace Chetwin, *On All Hallow's Eve*, 1984
  Two sisters on their way home from a party step into another time period, where the forces of Good and Evil involve them in a life or death adventure.
Paul R. Fisher, *The Princess and the Thorn*, 1980
  Mole finds himself drawn into a battle between Good and Evil in which all the powers of the world seem to gather around him and the lost Great Sword.
Alan Garner, *The Weirdstone of Brisingamen: A Tale of Alderley*, 1960
  A girl and her brother are catapulted into a battle between Good and Evil for possession of a magical stone of great power that is in her braclet.
Shirley Rousseau Murphy, *Medallion of the Black Hound*, 1989
  The power of the Medallion of the Black Hound brings David into a world called Meryn where he must join the battle of good versus evil.
Walter Wangerin, *The Book of the Dun Cow*, 1978
  Good struggles with evil as Chaunteclear the rooster fights against the mysterious Wyrm.

1371

James Otis
Illustrator: George Wilson

Toby Tyler: or Ten Weeks with a Circus (Cleveland: World, 1947)

Age range: Grades 4-6

Subject(s): Circus; Runaways

Major character(s): Toby Tyler, Runaway, Worker (circus worker)

Time period(s): 1800s

Locale(s): United States

What the book is about: The story of a little boy who really does run away to join the fun and misery of circus life. After making new friends and learning he is a valuable and skilled person in his own right, Toby is reunited with his aunt and uncle who miss him and want him to return home.

Where it's reviewed:
Hornbook, February 1981, page 83
Times Literary Supplement, October 22, 1971, page 1332

Other books you might like:
Vivien Alcock, *Travelers by Night*, 1983
  To save an elephant from the slaughterhouse, two circus children kidnap the animal and begin a journey to take the elephant to a safe safari park.
Michael Morpurgo, *Mr. Nobody's Eyes*, 1989
  Follows the adventures of an extraordinary pair on the run: an escaped circus monkey and an ostracized young English boy named Harry.
Wilson Rawls, *Summer of the Monkeys*, 1976
  A fourteen year old Ozark mountain boy spends the summer trying to recapture some monkeys and one very smart chimp escaped from a traveling circus.
Barbara Smucker, *Incredible Jumbo: A Novel*, 1990
  A boy helps care for an African elephant that is the London Zoo's feature attraction and accompanies him to America to be part of P.T Barnam's circus.
Augusta Stevenson, *P.T. Barnum, Circus Boy*, 1964
  The boyhood of the showman, operator of a popular museum in New York, and a three ring circus known as "the greatest show on earth."

P

1372

Edward Packard

Illustrator: Larry Ross

ESP McGee (New York: Avon, 1983)

Age range: Grades 5-7

Series: ESP McGee

Subject(s): Mystery and Detective Stories

Major character(s): Matt Terrell, Teenager; Edward Samuel "ESP" McGee, Genius, Teenager; Nina Ravinsky, Teenager

Time period(s): 1980s

Locale(s): Greenport, Connecticut

What the book is about: The first of many books about mystery solver ESP McGee and his sidekick, Matt Terrell. When Matt, new to the neighborhood, makes friends with ESP, a supposed genius with extrasensory perception, they become involved with terrorists interested in sabotaging a nuclear plant.

Where it's reviewed:
School Library Journal, December 1983, page 82

Other books by the author:
The Forest of the King, 1987
ESP McGee and the Dolphin's Message, 1984
ESP McGee to the Rescue, 1984
ESP McGee and the Haunted Mansion, 1983

Other books you might like:
Anne Fine, *My War with Goggle-Eyes*, 1989
Kitty doesn't like her mother's boyfriend until unexpected events prompt her to help him find his place in the family.
Annabel Johnson, *Finders, Keepers*, 1981
A boy and his rebellious sister flee Denver following a catastrophic explosion at a nearby nuclear power plant, hoping to survive in the mountains.
Cynthia K. Lukas, *Center Stage Summer*, 1988
Johanna risks losing her college scholarship from the Byron company when she joins her sister in opposing the building of a nuclear reactor.
Louise Moeri, *Downwind*, 1984
When Ephraim and his family flee their home after a possible radiation leak, they find themselves in circumstances perhaps even more threatening.
Robert E. Swindells, *A Serpent's Tooth*, 1988
Chaos spreads when a workman falls ill on the site of a proposed nuclear waste dump, an area which is a burial ground for victims of the Black Death.

1373

Dora Pantell

Illustrator: Charles Geer

Miss Pickerell and the War of the Computers (New York: Watts, 1984)

Age range: Grades 4-6

Subject(s): Computers; Mystery and Detective Stories

Major character(s): Miss Lavinia Pickerell, Private Detective; Euphus, Computer Expert (Miss Pickerell's nephew); Mrs. Broadribb, Neighbor

Time period(s): 1980s

Locale(s): Square Toe City, Earth

What the book is about: Miss Pickerell, with her nephew, Euphus, an aspiring computer analyst, gets involved in computer pricing and a plot to overthrow the United States Government when she investigates the rising cost of cat food. (Series originated by Ellen MacGregor)

Where it's reviewed:
Booklist, January 15, 1985, page 722
School Library Journal, February 1985, page 78

Other books by the author:
Miss Pickerell and the Lost World, 1986
Miss Pickerell Goes on a Dig, 1966
Miss Pickerell on the Moon, 1965

Other books you might like:
Milton Dank, *The Computer Caper*, 1983
Attempting to help the family of their new Vietnamese friend to retrieve their savings, the Galaxy Gang takes on a money swindling operation.
Ellen MacGregor, *Miss Pickerell and the Weather Satellite*, 1971
Miss Pickerell tries to avert disaster caused by a faulty weather satellite.
Ellen MacGregor, *Miss Pickerell Tackles the Energy Crisis*, 1980
Miss Pickerell campaigns for the use of her nephew's fuel substitute when the antique car fair parade is cancelled because of the energy crisis.
Ian McMahan, *Lake Fear*, 1985
During an investigation of a strange diease, Ricky and his computer sidekick, ALEC, uncover computer fraud, chemical pollution and illegal explosives.
Walter G. Oleksy, *Bug Scanner and the Computer Mystery*, 1983

Bug Scanner, his dog, Print, and his pal, Millie, try to track down the thief of an experimental and very secret microchip.

Peggy Parish

Amelia Bedelia (New York: Harper, 1963)

Age range: Grades 1-3

Subject(s): Humor; Servants

Major character(s): Amelia Bedelia, Servant (maid); Mrs. Rogers, Employer; Mr. Rogers, Employer

Time period(s): Indeterminate

Locale(s): Fictional Country

What the book is about: Amelia Bedelia works as a maid and takes everything literally. When instructed to "dust" the house, she scatters "dusting" powder all over, and so on. A great favorite with newly independent readers who love to laugh.

Where it's reviewed:
Los Angeles Times Book Review, June 26, 1983
Reading Teacher, November 1978, page 148
Reading Teacher, December 1984, page 276

Other books by the author:
Amelia Bedelia Goes Camping, 1985
Good Work, Amelia Bedelia, 1976
Amelia Bedelia and the Surprise Shower, 1966
Thank You, Amelia Bedelia, 1964

Other books you might like:
Robert E. Barry, *Mr. Willowby's Christmas Tree*, 1991
 Mr. Willowby's Christmas tree is too tall, so he cuts the top and gives it to the maid for a tree; she finds it too tall, so she cuts the top, etc.
Rose Impey, *Who's a Bright Girl?*, 1985
 A little girl becomes leader of a gang of pirates after they try to make her their maid, cook and seamstress.
Anita Lobel, *The Straw Maid*, 1983
 Forced to cook and clean for three robbers, a little girl tricks them and escapes with their booty.
Audrey Wood, *Rude Giants*, 1993
 Beatrix the butter maid saves Gerda the cow and transforms rude giants into good neighbors.
Paul O. Zelinsky, *The Maid and the Mouse and the Odd-Shaped House*, 1981
 An oddly-shaped house takes on the appearance of a cat as the maid and the mouse who live there make various changes in it.

Peggy Parish

Illustrator: James Watts

Good Hunting, Blue Sky (New York: Harper and Row, 1988)

Age range: Grades 1-3

Subject(s): Humor; Hunting; Indians of North America

Major character(s): Blue Sky, Child, Indian

Time period(s): Indeterminate Past

Locale(s): United States

What the book is about: Blue Sky intends to bring home some meat with his new bow and arrow but the food brings him home instead.

Where it's reviewed:
Booklist, December 1, 1988, page 657
School Library Journal, March 1989, page 168

Other books by the author:
Scruffy, 1988
Mr. Adam's Mistake, 1982
No More Monsters for Me!, 1981
Too Many Rabbits, 1974

Other books you might like:
Roald Dahl, *The Magic Finger*, 1966
 Angered by a neighboring family's sport hunting, an eight year old girl turns her magic finger on them and changes them into birds.
Adele De Leeuw, *Uncle Davy Lane, Mighty Hunter*, 1970
 Five tales about the exploits of the mightiest hunter in North Carolina.
Oren Lyons, *Dog Story*, 1973
 An Indian boy recounts his relationship with the unusual dog that becomes his hunting partner.
Lynn Sweat, *The Wonderful Hunting Dog*, 1973
 The hunting dog is not fast enough to catch a rabbit, but his sensible owner, a lady in a striped cap, finds a way to resolve the problem.
Lynd Ward, *The Biggest Bear*, 1952
 Johnny goes hunting for a bearskin to hang on his family's barn and returns with a small bundle of trouble.

Barbara Park

Almost Starring Skinnybones (New York: Knopf, 1988)

Age range: Grades 4-6

Subject(s): Schools; Humor

Major character(s): Alex "Skinnybones" Frankovitch, Child

Time period(s): 1980s

What the book is about: Alex "Skinnybones" Frankovitch hopes that starring in a national TV commercial will help him shed his hated nickname and gain the respect he craves.

Where it's reviewed:
Booklist, March 1, 1988, page 1185
School Library Journal, April 1988, page 103

Other books by the author:
Don't Make Me Smile, 1981
The Kid in the Red Jacket, 1987
My Mother Got Married and Other Disasters, 1989

Other books you might like:
Marlene Fanta Shyer, *Adorable Sunday*, 1983
 13 year old Sunday Donaldson finds that being a successful actress and model is not all she expected.
Barbara A. Steiner, *Oliver Dibbs to the Rescue*, 1985
 10 year old Ollie creates one disaster after another trying to raise money for wildlife preservation.

Gordon Korman, *Zucchini Warriors*, 1988
  The students at MacDonald Hall school find themselves with a football stadium and a gungho fried zucchini stick sponsor.

Patricia Maclachlan, *Arthur, for the Very First Time*, 1980
  Arthur learns a whole new way of life when he is sent to spend the summer with his eccentric great-aunt and great-uncle.

Gene Kemp, *The Turbulent Term of Tyke Tyler*, 1977
  Tyke Tyler specializes in getting into scrapes and turning his school into turmoil.

1377

Barbara Park

Buddies (New York: Knopf, 1985)

Age range: Grades 5-8

Subject(s): Camps and Camping; Friendship; Popularity

Major character(s): Dinah Feeney, Teenager; Cassandra Barnhill, Teenager; Fern Wadley, Teenager

Time period(s): 1980s

Locale(s): Illinois

What the book is about: Dinah goes to Camp Miniwawa longing to be popular, and to be friends with Cassandra and Marilyn, but she is hampered by an unattractive fellow camper, Fern, who wants to be her best friend. Fern's mom is obnoxious, which explains a lot about Fern, camp nerd and cabin mate.

Where it's reviewed:
Booklist, April 15, 1985, page 1198
Center for Children's Books Bulletin, May 1985, page 173
School Library Journal, May 1985, page 94

Other books by the author:
Beanpole, 1983
Skinnybones, 1982
Operation Dump the Chump, 1982
Don't Make Me Smile, 1981

Other books you might like:
Mary Anderson, *Who Says Nobody's Perfect?*, 1987
  When Ingvild arrives in New York as an exchange student, she shares a with Jennifer who becomes jealous of Ingvild's beauty and popularity at school.
Judy Baer, *Camp Pinetree Pals*, 1991
  Becky's plans for summer camp popularity nearly backfire.
Caroline B. Cooney, *The Return of the Vampire*, 1991
  Devnee makes a bargain with the vampire to gain beauty and brains, at the expense of her friends.
Lisa Norby, *The Holly Hudnut Admiration Society*, 1989
  Rejected by Holly and the other popular girls, Jan and her friends form their own club and find that there are more valuable things than popularity.
Susan Beth Pfeffer, *April Upstairs*, 1990
  April has trouble making friends at her new middle school, until her father's friendship with a rock star catapults her into sudden popularity.

1378

Barbara Park

The Kid in the Red Jacket (New York: Knopf, 1987)

Age range: Grades 4-6

Subject(s): Moving, Household; Friendship; Humor

Major character(s): Howard Jeeter, Child; Molly Vera Thompson, Child

Time period(s): 1980s

Locale(s): Massachusetts

What the book is about: Howard has just moved from Arizona with a bawling baby brother and a smelly basset hound into a 200-year-old house on Chester Pewe Street. Molly, a neighbor, is a first grader with red hair styled like Bozo the Clown. When Howard has trouble making friends, Molly takes a liking to him and things begin to change.

Where it's reviewed:
Center for Children's Books Bulletin, March 1987, page 133

Other books by the author:
Maxie, Rosie and Earl, 1990
My Mother Got Married.and Other Disasters, 1989
Almost Starring Skinnybones, 1988
Marie, Rosie and Earl: Partners in Grime, 1980

Other books you might like:
Emily Rhoads Johnson, *Spring and the Shadow Man*, 1984
  Spring Weldon's family moves the summer before her sixth grade year and she learns a great deal from a blind neighbor.
Alfred Slote, *Moving In*, 1988
  11 year old Robby Miller faces moving for the thrid time since his mother's death.
Patricia Hermes, *Kevin Corbett Eats Flies*, 1986
  Finally in a happy situation for the first time in a long time, Kevin plays Cupid to try to keep his father from moving again.
Patricia Hermes, *Heads, I Win*, 1988
  Fifth grader Bailey, shunted from one foster home to another, tries to become class president.
Betty Bates, *That's What T.J. Says*, 1982
  Just when Mouse finds a friend in the school orchestra, her father announces they are moving to Sioux City.

1379

Barbara Park

Illustrator: Alexander Strogart

Maxie, Rosie, and Earl - Partners in Grime (New York: Knopf, 1990)

Age range: Grades 4-6

Subject(s): Behavior; Schools

Major character(s): Earl Wilbur, Preteen; Rosie Swanson, Preteen; Maxie Zuckerman, Preteen

Time period(s): 1990s

Locale(s): United States

What the book is about: When their disciplinary meetings with the principal are postponed, three students skip school. Earl acts ridiculous whenever he's nervous, Rosie believes she was put on earth to tattle and Maxie is just too smart for his own good. Together they not only skip school, but land in a dumpster and become fugitives from justice. Even though they are very different, they wind up good friends.

Where it's reviewed:
Booklist, March 1, 1990, page 1348
Kirkus Reviews, March 15, 1990, page 428
School Library Journal, August 1990, page 149

Other books by the author:
Rosie Swanson: Fourth Grade Geek for President, 1991
My Mother Got Married and Other Disasters, 1989
Operation Dump the Chump, 1982
Skinnybones, 1982

Other books you might like:
Betsy Byars, *The Blossoms and the Green Phantom*, 1987
 Vern dreads letting a new friend meet his family. Pap has fallen into a dumpster and can't get out and Junior is working on a weird secret invention.
Joyce Hansen, *Yellow Bird and Me*, 1986
 Doris becomes friends with Yellow Bird as she helps him with his studies and his part in the school play and discovers that he is dyslexic.
Betty Hyland, *The Girl with the Crazy Brother*, 1987
 Dana's fears about moving across the country and making friends are made worse when her older brother is diagnosed as schizophrenic.
Emily Moore, *Something to Count On*, 1980
 Lorraine's behavior problems at school are aggravated by her family situation and eased by an understanding teacher.
Louis Sacher, *There's a Boy in the Girls' Bathroom*, 1990
 An unmanageable misfit learns to believe in himself when he gets to know the new school counselor, who is sort of a misfit too.

1380

Barbara Park

My Mother Got Married and Other Disasters (New York: Knopf, 1989)

Age range: Grades 4-6

Subject(s): Stepfamilies

Major character(s): Charles "Charlie" Hickle, Preteen; Lydia Russo, Teenager; Ben Russo, Step-Parent

Time period(s): 1980s

Locale(s): United States

What the book is about: Twelve year old Charlie experiences many difficulties in adjusting to a new stepfather, stepsister, and stepbrother. Things start out poorly when Charlie's first meeting with his relatives-to-be finds him hiding in the broom closet in his Superman pajamas.

Where it's reviewed:
Booklist, March 1, 1989, page 1195
School Library Journal, March 1989, page 178

Other books by the author:
Rosie Swanson: Fourth Grade Geek for President, 1991
Beanpole, 1983
Playing Beatie Bow, 1982
Don't Make Me Smile, 1981

Other books you might like:
Bruce Brooks, *What Hearts*, 1992
 After his mother divorces his father and remarries, Asa's sharp intellect and capacity for forgiveness help him deal with the adjustment.
Ilene Cooper, *Mean Streak*, 1991
 Alienating her best friend, Robin, eleven year old Veronica has no one to turn to for support when it appears that her divorced father may remarry.
Anne Lindbergh, *Travel Far, Pay No Fair*, 1992
 When 12 year old Owen finds his cousin has a magic bookmark, he joins her in hopes of finding a way to prevent their parents' upcoming marriage.
Berniece Rabe, *Tall Enough to Own the World*, 1989
 Unable to read, ten year old Joey is often in trouble at school, until a neighbor, a cat, and his new stepfather help him conquer his problem.
J.P. Reading, *The Summer of Sassy Jo*, 1989
 Almost fourteen, Sara Jo tries to cope with her emotions as she goes to spend time with her mother, a former alcoholic who abandoned her as a child.

1381

Barbara Park

Illustrator: Rob Sauber

Operation Dump the Chump (New York: Knopf, 1982)

Age range: Grades 4-6

Subject(s): Brothers and Sisters

Major character(s): Oscar Winkle, Preteen; Robert Winkle, Child

Time period(s): 1980s

Locale(s): United States

What the book is about: Eleven year old Oscar devises an elaborate plan to get rid of his little brother, Robert, who does things like taking Oscar's underwear to school for show and tell, and dumping a box of spiders on Oscar's bedroom floor.

Where it's reviewed:
Booklist, March 1, 1982, page 899
School Library Journal, May 1982, page 136

Awards the book has won:
Young Hoosier Book Award 1985

Other books by the author:
The Kid in the Red Jacket, 1987
Beanpole, 1983
Skinnybones, 1982
Don't Make Me Smile, 1981

Other books you might like:
Allan Baillie, *Adrift*, 1992
 While playing in an old crate on the beach, a young boy, his little sister, and a cat find themselves adrift on the sea.
Barbara Baker, *N-O Spells No!*, 1990
 During the events of one weekend, Walter and his little sister come to appreciate each other.
Judy Delton, *Back Yard Angel*, 1983
 Ten year old Angel gets weary of taking care of her little brother, Rags.
Michael Dorris, *Morning Girl*, 1992

Morning Girl loves the day and her brother, Star Boy, loves the night, as they take turns describing their life in pre-Columbian America.

Morris Gleitzman, *Two Weeks with the Queen*, 1991
　　Sent to live with relatives in England when his little brother develops cancer, Colin tries to see the Queen to help find a cure for him.

1382

Ruth Park

Playing Beatie Bow (New York: Atheneum, 1982)

Age range: Grades 5-7

Subject(s): Family Life; Space and Time

Major character(s): Abigail Kirk, Teenager; Natalie Crown, Child; Kathy Kirk, Parent (mother)

Time period(s): 1980s

Locale(s): Sydney, Australia

What the book is about: When Lynette's parents are divorced, she is so angry at her father she refuses to answer to any of the names he calls her, and chooses Abigail because it sounds like a witch's name. In the midst of dealing with her parents' reconciliation, Abigail is drawn back to a poor Sydney slum of the 1870s. She learns the history behind the children's game, "Beatie Bow" and later falls in love with a Bow descendant.

Where it's reviewed:
Horn Book, August 1982, page 407
School Library Journal, May 1982, page 65

Awards the book has won:
Boston Globe/Horn Book Award - Fiction Honor
Australian Children's Book of the Year Award 1981

Other books by the author:
Things in Corners, 1989
My Sister Sif, 1986
When the Winds Changed, 1982
The Gigantic Balloon, 1975

Other books you might like:
Patricia Beatty, *Jonathan Down Under*, 1982
　　After his father is killed in a mine cave-in, Jonathan must find a way to survive down under.
Laurence R. Kittleman, *Canyons Beyond the Sky*, 1985
　　Nothing can prepare Evan for the experience of being transported 5,000 years back in time and befriending an Indian boy from an ancient culture.
Jane Langton, *The Astonishing Stereoscope*, 1971
　　By discovering they can enter the three-dimensional world of the stereoscope, two children learn something about reality.
Cynthia Voigt, *Building Blocks*, 1984
　　In a trip back in time, Brann meets his father as a ten year old boy, and learns for the first time to love and understand him.
David Wiseman, *Adam's Common*, 1984
　　As a fourteen year old American attempts to preserve a piece of land in England, she makes contact with a boy of the 19th century.

1383

Richard Parker

He Is Your Brother (New York: Nelson, 1976)

Age range: Grades 5-6

Subject(s): Learning Disabilities; Family Life

Major character(s): Lawrence "Orry", Child, Handicapped (autistic); Mike, Preteen, Relative (brother)

Time period(s): 1970s

Locale(s): United States

What the book is about: Orry is an autistic child. His eleven year old brother, Mike, pays little attention to him until he discovers that Orry is also interested in trains. Mike takes Orry on outings and begins to go to therapy with him. As Orry improves, the family begins to change as well.

Where it's reviewed:
Kirkus Reviews, June 1, 1976, page 634
School Library Journal, September 1976, page 123

Other books by the author:
Hugo Takes Off, 1976
Quarter Boy, 1976

Other books you might like:
Karen Ackerman, *The Broken Boy*, 1991
　　Solly recounts his friendship with a mentally disturbed boy.
Jim Arter, *Cruel and Unusual Punishment*, 1991
　　Arnold specializes in anti-social behavior until a teacher he calls "Apeface" takes a special interest in him.
Louise Dickinson Rich, *Three of a Kind*, 1970
　　An orphan girl in a foster home and a tailless kitten help an emotionally disturbed four year old boy get well.
Eleanor Spence, *The Devil Hole*, 1976
　　The birth of an autistic child changes the lives of a once happy Australian family.
Susan Terris, *The Drowning Boy*, 1972
　　A twelve year old boy feels he is a complete idiot until he begins to help a six year old schizophrenic who is staying with a neighboring family.

1384

Francine Pascal

The Hand-Me-Down Kid (New York: Viking, 1980)

Age range: Grades 4-6

Subject(s): Honesty; Guilt

Major character(s): Arianne "Ari" Jacobs, Preteen; Rhona Finkelstein, Preteen; Jane Richardson, Preteen

Time period(s): 1980s

Locale(s): New York, New York (Greenwich Village)

What the book is about: Ari, eleven and the youngest of three, finds herself picked on all the time, and gets in trouble when she lends her sister's bike without permission in order to keep a friendship. The bike is stolen. A new girl in school, Jane Richardson, also has older siblings and has learned to hold her own and not let others push her around. Together, Ari and Jane find the stolen bike and nail the thief.

Where it's reviewed:
Horn Book, June 1980, page 302

School Library Journal, September 1980, page 76

Awards the book has won:
Dorothy Canfield Fisher Children's Book Award 1982

Other books by the author:
Love and Betrayal and Hold the Mayo!, 1985
My First Love and Other Disasters, 1979
Hangin' Out with Cici, 1977

Other books you might like:
Carole S. Adler, *A Tribe for Lexi*, 1991
    While spending the summer at her cousin's farm in upstate New York, Lexi finds Jeb to be the only one to offer friendship and she decides to help him.
Matt Christopher, *Undercover Tailback*, 1992
    Parker is a notorious liar. Now he has to convince his team that he saw a mysterious stranger stealing football plays from the coach's playbook.
Sheila Greenwald, *Rosy Cole's Great American Guilt Club*, 1985
    Rosy forms a club which will allow her rich friends to give her their surplus clothes, sports gear and jewelry.
Elizabeth-Ann Sachs, *Just Like Always*, 1981
    Two girls become best friends while in the hospital, despite their differences.
Susan Wojcieshowski, *Promises to Keep*, 1991
    Patty makes a New Year's resolution to beome friends with the popular and rich Penni.

1385

Francine Pascal

Hangin' Out with Cici (New York: Simon & Schuster, 1977)

Age range: Grades 6-8

Subject(s): Schools/Boarding Schools; Mothers and Daughters; Time Travel

Major character(s): Victoria, Teenager (Time Traveller); Cici, Parent

Time period(s): 1970s; 1940s (1944)

Locale(s): New York, New York

What the book is about: Victoria has just been kicked out of school, and then is caught smoking pot at her cousin's birthday party. She heads home to New York City, dreading seeing her mother. But Victoria has an accident on the train and enters a time warp, which takes her back to 1944. Is that oddly familiar girl she meets at Penn Station really her mother?

Where it's reviewed:
Booklist, May 1, 1977, page 1355
Hornbook, October 1977, page 541
Kirkus Reviews, February 1, 1977, page 99

Other books by the author:
The Hand Me-Down Kid, 1980

Other books you might like:
Helen Cresswell, *Moondial*, 1987
    While staying with her mother's godmother, Minty is drawn to a sundial which takes her back in time and links her life to that of two unhappy children
Amy Ehrlich, *The Dark Card*, 1993

After her mother's death, Laura is lured by the glamour of Atlantic City, where she uses her mother's jewelry and makeup to create a new identity.
Jamie Suzanne, *Brooke and Her Rock Star Mom*, 1991
    Brooke's mom is the incredible new rock singer, Coco. Brooke must keep her mother's identity secret because having a family could ruin Coco's career.
Kathryn Reiss, *Time Windows*, 1991
    Miranda moves with her family to a small town and a new house in which a mysterious dollhouse allows her to see into the past.
Nicholas Wilde, *Down Came a Blackbird*, 1991
    James withdraws into himself when sent to his uncle while his alcoholic mother is in the hospital. Strange dreams help him rediscover his emotions.

1386

Katherine Paterson

Illustrator: Diane Diamond

Bridge to Terabithia (New York: Crowell, 1977)

Age range: Grades 5-7

Subject(s): Friendship; Death

Major character(s): Jess Aarons, Preteen (5th Grader); Leslie Burke, Preteen (5th Grader); Miss Edmonds, Teacher

Time period(s): 1970s

Locale(s): Virginia

What the book is about: Jess has practiced all summer to be the fastest runner in the fifth grade and is shocked when Leslie, a new student and a girl, beats him. Despite the competition, they become good friends and create a secret place they name Terabithia. Jess's friendship with Leslie, who comes from a much different background, opens up new worlds of imagination to him and changes his outlook greatly. Then he must struggle to accept her unexpected death.

Where it's reviewed:
School Librarian, June 1979, page 165
School Library Journal, November 1977, page 61

Awards the book has won:
Newbery Medal 1978
Blue Spruce Award 1986

Other books by the author:
Lyddie, 1991
Come Sing, Jimmy Jo, 1985
Jacob Have I Loved, 1980
The Great Gilly Hopkins, 1978

Other books you might like:
Judie Angell, *Ronnie and Rosy*, 1977
    Just when things are looking up for thirteen year old Ronnie, her father dies, creating a void she and her mother have trouble filling.
Margery Evernden, *The Kite Song*, 1984
    After his mother's death, 11 year old Jamie is put in the care of his half-brother; with the help of a special education teacher, he begins to adjust.
Betty Miles, *The Trouble with Thirteen*, 1973
    12 year old Annie is unwilling to face some major changes in her life.
Doris Buchanan Smith, *A Taste of Blackberries*, 1973

A young boy recounts his efforts to adjust to the accidental death of his best friend.

Ellen Emerson White, *Life Without Friends*, 1987
  After the drug overdose of a fellow student, Beverly breaks away from the fast crowd, but finds herself friendless and full of guilt.

1387

Katherine Paterson

Come Sing, Jimmy Jo (New York: Dutton, 1985)

Age range: Grades 5-8

Subject(s): Country Music; Family Life; Musicians

Major character(s): James "Jimmy Jo" Johnson, Musician; Olive Johnson, Musician (Jimmy's Mother); Jerry Lee Johnson, Musician (Jimmy's father)

Time period(s): 1980s

Locale(s): West Virginia

What the book is about: James has learned the Appalachian blue grass songs from his grandmother, but at eleven, still watches from the wings when his whole family performs country music. When he finally takes his place with the group, he becomes a hit, and finds coping with being famous, and having friends with the kind of schedule his family keeps, can be as much of a challenge as being left out.

Where it's reviewed:
Center for Children's Books Bulletin, June 1985, page 191
School Library Journal, April 1985, page 91

Other books by the author:
Lyddie, 1991
Jacob Have I Loved, 1980
The Great Gilly Hopkins, 1978
Bridge to Terebithia, 1977

Other books you might like:
Judie Angell, *The Buffalo Nickel Blues Band*, 1982
  Eddie Levy relates how he and his four friends who are involved in a blues band change as their music does, or is it the other way around?
Mary S. Bell, *Sonata for Mind and Heart*, 1992
  Sixteen year old Ron, living in Toronto, is determined to go to New York to try for an important music scholarship despite his mother's disapproval.
Mary Blount Christian, *Singin' Somebody Else's Song*, 1988
  Tormented by his feelings of responsibility for his best friend's suicide, Gideon tries to fulfill their shared dream of breaking into country music.
Erika Tamar, *Blues for Silk Garcia*, 1983
  After her father's death, fifteen year old Linda, who has her father's looks and his gift for music, seeks the truth about him and her musical interest
Cynthia Voigt, *Orfe*, 1992
  Emmy tells of her relationship with Orfe, an unusually talented musician, and the relationship between Orfe and Yuri, a recovering drug addict.

1388

Katherine Paterson

The Great Gilly Hopkins (New York: Crowell, 1978)

Age range: Grades 5-6

Subject(s): Foster Homes; Friendship

Major character(s): Gilly Hopkins, Preteen; Maime Trotter, Foster Parent

Time period(s): 1980s

Locale(s): United States

What the book is about: An eleven year old foster child tries to cope with her longings and fears as she schemes against everyone who tries to be friendly, until she meets Maime, who is able to reach her.

Where it's reviewed:
Book World, December 3, 1978, page E4
Publisher's Weekly, June 18, 1979, page 94

Other books by the author:
Lyddie, 1991
Park's Quest, 1988
Come Sing, Jimmie Jo, 1985
Bridge to Terabithia, 1977

Other books you might like:
Carole S. Adler, *The Silver Coach*, 1979
  A summer away from her mother, and an eye-opening visit with her father give Chris a chance to gain a new perspective on the changes in her life.
Susan Terris, *No Scarlet Ribbons*, 1981
  Close to harming her mother's recent marriage, Rachel finally accepts her stepfather's affection and her own need to make peace with her family.
Ella Thorp Ellis, *Sleepwalker's Moon*, 1980
  Anna discovers that the "perfect family" she is staying with until her father returns from war, is far from perfect.
Harriet Gilbert, *Running Away*, 1979
  The family troubles of a friend help Jane see that discord and conflict exist in many people's lives.
Brenda Scott Wilkinson, *Ludell's New York Time*, 1980
  Ludell leaves everything she has ever known in Georgia to live with her mother in New York City.

1389

Katherine Paterson

Jacob Have I Loved (New York: Crowell, 1980)

Age range: Grades 5 and Up

Subject(s): Twins; Jealousy; Identity

Major character(s): Louise Bradshaw, Teenager; Caroline Bradshaw, Teenager

Time period(s): 1930s (1930s-1940s)

Locale(s): Rass Island, Maryland; Virginia

What the book is about: Louise, a tomboy growing up in the 1940s fights to gain recognition beside her pretty and talented twin sister, whom everyone seems to prefer. Louise befriends a "heathen" who moves in with the family after a hurricane destroys his home. He helps Louise reach her goal of becoming a nurse-midwife, and establishing her own identity.

Where it's reviewed:
Horn Book, December 1980, page 622
New York Times Book Review, December 21, 1980
School Librarian, December 1981, page 349

Awards the book has won:
Newbery Medal 1981
Crabbery Honor 1981

Other books by the author:
King's Equal, 1992
Lyddie, 1991
Come Sing, Jimmy Jo, 1985
Bridge to Terebithia, 1977

Other books you might like:
Carol Ryrie Brink, *Caddie Woodlawn*, 1988
    The adventures of an eleven year old tomboy growing up on the Wisconsin frontier in the mid 19th century.
Dorothy Guck, *Danger Rides the Forest*, 1968
    Endangering her life fighting forest fires and rounding up rustlers and poachers, the forest ranger's tomboy daughter, Jonnie, lives up to her name.
M.E. Kerr, *The Son of Someone Famous*, 1974
    Living under a pseudonym with his grandfather in a small town, the son of a celebrity grows up with the local tomboy.
Jane Langton, *The Boyhood of Grace Jones*, 1972
    A young girl persists in being a tomboy despite the disapproval of her parents and classmates.
Marilyn Sachs, *Peter and Veronica*, 1969
    A twelve year old Jewish boy struggles to maintain his friendship with his tomboy classmate, Veronica, despite the opposition of others.

1390

Katherine Paterson

Lyddie (New York: Dutton, 1991)

Age range: Grades 6 and Up

Subject(s): Self-Reliance; Work; Factories

Major character(s): Lyddie Worthen, Teenager, Worker; Charles Worthen, Child; Mattie Worthen, Parent

Time period(s): 1840s

Locale(s): Lowell, Massachusetts

What the book is about: Her parents are gone and her brothers and sisters sent to live with other people. Lyddie is on her own. When she hears about the mill jobs in Lowell, she heads there with the goal of earning enough money to reunite her family. When the working conditions begin to affect her friends' health, she has to make a choice. Will she speak up for better working conditions and risk her job and her dream? Or will she stay quiet until it is perhaps too late?

Where it's reviewed:
Booklist, January 1, 1991, page 920
School Library Journal, February 1991, page 82

Other books by the author:
Park's Quest, 1988
Jacob Have I Loved, 1980
The Great Gilly Hopkins, 1978
Bridge to Terabithia, 1977

Other books you might like:
Patricia Beatty, *Sarah and Me and the Lady From the Sea*, 1989
    In 1895, their father's business failure forces the family to live in their beach home, and 12 year old Marcella finds the experience rewarding.
Mabel Esther Allan, *The Mills Down Below*, 1980
    In England in the summer of 1914, a young girl tries to win some women's rights from her Victorian father.
F.N. Monjo, *Slater's Mill*, 1972
    A fictional story of a young immigrant's effort to build America's first automated spinning mill entirely from memory of similar factories in England.
Scott O'Dell, *Island of the Blue Dolphins*, 1987
    The courage and self-reliance of an Indian girl who lives alone for eighteen years on an isolated island off the California coast.
Jill Paton Walsh, *A Chance Child*, 1978
    Christopher, while searching for his half brother, locates Parliamentary Papers describing working conditions during the Industrial Revolution.

1391

Jill Paton Walsh

A Chance Child (New York: Farrar, Straus, and Giroux, 1978)

Age range: Grades 6-9

Subject(s): Labor Conditions; Historical; Space and Time

Major character(s): Creep, Abuse Victim, Time Traveller; Christopher, Relative (half brother)

Time period(s): 1800s

Locale(s): England

What the book is about: An unwanted and mistreated child, Creep is locked in a closet by his abusive mother, and emerges into 19th century England, still a victim, this time of the child labor practices of the time. He finds friends among other abused children and chooses not to return home. A sub-plot involves Creep's half-brother who traces him through old Parliamentary records of child labor. Great writing and great history.

Where it's reviewed:
Booklist, April 1, 1979, page 1222
Hornbook, February 1979, page 64
Kirkus Reviews, December 15, 1978, page 1359

Other books by the author:
Gaffer Sampson's Luck, 1984
Parcel of Patterns, 1983
The Green Book, 1982
The Dolphin Crossing, 1967

Other books you might like:
Patricia Beatty, *Turn Homeward, Hannalee*, 1984
    Hannalee, forced to relocate along with other Georgia mill-workers during the Civil War, leaves her mother, promising to return home at the war's end.
Rhoda Cahn, *No Time for School, No Time for Play*, 1972
    Describes the lives of working children in the United States before the passage of child labor laws. (Non-Fiction)
Ruth Robins Holland, *Mill Child*, 1970

Traces the history of child labor in the United States from the early nineteenth century to the present day.

Katherine Paterson, *Lyddie*, 1991

A Vermont farm girl Lyddie Worthen is determined to gain her independence by becoming a factory worker in Massachusetts in the 1840s.

R. Conrad Stein, *The Story of Child Labor Laws*, 1984

Traces the history of laws passed during the early 1900's to end the exploitation of child laborers.

1392

Jill Paton Walsh

Illustrator: Robin Eaton

Children of the Fox (New York: Farrar, 1978)

Age range: Grades 5-8

Subject(s): Short Stories

Major character(s): Themistokles, Hero, Historical Figure; Demeas, Hero

Time period(s): 5th century B.C.

Locale(s): Athens, Greece

What the book is about: The setting is the Persian Wars and the shifting political scene between Athens and Sparta. Three young people tell their stories about the Athenian hero, Themistokles. A princess helps him reach Persia and safety from both the Spartans and Athenians, Demeas runs from Sparta and Aster is involved in the Athenian flight to Salamis.

Where it's reviewed:
Hornbook, October 1978, page 520
Kirkus, July 1, 1978, page 690
School Library Journal, September 1978, page 165

Other books by the author:
Torch, 1988
A Parcel of Patterns, 1983
The Island Sunrise, 1976
The Huffler, 1975

Other books you might like:
Jacqueline Dineen, *The Greeks*, 1992
Surveys the civilization of Ancient Greece, including information about its history, government, religion, family life, social structure, and culture.
Michael Gibson, *Gods, Men and Monsters from the Greek Myths*, 1977
A collection of myths relating the exploits and adventures of the gods and heroes of ancient Greece.
Margaret Hodges, *The Avenger*, 1982
Alexis, son of the ruling family of the ancient Greek city of Asini, becomes obsessed with his quest for vengence against his family's enemies.
Charles Sakellariou, *Themistokles*, 1970
A biography of the heroic 5th century BC Greek general and statesman.
Henry Treece, *The Windswept City*, 1967
A boy, slave to Helen of Troy, witnesses the events leading to t he downfall of Troy.

1393

Jill Paton Walsh

Illustrator: Lloyd Bloom

The Green Book (New York: Farrar Straus & Giroux, 1982)

Age range: Grades 4-6

Subject(s): Science Fiction

Major character(s): Pattie, Child; Jason, Child

Time period(s): Indeterminate Future

Locale(s): Shine, Planet—Imaginary

What the book is about: A child settler's account of the hazardous colonization of a new planet. Pattie's family is one of the last to leave the dying Earth, and their choice of destination is limited by the poor ship they are in. They find a hospitable planet and name it Shine. As they struggle with plants that grow up and turn into crystals, giant moths and frequent arguements, Pattie keeps a journal in the blank book she chose as the one thing she could bring on the trip. It is ultimately the children who find a way to make the planet's strange ecosystem support humans.

Where it's reviewed:
Horn Book, December 1982, page 651
School Library Journal, October 1982, page 156

Other books by the author:
Gaffer Sampson's Luck, 1984
The Huffler, 1975
Toolmaker, 1974
Goldengrove, 1972

Other books you might like:
Umberto Eco, *The Three Astronauts*, 1989
Three astronauts from different countries land on Mars, meet a strange Martian, and make an amazing discovery about the nature of humanity.
Jonathan Etra, *Aliens for Breakfast*, 1988
Finding an intergalactic special agent in his cereal box, Richard joins the fight to save Earth from the Dranes.
Gery Greer, *Jason and the Aliens Down the Street*, 1991
Jason meets Cooper Vor and Lootna, aliens from space, and travels with them to a distant planet to retrieve a stolen energy crystal.
Hazel Hutchins, *Anastasia Morningstar*, 1990
Sarah and Ben decide Anastasia Morningstar's uncanny magical powers would be the perfect subject for their science project.
Jenny Pausacker, *Fast Forward*, 1991
With his grandmother's Anti-Boredom Machine, twelve year old Kieran finds he can speed up time or travel in the past.

1394

Jill Paton Walsh

Illustrator: Juliette Palmer

The Huffler (New York: Farrar, 1975)

Age range: Grades 5-8

Subject(s): Canals

Major character(s): Bess Jebb, Servant; Ned Jebb, Child

Time period(s): Indeterminate Past

Locale(s): England

What the book is about: A ruffled, proper English miss runs away and poses as a servant in order to fit into a canal boat family. Young Bess and Ned are delivering cargo alone because of a family crisis. The tales of the canal folk, the intricacies of the locks, and the friendliness of the canal travelers fill the book.

Where it's reviewed:
Booklist, February 15, 1976, page 858
Hornbook, April 1976, page 159
School Library Journal, December 1975, page 55

Other books by the author:
Grace, 1992
Torch, 1988
A Parcel of Patterns, 1983
Unleaving, 1976

Other books you might like:
Richard Church, *The White Doe*, 1968
   The friendship between two boys of different social classes is threatened by an insensitive, class-conscious youth who moves in their neighborhood.
Jane Louise Curry, *What the Dickens!*, 1991
   Twins whose father runs a boat on the Juniata Canal learn of a bookseller's plan to steal Charles Dickens' new novel while he tours the US.
Len Hilts, *Timmy O'Dowd and the Big Ditch*, 1988
   In the late 1800s Timmy and his "city boy" cousin must forget their differences and pool their energies when the Erie Canal is damaged by storms.
John Rowe Townsend, *Tom Tiddler's Ground*, 1986
   Amid the backwater canals of an English industrial town, five children unravel a mystery about a half-sunken canalboat and its hidden treasure.
Elizabeth M. Wilton, *Riverboat Family*, 1967
   An Australian family decides to restore a sunken paddlewheeler to use as a trading boat on the river, but the success of their venture is threatened.

1395

Jill Paton Walsh

Illustrator: Mary Rayner

Lost and Found (London: Deutsch, 1984)

Age range: Grades 2-4

Subject(s): Grandparents

Time period(s): Indeterminate Past

Locale(s): England

What the book is about: Through several historical periods, children are sent on an errand to hand over a certain object to a grandparent. Each time the object is lost, only to be replaced by another found by chance, one of the artifacts lost by children in previous centuries.

Where it's reviewed:
Growing Point, May 1985, page 4431
School Library Journal, September 1985, page 140

Other books by the author:
The Dolphin Crossing, 1990
A Chance Child, 1978
Children of the Fox, 1978

Fireweek, 1969

Other books you might like:
Rumer Godden, *The Dragon of Og*, 1981
   For centuries the Dragon of Og has taken for food two bullocks a monthfrom the lord's herd, but a new lord tries to end the custom.
Kathryn Meyrick, *The Lost Music: Gustav Mole's War on Noise*, 1991
   Sad in a world of nasty noise, Gustav Mole and his children search the world to retrieve their music among animals playing many kinds of instruments.
Beatrix Potter, *The Tale of Mrs. Tiggy-Winkle*, 1991
   Lucie visits the laundry of Mrs. Tiggy-Winkle, a hedgehog, and finds her lost handkerchiefs.
Ann Warren Turner, *Heron Street*, 1989
   Over the centuries, as people settle near the marsh by the sea, herons and other animals are displaced.
Audrey Wood, *Scaredy Cats*, 1980
   Two scaredy cats on an errand imagine all the hideous things that might happen to them during their trip.

1396

Jill Paton Walsh

Unleaving (New York: Farrar, 1976)

Age range: Grades 5 and Up

Subject(s): Death

Major character(s): Madge, Teenager, Heiress

Time period(s): 1970s

Locale(s): Cornwall, England

What the book is about: The recent heir to her grandmother's house, a young girl rents it for the summer to a professor and a group of students whose long, abstract philosophical discussions become meaningful to her as the summer wears on.

Where it's reviewed:
Horn Book, August 1976, page 408
Kirkus Reviews, May 15, 1976, page 601

Other books by the author:
Lapsing, 1987
Gaffer Sampson's Luck, 1984
A Chance Child, 1978
Children of the Fox, 1978

Other books you might like:
Eve Bunting, *The Happy Funeral*, 1982
   Laura tells of the Chinese-American family traditions celebrated when her grandfather died, and how the customs helped them deal with the loss.
Betsy Byars, *Goodbye, Chicken Little*, 1979
   Jimmie has called himself Chicken Little ever since his father's death in a mine accident. Now he must deal with the death of his Uncle Pete.
Vera Cleaver, *Belle Pruitt*, 1988
   When her adored baby brother dies, Belle's family starts to fall apart as she struggles to bring them back to normal.
Patricia Reilly Giff, *The Gift of the Pirate Queen*, 1982
   Grace is overwhelmed by responsibilities after her mother's unexpected death. Tales of a 15th century pirate queen help her find courage and strength.

Jan Greenberg, *A Season In-Between*, 1979
  Carrie's isolation at her exclusive private school is made worse when she finds that her father has cancer and is close to death.

1397

Gary Paulsen

Dogsong (New York: Bradbury, 1985)

Age range: Grades 5-7

Subject(s): Eskimos

Major character(s): Russell Susskit, Teenager, Eskimo (Inuit); Oogruk, Shaman

Time period(s): 1980s

Locale(s): Arctic

What the book is about: Russell Suslatt wants to escape the modernization of his Eskimo village, so he takes a dog sled across country on a 1400 mile journey to learn the ways of the North for himself and find his own ''song'' to sing.

Where it's reviewed:
Horn Book, July 1985, page 456
School Library Journal, April 1985, page 78

Awards the book has won:
Newbery Honor 1986
Parents' Choice (literature) 1985

Other books by the author:
The Voyage of the Frog, 1989
Island, 1988
Hatchet, 1987
Tracker, 1984

Other books you might like:
Terri Cohlene, *Ka-ha-si and the Loon: An Eskimo Legend*, 1990
  Ka-ha-si acquired great strength and boldness and uses them to rescue his people in times of peril. Good source of information on Eskimo culture.
Jean Craighead George, *Water Sky*, 1987
  A boy who goes to Barrow, Alaska, to live with friends of his father for awhile learns the importance of whaling to the Eskimo culture.
James A. Houston, *Drifting Snow: An Arctic Legend*, 1992
  A teenager who was taken from her home as a tiny child returns to look for her parents and her lost Eskimo heritage.
Aylette Jenness, *In Two Worlds: A Yup'ik Eskimo Family*, 1989
  Documents the life of a Yup'ik Eskimo family on the coast of the Bering Sea, showing the great changes that have taken place in the past fifty years.
Nancy Luenn, *Arctic Unicorn*, 1986
  Thirteen year old Kala finds her life in a remote Eskimo village disrupted when a young hunter arrives and she discovers her powers as a shaman.

1398

Gary Paulsen

Hatchet (New York: Bradbury, 1987)

Age range: Grades 5-6

Subject(s): Survival; Divorce

Major character(s): Brian Robeson, Teenager

Time period(s): 1980s

Locale(s): Canada

What the book is about: When Brian is going to spend time with his father after a divorce, the pilot he is riding with suffers a heart attack and dies and Brian goes down in the plane crash. His own determination and a small hatchet his mother had given him are the only things that allow him to survive 54 days in the wilderness.

Where it's reviewed:
Booklist, July 1988, page 1930
School Library Journal, December 1988, page 103

Awards the book has won:
Newbery Honor

Other books by the author:
Island, 1988
Tracker, 1984
The Voyage of the Frog, 1989

Other books you might like:
Gary L. Blackwood, *Wild Timothy*, 1987
  13 year old Timothy must learn the ways of the wilderness to survive when he becomes lost.
John Christopher, *Empty World*, 1978
  Neil and two girls he finds in London are the only survivors of a terrible plague.
Thomas A. Dyer, *Way of His Own*, 1981
  A crippled boy and a slave girl struggle to survive when they are left behind by the family.
Adrienne Jones, *Hawks of Chelney*, 1978
  Siri flees to the cliffs to avoid helping to capture the ospreys that villagers believe are responsbile for poor fishing.
Jim Kjelgaard, *Wild Trek*, 1981
  The dog, Chiri, helps Link Stevens find and rescue two men lost in the Canadian wilderness.

1399

Gary Paulsen

The Voyage of the Frog (New York: Orchard, 1989)

Age range: Grades 5-8

Subject(s): Sea Stories; Survival; Aunts and Uncles

Major character(s): David Alspeth, Sailor; Owen Alspeth, Relative (David's uncle)

Time period(s): 1980s

Locale(s): Pacific Ocean

What the book is about: When David goes out on his sailboat to scatter his recently deceased uncle's ashes to the wind, he is caught in a fierce storm and must survive many days on his own as he works out his feelings about life and about his uncle's death.

Where it's reviewed:
Booklist, March 1, 1989, page 1195
Hornbook, March 1989, page 219
Kirkus Reviews, December 15, 1988, page 1814

Other books by the author:
Amos Gets Famous, 1993
The Case of the Dirty Birds, 1992

The Boy Who Owned the School, 1990
Canyons, 1990

Other books you might like:
Leonard Everett Fisher, *The Death of the Evening Star: The Diary of a Young New England Whaler*, 1972
A boy keeps a diary of his experience on his first voyage aboard a sinister whaling ship.
Basil Heatler, *Wreck Ashore!*, 1969
After his father's death, Matt chooses to accompany his Uncle Nat to the wild and lawless waters of the Florida Keys in the mid 1700s.
Armstrong Sperry, *Call It Courage*, 1940
Young Mafatu, a Polynesian boy whose name means Stout Heart, overcomes his terrible fear of the sea and proves his courage to himself and his people.
Colin Thiele, *Shadow Shark*, 1985
Two cousins join a group of fishermen in pursuit of a massive shark off the coast of southern Arabia.
John Frederick Waters, *Victory Chimes*, 1976
A young boy leaves his foster home for the summer to work on Cape Cod where he becomes involved in an attempt to salvage a stranded cargo ship.

1400

Gary Paulsen

The Winter Room (New York: Orchard, 1989)

Age range: Grades 4-6

Subject(s): Family Life; Farm Life

Major character(s): Eldon, Preteen; Wayne, Teenager; David, Relative (uncle)

Time period(s): Indeterminate

Locale(s): Minnesota

What the book is about: A quiet, reflective portrait of four seasons on a Minnesota farm. Eleven year old Eldon narrates the story of his family, mother and father, Eldon and Wayne, Uncle David and Nels. In addition to vivid descriptions of all the work (and a little bit of play) on the farm, we see a special relationship between Uncle David and the family as he spins tales of logging from the old days. A powerful concluding chapter focuses on David's stories and how they affect his relationship with the boys, and his own self-esteem.

Where it's reviewed:
Booklist, November 1, 1984, page 556
Center for Children's Books Bulletin, January 1940, page 118
Hornbook, March 1940, paege 209

Awards the book has won:
Newbery Honor 1990

Other books by the author:
Canyons, 1990
Woodsong, 1990
Hatchet, 1987
Dogsong, 1985

Other books you might like:
Nina Ring Aamundsen, *Two Short and One Long*, 1990
Norweigian Jonas and Einar must come to terms with each other and their prejudices when an Afghanistani family moves into their neighborhood.
Ann Nolan Clark, *All This Wild Land*, 1976

Arriving in Minnesota in the late 1800s with plans to homestead, a Finnish family is faced with problems of starting a new life.
Richard Graber, *A Little Breathing Room*, 1978
A teen growing up in Minnesota in 1935 is frustrated in his attempts to contend with his manipulative family.
Walter Havighurst, *Song of the Pines*, 1949
A story of Norwegian lumbering in Wisconsin.
Kenneth Thomasma, *Kunu: Escape on the Missouri*, 1989
Following the forced removal of his people from Minnesota to Crow Creek, South Dakota, a Winnebago Indian boy embarks on a dangerous journey.

1401

Philippa Pearce

Tom's Midnight Garden (Philadelphia: Lippincott, 1958)

Age range: Grades 5-6

Subject(s): Space and Time

Major character(s): Tom Long, Child; Harriet "Hatty" Melbourne, Child

Time period(s): 1950s; 1890s

Locale(s): Castleford, England

What the book is about: While his brother recovers from an illness, Tom is sent to stay with an aunt and uncle. Their apartment offers very little for Tom to do until he discovers that when the old grandfather clock in the hall strikes thirteen, the parking lot in back becomes a beautiful garden. He meets Hatty and they become good friends. Each time he visits the garden, years have passed for Hatty but only days for Tom. An engaging time travel story.

Where it's reviewed:
Junior Bookshelf, December 1958, page 333
School Library Journal, July 1959, page 399

Awards the book has won:
Carnegie Medal 1958
Lewis Carroll Shelf 1963

Other books by the author:
The Shadow Cage, 1977
Who's Afraid? And Other Strange Stories, 1987

Other books you might like:
Margaret Jean Anderson, *In the Circle of Time*, 1979
Robert and Jennifer are projected forward into the 22nd century when the glaciers have melted and coastal cities are flooded.
John Christopher, *Fireball*, 1981
When Simon and Brad are thrown by a fireball into Roman Britain, they are actually in a parallel universe where Roman Britain lasted 2000 years.
Eric Houghton, *Steps out of Time*, 1980
Whenever the mist appears, Jonathan finds himself in a different time/place when he opens the door to his house.
Alison Uttley, *Traveller in Time*, 1939
Penelope travels to the 16th century when Sir Anthony Babington plotted to free the imprisoned Mary, Queen of Scots.
Jane Yolen, *The Devil's Arithmetic*, 1988

When Hannah opens the door for Elijah during the Passover Seder, she finds herself back in 1942 where she experiences the Holocaust first hand.

| 1402 |

Philippa Pearce

Illustrator: Charlotte Voake

The Way to Sattin Shore (New York: Greenwillow, 1984)

Age range: Grades 5-8

Subject(s): Fathers and Daughters; Mystery and Detective Stories

Major character(s): Kate Trantor, Student

Time period(s): 1980s

Locale(s): England

What the book is about: Kate learns that the man buried in the family plot is not her father as she has always believed. When the tombstone with her father's name suddenly disappears from the graveyard, Kate witnesses the unraveling of a mystery surrounding the death of her father.

Where it's reviewed:
Center for Children's Books Bulletin, May 1984, page 172
School Library Journal, April 1984, page 117

Other books by the author:
Fresh, 1988
Who's Afraid? And Other Strange Stories, 1987
The Shadow Cage, 1977
Tom's Midnight Garden, 1958

Other books you might like:
John W. Chambers, *Footlight Summer*, 1983
 A teenage girl working at a summer theater can't understand her mother's aversion to theater until she learns the truth about her "dead" father.
Valerie A. Lutters, *The Haunting of Julie Unger*, 1977
 The vivid memory of her dead father threatens to isolate a preteen girl from the rest of her family and push her to the brink of madness.
Charlette McLeod, *Cirak's Daughter*, 1982
Margaret A. Robinson, *A Woman of Her Tribe*, 1990
 Annette, whose dead father was Indian and who lives with her mother in British Columbia, must decide herself in which cultural heritage she belongs.
Jane Yolen, *The Stone Silenus*, 1984
 A year after her father has been found dead in a motel swimming pool, a strange faun-boy appears to Melissa, seeming to be her beloved father's spirit

| 1403 |

Susan Pearson

Illustrator: Steven Kellogg

Molly Moves Out (New York: Dial, 1979)

Age range: Grades 1-2

Subject(s): Friendship; Animals/Rabbits; Brothers and Sisters

Major character(s): Molly, Rabbit

Time period(s): Indeterminate Past

Locale(s): United States

What the book is about: Molly, a young rabbit with six siblings, decides to move out when the uproar becomes too much for her. She moves into a place alone, and though she enjoys it at first, she soon misses the companionship of her family.

Where it's reviewed:
Kirkus Reviews, October 1, 1979, page 1144
New York Times Book Review, November 11, 1979, page 55

Other books by the author:
The Bogeyman Caper, 1990
Well, I Never!, 1990
Monday I Was an Alligator, 1979
Everybody Knows That!, 1978

Other books you might like:
Tomie De Paola, *Too Many Hopkins*, 1989
 The rabbit family of Mr. and Mrs. Hopkins and their fifteen children work together to plant a garden.
Maryann Macdonald, *Rosie Runs Away*, 1990
 When her mother scolds her for taking her little brother on an adventure, Rosie decides to run away.
Robert M. Quackenbush, *Funny Bunnies on the Run*, 1989
 When all the lights go out, the bunny family flips every switch with no success, until the power returns and all the appliances go on at once.
Bethany Roberts, *Waiting-for-Spring Stories*, 1991
 As the family passes the winter in their cozy home, Papa Rabbit tells them stories.
Jerry Smath, *Pretzel and Pop's Closetful of Stories*, 1991
 Pop tells Pretzel humorous stories about family members.

| 1404 |

Richard Peck

Are You in the House Alone? (New York: Viking, 1976)

Age range: Grades 5-6

Subject(s): Rape

Major character(s): Gail, Teenager

Time period(s): 1970s

Locale(s): United States

What the book is about: As the recipient of threatening notes and phone calls, a high school girl becomes aware that she is under constant observation. Her nightmare becomes fact when she is raped by a classmate.

Where it's reviewed:
Kirkus Reviews, September 1, 1976, page 982
Publisher's Weekly, September 13, 1976, page 99

Awards the book has won:
Edgar Allan Poe Award

Other books by the author:
Voices After Midnight, 1990
The Ghost Belonged to Me, 1989
Father Figure, 1978
Monster Night at Grandma's House, 1977

Other books you might like:
Bernard Ashley, *A Kind of Wild Justice*, 1979
 Ronnie overcomes the paralyzing power of fear and learns to act, saving himself and other victims of terror.

Myron Levoy, *A Shadow Like a Leopard*, 1981
A Puerto Rican-American boy in New York finds his own definition of "macho" with the help of an artist and the discipline of keeping a journal.

Gloria D. Miklowitz, *Did You Hear What Happened to Andrea?*, 1979
Andrea knows she will never be the same, nor will those who love her. The man who raped her is in jail and she feels a strange new sense of freedom.

Crystal Thrasher, *Between Dark and Daylight*, 1979
Seely knows a great deal about family discord, violence and death in 1940s Indiana in this middle book of a trilogy.

Judie Wolkoff, *Where the Elf King Sings*, 1980
Marcie watches her world fall apart as her father re-experiences the horrors of Vietnam and alcoholic rages.

1405

Richard Peck

The Ghost Belonged to Me (New York: Viking, 1975)

Age range: Grades 5-9

Subject(s): Ghosts; Humor

Major character(s): Blossom Culp, Spirit; Alexander, Preteen; Uncle Miles, Adventurer

Time period(s): 1970s

Locale(s): United States

What the book is about: A series of hair-raising adventures with Blossom, a young ghost, Alexander, and 87 year old "Uncle Miles." After getting out of one scrape after another, Alexander and Uncle Miles manage to put the ghost to rest with the rest of her family. Lots of high adventure and great humor. But don't count Blossom out. There are more books about her.

Where it's reviewed:
Booklist, July 1, 1975, page 1129
Hornbook, October 1975, page 471
Kirkus Reviews, April 15, 1975, page 456

Other books by the author:
Voices After Midnight, 1989
Blossom Culp and the Sleep of Death, 1986
The Dreadful Future of Blossom Culp, 1983
Ghosts I Have Been, 1977

Other books you might like:
Avi, *Devil's Race*, 1984
John Proud is tormented by the ghost of an evil ancestor, with his own name and his own face, who was hanged in 1854 for being a demon.

Eve Bunting, *The Haunting of Safekeep*, 1985
Sara takes a summer job as caretaker at a Victorian restoration site and encounters a foundling and two ghosts.

E.W. Hildick, *The Ghost Squad and the Halloween Conspiracy*, 1985
Four young ghosts uncover a plot by a senator's stepson to have his stepfather unwittingly pass out candy embedded with needles at a Halloween party.

Andre Norton, *House of Shadows*, 1984
Mike and Susan feel a mounting sense of urgency and terror as they try to protect their brother who is threatened by an invisible and powerful force.

Edward Packer, *Ghost Hunter*, 1985

The reader is invited to help determine the plot and solve the mystery with the ghost hunter.

1406

Richard Peck

Voices After Midnight (New York: Delacorte, 1989)

Age range: Grades 6-9

Subject(s): Brothers and Sisters; Time Travel

Major character(s): Heidi, Preteen; Luke, Preteen; Chad, Child

Time period(s): 1980s (1988); 1880s (1888)

Locale(s): New York, New York (Manhattan)

What the book is about: When their father's business takes the family from California to Manhattan, Chad, his older sister, Heidi, and his little brother, Luke, find themselves living in a one hundred year old house alive with memories and dim voices which they can only hear after midnight. The voices summon them to the year 1888 where they save people from the great blizzard of the year. Suspenseful and fast paced, this is a good read aloud.

Where it's reviewed:
Booklist, October 1, 1989, page 353
School Library Journal, September 1989, page 276

Other books by the author:
Anonymously Yours, 1991
Father Figure, 1988
Ghosts I Have Been, 1979
Are You in the House Alone?, 1976

Other books you might like:
Grace Chetwin, *Friends in Time*, 1992
Unhappy about her family's upcoming move, Emma wishes for a friend and suddenly confronts a spoiled, lonely girl sent from the 1850s by a strange doll

Pam Conrad, *Stonewords: A Ghost Story*, 1990
Zoe discovers that her house is occupied by the ghost of a girl who carries her back to the day of her death in 1870 to try to alter that tragic event

Betty Levin, *Mercy's Mill*, 1992
While trying to deal with her new stepfather and a younger foster sister, Sarah meets a boy who claims to have traveled forward in time from the 1800s

John Peel, *Uptime, Downtime*, 1992
When Karyn and her brother, Mike, discover that they can time travel just by thinking, they meet other time travelers and have strange adventures.

William Sleator, *Strange Attractors*, 1991
Max finds himself in possession of a time travel device which is eagerly sought by the scientist who invented it and his alter ego from another time.

1407

Robert Newton Peck

Illustrator: Andrew Glass

Banjo (New York: Knopf, 1982)

Age range: Grades 3-6

Subject(s): Mountain Life; School Life

Major character(s): Alvin, Child; Banjo Byler, Child, Musician; Jake Horse, Recluse

Time period(s): 1980s

Locale(s): United States

What the book is about: Alvin's choice of Banjo Byler, a dirty, poor and unpopular boy as his partner in a school assignment leads him into unexpected adventure. Banjo wants to write about a local hermit, Jake Horse, and on their journey to find Jake, they stop to climb abandoned spar mine silos. Banjo falls in, alive, hurt and frightened. Banjo plays his banjo to attract attention. Rescued by Jake Horse, for whom the experience renews an interest in life, the boys return heroes.

Where it's reviewed:
New York Times Book Review, January 16, 1983, page 81
School Library Journal, October 1983, page 81

Other books by the author:
Higbee's Halloween, 1990
Basket Case, 1979
Fawn, 1975
A Day No Pigs Would Die, 1973

Other books you might like:
Patricia Beatty, *Charley Skedaddle*, 1987
 During the Civil War, a twelve year old boy from New York City joins the Union Army as a drummer, deserts during a battle, and meets a hostile woman.
Robbie Branscum, *The Adventures of Johnny May*, 1984
 As poor as any in the Arkansas hills, Johnny May struggles against great odds to provide her grandparents with a real Christmas.
Robbie Branscum, *Cameo Rose*, 1989
 Fourteen year old Cameo Rose's curiosity about the murder of a local ne'er-do-well gets her in trouble with her neighbors in the Arkansas hills.
Clyde Robert Bulla, *White Bird*, 1990
 A lonely boy is found and reared by a hermit in the wilderness of the Tennessee mountains in the 1880s.
Jane Yolen, *Uncle Lemon's Spring*, 1981
 Uncle Lemon gets his spring in the middle of the driest summer on record and it has troublesome consequences.

1408

Robert Newton Peck

A Day No Pigs Would Die (New York: Knopf, 1972)

Age range: Grades 5 and Up

Subject(s): Farm Life; Fathers and Sons

Major character(s): Rob, Teenager; Pinky, Pig

Time period(s): 1920s

Locale(s): Vermont

What the book is about: Rob comes of age on a Shaker farm, as his pig grows, wins a Blue Ribbon at the Rutland Fair, and eventually has to be slaughtered to feed the family. Rob learns to take on the duties of adulthood.

Where it's reviewed:
Horn Book, October 1973, page 472
Library Journal, March 15, 1973, page 1022

Other books by the author:
Soup in Love, 1992
Higbee's Halloween, 1990
Arly, 1989
Path of Hunters, 1973

Other books you might like:
Patricia Goehner Baehr, *Louisa Eclipsed*, 1988
 Louisa's return to her grandfather's farm is spoiled by news of the farm's financial troubles.
Betty Bates, *Hey There, Owlface*, 1991
 Brad forms a special relationship with the owls roosting in his family barn and has to protect them from a triggerhappy neighbor.
Larry Callen, *Pinch*, 1975
 A boy growing up in a country town becomes involved with a pig he trains to hunt, and a mean, crafty gentleman who teaches him the art of trickery.
Katherine Paterson, *Lyddie*, 1991
 A Vermont farm girl is determined to escape the farm by becoming a factory worker in Lowell, Massachusetts.
Carolyn Reeder, *Grandpa's Mountain*, 1991
 Carrie makes her annual summer visit to relatives in the Blue Ridge Mountains and watches her grandfather fight the government to save his farm.

1409

Robert Newton Peck

Illustrator: Charles Gehm

Soup (New York: Knopf, 1974)

Age range: Grades 3-6

Subject(s): Friendship

Major character(s): Robert "Rob" Peck, Child; Janice Riker, Preteen

Time period(s): 1930s

Locale(s): Vermont

What the book is about: Soup and his pal, Rob, get into trouble every time they turn around. They talk back to their teacher, roll down hills in a barrel, and try cheating the store keeper. Once you meet Soup and Rob, you'll want to read all the books about them.

Where it's reviewed:
Booklist, April 1, 1974, page 878
Center for Children's Books Bulletin, October 1974, page 35

Other books by the author:
Soup in Love, 1992
Soup on Fire, 1987
Soup for President, 1978
Fawn, 1975

Other books you might like:
Ellen Conford, *What's Cooking, Jenny Archer?*, 1989
 Jenny Archer goes into the business of preparing lunches for her friends at school with comic results.
Crescent Dragonwagon, *Dear Miss Moshki*, 1986
 Banished to the hallway for poor behavior when an author is visiting, Chris and Jeremy write the most outlandish apologies they can think of.
Sheila Greenwald, *Mat Pit and the Tunnel Tenants*, 1972

A boy and his friends rescue their rodent pets from probable extermination and build a zoo where the animals can live safely.

Elizabeth Starr Hill, *Fangs Aren't Everything*, 1985
Victim of an ancient family curse that turns him into a wolfman when the moon is full, a young man tries to hide his affliction from his friends.

Jeffrey Kelly, *Tramp Steamer and the Silver Bullet*, 1984
Two boys, Tramp and Silver, become involved with haunted houses, eccentric ladies, spiders, meat-eating plants and secret tunnels.

1410

Sylvia Peck

Illustrator: Robert Andrew Parker

Seal Child (New York: Morrow, 1989)

Age range: Grades 4-7

Subject(s): Animals/Seals and Sea Lions

Major character(s): Molly, 6th Grader; Douglas, Child (Molly's brother); Meara, Mythical Creature (selkie)

Time period(s): 1980s

Locale(s): Maine

What the book is about: Molly is a lonely sixth grader who finds a skinned seal with a pup crying nearby. Soon after, an old neighboring woman takes in a strange girl, Meara, who is not quite human.

Where it's reviewed:
Booklist, September 15, 1989, page 188
Horn Book, January/February 1990, page 65

Other books by the author:
Kelsey's Raven, 1992

Other books you might like:
Deborah Davis, *The Secret of the Seal*, 1989
Kyo, an Eskimo boy, faces a difficult moral choice between friendship for a seal and loyalty to his family.
Nancy Garden, *My Sister, the Vampire*, 1992
A beautiful Maine summer turns deadly for Sarah, Tim, Jenny and the neighbors as they learn the truth about the strange new owners of Spool Island.
Mollie Hunter, *A Stranger Came Ashore: A Story of Suspense*, 1975
Robbie is convinvced that the stranger befriended by his family is one of the Selkie Folk and seeks help against his magic powers from a local wizard.
Jackie French Koller, *The Last Voyage of the Misty Day*, 1992
Moving to Maine after her father's death in Manhattan, Denise forms a healing friendship with a boat owner surrounded by considerable mystery.
Liza Ketchum Murrow, *The Ghost of Lost Island*, 1991
Helping his grandfather herd and shear sheep on a small coastal Maine island, Gabe meets a strange woman who may be the ghost of a drowned milkmaid.

1411

Bill Peet, Author/Illustrator

Big Bad Bruce (Boston: Houghton Mifflin, 1977)

Age range: Grades 2-3

Subject(s): Animals/Bears; Witches and Witchcraft

Major character(s): Bruce, Bear

Time period(s): Indeterminate

Locale(s): United States

What the book is about: Bruce is a big bully. He never picks on anyone his own size. He is diminished in more ways than one by a small but very independent witch.

Where it's reviewed:
Horn Book, June 1977, page 302
Kirkus Reviews, February 15, 1977, page 163

Awards the book has won:
California Young Reader Medal 1980

Other books by the author:
Cock-a-Doodle Dudley, 1990
Jethro and Joel Were a Troll, 1987
Farewell to Shady Glade, 1984
Randy's Dandy Lions, 1964

Other books you might like:
Larry Dane Brimner, *Cory Colman, Grade 2*, 1990
Corey's birthday party is ruined by the class bully, who turns out not to be such a bully in the end.
Joanna Cole, *Bully Trouble*, 1989
Arlo and Robby, finding themselves the victims of a neighborhood bully, work out a red-hot scheme for discouraging him.
Doug Cushman, *Camp Big Paw*, 1990
Cyril and his cabin mates, Ben and Obie, run into trouble with the camp bully during Field Day at Camp Big Paw.
Marjorie Weinman Sharmat, *The Bully on the Bus*, 1991
Brian the bully took away Marvin's lunch and stole Aaron's baseball cap, but when he fights with Max, he won't get away with it.
Elizabeth Winthrop, *Luke's Bully*, 1990
Skinny, shy Luke cannot hide from Arthur, his personal bully, until it is time to pick roles for the class play.

1412

Bill Peet, Author/Illustrator

Cyrus, the Unsinkable Sea Serpent (Boston: Houghton Mifflin, 1975)

Age range: Grades 1-3

Subject(s): Monsters

Major character(s): Cyrus, Sea Serpent

Time period(s): Indeterminate

Locale(s): At Sea

What the book is about: Cyrus is a shy and friendly sea serpent. He becomes a hero by helping voyagers through a storm and doing-in some terrible pirates.

Where it's reviewed:
Kirkus Reviews, March 1, 1975, page 237
School Library Journal, September 1975, page 88

Awards the book has won:
Little Archer Award 1977

Other books by the author:
Zella, Zack and Zodiac, 1986
Pamela Camel, 1984
Eli, 1978
Kermit the Hermit, 1965

Other books you might like:
Kady MacDonald Denton, *Granny Is a Darling*, 1988
  Billy is worried about Granny's visit because she is staying in his room and he knows monsters come there every night.
Rose Impey, *Who's a Bright Girl?*, 1985
  A little girl becomes leader of a gang of pirates after they try to make her their maid, cook and seamstress.
Virginia Kahl, *How Do You Hide a Monster?*, 1971
  The townspeople must figure out a way to save Phinney, the friendly serpent in the lake, from hunters that are sent to kill the "monster."
Yasuko Kimura, *Fergus and the Sea Monster*, 1976
  Fergus doesn't know what to do with the funny blue monster who is growing bigger and bigger, following him everywhere.
Dave Ross, *Gorp and the Space Pirates*, 1983
  Gorp, the space monster, helps a space freighter fight space pirates.

1413

Bill Peet, Author/Illustrator

How Droofus the Dragon Lost His Head (Boston: Houghton Mifflin, 1971)

Age range: Grades 1-3

Subject(s): Dragons

Major character(s): Droofus, Dragon

Time period(s): Indeterminate

Locale(s): Alternate Earth

What the book is about: Droofus is lost in the fog when he is only four. On his own, he swears off eating people and critters and grows up to be a gentle vegetarian and the handy-dandy dragon for a farmer.

Where it's reviewed:
Horn Book, June 1971, page 179
Library Journal, May 15, 1971, page 1798

Other books by the author:
Cock-a-Doodle Dudley, 1990
Zella, Zack, and Zodiac, 1986
Kweeks of Kookatumdee, 1985
Cyrus the Unsinkable Sea-Serpent, 1971

Other books you might like:
Klaus Baumgart, *Anna and the Little Green Dragon*, 1992
  Anna finds a little green dragon in her box of cornflakes.
Fernando Krahn, *The Secret in the Dungeon*, 1983
  A child touring an old castle gets separated from the group and stumbles upon a sleeping dragon in the dungeon.
Margaret Leaf, *The Eyes of the Dragon*, 1987
  An artist paints a dragon mural and amazing things happen when he paints in the eyes.
Dav Pilkey, *Dragon's Fat Cat: Dragon's Fourth Tale*, 1992
  Dragon finds a fat cat in the snow, brings it inside and soon has formed a family.
Jane Thayer, *The Popcorn Dragon*, 1989

A young dragon learns that showing off does not make friends.

1414

Anne Pellowski

Illustrator: Wendy Watson

Willow Wind Farm: Betsy's Story (New York: Putnam, 1981)

Age range: Grades 3-5

Subject(s): Farm Life

Major character(s): Betsy, Child

Time period(s): Indeterminate Past

Locale(s): Wisconsin

What the book is about: The story of Betsy and her large family growing up on their small Wisconsin farm. Other books follow in the series and each focuses on a different daughter in the family.

Where it's reviewed:
Hornbook, October 1981, page 537
Kirkus Reviews, October 1, 1981, page 1236
School Library Journal, December 1981, page 67

Other books by the author:
Betsy's Up and Down Year, 1983
First Farm in the Valley: Annie's Story, 1982
Stairstep Farm: Anne Rose's Story, 1981

Other books you might like:
Carol Ryrie Brink, *Magical Melons*, 1990
  Fourteen tales relating the further adventures of ten year old Caddie and her six siblings living on the Wisconsin frontier in the 1860s.
Barbara M. Joosse, *Pieces of the Picture*, 1989
  Unhappy at moving from Chicago to Wisconsin after her father death, Emily tries to understand her calm, hard-working mother and her own mixed feelings
Edith S. McCall, *Better than a Brother*, 1988
  A young girl grows up at the turn of the century on the shores of a Madison, Wisconsin lake, where her family runs a boarding house for ice cutters.
A.M. Monson, *The Deer Stand*, 1992
  When her family moves from Chicago to rural Wisconsin and Bits has trouble making new friends at school, she spends her time trying to tame a deer.
Joan T. Zeier, *The Elderberry Thicket*, 1990
  In 1938 Wisconsin, when Franny's father loses his job, the family members doubt their self-reliance as they once again must face hard times.

1415

Kathy Pelta

Illustrator: Leslie Morrill

The Blue Empress (New York: Henry Holt, 1988)

Age range: Grades 4-6

Subject(s): Humor; Mystery and Detective Stories

Major character(s): Margaret Drusilla Kincaid, Child; Dru, Aged Person (Margaret's great-aunt)

Time period(s): 1980s

Locale(s): Riverbank, Texas

What the book is about: When Great Aunt Dru sprains her ankle, eleven year old Margaret flies with her mother down to Texas to help out so she will not have to go to a nursing home. Margaret gets involved in a mystery when a valuable lapis lazuli necklace is missing. The sleepy town of Riverbank turns out to be much more exciting once Detective Kincaid gets to work. Action, danger, and laughter all follow.

Where it's reviewed:
Booklist, April 15, 1988, page 1436
Kirkus Reviews, January 15, 1988, page 126
School Library Journal, August 1988, page 97

Other books by the author:
Discovering Christopher Columbus, 1991
The Parrot Man Mystery, 1987

Other books you might like:
Eve Bunting, *The Ghost Children*, 1989
    Matt's investigation of vandalism of life-sized dolls belonging to his aunt takes him to the art world of Los Angeles.
Eileen Dunlop, *The House on the Hill*, 1987
    Cousins visiting Great-Aunt Jane in her spooky Victorian house come upon a fifty year old mystery which reveals a tragic story in Jane's past.
Elizabeth Muskopf, *The Revenge of Jeremiah Plum*, 1987
    Darcy anticipates a dull summer at Aunt Prunella's boarding house until she meets J.P., a ghost who is determined to find out who murdered him.
Luke Wallin, *Blue Wings*, 1982
    While attempting to help her US Customs agent aunt, fourteen year old Mandy becomes an unwitting guest of the king of parrot smugglers.
Gertrude Chandler Warner, *The Old Motel Mystery*, 1992
    Someone is trying to put Aunt Jane's motel out of business, but the Alden children aren't going to let that happen.

1416

Patricia Pendergraft

Brushy Mountain (New York: Philomel, 1989)

Age range: Grades 4-6

Subject(s): Country Life; Twins; Animals/Wolves

Major character(s): Arney Burdette, Teenager; Tice Hooker, Bully; Sal Burdette, Midwife (Arney's sister)

Time period(s): 1940s

Locale(s): Weedpatch

What the book is about: Arney finds himself in the position of saving the life of the meanest man in town. Arney hates old man Hooker with a passion so strong he fantasizes killing him, and even tries once to do it. Instead, he ends up saving Hooker's life three times. Arney also helps his sister, Sal, deliver Hooker's twin grandsons in a terrible storm during which wolves surround the shack.

Where it's reviewed:
Booklist, April 15, 1989, page 1470
School Library Journal, June 1989, page 18

Other books by the author:
As Far as Mill Springs, 1991
The Legend of Daisy Flowerdew, 1990
Hear the Wind Blow, 1988
Miracle at Clement's Pond, 1988

Other books you might like:
Dennis Haseley, *Shadows*, 1991
    Jamie's lonely life with his aunt and uncle in rural West Virginia changes when Grandpa comes to visit and teaches him to make shadow pictures.
Herb Karl, *The Toom County Mud Race*, 1992
    Jackie Lee relates the events leading up to the big Toom County Mud Race and how he and his friends, Snake and Bonnie, outsmart the Slocum boys.
Sheila Solomon Klass, *Kool Ada*, 1991
    When Ada, a street-fighting girl from coal mining country, moves to Chicago, she learns from a tough teacher she has other options besides fighting.
Edith Nesbit, *The Railway Children*, 1992
    When their father is sent away to prison, three London children move to the country where they keep busy preventing accidents on the nearby railway.
Harvey Watson, *Bob War and Poke*, 1991
    Hired as a chauffeur and cook to a rich couple passing through town, two young back-country brothers have many adventures.

1417

Patricia Pendergraft

Hear the Wind Blow (New York: Putnam, 1988)

Age range: Grades 5-7

Subject(s): Dancing; Friendship; Religion

Major character(s): Isadora Clay, Preteen; Haskell Moore, Preteen; Maybelle, Preteen (fundamentalist)

Time period(s): 1910s

Locale(s): United States

What the book is about: Isadora watches as her deeply religious best friend, Maybelle, tries to reform the school troublemaker, Haskell, who enjoys teasing Isadora about her dancing aspirations.

Where it's reviewed:
Horn Book, September/October 1988, page 627
School Library Journal, September 1988, page 184

Other books by the author:
As Far as Mill Springs, 1991
The Legend of Daisy Flowerdew, 1990
Brushy Mountain, 1989
Miracle at Clement's Pond, 1987

Other books you might like:
T. Ernesto Bethancourt, *Instruments of Darkness*, 1979
    Strange events involving a religious cult led by a mysterious Rumanian mystic with great powers lead authorities to fear a plot to control the world.
Jean Little, *Kate*, 1971
    Product of a Jewish-Protestant marriage, Kate finds her dilemma over her religious leanings threatening her relationship with her best friend.

Les Martin, *Young Indiana Jones and the Princess of Peril*, 1991
In 1913 Russia, Indy befriends a young Georgian princess involved in a freedom movement and is chased by secret police and agents of an evil fanatic.

Robert Newton Peck, *Arly's Run*, 1991
Arly, an orphan seeking a home and family, escapes from a brutal migrant labor camp, joins a traveling religious show, and battles a Florida hurricane

Jill Pinkwater, *The Disappearance of Sister Perfect*, 1987
Sherelee Holmes, claiming descent from Sherlock, investigates the odd behavior of her older sister and infiltrates a dangerous religious cult.

1418

Patricia Pendergraft

Miracle at Clement's Pond (New York: Philomel, 1987)

Age range: Grades 6-9

Subject(s): City Life; Fathers and Sons

Major character(s): Sylvie, Preteen; Justin, Preteen; Lyon, Teenager

Time period(s): 1980s

Locale(s): South (rural South)

What the book is about: When Sylvie, Justin and Lyon are looking for frogs, they find an abandoned baby at the pond. Since they know that Miss Adeline has always prayed for a baby, they leave the child on her porch. When the whole town interprets this as a miracle from God, worse problems follow. A warm story of small town life.

Where it's reviewed:
Center for Children's Books Bulletin, September 1987, page 16
School Library Journal, August 1987, page 97

Other books by the author:
As Far as Mill Springs, 1991
The Legend of Daisy Flowerdew, 1990
Brushy Mountain, 1989
Hear the Wind Blow, 1988

Other books you might like:
Eve Bunting, *Sharing Susan*, 1991
Twelve year old Susan is shocked to find she was switched at birth andthe parents who raised her may have to give her up to her biological parents.

Bess Clayton, *Story for a Black Night*, 1982
An African father tells his son about the disaster that followed the night a baby with smallpox was abandoned in his family's house.

Leon Garfield, *The Strange Affair of Adelaide Harris*, 1971
An experiment to see if a wolf will suckle an abandoned baby turns desperate for two boys when the child is rescued by two well meaning passersby.

Betsy Haynes, *Taffy Sinclair, Baby Ashley and Me*, 1987
Two sixth grade girls find a baby girl abandoned on the front steps of their school.

Kim Piowaty, *Don't Look Her in the Eyes*, 1983
Abandoned by his psychotic mother, twelve year old Jason struggles to provide for himself and his baby brother while fearing their separation.

1419

Lila Perl

Hey, Remember Fat Glenda? (New York: Clarion, 1981)

Age range: Grades 5-6

Subject(s): Weight Control; Friendship

Major character(s): Glenda Waite, Teenager; Sara, Friend; Mr. Hartley, Teacher

Time period(s): 1980s

Locale(s): United States

What the book is about: Glenda is starting eighth grade and has struggled all summer to lose weight. Her eating problems come and go as she deals with friends' reactions, disappointments at school, and recovering from a crush on a teacher who exploits her willingness to work hard.

Where it's reviewed:
Center for Children's Books Bulletin, April 1982, page 156
School Library Journal, November 1981, page 97

Other books by the author:
Fat Glenda Turns Fourteen, 1991
Fat Glenda's Summer Romance, 1986
Pieface and Daphne, 1980
Me and Fat Glenda, 1972

Other books you might like:
Barthe DeClements, *Nothing's Fair in Fifth Grade*, 1981
A fifth grade class with negative feelings about a new, overweight student, finally learns to accept her.

Mary Oldham, *The White Pony*, 1981
An overweight girl becomes attached to a nearly blind white pony who inspires her to develop her writing talent.

Nancy Saxon, *Panky and William*, 1983
Ten year old Frances, overweight and lonely after a move to the suburbs, becomes interested in a horse that needs her help.

Doris Buchanan Smith, *Last Was Lloyd*, 1981
A friendless, overweight twelve year old begins to change the monotonous pattern of his life.

Robert Kimmel Smith, *Jelly Belly*, 1981
The fattest kid in fifth grade wants to lose weight, but not badly enough to starve.

1420

Lila Perl

The Telltale Summer of Tina C. (New York: Seabury, 1975)

Age range: Grades 4-6

Subject(s): Divorce

Major character(s): Tina Carstairs, Preteen; Arthur Carstairs, Child; Nana Tess, Child-Care Giver

Time period(s): 1970s

Locale(s): New York

What the book is about: Twelve year old Tina is tall and self-conscious. Her father has just announced he is going to marry a woman Tina dislikes. She and her mother are getting reacquainted. Her mother has married soon after divorcing Tina's father, and Tina learns to really like her new stepfather.

She meets a Dutch boy who has a crush on her, and grows in self-confidence.

Where it's reviewed:
Kirkus Reviews, November 15, 1975, page 1288
School Library Journal, January 1976, page 49

Other books by the author:
Remember Fat Glenda?, 1981
Pieface and Daphne, 1980
America Goes to the Fair, 1975
That Crazy April, 1974

Other books you might like:
Paula Danziger, *The Divorce Express*, 1982
    Resentful of her parents' divorce, a young girl tries to fit into their lives and find a place for herself.
Johanna Hurwitz, *DeDe Takes Charge!*, 1984
    A year after her father has left home for good, fifth grader DeDe helps her mother cope with life after divorce.
Kevin Major, *Dear Bruce Springsteen: A Novel*, 1987
    Terry reveals his musical ambitions and his problems with his parents' separation in letters to his favorite rock star.
Winifred Morris, *Dancer in the Mirror*, 1987
    Carole is devastated by her parents' divorce and is grateful for a good friend.
Susan Beth Pfeffer, *Dear Dad, Love Laurie*, 1989
    Laurie's letter to her divorced father tells about her year in sixth grade and her efforts to enter the school's program for the gifted and talented.

1421

P.J. Petersen

Going for the Big One (New York: Delacorte, 1986)

Age range: Grades 5-8

Subject(s): Brothers and Sisters; Drugs; Survival

Major character(s): Jefferson Bates, Teenager; Annie Bates, Teenager (Jefferson's sister); Lucky Bates, Parent

Time period(s): 1980s

Locale(s): Alaska

What the book is about: The teenage Bates kids decide to hike across the Sierras hoping to meet their father, who is looking for work in Alaska. Jefferson, Annie and Dave are abandoned by their new stepmother Grace. Robbed of all their possessions by Grace and fearing another foster home, the trio decide to find their adventuring father.

Where it's reviewed:
Center for Children's Books Bulletin, September 1986, page 16
School Library Journal, September 1986, page 146

Other books by the author:
Corky and the Brothers Cool, 1986
The Boll Weevil Express: A Novel, 1983
Nobody Else Can Walk It for You, 1982
Would You Settle for Improbable?, 1982

Other books you might like:
Robbie Branscum, *The Girl*, 1986
    Left with her four brothers and sisters in the care of a cruel grandmother, an eleven year old girl struggles for survival in the poor community.

Eth Clifford, *The Curse of the Moonraker: A Tale of Survival*, 1977
    The survivors of a shipwreck in the Auckland Islands fight for survival under seemingly hopeless conditions.
Jean Craighead George, *On the Far Side of the Mountain*, 1990
    Sam's peaceful existence in his wilderness home is disrupted when his sister runs away and his pet falcon is confiscated by a conservation officer.
Hilary H. Milton, *Mayday! Mayday!*, 1979
    After their airplane crashes, two young people must find their way down a mountain in order to bring help to the survivors.
Gloria Skurzynski, *Caught in the Moving Mountains*, 1984
    On a 3 day hike in the wilderness, 13 year old brothers use all of their skill to survive when they find an injured drug dealer during an earthquake.

1422

Jeanne Whitehouse Peterson

Illustrator: Deborah K. Ray

That Is That (New York: Harper, 1979)

Age range: Grades 2-4

Subject(s): Divorce; Single Parent Families

Major character(s): Emma Rose LaRue, Child; Meko LaRue, Child

Time period(s): 1970s

Locale(s): United States

What the book is about: Only time can heal the hurt when a girl's father leaves home, but Emma Rose and Meko devise their own ways of remembering and understanding. A gentle story to read aloud to primaries. Those who can read it alone have many other books on the subject to choose from.

Where it's reviewed:
Hornbook, August 1979, page 408
Kirkus Reviews, March 15, 1979, page 325
School Library Journal, March 1979, page 128

Other books by the author:
Sometimes I Dream Horses, 1987
While the Moon Shines Bright, 1981
I Have a Sister: My Sister Is Deaf, 1977

Other books you might like:
Crescent Dragonwagon, *Always, Always*, 1984
    A little girl discovers that although her parents are divorced, it in no way changes their love for her.
Jeannette Franklin, *Daddy*, 1977
    A child of separated parents describes the special activities she share with her dad on Saturdays.
Steven Kroll, *Annie's Four Grannies*, 1986
    While divorce and remarriage have given Annie four grandmothers, entertaining them all at once presents some problems.
Marcia Newfield, *A Book for Jodan*, 1975
    Upon learning that her parents are separating, Jodan wonders is she is to blame for their decision and what can be done to keep them together.
Jane Werner Watson, *Sometimes a Family Has to Split Up*, 1988

A young boy describes his feelings of fear and guilt and confusion when he discovers his parents are getting a divorce.

| 1423 |

Ann Petry

Tituba of Salem Village (New York: Crowell, 1964)

Age range: Grades 5 and Up

Subject(s): Witches and Witchcraft; Slavery; African Americans

Major character(s): Tituba, Slave, Historical Figure; Abigail Williams, Child; Reverend Samuel Parris, Religious

Time period(s): 17th century (1692)

Locale(s): Boston, Massachusetts, American Colonies

What the book is about: Tituba and her husband, John, are sold to pay a gambling debt and go to Boston with Rev. Parris and his family. Tituba cares for the family and enchants visitors with West Indian folk tales, but is accused of being a witch when villagers are looking for someone to blame for ''fits'' afflicting the indentured girls.

Where it's reviewed:
Horn Book, February 1965, page 65
Library Journal, September 15, 1964, page 3498

Other books by the author:
Legends of the Saints, 1970
Harriet Tubman, 1955

Other books you might like:
Eileen Dunlop, *The Valley of Deer*, 1989
    After finding an old family Bible, Anne tries to solve the mystery of the 1726 death of a young Scottish woman accused of witchcraft.
Evelyn White Minshull, *The Dune Witch*, 1972
    Newly arrived in the Massachusetts colony, Priss is accused of being a witch because of her friendship with a strange girl who appears on the dunes.
Phyllis Reynolds Naylor, *The Witch Returns*, 1992
    Convinced that the new woman in the neighborhood is really the ''dead'' Mrs. Tuggle, Lynn and Mouse try to understand her.
Zilpha Keatley Snyder, *The Witches of Worm*, 1972
    A lonely twelve year old is convinced that the cat she finds is possessed by a witch and is responsible for her own strange behavior.
Ann Warren Turner, *Rosemary's Witch*, 1991
    Rosemary discovers that the woods near her home conceal a 150 year old witch who once lived in the house and is trying to get it back by magic.

| 1424 |

Stella Pevsner

And You Give Me a Pain, Elaine (Boston: Seabury, 1978)

Age range: Grades 5-6

Subject(s): Family Problems; Death

Major character(s): Andrea, Teenager; Elaine, Teenager; Joe, Teenager

Time period(s): 1970s

Locale(s): United States

What the book is about: Andrea is the youngest, Joe is away at college and sixteen year old Elaine is an obnoxious rebel who can't get along with anyone in the family. Elaine is the center of attention when she defies their parents. Joe is killed in a motorcycle accident. Andrea grows in compassion and tolerance.

Where it's reviewed:
Center for Children's Books Bulletin, January 1979, p 86
Children's Book Review Service, February 1979, page 69

Awards the book has won:
Golden Kite Fiction Award 1978

Other books by the author:
How Could You Do It, Diane?, 1989
Cute Is a Four Letter Word, 1980
A Smart Kid Like You, 1975
Call Me Heller, That's My Name, 1973

Other books you might like:
Terry Farish, *Why I'm Already Blue*, 1989
    A girl tries to get a better understanding of her family and their problems, and to gain perspective on her relationship with the boy next door.
Harry Mazer, *When the Phone Rang*, 1985
    When their parents are killed in a plane crash, three kids try to keep the family together despite overwhelming personal and financial problems.
Jim Naughton, *My Brother Stealing Second*, 1989
    After his brother is killed in a car accident, Bobby tries to come to terms with some disturbing truths about his family and life.
Phyllis Reynolds Naylor, *The Solomon System*, 1983
    Ted and Nory have always been a team until the summer family problems make them look at their relationships and the expectations.
Stephen Schwandt, *Holding Steady*, 1988
    Brendon tries to come to terms with grief, anger and guilt during the first family vacation after the death of his father.

| 1425 |

Stella Pevsner

Cute Is a Four Letter Word (New York: Clarion, 1980)

Age range: Grades 5-6

Subject(s): Identity; Friendship; Dating (Social Customs)

Major character(s): Clara Conrad, Teenager; Skip Svoboda, Sports Figure

Time period(s): 1980s

Locale(s): United States

What the book is about: Clara Conrad begins eighth grade determined to find her own identity. She is happy to be Pom-Pom squad captain and dating the captain of the football team, until she finds that he engineered her victory because he only dates ''winners.'' Clara begins to sort out her values and decides being cute is not the most important thing.

Where it's reviewed:
Center for Children's Books Bulletin, September 1980, page 181

Horn Book, August 1980, page 410

Other books by the author:
The Night the Whole Class Slept Over, 1991
Sister of the Quints, 1987
And You Give Me a Pain, Elaine, 1978
A Smart Kid Like You, 1974

Other books you might like:
Mary Jane Auch, *Glass Slippers Give You Blisters*, 1989
 Kelly's involvement in drama club and her grandmother's encouragement help her discover her own artistic identity.
Lorna Baxter, *The Eggchild*, 1978
 In a country ruled by four families with special powers, a boy and girl find a mysterious Eggchild and try to protect it and discover its identity.
Sheila Greenwald, *All the Way to Wits End*, 1979
 Eleven year old Drucilla longs to rid herself of her dusty traditional family heritage but finds the price of conformity more than she wants to pay.
Katherine Paterson, *Jacob Have I Loved*, 1980
 Feeling deprived all her life of schooling, friends, and even her name by her twin sister, Louise begins to fight back and become her own person.
Joan Talmage Weiss, *Home for a Stranger*, 1980
 A young Mexican girl has no clear memories except of the orphanage where she grew up until she is taken to California for a special operation.

1426

Stella Pevsner

A *Smart Kid Like You* (New York: Seabury, 1975)

Age range: Grades 5-6

Subject(s): Divorce; Remarriage

Major character(s): Nina, Preteen, Student (transfer)

Time period(s): 1970s

Locale(s): United States

What the book is about: Nina is a transfer student from a private school. The teacher of her accelerated math class turns out to be her father's new wife! Nina hasn't adjusted to her parents' divorce yet, and now her mother has a new boyfriend.

Where it's reviewed:
Kirkus Reviews, April 1, 1975, page 375
School Library Journal, May 1975, page 58

Awards the book has won:
Dorothy Canfield Fisher Children's Book Award 1977

Other books by the author:
How Could You Do It, Diane?, 1992
The Night the Whole Class Slept Over, 1991
Footsteps on the Stairs, 1984
And You Give Me a Pain, Elaine, 1978

Other books you might like:
Anne Fine, *Alias Madame Doubtfire*, 1987
 Miranda's three children enjoy their huge baby-sitter/cleaning-woman who is actually their father in disguise.
Constance C. Greene, *Ask Anybody*, 1983
 The daughter of divorced parents befriends an eccentric new girl who is full of unexpected surprises.
Anna Grossnickle Hines, *Boys Are Yucko!*, 1989

Hoping her divorced father will come from California for her birthday, Cassie reluctantly agrees to a friend's suggestion to have a boy/girl party.
Hadley Irwin, *Bring to a Boil and Separate*, 1980
 Katie's world begins to fall apart when her parents, both veterinarians, decide to divorce.
Marilyn Sachs, *At the Sound of the Beep*, 1990
 Distraught at the thought of their parents divorcing, a brother and sister run away and live in Golden Gate Park.

1427

K.M. Peyton

Illustrator: Victor G. Ambrus

Flambards (New York: Oxford, 1967)

Age range: Grades 6 and Up

Subject(s): Hunting

Major character(s): Christina, Orphan, Hunter; Russell, Relative (uncle), Handicapped (disabled); Mark, Preteen

Time period(s): 1910s

Locale(s): England

What the book is about: Christina is sent to live with her cruel uncle who was crippled in a hunting accident. She loves hunting but hates the mindless world of the hunters. The story shows a struggle between a dying culture and a new one being born.

Where it's reviewed:
Horn Book, December 1968, page 701
Times Literary Supplement, November 30, 1967

Awards the book has won:
Boston Globe/Horn Book Award - Honor Book 1969

Other books by the author:
Darkling, 1990
Who, Sir? Me, Sir?, 1983
Flambards Divided, 1982
Thunder in the Sky, 1967

Other books you might like:
Peter Zachary Cohen, *Deadly Game at Stony Creek*, 1978
 A pack of wild killer dogs is hunted down by two teenage boys.
Anne Eliot Crompton, *Deer Country*, 1973
 The members of the Strong family hunt for different reasons, but their goal is the same - a huge ten point buck.
Wayne Dodd, *A Time of Hunting*, 1975
 An adolescent changes his values and perceptions during the Depression in Oklahoma, especially regarding his only way to earn money - hunting.
Moses L. Howard, *The Ostrich Chase*, 1974
 Although women are forbidden to hunt, a young Bushman girl is determined to hunt an ostrich.
Kay Smith, *Skeeter*, 1989
 The adventures of two young boys befriended by an old black man who is a legendary hunter.

$\boxed{1428}$

K.M. Peyton

Marion's Angels (New York: Oxford University Press, 1979)

Age range: Grades 5 and Up

Subject(s): Death; Supernatural; Emotional Problems

Major character(s): Marion, Preteen; Patrick Pennington, Musician; Ephraim Voight, Musician

Time period(s): 1970s

Locale(s): England

What the book is about: Marion is the caretaker of St. Michael's, a medieval church. Her mother was a historian, and before she died she taught Marion the history of the church. The church needs restoration, so Marion arranges a benefit concert. She learns a great deal about her own emotions, hopes, and expectations.

Where it's reviewed:
Center for Children's Books Bulletin, March 1980, p 1391
Horn Book, April 1980, page 177

Other books by the author:
Darkling, 1990
Who, Sir? Me, Sir?, 1983
Beethoven Medal, 1972
The Edge of the Cloud, 1969

Other books you might like:
Eve Bunting, *The Haunting of Safekeep*, 1985
    While trying to understand her mother, Sara takes a summer job as caretaker at a Victorian restoration site and encounters a foundling and two ghosts.
Jan O'Donnell Klaveness, *The Griffin Legacy*, 1983
    Amy Enfield becomes involved with the spirit of her ancestor, Lucy Griffin, and undertakes a quest for silver stolen from the parish church.
Margaret Mahy, *The Tricksters*, 1986
    While gathered together for Christmas, a large New Zealand family and their guests find their lives invaded by some fascinating but sinister brothers.
Karin N. Mango, *Just for the Summer*, 1990
    Working as a lifeguard at a New Hampshire beach, Jenny finds herself falling in love with a reclusive boy tormented by the death of his father.
Eleanora E. Tate, *The Secret of Gumbo Grove*, 1987
    While helping restore the cemetary of an old Baptist church, Raisin solves the mystery surrounding the founding of her home.

$\boxed{1429}$

K.M. Peyton, Author/Illustrator

The Team (New York: Crowell, 1975)

Age range: Grades 6-8

Subject(s): Animals/Horses

Major character(s): Ruth, Teenager, Equestrian; Peter, Teenager, Equestrian

Time period(s): 1970s

Locale(s): England

What the book is about: Ruth acquires what is considered an unsuitable pony and determines to train him so that she can become a member of the Pony Club. Ruth's position on the team is uncertain, particularly because of Peter's competition.

Where it's reviewed:
Center for Children's Books Bulletin, November 1976, page 46
Kirkus Reviews, June 15, 1976, page 691
School Library Journal, May 1981, page 27

Other books by the author:
Marion's Angels, 1979
If Ever I Marry, 1974 (Original title, *The Beethovan Medal*)
Fly by Night, 1968
The Plan for Birdsmarsh, 1966

Other books you might like:
Valerie Beales, *Emma and Freckles*, 1992
    Emma tries to rescue a spirited pony from a riding school where the owner mistreats animals.
Bonnie Bryant, *Horse Power*, 1989
    Stevie is less than thrilled when she discovers that her older brother, Chad, wants to learn to ride.
Patricia Leitch, *The Fields of Praise*, 1975
    A thirteen year old girl is given the chance to ride and show her neighbor's spirited pony which is being groomed for national competition.
Candice Ransom, *My Sister, the Traitor*, 1989
    When her older sister gets a summer job at a local amusement park, Jackie feels left out until she develops a crush on a boy who runs the pony rides.
Sam Savitt, *Vicki and the Black Horse*, 1964
    Vicki loves taking care of her father's beautiful horse, Pat. When she finds a neglected Shetland pony that nobody wants, he and Pat become friends.

$\boxed{1430}$

K.M. Peyton

Who, Sir? Me, Sir? (New York: Oxford University Press, 1983)

Age range: Grades 5-8

Subject(s): Contests; Sports

Major character(s): Sam Sylvester, Teacher; Deirdre "Nutty" McTavish, Teenager; Hoomey Rossiter, Teenager

Time period(s): 1980s

Locale(s): England

What the book is about: A group of children at the Hawkwood Comprehensive school are told by their form-master, Sam Sylvester, that they must complete in a tetrathlon in a competition against the poshest school in the neighborhood, and they have never done any of the events before.

Where it's reviewed:
Booklist, March 1, 1984, page 994
Center for Children's Books Bulletin, February 1984, page 115
School Library Journal, August 1984, page 86

Other books by the author:
Poor Badger, 1992
Darkling, 1990
Sea Fever, 1980

The Right Hand Man, 1977

Other books you might like:

Joan Davenport Carris, *Hedgehogs in the Closet*, 1988
Unhappy at first with his family's move to England, Nick slowly begins to thrive in the very British setting of his new home and school.

Meredith Daneman, *Francie and the Boys*, 1988
Despite her parents' objections, Francie becomes involved in a play at Dubbs' School for Boys, winning the lead role and the attention of two actors.

Leon Garfield, *Young Nick and Jubilee*, 1989
A meeting with a pickpocket and a pupil from a charity school changes the lives of an orphaned brother and sister living on the streets of London.

Jan Mark, *Under the Autumn Garden*, 1977
A young boy's efforts to excavate a historical relic for a school project prove futile until, too late for the project, he makes an amazing discovery.

Jill Paton Walsh, *Gaffer Sampson's Luck*, 1984
James' difficulty in adjusting to a new school and life in the Fens is further complicated by the dangerous effort to find a neighbor's lucky piece.

1431

Susan Beth Pfeffer

Illustrator: Lorna Tomei

Just Between Us (New York: Delacorte Press, 1980)

Age range: Grades 5-6

Subject(s): Friendship; Divorce; Adoption

Major character(s): Cass Miller, Preteen; Jenny, Preteen; Robin, Child, Adoptee

Time period(s): 1980s

Locale(s): United States

What the book is about: Cass cannot keep a secret. Robin tells her that she was adopted. Cass tries to keep this secret. Jenny is spiteful and bitter over her own parents' divorce. Jenny tries to figure out why Robin doesn't look like either of her parents. The three young girls learn the importance of trust.

Where it's reviewed:

Kirkus Reviews, September 1, 1980, page 1164
School Library Journal, August 1980, page 69

Other books by the author:

Starting with Melodie, 1982
What Do You Do When Your Mouth Won't Open?, 1981
About David, 1980
Starring Peter and Leigh, 1979

Other books you might like:

Liza Fosburgh, *Mrs. Abercorn and the Bunce Boys*, 1986
A retired mystery writer takes two boys under her wing and teaches them about trust and friendship.

Gene Kemp, *Gowie Corby Plays Chicken*, 1976
Gowie can trust no one and he wants no friends until he meets Rosie Angela Lee.

Mary Jane Miller, *Me and My Name*, 1990
Erin faces difficult decisions about adoption by her stepfather, two boys at school, and a game of truth or dare at a slumber party.

Joan Lowery Nixon, *Caught in the Act*, 1988

Michael is sent to a foster home on a Missouri farm with a sadistic owner, a bullying son, and a number of secrets, one of which may be murder.

Susan Richards Shreve, *Family Secrets*, 1979
Five very important stories about death, divorce, suicide, a terminally ill grandmother, and cheating on a school test.

1432

Susan Beth Pfeffer, Author/Illustrator

Kid Power (New York: Watts, 1977)

Age range: Grades 4-6

Subject(s): Employment; Family Life

Major character(s): Jamie, Preteen; Carol, Preteen

Time period(s): 1970s

Locale(s): United States

What the book is about: Jamie's mom loses her job and the family budget gets tight. Jamie starts to save her allowance for the bike her dad says they can no longer afford. Jamie organizes "Kid Power," doing odd jobs, hiring her friends and her sister, Carol. Mom decides she is going to do the same thing for adults.

Where it's reviewed:

Center for Children's Books Bulletin, January 1978, page 85
School Library Journal, November 1977, page 62
Dorothy Canfield Fisher Children's Book Award, 1979

Other books by the author:

Kid Power Strikes Back, 1984
Marly the Kid, 1975
The Beauty Queen, 1974

Other books you might like:

Patricia Beatty, *Turn Homeward, Hannalee*, 1984
Hannalee must move to Indiana with other Georgia mill-workers during the Civil War, leaving her mother with a promise to return when the war ends.

Kristi Holl, *Hidden in the Fog*, 1989
Nikki's family runs a Mississippi steamboat tourist attraction and she tries various schemes to make money when financial hard times hit.

Naomi Mitchison, *The Family at Ditlabeng*, 1970
During a long drought in Botswana, a young girl discovers her skill for making pottery is the key to her being able to attend school.

Willo Davis Roberts, *The Pet-Sitting Peril*, 1983
A boy who does odd jobs becomes involved with a gang of arsonists hired by the building's owner.

Judy Van der Veer, *Long Trail for Francisco*, 1974
A sixteen year old Mexican boy goes to California to earn money for his needy family.

1433

Susan Beth Pfeffer

Truth or Dare (New York: Macmillan, 1984)

Age range: Grades 5-7

Subject(s): Schools; Family Life; Conformity

Major character(s): Cathy, Preteen; Jessica, Preteen; Paul, Preteen, Dancer (ballet)

Time period(s): 1980s

Locale(s): United States

What the book is about: Cathy is just starting junior high. She misses her two best friends who have transferred to another school, and begins a campaign to get Jessica to like her. Jessica, however, is interested in Cathy's brother, Paul

Where it's reviewed:
Booklist, June 1, 1984, page 1400
Center for Children's Books Bulletin, page 172
Hornbook, August 1984, page 469

Other books by the author:
April Upstairs, 1990
Courage Dana, 1983
About David, 1980
Awful Evelina, 1979

Other books you might like:
Betsy Byars, *Bingo Brown's Guide to Romance*, 1992
    Bingo Brown's work hits a snag when his long-distance girlfriend Melissa returns unexpectedly from Oklahoma.
Laura Hawkins, *The Cat That Could Spell Mississippi*, 1992
    Anxious to prove that she is special at her new school, Linda makes everything more difficult for herself when she cheats on a spelling bee.
Claudia Mills, *Dinah for President*, 1992
    Dinah, now in middle school, struggles to become a big fish in an ocean, and in the process discovers recycling and of friendship of the elderly.
Bonnie Pryor, *Horses in the Garage*, 1992
    Samantha finds a way to cope with her difficulties in adjusting to a new stepfather, a new home and school when she makes friends with Jasmine.
Susan Richards Shreve, *Joshua T. Bates Takes Charge*, 1993
    Joshua, worried about fitting in at school, feels awkward when the new student he is supposed to be helping becomes the target of the bully.

| 1434 |

Terry Wolfe Phelan

Illustrator: Joel Schick

The Week Mom Unplugged the TVs (New York: Four Winds, 1979)

Age range: Grades 3-5

Subject(s): Family Life; Television

Major character(s): Steve, Child; Beth, Child; Stacey, Child

Time period(s): 1970s

Locale(s): United States

What the book is about: Mom unplugs the TVs for one whole school week. On the first day, Steve invites all his friends over. When they leave, the silence is overwhelming until he hears crickets for the first time. The second night he goes to bed two hours earlier and notices a comet. Day three he spends making a telescope, which opens a new world for Steve and his sisters.

Where it's reviewed:
Center for Children's Books Bulletin, June 1979, page 182

Kirkus Reviews, March 1, 1979, page 263

Other books by the author:
The S.S. Valentine, 1979

Other books you might like:
Betsy Byars, *The TV Kid*, 1976
    To escape failure, boredom, and loneliness, a young boy plunges with all his imagination into the world of television.
Betsy Haynes, *Taffy Sinclair Goes to Hollywood*, 1990
    Taffy has just landed a role in the TV movie about a beautiful girl whose life at school is made miserable by friends who despise her.
Kathleen Krull, *Alex Fitzgerald, TV Star*, 1991
    Alex's new friendships in California are endangered when her chance to appear in a rock video brings her glamour and an inflated ego.
Nancy Smiler Levinson, *The Ruthie Greene Show*, 1985
    Ruthie, feeling her intelligence and creativity are underrated, finds a sympathetic television producer as a mentor and helps on a TV production.
Joel L. Schwartz, *How to Get Rid of Your Older Brother*, 1992
    It hasn't been easy being Louis's younger brother. Then one fated night Louis refuses to give up the remote control, and it's Jay's turn to get even.

| 1435 |

Joan Phillips

Illustrator: Lynn Munsinger

My New Boy (New York: Random, 1986)

Age range: Grades 1-2

Series: Step Into Reading

Subject(s): Animals/Dogs

Time period(s): Indeterminate

Locale(s): United States

What the book is about: A pet store puppy searches for just the right owner. The little black puppy acquires a boy, teaches him some tricks and finds him when he is lost.

Where it's reviewed:
Booklist, December 1, 1986, page 583
Center for Children's Books Bulletin, January 1987, page 95
School Library Journal, December 1986, page 124

Other books by the author:
Lucky Bear, 1987
Tiger Is a Scaredy Cat, 1986
Gretchen and the Lost Carousel, 1982

Other books you might like:
Byrd Baylor, *Amigo*, 1963
    Desperately wanting a pet to love, a boy decides to tame a prairie dog who has already decided to tame the boy for his own pet.
Margaret Hillert, *A Friend for Dear Dragon*, 1985
    A boy and his pet dragon make friends with their new neighbors, a girl and her unicorn.
Jeffrey Moss, *Bob and Jack: A Boy and His Yak*, 1992
    Jack and his pet yak become inseparable friends, playing together, protecting each other, and occasionally running into trouble.
Zilpha Keatley Snyder, *The Changing Maze*, 1985

A shepherd boy braves the evil magic of a wizard's maze to save his pet lamb.

Tricia Springstubb, *The Magic Guinea Pig*, 1982
A small boy who wants a puppy more than anything else meets a witch who provides him with an unexpected pet.

1436

Mildred Kantrowitz Phillips

Illustrator: Margot Zemach

The Sign in Mendel's Window (New York: Macmillan, 1985)

Age range: Grades 1-2

Subject(s): City Life

Major character(s): Mendel, Butcher

Time period(s): Indeterminate Past

Locale(s): Kosnov, Russia

What the book is about: When a stranger comes to Kosnov and accuses Mendel the butcher of stealing his money, the whole town joins in to show the police who he really is.

Where it's reviewed:
Children's Book Review Service, October 1985, page 17
Center for Children's Books Bulletin, October 1985, page 35
School Library Journal, November 1985, page 76

Other books by the author:
Willy Bear, 1976
When Violet Died, 1973
I Wonder If Herbie's Home Yet, 1971
Maxie, 1970

Other books you might like:
Denys Cazet, *Mud Baths for Everyone*, 1981
When three little pigs are frightened by Bobble Bigpig, they seek revenge disguised as a butcher.
Guy Daniels, *The Tsar's Riddles: or, The Wise Little Girl*, 1967
In a dispute concerning the birth of a colt from her father's mare, the daughter of a poor peasant gives the Tsar answers as clever as his riddles.
Robert Kobayashi, *Maria Marzaretti Loves Spaghetti*, 1991
Two adventures in the life of an unusual old lady butcher, one involving a hungry mouse and the other a magic plant.
Irene Mirkovic, *The Greedy Grasshopper*, 1980
When Ivo returns a money pouch to the wealthy merchant who lost it, he is accused of stealing one of the gold coins in the pouch.
Arthur Yorinks, *Louis the Fish*, 1980
An unhappy butcher from Flatbush finally achieves happiness.

1437

Joan Phipson

The Horse with Eight Hands (New York: Atheneum, 1974)

Age range: Grades 5-6

Major character(s): Horst, Immigrant

Time period(s): 1970s

Locale(s): Australia

What the book is about: "Horse" is an German immigrant, the eight hands belong to four Australian children who take him under their wings. Horst turns an old house into an antique shop. A motorcycle gang hassles Horst and the kids try to protect him.

Where it's reviewed:
Kirkus Reviews, August 1, 1974, page 805
Library Journal, October 15, 1974, page 2748

Other books by the author:
A Tide Flowing, 1981
When the City Stopped, 1978
The Family Conspiracy, 1974
Polly's Tiger, 1974

Other books you might like:
Diana Kidd, *Onion Tears*, 1991
A Vietnamese girl tries to come to terms with her grief over the loss of her family and her new life with the Australian family who has taken her in.
William Mayne, *Salt River Times*, 1980
Twenty-one interlocking stories about the lives of people in a small community along Australia's Salt River.
Eleanor Spence, *The Devil Hole*, 1976
The birth of an autistic child changes the lives of a once happy Australian family.
Colin Thiele, *Jodie's Journey*, 1990
Jodie, disabled by arthritis and no longer able to ride her beloved horse, faces a crisis when they are alone at her remote Australian home.
Patricia Wrightson, *The Nargun and the Stars*, 1974
An ancient stone creature threatens the lives of a family on a lonely sheep farm in Australia.

1438

Joan Phipson

Polly's Tiger (New York: Dutton, 1974)

Age range: Grades 2-3

Subject(s): Animals/Tigers

Major character(s): Polly, Child

Time period(s): 1970s

Locale(s): Australia

What the book is about: Polly has come to a small settlement where her father has a job. The kids are not very friendly, so Polly has an imaginary companion - the tiger she saw at the zoo.

Where it's reviewed:
Booklist, April 1, 1974, page 878
Kirkus Reviews, February 1, 1974, page 110

Other books by the author:
A Tide Flowing, 1981
When the City Stopped, 1978
The Way Home, 1973

Other books you might like:
Richard Adams, *The Tyger Voyage*, 1976
The adventures of two young tygers who set out from Victorian England into the timeless unknown.
Helen Cowcher, *Tigress*, 1991

Herdsmen work with a wildlife sanctuary ranger to keep their animals safe from a marauding tigress.

Kay D. Oana, *Timmy Tiger and the Butterfly Net*, 1981
Tommy has trouble with bees, but his brother, Timmy, rescues him with a butterfly net.

Jack Prelutsky, *The Terrible Tiger*, 1970
A very hungry tiger eats the grocer, the baker, and the farmer, but makes a mistake when he eats the tailor.

Alex Whitney, *The Tiger That Barks*, 1978
A young boy raises a Siberian tiger cub with a German Shepherd. (Non-Fiction)

1439

Joan Phipson

The Watcher in the Garden (New York: Atheneum, 1982)

Age range: Grades 5 and Up

Subject(s): Mystery and Detective Stories; Blind; Gardens and Gardening

Major character(s): Kitty, Teenager; Mr. Lovett, Handicapped (blind), Aged Person; Terry, Teenager

Time period(s): 1980s

Locale(s): United States

What the book is about: Kitty and a young hoodlum battle to influence each others minds. Kitty becomes friendly with an elderly blind man, Mr. Lovett, after she trespasses in his hilltop garden. She learns that there is an evil presence in the garden. Terry is plotting Mr. Lovett's death.

Where it's reviewed:
Center for Children's Books Bulletin, December 1982, page 75
School Library Journal, November 1982, page 89

Other books by the author:
Bianca, 1988
A Tide Flowing, 1981
Fly into Danger, 1977
Cross Currents, 1967

Other books you might like:
Frances Hodgson Burnett, *The Secret Garden*, 1987
Mary comes to live in a lonely house on the Yorkshire moors and discovers an invalid cousin and a locked garden.

Sheila Hayes, *Speaking of Snapdragons*, 1982
Heather forms a friendship with an old, reclusive man who spends his days tending his garden.

Rudyard Kipling, *Rikki-Tikki-Tavi*, 1992
A courageous mongoose thwarts the evil plans of Nag and Nagaina, the two black cobras who live in the garden.

Judith St. George, *The Mysterious Girl in the Garden*, 1981
While visiting Kew Gardens, an American girl travels in time to 1805, where she meets the girl who will be queen.

Alison Smith, *Reserved for Mark Anthony Crowder*, 1978
A sixth grader believes his whole family thinks he is weird. He spends the summer cultivating his garden and his self-esteem.

1440

Tamora Pierce

Alanna: The First Adventure (New York: Atheneum, 1983)

Age range: Grades 5-8

Series: Song of the Lioness

Subject(s): Fantasy; Middle Ages; Sex Roles

Major character(s): Alanna, Preteen, Twin; Alan, Preteen, Twin; Jonathan, Royalty (prince)

Time period(s): Indeterminate Past (Middle Ages)

Locale(s): Fictional Country

What the book is about: Neither Alanna, who aspires to be a knight even though she is a girl, nor Thom, are happy with their father's decision to send Alanna to a convent and Thom to court. The two decide to switch places and Alanna, posing as Alan, becomes a page at court, while Thom goes to the convent to learn sorcery. Alanna finds life as a page hard, particularly as she is lighter and smaller than the other pages, but she struggles hard to overcome these disadvantages. She makes many friends at court, including Prince Jonathan, whose life she saves using her magical gift of healing. Many more books about Alanna follow.

Where it's reviewed:
Center for Children's Books Bulletin, February 1984, page 115
School Library Journal, February 1984, page 84

Other books by the author:
Wild Magic: The Immortals, 1992 (The Immortals, Book One)
Lioness Rampant, 1988
The Woman Who Rides Like a Man, 1986
In the Hand of the Goddess, 1984

Other books you might like:
Lloyd Alexander, *The Remarkable Journey of Prince Jen*, 1991
Bearing six unusual gifts, Prince Jen starts on a perilous quest, has exciting adventures, and learns about friendship, trust, and himself.

Lucy Cullyford Babbitt, *The Oval Amulet*, 1985
Paragrin discovers the importance of an iron oval amulet she possesses and uses it to make the world a place where men and women rule as equals.

Ruth Nichols, *A Walk out of the World*, 1969
A brother and sister walk into a world whose inhabitants are convinced that the girl is a descendant of a revered but nearly extixt line of kings.

Elizabeth Winthrop, *The Castle in the Air*, 1985
A gift of a toy castle, complete with a silver knight, introduces William to an adventure involving magic and a personal quest.

Jane Yolen, *Wren's Quest*, 1993
When Wren and Prince Connor set off to discover her birth family, a wizard creates havoc back home in Cantimoor.(Sequel to *Wren to the Rescue*)

1441

Robert Pierik

Illustrator: Beth Krush

Rookfleas in the Cellar (Philadelphia: Westminster Press, 1979)

Age range: Grades 3-6

Subject(s): Death

Major character(s): Danny Van Doren, Preteen; Stevie Van Doren, Preteen; Carrie Van Doren, Preteen

Time period(s): 1970s

Locale(s): Pinewood

What the book is about: Danny tries to become the man of the house after his father dies of emphysema. When their mom decides to sell the house, the three kids make up stories about high crime, the murder of a neighbor, leaks and rookfleas in the basement to scare off potential buyers. The three children struggle to accept their father's death and the inevitability of change.

Where it's reviewed:
School Library Journal, September 1979, page 146

Other books by the author:
Archy's Dream World, 1972

Other books you might like:
Sandy Asher, *Missing Pieces*, 1984
 Heather's year brings many changes, but it is the tragic death of her father that enables her to change her relationship with her mother.
Cynthia DeFelice, *Devil's Bridge*, 1992
 Ben must cope with the loss of his father, who died the year before, ana his mother's overprotectiveness when he enters the annual Striped Bass Derby.
Ann M. Martin, *With You and Without You*, 1986
 A girl faces the fact that her father is dying, and then his death, but dealing with the emptiness afterwards is hardest of all.
Mary Pope Osborne, *Run, Run as Fast as You Can*, 1982
 Hallie worries about popularity and faces an unexpected tragedy when her family moves to Virginia.
Jacqueline Woodson, *Last Summer with Maizon*, 1990
 Margaret tries to accept the inevitable changes that come one summer when her father dies and her best friend goes away to a private boarding school.

1442

Daniel Manus Pinkwater

Alan Mendelsohn, the Boy From Mars (New York: Dutton, 1979)

Age range: Grades 5-8

Subject(s): Humor; Schools; Science Fiction

Major character(s): Alan Mendelsohn, Alien; Leonard, Friend

Time period(s): 1970s

Locale(s): United States

What the book is about: Leonard's life at his new junior high school is just barely tolerable until he becomes friends with the unusual Alan and shares an extraordinary adventure with him.

Where it's reviewed:
Hornbook, August 1979, page 416

Kirkus Reviews, June 15, 1979, page 690
School Library Journal, May 1979, page 36

Other books by the author:
Jolly Roger: A Dog of Hoboken, 1985
The Snarkout Boys and the Avacado of Death, 1982
Attilla the Pun, 1981
Lizard Music, 1976

Other books you might like:
Janet Asimov, *Norby, the Mixed-Up Robot*, 1983
 Jeff Wells, a Space Academy student, and Norby, a robot with unusual skills, become involved in the plans of Ing the Ingrate to take over the universe
Walter R. Brooks, *Freddy and the Men From Mars*, 1987
 Freddy the Pig's sleuthing skills are put to the test by conniving rats and a band of rabbits masquerading as Martians.
Margaret Goff Clark, *Barney on Mars*, 1983
 When Barney's young friend's dog is taken to Mars, extraterrestrial acquaintance Tibbo helps them try to get it back.
Mel Gilden, *The Return of Captain Conquer*, 1986
 Watson Congruent and a group of fans dedicated to an old science fiction TV series discover an alien plot to conquer the world.
Harry Harrison, *The Men From P.I.G and R.O.B.O.T.*, 1974
 Humorous accounts of specially trained and bred pigs and of the Robot Obtrusion Batallion give new space policemen insight into possible assignments.

1443

Daniel Manus Pinkwater

Fat Men from Space (New York: Dodd, 1977)

Age range: Grades 3-6

Subject(s): Food; Aliens; Humor

Major character(s): William, Child; Mr. Wendel, Teacher

Time period(s): 1970s

Locale(s): United States

What the book is about: William can hear radio programs on the new filling in his tooth. He encounters invaders from space who plunder all the junk food on Earth and disappear in search of a giant potato pancake. William, and everyone else, has to survive on lean meat, fresh produce, and other healthy food.

Where it's reviewed:
Kirkus Reviews, September 1, 1977, page 934
School Library Journal, November 1977, page 62

Other books by the author:
The Wuggie Norple Story, 1980
The Big Orange Splot, 1977
The Hoboken Chicken Emergency, 1977
Around Fred's Bed, 1976

Other books you might like:
Peggy Bacon, *The Magic Touch*, 1968
 Bored with the housekeeper's fancy food, the three Lurie children and their friend try doing their own cooking using magic recipes.
William Pene Du Bois, *Porko Von Popbutton*, 1969

A two-hundred-seventy-four pound thirteen year old boy whose sole passion is food is miserable until he accidentally makes the hockey team at school.

Timothy Foote, *The Great Ringtail Garbage Caper*, 1980
  A group of desperate and daring raccoons organize a bold hijacking scheme when efficient young garbage collectors threaten their lush food supply.

Stephen Manes, *Chocolate-Covered Ants*, 1990
  Max and his sister make a bet about eating bugs.

Jean Van Leeuwen, *Benjy and the Power of Zingies*, 1982
  Tired of being small for his age, Benjy decides to eat the cereal of sports stars.

1444

Daniel Manus Pinkwater

The Hoboken Chicken Emergency (Englewood Cliffs, NJ: Prentice Hall, 1977)

Age range: Grades 3-5

Subject(s): Animals/Birds; Humor

Major character(s): Arthur Bobowicz, Hero; Henrietta, Chicken

Time period(s): 1970s

Locale(s): Hoboken, New Jersey

What the book is about: Arthur goes to pick up the turkey for Thanksgiving dinner at Murphy's Meat Market, but somehow the turkey reserved for the family has been lost. He comes back with a 260 pound chicken he purchased from Professor Mazzocchi. Since no one can face trying to eat a 260 pound chicken, the Bobowicz children acquire a new pet, which they enjoy greatly until she gets away and wanders around Hoboken.

Where it's reviewed:
Booklist, April 15, 1977, page 1268
Hornbook, June 1977, page 316
Kirkus Reviews, February 15, 1977, page 166

Other books by the author:
Author's Day, 1993
The Blue Thing, 1977
Fat Men from Space, 1977
Blue Moose, 1975

Other books you might like:
John R. Erickson, *The Original Adventures of Hank the Cowdog*, 1988
  Hank the Cowdog, Head of Ranch Security, is framed for the murder of a chicken and becomes an outlaw with the coyotes.
Constance C. Greene, *Odds on Oliver*, 1993
  Oliver's attempts to be a hero result in such humorous disasters as going up a tree to rescue a cat and getting stuck there himself.
Johanna Hurwitz, *Ali Baba Bernstein, Lost and Found*, 1992
  Ten year old David "Ali Baba" Bernstein spends most of his time thinking about becoming a detective and getting a dog.
Ellen Leroe, *Leap Frog Friday*, 1992
  Nine year old Oliver has a big problem one memorable Friday when he uses his new magic rocks and inadvertently changes his brother into a frog.
Janice Lee Smith, *Nelson in Love: An Adam Joshua Valentine's Day Story*, 1992

Adam Joshua's Valentine's Day is extremely complicated, and it doesn't help that his best friend, Nelson, and his dog, George, are both in love.

1445

Daniel Manus Pinkwater

Lizard Music (New York: Dodd, Mead & Co., 1976)

Age range: Grades 4-6

Subject(s): Humor; Fantasy; Science Fiction

Major character(s): Victor, Child; Horace Kopeckie, Eccentric

Time period(s): 1970s

Locale(s): McDonaldsville

What the book is about: When 11-year-old Victor's older sister takes off with friends and leaves him alone for two weeks, he can't wait to stay up all night watching TV. He sees a band made up of lizards and decides to track them down. He gets help from the Chicken Man, and visits Diamond Hard, the invisible island where the lizards live.

Where it's reviewed:
Booklist, September 1, 1976, page 41
School Library Journal, October 1976, page 110

Other books by the author:
Alan Mendelsohn, the Boy From Mars, 1979
Attila the Pun, 1988
Fat Men from Space, 1977
Jolly Roger: A Dog of Hoboken, 1985

Other books you might like:
Mel Gilden, *M Is for Monster*, 1987
  A monster story which begins with strange new students in a fifth grade class.
Louise Hawes, *Nelson Malone Meets the Man From Mush-Nut*, 1986
  Nelson's dream of glory begins when he takes his piano teacher's magical snake to his school's annual pet day.
Robert Newman, *Merlin's Mistake*, 1970
  Tertius is given knowledge at birth of future events and inventions and sets off on his quest with his friend, Brian.
Richard Peck, *The Ghost Belonged to Me*, 1975
  Alexander, his friend, Blossom, and 87 year old Uncle Miles succeed in laying to rest an errant ghost.
Judith Spearing, *Ghost Who Went to School*, 1966
  The teachers are amazed and the children delighted when two ghosts show up for school.

1446

Jill Pinkwater

Illustrator: Irene Brady

Cloud Horse (New York: Lothrop, 1983)

Age range: Grades 5-7

Subject(s): Animals/Horses; Vikings; Space and Time

Major character(s): Arnora, Teenager (viking); Kate, Teenager

Time period(s): Indeterminate Past

Locale(s): Ketilness, Maine; Fictional Country

What the book is about: Two dreamers, Arnora, a Viking girl of the distant past, and Kate, a modern American, both love and dream of the spirited horses of Iceland. The girls are brought together through time and they share an adventure rich in fantasy, adventure and discovery.

Where it's reviewed:
Booklist, January 15, 1984, page 750
Center for Children's Books Bulletin, December 1983, page 76
School Library Journal, December 1983, page 76

Other books by the author:
Buffalo Brenda, 1989
Tails of the Bronx: A Tale of the Bronx, 1989
The Disappearance of Sister Perfect, 1987

Other books you might like:
Caroline Baxter, *The Stolen Telesm*, 1975
    Two children are drawn into a battle with the evil forces of Darkness after they find a winged horse and an ancient stone.
Nathaniel Benchley, *Beyond the Mists*, 1975
    11th century Scandinavian life is portrayed through the eyes of an adventurous youth who travels to Vinland with Leif Eriksson.
Molly Holden, *The Unfinished Feud*, 1970
    An Icelandic youth faces great adversity when he attempts to end a family feud by atonement rather than killing.
Lee Kingman, *Escape From the Evil Prophecy*, 1973
    A brother and sister in 11th century Iceland try to escape the prophecy of a sorceress.
Nancy Luenn, *Arctic Unicorn*, 1986
    Kala's life in a remote Eskimo village on Baffin Island is disrupted by the arrival of a young hunter and her discovery that she has special powers.

1447

Jill Pinkwater

Tails of the Bronx: A Tale of the Bronx (New York: Macmillan, 1991)

Age range: Grades 6-9

Subject(s): City Life; Homeless; Neighbors and Neighborhoods

Major character(s): Loretta Bernstein, Preteen (Afro-American Jew)

Time period(s): 1990s

Locale(s): New York, New York (the Bronx)

What the book is about: The children of Burnbridge Avenue live in a dangerous area, but thanks to a good, strong neighborhood, they help and support each other, children and adults alike. When all the cats in the neighborhood are missing, the children set out to search for them, and find both the cats and two homeless persons. The children take care of the cats and help the homeless to find a place to live. An excellent choice for reading aloud.

Where it's reviewed:
Booklist, April 1, 1991, page 1568
School Library Journal, June 1991, page 112

Other books by the author:
Buffalo Brenda, 1989
The Disappearance of Sister Perfect, 1987
Cloud Horse, 1983

Other books you might like:
May Anderson, *The Unsinkable Molly Malone*, 1991
    Molly, a socially conscious struggling artist living in New York, befriends a group of children living in a welfare hotel.
Vicki Grove, *The Fastest Friend in the West*, 1990
    When her best friend dumps her to be with the popular kids, overweight Lori shares an unusual friendship with a homeless girl.
Alison Cragin Herzig, *Sam and the Moon Queen*, 1990
    Sympathetic to a homeless girl's plight, Sam tries to help her find food for herself and medical care for her dog.
Theresa Nelson, *The Beggar's Ride*, 1992
    Twelve year old Clare flees an unhappy home life and tries to survive on the streets of Atlantic City with a small gang of homeless kids.
Susan Wojciechowski, *Patty Dillman of Hot Dog Fame*, 1989
    Eight grader Patty becomes involved in working at a shelter for the homeless where she gains a new friend.

1448

Paul Pitts

Racing the Sun (New York: Avon, 1988)

Age range: Grades 5-7

Subject(s): Indians of North America; Grandparents

Major character(s): Brandon Rogers, Preteen, Indian (Navajo)

Time period(s): 1980s

Locale(s): Arizona

What the book is about: Twelve year old Brandon Rogers has known only contemporary suburban life. When his grandfather comes to live with the family, Brandon learns from him the importance of staying true to the Navajo heritage and finds himself in conflict with the white, contemporary culture in which he has been raised.

Where it's reviewed:
Booklist, September 15, 1988, page 169
Los Angeles Times Review, September 25, 1988, page 13
Publisher's Weekly, August 26, 1988, page 90

Other books you might like:
Nathan Aaseng, *Navajo Code Talkers*, 1992
    Describes how the American military in WWII used a group of Navajo Indians to create an indecipherable code based on their language. (Non-fiction)
A.E. Cannon, *The Shadow Brothers*, 1990
    Marcus feels his entire world changing as Henry, his Navajo foster brother, starts to wonder if her should return to his family's reservation.
Lynne Gessner, *Brother to the Navajo*, 1979
    Stranded in the desert, Paul and his family find refuge at a trading post on a Navajo reservation.
Tony Hillerman, *The Blessing Way*, 1970
    When Lt. Joe Leaphorn of the Navajo Tribal Police discovers a corpse at a crime scene without any clues, he is ready to suspect a supernatural killer.
Annabel Johnson, *Gamebuster*, 1990

A high school senior becomes involved in a fight against dispossessing the Navajos of their land forever.

1449

Kin Platt

Illustrator: Robert Lopshire

Big Max (New York: Harper, 1965)

Age range: Grades 1-2

Series: Mystery I Can Read Book

Subject(s): Animals/Elephants; Mystery and Detective Stories

Major character(s): Big Max, Private Detective; Jumbo, Elephant

Time period(s): Indeterminate

Locale(s): Fictional Country (Pooka Pooka)

What the book is about: A detective unravels the case of the king's missing elephant. Big Max follows Jumbo's tracks and discovers he has gone to his own birthday party. The king promises to give him a party in the future and invite all his relatives. The clue to Jumbo's escape is obvious enough for young readers to take their own guesses.

Where it's reviewed:
Booklist, September 15, 1965, page 100
Hornbook, October 1965, page 498
Kirkus Reviews, August 1, 1965, page 750

Other books by the author:
Big Max in the Mystery of the Missing Moose, 1977

Other books you might like:
Laura Jean Allen, *Rollo and Tweedy and the Ghost at Dougal Castle*, 1992
    Lord Dougal asks the detective Tweedy and his assistant, Rollo, to solve the mystery of the ghost that haunts Dougal Castle.
Doug Cushman, *Aunt Eater's Mystery Vacation*, 1992
    A mystery loving anteater has a chance to solve several mysteries during his vacation at the Hotel Bathwater.
Lillian Hoban, *The Case of the Two Masked Robbers*, 1986
    Raccoon twins Arabella and Albert track down the robbers who stole Mrs. Turtle's eggs.
Thomas P. Lewis, *Mr. Sniff and the Motel Mystery*, 1984
    The famous detective hound discovers why guests are being frightened away from a beach hotel.
Joan M. Lexau, *The Homework Caper*, 1966
    One morning Bill arrives at school to find his homework has vanished. He and his friend, Ken, try to catch the culprit before it is too late.

1450

Kin Platt

Chloris and the Creeps (Philadelphia: Chilton, 1973)

Age range: Grades 5-6

Subject(s): Remarriage; Family Life

Major character(s): Chloris, Preteen; Jenny, Relative (sister); Fidel Mancha, Step-Parent

Time period(s): 1970s

Locale(s): United States

What the book is about: Chloris has idealized her dead father. Any man who wants to marry her mom is a creep, she decides. Slowly, Chloris changes her mind about Fidel Mancha, her mom's new husband.

Where it's reviewed:
Kirkus Reviews, February 15, 1973, page 188
Library Journal, April 15, 1973, page 1389

Other books by the author:
Darwin and the Great Beasts, 1992
Chloris and the Freaks, 1975
Hey, Dummy, 1973
The Princess Stakes Murder, 1972

Other books you might like:
Ann M. Martin, *Bummer Summer*, 1983
    Twelve year old Kammy has trouble accepting her new family, but a summer at camp helps her see things differently.
Eloise Jarvis McGraw, *Hideaway*, 1983
    When his father forgets to come for him, twelve year old Jerry runs to his grandparents' house, but they don't live there anymore.
Ruth Riddell, *Ice Warrior*, 1992
    When his mother's remarriage moves him from California to Minnesota, twelve year old Rob feels out of place until he discovers ice boating.
Alfred Slote, *A Friend Like That*, 1988
    Eleven year old Robby takes drastic steps to stop his widowed father from developing a new love interest.
Judie Wolkoff, *Happily Ever After.Almost: A Novel*, 1982
    Eleven year old Kitty and her sister look forward to their mother's remarriage but not to getting a stepbrother.

1451

Kin Platt

Frank and Stein and Me (New York: Watts, 1982)

Age range: Grades 5-8

Subject(s): Crime and Criminals; Smuggling

Major character(s): Jack Hook, Sports Figure (basketball player)

Time period(s): 1980s

Locale(s): Paris, France

What the book is about: Jack, a young American basketball player wins a free trip to Paris where he encounters a smuggling ring and the strange Dr. Stein. Before he leaves for Paris, he is asked to deliver a cake to someone's mother. Unfortunately, the cake is loaded with marijuana.

Where it's reviewed:
Booklist, August 1982, page 1531
Children's Book Review Service, July 1982, page 129
School Library Journal, January 1983, page 87

Other books by the author:
Crocker, 1983
Brogg's Brain, 1981
Dracula, Go Home!, 1976
The Blue Man, 1961

Other books you might like:
Jim Hausman, *Mystery at Sans Souci*, 1978
  A number of unrelated incidents lead an American family to conclude that someone wants them out of their rented house in a small town outside Paris.
Elizabeth Howard, *The Mystery of the Deadly Diamond*, 1987
  In Paris at the turn of the century, an American girl uses an experimental diving bell in the Seine and finds a trunk possibly linked to a theft.
Pat Hutchins, *The Mona Lisa Mystery*, 1981
  Class 3 of Hampstead Primary School takes a school trip to Paris and lands right in the middle of a mystery.
Ivan Kusan, *The Mystery of the Stolen Painting*, 1975
  Two Yugoslav boys visiting Paris become involved with the theft of the Mona Lisa.
Gaston Leroux, *The Phantom of the Opera*, 1988
  A viscount seeks to unravel the mystery of the Paris Opera House and rescue the woman he loves from the threat of the phantom of the opera.

1452

Kin Platt

Sinbad and Me (New York: Chilton, 1966)

Age range: Grades 4-6

Subject(s): Mystery and Detective Stories; Animals/Dogs

Major character(s): Steve Forrester, Preteen; Sinbad, Dog (bulldog); Mr. Snowden, Teacher

Time period(s): 1960s

Locale(s): Hampton, New York

What the book is about: Steve Forrester narrates this exciting and humorous mystery. Steve and his bulldog, Sinbad, find a million dollars and Steve winds up in jail, trying to explain that he did not steal it. Platt's sense of humor comes through in this fast-paced mystery.

Where it's reviewed:
Kirkus Reviews, July 1, 1966, page 630
Young Readers Review, October 1966, page 1

Awards the book has won:
Edgar Allan Poe Award 1967

Other books by the author:
Darwin and the Great Beasts, 1992
Brogg's Brain, 1981
Dracula, Go Home!, 1979
The Boy Who Could Make Himself Disappear, 1968

Other books you might like:
David A. Adler, *The Fourth Floor Twins and the Sand Castle Contest*, 1988
  Two sets of twins resolve the mystery of the disappearance of a rich woman's dog.
Eve Bunting, *Jane Martin, Dog Detective*, 1984
  A young girl solves three cases involving dogs.
Marilyn Singer, *Where There's a Will, There's a Wag*, 1986
  Philip and his dog, Sam Spayed, are hired to investigate a will.
Mary Stolz, *Deputy Shep*, 1991
  Deputy Jack Shep is the laziest police dog to ever wear a badge in Cansville.

Jane Yolen, *The Bot and Rebecca and the Missing Owser*, 1981
  Rebecca and her robot investigate the disappearance of two dog-like creatures called Owsers.

1453

Patricia Polacco

Just Plain Fancy (New York: Bantam, 1990)

Age range: Grades 2-3

Subject(s): Amish; Animals/Birds; Farm Life

Major character(s): Naomi Vlecke, Child; Ruth Vlecke, Child; Kaleb Vlecke, Parent

Time period(s): 1990s

Locale(s): Pennsylvania

What the book is about: Two Amish girls find an unusual egg while tending their chickens. They secretly hatch and raise the remarkable peacock chick, much to their community's surprise. A celebration of the simple life, with just a bit of fancy tossed in.

Where it's reviewed:
Publisher's Weekly, October 12, 1990, page 62
School Library Journal, December 1990, page 24

Other books by the author:
Babushka's Doll, 1990
Thunder Cake, 1990
Uncle Vova's Tree, 1989
The Keeping Quilt, 1988

Other books you might like:
Sue Alexander, *Peacocks Are Very Special*, 1976
  Caught in Jackal's snare, Peacock manages to outwit him and stay out of his cooking pot.
Candace Christeiansen, *Calico and Tin Horns*, 1992
  Hannah sounds the warning signal when a posse comes after her father and other farmers rebelling against an unfair landlord.
Bill Peet, *The Spooky Tail of Prewitt Peacock*, 1972
  When Prewitt's tail begins to look like a greeneyed monster, the other peacocks decide it has to go.
Florence Wightman Rowland, *Amish Boy*, 1970
  An Amish boy helps rescue animals from the family's burning barn, and later participates in the raising of the new barn.
Margaret Wild, *The Very Best of Friends*, 1989
  William, the cat, wonders if he is still welcome on the farm after his owner's death.

1454

Penny Pollack

Illustrator: Gail Owens

Stall Buddies (New York: Putnam, 1984)

Age range: Grades 3-4

Subject(s): Animals; Fantasy; Sports

Major character(s): Scarlett, Horse; Rufus Jones, Rooster; Merabel, Goat

Time period(s): Indeterminate

Locale(s): Hiram, Ohio

What the book is about: An engaging fantasy of a skittish filly named Scarlett and a baby goat named Merabel, who gives Scarlett peace of mind, and a rooster named Rufus Jones III who gives her a piece of his mind as her sulky racing coach.

Where it's reviewed:
Booklist, February 15, 1985, page 848
Center for Children's Books Bulletin, February 1985, page 115
School Library Journal, March 1985, page 170

Other books by the author:
Keeping It Secret, 1982
Garlanda, 1980
The Slug Who Thought He Was a Snail, 1980
Ants Don't Get Sunday Off, 1978

Other books you might like:
Raymond James, *Gulliver's Travels*, 1990
  The voyage of an Englishman carried to all sorts of strange places. (Abridged version of Jonathon Swift's 1726 classic)
Jacky Jeter, *The Cat and the Fiddler*, 1968
  The fiddler won't sell his dancing cat so the king gets the animal by force, but discovers that without the fiddler the cat is a dancing pied piper.
Theodora Kroeber, *Carrousel*, 1977
  The winged carousel horse has a wildness carved in his wings, and it takes more than courage to rescue him.
Elizabeth A. Lynn, *The Silver Horse*, 1984
  Susannah follows her brother and his beautiful silver horse to the Land of Lost Toys, where she finds herself in the middle of a fantastic adventure.
Jean Marzollo, *Blue Sun Ben*, 1984
  In a world of two suns, Ben falls into the clutches of the Animal Singer, an evil man who changes people into shapes to suit his own purposes.

| 1455 |

Penny Pollock

Illustrator: Donna Diamond

Keeping it Secret (New York: Putnam, 1982)

Age range: Grades 4-6

Subject(s): Physically Handicapped

Major character(s): Mary Lou "Wisconsin" Spangler, Preteen, Handicapped (hearing-impaired); Jason Wainwright, Preteen; Marcia Maracosa, Preteen

Time period(s): 1980s

Locale(s): New Jersey

What the book is about: Mary Lou has just moved to New Jersey from Wisconsin. When Jason teases and humiliates her, she concentrates on avoiding him and somehow getting even. Jason has a crush on her, but has no clue how to let her know. Mary Lou has a hearing loss, and Marcia's life is not nearly as perfect as it looks.

Where it's reviewed:
Center for Children's Books Bulletin, January 1983, p 95
Horn Book, February 1983, page 48

Other books by the author:
Stall Buddies, 1984

The Slug Who Thought He Was a Snail, 1980

Other books you might like:
Mary Blount Christian, *Mystery at Camp Triumph*, 1986
  Recently blinded in an accident, Angie adjusts to her handicaps as she tries to find out who is sabotaging the summer camp for disabled children.
Jaap ter Haar, *The World of Ben Lightfoot*, 1977
  Blinded by an accident, a young boy decides he won't let his handicap keep him from his friends and family.
Elisabeth MacIntyre, *The Purple Mouse*, 1975
  A girl with a hearing problem learns that her struggle to overcome her handicap has made her a stronger and happier person.
Susan Richards Shreve, *The Gift of the Girl Who Couldn't Hear*, 1991
  Two friends, one of whom is deaf, help each other when tryouts are held for a seventh grade production of "Annie."
Susan Terris, *Wings and Roots*, 1982
  During the summer she works with polio victims, Jeannie meets a young climber who, like herself, needs to overcome a handicap and take risks.

| 1456 |

Elizabeth Marie Pope

Illustrator: Richard Cuffari

Perilous Gard (Boston: Houghton Mifflin, 1974)

Age range: Grades 6 and Up

Subject(s): Fantasy

Major character(s): Kate Sutton, Child; Elizabeth, Royalty (princess); Alicia, Royalty (princess)

Time period(s): 16th century (Tudor England)

Locale(s): Derbyshire, England

What the book is about: Perilous Gard is the last stronghold of the Fairy Folk (or People of the Hill). Kate is punished for a letter that her sister sends to Queen Mary and is sent to be kept locked in the Gard, a mysterious castle in a remote part of England. Kate is involved in a strange series of events which eventually return the Fairy Folk to domination.

Where it's reviewed:
Horn Book, June 1974, page 287
Library Journal, May 15, 1974, page 1484

Awards the book has won:
Newbery Honor 1975
Children's Book Showcase 1975

Other books by the author:
The Sherwood Ring, 1958

Other books you might like:
Godfried Bomans, *The Wily Witch and All the Other Fairy Tales and Fables*, 1977
  Collected tales of kings and queens, wizards and witches, spells and other magic.
Mollie Hunter, *The Stronghold*, 1974
  Crippled in a Roman raid on his native Scotland, Coll spends many years planning an impregnable defense but has to overcome many obstacles.
Washington Irving, *Castles in Spain: From the Alhambra*, 1971

Four legends of Moorish and Christian Spain abstracted from ''The Alhambra.''
Deborah Nourse Lattimore, *The Winged Cat: A Tale of Ancient Egypt*, 1992
  In ancient Egypt, a servant girl and a High Priest must find the right magic spells that open the twelve gates of the Netherworld.
Beth Smith, *Castles*, 1988
  Discusses the design and use of European castles from 500 A.D., relates what daily life was like inside, and presents legends linked with castles.

1457

Maureen Pople

The Other Side of the Family (New York: Holt, 1986)

Age range: Grades 5-6

Subject(s): World War II; Grandparents

Major character(s): Katherine ''Kate'' Tucker, Teenager; Grandmother Tucker, Grandparent

Time period(s): 1940s

Locale(s): London, England; Sydney, Australia

What the book is about: Katherine is sent to Australia to escape the bombing of London during WWII. She lives with her grandmother, who is known to hate her family. Discovering the ''other side'' of her family leads to a positive relationship with her grandmother, and she learns that her family's history is really legendary.

Where it's reviewed:
Center for Children's Books Bulletin, October 1988, page 50
School Library Journal, December 1988, page 27

Other books by the author:
A Nugget of Gold, 1989

Other books you might like:
Alan Collins, *Jacob's Ladder*, 1989
  Jacob and Solly are orphaned and put in a Sydney children's home where other refugee Jewish children are housed as Hitler rises to power.
George Ella Lyon, *Borrowed Children*, 1988
  Twelve year old Amanda has a holiday in Memphis after being caretaker for her sick mother in their Kentucky mountain home.
William Mayne, *Salt River Times*, 1980
  Twenty-one related stories about the lives of people in a small community along Australia's Salt River.
Joan Phipson, *When the City Stopped*, 1978
  A young boy and his sister escape from their Australian city being torn apart by strikes and riots.
Colin Thiele, *Rotten Egg Paterson to the Rescue*, 1991
  Danny rescues an emu egg in the Australian scrublands and is determined to hatch it, despite a series of near disasters.

1458

Barbara Ann Porte

Illustrator: Maxie Chambliss

Fat Fanny, Beanpole Bertha and the Boys (New York: Orchard, 1991)

Age range: Grades 3-5

Subject(s): Divorce; Humor; Friendship

Major character(s): Bertha, Preteen; Fanny, Preteen

Time period(s): 1990s

Locale(s): United States

What the book is about: This is the story of two best friends, filled with both humor and tragedy. When Bertha's father vanishes in the Bermuda Triangle, and Fanny's theater agent parents are secretly divorced, the girls decide to teach Fanny's triplet brothers to tap dance to raise money. The story is filled with well developed characters that seem unusual but very real.

Where it's reviewed:
Booklist, March 1, 1991, page 1388
School Library Journal, February 1991, page 82

Other books by the author:
Harry in Trouble, 1989
Ruthann and Her Pig, 1989
I Only Made Up the Roses, 1987
The Kidnapping of Aunt Elizabeth, 1985

Other books you might like:
Tom Birdseye, *Tucker*, 1990
  Eleven year old Tucker is happy living with his divorced dad until his sister moves in with them and claims their mother wants to reunite the family.
Elfie Donnelly, *Tina into Two Won't Go*, 1983
  Eleven year old Tina is delighted when her father, whom she seldom sees, takes her to Teneriffe for Christmas, but her mother informs the police.
Johanna Hurwitz, *DeDe Takes Charge*, 1992
  A year after her father has left home, fifth grader DeDe helps her mother cope with the realities of life after divorce.
Marilyn Kaye, *The Problem with Parents*, 1991
  Trina, still hoping her parents will reunite, gets upset when her mother shows interest in the widowed dad of Sarah, a girlfriend Trina met at camp.
Elizabeth-Ann Sachs, *Shyster*, 1985
  Becky's experience in owning a cat helps her in dealing with the departure of her father and the new man in her mother's life.

1459

Barbara Ann Porte

Illustrator: Yossi Abolafia

Harry in Trouble (New York: Greenwillow, 1989)

Age range: Grades 1-2

Subject(s): Libraries

Major character(s): Harry, Child; Dorcas, Child; Mrs. Katz, Librarian

Time period(s): 1980s

Locale(s): United States

What the book is about: Harry's third library card has dissappeared and he panics, thinking he can never get another one. He feels better when he learns that his father and his friend Dorcas sometimes lose things, too. The librarian understands and suggests she keep Harry's card at the library desk for him.

Where it's reviewed:
Booklist, March 1, 1989, page 1199
Hornbook, May 1989, page 391
Kirkus Reviews, January 1, 1989, page 53

Other books by the author:
Ruthann and Her Pig, 1989
Harry's Mom, 1985
Harry's Dog, 1984
Harry's Visit, 1983

Other books you might like:
Rose Blue, *A Quiet Place*, 1969
　　A little boy who loves books is desolate when the local library closes for reconstruction and he can find no quiet place at home to read.
Eric A. Kimmel, *I Took My Frog to the Library*, 1990
　　A young girl brings her pets to the library with predictably disasterous results.
Lucinda Landon, *Meg Mackintosh and the Mystery of the Locked Library*, 1993
　　Meg investigates the theft of a rare book from a locked library. A Solve-it-Yourself Mystery
Tanya Shpakow, *On the Way to Christmas*, 1991
　　Relates the journey of a lost teddy bear as he makes his way back to his little boy on the night before Christmas.
Barry Smith, *Cumberland Road*, 1988
　　The reader is asked to find, in the illustrations, objects lost by the residents of Cumberland Road.

| 1460 |

Barbara Ann Porte

Illustrator: Sucie Stevenson

Ruthann and Her Pig (New York: Orchard Books, 1989)

Age range: Grades 2-4

Subject(s): Cousins; Humor; Animals/Pigs

Major character(s): Ruthann Packer, Child; Frank, Cousin; Henry Brown, Pig

Time period(s): 1980s

Locale(s): United States

What the book is about: Each chapter about the Packer family details another zany episode involving Ruthann and her pet pig. When her cousin, Frank, comes to visit, he decides that her pet pig, Henry Brown, would be the perfect school bus companion for protection against wild older kids.

Where it's reviewed:
Booklist, October 1, 1989, page 354
School Library Journal, October 1989, page 121

Other books by the author:
Harry in Trouble, 1989
Take Along Dog, 1989
Harry's Dog, 1984
Jesse's Ghost and Other Stories, 1983

Other books you might like:
Hila Colman, *Benny, the Misfit*, 1973

Although Benny's parents consider themselves liberal minded, they are perturbed when he demonstrates for the rights of his new friends.
Barbara Park, *Junie B. Jones and the Stupid Smelly Bus*, 1992
　　A kindergarten girl describes what she does when she decides not to ride the school bus home.
Roberta Simon, *Somebody Else's Child*, 1976
　　As a result of his friendship with his school bus driver, Peter gains a greater understanding of what it means to be adopted.
1992 Gary Soto, *The Skirt*, 1992
　　Miata leaves the skirt she needs for a dance performance on the school bus. She must get it back in time and not get in trouble with her parents.
Virginia Vail, *All the Way Home*, 1987
　　Val rescues Tiny, a runt piglet, and raises him as a pet.

| 1461 |

Elsa Posell

Homecoming (New York: Harcourt Brace Jovanovich, 1987)

Age range: Grades 6-9

Subject(s): Jews; Refugees

Major character(s): Olya Koshansky, Refugee

Time period(s): 1910s (1917)

Locale(s): Ukraine

What the book is about: Posell describes the effect of the Bolshevik Revolution on a young girl, Olya, and her family in the Ukraine. After the Tsar is deposed, their lives are dramatically changed. They lose their home, belongings, friends, their entire life style. They cope with constant deprivation and danger. After their mother's death, they escape to America.

Where it's reviewed:
Horn Book, March/April 1988, page 211
School Library Journal, December 1987, page 104

Other books you might like:
Leonard Everett Fisher, *A Russian Farewell*, 1981
　　The story shows the anti-Semitic terror that finally drives Benjamin Shapiro and family out of Czarist Russia to America in the early 1900's.
Anita Heyman, *Exit From Home*, 1978
　　A Jewish youth, training to become a rabbi in turn of the century Russia, is exposed to "worldly" ideas which change his views on religion and country
Nancy Pitt, *Beyond the High White Wall*, 1986
　　Witnessing a murder in the Russian Ukraine in 1903, 13 year old Libby triggers hatred against her Jewish family and thoughts of emigration to the U.S.
Marilyn Sachs, *Call Me Ruth*, 1982
　　The daughter of a Russian immigrant family, newly arrived in Manhattan in 1908, feels confused about her mother's radical union involvement.
Yuri Suhl, *Uncle Misha's Partisans*, 1973
　　During WWII in the Ukraine, an orphaned Jewish boy joins a band of partisans who give him an important assignment against the Nazis.

1462

Marian Potter

Mark Makes His Move (New York: Morrow, 1986)

Age range: Grades 6-9

Subject(s): Bullies

Major character(s): Mark, Preteen; Mrs. McSwiggen, Friend

Time period(s): 1980s

Locale(s): United States

What the book is about: Mark has good intentions, but they usually backfire. He tries to find an answer to two of his most pressing problems—how to stop the Skinner brothers from bullying him and how to save his friend, Mrs. McSwiggen's property from developers.

Where it's reviewed:
Booklist, October 1, 1986, page 274

Other books by the author:
A Chance Wild Apple, 1982
Blatherskite, 1980
The Shared Room, 1979

Other books you might like:
Robert Cormier, *The Chocolate War: A Novel*, 1974
    A high school freshman learns the consequences of refusing to join the school's annual fund raising drive and arousing the wrath of the school bullies
Christopher Leach, *The Great Book Raid*, 1979
    Heroic literary figures assemble to help Jim and his mother keep their coastal property in Cornwall out of the hands of a land develoiper.
Don Moser, *A Heart to the Hawks*, 1975
    Mike's love for natural history leads him to fight a land developer's destruction of his woodland haven first with persuasion and then with violence.
Cecily Stern, *A Different Kind of Gold*, 1981
    A young girl in the Alaskan wilderness helps her family save the land from developers.
Virginia Vail, *Horse Play*, 1990
    Emily and others at Websters' Country Horse Camp fear the owner will sell his land, so they tell the developer of imaginary hazards on the property.

1463

Barbara Power

Illustrator: Marylin Hafner

I Wish Laura's Mommy Was My Mommy (New York: Lippincott, 1979)

Age range: Grades 1-2

Subject(s): Family Life; Working Mothers

Major character(s): Jennifer, Child; Laura, Child

Time period(s): 1970s

Locale(s): United States

What the book is about: Jennifer learns to accept her own home and mom when her friend's "perfect mom" becomes her babysitter. Jennifer can actually teach her friend, Laura, a couple of things. Although Laura's mother is wonderful, Jenni-

fer decides she is actually glad that her real mommy is her mommy after all.

Where it's reviewed:
Center for Children's Books Bulletin, February 1980, page 116
School Library Journal, March 1980, page 124

Other books you might like:
Arlene Alda, *Sonya's Mommy Works*, 1982
    With her mother working, a little girl has many adjustments to make.
Lawrence Balter, *A.J.'s Mom Gets a New Job*, 1990
    When A.J.'s mom takes a job outside the home, he is upset and attempts to adjust to the changes in family routine.
Dorothy Molnar, *Who Will Pick Me Up When I Fall?*, 1991
    A young child with a working mother needs Mommy's reassurance of love.
Miriam Stecher, *Daddy and Ben Together*, 1981
    Ben and Daddy fend for themselves while Mommy is on a business trip.
Harriet Ziefert, *Good Night, Lewis*, 1986
    Mama finally figures out that Lewis doesn't like to go to bed because he is afraid of the dark.

1464

Terry Pratchett

Truckers (New York: Delacorte, 1990)

Age range: Grades 4-5

Subject(s): Gnomes; Department Stores; Fantasy

Major character(s): Masklin, Mythical Creature (gnome)

Time period(s): Indeterminate

Locale(s): United States

What the book is about: Masklin is the leader of a community of small people called "nomes." When they are threatened, he loads everyone into a truck and moves them underneath the floorboards of Arnold Brothers Department Store. When the store is to be demolished, they must save themselves again. High humor and adventure.

Where it's reviewed:
Booklist, March 15, 1990, page 1457
Kirkus Reviews, January 1, 1990, page 49

Other books by the author:
Diggers, 1991
Wings: Last Book of the Bromeliad, 1991

Other books you might like:
Robert C. O'Brien, *Mrs. Frisby and the Rats of NIMH*, 1971
    A community of intelligent rats save Mrs. Frisby and her family and create a new home for themselves.
Thomas Rockwell, *Squwwwk!*, 1972
    An enormous bird who grew from a speck in a school reader fascinates the children and terrifies the adults of a small town.
Lisa J. Smith, *The Night of the Solstice*, 1987
    Four children set out to rescue a sorceress held captive in a parallel world.
John Verney, *Seven Sunflower Seeds*, 1968
    The Callendar family tries to find out why a breakfast mix has such a fantastic effect on race horses.
Nancy Willard, *The Firebrat*, 1988

Molly and Sean exit from the subway to the Crystal Empire and try to save the world from the Firebrat.

1465

Jack Prelutsky

Illustrator: James Stevenson

Something Big Has Been Here: Poems (New York: Greenwillow, 1990)

Age range: Grades 4-6

Subject(s): Humor; Poetry

Time period(s): Indeterminate

Locale(s): United States

What the book is about: An illustrated collection of humorous poems on a variety of topics. Prelutsky is at his best, from birthdays to baked potatoes, the Know-Nothing Neibies, Powdered Elephant Ears and more. Good fun.

Where it's reviewed:
Booklist, September 1, 1990, page 50
Kirkus Reviews, August 1, 1990, page 1090
School Library Journal, October 1990, paege 112

Other books by the author:
Beneath a Blue Umbrella, 1990
Ride a Purple Pelican, 1986
The New Kid on the Block: Poems, 1984
Zoo Doings: Animal Poems, 1983

Other books you might like:
John Ciardi, *The Hopeful Trout and Other Limericks*, 1989
  A collection of limericks about such fine characters as the Elephant Boy, the fast fiddler from Middletown, and the silly old skinflint named Quince.
Margaret Mahy, *Bubble Trouble and Other Poems and Stories*, 1991
  A collection of humorous stories and poems featuring a baby flying in a bubble, a lovestruck crocodile, and a grandmother who is tired of winter.
Colin McNaughton, *There's an Awful Lot of Weirdos in Our Neighborhood & Other Poems*, 1987
  A collection of humorous poems about eccentric characters.
Eve Merriam, *Chortles: New and Selected Wordplay Poems*, 1989
  A collection of poems focusing on unusual words and plays on words.
Jeffrey Moss, *The Other Side of the Door: Poems*, 1991
  A collection of humorous and fanciful poetry about a variety of subjects both real and imaginary.

1466

Otfried Preussler

The Satanic Mill (New York: Collier, 1972)

Age range: Grades 5-8

Subject(s): Fantasy; Occult; Mills and Millwork

Major character(s): Krabat, Teenager, Apprentice

Time period(s): 17th century

Locale(s): Schwarzkollm, Germany

What the book is about: A young apprentice outwits a strange magician at a mysterious mill that is a school for black magic. Krabat commits the inexcusable - he falls in love. His only chance for freedom lies in the strength of that power and the girl's help.

Where it's reviewed:
Booklist, July 15, 1973, page 1073
Hornbook, April 1973, page 147
Kirkus Reviews, January 15, 1973, page 61

Other books by the author:
The Tale of the Unicorn, 1989
The Further Adventures of the Robber Hotzenplotz, 1971
The Adventures of Strong Vanya, 1970
The Little Witch, 1961

Other books you might like:
Mildred Ames, *Conjuring Summer In*, 1986
  Unhappy with her family's move to California, Bernadette dabbles with psychic forces and black magic, resulting in murder and threats on her own life.
Wilanne Schneider Belden, *The Rescue of Ranor*, 1983
  Having no magic powers of his own, Sven Pentalion enlists the help of a white witch to help rescue his brother from a powerful Black Enchanter.
James Lincoln Collier, *The Clock*, 1992
  Trapped in a gruelling job in the mills to pay her father's debts, Annie becomes the victim of a cruel overseer and plots revenge against him.
Tanith Lee, *Black Unicorn*, 1991
  Tanaquil brings to life a unicorn which lures her away from her fortress home and sorceress mother to find the way to a perfect world.
Gloria Skurzynski, *Goodbye, Billy Radish*, 1992
  As the US enters WWI, Hank sees change all around him in his Pennsylvania steel mill town and feels his older Ukrainian friend, Billy, drifting away.

1467

Leontyne Price

Illustrator: Leo Dillon

Aida (San Diego: Harcourt, 1990)

Age range: Grades 5-7

Subject(s): Opera

Major character(s): Aida, Royalty (princess); King Amonasro, Parent, Ruler; Radames, Military Personnel

Time period(s): Indeterminate Past

Locale(s): Egypt

What the book is about: Retells the story of Verdi's opera in which the love of the enslaved Ethiopian princess for an Egyptian general brings tragedy to all involved. Aida is captured by Egyptian soldiers and forced into slavery. When she falls in love with the leader of the Egyptian army, she faces a terrible emotional struggle.

Where it's reviewed:
Booklist, October 1, 1990, page 331
Kirkus Reviews, October 1, 1990, page 1397
Publishers Weekly, September 14, 1990, page 123

Awards the book has won:
Coretta Scott King Award 1991

Other books you might like:
Cecil Bodker, *The Leopard*, 1975
An Ethiopian boy finds his life endangered when he learns that a disguised blacksmith, not a leopard, is responsible for a great many missing cattle.
Gillian Bradshaw, *The Land of Gold*, 1992
After the murder of her parents, a Nubian princess is helped to her rightful place on the throne by two friendly Egyptians and the dragon, Hathor.
Gloria Duran, *Malinche, Slave Princess of Cortez*, 1993
A biography of La Malinche, the Aztec noblewoman who was translator, interpreter and mistress to Cortez during the Spanish conquest of Mexico in 1520.
Elizabeth Laird, *The Miracle Child*, 1985
A 13th century Ethiopian, Takla St. Haymanot, performs many miracles for his people, feeding the hungry during a famine and raising the dead to life.
Jane Rosenberg, *Sing Me a Story*, 1989
Presents the stories of fifteen well-known operas.

1468

Susan Price

The Ghost Drum: A Cat's Tale (New York: Farrar, 1987)

Age range: Grades 4-6

Subject(s): Fantasy; Witches and Witchcraft; Wizards

Major character(s): Guidon, Ruler (czar); Safa, Royalty (prince); Chingis, Cat, Witch

Time period(s): Indeterminate

Locale(s): Czardom, Russia

What the book is about: A gifted shaman meets a Czar's son who has been imprisoned in his windowless room. The two join forces to fight fearful enemies. Out in the frozen wastes, in her magic hut that can run on chicken legs, Chingis has gained the ability to wander on many worlds and to understand the messages of the ghost drum.

Where it's reviewed:
Kirkus Reviews, June 15, 1987, page 929
School Library Journal, September 1987, page 182

Other books by the author:
Ghosts at Large, 1984

Other books you might like:
Emily Perl Kingsley, *An American Tail*, 1986
In 1885, the Mouskewitz family leave Russia for America and young Fieval is separated from them during the voyage.
Kathryn Lasky, *The Night Journey*, 1981
Rache ignores her parents' wishes and persuades her great-grandmother to tell the story of her escape from Czarist Russia.
Robert San Souci, *Short and Shivery: Thirty Chilling Tales*, 1987
Short and spooky tales from the folklore of Russia and other areas of the world.
Ruth Manning-Sanders, *A Book of Sorcerers and Spells*, 1973
Tales of magic from around the world.
Alki Zei, *The Sound of Dragon's Feet*, 1979
Ten year old Sasha's eyes are opened to more of life in turn-of-the-century Russia than her sheltered life has prepared her for.

1469

Susan Price

Illustrator: Alison Price

Ghosts at Large (Boston: Faber, 1984)

Age range: Grades 4-6

Subject(s): Ghosts

Time period(s): Indeterminate

Locale(s): Earth

What the book is about: A wonderful resource for campfire storytelling, these twelve stories include all moods from the lightly humorous to the macbre.

Where it's reviewed:
Booklist, April 15, 1985, page 1199
School Library Journal, April 1985, page 99
Times Educational Supplement, February 15, 1985, page 27

Other books by the author:
Ghost's Song, 1992
The Ghost Drum: A Cat's Tale, 1987
The Devil's Piper, 1973

Other books you might like:
Daniel Cohen, *The Ghosts of War*, 1990
Recounts supposedly true stories about ghosts connected in some way with war, from haunted battlefields to soldiers' premonitions of death.
Pat McKissack, *The Dark-Thirty: Southern Tales of the Supernatural*, 1992
A collection of ghost stories with African-American themes.
Q.L. Pearce, *More Scary Stories for Sleep-Overs*, 1992
A collection of eleven scary stories.
Alvin Schwartz, *In a Dark, Dark Room, and Other Scary Tales*, 1984
Seven scary stories to tell at night in front of a fire or in the dark, based on traditional stories and folktales from various countries.
Betty Ren Wright, *The Ghost of Popcorn Hill*, 1993
Martin and Peter acquire a mischievous new dog and two lonely ghosts.

1470

Alison Prince, Author/Illustrator

How's Business? (New York: Four Winds, 1988)

Age range: Grades 4-6

Subject(s): Survival; World War II

Major character(s): Howard "How", Teenager

Time period(s): 1940s

Locale(s): Lincolnshire, England

What the book is about: Howard is sent to the country from London during WWII to live with relatives. It seems a sensible idea to Howard's mother, but for How it is an experience in coping with local gangs in a strange environment. Relationships and courage are dealt with in a powerful way which will give mature readers insight into the less obvious effects of the war.

Where it's reviewed:
Growing Point, January 1988, page 4910

Kirkus Reviews, July 1988, page 1063
School Library Journal, September 1988, page 185

Other books by the author:
The Type One Super Robot, 1988
Night Landings, 1984
The Sinister Airfield, 1983
The Red Jaguar, 1972

Other books you might like:
Hester Burton, *In Spite of All Terror*, 1968
In 1940, an orphan girl from the London slums is evacuated to the country to live with an aristocratic family.
Malcolm Carrick, *I'll Get You*, 1979
A young boy growing up in post-war London tries to fit in with his neighboring friends.
Peggy Donaldson, *The Moon's on Fire*, 1980
Having escaped from Nazi-occupied France, Janey, Tadek and Stefek are placed in the care of Janey's uncle whom they suspect of being an enemy spy.
Jill Paton Walsh, *Fireweek*, 1969
Two teenage runaways who refuse to be evacuated from London struggle to survive the blitz of 1940.
Noel Streatfeild, *When the Sirens Wailed*, 1976
Rather than stay with a new family, three young evacuees try to return to their home in London after their country host dies suddenly.

1471

Alison Prince

Illustrator: Ellen Thompson

The Sinister Airfield (New York: Morrow, 1983)

Age range: Grades 5-7

Subject(s): Mystery and Detective Stories; Robbers and Outlaws

Major character(s): Harrie Armstrong, Preteen; Ian Armstrong, Preteen (Harry's brother); Neil Grey, Preteen

Time period(s): 1980s

Locale(s): England

What the book is about: Three youngsters find a body in the woods in this English thriller. When the police go to investigate, the body is gone. They become suspicious that rustlers working in the area may be local people. The newly employed gamekeeper is acting very strange and the nearby deserted airfield is reputed to be haunted.

Where it's reviewed:
Center for Children's Books Bulletin, May 1983, page 175
Kirkus Reviews, February 15, 1983, page 185
School Library Journal, May 1983, page 93

Other books by the author:
How's Business, 1988
The Type One Super Robot, 1988
Night Landings, 1984
The Red Jaguar, 1972

Other books you might like:
Janice Brown, *Sweet 'n Sour Summer*, 1988
Joanne insists that she has witnessed a murder on the ferry that brought her to the Scottish island where she is on holiday.
Patricia Miles, *A Disturbing Influence*, 1979

Andrew questions the future until he is drawn into a mystery involving a rock festival, forged bills, a runaway neighbor, a deserted farmhouse.
Robert Newman, *The Case of the Threatened King*, 1982
When Sara and a friend disappear, Andrew and Inspector Wyatt investigate and discover that the kidnappings are part of a plot against a visiting king.
Norah Smaridge, *The Mystery at Greystone Hall*, 1979
While vacationing in England, a young sleuth becomes involved in a mystery at Greystone Hall.
Robert Westall, *Stormsearch*, 1992
Tim's discovery of an antique model ship leads him to an unsolved family mystery involving a London heiress, a drunkard, and the miser Black Idris.

1472

Alison Prince, Author/Illustrator

The Type One Super Robot (New York: Macmillan, 1988)

Age range: Grades 4-6

Subject(s): Humor; Robots; Aunts and Uncles

Major character(s): Humbert, Preteen; Mandus, Robot

Time period(s): Indeterminate Future

Locale(s): London, England

What the book is about: While spending the summer together, a boy and his uncle acquire a household robot with a mind of its own. An overbearing neighbor "borrows" Mandus and Humbert has to figure out a way to get his robot out of Mrs. Panton-Perkins' clutches.

Where it's reviewed:
Booklist, July 1988, page 1841
Kirkus Reviews, March 15, 1988, page 457
School Library Journal, September 1988, page 185

Other books by the author:
Night Landings, 1984
The Sinister Airfield, 1983
The Turkey's Nest, 1980
The Red Jaguar, 1972

Other books you might like:
Mike Carr, *Robbers and Robots*, 1983
The reader, as Terry Morton, becomes involved in an attempt to steal the plans for a top secret security robot from his uncle's electronics factory.
Norma Fox Mazer, *Mrs. Fish, Ape, and Me, the Dump Queen*, 1980
A friendless girl, teased mercilessly at school because her uncle manages the town dump, finds a friend in Mrs. Fish, the school custodian.
Iris Schweitzer, *Tiglis and the Bird-Machine*, 1980
Tiglis convinces her parents to take a flight in her uncle's bird-machine.
Kathleen Thomas, *Nifkin*, 1982
Jeannie and Justin move in with their eccentric inventor uncle and make friends with a small boy who comes through a screen from another planet.
Leonard Wibberley, *The Crime of Martin Coverly*, 1980
After being visited by a man dressed in 18th century clothes and resembling his uncle, Nick finds himself on his uncle's pirate ship in the 1720's.

1473

Gary Provost

David and Max (Philadelphia: Jewish Publication Society, 1988)

Age range: Grades 5-8

Subject(s): Grandparents; Holocaust

Major character(s): David, Preteen; Max, Grandparent, Survivor (of the Holocaust)

Time period(s): 1950s; 1960s

Locale(s): United States

What the book is about: David spends a summer at the beach with his grandfather, Max, a Holocaust survivor, and learns lessons in strength and the ability to overcome grief. David helps Max search for a friend believed to have perished in the Holocaust.

Where it's reviewed:
Publisher's Weekly, October 28, 1988, page 81
Booklist, January 1, 1989, page 794
Kirkus, November 15, 1988, page 1678

Other books by the author:
Fatal Dosage, 1985
Popcorn, 1985
Good If It Goes, 1984
The Porkchop War, 1982

Other books you might like:
Tamar Bergman, *The Boy From Over There*, 1988
    Avramik, a young Holocaust survivor, has difficulties adjusting to life on a kibbutz in the days before the first Arab-Israeli War.
Mel Glenn, *Squeeze Play: A Baseball Story*, 1989
    Aided by gentle Mr. Janowicz, a Holocaust survivor, Jeremy speaks up against his bullying sixth grade teacher and his mandatory after-school ballgames
Judith Magyar Isaacson, *Seeds of Sarah*, 1990
    The memoirs of a survivor of Auschwitz from the Hungarian ghettos of Kaposvar.
Ruth Minsky Sender, *To Life*, 1988
    A Holocaust survivor recounts her liberation from a Nazi concentration camp, search for surviving family, and the ordeal of emigrating to America.
Ida Vos, *Anna Is Still Here*, 1993
    Anna, who was a ''hidden child'' in Nazi-occupied Holland during WWII, gradually learns to deal with the realities of being a survivor.

1474

Bonnie Pryor

Illustrator: J. Winslow Higginbottom

Rats, Spiders, and Love (New York: Morrow, 1986)

Age range: Grades 4-6

Subject(s): Family Life; Individuality; Remarriage

Major character(s): Samantha ''Sam'' Tate, Preteen; Julia Tate, Teenager; Kevin Tate, Child (gifted)

Time period(s): Indeterminate

Locale(s): Seal Point, Oregon

What the book is about: Samantha, a middle child who already feels lost between the beauty of her older sister and the genius intelligence of her younger brother, discovers her mother is planning to remarry and schemes to prevent it.

Where it's reviewed:
Booklist, August 1986, page 1692
Kirkus Reviews, May 1, 1986, page 717
School Library Journal, April 1986, page 91

Other books by the author:
Jumping Jenny, 1992
The Plum Tree War, 1989
Seth of the Lion People, 1988
Vinegar Pancakes and Vanishing Cream, 1987

Other books you might like:
Patricia Harrison Easton, *Summer's Chance*, 1988
    While spending the summer at her grandmother's farm, Elizabeth gains a clearer sense of her own individuality as she learns about her dead mother.
Leslie McGuire, *Is There Life After Sixth Grade?*, 1990
    When her eccentric dress keeps her out of the class yearbook picture, Amy decides to create a yearbook with candid shots of faculty and classmates.
Claudia Mills, *The One and Only Cynthia Jane Thornton*, 1982
    Ten year old Cynthia who is trying to find her own identity, copes with a very competitive classmate and a bright and challenging younger sister.
Emily Moore, *Whose Side Are You On?*, 1988
    When Barbara's friend and sixth grade math tutor T.J., disappears from school, she sets out to rescue him.
Mary E. Ryan, *Me, My Sister, and I*, 1992
    Mattie seeks independence from her identical twin sister by helping her mother manage the campaign of a candidate for city council.

1475

Bonnie Pryor

Seth of the Lion People (New York: Morrow, 1988)

Age range: Grades 5-7

Subject(s): Man, Prehistoric; Physically Handicapped; Storytelling

Major character(s): Seth, Prehistoric Human, Handicapped

Time period(s): Indeterminate Past

Locale(s): Earth

What the book is about: Although Seth, a young teen with a twisted leg, is only tolerated by his tribe for his storytelling abilities, he senses his people are on the brink of a transition from hunters to artisans and farmers, if only he can become their leader.

Where it's reviewed:
Booklist, November 15, 1988, page 582
Kirkus Reviews, September 15, 1988, page 1406

Other books by the author:
Horses in the Garage, 1992
Jumping Jenny, 1992
The Plum Tree War, 1989
The Twenty-Four-Hour Lipstick Mystery, 1989

Other books you might like:

J.H. Brennan, *Shiva: An Adventure of the Ice Age*, 1989
  A Cro-Magnon tribe is forced to confront its fear of the Neanderthal people they call ogres.

Patrick Skene Catling, *John Midas in the Dreamtime*, 1986
  While visiting a sacred cave painting, John Midas slips back thousands of years and finds himself among a prehistoric aboriginal tribe.

Sherryl Jordan, *A Time of Darkness*, 1990
  A teenage boy with unusual powers faces the challenge of his life when he's transported to a primitive society.

Chester G. Osborne, *The Memory String*, 1984
  Darath and his sister spend a winter on the Siberian penisula learning how to survive and search for a legendary land with no people or game.

Ann Turnbull, *Maroo of the Winter Caves*, 1984
  Maroo, a girl of the late Ice Age, must lead the family to safety through a blizzard after her father is killed.

1476

Bonnie Pryor

Illustrator: Sheila Hamanaka

The Twenty-Four-Hour Lipstick Mystery (New York: Morrow, 1989)

Age range: Grades 4-6

Subject(s): Mystery and Detective Stories; Haunted Houses

Major character(s): Cassie Adams, Preteen; Miss Murdock, Employer; Victoria Presser, Secretary

Time period(s): 1980s

Locale(s): Lexington, Kentucky

What the book is about: Cassie feels like a frog. She'd give anything to be changed into a princess at Mrs. DuPrey's School of Beauty and Charm, even if it means working for spooky Miss Murdock. The house has a secret room, a sinister gardener and floating night lights.

Where it's reviewed:
Booklist, November 1, 1989, page 557
School Library Journal, November 1989, page 114

Other books by the author:
Jumping Jenny, 1992
The Plum Tree War, 1989
Vinegar Pancakes and Vanishing Cream, 1987
Rats, Spiders and Love, 1986

Other books you might like:
Avi, *The Man Who Was Poe*, 1989
  In Providence, Rhode Island, in 1848, Edgar Allan Poe reluctantly investigates the problems of eleven year old Edmund, whose family has disappeared.

Eth Clifford, *I Hate Your Guts, Ben Brooster*, 1989
  11 year old Charlie's cousin, Ben, arrives from Japan and irritates Charlie with his intelligence, but they are drawn into a mystery together.

Willo Davis Roberts, *Megan's Island*, 1988
  Megan is astonished when her mother insists on going up to the lake cottage before school is out. Then they find a mysterious stranger following them.

Kathy Pelta, *The Parrot Man Mystery*, 1989
  While operating a pet-sitting business, Margaret, Wil and Denise uncover a parrot-smuggling operation in Malibu, California.

Mary Francis Shura, *Don't Call Me Toad!*, 1987
  A friendship with the strange, constantly angry new girl in her neighborhood leads Janie Potter to discover a hidden cache of money and stolen jewels.

1477

Alexander Pushkin

The Tale of the Golden Cockerel (New York: Crowell, 1975)

Age range: Grades 3-5

Subject(s): Magic

Major character(s): Dadon, Ruler (czar)

Time period(s): Indeterminate Past

Locale(s): Russia

What the book is about: The Czar's kingdom had been protected by warnings from the golden cockerel. He had promised to grant a wish to the sorcerer who had given him the bird. The Czar goes back on his promise, with tragic consequences.

Where it's reviewed:
Horn Book, October 1975, page 455
School Library Journal, October 1975, page 101

Other books by the author:
The Tale of Czar Saltan, 1975

Other books you might like:
Avi, *Bright Shadow*, 1985
  Having used 4 of the 5 wishes she is granted to make on behalf of her country's citizens, Morwena flees her realm to decide what to do with the last.

Arthur Ransome, *The Fool of the World and the Flying Ship*, 1968
  When the Czar proclaims he will give his daughter in marriage to the man who brings a flying ship, the Fool of the World sets out to try his luck.

Estelle Titiev, *How the Moolah was Taught a Lesson and Other Tales From Russia*, 1976
  This story joins "Chilbik and the Greedy Czar," "The Girl with the Silver Voice," and others in a collection of tales from Russia.

Joanne Webster, *Gypsy Gift*, 1981
  Cassie's part gypsy boyfriend, Rollo, gives her the gift of second sight, but when she breaks her promise to him, her visions show only disasters.

Anne Terry White, *Six Russian Tales*, 1969
  Tales from Russia including, "The Dead Princess," "The Seven Valiant Knights," "Fineas and the Bright Falcon," "Princess Frog," and others.

R

1478

Berniece Rabe

Illustrator: Lillian Hoban

The Balancing Girl (New York: Dutton, 1981)

Age range: Grades 1-2

Subject(s): School Life; Physically Handicapped

Major character(s): Margaret, Child, Handicapped (disabled); Tommy, Child, Bully; William, Child

Time period(s): 1980s

Locale(s): United States

What the book is about: Margaret gets around in a wheelchair, and in braces with crutches. She is an expert at balancing just about anything. Even contending with Tommy, a little bully who likes to make fun of Margaret and knock down her towers and castles, she is a happy child, functioning normally in a typical classroom.

Where it's reviewed:
Kirkus Reviews, October 15, 1981, page 1293
School Library Journal, October 1981, page 134

Other books by the author:
Where's Chimpy?, 1988

Other books you might like:
Barbara Aiello, *It's Your Turn at Bat*, 1988
  While researching sewing machines for a school report, a child with cerebral palsy learns that the money for his baseball team's jerseys is missing.
Nancy L. Carlson, *Arnie and the New Kid*, 1990
  When an accident requires Arnie to use crutches, he begins to understand the limits and possibilities of his new classmate, who has a wheelchair.
Nan Holcomb, *Andy Finds a Turtle*, 1987
  Andy's physical therapist calls him a turtle one day when he is feeling uncooperative, and thus begins a search to find a real turtle.
Marisabina Russo, *Alex Is My Friend*, 1992
  Even though Alex is a dwarf and sometimes has to use a wheelchair, he and his friend still have good times together.
Evelyn Witter, *Claw Foot*, 1976
  By learning to use his talents instead of dwelling on his handicap, Claw Foot, a lame Sioux Indian boy, earns a new name for himself.

1479

Berniece Rabe

The Girl Who Had No Name (New York: Dutton, 1977)

Age range: Grades 6-8

Subject(s): Identity; Family Life; Country Life

Major character(s): "Girlie" Webster, Preteen, Orphan; Wanda Webster, Teenager; Clark Gable, Cat

Time period(s): 1930s (1936)

Locale(s): Missouri

What the book is about: As she travels from sister to sister in search of a home after the death of their mother, a twelve year old country girl discovers many things about herself and her family, including why she was never given a name at birth.

Where it's reviewed:
Booklist, July 1, 1977, page 1654
School Library Journal, May 1977, page 71

Awards the book has won:
Golden Kite Fiction Award 1977

Other books by the author:
Rehearsal for the Big Time, 1988
The Orphans, 1978
Naomi, 1975
Rass, 1973

Other books you might like:
Caroline B. Cooney, *The Face on the Milk Carton*, 1990
  A photograph of a missing girl on a milk carton leads Janie on a search for her real identity.
Hadley Irwin, *Kim/Kimi*, 1987
  Despite a warm relationship with her mother, stepfather, and half-brother, 16 year old Kim wants to find answers about her Japanese-American father.
Gen LeRoy, *Cold Feet*, 1979
  Stuggling to take charge of her own life, Geneva poses as a boy and winds up getting involved in a smuggling ring.
Philip Pullman, *The Broken Bridge: A Novel*, 1992
  Over the course of a summer in Wales, Ginny, a girl of English and Haitian descent, finds she may have other living relatives.
Mary C. Ryan, *Frankie's Run*, 1987
  As she and her best friend grow up and start boy-watching, Mary Frances wonders if she should try to be like everyone else or do her own thing.

1480

Berniece Rabe

Naomi (New York: Nelson, 1975)

Age range: Grades 5-8

Subject(s): Farm Life; Family Life

Major character(s): Naomi Bradley, Preteen; Grace Bradley, Preteen; Sarah Mitchell, Nurse

Time period(s): 1930s

Locale(s): Missouri

What the book is about: A fortune teller tells eleven year old Naomi that she will die before her fourteenth birthday. As Naomi struggles with her mother's only plan for her - to get married as soon as possible so she is no longer a burden to the family, Sarah, a nurse, helps her discover medicine and she takes a job working for Dr. Foster. Naomi discovers that it is she, herself, who determines what happens to her.

Where it's reviewed:
Booklist, June 1, 1975, page 1016
Kirkus Reviews, June 1, 1975, page 612
School Library Journal, April 1975, page 69

Awards the book has won:
Golden Kite Honor Book 1975

Other books by the author:
Margaret's Moves, 1987
The Orphans, 1978
The Girl Who Had No Name, 1977
Rass, 1973

Other books you might like:
Joan Lowery Nixon, *Caught in the Act*, 1988
  Michael is sent to a Missouri foster home which has a sadistic owner, a bullying son, and a number secrets, one of which may be murder.
Marian Potter, *Blatherskite*, 1980
  A talkative ten year old living in 1930s, rural Missouri becomes the heroine of her family and community by putting her wagging tongue to good use.
Phyllis Rossiter, *Moxie*, 1990
  Thirteen year old Drew struggles to help keep his family on their drought striken farm during the dust storms of 1934.
Nancy Dingman Watson, *New Under the Stars*, 1970
  The adventures of a family traveling from their sharecropper's farm in Missouri to a new life in the state of Washington.
Laura Ingalls Wilder, *On the Way Home*, 1962
  Describes the sights and events a frontier family encounters traveling from South Dakota to Missouri in 1894.

1481

Ruth Yaffe Radin

Illustrator: Karl Swanson

Carver (New York: Macmillan, 1990)

Age range: Grades 3-5

Subject(s): Blind; Physically Handicapped; Artists and Art

Major character(s): Jon Bailey, Preteen, Handicapped (blind); Matt Nottingham, Preteen; Emmett Lewis, Artisan (woodcarver)

Time period(s): 1990s

Locale(s): Kellam's Landing

What the book is about: Ten year old Jon has been blind since the age of two, when an accident blinded him and killed his father. He and his mother have just moved back to Kellam's Landing where he was born. There will be no special schools for the blind and he will have to make new friends, but what Jon wants most is to be a carver like his father. He meets two friends who help him achieve his goal.

Where it's reviewed:
Booklist, May 15, 1990, page 1805
School Library Journal, July 1990, page 78

Other books by the author:
A Winter Place, 1990
High in the Mountains, 1989
Tac's Turn, 1987

Other books you might like:
Mary Blount Christian, *Mystery at Camp Triumph*, 1986
  Recently blinded, Angie begins to come to terms with her handicap when she tries to find out who is sabotaging the summer camp for disabled children.
James Duffy, *Uncle Shamus*, 1992
  Ten year old Akers and his friend are intrigued by the blind ex-convict who moves into their Oklahoma town and enlists their help in a secret plan.
Julia First, *The Absolute, Ultimate End*, 1985
  Maggie's new friendship with a blind girl leads her to fear that the program for the blind will be cut as budgets shrink.
Isabelle Holland, *The Unfrightened Dark*, 1990
  When her seeing eye dog is kidnapped, Jocelyn, orphaned and blind since age twelve, determines to solve the mystery surrounding his disappearance.
Jane Yolen, *Dream Weaver*, 1989
  For a penny a dream, the old, blind Dream Weaver weaves dreams for seven sets of passers-by.

1482

Ruth Yaffe Radin

Illustrator: Gail Owens

Tac's Island (New York: Macmillan, 1986)

Age range: Grades 3-5

Subject(s): Friendship; Vacations

Major character(s): Steve, Preteen; Thomas Andrew "TAC" Carter, Preteen

Time period(s): 1980s

Locale(s): Virginia (island off the coast of Virginia)

What the book is about: Steve's summer vacations on an island off the coast of Virginia consisted mostly of going to the beach. But this year, his sisters stay home and he meets TAC (Thomas Andrew Carter) who lives on the island year round and can show Steve lots more than the beach. They race bikes, go crabbing together, search for a child lost in the fog and develop a very special friendship.

Where it's reviewed:
Booklist, May 1, 1986, page 1316
Kirkus Reviews, March 1, 1986, page 388
School Library Journal, August 1986, page 96

Other books by the author:
Tac's Turn, 1986

Other books you might like:
LouAnn Gaeddert, *Your Former Friend, Matthew*, 1984
  Gail is devastated when her best friend, Matthew, ignores her after he returns from his summer vacation in the country.
Patricia Reilly Giff, *Love, From the Fifth-Grade Celebrity*, 1986
  Casey enjoys Tracy's company during summer vacation but becomes increasingly jealous of her new friend when she joins Casey's fifth grade class.
Johanna Hurwitz, *Yellow Blue Jay*, 1986
  Jay would rather spend his summer vacation at home in the city than share a rural Vermont house with his parents and some strangers.
Stephen Roos, *And the Winner Is.*, 1989
  Distraught over her family's finances, Phoebe sees her close friendship with Kit self-destructing as they both become involved in a local talent show.
Molly Mia Stewart, *Left-Out Elizabeth*, 1991
  On her first family ski vacation, Elizabeth Wakefield brings a friend,Todd Wilkins, but she becomes jealous of Todd's friendship with a boy he meets.

1483

Gail Radley

Nothing Stays the Same Forever (New York: Crown, 1981)

Age range: Grades 4-6

Subject(s): Fathers and Daughters; Remarriage; Old Age

Major character(s): Carrie Moyer, Preteen; Phyllis Moyer, Teenager; Grace Stebbins, Neighbor

Time period(s): 1980s

Locale(s): New York

What the book is about: Carrie's mom died when she was eight. Four years later her father is interested in a new woman. Phyllis likes Sharon and Carrie thinks she is being disloyal to their mother. Grace lets Carrie work in her garden to raise money for art classes. Grace is the only one that Carrie shares feelings with.

Where it's reviewed:
Booklist, January 15, 1982, page 652
Center for Children's Books Bulletin, June 1982, page 196
School Library Journal, January 1982, page 80

Other books by the author:
The Golden Days, 1991
C F in His Corner, 1984
The World Turned Inside Out, 1982

Other books you might like:
Carole S. Adler, *Footsteps on the Stairs: A Novel*, 1982
  Dodie and her new stepsister become friends as they investigate the sounds of footsteps which may be those of two sisters drowned in forty years ago.
Mildred Ames, *Cassandra-Jamie*, 1985
  Once deciding to arrange her father's marriage to the teacher she adores, Jamie discovers that people aren't always as they seem to be on the surface.
Bianca Bradbury, *Those Traver Kids*, 1972

Their mother's remarriage to a brutal man poses several serious problems for the four Traver children, especially for the older sister and brother.
Hila Colman, *Weekend Sisters*, 1985
  Amanda's weekends with her divorced father are disrupted when he announces plans to remarry, providing her with a stepsister her own age.
Judie Wolkoff, *Happily Ever After. Almost: A Novel*, 1982
  Eleven year old Kitty and her sister look forward to their mother's remarriage but not to getting a stepbrother.

1484

Candice Ransom

My Sister the Meanie (New York: Scholastic, 1988)

Age range: Grades 5-7

Subject(s): Sisters

Major character(s): Jackie Howard, Preteen, 7th Grader; Sharon Howard, Teenager

Time period(s): 1980s

Locale(s): Virginia

What the book is about: Trying to become more sophisticated and a seventh grade "somebody," Jackie goes too far in watching and copying her older sister, Sharon, and starts a war between them.

Where it's reviewed:
Kirkus Reviews, October 15, 1988, page 1533
Booklist, February 1, 1989, page 941
School Library Journal, November 1988, page 112

Other books by the author:
Millicent the Magnificent, 1989
My Sister the Creep, 1989
My Sister, the Traitor, 1989
Thirteen, 1986

Other books you might like:
Lynn Beach, *Stranger in the Mirror*, 1992
  Stacy is trapped in the past after being pulled through a mirror, while her twin, Tracy, must pretend to be both sisters while getting Stacy back.
Anne Fine, *The Book of the Banshee: A Novel*, 1992
  Will feels his sister, suddenly transformed into a teenage banshee, is responsible for turning the family home into a veritable war zone.
Constance Hiser, *Sixth Grade Star*, 1992
  Getting a part in the play doesn't keep Jill from being jealous of the attention her sister gets from her participation in beauty pageants.
Stacie Johnson, *Sort of Sisters*, 1992
  Sarah is looking forward to her junior year at Murphy High until her cousing Tasha moves in with her family.
Bonnie Pryor, *Jumping Jenny*, 1992
  The year that Jenny starts kindergarten, she has a busy time in the classroom and at home trying to adjust to some grown up changes.

1485

Arthur Ransome, Author/Illustrator

Swallows and Amazons (New York: Random, 1930)

Age range: Grades 5-9

Subject(s): Adventure and Adventurers; Sailing

Major character(s): John Walker, Child; Susan Walker, Child

Time period(s): 1930s

Locale(s): Holly Howe, England

What the book is about: The four Walker children get permission to take the sailboat, Swallow, and camp out on a nearby island. They meet other children in a boat called the Amazon and have great adventures. Ransome states that this story grew out of childhood memories and practically wrote itself. Of special interest to children who are interested in sailing and/or like really long books.

Where it's reviewed:
Hornbook, October 1983, page 601
New Statesman, May 24, 1968, page 693
School Library Journal, September 1984, page 201

Other books by the author:
We Didn't Mean to Go to Sea, 1938
Winter Holiday, 1933
Swallowdale, 1931

Other books you might like:
Avi, *Windcatcher*, 1991
 While learning to sail during a visit to his grandmother's in Connecticut, Tony becomes excited about the rumors of sunken treasure in the area.
Barbara Chamberlain, *Ride the West Wind*, 1979
 Nathan and his family join a group of other Quakers sailing to America, but the journey is plagued by suspicion, sickness and superstition.
Cynthia King, *Sailing Home*, 1982
 After running away, Paul returns home to finish school and to go sailing with the girlfriend whose father's false accusations caused him to leave.
Gary Paulsen, *The Voyage of the Frog*, 1989
 Caught in a fierce storm while sailing, David survives many days on his own while working out his feelings about life and his recently deceased uncle.
Caroline Tapley, *John Come Down the Backstay*, 1974
 A seaman tells of his experience on a sailing ship in the Artic which is searching for an exploring party lost twelve years earlier.

1486

Arthur Ransome, Author/Illustrator

We Didn't Mean to Go to Sea (London: J. Cape, 1937)

Age range: Grades 5-8

Subject(s): Sailing

Major character(s): John Walker, Sailor; Roger Walker, Sailor; Susan Walker, Sailor

Time period(s): 1930s

Locale(s): England; At Sea

What the book is about: While on holiday in East Anglia, the four Walker children whose previous sailing experience is limited to dinghies, accidentally drift out to the North Sea after the rising tide causes their cutter to drag anchor.

Where it's reviewed:
Books and Bookmen, August 1969, page 47
Reprint Bulletin—Book Reviews, issue #3, 1981, page 19

Other books by the author:
The Fool of the World and the Flying Ship, 1979
Swallows and Amazons, 1958
Old Peter's Russian Tales, 1916

Other books you might like:
J.S. Andrews, *The Green Hill of Nendrum*, 1970
 A fifteen year old boy sailing alone in Northern Ireland is suddenly transported back in time to a 10th century monastery threatened by a Viking raid.
Charles Boardman Hawes, *The Dark Frigate*, 1924
 A young man dares not return to England after his ship is taken over by pirates and he becomes a member of their crew.
Sesyle Joslin, *The Gentle Savages*, 1979
 Two youngsters flee their families when their cruise ship docks at a North African port and embark on a new life full of independence and adventure.
Rudyard Kipling, *Captains Courageous*, 1897
 After being washed overboard from an ocean liner, a spoiled millionaire's son is rescued by New England fishermen who put him to work on their boat.
Jill Paton Walsh, *The Dolphin Crossing*, 1967
 In wartime England two boys, too young to fight, take part in an evacuation from Dunkirk.

1487

Susan Lowry Rardin

Captives in a Foreign Land (Boston: Houghton Mifflin, 1984)

Age range: Grades 5-8

Subject(s): Antinuclear Movement; Kidnapping; Terrorism

Major character(s): Matt, Teenager (senator's son); Steve, Child, Captive

Time period(s): 1980s

Locale(s): Rome, Italy; Middle East

What the book is about: Six young Americans are kidnapped by a Pan-Islamic terrorist group called Tawbah, demanding unilateral American nuclear disarmament. When the government refuses to negotiate with the terrorists, the children must rely on theemselves to help tehir would-be rescuers locate them in an isolated spot in teh Middle East. Two of the six children are fully developed characters, and there is enough suspense and action to recommend it to older reluctant readers.

Where it's reviewed:
Horn Book, November/December 1984, page 766
School Library Journal, December 1984, page 94

Other books you might like:
Gillian Cross, *Wolf*, 1990

Casey is forced to stay with her mother in a squatters settlement of artists, where she learns that her "missing" father is a notorious terrorist.

Roger Elwood, *Sudden Fear*, 1991
   The teenage sons of an American diplomat find their lives in danger when they interrupt a terrorist's message.

Norma Johnson, *The Delphic Choice*, 1989
   Visiting Turkish relatives, Meredith tries to help free her uncle, a Quaker hostage negotiator, who has been taken hostage by Islamic terrorists.

Margot Merek, *Matt's Crusade*, 1988
   Seventh grader Matt Tyson wants to join his friend Allie in protestingArmy stockpiling of nuclear missiles near town despite a football game conflict.

Julian F. Thompson, *A Band of Angels*, 1986
   A group of teenagers decides to launch a kids' campaign against nuclear war, unaware that pursueing government agents are trying to kill them.

1488

Ellen Raskin

Figgs and Phantoms (New York: Dutton, 1974)

Age range: Grades 4-6

Subject(s): Family Life; Mystery and Detective Stories

Major character(s): Mona Lisa Newton, Preteen; Florence Italy Figg, Relative (uncle)

Time period(s): Indeterminate

Locale(s): Pineapple, Fictional Country

What the book is about: The adventures of the unusual Figg family after they leave show business and settle in the town of Pineapple. Mona is a Figg-Newton. All of her family have dreamed of Capri as their Utopia. When Uncle Florence dies, Mona is convinced she can find him in Capri.

Where it's reviewed:
Booklist, November 1, 1972, page 246
Hornbook, April 1972, page 138
Kirkus Reviews, February 1, 1972, page 132

Awards the book has won:
Children's Book Showcase 1975
Newbery Honor 1975

Other books by the author:
The Westing Game, 1978
The Tattooed Potato and Other Clues, 1975
The Mysterious Disappearance of Leon (I Mean Noel), 1971
A & The; or, William T.C. Baumgarten Comes to Town, 1970

Other books you might like:
Margaret E. Bechard, *Tory and Me and the Spirit of True Love*, 1992
   Cousins Tory and Emily go on a quest for secrets, romance and to learn about Aunt Louisa, who had not spoken to the family for years before her death.

Jane Louise Curry, *The Bassumtyte Treasure*, 1978
   When he goes to live with his cousin at the family's ancestral home, a boy finds a secret room and clues about the riddle of the family treasure.

Jim Hausman, *Mystery at Sans Souci*, 1978

A number of unrelated incidents lead an American family to conclude that someone wants them out of their rental house in a small town outside Paris.

Elizabeth Honness, *Mystery at the Villa Caprice*, 1969
   Darcy's first visit to her cousin in Capri becomes a dangerous adventure when the two girls wander into the wrong villa.

Ann Waldron, *The House on Pendleton Block*, 1975
   Chrissie is intrigued by many things about the old mansion her family rents, and she is especially interested about the former owner, now dead.

1489

Ellen Raskin

The Mysterious Disappearance of Leon (I Mean Noel) (New York: Dutton, 1971)

Age range: Grades 4-7

Subject(s): Humor; Mystery and Detective Stories

Major character(s): Caroline Fish, Child; Leon Carillion, Child

Time period(s): 1970s

Locale(s): United States

What the book is about: Caroline and Leon are married to each other at ages five and seven respectively, to insure the harmony of their two families in the business of marketing Pomato Soup. The disappearance of her husband is only one of the mysteries Mrs. Carillon must solve. Were Tina and Tony really Siamese twins? What were the glub-blubs? How was Leon's (I mean Noel's) last message decoded? Or was it? A great mystery/word puzzle with clues all along the way.

Where it's reviewed:
Kirkus Reviews, October 15, 1971, page 1122
Booklist, January 1, 1972, page 394
Center for Children's Books Bulletin, January 1972, page 79

Other books by the author:
The Westing Game, 1978
Figgs and Phantoms, 1974
Franklin Stein, 1972
The World's Greatest Freak Show, 1971

Other books you might like:
William Pene Du Bois, *The Three Policemen*, 1960
   Bottsford enables the three policemen of an isolated island to catch the thieves who have been stealing the islanders' fish and fishing nets.

John R. Erickson, *The Fiddle-Playing Fox*, 1989
   While working on a case involving disappearing eggs and a fiddle-playing fox named Frankie, Hand the cowdog falls for Miss Beulah, a beautiful collie.

Lynn Hall, *Murder in a Pig's Eye*, 1990
   Convinced that the owner of a farm has killed his sharp-tongued wife, Bodie searches for her body, until his detective work reaches a chaotic climax.

Jeffrey Kelly, *Tramp Steamer and the Silver Bullet*, 1984
   Tramp and Silver become involved with haunted houses, eccentric ladies, spiders, meat-eating plants and secret tunnels.

George Edward Stanley, *The Italian Spaghetti Mystery*, 1987

Miss Westminster and her pupils become entangled in the infamous Pasta Nostra when they entertain at Franco's Famous Italian Spaghetti Inn.

1490

Ellen Raskin

The Westing Game (New York: Dutton, 1978)

Age range: Grades 5-6

Subject(s): Inheritance; Mystery and Detective Stories

Major character(s): Samuel W. Westing, Wealthy (millionaire); Otis Amber, Worker (deliveryman)

Time period(s): 1970s

Locale(s): Westingtown, Wisconsin

What the book is about: A girl sneaks into the spooky old Westing Mansion and discovers the body of Samuel Westing. According to his will, sixteen people are paired and given clues to a riddle. The first to solve the riddle will inherit the Westing fortune.

Where it's reviewed:
Booklist, June 1, 1978, page 1555
Kirkus Reviews, April 15, 1978, page 438
School Library Journal, April 1978, page 87

Awards the book has won:
Newbery Medal 1979
Boston Globe/Horn Book Award 1978

Other books by the author:
The Mysterious Disappearance of Leon (I Mean Noel), 1980
The Tattooed Potato and Other Clues, 1975
Figgs and Phantoms, 1974

Other books you might like:
Thomas Baird, *Finding Fever*, 1982
  Benny and a classmate cooperate to solve the mystery when all the dogs along their road are stolen.
Patricia Elmore, *Susannah and the Blue House Mystery*, 1980
  Susannah and Lucy try to help Juliet find the missing will and inheritance left to her by a neighbor.
Madeleine L'Engle, *The Arm of the Starfish*, 1965
  Adam is involved in an adventure involving research on regeneration of organs based on work with starfish.
Philipa Pearce, *The Way to Sattin Shore*, 1983
  Kate Tranter tries to find the truth about the death of her father on the day she was born.
Mary Phraner Warren, *The Haunted Kitchen*, 1976
  Mark and his family are bothered by two mysteries, loss of belongings, and bicycle thieves.

1491

Marjorie Kinnan Rawlings

The Yearling (New York: Scribners, 1938)

Age range: Grades 5 and Up

Subject(s): Animals/Deer; Farm Life

Major character(s): Jody Baxter, Child; Ezra Baxter, Parent (Jody's father)

Time period(s): 1840s

Locale(s): Grahamsville, Florida

What the book is about: This classic of a boy and a fawn growing up together in the backwoods of Florida is perfect for reading aloud. It provides vivid pictures of rural life complete with dialect, and lots of excitement including the futile attempt to save a sow from Slewfoot, and hungry bear. Strong themes of father-son relationship, hunting, wandering in the beauty of the woods, and trading with neighbors.

Other books by the author:
Cross Creek, 1961
The Marjorie Rawlings Reader, 1956
The Sojourner, 1953
South Moon Under, 1933

Other books you might like:
Walter Farley, *The Black Stallion's Ghost*, 1969
  Alec's life is changed after he spends a night in the Everglades with a deranged Frenchman who is helping him search for a runaway black stallion.
Lois Lenski, *Strawberry Girl*, 1945
  Set in a little-known backwoods of Florida, this is the story of a little girl growing up in this region.
Robert Newton Peck, *Arly*, 1989
  Although Arly seems bound to follow in his father's footsteps as a field worker, his world seems larger when a schoolteacher comes to town.
Luke Wallin, *Ceremony of the Panther*, 1987
  John, a Miccosukee Indian, is torn between the shiftless life in the Everglads and his father's ambitions for him to carry on the shaman tradition.
Dorothy Raymond Whittaker, *Angels of the Swamp*, 1992
  Taffy, an orphan, joins two boys who have been forced leave their homes and the three of them try to survive the summer of 1932.

1492

Wilson Rawls

Summer of the Monkeys (New York: Doubleday, 1976)

Age range: Grades 4-6

Subject(s): Farm Life; Animals/Monkeys; Humor

Major character(s): Jay Berry Lee, Teenager; Daisy Lee, Child, Handicapped

Time period(s): 1890s

Locale(s): Oklahoma

What the book is about: When a train full of circus monkeys and one clever chimp escape from a circus train, Jay Berry Lee's summer becomes one hilarious incident after another as he sets out to round them up. He learns as much about life and family as he does about monkeys.

Where it's reviewed:
Booklist, July 1, 1976, page 1523

Awards the book has won:
California Young Reader Medal 1981
Golden Archer Award 1979

Other books by the author:
Where the Red Fern Grows, 1961

Other books you might like:
Susan Fleming, *The Pig at 37 Pinecrest Drive*, 1981

Crazy things begin to happen when Terry's mother brings home a pig for a pet as an educational experiment.
Wilson Gage, *My Stars, It's Mrs. Gaddy*, 1991
  Life on Mrs. Gaddy's farm is made more exciting by a ghost in her kitchen, a war with a perky crow and a vine that will not stop growing.
Saru Kani, *The Monkey and the Crab*, 1985
  A Japanese folk tale about Mr. Monkey who tricks Mrs. Crab out of her rice ball, and the way justice prevails.
Astrid Lindgren, *Emil's Pranks*, 1971
  Chaos follows a Swedish farm boy everywhere he goes in the community.
Stephen Manes, *The Great Gerbil Roundup*, 1988
  McBeth and Elton try to put their town on the map by creating the First National Drive-Through Museum of American Sightseeing and Clean Rest Rooms.

1493

Wilson Rawls

Where the Red Fern Grows (Garden City, New York: Doubleday, 1961)

Age range: Grades 4-6

Subject(s): Animals/Dogs; Farm Life; Mountain Life

Major character(s): Billy Colman, Preteen, Animal Trainer; Old Dan, Dog; Little Ann, Dog

Time period(s): Indeterminate Past

Locale(s): Oklahoma (Ozark Mountains)

What the book is about: A young boy living in the Ozarks achieves his heart's desire when he becomes the owner of two redbone hounds and teaches them to be champion hunters. When the big moment comes, Billy and his dogs upset the champions and win the coveted gold cup in the annual coonhunt contest, but tragedy awaits the pups in this well loved classic tear jerker.

Where it's reviewed:
School Library Journal, September 1984, page 48
New York Times Book Review, September 8, 1974, page 38
Best Sellers, October 1, 1974, page 311

Other books by the author:
Summer of the Monkeys, 1976

Other books you might like:
Vera Cleaver, *The Whys and Wherefores of Littabelle Lee*, 1973
  When adversity makes Littabelle the sole support of her aged grandparents, her situation teaches her about law, human nature, and her future.
John Donovan, *Wild in the World*, 1971
  When his entire family dies, John is left alone on the remote New Hampshire farm with only a wolf-dog for company.
Cena Christopher Draper, *The Worst Hound Around*, 1979
  A boy, his father, and his dog are living a happy bachelor existence until his mother's cousin with three daughters descends on them for a long visit.
Mark Taylor, *Old Blue, You Good Dog, You*, 1970
  Old Blue is the laziest hound dog in four counties except when it comes to his feud with Old Possum. Includes melody and words to "Old Blue."

1494

Deborah Kogan Ray

Illustrator: Debora K Ray

My Daddy Was a Soldier (New York: Holiday House, 1990)

Age range: Grades 3-4

Subject(s): World War II; Fathers; Family Life

Major character(s): Jeannie, Child

Time period(s): 1940s

Locale(s): Philadelphia, Pennsylvania

What the book is about: Jeannie's dad leaves home in 1943 for boot camp and then the war in the Pacific. She and her mom experience war on the home front. Jeannie helps her class collect scrap metal and her mom becomes a welder. Food shortages, victory gardens, blackouts and rationing fill their lives as they fear for Dad's safety.

Where it's reviewed:
Center for Children's Books Bulletin, June 1990, p 250
Kirkus Reviews, March 15, 1990, page 430

Other books by the author:
Ghosts and Goosebumps: Poems to Chill Your Bones, 1991
The Cloud, 1984

Other books you might like:
Paul Gallico, *The Snow Goose*, 1991
  Against the backdrop of WWII, a friendship develops between a lonely, crippled painter and a village girl as they care for an injured goose.
Natalie Kinsey-Warnock, *The Night the Bells Rang*, 1991
  A Vermont farm boy sees an older boy go off to war during the last year of WWI.
Toshi Maruki, *Hiroshima No Pika*, 1980
  A vivid disturbing picture book account of the experience of a mother and child during the flash that destroyed Hiroshima in 1945.
Shulamith Oppenheim, *The Lily Cupboard*, 1992
  A young Jewish girl is forced to leave her parents and hide with strangers during the German occupation of Holland.
Jane Yolen, *All Those Secrets of the World*, 1991
  When Janie's father goes to war and her family moves to her grandparent's, Janie learns a secret that helps her understand his absence.

1495

Jim Razzi

The Search for King Pup's Tomb (New York: Bantam, 1985)

Age range: Grades 3-5

Series: Sherluck Bones

Subject(s): Animals/Dogs; Mystery and Detective Stories

Major character(s): Sherluck Bones, Detective, Dog; Scotson, Assistant; Professor Morty Mutty, Teacher

Time period(s): Indeterminate

Locale(s): Fictional Country ("Far away country")

What the book is about: Sherluck Bones, master canine sleuth, is off to find the lost treasure of King Pup's tomb. He and

Scotson are deep inside a pyramid, looking at the strange writing on the walls, when they encounter the mummy of King Pup himself. Each chapter ends with a clue to help the reader solve the mystery of the mummy and treasure along with Sherluck.

Where it's reviewed:
Booklist, May 15, 1985, page 1337
School Library Journal, May 1985, page 110

Other books by the author:
Creature Feature, 1990
Bambi's Woodland Adventure, 1987
The Sherluck Bones Mystery Detective Book, 1984
The Dennis Bones Mystery Book, 1978

Other books you might like:
David A. Adler, *Cam Jansen and the Mystery of the Television Dog*, 1981
    Cam uses her photographic memory, with help from her friend, and his twin sisters, to solve the mystery of Poochie, a famous canine television star.
Mary Blount Christian, *Sebastian (Super Sleuth) and the Mystery Patient*, 1991
    Sebastian helps his master protect a patient at city hospital, at a time when an attempted coup has just occurred in a nation friendly to the U.S.
Terrance Dicks, *Goliath Goes to Summer School*, 1987
    David's big dog, Goliath, follows him to summer school on a farm and helps him to solve a ghostly mystery.
Denise Ortman Pomeraning, *The Great Dog Disaster*, 1989
    Andy McMandy, neighborhood detective, investigates the disappearance of Keegan's dog, Wizzer.
Marjorie Weinman Sharmat, *Nate the Great and the Boring Beach Bag*, 1987
    Oliver's boring blue beach bag is gone. Nate and his dog, Sludge, try to find clues to find the beach bag.

1496

Carolyn Reeder

Shades of Gray (New York: Macmillan, 1989)

Age range: Grades 5-6

Subject(s): Civil War; Orphans

Major character(s): Will Page, Preteen, Orphan; Jed Jones, Relative (uncle), Guardian; Meg Jones, Cousin

Time period(s): 1860s

Locale(s): Virginia

What the book is about: Will's father and brother were killed by Yankees in the Civil War. His little sisters died from the diseases spread by the conditions of war, and his mother "turned her head to the wall and slowly died of grief." Now Will must live with his uncle whom he considers a traitor because he did not fight the Yankees. Just as Will begins to adjust, his uncle allows a traveling Yankee to rest on the farm and re-ignites all Will's anger.

Where it's reviewed:
Booklist, January 15, 1990, page 1008
Kirkus Reviews, October 1, 1989, page 1480

Awards the book has won:
Jane Addams Children's Book Award 1990 Honor Book

Other books by the author:
Grandpa's Mountain, 1991

Other books you might like:
Isabelle Holland, *The Journey Home*, 1990
    Two orphan sisters in the late 1800s leave New York on the orphan train to seek a new home in the West.
Felice Holman, *The Wild Children*, 1983
    When his family is arrested during the Bolshevik Revolution, Alex joins a gang of homeless children, but never loses his hope for a better life.
Robin Moore, *The Bread Sister of Sinking Creek*, 1990
    Maggie has a special talent for making bread and she struggles to survive on the Pennsylvania frontier in the late 1700s.
Theodore Taylor, *Walking Up a Rainbow*, 1986
    In 1852, an orphan and her guardian, a tough drover and his crew take thousands of sheep from Iowa to California to raise money to save her home.
Cynthia Voigt, *The Callender Papers*, 1983
    In the 19th century, Jean is hired to sort out the papers of an artist and becomes curious about the death of his wife and disappearance of his child.

1497

Lynne Reid Banks

Illustrator: Terry Riley

I, Houdini: The Autobiography of a Self-Educated Hamster (New York: Doubleday, 1988)

Age range: Grades 4-6

Major character(s): Guy, Child; Mark, Child; Houdini "Goldy", Hamster

Time period(s): 1980s

Locale(s): United States

What the book is about: First person narration of a self-educated hamster searching for the great outdoors. The boastful hamster recounts his experiences chewing, wriggling, or squeezing his way out of various closed areas in his quest for the great outside. The family changes his name from Goldy to Houdini.

Other books by the author:
The Adventures of King Midas, 1992
The Fairy Rebel, 1985
The Indian in the Cupboard, 1980
The Farthest Away Mountain, 1976

Other books you might like:
Frank Asch, *Pearl's Promise*, 1984
    With her brother in the clutches of a python in a pet shop, Pearl, a mouse, goes through hair-raising adventures to rescue him.
Michael Bond, *The Tales of Olga da Polga*, 1971
    Recounts the adventures of an unusual guinea pig that specializes in tall tales.
Kathryn Kilby Borland, *Harry Houdini: Young Magician*, 1991
    A biography of Harry Houdini concentrating on his earlier years and the training that made him a master magician and escape artist.
Ann M. Martin, *Jessi Ramsey, Pet-Sitter*, 1989
    With snakes on the loose and sick hamsters, Jessi's got plenty of pet-sitting troubles.

Caroline Rush, *Eight Tales of Mr. Pengachoosa*, 1971
Hammy the hamster returns to his old home with more stories of his grandfather's adventures.

1498

Lynne Reid Banks

Illustrator: Brock Cole

The Indian in the Cupboard (New York: Doubleday, 1980)

Age range: Grades 4-6

Subject(s): Indians of North America; Magic; Toys

Major character(s): Omri, Child; Little Bear, Indian; Boone, Cowboy

Time period(s): 1980s

Locale(s): England

What the book is about: Omri receives a small cupboard as a birthday present and discovers accidentally that with a special key, the cupboard brings plastic figures to life. He brings an Indian figure to life, then expects peace and harmony when a cowboy is added to the equation. He expects to have a wonderful time with this magic, but he finds that being responsible for the life of another can be a tremendous burden.

Where it's reviewed:
Center for Children's Books Bulletin, October 1981, p22
School Library Journal, December 1981, page 59

Awards the book has won:
California Young Reader Medal 1985

Other books by the author:
Houdini: The Autobiography of a Self-Educated Hamster, 1988
The Fairy Rebel, 1988

Other books you might like:
John Bibee, *The Toy Campaign*, 1987
Armed with only her magic Spirit Fire bicycle, Susan takes on the owner of a toy store who offers free toys to lure children into the Deeper World.
Rumer Godden, *The Rocking Horse Secret*, 1978
Tibby finds something hidden in a gift rocking horse but isn't sure she should reveal the secret.
Russell Hoban, *The Mouse and His Child*, 1967
A toy mouse and his son are captured by a rat, then embark on a quest to find their friends.
Elizabeth Levy, *Dracula Is a Pain in the Neck*, 1983
Robert regrets taking his Dracula doll and security pillow to camp.
Margery Williams, *The Velveteen Rabbit*, 1983
A toy rabbit longs to be real and finds that the only way is to be loved.

1499

Johanna Reiss

Illustrator: Bruce Degen

The Upstairs Room (New York: Crowell, 1972)

Age range: Grades 5 and Up

Subject(s): World War II; Jews

Major character(s): Annie De Leeuw, Child, Refugee; Sini De Leeuw, Relative (sister), Refugee

Time period(s): 1940s

Locale(s): Netherlands

What the book is about: The author's true story of the two and a half years she and her sister spent hiding in a family farmhouse while German soldiers occupied the farm. She discovers concentration camp horrors and waits for liberation. (Autobiography)

Where it's reviewed:
Horn Book, February 1973, page 50
Saturday Review, April 14, 1973, page 87

Awards the book has won:
Jane Addams Children's Book Award 1973

Other books by the author:
The Journey Back, 1976 (Sequel to *Upstairs Room*)

Other books you might like:
Anne Frank, *Diary of a Young Girl*, 1977
The story of a young Jewish refugee during two years of hiding from the Germans in the Netherlands during WWII.
Gertie Evenhuis, *What about Me?*, 1976
A young boy searches for a way to help the resistance in Amsterdam during the German occupation.
Els Pelgrom, *The Winter When Time Was Frozen*, 1980
In Holland during the last months of WWII, a girl and her father find shelter with a farm family who courageously give sanctuary.
Hilda Van Stockum, *The Borrowed House*, 1975
During WWII, a young German girl, member of the Hitler Youth, goes to live with her parents in occupied Amsterdam and learns the truth about war.
Ida Vos, *Hide and Seek*, 1991
A young Jewish girl living in Holland tells of her experiences during the Nazi occupation, her years in hiding, and the after shock when the war ends.

1500

Beverly Hollett Renner

Illustrator: Ruth Sanderson

The Hideaway Summer (New York: Harper, 1978)

Age range: Grades 5-7

Subject(s): Brothers and Sisters; Survival

Major character(s): Adelaide "Addie" Carver, Preteen; Clay Carver, Preteen; Mrs. Groton, Businesswoman (Storekeeper)

Time period(s): 1970s

Locale(s): United States

What the book is about: Addie takes her younger brother off the bus to camp to show him a special hideaway she shared with their grandma for many years. They call their dad once a week, and he thinks they are still at camp. They have an adventurous summer exploring the woods. At the end of the summer, Addie finds out that Mrs. Groton, the storekeeper, has known her secret all along and has been keeping an eye on them.

Where it's reviewed:
Booklist, March 15, 1978, page 1197
Hornbook, June 1978, page 280
Kirkus Reviews, April 1, 1978, page 376

Other books you might like:
William Bell, *Crabbe's Journey*, 1986
Feeling misunderstood at home and at school, Crabbe runs off to live in the woods where he meets a woman who teachs him about survival.
Gary L. Blackwood, *Wild Timothy*, 1987
Timothy, more interested in reading than in physical activity, accompanies his father on a trip and, when he becomes lost, has to survive on his own.
Beverly Butler, *My Sister's Keeper*, 1980
In the north woods of Wisconsin following a forest fire that destroys their town in 1871, Mary James forms a new respect for her older sister.
Scott O'Dell, *Sarah Bishop*, 1980
Sarah struggles to shape a new life for herself in the wilderness after her father and brother die on opposite sides in the War for Independence.
Gary Paulsen, *The River*, 1991
After surviving alone in the wilderness for fifty-four days, Brian is asked to undergo a similar experience to help scientists understand survival.

1501

Margret Rettich

The Silver Touch and Other Family Christmas Stories
(New York: Morrow, 1978)

Age range: Grades 4-6

Subject(s): Christmas; Short Stories

Time period(s): Indeterminate

Locale(s): Germany

What the book is about: A nice collection of Christmas stories, some tender and some funny. Boastful relatives, thank you notes, staying up late, a household disaster and comparing Christmas dolls, and other delights of the season fill this book.

Where it's reviewed:
Center for Children's Books Bulletin, November 1978, page 3
Kirkus Reviews, November 15, 1978, page 1249
School Library Journal, October 1978, page 112

Other books by the author:
Suleiman the Elephant, 1986
The Voyage of the Jolly Boat, 1981
Tightwad's Curse and Other Pleasantly Chilling Stories, 1979

Other books you might like:
Joan Aiken, *Up the Chimney Down and Other Stories*, 1984
Eleven short Christmas stories by one of the best storytellers in the business.
Charles Dickens, *Christmas Stories*, 1946
Includes "A Christmas Carol", "The Chimes", and "The Cricket on the Hearth."
Martin Greenberg, *A Newbery Christmas*, 1991
A collection of Christmas stories by Newbery Award winning authors; including E.L. Konigsburg, Madeleine L'Engle, and Katherine Paterson.

Katherine Paterson, *Angels and Other Stories: Family Christmas Stories*, 1979
Nine Christmas stories by Newbery Award winning author Katherine Paterson.

1502

Bjarne B. Reuter

Buster, the Sheikh of Hope Street (New York: Dutton, 1991)

Age range: Grades 6-8

Subject(s): Imagination; Theater

Major character(s): Buster Mortensen, Child; Willy Valdi, Teacher; Ingeborg Mortensen, Child

Time period(s): 1980s

Locale(s): Copenhagen, Denmark

What the book is about: Buster's school is putting on a play and he hopes to win the lead, the part of dashing Arab Sheikh Suleiman. When he is only a last minute stagehand, he gets fired from his job for drawing on the grocery cartons, and his broomstick horselands a lady on top of the Italian tomatoes, you'd think he might be discouraged, but not Buster! He carries on cheerfully and eventually does wind up in the play.

Where it's reviewed:
Booklist, January 15, 1992, page 941
School Library Journal, February 1992, page 89

Other books by the author:
Buster's World, 1989
Princess and the Sun, Moon and Stars, 1986

Other books you might like:
Elizabeth Starr Hill, *Broadway Chances*, 1992
Twelve year old Fitzi, finally in a settled life after years of street performances with her parents, gets a chance to star in a Broadway musical.
Beverly Keller, *Fowl Play, Desdemona*, 1989
While checking out her father's new girl friend, Dez teams up with Sherman to design new posters for the school play, with hilarious results.
Noel Streatfeild, *Theater Shoes, or Other People's Shoes*, 1945
When their father is captured during the war, three children live with their grandmother and join the talented family in a school for stage training.
Susan Terris, *Stage Brat*, 1980
Twelve year old Linnet Purcell learns a lot about the theater and herself when she is chosen to play the role of Peter Pan in a repertory production.
Jean Ure, *Supermouse*, 1984
When her talented younger sister becomes her rival for a role in a local show, Nicola steps aside but finds her own talent has not gone unnoticed.

1503

Margaret Reuter

Illustrator: Joe Weinshel

You Can Depend on Me (Chicago: Children's Press, 1980)

Age range: Grades 1-2

Subject(s): Family Life; Responsibility; Brothers and Sisters

Major character(s): David, Child; Dan, Child; Mrs. Beck, Neighbor

Time period(s): 1980s

Locale(s): United States

What the book is about: David can help his mom and dad with no problem. Dan feels he never gets to do anything important. He always makes mistakes and gets yelled at. When the Becks go out of town, Dan gets to take care of their dog, Honey. He is glad for the responsibility.

Other books by the author:
My Mother Is Blind, 1979

Other books you might like:
Lonzo Anderson, *Izzard*, 1973
  Jamie finds both fun and responsibility when Izzard the lizard adopts him for a mother.
Judy Delton, *The Best Mom in the World*, 1979
  A youngster feels angry and betrayed when his doting mother begins asking him to do things for himself.
Jane Duncan, *Janet Reachfar and Chickabird*, 1978
  Because of her own carelessness, a young girl must decide the fate of an injured chicken.
Ann Grifalconi, *Flyaway Girl*, 1991
  Sent to the edge of the Niger to gather rushes for the Ceremony of the Beginnings, Nsia is guided by her ancestors' spirits on her way to wisdom.
Juanita Havill, *The Magic Fort*, 1991
  Playing in their "magic fort" in a tree, Kevin's brother Joseph breaks his arm, teaching them both a lesson about responsibility and togetherness.

1504

Eve Rice, Author/Illustrator

Papa's Lemonade and Other Stories (New York: Greenwillow, 1976)

Age range: Grades 1-2

Subject(s): Family Life; Short Stories

Major character(s): Mama, Dog; Papa, Dog

Time period(s): Indeterminate

Locale(s): United States

What the book is about: Five short chapters about a family of dogs, Mama, Papa, and their five puppies, who easily adjust to any situation.

Where it's reviewed:
Hornbook, February 1977, page 44
Kirkus Reviews, July 15, 1976, page 793
School Library Journal, December 1976, page 64

Other books by the author:
At Grammy's House, 1990
Peter's Pockets, 1989
Aren't You Coming Too?, 1988
New Blue Shoes, 1975

Other books you might like:
Ann Bradford, *The Mystery of the Midget Clown*, 1980

When Steve, the midget, fails to show up for his job as clown at the circus, five children set out to find him.
Natalie Savage Carlson, *Marie Louise's Heyday*, 1975
  Marie Louise babysits for five possum children and, while finding it an exhausting experience, realizes it is not without rewards.
Edith Holden Cooke, *The Bratchets*, 1936
  The five unruly Bratchet children leave home in anger, but when they make a bigger home in a hollow tree, the family is reunited.
Elisabeth Nardine, *Daydreams and Night*, 1976
  The imaginings of five children are induced by the reality of the moment.
Bernard Waber, *Goodbye, Funny Dumpy-Lumpy*, 1977
  Five vignettes reveal how a mother, father, and their three children negotiate common family problems.

1505

Eve Rice

The Remarkable Return of Winston Potter Crisply (New York: Greenwillow, 1978)

Age range: Grades 5-7

Subject(s): Mystery and Detective Stories

Major character(s): Becky Crisply, Preteen; Max Crisply, Teenager; Winston Potter Crisply, Student

Time period(s): 1970s

Locale(s): New York, New York

What the book is about: Becky and Max trail their brother who is supposed to be at Harvard in Cambridge, Massachusetts. Instead, he mysteriously appears on the streets of New York City. They decide to do some investigating to see what is really going on with him.

Where it's reviewed:
Booklist, September 1, 1978, page 52
Kirkus Reviews, April 15, 1978, page 438
School Library Journal, May 1978, page 85

Other books you might like:
Betty Baker, *The Night Spider Case*, 1984
  In the 1890s in New York City, eleven year old Lambert Grew reluctantly joins with his neighbor, Frances Ward to investigate the empty house next door
James Lincoln Collier, *Who Is Carrie?*, 1984
  A young black girl in New York City in the late 18th century observes the historic events around her and also solves the mystery of her own identity.
Milton Dank, *The Treasure Code*, 1985
  Six junior high school friends search for a treasure buried in Philadelphia by a local author whose book contains clues to the treasure's location.
Richard Peck, *Voices After Midnight*, 1989
  Two brothers, Chad and Luck, traveling back in time to 1888, uncover a mystery involving former tenants of a New York City house their family rents.
Patricia Windsor, *Killing Time*, 1980
  A teenager moves with his father from New York City to a small town where strange happenings begin to convince them they're not wanted.

1506

Conrad Richter

The Light in the Forest (New York: Knopf, 1953)

Age range: Grades 5 and Up

Subject(s): Indians of North America

Major character(s): John Butler, Captive; Cuyloga, Indian; Half Arrow, Indian

Time period(s): Indeterminate Past

Locale(s): Pennsylvania

What the book is about: John Butler was taken from a small Pennsylvania frontier town by the Lenni Lenape Indians when he was four years old. One of their greatest warriors, Cuyloga, renamed him "True Son" and raised him as his own son. He loves his people and the way of the woods. When he is fifteen, a treaty is signed and word reaches his village that all Lenni Lenape and Shawanose Indians must return all white prisoners. True Son cannot believe it applies to him. He is forced to return to his parents and is caught between loyalty to his Indian family, the love of the free Indian life, and the many restrictions and the different life of the white settlers.

Where it's reviewed:
Booklist, January 1, 1967, page 493
Hornbook, April 1967, page 222
Booklist, October 15, 1972, page 178

Other books by the author:
A Country of Strangers, 1975
The Fields, 1946
The Free Man, 1943
The Trees, 1940

Other books you might like:
James Lincoln Collier, *The Bloody Country,* 1976
In the mid-eighteenth century a family moves from Connecticut to Pennsylvania and becomes involved in the property conflict between the two states.
Ann Finlayson, *Greenhorn on the Frontier,* 1974
Just before the Revolutionary War, Harry and his sister Sukey move their few possessions by hand cart to start their own farm in Pennsylvania.
Jean Fritz, *The Cabin Faced West,* 1958
Ann overcomes loneliness and learns to appreciate the importance of her role in settling the wilderness of western Pennsylvania.
Robin Moore, *Maggie Among the Seneca,* 1987
Maggie journeys across the Pennsylvania frontier to find her kin. While reaching her destination, she is kidnaped by a band of Seneca warriors.
Elizabeth George Speare, *Calico Captive,* 1957
Miraim and her sister's family are captured in an Indian raid and are sold to the French, where they are held for ransom. Based on actual events.

1507

Hans Peter Richter

Friedrich (New York: Holt, 1970)

Age range: Grades 4-8

Subject(s): Jews

Major character(s): Friedrich Schneider, Child; Johann Resch, Landlord; Herr Neudorf, Teacher

Time period(s): 1930s

Locale(s): Germany

What the book is about: The unnamed narrator begins his story in Germany in 1925 when he and his friend, Friedrich, are four years old. We see their friendship form and the devastating effect of the Nazi regime on the Jews from the boys' point of view as they grow and the rights of the Schneiders and all Jews are taken away. It happens slowly at first, then later with alarming speed and cruelty. A chronology of dates is given for laws, decrees and regulations affecting the Jews. A powerful book for independent reading or group study.

Where it's reviewed:
Booklist, April 1, 1971, page 665
Hornbook, April 1971, page 173
Kirkus Reviews, October 15, 1970, page 1163

Awards the book has won:
Mildred L. Batchelder Award 1972
German Children's Book Prize 1962

Other books by the author:
I Was There, 1972

Other books you might like:
Edith Baer, *A Frost in the Night,* 1980
Relates the experiences of a young Jewish girl growing up in a city in southern Germany during the period of Hitler's rise to power.
Lucy S. Dawidowicz, *From That Place and Time: A Memoir, 1938-1947,* 1989
Personal narrative of life for a Lithuanian Jew during Hitler's rise to power and WWII and the aftermath, for very advanced readers.
Olga Levy Drucker, *Kindertransport,* 1992
Describes the author's experiences as a Jewish child taken from Germany to England for safety during WWII.
Ruth Minsky Sender, *To Life,* 1988
A Jewish woman recounts her liberation from a Nazi concentration camp, search for surviving family members and the ordeal of immigrating to America.
Aranka Siegal, *Grace in the Wilderness: After the Liberation, 1945-1948,* 1985
Liberated from a concentration camp at the end of World War II but haunted by the memory of her ordeal, Piri starts a new life as a Jew in Sweden.

1508

Mary Riskind

Wildcat Summer (Boston: Houghton Mifflin, 1985)

Age range: Grades 5-7

Subject(s): Animals/Wild Cats; Country Life; Grandparents

Major character(s): Lynn, Preteen; Vicky, Preteen; Skip, Preteen

Time period(s): 1940s

Locale(s): New Hampshire

What the book is about: Lynn, Vicky and Skip become involved in caring for wild kittens, which turn out to be bobcats.

Vicky learns that you cannot change the nature of animals or people to suit your own purposes. Good characterization and interesting story.

Where it's reviewed:
Center for Children's Books Bulletin, August 1985, page 15
School Library Journal, August 1985, page 69

Other books by the author:
Follow That Mom!, 1986
Apple Is My Sign, 1981

Other books you might like:
Clare Bell, *Clan Ground*, 1984
   The stranger Orange-Eyes, recognizing that the one who controls fire can become absolute ruler, challenges Ratha's authority over the Named.
John R. Erickson, *Lost in the Dark Uncharted Forest*, 1991
   Fearless Hank the cowdog, head of ranch security, enters the "dark uncharted forest" to rescue his master's son from Sinister, the bobcat.
Rutherford George Montgomery, *Rufus*, 1973
   A young bobcat struggles against hunters, a flash flood, an avalanche, and the laws of nature in his efforts to live a happy life.
Virginia Frances Voight, *Bobcat*, 1978
   This story follows the experience of a bobcat in his first year of life.
William J. Weber, *Wild Orphan Babies*, 1978
   A handbook offering instruction on the housing, feeding and general care of orphaned wild animal babies and how to prepare them for life in the wild.

│1509│

Willo Davis Roberts

Illustrator: Ruth Sanderson

Don't Hurt Laurie! (New York: Atheneum, 1977)

Age range: Grades 4-6

Subject(s): Child Abuse

Major character(s): Laurie, Preteen, Abuse Victim; Jack, Step-Parent; Annabelle, Parent

Time period(s): 1970s

Locale(s): United States

What the book is about: Annabelle moves each time Laurie makes a good friend, or is taken to the emergency room too many times because she fears someone will discover that she beats her daughter. Tim, her stepbrother, witnesses a beating that leaves Laurie unconscious. They escape to his grandmother's while Jack takes Annabelle away for treatment.

Where it's reviewed:
Hornbook, August 1977, page 444
Kirkus Reviews, April 15, 1977, page 427
School Library Journal, April 1977, page 70

Other books by the author:
What Are We Going to Do about David?, 1993
To Grandmother's House We Go, 1990
What Could Go Wrong?, 1989
The View From the Cherry Tree, 1975

Other books you might like:
Carole S. Adler, *Fly Free*, 1984

Shy, thirteen year old Shari, abused at home by a mother who resents her, is befriended by a neighbor who shares her love of birds and the outdoors.
Charlotte Culin, *Cages of Glass, Flowers of Time: A Novel*, 1979
   Claire, a victim of child abuse, gradually finds love in the world with the help of two unlikely friends.
Irene Hunt, *The Lottery Rose: A Novel*, 1976
   A young victim of child abuse gradually overcomes his fears and suspicions when placed in a home with other boys.
Louise Moeri, *The Girl Who Lived on the Ferris Wheel*, 1979
   Til realizes with increasing urgency that her divorced mother's violently abusive behavior is getting more and more out of control.
Marilyn Sachs, *A December Tale*, 1976
   A lonely foster child is weakened by the bribes of an abusive foster mother, yet strengthened by imaginary conversations with Joan of Arc.

│1510│

Willo Davis Roberts

The Girl with the Silver Eyes (New York: Atheneum, 1980)

Age range: Grades 4-6

Subject(s): Extrasensory Perception

Major character(s): Katie Walker, Preteen; Monica Walker, Parent (Katie's mother); Annie Michaelmas, Neighbor

Time period(s): 1980s

Locale(s): United States

What the book is about: Katie knows she's different, odd. She has silver eyes, can move objects with her mind, and communicate with animals. But her powers upset people so she and her mother move to make a new start. The mysterious Mr. Cooper moves into the same building and starts asking questions. Katie fears he will arrest her. Should she use her powers to save herself?

Where it's reviewed:
Booklist, November 1, 1980, page 408
Kirkus Reviews, November 15, 1980, page 1466
School Library Journal, November 1980, page 79

Awards the book has won:
Crabbery Award 1981
California Young Reader Medal

Other books by the author:
Scared Stiff, 1992
Dark Secrets, 1991
The Minden Curse, 1990
Megan's Island, 1988

Other books you might like:
Laurence F. Abrams, *Mysterious Powers of the Mind*, 1982
   Discusses mental telepathy, psychokinesis, levitation, clairvoyance and other manifestations of ESP.
Edward Packard, *ESP McGee*, 1983
   Matt and McGee become involved with terrorists interested in sabotaging a nuclear plant.
Lila Perl, *Annabelle Starr, E.S.P.*, 1983
   Annabelle has second thoughts about her "gift" when she sees the fear a prediction causes in her brother.

William Sleator, *Into the Dream*, 1979
When two youngsters realize they are having the same dream, they begin searching for an explanation for this coincidence.
Mary Towne, *Paul's Game*, 1983
An experiment in ESP becomes terrifying for two girls when one comes under the influence of a strange boy with mysterious purposes of his own.

1511

Willo Davis Roberts

The Magic Book (New York: Atheneum, 1986)

Age range: Grades 4-6

Subject(s): Bullies; Magic

Major character(s): Alexander William "Alex" Graden, Student; Norm Winthrop, Bully

Time period(s): 1980s

Locale(s): Seattle, Washington

What the book is about: Alex finds a book of spells and potions at the library book sale. He and his friends decide to use it to get back at the school bully. The spells in the book work, sort of. The things they had hoped would happen did happen, but never quite in the way they had thought.

Where it's reviewed:
Booklist, May 15, 1986, page 1400
Center for Children's Books Bulletin, June 1986, page 195
Kirkus Reviews, June 1, 1986, page 866

Other books by the author:
Dark Secrets, 1991
What Could Go Wrong?, 1989
Eddie and the Fairy Godpuppy, 1984
The Girl with the Silver Eyes, 1980

Other books you might like:
Polly Berrien Berends, *Ozma and the Wayward Wand*, 1985
While Dorothy is visiting the magic land of Oz, the royal gardener's son borrows Queen Ozma's wand without permission and endangers the Emerald City.
Robert Graves, *The Big Green Book*, 1962
A little boy finds a big green book in the attic and learns many handy magic spells that he uses with surprising results.
Phyllis Green, *Eating Ice Cream with a Werewolf*, 1983
A wacky baby sitter and her book of spells keep a twelve year old and his little sister guessing while their parents are away.
Ivan Southall, *Head in the Clouds*, 1972
An accident prone boy decides to work some magic spells to punish his friends who have forgotten him while he is recovering from his latest mishap.
Pamela Stearns, *Into the Painted Bear Lair*, 1976
Entering another world through a toy store, Gregory joins Sir Rosemary and a gourmet named Bear on a journey involving princesses and magic spells.

1512

Willo Davis Roberts

Megan's Island (New York: Atheneum, 1988)

Age range: Grades 5-8

Subject(s): Kidnapping; Mystery and Detective Stories; Prisoners and Prisons

Major character(s): Megan, Preteen; Sandy, Preteen; Ben, Neighbor

Time period(s): 1980s

Locale(s): Lakewood, Minnesota

What the book is about: Eleven year old Megan and her brother, Sandy, are alarmed to discover that someone is following their family. The children have been moved suddenly to stay with their grandfather, and learn that their father, presumed long dead, only recently died in prison. Their other grandfather had tried to get custody and men seeking the reward he offered try to kidnap Megan and Sandy.

Where it's reviewed:
Center for Children's Books Bulletin, April 1988, page 166
School Library Journal, April 1988, page 104

Other books by the author:
What Could Go Wrong?, 1989
The Pet-Sitting Peril, 1983
The Minden Curse, 1978
The View From the Cherry Tree, 1975

Other books you might like:
Vivien Alcock, *A Kind of Thief*, 1991
When her father is suddenly arrested and put in prison, thirteen year old Elinor has to face many unpleasant truths about him and their way of life.
Barthe DeClements, *Breaking Out*, 1991
As Jerry enters junior high he continues to adjust to the fact that his father is in prison for theft. Third book in a sequel.
Lynn Hall, *The Solitary*, 1986
With her mother in prison for killing her father, seventeen year old Jane, finally on her own and free from abuse, returns home to make a new life.
Carolyn Meyer, *Wild Room*, 1989
When her escaped convict father takes fifteen year old Andy into a remote and harsh wilderness, they make some shocking discoveries about each other.
Walter Dean Myers, *Somewhere in the Darkness*, 1992
A teen boy accompanies his father, recently escaped from prison, on a trip that turns out to be a painful time of discovery for both of them.

1513

Willo Davis Roberts

The View From the Cherry Tree (New York: Atheneum, 1976)

Age range: Grades 4-6

Subject(s): Mystery and Detective Stories; Murder

Major character(s): Rob Mallory, Preteen; S.O.B., Cat; Mrs. Calloway, Neighbor

Time period(s): 1970s

Locale(s): United States

What the book is about: Rob sees the murder of Mrs. Calloway while perched in a cherry tree. However, his sister's wedding takes everyone's attention while he screams "Murder!" Cousins by the dozens fill up his house, Rob gets shot at, attacked by flower pots, and the only one who knows what really happened is S.O.B., the cat.

Where it's reviewed:
Center for Children's Books Bulletin, January 1976, p 85
School Library Journal, December 1975, page 66

Other books by the author:
What Could Go Wrong?, 1989
Megan's Island, 1988
The Girl with the Silver Eyes, 1980
Don't Hurt Laurie!, 1977

Other books you might like:
Natalie Babbitt, *Tuck Everlasting*, 1975
    Winnie Foster is involved in kidnapping, murder, and a jailbreak, and must make a decision about a spring which gives everlasting life.
Robbie Branscum, *The Murder of Hound Dog Bates*, 1982
    Sassafras Bates believes one of his aunts killed his favorite dog and sets out to solve the mystery.
James Howe, *What Eric Knew*, 1985
    Sebastian and his friends solve a mystery involving cocaine. (A Sebastian Barth Mystery)
Ellen Raskin, *The Tattooed Potato and Other Clues*, 1975
    An art student takes a job assisting a portrait painter and becomes involved in theft, forgery, and murder.
John Rowe Townsend, *Tom Tiddler's Ground*, 1986
    Five children discover treasure in a sunken canalboat.

1514

Keith Robertson

Illustrator: Robert McCloskey

Henry Reed's Baby-Sitting Service (New York: Viking, 1966)

Age range: Grades 4-6

Subject(s): Babysitters; Money

Major character(s): Henry Reed, Preteen; Midge, Preteen

Time period(s): 1960s

Locale(s): Grover's Corners, New Jersey

What the book is about: Back in Grover's Corners, New Jersey, for the summer, Henry and his partner, Midge, establish a baby-sitting service and find a disappearing child and a peacock among their charges.

Where it's reviewed:
Booklist, July 15, 1979, page 1635

Other books by the author:
Henry Reed's Think Tank, 1986
Henry Reed's Big Show, 1970
Henry Reed's Journey, 1963
Henry Reed, Inc., 1958

Other books you might like:
Brenda Guiberson, *Instant Soup*, 1991
    Darlene plans to spend her winter break at the mall with best friend Stacy until Mom gives Darlene the job of babysitting her four year old cousin.
Ann Hodgman, *My Babysitter Is a Vampire*, 1991
    Meg is not happy that her mother insists on hiring a babysitter for her and her brother, especially one that likes to bite people's necks.

Ann M. Martin, *Kristy for President*, 1992
    Kristy is not happy with things at Stoneybrook Middle School, so she runs for class president, but can she babysit and be president?
Colleen O'Shaughnessy McKenna, *Mother Murphy*, 1992
    When Mrs. Murphy has to get off her feet because she's expecting a baby, Collette takes over with surprising results.
Suzanne Weyn, *Liza's Lucky Break*, 1991
    Working as a babysitter at the exclusive Palm Pavilion Hotel, Liza risks her job when she tries to get a part in a movie being filmed at the hotel.

1515

Harriette Robinet

Illustrator: David Brown

Ride the Red Cycle (Boston: Houghton Mifflin, 1980)

Age range: Grades 2-4

Subject(s): Courage; Physically Handicapped; Brothers and Sisters

Major character(s): Jerome Johnson, Handicapped; Tilly Johnson, Teenager

Time period(s): 1980s

Locale(s): United States

What the book is about: Jerome wears thick glasses, special shoes, and leg braces. A viral infection left him brain damaged and crippled. He resolves to make his legs work on their own. With courage, determination, and the loving help of his sister, Tilly, Jerome accomplishes some amazing things.

Where it's reviewed:
Hornbook, June 1980, page 303
Kirkus Reviews, July 15, 1980, page 911
School Library Journal, August 1980, page 69

Other books by the author:
Children of the Fire, 1991
Jay and the Marigold, 1976

Other books you might like:
Nancy L. Carlson, *Arnie and the New Kid*, 1990
    When an accident requires Arnie to use crutches, he begins to understand the limits and possibilities of his new classmate, who uses a wheelchair.
Jane Cowen-Fletcher, *Mama Zooms*, 1993
    A boy's wonderful mama takes him zooming everywhere with her because her wheelchair is a zooming machine.
Ken Kesey, *The Sea Lion: A Story of the Sea Cliff People*, 1991
    Although taunted for his small size and bad leg, Eemook proves his worth by saving his tribe from an evil and powerful spirit that comes one night.
Marisabina Russo, *Alex Is My Friend*, 1992
    Even though Alex is a dwarf and sometimes has to use a wheelchair, his friend does not mind because they still have good times together.
Joel Vecere, *A Story about Courage*, 1992
    Jarrod, a new student who's confined to a wheelchair, tries out for the school basketball team.

1516

Joan Robins

Illustrator: Sue Truesdell

Addie Meets Max (New York: Harper, 1985)

Age range: Grades 1-2

Series: An Early I Can Read Book

Subject(s): Friendship; Neighbors and Neighborhoods

Major character(s): Addie, Child; Max, Child; Ginger, Dog

Time period(s): 1980s

Locale(s): United States

What the book is about: When Max moves into the neighborhood, his dog terrifies Addie, and she and Max have a bicycle crash. Addie decides he is a terror to be avoided at all costs. But once Addie's mother invites Max over for pizza, Addie decides he might be a good friend after all. She helps Max bury the tooth he lost when their bikes crashed.

Where it's reviewed:
Booklist, April 15, 1985, page 1202
Kirkus Reviews, March 1, 1985, page J11
School Library Journal, May 1985, page 107

Other books by the author:
Addie Runs Away, 1989
My Brother, Will, 1986

Other books you might like:
Franz Brandenberg, *Nice New Neighbors*, 1977
  The Fieldmouse children find a way to make new friends when they move to a new house.
Johanna Hurwitz, *New Neighbors for Nora*, 1979
  Describes the further adventures of an inquisitive seven year old and her new neighbors in a New York City apartment building.
Ida Luttrell, *The Bear Next Door*, 1991
  Three episodes in the developing friendship of Vic Bear and Arlo Gopher demonstrate how they are good neighbors.
Colin McNaughton, *Guess Who's Just Moved in Next Door?*, 1991
  A tour through a popular neighborhood where an assortment of monsterous neighbors react to the arrival of their new neighbors, a normal human family.
Audrey Wood, *Rude Giants*, 1993
  Beatrix the butter maid saves Gerda the cow and transforms two rude giants into good neighbors.

1517

Barbara Robinson

Illustrator: Judith Gwyn Brown

The Best Christmas Pageant Ever (New York: Harper, 1972)

Age range: Grades 3-5

Subject(s): Christmas; Humor

Major character(s): Claude Herdman, Child; Imogene Herdman, Child; Alice Wendleken, Child

Time period(s): 1970s

Locale(s): United States

What the book is about: The six Herdman children have a terrible reputation. They lie, steal, smoke cigars and talk dirty. When they decide to take part in the town's Christmas pageant, everyone is surprised. The Herdmans come because they heard that you get treats to eat when you go to Sunday School. The result is both hilarious and thought provoking.

Where it's reviewed:
Booklist, March 1, 1973, page 650
Hornbook, December 1972, page 582
Kirkus Reviews, November 1, 1972, pagss 1240

Awards the book has won:
Georgia Children's Book Award 1976

Other books by the author:
My Brother Louis Measures Worms and Other Louis Stories, 1988
Temporary Times, Temporary Places, 1982
Trace through the Forest, 1965

Other books you might like:
Tomie De Paola, *The Christmas Pageant*, 1978
  The story of the nativity as performed in a children's Christmas pageant.
Shirley Hughes, *Another Helping of Chips*, 1986
  Four humorous episodes in the adventures of Chips and his friend, Jessie, including one about the excitement of Christmas.
Madeleine L'Engle, *The 24 Days Before Christmas: An Austin Family Story*, 1984
  Seven year old Vicky Austin recounts the events of the 24 days before Christmas as she prepares for her role as an angel in the Christmas pageant.
Alice Parker, *The Get Along Gang and the Christmas Thief*, 1984
  The Get Along Gang's plans for the Christmas pageant go awry when their presents for needy children disappear.
Robert Newton Peck, *Soup on Ice*, 1985
  Robert and Soup engineer an incredible appearance by Santa and his sleigh in their small Vermont town.

1518

Mary Robinson

The Amazing Valvano and the Mystery of the Hooded Rat (Boston: Houghton Mifflin, 1988)

Age range: Grades 4-6

Subject(s): Magicians; Mystery and Detective Stories

Major character(s): Maria Cecelia Valvano, Magician; Joey Perrella, Boyfriend (Maria's); Lester, Rat

Time period(s): 1980s

Locale(s): United States

What the book is about: Maria's plans for her great magic act are going great. She has persuaded her friends Joey and Maxine to assist her and her ex-pet rat, Lester, now owned by Joey, is to be the hit of the show, dressed up as a rabbit. When Lester disappears, the act is in jeopardy and Maria and friends set out to solve the mystery.

Where it's reviewed:
Children's Book Review Service, October 1988, page 22
School Library Journal, April 1988, page 104
Kirkus Reviews, February 15, 1988, page 283

Other books by the author:
Give It Up, Mom, 1989

Other books you might like:
Michael Bedard, *A Darker Magic*, 1989
Three people find their lives in danger when a ghostly magician haunts them with visions of an extraordinary, deadly magic show.
I.G. Edwards, *The Magic Dog*, 1982
Traces the career of the magician known as The Great Lafayette and his partner, an extraordinary dog named Beauty.
Pat Hutchins, *Rats!*, 1989
Sam's insistence on getting a pet rat eventually changes his family's entire daily routine and brings an exciting surprise.
Sonia Levitin, *Rita, the Weekend Rat*, 1971
Describes the events in Cynthia's life as she tries to prove she can provide a good home for the school's pet rat.
Tom McGowen, *The Magician's Company*, 1988
Armindor and his young apprentice, Tigs, return from the wild lands to warn the world that creatures know as reen will rise up and destroy all humans.

1519

Nancy K. Robinson

Oh Honestly, Angela! (New York: Scholastic, 1985)

Age range: Grades 2-4

Subject(s): Poverty; Family Life; Homeless

Major character(s): Tina Steele, Preteen; Angela Steele, Child, Kindergartner; Nathaniel Steele, Child

Time period(s): 1980s

Locale(s): United States

What the book is about: Eleven year old Tina feels her family is poor and everyone else in the world probably has all the material things she wishes she had. A fund raiser for the Rescue the Children Program exposes her to real poverty and want, and she then sees a homeless man searching for food in the trash. She mounts a campaign to "adopt" an orphan. Meanwhile, her little sister Angela doesn't quite get the concept yet. She takes a favorite toy elephant to her kindergarten, she thinks for show and tell, not understanding about the collection of toys for the poor.

Where it's reviewed:
Horn Book, March/April 1986, page 202
School Library Journal, October 1985, page 176

Other books by the author:
The Ghost of Whispering Rock, 1992
Angela, Private Citizen, 1989
Mom, You're Fired, 1983
Veronica, the Show-Off, 1982

Other books you might like:
M.S. Craig, *The Gray Ghosts of Taylor Ridge*, 1978
Nat's pesty little sister, Nan, blackmails him into going out to Taylor Ridge where ghosts are said to lurk after dark.
Astrid Lindgren, *Emil in the Soup Tureen*, 1970
Emil's exploits include stranding his little sister at the top of a flagpole and getting his head stuck in the soup tureen, not once, but twice.
Janet Lorimer, *The Trouble with Buster*, 1990

Danny is responsible for his little sister, Bernice, who is always getting into trouble with her school friend, Buster.
Stephen Manes, *Monstra vs. Irving*, 1989
Irving's plan to scare his bratty little sister, Claire, backfires when she drinks his mail order magic potion and turns into a monster.
Janny Bell White, *Adelaide Stories*, 1972
The story of a little girl and her older sister and baby brother growing up in the early 20th century in Pennsylvania.

1520

Nancy K. Robinson

Veronica Meets Her Match (New York: Scholastic, 1990)

Age range: Grades 3-5

Subject(s): Friendship

Major character(s): Veronica, Child; Crystal Webb, Neighbor

Time period(s): 1990s

Locale(s): United States

What the book is about: Veronica desperately wants to be liked by her new neighbor. They get along great, until Crystal becomes a hit on her own at school. Veronica's friend, Chris, helps her work things out. They work together trying to save their branch library from closing.

Where it's reviewed:
Kirkus Reviews, August 15, 1990, page 1178
School Library Journal, December 1990, page 106

Other books by the author:
Angela and the Broken Heart, 1991
Angela, Private Citizen, 1990
Veronica, the Show-Off, 1982

Other books you might like:
Anne Eliot Crompton, *The Snow Pony*, 1991
Janie eases her lonliness in her new, small town home, by taking a job with "the mad hermit of Winterfield."
Sarah Ellis, *Next-Door Neighbors*, 1990
Peggy is lonely and uncomfortable after a move to a new town until she finds two unusual friends.
Alice Mulcahey Fleming, *Welcome to Grossville*, 1985
After a divorce and move to a new neighborhood, Michael learns the meaning of friendship and finds new values in his rapidly changing life.
Larry King, *Because of Lozo Brown*, 1988
A little boy is afraid to meet his new neighbor but they eventually meet and become friends. (Related picture book)
Mary Stolz, *Cider Days*, 1978
A young girl's persistant overtures to a new neighbor finally pay off and result in a strong friendship.

1521

Nancy K. Robinson

Illustrator: Ingrid Fetz

Wendy and the Bullies (New York: Hastings House, 1980)

Age range: Grades 2-4

Subject(s): Bullies; Communication; Friendship

Major character(s): Wendy, Child; Pat, Bully; Stanley Kane, Bully

Time period(s): 1980s

Locale(s): United States

What the book is about: A young girl is terrorized by several bullies and becomes too scared to ask for help. Finally, she talks to her parents and they share their own childhood experiences with her.

Where it's reviewed:
Children's Book Review Service, September 1980, page 5
Center for Children's Books Bulletin, November 1980, page 63
School Library Journal, January 1981, page 54

Other books by the author:
The Ghost of Whispering Rock, 1992
Angela and the Broken Heart, 1991
Veronica the Show-Off, 1982
Just Plain Cat, 1981

Other books you might like:
Lynley Dodd, *Hairy Maclary From Donaldson's Dairy*, 1983
    A small black dog and his canine friends are terrorized by the local tomcat.
Jayne Harvey, *Great-Uncle Dracula*, 1992
    Emily Normal must adjust to a new town, Transylvania, USA, populated by vampires, witches and the like, and also to a bullying classmate.
Constance Hiser, *Ghosts in Fourth Grade*, 1991
    James and his friends turn the old Hathaway house into a haunted house to scare Mean Mitchell, the class bully, on Halloween night.
Liz Rosenberg, *Monster Mama*, 1993
    Patrick Edward's fierce monster mother helps him deal with some obnoxious bullies.
Harriet May Savitz, *The Bullies and Me*, 1991
    As the new kid in town, Allan is grateful when Tony and Pete befriend him. When they throw rocks at birds, Allan has second thoughts about Them.

1522

Nancy Robison

Illustrator: Karen Loccisano

Ballet Magic (Chicago: Whitman, 1981)

Age range: Grades 4-6

Subject(s): Ballet; Dancing; Self-Acceptance

Major character(s): Stacey, Teenager; Mrs. Fremple, Friend

Time period(s): 1980s

Locale(s): United States

What the book is about: Stacey is self-conscious about her height. She has grown three inches in the last three months. Mrs. Fremple is a short, chubby woman Stacey can tell her troubles to. Maria gets the part Stacey had hoped for. Maria carefully trains her for next year. Stacey becomes the production assistant and saves the day of the performance.

Where it's reviewed:
Booklist, April 1, 1982, page 1022
Children's Book Review Service, May 1982, page 95

School Library Journal, April 1982, page 75

Other books by the author:
Cheeerleading, 1980

Other books you might like:
Miriam Cohen, *Born to Dance Samba*, 1984
    At Carnival time in Brazil, a girl who has spent her life wishing to be chosen queen must cope with the jealousy of her only competitor.
R. Rozanne Knudson, *Zanballer*, 1972
    Zan Hagen, whose principal opposes her un-feminine activities, leads her dance class onto the athletic field to form a girl's football team.
Martha Tolles, *Darci and the Dance Contest*, 1985
    Anxious to make friends in her new school, Darci finds herself drawn into an uneasy relationship with the capricious Lisa and her circle of friends.
Jean Van Leeuwen, *Dear Mom, You're Ruining My Life*, 1989
    Samantha Slayton's eleventh year includes losing her last baby teeth, towering over every boy in dance school, and being mortified by her mother.
Rita Garcia-Williams, *Blue Tights*, 1988
    Growing up in a city neighborhood, Joyce, unsure of herself and not quite comfortable with her maturing body, tries to find solace through dance.

1523

Gail Rock

Illustrator: Charles C. Gehm

The House Without a Christmas Tree (New York: Knopf, 1974)

Age range: Grades 4-6

Subject(s): Christmas; Death; Grief

Major character(s): Addie, Child

Time period(s): 1940s (1946)

Locale(s): United States

What the book is about: Addie can't understand why her father refuses to have a Christmas tree. She defiantly brings the school tree home. When her father becomes furious, she takes the tree to a classmate's home where they are too poor to afford one. Finally, Addie and her dad can talk about her mother's death for the first time.

Where it's reviewed:
Booklist, February 1, 1975, page 572
Center for Children's Books Bulletin, December 1974, page 68
Kirkus Reviews, December 15, 1974, page 1305

Other books by the author:
Addie and the King of Hearts, 1976
A Dream for Addie, 1975
Thanksgiving Treasure, 1974

Other books you might like:
Eve Bunting, *The Day Before Christmas*, 1992
    After her mother's death, seven year old Allie sees "The Nutcracker" with her grandfather who tells about taking her mother to her first Nutcracker.
Fyodor Dostoyevsky, *The Heavenly Christmas Tree*, 1993

A poor boy freezing to death on Christmas Eve finds himself before Christ's Christmas tree with the spirits of other children who have gone to heaven.

Tom T. Hall, *Christmas and the Old House*, 1989
Bobby and Brenda learn about forgiveness and the Christmas spirit when they sneak into an abandoned house to decorate a tree growing through the floor

Rosalie Maggio, *The Music Box Christmas*, 1990
Despite his grandmother's recent death and the return of his troublesome father, Nick is determined that the family have a real Christmas celebration.

Gloria Pushker, *Toby Belfer Never Had a Christmas Tree*, 1991
Living in a small Louisiana town where hers is the only Jewish family, Toby Belfer gives a party for her friends to explain her Hannukah traditions.

1524

Joanne Rocklin

Illustrator: Eileen McKeating

Dear Baby (New York: Macmillan, 1988)

Age range: Grades 5-6

Subject(s): Pregnancy; Letters; Remarriage

Major character(s): Farla, Preteen; Lorraine, Preteen; Charlie, Step-Parent

Time period(s): 1980s

Locale(s): Los Angeles, California

What the book is about: While her mother is pregnant, Farla writes letters to the unborn baby. She tells the baby about her sadness at a fight with her best friend, Lorraine, her worries about not having a curvy figure as soon as some of her girlfriends, and the difficulties with adjusting to her stepfather. The family relationships are nicely drawn, and when the nine months have passed, Farla is ready to welcome the new member of the family.

Where it's reviewed:
Horn Book, September 1988, page 628
School Library Journal, June 1988, page 106

Other books by the author:
Discovering Martha, 1991
Jace the Ace, 1990
Sonia Begonia, 1986

Other books you might like:
Sarah Ellis, *A Family Project*, 1986
Eleven year old Jessica and her family prepare for the changes a new baby will bring to their lives.

Patricia Hermes, *A Place for Jeremy*, 1987
While staying with her grandparents, Jeremy is upset when her parents call from overseas and say they are adopting a new baby sister for her.

Ann M. Martin, *Karen's Baby*, 1992
Karen's friend is going to be a big sister soon, and the two of them eagerly await the baby's arrival. Includes activities to share with babies.

Cynthia Rylant, *A Kindness*, 1988
Chip is upset when his mother becomes pregnant, refuses to name the father, and confronts him with his own possessiveness.

Susan Saunders, *Twin Trouble*, 1989
A new baby compounds Sara's already shaky problem of identity as a twin in a growing family.

1525

Joanne Rocklin

Illustrator: Diane De Groat

Jace the Ace (New York: Macmillan, 1990)

Age range: Grades 3-5

Subject(s): Moving, Household; Photography; Honesty

Major character(s): Jason, Child; Earl, Child

Time period(s): 1990s

Locale(s): Los Angeles, California

What the book is about: Jason moves to Los Angeles with his family. He hopes to have many new friends. He plans on becoming a counterintelligence spy. He wanders around the library with his 5 year old brother, Earl, telling him wildly exaggerated stories about his future career.

Where it's reviewed:
Kirkus Reviews, August 15, 1990, page 1172
School Library Journal, December 1990, page 111

Other books by the author:
Discovering Martha, 1991
Dear Baby, 1988
Sonia Begonia, 1986

Other books you might like:
Linda Gondosch, *The Best Bet Gazette*, 1989
Judy Oliver deals with competition in producing a neighborhood newspapers, and a friend's case of polio in the summer of 1954.

Clifford B. Hicks, *Alvin Fernald, TV Anchorman*, 1980
When Alvin takes a regular spot on a news show, he helps solve an 11 year old crime.

Rebecca C. Jones, *Germy Blew the Bugle*, 1990
Jeremy Bluett starts a school paper with dreams of making a fortune, but his plans backfire.

Marjorie Weinman Sharmat, *Mysteriously Yours, Maggie Marmelstein*, 1982
Named the mystery column writer for the school newspaper, Maggie revels in the power she can wield.

1526

Joanne Rocklin

Illustrator: Julie Downing

Sonia Begonia (New York: Macmillan, 1986)

Age range: Grades 4-6

Subject(s): Humor; Self-Acceptance

Major character(s): Sonia Begley, Preteen; Jason, Preteen

Time period(s): 1980s (1986)

Locale(s): United States

What the book is about: Sonia Begley wants to follow in her family's footsteps and open her own business, which she does with some amusing results when she opens a house-watching service in a robbery-plagued neighborhood. She and her friend, Jason, open Sonia's Safety Sentinel Service. She encounters one disaster after another and discovers that success in business isn't everything, and one can profit from even the worst disasters.

Where it's reviewed:
Booklist, March 15, 1986, page 1087
Center for Children's Books Bulletin, September 1986, page 17
Kirkus Reviews, February 1, 1986, page 213

Other books by the author:
Discovering Martha, 1991
Jace the Ace, 1990
Dear Baby, 1988

Other books you might like:
Alice E. Christgau, *The Laugh Peddler: A Story*, 1968
  After his parents' death a boy has difficulty adjusting to life until an amiable peddler helps him find self-confidence and family acceptance.
Louis Sacher, *Someday Angeline*, 1983
  As an eight year old genius in sixth grade, Angeline is not too popular, but she tries to adjust to being different.
Doris Buchanan Smith, *Best Girl*, 1993
  As she struggles to cope with a difficult mother and finding her place in the world, Nealy finds solace in the safety beneath her neighbor's porch.
Mary Stolz, *The Explorer of Barkham Street*, 1985
  Reformed bully Martin fantasizes about heroic adventures as an explorer and a sports star, until his real life becomes as exciting as his daydreams.
Alexandra Whitaker, *Dream Sister*, 1986
  Ann is haunted by fears of failure, jealousy of her little sister, and a recurring dream in which a phantom sister tries to communicate with her.

1527

Anne Rockwell

The Gollywhopper Egg (New York: Macmillan, 1974)

Age range: Grades 1-2

Series: Ready to Read

Subject(s): Humor

Major character(s): Timothy Todd, Peddler; Mr. Foote, Farmer

Time period(s): Indeterminate

Locale(s): United States

What the book is about: Timothy Todd tries and tries to pedal a coconut and finally gets Farmer Foote to take it off his hands by telling him it is a Gollywhopper egg, and making extravagant promises about all the things Gollywhoppers can do for a farmer. Farmer Foote trys for a long time to hatch a coconut!

Where it's reviewed:
Kirkus Reviews, January 1, 1974, page 4
Hornbook, April 1974, page 142
Library Journal, May 15, 1974, page 1485

Other books by the author:
Come to Town, 1987
Emergency Room, 1985

Honk Honk!, 1980
The Story Snail, 1974

Other books you might like:
Eve Bunting, *Monkey in the Middle*, 1984
  When Hashim and Mohammed, two coconut pickers who were once friends, quarrel over a bicycle, Mohammed's monkey finds a way to make peace.
Ikuyo Isami, *The Fox's Egg*, 1988
  Fox discovers an egg and decides it would be tastier hatched. Sitting on the egg makes the fox feel protective and gives him some unexpected problems.
Lee Lorenz, *Dinah's Egg*, 1990
  A cumulative series of slapstick near-disasters befalls a dinosaur egg before it lands safely in its mother's nest in time to hatch.
Robert M. Quackenbush, *Sherlock Chick and the Giant Egg Mystery*, 1988
  Sherlock tries to solve the mystery of the giant egg that arrives at the farm.
Chyng Feng Sun, *Square Beak*, 1993
  Square Beak, famous for the beautiful and unusual eggs she lays, abandons an egg-laying contest to return to what she loves, traveling and dreaming.

1528

Thomas Rockwell

Illustrator: Emily Arnold McCully

How to Eat Fried Worms (New York: Watts, 1973)

Age range: Grades 3-5

Subject(s): Food; Humor; Animals/Worms

Major character(s): Billy Forrester, Child; Alan, Friend (challenger)

Time period(s): 1970s

Locale(s): United States

What the book is about: Billy Forrester bets a friend, Alan, $50 that he can eat fifteen worms, one a day for fifteen days. The biggest challenge is finding new and different ways to fix them. Billy tries worm pie, worm loaf, Alsatian smothered worms, and your basic fried worms. When he realizes he is going to lose his money, Alan does everything he can to keep Billy from finishing his planned meals.

Where it's reviewed:
Booklist, November 15, 1973, paage 342
Kirkus Reviews, August 15, 1973, page 883
School Library Journal, August 1980, page 70

Awards the book has won:
California Young Reader Medal 1975

Other books by the author:
How to Get Fabulously Rich, 1990
How to Fight a Girl, 1987
The Thief, 1977
Neon Motorcycle, 1973

Other books you might like:
Eleanor Clymer, *Hamburgers - And Ice Cream for Desert*, 1975
  Two families are stranded on a desert island and discover that there are other things to eat besides hamburgers, mash potatoes, peas, and ice cream.

Martyn N. Godfrey, *I Spent My Summer Vacation Kidnapped into Space*, 1990
> Reeann and her best friend, Jared, are kidnapped by Torkan aliens and taken to the planet of Freetal to fight Andovian slime worms.

Daniel Manus Pinkwater, *Slaves of Spiegel: A Magic Moscow Story*, 1982
> Steve Nickelson, his assistant Norman, and the Magic Moscow restaurant are sent through space to compete in an intergalactic junk food cooking contest

Barbara Robinson, *My Brother Louis Measures Worms and Other Louis Stories*, 1988
> Young Mary Elizabeth relates the humorous misadventures of her brother, Louis, and the other wacky members of her unpredictable, very odd family.

Jean Van Leeuwen, *Benjy and the Power of Zingies*, 1982
> Benjy, tired of being small for his age, decides to build up his body by eating the breakfast cereal of the sports stars.

1529

Emily Rodda

Illustrator: Noela Young

Finders Keepers (New York: Greenwillow, 1991)

Age range: Grades 4-7

Subject(s): Space and Time; Fantasy; Computers

Major character(s): Patrick, Child; Lucky Lamont, Robot; Estelle, Babysitter

Time period(s): 1990s

Locale(s): United States

What the book is about: Patrick gets an invitation while playing a computer game at the store. He turns to channel eight the following Saturday and finds himself a contestant on a game show in a parallel universe. He must find three lost items to win fabulous prizes. Great fantasy!

Where it's reviewed:
Booklist, November 15, 1991, page 625

Other books by the author:
The Best Kept Secret, 1990
Pigs Are Flying!, 1988
Something Special, 1984

Other books you might like:
Janet Asimov, *Norby and the Queen's Necklace*, 1986
> Jeff and Norby are transported back to France in 1785 and become involved in the creation of alternate futures for Earth.

Sandy Landsman, *The Gadget Factor*, 1984
> Two students create the ultimate computer game - their own universe.

Madeleine L'Engle, *Many Waters*, 1986
> The Murray twins are accidentally sent back to the time when a man named Noah is building a hugh boat.

Ruth Nichols, *The Marrow of the World*, 1972
> Philip and Linda become involved in a world of witches and evil forces while exploring an ancient castle.

Sally Farrell Odgers, *Drummond: The Search for Sarah*, 1990
> A teddy bear comes to life and begins a search for his original owner.

1530

Emily Rodda

Illustrator: Noela Young

The Pigs Are Flying! (New York: Greenwillow, 1988)

Age range: Grades 3-6

Subject(s): Adventure and Adventurers; Fantasy; Animals/Pigs

Major character(s): Rachel, Child; Burt, Child

Time period(s): 1980s

Locale(s): Australia

What the book is about: Rachel's friend Burt, who has come to cheer her up when she is sick with a bad cold and complaining that her life is boring, makes her believe the impossible. Rachel finds herself transported to a peculiar town where periodic storms appear and cause strange events. Pigs fly and people run for cover.

Where it's reviewed:
Horn Book, November/December 1988, page 784
School Library Journal, September 1988, page 185

Awards the book has won:
Australian Children's Book of the Year Award 1986

Other books by the author:
The Best Kept Secret, 1990
Finders Keepers, 1990
Something Special, 1984

Other books you might like:
Carole S. Adler, *Help, Pink Pig!*, 1990
> A lonely girl, recently moved to California with her mother, escapes both boredom and the local bully by entering a fantasy world.

Walter R. Brooks, *Freddy and the Perilous Adventure*, 1942
> A ballooning accident sends Freddy the pig and his friends on the trail of a blackmailing scheme and into the boxing ring.

Arthur Geisert, *Pa's Balloon and Other Pig Tales*, 1984
> A pig family take their new balloon for a ride, race it, and eventually fly it over the North Pole.

Dick King-Smith, *Pigs Might Fly: A Novel*, 1990
> A runt piglet with deformed front feet becomes a hero when the farm is flooded.

Carl Sandburg, *Rootabaga Stories*, 1974
> A collection of Sandburg's fantasy about the Rootabaga Country, where there are many amazing sights, including checkered and polka-dotted pigs.

1531

Mary Rodgers

A Billion for Boris (New York: Harper and Row, 1974)

Age range: Grades 5-7

Subject(s): Television; Magic; Fantasy

Major character(s): Boris Harris, Teenager; Annabel Andrews, Teenager; Ben "Ape Face" Andrews, Child

Time period(s): 1970s

Locale(s): New York, New York

What the book is about: When they discover an old TV that plays tomorrow's programs, fourteen year old Annabel and her fifteen year old boyfriend, Boris, try to use it to earn money to renovate Boris' eccentric mother. Meanwhile, Ape Face, (Annabel's little brother, Ben) trades away the magic TV for something he wants more.

Where it's reviewed:
Kirkus Reviews, October 15, 1974, page 1104
Booklist, October 1, 1974, page 180
Center for Children's Books Bulletin, April 1975. page 136

Other books by the author:
Summer Switch, 1982
Freaky Friday, 1972

Other books you might like:
Barbara Dillon, *A Mom by Magic*, 1990
  Jessica's wish for a mother results in some wacky, yet endearing adventures with a mannequin mom brought alive by magic power.
Beatrice Gormley, *More Fifth Grade Magic*, 1989
  Wishing she could be more assertive with her domineering mother, Amy Sacher finds a magic calendar that can change her life.
Kathleen Krull, *Alex Fitzgerald, TV Star*, 1991
  Alex's new friendships in California are endangered when her chance to appear in a rock video brings her glamour and an inflated ego.
Joel L. Schwartz, *How to Get Rid of Your Older Brother*, 1992
  It hasn't been easy being for Jay being Louis' brother. One night, Louis refuses to give up the remote TV control, and it's Jay's turn to get even.
Elvira Woodruff, *The Summer I Shrank My Grandmother*, 1990
  Nelly uses a magic chemistry set to make her grandmother young again, but is unable to stop the process. when the woman becomes a baby.

1532

Mary Rodgers

A Billion for Boris (New York: Harper, 1974)

Age range: Grades 4-6

Subject(s): Mothers and Sons; Television; Fantasy

Major character(s): Boris, Teenager; Annabel, Teenager

Time period(s): 1970s

Locale(s): England

What the book is about: Boris has an old TV set that gives the next day's news, which give him an extra edge on crime, races, and the stock market. His mother is a little eccentric and Boris really wants to change her life. When is mom is away, Boris completely redoes their apartment, which brings quite a reaction from her.

Where it's reviewed:
Center for Children's Books Bulletin, April 1975, page 136
Hornbook, October 1974, page 144
Kirkus Reviews, October 15, 1974, page 1104

Other books by the author:
Summer Switch, 1982
Freaky Friday, 1972

Other books you might like:
Kevin Henkes, *Return to Sender*, 1984
  When Whitaker writes a letter to Frogman, TV super hero, his family laughs, but they stop laughing and start wondering when he receives an answer.
Clifford B. Hicks, *Alvin Fernald, TV Anchorman*, 1980
  When Alvin takes a regular spot on a news show, he helps solve an eleven year old crime.
Charles Land, *Calling Earth*, 1978
  Two teenagers are asked to meet the sender of an intergalactic radio message inside the Great Caverns in exaclty eight hours.
Joel L. Schwartz, *How to Get Rid of Your Older Brother*, 1992
  Being Louis's younger brother hasn't been easy. Then one fated night Louis refuses to give up the remote control, and it's Jay's turn to get even.
Isaac Asimov, *Tomorrow's TV*, 1982
  Four stories from science fiction masters. Isaac Asimov, Jack C. Haldeman, II, Ray Bradbury and Robert Bloch contribute short stories.

1533

Mary Rodgers

Freaky Friday (New York: Harper and Row, 1972)

Age range: Grades 4-6

Subject(s): Fantasy; Identity; Mothers and Daughters

Major character(s): Annabel Andrews, Teenager; Benjamin "Ape Face" Andrews, Child; Ellen Jean Andrews, Parent

Time period(s): 1970s

Locale(s): New York, New York

What the book is about: A thirteen year old girl gains a much more sympathetic understanding of her relationship with her mother when she has to spend a day in her mother's body. Mother is in Annabel's body and has to go to school, while Annabel hilariously handles adult responsibilities.

Where it's reviewed:
Booklist, June 15, 1972, page 910
Kirkus Reviews, March 1, 1972, page 267
Hornbook, August 1972, page 378

Other books by the author:
Summer Switch, 1982
A Billion for Boris, 1974
The Mad Show: A Musical Based on Mad Magazine, 1966

Other books you might like:
Eve Bunting, *The Cloverdale Switch*, 1979
  John begins to suspect that his girlfriend and several other Cloverdale citizens are really alien beings.
Matt Christopher, *The Great Quarterback Switch*, 1984
  Michael, confined to a wheel chair, uses mental telepathy to communicate football plays to his twin brother, then finds himself on the field himself.
Amy Ehrlich, *The Dark Card*, 1993
  After her mother's death, Laura is lured by Atlantic City's casinos, and uses her mother's jewelry and makeup to create a new identity for herself.
Jesse Harris, *The Possession*, 1992
  McKenzie must use her special psychic power to save herself and her friends when a Halloween costume leads to a deadly new identity for Lilicat.

Anne Lindbergh, *Three Lives to Live*, 1992
Garet's quiet life with her grandmother is changed when down the laundry chute comes Garet's "twin," Daisy, whose true identity comes as a surprise.

1534

Bella Rodman

Lions in the Way (Chicago: Follett, 1966)

Age range: Grades 5 and Up

Subject(s): Race Relations

Major character(s): Robby Jones, Teenager

Time period(s): 1960s

Locale(s): South

What the book is about: This is the story of what it was like for eight black students who first integrated a white school.

Where it's reviewed:
Library Journal, July 1966, page 3546
Saturday Review of Literature, November 12, 1966, page 54

Awards the book has won:
Nancy Bloch Memorial Award 1966

Other books by the author:
Fiorella La Guardia, 1962 (adult biography)

Other books you might like:
Ann Waldron, *Integration of Mary-Larkin Thornhill*, 1975
A southern girl enters junior high at the beginning of school integration.
Robert Coles, *Saving Face*, 1972
A school incident with racial overtones creates problems within a white policeman's family.
Jacqueline Woodson, *Last Summer with Maizon*, 1990
11 year old Margaret must accept the inevitable when her father dies and her best friend goes away.
Kay Brown, *Willy's Summer Dream*, 1989
Willy faces another dull summer until tutoring from an older girl helps him develop self-esteem.
Jane Claypool Miner, *Tough Guy: Black in a White World*, 1982
When Larry's family moves, he is one of six black students in his new school, and he must deal with prejudice, as well as reflect on his own behavior.

1535

Maia Rodman

Shadow of a Bull (New York: Atheneum, 1964)

Age range: Grades 5 and Up

Subject(s): Bullfighting

Major character(s): Manolo Olivar, Child; Juan Olivar, Bullfighter

Time period(s): 1940s

Locale(s): Arcangel, Spain

What the book is about: Against his silent wishes, the surviving son of a great bullfighter is expected to follow in his father's footsteps. Manolo doubts his courage. Finally he has

the opportunity to prove his courage and confess that he doesn't wish to become a bullfighter.

Where it's reviewed:
Horn Book, June 1964, page 293
New York Times Book Review, March 22, 1964, page 22

Other books by the author:
The Life and Death of a Brave Bull, 1972
Don't Play Dead Before You Have To, 1970
Kingdom in a Horse, 1966

Other books you might like:
Helen Griffith, *Dancing Horses*, 1981
Francisco loves the golden colt, Gavilan, and dreams of riding him in the rejoneo, the mounted bullfighting.
Zibby Oneal, *In Summer Light*, 1985
Kate spends the summer with her strong-willed artist father and has the courage to pursue her own artistic goals.
Robert Vaura, *Felipe, the Bullfighter*, 1968
A young boy from a long line of matadors gets his first chance to fight a bull. (Related picture book)
Claudia Von Canon, *Inheritance*, 1983
A young nobleman in Padua goes home to Spain and is plunged into the treachery of the Inquisition.

1536

Colby Rodowsky

Illustrator: Kathleen Collins Howell

Dog Days (New York: Farrar Strauss and Giroux, 1990)

Age range: Grades 4-6

Subject(s): Friendship

Major character(s): Rosy Riggs, Preteen

Time period(s): 1980s

Locale(s): United States

What the book is about: Rosy is bored, with her best friend and favorite babysitter both gone and her mother now working full time. A new classmate, whom Rosy calls Skinnybones, is her only diversion. Predictably, Rosy begins to see beyond outward appearances and readers will enjoy this budding friendship.

Where it's reviewed:
Booklist, January 1, 1991, page 928
Hornbook, March 1991, page 202
Kirkus Reviews, December 1, 1990, page 1677

Other books by the author:
Sydney, Herself, 1989
The Gathering Room, 1981
Evy-Ivy-Over, 1978
P.S. Write Soon: A Novel, 1978

Other books you might like:
Sheila Cole, *Meaning Well*, 1974
A sixth grader learns the meaning of friendship too late to help a classmate who desperately needed a friend.
Nancy J. Hopper, *The Queen of Put-Down*, 1991
When she tries to befriend Sabrina, a new girl in class, Cassie finds the biggest obstacle is Sabrina's personality.
Thomas Rockwell, *How to Fight a Girl*, 1987

Joe and Alan's plan to get revenge on Billy backfires when their secret weapon, a girl in their class, becomes Billy's friend instead.

Maggie Twohill, *Valentine Frankenstein*, 1991
Amanda plans to boost her friend Walter's popularity by stuffing the Valentine Day Box, but her plan works so well she wonders if it was a mistake.

Joan T. Zier, *Stick Boy*, 1993
Skinny, self-conscious Eric, a misfit and the victim of the school bully, befriends Cynthia, a spirited black girl who is disabled.

1537

Colby Rodowsky

The Gathering Room (New York: Farrar, 1981)

Age range: Grades 4-6

Subject(s): Family Life; Cemeteries

Major character(s): Mudge Stokes, Child; Ned Stokes, Parent, Worker (graveyard caretaker); Dorro, Spirit

Time period(s): 1980s

Locale(s): United States

What the book is about: In the graveyard where his parents are caretakers, Mudge grows up surrounded by ghosts. Overseen by his reclusive parents, he is unfamiliar with the world outside the cemetery. When Mudge finally and reluctantly enters the outside world, his Aunt Ernestus helps restore family ties and eases his adjustment to the living.

Where it's reviewed:
Horn Book, October 1981, page 537
School Library Journal, December 1981, page 146

Other books by the author:
Sydney, Herself, 1989 (young adult fiction)
Julie's Daughter, 1985 (young adult fiction)
Evy-Ivy-Over, 1978
P.S. Write Soon: A Novel, 1978

Other books you might like:
Joan Aiken, *Return to Harken House*, 1988
In the 1930s, 11-year-old Julia spends the summer with her father and is haunted by strange voices.

Pam Conrad, *Stonewords: A Ghost Story*, 1990
Zoe discovers an 11-year-old girl ghost who takes her back to 1870 and the day of her death.

Sid Fleischman, *The Midnight Horse*, 1990
A ghostly magician helps Touch stay out of the orphanage and thwart his great-uncle's foul plans.

Jean Karl, *Beloved Benjamin Is Waiting*, 1978
Lucinda hides in the caretaker's house of a local cemetery where she makes contacts with beings from another planet.

Eleanora E. Tate, *The Secret of Gumbo Grove*, 1987
11-year-old Raisin helps restore a church cemetery and solves a mystery about the founding of her town.

1538

Colby Rodowsky

H, My Name Is Henley (New York: Farrar, Straus and Giroux, 1982)

Age range: Grades 5-6

Subject(s): Mothers and Daughters; Single Parent Families

Major character(s): Henley, Preteen; Patti, Parent; Mercy, Relative (aunt)

Time period(s): 1980s

Locale(s): Baltimore, Maryland; New York, New York

What the book is about: Patti and her daughter, Henley, are always on the move. Happiness is always right around the next corner. Patti uses up nearly all of the $1,000 Henley's paternal grandparents gave her when her dad died, leaving only $50 for emergencies. Aunt Mercy takes them in. Henley becomes tired of following her irresponsible mother around and makes her own secure world.

Where it's reviewed:
Hornbook, April 1983, page 167
Kirkus Reviews, November 15, 1982, page 1236
School Library Journal, January 1983, page 87

Other books by the author:
Dog Days, 1990
Fitchett's Folly, 1987
The Gathering Room, 1981
A Summer's Worth of Shame, 1980

Other books you might like:
Peter Dickinson, *The Devil's Children*, 1986
After the Changes begin, Nicola finds herself abandoned and wandering in an England where everyone has suddenly developed a hatred for machines.

Faye Gibbons, *Mighty Close to Heaven*, 1985
When Dave runs away from his grandparents' farm and makes his way through the mountains to rejoin his wandering father, he finds disappointment.

Lynn Hall, *Nobody's Dog*, 1973
After months of wandering a huge, ugly strange dog is finally befriended by an unhappy misfit of a boy to the benefit of both.

Mollie Hunter, *Cat, Herself*, 1985
Growing up in a family of wandering tinkers in Scotland, Cat McPhie fights for the right to be her own person and live the kind of life she wants.

Joan Phipson, *Bianca*, 1988
Finding Bianca wandering in a state of amnesia after a devestating scene with her mother, Hubert and his sister take her home to live in their home.

1539

Jean Rogers

Illustrator: Rie Munoz

Goodbye, My Island (New York: Greenwillow, 1983)

Age range: Grades 4-5

Subject(s): Eskimos

Major character(s): Esther Atoolik, Preteen (Eskimo); Dixon, Friend; Father Thomas, Religious (pastor)

Time period(s): 1960s (1964)

Locale(s): King Island, Alaska

What the book is about: Esther Atoolik tells of the last winter her people spend on King Island, Alaska in the early

1960s. In the middle of the Bering Sea, the island is ice-bound and inaccessible all winter. There is one school, one church, and one tiny store in the community.

Where it's reviewed:
Booklist, April 15, 1983, page 1098
Hornbook, August 1983, page 447
Kirkus, May 1, 1983, page 525

Other books by the author:
Raymond's Best Summer, 1990
Dinosaurs Are 568, 1988
King Island Christmas, 1985
The Secret Moose, 1985

Other books you might like:
Roxanne Chadwick, *Don't Shoot*, 1978
    Nick, the Eskimo boy, loves the wild creatures of his land and hates the outsiders who come to kill. A good story for reluctant readers.
Arnold A. Griese, *The Wind Is Not a River*, 1978
    As the only ones not captured when the Japanese take over their Aleutian island village during World War Two, two children must survive on their own.
James A. Houston, *The Falcon Bow*, 1986
    Kungo, a young Inuit, seeks to prevent a bloody feud when his people and a rival tribe find themselves in competition for dwindling food supplies.
Guenn Martin, *Remember the Eagle Day*, 1984
    Accompanying her parents to an Alaskan island to run a fishing business, Melanie's outlook changes after befriending a helpful old man who soon dies.
Carter Wilson, *On Firm Ice*, 1969
    A series of tales about the life of a Netsilik Eskimo family during the long winter of Northern Canada.

1540

Jean Rogers

Illustrator: Marylin Hafner

Raymond's Best Summer (New York: Greenwillow, 1990)

Age range: Grades 2-3

Subject(s): Summer; Sports/Swimming

Major character(s): Raymond, Child

Time period(s): 1990s

Locale(s): United States

What the book is about: There are surprises in store for Raymond the summer between first and second grade. He does well in his swimming class and he's the key witness leading to the capture of a ring of thieves. He is invited to California to visit his grandmother where he sees a whale exhibition.

Where it's reviewed:
Kirkus Reviews, July 1, 1990, page 1752
School Library Journal, December 1990, page 86

Other books by the author:
Dinosaurs Are 568, 1988
King Island Christmas, 1985
The Secret Moose, 1985
Goodbye, My Island, 1983

Other books you might like:
Ellen Conford, *A Job for Jenny Archer*, 1988
    9 year old Jenny is determined to make money, thinking her family poor because her parents refuse to get her a horse or a swimming pool.
Leonard Kessler, *Last One in Is a Rotten Egg*, 1969
    After Freddy is pushed into deep water by a couple of bullies, he decides to learn to swim.
Jean Marzollo, *Cannonball Chris*, 1987
    Chris tries to overcome his fear of jumping into deep water in time for the second grade swimming party.
Leonard Shortall, *Tony's First Dive*, 1872
    Tony learns to swim and dive with the help of a face mask.
Valerie Tripp, *Molly Saves the Day*, 1988
    Molly conquers her fear of swimming underwater when she and some other campers play "Color War."

1541

Jean Rogers

Illustrator: Jim Fowler

The Secret Moose (New York: Greenwillow, 1985)

Age range: Grades 3-4

Subject(s): Animals/Moose; Wildlife Rescue

Major character(s): Gerald, Child; Anita, Child

Time period(s): 1980s

Locale(s): Fairbanks, Alaska

What the book is about: A young boy living in Alaska develops an interest in moose and their habits after he sees a moose in his backyard and decides to follow her and finds her injured. He nurses her back to health and she shares the birth of her calf with him.

Where it's reviewed:
Booklist, August 1985, page 1670
Kirkus, May 15, 1985, page J35
School Library Journal, October 1985, page 176

Other books by the author:
Raymond's Best Summer, 1990
Runaway Mittens, 1988
King Island Christmas, 1985
Goodbye, My Island, 1983

Other books you might like:
David R. Collins, *Hali's Amazing Wings*, 1987
    Recounts the life of a bald eagle in Alaska from birth to first flight, mating, and forty years later, death.
Justin F. Denzel, *Black Kettle: King of the Wild Horses*, 1974
    A wild black stallion, coveted by all who see him, is protected from capture by an Indian youth.
Lillian Nordlicht, *The Call of the Wild*, 1980
    An unusual dog, part St. Bernard, part Scotch shepherd, is forcibly taken to Alaska where he eventually becomes leader of a wolf pack.
Daniel Manus Pinkwater, *Blue Moose*, 1975
    Mr. Breton runs a restaurant on the edge of the big north woods. One day he meets a talking blue moose who drops in to get warm and then stays on.
Miriam Schlein, *The Year of the Panda*, 1990

A Chinese boy rescues a starving baby panda, and, in the process, learns why pandas are endangered, and what the government is doing to save them.

Pamela Rogers

The Rare One (Nashville, Tennessee: T. Nelson, 1974)

Age range: Grades 4-6

Subject(s): Friendship; Self-Respect

Major character(s): Toby Grant, Teenager; Josh Penfold, Recluse

Time period(s): 1970s

Locale(s): England

What the book is about: Unhappy about his father's re-marriage, thirteen year old Toby finds friendship with an old man living alone in the woods in a well-hidden dugout hut. When the relationship ends with the old man's death, Toby's grief and guilt bring him closer to his own family.

Where it's reviewed:
Center for Children's Books Bulletin, May 1975, page 155
Kirkus Reviews, October 15, 1974, page 1105
Library Journal, October 15, 1974, page 2742

Other books by the author:
The Stone Angel, 1975
The Weekend, 1973

Other books you might like:
Dana Brenford, *Tracks in the North Woods*, 1988
When twins Peter and Jason and their stepsister Kim visit Canada's North Woods, they investigate the disappearance of an elderly woman hermit.
Anne Eliot Crompton, *The Snow Pony*, 1991
Moving to a small Massachusetts town and finding it hard to make friends, Jannie takes a job with Mr. Flower, "the mad hermit of Winterfield."
Anne Merrick Epstein, *Good Stones*, 1977
An aging ex-con who lives as a hermit joins with an orphan, and together they make a life for themselves, surviving the rejection of society.
David Roth, *The Hermit of Fog Hollow Station*, 1980
Lonely after his family moves from Boston to the country, twelve year old Alex befriends an old hermit.
Colin Thiele, *The Shadow on the Hills*, 1977
A young boy is caught in a dilemma when his friend, an old hermit, is accused of burning down their small Australian farming community.

Pamela Rogers

The Stone Angel (Nashville, Tennessee: Nelson, 1975)

Age range: Grades 4-6

Subject(s): Saints

Major character(s): Rab Banerjee, Immigrant; Susan Banerjee, Animal Lover

Time period(s): 1970s

Locale(s): England

What the book is about: Susan's father is a gravedigger and her mother is distracted with Susan's sister who is pregnant. A gravestone angel points the way for Susan. She could be a saint! Like St. Francis, Susan is sure she can tame animals by love.

Where it's reviewed:
Center for Children's Books Bulletin, December 1976, page 65
Kirkus Reviews, May 15, 1976, page 594
School Library Journal, September 1976, page 124

Other books by the author:
The Rare One, 1974

Other books you might like:
Vivien Alcock, *The Stonewalkers*, 1981
A statue of Belladonna, brought to life by a flash of lightning, gather a stone army from gardens and churches as Poppy and her friend Emma watch.
Tomie De Paola, *Francis, the Poor Man of Assisi*, 1982
A biography of the wealthy young Italian who gave away all his possessions to become a wandering preacher and protector of animals.
Betsy Haynes, *The Ghost of the Gravestone Hearth*, 1977
Charley's summer at the beach promises to be uneventful until the ghost of a sailor who died in 1712 persuades him to help dig for buried treasure.
Theodora Kroeber, *Carrousel*, 1977
The winged carrousel horse has wildness carved in his wings, and it takes more than courage to rescue him from the danger of becoming a mere statue.
Barbara Wersba, *The Crystal Child*, 1982
A young boy is haunted by, and later falls in love with, a crystal statue of a young girl of long ago.

Peter Roop

Illustrator: Peter E. Hansom

Keep the Lights Burning, Abbie (Minneapolis: Carolrhoda, 1985)

Age range: Grades 1-3

Subject(s): Lighthouses; Biography

Major character(s): Abbie Burgess, Lighthouse Keeper, Historical Figure

Time period(s): 1850s (1856)

Locale(s): Maine

What the book is about: Abbie's father is a lighthouse keeper trapped on the mainland during a bad storm and Abbie keeps the light on in the lighthouse for four weeks while caring for her two sisters and invalid mother. Good historical fiction for beginning readers.

Where it's reviewed:
Center for Children's Books Bulletin, January 1985, page 92
School Library Journal, December 1984, page 94

Other books by the author:
Ahyoka and the Talking Leaves, 1992
One Earth, a Multitude of Creatures, 1992
I, Columbus: My Journal 1492-1493, 1990

Buttons for General Washington, 1986

Other books you might like:

Edward Ardizonne, *Tim to the Lighthouse*, 1968
   One stormy night the lighthouse is dark, so Tim awakens Captain McFee and they row out to see what has happened to the keeper and the light.

Debby L. Carter, *Clipper*, 1981
   During a terrible storm, a lonely lighthouse keeper has a visitor who turns out to be just the friend he is looking for.

Dorothy Holder Jones, *Abbie Burgess, Lighthouse Heroine*, 1969
   A fictionalized biography for older readers and also a good resource for gifted readers or teachers using the beginning reader with students.

Sonia Levitin, *All the Cats in the World*, 1982
   An old woman is taunted by the lighthouse keeper for feeding the abandoned cats that live nearby, but when she falls ill, he has a change of heart.

Hildegarde Hoyt Swift, *The Little Red Lighthouse and the Great Gray Bridge*, 1942
   A little lighthouse on the Hudson River regains its pride when it finds out that it is still useful and has an important job to do.

1545

Stephen Roos

Illustrator: Dee DeRosa

My Favorite Ghost (New York: Atheneum, 1988)

Age range: Grades 6-8

Subject(s): Ghosts; Islands; Money

Major character(s): Derek Malloy, Teenager; Margo Malloy; Kit Malloy

Time period(s): 1980s

Locale(s): Plymouth Island (New England)

What the book is about: Derek does not believe there are ghosts on Plymouth Island, or anywhere else. But realizing that many others believe in them, Derek dupes his friends into paying admission to a "haunted house" involving the legend of a local ghost. A Plymouth Island Story.

Where it's reviewed:
Booklist, April 15, 1988, page 1437
Kirkus Reviews, February 15, 1988, page 284
School Library Journal, April 1988, page 104

Other books by the author:
And the Winner Is., 1989
Thirteenth Summer, 1987
Confessions of a Wayward Preppie, 1986
Horrible Secret, 1983

Other books you might like:

Avi, *Something Upstairs: A Tale of Ghosts*, 1988
   Kenny discovers that his new home is haunted by the spirit of a boy who asks him to return to the 19th century to prevent his murder by slave traders.

Eilis Dillon, *The Island of Ghosts*, 1989
   Before leaving for school in Galway, two boys visit their tutor who has moved to a haunted island and has plans to keep them there forever.

Sonia Levitin, *Roanoke: A Novel of the Lost Colony*, 1973

An English youth and an Indian girl are caught up in the events leading to the mysterious disappearance of the colony at Roanoke, Virginia.

Liza Ketchum Murrow, *The Ghosts of Lost Island*, 1991
   While helping his grandfather herd and shear his flock of sheep, Gabe encounters a mysterious woman who may be the ghost of a drowned milkmaid.

L.B. Taylor, *Haunted Houses*, 1983
   Describes thirteen documented cases involving haunted houses and ghost in the U.S., Canada, and England.

1546

Robert Roper

In Caverns of Blue Ice (Boston: Little Brown, 1991)

Age range: Grades 5-9

Subject(s): Mountaineering

Major character(s): Louise DeMaistre, Mountaineer; Lawrence Darnley, Mountaineer

Time period(s): 1960s

Locale(s): Asia (Himalaya Mountains)

What the book is about: Fiction which reads like a documentary of mountain climbing with a budding romance thrown in. We see the main character, Louise DeMaistre face avalanches, frostbite, and all the dangers of the Himalayan Mountains. Louise becomes interested in Lawrence, a Canadian mountain climber. Good adventure with a "happily ever after" ending. Good read aloud.

Where it's reviewed:
Booklist, April 1, 1991, page 1560
School Library Journal, June 1991, page 112

Other books by the author:
Trespassers, 1992 (adult fiction)
Mexico Days, 1991 (adult fiction)
On Spider Creek, 1978 (adult fiction)
Royo County, 1973 (adult fiction)

Other books you might like:

Judy Corbalis, *The Ice Cream House*, 1989
   Delivering an ice pick to his mother in the Himalyas, Oskar and his friend Henrietta meet abominable snowmen and are held in a palace of ice cream.

Jean Craighead George, *On the Far Side of the Mountain*, 1990
   Sam's peaceful existence in his wilderness home is disrupted when his sister runs away and his pet falcon is confiscated by a conservation officer.

Betty Levine, *Hawk High*, 1980
   Toni's plan to climb to a hawk's next to prove her maturity backfires when she is caught in a storm at night on the mountain.

Gloria Skurzynski, *Caught in the Moving Mountains*, 1984
   On a hike in the mountains, two brothers must use their skill to survive when they are confronted with an earthquake and an injured drug dealer.

James Ramsey Ullman, *Banner in the Sky*, 1954
   Rudi's growth from boy to man centers around his desire to climb the great Matterhorn and his mother's fears for his safety.

1547

Joseph Rosenbloom

Maximilian, You're the Greatest (New York: Lodestar, 1979)

Age range: Grades 4-6

Subject(s): Mystery and Detective Stories

Major character(s): Maximilian Augustus Adams, Detective; Peter, Detective; Jessica, Detective

Time period(s): 1970s

Locale(s): New York, New York

What the book is about: Each chapter of this detective story is a new case. They relate the adventures of twelve year old Max and his friends, Peter and Jessica, as they help the police officers of the mid-Manhattan precinct solve a variety of crimes. Solutions are provided at the end of the book. Except for the sequel, Maximilian Does It Again, most of Rosenbloom's books are jokes and riddles.

Where it's reviewed:
Booklist, July 15, 1979, page 1629
School Library Journal, May 1979, page 82
School Library Journal, April 1981, page 131

Other books by the author:
101 Summer Jokes and Riddles, 1988
Maximilian Does It Again, 1983
Official Wild West Joke Book, 1983
Sports Riddles, 1982

Other books you might like:
John Bellairs, *The Chessmen of Doom*, 1989
  A strange will requests that Johnny, Fergy, and Professor Childermass spend the summer at an estate where a madman is bent on destroying the world.
Franklin W. Dixon, *Bad Rap*, 1993
  Frank and Joe think they have solved the case of record counterfeiting by hustler Jack Martinelli, until Martinelli turns up dead.
E.W. Hildick, *Manhattan Is Missing*, 1969
  A boy and his family sublet an apartment in New York on the condition they care for the owner's prized Siamese cat, but suddenly the cat disappears.
Kristi Holl, *Cast a Single Shadow*, 1986
  With her mom arrested as a thief and the police not looking any further for the real criminal, Tracy searches for the dangerous thief alone.
Johanna Hurwitz, *Ali Baba Bernstein, Lost and Found*, 1992
  Throughout a series of adventures, David "Ali Baba" Bernstein spends most of his time thinking about becoming a detective and getting a dog.

1548

Pat Ross

Illustrator: Marylin Hafner

M & M and the Big Bag (New York: Pantheon, 1981)

Age range: Grades 1-3

Subject(s): Shopping; Friendship

Major character(s): Mandy, Child; Mimi, Child; Maxi, Dog

Time period(s): Indeterminate

Locale(s): United States

What the book is about: Mandy and Mimi are best friends who pretend to be twins. They go alone to the supermarket for the first time. Maxi, Mimi's dog, insists on going along. They lose the shopping list, which somehow has made its way into Maxi's mouth.

Where it's reviewed:
Booklist, November 15, 1981, page 448
Kirkus Reviews, October 15, 1981, page 1296
School Library Journal, December 1981, page 75

Other books by the author:
M & M and the Super Child Afternoon, 1987
M & M and the Santa Secrets, 1985
M & M and the Haunted House Game, 1980
Meet M & M, 1980

Other books you might like:
Linda Edwards, *The Downtown Day*, 1983
  Linda's two aunts take her downtown to shop for school clothes, but the only thing she really wants is a red sweater.
Bill Grossman, *Tommy at the Grocery Store*, 1989
  Tommy is mistaken for items in a grocery store until his mother comes to the rescue.
Lisa Passen, *Uncle's New Suit: A Sort of True Story*, 1992
  When Uncle Carmen gets a new job, a close-knit Italian family celebrates by taking him shopping for a new suit.
Nancy Shaw, *Sheep in a Shop*, 1991
  Sheep hunt for a birthday present and make havoc of the shop, only to discover they haven't the money to pay for things.
Harriet Ziefert, *Follow Me!*, 1990
  Lee goes shopping with his mother and follows her until the elevator door closes and he is left alone on the second floor.

1549

Phyllis Rossiter

Moxie (New York: Four Winds, 1990)

Age range: Grades 4-6

Subject(s): Depression (Economic); Drought; Farm Life

Major character(s): Drew Ralston, Teenager; Poke Ralston, Teenager

Time period(s): 1930s

Locale(s): Kansas

What the book is about: Thirteen year old Drew, determined to help his family hold on to their farm in the drought stricken Dust Bowl of 1934, stubbornly tends his livestock and refuses to give up hope.

Where it's reviewed:
Hornbook, July 1990, page 80
School Library Journal, December 1990, page 111
Children's Bookwatch, March 1991, page 3

Other books you might like:
Robert Burch, *Tyler, Wilkin, and Skee*, 1963
  Chronicles one year in the lives of three brothers growing up on a farm during the Depression.
Anna Myers, *Red-Dirt Jessie*, 1992
  Jessie, a young girl living in the Oklahoma dust bowl during the Depression, tries to tame a wild dog and help her father recover from a breakdown.

Violet Olsen, *The Growing Season*, 1982
　　Marie, living on her family's farm in Iowa, learns to face and overcome Depression poverty, family problems, and her own childhood fears.
Violet Olsen, *The View From the Pighouse Roof*, 1987
　　Marie, living with her widowed mother, brothers, and younger sister on a farm during the Depression, tries to cope with the problems of growing up.
Berniece Rabe, *Rass*, 1973
　　Chronicles a young boy's continuing conflict with his father while growing up on a Missouri farm during the Depression.

1550

Margaret I. Rostkowski

After the Dancing Days (New York: Harper, 1986)

Age range: Grades 6 and Up

Subject(s): World War I; Hero; Physically Handicapped

Major character(s): Annie Metcalf, Teenager; Andrew, Veteran

Time period(s): 1910s

Locale(s): Kansas

What the book is about: Annie struggles to love the unlovable and come to terms with the continuing effects of war. At the veterans' hospital where her father, a doctor, works, Annie meets Andrew, a badly burned, bitter young man whom she helps in his adjustment to a new life. An excellent novel for mature readers showing a girl's growth into womanhood in the midst of war.

Where it's reviewed:
Horn Book, January/February 11987, page 61
School Library Journal, October 1986, page 121

Awards the book has won:
Golden Kite Award 1986
International Reading Association Children's Book Award 1986

Other books by the author:
The Best of Friends, 1989

Other books you might like:
John Louis Beatty, *King's Knight's Pawn*, 1971
　　Christopher becomes involved in events that lead to the Roundhead Massacre of the Irish and their Cavalier defenders at Drogheda, in the mid-1600s.
Adele Geras, *The Girls in the Velvet Frame*, 1978
　　In Jerusalem just before WWI, five sisters send their photograph to a New York newspaper hoping to find their brother.
Janet Hickman, *The Stones*, 1976
　　While his father is fighting in Europe, an American boy, motivated by patriotism, harasses an old man who has a German name.
Kathleen Kudlinski, *Pearl Harbor Is Burning*, 1991
　　Frank is unhappy when his family moves to Hawaii in 1941 until he meets a Japanese-American boy who becomes his friend - then Pearl Harbor is bombed.
Elsie McCutcheon, *Summer of the Zeppelin*, 1985
　　During WWI in Britain, twelve year old Elvira promises to help a German prisoner escape.

1551

David Roth

The Hermit of Fog Hollow Station (New York: Beaufort, 1980)

Age range: Grades 4-6

Subject(s): Friendship; Hermits; Moving, Household

Major character(s): Alex, Preteen; Fritz, Preteen; Benny, Preteen

Time period(s): Indeterminate

Locale(s): Boston, Massachusetts

What the book is about: A lonely boy offers friendship to an eccentric old man, Mr. Turner, who lives in the woods. Fritz and Benny think the old man is crazy. They beat up on Alex for befriending the old man. Alex learns that friendship has nothing to do with age and everything to do with loyalty and caring.

Where it's reviewed:
Booklist, March 1, 1981, page 968
Children's Book Review Service, December 1980, page 30
School Library Journal, February 1981, page 70

Other books by the author:
Best of Friends, 1983
The Girl in the Grass, 1982
A World for Joey Carr, 1981

Other books you might like:
Dana Brenford, *Tracks in the North Woods*, 1988
　　When twins Peter and Jason and their stepsister Kim visit Canada's Nort Woods, they investigate the disappearance of an elderly woman hermit.
Clyde Robert Bulla, *White Bird*, 1990
　　A lonely boy is found and reared by a hermit in the wilderness of the Tennessee mountains in the 1990s
Elizabeth Coatsworth, *Grandmother Cat and the Hermit*, 1970
　　On an exploring trip up an arroyo, a young boy and his cat discover the well-hidden home of a hermit who is a friend of all the animals.
Anne Eliot Crompton, *The Snow Pony*, 1991
　　After moving to Massachusetts, Jannie who finds it hard to make friends, takes a job with Mr. Flower, a hermit, helping him train and groom a pony.
Pieter Van Raven, *The Great Man's Secret*, 1989
　　When a recluse novelist , Paul Bernard, is interviewed by student reporter Jerry, Paul writer's block is broken.

1552

Renee Roth-Hano

Touch Wood: A Girlhood in Occupied France (New York: Four Winds, 1988)

Age range: Grades 6-8

Subject(s): Holocaust; Jews

Major character(s): Renee Roth-Hano, Refugee

Time period(s): 1940s

Locale(s): France

What the book is about: An autobiographical novel in diary form written by Renee, beginning in 1940 when she is nine years old. As Hitler's rise to power begins, the family flees from Alsace to Paris. As arrests and deportation of Jews become commonplace, Renee and her two younger sisters are sent to a community of Catholic nuns in Normandy. The strength of the book is in the vivid picture of people and their reactions. A good complement to *Upon the Head of the Goat* (Siegal, 1982) giving more of the French perspective.

Where it's reviewed:
Horn Book, January/February 1989, page 81
School Library Journal, June/July 1988, page 128

Other books you might like:
Miriam Chaikin, *Lower! Higher! You're a Liar!*, 1984
　　Ten year old Molly, daughter of Palestinian parents, organizes a club to boycott the neighborhood bully during a summer in Brooklyn during WWII.
Eilis Dillon, *Children of Bach*, 1992
　　A Hungarian Jewish family of talented musicians escapes Nazi persecution during WWII.
Erwin Herman, *The Yanov Torch*, 1985
　　Jews in a work camp in Yanov during the Nazi occupation of L'vov, Poland, smuggle in a Torah, piece by piece, despite enormous personal danger.
Yuri Suhl, *On the Other Side of the Gate*, 1975
　　Relates the experiences of a young Jewish couple when they are confined to a ghetto during the German occupation of Poland in WWII.
Ida Vos, *Anna Is Still Here*, 1993
　　Thirteen year old Anna who was a "hidden child" in Nazi occupied Holland during WWII, gradually learns to deal with the realities of being a survivor.

1553

Glen Rounds, Author/Illustrator

Blind Outlaw (New York: Holiday House, 1980)

Age range: Grades 3-5

Subject(s): Animals/Horses; Mutism; Physically Handicapped

Major character(s): Blind Outlaw, Horse, Handicapped (blind); Unnamed Character, Handicapped (mute), Child

Time period(s): Indeterminate Past

Locale(s): Montana

What the book is about: The story of a blind horse and a mute boy who tames him. The horse has been mistreated and badly spooked, and only "the boy" can reach him. The horse and his boy, both handicapped, respond to each other and form a lasting bond. The characters all remain nameless. Companion to *The Blind Colt* and *The Stolen Pony*.

Where it's reviewed:
Booklist, October 1, 1980, page 257
Kirkus, February 1, 1981, page 142
School Library Journal, December 1980, page 62

Other books by the author:
Once We Had a Horse, 1971
The Blind Colt, 1960
Lone Muskrat, 1953
Buffalo Harvest, 1952
The Stolen Pony, 1948

Other books you might like:
C.W. Anderson, *The Blind Connemara*, 1971

A young girl is determined that her pony's blindness is not going to keep him from earning the blue ribbon in a horse show.
Diane Johnston Hamm, *Bunkhouse Journal*, 1990
　　Sandy spends the winter helping his cousins on their ranch recording his first love and attempting to sort out his confused feelings for his father.
Mary O'Hara, *My Friend Flicka*, 1941
　　A Wyoming boy begins to learn about responsibility and gain a better understanding of his father through his intense devotion to the foal, Flicka.
Sam Savitt, *Wild Horse Running*, 1973
　　A teen finds an injured mustang and is torn by his desire to keep him and his conviction that wild horses should be protected in their natural state.
Elizabeth Van Steenwyk, *The Secret of the Spotted Horse*, 1983
　　When Reddy goes to visit his aunt and uncle, he is determined to become a rodeo champion, but then someone tries to steal his horse, Ruff.

1554

Glen Rounds

The Day the Circus Came to Lone Tree (New York: Holiday, 1973)

Age range: Grades 2-4

Subject(s): Circus

Major character(s): Linda, Animal Trainer (lion tamer); Dan Dangerfield, Lawman (sheriff); Clyde Jones, Hunter

Time period(s): 19th century

Locale(s): Lone Tree County, West

What the book is about: This book tells the story of why the circus no longer comes to Lone Tree, ever! The circus came once. People came from miles around and were a terrific and awed audience. Most of them had never seen anything like it. But then Linda, the Lady Lion Tamer fired a pistol at a lion, the cowboys thought she was in danger and pandemonium ensued. Animals scattered everywhere and cowboys tried to treat them like cattle. When the circus folks got them rounded up, they left without even waving goodbye.

Where it's reviewed:
Booklist, January 15, 1974, page 545
Kirkus Reviews, October 15, 1973, page 1155
Center for Children's Books Bulletin, January 1974, page 85

Other books by the author:
Four Dollars and Fifty Cents, 1990
Charlie Drives the Stage, 1989
Hanna's Hog, 1988
Mr. Yowder and the Steamboat, 1977

Other books you might like:
David A. Adler, *Cam Jansen and the Mystery of the Circus Clown*, 1983
　　Cam Jansen uses her photographic memory to help find a pickpocket at the circus.
Mercer Mayer, *Liverwurst Is Missing*, 1981
　　When Liverwurst, the baby rhinosterwurst disappears, people join the circus calvery to save him from a tycoon who wants to create Rhino-burgers.
Gary Paulsen, *Dunc and Amos Hit the Big Top*, 1993

In order to impress Melissa, the girl of his dreams, Amos Binder decides to perform on the trapeze at the visiting circus.

Martin Waddell, *Harriet and the Haunted School*, 1984
When Harriet hides a circus horse in the closet at school, its nocturnal wanderings start a rumor that the building is haunted.

Bernard Wiseman, *Morris and Boris at the Circus*, 1988
Morris and Boris go to the circus as spectators and end up being part of the action.

1555

Glen Rounds, Author/Illustrator

Wild Appaloosa (New York: Holiday, 1983)

Age range: Grades 3-5

Subject(s): Animals/Horses

Major character(s): Bert, Preteen

Time period(s): 1980s

Locale(s): United States

What the book is about: An Appaloose filly runs with a herd of wild horses which attracts horse hunters, as well as a young boy named Bert. The hunters capture the herd, but the filly escapes and finds her way into a group of range horses and eventually into Bert's corral. Lots of description of the filly's wanderings. For all horse lovers, and a good read aloud.

Where it's reviewed:
Center for Children's Books Bulletin, December 1983, page 77
School Library Journal, August 1983, page 70

Other books by the author:
Blind Outlaw, 1980
The Blind Colt, 1960
Hunted Horses, 1951
The Stolen Pony, 1948

Other books you might like:
Glenn Balch, *A Horse of Two Colors*, 1962
A Nez Perce Indian escapes from a Spanish settlement, taking with him the stallion that sires the first of the Appaloosa breed.
Paul Goble, *The Girl Who Loved Wild Horses*, 1978
Though she is fond of her people, a girl prefers living among the wild horses where she is truly happy and free.
Amy Hagstrom, *Strong and Free*, 1987
With the help of an Indian friend and his own understanding of wild Appaloosas, a young boy finds the courage to save the herd from horse thieves.
Amy C. Laundrie, *Whinny of the Wild Horses*, 1990
Follows the adventures of a wild colt living on the Wyoming range from his birth to the time when he is a full grown stallion.
Jean Thompson, *Ghost Horse of the Palisades*, 1986
Molly's quiet life on the ranch with her widowed father is enlivened by the reappearance of a mysterious white stallion no one has ever captured.

1556

Ron Roy

Illustrator: Robert McLean

Avalanche! (New York: Dutton, 1981)

Age range: Grades 4-6

Subject(s): Brothers; Divorce; Survival

Major character(s): Scott Turner, Teenager; Tony Turner, Young Man (Scott's brother)

Time period(s): 1980s

Locale(s): Colorado

What the book is about: Scott's parents are sending him to Aspen, Colorado, while they go to St. Thomas to work out the details of the divorce. Tony had left Connecticut suddenly six years earlier, but he is glad to see his younger brother. They become buried alive in an avalanche while skiing off limits. They survive and their love for each other gives Scott the strength he needs.

Where it's reviewed:
Booklist, February 1, 1982, page 708
Center for Children's Books Bulletin, May 1982, page 177
School Library Journal, February 1982, page 79

Other books by the author:
Million Dollar Jeans, 1983
Nightmare Island, 1981
Franking Is Staying Back, 1981

Other books you might like:
Marion Dane Bauer, *Face to Face*, 1991
Michael confronts his fears during a trip to Colorado to see his father, a whitewater rafting guide whom Michael hasn't seen for eight years.
Jeffrey Carroll, *Climbing to the Sun*, 1977
Following an avalanche in Montana, an Indian boy's concern for a wild mountain goat reveals much more about life to him.
Annabel Johnson, *Finders, Keepers*, 1981
A boy and his rebellious sister flee Denver following a catastrophic explosion at a nearby nuclear power plant, hoping to survive in the mountains.
Susan Saunders, *Ice Cave*, 1985
You are a boy on a cross-country ski trip trapped in an ice cave by an avalanche, and you select the options leading to eight different outcomes.
Priscilla Turner, *Captives of Endless Snow*, 1980
Three teenagers who set out to climb to the summit of Oregon's Mount hood encounter snowstorms, an avalanche, and starvation.

1557

Ron Roy

Illustrator: Walter Kessell

Frankie Is Staying Back (New York: Clarion, 1981)

Age range: Grades 3-5

Subject(s): Friendship; Self-Confidence; Schools

Major character(s): Jonas, Child, 3rd Grader; Frankie Giordano, Child, 3rd Grader

Time period(s): 1970s

Locale(s): United States

What the book is about: Jonas and Frankie have been best friends for years. At the end of third grade, Frankie has to tell Jonas that he is not going on to fourth grade. Frankie's dad has recently left the family and Frankie is having trouble with math and reading. He has a chance to go on if he does well in summer school

Where it's reviewed:
Booklist, November 15, 1981, page 442
Kirkus, November 15, 1981, page 1409
School Library Journal, December 1981, page 57

Other books by the author:
The Chimpanzee Kid, 1985
Million Dollar Jeans, 1983
I Am a Thief, 1982
Avalanche!, 1981

Other books you might like:
Patricia Reilly Giff, *Sunny Side Up*, 1986
    Summer for Richard Best, nicknamed Beast, means facing the two ordeals of summer school and losing his best friend who is moving away.
Mona Kerby, *38 Weeks Til Summer Vacation*, 1989
    Nora Jean Simpson and her friends at R.B. Nolen Elementary School cope with a snake in the bathroom, a scary Halloween house and a library pizza party
James Marshall, *The Cut-Ups Cut Loose*, 1987
    Spud and Joe eagerly return to school in the fall for more practical jokes, unaware that Assistant Principal Lamar J. Spurgle is back and awaits them.
Alan Ritchie, *Erin McEwan: Your Days Are Numbered*, 1990
    If Erin doesn't start doing better in her math class, she may have to repeat the whole year.
Susan Richards Shreve, *The Flunking of Joshua T. Bates*, 1984
    Driving home from the beach on Labor Day, Joshua receives the shocking news from his mother that he must repeat third grade.

1558

Gillian Rubinstein

Space Demons (New York: Dial, 1988)

Age range: Grades 5-8

Subject(s): Computer Games; Science Fiction

Major character(s): Andrew, Preteen; Ben, Preteen; Elaine, Preteen

Time period(s): 1980s

Locale(s): Australia

What the book is about: Twelve year old Andrew gets a computer game from Japan as a gift from his father. He and his friend, Ben, and classmates Elaine and Mario, become obsessed with it and find themselves drawn into the game and into a dangerous world. In an environment filled with hate, they must learn to love and care for each other. Rubinstein deals with the same ethical questions as Sleator's *House of Stairs*, but from a different perspective.

Where it's reviewed:
Horn Book, September/October 1988, page 635
School Library Journal, August 1988, page 98

Other books by the author:
Skymaze, 1991
Beyond the Labyrinth, 1990

Other books you might like:
Sandy Landsman, *The Gadget Factor*, 1984
    Two students create a universe of their own within a computer game, and the formulas they have created for time travel also work in the real world.
Elisabeth Mace, *Under Seige*, 1990
    Morris is having trouble dealing with his parents' divorce, so he escapes into his computer fantasy where he can play God.
Clem Philbrook, *Ollie's Team and the Football Computer*, 1968
    When Ollie lets the school's computer help quarterback the football games, the results surprise even him.
William Sleator, *House of Stairs*, 1974
    Five teens, all orphans, are placed in a house of endless stairs as subjects for psychological experiments.
Vivian Vande Velde, *User Unfriendly*, 1991
    Arvin and his friends use an unpredictable and dangerous computer role playing game in which they actually become characters in a fantasy world.

1559

Ivy Ruckman

Night of the Twisters (New York: Crowell, 1984)

Age range: Grades 4-6

Subject(s): Weather

Major character(s): Dan Hatch, Preteen; Arthur Darlington, Preteen; Ryan Hatch, Child

Time period(s): 1980s (1980)

Locale(s): Grand Island, Nebraska

What the book is about: The harrowing story of the night seven tornadoes hit Grand Island, Nebraska, June 4, 1980. Dan and his friend, Arthur, had enjoyed a typical summer day when things went bad. This first person account of the disaster is riveting as Dan and Arthur save Ryan's life (and their own) help a woman trapped in her basement, and wonder if their families are alive. Read this aloud to any who think tornado drills are a waste of time.

Where it's reviewed:
Center for Children's Books Bulletin, November 1984, page 54
School Library Journal, December 1984, page 86

Awards the book has won:
Golden Sower Award 1986

Other books by the author:
No Way Out, 1988
The Hunger Scream, 1983
Melba the Brain, 1979
Encounter, 1978

Other books you might like:
Robbie Branscum, *Cheater and Flitter Dick*, 1983
    Fourteen year old Cheater lives with her alcoholic father on an Arkansas farm, when a tornado forces her to take in the farm owner's family.
Meindert DeJong, *A Horse Came Running*, 1970

After a devastating tornado passes, a young boy finds himself all alone with two horses, one dying and the other badly injured.

Nancy Hale, *The Night of the Hurricane*, 1978

A young boy, his friends and family discover many things about each other during a hurricane on the Massachusetts coast.

Robert Newton Peck, *Arly's Run*, 1991

Arly, an orphan in search of a home and family, escapes from a brutal migrant labor camp, joins a traveling religious show, and battles a hurricane.

Marian Rumsey, *Carolina Hurricane*, 1977

Lost in a crab boat in the middle of a South Carolina salt marsh, twelve year old Morgan endures the full brunt of a hurricane.

1560

John Ruskin

Illustrator: Krystyna Turska

King of the Golden River (New York: Greenwillow, 1978)

Age range: Grades 5-8

Subject(s): Fairy Tale; Fantasy; Folk Tales

Major character(s): Gluck, Preteen, Hero; Schwartz, Teenager, Bully; Hans, Teenager, Bully

Time period(s): Indeterminate

Locale(s): Fictional Country

What the book is about: Two cruel brothers incur the wrath of the South-West Wind, Esquire. Through kindness, Gluck regains for himself the treasure his mean older brothers lost through rudeness.

Where it's reviewed:
Booklist, September 15, 1978, page 225
Hornbook, October 1978, apge 520

Other books by the author:
Dame Wiggins of Lee and Her Seven Wonderful Cats, 1963

Other books you might like:
Monica Hughes, *The Promise*, 1992

A promise made by her parents before she was born sends Princess Raina to the desert to learn mastery of the wind and rain from an old woman.

Stephen Krensky, *The Dragon Circle*, 1977

The magical Wynd family becomes involved with dragons needing help in recovering treasure lost centuries before at the bottom of a lake.

Freya Littledale, *Peter and the North Wind*, 1988

The North Wind's magical gifts to Peter mysteriously lose their magic before Peter gets them home.

Marguerita Rudolph, *I Am Your Misfortune*, 1968

When the poorer of two brothers captures his misfortune in a box, his luck changes and so does that of his mean rich brother.

Brad Strickland, *Dragon's Plunder*, 1992

Having been kidnapped by former pirates because he can "whistle up the wind," Jamie agrees to help them find the dragon of Windrose Island.

1561

Dorotha Ruthstrom

Illustrator: Lillian Hoban

The Big Kite Contest (New York: Pantheon Books, 1980)

Age range: Grades 1-3

Series: An I Am Reading Book

Subject(s): Business Enterprises; Toys; Problem Solving

Major character(s): Stephen, Child

Time period(s): Indeterminate

Locale(s): United States

What the book is about: Stephen's kite is ruined when it crashes into a tree. A new kite costs two dollars but he only has ten cents. He buys lemonade mix, makes 50 cents and then buys soap. He offers to "wash anything" for 10 cents. He washes five bikes, two tricycles, two wagons and his little sister, but still only has one dollar. He's only half way to his goal, but he's not about to give up.

Where it's reviewed:
Booklist, January 15, 1981, page 706
Kirkus Reviews, October 1, 1980, page 1298
School Library Journal, December 1980, page 67

Other books you might like:
Margret Rey, *Curious George Flies a Kite*, 1958

A little monkey needs to be rescued when he tries to fly a kite.

Nancy Robison, *The Missing Ball of String*, 1977

The mysterious disappearance of a ball of kite string thwarts a boy's kiting fun but leads him into the discovery of a robin's nestbuilding activities

Eve Titus, *Anatole over Paris*, 1961

A giant kite lifts Anatole the mouse and his family into the sky over Paris, and only his ingenuity can bring them safely home again.

Yoshiko Uchida, *Sumi's Prize*, 1964

Seven year old Sumi longs to do something well enough to win a prize. Opportunity arises when she enters the kite flying contest in her village.

Marcia K. Vaughan, *The Sea-Breeze Hotel*, 1992

A fierce offshore wind discourages the guests from the Sea-Breeze Hotel until a boy makes kite-flying the major attraction.

1562

Mary C. Ryan

Illustrator: Rob Sauber

Me Two (Boston: Little Brown, 1991)

Age range: Grades 4-6

Subject(s): Cloning; Science Fiction; Scientific Experiments

Major character(s): Wilfred "Wilf" Farcus, Teenager; Rosemary Farcus, Parent; Chuckie Mounce, Teenager

Time period(s): 1990s

Locale(s): Gatesburg

What the book is about: Wilf's grades are so bad he expects to be grounded forever, so he plans a special science experiment which he is sure will bring up his grade. But lazy thirteen year old Wilf accidentally clones himself, and the clone turns out to be excellent. He goes to class, does homework, behaves well and pleases Wilf's parents. But after a while, Wilf is not sure which boy is really Wilf and decides to run away. For a younger audience and lighter, but similar in theme to William Sleator's *The Duplica te*.

Where it's reviewed:
Booklist, July 1991, page 2046
Kirkus, May 1, 1991, page 609
School Library Journal, June 1991, page 112

Other books by the author:
Who Says I Can't, 1988
Frankie's Run, 1987
The Voice From Mendelsohn's Maple, 1985

Other books you might like:
Mildred Ames, *Anna to the Infinite Power*, 1981
    A girl learns that she is a clone, part of an experiment gone awry, and the government is out to "recall" all clones produced in the experiment.
Margaret E. Bechard, *My Sister, My Science Report*, 1990
    Though Tess is stuck with the class nerd for a partner in a science project, they become good friends as they study their subject, Tess' older sister.
Mark Harris, *The Doctor Who Technical Manual*, 1983
    A guide to technological fantasies including weapons, computers, spaceships, robots and lifelike human clones from the TV series, "Dr. Who."
William Sleator, *The Duplicate*, 1988
    David, finding a machine that creates replicas of living organisms, duplicates himself and suffers the consequences when the duplicates turn on him.
Alfred Slote, *The Clone Catcher*, 1982
    Arthur Dunn is summoned to Australia to track down a runaway clone urgently needed to provide vital organ transplants for her mother.

1563

Cynthia Rylant

A Blue-Eyed Daisy (New York: Bradbury, 1985)

Age range: Grades 4-5

Subject(s): Alcoholism; Family Life

Major character(s): Ellie Farley, Preteen; Bullet, Dog (Beagle); Okey Farley, Parent (Ellie's father), Alcoholic

Locale(s): West Virginia

What the book is about: Relates the episodes in the life of eleven year old Ellie and her family who live in a coal mining town in West Virginia. She sees an uncle go off to war, a boy in her class has a fit in the middle of geography class, and another is accidentally killed while target shooting. One day, her father brings home a beagle and even stops drinking long enough to build a doghouse.

Where it's reviewed:
Booklist, June 15, 1985, page 1461
Hornbook, July 1985, page 450
School Library Journal, April 1985, page 92

Other books by the author:
A Couple of Kooks and Other Stories about Love, 1990
But I'll be Back Again: An Album, 1989
Children of Christmas, 1987

Every Living Thing, 1985

Other books you might like:
Tatyana Bylinsky, *Before the Wildflowers Bloom*, 1989
    Set in the coal mining town of Hastings, Colorado, Carm and her family learn to cope after the death of her father in a tragic accident.
James D. Forman, *A Ballad for Hogskin Hill*, 1979
    A teenage boy and his family attempt to stop the strip mining that threatens their home in the Kentucky mountains.
Dennis Haseley, *Shadows*, 1991
    Jamie's lonely life with his aunt and uncle in rural West Virginia changes when Grandpa comes to visit and teaches him to make shadow pictures.
Sheila Solomon Klass, *Kool Ada*, 1991
    Street fighting Ada learns that there are other ways to stand up for yourself when she moves to Chicago and gets Ms. Walker for a teacher.
Phyllis Reynolds Naylor, *Shiloh*, 1991
    When he finds a lost beagle behind his West Virginia home, Marty tries to hide it from his family and the dog's neglectful, real owner.

1564

Cynthia Rylant

Illustrator: S.D. Schindler

Children of Christmas (New York: Orchard, 1987)

Age range: Grades 3-5

Subject(s): Christmas; Short Stories

Major character(s): Garnet Ash, Businessman

Time period(s): Indeterminate

Locale(s): United States

What the book is about: Short stories for Christmas: "The Christmas Tree Man", "Halfway Home", "For Being Good", "Ballerinas and Bears", "Silver Packages", and "All the Stars in the Sky." Short and sweet, good tales for reading during the holidays. One crisp, detailed full page black and white picture for each story makes this appealing for reading aloud.

Where it's reviewed:
Booklist, September 1, 1987, page 71
Kirkus Review, August 1, 1987, page 1162
School Library Journal, October 1987, page 34

Other books by the author:
Henry and Mudge and the Forever Sea, 1989
But I'll Be Back Again: An Album, 1988
Henry and Mudge in the Sparkle Days, 1988
Birthday Presents, 1987

Other books you might like:
Joan Walsh Anglund, *Teddy Bear Tales*, 1985
    Brief tales relate the adventures of teddy bears at play, learning about numbers, colors, and traveling with Santa Claus on Christmas Eve.
May Justus, *Holidays in No-End Hollow*, 1970
    Four short stories tell how Thanksgiving, Christmas, a housewarming and a school's birthday are celebrated in Tenessee's Great Smoky Mountains.
Patrick T. McRae, *A Child's Book of Christmas*, 1988
    A magical store of favorite Christmas traditions.
Ethel Pochocki, *The Attic Mice*, 1990

A family of mice go shopping in the human's kitchen, discover useful items in the attic and celebrate Christmas.

Michael J. Rosen, *Elijah's Angel: A Story for Chanukah and Christmas*, 1992

During holiday time, a Christian woodcarver gives a carved angel to a young Jewish friend, who struggles with accepting the Christmas gift.

1565

Cynthia Rylant

A Fine White Dust (New York: Bradbury, 1986)

Age range: Grades 5-7

Subject(s): Religion; Friendship; Interpersonal Relations

Major character(s): Peter Cassidy, Teenager; James W. Carson, Religious (preacher)

Time period(s): 1940s

Locale(s): North Carolina

What the book is about: Thirteen year old Pete is very serious about his religion and is captivated when a charismatic "Preacher Man" comes to town. His atheistic friend, Rufus, remains loyal to him as Pete first devotes himself to the preacher and then copes with disillusionment.

Where it's reviewed:
Kirkus Reviews, July 1, 1986, page 1023
School Library Journal, September 1986, page 138

Awards the book has won:
Newbery Honor

Other books by the author:
A Couple of Kooks and Other Stories about Love, 1990
Children of Christmas, 1987
Every Living Thing, 1985
A Blue-Eyed Daisy, 1985

Other books you might like:
Judy Blume, *Are You There, God? It's Me, Margaret*, 1970
Faced with the difficulties of growing up and choosing a religion, Margaret talks over her problems with her own private God.
Elizabeth Coatsworth, *The Wanderers*, 1972
Father Ambrosius, the orphan Michael, an outcast, and a dog wander througout Ireland leaving everyone they meet touched by their joy and wisdom.
Erik Christian Haugaard, *The Rider and His Horse*, 1968
Involved in the tragedy of the fall of Jerusalem, a young survivor of Masada tells the story of cruelty, disillusionment and courage.
Sulamith Ish-Kishor, *Our Eddie*, 1969
Two young people relate the difficulties the family suffers at the hands of a religious and loving father who cannot understand his family's needs.
Jill Paton Walsh, *Gaffer Sampson's Luck*, 1984
James does not fit in at school, and when he dares ten village boys to cross a rain swollen weir, the results are almost fatal.

1566

Cynthia Rylant

A Fine White Dust (New York: Bradbury, 1986)

Age range: Grades 5 and Up

Subject(s): Religion; Clergy

Major character(s): Preacher Man, Religious (evangelist); Peter, Teenager

Time period(s): 1980s

Locale(s): North Carolina

What the book is about: Peter struggles with his own deeply-held beliefs and the lack of faith within his family and among his friends. His devotion to the church is shaken when he idolizes a visiting Preacher Man who betrays him.

Where it's reviewed:
Horn Book, November/December 1986, page 746
School Library Journal, September 1986, page 138

Other books by the author:
A Blue-Eyed Daisy, 1985
Every Living Thing, 1985
Waiting to Waltz, 1984

Other books you might like:
Judy Blume, *Are You There, God? It's Me, Margaret*, 1970
The story of the emotional, physical and spiritual ups and downs of a twelve year old girl of Jewish and Protestant parents.
William H. Hooks, *Circle of Fire*, 1982
Harrison is an eleven year old white boy growing up in 1936 in rural North Carolina. He begins to suspect that his father is involved with the KKK.
Rebecca C. Jones, *The Believers*, 1989
Tibby knows that she should stay away from the religious sect, but she is drawn by her friendship with Veri and her own hopes for a miracle.
Elizabeth George Speare, *The Bronze Bow*, 1961
A story about a young Jewish rebel, Daniel, who is drawn to the Rabbi, Jesus, in the earliest day of Christianity.
Cynthia Voigt, *Come a Stranger*, 1986
Mina's deep love for a grown minister drives her to seek a way to give him an unforgettable remembrance.

1567

Cynthia Rylant

Illustrator: Sucie Stevenson

Henry and Mudge and the Happy Cat (New York: Bradbury, 1990)

Age range: Grades 1-2

Subject(s): Animals/Cats; Animals/Dogs

Major character(s): Henry, Child; Mudge, Dog

Time period(s): 1980s

Locale(s): United States

What the book is about: A bedraggled stray cat moves into Henry's family and adopts their huge hound, Mudge. The cat teaches Mudge how to behave with proper "catiquette."

Where it's reviewed:
Booklist, June 1, 1990, page 1906
School Library Journal, August 1990, page 134

Other books by the author:
Henry and Mudge and the Long Weekend, 1992
Soda Jerk, 1990 (poetry)

Mr. Grigg's Work, 1989
Henry and Mudge: Their First Adventures, 1987

Other books you might like:
Mary Calhoun, *High-Wire Henry*, 1991
    Henry the cat learns tightrope walking to get his humans to pay attention to him instead of the new puppy in the family.
Mordicai Gerstein, *The New Creatures*, 1991
    An old man tells his grandchildren about a sheep dog named Herman who discovered the first humans in the days when dogs and cats ruled the world.
Nancy Gurney, *Impossible Dogs and Troublesome Cats*, 1970
    Pictures, cartoons, stories, rhymes and ABCs featuring dogs and cats.
Graham Oakley, *The Church Mice and the Ring*, 1992
    The church mice make a plan to find a home for their new friend, Percy, a stray dog.
Mark Saltzman, *The Adventures of Milo and Otis*, 1988
    A young dog and cat wander away from the farm, have harrowing adventures, and make new friends.

1568

Cynthia Rylant

Missing May (New York: Orchard, 1992)

Age range: Grades 4-8

Subject(s): Aunts and Uncles; Death; Grief

Major character(s): Summer, 7th Grader, Orphan; Ob, Relative (uncle); Cletus Underwood, Preteen (7th Grader)

Time period(s): 1990s

Locale(s): Deep Water, West Virginia

What the book is about: Summer lost her mother when she was six and bounced from relative to relative until Aunt May and Uncle Ob met her and took her home at once and became a family. Six years later, Aunt May dies and Summer and Ob are lost without her. One day Uncle Ob "hears from" Aunt

May in the spirit world. Summer, Ob, and Cletus Underwood, another seventh grader in Summer's class, search for a way to contact the spirits, travel to Putnam County to see a medium, (The Rev. Miriam B. Conklin, Small Medium at Large) and find something more important.

Where it's reviewed:
Booklist, February 15, 1992, page 1105
Horn Book, March/April 1992, page 206

Awards the book has won:
Newbery Medal 1993

Other books by the author:
A Couple of Kooks and Other Stories about Love, 1990
A Blue-Eyed Daisy, 1985
Every Living Thing, 1985
Miss Maggie, 1983

Other books you might like:
Margaret E. Bechard, *Tory and Me and the Spirit of True Love*, 1992
    Tory and Emily embark on a quest into the past of their mysterious Aunt Louisa who had not talked to the family for years before her death.
Louise Lawrence, *Sing and Scatter Daisies*, 1977
    A rebellious youth learns to deal with the approaching death of a beloved aunt after his involvement with the ghost of a young man.
Elisabet McHugh, *Beethoven's Cat*, 1988
    A cat named Ludwig finds out he resembles Ludwig von Beethovan's cat and suspects that he has become possessed by the spirit of the composer.
Joan Lowery Nixon, *Whispers From the Dead*, 1989
    After making contact with the spirit world during a near-death experience, Sarah receives otherworldly messages about a murder comitted in her house.
Jane Yolen, *The Stone Silenus*, 1984
    A year after her father dies, a strange faun-boy appears to Melissa, seeming to be the reincarnation of her father's spirit.

S

1569

Louis Sachar

Sixth Grade Secrets (New York: Scholastic, 1987)

Age range: Grades 4-6

Subject(s): Clubs; Humor; Schools

Major character(s): Laura Sibbie, Preteen, 6th Grader; Gabriel, Preteen, 6th Grader; Mr. Doyle, Teacher

Time period(s): 1980s

Locale(s): United States

What the book is about: When Laura Sibbie finds a hat that says PIG CITY, she starts a club called Pig City, and incites a near-war among her sixth grade classmates. A rival club forms that has designs on Pig City's precious secrets. Little does anyone know what treasures members have to give Laura to get into the club. They would die of embarrassment if they were found out. And Gabriel's club, Monkey Town, just might blow their cover.

Where it's reviewed:
Publisher's Weekly, August 28, 1987, page 80
School Library Journal, September 1987, page 182

Other books by the author:
Marvin Redpost: Kidnapped at Birth?, 1992
Dogs Don't Tell Jokes, 1991
The Boy Who Lost His Face, 1989
Johnny's in the Basement, 1981

Other books you might like:
Ilene Cooper, *The Queen of the Sixth Grade*, 1988
  After helping her supposed best friend, Veronica, found a secret club, Robin accedentally gets on her wrong side and finds Veronica cruel and bossy.
Merrill Joan Gerber, *I'd Rather Think about Robby*, 1989
  Marilyn is somewhat attracted to her precocious classmate Robby, but is confused by him and struggles to maintain her own values.
Betsy Haynes, *Taffy Sinclair and the Secret Admirer Epidemic*, 1988
  Jana Morgan and her club, the Fabulous Five, set out to uncover the identity of Jana's secret admirer.
Anna Grossnickle Hines, *Tell Me Your Best Thing*, 1991
  Sophie reluctantly joins the new club formed by Charlotte, the class bully, and is hurt when her best friend tells Sophie's darkest secret.
Carol K. Scism, *Secret Emily*, 1972

Emily is torn between wanting to be a member of the elite Clique-Claque Club and wanting to be friends with a girl disapproved of by club members.

1570

Louis Sachar

Illustrator: Barbara Samuels

Someday Angeline (New York: Knopf, 1983)

Age range: Grades 4-6

Subject(s): Gifted Children; Schools; Self-Acceptance

Major character(s): Angeline Persopolis, Genius, 6th Grader; Mrs. Hardlick, Teacher

Time period(s): 1980s

Locale(s): United States

What the book is about: Angelina can't help it if she's a genius, but the kids at school call her Freak, her teacher is always mean to her, and even her father treats her as if she's from Mars. She's eight years old and in the sixth grade.

Where it's reviewed:
Booklist, September 1, 1983, page 91
School Library Journal, November 1983, page 82
Publisher's Weekly, July 29, 1983, page 71

Other books by the author:
The Boy Who Lost His Face, 1989
There's a Boy in the Girls' Bathroom, 1987
Johnny's in the Basement, 1981
Sideways Stories From Wayside School, 1978

Other books you might like:
Jerome Brooks, *Knee Holes*, 1992
  Hope becomes spokesperson for the gifted students when trouble appears to be simmering between that teacher and another in the program.
Patricia Hermes, *I Hate Being Gifted*, 1990
  KT's friendship with her two best friends is threatened when she is selected for the talented and gifted program at school.
Ann M. Martin, *Yours Truly, Shirley*, 1990
  Shirley struggles with feelings of inferiority as she compares herself to her intellectually gifted older brother and her adopted Vietnamese sister.
Susan Beth Pfeffer, *Dear Dad, Love Laurie*, 1989
  Laurie's letter to her divorced father chronicles her year in the sixth grade and her efforts to enter her school's program for the gifted.

Jacqueline Woodson, *Maizon at Blue Hill*, 1992
Maizon finds herself one of only five blacks at an academically challenging boarding school and wonders if she will ever fit in.

1571

Louis Sacher

Sidewise Stories From Wayside School (New York: Lothrop, 1989)

Age range: Grades 3-6

Subject(s): Schools; Humor

Major character(s): Mrs. Gorf, Teacher; Mrs. Jules, Teacher; Joe, Child

Time period(s): 1980s

Locale(s): United States

What the book is about: When a school is built with 30 classrooms, one on top of another, a very strange school results, beginning with a teacher who turns all the kids into apples.

Where it's reviewed:
Booklist, May 1, 1989, page 1553
School Library Journal, May 1989, page 111

Other books by the author:
The Boy Who Lost His Face, 1989
Dogs Don't Tell Jokes, 1991
There's a Boy in the Girls' Bathroom, 1987
Wayside School Is Falling Down, 1989

Other books you might like:
Ellen Conford, *What's Cooking, Jenny Archer?*, 1989
Jenny runs into funny situations when she starts preparing lunches for her friends at school.
John D. Fitzgerald, *The Great Brain at the Academy*, 1972
In turn of the century Mormon Utah, the Great Brain faces the challenge of a Catholic boarding school with daring exploits and money making schemes.
Louis Phillips, *Louis Phillips Looseleaf*, 1990
A collection of humorous sayings, definitions and stories arranged in the form of a school notebook. (Non-fiction)
Franklyn E. Meyer, *Me and Caleb Again*, 1969
An Ozark mountain boy and his little brother Caleb have funny adventures at home and at school.
Larry Bograd, *Bernie Entertaining*, 1987
10 year old Bernie's comic misadventures at home and at school do not seem funny to him.

1572

Elizabeth-Ann Sachs

Just Like Always (New York: Atheneum, 1981)

Age range: Grades 5 and Up

Subject(s): Hospitals; Friendship

Major character(s): Jamie Tannenbaum, Child, Patient; Courtney Ann Schaeffer, Child, Patient

Time period(s): 1940s

Locale(s): United States

What the book is about: Two girls in the hospital become pals. Jamie is being treated for scoliosis. Her parents can visit only on weekends. Courtney has an imaginary kingdom. They share adventures and plots against the nursing staff. They throw their hospital food out the window and eat only the snacks their parents bring. Surgery separates them, but if friendship is real, it will be just like always.

Where it's reviewed:
Booklist, September 15, 1981, page 111
School Library Journal, September 1981, page 129

Other books by the author:
Kiss Me, Janie Tannenbaum, 1992
Shyster, 1985
Where Are You, Cow Patty?, 1984

Other books you might like:
Thomas Bertman, *On Our Own Terms*, 1989
Describes activity at the Caroline Hospital in Stockholm where children with physical disabilities receive training and physiotherapy. (Non-fiction)
Judy Blume, *Deenie*, 1973
A thirteen year old girl, seemingly destined for a modeling career finds she has a deformation of the spine called scoliosis.
James Howe, *A Night Without Stars*, 1983
When Maria has to go to the hospital for open-heart surgery, she finds strength in her friendship with a badly scarred burn victim.
Rebecca C. Jones, *Angie and Me*, 1981
During her stay at a children's hospital where she is treated for juvenile rheumatoid arthritis, Jenna comes to terms with her illness.
Marilyn Singer, *It Can't Hurt Forever*, 1978
Ellie describes her experiences during twelve days of hospitalization for heart surgery.

1573

Marilyn Sachs

At the Sound of the Beep (New York: Dutton, 1990)

Age range: Grades 4-7

Subject(s): Divorce; Homeless; Runaways

Major character(s): Matthew Green, Twin; Mathilda Green, Twin

Time period(s): 1990s

Locale(s): San Francisco, California

What the book is about: When Matthew and Mathilda discover they will be separated upon their parents' divorce, the run away to San Francisco where their Uncle Ben lives. Unfortunately, only his answering machine is at home when they call. So they take up residence across the street in Golden Gate Park. As the days pass and Uncle Ben still does not return, the pair is drawn deeper into the lives of the park's homeless inhabitants and the mystery of the murderer who stalks them all.

Where it's reviewed:
Booklist, April 15, 1990, page 1636
School Library Journal, May 1990, page 113

Other books by the author:
Circles, 1991
Baby Sister, 1986

Bus Ride, 1980
Class Pictures, 1980

Other books you might like:
Barbara Corcoran, *Stay Tuned*, 1991
En route to stay with a relative she has never seen, fourteen year old Stevie meets three other young people with no place to live and takes a detour.
Adrienne Jones, *Street Family: A Novel*, 1987
Sheltering beneath a Los Angeles freeway overpass, a group of street people to grow into an unlikely family.
Walter Macken, *The Flight of the Doves*, 1992
A twelve year old English boy and his seven year old sister run away from their abusive stepfather and set out to reach their grandmother in Ireland.
Ben Mikaelsen, *Rescue Josh McGuire*, 1991
When thirteen year old Josh runs away to the mountains of Montana with an orphaned bear cub, they must both fight for their lives in a snowstorm.
Theresa Nelson, *The Beggar's Ride*, 1992
Twelve year old Clare flees an unhappy homelife and tries to survive on the streets of Atlantic City with a small gang of homeless kids.

| **1574** |

Marilyn Sachs

The Bear's House (New York: Dutton, 1987)

Age range: Grades 3-5

Subject(s): Schools; Single Parent Families

Major character(s): Fran Ellen Smith, Child; Miss Thompson, Teacher

Time period(s): 1980s

Locale(s): United States

What the book is about: Fran Ellen loves the Bear House more than anything in the world. It sat in the back of her classroom and had wonderful furniture, windows with real glass, soft carpets on the floor and beautiful clothes in the closet. On the last day of class, Miss Thompson said she would give the Bear's House to the most deserving student.

Where it's reviewed:
Booklist, June 1, 1987, page 1526
New York Times Book Review, September 27, 1987, page 26
Wilson Library Bulletin, June 1987, page 64

Other books by the author:
Baby Sister, 1986
Thunderbird, 1985
Underdog, 1985
The Fat Girl, 1984

Other books you might like:
Kay Brown, *Willy's Summer Dream*, 1989
Willy is slow in school and ridiculed by the other boys in the neighbohood until tutoring from an older girl helps him develop some self-confidence.
Kathryn Ewing, *A Private Matter*, 1975
In her longing for a father, Marcy becomes extremely attached to the kind man next door.
Norma Klein, *Blue Trees, Red Sky*, 1975

Ten episodes in the life of an eight year old girl, who, because he father is dead, lives with just her mother and brother.
Doris Orgel, *My War with Mrs. Galloway*, 1985
Rebecca, whose divorced mother is a doctor, has an ongoing war with her babysitter, Mrs. Galloway, until one day the two reach an unexpected truce.
Margaret Teibl, *Davey Come Home*, 1979
A young boy yearns for a mother figure to make their home a welcoming place for him and his father.

| **1575** |

Marilyn Sachs

Class Pictures (New York: Dutton, 1980)

Age range: Grades 5-6

Subject(s): Friendship

Major character(s): Patricia "Pat" Maddox, Teenager; Lorraine "Lolly" Scheiner, Teenager

Time period(s): 1980s

Locale(s): United States

What the book is about: Best friends with Pat since kindergarten, Lolly is from a wealthy family. Pat lives with her mother, Grandma, and two brothers over a store. She learns her real dad is not the man who raised her. Lolly becomes a beauty - Pat used to protect her from the other kids. All of a sudden, Lolly doesn't need Pat to protect her anymore. Two girls and how they grow.

Where it's reviewed:
Center for Children's Books Bulletin, February 1981, p 118
Horn Book, October 1980, page 528

Other books by the author:
Beach Towels, 1982
Bus Ride, 1980
Hello.Wrong Number, 1981
A Summer's Lease, 1979

Other books you might like:
Rebecca Busselle, *Bathing Ugly*, 1991
Chosen to compete in the camp's Bathing Ugly contest because of her weight, Betsy forces the others to re-think their ideas about outward appearances.
Caroline B. Cooney, *The Return of the Vampire*, 1991
Devnee makes a bargain with a vampire to gain beauty and brains, at the expense of her friends.
Constance Hiser, *Sixth-Grade Star*, 1992
Getting a part in the school play doesn't help Jill with her jealousy toward her younger sister and the beauty pageants her sister is in.
Nancy J. Hopper, *The Seven and One-Half Sins of Stacey Kendall*, 1982
Wanting to become beautiful, Stacy devises a money-making scheme to purchase a Bustter-sizer, and learns in the process that beauty is only skin deep.
Ellen Leroe, *The Plot Against the Pom-Pom Queen*, 1985
Kelsey risks true friendship and integrity in her determination to get even with the school's reigning beauty for playing a cruel joke on her.

1576

Marilyn Sachs

Illustrator: Anne Sachs

Dorrie's Book (New York: Doubleday, 1975)

Age range: Grades 5-6

Subject(s): Family Life; Foster Families

Major character(s): Dorrie O'Brien, Preteen; Charles O'Brien, Teacher, Parent; Maureen O'Brien, Parent

Time period(s): 1970s

Locale(s): San Francisco, California

What the book is about: Dorrie has been an only child for eleven years. Suddenly she is a sister to triplets! The family moves from their beautiful apartment to an old, large house. When two foster children move in, her parents let Dorrie decide whether they can become part of the suddenly enlarged family.

Where it's reviewed:
Booklist, November 1, 1975, page 372
Center for Children's Books Bulletin, March 1976, page 117
Hornbook, February 1976, page 53

Awards the book has won:
Garden State Children's Book Award 1978

Other books by the author:
Baby Sister, 1986
Call Me Ruth, 1982
A Pocketfull of Seeds, 1973
The Truth about Mary Rose, 1973

Other books you might like:
Pat Kibbe, *The Hocus-Pocus Dilemma*, 1979
     Convinced that she has psychic powers, a girl makes predictions for the members of her large family which seem to come true.
Margaret Mahy, *The Tricksters*, 1986
     A large New Zealand family and their guests find their lives invaded by three sinister brothers, and by New Year's Day, nothing is the same.
Phyllis Reynolds Naylor, *Maudie in the Middle*, 1990
     Maudie seems to attract nothing but trouble until a crisis hits the family and she is noticed in the best way possible.
Anne Pellowski, *Betsy*, 1981
     Follows a year in the life of Betsy and her large family on their Wisconsin farm.
Stella Pevsner, *Sister of the Quints*, 1988
     Natalie's life undergoes chaotic changes when her stepbrother has quintuplets and their roomy Chicago home becomes a huge nursery.

1577

Marilyn Sachs

Fourteen (New York: Dutton, 1983)

Age range: Grades 5-8

Subject(s): Friendship; Mothers and Daughters; Prisoners and Prisons

Major character(s): Rebecca, Teenager; Jason, Teenager

Time period(s): 1980s

Locale(s): United States

What the book is about: Having to contend with a suffering poet-father and an author-mother who uses her daughter's life as material for her popular books, Rebecca finds her life is further disrupted by Jason, the new boy next door and his enigmatic family. Knowing her mother's special interest in her personal life, Rebecca conceals her budding romance with Jason, finds out that his father is in jail, and helps his family to cope with that reality.

Where it's reviewed:
Horn Book, August 1983, page 117
School Library Journal, April 1983, page 154

Other books by the author:
Circles, 1991
Just Like a Friend, 1989
Almost Fifteen, 1987
Class Pictures, 1980

Other books you might like:
Ossie Davis, *Just Like Martin*, 1992
     After the deaths of two classmates in an explosion at his Alabama church, fourteen year old Stone organizes a children's civil rights march in 1963.
Paul Fleischman, *Saturnalia*, 1990
     In 1681 in Boston, fourteen year old William, a captured indian, works as a printer's apprentice, but wants to make connections with his indian past.
Barbara Hall, *Dixie Storms*, 1990
     Dutch Peyton learns about growing up as her family struggles with a crippling drought and a painful past.
Will Hobbs, *The Big Wander*, 1992
     As he searches for his uncle in the rugged southwest canyon country, Clay becomes involved with Indians trying to save some of remaining wild mustangs
Lynne Reid Banks, *One More River*, 1992
     Lesley is upset when her parents abandon their comfortable life in Canada for a kibbutz in Israel prior to the 1967 war.

1578

Marilyn Sachs

Fran Ellen's House (New York: Dutton, 1987)

Age range: Grades 4-6

Subject(s): Dolls and Dollhouses; Family Life; Mental Illness

Major character(s): Fran Ellen, Child; Flora, Child; Felice, Child

Time period(s): 1980s

Locale(s): United States

What the book is about: In this sequel to *The Bear's House*, a mother and her children are reuni ted after the mother spends a year being treated for depression while the child ren were in separate foster homes. Picking up the pieces of their lives is not easy. Seven year old Felice begins to work on restoring the Bear's House, a dol lhouse. Gradually everyone becomes involved and the project becomes a symbol of the rebuilding of the family.

Where it's reviewed:
Kirkus Reviews, September 15, 1987, page 1397
School Library Journal, October 1987, page 129

Other books by the author:
At the Sound of the Beep, 1990
Baby Sister, 1986
Beach Towels, 1982
The Bear's House, 1971

Other books you might like:
Martha Derman, *And Phillipa Makes Four*, 1983
  Phillipa feels her life becoming intolerable as her widowed father becomes interested in the mother of her worst enemy at school.
Morris Gleitzman, *Worry Warts*, 1993
  Keith decides to help the family financial situation and stop his parents' constant fighting by picking up a fortune in Australia's opal fields.
Mary Francis Shura, *The Sunday Doll*, 1988
  Emmy finds herself sheltered from her family's problems when she is sent away for the summer because of some unknown problem with her older sister.
Doris Buchanan Smith, *Best Girl*, 1993
  Nealy Compton finds a "safe place" under a neighbor's porch as she copes with a difficult family situation.
Arvella Whitmore, *The Bread Winner*, 1990
  Sarah Ann Puckett helps her unemployed parents survive the Great Depression by selling her prizewinning homemade bread.

1579

Marilyn Sachs

Illustrator: Ben Stahl

A Pocket Full of Seeds (1973)

Age range: Grades 5-7

Subject(s): Jews; World War II

Major character(s): Nicole Nieman, Child

Time period(s): 1930s; 1940s

Locale(s): France

What the book is about: Nicole and her little sister are reunited with their parents when Nicole is eight. They are finally able to afford a home for the family. Many of her classmates are hostile towards her. Nicole's parents are taken away by the Nazis and Nicole returns to her foster parents and finally finds compassion from a teacher she at first dislikes.

Where it's reviewed:
Booklist, December 1, 1973, page 388
Center for Children's Books Bulletin, March 1974, page 117
Kirkus Reviews, November 1, 1973, page 1202

Other books by the author:
Almost Fifteen, 1987
Call Me Ruth, 1982
Dorrie's Book, 1975
The Truth about Mary Rose, 1973

Other books you might like:
Claire Hutchet Bishop, *Twenty and Ten*, 1952
  Twenty school children hide ten Jewish children from the Nazis occupying France during WWII.
Lois Lowry, *Number the Stars*, 1989
  During the German occupation of Denmark, Annemarie learns how to be brave and courageous when she helps shelter her Jewish friend from the Nazis.

Johanna Reiss, *The Journey Back*, 1976
  After spending three years hiding from the Nazis, a Jewish family is reunited and begins the job of rebuilding their country and family.
Renee Roth-Hano, *Touch Wood: A Girlhood in Occupied France*, 1988
  A young Jewish girl and her family flee her family their home in Alsace and live a precarious life in Paris until Renee and her sister escape.
Nelly S. Toll, *Behind the Secret Window: A Memoir of a Hidden Childhood During World War Two*, 1993
  The author recalls her experiences when she and her mother were hidden from the Nazis by a Gentile couple in Lwow, Poland, during World War Two.

1580

Marilyn Sachs

Underdog (Garden City, NJ: Doubleday, 1985)

Age range: Grades 5-7

Subject(s): Animals/Dogs; Orphans; Schools/Boarding Schools

Major character(s): Isabelle "Izzy" Cummings, Preteen, Orphan; Alice, Guardian (aunt); Roger Cummings, Guardian (uncle)

Time period(s): 1980s

Locale(s): California

What the book is about: When her father dies, Izzy is sent to California to stay with an aunt and uncle she's never met. They try to be kind, but would really rather send Izzy to boarding school. Then Izzy finds a picture of gus, a little black dog her family owned when she was little. She sets out to find Gus. She needs him because they are both underdogs, even if it means skipping school and disobeying her aunt to find him.

Where it's reviewed:
Booklist, February 15, 1986, page 871
School Library Journal, February 1986, page 89
Publisher's Weekly, December 20, 1985, page 65

Awards the book has won:
Christopher Award 1986

Other books by the author:
At the Sound of the Beep, 1990
The Big Book for Peace, 1990
Baby Sister, 1986
Dorrie's Book, 1975

Other books you might like:
Hila Colman, *The Double Life of Angela Jones*, 1988
  Angela learns not to judge people by their socio-economic class after she reluctantly accepts a scholarship to a fancy boarding school.
Ellen Conford, *Dear Mom, Get Me Out of Here!*, 1992
  Trapped in a dreadful boarding school, Paul joins his classmates in attempting to uncover the shocking past of their headmaster, Mr. Pickles.
Isabelle Holland, *The Man Without a Face*, 1972
  A fatherless boy develops an unusual relationship with a man living near his summer home who helps him prepare his entrance exams to boarding school.
George Ella Lyon, *Red Rover, Red Rover*, 1989

When Sumi's brother leaves for boarding school, her grandfather dies, and her mother withdraws into grief, Sumi finds herself alone and afraid.

Jacqueline Woodson, *Maizon at Blue Hill*, 1992
  Maizon finds herself one of only five blacks at an academically challenging boarding school and wonders if she will ever fit in.

1581

Antoine de Saint-Exupery, Author/Illustrator

The Little Prince (New York: Harcourt Brace and World, 1943)

Age range: Grades 3-6

Subject(s): Conduct of Life; Fantasy; Space Travel

Major character(s): Little Prince, Traveller, Royalty

Time period(s): 1930s (1937)

Locale(s): Asteroid B-612, Asteroid; Earth

What the book is about: The Little Prince lives alone on a tiny planet no larger than a house. He possesses three volcanoes and a flower of inordinate pride. It was this pride that ruins the serenity of the Little Prince's world and starts him on his travels which finally bring him to Earth.

Where it's reviewed:
Book World, December 9, 1973, page 7
New York Times Book Review, November 4, 1973, page 54

Other books by the author:
Wind, Sand, and Stars, 1968
Southern Mail, 1972
Flight to Arras, 1942
Night Flight, 1942

Other books you might like:
Lloyd Alexander, *The Remarkable Journey of Prince Jen*, 1991
  Bearing six unusual gifts, young Prince Jen embarks on a perilous quest and learns and teaches many lessons during his journey.
Victor Appleton, *Ark Two*, 1982
  Tom Swift and his crew travel to the planet Aquilla to recover SeaGlobe, an ecological system stolen from the space colony New America.
Isaac Asimov, *Norby and the Oldest Dragon*, 1990
  Jeff Wells and his personal robot, Norby, find adventure when they travel to the planet Jamyn to attend the Grand Dragon's birthday party.
C.S. Lewis, *Prince Caspian*, 1951
  Four children first introduced in *The Lion, the Witch and the Wardrobe*, help Prince Caspian and his army of beasts to free Narnia from evil.
Patricia A. McKillip, *The Changeling Sea*, 1988
  A floor scrubber and a magician try to help a prince return to his home under the sea and help a his half brother return to the land.

1582

Felix Salten

Illustrator: Kurt Wiese

Bambi (Cutchogue, New York: Buccaneer, 1929)

Age range: Grades 5-8

Subject(s): Animals/Deer; Nature

Major character(s): Bambi, Deer; Feline, Deer; Gobo, Deer

Time period(s): Indeterminate Past

Locale(s): Austria

What the book is about: A young fawn grows up in the woods, learning from his mother and all the forest animals with his constant questions. Salten's detailed observations make this a treasure for nature lovers of any age. Many editions available.

Where it's reviewed:
Kirkus Reviews, October 15, 1970, page 1150
Booklist, February 1, 1971, page 455
Bookwatch, March 11, 1979, page F2

Other books by the author:
Fifteen Rabbits, 1976
Bambi's Children, 1969
Perri, 1938

Other books you might like:
Jim Arnosky, *Long Spikes*, 1992
  Long Spikes, a deer who is orphaned when his mother is killed, grows to maturity and displaces old one-eyed buck from his position as dominant male.
A.M. Monson, *The Deer Stand*, 1992
  When her family moves from Chicago to Wisconsin, Bits has trouble making new friends. She spends her time trying to tame a deer near her home.
Gary Paulsen, *The Night the White Deer Died*, 1978
  A teenage girl and an old Indian are brought together by the same haunting dream.
Marcia Polese, *Frankie and the Fawn*, 1974
  An injured fawn has the good fortune to be found by two youngsters whose mother is a veterinarian.
Marjorie Kinnan Rawlings, *The Yearling*, 1938
  A young boy in the Florida backwoods is forced to decide the fate of the fawn he has lovingly raised as a pet.

1583

Lance Salway

Illustrator: Jeremy Ford

A Nasty Piece of Work and Other Ghost Stories (New York: Clarion, 1985)

Age range: Grades 5-8

Subject(s): Ghosts

Time period(s): Indeterminate

Locale(s): England

What the book is about: Seven original horror stories guaranteed to give chills down the spine. All six stories create great suspense that ghost story fans will love. All protagonists are about twelve years old, and each story seems like realistic fiction until a ghostly figure appears at a crucial point in the action.

Where it's reviewed:
School Library Journal, September 1985, page 138
Voice of Youth Advocates, June 1985, page 134

Other books you might like:
Isaac Asimov, *Young Ghosts*, 1985
　Includes twelve tales involving young ghosts by a variety of authors.
Eth Clifford, *Never Hit a Ghost with a Baseball Bat*, 1993
　While exploring a museum, Mary Rose and JoBeth hear voices from nowhere and other strange events make them think the museum is haunted.
Phyllis Reynolds Naylor, *Bernie and the Besseldorf Ghost*, 1990
　Living at the Besseldorf hotel, Bernie tries to help a young, troubled ghost who wanders the halls of the hotel at night.
Robert San Souci, *Short and Shivery: Thirty Chilling Tales*, 1987
　A collection of thirty short and spooky tales from around the world.
Frances Wosmek, *Never Mind Murder*, 1977
　A young girl and her mother rent an old Victorian house in a small Massachusetts town and are haunted by the ghost of a young artist who was murdered.

| 1584 |

Carl Sandburg

Illustrator: Maud Petersham

Rootabaga Stories (New York: Harcourt Brace and World, 1922)

Age range: Grades 4-8

Subject(s): Fairy Tale; Fantasy; Short Stories

Major character(s): Gimme-the-Ax, Parent; Potato Face, Musician (accordian player), Handicapped (blind)

Time period(s): Indeterminate

Locale(s): Rootabaga Country; Fictional Country (Rootabaga Country)

What the book is about: A wonderful collection of tales full of Sandburg's lively imaginative language and characters all journeying through the Rootabaga Country. Meet Gimme the Ax, his children who named themselves with the first words out of their mouths, "Please Gimme" and "Ax Me No Questions," the Potato Face Blind Man who plays the accordian, and many more. A classic of great stories for reading or telling aloud.

Where it's reviewed:
Hornbook, June 1983, page 271
New York Times Book Review, May 12, 1974, page 28

Other books by the author:
Fables, Foibles and Foobles, 1988
Rainbows Are Made: Poems, 1982
Prairie-Town Boy, 1955 (autobiography)
Early Moon, 1930

Other books you might like:
L. Frank Baum, *Little Wizard of Oz Stories*, 1985
　Six tales present the further adventures of Dorothy and Toto, Ozma, Tiktok, Jack Pumpkinhead, the Tin Woodman, and others from the land of Oz.
Peter Dickinson, *Merlin Dreams*, 1988
　Nine stories of blood, magic, and fabulous creatures, set in form of dreams coming to the enchanted wizard Merlin as he is imprisoned under a stone.

Diana Wynne Jones, *Warlock at the Wheel and Other Stories*, 1984
　Eight stories from one of the best writers of fantasy for children; "Warlock at the Wheel," "The Plague of Peacocks" and six others.
C.S. Lewis, *Boxen: The Imaginary World of the Young C.S. Lewis*, 1985
　A collection of maps, histories, sketches, and stories created by C.S. Lewis as a child to describe his fantasy world, known as Animal-Land or Boxen.
Jane Yolen, *The Faery Flag*, 1989
　A collection of stories and poems on various fairy tale, ghost, or supernatural themes.

| 1585 |

Scott R. Sanders

Illustrator: Jill Kastner

Aurora Means Dawn (New York: Bradbury, 1989)

Age range: Grades 2-5

Subject(s): Frontier and Pioneer Life

Time period(s): 1800s (1800)

Locale(s): Ohio

What the book is about: After traveling from Connecticut to Ohio in 1800 to start a new life in the settlement of Aurora, and facing a destructive thunderstorm, the Sheldons find that they are the first family to arrive there, and realize that they will be starting a new community by themselves. Spare text and full page watercolor illustrations make this a good choice as a read aloud for units on frontier life.

Where it's reviewed:
Booklist, September 15, 1989, page 190
Horn Book, September/October 1989, page 616

Other books by the author:
Bad Man Ballad, 1986
The Visionary, 1984
Wilderness Plots, 1983
Warm as Wool, 1972

Other books you might like:
Karen Ackerman, *Araminta's Paint Box*, 1990
　When her family moves from Boston to California in 1847, Araminta and her paintbox become separated but, through a series of owners, become reunited.
Mary Holmes, *Year of the Sevens*, 1992
　In 1777, Polly and her family face great danger after they move to the Kentucky frontier.
Ellen Howard, *The Chicken House House*, 1991
　When Alena and her family move onto new prairie farmland, they must live in the chicken house because there is not time to build a home before winter.
Janet Beeler Shaw, *Kirsten Saves the Day: A Summer Story*, 1988
　Kirsten is proud and excited when she finds a bee tree full of honey, one of the natural treasures of her Minnesota frontier world.
Martin Waddell, *Little Obie and the Flood*, 1992
　Through hardships and good times, Little Obie, Grandad, Effie and newly adopted Marty grow to become a real family.

1586

Pamela Sargent

Earthseed: A Novel (New York: Harper and Row, 1983)

Age range: Grades 6-9

Subject(s): Science Fiction

Major character(s): Zohert, Space Explorer

Time period(s): Indeterminate Future

Locale(s): Outer Space

What the book is about: A computerized space ship programmed to find a habitable planet and bring children to life from genetic material stored aboard, hurdles through space. As it nears a planet, children are grown and nurtured. However, when the children are faced with total responsibility for their own survival, they do not know how to live on a planet or work cooperatively, having spent their whole lives on the space ship.

Where it's reviewed:
Center for Children's Books Bulletin, July/August 1983, page 217
School Library Journal, August 1983, page 79

Other books by the author:
Venus of Shadows, 1990
Alien Child, 1988
Shore of Women, 1987
Eye of the Comet, 1984

Other books you might like:
Ben Bova, *End of Exile,* 1975
  Born and brought up on a space ship that is slowly deteriorating, Linc discovers its secrets and how to get the remaining people to their destination.
Clare Cooper, *Ashar of Qarius,* 1988
  When alien creatures attack the Earth colony on the planet Plioctis, stranded children must depend on an artificial intelligence in their computer.
Lester Del Rey, *Moon of Mutiny,* 1982
  A rebellious cadet is dismissed from the Goddard Space Academy and seeks to join the moon colony.
Douglas Arthur Hill, *ColSec Rebellion,* 1985
  A band of teenagers exiled by Earth's despotic government returns to lead a rebellion against that organization's strangle hold on the space colonies.
George Zebrowski, *Sunspacer,* 1984
  Joe Sorby has a longing for faraway places that eventually takes him to a life of hardship and danger on Mercury and in the rings of Saturn.

1587

Sarah Sargent

Jonas McFee, A.T.P. (New York: Bradbury, 1989)

Age range: Grades 4-7

Subject(s): Science Fiction

Major character(s): Jonas McFee, 5th Grader; Sean, Bully, 5th Grader; Jacobious, Scientist

Time period(s): Indeterminate Future

Locale(s): Earth

What the book is about: Fifth grader Jonas McFee faces the temptation of becoming the Awful Terrible Powerful One when he accidentally acquires a blue crystal from outer space, giving him the power to get China on his television and make his car fly.

Where it's reviewed:
Booklist, April 15, 1989, page 1471
School Library Journal, May 1989, page 112

Other books by the author:
Watermusic, 1986
Lure of the Dark, 1984
Secret Lies, 1981
Edward Troy and the Witch Cat, 1978

Other books you might like:
Dean Hughes, *Nutty Knows All,* 1988
  Nutty Nutshell produces a memorable science fair project when his partner, William, transfers photons of light to Nutty's brain.
O.T. Nelson, *The Girl Who Owned a City,* 1975
  When a plague sweeps over the Earth, killing everyone except children under twelve, ten year old Lisa organizes a group to rebuild a new way of life.
Kenneth Appel, *Colin's Fantastic Video Adventure,* 1985
  Colin discovers that the spaceships in his favorite video game are actually controlled by tiny men, who promise to help him in an upcoming contest.
Susan Beth Pfeffer, *Future Forward,* 1989
  Keeping the secret that their VCR sends people back in time, Scott and Kelly continue to search for the best way to use that power.
Ivy Ruckman, *Melba the Brain,* 1979
  A young genius's experiments with spliced energies acquaint her with a cat and hurtle her light years beyond Earth to a planet ruled by animals.

1588

Sarah Sargent

Weird Henry Berg (New York: Crown, 1980)

Age range: Grades 4-6

Subject(s): Fantasy; Death; Dragons

Major character(s): Henry Berg, Child; Millie Levenson, Aged Person

Time period(s): 1980s

Locale(s): Oshkosh, Wisconsin; Wales

What the book is about: Underachiever Henry is visited by a lost dragon hatchling. The baby dragon is tracked to Oshkosh by his full grown Welsh relative. The lives of Henry and a lonely old woman are drastically changed.

Where it's reviewed:
Horn Book, October 1980, page 642
School Library Journal, September 1980, page 78

Other books by the author:
Watermusic, 1986 (Young Adult)
Lure of the Dark, 1984 (Young Adult)
Secret Lies, 1981 (Young Adult)
Edward Troy and the Witch Cat, 1978

Other books you might like:
Carole S. Adler, *Eddie's Blue-Winged Dragon,* 1988

Eddie's brass dragon helps him out in some of his battles with cerebral palsy.

June Counsel, *A Dragon in Class Four*, 1984
  A dragon joins a nursery school class and the children love it.

E.W. Hildick, *The Dragon That Lived Under Manhattan*, 1970
  Jimmy finds a prince who has come to rescue a shy, lovable dragon hiding out in the subways of Manhattan.

Seymour Reit, *Benvenuto*, 1974
  Paolo brings a pet dragon home from camp to his home in New York City.

Oliver G. Selfridge, *The Trouble with Dragons*, 1978
  Three sisters take turns at slaying a dragon in order to win the hand of the prince.

1589

Susan Saunders

Illustrator: Melodye Rosales

Mystery of the Hard Luck Rodeo (New York: Random, 1989)

Age range: Grades 2-4

Series: Stepping Stone Book

Subject(s): Mystery and Detective Stories; Rodeos

Major character(s): Tommy Price, Preteen; Bonnie Sue, Preteen; Mel Jones, Musician

Time period(s): 1980s

Locale(s): United States

What the book is about: Ten year old Junior and his friend, Bonnie Sue, whose families work for area rodeos, are in the middle of strange happenings on the rodeo circuit that threaten to close down Red Bluffs rodeo and stop country singer Mel Jones from performing.

Where it's reviewed:
Booklist, June 15, 1989, page 1828
Kirkus Reviews, June 15, 1989, page 920
School Library Journal, July 1989, page 83

Other books by the author:
The Daring Rescue of Marlon the Swimming Pig, 1987
The Golden Goose, 1987
The Green Slime, 1982
A Sniff in Time, 1982

Other books you might like:
Eleanor Clymer, *The Horse in the Attic*, 1983
  Caroline's discovery of a painting leads to her father's restoration of the portrait of Sprite, a filly in the Racehorse Hall of Fame.
Jean Slaughter Doty, *Yesterday's Horses*, 1985
  Kelly finds a foal that seems to belong to a breed, supposedly extinct for thousands of years, which holds the secret to a medical mystery.
Robert M. Quackenbush, *Texas Trail to Calamity: A Miss Mallard Mystery*, 1986
  When her horse runs away with her across the desert, Miss Mallard, the famous ducktective, finds herself at a ranch where her safety is threatened.
Elizabeth Van Steenwyk, *The Secret of the Spotted Horse*, 1983

When Reddy goes to Montana, he is determined to become a rodeo champion before the summer is over, the then someone tries to steal his horse, Ruff.

Gertrude Chandler Warner, *The Amusement Park Mystery*, 1992
  The Aldens search for carousel horses that have disappeared from an amusement park.

1590

Ruth Sawyer

Illustrator: Valenti Angelo

Roller Skates (New York: Viking, 1936)

Age range: Grades 4-6

Subject(s): Friendship

Major character(s): Lucinda Wyman, Child; Patrick Gilligan, Driver (carriage driver); Vittore Coppicco, Peddler (fruit vendor)

Time period(s): 1890s

Locale(s): New York, New York

What the book is about: 10 year old Lucinda explores New York City on roller skates. She makes friends of all ages and experiences the death of a friend.

Where it's reviewed:
Booklist, December 1936, page 128
Horn Book, November 1936, page 359

Awards the book has won:
Newbery Medal 1937
Lewis Carroll Shelf 1964

Other books by the author:
Daddles, 1964
Enchanted Schoolhouse, 1956
Journey Cake, Ho!, 1953
Long Christmas, 1941

Other books you might like:
Osmond Molarsky, *Good Guys and the Bad Guys*, 1973
  Doug and Parker use their detective skills to solve the mystery of disappearing roller skates.
Eleanor Clymer, *Luke Was There*, 1973
  Julius, a child who lives in a shelter in the city, gets support and encouragement from Luke, a counselor.
Avi, *Sometimes I Think I Hear My Name*, 1982
  Conrad meets a new friend and they make plans for his visit to his parents in New York City.
Felice Holman, *Slake's Limbo*, 1974
  13 year old Aremis flees the gang members chasing him and hides in a subway tunnel for 121 days.
Harry Mazer, *Cave under the City*, 1986
  Tolley and Bubber survive on the streets of New York City during the Depression.

1591

Susan Fromberg Schaeffer

Illustrator: Darcy May

The Dragons of North Chittendon (New York: Simon and Schuster, 1986)

Age range: Grades 5-7

Subject(s): Dragons

Major character(s): Arthur, Dragon; Regina White Dragoness, Dragon; Patrick Witherspoon, Child

Time period(s): Indeterminate

Locale(s): North Chittendon, Vermont

What the book is about: Arthur, an unruly dragon and his extrasensory perception relationship with the boy, Patrick, in a story of humans and dragons. It is well know that humans are afraid of dragons. It is less well known that dragons are terrified of humans. Together, Arthur and Patrick try to improve relations between dragons and people.

Where it's reviewed:
Booklist, August 1986, page 1694
Publisher's Weekly, June 27, 1986, page 139
School Library Journal, September 1986, page 139

Other books by the author:
Buffalo Afternoon, 1990
Anya: A Novel, 1976
Falling, 1973

Other books you might like:
Rose Estes, *The Children of the Dragon*, 1985
    In the mythical kingdom of Gallardia, the Dragonlord's three children must fight to save themselves and the one remaining egg of the guardian dragon.
Susan Fletcher, *Dragon's Milk*, 1989
    Kaeldra possesses the power to understand dragons and uses this power to try to save her sister, who needs dragon's milk to recover from an illness.
Terry Jones, *Nicobobinus*, 1985
    Nicobobinus and his friend, Rosie, go in search of the Land of Dragons and find more adventures than they bargain for.
Shirley Rousseau Murphy, *The Ivory Lyre*, 1987
    With the help of four, dragonbards Tebriel and Kiri are instumental in inciting an uprising against the Dark and in locating the magical ivory lyre.
Jane Yolen, *A Sending of Dragons*, 1987
    When Jakkin and Akki are sent out to certain death, Jakkin's dragon and her offspring help them survive and gain unusual powers and insights.

1592

Alice Schick

Illustrator: Joel Schick

The Remarkable Ride of Israel Bissell (New York: Lippincott, 1976)

Age range: Grades 3-4

Subject(s): Revolutionary War

Major character(s): Israel Bissel, Historical Figure (post rider)

Time period(s): 1770s

Locale(s): Lexington, Massachusetts, American Colonies; Philadelphia, Pennsylvania; American Colonies

What the book is about: Based on a true story of the Revolutionary War. The story is told by Bissell's pet crow. Israel is a post rider who galloped from Boston to Philadelphia via

New York. He was spreading a document known as the Call to Arms.

Where it's reviewed:
Booklist, March 1, 1976, page 982
Kirkus Reviews, March 1, 1976, page 254
School Library Journal, April 1976, page 64

Other books by the author:
Santaberry and the Snard, 1979
Just This Once, 1978
Viola Hates Music, 1977
The Siamang Gibbons, 1976

Other books you might like:
Peter Burchard, *Whaleboat Ride*, 1977
    A sixteen year old boy guides a flotilla of American whaleboats across Long Island Sound to raid British-occupied Sag Harbor.
Clyde Robert Bulla, *Charlie's House*, 1983
    A poor, friendless, shipped to America as an indentured servant, runs away from a cruel master and dreams of building his own home.
Katherine Marko, *Away to Fundy Bay*, 1985
    Doone flees to the Bay of Fundy side of Nova Scotia to escape the British press gangs and joins the rebels in the fight for independence.
F.N. Monjo, *King George's Head Was Made of Lead*, 1974
    The statue of King George III tells his version of the events leading to the American Revolution.
Seymour Reit, *Guns for General Washington*, 1990
    Frustrated with life under seige in George Washington's army, Will Knox and his brother Colonel Henry Knox undertake the task of moving 183 cannons.

1593

Eleanor Schick

Home Alone (New York: Dial, 1980)

Age range: Grades 2-3

Series: Easy to Read

Subject(s): Latchkey Children; Mothers and Sons

Major character(s): Andy, Child (latchkey); Bisquits, Cat; Mrs. Scott, Neighbor

Time period(s): 1980s

Locale(s): United States

What the book is about: A boy manages his time when he gets out of school until his mother gets home from work. At first, it is a little scary, being home alone, but he and Bisquits have each other for company and there's still time to play.

Where it's reviewed:
Booklist, April 15, 1980, page 1211
Center for Children's Books Bulletin, September 1980, page 20
Hornbook, October 1980, page 516

Other books by the author:
Joey on His Own, 1982
Rainy Sunday, 1981
Summer at the Sea, 1979
Neighborhood Knight, 1976

Other books you might like:
Arlene Alda, *Sonya's Mommy Works*, 1982
  With Sonya's mother working, Sonya has adjustments to make, not all of which are easy.
Phyllis Rose Eisenberg, *You're My Nikki*, 1992
  Nikki needs reassurance that her mother won't forget her when she goes out to work.
Susan Saunders, *Lauren Takes Charge*, 1989
  Lauren's mother gets a job, so Lauren has extra responsibilities and more allowance, but she seems to be doing all the cleaning up after sleepovers.
Susan Richards Shreve, *How I Saved the World on Purpose*, 1985
  Miranda starts a club to take care of latchkey children and finds herself competing with the president of a rival club for publicity and support.
Muriel Stanek, *All Alone after School*, 1985
  When his mother must take a job and can't afford a babysitter, a young boy gradually develops confidence about staying home alone after school.

| 1594 |

Ann Schlee

Ask Me No Questions (New York: Holt, 1976)

Age range: Grades 5-8

Subject(s): Child Abuse; Orphans

Major character(s): Laura, Preteen; Barty, Preteen

Time period(s): 1840s (1848)

Locale(s): England (Seven miles from London)

What the book is about: Laura and Barty are sent to live with their aunt in the country to escape the cholera in London in 1848. Their whole life at Aunt Bolinger's seems composed of secrets. There are children at Drouet's asylum nearby, and Laura finds the neglected children eating pigs' food in her uncle's barn. She and Barty take on the task of finding out what is happening to the children at Drouet's, and they find real evil.

Where it's reviewed:
Growing Point, December 1976, page 3019
Times Literary Supplement, October 1, 1976, page 1249

Awards the book has won:
Boston Globe/Horn Book Award - Honor Book 1982

Other books by the author:
The Proprietor, 1983
The Vandal, 1979
The Consul's Daughter, 1972

Other books you might like:
John Louis Beatty, *1972*, Holdfast
  An Irish orphan, separated from her wolfhound when they are captured and taken to England, yearns for her dog and her homeland.
Gilbert B. Cross, *A Hanging at Tyburn*, 1983
  A fourteen year old orphan with a mysterious past is sentenced to death during the turmoil of building the first cross country canal in England.
Rumer Godden, *Listen to the Nightingale*, 1992
  When she wins a scholarship to a famous ballet school, Lottie is torn between a lifelong dream and her love for a puppy.

Michelle Magorian, *Good Night, Mr. Tom*, 1981
  A battered child learns to embrace life when he is adopted by an old man in the English countryside during WWII.
Noel Streatfeild, *Thursday's Children*, 1986
  Proud of her unusual history, a nameless orphan faces with spirit the unbearable conditions of an early 20th century English orphanage.

| 1595 |

Miriam Schlein

Illustrator: Erik Hilgerdt

I, Tut: The Boy Who Became Pharoah (New York: Four Winds, 1979)

Age range: Grades 3-5

Subject(s): Egyptian Antiquities; Historical

Major character(s): Tutankhaton, Royalty, Historical Figure; Hekenefer, Friend; Akhenaton, Royalty, Historical Figure

Time period(s): 14th century B.C.

Locale(s): Thebes, Egypt

What the book is about: Hekenefer, a friend of Tutankhaton, tells the story of the life and death of the young pharoah, later known as Tutankhamon, whose tomb in the Valley of the Kings amazed the world when it was discovered in 1922.

Where it's reviewed:
Center for Children's Books Bulletin, March 1979, page 126
Kirkus Reviews, March 1, 1979, page 266
School Library Journal, April 1979, page 62

Other books by the author:
I Sailed with Columbus, 1991
Little Rabbit the High Jumper, 1957
Deer in the Snow, 1956
Elephant Herd, 1954

Other books you might like:
Erick Berry, *Honey of the Nile*, 1963
  Intrigue abounds in the court of Ankhesenpaaton and Tutankhamun as opposing religious groups vie for leadership of ancient Egypt. (Advanced Readers)
Dorothy Sharp Carter, *His Majesty, Queen Hatshepsut*, 1987
  A fictionalized account of the life of Hatshepsut, a queen in ancient Egypt who declared herself king and ruled as such for more than twenty years.
Deborah Nourse Lattimore, *The Winged Cat: a Tale of Ancient Egypt*, 1992
  In ancient Egypt, a servant girl and a High Priest must find the spells from the Book of the Dead to find the truth behind the death of a sacred cat.
Naomi Mitchison, *Sun and Moon*, 1973
  Recounts the adventure of Sun and Moon, the twin children of Cleopatra and Mark Antony.
Mary Stolz, *Zekmet, the Stone Carver*, 1988
  Chosen to design a magnificent monument for a vain and demanding Pharoah, an Egyptian stone carver conceives of and begins to work on the Sphinx.

1596

Roni Schotter

Rhoda, Straight and True (New York: Lothrop, 1986)

Age range: Grades 5-7

Subject(s): Friendship; Schools

Major character(s): Rhoda, Preteen; Fig, Preteen

Time period(s): 1950s (1953)

Locale(s): New York, New York (Brooklyn)

What the book is about: In Brooklyn of the 1950s, sixth grader Rhoda learns to trust her own feelings as she befriends Fig, a girl ridiculed by her classmates.

Where it's reviewed:
Center for Children's Books Bulletin, October 1986, page 36
School Library Journal, December 1986, page 108

Other books by the author:
Hanukkah!, 1990
Efan the Great, 1986
Northern Fried Chicken, 1983

Other books you might like:
Miriam Chaikin, *Friends Forever*, 1988
    As news of German victories and Nazi atrocities comes over the radio, Mollie faces important decisions as she and her friends enter junior high.
Paige Dixon, *Promises to Keep*, 1974
    Sensitive to his hometown's reactions, an insecure boy is sure he willbe ridiculed when his orphaned Vietnamese cousin comes to live with them.
P.J. Petersen, *Would You Settle for Improbable?*, 1981
    The arrival of Arnold, who has spent much of his life in juvenile detention centers, has a great impact on Mike and his ninth grade classmates.
Mary Francis Shura, *The Search for Grissi*, 1985
    Peter feels uncomfortable at home and school after his family moves to Brooklyn, until the search for his sister's cat opens up a whole new life.
Vladimir Zheleznikov, *Scarecrow*, 1990
    Lena comes to live with her eccentric grandfather in a small village and finds herself mocked and persecuted by classmates at her new school.

1597

Alan Schroeder

Illustrator: Bernie Fuchs

Ragtime Tumpie (Boston: Little Brown, 1989)

Age range: Grades 2-3

Subject(s): Biography; African Americans; Dancing

Major character(s): Josephine ''Tumpie'' Baker, Musician (dancer), Historical Figure

Time period(s): 1910s (1915)

Locale(s): St. Louis, Missouri

What the book is about: Tumpie, a young black girl living in St. Louis in 1915, is drawn by the rhythm of the ragtime music she hears from the ragtime band in which her father plays. She dares to enter a dance contest meant for adults. When she wins the contest, she decides that dancing is her

calling. For more information, see Schroeder's longer biography, *Josephine Baker.*

Where it's reviewed:
Booklist, October 1, 1989, page 356
Center for Children's Books Bulletin, October 1989, page 43

Other books by the author:
Booker T. Washington, 1992
Jack London, 1992
Josephine Baker, 1991

Other books you might like:
Lucille Clifton, *Everett Anderson's Year*, 1974
    The story, in verse, of the activities of seven year old Everett Anderson throught the seasons.
Elizabeth Howard Fitzgerald, *Mac and Marie and the Train Toss Surprise*, 1993
    A brother and sister eagerly await the coming of the train, bringing their uncle who usually brings them presents.
Virginia Kroll, *Africa Brothers and Sisters*, 1993
    Daddy and Jesse play their favorite game: a question and answer game about people who live in Africa and how they are connected to Jesse.
Gloria Pinkney, *Back Home*, 1992
    Eight year old Ernestine returns to visit relatives on the North Caroline farm where she was born.
Faith Ringgold, *Aunt Harriet's Underground Railroad in the Sky*, 1992
    With Harriet Tubman as her guide, Cassie retraces the steps escaping slaves took on the Underground Railway in order to reunite with her brother.

1598

Janet Schulman

Illustrator: Lillian Hoban

The Big Hello (New York: Greenwillow, 1976)

Age range: Grades 1-2

Subject(s): Dolls and Dollhouses; Moving, Household

Major character(s): Sara, Toy (doll); Snoopy, Dog; Jane, Friend

Time period(s): 1970s

Locale(s): Los Angeles, California

What the book is about: A little girl chatters to everyone and everything around her, including her mother, her dog and her doll, while adjusting to her new life in California.

Where it's reviewed:
Booklist, March 15, 1976, page 1052
Kirkus, March 15, 1976, page 320
School Library Journal, May 1976, page 75

Other books by the author:
Camp Keewee's Secret Weapon, 1979
The Great Big Dummy, 1979
Jenny and the Tennis Nut, 1978
Jack the Bum and the Halloween Handout, 1977

Other books you might like:
Alma Flor Ada, *My Name Is Maria Isabel*, 1993
    Third grader Maria, born in Puerto Rico, wants badly to fit into her new school in the United States.
Angela Johnson, *The Leaving Morning*, 1992

A child watches for the moving men, has cocoa in the deli across the street and leaves lip marks on the apartment window before moving to a new home.

Alice McLerran, *I Want to Go Home*, 1992

A new cat named Sammy helps Marta adjust to the move to a new house.

Mattie Lou O'Kelley, *Moving to Town*, 1991

A rural family moves from their old farm house to a house in the big city.

Ann Warren Turner, *Stars for Sarah*, 1991

Lying in bed at night, Sarah wonders what life will be like when she moves to her new home.

| **1599** |

Janet Schulman

Illustrator: Marilyn Hofner

Jenny and the Tennis Nut (New York: Greenwillow, 1978)

Age range: Grades 2-4

Subject(s): Sports/Gymnastics; Sports/Tennis

Major character(s): Jennifer "Jenny", Sports Figure (gymnast); Mrs. Wister, Neighbor

Time period(s): 1970s

Locale(s): United States

What the book is about: Jenny's dad is a tennis nut who wants to share his love of the game with his daughter. However, Jennjy has already found the sport she enjoys. She shows her dad the cartwheels and other gymnastic tricks she has taught herself. Dad hopes that someday Jenny will want to try tennis, but for now he encourages her gymnastics.

Where it's reviewed:
Booklist, April 15, 1978, page 1357
Kirkus, March 15, 1978, page 304
School Library Journal, May 1978, page 82

Other books by the author:
Camp Keewee's Secret Weapon, 1979
The Great Big Dummy, 1979
Jack the Bum and the UFO, 1978
The Big Hello, 1976

Other books you might like:
Peter Firmin, *Basil Brush on the Trail*, 1979
When tennis star Nora Nett's trophies begin disappearing, her house-sitters, Basil Brush and Harry the Mole, turn into super sleuths.
Evelyn Lunemann, *Tennis Champ*, 1972
Although she wants to please her father and win the tennis tournament, Mattie finds a sick child's needs more important.
Bill Powers, *Flying High*, 1978
Karen wants desperately to win the gymnastics championship but she is her own worst enemy.
Nancy Robison, *On the Balance Beam*, 1978
Andrea's dream of becoming an accomplished gymnast is threatened by her own impulsiveness and a jealous member of her gym team.
H.R. Sheffer, *Two at the Net*, 1981

An excellent tennis player, Dee must decide whether to devote her life to the game or make time for some of the things other girls enjoy.

| **1600** |

Amy Schwartz

Oma and Bobo (New York: Bradbury, 1987)

Age range: Grades 1-3

Subject(s): Animals/Dogs; Grandparents

Major character(s): Alice, Child; Oma, Grandparent

Time period(s): 1980s

Locale(s): United States

What the book is about: Alice gets a dog for her birthday, but her grandmother is not pleased. Bobo and Alice get sent to obedience school and Oma helps them when she realizes how important Bobo is to Alice.

Where it's reviewed:
Booklist, April 1, 1987, page 1210
School Library Journal, March 1987, page 150

Other books by the author:
Albert Goes Hollywood, 1992
Magic Carpet, 1991
Wanted.Warm Fuzzy Friend, 1990
How I Captured a Dinosaur, 1989

Other books you might like:
Steven Kellogg, *Can I Keep Him?*, 1971
A boy wants a pet but nothing seems quite right until a new boy moves into the neighborhood.
Steven Kellogg, *Pinkerton, Behave!*, 1979
Pinkerton gets into so much trouble that he is sent to obedience school and creates chaos.
Ezra Jack Keats, *Hi, Cat!*, 1970
A cat follows Archie and Peter around their neighborhood.
Arnold Lobel, *Frog and Toad Together*, 1971
Five stories about the everyday activities of two good friends.
Barbara Ann Porte, *Harry's Dog*, 1984
Harry's dad is allergic to his dog, but his Aunt Rose helps solve the problem.

| **1601** |

Jon Scieszka

Illustrator: Lane Smith

Knights of the Kitchen Table (New York: Viking, 1991)

Age range: Grades 4-6

Subject(s): Arthurian Legend; Knights and Knighthood; Time Travel

Major character(s): Joe, Preteen; Sam, Preteen; Fred, Preteen

Time period(s): 1990s

Locale(s): Earth

What the book is about: The gift Joe receives from his uncle, the magician, turns out to be neither a magical coin nor a cloak, just a dumb book. Joe and his friends, Sam and Fred, are not impressed. However, the old blue book with the stars, moons and designs gives off a green mist that sends the boys back to the time of King Arthur. There they must overcome an evil knight and outwit a smelly giant and a menacing dragon.

Where it's reviewed:
Booklist, May 1, 1991, page 1716
Center for Children's Books Bulletin, July/August 1991, page 274

Other books by the author:
The Good, the Bad, and the Goofy, 1992
Stinky Cheese Man, 1992
Frog Prince Continued, 1991
The Not So Jolly Roger, 1991

Other books you might like:
Susan Cooper, *Over Sea, Under Stone*, 1965
    Three children on a Cornwall holiday find an ancient manuscript that sends them on a dangerous quest that would reveal the true story of King Arthur.
Ann Curry, *The Book of Brendan*, 1989
    The evil magician Myrddin battles Fr. Brendan of Holybury Abbey and his young friends who are helped by magical beasts, Arthur, Guinevere, and Merlin.
Margaret Hodges, *The Kitchen Knight*, 1990
    A retelling of the Arthurian legends of how Sir Gareth becomes a knight and rescues the lady imprisoned by the fearsome Red Knight of the Red Plain.
William McCay, *Young Indiana Jones and the Ghostly Riders*, 1991
    In 1913, young Indiana Jones finds a ring that may have belonged to King Arthur, investigates sabotage of some coal mines, and travels back in time.
James Riordan, *Tales of King Arthur*, 1982
    Twelve of the best known tales of King Arthur and his knights, retold from Malory's "Morte d'Arthur" and other medieval sources.

1602

Ouida Sebestyen

Words by Heart (Boston: Little Brown, 1979)

Age range: Grades 5-8

Subject(s): Prejudice; Fathers and Daughters; Race Relations

Major character(s): Lena Sills, Preteen (Afro-American); Claudie, Step-Parent; Tater Haney, Bully

Time period(s): 1910s (1910)

Locale(s): Bethel Springs, Mississippi

What the book is about: The Sills family is from Scatter Creek, an all-black town. Lena Sills wins first prize in a scripture memory contest, ahead of a popular white boy. When the Sills return home, they find a butcher knife stabbed through a fresh loaf of bread into the table. Papa says she can't hold the people of Bethel Springs responsible. Lena learns what "love your enemies" really means and how hard it can be to put into practice.

Where it's reviewed:
Horn Book, June 1979, page 303
School Library Journal, May 1979, page 76

Other books by the author:
The Girl in the Box, 1988
On Fire, 1985
IOU's, 1982
Far From Home, 1980

Other books you might like:
Eloise Greenfield, *Koya DeLaney and the Good Girl Blues*, 1992
    Koya DeLaney, an eleven year old African-American girl, has trouble expressing anger until her cousin, a popular male singer, comes to town.
Joyce Hansen, *Which Way Freedom?*, 1986
    Obi escapes from slavery during the Civil War, joins a black Union regiment, and becomes involved in the bloody fighting at Fort Pillow, Tennessee.
Hadley Irwin, *I Be Somebody*, 1984
    A young black boy in the 1900s hears his community talk about moving to Canada to escape the prejudices and problems they face in the United States.
Mildred D. Taylor, *Roll of Thunder, Hear My Cry*, 1976
    A black family living in the South of the 1930s is faced with prejudice and discrimination which the children do not understand.
Brenda Scott Wilkinson, *Not Separate, Not Equal*, 1987
    Malene, one of a group of six blacks to integrate a Georgia public high school in the mid-sixties, experiences hatred and racism in her life.

1603

Catherine Sefton

Illustrator: Jill Bennett

The Emma Dilemma (London: Faber, 1983)

Age range: Grades 3-5

Subject(s): Accidents; Fantasy

Major character(s): Emma Kirstie Small, Child; William Small, Child; Dr. Small, Dentist

Time period(s): 1980s (1982)

Locale(s): Balmayne, England

What the book is about: A fantasy involving a girl and her transparent twin. Emma falls down the steps, hits her head and meets her own self when her head stops spinning. This other Emma is a bossy boots troublemaker. What is Emma going to do with her?

Where it's reviewed:
Children's Book Review Service, July 1983, page 134
Center for Children's Books Bulletin, October 1983, page 37
School Library Journal, May 1983, page 77

Other books by the author:
Island of the Strangers, 1985
The Haunting of Ellen, 1974
In a Blue Velvet Dress, 1973

Other books you might like:
Ruth Christoffer Carlsen, *Half-Past Tomorrow*, 1973
    After an injury to his head, a boy discovers he has the frustrating, frightening and dangerous ability to read tomorrow's newspaper.
Morris Gleitzman, *Misery Guts*, 1993

Keith tries to cheer up his parents by painting their shop and convincing them to move from gloomy England to a place called Paradise in Australia.

E.W. Hildick, *My Kid Sister*, 1971
    A boy tries to solve the dilemma of having a little sister who cries constantly.

Pat Kibbe, *The Hocus-Pocus Dilemma*, 1979
    Convinced that she has psychic powers, a ten year old girl makes predictions that seem to come true.

David Lloyd, *The Ridiculous Story of Gammer Gurton's Needle*, 1987
    The village troublemaker sets neighbor against neighbor when Gammer Gurton loses her needle while stitching a rip in her servant's trousers.

1604

Catherine Sefton

Illustrator: Eros Keith

In a Blue Velvet Dress (New York: Harper, 1972)

Age range: Grades 4-7

Subject(s): Vacations; Literature

Major character(s): Jane Reid, Preteen; Albert Hildreth, Firefighter; William Smollet, Preteen

Time period(s): 1970s

Locale(s): Rathard, England (seacoast town)

What the book is about: Eleven year old Jane Reid, certifiable bookworm, takes a suitcase full of books when she goes to visit an aunt and uncle while her parents are in Scotland. When she arrives, she finds she has picked up her father's case of rock samples instead of her books. The thought of even a few days without something to read is awful. But on her first night with the Hildreths, a book appears at her bedside. In the morning, it is gone. Someone knows what Jane needs, but who is it?

Where it's reviewed:
Kirkus Reviews, May 15, 1973, page 561
Library Journal, December 15, 1973, page 3718
Times Educational Supplement, December 14, 1979, page 21

Other books by the author:
Island of the Strangers, 1985
The Ghost of Bertie Boggin, 1980
The Haunting of Ellen, 1974

Other books you might like:
June Foley, *It's No Crush, I'm in Love!*, 1982
    Annie Cassidy, following the book *Pride and Prejudice*, imagines how Elizabeth Bennet would act when she falls in love with her English teacher

Sheila Greenwald, *It All Began with Jane Eyre, or, The Secret Life of Fanny Dillman*, 1980
    Avid reading and a vivid imagination get Franny Dillman into hot water when she turns from the classics to modern teen novels.

Nancy Hayashi, *Cosmic Cousin*, 1988
    While at the public library, Eunice tries to learn the identity of Cosmic Cousin, who like her loves science fiction and who is leaving notes in books

Michael Mason, *The Book that Jason Wrote*, 1968

Stranded on a desert island without anything to read, an avid reader writes his own story. (Related picture book)

Gary Paulsen, *Nightjohn*, 1993
    Twelve year old Sarny's brutal life as a slave becomes even more dangerous when a newly arrived slave offers to teach her how to read.

1605

Jerry Segal

Illustrator: Dav Pilkey

The Place Where Nobody Stopped (New York: Orchard, 1991)

Age range: Grades 6-10

Subject(s): Jews

Major character(s): Mordecai ben Yahbahbai, Scholar; Yosip, Cook (baker)

Time period(s): 1890s

Locale(s): Russia

What the book is about: In turn-of-the-century Russia, the scholar Mordecai and his family move in with Yosip, the baker, while they wait for Mordecai's brother who has taken their life savings to get passports to America. The brother's character is less than pure he has been a liar and a thief. Each year, they must hide from the cossacks who come marauding and forcing recruits into the Czar's army. For readers who enjoy thought processes and internal dialogue more than action. Projected to be a trilogy.

Where it's reviewed:
Booklist, February 15, 1991, page 1188
School Library Journal, March 1991, page 216

Other books by the author:
One on One, 1977 (Book based on a screenplay)

Other books you might like:
Judie Angell, *One-Way to Ansonia*, 1985
    Rose immigrates from Russia to America and finds that her emergence into adolescence brings employment, marriage, motherhood and self-determination.

Marge Blain, *Dvora's Journey*, 1976
    After fleeing Russia in 1904, twelve year old Dvora and her family face unexpected problems.

Anita Heyman, *Exit From Home*, 1977
    A Jewish youth, training to become a rabbi in Russia, becomes exposed to "worldy" ideas which alter his attitude toward religion and his country.

Efraim Sevela, *We Were Not Like Other People*, 1989
    Separated from his family when the Germans invade Russia during WWII, a young boy learns to fend for himself and earn a living whenever he can.

Fannie Steinberg, *Birthday in Kishinev*, 1978
    Sarah believes her birthday to be the happiest day of her life in Russia, but it becomes the most frightening when the Jewish population is attacked.

1606

Tor Seidler

Illustrator: Fred Marcellino

A Rat's Tale (New York: Farrar, Straus and Giroux, 1986)

Age range: Grades 4-6

Subject(s): Artists and Art; Animals/Rats

Major character(s): Montague, Rat, Artist; Elizabeth, Rat, Relative (aunt); Isabel, Rat, Girlfriend

Time period(s): Indeterminate

Locale(s): New York, New York (Central Park)

What the book is about: The rat community under New York City is threatened with extermination, but young Montague, looked down upon for working with his paws, offers to donate his paintings to help further the cause of ratdom, at least in Central Park.

Where it's reviewed:
Kirkus Reviews, October 1, 1986, page 1511
Booklist, January 15 1987, page 788
School Library Journal, January 1987, page 79

Other books by the author:
The Steadfast Tin Soldier, 1992
The Tar Pit, 1987
The Dulcimer Boy, 1979

Other books you might like:
Jane Leslie Conly, *Racso and the Rats of NIMH*, 1986
  Timothy, a field mouse, teams with adventurous rat Rasco to try to prevent the destruction of a secret community of rats that can read and write.
Dan Elish, *The Great Squirrel Uprising*, 1992
  With the help of Sally, a sympathetic ten year old human, Scruff the squirrel leads squirrels and birds in the blockade of Central to protest litter.
E.W. Hildick, *The Dragon That Lived under Manhattan*, 1970
  Jimmy finds a prince who has come to rescue a shy, loveable dragon hiding out in the subway tunnels of Manhattan.
Wil Huygen, *Secrets of the Gnomes*, 1982
  A first-hand account of the life of gnomes by the author and artist who, themselves turned into gnomes, visited with the gnomes of Lapland and Siberia
Shirley Rousseau Murphy, *The Flight of the Fox*, 1978
  Rory, a wandering kangaroo rat, restores a model airplane to fly on his travels and foils a flock of starlings that have overrun his town.

1607

Tor Seidler

The Tar Pit (New York: Farrar, 1987)

Age range: Grades 5-8

Subject(s): Behavior; Fantasy; Dinosaurs

Major character(s): Edward Small, Preteen

Time period(s): 1980s

Locale(s): United States

What the book is about: Edward is short and shy, lousy at baseball and failing math. Trying to skip math class, Edward retreats to an old tar pit and discovers a dinosaur jawbone, but no one will believe him. After a terrible nightmare in which Edward's dinosaur destroys everything in sight, Edward realizes he is his own worst enemy, changes his behavior and finally reaps the rewards of his discovery.

Where it's reviewed:
Center for Children's Books Bulletin, July/August 1987, page 217
School Library Journal, August 1987, page 130

Other books by the author:
The Steadfast Tin Soldier, 1992
A Rat's Tale, 1986
The Dulcimer Boy, 1979

Other books you might like:
Pam Conrad, *My Daniel*, 1989
  Ellie and Stevie learn about a family legacy when their grandmother tells them stories of her brother's quest for dinosaur bones on their farm.
Bruce Coville, *The Dinosaur That Followed Me Home*, 1990
  Stuart looks forward to another adventurous summer at camp but he and a friend wind up traveling into the past to the time of the dinosaurs.
Jessica Hatchigan, *Dinosaurs Aren't Forever*, 1991
  Molly and her friends find themselves in a race against time to save a big cement dinosaur from destruction.
Barry Longyear, *The Homecoming*, 1989
  Highly intelligent dinosaurs come back to reclaim the earth as their home.
Kin Platt, *Darwin and the Great Beasts*, 1992
  During a visit to the LaBrea Tar Pits, a Darwin imagines what it would be like to live in prehistoric times and try to outwit the dangerous beasts.

1608

George Selden

Illustrator: Garth Williams

The Cricket in Times Square (New York: Farrar, Straus and Giroux, 1960)

Age range: Grades 4-6

Subject(s): Animals; Animals/Insects

Major character(s): Chester, Cricket; Tucker, Mouse; Harry, Cat

Time period(s): 1960s

Locale(s): New York, New York

What the book is about: Chester, a musical cricket from Connecticut, with his friends Tucker the Mouse and Harry the cat, help bring success to a newsstand in Times Square.

Where it's reviewed:
New York Times Book Review, November 8, 1970, page 6
Publisher's Weekly, October 19, 1970, page 56
Times Literary Supplement, July 23, 1982, page 798

Awards the book has won:
Newbery Honor 1961

Other books by the author:
Chester Cricket's New Home, 1983
Chester Cricket's Pigeon Ride, 1981
The Genie of Sutton Place, 1973
The Garden under the Sea, 1957

Other books you might like:
Edward Bartholic, *Cricket and Sparrow: Four Stories*, 1979
  In four encounters Cricket and Sparrow meet, pretend, visit, and picnic.

Otto Coontz, *Hornswoggle Magic*, 1981
Using seemingly magical methods, a strange "bag lady" helps two children save one's father's newsstand, threatened by a huge new vending machine.

Felice Holman, *The Cricket Winter*, 1967
A little boy exchanges messages with the cricket that lives in his house and together they trap the rat that has been plaguing the boy's father.

William MacKellar, *Alfie and Me and the Ghost of Peter Stuyvesant*, 1974
Billy's encounter with the ghost of Peter Stuyvesant leads to a sensational treasure find in the heart of Times Square.

Barbara Reid, *Carlo's Cricket*, 1967
At the spring festival of the crickets, a young Italian boy buys a good luck cricket, loses it, and sets out to find his own special cricket again.

1609

George Selden

The Genie of Sutton Place (New York: Farrar Straus and Giroux, 1973)

Age range: Grades 4-6

Subject(s): Genies; Magic

Major character(s): Tim Fan, Child; Abdullah "Dooley", Spirit; Madame Sosostris, Antiques Dealer

Time period(s): 1970s

Locale(s): New York, New York

What the book is about: Magic come to Sutton Place, a very special magic worked by Tim's own special genie, Abdullah. "Dooley" is an authentic Arabian genie and Tim needs his help badly.

Other books by the author:
Old Meadow, 1987
Irma and Jerry, 1982
Tucker's Countryside, 1970
The Cricket in Times Square, 1960

Other books you might like:
Bill Brittain, *The Wish Giver: Three Tales of Coven Tree*, 1983
A little man comes to the Coven Tree Church Social allowing three belilevers to each make a wish that comes true in a way they wish it hadn't.

Jeff Brown, *A Lamp for the Lambchops*, 1983
A genie in training provides madcap adventures for the Lambchops until they realize it is best to unwish their wishes.

Ellen Conford, *Genie with the Light Blue Hair*, 1989
Jean finds a genie in the lamp she receives for her birthday, and discovers that having all her wishes come true isn't as wonderful as she expected.

Joanne Webster, *The Love Genie*, 1978
Much to her surprise, Jennie finds that having her own genie complicates her life.

Maeve Henry, *A Gift for the Gift*, 1992
Fran, a British teen from a troubled home meets a mysterious man who holds the power to fulfill all of her wishes.

1610

George Selden

Illustrator: Garth Williams

Harry Cat's Pet Puppy (New York: Farrar, Straus and Giroux, 1974)

Age range: Grades 3-6

Subject(s): Animals/Dogs; Trains

Major character(s): Harry, Cat; Tucker, Mouse

Time period(s): Indeterminate

Locale(s): New York, New York

What the book is about: Harry and Tucker still live happily in a drainpipe in a Times Square subway station. They adopt a bedraggled puppy who soon outgrows the drainpipe. Harry is convinced that the pup will fall in with a rowdy crowd of strays that hang out in Bryant Park.

Where it's reviewed:
Booklist, January 1, 1975, page 463
Hornbook, October 1974, page 139
Kirkus Reviews, December 15, 1974, page 1305

Other books by the author:
Chester Cricket's New Home, 1983
The Genie of Sutton Place, 1973
Tucker's Countryside, 1969
The Cricket in Times Square, 1960

Other books you might like:
Evelyn Wilde Mayerson, *Coydog: A Novel*, 1982
The lives of the son of a Greek immigrant and a half-dog, half-coyote puppy cross as each struggles with the problems of survival in New York City.

Robert Scott McKinnon, *Moose, Bruce and the Goose*, 1969
An abandoned greyhound puppy and a wounded Canada goose form a partnership that becomes famous throughout Montana.

Willo Davis Roberts, *Eddie and the Fairy Godpuppy*, 1984
Eddie, an orphan, hopes the puppy he finds in the orphanage is a fairy godpuppy that will bring him a family and a real home.

E.W. Hildick, *The Dragon That Lived Under Manhattan*, 1970
Jimmy finds a prince who has come to rescue a shy, loveable dragon hiding out in the subway tunnels of Manhattan.

Era Zistel, *Hi Fella*, 1977
Relates the adventures of a lost puppy and how he finds a new home.

1611

George Selden

Illustrator: Garth Williams

Tucker's Countryside (New York: Farrar, Straus and Giroux, 1969)

Age range: Grades 3-6

Subject(s): Animals; Fantasy

Major character(s): Tucker, Mouse; Chester, Cricket; Harvey, Cat

Time period(s): Indeterminate

Locale(s): Connecticut

What the book is about: The adventures of a city bred cat and mouse when they go to the country in Connecticut to visit their friend, Chester Cricket. A sequel to *Cricket in Times Square*.

Where it's reviewed:
Times Literary Supplement, April 2, 1971, page 388

Awards the book has won:
Christopher Award 1970

Other books by the author:
Harry Kitten and Tucker Mouse, 1986
Irma and Jerry, 1982
Harry Cat's Pet Puppy, 1974
Sparrow Socks, 1965

Other books you might like:
Ursula Le Guin, *Catwings Return*, 1989
 Two winged cats leave their new country home and return to the city, where they discover a winged kitten in a building slated to be demolished.
Lilian Moore, *Don't Be Afraid, Amanda*, 1992
 Having entertained her country pen pal Adam in the city, town mouse Amanda overcomes her fears of the dangers of the country to visit him.
Bill Peet, *Fly, Homer, Fly*, 1969
 A country pigeon is talked into visiting a city park by a sparrow. After he injures a wing he is helped home by the sparrow and his friends.
Mary Riskind, *Wildcat Summer*, 1985
 While in the country, two city children find a litter of kittens and are determined to take care of them, not realizing they are bobcats.
Margery Sharp, *Bernard the Brave: A Miss Bianca Story*, 1977
 Bernard, secretary of the Mouse Prisoner's Aid Society, and his teddy bear ally, Algernon, attempt to rescue an orphan heiress who has been kidnapped.

1612

Oliver G. Selfridge

Illustrator: Shirley Hughes

The Trouble with Dragons (Reading, Massachusetts: Addison-Wesley, 1978)

Age range: Grades 5-6

Subject(s): Fairy Tale; Princes and Princesses

Major character(s): Celia, Royalty (princess); Amanda, Royalty (princess); Belinda, Royalty (princess)

Time period(s): Indeterminate Past

Locale(s): Fictional Country (Kingdom by the Sea)

What the book is about: Three sisters, princesses, vie for the hand of a prince by attempting to slay dragons. The first, Amanda, goes off to earn his hand and is eaten by the dragon. Belinda tries next and never returns. Celia now has to turn in her blue jeans for shining armor. But first she goes to the library to learn everything she possibly can about dragons. Celia succeeds where the others failed. A very "happily ever after" ending.

Where it's reviewed:
Booklist, June 1, 1978, page 1556
Center for Children's Books Bulletin, July 1978, page 184
School Library Journal, September 1978, page 148

Other books you might like:
Mary Margaret Kaye, *The Ordinary Princess*, 1984
 At her christening, a princess is given the gift of "ordinariness" by a fairy. When she becomes a 14th assistant kitchen maid, she meets her prince.
Tanith Lee, *Princess Hynchatti and Some Other Surprises*, 1972
 Twelve fairy tales about princes and princesses in which the wizards, fairy godmothers, dragons and the like don't always play the traditional parts.
Mary Norton, *Are All the Giants Dead?*, 1975
 Finding himself in a land peopled with fairy tale characters, James attempts to help Princess Dulcibel who is destined to marry a toad.
Sally Scott, *The Elf King's Bride*, 1981
 Before Prince Armandel can claim Princess Florelise as his bride, he must break the fatal spell of the Elf King.
Patricia C. Wrede, *Searching for Dragons*, 1991
 Princess Cimorene rescues the dragon Kazul and saves the enchanted forest from a band of wicked wizards.

1613

Kate Seredy, Author/Illustrator

The White Stag (New York: Viking, 1937)

Age range: Grades 5 and Up

Subject(s): Folk Tales

Major character(s): Hunor, Twin; Magyar, Twin; Bendeguz, Parent

Time period(s): 5th century (400s)

Locale(s): Hungary

What the book is about: Attila the Hun leads the Hungarians to new lands in this Hun-Magyar legend. The mighty God Hadur sends the White Stag and the Red Eagle to lead the way.

Where it's reviewed:
Library Journal, January 1, 1938, page 34
New York Times Book Review, December 12, 1937, page 10

Awards the book has won:
Newbery Medal 1938
Lewis Carroll Shelf 1959

Other books by the author:
Lazy Tinka, 1962
Philomena, 1955
The Singing Tree, 1939
The Good Master, 1935

Other books you might like:
Linda Atkinson, *In Kindling Flame: The Story of Hannah Senesh*, 1985
 A biography of a Jewish heroine whose resistance work during WWII made her a martyr and an inspiration.
Val Biro, *Hungarian Folk-Tales*, 1980
 An adaptation from the works of Emil Koloysvari Grandpierre and Gyula Illyes.
Laszlo Hamori, *Dangerous Journey*, 1966
 A dramatic escape story of two Hungarian boys who jump the iron curtain to Austria.
Andrew Lang, *The Yellow Fairy Book*, 1980

A collection of more than forty tales from the folklore of Eastern Europe and America.

Aranka Siegal, *Upon the Head of the Goat: A Childhood in Hungary, 1939-1944*, 1981

Recounts the bewilderment of being a Jewish child in Hungary between 1939 and 1944, and relates the ordeal of survival in the ghetto.

| 1614 |

Pamela F. Service

Stinker From Space (New York: Scribner, 1988)

Age range: Grades 3-5

Subject(s): Science Fiction; Aliens; Animals

Major character(s): Ts yng Stinker, Alien, Spy; Karen Blake, Child; Jonathan Waldron, Child

Time period(s): 1980s

Locale(s): United States

What the book is about: An agent of the Sylon Confederacy, fleeing from enemy ships, crashes on Earth, transfers his mind to that of a skunk, and enlists the aid of two children to get back to his home planet. Before it's all over, Karen and Jon have learned to communicate with Stinker, and make a plan to use the space shuttle to return him to space. Problems develop when Stinker is taken away by a woman who claims he is her pet skunk. Good science fiction and high humor.

Where it's reviewed:
Center for Children's Books Bulletin, May 1988, page 144
School Library Journal, April 1988, page 104

Awards the book has won:
Arizona Young Readers Award

Other books by the author:
Being of Two Minds, 1991
Stinker's Return, 1991
Under Alien Stars, 1990
Vision Quest, 1989

Other books you might like:
Jonathan Etra, *Aliens for Lunch*, 1991
When their bag of popcorn explodes and a space alien emerges, Richard and Henry join him on an interstellar mission to save the universe's desserts.
Beatrice Gormley, *Wanted, UFO*, 1990
Fifth grader Elise is thrilled when a UFO appears in her friend Nick's backyard, but is shocked by the aliens' reason for coming to Earth.
Gery Greer, *Jason and the Aliens Down the Street*, 1991
Jason meets Cooper Vor and Lootna, aliens from space now living on Earth, and travels with them to a distant planet to rescue a stolen energy crystal.
Amy Lawson, *Star Baby*, 1992
Nine year old Allie, an only child, wishes on a falling star for a baby sister and receives a star baby instead.
Dyan Sheldon, *Harry the Explorer*, 1991
Chicken's cat, Harry, who is actually an alien from the planet Arcana, takes her on an adventure that gets her into all kinds of trouble.

| 1615 |

Pamela F. Service

Vision Quest (New York: Atheneum, 1989)

Age range: Grades 6-9

Subject(s): Indians of North America; Space and Time

Major character(s): Kate Elliot, Time Traveller; Wadat, Shaman, Indian; Jimmy Fong, Classmate

Time period(s): 1980s

Locale(s): Argentum, Nevada

What the book is about: Even though she is a military brat, used to moving, Kate finds life dreary in her small, Nevada desert town where she and her mother landed when her father died. Then contact with an Indian artifact sends her visions of a restless shaman from the past, visions which eventually drag her and her friend Jimmy Fong into that far time-distant Nevada and she gains the vision to free herself from the past.

Where it's reviewed:
Booklist, April 15, 1989, page 1471
School Library Journal, May 1989, page 202

Other books by the author:
Weirdos of the Universe, Unite!, 1992
When the Night Wind Howls, 1987
A Question of Destiny, 1986
Winter of Magic's Return, 1985

Other books you might like:
John Christopher, *New Found Land*, 1983
Encountering a crossing point between their world and another, two boys face Indians, Vikings, and Aztecs in their attempts to reach California.
Jane Louise Curry, *The Daybreakers*, 1970
While exploring what they think is an underground passage, three children are transported back in time to an ancient Indian civilization.
J. Allison James, *Sing for a Gentle Rain*, 1990
A boy's search for an explanation to a dream leads him to an Anasazi village, 700 years ago, where he helps insure the survival of the Indian people.
William E. Oldenbrug, *Potawatomi Indian Summer*, 1975
Six children find themselves transported back several centuries to a time in which the forests around their home were inhabited by Potowatomi Indians.
Jay Williams, *The Hawkstone*, 1971
A young New Englander is unaware of the strange power in the Indian relic, a stone-carved bird, he finds buried in a cave.

| 1616 |

Pamela F. Service

Winter of Magic's Return (New York: Atheneum, 1985)

Age range: Grades 5-9

Subject(s): Arthurian Legend; Fantasy; Wizards

Major character(s): Welly, Teenager; Heather, Teenager; Earl, Teenager

Time period(s): Indeterminate Future

Locale(s): England

What the book is about: After 500 years of nuclear winter, Britain is beginning to come alive again, and three teenagers believe the next age will be one of magic rather than technology. One of the teens is Merlin in the body of a fourteen year old. The blending of post-holocaust future and Arthurian legends of the past is unique as two friends set out to bring King Arthur back to the land. The good characterization and excellent satirical humor will appeal to mature readers.

Where it's reviewed:
Horn Book, November/December 1985, page 742
School Library Journal, December 1985, page 94

Other books by the author:
Weirdos of the Universe, Unite!, 1992
Being of Two Minds, 1991
Tomorrow's Magic, 1987 (Sequel to *Winter of Magic's Return*)
A Question of Destiny, 1986

Other books you might like:
Victor Appleton, *Crater of Mystery*, 1983
    Tom Swift and his crew are instrumental in delivering the planet Verita from a nuclear holocaust.
Monica Hughes, *Beyond the Dark River*, 1979
    In a now primitive Canada after a nuclear war, a boy from the secluded Hutterite community and an Indian girl seek a cure for a mysterious illness.
Annabel Johnson, *The Danger Quotient*, 1984
    A super-genius in a small colony of survivors of nuclear war, Casey travels back to the 20th century to discover how to save all the dying survivors.
Louise Lawrence, *Children of the Dust*, 1985
    After a nuclear war devastates the Earth, a small band of people struggles for survival in a new world where children are born with strange mutations.
Gregory Maguire, *I Feel Like the Morning Star*, 1989
    Three teens in a post holocaust survival colony find that their shelter has become a prison and decide to break out.

1617

Dr. Seuss

The Cat in the Hat (New York: Random, 1957)

Age range: Grades 1-2

Subject(s): Animals/Cats; Weather

Major character(s): Sally, Child; Cat in the Hat, Cat

Time period(s): 1950s

Locale(s): United States

What the book is about: A boy narrates the story of the rainy day when his mother leaves him and his sister Sally home alone. They are visited by a fabulous cat who shows them a good time and turns the house into a disaster area.

Other books by the author:
I Can Read with My Eyes Shut, 1978
Hop on Pop, 1963
Green Eggs and Ham, 1960
The Cat in the Hat Comes Back, 1958

Other books you might like:
Lenore Blegvad, *Rainy Day Kate*, 1987
    A child's anticipation of fun when Kate comes to play are dashed by a rainy day cancellation of Kate's visit, but the fun is not permanently spoiled.

Ida DeLage, *The Squirrel's Tree Party*, 1978
    With nothing to do on a rainy day, the squirrel children plan a sunny day party.
Elizabeth Miller, *Cat and Dog Raise the Roof*, 1980
    When the rain makes the roof on Pig's house fall in, Cat and Dog get all their friends to help raise the roof and make the house whole again.
Eleanor Schick, *Rainy Sunday*, 1981
    A young girl enjoys some unexpected pleasures on a rainy day.
Martha Sanders, *Alexander and the Magic Mouse*, 1969
    The Old Lady, a Magical Mouse, a cat, a yak, and Alexander, the smiling alligator, live on a hill without friends until rain endangers the town below.

1618

Anna Sewell

Black Beauty: The Autobiography of a Horse (New York: Crowell, 1895)

Age range: Grades 5-9

Subject(s): Animals/Horses

Major character(s): Squire Gordon, Gentleman; Black Beauty, Horse; Reuben Smith, Worker (groomer)

Time period(s): 1800s

Locale(s): England

What the book is about: A beautiful and spirited thoroughbred horse begins life as a pampered favorite in the stable of a fine gentleman. His career comes to an end when his knees are broken by a drunken groom. From then on his life is a succession of cruel misfortunes until the day when a wonderful stroke of luck brings him the happiness and contentment he had always longed for.

Other books by the author:
Black Beauty - His Grooms and Companions, 1990
Black Beauty Grows Up, 1983
Black Beauty and the Runaway Horse, 1983
The Courage of Black Beauty, 1983

Other books you might like:
Glenn Balch, *Indian Paint, the Story of an Indian Pony*, 1942
    Permitted to select a horse from his father's herd, the son of a cheif chooses a black mare whose foal he raises, to be a fine, swift horse.
Kathleen N. Daly, *Mustang: From the Walt Disney Productions' Film Based on the Story by Calvin Clements*, 1975
    A young boy's love for a mustang prevents the execution of the wild horse.
Marguerite Henry, *Mustang: Wild Spirit of the West*, 1966
    Annie Johnston, a Nevada woman fights to protect the mustang from extinction by professional killers who capture the horses for use in dog food.
Manly Wade Wellman, *Brave Horse: The Story of Janus*, 1968
    A fictionalized account of a thoroughbred who, though lame, thrived under intensive care and became the foundation sire of the American Quarter Horse.
Frances Wilbur, *A Horse Called Holiday*, 1992
    Middie gets the opportunity to ride and show a thoroughbred, but then discovers the horse is deaf and scared, requiring more care than she expected.

| 1619 |

Monica Shannon

Dobry (New York: Viking, 1934)

Age range: Grades 5-7

Subject(s): Grandparents; Artists and Art

Major character(s): Dobry, Child

Time period(s): 1930s

Locale(s): Sofia, Bulgaria

What the book is about: A young Bulgarian boy, living with his practical mother and his sympathetic grandfather, learns of his love and talent for art. The grandfather, a master storyteller, guides Dobry to fulfil his ambition.

Where it's reviewed:
Booklist, January 1935, page 178
Horn Book, November 1934, page 363

Awards the book has won:
Newbery Medal 1935

Other books by the author:
Bean Boy, 1927
California Fairy Tales, 1927

Other books you might like:
Gillian Cross, Wolf, 1991
    Cassy is forced to stay with her mother in a squatters settlement of artists and gains disturbing information about her father.
Vladimir Zheleznikov, Scarecrow, 1990
    12 year old Lena comes to live with her eccentric grandfather in a small Russian town and encounters prejudice at school.
Alfred Slote, The Trading Game, 1990
    11 year old Andy spends the summer trading baseball cards and making interesting discoveries about his grandfather, a former baseball player.
T.A. Baron, Heartlight, 1990
    Kate and her grandfather travel faster than light to save the sun from dying.
Gary Provost, David and Max, 1988
    Max and his grandfather search for a friend believed dead in the Holocaust in Nazi Germany.

| 1620 |

Marjorie Weinman Sharmat

Illustrator: Marc Simont

Nate the Great (New York: Putnam, 1972)

Age range: Grades 1-3

Subject(s): Artists and Art; Mystery and Detective Stories

Major character(s): Nate, Detective; Annie, Friend

Time period(s): Indeterminate

Locale(s): United States

What the book is about: When a painting of Fang is discovered missing, Nate the boy detective, puts on his Sherlock Holmes outfit and sets out to solve the mystery.

Where it's reviewed:
Booklist, May 1, 1973, page 860
Kirkus Reviews, October 1, 1972, page 1142

New York Times Book Review, November 5, 1972, page 34

Other books by the author:
Nate the Great and the Snowy Trail, 1982
Nate the Great and the Sticky Case, 1978
Nate the Great and the Lost List, 1975
Nate the Great Goes Undercover, 1974

Other books you might like:
Mary Blount Christian, Sebastian (Super Sleuth) and the Impossible Crime, 1992
    Clever canine cop Sebastian and his human, John, take on the finding of an art masterpiece stolen in the very presence of the chief of police.
Dan Cohen, The Mystery of the Mellafeller Elephant, 1980
    When a valuable piece of art disappears from a museum, Ruthann and her sister Polly help Officer Greenwood solve the mystery.
Hila Colman, The Case of the Stolen Bagels, 1977
    When Paul is wrongly accused of stealing bagels intended for an art project in his classroom, he sets out to find the real culprit.
Jacqueline Cooper, Angus and the Mona Lisa, 1981
    Angus the cat helps thwart the theft of the famous Mona Lisa.
Lisa Eisenberg, Fast-food King, 1980
    Someone has poisoned Reginald Bumpo with his own hamburger sauce, and investigator Laura Brewster comes to Australia to find the murderer.

| 1621 |

Marjorie Weinman Sharmat

Illustrator: Denise Brunkus

The Pizza Monster (New York: Delacorte, 1989)

Age range: Grades 3-4

Subject(s): Friendship; Self-Perception

Major character(s): Olivia Sharp, Preteen, Detective—Amateur

Time period(s): 1980s

Locale(s): United States

What the book is about: Olivia's first case as an "agent for secrets" involves finding out why Duncan's best friend, Desiree, dropped him. As Olivia probes into the matter, she learns that Duncan is so negative that he doesn't know how to keep a friend. Olivia decides she has to teach him how to laugh. The story is presented as a TV show.

Where it's reviewed:
Booklist, June 1989, page 1727
School Library Journal, September 1989, page 234

Other books by the author:
The Bully on the Bus, 1991
Cooking Class, 1991
Green Toenails Gang, 1991
Attila the Angry, 1985

Other books you might like:
Betty Bates, Tough Beans, 1988
    With the help of his best friend, Cassie, Nat comes to terms with his diabetes and a bully named Jasper.
Kathleen Krull, Alex Fitzgerald, TV Star, 1991

Alex's new friendships in California are in jeopardy when her chance to appear in a rock video does a number on her ego.
Phyllis Reynolds Naylor, *Josie's Troubles*, 1992
Josie and Sarah break one of the legs of Sarah's mother's piano bench and desperately look for odd jobs in order to make enough money to repair it.
Jerry Spinelli, *Fourth Grade Rats*, 1991
Suds learns that his best friend is wrong - you don't have to be a "tough guy" to get along in fourth grade.
Cheryl Zach, *Benny and the No Good Teacher*, 1992
Fourth grade is off to a bad start for Benny - his friends are in a different class and he draws the strictest fourth grade teacher in the school.

1622

Marjorie Weinman Sharmat

Illustrator: Lillian Hoban

Sophie and Gussie (New York: Macmillan, 1973)

Age range: Grades 1-3

Series: Ready-to-Read

Subject(s): Animals/Squirrels; Friendship; Poetry

Major character(s): Sophie, Squirrel; Gussie, Squirrel

Time period(s): Indeterminate

Locale(s): United States

What the book is about: A beginning reader about the adventures of two squirrels who spend the weekend together, exchange presents, plan a party and trade hats. They are just the very best of friends.

Where it's reviewed:
Hornbook, August 1973 Page 375
Kirkus Reviews, April 1, 1973, page 381
Library Journal, May 15, 1973, page 1696

Other books by the author:
Who's Afraid of Ernestine?, 1986
Attila the Angry, 1985
The Story of Bentley Beaver, 1984
Two Ghosts on a Bench, 1984

Other books you might like:
Ted Allan, *Willie the Squowse*, 1973
Son of a squirrel and a mouse, Willie, resident of an apartment house wall, links the lives of two neighboring families in a very unusual way.
V.H. Drummond, *Phewtus the Squirrel*, 1987
A knitted squirrel has a chance to become real for a while and learns he vastly prefers life as a toy.
Sachiko Komoto, *Chessie the Long Island Squirrel*, 1992
Follow Chessie the squirrel through the four seasons, from infancy to motherhood.
Beatrix Potter, *The Tale of Squirrel Nutkin*, 1987
When the other squirrels are busy gathering nuts, bad little Nutkin asks Old Mr. Brown Squirrel so many riddles that he at last becomes angry.
Laurence Yep, *The Curse of the Squirrel*, 1987
When a giant squirrel curses a farmer's best hunting dog, things change around the farm, and hunting little animals ceases to be a sport.

1623

Margery Sharp

The Rescuers (New York: Dell, 1959)

Age range: Grades 3-6

Subject(s): Animals/Mice; Rescue Work

Major character(s): Miss Bianca, Mouse; Nils Norwegian, Mouse; Bernard Brave, Mouse

Time period(s): Indeterminate

Locale(s): Fictional Country

What the book is about: At the Prisoners' Aid Society meeting, it is decided that the first priority is the rescue of a Norwegian poet from a dungeon in the Black Castle. Miss Bianca is the obvious choice, since she lives in the embassy and is free to travel in the diplomatic bag. She finds Nils, a Norwegian sea mouse and cannot resist joining him and Bernard in their mission.

Where it's reviewed:
Booklist, February 15, 1980, page 841

Other books by the author:
Miss Bianca in the Orient, 1978
Bernard the Brave: A Miss Bianca Story, 1977
Miss Bianca, 1974
The Turret, 1974

Other books you might like:
Barbara Alexander, *A Little Bigalow Story*, 1985
In the world of T.J.'s and Katie's imaginations, Bigalow, the pantry mouse, begins a new life as he takes a ride on a helium-filled balloon.
Frank Asch, *Pearl's Promise*, 1984
With her brother in the clutches of a python in a pet shop, Pearl, a mouse, goes through hair-raising adventures to rescue him.
Roald Dahl, *The Witches*, 1983
A boy and his grandmother, who is an expert on witches, foil a witches' plot to destroy the world's children by turning them into mice.
Mary DeBall Kwitz, *Shadow over Mousehaven Manor*, 1989
Minabell Mouse's animal friends come to her rescue when she becomes ensnarled with a gang of vicious rats determined to take over the family home.
Carol Beach York, *The Good Day Mice*, 1968
Big dogs, little boys, and twenty-eight orphan girls add to the problems of mother and father mouse after they move their family to the cellar.

1624

Nancy Shaw

Illustrator: Margot Apple

Sheep in a Jeep (Boston: Houghton Mifflin, 1986)

Age range: Grades 1-2

Subject(s): Animals/Sheep

Time period(s): Indeterminate

Locale(s): Fictional Country

What the book is about: Slapstick for young readers. The sheep, jeep and all, fall down and land in a muddy pool

Where it's reviewed:
Booklist, September 15, 1986, page 136

Other books by the author:
Sheep out to Eat, 1992
Sheep in a Shop, 1991
Sheep on a Ship, 1989

Other books you might like:
Tomie De Paola, *Haircuts for the Woolseys*, 1989
    Although recent haircuts have a sheep family shivering in an untimely snowstorm, Granny helps with newly-knit wool sweaters, made from their own hair.
Betsy Maestro, *Lambs for Dinner*, 1978
    Mr. Wolf keeps insisting he would like to have the lambs for dinner, but Mama and her four little lambs are naturally wary.
Marshall McClintock, *A Fly Went By*, 1958
    A sheep with its foot caught in a tin can sets off a chase with a fly in the lead.
Anne Rockwell, *Big Bad Goat*, 1982
    When Big Strong Dog, Big Strong Sheep, and Big Strong Horse fail to help Tommy, Little Bee succeeds in getting Big Bad Goat out of Tommy's yard.
Lionel Wilson, *The Mule Who Refused to Budge*, 1975
    A hen, goose, sheep, cow and bee are too busy to be friends until they are confronted with an obnoxious singing mule who won't leave them in peace.

1625

Ben Shecter

Hester the Jester (New York: Harper, 1977)

Age range: Grades 1-2

Series: Early I Can Read Book

Subject(s): Sex Roles

Major character(s): Hester, Child

Time period(s): Indeterminate Past

Locale(s): Fictional Country

What the book is about: When Hester announces she wants to be a jester like her father, her parents tell her a girl cannot be a jester. But when her father cannot make the king laugh, he allows Hester to try and she is a smash hit. She then tries knighthood and does the work of a king.

Where it's reviewed:
Booklist, October 15, 1977, page 382
Kirkus, October 1, 1977, page 1048
School Library Journal, December 1977, page 60

Other books by the author:
The Big Stew, 1991
Cheer Up, Pig, 1975
Clean as a Whistle, 1969
Every Day a Dragon, 1967

Other books you might like:
Remy Charlip, *Harlequin and the Gifts of Many Colors*, 1973
    Due to the generosity of his friends, Harlequin gets a new patchwork suit for Carnival.
M.L. Miller, *Dizzy From Fools*, 1985
    A young girl becomes a court jester despite her father's objections.

Richard Scarry, *Richard Scarry's Peasant Pig and the Terrible Dragon: with Lowly Worm the Jolly Jester*, 1980
    When Princess Lily is captured by a dragon, Peasant Pig bravely attempts her rescue.
Jaquelin Singh, *Fat Gopal*, 1984
    A clever court jester helps his master solve a seemingly impossible task given him by the Nawab.
James Thurber, *Many Moons*, 1970
    Though many try, only the court jester is able to fulfill Princess Lenore's wish for the moon.

1626

Louisa R. Shotwell

Illustrator: Peter Burchard

Roosevelt Grady (Cleveland: World, 1963)

Age range: Grades 4-6

Subject(s): African Americans; Migrant Labor; Friendship

Major character(s): Roosevelt Grady, Child; Miss Gladys, Teacher; Cap Jackson, Worker

Time period(s): 1950s

Locale(s): United States

What the book is about: Roosevelt is the child of migrant workers. Although secure in the knowledge of his parents' love for him, his home is where the crops are ripe and just as he reaches for new friendships and learning at school it is time to move on. Roosevelt dreams of living in one place where he can make friends and not be an outsider.

Where it's reviewed:
Library Journal, November 15, 1963, page 4469
Saturday Review of Literature, November 9, 1963, page 62

Awards the book has won:
Nancy Bloch Memorial Award 1963

Other books by the author:
Magdalena, 1971
Adam Bookout, 1967
Harvesters: The Story of Migrant People, 1961

Other books you might like:
Jeanne Betancourt, *Not Just Party Girls*, 1989
    16 year old Anne threatens to quit a money-making business with her friends. Then she sees the horrible conditions in a migrant worker camp.
Sue Ellen Bridgers, *Home Before Dark*, 1977
    Returning with her migrant family to her father's childhood home, a fourteen year old struggles with her new stationary life.
Nancy Covert Smith, *Josie's Handful of Quietness*, 1975
    Used to migrant life, Josie finally realizes her dreams of a permanent home and school.
Robert Newton Peck, *Arly's Run*, 1991
    Arly, an orphan in search of a family, escapes from a brutal migrant labor camp, joins a traveling religious show and battles a Florida hurricane.
Sherley Anne Williams, *Working Cotton*, 1992
    A young black girl relates the daily events of her family's migrant life in the cotton fields of California. The text is based on poems by Williams.

1627

Ellen H. Showell

The Ghost of Tillie Jean Cassaway (New York: Four Winds, 1978)

Age range: Grades 5-7

Subject(s): Ghosts

Major character(s): Willy Barbour, Preteen; Tillie Jean Cassaway, Spirit; Hilary Barbour, Child

Time period(s): Indeterminate

Locale(s): Mauvy, Appalachians

What the book is about: Tillie Jean drowned in the river. But people say that her ghost still roams the hills and hollows near her home. (Is Tillie trying to lure another child into the river?) The longer Willy gazes into the depths of the river, the more he sees. He can almost imagine he sees a face down there.

Where it's reviewed:
Booklist, September 15, 1978, page 225
Kirkus Reviews, October 15, 1978, page 1139
School Library Journal, September 1978, page 148

Awards the book has won:
South Carolina Children's Book Award 1978

Other books by the author:
Trickster Ghost, 1992
Our Mountain, 1991
Cecelia and the Blue Mountain Boy, 1983

Other books you might like:
Carole S. Adler, *Footsteps on the Stairs: A Novel*, 1982
    Dodie and her new stepsister Anne investigate sounds which may be coming from the ghosts of two sisters who drowned nearly forty years earlier.
Gail Freeman, *Alien Thunder*, 1982
    Walker discovers the alarming significance of the ominous thunder that his younger brother heard when their mother nearly drowned in the lake.
Liza Ketchum Murrow, *The Ghost of Lost Island*, 1991
    While helping his grandfather herd a flock of sheep on a small island, Gabe encounters a mysterious woman who may be the ghost of a drowned milkmaid.
Virginia Euwer Wolff, *Probably Still Nick Swansen*, 1988
    Nick, who is learning disabled, struggles as other kids taunt him and he is haunted by the memory of his sister who drowned while he was watching.
Betty Ren Wright, *The Pike River Phantom*, 1988
    Rachel and Charlie become linked with the ghost of a fierce old lady who is eerily involved in the Sunbonnet Queen contest about which Rachel dreams.

1628

Susan Richards Shreve

Illustrator: Diane De Groat

The Bad Dreams of a Good Girl (New York: Knopf, 1982)

Age range: Grades 3-5

Subject(s): Family Life; Schools; Short Stories

Major character(s): Carlotta "Lotta" McDaniel, Child; Kathy Sanders, Child; Nicholas McDaniel, Preteen

Time period(s): 1980s

Locale(s): United States

What the book is about: Lotty is a good child who is often teased by her boisterious older brothers. In this awful year, an "I Hate Lotty club" at school and her mother going back to work cause her to have bad dreams in which she acts out revenge fantasies. When one dream comes true, Lotty resolves, no more bad dreams. Four short, interrelated stories tell the tale.

Where it's reviewed:
Center for Children's Books Bulletin, April 1982, p 158
School Library Journal, April 1982, page 76

Other books by the author:
Wait for Me, 1992
The Masquerade, 1980
Family Secrets, 1979
The Nightmares on Geranium Street, 1977

Other books you might like:
Rose Impey, *Desperate for a Dog*, 1990
    Two sisters are eager to get a dog but their father is against the idea until they take care of a neighbor's dog for several weeks.
Norma Fox Mazer, *D, My Name Is Danita*, 1991
    Danita finds out she has an older half brother and she re-examines the way she sees her father and her family.
Ellen Kindt McKenzie, *The King, the Princess and the Tinker*, 1992
    A good-hearted tinker and a curious princess show a narrow-minded king that there is more to life than treasure.
Deborah Moulton, *Summer Girl*, 1992
    Because her mother is dying, Tommy is sent to live with her estranged father, and she gradually understands him and the death of the woman they love.
Barbara Ann Porte, *Fat Fanny, Beanpole Bertha and the Boys*, 1991
    Bertha's dad disappears in the Bermuda Triangle and Fanny's parents' secretly divorce. Fanny's triplet brothers are taught to tap dance to earn money.

1629

Susan Richards Shreve

Lucy Forever and Miss Rosetree, Shrinks (New York: Holt, 1987)

Age range: Grades 5-6

Subject(s): Psychology; Child Abuse

Major character(s): Rosy Treeman, Preteen; Lucy Childs, Preteen; Cinder, Orphan

Time period(s): 1980s

Locale(s): Charlottesville, Virginia

What the book is about: Lucy is the daughter of a psychiatrist and she and her friend, Rosy, make up patients for their practice, Shrinks, Incorporated. They come upon a small, mute child from an orphanage who is a patient of Lucy's father. They are determined they are going to find out what is wrong and help her to talk again. Lucy takes great risks to find out what is wrong with Cinder and winds up confronting the villain and almost losing her own life. A vivid portrayal of family, friendship, child abuse, and determination.

Where it's reviewed:
Horn Book, November 1987, page 739
Childhood Education, December 1987, page 119

Other books by the author:
Country of Strangers, 1990
The Flunking of Joshua T. Bates, 1984
The Bad Dreams of a Good Girl, 1982
Children of Power, 1979

Other books you might like:
Catherine Cookson, *Our John Willie*, 1974
    Two orphans, one deaf and mute, struggle to stay alive by relying on their own wits and stolen food from a formidable recluse.
Paul Fleischman, *The Half-a-Moon Inn*, 1980
    Mute Aaron goes out in a blizzard to search for his mother and is trapped by the evil Miss Grackle at the Half-a-Moon Inn.
Kaye Gibbons, *Ellen Foster*, 1987
    Having suffered abuse and misfortune for much of her life, a child searches for a better life and finally gets a break.
Helen Griffith, *The Mysterious Appearance of Agnes*, 1975
    A small child, who mysteriously appears in a remote 16th century German village becomes emotionally disturbed and is accused of witchcraft.
Lila Hopkins, *Eating Crow*, 1988
    In order to befriend Zeke, a mute boy who is new in town, Croaker must swallow his pride. Then an attack on Zeke's pet crow tests their friendship.

1630

Elizabeth Shub

Illustrator: Rachel Isadora

Cutlass in the Snow (New York: Greenwillow, 1986)

Age range: Grades 2-5

Subject(s): Grandparents; Treasure

Major character(s): Sam, Child

Time period(s): 1790s (1797)

Locale(s): New York

What the book is about: When they set sail to Fire Island to gather holly for Christmas, a snow storm forces Sam and Grandpa to spend the night there, and talk of pirates keeps them up all night. In the morning, they find a pirate's cutlass in the snow and a buried treasure. A concluding chapter tells how Sam's descendants discover the story is true.

Where it's reviewed:
Horn Book, May/June, 1986, page 325
School Library Journal, April 1986, page 59

Other books by the author:
The White Stallion, 1982
Seeing Is Believing, 1979
The Adventures of Little Mouk, 1974
Clever Kate, 1973

Other books you might like:
Hope Campbell, *Mystery at Fire Island*, 1978

While spending the summer on Fire Island, a promising eleven year old cartoonist and her father observe the mysterious activities of their neighbor.
John W. Chambers, *Finder*, 1981
    Jenny and her friends are curious about the mysterious house on Fire Island after she finds an abandoned dog that seems to have belonged there.
John W. Chambers, *Fritzi's Winter*, 1979
    Separated from her family during their last weekend visit to Fire Island, a Siamese cat struggles to survive on her own during the long winter months.
Eleanor Estes, *Pinky Pye*, 1958
    While spending a bird-watching summer on Fire Island, the Pye family acquires a small black kitten that can use a typewriter.
Ann M. Martin, *Eleven Kids, One Summer*, 1991
    Adventures of a family with eleven children as they summer on the beach at Fire Island.

1631

Elizabeth Shub

Illustrator: Rachel Isadora

The White Stallion (New York: Greenwillow, 1982)

Age range: Grades 2-4

Subject(s): Animals/Horses; American West

Time period(s): 1840s (1845)

Locale(s): Texas

What the book is about: Gretchen is saved by a mysterious stallion when she is carried away from her wagon train by the old mare she is riding.

Where it's reviewed:
Booklist, October 1, 1982, page 249
Kirkus Reviews, August 15, 1982, page 937

Other books by the author:
Cutlass in the Snow, 1986
Hanukah Money, 1978
The Adventures of Little Mouk, 1974
Uncle Harry, 1972

Other books you might like:
Marion Dane Bauer, *Touch the Moon*, 1987
    When a gift is magically transformed into a real horse, Jennifer has an evening of exciting adventures.
Sherry Garland, *Best Horse on the Force*, 1991
    When Brandon and Wayne try to take revenge on a rookie mounted policeman, their joke backfires on their favorite horse, Skyjacker.
Amy C. Laundrie, *Whinny of the Wild Horses*, 1990
    Follows the adventures of a wild colt living on the Wyoming range from his birth to adulthood.
Penny Pollock, *Stall Buddies*, 1984
    Scarlett, a young filly, finds a home on a rundown farm in Ohio, but never forgets her ambition to be a harness racer.
Marcia Sewall, *Ridin' That Strawberry Roan*, 1985
    A brave but foolhardy bronco-buster meets his match, the "Strawberry Roan." Based on an old folk song.

1632

Uri Shulevitz, Author/Illustrator

The Strange and Exciting Adventures of Jeremiah Hush (New York: Farrar Straus and Giroux, 1986)

Age range: Grades 3-5

Subject(s): Animals/Monkeys

Major character(s): Jeremiah Hush, Writer (poet), Monkey; Winchester Bone, Detective

Time period(s): Indeterminate

Locale(s): Orangutanville County, Fictional Country

What the book is about: Jeremiah the lonely monkey spends a disappointing evening in a single's club, investigates the disappearance of his umbrella, and goes to a county fair. Jeremiah takes on the shifty-eyed champion pie-eater of all time.

Where it's reviewed:
Booklist, February 1987, page 846
Kirkus Reviews, December 1, 1986, page 1795
School Library Journal, February 1987, page 84

Other books by the author:
The Diamond Tree, 1991
Toddlecreek Post Office, 1990
Oh What a Noise, 1971
One Monday Morning, 1967

Other books you might like:
Eth Clifford, *Harvey's Marvelous Monkey Mystery*, 1987
   Harvey finds himself embroiled in a mystery when a monkey appears at his bedroom window in the middle of the night.
John S. Goodall, *Jacko*, 1971
   After escaping his organ-grinder master, Jacko, a monkey, embarks on a perilous journey on a sailing ship.
Randall Jarrell, *The Bat-Poet*, 1964
   A bat who can't sleep days makes up poems about the woodland creatures he now perceives for the first time.
Michael Morpurgo, *Mr. Nobody's Eyes*, 1989
   Follows the adventures of an extraordinary pair on the run: an escaped circus monkey and an ostracized young English boy named Harvey.
Martha Bennett, *Tana and the Useless Monkey*, 1979
   Tana tries to demonstrate the usefulness of her mischievous pet monkey.

1633

Mary Francis Shura

Illustrator: Gene Sparkman

The Berkley Street Six Pack (New York: Dodd Mead, 1979)

Age range: Grades 3-5

Subject(s): Friendship; Magic

Major character(s): Natalie Lowery, Child, Occultist; Jane Todd, Child; Steve Jarvis, Neighbor

Time period(s): 1970s

Locale(s): United States

What the book is about: When ''best'' friend Natalie moves away, Jane is devastated to relize how harmful their relationship has been to her. With tremendous effort, Jane begins to make friends with some of the Barkley Street kids alienated by Natalie.

Where it's reviewed:
Center for Children's Books Bulletin, February 1980, page 118
School Library Journal, December 1979, page 89

Other books by the author:
Polly Panic, 1990
Diana, 1988
The Josie Gambit, 1986
Chester, 1980

Other books you might like:
Cynthia D. Grant, *Joshua Fortune*, 1980
   A boy dreams of a life much different from the counterculture in which he and his sister live with their divorced mother and her friends.
Myron Levoy, *Three Friends*, 1984
   Three very different classmates find their friendship tested by the pressures of growing up.
Margaret Poynter, *What's One More?*, 1985
   Margaret is a pet rescuer, sharing her home with stray, unwanted and abused dogs, nursing sick dogs back to health, and finding new homes for them.
Marjorie Reynolds, *A Horse Called Mystery*, 1964
   A nearsighted boy with a limp finds his outlook very different at the end of a summer when he acquires and cares for a lame horse.
Janice Lee Smith, *The Kid Next Door and Other Headaches*, 1984
   Two boys who are best friends share different viewpoints about neatness, pets, heroes, horrible cousins, and what an overnight guest is entitled to.

1634

Mary Francis Shura

Illustrator: Syd Hoff

Chester (New York: Dodd Meade, 1980)

Age range: Grades 2-4

Subject(s): Friendship; Neighbors and Neighborhoods

Major character(s): Jamie, Child; Wally Parsons, Bully; Chester, Child

Time period(s): 1980s

Locale(s): United States

What the book is about: Jamie has more freckles than any kid in the world. Amy is the oldest of the largest family in the world. George is the fastest runner. Eddie's family has the baldest baby, and Zach has the greatest home zoo. Until they meet Chester! Nobody believed that one kid could change the whole neighborhood in one week.

Where it's reviewed:
Center for Children's Books Bulletin, October 1980, p 40
Horn Book, October 1980, page 522

Other books by the author:
Don't Call Me Toad!, 1987
The Josie Gambit, 1986
Jefferson, 1984
Happles and Cinnamunger, 1981

Other books you might like:

Franz Brandenberg, *Nice New Neighbors*, 1977
  The Fieldmouse children find a way to make new friends when they move to a new house.
Johanna Hurwitz, *New Neighbors for Nora*, 1979
  The adventures of an inquisitive seven year old and her neighbors in a New York City apartment building.
Astrid Lindgren, *Lotta on Troublemaker Street*, 1984
  Because everyone is so mean to her at home, Lotta takes her favorite toy and goes to live in a neighbor's attic.
Ida Luttrell, *The Bear Next Door*, 1991
  Vic Bear and Arlo Gopher show they are not only good neighbors, but good friends as well.
Colin McNaughton, *Guess Who's Just Moved in Next Door?*, 1991
  A tour through a very peculiar neighborhood where monstrous neighbors react to the arrival of their new neighbors, a normal human family.

1635

Mary Francis Shura

The Josie Gambit (New York: Dodd, Mead, 1986)

Age range: Grades 5-7

Subject(s): Games; Friendship

Major character(s): Greg Farrell, Preteen, Sports Figure (chess player); Tory Mitchell, Preteen; Josie Nolan, Preteen

Time period(s): 1980s

Locale(s): Pineville, Illinois

What the book is about: Shy, twelve year old, chess-playing Greg is not happy with the idea of spending six months with his grandmother in a small town in Illinois while his mother is in Europe. He is a chess champion and knows that a gambit means giving up something in hopes of getting something better later. Until his relationship with the Nolan family, he doesn't believe anyone would try a "gambit" in real life. But his relationship with Josie opens him up to loyalty and friendship with people who really count.

Where it's reviewed:
Kirkus Reviews, July 1, 1986, page 1018
School Library Journal, September 1986, page 139

Other books by the author:
Our Teacher Is Missing, 1992
Gentle Annie, 1991
Diana, 1988
Don't Call Me Toad!, 1987

Other books you might like:
Rosa Guy, *The Ups and Downs of Carl Davis III*, 1989
  12 year old Carl Davis tells of his anger and confusion as well as his gradual change of heart about being sent to live with his grandmother.
Elizabeth Levy, *The Computer That Said Steal Me*, 1983
  A sixth grader's consuming desire for a computer chess game leads him into serious trouble.
Jean Davies Okimoto, *Take a Chance, Gramps!*, 1990
  Twelve year old Jane and her grandfather, both of whom have suffered losses, help each other reach out, make new friends, and change their lives.
Ken Radford, *Haunting at Mill Lane*, 1983

When twelve year old Sarah develops a close friendship with a ghost in turn-of-the-century Wales, their identities become confused.

1636

Mary Francis Shura

The Search for Grissi (New York: Dodd, Mead, 1985)

Age range: Grades 4-6

Subject(s): Animals/Cats; Schools

Major character(s): Peter Gregory, Preteen; Dee Dee Gregory, Child; Grissi, Cat

Time period(s): 1980s

Locale(s): New York, New York (Brooklyn)

What the book is about: Eleven year old Peter feels uncomfortable at home and at school after his family moves to Brooklyn, until a search for his sister's missing cat, Grissi, opens up a whole new life for him in his new neighborhood.

Where it's reviewed:
Booklist, March 15, 1985, page 1061
Publisher's Weekly, January 25, 1985, page 94
School Library Journal, May 1985, page 97

Awards the book has won:
Carl Sandburg Award 1985

Other books by the author:
Polly Panic, 1990
Marilee, 1985
Mr. Wolf and Me, 1979
Shoefull of Shamrock, 1965

Other books you might like:
T. Ernesto Bethancourt, *New York City, Too Far From Tampa Blues*, 1975
  A young Spanish American boy tells of his experiences living in Brooklyn and his friendship with an Italian boy who shares his passion for music.
Kay Brown, *Willy's Summer Dream*, 1989
  Willy faces another dull summer with his mother until tutoring from an older girl helps him develop a sense of self-confidence.
Eth Clifford, *Will Somebody Please Marry My Sister?*, 1992
  In 1920s' Brooklyn, Abel and friend Hilda try to find a husband for Abel's doctor sister to marry.
Miriam Cohen, *Robert and Dawn Marie 4 Ever*, 1986
  A boy in Brooklyn discovers respect and love with a parochial school girl and with the eccentric couple who take him in.
Jacqueline Woodson, *Last Summer with Maizon*, 1990
  Margaret tries to accept the inevitable changes that come one summer when her father dies and her best friend, Maizon, goes away to boarding school.

1637

Marlene Fanta Shyer

Grandpa Ritz and the Lucious Lovelies (New York: Scribners, 1985)

Age range: Grades 5-7

Subject(s): Grandparents; Old Age

Major character(s): Philip, Teenager; Al, Grandparent, Widow(er)

Time period(s): Indeterminate

Locale(s): United States

What the book is about: Philip is not at all happy when his parents send him to stay with his grandfather, who is living in a retirement community. Several elderly women are pursuing Grandpa, who has just recently lost his wife, is still depressed and definitely not interested. The "lucious lovelies" treat Philip royally and he has a fantastic summer.

Where it's reviewed:
Booklist, June 15, 1985, page 1461
School Library Journal, September 1985, page 189

Other books by the author:
Me and Joe Pinstripe, the King of Rock, 1988
Adorable Sunday, 1983
My Brother, the Thief, 1980
Blood in the Snow, 1975

Other books you might like:
Corinne Gerson, *My Grandfather the Spy*, 1990
    An elderly man's mysterious past is revealed after Mark and his friends nominate him for "Grandfather of the Year."
Janice Jones, *Secrets of a Summer Spy*, 1990
    Ronnie, growing apart from her best friends Amy and Jimmy, finds solace with the island's eccentric, cat-loving, eighty-three year old retired pianist
Norma Fox Mazer, *A Figure of Speech*, 1973
    The very special relationship between Jenny and her grandfather leads to tragedy when Jenny's parents want to place the man in an old age home.
Mary Stolz, *Stealing Home*, 1992
    Though they still listen to baseball and go fishing, Thomas and his grandfather's life in their Florida home changes when Great-aunt Linzy moves in.
Mary Towne, *Their House*, 1990
    Moving into their new, bigger house, Molly's parents regret letting the former owners, an elderly couple, stay on until they find a place of their own

---

1638

Marlene Fanta Shyer

Welcome Home, Jellybean (New York: Scribner, 1978)

Age range: Grades 5-7

Subject(s): Brothers and Sisters; Mentally Handicapped

Major character(s): Neil Oxley, Preteen; Geraldine "Gerri" Oxley, Teenager, Handicapped; Joe Newbolt, Friend, Handicapped (mentally retarded)

Time period(s): 1970s

Locale(s): United States

What the book is about: Neil's sister, Gerri, has come home after years in institutions for the retarded and Neil's life is turned upside down. The home is disrupted with Gerri's screaming, the late night noise of her rocking and banging her head, and the messes she makes. Neil is ready to move out, along with his father, until he realizes that he is helping Gerri improve.

Where it's reviewed:
Booklist, June 15, 1978, page 1619
Center for Children's Books Bulletin, September 1978, page 19
Publisher's Weekly, July 10, 1978, page 136

Other books by the author:
Grandpa Ritz and Our Lucious Lovelies, 1985
Here I Am an Only Child, 1985
Adorable Sunday, 1983
Blood in the Snow, 1975

Other books you might like:
Jane Leslie Conly, *Crazy Lady!*, 1993
    As he tries to come to terms with his mother's death, Vernon finds solace in a relationship with the neighborhood outcasts, an alcoholic and her son.
Donna Hill, *First Your Penny*, 1985
    Richard, a retarded teen, takes to the streets looking for a job in an attempt to make his family understand his need to fulfill himself.
Daniel Keyes, *Flowers for Algernon*, 1988
    Mentally retarded Charlie Gordon participates in an experiment which turns him into a genius - temporarily.
Joseph McNair, *Commander Coatrack Returns*, 1989
    When Lisa's retarded brother starts becoming more independent and growing away from her, she begins a game of make believe with a new boy at school.
Betty Ren Wright, *The Dollhouse Murders*, 1983
    A dollhouse filled with a ghostly light and dolls that move lead Amy and her retarded sister to unravel the mystery surrounding grisly murders.

1639

Margaret Sidney

Illustrator: Harriet Lothrop

The Five Little Peppers and How They Grew (New York: Grosset, 1948 (First edition, 1880))

Age range: Grades 3-6

Subject(s): Family Life

Major character(s): Ben Pepper, Preteen; Polly Pepper, Preteen; Phronsie Pepper, Child

Time period(s): 1880s

Locale(s): United States

What the book is about: A fatherless family, happy in spite of its poverty, is befriended by a very rich gentleman. Mrs. Pepper is bringing up five children in The Little Brown House, supporting them by sewing for others. The kind and loving family gets some very special help when they need it most. Originally published in 1880.

Where it's reviewed:
Booklist, November 15, 1976, page 480
Kirkus Reviews, November 15, 1976, page 1222
Publishers Weekly, October 18, 1976, page 64

Other books by the author:
Five Little Peppers at School, 1903
Five Little Peppers Midway, 1892
Five Little Peppers Abroad, 1902
Five Little Peppers Grown-Up, 1892

Other books you might like:
Louisa M. Alcott, *Little Women: or, Meg, Jo, Beth and Amy*, 1868
> The joys and sorrows of the fou rMarch sisters as they grow to maturity in 19th century New England.

Joan W. Blos, *A Gathering of Days: A New England Journal, 1830-1832*, 1979
> The journal of a girl, kept the last year she lived on a farm, records events in her small town, her father's remarriage and best friend's death.

Marilyn Cram Donahue, *Straight Along a Crooked Road*, 1985
> As her family travel from Vermont to California, Luanna learns to accept life for what it is, no matter where she is living.

Ellen Howard, *Sister*, 1990
> Alena, the eldest child of a large family, remains hopeful despite the hardships of growing up on a farm in the late 1800s.

Johann David Wyss, *The Swiss Family Robinson*, 1812
> Relates the fortunes of a shipwrecked family as they adapt to life on an island.

| 1640 |

Diane Siebert

Illustrator: Wendell Minor

Heartland (New York: Crowell, 1989)

Age range: Grades 5-6

Subject(s): Poetry

Time period(s): Indeterminate

Locale(s): Midwest

What the book is about: Evokes the land, animals and people of the Middle West in poetic text and illustration. The book is dedicated to the American farmer.

Where it's reviewed:
Booklist, March 11, 1989, page 1196
School Library Journal, May 1989, page 101

Other books by the author:
Sierra, 1991
Train Song, 1990
Mojave, 1988
Truck Song, 1984

Other books you might like:
Ann Nolan Clark, *In My Mother's House*, 1969
> A young Tewa Indian describes the homes, customs, work and strong communal spirit of his people.

Mary Ann Coleman, *The Dreams of Hummingbirds: Poems From Nature*, 1993
> Eighteen poems of nature and ecology.

Gary Soto, *Neighborhood Odes*, 1992
> Twenty-one poems about growing up in a Hispanic neighborhood, including the delights in items like sprinklers, the park, the library and pomegranates.

William Stafford, *The Animal That Drank Up Sound*, 1992
> When a mysterious animal drinks up all sound and leaves the earth frozen and cold, a hidden cricket ushers in the return of spring.

Ann Warren Turner, *Grass Songs*, 1993

A collection of poems describing the experience of traveling West during the 1800s, as seen through the eyes of pioneer women.

| 1641 |

Aranka Siegal

Upon the Head of the Goat: A Childhood in Hungary, 1939-1944 (New York: Farrar, 1981)

Age range: Grades 5-9

Subject(s): Jews; Holocaust; World War II

Major character(s): Piri Davidowitz, Child; Rozsi Davidowitz, Preteen; Fage "Babi" Rosner, Grandparent (Grandmother)

Time period(s): 1930s (1939)

Locale(s): Komajaty, Union of Soviet Socialist Republics (Ukraine); Hungary

What the book is about: To nine year old Piri, war was not real until the soldiers came, closing the borders and turning her summer vacation into a year long stay in the Ukraine at her grandmother's farm. Suddenly the war is very real. When she returns to Hungary, she learns quickly that life will not be the same, for Hitler is in power and no place is safe for Jews.

Where it's reviewed:
Booklist, October 1, 1984, page 214
Hornbook, April 1982, page 183
School Library Journal, December 1981, page 73

Awards the book has won:
Newbery Honor 1982
Boston Globe/Horn Book Award

Other books by the author:
Grace in the Wilderness: After the Wilderness, 1945-1948, 1985 (Sequel)

Other books you might like:
Linda Atkinson, *In Kindling Flame: The Story of Hannah Senesh*, 1985
> A biography of a Jewish heroine whose resistance work during WWII made her a matyr and an inspiration to those with whom she worked.

Eilis Dillon, *Children of Bach*, 1992
> A Hungarian Jewish family of talented musicians escapes Nazi persecution during WWII.

Judith Magyar Isaacson, *Seed of Sarah*, 1990
> Memories of a survivor of the persecution of Hungarian Jews during WWII, with a look at the Polish concentration camp, Auschwitz.

Candice Ransom, *So Young to Die*, 1993
> The story of Hannah Senesh and the underground movement of Hungarian Jews during WWII.

Maxine Schur, *Hannah Szenes: A Song of Light*, 1986
> A biography of the Jewish heroine whose mission to help rescue European Jews in WWII cost her her life.

| 1642 |

Maida Silverman

Illustrator: David Small

Anna and the Seven Swans (New York: Morrow, 1984)

Age range: Grades 1-3

Subject(s): Witches and Witchcraft; Legends

Major character(s): Anna, Child; Ivan, Child; Baba Yaga, Witch

Time period(s): Indeterminate Past

Locale(s): Russia

What the book is about: When her little brother is taken away by the swans belonging to the terrible witch, Baba Yaga, Anna searches for him in the great dark forest. Anna saves him from the witch who lives in one of the best chicken-legged cottages in the neighborhood. A stove, an apple tree and a river of milk help Anna defeat Baba Yaga.

Where it's reviewed:
Center for Children's Books Bulletin, September 1984, page 15
School Library Journal, December 1984, page 35

Other books by the author:
The Glass Menorah and Other Stories for Jewish Holidays, 1992
The Magic Well, 1989

Other books you might like:
Becky Ayers, *Matreshka*, 1992
   Kata's little wooden doll saves her life when she is captured by Baba Yaga.
Gregory Maguire, *The Dream Stealer*, 1983
   A village of peasants rebuild their homes on a train to flee a wolf only to be saved by a little girl's dream and knowledge of the witch, Baba Yaga.
Elsa Okon Rael, *Marushka's Egg*, 1993
   Nine year old Marushka is sucked into a magic egg where she is forced to be a housekeeper for the witch, Baba Yaga.
Ann Tompert, *The Tzar's Bird*, 1990
   A tzar's fear of going to the edge of the world grows when Baba Yaga threatens him, but he learns that fear of the unknown is a senseless fear.
Elizabeth Winthrop, *Vasilissa the Beautiful*, 1991
   A retelling of the old Russian fairy tale in which beautiful Vasilissa uses the help of her doll to escape from the witch, Baba Yaga.

Herma Silverstein

Mad, Mad Monday (New York: Dutton, 1988)

Age range: Grades 6-8

Subject(s): Ghosts; Magic; Revenge

Major character(s): Miranda Taylor, Teenager; Michael Oliver Newberry, Spirit (ghost); Stormy Kincaid, Teenager

Time period(s): 1980s (1988)

Locale(s): United States

What the book is about: In trying to cast a spell with a love potion designed to bewitch handsome but conceited Stormy, Miranda actually conjures up the ghost of a boy who died in 1958. Having a ghost around is disconcerting, especially when Monday tells Miranda he wants to get revenge on his old girlfriend for marrying someone else after he died. Miranda

helps Monday with his plans, but they both discover that there are more important things than revenge.

Where it's reviewed:
Booklist, April 1, 1988, page 1353
Kirkus Reviews, December 15, 1988, page 1738
School Library Journal, February 1988, page 74

Other books by the author:
The Alamo, 1992
David Ben Gurion, 1988
Scream Machines, 1986
Mary Lou Retton, 1985

Other books you might like:
Daniel Cohen, *Ghostly Tales of Love and Revenge*, 1992
   A collection of ghost stories about such spirits as "The Demon Lover," "The Lady in Black," and "The Empire State Building Ghost."
Judith Winship Hollands, *The Like Potion*, 1986
   Beverly concocts a magic love potion to lure back her boyfriend, only to have it change the behavior of the teacher who accidentally consumes it.
Mollie Hunter, *The Haunted Mountain*, 1972
   After angering the fairy creatures of the Highlands, a stubborn Scot is thirteen years bringing an end to their terrible revenge against him.
Elizabeth Muskopf, *The Revenge of Jeremiah Plum*, 1987
   Darcy's summer becomes filled with exciting activity when she meets Jeremiah Plum, a ghost determined to find out who murdered him fifty years ago.
Betty Ren Wright, *A Ghost in the House*, 1991
   Strange things happen when Sarah is alone in the house with Great Aunt Margaret, who is the victim of a ghost seeking revenge for death in the past.

Shel Silverstein

The Giving Tree (New York: Harper and Row, 1964)

Age range: Grades 1-3

Time period(s): Indeterminate

Locale(s): United States

What the book is about: The lifetime of a boy and a tree are shared in this book that can be handled by beginning readers, but has a message for all ages. When the boy and tree are young, the boy swings on her branches, eats her apples, and plays in her shade. As they age, the tree keeps giving happiness to the boy until she has nothing left to give.

Where it's reviewed:
Book World, May 14, 1978, page G2
New Catholic World, March 1979, page 92
New York Times Book Review, September 9, 1973, page 8

Other books by the author:
The Missing Piece Meets the Big O, 1981
The Missing Piece, 1976
A Giraffe and a Half, 1964
Who Wants a Cheap Rhinoceros?, 1964

Other books you might like:
Corinne Demas Bliss, *Matthew's Meadow*, 1992

Every year at blackberry time, the red-tailed hawk in the black walnut tree teaches Matthew to use his senses to fully appreciate nature.

Tom T. Hall, *Christmas and the Old House*, 1989
    When Bobby and Brenda decorate a tree growing through the floor of an abandoned house they learn a lesson about forgiveness and the Christmas spirit.

Tony Johnston, *Yonder*, 1988
    As the plum tree changes in the passing seasons, so do the lives of three generations of a farm family.

Leo Lionni, *A Busy Year*, 1992
    Mouse twins befriend a tree and watch it grow and change throughout each month of the year.

Lynn Reiser, *Christmas Counting*, 1992
    Ten successive Christmases in a clearing in the forest witness the simultaneous growth of a tiny fir tree and a family.

| 1645 |

Shel Silverstein

Lafcadio, the Lion Who Shot Back (New York: Harper, 1963)

Age range: Grades 3-5

Subject(s): Humor; Animals/Lions

Major character(s): Lafcadio, Lion

Time period(s): Indeterminate

Locale(s): Chicago, Illinois

What the book is about: His markmanship makes him a success, but Lafcadio discovers it's not to his liking. After leaving the jungle for the circus and a life of fame and wealth, the lion who taught himself to be the best shot in the world discovers that he's not really a lion anymore, and not a human being either.

Where it's reviewed:
Reading Teacher, January 1984, page 435

Other books by the author:
A Light in the Attic, 1981
The Missing Piece, 1976
A Giraffe and a Half, 1964
Giving Tree, 1964

Other books you might like:
Frank Asch, *I Met a Penguin*, 1972
    No one considers the lion a great fisherman except the special penguin brought into his life by a storm.
Clifford B. Hicks, *Pop and Peter Potts*, 1984
    A boy describes his life with his grandpa who devotes his time to such hobbies as lion taming, hypnotizing chickens, and inventing a Great Stone Man.
Edith Thacher Hurd, *Johnny Lion's Book*, 1965
    When his parents go out hunting, Johnny Lion stays home and reads his book, about another little lion who goes out into the world and gets lost.
C.S. Lewis, *The Lion, the Witch, and the Wardrobe*, 1981
    Four schoolchildren find their way through the back of a wardrobe into the magic land of Narnia and assist a golden lion to triumph over White Witch.
Gerald McDermott, *The Knight of the Lion*, 1979
    A retelling of the adventure of Sir Yvain and his faithful lion, as the knight goes through several trials to prove himself worthy of a great triumph.

| 1646 |

Shel Silverstein, Author/Illustrator

Where the Sidewalk Ends (New York: Harper & Row, 1974)

Age range: Grades 3-6

Subject(s): Humor; Poetry

Time period(s): Indeterminate

What the book is about: Comic cartoon drawings and humorous poems express the fears, fun and dreams of kids everywhere. A boy turns into a TV set and a girl eats a whale. Great fun for reading aloud and for independent readers in the middle grades.

Where it's reviewed:
Booklist, January 15, 1975, page 509
Hornbook, April 1975, page 162
School Library Journal, April 1975, page 47

Awards the book has won:
Michigan Young Readers Award 1981
New York Times Outstanding Books 1974

Other books by the author:
Who Wants a Cheap Rhinoceros?, 1983
A Light in the Attic, 1981
The Missing Piece, 1976
A Giraffe and a Half, 1964

Other books you might like:
Karla Kuskin, *Something Sleeping in the Hall: Poems*, 1985
    Humorous poems about animals, nature, friends, and experiences.
Edward Lear, *The Nonsense Verse of Edward Lear*, 1984
    A collection of 236 limericks and other nonsense poems.
Ogden Nash, *Custard and Company: Poems*, 1980
    An illustrated collection of humorous poems on a variety of topics.
Jack Prelutsky, *My Parents Think I'm Sleeping: Poems*, 1985
    Funny poems about bedtime.
Joseph Rosenbloom, *Silly Verse (and Even Worse)*, 1979
    Contains more than 200 short, humorous poems from anonymous sources.

| 1647 |

Norma Simon

Illustrator: Joe Lasker

How Do I Feel? (Chicago: Whitman, 1970)

Age range: Grades 1-3

Subject(s): Emotional Problems; Self-Acceptance; Twins

Major character(s): Eddie Freeman, Twin; Carl Freeman, Twin; Mike Freeman, Child (Carl and Eddie's brother)

Time period(s): Indeterminate

Locale(s): United States

What the book is about: Carl has tangled emotional problems with his twin and his older brother. Carl feels his mistakes deeply and looks to his older brother, Mike, as someone who really has his act together. Then he focuses on the things he does well, the way he helps Grandma and his twin, Eddie, and he feels better.

Where it's reviewed:
Center for Children's Books Bulletin, April 1971, page 129
Library Journal, July 1971, page 2361

Other books by the author:
I Am Not a Crybaby, 1989
I'm Busy, Too, 1980
All Kinds of Families, 1976
Benjy's Bird, 1965

Other books you might like:
Aliki, *Jack and Jake*, 1986
    A sister complains about the way everyone confuses her twin brothers.
Kristine Church, *My Brother John*, 1991
    A younger sister describes her almost fearless older brother.
Beverly Cleary, *Janet's Thingamajigs*, 1987
    Jimmy is envious of the special treasures Janet hoards in her crib, until the arrival of real beds reminds them that they are both growing up.
Virginia Kroll, *Helen the Fish*, 1992
    When Hannah's beloved goldfish dies after a relatively long life, she seeks comfort from her big brother, Seth.
P.K. Roche, *Good-bye, Arnold!*, 1979
    Webster Mouse is delighted when his older brother goes away for a week and Webster has the house and their parents to himself.

1648

Seymour Simon

Illustrator: Steve Miller

Chip Rogers, Computer Whiz (New York: Morrow, 1984)

Age range: Grades 4-6

Subject(s): Computers; Mystery and Detective Stories

Major character(s): Chip Rogers, Computer Expert; Katie, Child

Time period(s): 1980s

Locale(s): United States

What the book is about: Chip and Katie track the action of a mysterious jewel thief they encountered in the museum where their computer club meets. The programs they use are printed in the book. You can follow the story without running the programs but if you have a computer available, it's fun to enter and run them yourself.

Where it's reviewed:
Booklist, December 15, 1984, page 592
Learning, November 1984, page 71
School Library Journal, January 1985, page 80

Other books by the author:
Einstein Anderson Goes to Bat, 1982
Einstein Anderson Makes Up for Lost Time, 1981
Ghosts, 1976 (non-fiction)
Meet the Computer, 1985 (non-fiction)

Other books you might like:
Fred D'Ignazio, *Chip Mitchell: Case of the Robot Warriors*, 1984
    Chip, his friend, Legs, and his robot Sherwin, solve a series of mysteries.
E.W. Hildick, *The Ghost Squad Breaks Through*, 1984

Four ghosts and two live friends, using a word processor to communicate, go after a bully and prevent a robbery.
Claire Mackay, *Minerva Program*, 1984
    Minerva is crushed when she is banned from using the school computers but she finds a way to use them anyway, to solve a mystery and clear herself.
Ian McMahan, *The Lost Forest*, 1985
    Ricky Foster's computer sidekick, Alec, is threatened by a shutdown as Ricky is attempting to rescue his mother who has disappeared.
Dean Marney, *The Computer That Ate My Brother*, 1985
    12-year-old Harry receives a computer for his birthday. Its former owner, Imogene Cuniformly, helps him discover the strange powers the machine has.

1649

Seymour Simon

Illustrator: Fred Winkowski

Einstein Anderson, Science Sleuth (New York: Viking, 1980)

Age range: Grades 3-6

Series: Einstein Anderson, Science Sleuth

Subject(s): Science Fiction; Mystery and Detective Stories; Scientific Experiments

Major character(s): Adam "Einstein" Anderson, Preteen, Detective; Dennis Anderson, Child

Time period(s): 1980s

Locale(s): United States

What the book is about: Einstein Anderson uses his knowledge of science to discover the cause of a shrinking table, win a bet with Pat the Brat, uncover a UFO hoax, and solve other scientific riddles.

Where it's reviewed:
Booklist, October 1, 1980, page 257
Kirkus Reviews, December 1, 1980, page 1517
School Library Journal, November 1980, page 79

Other books by the author:
Einstein Anderson Sees through the Invisible Man, 1983
Einstein Anderson Goes to Bat, 1982
Einstein Anderson Makes Up for Lost Time, 1981
Einstein Anderson Tells a Comet's Tale, 1981

Other books you might like:
Harriet Sheffer Abels, *Mystery on Mars*, 1979
    The crew of Emergency Spaceship EM 88 helps to rescue miners trapped by an earthquake on a Mars colony.
Janet Asimov, *Norby and the Court Jester*, 1991
    While visiting the toy and game fair on planet Izz, Jeff and Norby search for a missing robot and the villain responsible for sabotaging the planet's
Brian Earnshaw, *Dragonfall 5 and the Empty Planet*, 1973
    When their classmates disappear from the circle of singing stones on the Empty Planet, Tim and Sanchez try to solve the mystery.
Joan Lowery Nixon, *Mystery Dolls From Planet Urd*, 1981
    A container of lifelike dolls, a gift from the planet Urd, seems to be tied in with a mysterious warning that the planet Durth will be invaded.
Harriette Ziefert, *Mystery Day*, 1989

Mr. Rose's class experiment in identifying "mystery powders" turns into a delicious chemistry lesson.

| 1650 |

Tom Sinclair

Illustrator: John Wallner

Tales of a Wandering Warthog (Niles, Illinois: Whitman, 1985)

Age range: Grades 4-6

Subject(s): Fantasy; Science Fiction; Space Travel

Major character(s): Mr. Warthog, Warthog; Troy Armstrong, Teenager; Adam Armstrong, Teenager

Time period(s): 1950s; 1960s

Locale(s): Earth; Outer Space

What the book is about: A genteel warthog joins the human world and recounts his adventures. Born in the African bush with the ability to speak, the warthog joins his new human friends, Adam and Troy on adventures that span the globe and reach beyond. While witnessing a rocket launch, Troy, Adam and Mr. Warthog wind up taking off with it, and their adventures continue.

Where it's reviewed:
Booklist, June 1, 1985, page 1405
Children's Book Review Service, Spring 1985, page 134
School Library Journal, August 1985, page 69

Other books you might like:
Jonathan Etra, *Aliens for Lunch*, 1991
    When their bag of popcorn explodes and an alien emerges, Richard and Henry join him on an interstellar mission to save the desserts of the universe.
Thomas P. Lewis, *The Blue Rocket Fun Show, or, Friends Forever!*, 1986
    Leslie visits her new best friend Niki's carnival home, but it isn't until the carnival is ready to leave that she learns about Nikki's real home.
Pamela F. Service, *Weirdos of the Universe, Unite!*, 1992
    Dedicated weirdos Mandy and Owen accidentally summon up five mythological beings, who need their aid in defending the Earth from space invaders.
Barbara B. Simons, *A Visit to the Ocean*, 1978
    Three children enjoying the plant and animal life near the ocean shore encounter a talking dolphin who emphasizes the importance of conservation.
Marilyn Singer, *Horsemaster*, 1985
    Jessica learns to summon her dream horse, on which she flies through time and space to fulfill her destiny in a distant, war-torn land.

| 1651 |

Bill Singer

Illustrator: Dennis Kendrich

The Fox with Cold Feet (New York: Parents, 1980)

Age range: Grades 1-2

Subject(s): Animals/Foxes; Winter

Time period(s): Indeterminate

Locale(s): Fictional Country

What the book is about: A fox looks for a pair of boots to keep his cold paws warm. He collects an odd assortment of make-shift boots from his animal friends for doing them favors, but just who benefits more is questionable.

Where it's reviewed:
Booklist, November 15, 1980, page 433
Kirkus Reviews, January 1, 1981, page 5

Other books you might like:
Yossi Abolafia, *Fox Tale*, 1991
    Donkey, Crow and Rabbit join forces to prevent Fox from swindling Bear out of a jar of honey.
Kathy Caple, *Fox and Bear*, 1992
    Fox and Bear, mismatched friends, find that they can get along with each other very well despite their differences.
Nonny Hogrogian, *One Fine Day*, 1989
    After the old woman cuts off his tail when he steals her milk, the fox must go through a series of transactions before she will sew it back on again.
Ikuyo Isami, *The Fox's Egg*, 1988
    Fox discovers an egg and decides it would be tastier hatched, but sitting on the egg makes the fox feel protective and creates unexpected problems.
Amy MacDonald, *Little Beaver and the Echo*, 1990
    Unaware that the lonely voice from across the pond is his echo, a little sets out to make a friend of the voice, encountering real friends on the way.

| 1652 |

Isaac Bashevis Singer

Illustrator: Margot Zemach

Alone in the Wild Forest (New York: Farrar, 1971)

Age range: Grades 4-6

Subject(s): Angels; Folk Tales; Jews

Major character(s): Joseph, Orphan; Maltuch, Royalty; Chassidah, Royalty

Time period(s): Indeterminate

Locale(s): Fictional Country

What the book is about: A magical tale about Joseph, who with the help of an angel's amulet, wins the hand of a princess.

Where it's reviewed:
Center for Children's Books Bulletin, February 1972, page 97
Kirkus Reviews, September 15, 1971, page 1015
Publisher's Weekly, September 6, 1971, page 50

Other books by the author:
Elijah the Slave, 1970
Joseph and Koza or the Sacrifice to the Vistula, 1970
A Day of Pleasure, 1969
Mazel and Shlimazel or the Milk of a Lioness, 1967

Other books you might like:
Roger Bradfield, *Pickle-Chiffon Pie*, 1967
    Three princes seeking to win the hand of the princess go into the forest to see who can bring back the most wonderful thing and marry the princess.
Miriam Chaikin, *Yossi Asks the Angels for Help*, 1985

When he loses the Hannukah money he planned to use for presents for his sister and parents, Yossi prays to the angels for help.

Pat Cummings, *C.L.O.U.D.S.*, 1986
  Chuku the angel is given the job of painting the skies of New York City, an assignment he approaches with reluctance, but grows to love.

Esther Hautzig, *Riches*, 1992
  After following the advice of the wisest rabbi in the area, a rich storekeeper discovers that giving of himself is better than merely giving money.

Shari Lewis, *One-Minute Jewish Stories*, 1989
  Twenty stories from various aspect of Jewish life - the Talmud, folklore, history, all in a format for reading in one minute.

1653

Isaac Bashevis Singer

Stories for Children (New York: Farrar Straus and Giroux, 1984)

Age range: Grades 4-8

Subject(s): Folk Tales; Short Stories; Storytelling

Time period(s): Indeterminate Past

Locale(s): Earth

What the book is about: Thirty-six tales for children to enjoy, including the eight tales from Naftali the *Storyteller and His Horse Sus*, *When Shlemiel Went to Warsaw*, and *The Power of Light*, as well as Singer's essay, "Are Children the Ultimate Literary Critics?" Excellent as a resource for storytelling.

Where it's reviewed:
Horn Book, March/April 1985, page 183
School Library Journal, December 1984, page 86

Other books by the author:
Naftali the Storyteller and His Horse, Sus, 1976
Fools of Chelm and Their History, 1973
Alone in the Wild Forest, 1971
Gimpel the Fool and Other Stories, 1957

Other books you might like:
Tony Fairman, *Bury My Bones but Keep My Words: African Tales for Retelling*, 1991
  A collection of African folktales, especially good for storytelling collections.
Ann Pilling, *Realms of Gold: Myths and Legends From around the World*, 1993
  Collection of fourteen myths from Greece, West Africa, Russia, and other parts of the world.
Henri Pourrat, *French Folktales*, 1989
  French folktales from the collection of Henry Pourrat
Laurence Yep, *The Rainbow People*, 1989
  A collection of twenty Chinese folktales that were passed on for generations, as told by Chinese newly settled in the United States.
Richard Young, *Stories From the Days of Christopher Columbus: A Multicultural Collection for Young Readers*, 1991
  A collection of traditional tales, fables and legends from the Spanish, Portuguese, Italian, and Native American cultures.

1654

Marilyn Singer

Illustrator: Judy Glasser

The Case of the Cackling Car: A Sam and Dave Mystery Story (New York: Harper, 1985)

Age range: Grades 3-5

Subject(s): Kidnapping; Twins; Mystery and Detective Stories

Major character(s): Sam Bean, Detective, Twin; Dave Bean, Detective, Twin

Time period(s): 1980s

Locale(s): Texas

What the book is about: Sam and Dave encounter a kidnapping in a small Texas town that involves a "cackling green Chevy."

Where it's reviewed:
Booklist, July 1985, page 1560
Kirkus Reviews, May 15, 1985, page J36
School Library Journal, May 1985, page 110

Other books by the author:
The Case of the Fixed Election, 1989
The Hoax on You, 1989
A Clue in Code, 1985
The Case of the Sabotaged School Play, 1984

Other books you might like:
David A. Adler, *The Fourth Floor Twins and the Sand Castle Contest*, 1988
  After winning a sand castle contest, two sets of twins resolve the mystery of the disappearance of a rich woman's dog.
Dana Brenford, *Tracks in the North Woods*, 1988
  When twins Peter and Jason and their stepsister, Kim, visit Canada's North Woods, they investigate the disappearance of an elderly woman.
Lillian Hoban, *The Case of the Two Masked Robbers*, 1986
  Raccoon twins Arabella and Albert track down the robbers who stole Mrs. Turtle's eggs.
Marion M. Markham, *The April Fool's Day Mystery*, 1991
  The Dixon twins try to discover who put the snake in the school cafeteria on April Fool's Day.
Jamie Suzanne, *The Haunted House*, 1990
  Twins Elizabeth and Jessica think that the Mercandy house is haunted until Elizabeth solves the mystery.

1655

Marilyn Singer

No Applause, Please (New York: Dutton, 1977)

Age range: Grades 5-8

Subject(s): Friendship; Schools/High School; Musicians

Major character(s): Shelley Sugarman, Actress (snob); Ruthie Zeiler, Musician; Laurie Garnett, Musician

Time period(s): 1970s

Locale(s): West Hempstead, New York

What the book is about: A teen poet and singer rethinks her career aspirations and friendships when her stage-struck partner makes other plans.

Where it's reviewed:
Booklist, September 15, 1977, page 199
Kirkus Reviews, May 1, 1977, page 493
School Library Journal, May 1977, page 72

Other books by the author:
Charmed, 1990
Ghost Host, 1987
The Course of True Love Never Did Run Smooth, 1983
The First Few Friends, 1981

Other books you might like:
Judie Angell, *The Buffalo Nickel Blues Band*, 1982
  Eddie Levy relates how he and his four friends who are involved in a blue band change as their music does.
Mary S. Bell, *Sonata for Mind and Heart*, 1992
  Ron is determined to go to New York to compete for a music scholarship despite his mother's disapproval of his passion for the violin.
James David Landis, *The Band Never Dances*, 1989
  Working through the anguish of her brother's suicide and trying to forge an identity of her own, Judy goes on tour as drummer for a hot new rock band.
Berniece Rabe, *Rehearsal for the Bigtime*, 1988
  Margo, always thought of as just a sweet little angel, gains confidence and people's admiration when she joins the band a starts music lessons.
Virginia Euwer Wolff, *The Mozart Season*, 1991
  Allegra spends her twelfth summer practicing a Mozart concerto for a violin competition and finding many significant connections in her world.

1656

Harriet Sirof

Illustrator: Jan Albrecht

Save the Dam! (New York: Crestwood House, 1981)

Age range: Grades 4-6

Subject(s): Imagination; Honesty; Terrorism

Major character(s): Cathy, Child; Ms. Taylor, Teacher

Time period(s): 1980s

Locale(s): United States

What the book is about: Cathy makes up stories about why Ms. Taylor suddenly left town. She stumbles on the truth, and no one can believe her anymore. She discovers a radical terrorist group threatening to blow up the dam. The leader is Ms. Taylor's brother.

Where it's reviewed:
Booklist, March 15, page 965
School Library Journal, March 1982, page 158

Other books by the author:
The Real World: A Novel, 1985
The If Machine, 1978

Other books you might like:
Laura Hawkins, *The Cat That Could Spell Mississippi*, 1992
  Anxious to prove she is special at her new school, fourth grader Linda makes everything difficult for herself when she cheats on a spelling bee.
Eddie Iroh, *Without a Silver Spoon*, 1981

Ure Chokwe comes from a poor, honest family. He is accused of stealing money but proves that honest is the best policy.
Catherine Frey Murphy, *Alice Dodd and the Spirit of Truth*, 1993
  While spending the summer in a cabin with her aunt and cousin, a young girl finds herself involved in a series of lies and deceptions.
Julie Ann Peters, *The Stinky Sneakers Contest*, 1992
  Earl and Damien jeopardize their friendship when they compete in a contest to see who has the smelliest sneakers.
Joanne Rocklin, *Jace the Ace*, 1990
  When Jason moves from New York to Los Angeles, he finds himself telling stories about being a junior photojournalist and investigative reporter.

1657

Mindy Skolsky

Illustrator: Karen Weinhaus

Carnival and Kopeck and More About Hannah (New York: Harper and Row, 1979)

Age range: Grades 2-4

Subject(s): Grandparents; Promises; Self-Discipline

Major character(s): Hannah, Child

Time period(s): 1930s (1932)

Locale(s): United States

What the book is about: Hannah's grandmother is coming from New York City to Hannah's home town. Hannah gets very excited and usually ends up going too far. She gets into an argument with Grandma over the carnival. People who love each other don't always get along.

Where it's reviewed:
Kirkus Reviews, June 1, 1979, page 639
School Library Journal, March 1979, page 133

Other books by the author:
Hannah and the Best Father on Route 9W, 1982
Hannah Is a Palindrome, 1980
Whistling Teakettle, 1977

Other books you might like:
David A. Adler, *Cam Jansen and the Mystery of the Carnival Prize*, 1984
  Cam uses her photographic memory to investigate the disappearance of the best prizes at the school carnival.
Amy Hest, *Travel Tips From Harry*, 1989
  Harry explains to his favorite cousin, Sam, what he can expect spending vacation at their grandparents' home in Florida.
Patricia MacLachlan, *Journey*, 1991
  When their mother leaves them at their grandparents' house, only grandfather can restore two children's past.
H.M. Menino, *Pandora: A Raccoon's Journey*, 1985
  A young raccoon wanders from her den, is adopted by a girl and travels around with the carnival.
Liza Ketchum Murrow, *Dancing on the Table*, 1990
  Jenny doesn't want her grandmother to get married, so she makes two wishes on her lucky rabbit's foot to ruin Nana's plans.

1658

Gloria Skurzynski

Illustrator: Ellen Thompson

Caught in the Moving Mountains (New York: Lothrop, 1984)

Age range: Grades 4-7

Subject(s): Survival; Earthquakes; Drugs

Major character(s): Paul, Teenager; Lance, Teenager; Rex Tole, Pilot, Smuggler

Time period(s): 1980s

Locale(s): White Cloud Mountains, Idaho

What the book is about: Paul and his brother are sent backpacking through Idaho's primitive forests. One night, a pilot on a drug smuggling run from Mexico City in a stolen plane crosses paths with the boys, and the excitement begins. A survival tale blending wilderness adventure with aerospace, wrapped in vivid description of the Idaho mountain country.

Where it's reviewed:
Booklist, November 1, 1984, page 375
Center for Children's Books Bulletin, December 1984, page 74
School Library Journal, November 1984, page 138

Other books by the author:
Dangerous Ground, 1989
The Minstrel in the Tower, 1988
Trapped in Slickrock Canyon, 1984
Lost in the Devil's Desert, 1982

Other books you might like:
Carole S. Adler, *Shadows on Little Reef Bay*, 1984
    Defending her friend when he is arrested on a drug charge, Stacy stumbles onto a smuggling network that includes her mother's boyfriend.
Thomas Baird, *Walk out a Brother*, 1983
    Don runs away from the domination of his brother when his father dies and crosses paths with a murderer high in the Rocky Mountains.
Wilanne Schneider Belden, *Mind Hold*, 1987
    After an earthquake, Carson is responsible for his survival and that of his sister, who hates him for sharing mental powers that make him dangerous.
Lynne Reid Banks, *The Writing on the Wall*, 1981
    A teenage girl takes a journey of self-discovery with her boyfriend and unwittingly becomes involved in drug smuggling.
Marian Rumsey, *Lion on the Run*, 1973
    A preteen boy tries to return the mountain lion he's raised from a cub to her native habitat in the Idaho mountains.

1659

Gloria Skurzynski

What Happened in Hamelin? (New York : Four Winds, 1979)

Age range: Grades 5 and Up

Subject(s): Middle Ages; Legends

Major character(s): Albert "Geist", Teenager (Assistant); Master Herman, Baker; Gast, Musician (piper; stranger)

Time period(s): 13th century (1284)

Locale(s): Hamelin, Germany

What the book is about: A novel of the Pied Piper legend told from the viewpoint of Albert, called "Geist" (ghost) because he is a baker's assistant and always white because he is coverd with flour. He dreams of freedom from his harsh medieval life and of a new life with the piper. Explains how the real piper lured the children, and how Geist was caught up in the stranger's spell so completely.

Where it's reviewed:
Booklist, January 1, 1980, page 669
Hornbook, February 1980, page 57
Kirkus Reviews, December 1, 1979, page 1376

Awards the book has won:
Christopher Award

Other books by the author:
The Minstrel in the Tower, 1988
Swept in the Wave of Terror, 1985
Two Fools and a Faker: Three Lebanese Folk Tales, 1977
The Poltergeist of Jason Morey, 1975

Other books you might like:
Julia Cunningham, *Wolf Roland*, 1983
    After losing his beloved donkey to a ravenous wolf, a poor man is roused to such sorrow and anger that he challenges the beast.
Daniel Curley, *Billy Beg and the Bull*, 1978
    In Ireland in the days of the heroes, the son of a king and his bull set out to find a new life away from the boy's stepmother.
Katherine Marcuse, *The Devil's Workshop*, 1979
    In the mid 1400s in Mainz, Germany, a twelve year old boy becomes apprenticed to Johann Gutenberg, who is believed to be in league with the devil.
Howard Pyle, *Otto of the Silver Hand*, 1967
    The gentle son of a medieval German robber baron, raised in the calm and thoughtful quiet of a monastery, grows to honor and manhood.
Robert Westall, *The Cats of Seroster*, 1984
    In medieval France, huge cats and a magic dagger help Cam, through a series of unusual and dangerous adventures.

1660

William Sleator

Illustrator: Trina Schart Hyman

Among the Dolls (New York: Dutton, 1975)

Age range: Grades 5-8

Subject(s): Child Abuse; Dolls and Dollhouses; Fantasy

Major character(s): Vicky, Child, Abuse Victim; Danderoo, Toy (doll); Ganglia, Toy (doll), Parent (abusive father)

Time period(s): Indeterminate

Locale(s): Fictional Country

What the book is about: Vicky is shrunken to doll size and forced to live in her dollhouse with the malicious dolls whose personalities she has created to reflect of the pain in her own family. First, she must get out of the dollhouse. Then she struggles to get a tiny copy of her own house out of the dollhouse to prevent her being captured again.

Where it's reviewed:
Booklist, January 1, 1976, page 628
Hornbook, February 1976, page 53
Kirkus Reviews, October 15, 1975, page 1186

Other books by the author:
The Green Futures of Tycho, 1981
Into the Dream, 1979
House of Stairs, 1974
Blackbriar, 1972

Other books you might like:
Carole S. Adler, *Fly Free*, 1984
  Shy Shari, abused at home by a mother who resents her, is befriended by a neighbor who shares her love of birds and the outdoors.
Sylvia Cassedy, *Lucie Babbidge's House*, 1989
  Having found a dollhouse full of dolls in the orphanage where she leads an unhappy existence, Lucie creates a secret life for herself.
Florence Parry Heide, *The Shrinking of Treehorn*, 1971
  A boy discovers that he is shrinking but does not know the cause or the cure.
Louise Moeri, *The Girl who Lived on the Ferris Wheel*, 1979
  Til realizes with increasing urgency that her divorced mother's violently abusive behavior is getting more and more out of control.
Marilyn Sachs, *A December Tale*, 1976
  A child struggling to change her unhappy life is weakened by an abusive foster mother, yet strengthened by imaginary conversations with Joan of Arc.

| **1661** |

William Sleator

The Duplicate (New York: Dutton, 1988)

Age range: Grades 6-8

Subject(s): Science Fiction; Cloning

Major character(s): David, Teenager

Time period(s): 1980s

Locale(s): United States

What the book is about: Sixteen year old David finds a strange object labelled Spee-Dee-Dupe on the beach. He finds that it duplicates only human beings. What a godsend, just when he needs to be in two places at once! The duplicate seems to be David in every way, including memories and personality. When a second duplicate is produced, things begin to get out of hand. It's hard to decide who will be where, when, and worse still, all three claim to be the real David and subtle differences emerge among the three.

Where it's reviewed:
Horn Book, May/June 1988, page 362
School Library Journal, April 1988, page 113

Other books by the author:
Strange Attractors, 1990
Fingers, 1983
The Green Futures of Tycho, 1981
Into the Dream, 1979

Other books you might like:
Mildred Ames, *Anna to the Infinite Power*, 1981

A twelve year old math whiz accidentally learns the startling facts about her true identity as a clone and her role in a secret experiment.
Margaret C. Cooper, *Solution: Escape*, 1980
  In the 21st century, Stefan goes to a scientific research station where he discovers he is part of a scheme to control the government.
Anne Lindbergh, *Three Lives to Live*, 1992
  Thirteen year old Garet's quiet life with her grandmother is changed when Garet's "twin" Daisy enters his life, a complete surprise.
Mary C. Ryan, *Me Two*, 1991
  Thirteen year old Will accidentally clones himself when a science experiment goes awry, and the clone proves to be more of a help than a hindrance.
Alfred Slote, *The Clone Catcher*, 1982
  Arthur Dunn is summoned to Australia to find a runaway clone urgently needed to provide a vital organ for her mother's transplant.

| **1662** |

William Sleator

House of Stairs (New York: Dutton, 1974)

Age range: Grades 5-9

Subject(s): Science Fiction; Psychology Experiments

Time period(s): 1980s

Locale(s): United States

What the book is about: Five fifteen year old orphans of widely varying personality characteristics are forced into a house of endless stairs as subjects for a psychological experiment on conditioned human response. The only sources of food are machines that dispense or not depending on their behavior toward one another.

Where it's reviewed:
Booklist, June 1, 1974, page 1101
Horn Book, August 1974, page 386

Other books by the author:
The Duplicate, 1988
The Green Futures of Tycho, 1981
Into the Dream, 1979
Run, 1973

Other books you might like:
Dale Bick Carlson, *The Mystery of the Shining Children*, 1983
  Jenny Dean, teenage detective, suspects that a doctor's experiments on children at a private foundation are part of a plot to achieve mind control.
Nicholas Fisk, *A Rag, a Bone, and a Hank of Hair*, 1980
  In the 23rd century, when children have become scarce, an unusually bright boy is sent to live with an experimental family of reborn 1940 Londoners.
Helen V. Griffith, *Journal of a Teenage Genius*, 1987
  Through journal entries, a young scientist describes his less than successful experiments and trips into the past using his neighbor's time machine.
Bernice Grohskopf, *Notes on the Hauter Experiment: A Journey Through the Inner World of Evelyn B. Chestnut*, 1975
  It was a strange school, with no exits, no teachers and a day controlled by lights and screens. Evelyn wondered how she got here and how to get out.

Bernal C. Payne, *Experiments in Terror*, 1987
  As his friends mysteriously disappear one by one in the middle of the night, Steve finds himself developing terrifying powers.

1663

William Sleator

Interstellar Pig (New York: Dutton, 1984)

Age range: Grades 6-9

Subject(s): Science Fiction; Aliens; Mystery and Detective Stories

Major character(s): Barney, Preteen

Time period(s): Indeterminate Future

Locale(s): United States

What the book is about: Barney is terribly bored with summer vacation until he gets to know new neighbors - three exotic characters addicted to a game they call "Interstellar Pig." Readers will figure out that they are aliens before Barney does. Sleator leaves clues along the way that Barney may not be seeing things exactly as they are, but readers will enjoy the "Star Wars" type space battles nevertheless. For science fiction, fantasy, and/or mystery fans.

Where it's reviewed:
Horn Book, September/October 1984, page 599
School Library Journal, September 1984, page 134

Other books by the author:
The Duplicate, 1988
The Boy Who Reversed Himself, 1986
Fingers, 1983
Blackbriar, 1972

Other books you might like:
Grace Chetwin, *Collidescope*, 1990
  When his spaceship crashes to Earth, a highly advanced alien interferes with the lives of two teens living in Manhattan during different centuries.
Peni R. Griffin, *Otto From Otherwhere*, 1992
  A ten year old alien boy travels through a door in space to enter the lives of Paula and her family for a year.
Margaret Mahy, *Aliens in the Family*, 1986
  Jake Raven, expecting to dislike her new stepsister and brother, ends up helping them protect an alien as he flees from mysterious pursuers.
Gillian Rubinstein, *Beyond the Labyrinth*, 1988
  Fourteen year old Brenton questions the choices in his life when an alien anthropologist comes to study an ancient tribe that once lived in the area.
Pamela F. Service, *Under Alien Stars*, 1990
  Jason resents his mother's friendliness toward the military commander of the alien forces ruling Earth, until they unite against a much deadlier race.

1664

William Sleator

Illustrator: Steven Kellogg

Once, Said Darlene (New York: Dutton, 1979)

Age range: Grades 1-3

Subject(s): Imagination

Major character(s): Darlene, Storyteller; Peter, Friend; Amy, Friend

Time period(s): 1970s

Locale(s): United States

What the book is about: Darlene tells too many tall tales and her friends revolt, all except Peter. Peter is able to use his imagination almost as well as Darlene can and understands the difference between telling stories and telling lies.

Where it's reviewed:
Booklist, October 1979, page 4
Kirkus Reviews, March 1, 1979, page 262
School Library Journal, May 1979, page 78

Other books by the author:
That's Silly, 1981
The Angry Moon, 1970

Other books you might like:
Ezra Jack Keats, *Regards to the Man in the Moon*, 1981
  With the help of his imagination, his parents, and a few scraps of junk, Louis and his friends travel through space.
Beverly Keller, *Pimm's Place*, 1978
  A timorous young boy teaches his rowdy cousins the value of being quiet and using one's imagination.
Theo LeSieg, *I Wish That I Had Duck Feet*, 1965
  A boy imagines what it would be like if he had such things as duck feet, a whale spout, and an elephant's trunk.
Romeo Muller, *Puff in the Land of the Living Lies*, 1982
  Sandy has a vivid imagination, but her stories become lies and no one believes anything she says. Puff the magic dragon helps her find truth.
Evaline Ness, *Sam, Bangs, and Moonshine*, 1966
  The experiences of a little girl who learns the difference between make believe and reality, and how important that can be when safety is concerned.

1665

Jan Slepian

Alfred Summer (New York: Macmillan, 1980)

Age range: Grades 5-6

Subject(s): Physically Handicapped; Friendship; Courage

Major character(s): Lester, Handicapped, Child; Alfred, Handicapped, Child

Time period(s): 1930s (1937)

Locale(s): New York, New York (Brooklyn)

What the book is about: Four friends spend the summer building a boat, learning about "US" and "THEM." They all grow stronger and happier in their friendship with each other and with their families.

Where it's reviewed:
Horn Book, August 1980, page 411
School Library Journal, April 1980, page 128

Awards the book has won:
Boston Globe/Horn Book Award - Honor Book

Other books by the author:
Risk n' Roses, 1990

Something Beyond Paradise, 1987
Lester's Turn, 1981
The Night of the Bozos, 1983

Other books you might like:
Larry Callen, *Sorrow's Song*, 1979
Sorrow Nix, a mute, finds solace in protecting an injured whooping crane.
James Howe, *A Night Without Stars*, 1983
11 year old Maria has open heart surgery and finds strength in her friendship with another patient who has been badly burned.
Anne Knowles, *Under the Shadow*, 1983
Cathy shares the sense of freedom when she finds a horse for her disabled friend to ride.*SFN Sam
Sam Teague, *King of Hearts' Heart*, 1987
13 year old Harold is trying to make the track team and neglects his brain damaged friend, Billy, until a crisis intervenes.
Jane Yolen, *The Mermaid's Three Wisdoms*, 1978
A mermaid who cannot speak is banished from the sea and is found by a 12 year old girl with a hearing impairment.

1666

Jan Slepian

Rish n' Roses (New York: Philomel, 1990)

Age range: Grades 5-7

Subject(s): Friendship; Mentally Handicapped; Moving, Household

Major character(s): Skip, Preteen; Angela, Handicapped (mentally)

Time period(s): 1940s (1948)

Locale(s): New York, New York (the Bronx)

What the book is about: In 1948, newly moved to the Bronx, eleven year old Skip resents the constant responsiblity of her mentally handicapped older sister, Angela. Skip has met Jean, who seems to be the boss of the neighborhood and would much rather spend time with her. Jean turns out to be a bad choice for a role model, and the heartless way she treats Angela poses a difficult challenge for Skip. This story offers the reader a chance to see the pain that can be involved in growth.

Where it's reviewed:
Booklist, October 1, 1990, page 331
Horn Book, January/February 1991, page 70

Other books by the author:
The Broccoli Tapes, 1988
Getting on with It, 1985
The Night of the Bozos, 1983
Lester's Turn, 1981

Other books you might like:
1978 Anne Norris Baldwin, *A Little Time*, 1978
A ten year old begins to understand her feelings toward her younger brother who has Down's Syndrome.
Dawna Lisa Buchanan, *The Falcon's Wing*, 1992
After her mother's death, twelve year old Bryn and her father move to Canada to live with her aunt and cousin, a loving girl with Down's syndrome
Bo Gustaf Bertelsson Carpelan, *Bow Island: The Story of a Summer That Was Different*, 1971

An eleven year old boy learns about human relationships and mental handicaps during a summer spent on a Baltic island.
Vera Cleaver, *Me Too*, 1973
Hoping to get rid of the neighborhood prejudice and improve the situation, a twelve year old desperately tries to teach her retarded twin.
Nancy Hope Wilson, *Bringing Nettie Back*, 1992
Eleven year old Clara is enriched by her friendship with the vibrant Nettie, but then a serious brain condition threatens to change Nettie forever.

1667

Carolyn Sloan

The Sea Child (New York: Holiday, 1988)

Age range: Grades 5-7

Subject(s): Fantasy; Intolerance

Major character(s): Jessie, Child (10 years old); Danny, Parent (father); Lisa, Child

Time period(s): Indeterminate Past

Locale(s): Earth

What the book is about: Jessie and her father live alone on an island and she has never seen another human being. On her tenth birthday, her father shows her a dangerous secret passage leading to the mainland. For the first time in her life, Jessie meets another child.

Where it's reviewed:
Horn Book, January/February, 1989, page 75
School Library Journal, October 1988, page 148

Other books by the author:
The Friendly Robot, 1986

Other books you might like:
Jennifer Austin, *Treasure Beach*, 1990
Cassie joins Alexandra on a tropical island where strange events threaten a crew searching for sunken treasure.
Eileen Dunlop, *Finn's Island*, 1991
A boy's visit a remote Scottish Island, romanticized by his grandfather, gives him a dose of reality and helps him heal his relationship with his dad.
Patricia A. McKillip, *The Changeling Sea*, 1988
A floor scrubber and a magician try to help a prince return to his home beneath the sea, and help his half-brother.
Ruth Park, *My Sister Sif*, 1986
Riko and her delicate older sister, Sif, go to their remote Pacific island home, where it is discovered Sif has connections with an underwater race.
Pamela Powell, *The Turtle Watchers*, 1992
Sisters Esther, Philomena and Amelia work to protect a nest of leatherback turtle eggs from both human and natural enemies.

1668

Louis Slobodkin

The Spaceship Returns to the Apple Tree (New York: Macmillan, 1972)

Age range: Grades 3-5

Subject(s): Farm Life; Grandparents; Aliens

Major character(s): Eddie Blow, Preteen; Martin E. "Marty" Ann, Alien, Scientist

Time period(s): 1970s

Locale(s): Albany, New York

What the book is about: When a little spaceman becomes earthbound because he loses or mislays the power which made his spaceship fly (Secret Power 2 - short for Zurianomatichrome) Eddie takes him fishing, to a Boy Scout Jamboree, and through many adventures on his grandmother's farm, just outside Albany.

Where it's reviewed:
Grade Teacher, January 1965, page 30

Other books by the author:
The Spaceship in the Park, 1972
The Hundred Dresses, 1971
Rountrip Spaceship, 1968
The Three Seated Spaceship, 1962

Other books you might like:
Jane Louise Curry, *The Lost Farm*, 1974
    When their farm and everything in it is reduced to a miniature by a mysterious machine, Pete and his grandmother do all they can to keep themselves an
Mel Gilden, *Outer Space, and All That Junk*, 1989
    A boy works for his uncle one summer only to discover him collecting junk in the belief he is helping aliens return to their home in outer space.
Gery Greer, *Jason and the Aliens Down the Street*, 1991
    Jason meets Cooper Vor and Lootna, aliens from space now living on Earth, and travels with them to a distant planet in an attempt to retrieve a stolen
Andre Norton, *The Day of the Ness*, 1975
    Hal traces a frantic SOS to a group of friendly space aliens held captive inside a mountain by the evil Ness who plans to take over the world.
Natalie Standiford, *Space Dog and Roy*, 1990
    When a spaceship crashes in his backyard, Roy gets what he's always wanted, a dog of his very own. Space Dog soon sets Roy straight. He's an explorer

---

1669

Alfred Slote

Finding Buck McHenry (New York: HarperCollins, 1991)

Age range: Grades 4-6

Subject(s): African Americans; Sports/Baseball; Prejudice

Major character(s): Jason, Preteen (baseball fan), Sports Figure (Little Leaguer); Mack Henry, Maintenance Worker (custodian)

Time period(s): 1990s

Locale(s): United States

What the book is about: Eleven year old Jason thinks that the school custodian, Mack Henry, is really Buck McHenry, a baseball player who pitched in the old Negro leagues. Jason thinks it would be terrific to get him to coach his Little League team. In addition to the story line, there is lots of information here for serious baseball fans, especially about the treatment of the black players by the whites.

Where it's reviewed:
Booklist, March 15, 1991, page 1493
School Library Journal, May 1991, page 95

Other books by the author:
The Trading Game, 1990
Make-Believe Ball Player, 1989
Rabbit Ears, 1982
Hang Tough, Paul Mather, 1973

Other books you might like:
Nancy Baron, *Tuesday's Child*, 1984
    Grace intends to be the first female in the big leagues, but her mother insists she take ballet at the time her baseball team practices and plays.
Matt Christopher, *Look Who's Playing First Base*, 1971
    Mike Hagin offers his new friend from Russia the first baseman's position on the Little League team and then learns the boy has never played baseball.
Dean Hughes, *Superstar Team*, 1991
    The Angel Park Dodgers survive their second season in Little League as they discuss Jonathan Swingle, the new super star who is also super obnoxious.
E.L. Konigsburg, *About the B'nai Bagels*, 1985
    Mark Setzer tells about all sorts of troubles but especially the woes of having his mother managing and his brother coaching his Little League team.
R. Parker McVey, *Mystery at the Ball Game*, 1985
    In this "plot-your-own" story, the reader learns of a plot to kidnap a millionaire's son at a Little League game and must decide what to do about it.

1670

Alfred Slote

A Friend Like That (New York: Lippincott, 1988)

Age range: Grades 4-6

Subject(s): Fathers and Sons; Remarriage; Single Parent Families

Major character(s): Robby, Preteen; Beth, Friend

Time period(s): 1980s

Locale(s): United States

What the book is about: When Robby takes drastic steps to stop his widowed father from developing a love interest, his friend Beth has to step in and help him come to terms with the situation.

Where it's reviewed:
Booklist, January 15, 1989, page 874
Horn Book, January/February 1989, page 74

Other books by the author:
Make-Believe Ball Player, 1989
Moving In, 1988
Love and Tennis, 1979
Matt Gargan's Boy, 1979

Other books you might like:
Bruce Brooks, *What Hearts*, 1992
    After his mother and father divorce and she remarries, Asa's sharp intellect and forgiveness help him deal with the instabilities in his new home.
Ilene Cooper, *Mean Streak*, 1991

Having alienated her best friend, Veronica has no one left to turn to for sympathy and support when it appears that her divorced father might remarry.

A.M. Monson, *The Secret of Sanctuary Island*, 1991
While still becoming accustomed to his father's remarriage, Todd and a friend set out to prove they observed a burglary no one believes happened.

Jayne Pettit, *My Name Is San Ho*, 1992
A Vietnamese boy relates his experiences as he tries to adjust to his new life in the United States with his mother and American marine stepfather.

Ruth Riddell, *Ice Warrior*, 1992
When his mother's remarriage moves him from California to Minnesota, Rob feels out of place until he discovers iceboating.

1671

Alfred Slote

Hang Tough, Paul Mather (Philadelphia: Lippincott, 1973)

Age range: Grades 4-7

Subject(s): Sports/Baseball; Cancer; Moving, Household

Major character(s): Paul Mather, Sports Figure (baseball player); Dr. Kinsella, Doctor

Time period(s): 1970s

Locale(s): United States

What the book is about: Paul was the star batter on two Little League teams, and he has just moved to a new town. Paul has leukemia, and he knows it. He can't resist the chance to play ball again, even though it exhausts him. The relationship he has with his doctor and his younger brother are well developed.

Where it's reviewed:
Booklist, May 15, 1973, page 910
Center for Children's Books Bulletin, June 1973, page 162
Kirkus Reviews, February 1, 1973, page 116

Other books by the author:
Finding Buck McHenry, 1991
A Friend Like That, 1988
Matt Gargan's Boy, 1975
The Biggest Victory, 1972

Other books you might like:
Gunnel Beckman, *Admission to the Feast*, 1971
A nineteen year old girl, dying of leukemia, writes a long letter to a friend in an attempt to stabilize her crumbling world.

Monica Hughes, *Hunter in the Dark*, 1982
A teenage boy goes on a secret hunting trip alone in an effort to come to terms with his leukemia and to test his strength in battling the elements.

Peg Kehret, *Sisters, Long Ago*, 1990
When Willow Paige nearly drowns, she envisions scenes from a past life which lead her to an exploration of reincarnation and mental telepathy.

Madeleine L'Engle, *A Ring of Endless Light*, 1980
During the summer her grandfather is dying of leukemia and death seems all around, Vicky finds comfort with the pod of dolphins she is researching.

Jane Claypool Miner, *This Day Is Mine: Living with Leukemia*, 1982
Hospitalized for a mysterious cause, Cheryl discovers that she has leukemia and tries to come to terms with the implications of her illness.

1672

Alfred Slote

Jake (New York: Harper, 1971)

Age range: Grades 5-6

Subject(s): African Americans; Sports/Baseball

Major character(s): Jake Wrather, Preteen; Lenny, Relative (Uncle), Musician; John Fulton, Sports Figure

Time period(s): 1960s

Locale(s): Detroit, Michigan

What the book is about: Nobody's father has time to be the coach of Jake's Little League team. The chances of convincing Uncle Lenny to become their coach seem mighty slim. He had been a hot shot college athlete but now he seems interested only in music.

Where it's reviewed:
Booklist, November 15, 1971, page 295
Kirkus, July 15, 1971, page 740
Center for Children's Books Bulletin, March 1972, page 115

Other books by the author:
Finding Buck McHenry, 1991
Rabbit Ears, 1982
Matt Gargan's Boy, 1975
Tony and Me, 1974

Other books you might like:
Barbara Hood Burgess, *Oren Bell*, 1991
Oren and his twin sister Latonga come to terms with the house next door which they believe is haunted and responsible for tragedies in their lives.

Suzy Kline, *Herbie Jones and the Monster Ball*, 1988
Strike-out king Herbie Jones feels that the summer is ruined when his uncle arrives to coach a baseball team and asks Herbie to join up.

Marjorie Lewis, *Wrong Way Applebaum*, 1984
Applebaum has found both a coach and a sponsor for his team; now if he can only find his grandmother's talent.

Vaunda Micheaux Nelson, *Mayfield Crossing*, 1993
School in Mayfield Crossing is closed and students are sent to schools where black kids encounter prejudice, but baseball brings people together.

Leonard Wibberley, *Little League Family*, 1978
When two brothers become members of the Little League, the whole family becomes involved in baseball.

1673

Alfred Slote

Illustrator: Joel Schick

My Robot Buddy (New York: Harper, 1975)

Age range: Grades 4-6

Subject(s): Birthdays; Robots; Science Fiction

Major character(s): Jack Jameson, Child; Frank Jameson, Parent (Jack's father); Danny One, Robot

Time period(s): Indeterminate Future

Locale(s): Metropolis VII

What the book is about: For his tenth birthday, Jack wants a robot so he'll have someone to play with. When he and his parents take a tour of the big robot factory, they leave with Danny One, Jack's new robot buddy.

Where it's reviewed:
Booklist, November 15, 1975, page 460
Center for Children's Books Bulletin, February 1976, page 102
Kirkus Reviews, September 1, 1975, page 999

Other books by the author:
The Trouble on Janus, 1985
Omega Station, 1983
C.O.L.A.R.: A Tale of Outer Space, 1981
My Trip to Alpha I, 1978

Other books you might like:
Victor Appleton, *The Rescue Mission*, 1981
    Tom and his friends find themselves in the hands of unfriendly robots who are trying to eliminate all biological life from their planet.
Janet Asimov, *Norby and the Invaders*, 1985
    Jeff and his mixed-up robot, Norby, get involved in new adventures on a strange planet.
Alison Prince, *The Type One Super Robot*, 1986
    While spending the summer together, a boy and his uncle acquire a household robot with a mind of its own.
Cara Lockhart Smith, *Parchment House*, 1989
    In a desolate orphanage in futuristic Britain, orphan Johnnie pits his wits against those of the orphanage director, the cruel Reverend Slipper.
Martin Waddell, *Harriet and the Robot*, 1987
    Harriet gives her dear friend Anthea a doll for her birthday - a large robot she has made herself and is not quite able to control.

1674

Alfred Slote

Illustrator: Harold Berson

My Trip to Alpha I (New York: Lippincott, 1978)

Age range: Grades 3-6

Subject(s): Miners and Mining; Mystery and Detective Stories; Science Fiction

Major character(s): Jack, Traveller (space); Katherine, Wealthy, Mine Owner; Frank Arbo, Servant

Time period(s): Indeterminate Future

Locale(s): New Jersey; Alpha I, Planet—Imaginary

What the book is about: Jack is sent to Alpha I to help his Aunt Katherine pack and return to Earth. She is a wealthy mine owner, who changes her mind about moving and turns her mine over to two treacherous servants. Jack travels by VOYACODE, an interplanetary system that allows him to sleep in New Jersey while a duplicate is "FAXED" to Alpha I.

Where it's reviewed:
Center for Children's Books Bulletin, January 1979, page 88

Kirkus Reviews, November 15, 1978, page 1249
School Library Journal, October 1978, page 150

Other books by the author:
The Trading Game, 1990
A Friend Like That, 1988
Matt Gargan's Boy, 1975
Hang Tough, Paul Mather, 1973

Other books you might like:
Gene DeWeese, *Whatever Became of Aunt Margaret?*, 1990
    David and Julie discover a secret about Aunt Margaret when they try to help her protect an elderly animal lover from being "podified" by aliens.
Nicholas Fisk, *Grinny: A Novel of Science Fiction*, 1974
    Tim records the strange events that occur during Great Aunt Emma's visit and his growing conviction about her true identity.
Madeleine L'Engle, *A Wrinkle in Time*, 1962
    When Meg, her brother Charles, and Calvin go searching for her missing father, they experience traveling in time and space by "tessering."
William Sleator, *The Duplicate*, 1988
    David, finding a strange machine that creates clones, he duplicates himself and suffers the consequences when the duplicate turns against him.
Alison Smith, *A Trap of Gold*, 1985
    Margaret finds a mysterious, shadowy figure watching her as she searches for a lost gold nugget from an abandoned mine.

1675

Alfred Slote

The Trading Game (New York: Lippincott, 1990)

Age range: Grades 4-6

Subject(s): Sports/Baseball; Fathers and Sons; Grandparents

Major character(s): Andy Harris, Preteen; Tubby Watson, Preteen; Jim Harris, Grandparent, Sports Figure (ex-baseball player)

Time period(s): 1980s

Locale(s): United States

What the book is about: During a summer of baseball and baseball card trading, eleven year old Andy makes discoveries about his father, his grandfather, who played professional baseball, and himself. The only card he really wants features his grandfather. Tubby Watson owns that card and he's willing to trade for the Mickey Mantle worth $2500 in Andy's deceased father's collection. Grandfather comes to town and offers to coach Andy's team. Andy is delighted although Mrs. Harris cautions Andy that Grandpa can be a severe taskmaster. It caused a great deal of friction between Grandpa and Andy's father.

Where it's reviewed:
Booklist, March 15, 1990, page 1459
School Library Journal, May 1990, page 113

Other books by the author:
Finding Buck McHenry, 1991
Hang Tough, Paul Mather, 1973
The Biggest Victory, 1972

Jake, 1971

Other books you might like:
Matt Christopher, *Centerfield Ballhawk*, 1992
    Baseball player Jose Mendez worries about his poor batting and fears disappointing his father, a former ballplayer with a great batting average.
Donald Honig, *Way to Go, Teddy*, 1973
    Entering professional baseball against his father's will, Ted can't keep a good relationship with his father as his batting average soars then falls.
Davis Klass, *The Atami Dragons*, 1984
    After the death of Jerry's mother, his father takes the family to Japan for a summer, where Jerry's boredom is cured by a high school baseball team.
Jackson Volney Scholz, *Batter Up*, 1993
    Marty Shane, a powerful hitter and part owner of a major league baseball team, wants to use his talents, not his connections, to play professionally.
Robert Kimmel Smith, *Bobby Baseball*, 1989
    Ten year old Bobby loves baseball and is convinced that he is a great player, but he never seems to get a chance to prove this to his father.

| 1676 |

Alison Smith

Billy Boone (New York: Scribner's, 1989)

Age range: Grades 4-6

Subject(s): Grandparents; Music; Sex Roles

Major character(s): Billy Boone, Musician (trumpeter); Dixie, Grandparent

Time period(s): 1980s

Locale(s): United States (The South)

What the book is about: Billy wants to play the trumpet in the school band. Her grandmother is very supportive, but her mother thinks any well-bred Southern lady plays the piano. Billy's music teacher is not very sure that a girl should play the trumpet either. But, Billy persists in her dream and goes to work in her father's office to pay for her trumpet.

Where it's reviewed:
Center for Children's Books Bulletin, March 1989, page 182
Kirkus Reviews, April 1, 1989, page 554
School Library Journal, May 1989, page 112

Other books by the author:
Come Away Home, 1989
A Trap of Gold, 1985
Help! There's a Cat Washing in Here, 1981
Reserved for Mark Anthony Crowder, 1979

Other books you might like:
William Crane, *Encore*, 1983
    Darlene and Sheryle help their band teacher overcome the principal's prejudice against him and the band.
Judith Groch, *Play the Bach, Dear!*, 1978
    Hilary, who detests playing the piano, receives some remarkable assistance from her instructor at a recital.
Norma Klein, *Tomboy*, 1989
    Somewhat apprehensive about growing up, ten year old Antonia tries to cope with changes in herself and her friends.
Gloria D. Miklowitz, *Closer to the Edge*, 1985

Jenny sees little point in life until she volunteers to play the piano for a senior citizens' band and receives the benefit of elderly wisdom.
Gary Provost, *Popcorn*, 1985
    Three twelve year olds work for fame in the pop music world, receiving inspiration from a martial arts teacher.

| 1677 |

Alison Smith

Reserved for Mark Anthony Crowder (New York: Dutton, 1978)

Age range: Grades 4-6

Subject(s): Family Life; Gardens and Gardening

Major character(s): Mark Anthony Crowder, Preteen (6th grader), Gardener; Earl Jones, Preteen; Georgette Crowder, Child

Time period(s): 1970s

Locale(s): Ridgedale

What the book is about: A sixth grader who believes everyone, including his family, thinks he's odd, spends his summer tending the family garden and cultivating his self-esteem. Mark is looking for a private place where he won't feel too tall, too nearsighted, or too clumsy, as he does around his athletic coach father. He is teased about collecting Indian artifacts, but it turns out to be one of his strengths.

Where it's reviewed:
Horn Book, December 1978, page 642
Kirkus Reviews, October 1, 1978, page 1072

Awards the book has won:
International Reading Association Children's Book Award 1979

Other books by the author:
Come Away Home, 1991
Billy Boone, 1989
A Trap of Gold, 1985
Help! There's a Cat Washing in Here!, 1981

Other books you might like:
Thomas J. Dygard, *Halfback Tough*, 1986
    New at Graham High, Joe joins the football team and begins to change his tough guy outlook as he becomes absorbed by the game and gains self-esteem.
Franklin Folsom, *The Hidden Ruin*, 1966
    Two boys set out to discover the source of a restaurant owner's supply of Indian artifacts and find themselves able to prove charges against him.
Sheila Hayes, *Speaking of Snapdragons*, 1982
    During the summer while she is own her own, Heather forms a friendship with an old, reclusive man who spends his days tending his garden.
Salley Kelly, *Summer Growing Time*, 1971
    June and her grandmother live in their own world absorbed in gardening until racial unrest intrudes on their lives.
Marilyn Sachs, *Marv*, 1970
    Marv is a genius builder who seems to contruct only useless things, but they make sense to him.

1678

Carole Smith

Illustrator: Marie De John

The Hit-and-Run Connection (Chicago: Whitman, 1982)

Age range: Grades 3-6

Subject(s): Accidents; Sports/Baseball; Accidents

Major character(s): Ted Nichols, Preteen; Jeff Lindsey, Preteen; Andy Ferguson, Preteen

Time period(s): 1980s

Locale(s): Midwest

What the book is about: When Ted is injured by a hit-and-run driver, his friends Jeff and Andy set out to find the culprit, only to discover he is a star on their favorite baseball team.

Where it's reviewed:
Booklist, April 1, 1982, page 1023
School Library Journal, May 1982, page 86

Other books by the author:
Who Burned the Hartley House?, 1985
Danger at the Golden Dragon, 1983
The Kidnapping of Anna, 1979

Other books you might like:
Patricia Hermes, *Nobody's Fault*, 1981
  Emily likes to play baseball and tease her brother, but her happy life is interrupted when her brother has a fatal accident.
Jim Naughton, *My Brother Stealing Second*, 1989
  After his brother is killed, Bobby tries to come to terms with some disturbing truths about his family, their home town and his profound grief.
Joan Phipson, *Hit and Run*, 1985
  Roland's hit and run accident in a borrowed car sends him fleeing into the Australian countryside, where he struggles for survival and self-respect.
Laurence Yep, *Liar, Liar*, 1983
  Branded in the past as a liar, a boy trying to prove his friend's death was no accident finds himself stalked by a seemingly respectable businessman.
Jane Zirpoli, *Roots in the Outfield*, 1988
  Josh leaves California to live with his father's new family in Milwaukee he gets involved in a mystery involving his favorite professional player.

1679

Dodie Smith

Illustrator: Janet Grahme-Johnstone

The Hundred and One Dalmatians (New York: Viking, 1956)

Age range: Grades 3-5

Subject(s): Animals/Dogs; Kidnapping

Major character(s): Pongo, Dog; Missis, Dog; Cruella de Vil, Villain

Time period(s): Indeterminate Past

Locale(s): St. John's Wood, England

What the book is about: All over the country, Dalmatian puppies are disappearing into the hands of a cruel villainess. Only Pongo and Missis can save their fifteen puppies.

Where it's reviewed:
Best Sellers, March 1, 1967, page 443
Publishers Weekly, November 28, 1966, page 66

Other books by the author:
Starlight Barking, 1970

Other books you might like:
Sheila Burnford, *Bel Ria*, 1977
  Follows the wanderings of a little performing dog in France, England, and at sea during World War II.
Anna Coates, *Dog Magic*, 1991
  Matt is shocked when one day when his dog Toby speaks. Toby needs Matt's help to rescue his newborn puppies from a laboratory in the city.
Marilynne K. Roach, *Presto, or, The Adventures of a Turnspit Dog*, 1979
  A young dog escapes the drudgery of an inn's turnspit to become part of the colorful street life of 18th century London.
Jane Trahey, *The Clovis Caper*, 1990
  When a family moves to England, it looks like their dog, Clovis, will have to stay behind, until Aunt Horty comes up with an act of magic.
Robert Westall, *The Kingdom by the Sea*, 1991
  During World War II, Harry and a stray dog travel through war-torn England in search of safety.

1680

Doris Buchanan Smith

Illustrator: Alan Tiegreen

Kelly's Creek (New York: Crowell, 1975)

Age range: Grades 4-6

Subject(s): Physically Handicapped; Swamps; Self-Confidence

Major character(s): Kelly O'Brien, Child, Handicapped; Phillip, Student

Time period(s): Indeterminate

Locale(s): United States

What the book is about: Kelly has a physiological malfunction that makes him awkward and the brunt of his classmates' teasing. Only Phillip, a biology student at the local college, accepts Kelly as he is. Phillip shares the discoveries he made while studying marsh life. Kelly begins to develop self confidence as the friendship grows.

Where it's reviewed:
Booklist, November 1, 1975, page 373
Kirkus Reviews, August 15, 1975, page 919
School Library Journal, September 1975, page 112

Other books by the author:
Last Was Lloyd, 1981
Kick a Stone Home, 1974
Tough Chauncey, 1974
A Taste of Blackberries, 1973

Other books you might like:
Patricia Goehner Baehr, *Summer of the Dodo*, 1990

Tall, and ackward, Dodo worries about entering sixth grade, but a summer spent teaching a real dodo to survive helps her learn many things.

Elizabeth T. Billington, *Part-Time Boy*, 1980
   Jamie, a quiet individualist in a noisy family, finds friendship, understanding, and self-confidence during the summer he spends in the country.

Dana Brenford, *A Case of Poison*, 1988
   A chemical smell in the swamp and suspicious behavior on their neighbors' property alert Peter, Jason and Kim to a possible threat to the environment.

Sarah Sargent, *Seeds of Change*, 1989
   Rachel discovers the beauties and dangers of a swamp when she travels to Georgia with her father who plans to convert the swamp into a theme park.

Dorothy Raymond Whittaker, *Angels of the Swamp*, 1992
   Taffy, an orphan, joins two boys who have been forced to leave their homes and the three of them try to survive the summer of 1932.

1681

Doris Buchanan Smith

Last Was Lloyd (New York: Viking, 1981)

Age range: Grades 4-6

Subject(s): Self-Respect; Schools; Weight Control

Major character(s): Lloyd, Preteen; Kirby, Preteen; Ancil, Preteen

Time period(s): 1980s

Locale(s): United States

What the book is about: Lloyd is an unhappy, overweight twelve year old. His mother has let him skip sixty-four days of school and defends him from the truant officer. Kirby discovers Lloyd's hidden talent. Kirby refuses an invitation to a birthday party unless Lloyd is invited. Lloyd reaches out to another outcast.

Where it's reviewed:
Center for Children's Books Bulletin, July/August 1981, page 219
Horn Book, June 1981, page 305

Other books by the author:
The Pennywhistle Tree, 1991
Salted Lemons, 1980
Dreams and Drummers, 1978
A Taste of Blackberries, 1973

Other books you might like:
Betsy Byars, *After the Goat Man*, 1974
   An overweight, sensitive boy gains the insight and strength to overcome his problems through his search for and discovery of a friend's grandfather.
Vicki Grove, *The Fastest Friend in the West*, 1990
   When her best friend dumps her, Lori shares an unusual but brief friendship with a homeless girl.
Virginia Hamilton, *The Planet of Junior Brown*, 1971
   Buddy protects his overweight, emotionally disturbed friend with whom he has been playing hooky all semester.
Robert Lipsyte, *One Fat Summer*, 1977
   An overweight fourteen year old boy experiences a turning point summer in which he learns to stand up for himself.
Stephen Manes, *Slim Down Camp*, 1981

Sent to a camp for overweight children, a boy and girl rebel and discover their own effective method of losing weight.

1682

Doris Buchanan Smith

Return to Bitter Creek (New York: Viking Kestral, 1986)

Age range: Grades 6-10

Subject(s): Mothers and Daughters; Family Life; Unmarried Mothers

Major character(s): Lacey, Preteen; Campbell, Artisan (Leatherworker), Parent (Lacey's mother); David, Blacksmith (Campbell's boyfriend)

Time period(s): 1980s

Locale(s): United States

What the book is about: Twelve year old Lacey wants to "fit in" like any other child, but her unmarried mother's lifestyle and strange family makes it difficult. Lacey, her mother Campbell, and Campbell's boyfriend, David, move back to a small town in Appalachia which Campbell ran away from when Lacey was a baby. David's untimely death affects everyone profoundly and both the emotional depth and beauty of the setting will draw readers into the story.

Where it's reviewed:
Booklist, July 1986, page 1613
School Library Journal, September 1986, page 140

Other books by the author:
The Pennywhistle Tree, 1991
Voyages, 1989
Karate Dancer, 1987
Tough Chauncey, 1974

Other books you might like:
Kathryn Kilby Borland, *Good-By to Stony Crick*, 1975
   When a family is forced to leave their Appalachian home, Jeremy finds city life in Chicago hard to cope with.
Sarah Ellis, *Pick-Up Sticks*, 1992
   Thirteen year old Polly's rebellion against her unmarried, fiercely independent mother comes to a head when they must find a new apartment.
Jim Wayne Miller, *Newfound*, 1989
   A boy growing up in his grandparents' house in the Appalachians learns about the town and the people around him, their habits, stories and lore.
Ellen Harvey Showell, *The Ghost of Tillie Jean Cassaway*, 1978
   Twelve year old Willy Barbour and his sister follow different trails as they pursue the ghost of a young girl who died in their Appalachian community.
Jacqueline Woodson, *The Dear One*, 1991
   Twelve year old Feni has to adjust when the pregnant daughter of an old friend of her mother's comes to stay with them.

1683

Doris Buchanan Smith

Salted Lemons (New York: Four Winds, 1980)

Age range: Grades 4-6

Subject(s): Prejudice; Moving, Household

Major character(s): Darby Bannister, Child; Miss Hardy, Teacher; Yoko Sasaki, Child

Time period(s): 1940s

Locale(s): Atlanta, Georgia

What the book is about: Darby has moved from Washington, D.C. to Atlanta during WWII. Her neighbor, Yoko, is treated badly by the other kids. Mr. Kaigler, the grocer, speaks with a heavy German accent and is accused of being a spy by most of the children. Darby is faced with the irrational behavior of people who suspect anyone who is "different."

Where it's reviewed:
Center for Children's Books Bulletin, March 1981, p 140
Horn Book, February 1981, page 53

Other books by the author:
Karate Dancer, 1987
The First Hard Times, 1983
Last Was Lloyd, 1981
Dreams and Drummers, 1978

Other books you might like:
Audree Distad, Dakota Sons, 1972
　Tad learns the meaning of friendship when he begins to feel the town's prejudice toward his new friend from the Indian school.
Toeckey Jones, Skindeep, 1986
　Living in a society where racial prejudice is the national law, a South African teen is stunned by a secret from her boyfriend's past.
Mary Ann Marger, Justice at Peachtree, 1980
　Cary takes a job at her father's newspaper and becomes more aware of the racial prejudice in her home town.
Harry W. Paige, The Summer War, 1983
　While at camp in the Adirondacks, Ely discovers a buried skeleton and the hatred that had swirled around German-Americans during WWII.
John R. Tunis, Keystone Kids, 1990
　Two brothers join the Brooklyn Dodgers. One becomes the team manager faced with the task of uniting the team torn apart by religious prejudice.

1684

Doris Buchanan Smith

Illustrator: Charles Robinson

A Taste of Blackberries (New York: Crowell, 1973)

Age range: Grades 3-5

Subject(s): Allergies; Animals/Bees; Death

Major character(s): Jamie, Child

Time period(s): 1970s

Locale(s): United States

What the book is about: Because Jamie often exaggerates and dramatizes, when he falls to the ground and screams after a bee sting, his best friends think he is "crying wolf." When Jamie dies because of an unknown allergy, his unnamed friend must cope with the guilt.

Where it's reviewed:
Booklist, March 15, 1974, page 827

Hornbook, December 1973, page 594
Kirkus Reviews, May 15, 1973, page 561

Awards the book has won:
Georgia Children's Book Award 1975

Other books by the author:
Laura-Upside-Down, 1984
The First Hard Times, 1983
Last Was Lloyd, 1981
Kelly's Creek, 1975

Other books you might like:
Achim Broger, The Day Chubby Became Charles, 1990
　Afraid that her grandmother might be dying, Julia discovers a new friend with whom she can talk about her fears.
Bruce Brooks, Everywhere, 1990
　Afraid that his grandfather will die after suffering a heart attack, a boy agrees to join his friend in performing a ritual called soul switching.
Virginia Hamilton, Cousins, 1990
　Concerned that her grandmother may die, Cammy is unprepared for the accidental death of another relative.
Sandy E. Powell, Geranium Morning, 1990
　Two friends who lose parents, one suddenly in an accident and one by illness, learn to deal with their grief.
Hans Stolp, The Golden Bird, 1990
　Engaged in a losing battle with cancer, Daniel is comforted by many people, but finds his greatest solace in the visits of a phoenix-like golden bird.

1685

Doris Buchanan Smith

Tough Chauncey (New York: Morrow, 1974)

Age range: Grades 6-8

Subject(s): Family Life; Family Problems

Major character(s): Chauncey Childs, Teenager (13-Years-Old); Black Jack Levitt, Teenager

Time period(s): 1970s

Locale(s): Rambleton, Georgia

What the book is about: Abused by his grandfather and neglected by his mother, "tough" Chauncey is headed for trouble. He sees running away as the only solution to changing his life until a friend opens his eyes to an alternative.

Where it's reviewed:
Booklist, May 1, 1974, page 1006
Library Journal, September 15, 1974, page 2278

Awards the book has won:
Boston Globe/Horn Book Award - Honor Book 1974

Other books by the author:
Voyages, 1989
Return to Bitter Creek, 1986
Kelly's Creek, 1975
A Taste of Blackberries, 1973

Other books you might like:
Bruce Brooks, No Kidding, 1989
　In 21st century society, Sam is allowed to decide the fate of his family after his mother is released from an alcohol rehabilitation center.
Frederick Buechner, The Wizard's Tide, 1990

A preteen boy describes the joys and sorrows of growing up in a dysfunctional family with a jobless, alcoholic father during the Great Depression.

Terry Farish, *Why I'm Already Blue*, 1989
  A girl tries to understand her troubled family and to gain a perspective on her relationship with the physically challenged boy next door.

Jim Naughton, *My Brother Stealing Second*, 1989
  Bobby tries to come to terms with some disturbing truths about his family and the political corruption in his home town after his brother is killed.

Stephen Schwandt, *Holding Steady*, 1988
  Berndon tries to come to terms with his grief, anger, and guilt during the first family vacation after the accidental death of his father.

| 1686 |

Emma Smith

No Way of Telling (New York: Atheneum, 1972)

Age range: Grades 5-7

Subject(s): Mystery and Detective Stories; Weather

Major character(s): Amy Bowen, Preteen; Gran Bowen, Grandparent; Tom Protheroe, Shepherd

Time period(s): 1970s

Locale(s): Radnorshire, Wales (hill country)

What the book is about: Though they have stocked up on supplies and expect to be safe even in the threatening weather, Amy and Gran have a hard time telling who the good guys are as they are trapped in a four day snowstorm with a fugitive and two men who claim to be policemen.

Where it's reviewed:
Horn Book, October 1972, page 468
Library Journal, December 15, 1972, page 4086

Other books by the author:
The Opportunity of a Lifetime, 1978
Emily's Voyage, 1966

Other books you might like:
Jeannette Eyerly, *The Leonardo Touch: A Novel of Suspense*, 1976
  When a seemingly simple trip to Wales to choose a painting for her father involves Elizabeth with theft and murder, everyone she knows becomes suspect.

Carol J. Farley, *Mystery of the Melted Diamonds*, 1986
  Kipper and his cousin, Larry, get caught in a Kansas snowstorm and become involved in the search for diamonds stolen from a jewelry store in town.

Roderic Jeffries, *Trapped*, 1972
  Hampered by darkness and a heavy snowstorm, the river patrol tries to locate two boys trapped on the mudflats before high tide sweeps them off.

Elinor Lyon, *Green Grow the Rushes*, 1964
  A London girl, vacationing on the Welsh coast with a spoiled companion, joins with three new friends in a search for the track of an old Roman road.

Ben Mikaelsen, *Rescue Josh McGuire*, 1991
  When Josh runs away to the mountains of Montana with an bear cub destined for laboratory testing, they both face danger in a sudden snowstorm.

| 1687 |

Gene Smith

Illustrator: Ted Lewin

The Hayburners (New York: Delacorte, 1974)

Age range: Grades 4-7

Subject(s): Animals/Horses; Mentally Handicapped

Major character(s): Will, Preteen; Joey, Handicapped (mentally ill)

Time period(s): 1970s

Locale(s): United States

What the book is about: A "hayburner" is, literally, a second rate racehorse. In this story the ones who are considered second rate are Will's 4H steer and Joey, a retarded hired hand. Will learns to treat both with love and respect.

Where it's reviewed:
Booklist, May 1, 1974, page 1006
Center for Children's Books Bulletin, September 1974, page 17
Kirkus Reviews, February 1, 1974, page 121

Other books you might like:
Carol Carrick, *Stay Away from Simon!*, 1985
  Lucy and her younger brother examine their feelings about a mentally handicapped boy they both fear when he follows them home one snowy day.

Florence Parry Heide, *Secret Dreamer, Secret Dreams*, 1978
  Reveals the inner world of a thirteen year old mentally handicapped girl.

Patricia Hermes, *Who Will Take Care of Me?*, 1983
  Terrified that the death of the grandmother who was their guardian will separate them, Mark decides to run away with his retarded younger brother.

Daniel Keyes, *Flowers for Algernon*, 1988
  Mentally retarded Charlie Gordon participates in an experiment which turns him into a genius, but only temporarily.

Robert Newton Peck, *Clunie*, 1979
  A teenage boy risks his own popularity to give friendship and support to a retarded girl who is harrassed by her classmates.

| 1688 |

Janice Lee Smith

Illustrator: Dick Gackenbach

The Monster in the 3rd Dresser Drawer and Other Stories about Adam Joshua (New York: Harper & Row, 1981)

Age range: Grades 2-3

Subject(s): Family Life; Moving, Household

Major character(s): Adam Joshua, Child; Emily, Relative (great-aunt); Amanda Jane, Babysitter

Time period(s): 1980s

Locale(s): United States

What the book is about: Adam Joshua can't understand why his parents would want to move. He certainly doesn't! Who will Peter collect ants with, or play Star Commander and Frankenstein with? There's a new baby in store for him, monsters in the night, loose teeth, new friends, dinners with Great-Aunt Emily and lots more!

Where it's reviewed:
Booklist, December 1, 1981, page 503
Kirkus Reviews, January 1, 1982, page 7
School Library Journal, 1982, page 70

Other books by the author:
There's a Ghost in the Coatroom, 1991
It's Not Easy Being George, 1989
Show and Tell War, 1988
The Kid Next Door and Other Headaches, 1984

Other books you might like:
Alma Flor Ada, *My Name Is Maria Isabel*, 1993
   Maria wants badly to fit in at school. Her teacher's writing assignment, ''My Greatest Wish'' gives her that opportunity.
Sylvia Cassedy, *The Best Cat Suit of All*, 1991
   When Mike has a cold and can't go out in his cat suit for Halloween, the only one that can cheer him up is wearing the best cat suit of all.
Lucy Diggs, *Selene Goes Home*, 1989
   Selene the cat does not like her mistress' new home aboard a houseboat and returns to her old home with the help of a pesky sea gull.
Diana Engel, *Fishing*, 1993
   When Loretta moves to a new town, she misses her grandfather and the love of fishing they shared.
Jayne Harvey, *Great-Uncle Dracula*, 1992
   Emily Normal finds it hard enough adjusting to a new town populated by vampires, witches, and the like, without being bullied by other third graders.

1689

Nancy Covert Smith

The Falling-Apart Winter (New York: Walker, 1982)

Age range: Grades 5-6

Subject(s): Family Problems; Mental Illness; Depression

Major character(s): Addam Hanley, Preteen; Dr. Collier, Psychologist

Time period(s): 1980s

Locale(s): Virginia

What the book is about: Addam tries to make sense of his changing family situation. They have moved from Ohio to Virginia. Addam's mother is struggling with a severe episode of depression. His father withdraws and Addam is left to struggle with a new school and an angry bully on his own. He learns to deal with his own negative feelings about his mom's illness, and to turn them around and begin a positive life.

Where it's reviewed:
Booklist, September 1, 1982, page 48
School Library Journal, September 1982, page 127

Other books by the author:
Josie's Handful of Quietness, 1975

Other books you might like:
Spring Hermann, *Flip City*, 1988
   Four girls whose family lives are difficult compete in gymnastics for their gym, Flip City, the place where they feel most at home.
Betty Hyland, *The Girl with the Crazy Brother*, 1987

Dana's fears and worries about moving across country and making friends at school are made worse when her brother is diagnosed as schizophrentic.
Paul Kropp, *Wilted: A Novel*, 1980
   His family problems, his first girlfriend, and a class bully leave a fourteen year old in a state of confusion.
Jean McCord, *Turkeylegs Thompson*, 1979
   Betty Ann's childhood ends when her father abandons the family and her mother goes to work, making her responsible for her younger brother and sister.
Phyllis Rossiter, *Moxie*, 1990
   Drew, determined to help his family hold on to their farm in the Dust Bowl of 1934, stubbornly tends the livestock and refuses to give up hope.

1690

Robert Kimmel Smith

Illustrator: Gioia Fiammenghi

Chocolate Fever (New York: Dell, 1978)

Age range: Grades 3-4

Subject(s): Food

Major character(s): Henry Green, Child; Enid Green, Parent (Henry and Mark's mother); Mark Green, Child

Time period(s): Indeterminate

Locale(s): United States

What the book is about: Henry Green was a boy who loved chocolate. He liked it bitter, sweet, dark, light and daily. Since it didn't make him overweight or sick, or give him bad skin, his parents let him have all he wanted, for breakfast, lunch, dinner and snacks. One day Henry woke not feeling well, and he began to break out with little brown spots all over. He had made medical history with the first recorded case of chocolate fever.

Where it's reviewed:
Center for Children's Books Bulletin, December 1972, page 65
Kirkus Reviews, April 1, 1972, page 403
Library Journal, February 15, 1973, page 648

Awards the book has won:
Massachusetts Childrens Book Award 1980

Other books by the author:
The Squeaky Wheel, 1990
Bobby Baseball, 1989
Mostly Michael, 1987
Jelly Belly, 1981

Other books you might like:
Crosby Bonsall, *Twelve Bells for Santa*, 1977
   Three children, off to the North Pole to deliver twelve chocolate bells to Santa for winning a contest, become very hungry along the way.
Patrick Skene Catling, *The Chocolate Touch*, 1952
   A boy acquires a magical gift that turns everything his lips touch into chocolate.
Roald Dahl, *Charlie and the Chocolate Factory*, 1964
   Each of five children lucky enough to discover an entry ticket into Mr. Willy Wonka's mysterious chocolate factory takes advantage of the situation.
Patricia Reilly Giff, *The Candy Corn Contest*, 1986

Richard is determined to win the Candy Corn Contest by guessing the correct number of candies in the jar, but eats three big pieces by mistake.

Mike Thaler, *It's Me, Hippo!*, 1983
  With the help of his animal friends, Hippo builds a house, paints a picture, breaks out in spots, and celebrates a birthday.

1691

Robert Kimmel Smith

Illustrator: Juan Wijngaard

Jelly Belly (New York: Delacorte, 1981)

Age range: Grades 5-6

Subject(s): Family Life; Weight Control

Major character(s): Ned Robbins, Preteen; Richard, Camper

Time period(s): 1980s

Locale(s): United States

What the book is about: Ned is thirty pounds overweight. His classmates call him Blimpie, Tubby, Piggie, Lard-Butt and Jelly Belly. His parents send him to camp Lean-Too. By the first day of camp, he has gained another seven pounds. His best friend at camp is Richard, the only other kid who sneaks food into camp. Only when Ned decides he wants to lose weight for himself is he ever successful.

Where it's reviewed:
Kirkus Reviews, April 15, 1981, page 505
School Library Journal, May 1981, page 66

Other books by the author:
The Squeaky Wheel, 1990
Bobby Baseball, 1989
Mostly Michael, 1987
The War with Grandpa, 1984

Other books you might like:
John Bellairs, *The Figure in the Shadows*, 1975
  A painfully overweight sixth grade boy receives a magic amulet which brings him luck, but also terrifying side effects.
Barthe DeClements, *Nothing's Fair in Fifth Grade*, 1981
  A fifth grade class ostracizes a new student who is overweight and has serious problems at home, but finally learns to accept her.
Harry Mazer, *The Dollar Man*, 1874
  Raised by his mother, an overweight boy feels he must find his father in order to establish his own identity.
Lila Perl, *Fat Glenda's Summer Romance*, 1986
  Glenda finds her weight problem returning to haunt her after friendship and romance turn sour during a summer that looked promising at the beginning.
Doris Buchanan Smith, *Last Was Lloyd*, 1981
  A friendless, overweight boy with an overprotective mother begins to change the pattern of his life through his own efforts and determination.

1692

Robert Kimmel Smith

Illustrator: Richard Lauter

The War with Grandpa (New York: Delacorte, 1984)

Age range: Grades 4-6

Subject(s): Family Life; Grandparents

Major character(s): Peter Stokes, Preteen (Fifth grader); Jennifer Stokes, Child; Billy Alston, Preteen

Time period(s): 1980s

Locale(s): United States

What the book is about: Peter is thrilled that Grandpa is coming to live with his family, until he realizes that Grandpa is getting his room and he has to move upstairs. Grandpa cannot handle the steps, but that does not matter much to Peter at this point in his resentment. Peter declares war and enlists the help of his friends to make a plan to force Grandpa to give up the room. Grandpa does not give up easily, but tries to get even. They play all kinds of tricks on each other as Peter is determined to win the war. The outcome is both satisfying and realistic.

Where it's reviewed:
Center for Children's Books Bulletin, March 1984, page 135
School Library Journal, April 1984, page 198

Awards the book has won:
Dorothy Canfield Fisher Children's Book Award 1986
Golden Sower Award 1984

Other books by the author:
The Squeaky Wheel, 1990
Bobby Baseball, 1989
Mostly Michael, 1987
Jelly Belly, 1981

Other books you might like:
Ann R. Blakeslee, *After the Fortune Cookies*, 1989
  The summer Allison turns 12 brings many disturbing changes, as she tries to protect her beloved grandfather from the schemes of other family members.
Kristi Holl, *No Strings Attached*, 1988
  June finds sharing a house with her mother and her foster grandfather requires a difficult adjustment.
Scott O'Dell, *Alexandra*, 1984
  While helping her crippled grandfather by diving for sponges, Alexandra finds someone is using their sponges for illegal activities.
Kathleen Stevens, *Eddie's Luck*, 1992
  11 year old Eddie is upset to have to share his room with his 83 year old grandfather while he recovers from a stroke, until they form a special bond.
Hilma Wolitzer, *Wish You Were Here*, 1984
  When his widowed mother meets a man she wants to marry, thirteen year old Bernie decides he will go to live with his grandfather in Florida.

1693

Virginia Driving Hawk Sneve

Betrayed (New York: Holiday House, 1974)

Age range: Grades 5-7

Subject(s): Indians of North America; Civil War

Major character(s): White Lodge, Chieftain, Indian

Time period(s): 1860s

Locale(s): Lake Shetek, Minnesota

What the book is about: Based on a true Civil War incident, this is a story of Indian-white conflict. Impoverished and starving, the Santee Indians raid a Minnesota settlement, killing the men they catch and taking women and children prisoners. A band of Teton braves barter for the prisoners.

Where it's reviewed:
Booklist, November 15, 1974, page 345
Kirkus Reviews, November 15, 1974, page 1203
School Library Journal, January 1975, page 57

Other books by the author:
When Thunder Spoke, 1974

Other books you might like:
Jamake Highwater, *Eyes of Darkness: A Novel*, 1985
    Yesa, a Sioux Indian, after being taken at seventeen to live among whites, becomes a doctor and then returns to the reservation to live traditionally.
Sollace Hotze, *A Circle Unbroken*, 1988
    Captured by Sioux Indians and brought up as the chief's daughter, Rachel is recaptured by her white family but wants to return to the tribe.
Dorothy M. Johnson, *All the Buffalo Returning*, 1979
    A fictionalized account of the Hunkpapa and Oglala Sioux from the battle of the Little Bighorn in 1876 to Wounded Knee in 1890.
Kathryn Lasky, *The Bone Wars*, 1988
    In the mid 1870s, young teenage scout Thad Longsworth, blood brother to the Sioux visionary Black Elk, finds his destiny linked with that of three riv
Louise Moeri, *Save Queen of Sheba*, 1981
    After miraculously surviving a Sioux Indian raid on the trail to Oregon, a brother and sister set out with few provisions to find the rest of the sett

---

1694

Carol Snyder

The Leftover Kid (New York: Pacer Books, 1986)

Age range: Grades 5 and Up

Subject(s): Family Life; Grandparents

Major character(s): Wendy, Teenager

Time period(s): 1980s

Locale(s): United States

What the book is about: Now that all her siblings are gone, Wendy is delighted that the house is now all hers. She can come home to an empty house, eat junk food, watch TV and sing at the top of her lungs. Then it all disappears when her brother and sister-in-law and her baby nephew return home, along with her grandparents and a computer.

Where it's reviewed:
Center for Children's Books Bulletin, September 1986, page 19
School Library Journal, September 1986, page 146

Other books by the author:
Dear Mom and Dad, Don't Worry, 1989
Leave Me Alone, Ma, 1987
Ike and Mama and the Seven Surprises, 1985
Memo: To Myself When I Have a Teenage Kid, 1983

Other books you might like:
Carole s. Adler, *One Sister Too Many*, 1989
    The family is thrown into turmoil by 3 month old Meredith's constant crying. Only Cass notices that Meredith's babysitter is behaving oddly.
Elizabeth T. Billington, *Part-Time Boy*, 1980
    Jamie, a quiet individual, finds friendship, understanding and a new self-confidence during the summer he spends in the country with an unusual woman.
Anne Lindbergh, *Three Lives to Live*, 1992
    Thirteen year old Garet's quiet life with her grandmother is changed when Daisy comes down the laundry chute.
Elisabet McHugh, *Karen's Sister*, 1983
    Karen's mother adopts a second Korean child and finds a husband with three children of his own.
John Rowe Townsend, *The Persuading Stick*, 1987
    A quiet English girl becomes more assertive with the help of a magic stick.

1695

Zilpha Keatley Snyder

Illustrator: Alton Raible

Below the Root (New York: Atheneum, 1975)

Age range: Grades 5-7

Subject(s): Fantasy; Science Fiction

Major character(s): Raamo, Teenager

Time period(s): Indeterminate Future

Locale(s): Green Sky, Planet—Imaginary

What the book is about: When the planet of Green Sky was settled, the people broke into two factions. One believed they should tell children the truth about the war that destroyed their home on Earth. The others believed that if children were never told about any sort of negative feelings, they would never experience sadness, fear, hate or conflict. The former group is exiled "Below the Root," the huge, thick interlacing of roots that cover the planet. When thirteen year old Raamo is chosen as a leader, he questions the past and the truths that have been hidden. Exciting action and great springboard for discussion. Sequels are *And All Between* (1976), and *Until the Celebration* (1977).

Where it's reviewed:
Booklist, March 15, 1974, page 764
School Library Journal, September 1975, page 112

Other books by the author:
Until the Celebration, 1977
And All Between, 1976
Changeling, 1970
Black and Blue Magic, 1966

Other books you might like:
H.M. Hoover, *Only Child*, 1992
    Cody discovers that the Terran Corporation, in colonizing the planet Patma, is destroying the intelligent native inhabitants.
Monica Hughes, *The Guardian of Isis*, 1982
    The settlers on the planet Isis, under the dominance of an absolute ruler, have lost all technology and reverted to a society of myths and taboos.
Paul Samuel Jacobs, *Born into the Light*, 1988

When a group of "feral children" are found in a New England town during the Depression, only young Roger suspects they are not earthly creatures.

Madeleine L'Engle, *A Wind in the Door*, 1973
  With Meg's help, the dragons that her brother saw in the vegetable garden play an important part in his struggle between life and death.

Donald J. Sobol, *The Amazing Power of Ashur Fine*, 1986
  Endowed with extra powers by an ancient African elephant, Ashur Fine finds himself relying on them as he tries to bring his aunt's mugger to justice.

1696

Zilpha Keatley Snyder

Illustrator: Alton Raible

Changeling (New York: Atheneum, 1970)

Age range: Grades 5-8

Subject(s): Fantasy; Friendship

Major character(s): Martha Abbott, Teenager; Ivy Carson, Eccentric; Thomas Abbott, Lawyer

Time period(s): 1970s

Locale(s): United States

What the book is about: Martha looks back at her relationship with Ivy Carson when the Carsons move back to town but Ivy is not with them. Though very different, Martha and Ivy had an intense relationship involving great fantasies and a game about the Land of Green Sky and the Doorway to Space. Ivy's family is usually in trouble and moves in and out of town. At one point, Ivy told Martha that she was a changeling and Martha never quite knew if she was kidding. Ivy is certainly unique. Often overlooked among Snyder's prolific works, this is worth the time for readers who love stories of deep friendship and great fantasy.

Where it's reviewed:
Booklist, October 15, 1970, page 196
Library Journal, November 15, 1970

Awards the book has won:
Christopher Award 1971

Other books by the author:
Song of the Gargoyle, 1991
Libby on Wednesday, 1990
Janie's Private Eyes, 1989
The Egypt Game, 1967

Other books you might like:
Jeanne Betancourt, *Not Just Party Girls*, 1989
  Anne wants to quit the money-making business she started with her friends when she feels guilty about the bad conditions at the migrant workers' camp.
Constance C. Greene, *Ask Anybody*, 1983
  The daughter of divorced parents befriends an eccentric new girl who is full of surprises.
Barbara Ware Holmes, *Charlotte Shakespeare and Annie the Great*, 1989
  After persuading her best friend to try out for the lead in the play she's written, Char feels she's losing control of her own play.
Janice Jones, *Secrets of a Summer Spy*, 1990

Ronnie, part of a trio of best friends that seems to be falling apart, finds solace in the company of an eccentric 83 year old retired pianist.

Janet Taylor Lisle, *Afternoon of the Elves*, 1989
  As Hilary works in a miniature village allegedly built by elves in Sara-Kate's backyard, she becomes curious about Sara-Kate's life and family.

1697

Zilpha Keatley Snyder

Illustrator: Alton Raible

The Egypt Game (New York: Atheneum, 1967)

Age range: Grades 5-6

Subject(s): Murder

Major character(s): Melanie Ross, Child; April Hall, Child

Time period(s): 1960s

Locale(s): California (in a large university town)

What the book is about: Melanie and her friend, April, convert an abandoned junk yard into an Egyptian temple where they have fun and "fit in" in a way they never can do at school. When it is revealed that a murderer is roaming the neighborhood, they have more excitement than they bargained for.

Where it's reviewed:
Book Week, May 7, 1967, page 14
Library Journal, April 15, 1967, page 1742

Awards the book has won:
Newbery Honor

Other books by the author:
Changing Maze, 1985
Changeling, 1986
The Headless Cupid, 1971
The Witches of Worm, 1965

Other books you might like:
Leona Ellerby, *King Tut's Game Board*, 1980
  On vacation in Cairo, Justin meets Nate, a distant relative who leads him into a mystery and finally reveals his secret identity.
Pamela F. Service, *The Reluctant God*, 1988
  In this time travel fantasy, two friends set out to reclaim a stolen urn from a gang of theives.
Mansfield Kirby, *The Secret of Thut-Mouse ****or Basil Beaudesert's Revenge*, 1985
  This story of two clever mice who plan revenge on the museum cat will appeal to readers interested in ancient Egypt.
Dorothy Sharp Carter, *His Majesty, Queen Hatshepsut*, 1987
  A fictionalized account of Hatshepsut, a queen in ancient Egypt who declared herself king and ruled as such for more than 20 years.
Erick Berry, *Honey of the Nile*, 1963
  Intrigue flourishes in the court of Ankhesenpanton and Tutankhamun as opposing religious groups fight for the leadership of ancient Egypt.

1698

Zilpha Keatley Snyder

Illustrator: Alton Raible

The Headless Cupid (New York: Atheneum, 1971)

Age range: Grades 4-6

Subject(s): Stepfamilies; Occult; Extrasensory Perception

Major character(s): Amanda, Child, Occultist; David Stanley, Child; Molly, Step-Parent

Time period(s): 1970s

Locale(s): United States

What the book is about: David and the three younger children have moved into an old house with their father and new mother, Molly. David is worried about how Molly's daughter, Amanda, will fit into the new family. Amanda studies the occult and proceeds to put all the children through a series of tests and an initiation rite. When there are signs of a poltergeist, suspense builds. Great characters and plenty of action.

Where it's reviewed:
Horn Book, October 1971, page 485
Kirkus Reviews, July 1, 1971, page 678

Awards the book has won:
Christopher Award 1972
Newbery Honor

Other books by the author:
Janie's Private Eyes, 1989
The Famous Stanley Kidnapping Case, 1985
Blair's Nightmare, 1984

Other books you might like:
Betty Bates, *Bugs in Your Ears*, 1977
  Carrie has difficulty adjusting to her new family until she realizes her new stepbrothers and stepsister are having difficulty too.
Mary Downing Hahn, *Wait Until Helen Comes*, 1986
  Molly and Michael dislike their new stepsister but realize they must protect Heather when she seems ready to follow a ghost child to her doom.
Richard M. Koff, *Christopher*, 1981
  In a haunted house, Christopher goes through a series of occult lessons with a strange old man.
Marianna Mayer, *Noble-Hearted Kate*, 1990
  Using elements of Celtic lore, this is the story of Kate helping her stepsister, Meghan, break the spell that has given her the head of a sheep.
Willo Davis Roberts, *The Girl with the Silver Eyes*, 1980
  Katie's silver eyes mark her as one of a group of children with psychokinetic powers, but she does not know there are others.

1699

Zilpha Keatley Snyder

Janie's Private Eyes (New York: Delacorte, 1989)

Age range: Grades 5-6

Subject(s): Mystery and Detective Stories

Major character(s): David Stanley, Teenager; Janie Stanley, Child; Thuy Tran, Child

Time period(s): 1980s

Locale(s): Steven's Corners

What the book is about: In this fourth book about the eccentric but believable Stanleys, eight year old Janie forms a detective agency to investigate the rash of dog disappearances. She involves her friends and unwilling family in tracing clues and suspects. The mystery is credibly solved and the humor and fast pace make this attractive.

Where it's reviewed:
Booklist, March 15, 1989, page 1304
School Library Journal, February 1989, page 83

Other books by the author:
Song of the Gargoyle, 1991
Libby on Wednesday, 1990
The Headless Cupid, 1985
The Velvet Room, 1965

Other books you might like:
M.S. Craig, *The Mystery at Wolf River*, 1989
  Kate and Bugs solve a mystery surrounding a drowning dog and a mansion and in the process, Kate and her little brother become friends.
Lynn Hall, *The Tormentors*, 1990
  When his beloved German Shepherd vanishes, Sox sets out to find the thief and becomes involved with a ring of dangerous dog trainers.
Isabelle Holland, *The Unfrightened Dark*, 1990
  When her beloved seeing-eye dog is kidnapped, Jocelyn, orphaned and blind since the age of twelve, determines to solve the mystery.
James Howe, *Howliday Inn*, 1982
  Harold and Chester are boarded at Chateau Bow-Wow. While the family is away, Chester becomes alarmed by the strange behavior of his fellow guests.
Willo Davis Roberts, *The Minden Curse*, 1978
  When Danny goes to live with his aunt and grandfather in a small village, it becomes apparant that he and his dog are afflicted with a curse.

1700

Zilpha Keatley Snyder

Libby on Wednesday (New York: Delacorte, 1990)

Age range: Grades 5-6

Subject(s): Friendship; Authorship; Schools

Major character(s): Libby, Child

Time period(s): 1990s

Locale(s): United States

What the book is about: Libby had been taught at home by a rather eccentric family. When she finally attends public school, she is exposed to her classmates' wisecracks. After a rough start, Libby makes a few friends and learns to have compassion for the others. She makes some highly original friends in a writing workshop.

Where it's reviewed:
Booklist, February 1, 1990, page 1095
Horn Book, May 1990, page 336

Other books by the author:
Janie's Private Eyes, 1989

Squeak Saves the Day, 1988
And Condors Danced, 1987
Below the Root, 1975

Other books you might like:
Mary Oldham, *The White Pony*, 1981
An overweight girl becomes attached to a nearly blind white pony who inspires her to develop her writing talent and solve other problems as well.
Susan Beth Pfeffer, *April Upstairs*, 1990
April has trouble making friends at her new school until her father's friendship with a missing rock star makes her suddenly popular.
Enid Richemont, *The Time Tree*, 1989
Rachel and Joanna experience the merging of past and present as a mysterious girl in old fashioned clothing appears and disappears.
Marilyn Singer, *Lizzie Silver of Sherwood Forest*, 1986
Inspired by the example of her latest obsession, Robin Hood, Lizzie begins to scheme to follow her best friend, Tessa, into music school.
Rachel Vail, *Wonder*, 1991
Everything changes for Jessica when she enters junior high and finds herself ignored by all her former friends.

| 1701 |

Zilpha Keatley Snyder

The Witches of Worm (New York: Atheneum, 1972)

Age range: Grades 5-7

Subject(s): Demons; Witches and Witchcraft; Animals/Cats

Major character(s): Jessica Ann Porter, Preteen (12 years old); Joy Porter, Parent (mother); Brandon Doyle, Preteen

Time period(s): 1980s

Locale(s): United States

What the book is about: Jessica is both lonely and jealous when her mother leaves her alone evenings to go out with her boyfriend, Allan. In the back of a cave, Jessica finds a half dead kitten who seems to be much more than just a regular cat. As Jessica's anger deepens and her behavior worsens, she is certain that it is Worm, the cat, who is responsible. She performs an exorcism on Worm in an attempt to change her own behavior. Finding out what made Worm the cat he was was the answer to Jessica's problems, but it was not the answer she expected or wanted.

Where it's reviewed:
Horn Book, December 1972, page 596
Library Journal, November 15, 1972, page 183

Awards the book has won:
Newbery Honor 1973
New York Times Outstanding Books 1972

Other books by the author:
Libby on Wednesday, 1990
And Condors Danced, 1987
The Truth about Stone Hollow, 1974
Changeling, 1970

Other books you might like:
Joan Davenport Carris, *Witch-Cat*, 1986
A down-to-earth girl is made to see that she is a witch through the efforts of a magical cat.

Ruth Chew, *The Witch and the Ring*, 1989
A sister and brother find a ring that brings a special cat, a witch, and a series of adventures into their lives.
Barbara Corcoran, *Which Witch Is Which?*, 1983
After a series of neighborhood catnappings, inquisitive twins follow a frightening old woman to an abandoned house where they both danger and cats.
E.E. Cummings, *Hist Whist*, 1989
The famous poet presents ghosts, goblins, and witches in poems with beautiful illustrations. A book to share.
Phyllis Reynolds Naylor, *Witch Weed*, 1991
A series of mysterious events convince Lynn and her friend that the destructive power of a dead witch is still very much alive.

| 1702 |

Donald J. Sobol

Angie's First Case (New York: Four Winds, 1981)

Age range: Grades 4-7

Subject(s): Brothers and Sisters; Mystery and Detective Stories

Major character(s): Angie Zane, Preteen, Detective; Kit Zane, Police Officer; Jess Berg, Preteen

Time period(s): 1980s

Locale(s): Dadesville, Florida

What the book is about: To help her police officer sister, 12 year old Angie tracks the Wolfpack, a gang of teenagers who have broken into a dozen homes in the city. While on the trail of the house thieves, Angie and Jess become involved with counterfeiters and are kidnapped.

Where it's reviewed:
Booklist, September 15, 1981, page 111
Kirkus Reviews, July 1, 1981, page 801
School Library Journal, December 1981, page 68

Other books by the author:
The Amazing Power of Ashur Fine, 1987
Encyclopedia Brown Solves Them All, 1977
Great Sea Stories, 1975
True Sea Adventures, 1975

Other books you might like:
Ruth Hallman, *Search Without Fear*, 1987
Dee goes to live with her brother, a state trooper in Virginia, where one dangerous adventure follows another.
Kristi Holl, *Cast a Single Shadow*, 1986
With her mom arrested as a thief and the police not looking any further for the real criminal, Tracy searches for the dangerous thief alone.
Elizabeth Levy, *The Dani Trap*, 1984
After Dani agrees to work in a police investigation of illegal liquor sales to teens, she finds herself being framed in a liquor store holdup.
Jim Murphy, *Death Run*, 1982
An incident in a park leads to an accidental death, but a detective wonders if it was an accident, or murder!
R.L. Stine, *Lights Out*, 1991
Acts of vandalism, where a red feather is left behind, are occuring at Camp Nightwing. Suddenly a counselor is dead and Holly has a dangerous secret.

1703

Donald J. Sobol

Illustrator: Leonard Shortall

Encyclopedia Brown, Boy Detective (Nashville, Tennessee: T. Nelson, 1963)

Age range: Grades 4-6

Series: Encyclopedia Brown

Subject(s): Mystery and Detective Stories

Major character(s): Leroy "Encyclopedia" Brown, Detective, 5th Grader

Time period(s): 1960s

Locale(s): United States

What the book is about: Fifth grader "Encyclopedia" Leroy Brown solves ten mysteries and challenges readers to try their own skill at solving as they read. Solutions are provided at the back of the book. First of a popular and prolific author's series.

Where it's reviewed:
New York Times Book Review, March 26, 1978, page 29
Teacher, October 1978, page 175

Other books by the author:
Encyclopedia Brown and the Case of the Disgusting Sneakers, 1990
Angie's First Case, 1981
Case of the Dead Eagles, 1975
Encyclopedia Brown Solves Them All, 1968

Other books you might like:
David A. Adler, *Cam Jansen and the Mystery of the Carnival Prize*, 1984
  When Cam notices that the prizes for the most difficult game at the carnival are disappearing, she uses her photographic memory to investigate.
John Bellairs, *The Figure in the Shadows*, 1975
  A painfully overweight sixth grade boy receives a magic amulet which brings him luck, but also terrifying side effects.
Paul Fleischman, *Phoebe Danger, Detective, in the Case of the Two-Minute Cough*, 1983
  The first case to come to Phoebe's detective agency involves a cough syrup bottle, Canadian ornithologists, and a shop specializing in curios.
Sarah Sargent, *Jerry's Ghosts: The Mystery of the Blind Tower*, 1992
  Jerry discovers two ghostly children, trapped with their mad scientist uncle, in the mansion that was their former home, and sets them free.
Drew Stevenson, *The Case of the Horrible Swamp Monster*, 1984
  When the sixth grade decides to film a monster movie as a class project, the camera reveals something unexpected.

1704

Harriet Langsam Sobol

Illustrator: Patricia Agre

My Other Mother, My Other Father (New York: Macmillan, 1979)

Age range: Grades 2-4

Subject(s): Divorce; Remarriage

Major character(s): Andrea Hayes, Preteen; Mrs. Burns, Teacher

Time period(s): 1970s

Locale(s): United States

What the book is about: There are both advantages and disadvantages to not having a regular family. Andrea has many feelings about her parents' divorce and later remarriages. She is not without sadness and confusion, but she does learn to make the best of a complicated family life.

Where it's reviewed:
Center for Children's Books Bulletin, September 1979, page 19
School Library Journal, May 1979, page 55

Other books by the author:
The Interns, 1981
Grandpa: A Young Man Grown Old, 1980
Pete's House, 1978
My Brother Steven Is Retarded, 1977

Other books you might like:
Lawrence Balter, *The Wedding*, 1989
  A child experiences the bewildering set of life changes upon the remarriage of one parent after a divorce.
Claire Berman, *What Am I Doing in a Stepfamily?*, 1992
  Advice for children of divorced or remarried parents on adjusting to life with a stepfamily. (Non-fiction)
Crescent Dragonwagon, *Always, Always*, 1984
  A little girl realizes that ther parents' divorce doesn't change their feelings about her.
Linda Walvoord Girard, *At Daddy's on Saturdays*, 1987
  Katie feels anger, confusion, and sadness over her parents' divorce; she discovers she can keep her loving relationship with her father.
Amy Hest, *Where in the World Is the Perfect Family?*, 1989
  Cornie has divorced parents and a new baby half-sister which gives her and Megan an idea for a school project.

1705

Robert Somerlott

Blaze (New York: Viking, 1981)

Age range: Grades 6 and Up

Subject(s): Animals; Grandparents

Major character(s): David Holland, Orphan; Cappy Holland, Grandparent; Arthur, Guardian

Time period(s): 1980s

Locale(s): Rancho San Pasqual, Arizona; San Francisco, California

What the book is about: Orphaned ten year old David has been living in California with his aunt and uncle. Cappy, his grandfather, raises German Shepherds on a ranch in the Rockies. He sends David a puppy (Blaze) but his uncle gives the pup away to a man who mistreats him. David stows away in his grandfather's truck when Cappy rescues Blaze.

Where it's reviewed:
Horn Book, June 1981, page 305
School Library Journal, August 1981, page 71

Other books you might like:

Betsy Byars, *The House of Wings*, 1972
  Sammy learns to respect and love his grandfather as they care for an injured crane together.

Roderic Jeffries, *Police Dog*, 1965
  Combination dog and detective story written as a police account of the methods used in England for training police dogs.

Norma Fox Mazer, *A Figure of Speech*, 1973
  The special relationship between Jenny and her grandfather leads to tragedy when her parents want to place him in a retirement home.

Katy Peake, *The Indian Heart of Carrie Hodges*, 1972
  Convinced that she has found her own animal spirit, Carrie calls on that spirit to save the coyotes in the valley from extermination by ranchers.

Bill Wallace, *Trapped in Death Cave*, 1984
  A letter about buried treasure convinces Gary that his grandfather didn't die a natural death. With Brian, he tries to find both killer and treasure.

1706

Virginia Sorensen

Illustrator: Beth Krush, Joe Krush

Miracles on Maple Hill (New York: Harcourt, Brace & World, 1956)

Age range: Grades 4-6

Subject(s): Country Life; Family Life

Major character(s): Joe, Child; Marly, Child; Dad, Prisoner (ex-POW)

Time period(s): 1950s

Locale(s): Pittsburgh, Pennsylvania

What the book is about: A troubled family moves to the country for a year. The father adjusts to being an ex-prisoner of war. 12 year old Joe befriends a hermit. 10 year old Marly discovers the wonders of nature. The entire family becomes closer as they work together to save a maple sugar crop.

Where it's reviewed:
Booklist, September 1, 1956, page 30
Library Journal, September 15, 1956, page 2045

Awards the book has won:
Newbery Medal 1957

Other books by the author:
Around the Corner, 1971
Curious Missie, 1953
Lotte's Locket, 1964
Plain Girl, 1955

Other books you might like:

Barbara Corcoran, *Potato Kid*, 1989
  Ellis thinks her summer is ruined when her family takes in 10 year old Lilac.

Betty Hyland, *The Girl with the Crazy Brother*, 1987
  Dana's fears about moving are made worse when her brother is diagnosed as schizophrenic.

Johanna Hurwitz, *Yellow Blue Jay*, 1986
  Jay is unhappy about his parents' plan to vacation in the Vermont woods and share a house with another family.

Marian Potter, *Blatherskite*, 1980
  A talkative 10 year old in rural Missouri becomes a community hero by putting her wagging tongue to good use.

Walt Morey, *Year of the Black Pony*, 1976
  A boy growing up in the Oregon country in the early 1900s attains his dream.

1707

Ivan Southall

Illustrator: Ingrid Fetz

Benson Boy (London: Methuen, 1972)

Age range: Grades 5-6

Subject(s): Accidents; Family Life; Birth

Major character(s): Perry Benson, Preteen; Denis Benson, Parent (Perry's father); Mr. Morgan, Neighbor

Time period(s): Indeterminate

Locale(s): England

What the book is about: Perry wakes in the middle of a stormy night. His mother is about to have a baby. Perry's dad falls over a wagon, hits his head and lies in the rain unconscious. Perry must get his dad to shelter and get help for his mother. The nearest phone is at Mr. Morgan's, a half-mile away through the rain and darkness.

Where it's reviewed:
Booklist, July 15, 1973
Hornbook, June 1973, page 273
Kirkus Reviews, February 1, 1973, page 117

Other books by the author:
Blackbird, 1988
The Golden Goose, 1981
Ash Road, 1965
Hills End, 1962

Other books you might like:

Vivien Alcock, *The Cuckoo Sister*, 1985
  A scruffy teenager appears at the door of Kate's parents' home bearing a note that she is their long-lost child, stolen from her pram as a baby.

Susan McLean, *Pennies for the Piper*, 1981
  A ten year old, known for her emotional strength, takes it upon herself to provide her mother with a proper funeral.

Hilary H. Milton, *Tornado!*, 1983
  Paul exhibits heroism while stranded by a flood and tornadoes.

Elizabeth-Ann Sachs, *Where Are You, Cow Patty?*, 1984
  When her friends begin dating each other Janie feels left out but then has a chance to witness the birth of a calf, which matures her in her own way.

William Taylor, *Knitwits*, 1992
  Nine year old Charlie Kenny's life becomes chaotic when he gets himself into a bet that he can knit something for the baby his mother is expecting.

1708

Elizabeth George Speare

The Bronze Bow (Boston: Houghton Mifflin, 1961)

Age range: Grades 6 and Up

Subject(s): Jews; Christian Life; Religion

Major character(s): Daniel bar Jamin, Zealot; Sampson, Slave; Joel bar Hezron, Zealot

Time period(s): 1st century

Locale(s): Israel

What the book is about: Daniel, a Jewish boy in first century Galilee, longs for freedom from the hated Romans. He runs away from the cruel blacksmith to whom he was apprenticed and joins the outlaw, Rosh, in hopes of defeating the Romans. When he returns home to care for his sister and meets Jesus, he finds himself torn between his desire for military power to defeat the Romans and Jesus' message that love is the way to the kingdom he seeks.

Where it's reviewed:
Horn Book, October 1961, page 432
Kirkus Service, July 16, 1961, page 615

Awards the book has won:
Newbery Medal 1962

Other books by the author:
The Sign of the Beaver, 1983
The Witch of Blackbird Pond, 1958
Calico Captive, 1957
Life in Colonial America, 1963

Other books you might like:
Tamar Bergman, *The Boy From Over There*, 1988
    Two children experience life in a kibbutz after the modern state of Israel is reborn.
Eric A. Kimmel, *Nicanor's Gate*, 1980
    Nicanor joins with other Jews to rebuild the temple in Jerusalem.
Jane Yolen, *The Devil's Arithmetic*, 1988
    13 year old Hannah Stern is taken back in time to 1942 when she opens the door for Elijah during the Passover Seder.
Eric P. Kelly, *Trumpeter of Krakow*, 1966
    A young boy sounds a warning when the ancient city of Krakow is under attack in Medieval Poland.

1709

Elizabeth George Speare

The Sign of the Beaver (Boston: Houghton Mifflin, 1983)

Age range: Grades 3-6

Subject(s): Indians of North America; Frontier and Pioneer Life; Survival

Major character(s): Matt, Teenager, Settler; Saknis, Indian; Attean, Indian, Teenager

Time period(s): 1700s

Locale(s): Maine

What the book is about: Matt is left alone in a newly built cabin while his father leaves to bring the rest of the family into the wilderness. A wanderer steals his rifle, a bear steals his flour and molasses and he is attacked by bees while collecting honey. It is Attean and Saknis who save his life. He learns to respect the Native Americans as they help him and teach him what he needs to survive. His "thank you" to Saknis is teaching Attean to read, and the two boys form a close yet tense bond.

When his father is late in returning, he is invited to go with Saknis and Attean and join their family.

Where it's reviewed:
School Library Journal, December 1983, page 30

Other books by the author:
Life in Colonial America, 1963
The Bronze Bow, 1962
The Witch of Blackbird Pond, 1959
Calico Captive, 1957

Other books you might like:
Anne Merrick Epstein, *Good Stones*, 1977
    An aging ex-con who lives as a hermit joins with a twelve year old half-breed orphan as they survive the elements and the rejection of society.
Donn Fendler, *Lost on a Mountain in Maine*, 1992
    A twelve year old describes his nine day struggle to survive after being separated from his companions in the mountains of Maine.
Danita Ross Haller, *Not Just Any Ring*, 1982
    Jessie's grandfather buys her a special ring, but she must depend on herself, not the ring, when she and her grandfather are stranded in the desert.
Honore Morrow, *On to Oregon!*, 1954
    Based on the actual mid-nineteenth century journey by wagon of seven children through 2000 miles of wilderness and hardship from Missouri to Oregon.
Ann Warren Turner, *Grasshopper Summer*, 1989
    In 1874, Sam and his family move from Kentucky to the Dakota territory where harsh conditions and a plague of grasshoppers threaten their survival.

1710

Elizabeth George Speare

The Witch of Blackbird Pond (Boston: Houghton Mifflin, 1958)

Age range: Grades 5 and Up

Subject(s): Puritans; Witches and Witchcraft

Major character(s): Katherine "Kit" Tyler, Orphan; Hannah Tupper, Widow(er); Nathaniel Eaton, Sailor

Time period(s): 17th century

Locale(s): Wethersfield, Connecticut

What the book is about: A free-spirited girl from Barbados goes to live with Puritanical relatives in Connecticut in the late 1600s. Although she tries to tone down her clothing and her approach to life in general, she cannot ignore a lonely widow whom the villagers shun because they think she is a witch. By befriending others, Kit get herself in trouble and she is accused of being a witch.

Where it's reviewed:
Horn Book, August 1959, page 271
Library Journal, April 15, 1959, page 1291
New York Herald Tribune Book Review, November 2, 1958, page 20

Awards the book has won:
Newbery Medal 1959

Other books by the author:
Calico Captive, 1957
The Bronze Bow, 1961

Life in Colonial America, 1963
The Sign of the Beaver, 1983

Other books you might like:
Jay Williams, *Magic Grandfather,* 1979
Sam interrupts a spell cast by his "enchanter" grandfather, who is sent to another world. Sam and his cousin Sarah delve into magic to get him back.
Ann Petry, *Tituba of Salem Village,* 1964
Tituba is brought to trial for witchcraft.
Carol Carrick, *The Elephant in the Dark,* 1988
Will, an orphan, crosses paths with Toong Talong, the first elephant seen in Massachusetts of the 1830s.
Mary Downing Hahn, *The Time of the Witch,* 1982
Laura tells an old woman of her wish that her parents were back together again without realizing that she is speaking to a real witch.
Barthe DeClements, *No Place for Me,* 1987
Copper Jones is sent to live with her Aunt Maggie who is a witch.

1711

Armstrong Sperry, Author/Illustrator

All Sail Set: A Romance of the Flying Cloud (Chicago: Winston, 1935)

Age range: Grades 5-7

Subject(s): Ships; Sea Stories

Major character(s): Enoch Thacher, Sailor; Josiah Perkins Creesy, Sea Captain

Time period(s): 19th century (1851-1874)

Locale(s): New York, New York; At Sea

What the book is about: When his father loses his fortune, Enoch is taken on by a famous shipbuilder and eventually makes a maiden, record-breaking trip around Cape Horn on the *Flying Cloud.* A wonderful story for readers interested in the details of a clipper ship. Includes a nautical glossary.

Other books by the author:
Great River, Wide Land, 1967
Hull Down for Action, 1945
Call it Courage, 1940
One Day with Manu, 1933

Other books you might like:
Peter Burchard, *Ocean Race,* 1978
Presents an account of a voyage aboard a sailboat during the biennial Newport to Bermuda race.
Joe Lasker, *The Strange Voyage of Neptune's Car,* 1977
Young Mary Ann Patten commands a clipper ship rounding Cape Horn when her her husband, the captain, falls ill. Based on actual event.
John J. Loeper, *The Golden Dragon,* 1978
The account of a boy's journey by clipper ship from New York, around Cape Horn, to San Francisco in 1850.
Tim McNeese, *Clippers and Whaling Ships,* 1993
Surveys the history of clippers and whaling ships and examines their significance in America's growth as a nation. (Non-fiction)
Caroline Tapley, *John Come Down the Backstay,* 1974
A young sailor's experiences on the sailing ship *Fox* during two years in the Arctic searching for a lost exploration party.

1712

Armstrong Sperry, Author/Illustrator

Call It Courage (New York: Macmillan, 1940)

Age range: Grades 5-6

Subject(s): Courage; Adventure and Adventurers

Major character(s): Mafutu, Child

Time period(s): Indeterminate Past

Locale(s): Hikueru, French Polynesia

What the book is about: Tired of being called a coward and shaming his family, a young Polynesian boy who is terrified of water, embarks on a journey in a canoe in the South Seas. Mafutu takes his pets, a dog and an albatross, for company. Their adventures include battles with cannibals and a savage boar.

Where it's reviewed:
Booklist, April 1, 1940, page 309
Horn Book, July 1940, page 271

Awards the book has won:
Newbery Medal 1941

Other books by the author:
Danger to Windward, 1942
Little Eagle, Navajo Boy, 1938
Frozen Fire, 1956
Great River, Wide Land, 1967

Other books you might like:
Penina Keen Spinka, *White Hare's Horses,* 1991
In 16th century California, a young Chumash Indian must find the courage to save her people from Aztec invaders.
G. Clifton Wisler, *Red Cap,* 1991
A young Yankee drummer boy displays great courage when he is captured and sent to Andersonville Prison.
Stephanie S. Tolan, *Good Courage,* 1988
14 year old Ty is dragged from one commune to another as she searches for a place to belong.
Michael Morpurgo, *King of the Cloud Forests,* 1987
After being rescued by a tribe who thinks he's a god, Ashley must choose between returning his violent village and the tribe's tests of his "godhood."
Amy Hagstrom, *Strong and Free,* 1987
With the help of an Indian friend and through his love and understanding of Appaloosas, a boy finds the courage to save a herd from horse thieves.

1713

Peter Spier, Author/Illustrator

Oh, Were They Ever Happy! (New York: Doubleday, 1978)

Age range: Grades 1-3

Subject(s): Surprises

Time period(s): 1970s

Locale(s): United States

What the book is about: One Saturday morning while their parents are away, the three Noonan children decide to paint the house. It starts out pretty messy, but when they decide to clean up, it gets even worse.

Where it's reviewed:
Booklist, June 1, 1978, page 1557
Kirkus Reviews, May 1, 1978, page 495
School Library Journal, April 1978, page 78

Awards the book has won:
Little Archer Award 1978

Other books by the author:
Dreams, 1986
Bored-Nothing to Do!, 1978
Tin-Lizzie, 1975
The Fox Went Out on a Chilly Night, 1961

Other books you might like:
Deborah Hautzig, *Get Well, Granny Bird*, 1989
    Though Big Bird makes a mess trying to help Granny get well, she appreciates the fact that he came.
Peggy Kahn, *The Handy Girls Can Fix It!*, 1984
    A group of girls whose "fix it" shop specializes in painting, repairing, and gardening, help two preschoolers by building them a clubhouse.
Liz Matthews, *Teeny Witch and the Terrible Twins*, 1971
    Teeny Witch tries to watch her aunt's house and babysit some terrible twins at the same time, resulting in horrible chaos.
Glen Rounds, *Mr. Yowder and the Windwagon*, 1983
    Mr. Yowder tries to make his fortune by inventing a real prairie schooner from sails, a mast, a rudder and an old wagon, but makes a mess instead.
Ann Tompert, *Sue Patch and the Crazy Clocks*, 1989
    All of the clocks in the King of Tango's palace are set at different times and are driving him nuts, so he appeals to Sue Patch who can fix anything.

1714

Jerry Spinelli

Dump Days (Boston: Little Brown, 1988)

Age range: Grades 4-7

Subject(s): Friendship; Vacations

Major character(s): Duke, Preteen; J.D. Kidd, Preteen; Bertie Kidd, Child

Time period(s): 1980s

Locale(s): United States

What the book is about: Duke and J.D. promise themselves one perfect day before the summer ends and seventh grade begins. Strawberry milk, their favorite sandwiches, a movie, and a bike ride - all the best things all in one day, so they make plans to raise money to pay for their day, down in the dumps.

Where it's reviewed:
Horn Book, May/June 1988, page 355
School Library Journal, August 1988, page 99

Other books by the author:
Do the Funky Pickle, 1992
Fourth Grade Rats, 1991
Maniac Magee, 1991
Bathwater Gang, 1990

Other books you might like:
Helen Cresswell, *Bagthorpes Abroad*, 1984

The irrepresible Bagthorpes vacation in a reputedly haunted house in Wales.
Judy Delton, *The Mystery of the Haunted Cabin*, 1986
    Three children spending the summer in an old cottage on a lake try to solve the mystery of a ghost who seems to be haunting the place.
Catherine Frey Murphy, *Alice Dodd and the Spirit of Truth*, 1993
    While spending the summer vacation with her aunt and three year old cousin, a girl finds herself caught in a series of lies and deceptions.
Mary Towne, *Steve the Sure*, 1990
    Steve is confident of his problem solving ability. While on vacation with his family at a resort, he helps solve the resort's financial problems.
Mary Towne, *Wanda the Worrywart*, 1989
    Wanda's worries become greater than usual during her family's vacation when her divorced step-grandmother is interested in a prospective new husband.

1715

Jerry Spinelli

Maniac Magee (Boston: Little, Brown, 1990)

Age range: Grades 4-6

Subject(s): Orphans; Race Relations; Sports/Baseball

Major character(s): Jeffrey "Maniac" Magee, Orphan, Runaway; Mr. Grayson, Maintenance Worker (Groundskeeper)

Time period(s): 1990s

Locale(s): Two Mills, Pennsylvania

What the book is about: Jeffrey Magee, orphan, then runaway, blazes his own trail through Two Mills, Pennsylvania. His courage is amazing, his knowledge impressive, and his athletic feats legendary. Jeffrey becomes known as "Maniac" because nothing stops him, not even haunted houses or the worst bully. No one knows where he belongs, least of all, Maniac himself.

Where it's reviewed:
Booklist, July 1, 1990, page 1902
Horn Book, May 1990, page 340
School Library Journal, June 1990, page 138

Awards the book has won:
Newbery Medal 1991

Other books by the author:
Dump Days, 1988
Jason and Marceline, 1986
Night of the Whale, 1985
Who Put That Hair in My Toothbrush?, 1984

Other books you might like:
Felice Holman, *Slake's Limbo*, 1974
    13 year old Aremis survives in the subway for 121 days.
Harry Mazer, *Cave under the City*, 1986
    During the depression, brothers Tolley and Bubber survive on the streets of New York while father is out of town and mother is in the hospital.
Anne Lindbergh, *Worry Week*, 1985
    Allegra, Edith and Alice find that a week alone at their cottage in Maine is not a easy as they thought it would be.

Laurence R. Kittleman, *Canyons Beyond the Sky*, 1985
    An archeological dig turns into a time-travel test of survival for 12-year-old Evan.
Rodgers Raboo, *Magnam Fault*, 1984
    Searching for Jill's father, Jill and Cody find a mystery and a test of their own ability to survive.

Gretchen Sprague

Signpost to Terror (New York: Dodd Mead, 1967)

Age range: Grades 5 and Up

Subject(s): Robbers and Outlaws; Hiking

Major character(s): Gail, Teenager, Sports Figure (hiker); Lew, Criminal, Sports Figure (hiker)

Time period(s): 1960s

Locale(s): New York (Adirondack Mountains)

What the book is about: Within a the span of just few hours, Gail experiences the peace of a solitary hiker who has escaped a quarrelsome family, and the terror of a victim, when she meets a fellow outdoorsman who is not what he seems to be. Recommended for reluctant readers.

Where it's reviewed:
Christian Science Monitor, November 16, 1967, page 15
Library Journal, September 15, 1967, page 3205

Awards the book has won:
Edgar Allan Poe Award 1968

Other books you might like:
Thomas Baird, *Where Time Ends*, 1988
    While camping in the Adirondacks, Doug and Loop fall in with Ernie and her belligerent brother, as the world plummets into a devastating war.
Michael French, *Pursuit: A Novel*, 1982
    After a boy falls to his death on a hiking trip, his brother is pursued through the wilderness by the man he believes responsible.
Carolyn Lane, *Ghost Island*, 1985
    Four campers are marooned on Ghost Island where Sally becomes convinced that its name is for real.
Gregory Maguire, *The Lightning Time*, 1978
    After the illness of his grandmother, David moves to her home in northern New York state.
Ivy Ruckman, *No Way Out*, 1988
    Hiking along the Virgin River in Utah, Amy and her fiance, and four friends battle a flash flood.

Nancy Springer

A Horse to Love (New York: Harper, 1987)

Age range: Grades 5-7

Subject(s): Animals/Horses

Major character(s): Erin Callahan, Teenager, Equestrian; Mike Calahan, Teenager; Lexie Bromer, Relative (aunt)

Time period(s): 1980s

Locale(s): Pennsylvania

What the book is about: Shy Erin gains confidence when she gets a horse and learns to care for the animal. She finds that her dream horse can be both rewarding and frustrating. Since Spindrift is cranky, Erin is not allowed to let other kids ride, so they think her stuckup. But in getting to know her horse, Erin comes to know herself better and begins to reach out to friends.

Where it's reviewed:
Booklist, March 15, 1987, page 1130
Kirkus Reviews, December 1, 1986, page 1795
School Library Journal, March 1987, page 166

Other books by the author:
Colt, 1991
Red Wizard, 1989
They're All Named Wildfire, 1989
Not on a White Horse, 1988

Other books you might like:
Patricia Calvert, *The Money Creek Mare*, 1981
    Sharing her father's dream of having a champion horse farm, Elle Rae secretly takes his crippled red mare to mate with a famous stallion.
Barbara Corcoran, *A Horse Named Sky*, 1986
    Georgia's one goal when she and her mother move to Montana is to own a hourse, a dream that seems remote until her neighbor wants to sell her horse.
Jean Slaughter Doty, *Dark Horse*, 1983
    A special brown horse helps Abby realize her dream of taking part in a first class riding competition.
Jo Ann Simon, *Star*, 1989
    Shy, overweight Toni loses her feelings of self-consciousness when she forges a bond with a horse during riding lessons and succeeds a horse show.
Phillip Viereck, *Sue's Secondhand Horse*, 1973
    A thirteen year old girl's dream is realized when she receives a mare for Christmas, an event that changes the lives of all her family in many ways.

Nancy Springer

They're All Named Wildfire (New York: Macmillan, 1989)

Age range: Grades 4-6

Subject(s): Friendship; Animals/Horses; Racism

Major character(s): Jenny Wetzel, Preteen; Shanteray Lucas, Friend

Time period(s): 1980s

Locale(s): United States

What the book is about: Jenny loses most of her friends and suffers the verbal abuse of classmates when she befriends a black girl who has moved with her family into Jenny's duplex and shares her interest in horses.

Where it's reviewed:
Horn Book, May/June 1989, page 373
School Library Journal, April 1989, page 104

Other books by the author:
Friendship Song, 1992
Colt, 1991
Red Wizard, 1990

A Horse to Love, 1987

Other books you might like:
Ken Adler, *The White Bus*, 1987
Ira deals with disapproval and prejudice on both sides of the color line when he rejects private school to attend his black friend's high school.
Larry Bograd, *The Fourth-Grade Dinosaur Club*, 1989
Billy feels everything in his life is wrong, with a hectic homelife, the bullies at school, and the prejudice his friend Juan is experienceing.
John Craig, *No Word for Goodbye*, 1969
A white boy and an Ojibway Indian youth become close friends but find their friendship vulnerable to prejudice and misunderstanding.
Barbara Girion, *Indian Summer*, 1990
Joni spends the summer on an Indian reservation and has to cope with Sarah and her friends, who blame Joni for the prejudice they experience.
Joan Kane Nichols, *All but the Right Folks*, 1985
A young black boy discovers that the mother he never knew was white and spends an unforgettable summer with his white grandmother in New York City.

1719

Tricia Springstubb

Eunice (the Egg Salad) Gottlieb (New York: Delacorte, 1988)

Age range: Grades 4-6

Subject(s): Friendship; Sports/Gymnastics; Self-Acceptance

Major character(s): Eunice Gottlieb, Child (10 years old), Sports Figure (gymnast); Joy McKenzie, Preteen, Sports Figure (gymnast); Mr. Cruikshank, Coach

Time period(s): 1980s

Locale(s): United States

What the book is about: In the midst of assorted crises involving her brother and sister, Eunice struggles to master the vault for her school's upcoming gymnastics exhibition, a project that has damaged her sense of self-worth and threatens to end her friendship with the athletically talented Joy.

Where it's reviewed:
Booklist, January 15, 1988, page 868
School Library Journal, February 1988, page 75

Other books by the author:
Two Plus One Makes Trouble, 1991
With a Name Like Lulu, Who Needs More Trouble?, 1989
Eunice Gottlieb and the Unwhitewashed Truth about Life, 1987
Give and Take, 1981

Other books you might like:
Alice Bach, *The Meat in the Sandwich*, 1975
Mike feels his decision of becoming a star athlete is threatened by his older and younger sisters, until he is befriended by another athlete.
Spring Hermann, *Flip City*, 1988
Four girls whose family lives are difficult, compete in gymnastics for their gym, the place they feel most "at home."
Jean Davies Okimoto, *Norman Schnurman, Average Person*, 1982

Norman doesn't like sports. He wishes he could find something to do that would make his college-football-star dad proud of him.
Sheri Cooper Singkin, *Shrimpboat and Gym Bags*, 1990
Bo copes with the pressures of moving from California, keeping his grades high, and competing against a talented but temperamental teammate.
Victoria Whitehead, *Chimney Witch Chase*, 1988
Ellen's efforts to get chosen for competition are complicated by the witch boy who lives in her chimney.

1720

Johanna Spyri

Heidi (New York: Grossett, 1945)

Age range: Grades 3-7

Subject(s): Grandparents; Mountain Life; Orphans

Major character(s): Heidi, Orphan; Peter, Preteen; Grandfather, Grandparent

Time period(s): Indeterminate Past

Locale(s): Mayenfield, Switzerland

What the book is about: Heidi comes to live with her reclusive grandfather in the Swiss Alps. She loves the mountains and the goats they care for. She would prefer to stay forever, but is sent to the city to be a companion to the crippled girl, Clara. Beautiful descriptions of the glory of the Swiss Alps, available in many different editions.

Where it's reviewed:
Books & Bookmen, August 1969, page 46
Grade Teacher, February 1972, page 96

Other books by the author:
Heidi's Children, 1989
New Adventures of Heidi, 1980
Heidi Grows Up, 1966

Other books you might like:
Paige Dixon, *Summer of the White Goat*, 1977
A young man observes a mountain goat living in the boundaries of Glacier National Park in Montana as it deals with the various problems of survival.
Jean Craighead George, *On the Far Side of the Mountain*, 1990
Sam's peaceful existence in his wilderness home is disrupted when his sister runs away and his pet falcon is confiscated by a conservation officer.
William MacKellar, *The Silent Bells*, 1978
A Swiss girl dreams of the Christmas Day when a special gift is presented at the creche, causing the cathedral bells to break their long silence.
Olive M. Price, *The Dog That Watched the Mountain*, 1967
A Swiss youth persues the loyalty, love, and obedience of an unaffectionate St. Bernard he has selected to assist him in his ski classes.
Stephanie S. Tolan, *The Great Skinner Homestead*, 1988
Jenny relates her family's misadventures homesteading in the Adirondack mountains during the summer.

1721

Wylly Folk St. John

Illustrator: Frank Aloise

Mystery of the Gingerbread House (New York: Viking, 1969)

Age range: Grades 5-7

Subject(s): Mystery and Detective Stories

Major character(s): Ron Jameson, Detective; Greg Jameson, Detective; Evie, Handicapped

Time period(s): 1960s

Locale(s): Atlanta, Georgia

What the book is about: Two boys solve a mystery involving an abandoned body and missing jewels in Atlanta and try to help a handicapped child and her baby sister find their grandmother. The only thing the girl recalls about her grandmother is that she lives in a gingerbread house with a yellow rose at one end and a stained glass window on the stair landing.

Where it's reviewed:
Kirkus, May 1, 1969, page 505
Library Journal, May 15, 1969, page 2123

Other books by the author:
The Secrets of Hidden Creek, 1976
The Secret of the Seven Crows, 1973
The Mystery of the Other Girl, 1971
The Secrets of the Pirate Inn, 1968

Other books you might like:
Lynn Hall, *Murder in a Pig's Eye*, 1990
 Convinced a neighboring farmer has murdered his wife, Bobie searches for her body until his detective work reaches a chaotic and humorous climax.
Daniel Hayes, *The Trouble with Lemons*, 1991
 Tyler and Lymie, 8th grade misfits, discover a dead body in a quarry and work to solve the mystery behind it.
Florence Parry Heide, *Body in the Brillstone Garage*, 1980
 Liza finds a body wearing Mr. Greening's jacket, but when she returns to the scene with a friend, the body is gone. Later, Mr. Greening is wearing it.
Willo Davis Roberts, *Nightmare*, 1991
 When a falling body strikes Nick's car as he drives under an overpass, the police call it suicide, but Nick suspects murder.
Otto R. Salassi, *And Nobody Knew They Were There*, 1984
 Two boys try to track down some missing marines.

1722

Joyce St. Peter

Illustrator: Elise Primavera

Always Abigail (New York: Harper, 1981)

Age range: Grades 4-6

Subject(s): Diaries; Ranch Life; Weight Control

Major character(s): Abigail John, Preteen (overweight); Aunt Bess, Journalist

Time period(s): 1970s

Locale(s): Westlyn, California

What the book is about: Abigail not only survives but also unexpectedly enjoys a summer with her aunt. After Abigail gets expelled from "fat camp," she and Aunt Bess pack off to the Tenderfoot Farm together, and Abigail realizes that being "almost twelve" is not so bad after all.

Where it's reviewed:
Booklist, October 1, 1981, page 239
Kirkus, November 15, 1981, page 1410
School Library Journal, October 1981, page 146

Other books you might like:
Hila Colman, *Diary of a Frantic Kid Sister*, 1973
 By recording her feelings in a diary, an eleven year old girl comes to terms with her lack of self confidence and mixed feelings about her sister.
Eleanor Frances Lattimore, *The Two Helens*, 1967
 Young Helen meets and tames Great-Aunt Helen whom her parents refer to as "The Dragon."
Colleen O'Shaughnessy McKenna, *Eenie, Meanie, Murphy, NO!*, 1990
 While at camp, Collette is desperate to retrieve her secret diary, which has been stolen and read out loud.
Lila Perl, *The Secret Diary of Katie Dinkerhoff*, 1987
 Katie lies to her diary, writing what she wished would happen, rather than what did happen, and learns how to make wishful thinking a reality.
Robert Kimmel Smith, *Mostly Michael*, 1987
 Michael's diary reflects his eleventh year, as he copes with braces, relatives, a little sister, the school play and a spelling bee.

1723

John Stadler, Author/Illustrator

Snail Saves the Day (New York: Crowell, 1985)

Age range: Grades 1-3

Subject(s): Animals; Sports/Football

Major character(s): Snail, Snail, Sports Figure (football player); Dog, Dog, Sports Figure (football player)

Time period(s): Indeterminate

Locale(s): Fictional Country

What the book is about: When two football teams are badly mismatched, it is snail who must get to the stadium in time to save his team by catching the winning touchdown.

Where it's reviewed:
School Library Journal, December 1985, page 110
Publisher's Weekly, August 2, 1985, page 66

Other books by the author:
Cat at Bat, 1988
Three Cheers for Hippo!, 1987
Hooray for Snail, 1984
Hector the Accordion-Nosed Dog, 1983

Other books you might like:
John Carroll, *Donkey Nina and the Giant*, 1989
 Donkey Nina and her friend the snail set out to protect the world from monsters.
Paula Franklin, *The Snail who Flew*, 1983
 When two caterpillars become butterflies, they offer snail a chance to fly.
John Himmelman, *Simpson Snail Sings*, 1992

Simpson Snail goes to a costume party, makes a new friend, learns to sing, and sleeps over at Tucker Turtle's house.

Leo Lionni, *The Biggest House in the World*, 1968
A snail's father advises him to keep his house small and tells him what happened to a snail that grew a large and spectacular shell.

Anne Rockwell, *The Story Snail*, 1974
John can do nothing well until a snail gives him one hundred stories to tell. But even they wear thin and he goes in search of the snail again.

1724

Ben Stahl

Blackbeard's Ghost (Boston: Houghton Mifflin, 1965)

Age range: Grades 6 and Up

Subject(s): Pirates

Major character(s): Edward "Blackbeard" Teach, Pirate, Historical Figure

Time period(s): 1960s

Locale(s): Godolphin, North Carolina

What the book is about: The poltergeist of Blackbeard is accidentally summoned by two boys, and the ghost harrasses the boys and the demolition gang that is hard at work wrecking the Boar's Head Tavern to make way for a gas station. Suspense, humor and history in an imaginative tale.

Where it's reviewed:
Hornbook, August 1965, page 393
Kirkus Reviews, March 1, 1965, page 244
Library Journal, June 15, 1965, page 2897
New York Review of Books, March 21, 1965, page 26

Awards the book has won:
Sequoyah Children's Book Award 1969

Other books by the author:
Secret of Red Skull, 1971

Other books you might like:
Sid Fleischman, *The Ghost in the Noonday Sun*, 1965
Oliver Finch is shanghaied by a pirate band and manages to outwit the infamous Captain Scratch.

Richard Kennedy, *Amy's Eyes*, 1985
Amy is the mascot on a ship hunting for pirate treasure. Complex but rewarding.

Margaret Mahy, *Great Piratical Rumbustificaion*, 1978
Two wild stories which present pirates, robbers, and librarians in a new light.

Robert Louis Stevenson, *Treasure Island*, 1980
Classic treasure hunt story of the crew of Black Dog and Long John Silver.

Leonard Wibberley, *The Crime of Martin Coverly*, 1980
When Nick discovers he has a famous pirate ancestor, he is drawn into the past, sails with Martin's crew, and is captured.

1725

Muriel Stanek

Illustrator: Judith Friedman

I Speak English for My Mom (Chicago: Whitman, 1989)

Age range: Grades 2-5

Subject(s): Literacy; Emigration and Immigration; Mexican Americans

Major character(s): Lupe Gomez, Child; Mrs. Gomez, Parent

Time period(s): 1980s

Locale(s): United States

What the book is about: A young Mexican-American translates for her mother who cannot speak English. This book provides positive reinforcement to the increasingly important role in which many children, particularly recent immigrants, find themselves.

Where it's reviewed:
Booklist, March 1, 1989, page 1196
Center for Children's Books Bulletin, February 1989, page 158

Other books by the author:
My Mom Can't Read, 1986
My Little Foster Sister, 1981
Growl When You Say "R", 1979
I Won't Go with My Father, 1972

Other books you might like:
Larry Bograd, *The Fourth-Grade Dinosaur Club*, 1989
Billy feels that his life is all wrong, from his hectic home life to the school bullies, and the spoiled friendship with his best friend, Juan.

Juanita Havill, *Treasure Map*, 1992
One afternoon when it is too hot to sleep, a young girl asks for the story of how her great-great-grandmother came to the U.S. with a special treasure

Joan Hewett, *Hector Lives in the United States Now*, 1990
Text and photos of the daily happenings and milestones in the life of a young Mexican boy whose family seeks amnesty in America. (Non-fiction)

Gary Soto, *Local News*, 1993
A collection of thirteen short stories about the everyday lives of Mexican-American young people in California's Central Valley.

Theodore Taylor, *Maria, a Christmas Story*, 1992
Maria and her family are the first Mexican-Americans to enter a float in the annual Christmas parade in San Lazaro, California.

1726

Suzanne Fisher Staples

Shabanu, Daughter of the Wind (New York: Knopf, 1989)

Age range: Grades 6-9

Subject(s): Parent and Child; Sex Roles

Major character(s): Shabanu, Nomad, Preteen

Time period(s): 1980s

Locale(s): Cholistan Desert, Pakistan

What the book is about: When Shabanu, the daughter of a nomad in the Cholistan Desert of modern Pakistan, is pledged in marriage to an older man whose wealth will bring prestige to the family, she must either accept the decision or defy her father. A vivid picture of a loving family in conflict, as well as a portrait of the people and customs of the culture.

Where it's reviewed:
Center for Children's Books Bulletin, October 1989, page 45
Hornbook, January 1990, page 72
School Library Journal, November 1989, page 128

Other books you might like:
Jean Bothwell, *Defiant Bride*, 1969
In 17th century India, the destiny of a Nomad girl is changed when the powerful ruler Akbar decides to annex the hill country where her people wander.
Mavis Thorpe Clark, *The Hundred Islands*, 1976
Greg's concern with preserving the wildlife of the hundred islands in Australia's Bass Strait leads him to defy his father and set out on his own path
Judith Gorog, *Winning Scheherazade*, 1991
No longer a storyteller and doomed bride of the Sultan, Scheherazade is sent by a mysterious visitor into dangerous adventures in the desert.
Sam B. Hobson, *The Lion of the Kalahari*, 1976
Bushmen driven from their tribe when a new leader takes command struggle to survive on their own in the Kalahari.
Susan Sussman, *Casey the Nomad*, 1985
Casey is fascinated by nomads, but he's distressed to learn that his own father will be traveling the country for two years on business.

1727

Marion Lena Starkey

Illustrator: Charles Mikolaycak

The Tall Man From Boston (New York: Crown, 1975)

Age range: Grades 3-5

Subject(s): Witches and Witchcraft

Major character(s): Tituba, Slave, Historical Figure; John Alden, Settler

Time period(s): 17th century (1690s)

Locale(s): Salem, Massachusetts, American Colonies

What the book is about: The story of the Salem witch hunts of Colonial America, told for the middle grades. Background information is given about the long winter boredom, piety and superstition, and guilt that led to the famous witch hunts. John Alden is accused at random by a group of troubled girls.

Where it's reviewed:
Booklist, December 15, 1975, page 581
Kirkus Reviews, October 15, 1975, page 1191
School Library Journal, December 1975, page 55

Other books by the author:
The Visionary Girls: Witchcraft in Salem Village, 1973

Other books you might like:
Rose Blue, *My Mother, the Witch*, 1980
In Chatham, Massachusetts, in 1697, ten year old Betsy feels sick with fear as more and more incidents seem to indicate that her mother is a witch.
Alice Dickinson, *The Salem Witchcraft Delusion, 1692*, 1974
Discusses the social and religious climate that led to the Salem witch hunts and describes the trials and their aftermath.

William H. Hooks, *The Legend of the White Doe*, 1988
After the destruction of the English colony on Roanoke Island by hostile Indians forces the survivors to live with a friendly tribe, Virginia Dare fin
Stephen Krensky, *Witch Hunt: It Happened in Salem Village*, 1989
An account of the madness that overtook Salem Massachusetts, when several young girls accused a number of adults in the community of being witches.
F.N. Monjo, *The House on Stink Alley: A Story about the Pilgrims in Holland*, 1977
Young Love Brewster describes the experiences of his family living in Leyden in the years before the *Mayflower* sails for the New World.

1728

Mary Q. Steele

Journey Outside (New York: Viking, 1969)

Age range: Grades 5-8

Subject(s): Fantasy

Major character(s): Dilar, Young Man; Gimal, Fisherman

Time period(s): Indeterminate

Locale(s): Fictional Country

What the book is about: Young Dilar, believing that his Raft People in seeking a "better place" have been circling endlessly, sets out to discover the origin and fate of his kind. He leaves the rafts behind and journeys into knowledge of the land.

Where it's reviewed:
Booklist, July 15, 1969, page 1276
Hornbook, June 1969, page 309
Kirkus Reviews, May 1, 1969, page 506

Other books by the author:
The True Men, 1976
Because of the Sand Witches There, 1975
The Eye in the Forest, 1975

Other books you might like:
Natalie Babbitt, *Tuck Everlasting*, 1975
A family is confronted with a choice when they discover that a girl and a stranger know about a spring whose water prevents people from growing old.
Lorna Baxter, *The Eggchild*, 1978
A boy and girl find a mysterious Eggchild and feel compelled to protect it and discover its true identity.
Tom McGowen, *Odyssey From River Bend*, 1975
Some of the animals of River Bend risk the dangers of a journey to the Haunted Land in search of the secret to the magic of the Long Ago Ones.
Patricia A. McKillip, *The Moon and the Face*, 1985
Kyreol's mission to another planet and Terje's trip to observe their old river home both meet with unexpected dangers.
Marilyn Singer, *Charmed*, 1990
Miranda and her companion, Bastable, discover that they are part of a team that must stop the evil Charmer from taking over the universe.

1729

William O. Steele

Man with the Silver Eyes (New York: Harcourt Brace Jovanovich, 1976)

Age range: Grades 5-6

Subject(s): Fathers and Sons; Indians of North America; Revolutionary War

Major character(s): Shinn, Quaker; Talatu, Preteen, Indian

Time period(s): 1780s

Locale(s): American Colonies

What the book is about: Eleven year old Talatu is sent from his Cherokee village to live with a white man. Talatu hates whites because of their constant raids on his village, and cannot understand why he was sent to live with Shinn, whose silver eyes and Quaker ways are strange to him. When Shinn is critically wounded saving Talatu's life, he reveals that he is the boy's father.

Where it's reviewed:
Booklist, November 1, 1976, page 412
Center for Children's Books Bulletin, May 1977, page 150
Hornbook, October 1976, page 500

Other books by the author:
Triple Trouble for Hound Dog Zip, 1972
Trail through Danger, 1965
Wayah of the Real People, 1964
The Perilous Road, 1958

Other books you might like:
Weyman B. Jones, *Edge of Two Worlds*, 1968
   Sole survivor of a Comanche raid on the wagon train taking him East to school, a boy wanders until he meets an unusual old Cherokee.
Harold Keith, *The Obstinate Land*, 1977
   During a hard winter the father of a pioneering German family in Oklahoma freezes to death and his fourteen year old son must assume responsibility.
Lois Gladys Leppard, *Mandie and the Cherokee Legend*, 1983
   Mandy is bewildered by the unhappy reaction of some of her Cherokee friends to her discovery of gold inside a cave.
Joyce Rockwood, *Groundhog's Horse*, 1978
   An eleven year old Cherokee sets off on a one-boy raid of a Creek town to rescue his "unusual" horse.
Joyce Rockwood, *To Spoil the Sun*, 1979
   Forewarned by omens, an Indian village is struck by an "invisible fire" which actually is smallpox brought to America by European explorers.

1730

Cathy Stefanec-Ogren

Illustrator: Priscilla P. Circolo

Sly, P.I.: The Case of the Missing Shoes (New York: Harper, 1989)

Age range: Grades 2-3

Subject(s): Ballet; Animals/Pigs; Mystery and Detective Stories

Major character(s): Sly Fox, Private Detective; Lotta Oink, Pig, Dancer; Yuri Wolfruff, Dancer

Time period(s): Indeterminate

Locale(s): United States

What the book is about: It is time for Lotta to perform, and all her toe shoes and costumes are gone. Her friend, Sly P.I., is on the case. When he finds some rats using one shoe to rock their babies in, he thinks he has found the culprits, but they have only one shoe, which they thought had been thrown away. The case is solved when Sly runs into Messy Face Elmo who has all the goods hidden in a cello case.

Where it's reviewed:
Booklist, May 1, 1989, page 1555
Center for Children's Books Bulletin, April 1989, page 206
School Library Journal, June 1989, page 95

Other books you might like:
Eth Clifford, *Flatfoot Fox and the Case of the Missing Eye*, 1990
   Detective Fox uncovers the thief who stole Fat Cat's glass eye.
Geoffrey Hayes, *The Secret of Foghorn Island*, 1988
   Otto and Uncle Tooth, detectives, investigate a series of shipwrecks, which brings them into contact with the dangerous Sid Rat.
Jon Scieszka, *The True Story of the Three Little Pigs*, 1989
   The wolf gives his own outlandish version of what happened when he tangled with the three little pigs.
John Stadler, *The Ballad of Wilbur and the Moose*, 1989
   A cowboy and a big blue moose work their way through the Wild West where rustlers steal pigs and the card dealer may well be a crocodile.
Jean Van Leeuwen, *Amanda Pig on her Own*, 1991
   When her brother goes off to school, Amanda finds new things to do, including ballet dancing, with the help of hugs from her mother.

1731

William Steig

Abel's Island (New York: Farrar, 1976)

Age range: Grades 5-6

Subject(s): Islands; Animals/Mice; Survival

Major character(s): Abelard Mouse, Survivor; Amanda Mouse, Spouse (Able's wife)

Time period(s): Indeterminate

Locale(s): Fictional Country

What the book is about: Abel loved his pampered, cozy life in the little community of Mossville, until the day a furious summer storm swept him off to a lonely river island.

Where it's reviewed:
Booklist, September 15, 1976, page 181
Hornbook, October 1976, page 500
Kirkus Reviews, June 15, 1976, page 686

Awards the book has won:
Newbery Honor 1977

Other books by the author:
The Real Thief, 1973
Dominic, 1972
Amos and Boris, 1971
Sylvester and the Magic Pebble, 1969

Other books you might like:

Liza Fosburgh, *Bella Arabella*, 1985
  Arabella thinks that by becoming a cat, she can avoid being sent to boarding school, but she finds her new life is not how she expected it to be.

Ruth Stiles Gannett, *My Father's Dragon*, 1948
  A young boy determines to rescue a poor baby dragon who is being used by a group of lazy wild animals to ferry them across the river on Wild Island.

Belinda Hurmence, *A Girl Called Boy*, 1982
  A pampered young black girl who has been mysteriously transported back to the days of slavery, struggles to escape bondage.

Anne Knowles, *The Halcyon Island*, 1980
  While on summer vacation, a boy overcomes his fear of the river with the help of a mysterious friend.

John Rowe Townsend, *Pirate's Island*, 1968
  A boy lets a highly imaginative girl talk him into friendship and a search for pirates' treasure on an island in the river that boarders their slum.

1732

William Steig

Brave Irene (New York: Farrar, Strauss and Giroux, 1986)

Age range: Grades 1-3

Subject(s): Weather; Courage; Mothers and Daughters

Major character(s): Irene Bobbin, Child; Mrs. Bobbin, Seamstress

Time period(s): Indeterminate

Locale(s): United States

What the book is about: This is a story of bravery and success through hard work. Irene's mother is too sick to deliver the dress she has sewn for the duchess. Irene faces a winter storm and a fierce wind to make the delivery. For her bravery and determination she receives exciting rewards as well as medical help for her mother and returns home in triumph.

Where it's reviewed:
Booklist, November 1, 1986, page 414
Kirkus Reviews, October 15, 1986, page 1580

Other books by the author:
The Amazing Bone, 1986
Caleb and Kate, 1986
Doctor De Soto, 1982
Gorky Rises, 1980

Other books you might like:

Amy Aitken, *Ruby the Red Knight*, 1983
  After visiting the museum, Ruby imagines that she is a knight who breaks the enchantment of the wizard.

Ellen Conford, *Eugene the Brave*, 1978
  Eugene the possum learns to overcome his fear of the dark.

Bill Peet, *Cowardly Clyde*, 1979
  Clyde is a huge war horse who pretends to be brave but isn't. In spite of his fear, he rescues his master and becomes a hero.

Mark Taylor, *Henry the Explorer*, 1966
  Henry and his dog go off on an adventure that is full of surprises.

David Wiesner, *The Loathsome Dragon*, 1987

Childe Wynd must rescue his sister from the spell of the evil enchantress.

1733

William Steig, Author/Illustrator

Dominic (New York: Farrar, Straus and Giroux, 1972)

Age range: Grades 4-7

Subject(s): Adventure and Adventurers; Fantasy

Major character(s): Dominic, Dog; Bartholomew Badger, Pig; Elijah Hogg, Mule

Time period(s): Indeterminate

Locale(s): Fictional Country

What the book is about: Dominic, an adventurous dog, locks his house, buries the key and sets off to see the world. He politely refuses the offer of an alligator witch to tell his fortune, but he does take her advice about which fork in the road leads to adventure. He is soon trapped by the Doomsday Gang, a fox, ferret and a weasel, and his adventure is underway. Before all is done, Dominic comes into a fortune, makes many friends, and finds a lifetime companion, Evelyn Dog.

Where it's reviewed:
Center for Children's Books Bulletin, October 1972, page 31
Hornbook, October 1972, page 470
Kirkus Reviews, December 15, 1972, page 1414

Awards the book has won:
Christopher Award 1973

Other books by the author:
Abel's Island, 1976
The Amazing Bone, 1976
The Real Thief, 1973
Sylvester and the Magic Pebble, 1969

Other books you might like:

Betty Brock, *No Flying in the House*, 1970
  A tiny talking dog arrives at the home of rich Mrs. Vancourt and asks for shelter for herself and her companion, a little girl.

Scott Corbett, *The Hairy Horror Trick*, 1969
  Two boys mix a startling potion with a secret chemistry set that unexpectly grows hair on their faces and makes the dog hairless.

Elizabeth Goudge, *The Little White Horse*, 1946
  Newly orphaned Maria, her governess, and dog arrive at her ancestral home in an enchanted village where the people's bliss is marred by a dark shadow.

Fran Grace, *Branigan's Dog: A Novel*, 1981
  Casey, having talked to the world through his dog, must emerge from his fantasy life when the dog dies.

Diana Wynne Jones, *Dogsbody*, 1975
  Sirius, the dog star, is reborn on earth as a puppy with a mission to search for the lost Zoi, murder weapon of the stars.

1734

William Steig

Dr. De Soto (New York: Farrar, 1982)

Age range: Grades 2-4

Subject(s): Dentistry; Animals/Foxes; Animals/Mice

Major character(s): Doctor De Soto, Mouse, Dentist

Time period(s): Indeterminate

Locale(s): Fictional Country

What the book is about: Dr. De Soto, the dentist, did very good work for animals large and small. He was anxious, however, about cats and other dangerous animals - dangerous to mice, that is. When a fox tries to take advantage of him, Dr. De Soto outsmarts him.

Where it's reviewed:
Booklist, January 1, 1983, page 621
Hornbook, April 1983, page 162
Kirkus Reviews, November 1, 1982, page 1191

Awards the book has won:
Newbery Honor 1983
American Book Award 1983

Other books by the author:
Gorky Rises, 1980
Caleb and Kate, 1977
Abel's Island, 1976
Roland, the Minstrel Pig, 1968

Other books you might like:
Mary Jane Auch, *Peeping Beauty*, 1993
    Poulette, the dancing hen, falls into the clutches of a hungry fox, who exploits her desire to become a great ballerina.
Diane De Groat, *Alligator's Toothache*, 1977
    It is a serious problem when an alligator gets a toothache, especially when it is afraid of the dentist.
Ida Lutrell, *Milo's Toothache*, 1992
    Milo Pig plans to visit the dentist about his toothache, but his friends overreact and make the outing into a big problem.
David M. McPhail, *The Bear's Toothache*, 1972
    When he discovers a bear with a toothache outside his window, a little boy tries to think of ways of removing the tooth.
Annie Mitra, *Tusk! Tusk!*, 1990
    Waking up on his birthday with a toothache, Elephant visits the dentist and learns about proper tooth care.

1735

William Steig, Author/Illustrator

The Real Thief (New York: Farrar, Straus and Giroux, 1973)

Age range: Grades 3-5

Subject(s): Robbers and Outlaws

Major character(s): Gawain, Goose, Guard; Derek, Mouse, Thief; King Basil, Bear, Royalty

Time period(s): Indeterminate

Locale(s): Fictional Country

What the book is about: When Gawain the goose is deserted by his friends after being unjustly convicted of stealing from his beloved king, the real thief is tortured by his conscience.

Where it's reviewed:
Booklist, October 15, 1973, page 242
Hornbook, December 1973, page 595

Kirkus Reviews, July 15, 1973, page 756

Other books by the author:
Dr. De Soto, 1982
Dominic, 1972
Amos and Boris, 1971
Slyvester and the Magic Pebble, 1969

Other books you might like:
Alan Coren, *Arthur the Kid*, 1977
    Ten year old Arthur the Kid takes over an outlaw gang and changes their lives forever.
Terry Deary, *The Custard Kid*, 1980
    The Custard Kid, who wants only to be a Hollywood stunt man, finds himself accidentally pursuing an outlaw career instead.
Berniece Freschet, *Bernard of Scotland Yard*, 1978
    An enterprising Bostonian mouse assists his cousin, a Scotland Yard inspector, in apprehending a gang of jewel thieves.
Astrid Lindgren, *Ronia, the Robber's Daughter*, 1983
    Ronia, who lives with her father and his band of robbers causes trouble when she befriends the son of a rival robber chieftain.
George Shannon, *The Gang and Mrs. Higgins*, 1981
    When the Anderson gang raids the pioneer trading post in Kansas, Mrs. Higgins uses their own bad habits to save the gold.

1736

William Steig

Shrek! (New York: Farrar, 1990)

Age range: Grades 2-4

Subject(s): Monsters; Princes and Princesses

Major character(s): Shrek, Monster

Time period(s): Indeterminate

Locale(s): Earth

What the book is about: A love-hungry, ugly, fire-breathing monster sets off on a romantic quest. He yearns for an ugly princess that he can live "horribly ever after" with.

Where it's reviewed:
Kirkus Reviews, October 1, 1990, page 1402
School Library Journal, December 1990, page 25

Other books by the author:
Solomon and the Rusty Nail, 1985
Dr. DeSoto, 1982
The Amazing Bone, 1976
Sylvester and the Magic Pebble, 1969

Other books you might like:
Jackie French Koller, *The Dragonling*, 1990
    Finding a baby dragon left alive after his older brother's dragon quest, Darek risks death and the anger of his people in trying to return it safely.
Rosemary Sutcliff, *The Minstrel and the Dragon Pup*, 1993
    When a minstrel's adopted dragon pup is stolen by a wicked showman, the minstrel's songs suffer terribly.
Stephanie S. Tolan, *Marcy Hooper and the Greatest Treasure in the World*, 1991

Marcy, who can't seem to do anything right, has an adventure involving a dragon and treasure, which bolsters her self-esteem.

Caryn Yacowitz, *The Jade Stone*, 1992
The Emperor of all China gives the command to carve a dragon, but Chan Lo discovers the stone wants to be something else.

Jane Yolen, *Dove Isabeau*, 1989
Young, beautiful Dove Isabeau is turned into a fire-breathing dragon by her evil stepmother and is saved from the spell by her true love, Kemp Owain.

1737

William Steig

Illustrator: William Steig

Spinky Sulks (New York: Farrar Strauss and Giroux, 1988)

Age range: Grades 1-5

Subject(s): Behavior

Major character(s): Spinky, Child

Time period(s): 1980s

Locale(s): United States

What the book is about: Spinky goes into a massive sulk because of the way his family treats him, especially calling him "Stinky." The story is a child's favorite dream of being able to manipulate others into trying to placate him for real or imagined wrongs. He gets lunch on a tray, his favorite candy and ice cream and wins concessions from his brother in arguments. He begins to realize he will have to begin to behave better, but wants to keep the self-respect he has gained.

Where it's reviewed:
Booklist, January 15, 1989, page 874
Horn Book, March/April 1989, page 204

Other books by the author:
Dr. DeSoto Goes to Africa, 1992
Dr. DeSoto, 1982
The Amazing Bone, 1976
Amos and Boris, 1971

Other books you might like:
Margery Cuyler, *Baby Dot: A Dinosaur Story*, 1990
Spoiled dinosaur Baby Dot returns to the cave after a tantrum and finds another young dinosaur even more obnoxious than she is.

Rumer Godden, *Candy Floss*, 1991
A doll named Candy Floss is very happy serving as Jack's lucky charm at his stall at the fair until a spoiled rich girl steals them.

James McEwan, *The Story of Grump and Pout*, 1988
When a human comes to the forest and sells custom made shoes to the monsters, bringing them comfort, Grump no longer grumps and Pout no longer pouts.

Marilyn Sadler, *P.J. the Spoiled Bunny*, 1986
P.J. finally learns that if he wants people to play with him he can't always have his own way.

Yoshiko Uchida, *The Birthday Visitor*, 1975
Emi is convinced that her seventh birthday will be spoiled by yet another of her parents' dull visitors from Japan.

1738

John Steinbeck

The Red Pony (New York: Viking, 1945)

Age range: Grades 5-8

Subject(s): Animals/Horses; Ranch Life

Major character(s): Jody Tifflin, Child; Billy Buck, Cowboy; Carl Tifflin, Parent

Time period(s): 1920s

Locale(s): California (Pastures of Heaven)

What the book is about: Jody dreamed great dreams of the sorrel pony. The red colt was standing in the stall, his tense ears were forward and a light of disobedience was in his eyes. When Jody learned the colt was his, he reached out towards him and the colt closed his strong teeth on his fingers. Sometimes, that's the way love begins.

Other books by the author:
The Moon Is Down, 1976
The Pearl, 1963
Travels with Charley, 1963
The Wayward Bus, 1947

Other books you might like:
Gary Paulsen, *The Haymeadow*, 1992
John comes of age and gains self-reliance during the summer he spends up in the Wyoming mountains tending his father's herd of sheep.

Robert Newton Peck, *Spanish Hoof*, 1985
The year she turns twelve on Spanish Hoof, her family's beloved ranch in Florida, Harry gets a pony and learns some hard lessons about life.

Zilpha Keatley Snyder, *And Condors Danced*, 1987
Carly plays detective, watches condors, observes a fierce feud involving her family's Southern California ranch, and copes with unexpected tragedies.

Zane Spencer, *The Cry of the Wolf*, 1977
Crippled from an auto accident, Jim must rise above his sense of guilt and worthlessness to assume some of the responsibilities on the family's ranch.

Ester Wier, *The Long Year*, 1969
A boy retreats to the mountains with his half-wild wolf where he realizes the greatest changes are within himself.

1739

Barbara A. Steiner

Illustrator: Eileen Christelow

Dolby and the Woof-Off (New York: Morrow, 1991)

Age range: Grades 4-6

Subject(s): Animals/Dogs; Humor

Major character(s): Bo Dibbs, Child; Dolby, Dog; Oliver "Ollie" Dibbs, Child (brother)

Time period(s): 1980s

Locale(s): Boulder, Colorado

What the book is about: Bo teaches his dog, Dolby, some unusual tricks in an attempt to win the woof-off contest, sponsored by Woofies Dog Food. Dolby ends up being a hero, learning how to answer the phone, saving a little girl's eyesight.

Where it's reviewed:
Booklist, March 15, 1991, page 1494
Kirkus Reviews, April 15, 1991, page 539
School Library Journal, June 1991, page 112

Other books by the author:
The Steamstalker, 1992
Tessa, 1988
Oliver Dibbs and the Dinosaur Cause, 1986
Oliver Dibbs to the Rescue, 1985

Other books you might like:
Betty Cavanna, *Petey*, 1973
 A young boy has some unusual adventures with his Great Dane when they move from a farm to a small house in a development.
Betsy Duffey, *A Boy in the Doghouse*, 1991
 George is faced with the task of training his new puppy, Lucky.
Lynn Hall, *The Soul of the Silver Dog*, 1992
 Rejected by her family after her sister's death, Cory adopts a show dog and tries to bring back some of his championship glory.
Dick King-Smith, *The Invisible Dog*, 1993
 Events conspire to turn Janie's imaginary harlequin Great Dane into a real dog.
Elizabeth Levy, *Something Queer Is Going On: A Mystery*, 1973
 The kidnapping of a Bassett hound, leads Jill and Gwen on a frantic search that ends up in front of a TV camera shooting a dog food commercial.

1740

John Steptoe

Illustrator: John Steptoe

The Story of Jumping Mouse (New York: Lothrop, 1984)

Age range: Grades 2-4

Subject(s): Indians of North America

Major character(s): Magic, Frog; Jumping Mouse, Mouse

Time period(s): Indeterminate

Locale(s): United States

What the book is about: In order to reach a far-off land, a young mouse has to keep hope alive within himself. A retelling of an ancient Native American tribal legend. Jumping Mouse faces many obstacles, loses his sight and sense of smell (giving them to others) and he is transformed into a wonderful eagle.

Where it's reviewed:
Center for Children's Books Bulletin, April 1984, page 156
Horn Book, August 1984, page 160

Awards the book has won:
Caldecott Honor Book 1985

Other books by the author:
Baby Says, 1988
Mufaro's Beautiful Daughter, 1987
Stevie, 1969

Other books you might like:
Olaf Baker, *Where the Buffaloes Begin*, 1981
 Little Wolf is fascinated by the tribal legend of a lake to the south, a sacred spot where the buffalo are said to originate.

Byrd Baylor, *When Clay Sings*, 1972
 A lyrical tribute to an almost forgotten time of the prehistoric Indian of the desert West shows bits of pottery from this ancient time. (non-fiction)
Paul Goble, *Dream Wolf*, 1990
 When two Plains Indian children become lost, they are cared for and guided safely home by a wolf.
Bill Martin, *Knots on a Counting Rope*, 1987
 Boy-Strength-of-Blue-Horses begs his grandfather to tell him again the story of the night he was born.
Jane Yolen, *Sky Dogs*, 1990
 Drawn from Blackfoot legend, an old man tells of the coming of horses to his tribe, "Sky Dogs" from across the plains.

1741

Dorothy Sterling

Captain of the Planters: The Biography of Robert Smalls (Garden City: Doubleday, 1958)

Age range: Grades 5-6

Subject(s): Civil War; African Americans

Major character(s): Robert Smalls, Military Personnel, Historical Figure

Time period(s): 19th century

Locale(s): Charleston, South Carolina

What the book is about: Smalls was the first Black commissioned officer in the Union Army and a legislator. He helped rebuild his state and nation during the reconstruction. He later captained The Planter, a paddle-wheeled steamer from Charleston.

Where it's reviewed:
Horn Book, August 1958, page 283
Kirkus Reviews, January 1, 1958, page 4

Awards the book has won:
Nancy Bloch Memorial Award 1958

Other books by the author:
Forever Free, 1963
Freedom Train, 1954
It Started in Montgomery, 1972
Tender Warriors, 1958

Other books you might like:
Philip Sterling, *Four Took Freedom*, 1967
 The lives of Harriet Tubman, Frederick Douglass, Robert Smalls and Blanche K. Bruce
Yvette Moore, *Freedom Songs*, 1991
 Cheryl's uncle joins a freedom movement in the sixties and she organizes a concert to help him.
Henriette Robinet, *Children of the Fire*, 1991
 A young black girl lives through the Great Chicago Fire.
Eleanora E. Tate, *Thank You, Dr. Martin Luther King, Jr.!*, 1990
 A class at Gumbo Grove Elementary discovers many famous Afro-Americans.
Candy Dawson Boyd, *Breadsticks and Blessing Places*, 1985
 A young black girl, preparing for entrance exams to a private school, is devastated when her best friend is killed.

1742

Dorothy Sterling

Mary Jane (Garden City, NY: Doubleday, 1959)

Age range: Grades 4-6

Subject(s): Race Relations; Friendship

Major character(s): Mary Jane, Child; Sally Green, Child

Time period(s): 1950s

Locale(s): United States

What the book is about: Mary Jane enters a large Southern junior high, integrated for the first time. The balanced philosophy of her grandfather helps her to accept interracial friendship. She and Sally rescue a squirrel and try to hide him at school.

Where it's reviewed:
Horn Book, June 1959, page 216
Library Journal, May 15, 1959, page 1700

Other books by the author:
Silver Spoon Mystery, 1959
We Are Your Sisters, 1984 (non-fiction)

Other books you might like:
Mildred D. Taylor, *The Friendship*, 1987
    Four children witness a confrontation between an elderly man and a white storekeeper in rural Mississippi in the 1930s.
Nancy Springer, *They're All Named Wildfire*, 1989
    Jenny loses most of her friends when she befriends a Black girl who shares her interest in horses.
Sheila Gordon, *The Middle of Somewhere: A Story of South Africa*, 1990
    9-year-old Rebecca, living in a South African village for Blacks, is threatened with losing her home to make room for whites.
Dirlie Herlihy, *Ludie's Song*, 1988
    A bi-racial friendship in Georgia in the 1950s exposes both families to danger.
Nancy Garden, *What Happened in Marston*, 1971
    A middle class white boy and a Black boy from the slums find their friendship in jeopardy when a race war erupts in the city.

1743

Betsy Sterman

Illustrator: Judy Glasser

Too Much Magic (New York: Lippincott, 1987)

Age range: Grades 4-6

Subject(s): Brothers; Magic; Science Fiction

Major character(s): Jeff Hasting, Child; Bill Hasting, Preteen; Mark Jackson, Coach, Scientist

Time period(s): 1980s

Locale(s): Clinton

What the book is about: When yucky broccoli turns into a sizzling ball park hot dog, and a window broken by a soccer ball is suddenly whole again, Bill knows something weird is going on with his brother, Jeff. Jeff has found a "wishing cube" that produces everything the boys wish for. When they wish for money to buy Dad a birthday present, the money appears, but the exact same amount is missing from the bank where their father works, and that's just the beginning of their wishing troubles. A new teacher, Mr. Jackson, knows the answer, but it is not what the boys want to hear. A good first science fiction story for middle graders.

Where it's reviewed:
Booklist, March 15, 1987, page 1130
Kirkus Reviews, December 1, 1986, page 1796
School Library Journal, February 1987, page 85

Other books you might like:
Bill Brittain, *The Wish Giver*, 1983
    A strange little man comes to a church social promising to grant people's wishes. The wishes of three young believers come true in unexpected ways.
Ellen Conford, *Genie with the Light Blue Hair*, 1989
    Jean finds a genie in a lamp she receives for her birthday, and discovers that having all her wishes come true isn't as great as she thinks it will be
Jackie French Koller, *If I Had One Wish*, 1991
    Alec wishes his little brother had never been born, but when his wish comes true, his whole life changes, and not for the better.
Mary Downing Hahn, *The Time of the Witch*, 1982
    Laura tells an old woman of her wish that her parents were back together again, without realizing that she is speaking to a real witch.
Mary Q. Steele, *Wish, Come True*, 1979
    A ring that belonged to their great-grandfather has more magical powers than Megan and her older brother realize.

1744

Carla Stevens

Lily and Miss Liberty (New York: Scholastic, 1992)

Age range: Grades 2-3

Subject(s): Monuments

Major character(s): Lily Lafferty, Child; Rachel, Child

Time period(s): 1880s (1885)

Locale(s): New York, New York

What the book is about: Children in Lily's class are collecting money to pay for the Statue of Liberty's pedestal, in the weeks just prior to its arrival from France. Lily has no money to contribute but makes crowns and sells them. She, her father, and her friend, Rachel, go to see the Isere, the ship which is bringing Miss Liberty to America.

Where it's reviewed:
Center for Children's Books Bulletin, March 1992, page 194
Kirkus Reviews, May 15, 1992, page 100

Other books by the author:
Anna, Grandpa and the Big Storm, 1982
Sara and the Pinch, 1980
Pig and the Blue Flag, 1977
Hooray for Pig, 1974

Other books you might like:
Jeffrey Eger, *The Statue in the Harbor: A Story of Two Apprentices*, 1985

10 year old Philippe apprentices as a coppersmith to his dad in the Parisian foundry where the Statue of Liberty is being constructed. (Older readers)

Susan Lee, *The Battle for Long Island and New York*, 1975
Unwilling to side with the rebels or loyalists, two brothers make up their minds at the Battle of Long Island, during the Revolutionary War.

Betsy Maestro, *The Story of the Statue of Liberty*, 1986
Describes the creation of the statue and its erection in New York Harbor as a symbol of liberty.

Susan Saunders, *The Miss Liberty Caper*, 1986
You're visiting the Statue of Liberty with your day camp when Charley, your pet flying squirrel, is lost from your backpack. How do you find Charley?

Ann Warren Turner, *Katie's Trunk*, 1992
Katie's parents do not side with the rebels in the American Revolution, so she hides in her mother's wedding trunk when they invade her home.

1745

Drew Stevenson

Illustrator: Susan Swan

The Case of the Horrible Swamp Monster (New York: Putnam, 1984)

Age range: Grades 4-6

Subject(s): Crime and Criminals; Monsters

Major character(s): Raymond Almond, Filmmaker; Verna Wilkes, Friend; J. Huntley English, M.H., Detective (monster hunter)

Time period(s): Indeterminate

What the book is about: When Ray and Verna go to spooky Lost Swamp to film a monster movie for school, they don't expect to find a real monster! When they develop the film, the see a shiny green thing rising out of the swamp and hobbling away.

Where it's reviewed:
Booklist, January 1, 1985, page 643
Center for Children's Books Bulletin, April 1985, page 156
School Library Journal, January 1985, page 80

Other books by the author:
The Case of the Wandering Werewolf, 1987
Case of the Visiting Vampire, 1986

Other books you might like:
Nicholas Fish, *Monster Maker*, 1979
For Matt, working at a studio where movie monsters are made, fantasy turns into a nightmare when vandalism seems to bring the monsters to life.

Mercer Mayer, *Liza Lou and the Yeller Belly Swamp*, 1976
Liza Lou manages to outwit all the haunts, gobblygooks, witches and devils in the Yeller Belly Swamp.

Stephen Mooser, *The Fright-Face Contest*, 1989
Rosa and the bullies led by Zack Morton all want a monster trading card. Whoever snaps a photo of the best frightened face will win the card.

Philip Ridley, *Krindlekrax*, 1991
Ruskin believes he is born to be a hero and sets out to prove it by delivering his beloved Lizard Street from the menace of Krindlekrax.

Sarah Sargent, *Seeds of Change*, 1989

Rachel discovers the beauties and dangers of a swamp when she travels to Georgia with her father who plans to convert the swamp into a theme park.

1746

James Stevenson

Fast Friends: Two Stories (New York: Greenwillow, 1979)

Age range: Grades 1-3

Subject(s): Friendship; Short Stories; Animals/Turtles

Major character(s): Murray, Turtle; Fred, Snail; Thomas, Mouse

Time period(s): Indeterminate

Locale(s): United States

What the book is about: Two short stories involving friendless turtles, "Murray and Fred" and "Thomas and Clem." In the first, a turtle and a snail make some friends with the help of a skateboard. In the second, a mouse and a snail have a rocky relationship but learn to be friends.

Where it's reviewed:
Booklist, February 15, 1980, page 838
Hornbook, October 1979, page 530
Kirkus Reviews, November 1, 1979, page 1262

Other books by the author:
Could Be Worse!, 1987
Are We Almost There?, 1985
"Help!" Yelled Maxwell, 1978
The Bear Who Had No Place to Go, 1972

Other books you might like:
Phylliss Adams, *The Shy Little Turtle*, 1985
Sandy, a turtle, is too shy to start a friendship until she discovers some good ways to make friends.

Lillian Hoban, *Stick-in-the-Mud Turtle*, 1977
Fred Turtle's family must decide weather they want to live like the ritzy new family in the pond, or stick to the simpler things in life.

Leonard Kessler, *The Worst Team Ever*, 1985
Old Turtle and Melvin Moose help the worst baseball team in the swamp win the final game of the season.

Morgan Matthews, *Which Way, Hugo?*, 1986
An elephant with sore feet tries flying like a bird, hopping like a kangaroo, and digging like a mole as ways of going places. Then a turtle gives him

Mary Elise Monsell, *Toohy and Wood*, 1992
After he loses his home and his friends in a fire, a fence lizard is taken in by a poetry-writing turtle who helps him deal with his loss.

1747

Jocelyn Stevenson

Illustrator: Sue Truesdell

O'Diddy (New York: Random, 1988)

Age range: Grades 2-4

Subject(s): Fantasy; Imagination

Major character(s): O'Diddy, Friend (imaginary); Beatrice Odile Olivia "Boon" Noodleman, Child

Time period(s): Indeterminate

Locale(s): United States

What the book is about: O'Diddy is Boon's imaginary friend, but he feels left out, now that she is eight and a half and has a human friend, Cassie, next door.

Where it's reviewed:
Booklist, July 1988, page 1842
Kirkus Reviews, May 15, 1988, page 768
School Library Journal, October 1988, page 129

Other books by the author:
When I'm as Big as Freddy, 1987
Booker Fraggle's Giant Wish, 1986
Best Friends, 1984
Red and the Pumpkins, 1983

Other books you might like:
Isabelle Holland, *God, Mrs. Muskrat, and Aunt Dot*, 1983
    In a letter to God, orphaned Rebecca tells how lonely she is living with her aunt and uncle and how helpful her imaginary friend has been.
Cynthia King, *The Year of Mr. Nobody*, 1978
    A little boy gradually outgrows his dependence on his imaginary friend.
Lois Osborn, *My Dad Is Really Something*, 1983
    When they compare fathers, Harry finds that his father just doesn't stack up against Ron's, until he finds out that Ron is describing a fantasy.
Judith St. George, *The Halloween Pumpkin Smasher*, 1978
    Mary Grace and her imaginary friend, Nellie, plan to find out who has been smashing all the jack-o-lanterns the week before Halloween.
Nicki Weiss, *Menj!*, 1981
    Francine argues with her sister, makes a collection with a neighbor boy, bakes chocolate chipless cookies and talks with her imaginary friend.

| 1748 |

Robert Louis Stevenson

Kidnapped (New York: Scribners, 1913)

Age range: Grades 5-9

Subject(s): Adventure and Adventurers; Kidnapping

Major character(s): David Balfour, Heir; Ebenezer Shaw, Villain (David's uncle)

Time period(s): 1750s

Locale(s): Scotland

What the book is about: David Balfour's villainous uncle, Ebenezer Shaw, who wants to inherit David's fortune, fails in an attempt on David's life, so has him kidnapped and put aboard the ship Covenant to be sold into slavery. On board ship, David meets Alan Breck Stewart, a Jacobite, and the two have many adventures until David finally returns and regains his inheritance. Classic adventures for advanced readers or to share aloud. Many editions available.

Other books by the author:
Dr. Jekyll and Mr. Hyde, 1967
Master of Ballantrae, 1957

The Black Arrow, 1949
Treasure Island, 1911

Other books you might like:
Margaret Jean Anderson, *The Druid's Gift*, 1989
    Druids give a girl on the island of Hirta the gift of seeing the future, and with this gift she is able to see the events that will shape its history.
Patricia Calvert, *Hadder MacColl*, 1985
    Loyal to her Highland heritage, Hadder can't understand when her brother returns from school, and no longer shares her belief in the Jacobite cause.
Eileen Dunlop, *The Valley of Deer*, 1989
    Finding an old family Bible in her house leads Anne on a quest to solve the mysterious death of a Scottish woman accused of witchcraft in 1726.
James D. Forman, *Prince Charlie's Year*, 1991
    In 1745, fourteen year old Colin joins his father to fight with Bonnie Prince Charlie in his attempt at the throne.
Rosemary Sutcliff, *Bonnie Dundee*, 1983
    Hugh Herriot recalls the exploits of his youth as a follower of Bonnie Dundee who tried to win back Scotland for the Catholic King James.

| 1749 |

Robert Louis Stevenson

Treasure Island (New York: Scribners, 1911)

Age range: Grades 6 and Up

Subject(s): Treasure; Sea Stories; Pirates

Major character(s): Jim Hawkins, Teenager; Long John Silver, Pirate

Time period(s): 18th century

Locale(s): At Sea

What the book is about: The classic treasure hunt story of the evil crew of the *Black Dog*. We meet young Jim Hawkins as he meets the sinister Blind Pew at the Admiral Benbow Inn. Long John Silver is the famous villain who sets the tone of this tale of treachery, greed and daring. Originally published in 1883.

Where it's reviewed:
Book World, September 17, 1972, page 15
Contemporary Review, October 1972, page 216
Kirkus Reviews, July 1, 1972, page 730

Other books by the author:
The Black Arrow, 1888
Kidnapped, 1886
A Child's Garden of Verses, 1885
Dr. Jekyll and Mr. Hyde, 1886

Other books you might like:
Rex Benedict, *Good Luck Arizona Man*, 1972
    A half-white, half-Apache boy sets out to solve the mystery of his own origins and the hiding place of a treasure in gold.
Sid Fleischman, *Jingo Django*, 1971
    A orphan boy resolves to follow a treasure map he finds inscribed on a whale's tooth.
Joseph Jay Deiss, *The Town of Hercules: A Buried Treasure Trove*, 1974

Reconstructs the day in 79 A.D. when the town of Herculaneum was destroyed by the eruption of Mount Vesuvius and the civilization that was buried.

Peggy Parish, *Hermit Dan*, 1977
Intrigued by stories of local pirates and buried treasure, three children decide to find out the truth about Hermit Dan and his ancestors.

Ann Waldron, *The Luckie Star*, 1977
A girl is not anticipating the family's summer in Florida, but a sunken treasure and her family's recognition of her as an anomaly make it worthwhile.

1750

Frank R. Stockton

Illustrator: Maurice Sendak

The Griffin and the Minor Canon (New York: Holt, 1963)

Age range: Grades 3-5

Subject(s): Monsters; Artists and Art

Major character(s): Minor Canon, Religious (priest); The Griffin, Mythical Creature (griffin)

Time period(s): Indeterminate Past

Locale(s): Fictional Country ("Faraway Land")

What the book is about: A town is terrified when a griffin arrives to view a stone likeness of himself over the church door. Only the Minor Canon has the courage to face the griffin. The people criticize the young priest for inviting the griffin into town to view the likeness, because they are afraid the griffin will stay forever. It takes clever thinking to resolve the situation.

Where it's reviewed:
New Yorker, December 2, 1972, page 205
Times Literary Supplement, April 2, 1976, page 376
Observer (London), August 4, 1968, page 22

Other books by the author:
The Lady or the Tiger?, 1983
The Bee-Man of Orn, 1964

Other books you might like:
Jeanne Bendick, *Scare a Ghost, Tame a Monster*, 1983
Discusses ghosts, monsters, and other scary components of folklore in countries around the world.

Tomie De Paola, *The Mysterious Giant of Barletta*, 1984
A giant statue is called upon to save a town from an army that is destroying all the towns and cities along the lower Adriatic coast.

John Gardner, *Gudgekin, the Thistle Girl, and Other Tales*, 1976
"Gudgekin, the Thistle Girl," "The Griffin and the Wise Old Philosopher," "The Shape Shifters of Shorm" and others.

Joan Marshall, *The Monster That Grew Small*, 1987
A retelling of an Egyptian folktale in which a timid boy finds courage by going after a monster that seems to shrink when confronted.

Alison Lurie, *Fabulous Beasts*, 1981
Describes the habits and characteristics of strange beasts and birds, including the unicorn, griffin, phoenix and basilisk.

1751

Mary Stolz

Illustrator: Beni Montresar

Belling the Tiger (New York: Harper, 1961)

Age range: Grades 1-3

Subject(s): Animals/Mice; Animals/Tigers

Time period(s): Indeterminate

Locale(s): Earth

What the book is about: The story of the two timid mice who are appointed to bell the cat and somehow end up in a jungle where they bell a nearby tiger instead.

Where it's reviewed:
Booklist, June 15, 1961, page 644
Horn Book, August 1961, page 339

Awards the book has won:
Newbery Honor

Other books by the author:
Storm in the Night, 1988
Cat Walk, 1983
Fredou, 1962
The Great Rebellion, 1962

Other books you might like:
Syd Hoff, *Baseball Mouse*, 1969
Bernard is a field mouse - an infield mouse, who more than anything else wants to help the losing team win the pennant.

Emily Perl Kingsley, *An American Tail*, 1986
Separated from his family on a trip from Russia to America, a young mouse arrives alone in New York City.

Margery Sharp, *Bernard into Battle*, 1978
Miss Bianca's faithful lieutenant, Bernard, directs an operation that repulses an army of rats.

William Steig, *Abel's Island*, 1976
Castaway on an uninhabited island, the mouse, Abel, finds himself tested as he struggles to survive and return to his home.

Eve Titus, *Basil and the Pigmy Cats: A Basil of Baker Street Mystery*, 1971
The famous English mouse detective sets out to solve the mystery concerning the existence of pygmy cats.

1752

Mary Stolz

The Cat in the Mirror (New York: Harper, 1975)

Age range: Grades 6-8

Subject(s): Egyptian Antiquities; Space and Time; Time Travel

Major character(s): Erin "Irun" Gandy, Child; Seti Gammel, Child; Flora Todd, Housekeeper

Time period(s): 1970s

Locale(s): New York, New York; Egypt

What the book is about: Erin, frustrated with her life and her family, escapes to another point in time. She becomes Irun, a wealthy girl in ancient Egypt. All the major figures in her life are duplicated as well, including her cat. In both of her worlds, she has the same friend, Seti, an Egyptian boy. Rich in detail, this is a gold mine for readers interested in ancient Egypt.

Where it's reviewed:
Booklist, January 1, 1976, page 628
Hornbook, December 1975, page 597
Kirkus Reviews, September 1, 1975, page 999

Other books by the author:
Bartholomew Fair, 1990
Pangur Ban, 1988
The Edge of Next Year, 1974
By the Highway Home, 1971

Other books you might like:
Erick Berry, *Honey of the Nile*, 1963
  Intrigue flourishes in the court of Ankhesenpanton and Tutankhamun as opposing religious groups vie for the leadership of ancient Egypt.
Gillian Bradshaw, *The Dragon and the Thief*, 1991
  In ancient Egypt, an unlucky young man meets a wealthy dragon and together they find dangerous, exciting adventure.
Catherine Dexter, *The Gilded Cat*, 1992
  Maggie buys a mummified cat at a yard sale and is drawn into a frightening world of ancient Eygptian magic.
Leona Ellerby, *King Tut's Game Board*, 1980
  With a myserious friend he meets while vacationing in Egypt, Justin makes astonishing discoveries about two ancient civilizations.
Elsa Marston, *The Cliffs of Cairo*, 1981
  Buying an ancient icon from a street merchant in Cairo opens a Pandora's box of intrigue and peril for a teenage girl at odds with her family.

1753

Mary Stolz

A Dog on Barkham Street (New York: Harper and Row, 1960)

Age range: Grades 4-6

Subject(s): Bullies; Animals/Dogs

Major character(s): Edward Frost, Child; Martin Hastings, Bully; Uncle John, Streetperson

Time period(s): 1960s

Locale(s): St. Louis, Missouri

What the book is about: More than anything in the world Edward wants a dog, and to be left alone by the bully of Barkham Street. Into the heart of these problems comes Uncle Josh, a hobo, and Argess, a collie. Edward sets out to convince his parents that he is responsible enough to have a pet.

Where it's reviewed:
Hornbook, February 1965, page 74

Other books by the author:
Bartholomew Fair, 1990
The Cat in the Mirror, 1975
The Edge of Next Year, 1974
The Bully of Barkham Street, 1963

Other books you might like:
Dana Brookins, *Rico's Cat*, 1976

In St. Louis during WWII, a boy determines to hide and raise his cat and her kittens, despite the landlord's firm rule against pets on the premises.
Barbara Campbell, *A Girl Called Bob and a Horse Called Yoki*, 1982
  In St. Louis during the Second World War, Bob makes secret plans to save the life of an old horse that pulls the milk delivery wagon.
Lynn Hall, *Danger Dog*, 1986
  Having failed once to show responsibility as a pet owner, David is determined to save a Doberman Pinscher by deprogramming his attack training.
Theresa Nelson, *Devil Storm*, 1987
  A brother and sister living off the Texas Gulf Coast befriend Tom the Tramp who becomes a hero during the Great Storm of 1900.
Zilpha Keatley Snyder, *Blair's Nightmare*, 1984
  The Stanley kids try to keep secret a dog that Blair finds, keep David out of the clutches a school bully, and find out if some convicts are nearby.

1754

Mary Stolz

The Edge of Next Year (New York: Harper, 1974)

Age range: Grades 5-8

Subject(s): Alcoholism; Automobile Accidents; Grief

Major character(s): Orin Woodward, Teenager; Victor Woodward, Child; Jeanie Sager, Friend

Time period(s): Indeterminate

Locale(s): United States

What the book is about: A driver was in the wrong lane and the Woodward's car skidded after avoiding the on-coming driver. Orin and Victor's mother was killed that October day. After she died, their dad began to drink more and more, until he realized that he had to get help.

Where it's reviewed:
Booklist, September 15, 1974, page 102
Hornbook, October 1974, page 144
Kirkus Reviews, October 15, 1974, page 1111

Other books by the author:
Cider Days, 1978
Ferris Wheel, 1977
The Cat in the Mirror, 1975
Leap Before You Look, 1972

Other books you might like:
Bruce Brooks, *No Kidding*, 1989
  In his 21st century society, Sam is allowed to decide the fate of his family after his mother is released from an alcohol rehabilitation center.
Alden R. Carter, *Up Country*, 1991
  When his mother's drinking problem causes him to spend several months with relatives, Carl begins to build a new life for himself.
Robert Cormier, *We All Fall Down: A Novel*, 1991
  After Buddy vandalizes a home, he increases his drinking in order to cope with his parents' seperation and obsession with the homeowner's daughter.
Cynthia D. Grant, *Shadow Man*, 1992

Charming but reckless Gabe, drunk as usual, smashes his truck into a tree and dies, sending waves of shock and grief through his small town.

Stephen Roos, *You'll Miss Me When I'm Gone*, 1988
Disgusted with the relationship between his separated parents, Marcus finds that a vodka bottle is the only thing that gets him from day to day.

Mary Stolz

Go and Catch a Flying Fish (New York: Harper, 1979)

Age range: Grades 5 and Up

Subject(s): Family Life; Family Problems

Major character(s): Jem Reddick, Child; Taylor Reddick, Teenager; Tony Reddick, Parent, Cook (chef)

Time period(s): 1970s

Locale(s): Florida

What the book is about: A family breaks up when the parents are unwilling and unable to compromise. Tony insists that his wife, Junie, be a traditional homemaker. Junie loves the children, but is irresponsible about taking care of them. Thirteen year old Taylor tries to remain neutral as their parents pull apart. She and her brother Jem grow closer and more protective of their baby brother, BJ.

Where it's reviewed:
Horn Book, August 1979, page 424
School Library Journal, September 1979, page 148

Other books by the author:
What Time of Night Is It?, 1981 (Sequel)
By the Highway Home, 1974
The Edge of Next Year, 1974
Land's End, 1973

Other books you might like:
Stephanie Jona Buehler, *There's No Surf in Cleveland*, 1993
Having moved with his mother to Los Angeles after his parents' divorce, Phillip finds that he hates California and wants to go back to Ohio.
Vicki Grove, *Junglerama*, 1989
Three twelve year old boys dream of creating a "Junglerama" with rare animals, but other things seem to consume most of their time.
Joan Lowery Nixon, *In the Face of Danger*, 1988
Deeply unhappy about her family's separation because of poverty, Megan gradually finds contentment and purpose in her new home.
Ray Prather, *Fish and Bones*, 1992
Thirteen year old Bones, intent on collecting the reward for finding a bank robber, discovers some of the ugly secrets hidden in his small town.
Marc Talbert, *Pillow of Clouds*, 1991
Angry at being forced to decide which of his divorcing parents will get custody, Chester is further burdened with guilt about the decision.

Mary Stolz

Illustrator: Pat Cummings

Go Fish (New York: HarperCollins, 1991)

Age range: Grades 2-4

Subject(s): Fishing; Grandparents; African Americans

Major character(s): Thomas, Child

Time period(s): Indeterminate

Locale(s): United States (Gulf of Mexico)

What the book is about: After spending the day fishing in the Gulf of Mexico, Thomas and his grandfather spend a quiet evening on the proch hearing about his African heritage. A good chapter book which shows a warm family relationship through poetic description and realistic dialogue.

Where it's reviewed:
Booklist, May 15, 1991, page 1800
School Library Journal, May 1991, page 84

Other books by the author:
King Emmett the Second, 1991
Storm in the Night, 1988
The Scarecrows and Their Child, 1987
The Leftover Elf, 1952

Other books you might like:
Eve Bunting, *Magic and the Night River*, 1978
A Japanese boy and his grandfather fish successfully with their cormorants because they have treated the birds with kindness.
Bonnie Dobkin, *I Love Fishing*, 1993
A young fisher expresses enthusiasm for the sport while asknowledging the many distractions.
Pat McKissack, *A Million Fish, More or Less*, 1992
A boy learns the truth is often stretched on the Bayou Clapateaux, and gets the chance to tell his own version of a bayou tale when he goes fishing.
Peter Parnall, *The Great Fish*, 1973
An Indian's boy's grandfather tells him of when the mothers' tears for their hungry children brought salmon to now polluted and lifeless waters.
Jan Wahl, *The Fisherman*, 1969
A little girl goes fishing with her grandfather and although they catch no fish, they find a bigger treasure.

Mary Stolz

Illustrator: Dennis Hermanson

Land's End (New York: Harper, 1973)

Age range: Grades 5-8

Subject(s): Humor; Single Parent Families

Major character(s): Joshua Redmond, Naturalist, Preteen; Doctor Arthur, Neighbor

Time period(s): 1970s

Locale(s): Land's End, Florida

What the book is about: Josh is a sailor, fisherman, and lover of pelicans and porpoises. An only child, he feels isolated. His summer becomes a discovery voyage through a variety of human feelings and expressions. He finds an intriguing contrast between his own family structure, and the casual, relaxed life-style of his new neighbors, the Arthurs.

Where it's reviewed:
Booklist, January 15, 1974, page 546
Center for Children's Books Bulletin, April 1974, page 136
Kirkus Reviews, September 1, 1973, page 973

Other books by the author:
Ivy Larkin, 1986
The Cat in the Mirror, 1975
The Bully of Barkham Street, 1963
A Dog on Barkham Street, 1960

Other books you might like:
Paula Fox, *Portrait of Ivan*, 1969
  An eleven year old boy gains a new understanding of himself and his father after a trip to Florida with unusual people.
Jean Craighead George, *The Talking Earth*, 1983
  Billie ventures out into the Everglades to test the legends of her Indian ancestors and learns the importance of listening to the Earth's messages.
Lois Lenski, *Strawberry Girl*, 1973
  Set in a little-known backwoods region of Florida, Strawberry Girl is the first of the Lenski regional books and a Newbery Medal winner.
Phyllis Reynolds Naylor, *To Walk the Sky Path*, 1973
  Billie, a Seminole Indian, is caught between cultures when his family moves away from the Florida Everglades and nearer the white man's civilization.
Bryce Walton, *Hurricane Reef*, 1970
  A teen who has always wanted to be a marine scientist discovers in the Florida Keys the challenges of the profession he has chosen.

1758

Mary Stolz

Illustrator: Louis S. Glanzman

Noonday Friends (New York: Harper and Row, 1965)

Age range: Grades 4-6

Subject(s): Friendship; Race Relations

Major character(s): Franny Davis, Child; Simone, Child; Lila Wembleton, Child

Time period(s): 1960s

Locale(s): New York, New York (Greenwich Village)

What the book is about: 11 year old Franny Davis cares for her little brother and tolerates her twin while mom works. Her best friend, Simone, has seven brothers and sisters, so they have little time to play together, but always share lunch and become "Noonday Friends."

Where it's reviewed:
Horn Book, October 1965, page 503
Library Journal, July 1965, page 3128

Awards the book has won:
Newbery Honor

Other books by the author:
Bartholomew Fair, 1990
Cat Walk, 1983

The Explorer of Barkham Street, 1985
Ivy Larkin, 1986

Other books you might like:
Brenda Scott Wilkinson, *Not Separate, Not Equal*, 1987
  Malene experiences hatred and racism at the beginning of the Civil Rights movement.
Erin Jolly, *Summer Growing Time*, 1971
  June and her grandmother live absorbed in their own world until racial conflict intrudes on their lives.
Pat Edwards, *Little John and Plutie*, 1988
  John learns how difficult it is to have a close friendship with a black child in the rural south.
Ouida Sebestyen, *Words by Heart*, 1979
  A young girl struggles for success in the southwestern town where she and her family are the only Blacks.
Nancy Garden, *What Happened in Marston*, 1971
  Close friends find their friendship tested when race war breaks out in their city.

1759

Mary Stolz

Illustrator: Pamela Johnson

Quentin Corn (Boston: Godine, 1985)

Age range: Grades 4-6

Subject(s): Animals/Pigs

Major character(s): Quentin Corn, Pig; Mrs. Benway, Landlord

Time period(s): 1980s

Locale(s): United States

What the book is about: Quentin refuses to become pork chops and spare ribs. He puts on human clothing and runs away. Disguised as a boy, Quentin makes friends with a little girl and begins his life as a boarder at Mrs. Benway's boarding house.

Where it's reviewed:
Center for Children's Books Bulletin, December 1985, page 80
School Library Journal, September 1985, page 140

Other books by the author:
Deputy Shep, 1991
Go Fish, 1991
The Explorer of Barkham Street, 1985
Cat Walk, 1983

Other books you might like:
Michael Bond, *Olga Takes Charge*, 1982
  Olga, the guinea pig, saves the Sawdust family from disaster and takes up jogging.
Dick King-Smith, *Ace, the Very Important Pig*, 1990
  Farmer Tubbs' amazing pig, Ace of Clubs, winds up on television because he is so clever.
Dick King-Smith, *Pigs Might Fly: A Novel*, 1982
  A runt piglet born with deformed front feet is coached in swimming by a duck and an otter, and becomes a hero when the farm is flooded.
Cathy Stefanec-Ogren, *Sly, P.I.: The Case of the Missing Shoes*, 1989
  When ballet star Lotta Oink's toe shoes disappear on opening night, fox and old friend, Sly, P.I., solve the case.

Will Watkins, *Sid Seal, Houseman*, 1989
  Waltham de Swine, a wealthy young pig, finds his life changed when a seal comes to work for his family.

1760

Mary Stolz

Illustrator: Louis S. Glanzman

A Wonderful, Terrible Time (New York: HarperCollins, 1967)

Age range: Grades 4-6

Subject(s): African Americans; Camps and Camping

Major character(s): Mady Guthrie, Preteen; Sue Ellen Forrest, Preteen

Time period(s): 1960s

Locale(s): New York, New York

What the book is about: Mady and Sue Ellen live across the hall from each other in a racially mixed neighborhood. They are inseparable and every morning they plan their day together. They are able to leave the hot city for a camp vacation and more fun together.

Where it's reviewed:
Booklist, December 15, 1976, page 504
Hornbook, December 1967, page 754
Kirkus Reviews, September 15, 1967, page 1136

Other books by the author:
Leap Before You Look, 1972
Noonday Friends, 1965
Fredou, 1962
And Love Replied, 1958

Other books you might like:
Alan Brown, *Lost Boys Never Say Die*, 1989
  Scheduled to go to summer camp while his parents are away, Lewis breaks back into the house and lives a secret life for eight weeks.
Jamie Gilson, *Hobie Hanson, You're Weird*, 1987
  With his best friend away at computer camp, Hobie reluctantly shares adventures with a girl classmate the summer after fourth grade.
Nancy Smiler Levinson, *Your Friend, Natalie Popper*, 1991
  In the summer of 1946, Natalie looks forward to going to camp and being with her friend Corinne, but things do not turn out as she anticipates.
Kate McMullan, *Great Advice From Lila Fenwick*, 1988
  Lila and her friend spend two weeks at a Boy Scout camp, where Lila's father is camp doctor, having a wonderful time learning about boys and nature.
Sheri Cooper Sinykin, *The Buddy Trap*, 1991
  Korean American Cam endures the antagonism of tentmates and keeps his love for the flute a secret while spending the summer at a war games camp.

1761

Celia Strang

Foster Mary (New York: McGraw-Hill, 1979)

Age range: Grades 5-6

Subject(s): Foster Homes; Migrant Labor; Child Abuse

Major character(s): Wallace "Bud" Meekin, Child (foster child); Foster Mary, Foster Parent; Alonzo, Foster Parent

Time period(s): 1950s (1959)

Locale(s): Yakima, Washington

What the book is about: Foster Mary and Alonzo have taken in abandoned children, including Bud, Bennie, Amelia, and recently, Lonnie. Mary can make a home out of anything. They are migrant workers who take the kids wherever they go. College is Mary's goal for all of the children. Bud isn't very sure about going to school full time. Liz, a friend, helps him find a way out of migrant farming.

Where it's reviewed:
Horn Book, August 1979, page 417
School Library Journal, September 1979, page 162

Other books by the author:
This Child Is Mine, 1981

Other books you might like:
E. Sandy Powell, *Daisy*, 1991
  A young girl deals with the emotional and physical problems of being a victim of child abuse.
Willo Davis Roberts, *Don't Hurt Laurie!*, 1977
  Laurie is abandoned by her mother. Can she escape? Will anyone believe her?
Ann Schlee, *Ask Me No Questions*, 1982
  Laura tries to help the neglected children she finds eating the pigs' food in her uncle's barn in 1848.
Oralee Wachter, *No More Secrets for Me*, 1983
  In four stories, young victims express their feelings to a person they trust.
Linda Woolverton, *Running Before the Wind*, 1987
  Kelly finds running the only outlet for her confused feelings about her abusive father.

1762

Noel Streatfeild

Illustrator: Richard Floethe

Ballet Shoes (New York: Random House, 1937)

Age range: Grades 5-8

Subject(s): Ballet; Dancing

Major character(s): Pauline Fossil, Preteen; Petrovna Fossil, Child; Posy Fossil, Child

Time period(s): 1930s

Locale(s): London, England

What the book is about: When great-uncle Matthew disappears on an extended voyage and funds grow short, his three adopted children are sent to become dancers at the Academy of Dancing and Stage Training.

Where it's reviewed:
Book World, November 18, 1979, page 13
Hornbook, April 1978, page 191
Library Journal, October 15, 1973, page 3123

Other books by the author:
A Young Person's Guide to Ballet, 1975
Theatre Shoes, or Other People's Shoes, 1973
The Children on the Top Floor, 1965

Circus Shoes, 1939

Other books you might like:
Jane Gardam, *A Long Way From Verona*, 1971
   A young girl aspiring to be a writer recounts her experiences growing up in England during the Second World War.
Rumer Godden, *Listen to the Nightingale*, 1992
   After winning a scholarship to a famous ballet school, Lottie is torn between her lifelong dream and her love for a dog.
Patricia Pendergraft, *Hear the Wind Blow*, 1988
   Isadora watches as her deeply religious best friend tries to reform the school troublemaker who enjoys teasing Isadora about her dancing aspirations.
Jean Ure, *You Win Some, You Lose Some*, 1984
   Jamie's decision to leave school and become a ballet dancer brings him problems but strengthens his character.
Barbara Willard, *The Country Maid*, 1978
   A sixteen year old, who has left her home in the English countryside to work for a London family, gradually realizes what she really wants.

1763

Noel Streatfeild

Illustrator: Judith Gwyn Brown

When the Sirens Wailed (New York: Random House, 1976)

Age range: Grades 4-6

Subject(s): Evacuees; World War II

Major character(s): Laura Clark, Child; Andy Clark, Child; Tim Clark, Child

Time period(s): 1940s

Locale(s): London, England; Dorset, England

What the book is about: The three Clark children are sent to the countryside during the London Blitz of WWII. Mum gets a job in a factory and Dad serves in the Royal Navy. When their sponsor dies, the children, ages nine, seven and five, run away from their second sponsor and return to London to find their parents.

Where it's reviewed:
Junior Bookshelf, April 1975, page 136
Times Literary Supplement, April 4, 1975, page 361
Observer, December 8, 1974, page 30

Other books by the author:
Thursday's Child, 1970
The Family at Caldicott Place, 1968
The Children on the Top Floor, 1965
Queen Victoria, 1958

Other books you might like:
Hester Burton, *In Spite of All Terror*, 1968
   In 1940, an orphan girl from the London slums is evacuated to the country to live with an aristocratic family.
Malcolm Carrick, *I'll Get You!*, 1979
   A young boy growing up in post-war London tries to fit in with his neighborhood friends.
Richard Lidz, *Many Kinds of Courage*, 1980
   A collection of personal narratives describing the London Blitz, the attack on Pearl Harbor, the Normandy Invasion, and other events of WWII.
Jill Paton Walsh, *Fireweed*, 1969

Two teen runaways who refuse to be evacuated from London struggle to survive the Blitz of 1940.
Alison Prince, *How's Business?*, 1987
   A story of wartime England written by the author in collaboration with children from Horbling Brown's Church of England Primary School, Lincolnshire.

1764

Patti Stren

There's a Rainbow In My Closet (New York: Harper, 1979)

Age range: Grades 3-5

Subject(s): Identity; Grandparents

Major character(s): Emma, Child; Edgar, Child; Gramma, Grandparent, Immigrant (Russian)

Time period(s): 1970s

Locale(s): Canada

What the book is about: Emma feels abandoned, hurt, and angry when her mom tours Europe for two months with a ballet company. Gramma, from Florida, is not at all what Emma expects. Gramma keeps a hat with feathers and fruit on her dresser just because it makes her feel alive. They have a special tea party, go fishing with Emma's friend, Edgar. Gramma makes a rainbow in Emma's closet.

Where it's reviewed:
Center for Children's Books Bulletin, February 1980, page 120
School Library Journal, September 1979, page 149

Other books by the author:
I Was a Fifteen Year Old Blimp, 1985
Mountain Rose, 1982

Other books you might like:
Warwick Downing, *Kid Curry's Last Ride*, 1989
   Spending a summer with his grandmother in a small town in the 1930s, Alex meets an old man who says he's Kid Curry, a member of Butch Cassidy's gang.
Anne Lindbergh, *Three Lives to Live*, 1992
   Garet's quiet life with her grandmother is changed when down the laundry chute comes Garet's "twin" Daisy, whose true identity comes as a surprise.
Maureen Pople, *The Other Side of the Family*, 1986
   Sent to Australia during WWII for safety, Katherine discovers a totally unexpected character in the grandmother known to hate her family.
Willo Davis Roberts, *What Are We Going to Do about David?*, 1993
   Upset that his parents ignore him, David becomes even more worried when they deposit him with a grandmother he hardly knows.
Alison Smith, *Billy Boone*, 1989
   Billy fights for her right to take trumpet lessons and spend time with her unorthodox grandmother, even though her parents object.

1765

Rodie Sudbery

The Silk and the Skin (London: Deutsch, 1976)

Age range: Grades 5-8

Subject(s): Animals; Gangs

Major character(s): Guy Carmichael, Preteen; Ralph, Bully (classmate); Simon Carmichael, Handicapped (mentally)

Time period(s): 1970s

Locale(s): England

What the book is about: Guy wanted to join Ralph's graveyard gang. Then, his slightly retarded younger brother becomes master of a magical bat that contains a powerful force.

Where it's reviewed:
Booklist, October 15, 1982, page 316
Hornbook, October 1982, page 523
School Library Journal, November 1982, page91

Other books by the author:
A Sound of Crying, 1970

Other books you might like:
Roy Brown, *Escape the River*, 1970
  A boy and his retarded brother, products of an unhappy home, become involved with crooks on the Thames River.
Annabel Farjeon, *The Siege of Trapp's Mill*, 1972
  A group of boys spending the night in an abandoned mill find their fun threatened when they are attacked by another gang.
Alison Cragin Herzig, *A Season of Secrets*, 1982
  Brooke worries about her brother's fainting spells, which her parents will not explain, and has difficulty understanding his fondness for a pet bat.
Norma Johnson, *Bats on the Bedstead*, 1987
  When his family moves into an old house, Ricky is threatened by a flock of evil bats who want to regain possession of the house.
Philippa Pearce, *The Way to Sattin Shore*, 1983
  When her father's tombstone disappears from the graveyard, a school girl witnesses the unraveling of a mystery surrounding the death of her father.

1766

Yuri Suhl

Illustrator: Thomas Di Grazia

The Merrymaker (New York: Four Winds, 1975)

Age range: Grades 3-5

Subject(s): Jews

Major character(s): Shloimeh, Child

Time period(s): 1910s

Locale(s): Europe

What the book is about: Ten year old Shloimeh's family is so poor they can hardly feed the three of them. A stranger's presence makes them question whether they can afford hospitality. The stranger is a badchen, a merrymaker. He entertains at weddings with his impromptu rhyming.

Where it's reviewed:
Booklist, May 1, 1975, page 918
Hornbook, August 1975, page 384
Kirkus Reviews, April 15, 1975, page 458

Other books by the author:
The Purim Goat, 1980
Simon Boom Gets a Letter, 1976
On the Other Side of the Gate, 1975
Uncle Misha's Partisans, 1973

Other books you might like:
Adele Geras, *My Grandmother's Stories*, 1990
  A collection of tales from Jewish history and folklore.
Michael Mark, *Toba*, 1984
  Nine stories about ten year old Toba and her family, presenting a picture of Jewish life in Poland around 1910.
Patricia Polacco, *The Keeping Quilt*, 1988
  A homemade quilt ties together the lives of four generations of an immigrant Jewish family, remaining a symbol of their enduring faith and love.
Laurence Salzmann, *A Family Passover*, 1980
  A ten year old girl describes how her family celebrates Passover.
Steve Sanfield, *The Feather Merchants and Other Tales of the Fools of Chelm*, 1991
  Thirteen traditional Eastern European Jewish tales of the town of Chelm and its silly citizens.

1767

Yuri Suhl

Uncle Misha's Partisans (New York: Four Winds, 1973)

Age range: Grades 5-9

Subject(s): Jews; Music; World War II

Major character(s): Motele "Mitek", Preteen (partisan), Musician (violinist); Yoshke, Resistance Fighter (partisan)

Time period(s): 1940s

Locale(s): Klynov, Union of Soviet Socialist Republics (Ukraine)

What the book is about: A colony of Jewish partisans live in a Ukrainian forest during WWII. Motele is a twelve year old violinist who turns to his Uncle Misha when his family is killed. He uses his Ukrainian name, Mitek, to pose as a peasant boy, and becomes established as a musician at German Headquarters. He is used as the inside man in a plot to blow up the building.

Where it's reviewed:
Booklist, November 1, 1972, page 294
Center for Children's Books Bulletin, January 1974, page 87
Hornbook February 1974, page 54

Other books by the author:
The Merrymaker, 1975
On the Other Side of the Gate, 1975
Simon Boom Gives a Wedding, 1972

Other books you might like:
Carol Matas, *Lisa's War*, 1987
  During the Nazi occupation of Denmark, teenage Jews become involved in an underground resistance movement and eventually must flee for their lives.
Nancy Pitt, *Beyond the High White Wall*, 1986

Witnessing the murder of a peasant, Libby triggers a wave of hate against her Jewish family, prompting them to consider emigrating to American.

Elsa Posell, *Homecoming*, 1987
  The six Koshansky children and their mother struggle to survive in an increasingly hostile environment of the 1917 Russian Revolution.

Aranka Siegal, *Upon the Head of the Goat: A Childhood in Hungary, 1939-1944*, 1981
  Recounts the bewilderment of being a Jewish child in Hungary between 1939 and 1944, and relates the ordeal of survival in the ghetto.

Nelly S. Toll, *Behind the Secret Window: A Memoir of a Hidden Childhood During World War Two*, 1993
  The author recalls her experiences when she and her mother were hidden from the Nazis by a Gentile couple in Lwow, Poland, during WWII.

1768

Mary W. Sullivan

Earthquake 2099 (New York: Lodestar, 1982)

Age range: Grades 5-9

Subject(s): Earthquakes; Survival

Major character(s): Philip, Preteen; Vita, Cousin

Time period(s): Indeterminate Future

Locale(s): California (Tower 117, Shark Tooth Mountain Wildlife Preserve)

What the book is about: Philip has spent his entire life in the controlled environment of an Urban Complex Tower. Suddenly, following an earthquake, he and his cousin, Vita, must learn to survive among wild animals and wild people in the wildlife preserve.

Where it's reviewed:
Booklist, August 1982, page 1529
Center for Children's Books Bulletin, November 1982, page 56
School Library Journal, September 1982, page 128

Other books by the author:
What's This about Pete?, 1981
The VW Connection, 1980
Brian Foot-in-the-Mouth, 1978

Other books you might like:
Clare Cooper, *Ashar of Qarius*, 1988
  A small band of children must depend on an unknown artificial intelligence when alien creatures attack their Earth colony on the planet Plioctis.
Douglas Arthur Hill, *The Caves of Klydor*, 1985
  After their exile to the planet Klydor, five young people suspect that their struggle is linked to an uprising against Earth's authoritarian regime.
Madeleine L'Engle, *A Wind in the Door*, 1973
  With Meg's help, the dragons her six year old brother sees in the vegetable garden play an important part in his struggle between life and death.
Caroline Stevermer, *River Rats*, 1992
  Years after the Flash destroyed civilization, Tomcat and a group of orphans face a dangerous trip in an old steamboat over the toxic Mississippi River
Adrien Stoutenburg, *Out There*, 1971

Five children and their nature-loving aunt leave the domed city to search for signs of life in a land made barren by disasters of misused technology.

1769

Susan Sussman

Illustrator: Joelle Shefts

Casey the Nomad (Niles, Illinois: Whitman, 1985)

Age range: Grades 3-5

Subject(s): Fathers and Sons; Sports/Swimming

Major character(s): Casey Cooper, Child; Rosey Cooper, Child (Casey's sister); Art Pepper, Friend

Time period(s): 1980s

Locale(s): Los Angeles, California

What the book is about: Casey loves studying Nomads in school. He and his little sister, Rosey, dress like Nomads, build tents and have a wonderful time. But when Casey finds out his father will spend most of the next two years traveling on business, nomad takes on a whole new meaning. His dad can no longer help Casey train for the Cub Scout Olympics.

Where it's reviewed:
Booklist, December 1, 1985, page 576
School Library Journal, March 1986, page 171

Other books by the author:
Big Friend, Little Friend, 1989
Hanukkah, 1988
Lies People Believe about Animals, 1987
There's No Such Thing as a Chanukah Bush, Sandy Goldstein, 1983

Other books you might like:
Janet Adele Bloss, *The Girl with the Green Hair*, 1989
  Cassie joins the swim club to make her parents proud of her, but her life becomes overshadowed by a problem with her hair.
Chris Crutcher, *Stotan!*, 1986
  A high school coach invites members of his swimming team to a week of rigorous training that tests their moral fiber as well as physical stamina.
Tessa Duder, *Alex in Rome*, 1991
  As a member of the 1960 Olympic swim team, Alex gets her first taste of independence as she faces the challenges of competition.
Diana Gregory, *There's a Caterpillar in My Lemonade*, 1980
  Samantha has difficulty coping with her mother's impending remarriage and tried to evade the situation by involving herself with the swim team.
Ingrid Tomey, *Neptune Princess*, 1992
  A broken leg means Poppy won't compete in the swimming events to be "Neptune Princess" but another challenge comes her way that summer.

1770

Rosemary Sutcliff

Tristan and Iseult (New York: Dutton, 1971)

Age range: Grades 5-8

Subject(s): Celts; Legends; Romance

Major character(s): Iseult, Teenager, Royalty (princess); Tristan, Teenager, Royalty (prince); Marc, Ruler (king)

Time period(s): 12th century (1100s)

Locale(s): England

What the book is about: The tale of the love of Tristan for the red-haired Iseult, the princess of Ireland. The story begins as a Celtic legend, first known written version 1150. Tristan, at sixteen, has mastered all the arts and bested everyone in Lothian at every skill. He puts to sea to see the world. It is a story of love and war, of high adventures and deeds of bravery in epic style.

Where it's reviewed:
Booklist, February 1, 1971, page 454
Hornbook, December 1970, page 621
Kirkus Reviews, November 1, 1970, page 1201

Awards the book has won:
Boston Globe/Horn Book Award 1972

Other books by the author:
Blue Remembered Hills, 1983
Bonnie Dundee, 1983
Blood Feud, 1976
Beowulf, 1961

Other books you might like:
Proinsias Mac Cana, *Celtic Mythology*, 1983
    Describes the gods, myths, and epic legends of the Celts, discussing their relationship with Celtic history and the influence of the Romans.
Robin Place, *The Celts*, 1977
    Describes the origins, history, culture and day-to-day life of the Celts, whose civilization flourished in the 500 years before Christ.
Mary Tannen, *The Wizard Children of Finn*, 1981
    Two children are transported back in time to ancient Ireland where they share amazing adventures with the boy who claims leadership of the Fianna.
Peter Vansittart, *The Dark Tower: Tales from the Past*, 1965
    Eleven tales of Celtic origin interspersed with traditional poems and ballads tell of deeds of courage and treachery, magical powers, elfs and gods.
Mary Alexander Walker, *The Scathach and Maeve's Daughters*, 1990
    In the 8th century, Scathach appears to Maeve Moira, daughter of a Celtic High King and promises that Maeve's offspring will have her qualities.

1771

Margaret Sutherland

Illustrator: Jane Paton

Hello, I'm Karen (New York: Coward, 1976)

Age range: Grades 2-3

Subject(s): Friendship; Maoris; Race Relations

Major character(s): Karen, Child; Henri, Child

Time period(s): Indeterminate

Locale(s): New Zealand

What the book is about: Karen is a small New Zealand girl. Her best friend, Henri, is a Maori. Her activities are familiar ones; playing with a friend, going on errands, being part of a family. Each chapter is a story of its own, for young, independent readers.

Where it's reviewed:
Center for Children's Books Bulletin, June 1976, page 165
Kirkus Reviews, January 15, 1976, page 72
School Library Journal, April, 1976, page 66

Other books you might like:
Graeme Base, *My Grandma Lived in Gooligulch*, 1990
    Grandma, who lives with a large collection of animals in her small Australian town, takes a disasterous trip to the seaside.
Anne Rockwell, *Tuhurahura and the Whale*, 1971
    Left to drown in the sea, a Maori boy is saved by a whale who returns him to shore.
Kiri Te Kanawa, *Land of the Long White Cloud*, 1989
    A collection of Maori stories that the author heard during her childhood as a member of a Maori tribe.
Colin Thiele, *Storm Boy*, 1963
    A boy living on a desolate beach in Australia rescues a baby pelican that becomes his constant companion.
Gordon Winch, *Enoch, the Emu*, 1988
    As emus really do, Enoch sits on the nest for weeks till the nine eggs laid by his wife hatch, and then he proudly shows off the new family.

1772

Jane Sutton

Illustrator: Sandy Kossin

Me and the Weirdos (Boston: Houghton Mifflin, 1987)

Age range: Grades 3-5

Subject(s): Family Life; Individuality; Parent and Child

Major character(s): Cindy Krinkle, Preteen; Roger Snooterman, Newspaper Carrier; Smith Krinkle, Parent

Time period(s): Indeterminate

Locale(s): Chesterville

What the book is about: Ten year old Cindy is constantly embarrassed by her weird family. Her mother wears red sneakers, year round, every day, and can be found polishing the gum ball machine and drinking fountain in the Krinkle living room. And of course, Squirrel *is* an unusual name for a mom, and her father is the only dad around who *plants* dandelions instead of trying to kill them off.

Other books by the author:
Definitely Not Sexy, 1988
Not Even Mrs. Mazursky, 1984
What Should a Hippo Wear?, 1979

Other books you might like:
Patricia MacLachlan, *The Facts and Fictions of Minna Pratt*, 1988
    An eleven year old cellist learns about life from her eccentric family, her first boyfriend, and Mozart.
Noel Streatfeild, *The Magic Summer*, 1967
    An adventurous summer with four children visiting their eccentric aunt in the Irish countryside.
Judy Delton, *Brimhall Comes to Stay*, 1978

Bear welcomes the arrival of his cousin Brimhall to live with him, but Brimhall's eccentric habits soon tax Bear's hospitality.

Helen Cresswell, *Ordinary Jack*, 1977
  Jack, the only "ordinary" member of the eccentric Bagthorpe family, concocts a scheme with his uncle to distinguish himself as a modern-day prophet.

Diana Wynne Jones, *The Ogre Downstairs*, 1974
  When a disagreeable man with two boys marries a widow with three children, family adjustments are complicated by two magic chemistry.

| 1773 |

David Warren Swartley

Illustrator: James Converse

My Friend, My Brother (Scottdale, Pennsylvania: Herald Press, 1980)

Age range: Grades 4-7

Subject(s): Adoption; Child Abuse

Major character(s): Eric, Preteen; Jon Simon, Preteen, Abuse Victim

Time period(s): 1980s

Locale(s): Indiana

What the book is about: Jon parents were killed when he was a baby and he lives with an aunt and uncle. Eric, a Mennonite boy who is Jon's friend, discovers bruises on Jon's back. Eventually Eric's family adopts Jon, but first he suffers a great deal of abuse.

Where it's reviewed:
School Library Journal, May 1980, page 72

Other books you might like:
Monica Hughes, *Beyond the Dark River*, 1979
  In a Canada devoid of technological knowledge and equipment because of a nuclear war, a boy and girl seek a cure for a mysterious illness.

Ruth Nulton Moore, *The Ghost Bird Mystery*, 1977
  A Mennonite brother and sister move with their parents to a reputedly haunted house in Pennsylvania and resolve several mysteries.

Steven Schnur, *Hannah and the Cyclops*, 1990
  Everyone in Mrs. Hamilton's class thinks Rafi is the clumsiest boy in the fifth grade. Rafi's friend, Hannah, suspects another cause of the bruises.

Esther Loewen Vogt, *Harvest Gold*, 1978
  The further experiences of Martha and her family as they face the hardships and the rewards of life on the Kansas prairie in the 1870s.

Jeanne Williams, *Winter Wheat*, 1975

In 1874, sixteen year old Cobie leaves Russia with her five sisters and Mennonite parents to settle on the harsh Kansas prairies and build a new life.

| 1774 |

Robert E. Swindells

Illustrator: Reg Sandland

The Moonpath and Other Tales of the Bizarre (Minneapolis: Carolrhoda, 1979)

Age range: Grades 4-8

Subject(s): Occult; Short Stories

Time period(s): Indeterminate

Locale(s): United States

What the book is about: Five stories of the occult and mysterious, all with an ironic twist at the end: "The Moonpath," "The Plastic-Eaters," "The Rajah," "The Mermaid," and "The Fell-Dog."

Where it's reviewed:
Booklist, April 1, 1984, page 1122
School Library Journal, April 1984, page 120
Children's Book Review Service, March 1984, page 88

Other books by the author:
Following a Shadow, 1990
A Serpent's Tooth, 1989
Staying Up, 1986
Brother in the Land, 1985

Other books you might like:
Isaac Asimov, *The Disappearing Man and Other Mysteries*, 1985
  Five short mystery tales: " The D Man," "Lucky Seven," "The Christmas Solution," "The Twins," and "The Man in the Park."

M. Masters, *The Case of the Chocolate Snatchers and Other Mysteries*, 1983
  Nine short mystery tales starring Hawkeye Collins and Amy Adams, two sleuths who solve mysteries using Hawkeye's sketches of importantant sleuths.

Murray Shaw, *The Adventures of the Abbey Grange*, 1991
  Two Sherlock Holmes adventures with extensive explanations of clues presented and how Sherlock Holmes used each one to reason his way to the solution.

Lawrence Treat, *The Clue Armchair Detective*, 1983
  Characters from the Clue board game appear in these short mysteries which the reader solves with the aid of visual clues.

Carol Beach York, *Ghost Story Mysteries*, 1982
  Short stories involving ghostly mysteries which the reader is invited to solve.

T

1775

Shizuye Takashima

A Child in Prison Camp (New York: Morrow, 1971)

Age range: Grades 4-6

Subject(s): World War II

Major character(s): Shizuye Takashima, Child

Time period(s): 1940s (1941-1944)

Locale(s): Vancouver, British Columbia, Canada

What the book is about: The Takashima family spend three years in a Japanese relocation camp in Canada during World War II. The prisoners must protest to gain even the necessities of life, food and water. Told from a child's point of view.

Where it's reviewed:
Center for Children's Books Bulletin, November 1974, page 55
Kirkus Reviews, May 15, 1974, page 536
Publisher's Weekly, July 8, 1974, page 75

Other books you might like:
James D. Forman, *Ring the Judas Bell*, 1965
   Taken from their homes by guerrillas during the civil war, a group of Greek children try to return from a prison camp in the Yugoslav mountains.
Florence Crannel Means, *The Moved Outers*, 1945
   A novel based on the life of a Japanese-American family in California after the attack on Pearl Harbor.
Ken Mochizuki, *Baseball Saved Us*, 1993
   A Japanese American boy learns to play baseball in an internment camp during World War II, and his ability to play helps him after the war is over.
Zane Spencer, *Branded Runaway*, 1980
   Instead of prison camp or another foster home, Reese is made a camp counselor for problem city kids and for the first time finds he cares about others
Yoshiko Uchida, *The Invisible Thread*, 1991
   Yoshiko Uchida describes growing up in Berkeley, California and her family's internment in a Nevada relocation center during the World War II.

1776

Marc Talbert
Illustrator: Toby Gowing

Double or Nothing (New York: Dial, 1990)

Age range: Grades 3-6

Subject(s): Aunts and Uncles; Magic; Death

Major character(s): Sam, Preteen; Frank, Magician

Time period(s): 1980s

Locale(s): United States

What the book is about: Sam acquires a knowldege of magic from his Uncle Frank, and we see Sam successfully give his first public magic show in the park. Through only one day in Sam's life, we see much of the warm relationship with his uncle through flashbacks. Even after his uncle's death, he remembers his uncle's lesson: "Believe in magic and you'll see magic. Believe in beauty and you'll see beautiful things."

Where it's reviewed:
Booklist, October 1, 1990, page 333
Horn Book January/February 1991, page 71

Other books by the author:
Pillow of Clouds, 1991
The Paper Knife, 1988
Thin Ice, 1987
Dead Birds Singing, 1986

Other books you might like:
Jane Cutler, *Family Dinner*, 1991
   Great-Uncle Benson prepares exotic food dishes in order to lure Rachel's family to a communal dinner.
Nancy Farmer, *Do You Know Me?*, 1993
   Tapiwa's uncle becomes her best friend when he comes to live with her family in Harare, Zimbawe.
Johanna Hurwitz, *The Up and Down Spring*, 1993
   Eleven year old Rory tries to hide his fear of flying when he is asked to take a trip in his uncle's airplane.
David Kherdian, *A Song for Uncle Harry*, 1989
   A young boy relates his special friendship with his uncle.
Russell Stannard, *The Time and Space of Uncle Albert*, 1989
   Gedanken's eccentric uncle sends her into out space in a spacecraft to help him conduct experiments regarding the law of relativity.

1777

Mary Tannen
Illustrator: Rob Sauber

Huntly, Nutley and the Missing Link (New York: Knopf, 1983)

Age range: Grades 4-6

Subject(s): Humor; Man, Prehistoric; Single Parent Families

Major character(s): Huntley Nutley, Preteen; Baby Beau Nutley, Child; Orson Forest, Bully

Time period(s): 1980s

Locale(s): Wolcott

What the book is about: Huntley discovers a living creature, the ape-human missing link, and brings him into the household. He and his brother, Baby Beau, try to hide ''Link'' fearing that if he is found, he will become an experiment in their father's laboratory. They disguise him as a new housekeeper, Mrs. Link. One day Link gets tired of hiding and decides to take off on his own.

Where it's reviewed:
Booklist, July 1983, page 1405
Children's Book Review Service, Spring 1983, page 121
Center for Children's Books Bulletin, July 1983, page 219

Other books by the author:
The Lost Legend of Finn, 1982
The Wizard Children of Finn, 1981

Other books you might like:
William Bence, *People of the Bison*, 1966
    A boy, a cave painter, is found by a less advanced people, some of whom accept him, but others fear his artistic talents.
Oliver Butterworth, *The Narrow Passage*, 1973
    Two boys on an expedition in southern France decide to protect the prehistoric cave they discover from desecration and public scrutiny.
Hal George Evarts, *Jay-Jay and the Peking Monster*, 1978
    A southern California boy finds a box of bones that may be the remains of prehistoric Peking Man which have been missing from a museum since WWII.
Rosalie K. Fry, *Mungo*, 1972
    A youngster's lonliness comes to an end when he discovers a prehistoric sea monster off the Scottish coast.
William L. Heath, *The Earthquake Man*, 1980
    When a troll gives the O'Grady family a lot of misery, a peculiar man appears and vows to rid the family of the troll.

1778

Kathy Kennedy Tapp

The Scorpio Ghosts and the Black Hole Gang (New York: Harper, 1987)

Age range: Grades 5-7

Subject(s): Brothers and Sisters; Ghosts

Major character(s): Ryan, Preteen; C.C., Spirit; Aunt Vira, Spirit

Time period(s): 1980s

Locale(s): Madison, Wisconsin

What the book is about: Ryan and his brother and sisters are not thrilled with the idea of helping renovate an old schoolhouse in a Wisconsin cornfield. But adventure begins for them when they help free two modern day ghosts from a haunt pattern that has them trapped in a time loop in their bookmobile.

Where it's reviewed:
Booklist, March 1, 1987, page 1057
Kirkus Reviews, February 1, 1987, page 225

School Library Journal, April 1987, page 105

Other books by the author:
The Sacred Circle of the Hula Hoop, 1989
Flight of the Moth-Kin, 1987
The Ghostmobile, 1987
Moth-Kin Magic, 1983

Other books you might like:
Shirley Climo, *T.J.'s Ghost*, 1989
    A girl helps the ghost of a 19th century stowaway find a ring that will help free him to his future.
Florence Parry Heide, *Mystery of the Bewitched Bookmobile*, 1975
    The Spotlight Club tries to unravel the mystery of someone who breaks into the bookmobile but does not steal anything.
Eva Ibbotson, *The Great Ghost Rescue*, 1975
    A young boy decides to establish a sanctuary for an bunch of ghosts when the homes they haunted are replaced by highways and other modern improvements
Sarah Sargent, *Jerry's Ghosts: The Mystery of the Blind Tower*, 1992
    Jerry discovers two ghostly children trapped with their mad scientist uncle in the 19th century mansion that was their former home and sets them free.
Sarah Sargent, *Lure of the Dark*, 1984
    Chaos and disorder generated by the Norse god Loki pervade the life of a girl whose personal problems have left her in a vulnerable state.

1779

Eleanora E. Tate

Just an Overnight Guest (New York: Dial, 1980)

Age range: Grades 4-6

Subject(s): African Americans; Cousins; Family Problems

Major character(s): Margie Carson, Child; Ethel Hardison, Child; Luvenia Carson, Teacher

Time period(s): 1980s

Locale(s): Nutbrush, Mississippi

What the book is about: Margie likes softball, fishing, and the times her daddy is home from his job as a mover. She doesn't like Ethel, who is a wild, half-black half-white child. Margie's mom insists on taking Ethel into their family to keep her out of the Home. Ethel wets Margie's bed, breaks a precious shell collection and causes all sorts of trouble. Margie begins to suspect she is in so much trouble because she has never been loved.

Where it's reviewed:
Center for Children's Books Bulletin, October 1980, page 42
Horn Book, December 1980, page 643

Other books by the author:
Front Porch Stories at the One Room School, 1992
Thank You, Dr. Martin Luther King, Jr., 1990
The Secret of Gumbo Grove, 1987

Other books you might like:
Brenda Guiberson, *Instant Soup*, 1991
    Darlene's plans to spend her winter break at the mall with Stacy are interrupted when Mom asks Darlene to babysit for her four year old cousin.
Barbara Hall, *Dixie Storms*, 1990

Dutch Peyton learns about growing up as her family struggles with a crippling drought and a painful past.

Virginia Hamilton, *Cousins*, 1990
Concerned that her grandmother may die, Cammy is unprepared for the accidental death of another relative.

Christel Kleitsch, *Cousin Markie and Other Disasters*, 1992
Ben doesn't get along with his younger cousin and he is certain that having him spend the weekend will ruin his plans to get a skateboard.

Susan Beth Pfeffer, *Darcy Downstairs*, 1990
When Darcy's cousin moves into the upstairs apartment and they become inseparable, Darcy has trouble with her former best friend and her schoolwork.

1780

Eleanora E. Tate

The Secret of Gumbo Grove (New York: Watts, 1987)

Age range: Grades 5-8

Subject(s): African Americans; Mystery and Detective Stories

Major character(s): Raisin Stackhouse, Preteen (11 years old); Effie Pfluggins, Widow(er); Maizell Stackhouse, Preteen

Time period(s): 1980s

Locale(s): Gumbo Grove, South Carolina

What the book is about: When Raisin asks her teacher, Miz Gore, why they don't study about anybody Black, her teacher tells her, "Nobody Black around here ever did anything worth talking about." Raisin disagrees, and while helping restore the cemetary of the Old Baptist Church, she solves the mystery surrounding the founding of her home town and gains pride in her family's past.

Where it's reviewed:
Kirkus Reviews, March 1, 1987, page 380
School Library Journal, March 1987, page 167

Other books by the author:
Front Porch Stories at the One Room School, 1992
Thank You, Dr. Martin Luther King, Jr.!, 1990
Just an Overnight Guest, 1980

Other books you might like:
Gary W. Barger, *Life. Is. Not. Fair.*, 1984
In 1958, Louis and his aunt are upset when a black family moves next door, but Louis soon learns his new neighbor is a better friend than anyone else.

Virginia Hamilton, *A Little Love*, 1984
Though she has been raised lovingly by her grandparents, a black teen goes in search of her father.

Dori Sanders, *Clover: A Novel*, 1990
After her father dies within hours of being married to a white woman, a ten year old black girl learns to overcome grief and adjust to her new life.

Mildred D. Taylor, *Let the Circle Be Unbroken*, 1981
4 black children growing up in rural Mississippi during the Depression experience racial antagonisms and hard times, but learn pride and self respect.

Mildred Pitts Walter, *Because We Are*, 1983
After a misunderstanding with a teacher, honor student Emma is transferred from the integrated high school where she excelled to a segregated school.

1781

Joan Tate

Illustrator: Judith Gwyn Brown

Ben and Annie (Garden City, NY: Doubleday, 1974)

Age range: Grades 4-6

Subject(s): Friendship; Physically Handicapped

Major character(s): Ben, Preteen; Annie, Teenager, Handicapped (disabled)

Time period(s): 1970s

Locale(s): England

What the book is about: Ben lives downstairs from Annie, a thirteen year old confined to a wheelchair. He takes her to the store, plays checkers and talks with her on the intercom his dad has installed for them. He takes her to play with his friends and bystanders misunderstand.

Where it's reviewed:
Center for Children's Books Bulletin, November 1974, page 55
Hornbook, December 1974, page 694
Kirkus Reviews, July 15, 1974, page 744

Other books by the author:
Grandpa and My Sister Bee, 1976
Jock and the Rock Cakes, 1976
Wild Boy, 1973
Admission to the Feast, 1969

Other books you might like:
Matt Christopher, *The Great Quarterback Switch*, 1984
Michael uses mental telepathy to communicate plays to his quarterback brother, then suddenly finds himself on the field in his brother's place.

Phyllis Green, *Walkie-Talkie*, 1978
Hyperactive Richie and Norman, who is confined to a wheelchair, share a brief friendship during the summer before they enter junior high school.

Berniece Rabe, *Margaret's Moves*, 1987
Margaret, confined to a wheelchair, longs for a lightweight "sportsmodel" chair so she can speed as fast as her brother.

Harriet May Savitz, *Run, Don't Walk: A Novel*, 1979
When a teenager returns to school in a wheelchair, she wants to be left alone. However, a handicapped activist insists she join his crusade.

Simon Watson, *The Partisan*, 1973
Two English boys discover their garden ruled by a boy in a wheelchair who becomes their leader.

1782

Joan Tate

Illustrator: Susan Jeschke

Wild Boy (New York: Harper, 1973)

Age range: Grades 5-7

Subject(s): Feral Children

Major character(s): Will, Preteen; Martin "Mart", Teenager; Rory, Dog

Time period(s): Indeterminate

Locale(s): Yorkshire, England (Yorkshire Moors)

What the book is about: Will's whole life has been spent in the small Yorkshire town where he was born. He and his dog wanders the Moors endlessly. Will wishes he could stay there all the time. One day he and Rory meet Mart, a boy who lives on the moors in a small shelter. Through Will and his family, Mart learns to relate to people again and eventually makes the choice to return to London.

Where it's reviewed:
Booklist, December 1, 1973, page 389
Hornbook, December 1973, page 596
Kirkus Reviews, September 15, 1973, page 1045

Other books by the author:
Luke's Garden and Gramp: Two Novels, 1981
Ben and Annie, 1974
Tina and David, 1973
Admission to the Feast, 1969

Other books you might like:
John R. Burger, *Children of the Wild*, 1978
    A collection of true stories and legends about children who were raised by animals.
Paul Samuel Jacobs, *Born into the Light*, 1988
    When a number of "feral children" are found, only Roger suspects they are not earthly creatures, but can't figure out the nature of their mission.
Rudyard Kipling, *The Jungle Book*, 1984
    The adventures of Mowgli, a boy reared by a pack of wolves and the wild animals of the jungle.
Willaim Mayne, *Antar and the Eagles*, 1990
    Abducted and raised by eagles, a young boy is sent on a mission to rescue a lost egg and, in the process, save the race of eagles.
Gary Paulsen, *Dunc Breaks the Record*, 1992
    Dunc and Amost crash in the wilderness while hang gliding but things go from bad to worse when they are captured by a wild man.

1783

Mark Taylor

Illustrator: Nancy Kincade

Mr. Pepper Stories (New York: Macmillan, 1984)

Age range: Grades 2-3

Subject(s): Humor

Major character(s): Mr. Pepper, Handyman; Mrs. Sunshine, Neighbor

Time period(s): Indeterminate

Locale(s): United States

What the book is about: The misadventures of two elderly friends, Mr. Pepper and Mrs. Sunshine. Mr. Pepper is always sure he is doing the right thing, even though he is wrong most of the time. But Mr. Pepper has fun, and so does his neighbor and best friend, Mrs. Sunshine.

Where it's reviewed:
Kirkus Reviews, September 1, 1984, page J73
Booklist, January 1, 1985, page 644
School Library Journal, January 1985, page 69

Other books by the author:
The Secret Life of Angus, 1985
Pippin's Lucky Penny, 1983

Henry the Castaway, 1977
Henry the Explorer, 1966

Other books you might like:
William Corbin, *The Pup with the Up-and-Down Tail*, 1972
    Due to an accident, the service station crew's dog becomes famous and acquires a tail that wags in the wrong direction.
Stephen Mooser, *Crazy Mixed-Up Valentines*, 1990
    Valentine's Day is his birthday, but not one of his Creepy Creature Club friends seems to care. In addition, he's afraid to talk to the girl he likes.
Bernice Myers, *The Extraordinary Invention*, 1984
    Sally and her father, who love to invent things together, make a time machine as a present for Sally's mother, only something goes terribly wrong.
Louis Phillips, *The Brothers Wrong and Wrong Again*, 1979
    Two foolish brothers, an attack by soldiers, and a fire-breathing dragon blend to create confusion in the town of Tsk.
Ellen Weiss, *The Tiny Parents*, 1989
    When an experiment goes wrong and their inventor parents shrink, it's up to Marie and Eddie to figure out how to get them back to normal.

1784

Mildred D. Taylor

Illustrator: Max Ginsburg

The Friendship (New York: Dial, 1987)

Age range: Grades 3-6

Subject(s): Race Relations; Prejudice; African Americans

Major character(s): Tom Bee, Farmer (sharecropper), Fisherman; Stacey Logan, Preteen; John Wallace, Store Owner

Time period(s): 1930s (1933)

Locale(s): Mississippi

What the book is about: Poor black children witness a confrontation between an elderly black man and a white storekeeper in rural Mississippi in the 1930s. Tom Bee, the black man, dares to refer to the owner of the store, Tom Wallace, as "John," not acceptable behavior to whites in Mississippi of the 1930s. The courage Tom shows and the way he holds John to a promise made long ago, even in the face of a shotgun blast, makes a powerful statement. A book all children should read or hear.

Where it's reviewed:
Booklist, December 15, 1987, page 713
Kirkus Reviews, October 1, 1987, page 1468

Awards the book has won:
Boston Globe/Horn Book Award
Coretta Scott King Award

Other books by the author:
The Road to Memphis, 1990
The Gold Cadillac, 1987
Let the Circle Be Unbroken, 1981
Roll of Thunder, Hear My Cry, 1976

Other books you might like:
Leigh Dean, *Rufus Gideon Grant*, 1970
    Unlike his father who sees their existence as little more than slavery, Rufus views the fields and animals as part of his dream for the future.
Pat Edwards, *Little John and Plutie*, 1988

Courageous Plutie is his first real friend, but John soon realizes their rural South environment discourages relationships between blacks and whites.

Winifred Madison, *Maria Luisa*, 1971
Maria Luisa encounters prejudice against Chicanos when she and her brother move to San Francisco to live with an aunt.

Barbara Murphy, *Home Free*, 1970
During summer vacation in South Carolina a white boy from New York and his black friend learn firsthand about the violence of racial prejudice.

Crystal Thrasher, *Between Dark and Daylight*, 1979
In rural Indiana at the end of the Depression, Seely's world is forever changed when an ominous threat from the Fender twins explodes into violence.

| 1785 |

Mildred D. Taylor

Illustrator: Max Ginsburg

Mississippi Bridge (New York: Dial, 1990)

Age range: Grades 4-6

Subject(s): African Americans; Prejudice; Race Relations

Major character(s): Jeremy Simms, Preteen; Stacey Logan, Preteen; Josias Williams, Lumberjack

Time period(s): 1930s

Locale(s): Mississippi

What the book is about: During a heavy rainstorm in 1930s rural Mississippi, a ten year old white boy sees a bus driver order all the black passengers off a crowded bus to make room for later-arriving white passengers and then sets off across the raging Rose Lee River.

Where it's reviewed:
Booklist, September 15, 1990, page 164
Kirkus Reviews, August 15, 1990, page 1174

Other books by the author:
The Road to Memphis, 1990
The Gold Cadillac, 1987
Roll of Thunder, Hear My Cry, 1976
Song of the Trees, 1975

Other books you might like:
Larry Bograd, *The 4th Grade Dinosaur Club*, 1989
Billy feels that everything in his life is wrong, with a hectic homelife, bullies at school, and the prejudice his friend Juan is experiencing.

Lucile Watkins Ellison, *Butter on Both Sides*, 1979
A year in the life of a close-knit family living in Alabama in the early 1900s as seen by eight year old Lucy.

Rachel Krantz, *Straight Talk about Prejudice*, 1992
Discusses prejudice and sterotyping and how such thinking leads to discrimination against women, ethnic groups, homosexuals, the aging, and others.

Robert Lipsyte, *The Summerboy*, 1992
When Bobby takes a summer job in a laundry, he gets more than he bargained for: prejudice, unrequited love and other hazards.

Pamela Melnikoff, *Plots and Players*, 1988

Robin, Philip and Frances, exiled Portugese Jews secretly practicing their faith in intolerant 16th century London, fight against prejudice there.

| 1786 |

Mildred D. Taylor

Illustrator: Jerry Pinkney

Roll of Thunder, Hear My Cry (New York: Dial, 1976)

Age range: Grades 5-6

Subject(s): African Americans; Depression (Economic); Race Relations

Major character(s): Cassie Logan, Child; Clayton "Little Man" Logan, Child; Mary Logan, Teacher

Time period(s): 1930s

Locale(s): Mississippi

What the book is about: The Logans, a Black family, struggle to maintain their pride and independence during the Depression. Cassie is humiliated and seeks revenge. A friend of the family is injured in a robbery and seeks their help. A sudden fire saves her brother from a lynch mob.

Where it's reviewed:
Horn Book, December 1976, page 627
Interracial Books for Children Bulletin #7, 1976, page 18

Awards the book has won:
Newbery Medal 1977
Young Reader's Choice Award 1979

Other books by the author:
Let the Circle Be Unbroken, 1981 (sequel to *Roll of Thunder, Hear My Cry*.)
The Friendship, 1987 (more about the Logan family.)
Song of the Trees, 1975 (precedes Roll of *Thunder, Hear My Cry*.)

Other books you might like:
Eth Clifford, *The Man Who Sang in the Dark*, 1987
A widowed mother and her two children cope with life in the difficult times of the Depression.

Paul Fleischman, *The Borning Room*,
Georgina, born in 1851, reflects on how events such as the Underground Railroad movement and the Civil War impacted individuals.

Evelyn Slaatten, *Good, the Bad, and the Rest of Us*, 1980
10 year old Katie grows up in a Hudson River town during the Depression.

Mary Stolz, *A Wonderful, Terrible Time*, 1967
Mady and Sue Ellen have adventures in their apartment house in the city and spend two weeks at summer camp.

Mary Stolz, *Ivy Larkin*, 1986
The Depression forces the Larkins to move to ever smaller and smaller apartments and makes life very difficult for 14 year old Ivy.

| 1787 |

Sydney Taylor
All-of-a-Kind Family (Chicago: Follett, 1951)
Age range: Grades 3-6

Subject(s): Family Life; Jews

Major character(s): Henrietta, Preteen; Ella, Preteen; Sarah, Child

Time period(s): 1900s (1901)

Locale(s): New York, New York (Lower East Side)

What the book is about: There isn't much money in this family of five girls, but there is a great deal of companionship, lots of books, outings, games and friends, and understanding and loving parents.

Other books by the author:
Danny Loves a Holiday, 1980
All-of-a-Kind Family Downtown, 1972
Mr. Barney's Beard, 1961
More All-of-a-Kind Family, 1954

Other books you might like:
Malka Drucker, *Shabbat: A Peaceful Island*, 1983
  Discusses the origins, rituals, and evening meal of the Sabbath holiday and special Sabbaths that occur during the year. (Non-Fiction)
Judith E. Greenberg, *Jewish Holidays*, 1984
  Briefly describes the yearly cycle of Jewish holidays. (Non-Fiction)
Semadar Shir, *The Dreidle Champ and Other Holiday Stories*, 1987
  A collection of stories for each of the seven major Jewish holidays.
Sholem Aleichem, *Around the Table: Family Stories of Sholom Aleichem*, 1991
  Presents retellings of five Sholom Aleichem stories which depict families observing the rituals and traditions of Jewish holidays together.
Maida Silverman, *The Glass Menorah and Other Stories for Jewish Holidays*, 1992
  Eight stories describing the way the Berg family celebrates various Jewish holidays.

1788

Theodore Taylor

The Cay (New York: Doubleday, 1969)

Age range: Grades 5-8

Subject(s): Blind; Survival; Race Relations

Major character(s): Phillip Enright, Survivor, Handicapped (blind); Timothy, Survivor

Time period(s): 1940s (1942)

Locale(s): Caribbean

What the book is about: As Phillip and his mother are fleeing Curacao for the United States in 1942, the freighter on which they are traveling is torpedoed, and Phillip finds himself on a raft with an old West Indian man named Timothy. Phillip has been blinded by a blow on the head, and he and Timothy are cast up on a barren cay. Phillip not only adjusts to his blindness, but comes to know the wise and loving man who is his only link to survival.

Where it's reviewed:
Booklist, July 15, 1969, page 1277
Hornbook, October 1969, page 537
Kirkus Reviews, May 15, 1969, page 560

Other books by the author:
Sniper, 1989
The Hostage, 1987
The Maldonado Miracle, 1973
The Children's War, 1971

Other books you might like:
Joel Matus, *Leroy and the Caveman*, 1993
  Driven by bullies into Dead Man's Canyon, Leroy discovers a living Neanderthal man and is entangled in an adventure involving German spies in 1942.
Jean Thesman, *Molly Donnelly*, 1993
  Molly, who lives next door to a Japanese-American family and whose cousin is a nurse in the Phillipines, experiences many changes as WWII begins.
Pieter Van Raven, *Harpoon Island*, 1989
  A teacher's attempt to start a new life on a sparsely populated island is threatened when WWI breaks out and his German heritage is discovered.
Yoko Kawashima Watkins, *So Far From the Bamboo Grove*, 1986
  A fictionalized autobiography in which eight year old Yoko escapes from Korea to Japan with her mother and sister at the end of WWII.
Nicholas Wilde, *Into the Dark*, 1987
  A lonely boy's new friend has a frightening secret in this story of ghosts, friendship, blindness and time travel.

1789

Theodore Taylor

The Hostage (New York: Delacorte, 1987)

Age range: Grades 5-8

Subject(s): Animals/Whales; Environmental Problems

Major character(s): Jamie Tidd, Teenager; Angie, Teenager; Zachary Cooke, Businessman

Time period(s): 1980s

Locale(s): Vancouver, British Columbia, Canada

What the book is about: Fourteen year old Jamie is stunned when his efforts to capture a trapped whale are misinterpreted. The $100,000 the marine park is offering is compelling, but so is Angie's environmental argument.

Where it's reviewed:
Booklist, February 15, 1988, page 1003
School Library Journal, March 1988, page 200

Other books by the author:
Rocket Island, 1985
Battle in the Arctic Seas, 1976
The Maldonado Miracle, 1973
The Children's War, 1971

Other books you might like:
Nathaniel Benchley, *Kilroy and the Gull*, 1977
  Captured and trained to be a marineland sensation, Kilroy, a killer whale, escapes to life on the open sea with his friend Morris the seagull.
Midas Dekkers, *Arctic Adventure*, 1987
  Exploring an ancient whaling station in the Arctic circle, two Dutch brothers risk their lives to stop a whaling boat from harpooning a whale.
Diane Duane, *Deep Wizardry*, 1985

During a summer vacation at the beach, thirteen year old wizard Nita and her friend Kit assist the whale-wizard S'ree in combating an evil power.

Jerry Spinelli, *Night of the Whale*, 1985
  6 rowdy high school seniors studying at a beach house for the summer are determined to just party, but then they encounter a group of beached whales.

Robin A. Thrush, *The Gray Whales Are Missing*, 1987
  Pence is trying to match up his father and his favorite teacher when he becomes involved in investigating the gray whales by the California coast.

1790

Theodore Taylor

Illustrator: Richard Cuffari

Teetoncey (Garden City, New York: Doubleday, 1974)

Age range: Grades 5-8

Subject(s): Survival

Major character(s): Ben O'Neal, Preteen; John O'Neal, Parent; Teetoncey, Survivor, Handicapped (mute)

Time period(s): 1890s (1898)

Locale(s): Heron Head, North Carolina (Outer Banks of North Carolina)

What the book is about: In this first novel of a trilogy, eleven year old Ben rescues a frail, young English girl from a shipwreck off the Outer Banks of North Carolina. Though she becomes part of his family, the shipwreck and resulting trauma have left her without speech. Since she cannot tell anyone who she is, they name her Teetoncey, island dialect for "small." The relationship between Ben and Teetoncey continues in *Teetoncey and Ben O'Neal* and *The Odyssey of Ben O'Neal*.

Where it's reviewed:
Booklist, September 1, 1974, page 47
Hornbook, October 1974, page 145
Kirkus, July 15, 1974, page 744

Other books by the author:
Sniper, 1989
The Odyssey of Ben O'Neal, 1977
Teetoncey and Ben O'Neal, 1975
The Maldonado Miracle, 1973

Other books you might like:
Joan Davenport, *A Ghost of a Chance*, 1992
  Punch and friends spend a summer in North Carolina, looking at dolphins, hunting for Blackbeard's treasure, and watching for the famed pirate's ghost.
Gloria Houston, *Littlejim*, 1990
  Littlejim, a bookish boy from in rural North Carolina at the turn of the century, hopes to win an essay contest and gain the respect of his father.
Eleanor Frances Lattimore, *Fair Boy*, 1958
  A girl visiting her great-aunt on a South Carolina island goes for a horseback ride and discovers that the island is just the way it was in the 1890s.
Brenda Seabrooke, *The Bridges of Summer*, 1992
  When she reluctantly comes to stay on a small South Carolina island, Zarah gradually accepts her grandmother's traditions and different way of life.
Wilma Yeo, *The Mystery of the Third Twin*, 1972

Newly arrived in North Carolina, fraternal twins are intrigued by the appearance of a mysterious girl who seems physically identical to one of them.

1791

Theodore Taylor

The Trouble with Tuck (New York: Doubleday, 1981)

Age range: Grades 4-6

Subject(s): Animals/Dogs; Blind

Major character(s): Helen Ogden, Preteen; Friar Tuck, Dog; Dr. Douglas Tobin, Veterinarian

Time period(s): 1950s

Locale(s): Los Angeles, California

What the book is about: A young girl trains her blind dog to follow and trust a seeing-eye companion dog.

Where it's reviewed:
Horn Book, April 1982, page 170
School Library Journal, January 1982, page 82

Awards the book has won:
California Young Reader Medal (Intermediate) 1984

Other books by the author:
Tuck Triumphant, 1991
The Hostage, 1987
The Maldonado Miracle, 1973
The Cay, 1969

Other books you might like:
Caroline Arnold, *A Guide Dog Puppy Grows Up*, 1991
  Follows the career of a guide dog from its raising as a puppy, through the training process and placement with a blind person.
Beverly Butler, *Maggie by My Side*, 1987
  The author describes her experiences at Pilot Dogs, a facility in Ohio where she trained with a guide dog.
Patricia Curtis, *Greff, the Story of a Guide Dog*, 1982
  Traces the life of a Labrador Retriever from birth through training at the Guide Dog Foundation.
Richard B. McFee, *Tom and Bear*, 1981
  The author tells of his twenty-six days observing a young blind man training with a guide dog at Guiding Eyes for the Blind, a school in New York.
Bernard Wolf, *Connie's New Eyes*, 1976
  Photographic essay about a 22 year old blind woman and her guide dog, Blythe.

1792

Margaret Teibl

Illustrator: Jacqueline B. Smith

Davey Come Home (New York: Harper and Row, 1979)

Age range: Grades 2-4

Subject(s): Single Parent Families; Loneliness

Major character(s): Davey, Child; Ruth Summers, Housekeeper

Time period(s): 1970s

Locale(s): United States

What the book is about: Davey lives alone with his busy, but caring, father. His teenage babysitter ignores him. His mom lives far away and calls only once in a great while. Then his dad hires Mrs. Summers to be their housekeeper. She packs his lunch, bakes pies and zips his jacket, but will she call him in for supper like his friend's mom's do?

Where it's reviewed:
Booklist, September 1, 1979, page 48
School Library Journal, October 1979, page 156

Other books you might like:
Mildred Amers, *Grandpa Jake and the Grand Christmas*, 1990
    Lizzie's family has hit on hard times until Grandpa Jake appears on their doorstep.
Kathryn Ewing, *A Private Matter*, 1975
    In her longing for a father, Marcy becomes attached to the kind man who lives next door.
Norma Klein, *Blue Trees, Red Sky*, 1975
    An eight year old girl lives alone with her mother and brother because her father has died.
Doris Orgel, *My War with Mrs. Galloway*, 1985
    Rebecca has an on-going war with her babysitter, until they make a truce.
Muriel Stanek, *I Won't Go Without a Father*, 1972
    Steve is reluctant to go to the school open-house because he has no father.

1793

Jan Terlouw

How to Become King (Rotterdam: Lemniscaat, 1971)

Age range: Grades 4-6

Subject(s): Adventure and Adventurers; Kings, Queens, Rulers

Major character(s): Stark, Teenager (royal contender); Gervaas, Servant (royal butler)

Time period(s): Indeterminate

Locale(s): Wiss, Fictional Country (Katoren)

What the book is about: Seventeen year old Stark was born the night the king of Katoren died. His loving uncle dreams that Stark will become king. Stark must perform seven impossible tasks. These are not ordinary tasks of fairy tales, but rather they are difficult, devious, and totally unethical tasks.

Where it's reviewed:
Booklist, March 1, 1978, page 1111
Center for Children's Books Bulletin, April 1978, page 135
School Library Journal, March 1978, page 134

Awards the book has won:
Austrian Juvenile Prize 1973
Children's Book of the Year, Holland 1972

Other books by the author:
Winter in Wartime, 1976
Pjotr, 1970

Other books you might like:
Bill Brittain, *My Buddy, the King: A Novel*, 1989

When King Tokab of Mokobway is saved from choking on a frankfurter by Tim, they become fast friends and together outwit a plan to do in the king.
Matt Christopher, *The Hit-Away Kid*, 1988
    A batter for the Peach Street Mudders enjoys winning so much that he has a tendency to bend the rules; dirty tactics on another team make him think.
Dean Hughes, *Millie Willenheimer and the Chestnut Corporation*, 1983
    Millie uses her ingenuity to corner the market on chestnuts before she is forced to question her own ethics and business practices.
Pamela F. Service, *Being of Two Minds*, 1991
    Connie's ability to share "mental visits" with the prince of Thulgaria proves useful when he's mysteriously kidnapped.
Jonathan Swift, *Gulliver's Travels*, 1947
    The travels of Gulliver include adventures in a land where people are only inches tall, a land of giants, a floating island, and a land run by horses.

1794

Susan Terris

The Latchkey Kids (New York: Farrar, 1986)

Age range: Grades 4-7

Subject(s): Brothers and Sisters; Latchkey Children; Family Problems

Major character(s): Callie Hoveler, Preteen; Rex Hoveler, Preteen

Time period(s): 1980s

Locale(s): San Francisco, California

What the book is about: Callie and Rex move from the suburbs to an apartment in San Francisco. They have to cope with a new home, new school, a working mother and a father who is suffering from depression. Nora is another latchkey kid who becomes not only a good friend but a mischief partner for Callie. Together they brush against real danger.

Where it's reviewed:
Center for Children's Books Bulletin, March 1986, page 1381
School Library Journal, June 1986, page 84

Other books by the author:
Author! Author!, 1990
Baby-Snatcher, 1984
No Scarlet Ribbons, 1981
The Chicken Pox Papers, 1976

Other books you might like:
Eve Bunting, *Is Anybody There?*, 1988
    After discovering the disappearance of several household items, Marcus fears a stranger may be prowling around his house.
Margaret Goff Clark, *The Latchkey Mystery*, 1985
    Eleven year old Minda forms a group to watch for a burglar who is breaking into houses.
Brenda Seabrooke, *Jerry on the Line*, 1990
    Aspiring soccer star Jerry starts an unusual friendship with a younger latchkey kid when she calls his phone number by accident.
Susan Richards Shreve, *How I Saved the World on Purpose*, 1985

Miranda starts a club taking care of latchkey kids and finds herself competing with the president of a rival club for publicity and local support.

Todd Strasser, *Home Alone: A Novelization*, 1990
Kevin McCallister regrets his wish to live alone when he is accidentlly left behind and must defend his home against burglars.

1795

Susan Terris

Octopus Pie (New York: Farrar, Strauss and Giroux, 1983)

Age range: Grades 4-6

Subject(s): Humor; Animals; Sisters

Major character(s): Kristin "Kris" Hart, Preteen; Mari, Preteen; Dorf, Worker (library aide)

Time period(s): 1970s

Locale(s): Terra Vista, California

What the book is about: Eleven year old Kris relates the events in her household when her father brings home a live octopus. Mari insists on moving the octopus to their classroom at school, and the octopet is octonapped!

Where it's reviewed:
Booklist, September 1, 1983, page 92
Kirkus, September 1, 1983, page J166
School Library Journal, October 1983, page 162

Other books by the author:
No Scarlet Ribbons, 1981
Stage Brat, 1980
Two P's in a Pod, 1977
The Pencil Families, 1975

Other books you might like:
Barbara Cohen, *The Carp in the Bathtub*, 1972
Two children try to rescue the carp their mother plans to make into gefilte fish for the Seder.
Patricia Hermes, *I Hate Being Gifted*, 1990
KT's friendship with her two best friends is threatened when she is selected for the gifted and talented program at her school.
Susan Beth Pfeffer, *Dear Dad, Love Laurie*, 1989
Laurie's letters to her divorced father chronicle her year in the 6th grade and her efforts to enter her school's program for the gifted and talented.
Jane Sutton, *Confessions of an Orange Octopus*, 1983
Clarence, also known as Chooch, enlivens a boring summer by teaching himself to juggle oranges and performing as the Orange Octopus.
Virginia Vail, *Petnapped!*, 1990
Valentine Taylor, the daughter of a veterinarian, investigates reports of missing pets.

1796

Susan Terris

Whirling Rainbows (Garden City, New York: Doubleday, 1974)

Age range: Grades 5-7

Subject(s): Camps and Camping; Jews; Indians of North America

Major character(s): Leah Friedman, Teenager

Time period(s): 1970s

Locale(s): Wisconsin

What the book is about: Leah describes herself as a "fat, blue-eyed Jewish Indian." Leah's dad is Polish and her mother is Chippewa. She was adopted by the Friedmans when she was a baby. When Leah and her cousin, Torie, go to camp in Wisconsin, Leah begins to explore her Native American heritage.

Where it's reviewed:
Center for Children's Books Bulletin, January 1975, page 86
Kirkus, June 1, 1974, page 588
Library Journal, October 15, 1974, page 2742

Other books by the author:
Author! Author!, 1990
The Latchkey Kids, 1986
Wings and Roots, 1982
Tucker and the Horse Thief, 1979

Other books you might like:
Alan Brown, *Lost Boys Never Say Die*, 1989
Scheduled to go to camp to work on his stuttering, Lewis sneaks back to his house, meets a new friend, and learns a new approach to his problems.
Patricia Lee Gauch, *Night Talks*, 1983
Three well intentioned classmates from an upper class Detroit suburb share a summer camp tent with an inner city girl, with unpredictable results.
Mort Grossman, *The Summer Ends Too Soon*, 1975
The growing involvement between the only female Gentile counselor at a Jewish camp and the drama coach considerably upsets both sets of parents.
Nancy Smiler Levinson, *Your Friend, Natalie Popper*, 1991
In the summer of 1946, Natalie looks forward to going to camp for the first time with her friend, Corinne, but things do not turn out as she expects.
Sheri Cooper Sinykin, *The Buddy Trap*, 1991
Forced to spend the summer at a camp dominated by wargames, Cam endures the hostility of tentmates and keeps secret his love of for playing the flute.

1797

Mike Thaler

Illustrator: Bruce Degen

In the Middle of the Puddle (New York: Harper and Row, 1988)

Age range: Grades 1-2

Subject(s): Animals/Frogs and Toads; Animals/Turtles; Weather

Major character(s): Fred, Frog; Ted, Turtle

Time period(s): Indeterminate

Locale(s): United States

What the book is about: A frog and turtle watch the rain turn their puddle into an ocean before the sun comes along and returns things to normal.

Where it's reviewed:
Booklist, June 1, 1988, page 1678
Children's Book Review Service, September 1988, page 5

Other books by the author:
Come and Play, 1991
The Teacher From the Black Lagoon, 1989
The Clown's Smile, 1982
A Hippopotamus Ate the Teacher!, 1981

Other books you might like:
Gail Hartman, *For Sand Castles on Seashells*, 1990
   Depicts the alternative uses of such places as a tree stump, a busy street, and a rain puddle.
Charlotte Pomerantz, *The Piggy in the Middle*, 1974
   Unable to persuade a young pig from frolicing in the mud, her family joins her for a mud party.
Beatrix Potter, *The Tale of Jemima Puddle Duck*, 1992
   Jemima Puddle Duck foolishly allows the fox to help her find a "safe" nest.
Anslie Pryor, *A Baby Blue Cat and the Dirty Dog Brothers*, 1987
   Baby Blue Cat has a good time playing with the Dirty Dog Brothers in the sooty ashes and the very big mud puddle.
John Schindel, *I'll Meet You Halfway*, 1993
   After not seeing one another for a long time, two friends, Titus Turtle and Fuller Frog, each bring a special gift to the other.

1798

Mike Thaler

Illustrator: Maxie Chambliss

It's Me, Hippo! (New York: Harper, 1983)

Age range: Grades 1-3

Subject(s): Animals

Time period(s): Indeterminate

Locale(s): Fictional Country

What the book is about: Four short stories about a friendly hippo. With the help of his animal friends, Giraffe, Parrot, Mole, Lion and others, Hippo builds a house, paints a picture, breaks out in sports and celebrates a birthday.

Where it's reviewed:
Booklist, September 15, 1983, page 176
Kirkus Reviews, September 1, 1983, page J158
School Library Journal, December 1983, page 80

Other books by the author:
Pack 109, 1988
Moonkey, 1982
Owly, 1982
My Puppy, 1980

Other books you might like:
Alice Bach, *Warren Weasel's Worse than Measels*, 1980
   The smartest bear in the world makes a winner out of a loser weasel.
Tony Bradman, *Dilly Tells the Truth*, 1988
   Dilly the dinosaur gets sick, decides to tell the exact truth regardless of the consequences, holds his own Dinolympics, and gets lost.
James Marshall, *George and Martha Round and Round*, 1988

Five episodes chronicle the ups and downs of a special friendship.
Lillian Nordlicht, *The Alligator with the Lean Mean Smile*, 1985
   Small Hippo and Big Rhino face a hungry alligator who engages them in a riddle-solving battle of wits.
Derek Radford, *Harry Builds a House*, 1990
   Harry Hippo and his friends build a house, step-by-step, from digging a ditch for the pipes to putting in the last joints and plugs.

1799

Colin Thiele

February Dragon (New York: Harper, 1976)

Age range: Grades 5-6

Subject(s): Fires

Major character(s): Resin Pine, Child; Turpo Pine, Child; Columbine Pine, Child

Time period(s): 1970s

Locale(s): Upper Gumbowie, Australia

What the book is about: During the hot, dry summer in Australia, there is always a danger of a bush fire, called the "dragon" of February. A picnicker starts a fire that costs the Pine family and their neighbors their crops, homes and most of their pets. Aunt Hester takes in the family, completely unaware that she is the one who carelessly started the fire.

Where it's reviewed:
Booklist, September 15, 1976, page 181
Center for Children's Books Bulletin, November 1976, page 49
Hornbook, October 1976, page 501
Kirkus Reviews, July 1, 1976, page 733

Other books by the author:
Jodie's Journey, 1990
Shadow Shark, 1985
Fight Against Albatross Two, 1976
The Fire in the Stone, 1974

Other books you might like:
Anne De Roo, *Scrub Fire*, 1980
   Michelle and her younger brothers, separated from their aunt and uncle during a camping trip in New Zealand, must find their way back to civilization.
Maurice Gee, *The Fire-Raiser*, 1986
   In 1915, Kitty Wix and her friends try to stop the arsonist who is terryfying their small New Zealand town.
Harriette Robinet, *Children of the Fire*, 1991
   A young black girl named Hallelujah lives through the great Chicago fire with courage and resourcefulness.
Robb White, *Fire Storm: A Novel*, 1979
   A raging forest fire in the National Parks area of the Sierras traps a forest ranger and a young boy he suspects is an arsonist.
Laura Ingalls Wilder, *Little House on the Prairie*, 1935
   A family moves from the woods of Wisconsin to the prairie where they bbuild a house, meet neighboring Indians, dig a well and fight a prairie fire.

1800

Colin Thiele

The Hammerhead Light (New York: Harper, 1976)

Age range: Grades 5-6

Subject(s): Lighthouses; Sea Stories

Major character(s): Alex Jorgenson, Aged Person; Tessa, Child

Time period(s): Indeterminate

Locale(s): Australia

What the book is about: A small Australia town tries to preserve an old lighthouse. After Alex's house blows down, he moves into the lighthouse. He and Tessa use the old lighthouse to guide Tessa's father to shore when there is a storm at sea.

Where it's reviewed:
Booklist, March 15, 1977, page 1096
Hornbook, August 1977, page 445
Kirkus Reviews, March 15, 1977, page 286

Other books by the author:
The Shadow on the Hills, 1978
February Dragon, 1976
Fight Against Albatross Two, 1976
The Fire in the Stone, 1974

Other books you might like:
Dorothy Holder Jones, *Abbie Burgess, Lighthouse Heroine*, 1969
  A fictionalized biography of teenage lighthouse heroine Abbie Burgess who became a legend for her vigil on Matinicus Rock, a Maine coastal island.
Reginald Ottley, *No More Tomorrow*, 1971
  A faithful dog accompanies his old master on travels through the Australian outback.
Joan Phipson, *Six and Silver*, 1971
  The adventures of a young city girl spending her first summer with country friends on their Australian farm.
Eleanor Spence, *The Switherby Pilgrims*, 1967
  A young English lady moves her ten orphan children to Australia where they carve out a new life for themselves in the austere Australian bush.
Wallace White, *The Storm*, 1982
  Mike, suspected of setting a fire at a marina, survives a storm at sea and learns to accept responsibility for his own life.

1801

Colin Thiele

The Shadow on the Hills (New York: Harper, 1978)

Age range: Grades 5-8

Subject(s): Farm Life; Friendship

Major character(s): Bodo Schneider, Preteen; Ebenezer Blitz, Recluse; Moses Mibus, Farmer

Time period(s): 20th century

Locale(s): Gonunda, Australia

What the book is about: Bodo Schneider is from a German family which settles in South Australia. He grows up learning about the world around him and coping with the strict rules which govern his family and church. He becomes friends with Ebenezer Blitz, an old hermit who preaches from hilltops, always accompanied by his wild dog, Elijah. Bodo becomes involved in the mysteries and madness that seem to permeate the community.

Where it's reviewed:
Booklist, April 1, 1978, page 1262
Hornbook, August 1978, page 398
Kirkus Reviews, March 1, 1978, page 248

Other books by the author:
Blue Fin, 1974
Fight Against Albatross Two, 1974
The Fire in the Stone, 1973
February Dragon, 1966

Other books you might like:
Anne De Roo, *Cinnamon and Nutmeg*, 1974
  A young girl growing up on an Australia farm finds two orphans in the bush, a kid and a newborn calf, and tries to raise them secretly.
Beverley Dunlop, *The Poetry Girl*, 1983
  Growing up in New Zealand following WWII, Natalia uses poetry to escape from her problems at home and at school.
William Mayne, *Salt River Times*, 1980
  Twenty-one interlocking stories about the lives of the people living in a small community along Australia's Salt River.
Reginald Ottley, *The War on William Street*, 1973
  Rescuing a girl from a shark at a Sydney, Australia beach changes the lives of three newsboys in the 1930s.
Katherine Susannah Prichard, *The Wild Oats of Han*, 1973
  Chronicles the adventures of a young girl and her brothers growing up in a small Australian town in the late 1800s.

1802

Colin Thiele

Illustrator: John Schoenherr

Storm Boy (New York: Harper, 1978)

Age range: Grades 4-6

Subject(s): Friendship; Animals/Birds

Major character(s): Storm Boy, Preteen; Hideaway Tom, Beachcomber, Parent; Mr. Percival, Pelican

Time period(s): Indeterminate

Locale(s): Australia

What the book is about: Storm Boy lives with Hideaway Tom, his father, in a shack on the southern coast of Australia. An aborigine friend, Fingerbone Bill, teaches Storm Boy all about the rich plant and animal life that surrounds them, and so Storm Boy is a friend to the animals. One day two men invade a pelican's next, killing the adults and smashing the eggs. Storm Boy finds three baby pelicans who survived and rescues them. When they are well, two of them go on their way, but one remains and becomes Storm Boy's special friend, Mr. Percival.

Where it's reviewed:
Booklist, January 15, 1979, page 814
Hornebook, October 1978, page 523
Kirkus Reviews, January 15, 1979, page 67

Other books by the author:
Pinquo, 1983
The Hammerhead Light, 1976
Magpie Island, 1974
February Dragon, 1966

Other books you might like:
Graeme Base, *My Grandma Lived in Gooligulch*, 1983
  Grandma, who lives with a large collection of animals in her small Australian town, takes a disastrous trip to the seaside.
Felicia Cotich, *Valda*, 1983
  During the Depression in a small town in Australia, a grindingly poor family tries to work out its problems.
Reginald Ottley, *No More Tomorrow*, 1971
  A faithful dog accompanies his old master on travels through the Australian outback.
Michael F. Page, *The Great Bullocky Race*, 1984
  Two competitive Australian bullockies undertake a fierce race, accompanied by their children, to prove their superiority in driving teams of cattle.
Nadia Wheatley, *My Place*, 1987
  The story of Australia's history as it might have been seen by children from 1788 to 1988.

1803

Dylan Thomas

Illustrator: Trina S. Hyman

A Child's Christmas in Wales (New York: Holiday, 1985)

Age range: Grades 3 and Up

Subject(s): Christmas

Time period(s): Indeterminate Past

Locale(s): Wales

What the book is about: Thomas' lyrical writing can be very difficult for American children, used to fast paced stories. But for those reflective moments, this is a beautiful recollection of Christmas memories, well shared, adult to child, or for the mature reader.

Where it's reviewed:
Horn Book, November/December 1985, page 722
School Library Journal, October 1985, page 192

Other books you might like:
Stefan Czernecki, *Pancho's Pinata*, 1992
  On Christmas Eve, Pancho rescues a star from a cactus, and receives the gift of happiness.
Fyodor Dostoyevsky, *The Heavenly Christmas Tree*, 1993
  A poor boy freezing on Christmas Eve finds himself before Christ's Christmas tree, with the spirits of other children who have died and gone to heaven
Rosalie K. Fry, *Snowed Up*, 1970
  Although being snowbound in a Welsh farmhouse is at first a great adventure, three children must soon concentrate on finding food, fuel, and help.
Patricia Polacco, *Uncle Vova's Tree*, 1989
  Grandparents, aunts and uncles, and children gather at a farm house to celebrate Christmas in the Russian tradition.
Robina Beckles Willson, *Merry Christmas*, 1983
  Presents Christmas traditions, legends, carols and recipes from many countries around the world.

1804

Jane Resh Thomas

Illustrator: Troy Howell

The Comeback Dog (New York: Clarion Books, 1981)

Age range: Grades 3-5

Subject(s): Animals/Dogs

Major character(s): Daniel, Child

Time period(s): 1980s

Locale(s): United States

What the book is about: Daniel is a farm boy who has recently faced the death of his dog, Captain. He finds an English setter nearly starved to death in a ditch. Daniel nurses Lady back to health. She is in no way like his dog, Captain. They get a second chance to become pals when she runs away and comes back to Daniel really needing his help again.

Where it's reviewed:
Horn Book, August 1981, page 427
School Library Journal, December 1981, page 69

Other books by the author:
The Princess in the Pigpen, 1989
Saying Goodbye to Grandma, 1988
Fox in a Trap, 1987
Courage at Indian Deep, 1984

Other books you might like:
Jim Arnosky, *Gray Boy*, 1988
  Despite his attachment to the boy who raised him, Gray Boy follows his natural instincts and returns to the wild.
Beverly Cleary, *Strider*, 1991
  Leigh tells how he comes to terms with his parents' divorce, acquires joint custody of an abandoned dog and joins the track team at school.
Barbara Corcoran, *Annie's Monster*, 1990
  Delighted when her prayers for an Irish Wolfhound are answered, Annie soon finds herself in trouble, along with the huge, curious dog, in her town.
Sid Fleischman, *Jim Ugly*, 1992
  Jake and Jim Ugly - his father's part mutt/part wolf dog, travel through the Old West trying to find out what happened to Jake's father.
Gary Paulsen, *Woodsong*, 1990
  For a rugged family living in Minnesota, life is a wild experience full of wolves, deer and sled dogs.

1805

Jane Resh Thomas

Courage at Indian Deep (Boston: Houghton Mifflin, 1984)

Age range: Grades 5-7

Subject(s): Winter; Survival

Major character(s): Cass Kennedy, Child (rescuer)

Time period(s): Indeterminate Past

Locale(s): Indian Deep, Minnesota

What the book is about: Forced to move to northern Minnesota from a comfortable life in Minneapolis, a family finds they need to make some big adjustments. But there is no lack of excitement, as Cass must help save a ship caught in a sudden blizzard on Lake Superior.

Where it's reviewed:
Booklist, May 1, 1984, page 1254
Kirkus Reviews, March 1, 1984, page J18

School Library Journal, August 1984, page 78

Other books by the author:
The Princess in the Pigpen, 1989
Fox in a Trap, 1987
The Comeback Dog, 1981

Other books you might like:
Mel Ellis, *An Eagle to the Wind*, 1978
    In the forests along Lake Superior, a teenage boy watches the activities of a pair of eagles that become symbols of his own passage to adulthood.
James Nichols, *Boundary Waters*, 1985
    Working at a camp among the lakes of northern Minnesota, Dave finds the search for loot from a hijacked airplane drawing him into danger.
Gary Paulsen, *The Foxman*, 1977
    A town boy sent to live on a remote wilderness farm forms a friendship with an elderly, disfigured man who teaches him many things.
Ruth Riddell, *Ice Warrior*, 1992
    When his mother's remarriage moves him, Rob feels out of place until he discovers iceboating, which he hopes will draw him closer to his father.
Eleanor Wong Telemaque, *It's Crazy to Stay Chinese in Minnesota*, 1978
    A Chinese-American in Minnesota and her family tread a balance between the Far East and the Middle West.

| 1806 |

Jane Resh Thomas

Illustrator: Troy Howell

Fox in a Trap (New York: Ticknor, 1987)

Age range: Grades 3-5

Subject(s): Animals/Foxes; Hunting

Major character(s): Daniel, Child; Pete, Writer

Time period(s): Indeterminate

Locale(s): Michigan

What the book is about: Daniel looks forward to helping his Uncle Pete set traps for the foxes that have been plaguing the family farm, until the use of kittens for bait and the discovery of a severed fox paw makes him seriously question what he and his uncle are doing.

Where it's reviewed:
Booklist, April 1, 1987, page 1210
Kirkus Reviews, April 15, 1987, page 645
School Library Journal, June 1987, page 102

Other books by the author:
Wheels, 1986
Courage at Indian Deep, 1984
The Comeback Dog, 1981
Elizabeth Catches a Fish, 1977

Other books you might like:
E.J. Bird, *The Blizzard of 1896*, 1990
    Uncle Tim tells in his own words the amazing things that happened to people and animals during the powerful snowstorm in the West in 1896.
James I. Clark, *Shortcut to Peril*, 1980

Relates the adventures of a beaver trapper who survived for fifty-seven days after becoming lost in the wilderness of British Columbia.
Dennis Haseley, *Shadows*, 1991
    Jamie's lonely life with his aunt and uncle in rural West Virginia changes when Grandpa comes to visit and teaches him to make shadow pictures.
Juanita Havill, *It Always Happens to Leona*, 1989
    Feeling left out between her older sister and younger brother, Leona decides to run away with Uncle Rosco, a motorcycle racer.
Susan Price, *Ghost Song*, 1992
    When a magical shaman tries to claim his son Ambrosi, he finds himself tempted to renounce his mortality and learn his true identity.

| 1807 |

Ruth Thomas

The Runaways (New York: Harper, 1989)

Age range: Grades 5-7

Subject(s): Runaways

Major character(s): Julia, Preteen, Runaway; Nathan, Preteen, Runaway

Time period(s): 1940s

Locale(s): London, England

What the book is about: Having found an enormous sum of money and been threatened by their parents with punishment for not turning it in to the police, Julia and Nathan flee London for Brighton and the open countryside. The two misfits teach each other how to overcome their problems.

Where it's reviewed:
Horn Book, July/August 1989, page 484
School Library Journal, May 1989, page 112

Other books you might like:
Mavis Thorpe Clark, *The Sky Is Free*, 1974
    Two boys, each on his own quest, run away to a rugged opal mining town in the Australian outback.
E.L. Konigsburg, *From the Mixed-Up Files of Mrs. Basil E. Frankweiler*, 1967
    Claudia and her younger brother run away to the Metropolitan Museum of Art and set up housekeeping there, hiding from the guards at night.
Laurie Lawlor, *George on His Own*, 1993
    Addie's twelve year old brother, George, decides to runaway from home when he feels no one appreciates his musical talent.
Stephen Moser, *The Hitchhiking Vampire*, 1989
    Jamie and her brother pick-up a hitchhiker with a bag of money and soon find themselves helping to place a $12,000 bet in Las Vegas.
Adrian Stoutenburg, *Where to Now, Blue?*, 1978
    Blueberry's attempt to run away from her poor home in Minnesota with a six year old tagalong from the orphanage is not successful, but enlightening.

1808

Jean Thompson

Illustrator: Margot Apple

Don't Forget Michael (New York: Morrow, 1979)

Age range: Grades 2-4

Subject(s): Family Life; Privacy

Major character(s): Michael McBride, Child; Kevin McBride, Child; Grandma Cameron, Grandparent

Time period(s): 1970s

Locale(s): United States

What the book is about: Michael lives with mom and dad, five brothers and sisters, three grandparents, various aunts and uncles, twenty-five cousins, and a lot of pets. Sometimes he feels overlooked. When he gets left at a family picnic site, he hears silence for the first time in his live. Grandma Cameron and Captain Kid, the parrot, provide an evening's entertainment.

Where it's reviewed:
Booklist, October 15, 1979, page 358
Kirkus Reviews, September 15, 1979, page 1069

Other books by the author:
Brother of the Wolves, 1978

Other books you might like:
Elizabeth T. Billington, *Part-Time Boy*, 1980
　Jamie is a quiet boy in a noisy family who spends the summer with an understanding young woman.
Betty Horvath, *The Cheerful Quiet*, 1969
　Patrick searches for a quiet place away from his large, noisy family.
Johanna Hurwitz, *Nora and Mrs. Mind-Your-Own Business*, 1977
　Because they live in an apartment building, Nora and her brother have problems with privacy, where to play, and how to make friends.
Marjorie Weinman Sharmat, *Mr. Jameson and Mr. Phillips*, 1979
　Two friends go searching for a quiet place away from the city, but find it very hard to get away from it all.
Virginia Sicotte, *A Riot of Quiet*, 1969
　Sounds you won't hear if you twitch your nose or wiggle your ears, told in verse.

1809

Crystal Thrasher

End of a Dark Road (New York: Atheneum, 1982)

Age range: Grades 4-6

Subject(s): Child Abuse; Depression (Economic)

Major character(s): Seely, Teenager, Clerk; Russell, Abuse Victim, Teenager; Peedle, Handicapped (mentally retarded), Child

Time period(s): 1930s

Locale(s): Indiana

What the book is about: Seely sees her family through her father's death to the promise of a better future. She is concerned about Russell, whose stepfather abuses him, and

Peedle, a retarded boy. Seely works for Mr. and Mrs. Avery in their store in town.

Where it's reviewed:
Horn Book, October 1982, page 518
School Library Journal, September 1982, page 129

Other books by the author:
Taste of Daylight, 1984
Julie's Summer, 1982
Between Dark and Daylight, 1979
Dark Didn't Catch Me, 1975

Other books you might like:
Emily Crofford, *Stories from the Blue Road*, 1982
　Five episodes from the life of a family in Arkansas during the Depression.
George Ella Lyon, *Borrowed Children*, 1988
　12 year old Amanda has a holiday in Memphis, and excapes the Depression drudgery of her family's life in the mountains.
Patricia Pendergraft, *As Far as Mill Springs*, 1991
　Tired of foster homes, Robert begins a journey to find his mother in time to celebrate Christmas.
Ann Waldron, *Scaredy Cat*, 1978
　10 year old Jane, living during the Depression, is afraid of being kidnapped.
Linda Woolverton, *Running Before the Wind*, 1987
　13 year old Kelly finds running her only outlet for her feelings about her abusive father.

1810

Marcella Thum

Mystery at Crane's Landing (New York: Dodd, Mead, 1964)

Age range: Grades 6-9

Subject(s): Mystery and Detective Stories

Major character(s): Paula Jordan, Teenager; Lucy Crane, Teenager; Dave Rawlings, Friend

Time period(s): 1960s

Locale(s): New Madrid, Missouri

What the book is about: Paula goes to visit her school roommmate, Lucy, at Crane's Landing for the last half of spring break, to relax. When Lucy falls from a horse, Paula wonders if it is really an accident. Why does Lucy send Paula a desperate message about a hidden photograph? Full of fear, Paula sets out to solve the mystery at Crane Landing and runs into serious trouble herself.

Awards the book has won:
Edgar Allan Poe Award 1965

Other books you might like:
Bonnie Bryant, *Horse Shy*, 1988
　Three friends go on an overnight ride. They are having such a good time that a snobbish girl can't spoil the fun, until she causes an accident.
Lynn Hall, *Tin Can Tucker*, 1982
　A sixteen year old girl runs away from her foster home in Missouri, planning to make a name for herself on the rodeo circuit.
Marian Potter, *A Chance Wild Apple*, 1982

On a Missouri farm in the midst of the Depression, eleven year old Maureen has a bit of good luck when she finds a special wild apple tree.

Diane Walker, *Mother Wants a Horse*, 1978
When a riding accident grounds her for a year, a headstrong sixteen year old girl decides to give riding lessons.

Kate William, *Spring Fever*, 1987
The Wakefield twins spend spring break with relatives in a Kansas farming community.

1811

James Thurber

Illustrator: Louis Slobodkin

Many Moons (New York: Harcourt, Brace Jovanovich, 1943)

Age range: Grades 2-3

Subject(s): Princes and Princesses; Wishes; Wizards

Major character(s): Lenore, Royalty (princess)

Time period(s): Indeterminate Past

Locale(s): Fictional Country

What the book is about: Princess Lenore wants the moon and her royal father demands that the Royal Chamberlain, the Royal Wizard and the Royal Mathematician provide her with it. She is so distraught she will surely wither and die without it. Only the court jester is wise enough to give her the moon in a meaningful way.

Where it's reviewed:
Bookwatch, May 13, 1973, page 7
Times Literary Supplement, July 11, 1975, page 770
New Yorker, December 3, 1973, page 198

Awards the book has won:
Caldecott Medal 1971

Other books by the author:
The Thirteen Clocks, 1990
The Night the Ghost Got It, 1983
The Secret Life of Walter Mitty, 1983
The Great Quillow, 1944

Other books you might like:
Tomie De Paola, *The Prince of the Dolomites: An Old Italian Tale*, 1980
Because of Prince Pazzo's love for Princess Lucia of the Moon, the black peaks of the Dolomite mountains are changed to glimmering colors.

Sally Fisher, *The Tale of the Shining Princess*, 1980
An extraordinarily beautiful moon princess who is sent to Earth for punishment temporarily becomes the daughter of a poor bamboo cutter and his wife.

Judith Berry Griffin, *The Magic Mirrors*, 1971
With the help of her friends the sun and moon, an African princess overcomes the evil of the only one of her father's 53 wives who doesn't love her.

Daisaku Ikeda, *The Princess and the Moon*, 1991
Sophie, a bad-tempered and unhappy child, is taken to the moon by the Great Moon Rabbit and shown how pleasant and happy people can be.

Mercer Mayer, *East of the Sun and West of the Moon*, 1980

The Moon, Father Forest, Great Fish of the Sea, and North Wind help a maiden rescue her true love from a troll princess in a faraway kingdom.

1812

Nancy Tilly

Golden Girl (New York: Farrar Strauss and Giroux, 1985)

Age range: Grades 5-8

Subject(s): Friendship

Major character(s): Penny, Preteen

Time period(s): 1980s

Locale(s): South (small, coastal town)

What the book is about: Twelve year old Penny is envious of the wealth and families of her two best friends, not realizing they both believe she is luckier than they. Penny is worried about her friend, Tracey and her family problems, and lots of subplots, including shoplifting and a boat race, keep the action moving.

Where it's reviewed:
Center for Children's Books Bulletin, April 1986, page 160
School Library Journal, March 1986, page 172

Other books you might like:
Elizabeth Helfman, *On Being Sarah*, 1993
Even though life with cerebral palsy isn't easy for twelve year old Sarah, she manages with the help of a loving family and several new friends.

Jean Davies Okimoto, *Take a Chance, Gramps!*, 1990
Twelve year old Jane and her grandfather, both of whom have suffered losses, help each other reach out, make new friends, and change their lives.

Joan Price, *Truth Is a Bright Star*, 1982
Understanding and finally friendship develop between a twelve year oldHopi Indian boy and the fur trapper who buys him from Spanish soldiers in 1832.

Rachel Vail, *Wonder*, 1991
Everything changes for twelve year old Jessica when she goes to junior high and finds herself an outcast, ignored by all her former friends.

Betty Ren Wright, *The Summer of Mrs. MacGregor*, 1986
Torn between devotion for and jealousy of her invalid sister, Caroline's self-image begins to change when she meets Mrs. MacGregor.

1813

Estelle Titiev

Illustrator: Ray Cruz

How the Moolah Was Taught a Lesson and Other Tales from Russia (New York: Dial, 1976)

Age range: Grades 3-5

Subject(s): Folk Tales

Time period(s): Indeterminate Past

Locale(s): Russia

What the book is about: Four stories from the former Soviet Union; northern Siberia, the Caucasus and the Volga

Steppes, carry the morals of Russian culture—be kind, faithful and ingenious.

Where it's reviewed:
Booklist, April 1, 1976, page 1118
Hornbook, June 1976, page 286
Kirkus Reviews, April 15, 1976, page 480

Other books you might like:
A.N. Afanas'ev, *The Three Kingdoms*, 1985
A collection of traditional Russian tales including "Ivan the Fool," "The Fire-Bird Princess Vassilissa," and "The Wise Maid and the Seven Robbers."
Mirra Ginsburg, *The Night It Rained Pancakes*, 1980
Because he wants to keep the pot of gold he found, Ivan must outwit the lord of the manor who wants the gold for himself.
Cynthia Jameson, *The Clay Pot Boy*, 1973
Wanting a son, the old man and woman make a clay pot boy who comes to life and begins eating everything in sight.
Michael McCurdy, *The Devils Who Learned to Be Good*, 1987
An old Russian soldier receives a magical flour sack and a deck of playing cards which help him to remove some pesky devils from the Tsar's palace.
Dmitrii Nagishkin, *Folktales of the Amur*, 1980
A collection of thirty-one traditional tales from that far eastern part of Russia that lies along the banks of the Amur River.

1814

Eve Titus

Illustrator: Paul Galdone

Basil in Mexico (New York: McGraw-Hill, 1976)

Age range: Grades 3-5

Subject(s): Animals/Mice; Mystery and Detective Stories

Major character(s): Basil, Mouse; Dr. Dawson, Mouse

Time period(s): Indeterminate

Locale(s): Mexico

What the book is about: Where is the real *Mousa Lisa*? The original has been stolen from a Mexican museum and a forgery put in its place. The great detective, Basil, comes to the rescue of Dawson when he is mousenapped. The Pandero Street Irregulars, a group of seven mice, help Basil solve the mystery.

Where it's reviewed:
Booklist, July 1, 1976, page 1529
Kirkus Reviews, May 1, 1976, page 536
School Library Journal, September 1976, page 106

Other books by the author:
Anatole in Italy, 1973
Mr. Shaw's Shipshape Shoeshop, 1970
Basil of Baker Street, 1958
Anatole, 1956

Other books you might like:
Laura Jean Allen, *Where Is Freddy?*, 1986
Famous mouse detective Tweedy and his assistant Rollo investigate the case of wealthy Mrs. Twombly's missing grandson.
Doug Cushman, *Aunt Eater's Mystery Vacation*, 1992
A mystery loving anteater has a chance to solve several mysteries during her vacation at the Hotel Bathwater.
James Duffy, *The Christmas Gang: A May Gray Mystery*, 1989

While celebrating Christmas together, May's family asks her to tell them again about her first assignment as a police officer.
Mary Pope Osborne, *Spider Kane and the Mystery under the May-Apple*, 1992
With the help of a spider, a moth, and two ladybug friends, a butterfly tries to solve the mystery of a gossamer-winged butterfly that he loves.
Mary Stolz, *Deputy Shep*, 1991
Deputy Jack Shep, the laziest police dog to ever wear a badge, is called upon to investigate a wave of burglaries in the sleepy village of Canoville.

1815

Tobi Tobias

Illustrator: Carole Byard

Arthur Mitchell (New York: Crowell, 1975)

Age range: Grades 3-5

Subject(s): African Americans; Biography; Ballet

Major character(s): Arthur Mitchell, Dancer

Time period(s): 1930s; 1940s

Locale(s): New York, New York (Harlem)

What the book is about: Arthur always wanted to be a dancer. Black ballet dancers are very rare. After studying with the New York City Ballet Co., Mitchell grows up to become the director of the Dance Theatre of Harlem. This is the story of his childhood and young adulthood.

Where it's reviewed:
Booklist, July 1, 1975, page 1130
Kirkus Reviews, June 1, 1975, page 611
School Library Journal, September 1975, page 92

Other books by the author:
How Your Mother Met Your Father, 1978
Petey, 1978
Jane Wishing, 1977
Isamu Noguchi: Life of a Sculptor, 1974

Other books you might like:
Birdie Ballenberg, *Looking at Ballet*, 1989
Explores the world of ballet, discussing choreography, dancers, ballet companies, rehearsals, sets, costumes and famous ballets. (Non-Fiction)
Robert Maiorano, *Worlds Apart: The Autobiography of a Dancer from Brooklyn*, 1980
A soloist with the New York City Ballet recounts his rise from poverty and the streets of Brooklyn to success in the world of dance. (Non-Fiction)
Dindga McCannon, *Peaches*, 1974
A young black girl growing up in Harlem tells about her life with her family and her ambition to be an artist.
Ann Morris, *On Their Toes: A Russian Ballet School*, 1991
A behind-the-scenes look at the Kirov Ballet Academy, a training school for young dancers in the Soviet Union. (Non-Fiction)
Charnan Simon, *Evelyn Cisneros, Prima Ballerina*, 1990
Describes the life, training and accomplishments of the Mexican American dancer who is the prima ballerina for the San Francisco Ballet. (Non-Fiction)

1816

Stephanie S. Tolan

Grandpa and Me (New York: Scribner, 1978)

Age range: Grades 5-8

Subject(s): Old Age; Grandparents; Suicide

Major character(s): Kerry, Preteen

Time period(s): 1970s

Locale(s): United States

What the book is about: Kerry tells the story of her grandpa's aging and growing senile. He has lived with the family for many years. Because both of her parents work, Grandpa has been a big help for Kerry and her brother. Kerry tries to protect Grandpa from the possibility he might be sent away. Grandpa takes matters into his own hands.

Where it's reviewed:
Booklist, June 1, 1978, page 1558
Center for Children's Books Bulletin, July 1978, page 187
Kirkus Reviews, April 1, 1978, page 376

Other books by the author:
Good Courage, 1988
The Great Skinner Getaway, 1987
No Safe Harbors, 1981
Last of Eden, 1980

Other books you might like:
Margaret Oldroyd Hyde, *Meeting Death*, 1989
  Gives information on how to acceptance the concept of death and the treatment of death in various cultures. (Nonfiction)
Sandra McCuaig, *Blindfold*, 1990
  Benji and his blind older brother Joel share a very special bond until their suicide, leaving feelings of grief and guilt with their friend, Sally.
Lygia Bojunga Nunes, *My Friend, the Painter*, 1991
  A boy in Brazil becomes friends with the artist who lives upstairs and tries hard to understand when his friend commits suicide.
Kin Platt, *Chloris and the Freaks*, 1975
  Adjusting to her father's suicide and her mother's remarriage leads a young girl to astrology which she uses to sort out her family problems.
Judy Carole Rhodes, *The King Boy*, 1991
  Benjy's childhood is enriched by the times he spends with his grandfather. It is not until grandfather's death that he learns of an old family secret.

1817

Stephanie S. Tolan

The Great Skinner Strike (New York: Macmillan, 1983)

Age range: Grades 3-6

Subject(s): Labor Conditions

Major character(s): Jenny Skinner, Teenager (narrator); Mrs. Skinner, Librarian (PTA mother); Marcia Skinner, Child

Time period(s): 1980s

Locale(s): United States

What the book is about: When fourteen year old Jenny Skinner's mother goes on strike for better working conditions in the home, and as a result polarizes much of their community, Jenny, her three younger siblings, and their father come to some surprising conclusions. They form CHAOS, Children and Husbands Against Offensive Strikers. Then Jenny and her sister, Marcia, instigate a strike of their own. A funny story with a serious theme that will help kids understand labor/management relations.

Where it's reviewed:
Center for Children's Books Bulletin, May 1983, page 180
School Library Journal, May 1983, page 86

Awards the book has won:
Crabbery Honor 1984

Other books by the author:
The Great Skinner Homestead, 1988
The Great Skinner Getaway, 1987
The Great Skinner Enterprise, 1986
Grandpa and Me, 1978

Other books you might like:
James Lincoln Collier, *The Winchesters*, 1988
  Chris, a poor relation of the wealthy Winchesters, must choose between management and labor when his classmates' parents go on strike at the mill.
Barbara Corcoran, *Strike!*, 1983
  A teachers' strike upsets the life of a high school student who has good friends among the teachers and a father on the school board.
Athena V. Lord, *A Spirit to Ride the Whirlwind*, 1981
  Binnie, whose mother runs a boarding house in Lowell, Massachusetts, begins working in a textile mill and is caught up in the strike of women workers.
Doreen Rappaport, *Trouble at the Mines*, 1987
  Rosie and her family are caught up in the Arnot, Pennsylvania mining strike of 1899-1900, led by the union organizer, Mother Jones.
Ouida Sebestyen, *On Fire*, 1985
  Involved in a dangerous strike in a frontier town in 1911, Sammy finds his feelings changing toward the older brother he has always idolized.

1818

J.R.R. Tolkien, Author/Illustrator

The Hobbit (Boston: Houghton Mifflin)

Age range: Grades 5 and Up

Subject(s): Fantasy

Major character(s): Bilbo Baggins, Mythical Creature (hobbit); Gandalf, Wizard

Time period(s): Indeterminate

Locale(s): Fictional Country

What the book is about: Bilbo, a respectable, home-loving hobbit, is quite happy to stay at home until he meets the wizard, Gandalf, and is enticed/cajoled/encouraged into an adventure in which he becomes an "Expert Treasure Hunter" after encountering many monsters and dangers in search of gold. There are many editions of this classic, originally published in 1937, that every child should read or hear.

Where it's reviewed:
Center for Children's Books Bulletin, January 1985, page 96
School Library Journal, December 1984, page 86

Other books by the author:
The Silmarillion, 1977
The Fellowship of the Ring, 1965
Return of the King, 1965
The Two Towers, 1965

Other books you might like:
Lloyd Alexander, *The Remarkable Journey of Prince Jen*, 1991
  Bearing six unusual gifts, young Prince Jen embarks on a perilous quest and emerges triumphantly into manhood (with a little help from his friends.)
John Kendall, *Under Dragon's Wing*, 1984
  Prince Treon must find a way, with the help of a magical dragon ring and an ancient sorcery book, to rid the country of the evil Crimson Wizard.
Terry Jones, *Nicobobinus*, 1985
  Nicobobinus and his friend, Rosie, go in search of the land of Dragons and find more adventure than they bargained for.
John Masefield, *The Box of Delights*, 1984
  Kay finds himself involved in a fantastic adventure when he becomes guardian of the mysterious Box of Delights.
Tom McGowen, *The Magician's Apprentice*, 1987
  A young pickpocket becomes apprenticed to a magician who opens a new world for the boy, not only of magic and healing, but of kindness and adventure.

1819

John Rowe Townsend

Illustrator: Graham Humphreys

Intruder (New York: Lippincott, 1969)

Age range: Grades 6-9

Subject(s): Mystery and Detective Stories

Major character(s): Arnold Haithwaite, Teenager; Ernest Haithwaite, Foster Parent

Time period(s): 1960s

Locale(s): Skirlston, England

What the book is about: The life of Arnold, a sixteen year old English boy, begins to change when a stranger claiming to be a relative appears in the village. At times, the stranger behaves violently toward Arnold, then acts as if nothing strange has happened at all. When the health of Arnold's foster father, Ernest, begins to fail, the stranger hangs like a dark cloud and threatens Arnold's identity.

Where it's reviewed:
Booklist, June 1970, page 617
Kirkus Reviews, February 1, 1970, page 112
Center for Children's Books Bulletin, July 1970, page 186

Awards the book has won:
Boston Globe/Horn Book Award 1970
Edgar Allan Poe Award 1971

Other books by the author:
Dan Alone, 1983
The Islanders, 1981
Good Night, Prof, Dear, 1970
Good-bye to the Jungle, 1965

Other books you might like:
Jennifer Austin, *Ticket to Danger*, 1990

When Cassie arrives in London, she discovers that Alexadra has been kidnapped, and even Scotland Yard has no clue as to her whereabouts.
Harriet Graham, *The Chinese Puzzle*, 1987
  Two children set out to find their guardian who has disappeared along with his friend, and find themselves held captive by some dangerous characters.
Robert Newman, *The Case of the Threatened King*, 1982
  When Sara and her friend disappear, Andrew and Inspector Wyatt discover that the kidnappings are part of a plot against a visiting king.
Philip Pullman, *Shadow in the North*, 1988
  Sally and her companions try to solve the mystery surrounding the unexpected collapse of a shipping firm and its ties to a sinsiter company.
Robert Westall, *Stormsearch*, 1992
  Tim's discovery of an antique model ship leads him to an unsolved mystery involving a London heiress, a heartbroken drundard and a frantic miser.

1820

John Rowe Townsend

Illustrator: Mark Peppe

Tom Tiddler's Ground (New York: Lippincott, 1986)

Age range: Grades 4-7

Subject(s): Treasure; Canals; Mystery and Detective Stories

Major character(s): Vic, Preteen

Time period(s): Indeterminate Past

Locale(s): England

What the book is about: Amid the backwater canals of an English industrial town, Vic and his friends discover a half-sunken canal boat and set out to find the owner. The ancient boat has lain on a bit of land known as Tom Tiddler's Ground, though no one seems to know just why. The children explore the greasy, murky waters of English canals and the streets and lanes of Claypits. The well defined characters' adventure is full of suspense and humor, and the cross-generational sparring with Gran adds to the fun.

Where it's reviewed:
Horn Book, January/February 1987, page 57
School Library Journal, December 1986, page 110

Other books by the author:
The Persuading Stick, 1987
Rob's Place, 1987
Dan Alone, 1983
Trouble in the Jungle, 1969

Other books you might like:
Avi, *Windcatcher*, 1991
  Eleven year old Tony becomes excited about the rumors of sunken treasures while learning to sail along the Connecticut shore.
Jane Louise Curry, *What the Dickens!*, 1991
  Twins whose father runs a boat in Pennsylvania, learn of a bookseller's plan to steal Charles Dickens' newly finished novel while he tours the U.S.
Peni R. Griffin, *The Treasure Bird*, 1992

With clues from a talking parrot, Jessy and her stepbrother, Matt, discover the whereabouts of a hidden treaure in Uncle Matthew's old house in Texas.

Kathleen Karr, *Gideon and the Mummy Professor*, 1993
Gideon and his father travel down the Mississippi River in a second rate vaudeville act about life in Egypt, with a mummy that has a special secret.

Sarita Kendall, *The Bell Reef*, 1990
Anxious to recover the sunken treasure of a famous pirate ship, two teenagers enlist the help of a trained dolphin.

1821

Maryann Townsend

Pop's Secret (Reading, Massachusetts: Addison-Wesley, 1980)

Age range: Grades 1-2

Subject(s): Death; Grandparents

Major character(s): Mark, Child; Pop, Grandparent

Time period(s): 1980s

Locale(s): United States

What the book is about: With the aid of family photographs, Mark tells the story of his recently deceased grandfather's life, noting family resemblances and the common interests of three generations.

Where it's reviewed:
Kirkus Reviews, November 1, 1980, page 1394
School Library Journal, February 1981, page 60

Other books you might like:
Aliki, *The Two of Them*, 1979
Describes the relationship of a grandfather and his granddaughter from her birth to his death.

Elfie Donnelly, *So Long, Grandpa*, 1980
A Viennese boy describes his close relationship with his seventy-nine year old grandfather, and how he copes with the old man's illness and death.

Joan Fassler, *My Grandpa Died Today*, 1971
A little boy tries to understand and accept the death of his grandfather.

Ingrid Tomey, *Grandfather's Day*, 1992
A spirited young girl tries to help her grandfather overcome his sadness due to his wife's recent death.

Judith Vigna, *Saying Goodbye to Daddy*, 1991
Frightened, lonely and angry after her father is killed in a car accident, Clare is helped through the grieving process by her mother and grandmother.

1822

Henry Treece

Viking's Dawn (New York: Phillips, 1956)

Age range: Grades 4-6

Subject(s): Sea Stories; Shipwrecks; Vikings

Major character(s): Harald, Pirate (Viking); Thorkell Fairhair, Pirate (Viking captain); Ragmar, Pirate (Viking lieutenant)

Time period(s): 8th century (780)

Locale(s): Scandinavia

What the book is about: A thrilling saga of the Vikings, as they lived and talked, fought and died. They were ready to give their lives for a comrade, as they were prepared to take the life of an enemy in battle.

Other books by the author:
The Dream Time, 1968
The Last Viking, 1964
Man with a Sword, 1962
Men of the Hills, 1958

Other books you might like:
John Christopher, *New Found Land*, 1983
Encountering a crossing point between their world and another one on a different probability track, two boys face Indians, Vikings, and Aztecs.

Bruce Clements, *Prison Window, Jerusalem Blue*, 1977
In 831, an English brother and sister, members of a family of entertainers, are kidnapped in a raid and taken as slaves to the land of their captors.

Terry Jones, *The Saga of Erik the Viking*, 1983
A Viking warrior who lived hundreds of years ago sets sail with his men on the Golden Dragon to find the land where the sun goes at night.

Jill Pinkwater, *Cloud Horse*, 1983
Kate aquires understanding and love for the free-spirited cloud horses of Iceland from a Viking girl from the shores of Vinland.

Rosemary Sutcliff, *Blood Feud*, 1976
Sold into slavery in the 10th century, a young English man becomes involved in a blood feud which leads him to Constantinople and a new way of life.

1823

Elizabeth Borton de Trevino

I, Juan de Pareja (New York: Farrar, Straus and Giroux, 1965)

Age range: Grades 6 and Up

Subject(s): Artists and Art

Major character(s): Juan de Pareja, Slave; Diego Velazquez, Artist (painter), Historical Figure

Time period(s): 17th century

Locale(s): Spain

What the book is about: The black slave of the painter Velazquez wishes to become a painter and a free man. Through the help of Velazquez, Juanico shows one of his paintings to King Philip IV. He achieves his goal and becomes Juan de Pareja even though there is a Spanish law which forbids slaves to practice the arts.

Where it's reviewed:
Booklist, October 1965, page 163
Horn Book, October 1965, page 507
Kirkus Reviews, June 1965, page 579

Awards the book has won:
Newbery Medal 1966

Other books by the author:
Carpets of Flowers, 1955
Casilda of the Rising Moon, 1967
Nacar the White Deer, 1963

Turi's Papa, 1968

Other books you might like:
Johnny Alcorn, *Rembrandt's Beret or the Painter's Crown*, 1991
    Tiberius tells how paintings came alive one day in a museum. (Related picture book)
Scott O'Dell, *My Name Is Not Angelica*, 1989
    A young Senegalese girl is brought as a slave to the island of St. John and takes part in the slave revolt of 1733-34.
Milton Meltzer, *Underground Man*, 1990
    A courageous white man aids slaves escaping from Kentucky in pre-Civil War days.
Patricia Beatty, *Jayhawker*, 1991
    Teenage Lije Tulley becomes an abolitionist raider and goes underground as a spy.
Elizabeth Witheridge, *And What of You, Josephine Charlotte?*, 1969
    A young Maryland slave girl fears for her future when her mistress is to be married.

1824

Wallace Tripp, Author/Illustrator

Sir Toby Jingle's Beastly Journey (New York: Coward, 1976)

Age range: Grades 3-5

Subject(s): Castles; Magic; Knights and Knighthood

Major character(s): Sir Toby Jingle, Knight

Time period(s): Indeterminate Past (medieval times)

Locale(s): Fictional Country

What the book is about: Sir Toby's long record as an aggressive knight has led the animals to believe he has magic powers. They decide to work together and trap him. He keeps slipping away from them, completely unaware that the animals are after him. They end up trapped in Sir Toby's castle courtyard.

Where it's reviewed:
Booklist, June 15, 1976, page 1469
Kirkus Reviews, May 15, 1976, page 590
School Library Journal, September 1976, page 106

Other books by the author:
A Great Big Ugly Man Came Up and Tied His Horse to Me, 1973

Other books you might like:
Lee Grimes, *Fortune Cookie Cattle*, 1990
    Cap and Lisa encounter monsters, ghosts, and secret passageways when they try to help Duke Lothrio free his castle from an evil spell.
Margaret Hodges, *Don Quixote and Sancho Panza*, 1992
    An abridged version of the adventures of an eccentric country gentleman and his faithful companion who set out to right wrongs and punish evil.
Ali Mitgutsch, *A Knight's Book*, 1991
    Young Wolflieb relates the medieval adventures of his poor but brave master, Sir Frank von Fidelstein, participating in a tournament and a duel.
Donald J. Sobol, *Greta the Strong*, 1970
    Through a number of trials, Greta proves that she is the only person qualified to replace the long-dead Arthur.

Nicholas Wilde, *Sir Bertie and the Wyvern*, 1982
    Sir Bertie the Bold accompanies his clever son Jop on a quest for the fierce Wyvern when he needs a dragon to pose for the family coat of arms.

1825

Edwin Tunis, Author/Illustrator

The Tavern at the Ferry (New York: Crowell, 1973)

Age range: Grades 4-6

Subject(s): Revolutionary War; Quakers

Time period(s): 1770s (1776)

Locale(s): New Jersey, American Colonies

What the book is about: A New Jersey ferry and tavern belong to a Quaker family during Colonial times. The events leading up to the Battle of Trenton are described, as is the battle itself. The story helps us look at the changes in the family and the property itself during this important time in American history.

Where it's reviewed:
Booklist, November 15, 1973, page 335
Kirkus Reviews, September 1, 1973, page 978
Hornbook, December 1973, page 600

Other books by the author:
Shaw's Fortune, 1966
Colonial Craftsmen, 1965
Colonial Living, 1957
Oars, Sails and Steam, 1952

Other books you might like:
Avi, *The Fighting Ground*, 1984
    Thirteen year old Jonathon goes off to fight in the Revolutionary War and discovers the real war is being fought within himself.
Patricia Edwards Clyne, *The Corduroy Road*, 1973
    A young patriot's plans to escape from his uncle are complicated by Redcoats swarming through the area and his discovery of a critically ill American.
Dorothea Jensen, *The Riddle of Penncroft Farm*, 1989
    When Lars moves to a farm near Valley Forge, he encounters the ghost of an 18th century ancestor, who recounts his adventures during the Revolution.
Beverly Haskell Lee, *The Secret of Van Rink's Cellar*, 1979
    While searching for a ghost that haunts the house in which their mother is a maid, Sarah and Stephen become involved in the Revolutionary War.
Ann Rinaldi, *A Ride into Morning*, 1991
    When unrest spreads a Morristown camp, a young woman cleverly hides her horse from soldiers who have need for it.

1826

John R. Tunis

Highpockets (New York: Morrow, 1948)

Age range: Grades 4-6

Subject(s): Automobile Accidents; Sports/Baseball

Major character(s): Cecil "Highpockets" McDade, Sports Figure (baseball player); Dean Kennedy, Collector (stamp collector)

Time period(s): 1940s

Locale(s): New York, New York (Brooklyn)

What the book is about: Highpockets is not a team player, thinking only of himself. When the fans from his home town give him a car, he accidentally runs over a boy the first time he drives it. During many anxious hours in and out of the boy's hospital room, Highpockets learns a lot about life and reaching out to others.

Other books by the author:
His Enemy, His Friend, 1967
Go, Team, Go!, 1954
Young Razzle, 1954
The Kid Comes Back, 1946

Other books you might like:
Susan E. Kirby, *Shadow Boy*, 1991
    After Arnie suffers a closed-head wound in a car accident, adjustment and recovery are difficult for him, his sister, Cozy, and the whole family.
Joan Phipson, *Hit and Run*, 1985
    Roland's hit and run accident in a borrowed car sends him fleeing into the countryside where he struggles for both survial and self-respect.
Marc Talbert, *Dead Birds Singing*, 1985
    After his mother is killed and his sister is badly injured in a car accident, Matt faces life with a new family and a deep feeling of anger.
Cynthia Voigt, *Izzy, Willy-Nilly*, 1986
    A car accident causes Izzy to lose one leg and face the need to start building a new life as an amputee.
Laurence Yep, *Liar, Liar*, 1983
    A teenage boy trying to prove his friend's death in a car crash was no accident, finds himself stalked by a businessman for a similar fate.

【1827】

John R. Tunis

The Kid Comes Back (New York: Morrow, 1946)

Age range: Grades 4-7

Subject(s): Sports/Baseball; Veterans; World War II

Major character(s): Bobby "Spike" Russell, Sports Figure (baseball player), Manager (Sports); Roy Tucker, Sports Figure (baseball player), Veteran (war hero)

Time period(s): 1940s

Locale(s): New York, New York (Brooklyn)

What the book is about: On baseball teams before 1950, it was not unusual for the team's manager to also play one of the positions on the field. Spike is both the Dodger's manager and shortstop. This is the story of the returning vets from WWII, as they try to return to their real lives after the war.

Where it's reviewed:
New York Times Book Review, September 11, 1977, page 61

Other books by the author:
His Friend, His Enemy, 1967
Silence over Dunkirque, 1962

Schoolboy Johnson, 1958
Buddy and the Old Pro, 1955

Other books you might like:
Matt Christopher, *Catcher with a Glass Arm*, 1964
    A baseball player struggles to overcome his fear of a pitched ball, improve his throwing, and somehow redeem himself in the eyes of his teammates.
Zane Grey, *The Shortstop*, 1992
    Chase relies on his talent and inner resources as he struggles to succeed as a professional baseball player.
Mary Downing Hahn, *December Stillness*, 1988
    Kelly tries to befriend a disturbed Vietnam War veteran who spends his days in her library, though he makes it clear he wants to be left alone.
Shannon Kennedy, *Daddy, Please Tell Me What's Wrong*, 1988
    Jenny tries to understand the strange behavior of her father, a Vietnam War veteran.
Phyllis Anderson Wood, *Song of the Shaggy Canary*, 1974
    A divorced woman and a young veteran hurt by a broken engagement want friendship without commitment, but find themselves committed to each other.

【1828】

John R. Tunis

The Kid from Tomkinsville (New York: Harcourt, 1940)

Age range: Grades 5-8

Subject(s): Sports/Baseball

Major character(s): Roy Tucker, Sports Figure; Gus Spencer, Manager

Time period(s): 1930s

Locale(s): New York, New York (Brooklyn)

What the book is about: The Dodgers lead the Giants 4-3; giants at bat, tying run on third, winning run on second. Crack! It's a sure home run. Can Tucker spear the ball, save the game and clinch the pennant? If he smashes into the fence he has a chance. Will the kid from Tomkinsville, Connecticut ever shake the nickname "Bad News Tucker?"

Where it's reviewed:
Booklist, August 1987, page 1753
Book World, June 14, 1987, page 8

Other books by the author:
Keystone Kids, 1987
World Series, 1987
The Kid Comes Back, 1946
Rookie of the Year, 1944

Other books you might like:
Matt Christopher, *Pressure Play*, 1993
    Travis would like to split his time between baseball and other hobbies, but he receives anonymous threats warning him to concentrate on baseball.
Zane Grey, *The Shortstop*, 1992
    Chase relies on his talent and inner resources as he struggles to succeed as a professional baseball player.
Dean Hughes, *All Together Now*, 1991
    The Dodgers make their way to the regional championship, up against the toughest team in California.
Jackson Volney Scholz, *Batter Up*, 1946

Marty Shane, a powerful hitter and part owner of a major league baseball club, is determined to use his talent, not his connections, to play pro ball.

Alfred Slote, *Make-Believe Ball Player*, 1989
  Although he's not very good at baseball, Henry uses his imagination to become a better ball player.

1829

Brinton Turkle

Adventures of Obadiah (New York: Viking, 1972)

Age range: Grades 2-4

Subject(s): Quakers; Animals/Sheep

Major character(s): Obadiah Starbuck, Child; Rachel Starbuck, Child; Eliza Gardner, Teacher

Time period(s): Indeterminate

Locale(s): Nantucket, Massachusetts

What the book is about: No one in Obadiah's strict Quaker family appreciates his vivid imagination. For every letter of the alphabet he has an absurd adventure to relate. Because he is always making up stories, no one in the family believes Obadiah's adventure at the sheep shearing squantum, but a neighbor verifies his story and Obadiah is suddenly the center of attention.

Where it's reviewed:
Booklist, November 15, 1972, page 303
Hornbook, February 1973, page 39
Kirkus Reviews, August 15, 1972, page 938

Awards the book has won:
Christopher Award 1973

Other books by the author:
Rachel and Obadiah, 1978
Deep in the Forest, 1976
Thy Friend, Obadiah, 1969
Obadiah the Bold, 1965

Other books you might like:
Mary Blount Christian, *Goody Sherman's Pig*, 1991
  In Massachusetts in 1636, Goody Sherman begins a legal battle over her pig that winds up dividing the legislative department in two.
F.N. Monjo, *Zenas and the Shaving Mill*, 1976
  A young Quaker boy relates how he eludes the ships of both the British and the rebels while sailing to Nantucket with supplies.
Carol Partridge Ochs, *When I'm Alone*, 1992
  A little girl tries to explain that it was an assortment of animals who made the mess for which she is blamed.
Ruth Eitzen, *The White Feather*, 1987
  A Quaker family living in Ohio in the early 1800s makes peace with a Shawnee Indian tribe during a very troubled time.
Jane Yolen, *Letting Swift River Go*, 1992
  Sally experiences changing times in America as she lives through the drowning of the Swift River towns in Massachusetts to form the Quabbin Reservoir.

1830

Brinton Turkle

Rachel and Obadiah (New York: Dutton, 1978)

Age range: Grades 3-4

Subject(s): Quakers; Ships

Major character(s): Rachel Starbuck, Child; Obadiah Starbuck, Child

Time period(s): Indeterminate Past

Locale(s): Nantucket, Massachusetts

What the book is about: Obadiah's friend received a silver coin for letting a captain's wife know when his ship sailed into port. Rachel and Obadiah compete to get a coin when the next ship comes into port. The winner gets two coins when the other gets distracted by a berry patch.

Where it's reviewed:
Booklist, November 15, 1978, page 551
Kirkus Reviews, December 15, 1978, page 1354
School Library Journal, December 1978, page 47

Other books by the author:
Do Not Open, 1981
Deep in the Forest, 1976
Adventures of Obadiah, 1972
Thy Friend, Obadiah, 1969

Other books you might like:
Patricia Daniels, *Moby Dick*, 1982
  Melville's classic tale of the seaman who joins the crew of the whaling ship Pequod, captained by the fanatical Ahab, abridged for young readers.
Adele DeLeeuw, *Horseshoe Harry and the Whale*, 1976
  A cowboy eager to see the sea is shanghaied onto a whaling ship whose captain is only interested in playing the basoon.
Marguerite Henry, *Benjamin West and His Cat Grimalkin*, 1947
  Even though his Quaker faith looks upon painting as a waste of time, Benjamin West longs to be an artist.
Rudyard Kipling, *The Crab that Played with the Sea*, 1982
  Relates how the crab came to live both in the sea and on the land and to lose its hard shell once a year.
F.N. Monjo, *Zenas and the Shaving Mill*, 1976
  A young Quaker boy relates how he eludes the ships of both the British and the rebels while sailing to Nantucket with supplies.

1831

Ann Turnbull

Maroo of the Winter Caves (New York: Clarion, 1984)

Age range: Grades 4-7

Subject(s): Man, Prehistoric; Survival

Major character(s): Maroo, Prehistoric Human

Time period(s): Indeterminate Past

Locale(s): Earth

What the book is about: Maroo, a girl of the late Ice Age, must take charge after her father is killed and lead her little brother, mother and aged grandmother to the safety of the winter camp before the first blizzards strike. A survival story just as exciting as those set in the present day.

Where it's reviewed:
Booklist, January 15, 1985, page 725
Horn Book, January 1985, page 56

Other books by the author:
The Tapestry Cat, 1992
The Sand Horse, 1989
The Queen Cat, 1989
The Wolf King, 1975

Other books you might like:
William Bence, *People of the Bison*, 1966
  A young picture maker is found by less advanced people, some of whom accept him, but others fear his artistic talent and belittle his lack of prowess.
Hal George Evarts, *Jay-Jay and the Peking Monster*, 1978
  A southern California boy finds a box of bones that may be the remains of prehistoric Peking Man, which have been missing from a museum since WWII.
Ross E. Hutchins, *Tonka, the Cave Boy*, 1973
  Recounts the adventures of a boy living 8000 years ago in an Alabama cave as he hunts, copes with the death of his father, and tames a wolf cub.
William O. Steele, *The Magic Amulet*, 1979
  Left to die by his prehistoric family band, a wounded young hunter must find and join a new group if he is to survive.
Henry Treece, *The Dream Time*, 1968
  A boy finds that his gifts for drawing and shaping from clay result in his being ostrasized from his people.

| 1832 |

Ann Warren Turner

Grasshopper Summer (New York: Macmillan, 1989)

Age range: Grades 4-6

Subject(s): Frontier and Pioneer Life

Major character(s): Sam White, Preteen; William "Billy" White, Preteen; Ellen White, Parent (mother)

Time period(s): 1870s (1874)

Locale(s): Dakota Territory

What the book is about: Ten year old Billy is teaching Harold, an ex-slave, to read. Harold sees Billy's pa's restlessness and knows the family is moving before the children do. They move from Kentucky to the southern Dakota Territory, where harsh conditions and a plague of hungry grasshoppers threaten their chances of survival. The Whites are one of the few families to make it through.

Where it's reviewed:
Booklist, June 15, 1989, page 1829
Horn Book, September 1989, page 624

Other books by the author:
Katie's Trunk, 1992
Nettie's Trip South, 1987
Dakota Dugout, 1985
A Hunter Comes Home, 1980

Other books you might like:
Patricia Beatty, *Jonathon Down Under*, 1982

Jonathan accompanies his luckless father to the gold fields of Australia, where he learns to be his own man in rough-and-tumble 19th century Victoria.
William Heuman, *Buffalo Soldier*, 1969
  An ex-Confederate soldier goes west where he meets and becomes friends with Trooper Joel Tibbs, the son of a former slave.
Annabel Johnson, *Torrie*, 1960
  A story of westward migration from St. Louis to California on a wagon train and the process of a young girl's growing up.
Laurie Lawlor, *Addie's Dakota Winter*, 1989
  In her new pioneer home of Dakota, Addie finds an unlikely friend and, stranded alone during a blizzard, learns about courage.
Nancy Veglahn, *Follow the Golden Goose*, 1970
  In 1876, a phony gold rush in Dakota Territory influences the lives of a fourteen year old boy and his father who have just come west.

| 1833 |

Ann Warren Turner

Rosemary's Witch (New York: HarperCollins, 1991)

Age range: Grades 4-7

Subject(s): Fantasy; Witches and Witchcraft

Major character(s): Rosemary, Preteen; Mathilda, Witch

Time period(s): 1980s

Locale(s): United States (small Northeastern town)

What the book is about: After moving into an old house in a small New England town, nine year old Rosemary discovers that the nearby woods conceal Mathilda, a 150 year old witch who once lived in the house, and is trying to use her magic to take it back. The point-of-view shifts from Rosemary to Mathilda, so we see both sides of the story. However, readers will identity with Rosemary and cheer her on in her battle to keep her home.

Where it's reviewed:
Booklist, April 1, 1991, page 1569
School Library Journal, May 1991, page 95

Other books by the author:
Grasshopper Summer, 1989
Time of the Bison, 1987
Third Girl From the Left, 1986
A Hunter Comes Home, 1980

Other books you might like:
Ruth Chew, *Earthstar Magic*, 1979
  Ellen and Ben meet a friendly witch who reveals the magic power of the earthstar to them.
Roald Dahl, *The Witches*, 1983
  A boy and his grandmother foil a witches' plot to turn all of the children of the world into mice.
Claudia Paley, *Benjamin the True*, 1969
  The witch Benjamin finds in a neighbor's cellar isn't good or bad, just powerful. But one day she is not strong enough and must ask Benjamin for help.
Marian T. Place, *The First Astrowitches*, 1984
  Two witches stow away on a space mission in an effort to contact a witches' space exploring expedition that has not been heard from for a long time.
Theresa Tomlinson, *Summer Witches*, 1989

Two friends convert an old air raid shelter into a den and help an old woman overcome her painful memories of WWII.

Mark Twain

The Adventures of Tom Sawyer (Connecticut: American Pub. Co., 1876)

Age range: Grades 5 and Up

Subject(s): Adventure and Adventurers; Friendship

Major character(s): Tom Sawyer, Hero, Preteen; Polly, Relative (aunt); Becky Thatcher, Friend

Time period(s): 19th century

Locale(s): Hannibal, Missouri

What the book is about: The classic hero, Tom Sawyer, suffers through school, plots mischief with his pal, Huckleberry Finn, cons Ben into whitewashing a fence, shows off in Sunday school, meets Becky Thatcher, skulks through a graveyard and hunts for buried treasure. Many, many editions available.

Other books by the author:
A Boy's Adventure, 1928

The Celebrated Jumping Frog of Calaveras County, 1865
The Gilded Age: A Tale of Today, 1873
Connecticut Yankee in King Arthur's Court, 1889

Other books you might like:
Clyde Robert Bulla, *Down the Mississippi*, 1954
    A Minnesota farm boy gets a much longed for opportunity to go down the Mississippi on a raft as the cook's helper.
Kristi Holl, *Hidden in the Fog*, 1989
    Financial problems endanger the future of a Mississippi steamboat tourist ride run by Nikki's family. She learns there's more to life than worrying.
F.N. Monjo, *Willie Jasper's Golden Eagle*, 1976
    An account of the 1870 race down the Mississippi between the *Natchez* and the *Robert E. Lee*, told by a boy aboard the *Natchez*.
A.L. Singer, *Davy Crockett and the King of the River*, 1991
    Davy and his trusted friend, Georgie Russel, are in for a wild ride down the mighty Mississippi in a race with Mike Fink, King of the River.
Gertrude Chandler Warner, *The Haunted Cabin Mystery*, 1991
    The Alden children travel on a steamboat to visit a friend in his cabin near Hannibal Missouri, and investigate mysterious activities near the house.

U

1835

Yoshiko Uchida

The Best Bad Thing (New York: Atheneum, 1983)

Age range: Grades 4-6

Subject(s): Japanese Americans; Poverty; Family Life

Major character(s): Rinko, Preteen; Mrs. Hata, Widow(er)

Time period(s): 1930s

Locale(s): California

What the book is about: The details of Japanese-American family life in 1930s California come to life. Rinko goes to help a family friend, "Aunt" Hata, who has been recently widowed and is struggling with her cucumber farm. The prejudice Rinko and all Japanese-Americans faced in prewar America is touched upon. Sequel to *A Jar of Dreams*.

Where it's reviewed:
Horn Book, October 1983, page 578
School Library Journal, November 1983, page 83

Other books by the author:
The Happiest Ending, 1985
A Jar of Dreams, 1981
Hisako's Mysteries, 1969
In-Between Miya, 1967

Other books you might like:
Elizabeth Coatsworth, *The Cat Who Went to Heaven*, 1958
  Watched by his cat, a Japanese artist paints a picture of the Buddha receiving homage from animals. He dares to include the cat, contrary to custom.
Daniel S. Davis, *Behind Barbed Wire: The Imprisonment of Japanese-Americans During World War II*, 1982
  This is the history of anti-Asian feelings behind the incarceration of 120,000 Japanese and Japanese Americans. (nonfiction)
Thomas Hoobler, *Aloha Means Come Back*, 1991
  Laura and her mother join her Navy father in 1941 in the expectation that the US and Japan will go to war.
Katherine Paterson, *The Master Puppeteer*, 1976
  As Jiro works to learn the art of the puppeteer in 18th century Japan, he travels among the savage bands of night rovers in search of his parents.
Yoko Kawashima Watkins, *So Far From the Bamboo Grove*, 1986
  Yoko and his sister Ko escape from Korea to Japan at the end of WWII. Their courage and ingenuity summon respect for the resources of human spirit.

1836

Yoshiko Uchida

A Jar of Dreams (New York: Atheneum, 1981)

Age range: Grades 4-6

Subject(s): Japanese Americans; Prejudice; Race Relations

Major character(s): Rinko Tsujimura, Preteen; Waka, Relative (aunt); Tami Nukaga, Friend

Time period(s): 1930s (1935)

Locale(s): Berkeley, California

What the book is about: A young girl grows up in a closely knit Japanese-American family in California during the 1930s, a time of great prejudice against the Japanese. When Aunt Waka comes to visit from Japan, she helps both Rinko and her younger brother Joji discover their own strengths.

Where it's reviewed:
Booklist, October 15, 1981, page 312
Kirkus, November 1, 1981, page 1345
School Library Journal, August 1981, page 72

Other books by the author:
The Invisible Thread, 1991
The Best Bad Thing, 1983
Journey to Topaz, 1971
The Dancing Kettle, 1949

Other books you might like:
Margaret Scrogin Chang, *In the Eye of War*, 1990
  During the final days of the Japanese occupation of China, Shao-Shao celebrates his 10th birthday and befriends the daughter of a traitor.
Thomas Hoobler, *Aloha Means Come Back*, 1991
  Laura and her mother join her Navy father in Hawaii in 1941, where suspicion against the Japanese American residents runs high.
Ken Mochizuki, *Baseball Saved Us*, 1993
  During his forced stay in a WWII internment camp, a Japanese-American boy learns to play baseball. His abilities help him when the war is over.
Barbara Murphy, *Home Free*, 1970
  During summer vacation in South Carolina, a white boy from New York and his black friend learn firsthand about the violence of racial prejudice.
R. Conrad Stein, *The Nisei Regiment*, 1985
  History of the 442nd Regiment which consisted of Japanese-American men and received more medals for bravery than any other American unit in WWII.

1837

Yoshiko Uchida

Illustrator: Donald Carrick

Journey to Topaz (New York: Scribner, 1971)

Age range: Grades 4-6

Subject(s): Deserts; Japanese Americans; World War II

Major character(s): Yuki Chan, Preteen; Kenichi "Ken" Chan, Child; Emiko "Emi" Kurihara, Friend

Time period(s): 1940s

Locale(s): San Francisco, California; Topaz, Utah

What the book is about: After the Pearl Harbor attack, a Japanese-American girl and her family are forced to go to an enemy alien's camp in Utah. This is the story of one family and what happened to them in America during WWII.

Where it's reviewed:
Booklist, January 1, 1972, page 395
Center for Children's Books Bulletin, April 1979, page 146
School Library Journal, January 1979, page 58

Other books by the author:
The Happiest Ending, 1985
Desert Exile, 1982
A Jar of Dreams, 1981
Journey Home, 1978

Other books you might like:
Shiela Garrigue, The Eternal Spring of Mr. Ito, 1985
    The fate of a bonsai tree is decided by a girl and an old Japanese Canadian gardener who resists being imprisoned in an internment camp.
Angela Johnson, Toning the Sweep: A Novel, 1993
    On a visit to her grandmother, who is dying of cancer, Emmie hears many stories about the past and her family history.
Marcia Savin, The Moon Bridge, 1992
    The friendship between Mitzi Ruthie is changed when WWII begins and Mitzi and her family are forced to go into an internment camp.
Aranka Siegal, Grace in the Wilderness: After the Liberation, 1945-1948, 1985
    Liberated from a German concentration camp at the end of WWII, but haunted by the memory of her ordeal, Piri starts a strange new life.
Theodore Taylor, The Cay, 1969
    When the freighter on which they are traveling is torpedoed by a German submarine during WWII, a blind boy and a black man are stranded on an island.

1838

Yoshiko Uchida

Illustrator: Charles Robinson

The Rooster Who Understood Japanese (New York: Scribner, 1976)

Age range: Grades 3-4

Subject(s): Japanese Americans; Animals/Birds

Major character(s): Mrs. Kitamura, Neighbor, Child-Care Giver; Mr. Lincoln, Rooster; Miyo, Child

Time period(s): Indeterminate

Locale(s): United States

What the book is about: Mr. Lincoln's loud early moring cfrowing causes a neighbor to compalin to the police, who regretfully order the rooster's owner, Mrs. Kitamura, to get rid of him. Miyo, the your girl Mrs. Kitamura watches after school, writes an ad in her school newspaper and findsa the rooster a new home. Nice portrayal of Japanese-American families.

Where it's reviewed:
Booklist, September 15, 1976, page 182
Kirkus Reviews, August 15, 1976, page 905
School Library Journal, November 1976, page 52

Other books by the author:
Journey Home, 1978
The Birthday Visitor, 1975
Journey to Topaz, 1971

Other books you might like:
Victor G. Ambrus, The Little Cockerel, 1968
    A poor old woman's pet fowl cleverly recovers a gold coin unjustly taken from his mistress by the Turkish Sultan.
Henry Chafetz, Chanticleer: The Story of a Proud Rooster, 1968
    Chanticleer, the vain rooster, believes the sun cannot rise without his call, until he learns his place in the universe from the nightingale's song.
Mirra Ginsburg, The Magic Stove, 1983
    An old man, his wife, and their rooster enjoy the delicious pies their magic stove bakes for them, until a greedy king comes to visit.
Bill Peet, Cock-a-Doodle Dudley, 1990
    Dudley the rooster's ability to make the sun rise with his crowing is questioned by a spiteful goose, whose malice almost destroys the popular rooster
Ursel Scheffler, Stop Your Crowing, Kasimir!, 1986
    Katy's neighbors appeal to the authorities to silence her extremely loud rooster, but the final result is very different from what they had in mind.

V

1839

Hannelore Valencak

A Tangled Web (New York: Morrow, 1978)

Age range: Grades 5-6

Subject(s): Dishonesty; Bullies

Major character(s): Annie, Preteen; Josepha, Bully (gossip)

Time period(s): 1970s

Locale(s): Austria

What the book is about: Annie tells the bully Josepha that she can work a magic spell, a fantasy she sw ears is true, but then becomes afraid that Josepha will tell everyone that Anni e is a witch.

Where it's reviewed:
Booklist, December 15, 1978, page 691
Kirkus Reviews, October 1, 1978, page 1072
School Library Journal, October 1978, page 151

Other books you might like:
Avi, *The History of Helpless Harry*, 1980
  When his parents go away, leaving him with young woman, Harry's adventures begin and they include lies, attempted robbery and a possible murder.
Lucy Cullyford Babbitt, *Where the Truth Lies: A Novel*, 1993
  Three young people from different backgrounds, set out on a mission to end the war that has been perpetuated by their disparate beliefs.
Barbara Ware Holmes, *Charlotte Cheetham, Master of Disaster*, 1985
  Charlotte, in her desperation to be included by a group of girls in her class, tells the most outlandish tale ever.
Willo Davis Roberts, *The Magic Book*, 1986
  When Alex and his friends try the spells in an old book, things don't happen quite the way they thought.
Thomas Rockwell, *How to Get Fabulously Rich*, 1990
  After Billy wins $410,000, his friends claim that he owes them a share for helping him play, creating a tangle of lies, memory and money.

1840

Chris Van Allsburg, Author/Illustrator

Jumanji (Boston: Houghton Mifflin, 1981)

Age range: Grades 1-8

Subject(s): Play; Games; Fantasy

Major character(s): Peter, Child; Judy, Child

Time period(s): 1980s

Locale(s): United States

What the book is about: Peter and Judy are bored at home alone and take a walk in the park. They find a board game called Jumanji: A Jungle Adventure, and bring it home to play. The board is filled with jungle creatures and scenes, and as the children play, the scenes come alive in their living room. There is a lion on the piano, monkeys in the kitchen, and a snake on the mantle. Stunning black and white illustrations bring the reader right into this multiple award winning fantasy.

Where it's reviewed:
Horn Book, August 1981, page 416
School Library Journal, May 1981, page 60

Awards the book has won:
Caldecott Medal 1982
Boston Globe/Horn Book Award - Illustration Honor 1981

Other books by the author:
The Wretched Stone, 1991
The Polar Express, 1985
Ben's Dream, 1982
The Garden of Abdul Gasazi, 1980

Other books you might like:
John Bibee, *Bicycle Hills*, 1989
  Secret games in a new amusement park lead the young cyclists into an adventure of magic and a battle against evil.
Hal Higdon, *The Electronic Olympics*, 1971
  Opposed to mechanized sports, a young photographer and his friend try to foil the computerized Olympics in which the athletes are programmed.
Alexander Key, *The Magic Meadow*, 1975
  Five crippled children find a way to escape to a strange new place.
Gillian Rubinstein, *Space Demons*, 1988
  Andrew becomes obsessed with a strange new computer game, which has the power to zap him and his friends into a dangerous world of space warriors.
Pamela Stearns, *Into the Painted Bear Lair*, 1976
  Entering another world through a toy store, Gregory joins Sir Rosemary and a Bear on a journey involving princesses, magic spells and hidden passages.

1841

Chris Van Allsburg

Just a Dream (Boston: Houghton Mifflin, 1990)

Age range: Grades 2-4

Subject(s): Pollution; Dreams and Nightmares; Environmental Problems

Major character(s): Walter, Child

Time period(s): 1990s

Locale(s): United States

What the book is about: Walter is totally ignorant about the environment. He is careless and scornful of recycling and planting trees. Walter has two dreams, one of the earth destroyed and filthy, the other of the planet renewed. He begins to understand the importance of taking care of the earth.

Where it's reviewed:
Publisher's Weekly, September 28, 1990, page 99
School Library Journal, December 1990, page 88

Other books by the author:
The Mysteries of Harris Burdick, 1984
The Wreck of the Zephyr, 1983
Ben's Dream, 1982
The Garden of Abdul Gasazi, 1979

Other books you might like:
Graeme Base, *The Sign of the Seahorse*, 1992
    The inhabitants of a coral reef are threatened when a shady real estate deal floods their home with poisonous waste.
Joanne Fink, *Jack, the Seal, and the Sea*, 1988
    Jack sails and fishes, ignoring the pollution in the water, until he finds an ailing seal and receives a message from the sea itself.
Jo Polseno, *This Hawk Belongs to Me*, 1976
    An 11 year old boy in New York finds a dying baby kestral in the marshes of Long Island and cares for it, so he can return it to its own environment.
Jan Wahl, *The Very Peculiar Tunnel*, 1972
    Passengers on a zoo train find a tunnel leads them to a jungle where they can observe animals in their natural environment.
Brian Wildsmith, *Professor Noah's Spaceship*, 1980
    As the forest begins to change, the animals fly away in Professor Noah's amazing spaceship.

1842

Chris Van Allsburg

The Mysteries of Harris Burdick (Boston: Houghton Mifflin, 1984)

Age range: Grades 1-9

Subject(s): Mystery and Detective Stories

Major character(s): Peter Wenders, Publisher; Harris Burdick, Writer, Artist

Time period(s): 1980s

Locale(s): United States

What the book is about: One of the most unusual books from Chris Van Allsburg, who has a well deserved reputation for the unique. Fourteen unrelated pictures are presented with the introduction saying they were left with a publisher by the artist, who promised to return with the stories, but never did. The possibilites for using the book with any age are unlimited.

Where it's reviewed:
Horn Book, September/October 1984, page 585
School Library Journal, October 1984, page 152

Other books by the author:
Just a Dream, 1990
The Stranger, 1986
The Polar Express, 1985
The Garden of Abdul Gasazi, 1979

Other books you might like:
Wolfgang Ecke, *The Stolen Paintings*, 1979
    Contains seventeen mysteries for the reader to solve with explanations and solutions in the back of the book.
Thomas Locker, *The Young Artist*, 1989
    An artist commanded to paint the king's courtiers struggles with his sense of integrity which demands honest portraiture.
David Macauley, *Black and White*, 1990
    Four brief stories about parents, trains, and cows, or is it really all one story?
Cynthia Rylant, *An Angel for Solomon Singer*, 1992
    A lonely New York City resident finds companionship and good cheer at the West Way Cafe where dreams come true.
Max Velthuijs, *Crocodile's Masterpiece*, 1991
    Croc is inspired to even greater heights by elephant's enthusiasm for his paintings.

1843

Chris Van Allsburg, Author/Illustrator

The Polar Express (Boston: Houghton Mifflin, 1985)

Age range: Grades 1-6

Subject(s): Christmas; Santa Claus

Time period(s): Indeterminate

Locale(s): United States

What the book is about: A magical ride, filled with Van Allsburg's stunning paintings, takes a boy to the North Pole to receive a special gift from Santa Claus. Santa is a true mythic image, and the North Pole is not one of commercial cuteness, but rather drawn from the deep tales of folklore. The ending message for all ages - "Though I've grown old, the bell still rings for me as it does for all who believe."

Where it's reviewed:
Horn Book, November/December 1985, page 723
School Library Journal, October 1985, page 164

Other books by the author:
The Widow's Broom, 1992
The Wretched Stone, 1991
The Stranger, 1986
Jumanji, 1981

Other books you might like:
Arthur Dorros, *Abuela*, 1991
    While riding on a bus with her grandmother, a little girl imagines that they are carried up into the sky and fly over the sights of New York City.
Ann Jonas, *Round Trip*, 1983
    A trip to the city and back again is accomplished by reading this book forward for the daytime trip to the city, then backwards on the way home.

William Joyce, *A Day with Wilbur Robinson*, 1990
  Wilbur's best friend joins in the search for Grandfather Robinson's missing false teeth and meets one wacky relative after another.
Michael Elsohn Ross, *Become a Bird and Fly*, 1992
  Using his imagination, Nicky changes into a bird and takes flight.
David Wiesner, *Tuesday*, 1991
  Frogs rise on their lily pads, float through the air and explore the nearby houses while their inhabitants sleep.

1844

Chris Van Allsburg

The Stranger (Boston: Houghton Mifflin, 1986)

Age range: Grades 2-4

Subject(s): Seasons; Farm Life

Major character(s): Farmer Bailey, Farmer

Time period(s): Indeterminate

Locale(s): United States

What the book is about: A picture book that tells why, one year, autumn did not come to the Bailey farm. Farmer Bailey's truck runs into a stranger, who then stays on at the farm to help with the harvest. When leaves begin to turn everywhere but on the farm, the stranger remembers his mission blows on a leaf and disappears, and autumn comes as usual. Another from Van Allsburg that can be used with all ages, although the youngest may miss the clues to the stranger's identity.

Where it's reviewed:
Horn Book, November/December 1986, page 741
School Library Journal, November 1986, page 84

Other books by the author:
Just a Dream, 1990
Two Bad Ants, 1988
Jumanji, 1981
The Garden of Abdul Gasazi, 1979

Other books you might like:
Lily Toy Hong, *Two of Everything*, 1993
  A poor old Chinese farmer finds a magic pot that duplicates whatever is placed inside it, but his efforts to become wealthy lead to complications.
Carlos Llerena, *The Fair at Kanta: A Story From Peru*, 1975
  A young Peruvian boy living in the Andes with his grandmother takes his first harvest to market with the aid of a magic flute.
Mercer Mayer, *Appelard and Liverwurst*, 1978
  Aided by a wayward rhinoceros, Appelard and his motley farm animals finally have a successful harvest.
Sharon Peters, *Here Comes Jack Frost*, 1981
  When the wind blows on a cold night, Jack Frost goes to work.
David L. Weitzman, *Thrashin' Time: Harvest Days in the Dakotas*, 1991
  A young boy describes his life on the family farm in North Dakota in 1912, particularly the arrival of a new steam-powered threshing machine.

1845

Jean Van Leeuwen

Illustrator: Gail Owens

Benjy the Football Hero (New York: Dial, 1985)

Age range: Grades 3-5

Subject(s): Humor; Sports/Football

Major character(s): Clayton "The Ace" Case, Sports Figure (football player), 4th Grader; Benjy, Sports Figure (football player), 4th Grader; Kelly "Killer" Kramer, Sports Figure (football player), 4th Grader

Time period(s): 1980s

Locale(s): New York

What the book is about: Benjy discovers that brains work better than brawn when it comes to beating the other fourth grade class's football team.

Where it's reviewed:
Booklist, September 1, 1985, page 72
School Library Journal, May 1985, page 111

Other books by the author:
The Great Rescue Operation, 1982
Tales of Oliver Pig, 1979
Too Hot for Ice Cream, 1974
I was a 98-Pound Duckling, 1972

Other books you might like:
Judy Blume, *Tales of a Fourth Grade Nothing*, 1972
  Peter finds his demanding two year old brother an ever increasing problem.
Joan Davenport Carris, *The Greatest Idea Ever*, 1990
  Fourth grade is a time of turmoil for Gus, whose ideas get him into trouble as he tries to train a dog, organizes an art show, and battles his enemy.
Thomas J. Dygard, *Winning Kicker*, 1978
  Relates what happens when a girl place-kicker joins a champion high school football team.
William Heuman, *Horace Higby and the Gentle Fullback*, 1970
  Horace Higby comes to the rescue of his school's football team as the "secret weapon" on the offense.
Robert Newton Peck, *Soup's Hoop*, 1990
  Soups plan to help the basketball team to victory includes constructing an instrument called a spitzentootle and snaring the evil Janice Riker.

1846

Jean Van Leeuwen

Dear Mom, You're Ruining My Life (New York: Dial, 1989)

Age range: Grades 4-7

Subject(s): Mothers and Daughters; Gifted Children; Humor

Major character(s): Samantha Slayton, Preteen (gifted); Brian Finnegan, Preteen, Classmate; Dr. Jerome Slayton, Scientist (mathematician), Researcher

Time period(s): 1980s

Locale(s): United States

What the book is about: Eleven year old Samantha is definitely on the brink of adolescence. She is coping with being moved to a program for gifted students, being taller than every boy in her dance class, her a crush on a classmate, and her two perfectly delightful parents who cause her constant embarrassment in public. A family story told with love and good humor.

Where it's reviewed:
Booklist, May 1, 1989, page 1555
School Library Journal, June 1989, page 109

Other books by the author:
The Great Summer Camp Conspiracy, 1992
Benjy in Business, 1983
Seems Like This Road Goes on Forever, 1979
A Time of Growing, 1967

Other books you might like:
Eve Bunting, *Face at the Edge of the World*, 1985
 Haunted by the suicide of a gifted young black writer who was his best friend, Jed tries to find out the reasons behind the tragedy.
Margery Evernden, *The Dream Keeper*, 1985
 Her parents' separation leads a thirteen year old to discover the story her great-grandmother's immigration to America from a Jewish shtetl in Poland.
Patricia Hermes, *I Hate Being Gifted*, 1990
 KT's friendship with her two best friends is threatened when she is selected for the gifted and talented program at her school.
Barbara Morgenroth, *Tramps Like Us*, 1979
 Feeling tied down by her school and hometown, a gifted girl seeks her own identity through a relationship with a musically dedicated boy.
Jacqueline Woodson, *Maizon at Blue Hill*, 1992
 After winning a scholarship to a school for academically gifted students, Maizon finds herself one of only five black students there.

1847

Jean Van Leeuwen

Illustrator: Steven Kellogg

The Great Christmas Kidnapping Caper (New York: Dial, 1975)

Age range: Grades 3-5

Subject(s): Department Stores; Christmas; Animals/Mice

Major character(s): Marvin the Magnificent, Mouse; Fats, Mouse; Raymond, Mouse, Scholar

Time period(s): 1970s

Locale(s): New York, New York

What the book is about: Marvin lives in a dollhouse in Macy's toy department. He invites his pals Fats and Raymond to join him. They become fond of the department's Santa Claus and become detectives when the old gentleman disappears.

Where it's reviewed:
Booklist, September 15, 1975, page 169
Kirkus Reviews, July 15, 1975, page 778
Center for Children's Books Bulletin, November 1975, page 54

Other books by the author:
The Great Summer Camp Catastrophe, 1992
Going West, 1992
Benjy and the Power of Zingies, 1982
The Great Rescue Operation, 1982

Other books you might like:
Mary Blount Christian, *Sebastian (Super Sleuth) and the Santa Claus Caper*, 1984
 Sebastian goes undercover as Santa Clause to unravel a mystery at a department store.
Marguerite DeAngeli, *The Lion in the Box*, 1975
 Retells the story of a special Christmas for a poor family in New York City at the turn of the century.
Shirley Rousseau Murphy, *The Song of the Christmas Mouse*, 1970
 Rick's efforts at capturing a beautiful wild mouse for a pet seem constantly thwarted by his willful cousin who has come to stay for Christmas.
Ethel Pochocki, *The Attic Mice*, 1990
 A family of mice prepare for the Christmas holiday.
Eve Titus, *Basil in Mexico*, 1976
 Basil, mouse and master detective, seeking the truth behind the disappearance of the Mousa Lisa, must solve the mystery of his missing companion.

1848

Jean Van Leeuwen

Illustrator: Ann Schweninger

More Tales of Amanda the Pig (New York: Dial, 1985)

Age range: Grades 1-3

Subject(s): Animals/Pigs

Major character(s): Amanda, Pig

Time period(s): Indeterminate

Locale(s): United States

What the book is about: These five tales of Amanda Pig involve a game of pretend that deals with the turmoil of visiting relatives, noisy cousins who come to visit and boisterous sibling rivalry in a warm and happy family. Good, easy to read dialogue.

Where it's reviewed:
Horn Book, March/April 1986, page 199
School Library Journal, December 1985, page 110

Other books by the author:
Amanda Pig on Her Own, 1991
Dear Mom, You're Ruining My Life, 1989
Oliver, Amanda and Grandmother Pig, 1987
Benjy and the Power of Zingies, 1982

Other books you might like:
Teresa Noel Celsi, *The Fourth Little Pig*, 1990
 The sister of the three little pigs tries to persuade her brothers, who have been hermits since an episode with a wolf, to overcome fears.
Ida Luttrell, *Milo's Toothache*, 1992
 Milo Pig plans to visit the dentist about his toothache, but his friends overreact and make the outing into a big problem.
Karen Nagel, *Two Crazy Pigs*, 1992

Two pigs drive a farmer and his wife crazy with their silliness and pranks. When they move to a new farm, they are missed by all when they leave.

Mary Rayner, *Garth Pig Steals the Show*, 1993
  During a musical concert for the mayor, the family Pig Players discover that their new member, a lady sousaphonist, likes pigs just a little too much.

David Vozar, *Yo, Hungry Wolf!: A Nursery Rap*, 1993
  A retelling in rap verse of "The Three Little Pigs," "Little Red Riding Hood," and "The Boy Who Cried Wolf."

1849

Elizabeth Van Steenwyk

Illustrator: Rondi Anderson

Rivals on Ice (Chicago: Whitman, 1979)

Age range: Grades 4-6

Subject(s): Sports/Ice Skating

Major character(s): Tucker Cameron, Sports Figure (skater); Sara Mars, Sports Figure (skater)

Time period(s): 1970s

Locale(s): South Bay

What the book is about: Tucker is an ice skater. She loves figure skating. She is the best at the South Bay Skating Club and dreams of winning the regional competition. Maybe her mom will notice her again. Sara has everything. She has money, talent, looks, and a mother who is deeply involved in her daughter's activities. Sara is the reigning Midwest Novice Champion.

Where it's reviewed:
Center for Children's Books Bulletin, December 1979, page 831
School Library Journal, December 1979, page 100

Other books by the author:
The Ghost in the Gym, 1983
Dance with a Stranger, 1982
Mystery at Beach Bay, 1980
Fly Like an Eagle, 1979

Other books you might like:
Peter Carver, *Bury the Dead*, 1986
  As East Berliner Erika is preparing for an important track competition, several incidents suggest her family may have had Nazi ties.
Barbara Douglass, *Sizzle Wheels*, 1981
  Tori wants her gang to win the street skating competition so she can one-up her sister.
Elizabeth Levy, *Cold as Ice*, 1988
  Working at the Dome during a pre-Olympic skating exhibition, Kelly meets two skaters whose lives become threatened by a string of accidents.
Barbara J. Mumma, *Breaking the Ice*, 1988
  Clair Glass auditions for the Lake Placid Skating School and discovers what it really takes to be a champion.
Noel Streatfeild, *Skating Shoes*, 1983
  A girl goes ice-skating to strengthen her legs, befriends the orphaned daughter of a great skater, and finds encouragement to become a great champion.

1850

Hilda Van Stockum

The Borrowed House (New York: Farrar, 1975)

Age range: Grades 5-8

Subject(s): World War II

Major character(s): Janna, Preteen

Time period(s): 1940s

Locale(s): Amsterdam, Netherlands; Germany

What the book is about: Janna misses her parents who are on a tour with a theatrical group. She becomes a Hitler Youth and is reluctant to join her parents in Amsterdam. A German officer falls in love with Janna's mother. She observes the cruelty of others and becomes acquainted with a boy in the Dutch underground.

Where it's reviewed:
Booklist, September 15, 1975, page 169
Center for Children's Books Bulletin, November 1975, page 55
Kirkus Reviews, June 1, 1975, page 606

Other books by the author:
Mogo's Flute, 1966
The Winged Watchman, 1962

Other books you might like:
T. Degans, *The Visit*, 1982
  At a family reunion in Berlin, Kate relives some of the events described in the diary of a dead aunt who was a member of the Hitler Youth movement.
Evert Hartman, *War Without Friends*, 1982
  Arnold, a member of the Hitler Youth, feels trapped between his father's support of the Nazi party and his classmates' hostile opposition.
Mara Kay, *In Face of Danger*, 1976
  While living with a German family, Ann discovers that Fran, whose son is a member of the Hitler Youth, is hiding two Jewish girls in the attic.
Hans Peter Richter, *I Was There*, 1972
  A young German boy narrates his experiences in the Hitler Youth movement during the early years of the Third Reich.
R. Conrad Stein, *Hitler Youth*, 1985
  Describes the origin and growth of the Nazi Youth organization known as Hitler Jugend, its rigorous training and testing of German girls and boys and

1851

Dorothy Van Woerkom

Becky and the Bear (New York: Putnam, 1975)

Age range: Grades 2-3

Subject(s): Animals/Bears

Major character(s): Becky, Child

Time period(s): 18th century

Locale(s): Maine, American Colonies

What the book is about: Becky's father and brother are off hunting, Grandmother is gone tending an injured neighbor, and Becky has to deal with a bear. She runs away from the bear to the cabin. The bear keeps scratching, but Becky has a plan to keep herself safe.

Where it's reviewed:
Booklist, September 1, 1975, page 46
Hornbook, October 1975, page 457
School Library Journal, September 1975, page 93

Other books by the author:
Alexandra the Rock-Eater, 1978
Friends of Abu Ali and More, 1978
Abu Ali: Three Tales of the Middle East, 1976
The Queen Who Couldn't Bake Gingerbread, 1975

Other books you might like:
Clyde Robert Bulla, *Charlie's House*, 1983
    A poor, friendless English boy, shipped to Colonial America as an indentured servant, runs away from his cruel master.
Rosalys Haskell Hall, *The Bright and Shining Breadboard*, 1969
    A young man in Colonial America sets out to find a bride who can show a clean breadboard.
Mary Holmes, *Year of the Sevens*, 1992
    In 1777, Polly and her family face great danger after they move to the Kentucky frontier.
Doreen Rappaport, *The Boston Coffee Party*, 1988
    During the Revolutionary War, two young sisters help a group of Boston women get coffee from a greedy merchant.
Cyndy Szekeres, *Long Ago*, 1977
    Depicts everyday activities and special occasions in Colonial America.

1852

Jules Verne

Around the World in Eighty Days (1873)

Age range: Grades 5 and Up

Subject(s): Adventure and Adventurers

Major character(s): Phileas Fogg, Traveller; Jean Passepartout, Servant, Entertainer

Time period(s): 1870s (1872)

Locale(s): Earth

What the book is about: Wealthy, independent Phileas Fogg makes a bet that he can circle the globe in eighty days, arriving back in London on Saturday, December 2, 1872 (at 8:45 pm - he is always on time). He and his manservant, Passepartout, travel by train, steamship, carriage, yacht, elephant and sled in this classic adventure. Many editions available, including controlled vocabulary (Scott Foresman, 1952)

Where it's reviewed:
School Library Journal, August 1980, page 72
Publishers Weekly, June 6, 1980, page 82
Kliatt, Fall 1983, page 18

Other books by the author:
A Journey to the Center of the Earth, 1864
The Mysterious Island, 1874
From Earth to the Moon, 1865
20,000 Leagues Under the Sea, 1870

Other books you might like:
William Pene Du Bois, *The Twenty-One Balloons*, 1947
    William Sherman sets off in a balloon across the Pacific, survives a volcanic eruption and is finally picked up in the Atlantic, but with a big secret
Sonia Levitin, *A Season for Unicorns*, 1986

Disillusioned by her father's infidelity, Inky abandons her family to seek courage and honesty in a household operating a hot air balloon launch.
Hugh Lofting, *The Voyages of Dr. Doolittle*, 1922
    The story of the good doctor who learned to talk to the animals and had marvelous and exciting adventures.
Thom. Roberts, *The Atlantic Free Balloon Race*, 1986
    Ned joins his eccentric relative, Mr. T. Gray and a pet kangaroo in a balloon race from New York to London.
Kathleen Thomas, *Goats Are Better than Worms*, 1984
    When Jake the goat wins a balloon ride in a drawing, Ellen accompanies him on what turns out to be a magical trip to a fantastic island.

1853

Jules Verne

Twenty Thousand Leagues Under the Sea (New York: World Publishing, 1946)

Age range: Grades 6-9

Subject(s): Adventure and Adventurers; Sea Stories; Submarines

Major character(s): Captain Nemo, Sea Captain

Time period(s): 1960s

Locale(s): Submarine

What the book is about: The adventures of a French scientist and his companions who travel the seven seas in the mid 19th century as prisoners in Captain Nemo's mysterious electric submarine, which anticipates many of the discoveries and scientific achievements of the 20th century. Originally published in 1870.

Where it's reviewed:
Booklist, February 1, 1977, page 838
Library Journal, November 1, 1976, page 2283
Publisher's Weekly, January 3, 1977, page 69

Other books by the author:
From the Earth to the Moon, 1865
The Mysterious Island, 1874
A Journey to the Center of the Earth, 1864
Around the World in Eighty Days, 1873

Other books you might like:
Avi, *The True Confessions of Charlotte Doyle*, 1990
    As the lone "young lady" on a translantic voyage in 1832, Charlotte learns that the captain is murderous and the crew rebellious.
Jonathan Gathorne-Hardy, *Operation Peeg*, 1972
    Jarred loose by an explosion, an island occupied by a young girl and two companions floats to sea led by two British sailors still fighting WWII.
James A. Houston, *Ice Swords: An Undersea Adventure*, 1985
    Two boys, spending a summer at an Arctic research station to study whale migration, learn deep sea diving and encounter dangerous adventure.
Marguerite Murray, *The Sea Bears*, 1984
    Jeanine, spending the summer on the Nova Scotia coast while her father works on a secret project, believes someone is helping enemy submarines.
Robert M. Quackenbush, *Who Said There's No Man on the Moon?*, 1985

A biography of Jules Verne, the 19th century author whose science fiction novels predicted space travel, the submarine, and other modern achievements.

1854

Anne Vestly

Illustrator: Leonard Kessler

Aurora and Socrates (New York: Crowell, 1977)

Age range: Grades 3-5

Subject(s): Babysitters; Family Life; Working Mothers

Major character(s): Aurora, Child; Socrates, Child

Time period(s): 1970s

Locale(s): Norway

What the book is about: Dad is working on his doctoral dissertation. He stays home and takes care of the house and kids while mom works as a lawyer. Since Dad needs lots of time to study, friends come in to take care of Aurora and Socrates. Separation anxiety, peer jealousy, losing a friend, and arguing parents are all part of the family picture.

Where it's reviewed:
Center for Children's Books Bulletin, March 1978, page 120
Hornbook, February 1978, page 50
Kirkus Reviews, July 1, 1977, page 670

Other books by the author:
Hello Aurora, 1974

Other books you might like:
Betsy Byars, *Wanted.Mud Blossom*, 1991
  Convinced that Mud is responsible for the disappearance of the school hamster, Junior is determined Mud should be tried for his crime.
Vera Cleaver, *Sweetly Sings the Donkey*, 1985
  When Lily and her family move to Florida, it falls to her to keep her family together and start a new life.
Johanna Hurwitz, *Aldo Peanut Butter*, 1992
  Peanut and Butter, the two dogs Aldo gets for his eleventh birthday, create chaos while his parents are out of town.
Joan Lowery Nixon, *Maggie, Too*, 1985
  A defensive girl comes to understand her father, a Hollywood director planning to remarry, after she is exiled for the summer to her grandma's house.
Stephanie S. Tolan, *The Great Skinner Getaway*, 1987
  Jennifer recounts the adventures of the Skinner family as they set off across the United States in a motor home.

1855

Phillip Viereck

The Summer I Was Lost (New York: Harper, 1965)

Age range: Grades 5-7

Subject(s): Survival

Major character(s): Paul Griffin, Preteen, Camper (wilderness survivor); Hank Tracy, Counselor (camp)

Time period(s): 1960s

Locale(s): Rhode Island; New Hampshire

What the book is about: A boy survives a harrowing ordeal when he is lost on a mountain. A panicked camp counselor runs for his own life when a thunderstorm strikes the mountain in New Hampshire. Without food or compass how can Paul survive and find his way out?

Where it's reviewed:
Kirkus Reviews, February 15, 1965, page 179
Library Journal, March 15, 1965, page 1563
Book Shelf, March 15, 1965, page 495

Other books by the author:
Sue's Secondhand Horse, 1973
Terror on the Mountains, 1972

Other books you might like:
Peter Zachary Cohen, *Morena*, 1970
  A Boy Scout lost in the hills and an abandoned old mare depend on each other for survival during a snow storm and the freezing weather that follows.
Jean Craighead George, *My Side of the Mountain*, 1988
  A young boy relates his adventures during the year he spends living alone in the Catskill Mountains.
David Mathieson, *Trial by Wilderness*, 1985
  A girl survives a plane crash off the coast of British Columbia, and then faces survival in the wilderness.
Hilary H. Milton, *Mayday! Mayday!*, 1979
  After their plane crashes, two young people must find their way down a mountain in order to bring help to the survivors.
Elaine Macmann Willoughby, *Mystery of the Island Fires*, 1991
  Annie, Wallace and Dave investigate the mystery of who is setting fires on the New Hampshire island where they are spending their summer vacation.

1856

Judith Viorst

Illustrator: Ray Cruz

Alexander, Who Used to Be Rich Last Sunday (New York: Atheneum, 1978)

Age range: Grades 1-2

Subject(s): Money

Major character(s): Anthony, Child; Nicholas, Child; Alexander, Child

Time period(s): 1970s

Locale(s): United States

What the book is about: Alexander has a dollar to spend, and every penny seems to go for foolishness. Yet, he realizes there are many things a dollar can do.

Where it's reviewed:
Booklist, April 1, 1978, page 1262
Hornbook, June 1978, page 269
Kirkus Reviews, April 1978, page 369

Other books by the author:
Earrings!, 1990
The Good-Bye Book, 1988
Rosie and Michael, 1974
I'll Fix Anthony, 1969

Other books you might like:
Stan Berenstain, *The Berenstain Bears' Trouble with Money*, 1983
  Brother and Sister Bear learn some important lessons about earning and spending money.
Johanna Hurwitz, *Aldo Ice Cream*, 1981
  Aldo discovers the pleasures of doing volunteer work to help the older citizens of the community and the satisfactions of earning money on his own.
Patrick E. King, *Down on the Funny Farm*, 1986
  A farmer thinks he is getting a bargain when he buys a farm for a dollar, until he finds all the animals mixed up about what they are supposed to do.
Melanie Martin, *Morris, the Millionaire Mouse*, 1989
  Overjoyed when he wins the million dollar raffle, Morris Mouse decides to quit his job and buy everything he's ever wanted.
Louis Phillips, *The Million Dollar Potato*, 1991
  A eight year old boy inherits a million dollars on the condition that he spend the same amount in twenty-four hours.

1857

Jackie Vivelo

Beagle in Trouble: 12 Solve It Yourself Mysteries (New York: Putnam, 1986)

Age range: Grades 4-6

Subject(s): Mystery and Detective Stories; Literature

Major character(s): Ellen, Detective; Charlie "Beagle" Beaghley, Detective

Time period(s): 1980s

Locale(s): United States

What the book is about: Solve the mysteries with Ellen and Charlie as they take on "Unmasking the Vandals" and "The Big Pig Problem."

Where it's reviewed:
Booklist, November 1, 1986, page 415

Other books by the author:
Super Sleuth and the Bare Bones, 1988
A Trick of the Light, 1987
Super Sleuth: 12 Solve It Yourself Mysteries, 1985
We Wait in the Darkness, 1974

Other books you might like:
Fred D'Ignazio, *Chip Mitchell: The Case of the Chocolate Covered Bugs*, 1985
  The reader is asked to supply the answers to ten more cases which are solved by young computer whiz, Chip Mitchell.
Jamie Gilson, *Soccer Circus*, 1993
  While spending the night at a motel during a soccer tournament, Hobie Hanson and his friends help a mystery buff solve a fictitious case.
Robert M. Quackenbush, *Investigator Ketchem's Crime Book*, 1984
  The reader matches wits with Investigator Ketchem by trying to solve the twenty mysteries before she does.
Donald J. Sobol, *Encyclopedia Brown and the Case of the Disgusting Sneakers*, 1990
  America's Sherlock Holmes in sneakers continues his war on crime in ten more cases, the solutions to which are found in the back of the book.

Falcon Travis, *Super Sleuth: Mini-Mysteries for You to Solve*, 1985
  Describes 43 crime puzzles, which the reader tries to solve with the aid of clues, codes, alibis, and other evidence.

1858

Ilse-Margret Vogel

Farewell, Aunt Isabell (New York: Harper and Row, 1979)

Age range: Grades 4-5

Subject(s): Mental Illness; Twins

Major character(s): Erika, Twin; Inge, Twin; Isabell, Relative (aunt), Mentally Ill Person

Time period(s): 1970s

Locale(s): Germany

What the book is about: Erika and Inge are twins whose Aunt Isabell is being brought home from a year in the hospital. Aunt Isabell does some rather bizarre things. Mother, Grandmother, and Nurse Amelia think that all Aunt Isabell needs is to be kept happy. When Magda, the curious neighbor girl surprises her, Aunt Isabell attacks her.

Where it's reviewed:
Center for Children's Books Bulletin, February 1980, page 122
School Library Journal, September 1979, page 149
Kirkus Reviews, October 15, 1979, page 1211

Other books by the author:
Tikhon, 1984
My Summer Brother, 1981
Dodo Every Day, 1977
My Twin Sister, Erika, 1976

Other books you might like:
Carole S. Adler, *The Shell Lady's Daughter*, 1983
  When Kelly is sent to Florida after her mother's nervous breakdown, she learns the meaning of love and support.
Ella Thorp Ellis, *Celebrate the Morning*, 1972
  A teen's struggle with poverty and her mother's schizophrenia is eased by an old man, a social worker and two school friends.
Barbara Morgenroth, *Demons At My Door*, 1980
  A young girl drives herself into a nervous breakdown by striving to live up to other's standards.
Phyllis Reynolds Naylor, *The Keeper*, 1986
  Junior high student Nick must face the fact that his father is plunging into serious mental illness.
Peter Silsbee, *The Big Way Out*, 1984
  Paul tries to pull his family back together after it is split apart over his father's inevitable return to a mental hospital.

1859

Ilse-Margret Vogel, Author/Illustrator

My Summer Brother (New York: Harper and Row, 1981)

Age range: Grades 3-5

Subject(s): Friendship; Death; Family Life

Major character(s): Erika, Twin; Inge, Twin; Dieter, Student

Time period(s): Indeterminate

Locale(s): Germany

What the book is about: Six weeks after Erika dies, nine year old Inge meets Dieter. He becomes her "big brother" and a wonderful friendship begins. Inge finds her mother crying not only for Erika but about Papa's preoccupation with work. Inge is hurt in a hotel fire, worried that her friend, Dieter, is attracted to her mother.

Where it's reviewed:
Kirkus Reviews, June 15, 1981, page 741
School Library Journal, May 1981, page 70

Other books by the author:
Tikhon, 1984
Farewell, Aunt Isabell, 1979
My Twin Sister, Erika, 1976
The Rainbow Dress and Other Tollush Tales, 1975

Other books you might like:
Bruce Brooks, *Everywhere*, 1990
　　Afraid that his grandfather will die after suffering a heart attack, a boy agrees to a ritual called "soul-switching" to save his life.
Eth Clifford, *The Remembering Box*, 1985
　　Joshua's weekly visits to grandma on the Sabbath help him understand his family's Jewish traditions and the love which helps him cope with her death.
Mavis Jukes, *Blackberries in the Dark*, 1985
　　Austin visits his grandmother the summer after his grandfather dies and together, they cope with the loss.
Karin Lorentzen, *Stine Stankelben*, 1982
　　Nine year old Di, busy taking care of a litter of new puppies, must also face the knowledge that her little brother will not live much longer.
Ruth Wallace-Brodeur, *The Kenton Year*, 1980
　　After the death of her father, Mandy and her mother move to Vermont, where they finally learn to let go of the past and begin a new life.

1860

Cynthia Voigt

Building Blocks (New York: Atheneum, 1984)

Age range: Grades 4-6

Subject(s): Fathers and Sons; Child Abuse; Space and Time

Major character(s): Brann Connell, Preteen, Time Traveller

Time period(s): 1970s (1974); 1930s

Locale(s): United States

What the book is about: Brann is able to travel back to his father's childhood with his dad's set of building blocks. He sees his father's brutal experiences and returns to the present with a new respect for the man his father became.

Where it's reviewed:
Center for Children's Books Bulletin, April 1984, page 158
School Library Journal, May 1984, page 85

Other books by the author:
David and Jonathan, 1992
The Callender Papers, 1983
Dicey's Song, 1982
Homecoming, 1981

Other books you might like:
Annabel Johnson, *A Golden Touch*, 1963
　　A thirteen year old boy travels West to join his father, a poker dealer who has been thrown out of town.
Harold Keith, *The Obstinate Land*, 1977
　　A fourteen year old boy must assume the responsibility for his family after his father's death.
Alfred Slote, *Matt Gargan's Boy*, 1975
　　A baseball player's son is uncomfortable when a girl tries out for his baseball team and his divorced mother becomes interested in the girl's father.
Marya Smith, *Winter-Broken*, 1990
　　A timid twelve year old, abused by an alcoholic father, finds friendship with a horse named Wildfire.
Linda Woolverton, *Running Before the Wind*, 1987
　　Kelly finds running her only outlet for her confused feelings about her abusive father.

1861

Cynthia Voigt

Callender Papers (New York: Atheneum, 1983)

Age range: Grades 5-8

Subject(s): Mystery and Detective Stories; Orphans

Major character(s): Jean Wainwright, Orphan; Oliver "Mac" McWilliams, Teenager; Daniel Thiel, Artist

Time period(s): 1890s (1894)

Locale(s): Marlborough, Massachusetts (Berkshire Mountains)

What the book is about: In 19th century Massachusetts, orphan Jean is employed to sort out the family papers of a reclusive artist. She becomes curious about the mysterious, long-ago death of his wife and the subsequent disappearance of their young child. As she continues through papers and letters, Jean begins to think there may have been a murder committed. Her discoveries impact her own life more than she could ever have imagined.

Where it's reviewed:
Horn Book, August 1983, page 458
Kirkus Reviews, March 15, 1983

Awards the book has won:
Edgar Allan Poe Award 1984

Other books by the author:
David and Jonathan, 1992
Jackaroo, 1985
Dicey's Song, 1982
Homecoming, 1981

Other books you might like:
Avi, *Punch with Judy*, 1993
　　An boy, orphaned by the Civil War is taken in by the owner of a traveling medicine show and later proves the man was wise to have faith in him.
Barbee Oliver Carleton, *The Secret of Saturday Cove*, 1961
　　David searches for a treasure long thought to have been hidden by his ancestors during the Revolutionary War, in his Massachusetts town.
Leonard Everett Fisher, *The Warlock of Westfall*, 1974

A lonely old recluse is accused by his fellow villagers of being the devil's disciple when they discover he has invented an imaginary friend.

Carolyn Reeder, *Shades of Gray*, 1989

At the end of the Civil War, twelve year old Will reluctantly leaves his city home to live in the Virginia countryside with an uncle.

Leonard Wibberley, *Leopard's Prey*, 1971

An orphan is pressed into service as a powderboy on a British ship and later into service on a Haitian pirate ship before he finally returns to Salem.

1862

Cynthia Voigt

Come a Stranger (New York: Atheneum, 1986)

Age range: Grades 5 and Up

Subject(s): African Americans; Ballet

Major character(s): Mina Smith, Teenager, Dancer (ballet); Tamer Shipp, Religious

Time period(s): 1980s

Locale(s): United States

What the book is about: The story of a determined, intelligent young black woman who learns who she is and leaves behind the stranger she was. She is a ballet dancer and the daughter of a minister. Her world view is changed by a young pastor, Tamer Shipp. An adjunct to the Tillerman saga.

Where it's reviewed:
Horn Book, November/December 1986, page 749
School Library Journal, October 1986, page 184

Other books by the author:
Building Blocks, 1984
The Callender Papers, 1983
A Solitary Blue, 1983
Dicey's Song, 1982

Other books you might like:
Rose Blue, *The Preacher's Kid*, 1975
When her father supports a school busing issue, Linda must look at her own values.
Barbara Corcoran, *Annie's Monster*, 1990
The daughter of an Episcopal minister finds herself in trouble when her prayers are answered.
Virginia Hamilton, *Arilla Sun Down*, 1976
A young girl, half black and half Indian, follows her own cultural values, even as her brother goes in another direction.
Jacqueline Roy, *Soul Daddy*, 1990
Life changes for Hannah her twin Rosie, and thier white mother when their black, rock star father and his daughter move into the family's home.
Jean Ure, *The Most Important Thing*, 1986
Nicola begins to pursue ballet seriously even though she has doubts about her long term commitment.

1863

Cynthia Voigt

Dicey's Song (New York: Atheneum, 1982)

Age range: Grades 5-6

Subject(s): Brothers and Sisters; Family Life

Major character(s): Dicey Tillerman, Teenager; Gram Tillerman, Grandparent

Time period(s): 1980s

Locale(s): United States

What the book is about: Dicey adjusts to her new way of life with Gram. Dicey struggles with a job, school, repairing a boat and responsibility for her brothers and sister. Gram legally adopts the children but Dicey doesn't feel the weight lifted until her mother dies.

Where it's reviewed:
Booklist, September 1982, page 49

Awards the book has won:
Newbery Medal 1983
Boston Globe/Horn Book Award - Fiction Honor 1983

Other books by the author:
Homecoming, 1981 (Precedes *Dicey's Song*)
A Solitary Blue, 1983 (More about Dicey, though she is not the main character)
Building Blocks, 1984
On Fortune's Wheel, 1990

Other books you might like:
Gary L. Blackwood, *Wild Timothy*, 1987
13 year old Timothy becomes lost while camping with his father and must learn to survive in the wilderness.
Beverly Butler, *My Sister's Keeper*, 1980
Two sisters face family squabbles and battle a forest fire in the deep woods of Wisconsin.
Myrtle Archer, *Young Boys Gone*, 1978
Thad and his family flee to the Ozarks to escape Quantril and his marauders.
Eleanor Cameron, *To the Green Mountains*,
Kathe and her mother long to return "to the green mountains" and Grandmother's home there.
Elfie Donnelly, *Offbeat Friends*, 1982
Mari meets the strange mrs. Panacek and tries to help when the old woman runs away from the mental hospital where she lives.
Sheila Greenwald, *Will the Real Gertrude Hollings Please Stand Up?*, 1983
In spite of her learning disabilities, Gertrude finds she has something to teach her very successful cousin, Albert.
Irene Hunt, *The Everlasting Hills*, 1985
When a mountain man rejects his mentally handicapped son, the boy wanders into the wilderness and finds a new father figure.

1864

Cynthia Voigt

Homecoming (New York: Atheneum, 1981)

Age range: Grades 5-8

Subject(s): Family Problems; Mental Illness; Survival

Major character(s): Dicey Tillerman, Teenager, Abandoned Child; Cilla, Relative (great-aunt); Maybeth Tillerman, Abandoned Child

Time period(s): 1980s

Locale(s): Connecticut

What the book is about: Abandoned in a shopping center parking lot with a crumped-up address of a relative and less than ten dollars, Dicey tries to reach her great-aunt Cilla with her little sister and two younger brothers. The only way they can reach her is to walk - and they do - the entire length of the Connecticut coastline, along Route 1. They scrape together enough food to keep going and search for a place to call home. Great-Aunt Cilla takes them in, but it is clear she considers it a duty and no pleasure, and Dicey realizes they cannot stay there for long. The sequel is *Dicey's Song*, and the Tillermans show up in many other Voigt novels.

Where it's reviewed:
Booklist, April 1, 1981, page 1109
Hornbook, August 1981, page 438
Kirkus Reviews, August 1, 1981, page 935

Other books by the author:
David and Jonathan, 1992
Come a Stranger, 1986
The Callender Papers, 1983
Dicey's Song, 1982

Other books you might like:
James Lincoln Collier, *The Clock*, 1992
  Trapped in a gruelling job in the textile mill to pay her father's debts, Annie becomes the victim of a cruel overseer, and plots revenge against him.
James Lincoln Collier, *War Comes to Willy Freeman*, 1983
  A free black girl is caught in the horror of the Revolutionary War and faces return to slavery when her father is killed and her mother disappears.
Cynthia D. Grant, *Kumquat May, I'll Always Love You*, 1986
  Abandoned by her mother, Livvy decides she is smart and self-reliant enough to live by herself, if she can only keep her situation a secret.
Alison Cragin Herzig, *The Ten-Speed Babysitter*, 1987
  In a town in Connecticut, a babysitter's job is filled with surprises when his employer jets to the Caribbean and leaves him with a toddler.
Brigette Roux-Lough, *The Fresh Air Kid*, 1990
  Leigh, a street-smart teen living in a tenement building in the Bronx, spends the summer in suburban Connecticut.

1865

Cynthia Voigt

A Solitary Blue (New York: Atheneum, 1983)

Age range: Grades 5-8

Subject(s): Divorce; Fathers and Sons

Major character(s): Jeff Greene, Teenager; Thomas, Religious; Melody Greene, Parent (mother)

Time period(s): 1980s

Locale(s): Charleston, South Carolina

What the book is about: Jeff's charming but unstable mother deserts the family when he is six, and he is brought up by his silent, remote father. When Jeff's mother reenters his life, the conflict he feels between mother and father is finely drawn. Finally, Jeff and his father move to the Maryland shore where he becomes friends with Dicey Tillerman from *Dicey's Song*. Fans of the Tillermans will want to branch out in this direction.

Where it's reviewed:
Center for Children's Books Bulletin, September 1983, page 19
School Library Journal, September 1983, page 139

Awards the book has won:
Boston Globe/Horn Book Award - Fiction Honor 1984
Newbery Honor 1984

Other books by the author:
Tree by Leaf, 1988
Sons from Afar, 1987
Come a Stranger, 1986
The Runner, 1985

Other books you might like:
Tom Birdseye, *Tucker*, 1990
  Tucker likes life with his divorced father until the nine year old sister he has not seen in years moves in with them.
Paul Kropp, *Moonkid and Liberty*, 1990
  While Libby and Ian, who live with their father, experience the problems of starting at a new school, their mother reappears and wants them to move.
Norma Fox Mazer, *Taking Terri Mueller*, 1981
  Terri remembers only life with her father, then she discovers that he kidnapped her from her mother after a divorce and her mother is still alive.
Eloise Jarvis McGraw, *Hideaway*, 1990
  When his father forgets to come for him after his mother leaves on her wedding trip with her new husband, Jerry runs away from both of them.
Richard Peck, *Unfinished Portrait of Jessica*, 1991
  In Mexico to visit her father, Jessica realizes certain illusions she had about him, and she is able to improve her relationship with her mother.

W

1866

Bernard Waber

I Was All Thumbs (Boston: Houghton Mifflin, 1975)

Age range: Grades 1-2

Subject(s): Animals/Squid, Octopus

Major character(s): Legs, Octopus

Time period(s): Indeterminate

Locale(s): At Sea

What the book is about: Legs is suddenly "returned" to the sea after being raised in a lab tank. Ignorant of how to get along in the ocean, he at first does all the wrong things. When he finds a friend, things start to look brighter.

Where it's reviewed:
Booklist, October 15, 1975, page 306
Hornbook, February 1976, page 1125
Kirkus, October 1, 1975, page 57

Other books by the author:
Bernard, 1982
The Snake, A Very Long Story, 1978
Mice on My Mind, 1977
Lyle Finds His Mother, 1974

Other books you might like:
Franz Brandenburg, *Otto Is Different*, 1985
  Otto learns the advantage of being an octopus and having eight arms instead of only two.
Robert Kraus, *Herman the Helper*, 1987
  Herman the helpful octopus is always willing to assist anyone who needs his help, old or young, friend or enemy.
Leo Lionni, *Swimmy*, 1963
  A little black fish in a school of red fish figures out a way of protecting them all from their natural enemies.
Bernard Most, *My Very Own Octopus*, 1980
  A boy imagines what fun he would have with a pet octopus.
Tomi Ungerer, *Emile*, 1989
  A story of an octopus who decides to try living on land and how he becomes a hero.

1867

Bernard Waber, Author/Illustrator

Mice on My Mind (Boston: Houghton Mifflin, 1977)

Age range: Grades 2-4

Subject(s): Animals/Cats; Animals/Mice

Time period(s): Indeterminate

Locale(s): Fictional Country

What the book is about: A cat is obsessed with mice, but there are none around. He tries scattering cheese around the house and drilling holes in the baseboards, all to no avail. Even the psychiatrist the cat consults cannot help him to get mice off his mind.

Where it's reviewed:
Center for Children's Books Bulletin, February 1978, page 103
Hornbook, October 1977, page 526
Kirkus, October 1, 1977, page 1045

Other books by the author:
Bernard, 1982
The Snake, A Very Long Story, 1978
I Was All Thumbs, 1975
Lyle Finds His Mother, 1974

Other books you might like:
Lisa Campbell Ernst, *The Rescue of Aunt Pansy*, 1987
  When Russell the cat receives a new toy mouse, Joanne the mouse thinks the toy is her Aunt Pansy and is determined to save her.
Barbara Shook Hazen, *The Fat Cats, Cousin Scraggs and the Monster Mice*, 1985
  Relates how Cousin Scraggs saves the Fat Cat family from an attack by monster mice, and eventually, leads them to a simpler but happier life.
Susan Jeschke, *Lucky's Choice*, 1987
  Lucky, a comfortable but unloved cat, risks his home when he refuses to kill a mouse he has befriended.
Dick King-Smith, *Martin's Mice*, 1988
  A farm cat who doesn't want to catch mice keeps a family of them as pets, but then he is given away to a townswoman and acquires a new perspective.
Eve Titus, *Basil and the Pygmy Cats*, 1971
  The famous English mouse detective sets out to solve the mystery concerning the existence of pygmy cats.

1868

Jane Wagner

Illustrator: Gordon Parks

J.T. (New York: Van Nostrand, 1969)

Age range: Grades 3-6

Subject(s): African Americans; City Life

Major character(s): J.T. Gamble, Child; Rodeen Gamble, Parent (mother); Bones, Cat

Time period(s): 1960s

Locale(s): New York, New York

What the book is about: J.T. begins to change when he discovers there is more satisfaction in caring for an injured cat than in listening to a stolen transister radio. J.T. makes a home for the cat, feeds it, and even makes a patch for its injured eye. When Boomer and Claymore come after J.T., the cat runs into the street and is killed by a car. A loving family relationship helps J.T. through the loss. Dramatic black and white photos.

Where it's reviewed:
Kirkus Reviews, December 1, 1969, page 1254
Saturday Review, December 20, 1969, page 29

Awards the book has won:
Georgia Children's Book Award 1972

Other books by the author:
The Search for Signs of Intelligent Life in the Universe, 1986 (Adult)

Other books you might like:
Lloyd Alexander, *The Cat Who Wished to Be a Man*, 1973
    When he begins dealing with humanity, Lionel the cat begins to understand why his wizard master was reluctant to change him into a man.
Lynn Beach, *Scream of the Cat*, 1992
    Weird things are happening in Phantom Valley and Tamara Hunt wants to know why.
Clare Bell, *Ratha and Thistle-Chaser*, 1990
    Tortured by nightmares, Newt, a solitary cat, finds a new life for herself with the strange creatures of the seashore until forced to face her past.
Patricia Reilly Giff, *Matthew Jackson Meets the Wall*, 1990
    Matthew's family's move from New York to Ohio is rough enough, but the disappearance of his cat and a neighbor makes it even worse.
Robert Westall, *Yaxley's Cat*, 1991
    After Yaxley disappears, the inhabitants of an English village fear that his ugly old cat will uncover the truth about the secret they are hiding.

1869

Ann Waldron

The Integration of Mary-Larkin Thornhill (New York: Dutton, 1977)

Age range: Grades 5-7

Subject(s): Race Relations

Major character(s): Mary-Larkin Thornhill, Student; Rev. Thornhill, Religious; Vanella, Student

Time period(s): 1960s

Locale(s): United States

What the book is about: A group of white, southern children must go to a black junior high. Mary-Larkin's parents feel strongly that integration is right. Her dad wishes the members of his church would welcome black people. Mary-Larkin's first experiences at Wheatley Junior High are discouraging, until she makes friends with a girl named Vanella.

Where it's reviewed:
Booklist, November 1, 1975, page 374
Hornbook, April 1976, page 89
Kirkus Reviews, September 15, 1975, page 1075

Other books by the author:
Bluebury Collection, 1981
Scaredy Cat, 1978
The Luckie Star, 1977
The House on Pendleton Block, 1975

Other books you might like:
Barbara Corcoran, *Making It*, 1980
    Just as she begins to take charge of her life, the daughter of a small town minister is forced to face the truth about the sister she idolizes.
James Geibel, *The Blond Brother*, 1979
    Racial tension in his new junior high school undermines Rich Gaskin's efforts to help his team in the state basketball championship.
Mary Ann Marger, *Justice at Peachtree*, 1980
    When Cary Bowen takes a job with her father's newspaper, she becomes more aware of the racial prejudice in her small town of Peachtree, SC in 1950.
Betty Underwood, *The Forge and the Forest*, 1975
    An orphaned girl's life is filled with conflicting emotions toward her guardian, the growing abolitionist movement and women's roles in society.
Mildred Pitts Walter, *The Girl on the Outside*, 1982
    A fictionalized recreation of the 1957 integration of Little Rock's Central High School, focusing on the experience of one black girl and one white.

1870

Alice Walker

Illustrator: Don Miller

Langston Hughes, American Poet (New York: Crowell, 1974)

Age range: Grades 2-4

Subject(s): African Americans; Biography; Poetry

Major character(s): Langston Hughes, Child, Historical Figure

Locale(s): Mexico

What the book is about: When Langston was six, he visited his father in Mexico and his mother returned to the United States without her husband. Close attention is paid to the relationship Langston had with his bitter, biased father.

Where it's reviewed:
Center for Children's Books Bulletin, December 1974, page 71
Kirkus Reviews, March 15, 1974, page 307
Library Journal, October 15, 1974, page 2743

Other books by the author:
Finding the Green Stone, 1991
To Hell with Dying, 1987

Other books you might like:
Tony Gentry, *Paul Laurence Dunbar*, 1989
    Examines the life of the poet and novelist who battled racism and accepted the challenge of depicting the black experience in America.

Wade Hudson, *Pass It On: African-American Poetry for Children*, 1993
 An illustrated collection of the poetry of Langston Hughes, Nikki Giovanni, Eloise Greenfield and Lucille Clifton.
Pat McKissack, *Langston Hughes, Great American Poet*, 1992
 Simple text describes the life of the Harlem poet whose work gave voice to the joy and pain of the black experience in America.
Merle A. Richmond, *Phillis Wheatley*, 1988
 The life of the Black American poet born in Africa in 1753, brought to New England as a slave and published her first poem as a teen in Boston.
Deborah Slier, *Make a Joyful Noise*, 1991
 A collection of poems for children by African-American poets.

1871

Barbara Brooks Wallace

Illustrator: Blanche Sims

The Interesting Thing That Happened at Perfect Acres, Inc. (New York: Atheneum, 1988)

Age range: Grades 4-6

Subject(s): Fantasy

Major character(s): Perfecta D. Jones, Preteen; Puck, Friend

Time period(s): Indeterminate

Locale(s): United States

What the book is about: Perfecta Jones and her friend, Puck, outsmart the nasty man who owns the housing development where they live. They climb a ladder to the stars, acquire covers that make them invisible, and deal with evil Mr. Snoot who is trying to change the characters in children's books.

Where it's reviewed:
Booklist, March 15, 1988, page 1269
Kirkus Reviews, February 15, 1988, page 287
School Library Journal, April 1988, page105

Other books by the author:
The Barrell in the Basement, 1985
Peppermints in the Parlor, 1984
Miss Switch to the Rescue, 1981
Andrew, the Big Deal, 1970

Other books you might like:
M.J. Engh, *The House in the Snow*, 1987
 Nine boys outwit the invisible robbers who have inhabited the house in the snow for generations, by using the robber's own cloaks of invisibility.
Nancy Garden, *The Door Between*, 1987
 When her father announces plans for a housing development in the woods considered sacred by the mysterious hermit, the village is attacked.
Anne Lindbergh, *The People in Pineapple Place*, 1982
 August Brown adjusts to his new home in Washington, D.C., with the help of seven children of Pineapple Place, invisible to everyone but him.
Penelope Lively, *The Revenge of Samuel Stokes*, 1981
 When positively uncanny things begin happening in the new housing development, Tim and his grandfather realize they must do something to stop them.
R.L. Stine, *Let's's Get Invisible!*, 1993

On Max's birthday, he finds a magic mirror in the attic that can make him become invisible.

1872

Barbara Brooks Wallace

Illustrator: Lawrence Di Fiori

Palmer Patch (Chicago: Follett, 1976)

Age range: Grades 4-6

Subject(s): Trust; Animals

Major character(s): Palmer, Skunk; Jonathon Patch, Child

Time period(s): Indeterminate

Locale(s): United States

What the book is about: Palmer is adopted by the Patch family, after he has been descented. He is quickly accepted by the other pets; a duck, a goat, two dogs and a cat. Palmer is reluctant to trust Jonathon and his family. He unites the critters when he misunderstands the humans' intentions.

Where it's reviewed:
Booklist, January 1, 1977, page 671
Center for Children's Books Bulletin, March 1977, page 116
School Library Journal, April 1977, page 72

Other books by the author:
Argyle, 1987
The Contest Kid Strikes Again, 1980
The Secret Summer of L.E.B., 1974
Hawkins, 1971

Other books you might like:
Richard Kennedy, *The Mouse God*, 1979
 A cat makes a coat of mouse skins to protect his fur while chasing mice. The mice consider him their god and trust him to send them to heaven.
Liza Ketchum Murrow, *Allergic to My Family*, 1992
 Living with five brothers and sisters, a pet skunk and two nutty parents, Rosie sometimes feels that her family is too busy to appreciate her.
Clem Philbrook, *Ollie's Team and the Basketball Computer*, 1969
 A computer and a skunk help spur the Willowdale Regional School basketball team to the championship.
Pamela F. Service, *Stinker's Return*, 1993
 Alien agent Tsyng Yr, inhabiting a skunk's body, returns to Earth and enlists Jonathan and Karen's help in finding a souvenir from Washington D.C.
Susanne Santoro Whayne, *Watch the House*, 1992
 The family pets, two cats, a dog, a guinea pig and a canary, venture outside and have a series of experiences that make them appreciate indoor life.

1873

Barbara Brooks Wallace

Peppermints in the Parlor (New York: Atheneum, 1980)

Age range: Grades 4-7

Subject(s): Horror; Nursing Homes

Major character(s): Emily Luccock, Heiress, Servant; Mrs. Plumley, Actress; Kipper, Child

Time period(s): 1800s

Locale(s): San Francisco, California

What the book is about: What has happened to Uncle Twice? Why is Aunt Twice the frightened cook in her own house? Why is Sugar Hill Hall now a spooky old folks home under the hard direction of Mrs. Meeding? How can Emily, who arrives as an heiress and is transformed into a kitchen slave, find all of the answers?

Where it's reviewed:
Booklist, September 15, 1980, page 122
Kirkus Reviews, December 1, 1980, page 1519
School Library Journal, October 1980, page 152

Awards the book has won:
William Allen White Children's Book Award 1983

Other books by the author:
The Barrel in the Basement, 1985
The Contest Kid and the Big Prize, 1977
Andrew, the Big Deal, 1970
Claudia, 1969

Other books you might like:
T. Ernesto Bethancourt, *The Tomorrow Connection*, 1984
  A time travel fantasy involving Harry Houdini and the Great San Francisco earthquake.
Patricia Elmore, *Susannah and the Purple Mongoose Mystery*, 1992
  Susannah and her friends investigate a series of fires in their San Francisco neighborhood.
P.J. Petersen, *The Boll Weevil Express: A Novel*, 1983
  A northern California farm boy and a brother and sister from an orphanage decide to flee to Idaho but find themselves down and out in San Francisco.
Bill Wallace, *Buffalo Gal*, 1992
  Amanda's life is disrupted when she grudgingly accompanies her mother to the Oklahoma Territory on a crusade to save the buffalo.
Laurence Yep, *The Tom Sawyer Files*, 1984
  The narrator relates how cub reporter Mark Twain and fire fighter Tom Sawyer uncover the plot of a Southern arsonist during the Civil War.

1874

Bill Wallace

Beauty (New York: Holiday House, 1988)

Age range: Grades 4-6

Subject(s): Farm Life; Animals/Horses

Major character(s): Luke, Preteen; Carol, Parent; Mike Garrison, Rancher

Time period(s): 1980s

Locale(s): Chickasha, Oklahoma

What the book is about: Unhappy about his parents splitting up and moving from Denver with his mother to Grandpa's farm in Oklahoma, Luke finds comfort in riding and caring for a 27 year old horse named Beauty. Luke is warned to be careful and not run Beauty because she is so old, but he doesn't listen. One night during a terrible storm, Beauty spooks and runs through the barn doors Luke forgot to close. He runs into the storm to try to save his best friend.

Where it's reviewed:
School Library Journal, October 1988, page 149
Booklist, February 1, 1989, page 943
Center for Children's Books Bulletin, November 1988, page 88

Other books by the author:
The Biggest Klutz in Fifth Grade, 1992
The Christmas Spurs, 1990
Red Dog, 1987
Shadow on the Snow, 1985

Other books you might like:
Max Evans, *My Pardner*, 1972
  Accompanied by a deceitful cowboy who teaches him some ingenious methods of survival, a Texas boy drives his father's horses to Oklahoma in the 1930s.
Mary A. Hancock, *The Thundering Prairie*, 1969
  When the Cherokee Strip is opened in 1893, thirteen year old Benjy Bryan must race for the homestead claim on which his family has gambled.
Harold Keith, *Susy's Scoundrel*, 1974
  An Amish girl in Oklahoma adopts two coyote pups, but their mother takes them back and their subsequent activities put them in deadly peril.
Tunie Munson, *A Fistful of Sun*, 1974
  Newly-moved to the country, a lonely city girl finds solace in a barn loft where an equally lonely boy raises pigeons.
Anna Myers, *Red-Dirt Jessie*, 1992
  Jessie, a young girl in the Oklahoma dust bowl during the Depression, tries to tame a wild dog and help her father recover from a nervous breakdown.

1875

Bill Wallace

Danger in Quicksand Swamp (New York: Holiday House, 1989)

Age range: Grades 4-5

Subject(s): Treasure; Swamps

Major character(s): Ben, Preteen; Jake, Preteen; Lisa, Child

Time period(s): 1980s

Locale(s): Oklahoma

What the book is about: Ben and Jake are excited enough when they dig up a sunken boat from the river behind their houses. When they discover a treasure map in an old jar under the seat, they have no idea that they will have to battle alligators, quicksand, and a murderer when they search for the treasure on a island in a swamp.

Where it's reviewed:
School Library Journal, October 1989, page 122
Booklist, January 1, 1990, page 922
Kirkus Reviews, December 15, 1989, page 1831

Other books by the author:
Never Say Quit, 1993
Buffalo Gal, 1992
Danger on Panther Peak, 1985
Trapped in Death Cave, 1984

Other books you might like:
Joan Davenport Carris, *A Ghost of a Chance*, 1992

Punch and his friends spend a summer in North Carolina looking at dolphins, hunting for Blackbeard's buried treasure, and watching out for his ghost.

Peni R. Griffin, *The Treasure Bird*, 1992
With clues from a talking parrot, Jessy and her stepbrother Matt discover the whereabouts of a hidden treasure in Uncle Matthew's old house in Texas.

Anne Lindbergh, *The Worry Week*, 1985
Alone for a week in the family's summer house on a Maine island, Allegra and her two sisters scrounge for food and search for supposed treasure.

Mary Francis Shura, *Don't Call Me Toad!*, 1987
An uneasy friendship with the strange, constantly angry new girl in her neighborhood leads Janie to find a hidden cache of money and stolen jewelry.

John Rowe Townsend, *Tom Tiddler's Ground*, 1986
Amid the backwater canals of an English industrial town, five children solve a fifty year old mystery about a half-sunken boat and its hidden treasure

---

1876

Bill Wallace

A Dog Called Kitty (New York: Holiday House, 1980)

Age range: Grades 4-6

Subject(s): Animals/Dogs; Farm Life; Fear

Major character(s): Ricky, Preteen; Brad McNeil, Preteen; Sammy Darlinger, Bully

Time period(s): 1980s

Locale(s): Chickasha, Oklahoma

What the book is about: Afraid of dogs since he was attacked by a mad one, Ricky resists taking in a homeless pup that shows up on the farm. Ricky is ready to ignore the pup, but when he sees it in the barn starved almost to death, something stronger than fear is wakened in him and he sneaks out to the barn at midnight with milk and bologna scraps. Before the story is over, both Ricky and the dog have proven their courage beyond doubt.

Where it's reviewed:
Booklist, February 1, 1981, page 755
Center for Children's Books Bulletin, January 1981, page 102
School Library Journal, February 1981, page 71

Awards the book has won:
Golden Sower Award 1985

Other books by the author:
Totally Disgusting, 1991
Snot Stew, 1989
Red Dog, 1987
Ferret in the Bedroom, Lizards in the Fridge, 1986

Other books you might like:
Barbara Dana, *Zucchini*, 1982
A painfully shy young boy befriends a homeless baby ferret and gets as much comfort as he gives.

Betsy Duffey, *Puppy Love*, 1992
When Evie and Megan start the Pet Patrol to solve animal problems, they soon have their hands full taking care of an army of homeless puppies.

Alison Cragin Herzig, *Sam and the Moon Queen*, 1990

Sympathetic to a homeless girl's plight, Sam tries to help her find food for herself and medical aid for her dog.

Judith Bernie Strommen, *Champ Hobarth*, 1993
Marty's love for a stray dog takes him to the local animal shelter where he discovers the plight of the many homeless pets there.

Theodore Taylor, *Tuck Triumphant*, 1991
Blind dog Friar Tuck and his owners face challenges when discovering the Korean boy they've adopted is deaf. Sequel to *The Trouble with Tuck*.

1877

Bill Wallace

Red Dog (New York: Holiday House, 1987)

Age range: Grades 5-6

Subject(s): Courage; Animals/Dogs; Frontier and Pioneer Life

Major character(s): Adam, Preteen; Jenny, Child; Laurie, Child

Time period(s): 1860s

Locale(s): Wyoming

What the book is about: Living with his family in the rugged often dangerous Wyoming mountains in the 1860s, twelve year old Adam finds his courage put to the test when he is left in charge of the household during his stepfather's absence. Everything goes smoothly until three gold prospectors break into the cabin and hold the family at gunpoint. Adam manages to escape but the men let Ruff loose and he follows Adam. Will Ruff lead the men to Adam, or can Adam and Ruff save the family?

Where it's reviewed:
Booklist, June 1, 1987, page 1526
School Library Journal, June 1987, page 102
Publisher's Weekly, April 24, 1987, page 70

Other books by the author:
The Biggest Klutz in Fifth Grade, 1992
The Christmas Spurs, 1990
Beauty, 1988
Shadow in the Show, 1985

Other books you might like:
Esther Silverstein Blanc, *Berchick*, 1989
An orphaned cat becomes the pet of a Jewish family homesteading in Wyoming in the early 1900s.

Marilyn Cram Donahue, *The Valley in Between*, 1987
Traveling with her family from Vermont to California in the early 1850s, Luanna grows and finds new experiences in their pioneer community.

Warwick Downing, *Kid Curry's Last Ride*, 1989
During a summer in the 1930s with his grandmother in a small Wyoming town, Alex meets an old man who claims to be Kid Curry from Butch Cassidy's gang.

Harold Keith, *The Obstinate Land*, 1977
During a hard winter the father of a German family, settling the Cherokee Strip in Oklahoma, freezes to death and his son must take over the family.

Gloria Skurzynski, *Dangerous Ground*, 1989
Angela enjoys living with her seventy-eight year old great aunt, until Hil, acting strangely, rents a camper for an unplanned Wyoming vacation.

1878

Bill Wallace

Trapped in Death Cave (New York: Holiday, 1984)

Age range: Grades 5-8

Subject(s): Treasure; Mystery and Detective Stories

Major character(s): Gary Marler, Detective; Brian, Friend

Time period(s): Indeterminate

Locale(s): Medicine Park, Oklahoma

What the book is about: Gary is convinced his grandfather was murdered to secure a treasure map leading to gold. With his friend, Brian, he sets out to find both the treasure and his grandfather's killer, braving the curse of an Indian shaman.

Where it's reviewed:
Booklist, June 15, 1984, page 1488
School Library Journal, May 1984, page 102
Children's Book Review Service, April 1984, page 98

Other books by the author:
Never Say Quit, 1993
Biggest Klutz in Fifth Grade, 1992
Danger in Quicksand Swamp, 1989
A Dog Called Kitty, 1980

Other books you might like:
Patricia Edwards Clyne, The Curse of Camp Gray Owl, 1981
    Five friends explore an old Army camp that has been cursed by an Indian.
Betty Hager, Old Jake and the Pirate's Treasure, 1980
    Four Alabama children look for pirate treasure using a map belonging to an old Cajun fisherman.
Robert Newman, The Case of the Indian Curse, 1986
    While Inspector Wyatt and Andrew's mother are on their honeymoon, Andrew and Sara investigate a mysterious statue that produces light and sound.
Pamela F. Service, Vision Quest, 1989
    Kate's dreary life in a small Nevada town is shaken by an Indian artifact that puts her in contact with a shaman and drags her into the distant past.
Judith St. George, The Shadow of the Shaman, 1977
    His father hospitalized after a serious accident, Jay finds himself alone in a remote Oregon lodge. Its owner is threatened by mysterious enemies.

1879

Ruth Wallace-Brodeur

The Kenton Year (New York: Atheneum, 1980)

Age range: Grades 4-6

Subject(s): Death; Moving, Household; Mothers and Daughters

Major character(s): Mandy McPherson, Child; Martin Wechsler, Editor

Time period(s): 1980s

Locale(s): Kenton, Vermont; Boston, Massachusetts

What the book is about: Nine year old Mandy's father is hit and killed by a truck. Mandy's mother returns to the small town she herself had grown up in. They make new friends including the editor of the town paper and his brother, Shandee. Mandy has natural skiing ability and trains for the

Crawford County Winter Carnival. On the anniversary of her father's death, she and her mom dedicate a memorial to him.

Where it's reviewed:
Kirkus Reviews, November 1, 1980
School Library Journal, November 1980, page 80

Other books by the author:
Stories From the Big Chair, 1989
Steps in Time, 1986
Callie's Way, 1984
One April Vacation, 1981

Other books you might like:
Johanna Hurwitz, The Rabbi's Girls, 1982
    Moving to a new town, the birth of a sister and the death of her father makes 1923 a bittersweet year for Carrie Levin.
Eda J. LeShan, When a Parent Is Very Sick, 1986
    This non-fiction title discusses a child's feelings when a parent is ill, how this affects the whole family, and suggests coping skills.
Valerie A. Lutters, The Haunting of Julie Unger, 1977
    The vivid memory of her dead father threatens to isolate Julie from the rest of her family and push her to the brink of insanity.
Deborah Moulton, Summer Girl, 1992
    When her mother is dying, Tommy goes to live with her estranged father, and she gradually understands him and the death of the woman they both love.
Catherine Petroski, The Summer That Lasted Forever, 1984
    Molly approaches her twelfth birthday still trying to accept the death of her mother and facing the imminent sale of her beloved pony.

1880

Mildred Pitts Walter

Illustrator: Catherine Stock

Justin and the Best Biscuits in the World (New York: Lothrop Lee and Shepard, 1986)

Age range: Grades 3-6

Subject(s): African Americans; Ranch Life; Sex Roles

Major character(s): Justin, Preteen

Time period(s): 1980s

Locale(s): United States

What the book is about: Justin spends time at his grandfather's ranch and learns many things. He gets a history of Black cowboys in the West. He learns how to tend livestock and ride horses, but balks when Grandpa asks him to help make biscuits because Justin thinks it's "woman's work." With understanding, humor, and no lecturing, Grandpa changes Justin's mind when he proudly displays the blue ribbon he won at the county fair for the best biscuits.

Where it's reviewed:
Center for Children's Books Bulletin, December 1986, page 78
School Library Journal, November 1986, page 94

Other books by the author:
Mariah Keeps Cool, 1990
The Girl on the Outside, 1982
Lillie of Watts Takes a Giant Step, 1971
Lillie of Watts: A Birthday Discovery, 1969

Other books you might like:
Augusta Fink, *To Touch the Sky*, 1971
When he discovers the ranch promised to his father has been given to someone else, a boy commits an act which changes his entire life.
Dick King-Smith, *Lady Daisy*, 1993
Nine year old Ned faces a lot of teasing when he decides to keep a Victorian doll that speaks only to him.
Osmond Molarsky, *Robbery in Right Field*, 1978
Young Cynthia Rose, the Little League's best player, does a little coaching with tremendous results.
Zibby Oneal, *A Long Way to Go*, 1990
An eight year old girl deals with the women's suffrage movement that rages during WWI.
Alison Smith, *Billy Boone*, 1989
Billy fights for her right to take trumpet lessons and spends time with her unorthodox grandmother, even though her parents think this is unladylike.

1881

Mildred Pitts Walter

Mariah Loves Rock (New York: Bradbury, 1988)

Age range: Grades 3-6

Subject(s): African Americans; Family Life; Stepfamilies

Major character(s): Mariah, 5th Grader, Preteen (Afro-American); Sheik Bashara, Musician (rock star); Lynn, Preteen

Time period(s): 1980s

Locale(s): United States

What the book is about: Mariah is crazy about rock star Sheik Bashara. Her family is being turned upside down by the impending arrival of her father's daughter from a previous marriage. A fine family story with lots of emotional ups and downs.

Where it's reviewed:
Horn Book, April 1989, page 212
School Library Journal, December 1988, page 113

Other books by the author:
Mariah Keeps Cool, 1990
Justin and the Best Biscuits in the World, 1986
Because We Are, 1983
The Girl on the Outside, 1982

Other books you might like:
James Duffy, *Uncle Shamus*, 1992
Ten year old Akers and his friend, Marleena, get to know a blind ex-convict who moves into their poor Oklahoma town and asks them for help.
Virginia Hamilton, *Willie Bea and the Time the Martians Landed*, 1983
In October, 1938, on their farm in Ohio, a black family is caught up in the fear caused by the Orson Wells "Martians Have Landed" broadcast.
Lila Hopkins, *Talking Turkey*, 1989
A seventh grader with a talent for mischief tries to prove his innocence of involvement in a series of thefts.
Johnniece Marshall, *Robin on His Own*, 1990
A black boy whose family is in transition tries to cope with the death of his mother.
Camille Yarbrough, *The Shimmershine Queens*, 1989

Two fifth graders try to lift themselves and their classmates out of their environment by encouraging them to keep their eyes on their dreams.

1882

Walter Wangerin

The Book of the Dun Cow (New York: Harper, 1978)

Age range: Grades 5-8

Subject(s): Animals; Fantasy; Good and Evil

Major character(s): Chauntecleer, Rooster; John Wesley, Weasel; Mundo Cani, Dog

Time period(s): Indeterminate

Locale(s): Fictional Country

What the book is about: A battle between good and evil is waged. Chantecleer and his subjects fight against the huge, evil Wyrm. The Dun Cow is a great-mother figure, who gives comfort and aid during the struggle.

Where it's reviewed:
Booklist, February 15, 1979, page 927
Kirkus Reviews, November 15, 1978, page 1255
School Library Journal, October 1978, page 160

Other books by the author:
Elisabeth and the Water Troll, 1991
The Book of Sorrows, 1985
Thistle, 1983
The Bible for Children, 1981

Other books you might like:
Richard Adams, *Watership Down*, 1972
Chronicles the adventures of a group of rabbits searching for a safe place to establish a new warren where they can live in peace.
Grace Chetwin, *On All Hallow's Eve*, 1984
Two sister on their way home from a party step into another time period, where the forces of good and evil involve them in a life or death adventure.
Hilary H. Milton, *Two From the Dead*, 1983
Two teenagers, after experiencing clinical death in separate incidents, return to life, endowed with supernatural powers, one good, the other evil.
Shirley Rousseau Murphy, *Medallion of the Black Hound*, 1989
The power of the Medallion of the Black Hound brings David to a world called Meryn where he must join in the battle of good against evil.
Andre Norton, *Here Abide Monsters*, 1973
Taking an abandoned road, two teenagers are transported back in time to Avalon where they are embroiled in a battle between good and evil.

1883

Walter Wangerin

Illustrator: Marcia Sewall

Thistle (New York: Harper, 1983)

Age range: Grades 2-4

Subject(s): Witches and Witchcraft; Courage

Major character(s): Thistle, Child

Time period(s): 1980s

Locale(s): United States

What the book is about: Through kindness, a little girl saves her family from the giant potato who has eaten them. Only the ugly witch can help them, and only Thistle has the courage to deal with the witch.

Where it's reviewed:
Center for Children's Books Bulletin, December 1983, page 80
School Library Journal, November 1983, page 84

Other books by the author:
The Book of Sorrows, 1985
Potter, Come Fly to the First of the Earth, 1985

Other books you might like:
Bruce Coville, *The Foolish Giant*, 1978
  In spite of not being too bright, a giant named Harry saves a town from a wicked wizard.
Roald Dahl, *The BFG*, 1982
  Sophie is saved by the BFG (Big Friendly Giant) and finds herself in a strange environment.
Ross Martin Madsen, *Perrywinkle and the Book of Magic Spells*, 1986
  Perrywinkle is a wizard-in-training, but his education is rife with pitfalls and he falls into all of them.
Carl Sandburg, *Rootabaga Stories*, 1988
  Fanciful, funny short stories including Potato Face, The Blue Wind Boy and others. Good read aloud.
Anne Rockwell, *The Gollywhopper Egg*, 1986
  A gullible farmer tries to hatch a coconut, thinking that it is a gollywhopper's egg.

1884

Lynd Ward, Author/Illustrator

The Silver Pony (Boston: Houghton Mifflin, 1973)

Age range: Grades 1-6

Subject(s): Loneliness; Mythology

Time period(s): 1960s

Locale(s): United States (Midwest Farm)

What the book is about: Recounts without words, the adventure of a boy and his winged horse. The boy imagines a winged silver pony that takes him on an adventurous flight to far points of the world. A beautiful picture book with many uses.

Where it's reviewed:
Booklist, May 15, 1973, page 911
Hornbook, June 1973, page 280
Kirkus Reviews, November 1, 1965, page 112 .

Other books by the author:
Gods' Man: A Novel in Woodcuts, 1978
The Biggest Bear, 1952

Other books you might like:
Mitsumasa Anno, *Anno's Britain*, 1981
  The illustrations lead the reader on a journey through Great Britain moving freely through time and space.
Craig McFarland Brown, *The Patchwork Farmer*, 1989

After ripping his overalls again and again in the course of his daily work, a farmer ends up with a colorful patchwork pair.
Chris L. Demarest, *Orville's Odyssey*, 1986
  Orville's fishing expedition becomes a strange adventure when a large fish pulls him into a puddle and he struggles to escape.
Robin Michal Koontz, *Dinosaur Dream*, 1988
  A boy who loves dinosaurs is taken on a journey to their land one special night.
Colin Robinson, *Sunrise*, 1992
  Illustrations reveal the activities in a country village as the sun slowly dawns.

1885

Leon Ware

Mystery of 22 East (Philadelphia: Westminster, 1965)

Age range: Grades 5-8

Subject(s): Sea Stories

Major character(s): Tom Cameron, Teenager; Captain Altman, Sea Captain; Ben Cameron, Relative (uncle)

Time period(s): Indeterminate

Locale(s): At Sea

What the book is about: Tom Cameron is traveling alone aboard the German freighter, *Hornbill*, on his way to England to meet his father. A hidden package of microfilm, a circus monkey, a storm and a new friend lead him into mystery and adventure on the high seas.

Where it's reviewed:
Kirkus Reviews, August 15, 1965, page 835
School Library Journal, February 1978, page 35

Awards the book has won:
Edgar Allan Poe Award 1966

Other books by the author:
The Jade Monkey Mystery, 1969
Phantom of the Bridge, 1954

Other books you might like:
Joan Aiken, *The Stolen Lake*, 1981
  Sailing to England from Nantucket on a British Man-o'-War, Dido has many adventures when the ship is taken to New Cumbria, in the southern hemisphere.
Franklin W. Dixon, *The Phantom Freighter*, 1970
  The Hardy Boys embark on a freighter trip under mysterious circumstances and find themselves involved with a smuggling ring.
Sesyle Joslin, *The Gentle Savages*, 1979
  Two English children run away when their cruise ship docks at a North African port and lead a new life of freedom, adventure, discomfort, and danger.
Joel Matus, *Leroy and the Caveman*, 1993
  In 1942, having been driven by bullies into Dead Man's Canyon, Leroy discovers a living Neanderthal man and has an adventure involving German spies.
Theodore Taylor, *The Cay*, 1990
  Their freighter is torpedoed by a German submarine during WWII, leaving a white teenager and a black man stranded on a Caribbean island.

| 1886 |

William E. Warren

Illustrator: Edward Frascino

The Graveyard: And Other Not-So-Scary Stories
(Englewood Cliffs, New Jersey: Prentice Hall, 1984)

Age range: Grades 4-6

Subject(s): Horror; Humor; Short Stories

Time period(s): Indeterminate

Locale(s): United States

What the book is about: Four stories that involve reader participation. Each is presented in a split sequence: the first leaves the reader on the verge of horror; the second presents an ordinary explanation for the situation.

Where it's reviewed:
Booklist, September 15, 1984, page 136
School Library Journal, November 1984, page 129

Other books by the author:
The Screaming Skull, 1987
Footsteps in the Fog, 1985
The Thing in the Swamp, 1984

Other books you might like:
Rita Golden Gelman, *Vampires and Other Creatures of the Night*, 1991
 Contains "Out of the Night," "Vampires," "Werewolves," and "Personal Monsters."
Barbara Griffiths, *Frankenstein's Hamster*, 1992
 A collection of ten scary stories featuring a school boy with a talent for taxidermy, the highwayman of death and other disturbing characters.
Collin McDonald, *Nightwaves: Scary Tales for After Dark*, 1990
 A collection of horror stories featuring a spirit hunter from ancient Egypt, two ghosts at a dangerous dam and a mad killer in the woods.
Alvin Schwartz, *Scary Stories 3: More Tales to Chill Your Bones*, 1991
 More traditional and modern-day stories of ghosts, haunts, superstitions, monsters and horrible scary things.
George Ulrich, *The Spook Matinee*, 1992
 A collection of short poems about ghosts, spiders, aliens, vampires and horror movies.

| 1887 |

Maureen Crane Wartski

A Boat to Nowhere (Philadelphia: Westminster Press, 1980)

Age range: Grades 6 and Up

Subject(s): Courage; Refugees

Major character(s): Mai, Preteen, Refugee; Loc, Preteen, Refugee; Kien Ho, Preteen, Refugee

Time period(s): 1970s

Locale(s): Vietnam; Thailand

What the book is about: Mai and Loc are Vietnamese war orphans. They flee with their grandfather to the southern tip of Vietnam. Kien is a fourteen year old refugee who lives by his wits. He tells of resettlement camps and economic zones. Kien helps Mai, Loc and their grandfather escape and set sail for Thailand, then Malaysia. They reach land on Outcast Island run by an outlaw. Kien takes responsiblity for the family.

Where it's reviewed:
Center for Children's Books Bulletin, December 1980, page 82
School Library Journal, April 1980, page 118

Other books by the author:
The Lake Is on Fire, 1981
A Long Way From Home, 1981 (Sequel to *A Boat to Nowhere*)
My Brother Is Special, 1979

Other books you might like:
Huynh Quang Nhuong, *The Land I Lost*, 1982
 The story of a boy's growing up in rural Vietnam before the war.
Sonia Levitin, *Journey to America*, 1970
 A family fleeing Nazi Germany in 1938 endures a great deal before they are reunited.
Iris Noble, *Mahmud's Story*, 1976
 From the time he is ten until he is a college student, a Palestinian Arab refugee grows in his understanding of the Middle East conflict.
Jean Davies Okimoto, *Jason's Women*, 1986
 Jason finds self-confidence and new purpose in his lonely life when he answers a job ad and meets Bertha Jane and the Vietnamese refugee at her place.
Katherine Paterson, *Park's Quest*, 1988
 11 year old Park travels to his grandfather's farm in Virginia, learns about his father's death in Vietnam, and meets a Vietnamese-American girl.

| 1888 |

Maureen Crane Wartski

The Lake Is on Fire (Philadelphia: Westminster, 1981)

Age range: Grades 5-8

Subject(s): Animals; Blind; Suicide

Major character(s): Ricky, Teenager; Deidre, Friend; King, Dog (German Shepherd)

Time period(s): 1980s

Locale(s): New Hampshire

What the book is about: Ricky is in a car accident that blinds him and kills his best friend. He attempts suicide. Sol and Deirder, family friends, take Ricky to their mountain home. Their latest "orphan" is an abused German Shepherd, King. Caught in a terrible storm and forest fire, King and Ricky have to rely on each other, as Ricky overcomes his fear of the dog.

Where it's reviewed:
School Library Journal, November 1981, page 112

Other books by the author:
A Long Way From Home, 1981
A Boat to Nowhere, 1980
My Brother Is Special, 1979

Other books you might like:
Eth Clifford, *The Man Who Sang in the Dark*, 1987
 Leah, her brother and recently widowed mother begin forming a new life through friendship with a blind man in their Deprssion Era boarding house.
James Duffy, *Uncle Shamus*, 1992

Akers and Marleena are intrigued by the blind, black ex-convict who moves into their Oklahoma shanty town and enlists their help in a secret plan.

Emily Rhoads Johnson, *Spring and the Shadow Man*, 1984
  Through helping a blind neighbor, Spring learns that having an overactive imagination is someting to be treasured.

Sandra McCuaig, *Blindfold*, 1990
  Benji and his blind brother, Joel, share a very special bond until their suicide, leaving feelings of grief and guilt with their friend, Sally.

Kin Platt, *Chloris and the Freaks*, 1975
  Adjusting to her father's suicide and mother's remarriage leads a girl to astrology which she uses to sort out her family problems.

1889

Will Watkins

Illustrator: Toni Goffe

Sid Seal, Houseman (New York: Orchard, 1989)

Age range: Grades 1-3

Subject(s): Animals/Pigs; Animals/Seals and Sea Lions

Major character(s): Waltham de Swine, Pig; Sid, Seal

Time period(s): Indeterminate

Locale(s): Boston, Massachusetts

What the book is about: Waltham de Swine is a pig in a wealthy, upper class Boston family and the course of his days changes drastically when a seal named Sid comes to the household to work as a servant. Sid stirs up all sorts of adventures from getting stranded in a candy shop by a snowstorm, to encountering a hard hearted landlord who torches his own building for the insurance money. Lots of magic and fun in chapters begging to be read aloud to primary listeners, only a few of whom can read it on their own.

Where it's reviewed:
Booklist, July 1989, page 1908
School Library Journal, September 1989, page 235

Other books you might like:
Caroline Fairless, *Hambone*, 1980
  Jeremy's memorial to Hambone, his pet pig, is a big success because of the love put into it.

John Jiler, *Wild Berry Moon*, 1982
  A pig escapes into the forest to give birth to her piglets and with the help of a snake, saves them from the fate the farmer has planned for them.

Ida Luttrell, *Milo's Toothache*, 1992
  Milo Pig plans to visit the dentist about his toothache, but his friends overreact and make the situation into a big problem.

Zibby Oneal, *The Improbable Adventures of Marvelous O'Hara Soapstone*, 1972
  The Soapstone family finds it very difficult to cope with their pig when she falls in love with the cement dolphin in the park lily pond.

Jean Van Leeuwen, *Oliver and Amanda's Halloween*, 1992
  Oliver and Amanda Pig's activities include making costumes, getting a pumpkin and going trick-or-treating.

1890

Eiveen Weiman

It Takes Brains (New York: Atheneum, 1982)

Age range: Grades 3-5

Subject(s): Loneliness; Schools

Major character(s): Barbara Brainard, Preteen; Ned Ferris, Preteen; Margery, Preteen

Time period(s): 1980s

Locale(s): Ohio

What the book is about: Barbara's parents are both doctors and seldom home. They move to Ohio from California. Barbara's new teacher suspects that she is gifted. Ned invites her sledding and Margery has her over for a slumber party. Barbara has found a place to belong.

Where it's reviewed:
Booklist, May 1, 1982, page 1166
Center for Children's Books Bulletin, July 1982, page 218

Other books by the author:
Which Way Courage

Other books you might like:
Betty Bates, *That's What T.J. Says*,
  Meeting another lonely person helps a young girl face her problems and begin to grow up.

Betsy Byars, *The TV Kid*, 1976
  A young boy escapes from his loneliness by watching television and soon he can't tell fantasy from reality.

Jean Little, *Lost and Found*, 1986
  Moving to a new home worries Lucy as she thinks about making new friends and going to a new school.

Uri Shulevitz, *The Strange and Exciting Adventures of Jeremiah Hush.*, 1986
  Jeremiah is a lonely monkey who has an awful evening trying not to be lonely.

Janwillem Van De Wetering, *Hugh Pine and the Good Place*, 1986
  Hugh the porcupine searches for a secluded spot, then realizes being alone is not what he expected.

1891

Patricia Welch, Author/Illustrator

The Day of the Muskie (Boston: Faber, 1984)

Age range: Grades 2-4

Subject(s): Boats and Boating; Fishing

Major character(s): Norm, Fisherman; Pete, Dog

Time period(s): 1980s

Locale(s): Moose Lake ("North Country")

What the book is about: Norm wants desperately to catch a large muskie, and win a new boat to improve his sagging business as a fishing guide. As he and his dog, Pete, are eating lunch on the pier, Norm tosses a last bite of tuna into the water and it is grabbed by a beautiful, large muskie. The fish becomes their friend and Norm feeds it regularly, called "chumming a fish" if you later catch it. Even though a disaster occurs with his old boat, and Norm catches the huge muskie he has come to know, he cannot end its life. He must think of another way to get a new boat.

Where it's reviewed:
School Library Journal, December 1984, page 87

Other books you might like:
Sally Hobart Alexander, *Maggie's Whopper*, 1992
While fishing with her great-uncle Ezra, seven year old Maggie sacrifices her prize catch to save her uncle from a hungry bear.
Jamie Gilson, *You Cheat!*, 1992
Nathan bribes his older brother to go fishing, and then wishes he had never brought up the idea.
David Kherdian, *The Great Fishing Contest*, 1991
After painstaking preparations with his friend, jason enters the fishing contest and plans to discover where the biggest fish in the pond are hiding.
Steven Kroll, *Gone Fishing*, 1990
At their summer house, a young boy and his father go off by themselves on a special fishing trip.
Jean Marzollo, *Amy Goes Fishing*, 1980
A young girl goes fishing for the first time with her father.

1892

Valerie Weldrick

Illustrator: Ron Brooks

Time Sweep (New York: Lothrop, 1978)

Age range: Grades 5-8

Subject(s): Time Travel; Space and Time

Major character(s): Laurie, Preteen, Time Traveller; Clare, Friend; Frank, Friend

Time period(s): 1970s (1978); 1860s (1862)

Locale(s): Sydney, Australia; London, England

What the book is about: Twelve year old Laurie is an Australian boy who time travels in an old bed. Frank is a friend he meets in 1862 London. Laurie teaches the boy to read. They happen to overhear a planned burglary, which they prevent. Clare and Laurie meet Frank's descendent, now living in Austrailia, because of Frank's friendship with Laurie during time travel.

Where it's reviewed:
Hornbook, April 1979, page 196
Kirkus, January 1, 1979, page 7
School Library Journal, January 1979, page 58

Other books you might like:
John Bellairs, *The Ghost in the Mirror*, 1993
Rose Rita Pottinger and Mrs. Zimmerman are transported back to 1828 to save the Weiss family from being destroyed.
Virginia Hamilton, *Dustland*, 1980
Four children, all possessing extraordinary mental powers, are projected into the far future to a bleak region called Dustland.
Sherryl Jordan, *A Time of Darkness*, 1990
A teenage boy with unusual powers faces the challenge of his life when he's transported to a primitive society.
Pamela F. Service, *All's Faire*, 1993
Kevin meets a gypsy girl while touring with his parents in a medieval show, and they travel back to medieval times.
William Sleator, *Strange Attractors*, 1990

Max has a time travel device which is sought by two desperate men, the scientist who invented it and his alter ego from a different timeline.

1893

Rosemary Wells

The Man in the Woods (New York: Dial, 1984)

Age range: Grades 6-9

Subject(s): Drugs; Mystery and Detective Stories

Major character(s): Helen, Teenager; Pinky, Teenager

Time period(s): 1980s

Locale(s): United States

What the book is about: Helen and Pinky witness a car accident caused by the Punk Rock Thrower in the woods. They follow someone in the woods but lose him. As she investigates what she considers the false arrest of a friend, Helen finds she is being followed but no one will believe her. She and Pinky, by delving into the town's history, discover the truth and Helen is nearly killed herself. A fascinating mystery-within-a-mystery with lots of humor.

Where it's reviewed:
Horn Book, Spetember/October 1984, page 601
School Library Journal, May 1984, page 104

Other books by the author:
Through the Hidden Door, 1987
Leave Well Enough Alone, 1977
None of the Above, 1974
The Fog Comes on Little Cat Feet, 1972

Other books you might like:
Avi, *Shadrach's Crossing*, 1983
Living on an island in 1932, a boy determines to identify and somehow bring to justice, the liquor smugglers who have been terrorizing the island.
Margaret Mahy, *Memory*, 1987
Johnny Dart goes in search of the only other witness to the fatal accident which killed his sister.
Virginia Masterman-Smith, *The Great Egyptian Heist*, 1982
Angel Wilson and her two friends find a cache of diamonds in an Egyptian coffin.
Alison Prince, *Night Landings*, 1984
Harriet and her brother, Ian, become convinced that smugglers are operating from the airfield near their English farm home.
Rosemary Sutcliff, *Flame-Colored Taffeta*, 1986
Damaris and her friends become involved with smugglers and a young man who may be a spy, in a rural community near the south coast of England.

1894

Robert Westall

The Machine Gunners (New York: Greenwillow, 1976)

Age range: Grades 5-6

Subject(s): World War II

Major character(s): Charles McGill, Teenager

Time period(s): 1940s (1941)

Locale(s): Garmouth, England

What the book is about: After an air raid, Chas McGill and his friends find a German machine gun and hide it. The kids are exposed to daily air raids and build a secret emplacement for the gun. The authorities are unable to trace the gun until the boys, tragically, put it to use. A real cliff hanger.

Where it's reviewed:
Booklist, November 1, 1976, page 413
Hornbook, February 1977, page 61
Kirkus, Reviews, September 15, 1976, page 1046

Awards the book has won:
Boston Globe/Horn Book Award

Other books by the author:
The Kingdom by the Sea, 1991
Blitzcat, 1989
Echoes of War, 1989
Fathom Five, 1979

Other books you might like:
Jane Gardam, *A Long Way From Verona*, 1971
A young girl aspiring to be a writer recounts her experiences growing up in England during the Second World War.
Richard Alexander Hough, *Razor Eyes*, 1981
More than forty years after the fact, a farmer details his experiences as a British pilot in WWII and the maturing effect they had on him.
Elisabeth Mace, *Brother Enemy*, 1981
Sent from Nazi Germany to England to spend the war years with his Jewish father, Andreas yearns for his home and make plans for his return.
Jill Paton Walsh, *Fireweed*, 1969
Two teenage runaways who refuse to be evacuated from London struggle to survive the Blitz of 1940.
David Rees, *The Exeter Blitz*, 1978
On top of the Exeter cathedral when a Nazi bombin raid begins, Colin Lockwood survives the attack and searches for the rest of his family.

1895

Robert Westall

The Machine Gunners (New York: Greenwillow, 1976)

Age range: Grades 5-9

Subject(s): Children and War; World War II

Major character(s): Charles, Child; Rudi, Military Personnel (German soldier)

Time period(s): 1940s

Locale(s): England

What the book is about: Charles finds a machine gune in a German plane that has crashed over England. He and his friends hide the gun. Rudi is a German soldier who is hiding in the countryside. He becomes friends with Charles, teaching him and his friends about the gun in exchange for an escape boat.

Where it's reviewed:
Booklist, November 1, 1976, page 413
Hornbook, February 1977, page 61
Kirkus Reviews, September 15, 1976, page 1046

Awards the book has won:
Carnegie Medal 1976

Other books by the author:
Echoes of War, 1991
Blitzcat, 1989
The Watch House, 1978
The Wind Eye, 1977

Other books you might like:
Malcolm Carrick, *I'll Get You!*, 1979
A young boy growing up in post-war London tries to fit in with his neighborhood friends.
James D. Forman, *Horses of Anger*, 1967
In the last days of WWII, a German soldier begins to question the Nazis as he sees more and more discrepancies between facts and official statements.
Jill Paton Walsh, *The Dolphin Crossing*, 1967
In wartime England, two boys, too young to fight, take part in the evacuation from Dunkirk.
Susan Sallis, *A Time for Everything*, 1979
A young girl grows up amid many family problems in a small English village during WWII.
Eileen Van Kirk, *A Promise to Keep*, 1990
Ellie falls in love with a handsome Austrian refugee and faces a conflict of loyalties when he reveals that he is sympathetic to the German army.

1896

Robert Westall

The Wind Eye (New York: Greenwillow, 1977)

Age range: Grades 5-8

Subject(s): Space and Time; Vikings

Major character(s): Mike, Child, Time Traveller; Sally, Child, Time Traveller; Beth, Child, Time Traveller

Time period(s): 7th century (600s)

Locale(s): Northumberland, England

What the book is about: Mike, Sally and Beth find an old boat on the English coast. which they use to time travel back to the Middle Ages where they meet St. Cuthbert. Sally becomes marooned in St. Cuthbert's time, but when she is rescued, her crippled hand has been healed. Mike's father, a professor, travels back into the midst of a Viking raid.

Where it's reviewed:
Booklist, October 15, 1977, page 6
Kirkus Reviews, October 15, 1977, page 1104
School Library Journal, November 1977, page 77

Other books by the author:
Stormsearch, 1992
Urn Burial, 1987
The Watch House, 1978
The Machine Gunners, 1975

Other books you might like:
J.S. Andrews, *The Green Hill of Nendrum*, 1970
A 20th century boy sailing alone in Northern Ireland is suddenly transported back in time to a 10th century monastery threatened by a Viking raid.
Bruce Clements, *Prison Window, Jerusalem Blue*, 1977

In 831, members of a family of entertainers are kidnapped in a Viking raid and taken as slaves to the land of their captors.
Betty Levin, *A Griffon's Nest*, 1975
  Two 20th century children yield to the power of the bronze sword that leads them back in time to the Orkney Islands in the 7th and 10th centuries.
Howard Pyle, *Otto of the Silver Hand*, 1967
  The son of a medieval German robber baron returns to his father's castle and, despite great suffering and blood-feuds, grows to honor and manhood.
Mary Stolz, *Pangur Ban*, 1988
  Cormac leaves his family in 9th century Ireland and joins a monastery, where he creates an illuminated manuscript to be treasured by generations.

1897

Gloria Whelan

Illustrator: Stephen Marchesi

Silver (New York: Random House, 1988)

Age range: Grades 2-4

Subject(s): Animals/Dogs; Eskimos; Sports/Dog Sled Racing

Major character(s): Rachel, Child; Silver, Dog (Siberian Husky); Mary Sue, Neighbor

Time period(s): 1980s

Locale(s): Alaska (halfway between Anchorage and Fairbanks)

What the book is about: Rachel wants to compete in the Alaska Iditarod Sled Race, and she thinks she can do it with her lead dog, Silver. Even though he is the runt of the litter from her father's prize sled racing dog, Rachel is determined to track him down when he mysteriously disappears.

Where it's reviewed:
Booklist, July 1988, page 1842
Kirkus Reviews, May 15, 1988, page 768
School Library Jouranal, October 1988, page 129

Other books by the author:
Bringing the Farmhouse Home, 1992
Hannah, 1991
The Secret Keeper, 1990
Next Spring, an Oriole, 1987

Other books you might like:
Raymond Creekmore, *Lokoshi Learns to Hunt Seals*, 1946
  Lokoshi, an Eskimo boy, goes on a seal hunt with his Papa, before civilization has a chance to change their culture and traditions.
Mischa Damjan, *Atuk*, 1990
  Atuk's best friend, a husky puppy, is killed by a wolf. Atuk vows to kill the wolf, but he learns that revenge is not necessarily a good thing.
James A. Houston, *Wolf Run: A Caribou Eskimo Tale*, 1971
  When the caribou herds fail to return in the spring, famine becomes so acute that a young Eskimo boy sets out alone in search of food.
Robert A. Ruttan, *The Adventures of Oolakuk*, 1969
  Describes the life of an Eskimo boy, as he goes on his first hunt, goes to school and helps his father build an igloo.
Carter Wilson, *On Firm Ice*, 1969

A series of tales about the life of a Netsilik Eskimo family during the long winter of northern Canada.

1898

Gloria Whelan

A Time to Keep Silent (New York: Putnam, 1979)

Age range: Grades 5 and Up

Subject(s): Child Abuse; Mutism; Death

Major character(s): Clair Lothrop, Teenager, Handicapped (mute); Reverend Lothrop, Parent, Religious; Dorrie Norcher, Teenager, Abuse Victim

Time period(s): 1970s

Locale(s): United States

What the book is about: Clair becomes mute when her mother dies. Her father is pastor of a large, suburban church. He transfers to a mission in the isolated northern part of their state. Despite her muteness, she becomes friends with Dorrie Norcher. Dorrie's mom is also dead and her father beats her. Dorrie has a hideout in the woods.

Where it's reviewed:
Kirkus Reviews, November 15, 1979, page 1332
School Library Journal, December 1979, page 92

Other books by the author:
Hannah, 1991
Playing with Shadows, 1988
Next Spring, an Oriole, 1987
A Clearing in the Forest, 1978

Other books you might like:
Robbie Branscum, *The Ugliest Boy*, 1978
  Unexpected romance and a cult prompt the son of an Arkansas preacher to reconsider his negative feelings about himself and his family.
Hugh Barnett Cave, *Conquering Kilmarnie*, 1989
  Peter and his father are still mourning the death of his mother and brother when a determined black boy arrives on their Jamaican coffee plantation.
Nancy Garden, *Lark in the Morning*, 1991
  Gillian discovers that the thieves who broke into her parents' house are really two runaways terrified of being returned to their abusive parents.
Lee Pennock Huntington, *Maybe a Miracle*, 1984
  Life as a minister's daughter is good and bad. Dorcas experiences the best of her year when she prays for a miracle for a friend.
Phyllis Reynolds Naylor, *A String of Chances*, 1982
  The sixteen year old daughter of a small town preacher not only discovers secrets that divide her family, but experiences uncertainties about her own

1899

E.B. White

Illustrator: Garth Williams

Charlotte's Web (New York: Harper, 1952)

Age range: Grades 3-6

Subject(s): Animals; Fantasy

Major character(s): Charlotte, Spider; Wilbur, Pig; Fern Zuckerman, Child

Time period(s): 1950s

Locale(s): United States

What the book is about: Wilbur, the pig, is desolate when he discovers that he is destined to be the farmer's Christmas dinner, until his spider friend, Charlotte, decides to help him. By weaving words about Wilbur into her web, she makes him the "miracle" of the county, and the farmer will keep him healthy and happy as long as possible.

Where it's reviewed:
Booklist, September 1, 1983, page 96
Hornbook, October 1982, page 489
School Library Journal, March 1984, page 119

Awards the book has won:
Newbery Honor 1953

Other books by the author:
The Trumpet of the Swan, 1970
Stuart Little, 1945

Other books you might like:
Larry Callen, *Pinch*, 1975
    A boy growing up in a country town becomes involved with a pig he trains to hunt, and a mean, crafty gentleman who teaches him the art of trickery.
Janet Chenery, *Wolfie*, 1969
    Two boys find a wolf spider and through observing it and consulting a woman at the nature center, they learn its habits and needs.
Jeffrey Kelly, *Tramp Steamer and the Silver Bullet*, 1984
    Two boys become involved with haunted houses, eccentric ladies, spiders, meat-eating plants, and secret tunnels.
Shirley Rousseau Murphy, *The Pig Who Could Conjure the Wind*, 1978
    A witch's one passion in life, to fly on the wind, is seriously endangered when a demon puts a spell on her.
Jane Yolen, *Spider Jane*, 1978
    Four episodes about a spider and a fly who become friends and decide to live together.

1900

E.B. White

Illustrator: Garth Williams

Stuart Little (New York: Harper and Row, 1945)

Age range: Grades 3-5

Subject(s): Friendship; Animals/Mice

Major character(s): Stuart Little, Mouse; George Little, Mouse; Frederick C. Little, Mouse, Parent

Time period(s): 19th century

Locale(s): New York, New York

What the book is about: The adventure of the debonaire mouse, Stuart Little, as he sets out in the world to seek out his dearest friend, a little bird who stayed a few days in his family's garden.

Where it's reviewed:
New York Times Book Review, November 5, 1967, page 54
New York Times Book Review, February 25, 1968, page 18

Publisher's Weekly, January 23, 1967, page 262

Other books by the author:
The Trumpet of the Swan, 1970
Charlotte's Web, 1952

Other books you might like:
Franz Brandenberg, *Nice New Neighbors*, 1977
    The Fieldmouse children find a way to make new friends when they move to a new house.
Beverly Cleary, *Runaway Ralph*, 1970
    Ralph runs away looking for freedom but winds up a prisoner at a summer camp.
Brian Jacques, *Mariel of Redwall*, 1991
    The mousemaid Mariel achieves a victory at sea for the animals of Redwall Abbey, fighting the savage pirate rat Gabool the Wild.
Eve Titus, *Basil in Mexico*, 1976
    Basil, mouse and master detective seeks the truth about the theft of the Mousa Lisa, and must also solve the mystery of his companion's disappearance.
Jean Van Leeuwen, *The Great Summer Camp Catastrophe*, 1992
    Three mice who live in a department store are dismayed when they are accidentally shipped in a care package to a boy at summer camp in Vermont.

1901

E.B. White

Illustrator: Edward Frascino

The Trumpet of the Swan (New York: Harper & Row, 1970)

Age range: Grades 3-6

Subject(s): Animals/Birds

Major character(s): Sam Beaver, Preteen; Louis, Swan

Time period(s): 1960s

Locale(s): Ontario, Canada; Billings, Montana

What the book is about: Sam keeps a journal of the trumpeter swan nest he finds while on a camping trip with his father in Canada. Each year, the birds migrate to the Red Rock Lakes area of Montana, where Sam lives on a ranch. Louis, an unusual bird who has no voice, comes to Sam's attention and communicates with him in a very special way.

Where it's reviewed:
Booklist, September 1, 1970, page 59
Hornbook, August, 1970, page 391
Kirkus Reviews, April 15, 1970, page 455

Awards the book has won:
William Allen White Children's Book Award 1973
Sequoyah Children's Book Award 1973

Other books by the author:
Charlotte's Web, 1952
Stuart Little, 1945

Other books you might like:
Jane Annixter, *Trumpeter*, 1973
    This narrative tells of Olor and his mate, Asa, and follows them through migration, courtship and mating.
Jeffrey Carroll, *Climbing to the Sun*, 1977

Following an avalanche in Montana, an Indian boy's concern for a wild mountain goat leads him into encounters which reveal much about life to him.

Eth Clifford, *The Killer Swan*, 1980
Lex's involvement with a family of swans headed by a crazed cob helps him work out the emotional problems following his father's suicide.

Paige Dixon, *Summer of the White Goat*, 1977
A young man observes a mountain goat living within the boundaries of Glacier Park in Montana as it deals with the various problems of survival.

Robert Scott McKinnon, *Moose, Bruce and the Goose*, 1969
A abandoned greyhound puppy and a wounded Canada goose form a partnership that becomes famous throughout Montana.

| **1902** |

Robb White

Deathwatch (New York: Doubleday, 1972)

Age range: Grades 5-8

Subject(s): Animals/Sheep; Hunting; Mystery and Detective Stories

Major character(s): Madec, Hunter; Ben, Guide, Student—College

Time period(s): 1970s

Locale(s): Death Valley, California

What the book is about: Ben detests the man he is paid to guide on a bighorn sheep hunt. Cruel and cold, Madec likes hurting things and he is dangerous with a gun. Suddenly, Ben is entangled in the death of a nameless old prospector.

Where it's reviewed:
Booklist, July 15, 1972, page 1000
Hornbook, October 1972, page 475
Kirkus Reviews, March 15, 1972, paege 336

Awards the book has won:
Edgar Allan Poe Award 1973

Other books by the author:
Fire Storm: A Novel, 1979
The Frogmen, 1973
The Survivor, 1964
Up Periscope, 1956

Other books you might like:
William Bence, *People of the Bison*, 1966
A picture maker from a cave painting stone age tribe, is found by a less advanced people. Some of them accept him, but other fear his artistic talent.

Paige Dixon, *Lion on the Mountain*, 1972
When his father announces they are taking a guest on their hunting trip, a boy suspects the newcomer is more interested in killing the animals.

Wayne Dodd, *A Time of Hunting*, 1975
Glimpses an adolescent's change of values and perceptions during Depression days, especially regarding hunting, his only way of earning money.

Robert Scott McKinnon, *To Yellowstone, a Journey Home*, 1975

A bull elk, his lifetime mate, and camel calf strayed from a circus show attempt to reach Yellowstone Park before hunting season opens.

William O. Steele, *The Lone Hunt*, 1956
A young Tennessee boy in the early 1800s goes on a buffalo hunt to prove his manhood.

| **1903** |

Phyllis A. Whitney

Illustrator: H. Tom Hall

Mystery of the Haunted Pool (Louisville, Kentucky: Westminster, 1960)

Age range: Grades 5-7

Subject(s): Mystery and Detective Stories

Major character(s): Susan Price, Preteen; Daniel Teague, Landlord; Edith Sperry, Antiques Dealer, Relative (aunt)

Time period(s): 1960s

Locale(s): Highland Crossing, New York

What the book is about: Aunt Edith runs an antique shop in Highland Crossing. She is trying to make a deal with Captain Teague for his house since Susan's father needs to move out of the dirty air in the city. Before long, Susan discovers a strange face that appears and disappears at the bottom of a pool. Could it be Sarah Teague?

Awards the book has won:
Edgar Allan Poe Award 1961

Other books by the author:
The Mystery of the Gulls, 1974
Mystery on the Isle of Skye, 1974
Secret of the Samurai Sword, 1958
Mystery of the Black Diamonds, 1954

Other books you might like:
Arthur Catherall, *Ten Fathoms Deep*, 1968
A boy joins his father, a tug master, in Singapore and finds himself opposing a group trying to prevent the salvage of a sunken ship.

Franklin W. Dixon, *Lethal Cargo*, 1992
While sailing a friend's yacht from Saint Martin to Florida, Frank and Joe Hardy become involved in a mystery involving a cargo ship.

Cynthia Harnett, *The Cargo of the Madalena*, 1984
Bendy solves the mystery when the master printer, William, fails to receive the paper shipped to him aboard the cargo ship *Madalena*.

Clifford B. Hicks, *Alvin's Swap Shop*, 1976
While running a swap shop, a group of youngsters become involved in the mystery of a sunken ship.

Joan Lowery Nixon, *Mystery of the Secret Stowaway*, 1968
Hoping to join his father who is working in Mexico, Joe stows away on a cruise ship boy passing as a member of a large family on board.

| **1904** |

Phyllis A. Whitney

Mystery of the Hidden Hand (New York: New American Library, 1963)

Age range: Grades 6-9

Subject(s): Mystery and Detective Stories

Major character(s): Gale Tyler, Preteen; Warren Tyler, Teenager; Alexandros Castelis, Hotel Owner (Gale and Warren's uncle)

Time period(s): 1960s

Locale(s): Rhodes, Greece

What the book is about: The first thing Gale and Warren see the morning after arriving at their uncle's hotel in Rhodes is a caped stranger dashing down the hall. They also have to identify an angry woman who identified their family as enemies. Their search for answers leads Gale and Warren into a plot engineered by their cousins, and to the discovery of a shameful family secret.

Where it's reviewed:
Center for Children's Books Bulletin, February 1965, page 95
School Library Journal, February 1978, page 35

Awards the book has won:
Edgar Allan Poe Award 1964

Other books by the author:
Secret of the Stone Face, 1977
Secret of Haunted Mesa, 1975
Mystery on the Isle of Skye, 1974
Secret of Goblin Glen, 1968

Other books you might like:
Catherine Dexter, The Oracle Doll, 1988
    Three youngsters discover how difficult their task will be when they become guardians of a talking doll that is actually the Oracle of Delphi.
Paula Fox, Lily and the Lost Boy, 1987
    Lily grows closer to her brother during the spring their family spends on the Greek island of Thasos, until an American boy disrupts their lives.
Carolyn Keene, The Greek Symbol Mystery, 1981
    Her friends Bess and George accompany Nancy Drew to Greece they encounter two mysteries.
Constance Leonard, Strange Waters, 1985
    Working on board a yacht in the Grecian islands, Tracy James becomes involved in a murder and the theft of priceless artifacts from a museum.
Mary Tyson Pickering, The Mystery of the Greek Icon, 1984
    With her only clue a small Greek icon, Marty's search for her father takes her to Portugal, Switzerland, and Greece.

1905

Phyllis A. Whitney

Secret of the Stone Face (Philadelphia: Westminster, 1977)

Age range: Grades 5-7

Subject(s): Mystery and Detective Stories; Stepfathers

Major character(s): Joanna "Jo" Baird, Preteen; Liza Prentice, Friend

Time period(s): 1970s

Locale(s): Laurel Mountain, New York (Catskill Mountains)

What the book is about: Trying to discredit the reputation of her mother's fiance, Jo encounters a mystery. She is staying with her mother in an old Victorian hotel, and becomes entangled in a mystery involving a dangerous old mill, a labyrinth, and faked antiques.

Where it's reviewed:
Booklist, September 1, 1977, page 45
Kirkus Reviews, April 1, 1977, page 353
School Library Journal, May 1977, page 78

Other books by the author:
Secret of the Spotted Shell, 1967
Secret of the Emerald Star, 1964
Secret of the Tiger's Eye, 1961
Secret of the Samurai Sword, 1958

Other books you might like:
Jean Bothwell, The Mystery Cup, 1968
    A family buys an old house but after their first visit the house is ransacked and local police and residents are reluctant to help catch the culprits.
Barbara Corcoran, The Person in the Potting Shed, 1980
    While vacationing with their mother and new stepfather in a semi-deserted plantation house outside New Orleans, a boy and girl discover a murder.
Peg Kehret, Nightmare Mountain, 1989
    Molly's visit to her aunt and uncle's llama ranch in Washington state leads her into unexpected danger and suspense.
Ruth Nulton Moore, The Ghost Bird Mystery, 1977
    A Mennonite family moves into a reputedly haunted house. Brother and sister solve several mysteries while helping their father set up a bird refuge.
Mary Jo Stephens, Witch of the Cumberlands, 1974
    The arrival of three children on Devil's Mountain enables an elderly woman whom villagers call a witch to unravel the old mystery of a mine disaster.

1906

David Wiesner

Hurricane (New York: Clarion, 1990)

Age range: Grades 2-3

Subject(s): Hurricanes

Major character(s): David, Child; George, Child

Time period(s): 1990s

Locale(s): United States

What the book is about: Brothers David and George experience a horrible storm that rages for most of a whole day. The only thing more unforgettable is the huge elm tree they find the next morning. The tree becomes a vehicle for hours of imaginative fantasies.

Where it's reviewed:
Booklist, December 15, 1990, page 863
School Library Journal, October 1990, page 104

Other books by the author:
June 29, 1999, 1992
Tuesday, 1991
Free Fall, 1990

Other books you might like:
Elizabeth Coatsworth, All-of-a-Sudden Susan, 1974
    When she is caught in a flood, a little girl copes with the situation with the help of her antique doll.
William Kotzwinkle, Dream of Dark Harbor, 1979

A farm boy sets out to see the world and battles a storm at the edge of the sea and encounters a crew of ghosts rising from the water.

Faith McNulty, *Hurricane*, 1983
John and his family prepare for and experience a hurricane on the East Coast.

Joan Balfour Payne, *The Piebald Princess*, 1954
A lazy and imperious cat, claiming to be a Siamese princess, saves the water rats from drowning in a flood, but then loses her regal disguise.

Elizabeth Winthrop, *Belinda's Hurricane*, 1984
While waiting out a fierce hurricane in her grandmother's house on Fox Island, Belinda has a chance to get to know her grandmother's neighbor.

1907

Kate Douglas Wiggin

Rebecca of Sunnybrook Farm (New York: Macmillan, 1903)

Age range: Grades 4-6

Subject(s): City Life

Major character(s): Rebecca Rowena Randall, Child; Miranda, Relative (aunt); Minnie Smellie, Bully (tattletale)

Time period(s): 19th century

Locale(s): Riverboro, Maine

What the book is about: Rebecca is a spunky, curious girl living in a quiet Maine community of the 19th century. She is smart as a whip and funny. She loves pink dresses and parasols, but she can't keep them out of wet paint and thunderstorms. She is sent to live with her two aunts in town and wins the hearts of everyone in the little Maine village. This classic is sometimes called a "girl's Tom Sawyer."

Where it's reviewed:
Reprint Bulletin-Book Reviews, October 1, 1978, page 30

Other books by the author:
The Fairy Ring, 1934
Mother Carey's Children, 1911
The Diary of a Goose Girl, 1902
Polly Oliver's Problem, 1893

Other books you might like:
Louisa M. Alcott, *Little Women*, 1868
Chronicles the joys and troubles of the four March sisters as they grow into young ladies and marry in 19th century New England.

Lewis Carroll, *Alice's Adventures in Wonderland*, 1865
By falling down a rabbit hole, Alice experiences unusual adventures with a variety of nonsensical characters.

Georgene Faulkner, *Melindy's Happy Summer*, 1949
A young Afro-American girl from Boston spends part of her summer on a farm in Maine.

Margaret Sidney, *The Five Little Peppers and How They Grew*, 1881
The classic story of five children growing up in a happy, noisy family.

Mark Twain, *The Adventures of Tom Sawyer*, 1876
The adventures of Tom and his friend, Huck Finn, in a Mississippi River town in the 19th century.

1908

Margaret Wild

Illustrator: Julie Vivas

Let the Celebrations Begin! (New York: Orchard, 1991)

Age range: Grades 2-6

Subject(s): Holocaust; Jews; Courage

Time period(s): 1940s

Locale(s): Bergan-Belsen, Germany (concentration camp)

What the book is about: A picture book which tells the story of women in the concentration camp of Nazi Germany, who used any scraps of fabric, some torn from their own slight clothing, to make stuffed toys for the few remaining children in the camp. By itself, the book will leave young children puzzled since the horrors of the camp are not shown and are barely mentioned, but is still a beautiful tribute to the human spirit.

Where it's reviewed:
Booklist, August 1991, page 2154
School Library Journal, July 1991, page 75

Other books by the author:
Queen's Holiday, 1992
Space Travelers, 1992
Mr. Nick's Knitting, 1989
There's a Sea in My Bedroom, 1987

Other books you might like:
David A. Daler, *The Number on my Grandfather's Arm*,
A little girl questions a number printed on her grandfather's arm and he explains how he received it in a Nazi concentration camp.

Margaretha Shemin, *The Little Riders*, 1988
An American girl living in Nazi-occupied Holland resents the presence of a German soldier quartered in her grandparents' home.

R. Conrad Stein, *The Holocaust*, 1986
A revelation of the atrocities committed against European Jews by Hitler and the Nazis during World War II.

Terry W. Treseder, *Hear O Israel: A Story of the Warsaw Ghetto*, 1990
A Jewish boy describes life in the Warsaw Ghetto and his family's ultimate transference to and decimation in the camp of Treblinka.

1909

Laura Ingalls Wilder

Illustrator: Helen Sewell

By the Shores of Silver Lake (New York: Harper and Row, 1939)

Age range: Grades 4-6

Series: Little House Series

Subject(s): Animals/Wolves; Frontier and Pioneer Life

Major character(s): Laura Ingalls, Child, Settler; Carrie Ingalls, Child, Settler; Grace Ingalls, Child, Settler

Time period(s): 1860s

Locale(s): Silver Lake (Dakota Territory)

What the book is about: Laura and her family are moving west to the Dakota Territory. Pa has heard about a good job with the railroad and the family will be among the first settlers in a new town.

Where it's reviewed:
Times Literary Supplement, May 25, 1967, page 449
Booklist, December 15, 1986, page 656

Awards the book has won:
Newbery Honor 1940
Young Reader's Choice 1942

Other books by the author:
These Happy Golden Years, 1943
Little Town on the Prairie, 1941
The Long Winter, 1940
On the Banks of Plum Creek, 1937

Other books you might like:
Patricia Calvert, *The Snowbird*, 1980
    Willanna faces an uncertain future as she and her younger brother move from Tennessee to the Dakota Territory, where she trains her first horse.
Catherine E. Chambers, *Frontier Dream: Life on the Great Plains*, 1984
    A Norwegian family suffers great hardship as they try to establish a farm on the plains of the Dakota Territory in the 1870s.
Brett Harvey, *My Prairie Year*, 1986
    Elenore describes her experiences living with her family in the Dakota Territory in the late nineteenth century.
Laurie Lawlor, *Addie Across the Prairie*, 1986
    Unhappy to leave her home and friends, Addie accompanies her family to the Dakota Territory and slowly begins to adjust to life on the prairie.
Ann Warren Turner, *Grasshopper Summer*, 1989
    In 1874, Sam and his family move to the southern Dakota Territory, where harsh conditions and a plague of hungry grasshoppers threaten their survival.

1910

Laura Ingalls Wilder

Illustrator: Helen Sewell

Little Town on the Prairie (New York: Harper and Row, 1941)

Age range: Grades 4-6

Subject(s): Frontier and Pioneer Life

Major character(s): Laura Ingalls, Teenager; Mary Ingalls, Teenager, Handicapped (blind); Almanzo Wilder, Farmer, Boyfriend

Time period(s): 1870s; 1880s

Locale(s): DeSmet (Dakota Territory)

What the book is about: In the summer, Laura takes a grueling job - making shirtsfor long, hard hours. She wants to save enough money to send Mary, her blind sister, to the college for the blind in Vinton, Iowa.

Where it's reviewed:
Books and Bookmen, August 1969, page 47

Awards the book has won:
Newbery Honor 1942

Other books by the author:
The Long Winter, 1940

On the Banks of Plum Creek, 1937
Farmer Boy, 1933
Little House in the Big Woods, 1932

Other books you might like:
Kathleen Karr, *Oh, Those Harper Girls! or, Young and Dangerous*, 1992
    In West Texas in 1869, Lily and her five older sisters participate in a series of misguided schemes to save their father's ranch.
Jackie French Koller, *The Primrose Way*, 1992
    Rebekah, a missionary's daughter, befriends a Native American woman and begins to question whether the "savages" need saving after all.
Carolyn Meyer, *Where the Broken Heart Still Beats: The Story of Cnythia Ann Parker*, 1992
    Having been raised by Comanche Indians, 34 year old Cynthia Ann Parker is forcibly returned to her white relatives but longs for her Indian life.
Robin Moore, *The Bread Sister of Sinking Creek*, 1990
    Maggie Callahan, who has a special talent for making bread, struggles to survive on the Pennsylvania frontier in the late 1700s.
Honore Morrow, *On to Oregon!*, 1954
    Based on the actual mid 19th century journey by wagon of seven children through two thousand miles of wilderness and hardship from Missouri to Oregon.

1911

Laura Ingalls Wilder

Illustrator: Helen Sewell

On the Banks of Plum Creek (New York: Harper and Row, 1937)

Age range: Grades 5-6

Series: Little House Series

Subject(s): Frontier and Pioneer Life

Major character(s): Laura Ingalls, Child, Settler; Pa Ingalls, Parent, Settler; Caroline Ingalls, Parent, Settler

Time period(s): 1860s

Locale(s): Plum Creek, Minnesota

What the book is about: At first, the Ingalls live in a sod house in Minnesota. Then Pa builds a house on Plum Creek, hoping to pay for the materials with his harvest. Suddenly a plague of grasshoppers destroys everything in their path and there is no wheat crop at all.

Where it's reviewed:
Instructor, November 1990, page 24
Criticism, Winter 1988, page 47
Learning, February 1988, page 51

Awards the book has won:
Newbery Honor 1938

Other books by the author:
These Happy Golden Years, 1943
Little Town on the Prairie, 1941
The Long Winter, 1953
By the Shores of Silver Lake, 1939

Other books you might like:
Catherine E. Chambers, *Indiana Days: Life in a Frontier Town*, 1984
   In the 1840s, Kristi travels from her family's sod house on the Iowa prairie to an Indiana town to stay with relatives and get an education.
Ann Nolan Clark, *All This Wild Land*, 1976
   Arriving in Minnesota in the late 1800s with plans to homestead, a Finnish family is faced with the problems of starting a new life.
Stig Ericson, *Dan Henry in the Wild West*, 1976
   A young Swede who arrives in Minnesota hoping to homestead yields to the call of the West and sets out to seek his fortune.
Janet Beeler Shaw, *Kirsten's Surprise: A Christmas Story*, 1986
   Kirsten and her family celebrate the first Christmas in their new home on Uncle Olav's farm in mid 19th century Minnesota.
Stephanie S. Tolan, *The Great Skinner Homestead*, 1988
   Jenny relates her family's misadventures homesteading in the Adirondack Mountains during the summer.

1912

Marilyn Wilkes

Illustrator: Larry Ross

C.L.U.T.Z. and the Fission Formula (New York: Dial, 1982)

Age range: Grades 4-6

Subject(s): Robots; Science Fiction

Major character(s): Rodney Pentax, Preteen; C.L.U.T.Z., Robot; Arthur Pentax, Businessman (salesman)

Time period(s): 22nd century

Locale(s): United Fed. of North America, Fictional Country

What the book is about: Everything C.L.U.T.Z. tries to do becomes a disaster. When he talks, a spring goes boing! When he sneezes, he crashes into things. When he cooks, he burns the food. Rodney loves his housekeeper robot but his parents are fed up. Rodney has one week to turn C.L.U.T.Z. into the perfect housekeeper or it's the scrap heap for the robot.

Where it's reviewed:
Booklist, August 1982, page 1529
Kirkus Reviews, May 1, 1982, page 555
School Library Journal, May 1982, page 67

Other books by the author:
C.L.U.T.Z. and the Fission Formula, 1985

Other books you might like:
John Bellairs, *The Eyes of the Killer Robot*, 1986
   Johnny Dixon is put in jeopardy when he and Professor Childermass try to find a robot made many years ago by an evil wizard.
H.M. Hoover, *Orvis*, 1987
   On an Earth that is inhospitable, Toby and her friend find themselves lost in "the empty" with a robot who is their only hope for protection.
Alison Prince, *The Type One Super Robot*, 1986
   While spending the summer together, a boy and his uncle acquire a household robot with a mind of its own.
Alfred Slote, *Omega Station*, 1986

Jack Jameson and his robot twin, Danny One, must save the universe from a mad scientist.
Martin Waddell, *Harriet and the Robot*, 1987
   Harriet gives her friend Anthea a doll for her birthday - a large robot she has made herself and is not quite able to control.

1913

Brenda Scott Wilkinson

Ludell (New York: Harper, 1975)

Age range: Grades 5-8

Subject(s): African Americans; Family Life; Segregation

Major character(s): Ludell Wilson, Preteen, 5th Grader; Ruthie Mae, Friend

Time period(s): 1950s

Locale(s): Waycross, Georgia

What the book is about: Fifth grader Ludell Wilson knows there is a world beyond the small Georgia town of Waycross. She loves her best friend, Ruthie Mae, and gets a crush on Willie, the boy next door. But she experiences the prejudices and segregated schools of the south of the 1950s as well

Where it's reviewed:
Booklist, December 15, 1975, page 581
Hornbook, April 1976, page 160
Kirkus Reviews, September 15, 1975, page 1068

Other books by the author:
Not Separate, Not Equal, 1987
Ludell's New York Time, 1980
Ludell and Willie, 1977

Other books you might like:
Robert Burch, *Hut School and the Wartime Home-Front Heroes*, 1974
   Describes the reactions of a sixth grade class in Georgia to WWII and its effects on their lives.
Beth Bland Engel, *Big Words*, 1982
   Sandy befriends a young black man she finds hiding on her father's property after he has been accused of murdering a white woman in their Georgia town
Jesse Jackson, *Tessie*, 1968
   A young girl from Harlem wins a scholarship and becomes the first black student in an exclusive private school, which seems like a new world to her.
Frank Brown Latham, *The Rise and Fall of Jim Crow*, 1969
   Discusses events and court decisions that led to the creation, and finally the abolition of, the "Jim Crow" laws. (Nonfiction)
Doris Buchanan Smith, *Dreams and Drummers*, 1978
   Growing up is not quite so easy as she'd expected for a teenage girl in a small Georgia town.

1914

Nancy Willard

Illustrator: Richard Jesse Watson

The High Rise Glorious Skittle Skat Roarious Sky Pie Angel Food Cake (New York: Harcourt Brace Jovanovich, 1990)

Age range: Grades 2-4

Subject(s): Angels; Birthdays

Locale(s): United States

What the book is about: Three very special angels surprise a girl who is making an angel food cake for her mother's birthday. The angels consist of a white-haired male in patches, a beautiful Japanese woman and a black child. Watson's detailed, full color illustrations bring the story alive for both adults and children.

Where it's reviewed:
Booklist, September 1, 1990, page 52
Kirkus, July 15, 1990, page 1009
Publisher's Weekly, August 31, 1990, page 67

Other books by the author:
The Ballad of Biddy Early, 1989
Firebrat, 1988
Mountains of Quilt, 1987
Highest Hit, 1978

Other books you might like:
Debby Boone, *The Snow Angel*, 1991
   Rose and her grandfather are the only villagers left who can dream and experience the world's beauty, until a snow angel creates a wondrous event.
Jon Buller, *Fanny and May*, 1984
   Fanny, May and their mother live in a temptingly delicious house that is a pink cake, which Fanny takes a bite of once too often.
Miriam Chaikin, *Yossi Asks the Angels for Help*, 1985
   When he loses the Hanukkah money he planned to use for presents for his sister and parents, Yossi prays to the angels for help.
Barbara Dillon, *The Good-Guy Cake*, 1980
   When Martin eats a magic cake that makes him anxious to behave perfectly and please everyone, he finds that his new behavior has some drawbacks.
Charles Tazewell, *The Littlest Angel*, 1946
   A earth-sick little angel newly arrived in the celestial kingdom finds his recent transition from boy to cherub a difficult one.

1915

Nancy Willard

Illustrator: Marcia Sewall

The Marzipan Moon (New York: Harcourt, 1981)

Age range: Grades 3-4

Subject(s): Food; Magic; Wishes

Time period(s): Indeterminate Past

Locale(s): Fictional Country

What the book is about: A cracked pot given to a poor parish priest has miraculous powers. The almonds in the old, mended but magic crock produce a delicious, nourishing marzipan moon nightly for the priest until a visiting bishop decides the miraculous almonds need a more fitting home. But when the cracked pot is gone, so is the magic.

Where it's reviewed:
Booklist, June 1, 1981, page 1302
Hornbook, August 1981, page 418
Kirkus Reviews, April 1, 1981, page 428

Other books by the author:
Beauty and the Beast, 1992
East of the Sun and West of the Moon, 1989
Uncle Terrible: More Adventures of Anatole, 1982
The Highest Hit, 1978

Other books you might like:
Patricia Coombs, *The Magic Pot*, 1977
   A demon in the guise of a magic pot outwits a greedy, rich man and brings wealth and happiness to a poor old fellow and his wife.
Tomie De Paola, *Strega Nona: An Old Tale*, 1975
   When Strega Nona leaves him alone with her magic pasta pot, Big Anthony is determined to show the townspeople how it works.
Russell Hoban, *The Marzipan Pig*, 1986
   A chain of events occurs involving a grandfather clock, an owl, a bee, a flower, and the feelings of a mouse who eats a marzipan pig.
Lily Toy Hong, *Two of Everything*, 1993
   A poor old Chinese farmer finds a magic pot that duplicates anything put in it, but his efforts to make himself rich lead to unexpected complications.
Deborah Nourse Lattimore, *The Winged Cat: A Tale of Ancient Egypt*, 1992
   In ancient Egypt, a servant girl and a High Priest use magic spells to determine the truth about the death of the girl's sacred cat.

1916

Nancy Willard

Illustrator: Alice Provensen

A Visit to William Blake's Inn (New York: Harcourt Brace Jovanovich, 1981)

Age range: Grades 3 and Up

Subject(s): Poetry

Time period(s): Indeterminate

Locale(s): Fictional Country

What the book is about: The poems guide the reader through an inn managed by the poet, William Blake. Poems echo Blake's own. Magical creatures including the King of Cats and the Wise Cow inhabit the inn. Use from primary read aloud to college literature classes.

Where it's reviewed:
Booklist, September 1981, page 41
School Library Journal, December 1981, page 69

Awards the book has won:
Caldecott Honor Book 1982
Golden Kite Award 1981

Other books by the author:
Pish, Posh, Said Hieronymus Bosch, 1991
The Voyage of the Ludgate Hill: Travels with Robert Louis Stevenson, 1987
The Marzipan Moon, 1981
The Highest Hit, 1978

Other books you might like:
Richard Adams, *The Tyger Voyage*, 1976
   The adventures of two young, inexperienced Tygers who set out from Victorian England into the timeless unknown.

Bobbi Katz, *Poems for Small Friends*, 1989
  A collection of poems, including *Berry Picking*, *The Truth About Dogs*, *Conversation with a Kite*, and *My Travel Tree*.
Jean Marzollo, *In 1492*, 1991
  Rhyming text describes Christopher Columbus's first voyage to the New World.
Ann Warren Turner, *Grass Songs*, 1993
  A collection of seventeen poems describing the experience of traveling West during the 1800s, as seen through the eyes of pioneer women.

1917

Barbara Williams

Illustrator: Kay Chorao

Chester Chipmunk's Thanksgiving (New York: Dutton, 1978)

Age range: Grades 2-3

Subject(s): Holidays

Major character(s): Chester, Chipmunk; Oswald, Opossum; Archie, Chipmunk

Time period(s): Indeterminate

Locale(s): Fictional Country

What the book is about: On Thanksgiving Day, Chester appreciates his blessings, but worries about his Uncle Archie, not well and living in cramped quarters. When Chester invites Archie over, he has a dozen excuses why he can't come as do the Woodchuck family and the Cottontail family. What could turn out to be a lonely day becomes a wild party as all the invited guests change their minds and come to share Chester's pecan pies and bring Thanksgiving dinner with them.

Where it's reviewed:
Center for Children's Books Bulletin, Novmeber 1978, page 56
Kirkus Reviews, June 15, 1978, page 635
School Library Journal, October 1978, page 140

Awards the book has won:
Christopher Award 1979

Other books by the author:
The Author and Squinty Gritt, 1990
The Crazy Gang Next Door, 1990
Jeremy Isn't Hungry, 1978
Gary and the Very Terrible Monster, 1973

Other books you might like:
Eve Bunting, *A Turkey for Thanksgiving*, 1991
  Mr. and Mrs. Moose try to invite a turkey to their Thanksgiving feast.
Margery Cuyler, *Daisy's Crazy Thanksgiving*, 1990
  Wanting to spend a quiet Thanksgiving away from her parents' restaurant, Daisy discovers that her relatives lead even crazier lives than her own.
Dahlov Ipcar, *Hard Scrabble Harvest*, 1976
  Relates in rhyme the farmer's struggle against the odds from spring planting to full harvest and Thanksgiving dinner.
Steven Kroll, *The Squirrel's Thanksgiving*, 1991
  A brother and sister squirrel appreciate each other more after being exposed to their really naughty cousins at Thanksgiving dinner.
Edna Miller, *Mousekin's Thanksgiving*, 1985

Mousekin and his forest friends struggle to survive the winter together with a wild turkey.

1918

Barbara Williams

Illustrator: Emily Arnold McCully

Mitzi and the Terrible Tyranosaurus Rex (New York: Dutton, 1982)

Age range: Grades 2-5

Subject(s): Stepfamilies; Brothers and Sisters; Family Life

Major character(s): Mitzi, Child; Frederick, Preteen; Walter, Step-Parent

Time period(s): 1980s

Locale(s): United States

What the book is about: This is the story of eight year old Mitzi, whose archeologist mother is about to marry Walter, who has two boys, ages three and eleven. Things do not go well at first, as Mitzi is understandably jealous when her mother offers to take Frederick on a dig. We see genuinely caring people working out real problems as Mitzi finds positive ways to get her share of the attention.

Where it's reviewed:
Booklist, June 1, 1982, page 1316
Kirkus Reviews, April 15, 1982, page 492
School Library Journal, January 1982, page 82

Other books by the author:
The Crazy Gang Next Door, 1990
Donna Jean's Disaster, 1986
Brigham Young and Me, Clarissa, 1978
Albert's Toothache, 1974

Other books you might like:
Carol Lea Benjamin, *The Wicked Stepdog*, 1982
  When her father remarries, twelve year old Louise has to come to grips with an unwanted stepmother and a slobbering golden retriever.
Kathryn Ewing, *Things Won't Be the Same*, 1980
  Upset by her mother's coming remarriage, Marcy feels even worse when she learns she'll be staying with her father whom she hardly remembers.
Kevin Henkes, *Two under Par*, 1987
  When his mother's new marriage takes them into her new husband's house, Wedge struggles with feelings of resentment and dislike for his stepfather.
Mindy Schanback, *Does Third Grade Last Forever?*, 1990
  When her mother remarries, eight year old Tracy has to get used to a new school and a new obnoxious stepfather.
Susan Richards Shreve, *Family Secrets*, 1979
  Sammy deals with many difficult situations, including his brother's friend's suicide, the divorce of his aunt and uncle and the loss of his dog.

1919

Jay Williams

Illustrator: Paul Sagsoorian

Danny Dunn and the Universal Glue (New York: McGraw Hill, 1977)

Age range: Grades 4-6

Subject(s): Mystery and Detective Stories; Pollution; Science Fiction

Major character(s): Professor Euclid Bullfinch, Scientist; Danny Dunn, Inventor, Preteen; Irene Miller, Neighbor, Preteen

Time period(s): 1970s

Locale(s): Midston

What the book is about: Danny goes fishing, falls in the stream and discovers that the water tastes like lemonade. Is this caused by waste from a new factory? Danny is soon plunged into a wild adventure fighting water pollution and an emergency that threatens his whole town.

Where it's reviewed:
Booklist, January 15, 1978, page 816
Center for Children's Books Bulletin, February 1978, page 104
Shool Library Journal, January 1978, page 92

Other books by the author:
Danny Dunn and the Voice From Space, 1979
Danny Dunn and the Smallifying Machine, 1969
Danny Dunn and the Automatic House, 1965
Danny Dunn and the Homework Machine, 1958

Other books you might like:
Margaret E. Bechard, *My Sister, My Science Report*, 1990
    Tess feels stuck with the class nerd for a partner in a science project. But they become good friends as they study an unlikely subject, Tess' sister.
James Lincoln Collier, *When the Stars Begin to Fall*, 1986
    Angry that his entire family is considered to be poor trash, Harry defies his father and tries to prove that a factory is polluting their small town.
Kathryn Lasky, *Shadows in the Water*, 1992
    The two sets of Starbuck twins use their telepathic powers and the aid of some endangered dolphins to help their father track down toxic waste.
Robert Lipsyte, *The Chemo Kid*, 1992
    When drugs from his chemotherapy suddenly transform Fred from wimp into superhero, he and his friends plot to rid the town of lethal toxic waste.
John McNamara, *Revenge of the Nerd*, 1984
    A genius with a reputation for being a nerd wreaks revenge on his tormentors using his latest science project.

1920

Jay Williams

Illustrator: Brinton Turkle

Danny Dunn on the Ocean Floor (New York: McGraw-Hill, 1960)

Age range: Grades 4-6

Subject(s): Diving; Sea Stories

Major character(s): Professor Euclid Bullfinch, Scientist (chemist); Danny Dunn, Inventor (Preteen); Irene Miller, Neighbor (Preteen)

Time period(s): 1950s

Locale(s): Nomata, Mexico

What the book is about: Dr. Grimes is planning a remarkable project for the exploration of the ocean floor. He intends to build a bathyscape. The kids helped him "discover" plexiglas, so of course they get to go on the project. They travel through the Panama Canal and dive in the Pacific, based closed to Mazatlan.

Awards the book has won:
Young Reader's Choice Award 1963

Other books by the author:
The Burglar Next Door, 1976
Bag Full of Nothing, 1974
The Hawkstone, 1971
Danny Dunn and the Fossil Cave, 1961

Other books you might like:
Jean Craighead George, *Shark Beneath the Reef*, 1989
    On the Island of Coronado, a young Mexican fisherman comes of age as he becomes aware of the politics, corruption and changes around him.
Will Hobbs, *Changes in Latitudes*, 1993
    A trip changes a teenager's attitudes as he becomes exposed to his brother's consuming interest in endangered species and to his own selfishness.
Madeleine L'Engle, *The Arm of the Starfish*, 1965
    A student reporting to his summer job on an island near Portugal finds himself at the center of a struggle between his boss and a group of Americans.
Scott O'Dell, *The Black Pearl*, 1967
    In claiming as his own the magnificent black pearl he finds, a youth enrages the sea devil who legend says is its owner.
Nola Thacker, *Summer Stories*, 1988
    Beginning with a bus trip and ending with a sailboat ride, Red enjoys both independence and companionship as she visits the Gulf of Mexico.

1921

Jay Williams

Illustrator: Frisco Henstra

The Wicked Tricks of Tyl Uilenspiegel (New York: Four Winds, 1978)

Age range: Grades 3-5

Subject(s): Folk Tales; Hero

Major character(s): Tyl Uilenspiegel, Hero

Time period(s): 17th century

Locale(s): Netherlands

What the book is about: For several centuries, Tyl has been a popular Dutch folk hero. This story descr ibes how he outwits Spanish soldiers and misers, steals from the rich and gives to the poor, and lines his own pockets in the process.

Where it's reviewed:
Booklist, July 1, 1978, page 1682
Hornbook, June 1978, page 290
School Library Journal, May 1978, page 73

Other books by the author:
The Burgler Next Door, 1976
Everyone Knows What a Dragon Looks Like, 1976
The Hawkstone, 1971

The King with Six Friends, 1968

Other books you might like:
Kevin Crossley-Holland, *The Faber Book of Northern Legends*, 1983
Includes twenty-two tales drawn from Norse mythology, Germanic heroic legends and Icelandic sagas.
Roger Duvoisin, *The Three Sneezes and Other Swiss Tales*, 1941
Thirty-seven folk tales from the French and German areas of Switzerland.
F.N. Monjo, *The Sea Beggar's Son*, 1974
The story Piet Heyn, whose capture of Spanish ships carrying valuable cargo was helpful in Holland overthrowing Spanish rule in the 17th century.
Steve Sanfield, *The Adventures of High John the Conqueror*, 1989
Sixteen tales about High John the Conqueror, the traditional trickster hero of blacks during and immediately after the time of slavery in America.
Dorothy Van Woerkom, *The Queen Who Couldn't Bake Gingerbread*, 1975
When a king is unable to find a queen who bakes gingerbread, he realizes there are more important things to consider in selecting a wife.

⟦**1922**⟧

Karen Lynn Williams

Baseball and Butterflies (New York: Lothrop, 1990)

Age range: Grades 2-3

Subject(s): Sports/Baseball; Animals/Insects; Brothers

Major character(s): Joey, Child; Daniel, Child

Time period(s): 1990s

Locale(s): United States

What the book is about: At the end of third grade, Daniel looks forward to summer, but his little brother Joey is a better baseball player than he is, and a nuisance tattle tale. Daniel's butterflies are prettier flying free than they are in his collection. He learns new ways to enjoy butterflies and his brother.

Where it's reviewed:
Kirkus Reviews, July 15, 1990, page 1009
School Library Journal, December 1990, page 90

Other books by the author:
When Africa Was Home, 1991
Galimoto, 1990

Other books you might like:
Matt Christopher, *The Lucky Baseball Hat*, 1991
Marty loses his lucky baseball hat and his confidence along with it.
David Halecroft, *Championship Summer*, 1991
Rivalry between seventh and eighth grade players from Alden Junior High threatens playoff hopes.
Constance Hiser, *Dog on Third Base*, 1991
James and the gang are busy with spring baseball practice until the dog, Tag, who plays third base, disappears.
P.J. Petersen, *The Fireplug Is First Base*, 1990
A small baseball player surprises his bigger teammates when he finally gets his chance at bat.
Alfred Slote, *Make-Believe Ball Player*, 1989

Although he's not very good at baseball, ten year old Henry uses his imagination to become a better player.

⟦**1923**⟧

Margery Williams

The Velveteen Rabbit (Garden City, New Jersey: Doubleday, 1926)

Age range: Grades 3-5

Subject(s): Fantasy; Animals/Rabbits; Toys

Major character(s): Skin Horse, Toy, Horse; Velveteen Rabbit, Toy, Rabbit; The Boy, Child

Time period(s): Indeterminate

Locale(s): England

What the book is about: Even though he knows the boy has loved him, by the time the velveteen rabbit is dirty, worn out, and about to be burned, he has almost given up hope of ever finding the magic called Real. The old skin horse told him about it in the nursery long, long ago. A classic to be enjoyed at any age.

Where it's reviewed:
Hornbook, June 1975, page 289
New York Times Book Review, September 9, 1973, page 8
Publisher's Weekly, March 10, 1975, page 57

Other books you might like:
V.H. Drummond, *Phewtus the Squirrel*, 1987
A knitted squirrel has a chance to become real for a while and learns he vastly prefers life as a toy.
Don Freeman, *Beady Bear*, 1977
A toy bear goes off to a cave to live as a real bear should, only to find he needs something more to be truly happy.
Kathryn Osebold Galbraith, *Laura Charlotte*, 1990
A mother describes her love for a toy elephant she was given as a child, a gift she has now passed on to her daughter.
Consuelo Joerns, *The Midnight Castle*, 1983
A family of mice makes itself at home in a toy castle only to find that the castle and its medieval inhabitants become real at the stroke of midnight.
Leo Lionni, *Alexander and the Wind-up Mouse*, 1969
Alexander, a real mouse, wants to be a toy mouse like his friend, Willy, until he discovers Willy is to be thrown away.

⟦**1924**⟧

Ursula Moray Williams

Bogwoppit (Nashville: Nelson, 1978)

Age range: Grades 5-6

Subject(s): Orphans; Aunts and Uncles

Major character(s): Samantha, Orphan; Daisy, Relative (aunt)

Time period(s): 1970s

Locale(s): England

What the book is about: Samantha goes to live with Aunt Daisy when her Aunt Lily goes traveling. Bogwoppits are furry, cuddly critters in danger of extinction. They multiply and take Aunt Daisy prisoner in the drain.

Where it's reviewed:
Booklist, September 1, 1978, page 54
Center for Children's Books Bulletin, March 1979, page 128
Kirkus Reviews, August 15, 1978, page 879

Other books by the author:
Three Toymakers, 1971
Gobboliino the Witch's Cat, 1965
Moonball, 1965

Other books you might like:
Mary Anderson, *The Terrible Thing in the Bottle*, 1989
Cassie and Barney are cousins who detest each other and are thrown together for a year when an eccentric aunt takes them to England.
Nina Bawden, *The House of Secrets*, 1963
While staying at their aunt's in an English seaside town, the Mallory children find a secret passage into the mysterious old house next door.
Susan Meyers, *Melissa Finds a Mystery*, 1966
A young girl, spending the summer with her eccentric aunt, is confronted with a mystery involving the house her where her ancestors lived.
Doris Orgel, *Baron Munchausen*, 1971
Fifteen tall tales as the Baron fights the fiercest monsters, encounters flaming volcanoes, flys on eagles and off to the wild blue yonder and beyond.
Alvin Schwartz, *Kickle Snifters and Other Fearsome Critters*, 1976
Brief text and illustrations introduce such strange creatures from American folklore as the snawfus, billdad, lufferlang and tripodero.

1925

Vera B. Williams

Something Special for Me (New York: Greenwillow, 1983)

Age range: Grades 1-3

Subject(s): Birthdays

Major character(s): Rosa, Child; Mother, Parent; Grandmother, Grandparent

Time period(s): Indeterminate

Locale(s): United States

What the book is about: Rosa gets to buy her own special birthday present. She tries all sorts of things and decides an accordian is what she really wants. Rosa learns it is fun to be different than her friends.

Where it's reviewed:
Booklist, April 15, 1983, page 1098
Center for Children's Books Bulletin, March 1983, page 140
Hornbook, June 1983, page 296

Other books by the author:
Music, Music for Everyone, 1984
A Chair for My Mother, 1982

Other books you might like:
Jan Brett, *Annie and the Wild Animals*, 1985
The food Annie leaves out for her lost cat Taffy attracts many woodland animals instead.
Dennis Haseley, *The Old Banjo*, 1983

In this musical fantasy, the long forgotten instruments play a concert and fill the farm air with their own special sounds.
Amy Hest, *The Purple Coat*, 1986
Gabrielle knows she will feel special in an unusual new coat.
Leo Lionni, *Cornelius*, 1983
Cornelius is a crocodile who has seen the world and learned new things.
Eleanor Schick, *A Piano for Julie*, 1984
Julie loves the piano at her grandmother's house and she longs for one of her own.

1926

Willie Wilson

Illustrator: Karen Bertrand

Up Mountain One Time (New York: Orchard, 1987)

Age range: Grades 5-7

Subject(s): Animals

Major character(s): Viggo, Mongoose; Manteoba, Witch; Spike, Writer (poet), Iguana

Time period(s): Indeterminate

Locale(s): St. Thomas, Virgin Islands of the United States

What the book is about: Viggo the mongoose makes choices about whether to live in the wild or a populated area in this animal fantasy set on St. Thomas. He spends his childhood in a safe churchyard, but when his mother disappears, he sets off on his own, meets other island dwellers, and explores the hills and the sea.

Where it's reviewed:
Booklist, September 15, 1987, page 154
Kirkus Reviews, July 15, page 1076
School Library Journal, September 1987, page 184

Other books you might like:
James Berry, *The Future-Telling Lady and Other Stories*, 1993
Six children's stories from the West Indies of ghosts, magic, mules, a mongoose, and a hen.
Elizabeth Starr Hill, *Ever-After Island*, 1977
Two children accompany their scientist father on an expedition to a remote island inhabited by elves, mermaids, a wizard, and other magical creatures.
Rudyard Kipling, *Rikki-Tikki-Tavi*, 1992
A courageous mongoose thwarts the evil plans of Nag and Nagina, two black cobras who live in the garden.
Brinton Turkle, *Mooncoin Castle*, 1970
A ghost and a witch agree to help the jackdaws prevent the razing of Mooncoin Castle ruins to make way for a supermarket.
John Vigor, *Danger, Dolphins and Ginger Beer*, 1993
While camping on Crab Island, Sally and her two brothers rescue an injured dolphin and become involved in a dangerous adventure.

1927

Patricia Windsor

Mad Martin (New York: Harper, 1976)

Age range: Grades 5-6

Subject(s): Foster Homes; Grandparents

Major character(s): Martin, Child; Mr. Drivic, Grandparent; Mrs. Crimp, Neighbor

Time period(s): Indeterminate

Locale(s): London, England

What the book is about: Martin lives alone with his grandfather. He is a sad and lonely boy who is very shy. When Grandfather becomes ill, Martin is taken by his neighbor, Mrs. Crimp. From her, he learns how to be clean, how to play, and how to have a friend.

Where it's reviewed:
Booklist, November 15, 1976, page 478
Hornbook, October 1976, page 502
Kirkus Reviews, July 1, 1976, page 733

Other books by the author:
Two Weirdos and a Ghost, 1991
The Sandman's Eyes, 1985
Killing Time, 1980
Diving for Roses, 1976

Other books you might like:
Vera Cleaver, *Moon Lake Angel: A Novel*, 1987
  Kitty, whose mother does not want a child in her life, spends the summer with Aunt Petal and eventually learns to accept her mother's weakness.
Helen Cresswell, *Dear Shrink*, 1982
  Three English children suddenly find themselves in foster care and must use all their courage and ingenuity to cope with the situation.
Patricia Pendergraft, *As Far as Mill Springs*, 1991
  Tired of being bounced from one foster home to another, Robert sets out with Abiah on a long journey to find his mother by Christmas.
Diana J. Wieler, *Last Chance Summer*, 1986
  A troubled preteen with a history of running away from foster homes is given a last chance on a farm with other "tough kids" and a caring Englishman.
Phyllis Anderson Wood, *The Revolving Door Stops Here*, 1990
  Eric moves from one foster home to another, always wishing for a family of his own.

| 1928 |

Patricia Windsor

The Sandman's Eyes (New York: Delacorte, 1985)

Age range: Grades 6-10

Subject(s): Mystery and Detective Stories

Major character(s): Michael Thorn, Teenager

Time period(s): 1980s

Locale(s): United States

What the book is about: When Michael is sixteen, he witnesses a murder. He is so traumatized by the event, that when he is accused of the murder, he is unable to defend himself. Everyone but Michael's grandfather thinks he is guilty. After two years in a juvenile detention facility, Michael returns to his grandparents' home and begins to search for the killer. He finds out his mother, whom he thought dead, is alive and he searches for her as well.

Where it's reviewed:
Horn Book, September/October 1985, page 571
School Library Journal, May 1985, page 111

Awards the book has won:
Edgar Allan Poe Award 1986

Other books by the author:
How a Weirdo and a Ghost Can Change Your Entire Life, 1986
Killing Time, 1980
Mad Martin, 1976
The Summer Before, 1973

Other books you might like:
Jay Burnett, *The Dangling Witness*, 1974
  A young adult who witnesses a murder decides to keep quiet after he is threatened by the killer, but finds his silence increasingly hard to bear.
Jesse Harris, *The Witness*, 1992
  McKenzie Gold gets entangled in a string of babysitter murders when her special psychic power allows her to see through the eyes of the killer.
Jan Hayden, *Has Anyone Seen Allie?*, 1991
  After her best friend, Allie, disappears bearing a dangerous secret, Judy is stalked through her Wyoming town by a shadowy killer.
Ernest Pintoff, *Zachary: A Novel*, 1990
  Sole witness to the murder of a local war hero in a just after World War II, Zachary joins forces with the detective called to solve the crime.
Julian F. Thompson, *Discontinued*, 1985
  When his mother and brother are "discontinued" by a car bomb, Duncan begins a search for the killer and his motive.

| 1929 |

Henry Winterfeld

Illustrator: Charlotte Kleinert

Detectives in Togas (New York: Harcourt, 1956)

Age range: Grades 4-7

Subject(s): Historical; Mystery and Detective Stories

Major character(s): Mucias, Preteen, Detective—Amateur; Antonius, Preteen, Detective—Amateur; Rufus, Preteen, Detective—Amateur

Time period(s): Indeterminate Past

Locale(s): Rome, Italy

What the book is about: In an effort to save a boy wrongly accused, a group of young friends living in Ancient Rome search for the person who scrawled graffiti on the wall of the temple of Minerva. Rufus faces a sinister search for the real culprit, with his friends, as time gets shorter and the trail becomes more twisted and dangerous.

Where it's reviewed:
School Library Journal, February 1978, page 35

Other books by the author:
Mystery of the Roman Ransom, 1981
Castaways in Lilliput, 1960

Other books you might like:
Eilis Dillon, *The Shadow of Vesuvius*, 1977

A Greek slave of a Roman artisan plans his escape from the city of Pompeii amid ominous signs of the approaching eruption of Mt. Vesuvius.

Elizabeth Levy, *Running out of Time*, 1980
Three friends suddenly find themselves in the Roman Empire of 73 B.C. where they become catalysts in a slave revolt led by the gladiator, Spartacus.

Steven Rayson, *The Crows of War*, 1974
Captured and blinded during the Roman invasion of Britain in 43 A.D., a Celtic girl discovers that even the Romans have good people among them.

Rosemary Sutcliff, *Song for a Dark Queen*, 1978
The life of Boadicea queen of the Iceni, who led them and other British tribes in a valiant but futile revolt against the Romans in 6.2. A.D.

Chelsea Quinn Yarbro, *Four Horses for Tishtry*, 1985
Tishtry's wish to buy her family's freedom from slavery in the Roman Empire inspires her to perform dangerous feats of stunt riding.

1930

Elizabeth Winthrop

Illustrator: Wendy Watson

Belinda's Hurricane (New York: Dutton, 1984)

Age range: Grades 2-5

Subject(s): Grandparents; Hurricanes; Islands

Major character(s): Belinda, Child; Granny May, Grandparent

Time period(s): 1980s

Locale(s): Fox Island, Maine

What the book is about: Belinda experiences a hurricane on Fox Island with her Granny May, cranky Mr. Fletcher and his bulldog, Fishface. By the time the ferry is running again, Belinda will solve the mystery of the shell necklace, and find the perfect birthday gift for Granny May.

Where it's reviewed:
Booklist, January 1, 1985, page 645
Children's Center for Books Bulletin, March 1985, page 137
Schoool Library Journal, February 1985, page 80

Other books by the author:
Lizzie and Harold, 1986
Katharine's Doll, 1983
Journey to the Bright Kingdom, 1979
Marathon Miranda, 1979

Other books you might like:
Harriette Sheffer Abels, *September Storm*, 1981
Three young people stranded in a severe storm on an island draw upon all their resources to stay alive.

Lonzo Anderson, *The Day the Hurricane Happened*, 1974
On the Caribbean island of St. John, a family experiences the drama, danger, and destruction of a hurricane.

Judith Caseley, *Hurricane Harry*, 1991
Turning five years old, Harry faces the challenges of moving to a new house, acquiring a pet turtle, and starting kindergarten.

Matt Christopher, *Stranded*, 1974

Shipwrecked with his dog on an uninhabited Caribbean Island after a hurricane that washed his parents overboard, a blind boy struggles for survival.

Gertrude Chandler Warner, *Bus Station Mystery*, 1974
The Alden children, isolated in a storm at a small bus station, are led into a mystery centering on a polluted river.

1931

Elizabeth Winthrop

The Castle in the Attic (New York: Holiday, 1985)

Age range: Grades 4-6

Subject(s): Castles; Knights and Knighthood; Fantasy

Major character(s): William, Preteen; Mrs. Phillips, Housekeeper, Child-Care Giver; Sir Simon, Knight

Time period(s): Indeterminate Past

Locale(s): Earth

What the book is about: William is so upset when he learns his beloved nanny, Mrs. Phillips, is returning to England, he shrinks her to the size of the toy knight in her inherited wooden castle. To bring her back, William must become tiny himself and accompany Sir Simon, the knight, on an adventure to overthrow a wicked magician who long ago usurped the throne of Sir Simon's kingdom. Fantasy, gymnastics, and moral dilemmas abound.

Where it's reviewed:
Horn Book, March/April 1986, page 204
School Library Journal, February 1986, page 91

Awards the book has won:
Dorothy Canfield Fisher Children's Book Award 1987

Other books by the author:
The Battle for the Castle, 1993
Journey to the Bright Kingdom, 1979
Knock Knock, Who's There?, 1978
A Little Demonstration of Affection, 1975

Other books you might like:
Otto Coontz, *The Night Walkers*, 1982
When half of the children of Covendale get a mysterious illness, only two teens and a housekeeper suspect the infection is also destroying their souls

M.S. Craig, *Happles and Cinnamunger*, 1981
When the Taggart family's housekeeper wins a trip around the world, her replacement brings a troop of fairies into the house.

Mary Nash, *Mrs. Coverlet's Magicians*, 1961
While the housekeeper is away participating in a baking contest, Toad Persever resorts to his magic kit to get rid of the babysitter, Miss Penalty.

Mary Pope Osborne, *The Knight at Dawn*, 1993
Josh and his sister, Annie, use the magic treehouse to travel to the Middle Ages, where they explore a castle and are helped by a mysterious knight.

Tor Seidler, *The Tar Pit*, 1987
Shy Edward Small has only one real friend, a loving and brave dinosaur. They find adventure near a curious pond full of dark, oily goo and daydreams.

1932

Elizabeth Winthrop

Marathon Miranda (New York: Holiday House, 1979)

Age range: Grades 4-6

Subject(s): Asthma; Adoption; Fear

Major character(s): Miranda, Teenager (asthmatic); Phoebe, Teenager, Adoptee

Time period(s): 1970s

Locale(s): Vermont

What the book is about: Miranda has frequent asthma attacks. Phoebe convinces her to try running to strengthen her lungs. Miranda finds she loves running, and trains for a marathon, overcoming her asthma. She, in turn, helps Phoebe face the fact that she was adopted.

Where it's reviewed:
Horn Book, August 1979, page 419
School Library Journal, September 1979, page 151

Other books by the author:
Miranda in the Middle, 1980 (Sequel to Marathan Miranda)
Sloppy Kisses, 1980
Are You Sad, Mama?, 1979
Journey to the Bright Kingdom, 1979

Other books you might like:
Rose Blue, *Seven Years From Home*, 1976
    Follows an adopted boy's emotional struggle to find his "real" parents and ultimately, himself.
David Getz, *Thin Air*, 1990
    Jacob struggles to overcome asthma and his overprotective brother as he tries to fit in with his peers.
Miska Miles, *Aaron's Door*, 1977
    Unable to adjust to the idea of being adopted, Aaron locks his door against the world.
Walter Dean Myers, *Mop, Moondance, and the Nagasaki Knights*, 1992
    After TJ and his brothers are adopted, their biggest challenge is the international baseball tournament and a homeless teammate.
Gunilla Brodde Norris, *The Top Step*, 1970
    A youngster who has been told that he'll outgrow his asthma anxiously awaits the arrival of that moment.

1933

Elizabeth Winthrop

Illustrator: Noelle Massena

Walking Away (New York: Harper, 1973)

Age range: Grades 5-7

Subject(s): Grandparents; Farm Life

Major character(s): Emily, Vacationer; Nina, Friend

Time period(s): 1970s

Locale(s): United States

What the book is about: Emily loves summers on Grandfather's farm. When her friend, Nina, comes to visit, she and Grandfather don't get along at all. Nina takes up all of Emily's time, smuggles in cigarettes, looks down on the local people, and goes where she isn't supposed to go. A story of changing relationships.

Where it's reviewed:
Booklist, July 15, 1973, page 1074
Center for Children's Books Bulletin, December 1973, page 72
Kirkus Reviews, April 1, 1973, page 386

Other books by the author:
The Battle for the Castle, 1993
Luke's Bully, 1990
The Castle in the Attic, 1985
Belinda's Hurricane, 1984

Other books you might like:
Jacqueline Turner Banks, *Project Wheels*, 1993
    While helping to raise money for Wayne's motorized wheelchair, Angela finds her relationships with her four best friends changing.
Paula Danziger, *It's an Aardvark-Eat-Turtle World*, 1985
    When Rosie, her mother, her best friend, and her best friend's father form a new family and find it takes a lot of work to make a family.
Christine McDonnell, *Friends First*, 1990
    An eighth grade girl faces evolving relationships, complex changes and feelings arising from her first steps into adulthood.
Georgess McHargue, *The Horseman's Word*, 1981
    When Leigh goes to help her aunt and uncle with the horses on their farm and becomes involved with a local boy and the grandfather who blackmails him.
Andrea Wyman, *Red Sky at Morning*, 1991
    In 1909 in Indiana, Callie finds that she must grow up quickly when she is left alone on the farm with her ailing grandfather.

1934

Bernard Wiseman, Author/Illustrator

The Lucky Runner (New Canaan, CT: Garrard, 1979)

Age range: Grades 2-3

Subject(s): Superstition; Talent

Major character(s): Buddy, Child, Sports Figure (runner); Chub, Child

Time period(s): 1970s

Locale(s): United States

What the book is about: Buddy is a very good runner, but he always says that his lucky socks make him win. When the state championship race comes, his coach gives him a new pair of shoes. Buddy can't find his lucky socks. He hopes his mom can get his socks to him in time.

Where it's reviewed:
Children's Book Review Service, December 1979, page 35
School Library Journal, December 1979, page 97

Other books by the author:
Morris Has a Cold, 1979
Morris Tells Boris Mother Goose, 1979
My Googoo, 1979
Quick Quackers, 1979

Other books you might like:
Mary Blount Christian, *The Lucky Man*, 1979

The catastrophes of hard-luck Felix land him in court where a wise judge's decisions prove him to be a lucky man.

Kathlyn Gay, *They Don't Wash Their Socks*, 1990
Superstitions held by individuals or teams in all the major sports.(Non-fiction)

Joanne Robertson, *Sea Witches*, 1991
A Scottish grandmother explains the legend behind old superstitions to her grandson.

Diane Stanley, *The Good Luck Pencil*, 1986
A magic pencil brings Mary Ann more good luck than she can handle.

Yoshiko Uchida, *Makoto, the Smallest Boy*, 1970
With the help of his father's good-luck cap and a gift from his friend, Makoto finally finds something in which he can be first.

1935

Bernard Wiseman

Morris and Boris at the Circus (New York: Harper, 1988)

Age range: Grades 1-2

Subject(s): Circus; Animals

Major character(s): Morris, Moose; Boris, Bear

Time period(s): Indeterminate

Locale(s): United States

What the book is about: Two friends, Morris the Moose and Boris the Bear, attend the circus, and end up being part of the action.

Other books by the author:
Barber Bear, 1987
Handy Hound, 1987
Morris and Boris, 1970
Morris Goes to School, 1970

Other books you might like:
Lois Ehlert, *Circus*, 1992
Leaping lizards, marching snakes, a bear on the high wire and others perform in a very unusual circus.

Michael Garland, *Circus Girl*, 1993
Alice and members of her family spend a busy day working in a circus as it travels from town to town.

Marilyn Kaye, *Gonzo the Great*, 1989
Gonzo searches for an act that will cause people to call him "Gonzo the Great" and discovers he has to choose between friends and the circus.

Alice Low, *Zena and the Witch Circus*, 1990
A magically untalented witch is barred from performing in the Witch Circus until one day when she becomes a hero.

Barbara Westman, *Dancing Dogs: Charlotte and Emilio at the Circus*, 1991
Stage-struck dogs Charlotte and Emilio become dancing stars in their uncle's traveling circus.

1936

Bernard Wiseman, Author/Illustrator

Morris Has a Cold (New York: Dodd, 1978)

Age range: Grades 1-3

Subject(s): Illness; Humor; Animals

Major character(s): Morris, Moose; Boris, Bear

Time period(s): Indeterminate

Locale(s): United States

What the book is about: Morris is a moose with a bad head cold. His friend, Boris, a bear, tries to help him but soon gets awfully tired of Morris. Fun reading for newly independent readers.

Where it's reviewed:
Booklist, February 15, 1978, page 1013
Kirkus Reviews, February 1978, page 106
School Library Journal, May 1978, page 82

Other books by the author:
Morris the Moose, 1989
Dr. Duck and Nurse Swan, 1984
Christmas with Morris and Boris, 1983
Iglooks Seal, 1977

Other books you might like:
Eve Bunting, *A Turkey for Thanksgiving*, 1991
Mr. and Mrs. Moose try to invite a turkey to their Thanksgiving feast.

Leonard Kessler, *The Worst Team Ever*, 1985
Old Turtle and Melvin Moose help the worst baseball team in the swamp win the final game of the season.

Lorenz Lee, *A Weekend in the City*, 1991
As Pig and Duck describe to Moose what they've planned for his visit to the city, Moose is reminded of outrageous experiences in the country.

Laura Joffe Numeroff, *If You Give a Moose a Muffin*, 1991
Chaos can ensue if you give a moose a muffin and start him on a cycle of urgent requests.

Thor Wickstrom, *The Big Night Out*, 1993
Bear, Moose and Goose go out for a night on the town.

1937

David Wiseman

Adam's Common (Boston: Houghton Mifflin, 1984)

Age range: Grades 4-7

Subject(s): Fantasy; Space and Time

Major character(s): William Trafford, Teenager; Peggy Donaldson, Teenager

Time period(s): 1840s (1849); 1980s (1984)

Locale(s): Traverton, England

What the book is about: Peggy, transplanted from Boston to Traverton, England, hates her new world except for Adam's Common which is beautiful. When she finds out that its lovely woods and meadows are to become an industrial park, she launches a campaign to save it. But she has little chance of success until she makes contact with William Trafford, living in cholera-plagued Traverton of 1849. William has information vital to Peggy's effort to discover the history of Adam's Common.

Where it's reviewed:
Center for Children's Books Bulletin, January 1985, page 97
Kirkus Reviews, November 1, 1984, page J98
School Library Journal, November 1984, page 129

Other books by the author:
Thimbles: A Novel, 1992

A Tie to the Past, 1989
Blodwen and the Guardians, 1983
Jeremy Visick, 1981

Other books you might like:
Elisabeth Beresford, *Curious Magic*, 1980
   A boy's vacation brings him in contact with a white witch, a girl with increasing magic powers, a boy from the sea and travel backwards in time.
Nancy Bond, *Another Shore*, 1988
   Lyn, working in a reconstructed colonial settlement, finds herself transported back to 1744, when French inhabitants are at war with England.
Phyllis Reynolds Naylor, *Faces in the Water*, 1981
   During Daniel's summer visit with his grandmother, characters and events from his visit to York England, appear and reappear mysteriously.
Colby Rodowsky, *Keeping Time*, 1983
   Drew, a member of a band of street performers, finds himself slipping back in time, where he acquires the strength to deal with his unusual lifestyle.
Robert Westall, *The Devil on the Road*, 1978
   While seeking shelter from a sudden rainstorm, a motorcyclist finds himself catapulted into a mid-17th century England troubled by witch hunts.

1938

G. Clifton Wisler

The Antrian Messenger (New York: Dutton, 1986)

Age range: Grades 4-7

Subject(s): Aliens; Gifted Children; Science Fiction

Major character(s): Scott Childers, Teenager, Alien; Brian Childers, Preteen; Tiaf, Antiques Dealer

Time period(s): 1980s

Locale(s): Texas

What the book is about: Fourteen year old Scott Childers has a hard time dealing with his "gifts." Being very smart can be trouble enough, but having eyes that literally see more than everyone else, and having frightening precognitive dreams of disasters have badly upset him. When two strange men start following him, even his parents become alarmed. Then he meets Tiaf, a strange man who knows more about him than even his family, and his parents then tell him he was found in an air crash and never identified, so they adopted him. Who is Scott?

Where it's reviewed:
Booklist, April 15, 1986, page 1228
School Library Journal, September 1986, page 141
Children's Book Review Service, Spring 1986, page 137

Other books by the author:
Red Cap, 1991
Piper's Ferry, 1990
The Seer, 1988
Buffalo Moon, 1984

Other books you might like:
Joan Bodger, *Clever-Lazy, the Girl Who Invented Herself*, 1979

A fledgling inventor concentrates so hard on developing her genius that she almost forgets the teachings of the Goddess in the Dancing Mountains.
Grace Chetwin, *Collidescope*, 1990
   When his spaceship crashes to Earth, a highly advanced alien interferes in the lives of two teens, both from Manhattan, but from difference centuries.
Gene DeWeese, *Black Suits From Outer Space*, 1985
   Two young people meet a visitor from outer space who badly needs their help.
Ken Follett, *The Power Twins*, 1990
   Uncle Gregorian, an alien, takes the Price twins to the capital of the Galactic Empire where they serve as arbitrators in the Worm War.
Mark Jonathan Harris, *Solay*, 1993
   Unhappy in her new school where she is the target of bullies, Melissa finds comfort and self-confidence through her friendship with an alien visitor.

1939

Maia Wojciechowska

Illustrator: Joan Sandin

Hey, What's Wrong with This One? (New York: Harper, 1969)

Age range: Grades 3-5

Subject(s): Fathers and Sons; Single Parent Families

Major character(s): Mott Elliott, Child; Davidson Elliot, Preteen; Harley Elliott, Preteen

Time period(s): 1960s

Locale(s): New York

What the book is about: Mott, the youngest of the three motherless Elliott boys decides his father is not doing enough to find the family a mother, so he is going to do it himself. Three boys, three ponies and a sheepdog have proven too much for a long succession of housekeepers. How can Mott find someone who wants to stay permanently? Amazingly enough, Mott's strange behavior in the supermarket (grabbing women by the hand, taking them to his dad and shouting "What's wrong with this one?") actually results in Dad meeting someone who has definite possibilities in the mother department.

Where it's reviewed:
Center for Children's Books Bulletin, July 1969, page 185
Kirkus Reviews, May 1, 1969, page 507
School Library Journal, December 1978, page 33

Awards the book has won:
Georgia Children's Book Award 1973

Other books by the author:
How God Got Christian in Trouble, 1984
The Life and Death of a Brave Bull, 1972
Single Light, 1968
Kingdom in a Horse, 1965

Other books you might like:
Kathryn Ewing, *A Private Matter*, 1975
   In her longing for a father, Marcy becomes extremely attached to the kind man next door.
Janice Marriott, *Letters to Lesley*, 1991
   Henry plots to solve all his problems by marrying off his eccentric mother to his pen pal's father.

Theresa Nelson, *The 25iracle*, 1986
  Motherless Elvira looks for a mother and finds instead the father she hardly knew she had.
Mary Tannen, *Huntley, Nutley and the Missing Link*, 1983
  A boy finds an australopithecine in a ravine during the winter and brings him home where his father, a befuddled scientist, thinks it's a new maid.
Margaret Teibl, *Davy Come Home*, 1979
  A boy yearns for a mother to make their home a welcoming place for him and his father.

1940

Susan Wojciechowski

Patty Dillman of Hot Dog Fame (New York: Orchard, 1989)

Age range: Grades 5-8

Subject(s): Homeless; Humor

Major character(s): Patty Dillman, Writer, 8th Grader; Tracy Gilmore, Friend, 8th Grader; Alex Henley, Teenager

Time period(s): 1980s

Locale(s): United States

What the book is about: Patty and Tracy are eighth grade buddies who manage to have wonderful times and get into all sorts of trouble together. Patty is most interested in Tim Shokow, whose whole live revolves around sports, especially skiing. Patty gets very tired of trying to either pry him away from the slopes or work up an interest in skiing herself. When she reluctantly helps her mother at a shelter for the homeless, she meets Alex Henley, a person she discovers is far more sensitive and interesting than Tim, and her world view enlarges considerably.

Where it's reviewed:
Children's Book Review Service, June 1989, page 128
Kirkus Reviews, June 1, 1989, page 842
School Library Journal, June 1989, page 110

Other books by the author:
Promises to Keep, 1991
And the Other Gold, 1987

Other books you might like:
Eth Clifford, *Never Hit a Ghost with a Baseball Bat*, 1993
  While exploring a trolley car museum, Mary, Rose, and Jo Beth encounter voices and other strange events that make them think the museum is haunted.
Paula Fox, *Monkey Island*, 1991
  Forced to live on the streets of New York after his mother disappears from their hotel room, Clay is befriended by two men who help him survive.
Jean Craighead George, *The Missing 'Gator of Gumbo Limbo: An Ecological Mystery*, 1992
  Liza K., homeless and living in a south Florida forest, looks for a missing alligator destined for extermination and studies the fragile local ecology
James Howe, *Dew Drop Dead: A Sebastian Barth Mystery*, 1990
  While setting up a homeless shelter at the church, Sebastian and his friends solve the mystery of a dead man found in an abandoned inn.
Barbara Wersba, *Just Be Gorgeous: A Novel*, 1988

Feeling unattractive, untalented and misunderstood, a New York City teenager develops self-respect through friendship with a homeless street performer

1941

Bernard Wolf

Anna's Silent World (New York: Lippincott, 1977)

Age range: Grades 2-4

Subject(s): Deafness; Communication

Major character(s): Anna, Handicapped (deaf), Child

Time period(s): 1970s

Locale(s): United States

What the book is about: Six year old Anna was born deaf. This story shows how a deaf child learns to talk. With therapy and special equipment, Anna attends classes with children who have normal hearing.

Where it's reviewed:
Booklist, April 15, 1977, page 1270
Hornbook, October 1977, page 546
Kirkus Reviews, April 15, 1977, page 434

Other books by the author:
Amazing Grace, 1986
Connie's New Eyes, 1976
Don't Feel Sorry for Paul, 1974
Tinker and the Medicine Man, 1973

Other books you might like:
Catherine Arthur, *My Sister's Silent World*, 1979
  A child describes her sister's hearing problem and the family's birthday visit to the zoo.
Karen Hirsh, *Becky*, 1981
  A deaf child lives with a hearing family while she attends school and enables them to become conscious of the problems facing the deaf.
Jeanne M. Lee, *Silent Lotus*, 1991
  Although she cannot speak or hear, Lotus trains as a Shmer Court dancer and becomes eloquent in dancing out the legends of the gods.
Susan Richards Shreve, *The Gift of the Girl Who Couldn't Hear*, 1991
  Two friends, one of whom is deaf, help each other when tryouts are held for "Annie."
Linda Yeatman, *Buttons: The Dog Who Was More Than a Friend*, 1985
  The story of hearing-ear dog, Buttons.

1942

Bernard Wolf, Author/Illustrator

Don't Feel Sorry for Paul (New York: Lippincott, 1974)

Age range: Grades 3-6

Subject(s): Physically Handicapped

Major character(s): Paul Jockimo, Child, Handicapped

Time period(s): 1970s

Locale(s): United States

What the book is about: Paul is a seven year old who was born with malformed feet and hands. He has three prosthetic devices to help him at home and at school. He takes riding lessons and wins a ribbon in a show. On his birthday, he visits with prosthetic specialists, doctors and rehabilitation therapists. He's a tough little kid!

Where it's reviewed:
Booklist, November 1, 1974, page 296
Kirkus Reviews, November 15, 1974, page 1205
School Library Journal, March 1975, page 90

Other books by the author:
Amazing Grace, 1986
Anna's Silent World, 1977
Connie's New Eyes, 1976
Tinker and the Medicine Man, 1973

Other books you might like:
Thomas Bergman, *On Our Own Terms*, 1989
 Describes the activities at the Caroline Hospital in Stockholm, where children with congenital handicaps receive training and psysiotherapy.
Eloise Greenfield, *Alesia*, 1981
 A physically handicapped girl discusses her daily activities, the accident which left her crippled, and her feelings about her disability.
Suzanne Haldane, *Helping Hands*, 1991
 A photo-essay illustrating how capuchin monkeys are trained to provide help and companionship to people who are disabled.
Katherine Elliott Wilkie, *Helen Keller: From Tragedy to Triumph*, 19647
 A biography, focusing on the childhood years of the blind and deaf woman who overcame handicaps with the help of her teacher, Annie Sullivan.
David Wisniewski, *Sundiata: Lion King of Mali*, 1992
 The story of Sundiata, who overcame physical handicaps, social disgrace and strong opposition to rule in Mali in the 13th century.

1943

Hilma Wolitzer

Toby Lived Here (New York: Farrar Straus and Giroux, 1978)

Age range: Grades 5-6

Subject(s): Foster Homes; Single Parent Families; Mental Illness

Major character(s): Toby, Preteen; Anne, Child

Time period(s): 1970s

Locale(s): New York, New York (Brooklyn)

What the book is about: Toby and her sister, Anne, are sent away to live with a foster family, the Selwyns, when their mom has a nervous breakdown. Toby doesn't want to accept the Selwyns, even though Anne is happy there. When the time comes for Toby and Anne to return to their mother, she has learned to feel secure and safe at the Selwyn home.

Where it's reviewed:
Booklist, June 15, 1978, page 1620
Hornbook, August 1978, page 399
Kirkus Reviews, May 1, 1978, page 498

Other books by the author:
Hearts, 1980
Out of Love, 1979
Wish You Were Here, 1978
Introducing Shirley Braverman, 1975

Other books you might like:
Patricia Calvert, *When Morning Comes*, 1989
 Cat finds herself stuck on a farm with an elderly beekeeper after being unable to fit into one foster home after another.
Gudrun Mebs, *Sunday's Child*, 1989
 Jenny's foster mother doesn't live up to her expectations until she discovers there are more important things in a life than material things.
Joan Lowery Nixon, *A Place to Belong*, 1989
 Having traveled with his sister from a foster home to a farm in Missouri, Danny plots to get his foster father to send for and marry his mother.
Patricia Pendergraft, *As Far as Mill Springs*, 1991
 Tired of being bounced from one foster home to another, Robert sets out with Abiah to find his mother by Christmas.
Patricia Windsor, *Mad Martin*, 1976
 Martin is sad, lonely and shy until Mrs. Crimp teaches him how to be clean, to play, and to have a friend.

1944

Hilma Wolitzer

Wish You Were Here (New York: Farrar, Straux and Giroux, 1984)

Age range: Grades 5-8

Subject(s): Family Life; Jews; Remarriage

Major character(s): Bernard Martin "Bernie" Segal, Teenager (asthmatic); Grace Segal, Child; Nat Greenberg, Step-Parent

Time period(s): 1980s

Locale(s): New York, New York (Long Island)

What the book is about: When his widowed mother meets a man she wants to marry, Bernie decides to move to Florida and live with his grandfather rather than live in the same house as his new stepfather. This is a funny and sad story of Bernie's struggle to get what he wants and his discovery that he can learn to want what he gets.

Where it's reviewed:
Center for Children's Books Bulletin, December 1984, page 76
Horn Book, January/February 1985, page 63
Booklist, September 15, 1984, page 136

Other books by the author:
Toby Lived Here, 1978
Out of Love, 1976
Introducing Shirley Braverman, 1975

Other books you might like:
Mary Jane Auch, *Seven Long Years Until College*, 1991
 When her stepfather restricts her daily life, and her friend prepares to move, Natalie takes drastic steps to stem the tide of change in her life.
Barbara Dillon, *My Stepfather Shrank!*, 1992

Mallory discovers that her new stepfather has been shrunk accidentally and tries to return him to normal size before her mother gets home.

Betty Levin, *Mercy's Mill*, 1992

While trying to deal with her new stepfather and younger foster sister, Sarah encounters a strange boy who claims to have traveled forward in time.

Jayne Pettit, *My Name Is San Ho*, 1992

A Vietnamese boy relates his experiences as he tries to adjust to his new life in the United States with his mother and American Marine stepfather.

Bonnie Pryor, *Horses in the Garage*, 1992

Samantha finds a way to cope with her difficulties in adjusting to a new stepfather, a new home and a new school when she makes friends with Jasmine.

1945

Judie Wolkoff

Happily Ever After.Almost (Scarsdale, New York: Bradbury Press, 1982)

Age range: Grades 5-6

Subject(s): Divorce; Remarriage

Major character(s): Kitty Birdsall, Child; Sarah Birdsall, Child; Seth Krampner, Step-Parent

Time period(s): 1980s

Locale(s): New York, New York

What the book is about: Seth has a difficult son, RJ, from an earlier marriage. When Seth and Kitty's mother marry, Kitty and RJ take an instant dislike to each other. Their new family moves into the loft of a huge old shoe factory. Kitty and Sarah's father has remarried also, and is now expecting a new baby. RJ's mother tries to take him away from the custody of his father.

Where it's reviewed:
Center for Children's Books Bulletin, November 1982, page 59
School Library Journal, November 1982, page 92

Other books by the author:
In a Pig's Eye, 1986
Ace Hits Rock Bottom, 1985
Ace Hits the Big Time, 1981
Where the Elf King Sings, 1980

Other books you might like:
Elizabeth Starr Hill, *When Christmas Comes*, 1989
Callie is drawn into a confrontation about the meaning of family when his father decides to remarry.
A.M. Monson, *The Secret of Sanctuary Island*, 1991
While adjusting to his father's remarriage, thirteen year old Todd and a friend set out to prove they observed a burglary no on believes happened.
Jean Davies Okimoto, *It's Just Too Much*, 1980
When her mother remarries, twelve year old Cynthia faces a new family and a new school at the same time.
Marilyn Sachs, *At the Sound of the Beep*, 1990
In a panic about their parents' divorce, a brother and sister run away and live live among the homeless in Golden Gate Park.
Marc Talbert, *Pillow of Clouds*, 1991

Angry at being forced to decide which of his parents he will live with, Chester feels burdened with guilt no matter which choice he makes.

1946

Audrey Wood

Illustrator: Don Wood

Heckedy Peg (New York: Harcourt, Brace, Jovanovich, 1987)

Age range: Grades 2-3

Subject(s): Fairy Tale; Witches and Witchcraft

Time period(s): Indeterminate Past

Locale(s): Alternate Earth

What the book is about: A witch turns seven children into different kinds of food. Only their mother can save them and she must solve a riddle.

Where it's reviewed:
Kirkus Reviews, August 1, 1987, page 1166
School Library Journal, December 1987, page 39

Other books by the author:
Detective Valentine, 1987
Moonflute, 1987
Three Sisters, 1986

Other books you might like:
Paul Buckley, *Amy Belligera and the Fireflies*, 1987
The story behind the light of fireflies whose "lanterns" came from a remorseful witch.
Maggie S. Davis, *Rickety Witch*, 1984
An old witch finally gets even with two young witches who have been intimidating her.
Joanne Robertson, *Sea Witches*, 1991
A Scottish grandmother explains the legend behind the superstition of always crumbling eggshells.
Ben Shecter, *The Big Stew*, 1991
Two people get carried away making stew and turn into witches.
Erica Silverman, *Big Pumpkin*, 1991
A witch trying to pick a big pumpkin on Halloween discovers the value of cooperation.

1947

Audrey Wood

Illustrator: Rosecrantz Hoffman

The Horrible Holidays (New York: Dial, 1988)

Age range: Grades 1-3

Subject(s): Holidays; Christmas

Major character(s): Alf, Child; Mert, Cousin

Time period(s): 1980s

Locale(s): United States

What the book is about: Three stories about Alf, a dog child, who considers his cousin a royal pain. One of the holiday books that tells it like it is. Alf squabbles with his relatives especially cousin Mert, and they vie to see who can get the other in trouble at Thanksgiving, Christmas and New Years. A great book to share when post-holiday crankiness sets in.

Where it's reviewed:
Horn Book, November/December 1988, page 766
School Library Journal, January 1989, page 68

Other books by the author:
Heckedy Peg, 1987
Moonflute, 1986
Three Sisters, 1986
Magic Shoelaces, 1980

Other books you might like:
Patricia Reilly Giff, *December Secrets*, 1984
  Each student in Ms. Rooney's room celebrates the December holidays by being a secret pal to a classmate.
Esther Hautzig, *A Gift for Mama*, 1981
  Sick and tired of making presents for various holidays and occasions, Sara decides that for this Mother's Day she will do something different.
May Justus, *Holidays in No-End Hollow*, 1970
  Four short stories tell how Thanksgiving, Christmas, a house-warming, and a school's birthday are celebrated in Tennessee's Great Smoky Mountains.
Suzy Kline, *Horrible Harry and the Christmas Surprise*, 1991
  Horrible Harry and the rest of Miss Mackle's class at South School promise fun for the holidays, starting when Miss Mackle's chair collapses under her
Tony Ross, *Hugo and the Bureau of Holidays*, 1982
  When Hugo the mouse receives an Easter egg instead of a blackboard for a Christmas present, he goes to the Bureau of Holidays to try to fix the mixup.

1948

Audrey Wood

Illustrator: Don Wood

King Bidgood's in the Bathtub (San Diego: Harcourt Brace Jovanovich, 1985)

Age range: Grades 2-4

Subject(s): Kings, Queens, Rulers

Major character(s): King Bidgood, Ruler

Time period(s): Indeterminate

Locale(s): Fictional Country

What the book is about: The entire court tries to convince the king to get out of his bathtub and rule his kingdom. The court gets all of its starch taken out of it by a red-haired romping, royal master. The duke gets more than he's fishing for.

Where it's reviewed:
Bulletin for the Center for Children's Books Bulletin, January 1986, p
School Library Journal, November 1985, page 79

Other books by the author:
Silly Sally, 1992
Oh My Baby Bear!, 1990
Heckedy Peg, 1987
The Napping House, 1984

Other books you might like:
Ellen B. Jackson, *The Bear in the Bathtub*, 1981
  Andrew doesn't like to take baths, but when a bear comes to stay in the bathtub, he actually misses them.
C. Imbior Kudrna, *To Bathe a Boa*, 1986
  At bathtime, a younster has to struggle to get his pet boa into the tub.
Kathleen Stevens, *The Beast in the Bathtub*, 1985
  Lewis gets into mischief with an imaginary beast in the bathtub while his parents are watching television.
Sarah Wilson, *Uncle Albert's Flying Birthday*, 1991
  Jennifer and her brother William must take their baths after all when a sleepy baker puts soap powder instead of flour in their uncle's birthday cake.
Harriet Ziefert, *Harry's Bath*, 1990
  Harry tries to expalin to his mother how various animals in the bathtub are preventing him from taking a bath himself.

1949

Audrey Wood

Illustrator: Don Wood

The Napping House (New York: Harcourt, 1984)

Age range: Grades 1-2

Subject(s): Sleep; Animals

Time period(s): Indeterminate

Locale(s): Fictional Country

What the book is about: Granny, child, dog, cat, and mouse pile on top of each other while taking a nap on a rainy afternoon. All is peaceful until a flea reverses the order and everyone wakes up.

Where it's reviewed:
Center for Children's Books Bulletin, September 1984, page 18
School Library Journal, August 1984, page 67

Other books by the author:
The Horrible Holidays, 1988
Detective Valentine, 1987
Heckedy Peg, 1987
Balloonia, 1981

Other books you might like:
Lisa Bassett, *Beany and Scamp*, 1987
  Just as Beany Bear is ready for his long winter's nap, his friend Scamp Squirrel asks his help in searching for his misplaced winter nut supply.
Fred Burstein, *Rebecca's Nap*, 1988
  Rebecca, Daddy, and Mommy have different ideas about naptime.
William Kotzwinkle, *The Nap Master*, 1979
  Herman refuses to take a nap until the Nap Master takes him to the land of dreams.
Dianne Snyder, *The Boy of the Three-Year Nap*, 1988
  A poor Japanese woman maneuvers events to change the lazy habits of her son.
Cindy Wheeler, *Marmalade's Nap*, 1983
  Marmalade looks for a quiet place in the barn to sleep, away from all the baby animals.

1950

Marcia Wood

The Search for Jim McGwynn (New York: Atheneum, 1989)

Age range: Grades 5-8

Subject(s): Alcoholism; Mystery and Detective Stories

Major character(s): Jamie, Teenager; Shelby, Teenager

Time period(s): 1980s

Locale(s): United States

What the book is about: Jamie spends the summer working for an eccentric neighbor. Through his diary we discover that he and his friend, Shelby, are great fans of Jim McGwynn, a hero of a series of spy novels. They learn that P.J. Ross, the author of the series, lives in their town. They set out to find him, and Jamie, who lives with a quick-tempered, alcoholic father, makes an idealized father figure of Ross to try to escape the painful relationship with his own father. A vivid portrait of living with alcoholism.

Where it's reviewed:
Booklist, September 15, 1989, page 191
School Library Journal, October 1989, page 138

Other books by the author:
The Secret Life of Hilary Thorne, 1988

Other books you might like:
Paula Fox, *The Moonlight Man*, 1986
   Catherine and her father take their first vacation together in Nova Scotia and finally get to know each other.
Marilyn Halvorson, *Cowboys Don't Cry*, 1984
   Still suffering from his mother's death and his father's alcoholism, Shane hopes things will be better when they go to live on a farm in Alabama.
Jane Claypool Miner, *A Day at a Time: Dealing with an Alcoholic*, 1982
   When her father seems unable to stop drinking, Ellen decides to attend an Alateen meeting to help her cope with his alcoholism.
Helen K. Passey, *Speak to the Rain*, 1989
   After her mother's recent death, Janna's life becomes a nightmare as her father starts drinking heavily and her sister is possessed by spirits.
Judie Wolkoff, *A Stranger in the Family*, 1980
   Deeply disturbed by his Vietnam experience, twelve year old Marcie's father drinks heavily and terrorizes his family.

1951

Elvira Woodruff

Illustrator: Will Hillenbrand

Awfully Short for the Fourth Grade (New York: Holiday, 1989)

Age range: Grades 3-6

Subject(s): Schools; Wishes

Major character(s): Noah Murphy, Preteen; Jess Murphy, Child; Commander Falcon, Military Personnel (soldier)

Time period(s): 1980s

Locale(s): United States

What the book is about: Noah wants to try out the magic wishing powder he got from the miniature-toy machine at the supermarket. He disrupts the school when his wish comes true and he becomes small and his miniature toy men come to life. Commander Falcon, his sidekick Sergeant Gordy and three headless green aliens become real.

Where it's reviewed:
Booklist, January 1, 1990, page 941
Kirkus Reviews, September 1, 1989, page 1335

Other books by the author:
Back in Action, 1991 (Sequel to Awfully Short for the Fourth Grade)
George Washington's Socks, 1991
The Summer I Shrank My Grandmother, 1990

Other books you might like:
Rosalind Barden, *TV Monster*, 1988
   A boy turns into a TV monster and is mistaken for Colonel Bop by aliens who take him aboard their flying saucer and into outer space.
Jonathan Etra, *Aliens for Breakfast*, 1988
   Finding an intergalactic agent in his cereal box, Richard joins the alien in a fight to save Earth from Dranes, one of whom is posing as a classmate.
Maxine Kumin, *The Wizard's Tears*, 1975
   The new wizard tries to solve all the town's problems, but carelessness with his own magic creates a tragedy instead.
Edith Nesbit, *The Enchanted Castle*, 1992
   Four English children find a wonderful world of magic through an enchanted wishing ring.
Elizabeth Winthrop, *The Castle in the Attic*, 1985
   A gift of a toy castle, complete with silver knight, introduces William to an adventure involving magic and an personal quest.

1952

Frances Wosmek

Illustrator: Ted Lewin

A Brown Bird Singing (New York: Lothrop, 1986)

Age range: Grades 4-6

Subject(s): Family Life; Indians of North America

Time period(s): Indeterminate Past

Locale(s): Minnesota

What the book is about: Left by her father to be raised by his white friends in a small Minnesota town, a Chippewa Indian girl is afraid he will return and take her away from the only family she has ever known.

Where it's reviewed:
Children's Book Review Service, August 1986, page 159
Center for Children's Books Bulletin, June 1986, page 199
Kirkus Reviews, July 1, 1986, page 1019

Other books by the author:
Mystery of the Eagle's Claw, 1979
A Bowl of Sun, 1976

Other books you might like:
L.E. Blair, *The Ghost of Eagle Mountain*, 1990
   A ski trip becomes a journey into Allison's Native American heritage when she and her three best friends begin to live the legend of Eagle Mountain.

Carolyn Meyer, *Where the Broken Heart Still Beats: The Story of Cynthia Ann Parker*, 1992
  Having been taken as a child and raised by Comanche Indians, Cynthia Ann is returned to her white relatives, where she longs for her Indian life.
Walter O'Meara, *The Sioux Are Coming*, 1971
  A Chippewa family's flight from their enemy, the Sioux, presents the son of the family with many opportunities to test his resourcefulness.
Virginia Driving Hawk Sneve, *Betrayed*, 1974
  Relates the events of the Santee Indian raid on the Lake Shetek, Minnesota, settlement and the subsequent fate of the captives.
Kenneth Thomasma, *Kunu: Winnebago Boy Escapes*, 1992
  Following the forced removal of his people from Minnesota to Crow Creek, an Indian boy embarks on a journey to return his grandfather to his homeland.

1953

Patricia C. Wrede

Dealing with Dragons (San Diego: Harcourt Brace Jovanovich, 1990)

Age range: Grades 4-6

Series: Enchanted Forest Chronicles

Subject(s): Dragons; Wizards; Princes and Princesses

Major character(s): Cimorene, Royalty (princess); Kazul, Dragon

Time period(s): Indeterminate Past

Locale(s): Linderwall, Fictional Country (Mountains of Morning)

What the book is about: A princess with a mind of her own, tired of embroidery and keeping house, prefers to volunteer as a dragon's servant and companion than go through royalty training. Magic, wizardry and the triumph of good over evil make this fun reading.

Where it's reviewed:
Booklist, June 15, 1991, page 1965
School Library Journal, December 1990, page 112

Other books by the author:
Searching for Dragons, 1991 (Enchanted Forest Chronicles Book 2)
Snow White and Rose Red, 1989
Sorcery and Celia, 1988
Talking to Dragons, 1985

Other books you might like:
Bruce Coville, *Jeremy Thatcher, Dragon Hatcher*, 1991
  Jeremy unknowingly buys and hatches a dragon's egg.
Beverly Keller, *A Small, Elderly Dragon*, 1984
  When a sorcerer takes over the kingdom, Princess Dorma helps an old dragon find his power.
Jon Scieszka, *Knights of the Kitchen Table*, 1991
  Joe, Fred and Sam are transported to a time when evil knights, fire-breathing dragons and vile-smelling giants roamed the land.
Oliver G. Selfridge, *The Trouble with Dragons*, 1978
  Three sisters take turns at slaying a dragon to win the hand of the prince.
Jane Zaring, *The Return of the Dragon*, 1981

A dragon, exiled from Wales, reforms and must do twelve good deeds in a year in order to return home.

1954

Betty Ren Wright

The Dollhouse Murders (New York: Holiday, 1983)

Age range: Grades 5-7

Subject(s): Dolls and Dollhouses; Ghosts; Mentally Handicapped

Major character(s): Amy Treloar, Preteen; Louann Treloar, Handicapped (mentally retarded)

Time period(s): 1980s

Locale(s): Claiborne, Illinois

What the book is about: A dollhouse filled with a ghostly light in the middle of the night, and dolls that move from where she last left them lead Amy and her retarded sister to unravel a mystery surrounding grisly murders that took place years ago.

Where it's reviewed:
Booklist, October 1, 1983, page 301
Hornbook, December 1983, page 713
School Library Journal, November 1983, page 84

Awards the book has won:
California Young Reader Medal 1957
Edgar Allan Poe Award - Runner-up

Other books by the author:
A Ghost in the House, 1991
The Ghost of Ernie P., 1990
A Ghost in the Window, 1987
Christina's Ghost, 1985

Other books you might like:
Betsy Byars, *The Summer of the Swans*, 1970
  A teenage girl gains new insight into herself and her family when her mentally handicapped brother gets lost.
Vera Cleaver, *Me Too*, 1973
  Hoping to expunge neighborhood prejudice and do something everyone else has failed to do, a 12 year old desperately tries to teach her retarded twin.
Theodora Koob, *The Deep Search*, 1969
  A girl feels resentful when she finds herself in the middle of her parents' disagreement about the future of her retarded ten year old brother.
Kin Platt, *Hey, Dummy*, 1971
  Despite the opposition of his family and friends, Neil befriends the brain-damaged boy newly-arrived in the neighborhood.
C.L. Rinaldo, *Dark Dreams*, 1974
  An insecure boy with a weak heart finds new courage and strength through his friendship with a mentally retarded man.

1955

Betty Ren Wright

Getting Rid of Marjorie (New York: Scholastic, 1984)

Age range: Grades 4-6

Subject(s): Grandparents; Stepfamilies

Major character(s): Emily, Preteen; Mr. Walker, Grandparent; Marjorie Walker, Spouse (of Emily's grandfather)

Time period(s): 1980s

Locale(s): United States

What the book is about: Emily is looking forward to her grandfather's return from California so there will be someone around to pay attention to her. When he returns with his new bride, Marjorie, Emily is disappointed and resentful. She invents a variey of schemes to get rid of her new step-grandmother, since Emily sees her as a threat to the close relationship she has with her grandfather. When Emily tries to scare Marjorie by creating "burglar noises" she is faced with actually getting to know her as a person.

Where it's reviewed:
Booklist, October 15, 1981, page 313
Children's Book Review Service, December 1981, page 40
School Library Journal, January 1982, page 82

Other books by the author:
A Ghost in the House, 1991
The Scariest Night, 1991
Ghosts Beneath Our Feet, 1984
The Dollhouse Murders, 1983

Other books you might like:
Nina Bawden, Kept in the Dark, 1982
 When a mysterious eighteen year old comes to live with his grandparents and three half-cousins, sinister things begin to happen to a young boy.
Roger Carr, The Clinker, 1989
 Having come to spend the summer in Australia with his great-grandparents, Rust worries that he can live up to the responsibilities they lay on him.
Kimberly Olson Fakih, Grandpa Putter and Granny Hoe, 1992
 Twins Jazz and Roo find themselves in the middle of a nonstop war of one-upsmanship as their bickering grandparents vie for their attention.
Evelyn Slaatten, In the Captain's Shoes, 1978
 An orphaned boy goes to live with his unusual grandfather, subsequently sharing many adventures and learning the meaning of friendship.
Carol Snyder, The Great Condominium Rebellion, 1981
 Stacy and Marc visit their newly retired Jewish grandparents in their Florida condominium where the restrictive rules stir them to rebel.

1956

Betty Ren Wright

A Ghost in the Window (New York: Holiday, 1987)

Age range: Grades 5-8

Subject(s): Supernatural

Major character(s): Meg Korshak, Teenager; Caleb Larsen, Teenager

Time period(s): 1980s

Locale(s): United States

What the book is about: Meg wants her parents reunited, but during a summer with her father she learns that she is her own person and cannot be held responsible for her parents. Meg has dreams that come true, and give her a window to the future. They soon involve her in the mystery surrounding a

death, and she learns some hard truths about herself, her family, and her parents' impending divorce.

Where it's reviewed:
Center for Children's Books Bulletin, February 1988, page 128
School Library Journal, October 1987, page 130

Other books by the author:
A Ghost in the House, 1991
Christina's Ghost, 1985
The Dollhouse Murders, 1983
The Secret Window, 1982

Other books you might like:
Margaret Buffie, The Warnings, 1989
 Rachel leads a lonely life with the old people she calls the Fossils until she starts getting strange psychic messages about a grave threat.
Robert Cormier, Fade, 1988
 Paul Moreaux, son of French Canadian immigrants, inherits the ability to become invisible, but this power leads to death, destruction and no escape.
Susan Gates, The Burnhope Wheel, 1989
 After finding old photographs involving the abandoned mines near her English village, Ellen is tempted by dreams and images to reenact an old tragedy.
Margaret Mahy, The Haunting, 1982
 After a shy child begins receiving frightening supernatural immages and messages, he learns about a family legacy which could be a curse or a gift.
William Sleator, The Spirit House, 1991
 Julie investigates the odd behavior of the Thai student staying with her family and comes to believe in a spirit who has followed her across the sea.

1957

Betty Ren Wright

Illustrator: Betsy Day

My New Mom and Me (Milwaukee: Raintree, 1981)

Age range: Grades 2-4

Subject(s): Death; Remarriage; Stepfamilies

Major character(s): "Girl", Child; Elena, Step-Parent

Time period(s): 1980s

Locale(s): United States

What the book is about: The girl has no name. Her mother died two summers ago when she was about seven. Her father decides to marry Elena. The girl withdraws from the affection her stepmother offers. When Elena helps save CAT when he becomes trapped, the girl begins to think that Elena may not be so bad after all.

Where it's reviewed:
School Library Journal, March 1982, page 142

Other books by the author:
Why Do I Daydream?, 1982
The Day Our TV Broke, 1981
Getting Rid of Marjorie, 1981
My Sister Is Different, 1981

Other books you might like:
Lizi Boyd, The Not-So-Wicked Stepmother, 1987

Expecting her new stepmother to be mean, ugly, and horrible, Hessie is surprised and confused to find her not wicked at all.

Lizi Boyd, *Sam Is My Half-Brother*, 1990
A young girl, fearful that her newborn half-brother will get all of the attention, is reassured of her father's love.

Steven Kroll, *Queen of the May*, 1993
Because of Sylvie's goodness, her wicked stepsisters are vanquished and she becomes Queen of the May.

Jean Marzollo, *Pizza Pie Slugger*, 1989
Billy, baseball, and Billy's stepsister are at the center of this warm, easy to read family story.

Marguerita Rudolph, *The Good Stepmother*, 1992
Princess Elena, lonely for a mother, persuades her father to let her choose the woman he will marry.

| 1958 |

Patricia Wrightson

A Little Fear (New York: Atheneum, 1983)

Age range: Grades 5-8

Subject(s): Old Age; Gnomes; Supernatural

Major character(s): Mrs. Tucker, Aged Person; Hector, Dog; Njimbin, Mythical Creature (gnome)

Time period(s): Indeterminate Past

Locale(s): Australia

What the book is about: When elderly Mrs. Tucker inherits a cottage from her brother, she takes the opportunity to run away from Sunset House, the old people's home where she has been living, and takes possession of the cottage. Unfortunately, a creature called Njimbin resents the intrusion and a struggle ensues with the old gnome calling up powers beyond the old woman's ability to defy. The monster will scare some readers, but frightening or not, Wrighson's vivid prose makes the story worthwhile.

Where it's reviewed:
Horn Book, February 1984, page 66
School Library Journal, November 1983, page 948

Awards the book has won:
Boston Globe/Horn Book Award 1984

Other books by the author:
Balyet, 1989
Journey Behind the Wind, 1981
The Ice Is Coming, 1977
Down to Earth, 1965

Other books you might like:
Kenneth Ethridge, *Viola, Furgy, Bobbi and Me*, 1989
Three friends try to protect Viola, a wealthy seventy-eight year woman, from her abusive daughters who want to send Viola to a nursing home.

Liza Fosburgh, *The Wrong Way Home*, 1990
Bent resents her father, who deserted her and her mother, for attempting to put her mother, who suffers from Huntington's Chorea, in a nursing home.

JoAnn Bren Guernsey, *Journey to Almost There*, 1985
To prevent her grandfather's going to a nursing home, Alison drives him from Minnesota to Massachusetts where her estranged artist father lives.

Louis Sacher, *The Boy Who Lost His Face*, 1989

David receives a curse from an elderly woman whom he has helped his schoolmates attack, and he learns to regret his weakness.

Liesel Moak Skorpen, *Grace*, 1984
Sara, a lonely sixth grader, forms a friendship with a proud old woman who is afraid her daughter will put her in a nursing home.

| 1959 |

Patricia Wrightson

The Nargun and the Stars (New York: Atheneum, 1974)

Age range: Grades 5-6

Subject(s): Fantasy

Major character(s): Simon, Orphan; Charlie, Aged Person; Edie, Aged Person

Time period(s): Indeterminate

Locale(s): Australia (sheep station in Australia)

What the book is about: Charlie and Edie are elderly cousins that Simon is sent to live with on their sheep station. Simon is miserable until he finds a swamp with a mysterious water creature living in it, the Potkoorok. Then he discovers a creature born of fire, a thing of stone that kills, the Nargun. Charlie and Edie have met the Potkoorok and the Turong and Nyol elves. Together they deal with the Nargun.

Where it's reviewed:
Booklist, June 1, 1974, page 1108
Hornbook, August 1974, page 382
Kirkus Reviews, March 15, 1974, page 302

Other books by the author:
Balyet, 1989
Moon Dark, 1988
A Little Fear, 1983
Journey Behind the Wind, 1981

Other books you might like:
Patrick Skene Catling, *John Midas in the Dreamtime*, 1986
While visiting the site of sacred cave paintings, John slips back thousands of years and finds himself among a prehistoric Aboriginal tribe.

James Clavell, *Thrump-o-moto*, 1986
When a tiny wizard whisks Patricia and her crutches away from her home, where she meets his family, an evil ghoul, and a magic cure for her handicap.

Louise Munro Foley, *Australia - Find the Flying Foxes*, 1988
The reader travels back 2000 years with an inspector trying to find the real meaning of a legen involving the white settlers and native Australians.

Nancy Sheppard, *Alitji in Dreamland*, 1992
In this retelling of the Alice in Wonderland story set in Australia, the white rabbit becomes a white kangaroo and the red queen is a witch spirit.

Edna Wignell, *Escape by Deluge*, 1989
Shelley encounters a time of searching and terror as something booms and wails in the basement of her building.

1960

Andrea Wyman

Red Sky at Morning (New York: Holiday, 1991)

Age range: Grades 4-6

Subject(s): Frontier and Pioneer Life; Grandparents

Major character(s): Callie Common, Preteen; Opa, Grandparent (grandfather), Farmer; Katherine Common, Teenager

Time period(s): 1900s (1909)

Locale(s): Indiana

What the book is about: Callie and her grandfather, Opa, try to take care of the farm while fifteen year old Katherine goes to work at Aunt Mary's boarding house to help with finances. The girls' mother has died in childbirth and their father has run off with Opa's money. A dramatic tale of a family struggling to survive.

Where it's reviewed:
Kirkus Reviews, September 15, 1991, page 1230
School Library Journal, September 1991, page 260

Other books you might like:
Eth Clifford, *The Year of the Three Legged Deer*, 1972
    The story of one year in the life of a white man and his Indian family on the Indiana frontier.
Kristiana Gregory, *The Legend of Jimmy Spoon*, 1990
    The adventures of a young white boy living among the Shoshoni Indians during the early frontier days.
Brett Harvey, *Cassie's Journey: Going West in the 1860's*, 1988
    A young girl relates the hardships and dangers of traveling with her family in a covered wagon from Illinois to California.
Joanne Landers Henry, *Log Cabin in the Woods*, 1988
    The true story of eleven year old Oliver Johnson's experiences living in the densely forested wilderness of 19th century central Indiana.
Jean Van Leeuwen, *Going West*, 1992
    Follows a family's emigration by prairie schooner from the East, across the plains to Kansas.

1961

Johann David Wyss

The Swiss Family Robinson (New York: World, 1947)

Age range: Grades 5-6

Subject(s): Family Life; Survival

Major character(s): Pastor Robinson, Religious (Missionary), Castaway; Fritz Robinson, Teenager

Time period(s): 1700s

Locale(s): Fictional Country (New Switzerland)

What the book is about: Relates the fortunes of a shipwrecked family as they imaginatively adapt to life on an island abundantly inhabited by animal and plant life. Missionaries, at sea, they are resourceful, inventive and courageous as they create a home on the wild island.

Other books you might like:
Eth Clifford, *The Curse of the Moonraker: A Tale of Survival*, 1977
    The survivors of a strange shipwreck in the Auckland Islands fight for survival under seemingly hopeless conditions.
Daniel Defoe, *Robinson Crusoe*, 1983
    During one of his voyages in the 1600s, an English man becomes the sole survivor of a shipwreck and lives for thirty years on a deserted island.
Felice Holman, *The Wild Children*, 1983
    After the Bolshevik Revolution, Alex falls in with a gang of other desperate, homeless children, but never loses his hope for a better life.
Harry Mazer, *The Island Keeper*, 1981
    Cleo runs away from her overprotective and oppressive family and goes to a remote island where she is the only human inhabitant.
Theodore Taylor, *Teetoncey and Ben O'Neal*, 1976
    When a recovered shipwreck victim reveals that two chests full of silver went down with the ship, young boys try to recover them without suspicion.

Y

1962

Elizabeth Yates

Illustrator: Nora S. Unwin

Amos Fortune, Free Man (New York: Dutton, 1950)

Age range: Grades 6 and Up

Subject(s): Biography; Slavery; African Americans

Major character(s): Amos Fortune, Slave

Time period(s): 18th century

Locale(s): Jaffrey, New Hampshire

What the book is about: Amos is born a prince in Africa and is brought to America by slave traders at age 15. He gains freedom at age 50, and helps other slaves to do the same. He is a man of patience, courage and great vision. He dies in 1801.

Where it's reviewed:
Booklist, May 1, 1959, page 279
Horn Book, May 1950, page 202

Awards the book has won:
Newbery Medal 1951

Other books by the author:
Children of the Bible, 1951
Guardian Heart, 1950

Other books you might like:
Edward Beecher Claflin, *Sojourner Truth and the Struggle for Freedom*, 1987
    Biography of Sojourner Truth who spoke out courageously for freedom and equality.
Jan Gleiter, *Booker T. Washington*, 1988
    Born a slave, Booker T. Washington gained an education and founded the Tuskegee Institute.
Alice Walker, *Langston Hughes, American Poet*, 1974
    Langston Hughes began writing as a boy and became one of the most famous American writers of poems, stories, novels and plays.
Richard Scott, *Jackie Robinson*, 1987
    The life of Jackie Robinson, ''baseball's great experiement,'' who proved a man should be judged by ability, not race.

1963

Paul Yee

Illustrator: Simon Ng

Tales From Gold Mountain: Stories of the Chinese in the New World (New York: Macmillan, 1989)

Age range: Grades 4-9

Subject(s): Chinese Americans; Short Stories

Time period(s): Indeterminate Past

Locale(s): Canada; United States

What the book is about: Eight separate stories reflect the experiences of Chinese immigrants to the United States and Canada. Many different settings are depicted and the stories reflect traditions and beliefs, the separation of families, clashes between old culture and new attitudes and exploitation of immigrants on the gold fields, farms and railroads. Family loyalty is valued throughout.

Where it's reviewed:
Booklist, March 5, 1990, page 1464
School Library Journal, May 1990, page 121
Kirkus, February 15, 1990, page 272

Other books by the author:
Roses Sing on New Snow, 1991

Other books you might like:
Eleanor Estes, *The Lost Umbrella of Kim Chu*, 1978
    Nine year old Kim Chu searches for her father's special umbrella which she left in a library umbrella stand.
Daniel Manus Pinkwater, *Wingman*, 1975
    To escape his problems, Donald begins to cut school and climb the George Washington Bridge where he meets Wingman, a sort of Chinese Superman.
Dian Curtis Regan, *The Curse of the Trouble Dolls*, 1992
    Angie Wu finds herself at the center of attention in the fourth grade when she starts sharing her Guatemalan trouble dolls.
Eleanor Wong Telemaque, *It's Crazy to Stay Chinese in Minnesota*, 1978
    A Chinese-American girl in Minnesota and her family tread a balance between the Far East and the Middle West.
Laurence Yep, *The Star Fisher*, 1991
    Joan Lee and her family find the adjustment hard when they move from Ohio to West Virginia in the 1920s.

1964

Laurence Yep

Illustrator: Julia Noonan

Sweetwater (New York: Harper, 1973)

Age range: Grades 6-8

Subject(s): Music; Science Fiction

Major character(s): Tyree, Religious (priest), Settler; Caley, Settler; Jafer Purdy, Settler

Time period(s): 22nd century

Locale(s): Harmony, Planet—Imaginary

What the book is about: Tyree and the other inhabitants of Old Sion are descendants of the starship crew that first brought a human colony to the planet. They live peacefully, trying to preserve their old way of life, but sudden events threaten the existence of the city and its people.

Where it's reviewed:
Booklist, October 15, 1973, page 243
Kirkus Reviews, May 1, 1973, page 522
Publisher's Weekly, April 16, 1973, page 55

Other books by the author:
Dragon Cauldron, 1991
The Lost Garden, 1991
The Star Fisher, 1991
Tongues of Jade, 1991

Other books you might like:
Victor Appleton, *The City in the Stars*, 1981
    Despite attempts to sabotage his fusion drive spacecraft, a scientist investigates the head of the space colony hiding flaws in his own new craft.
Jerome Beatty, *Matthew Looney in the Outback: A Space Story*, 1969
    Because of the tense conditions between moonsters and earthlings, moonman Looney is sent to establish a peaceful colony on a new planet.
H.M. Hoover, *Another Heaven, Another Earth*, 1981
    A space colony is discovered by an exploratory expedition from Earth whose technology threatens to destroy the colony's civilization.
Anne McCaffrey, *Dragonsinger*, 1977
    Pursuing her dream to be a Harper of Pern, Menolly studies under the Masterharper learning that more is required than music and clever words.
Sarah Sargent, *Watermusic*, 1986
    Laura's job of playing the flute for Mrs. Urhlander involves her in an attempt to revive an ancient batlike creature from its suspended animation.

1965

Lawrence Yep

Child of the Owl (New York: Harper and Row, 1977)

Age range: Grades 6-9

Subject(s): Chinese Americans; Grandparents

Major character(s): Casey, Preteen; Barney, Gambler, Parent (Casey's father)

Time period(s): 1970s

Locale(s): San Francisco, California

What the book is about: When Casey's gambler, dreamer father, Barney, is hospitalized, she goes to live with a grandmother she hardly knows in Chinatown. Her discovery of her Chinese heritage is beautifully told, and she comes to regard herself as a "Child of the Owl," a reference to an old folktale.

Where it's reviewed:
Booklist, April 1, 1977, page 1173
Hornbook, August 1977, page 447
Kirkus Reviews, February 1, 1977, page 99

Awards the book has won:
Boston Globe/Horn Book Award

Other books by the author:
Dragon Cauldron, 1991
The Lost Garden, 1991
Dragon of the Lost Sea, 1982
Dragonwings, 1975

Other books you might like:
Frances Carpenter, *Tales of a Chinese Grandmother*, 1973
    An aged Chinese grandmother tells some Chinese folk tales and legends to her grandchildren.
Cora Cheney, *Tales from a Taiwan Kitchen*, 1976
    A collection of traditional Taiwanese tales that reflect the varied cultural heritage of the island.
Dorothy Dowdell, *The Chinese Helped Build America*, 1972
    Describes Chinese immigrants' efforts to make valuable contributions to America's cultural heritage while overcoming prejudice and hardship.
Ellen Howard, *Her Own Song*, 1988
    When her adoptive father is hospitalized, Mellie is befriended by Gemm-Wah who holds the key to the events surrounding Mellie's birth.
Eleanor Wong Telemaque, *It's Crazy to Stay Chinese in Minnesota*, 1978
    A seventeen year old Chinese American in Minnesota and her family tread a balance between the Far East and Middle West.

1966

Lawrence Yep

Dragonwings (New York: Harper and Row, 1975)

Age range: Grades 6 and Up

Subject(s): Chinese Americans

Major character(s): Moon Shadow, Child; Miss Whitlaw, Neighbor; Robin, Child

Time period(s): 1900s (1906)

Locale(s): San Francisco, California

What the book is about: Eight year old Moon Shadow comes to join his father in San Francisco's Chinatown. With Miss Whitlaw and her neice, Robin, he does rescue work after the great earthquake. An added element to the story is Moon Shadow's father, who is determined to build and fly an airplane.

Where it's reviewed:
Booklist, November 1, 1975, page 375
Hornbook, October 1975, page 472
Kirkus Reviews, July 1, 1975, page 719

Awards the book has won:
Boston Globe/Horn Book Award - Honor Book
Carter G. Woodson Book Award 1976

Other books by the author:
Dragon War, 1992
Dragon Cauldron, 1991
The Star Fisher, 1991

Kind Hearts and Gentle Monsters, 1982

Other books you might like:
Heidi Chang, *Elaine, Mary Lewis, and the Frogs*, 1988
 Chinese-American Elaine feels outcast after moving to Iowa, until she shares a new friendship and science project with a girl who loves frogs.
Sonia Levitin, *The Golem and the Dragon Girl*, 1993
 Jonathon, a Jewish boy, and Laurel, a Chinese-American girl, become friends as they deal with ancestral spirits and changing family relationships.
Andre Norton, *Dragon Magic*, 1972
 Four boys of Scandinavian, Welsh, Chinese, and African origin find a magic puzzle which takes each of them back to their own ancestral heritage.
Leo Politi, *Mr. Fong's Toy Shop*, 1978
 A toymaker and his young friends prepare a shadow puppet play for the Moon Festival in Los Angeles' Chinatown.
Judith St. George, *The Chinese Puzzle of Shag Island*, 1976
 What seems a harmless trip to the family's ancestral home on a Maine island turns into something much more dangerous for Kim.

1967

Jane Yolen

Illustrator: Susanna Natti

The Acorn Quest (New York: Crowell, 1981)

Age range: Grades 2-4

Subject(s): Animals; Fantasy

Major character(s): Squirrelin, Wizard; King Earthor, Owl; Sir Tarryhere, Turtle, Knight

Time period(s): Indeterminate Past

Locale(s): Fictional Country (Woodland)

What the book is about: When the happy kingdom of Woodland is threatened with hunger, King Earthor chooses four of his faithful knights, Sir Tarryhere the Turtle, Sir Belliful the Groundhog, Sir Gimmemore the Rabbit, and Sir Runsalot the Mouse, to accompany Squirrelin the Wizard.

Where it's reviewed:
Booklist, November 15, 1981, page 444
Hornbook, February 1982, page 48
Kirkus Reviews, November 1, 1981, page 1346

Other books by the author:
The Seeing Stick, 1977
The Moon Ribbon, 1976
The Transfigured Hart, 1975
The Girl Who Cried Flowers, 1974

Other books you might like:
Constance B. Hieatt, *Sir Gawain and the Green Knight*, 1967
 The quest of Sir Gawain for the Green Knight teaches him a lesson in pride, humility and honor.
Brian Jacques, *Mossflower*, 1988
 Martin the warrior mouse and Gonff the mousethief search for a missing ruler, while the other animals of the woodland rebel against the evil wildcat.
Emily Lampert, *The Unusual Jam Detective*, 1978
 Pig's breakfast jam (or was it?) changes his appearance and starts him on a fantastical quest to rescue jam.
Jean Marzollo, *Blue Sun Ben*, 1984

In a world of two suns, Ben falls into the clutches of the Animal Singer, an evil man who changes animals into shapes to suit his own purposes.
William Wise, *Monsters of the Middle Ages*, 1971
 Describes the various creatures that were believed to exist during the Middle Ages.

1968

Jane Yolen

Illustrator: Bruce Degen

Commander Toad and the Intergalactic Spy (New York: Coward McCann, 1986)

Age range: Grades 1-3

Series: Commander Toad

Subject(s): Space Travel; Science Fiction

Major character(s): Commander Toad, Spaceship Captain; Jake Skyjumper, Computer Expert; Lieutenant Lily, Pilot

Time period(s): Indeterminate

Locale(s): Eden, Planet—Imaginary

What the book is about: Commander Toad is after the intergalactic spy called Tip-Toad, a master of disguises, and Toad's cousin! They end up in a tiptoe through the tulips.

Where it's reviewed:
Booklist, August 1986, page 1695
School Library Journal, September 1986, page 129

Other books by the author:
Commander Toad and the Space Pirates, 1987
Commander Toad and the Dis-asteroid, 1985
Commander Toad and the Big Black Hole, 1983
Commander Toad and the Planet of the Grapes, 1982

Other books you might like:
Chris L. Demarest, *The Lunatic Adventure of Kitman and Willy*, 1988
 Kitman and Willy's space adventures result in the displacement of the moon and several stars. They have to try to put them back where they belong.
Jonathan Etra, *Aliens for Breakfast*, 1988
 Finding an intergalactic spy in his cereal box, Richard joins the extraterrestrial Dranes, one of whom is masquerading as a student in Richard's class
Ezra Jack Keats, *Regards to the Man in the Moon*, 1981
 With the help of his imagination, his parents and a few scraps of junk, Louis and his friends travel through space.
Lynn Marie Luderer, *The Toad Intruder*, 1982
 Although Monica would like her toad Schultz to need her as much as her dog and hamster do, she comes to believe he would be happier in the woods.
Robert M. Quackenbush, *The Most Welcome Visitor*, 1978
 Fred Horny Toad endures visiting relatives all year long, but on Christmas Day, after the visit of Santa Claus, the relatives are all anxious to leave

---

1969

Jane Yolen

The Dragon's Boy (New York: Harper and Row, 1990)

Age range: Grades 4-7

Subject(s): Arthurian Legend

Major character(s): Artos, Servant (kennel boy); Merlinnus, Apothecary; Sir Ector, Knight

Time period(s): Indeterminate Past

Locale(s): England

What the book is about: In this original story created from bits and pieces of Arthurian legends, young Artos, a kennel boy in the household of Sir Ector, finds a secret cave and hears the voice of a grouchy, though wise, old dragon. In exchange for the food which Artos brings him, the dragon becomes his mentor and he grows toward manhood. After a long absence, Artos returns to the cave and finds the voice weakened, and belonging not to a dragon but the apothecary, Merlinnus.

Where it's reviewed:
Booklist, September 15, 1990, page 165
Kirkus, August 15, 1990, page 1175
School Library Journal, October 1990, page 122

Other books by the author:
Children of the Wolf: A Novel, 1984
Heart's Blood, 1984
Dragon's Blood, 1982
The Gift of Sarah Barker, 1981

Other books you might like:
Paul Doherty, *King Arthur*, 1987
  A biography of the legendary king of medieval Britain who became the main figure in tales describing his own heroic deeds and those of his knights.
Gwen Gross, *Knights of the Round Table*, 1985
  Retells the exploits of King Arthur and the Knights of the Round Table.
Margaret Hodges, *Of Swords and Sorcerers*, 1993
  Nine episodes in the Arthurian cycle, from the placing of the boy Arthur in Merlin's care to Arthur's departure for Avalon.
Robin Lister, *The Legend of King Arthur*, 1988
  A retelling of fourteen tales from the legend of King Arthur, from the wizard Merlin to the departure of Arthur for the magical isle of Avalon.
Neil Philip, *The Tale of Sir Gawain*, 1987
  The knight Gawain tells the adventures of King Arthur and the Round Table, his own battle with the Green Knight, his marriage, and the end of Camelot.

1970

Jane Yolen

The Robot and Rebecca: The Mystery of the Code Carrying Kids (New York: Knopf, 1980)

Age range: Grades 3-5

Subject(s): Mystery and Detective Stories; Robots; Science Fiction

Major character(s): Rebecca Jasons, Child; Watson II, Robot; Snar Sizzlegridian, Friend

Time period(s): 22nd century (2121)

Locale(s): Bosyork (East Coast America)

What the book is about: Rebecca uses the robot she receives for her ninth birthday to solve a mystery in Bosyork, biggest metroplex of East Coast America in 2121. Two lost

children and a mysterious code lead the detective team toward an exciting ending.

Other books by the author:
Encounter, 1992
2041, 1991
Wizard's Hall, 1991
Dinosaur Dances, 1990

Other books you might like:
Patricia Coombs, *Dorrie and the Witches' Camp*, 1983
  Big Witch, Dorrie's mother, is turned into a robot by Morzo, the Magician of Machines.
Roger Elwood, *Children of Infinity*, 1973
  Ten science fiction stories about young people of the future.
Cara Lockhart Smith, *Parchment House*, 1989
  In a desolate orphanage in futuristic Britain, orphan Johnnie Rattle pits his wits against those of the cruel orphanage director.
Barbara Rinkoff, *The Case of the Stolen Code Book*, 1971
  When he is not asked to join the Secret Agents Club, the new boy next door sets out to prove that he would be a worthy member. (Includes codes.)
Martin Waddell, *Harriet and the Robot*, 1987
  Harriet gives her friend Anthea a doll for her birthday—a large robot she has made herself and is not quite able to control.

1971

Jane Yolen

Illustrator: Anthony Rao

Shirlick Holmes and the Case of the Wandering Wardrobe (New York: McCann and Geohegan, 1981)

Age range: Grades 3-6

Subject(s): Mystery and Detective Stories

Major character(s): Shirlick Holmes, Detective; George Parker, Neighbor; Candy, Friend

Time period(s): 1970s

Locale(s): United States

What the book is about: "The Seekers," Shirli and the three friends, determine to solve the mystery of vanishing antiques that has baffled the chief of police in their small town. Someone is breaking into summer homes and stealing furniture. Detective work for Shirli becomes scary and dangerous.

Where it's reviewed:
Booklist, May 1, 1981, page 3
Kirkus Reviews, May 1, 1981, page 284
School Library Journal, September 1978, page 167

Other books by the author:
The Robot and Rebecca and the Missing Owser, 1981
Mice on Ice, 1980
The Robot and Rebecca: The Mystery of the Code Carrying Kids, 1980
The Inway Investigators: or, The Mystery at McCracken's Place, 1969

Other books you might like:
Jean Bothwell, *The Mystery Cup*, 1968
  A family buys an old house filled with antiques. After the house is ransacked, they find townspeople reluctant to help apprehend the culprit.

Nancy J. Hopper, *Ape Ears and Beaky*, 1984
  Scott struggles to learn to control his temper, but not before it leads to all sorts of troubles.
Gary Paulsen, *Amos Gets Famous*, 1993
  Amos and Dunc stumble upon a burglary ring when they decipher a code they find in a library book.
Donald J. Sobol, *Encyclopedia Brown Carries On*, 1980
  Ten more mysteries for ten year old detective Encyclopedia Brown as he helps his police chief father solve case after case.
Phyllis A. Whitney, *Secret of the Stone Face*, 1977
  While staying with her mother in an old hotel, a girl becomes entangled in a mystery involving a dangerous old mill, a labyrinth and faked antiques.

| 1972 |

Jane Yolen

Illustrator: Donna Diamond

Transfigured Hart (New York: Crowell, 1975)

Age range: Grades 3-5

Subject(s): Magic; Unicorns

Major character(s): Richard Plante, Preteen; Heather Fielding, Preteen

Time period(s): Indeterminate

Locale(s): Fictional Country

What the book is about: An albino deer is born in the Five Mile Wood, and though small and weak, lives and grows into a magnificent animal. Two twelve year olds, Richard and Heather, separately discover the animal and the placid pool where it can be found. Though very different, Richard and Heather find common ground in their love for the animal, which Richard believes is a unicorn. After a disastrous evening when Richard comes to dinner and Heather lets slip information about the deer, they both sneak out at midnight, knowing opening day of hunting season will spell disaster for the deer. They experience the beauty of the unicorn, and desolation when it flees.

Where it's reviewed:
Kirkus Reviews, June 15, 1975, page 662
Publisher's Weekly, August 11, 1975, page 117
School Library Journal, September 1975, page 115

Awards the book has won:
Golden Kite Honor Book 1975

Other books by the author:
The Dragon's Boy, 1990
The Acorn Quest, 1981
Brothers of the Wind, 1981
The Girl Who Cried Flowers, 1974

Other books you might like:
Jim Arnosky, *Long Spikes*, 1992
  Long Spikes, a deer who is orphaned as a yearling when his mother is killed, grows up and displaces the old one-eyed buck as dominant male of the herd
Frederic Bell, *Jenny's Corner*, 1974
  A little girl's love for deer results in the prohibition of hunting in the valley.
Wayne Dodd, *A Time of Hunting*, 1975

Glimpses a teen's changes of values and perceptions during the Depression days in Oklahoma, especially about hunting, his only way of earning money.
Nancy Luenn, *Unicorn Crossing*, 1987
  Jenny hopes to fulfill her desire to see a real unicorn on her vacation when she helps old Mrs. Donovan pick roses one misty morning.
Louise Moeri, *The Unicorn and the Plow*, 1982
  A poor starving farmer is persuaded by his oxen to wait one more day before he sells one animal and kills the other for food.

| 1973 |

Jane Yolen

Illustrator: Glen Rounds

Uncle Lemon's Spring (New York: Dutton, 1981)

Age range: Grades 3-6

Subject(s): Mountain Life

Major character(s): Lemon Clarkson Cleary, Criminal (poacher); Letty Cleary, Heroine

Time period(s): Indeterminate

Locale(s): United States (Back Fork River)

What the book is about: Uncle Lemon and Letty outwit the mean Preacher Morton in this mountain tale. Uncle Lemon got his spring in the middle of the driest summer on record, and troublesome consequences followed.

Where it's reviewed:
Hornbook, August 1981, page 428
Kirkus Reviews, May 15, 1981, page 634
School Library Journal, September 1981, page 132

Other books by the author:
Wizards's Hall, 1991
The Stone Silenus, 1984
The Seeing Stick, 1977
Hobo Toad and the Motorcycle Gang, 1970

Other books you might like:
Robbie Branscum, *Cameo Rose*, 1989
  Cameo Rose's insatiable curiosity about the murder of a local ne'er-do-well gets her in trouble with her taciturn neighbors in the Arkansas hills.
Mary Calhoun, *Old Man Whickutt's Donkey*, 1975
  In this fable, a man, a boy and a donkey, enroute to the miller with a sack of corn, are criticized by their neighbors no matter who walks or rides.
Brinton Turkle, *The Fiddler of High Lonesome*, 1968
  The Fogle brothers don't believe that Lysander is related to them, but welcome him to the family when they learn his fiddle can charm the animals.
Alice Wellman, *Small-Boy Chuku*, 1973
  As the youngest son, Chuku feels the least important, but when drought plagues his African village, he is able to prove himself a "most important son.
Jay Williams, *The Water of Life*, 1980
  A kindly fisherman is sent by the king to find the Water of Life, but gives away all his magic implements to needy creatures he meets along the way.

1974

Arthur Yorinks

Illustrator: Richard Egielski

It Happened in Pinsk (New York: Farrar Strauss, 1983)

Age range: Grades 1-3

Subject(s): Humor

Major character(s): Irv Irving, Hero

Time period(s): Indeterminate

Locale(s): Fictional Country

What the book is about: Irv seems to have it all but he still isn't happy. He really loses his head, his wife makes a new one for him, but he needs to look for his own head. Imaginative and funny tale for beginning readers.

Where it's reviewed:
Horn Book, April 1984, page 191
Kirkus Reviews, March 1, 1984

Other books by the author:
Ugh, 1990
Bravo, Minski, 1988
Hey, Al, 1986
Louis the Fish, 1980

Other books you might like:
Kay Chorao, *Molly's Moe*, 1976
    Molly has problems because she is always losing something.
Martin Handford, *Where's Waldo?*, 1987
    Waldo is not really lost, he is hiding on every page of this immensely popular book.
Steven Kellogg, *The Mystery of the Missing Red Mitten*, 1974
    Annie has lost her mitten (again!) and imagines where it might be.
Bill Peet, *How Droofus the Dragon Lost His Head*, 1971
    Droofus is unhappy until he finds a way to be useful.
Shel Silverstein, *Where the Sidewalk Ends*, 1974
    Popular poetry of Shel Silverstein, including "The Loser," who loses his head.

1975

Carol Beach York

Illustrator: Catherine Stock

Miss Know-It-All and the Three Ring Circus (New York: Bantam, 1988)

Age range: Grades 3-5

Subject(s): Circus; Orphans

Major character(s): Kate, Orphan (Tomboy); Miss Lavender, Guardian; Miss Plum, Guardian

Time period(s): 1960s

Locale(s): East Bridge

What the book is about: The twenty-eight girls at Good Day Home have received a wonderful surprise - tickets to a traveling circus. The girls have such a good time they decide to put on their own circus right in the backyard.

Where it's reviewed:
Booklist, August 1988, page 1933
School Library Journal, March 1989, page 172

Other books by the author:
Miss Know-It-All and the Wishing Lamp, 1987
Good Charlotte, 1983
The Christmas Dolls, 1967
Ghost of the Isherwoods, 1966

Other books you might like:
Dean Hughes, *Jelly's Circus*, 1986
    A person with a million ideas, most of which don't work, Jelly's latest is to have a circus, only his friends have problems with learning their roles.
Janet Taylor Lisle, *The Dancing Cats of Applesap*, 1984
    A shy 10 year old gets together with 100 remarkable cats to bring notoriety to Applesap, New York, and to save their beloved Rigg's Drug Store.
Claudia Mills, *The Secret Carousel*, 1983
    When her older sister goes to New York to be a ballet dancer, Lindy chafes at the dullness of life with her grandparents in a small Iowa town.
L.M. Montgomery, *Anne of Green Gables*, 1989
    An orphan is sent to live with a lonely, middle-aged brother and sister on a Prince Edward Island farm and proceeds to make an indelible mark.
Noel Streatfeild, *Circus Shoes*, 1939
    Threatened with life in separate orphanages, two children run away to look for their uncle who works for a circus and consider joining the circus.

1976

Carol Beach York

Remember Me When I Am Dead (New York: Elsevier/Nelson Books, 1980)

Age range: Grades 3-5

Subject(s): Death; Stepmothers; Jealousy

Major character(s): Jenny Loring, Child; Margaret Loring, Step-Parent; Sara Loring, Teenager

Time period(s): 1980s

Locale(s): United States

What the book is about: Deeply jealous of her younger sister, Sara hatches a plan to get rid of Jenny. Their mother died a year ago at Christmas time. Jenny has had a difficult time accepting her death. Their father married Margaret only a month ago. Sara gets caught up in her own mean plan.

Where it's reviewed:
Kirkus Reviews, August 1, 1980, page 980
School Library Journal, October 1980, page 165

Other books by the author:
Once upon a Dark November, 1989
When Midnight Comes, 1979
Beware of This Shop, 1977
I Will Make You Disappear, 1974

Other books you might like:
Betsy Hearne, *Eli's Ghost*, 1987
    Eli searches for the mother he'd long assumed dead in a huge swamp, where he is sustained by ghosts of friends from earlier days.
Patricia Hermes, *You Shouldn't Have to Say Good-bye*, 1982
    During the autumn of the year, Sarah learns that her mother is dying of cancer.

Ouida Sebestyen, *Far From Home*, 1990
  After the death of his mother, thirteen year old Salty goes to take his place working at the Buckley Arms Hotel where he learns about love and family.
Marya Smith, *Across the Creek*, 1989
  Rye's friendship with a mysterious girl across the creek helps him cope with the death of his mother.

1977

Ed Young, Author/Illustrator

Lon Po Po: A Red Riding Hood Story From China (New York: Philomel, 1989)

Age range: Grades 2-3

Subject(s): Fairy Tale

Major character(s): Shang, Child; Tao, Child; Paotze, Child

Time period(s): Indeterminate Past

Locale(s): China

What the book is about: This Red Riding Hood tale from Chinese folklore involves three little sisters who allow the wolf (Lon in Cantonese) into the house, thinking he is their grandmother (Po Po). The eldest finally realizes it is the wolf and tricks him into letting them go outside to pick gingko nuts. Beautiful illustrations beg to be shared.

Where it's reviewed:
Booklist, November 15, 1989, page 672
Horn Book, January/February 1990, page 79

Other books by the author:
Dreamcatcher, 1992
All of You Was Singing, 1990
High in the Mountains, 1989
Emperor and the Kite, 1967

Other books you might like:
Fred Ehrlich, *A Class Play with Ms. Vanilla*, 1989
  When Ms. Vanilla's class puts on a play of Little Red Riding Hood, Ms. Vanilla plays the wolf.
Loreen Leedy, *The Bunny Play*, 1988
  When the little bunnies decide to put on a musical stage version of Little Red Riding Hood, they all work hard in the many aspect of producing a play.
Ann Morris, *Little Red Riding Hood: A Rebus Book*, 1987
  A rebus version of the fairy tale in which pictures are substituted for some of the words.
Lydia Very, *Little Red Riding Hood*, 1985
  A verse adaptation of Little Red Riding Hood housed in a book cut in the shape of the standing girl herself.
David Vozar, *Yo, Hungry Wolf!: A Nursery Rap*, 1993
  A retelling in rap verse of *The Three Little Pigs*, *Little Red Riding Hood* and *The Boy Who Cried Wolf*.

1978

Helen Young

Illustrator: Quentin Blake

What Difference Does It Make, Danny? (London: Andre Deutsch, 1980)

Age range: Grades 4-6

Subject(s): Epilepsy; Schools

Major character(s): Danny Blane, Child; Mr. Masterson, Coach

Time period(s): 1980s

Locale(s): England

What the book is about: Danny loves sports. Mr. Masterson, the new games master at Danny's English school, admires Danny's athletic ability, until he learns of his epilepsy. Masterson is afraid that any stress could trigger a seizure. Danny becomes troublesome at school. One day, while skipping school, he rescues a small boy who has fallen into a canal.

Where it's reviewed:
Booklist, November 15, 1980, page 462
Kirkus Reviews, March 1, 1981, page 284
Center for Children's Books Bulletin, January 1981, page 104

Other books by the author:
Throne for Sesame, 1977
Wide Awake Jake, 1975

Other books you might like:
Barbara Aiello, *Trick or Treat or Trouble*, 1989
  Just as friends misunderstand his epilepsy, Brian's misconceptions about mortuaries are cleared up on Halloween.
Barbara Corcoran, *Child of the Morning*, 1982
  A teen joins a theatre group and aspires to be an actress but fears having an epileptic seizure on stage.
Alison Cragin Herzig, *A Season of Secrets*, 1982
  Brooke worries about her brother's fainting spells, which her parents won't explain, and has trouble understanding his attachment to a pet bat.
Zoa Sherburne, *Why Have the Birds Stopped Singing?*, 1976
  During a seizure, Katie time-travels and is mistaken for her great-great-grandmother, who also had epilepsy when the disease was greatly misunderstood
Alvin Silverstein, *Epilepsy*, 1975
  The causes, symptoms, effects and treatment of the various forms of epilepsy.

1979

Miriam Young

Truth or Consequences (New York: Four Winds, 1975)

Age range: Grades 4-6

Subject(s): Friendship; Honesty

Major character(s): Kim Jones, Preteen

Time period(s): 1970s

Locale(s): United States

What the book is about: Kim is bothered by lies. She vows to tell only the truth and loses her best friend, Alison. Should she tell her little brother the "truth" about Santa Claus? She hates getting in trouble when she lies and she doesn't respect the adults around her who tell social lies.

Where it's reviewed:
Booklist, May 1, 1975, page 918
Hornbook, August 1975, page 387
Kirkus Reviews, March 1, 1975, page 241

Other books by the author:
No Place for Mitty, 1976
A Witch's Garden, 1973
Christy and the Cat Jail, 1972
The Secret of Stone House Farm, 1963

Other books you might like:
Ann M. Martin, *Karen's Pen Pal*, 1992
  Karen thinks having a pen pal in New York City is very cool. But when her pal Maxie turns out to be a big bragger, Karen starts to make up stories.
P.J. Petersen, *Liars*, 1992
  In the remote town of Alder Creek, California, Sam and his friends have many adventures because of his new ability to tell when a person is lying.
Laura Hawkins, *The Cat That Could Spell Mississippi*, 1992
  Anxious to prove that she is special at her new school, Linda makes everything more difficult for herself when she cheats in a spelling bee.
Barbara Ware Holmes, *Charlotte Cheetham, Master of Disaster*, 1985
  Trying to become popular in fifth grade, Charlotte discovers that her talent for exaggeration and downright lying causes her a lot of trouble.
Lois Lowry, *Your Move, J.P.!*, 1990
  Lovestruck J.P. does all sorts of weird things to impress his new interest but his life becomes very complicated when a simple lie gets out of control

---

1980

Miriam Young

Illustrator: Charles Robinson

A Witch's Garden (New York; Atheneum, 1973)

Age range: Grades 5-6

Subject(s): Witches and Witchcraft; Prejudice

Major character(s): Jenny Henderson, Preteen; Meeghan Matthews, Eccentric; Russell Petit, Businessman, Bigot

Time period(s): 1970s

Locale(s): Clover Lake

What the book is about: The club members of Clover Lake are a bunch of WASPs as far as Jenny is concerned. They talk nicely about the Greens, but "let one Jewish family in." Jenny is furious. Then the Matthews move in. Mrs. Matthews has a pet rat, grows poisonous plants in her garden, and takes credit for any mishaps the Clover Lake Community members experience. Jenny and the reader are left wondering if Mrs. Matthews is a powerful witch or just an eccentric involved in lots of coincidental events.

Other books by the author:
No Place for Mitty, 1976
Truth or Consequences, 1975
Christy and the Jail Cat, 1972
The Secret of Stone House Farm, 1963

Other books you might like:
Vera Cleaver, *Moon Lake Angel: A Novel*, 1987
  Kitty, whose mother does not want to deal with a child, spends the summer with Aunt Pearl and eventually learns to accept her mother's weaknesses.
Barbara Girion, *Indian Summer*, 1990
  Joni has a tough summer on an Indian reservation getting along with Sarah Birdsong and her friends, who blame her for the prejudice they experience.
Sara Gogol, *Vatsana's Lucky New Year*, 1992
  Torn between Laotian and American cultures, Vatsana faces prejudice from a boy at school as she helps her newly arrived Laotian cousin adjust.
Ruth Nichols, *The Marrow of the World*, 1972
  Philip and Linda, attempting to explore an ancient castle beneath the lake, becomes involved in another world.
Joan G. Robinson, *The Dark House of the Sea Witch*, 1979
  While they are home alone, Meg and her brother meet a neighbor they suspect is a witch.

Z

Joyce Audy Zarins, Author/Illustrator

Toasted Bagels (New York: Coward McCann, 1988)

Age range: Grades 1-3

Series: Break of Day

Subject(s): Animals/Mice; Talent

Major character(s): P.C., Baker; Scotter, Sports Figure (Biker); Yolanda, Artist

Time period(s): 1980s

Locale(s): Willow Cobble

What the book is about: P.C. would like to be the best at something, since all of his friends seem to have special talents. He loves to bake so P.C. invites everyone in to enjoy his bagels, but his friends have to help put out a fire.

Where it's reviewed:
Booklist, April 1, 1988, page 1356
School Library Journal, August, 1988, page 87

Other books by the author:
Gus Goes to School, 1982
Henri and the Loup-Garou, 1982
The Diviner, 1980
Sand Dollar, Sand Dollar, 1980

Other books you might like:
Melinda Green, *Bembelman's Bakery*, 1978
    Relates the way in which Saul Bembelman began baking bread.
Treska Lindsey, *When Batistine Made Bread*, 1985
    Batistine makes her own breakfast by milking the cow and making bread from scratch.
Marianna Mayer, *Marcel the Pastry Chef*, 1991
    A dishwasher practices pastry making in the palace kitchen each night. Then one night the king discovers one of his cream puffs.
Mary Elise Monsell, *Toohy and Wood*, 1992
    After he loses his home and his friends, a fence lizard, who is also a gourmet cook, is taken in by a turtle who helps him deal with his loss.
Kate Spohn, *Ruth's Bake Shop*, 1990
    Ruth, an octopus who loves to bake, spends so much time making shortbread, pies, cookies and cakes that she opens a bake shop.

Alki Zei

Petros' War (New York: Dutton, 1972)

Age range: Grades 5-8

Subject(s): Resistance Movements; World War II

Major character(s): Petros, Preteen, Resistance Fighter; Drossoula, Friend, Resistance Fighter; Antigone

Time period(s): 1940s

Locale(s): Piraeus, Greece

What the book is about: A ten year old boy and his family endure the Fascist occupation of Athens during WWII. He paints slogans on walls for the underground (Freedom or Death!) and liberates a dog from a German soldier. Greek resistance fighters win the first victories for the Allies in WWII, resist the Fascist invaders for four years and endure a savage occupation.

Where it's reviewed:
Booklist, September 15, 1972, page 103
Hornbook, October 1972, page 475
Kirkus Reviews, June 1, 1972, page 624

Awards the book has won:
Mildred L. Batchelder Award 1974

Other books by the author:
The Sound of Dragons Feet, 1979
Wildcat under Glass, 1968

Other books you might like:
Nathaniel Benchley, *Bright Candles: A Novel of the Danish Resistance*, 1974
    The experiences of a Danish boy during the German occupation of his country in WWII.
Arnold Elliott, *A Kind of Secret Weapon*, 1969
    Relates one family's contribution to the resistance movement in Nazi-occupied Denmark during WWII.
James D. Forman, *Ring the Judas Bell*, 1965
    Abducted by guerrillas during the Civil War, a group of Greek children try to make their way back from a prison camp in the Yugoslav mountains.
Charles Gelman, *Do Not Go Gentle*, 1989
    The story of the persecution of Russian Jews and the underground movement that developed during WWII. (Non-Fiction)
R. Conrad Stein, *Resistance Movements*, 1982
    Discusses the importance of resistance movements which sprang up in France, Russia, Greece and other countries under German occupation during WWII.

1983

Alki Zei

The Sound of Dragon's Feet (New York: Dutton, 1979)

Age range: Grades 4-6

Subject(s): Fathers and Daughters; Historical

Major character(s): Alexandra Sasha "Pippin" Velitsanskaya, Child; Igor "Sesame" Lvovitch, Parent, Doctor; Pavel Grigorevich Semyonov, Tutor

Time period(s): 1890s

Locale(s): St. Petersburg, Russia

What the book is about: Time spent with her "revolutionary" tutor opens ten year old Sasha's eyes to more of life in turn-of-the century Russia. She becomes aware of the inequities of class and privilege at the time of the birth of the Russian Revolution.

Where it's reviewed:
Center for Children's Books Bulletin, February 1980, page 124
Hornbook, October 1979, page 538
School Library Journal, September 1979, page 151

Awards the book has won:
Mildred L. Batchelder Award 1980

Other books by the author:
Petros' War, 1972
Wildcat under Glass, 1968

Other books you might like:
E.M. Almedingen, *Anna*, 1972
    Based on the journals and letters of the author's great-grandmother, this family chronicle tells of her life in 18th and 19th century Tsarist Russia.
Leonard Everett Fisher, *A Russian Farewell*, 1980
    Depicts the anti-Semitic terror that drives Benjamin, his wife and children out of Czarist Russia to America at the beginning of the 20th century.
Kathryn Lasky, *The Night Journey*, 1981
    A young girl ignores her parents' wishes and persuades her great-grandmother to relate the story of her escape from czarist Russia.
Les Martin, *Young Indiana Jones and the Princess of Peril*, 1991
    Indy befriends a Georgian princess involved in the Georgian independence movement and is pursued by secret police and agents of an evil fanatic.
Kyra Petrovskaya Wayne, *The Witches of Barguzin*, 1975
    A woman and her son, political exiles from St. Petersburg, try to adjust to the primitive life among hostile peasants in a Siberian village in Russia.

1984

Alki Zei

Wildcat under Glass (New York: Holt, 1968)

Age range: Grades 5-7

Subject(s): Resistance Movements

Major character(s): Melissa, Courier; Niko, Activist; Myrto, Relative (sister)

Time period(s): 1930s

Locale(s): Lamagari Island, Greece

What the book is about: The stuffed wildcat holds messages for the Greek underground in pre-WWII Greece. The story tells the tale of a nation longing for independence and dignity, and the meaning of freedom and democracy.

Where it's reviewed:
Horn Book, June 1968, page 326
Library Journal, April 15, 1968, page 1806

Other books by the author:
The Sound of Dragon's Feet, 1979
Petros' War, 1972

Other books you might like:
Gertie Evans, *What about Me?*, 1976
    A boy searches for a way to help the resistance movement in Amsterdam during the German occupation.
Paula Fox, *Lily and the Lost Boy*, 1987
    Jack, the "Lost Boy" appears suddenly during the Corey family stay on the Greek island of Thasos and causes chaos in the family.
Carol Matas, *Lisa's War*, 1989
    During the Nazi occupation of Denmark, teenage Jews become involved in an underground resistance movement and eventually must flee for their lives.
Arthur Prager, *World War ****Resistance Stories*, 1979
    Describes the secret activities of six members of resistance movements in Europe and Japan during WWII.
R. Conrad Stein, *Resistance Movements*, 1982
    Discusses the resistance movements which arose in Yugoslavia, France, Russia, Greece and other countries under German occupation during WWII.

1985

Joy Zelonky

Illustrator: Barbara Bejna

I Can't Always Hear You (Milwaukee: Raintree, 1980)

Age range: Grades 2-4

Subject(s): Deafness; Schools; Mainstreaming in Education

Major character(s): Kim, Handicapped (deaf); Mr. Davis, Teacher; Ms. Pinkowski, Principal

Time period(s): 1980s

Locale(s): United States

What the book is about: Kim is being mainstreamed in school for the first time. She is sure that she is the only one in school who is different. Ms. Pinkowski tells her that she, too, has a hearing aid. The other children begin to share their own differences with her.

Where it's reviewed:
Interracial Books for Children, 1982, page 10
School Library Journal, February 1981, page 57

Other books by the author:
My Best Friend Moved Away, 1980

Other books you might like:
George Ancona, *Handtalk Zoo*, 1989
    Words and sign language depict children at the zoo discovering how to sign the names of various animals and how to tell time.
Jean F. Andrews, *The Flying Fingers Club*, 1988

Entering a new school, Donald struggles with his learning disability and makes friends with a deaf boy.

Remy Charlip, *Handtalk Birthday: A Number and Story Book in Sign Language*, 1987
  Words and sign language depict friends helping a deaf woman celebrate her birthday.

Lilo Hess, *The Good Luck Dog*, 1985
  A Tibetan terrier named Kah-Loo is dognapped, sold to a research laboratory, and adopted by an unsuitable owner before finally finding a happy home.

Jeanne M. Lee, *Silent Lotus*, 1991
  Although she cannot speak or hear, Lotus trains as a Khmer court dancer and becomes eloquent in dancing out the legends of the gods.

1986

Harriet Ziefert

Illustrator: David Prebenna

A Clean House for Mole and Mouse (New York: Penguin, 1988)

Age range: Grades 1-3

Subject(s): Animals; Cleanliness

Major character(s): Mouse, Mouse; Mole, Mole

Time period(s): Indeterminate

Locale(s): Fictional Country

What the book is about: Mouse and Mole work hard cleaning and tidying their house and spend the rest of the day outside so the house will stay clean.

Where it's reviewed:
Booklist, July 1988, page 1844

Other books by the author:
Egg-Drop Day, 1988
Harry Takes a Bath, 1987
Mike and Tony: Best Friends, 1987
Trip Day, 1987

Other books you might like:
Ned Delaney, *A Worm for Dinner*, 1977
  Bird and Mole lose their appetites as a result of their cooperative efforts to locate some dinner.
Peter Firmin, *Basil Brush in the Jungle*, 1970
  Basil the fox and Harry the mole go to India to find an exotic pet to occupy the cage Basil has made.
Russell Hoban, *The Mole Family's Christmas*, 1969
  When the Mole family finds out about Christmas and the fat man in the red suit, they ask for a telescope to help them see the stars.
Richard J. Margolis, *Big Bear to the Rescue*, 1975
  A cumulative series of trades results when Big Bear tries to borrow a rope to rescue Mr. Mole.
Luis Murschetz, *Mister Mole*, 1976
  When Mister Mole's home is destroyed by men with steam shovels he must search for another meadow to live in.

1987

Harriet Ziefert

Illustrator: Anita Lobel

A New Coat for Anna (New York: Knopf, 1986)

Age range: Grades 1-3

Subject(s): Self-Reliance; Poverty

Major character(s): Anna, Child

Time period(s): 1940s

Locale(s): Europe

What the book is about: Anna's family is very poor after World War II. When winter comes and Anna needs a new coat, her mother trades cherished possessions - a gold watch, a garnet necklace, a teapot, and a lamp - to acquire the much-needed garment.

Where it's reviewed:
Kirkus Reviews, October 15, 1986
Publisher's Weekly, September 26, 1986, page 77

Other books by the author:
A Clean House for Mole and Mouse, 1988
Egg-Drop Day, 1988
Harry Takes a Bath, 1987
Mike and Tony: Best Friends, 1987

Other books you might like:
Charles Blood, *The Goat in the Rug*, 1976
  A goat named Geraldine describes the process of weaving a Navajo rug.
Elsa Maartman Beskow, *Pelle's New Suit*, 1929
  Each person he asks for help gives Pelle something to do, but eventually his new suit is finished.
Tomie De Paola, *Charlie Needs a Cloak*, 1973
  Charlie looks at his old tattered cloak and decides to make a new one.
June Jordan, *New Life, New Room*, 1975
  Children in a family expecting a new baby, living in a two room apartment, plan a way for six people to live comfortably.
Joan M. Lexau, *Striped Ice Cream*, 1968
  The conquest of poverty is realistically portrayed in this warm story about a fatherless black family as they work together.

1988

Jane Zirpoli

Roots in the Outfield (Boston: Houghton Mifflin, 1988)

Age range: Grades 5-6

Subject(s): Sports/Baseball; Stepfamilies

Major character(s): Josh "Roots" Morris, Preteen, Sports Figure (baseball player); Barbara Morris, Step-Parent; Slug Smith, Sports Figure (professional baseball player)

Time period(s): 1980s

Locale(s): Madison, Wisconsin; San Francisco, California

What the book is about: Criticized by his baseball teammates for being afraid of the ball, Josh leaves his mother in San Francisco to live with his father, but finds that his own problems with himself do not depend on whom he lives with.

Other books you might like:
Matt Christopher, *Man Out at First*, 1993
  After he gets hit by a fast ball, Turtleneck Jones loses his confidence on the diamond and sees his position at first base given to another player.

Johanna Hurwitz, *Baseball Fever*, 1981
　　Ezra tries to convince his scholarly father that his baseball fever is not wasting his mind.
Lensey Namioka, *Yang the Youngest and His Terrible Ear*, 1992
　　Musically untalented Yingtao must give a violin performance to attract new students for his father when he would rather be playing baseball.

Alfred Slote, *Make-Believe Ball Player*, 1989
　　Although he's not very good at baseball, Henry uses his imagination to become a better player.
Robert Kimmel Smith, *Bobby Baseball*, 1989
　　Bobby is passionate about baseball and convinced that he will be a great player, but he wants a chance to prove his skill to his father.

Award Index

This index lists major awards given to books featured in the entries. Books are listed alphabetically beneath the name of the award, with author name and entry number number also indicated.

Christopher Award

Adventures of Obadiah - Brinton Turkle 1829
Annie and the Old One - Miska Miles 1264
The Champion of Merrimack County - Roger W. Drury 538
Changeling - Zilpha Keatley Snyder 1696
Chester Chipmunk's Thanksgiving - Barbara Williams 1917
Dominic - William Steig 1733
Even If I Did Something Awful - Barbara Shook Hazen 840
First Snow - Helen Coutant 436
Frog and Toad All Year - Arnold Lobel 1139
The Headless Cupid - Zilpha Keatley Snyder 1698
How My Parents Learned to Eat - Ina R. Friedman 647
Hurry, Hurry, Mary Dear! And Other Nonsense Poems - N.M. Bodecker 161
Pocahontas and the Strangers - Clyde Robert Bulla 227
Tuck Everlasting - Natalie Babbitt 79
Tucker's Countryside - George Selden 1611
Underdog - Marilyn Sachs 1580
What Happened in Hamelin? - Gloria Skurzynski 1659
The Wheel of King Asoka - Ashok Davar 484
The Wolf - Michael W. Fox 635

Colorado Children's Book Award

Cloudy with a Chance of Meatballs - Judi Barrett 97
Cross-Country Cat - Mary Calhoun 272
The Great Green Turkey Creek Monster - James Flora 629
The Unicorn and the Lake - Marianna Mayer 1210

Commonwealth Club of California

Seabird - Holling Clancy Holling 905

Coretta Scott King Award

Aida - Leontyne Price 1467
The Friendship - Mildred D. Taylor 1784
A Long Hard Journey: The Story of the Pullman Porter - Pat McKissack 1245
Nathaniel Talking - Eloise Greenfield 755
Somewhere in the Darkness - Walter Dean Myers 1304
The Young Landlords - Walter Dean Myers 1305

Crabbery Award

The Animal, the Vegetable, and John D. Jones - Betsy Byars 256
The First Two Lives of Lukas Kasha - Lloyd Alexander 27
The Girl with the Silver Eyes - Willo Davis Roberts 1510
The Magic of the Glits - Carole S. Adler 9
Magnolia's Mixed-Up Magic - Joan Lowery Nixon 1340
Sport - Louise Fitzhugh 610
There's a Bat in Bunk Five - Paula Danziger 481
What If They Knew? - Patricia Hermes 865

Crabbery Honor

Banana Blitz - Florence Parry Heide 843
Be a Perfect Person in Just Three Days - Stephen Manes 1187
Captain Hook, That's Me - Ada B. Litchfield 1131
The Ghosts of Austwick Manor - Reby Edmond MacDonald 1166
The Great Skinner Strike - Stephanie S. Tolan 1817
Jacob Have I Loved - Katherine Paterson 1389

Danish Children's Book Prize

Days of Courage; A Medieval Adventure - Niels Jensen 973

Dorothy Canfield Fisher Children's Book Award

The 18th Emergency - Betsy Byars 255
Bones on Black Spruce Mountain - David Budbill 222
A Bundle of Sticks - Pat Rhoads Mauser 1209

Bunnicula: A Rabbit Tale of Mystery - Deborah Howe 923
The Castle in the Attic - Elizabeth Winthrop 1931
Flight of the White Wolf - Mel Ellis 568
The Hand-Me-Down Kid - Francine Pascal 1384
Kavik the Wolf Dog - Walt Morey 1286
Never Steal a Magic Cat - Donald E. Caufield 312
A Smart Kid Like You - Stella Pevsner 1426
Summer of Fear - Lois Duncan 550
The Toothpaste Millionaire - Jean Merrill 1259
The War with Grandpa - Robert Kimmel Smith 1692

Edgar Allan Poe Award

Alone in Wolf Hollow - Dana Brookins 208
Are You in the House Alone? - Richard Peck 1404
Callender Papers - Cynthia Voigt 1861
Danger at Black Dyke - Winifred Finlay 603
The Dangling Witness - Jay Bennett 136
Deathwatch - Robb White 1902
The House of Dies Drear - Virginia Hamilton 802
Intruder - John Rowe Townsend 1819
The Kidnapping of Christina Lattimore - Joan Lowery Nixon 1338
The Long Black Coat - Jay Bennett 137
The Murder of Hound Dog Bates - Robbie Branscum 189
Mystery at Crane's Landing - Marcella Thum 1810
Mystery of 22 East - Leon Ware 1885
Mystery of the Haunted Pool - Phyllis A. Whitney 1903
Mystery of the Hidden Hand - Phyllis A. Whitney 1904
Night Cry - Phyllis Reynolds Naylor 1316
Night Fall - Joan Aiken 17
Really Weird Summer - Eloise Jarvis McGraw 1230
The Sandman's Eyes - Patricia Windsor 1928
Signpost to Terror - Gretchen Sprague 1716
Sinbad and Me - Kin Platt 1452
Taking Terri Mueller - Norma Fox Mazer 1219
Z for Zachariah - Robert C. O'Brien 1348

Edgar Allan Poe Award - Runner-up

The Doggone Mystery - Mary Blount Christian 331
The Dollhouse Murders - Betty Ren Wright 1954
Miss Nelson Is Missing! - Harry Allard 34
On the Edge - Gillian Cross 449

Ehon Nippon Prize (Most excellent picture book of Japan)

Hiroshima No Pika - Toshi Maruki 1205

Ethical Culture School Book Award

In Summertime, It's Tuffy - Judie Angell 49
King Tut's Game Board - Leona Ellerby 567
A Word From Our Sponsor: Or, My Friend Alfred - Judie Angell 51

Friends of American Writers Juvenile Book Merit Award

Foal Creek - Peter Zachary Cohen 386

Garden State Children's Book Award

Dorrie's Book - Marilyn Sachs 1576
Nobody Has to Be a Kid Forever - Hila Colman 395
Ramona and Her Father - Beverly Cleary 354

Georgia Children's Book Award

The Best Christmas Pageant Ever - Barbara Robinson 1517
Doodle and the Go-Cart - Robert Burch 241
Hey, What's Wrong with This One? - Maia Wojciechowska 1939
J.T. - Jane Wagner 1868
Queenie Peavy - Robert Burch 244
Skinny - Robert Burch 245
A Taste of Blackberries - Doris Buchanan Smith 1684

German Children's Book Prize

Friedrich - Hans Peter Richter 1507
Oma - Peter Hartling 822

German Children's Book Prize, Runner-up

There, Far Beyond the River - Yuri Korinetz 1050

Golden Archer Award

Home Run Trick - Scott Corbett 425
My Sister's Keeper - Beverly Butler 253
Mystery of the Bewitched Bookmobile - Florence Parry Heide 845
Summer of the Monkeys - Wilson Rawls 1492
This School is Driving Me Crazy - Nat Hentoff 858

Golden Kite Award

After the Dancing Days - Margaret I. Rostkowski 1550
Children of the River - Linda Crew 447
The Garden Is Doing Fine - Carol J. Farley 586
Jenny of the Tetons - Kristiana Gregory 764
Little Little - M.E. Kerr 1017
One More Flight - Eve Bunting 234
Ralph S. Mouse - Beverly Cleary 353
A Visit to William Blake's Inn - Nancy Willard 1916

Golden Kite Fiction Award

And You Give Me a Pain, Elaine - Stella Pevsner 1424
Arthur, for the Very First Time - Patricia MacLachlan 1169
The Girl Who Had No Name - Berniece Rabe 1479

Golden Kite Fiction Honor Book

Devil in Vienna - Doris Orgel 1363
Foster Child - Marion Dane Bauer 107

Golden Kite Honor Book

Growing Anyway Up - Florence Parry Heide 844
The Half-a-Moon Inn - Paul Fleischman 615
Meaning Well - Sheila R. Cole 391
Naomi - Berniece Rabe 1480
The Path of the Pale Horse - Paul Fleischman 617
Red Rock over the River - Patricia Beatty 126
The Solitary - Lynn Hall 795
Transfigured Hart - Jane Yolen 1972

Golden Sower Award

A Dog Called Kitty - Bill Wallace 1876
Night of the Twisters - Ivy Ruckman 1559
The War with Grandpa - Robert Kimmel Smith 1692
Yours Till Niagara Falls, Abby - Jane O'Connor 1351

Guardian Award for Children's Fiction

Conrad's War - Andrew Davies 485
A Pack of Lies - Geraldine McCaughrean 1220

Guardian Award Runner Up

Me and My Million - Clive King 1027

Hans Christian Andersen Award

The Singing Hill - Meindert DeJong 506

International Reading Association Children's Book Award

After the Dancing Days - Margaret I. Rostkowski 1550
My Own Private Sky - Delores Beckman 127
Reserved for Mark Anthony Crowder - Alison Smith 1677

Jane Addams Children's Book Award

The Endless Steppe: Growing Up in Siberia - Esther Hautzig 830
A Long Hard Journey: The Story of the Pullman Porter - Pat McKissack 1245
Shades of Gray - Carolyn Reeder 1496
The Upstairs Room - Johanna Reiss 1499
The Wednesday Surprise - Eve Bunting 240

Jane Addams Children's Book Award, Honor Book

My Brother Sam Is Dead - James Lincoln Collier 392
Number the Stars - Lois Lowry 1153
Z for Zachariah - Robert C. O'Brien 1348

Time Period Index

This index chronologically lists the time settings in which the featured books take place. Main headings refer to a century; where no specific time is given, the headings INDETERMINATE PAST, INDETERMINATE FUTURE, and INDETERMINATE are used. The 18th through 21st centuries are broken down into decades when possible. (Note: 1800s, for example, refers to the first decade of the 19th century.) Featured titles are listed alphabetically beneath time headings, with author names, and entry numbers also provided.

1940s

The Adventures of Johnny May - Robbie Branscum 188
Alan and Naomi - Myron Levoy 1104
All the Children Were Sent Away - Sheila Garrigue 674
Arthur Mitchell - Tobi Tobias 1815
At the Back of the Woods - Claudia Mills 1267
Autumn Street - Lois Lowry 1152
Big Red - Jim Kjelgaard 1037
The Black Stallion - Walter Farley 587
Blue Willow - Doris Gates 675
The Borrowed House - Hilda Van Stockum 1850
Brushy Mountain - Patricia Pendergraft 1416
The Canada Geese Quilt - Natalie Kinsey-Warnock 1035
The Carp in the Bathtub - Barbara Cohen 381
Carrie's War - Nina Bawden 111
The Cay - Theodore Taylor 1788
A Child in Prison Camp - Shizuye Takashima 1775
Conrad's War - Andrew Davies 485
Crutches - Peter Hartling 820
Danza! - Lynn Hall 792
Destination Unknown - Dale Fife 599
Don't Say a Word - Barbara Gehrts 679
The Endless Steppe: Growing Up in Siberia - Esther Hautzig 830
A Fine White Dust - Cynthia Rylant 1565
The Garden Is Doing Fine - Carol J. Farley 586
Gay-Neck: The Story of a Pigeon - Dan Gopal Mukerji 1297
A Gift for Mama - Esther Hautzig 831
A Girl Called Bob and a Horse Called Yoki - Barbara Campbell 287
Good Night, Mr. Tom - Michelle Magorian 1177
Hangin' Out with Cici - Francine Pascal 1385
The Haunting - Margaret Mahy 1182
Henry - Nina Bawden 113
Hide Crawford Quick - Margaret Walden Froehlich 653
Highpockets - John R. Tunis 1826
Hiroshima No Pika - Toshi Maruki 1205
The House of Sixty Fathers - Meindert De Jong 494
The House with a Clock in Its Walls - John Bellairs 129
The House Without a Christmas Tree - Gail Rock 1523
How's Business? - Alison Prince 1470
I Should Worry, I Should Care - Miriam Chaikin 315
In the Year of the Boar and Jackie Robinson - Bette Bao Lord 1148
The Island on Bird Street - Uri Orlev 1364
Journey to America - Sonia Levitin 1103
Journey to Topaz - Yoshiko Uchida 1837
Just Like Always - Elizabeth-Ann Sachs 1572
The Kid Comes Back - John R. Tunis 1827
Lassie Come Home - Eric Knight 1042
The Last Mission - Harry Mazer 1215
Lenny Kendall, Smart Aleck - Ellen Conford 405
Let the Celebrations Begin! - Margaret Wild 1908
Little Fishes - Erik Christian Haugaard 828
A Long Day in November - Ernest J. Gaines 660
Love You, Soldier - Amy Hest 872
The Machine Gunners - Robert Westall 1894
The Machine Gunners - Robert Westall 1895
The Man From the Other Side - Uri Orlev 1365
Miss Hickory - Carolyn Sherwin Bailey 83
Misty of Chincoteague - Marguerite Henry 855
The Moved Outers - Florence Crannel Means 1252
Mr. Nobody's Eyes - Michael Morpurgo 1290
My Daddy Was a Soldier - Deborah Kogan Ray 1494
The Mystery of the Diamond in the Wood - David Kherdian 1021
The Mystery of the Haunted Cabin - Judy Delton 513
A New Coat for Anna - Harriet Ziefert 1987
Number the Stars - Lois Lowry 1153
Once I Was a Plum Tree - Johanna Hurwitz 954

The Other Side of the Family - Maureen Pople 1457
Petros' War - Alki Zei 1982
A Pocket Full of Seeds - Marilyn Sachs 1579
Randolph's Dream - Judith Mellecker 1256
The Remembering Box - Eth Clifford 364
The Ring and the Window Seat - Amy Hest 874
Rish n' Roses - Jan Slepian 1666
Rufus M. - Eleanor Estes 578
The Runaways - Ruth Thomas 1807
Salted Lemons - Doris Buchanan Smith 1683
The Saturdays - Elizabeth Enright 573
Shadow of a Bull - Maia Rodman 1535
A Sound of Chariots - Mollie Hunter 940
Stepping on the Cracks - Mary Downing Hahn 789
The Stones - Janet Hickman 875
The Three Wars of Billy Joe Treat - Robbie Branscum 190
The Times They Used to Be - Lucille Clifton 367
Touch Wood: A Girlhood in Occupied France - Renee Roth-Hano 1552
Uncle Misha's Partisans - Yuri Suhl 1767
The Upstairs Room - Johanna Reiss 1499
Waiting for Anya - Michael Morpurgo 1291
When the Sirens Wailed - Noel Streatfeild 1763
Wildcat Summer - Mary Riskind 1508
The Wind Is Not a River - Arnold A. Griese 767
With a Wave of the Wand - Mark Jonathan Harris 817

1950s

All Together Now - Sue Ellen Bridgers 197
Along Came a Dog - Meindert De Jong 493
.and Now Miguel - Joseph Krumgold 1057
Beezus and Ramona - Beverly Cleary 349
The Best Bet Gazette - Linda Gondosch 720
A Big Ball of String - Marion Holland 902
Black Stallion Mystery - Walter Farley 588
The Cat in the Hat - Dr. Seuss 1617
Charlotte's Web - E.B. White 1899
Danny Dunn on the Ocean Floor - Jay Williams 1920
David and Max - Gary Provost 1473
Ellen Tebbits - Beverly Cleary 351
The Enormous Egg - Oliver Butterworth 254
Family Under the Bridge - Natalie Savage Carlson 292
Follow My Leader - James B. Garfield 669
Foster Mary - Celia Strang 1761
Gone-Away Lake - Elizabeth Enright 572
How Pizza Came to Queens - Dayal Kaur Khalsa 1019
Hurry Home, Candy - Meindert DeJong 505
The Kid Who Batted 1000 - Bob Allison 35
Knock at the Door, Emmy - Florence Crannel Means 1251
Little Witch - Anna Elizabeth Bennett 135
Ludell - Brenda Scott Wilkinson 1913
Ludie's Song - Dirlie Herlihy 859
Mary Jane - Dorothy Sterling 1742
Miracles on Maple Hill - Virginia Sorensen 1706
The Mouse and His Child - Russell Hoban 892
My Side of the Mountain - Jean Craighead George 683
Next-Door Neighbors - Sarah Ellis 570
Nobody Listens to Andrew - Elizabeth Guilfoile 778
Old Yeller - Fred Gipson 707
Onion John - Joseph Krumgold 1058
Pippi Longstocking - Astrid Lindgren 1124
The Red Balloon - Albert Lamorisse 1063
Rhoda, Straight and True - Roni Schotter 1596
Roosevelt Grady - Louisa R. Shotwell 1626
Sadako and the Thousand Paper Cranes - Eleanor Coerr 378
The Secret of the Andes - Ann Nolan Clark 344
Seven-Day Magic - Edward Eager 556
Shadrach - Meindert De Jong 495
The Singing Hill - Meindert DeJong 506
Susan Cornish - Rebecca Caudill 311

Tales of a Wandering Warthog - Tom Sinclair 1650
Thank You, Jackie Robinson - Barbara Cohen 384
Thunder Pup - Janet Hickman 876
Tom's Midnight Garden - Philippa Pearce 1401
The Trouble with Tuck - Theodore Taylor 1791
What Happened to Mr. Forester? - Gary W. Barger 96
The Wheel on the School - Meindert DeJong 507
The Witch Family - Eleanor Estes 579

1960s

The 17th Street Gang - Emily Cheney Neville 1326
And One for All - Theresa Nelson 1321
Blackbeard's Ghost - Ben Stahl 1724
Catch That Pass! - Matt Christopher 337
A Certain Small Shepherd - Rebecca Caudill 310
Chitty-Chitty-Bang-Bang - Ian Fleming 627
The Cricket in Times Square - George Selden 1608
Danger at Black Dyke - Winifred Finlay 603
David and Max - Gary Provost 1473
The Day That Elvis Came to Town - Jan Marino 1193
A Dog on Barkham Street - Mary Stolz 1753
Don't Take Teddy - Babbis Friis-Baastad 648
Edgar Allan - John Neufeld 1325
The Egypt Game - Zilpha Keatley Snyder 1697
The Empty Schoolhouse - Natalie Savage Carlson 291
Encyclopedia Brown, Boy Detective - Donald J. Sobol 1703
Fantastic Voyage - Isaac Asimov 61
From the Mixed-Up Files of Mrs. Basil E. Frankweiler - E.L. Konigsburg 1045
Frozen Fire - James A. Houston 917
Gentle Ben - Walt Morey 1285
A Girl Called Al - Constance C. Greene 750
Goodbye, My Island - Jean Rogers 1539
The Grizzly - Annabel Johnson 974
Harriet the Spy - Louise Fitzhugh 608
Henry Reed's Baby-Sitting Service - Keith Robertson 1514
Hey, What's Wrong with This One? - Maia Wojciechowska 1939
The House of Dies Drear - Virginia Hamilton 802
How Many Miles to Babylon? - Paula Fox 636
In Caverns of Blue Ice - Robert Roper 1546
The Integration of Mary-Larkin Thornhill - Ann Waldron 1869
Intruder - John Rowe Townsend 1819
J.T. - Jane Wagner 1868
Jake - Alfred Slote 1672
Jazz Country - Nat Hentoff 857
Jennifer, Hecate, Macbeth, William McKinley and Me, Elizabeth - E.L. Konigsburg 1046
Kavik the Wolf Dog - Walt Morey 1286
Lions in the Way - Bella Rodman 1534
Manhattan Is Missing - E.W. Hildick 880
Meet the Austins - Madeleine +L'Engle 1089
The Midnight Fox - Betsy Byars 264
Mishmash - Molly Cone 399
Miss Know-It-All and the Three Ring Circus - Carol Beach York 1975
The Mouse and the Motorcycle - Beverly Cleary 352
My Brother Stevie - Eleanor Clymer 372
Mystery at Crane's Landing - Marcella Thum 1810
Mystery of the Fat Cat - Frank Bonham 172
Mystery of the Gingerbread House - Wylly Folk St. John 1721
Mystery of the Haunted Pool - Phyllis A. Whitney 1903
Mystery of the Hidden Hand - Phyllis A. Whitney 1904
Night Fall - Joan Aiken 17
Noonday Friends - Mary Stolz 1758
The Owl Service - Alan Garner 673
Phantom of Walkaway Hill - Edward Fenton 594
Portrait of Ivan - Paula Fox 640
Queenie Peavy - Robert Burch 244
Sasha, My Friend - Barbara Corcoran 432

Geographic Index

This index provides access to all featured books by geographic settings—such as countries, continents, oceans, and planets. States and provinces are indicated for the United States and Canada. Also interfiled are headings for fictional place names (Spaceships, Imaginary Planets, etc.). Sections are further broken down by city or the specific name of the imaginary locale. Book titles are listed alphabetically under headings, and author names and entry numbers are also provided.

AFRICA

Cow-Tail Switch and Other West Africa Stories - Harold Courlander 435
The First Morning: An African Myth - Margery Bernstein 142

Cameroons
The Village of Round and Square Houses - Ann Grifalconi 768

ALTERNATE EARTH

The First Two Lives of Lukas Kasha - Lloyd Alexander 27
Heckedy Peg - Audrey Wood 1946
How Droofus the Dragon Lost His Head - Bill Peet 1413
The Owlstone Crown - X.J. Kennedy 1016
The Search for Delicious - Natalie Babbitt 78
The Tombs of Atuan - Ursula Le Guin 1085
A Wizard of Earthsea - Ursula Le Guin 1086

AMERICAN COLONIES

I'm Deborah Sampson: A Soldier in the War of the Revolution - Patricia Clapp 342
Man with the Silver Eyes - William O. Steele 1729
The Remarkable Ride of Israel Bissell - Alice Schick 1592

CONNECTICUT

Redding
My Brother Sam Is Dead - James Lincoln Collier 392

MAINE

Becky and the Bear - Dorothy Van Woerkom 1851

MASSACHUSETTS

Boston
And Then What Happened, Paul Revere? - Jean Fritz 649
Ben and Me - Robert Lawson 1083
George the Drummer Boy - Nathaniel Benchley 132
Tituba of Salem Village - Ann Petry 1423

Lexington
The Remarkable Ride of Israel Bissell - Alice Schick 1592

Nantucket
Zenas and the Shaving Mill - F.N. Monjo 1276

Salem
The Tall Man From Boston - Marion Lena Starkey 1727

NEW JERSEY
The Tavern at the Ferry - Edwin Tunis 1825

NEW YORK

Long Island
Sarah Bishop - Scott O'Dell 1354

Tarry Town
The Legend of Sleepy Hollow - Washington Irving 964

PENNSYLVANIA
Greenhorn on the Frontier - Ann Finlayson 604

Philadelphia
Ben and Me - Robert Lawson 1083

VERMONT

Castleton
The Blue Cat of Castle Town - Catherine C. Coblentz 376

Randolph
Justin Morgan Had a Horse - Marguerite Henry 853

VIRGINIA

Jamestown
The Double Life of Pocahontas - Jean Fritz 650
Pocahontas and the Strangers - Clyde Robert Bulla 227

ANCIENT CIVILIZATION

Shiva: An Adventure of the Ice Age - J.H. Brennan 191

ARCTIC

Dogsong - Gary Paulsen 1397
Snowfoot: White Reindeer of the Arctic - Justin F. Denzel 514

ARMENIA

The Contest - Nonny Hogrogian 897

ASIA

In Caverns of Blue Ice - Robert Roper 1546

ASTEROID

Asteroid B-612
The Little Prince - Antoine de Saint-Exupery 1581

AT SEA

All Sail Set: A Romance of the Flying Cloud - Armstrong Sperry 1711
The Black Stallion - Walter Farley 587
Cyrus, the Unsinkable Sea Serpent - Bill Peet 1412
I Was All Thumbs - Bernard Waber 1866
The Journey of the Shadow Bairns - Margaret Jean Anderson 44
Mystery of 22 East - Leon Ware 1885
Pearl's Pirates - Frank Asch 58
Seabird - Holling Clancy Holling 905
Ship's Cook Ginger - Edward Ardizzone 54
Treasure Island - Robert Louis Stevenson 1749
The True Confessions of Charlotte Doyle - Avi 74
We Didn't Mean to Go to Sea - Arthur Ransome 1486

HMS Beagle
Darwin and the Voyage of the Beagle - Felicia Law 1078

R.M.S. Titanic
The Titanic: Lost.and Found - Judy Donnelly 530

ATLANTIC OCEAN

Destination Unknown - Dale Fife 599

AUSTRALIA

Enemies - Robin Klein 1040
The Hammerhead Light - Colin Thiele 1800
The Horse with Eight Hands - Joan Phipson 1437
I Am Susannah - Libby Gleeson 709
The Iron Giant: A Story in Five Nights - Ted Hughes 935
A Little Fear - Patricia Wrightson 1958
The Nargun and the Stars - Patricia Wrightson 1959
Ned Kelly and the City of the Bees - Thomas Keneally 1013
Onion Tears - Diana Kidd 1023
The Pigs Are Flying! - Emily Rodda 1530
Polly's Tiger - Joan Phipson 1438
Samantha on Stage - Susan Clement Farrar 590
Space Demons - Gillian Rubinstein 1558
Storm Boy - Colin Thiele 1802

Ballarat
Jonathan Down Under - Patricia Beatty 125

Gonunda
The Shadow on the Hills - Colin Thiele 1801

Opal Town
The Sky Is Free - Mavis Thorpe Clark 346

Queensland
Where the Forest Meets the Sea - Jeannie Baker 90

Sydney
The Other Side of the Family - Maureen Pople 1457

Playing Beatie Bow - Ruth Park   1382
Time Sweep - Valerie Weldrick   1892
The Tram to Bondi Beach - Elizabeth Hathorn   825

Upper Gumbowie
February Dragon - Colin Thiele   1799

AUSTRIA

Bambi - Felix Salten   1582
Konrad - Christine Nostlinger   1346
So Long, Grandpa - Elfie Donnelly   529
A Tangled Web - Hannelore Valencak   1839

Vienna
Crutches - Peter Hartling   820
Devil in Vienna - Doris Orgel   1363

BANGLADESH

Kukuri Mukuri Char
The Night the Water Came - Clive King   1028

BULGARIA

Sofia
Dobry - Monica Shannon   1619

CANADA

Brother Moose - Betty Levin   1096
Dr. Beaumont and the Man with the Hole in His Stomach - Sam Epstein   575
From Anna - Jean Little   1133
Hatchet - Gary Paulsen   1398
Hold Fast - Kevin Major   1185
Ida and the Wool Smugglers - Sue Ann Alderson   24
The Journey of the Shadow Bairns - Margaret Jean Anderson   44
Next-Door Neighbors - Sarah Ellis   570
Our Fathers Had Powerful Songs - Natalie Maree Belting   130
The Root Cellar - Janet Louise Lunn   1157
Squirrel in My Teacup! - Eileen Cade-Edwards   271
Tales From Gold Mountain: Stories of the Chinese in the New World - Paul Yee   1963
There's a Rainbow In My Closet - Patti Stren   1764

BRITISH COLUMBIA

Boy of Tache - Ann Blades   147

Vancouver
All the Children Were Sent Away - Sheila Garrigue   674
Call Me Danica - Winifred Madison   1174
A Child in Prison Camp - Shizuye Takashima   1775
The Hostage - Theodore Taylor   1789

MANITOBA

A Northern Nativity: Christmas Dreams of a Prairie Boy - William Kurelek   1061

Winnipeg
The Empty Chair - Bess Kaplan   993

NORTHWEST TERRITORIES

Frobisher Bay
Frozen Fire - James A. Houston   917

NOVA SCOTIA

The Baitchopper - Silver Donald Cameron   286

ONTARIO
The Incredible Journey - Sheila Burnford   250
The Trumpet of the Swan - E.B. White   1901
The Zucchini Warriors - Gordon Korman   1052

Lake Nipigon
Paddle-to-the-Sea - Holling Clancy Holling   904

Riverside
Look through My Window - Jean Little   1134

Windsor
King of the Wind - Marguerite Henry   854

PRINCE EDWARD ISLAND

Anne of Green Gables - L.M. Montgomery   1278

ROCKY MOUNTAINS

Wild Man of the Woods - Joan Clark   345

SASKATCHEWAN

Saskatoon
The Dog Who Wouldn't Be - Farley Mowat   1296

YUKON TERRITORY

Dawson
Bring to a Boil and Separate - Hadley Irwin   966

CARIBBEAN

The Cay - Theodore Taylor   1788
Jethro and the Jumbie - Susan Cooper   420
The Life and Strange and Surprising Adventures of Robinson Crusoe - Daniel Defoe   503

CHINA

The House of Sixty Fathers - Meindert De Jong   494
Lon Po Po: A Red Riding Hood Story From China - Ed Young   1977
Shen of the Sea - Arthur Bowie Chrisman   329

Chungking
Young Fu of the Upper Yangtze - Elizabeth Lewis   1111

Hankow
Homesick: My Own Story - Jean Fritz   652

DENMARK

Days of Courage; A Medieval Adventure - Niels Jensen   973
Hurry, Hurry, Mary Dear! And Other Nonsense Poems - N.M. Bodecker   161
Silas and Ben-Godik - Cecil Bodker   163
Those Foolish Molboes - Lillian Bason   101

Copenhagen
Buster, the Sheikh of Hope Street - Bjarne B. Reuter   1502
Number the Stars - Lois Lowry   1153

EARTH

All the Money in the World - Bill Brittain   202
Around the World in Eighty Days - Jules Verne   1852
BAAA - David Macaulay   1161
The Bat-Poet - Randall Jarrell   971
Belling the Tiger - Mary Stolz   1751
The Buried Moon and Other Stories - Molly Bang   93
The Castle in the Attic - Elizabeth Winthrop   1931

Danger in Dinosaur Valley - Joan Lowery Nixon   1332
The Devil's Donkey - Bill Brittain   203
The Devil's Storybook - Natalie Babbitt   75
Doctor Change - Joanna Cole   388
Dogsbody - Diana Wynne Jones   981
Eva - Peter Dickinson   521
George and Martha Back in Town - James Marshall   1199
Ghosts at Large - Susan Price   1469
Graven Images - Paul Fleischman   614
How the Witch Got Alf - Cora Annett   52
Ig Lives in a Cave - Carol Chapman   318
In the Beginning: Creation Stories from Around the World - Virginia Hamilton   803
Jeremiah in the Dark Woods - Janet Ahlberg   15
Jolly Roger and the Pirates of Abdul, the Skinhead - Colin McNaughton   1248
Jonas McFee, A.T.P. - Sarah Sargent   1587
Knights of the Kitchen Table - Jon Scieszka   1601
The Lemming Condition - Alan Arkin   55
Little Little - M.E. Kerr   1017
The Little Prince - Antoine de Saint-Exupery   1581
Magnolia's Mixed-Up Magic - Joan Lowery Nixon   1340
Maroo of the Winter Caves - Ann Turnbull   1831
Mazemaker - Catherine Dexter   517
Nightwaves: Scary Tales for After Dark - Collin McDonald   1223
Orvis - H.M. Hoover   914
Outside the Gates - Molly Gloss   711
The Planetoid of Amazement - Mel Glidden   710
The Sea Child - Carolyn Sloan   1667
Seth of the Lion People - Bonnie Pryor   1475
Shrek! - William Steig   1736
Spirit on the Wall - Ann O'Neal Garcia   664
Stonewords: A Ghost Story - Pam Conrad   411
Stories for Children - Isaac Bashevis Singer   1653
Tales of a Wandering Warthog - Tom Sinclair   1650
Tales of the Early World - Ted Hughes   936
Uncle Elephant - Arnold Lobel   1142
Watership Down - Richard Adams   4
Wish Again, Big Bear - Richard J. Margolis   1192
The Wolf's Chicken Stew - Keiko Kasza   998
Yankel the Fool - Shan Ellentuck   565

Dimpole
The Great Dimpole Oak - Janet Taylor Lisle   1130

East Gradwohl
The Dandelion Caper - Gene DeWeese   516

Square Toe City
Miss Pickerell and the War of the Computers - Dora Pantell   1373

EGYPT

Aida - Leontyne Price   1467
The Cat in the Mirror - Mary Stolz   1752
King Tut's Game Board - Leona Ellerby   567

Thebes
I, Tut: The Boy Who Became Pharoah - Miriam Schlein   1595

ENGLAND

Adam of the Road - Elizabeth Gray   735
Alice's Adventures in Wonderland - Lewis Carroll   305
Annerton Pit - Peter Dickinson   519
Archer's Goon - Diana Wynne Jones   978
Ask Me No Questions - Ann Schlee   1594
The Beachcombers - Helen Cresswell   441
Bedknob and Broomsticks - Mary Norton   1343
Ben and Annie - Joan Tate   1781
Benson Boy - Ivan Southall   1707
Beyond the Weir Bridge - Hester Burton   251
A Billion for Boris - Mary Rodgers   1532

The Half-Child - Kathleen Hersom 868
Only One Woof - James Herriot 867
The Secret Garden - Frances Hodgson Burnett 249
Wild Boy - Joan Tate 1782

ETHIOPIA

The Leopard - Cecil Bodker 162

EUROPE

The Adventures of Pinocchio - Carlo Collodi 394
Cakes and Miracles - Barbara Diamond Goldin 718
The Castle of the Red Gorillas - Wolfgang Ecke 558
Funnyman and the Penny Dodo - Stephen Mooser 1282
Journey to America - Sonia Levitin 1103
The Last Mission - Harry Mazer 1215
The Merrymaker - Yuri Suhl 1766
A Net to Catch the Wind - Margaret Greaves 741
A New Coat for Anna - Harriet Ziefert 1987

FICTIONAL CITY

My Father's Dragon - Ruth Stiles Gannett 663

Instep
Knee-Knock Rise - Natalie Babbitt 77

Tillbury Upper Village
Carrot Holes and Frisbee Trees - N.M. Bodecker 160

FICTIONAL COUNTRY

Abel's Island - William Steig 1731
The Acorn Quest - Jane Yolen 1967
Alanna: The First Adventure - Tamora Pierce 1440
The Alligator and His Uncle Tooth: A Novel of the Sea - Geoffrey Hayes 833
Alone in the Wild Forest - Isaac Bashevis Singer 1652
Amelia Bedelia - Peggy Parish 1374
Among the Dolls - William Sleator 1660
Andrew and the Alchemist - Barbara Ninde Byfield 269
Animal Family - Randall Jarrell 970
Arthur's Baby - Marc T. Brown 216
Arthur's Honey Bear - Lillian Hoban 888
Babar and the Ghost: An Easy to Read Version - Laurent De Brunhoff 219
Bedtime for Frances - Russell Hoban 891
The Best Dressed Bear - Mary Blocksma 149
Big Max - Kin Platt 1449
The Black Cauldron - Lloyd Alexander 25
A Book of Dragons - Hosie Baskin 100
The Book of the Dun Cow - Walter Wangerin 1882
Call for Mr. Sniff - Thomas P. Lewis 1114
Castle in the Air - Diana Wynne Jones 979
Charlie and the Chocolate Factory - Roald Dahl 464
Chester Chipmunk's Thanksgiving - Barbara Williams 1917
A Clean House for Mole and Mouse - Harriet Ziefert 1986
Cloud Horse - Jill Pinkwater 1446
Cloudy with a Chance of Meatballs - Judi Barrett 97
The Dawn Seekers - Carol Hamilton 798
December's Travels - Mischa Damjan 474
Dr. De Soto - William Steig 1734
Dominic - William Steig 1733
The Door in the Hedge - Robin McKinley 1240
Dorp Dead - Julia Cunningham 452
Euphonia and the Flood - Mary Calhoun 273
Flat Stanley - Jeff Brown 214

The Fox Busters - Dick King-Smith 1031
The Fox with Cold Feet - Bill Singer 1651
Frog and Toad Together - Arnold Lobel 1140
Gammage Cup - Carol Kendall 1012
Gom on Windy Mountain - Grace Chetwin 324
The Griffin and the Minor Canon - Frank R. Stockton 1750
Hello, Mrs. Piggle-Wiggle - Betty MacDonald 1164
The Hero and the Crown - Robin McKinley 1241
Hester the Jester - Ben Shecter 1625
The Hobbit - J.R.R. Tolkien 1818
It Happened in Pinsk - Arthur Yorinks 1974
It's Me, Hippo! - Mike Thaler 1798
Journey Outside - Mary Q. Steele 1728
King Bidgood's in the Bathtub - Audrey Wood 1948
King of the Golden River - John Ruskin 1560
The King, the Mice, and the Cheese - Nancy Gurney 779
The King's Fountain - Lloyd Alexander 30
Little Witch - Anna Elizabeth Bennett 135
The Little Witch and the Riddle - Bruce Degen 504
Lulu and the Witch Baby - Jane O'Connor 1350
The Magic Finger - Roald Dahl 467
Many Moons - James Thurber 1811
The Marzipan Moon - Nancy Willard 1915
Merlin Dreams - Peter Dickinson 523
Mice on My Mind - Bernard Waber 1867
Miss Pickerell and the Blue Whales - Ellen MacGregor 1167
Miss Plunkett to the Rescue - Jane Flory 630
Mo to the Rescue - Mary Pope Osborne 1369
Mrs. Brice's Mice - Syd Hoff 895
The Napping House - Audrey Wood 1949
Never Steal a Magic Cat - Donald E. Caufield 312
Nicobobinus - Terry Jones 984
Norby, the Mixed-Up Robot - Janet Asimov 62
Oaf - Julia Cunningham 454
Odyssey From River Bend - Tom McGowen 1227
Perrywinkle and the Book of Magic Spells - Ross Martin Madsen 1176
The Phantom Tollbooth - Norton Juster 990
Pig Pig and the Magic Photo Album - David M. McPhail 1250
Pippa Pops Out: Four Read-Aloud/Read Alone Stories - Betty Boegehold 164
Poor Stainless: A New Story about the Borrowers - Mary Norton 1345
Porcupine's Pajama Party - Terry Webb Harshman 818
Princess Bee and the Royal Goodnight Story - Sandy Asher 60
The Real Thief - William Steig 1735
The Red King - Victor Kelleher 1005
Redwall - Brian Jacques 967
The Rescuers - Margery Sharp 1623
Richard Kennedy: Collected Stories - Richard Kennedy 1014
Rootabaga Stories - Carl Sandburg 1584
The Search for King Pup's Tomb - Jim Razzi 1495
Seven Spells to Farewell - Betty Baker 86
The Shadowmaker - Ron Hansen 814
Sheep in a Jeep - Nancy Shaw 1624
Sidney Rella and the Glass Sneaker - Bernice Myers 1301
Sir Toby Jingle's Beastly Journey - Wallace Tripp 1824
Small Fur - Irina Korschunov 1053
Snail Saves the Day - John Stadler 1723
The Swiss Family Robinson - Johann David Wyss 1961
Ten Apples Up on Top - Theo LeSieg 1094
This Is the House Where Jack Lives - Joan Heilbroner 847
Tillie and Mert - Ida Luttrell 1158
Tomorrow's Wizard - Patricia Maclachlan 1172
Transfigured Hart - Jane Yolen 1972
The Trouble with Dragons - Oliver G. Selfridge 1612
The Unicorn and the Lake - Marianna Mayer 1210

A Visit to William Blake's Inn - Nancy Willard 1916
Where Is Freddy? - Laura Jean Johnson 976
The Whipping Boy - Sid Fleischman 625
Why the Chicken Crossed the Road - David Macaulay 1162
The Wishing People - Nina Beachcroft 121
The Wizard's Tears - Maxine Kumin 1060
The Worst Witch - Jill Murphy 1299

Damar
The Blue Sword - Robin McKinley 1239

Dogtown
Sherlick Hound and the Valentine Mystery - Kelly Goldman 719

Foghorn Island
The Secret of Foghorn Island - Geoffrey Hayes 834

Giantland
The BFG - Roald Dahl 463

Gotham
The Wise Men of Gotham - Malcolm Carrick 299

Hookywalker
The Blood and Thunder Adventure on Hurricane Peak - Margaret Mahy 1179

Jedera
The Jedera Adventure - Lloyd Alexander 29

Kamalant
Sandwriter - Monica Hughes 934

Land of Sweets
The Nutcracker - E.T.A. Hoffman 896

Linderwall
Dealing with Dragons - Patricia C. Wrede 1953

Market Chipping
Howl's Moving Castle - Diana Wynne Jones 982

Mythologia
The Talking Parcel - Gerald Durrel 552

Narnia
The Lion, the Witch, and the Wardrobe - C.S. Lewis 1110

Never-Never-Land
Peter Pan - James Barrie 98

Orangutanville County
The Strange and Exciting Adventures of Jeremiah Hush - Uri Shulevitz 1632

Pineapple
Figgs and Phantoms - Ellen Raskin 1488

Prydain
The High King - Lloyd Alexander 28

Thyrne
The Ice Bear - Betty Levin 1097

Treegap
Tuck Everlasting - Natalie Babbitt 79

United Fed. of North America
C.L.U.T.Z. and the Fission Formula - Marilyn Wilkes 1912

Waterpushin
Glom Gloom - Jo Dereske 515

Wiss
How to Become King - Jan Terlouw 1793

Wonderland
Alice's Adventures in Wonderland - Lewis Carroll 305

Yupitz
Harry Newberry and the Raiders of the Red Drink - Mel Gilden 700

Nigeria (continued)

Gideon Bay
Underrunners - Margaret Mahy   1183

Viridian
Dangerous Spaces - Margaret Mahy   1180

NIGERIA

Omoteji's Baby Brother - Mary-Joan Gerson   688

NORTH AMERICA

Drift - William Mayne   1213
Snorri and the Strangers - Nathaniel Benchley   134

ALASKA
At the Mouth of the Luckiest River - Arnold A. Griese   765

NORWAY

Aurora and Socrates - Anne Vestly   1854
Don't Take Teddy - Babbis Friis-Baastad   648
The Night Birds - Tormod Haugen   829
Ronia, the Robber's Daughter - Astrid Lindgren   1125
Two Short and One Long - Nina Ring Aamundsen   1

OUTER SPACE

Earthseed: A Novel - Pamela Sargent   1586
Ellsworth and the Cats from Mars - Patience Brewster   196
The Magic School Bus, Lost in the Solar System - Joanna Cole   389
Miss Pickerell and the Blue Whales - Ellen MacGregor   1167
The Package in Hyperspace - Janet Asimov   63
The Planetoid of Amazement - Mel Glidden   710
Ready, Set, Robot - Lillian Hoban   890
Tales of a Wandering Warthog - Tom Sinclair   1650

PACIFIC OCEAN

The Voyage of the Frog - Gary Paulsen   1399

PAKISTAN

Cholistan Desert
Shabanu, Daughter of the Wind - Suzanne Fisher Staples   1726

PERU

Cuzco
The Secret of the Andes - Ann Nolan Clark   344

PLANET—IMAGINARY

But We Are Not of Earth - Jean Karl   995

Alpha I
My Trip to Alpha I - Alfred Slote   1674

Eden
Commander Toad and the Intergalactic Spy - Jane Yolen   1968

Green Sky
Below the Root - Zilpha Keatley Snyder   1695

Harmony
Sweetwater - Laurence Yep   1964

Merkina
The Package in Hyperspace - Janet Asimov   63

Pleiste
Planet out of the Past - James Lincoln Collier   393

Shine
The Green Book - Jill Paton Walsh   1393

Vanaris
The Donkey Planet - Scott Corbett   423

Ziax II
The Humans of Ziax II - John Morressy   1292

POLAND

Krakow
Trumpeter of Krakow - Eric P. Kelly   1009

Vilma
A Gift for Mama - Esther Hautzig   831

Vilna
The Endless Steppe: Growing Up in Siberia - Esther Hautzig   830

Warsaw
The Island on Bird Street - Uri Orlev   1364
The Man From the Other Side - Uri Orlev   1365

PUERTO RICO

Danza! - Lynn Hall   792

RUSSIA

Anna and the Seven Swans - Maida Silverman   1642
How the Moolah Was Taught a Lesson and Other Tales from Russia - Estelle Titiev   1813
The Place Where Nobody Stopped - Jerry Segal   1605
The Tale of the Golden Cockerel - Alexander Pushkin   1477

Czardom
The Ghost Drum: A Cat's Tale - Susan Price   1468

Kosnov
The Sign in Mendel's Window - Mildred Kantrowitz Phillips   1436

Odessa
The Silver Crest: My Russian Boyhood - Kornei Chukovsky   341

St. Petersburg
The Sound of Dragon's Feet - Alki Zei   1983
Young Mark - E.M. Almedingen   36

SCANDINAVIA

Viking's Dawn - Henry Treece   1822

SCOTLAND

At the Back of the North Wind - George MacDonald   1165
Elizabeth, Elizabeth - Eileen Dunlop   551
The Ghosts of Austwick Manor - Reby Edmond MacDonald   1166
An Island in a Green Sea - Mabel Esther Allan   33
Kate Crackernuts - Katharine Mary Briggs   199
Kidnapped - Robert Louis Stevenson   1748
The Mermaid Summer - Mollie Hunter   939
Mr. McFadden's Hallowe'en - Rumer Godden   714
Operation Peeg - Jonathan Gathorne-Hardy   677
The Selchie's Seed - Shulamith Oppenheim   1361
A Sound of Chariots - Mollie Hunter   940
A Stranger Came Ashore: A Story of Suspense - Mollie Hunter   941

Cames
Beyond Silence - Eleanor Cameron   282

Highlands
Brave Janet Reachfar - Jane Duncan   547

SOUTH AFRICA

The Lion of the Kalahari - Esther Linfield   1127

Bophelong
Chain of Fire - Beverly Naidoo   1309

Johannesburg
Go Well, Stay Well - Toeckey Jones   985

Soweto
Go Well, Stay Well - Toeckey Jones   985

SOUTH AMERICA

Tales from Silver Lands - Charles J. Finger   602
Where Angels Glide at Dawn - Lori M. Carlson   290

SPAIN

Adventure in Granada - Walter Dean Myers   1302
I, Juan de Pareja - Elizabeth Borton de Trevino   1823
Just a Dog - Helen Griffith   769

Arcangel
Shadow of a Bull - Maia Rodman   1535

SUBMARINE

Twenty Thousand Leagues Under the Sea - Jules Verne   1853

SWEDEN

Grandpa's Maria - Hans-Eric Hellberg   848
Trust in the Unexpected - Gunnel Linde   1122

Noda Diseberga
The Glassblower's Children - Maria Gripe   774

Stockholm
The Battle Horse - Harry Kullman   1059

Villa Villekulla
Pippi Longstocking - Astrid Lindgren   1124

SWITZERLAND

Mayenfield
Heidi - Johanna Spyri   1720

THAILAND

A Boat to Nowhere - Maureen Crane Wartski   1887

TURKEY

The Adventures of Little Mouk - Wilhelm Hauff   826
The Road From Home: The Story of an Armenian Girl - David Kherdian   1022

UGANDA

Mukasa - John Nagenda   1308

UKRAINE

Homecoming - Elsa Posell   1461
The Mitten: An Old Ukranian Folk Tale - Jan Brett   195

Don't Forget Michael - Jean Thompson 1808

Don't Hurt Laurie! - Willo Davis Roberts 1509

Doodlebug - Irene Brady 185

Dorrie and the Pin Witch - Patricia Coombs 414

Double or Nothing - Marc Talbert 1776

Down in the Boondocks - Wilson Gage 659

Dracula Is a Pain in the Neck - Elizabeth Levy 1107

Dumb Old Casey Is a Fat Tree - Barbara Bottner 180

Dump Days - Jerry Spinelli 1714

The Duplicate - William Sleator 1661

Dupper - Betty Baker 85

The Ears of Louis - Constance C. Greene 749

Eating Ice Cream with a Werewolf - Phyllis Green 743

Eddie, Incorporated - Phyllis Reynolds Naylor 1314

Eddie's Valuable Property - Carolyn Haywood 838

The Edge of Next Year - Mary Stolz 1754

Edith Herself - Ellen Howard 920

Einstein Anderson, Science Sleuth - Seymour Simon 1649

Encyclopedia Brown, Boy Detective - Donald J. Sobol 1703

Eunice (the Egg Salad) Gottlieb - Tricia Springstubb 1719

Even If I Did Something Awful - Barbara Shook Hazen 840

Everett Anderson's Friend - Lucille Clifton 365

Everywhere - Bruce Brooks 209

Family Pose - Dean Hughes 930

A Family Project - Sarah Ellis 569

Fantastic Voyage - Isaac Asimov 61

Fast Friends: Two Stories - James Stevenson 1746

Fat Fanny, Beanpole Bertha and the Boys - Barbara Ann Porte 1458

Fat Men from Space - Daniel Manus Pinkwater 1443

Feldman Fieldmouse - Nathaniel Benchley 131

Felicia the Critic - Ellen Conford 402

Fifty Saves His Friend - Martin Baynton 120

Finders Keepers - Emily Rodda 1529

Finding Buck McHenry - Alfred Slote 1669

Fiona's Bee - Beverly Keller 1006

The Fireball Mystery - Mary Adrain 14

First Snow - Helen Coutant 436

Five-Finger Discount - Barthe DeClements 497

The Five Little Peppers and How They Grew - Margaret Sidney 1639

Flight of the White Wolf - Mel Ellis 568

Flossie and the Fox - Pat McKissack 1244

Foal Creek - Peter Zachary Cohen 386

Follow My Leader - James B. Garfield 669

Follow That Ghost! - Dale Fife 600

Following the Mystery Man - Mary Downing Hahn 788

Footprints in the Refrigerator - Selma Boyd 183

Foster Child - Marion Dane Bauer 107

Four on the Shore - Edward Marshall 1196

Fourteen - Marilyn Sachs 1577

The Fourth Floor Twins and the Sand Castle Contest - David A. Adler 11

Fourth Grade Celebrity - Patricia Reilly Giff 693

Fourth Grade Wizards - Barthe DeClements 498

Fox on the Job - James Marshall 1198

Fran Ellen's House - Marilyn Sachs 1578

Frank and Ernest - Alexandra Day 489

Frankie Is Staying Back - Ron Roy 1557

Freddy the Detective - Walter R. Brooks 212

The Freewheeling of Joshua Cobb - Margaret Hodges 894

A Friend Like That - Alfred Slote 1670

The Friendly Wolf - Paul Goble 712

Friends - Terry Berger 141

Frog and Toad All Year - Arnold Lobel 1139

Fudge - Charlotte Towner Graeber 728

The Gathering Room - Colby Rodowsky 1537

General Butterfingers - John Reynolds Gardiner 667

George Shrinks - William Joyce 987

The Get-Away Car - Eleanor Clymer 369

Getting Rid of Krista - Amy Hest 871

Getting Rid of Marjorie - Betty Ren Wright 1955

The Ghost Belonged to Me - Richard Peck 1405

The Ghost-Eye Tree - Bill Martin, Jr. 1203

A Ghost in the Window - Betty Ren Wright 1956

Ghost Island - Carolyn Lane 1068

Ghost Story - Genevieve Gray 736

The Ghost Upstairs - Lila McGinnis 1226

Gildaen: The Heroic Adventures of a Most Unusual Rabbit - Emilie Buchwald 221

The Girl with the Silver Eyes - Willo Davis Roberts 1510

Give Us a Great Big Smile, Rosy Cole - Sheila Greenwald 757

The Giving Tree - Shel Silverstein 1644

The Glad Man - Gloria Gonzalez 721

Glass Slippers Give You Blisters - Mary Jane Auch 65

Glass Slippers Give You Blisters - Mary Jane Auch 66

The Glory Girl - Betsy Byars 263

Go Fish - Mary Stolz 1756

Golden Daffodils - Marilyn Gould 726

The Gollywhopper Egg - Anne Rockwell 1527

Gone-Away Lake - Elizabeth Enright 572

Good-Bye Pink Pig - Carole S. Adler 7

Good Hunting, Blue Sky - Peggy Parish 1375

The Good Luck Dog - Lilo Hess 870

Goodbye, My Wishing Star - Vicki Grove 777

The Goof That Won the Pennant - Jonah Kalb 991

Grand Papa and Ellen Aroon - F.N. Monjo 1275

Grandaddy's Place - Helen V. Griffith 773

The Grandma Mix-Up - Emily Arnold McCully 1222

Grandpa and Me - Stephanie S. Tolan 1816

Grandpa Ritz and the Lucious Lovelies - Marlene Fanta Shyer 1637

Grandpa's Ghost Stories - James Flora 628

Grandpa's Slide Show - Deborah Gould 725

The Graveyard: And Other Not-So-Scary Stories - William E. Warren 1886

The Great Gilly Hopkins - Katherine Paterson 1388

The Great Skinner Strike - Stephanie S. Tolan 1817

The Great White Man-Eating Shark - Margaret Mahy 1181

The Green Ghost of Appleville - Jean Marzollo 1206

The Green Lion of Zion Street - Julia Fields 598

Grey Cloud - Charlotte Towner Graeber 729

Gumshoe Goose, Private Eye - Mary DeBall Kwitz 1062

Gwenda and the Animals - Tessa Dahl 470

Hail, Hail, Camp Timberwood - Ellen Conford 403

The Half-a-Moon Inn - Paul Fleischman 615

Halfway Up the Mountain - Theo E. Gilchrist 699

The Halloween Candy Mystery - Marion M. Markham 1194

The Halloween Tree - Ray Bradbury 184

Hang Tough, Paul Mather - Alfred Slote 1671

Harold and the Purple Crayon - Crockett Johnson 975

Harriet the Spy - Louise Fitzhugh 608

Harry in Trouble - Barbara Ann Porte 1459

Hattie Be Quiet, Hattie Be Good - Dick Gackenbach 654

The Haunted House - Dorothy Haas 782

The Haunting - Margaret Mahy 1182

Hawk, I'm Your Brother - Byrd Baylor 119

The Hayburners - Gene Smith 1687

He Is Your Brother - Richard Parker 1383

The Headless Cupid - Zilpha Keatley Snyder 1698

Heads, I Win - Patricia Hermes 862

Hear the Wind Blow - Patricia Pendergraft 1417

Henry and Mudge and the Happy Cat - Cynthia Rylant 1567

Henry and the Red Stripes - Eileen Christelow 330

Henry's Special Delivery - M.C. Delaney 508

Her Seven Brothers - Paul Goble 713

Herbie's Troubles - Carol Chapman 317

A Hero Ain't Nothin' but a Sandwich - Alice Childress 326

Hershel and the Hanukkah Goblins - Eric A. Kimmel 1026

He's My Brother - Joe Lasker 1070

Hey, Remember Fat Glenda? - Lila Perl 1419

Hi, Clouds - Carol Greene 747

The Hideaway Summer - Beverly Hollett Renner 1500

The High Rise Glorious Skittle Skat Roarious Sky Pie Angel Food Cake - Nancy Willard 1914

The Hockey Girls - Scott Corbett 424

Home Alone - Eleanor Schick 1593

Home Before Dark - Sue Ellen Bridgers 198

Home Run Trick - Scott Corbett 425

Honestly, Myron - Dean Hughes 931

The Horrible Holidays - Audrey Wood 1947

Horse Crazy - Bonnie Bryant 220

The House in the Snow - M.J. Engh 571

House of Stairs - William Sleator 1662

The House on Hackman's Hill - Joan Lowery Nixon 1337

The House Without a Christmas Tree - Gail Rock 1523

How Do I Feel? - Norma Simon 1647

How to Eat Fried Worms - Thomas Rockwell 1528

Hurricane - David Wiesner 1906

Hurricane Elaine - Johanna Hurwitz 952

Hurry Home, Candy - Meindert DeJong 505

I Am Rubber, You are Glue - Jane Morton 1293

I Am the Universe - Barbara Corcoran 430

I Can't Always Hear You - Joy Zelonky 1985

I Hate Being Gifted - Patricia Hermes 863

I Hate My Sister Maggie - Crescent Dragonwagon 535

I Hate Red Rover - Joan M. Lexau 1116

I Have Two Families - Doris Wild Helmering 849

I, Houdini: The Autobiography of a Self-Educated Hamster - Lynne Reid Banks 1497

I Speak English for My Mom - Muriel Stanek 1725

I Wish Laura's Mommy Was My Mommy - Barbara Power 1463

The Iceberg and Its Shadow - Jan Greenberg 745

I'll Meet You at the Cucumbers - Lilian Moore 1281

Impy for Always - Jackie French Koller 1044

In Summertime, It's Tuffy - Judie Angell 49

In the Middle of the Puddle - Mike Thaler 1797

In Trouble Again, Zelda Hammersmith - Lynn Hall 793

Incident at Hawk's Hill - Allan W. Eckert 559

The Integration of Mary-Larkin Thornhill - Ann Waldron 1869

The Interesting Thing That Happened at Perfect Acres, Inc. - Barbara Brooks Wallace 1871

Interstellar Pig - William Sleator 1663

Isaac Campion - Janni Howker 926

Isabelle the Itch - Constance C. Greene 752

Island of the Loons - Dayton O. Hyde 962

Itchy Richard - Jamie Gilson 704

It's Not the End of the World - Judy Blume 155

Ivan the Great - Isabel Langis Cusack 460

Jacob and Owl - Ada Graham 731

Jane Martin, Dog Detective - Eve Bunting 232

Jason and the Baseball Bear - Dan Elish 563

Jazz Country - Nat Hentoff 857

Jeffrey's Ghost and the Fifth Grade Dragon - David A. Adler 12

Jelly Belly - Robert Kimmel Smith 1691

Jenny and the Tennis Nut - Janet Schulman 1599

Jenny Archer to the Rescue - Ellen Conford 404

Joel and the Great Merlini - Eloise Jarvis McGraw 1228

Josie's Beau - Natalie Honeycutt 910

Jumanji - Chris Van Allsburg 1840

Just a Dream - Chris Van Allsburg 1841

Just Between Us - Susan Beth Pfeffer 1431

Just Like a Real Family - Kristi Holl 898

Just Like Always - Elizabeth-Ann Sachs 1572

Just My Luck - Emily Moore 1280

Justice and Her Brothers - Virginia Hamilton 804

Sidewise Stories From Wayside School - Louis Sacher　1571

The Silver Pony - Lynd Ward　1884

The Singing Hill - Meindert DeJong　506

Sister - Eloise Greenfield　756

Sixth Grade Secrets - Louis Sachar　1569

The Skates of Uncle Richard - Carol Fenner　593

Sly, P.I.: The Case of the Missing Shoes - Cathy Stefanec-Ogren　1730

A Smart Kid Like You - Stella Pevsner　1426

The Snake Horn - Morton Grosser　776

Snakes Are Nothing to Sneeze At - Gabrielle Charbonnet　319

Sneakers: Seven Stories about a Cat - Margaret Wise Brown　218

Soccer Sam - Jean Marzollo　1207

The Solid Gold Kid - Norma Fox Mazer　1218

Some Friend - Carol Carrick　296

Some of the Adventures of Rhode Island Red - Stephen Manes　1189

Someday Angeline - Louis Sachar　1570

Something Big Has Been Here: Poems - Jack Prelutsky　1465

Something Queer at the Library: A Mystery - Elizabeth Levy　1109

Something Special for Me - Vera B. Williams　1925

Something Suspicious - Kathryn Osebold Galbraith　662

The Song of the Christmas Mouse - Shirley Rousseau Murphy　1300

Song of the Horse - Richard Kennedy　1015

Sonia Begonia - Joanne Rocklin　1526

Sophie and Gussie - Marjorie Weinman Sharmat　1622

Sorrow's Song - Larry Callen　278

Space Case - Edward Marshall　1197

Spinky Sulks - William Steig　1737

Sport - Louise Fitzhugh　610

Step on a Crack - Mary Anderson　46

Stinker From Space - Pamela F. Service　1614

The Stone-Faced Boy - Paula Fox　642

The Stones - Janet Hickman　875

The Stories Julian Tells - Ann Cameron　281

The Story of Jumping Mouse - John Steptoe　1740

The Strange Night Writing of Jessamine Colter - Cynthia DeFelice　501

The Stranger - Chris Van Allsburg　1844

Strider - Beverly Cleary　356

Striped Ice Cream - Joan M. Lexau　1117

Sugar Blue - Vera Cleaver　359

A Summer Like Turnips - LouAnn Gaeddert　655

The Summer of the Swans - Betsy Byars　267

Superduper Teddy - Johanna Hurwitz　957

Susan Cornish - Rebecca Caudill　311

The Sweet Touch - Lorna Balian　92

Sweet Whispers, Brother Rush - Virginia Hamilton　806

Tackle-22 - Louise Munro Foley　631

Taking Terri Mueller - Norma Fox Mazer　1219

Tales From Gold Mountain: Stories of the Chinese in the New World - Paul Yee　1963

Tales of a Gambling Grandmother - Dayal Kaur Khalsa　1020

Tallahassee Higgins - Mary Downing Hahn　790

The Tar Pit - Tor Seidler　1607

A Taste of Blackberries - Doris Buchanan Smith　1684

That Is That - Jeanne Whitehouse Peterson　1422

There Are Two Kinds of Terrible - Peggy Mann　1190

There's a Caterpillar in My Lemonade - Diana Gregory　763

They're All Named Wildfire - Nancy Springer　1718

This Farm is a Mess - Leslie McGuire　1232

This Island Isn't Big Enough for the Four of Us! - Gery Greer　762

This School is Driving Me Crazy - Nat Hentoff　858

Thistle - Walter Wangerin　1883

Time at the Top - Edward Ormondroyd　1367

A Time to Keep Silent - Gloria Whelan　1898

The Times They Used to Be - Lucille Clifton　367

The Toad Hunt - Janet Chenery　322

Toby Tyler: or Ten Weeks with a Circus - James Otis　1371

Too Many Murphys - Colleen O'Shaughnessy McKenna　1236

Touch the Moon - Marion Dane Bauer　110

The Trading Game - Alfred Slote　1675

Treehorn's Treasure - Florence Parry Heide　846

The Trial of Anna Cotman - Vivien Alcock　22

Trouble with Mothers - Margery Facklam　583

The Trouble with Soap - Margery Cuyler　462

Truckers - Terry Pratchett　1464

Truth or Consequences - Miriam Young　1979

Truth or Dare - Susan Beth Pfeffer　1433

Tundra - William F. Hallstead　797

The Turtle Street Trading Company - Jill Ross Klevin　1041

Two Piano Tuners - M.B. Goffstein　716

Two Ways about It - Judy Frank Mearian　1253

Unclaimed Treasures - Patricia MacLachlan　1173

Uncle Foster's Hat Tree - Doug Cushman　461

Uncle Lemon's Spring - Jane Yolen　1973

Uncle Mike's Boy - Jerome Brooks　211

Ups and Downs with Oink and Pearl - Kay Chorao　328

Us and Uncle Fraud - Lois Lowry　1156

Veronica Meets Her Match - Nancy K. Robinson　1520

The Very Worst Monster - Pat Hutchins　961

The View From the Cherry Tree - Willo Davis Roberts　1513

Wait Till Helen Comes - Mary Downing Hahn　791

Walk the World's Rim - Betty Baker　88

Walking Away - Elizabeth Winthrop　1933

The War with Grandpa - Robert Kimmel Smith　1692

The Watcher in the Garden - Joan Phipson　1439

The Wednesday Surprise - Eve Bunting　240

The Week Mom Unplugged the TVs - Terry Wolfe Phelan　1434

Welcome Home, Jellybean - Marlene Fanta Shyer　1638

Wendy and the Bullies - Nancy K. Robinson　1521

What Happened to Heather Hopkowitz? - Charlotte Herman　861

What Is Papa Up To Now? - Miriam Anne Bourne　181

When the Boys Ran the House - Joan Davenport Carris　303

When Will I Read? - Miriam Cohen　385

Where Does the Teacher Live? - Paula Kurzband Feder　591

Where the Lilies Bloom - Vera Cleaver　360

The White Bicycle - Rob Lewis　1113

Who Would Want to Kill Hallie Panky's Cat? - G. Majors　1186

The Wicked Pigeon Ladies in the Garden - Mary Chase　321

Wild Appaloosa - Glen Rounds　1555

The Wish Giver: Three Tales of Coven Tree - Bill Brittain　206

Witch, Goblin and Sometimes Ghost: Six Read Alone Stories - Sue Alexander　32

Witch in Room 6 - Edith Battles　106

The Witches of Worm - Zilpha Keatley Snyder　1701

With You and Without You - Ann M. Martin　1201

The Wolf - Michael W. Fox　635

Woodruff and the Clocks - Elizabeth Bram　186

Worthington Botts and the Steam Machine - Betty Baker　89

Wrongway Applebaum - Marjorie Lewis　1112

Yonder - Tony Johnston　977

You Can Depend on Me - Margaret Reuter　1503

You Shouldn't Have to Say Goodbye - Patricia Hermes　866

Your Old Pal, Al - Constance C. Greene　753

Yours Till Niagara Falls, Abby - Jane O'Connor　1351

Yours Truly, Shirley - Ann M. Martin　1202

Z for Zachariah - Robert C. O'Brien　1348

The Zebra Wall - Kevin Henkes　852

Zeely - Virginia Hamilton　807

Appleton
The Worldwide Dessert Contest - Dan Elish　564

Bosyork
The Robot and Rebecca: The Mystery of the Code Carrying Kids - Jane Yolen　1970

Bramton
Who Knew There'd Be Ghosts? - Bill Brittain　205

Bridgeton
The Horse in the Attic - Eleanor Clymer　370

Camden Woods
Just the Beginning - Betty Miles　1262

Chester Falls
The Swing - Emily Hanlon　811

Chesterville
Me and the Weirdos - Jane Sutton　1772

Clinton
Too Much Magic - Betsy Sterman　1743

Clover Lake
A Witch's Garden - Miriam Young　1980

Dakota Territory
Grasshopper Summer - Ann Warren Turner　1832

DeSmet
Little Town on the Prairie - Laura Ingalls Wilder　1910

East Bridge
Miss Know-It-All and the Three Ring Circus - Carol Beach York　1975

Gatesburg
Me Two - Mary C. Ryan　1562

Gypsy Wild
Poopsie Pomerantz, Pick up Your Feet - Patricia Reilly Giff　696

High Flats
Left-Handed Shortstop - Patricia Reilly Giff　695

Hoosac
The Treasure of Alpheus Winterborn - John Bellairs　128

Humboldt
Welcome to Grossville - Alice Mulcahey Fleming　626

Kellam's Landing
Carver - Ruth Yaffe Radin　1481

Kennituck Falls
The Monster's Ring - Bruce Coville　438

La Grande
Charlie Drives the Stage - Eric A. Kimmel　1025

McDonaldsville
Lizard Music - Daniel Manus Pinkwater　1445

Metropolis VII
My Robot Buddy - Alfred Slote　1673

Midston
Danny Dunn and the Universal Glue - Jay Williams　1919

Monroe
The Leipzig Vampire - Mary Anderson　45

Moose Lake
The Day of the Muskie - Patricia Welch　1891

Oakdale
Dreams of Victory - Ellen Conford　401

Someone Is Hiding on Alcatraz Island - Eve Bunting 238
Things Won't Be the Same - Kathryn Ewing 582
Twenty-One Balloons - William Pene Du Bois 540

San Nicolas Island
Island of the Blue Dolphins - Scott O'Dell 1353

Sierra Nevada Mountains
Snowshoe Thompson - Nancy Smiler Levinson 1101

Terra Vista
Octopus Pie - Susan Terris 1795

Venice
With a Wave of the Wand - Mark Jonathan Harris 817

Westlyn
Always Abigail - Joyce St. Peter 1722

COLORADO

Avalanche! - Ron Roy 1556

Boulder
Dolby and the Woof-Off - Barbara A. Steiner 1739

Denver
The Moved Outers - Florence Crannel Means 1252

Hastings
Before the Wildflowers Bloom - Tatyana Bylinsky 270

Leadville
High Trail to Danger - Joan Lowery Nixon 1336

CONNECTICUT

Homecoming - Cynthia Voigt 1864
Just as Long as We're Together - Judy Blume 156
Rabbit Hill - Robert Lawson 1084
Tucker's Countryside - George Selden 1611

Butterfield
Seven-Day Magic - Edward Eager 556

Greenport
ESP McGee - Edward Packard 1372

New Milford
Courage of Sarah Noble - Alice Dalgliesh 473

West Hazardsville
The Ten-Speed Babysitter - Alison Cragin Herzig 869

Wethersfield
The Witch of Blackbird Pond - Elizabeth George Speare 1710

Whitmarsh Point
A Sudden Change of Family - Mary Jane Auch 67

DISTRICT OF COLUMBIA

Washington
The People in Pineapple Place - Anne Lindbergh 1120
The Wall - Eve Bunting 239
The Witch Family - Eleanor Estes 579

FLORIDA

Foxy - Helen V. Griffith 771
Go and Catch a Flying Fish - Mary Stolz 1755
Hazel Rye - Vera Cleaver 358
Portrait of Ivan - Paula Fox 640
Strawberry Girl - Lois Lenski 1091
The Talking Earth - Jean Craighead George 685

Dadesville
Angie's First Case - Donald J. Sobol 1702

Echo Bay
Fishman and Charly - Davis Gibbs 691

Grahamsville
The Yearling - Marjorie Kinnan Rawlings 1491

Land's End
Land's End - Mary Stolz 1757

Palmelo
A Gift of Magic - Lois Duncan 548

GEORGIA

Georgia Music - Helen V. Griffith 772
Ida Early Comes over the Mountain - Robert Burch 242
Ludie's Song - Dirlie Herlihy 859
Queenie Peavy - Robert Burch 244
Skinny - Robert Burch 245
Sounder - William Armstrong 57
Wilkin's Ghost - Robert Burch 246

Atlanta
Mystery of the Gingerbread House - Wylly Folk St. John 1721
Salted Lemons - Doris Buchanan Smith 1683

Harmony
The Day That Elvis Came to Town - Jan Marino 1193

Rambleton
Tough Chauncey - Doris Buchanan Smith 1685

Ripley
Doodle and the Go-Cart - Robert Burch 241

Waycross
Ludell - Brenda Scott Wilkinson 1913

GREAT LAKES

Paddle-to-the-Sea - Holling Clancy Holling 904

IDAHO

Buck, Wild - Glenn Balch 91
Jenny of the Tetons - Kristiana Gregory 764

White Cloud Mountains
Caught in the Moving Mountains - Gloria Skurzynski 1658

ILLINOIS

Across Five Aprils - Irene Hunt 937
Buddies - Barbara Park 1377
Do Bananas Chew Gum? - Jamie Gilson 702
Sister - Ellen Howard 922

Chicago
High Trail to Danger - Joan Lowery Nixon 1336
It Always Happens to Leona - Juanita Havill 832
Lafcadio, the Lion Who Shot Back - Shel Silverstein 1645
The Mysterious Cases of Mr. Pin - Mary Elise Monsell 1277
Somewhere in the Darkness - Walter Dean Myers 1304
Terror Train! - Gilbert B. Cross 448

Claiborne
The Dollhouse Murders - Betty Ren Wright 1954

Decatur
Judge Benjamin, Superdog - Judith Whitelock McInerney 1235

Evanston
New Friends - Dorothy Haas 783

New Salem
Lincoln: A Photobiography - Russell Freedman 644

Pineville
The Josie Gambit - Mary Francis Shura 1635

Stockton
Thirteen Ways to Sink a Sub - Jamie Gilson 705

Trout Lake
Thatcher Payne-in-the-Neck - Betty Bates 105

Woodvale
Babysitter on Horseback - Fern G. Brown 213

INDIANA

End of a Dark Road - Crystal Thrasher 1809
My Friend, My Brother - David Warren Swartley 1773
Red Sky at Morning - Andrea Wyman 1960
Witch Weed - Phyllis Reynolds Naylor 1319

Cowden's Creek
Witch's Sister - Phyllis Reynolds Naylor 1320

Gary
Raymond - Mark Geller 681

Indianapolis
Help! I'm a Prisoner in the Library - Eth Clifford 361

IOWA

Maudie in the Middle - Phyllis Reynolds Naylor 1315

KANSAS

After the Dancing Days - Margaret I. Rostkowski 1550
Amelia's Flying Machine - Barbara Shook Hazen 839
A Family Apart - Joan Lowery Nixon 1333
Jayhawker - Patricia Beatty 124
The Journey Home - Isabelle Holland 900
Moxie - Phyllis Rossiter 1549
Old Blue - Sibyl Hancock 810
Rifles for Watie - Harold Keith 1004
Sarah, Plain and Tall - Patricia MacLachlan 1170

Nicodemus
Wagon Wheels - Barbara Brenner 193

KENTUCKY

Borrowed Children - George Ella Lyon 1159
The Flying Fingers Club - Jean F. Andrews 47

Lexington
The Twenty-Four-Hour Lipstick Mystery - Bonnie Pryor 1476

LOUISIANA

The Empty Schoolhouse - Natalie Savage Carlson 291

Four Corners
Pinch - Larry Callen 277

New Orleans
The Mockingbird Song - Berthe Amoss 41
Secret Lives - Berthe Amoss 42
The Slave Dancer - Paula Fox 641

MAINE

Brother Moose - Betty Levin 1096
Calico Bush - Rachel Field 596
Child of the Morning - Barbara Corcoran 428
Fudge-a-Mania - Judy Blume 154

United States—New Hampshire (continued)

Little Women, or Meg, Jo, Beth and Amy - Louisa M. Alcott 23

Coven Tree
Dr. Dredd's Wagon of Wonders - Bill Brittain 204

Cranberry
Rufus M. - Eleanor Estes 578

Northridge
The One and Only Cynthia Jane Thornton - Claudia Mills 1269

NEW HAMPSHIRE

A Gathering of Days: A New England Girl's Journal, 1830-1832 - Joan W. Blos 150
The Lake Is on Fire - Maureen Crane Wartski 1888
Miss Hickory - Carolyn Sherwin Bailey 83
Mystery on Ice - Barbara Corcoran 431
The Summer I Was Lost - Phillip Viereck 1855
Wildcat Summer - Mary Riskind 1508

Freedom
The Enormous Egg - Oliver Butterworth 254

Jaffrey
Amos Fortune, Free Man - Elizabeth Yates 1962

Wingate
Missing - James Duffy 545

NEW JERSEY

Are You There, God? It's Me, Margaret - Judy Blume 152
Benny - Barbara Cohen 380
The Cat Ate My Gymsuit - Paula Danziger 477
Keeping it Secret - Penny Pollock 1455
Mail-Order Kid - Joyce McDonald 1224
My Trip to Alpha I - Alfred Slote 1674
Ride the Green Dragon - Andre Norton 1342
Ten Kids, No Pets - Ann M. Martin 1200
When the Rattlesnake Sounds: A Play - Alice Childress 327

Atlantic City
Fiddlestrings - Marguerite De Angeli 491

Elmwood
Hotel for Dogs - Lois Duncan 549

Grover's Corners
Henry Reed's Baby-Sitting Service - Keith Robertson 1514

Hoboken
The Hoboken Chicken Emergency - Daniel Manus Pinkwater 1444

Long Beach Island
The Orphan Game - Barbara Cohen 383

Longtree
Call Me Amanda - Dale Bick Carlson 289

Princeton
Superfudge - Judy Blume 158

Serenity
Onion John - Joseph Krumgold 1058

Woodside
The Cold and Hot Winter - Johanna Hurwitz 951
Tough-Luck Karen - Johanna Hurwitz 958

NEW MEXICO

Summer of Fear - Lois Duncan 550

Los Alamos
Tiger Eyes - Judy Blume 159

Taos
.and Now Miguel - Joseph Krumgold 1057

NEW YORK

And One for All - Theresa Nelson 1321
Bella Arabella - Liza Fosburgh 634
Benjy the Football Hero - Jean Van Leeuwen 1845
The Black Stallion - Walter Farley 587
Cutlass in the Snow - Elizabeth Shub 1630
A Girl Called Al - Constance C. Greene 750
Hey, What's Wrong with This One? - Maia Wojciechowska 1939
The Lightning Time - Gregory Maguire 1178
Mariah Delany's Author-of-the-Month Club - Sheila Greenwald 759
The Matchlock Gun - Walter D. Edmonds 560
Me and the Terrible Two - Ellen Conford 407
My Daniel - Pam Conrad 409
Nothing Stays the Same Forever - Gail Radley 1483
One-Eyed Cat - Paula Fox 639
The Saturdays - Elizabeth Enright 573
Signpost to Terror - Gretchen Sprague 1716
Silent Dancer - Bruce Hlibok 886
Six Impossible Things Before Breakfast - Norma Farber 584
Snow Bound - Harry Mazer 1216
The Telltale Summer of Tina C. - Lila Perl 1420
There's a Bat in Bunk Five - Paula Danziger 481
Today's Special: Z.A.P and Zoe - Athena V. Lord 1147
Who's in Charge of Lincoln? - Dale Fife 601

Adirondacks
Katy Did It - Victoria Boutis 182

Albany
The Spaceship Returns to the Apple Tree - Louis Slobodkin 1668

Applesap
The Dancing Cats of Applesap - Janet Taylor Lisle 1129

Birch Valley
Soccer Halfback - Matt Christopher 340

Catskills
My Side of the Mountain - Jean Craighead George 683

Cranbury
Ginger Pye - Eleanor Estes 576

Elyria
Tramp Steamer and the Silver Bullet - Jeffrey Kelly 1010

Fair Park
The Real Me - Betty Miles 1263

Flatbush
The Carp in the Bathtub - Barbara Cohen 381

Flushing
Baseball Fever - Johanna Hurwitz 948

Hampton
Sinbad and Me - Kin Platt 1452

Highland Crossing
Mystery of the Haunted Pool - Phyllis A. Whitney 1903

Kaatskill Mountains
Rip Van Winkle - Washington Irving 965

Katonah
Murder at the Spaniel Show - Lynn Hall 794

Lakeview
The Witching of Ben Wagner - Mary Jane Auch 68

Laurel Mountain
Secret of the Stone Face - Phyllis A. Whitney 1905

Long Island
Up From Jerico Tel - E.L. Konigsburg 1048

New Albany
The Thing in Kat's Attic - Charlotte Towner Graeber 730

New York
The 17th Street Gang - Emily Cheney Neville 1326
Alan and Naomi - Myron Levoy 1104
Alan and the Animal Kingdom - Isabelle Holland 899
Alfred Summer - Jan Slepian 1665
Alice and the Boa Constrictor - Laurie Adams 3
All-of-a-Kind Family - Sydney Taylor 1787
All Sail Set: A Romance of the Flying Cloud - Armstrong Sperry 1711
Anything for a Friend - Ellen Conford 400
Arthur Mitchell - Tobi Tobias 1815
A Billion for Boris - Mary Rodgers 1531
The Bronze King - Suzy McKee Charnas 320
Busybody Nora - Johanna Hurwitz 949
Captains of the City Street: A Story of a Cat Club - Esther Averill 69
The Cat in the Mirror - Mary Stolz 1752
Cat-Man's Daughter - Barbara Mattes Abercrombie 2
Cave under the City - Harry Mazer 1214
The Cricket in Times Square - George Selden 1608
The Dangling Witness - Jay Bennett 136
Dinnie Abbie Sister-R-RI - Riki Levinson 1102
The Divorce Express - Paula Danziger 478
Do-it-Yourself Magic - Ruth Chew 325
The Dog Days of Arthur Cane - T. Ernesto Bethancourt 144
Emma's Dilemma - Gen LeRoy 1093
Felita - Nicolasa Mohr 1274
Freaky Friday - Mary Rodgers 1533
From the Mixed-Up Files of Mrs. Basil E. Frankweiler - E.L. Konigsburg 1045
The Genie of Sutton Place - George Selden 1609
The Gift-Giver - Joyce Hansen 812
The Great Christmas Kidnapping Caper - Jean Van Leeuwen 1847
H, My Name Is Henley - Colby Rodowsky 1538
The Hand-Me-Down Kid - Francine Pascal 1384
Hangin' Out with Cici - Francine Pascal 1385
Happily Ever After.Almost - Judie Wolkoff 1945
Harry Cat's Pet Puppy - George Selden 1610
Hattie and the Wild Waves - Barbara Cooney 415
Have You Seen Hyacinth Macaw? - Patricia Reilly Giff 694
Highpockets - John R. Tunis 1826
The Horse in the Attic - Eleanor Clymer 370
How Many Miles to Babylon? - Paula Fox 636
How Pizza Came to Queens - Dayal Kaur Khalsa 1019
I and Sproggy - Constance C. Greene 751
I Should Worry, I Should Care - Miriam Chaikin 315
Immigrant Girl: Becky of Eldridge Street - Harvey Brett 194
In the Year of the Boar and Jackie Robinson - Bette Bao Lord 1148
It Ain't Always Easy - Kathleen Karr 996
It All Began with Jane Eyre, or the Secret Life of Franny Dillman - Sheila Greenwald 758
J.T. - Jane Wagner 1868
Jennifer, Hecate, Macbeth, William McKinley and Me, Elizabeth - E.L. Konigsburg 1046
Joseph on the Subway Train - Kathleen Benson 138
The Journey Home - Isabelle Holland 900
The Kid Comes Back - John R. Tunis 1827
The Kid from Tomkinsville - John R. Tunis 1828
The Kidnapping of Courtney Van Allen and What's-Her-Name - Joyce Cool 412
The Last Mission - Harry Mazer 1215
The Law of Gravity - Johanna Hurwitz 953
Leo, Zack and Emmie - Amy Ehrlich 561
Lily and Miss Liberty - Carla Stevens 1744
The Lion in the Box - Marguerite De Angeli 492
The Lost Umbrella of Kim Chu - Eleanor Estes 577
Love You, Soldier - Amy Hest 872

The Case of the Cackling Car: A Sam and Dave Mystery Story - Marilyn Singer 1654
Old Blue - Sibyl Hancock 810
Old Yeller - Fred Gipson 707
Quarterback Walk-On - Thomas J. Dygard 555
The White Stallion - Elizabeth Shub 1631

Calder
The Twenty-Five Cent Miracle - Theresa Nelson 1322

El Paso
Come the Morning - Mark Jonathan Harris 816

Houston
The Kidnapping of Christina Lattimore - Joan Lowery Nixon 1338

Marfa
The Winged Colt of Casa Mia - Betsy Byars 268

Mason County
Curly and the Wild Boar - Fred Gipson 706

Riverbank
The Blue Empress - Kathy Pelta 1415

Smilax
Journey to an 800 Number - E.L. Konigsburg 1047

UTAH

Nutty and the Case of the Ski-Slope Spy - Dean Hughes 932

Adenville
The Great Brain Reforms - John D. Fitzgerald 607

Grandview
Theo Zephyr - Dean Hughes 933

Monument Valley
Morning Arrow - Nanabah Chee Dodge 528

Topaz
Journey to Topaz - Yoshiko Uchida 1837

VERMONT

A Day No Pigs Would Die - Robert Newton Peck 1408
Marathon Miranda - Elizabeth Winthrop 1932
Soup - Robert Newton Peck 1409
Sugaring Time - Kathryn Lasky 1074
Understood Betsy - Dorothy Canfield Fisher 605

Burlington
Puppy Love - Jeanne Betancourt 143

Doe's Crossing
Pip and Emma - Katharine Bacon 80

Kenton
The Kenton Year - Ruth Wallace-Brodeur 1879

Miles Hill
The Canada Geese Quilt - Natalie Kinsey-Warnock 1035

North Chittendon
The Dragons of North Chittendon - Susan Fromberg Schaeffer 1591

VIRGINIA

Bridge to Terabithia - Katherine Paterson 1386
Eben Tyne: Powdermonkey - Patricia Beatty 123
The Falling-Apart Winter - Nancy Covert Smith 1689
Jacob Have I Loved - Katherine Paterson 1389
My Sister the Meanie - Candice Ransom 1484
Shades of Gray - Carolyn Reeder 1496
Spring Rider - John Shults Lawson 1082
Tac's Island - Ruth Yaffe Radin 1482

Arlington
Rinehart Lifts - R. Rozanne Knudson 1043

Charlottesville
Lucy Forever and Miss Rosetree, Shrinks - Susan Richards Shreve 1629

Chincoteague Island
Misty of Chincoteague - Marguerite Henry 855

Richmond
Runaway Balloon: The Last Flight of Confederate Air Force One - Burke Davis 486

WASHINGTON

Nightmare Mountain - Peg Kehret 1003

Cascade
Lake Fear - Ian McMahan 1247

Everett
No Place for Me - Barthe DeClements 499

Seattle
Her Own Song - Ellen Howard 921
The Magic Book - Willo Davis Roberts 1511
Rusty Fertlanger, Lady's Man - Christi Killien 1024

Tacoma
Mishmash - Molly Cone 399

Yakima
Foster Mary - Celia Strang 1761

WEST

Humbug Mountain - Sid Fleischman 622

Lone Tree County
The Day the Circus Came to Lone Tree - Glen Rounds 1554

WEST VIRGINIA

A Blue-Eyed Daisy - Cynthia Rylant 1563
Come Sing, Jimmy Jo - Katherine Paterson 1387
Shadows - Dennis Haseley 823

Deep Water
Missing May - Cynthia Rylant 1568

Friendly
Shiloh - Phyllis Reynolds Naylor 1318

Twillys' Green
The Watchers - Jane Louise Curry 458

WISCONSIN

Caddie Woodlawn - Carol Ryrie Brink 201
Whirling Rainbows - Susan Terris 1796

Willow Wind Farm: Betsy's Story - Anne Pellowski 1414

Esau's Valley
Thimble Summer - Elizabeth Enright 574

LaSalle
The Mystery of the Diamond in the Wood - David Kherdian 1021

Madison
Roots in the Outfield - Jane Zirpoli 1988
The Scorpio Ghosts and the Black Hole Gang - Kathy Kennedy Tapp 1778

Oshkosh
Weird Henry Berg - Sarah Sargent 1588

Peshtigo
My Sister's Keeper - Beverly Butler 253

Westingtown
The Westing Game - Ellen Raskin 1490

WYOMING

Berchick - Esther Silverstein Blanc 148
Bunkhouse Journal - Diane Johnston Hamm 809
Red Dog - Bill Wallace 1877

Jackson
Stone Fox - John Reynolds Gardiner 668

VIETNAM

A Boat to Nowhere - Maureen Crane Wartski 1887

VIRGIN ISLANDS OF THE UNITED STATES

St. Thomas
Up Mountain One Time - Willie Wilson 1926

WALES

A Child's Christmas in Wales - Dylan Thomas 1803
The Dark Is Rising - Susan Cooper 417
The Gift - Peter Dickinson 522
The Grey King - Susan Cooper 419
The Silver Cow: A Welsh Tale - Susan Cooper 422
The Snow Spider - Jenny Nimmo 1331
Star Lord - Louise Lawrence 1081
A String in the Harp - Nancy Bond 169
Through the Dolls' House Door - Jane Gardam 666
Weird Henry Berg - Sarah Sargent 1588

Aber
The Owl Service - Alan Garner 673

Druid's Bottom
Carrie's War - Nina Bawden 111

Radnorshire
No Way of Telling - Emma Smith 1686

YUGOSLAVIA

Plov
Finzel the Farsighted - Paul Fleischman 613

Subject Index

This index lists subjects which are covered in the featured titles. These can include such things as family life, animals, personal and social problems, historical events, ethnic groups, and story types, e.g. Mystery and Detective Stories. Beneath each subject heading, titles are arranged alphabetically with author names and entry numbers also indicated.

The Strange and Exciting Adventures of Jeremiah Hush - Uri Shulevitz　1632
Summer of the Monkeys - Wilson Rawls　1492

Animals/Moose
The Secret Moose - Jean Rogers　1541

Animals/Pigs
Ace, the Very Important Pig - Dick King-Smith　1029
Arthur, for the Very First Time - Patricia MacLachlan　1169
Babe: The Gallant Pig - Dick King-Smith　1030
Freddy the Detective - Walter R. Brooks　212
More Tales of Amanda the Pig - Jean Van Leeuwen　1848
The Peppermint Pig - Nina Bawden　115
Pig Pig and the Magic Photo Album - David M. McPhail　1250
The Pigs Are Flying! - Emily Rodda　1530
Pigs Might Fly: A Novel - Dick King-Smith　1033
Pinch - Larry Callen　277
Quentin Corn - Mary Stolz　1759
Ruthann and Her Pig - Barbara Ann Porte　1460
Sid Seal, Houseman - Will Watkins　1889
Sly, P.I.: The Case of the Missing Shoes - Cathy Stefanec-Ogren　1730
Ups and Downs with Oink and Pearl - Kay Chorao　328

Animals/Rabbits
ABC Bunny - Wanda Gag　656
The Bionic Bunny Show - Marc T. Brown　217
Bunnicula: A Rabbit Tale of Mystery - Deborah Howe　923
Gildaen: The Heroic Adventures of a Most Unusual Rabbit - Emilie Buchwald　221
Hare's Choice - Dennis Hamley　808
Hattie Be Quiet, Hattie Be Good - Dick Gackenbach　654
Henry and the Red Stripes - Eileen Christelow　330
Marshmallow - Clare Turlay Newberry　1327
Molly Moves Out - Susan Pearson　1403
Rabbit Hill - Robert Lawson　1084
Rabbit Spring - Tilde Michels　1261
Shadrach - Meindert De Jong　495
The Solitary - Lynn Hall　795
The Velveteen Rabbit - Margery Williams　1923
Watership Down - Richard Adams　4

Animals/Rats
Fifty Saves His Friend - Martin Baynton　120
Mrs. Frisby and the Rats of NIMH - Robert C. O'Brien　1347
A Rat's Tale - Tor Seidler　1606

Animals/Reptiles
Alice and the Boa Constrictor - Laurie Adams　3
Snakes Are Nothing to Sneeze At - Gabrielle Charbonnet　319
The Unicorn and the Lake - Marianna Mayer　1210

Animals/Seals and Sea Lions
Marra's World - Elizabeth Coatsworth　375
The Sea Egg - L.M. Boston　178
Seal Child - Sylvia Peck　1410
The Secret of the Seal - Deborah Davis　487
Sid Seal, Houseman - Will Watkins　1889

Animals/Sharks
Alfred Hitchcock and the Three Investigators in the Secret of Shark Reef - William Arden　53
The Great White Man-Eating Shark - Margaret Mahy　1181

Animals/Sheep
Adventures of Obadiah - Brinton Turkle　1829
.and Now Miguel - Joseph Krumgold　1057
BAAA - David Macaulay　1161
Brave Janet Reachfar - Jane Duncan　547
Deathwatch - Robb White　1902
Ida and the Wool Smugglers - Sue Ann Alderson　24

Only One Woof - James Herriot　867
The Reluctant Dragon - Kenneth Grahame　732
Sheep in a Jeep - Nancy Shaw　1624

Animals/Squid, Octopus
I Was All Thumbs - Bernard Waber　1866

Animals/Squirrels
Henry - Nina Bawden　113
Sophie and Gussie - Marjorie Weinman Sharmat　1622
Squirrel in My Teacup! - Eileen Cade-Edwards　271

Animals/Tigers
Belling the Tiger - Mary Stolz　1751
Polly's Tiger - Joan Phipson　1438

Animals/Turtles
Fast Friends: Two Stories - James Stevenson　1746
In the Middle of the Puddle - Mike Thaler　1797
Minn of the Mississipppi - Holling Clancy Holling　903
Old Turtle's Soccer Team - Leonard Kessler　1018

Animals/Whales
The Hostage - Theodore Taylor　1789
Kilroy and the Gull - Nathaniel Benchley　133
Miss Pickerell and the Blue Whales - Ellen MacGregor　1167

Animals/Wild Cats
Wildcat Summer - Mary Riskind　1508

Animals/Wolves
The Box of Delights - John Masefield　1208
Brushy Mountain - Patricia Pendergraft　1416
By the Shores of Silver Lake - Laura Ingalls Wilder　1909
Flight of the White Wolf - Mel Ellis　568
Julie of the Wolves - Jean Craighead George　682
Kavik the Wolf Dog - Walt Morey　1286
Sasha, My Friend - Barbara Corcoran　432
Wolf - Gillian Cross　450
The Wolf - Michael W. Fox　635
The Wolf's Chicken Stew - Keiko Kasza　998
The Wolves of Willoughby Chase - Joan Aiken　18

Animals/Worms
How to Eat Fried Worms - Thomas Rockwell　1528

Antinuclear Movement
Captives in a Foreign Land - Susan Lowry Rardin　1487

Anti-Semitism
The Man From the Other Side - Uri Orlev　1365

Anthropology
Java Jack - Luqman Keele　1002

Apartheid
Chain of Fire - Beverly Naidoo　1309
Go Well, Stay Well - Toeckey Jones　985

Apartments
Busybody Nora - Johanna Hurwitz　949
This Is the House Where Jack Lives - Joan Heilbroner　847

Apprentices
Young Fu of the Upper Yangtze - Elizabeth Lewis　1111

Archeology
Sebastian (Super Sleuth) and the Bone to Pick Mystery - Mary Blount Christian　333
The Turquoise Toad Mystery - Georgess McHargue　1233

Arson
The Case of the Weird Street Firebug - Carol Russell Law　1077

Arthurian Legend
The Book of Brendan - Ann Curry　456
The Dragon's Boy - Jane Yolen　1969
Knights of the Kitchen Table - Jon Scieszka　1601

Winter of Magic's Return - Pamela F. Service　1616

Artists and Art
Carver - Ruth Yaffe Radin　1481
The Chalk Box Kid - Clyde Robert Bulla　224
Daniel's Duck - Clyde Robert Bulla　225
Dobry - Monica Shannon　1619
Dupper - Betty Baker　85
From the Mixed-Up Files of Mrs. Basil E. Frankweiler - E.L. Konigsburg　1045
Glass Slippers Give You Blisters - Mary Jane Auch　66
Good Night, Mr. Tom - Michelle Magorian　1177
The Griffin and the Minor Canon - Frank R. Stockton　1750
Harold and the Purple Crayon - Crockett Johnson　975
Hattie and the Wild Waves - Barbara Cooney　415
The Horse in the Attic - Eleanor Clymer　370
I, Juan de Pareja - Elizabeth Borton de Trevino　1823
In Summer Light - Zibby Oneal　1360
Jemmy - Jon Francis Hassler　824
Maria's House - Jean Merrill　1258
Nate the Great - Marjorie Weinman Sharmat　1620
Nicky and the Joyous Noise - Mildred Ames　39
On the Frontier with Mr. Audubon - Barbara Brenner　192
Randall's Wall - Carol Fenner　592
A Rat's Tale - Tor Seidler　1606
Rusty Fertlanger, Lady's Man - Christi Killien　1024

Asian Americans
Children of the River - Linda Crew　447

Asthma
Marathon Miranda - Elizabeth Winthrop　1932
Thin Air - David Getz　689

Astronomy
The Magic School Bus, Lost in the Solar System - Joanna Cole　389

Atlantis
King Tut's Game Board - Leona Ellerby　567

Aunts and Uncles
The Alligator and His Uncle Tooth: A Novel of the Sea - Geoffrey Hayes　833
The Big Green Book - Robert Graves　734
Bogwoppit - Ursula Moray Williams　1924
Christmas Memory - Truman Capote　288
Double or Nothing - Marc Talbert　1776
A Few Fair Days - Jane Gardam　665
Losing Uncle Tim - Marykate Jordan　986
Missing May - Cynthia Rylant　1568
No Place for Me - Barthe DeClements　499
Seven Kisses in a Row - Patricia Maclachlan　1171
Sugar Blue - Vera Cleaver　359
Tallahassee Higgins - Mary Downing Hahn　790
The Type One Super Robot - Alison Prince　1472
Uncle Elephant - Arnold Lobel　1142
Us and Uncle Fraud - Lois Lowry　1156
The Village by the Sea - Paula Fox　643
The Voyage of the Frog - Gary Paulsen　1399
The Winged Colt of Casa Mia - Betsy Byars　268

Authorship
Anastasia Krupnik - Lois Lowry　1150
Dear Mr. Henshaw - Beverly Cleary　350
Harriet the Spy - Louise Fitzhugh　608
Julia and the Hand of God - Eleanor Cameron　284
Libby on Wednesday - Zilpha Keatley Snyder　1700
Mariah Delany's Author-of-the-Month Club - Sheila Greenwald　759
A Room Made of Windows - Eleanor Cameron　285
The Silver Crest: My Russian Boyhood - Kornei Chukovsky　341
A Sound of Chariots - Mollie Hunter　940
Strider - Beverly Cleary　356

You Can Depend on Me - Margaret Reuter   1503
Young Nick and Jubilee - Leon Garfield   672
Yours Truly, Shirley - Ann M. Martin   1202
The Zebra Wall - Kevin Henkes   852

Buddhism
The Boy and the Samurai - Erik Christian Haugaard   827

Bullfighting
Shadow of a Bull - Maia Rodman   1535

Bullies
The 18th Emergency - Betsy Byars   255
A Bundle of Sticks - Pat Rhoads Mauser   1209
A Dog on Barkham Street - Mary Stolz   1753
Five-Finger Discount - Barthe DeClements   497
Herbie's Troubles - Carol Chapman   317
The Magic Book - Willo Davis Roberts   1511
Mark Makes His Move - Marian Potter   1462
Mean and Mighty Me - Sally Christie   334
The Red Balloon - Albert Lamorisse   1063
So You Want to Be a Wizard - Diane Duane   541
Stepping on the Cracks - Mary Downing Hahn   789
A Tangled Web - Hannelore Valencak   1839
Wendy and the Bullies - Nancy K. Robinson   1521
Wild Man of the Woods - Joan Clark   345

Burglary
The Big Smith Snatch - Jane Louise Curry   457
Do-it-Yourself Magic - Ruth Chew   325
Gopher, Tanker, and the Admiral - Shirley Climo   368

Business Enterprises
The Big Kite Contest - Dorotha Ruthstrom   1561
No Coins, Please - Gordon Korman   1051

Camps and Camping
Buddies - Barbara Park   1377
Dracula Is a Pain in the Neck - Elizabeth Levy   1107
Foal Creek - Peter Zachary Cohen   386
The Freewheeling of Joshua Cobb - Margaret Hodges   894
Ghost Island - Carolyn Lane   1068
The Grizzly - Annabel Johnson   974
Hail, Hail, Camp Timberwood - Ellen Conford   403
In Summertime, It's Tuffy - Judie Angell   49
Jem's Island - Kathryn Lasky   1072
Katy Did It - Victoria Boutis   182
There's a Bat in Bunk Five - Paula Danziger   481
This Island Isn't Big Enough for the Four of Us! - Gery Greer   762
Whirling Rainbows - Susan Terris   1796
A Wonderful, Terrible Time - Mary Stolz   1760
Yours Till Niagara Falls, Abby - Jane O'Connor   1351

Canals
The Huffler - Jill Paton Walsh   1394
Tom Tiddler's Ground - John Rowe Townsend   1820

Cancer
Hang Tough, Paul Mather - Alfred Slote   1671
Mama's Going to Buy You a Mockingbird - Jean Little   1135
Sadako and the Thousand Paper Cranes - Eleanor Coerr   378
So Long, Grandpa - Elfie Donnelly   529
Two Ways about It - Judy Frank Mearian   1253
You Shouldn't Have to Say Goodbye - Patricia Hermes   866

Canoeing
Mean and Mighty Me - Sally Christie   334

Castles
Babar and the Ghost: An Easy to Read Version - Laurent De Brunhoff   219
The Castle in the Attic - Elizabeth Winthrop   1931

Meg Mackintosh and the Mystery at the Medieval Castle - Lucinda Landon   1066
Sir Toby Jingle's Beastly Journey - Wallace Tripp   1824

Cathedrals
A Murder for Her Majesty - Beth Hilgartner   881

Cave Dwellers
Ig Lives in a Cave - Carol Chapman   318
Spirit on the Wall - Ann O'Neal Garcia   664

Celts
Tristan and Iseult - Rosemary Sutcliff   1770

Cemeteries
Beloved Benjamin Is Waiting - Jean Karl   994
The Gathering Room - Colby Rodowsky   1537

Censorship
Trouble with Mothers - Margery Facklam   583

Cerebral Palsy
Golden Daffodils - Marilyn Gould   726
It's Your Turn at Bat - Barbara Aiello   16

Child Abuse
Almost a Hero - Clyde Robert Bulla   223
Among the Dolls - William Sleator   1660
Ask Me No Questions - Ann Schlee   1594
Building Blocks - Cynthia Voigt   1860
The Cat Ate My Gymsuit - Paula Danziger   477
Daphne's Book - Mary Downing Hahn   785
Don't Hurt Laurie! - Willo Davis Roberts   1509
End of a Dark Road - Crystal Thrasher   1809
An End to Perfect - Suzanne Newton   1330
Foster Child - Marion Dane Bauer   107
Foster Mary - Celia Strang   1761
Good Night, Mr. Tom - Michelle Magorian   1177
Lucy Forever and Miss Rosetree, Shrinks - Susan Richards Shreve   1629
Moondial - Helen Cresswell   445
My Friend, My Brother - David Warren Swartley   1773
The Night Birds - Tormod Haugen   829
Now Is Not Too Late - Isabelle Holland   901
The Owlstone Crown - X.J. Kennedy   1016
Raymond - Mark Geller   681
Squib - Nina Bawden   117
Step on a Crack - Mary Anderson   46
Stepping on the Cracks - Mary Downing Hahn   789
A Time to Keep Silent - Gloria Whelan   1898

Child Custody
Sport - Louise Fitzhugh   610

Children and War
The Machine Gunners - Robert Westall   1895

Chinese Americans
Chang's Paper Pony - Eleanor Coerr   377
Child of the Owl - Lawrence Yep   1965
Dragonwings - Lawrence Yep   1966
Her Own Song - Ellen Howard   921
In the Year of the Boar and Jackie Robinson - Bette Bao Lord   1148
The Lost Umbrella of Kim Chu - Eleanor Estes   577
Tales From Gold Mountain: Stories of the Chinese in the New World - Paul Yee   1963

Christian Life
The Bronze Bow - Elizabeth George Speare   1708

Christmas
The Bells of Christmas - Virginia Hamilton   800
The Best Christmas Pageant Ever - Barbara Robinson   1517
A Certain Small Shepherd - Rebecca Caudill   310
Children of Christmas - Cynthia Rylant   1564
A Child's Christmas in Wales - Dylan Thomas   1803
Christmas Memory - Truman Capote   288
December's Travels - Mischa Damjan   474

The Great Christmas Kidnapping Caper - Jean Van Leeuwen   1847
The Horrible Holidays - Audrey Wood   1947
The House Without a Christmas Tree - Gail Rock   1523
The Lion in the Box - Marguerite De Angeli   492
The Mouse and His Child - Russell Hoban   892
A Northern Nativity: Christmas Dreams of a Prairie Boy - William Kurelek   1061
Plain Lane Christmas - Cyril Walter Hodges   893
The Polar Express - Chris Van Allsburg   1843
Say Cheese - Betty Bates   104
School Can Wait - Tessa Dahl   471
The Silver Touch and Other Family Christmas Stories - Margret Rettich   1501
The Song of the Christmas Mouse - Shirley Rousseau Murphy   1300
We Three Kings - Janet McNeill   1249

Circus
The Day the Circus Came to Lone Tree - Glen Rounds   1554
Little Man - Erich Kastner   997
Miss Know-It-All and the Three Ring Circus - Carol Beach York   1975
Morris and Boris at the Circus - Bernard Wiseman   1935
Put Me in the Zoo - Robert Lopshire   1146
Toby Tyler: or Ten Weeks with a Circus - James Otis   1371
Travelers by Night - Vivien Alcock   21

City Life
The 18th Emergency - Betsy Byars   255
Best Town in the World - Byrd Baylor   118
Busybody Nora - Johanna Hurwitz   949
The Case of the Elevator Duck - Polly Berrien Berends   139
A Girl Called Al - Constance C. Greene   750
Have You Seen Hyacinth Macaw? - Patricia Reilly Giff   694
J.T. - Jane Wagner   1868
Miracle at Clement's Pond - Patricia Pendergraft   1418
Plain Lane Christmas - Cyril Walter Hodges   893
Rebecca of Sunnybrook Farm - Kate Douglas Wiggin   1907
Saturdays in the City - Ann Sharpless Bond   166
The Sign in Mendel's Window - Mildred Kantrowitz Phillips   1436
Superduper Teddy - Johanna Hurwitz   957
Tails of the Bronx: A Tale of the Bronx - Jill Pinkwater   1447
The Young Landlords - Walter Dean Myers   1305

Civil Rights
The Times They Used to Be - Lucille Clifton   367

Civil Rights Movement
Don't Ride the Bus on Monday: The Rosa Parks Story - Louise Meriwether   1257

Civil War
Across Five Aprils - Irene Hunt   937
Betrayed - Virginia Driving Hawk Sneve   1693
Captain of the Planters: The Biography of Robert Smalls - Dorothy Sterling   1741
Eben Tyne: Powdermonkey - Patricia Beatty   123
Little Women, or Meg, Jo, Beth and Amy - Louisa M. Alcott   23
Rifles for Watie - Harold Keith   1004
Runaway Balloon: The Last Flight of Confederate Air Force One - Burke Davis   486
Shades of Gray - Carolyn Reeder   1496
Spring Rider - John Shults Lawson   1082
Which Way Freedom? - Joyce Hansen   813

Cleanliness
A Clean House for Mole and Mouse - Harriet Ziefert   1986
This Farm is a Mess - Leslie McGuire   1232

Dew Drop Dead: A Sebastian Barth Mystery - James Howe 925

The Dog Food Caper - Joan M. Lexau 1115

The Doggone Mystery - Mary Blount Christian 331

Dogsbody - Diana Wynne Jones 981

Einstein Anderson, Science Sleuth - Seymour Simon 1649

Encyclopedia Brown, Boy Detective - Donald J. Sobol 1703

ESP McGee - Edward Packard 1372

Figgs and Phantoms - Ellen Raskin 1488

Follow That Bus! - Pat Hutchins 960

Follow That Ghost! - Dale Fife 600

Footprints in the Refrigerator - Selma Boyd 183

The Fourth Floor Twins and the Sand Castle Contest - David A. Adler 11

Freddy the Detective - Walter R. Brooks 212

Funnyman and the Penny Dodo - Stephen Mooser 1282

The Ghost Children - Eve Bunting 231

The Ghost Wore Gray - Bruce Coville 437

The Ghosts of Austwick Manor - Reby Edmond MacDonald 1166

Goody Hall - Natalie Babbitt 76

Graven Images - Paul Fleischman 614

Gumshoe Goose, Private Eye - Mary DeBall Kwitz 1062

Have You Seen Hyacinth Macaw? - Patricia Reilly Giff 694

High Trail to Danger - Joan Lowery Nixon 1336

The House of Dies Drear - Virginia Hamilton 802

I Am Susannah - Libby Gleeson 709

Interstellar Pig - William Sleator 1663

Intruder - John Rowe Townsend 1819

Jane Martin, Dog Detective - Eve Bunting 232

Janie's Private Eyes - Zilpha Keatley Snyder 1699

Jim Ugly - Sid Fleischman 623

Kept in the Dark - Nina Bawden 114

Knee-Knock Rise - Natalie Babbitt 77

Lake Fear - Ian McMahan 1247

The Long Black Coat - Jay Bennett 137

The Man in the Woods - Rosemary Wells 1893

Maximilian, You're the Greatest - Joseph Rosenbloom 1547

Meg Mackintosh and the Mystery at the Medieval Castle - Lucinda Landon 1066

Megan's Island - Willo Davis Roberts 1512

Miss Pickerell and the War of the Computers - Dora Pantell 1373

Miss Plunkett to the Rescue - Jane Flory 630

The Money Room - Eloise Jarvis McGraw 1229

Murder at the Spaniel Show - Lynn Hall 794

A Murder for Her Majesty - Beth Hilgartner 881

My Trip to Alpha I - Alfred Slote 1674

The Mysteries of Harris Burdick - Chris Van Allsburg 1842

The Mysterious Cases of Mr. Pin - Mary Elise Monsell 1277

The Mysterious Disappearance of Leon (I Mean Noel) - Ellen Raskin 1489

Mystery at Crane's Landing - Marcella Thum 1810

The Mystery at Peacock Place - M.F. Craig 439

Mystery Madness - Otto Coontz 416

Mystery of the Bewitched Bookmobile - Florence Parry Heide 845

The Mystery of the Diamond in the Wood - David Kherdian 1021

Mystery of the Fat Cat - Frank Bonham 172

Mystery of the Gingerbread House - Wylly Folk St. John 1721

Mystery of the Hard Luck Rodeo - Susan Saunders 1589

The Mystery of the Haunted Cabin - Judy Delton 513

Mystery of the Haunted Pool - Phyllis A. Whitney 1903

Mystery of the Hidden Hand - Phyllis A. Whitney 1904

Mystery of the Maya Jade - Elizabeth Honness 911

Mystery of the Metro - Elizabeth Howard 918

Mystery on Ice - Barbara Corcoran 431

Nate the Great - Marjorie Weinman Sharmat 1620

Night Fall - Joan Aiken 17

Nightmare Mountain - Peg Kehret 1003

No Flying in the House - Betty Brock 207

No Way of Telling - Emma Smith 1686

Nutty and the Case of the Ski-Slope Spy - Dean Hughes 932

On the Edge - Gillian Cross 449

The Over-the-Hill Ghost - Ruth Calif 276

P.J. Clover, Private Eye: The Case of the Missing Mouse - Susan Meyers 1260

Phantom of Walkaway Hill - Edward Fenton 594

Philo Potts, or, The Helping Hand Strikes Again - Mildred Ames 40

Pitch and Hasty Check It Out - Eric Deleon 509

Quacky and the Crazy Curve Ball - Walter G. Oleksy 1358

The Remarkable Return of Winston Potter Crisply - Eve Rice 1505

Ride the Green Dragon - Andre Norton 1342

The Robot and Rebecca: The Mystery of the Code Carrying Kids - Jane Yolen 1970

The Rocking Horse Secret - Rumer Godden 715

The Sandman's Eyes - Patricia Windsor 1928

The Search for Jim McGwynn - Marcia Wood 1950

The Search for King Pup's Tomb - Jim Razzi 1495

Sebastian (Super Sleuth) and the Bone to Pick Mystery - Mary Blount Christian 333

Secret Lives - Berthe Amoss 42

The Secret of Foghorn Island - Geoffrey Hayes 834

The Secret of Gumbo Grove - Eleanora E. Tate 1780

Secret of the Stone Face - Phyllis A. Whitney 1905

Sherlick Hound and the Valentine Mystery - Kelly Goldman 719

Shirlick Holmes and the Case of the Wandering Wardrobe - Jane Yolen 1971

Sinbad and Me - Kin Platt 1452

The Sinister Airfield - Alison Prince 1471

Sly, P.I.: The Case of the Missing Shoes - Cathy Stefanec-Ogren 1730

Something Suspicious - Kathryn Osebold Galbraith 662

Terror Train! - Gilbert B. Cross 448

Tom Tiddler's Ground - John Rowe Townsend 1820

Tramp Steamer and the Silver Bullet - Jeffrey Kelly 1010

Trapped in Death Cave - Bill Wallace 1878

Trouble in Bugland: A Collection of Inspector Mantis Mysteries - William Kotzwinkle 1055

Tuppenny - Julia Cunningham 455

The Turquoise Toad Mystery - Georgess McHargue 1233

The Twenty-Four-Hour Lipstick Mystery - Bonnie Pryor 1476

Underrunners - Margaret Mahy 1183

Up From Jerico Tel - E.L. Konigsburg 1048

The View From the Cherry Tree - Willo Davis Roberts 1513

The Watcher in the Garden - Joan Phipson 1439

The Way to Sattin Shore - Philippa Pearce 1402

The Westing Game - Ellen Raskin 1490

Where Is Freddy? - Laura Jean Johnson 976

Who Knew There'd Be Ghosts? - Bill Brittain 205

Who Really Killed Cock Robin? - Jean Craighead George 686

Who Would Want to Kill Hallie Panky's Cat? - G. Majors 1186

Mutism

Blind Outlaw - Glen Rounds 1553

The Half-a-Moon Inn - Paul Fleischman 615

King of the Wind - Marguerite Henry 854

Sorrow's Song - Larry Callen 278

A Time to Keep Silent - Gloria Whelan 1898

Nature

Bambi - Felix Salten 1582

Georgia Music - Helen V. Griffith 772

My Side of the Mountain - Jean Craighead George 683

Mythology

The First Morning: An African Myth - Margery Bernstein 142

The Golden Fleece and the Heroes Who Lived Before Achilles - Padraic Colum 397

The Hounds of the Morrigan - Pat O'Shea 1370

In the Beginning: Creation Stories from Around the World - Virginia Hamilton 803

The Oracle Doll - Catherine Dexter 518

The Silver Pony - Lynd Ward 1884

Neighbors and Neighborhoods

Addie Meets Max - Joan Robins 1516

Busybody Nora - Johanna Hurwitz 949

Chester - Mary Francis Shura 1634

Leo and Emily - Franz Brandenberg 187

Me and the Terrible Two - Ellen Conford 407

Tails of the Bronx: A Tale of the Bronx - Jill Pinkwater 1447

Newspapers

The Best Bet Gazette - Linda Gondosch 720

Isabelle the Itch - Constance C. Greene 752

Nuclear Warfare

Hiroshima No Pika - Toshi Maruki 1205

Sadako and the Thousand Paper Cranes - Eleanor Coerr 378

Nursing Homes

Borrowed Summer - Marion Walker Doren 531

Peppermints in the Parlor - Barbara Brooks Wallace 1873

Occult

Conjure Tales - Charles Chestnutt 323

The Headless Cupid - Zilpha Keatley Snyder 1698

Mojo and the Russians - Walter Dean Myers 1303

The Moonpath and Other Tales of the Bizarre - Robert E. Swindells 1774

The Satanic Mill - Otfried Preussler 1466

Old Age

Aunt Morbelia and the Screaming Skulls - Joan Davenport Carris 300

The Big Smith Snatch - Jane Louise Curry 457

Borrowed Summer - Marion Walker Doren 531

General Butterfingers - John Reynolds Gardiner 667

Gopher, Tanker, and the Admiral - Shirley Climo 368

Grandpa and Me - Stephanie S. Tolan 1816

Grandpa Ritz and the Lucious Lovelies - Marlene Fanta Shyer 1637

Just Like a Real Family - Kristi Holl 898

A Little Fear - Patricia Wrightson 1958

The Mockingbird Song - Berthe Amoss 41

Nothing Stays the Same Forever - Gail Radley 1483

Old John - Peter Hartling 821

Oma - Peter Hartling 822

Sea Swan - Kathryn Lasky 1073

Speaking of Snapdragons - Sheila Hayes 836

Opera

Aida - Leontyne Price 1467

Orchestra

Jellybean - Tessa Duder 542

Orphans

Alan and the Animal Kingdom - Isabelle Holland 899

Almost a Hero - Clyde Robert Bulla 223

Alone in Wolf Hollow - Dana Brookins 208

Ask Me No Questions - Ann Schlee 1594

Behind the Attic Wall - Sylvia Cassedy 307

Bogwoppit - Ursula Moray Williams 1924

Boy Without a Name - Penelope Lively 1136

Brother Moose - Betty Levin 1096

Subject Index

Character Name Index

This index alphabetically lists the major characters in each featured title. Each character name is followed by a description of the character. Citations also provide titles of the books featuring the character—listed alphabetically if there is more than one title—author names, and entry numbers.

A

Aaron (Handicapped)
The Half-a-Moon Inn - Paul Fleischman 615

Aarons, Jess (Preteen)
Bridge to Terabithia - Katherine Paterson 1386

Abbie (Child)
Dinnie Abbie Sister-R-R! - Riki Levinson 1102
Seven-Day Magic - Edward Eager 556

Abbott, Martha (Teenager)
Changeling - Zilpha Keatley Snyder 1696

Abbott, Thomas (Lawyer)
Changeling - Zilpha Keatley Snyder 1696

Abby (Preteen)
Dark Horse - Jean Slaughter Doty 534

Abby (Child; Orphan)
The Ghost Children - Eve Bunting 231

Abby (Preteen)
Me and Mr. Stenner - Evan Hunter 938

Abby (Child; Camper)
Yours Till Niagara Falls, Abby - Jane O'Connor 1351

Abdullah (Merchant)
Castle in the Air - Diana Wynne Jones 979

Abdullah "Dooley" (Spirit)
The Genie of Sutton Place - George Selden 1609

Abuelita (Grandparent)
Felita - Nicolasa Mohr 1274

Ace (Pig)
Ace, the Very Important Pig - Dick King-Smith 1029

Ackerman, Cybil (Preteen)
The Cybil War - Betsy Byars 262

Ada (Child)
Knee-Knock Rise - Natalie Babbitt 77

Adam (Child)
Adam of the Road - Elizabeth Gray 735
Chocolate-Covered Ants - Stephen Manes 1188

Adam (Preteen)
I and Sproggy - Constance C. Greene 751
Red Dog - Bill Wallace 1877

Adam (Scientist)
A Ring of Endless Light - Madeleine +L'Engle 1090

Adams, Arilla (Preteen; 7th Grader)
Arilla Sun Down - Virginia Hamilton 799

Adams, Cassie (Preteen)
The Twenty-Four-Hour Lipstick Mystery - Bonnie Pryor 1476

Adams, Maximilian Augustus (Detective)
Maximilian, You're the Greatest - Joseph Rosenbloom 1547

Adams, Mike (Preteen)
Follow My Leader - James B. Garfield 669

Adams, Sun (Parent)
Arilla Sun Down - Virginia Hamilton 799

Addie (Child)
Addie Meets Max - Joan Robins 1516
The House Without a Christmas Tree - Gail Rock 1523

Aerin (Royalty)
The Hero and the Crown - Robin McKinley 1241

Agnew, Addie (Preteen)
Secret Lives - Berthe Amoss 42

Agnew, Dan (Child)
We Three Kings - Janet McNeill 1249

Ah Mee (Child)
Shen of the Sea - Arthur Bowie Chrisman 329

Ahlenslagen, Heide Patricia (Child)
After Fifth Grade, the World - Claudia Mills 1266

Ahmed (Relative)
The Night the Water Came - Clive King 1028

Aida (Royalty)
Aida - Leontyne Price 1467

Ailsa (Child)
A Pack of Lies - Geraldine McCaughrean 1220

Airedale, Archibald (Dog)
Sherlick Hound and the Valentine Mystery - Kelly Goldman 719

Akela (Leader)
The Curse of the Egyptian Mummy - Pat Hutchins 959

Akhenaton (Royalty; Historical Figure)
I, Tut: The Boy Who Became Pharoah - Miriam Schlein 1595

Al (Grandparent; Widow(er))
Grandpa Ritz and the Lucious Lovelies - Marlene Fanta Shyer 1637

Al (Businessman)
Shoeshine Girl - Clyde Robert Bulla 228

Alan (Orphan)
Alan and the Animal Kingdom - Isabelle Holland 899

Alan (Preteen; Twin)
Alanna: The First Adventure - Tamora Pierce 1440

Alan (Friend)
How to Eat Fried Worms - Thomas Rockwell 1528

Alanna (Preteen; Twin)
Alanna: The First Adventure - Tamora Pierce 1440

Alba (Child)
Where Does the Teacher Live? - Paula Kurzband Feder 591

Alberoy, Priscilla Jane "PJ" (Preteen)
The Turtle Street Trading Company - Jill Ross Klevin 1041

Albert (Artisan)
The Glassblower's Children - Maria Gripe 774

Albert "Geist" (Teenager)
What Happened in Hamelin? - Gloria Skurzynski 1659

Alberta (Teenager)
Sister - Eloise Greenfield 756

Alcott, Louisa May (Historical Figure; Writer)
Invincible Louisa - Cornelia Meigs 1254

Alden, John (Settler)
The Tall Man From Boston - Marion Lena Starkey 1727

Aldo (Preteen)
Aldo Peanut Butter - Johanna Hurwitz 947

Aldo (Child)
Aldo Peanut Butter - Johanna Hurwitz 946

ALEC (Artificial Intelligence)
Lake Fear - Ian McMahan 1247

Alec (Preteen; Sports Figure)
The Luck of the Miss L. - Lee Kingman 1034

Aleson, Catherine (Preteen)
I Met a Traveller - Lillian Hoban 889

Alex (Dog)
Alex and the Cat - Helen V. Griffith 770

Alex (Horse Trainer)
The Crumb - Jean Slaughter Doty 533

Alex (Preteen)
The Hermit of Fog Hollow Station - David Roth 1551
The Island on Bird Street - Uri Orlev 1364

Alex (Child)
Like Jake and Me - Mavis Jukes 988

Alexander (Child)
Alexander, Who Used to Be Rich Last Sunday - Judith Viorst 1856

Alexander (Preteen)
The Ghost Belonged to Me - Richard Peck 1405

Alexander (Ruler)
Valentine and Orson - Nancy Ekholm Burkert 247

Alexandra "Al" (Teenager)
A Girl Called Al - Constance C. Greene 750

Alexandra "Al" (Preteen)
Your Old Pal, Al - Constance C. Greene 753

Alf (Child)
The Horrible Holidays - Audrey Wood 1947

Alf (Donkey)
How the Witch Got Alf - Cora Annett 52

Alfie (Preteen)
The Cartoonist - Betsy Byars 260

Alfred (Handicapped; Child)
Alfred Summer - Jan Slepian 1665

Alice (7th Grader)
Alice in Rapture, Sort Of - Phyllis Reynolds Naylor 1311

Alice (Child)
Alice's Adventures in Wonderland - Lewis Carroll 305
Oma and Bobo - Amy Schwartz 1600

Alice (Pig)
Quick Chick - Julia Hoban 887

Alice (Guardian)
Underdog - Marilyn Sachs 1580

Alicia (Royalty)
Perilous Gard - Elizabeth Marie Pope 1456

Alison (Teenager)
The Owl Service - Alan Garner 673

Alistant, Nathan (Teenager)
King Tut's Game Board - Leona Ellerby 567

Allan, Edgar (Child; Adoptee)
Edgar Allan - John Neufeld 1325

Allen, Austine (Child)
Ellen Tebbits - Beverly Cleary 351

Allen, Lauren (Teenager)
Can You Sue Your Parents for Malpractice? - Paula Danziger 476

Allen, Linda (Entertainer)
Can You Sue Your Parents for Malpractice? - Paula Danziger 476

Almond, Raymond (Filmmaker)
The Case of the Horrible Swamp Monster - Drew Stevenson 1745

Alonzo (Foster Parent)
Foster Mary - Celia Strang 1761

Alspeth, David (Sailor)
The Voyage of the Frog - Gary Paulsen 1399

Alspeth, Owen (Relative)
The Voyage of the Frog - Gary Paulsen 1399

Alston, Billy (Preteen)
The War with Grandpa - Robert Kimmel Smith 1692

Altman (Sea Captain)
Mystery of 22 East - Leon Ware 1885

Alvin (Child)
Banjo - Robert Newton Peck 1407

Amanda (Child)
Good-Bye Pink Pig - Carole S. Adler 7

Amanda (Child; Occultist)
The Headless Cupid - Zilpha Keatley Snyder 1698

Amanda (Pig)
More Tales of Amanda the Pig - Jean Van Leeuwen 1848

Amanda (Royalty)
The Trouble with Dragons - Oliver G. Selfridge 1612

Amanda Jane (Babysitter)
The Monster in the 3rd Dresser Drawer and Other Stories about Adam Joshua - Janice Lee Smith 1688

Amanda "Mandy" (Preteen)
Borrowed Children - George Ella Lyon 1159

Amaroq (Wolf)
Julie of the Wolves - Jean Craighead George 682

Amber (Neighbor)
Foxy - Helen V. Griffith 771

Amber, Otis (Worker)
The Westing Game - Ellen Raskin 1490

Amir (Preteen)
The Gift-Giver - Joyce Hansen 812

Amonasro (Parent; Ruler)
Aida - Leontyne Price 1467

Amos (Mouse)
Ben and Me - Robert Lawson 1083

Amy (Child)
Amy's Goose - Efner Tudor Holmes 909
It's Not the End of the World - Judy Blume 155

Amy (Relative)
Java Jack - Luqman Keele 1002

Amy (Friend)
Once, Said Darlene - William Sleator 1664

Amy (Child)
The Witch Family - Eleanor Estes 579

Anabeth (Preteen; 6th Grader)
The Iceberg and Its Shadow - Jan Greenberg 745

Ancil (Preteen)
Last Was Lloyd - Doris Buchanan Smith 1681

Anderson, Adam "Einstein" (Preteen; Detective)
Einstein Anderson, Science Sleuth - Seymour Simon 1649

Anderson, Anna (Child)
The Mermaid Summer - Mollie Hunter 939

Anderson, April (Time Traveller)
The People in Pineapple Place - Anne Lindbergh 1120

Anderson, Dennis (Child)
Einstein Anderson, Science Sleuth - Seymour Simon 1649

Anderson, Eric (Grandparent)
The Mermaid Summer - Mollie Hunter 939

Anderson, Everett (Child)
Everett Anderson's Friend - Lucille Clifton 365

Anderson, Grandpa (Grandparent)
Summer of the Stallion - June Andrea Hanson 815

Anderson, Janey (Preteen)
Summer of the Stallion - June Andrea Hanson 815

Anderson, Jon (Child)
The Mermaid Summer - Mollie Hunter 939

Anderson, Mark (Preteen)
Gentle Ben - Walt Morey 1285

Anderson, Retta (Child)
Night Swimmers - Betsy Byars 265

Anderson, Roy (Child)
Night Swimmers - Betsy Byars 265

Anderson, Shorty (Singer)
Night Swimmers - Betsy Byars 265

Anderson, Susan (Teenager)
The Root Cellar - Janet Louise Lunn 1157

Andrea (Teenager)
And You Give Me a Pain, Elaine - Stella Pevsner 1424

Andrea (Friend)
Homesick: My Own Story - Jean Fritz 652

Andreas, Christos (Captive)
The Rich Kid - Bill Gillham 701

Andrew (Child)
The 24-Hour Genie - Lila McGinnis 1225

Andrew (Veteran)
After the Dancing Days - Margaret I. Rostkowski 1550

Andrew (Orphan; Apprentice)
Andrew and the Alchemist - Barbara Ninde Byfield 269

Andrew (Child)
Nobody Listens to Andrew - Elizabeth Guilfoile 778

Andrew (Preteen)
Space Demons - Gillian Rubinstein 1558

Andrews, Annabel (Teenager)
A Billion for Boris - Mary Rodgers 1531
Freaky Friday - Mary Rodgers 1533

Andrews, Ben "Ape Face" (Child)
A Billion for Boris - Mary Rodgers 1531

Andrews, Benjamin "Ape Face" (Child)
Freaky Friday - Mary Rodgers 1533

Andrews, Bob (Detective)
Alfred Hitchcock and the Three Investigators in the Secret of Shark Reef - William Arden 53

Andrews, Diane (Preteen)
The Ivy Garland - John Hoyland 927

Andrews, Ellen Jean (Parent)
Freaky Friday - Mary Rodgers 1533

Andrews, Jamie (Child)
The Ivy Garland - John Hoyland 927

Andrews, Tim (Child)
The Fireball Mystery - Mary Adrain 14

Andrews, Vicki (Child)
The Fireball Mystery - Mary Adrain 14

Andy (Preteen)
The Deserter - Nigel Gray 738

Andy (Child)
Home Alone - Eleanor Schick 1593

Andy (6th Grader)
King Kong and Other Poets - Robert Burch 243

Andy (Teenager)
When the Tripods Came - John Christopher 335

Angel (Child)
Angel's Mother's Wedding - Judy Delton 510

Angela (Handicapped)
Rish n' Roses - Jan Slepian 1666

Angie (Teenager)
The Hostage - Theodore Taylor 1789

Angie (Cousin; Indian)
The Whipman Is Watching - Thomas A. Dyer 554

Angotti, Tony (Preteen)
The Cybil War - Betsy Byars 262

Anita (Child)
The Secret Moose - Jean Rogers 1541

Ann, Martin E. "Marty" (Alien; Scientist)
The Spaceship Returns to the Apple Tree - Louis Slobodkin 1668

B

Baba Yaga (Witch)
Anna and the Seven Swans - Maida Silverman 1642

Babar (Elephant)
Babar and the Ghost: An Easy to Read Version - Laurent De Brunhoff 219

Babbidge, Lucie (Orphan)
Lucie Babbidge's House - Sylvia Cassedy 308

Babe (Pig)
Babe: The Gallant Pig - Dick King-Smith 1030

Baby (Mouse)
The Pea Patch Jig - Thacher Hurd 942

Baby Sister (Indian)
Waterless Mountain - Laura Adams Armer 56

Bacon, Pam (Teenager)
Mystery of the Maya Jade - Elizabeth Honness 911

Badger, Bartholomew (Pig)
Dominic - William Steig 1733

Bagdad
Bagdad Ate It - Phyllis Green 742

Bagg, Stuart (Cockroach)
Shoebag - Mary James 968

Baggins, Bilbo (Mythical Creature)
The Hobbit - J.R.R. Tolkien 1818

Bagthorpe, Daisy (Cousin)
Ordinary Jack - Helen Cresswell 446

Bagthorpe, Jack (Preteen)
Ordinary Jack - Helen Cresswell 446

Bagthorpe, Parker (Relative)
Ordinary Jack - Helen Cresswell 446

Bailey (Preteen)
Last One Home - Mary Pope Osborne 1368

Bailey, Farmer (Farmer)
The Stranger - Chris Van Allsburg 1844

Bailey, Jenny (Child)
Welcome to Grossville - Alice Mulcahey Fleming 626

Bailey, Jon (Preteen; Handicapped)
Carver - Ruth Yaffe Radin 1481

Bailey, Michael (Preteen)
Welcome to Grossville - Alice Mulcahey Fleming 626

Bain, John (Child)
Stargone John - Ellen Kindt McKenzie 1237

Bain, Liza (Child)
Stargone John - Ellen Kindt McKenzie 1237

Baird, Joanna "Jo" (Preteen)
Secret of the Stone Face - Phyllis A. Whitney 1905

Baker, Howie (Preteen)
The Mystery of the Diamond in the Wood - David Kherdian 1021

Baker, Joey (Neighbor)
The Fireball Mystery - Mary Adrain 14

Baker, Josephine "Tumpie" (Musician; Historical Figure)
Ragtime Tumpie - Alan Schroeder 1597

Baker, Margaret (Child)
Stepping on the Cracks - Mary Downing Hahn 789

Baldwin, Glendon (Preteen)
Nightmare Mountain - Peg Kehret 1003

Baldwin, Karen (Relative)
Nightmare Mountain - Peg Kehret 1003

Balfour, David (Heir)
Kidnapped - Robert Louis Stevenson 1748

Bambi (Deer)
Bambi - Felix Salten 1582

Banerjee, Rab (Immigrant)
The Stone Angel - Pamela Rogers 1543

Banerjee, Susan (Animal Lover)
The Stone Angel - Pamela Rogers 1543

Bankhead, Tallulah (Spirit; Actress)
Up From Jerico Tel - E.L. Konigsburg 1048

Banks, Will "Loony Willy" (Neighbor)
A Summer to Die - Lois Lowry 1155

Bannister, Darby (Child)
Salted Lemons - Doris Buchanan Smith 1683

Bannock, Jake (Child)
Jim Ugly - Sid Fleischman 623

Bannock, Sam (Actor; Parent)
Jim Ugly - Sid Fleischman 623

bar Hezron, Joel (Zealot)
The Bronze Bow - Elizabeth George Speare 1708

bar Jamin, Daniel (Zealot)
The Bronze Bow - Elizabeth George Speare 1708

Barbara (Step-Parent)
Shelter from the Wind - Marion Dane Bauer 109

Barbara "Bob" (Preteen)
A Girl Called Bob and a Horse Called Yoki - Barbara Campbell 287

Barbour, Hilary (Child)
The Ghost of Tillie Jean Cassaway - Ellen H. Showell 1627

Barbour, Willy (Preteen)
The Ghost of Tillie Jean Cassaway - Ellen H. Showell 1627

Bargle, Argie (Hero)
The Great Green Turkey Creek Monster - James Flora 629

Barleylove (Pig)
Pigs Might Fly: A Novel - Dick King-Smith 1033

Barnaby (Inventor)
Seven-Day Magic - Edward Eager 556

Barnard, George (Stock Broker)
Night Fall - Joan Aiken 17

Barnavelt, Lewis (Child; Ward)
The House with a Clock in Its Walls - John Bellaris 129

Barnes, Frank (Scientist; Detective)
The Donkey Planet - Scott Corbett 423

Barney (Gambler; Parent)
Child of the Owl - Lawrence Yep 1965

Barney (Preteen)
Interstellar Pig - William Sleator 1663

Barnhill, Cassandra (Teenager)
Buddies - Barbara Park 1377

Barrett, Kathy (Preteen)
Now Is Not Too Late - Isabelle Holland 901

Barrows, Louie (Cousin)
Wild Man of the Woods - Joan Clark 345

Bart (Orphan)
Alone in Wolf Hollow - Dana Brookins 208

Barth, Sebastian (Detective)
Dew Drop Dead: A Sebastian Barth Mystery - James Howe 925

Bartolotti (Guardian)
Konrad - Christine Nostlinger 1346

Barton, Bentley "Bart" (Child; Sports Figure)
I Am Rubber, You are Glue - Jane Morton 1293

Barton, Jane (Twin; Sports Figure)
Racing in Her Blood - Millys N. Altman 37

Barton, Jay (Twin)
Racing in Her Blood - Millys N. Altman 37

Barton, John (Parent)
Racing in Her Blood - Millys N. Altman 37

Barty (Preteen)
Ask Me No Questions - Ann Schlee 1594

Basha (Parent; Baker)
Cakes and Miracles - Barbara Diamond Goldin 718

Bashara, Sheik (Musician)
Mariah Loves Rock - Mildred Pitts Walter 1881

Basil (Mouse)
Basil in Mexico - Eve Titus 1814

Basil (Bear; Royalty)
The Real Thief - William Steig 1735

Basini, Jackie (Child)
Yours Truly, Shirley - Ann M. Martin 1202

Basini, Joe (Student—College)
Yours Truly, Shirley - Ann M. Martin 1202

Basini, Shirley (Preteen; Handicapped)
Yours Truly, Shirley - Ann M. Martin 1202

Bat (Bat)
The Bat-Poet - Randall Jarrell 971

Bates, Agatha (Police Officer)
Missing - James Duffy 545

Bates, Annie (Teenager)
Going for the Big One - P.J. Petersen 1421

Bates, Jefferson (Teenager)
Going for the Big One - P.J. Petersen 1421

Bates, Lucky (Parent)
Going for the Big One - P.J. Petersen 1421

Bates, Sassafras (Teenager)
The Murder of Hound Dog Bates - Robbie Branscum 189

Baxter, Ezra (Parent)
The Yearling - Marjorie Kinnan Rawlings 1491

Baxter, Jody (Child)
The Yearling - Marjorie Kinnan Rawlings 1491

Bayard (Toy)
Gentleman Bear - William Pene Du Bois 539

Baylis (Teacher)
Silent Dancer - Bruce Hlibok 886

BB-9 (Alien)
The Computer Nut - Betsy Byars 261

Bea (Relative)
The Village by the Sea - Paula Fox 643

Beaghley, Charlie "Beagle" (Detective)
Beagle in Trouble: 12 Solve It Yourself Mysteries - Jackie Vivelo 1857

Beaky (Teenager)
Ape Ears and Beaky - Nancy J. Hopper 916

Bean (Farmer)
Freddy the Detective - Walter R. Brooks 212

Bonnie Sue (Preteen)
Mystery of the Hard Luck Rodeo - Susan Saunders 1589

Bony-Legs (Witch)
Bony-legs - Joanna Cole 387

Booklouse, Channing (Teacher; Insect)
Trouble in Bugland: A Collection of Inspector Mantis Mysteries - William Kotzwinkle 1055

Boone (Cowboy)
The Indian in the Cupboard - Lynne Reid Banks 1498

Boone, Billy (Musician)
Billy Boone - Alison Smith 1676

Boone, Daniel (Frontiersman; Historical Figure)
Daniel Boone - James Daugherty 483

Boots (Student)
The Zucchini Warriors - Gordon Korman 1052

Boris (Teenager)
A Billion for Boris - Mary Rodgers 1532

Boris (Bear)
Morris and Boris at the Circus - Bernard Wiseman 1935
Morris Has a Cold - Bernard Wiseman 1936

Borman, Mose (Sports Figure)
Soccer Halfback - Matt Christopher 340

Boruch (Manager)
The Island on Bird Street - Uri Orlev 1364

Botkin, Ussiah (Benefactor)
The Path of the Pale Horse - Paul Fleischman 617

Botts, Leigh (Child)
Dear Mr. Henshaw - Beverly Cleary 350

Botts, Leigh (Teenager; Writer)
Strider - Beverly Cleary 356

Botts, Worthington (Inventor)
Worthington Botts and the Steam Machine - Betty Baker 89

Bowditch, Nathaniel (Sailor; Historical Figure)
Carry On, Mr. Bowditch - Jean Lee Latham 1075

Bowen, Amy (Preteen)
No Way of Telling - Emma Smith 1686

Bowen, Cassie (Child)
Cassie Bowen Takes Witch Lessons - Anna Grossnickle Hines 884

Bowen, Gran (Grandparent)
No Way of Telling - Emma Smith 1686

Boy (Child)
The Wall - Eve Bunting 239
The Velveteen Rabbit - Margery Williams 1923

Boy-Strength-of-Blue-Horses (Indian)
Knots on a Counting Rope - Bill Martin, Jr. 1204

Boyd (Teenager; 7th Grader)
Just Good Friends - Dean Marney 1195

Boyd, Blanche (Preteen)
Mystery Madness - Otto Coontz 416

Boyd, Jamie (Preteen)
The Over-the-Hill Ghost - Ruth Calif 276

Boyd, Murray (Preteen)
Mystery Madness - Otto Coontz 416

Boyer, Birdie (Child)
Strawberry Girl - Lois Lenski 1091

Bradford (Spirit)
Jeffrey's Ghost and the Fifth Grade Dragon - David A. Adler 12

Bradley, Grace (Preteen)
Naomi - Berniece Rabe 1480

Bradley, Naomi (Preteen)
Naomi - Berniece Rabe 1480

Bradley, Roger (Teenager)
The Owl Service - Alan Garner 673

Bradshaw, Caroline (Teenager)
Jacob Have I Loved - Katherine Paterson 1389

Bradshaw, Louise (Teenager)
Jacob Have I Loved - Katherine Paterson 1389

Brainard, Barbara (Preteen)
It Takes Brains - Eiveen Weiman 1890

Bramble, Adam (Child)
The Gods in Winter - Patricia Miles 1265

Bramble, Ryan (Child)
Ralph S. Mouse - Beverly Cleary 353

Branch, Steven "Silver Bullet" (Child)
Tramp Steamer and the Silver Bullet - Jeffrey Kelly 1010

Branigan, Casey (Teenager)
Branigan's Dog: A Novel - Fran Grace 727

Brant, Bethany (Preteen)
Behave Yourself, Bethany Brant - Patricia Beatty 122

Brave, Bernard (Mouse)
The Rescuers - Margery Sharp 1623

Breen, Orville (Animal Lover)
Grey Cloud - Charlotte Towner Graeber 729

Brendan (Religious)
The Book of Brendan - Ann Curry 456

Brewer, Marcus (Artist)
In Summer Light - Zibby Oneal 1360

Brian (Child)
The Gift - Joan Lowery Nixon 1334

Brian (Teenager)
It Must've Been the Fish Sticks - Betty Bates 102

Brian (Friend)
Trapped in Death Cave - Bill Wallace 1878

Bridger, Jim (Mountain Man)
Hugh Glass, Mountain Man - Robert McClung 1221

Bright, Lustre (Preteen)
Honestly, Myron - Dean Hughes 931

Bright Dawn (Teenager; Sports Figure)
Black Star, Bright Dawn - Scott O'Dell 1352

Bright Eyes (Indian)
The Friendly Wolf - Paul Goble 712

Bright Morning (Indian)
Sing Down the Moon - Scott O'Dell 1355

Brigit (Child)
The Hounds of the Morrigan - Pat O'Shea 1370

Brigitte (Orphan)
The Happy Orpheline - Natalie Savage Carlson 294

Brimhall, Gil (Child)
Theo Zephyr - Dean Hughes 933

Briskly (Broom)
Euphonia and the Flood - Mary Calhoun 273

Broadribb (Neighbor)
Miss Pickerell and the War of the Computers - Dora Pantell 1373

Bromer, Lexie (Relative)
A Horse to Love - Nancy Springer 1717

Bronka (Rescuer)
Crutches - Peter Hartling 820

Brooks, Suzanna (6th Grader; Collector)
Harvey, the Beer Can King - Jamie Gilson 703

Brother (Bear)
Bears in the Night - Stan Berenstain 140

Brown, Abner (Magician)
The Box of Delights - John Masefield 1208

Brown, Amazon (Coach)
When the Boys Ran the House - Joan Davenport Carris 303

Brown, August (Child)
The People in Pineapple Place - Anne Lindbergh 1120

Brown, Bingo (Child)
Burning Questions of Bingo Brown - Betsy Byars 259

Brown, Clara (Child)
The Doggone Mystery - Mary Blount Christian 331

Brown, Ezra (Sailor)
Seabird - Holling Clancy Holling 905

Brown, Great-Granny (Grandparent)
Miss Hickory - Carolyn Sherwin Bailey 83

Brown, Henry (Pig)
Ruthann and Her Pig - Barbara Ann Porte 1460

Brown, Jason (Child)
The Doggone Mystery - Mary Blount Christian 331

Brown, Junior (Teenager)
The Planet of Junior Brown - Virginia Hamilton 805

Brown, Leroy "Encyclopedia" (Detective; 5th Grader)
Encyclopedia Brown, Boy Detective - Donald J. Sobol 1703

Brown, Velvet (Equestrian)
National Velvet - Enid Bagnold 82

Browne-Browne, Billy (Child)
Gentleman Bear - William Pene Du Bois 539

Browne-Browne, Peter (Parent)
Gentleman Bear - William Pene Du Bois 539

Brownell, Betsy (Friend)
The Horse in the Attic - Eleanor Clymer 370

Browser (Teacher)
Invasion of the Comet People - Philip Curtis 459

Bruce (Bear)
Big Bad Bruce - Bill Peet 1411

Bruno (Student)
The Zucchini Warriors - Gordon Korman 1052

Bruno, Brian (Preteen)
Make Like a Tree and Leave - Paula Danziger 479

Bryan, John Randolph (Military Personnel)
Runaway Balloon: The Last Flight of Confederate Air Force One - Burke Davis 486

Bryant, Rachel (Teenager)
Summer of Fear - Lois Duncan 550

Bubber (Child)
Cave under the City - Harry Mazer 1214

Bubber (Lemming)
The Lemming Condition - Alan Arkin 55

Bubbie (Grandparent)
Our Snowman Had Olive Eyes - Charlotte Herman 860

Buck (Horse)
Buck, Wild - Glenn Balch 91

Buck, Billy (Cowboy)
The Red Pony - John Steinbeck   1738

Buck, Tuffy (Bully)
Shoebag - Mary James   968

Bucket, Charlie (Hero)
Charlie and the Chocolate Factory - Roald
   Dahl   464

Buddy (Child; Sports Figure)
The Lucky Runner - Bernard Wiseman   1934

Buddy (Teenager; Runaway)
Monkey Island - Paula Fox   638

Buder, Stanley (Historian)
*A Long Hard Journey: The Story of the Pullman
   Porter* - Pat McKissack   1245

Bugle, Wicker (Aged Person)
Glom Gloom - Jo Dereske   515

Bullet (Dog)
A Blue-Eyed Daisy - Cynthia Rylant   1563

Bullfinch, Euclid (Scientist)
Danny Dunn and the Universal Glue - Jay
   Williams   1919
Danny Dunn on the Ocean Floor - Jay
   Williams   1920

Bullfrog (Frog)
Bullfrog Grows Up - Rosamond Dauer   482

Bunnicula (Rabbit)
Bunnicula: A Rabbit Tale of Mystery - Deborah
   Howe   923

Burden, Ann (Child)
Z for Zachariah - Robert C. O'Brien   1348

Burdette, Arney (Teenager)
Brushy Mountain - Patricia Pendergraft   1416

Burdette, Sal (Midwife)
Brushy Mountain - Patricia Pendergraft   1416

Burdick, Harris (Writer; Artist)
The Mysteries of Harris Burdick - Chris Van
   Allsburg   1842

Burgess, Abbie (Lighthouse Keeper; Historical
   Figure)
Keep the Lights Burning, Abbie - Peter Roop   1544

Burgmeister (Principal)
The Silver Crest: My Russian Boyhood - Kornei
   Chukovsky   341

Burke, Leslie (Preteen)
Bridge to Terabithia - Katherine Paterson   1386

Burkis, Petie (Friend)
The Midnight Fox - Betsy Byars   264

Burns (Teacher)
My Other Mother, My Other Father - Harriet
   Langsam Sobol   1704

Burns, Toby (Teenager)
Mystery of the Maya Jade - Elizabeth Honness   911

Burr (Survivor)
Medicine Walk - Ardath Mayhar   1212

Burra (Alien)
A Box of Nothing - Peter Dickinson   520

Burt (Child)
The Pigs Are Flying! - Emily Rodda   1530

Bussey, Jeff (Teenager; Military Personnel)
Rifles for Watie - Harold Keith   1004

Buster (Child)
Buster Loves Buttons - Fran Manushkin   1191

Butler, John (Captive)
The Light in the Forest - Conrad Richter   1506

Butter (Dog)
Aldo Peanut Butter - Johanna Hurwitz   947

Buttercup, Susan (Friend)
The Chocolate Touch - Patrick Skene Catling   309

Butterman, Polly "Peanut" (Child)
New Friends - Dorothy Haas   783

Byler, Banjo (Child; Musician)
Banjo - Robert Newton Peck   1407

C

C.C. (Spirit)
The Scorpio Ghosts and the Black Hole Gang -
   Kathy Kennedy Tapp   1778

C.L.U.T.Z. (Robot)
C.L.U.T.Z. and the Fission Formula - Marilyn
   Wilkes   1912

Cafferty, Mickey (Child)
The Voyage Begun - Nancy Bond   170

Cahill, Jane (Teenager)
The Solitary - Lynn Hall   795

Calahan, Mike (Teenager)
A Horse to Love - Nancy Springer   1717

Caley (Settler)
Sweetwater - Laurence Yep   1964

Calkins, Quint (6th Grader; Magician)
Harvey, the Beer Can King - Jamie Gilson   703

Callahan, Erin (Teenager; Equestrian)
A Horse to Love - Nancy Springer   1717

Callahan, Heather (Girlfriend)
Henry's Special Delivery - M.C. Delaney   508

Calloway (Neighbor)
The View From the Cherry Tree - Willo Davis
   Roberts   1513

Calvin (Teacher; Streetperson)
Monkey Island - Paula Fox   638

Cameron (Veterinarian)
Pets, Vets, and Marty Howard - Joan Davenport
   Carris   302

Cameron, Ben (Relative)
Mystery of 22 East - Leon Ware   1885

Cameron, Grandma (Grandparent)
Don't Forget Michael - Jean Thompson   1808

Cameron, Tom (Teenager)
Mystery of 22 East - Leon Ware   1885

Cameron, Tucker (Sports Figure)
Rivals on Ice - Elizabeth Van Steenwyk   1849

Cames, Alexander (Parent)
Beyond Silence - Eleanor Cameron   282

Cames, Andy (Teenager)
Beyond Silence - Eleanor Cameron   282

Cammy (Teenager)
Cousins - Virginia Hamilton   801

Campbell (Artisan; Parent)
Return to Bitter Creek - Doris Buchanan Smith   1682

Campion, Dan (Teenager)
Isaac Campion - Janni Howker   926

Campion, Isaac (Child)
Isaac Campion - Janni Howker   926

Candice "Candy" (Teenager)
Go Well, Stay Well - Toeckey Jones   985

Candlelight (Horse)
Can I Get There by Candlelight? - Jean Slaughter
   Doty   532

Candy (Dog)
Hurry Home, Candy - Meindert DeJong   505

Candy (Friend)
*Shirlick Holmes and the Case of the Wandering
   Wardrobe* - Jane Yolen   1971

Cane, Arthur (Dog)
The Dog Days of Arthur Cane - T. Ernesto
   Bethancourt   144

Canfield, Emily (Spirit)
Jane-Emily - Patricia Clapp   343

Cani, Mundo (Dog)
The Book of the Dun Cow - Walter
   Wangerin   1882

Cannon, Roscoe (Neighbor)
Babysitter on Horseback - Fern G. Brown   213

Capote, Truman (Child; Historical Figure)
Christmas Memory - Truman Capote   288

Captain Cook (Penguin)
Mr. Popper's Penguins - Richard Atwater   64

Carillion, Leon (Child)
*The Mysterious Disappearance of Leon (I Mean
   Noel)* - Ellen Raskin   1489

Carl (Patient)
Borrowed Summer - Marion Walker Doren   531

Carlie (Teenager; Abuse Victim)
The Pinballs - Betsy Byars   266

Carlin (Friend)
Rusty Fertlanger, Lady's Man - Christi Killien   1024

Carmela "Carm" (Immigrant)
Before the Wildflowers Bloom - Tatyana
   Bylinsky   270

Carmen (Frog)
Fox on the Job - James Marshall   1198

Carmichael, Guy (Preteen)
The Silk and the Skin - Rodie Sudbery   1765

Carmichael, Quentin (Rat)
The Dawn Seekers - Carol Hamilton   798

Carmichael, Simon (Handicapped)
The Silk and the Skin - Rodie Sudbery   1765

Carmody, Alfred J. (Landlord)
Home Run Trick - Scott Corbett   425

Carmody, Jordan (Parent)
Hello, Mrs. Piggle-Wiggle - Betty
   MacDonald   1164

Carmody, Philip (Child)
Hello, Mrs. Piggle-Wiggle - Betty
   MacDonald   1164

Caro, Alfred (Scientist; Preteen)
A Word From Our Sponsor: Or, My Friend Alfred -
   Judie Angell   51

Carol (Parent)
Beauty - Bill Wallace   1874

Carol (Preteen)
Kid Power - Susan Beth Pfeffer   1432

Carpenter, Jacob (Restauranteur)
The Strange Night Writing of Jessamine Colter -
   Cynthia DeFelice   501

Carraclough, Joe (Child)
Lassie Come Home - Eric Knight   1042

Carraclough, Sam (Parent)
Lassie Come Home - Eric Knight   1042

Carrie (Orphan)
Carrie's War - Nina Bawden 111

Carrie (Teenager)
The Spirit Is Willing - Betty Baker 87

Carson, Ivy (Eccentric)
Changeling - Zilpha Keatley Snyder 1696

Carson, James W. (Religious)
A Fine White Dust - Cynthia Rylant 1565

Carson, Kit (Frontiersman; Historical Figure)
Sing Down the Moon - Scott O'Dell 1355

Carson, Luvenia (Teacher)
Just an Overnight Guest - Eleanora E. Tate 1779

Carson, Margie (Child)
Just an Overnight Guest - Eleanora E. Tate 1779

Carstairs, Arthur (Child)
The Telltale Summer of Tina C. - Lila Perl 1420

Carstairs, Tina (Preteen)
The Telltale Summer of Tina C. - Lila Perl 1420

Carter, Alan (Military Personnel)
Fantastic Voyage - Isaac Asimov 61

Carter, Glenn (Child)
Doodle and the Go-Cart - Robert Burch 241

Carter, Jimmy (Preteen)
Follow My Leader - James B. Garfield 669

Carter, Noah (Child; 4th Grader)
Saturdays in the City - Ann Sharpless Bond 166

Carter, Thomas Andrew "TAC" (Preteen)
Tac's Island - Ruth Yaffe Radin 1482

Carver, Adelaide "Addie" (Preteen)
The Hideaway Summer - Beverly Hollett
Renner 1500

Carver, Clay (Preteen)
The Hideaway Summer - Beverly Hollett
Renner 1500

Case, Clayton "The Ace" (Sports Figure; 4th
Grader)
Benjy the Football Hero - Jean Van Leeuwen 1845

Casey (Preteen)
Child of the Owl - Lawrence Yep 1965

Casey (Teenager)
Wolf - Gillian Cross 450

Cassaway, Tillie Jean (Spirit)
The Ghost of Tillie Jean Cassaway - Ellen H.
Showell 1627

Cassidy, Peter (Teenager)
A Fine White Dust - Cynthia Rylant 1565

Cassie (Teenager)
Daphne - Marilyn Kaye 1001

Castelis, Alexandros (Hotel Owner)
Mystery of the Hidden Hand - Phyllis A.
Whitney 1904

Cat in the Hat (Cat)
The Cat in the Hat - Dr. Seuss 1617

Cathy (Child)
Save the Dam! - Harriet Sirof 1656

Cathy (Preteen)
There's a Caterpillar in My Lemonade - Diana
Gregory 763
Truth or Dare - Susan Beth Pfeffer 1433

Catt, Tristram "Tris" (Preteen)
Underrunners - Margaret Mahy 1183

Ceci (Preteen)
New Friends - Dorothy Haas 783

Celeste (Elephant)
Babar and the Ghost: An Easy to Read Version -
Laurent De Brunhoff 219

Celia (Child)
I Should Worry, I Should Care - Miriam
Chaikin 315

Celia (Royalty)
The Trouble with Dragons - Oliver G.
Selfridge 1612

Celia (Activist; Worker)
When the Rattlesnake Sounds: A Play - Alice
Childress 327

CG (Child)
The Empty Window - Anne Evelyn Bunting 229

Chad (Child)
The Cat That Was Left Behind - Carole S. Adler 6
Fudge - Charlotte Towner Graeber 728
Voices After Midnight - Richard Peck 1406

Chakoh (Child; Indian)
Walk the World's Rim - Betty Baker 88

Chalmers, Margaret "Meg" (Teenager)
A Summer to Die - Lois Lowry 1155

Chalmers, Molly (Teenager)
A Summer to Die - Lois Lowry 1155

Champion, Darla (Child)
Thunder Pup - Janet Hickman 876

Chan, Kenichi "Ken" (Child)
Journey to Topaz - Yoshiko Uchida 1837

Chan, Yuki (Preteen)
Journey to Topaz - Yoshiko Uchida 1837

Chang (Child)
Chang's Paper Pony - Eleanor Coerr 377

Change (Wizard)
Doctor Change - Joanna Cole 388

Chant, Eric "Cat" (Child)
Charmed Life - Diana Wynne Jones 980

Chant, Gwendolyn (Child)
Charmed Life - Diana Wynne Jones 980

Chapman, Derek (Captive)
The Solid Gold Kid - Norma Fox Mazer 1218

Chapman, Otis (Artist)
Jemmy - Jon Francis Hassler 824

Char (Researcher)
Planet out of the Past - James Lincoln Collier 393

Charles (Child)
Autumn Street - Lois Lowry 1152
The Machine Gunners - Robert Westall 1895

Charley (Entertainer)
Travelers by Night - Vivien Alcock 21

Charlie (Hunter; Indian)
Boy of Tache - Ann Blades 147

Charlie (Step-Parent)
Dear Baby - Joanne Rocklin 1524

Charlie (Aged Person)
The Nargun and the Stars - Patricia
Wrightson 1959

Charlie (Relative)
Alone in Wolf Hollow - Dana Brookins 208

Charlip, Vicki (Preteen)
Our Sixth-Grade Sugar Babies - Eve Bunting 235

Charlotte (Spider)
Charlotte's Web - E.B. White 1899

Charlotte (Child)
Snakes Are Nothing to Sneeze At - Gabrielle
Charbonnet 319

Charlton, Tim (Preteen)
Danger at Black Dyke - Winifred Finlay 603

Charrington, Jane (Preteen)
Operation Peeg - Jonathan Gathorne-Hardy 677

Chase, Frank (Step-Parent)
Year of the Black Pony - Walt Morey 1288

Chassidah (Royalty)
Alone in the Wild Forest - Isaac Bashevis
Singer 1652

Chauntecleer (Rooster)
The Book of the Dun Cow - Walter
Wangerin 1882

Chavez, Miguel (Child)
.and Now Miguel - Joseph Krumgold 1057

Cheryl Suzanne (Apprentice; Witch)
Witch in Room 6 - Edith Battles 106

Chester (Cat)
Bunnicula: A Rabbit Tale of Mystery - Deborah
Howe 923

Chester (Child)
Chester - Mary Francis Shura 1634

Chester (Chipmunk)
Chester Chipmunk's Thanksgiving - Barbara
Williams 1917

Chester (Cricket)
The Cricket in Times Square - George Selden 1608
Tucker's Countryside - George Selden 1611

Chiefie (Abuse Victim; Orphan)
Almost a Hero - Clyde Robert Bulla 223

Child, Kristi
The Doll in the Garden - Mary Downing Hahn 787

Childers, Brian (Preteen)
The Antrian Messenger - G. Clifton Wisler 1938

Childers, Scott (Teenager; Alien)
The Antrian Messenger - G. Clifton Wisler 1938

Childs, Chauncey (Teenager)
Tough Chauncey - Doris Buchanan Smith 1685

Childs, Lucy (Preteen)
Lucy Forever and Miss Rosetree, Shrinks - Susan
Richards Shreve 1629

Chingis (Cat; Witch)
The Ghost Drum: A Cat's Tale - Susan Price 1468

Chloris (Preteen)
Chloris and the Creeps - Kin Platt 1450

Chris (Teenager; Detective)
Adventure in Granada - Walter Dean Myers 1302

Chris (Child)
The Magic Stone - Leonie Kooiker 1049
Year of the Black Pony - Walt Morey 1288

Chrissy (Preteen)
I Hate Being Gifted - Patricia Hermes 863

Christina (Orphan; Hunter)
Flambards - K.M. Peyton 1427

Christina "Teeny" (Preteen)
Impy for Always - Jackie French Koller 1044

Christine "Chris" (Preteen)
The Deserter - Nigel Gray 738

Christopher (Relative)
A Chance Child - Jill Paton Walsh 1391

Christopher Robin (Child)
The House at Pooh Corner - A.A. Milne   1270
Winnie-the-Pooh - A.A. Milne   1271

Chu, Kim (Child)
The Lost Umbrella of Kim Chu - Eleanor Estes   577

Chub (Child)
The Lucky Runner - Bernard Wiseman   1934

Chub (Sports Figure; Child)
Tackle-22 - Louise Munro Foley   631

Chuck (Detective; Child)
Follow That Ghost! - Dale Fife   600

Chuckie (Military Personnel)
The Last Mission - Harry Mazer   1215

Chukovsky, Kornei (Outcast; Bastard Son)
The Silver Crest: My Russian Boyhood - Kornei Chukovsky   341

Chuto (Indian)
The Secret of the Andes - Ann Nolan Clark   344

Cici (Parent)
Hangin' Out with Cici - Francine Pascal   1385

Cilla (Relative)
Homecoming - Cynthia Voigt   1864

Cimorene (Royalty)
Dealing with Dragons - Patricia C. Wrede   1953

Cinder (Orphan)
Lucy Forever and Miss Rosetree, Shrinks - Susan Richards Shreve   1629

Cindy (Teenager)
The Crumb - Jean Slaughter Doty   533

Cinnamon, Sydney (Dwarf; Teenager)
Little Little - M.E. Kerr   1017

Claire (Child)
Sea Swan - Kathryn Lasky   1073

Claire (Relative)
The Song of the Christmas Mouse - Shirley Rousseau Murphy   1300

Claire (Child)
Through the Dolls' House Door - Jane Gardam   666

Clancy (Farmer)
Clancy's Coat - Eve Bunting   230

Clancy, Nancy (Preteen)
Ned Kelly and the City of the Bees - Thomas Keneally   1013

Clara (Child; Vacationer)
The Animal, the Vegetable, and John D. Jones - Betsy Byars   256

Clara (Child)
Clara and the Bookwagon - Nancy Smiler Levinson   1100

Clare (Friend)
Time Sweep - Valerie Weldrick   1892

Clarissa (Child)
The Witch Family - Eleanor Estes   579

Clarisse (Child; Handicapped)
At the Back of the Woods - Claudia Mills   1267

Clark (Neighbor)
Gopher, Tanker, and the Admiral - Shirley Climo   368

Clark, Andy (Child)
When the Sirens Wailed - Noel Streatfeild   1763

Clark, Buddy (Teenager)
The Planet of Junior Brown - Virginia Hamilton   805

Clark, Jeffrey (Preteen; 5th Grader)
Jeffrey's Ghost and the Fifth Grade Dragon - David A. Adler   12

Clark, Laura (Child)
When the Sirens Wailed - Noel Streatfeild   1763

Clark, Tim (Child)
When the Sirens Wailed - Noel Streatfeild   1763

Clarke, Benjie (Child)
Manhattan Is Missing - E.W. Hildick   880

Clarke, Peter (Preteen)
Manhattan Is Missing - E.W. Hildick   880

Claude (Relative)
Us and Uncle Fraud - Lois Lowry   1156

Claudia (Preteen; Runaway)
From the Mixed-Up Files of Mrs. Basil E. Frankweiler - E.L. Konigsburg   1045

Claudia (Relative)
Shoeshine Girl - Clyde Robert Bulla   228

Claudie (Step-Parent)
Words by Heart - Ouida Sebestyen   1602

Clay, Isadora (Preteen)
Hear the Wind Blow - Patricia Pendergraft   1417

Claypool, Fenton (Child)
Home Run Trick - Scott Corbett   425

Cleary, Lemon Clarkson (Criminal)
Uncle Lemon's Spring - Jane Yolen   1973

Cleary, Letty (Heroine)
Uncle Lemon's Spring - Jane Yolen   1973

Clem (Farmer)
The Pea Patch Jig - Thacher Hurd   942

Clemmons (Inventor)
Eddie, Incorporated - Phyllis Reynolds Naylor   1314

Clock, Arrietty (Mythical Creature)
The Borrowers - Mary Norton   1344

Clock, Homily (Mythical Creature)
The Borrowers - Mary Norton   1344

Clock, Pod (Mythical Creature)
The Borrowers - Mary Norton   1344

Clover, Pamela Jean "P.J." (Detective)
P.J. Clover, Private Eye: The Case of the Missing Mouse - Susan Meyers   1260

Clutchett (Neighbor)
Time at the Top - Edward Ormondroyd   1367

Clutterworth, Mary-Anna (Child)
Enemies - Robin Klein   1040

Coatsworth (Driver)
Follow That Bus! - Pat Hutchins   960

Cobb, Joshua (Preteen; Camper)
The Freewheeling of Joshua Cobb - Margaret Hodges   894

Cole (Teacher)
The Agony of Alice - Phyllis Reynolds Naylor   1310

Cole, Jonathan (Teenager)
Jonathan Down Under - Patricia Beatty   125

Cole, Raymond (Runaway)
Raymond - Mark Geller   681

Cole, Rosy (Child)
Give Us a Great Big Smile, Rosy Cole - Sheila Greenwald   757

Coleman (Neighbor)
At the Back of the North Wind - George MacDonald   1165

Collier (Psychologist)
The Falling-Apart Winter - Nancy Covert Smith   1689

Collins, Alice (Relative)
Hotel for Dogs - Lois Duncan   549

Collins, Coot (Stuntman; Rancher)
The Winged Colt of Casa Mia - Betsy Byars   268

Colman, Billy (Preteen; Animal Trainer)
Where the Red Fern Grows - Wilson Rawls   1493

Colter, Jessamine (Widow(er); Artist)
The Strange Night Writing of Jessamine Colter - Cynthia DeFelice   501

Comfort (Preteen)
Comfort Herself - Geraldine Kaye   1000

Common, Callie (Preteen)
Red Sky at Morning - Andrea Wyman   1960

Common, Katherine (Teenager)
Red Sky at Morning - Andrea Wyman   1960

Conger, Conrad (Twin)
Me and the Terrible Two - Ellen Conford   407

Conger, Haskell (Twin)
Me and the Terrible Two - Ellen Conford   407

Congruent, Rodney (Teenager)
The Planetoid of Amazement - Mel Glidden   710

Connell, Brann (Preteen; Time Traveller)
Building Blocks - Cynthia Voigt   1860

Connolly, Sara Kate (Preteen)
Afternoon of the Elves - Janet Taylor Lisle   1128

Conrad, Clara (Teenager)
Cute Is a Four Letter Word - Stella Pevsner   1425

Considine, Rafe (Teenager)
Drift - William Mayne   1213

Constance (Badger)
Redwall - Brian Jacques   967

Cooke, Zachary (Businessman)
The Hostage - Theodore Taylor   1789

Cookee (Cook; Parent)
Jolly Roger and the Pirates of Abdul, the Skinhead - Colin McNaughton   1248

Cooper, Casey (Child)
Casey the Nomad - Susan Sussman   1769

Cooper, Franklin (Aged Person)
Just Like a Real Family - Kristi Holl   898

Cooper, Rosey (Child)
Casey the Nomad - Susan Sussman   1769

Coopersmith, Leah (Friend)
Mariah Delany's Author-of-the-Month Club - Sheila Greenwald   759

Coppicco, Vittore (Peddler)
Roller Skates - Ruth Sawyer   1590

Corbett, Kevin (Preteen)
Heads, I Win - Patricia Hermes   862

Corduroy (Alligator)
The Alligator and His Uncle Tooth: A Novel of the Sea - Geoffrey Hayes   833

Corn, Quentin (Pig)
Quentin Corn - Mary Stolz   1759

Cornish, Susan (Teenager)
Susan Cornish - Rebecca Caudill   311

Cosette, Bryant (Archaeologist)
The Turquoise Toad Mystery - Georgess McHargue   1233

Costue (Insurance Agent)
Best Friend Insurance - Beatrice Gormley 723

Cotman, Anna (Teenager)
The Trial of Anna Cotman - Vivien Alcock 22

Cott, Lucas (Child; 3rd Grader)
Class Clown - Johanna Hurwitz 950

Cowlander (Milkman)
The Ghost-Eye Tree - Bill Martin, Jr. 1203

Cox, Dawn (Single Parent)
Tough Tiffany - Belinda Hurmence 945

Cox, Tiffany (Preteen)
Tough Tiffany - Belinda Hurmence 945

Craig, Butler (Step-Parent)
A Hero Ain't Nothin' but a Sandwich - Alice
  Childress 326

Craigie, Andrew (Orphan)
*The Case of the Baker Street Irregular: A Sherlock
  Holmes Story* - Robert Newman 1328

Crane (Preteen; Camper)
The Freewheeling of Joshua Cobb - Margaret
  Hodges 894

Crane, Ichabod (Teacher)
The Legend of Sleepy Hollow - Washington
  Irving 964

Crane, Lucy (Teenager)
Mystery at Crane's Landing - Marcella Thum 1810

Crane, Stogie (Preteen)
Shortstop From Tokyo - Matt Christopher 339

Crannaker, Russell (Monster; Preteen)
The Monster's Ring - Bruce Coville 438

Craven, Colin (Orphan; Handicapped)
The Secret Garden - Frances Hodgson Burnett 249

Crawford, Elizabeth (Child)
Stepping on the Cracks - Mary Downing
  Hahn 789

Creep (Abuse Victim; Time Traveller)
A Chance Child - Jill Paton Walsh 1391

Creesy, Josiah Perkins (Sea Captain)
All Sail Set: A Romance of the Flying Cloud -
  Armstrong Sperry 1711

Creighton, Ellen (Parent)
Across Five Aprils - Irene Hunt 937

Creighton, Jethro (Child)
Across Five Aprils - Irene Hunt 937

Crenshaw, Pete (Detective)
*Alfred Hitchcock and the Three Investigators in the
  Secret of Shark Reef* - William Arden 53

Crew, Harry (Warrior)
The Blue Sword - Robin McKinley 1239

Crewe, Sara (Orphan)
Sara Crewe - Frances Hodgson Burnett 248

Cricket (Child)
Cricket and the Crackerbox Kid - Alane
  Ferguson 595

Crimp (Neighbor)
Mad Martin - Patricia Windsor 1927

Crinkley, Elissa (Preteen)
Be a Perfect Person in Just Three Days - Stephen
  Manes 1187

Crinkley, Milo (Child)
Be a Perfect Person in Just Three Days - Stephen
  Manes 1187

Crisply, Becky (Preteen)
The Remarkable Return of Winston Potter Crisply -
  Eve Rice 1505

Crisply, Max (Teenager)
The Remarkable Return of Winston Potter Crisply -
  Eve Rice 1505

Crisply, Winston Potter (Student)
The Remarkable Return of Winston Potter Crisply -
  Eve Rice 1505

Cristabel (Preteen)
Philo Potts, or, The Helping Hand Strikes Again -
  Mildred Ames 40

Crow (Crow)
The Lemming Condition - Alan Arkin 55

Crowder, Georgette (Child)
Reserved for Mark Anthony Crowder - Alison
  Smith 1677

Crowder, Mark Anthony (Preteen; Gardener)
Reserved for Mark Anthony Crowder - Alison
  Smith 1677

Crowell, Bruce (Preteen)
The Red Room Riddle - Scott Corbett 427

Crown, Natalie (Child)
Playing Beatie Bow - Ruth Park 1382

Cruikshank (Coach)
Eunice (the Egg Salad) Gottlieb - Tricia
  Springstubb 1719

Crusoe, Robinson (Castaway)
*The Life and Strange and Surprising Adventures of
  Robinson Crusoe* - Daniel Defoe 503

Crutches (Veteran)
Crutches - Peter Hartling 820

Cuffy (Housekeeper; Child-Care Giver)
The Saturdays - Elizabeth Enright 573

Culp, Blossom (Spirit)
The Ghost Belonged to Me - Richard Peck 1405

Cultus (Teenager; Indian)
The Whipman Is Watching - Thomas A. Dyer 554

Cumbers, Merrily (Adventurer)
Glom Gloom - Jo Dereske 515

Cummings, Isabelle "Izzy" (Preteen; Orphan)
Underdog - Marilyn Sachs 1580

Cummings, Roger (Guardian)
Underdog - Marilyn Sachs 1580

Curry, Derek (Preteen; 5th Grader)
The Cold and Hot Winter - Johanna Hurwitz 951

Curtis, Tom (12th Grader; Musician)
Jazz Country - Nat Hentoff 857

Cusi (Indian)
The Secret of the Andes - Ann Nolan Clark 344

Cutter, Charles (Preteen)
The Winged Colt of Casa Mia - Betsy Byars 268

Cuyloga (Indian)
The Light in the Forest - Conrad Richter 1506

Cynthia (Teenager)
Thin Air - David Getz 689

Cyril (Child)
Five Children and It - Edith Nesbit 1323

Cyrus (Sea Serpent)
Cyrus, the Unsinkable Sea Serpent - Bill Peet 1412

D

D-Dog (Dog)
Branigan's Dog: A Novel - Fran Grace 727

D.W. (Child)
Arthur's Baby - Marc T. Brown 216

da Polga, Olga (Guinea Pig)
Olga Carries On - Michael Bond 168

Dab (Handicapped)
Sweet Whispers, Brother Rush - Virginia
  Hamilton 806

Dad (Prisoner)
Miracles on Maple Hill - Virginia Sorensen 1706

Dadon (Ruler)
The Tale of the Golden Cockerel - Alexander
  Pushkin 1477

Dagda (Spirit)
The Hounds of the Morrigan - Pat O'Shea 1370

Dailey, Henry (Horse Trainer)
The Black Stallion - Walter Farley 587
Black Stallion Mystery - Walter Farley 588

Daisy (Relative)
Bogwoppit - Ursula Moray Williams 1924

Dake, Thomas (Carpenter)
The Blue Cat of Castle Town - Catherine C.
  Coblentz 376

Dale (Child)
Good-Bye Pink Pig - Carole S. Adler 7

Dallaker, Fiony (Scavenger)
The Beachcombers - Helen Cresswell 441

Dan (Child)
You Can Depend on Me - Margaret Reuter 1503

Dandelion (Spy; Alien)
The Dandelion Caper - Gene DeWeese 516

Danderoo (Toy)
Among the Dolls - William Sleator 1660

Dandylion (Dog)
Never Steal a Magic Cat - Donald E. Caufield 312

Dangerfield, Dan (Lawman)
The Day the Circus Came to Lone Tree - Glen
  Rounds 1554

Danica (Preteen)
Call Me Danica - Winifred Madison 1174

Daniel (Child)
Baseball and Butterflies - Karen Lynn
  Williams 1922

Daniel (Preteen; Camper)
Bones on Black Spruce Mountain - David
  Budbill 222

Daniel (Child)
The Comeback Dog - Jane Resh Thomas 1804
Fox in a Trap - Jane Resh Thomas 1806

Daniel (Genius; 3rd Grader)
I Am the Universe - Barbara Corcoran 430

Daniel (Child)
Losing Uncle Tim - Marykate Jordan 986

Daniel (Teenager; Archaeologist)
My Daniel - Pam Conrad 409

Daniel (Time Traveller; Servant)
The Stove Haunting - Bel Mooney 1279

Dan'l (Child; Donkey)
The Devil's Donkey - Bill Brittain 203

Dumehjian, Apkar (Refugee; Child)
The Road From Home: The Story of an Armenian Girl - David Kherdian 1022

Dumehjian, Vernon (Refugee)
The Road From Home: The Story of an Armenian Girl - David Kherdian 1022

Dumehjian, Yeghsa (Refugee; Child)
The Road From Home: The Story of an Armenian Girl - David Kherdian 1022

Dunbar, Alison (Child)
Marra's World - Elizabeth Coatsworth 375

Dunbar, Donald (Child)
The Flying Fingers Club - Jean F. Andrews 47

Dunbar, Susan (Newspaper Carrier)
The Flying Fingers Club - Jean F. Andrews 47

Dunn, Danny (Inventor; Preteen)
Danny Dunn and the Universal Glue - Jay Williams 1919

Dunn, Danny (Inventor)
Danny Dunn on the Ocean Floor - Jay Williams 1920

Dunn, Rory (Preteen; 5th Grader)
The Cold and Hot Winter - Johanna Hurwitz 951

Dupper (Prairie Dog)
Dupper - Betty Baker 85

Dusty (Teenager; Camper)
The Freewheeling of Joshua Cobb - Margaret Hodges 894

Dusty (Dog)
No-Name Dog - Rose Impey 963

Duval, Peter Lawrence (Doctor)
Fantastic Voyage - Isaac Asimov 61

E

Eagle, Chuck (Scientist)
Mak - Belle Coates 373

Earhart, Amelia (Child; Historical Figure)
Amelia's Flying Machine - Barbara Shook Hazen 839

Earl (Child)
Jace the Ace - Joanne Rocklin 1525

Earl (Teenager)
Winter of Magic's Return - Pamela F. Service 1616

Earl, James (Parent)
Home Before Dark - Sue Ellen Bridgers 198

Earl, Stella (Teenager)
Home Before Dark - Sue Ellen Bridgers 198

Early, Ida (Child-Care Giver)
Ida Early Comes over the Mountain - Robert Burch 242

Earthor (Owl)
The Acorn Quest - Jane Yolen 1967

Easter (Duck)
The Case of the Elevator Duck - Polly Berrien Berends 139

Eaton, Nathaniel (Sailor)
The Witch of Blackbird Pond - Elizabeth George Speare 1710

Ecklund, Junior (Teenager)
The Something Special Horse - Lynn Hall 796

Ector (Knight)
The Dragon's Boy - Jane Yolen 1969

Eddie (Child)
Eddie's Valuable Property - Carolyn Haywood 838

Eddie (Parent)
A Long Day in November - Ernest J. Gaines 660

Eddie (Bully)
The Monster's Ring - Bruce Coville 438

Edgar (Child)
There's a Rainbow In My Closet - Patti Stren 1764

Edie (Aged Person)
The Nargun and the Stars - Patricia Wrightson 1959

Edith (Child; Orphan)
Edith Herself - Ellen Howard 920

Edmonds (Teacher)
Bridge to Terabithia - Katherine Paterson 1386

Edwards, Julie "Miyax Kapugen" (Teenager)
Julie of the Wolves - Jean Craighead George 682

Edwin (Preteen)
Katie John and Heathcliff - Mary Calhoun 274

Eel (Villain)
Flight of the Sparrow - Julia Cunningham 453

Eeyore (Toy; Donkey)
The House at Pooh Corner - A.A. Milne 1270
Winnie-the-Pooh - A.A. Milne 1271

Egan (Child)
Knee-Knock Rise - Natalie Babbitt 77

Ehleezah (Fiance(e))
The Contest - Nonny Hogrogian 897

Eilonwy (Heroine; Royalty)
The High King - Lloyd Alexander 28

Einar (Child)
Two Short and One Long - Nina Ring Aamundsen 1

Eirlyo (Spirit)
The Snow Spider - Jenny Nimmo 1331

Eklund, Chris (Musician; Equestrian)
The Something Special Horse - Lynn Hall 796

Elaine (Teenager)
And You Give Me a Pain, Elaine - Stella Pevsner 1424

Elaine (Preteen)
Space Demons - Gillian Rubinstein 1558

Elda (Guardian)
Arthur, for the Very First Time - Patricia MacLachlan 1169

Elder Brother (Indian)
Waterless Mountain - Laura Adams Armer 56

Eldon (Preteen)
The Winter Room - Gary Paulsen 1400

Elena (Step-Parent)
My New Mom and Me - Betty Ren Wright 1957

Elephant (Elephant)
Uncle Elephant - Arnold Lobel 1142

Elevator, Elmer (Child)
My Father's Dragon - Ruth Stiles Gannett 663

Eliza (Parent)
Boy Without a Name - Penelope Lively 1136

Elizabeth (Child)
Autumn Street - Lois Lowry 1152

Elizabeth (Time Traveller)
Elizabeth, Elizabeth - Eileen Dunlop 551

Elizabeth (5th Grader)
Jennifer, Hecate, Macbeth, William McKinley and Me, Elizabeth - E.L. Konigsburg 1046

Elizabeth (Artist)
Now Is Not Too Late - Isabelle Holland 901

Elizabeth (Royalty)
Perilous Gard - Elizabeth Marie Pope 1456

Elizabeth (Rat; Relative)
A Rat's Tale - Tor Seidler 1606

Elizabeth Ann "Betsy" (Orphan)
Understood Betsy - Dorothy Canfield Fisher 605

Ella (Preteen)
All-of-a-Kind Family - Sydney Taylor 1787

Ella (Recluse)
Shelter from the Wind - Marion Dane Bauer 109

Ella (Child)
Sugar Blue - Vera Cleaver 359

Ellen (Detective)
Beagle in Trouble: 12 Solve It Yourself Mysteries - Jackie Vivelo 1857

Ellen (Teenager)
Night Cry - Phyllis Reynolds Naylor 1316

Ellen Grae (Preteen)
Ellen Grae - Vera Cleaver 357

Ellie (Child)
The Ghost-Eye Tree - Bill Martin, Jr. 1203

Ellie (Preteen; 6th Grader)
Our Sixth-Grade Sugar Babies - Eve Bunting 236

Elliot (Relative)
Seven Kisses in a Row - Patricia Maclachlan 1171

Elliot, Davidson (Preteen)
Hey, What's Wrong with This One? - Maia Wojciechowska 1939

Elliot, Kate (Time Traveller)
Vision Quest - Pamela F. Service 1615

Elliott, Arthur Livingston (Preteen)
My Own Private Sky - Delores Beckman 127

Elliott, Harley (Preteen)
Hey, What's Wrong with This One? - Maia Wojciechowska 1939

Elliott, Mott (Child)
Hey, What's Wrong with This One? - Maia Wojciechowska 1939

Ellsworth (Cat)
Ellsworth and the Cats from Mars - Patience Brewster 196

Elmer (Spirit)
The Over-the-Hill Ghost - Ruth Calif 276

Elsie (Preteen; Tutor)
Nothing's Fair in Fifth Grade - Barthe DeClements 500

Elvis (Teenager)
Me and My Million - Clive King 1027

Emerson, Lucy (Preteen)
The Half-Child - Kathleen Hersom 868

Emerson, Sarah (Child; Handicapped)
The Half-Child - Kathleen Hersom 868

Emily (Child)
At the Back of the Woods - Claudia Mills 1267

Emily (Preteen)
Getting Rid of Marjorie - Betty Ren Wright 1955

Emily (Child)
Leo and Emily - Franz Brandenberg 187

Emily (Relative)
The Monster in the 3rd Dresser Drawer and Other Stories about Adam Joshua - Janice Lee Smith 1688

Emily (Vacationer)
Walking Away - Elizabeth Winthrop 1933

Emma (Teenager)
Emma's Dilemma - Gen LeRoy 1093

Emma (Servant)
The Empty Schoolhouse - Natalie Savage Carlson 291

Emma (Preteen)
Nobody's Family Is Going to Change - Louise Fitzhugh 609
Pip and Emma - Katharine Bacon 80

Emma (Child)
Seven Kisses in a Row - Patricia Maclachlan 1171
There's a Rainbow In My Closet - Patti Stren 1764
The Village by the Sea - Paula Fox 643

Emmy (Camper)
Ghost Island - Carolyn Lane 1068

Endersby, Laurie (Teenager)
The Trouble with Soap - Margery Cuyler 462

English, M.H., J. Huntley (Detective)
The Case of the Horrible Swamp Monster - Drew Stevenson 1745

Enright, Phillip (Survivor; Handicapped)
The Cay - Theodore Taylor 1788

Entsminger, Kathy (Preteen; Traveller)
The Dandelion Caper - Gene DeWeese 516

Ephraim (Preteen)
Downwind - Louise Moeri 1273

Eric (Child)
The Book of Brendan - Ann Curry 456

Eric (Preteen)
My Friend, My Brother - David Warren Swartley 1773

Erica (Teenager)
Early Rising - Joan Clarke 347

Erika (Twin)
Farewell, Aunt Isabell - Ilse-Margret Vogel 1858
My Summer Brother - Ilse-Margret Vogel 1859

Ernest (Elephant)
Frank and Ernest - Alexandra Day 489

Eskoril (Tutor)
Sandwriter - Monica Hughes 934

Esteban (Slave)
Walk the World's Rim - Betty Baker 88

Estelle (Babysitter)
Finders Keepers - Emily Rodda 1529

Esther (Preteen)
The Law of Gravity - Johanna Hurwitz 953

Esther (Grandparent)
A Mitzvah Is Something Special - Phyllis Rose Eisenberg 562

Estrada, Eduardo (Artist)
Nicky and the Joyous Noise - Mildred Ames 39

Etta (Professor; Relative)
The Ghost on Saturday Night - Sid Fleischman 621

Euphonia (Rescuer)
Euphonia and the Flood - Mary Calhoun 273

Euphus (Computer Expert)
Miss Pickerell and the War of the Computers - Dora Pantell 1373

Eva (Experimental Subject)
Eva - Peter Dickinson 521

Evans, Andy (Child; Animal Lover)
Kavik the Wolf Dog - Walt Morey 1286

Evelyn (Relative; Child-Care Giver)
The Believers - Rebecca C. Jones 983

Evelyn (Relative)
Seven Kisses in a Row - Patricia Maclachlan 1171

Evie (Handicapped)
Mystery of the Gingerbread House - Wylly Folk St. John 1721

Evon (Child)
Gildaen: The Heroic Adventures of a Most Unusual Rabbit - Emilie Buchwald 221

Ezel (Child)
Mirandy and Brother Wind - Pat McKissack 1246

Ezzy (Child)
The 18th Emergency - Betsy Byars 255

F

Face, Potato (Musician; Handicapped)
Rootabaga Stories - Carl Sandburg 1584

Fairhair, Thorkell (Pirate)
Viking's Dawn - Henry Treece 1822

Falcon (Military Personnel)
Awfully Short for the Fourth Grade - Elvira Woodruff 1951

Fan, Tim (Child)
The Genie of Sutton Place - George Selden 1609

Fanny (Preteen)
Fat Fanny, Beanpole Bertha and the Boys - Barbara Ann Porte 1458

Farcus, Rosemary (Parent)
Me Two - Mary C. Ryan 1562

Farcus, Wilfred "Wilf" (Teenager)
Me Two - Mary C. Ryan 1562

Farisee (Housekeeper)
No Beasts! No Children! - Beverly Keller 1007

Farla (Preteen)
Dear Baby - Joanne Rocklin 1524

Farley (Preteen)
The Dog Who Wouldn't Be - Farley Mowat 1296

Farley, Ellie (Preteen)
A Blue-Eyed Daisy - Cynthia Rylant 1563

Farley, Okey (Parent; Alcoholic)
A Blue-Eyed Daisy - Cynthia Rylant 1563

Farmer, Lincoln (Child)
Who's in Charge of Lincoln? - Dale Fife 601

Farrell, Greg (Preteen; Sports Figure)
The Josie Gambit - Mary Francis Shura 1635

Father (Parent)
Best Town in the World - Byrd Baylor 118

Father (Mouse)
The Mouse and His Child - Russell Hoban 892

Father (Parent)
The Wall - Eve Bunting 239

Fatly (Pig)
Euphonia and the Flood - Mary Calhoun 273

Fats (Mouse)
The Great Christmas Kidnapping Caper - Jean Van Leeuwen 1847

Fatso (Child)
Joseph on the Subway Train - Kathleen Benson 138

Faulk, Sook (Cousin)
Christmas Memory - Truman Capote 288

Feeney, Dinah (Teenager)
Buddies - Barbara Park 1377

Felange, Johnny (Bully)
The Empty Chair - Bess Kaplan 993

Feldman (Doctor; Parent)
Baseball Fever - Johanna Hurwitz 948

Feldman, Ezra (Sports Figure; Child)
Baseball Fever - Johanna Hurwitz 948

Feldman, Harris (Child; Student)
Baseball Fever - Johanna Hurwitz 948

Felice (Child)
Fran Ellen's House - Marilyn Sachs 1578

Felicia (Child)
Felicia the Critic - Ellen Conford 402

Felicity (Child)
Best Enemies - Kathleen Leverich 1095

Felicity (Duck)
Pigs Might Fly: A Novel - Dick King-Smith 1033

Feline (Deer)
Bambi - Felix Salten 1582

Felipe (Child)
How Far, Felipe? - Genevieve Gray 737

Felita (Child)
Felita - Nicolasa Mohr 1274

Feltwright, Hercules (Actor; Tutor)
Goody Hall - Natalie Babbitt 76

Ferguson, Amy (Twin; Detective)
The Leipzig Vampire - Mary Anderson 45

Ferguson, Andy (Preteen)
The Hit-and-Run Connection - Carole Smith 1678

Ferguson, Jamie (Twin; Detective)
The Leipzig Vampire - Mary Anderson 45

Ferlanger, Rusty (Artist; Teenager)
Rusty Fertlanger, Lady's Man - Christi Killien 1024

Fernald, Alvin (Preteen)
Alvin Fernald, Master of a Thousand Disguises - Clifford B. Hicks 877

Ferris, Ned (Preteen)
It Takes Brains - Eiveen Weiman 1890

Fibbey, Raymond (Adventurer)
Glom Gloom - Jo Dereske 515

Fickett (Religious)
Edgar Allan - John Neufeld 1325

Fickett, Mary Nell (Teenager)
Edgar Allan - John Neufeld 1325

Fielding, Heather (Preteen)
Transfigured Hart - Jane Yolen 1972

Fieldmouse, Feldman (Mouse)
Feldman Fieldmouse - Nathaniel Benchley 131

Fifty (Tractor)
Fifty Saves His Friend - Martin Baynton 120

Fig (Preteen)
Rhoda, Straight and True - Roni Schotter 1596

Figg, Florence Italy (Relative)
Figgs and Phantoms - Ellen Raskin 1488

Filomena (Donkey)
How Far, Felipe? - Genevieve Gray 737

Finch (Social Worker)
The Boy Who Wanted a Family - Shirley Gordon 722

Finch, Becky (Preteen)
The Bongleweed - Helen Cresswell 442

Finch, June (Preteen)
Just Like a Real Family - Kristi Holl 898

Finch, Oliver (Child)
The Ghost in the Noonday Sun - Sid Fleischman 620

Finkelstein, Rhona (Preteen)
The Hand-Me-Down Kid - Francine Pascal 1384

Finley, Flossie (Child)
Flossie and the Fox - Pat McKissack 1244

Finnegan, Brian (Preteen; Classmate)
Dear Mom, You're Ruining My Life - Jean Van Leeuwen 1846

Finney, Barbara (Teacher)
The Cat Ate My Gymsuit - Paula Danziger 477

Finxel (Psychic; Handicapped)
Finzel the Farsighted - Paul Fleischman 613

Fiona (Child)
Fiona's Bee - Beverly Keller 1006

Firebone, Selsey (Spy)
Underrunners - Margaret Mahy 1183

Firestone, Terri (Librarian)
Mystery of the Bewitched Bookmobile - Florence Parry Heide 845

Fish (Child)
A Boy Called Fish - Alison Morgan 1289

Fish, Caroline (Child)
The Mysterious Disappearance of Leon (I Mean Noel) - Ellen Raskin 1489

Fisher, Barbara (Preteen)
The Real Me - Betty Miles 1263

Fisher, George (Neighbor)
The Luck of Pokey Bloom - Ellen Conford 406

Fisher, Kitty (Preteen)
Circle of Fire - William H. Hooks 913

Fisher, Marion (Journalist)
The Real Me - Betty Miles 1263

Fisher, Richard (Teenager)
The Real Me - Betty Miles 1263

Fisher, Scrap (Preteen)
Circle of Fire - William H. Hooks 913

Fiske, Adam (Child)
The Wish Giver: Three Tales of Coven Tree - Bill Brittain 206

Fitzgerald, Arabella (Preteen)
Bella Arabella - Liza Fosburgh 634

Fitzgerald, John D. (Preteen)
The Great Brain Reforms - John D. Fitzgerald 607

Fitzgerald, Sweyn (Teenager)
The Great Brain Reforms - John D. Fitzgerald 607

Fitzgerald, Tom (Teenager)
The Great Brain Reforms - John D. Fitzgerald 607

Fitzi (Child; Entertainer)
The Street Dancers - Elizabeth Starr Hill 882

Fitzroy, Captain (Sea Captain)
Darwin and the Voyage of the Beagle - Felicia Law 1078

Fiver (Rabbit; Psychic)
Watership Down - Richard Adams 4

Fizz (Child)
The Green Ghost of Appleville - Jean Marzollo 1206

Flagg, Jack (Orphan; Adventurer)
By the Great Horn Spoon - Sid Fleischman 619

Flam, Fflewddur (Minstrel)
The High King - Lloyd Alexander 28

Flam, Gerry (Child)
Once I Was a Plum Tree - Johanna Hurwitz 954

Flanagan, Casey (Teenager)
All Together Now - Sue Ellen Bridgers 197

Flitter (Babysitter)
The Robot Birthday - Eve Bunting 237

Flood, Crobar (Teenager; Friend)
River Rats, Inc. - Jean Craighead George 684

Flora (Cousin)
Dangerous Spaces - Margaret Mahy 1180

Flora (Child)
Fran Ellen's House - Marilyn Sachs 1578

Floss (Dog)
A Boy Called Fish - Alison Morgan 1289

Flower-in-the-Night (Royalty)
Castle in the Air - Diana Wynne Jones 979

Flowers, Poppy (Child; Animal Lover)
Poppy and the Outdoor Cat - Dorothy Haas 784

Fly (Fly)
The First Morning: An African Myth - Margery Bernstein 142

Fogg, Phileas (Traveller)
Around the World in Eighty Days - Jules Verne 1852

Folsom, Alex (Wanderer)
Wilkin's Ghost - Robert Burch 246

Fong, Jimmy (Classmate)
Vision Quest - Pamela F. Service 1615

Fooley (Balloonist)
Gammage Cup - Carol Kendall 1012

Foote (Farmer)
The Gollywhopper Egg - Anne Rockwell 1527

Forest (Squirrel)
Squirrel in My Teacup! - Eileen Cade-Edwards 271

Forest, Orson (Bully)
Huntly, Nutley and the Missing Link - Mary Tannen 1777

Forrest, Sue Ellen (Preteen)
A Wonderful, Terrible Time - Mary Stolz 1760

Forrester, Billy (Child)
How to Eat Fried Worms - Thomas Rockwell 1528

Forrester, Steve (Preteen)
Sinbad and Me - Kin Platt 1452

Forster, Jack (Teacher)
What Happened to Mr. Forester? - Gary W. Barger 96

Fortune, Amos (Slave)
Amos Fortune, Free Man - Elizabeth Yates 1962

Foskett, Arthur William (Detective; Child)
Arthur the Kid - Alan Coren 433

Foss, Mark Oliver "Mark-O" (Child)
The Magic Moth - Virginia Lee 1088

Foss, Maryanne (Preteen)
The Magic Moth - Virginia Lee 1088

Fossil, Pauline (Preteen)
Ballet Shoes - Noel Streatfeild 1762

Fossil, Petrovna (Child)
Ballet Shoes - Noel Streatfeild 1762

Fossil, Posy (Child)
Ballet Shoes - Noel Streatfeild 1762

Foster (Child)
Gone-Away Lake - Elizabeth Enright 572

Foster, Ricky (Detective)
Lake Fear - Ian McMahan 1247

Foster, Winnie (Child)
Tuck Everlasting - Natalie Babbitt 79

Foster Mary (Foster Parent)
Foster Mary - Celia Strang 1761

Found Arrow (Indian)
Dawn Rider - Jan Hudson 929

Fowler, Molly (Child)
Weasel - Cynthia DeFelice 502

Fowler, Nathan (Preteen)
Weasel - Cynthia DeFelice 502

Fox (Fox)
Fox on the Job - James Marshall 1198

Fox, Fat (Villain)
Gumshoe Goose, Private Eye - Mary DeBall Kwitz 1062

Fox, Sly (Private Detective)
Sly, P.I.: The Case of the Missing Shoes - Cathy Stefanec-Ogren 1730

Foxglove, Melody (Child)
Hello, Mrs. Piggle-Wiggle - Betty MacDonald 1164

Fraley, Robert (Rancher)
Big Red - Jim Kjelgaard 1037

Fran (Preteen)
You've Been Away All Summer - Sheila Hayes 837

Fran Ellen (Child)
Fran Ellen's House - Marilyn Sachs 1578

Frances (Badger)
Bedtime for Frances - Russell Hoban 891

Francie (Handicapped)
Circle of Giving - Ellen Howard 919

Francie (Sports Figure)
Running out of Magic with Houdini - Elizabeth Levy 1108

Frank (Magician)
Double or Nothing - Marc Talbert 1776

Frank (Bear)
Frank and Ernest - Alexandra Day 489

Frank (Teenager)
Remember Me to Harold Square - Paula Danziger 480

Frank (Cousin)
Ruthann and Her Pig - Barbara Ann Porte 1460

Frank (Friend)
Time Sweep - Valerie Weldrick 1892

Franklin, Benjamin (Historical Figure; Inventor)
Ben and Me - Robert Lawson 1083

Franklin, Benjamin (Inventor; Historical Figure)
What Is Papa Up To Now? - Miriam Anne Bourne 181

Franklin, Sally (Child)
What Is Papa Up To Now? - Miriam Anne Bourne 181

Frankovitch, Alex "Skinnybones" (Child)
Almost Starring Skinnybones - Barbara Park 1376

Frankweiler, Basil E. (Wealthy; Widow(er))
From the Mixed-Up Files of Mrs. Basil E. Frankweiler - E.L. Konigsburg   1045

Frazer, Meg (Artist; Young Woman)
Night Fall - Joan Aiken   17

Fred (Snail)
Fast Friends: Two Stories - James Stevenson   1746

Fred (Frog)
In the Middle of the Puddle - Mike Thaler   1797

Fred (Preteen)
Knights of the Kitchen Table - Jon Scieszka   1601

Fred (Mole)
So You Want to Be a Wizard - Diane Duane   541

Freddy (Pig)
Freddy the Detective - Walter R. Brooks   212

Frederick (Preteen)
Mitzi and the Terrible Tyranosaurus Rex - Barbara Williams   1918

Fredericka (Child)
Seven-Day Magic - Edward Eager   556

Free, Nathaniel B. (Child; Writer)
Nathaniel Talking - Eloise Greenfield   755

Freebaker, Missy (Friend)
The Monster's Ring - Bruce Coville   438

Freeman, Carl (Twin)
How Do I Feel? - Norma Simon   1647

Freeman, Eddie (Twin)
How Do I Feel? - Norma Simon   1647

Freeman, Mike (Child)
How Do I Feel? - Norma Simon   1647

Fremple (Friend)
Ballet Magic - Nancy Robison   1522

Friar Tuck (Dog)
The Trouble with Tuck - Theodore Taylor   1791

Friday (Servant)
The Life and Strange and Surprising Adventures of Robinson Crusoe - Daniel Defoe   503

Friedman, Leah (Teenager)
Whirling Rainbows - Susan Terris   1796

Friend, Jinnie (Child)
Gran at Coalgate - Winifred Cawley   313

Frisby (Mouse; Parent)
Mrs. Frisby and the Rats of NIMH - Robert C. O'Brien   1347

Frito, Dave (Coatimundi)
The Turquoise Toad Mystery - Georgess McHargue   1233

Fritz (Preteen)
The Hermit of Fog Hollow Station - David Roth   1551

Frizzle (Teacher)
The Magic School Bus, Lost in the Solar System - Joanna Cole   389

Frog (Frog)
Frog and Toad All Year - Arnold Lobel   1139
Frog and Toad Together - Arnold Lobel   1140

Froggatt, Linda (Preteen)
The Ivy Garland - John Hoyland   927

Frost, Edward (Child)
A Dog on Barkham Street - Mary Stolz   1753

Fuchs, Barney (Child)
Golden Daffodils - Marilyn Gould   726

Fudge (Dog)
Fudge - Charlotte Towner Graeber   728

Fudge (Child)
Superfudge - Judy Blume   158

Fuller, Tex (Friend)
The Friends of the Loony Lake Monster - Frank Bonham   171

Fulton, John (Sports Figure)
Jake - Alfred Slote   1672

Funny Little Woman (Heroine)
The Funny Little Woman - Arlene Mosel   1294

Funnyman (Detective)
Funnyman and the Penny Dodo - Stephen Mooser   1282

Furball (Royalty)
Princess Furball - Charlotte S. Huck   928

G

Gable, Clark (Cat)
The Girl Who Had No Name - Berniece Rabe   1479

Gabriel (Preteen; 6th Grader)
Sixth Grade Secrets - Louis Sachar   1569

Gaddy (Housewife)
The Crow and Mrs. Gaddy - Wilson Gage   658

Gail (Teenager)
Are You in the House Alone? - Richard Peck   1404

Gail (Teenager; Sports Figure)
Signpost to Terror - Gretchen Sprague   1716

Gallagher, Mike (Teenager)
Summer of Fear - Lois Duncan   550

Gallgnat, Adrian C. (Criminal; Insect)
Trouble in Bugland: A Collection of Inspector Mantis Mysteries - William Kotzwinkle   1055

Gamble, J.T. (Child)
J.T. - Jane Wagner   1868

Gamble, Rodeen (Parent)
J.T. - Jane Wagner   1868

Gami (Magician)
Perfect Crane - Anne Laurin   1076

Gammel, Seti (Child)
The Cat in the Mirror - Mary Stolz   1752

Gandalf (Wizard)
The Hobbit - J.R.R. Tolkien   1818

Gandy, Erin "Irun" (Child)
The Cat in the Mirror - Mary Stolz   1752

Ganglia (Toy; Parent)
Among the Dolls - William Sleator   1660

Gardner, Eliza (Teacher)
Adventures of Obadiah - Brinton Turkle   1829

Garing, Jemima (Friend)
Operation Peeg - Jonathan Gathorne-Hardy   677

Garmouche, Tony (Businessman)
Pinch - Larry Callen   277

Garnett, Laurie (Musician)
No Applause, Please - Marilyn Singer   1655

Garrett (Child)
The Stones - Janet Hickman   875

Garrett, Brinton "Brinnie" (Guardian)
The Jedera Adventure - Lloyd Alexander   29

Garrett, Elizabeth (Parent)
A Gift of Magic - Lois Duncan   548

Garrett, Kirby (Dancer)
A Gift of Magic - Lois Duncan   548

Garrett, Nancy (Psychic)
A Gift of Magic - Lois Duncan   548

Garrison, Mike (Rancher)
Beauty - Bill Wallace   1874

Garrity, Clay (Preteen; Runaway)
Monkey Island - Paula Fox   638

Garth, Matthew (Teenager)
The Dangling Witness - Jay Bennett   136

Gary (Twin)
The Fourth Floor Twins and the Sand Castle Contest - David A. Adler   11

Gast (Musician)
What Happened in Hamelin? - Gloria Skurzynski   1659

Gawain (Goose; Guard)
The Real Thief - William Steig   1735

Ged (Wizard)
The Tombs of Atuan - Ursula Le Guin   1085

"Gee" (Grandparent)
Pip and Emma - Katharine Bacon   80

Geem-Wah (Worker)
Her Own Song - Ellen Howard   921

Gentle Ben (Bear)
Gentle Ben - Walt Morey   1285

Gentle Tom (Mountain Man)
The Adventures of Johnny May - Robbie Branscum   188

George (Child)
A Boy in the Doghouse - Betsy Duffey   543

George (Hippopotamus)
George and Martha Back in Town - James Marshall   1199

George (Child)
George Shrinks - William Joyce   987

George (Military Personnel)
George the Drummer Boy - Nathaniel Benchley   132

George (Child)
Hurricane - David Wiesner   1906

George (Knight)
The Reluctant Dragon - Kenneth Grahame   732

Georgie (Preteen)
The Power of the Rellard - Carolyn F. Logan   1145

Gerald (Child)
The Secret Moose - Jean Rogers   1541

Geraldine (Preteen)
And One for All - Theresa Nelson   1321
Jellybean - Tessa Duder   542

Gerda (Relative; Guardian)
The Ghost Children - Eve Bunting   231

Gervaas (Servant)
How to Become King - Jan Terlouw   1793

Gian-Piero (Orphan)
In the Company of Clowns - Martha Bacon   81

Gibson, Ben (Streetperson; Teenager)
Come the Morning - Mark Jonathan Harris   816

Gifford, Agatha (Child)
Cassie Bowen Takes Witch Lessons - Anna Grossnickle Hines   884

Gifford, Arden (Preteen)
An End to Perfect - Suzanne Newton   1330

Gifford, Hill (Teenager)
An End to Perfect - Suzanne Newton   1330

Gilbert (Child)
The Case of the Elevator Duck - Polly Berrien
   Berends   139

Gildaen (Rabbit)
*Gildaen: The Heroic Adventures of a Most Unusual
   Rabbit* - Emilie Buchwald   221

Gillian "Gillie" (Child)
Getting Rid of Krista - Amy Hest   871

Gilligan, Patrick (Driver)
Roller Skates - Ruth Sawyer   1590

Gilmore, Tracy (Friend; 8th Grader)
Patty Dillman of Hot Dog Fame - Susan
   Wojciechowski   1940

Gimal (Fisherman)
Journey Outside - Mary Q. Steele   1728

Gimme-the-Ax (Parent)
Rootabaga Stories - Carl Sandburg   1584

Ginger (Dog)
Addie Meets Max - Joan Robins   1516

Ginger (Child)
Ship's Cook Ginger - Edward Ardizzone   54

Ginger (Child; Camper)
There's a Bat in Bunk Five - Paula Danziger   481

Giordano, Frankie (Child; 3rd Grader)
Frankie Is Staying Back - Ron Roy   1557

"Girl" (Child)
My New Mom and Me - Betty Ren Wright   1957

Girl (Child)
The Magic Finger - Roald Dahl   467

Gitter (Paranormal Investigator)
The Gitter, the Googer and the Ghost - Stephen
   Ryan Oliver   1359

Glad Man (Streetperson)
The Glad Man - Gloria Gonzalez   721

Gladstone, Henry Lincoln "Squib" (Child)
Squib - Nina Bawden   117

Gladys (Teacher)
Roosevelt Grady - Louisa R. Shotwell   1626

Glass, Hugh (Trapper; Mountain Man)
Hugh Glass, Mountain Man - Robert
   McClung   1221

Gloria (Dog)
No Flying in the House - Betty Brock   207

Glorietta (Child)
Humbug Mountain - Sid Fleischman   622

Glory (Client; Child)
Follow That Ghost! - Dale Fife   600

Glory, Anna (Preteen)
The Glory Girl - Betsy Byars   263

Glory-of-the-Republic (Pig)
The House of Sixty Fathers - Meindert De Jong   494

Glover, Jeff (Preteen)
Terror Train! - Gilbert B. Cross   448

Gluck (Preteen; Hero)
King of the Golden River - John Ruskin   1560

Gobo (Deer)
Bambi - Felix Salten   1582

Goddard, Ed (Thief)
Man From the Sky - Avi   70

Godfrey, Charlie (Child)
The Summer of the Swans - Betsy Byars   267

Godfrey, Sarah (Child)
The Summer of the Swans - Betsy Byars   267

Gold, Eileen (Writer)
Like Everybody Else - Barbara Girion   708

Gold, Samantha "Sam" (Preteen)
Like Everybody Else - Barbara Girion   708

Goldie (Parent)
Wolf - Gillian Cross   450

Golding (Grandparent)
The Remembering Box - Eth Clifford   364

Gom (Wizard; Telepath)
Gom on Windy Mountain - Grace Chetwin   324

Gomez (Parent)
I Speak English for My Mom - Muriel Stanek   1725

Gomez, Lupe (Child)
I Speak English for My Mom - Muriel Stanek   1725

Good Fortune (Cat)
The Cat Who Went to Heaven - Elizabeth
   Coatsworth   374

Goodall, Philip (Child)
Plain Lane Christmas - Cyril Walter Hodges   893

Goodall, Sue (Child)
Plain Lane Christmas - Cyril Walter Hodges   893

Goody (Parent)
Goody Hall - Natalie Babbitt   76

Goody, Willet (Child)
Goody Hall - Natalie Babbitt   76

Googer (Paranormal Investigator)
The Gitter, the Googer and the Ghost - Stephen
   Ryan Oliver   1359

Goose (Detective; Parent)
Gumshoe Goose, Private Eye - Mary DeBall
   Kwitz   1062

Goose, Ellery "Gumshoe" (Detective)
Gumshoe Goose, Private Eye - Mary DeBall
   Kwitz   1062

Gordon (Gentleman)
Black Beauty: The Autobiography of a Horse - Anna
   Sewell   1618

Gordon, Amanda (Preteen; 6th Grader)
Call Me Amanda - Dale Bick Carlson   289

Gordon, Dana (Writer; Parent)
Call Me Amanda - Dale Bick Carlson   289

Gorf (Teacher)
Sidewise Stories From Wayside School - Louis
   Sacher   1571

Goss, Joel (Student)
Justin Morgan Had a Horse - Marguerite
   Henry   853

Gottlieb, Eunice (Child; Sports Figure)
Eunice (the Egg Salad) Gottlieb - Tricia
   Springstubb   1719

Gowan, Brad (Preteen)
Eating Ice Cream with a Werewolf - Phyllis
   Green   743

Gowan, Nancy (Child)
Eating Ice Cream with a Werewolf - Phyllis
   Green   743

Grabseth, Mikkel (Teenager; Runaway)
Don't Take Teddy - Babbis Friis-Baastad   648

Grabseth, Teddy (Teenager; Handicapped)
Don't Take Teddy - Babbis Friis-Baastad   648

Grace (Relative)
How Many Miles to Babylon? - Paula Fox   636

Grackle (Innkeeper)
The Half-a-Moon Inn - Paul Fleischman   615

Graden, Alexander William "Alex" (Student)
The Magic Book - Willo Davis Roberts   1511

Grady, Danny (Teenager)
The Swing - Emily Hanlon   811

Grady, Roosevelt (Child)
Roosevelt Grady - Louisa R. Shotwell   1626

Graham (Parent; Writer)
The Boy Who Wanted a Family - Shirley
   Gordon   722

Gram (Grandparent; Patient)
Borrowed Summer - Marion Walker Doren   531

Gramma (Grandparent; Immigrant)
There's a Rainbow In My Closet - Patti Stren   1764

Gramps (Grandparent)
A Summer Like Turnips - LouAnn Gaeddert   655

Gran (Grandparent)
Gran at Coalgate - Winifred Cawley   313

Grandfather (Grandparent)
Heidi - Johanna Spyri   1720

Grandmother (Grandparent)
Something Special for Me - Vera B. Williams   1925

Grandmother (Storyteller)
The Village of Round and Square Houses - Ann
   Grifalconi   768

Grandpa (Grandparent)
Cloudy with a Chance of Meatballs - Judi
   Barrett   97
Grandpa's Maria - Hans-Eric Hellberg   848
Grandpa's Slide Show - Deborah Gould   725

Granger, Aviva (Teenager; 8th Grader)
Puppy Love - Jeanne Betancourt   143

Granny May (Grandparent)
Belinda's Hurricane - Elizabeth Winthrop   1930

Grant, Gussie (Child)
The Friends of the Loony Lake Monster - Frank
   Bonham   171

Grant, Martha (Preteen)
The Wishing People - Nina Beachcroft   121

Grant, Toby (Teenager)
The Rare One - Pamela Rogers   1542

Gray (Wolf)
Flight of the White Wolf - Mel Ellis   568

Gray (Relative)
Spring Rider - John Shults Lawson   1082

Gray, May (Dog)
The Revolt of the Teddy Bears: A May Gray Mystery
   - James Duffy   546

Gray, Victor (Dog)
The Revolt of the Teddy Bears: A May Gray Mystery
   - James Duffy   546

Grayson (Maintenance Worker)
Maniac Magee - Jerry Spinelli   1715

Grayson, Peter (Teenager)
Canyon Winter - Walt Morey   1284

Green (Social Worker)
Raymond - Mark Geller   681

Green, Curley (Artist)
Gammage Cup - Carol Kendall   1012

Hanny (Spirit)
A Haunting Air - Barbara Constance Freeman 645

Hans (Teenager; Bully)
King of the Golden River - John Ruskin 1560

Hansen, Erik (Parent)
The Night Birds - Tormod Haugen 829

Hansen, Jake (Child)
The Night Birds - Tormod Haugen 829

Hansen, Linda (Parent)
The Night Birds - Tormod Haugen 829

Hanson, Carole (Preteen; Equestrian)
Horse Crazy - Bonnie Bryant 220

Hanson, Hobie (Child)
Thirteen Ways to Sink a Sub - Jamie Gilson 705

Happ (Witch)
The Dog Food Caper - Joan M. Lexau 1115

Harald (Child)
Harald and the Great Stag - Donald Carrick 298

Harald (Pirate)
Viking's Dawn - Henry Treece 1822

Haraz, Fawzi (Mythical Creature)
A Lamp for the Lambchops - Jeff Brown 215

Hardbroom (Teacher)
The Worst Witch - Jill Murphy 1299

Hardison, Ethel (Child)
Just an Overnight Guest - Eleanora E. Tate 1779

Hardlick (Teacher)
Someday Angeline - Louis Sachar 1570

Hardy (Teacher)
Salted Lemons - Doris Buchanan Smith 1683
Theo Zephyr - Dean Hughes 933

Hardy, Bruce (Preteen)
A Summer Like Turnips - LouAnn Gaeddert 655

Harker, Kay (Hero)
The Box of Delights - John Masefield 1208

Harmsworth, Nina (Child)
The Court of the Stone Children - Eleanor Cameron 283

Harold (Child; Artist)
Harold and the Purple Crayon - Crockett Johnson 975

Harold (Child)
The Secret Life of Harold the Birdwatcher - Hila Colman 396

Harper (Scientist)
The Bongleweed - Helen Cresswell 442

Harriet (Relative)
Behind the Attic Wall - Sylvia Cassedy 307
Cat's Magic - Margaret Greaves 740

Harris (Veterinarian)
Alan and the Animal Kingdom - Isabelle Holland 899

Harris, Andy (Preteen)
The Trading Game - Alfred Slote 1675

Harris, Boris (Teenager)
A Billion for Boris - Mary Rodgers 1531

Harris, Brad (Sports Figure)
Short Season - Scott Eller 566

Harris, Dean (Sports Figure)
Short Season - Scott Eller 566

Harris, Jim (Grandparent; Sports Figure)
The Trading Game - Alfred Slote 1675

Harris, Lisa (Child)
Short Season - Scott Eller 566

Harrison, Barry (Child)
The Mystery of the Haunted Cabin - Judy Delton 513

Harrison, James (Preteen)
The Ghost of Thomas Kempe - Penelope Lively 1137

Harrison, Robin (Preteen)
The Mystery of the Haunted Cabin - Judy Delton 513

Harrity, Maureen (Preteen)
Best Friend Insurance - Beatrice Gormley 723

Harry (Cat)
The Cricket in Times Square - George Selden 1608

Harry (Centipede)
The Dawn Seekers - Carol Hamilton 798

Harry (Dog)
The Dog That Pitched a No-Hitter - Matt Christopher 338

Harry (Cat)
Harry Cat's Pet Puppy - George Selden 1610

Harry (Child)
Harry in Trouble - Barbara Ann Porte 1459
I Hate My Sister Maggie - Crescent Dragonwagon 535

Harry (Preteen)
Mr. Nobody's Eyes - Michael Morpurgo 1290

Harry (Dog)
Thunder Pup - Janet Hickman 876

Hart, Kristin "Kris" (Preteen)
Octopus Pie - Susan Terris 1795

Hartley (Teacher)
Hey, Remember Fat Glenda? - Lila Perl 1419

Harvey (Child)
The Carp in the Bathtub - Barbara Cohen 381

Harvey (Teenager; Handicapped)
The Pinballs - Betsy Byars 266

Harvey (Cat)
Tucker's Countryside - George Selden 1611

Harvey, Albert (Gambler)
Big Diamond's Boy - Ellen H. Goins 717

Harvey, Albert "Cotton" (Child)
Big Diamond's Boy - Ellen H. Goins 717

Harwood, Jamie (Teenager)
Tundra - William F. Hallstead 797

Harwood, Marjorie (Parent)
Tundra - William F. Hallstead 797

Hasting, Bill (Preteen)
Too Much Magic - Betsy Sterman 1743

Hasting, Jeff (Child)
Too Much Magic - Betsy Sterman 1743

Hastings, Martin (Bully)
A Dog on Barkham Street - Mary Stolz 1753

Hasty (Preteen; Detective—Amateur)
Pitch and Hasty Check It Out - Eric Deleon 509

Hata (Widow(er))
The Best Bad Thing - Yoshiko Uchida 1835

Hatch, Dan (Preteen)
Night of the Twisters - Ivy Ruckman 1559

Hatch, Ryan (Child)
Night of the Twisters - Ivy Ruckman 1559

Hatcher, Farley "Fudge" (Child)
Fudge-a-Mania - Judy Blume 154

Hatcher, Peter "Pete" (Preteen)
Fudge-a-Mania - Judy Blume 154

Hatfield (Administrator)
Almost a Hero - Clyde Robert Bulla 223

Hattie (Child; Wealthy)
Hattie and the Wild Waves - Barbara Cooney 415

Hattie (Child)
Hattie Be Quiet, Hattie Be Good - Dick Gackenbach 654

Hattie Lou (Cousin)
The Song of the Christmas Mouse - Shirley Rousseau Murphy 1300

Hauser, Citronella (Child)
Thimble Summer - Elizabeth Enright 574

Hawkins (Parent)
Fishman and Charly - Davis Gibbs 691
The Ghost in the Lagoon - Natalie Savage Carlson 293
The Ghost in the Lagoon - Natalie Savage Carlson 293

Hawkins, Charlene "Charly" (Relative)
Fishman and Charly - Davis Gibbs 691

Hawkins, Harrison (Preteen)
Circle of Fire - William H. Hooks 913

Hawkins, Jim (Teenager)
Treasure Island - Robert Louis Stevenson 1749

Hawkins, Timmy (Child)
The Ghost in the Lagoon - Natalie Savage Carlson 293

Hawkins, Tyler "Fishman" (Preteen; Animal Lover)
Fishman and Charly - Davis Gibbs 691

Hayden, Josie (Immigrant; Preteen)
I Met a Traveller - Lillian Hoban 889

Hayes, Andrea (Preteen)
My Other Mother, My Other Father - Harriet Langsam Sobol 1704

Hayes, Bucky (Sports Figure)
Catch That Pass! - Matt Christopher 337

Hayward, John (Preteen)
The Warlock of Westfall - Leonard Everett Fisher 606

Hazel (Rabbit)
Watership Down - Richard Adams 4

Hazell (Businessman)
Danny, the Champion of the World - Roald Dahl 465

Heather (Handicapped)
The Good Luck Dog - Lilo Hess 870

Heather (Child)
Wait Till Helen Comes - Mary Downing Hahn 791

Heather (Teenager)
Winter of Magic's Return - Pamela F. Service 1616

Heck (Store Owner)
The Alligator and His Uncle Tooth: A Novel of the Sea - Geoffrey Hayes 833

Hector (Dog)
A Little Fear - Patricia Wrightson 1958

Heidi (Orphan)
Heidi - Johanna Spyri 1720

Heidi (Preteen)
Voices After Midnight - Richard Peck 1406

Hekenefer (Friend)
I, Tut: The Boy Who Became Pharoah - Miriam Schlein 1595

Helen (Teenager)
The Man in the Woods - Rosemary Wells 1893

Hen, Jenny (Chicken)
Quick Chick - Julia Hoban 887

Henderson, Jenny (Preteen)
A Witch's Garden - Miriam Young 1980

Henley (Preteen)
H, My Name Is Henley - Colby Rodowsky 1538

Henley, Alex (Teenager)
Patty Dillman of Hot Dog Fame - Susan Wojciechowski 1940

Henri (Child)
Hello, I'm Karen - Margaret Sutherland 1771

Henrietta (Preteen)
All-of-a-Kind Family - Sydney Taylor 1787

Henrietta (Chicken)
The Hoboken Chicken Emergency - Daniel Manus Pinkwater 1444

Henry (Worker)
Busybody Nora - Johanna Hurwitz 949

Henry (Child)
Cloudy with a Chance of Meatballs - Judi Barrett 97

Henry (Cat)
Cross-Country Cat - Mary Calhoun 272

Henry (Squirrel)
Henry - Nina Bawden 113

Henry (Child)
Henry and Mudge and the Happy Cat - Cynthia Rylant 1567

Henry, Mack (Maintenance Worker)
Finding Buck McHenry - Alfred Slote 1669

Henshaw, Boyd (Writer)
Dear Mr. Henshaw - Beverly Cleary 350

Herbie (Child)
Emma's Dilemma - Gen LeRoy 1093

Herbie (1st Grader)
Herbie's Troubles - Carol Chapman 317

Herbie (Classmate)
Isabelle the Itch - Constance C. Greene 752

Herbie (Child)
Tackle-22 - Louise Munro Foley 631

Herdman, Claude (Child)
The Best Christmas Pageant Ever - Barbara Robinson 1517

Herdman, Imogene (Child)
The Best Christmas Pageant Ever - Barbara Robinson 1517

Herman (Baker)
What Happened in Hamelin? - Gloria Skurzynski 1659

"Herself" (Grandparent)
Brave Janet Reachfar - Jane Duncan 547

Hershel (Handicapped; Baker)
Cakes and Miracles - Barbara Diamond Goldin 718

Hershel (Child)
Hershel and the Hanukkah Goblins - Eric A. Kimmel 1026

Hester (Child)
Hester the Jester - Ben Shecter 1625

Hickle, Charles "Charlie" (Preteen)
My Mother Got Married and Other Disasters - Barbara Park 1380

Hickory (Toy)
Miss Hickory - Carolyn Sherwin Bailey 83

Hideaway Tom (Beachcomber; Parent)
Storm Boy - Colin Thiele 1802

Higgins, Tally (Preteen)
Tallahassee Higgins - Mary Downing Hahn 790

Higgs, Louise Genevieve (Orphan)
Cat's Magic - Margaret Greaves 740

Hilary (Child)
Afternoon of the Elves - Janet Taylor Lisle 1128
Devil by the Sea - Nina Bawden 112

Hilary (Preteen)
Play the Bach, Dear! - Judith Groch 775

Hildreth, Albert (Firefighter)
In a Blue Velvet Dress - Catherine Sefton 1604

Hill, Brad (Child)
Theo Zephyr - Dean Hughes 933

Hill, Carrie (Teenager; Orphan)
Jenny of the Tetons - Kristiana Gregory 764

Hines, Sue (Sports Figure)
Rusty Fertlanger, Lady's Man - Christi Killien 1024

Hirsch, Stephanie (Preteen; 7th Grader)
Just as Long as We're Together - Judy Blume 156

Hitty (Toy)
Hitty: Her First Hundred Years - Rachel Field 597

Ho, Kien (Preteen; Refugee)
A Boat to Nowhere - Maureen Crane Wartski 1887

Hogan, Harry (Preteen)
Our Sixth-Grade Sugar Babies - Eve Bunting 235

Hogarth (Child)
The Iron Giant: A Story in Five Nights - Ted Hughes 935

Hogg, Elijah (Mule)
Dominic - William Steig 1733

Hogget (Farmer)
Babe: The Gallant Pig - Dick King-Smith 1030

Holbein, Henry (Journalist)
The Robbers - Nina Bawden 116

Holbein, Philip (Child)
The Robbers - Nina Bawden 116

Hold-Your-Nose Billy (Outlaw)
The Whipping Boy - Sid Fleischman 625

Holdsworth, Harry (Preteen)
Harry's Mad - Dick King-Smith 1032

Holland, Cappy (Grandparent)
Blaze - Robert Somerlott 1705

Holland, David (Orphan)
Blaze - Robert Somerlott 1705

Holloway, Melinda "Lindy" (Child)
The Money Room - Eloise Jarvis McGraw 1229

Holloway, Scott "Scotty" (Teenager)
The Money Room - Eloise Jarvis McGraw 1229

Holly (Child)
The Thing in Kat's Attic - Charlotte Towner Graeber 730

Holly, Vesper (Heroine)
The Jedera Adventure - Lloyd Alexander 29

Holmes, Diggery (Preteen)
Hedgehogs in the Closet - Joan Davenport Carris 301

Holmes, Shirlick (Detective)
Shirlick Holmes and the Case of the Wandering Wardrobe - Jane Yolen 1971

Holt, Amy (Preteen)
Haunted Island - Joan Lowery Nixon 1335

Holt, Chris (Teenager)
Haunted Island - Joan Lowery Nixon 1335

Holt, Elizabeth (Parent)
Haunted Island - Joan Lowery Nixon 1335

Homer (Panda)
Henry's Special Delivery - M.C. Delaney 508

Homer (Pig)
Pinch - Larry Callen 277

Homily (Parent)
Poor Stainless: A New Story about the Borrowers - Mary Norton 1345

Honey (Child)
A Certain Small Shepherd - Rebecca Caudill 310

Honey (Teacher)
Matilda - Roald Dahl 468

Honor (Preteen)
Always and Forever Friends - Carole S. Adler 5

Hood, Robin (Hero; Outlaw)
The Outlaws of Sherwood - Robin McKinley 1242

Hook, Jack (Sports Figure)
Frank and Stein and Me - Kin Platt 1451

Hooker, Tice (Bully)
Brushy Mountain - Patricia Pendergraft 1416

Hooper, Christy (Preteen; 5th Grader)
Say Cheese - Betty Bates 104

Hope (Teenager)
My Mom, the Money Nut - Betty Bates 103

Hopkins, Gilly (Preteen)
The Great Gilly Hopkins - Katherine Paterson 1388

Hopkowitz, Heather (Teenager)
What Happened to Heather Hopkowitz? - Charlotte Herman 861

Horace "Brat" (Royalty)
The Whipping Boy - Sid Fleischman 625

Horse, Jake (Recluse)
Banjo - Robert Newton Peck 1407

Horst (Immigrant)
The Horse with Eight Hands - Joan Phipson 1437

Houdini "Goldy" (Hamster)
I, Houdini: The Autobiography of a Self-Educated Hamster - Lynne Reid Banks 1497

Hound, Sherlick (Detective)
Sherlick Hound and the Valentine Mystery - Kelly Goldman 719

Hovanec, Clem (Cousin)
The Kite Song - Margery Evernden 581

Hovanec, Jamie (Child)
The Kite Song - Margery Evernden 581

Hovanec, Ron (Veteran)
The Kite Song - Margery Evernden 581

Hoveler, Callie (Preteen)
The Latchkey Kids - Susan Terris 1794

Hoveler, Rex (Preteen)
The Latchkey Kids - Susan Terris 1794

Howard, Jackie (Preteen; 7th Grader)
My Sister the Meanie - Candice Ransom   1484

Howard, Justice "Jut" (Teenager)
Pets, Vets, and Marty Howard - Joan Davenport
Carris   302

Howard, Justin "Jut" (Preteen)
When the Boys Ran the House - Joan Davenport
Carris   303

Howard, Marty (Teenager)
Hedgehogs in the Closet - Joan Davenport
Carris   301

Howard, Marty (Preteen)
Pets, Vets, and Marty Howard - Joan Davenport
Carris   302

Howard, Marty (Child)
When the Boys Ran the House - Joan Davenport
Carris   303

Howard, Nick (Preteen)
Hedgehogs in the Closet - Joan Davenport
Carris   301

Howard, Sharon (Teenager)
My Sister the Meanie - Candice Ransom   1484

Howard "How" (Teenager)
How's Business? - Alison Prince   1470

Howl (Wizard)
Howl's Moving Castle - Diana Wynne Jones   982

Hubble, Mildred (Witch)
The Worst Witch - Jill Murphy   1299

Huey (Child)
The Stories Julian Tells - Ann Cameron   281

Huggins (Teacher)
Do Bananas Chew Gum? - Jamie Gilson   702

Huggins, Dorothy JoAnna "DorJo" (Friend)
An End to Perfect - Suzanne Newton   1330

Huggins, Henry (Child)
Beezus and Ramona - Beverly Cleary   349

Hugh (Child)
A Game of Catch - Helen Cresswell   444

Hugh (Friend)
Manhattan Is Missing - E.W. Hildick   880

Hughes, Langston (Child; Historical Figure)
Langston Hughes, American Poet - Alice
Walker   1870

Humbert (Preteen)
The Type One Super Robot - Alison Prince   1472

Humphrey (Pig)
Seven Spells to Farewell - Betty Baker   86

Hunor (Twin)
The White Stag - Kate Seredy   1613

Hunter (Wealthy)
Kavik the Wolf Dog - Walt Morey   1286

Hunter, Jeff (Child)
Runaway Stallion - Walt Morey   1287

Hush, Jeremiah (Writer; Monkey)
*The Strange and Exciting Adventures of Jeremiah
Hush* - Uri Shulevitz   1632

Huw (Musician)
The Silver Cow: A Welsh Tale - Susan Cooper   422

Hylyard (Businesswoman)
The Curse of the Egyptian Mummy - Pat
Hutchins   959

I

Ida (Child; Shepherd)
Ida and the Wool Smugglers - Sue Ann
Alderson   24

Ig (Prehistoric Human)
Ig Lives in a Cave - Carol Chapman   318

Imogene (Parent)
It Must've Been the Fish Sticks - Betty Bates   102

Imogene "Impy" (Child)
Impy for Always - Jackie French Koller   1044

Ingalls, Caroline (Parent; Settler)
On the Banks of Plum Creek - Laura Ingalls
Wilder   1911

Ingalls, Carrie (Child; Settler)
By the Shores of Silver Lake - Laura Ingalls
Wilder   1909

Ingalls, Grace (Child; Settler)
By the Shores of Silver Lake - Laura Ingalls
Wilder   1909

Ingalls, Laura (Child; Settler)
By the Shores of Silver Lake - Laura Ingalls
Wilder   1909

Ingalls, Laura (Teenager)
Little Town on the Prairie - Laura Ingalls
Wilder   1910

Ingalls, Laura (Child; Settler)
On the Banks of Plum Creek - Laura Ingalls
Wilder   1911

Ingalls, Mary (Teenager; Handicapped)
Little Town on the Prairie - Laura Ingalls
Wilder   1910

Ingalls, Pa (Parent; Settler)
On the Banks of Plum Creek - Laura Ingalls
Wilder   1911

Inge (Twin)
Farewell, Aunt Isabell - Ilse-Margret Vogel   1858
My Summer Brother - Ilse-Margret Vogel   1859

The Ingrate, Ing (Villain)
Norby, the Mixed-Up Robot - Janet Asimov   62

Ingrid (Friend)
Bailey's Window - Anne Lindbergh   1119

Ira (Recluse)
Ellen Grae - Vera Cleaver   357

Irma (Teenager)
The Hockey Girls - Scott Corbett   424

Iron (Mythical Creature)
The Iron Giant: A Story in Five Nights - Ted
Hughes   935

Irving, Irv (Hero)
It Happened in Pinsk - Arthur Yorinks   1974

Isabel (Rat; Girlfriend)
A Rat's Tale - Tor Seidler   1606

Isabell (Relative; Mentally Ill Person)
Farewell, Aunt Isabell - Ilse-Margret Vogel   1858

Isabelle "Izzy" (Newspaper Carrier)
Isabelle the Itch - Constance C. Greene   752

Iseult (Teenager; Royalty)
Tristan and Iseult - Rosemary Sutcliff   1770

Isidora, Tony (Activist; 8th Grader)
Who Really Killed Cock Robin? - Jean Craighead
George   686

Ivan (Child)
Anna and the Seven Swans - Maida
Silverman   1642

Ivan (Parrot)
Ivan the Great - Isabel Langis Cusack   460

Ivan (Preteen)
Portrait of Ivan - Paula Fox   640

Ivanovich, Svetlana (Teacher)
Thirteen Ways to Sink a Sub - Jamie Gilson   705

Ivy (Preteen)
Something Suspicious - Kathryn Osebold
Galbraith   662

Izzy (Grandparent)
After the Rain - Norma Fox Mazer   1217

J

Jack (Child)
The Big Green Book - Robert Graves   734
The Birthday Tree - Paul Fleischman   611

Jack (Step-Parent)
Don't Hurt Laurie! - Willo Davis Roberts   1509

Jack (Child)
Fourth Grade Wizards - Barthe DeClements   498

Jack (Traveller)
My Trip to Alpha I - Alfred Slote   1674

Jack (Child)
School Can Wait - Tessa Dahl   471

Jack (Vagrant)
The Stones - Janet Hickman   875

Jack (Child)
This Is the House Where Jack Lives - Joan
Heilbroner   847

Jackson, Cap (Worker)
Roosevelt Grady - Louisa R. Shotwell   1626

Jackson, Ian (Student)
In Summer Light - Zibby Oneal   1360

Jackson, Mark (Coach; Scientist)
Too Much Magic - Betsy Sterman   1743

Jackson, Matthew (Child)
Purple Climbing Days - Patricia Reilly Giff   697

Jackson, Simon "Spikey" (Preteen)
Invasion of the Comet People - Philip Curtis   459

Jacob (Preteen)
Jacob and Owl - Ada Graham   731

Jacob (Friend)
Maurice's Room - Paula Fox   637

Jacob (Child)
Spring Rider - John Shults Lawson   1082

Jacob (Spirit)
The Trouble with Jacob - Eloise Jarvis
McGraw   1231

Jacobious (Scientist)
Jonas McFee, A.T.P. - Sarah Sargent   1587

Jacobs, Ambrose "Bosie" (Child)
Kept in the Dark - Nina Bawden   114

Jacobs, Arianne "Ari" (Preteen)
The Hand-Me-Down Kid - Francine Pascal   1384

Jacobs, Clara (Child)
Kept in the Dark - Nina Bawden   114

Jacobs, Noel (Child)
Kept in the Dark - Nina Bawden   114

Jake (Preteen)
Danger in Quicksand Swamp - Bill Wallace   1875

Jake (Child)
A Few Fair Days - Jane Gardam   665

Jake (Preteen; Sports Figure)
The Hour of the Wolf - Patricia Calvert   279

Jake (Step-Parent)
Like Jake and Me - Mavis Jukes   988

James (Preteen)
A Box of Nothing - Peter Dickinson   520
The Ghosts - Antonia Barber   94

James (Child)
No Bean Sprouts, Please! - Constance Hiser   885
The Toothpaste Millionaire - Jean Merrill   1259

James, Clint (Boarder)
Following the Mystery Man - Mary Downing
   Hahn   788

James, Mary (Child; Settler)
My Sister's Keeper - Beverly Butler   253

Jameson, Frank (Parent)
My Robot Buddy - Alfred Slote   1673

Jameson, Greg (Detective)
Mystery of the Gingerbread House - Wylly Folk St.
   John   1721

Jameson, Jack (Child)
My Robot Buddy - Alfred Slote   1673

Jameson, Ron (Detective)
Mystery of the Gingerbread House - Wylly Folk St.
   John   1721

Jamie (Child; Handicapped)
A Certain Small Shepherd - Rebecca Caudill   310

Jamie (Child)
Chester - Mary Francis Shura   1634

Jamie (Child; Runaway)
From the Mixed-Up Files of Mrs. Basil E. Frankweiler
   - E.L. Konigsburg   1045

Jamie (Child)
He's My Brother - Joe Lasker   1070

Jamie (Preteen)
Kid Power - Susan Beth Pfeffer   1432

Jamie (Child)
Part-Time Boy - Elizabeth T. Billington   146

Jamie (Preteen)
Rattlesnake Cave - Evelyn Sibley Lampman   1064

Jamie (Teenager)
The Search for Jim McGwynn - Marcia
   Wood   1950

Jamie (Child)
Shadows - Dennis Haseley   823
A Taste of Blackberries - Doris Buchanan
   Smith   1684

Jan (Preteen)
Borrowed Summer - Marion Walker Doren   531

Jane (Friend)
The Big Hello - Janet Schulman   1598

Jane (Child)
Five Children and It - Edith Nesbit   1323

Jane (Dinosaur)
The Friends of the Loony Lake Monster - Frank
   Bonham   171

Jane (Child)
The Green Ghost of Appleville - Jean
   Marzollo   1206
Jane-Emily - Patricia Clapp   343

Jane (Relative)
Liza Lou and the Yeller Belly Swamp - Mercer
   Mayer   1211

Jane (Classmate)
Randall's Wall - Carol Fenner   592

Janet (Teenager)
Devil by the Sea - Nina Bawden   112

Janetta (Child)
Grandaddy's Place - Helen V. Griffith   773

Janey (Preteen)
Blue Willow - Doris Gates   675

Janey (Friend)
Dreams of Victory - Ellen Conford   401

Janna (Preteen)
The Borrowed House - Hilda Van Stockum   1850

Jansen, Jennifer "Cam" (Detective)
Cam Jansen and the Mystery at the Monkey House -
   David A. Adler   10

Jarvis, Steve (Neighbor)
The Berkley Street Six Pack - Mary Francis
   Shura   1633

Jason (Child)
The Bells of Christmas - Virginia Hamilton   800
The Bongleweed - Helen Cresswell   442

Jason (Preteen; Sports Figure)
Finding Buck McHenry - Alfred Slote   1669

Jason (Detective; Child)
Follow That Ghost! - Dale Fife   600

Jason (Teenager)
Fourteen - Marilyn Sachs   1577

Jason (Hero)
*The Golden Fleece and the Heroes Who Lived
   Before Achilles* - Padraic Colum   397

Jason (Child)
The Green Book - Jill Paton Walsh   1393
Jace the Ace - Joanne Rocklin   1525

Jason (Preteen)
Katie John and Heathcliff - Mary Calhoun   274
Sonia Begonia - Joanne Rocklin   1526

Jasons, Rebecca (Child)
*The Robot and Rebecca: The Mystery of the Code
   Carrying Kids* - Jane Yolen   1970

Jean (Child)
Homesick: My Own Story - Jean Fritz   652

Jeanne (Parent)
The Grizzly - Annabel Johnson   974

Jeannie (Child)
My Daddy Was a Soldier - Deborah Kogan
   Ray   1494

Jebb, Bess (Servant)
The Huffler - Jill Paton Walsh   1394

Jebb, Ned (Child)
The Huffler - Jill Paton Walsh   1394

Jed (Handyman)
The Rocking Horse Secret - Rumer Godden   715

Jeeter, Howard (Child)
The Kid in the Red Jacket - Barbara Park   1378

Jeff (Child)
Daniel's Duck - Clyde Robert Bulla   225
Foxy - Helen V. Griffith   771
The House on Hackman's Hill - Joan Lowery
   Nixon   1337

Jeff (Teenager)
It's Not the End of the World - Judy Blume   155

Jefferson, Thomas (Grandparent; Historical
   Figure)
Grand Papa and Ellen Aroon - F.N. Monjo   1275

Jella (Child)
The Wheel on the School - Meindert DeJong   507

Jem (Camper)
Jem's Island - Kathryn Lasky   1072

Jemmy (Servant)
The Whipping Boy - Sid Fleischman   625

Jenner, Annie (Preteen)
My Brother Stevie - Eleanor Clymer   372

Jenner, Stevie (Preteen)
My Brother Stevie - Eleanor Clymer   372

Jennie (Child)
Dinnie Abbie Sister-R-R! - Riki Levinson   1102

Jennifer (Child)
I Wish Laura's Mommy Was My Mommy - Barbara
   Power   1463

Jennifer (Witch; 5th Grader)
*Jennifer, Hecate, Macbeth, William McKinley and
   Me, Elizabeth* - E.L. Konigsburg   1046

Jennifer (Preteen)
Nothing's Fair in Fifth Grade - Barthe
   DeClements   500

Jennifer (Child)
Touch the Moon - Marion Dane Bauer   110

Jennifer "Jenny" (Sports Figure)
Jenny and the Tennis Nut - Janet Schulman   1599

Jenny (Preteen)
A Certain Magic - Doris Orgel   1362

Jenny (Relative)
Chloris and the Creeps - Kin Platt   1450

Jenny (Preteen)
Just Between Us - Susan Beth Pfeffer   1431

Jenny (Child)
My Dog and the Birthday Mystery - David A.
   Adler   13
Red Dog - Bill Wallace   1877

Jeremy (Child; Sports Figure)
The Backyard Basketball Superstar - Monica
   Klein   1038

Jeremy (Child; Babysitter)
The Magic of the Glits - Carole S. Adler   9

Jeremy (Child)
Mama's Going to Buy You a Mockingbird - Jean
   Little   1135
Sea Swan - Kathryn Lasky   1073
What If They Knew? - Patricia Hermes   865
With a Wave of the Wand - Mark Jonathan
   Harris   817

Jeroboam (Jerboa)
The Dawn Seekers - Carol Hamilton   798

Jerome (Teenager)
The Moves Make the Man: A Novel - Bruce
   Brooks   210

Jessica (Writer)
Daphne's Book - Mary Downing Hahn   785

Jessica (Preteen)
A Family Project - Sarah Ellis   569

Jessica (Detective)
Maximilian, You're the Greatest - Joseph
   Rosenbloom   1547

Jessica (Preteen)
Truth or Dare - Susan Beth Pfeffer   1433

Jessie (Child; Dancer)
Maybe She Forgot - Ellen Kandoian 992

Jessie (Child)
The Sea Child - Carolyn Sloan 1667

Jessie (Guardian)
Alan and the Animal Kingdom - Isabelle Holland 899

Jethro (Child)
Jethro and the Jumbie - Susan Cooper 420

Jiggs (Store Owner)
The Dancing Cats of Applesap - Janet Taylor Lisle 1129

Jill (Preteen)
Blubber - Judy Blume 153

Jill (Child)
I Hate Red Rover - Joan M. Lexau 1116
Something Queer at the Library: A Mystery - Elizabeth Levy 1109

Jim (Teenager)
Barefoot a Thousand Miles - Patsey Gray 739

Jim (Child)
Shipwreck - Vera G. Cumberlege 451
When Will I Read? - Miriam Cohen 385

Jimmie (Child)
Eddie's Valuable Property - Carolyn Haywood 838

Jimmy (Child)
Amelia's Flying Machine - Barbara Shook Hazen 839
A Boy Called Fish - Alison Morgan 1289

Jimmy (Captive)
Island of the Loons - Dayton O. Hyde 962

Jimmy Joe (Bully; 1st Grader)
Herbie's Troubles - Carol Chapman 317

Jingle, Toby (Knight)
Sir Toby Jingle's Beastly Journey - Wallace Tripp 1824

Jinny (Teenager)
On the Edge - Gillian Cross 449

Jinx (Cat)
Freddy the Detective - Walter R. Brooks 212

Jo (Mythical Creature)
The 24-Hour Genie - Lila McGinnis 1225

Jo (Captive)
The Rich Kid - Bill Gillham 701

Jo (Shepherd)
Waiting for Anya - Michael Morpurgo 1291

Jockimo, Paul (Child; Handicapped)
Don't Feel Sorry for Paul - Bernard Wolf 1942

Jodi (Child)
In Our House, Scott Is My Brother - Carole S. Adler 8

Jodril (Royalty)
Sandwriter - Monica Hughes 934

Joe (Teenager)
And You Give Me a Pain, Elaine - Stella Pevsner 1424

Joe (Grandparent; Indian)
Brother Moose - Betty Levin 1096

Joe (Fish)
The Carp in the Bathtub - Barbara Cohen 381

Joe (Child; Invalid)
The Empty Window - Anne Evelyn Bunting 229

Joe (Preteen)
Knights of the Kitchen Table - Jon Scieszka 1601

Joe (Child)
Miracles on Maple Hill - Virginia Sorensen 1706
The Sea Egg - L.M. Boston 178
Sidewise Stories From Wayside School - Louis Sacher 1571

Joel (Friend)
The Bronze King - Suzy McKee Charnas 320

Joel (Child)
On My Honor - Marion Dane Bauer 108

Joey (Child)
Baseball and Butterflies - Karen Lynn Williams 1922

Joey (Handicapped)
The Hayburners - Gene Smith 1687

Joey (Child)
Trust in the Unexpected - Gunnel Linde 1122

Johansen, Annemarie (Preteen)
Number the Stars - Lois Lowry 1153

Johansen, Kirsti (Child)
Number the Stars - Lois Lowry 1153

Joher, Nuell (Explorer)
Planet out of the Past - James Lincoln Collier 393

John (Child)
All Because I'm Older - Phyllis Reynolds Naylor 1312

John (Artisan)
Boy Without a Name - Penelope Lively 1136

John (Streetperson)
A Dog on Barkham Street - Mary Stolz 1753

John, Abigail (Preteen)
Always Abigail - Joyce St. Peter 1722

Johnnie (Pig)
The Peppermint Pig - Nina Bawden 115

Johnson, Bunny (Child)
Captain Hook, That's Me - Ada B. Litchfield 1131

Johnson, James "Jimmy Jo" (Musician)
Come Sing, Jimmy Jo - Katherine Paterson 1387

Johnson, Jerome (Handicapped)
Ride the Red Cycle - Harriette Robinet 1515

Johnson, Jerry (Child)
Five-Finger Discount - Barthe DeClements 497

Johnson, Jerry Lee (Musician)
Come Sing, Jimmy Jo - Katherine Paterson 1387

Johnson, Joe (Military Personnel)
Runaway Balloon: The Last Flight of Confederate Air Force One - Burke Davis 486

Johnson, Joey (Child)
Cave-in at Mason's Mine - Bessie Holland Heck 842

Johnson, Judy (Handicapped)
Captain Hook, That's Me - Ada B. Litchfield 1131

Johnson, Olive (Musician)
Come Sing, Jimmy Jo - Katherine Paterson 1387

Johnson, Sylvester "Scooter" (Friend)
The Over-the-Hill Ghost - Ruth Calif 276

Johnson, Tilly (Teenager)
Ride the Red Cycle - Harriette Robinet 1515

Jon (Preteen)
Destination Unknown - Dale Fife 599

Jonas (Child; 3rd Grader)
Frankie Is Staying Back - Ron Roy 1557

Jonas (Child)
Two Short and One Long - Nina Ring Aamundsen 1

Jonathan (Royalty)
Alanna: The First Adventure - Tamora Pierce 1440

Jonathan (Child)
Bears on Hemlock Mountain - Alice Dalgliesh 472

Jonathan (Preteen)
The Wishing People - Nina Beachcroft 121

Jonathan (Wizard)
The House with a Clock in Its Walls - John Bellaris 129

Jones, A. Roberta "Abby" (Detective)
Have You Seen Hyacinth Macaw? - Patricia Reilly Giff 694

Jones, Clyde (Hunter)
The Day the Circus Came to Lone Tree - Glen Rounds 1554

Jones, Copper (Preteen)
No Place for Me - Barthe DeClements 499

Jones, Darcy (Streetperson)
The Robbers - Nina Bawden 116

Jones, Earl (Preteen)
Reserved for Mark Anthony Crowder - Alison Smith 1677

Jones, Jed (Relative; Guardian)
Shades of Gray - Carolyn Reeder 1496

Jones, Jeremiah (Child)
Jeremiah in the Dark Woods - Janet Ahlberg 15

Jones, John D. (Child; Vacationer)
The Animal, the Vegetable, and John D. Jones - Betsy Byars 256

Jones, John Quincy (Detective)
Sebastian (Super Sleuth) and the Bone to Pick Mystery - Mary Blount Christian 333

Jones, Jupiter (Detective)
Alfred Hitchcock and the Three Investigators in the Secret of Shark Reef - William Arden 53

Jones, Kim (Preteen)
Truth or Consequences - Miriam Young 1979

Jones, Maggie "Margo" (Witch)
No Place for Me - Barthe DeClements 499

Jones, Meg (Cousin)
Shades of Gray - Carolyn Reeder 1496

Jones, Mel (Musician)
Mystery of the Hard Luck Rodeo - Susan Saunders 1589

Jones, Perfecta D. (Preteen)
The Interesting Thing That Happened at Perfect Acres, Inc. - Barbara Brooks Wallace 1871

Jones, Peter (Friend)
The Box of Delights - John Masefield 1208

Jones, Robby (Teenager)
Lions in the Way - Bella Rodman 1534

Jones, Rufus (Rooster)
Stall Buddies - Penny Pollack 1454

Jones, Stacy (Preteen)
P.J. Clover, Private Eye: The Case of the Missing Mouse - Susan Meyers 1260

Jones, Weddy (Explorer)
Planet out of the Past - James Lincoln Collier 393

Jones, William (Child)
Footsteps - Leon Garfield 670

Joralemon, Jerry (Friend)
One of Us - Nikki Amdur 38

Jordan, Katy (Preteen)
A Sudden Change of Family - Mary Jane Auch 67

Jordan, Linda (Parent)
A Sudden Change of Family - Mary Jane Auch 67

Jordan, Nip (Maintenance Worker)
The Great Ringtail Garbage Caper - Timothy Foote 632

Jordan, Paula (Teenager)
Mystery at Crane's Landing - Marcella Thum 1810

Jorgenson, Alex (Aged Person)
The Hammerhead Light - Colin Thiele 1800

Joseph (Orphan)
Alone in the Wild Forest - Isaac Bashevis Singer 1652

Joseph (Child; 2nd Grader)
Joseph on the Subway Train - Kathleen Benson 138

Joseph (Teenager)
Trumpeter of Krakow - Eric P. Kelly 1009

Josepha (Bully)
A Tangled Web - Hannelore Valencak 1839

Josh (Cat)
Beethoven's Cat - Elisabet McHugh 1234

Joshua (Slave)
The Ballad of Belle Dorcas - William H. Hooks 912

Joshua, Adam (Child)
The Monster in the 3rd Dresser Drawer and Other Stories about Adam Joshua - Janice Lee Smith 1688

Josiah (Child)
Stay Away From Simon! - Carol Carrick 297

Josie (Preteen)
Josie's Beau - Natalie Honeycutt 910

Josie (Friend)
Step on a Crack - Mary Anderson 46

Joss (Child)
Beat the Turtle Drum - Constance C. Greene 748

Jozek (Refugee)
The Man From the Other Side - Uri Orlev 1365

Juan (Child; Immigrant)
Maria Luisa - Winifred Madison 1175

Juan (Child)
The Most Beautiful Place in the World - Ann Cameron 280

Jubilee (Child)
Young Nick and Jubilee - Leon Garfield 672

Judd-Sprocket, Quincey (Industrialist)
The Blood and Thunder Adventure on Hurricane Peak - Margaret Mahy 1179

Judge Benjamin (Dog)
Judge Benjamin, Superdog - Judith Whitelock McInerney 1235

Judy (Child)
Jumanji - Chris Van Allsburg 1840

Jules (Teacher)
Sidewise Stories From Wayside School - Louis Sacher 1571

Julia (Grandparent)
My Daniel - Pam Conrad 409

Julia (Preteen; Runaway)
The Runaways - Ruth Thomas 1807

Julia (Teenager)
Summer of Fear - Lois Duncan 550

Julian (Child)
Gone-Away Lake - Elizabeth Enright 572
The Stories Julian Tells - Ann Cameron 281

Julius (Child)
Luke Was There - Eleanor Clymer 371

Jumbo (Elephant)
Big Max - Kin Platt 1449

Jumping Mouse (Mouse)
The Story of Jumping Mouse - John Steptoe 1740

Justin (Preteen)
Justin and the Best Biscuits in the World - Mildred Pitts Walter 1880
Miracle at Clement's Pond - Patricia Pendergraft 1418

Justin (Nobleman; Knight)
A Tournament of Knights - Joe Lasker 1071

K

Kaila (Handicapped)
The Ice Bear - Betty Levin 1097

Kalle (Child; Orphan)
Oma - Peter Hartling 822

Kane, Minty (Witch)
Moondial - Helen Cresswell 445

Kane, Stanley (Bully)
Wendy and the Bullies - Nancy K. Robinson 1521

Kano (Hunter; Indian)
The Way of Our People - Arnold A. Griese 766

Karana (Indian)
Island of the Blue Dolphins - Scott O'Dell 1353

Karen (Child; Runaway)
Foster Child - Marion Dane Bauer 107

Karen (Child)
Hello, I'm Karen - Margaret Sutherland 1771

Karen (Preteen)
It's Not the End of the World - Judy Blume 155

Karsten (Neighbor)
The House on Hackman's Hill - Joan Lowery Nixon 1337

Kasha, Lukas (Teenager; Apprentice)
The First Two Lives of Lukas Kasha - Lloyd Alexander 27

Kate (Child)
Arthur's Baby - Marc T. Brown 216

Kate (Preteen)
Beat the Turtle Drum - Constance C. Greene 748

Kate (Preteen; Detective—Amateur)
The Case of the Mind Reading Mommies - Elizabeth Levy 1106

Kate (Teenager)
Cloud Horse - Jill Pinkwater 1446

Kate (Child; Computer Expert)
The Computer Nut - Betsy Byars 261

Kate (Cat)
Digby and Kate - Barbara Baker 84

Kate (Child)
Doctor Change - Joanna Cole 388
A Game of Catch - Helen Cresswell 444

Kate (Orphan)
Miss Know-It-All and the Three Ring Circus - Carol Beach York 1975

Kate (Preteen)
The Toothpaste Millionaire - Jean Merrill 1259

Katherine (Wealthy; Mine Owner)
My Trip to Alpha I - Alfred Slote 1674

Kathleen (Child)
Dogsbody - Diana Wynne Jones 981

Katie (Child)
Chip Rogers, Computer Whiz - Seymour Simon 1648
Love You, Soldier - Amy Hest 872
Trust in the Unexpected - Gunnel Linde 1122

Katrin (Relative)
Step on a Crack - Mary Anderson 46

Katy (Child)
My Mother's Getting Married - Joan Drescher 537

Katy (Innkeeper)
The Ghost in the Noonday Sun - Sid Fleischman 620

Katz (Librarian)
Harry in Trouble - Barbara Ann Porte 1459

Katz, Alex (Scavenger)
The Amazing Memory of Harvey Bean - Molly Cone 398

Katz, Dottie (Spouse)
The Amazing Memory of Harvey Bean - Molly Cone 398

Katz, Isaac (Teenager)
Thin Air - David Getz 689

Katz, Jacob (Teenager)
Thin Air - David Getz 689

Kavik (Dog)
Kavik the Wolf Dog - Walt Morey 1286

Kayak (Eskimo)
Frozen Fire - James A. Houston 917

Kazul (Dragon)
Dealing with Dragons - Patricia C. Wrede 1953

Kearns, Jennifer Wingford "Jenny" (Neighbor)
My Own Private Sky - Delores Beckman 127

Keating, Caroline (Preteen)
The Horse in the Attic - Eleanor Clymer 370

Keiran (Child)
The Tram to Bondi Beach - Elizabeth Hathorn 825

Keith (Child; Vacationer)
The Mouse and the Motorcycle - Beverly Cleary 352

Kellerman, Adie (Child)
A Room Made of Windows - Eleanor Cameron 285

Kelly (Child)
December Stillness - Mary Downing Hahn 786
Glass Slippers Give You Blisters - Mary Jane Auch 66

Kelly, Bob (Miner)
The Sky Is Free - Mavis Thorpe Clark 346

Kelly, Frances (Child)
A Family Apart - Joan Lowery Nixon 1333

Kelly, Mary Beth (Child)
Cookies and Crutches - Judy Delton 511

Kelly, Ned (Student)
Ned Kelly and the City of the Bees - Thomas Keneally 1013

Kelly, Petey (Child)
A Family Apart - Joan Lowery Nixon 1333

Kelly, Suzanne (Child)
Dynamite Dinah - Claudia Mills 1268

Kemp, Polly (Child)
The Wish Giver: Three Tales of Coven Tree - Bill Brittain 206

Ken (Teenager; Detective)
Adventure in Granada - Walter Dean Myers 1302

Ken (Teenager)
Hold Fast - Kevin Major 1185

Kendra (Teenager)
Remember Me to Harold Square - Paula Danziger 480

Kennedy, Cass (Child)
Courage at Indian Deep - Jane Resh Thomas 1805

Kennedy, Dean (Collector)
Highpockets - John R. Tunis 1826

Kenny (Teenager)
Don't Call Me Orphan - Michael Leach 1087

Kenny (Child)
Some Friend - Carol Carrick 296
Something Upstairs: A Tale of Ghosts - Avi 72

Kerne, Ned (Tourist)
The Beachcombers - Helen Cresswell 441

Kerry (Preteen)
Grandpa and Me - Stephanie S. Tolan 1816

Kerry (Twin)
The Robot Birthday - Eve Bunting 237

Kidd, Bertie (Child)
Dump Days - Jerry Spinelli 1714

Kidd, J.D. (Preteen)
Dump Days - Jerry Spinelli 1714

Kiki (Step-Parent)
Maggie Forevermore - Joan Lowery Nixon 1339

Kilroy (Whale)
Kilroy and the Gull - Nathaniel Benchley 133

Kim (Preteen)
I Am Susannah - Libby Gleeson 709

Kim (Handicapped)
I Can't Always Hear You - Joy Zelonky 1985

Kim (Preteen)
Mystery on Ice - Barbara Corcoran 431

Kimball, Dorrie (Preteen)
Me and the Terrible Two - Ellen Conford 407

Kincaid, Margaret Drusilla (Child)
The Blue Empress - Kathy Pelta 1415

Kincaid, Stormy (Teenager)
Mad, Mad Monday - Herma Silverstein 1643

King (Dog)
The Lake Is on Fire - Maureen Crane Wartski 1888

King, Dave (Teenager; Sports Figure)
The Kid Who Batted 1000 - Bob Allison 35

King, John Fitzgerald "Jay" (Sports Figure)
Showboat in the Backcourt - William Campbell Gault 678

Kinsella (Doctor)
Hang Tough, Paul Mather - Alfred Slote 1671

Kipp (Badger)
Odyssey From River Bend - Tom McGowen 1227

Kipper (Child)
Peppermints in the Parlor - Barbara Brooks Wallace 1873

Kippy (Child)
Buster Loves Buttons - Fran Manushkin 1191

Kirby (Preteen)
Last Was Lloyd - Doris Buchanan Smith 1681

Kirk (Child)
Everett Anderson's Friend - Lucille Clifton 365

Kirk, Abigail (Teenager)
Playing Beatie Bow - Ruth Park 1382

Kirk, Kathy (Parent)
Playing Beatie Bow - Ruth Park 1382

Kit (Teenager; Care Giver)
I Am the Universe - Barbara Corcoran 430

Kit (Preteen)
So You Want to Be a Wizard - Diane Duane 541

Kit (Child)
The Thing in Kat's Attic - Charlotte Towner Graeber 730

Kit Fox (Indian)
Dawn Rider - Jan Hudson 929

Kitamura (Neighbor; Child-Care Giver)
The Rooster Who Understood Japanese - Yoshiko Uchida 1838

Kitty (Relative)
A Few Fair Days - Jane Gardam 665

Kitty (Teenager)
The Watcher in the Garden - Joan Phipson 1439

Klara (Child)
The Glassblower's Children - Maria Gripe 774

Klas (Child)
The Glassblower's Children - Maria Gripe 774

Knockwurst, Burton Bell Whitney (Child)
Burton's Zoom Zoom Va-Room Machine - Dorothy Haas 781

Knockwurst, Edisonia (Child)
Burton's Zoom Zoom Va-Room Machine - Dorothy Haas 781

Knockwurst, Newton (Child)
Burton's Zoom Zoom Va-Room Machine - Dorothy Haas 781

Kobalt (Carpenter)
Dorp Dead - Julia Cunningham 452

Konrad (Android; Child)
Konrad - Christine Nostlinger 1346

Kopeckie, Horace (Eccentric)
Lizard Music - Daniel Manus Pinkwater 1445

Korngold (Housekeeper)
The Gods in Winter - Patricia Miles 1265

Korshak, Meg (Teenager)
A Ghost in the Window - Betty Ren Wright 1956

Koshansky, Olya (Refugee)
Homecoming - Elsa Posell 1461

Kossan (Child)
The Battle Horse - Harry Kullman 1059

Kozodoy (Teacher)
This School is Driving Me Crazy - Nat Hentoff 858

Krabat (Teenager; Apprentice)
The Satanic Mill - Otfried Preussler 1466

Kramer, Kelly "Killer" (Sports Figure; 4th Grader)
Benjy the Football Hero - Jean Van Leeuwen 1845

Krampner, Seth (Step-Parent)
Happily Ever After.Almost - Judie Wolkoff 1945

Krinkle, Cindy (Preteen)
Me and the Weirdos - Jane Sutton 1772

Krinkle, Smith (Parent)
Me and the Weirdos - Jane Sutton 1772

Krock, Jonah (Student)
Banana Blitz - Florence Parry Heide 843

Krupnik, Anastasia (Teenager)
Anastasia, Ask Your Analyst - Lois Lowry 1151

Krupnik, Anastasia (Child)
Anastasia Krupnik - Lois Lowry 1150

Krupnik, Sam (Child)
All About Sam - Lois Lowry 1149

KT (Preteen)
I Hate Being Gifted - Patricia Hermes 863

Kudlah (Parent)
The Secret of the Seal - Deborah Davis 487

Kurihara, Emiko "Emi" (Friend)
Journey to Topaz - Yoshiko Uchida 1837

Kwami (Preteen)
Mojo and the Russians - Walter Dean Myers 1303

Kyo (Preteen; Hunter)
The Secret of the Seal - Deborah Davis 487

L

La Belle, Little Little (Dwarf; Teenager)
Little Little - M.E. Kerr 1017

Lacey (Preteen)
Return to Bitter Creek - Doris Buchanan Smith 1682

Lacey, Jonathon (Child)
Sugaring Time - Kathryn Lasky 1074

Lady Sharon (Dog)
Sebastian (Super Sleuth) and the Bone to Pick Mystery - Mary Blount Christian 333

Ladybug, Lewis O. (Detective)
The Owlstone Crown - X.J. Kennedy 1016

Lafcadio (Lion)
Lafcadio, the Lion Who Shot Back - Shel Silverstein 1645

Lafferty, Lily (Child)
Lily and Miss Liberty - Carla Stevens 1744

Lake, Stevie (Preteen; Equestrian)
Horse Crazy - Bonnie Bryant 220

Lamb, Louis (Preteen; 6th Grader)
What Happened to Mr. Forester? - Gary W. Barger 96

Lambchop, Arthur (Child)
A Lamp for the Lambchops - Jeff Brown 215

Lambchop, Stanley (Child)
A Lamp for the Lambchops - Jeff Brown 215

Lambert, Beth (Preteen)
Philip Hall Likes Me, I Reckon Maybe - Bette Greene 746

Lambert, Lynette (Child)
After Fifth Grade, the World - Claudia Mills 1266

Lambert, Mary Ann (Activist; 8th Grader)
Who Really Killed Cock Robin? - Jean Craighead George 686

Lamont, Lucky (Robot)
Finders Keepers - Emily Rodda 1529

Lisa (Preteen)
With You and Without You - Ann M. Martin 1201

Little, Amanda (Writer)
Phantom of Walkaway Hill - Edward Fenton 594

Little, Cephus "Crab" (Parent; Criminal)
Somewhere in the Darkness - Walter Dean Myers 1304

Little, Frederick C. (Mouse; Parent)
Stuart Little - E.B. White 1900

Little, George (Mouse)
Stuart Little - E.B. White 1900

Little, Jimmy (Teenager)
Somewhere in the Darkness - Walter Dean Myers 1304

Little, Stuart (Mouse)
Stuart Little - E.B. White 1900

Little Ann (Dog)
Where the Red Fern Grows - Wilson Rawls 1493

Little Bear (Indian)
The Indian in the Cupboard - Lynne Reid Banks 1498

Little Bear (Bear)
Little Bear - Else Holmelund Minarik 1272

Little Black (Horse)
Little Black, a Pony - Walter Farley 589

Little Bub (Horse)
Justin Morgan Had a Horse - Marguerite Henry 853

Little Cigarette (Orphan)
Flight of the Sparrow - Julia Cunningham 453

Little Cloud (Indian)
The Friendly Wolf - Paul Goble 712

Little Prince (Traveller; Royalty)
The Little Prince - Antoine de Saint-Exupery 1581

Liza (Orphan)
The Clown - Barbara Corcoran 429

Liza Lou (Child)
Liza Lou and the Yeller Belly Swamp - Mercer Mayer 1211

Lizard, Granny (Witch)
The Ballad of Belle Dorcas - William H. Hooks 912

Lizzie (Preteen)
Something Suspicious - Kathryn Osebold Galbraith 662

Lloyd (Preteen)
Last Was Lloyd - Doris Buchanan Smith 1681

Loc (Preteen; Refugee)
A Boat to Nowhere - Maureen Crane Wartski 1887

Lof (Animal; Alien)
The Package in Hyperspace - Janet Asimov 63

Logan, Cassie (Child)
Roll of Thunder, Hear My Cry - Mildred D. Taylor 1786

Logan, Clayton "Little Man" (Child)
Roll of Thunder, Hear My Cry - Mildred D. Taylor 1786

Logan, Mary (Teacher)
Roll of Thunder, Hear My Cry - Mildred D. Taylor 1786

Logan, Stacey (Preteen)
The Friendship - Mildred D. Taylor 1784
Mississippi Bridge - Mildred D. Taylor 1785

Long, Tom (Child)
Tom's Midnight Garden - Philippa Pearce 1401

Long Arrow (Naturalist)
The Voyages of Dr. Doolittle - Hugh Lofting 1144

Longstocking, Pippi (Orphan)
Pippi Longstocking - Astrid Lindgren 1124

Loomis, John (Engineer)
Z for Zachariah - Robert C. O'Brien 1348

Lord, Randall (Preteen)
Randall's Wall - Carol Fenner 592

Loring, Jenny (Child)
Remember Me When I Am Dead - Carol Beach York 1976

Loring, Margaret (Step-Parent)
Remember Me When I Am Dead - Carol Beach York 1976

Loring, Sara (Teenager)
Remember Me When I Am Dead - Carol Beach York 1976

Lorraine (Preteen)
Dear Baby - Joanne Rocklin 1524

Lothrop (Parent; Religious)
A Time to Keep Silent - Gloria Whelan 1898

Lothrop, Clair (Teenager; Handicapped)
A Time to Keep Silent - Gloria Whelan 1898

Lott, Georgina (Narrator)
The Borning Room - Paul Fleischman 612

Lott, Titus (Teenager)
The Borning Room - Paul Fleischman 612

Lou (Preteen)
Two Ways about It - Judy Frank Mearian 1253

Louella "Lou" (Teenager; 7th Grader)
Just Good Friends - Dean Marney 1195

Louis (Child)
The Ears of Louis - Constance C. Greene 749

Louis (Swan)
The Trumpet of the Swan - E.B. White 1901

Louisa (Orphan)
Brother Moose - Betty Levin 1096

Louisa (Child)
Prairie Songs - Pam Conrad 410

Louise (Fox)
Fox on the Job - James Marshall 1198

Louise (Child)
Lionel at Large - Stephen Krensky 1056

Louise (Friend)
Love You, Soldier - Amy Hest 872

Louise (Child)
Us and Uncle Fraud - Lois Lowry 1156

Lovett (Handicapped; Aged Person)
The Watcher in the Garden - Joan Phipson 1439

Lowery, Natalie (Child; Occultist)
The Berkley Street Six Pack - Mary Francis Shura 1633

Luath (Dog)
The Incredible Journey - Sheila Burnford 250

Lucas, Shanteray (Friend)
They're All Named Wildfire - Nancy Springer 1718

Luccock, Emily (Heiress; Servant)
Peppermints in the Parlor - Barbara Brooks Wallace 1873

Lucie (Child)
A Family Project - Sarah Ellis 569

Lucinda (Child)
Beloved Benjamin Is Waiting - Jean Karl 994

Lucky (Dog)
A Boy in the Doghouse - Betsy Duffey 543

Lucy (Child)
Emma's Dilemma - Gen LeRoy 1093
A Few Fair Days - Jane Gardam 665

Lucy (Preteen)
The Ghosts - Antonia Barber 94

Lucy (Child)
The Power of the Rellard - Carolyn F. Logan 1145

Lucy (Teenager)
Stay Away From Simon! - Carol Carrick 297

Ludie (Teenager; Abuse Victim)
Ludie's Song - Dirlie Herlihy 859

Ludwig "Wiggie" (Cat)
Beethovan's Cat - Elisabet McHugh 1234

Luke (Preteen)
Beauty - Bill Wallace 1874

Luke (Child)
Days of Courage; A Medieval Adventure - Niels Jensen 973

Luke (Social Worker)
Luke Was There - Eleanor Clymer 371

Luke (Preteen)
Voices After Midnight - Richard Peck 1406

Luke (Religious)
The Door in the Wall - Marguerite De Angeli 490

Lullah (Child)
The Empty Schoolhouse - Natalie Savage Carlson 291

Lulu (Witch)
Lulu and the Witch Baby - Jane O'Connor 1350

Lundy, Jethro (Parent)
San Domingo, the Medicine Hat Stallion - Marguerite Henry 856

Lundy, Peter (Horse Trainer)
San Domingo, the Medicine Hat Stallion - Marguerite Henry 856

Lurie, Gillian (Preteen)
Man From the Sky - Avi 70

Luther (Healer)
The Hero and the Crown - Robin McKinley 1241

Luther, Mary Call (Teenager)
Where the Lilies Bloom - Vera Cleaver 360

Lvovitch, Igor "Sesame" (Parent; Doctor)
The Sound of Dragon's Feet - Alki Zei 1983

Lydia (Teenager)
Daphne - Marilyn Kaye 1001

Lynn (Preteen)
Mariah Loves Rock - Mildred Pitts Walter 1881
Wildcat Summer - Mary Riskind 1508

Lyon (Teenager)
Miracle at Clement's Pond - Patricia Pendergraft 1418

M

M.J. (Preteen)
The Peanut Butter Poltergeist - Ellen Leroe 1092

Mabel (Goat)
Quick Chick - Julia Hoban 887

Macadoo (Farmer)
The Wizard's Tears - Maxine Kumin 1060

MacDonald, Ben (Child)
Incident at Hawk's Hill - Allan W. Eckert 559

MacDonald, Donald (Teenager)
The Ghosts of Austwick Manor - Reby Edmond
MacDonald 1166

MacDonald, Elspeth (Orphan; Teenager)
The Journey of the Shadow Bairns - Margaret Jean
Anderson 44

MacDonald, Heather (Child)
The Ghosts of Austwick Manor - Reby Edmond
MacDonald 1166

MacDonald, Hillary (Preteen)
The Ghosts of Austwick Manor - Reby Edmond
MacDonald 1166

MacDonald, Kelly (Preteen; Student)
Glass Slippers Give You Blisters - Mary Jane
Auch 65

MacDonald, Robbie (Orphan; Child)
The Journey of the Shadow Bairns - Margaret Jean
Anderson 44

MacKenzie, Paris (Detective; Teenager)
Mystery of the Metro - Elizabeth Howard 918

Mackintosh, Meg (Detective)
*Meg Mackintosh and the Mystery at the Medieval
Castle* - Lucinda Landon 1066

Maddox, Patricia "Pat" (Teenager)
Class Pictures - Marilyn Sachs 1575

Madec (Hunter)
Deathwatch - Robb White 1902

Madge (Teenager; Heiress)
Unleaving - Jill Paton Walsh 1396

Madigan (Preteen; 6th Grader)
Following the Mystery Man - Mary Downing
Hahn 788

Madison (Parrot)
Harry's Mad - Dick King-Smith 1032

Mafutu (Child)
Call It Courage - Armstrong Sperry 1712

Magee, Jeffrey "Maniac" (Orphan; Runaway)
Maniac Magee - Jerry Spinelli 1715

Maggic (Child; Orphan)
Almost a Hero - Clyde Robert Bulla 223

Maggie (Orphan)
Behind the Attic Wall - Sylvia Cassedy 307

Maggie (Preteen; Runaway)
The Get-Away Car - Eleanor Clymer 369

Maggie (Child)
I Hate My Sister Maggie - Crescent
Dragonwagon 535
She and the Dubious Three - Dorothy Crayder 440

Magic (Frog)
The Story of Jumping Mouse - John Steptoe 1740

Mago (Hero)
Flight of the Sparrow - Julia Cunningham 453

Magus (Wizard)
A Net to Catch the Wind - Margaret Greaves 741

Magyar (Twin)
The White Stag - Kate Seredy 1613

Mai (Preteen; Refugee)
A Boat to Nowhere - Maureen Crane
Wartski 1887

Maid Marion (Noblewoman)
The Outlaws of Sherwood - Robin McKinley 1242

Maiden (Maiden; Indian)
Her Seven Brothers - Paul Goble 713

Mairi (Preteen)
An Island in a Green Sea - Mabel Esther Allan 33

Makarov, Timosha (Child)
The Silver Crest: My Russian Boyhood - Kornei
Chukovsky 341

Malachi (Bee)
The Witch Family - Eleanor Estes 579

Malcolm, Johnny (Teacher)
Sister - Ellen Howard 922

Maleesh (Magician)
The Jedera Adventure - Lloyd Alexander 29

Malley, Joe (Child)
The Summer of the Swans - Betsy Byars 267

Mallixxan (Parent; Military Personnel)
The Humans of Ziax II - John Morressy 1292

Mallixxan, Toren (Settler)
The Humans of Ziax II - John Morressy 1292

Mallory, Heather (Preteen)
Speaking of Snapdragons - Sheila Hayes 836

Mallory, Makosica "Mike" (Teenager)
Mak - Belle Coates 373

Mallory, Rob (Preteen)
The View From the Cherry Tree - Willo Davis
Roberts 1513

Malloy, Derek (Teenager)
My Favorite Ghost - Stephen Roos 1545

Malloy, Kit
My Favorite Ghost - Stephen Roos 1545

Malloy, Margo
My Favorite Ghost - Stephen Roos 1545

Maltuch (Royalty)
Alone in the Wild Forest - Isaac Bashevis
Singer 1652

Mama (Spirit)
Ghost Story - Genevieve Gray 736

Mama (Thief)
Mama - Lee Bennett Hopkins 915

Mama (Dog)
Papa's Lemonade and Other Stories - Eve
Rice 1504

Mama (Preteen)
The Times They Used to Be - Lucille Clifton 367

Mancha, Fidel (Step-Parent)
Chloris and the Creeps - Kin Platt 1450

Manderby (Model)
Portrait of Ivan - Paula Fox 640

Mandus (Robot)
The Type One Super Robot - Alison Prince 1472

Mandy (Runaway; Abuse Victim)
It Ain't Always Easy - Kathleen Karr 996

Mandy (Child)
M & M and the Big Bag - Pat Ross 1548

Manheim, Gustav (Scientist)
The Leipzig Vampire - Mary Anderson 45

Mannie (Rat)
The Mouse and His Child - Russell Hoban 892

Manning, Molly (Householder)
Six Impossible Things Before Breakfast - Norma
Farber 584

Mannis, Bruce (Preteen)
King Shoes and Clown Pockets - Faye
Gibbons 690

Mannix, Sandy (Teenager; Runaway)
Bunkhouse Journal - Diane Johnston Hamm 809

Mansfield (Judge)
Smith - Leon Garfield 671

Mansfield, Melissa (Teenager; Babysitter)
Babysitter on Horseback - Fern G. Brown 213

Manteoba (Witch)
Up Mountain One Time - Willie Wilson 1926

Mantis (Detective; Insect)
*Trouble in Bugland: A Collection of Inspector Mantis
Mysteries* - William Kotzwinkle 1055

Maracosa, Marcia (Preteen)
Keeping it Secret - Penny Pollock 1455

Marc (Ruler)
Tristan and Iseult - Rosemary Sutcliff 1770

March (Child)
December's Travels - Mischa Damjan 474

March, Beth (Teenager)
Little Women, or Meg, Jo, Beth and Amy - Louisa M.
Alcott 23

March, Jo (Teenager)
Little Women, or Meg, Jo, Beth and Amy - Louisa M.
Alcott 23

March, Meg (Teenager)
Little Women, or Meg, Jo, Beth and Amy - Louisa M.
Alcott 23

Marcia (Preteen)
You've Been Away All Summer - Sheila Hayes 837

Marco (Child)
Soccer Sam - Jean Marzollo 1207

Marconi, Kate (Computer Expert)
Chip Mitchell: The Case of the Robot Warriors -
Fred D'Ignazio 525

Marcus (Child)
Us and Uncle Fraud - Lois Lowry 1156

Marcy (Teenager; Counselor)
There's a Bat in Bunk Five - Paula Danziger 481

Marcy (Child)
Things Won't Be the Same - Kathryn Ewing 582

Marek (Teenager)
The Man From the Other Side - Uri Orlev 1365

Margaret (Preteen)
Are You There, God? It's Me, Margaret - Judy
Blume 152

Margaret (Child; Handicapped)
The Balancing Girl - Berniece Rabe 1478

Margaret (Cat; Alien)
Ellsworth and the Cats from Mars - Patience
Brewster 196

Margery (Preteen)
It Takes Brains - Eiveen Weiman 1890

Margola (Relative)
A Gift for Mama - Esther Hautzig 831

Marguerite (Child)
Circle of Giving - Ellen Howard 919

Mari (Preteen)
Octopus Pie - Susan Terris 1795

Maria (Child)
Everett Anderson's Friend - Lucille Clifton   365
Grandpa's Maria - Hans-Eric Hellberg   848
Maria's House - Jean Merrill   1258

Maria (Worker)
Mystery Madness - Otto Coontz   416

Maria (Preteen)
A Stitch in Time - Penelope Lively   1138

Maria Luisa (Child; Immigrant)
Maria Luisa - Winifred Madison   1175

Mariah (5th Grader; Preteen)
Mariah Loves Rock - Mildred Pitts Walter   1881

Marianne (Child)
Fourth Grade Wizards - Barthe DeClements   498

Marianne (Preteen)
Now Is Not Too Late - Isabelle Holland   901

Marica (Teenager; 7th Grader)
Just Good Friends - Dean Marney   1195

Marie (Child)
The Nutcracker - E.T.A. Hoffman   896

Marigold (Child)
The Case of the Double Cross - Crosby
   Bonsall   174

Marilyn (6th Grader; Writer)
King Kong and Other Poets - Robert Burch   243

Marion (Preteen)
Marion's Angels - K.M. Peyton   1428

Mark (Preteen)
Flambards - K.M. Peyton   1427

Mark (Parent; Camper)
The Grizzly - Annabel Johnson   974

Mark (Child)
*I, Houdini: The Autobiography of a Self-Educated
   Hamster* - Lynne Reid Banks   1497

Mark (Preteen)
Mark Makes His Move - Marian Potter   1462

Mark (Child)
Pop's Secret - Maryann Townsend   1821
The Secret Three - Mildred Myrick   1306

Marlee (Preteen; 5th Grader)
With a Wave of the Wand - Mark Jonathan
   Harris   817

Marler, Gary (Detective)
Trapped in Death Cave - Bill Wallace   1878

Marly (Child)
Miracles on Maple Hill - Virginia Sorensen   1706

Maroo (Prehistoric Human)
Maroo of the Winter Caves - Ann Turnbull   1831

Marra (Child)
Marra's World - Elizabeth Coatsworth   375

Mars, Sara (Sports Figure)
Rivals on Ice - Elizabeth Van Steenwyk   1849

Marsh, Tina Valentine (Hero)
The Bronze King - Suzy McKee Charnas   320

Marsha (Child)
The Skates of Uncle Richard - Carol Fenner   593

Marshmallow (Rabbit)
Marshmallow - Clare Turlay Newberry   1327

Marta (Dancer)
The Whipman Is Watching - Thomas A. Dyer   554

Martha (Hippopotamus)
George and Martha Back in Town - James
   Marshall   1199

Martha (Teenager)
Ludie's Song - Dirlie Herlihy   859

Martin (Child)
Mad Martin - Patricia Windsor   1927

Martin (Relative)
The Singing Hill - Meindert DeJong   506

Martin, Gary (Pilot)
The Last Mission - Harry Mazer   1215

Martin, Jane (Detective)
Jane Martin, Dog Detective - Eve Bunting   232

Martin, Matthew (Preteen; 6th Grader)
Make Like a Tree and Leave - Paula Danziger   479

Martin "Mart" (Teenager)
Wild Boy - Joan Tate   1782

Marty (Child)
Jemmy - Jon Francis Hassler   824
The Math Whiz - Betsy Duffey   544

Marvin the Magnificent (Mouse)
The Great Christmas Kidnapping Caper - Jean Van
   Leeuwen   1847

Mary (Child)
Mary, Mary - Sarah Hayes   835

Mary (Relative)
Moondial - Helen Cresswell   445

Mary (Child)
Through the Dolls' House Door - Jane Gardam   666

Mary Eliza (Friend)
Isabelle the Itch - Constance C. Greene   752

Mary Jane (Child)
Mary Jane - Dorothy Sterling   1742

Mary Kate (Child)
The Green Ghost of Appleville - Jean
   Marzollo   1206

Mary Sue (Neighbor)
Silver - Gloria Whelan   1897

Mash (Dog)
Dorp Dead - Julia Cunningham   452

Masklin (Mythical Creature)
Truckers - Terry Pratchett   1464

Mason, John (Murderer)
Tuppenny - Julia Cunningham   455

Mason, Joseph (Teenager)
On the Frontier with Mr. Audubon - Barbara
   Brenner   192

Mason, Thomas (Child; Apprentice)
Boy Without a Name - Penelope Lively   1136

Masterson (Coach)
What Difference Does It Make, Danny? - Helen
   Young   1978

Mat-Maw (Prehistoric Human)
Spirit on the Wall - Ann O'Neal Garcia   664

Mather, Paul (Sports Figure)
Hang Tough, Paul Mather - Alfred Slote   1671

Matheson, Dave (Preteen)
The Brain on Quartz Mountain - Margaret Jean
   Anderson   43

Mathilda (Witch)
Rosemary's Witch - Ann Warren Turner   1833

Matilda (Genius)
Matilda - Roald Dahl   468

Matson, Tracy (Friend)
Poopsie Pomerantz, Pick up Your Feet - Patricia
   Reilly Giff   696

Matt (Teenager)
Captives in a Foreign Land - Susan Lowry
   Rardin   1487

Matt (Preteen; Orphan)
The Ghost Children - Eve Bunting   231

Matt (Thief)
Ronia, the Robber's Daughter - Astrid
   Lindgren   1125

Matt (Teenager; Settler)
The Sign of the Beaver - Elizabeth George
   Speare   1709

Matthew (Child)
The Ears of Louis - Constance C. Greene   749

Matthews, Jillian "Jilly" (Preteen)
The Haunted House - Dorothy Haas   782
New Friends - Dorothy Haas   783

Matthews, Meeghan (Eccentric)
A Witch's Garden - Miriam Young   1980

Matthews, Polly "Peanut" (Preteen)
The Haunted House - Dorothy Haas   782

Maud (Witch)
The Worst Witch - Jill Murphy   1299

Maurice (Child)
Maurice's Room - Paula Fox   637

Maurice (Cat)
Never Steal a Magic Cat - Donald E. Caufield   312

Max (Child)
Addie Meets Max - Joan Robins   1516

Max (Preteen; Detective—Amateur)
The Case of the Mind Reading Mommies - Elizabeth
   Levy   1106

Max (Child)
Chocolate-Covered Ants - Stephen Manes   1188

Max (Grandparent; Survivor)
David and Max - Gary Provost   1473

Max (Child)
Max and Me and the Time Machine - Gery
   Greer   761

Max (Dog)
No One Is Going to Nashville - Mavis Jukes   989

Maxi (Dog)
M & M and the Big Bag - Pat Ross   1548

Maxwell, Kate (Child)
Kate Crackernuts - Katharine Mary Briggs   199

Maxwell, Kerby (Child)
Home Run Trick - Scott Corbett   425

May, April (Boarder)
The Day That Elvis Came to Town - Jan
   Marino   1193

May, Johnny (Hunter)
The Adventures of Johnny May - Robbie
   Branscum   188

Maybelle (Preteen)
Hear the Wind Blow - Patricia Pendergraft   1417

Mayflower, Rufus (Child)
The Toothpaste Millionaire - Jean Merrill   1259

McAllister, Kate (Teenager)
Cat-Man's Daughter - Barbara Mattes
   Abercrombie   2

McAllister, Riley (Grandparent)
Cat-Man's Daughter - Barbara Mattes
   Abercrombie   2

McBride, Kevin (Child)
Don't Forget Michael - Jean Thompson   1808

Milonas, Katy (Child)
Katy Did It - Victoria Boutis   182

Mimi (Child)
M & M and the Big Bag - Pat Ross   1548
What If They Knew? - Patricia Hermes   865

Mindy (Preteen; 6th Grader)
The Iceberg and Its Shadow - Jan Greenberg   745

Minh, Chu (Cook)
Onion Tears - Diana Kidd   1023

Minn (Turtle)
Minn of the Mississipppi - Holling Clancy
   Holling   903

Minor Canon (Religious)
The Griffin and the Minor Canon - Frank R.
   Stockton   1750

Mirabelle (Royalty)
A Net to Catch the Wind - Margaret Greaves   741

Miranda (Cat)
Bella Arabella - Liza Fosburgh   634

Miranda (Teenager)
Marathon Miranda - Elizabeth Winthrop   1932

Miranda (Child)
The Orphan Game - Barbara Cohen   383

Miranda (Relative)
Rebecca of Sunnybrook Farm - Kate Douglas
   Wiggin   1907

Mirandy (Child)
Mirandy and Brother Wind - Pat McKissack   1246

Misha (Child)
There, Far Beyond the River - Yuri Korinetz   1050

Mishmash (Dog)
Mishmash - Molly Cone   399

Miss Bossy (Toy)
Through the Dolls' House Door - Jane Gardam   666

Missis (Dog)
The Hundred and One Dalmatians - Dodie
   Smith   1679

Mitchell, Arthur (Dancer)
Arthur Mitchell - Tobi Tobias   1815

Mitchell, Chip (Computer Expert)
Chip Mitchell: The Case of the Robot Warriors -
   Fred D'Ignazio   525

Mitchell, Mean (Child)
No Bean Sprouts, Please! - Constance Hiser   885

Mitchell, Sarah (Nurse)
Naomi - Berniece Rabe   1480

Mitchell, Tory (Preteen)
The Josie Gambit - Mary Francis Shura   1635

Mitzi (Child)
Mitzi and the Terrible Tyranosaurus Rex - Barbara
   Williams   1918

Miyo (Child)
The Rooster Who Understood Japanese - Yoshiko
   Uchida   1838

Mo (Lawman; Beaver)
Mo to the Rescue - Mary Pope Osborne   1369

Moffat, Rufus (Child)
Rufus M. - Eleanor Estes   578

Mohlen, Gordon (Student—High School)
Summer of the White Goat - Paige Dixon   527

Mole (Mole)
A Clean House for Mole and Mouse - Harriet
   Ziefert   1986
The Wind in the Willows - Kenneth Grahame   733

Moles, Walter (Preteen)
Fourth Grade Celebrity - Patricia Reilly Giff   693

Moles, Walter (Activist)
Left-Handed Shortstop - Patricia Reilly Giff   695

Moller, Andy (Child)
Beetles, Lightly Toasted - Phyllis Reynolds
   Naylor   1313

Molly (Step-Parent)
The Headless Cupid - Zilpha Keatley Snyder   1698

Molly (Child)
I Should Worry, I Should Care - Miriam
   Chaikin   315

Molly (Mole)
Molly in Danger - Anne Carter   306

Molly (Rabbit)
Molly Moves Out - Susan Pearson   1403

Molly (Child; Immigrant)
Molly's Pilgrim - Barbara Cohen   382

Molly (6th Grader)
Seal Child - Sylvia Peck   1410

Molly (Child)
Wait Till Helen Comes - Mary Downing Hahn   791

Mom (Parent)
Cloudy with a Chance of Meatballs - Judi
   Barrett   97

Monnie (Monster)
The Monster Garden - Vivien Alcock   20

Monroe, Harold (Dog)
Bunnicula: A Rabbit Tale of Mystery - Deborah
   Howe   923

Monster, Billy (Monster)
The Very Worst Monster - Pat Hutchins   961

Monster, Hazel (Monster)
The Very Worst Monster - Pat Hutchins   961

Montague (Rat; Artist)
A Rat's Tale - Tor Seidler   1606

Moody, Delbert (Neighbor)
The Wicked Pigeon Ladies in the Garden - Mary
   Chase   321

Moomintroll (Mythical Creature)
Finn Family Moomintroll - Tove Jansson   969

Moon Shadow (Child)
Dragonwings - Lawrence Yep   1966

Moonseeker China (Horse)
Touch the Moon - Marion Dane Bauer   110

Moore (Recluse)
A Room Made of Windows - Eleanor
   Cameron   285

Moore, Haskell (Preteen)
Hear the Wind Blow - Patricia Pendergraft   1417

Moore, Olive (Child-Care Giver)
Hide Crawford Quick - Margaret Walden
   Froehlich   653

Mopey (Dog)
Philo Potts, or, The Helping Hand Strikes Again -
   Mildred Ames   40

Morbelia (Relative; Aged Person)
Aunt Morbelia and the Screaming Skulls - Joan
   Davenport Carris   300

Morgan (Student)
Follow That Bus! - Pat Hutchins   960

Morgan (Neighbor)
Benson Boy - Ivan Southall   1707

Morgan, Becky (Child)
A String in the Harp - Nancy Bond   169

Morgan, Hobie (Preteen)
The Mystery at Peacock Place - M.F. Craig   439

Morgan, Jen (Teenager)
A String in the Harp - Nancy Bond   169

Morgan, Justin (Teacher)
Justin Morgan Had a Horse - Marguerite
   Henry   853

Morgan, Matthew "Mattoosie" (Preteen)
Frozen Fire - James A. Houston   917

Morgan, Peter (Preteen)
A String in the Harp - Nancy Bond   169

Morgenstern, Ruthie (Preteen)
Daughters of the Law - Sandy Asher   59

Morley, Judith (Preteen)
Witch's Sister - Phyllis Reynolds Naylor   1320

Morley, Lynn (Preteen)
Witch Weed - Phyllis Reynolds Naylor   1319

Morley, Lynn (Teenager)
Witch's Sister - Phyllis Reynolds Naylor   1320

Morning Star (Indian)
Morning Arrow - Nanabah Chee Dodge   528

Morris (Seagull)
Kilroy and the Gull - Nathaniel Benchley   133

Morris (Moose)
Morris and Boris at the Circus - Bernard
   Wiseman   1935
Morris Has a Cold - Bernard Wiseman   1936

Morris (Teacher)
Captain Hook, That's Me - Ada B. Litchfield   1131

Morris, Barbara (Step-Parent)
Roots in the Outfield - Jane Zirpoli   1988

Morris, Jarvis "Jabber" (Sports Figure)
Soccer Halfback - Matt Christopher   340

Morris, Josh "Roots" (Preteen; Sports Figure)
Roots in the Outfield - Jane Zirpoli   1988

Morris, Melba (Preteen)
The Dancing Cats of Applesap - Janet Taylor
   Lisle   1129

Morrison, Scott "Earthquake" (Sports Figure)
Quarterback Walk-On - Thomas J. Dygard   555

Morrissay, Will (Military Personnel)
The Root Cellar - Janet Louise Lunn   1157

Morrissey, Matt (Handicapped)
The Flying Fingers Club - Jean F. Andrews   47

Morrow, Sarah (Teenager)
You Shouldn't Have to Say Goodbye - Patricia
   Hermes   866

Mortensen, Buster (Child)
Buster, the Sheikh of Hope Street - Bjarne B.
   Reuter   1502

Mortensen, Ingeborg (Child)
Buster, the Sheikh of Hope Street - Bjarne B.
   Reuter   1502

Moscowitz, Becky (Immigrant)
Immigrant Girl: Becky of Eldridge Street - Harvey
   Brett   194

Moscowitz, Max (Immigrant)
Immigrant Girl: Becky of Eldridge Street - Harvey
   Brett   194

Motele "Mitek" (Preteen; Musician)
Uncle Misha's Partisans - Yuri Suhl   1767

Mother (Parent)
Something Special for Me - Vera B. Williams 1925

Mother Bear (Bear)
Little Bear - Else Holmelund Minarik 1272

Mott, Sam (Child)
Do Bananas Chew Gum? - Jamie Gilson 702

Mouk (Dwarf)
The Adventures of Little Mouk - Wilhelm Hauff 826

Mounce, Chuckie (Teenager)
Me Two - Mary C. Ryan 1562

Moundshround, Carapace Clavicle (Spirit)
The Halloween Tree - Ray Bradbury 184

Mouse (Child)
The 18th Emergency - Betsy Byars 255

Mouse (Mouse)
A Clean House for Mole and Mouse - Harriet Ziefert 1986
The First Morning: An African Myth - Margery Bernstein 142

Mouse, Abelard (Survivor)
Abel's Island - William Steig 1731

Mouse, Adam (Writer; Mouse)
I'll Meet You at the Cucumbers - Lilian Moore 1281

Mouse, Amanda (Spouse)
Abel's Island - William Steig 1731

Mouse, Amanda (Mouse)
I'll Meet You at the Cucumbers - Lilian Moore 1281

Mouse, Junius (Mouse)
I'll Meet You at the Cucumbers - Lilian Moore 1281

Mouse, Matthias (Hero; Mouse)
Redwall - Brian Jacques 967

Mouse, Timothy (Mouse)
Mrs. Frisby and the Rats of NIMH - Robert C. O'Brien 1347

Moyer, Carrie (Preteen)
Nothing Stays the Same Forever - Gail Radley 1483

Moyer, Phyllis (Teenager)
Nothing Stays the Same Forever - Gail Radley 1483

Mpala, Rebecca "Becky" (Teenager)
Go Well, Stay Well - Toeckey Jones 985

Mr. Lincoln (Rooster)
The Rooster Who Understood Japanese - Yoshiko Uchida 1838

Mr. Sniff (Dog)
Call for Mr. Sniff - Thomas P. Lewis 1114

Mucias (Preteen; Detective—Amateur)
Detectives in Togas - Henry Winterfeld 1929

Mud (Dog)
The Blossoms and the Green Phantom - Betsy Byars 258

Mudge (Dog)
Henry and Mudge and the Happy Cat - Cynthia Rylant 1567

Mueller, Phil (Parent)
Taking Terri Mueller - Norma Fox Mazer 1219

Mueller, Terri (Teenager)
Taking Terri Mueller - Norma Fox Mazer 1219

Mukasa (Child)
Mukasa - John Nagenda 1308

Muldie, Ed (Settler)
Wagon Wheels - Barbara Brenner 193

Muldie, Johnny (Child)
Wagon Wheels - Barbara Brenner 193

Munay, Conrad (Teenager)
Sometimes I Think I Hear My Name - Avi 73

Munson, Jason (Preteen; Sports Figure)
Jason and the Baseball Bear - Dan Elish 563

Murdoch (Apprentice)
Tomorrow's Wizard - Patricia Maclachlan 1172

Murdock (Employer)
The Twenty-Four-Hour Lipstick Mystery - Bonnie Pryor 1476

Murphy, Collette (Child; 3rd Grader)
Too Many Murphys - Colleen O'Shaughnessy McKenna 1236

Murphy, Jeff (Child)
Too Many Murphys - Colleen O'Shaughnessy McKenna 1236

Murphy, Jess (Child)
Awfully Short for the Fourth Grade - Elvira Woodruff 1951

Murphy, Laura (Child)
Too Many Murphys - Colleen O'Shaughnessy McKenna 1236

Murphy, Noah (Preteen)
Awfully Short for the Fourth Grade - Elvira Woodruff 1951

Murray (Turtle)
Fast Friends: Two Stories - James Stevenson 1746

Mustazza, Matt (Artist)
Portrait of Ivan - Paula Fox 640

Mutt (Dog)
The Dog Who Wouldn't Be - Farley Mowat 1296

Mutty, Morty (Teacher)
The Search for King Pup's Tomb - Jim Razzi 1495

My Dog (Dog)
My Dog and the Birthday Mystery - David A. Adler 13

Myers, Catherine "Cathy" (Teenager)
Just the Beginning - Betty Miles 1262

Myers, Clara (Parent)
Just the Beginning - Betty Miles 1262

Myers, Julia (Teenager)
Just the Beginning - Betty Miles 1262

Myrddin (Magician)
The Book of Brendan - Ann Curry 456

Myrto (Relative)
Wildcat under Glass - Alki Zei 1984

N

Nai Nai, Lin (Governess)
Homesick: My Own Story - Jean Fritz 652

Naledi (Teenager)
Chain of Fire - Beverly Naidoo 1309

Nam-Huong (Child)
Onion Tears - Diana Kidd 1023

Nana Tess (Child-Care Giver)
The Telltale Summer of Tina C. - Lila Perl 1420

Nancy (Child)
The Golden Name Day - Jennie D. Lindquist 1126

Nancy (Child; Handicapped)
Silent Dancer - Bruce Hlibok 886

Nancy (Child)
Where Does the Teacher Live? - Paula Kurzband Feder 591

Naomi (Teenager; Neighbor)
Alan and Naomi - Myron Levoy 1104

Napak (Hunter; Indian)
The Way of Our People - Arnold A. Griese 766

Nardi, Doug (Coach)
Catch That Pass! - Matt Christopher 337

Nardi, Jim (Sports Figure)
Catch That Pass! - Matt Christopher 337

Natasha (Neighbor)
Toughboy and Sister - Kirkpatrick Hill 883

Nate (Detective)
Nate the Great - Marjorie Weinman Sharmat 1620

Nathan (Preteen; Runaway)
The Runaways - Ruth Thomas 1807

Nell (Orphan)
Brother Moose - Betty Levin 1096

Nels (Preteen)
Really Weird Summer - Eloise Jarvis McGraw 1230

Nemo (Sea Captain)
Twenty Thousand Leagues Under the Sea - Jules Verne 1853

Nerea (Parent)
Marra's World - Elizabeth Coatsworth 375

Neudorf (Teacher)
Friedrich - Hans Peter Richter 1507

Neuman, Molly (Child)
Nightmare Mountain - Peg Kehret 1003

Newberry, Harry (Preteen)
Harry Newberry and the Raiders of the Red Drink - Mel Gilden 700

Newberry, Michael Oliver (Spirit)
Mad, Mad Monday - Herma Silverstein 1643

Newbolt, Joe (Friend; Handicapped)
Welcome Home, Jellybean - Marlene Fanta Shyer 1638

Newman, Kate (Preteen; Dancer)
Maybe Next Year - Amy Hest 873

Newt (Relative)
The Glory Girl - Betsy Byars 263

Newton, Mona Lisa (Preteen)
Figgs and Phantoms - Ellen Raskin 1488

Nguyen, Vo (Adoptee)
Terror Train! - Gilbert B. Cross 448

Nibbles (Chimpanzee)
Castaways on Chimp Island - Sandy Landsman 1067

Nicholas (Child)
Alexander, Who Used to Be Rich Last Sunday - Judith Viorst 1856

Nicholas (Religious)
Days of Courage; A Medieval Adventure - Niels Jensen 973

Nichols, Ted (Preteen)
The Hit-and-Run Connection - Carole Smith 1678

Nick (Dog)
Adam of the Road - Elizabeth Gray 735

Paul (Teenager)
The Young Landlords - Walter Dean Myers   1305

Paulo (Preteen)
Danza! - Lynn Hall   792

Payne, Thatcher (Preteen)
Thatcher Payne-in-the-Neck - Betty Bates   105

Payson, Big Lou (Parent)
Come by Here - Olivia Coolidge   413

Payson, Minty Lou (Child)
Come by Here - Olivia Coolidge   413

Peanut (Dog)
Aldo Peanut Butter - Johanna Hurwitz   947

Pearl (Mouse)
Pearl's Pirates - Frank Asch   58

Pearl (Pig)
Ups and Downs with Oink and Pearl - Kay Chorao   328

Pearly (Grandparent)
Good-Bye Pink Pig - Carole S. Adler   7

Peavy, Queenie (Child)
Queenie Peavy - Robert Burch   244

Peck, Robert "Rob" (Child)
Soup - Robert Newton Peck   1409

Pee Wee (Preteen)
Paris, Pee Wee, and Big Dog - Rosa Guy   780

Peedle (Handicapped; Child)
End of a Dark Road - Crystal Thrasher   1809

Peggy (Child)
The Sweet Touch - Lorna Balian   92

Pelligrino (Immigrant)
How Pizza Came to Queens - Dayal Kaur Khalsa   1019

Pendergast, Popoff (Manager (Sports))
The Kid Who Batted 1000 - Bob Allison   35

Penelope (Child)
The Talking Parcel - Gerald Durrel   552

Penfold, Josh (Recluse)
The Rare One - Pamela Rogers   1542

Penn, John (Settler)
Greenhorn on the Frontier - Ann Finlayson   604

Penney, Birdie (Neighbor; Handicapped)
Sasha, My Friend - Barbara Corcoran   432

Pennington, Patrick (Musician)
Marion's Angels - K.M. Peyton   1428

Penny (Preteen)
Golden Girl - Nancy Tilly   1812

Penny, Joel (Magician)
Joel and the Great Merlini - Eloise Jarvis McGraw   1228

Penny, Sammy (Child)
Joel and the Great Merlini - Eloise Jarvis McGraw   1228

Penrod (Porcupine)
Penrod's Pants - Mary Blount Christian   332

Pentax, Arthur (Businessman)
C.L.U.T.Z. and the Fission Formula - Marilyn Wilkes   1912

Pentax, Rodney (Preteen)
C.L.U.T.Z. and the Fission Formula - Marilyn Wilkes   1912

Pepper (Handyman)
Mr. Pepper Stories - Mark Taylor   1783

Pepper (Occultist)
The Ghost on Saturday Night - Sid Fleischman   621

Pepper, Art (Friend)
Casey the Nomad - Susan Sussman   1769

Pepper, Ben (Preteen)
The Five Little Peppers and How They Grew - Margaret Sidney   1639

Pepper, Phronsie (Child)
The Five Little Peppers and How They Grew - Margaret Sidney   1639

Pepper, Polly (Preteen)
The Five Little Peppers and How They Grew - Margaret Sidney   1639

Percival (Pelican)
Storm Boy - Colin Thiele   1802

Perrella, Joey (Boyfriend)
The Amazing Valvano and the Mystery of the Hooded Rat - Mary Robinson   1518

Perry, Elizabeth "Geeder" (Child)
Zeely - Virginia Hamilton   807

Perry, Matthew C. (Military Personnel; Historical Figure)
Commodore Perry in the Land of the Shogun - Rhoda Blumberg   151

Perry, Miranda Alexis (Preteen)
The Secret in Miranda's Closet - Sheila Greenwald   760

Perry, Olivia (Parent; Feminist)
The Secret in Miranda's Closet - Sheila Greenwald   760

Perrywinkle (Apprentice; Wizard)
Perrywinkle and the Book of Magic Spells - Ross Martin Madsen   1176

Persopolis, Angeline (Genius; 6th Grader)
Someday Angeline - Louis Sachar   1570

Pete (Dog)
The Day of the Muskie - Patricia Welch   1891

Pete (Writer)
Fox in a Trap - Jane Resh Thomas   1806

Peter (Child)
All Because I'm Older - Phyllis Reynolds Naylor   1312

Peter (Teenager)
A Fine White Dust - Cynthia Rylant   1566

Peter (Parent)
Ghost Vision - Jeanie Kortum   1054

Peter (Preteen)
Heidi - Johanna Spyri   1720

Peter (Child)
Jumanji - Chris Van Allsburg   1840
The Lion, the Witch, and the Wardrobe - C.S. Lewis   1110

Peter (Detective)
Maximilian, You're the Greatest - Joseph Rosenbloom   1547

Peter (Friend)
Once, Said Darlene - William Sleator   1664

Peter (Preteen)
The Railway Children - Edith Nesbit   1324

Peter (Child)
Superfudge - Judy Blume   158
The Talking Parcel - Gerald Durrel   552

Peter (Teenager; Equestrian)
The Team - K.M. Peyton   1429

Peter (Child)
This Island Isn't Big Enough for the Four of Us! - Gery Greer   762
The Toad Hunt - Janet Chenery   322

Peters (Leader)
Cookies and Crutches - Judy Delton   511

Peters, Jamie (Preteen)
Man From the Sky - Avi   70

Peters, John "Pete" (Preteen)
Mishmash - Molly Cone   399

Peterson, Andy (Twin)
The Trouble with Jacob - Eloise Jarvis McGraw   1231

Peterson, Kat (Twin)
The Trouble with Jacob - Eloise Jarvis McGraw   1231

Petie (Magician)
The Red King - Victor Kelleher   1005

Petit, Russell (Businessman; Bigot)
A Witch's Garden - Miriam Young   1980

Petros (Preteen; Resistance Fighter)
Petros' War - Alki Zei   1982

Pettifer, Penny (Child)
Plain Lane Christmas - Cyril Walter Hodges   893

Pettigrew, Henry (Artisan)
Daniel's Duck - Clyde Robert Bulla   225

Petya (Relative; Activist)
There, Far Beyond the River - Yuri Korinetz   1050

Pfluggins, Effie (Widow(er))
The Secret of Gumbo Grove - Eleanora E. Tate   1780

Phil (Teenager)
The Long Black Coat - Jay Bennett   137

Philip (Preteen)
Earthquake 2099 - Mary W. Sullivan   1768

Philip (Teenager)
Grandpa Ritz and the Lucious Lovelies - Marlene Fanta Shyer   1637

Phillip (Student)
Kelly's Creek - Doris Buchanan Smith   1680

Phillips (Housekeeper; Child-Care Giver)
The Castle in the Attic - Elizabeth Winthrop   1931

Philpotts, Hugh (Relative)
The Treasure of Alpheus Winterborn - John Bellairs   128

Phoebe (Teenager)
The Divorce Express - Paula Danziger   478

Phoebe (Teenager; Adoptee)
Marathon Miranda - Elizabeth Winthrop   1932

Phyllis (Grandparent)
If Phyllis Were Here - Gail Jarrow   972

Phyllis (Child)
The Railway Children - Edith Nesbit   1324

Pichelsteiner, Maxie (Orphan)
Little Man - Erich Kastner   997

Pickens, Dwayne (Handicapped)
All Together Now - Sue Ellen Bridgers   197

Pickerell, Lavinia (Traveller)
Miss Pickerell and the Blue Whales - Ellen MacGregor   1167

Pickerell, Lavinia (Private Detective)
Miss Pickerell and the War of the Computers - Dora Pantell   1373

Price, Davy (Preteen; Psychic)
The Gift - Peter Dickinson 522

Price, Ian (Teenager)
The Gift - Peter Dickinson 522

Price, Penny (Teenager)
The Gift - Peter Dickinson 522

Price, Susan (Preteen)
Mystery of the Haunted Pool - Phyllis A. Whitney 1903

Price, Tommy (Preteen)
Mystery of the Hard Luck Rodeo - Susan Saunders 1589

Priscilla (Child)
Best Enemies - Kathleen Leverich 1095

Pritchett, Nora (Writer)
One of Us - Nikki Amdur 38

Pritchett, Walt (Parent)
One of Us - Nikki Amdur 38

Protheroe, Tom (Shepherd)
No Way of Telling - Emma Smith 1686

Pruitt, Libby (Preteen)
If Phyllis Were Here - Gail Jarrow 972

Pryce, Clarissa (Child)
Hitty: Her First Hundred Years - Rachel Field 597

Puck (Friend)
The Interesting Thing That Happened at Perfect Acres, Inc. - Barbara Brooks Wallace 1871

Pudge (Child)
Uncle Mike's Boy - Jerome Brooks 211

Pullman, George Mortimer (Inventor; Historical Figure)
A Long Hard Journey: The Story of the Pullman Porter - Pat McKissack 1245

Pum-Hessel (Nobleman)
The Marvelous Misadventures of Sebastian - Lloyd Alexander 31

Purdy, Jafer (Settler)
Sweetwater - Laurence Yep 1964

Pursewig (Political Figure)
The Cat Who Wished to Be a Man - Lloyd Alexander 26

Putter (Dog)
The Thing in Kat's Attic - Charlotte Towner Graeber 730

Pye, Ginger (Dog)
Ginger Pye - Eleanor Estes 576

Pye, Jared "Jerry" (Child)
Ginger Pye - Eleanor Estes 576

Pye, Rachel (Child)
Ginger Pye - Eleanor Estes 576

Q

Quacky (Orphan; Preteen)
Quacky and the Crazy Curve Ball - Walter G. Oleksy 1358

Quick (Dog)
Barefoot a Thousand Miles - Patsey Gray 739

Quimby, Beatrice "Beezus" (Child)
Beezus and Ramona - Beverly Cleary 349
Ramona and Her Father - Beverly Cleary 354

Quimby, Ramona (Child)
Beezus and Ramona - Beverly Cleary 349

Quimby, Ramona (Child; 2nd Grader)
Ramona and Her Father - Beverly Cleary 354

Quimby, Ramona (Child)
Ramona Quimby, Age 8 - Beverly Cleary 355

Quinn, Turner (Animal Trainer)
Murder at the Spaniel Show - Lynn Hall 794

R

Raab, Bolivia (Preteen)
The Cold and Hot Winter - Johanna Hurwitz 951

Raab, Jack (Teenager; Military Personnel)
The Last Mission - Harry Mazer 1215

Raamo (Teenager)
Below the Root - Zilpha Keatley Snyder 1695

Rabbit, Wilbur (Television Personality)
The Bionic Bunny Show - Marc T. Brown 217

Rachel (Teenager)
After the Rain - Norma Fox Mazer 1217

Rachel (Preteen; 6th Grader)
The Iceberg and Its Shadow - Jan Greenberg 745

Rachel (Child)
Lily and Miss Liberty - Carla Stevens 1744
The Pigs Are Flying! - Emily Rodda 1530
Silver - Gloria Whelan 1897

Radames (Military Personnel)
Aida - Leontyne Price 1467

Ragmar (Pirate)
Viking's Dawn - Henry Treece 1822

Rahloo (Dog)
The Good Luck Dog - Lilo Hess 870

Rahm (Rabbit; Parent)
Rabbit Spring - Tilde Michels 1261

Ralph (Mouse)
The Mouse and the Motorcycle - Beverly Cleary 352

Ralph (Bully)
The Silk and the Skin - Rodie Sudbery 1765

Ralston, Drew (Teenager)
Moxie - Phyllis Rossiter 1549

Ralston, Poke (Teenager)
Moxie - Phyllis Rossiter 1549

Ramsey, Alec (Child)
The Black Stallion - Walter Farley 587

Ramsey, Alec (Teenager; Equestrian)
Black Stallion Mystery - Walter Farley 588

Randall, Rebecca Rowena (Child)
Rebecca of Sunnybrook Farm - Kate Douglas Wiggin 1907

Ras (Slave)
The Slave Dancer - Paula Fox 641

Rat (Rat)
The Wind in the Willows - Kenneth Grahame 733

Ratchett, Olga (Spy)
Mystery of the Bewitched Bookmobile - Florence Parry Heide 845

Ravinsky, Nina (Teenager)
ESP McGee - Edward Packard 1372

Rawlings, Dave (Friend)
Mystery at Crane's Landing - Marcella Thum 1810

Rawlings, Norris (Convict)
The Case of the Vanishing Villain - Carol J. Farley 585

Ray (Teenager)
The Watchers - Jane Louise Curry 458

Raymond (Mouse; Scholar)
The Great Christmas Kidnapping Caper - Jean Van Leeuwen 1847

Raymond (Child)
Raymond's Best Summer - Jean Rogers 1540

Raymond "Ray" (Child)
The Singing Hill - Meindert DeJong 506

Reachfar, Janet (Preteen)
Brave Janet Reachfar - Jane Duncan 547

Rebecca (Teenager)
Fourteen - Marilyn Sachs 1577

Rebecca (Preteen; Student)
Glass Slippers Give You Blisters - Mary Jane Auch 65

Red King (Villain)
The Red King - Victor Kelleher 1005

Reddick, Jem (Child)
Go and Catch a Flying Fish - Mary Stolz 1755

Reddick, Taylor (Teenager)
Go and Catch a Flying Fish - Mary Stolz 1755

Reddick, Tony (Parent; Cook)
Go and Catch a Flying Fish - Mary Stolz 1755

Redfern, Greg (Child)
Julia and the Hand of God - Eleanor Cameron 284

Redfern, Julia (Preteen)
Julia and the Hand of God - Eleanor Cameron 284

Redfern, Julia (Child)
A Room Made of Windows - Eleanor Cameron 285

Redmond, Joshua (Naturalist; Preteen)
Land's End - Mary Stolz 1757

Reed, Gunther "Goony" (Sports Figure)
Left-Handed Shortstop - Patricia Reilly Giff 695

Reed, Henry (Preteen)
Henry Reed's Baby-Sitting Service - Keith Robertson 1514

Reichert, Cindy (Hitchhiker)
Snow Bound - Harry Mazer 1216

Reid, Donald (Military Personnel)
Fantastic Voyage - Isaac Asimov 61

Reid, Jane (Preteen)
In a Blue Velvet Dress - Catherine Sefton 1604

Reilly, Andy (Child)
The Night the Monster Came - Mary Calhoun 275

Rella, Sidney (Child)
Sidney Rella and the Glass Sneaker - Bernice Myers 1301

Renny (Child; Runaway)
Foster Child - Marion Dane Bauer 107

Resch, Johann (Landlord)
Friedrich - Hans Peter Richter 1507

Revere, Paul (Patriot; Historical Figure)
And Then What Happened, Paul Revere? - Jean Fritz 649

Revis, Alesia (Teenager; Handicapped)
Alesia - Eloise Greenfield 754

Reynolds, Daisy (Child)
The Fox and the Kingfisher - Judith Mellecker 1255

Rourke, Hollis (Preteen)
The 17th Street Gang - Emily Cheney Neville   1326

Ruby (Grandparent)
Nicky and the Joyous Noise - Mildred Ames   39

Rudd, Maggie (Activist)
The Voyage Begun - Nancy Bond   170

Rudi (Military Personnel)
The Machine Gunners - Robert Westall   1895

Rudomin, Esther (Child; Refugee)
The Endless Steppe: Growing Up in Siberia - Esther Hautzig   830

Rudy (Child)
Hawk, I'm Your Brother - Byrd Baylor   119

Rudy (Friend)
A Word From Our Sponsor: Or, My Friend Alfred - Judie Angell   51

Ruffles (Dog)
The Doggone Mystery - Mary Blount Christian   331

Rufus (Preteen; Detective—Amateur)
Detectives in Togas - Henry Winterfeld   1929

Rusch, Andy (Child)
Onion John - Joseph Krumgold   1058

Rusche (Worker)
Outside the Gates - Molly Gloss   711

Rush (Step-Parent)
Branigan's Dog: A Novel - Fran Grace   727

Rush (Spirit)
Sweet Whispers, Brother Rush - Virginia Hamilton   806

Russ (Teenager)
Flight of the White Wolf - Mel Ellis   568

Russell (Abuse Victim; Teenager)
End of a Dark Road - Crystal Thrasher   1809

Russell (Relative; Handicapped)
Flambards - K.M. Peyton   1427

Russell (Child)
Rip-Roaring Russell - Johanna Hurwitz   955
Squirrel in My Teacup! - Eileen Cade-Edwards   271

Russell, Bobby "Spike" (Sports Figure; Manager (Sports))
The Kid Comes Back - John R. Tunis   1827

Russell, Priscille (Foster Parent)
The Journey Home - Isabelle Holland   900

Russo, Ben (Step-Parent)
My Mother Got Married and Other Disasters - Barbara Park   1380

Russo, Lydia (Teenager)
My Mother Got Married and Other Disasters - Barbara Park   1380

Ruth (Teenager; Equestrian)
The Team - K.M. Peyton   1429

Ruthie Mae (Friend)
Ludell - Brenda Scott Wilkinson   1913

Ruthy (Child)
Nobody Listens to Andrew - Elizabeth Guilfoile   778

Ryan (Preteen)
The Scorpio Ghosts and the Black Hole Gang - Kathy Kennedy Tapp   1778

Rye, Hazel (Preteen; Landlord)
Hazel Rye - Vera Cleaver   358

Rye, Millard (Parent; Farmer)
Hazel Rye - Vera Cleaver   358

S

S.O.B. (Cat)
The View From the Cherry Tree - Willo Davis Roberts   1513

Safa (Royalty)
The Ghost Drum: A Cat's Tale - Susan Price   1468

Sager, Jeanie (Friend)
The Edge of Next Year - Mary Stolz   1754

St. Clavi, Regina (Witch)
The Witching of Ben Wagner - Mary Jane Auch   68

St. Martin, Alexis (Patient)
Dr. Beaumont and the Man with the Hole in His Stomach - Sam Epstein   575

Saknis (Indian)
The Sign of the Beaver - Elizabeth George Speare   1709

Saleem (Child)
Smoke Over Golan - Uriel Ofek   1357

Sally (Friend)
Call Me Amanda - Dale Bick Carlson   289

Sally (Child)
The Cat in the Hat - Dr. Seuss   1617

Sally (Camper)
Ghost Island - Carolyn Lane   1068

Sally (Child; Time Traveller)
The Wind Eye - Robert Westall   1896

Salt, Verucca (Child)
Charlie and the Chocolate Factory - Roald Dahl   464

Saltz, Pete (Teenager; 8th Grader)
Romeo and Juliet - Together (and Alive!) at Last - Avi   71

Salvatore, Paul (Sports Figure)
Showboat in the Backcourt - William Campbell Gault   678

Sam (Activist)
And One for All - Theresa Nelson   1321

Sam (Child)
Cutlass in the Snow - Elizabeth Shub   1630

Sam (Preteen)
Double or Nothing - Marc Talbert   1776
Dracula Is a Pain in the Neck - Elizabeth Levy   1107

Sam (Child)
A Dragon in Class Four - June Counsel   434
Grandpa's Slide Show - Deborah Gould   725

Sam (Preteen)
Knights of the Kitchen Table - Jon Scieszka   1601

Sam (Runaway)
The Sky Is Free - Mavis Thorpe Clark   346

Sam (Child)
Soccer Sam - Jean Marzollo   1207
Thank You, Jackie Robinson - Barbara Cohen   384

Samantha (Orphan)
Bogwoppit - Ursula Moray Williams   1924

Samantha (Preteen; Dancer)
Samantha on Stage - Susan Clement Farrar   590

Samantha (Preteen; Sports Figure)
There's a Caterpillar in My Lemonade - Diana Gregory   763

Sampson (Slave)
The Bronze Bow - Elizabeth George Speare   1708

Sampson, Deborah (Military Personnel; Historical Figure)
I'm Deborah Sampson: A Soldier in the War of the Revolution - Patricia Clapp   342

Sampson, Radcliffe "Cliffie" (Preteen)
Rat Teeth - Patricia Reilly Giff   698

Samuel (Friend)
A Memory for Tino - Leo Buscaglia   252

San Domingo (Horse)
San Domingo, the Medicine Hat Stallion - Marguerite Henry   856

Sanders, Justin (Teenager)
King Tut's Game Board - Leona Ellerby   567

Sanders, Kathy (Child)
The Bad Dreams of a Good Girl - Susan Richards Shreve   1628

Sandowsky, Willie (Detective)
The Case of the Condemned Cat - E.W. Hildick   879

Sandpiper (Horse)
Dark Horse - Jean Slaughter Doty   534

Sands, Joey (Child)
Don't Call Me Orphan - Michael Leach   1087

Sandy (Preteen)
Megan's Island - Willo Davis Roberts   1512

Sara (Refugee)
All the Children Were Sent Away - Sheila Garrigue   674

Sara (Toy)
The Big Hello - Janet Schulman   1598

Sara (Friend)
Hey, Remember Fat Glenda? - Lila Perl   1419

Sarah (Child)
All-of-a-Kind Family - Sydney Taylor   1787
Family Farm - Thomas Locker   1143
Mama's Going to Buy You a Mockingbird - Jean Little   1135

Sarah (Abuse Victim)
Step on a Crack - Mary Anderson   46

Sarah (Preteen)
You've Been Away All Summer - Sheila Hayes   837

Sarah Ida (Child)
Shoeshine Girl - Clyde Robert Bulla   228

Sargent, Dolly (Wealthy)
Calico Bush - Rachel Field   596

Saro (Child)
A Certain Small Shepherd - Rebecca Caudill   310

Saru (Orphan)
The Boy and the Samurai - Erik Christian Haugaard   827

Sasaki, Sadako (Child)
Sadako and the Thousand Paper Cranes - Eleanor Coerr   378

Sasaki, Yoko (Child)
Salted Lemons - Doris Buchanan Smith   1683

Sasan (Child; Eskimo)
The Wind Is Not a River - Arnold A. Griese   767

Sasha (Child)
Bony-legs - Joanna Cole   387

Saunders, Craig (Preteen)
Mrs. Tooey and the Terrible Toxic Tar - Barbara Dillon   526

Shub, Sam "Terrific Hunk - THUNK"
(Teenager)
Our Sixth-Grade Sugar Babies - Eve Bunting　235

Shun (Indian)
Jaguar, My Twin - Betty Jean Lifton　1118

Sibbie, Laura (Preteen; 6th Grader)
Sixth Grade Secrets - Louis Sachar　1569

Sid (Rat)
The Secret of Foghorn Island - Geoffrey Hayes　834

Sid (Seal)
Sid Seal, Houseman - Will Watkins　1889

Sidak (Child; Eskimo)
The Wind Is Not a River - Arnold A. Griese　767

Silas (Entertainer)
Silas and Ben-Godik - Cecil Bodker　163

Silla (Rabbit; Parent)
Rabbit Spring - Tilde Michels　1261

Sills, Lena (Preteen)
Words by Heart - Ouida Sebestyen　1602

Silver (Dog)
Silver - Gloria Whelan　1897

Silver, Long John (Pirate)
Treasure Island - Robert Louis Stevenson　1749

Silverfish, K. Pinkerton (Writer)
Be a Perfect Person in Just Three Days - Stephen Manes　1187

Silverman, Alan (Teenager; Sports Figure)
Alan and Naomi - Myron Levoy　1104

Simmons, Gail (Equestrian; Time Traveller)
Can I Get There by Candlelight? - Jean Slaughter Doty　532

Simms (Coach; Sports Figure)
I Am Rubber, You are Glue - Jane Morton　1293

Simms, Jeremy (Preteen)
Mississippi Bridge - Mildred D. Taylor　1785

Simms, Maudie (Child)
Maudie in the Middle - Phyllis Reynolds Naylor　1315

Simms, Randy (Child)
I Am Rubber, You are Glue - Jane Morton　1293

Simon (Preteen; 5th Grader)
The Cybil War - Betsy Byars　262

Simon (Child)
Friends - Terry Berger　141

Simon (Orphan)
The Nargun and the Stars - Patricia Wrightson　1959

Simon (Teenager; Handicapped)
Stay Away From Simon! - Carol Carrick　297

Simon (Child)
The Talking Parcel - Gerald Durrel　552

Simon (Knight)
The Castle in the Attic - Elizabeth Winthrop　1931

Simon, Jon (Preteen; Abuse Victim)
My Friend, My Brother - David Warren Swartley　1773

Simone (Child)
Noonday Friends - Mary Stolz　1758

Sinbad (Cat; Vagrant)
Captains of the City Street: A Story of a Cat Club - Esther Averill　69

Sinbad (Dog)
Sinbad and Me - Kin Platt　1452

Sinclare, Edward (Fisherman)
The Selchie's Seed - Shulamith Oppenheim　1361

Sinclare, Marian (Preteen)
The Selchie's Seed - Shulamith Oppenheim　1361

Sinclare, Ursilla (Spouse)
The Selchie's Seed - Shulamith Oppenheim　1361

Sing (Gardener)
Next-Door Neighbors - Sarah Ellis　570

Singelmann, Anna (Teenager)
Don't Say a Word - Barbara Gehrts　679

Singer, Vanessa (Preteen)
Make Like a Tree and Leave - Paula Danziger　479

Singleton, Myron (Preteen)
Honestly, Myron - Dean Hughes　931

Sir Lancelot (Snake)
Alice and the Boa Constrictor - Laurie Adams　3

Sirius (Dog)
Dogsbody - Diana Wynne Jones　981

Sirow, Ed (Teenager; 8th Grader)
Romeo and Juliet - Together (and Alive!) at Last - Avi　71

Sister (Bear)
Bears in the Night - Stan Berenstain　140

Sister (Child; Indian)
Toughboy and Sister - Kirkpatrick Hill　883

Sizzlegridian, Snar (Friend)
The Robot and Rebecca: The Mystery of the Code Carrying Kids - Jane Yolen　1970

Skankwan (Chieftain; Teenager)
The Lion of the Kalahari - Esther Linfield　1127

Skellar, Dismas (Villain)
Gom on Windy Mountain - Grace Chetwin　324

Skin Horse (Toy; Horse)
The Velveteen Rabbit - Margery Williams　1923

Skinner (Librarian)
The Great Skinner Strike - Stephanie S. Tolan　1817

Skinner, Jenny (Teenager)
The Great Skinner Strike - Stephanie S. Tolan　1817

Skinner, Marcia (Child)
The Great Skinner Strike - Stephanie S. Tolan　1817

Skinny (Child)
The Case of the Scaredy Cats - Crosby Bonsall　175

Skinny (Orphan)
Skinny - Robert Burch　245

Skinny Jack (Handyman)
The Ghost of Skinny Jack - Astrid Lindgren　1123

Skip (Assistant)
The Curse of the Egyptian Mummy - Pat Hutchins　959

Skip (Preteen)
Rish n' Roses - Jan Slepian　1666
Wildcat Summer - Mary Riskind　1508

Skyjumper, Jake (Computer Expert)
Commander Toad and the Intergalactic Spy - Jane Yolen　1968

Slake, Aremis (Teenager; Streetperson)
Slake's Limbo - Felice Holman　908

Slayton, Jerome (Scientist; Researcher)
Dear Mom, You're Ruining My Life - Jean Van Leeuwen　1846

Slayton, Samantha (Preteen)
Dear Mom, You're Ruining My Life - Jean Van Leeuwen　1846

Slighcarp (Governess)
The Wolves of Willoughby Chase - Joan Aiken　18

Sloane, Alice (Teenager)
The Worry Week - Anne Lindbergh　1121

Sloane, Allegra "Legs" (Preteen)
The Worry Week - Anne Lindbergh　1121

Sloane, Edith "Minnow" (Child)
The Worry Week - Anne Lindbergh　1121

Slobodkin, George (Preteen)
Next-Door Neighbors - Sarah Ellis　570

Slocum, Bill (Preteen)
The Red Room Riddle - Scott Corbett　427

Slocum, Kib (Preteen)
Thatcher Payne-in-the-Neck - Betty Bates　105

Small (Dentist)
The Emma Dilemma - Catherine Sefton　1603

Small, Edward (Preteen)
The Tar Pit - Tor Seidler　1607

Small, Emma Kirstie (Child)
The Emma Dilemma - Catherine Sefton　1603

Small, Thomas (Teenager)
The House of Dies Drear - Virginia Hamilton　802

Small, William (Child)
The Emma Dilemma - Catherine Sefton　1603

Small Fur (Mythical Creature)
Small Fur - Irina Korschunov　1053

Smalls, Robert (Military Personnel; Historical Figure)
Captain of the Planters: The Biography of Robert Smalls - Dorothy Sterling　1741

Smart, Ralph (Mouse)
Ralph S. Mouse - Beverly Cleary　353

Smellie, Minnie (Bully)
Rebecca of Sunnybrook Farm - Kate Douglas Wiggin　1907

Smitch (Child)
The Case of the Scaredy Cats - Crosby Bonsall　175

Smith (Thief)
Smith - Leon Garfield　671

Smith, Beau (Neighbor)
The Solitary - Lynn Hall　795

Smith, Belinda Rainbow "Boo" (Preteen)
The Big Smith Snatch - Jane Louise Curry　457

Smith, Cisco (Child)
The Big Smith Snatch - Jane Louise Curry　457

Smith, Fran Ellen (Child)
The Bear's House - Marilyn Sachs　1574

Smith, Galen (Preteen)
Mystery on Ice - Barbara Corcoran　431

Smith, James Gregory Jr. (Child)
Phantom of Walkaway Hill - Edward Fenton　594

Smith, John (Settler; Historical Figure)
The Double Life of Pocahontas - Jean Fritz　650
Pocahontas and the Strangers - Clyde Robert Bulla　227

Smith, Josie (Child)
Josie Smith - Magdalen Nabb　1307

Smith, Mina (Teenager; Dancer)
Come a Stranger - Cynthia Voigt　1862

Stebbins, Grace (Neighbor)
Nothing Stays the Same Forever - Gail Radley 1483

Steele, Angela (Child; Kindergartner)
Oh Honestly, Angela! - Nancy K. Robinson 1519

Steele, Nathaniel (Child)
Oh Honestly, Angela! - Nancy K. Robinson 1519

Steele, Tina (Preteen)
Oh Honestly, Angela! - Nancy K. Robinson 1519

Stein (Teacher)
Maria Luisa - Winifred Madison 1175

Stein, Frances "Frankie" (Scientist)
The Monster Garden - Vivien Alcock 20

Stella (Preteen)
Mystery on Ice - Barbara Corcoran 431

Stella (Relative)
The Ring and the Window Seat - Amy Hest 874

Stenner (Step-Parent)
Me and Mr. Stenner - Evan Hunter 938

Stephanie (Child)
All Because I'm Older - Phyllis Reynolds Naylor 1312
The Case of the Weird Street Firebug - Carol Russell Law 1077

Stephanus, Magister (Wizard)
The Cat Who Wished to Be a Man - Lloyd Alexander 26

Stephen (Child)
The Big Kite Contest - Dorotha Ruthstrom 1561

Stephen (Preteen)
Wild Man of the Woods - Joan Clark 345

Sterling, Nancy (Teenager)
Sometimes I Think I Hear My Name - Avi 73

Sternwood, Stafford "Stuffy" (Preteen)
Anything for a Friend - Ellen Conford 400

Steve (Child; Captive)
Captives in a Foreign Land - Susan Lowry Rardin 1487

Steve (Child)
Max and Me and the Time Machine - Gery Greer 761

Steve (Preteen)
Tac's Island - Ruth Yaffe Radin 1482

Steve (Child)
The Week Mom Unplugged the TVs - Terry Wolfe Phelan 1434

Stewart, Candace (Preteen)
If Phyllis Were Here - Gail Jarrow 972

Stickley (Teacher)
Molly's Pilgrim - Barbara Cohen 382

Stig (Parent; Worker)
Gom on Windy Mountain - Grace Chetwin 324

Stinker, Ts yng (Alien; Spy)
Stinker From Space - Pamela F. Service 1614

Stinson, Luke (Child)
Doodle and the Go-Cart - Robert Burch 241

Stirkel, Florence (Preteen)
Growing Anyway Up - Florence Parry Heide 844

Stokes, Jennifer (Child)
The War with Grandpa - Robert Kimmel Smith 1692

Stokes, Mudge (Child)
The Gathering Room - Colby Rodowsky 1537

Stokes, Ned (Parent; Worker)
The Gathering Room - Colby Rodowsky 1537

Stokes, Peter (Preteen)
The War with Grandpa - Robert Kimmel Smith 1692

Stomper (Preteen; Sports Figure)
The Luck of the Miss L. - Lee Kingman 1034

Stone Fox (Sports Figure; Indian)
Stone Fox - John Reynolds Gardiner 668

Stoner, Casey (Child; Dancer)
Dumb Old Casey Is a Fat Tree - Barbara Bottner 180

Storm Boy (Preteen)
Storm Boy - Colin Thiele 1802

Stott, Jemmy (Teenager)
Jemmy - Jon Francis Hassler 824

Stout, Benjamin (Sailor)
The Slave Dancer - Paula Fox 641

Stover (Teacher)
My Brother Stevie - Eleanor Clymer 372

Stowe, Quentin (Child)
All the Money in the World - Bill Brittain 202

Strawspinner (Clerk)
Andrew and the Alchemist - Barbara Ninde Byfield 269

Strider (Dog)
Strider - Beverly Cleary 356

Stubbins, Tommy (Child)
The Voyages of Dr. Doolittle - Hugh Lofting 1144

Stubbs, Rainbow Maximilian (Preteen)
Journey to an 800 Number - E.L. Konigsburg 1047

Stubbs, Sarah (Parent)
Journey to an 800 Number - E.L. Konigsburg 1047

Stubbs, Woody (Parent; Entertainer)
Journey to an 800 Number - E.L. Konigsburg 1047

Sue Ellen (Child)
Like Everybody Else - Barbara Girion 708

Sugarman, Shelley (Actress)
No Applause, Please - Marilyn Singer 1655

Suggs, Dorrit L. (Villain)
The Money Room - Eloise Jarvis McGraw 1229

Summer (7th Grader; Orphan)
Missing May - Cynthia Rylant 1568

Summers, Ruth (Housekeeper)
Davey Come Home - Margaret Teibl 1792

Sun Run, Jack (Teenager)
Arilla Sun Down - Virginia Hamilton 799

Sunday, Gladys (Neighbor)
A Memory for Tino - Leo Buscaglia 252

Sunshine (Neighbor)
Mr. Pepper Stories - Mark Taylor 1783

Susan (Child)
The Lion, the Witch, and the Wardrobe - C.S. Lewis 1110

Susan (Preteen)
Meaning Well - Sheila R. Cole 391
Worlds Apart - Jill Murphy 1298

Susannah (Preteen)
I Am Susannah - Libby Gleeson 709

Susskit, Russell (Teenager; Eskimo)
Dogsong - Gary Paulsen 1397

Sutherland, Roger (Relative)
Look through My Window - Jean Little 1134

Sutton, Annie (Preteen)
The Well - Gene Kemp 1011

Sutton, Kate (Child)
Perilous Gard - Elizabeth Marie Pope 1456

Sutton, Randall (Child)
Ida Early Comes over the Mountain - Robert Burch 242

Sutton, Sandra (Child)
Enemies - Robin Klein 1040

Sutton, Tom (Preteen)
The Well - Gene Kemp 1011

Suzuki, Hideko "Sam" (Preteen)
Shortstop From Tokyo - Matt Christopher 339

Svoboda, Sam (Preteen)
The Mystery of the Diamond in the Wood - David Kherdian 1021

Svoboda, Skip (Sports Figure)
Cute Is a Four Letter Word - Stella Pevsner 1425

Swain, Joshua (Sea Captain)
By the Great Horn Spoon - Sid Fleischman 619

Swamp Haunt (Monster)
Liza Lou and the Yeller Belly Swamp - Mercer Mayer 1211

Swan, Elzibah (Grandparent)
Sea Swan - Kathryn Lasky 1073

Swanson, Maureen (Preteen)
The Wicked Pigeon Ladies in the Garden - Mary Chase 321

Swanson, Rosie (Preteen)
Maxie, Rosie, and Earl - Partners in Grime - Barbara Park 1379

Swanstrom, Eric (Orphan)
Thimble Summer - Elizabeth Enright 574

Sweeney (Child)
The Empty Window - Anne Evelyn Bunting 229

Sweep (Dog)
Only One Woof - James Herriot 867

Sweet, Ben (Servant)
Darwin and the Voyage of the Beagle - Felicia Law 1078

Sweet, Sylvester S. (Villain)
The Worldwide Dessert Contest - Dan Elish 564

Swenson, Mattie (Scientist)
Part-Time Boy - Elizabeth T. Billington 146

Swift, Samuel (Eccentric)
The Warlock of Westfall - Leonard Everett Fisher 606

Sykes, Anthea "Awful" (Child)
Archer's Goon - Diana Wynne Jones 978

Sykes, Howard (Teenager)
Archer's Goon - Diana Wynne Jones 978

Sylvester, Sam (Teacher)
Who, Sir? Me, Sir? - K.M. Peyton 1430

Sylvie (Preteen)
Miracle at Clement's Pond - Patricia Pendergraft 1418

T

Tabitha "Tabby" (Teenager)
Murder at the Spaniel Show - Lynn Hall 794

Tabor, Zeely (Neighbor)
Zeely - Virginia Hamilton   807

Tag (Dog)
No Bean Sprouts, Please! - Constance Hiser   885

Takashima, Shizuye (Child)
A Child in Prison Camp - Shizuye Takashima   1775

Talatu (Preteen; Indian)
Man with the Silver Eyes - William O. Steele   1729

Tanleven, Nina (Preteen; 6th Grader)
The Ghost Wore Gray - Bruce Coville   437

Tannenbaum, Jamie (Child; Patient)
Just Like Always - Elizabeth-Ann Sachs   1572

Tao (Cat)
The Incredible Journey - Sheila Burnford   250

Tao (Child)
Lon Po Po: A Red Riding Hood Story From China - Ed Young   1977

Taolo (Teenager)
Chain of Fire - Beverly Naidoo   1309

Taran (Farmer)
The Black Cauldron - Lloyd Alexander   25

Taran (Hero)
The High King - Lloyd Alexander   28

Taro (Military Personnel)
The Wind Is Not a River - Arnold A. Griese   767

Tarryhere (Turtle; Knight)
The Acorn Quest - Jane Yolen   1967

Tarzan (Chimpanzee)
Castaways on Chimp Island - Sandy Landsman   1067

Tassie (Preteen)
The Times They Used to Be - Lucille Clifton   367

Tate, Julia (Teenager)
Rats, Spiders, and Love - Bonnie Pryor   1474

Tate, Kevin (Child)
Rats, Spiders, and Love - Bonnie Pryor   1474

Tate, Samantha "Sam" (Preteen)
Rats, Spiders, and Love - Bonnie Pryor   1474

Tatie (Housekeeper)
Autumn Street - Lois Lowry   1152

Tatlek (Child; Handicapped)
At the Mouth of the Luckiest River - Arnold A. Griese   765

Tawena (Indian)
Drift - William Mayne   1213

Taylor (Teacher)
Save the Dam! - Harriet Sirof   1656

Taylor, Emily (Child)
Nobody's Fault - Patricia Hermes   864

Taylor, Jason (Alien)
Invasion of the Comet People - Philip Curtis   459

Taylor, Matthew "Monse" (Child)
Nobody's Fault - Patricia Hermes   864

Taylor, Mi (Horse Trainer)
National Velvet - Enid Bagnold   82

Taylor, Miranda (Teenager)
Mad, Mad Monday - Herma Silverstein   1643

Taylor, Tuck (Maintenance Worker)
The Great Ringtail Garbage Caper - Timothy Foote   632

Teach, Edward "Blackbeard" (Pirate; Historical Figure)
Blackbeard's Ghost - Ben Stahl   1724

Teague, Daniel (Landlord)
Mystery of the Haunted Pool - Phyllis A. Whitney   1903

Tebbits, Ellen (Child)
Ellen Tebbits - Beverly Cleary   351

Ted (Turtle)
In the Middle of the Puddle - Mike Thaler   1797

Ted (Teenager; Counselor)
There's a Bat in Bunk Five - Paula Danziger   481

Teddy (Child)
Russell Sprouts - Johanna Hurwitz   956

Teddy (Child; Kindergartener)
Superduper Teddy - Johanna Hurwitz   957

Teddy (Child)
The Toad Hunt - Janet Chenery   322

Tee (Child)
The Lucky Stone - Lucille Clifton   366

Teetoncey (Survivor; Handicapped)
Teetoncey - Theodore Taylor   1790

Temple, Cindy (Child)
Mystery of the Bewitched Bookmobile - Florence Parry Heide   845

Tenser, Gillian (Friend)
A Word From Our Sponsor: Or, My Friend Alfred - Judie Angell   51

Terrell, Matt (Teenager)
ESP McGee - Edward Packard   1372

Terry (Teenager)
The Watcher in the Garden - Joan Phipson   1439

Tessa (Child)
The Hammerhead Light - Colin Thiele   1800

Thacher, Enoch (Sailor)
All Sail Set: A Romance of the Flying Cloud - Armstrong Sperry   1711

Thaddeus (Survivor)
Orvis - H.M. Hoover   914

Thatcher, Becky (Friend)
The Adventures of Tom Sawyer - Mark Twain   1834

Thelma (Relative)
Tallahassee Higgins - Mary Downing Hahn   790

Themistokles (Hero; Historical Figure)
Children of the Fox - Jill Paton Walsh   1392

Thiel, Daniel (Artist)
Callender Papers - Cynthia Voigt   1861

Thing (Alien)
Space Case - Edward Marshall   1197

Thistle (Child)
Thistle - Walter Wangerin   1883

Thomas (Teenager)
Beyond the Weir Bridge - Hester Burton   251

Thomas (Child)
Crutches - Peter Hartling   820

Thomas (Mouse)
Fast Friends: Two Stories - James Stevenson   1746

Thomas (Child)
Go Fish - Mary Stolz   1756

Thomas
Jethro and the Jumbie - Susan Cooper   420

Thomas (Child)
The Pinballs - Betsy Byars   266
Porcupine Stew - Beverly Major   1184

Thomas (Religious)
A Solitary Blue - Cynthia Voigt   1865

Goodbye, My Island - Jean Rogers   1539

Thomas (Teacher)
Saturdays in the City - Ann Sharpless Bond   166

Thompson (Teacher)
The Bear's House - Marilyn Sachs   1574
No Place for Me - Barthe DeClements   499

Thompson, John (Postal Worker)
Snowshoe Thompson - Nancy Smiler Levinson   1101

Thompson, Molly Vera (Child)
The Kid in the Red Jacket - Barbara Park   1378

Thompson, Wade (Child)
213 Valentines - Barbara Cohen   379

Thorfinnsson, Snorri (Viking)
Snorri and the Strangers - Nathaniel Benchley   134

Thorn, Michael (Teenager)
The Sandman's Eyes - Patricia Windsor   1928

Thornhill (Religious)
The Integration of Mary-Larkin Thornhill - Ann Waldron   1869

Thornhill, Mary-Larkin (Student)
The Integration of Mary-Larkin Thornhill - Ann Waldron   1869

Thornton, Cynthia Jane (Preteen; 5th Grader)
The One and Only Cynthia Jane Thornton - Claudia Mills   1269

Thornton, Lucy (Child; 5th Grader)
The One and Only Cynthia Jane Thornton - Claudia Mills   1269

Thoroughgood (Teacher)
The Blood and Thunder Adventure on Hurricane Peak - Margaret Mahy   1179

Tiaf (Antiques Dealer)
The Antrian Messenger - G. Clifton Wisler   1938

Tibbs, Timothy (Twin; Orphan)
The Owlstone Crown - X.J. Kennedy   1016

Tibbs, Verity (Twin; Orphan)
The Owlstone Crown - X.J. Kennedy   1016

Tibby (Adoptee)
The Believers - Rebecca C. Jones   983

Tibeso (Worker)
The Leopard - Cecil Bodker   162

Tidd, Jamie (Teenager)
The Hostage - Theodore Taylor   1789

Tifflin, Carl (Parent)
The Red Pony - John Steinbeck   1738

Tifflin, Jody (Child)
The Red Pony - John Steinbeck   1738

Tillerman, Dicey (Teenager)
Dicey's Song - Cynthia Voigt   1863

Tillerman, Dicey (Teenager; Abandoned Child)
Homecoming - Cynthia Voigt   1864

Tillerman, Gram (Grandparent)
Dicey's Song - Cynthia Voigt   1863

Tillerman, Maybeth (Abandoned Child)
Homecoming - Cynthia Voigt   1864

Tillett, Andrew (Preteen)
The Case of the Murdered Players - Robert Newman   1329

Tillett, Verna (Actress; Parent)
The Case of the Murdered Players - Robert Newman   1329

Tillie (Skunk)
Tillie and Mert - Ida Luttrell 1158

Tilly (Animal Lover)
Marshmallow - Clare Turlay Newberry 1327

Tim (Relative)
Losing Uncle Tim - Marykate Jordan 986

Tim (Child)
Ship's Cook Ginger - Edward Ardizzone 54

Timkin (Acrobat)
The Red King - Victor Kelleher 1005

Timmer (Teenager)
One More Flight - Eve Bunting 234

Timothy (Survivor)
The Cay - Theodore Taylor 1788

Tingley (Coach)
The Hockey Girls - Scott Corbett 424

Tino (Child)
A Memory for Tino - Leo Buscaglia 252

Tippet, Margaret (Child)
Margaret and Taylor - Kevin Henkes 851

Tippet, Taylor (Child)
Margaret and Taylor - Kevin Henkes 851

Tippitt (Tailor)
Clancy's Coat - Eve Bunting 230

Tituba (Slave; Historical Figure)
The Tall Man From Boston - Marion Lena
    Starkey 1727
Tituba of Salem Village - Ann Petry 1423

Toad (Toad)
Frog and Toad All Year - Arnold Lobel 1139
Frog and Toad Together - Arnold Lobel 1140
The Wind in the Willows - Kenneth Grahame 733

Toad (Spaceship Captain)
Commander Toad and the Intergalactic Spy - Jane
    Yolen 1968

Tobin, Douglas (Veterinarian)
The Trouble with Tuck - Theodore Taylor 1791

Toby (Dog)
Katy Did It - Victoria Boutis 182

Toby (Survivor)
Orvis - H.M. Hoover 914

Toby (Child)
The Sea Egg - L.M. Boston 178

Toby (Preteen)
Toby Lived Here - Hilma Wolitzer 1943

Tock (Dog)
The Phantom Tollbooth - Norton Juster 990

Todd (Preteen)
Aunt Morbelia and the Screaming Skulls - Joan
    Davenport Carris 300

Todd (Toy)
The Dollhouse Caper - Jean S. O'Connell 1349

Todd, Flora (Housekeeper)
The Cat in the Mirror - Mary Stolz 1752

Todd, Jane (Child)
The Berkley Street Six Pack - Mary Francis
    Shura 1633

Todd, Timothy (Peddler)
The Gollywhopper Egg - Anne Rockwell 1527

Tole, Rex (Pilot; Smuggler)
Caught in the Moving Mountains - Gloria
    Skurzynski 1658

Tolly (Preteen)
Cave under the City - Harry Mazer 1214

Tom (Apprentice; Hero)
Doctor Change - Joanna Cole 388

Tom (Preteen)
Grey Cloud - Charlotte Towner Graeber 729

Tom (Child)
The Secret Three - Mildred Myrick 1306

Tomaro (Magician)
With a Wave of the Wand - Mark Jonathan
    Harris 817

Tommy (Child; Bully)
The Balancing Girl - Berniece Rabe 1478

Tomorrow's Wizard (Wizard)
Tomorrow's Wizard - Patricia Maclachlan 1172

Tony (Child)
The Midnight Fox - Betsy Byars 264
On My Honor - Marion Dane Bauer 108

Tony (Orphan)
The Sky Is Free - Mavis Thorpe Clark 346

Tooey, Alice (Babysitter; Witch)
Mrs. Tooey and the Terrible Toxic Tar - Barbara
    Dillon 526

Toong Talong (Elephant)
The Elephant in the Dark - Carol Carrick 295

Toonie (Clerk)
The Dancing Cats of Applesap - Janet Taylor
    Lisle 1129

Tooth (Detective; Dragon)
The Secret of Foghorn Island - Geoffrey Hayes 834

Tooth (Sea Captain)
*The Alligator and His Uncle Tooth: A Novel of the
    Sea* - Geoffrey Hayes 833

Tootsie (Child)
Superfudge - Judy Blume 158

Torcom (Musician)
My Mom, the Money Nut - Betty Bates 103

Torolov (Orphan)
Torolov the Fatherless - Pauline Clarke 348

Toughboy (Preteen; Indian)
Toughboy and Sister - Kirkpatrick Hill 883

Tracy, Hank (Counselor)
The Summer I Was Lost - Phillip Viereck 1855

Trafford, William (Teenager)
Adam's Common - David Wiseman 1937

Tran, Thuy (Child)
Janie's Private Eyes - Zilpha Keatley Snyder 1699

Trane, Lewis "Goober" (Student)
Banana Blitz - Florence Parry Heide 843

Trantor, Kate (Student)
The Way to Sattin Shore - Philippa Pearce 1402

Trapper Jack (Recluse)
The Mystery of the Diamond in the Wood - David
    Kherdian 1021

Travers, Judd (Hunter)
Shiloh - Phyllis Reynolds Naylor 1318

Travis (Teenager)
Old Yeller - Fred Gipson 707

Travis, Jan (Child; Captive)
*The Kidnapping of Courtney Van Allen and What's-
    Her-Name* - Joyce Cool 412

Tree (Teenager)
Sweet Whispers, Brother Rush - Virginia
    Hamilton 806

Treehorn (Child)
Treehorn's Treasure - Florence Parry Heide 846

Treeman, Rosy (Preteen)
Lucy Forever and Miss Rosetree, Shrinks - Susan
    Richards Shreve 1629

Treloar, Amy (Preteen)
The Dollhouse Murders - Betty Ren Wright 1954

Treloar, Louann (Handicapped)
The Dollhouse Murders - Betty Ren Wright 1954

Treloar, Septimus (Detective; Religious)
Septimus and the Danedyke Mystery - Stephen
    Chance 316

Tremain, Johnny (Apprentice)
Johnny Tremain - Esther Forbes 633

Tremalin (Knight)
Merlin Dreams - Peter Dickinson 523

Trevelyan, Toby (Businessman)
Night Fall - Joan Aiken 17

Tristan (Teenager; Royalty)
Tristan and Iseult - Rosemary Sutcliff 1770

Triton (Mythical Creature)
The Sea Egg - L.M. Boston 178

Trotter, James Henry (Orphan)
James and the Giant Peach - Roald Dahl 466

Trotter, Maime (Foster Parent)
The Great Gilly Hopkins - Katherine Paterson 1388

Troup (Neighbor)
No Beasts! No Children! - Beverly Keller 1007

Trowbridge, Gilbert (Friend; 5th Grader)
Say Cheese - Betty Bates 104

Troxell, Jeanmarie (Preteen)
Up From Jerico Tel - E.L. Konigsburg 1048

Troy, Luke (Teenager)
Trouble with Mothers - Margery Facklam 583

Troy, Maggie (Child)
Trouble with Mothers - Margery Facklam 583

Troy, Martha (Writer; Teacher)
Trouble with Mothers - Margery Facklam 583

Trudl (Refugee)
A Certain Magic - Doris Orgel 1362

True Blue (Cat)
Porcupine Stew - Beverly Major 1184

Trumble, Harvey William (6th Grader;
    Collector)
Harvey, the Beer Can King - Jamie Gilson 703

Trumbull, Elvira (Preteen)
The Twenty-Five Cent Miracle - Theresa
    Nelson 1322

Trumbull, Henry "Hank" (Parent)
The Twenty-Five Cent Miracle - Theresa
    Nelson 1322

Trunchbull (Principal)
Matilda - Roald Dahl 468

Tsujimura, Rinko (Preteen)
A Jar of Dreams - Yoshiko Uchida 1836

Tuatara (Hero)
Harry Newberry and the Raiders of the Red Drink -
    Mel Gilden 700

Vikki (Teenager; Detective)
The Bloodhound Gang and the Case of the Secret Message - Sid Fleischman 618

Violet (Chimpanzee)
Arthur's Honey Bear - Lillian Hoban 888

Vira (Spirit)
The Scorpio Ghosts and the Black Hole Gang - Kathy Kennedy Tapp 1778

Vita (Cousin)
Earthquake 2099 - Mary W. Sullivan 1768

Vlecke, Kaleb (Parent)
Just Plain Fancy - Patricia Polacco 1453

Vlecke, Naomi (Child)
Just Plain Fancy - Patricia Polacco 1453

Vlecke, Ruth (Child)
Just Plain Fancy - Patricia Polacco 1453

Vogel, Mark (Friend)
Dreams of Victory - Ellen Conford 401

Voight, Ephraim (Musician)
Marion's Angels - K.M. Peyton 1428

Von Pokus, Hokus (Magician)
Little Man - Erich Kastner 997

Vorlob, Adine (Preteen)
The Zebra Wall - Kevin Henkes 852

Vorlob, Bernice (Child)
The Zebra Wall - Kevin Henkes 852

Vorlob, Carla (Child)
The Zebra Wall - Kevin Henkes 852

Vren (Animal Lover)
Outside the Gates - Molly Gloss 711

W

Wadat (Shaman; Indian)
Vision Quest - Pamela F. Service 1615

Wade, Crockett "Crock" (Twin)
Lavender-Green Magic - Andre Norton 1341

Wade, Holly (Preteen)
Lavender-Green Magic - Andre Norton 1341

Wade, Judy (Twin)
Lavender-Green Magic - Andre Norton 1341

Wade, Pete (Child)
The Package in Hyperspace - Janet Asimov 63

Wadley, Fern (Teenager)
Buddies - Barbara Park 1377

Waggoner, Catfish (Parent)
Curly and the Wild Boar - Fred Gipson 706

Wagner, Ben (Preteen)
The Witching of Ben Wagner - Mary Jane Auch 68

Wagner, Susan (Child)
The Witching of Ben Wagner - Mary Jane Auch 68

Wagoner, Curly (Preteen)
Curly and the Wild Boar - Fred Gipson 706

Wainwright, Jason (Preteen)
Keeping it Secret - Penny Pollock 1455

Wainwright, Jean (Orphan)
Callender Papers - Cynthia Voigt 1861

Waite, Adam (Doctor)
Dark Venture - Audrey White Beyer 145

Waite, Dudley (Child; Vacationer)
Castaways on Long Ago - Edward Ormondroyd 1366

Waite, Glenda (Teenager)
Hey, Remember Fat Glenda? - Lila Perl 1419

Waite, Linda (Child; Vacationer)
Castaways on Long Ago - Edward Ormondroyd 1366

Waite, Richard (Child; Vacationer)
Castaways on Long Ago - Edward Ormondroyd 1366

Waka (Relative)
A Jar of Dreams - Yoshiko Uchida 1836

Waldron, Jonathan (Child)
Stinker From Space - Pamela F. Service 1614

Walker (Grandparent)
Getting Rid of Marjorie - Betty Ren Wright 1955

Walker, Bonnie (Coach)
The Rascals From Haskell's Gym - Frank Bonham 173

Walker, Bruce (Preteen; Animal Lover)
Hotel for Dogs - Lois Duncan 549

Walker, John (Child)
Swallows and Amazons - Arthur Ransome 1485

Walker, John (Sailor)
We Didn't Mean to Go to Sea - Arthur Ransome 1486

Walker, Katie (Preteen)
The Girl with the Silver Eyes - Willo Davis Roberts 1510

Walker, Liz (Preteen; Animal Lover)
Hotel for Dogs - Lois Duncan 549

Walker, Marjorie (Spouse)
Getting Rid of Marjorie - Betty Ren Wright 1955

Walker, Martha "Marti" (Friend)
Bring to a Boil and Separate - Hadley Irwin 966

Walker, Monica (Parent)
The Girl with the Silver Eyes - Willo Davis Roberts 1510

Walker, Rachel (Child)
Do-it-Yourself Magic - Ruth Chew 325

Walker, Roger (Sailor)
We Didn't Mean to Go to Sea - Arthur Ransome 1486

Walker, Scott (Child)
Do-it-Yourself Magic - Ruth Chew 325

Walker, Susan (Child)
Swallows and Amazons - Arthur Ransome 1485

Walker, Susan (Sailor)
We Didn't Mean to Go to Sea - Arthur Ransome 1486

Wallace (Neighbor)
A Sound of Chariots - Mollie Hunter 940

Wallace, John (Store Owner)
The Friendship - Mildred D. Taylor 1784

Wallis, Ned (Child)
One-Eyed Cat - Paula Fox 639

Walter (Preteen)
General Butterfingers - John Reynolds Gardiner 667

Walter (Child)
Just a Dream - Chris Van Allsburg 1841

Walter (Step-Parent)
Mitzi and the Terrible Tyranosaurus Rex - Barbara Williams 1918

Warbeak (Sparrow)
Redwall - Brian Jacques 967

Ward, Janis (Child)
Golden Daffodils - Marilyn Gould 726

Warner, Kathryn "Katie" (Teenager)
Bring to a Boil and Separate - Hadley Irwin 966

Warren, Amy (Neighbor)
Rat Teeth - Patricia Reilly Giff 698

Warrilow, Harry (Settler)
Greenhorn on the Frontier - Ann Finlayson 604

Warrilow, Sukey (Settler)
Greenhorn on the Frontier - Ann Finlayson 604

Warthog (Warthog)
Tales of a Wandering Warthog - Tom Sinclair 1650

Washington (Nurse)
Raymond - Mark Geller 681

Washington, Mercedes (Musician)
The Day That Elvis Came to Town - Jan Marino 1193

Wat (Baker)
The Ice Bear - Betty Levin 1097

Watie, Stand (Military Personnel)
Rifles for Watie - Harold Keith 1004

Watson, Tubby (Preteen)
The Trading Game - Alfred Slote 1675

Watson II (Robot)
The Robot and Rebecca: The Mystery of the Code Carrying Kids - Jane Yolen 1970

Waxweather, Myrna C. (Spirit; Entertainer)
The Magic of Myrna C. Waxweather - Sandra Dutton 553

Wayd, Ginnela "Ginn" (Preteen)
The Package in Hyperspace - Janet Asimov 63

Wayne (Teenager)
The Winter Room - Gary Paulsen 1400

Wayne, Jared (Preteen)
Ride the Green Dragon - Andre Norton 1342

Wayne, Tracy (Preteen)
Ride the Green Dragon - Andre Norton 1342

Weasel (Villain)
Weasel - Cynthia DeFelice 502

Webb, Crystal (Neighbor)
Veronica Meets Her Match - Nancy K. Robinson 1520

Weber (Duck)
Pippa Pops Out: Four Read-Aloud/Read Alone Stories - Betty Boegehold 164

Webster, "Girlie" (Preteen; Orphan)
The Girl Who Had No Name - Berniece Rabe 1479

Webster, Jane (Preteen)
Afternoon of the Elves - Janet Taylor Lisle 1128

Webster, Wanda (Teenager)
The Girl Who Had No Name - Berniece Rabe 1479

Wechsler, Martin (Editor)
The Kenton Year - Ruth Wallace-Brodeur 1879

Weems (Veteran)
December Stillness - Mary Downing Hahn 786

Weinstock, Reuben (Worker)
Two Piano Tuners - M.B. Goffstein 716

Wells (Teacher)
Rufus M. - Eleanor Estes 578

Wells, Jefferson "Jeff" (Teenager; Student)
Norby, the Mixed-Up Robot - Janet Asimov 62

Welly (Teenager)
Winter of Magic's Return - Pamela F. Service 1616

Welsch, Harriet (Child)
Harriet the Spy - Louise Fitzhugh 608

Wembleton, Lila (Child)
Noonday Friends - Mary Stolz 1758

Wemstock, Debbie (Child)
Two Piano Tuners - M.B. Goffstein 716

Wendel (Teacher)
Fat Men from Space - Daniel Manus
Pinkwater 1443

Wenders, Peter (Publisher)
The Mysteries of Harris Burdick - Chris Van
Allsburg 1842

Wendleken, Alice (Child)
The Best Christmas Pageant Ever - Barbara
Robinson 1517

Wendy (Preteen)
Always and Forever Friends - Carole S. Adler 5
Blubber - Judy Blume 153

Wendy (Teenager)
The Leftover Kid - Carol Snyder 1694

Wendy (Child)
Wendy and the Bullies - Nancy K. Robinson 1521

Wesley, John (Weasel)
The Book of the Dun Cow - Walter
Wangerin 1882

West, Daniel (Teenager)
Early Thunder - Jean Fritz 651

Westbrooke, Denny (Sports Figure)
Quarterback Walk-On - Thomas J. Dygard 555

Westing, Samuel W. (Wealthy)
The Westing Game - Ellen Raskin 1490

Wetzel, Jenny (Preteen)
They're All Named Wildfire - Nancy
Springer 1718

Wexler, Davey (Teenager)
Tiger Eyes - Judy Blume 159

Wexler, Gwendolyn (Parent)
Tiger Eyes - Judy Blume 159

Wexler, Jason (Child)
Tiger Eyes - Judy Blume 159

Wharton, Bailey (Preteen)
Heads, I Win - Patricia Hermes 862

Wheaton, Sarah (Mail Order Bride; Step-Parent)
Sarah, Plain and Tall - Patricia MacLachlan 1170

Whipple, Alice (Child)
Alice and the Boa Constrictor - Laurie Adams 3

White, Ellen (Parent)
Grasshopper Summer - Ann Warren Turner 1832

White, Otis (Spirit)
The Ghost Upstairs - Lila McGinnis 1226

White, Sam (Preteen)
Grasshopper Summer - Ann Warren Turner 1832

White, William "Billy" (Preteen)
Grasshopper Summer - Ann Warren Turner 1832

White Dragoness, Regina (Dragon)
The Dragons of North Chittendon - Susan Fromberg
Schaeffer 1591

White Fang (Indian)
Rattlesnake Cave - Evelyn Sibley Lampman 1064

White Lodge (Chieftain; Indian)
Betrayed - Virginia Driving Hawk Sneve 1693

Whitfield, Henry Barrett (Preteen)
Henry's Special Delivery - M.C. Delaney 508

Whiting, Anna (Child)
Sarah, Plain and Tall - Patricia MacLachlan 1170

Whiting, Caleb (Child)
Sarah, Plain and Tall - Patricia MacLachlan 1170

Whitlaw (Neighbor)
Dragonwings - Lawrence Yep 1966

Whitney (Bear)
Jason and the Baseball Bear - Dan Elish 563

Wilbur (Pig)
Charlotte's Web - E.B. White 1899

Wilbur (Mouse)
Pearl's Pirates - Frank Asch 58

Wilbur, Earl (Preteen)
Maxie, Rosie, and Earl - Partners in Grime - Barbara
Park 1379

Wilder, Almanzo (Farmer; Boyfriend)
Little Town on the Prairie - Laura Ingalls
Wilder 1910

Wiley (Child)
Humbug Mountain - Sid Fleischman 622

Wilfred (Snake)
Snakes Are Nothing to Sneeze At - Gabrielle
Charbonnet 319

Wilkes, Verna (Friend)
The Case of the Horrible Swamp Monster - Drew
Stevenson 1745

Wilkin (Teenager)
Wilkin's Ghost - Robert Burch 246

Wilkin (Farmer)
Only One Woof - James Herriot 867

Will (Orphan)
The Elephant in the Dark - Carol Carrick 295

Will (Preteen)
The Hayburners - Gene Smith 1687
Wild Boy - Joan Tate 1782

Willa (Child)
Unclaimed Treasures - Patricia MacLachlan 1173

Willard-Brown, T. (Cat)
Miss Hickory - Carolyn Sherwin Bailey 83

Willeford, Calvin (Preteen; Traveller)
The Dandelion Caper - Gene DeWeese 516

William (Child)
The Balancing Girl - Berniece Rabe 1478

William (Preteen)
The Castle in the Attic - Elizabeth Winthrop 1931

William (Child)
Fat Men from Space - Daniel Manus
Pinkwater 1443

William (Preteen)
*A Northern Nativity: Christmas Dreams of a Prairie
Boy* - William Kurelek 1061

Williams, Abigail (Child)
Tituba of Salem Village - Ann Petry 1423

Williams, Buddy (Preteen)
Mystery of the Fat Cat - Frank Bonham 172

Williams, Calamine "Callie" (Apprentice)
The Strange Night Writing of Jessamine Colter -
Cynthia DeFelice 501

Williams, Emmie (Child)
Leo, Zack and Emmie - Amy Ehrlich 561

Williams, Josias (Lumberjack)
Mississippi Bridge - Mildred D. Taylor 1785

Williams, Pop (Foster Parent)
Mak - Belle Coates 373

Willoughby-Green, Bonnie (Preteen)
The Wolves of Willoughby Chase - Joan Aiken 18

Willy (Child; Storyteller)
Four on the Shore - Edward Marshall 1196

Willy (Child)
Stone Fox - John Reynolds Gardiner 668

Wilson (Coach)
The Dog That Pitched a No-Hitter - Matt
Christopher 338

Wilson, Carey (Child)
Bedknob and Broomsticks - Mary Norton 1343

Wilson, Charles (Child)
Bedknob and Broomsticks - Mary Norton 1343

Wilson, Chuck (Preteen)
Follow My Leader - James B. Garfield 669

Wilson, Eli (Preteen)
Eli's Ghost - Betsy Hearne 841

Wilson, Lucy (Child)
The Oracle Doll - Catherine Dexter 518

Wilson, Ludell (Preteen; 5th Grader)
Ludell - Brenda Scott Wilkinson 1913

Wilson, Paul (Child)
Bedknob and Broomsticks - Mary Norton 1343

Wilson, Rose (Preteen)
The Oracle Doll - Catherine Dexter 518

Wind, Billie (Teenager; Indian)
The Talking Earth - Jean Craighead George 685

Wingate, Corrie (Preteen)
Dew Drop Dead: A Sebastian Barth Mystery - James
Howe 925

Wingford, David Ward "Pilgrim" (Parent;
Aged Person)
My Own Private Sky - Delores Beckman 127

Winkle, Oscar (Preteen)
Operation Dump the Chump - Barbara Park 1381

Winkle, Robert (Child)
Operation Dump the Chump - Barbara Park 1381

Winnie (Preteen; Time Traveller)
Mazemaker - Catherine Dexter 517

Winnie-the-Pooh (Toy; Bear)
The House at Pooh Corner - A.A. Milne 1270
Winnie-the-Pooh - A.A. Milne 1271

Winola (Orphan)
Underrunners - Margaret Mahy 1183

Winter (Teacher)
The Magic Finger - Roald Dahl 467
Meaning Well - Sheila R. Cole 391

Winterborn, Alpheus (Wealthy)
The Treasure of Alpheus Winterborn - John
Bellairs 128

Winters, Tabitha "Tibby" (Child)
The Rocking Horse Secret - Rumer Godden 715

Winthrop, Hallie (Teenager)
Sasha, My Friend - Barbara Corcoran 432

Winthrop, Norm (Bully)
The Magic Book - Willo Davis Roberts 1511

Wister (Neighbor)
Jenny and the Tennis Nut - Janet Schulman 1599

Wistrow, Waver (Friend)
But We Are Not of Earth - Jean Karl 995

Witch of the Waste (Witch)
Howl's Moving Castle - Diana Wynne Jones 982

Witherspoon, Abigail (Feminist)
The Manifesto and Me - Meg - Bobbi Katz 999

Witherspoon, Patrick (Child)
The Dragons of North Chittendon - Susan Fromberg Schaeffer 1591

Wolf (Dog)
Rip Van Winkle - Washington Irving 965

Wolfruff, Yuri (Dancer)
Sly, P.I.: The Case of the Missing Shoes - Cathy Stefanec-Ogren 1730

Wong, Shirley Temple (Child; Immigrant)
In the Year of the Boar and Jackie Robinson - Bette Bao Lord 1148

Woodlawn, Caddie (Child)
Caddie Woodlawn - Carol Ryrie Brink 201

Woodlawn, Tom (Teenager)
Caddie Woodlawn - Carol Ryrie Brink 201

Woodlawn, Warren (Child)
Caddie Woodlawn - Carol Ryrie Brink 201

Woodruff (Child; Collector)
Woodruff and the Clocks - Elizabeth Bram 186

Woodward, Orin (Teenager)
The Edge of Next Year - Mary Stolz 1754

Woodward, Victor (Child)
The Edge of Next Year - Mary Stolz 1754

Wook, Farmer (Farmer)
This Farm is a Mess - Leslie McGuire 1232

Worthen, Charles (Child)
Lyddie - Katherine Paterson 1390

Worthen, Lyddie (Teenager; Worker)
Lyddie - Katherine Paterson 1390

Worthen, Mattie (Parent)
Lyddie - Katherine Paterson 1390

Wrather, Jake (Preteen)
Jake - Alfred Slote 1672

Wrisby (Guardian)
Arthur, for the Very First Time - Patricia MacLachlan 1169

Wulf, Edgar (Child)
Once I Was a Plum Tree - Johanna Hurwitz 954

Wurmbrand (Widow(er); Neighbor)
Busybody Nora - Johanna Hurwitz 949

Wyatt, Peter (Police Officer)
The Case of the Murdered Players - Robert Newman 1329

Wyman, Lucinda (Child)
Roller Skates - Ruth Sawyer 1590

Y

Yale, Shadrach (Teacher)
Across Five Aprils - Irene Hunt 937

Yankel (Outcast; Criminal)
Yankel the Fool - Shan Ellentuck 565

Yanovitch, Mira (Immigrant)
I Met a Traveller - Lillian Hoban 889

Yoki (Horse)
A Girl Called Bob and a Horse Called Yoki - Barbara Campbell 287

Yolanda (Artist)
Toasted Bagels - Joyce Audy Zarins 1981

Yorick, Harold "Harry" (Child)
A Camel Called April - Diana Hendry 850

Yoshke (Resistance Fighter)
Uncle Misha's Partisans - Yuri Suhl 1767

Yosip (Cook)
The Place Where Nobody Stopped - Jerry Segal 1605

Young, Grubber (Alien)
The Planetoid of Amazement - Mel Glidden 710

Young Fu (Child)
Young Fu of the Upper Yangtze - Elizabeth Lewis 1111

Younger Brother (Indian)
Waterless Mountain - Laura Adams Armer 56

Z

Zach (Preteen; Detective)
The Bloodhound Gang and the Case of the Secret Message - Sid Fleischman 618

Zach (Preteen)
Today's Special: Z.A.P and Zoe - Athena V. Lord 1147

Zack (Child)
Leo, Zack and Emmie - Amy Ehrlich 561

Zane, Angie (Preteen; Detective)
Angie's First Case - Donald J. Sobol 1702

Zane, Kit (Police Officer)
Angie's First Case - Donald J. Sobol 1702

Zeiler, Ruthie (Musician)
No Applause, Please - Marilyn Singer 1655

Zenas (Teenager; Pacifist)
Zenas and the Shaving Mill - F.N. Monjo 1276

Zero, Joe (Teenager)
River Rats, Inc. - Jean Craighead George 684

Ziegler, Margaret (Child; Animal Lover)
Margaret Ziegler Is Horse Crazy - Crescent Dragonwagon 536

Ziegler, Rodney (Relative)
Margaret Ziegler Is Horse Crazy - Crescent Dragonwagon 536

Zimmer, Fritzi (Musician; Teenager)
My Mom, the Money Nut - Betty Bates 103

Zimmerman (Witch)
The House with a Clock in Its Walls - John Bellaris 129

Zinn, Muriel "Missy" (Aged Person)
A Morgan for Melinda - Doris Gates 676

Zoe (Preteen)
Stonewords: A Ghost Story - Pam Conrad 411

Zoe (Child)
Today's Special: Z.A.P and Zoe - Athena V. Lord 1147

Zoe Louise (Spirit)
Stonewords: A Ghost Story - Pam Conrad 411

Zohert (Space Explorer)
Earthseed: A Novel - Pamela Sargent 1586

Zona (Guardian)
What Happened to Mr. Forester? - Gary W. Barger 96

Zookey (Teacher)
Itchy Richard - Jamie Gilson 704

Zucchini (Ferret)
Zucchini - Barbara Dana 475

Zuchelli, Bertha (Preteen; 5th Grader)
The Magic of Myrna C. Waxweather - Sandra Dutton 553

Zuckerman, Fern (Child)
Charlotte's Web - E.B. White 1899

Zuckerman, Maxie (Preteen)
Maxie, Rosie, and Earl - Partners in Grime - Barbara Park 1379

Zwicker, Zachary (Student)
The Mysterious Zetabet - Scott Corbett 426

Zyzmund the Zeventh (Ruler)
The Mysterious Zetabet - Scott Corbett 426

Character Description Index

This index alphabetically lists descriptions of the major characters in featured titles. The descriptions may be occupations (astronaut, lawyer, etc.) or may describe persona (amnesiac, runaway, teenager, etc.). For each description, character names are listed alphabetically. Also provided are book titles, author names, and entry numbers.

Burdick, Harris
The Mysteries of Harris Burdick - Chris Van
Allsburg 1842

Chapman, Otis
Jemmy - Jon Francis Hassler 824

Colter, Jessamine
The Strange Night Writing of Jessamine Colter -
Cynthia DeFelice 501

Daphne
Daphne's Book - Mary Downing Hahn 785

Elizabeth
Now Is Not Too Late - Isabelle Holland 901

Estrada, Eduardo
Nicky and the Joyous Noise - Mildred Ames 39

Ferlanger, Rusty
Rusty Fertlanger, Lady's Man - Christi Killien 1024

Frazer, Meg
Night Fall - Joan Aiken 17

Green, Curley
Gammage Cup - Carol Kendall 1012

Gregory
The Chalk Box Kid - Clyde Robert Bulla 224

Harold
Harold and the Purple Crayon - Crockett
Johnson 975

Montague
A Rat's Tale - Tor Seidler 1606

Mustazza, Matt
Portrait of Ivan - Paula Fox 640

Thiel, Daniel
Callender Papers - Cynthia Voigt 1861

Velazquez, Diego
I, Juan de Pareja - Elizabeth Borton de
Trevino 1823

Yolanda
Toasted Bagels - Joyce Audy Zarins 1981

ASSISTANT

Scotson
The Search for King Pup's Tomb - Jim Razzi 1495

Skip
The Curse of the Egyptian Mummy - Pat
Hutchins 959

BABYSITTER

Amanda Jane
*The Monster in the 3rd Dresser Drawer and Other
Stories about Adam Joshua* - Janice Lee
Smith 1688

Anselmino, Eddie
Eddie, Incorporated - Phyllis Reynolds
Naylor 1314

Estelle
Finders Keepers - Emily Rodda 1529

Flitter
The Robot Birthday - Eve Bunting 237

Hadley, Phoebe
Eating Ice Cream with a Werewolf - Phyllis
Green 743

Jeremy
The Magic of the Glits - Carole S. Adler 9

Lewie
The Garden Is Doing Fine - Carol J. Farley 586

Mansfield, Melissa
Babysitter on Horseback - Fern G. Brown 213

Patterson, Tony
The Ten-Speed Babysitter - Alison Cragin
Herzig 869

Sheldon, Corrie
The Garden Is Doing Fine - Carol J. Farley 586

Sossi, Karen
Tough-Luck Karen - Johanna Hurwitz 958

Tooey, Alice
Mrs. Tooey and the Terrible Toxic Tar - Barbara
Dillon 526

BADGER

Constance
Redwall - Brian Jacques 967

Frances
Bedtime for Frances - Russell Hoban 891

Kipp
Odyssey From River Bend - Tom McGowen 1227

BAKER

Basha
Cakes and Miracles - Barbara Diamond
Goldin 718

Herman
What Happened in Hamelin? - Gloria
Skurzynski 1659

Hershel
Cakes and Miracles - Barbara Diamond
Goldin 718

Otter
Porcupine's Pajama Party - Terry Webb
Harshman 818

P.C.
Toasted Bagels - Joyce Audy Zarins 1981

Wat
The Ice Bear - Betty Levin 1097

BALLOONIST

Fooley
Gammage Cup - Carol Kendall 1012

BASTARD SON

Chukovsky, Kornei
The Silver Crest: My Russian Boyhood - Kornei
Chukovsky 341

BAT

Bat
The Bat-Poet - Randall Jarrell 971

BEACHCOMBER

Hideaway Tom
Storm Boy - Colin Thiele 1802

BEAR

Basil
The Real Thief - William Steig 1735

Big Bear
Wish Again, Big Bear - Richard J. Margolis 1192

Boris
Morris and Boris at the Circus - Bernard
Wiseman 1935
Morris Has a Cold - Bernard Wiseman 1936

Brother
Bears in the Night - Stan Berenstain 140

Bruce
Big Bad Bruce - Bill Peet 1411

Frank
Frank and Ernest - Alexandra Day 489

Gentle Ben
Gentle Ben - Walt Morey 1285

Griswold
Penrod's Pants - Mary Blount Christian 332

Little Bear
Little Bear - Else Holmelund Minarik 1272

Mother Bear
Little Bear - Else Holmelund Minarik 1272

Paddington
A Bear Called Paddington - Michael Bond 167

Sister
Bears in the Night - Stan Berenstain 140

Whitney
Jason and the Baseball Bear - Dan Elish 563

Winnie-the-Pooh
The House at Pooh Corner - A.A. Milne 1270
Winnie-the-Pooh - A.A. Milne 1271

BEAVER

Mo
Mo to the Rescue - Mary Pope Osborne 1369

BEE

Apis
Ned Kelly and the City of the Bees - Thomas
Keneally 1013

Malachi
The Witch Family - Eleanor Estes 579

BENEFACTOR

Botkin, Ussiah
The Path of the Pale Horse - Paul Fleischman 617

BIGOT

Petit, Russell
A Witch's Garden - Miriam Young 1980

BLACKSMITH

David
Return to Bitter Creek - Doris Buchanan Smith 1682

BOARDER

James, Clint
Following the Mystery Man - Mary Downing
Hahn 788

May, April
The Day That Elvis Came to Town - Jan
Marino 1193

BOYFRIEND

Perrella, Joey
*The Amazing Valvano and the Mystery of the
Hooded Rat* - Mary Robinson 1518

Wilder, Almanzo
Little Town on the Prairie - Laura Ingalls
Wilder 1910

BROOM

Briskly
Euphonia and the Flood - Mary Calhoun 273

BULL

Old Blue
Old Blue - Sibyl Hancock 810

BULLFIGHTER

Olivar, Juan
Shadow of a Bull - Maia Rodman 1535

BULLY

Bones, Brom
The Legend of Sleepy Hollow - Washington Irving 964

Buck, Tuffy
Shoebag - Mary James 968

Darlinger, Sammy
A Dog Called Kitty - Bill Wallace 1876

Eddie
The Monster's Ring - Bruce Coville 438

Felange, Johnny
The Empty Chair - Bess Kaplan 993

Forest, Orson
Huntly, Nutley and the Missing Link - Mary Tannen 1777

Greene, Josh
Puppy Love - Jeanne Betancourt 143

Hammerman, Marv
The 18th Emergency - Betsy Byars 255

Haney, Tater
Words by Heart - Ouida Sebestyen 1602

Hans
King of the Golden River - John Ruskin 1560

Hastings, Martin
A Dog on Barkham Street - Mary Stolz 1753

Hooker, Tice
Brushy Mountain - Patricia Pendergraft 1416

Jimmy Joe
Herbie's Troubles - Carol Chapman 317

Josepha
A Tangled Web - Hannelore Valencak 1839

Kane, Stanley
Wendy and the Bullies - Nancy K. Robinson 1521

Parsons, Wally
Chester - Mary Francis Shura 1634

Pat
Wendy and the Bullies - Nancy K. Robinson 1521

Ralph
The Silk and the Skin - Rodie Sudbery 1765

Roger
We Three Kings - Janet McNeill 1249

Schwartz
King of the Golden River - John Ruskin 1560

Sean
Jonas McFee, A.T.P. - Sarah Sargent 1587

Smellie, Minnie
Rebecca of Sunnybrook Farm - Kate Douglas Wiggin 1907

Tommy
The Balancing Girl - Berniece Rabe 1478

Winthrop, Norm
The Magic Book - Willo Davis Roberts 1511

BUSINESSMAN

Al
Shoeshine Girl - Clyde Robert Bulla 228

Ash, Garnet
Children of Christmas - Cynthia Rylant 1564

Ashford, Jan
The Crumb - Jean Slaughter Doty 533

Bill, Buffalo
The Battle Horse - Harry Kullman 1059

Cooke, Zachary
The Hostage - Theodore Taylor 1789

Diamond, Alfred
Footsteps - Leon Garfield 670

Garmouche, Tony
Pinch - Larry Callen 277

Hazell
Danny, the Champion of the World - Roald Dahl 465

Pentax, Arthur
C.L.U.T.Z. and the Fission Formula - Marilyn Wilkes 1912

Petit, Russell
A Witch's Garden - Miriam Young 1980

Trevelyan, Toby
Night Fall - Joan Aiken 17

BUSINESSWOMAN

Groton
The Hideaway Summer - Beverly Hollett Renner 1500

Hylyard
The Curse of the Egyptian Mummy - Pat Hutchins 959

BUTCHER

Mendel
The Sign in Mendel's Window - Mildred Kantrowitz Phillips 1436

CAMEL

April
A Camel Called April - Diana Hendry 850

CAMPER

Abby
Yours Till Niagara Falls, Abby - Jane O'Connor 1351

Artie
No Coins, Please - Gordon Korman 1051

Cobb, Joshua
The Freewheeling of Joshua Cobb - Margaret Hodges 894

Crane
The Freewheeling of Joshua Cobb - Margaret Hodges 894

Daniel
Bones on Black Spruce Mountain - David Budbill 222

David
The Grizzly - Annabel Johnson 974

Dusty
The Freewheeling of Joshua Cobb - Margaret Hodges 894

Emmy
Ghost Island - Carolyn Lane 1068

(continued)

Ginger
There's a Bat in Bunk Five - Paula Danziger 481

Griffin, Paul
The Summer I Was Lost - Phillip Viereck 1855

Jem
Jem's Island - Kathryn Lasky 1072

Mark
The Grizzly - Annabel Johnson 974

Richard
Jelly Belly - Robert Kimmel Smith 1691

Roberta
Yours Till Niagara Falls, Abby - Jane O'Connor 1351

Sally
Ghost Island - Carolyn Lane 1068

Seth
Bones on Black Spruce Mountain - David Budbill 222

CAPTIVE

Andreas, Christos
The Rich Kid - Bill Gillham 701

Bollier, Jessie
The Slave Dancer - Paula Fox 641

Butler, John
The Light in the Forest - Conrad Richter 1506

Chapman, Derek
The Solid Gold Kid - Norma Fox Mazer 1218

Jimmy
Island of the Loons - Dayton O. Hyde 962

Jo
The Rich Kid - Bill Gillham 701

Lattimore, Christina
The Kidnapping of Christina Lattimore - Joan Lowery Nixon 1338

Steve
Captives in a Foreign Land - Susan Lowry Rardin 1487

Travis, Jan
The Kidnapping of Courtney Van Allen and What's-Her-Name - Joyce Cool 412

Van Allen, Courtney
The Kidnapping of Courtney Van Allen and What's-Her-Name - Joyce Cool 412

CARE GIVER

Kit
I Am the Universe - Barbara Corcoran 430

CARPENTER

Antonio, Mastro "Cherry"
The Adventures of Pinocchio - Carlo Collodi 394

Dake, Thomas
The Blue Cat of Castle Town - Catherine C. Coblentz 376

Kobalt
Dorp Dead - Julia Cunningham 452

CASTAWAY

Crusoe, Robinson
The Life and Strange and Surprising Adventures of Robinson Crusoe - Daniel Defoe 503

Robinson
The Swiss Family Robinson - Johann David Wyss 1961

CAT

Bisquits
Home Alone - Eleanor Schick   1593

Bones
J.T. - Jane Wagner   1868

Cat in the Hat
The Cat in the Hat - Dr. Seuss   1617

Chester
Bunnicula: A Rabbit Tale of Mystery - Deborah Howe   923

Chingis
The Ghost Drum: A Cat's Tale - Susan Price   1468

Duke
Captains of the City Street: A Story of a Cat Club - Esther Averill   69

Ellsworth
Ellsworth and the Cats from Mars - Patience Brewster   196

Gable, Clark
The Girl Who Had No Name - Berniece Rabe   1479

Good Fortune
The Cat Who Went to Heaven - Elizabeth Coatsworth   374

Grissi
The Search for Grissi - Mary Francis Shura   1636

Harry
The Cricket in Times Square - George Selden   1608
Harry Cat's Pet Puppy - George Selden   1610

Harvey
Tucker's Countryside - George Selden   1611

Henry
Cross-Country Cat - Mary Calhoun   272

Jinx
Freddy the Detective - Walter R. Brooks   212

Josh
Beethoven's Cat - Elisabet McHugh   1234

Kate
Digby and Kate - Barbara Baker   84

Lionel
The Cat Who Wished to Be a Man - Lloyd Alexander   26

Ludwig "Wiggie"
Beethoven's Cat - Elisabet McHugh   1234

Margaret
Ellsworth and the Cats from Mars - Patience Brewster   196

Maurice
Never Steal a Magic Cat - Donald E. Caufield   312

Miranda
Bella Arabella - Liza Fosburgh   634

Oliver
Marshmallow - Clare Turlay Newberry   1327

Pandora
Never Steal a Magic Cat - Donald E. Caufield   312

Patchy Pete
Captains of the City Street: A Story of a Cat Club - Esther Averill   69

Presto
The Marvelous Misadventures of Sebastian - Lloyd Alexander   31

Rosetta
Witch-Cat - Joan Davenport Carris   304

S.O.B.
The View From the Cherry Tree - Willo Davis Roberts   1513

Selene
Selene Goes Home - Lucy Diggs   524

Sinbad
Captains of the City Street: A Story of a Cat Club - Esther Averill   69

Sneakers
Sneakers: Seven Stories about a Cat - Margaret Wise Brown   218

Tao
The Incredible Journey - Sheila Burnford   250

True Blue
Porcupine Stew - Beverly Major   1184

Willard-Brown, T.
Miss Hickory - Carolyn Sherwin Bailey   83

CENTIPEDE

Harry
The Dawn Seekers - Carol Hamilton   798

CHICKEN

Hen, Jenny
Quick Chick - Julia Hoban   887

Henrietta
The Hoboken Chicken Emergency - Daniel Manus Pinkwater   1444

CHIEFTAIN

Skankwan
The Lion of the Kalahari - Esther Linfield   1127

White Lodge
Betrayed - Virginia Driving Hawk Sneve   1693

CHILD

Abbie
Dinnie Abbie Sister-R-R! - Riki Levinson   1102
Seven-Day Magic - Edward Eager   556

Abby
The Ghost Children - Eve Bunting   231
Yours Till Niagara Falls, Abby - Jane O'Connor   1351

Ada
Knee-Knock Rise - Natalie Babbitt   77

Adam
Adam of the Road - Elizabeth Gray   735
Chocolate-Covered Ants - Stephen Manes   1188

Addie
Addie Meets Max - Joan Robins   1516
The House Without a Christmas Tree - Gail Rock   1523

Agnew, Dan
We Three Kings - Janet McNeill   1249

Ah Mee
Shen of the Sea - Arthur Bowie Chrisman   329

Ahlenslagen, Heide Patricia
After Fifth Grade, the World - Claudia Mills   1266

Ailsa
A Pack of Lies - Geraldine McCaughrean   1220

Alba
Where Does the Teacher Live? - Paula Kurzband Feder   591

Aldo
Aldo Peanut Butter - Johanna Hurwitz   946

Alex
Like Jake and Me - Mavis Jukes   988

Alexander
Alexander, Who Used to Be Rich Last Sunday - Judith Viorst   1856

Alf
The Horrible Holidays - Audrey Wood   1947

Alfred
Alfred Summer - Jan Slepian   1665

Alice
Alice's Adventures in Wonderland - Lewis Carroll   305
Oma and Bobo - Amy Schwartz   1600

Allan, Edgar
Edgar Allan - John Neufeld   1325

Allen, Austine
Ellen Tebbits - Beverly Cleary   351

Alvin
Banjo - Robert Newton Peck   1407

Amanda
Good-Bye Pink Pig - Carole S. Adler   7
The Headless Cupid - Zilpha Keatley Snyder   1698

Amy
Amy's Goose - Efner Tudor Holmes   909
It's Not the End of the World - Judy Blume   155
The Witch Family - Eleanor Estes   579

Anderson, Anna
The Mermaid Summer - Mollie Hunter   939

Anderson, Dennis
Einstein Anderson, Science Sleuth - Seymour Simon   1649

Anderson, Everett
Everett Anderson's Friend - Lucille Clifton   365

Anderson, Jon
The Mermaid Summer - Mollie Hunter   939

Anderson, Retta
Night Swimmers - Betsy Byars   265

Anderson, Roy
Night Swimmers - Betsy Byars   265

Andrew
The 24-Hour Genie - Lila McGinnis   1225
Nobody Listens to Andrew - Elizabeth Guilfoile   778

Andrews, Ben "Ape Face"
A Billion for Boris - Mary Rodgers   1531

Andrews, Benjamin "Ape Face"
Freaky Friday - Mary Rodgers   1533

Andrews, Jamie
The Ivy Garland - John Hoyland   927

Andrews, Tim
The Fireball Mystery - Mary Adrain   14

Andrews, Vicki
The Fireball Mystery - Mary Adrain   14

Andy
Home Alone - Eleanor Schick   1593

Angel
Angel's Mother's Wedding - Judy Delton   510

Anita
The Secret Moose - Jean Rogers   1541

Anna
Anna and the Seven Swans - Maida Silverman   1642
Anna's Silent World - Bernard Wolf   1941
From Anna - Jean Little   1133
A New Coat for Anna - Harriet Ziefert   1987
The Wednesday Surprise - Eve Bunting   240

Annabel
No Flying in the House - Betty Brock   207
Snakes Are Nothing to Sneeze At - Gabrielle Charbonnet   319

Anne
Toby Lived Here - Hilma Wolitzer   1943

Annie
Annie and the Old One - Miska Miles   1264
The Ring and the Window Seat - Amy Hest   874

Carson, Margie
Just an Overnight Guest - Eleanora E. Tate   1779

Carstairs, Arthur
The Telltale Summer of Tina C. - Lila Perl   1420

Carter, Glenn
Doodle and the Go-Cart - Robert Burch   241

Carter, Noah
Saturdays in the City - Ann Sharpless Bond   166

Cathy
Save the Dam! - Harriet Sirof   1656

Celia
I Should Worry, I Should Care - Miriam Chaikin   315

CG
The Empty Window - Anne Evelyn Bunting   229

Chad
The Cat That Was Left Behind - Carole S. Adler   6
Fudge - Charlotte Towner Graeber   728
Voices After Midnight - Richard Peck   1406

Chakoh
Walk the World's Rim - Betty Baker   88

Champion, Darla
Thunder Pup - Janet Hickman   876

Chan, Kenichi "Ken"
Journey to Topaz - Yoshiko Uchida   1837

Chang
Chang's Paper Pony - Eleanor Coerr   377

Chant, Eric "Cat"
Charmed Life - Diana Wynne Jones   980

Chant, Gwendolyn
Charmed Life - Diana Wynne Jones   980

Charles
Autumn Street - Lois Lowry   1152
The Machine Gunners - Robert Westall   1895

Charlotte
Snakes Are Nothing to Sneeze At - Gabrielle Charbonnet   319

Chavez, Miguel
.and Now Miguel - Joseph Krumgold   1057

Chester
Chester - Mary Francis Shura   1634

Chris
The Magic Stone - Leonie Kooiker   1049
Year of the Black Pony - Walt Morey   1288

Christopher Robin
The House at Pooh Corner - A.A. Milne   1270
Winnie-the-Pooh - A.A. Milne   1271

Chu, Kim
The Lost Umbrella of Kim Chu - Eleanor Estes   577

Chub
The Lucky Runner - Bernard Wiseman   1934
Tackle-22 - Louise Munro Foley   631

Chuck
Follow That Ghost! - Dale Fife   600

Claire
Sea Swan - Kathryn Lasky   1073
Through the Dolls' House Door - Jane Gardam   666

Clara
The Animal, the Vegetable, and John D. Jones - Betsy Byars   256
Clara and the Bookwagon - Nancy Smiler Levinson   1100

Clarissa
The Witch Family - Eleanor Estes   579

Clarisse
At the Back of the Woods - Claudia Mills   1267

Clark, Andy
When the Sirens Wailed - Noel Streatfeild   1763

Clark, Laura
When the Sirens Wailed - Noel Streatfeild   1763

Clark, Tim
When the Sirens Wailed - Noel Streatfeild   1763

Clarke, Benjie
Manhattan Is Missing - E.W. Hildick   880

Claypool, Fenton
Home Run Trick - Scott Corbett   425

Clutterworth, Mary-Anna
Enemies - Robin Klein   1040

Cole, Rosy
Give Us a Great Big Smile, Rosy Cole - Sheila Greenwald   757

Cooper, Casey
Casey the Nomad - Susan Sussman   1769

Cooper, Rosey
Casey the Nomad - Susan Sussman   1769

Cott, Lucas
Class Clown - Johanna Hurwitz   950

Crawford, Elizabeth
Stepping on the Cracks - Mary Downing Hahn   789

Creighton, Jethro
Across Five Aprils - Irene Hunt   937

Cricket
Cricket and the Crackerbox Kid - Alane Ferguson   595

Crinkley, Milo
Be a Perfect Person in Just Three Days - Stephen Manes   1187

Crowder, Georgette
Reserved for Mark Anthony Crowder - Alison Smith   1677

Crown, Natalie
Playing Beatie Bow - Ruth Park   1382

Cyril
Five Children and It - Edith Nesbit   1323

D.W.
Arthur's Baby - Marc T. Brown   216

Dale
Good-Bye Pink Pig - Carole S. Adler   7

Dan
You Can Depend on Me - Margaret Reuter   1503

Daniel
Baseball and Butterflies - Karen Lynn Williams   1922
The Comeback Dog - Jane Resh Thomas   1804
Fox in a Trap - Jane Resh Thomas   1806
Losing Uncle Tim - Marykate Jordan   986

Dan'l
The Devil's Donkey - Bill Brittain   203

Danny
Danny, the Champion of the World - Roald Dahl   465
Son for a Day - Corinne Gerson   687

Daphne
Alvin Fernald, Master of a Thousand Disguises - Clifford B. Hicks   877

Darling, John
Peter Pan - James Barrie   98

Darling, Peter
Peter Pan - James Barrie   98

Darling, Wendy
Peter Pan - James Barrie   98

d'Aulneaux, Roger
The Stones of Green Knowe - L.M. Boston   179

Davey
Davey Come Home - Margaret Teibl   1792

David
Hurricane - David Wiesner   1906
The Monster Garden - Vivien Alcock   20
You Can Depend on Me - Margaret Reuter   1503

Davidowitz, Piri
Upon the Head of the Goat: A Childhood in Hungary, 1939-1944 - Aranka Siegal   1641

Davie
Shadrach - Meindert De Jong   495

Davis, Franny
Noonday Friends - Mary Stolz   1758

Davy
Old Blue - Sibyl Hancock   810

De Angeli, Dailey
Fiddlestrings - Marguerite De Angeli   491

De Leeuw, Annie
The Upstairs Room - Johanna Reiss   1499

Debbie
The House on Hackman's Hill - Joan Lowery Nixon   1337

December
December's Travels - Mischa Damjan   474

Deenie
The Animal, the Vegetable, and John D. Jones - Betsy Byars   256

Delilah
Delilah - Carole Hart   819

Devine, Saul
The Empty Chair - Bess Kaplan   993

Diamond
At the Back of the North Wind - George MacDonald   1165

Dibbs, Bo
Dolby and the Woof-Off - Barbara A. Steiner   1739

Dibbs, Oliver "Ollie"
Dolby and the Woof-Off - Barbara A. Steiner   1739

Dinnie
Dinnie Abbie Sister-R-R! - Riki Levinson   1102

Dissel, Freddy
The One in the Middle Is the Green Kangaroo - Judy Blume   157

Dissell, Ellen
The One in the Middle Is the Green Kangaroo - Judy Blume   157

Dissell, Mike
The One in the Middle Is the Green Kangaroo - Judy Blume   157

Dobry
Dobry - Monica Shannon   1619

Domin, Sara
A Gift for Mama - Esther Hautzig   831

Dominic
Cricket and the Crackerbox Kid - Alane Ferguson   595

Dorado, Rosa
My Halloween Boyfriend - Stephen Mooser   1283

Dorcas
Harry in Trouble - Barbara Ann Porte   1459

Dorian, Georgie
The Fledgling - Jane Langton   1069

Dorrie
Dorrie and the Pin Witch - Patricia Coombs   414

Douglas
Grandpa's Slide Show - Deborah Gould   725
Seal Child - Sylvia Peck   1410

Douglas, James
How Many Miles to Babylon? - Paula Fox   636

The Green Ghost of Appleville - Jean Marzollo 1206
Jane-Emily - Patricia Clapp 343

Janetta
Grandaddy's Place - Helen V. Griffith 773

Jason
The Bells of Christmas - Virginia Hamilton 800
The Bongleweed - Helen Cresswell 442
Follow That Ghost! - Dale Fife 600
The Green Book - Jill Paton Walsh 1393
Jace the Ace - Joanne Rocklin 1525

Jasons, Rebecca
The Robot and Rebecca: The Mystery of the Code Carrying Kids - Jane Yolen 1970

Jean
Homesick: My Own Story - Jean Fritz 652

Jeannie
My Daddy Was a Soldier - Deborah Kogan Ray 1494

Jebb, Ned
The Huffler - Jill Paton Walsh 1394

Jeeter, Howard
The Kid in the Red Jacket - Barbara Park 1378

Jeff
Daniel's Duck - Clyde Robert Bulla 225
Foxy - Helen V. Griffith 771
The House on Hackman's Hill - Joan Lowery Nixon 1337

Jella
The Wheel on the School - Meindert DeJong 507

Jennie
Dinnie Abbie Sister-R-R! - Riki Levinson 1102

Jennifer
I Wish Laura's Mommy Was My Mommy - Barbara Power 1463
Touch the Moon - Marion Dane Bauer 110

Jenny
My Dog and the Birthday Mystery - David A. Adler 13
Red Dog - Bill Wallace 1877

Jeremy
The Backyard Basketball Superstar - Monica Klein 1038
The Magic of the Glits - Carole S. Adler 9
Mama's Going to Buy You a Mockingbird - Jean Little 1135
Sea Swan - Kathryn Lasky 1073
What If They Knew? - Patricia Hermes 865
With a Wave of the Wand - Mark Jonathan Harris 817

Jessie
Maybe She Forgot - Ellen Kandoian 992
The Sea Child - Carolyn Sloan 1667

Jethro
Jethro and the Jumbie - Susan Cooper 420

Jill
I Hate Red Rover - Joan M. Lexau 1116
Something Queer at the Library: A Mystery - Elizabeth Levy 1109

Jim
Shipwreck - Vera G. Cumberlege 451
When Will I Read? - Miriam Cohen 385

Jimmie
Eddie's Valuable Property - Carolyn Haywood 838

Jimmy
Amelia's Flying Machine - Barbara Shook Hazen 839
A Boy Called Fish - Alison Morgan 1289

Jockimo, Paul
Don't Feel Sorry for Paul - Bernard Wolf 1942

Jodi
In Our House, Scott Is My Brother - Carole S. Adler 8

Joe
The Empty Window - Anne Evelyn Bunting 229
Miracles on Maple Hill - Virginia Sorensen 1706
The Sea Egg - L.M. Boston 178
Sidewalk Stories From Wayside School - Louis Sachar 1571

Joel
On My Honor - Marion Dane Bauer 108

Joey
Baseball and Butterflies - Karen Lynn Williams 1922
Trust in the Unexpected - Gunnel Linde 1122

Johansen, Kirsti
Number the Stars - Lois Lowry 1153

John
All Because I'm Older - Phyllis Reynolds Naylor 1312

Johnson, Bunny
Captain Hook, That's Me - Ada B. Litchfield 1131

Johnson, Jerry
Five-Finger Discount - Barthe DeClements 497

Johnson, Joey
Cave-in at Mason's Mine - Bessie Holland Heck 842

Jonas
Frankie Is Staying Back - Ron Roy 1557
Two Short and One Long - Nina Ring Aamundsen 1

Jonathan
Bears on Hemlock Mountain - Alice Dalgliesh 472

Jones, Jeremiah
Jeremiah in the Dark Woods - Janet Ahlberg 15

Jones, John D.
The Animal, the Vegetable, and John D. Jones - Betsy Byars 256

Jones, William
Footsteps - Leon Garfield 670

Joseph
Joseph on the Subway Train - Kathleen Benson 138

Joshua, Adam
The Monster in the 3rd Dresser Drawer and Other Stories about Adam Joshua - Janice Lee Smith 1688

Josiah
Stay Away From Simon! - Carol Carrick 297

Joss
Beat the Turtle Drum - Constance C. Greene 748

Juan
Maria Luisa - Winifred Madison 1175
The Most Beautiful Place in the World - Ann Cameron 280

Jubilee
Young Nick and Jubilee - Leon Garfield 672

Judy
Jumanji - Chris Van Allsburg 1840

Julian
Gone-Away Lake - Elizabeth Enright 572
The Stories Julian Tells - Ann Cameron 281

Julius
Luke Was There - Eleanor Clymer 371

Kalle
Oma - Peter Hartling 822

Karen
Foster Child - Marion Dane Bauer 107
Hello, I'm Karen - Margaret Sutherland 1771

Kate
Arthur's Baby - Marc T. Brown 216
The Computer Nut - Betsy Byars 261
Doctor Change - Joanna Cole 388
A Game of Catch - Helen Cresswell 444

Kathleen
Dogsbody - Diana Wynne Jones 981

Katie
Chip Rogers, Computer Whiz - Seymour Simon 1648
Love You, Soldier - Amy Hest 872
Trust in the Unexpected - Gunnel Linde 1122

Katy
My Mother's Getting Married - Joan Drescher 537

Keiran
The Tram to Bondi Beach - Elizabeth Hathorn 825

Keith
The Mouse and the Motorcycle - Beverly Cleary 352

Kellerman, Adie
A Room Made of Windows - Eleanor Cameron 285

Kelly
December Stillness - Mary Downing Hahn 786
Glass Slippers Give You Blisters - Mary Jane Auch 66

Kelly, Frances
A Family Apart - Joan Lowery Nixon 1333

Kelly, Mary Beth
Cookies and Crutches - Judy Delton 511

Kelly, Petey
A Family Apart - Joan Lowery Nixon 1333

Kelly, Suzanne
Dynamite Dinah - Claudia Mills 1268

Kemp, Polly
The Wish Giver: Three Tales of Coven Tree - Bill Brittain 206

Kennedy, Cass
Courage at Indian Deep - Jane Resh Thomas 1805

Kenny
Some Friend - Carol Carrick 296
Something Upstairs: A Tale of Ghosts - Avi 72

Kidd, Bertie
Dump Days - Jerry Spinelli 1714

Kincaid, Margaret Drusilla
The Blue Empress - Kathy Pelta 1415

Kipper
Peppermints in the Parlor - Barbara Brooks Wallace 1873

Kippy
Buster Loves Buttons - Fran Manushkin 1191

Kirk
Everett Anderson's Friend - Lucille Clifton 365

Kit
The Thing in Kat's Attic - Charlotte Towner Graeber 730

Klara
The Glassblower's Children - Maria Gripe 774

Klas
The Glassblower's Children - Maria Gripe 774

Knockwurst, Burton Bell Whitney
Burton's Zoom Zoom Va-Room Machine - Dorothy Haas 781

Knockwurst, Edisonia
Burton's Zoom Zoom Va-Room Machine - Dorothy Haas 781

Knockwurst, Newton
Burton's Zoom Zoom Va-Room Machine - Dorothy Haas 781

McKay, Linnie
Thunder Pup - Janet Hickman 876

McPherson, Mandy
The Kenton Year - Ruth Wallace-Brodeur 1879

McShane, Bridie
A Sound of Chariots - Mollie Hunter 940

Meekin, Wallace "Bud"
Foster Mary - Celia Strang 1761

Melanie
Hail, Hail, Camp Timberwood - Ellen Conford 403

Melbourne, Harriet "Hatty"
Tom's Midnight Garden - Philippa Pearce 1401

Melendy, Miranda "Randy"
The Saturdays - Elizabeth Enright 573

Melissa
The Glad Man - Gloria Gonzalez 721

Mellie
Her Own Song - Ellen Howard 921

Michael
The Boy Who Wanted a Family - Shirley
    Gordon 722
I Have Two Families - Doris Wild Helmering 849
Wait Till Helen Comes - Mary Downing Hahn 791

Michaels, Elisa
Russell Sprouts - Johanna Hurwitz 956

Michaels, Russell
Russell Sprouts - Johanna Hurwitz 956

Midas, John
The Chocolate Touch - Patrick Skene Catling 309

Midas, Mary
The Chocolate Touch - Patrick Skene Catling 309

Mii
Hiroshima No Pika - Toshi Maruki 1205

Mike
Family Farm - Thomas Locker 1143
Some Friend - Carol Carrick 296
The Wind Eye - Robert Westall 1896

Miller, Dusty
Johnny Tremain - Esther Forbes 633

Milonas, Katy
Katy Did It - Victoria Boutis 182

Mimi
M & M and the Big Bag - Pat Ross 1548
What If They Knew? - Patricia Hermes 865

Miranda
The Orphan Game - Barbara Cohen 383

Mirandy
Mirandy and Brother Wind - Pat McKissack 1246

Misha
There, Far Beyond the River - Yuri Korinetz 1050

Mitchell, Mean
No Bean Sprouts, Please! - Constance Hiser 885

Mitzi
Mitzi and the Terrible Tyranosaurus Rex - Barbara
    Williams 1918

Miyo
The Rooster Who Understood Japanese - Yoshiko
    Uchida 1838

Moffat, Rufus
Rufus M. - Eleanor Estes 578

Moller, Andy
Beetles, Lightly Toasted - Phyllis Reynolds
    Naylor 1313

Molly
I Should Worry, I Should Care - Miriam
    Chaikin 315
Molly's Pilgrim - Barbara Cohen 382
Wait Till Helen Comes - Mary Downing Hahn 791

Moon Shadow
Dragonwings - Lawrence Yep 1966

Morgan, Becky
A String in the Harp - Nancy Bond 169

Mortensen, Buster
Buster, the Sheikh of Hope Street - Bjarne B.
    Reuter 1502

Mortensen, Ingeborg
Buster, the Sheikh of Hope Street - Bjarne B.
    Reuter 1502

Mott, Sam
Do Bananas Chew Gum? - Jamie Gilson 702

Mouse
The 18th Emergency - Betsy Byars 255

Mukasa
Mukasa - John Nagenda 1308

Muldie, Johnny
Wagon Wheels - Barbara Brenner 193

Murphy, Collette
Too Many Murphys - Colleen O'Shaughnessy
    McKenna 1236

Murphy, Jeff
Too Many Murphys - Colleen O'Shaughnessy
    McKenna 1236

Murphy, Jess
Awfully Short for the Fourth Grade - Elvira
    Woodruff 1951

Murphy, Laura
Too Many Murphys - Colleen O'Shaughnessy
    McKenna 1236

Nam-Huong
Onion Tears - Diana Kidd 1023

Nancy
The Golden Name Day - Jennie D. Lindquist 1126
Silent Dancer - Bruce Hlibok 886
Where Does the Teacher Live? - Paula Kurzband
    Feder 591

Neuman, Molly
Nightmare Mountain - Peg Kehret 1003

Nicholas
Alexander, Who Used to Be Rich Last Sunday -
    Judith Viorst 1856

Nicky
Nicky and the Joyous Noise - Mildred Ames 39

Nicobobinus
Nicobobinus - Terry Jones 984

Nidetzky, Linda
So Long, Grandpa - Elfie Donnelly 529

Nidetzky, Micky
So Long, Grandpa - Elfie Donnelly 529

Nieman, Nicole
A Pocket Full of Seeds - Marilyn Sachs 1579

Nilly, Willy
The Dog Food Caper - Joan M. Lexau 1115

Nix, Sorrow
Sorrow's Song - Larry Callen 278

Noble, Sarah
Courage of Sarah Noble - Alice Dalgliesh 473

Noodleman, Beatrice Odile Olivia "Boon"
O'Diddy - Jocelyn Stevenson 1747

Nora
Busybody Nora - Johanna Hurwitz 949
Superduper Teddy - Johanna Hurwitz 957

Norvin
The Great White Man-Eating Shark - Margaret
    Mahy 1181

Novak, Jimmy
One of the Third Grade Thonkers - Phyllis Reynolds
    Naylor 1317

Nutley, Baby Beau
Huntly, Nutley and the Missing Link - Mary
    Tannen 1777

O.K.
Remember Me to Harold Square - Paula
    Danziger 480

Oaf
Oaf - Julia Cunningham 454

O'Brien, Kelly
Kelly's Creek - Doris Buchanan Smith 1680

October
December's Travels - Mischa Damjan 474

O'Driscoll, Eily
Under the Hawthorne Tree - Marita Conlon-
    McKenna 408

O'Driscoll, Michael
Under the Hawthorne Tree - Marita Conlon-
    McKenna 408

O'Driscoll, Peggy
Under the Hawthorne Tree - Marita Conlon-
    McKenna 408

Olivar, Manolo
Shadow of a Bull - Maia Rodman 1535

Omoteji
Omoteji's Baby Brother - Mary-Joan Gerson 688

Omri
The Indian in the Cupboard - Lynne Reid
    Banks 1498

Onetree, JoBeth
Help! I'm a Prisoner in the Library - Eth
    Clifford 361

Onetree, Mary Rose
Help! I'm a Prisoner in the Library - Eth
    Clifford 361

Opie
The Ghost on Saturday Night - Sid Fleischman 621

O'Riley, Danny
Snowshoe Thompson - Nancy Smiler
    Levinson 1101

O'Riley, Kathleen
Judge Benjamin, Superdog - Judith Whitelock
    McInerney 1235

Packer, Ruthann
Ruthann and Her Pig - Barbara Ann Porte 1460

Palmer, Barney
The Haunting - Margaret Mahy 1182

Pao, Tien
The House of Sixty Fathers - Meindert De Jong 494

Paotze
Lon Po Po: A Red Riding Hood Story From China -
    Ed Young 1977

Pascal
The Red Balloon - Albert Lamorisse 1063

Patch, Jonathon
Palmer Patch - Barbara Brooks Wallace 1872

Patrick
Finders Keepers - Emily Rodda 1529

Pattie
The Green Book - Jill Paton Walsh 1393

Patty
I Have Two Families - Doris Wild Helmering 849

Payson, Minty Lou
Come by Here - Olivia Coolidge 413

Peavy, Queenie
Queenie Peavy - Robert Burch 244

Peck, Robert "Rob"
Soup - Robert Newton Peck 1409

Peedle
End of a Dark Road - Crystal Thrasher 1809

Go Fish - Mary Stolz　1756
The Pinballs - Betsy Byars　266
Porcupine Stew - Beverly Major　1184

Thompson, Molly Vera
The Kid in the Red Jacket - Barbara Park　1378

Thompson, Wade
213 Valentines - Barbara Cohen　379

Thornton, Lucy
The One and Only Cynthia Jane Thornton - Claudia
Mills　1269

Tifflin, Jody
The Red Pony - John Steinbeck　1738

Tim
Ship's Cook Ginger - Edward Ardizzone　54

Tino
A Memory for Tino - Leo Buscaglia　252

Tippet, Margaret
Margaret and Taylor - Kevin Henkes　851

Tippet, Taylor
Margaret and Taylor - Kevin Henkes　851

Toby
The Sea Egg - L.M. Boston　178

Todd, Jane
The Berkley Street Six Pack - Mary Francis
Shura　1633

Tom
The Secret Three - Mildred Myrick　1306

Tommy
The Balancing Girl - Berniece Rabe　1478

Tony
The Midnight Fox - Betsy Byars　264
On My Honor - Marion Dane Bauer　108

Tootsie
Superfudge - Judy Blume　158

Tran, Thuy
Janie's Private Eyes - Zilpha Keatley Snyder　1699

Travis, Jan
*The Kidnapping of Courtney Van Allen and What's-
Her-Name* - Joyce Cool　412

Treehorn
Treehorn's Treasure - Florence Parry Heide　846

Troy, Maggie
Trouble with Mothers - Margery Facklam　583

Tubby
The Case of the Scaredy Cats - Crosby
Bonsall　175

Tucker, Jens
Goodbye, My Wishing Star - Vicki Grove　777

Tyler, Adam
Saturdays in the City - Ann Sharpless Bond　166

Unnamed Character
Blind Outlaw - Glen Rounds　1553

Van Allen, Courtney
*The Kidnapping of Courtney Van Allen and What's-
Her-Name* - Joyce Cool　412

Van Alstyne, Edward
The Matchlock Gun - Walter D. Edmonds　560

Van Alstyne, Trudy
The Matchlock Gun - Walter D. Edmonds　560

Vaungaylen "Gaylen"
The Search for Delicious - Natalie Babbitt　78

Velitsanskaya, Alexandra Sasha "Pippin"
The Sound of Dragon's Feet - Alki Zei　1983

Veronica
Veronica Meets Her Match - Nancy K.
Robinson　1520

Vicky
Among the Dolls - William Sleator　1660

Victor
Lizard Music - Daniel Manus Pinkwater　1445

Vlecke, Naomi
Just Plain Fancy - Patricia Polacco　1453

Vlecke, Ruth
Just Plain Fancy - Patricia Polacco　1453

Vorlob, Bernice
The Zebra Wall - Kevin Henkes　852

Vorlob, Carla
The Zebra Wall - Kevin Henkes　852

Wade, Pete
The Package in Hyperspace - Janet Asimov　63

Wagner, Susan
The Witching of Ben Wagner - Mary Jane
Auch　68

Waite, Dudley
Castaways on Long Ago - Edward
Ormondroyd　1366

Waite, Linda
Castaways on Long Ago - Edward
Ormondroyd　1366

Waite, Richard
Castaways on Long Ago - Edward
Ormondroyd　1366

Waldron, Jonathan
Stinker From Space - Pamela F. Service　1614

Walker, John
Swallows and Amazons - Arthur Ransome　1485

Walker, Rachel
Do-it-Yourself Magic - Ruth Chew　325

Walker, Scott
Do-it-Yourself Magic - Ruth Chew　325

Walker, Susan
Swallows and Amazons - Arthur Ransome　1485

Wallis, Ned
One-Eyed Cat - Paula Fox　639

Walter
Just a Dream - Chris Van Allsburg　1841

Ward, Janis
Golden Daffodils - Marilyn Gould　726

Welsch, Harriet
Harriet the Spy - Louise Fitzhugh　608

Wembleton, Lila
Noonday Friends - Mary Stolz　1758

Wemstock, Debbie
Two Piano Tuners - M.B. Goffstein　716

Wendleken, Alice
The Best Christmas Pageant Ever - Barbara
Robinson　1517

Wendy
Wendy and the Bullies - Nancy K. Robinson　1521

Wexler, Jason
Tiger Eyes - Judy Blume　159

Whipple, Alice
Alice and the Boa Constrictor - Laurie Adams　3

Whiting, Anna
Sarah, Plain and Tall - Patricia MacLachlan　1170

Whiting, Caleb
Sarah, Plain and Tall - Patricia MacLachlan　1170

Wiley
Humbug Mountain - Sid Fleischman　622

Willa
Unclaimed Treasures - Patricia MacLachlan　1173

William
The Balancing Girl - Berniece Rabe　1478
Fat Men from Space - Daniel Manus
Pinkwater　1443

Williams, Abigail
Tituba of Salem Village - Ann Petry　1423

Williams, Emmie
Leo, Zack and Emmie - Amy Ehrlich　561

Willy
Four on the Shore - Edward Marshall　1196
Stone Fox - John Reynolds Gardiner　668

Wilson, Carey
Bedknob and Broomsticks - Mary Norton　1343

Wilson, Charles
Bedknob and Broomsticks - Mary Norton　1343

Wilson, Lucy
The Oracle Doll - Catherine Dexter　518

Wilson, Paul
Bedknob and Broomsticks - Mary Norton　1343

Winkle, Robert
Operation Dump the Chump - Barbara Park　1381

Winters, Tabitha "Tibby"
The Rocking Horse Secret - Rumer Godden　715

Witherspoon, Patrick
The Dragons of North Chittendon - Susan Fromberg
Schaeffer　1591

Wong, Shirley Temple
In the Year of the Boar and Jackie Robinson - Bette
Bao Lord　1148

Woodlawn, Caddie
Caddie Woodlawn - Carol Ryrie Brink　201

Woodlawn, Warren
Caddie Woodlawn - Carol Ryrie Brink　201

Woodruff
Woodruff and the Clocks - Elizabeth Bram　186

Woodward, Victor
The Edge of Next Year - Mary Stolz　1754

Worthen, Charles
Lyddie - Katherine Paterson　1390

Wulf, Edgar
Once I Was a Plum Tree - Johanna Hurwitz　954

Wyman, Lucinda
Roller Skates - Ruth Sawyer　1590

Yorick, Harold "Harry"
A Camel Called April - Diana Hendry　850

Young Fu
Young Fu of the Upper Yangtze - Elizabeth
Lewis　1111

Zack
Leo, Zack and Emmie - Amy Ehrlich　561

Ziegler, Margaret
Margaret Ziegler Is Horse Crazy - Crescent
Dragonwagon　536

Zoe
Today's Special: Z.A.P and Zoe - Athena V.
Lord　1147

Zuckerman, Fern
Charlotte's Web - E.B. White　1899

CHILD-CARE GIVER

Cuffy
The Saturdays - Elizabeth Enright　573

Early, Ida
Ida Early Comes over the Mountain - Robert
Burch　242

Evelyn
The Believers - Rebecca C. Jones　983

Kitamura
The Rooster Who Understood Japanese - Yoshiko
Uchida　1838

Moore, Olive
Hide Crawford Quick - Margaret Walden
Froehlich 653

Nana Tess
The Telltale Summer of Tina C. - Lila Perl 1420

Phillips
The Castle in the Attic - Elizabeth Winthrop 1931

CHIMPANZEE

Arthur
Arthur's Honey Bear - Lillian Hoban 888

Danny
Castaways on Chimp Island - Sandy
Landsman 1067

Nibbles
Castaways on Chimp Island - Sandy
Landsman 1067

Ocky
Mr. Nobody's Eyes - Michael Morpurgo 1290

Tarzan
Castaways on Chimp Island - Sandy
Landsman 1067

Violet
Arthur's Honey Bear - Lillian Hoban 888

CHIPMUNK

Archie
Chester Chipmunk's Thanksgiving - Barbara
Williams 1917

Chester
Chester Chipmunk's Thanksgiving - Barbara
Williams 1917

CLASSMATE

Finnegan, Brian
Dear Mom, You're Ruining My Life - Jean Van
Leeuwen 1846

Fong, Jimmy
Vision Quest - Pamela F. Service 1615

Herbie
Isabelle the Itch - Constance C. Greene 752

Jane
Randall's Wall - Carol Fenner 592

Sean
Witch in Room 6 - Edith Battles 106

CLERK

Bogwater
The Great Green Turkey Creek Monster - James
Flora 629

Seely
End of a Dark Road - Crystal Thrasher 1809

Strawspinner
Andrew and the Alchemist - Barbara Ninde
Byfield 269

Toonie
The Dancing Cats of Applesap - Janet Taylor
Lisle 1129

CLIENT

Glory
Follow That Ghost! - Dale Fife 600

COACH

Brown, Amazon
When the Boys Ran the House - Joan Davenport
Carris 303

Cruikshank
Eunice (the Egg Salad) Gottlieb - Tricia
Springstubb 1719

Dirkus, Bob
Shortstop From Tokyo - Matt Christopher 339

Jackson, Mark
Too Much Magic - Betsy Sterman 1743

Masterson
What Difference Does It Make, Danny? - Helen
Young 1978

Nardi, Doug
Catch That Pass! - Matt Christopher 337

Old Turtle
Old Turtle's Soccer Team - Leonard Kessler 1018

Pike, Ray
Soccer Halfback - Matt Christopher 340

Polk, Wally
Quarterback Walk-On - Thomas J. Dygard 555

Simms
I Am Rubber, You are Glue - Jane Morton 1293

Sophie
Wrongway Applebaum - Marjorie Lewis 1112

Tingley
The Hockey Girls - Scott Corbett 424

Venuti
The Goof That Won the Pennant - Jonah Kalb 991

Walker, Bonnie
The Rascals From Haskell's Gym - Frank
Bonham 173

Wilson
The Dog That Pitched a No-Hitter - Matt
Christopher 338

COATIMUNDI

Frito, Dave
The Turquoise Toad Mystery - Georgess
McHargue 1233

COCKROACH

Bagg, Stuart
Shoebag - Mary James 968

COLLECTOR

Brooks, Suzanna
Harvey, the Beer Can King - Jamie Gilson 703

Kennedy, Dean
Highpockets - John R. Tunis 1826

Trumble, Harvey William
Harvey, the Beer Can King - Jamie Gilson 703

Woodruff
Woodruff and the Clocks - Elizabeth Bram 186

COMPUTER EXPERT

Euphus
Miss Pickerell and the War of the Computers - Dora
Pantell 1373

Kate
The Computer Nut - Betsy Byars 261

Marconi, Kate
Chip Mitchell: The Case of the Robot Warriors -
Fred D'Ignazio 525

Mitchell, Chip
Chip Mitchell: The Case of the Robot Warriors -
Fred D'Ignazio 525

Rogers, Chip
Chip Rogers, Computer Whiz - Seymour
Simon 1648

Skyjumper, Jake
Commander Toad and the Intergalactic Spy - Jane
Yolen 1968

CONVICT

Rawlings, Norris
The Case of the Vanishing Villain - Carol J.
Farley 585

Riggs
Island of the Loons - Dayton O. Hyde 962

COOK

Applefeller, John
The Worldwide Dessert Contest - Dan Elish 564

Cookee
Jolly Roger and the Pirates of Abdul, the Skinhead -
Colin McNaughton 1248

Davy
Thank You, Jackie Robinson - Barbara Cohen 384

Minh, Chu
Onion Tears - Diana Kidd 1023

Reddick, Tony
Go and Catch a Flying Fish - Mary Stolz 1755

Yosip
The Place Where Nobody Stopped - Jerry
Segal 1605

COUNSELOR

Dennis
No Coins, Please - Gordon Korman 1051

Marcy
There's a Bat in Bunk Five - Paula Danziger 481

Rob
No Coins, Please - Gordon Korman 1051

Ted
There's a Bat in Bunk Five - Paula Danziger 481

Tracy, Hank
The Summer I Was Lost - Phillip Viereck 1855

COURIER

Melissa
Wildcat under Glass - Alki Zei 1984

COUSIN

Angie
The Whipman Is Watching - Thomas A. Dyer 554

Anna
Bailey's Window - Anne Lindbergh 1119

Avataq
Ghost Vision - Jeanie Kortum 1054

Bagthorpe, Daisy
Ordinary Jack - Helen Cresswell 446

Barrows, Louie
Wild Man of the Woods - Joan Clark 345

David
One of the Third Grade Thonkers - Phyllis Reynolds
Naylor 1317

Faulk, Sook
Christmas Memory - Truman Capote 288

Flora
Dangerous Spaces - Margaret Mahy 1180

Frank
Ruthann and Her Pig - Barbara Ann Porte 1460

Green, Sylvia
The Wolves of Willoughby Chase - Joan Aiken 18

Hattie Lou
The Song of the Christmas Mouse - Shirley Rousseau Murphy 1300

Hovanec, Clem
The Kite Song - Margery Evernden 581

Jones, Meg
Shades of Gray - Carolyn Reeder 1496

Mert
The Horrible Holidays - Audrey Wood 1947

Patty Ann
Cousins - Virginia Hamilton 801

Polko
Rabbit Spring - Tilde Michels 1261

Vita
Earthquake 2099 - Mary W. Sullivan 1768

COWBOY

Boone
The Indian in the Cupboard - Lynne Reid Banks 1498

Buck, Billy
The Red Pony - John Steinbeck 1738

CRICKET

Chester
The Cricket in Times Square - George Selden 1608
Tucker's Countryside - George Selden 1611

CRIMINAL

Cleary, Lemon Clarkson
Uncle Lemon's Spring - Jane Yolen 1973

Gallgnat, Adrian C.
Trouble in Bugland: A Collection of Inspector Mantis Mysteries - William Kotzwinkle 1055

Lew
Signpost to Terror - Gretchen Sprague 1716

Little, Cephus "Crab"
Somewhere in the Darkness - Walter Dean Myers 1304

Yankel
Yankel the Fool - Shan Ellentuck 565

CROW

Crow
The Lemming Condition - Alan Arkin 55

DANCER

Garrett, Kirby
A Gift of Magic - Lois Duncan 548

Jessie
Maybe She Forgot - Ellen Kandoian 992

Leonard, Lily
The Sisters Impossible - James David Landis 1065

Leonard, Saundra
The Sisters Impossible - James David Landis 1065

Marta
The Whipman Is Watching - Thomas A. Dyer 554

Meredith, Meredith
The Sisters Impossible - James David Landis 1065

Mitchell, Arthur
Arthur Mitchell - Tobi Tobias 1815

Newman, Kate
Maybe Next Year - Amy Hest 873

Oink, Lotta
Sly, P.I.: The Case of the Missing Shoes - Cathy Stefanec-Ogren 1730

Paul
Truth or Dare - Susan Beth Pfeffer 1433

Pomerantz, Poopsie
Poopsie Pomerantz, Pick up Your Feet - Patricia Reilly Giff 696

Robinson, Peter
Maybe Next Year - Amy Hest 873

Samantha
Samantha on Stage - Susan Clement Farrar 590

Smith, Mina
Come a Stranger - Cynthia Voigt 1862

Stoner, Casey
Dumb Old Casey Is a Fat Tree - Barbara Bottner 180

Wolfruff, Yuri
Sly, P.I.: The Case of the Missing Shoes - Cathy Stefanec-Ogren 1730

DEER

Bambi
Bambi - Felix Salten 1582

Feline
Bambi - Felix Salten 1582

Gobo
Bambi - Felix Salten 1582

DENTIST

De Soto
Dr. De Soto - William Steig 1734

Small
The Emma Dilemma - Catherine Sefton 1603

DETECTIVE

Adams, Maximilian Augustus
Maximilian, You're the Greatest - Joseph Rosenbloom 1547

Anderson, Adam "Einstein"
Einstein Anderson, Science Sleuth - Seymour Simon 1649

Andrews, Bob
Alfred Hitchcock and the Three Investigators in the Secret of Shark Reef - William Arden 53

Barnes, Frank
The Donkey Planet - Scott Corbett 423

Barth, Sebastian
Dew Drop Dead: A Sebastian Barth Mystery - James Howe 925

Beaghley, Charlie "Beagle"
Beagle in Trouble: 12 Solve It Yourself Mysteries - Jackie Vivelo 1857

Bean, Dave
The Case of the Cackling Car: A Sam and Dave Mystery Story - Marilyn Singer 1654

Bean, Sam
The Case of the Cackling Car: A Sam and Dave Mystery Story - Marilyn Singer 1654

Binky, Dinky
Binky Brothers, Detectives - James Duncan Lawrence 1080

Binky, Pinky
Binky Brothers, Detectives - James Duncan Lawrence 1080

Bone, Winchester
The Strange and Exciting Adventures of Jeremiah Hush - Uri Shulevitz 1632

Bones, Sherluck
The Search for King Pup's Tomb - Jim Razzi 1495

Brown, Leroy "Encyclopedia"
Encyclopedia Brown, Boy Detective - Donald J. Sobol 1703

Chris
Adventure in Granada - Walter Dean Myers 1302

Chuck
Follow That Ghost! - Dale Fife 600

Clover, Pamela Jean "P.J."
P.J. Clover, Private Eye: The Case of the Missing Mouse - Susan Meyers 1260

Crenshaw, Pete
Alfred Hitchcock and the Three Investigators in the Secret of Shark Reef - William Arden 53

Ellen
Beagle in Trouble: 12 Solve It Yourself Mysteries - Jackie Vivelo 1857

English, M.H., J. Huntley
The Case of the Horrible Swamp Monster - Drew Stevenson 1745

Ferguson, Amy
The Leipzig Vampire - Mary Anderson 45

Ferguson, Jamie
The Leipzig Vampire - Mary Anderson 45

Foskett, Arthur William
Arthur the Kid - Alan Coren 433

Foster, Ricky
Lake Fear - Ian McMahan 1247

Funnyman
Funnyman and the Penny Dodo - Stephen Mooser 1282

Goose
Gumshoe Goose, Private Eye - Mary DeBall Kwitz 1062

Goose, Ellery "Gumshoe"
Gumshoe Goose, Private Eye - Mary DeBall Kwitz 1062

Grieg, Wanda
The Case of the Condemned Cat - E.W. Hildick 879

Holmes, Shirlick
Shirlick Holmes and the Case of the Wandering Wardrobe - Jane Yolen 1971

Hound, Sherlick
Sherlick Hound and the Valentine Mystery - Kelly Goldman 719

Jameson, Greg
Mystery of the Gingerbread House - Wylly Folk St. John 1721

Jameson, Ron
Mystery of the Gingerbread House - Wylly Folk St. John 1721

Jansen, Jennifer "Cam"
Cam Jansen and the Mystery at the Monkey House - David A. Adler 10

Jason
Follow That Ghost! - Dale Fife 600

Jessica
Maximilian, You're the Greatest - Joseph Rosenbloom 1547

Little Ann
Where the Red Fern Grows - Wilson Rawls   1493

Luath
The Incredible Journey - Sheila Burnford   250

Lucky
A Boy in the Doghouse - Betsy Duffey   543

Mama
Papa's Lemonade and Other Stories - Eve
Rice   1504

Mash
Dorp Dead - Julia Cunningham   452

Max
No One Is Going to Nashville - Mavis Jukes   989

Maxi
M & M and the Big Bag - Pat Ross   1548

Mishmash
Mishmash - Molly Cone   399

Missis
The Hundred and One Dalmatians - Dodie
Smith   1679

Monroe, Harold
Bunnicula: A Rabbit Tale of Mystery - Deborah
Howe   923

Mopey
Philo Potts, or, The Helping Hand Strikes Again -
Mildred Ames   40

Mr. Sniff
Call for Mr. Sniff - Thomas P. Lewis   1114

Mud
The Blossoms and the Green Phantom - Betsy
Byars   258

Mudge
Henry and Mudge and the Happy Cat - Cynthia
Rylant   1567

Mutt
The Dog Who Wouldn't Be - Farley Mowat   1296

My Dog
My Dog and the Birthday Mystery - David A.
Adler   13

Nick
Adam of the Road - Elizabeth Gray   735

Old Dan
Where the Red Fern Grows - Wilson Rawls   1493

Old Yeller
Old Yeller - Fred Gipson   707

Papa
Papa's Lemonade and Other Stories - Eve
Rice   1504

Peanut
Aldo Peanut Butter - Johanna Hurwitz   947

Pete
The Day of the Muskie - Patricia Welch   1891

Pinkerton
Pinkerton, Behave! - Steven Kellogg   1008

Pongo
The Hundred and One Dalmatians - Dodie
Smith   1679

Poodle, Princess Penelope
Sherlick Hound and the Valentine Mystery - Kelly
Goldman   719

Pooky
Ride the Green Dragon - Andre Norton   1342

Putter
The Thing in Kat's Attic - Charlotte Towner
Graeber   730

Pye, Ginger
Ginger Pye - Eleanor Estes   576

Quick
Barefoot a Thousand Miles - Patsey Gray   739

Rahloo
The Good Luck Dog - Lilo Hess   870

Rory
Wild Boy - Joan Tate   1782

Ruffles
The Doggone Mystery - Mary Blount Christian   331

Searchlight
Stone Fox - John Reynolds Gardiner   668

Sebastian
*Sebastian (Super Sleuth) and the Bone to Pick
Mystery* - Mary Blount Christian   333

Shadow
The Mystery at Peacock Place - M.F. Craig   439

Shiloh
Shiloh - Phyllis Reynolds Naylor   1318

Silver
Silver - Gloria Whelan   1897

Sinbad
Sinbad and Me - Kin Platt   1452

Sirius
Dogsbody - Diana Wynne Jones   981

Snoopy
The Big Hello - Janet Schulman   1598

Sounder
Sounder - William Armstrong   57

Strider
Strider - Beverly Cleary   356

Sweep
Only One Woof - James Herriot   867

Tag
No Bean Sprouts, Please! - Constance Hiser   885

Toby
Katy Did It - Victoria Boutis   182

Tock
The Phantom Tollbooth - Norton Juster   990

Tundra
Tundra - William F. Hallstead   797

Wolf
Rip Van Winkle - Washington Irving   965

DONKEY

Alf
How the Witch Got Alf - Cora Annett   52

Dan'l
The Devil's Donkey - Bill Brittain   203

Eeyore
The House at Pooh Corner - A.A. Milne   1270
Winnie-the-Pooh - A.A. Milne   1271

Filomena
How Far, Felipe? - Genevieve Gray   737

DRAGON

Arthur
The Dragons of North Chittendon - Susan Fromberg
Schaeffer   1591

Droofus
How Droofus the Dragon Lost His Head - Bill
Peet   1413

Kazul
Dealing with Dragons - Patricia C. Wrede   1953

Otto
The Secret of Foghorn Island - Geoffrey Hayes   834

Scales
A Dragon in Class Four - June Counsel   434

Tooth
The Secret of Foghorn Island - Geoffrey Hayes   834

White Dragoness, Regina
The Dragons of North Chittendon - Susan Fromberg
Schaeffer   1591

DRIVER

Coatsworth
Follow That Bus! - Pat Hutchins   960

Drummond, Charlie
Charlie Drives the Stage - Eric A. Kimmel   1025

Gilligan, Patrick
Roller Skates - Ruth Sawyer   1590

DUCK

Easter
The Case of the Elevator Duck - Polly Berrien
Berends   139

Felicity
Pigs Might Fly: A Novel - Dick King-Smith   1033

Weber
*Pippa Pops Out: Four Read-Aloud/Read Alone
Stories* - Betty Boegehold   164

DWARF

Cinnamon, Sydney
Little Little - M.E. Kerr   1017

La Belle, Little Little
Little Little - M.E. Kerr   1017

Lionel, Knox
Little Little - M.E. Kerr   1017

Mouk
The Adventures of Little Mouk - Wilhelm Hauff   826

ECCENTRIC

Carson, Ivy
Changeling - Zilpha Keatley Snyder   1696

Kopeckie, Horace
Lizard Music - Daniel Manus Pinkwater   1445

Matthews, Meeghan
A Witch's Garden - Miriam Young   1980

Swift, Samuel
The Warlock of Westfall - Leonard Everett
Fisher   606

EDITOR

Wechsler, Martin
The Kenton Year - Ruth Wallace-Brodeur   1879

ELEPHANT

Babar
Babar and the Ghost: An Easy to Read Version -
Laurent De Brunhoff   219

Celeste
Babar and the Ghost: An Easy to Read Version -
Laurent De Brunhoff   219

Elephant
Uncle Elephant - Arnold Lobel   1142

Ernest
Frank and Ernest - Alexandra Day   489

Jumbo
Big Max - Kin Platt   1449

Toong Talong
The Elephant in the Dark - Carol Carrick   295

FRIEND

Alan
How to Eat Fried Worms - Thomas Rockwell 1528

Amy
Once, Said Darlene - William Sleator 1664

Andrea
Homesick: My Own Story - Jean Fritz 652

Annie
Nate the Great - Marjorie Weinman Sharmat 1620

Argos, Tracey
Best Friend Insurance - Beatrice Gormley 723

Becker, Tink
Poppy and the Outdoor Cat - Dorothy Haas 784

Beth
A Friend Like That - Alfred Slote 1670

Bings, Alec
The Phantom Tollbooth - Norton Juster 990

Brian
Trapped in Death Cave - Bill Wallace 1878

Brownell, Betsy
The Horse in the Attic - Eleanor Clymer 370

Burkis, Petie
The Midnight Fox - Betsy Byars 264

Buttercup, Susan
The Chocolate Touch - Patrick Skene Catling 309

Candy
Shirlick Holmes and the Case of the Wandering Wardrobe - Jane Yolen 1971

Carlin
Rusty Fertlanger, Lady's Man - Christi Killien 1024

Clare
Time Sweep - Valerie Weldrick 1892

Coopersmith, Leah
Mariah Delany's Author-of-the-Month Club - Sheila Greenwald 759

Davies, Bran
The Grey King - Susan Cooper 419

Dawson, Timothy
Jethro and the Jumbie - Susan Cooper 420

Deidre
The Lake Is on Fire - Maureen Crane Wartski 1888

Delia
Lucie Babbidge's House - Sylvia Cassedy 308

Dixon
Goodbye, My Island - Jean Rogers 1539

Dornenwald, Inge
Devil in Vienna - Doris Orgel 1363

Drew, Jane
Greenwitch - Susan Cooper 418

Drossoula
Petros' War - Alki Zei 1982

Dubrowski, Brenda
It's Your Turn at Bat - Barbara Aiello 16

Flood, Crobar
River Rats, Inc. - Jean Craighead George 684

Frank
Time Sweep - Valerie Weldrick 1892

Freebaker, Missy
The Monster's Ring - Bruce Coville 438

Fremple
Ballet Magic - Nancy Robison 1522

Fuller, Tex
The Friends of the Loony Lake Monster - Frank Bonham 171

Garing, Jemima
Operation Peeg - Jonathan Gathorne-Hardy 677

Gilmore, Tracy
Patty Dillman of Hot Dog Fame - Susan Wojciechowski 1940

Gurley, Chris
The Ghost Wore Gray - Bruce Coville 437

Hagen, Zan
Rinehart Lifts - R. Rozanne Knudson 1043

Halab, Bitsy
But We Are Not of Earth - Jean Karl 995

Hank
Getting Rid of Krista - Amy Hest 871

Hekenefer
I, Tut: The Boy Who Became Pharoah - Miriam Schlein 1595

Huggins, Dorothy JoAnna "DorJo"
An End to Perfect - Suzanne Newton 1330

Hugh
Manhattan Is Missing - E.W. Hildick 880

Ingrid
Bailey's Window - Anne Lindbergh 1119

Jacob
Maurice's Room - Paula Fox 637

Jane
The Big Hello - Janet Schulman 1598

Janey
Dreams of Victory - Ellen Conford 401

Joel
The Bronze King - Suzy McKee Charnas 320

Johnson, Sylvester "Scooter"
The Over-the-Hill Ghost - Ruth Calif 276

Jones, Peter
The Box of Delights - John Masefield 1208

Joralemon, Jerry
One of Us - Nikki Amdur 38

Josie
Step on a Crack - Mary Anderson 46

Kurihara, Emiko "Emi"
Journey to Topaz - Yoshiko Uchida 1837

Lane, Laura
Jeffrey's Ghost and the Fifth Grade Dragon - David A. Adler 12

Leonard
Alan Mendelsohn, the Boy From Mars - Daniel Manus Pinkwater 1442

Louise
Love You, Soldier - Amy Hest 872

Lucas, Shanteray
They're All Named Wildfire - Nancy Springer 1718

Mary Eliza
Isabelle the Itch - Constance C. Greene 752

Matson, Tracy
Poopsie Pomerantz, Pick up Your Feet - Patricia Reilly Giff 696

McSwiggen
Mark Makes His Move - Marian Potter 1462

Newbolt, Joe
Welcome Home, Jellybean - Marlene Fanta Shyer 1638

Nina
Walking Away - Elizabeth Winthrop 1933

Nukaga, Tami
A Jar of Dreams - Yoshiko Uchida 1836

O'Diddy
O'Diddy - Jocelyn Stevenson 1747

Partimkin, Jennifer
The Haunted House - Dorothy Haas 782

Pepper, Art
Casey the Nomad - Susan Sussman 1769

Peter
Once, Said Darlene - William Sleator 1664

Pickering, Jack
The Beachcombers - Helen Cresswell 441

Potsie
Have You Seen Hyacinth Macaw? - Patricia Reilly Giff 694

Prentice, Liza
Secret of the Stone Face - Phyllis A. Whitney 1905

Puck
The Interesting Thing That Happened at Perfect Acres, Inc. - Barbara Brooks Wallace 1871

Rawlings, Dave
Mystery at Crane's Landing - Marcella Thum 1810

Rita
Our Snowman Had Olive Eyes - Charlotte Herman 860

Robin
Squib - Nina Bawden 117

Rudy
A Word From Our Sponsor: Or, My Friend Alfred - Judie Angell 51

Ruthie Mae
Ludell - Brenda Scott Wilkinson 1913

Sager, Jeanie
The Edge of Next Year - Mary Stolz 1754

Sally
Call Me Amanda - Dale Bick Carlson 289

Samuel
A Memory for Tino - Leo Buscaglia 252

Sara
Hey, Remember Fat Glenda? - Lila Perl 1419

Segal, Randy
Gopher, Tanker, and the Admiral - Shirley Climo 368

Shelton, Eric
Cam Jansen and the Mystery at the Monkey House - David A. Adler 10

Shori
Alvin Fernald, Master of a Thousand Disguises - Clifford B. Hicks 877

Sizzlegridian, Snar
The Robot and Rebecca: The Mystery of the Code Carrying Kids - Jane Yolen 1970

Spencer
The Mystery of the Haunted Cabin - Judy Delton 513

Tenser, Gillian
A Word From Our Sponsor: Or, My Friend Alfred - Judie Angell 51

Thatcher, Becky
The Adventures of Tom Sawyer - Mark Twain 1834

Trowbridge, Gilbert
Say Cheese - Betty Bates 104

Valentine, Casey
Left-Handed Shortstop - Patricia Reilly Giff 695

Vesseley, Lieselotte
Devil in Vienna - Doris Orgel 1363

Vogel, Mark
Dreams of Victory - Ellen Conford 401

Walker, Martha "Marti"
Bring to a Boil and Separate - Hadley Irwin 966

Wilkes, Verna
The Case of the Horrible Swamp Monster - Drew Stevenson 1745

Wistrow, Waver
But We Are Not of Earth - Jean Karl 995

Turner, Granny
Tough Tiffany - Belinda Hurmence   945

Tut, Gram
Cousins - Virginia Hamilton   801

Walker
Getting Rid of Marjorie - Betty Ren Wright   1955

GUARD

Gawain
The Real Thief - William Steig   1735

GUARDIAN

Alice
Underdog - Marilyn Sachs   1580

Arthur
Blaze - Robert Somerlott   1705

Bartolotti
Konrad - Christine Nostlinger   1346

Cummings, Roger
Underdog - Marilyn Sachs   1580

Dennison, Herbert
The Case of the Baker Street Irregular: A Sherlock Holmes Story - Robert Newman   1328

Dorothy
Son for a Day - Corinne Gerson   687

Drume
All the Children Were Sent Away - Sheila Garrigue   674

Elda
Arthur, for the Very First Time - Patricia MacLachlan   1169

Garrett, Brinton "Brinnie"
The Jedera Adventure - Lloyd Alexander   29

Gerda
The Ghost Children - Eve Bunting   231

Jessie
Alan and the Animal Kingdom - Isabelle Holland   899

Jones, Jed
Shades of Gray - Carolyn Reeder   1496

Lavender
Miss Know-It-All and the Three Ring Circus - Carol Beach York   1975

Oma
Oma - Peter Hartling   822

Plum
Miss Know-It-All and the Three Ring Circus - Carol Beach York   1975

Sharp
Charmed Life - Diana Wynne Jones   980

Wrisby
Arthur, for the Very First Time - Patricia MacLachlan   1169

Zona
What Happened to Mr. Forester? - Gary W. Barger   96

GUIDE

Ben
Deathwatch - Robb White   1902

GUINEA PIG

da Polga, Olga
Olga Carries On - Michael Bond   168

HAMSTER

Houdini "Goldy"
I, Houdini: The Autobiography of a Self-Educated Hamster - Lynne Reid Banks   1497

HANDICAPPED

Aaron
The Half-a-Moon Inn - Paul Fleischman   615

Alfred
Alfred Summer - Jan Slepian   1665

Angela
Rish n' Roses - Jan Slepian   1666

Anna
Anna's Silent World - Bernard Wolf   1941

Annie
Ben and Annie - Joan Tate   1781

Bailey, Jon
Carver - Ruth Yaffe Radin   1481

Basini, Shirley
Yours Truly, Shirley - Ann M. Martin   1202

Bertold, Jake
Annerton Pit - Peter Dickinson   519

Blind Outlaw
Blind Outlaw - Glen Rounds   1553

Carmichael, Simon
The Silk and the Skin - Rodie Sudbery   1765

Clarisse
At the Back of the Woods - Claudia Mills   1267

Craven, Colin
The Secret Garden - Frances Hodgson Burnett   249

Dab
Sweet Whispers, Brother Rush - Virginia Hamilton   806

de Bureford, Robin
The Door in the Wall - Marguerite De Angeli   490

Emerson, Sarah
The Half-Child - Kathleen Hersom   868

Enright, Phillip
The Cay - Theodore Taylor   1788

Evie
Mystery of the Gingerbread House - Wylly Folk St. John   1721

Face, Potato
Rootabaga Stories - Carl Sandburg   1584

Finxel
Finzel the Farsighted - Paul Fleischman   613

Francie
Circle of Giving - Ellen Howard   919

Grabseth, Teddy
Don't Take Teddy - Babbis Friis-Baastad   648

Harvey
The Pinballs - Betsy Byars   266

Heather
The Good Luck Dog - Lilo Hess   870

Hershel
Cakes and Miracles - Barbara Diamond Goldin   718

Ingalls, Mary
Little Town on the Prairie - Laura Ingalls Wilder   1910

Jamie
A Certain Small Shepherd - Rebecca Caudill   310

Jockimo, Paul
Don't Feel Sorry for Paul - Bernard Wolf   1942

Joey
The Hayburners - Gene Smith   1687

Johnson, Jerome
Ride the Red Cycle - Harriette Robinet   1515

Johnson, Judy
Captain Hook, That's Me - Ada B. Litchfield   1131

Kaila
The Ice Bear - Betty Levin   1097

Kim
I Can't Always Hear You - Joy Zelonky   1985

Lawrence "Orry"
He Is Your Brother - Richard Parker   1383

Lee, Daisy
Summer of the Monkeys - Wilson Rawls   1492

Lester
Alfred Summer - Jan Slepian   1665

Lisa
Lisa and Her Soundless World - Edna S. Levine   1099

Lothrop, Clair
A Time to Keep Silent - Gloria Whelan   1898

Lovett
The Watcher in the Garden - Joan Phipson   1439

Margaret
The Balancing Girl - Berniece Rabe   1478

Morrissey, Matt
The Flying Fingers Club - Jean F. Andrews   47

Nancy
Silent Dancer - Bruce Hlibok   886

Newbolt, Joe
Welcome Home, Jellybean - Marlene Fanta Shyer   1638

Nix, Sorrow
Sorrow's Song - Larry Callen   278

O'Brien, Kelly
Kelly's Creek - Doris Buchanan Smith   1680

Oxley, Geraldine "Gerri"
Welcome Home, Jellybean - Marlene Fanta Shyer   1638

Peedle
End of a Dark Road - Crystal Thrasher   1809

Penney, Birdie
Sasha, My Friend - Barbara Corcoran   432

Pickens, Dwayne
All Together Now - Sue Ellen Bridgers   197

Revis, Alesia
Alesia - Eloise Greenfield   754

Riley, Mark
It's Your Turn at Bat - Barbara Aiello   16

Russell
Flambards - K.M. Peyton   1427

Seth
Seth of the Lion People - Bonnie Pryor   1475

Simon
Stay Away From Simon! - Carol Carrick   297

Spangler, Mary Lou "Wisconsin"
Keeping it Secret - Penny Pollock   1455

Tatlek
At the Mouth of the Luckiest River - Arnold A. Griese   765

Teetoncey
Teetoncey - Theodore Taylor   1790

Treloar, Louann
The Dollhouse Murders - Betty Ren Wright   1954

Tyree
The Dog Days of Arthur Cane - T. Ernesto Bethancourt   144

Unnamed Character
Blind Outlaw - Glen Rounds   1553

HANDYMAN

Jed
The Rocking Horse Secret - Rumer Godden   715

Pepper
Mr. Pepper Stories - Mark Taylor   1783

Skinny Jack
The Ghost of Skinny Jack - Astrid Lindgren   1123

HEALER

Luther
The Hero and the Crown - Robin McKinley   1241

HEALTH CARE PROFESSIONAL

Oliver
The Stone-Faced Boy - Paula Fox   642

HEIR

Balfour, David
Kidnapped - Robert Louis Stevenson   1748

HEIRESS

Luccock, Emily
Peppermints in the Parlor - Barbara Brooks
    Wallace   1873

Madge
Unleaving - Jill Paton Walsh   1396

HERO

Bargle, Argie
The Great Green Turkey Creek Monster - James
    Flora   629

Bobowicz, Arthur
The Hoboken Chicken Emergency - Daniel Manus
    Pinkwater   1444

Bucket, Charlie
Charlie and the Chocolate Factory - Roald
    Dahl   464

Demeas
Children of the Fox - Jill Paton Walsh   1392

Gluck
King of the Golden River - John Ruskin   1560

Harker, Kay
The Box of Delights - John Masefield   1208

Hood, Robin
The Outlaws of Sherwood - Robin McKinley   1242

Irving, Irv
It Happened in Pinsk - Arthur Yorinks   1974

Jason
*The Golden Fleece and the Heroes Who Lived
    Before Achilles* - Padraic Colum   397

Mago
Flight of the Sparrow - Julia Cunningham   453

Marsh, Tina Valentine
The Bronze King - Suzy McKee Charnas   320

Mouse, Matthias
Redwall - Brian Jacques   967

Sawyer, Tom
The Adventures of Tom Sawyer - Mark Twain   1834

Taran
The High King - Lloyd Alexander   28

Themistokles
Children of the Fox - Jill Paton Walsh   1392

Tom
Doctor Change - Joanna Cole   388

Tuatara
Harry Newberry and the Raiders of the Red Drink -
    Mel Gilden   700

Uilenspiegel, Tyl
The Wicked Tricks of Tyl Uilenspiegel - Jay
    Williams   1921

Unicorn
The Unicorn and the Lake - Marianna Mayer   1210

HEROINE

Archer, Jenny
Jenny Archer to the Rescue - Ellen Conford   404

Beauty
*Beauty: A Retelling of the Story of Beauty and the
    Beast* - Robin McKinley   1238

Cleary, Letty
Uncle Lemon's Spring - Jane Yolen   1973

Dorrie
Dorrie and the Pin Witch - Patricia Coombs   414

Eilonwy
The High King - Lloyd Alexander   28

Funny Little Woman
The Funny Little Woman - Arlene Mosel   1294

Holly, Vesper
The Jedera Adventure - Lloyd Alexander   29

HIPPOPOTAMUS

George
George and Martha Back in Town - James
    Marshall   1199

Martha
George and Martha Back in Town - James
    Marshall   1199

HISTORIAN

Buder, Stanley
*A Long Hard Journey: The Story of the Pullman
    Porter* - Pat McKissack   1245

HISTORICAL FIGURE

Akhenaton
I, Tut: The Boy Who Became Pharoah - Miriam
    Schlein   1595

Alcott, Louisa May
Invincible Louisa - Cornelia Meigs   1254

Aroon, Ellen
Grand Papa and Ellen Aroon - F.N. Monjo   1275

Audubon, John James
On the Frontier with Mr. Audubon - Barbara
    Brenner   192

Baker, Josephine "Tumpie"
Ragtime Tumpie - Alan Schroeder   1597

Bissel, Israel
The Remarkable Ride of Israel Bissel - Alice
    Schick   1592

Boone, Daniel
Daniel Boone - James Daugherty   483

Bowditch, Nathaniel
Carry On, Mr. Bowditch - Jean Lee Latham   1075

Burgess, Abbie
Keep the Lights Burning, Abbie - Peter Roop   1544

Capote, Truman
Christmas Memory - Truman Capote   288

Carson, Kit
Sing Down the Moon - Scott O'Dell   1355

Darwin, Charles
Darwin and the Voyage of the Beagle - Felicia
    Law   1078

Earhart, Amelia
Amelia's Flying Machine - Barbara Shook
    Hazen   839

Franklin, Benjamin
Ben and Me - Robert Lawson   1083
What Is Papa Up To Now? - Miriam Anne
    Bourne   181

Hughes, Langston
Langston Hughes, American Poet - Alice
    Walker   1870

Jefferson, Thomas
Grand Papa and Ellen Aroon - F.N. Monjo   1275

Lincoln, Abraham
Lincoln: A Photobiography - Russell Freedman   644

Parks, Rosa
Don't Ride the Bus on Monday: The Rosa Parks Story
    - Louise Meriwether   1257

Perry, Matthew C.
Commodore Perry in the Land of the Shogun - Rhoda
    Blumberg   151

Pocahontas
The Double Life of Pocahontas - Jean Fritz   650
Pocahontas and the Strangers - Clyde Robert
    Bulla   227

Powhatan
The Double Life of Pocahontas - Jean Fritz   650

Pullman, George Mortimer
*A Long Hard Journey: The Story of the Pullman
    Porter* - Pat McKissack   1245

Revere, Paul
And Then What Happened, Paul Revere? - Jean
    Fritz   649

Rolfe, John
Pocahontas and the Strangers - Clyde Robert
    Bulla   227

Sampson, Deborah
*I'm Deborah Sampson: A Soldier in the War of the
    Revolution* - Patricia Clapp   342

Smalls, Robert
*Captain of the Planters: The Biography of Robert
    Smalls* - Dorothy Sterling   1741

Smith, John
The Double Life of Pocahontas - Jean Fritz   650
Pocahontas and the Strangers - Clyde Robert
    Bulla   227

Teach, Edward "Blackbeard"
Blackbeard's Ghost - Ben Stahl   1724

Themistokles
Children of the Fox - Jill Paton Walsh   1392

Tituba
The Tall Man From Boston - Marion Lena
    Starkey   1727
Tituba of Salem Village - Ann Petry   1423

Tubman, Harriet
When the Rattlesnake Sounds: A Play - Alice
    Childress   327

Tutankhaton
I, Tut: The Boy Who Became Pharoah - Miriam
    Schlein   1595

Velazquez, Diego
I, Juan de Pareja - Elizabeth Borton de
    Trevino   1823

HITCHHIKER

Reichert, Cindy
Snow Bound - Harry Mazer   1216

HORSE

Big Red
Little Black, a Pony - Walter Farley   589

Black Beauty
Black Beauty: The Autobiography of a Horse - Anna Sewell   1618

Blind Outlaw
Blind Outlaw - Glen Rounds   1553

Buck
Buck, Wild - Glenn Balch   91

Candlelight
Can I Get There by Candlelight? - Jean Slaughter Doty   532

Doodlebug
Doodlebug - Irene Brady   185

Little Black
Little Black, a Pony - Walter Farley   589

Little Bub
Justin Morgan Had a Horse - Marguerite Henry   853

Moonseeker China
Touch the Moon - Marion Dane Bauer   110

San Domingo
San Domingo, the Medicine Hat Stallion - Marguerite Henry   856

Sandpiper
Dark Horse - Jean Slaughter Doty   534

Scarlett
Stall Buddies - Penny Pollack   1454

Skin Horse
The Velveteen Rabbit - Margery Williams   1923

Spirit
Song of the Horse - Richard Kennedy   1015

Ssprite
The Horse in the Attic - Eleanor Clymer   370

Yoki
A Girl Called Bob and a Horse Called Yoki - Barbara Campbell   287

HORSE TRAINER

Alex
The Crumb - Jean Slaughter Doty   533

Dailey, Henry
The Black Stallion - Walter Farley   587
Black Stallion Mystery - Walter Farley   588

Lundy, Peter
San Domingo, the Medicine Hat Stallion - Marguerite Henry   856

Taylor, Mi
National Velvet - Enid Bagnold   82

HOTEL OWNER

Bessie
Skinny - Robert Burch   245

Castelis, Alexandros
Mystery of the Hidden Hand - Phyllis A. Whitney   1904

HOTEL WORKER

Paul
Family Pose - Dean Hughes   930

HOUSEHOLDER

Manning, Molly
Six Impossible Things Before Breakfast - Norma Farber   584

Vancourt
No Flying in the House - Betty Brock   207

HOUSEKEEPER

Cuffy
The Saturdays - Elizabeth Enright   573

Deal
Operation Peeg - Jonathan Gathorne-Hardy   677

Dohr, Wanda Sue
The Day That Elvis Came to Town - Jan Marino   1193

Farisee
No Beasts! No Children! - Beverly Keller   1007

Korngold
The Gods in Winter - Patricia Miles   1265

Phillips
The Castle in the Attic - Elizabeth Winthrop   1931

Scher, Anna
The Lion in the Box - Marguerite De Angeli   492

Summers, Ruth
Davey Come Home - Margaret Teibl   1792

Tatie
Autumn Street - Lois Lowry   1152

Todd, Flora
The Cat in the Mirror - Mary Stolz   1752

HOUSEWIFE

Gaddy
The Crow and Mrs. Gaddy - Wilson Gage   658

Popper
Mr. Popper's Penguins - Richard Atwater   64

HUNTER

Charlie
Boy of Tache - Ann Blades   147

Christina
Flambards - K.M. Peyton   1427

Jones, Clyde
The Day the Circus Came to Lone Tree - Glen Rounds   1554

Kano
The Way of Our People - Arnold A. Griese   766

Kyo
The Secret of the Seal - Deborah Davis   487

Madec
Deathwatch - Robb White   1902

May, Johnny
The Adventures of Johnny May - Robbie Branscum   188

Napak
The Way of Our People - Arnold A. Griese   766

Travers, Judd
Shiloh - Phyllis Reynolds Naylor   1318

IGUANA

Spike
Up Mountain One Time - Willie Wilson   1926

IMMIGRANT

Banerjee, Rab
The Stone Angel - Pamela Rogers   1543

Carmela "Carm"
Before the Wildflowers Bloom - Tatyana Bylinsky   270

Gramma
There's a Rainbow In My Closet - Patti Stren   1764

Hayden, Josie
I Met a Traveller - Lillian Hoban   889

Horst
The Horse with Eight Hands - Joan Phipson   1437

Juan
Maria Luisa - Winifred Madison   1175

Maria Luisa
Maria Luisa - Winifred Madison   1175

Molly
Molly's Pilgrim - Barbara Cohen   382

Moscowitz, Becky
Immigrant Girl: Becky of Eldridge Street - Harvey Brett   194

Moscowitz, Max
Immigrant Girl: Becky of Eldridge Street - Harvey Brett   194

Onion John
Onion John - Joseph Krumgold   1058

Pelligrino
How Pizza Came to Queens - Dayal Kaur Khalsa   1019

Wong, Shirley Temple
In the Year of the Boar and Jackie Robinson - Bette Bao Lord   1148

Yanovitch, Mira
I Met a Traveller - Lillian Hoban   889

IMMORTAL

Stanton, Will
The Grey King - Susan Cooper   419

INDIAN

Angie
The Whipman Is Watching - Thomas A. Dyer   554

Annie
Annie and the Old One - Miska Miles   1264

Anpao
Anpao: An American Indian Odyssey - Jamake Highwater   878

Attean
The Sign of the Beaver - Elizabeth George Speare   1709

Baby Sister
Waterless Mountain - Laura Adams Armer   56

Blue Sky
Good Hunting, Blue Sky - Peggy Parish   1375

Boy-Strength-of-Blue-Horses
Knots on a Counting Rope - Bill Martin, Jr.   1204

Bright Eyes
The Friendly Wolf - Paul Goble   712

Bright Morning
Sing Down the Moon - Scott O'Dell   1355

Chakoh
Walk the World's Rim - Betty Baker   88

Charlie
Boy of Tache - Ann Blades   147

Chuto
The Secret of the Andes - Ann Nolan Clark   344

LAWYER

Abbott, Thomas
Changeling - Zilpha Keatley Snyder 1696

LEADER

Akela
The Curse of the Egyptian Mummy - Pat Hutchins 959

Peters
Cookies and Crutches - Judy Delton 511

LEMMING

Bubber
The Lemming Condition - Alan Arkin 55

LIBRARIAN

Firestone, Terri
Mystery of the Bewitched Bookmobile - Florence Parry Heide 845

Katz
Harry in Trouble - Barbara Ann Porte 1459

Skinner
The Great Skinner Strike - Stephanie S. Tolan 1817

LIGHTHOUSE KEEPER

Burgess, Abbie
Keep the Lights Burning, Abbie - Peter Roop 1544

LION

Aslan
The Lion, the Witch, and the Wardrobe - C.S. Lewis 1110

Lafcadio
Lafcadio, the Lion Who Shot Back - Shel Silverstein 1645

LUMBERJACK

Williams, Josias
Mississippi Bridge - Mildred D. Taylor 1785

MAGICIAN

Blinn, Thaddeus
The Wish Giver: Three Tales of Coven Tree - Bill Brittain 206

Brown, Abner
The Box of Delights - John Masefield 1208

Calkins, Quint
Harvey, the Beer Can King - Jamie Gilson 703

Dredd
Dr. Dredd's Wagon of Wonders - Bill Brittain 204

Frank
Double or Nothing - Marc Talbert 1776

Gami
Perfect Crane - Anne Laurin 1076

Gwyn
The Snow Spider - Jenny Nimmo 1331

Maleesh
The Jedera Adventure - Lloyd Alexander 29

Merlin
Merlin Dreams - Peter Dickinson 523

Merlini the Great
Joel and the Great Merlini - Eloise Jarvis McGraw 1228

Myrddin
The Book of Brendan - Ann Curry 456

Penny, Joel
Joel and the Great Merlini - Eloise Jarvis McGraw 1228

Petie
The Red King - Victor Kelleher 1005

Poinsettia
Mirandy and Brother Wind - Pat McKissack 1246

Tomaro
With a Wave of the Wand - Mark Jonathan Harris 817

Valvano, Maria Cecelia
The Amazing Valvano and the Mystery of the Hooded Rat - Mary Robinson 1518

Von Pokus, Hokus
Little Man - Erich Kastner 997

MAIDEN

Maiden
Her Seven Brothers - Paul Goble 713

MAIL ORDER BRIDE

Wheaton, Sarah
Sarah, Plain and Tall - Patricia MacLachlan 1170

MAINTENANCE WORKER

Benson, Josiah
The Worldwide Dessert Contest - Dan Elish 564

Bly, Jamie
The Red Room Riddle - Scott Corbett 427

Grayson
Maniac Magee - Jerry Spinelli 1715

Henry, Mack
Finding Buck McHenry - Alfred Slote 1669

Jordan, Nip
The Great Ringtail Garbage Caper - Timothy Foote 632

Pluto
The House of Dies Drear - Virginia Hamilton 802

Popper
Mr. Popper's Penguins - Richard Atwater 64

Taylor, Tuck
The Great Ringtail Garbage Caper - Timothy Foote 632

MANAGER

Boruch
The Island on Bird Street - Uri Orlev 1364

Spencer, Gus
The Kid from Tomkinsville - John R. Tunis 1828

MANAGER (SPORTS)

Pendergast, Popoff
The Kid Who Batted 1000 - Bob Allison 35

Russell, Bobby "Spike"
The Kid Comes Back - John R. Tunis 1827

MARTIAL ARTS EXPERT

Ben
A Bundle of Sticks - Pat Rhoads Mauser 1209

MENTALLY ILL PERSON

Isabell
Farewell, Aunt Isabell - Ilse-Margret Vogel 1858

MERCHANT

Abdullah
Castle in the Air - Diana Wynne Jones 979

MIDWIFE

Burdette, Sal
Brushy Mountain - Patricia Pendergraft 1416

MILITARY PERSONNEL

Bryan, John Randolph
Runaway Balloon: The Last Flight of Confederate Air Force One - Burke Davis 486

Bussey, Jeff
Rifles for Watie - Harold Keith 1004

Carter, Alan
Fantastic Voyage - Isaac Asimov 61

Chuckie
The Last Mission - Harry Mazer 1215

Dave
The Deserter - Nigel Gray 738

Falcon
Awfully Short for the Fourth Grade - Elvira Woodruff 1951

George
George the Drummer Boy - Nathaniel Benchley 132

Hannibal
Spring Rider - John Shults Lawson 1082

Johnson, Joe
Runaway Balloon: The Last Flight of Confederate Air Force One - Burke Davis 486

Mallixxan
The Humans of Ziax II - John Morressy 1292

Morrissay, Will
The Root Cellar - Janet Louise Lunn 1157

Perry, Matthew C.
Commodore Perry in the Land of the Shogun - Rhoda Blumberg 151

Raab, Jack
The Last Mission - Harry Mazer 1215

Radames
Aida - Leontyne Price 1467

Reid, Donald
Fantastic Voyage - Isaac Asimov 61

Rudi
The Machine Gunners - Robert Westall 1895

Sampson, Deborah
I'm Deborah Sampson: A Soldier in the War of the Revolution - Patricia Clapp 342

Smalls, Robert
Captain of the Planters: The Biography of Robert Smalls - Dorothy Sterling 1741

Taro
The Wind Is Not a River - Arnold A. Griese 767

Tyne, Eben
Eben Tyne: Powdermonkey - Patricia Beatty 123

Watie, Stand
Rifles for Watie - Harold Keith   1004

MILKMAN

Cowlander
The Ghost-Eye Tree - Bill Martin, Jr.   1203

MINE OWNER

Katherine
My Trip to Alpha I - Alfred Slote   1674

MINER

Big Pete
Chang's Paper Pony - Eleanor Coerr   377

Kelly, Bob
The Sky Is Free - Mavis Thorpe Clark   346

MINSTREL

Flam, Fflewddur
The High King - Lloyd Alexander   28

Roger
Adam of the Road - Elizabeth Gray   735

MODEL

Manderby
Portrait of Ivan - Paula Fox   640

MOLE

Fred
So You Want to Be a Wizard - Diane Duane   541

Mole
A Clean House for Mole and Mouse - Harriet Ziefert   1986
The Wind in the Willows - Kenneth Grahame   733

Molly
Molly in Danger - Anne Carter   306

MONGOOSE

Viggo
Up Mountain One Time - Willie Wilson   1926

MONKEY

Hush, Jeremiah
The Strange and Exciting Adventures of Jeremiah Hush - Uri Shulevitz   1632

MONSTER

Crannaker, Russell
The Monster's Ring - Bruce Coville   438

Monnie
The Monster Garden - Vivien Alcock   20

Monster, Billy
The Very Worst Monster - Pat Hutchins   961

Monster, Hazel
The Very Worst Monster - Pat Hutchins   961

Oni
The Funny Little Woman - Arlene Mosel   1294

Scipiod
Merlin Dreams - Peter Dickinson   523

Shrek
Shrek! - William Steig   1736

Swamp Haunt
Liza Lou and the Yeller Belly Swamp - Mercer Mayer   1211

MOOSE

Morris
Morris and Boris at the Circus - Bernard Wiseman   1935
Morris Has a Cold - Bernard Wiseman   1936

MOUNTAIN MAN

Bridger, Jim
Hugh Glass, Mountain Man - Robert McClung   1221

Gentle Tom
The Adventures of Johnny May - Robbie Branscum   188

Glass, Hugh
Hugh Glass, Mountain Man - Robert McClung   1221

MOUNTAINEER

Darnley, Lawrence
In Caverns of Blue Ice - Robert Roper   1546

DeMaistre, Louise
In Caverns of Blue Ice - Robert Roper   1546

MOUSE

Amos
Ben and Me - Robert Lawson   1083

Baby
The Pea Patch Jig - Thacher Hurd   942

Basil
Basil in Mexico - Eve Titus   1814

Bernard
Bernard Sees the World - Berniece Freschet   646

Bianca
The Rescuers - Margery Sharp   1623

Brave, Bernard
The Rescuers - Margery Sharp   1623

Dawson
Basil in Mexico - Eve Titus   1814

De Soto
Dr. De Soto - William Steig   1734

Derek
The Real Thief - William Steig   1735

Father
The Mouse and His Child - Russell Hoban   892

Fats
The Great Christmas Kidnapping Caper - Jean Van Leeuwen   1847

Fieldmouse, Feldman
Feldman Fieldmouse - Nathaniel Benchley   131

Frisby
Mrs. Frisby and the Rats of NIMH - Robert C. O'Brien   1347

Jumping Mouse
The Story of Jumping Mouse - John Steptoe   1740

Little, Frederick C.
Stuart Little - E.B. White   1900

Little, George
Stuart Little - E.B. White   1900

Little, Stuart
Stuart Little - E.B. White   1900

Marvin the Magnificent
The Great Christmas Kidnapping Caper - Jean Van Leeuwen   1847

Merle
Uncle Foster's Hat Tree - Doug Cushman   461

Mert
Tillie and Mert - Ida Luttrell   1158

Mouse
A Clean House for Mole and Mouse - Harriet Ziefert   1986
The First Morning: An African Myth - Margery Bernstein   142

Mouse, Adam
I'll Meet You at the Cucumbers - Lilian Moore   1281

Mouse, Amanda
I'll Meet You at the Cucumbers - Lilian Moore   1281

Mouse, Junius
I'll Meet You at the Cucumbers - Lilian Moore   1281

Mouse, Matthias
Redwall - Brian Jacques   967

Mouse, Timothy
Mrs. Frisby and the Rats of NIMH - Robert C. O'Brien   1347

Norwegian, Nils
The Rescuers - Margery Sharp   1623

O'Crispin
The Champion of Merrimack County - Roger W. Drury   538

Pearl
Pearl's Pirates - Frank Asch   58

Pippa
Pippa Pops Out: Four Read-Aloud/Read Alone Stories - Betty Boegehold   164

Ralph
The Mouse and the Motorcycle - Beverly Cleary   352

Raymond
The Great Christmas Kidnapping Caper - Jean Van Leeuwen   1847

Smart, Ralph
Ralph S. Mouse - Beverly Cleary   353

Son
The Mouse and His Child - Russell Hoban   892

Thomas
Fast Friends: Two Stories - James Stevenson   1746

Tucker
The Cricket in Times Square - George Selden   1608
Harry Cat's Pet Puppy - George Selden   1610
Tucker's Countryside - George Selden   1611

Tweedy
Where Is Freddy? - Laura Jean Johnson   976

Wilbur
Pearl's Pirates - Frank Asch   58

MULE

Hogg, Elijah
Dominic - William Steig   1733

MURDERER

Mason, John
Tuppenny - Julia Cunningham   455

MUSICIAN

Aviva
Aviva's Piano - Miriam Chaikin   314

Baker, Josephine "Tumpie"
Ragtime Tumpie - Alan Schroeder   1597

Bashara, Sheik
Mariah Loves Rock - Mildred Pitts Walter   1881

Bollier, Jessie
The Slave Dancer - Paula Fox   641

Boone, Billy
Billy Boone - Alison Smith   1676

Byler, Banjo
Banjo - Robert Newton Peck   1407

Curtis, Tom
Jazz Country - Nat Hentoff   857

De Angeli, Dailey
Fiddlestrings - Marguerite De Angeli   491

Eklund, Chris
The Something Special Horse - Lynn Hall   796

Face, Potato
Rootabaga Stories - Carl Sandburg   1584

Garnett, Laurie
No Applause, Please - Marilyn Singer   1655

Gast
What Happened in Hamelin? - Gloria
   Skurzynski   1659

Huw
The Silver Cow: A Welsh Tale - Susan Cooper   422

Johnson, James "Jimmy Jo"
Come Sing, Jimmy Jo - Katherine Paterson   1387

Johnson, Jerry Lee
Come Sing, Jimmy Jo - Katherine Paterson   1387

Johnson, Olive
Come Sing, Jimmy Jo - Katherine Paterson   1387

Jones, Mel
Mystery of the Hard Luck Rodeo - Susan
   Saunders   1589

Lenny
Jake - Alfred Slote   1672

Lipman, Isaac
Two Piano Tuners - M.B. Goffstein   716

Motele "Mitek"
Uncle Misha's Partisans - Yuri Suhl   1767

Nicky
Nicky and the Joyous Noise - Mildred Ames   39

Paavo
The Bronze King - Suzy McKee Charnas   320

Pennington, Patrick
Marion's Angels - K.M. Peyton   1428

Sebastian
The Marvelous Misadventures of Sebastian - Lloyd
   Alexander   31

Torcom
My Mom, the Money Nut - Betty Bates   103

Tyree
The Dog Days of Arthur Cane - T. Ernesto
   Bethancourt   144

Voight, Ephraim
Marion's Angels - K.M. Peyton   1428

Washington, Mercedes
The Day That Elvis Came to Town - Jan
   Marino   1193

Zeiler, Ruthie
No Applause, Please - Marilyn Singer   1655

Zimmer, Fritzi
My Mom, the Money Nut - Betty Bates   103

MYTHICAL CREATURE

Baggins, Bilbo
The Hobbit - J.R.R. Tolkien   1818

Big Friendly Giant
The BFG - Roald Dahl   463

Clock, Arrietty
The Borrowers - Mary Norton   1344

Clock, Homily
The Borrowers - Mary Norton   1344

Clock, Pod
The Borrowers - Mary Norton   1344

Dick, Hobberdy
Hobberdy Dick - Katherine Mary Briggs   200

Griffin
The Griffin and the Minor Canon - Frank R.
   Stockton   1750

Haraz, Fawzi
A Lamp for the Lambchops - Jeff Brown   215

Iron
The Iron Giant: A Story in Five Nights - Ted
   Hughes   935

Jo
The 24-Hour Genie - Lila McGinnis   1225

Leaper
The Wicked Pigeon Ladies in the Garden - Mary
   Chase   321

Masklin
Truckers - Terry Pratchett   1464

Meara
Seal Child - Sylvia Peck   1410

Moomintroll
Finn Family Moomintroll - Tove Jansson   969

Njimbin
A Little Fear - Patricia Wrightson   1958

Otto
The Little Witch and the Riddle - Bruce Degen   504

Small Fur
Small Fur - Irina Korschunov   1053

Sniff
Finn Family Moomintroll - Tove Jansson   969

Snufkin
Finn Family Moomintroll - Tove Jansson   969

Starlight
A Net to Catch the Wind - Margaret Greaves   741

Triton
The Sea Egg - L.M. Boston   178

NARRATOR

Lott, Georgina
The Borning Room - Paul Fleischman   612

NATURALIST

Long Arrow
The Voyages of Dr. Doolittle - Hugh Lofting   1144

Redmond, Joshua
Land's End - Mary Stolz   1757

NEIGHBOR

Amber
Foxy - Helen V. Griffith   771

Arthur
Land's End - Mary Stolz   1757

Baker, Joey
The Fireball Mystery - Mary Adrain   14

Banks, Will "Loony Willy"
A Summer to Die - Lois Lowry   1155

Beck
You Can Depend on Me - Margaret Reuter   1503

Bee
One More Flight - Eve Bunting   234

Beeble
The Ears of Louis - Constance C. Greene   749

Ben
Megan's Island - Willo Davis Roberts   1512

Benedict, Marshall
Speaking of Snapdragons - Sheila Hayes   836

Blue Lady
I Am Susannah - Libby Gleeson   709

Broadribb
Miss Pickerell and the War of the Computers - Dora
   Pantell   1373

Calloway
The View From the Cherry Tree - Willo Davis
   Roberts   1513

Cannon, Roscoe
Babysitter on Horseback - Fern G. Brown   213

Clark
Gopher, Tanker, and the Admiral - Shirley
   Climo   368

Clutchett
Time at the Top - Edward Ormondroyd   1367

Coleman
At the Back of the North Wind - George
   MacDonald   1165

Crimp
Mad Martin - Patricia Windsor   1927

Fisher, George
The Luck of Pokey Bloom - Ellen Conford   406

Gregg, Philip
The Magic Finger - Roald Dahl   467

Jarvis, Steve
The Berkley Street Six Pack - Mary Francis
   Shura   1633

Karsten
The House on Hackman's Hill - Joan Lowery
   Nixon   1337

Kearns, Jennifer Wingford "Jenny"
My Own Private Sky - Delores Beckman   127

Kitamura
The Rooster Who Understood Japanese - Yoshiko
   Uchida   1838

Leitstein
Love You, Soldier - Amy Hest   872

Mary Sue
Silver - Gloria Whelan   1897

Michaelmas, Annie
The Girl with the Silver Eyes - Willo Davis
   Roberts   1510

Miller, Irene
Danny Dunn and the Universal Glue - Jay
   Williams   1919
Danny Dunn on the Ocean Floor - Jay
   Williams   1920

Moody, Delbert
The Wicked Pigeon Ladies in the Garden - Mary
   Chase   321

Morgan
Benson Boy - Ivan Southall   1707

Naomi
Alan and Naomi - Myron Levoy   1104

Natasha
Toughboy and Sister - Kirkpatrick Hill   883

PELICAN

Percival
Storm Boy - Colin Thiele   1802

PENGUIN

Captain Cook
Mr. Popper's Penguins - Richard Atwater   64

Pin
The Mysterious Cases of Mr. Pin - Mary Elise
Monsell   1277

PIG

Ace
Ace, the Very Important Pig - Dick King-
Smith   1029

Alice
Quick Chick - Julia Hoban   887

Amanda
More Tales of Amanda the Pig - Jean Van
Leeuwen   1848

Babe
Babe: The Gallant Pig - Dick King-Smith   1030

Badger, Bartholomew
Dominic - William Steig   1733

Barleylove
Pigs Might Fly: A Novel - Dick King-Smith   1033

Brown, Henry
Ruthann and Her Pig - Barbara Ann Porte   1460

Corn, Quentin
Quentin Corn - Mary Stolz   1759

de Swine, Waltham
Sid Seal, Houseman - Will Watkins   1889

Dogfoot, Daggie
Pigs Might Fly: A Novel - Dick King-Smith   1033

Fatly
Euphonia and the Flood - Mary Calhoun   273

Freddy
Freddy the Detective - Walter R. Brooks   212

Glory-of-the-Republic
The House of Sixty Fathers - Meindert De Jong   494

Homer
Pinch - Larry Callen   277

Humphrey
Seven Spells to Farewell - Betty Baker   86

Johnnie
The Peppermint Pig - Nina Bawden   115

Oink
Ups and Downs with Oink and Pearl - Kay
Chorao   328

Oink, Lotta
Sly, P.I.: The Case of the Missing Shoes - Cathy
Stefanec-Ogren   1730

Pearl
Ups and Downs with Oink and Pearl - Kay
Chorao   328

Pig Pig
Pig Pig and the Magic Photo Album - David M.
McPhail   1250

Pinky
A Day No Pigs Would Die - Robert Newton
Peck   1408

Wilbur
Charlotte's Web - E.B. White   1899

PIGEON

Grey Cloud
Grey Cloud - Charlotte Towner Graeber   729

PILOT

Lily
Commander Toad and the Intergalactic Spy - Jane
Yolen   1968

Martin, Gary
The Last Mission - Harry Mazer   1215

Tole, Rex
Caught in the Moving Mountains - Gloria
Skurzynski   1658

PIRATE

Fairhair, Thorkell
Viking's Dawn - Henry Treece   1822

Harald
Viking's Dawn - Henry Treece   1822

Ragmar
Viking's Dawn - Henry Treece   1822

Scratch, Captain
The Ghost in the Noonday Sun - Sid
Fleischman   620

Silver, Long John
Treasure Island - Robert Louis Stevenson   1749

Teach, Edward "Blackbeard"
Blackbeard's Ghost - Ben Stahl   1724

POLICE OFFICER

Bates, Agatha
Missing - James Duffy   545

Gru
The Donkey Planet - Scott Corbett   423

Noir, Pierre
The Revolt of the Teddy Bears: A May Gray Mystery
- James Duffy   546

O'Kelly, Kelly
The Murder of Hound Dog Bates - Robbie
Branscum   189

Wyatt, Peter
The Case of the Murdered Players - Robert
Newman   1329

Zane, Kit
Angie's First Case - Donald J. Sobol   1702

POLITICAL FIGURE

DeCree
The Search for Delicious - Natalie Babbitt   78

Lincoln, Abraham
Lincoln: A Photobiography - Russell Freedman   644

McCorkle, Roscoe
Charlie Drives the Stage - Eric A. Kimmel   1025

Pursewig
The Cat Who Wished to Be a Man - Lloyd
Alexander   26

PORCUPINE

Penrod
Penrod's Pants - Mary Blount Christian   332

POSTAL WORKER

Thompson, John
Snowshoe Thompson - Nancy Smiler
Levinson   1101

PRAIRIE DOG

Dupper
Dupper - Betty Baker   85

PREHISTORIC HUMAN

Doban
Shiva: An Adventure of the Ice Age - J.H.
Brennan   191

Ig
Ig Lives in a Cave - Carol Chapman   318

Maroo
Maroo of the Winter Caves - Ann Turnbull   1831

Mat-Maw
Spirit on the Wall - Ann O'Neal Garcia   664

Seth
Seth of the Lion People - Bonnie Pryor   1475

Shiva
Shiva: An Adventure of the Ice Age - J.H.
Brennan   191

PRETEEN

Aarons, Jess
Bridge to Terabithia - Katherine Paterson   1386

Abby
Dark Horse - Jean Slaughter Doty   534
Me and Mr. Stenner - Evan Hunter   938

Ackerman, Cybil
The Cybil War - Betsy Byars   262

Adam
I and Sproggy - Constance C. Greene   751
Red Dog - Bill Wallace   1877

Adams, Arilla
Arilla Sun Down - Virginia Hamilton   799

Adams, Cassie
The Twenty-Four-Hour Lipstick Mystery - Bonnie
Pryor   1476

Adams, Mike
Follow My Leader - James B. Garfield   669

Agnew, Addie
Secret Lives - Berthe Amoss   42

Alan
Alanna: The First Adventure - Tamora Pierce   1440

Alanna
Alanna: The First Adventure - Tamora Pierce   1440

Alberoy, Priscilla Jane "PJ"
The Turtle Street Trading Company - Jill Ross
Klevin   1041

Aldo
Aldo Peanut Butter - Johanna Hurwitz   947

Alec
The Luck of the Miss L. - Lee Kingman   1034

Aleson, Catherine
I Met a Traveller - Lillian Hoban   889

Alex
The Hermit of Fog Hollow Station - David
Roth   1551
The Island on Bird Street - Uri Orlev   1364

Alexander
The Ghost Belonged to Me - Richard Peck   1405

Alexandra "Al"
Your Old Pal, Al - Constance C. Greene   753

Charlton, Tim
Danger at Black Dyke - Winifred Finlay 603

Charrington, Jane
Operation Peeg - Jonathan Gathorne-Hardy 677

Childers, Brian
The Antrian Messenger - G. Clifton Wisler 1938

Childs, Lucy
Lucy Forever and Miss Rosetree, Shrinks - Susan Richards Shreve 1629

Chloris
Chloris and the Creeps - Kin Platt 1450

Chrissy
I Hate Being Gifted - Patricia Hermes 863

Christina "Teeny"
Impy for Always - Jackie French Koller 1044

Christine "Chris"
The Deserter - Nigel Gray 738

Clancy, Nancy
Ned Kelly and the City of the Bees - Thomas Keneally 1013

Clark, Jeffrey
Jeffrey's Ghost and the Fifth Grade Dragon - David A. Adler 12

Clarke, Peter
Manhattan Is Missing - E.W. Hildick 880

Claudia
From the Mixed-Up Files of Mrs. Basil E. Frankweiler - E.L. Konigsburg 1045

Clay, Isadora
Hear the Wind Blow - Patricia Pendergraft 1417

Cobb, Joshua
The Freewheeling of Joshua Cobb - Margaret Hodges 894

Colman, Billy
Where the Red Fern Grows - Wilson Rawls 1493

Comfort
Comfort Herself - Geraldine Kaye 1000

Common, Callie
Red Sky at Morning - Andrea Wyman 1960

Connell, Brann
Building Blocks - Cynthia Voigt 1860

Connolly, Sara Kate
Afternoon of the Elves - Janet Taylor Lisle 1128

Corbett, Kevin
Heads, I Win - Patricia Hermes 862

Cox, Tiffany
Tough Tiffany - Belinda Hurmence 945

Crane
The Freewheeling of Joshua Cobb - Margaret Hodges 894

Crane, Stogie
Shortstop From Tokyo - Matt Christopher 339

Crannaker, Russell
The Monster's Ring - Bruce Coville 438

Crinkley, Elissa
Be a Perfect Person in Just Three Days - Stephen Manes 1187

Crisply, Becky
The Remarkable Return of Winston Potter Crisply - Eve Rice 1505

Cristabel
Philo Potts, or, The Helping Hand Strikes Again - Mildred Ames 40

Crowder, Mark Anthony
Reserved for Mark Anthony Crowder - Alison Smith 1677

Crowell, Bruce
The Red Room Riddle - Scott Corbett 427

Cummings, Isabelle "Izzy"
Underdog - Marilyn Sachs 1580

Curry, Derek
The Cold and Hot Winter - Johanna Hurwitz 951

Cutter, Charles
The Winged Colt of Casa Mia - Betsy Byars 268

Danica
Call Me Danica - Winifred Madison 1174

Daniel
Bones on Black Spruce Mountain - David Budbill 222

Danny
The Snake Horn - Morton Grosser 776

Daphne
Daphne - Marilyn Kaye 1001

Darlington, Arthur
Night of the Twisters - Ivy Ruckman 1559

David
David and Max - Gary Provost 1473
The Grizzly - Annabel Johnson 974

Davidowitz, Rozsi
Upon the Head of the Goat: A Childhood in Hungary, 1939-1944 - Aranka Siegal 1641

Davies, Peggy
Next-Door Neighbors - Sarah Ellis 570

Dean
Mojo and the Russians - Walter Dean Myers 1303

Delany, Mariah
Mariah Delany's Author-of-the-Month Club - Sheila Greenwald 759

Demba
Dark Venture - Audrey White Beyer 145

Devine, Rebecca "Becky"
The Empty Chair - Bess Kaplan 993

DeWitt, Louise
The 17th Street Gang - Emily Cheney Neville 1326

Dillman, Franny
It All Began with Jane Eyre, or the Secret Life of Franny Dillman - Sheila Greenwald 758

Dobson, Peter J. "Dobby"
One More Flight - Eve Bunting 234

Donahue, Tommy
Who Knew There'd Be Ghosts? - Bill Brittain 205

Doris
The Gift-Giver - Joyce Hansen 812

Doty, Philip "Flip"
Mail-Order Kid - Joyce McDonald 1224

Douglas, Justice "Ticey"
Justice and Her Brothers - Virginia Hamilton 804

Dove, Finn
The Flight of the Doves - Walter Macken 1168

Doyle, Brandon
The Witches of Worm - Zilpha Keatley Snyder 1701

Doyle, Charlotte
The True Confessions of Charlotte Doyle - Avi 74

Duke
Dump Days - Jerry Spinelli 1714

Dunn, Danny
Danny Dunn and the Universal Glue - Jay Williams 1919

Dunn, Rory
The Cold and Hot Winter - Johanna Hurwitz 951

Edwin
Katie John and Heathcliff - Mary Calhoun 274

Elaine
Space Demons - Gillian Rubinstein 1558

Eldon
The Winter Room - Gary Paulsen 1400

Ella
All-of-a-Kind Family - Sydney Taylor 1787

Ellen Grae
Ellen Grae - Vera Cleaver 357

Ellie
Our Sixth-Grade Sugar Babies - Eve Bunting 236

Elliot, Davidson
Hey, What's Wrong with This One? - Maia Wojciechowska 1939

Elliott, Arthur Livingston
My Own Private Sky - Delores Beckman 127

Elliott, Harley
Hey, What's Wrong with This One? - Maia Wojciechowska 1939

Elsie
Nothing's Fair in Fifth Grade - Barthe DeClements 500

Emerson, Lucy
The Half-Child - Kathleen Hersom 868

Emily
Getting Rid of Marjorie - Betty Ren Wright 1955

Emma
Nobody's Family Is Going to Change - Louise Fitzhugh 609
Pip and Emma - Katharine Bacon 80

Entsminger, Kathy
The Dandelion Caper - Gene DeWeese 516

Ephraim
Downwind - Louise Moeri 1273

Eric
My Friend, My Brother - David Warren Swartley 1773

Esther
The Law of Gravity - Johanna Hurwitz 953

Fanny
Fat Fanny, Beanpole Bertha and the Boys - Barbara Ann Porte 1458

Farla
Dear Baby - Joanne Rocklin 1524

Farley
The Dog Who Wouldn't Be - Farley Mowat 1296

Farley, Ellie
A Blue-Eyed Daisy - Cynthia Rylant 1563

Farrell, Greg
The Josie Gambit - Mary Francis Shura 1635

Ferguson, Andy
The Hit-and-Run Connection - Carole Smith 1678

Fernald, Alvin
Alvin Fernald, Master of a Thousand Disguises - Clifford B. Hicks 877

Ferris, Ned
It Takes Brains - Eiveen Weiman 1890

Fielding, Heather
Transfigured Hart - Jane Yolen 1972

Fig
Rhoda, Straight and True - Roni Schotter 1596

Finch, Becky
The Bongleweed - Helen Cresswell 442

Finch, June
Just Like a Real Family - Kristi Holl 898

Finkelstein, Rhona
The Hand-Me-Down Kid - Francine Pascal 1384

Finnegan, Brian
Dear Mom, You're Ruining My Life - Jean Van Leeuwen 1846

Fisher, Barbara
The Real Me - Betty Miles 1263

Quacky
Quacky and the Crazy Curve Ball - Walter G. Oleksy 1358

Raab, Bolivia
The Cold and Hot Winter - Johanna Hurwitz 951

Rachel
The Iceberg and Its Shadow - Jan Greenberg 745

Reachfar, Janet
Brave Janet Reachfar - Jane Duncan 547

Rebecca
Glass Slippers Give You Blisters - Mary Jane Auch 65

Redfern, Julia
Julia and the Hand of God - Eleanor Cameron 284

Redmond, Joshua
Land's End - Mary Stolz 1757

Reed, Henry
Henry Reed's Baby-Sitting Service - Keith Robertson 1514

Reid, Jane
In a Blue Velvet Dress - Catherine Sefton 1604

Rhoda
Rhoda, Straight and True - Roni Schotter 1596

Richardson, Jane
The Hand-Me-Down Kid - Francine Pascal 1384

Ricky
A Dog Called Kitty - Bill Wallace 1876

Rider, Daniel
The Lightning Time - Gregory Maguire 1178

Riggs, Rosy
Dog Days - Colby Rodowsky 1536

Riker, Janice
Soup - Robert Newton Peck 1409

Riley, Denise
Daughters of the Law - Sandy Asher 59

Rinehart, Arthur
Rinehart Lifts - R. Rozanne Knudson 1043

Ringo
Me and My Million - Clive King 1027

Rinko
The Best Bad Thing - Yoshiko Uchida 1835

Robbins, Ned
Jelly Belly - Robert Kimmel Smith 1691

Robby
A Friend Like That - Alfred Slote 1670

Roberta
The Railway Children - Edith Nesbit 1324

Robinson, Rachel
Just as Long as We're Together - Judy Blume 156

Robinson, Scott
Babysitter on Horseback - Fern G. Brown 213

Roger
Jolly Roger and the Pirates of Abdul, the Skinhead - Colin McNaughton 1248

Rogers, Brandon
Racing the Sun - Paul Pitts 1448

Rosemary
Ellen Grae - Vera Cleaver 357
Rosemary's Witch - Ann Warren Turner 1833

Rosen, Ellen
Number the Stars - Lois Lowry 1153

Rosso, Abbie
Ten Kids, No Pets - Ann M. Martin 1200

Rosso, Dagwood ''Woody''
Ten Kids, No Pets - Ann M. Martin 1200

Rourke, Hollis
The 17th Street Gang - Emily Cheney Neville 1326

Rufus
Detectives in Togas - Henry Winterfeld 1929

Ryan
The Scorpio Ghosts and the Black Hole Gang - Kathy Kennedy Tapp 1778

Rye, Hazel
Hazel Rye - Vera Cleaver 358

Sam
Double or Nothing - Marc Talbert 1776
Dracula Is a Pain in the Neck - Elizabeth Levy 1107
Knights of the Kitchen Table - Jon Scieszka 1601

Samantha
Samantha on Stage - Susan Clement Farrar 590
There's a Caterpillar in My Lemonade - Diana Gregory 763

Sampson, Radcliffe ''Cliffie''
Rat Teeth - Patricia Reilly Giff 698

Sandy
Megan's Island - Willo Davis Roberts 1512

Sarah
You've Been Away All Summer - Sheila Hayes 837

Saunders, Craig
Mrs. Tooey and the Terrible Toxic Tar - Barbara Dillon 526

Saunders, Margo
Mrs. Tooey and the Terrible Toxic Tar - Barbara Dillon 526

Sawyer, Tom
The Adventures of Tom Sawyer - Mark Twain 1834

Schirmers, Laura
Old John - Peter Hartling 821

Schneider, Bodo
The Shadow on the Hills - Colin Thiele 1801

Seth
Bones on Black Spruce Mountain - David Budbill 222

Seton, Andrew
Scrub Fire - Anne De Roo 496

Shabanu
Shabanu, Daughter of the Wind - Suzanne Fisher Staples 1726

Sharp, Olivia
The Pizza Monster - Marjorie Weinman Sharmat 1621

Sherman
The Gift-Giver - Joyce Hansen 812

Shook, Albert
The Ghost Upstairs - Lila McGinnis 1226

Sibbie, Laura
Sixth Grade Secrets - Louis Sachar 1569

Sills, Lena
Words by Heart - Ouida Sebestyen 1602

Simms, Jeremy
Mississippi Bridge - Mildred D. Taylor 1785

Simon
The Cybil War - Betsy Byars 262

Simon, Jon
My Friend, My Brother - David Warren Swartley 1773

Sinclare, Marian
The Selchie's Seed - Shulamith Oppenheim 1361

Singer, Vanessa
Make Like a Tree and Leave - Paula Danziger 479

Singleton, Myron
Honestly, Myron - Dean Hughes 931

Skip
Rish n' Roses - Jan Slepian 1666
Wildcat Summer - Mary Riskind 1508

Slayton, Samantha
Dear Mom, You're Ruining My Life - Jean Van Leeuwen 1846

Sloane, Allegra ''Legs''
The Worry Week - Anne Lindbergh 1121

Slobodkin, George
Next-Door Neighbors - Sarah Ellis 570

Slocum, Bill
The Red Room Riddle - Scott Corbett 427

Slocum, Kib
Thatcher Payne-in-the-Neck - Betty Bates 105

Small, Edward
The Tar Pit - Tor Seidler 1607

Smith, Belinda Rainbow ''Boo''
The Big Smith Snatch - Jane Louise Curry 457

Smith, Galen
Mystery on Ice - Barbara Corcoran 431

Smith, Rich
Mystery of the Fat Cat - Frank Bonham 172

Smollet, William
In a Blue Velvet Dress - Catherine Sefton 1604

Soo, Malcolm
Up From Jerico Tel - E.L. Konigsburg 1048

Sossi, Aldo
Hurricane Elaine - Johanna Hurwitz 952

Sossi, Karen
Tough-Luck Karen - Johanna Hurwitz 958

Spangler, Mary Lou ''Wisconsin''
Keeping it Secret - Penny Pollock 1455

Spencer, Richard
The Warlock of Westfall - Leonard Everett Fisher 606

Sport
Sport - Louise Fitzhugh 610

Spratt, Christopher ''Gopher''
Gopher, Tanker, and the Admiral - Shirley Climo 368

Sproggy
I and Sproggy - Constance C. Greene 751

Stackhouse, Maizell
The Secret of Gumbo Grove - Eleanora E. Tate 1780

Stackhouse, Raisin
The Secret of Gumbo Grove - Eleanora E. Tate 1780

Stanton, Will
The Dark Is Rising - Susan Cooper 417
Greenwitch - Susan Cooper 418

Steele, Tina
Oh Honestly, Angela! - Nancy K. Robinson 1519

Stella
Mystery on Ice - Barbara Corcoran 431

Stephen
Wild Man of the Woods - Joan Clark 345

Sternwood, Stafford ''Stuffy''
Anything for a Friend - Ellen Conford 400

Steve
Tac's Island - Ruth Yaffe Radin 1482

Stewart, Candace
If Phyllis Were Here - Gail Jarrow 972

Stirkel, Florence
Growing Anyway Up - Florence Parry Heide 844

Stokes, Peter
The War with Grandpa - Robert Kimmel Smith 1692

Stomper
The Luck of the Miss L. - Lee Kingman 1034

Storm Boy
Storm Boy - Colin Thiele   1802

Stubbs, Rainbow Maximilian
Journey to an 800 Number - E.L. Konigsburg   1047

Susan
Meaning Well - Sheila R. Cole   391
Worlds Apart - Jill Murphy   1298

Susannah
I Am Susannah - Libby Gleeson   709

Sutton, Annie
The Well - Gene Kemp   1011

Sutton, Tom
The Well - Gene Kemp   1011

Suzuki, Hideko "Sam"
Shortstop From Tokyo - Matt Christopher   339

Svoboda, Sam
The Mystery of the Diamond in the Wood - David Kherdian   1021

Swanson, Maureen
The Wicked Pigeon Ladies in the Garden - Mary Chase   321

Swanson, Rosie
Maxie, Rosie, and Earl - Partners in Grime - Barbara Park   1379

Sylvie
Miracle at Clement's Pond - Patricia Pendergraft   1418

Talatu
Man with the Silver Eyes - William O. Steele   1729

Tanleven, Nina
The Ghost Wore Gray - Bruce Coville   437

Tassie
The Times They Used to Be - Lucille Clifton   367

Tate, Samantha "Sam"
Rats, Spiders, and Love - Bonnie Pryor   1474

Thornton, Cynthia Jane
The One and Only Cynthia Jane Thornton - Claudia Mills   1269

Tillett, Andrew
The Case of the Murdered Players - Robert Newman   1329

Toby
Toby Lived Here - Hilma Wolitzer   1943

Todd
Aunt Morbelia and the Screaming Skulls - Joan Davenport Carris   300

Tolly
Cave under the City - Harry Mazer   1214

Tom
Grey Cloud - Charlotte Towner Graeber   729

Toughboy
Toughboy and Sister - Kirkpatrick Hill   883

Treeman, Rosy
Lucy Forever and Miss Rosetree, Shrinks - Susan Richards Shreve   1629

Treloar, Amy
The Dollhouse Murders - Betty Ren Wright   1954

Troxell, Jeanmarie
Up From Jerico Tel - E.L. Konigsburg   1048

Trumbull, Elvira
The Twenty-Five Cent Miracle - Theresa Nelson   1322

Tsujimura, Rinko
A Jar of Dreams - Yoshiko Uchida   1836

Tubman, Sheila
Fudge-a-Mania - Judy Blume   154

Tuffy
In Summertime, It's Tuffy - Judie Angell   49

Twitchell, Nate
The Enormous Egg - Oliver Butterworth   254

Tyler, Gale
Mystery of the Hidden Hand - Phyllis A. Whitney   1904

Underwood, Cletus
Missing May - Cynthia Rylant   1568

Valentine, Casey
Fourth Grade Celebrity - Patricia Reilly Giff   693

Van Doren, Carrie
Rookfleas in the Cellar - Robert Pierik   1441

Van Doren, Danny
Rookfleas in the Cellar - Robert Pierik   1441

Van Doren, Stevie
Rookfleas in the Cellar - Robert Pierik   1441

Vanderpane, Clement Charles "CC"
The 17th Street Gang - Emily Cheney Neville   1326

Vic
Tom Tiddler's Ground - John Rowe Townsend   1820

Vicki
Our Sixth-Grade Sugar Babies - Eve Bunting   236

Vicky
Wildcat Summer - Mary Riskind   1508

Vorlob, Adine
The Zebra Wall - Kevin Henkes   852

Wade, Holly
Lavender-Green Magic - Andre Norton   1341

Wagner, Ben
The Witching of Ben Wagner - Mary Jane Auch   68

Wagoner, Curly
Curly and the Wild Boar - Fred Gipson   706

Wainwright, Jason
Keeping it Secret - Penny Pollock   1455

Walker, Bruce
Hotel for Dogs - Lois Duncan   549

Walker, Katie
The Girl with the Silver Eyes - Willo Davis Roberts   1510

Walker, Liz
Hotel for Dogs - Lois Duncan   549

Walter
General Butterfingers - John Reynolds Gardiner   667

Watson, Tubby
The Trading Game - Alfred Slote   1675

Wayd, Ginnela "Ginn"
The Package in Hyperspace - Janet Asimov   63

Wayne, Jared
Ride the Green Dragon - Andre Norton   1342

Wayne, Tracy
Ride the Green Dragon - Andre Norton   1342

Webster, "Girlie"
The Girl Who Had No Name - Berniece Rabe   1479

Webster, Jane
Afternoon of the Elves - Janet Taylor Lisle   1128

Wendy
Always and Forever Friends - Carole S. Adler   5
Blubber - Judy Blume   153

Wetzel, Jenny
They're All Named Wildfire - Nancy Springer   1718

Wharton, Bailey
Heads, I Win - Patricia Hermes   862

White, Sam
Grasshopper Summer - Ann Warren Turner   1832

White, William "Billy"
Grasshopper Summer - Ann Warren Turner   1832

Whitfield, Henry Barrett
Henry's Special Delivery - M.C. Delaney   508

Wilbur, Earl
Maxie, Rosie, and Earl - Partners in Grime - Barbara Park   1379

Will
The Hayburners - Gene Smith   1687
Wild Boy - Joan Tate   1782

Willeford, Calvin
The Dandelion Caper - Gene DeWeese   516

William
The Castle in the Attic - Elizabeth Winthrop   1931
A Northern Nativity: Christmas Dreams of a Prairie Boy - William Kurelek   1061

Williams, Buddy
Mystery of the Fat Cat - Frank Bonham   172

Willoughby-Green, Bonnie
The Wolves of Willoughby Chase - Joan Aiken   18

Wilson, Chuck
Follow My Leader - James B. Garfield   669

Wilson, Eli
Eli's Ghost - Betsy Hearne   841

Wilson, Ludell
Ludell - Brenda Scott Wilkinson   1913

Wilson, Rose
The Oracle Doll - Catherine Dexter   518

Wingate, Corrie
Dew Drop Dead: A Sebastian Barth Mystery - James Howe   925

Winkle, Oscar
Operation Dump the Chump - Barbara Park   1381

Winnie
Mazemaker - Catherine Dexter   517

Wrather, Jake
Jake - Alfred Slote   1672

Zach
The Bloodhound Gang and the Case of the Secret Message - Sid Fleischman   618
Today's Special: Z.A.P and Zoe - Athena V. Lord   1147

Zane, Angie
Angie's First Case - Donald J. Sobol   1702

Zoe
Stonewords: A Ghost Story - Pam Conrad   411

Zuchelli, Bertha
The Magic of Myrna C. Waxweather - Sandra Dutton   553

Zuckerman, Maxie
Maxie, Rosie, and Earl - Partners in Grime - Barbara Park   1379

PRINCIPAL

Burgmeister
The Silver Crest: My Russian Boyhood - Kornei Chukovsky   341

Pinkowski
I Can't Always Hear You - Joy Zelonky   1985

Trunchbull
Matilda - Roald Dahl   468

Van Crockett
The Magic of Myrna C. Waxweather - Sandra Dutton   553

PRISONER

Dad
Miracles on Maple Hill - Virginia Sorensen   1706

RELIGIOUS

RESCUER

RESEARCHER

RESISTANCE FIGHTER

Drossoula
Petros' War - Alki Zei 1982

Petros
Petros' War - Alki Zei 1982

Yoshke
Uncle Misha's Partisans - Yuri Suhl 1767

RESTAURANTEUR

Carpenter, Jacob
The Strange Night Writing of Jessamine Colter - Cynthia DeFelice 501

ROBOT

C.L.U.T.Z.
C.L.U.T.Z. and the Fission Formula - Marilyn Wilkes 1912

Danny One
My Robot Buddy - Alfred Slote 1673

Lamont, Lucky
Finders Keepers - Emily Rodda 1529

Mandus
The Type One Super Robot - Alison Prince 1472

Norby
Norby, the Mixed-Up Robot - Janet Asimov 62

Orvis
Orvis - H.M. Hoover 914

Sol-1
Ready, Set, Robot - Lillian Hoban 890

Watson II
The Robot and Rebecca: The Mystery of the Code Carrying Kids - Jane Yolen 1970

ROOSTER

Chauntecleer
The Book of the Dun Cow - Walter Wangerin 1882

Jones, Rufus
Stall Buddies - Penny Pollack 1454

Mr. Lincoln
The Rooster Who Understood Japanese - Yoshiko Uchida 1838

ROYALTY

Aerin
The Hero and the Crown - Robin McKinley 1241

Aida
Aida - Leontyne Price 1467

Akhenaton
I, Tut: The Boy Who Became Pharoah - Miriam Schlein 1595

Alicia
Perilous Gard - Elizabeth Marie Pope 1456

Amanda
The Trouble with Dragons - Oliver G. Selfridge 1612

Antia
Sandwriter - Monica Hughes 934

Basil
The Real Thief - William Steig 1735

Beast
Beauty: A Retelling of the Story of Beauty and the Beast - Robin McKinley 1238

Bee
Princess Bee and the Royal Goodnight Story - Sandy Asher 60

Belinda
The Trouble with Dragons - Oliver G. Selfridge 1612

Bellisant
Valentine and Orson - Nancy Ekholm Burkert 247

Celia
The Trouble with Dragons - Oliver G. Selfridge 1612

Chassidah
Alone in the Wild Forest - Isaac Bashevis Singer 1652

Cimorene
Dealing with Dragons - Patricia C. Wrede 1953

Eilonwy
The High King - Lloyd Alexander 28

Elizabeth
Perilous Gard - Elizabeth Marie Pope 1456

Flower-in-the-Night
Castle in the Air - Diana Wynne Jones 979

Furball
Princess Furball - Charlotte S. Huck 928

Horace "Brat"
The Whipping Boy - Sid Fleischman 625

Iseult
Tristan and Iseult - Rosemary Sutcliff 1770

Jodril
Sandwriter - Monica Hughes 934

Jonathan
Alanna: The First Adventure - Tamora Pierce 1440

Lenore
Many Moons - James Thurber 1811

Little Prince
The Little Prince - Antoine de Saint-Exupery 1581

Maltuch
Alone in the Wild Forest - Isaac Bashevis Singer 1652

Mirabelle
A Net to Catch the Wind - Margaret Greaves 741

Safa
The Ghost Drum: A Cat's Tale - Susan Price 1468

Tristan
Tristan and Iseult - Rosemary Sutcliff 1770

Tutankhaton
I, Tut: The Boy Who Became Pharoah - Miriam Schlein 1595

RULER

Alexander
Valentine and Orson - Nancy Ekholm Burkert 247

Amonasro
Aida - Leontyne Price 1467

Arlbeth
The Hero and the Crown - Robin McKinley 1241

Asoka
The Wheel of King Asoka - Ashok Davar 484

Bidgood
King Bidgood's in the Bathtub - Audrey Wood 1948

Bindusara
The Wheel of King Asoka - Ashok Davar 484

Dadon
The Tale of the Golden Cockerel - Alexander Pushkin 1477

Guidon
The Ghost Drum: A Cat's Tale - Susan Price 1468

Gwidion
The Black Cauldron - Lloyd Alexander 25

Marc
Tristan and Iseult - Rosemary Sutcliff 1770

Zyzmund the Zeventh
The Mysterious Zetabet - Scott Corbett 426

RUNAWAY

Buddy
Monkey Island - Paula Fox 638

Claudia
From the Mixed-Up Files of Mrs. Basil E. Frankweiler - E.L. Konigsburg 1045

Cole, Raymond
Raymond - Mark Geller 681

David
Family Pose - Dean Hughes 930

Garrity, Clay
Monkey Island - Paula Fox 638

Grabseth, Mikkel
Don't Take Teddy - Babbis Friis-Baastad 648

Jamie
From the Mixed-Up Files of Mrs. Basil E. Frankweiler - E.L. Konigsburg 1045

Julia
The Runaways - Ruth Thomas 1807

Karen
Foster Child - Marion Dane Bauer 107

Laporte, Tony
Snow Bound - Harry Mazer 1216

Leona
It Always Happens to Leona - Juanita Havill 832

Magee, Jeffrey "Maniac"
Maniac Magee - Jerry Spinelli 1715

Maggie
The Get-Away Car - Eleanor Clymer 369

Mandy
It Ain't Always Easy - Kathleen Karr 996

Mannix, Sandy
Bunkhouse Journal - Diane Johnston Hamm 809

Nathan
The Runaways - Ruth Thomas 1807

Renny
Foster Child - Marion Dane Bauer 107

Sam
The Sky Is Free - Mavis Thorpe Clark 346

Stacy
Shelter from the Wind - Marion Dane Bauer 109

Tyler, Toby
Toby Tyler: or Ten Weeks with a Circus - James Otis 1371

SAILOR

Alspeth, David
The Voyage of the Frog - Gary Paulsen 1399

Bowditch, Nathaniel
Carry On, Mr. Bowditch - Jean Lee Latham 1075

Brown, Ezra
Seabird - Holling Clancy Holling 905

Doyle, Charlotte
The True Confessions of Charlotte Doyle - Avi 74

Eaton, Nathaniel
The Witch of Blackbird Pond - Elizabeth George Speare 1710

Old Bill
Pearl's Pirates - Frank Asch 58

SHEPHERD

Ida
Ida and the Wool Smugglers - Sue Ann Alderson 24

Jo
Waiting for Anya - Michael Morpurgo 1291

Protheroe, Tom
No Way of Telling - Emma Smith 1686

SIDEKICK

Rollo
Where Is Freddy? - Laura Jean Johnson 976

SINGER

Anderson, Shorty
Night Swimmers - Betsy Byars 265

SINGLE PARENT

Cox, Dawn
Tough Tiffany - Belinda Hurmence 945

SKUNK

Palmer
Palmer Patch - Barbara Brooks Wallace 1872

Tillie
Tillie and Mert - Ida Luttrell 1158

SLAVE

Demba
Dark Venture - Audrey White Beyer 145

Esteban
Walk the World's Rim - Betty Baker 88

Fortune, Amos
Amos Fortune, Free Man - Elizabeth Yates 1962

Joshua
The Ballad of Belle Dorcas - William H. Hooks 912

Obi
Which Way Freedom? - Joyce Hansen 813

Pareja, Juan de
I, Juan de Pareja - Elizabeth Borton de Trevino 1823

Ras
The Slave Dancer - Paula Fox 641

Sampson
The Bronze Bow - Elizabeth George Speare 1708

Tituba
The Tall Man From Boston - Marion Lena Starkey 1727
Tituba of Salem Village - Ann Petry 1423

SMUGGLER

Tole, Rex
Caught in the Moving Mountains - Gloria Skurzynski 1658

SNAIL

Fred
Fast Friends: Two Stories - James Stevenson 1746

Snail
Snail Saves the Day - John Stadler 1723

SNAKE

Sir Lancelot
Alice and the Boa Constrictor - Laurie Adams 3

Wilfred
Snakes Are Nothing to Sneeze At - Gabrielle Charbonnet 319

SOCIAL WORKER

Finch
The Boy Who Wanted a Family - Shirley Gordon 722

Green
Raymond - Mark Geller 681

Luke
Luke Was There - Eleanor Clymer 371

SORCERER

Delver, P.C.
Andrew and the Alchemist - Barbara Ninde Byfield 269

Grimald
Gildaen: The Heroic Adventures of a Most Unusual Rabbit - Emilie Buchwald 221

SORCERESS

Dru
Seven Spells to Farewell - Betty Baker 86

SPACE EXPLORER

Aric
Aliens for Breakfast - Jonathan Etra 580

Zohert
Earthseed: A Novel - Pamela Sargent 1586

SPACESHIP CAPTAIN

Toad
Commander Toad and the Intergalactic Spy - Jane Yolen 1968

SPARROW

Warbeak
Redwall - Brian Jacques 967

SPIDER

Charlotte
Charlotte's Web - E.B. White 1899

Spider
The First Morning: An African Myth - Margery Bernstein 142

SPIRIT

Abdullah "Dooley"
The Genie of Sutton Place - George Selden 1609

Bankhead, Tallulah
Up From Jerico Tel - E.L. Konigsburg 1048

Benjamin
Beloved Benjamin Is Waiting - Jean Karl 994

Bradford
Jeffrey's Ghost and the Fifth Grade Dragon - David A. Adler 12

C.C.
The Scorpio Ghosts and the Black Hole Gang - Kathy Kennedy Tapp 1778

Canfield, Emily
Jane-Emily - Patricia Clapp 343

Cassaway, Tillie Jean
The Ghost of Tillie Jean Cassaway - Ellen H. Showell 1627

Culp, Blossom
The Ghost Belonged to Me - Richard Peck 1405

Dagda
The Hounds of the Morrigan - Pat O'Shea 1370

Dorro
The Gathering Room - Colby Rodowsky 1537

Eirlyo
The Snow Spider - Jenny Nimmo 1331

Elmer
The Over-the-Hill Ghost - Ruth Calif 276

Hannibal
Spring Rider - John Shults Lawson 1082

Hanny
A Haunting Air - Barbara Constance Freeman 645

Jacob
The Trouble with Jacob - Eloise Jarvis McGraw 1231

Mama
Ghost Story - Genevieve Gray 736

Moundshround, Carapace Clavicle
The Halloween Tree - Ray Bradbury 184

Newberry, Michael Oliver
Mad, Mad Monday - Herma Silverstein 1643

North Wind
At the Back of the North Wind - George MacDonald 1165

Papa
Ghost Story - Genevieve Gray 736

Parnell, Essie
Who Knew There'd Be Ghosts? - Bill Brittain 205

Parnell, Horace
Who Knew There'd Be Ghosts? - Bill Brittain 205

Porcupine
Porcupine's Pajama Party - Terry Webb Harshman 818

Rush
Sweet Whispers, Brother Rush - Virginia Hamilton 806

Vira
The Scorpio Ghosts and the Black Hole Gang - Kathy Kennedy Tapp 1778

Waxweather, Myrna C.
The Magic of Myrna C. Waxweather - Sandra Dutton 553

White, Otis
The Ghost Upstairs - Lila McGinnis 1226

Zoe Louise
Stonewords: A Ghost Story - Pam Conrad 411

SPORTS FIGURE

Alec
The Luck of the Miss L. - Lee Kingman 1034

Applebaum, Stanley
Wrongway Applebaum - Marjorie Lewis 1112

Barton, Bentley "Bart"
I Am Rubber, You are Glue - Jane Morton 1293

Barton, Jane
Racing in Her Blood - Millys N. Altman 37

Stock Broker (continued)

Hall, Frederick
The Fledgling - Jane Langton　1069

Jack
Don't Hurt Laurie! - Willo Davis Roberts　1509

Jake
Like Jake and Me - Mavis Jukes　988

Kiki
Maggie Forevermore - Joan Lowery Nixon　1339

Krampner, Seth
Happily Ever After.Almost - Judie Wolkoff　1945

Loring, Margaret
Remember Me When I Am Dead - Carol Beach York　1976

Mancha, Fidel
Chloris and the Creeps - Kin Platt　1450

Mebin, Steve
The Killer Swan - Eth Clifford　362

Molly
The Headless Cupid - Zilpha Keatley Snyder　1698

Morris, Barbara
Roots in the Outfield - Jane Zirpoli　1988

Rush
Branigan's Dog: A Novel - Fran Grace　727

Russo, Ben
My Mother Got Married and Other Disasters - Barbara Park　1380

Stenner
Me and Mr. Stenner - Evan Hunter　938

Walter
Mitzi and the Terrible Tyranosaurus Rex - Barbara Williams　1918

Wheaton, Sarah
Sarah, Plain and Tall - Patricia MacLachlan　1170

STOCK BROKER

Barnard, George
Night Fall - Joan Aiken　17

STORE OWNER

Heck
The Alligator and His Uncle Tooth: A Novel of the Sea - Geoffrey Hayes　833

Jiggs
The Dancing Cats of Applesap - Janet Taylor Lisle　1129

Oliphant, Iva
The Solitary - Lynn Hall　795

Wallace, John
The Friendship - Mildred D. Taylor　1784

STORYTELLER

Darlene
Once, Said Darlene - William Sleator　1664

Grandmother
The Village of Round and Square Houses - Ann Grifalconi　768

Pacolet
Valentine and Orson - Nancy Ekholm Burkert　247

Scheherazade
Tales From the Arabian Nights - N.J. Dawood　488

Willy
Four on the Shore - Edward Marshall　1196

STREETPERSON

Armand
Family Under the Bridge - Natalie Savage Carlson　292

Calvin
Monkey Island - Paula Fox　638

Gibson, Ben
Come the Morning - Mark Jonathan Harris　816

Glad Man
The Glad Man - Gloria Gonzalez　721

John
A Dog on Barkham Street - Mary Stolz　1753

Jones, Darcy
The Robbers - Nina Bawden　116

Screamer
The Case of the Baker Street Irregular: A Sherlock Holmes Story - Robert Newman　1328

Slake, Aremis
Slake's Limbo - Felice Holman　908

STUDENT

Aravon, Frank
Foal Creek - Peter Zachary Cohen　386

Boots
The Zucchini Warriors - Gordon Korman　1052

Bruno
The Zucchini Warriors - Gordon Korman　1052

Crisply, Winston Potter
The Remarkable Return of Winston Potter Crisply - Eve Rice　1505

Dieter
My Summer Brother - Ilse-Margret Vogel　1859

Feldman, Harris
Baseball Fever - Johanna Hurwitz　948

Goss, Joel
Justin Morgan Had a Horse - Marguerite Henry　853

Graden, Alexander William "Alex"
The Magic Book - Willo Davis Roberts　1511

Jackson, Ian
In Summer Light - Zibby Oneal　1360

Kelly, Ned
Ned Kelly and the City of the Bees - Thomas Keneally　1013

Krock, Jonah
Banana Blitz - Florence Parry Heide　843

Lisa
Glass Slippers Give You Blisters - Mary Jane Auch　65

MacDonald, Kelly
Glass Slippers Give You Blisters - Mary Jane Auch　65

Morgan
Follow That Bus! - Pat Hutchins　960

Nina
A Smart Kid Like You - Stella Pevsner　1426

Phillip
Kelly's Creek - Doris Buchanan Smith　1680

Rebecca
Glass Slippers Give You Blisters - Mary Jane Auch　65

Roland
The Battle Horse - Harry Kullman　1059

Thornhill, Mary-Larkin
The Integration of Mary-Larkin Thornhill - Ann Waldron　1869

Trane, Lewis "Goober"
Banana Blitz - Florence Parry Heide　843

Trantor, Kate
The Way to Sattin Shore - Philippa Pearce　1402

Vanella
The Integration of Mary-Larkin Thornhill - Ann Waldron　1869

Wells, Jefferson "Jeff"
Norby, the Mixed-Up Robot - Janet Asimov　62

Zwicker, Zachary
The Mysterious Zetabet - Scott Corbett　426

STUDENT—COLLEGE

Basini, Joe
Yours Truly, Shirley - Ann M. Martin　1202

Ben
Deathwatch - Robb White　1902

STUDENT—HIGH SCHOOL

Mohlen, Gordon
Summer of the White Goat - Paige Dixon　527

STUNTMAN

Collins, Coot
The Winged Colt of Casa Mia - Betsy Byars　268

SURVIVOR

Apu
The Night the Water Came - Clive King　1028

Burr
Medicine Walk - Ardath Mayhar　1212

Enright, Phillip
The Cay - Theodore Taylor　1788

Max
David and Max - Gary Provost　1473

Mouse, Abelard
Abel's Island - William Steig　1731

Teetoncey
Teetoncey - Theodore Taylor　1790

Thaddeus
Orvis - H.M. Hoover　914

Timothy
The Cay - Theodore Taylor　1788

Toby
Orvis - H.M. Hoover　914

SWAN

Louis
The Trumpet of the Swan - E.B. White　1901

TAILOR

Larson, Finn
A Stranger Came Ashore: A Story of Suspense - Mollie Hunter　941

Tippitt
Clancy's Coat - Eve Bunting　230

TEACHER

Baylis
Silent Dancer - Bruce Hlibok　886

Beaver
Follow That Bus! - Pat Hutchins　960

TELEPATH

TELEVISION PERSONALITY

Dixon, Mickey
The Halloween Candy Mystery - Marion M. Markham 1194

Douglas, Lee
Justice and Her Brothers - Virginia Hamilton 804

Douglas, Thomas
Justice and Her Brothers - Virginia Hamilton 804

Erika
Farewell, Aunt Isabell - Ilse-Margret Vogel 1858
My Summer Brother - Ilse-Margret Vogel 1859

Ferguson, Amy
The Leipzig Vampire - Mary Anderson 45

Ferguson, Jamie
The Leipzig Vampire - Mary Anderson 45

Freeman, Carl
How Do I Feel? - Norma Simon 1647

Freeman, Eddie
How Do I Feel? - Norma Simon 1647

Gary
The Fourth Floor Twins and the Sand Castle Contest - David A. Adler 11

Green, Mathilda
At the Sound of the Beep - Marilyn Sachs 1573

Green, Matthew
At the Sound of the Beep - Marilyn Sachs 1573

Hunor
The White Stag - Kate Seredy 1613

Inge
Farewell, Aunt Isabell - Ilse-Margret Vogel 1858
My Summer Brother - Ilse-Margret Vogel 1859

Kerry
The Robot Birthday - Eve Bunting 237

Magyar
The White Stag - Kate Seredy 1613

Pam
The Robot Birthday - Eve Bunting 237

Peterson, Andy
The Trouble with Jacob - Eloise Jarvis McGraw 1231

Peterson, Kat
The Trouble with Jacob - Eloise Jarvis McGraw 1231

Shelton, Diane
The Fourth Floor Twins and the Sand Castle Contest - David A. Adler 11

Shelton, Donna
The Fourth Floor Twins and the Sand Castle Contest - David A. Adler 11

Tibbs, Timothy
The Owlstone Crown - X.J. Kennedy 1016

Tibbs, Verity
The Owlstone Crown - X.J. Kennedy 1016

Wade, Crockett "Crock"
Lavender-Green Magic - Andre Norton 1341

Wade, Judy
Lavender-Green Magic - Andre Norton 1341

VACATIONER

Anthony
The Escape of the Giant Hogstalk - Felice Holman 906

Clara
The Animal, the Vegetable, and John D. Jones - Betsy Byars 256

Deenie
The Animal, the Vegetable, and John D. Jones - Betsy Byars 256

Drew, Barney
Over Sea, Under Stone - Susan Cooper 421

Drew, Jane
Over Sea, Under Stone - Susan Cooper 421

Drew, Simon
Over Sea, Under Stone - Susan Cooper 421

Emily
Walking Away - Elizabeth Winthrop 1933

Jones, John D.
The Animal, the Vegetable, and John D. Jones - Betsy Byars 256

Keith
The Mouse and the Motorcycle - Beverly Cleary 352

Lawrence
The Escape of the Giant Hogstalk - Felice Holman 906

Waite, Dudley
Castaways on Long Ago - Edward Ormondroyd 1366

Waite, Linda
Castaways on Long Ago - Edward Ormondroyd 1366

Waite, Richard
Castaways on Long Ago - Edward Ormondroyd 1366

VAGRANT

Duke
Captains of the City Street: A Story of a Cat Club - Esther Averill 69

Jack
The Stones - Janet Hickman 875

Sinbad
Captains of the City Street: A Story of a Cat Club - Esther Averill 69

VETERAN

Andrew
After the Dancing Days - Margaret I. Rostkowski 1550

Crutches
Crutches - Peter Hartling 820

Hovanec, Ron
The Kite Song - Margery Evernden 581

Tucker, Roy
The Kid Comes Back - John R. Tunis 1827

Weems
December Stillness - Mary Downing Hahn 786

VETERINARIAN

Cameron
Pets, Vets, and Marty Howard - Joan Davenport Carris 302

Doolittle
The Voyages of Dr. Doolittle - Hugh Lofting 1144

Harris
Alan and the Animal Kingdom - Isabelle Holland 899

Tobin, Douglas
The Trouble with Tuck - Theodore Taylor 1791

VIKING

Thorfinnsson, Snorri
Snorri and the Strangers - Nathaniel Benchley 134

VILLAIN

de Vil, Cruella
The Hundred and One Dalmatians - Dodie Smith 1679

Eel
Flight of the Sparrow - Julia Cunningham 453

Fox, Fat
Gumshoe Goose, Private Eye - Mary DeBall Kwitz 1062

The Ingrate, Ing
Norby, the Mixed-Up Robot - Janet Asimov 62

Meduse
Mystery of the Metro - Elizabeth Howard 918

Red King
The Red King - Victor Kelleher 1005

Serpent
The Unicorn and the Lake - Marianna Mayer 1210

Shaw, Ebenezer
Kidnapped - Robert Louis Stevenson 1748

Skellar, Dismas
Gom on Windy Mountain - Grace Chetwin 324

Suggs, Dorrit L.
The Money Room - Eloise Jarvis McGraw 1229

Sweet, Sylvester S.
The Worldwide Dessert Contest - Dan Elish 564

Weasel
Weasel - Cynthia DeFelice 502

WAITER/WAITRESS

Dohr, Wanda Sue
The Day That Elvis Came to Town - Jan Marino 1193

WANDERER

Berkshire, MCC
A Pack of Lies - Geraldine McCaughrean 1220

Folsom, Alex
Wilkin's Ghost - Robert Burch 246

Tuppenny
Tuppenny - Julia Cunningham 455

WARD

Barnavelt, Lewis
The House with a Clock in Its Walls - John Bellaris 129

WARRIOR

Crew, Harry
The Blue Sword - Robin McKinley 1239

WARTHOG

Warthog
Tales of a Wandering Warthog - Tom Sinclair 1650

WEALTHY

Frankweiler, Basil E.
From the Mixed-Up Files of Mrs. Basil E. Frankweiler - E.L. Konigsburg 1045

Hattie
Hattie and the Wild Waves - Barbara Cooney 415

Hunter
Kavik the Wolf Dog - Walt Morey 1286

Age Index

This index groups books according to the grade levels for which they are most appropriate. Beneath each grade range book titles are listed alphabetically, followed by the author's name and the entry number.

GRADES 1-2

Addie Meets Max - Joan Robins 1516
Alexander, Who Used to Be Rich Last Sunday - Judith Viorst 1856
Are You My Mother? - P.D. Eastman 557
Arthur's Baby - Marc T. Brown 216
Bagdad Ate It - Phyllis Green 742
The Balancing Girl - Berniece Rabe 1478
Bears in the Night - Stan Berenstain 140
Bedtime for Frances - Russell Hoban 891
The Best Dressed Bear - Mary Blocksma 149
A Big Ball of String - Marion Holland 902
The Big Hello - Janet Schulman 1598
Big Max - Kin Platt 1449
Binky Brothers, Detectives - James Duncan Lawrence 1080
Call for Mr. Sniff - Thomas P. Lewis 1114
The Cat and Mouse Who Shared a House - Ruth Hurlimann 943
The Cat in the Hat - Dr. Seuss 1617
Chang's Paper Pony - Eleanor Coerr 377
Cookies and Crutches - Judy Delton 511
The Day I Had to Play with My Sister - Crosby Bonsall 176
Dorrie and the Pin Witch - Patricia Coombs 414
Even If I Did Something Awful - Barbara Shook Hazen 840
Everett Anderson's Friend - Lucille Clifton 365
Fifty Saves His Friend - Martin Baynton 120
Fiona's Bee - Beverly Keller 1006
Footprints in the Refrigerator - Selma Boyd 183
Four on the Shore - Edward Marshall 1196
Fox on the Job - James Marshall 1198
The Fox with Cold Feet - Bill Singer 1651
Frog and Toad All Year - Arnold Lobel 1139
Frog and Toad Together - Arnold Lobel 1140
George and Martha Back in Town - James Marshall 1199
George Shrinks - William Joyce 987
The Ghost-Eye Tree - Bill Martin, Jr. 1203
The Gollywhopper Egg - Anne Rockwell 1527
Gumshoe Goose, Private Eye - Mary DeBall Kwitz 1062
Harold and the Purple Crayon - Crockett Johnson 975
Harry in Trouble - Barbara Ann Porte 1459
Henry and Mudge and the Happy Cat - Cynthia Rylant 1567
Herbie's Troubles - Carol Chapman 317
Hester the Jester - Ben Shecter 1625
Hi, Clouds - Carol Greene 747
How Pizza Came to Queens - Dayal Kaur Khalsa 1019
I Have Two Families - Doris Wild Helmering 849
I Was All Thumbs - Bernard Waber 1866
I Wish Laura's Mommy Was My Mommy - Barbara Power 1463
In the Middle of the Puddle - Mike Thaler 1797
The King, the Mice, and the Cheese - Nancy Gurney 779
Leo and Emily - Franz Brandenberg 187
Leo, Zack and Emmie - Amy Ehrlich 561
Lionel at Large - Stephen Krensky 1056

Little Bear - Else Holmelund Minarik 1272
Magnolia's Mixed-Up Magic - Joan Lowery Nixon 1340
Maybe She Forgot - Ellen Kandoian 992
Mice at Bat - Kelly Oechsli 1356
The Missing Tooth - Joanna Cole 390
Molly in Danger - Anne Carter 306
Molly Moves Out - Susan Pearson 1403
Morris and Boris at the Circus - Bernard Wiseman 1935
Mrs. Brice's Mice - Syd Hoff 895
My Dog and the Birthday Mystery - David A. Adler 13
My New Boy - Joan Phillips 1435
The Napping House - Audrey Wood 1949
Old Turtle's Soccer Team - Leonard Kessler 1018
Owl at Home - Arnold Lobel 1141
Papa's Lemonade and Other Stories - Eve Rice 1504
Pop's Secret - Maryann Townsend 1821
Put Me in the Zoo - Robert Lopshire 1146
Russell Sprouts - Johanna Hurwitz 956
Sheep in a Jeep - Nancy Shaw 1624
The Sign in Mendel's Window - Mildred Kantrowitz Phillips 1436
Snowshoe Thompson - Nancy Smiler Levinson 1101
Soccer Sam - Jean Marzollo 1207
Ten Apples Up on Top - Theo LeSieg 1094
This Is the House Where Jack Lives - Joan Heilbroner 847
Uncle Foster's Hat Tree - Doug Cushman 461
When Will I Read? - Miriam Cohen 385
Where Does the Teacher Live? - Paula Kurzband Feder 591
Where Is Freddy? - Laura Jean Johnson 976
Woodruff and the Clocks - Elizabeth Bram 186
You Can Depend on Me - Margaret Reuter 1503

GRADES 1-3

Alex and the Cat - Helen V. Griffith 770
Amelia Bedelia - Peggy Parish 1374
Anna and the Seven Swans - Maida Silverman 1642
Arthur's Honey Bear - Lillian Hoban 888
Babar and the Ghost: An Easy to Read Version - Laurent De Brunhoff 219
The Backyard Basketball Superstar - Monica Klein 1038
Bears on Hemlock Mountain - Alice Dalgliesh 472
Belling the Tiger - Mary Stolz 1751
Bernard Sees the World - Berniece Freschet 646
The Big Kite Contest - Dorotha Ruthstrom 1561
Brave Irene - William Steig 1732
Bullfrog Grows Up - Rosamond Dauer 482
Buster Loves Buttons - Fran Manushkin 1191
Cakes and Miracles - Barbara Diamond Goldin 718
The Case of the Scaredy Cats - Crosby Bonsall 175
Clancy's Coat - Eve Bunting 230

A Clean House for Mole and Mouse - Harriet Ziefert 1986
Commander Toad and the Intergalactic Spy - Jane Yolen 1968
The Crow and Mrs. Gaddy - Wilson Gage 658
Cyrus, the Unsinkable Sea Serpent - Bill Peet 1412
Digby and Kate - Barbara Baker 84
The Dog Food Caper - Joan M. Lexau 1115
Euphonia and the Flood - Mary Calhoun 273
Fast Friends: Two Stories - James Stevenson 1746
The Funny Little Woman - Arlene Mosel 1294
The Giving Tree - Shel Silverstein 1644
Good Hunting, Blue Sky - Peggy Parish 1375
Grandaddy's Place - Helen V. Griffith 773
The Grandma Mix-Up - Emily Arnold McCully 1222
Hattie Be Quiet, Hattie Be Good - Dick Gackenbach 654
The Horrible Holidays - Audrey Wood 1947
How Do I Feel? - Norma Simon 1647
How Droofus the Dragon Lost His Head - Bill Peet 1413
How Far, Felipe? - Genevieve Gray 737
How My Parents Learned to Eat - Ina R. Friedman 647
Ida and the Wool Smugglers - Sue Ann Alderson 24
Ig Lives in a Cave - Carol Chapman 318
It Happened in Pinsk - Arthur Yorinks 1974
It's Me, Hippo! - Mike Thaler 1798
Jeremiah in the Dark Woods - Janet Ahlberg 15
Keep the Lights Burning, Abbie - Peter Roop 1544
Little Black, a Pony - Walter Farley 589
The Little Witch and the Riddle - Bruce Degen 504
Liza Lou and the Yeller Belly Swamp - Mercer Mayer 1211
Losing Uncle Tim - Marykate Jordan 986
Lulu and the Witch Baby - Jane O'Connor 1350
M & M and the Big Bag - Pat Ross 1548
Mo to the Rescue - Mary Pope Osborne 1369
More Tales of Amanda the Pig - Jean Van Leeuwen 1848
Morris Has a Cold - Bernard Wiseman 1936
Nate the Great - Marjorie Weinman Sharmat 1620
A New Coat for Anna - Harriet Ziefert 1987
Nobody Listens to Andrew - Elizabeth Guilfoile 778
Nonna - Jennifer Bartoli 99
Oh, Were They Ever Happy! - Peter Spier 1713
Old Blue - Sibyl Hancock 810
Oma and Bobo - Amy Schwartz 1600
Once, Said Darlene - William Sleator 1664
The Pea Patch Jig - Thacher Hurd 942
Penrod's Pants - Mary Blount Christian 332
Perrywinkle and the Book of Magic Spells - Ross Martin Madsen 1176
Pig Pig and the Magic Photo Album - David M. McPhail 1250
Porcupine's Pajama Party - Terry Webb Harshman 818
Ready, Set, Robot - Lillian Hoban 890
The Robot Birthday - Eve Bunting 237

Second Grade Dog - Laurie Lawlor 1079
The Secret Three - Mildred Myrick 1306
Sid Seal, Houseman - Will Watkins 1889
Snail Saves the Day - John Stadler 1723
Something Special for Me - Vera B. Williams 1925
Sophie and Gussie - Marjorie Weinman Sharmat 1622
This Farm is a Mess - Leslie McGuire 1232
Tillie and Mert - Ida Luttrell 1158
The Toad Hunt - Janet Chenery 322
Toasted Bagels - Joyce Audy Zarins 1981
The Tram to Bondi Beach - Elizabeth Hathorn 825
Uncle Elephant - Arnold Lobel 1142
Ups and Downs with Oink and Pearl - Kay Chorao 328
The Very Worst Monster - Pat Hutchins 961
The Village of Round and Square Houses - Ann Grifalconi 768
Wish Again, Big Bear - Richard J. Margolis 1192
Witch, Goblin and Sometimes Ghost: Six Read Alone Stories - Sue Alexander 32
Worthington Botts and the Steam Machine - Betty Baker 89

GRADES 1-4

The Bionic Bunny Show - Marc T. Brown 217
The Ghost of Skinny Jack - Astrid Lindgren 1123
Where the Forest Meets the Sea - Jeannie Baker 90

GRADES 1-5

Animal Family - Randall Jarrell 970
Spinky Sulks - William Steig 1737

GRADES 1-6

The House at Pooh Corner - A.A. Milne 1270
The Polar Express - Chris Van Allsburg 1843
The Silver Pony - Lynd Ward 1884

GRADES 1-8

Jumanji - Chris Van Allsburg 1840

GRADES 1-9

The Mysteries of Harris Burdick - Chris Van Allsburg 1842

GRADES 2-3

ABC Bunny - Wanda Gag 656
All Because I'm Older - Phyllis Reynolds Naylor 1312
Baseball and Butterflies - Karen Lynn Williams 1922
The Beast in Ms. Rooney's Room - Patricia Reilly Giff 692
Becky and the Bear - Dorothy Van Woerkom 1851
Best Enemies - Kathleen Leverich 1095
Big Bad Bruce - Bill Peet 1411
The Big Green Book - Robert Graves 734
A Boy in the Doghouse - Betsy Duffey 543
Busybody Nora - Johanna Hurwitz 949
A Camel Called April - Diana Hendry 850
Captain Hook, That's Me - Ada B. Litchfield 1131
The Case of the Double Cross - Crosby Bonsall 174
Cave-in at Mason's Mine - Bessie Holland Heck 842
Chester Chipmunk's Thanksgiving - Barbara Williams 1917
Clara and the Bookwagon - Nancy Smiler Levinson 1100
Come a Tide - George Ella Lyon 1160
Cross-Country Cat - Mary Calhoun 272

Danger in Dinosaur Valley - Joan Lowery Nixon 1332
December's Travels - Mischa Damjan 474
The Doggone Mystery - Mary Blount Christian 331
The First Morning: An African Myth - Margery Bernstein 142
Flossie and the Fox - Pat McKissack 1244
The Fox and the Kingfisher - Judith Mellecker 1255
The Friendly Wolf - Paul Goble 712
Friends - Terry Berger 141
Funnyman and the Penny Dodo - Stephen Mooser 1282
George the Drummer Boy - Nathaniel Benchley 132
Georgia Music - Helen V. Griffith 772
Grandpa's Ghost Stories - James Flora 628
The Green Ghost of Appleville - Jean Marzollo 1206
The Green Lion of Zion Street - Julia Fields 598
Halfway Up the Mountain - Theo E. Gilchrist 699
Harald and the Great Stag - Donald Carrick 298
Hattie and the Wild Waves - Barbara Cooney 415
Heckedy Peg - Audrey Wood 1946
Hello, I'm Karen - Margaret Sutherland 1771
Henry and the Red Stripes - Eileen Christelow 330
Home Alone - Eleanor Schick 1593
Hurricane - David Wiesner 1906
I Hate Red Rover - Joan M. Lexau 1116
Itchy Richard - Jamie Gilson 704
Jane Martin, Dog Detective - Eve Bunting 232
Jethro and the Jumbie - Susan Cooper 420
Joseph on the Subway Train - Kathleen Benson 138
Just Plain Fancy - Patricia Polacco 1453
Laura Charlotte - Kathryn Osebold Galbraith 661
Lily and Miss Liberty - Carla Stevens 1744
Lon Po Po: A Red Riding Hood Story From China - Ed Young 1977
The Lucky Runner - Bernard Wiseman 1934
The Lucky Stone - Lucille Clifton 366
Many Moons - James Thurber 1811
Margaret and Taylor - Kevin Henkes 851
Mary, Mary - Sarah Hayes 835
Mean and Mighty Me - Sally Christie 334
Millions of Cats - Wanda Gag 657
Mirandy and Brother Wind - Pat McKissack 1246
Miss Nelson Is Missing! - Harry Allard 34
The Mitten: An Old Ukranian Folk Tale - Jan Brett 195
The Monster in the 3rd Dresser Drawer and Other Stories about Adam Joshua - Janice Lee Smith 1688
Mother's Day Mice - Eve Bunting 233
Mr. Pepper Stories - Mark Taylor 1783
No-Name Dog - Rose Impey 963
Omoteji's Baby Brother - Mary-Joan Gerson 688
Only One Woof - James Herriot 867
Pinkerton, Behave! - Steven Kellogg 1008
Pippa Pops Out: Four Read-Aloud/Read Alone Stories - Betty Boegehold 164
Polly's Tiger - Joan Phipson 1438
Princess Bee and the Royal Goodnight Story - Sandy Asher 60
Princess Furball - Charlotte S. Huck 928
Purple Climbing Days - Patricia Reilly Giff 697
Quick Chick - Julia Hoban 887
Ragtime Tumpie - Alan Schroeder 1597
Randolph's Dream - Judith Mellecker 1256
Raymond's Best Summer - Jean Rogers 1540
The Ring and the Window Seat - Amy Hest 874
Rip-Roaring Russell - Johanna Hurwitz 955
The Secret of Foghorn Island - Geoffrey Hayes 834
Ship's Cook Ginger - Edward Ardizzone 54
Sly, P.I.: The Case of the Missing Shoes - Cathy Stefanec-Ogren 1730
Small Fur - Irina Korschunov 1053
Space Case - Edward Marshall 1197
Superduper Teddy - Johanna Hurwitz 957
The Sweet Touch - Lorna Balian 92
What Is Papa Up To Now? - Miriam Anne Bourne 181

The Wheel of King Asoka - Ashok Davar 484
The White Bicycle - Rob Lewis 1113
Who's in Charge of Lincoln? - Dale Fife 601
The Wild Horses of Sweetbriar - Natalie Kinsey-Warnock 1036
The Wolf's Chicken Stew - Keiko Kasza 998

GRADES 2-4

The Acorn Quest - Jane Yolen 1967
Adventures of Obadiah - Brinton Turkle 1829
All the Money in the World - Bill Brittain 202
Amelia's Flying Machine - Barbara Shook Hazen 839
Amy's Goose - Efner Tudor Holmes 909
Anna's Silent World - Bernard Wolf 1941
Aviva's Piano - Miriam Chaikin 314
A Bear Called Paddington - Michael Bond 167
Berchick - Esther Silverstein Blanc 148
Black and White - David Macauley 1163
Bony-legs - Joanna Cole 387
The Boy Who Wanted a Family - Shirley Gordon 722
Cam Jansen and the Mystery at the Monkey House - David A. Adler 10
Carnival and Kopeck and More About Hannah - Mindy Skolsky 1657
A Certain Small Shepherd - Rebecca Caudill 310
The Chalk Box Kid - Clyde Robert Bulla 224
Charlie Drives the Stage - Eric A. Kimmel 1025
Chester - Mary Francis Shura 1634
Class Clown - Johanna Hurwitz 950
Cloudy with a Chance of Meatballs - Judi Barrett 97
Daniel's Duck - Clyde Robert Bulla 225
Davey Come Home - Margaret Teibl 1792
The Day of the Muskie - Patricia Welch 1891
The Day the Circus Came to Lone Tree - Glen Rounds 1554
Dinnie Abbie Sister-R-R! - Riki Levinson 1102
Doctor Change - Joanna Cole 388
Dr. De Soto - William Steig 1734
The Dog That Pitched a No-Hitter - Matt Christopher 338
Don't Forget Michael - Jean Thompson 1808
Doodlebug - Irene Brady 185
Down in the Boondocks - Wilson Gage 659
Eddie's Valuable Property - Carolyn Haywood 838
Ellsworth and the Cats from Mars - Patience Brewster 196
Family Farm - Thomas Locker 1143
Feldman Fieldmouse - Nathaniel Benchley 131
Flat Stanley - Jeff Brown 214
Follow That Bus! - Pat Hutchins 960
Follow That Ghost! - Dale Fife 600
The Fourth Floor Twins and the Sand Castle Contest - David A. Adler 11
Frank and Ernest - Alexandra Day 489
The Ghost in the Lagoon - Natalie Savage Carlson 293
Go Fish - Mary Stolz 1756
The Good Luck Dog - Lilo Hess 870
Grand Papa and Ellen Aroon - F.N. Monjo 1275
Grandpa's Slide Show - Deborah Gould 725
The Great Green Turkey Creek Monster - James Flora 629
The Great White Man-Eating Shark - Margaret Mahy 1181
Gwenda and the Animals - Tessa Dahl 470
The Halloween Candy Mystery - Marion M. Markham 1194
Her Seven Brothers - Paul Goble 713
He's My Brother - Joe Lasker 1070
The High Rise Glorious Skittle Skat Roarious Sky Pie Angel Food Cake - Nancy Willard 1914
The Humans of Ziax II - John Morressy 1292
I Can't Always Hear You - Joy Zelonky 1985
I Hate My Sister Maggie - Crescent Dragonwagon 535

Danny Dunn on the Ocean Floor - Jay Williams 1920

Danny, the Champion of the World - Roald Dahl 465

Danza! - Lynn Hall 792

Dark Horse - Jean Slaughter Doty 534

Darwin and the Voyage of the Beagle - Felicia Law 1078

The Dawn Seekers - Carol Hamilton 798

Dealing with Dragons - Patricia C. Wrede 1953

Dear Mr. Henshaw - Beverly Cleary 350

The Deserter - Nigel Gray 738

Devil in Vienna - Doris Orgel 1363

Do Bananas Chew Gum? - Jamie Gilson 702

A Dog Called Kitty - Bill Wallace 1876

Dog Days - Colby Rodowsky 1536

A Dog on Barkham Street - Mary Stolz 1753

Dolby and the Woof-Off - Barbara A. Steiner 1739

The Doll in the Garden - Mary Downing Hahn 787

The Donkey Planet - Scott Corbett 423

Don't Hurt Laurie! - Willo Davis Roberts 1509

The Door in the Hedge - Robin McKinley 1240

The Door in the Wall - Marguerite De Angeli 490

Dorp Dead - Julia Cunningham 452

The Double Life of Pocahontas - Jean Fritz 650

Down the Mississippi - Clyde Robert Bulla 226

Dreams of Victory - Ellen Conford 401

Dupper - Betty Baker 85

Eddie, Incorporated - Phyllis Reynolds Naylor 1314

Edgar Allan - John Neufeld 1325

Edith Herself - Ellen Howard 920

Emma's Dilemma - Gen LeRoy 1093

Encyclopedia Brown, Boy Detective - Donald J. Sobol 1703

End of a Dark Road - Crystal Thrasher 1809

Eunice (the Egg Salad) Gottlieb - Tricia Springstubb 1719

Felita - Nicolasa Mohr 1274

A Few Fair Days - Jane Gardam 665

Figgs and Phantoms - Ellen Raskin 1488

Finding Buck McHenry - Alfred Slote 1669

Finn Family Moomintroll - Tove Jansson 969

The First Two Lives of Lukas Kasha - Lloyd Alexander 27

Five Children and It - Edith Nesbit 1323

Five-Finger Discount - Barthe DeClements 497

The Fledgling - Jane Langton 1069

Follow My Leader - James B. Garfield 669

Fourth Grade Wizards - Barthe DeClements 498

The Fox Busters - Dick King-Smith 1031

Foxy - Helen V. Griffith 771

Fran Ellen's House - Marilyn Sachs 1578

Freaky Friday - Mary Rodgers 1533

A Friend Like That - Alfred Slote 1670

The Friends of the Loony Lake Monster - Frank Bonham 171

From Anna - Jean Little 1133

From the Mixed-Up Files of Mrs. Basil E. Frankweiler - E.L. Konigsburg 1045

The Garden Is Doing Fine - Carol J. Farley 586

The Gathering Room - Colby Rodowsky 1537

Gay-Neck: The Story of a Pigeon - Dan Gopal Mukerji 1297

General Butterfingers - John Reynolds Gardiner 667

The Genie of Sutton Place - George Selden 1609

Gentle Ben - Walt Morey 1285

Getting Rid of Marjorie - Betty Ren Wright 1955

The Ghost Children - Eve Bunting 231

The Ghost Drum: A Cat's Tale - Susan Price 1468

Ghost Island - Carolyn Lane 1068

The Ghost of Thomas Kempe - Penelope Lively 1137

The Ghost Upstairs - Lila McGinnis 1226

The Ghost Wore Gray - Bruce Coville 437

The Ghosts - Antonia Barber 94

Ghosts at Large - Susan Price 1469

The Gift - Joan Lowery Nixon 1334

The Gift-Giver - Joyce Hansen 812

Gildaen: The Heroic Adventures of a Most Unusual Rabbit - Emilie Buchwald 221

A Girl Called Bob and a Horse Called Yoki - Barbara Campbell 287

The Girl with the Silver Eyes - Willo Davis Roberts 1510

The Glad Man - Gloria Gonzalez 721

The Glassblower's Children - Maria Gripe 774

Golden Daffodils - Marilyn Gould 726

Goody Hall - Natalie Babbitt 76

Gopher, Tanker, and the Admiral - Shirley Climo 368

Grasshopper Summer - Ann Warren Turner 1832

The Graveyard: And Other Not-So-Scary Stories - William E. Warren 1886

The Great Brain Reforms - John D. Fitzgerald 607

The Great Ringtail Garbage Caper - Timothy Foote 1510

The Green Book - Jill Paton Walsh 1393

Grey Cloud - Charlotte Towner Graeber 729

The Hand-Me-Down Kid - Francine Pascal 1384

Harriet the Spy - Louise Fitzhugh 608

Harry's Mad - Dick King-Smith 1032

Harvey, the Beer Can King - Jamie Gilson 703

Have You Seen Hyacinth Macaw? - Patricia Reilly Giff 694

The Headless Cupid - Zilpha Keatley Snyder 1698

Heads, I Win - Patricia Hermes 862

Henry Reed's Baby-Sitting Service - Keith Robertson 1514

The Hermit of Fog Hollow Station - David Roth 1551

High Trail to Danger - Joan Lowery Nixon 1336

Highpockets - John R. Tunis 1826

Hiroshima No Pika - Toshi Maruki 1205

Hobberdy Dick - Katherine Mary Briggs 200

The Hockey Girls - Scott Corbett 424

Home Run Trick - Scott Corbett 425

Homesick: My Own Story - Jean Fritz 652

Horse Crazy - Bonnie Bryant 220

The Horse in the Attic - Eleanor Clymer 370

Hotel for Dogs - Lois Duncan 549

The House in the Snow - M.J. Engh 571

The House on Hackman's Hill - Joan Lowery Nixon 1337

The House with a Clock in Its Walls - John Bellaris 129

The House Without a Christmas Tree - Gail Rock 1523

How to Become King - Jan Terlouw 1793

How's Business? - Alison Prince 1470

Humbug Mountain - Sid Fleischman 622

Huntly, Nutley and the Missing Link - Mary Tannen 1777

Hurry Home, Candy - Meindert DeJong 505

Hurry, Hurry, Mary Dear! And Other Nonsense Poems - N.M. Bodecker 161

I and Sproggy - Constance C. Greene 751

I Hate Being Gifted - Patricia Hermes 863

I, Houdini: The Autobiography of a Self-Educated Hamster - Lynne Reid Banks 1497

I Should Worry, I Should Care - Miriam Chaikin 315

Ida Early Comes over the Mountain - Robert Burch 242

If Phyllis Were Here - Gail Jarrow 972

In the Year of the Boar and Jackie Robinson - Bette Bao Lord 1148

In Trouble Again, Zelda Hammersmith - Lynn Hall 793

The Indian in the Cupboard - Lynne Reid Banks 1498

The Interesting Thing That Happened at Perfect Acres, Inc. - Barbara Brooks Wallace 1871

Isabelle the Itch - Constance C. Greene 752

An Island in a Green Sea - Mabel Esther Allan 33

Island of the Blue Dolphins - Scott O'Dell 1353

It's Not the End of the World - Judy Blume 155

The Ivy Garland - John Hoyland 927

Jaguar, My Twin - Betty Jean Lifton 1118

A Jar of Dreams - Yoshiko Uchida 1836

Johnny Tremain - Esther Forbes 633

The Journey Home - Isabelle Holland 900

Journey to Topaz - Yoshiko Uchida 1837

Judge Benjamin, Superdog - Judith Whitelock McInerney 1235

Julia and the Hand of God - Eleanor Cameron 284

Just an Overnight Guest - Eleanora E. Tate 1779

Just Like a Real Family - Kristi Holl 898

Just My Luck - Emily Moore 1280

Justin Morgan Had a Horse - Marguerite Henry 853

Katie John and Heathcliff - Mary Calhoun 274

Keeping it Secret - Penny Pollock 1455

Kelly's Creek - Doris Buchanan Smith 1680

The Kenton Year - Ruth Wallace-Brodeur 1879

The Kid in the Red Jacket - Barbara Park 1378

Kid Power - Susan Beth Pfeffer 1432

King of Wind - Marguerite Henry 854

The King's Fountain - Lloyd Alexander 30

Knights of the Kitchen Table - Jon Scieszka 1601

Konrad - Christine Nostlinger 1346

Lassie Come Home - Eric Knight 1042

Last Was Lloyd - Doris Buchanan Smith 1681

Left-Handed Shortstop - Patricia Reilly Giff 695

The Leopard - Cecil Bodker 162

Little Man - Erich Kastner 997

Little Town on the Prairie - Laura Ingalls Wilder 1910

Lizard Music - Daniel Manus Pinkwater 1445

Look through My Window - Jean Little 1134

The Luck of Pokey Bloom - Ellen Conford 406

Luke Was There - Eleanor Clymer 371

The Magic Book - Willo Davis Roberts 1511

The Magic Moth - Virginia Lee 1088

Man From the Sky - Avi 70

Manhattan Is Missing - E.W. Hildick 880

Maniac Magee - Jerry Spinelli 1715

The Manifesto and Me - Meg - Bobbi Katz 999

Marathon Miranda - Elizabeth Winthrop 1932

Mariah Delany's Author-of-the-Month Club - Sheila Greenwald 759

Mary Jane - Dorothy Sterling 1742

Maxie, Rosie, and Earl - Partners in Grime - Barbara Park 1379

Maximilian, You're the Greatest - Joseph Rosenbloom 1547

Maybe Next Year - Amy Hest 873

Me and the Terrible Two - Ellen Conford 407

Me Two - Mary C. Ryan 1562

A Memory for Tino - Leo Buscaglia 252

Merlin Dreams - Peter Dickinson 523

The Mermaid Summer - Mollie Hunter 939

The Midnight Fox - Betsy Byars 264

Minn of the Mississippi - Holling Clancy Holling 903

Miracles on Maple Hill - Virginia Sorensen 1706

Mishmash - Molly Cone 399

Miss Hickory - Carolyn Sherwin Bailey 83

Miss Pickerell and the War of the Computers - Dora Pantell 1373

Missing - James Duffy 545

Mississippi Bridge - Mildred D. Taylor 1785

Misty of Chincoteague - Marguerite Henry 855

The Monster's Ring - Bruce Coville 438

Morning Arrow - Nanabah Chee Dodge 528

The Mouse and His Child - Russell Hoban 892

The Mousehole Cat - Antonia Barber 95

Moxie - Phyllis Rossiter 1549

Mr. McFadden's Hallowe'en - Rumer Godden 714

Mrs. Frisby and the Rats of NIMH - Robert C. O'Brien 1347

Mukasa - John Nagenda 1308

Murder at the Spaniel Show - Lynn Hall 794

My Mother Got Married and Other Disasters - Barbara Park 1380

My Robot Buddy - Alfred Slote 1673

My Side of the Mountain - Jean Craighead George 683

My Sister's Keeper - Beverly Butler 253

Mystery of the Bewitched Bookmobile - Florence Parry Heide 845

GRADES 4-7

The Marvelous Misadventures of Sebastian - Lloyd Alexander 31

The Monster Garden - Vivien Alcock 20

My Friend, My Brother - David Warren Swartley 1773

The Mysterious Disappearance of Leon (I Mean Noel) - Ellen Raskin 1489

Old John - Peter Hartling 821

The Package in Hyperspace - Janet Asimov 63

Peppermints in the Parlor - Barbara Brooks Wallace 1873

Richard Kennedy: Collected Stories - Richard Kennedy 1014

River Rats, Inc. - Jean Craighead George 684

Rosemary's Witch - Ann Warren Turner 1833

San Domingo, the Medicine Hat Stallion - Marguerite Henry 856

Seal Child - Sylvia Peck 1410

The Snow Spider - Jenny Nimmo 1331

The Talking Parcel - Gerald Durrel 552

Tom Tiddler's Ground - John Rowe Townsend 1820

The Turtle Street Trading Company - Jill Ross Klevin 1041

The Well - Gene Kemp 1011

Wild Man of the Woods - Joan Clark 345

The Witch of Fourth Street and Other Stories - Myron Levoy 1105

The Worldwide Dessert Contest - Dan Elish 564

Zeely - Virginia Hamilton 807

GRADES 4-8

Alfred Hitchcock and the Three Investigators in the Secret of Shark Reef - William Arden 53

Alice's Adventures in Wonderland - Lewis Carroll 305

Ape Ears and Beaky - Nancy J. Hopper 916

Friedrich - Hans Peter Richter 1507

Java Jack - Luqman Keele 1002

Missing May - Cynthia Rylant 1568

The Moonpath and Other Tales of the Bizarre - Robert E. Swindells 1774

The Phantom Tollbooth - Norton Juster 990

Rootabaga Stories - Carl Sandburg 1584

Stories for Children - Isaac Bashevis Singer 1653

When the Tripods Came - John Christopher 335

The Wind in the Willows - Kenneth Grahame 733

GRADES 4-9

Strider - Beverly Cleary 356

Tales From Gold Mountain: Stories of the Chinese in the New World - Paul Yee 1963

GRADES 4 AND UP

Christmas Memory - Truman Capote 288

GRADES 5-6

Abel's Island - William Steig 1731

Adam of the Road - Elizabeth Gray 735

Alan and the Animal Kingdom - Isabelle Holland 899

Alfred Summer - Jan Slepian 1665

Anastasia Krupnik - Lois Lowry 1150

And You Give Me a Pain, Elaine - Stella Pevsner 1424

Are You in the House Alone? - Richard Peck 1404

Autumn Street - Lois Lowry 1152

Babe: The Gallant Pig - Dick King-Smith 1030

The Baitchopper - Silver Donald Cameron 286

Beetles, Lightly Toasted - Phyllis Reynolds Naylor 1313

Behind the Attic Wall - Sylvia Cassedy 307

Benson Boy - Ivan Southall 1707

Big Diamond's Boy - Ellen H. Goins 717

Blue Willow - Doris Gates 675

Bogwoppit - Ursula Moray Williams 1924

Borrowed Children - George Ella Lyon 1159

Buck, Wild - Glenn Balch 91

Burning Questions of Bingo Brown - Betsy Byars 259

Call It Courage - Armstrong Sperry 1712

Call Me Danica - Winifred Madison 1174

Captain of the Planters: The Biography of Robert Smalls - Dorothy Sterling 1741

The Case of the Vanishing Villain - Carol J. Farley 585

Cat-Man's Daughter - Barbara Mattes Abercrombie 2

The Cat Who Went to Heaven - Elizabeth Coatsworth 374

The Cave Beyond Time - Malcolm J. Bosse 177

Charmed Life - Diana Wynne Jones 980

Child of the Morning - Barbara Corcoran 428

Chloris and the Creeps - Kin Platt 1450

Class Pictures - Marilyn Sachs 1575

The Clown - Barbara Corcoran 429

Come by Here - Olivia Coolidge 413

Cow-Tail Switch and Other West Africa Stories - Harold Courlander 435

Cricket and the Crackerbox Kid - Alane Ferguson 595

The Crumb - Jean Slaughter Doty 533

Cute Is a Four Letter Word - Stella Pevsner 1425

Dark Venture - Audrey White Beyer 145

Daughters of the Law - Sandy Asher 59

Dear Baby - Joanne Rocklin 1524

December Stillness - Mary Downing Hahn 786

Devil by the Sea - Nina Bawden 112

Dew Drop Dead: A Sebastian Barth Mystery - James Howe 925

Dicey's Song - Cynthia Voigt 1863

The Divorce Express - Paula Danziger 478

Don't Call Me Orphan - Michael Leach 1087

Dorrie's Book - Marilyn Sachs 1576

Dynamite Dinah - Claudia Mills 1268

The Egypt Game - Zilpha Keatley Snyder 1697

The Elephant in the Dark - Carol Carrick 295

Elizabeth, Elizabeth - Eileen Dunlop 551

The Falling-Apart Winter - Nancy Covert Smith 1689

A Family Apart - Joan Lowery Nixon 1333

February Dragon - Colin Thiele 1799

Flight of the Sparrow - Julia Cunningham 453

Foster Child - Marion Dane Bauer 107

Foster Mary - Celia Strang 1761

Frozen Fire - James A. Houston 917

Gammage Cup - Carol Kendall 1012

The Ghost in the Noonday Sun - Sid Fleischman 620

Glass Slippers Give You Blisters - Mary Jane Auch 65

Glass Slippers Give You Blisters - Mary Jane Auch 66

The Gods in Winter - Patricia Miles 1265

Gone-Away Lake - Elizabeth Enright 572

Goodbye, My Wishing Star - Vicki Grove 777

The Great Gilly Hopkins - Katherine Paterson 1388

Greenwitch - Susan Cooper 418

Growing Anyway Up - Florence Parry Heide 844

H, My Name Is Henley - Colby Rodowsky 1538

Hail, Hail, Camp Timberwood - Ellen Conford 403

The Hammerhead Light - Colin Thiele 1800

Happily Ever After.Almost - Judie Wolkoff 1945

Hatchet - Gary Paulsen 1398

A Haunting Air - Barbara Constance Freeman 645

He Is Your Brother - Richard Parker 1383

Heartland - Diane Siebert 1640

Hedgehogs in the Closet - Joan Davenport Carris 301

Hey, Remember Fat Glenda? - Lila Perl 1419

Home Before Dark - Sue Ellen Bridgers 198

The Horse with Eight Hands - Joan Phipson 1437

The House of Sixty Fathers - Meindert De Jong 494

The Iceberg and Its Shadow - Jan Greenberg 745

In Our House, Scott Is My Brother - Carole S. Adler 8

The Island on Bird Street - Uri Orlev 1364

It Must've Been the Fish Sticks - Betty Bates 102

Jake - Alfred Slote 1672

Janie's Private Eyes - Zilpha Keatley Snyder 1699

Jelly Belly - Robert Kimmel Smith 1691

Jellybean - Tessa Duder 542

Julie of the Wolves - Jean Craighead George 682

Just a Dog - Helen Griffith 769

Just Between Us - Susan Beth Pfeffer 1431

Kavik the Wolf Dog - Walt Morey 1286

The Kid Who Batted 1000 - Bob Allison 35

The Killer Swan - Eth Clifford 362

King Shoes and Clown Pockets - Faye Gibbons 690

Lenny Kendall, Smart Aleck - Ellen Conford 405

Libby on Wednesday - Zilpha Keatley Snyder 1700

Like Everybody Else - Barbara Girion 708

Lucy Forever and Miss Rosetree, Shrinks - Susan Richards Shreve 1629

The Machine Gunners - Robert Westall 1894

Mad Martin - Patricia Windsor 1927

The Magic of the Glits - Carole S. Adler 9

Make Like a Tree and Leave - Paula Danziger 479

Man with the Silver Eyes - William O. Steele 1729

Maria Luisa - Winifred Madison 1175

Maudie in the Middle - Phyllis Reynolds Naylor 1315

The Mockingbird Song - Berthe Amoss 41

Mojo and the Russians - Walter Dean Myers 1303

A Morgan for Melinda - Doris Gates 676

My Daniel - Pam Conrad 409

The Mystery at Peacock Place - M.F. Craig 439

The Nargun and the Stars - Patricia Wrightson 1959

Night Cry - Phyllis Reynolds Naylor 1316

Night Swimmers - Betsy Byars 265

Nightmare Mountain - Peg Kehret 1003

Now Is Not Too Late - Isabelle Holland 901

On the Banks of Plum Creek - Laura Ingalls Wilder 1911

On the Edge - Gillian Cross 449

Onion John - Joseph Krumgold 1058

Ordinary Jack - Helen Cresswell 446

The Other Side of the Family - Maureen Pople 1457

Our Sixth-Grade Sugar Babies - Eve Bunting 235

The Peppermint Pig - Nina Bawden 115

Philip Hall Likes Me, I Reckon Maybe - Bette Greene 746

The Pinballs - Betsy Byars 266

The Planetoid of Amazement - Mel Glidden 710

Prairie Songs - Pam Conrad 410

Rabble Starkey - Lois Lowry 1154

Red Dog - Bill Wallace 1877

Roll of Thunder, Hear My Cry - Mildred D. Taylor 1786

A Room Made of Windows - Eleanor Cameron 285

Roots in the Outfield - Jane Zirpoli 1988

Scrub Fire - Anne De Roo 496

Seven-Day Magic - Edward Eager 556

Shades of Gray - Carolyn Reeder 1496

Slake's Limbo - Felice Holman 908

A Smart Kid Like You - Stella Pevsner 1426

Smoke Over Golan - Uriel Ofek 1357

The Snake Horn - Morton Grosser 776

Something Upstairs: A Tale of Ghosts - Avi 72

Sometimes I Think I Hear My Name - Avi 73

The Spirit Is Willing - Betty Baker 87

Stepping on the Cracks - Mary Downing Hahn 789

The Summer of the Swans - Betsy Byars 267

The Swiss Family Robinson - Johann David Wyss 1961

Tales from the Arabian Nights - N.J. Dawood 488

A Tangled Web - Hannelore Valencak 1839

There, Far Beyond the River - Yuri Korinetz 1050

There's a Bat in Bunk Five - Paula Danziger 481

The Three Wars of Billy Joe Treat - Robbie Branscum 190

The Times They Used to Be - Lucille Clifton 367

Illustrator Index

This index lists the illustrators of the featured titles. Illustrators are listed alphabetically, followed by the title, author, and entry number of the book or books in which the artist's work appears.

Yonder - Tony Johnston 977

Bobak, Cathy
Burton's Zoom Zoom Va-Room Machine - Dorothy Haas 781

Bodecker, N.M.
Hurry, Hurry, Mary Dear! And Other Nonsense Poems - N.M. Bodecker 161
Seven-Day Magic - Edward Eager 556

Bolognese, Don
George the Drummer Boy - Nathaniel Benchley 132
A Long Day in November - Ernest J. Gaines 660
Snorri and the Strangers - Nathaniel Benchley 134
Wagon Wheels - Barbara Brenner 193
The Wicked Pigeon Ladies in the Garden - Mary Chase 321

Boston, Peter
The Sea Egg - L.M. Boston 178
The Stones of Green Knowe - L.M. Boston 179

Bowman, Leslie
The Canada Geese Quilt - Natalie Kinsey-Warnock 1035
The House in the Snow - M.J. Engh 571
Shadows - Dennis Haseley 823

Brady, Irene
Cloud Horse - Jill Pinkwater 1446
Doodlebug - Irene Brady 185

Brett, Jan
The Mitten: An Old Ukranian Folk Tale - Jan Brett 195
Mother's Day Mice - Eve Bunting 233

Brewster, Patience
Ellsworth and the Cats from Mars - Patience Brewster 196

Brook, Judy
Darwin and the Voyage of the Beagle - Felicia Law 1078

Brooks, Ron
Time Sweep - Valerie Weldrick 1892

Brown, Anthony
Alice's Adventures in Wonderland - Lewis Carroll 305

Brown, David
Don't Ride the Bus on Monday: The Rosa Parks Story - Louise Meriwether 1257
Ride the Red Cycle - Harriette Robinet 1515

Brown, Judith Gwyn
Ben and Annie - Joan Tate 1781
The Best Christmas Pageant Ever - Barbara Robinson 1517
Lavender-Green Magic - Andre Norton 1341
The Treasure of Alpheus Winterborn - John Bellairs 128
When the Sirens Wailed - Noel Streatfeild 1763

Brown, Laurence K
The Bionic Bunny Show - Marc T. Brown 217

Brown, Marc T.
Arthur's Baby - Marc T. Brown 216

Brown, Margaret Wise
Sneakers: Seven Stories about a Cat - Margaret Wise Brown 218

Brunhoff, Laurent De
Babar and the Ghost: An Easy to Read Version - Laurent De Brunhoff 219

Brunkus, Denise
The Pizza Monster - Marjorie Weinman Sharmat 1621

Bryan, Ashley
Jethro and the Jumbie - Susan Cooper 420

Bucholtz-Ross, Linda
Magnolia's Mixed-Up Magic - Joan Lowery Nixon 1340

Burchard, Peter
Down the Mississippi - Clyde Robert Bulla 226
Pocahontas and the Strangers - Clyde Robert Bulla 227
Roosevelt Grady - Louisa R. Shotwell 1626

Burleson, Joe
Witch Weed - Phyllis Reynolds Naylor 1319

Butler, John
Molly in Danger - Anne Carter 306

Byard, Carole
Arthur Mitchell - Tobi Tobias 1815

Byars, Guy
The Computer Nut - Betsy Byars 261

C

Carrick, Donald
Doctor Change - Joanna Cole 388
The Elephant in the Dark - Carol Carrick 295
Harald and the Great Stag - Donald Carrick 298
Journey to Topaz - Yoshiko Uchida 1837
Some Friend - Carol Carrick 296
Stay Away From Simon! - Carol Carrick 297

Carrick, Malcolm
The Wise Men of Gotham - Malcolm Carrick 299

Carroll, Charles
Me and the Terrible Two - Ellen Conford 407

Carter, Abby
Snakes Are Nothing to Sneeze At - Gabrielle Charbonnet 319

Chalk, Gary
Redwall - Brian Jacques 967

Chambliss, Maxie
Fat Fanny, Beanpole Bertha and the Boys - Barbara Ann Porte 1458
It's Me, Hippo! - Mike Thaler 1798

Charlot, Jean
.and Now Miguel - Joseph Krumgold 1057
The Secret of the Andes - Ann Nolan Clark 344

Chartier, Normand
The Great Ringtail Garbage Caper - Timothy Foote 632

Chessare, Michele
The Owlstone Crown - X.J. Kennedy 1016
Who Knew There'd Be Ghosts? - Bill Brittain 205

Chew, Ruth
Do-it-Yourself Magic - Ruth Chew 325

Chhuy, Dorothy H.
Dark Horse - Jean Slaughter Doty 534

Chorao, Kay
Chester Chipmunk's Thanksgiving - Barbara Williams 1917

Christelow, Eileen
Alvin Fernald, Master of a Thousand Disguises - Clifford B. Hicks 877
Dolby and the Woof-Off - Barbara A. Steiner 1739
Henry and the Red Stripes - Eileen Christelow 330
The Mysterious Cases of Mr. Pin - Mary Elise Monsell 1277
Zucchini - Barbara Dana 475

Circolo, Priscilla P.
Sly, P.I.: The Case of the Missing Shoes - Cathy Stefanec-Ogren 1730

Clark, Matthew
The Magic of Myrna C. Waxweather - Sandra Dutton 553

Cleaver, Vera
Where the Lilies Bloom - Vera Cleaver 360

Coalson, Glo
At the Mouth of the Luckiest River - Arnold A. Griese 765
Operation Peeg - Jonathan Gathorne-Hardy 677
The Wind Is Not a River - Arnold A. Griese 767

Cober, Alan E.
The Dark Is Rising - Susan Cooper 417

Coconis, Ted
The Summer of the Swans - Betsy Byars 267

Coerr, Eleanor
Chang's Paper Pony - Eleanor Coerr 377

Cogancherry, Helen
Dinnie Abbie Sister-R-R! - Riki Levinson 1102

Cole, Brock
The Indian in the Cupboard - Lynne Reid Banks 1498

Converse, James
My Friend, My Brother - David Warren Swartley 1773

Coombs, Patricia
Dorrie and the Pin Witch - Patricia Coombs 414

Cooper, Floyd
Laura Charlotte - Kathryn Osebold Galbraith 661

Cosgrove, John O.
Carry On, Mr. Bowditch - Jean Lee Latham 1075

Coville, Katherine
The Monster's Ring - Bruce Coville 438

Craft, Kinuko
Bailey's Window - Anne Lindbergh 1119

Craig, Helen
Mary, Mary - Sarah Hayes 835

Croll, Carolyn
Clara and the Bookwagon - Nancy Smiler Levinson 1100

Cruz, Ray
Alexander, Who Used to Be Rich Last Sunday - Judith Viorst 1856
Baseball Fever - Johanna Hurwitz 948
Felita - Nicolasa Mohr 1274
How the Moolah Was Taught a Lesson and Other Tales from Russia - Estelle Titiev 1813
In Trouble Again, Zelda Hammersmith - Lynn Hall 793

Cuffari, Richard
The Cartoonist - Betsy Byars 260
Confessions of an Only Child - Norma Klein 1039
The Freewheeling of Joshua Cobb - Margaret Hodges 894
The Magic Moth - Virginia Lee 1088
Perilous Gard - Elizabeth Marie Pope 1456
The Stones - Janet Hickman 875
Teetoncey - Theodore Taylor 1790
Thank You, Jackie Robinson - Barbara Cohen 384
The Winged Colt of Casa Mia - Betsy Byars 268
Zenas and the Shaving Mill - F.N. Monjo 1276

Cummings, Pat
Go Fish - Mary Stolz 1756

Cushman, Doug
Aunt Morbelia and the Screaming Skulls - Joan Davenport Carris 300

Illustrator Index

Fouracre, Chantel
The Well - Gene Kemp   1011

Fowler, Jim
The Secret Moose - Jean Rogers   1541

Frace, Charles
The Wolf - Michael W. Fox   635

Frame, Paul
Mystery of the Maya Jade - Elizabeth Honness   911

Frascino, Edward
Delilah - Carole Hart   819
The Graveyard: And Other Not-So-Scary Stories -
   William E. Warren   1886
The Trumpet of the Swan - E.B. White   1901

Freschet, Gina
Bernard Sees the World - Berniece Freschet   646

Friedman, Judith
I Speak English for My Mom - Muriel Stanek   1725
Losing Uncle Tim - Marykate Jordan   986

Friedman, Marvin
Pinch - Larry Callen   277
Sorrow's Song - Larry Callen   278

Fuchs, Bernie
Ragtime Tumpie - Alan Schroeder   1597

G

Gackenbach, Dick
*The Monster in the 3rd Dresser Drawer and Other
   Stories about Adam Joshua* - Janice Lee
   Smith   1688
My Dog and the Birthday Mystery - David A.
   Adler   13
What Is Papa Up To Now? - Miriam Anne
   Bourne   181

Gaffney-Kessell, Walter
Lenny Kendall, Smart Aleck - Ellen Conford   405
One of the Third Grade Thonkers - Phyllis Reynolds
   Naylor   1317

Gag, Wanda
ABC Bunny - Wanda Gag   656
Millions of Cats - Wanda Gag   657

Galdone, Paul
Basil in Mexico - Eve Titus   1814
Home Run Trick - Scott Corbett   425

Gammell, Stephen
Come a Tide - George Ella Lyon   1160
The Great Dimpole Oak - Janet Taylor Lisle   1130
A Net to Catch the Wind - Margaret Greaves   741

Gampert, John
The Package in Hyperspace - Janet Asimov   63

Gannett, Ruth Stiles
Miss Hickory - Carolyn Sherwin Bailey   83
My Father's Dragon - Ruth Stiles Gannett   663

Garraty, Gail
The Tombs of Atuan - Ursula Le Guin   1085

Garrick, Donald
The Wednesday Surprise - Eve Bunting   240

Geer, Charles
Miss Pickerell and the Blue Whales - Ellen
   MacGregor   1167
Miss Pickerell and the War of the Computers - Dora
   Pantell   1373

Gehm, Charles
Soup - Robert Newton Peck   1409

Gehm, Charles C.
The House Without a Christmas Tree - Gail
   Rock   1523

Geiger, Paul
The Mystery of the Diamond in the Wood - David
   Kherdian   1021

George, Jean Craighead
My Side of the Mountain - Jean Craighead
   George   683

Gerlach, Geff
The Red Room Riddle - Scott Corbett   427

Gerstein, Mordicai
Something Queer at the Library: A Mystery -
   Elizabeth Levy   1109

Gilchrist, Jan S.
Nathaniel Talking - Eloise Greenfield   755

Gill, Margery
Over Sea, Under Stone - Susan Cooper   421

Ginsburg, Max
The Friendship - Mildred D. Taylor   1784
Mississippi Bridge - Mildred D. Taylor   1785

Giovanopoulos, Paul
How Many Miles to Babylon? - Paula Fox   636

Glanzman, Louis S.
Noonday Friends - Mary Stolz   1758
Pippi Longstocking - Astrid Lindgren   1124
A Wonderful, Terrible Time - Mary Stolz   1760

Glass, Andrew
Banjo - Robert Newton Peck   1407
The Devil's Donkey - Bill Brittain   203
Dr. Dredd's Wagon of Wonders - Bill Brittain   204
The Ghost in the Lagoon - Natalie Savage
   Carlson   293
The Gift - Joan Lowery Nixon   1334
Graven Images - Paul Fleischman   614
The Wish Giver: Three Tales of Coven Tree - Bill
   Brittain   206

Glasser, Judy
*The Case of the Cackling Car: A Sam and Dave
   Mystery Story* - Marilyn Singer   1654
Too Much Magic - Betsy Sterman   1743

Goble, Paul
The Friendly Wolf - Paul Goble   712

Goffe, Toni
Sid Seal, Houseman - Will Watkins   1889

Gorey, Edward
Treehorn's Treasure - Florence Parry Heide   846

Gowing, Toby
Double or Nothing - Marc Talbert   1776

Grahme-Johnstone, Janet
The Hundred and One Dalmatians - Dodie
   Smith   1679

Grant, Leigh
Shoeshine Girl - Clyde Robert Bulla   228

Grazia, Thomas Di
The Merrymaker - Yuri Suhl   1766

Greenwald, Sheila
The Secret in Miranda's Closet - Sheila
   Greenwald   760

Grifalconi, Ann
Everett Anderson's Friend - Lucille Clifton   365
How Far, Felipe? - Genevieve Gray   737
The Midnight Fox - Betsy Byars   264
The Village of Round and Square Houses - Ann
   Grifalconi   768

Gripe, Harold
The Glassblower's Children - Maria Gripe   774

Grossman, Robert
The 18th Emergency - Betsy Byars   255

Guitar, Jeremy
The Dawn Seekers - Carol Hamilton   798

Gurney, John Steven
The Worldwide Dessert Contest - Dan Elish   564

H

Hafner, Marylin
The Crow and Mrs. Gaddy - Wilson Gage   658
The Dog Food Caper - Joan M. Lexau   1115
I Wish Laura's Mommy Was My Mommy - Barbara
   Power   1463
M & M and the Big Bag - Pat Ross   1548
The Missing Tooth - Joanna Cole   390
Raymond's Best Summer - Jean Rogers   1540

Hague, Michael
Peter Pan - James Barrie   98
The Unicorn and the Lake - Marianna Mayer   1210

Hall, H. Tom
Mystery of the Haunted Pool - Phyllis A.
   Whitney   1903

Hamanaka, Sheila
Class Clown - Johanna Hurwitz   950
The Twenty-Four-Hour Lipstick Mystery - Bonnie
   Pryor   1476

Hansom, Peter E.
Keep the Lights Burning, Abbie - Peter Roop   1544

Harmuth, William
*The Bloodhound Gang and the Case of the Secret
   Message* - Sid Fleischman   618

Harness, Cheryl
Fudge - Charlotte Towner Graeber   728
Grandpa's Slide Show - Deborah Gould   725

Hasselriis, Else
Shen of the Sea - Arthur Bowie Chrisman   329

Haywood, Carolyn
Eddie's Valuable Property - Carolyn Haywood   838

Hedderwick, Mairi
Brave Janet Reachfar - Jane Duncan   547

Heinly, John
Tackle-22 - Louise Munro Foley   631

Helpern, Joan
The Carp in the Bathtub - Barbara Cohen   381

Hemmant, Lynette
Ace, the Very Important Pig - Dick King-
   Smith   1029

Henkes, Kevin
Margaret and Taylor - Kevin Henkes   851

Henstra, Frisco
The Wicked Tricks of Tyl Uilenspiegel - Jay
   Williams   1921

Hermanson, Dennis
Land's End - Mary Stolz   1757

Heslop, Michael
The Grey King - Susan Cooper   419

Hewitt, Kathryn
The Worry Week - Anne Lindbergh   1121

Higginbottom, J. Winslow
Rats, Spiders, and Love - Bonnie Pryor   1474

Hilgerdt, Erik
I, Tut: The Boy Who Became Pharoah - Miriam
   Schlein   1595

Hillenbrand, Will
Awfully Short for the Fourth Grade - Elvira Woodruff 1951

Himler, Ronald
Best Town in the World - Byrd Baylor 118
Curly and the Wild Boar - Fred Gipson 706
Edith Herself - Ellen Howard 920
Eli's Ghost - Betsy Hearne 841
Jem's Island - Kathryn Lasky 1072
Sadako and the Thousand Paper Cranes - Eleanor Coerr 378
The Wall - Eve Bunting 239

Hoban, Lillian
Arthur's Honey Bear - Lillian Hoban 888
The Balancing Girl - Berniece Rabe 1478
The Big Hello - Janet Schulman 1598
The Big Kite Contest - Dorotha Ruthstrom 1561
The Mouse and His Child - Russell Hoban 892
Quick Chick - Julia Hoban 887
Ready, Set, Robot - Lillian Hoban 890
Rip-Roaring Russell - Johanna Hurwitz 955
Russell Sprouts - Johanna Hurwitz 956
The Selchie's Seed - Shulamith Oppenheim 1361
Sophie and Gussie - Marjorie Weinman Sharmat 1622
When Will I Read? - Miriam Cohen 385
Where Does the Teacher Live? - Paula Kurzband Feder 591

Hoff, Syd
Chester - Mary Francis Shura 1634
Mrs. Brice's Mice - Syd Hoff 895

Hoffman, Rosecrantz
The Horrible Holidays - Audrey Wood 1947

Hofner, Marilyn
Jenny and the Tennis Nut - Janet Schulman 1599

Hogrogian, Nonny
The Contest - Nonny Hogrogian 897

Holland, Janice
The Blue Cat of Castle Town - Catherine C. Coblentz 376

Holland, Marion
A Big Ball of String - Marion Holland 902

Hollander, Carl
The Magic Stone - Leonie Kooiker 1049

Holling, Holling Clancy
Minn of the Mississipppi - Holling Clancy Holling 903
Seabird - Holling Clancy Holling 905

Hollinger, Deane
Andrew and the Alchemist - Barbara Ninde Byfield 269

Hoogendijk, Wouter
The Wily Witch and All the Other Fairy Tales and Fables - Godfried Bomans 165

Houston, James A.
Frozen Fire - James A. Houston 917

Howell, Kathleen Collins
Dog Days - Colby Rodowsky 1536

Howell, Troy
The Comeback Dog - Jane Resh Thomas 1804
The Donkey Planet - Scott Corbett 423
Fox in a Trap - Jane Resh Thomas 1806
Night Swimmers - Betsy Byars 265

Howland, Deborah
The Adventures of Johnny May - Robbie Branscum 188

Huffman, Tom
Be a Perfect Person in Just Three Days - Stephen Manes 1187

Hughes, George
Help! I'm a Prisoner in the Library - Eth Clifford 361

Hughes, Shirley
Squib - Nina Bawden 117
The Trouble with Dragons - Oliver G. Selfridge 1612

Humphreys, Graham
Intruder - John Rowe Townsend 1819

Hurlimann, Ruth
The Cat and Mouse Who Shared a House - Ruth Hurlimann 943

Hutchins, Laurence
The Curse of the Egyptian Mummy - Pat Hutchins 959
Follow That Bus! - Pat Hutchins 960

Hutchins, Pat
The Very Worst Monster - Pat Hutchins 961

Hutton, Warwick
The Silver Cow: A Welsh Tale - Susan Cooper 422

Hyman, Trina S.
A Child's Christmas in Wales - Dylan Thomas 1803
Hershel and the Hanukkah Goblins - Eric A. Kimmel 1026
A Room Made of Windows - Eleanor Cameron 285

Hyman, Trina Schart
Among the Dolls - William Sleator 1660

I

Ilsley, Velma
She and the Dubious Three - Dorothy Crayder 440
Son for a Day - Corinne Gerson 687

Ingraham, Erick
Cross-Country Cat - Mary Calhoun 272
Old Blue - Sibyl Hancock 810
Porcupine Stew - Beverly Major 1184

Isadora, Rachel
Cutlass in the Snow - Elizabeth Shub 1630
Flossie and the Fox - Pat McKissack 1244
The White Stallion - Elizabeth Shub 1631

J

Jacobi, Kathy
The Half-a-Moon Inn - Paul Fleischman 615
Tomorrow's Wizard - Patricia Maclachlan 1172

Jaques, Faith
The Box of Delights - John Masefield 1208

Jenkins, Jean
Jeffrey's Ghost and the Fifth Grade Dragon - David A. Adler 12
Today's Special: Z.A.P and Zoe - Athena V. Lord 1147

Jeschke, Susan
Busybody Nora - Johanna Hurwitz 949
A Mitzvah Is Something Special - Phyllis Rose Eisenberg 562
Superduper Teddy - Johanna Hurwitz 957
The Times They Used to Be - Lucille Clifton 367
Wild Boy - Joan Tate 1782

Johnson, Crockett
Harold and the Purple Crayon - Crockett Johnson 975

Johnson, Larry
Soccer Halfback - Matt Christopher 340

Johnson, Milton
Come by Here - Olivia Coolidge 413

Johnson, Pamela
Quentin Corn - Mary Stolz 1759

Joyce, William
George Shrinks - William Joyce 987
Some of the Adventures of Rhode Island Red - Stephen Manes 1189

K

Kallay, Dusan
December's Travels - Mischa Damjan 474

Kalthoff, Sandra Cox
The Best Dressed Bear - Mary Blocksma 149

Kaluta, Michael W.
Mystery of the Metro - Elizabeth Howard 918

Kamen, Gloria
Lisa and Her Soundless World - Edna S. Levine 1099

Kandoian, Ellen
Maybe She Forgot - Ellen Kandoian 992

Kastner, Jill
Aurora Means Dawn - Scott R. Sanders 1585

Kasza, Keiko
The Wolf's Chicken Stew - Keiko Kasza 998

Kaufmann, John
The Empty Schoolhouse - Natalie Savage Carlson 291

Kavanagh, Peter
Mean and Mighty Me - Sally Christie 334

Keats, Ezra Jack
The King's Fountain - Lloyd Alexander 30

Keith, Eros
The House of Dies Drear - Virginia Hamilton 802
In a Blue Velvet Dress - Catherine Sefton 1604

Kellogg, Steven
The Great Christmas Kidnapping Caper - Jean Van Leeuwen 1847
Leo, Zack and Emmie - Amy Ehrlich 561
Molly Moves Out - Susan Pearson 1403
Once, Said Darlene - William Sleator 1664

Kendrich, Dennis
The Fox with Cold Feet - Bill Singer 1651

Kessell, Walter
Frankie Is Staying Back - Ron Roy 1557

Kessler, Leonard
Aurora and Socrates - Anne Vestly 1854
Binky Brothers, Detectives - James Duncan Lawrence 1080
Old Turtle's Soccer Team - Leonard Kessler 1018

Khalsa, Dayal Kaur
Tales of a Gambling Grandmother - Dayal Kaur Khalsa 1020

Kidder, Harvey
Catch That Pass! - Matt Christopher 337
Shortstop From Tokyo - Matt Christopher 339

Kincade, Nancy
Even If I Did Something Awful - Barbara Shook Hazen 840
Mr. Pepper Stories - Mark Taylor 1783

Illustrator Index

Say, Allen
How My Parents Learned to Eat - Ina R. Friedman   647

Schick, Joel
Bagdad Ate It - Phyllis Green   742
My Robot Buddy - Alfred Slote   1673
The Remarkable Ride of Israel Bissell - Alice Schick   1592
The Week Mom Unplugged the TVs - Terry Wolfe Phelan   1434

Schindelman, Joseph
Charlie and the Chocolate Factory - Roald Dahl   464

Schindler, S.D.
Children of Christmas - Cynthia Rylant   1564

Schoenherr, John
Gentle Ben - Walt Morey   1285
Incident at Hawk's Hill - Allan W. Eckert   559
Julie of the Wolves - Jean Craighead George   682
Kilroy and the Gull - Nathaniel Benchley   133
Storm Boy - Colin Thiele   1802

Scholder, Fritz
Anpao: An American Indian Odyssey - Jamake Highwater   878

Schucker, James
Little Black, a Pony - Walter Farley   589

Schwartz, Amy
Jane Martin, Dog Detective - Eve Bunting   232

Schweninger, Ann
More Tales of Amanda the Pig - Jean Van Leeuwen   1848

Scott, Frances Gruse
Maria's House - Jean Merrill   1258

Scrofani, Joseph
Dr. Beaumont and the Man with the Hole in His Stomach - Sam Epstein   575

Sendak, Maurice
Along Came a Dog - Meindert De Jong   493
The Bat-Poet - Randall Jarrell   971
The Big Green Book - Robert Graves   734
The Griffin and the Minor Canon - Frank R. Stockton   1750
The House of Sixty Fathers - Meindert De Jong   494
Little Bear - Else Holmelund Minarik   1272
The Nutcracker - E.T.A. Hoffman   896
Shadrach - Meindert De Jong   495
The Singing Hill - Meindert DeJong   506

Seredy, Kate
The White Stag - Kate Seredy   1613

Servello, Joe
Trouble in Bugland: A Collection of Inspector Mantis Mysteries - William Kotzwinkle   1055

Sewall, Marcia
The Birthday Tree - Paul Fleischman   611
Finzel the Farsighted - Paul Fleischman   613
The Marzipan Moon - Nancy Willard   1915
Richard Kennedy: Collected Stories - Richard Kennedy   1014
Song of the Horse - Richard Kennedy   1015
Stone Fox - John Reynolds Gardiner   668
Thistle - Walter Wangerin   1883

Sewell, Helen
Bears on Hemlock Mountain - Alice Dalgliesh   472
By the Shores of Silver Lake - Laura Ingalls Wilder   1909
Little Town on the Prairie - Laura Ingalls Wilder   1910
On the Banks of Plum Creek - Laura Ingalls Wilder   1911

Sharp, Gene
Hi, Clouds - Carol Greene   747

Shecter, Ben
The Escape of the Giant Hogstalk - Felice Holman   906
The Toad Hunt - Janet Chenery   322

Shefts, Joelle
Casey the Nomad - Susan Sussman   1769
The Dancing Cats of Applesap - Janet Taylor Lisle   1129

Shell, Richard L.
Sasha, My Friend - Barbara Corcoran   432

Shepard, Ernest H.
The Wind in the Willows - Kenneth Grahame   733

Shimin, Symeon
Onion John - Joseph Krumgold   1058
Zeely - Virginia Hamilton   807

Shortall, Leonard
Encyclopedia Brown, Boy Detective - Donald J. Sobol   1703
Hotel for Dogs - Lois Duncan   549
Saturdays in the City - Ann Sharpless Bond   166

Shulevitz, Uri
The Strange and Exciting Adventures of Jeremiah Hush - Uri Shulevitz   1632

Silverstein, Shel
Where the Sidewalk Ends - Shel Silverstein   1646

Simeon, Michel
James and the Giant Peach - Roald Dahl   466

Simont, Marc
In the Year of the Boar and Jackie Robinson - Bette Bao Lord   1148
Nate the Great - Marjorie Weinman Sharmat   1620

Sims, Blanche
The Beast in Ms. Rooney's Room - Patricia Reilly Giff   692
Eddie, Incorporated - Phyllis Reynolds Naylor   1314
The Interesting Thing That Happened at Perfect Acres, Inc. - Barbara Brooks Wallace   1871
Miss Plunkett to the Rescue - Jane Flory   630
Purple Climbing Days - Patricia Reilly Giff   697
Running out of Magic with Houdini - Elizabeth Levy   1108
Soccer Sam - Jean Marzollo   1207

Singer, Gloria
Summer of the Stallion - June Andrea Hanson   815

Sis, Peter
The Ghost in the Noonday Sun - Sid Fleischman   620
Oaf - Julia Cunningham   454
The Whipping Boy - Sid Fleischman   625

Skardinski, Stan
The Humans of Ziax II - John Morressy   1292

Slobodkin, Louis
Many Moons - James Thurber   1811
Rufus M. - Eleanor Estes   578

Small, David
Anna and the Seven Swans - Maida Silverman   1642

Smith, Alvin
Mystery of the Fat Cat - Frank Bonham   172

Smith, Cat B.
General Butterfingers - John Reynolds Gardiner   667
Princess Bee and the Royal Goodnight Story - Sandy Asher   60

Smith, E. Boyd
The Life and Strange and Surprising Adventures of Robinson Crusoe - Daniel Defoe   503

Smith, Jacqueline B.
Davey Come Home - Margaret Teibl   1792

Smith, Jessie Wilcox
Little Women, or Meg, Jo, Beth and Amy - Louisa M. Alcott   23

Smith, Jos. A.
Jim Ugly - Sid Fleischman   623

Smith, Juliet Stanwell
The Rocking Horse Secret - Rumer Godden   715

Smith, Lane
Knights of the Kitchen Table - Jon Scieszka   1601

Smith, Wendy
The Blood and Thunder Adventure on Hurricane Peak - Margaret Mahy   1179

Spanfeller, James
Dorp Dead - Julia Cunningham   452

Sparkman, Gene
The Berkley Street Six Pack - Mary Francis Shura   1633

Spence, Jim
Say Cheese - Betty Bates   104

Sperry, Armstrong
All Sail Set: A Romance of the Flying Cloud - Armstrong Sperry   1711
Call It Courage - Armstrong Sperry   1712

Spier, Peter
Oh, Were They Ever Happy! - Peter Spier   1713

Spillman, Fredrika
Year of the Black Pony - Walt Morey   1288

Stadler, John
Jason and the Baseball Bear - Dan Elish   563
Snail Saves the Day - John Stadler   1723

Stahl, Ben
Almost a Hero - Clyde Robert Bulla   223
A Pocket Full of Seeds - Marilyn Sachs   1579

Steig, William
Dominic - William Steig   1733
The Real Thief - William Steig   1735
Spinky Sulks - William Steig   1737

Steptoe, John
The Story of Jumping Mouse - John Steptoe   1740

Stermer, Duguld
Ghost Vision - Jeanie Kortum   1054

Stevens, Mary
Nobody Listens to Andrew - Elizabeth Guilfoile   778

Stevenson, James
Georgia Music - Helen V. Griffith   772
Grandaddy's Place - Helen V. Griffith   773
Something Big Has Been Here: Poems - Jack Prelutsky   1465

Stevenson, Sucie
Henry and Mudge and the Happy Cat - Cynthia Rylant   1567
Ruthann and Her Pig - Barbara Ann Porte   1460

Stewart, Arvis
Felicia the Critic - Ellen Conford   402
A Gift of Magic - Lois Duncan   548

Stock, Catherine
Bella Arabella - Liza Fosburgh   634
Justin and the Best Biscuits in the World - Mildred Pitts Walter   1880

Miss Know-It-All and the Three Ring Circus - Carol Beach York   1975
Sea Swan - Kathryn Lasky   1073

Stone, David K.
The Snake Horn - Morton Grosser   776

Stone, Helen
Little Witch - Anna Elizabeth Bennett   135

Stren, Patti
Eating Ice Cream with a Werewolf - Phyllis Green   743

Strogart, Alexander
Maxie, Rosie, and Earl - Partners in Grime - Barbara Park   1379

Strugnell, Ann
Mr. McFadden's Hallowe'en - Rumer Godden   714
The Stories Julian Tells - Ann Cameron   281

Svend, Otto S.
Trust in the Unexpected - Gunnel Linde   1122

Swan, Susan
The Case of the Horrible Swamp Monster - Drew Stevenson   1745

Swanson, Karl
Carver - Ruth Yaffe Radin   1481

Sweat, Lynn
The Garden Is Doing Fine - Carol J. Farley   586

Szekers, Cyndy
Pippa Pops Out: Four Read-Aloud/Read Alone Stories - Betty Boegehold   164

T

Taback, Simms
Euphonia and the Flood - Mary Calhoun   273

Teskey, Donald
Under the Hawthorne Tree - Marita Conlon-McKenna   408

Thompson, Ellen
Caught in the Moving Mountains - Gloria Skurzynski   1658
The Sinister Airfield - Alison Prince   1471

Tiegreen, Alan
Cookies and Crutches - Judy Delton   511
Kelly's Creek - Doris Buchanan Smith   1680
Ramona and Her Father - Beverly Cleary   354
Ramona Quimby, Age 8 - Beverly Cleary   355

Tolkien, J.R.R.
The Hobbit - J.R.R. Tolkien   1818

Tomei, Lorna
Just Between Us - Susan Beth Pfeffer   1431

Tomes, Margot
And Then What Happened, Paul Revere? - Jean Fritz   649
Homesick: My Own Story - Jean Fritz   652
Sara Crewe - Frances Hodgson Burnett   248
The Shadowmaker - Ron Hansen   814
Those Foolish Molboes - Lillian Bason   101

Travis, Irene
The Fourth Floor Twins and the Sand Castle Contest - David A. Adler   11

Tripp, Wallace
No Flying in the House - Betty Brock   207
Sir Toby Jingle's Beastly Journey - Wallace Tripp   1824

Trivas, Irene
The Doggone Mystery - Mary Blount Christian   331

One-Eyed Cat - Paula Fox   639

Truesdell, Sue
Addie Meets Max - Joan Robins   1516
O'Diddy - Jocelyn Stevenson   1747

Tudor, Tasha
Amy's Goose - Efner Tudor Holmes   909

Tunis, Edwin
The Tavern at the Ferry - Edwin Tunis   1825

Turkle, Brinton
Danny Dunn on the Ocean Floor - Jay Williams   1920

Turska, Krystyna
King of the Golden River - John Ruskin   1560
Marra's World - Elizabeth Coatsworth   375

U

Ulrich, George
My Halloween Boyfriend - Stephen Mooser   1283

Unwin, Nora S.
Amos Fortune, Free Man - Elizabeth Yates   1962

V

Vachula, Monica
Cow-Tail Switch and Other West Africa Stories - Harold Courlander   435

Vainio, Pirkko
Josie Smith - Magdalen Nabb   1307

Van Allsburg, Chris
Jumanji - Chris Van Allsburg   1840
The Polar Express - Chris Van Allsburg   1843

Vasconcellos, Daniel
The Dog That Pitched a No-Hitter - Matt Christopher   338

Velasquez, Eric
Chain of Fire - Beverly Naidoo   1309

Vicary, Richard
The Ivy Garland - John Hoyland   927

Vivas, Julie
Let the Celebrations Begin! - Margaret Wild   1908
The Tram to Bondi Beach - Elizabeth Hathorn   825

Vo-Dinh
First Snow - Helen Coutant   436

Voake, Charlotte
The Way to Sattin Shore - Philippa Pearce   1402

Vogel, Ilse-Margret
My Summer Brother - Ilse-Margret Vogel   1859

Von Schmidt, Eric
The Ghost on Saturday Night - Sid Fleischman   621
Humbug Mountain - Sid Fleischman   622

W

Waber, Bernard
Mice on My Mind - Bernard Waber   1867

Wallner, John
Aldo Peanut Butter - Johanna Hurwitz   946
Gloomy Louis - Phyllis Green   744
Harvey, the Beer Can King - Jamie Gilson   703

Tales of a Wandering Warthog - Tom Sinclair   1650

Ward, Keith
The Black Stallion - Walter Farley   587

Ward, Lynd
The Cat Who Went to Heaven - Elizabeth Coatsworth   374
Early Thunder - Jean Fritz   651
Johnny Tremain - Esther Forbes   633
The Silver Pony - Lynd Ward   1884

Washburn, James K.
The Case of the Elevator Duck - Polly Berrien Berends   139

Watson, Richard Jesse
The High Rise Glorious Skittle Skat Roarious Sky Pie Angel Food Cake - Nancy Willard   1914

Watson, Wendy
Belinda's Hurricane - Elizabeth Winthrop   1930
Willow Wind Farm: Betsy's Story - Anne Pellowski   1414

Watts, James
Good Hunting, Blue Sky - Peggy Parish   1375

Wegner, Fritz
The Champion of Merrimack County - Roger W. Drury   538

Weihs, Erika
Cakes and Miracles - Barbara Diamond Goldin   718

Weil, Lisl
The Case of the Condemned Cat - E.W. Hildick   879

Weinhaus, Karen
Carnival and Kopeck and More About Hannah - Mindy Skolsky   1657

Weinshel, Joe
You Can Depend on Me - Margaret Reuter   1503

Weisgard, Leonard
Courage of Sarah Noble - Alice Dalgliesh   473

Welch, Patricia
The Day of the Muskie - Patricia Welch   1891

Wells, Haru
The Way of Our People - Arnold A. Griese   766

Wheeler, Cindy
The Kite Song - Margery Evernden   581

Wheeling, Lynn
A Lamp for the Lambchops - Jeff Brown   215

Wiese, Kurt
Bambi - Felix Salten   1582
Freddy the Detective - Walter R. Brooks   212

Wiesner, David
Man From the Sky - Avi   70

Wijngaard, Juan
Jelly Belly - Robert Kimmel Smith   1691

Wikland, Ilon
The Ghost of Skinny Jack - Astrid Lindgren   1123

Williams, Garth
Bedtime for Frances - Russell Hoban   891
Charlotte's Web - E.B. White   1899
The Cricket in Times Square - George Selden   1608
Family Under the Bridge - Natalie Savage Carlson   292
The Golden Name Day - Jennie D. Lindquist   1126
The Happy Orpheline - Natalie Savage Carlson   294
Harry Cat's Pet Puppy - George Selden   1610
Stuart Little - E.B. White   1900
Tucker's Countryside - George Selden   1611

Author Index

This index is an alphabetical listing of the authors of books featured in entries and those listed under "Other books by the author" and "Other books you might like." For each author, the titles of books written and entry numbers are also provided. Editors and co-authors are interfiled with Author names. Bold numbers indicate a featured main entry; other numbers refer to books recommended for further reading.

Author Index

You Hold Me and I'll Hold You 986

Carter, Alden R.
Sheila's Dying 1135
Shelia's Dying 1253
Up Country 1754

Carter, Anne
12 Dancing Princesses 306
Fisherwoman 306
Molly in Danger **306**
Ruff Leaves Home 306
Scurry's Treasure 306

Carter, Debby L.
Clipper 1544

Carter, Dorothy Sharp
His Majesty, Queen Hatshepsut 567,
   1595, 1697

Carver, Peter
Bury the Dead 1849

Carylon, Richard
The Dark Lord of Pengersick 25

Case, Dianne
Love, David 360, 985, 1117, 1127,
   1309

Caseley, Judith
Apple Pie and Onions 194
Hurricane Harry 1930
Starring Dorothy Kane 5

Caselli, Giovanni
A Viking Settler 134

Casely, Judith
Sophie and Sammy's Library
   Sleepover 1109

Cassedy, Sylvia
Behind the Attic Wall **307**, 308, 645
The Best Cat Suit of All 308, 524,
   1197, 1688
Birds, Frogs and Moonlight 308
Lucie Babbidge's House 307, **308**,
   597, 1660
M.E. and Morton 267, 307, 308
Pierino and the Bell 307

Castaneda, Omar S.
Among the Volcanoes 911

Caswell, Helen
Shadows From the Singing
   House 682

Catalanotto, Peter
Dylan's Day Out 1018

Cate, Dick
Old Dog, New Tricks 1011, 1256

Catherall, Arthur
The Big Tusker 295
Jungle Rescue 1028
Kalu and the Wild Boar 706
Kidnapped by Accident 1034
Last Horse on the Sands 185
Red Sea Rescue 303
Ten Fathoms Deep 1903

Catlin, Wynelle
Old Wattles 706

Catling, Patrick Skene
The Chocolate Touch **309**, 464,
   1690
John Midas in the Dreamtime 309,
   444, 1120, 1475, 1959

Caudill, Rebecca
The Best Loved Doll 310
A Certain Small Shepherd **310**
Contrary Jenkins 310
Far Off Land 311
House of the Fifers 311
My Appalachia 311
Pocket Full of Cricket 310

Saturday Cousins 310
Schoolhouse in the Woods 311
Susan Cornish **311**

Caufield, Donald E.
Never Steal a Magic Cat 26, **312**

Cavanna, Betty
Petey 1739
Stamp Twice for Murder 918
You Can't Take Twenty Dogs on a
   Date 794

Cave, Hugh Barnett
Conquering Kilmarnie 413, 1898
The Voyage 429

Cave, Kathryn
Out for the Count: A Counting
   Adventure 1094

Cawley, Winifred
Feast of the Serpent 313
Gran at Coalgate **313**

Cazet, Denys
Mud Baths for Everyone 1436

Cazzola, Gus
To Touch the Deer 970

Cebulash, Mel
Ruth Marini of the Dodgers 339

Celsi, Teresa Noel
The Fourth Little Pig 1848
Rosa Parks and the Montgomery Bus
   Boycott 1257

Cendrars, Blaise
Shadow 823

Chadwick, Roxanne
Don't Shoot 1539

Chafetz, Henry
Chanticleer: The Story of a Proud
   Rooster 1838

Chaikin, Miriam
Aviva's Piano **314**
Esther 314
Feathers in the Wind 314, 315,
   1187
Finders Weepers 315
Friends Forever 315, 1596
Getting Even 315
How Yossi Beat the Evil Urge 314
I Should Worry, I Should Care **315**,
   1102
Lower! Higher! You're a Liar! 872,
   1552
Make Noise, Make Merry 718
Yossi Asks the Angels for Help 202,
   1652, 1914
Yossi Tries to Help God 314

Chall, Marsha Wilson
Mattie 871

Chamberlain, Barbara
Ride the West Wind 1354, 1485

Chambers, Aidan
Present Takers 1209
Seal Secret 169

Chambers, Catherine E.
Frontier Dream: Life on the Great
   Plains 1909
Frontier Farmer: Kansas
   Adventure 148
Indiana Days: Life in a Frontier
   Town 1911
Texas Roundup : Life on the
   Range 810

Chambers, John W.
Finder 771, 1630
Footlight Summer 877, 1402
Fritzi's Winter 1630

Chance, Stephen
Septimus and the Danedyke
   Mystery **316**
The Stone of Offering 316

Chandler, Edna Walker
Almost Brothers 87
Indian Paintbrush 799
Popcorn Patch 706

Chang, Heidi
Elaine, Mary Lewis, and the
   Frogs 1148, 1315, 1966

Chang, Margaret Scrogin
In the Eye of War 652, 1836

Chapman, Carol
Barney Bipple's Magic Dandelion 584
Barney Bipple's Magic
   Dandelions 317, 318
Herbie's Troubles **317**, 318
Ig Lives in a Cave 317, **318**
The Tale of Meshka the Kvetch 317,
   318

Chapman, Vera
Miranty and the Alchemist 129

Charbonneau, Eileen
The Ghosts of Stony Clove 1147

Charbonnet, Gabrielle
Boodil My Dog 319
Else Marie and Her Seven Little
   Daffodils 319
Snakes Are Nothing to Sneeze At 3,
   319

Chardiet, Bernice
Martin and the Tooth Fairy 202, 390

Charles, Veronika Martenova
The Crane Girl 535

Charlip, Remy
Handtalk Birthday: A Number and
   Story Book in Sign Language 1985
Harlequin and the Gifts of Many
   Colors 1625

Charnas, Suzy McKee
The Bronze King **320**
The Golden Thread 320, 980
The Silver Glove 320, 541, 982
The Vampire Tapestry 320

Chase, Mary
Harvey 321
Mrs. McThing: A Play 321
The Wicked Pigeon Ladies in the
   Garden **321**
Wicked Wicked Ladies in the Haunted
   House 321

Cheetham, Ann
The Pit 670, 671

Chenery, Janet
Golden Book of Lost Worlds 322
Pickles and Jake 322
The Toad Hunt **322**
Wolfie 322, 1899

Cheney, Cora
The Mystery of the Disappearing
   Cars 80
Tales from a Taiwan Kitchen 1965
The Treasures of Lin Li-ti 447

Chestnutt, Charles
Conjure Tales **323**

Chetwin, Grace
Collidescope 63, 320, 1663, 1938
The Crystal Stair 324
Friends in Time 324, 1406
Gom on Windy Mountain **324**
On All Hallow's Eve 184, 324, 417,
   774, 1085, 1119, 1370, 1882
Out of the Dark World 324

Chew, Ruth
Do-it-Yourself Magic **325**
Earthstar Magic 1833
Mostly Magic 325
The Wishing Tree 121
The Witch and the Ring 304, 312,
   438, 740, 1701
The Would-Be-Witch 325
The Would-Be Witch 469

Childress, Alice
A Hero Ain't Nothin' but a
   Sandwich **326**, 327, 1305
Like One of the Family 326, 327
Rainbow Jordan 326, 327
Those Other People 96, 326, 327
When the Rattlesnake Sounds: A
   Play 326, **327**

Chittum, Ida
The Hermit Boy 607, 1021

Chlad, Dorothy
Animals Can Be Special Friends 271

Chorao, Kay
Cathedral Mouse 328, 598
Dracula's Cat 328
The Good-Bye Book 328
Lemon Moon 987
Molly's Moe 1974
Ralph and the Queen's Bathtub 1196
Ups and Downs with Oink and
   Pearl **328**

Chrisman, Arthur Bowie
Shen of the Sea **329**

Christeiansen, Candace
Calico and Tin Horns 1453

Christelow, Eileen
The Completed Hickory Dickory
   Dock 330
Five Little Monkeys Jumping on the
   Bed 330
Five Little Monkeys Sitting in a
   Tree 330
Gertrude the Bulldog Detective 330
Glenda Feathers Casts a Spell 1198
Henry and the Red Stripes **330**
The Robbery at the Diamond Dog
   Diner 489

Christensen, Gardell Dano
Colonial New York 964

Christgau, Alice E.
The Laugh Peddler: A Story 1526

Christian, Mary Blount
April Fool 331, 332
The Devil Take You, Barnabas
   Beane 331
The Devil Take You, Barnabas
   Beane! 874
The Doggone Mystery **331**
Go West, Swamp Monsters! 1211
Goody Sherman's Pig 1030, 1829
Growin' Pains 268, 1322
Linc 465, 974
The Lucky Man 331, 332, 1934
Mystery at Camp Triumph 669, 754,
   1455, 1481
No Dogs Allowed, Jonathan! 139,
   989
Penrod Again 332
Penrod's Pants **332**
Sebastian and the Baffling
   Bigfoot 275
Sebastian (Super Sleuth) and the Bone
   to Pick Mystery **333**
Sebastian (Super Sleuth) and the Hair
   of the Dog Mystery 333
Sebastian (Super Sleuth) and the
   Impossible Crime 1620

Hall, Rosalys Haskell *(cont.)*
Flash, Dog of Old Egypt 796
The Ghost of the Great River Inn 792
The Giver 1310
Half the Battle 496
Halsey's Pride 795, 920
Here Comes Zelda Claus and Other Holiday Disasters 793
The Horse Trader 792, 856
In Trouble Again, Zelda Hammersmith **793**
The Leaving 792
Megan's Mare 534, 867
Mrs. Portree's Pony 589, 1040, 1333
Murder at the Spaniel Show **794**
Murder in a Pig's Eye 1489, 1721
The Mystery of Pony Hollow 588, 1277
The Mystery of the Caramel Cat 239, 437, 486
The Mystery of the Lost and Found Hound 207, 232, 1318
Mystery of the Plum Park Pony 792
The Mystery of the Schoolhouse Dog 794, 876, 1237
Nobody's Dog 1538
Ride a Dark Horse 793
The Secret Life of Dagmar Schultz 110, 158, 793
The Solitary **795**, 1512
The Something Special Horse **796**
The Soul of the Silver Dog 569, 794, 795, 1739
Tin Can Tucker 1810
Too Near the Sun 440
The Tormentors 623, 1699
Troublemaker 543
Uphill All the Way 109
Windsong 794, 795

Hall, Rosalys Haskell
The Bright and Shining Breadboard 1851

Hall, Tom T.
Christmas and the Old House 1523, 1644
Christmas in the Old House 492

Haller, Danita Ross
Not Just Any Ring 92, 1709

Halliburton, Warren J.
Celebrations of African Heritage 142

Hallman, Ruth
Breakaway 234
Gimme Something, Mister! 70
Rescue Chopper 1028
Search Without Fear 1702
Tough Is Not Enough 698, 1072

Hallowell, Tommy
Duel on the Diamond 156
Last Chance Quarterback 337
Shot From Midfield 340, 1351

Hallstead, William F.
The Launching of Linda Bell 797
The Man Downstairs 797
Tundra 356, **797**

Halvorson, Marilyn
Cowboys Don't Cry 681, 801, 1950
Hold On, Geronimo 559

Hamberger, John
The Lazy Dog 1008

Hamilton, Carol
The Dawn Seekers **798**

Hamilton, Dorothy
Mindy 966

Hamilton, Gail
A Candle to the Devil 603

Hamilton, Morse
Big Sisters Are Bad Witches 535, 1350
Effie's House 790, 1321

Hamilton, Sue L.
Royal Mail Steamship Titanic 451, 530

Hamilton, Virginia
The All Jadhu Storybook 807
The All Jahdu Storybook 799, 803, 805, 806
Anthony Burns: The Defeat and Triumph of a Fugitive Slave 800
Arilla Sun Down **799**, 806, 1862
The Bells of Christmas **800**, 801
Cousins 799, **801**, 802, 803, 805, 806, 807, 899, 1684, 1779
The Dark Way 801
Dark Way Stories from the Spirit World 803
Drylongso 624, 773, 802
Dustland 522, 804, 1119, 1892
The Gathering 804
The House of Dies Drear 799
House of Dies Drear 800
The House of Dies Drear **802**
In the Beginning 800
In the Beginning: Creation Stories from Around the World **803**
Jahdu 823
Junius Over Far 802
Justice and Her Brothers 799, 801, **804**
A Little Love 804, 1780
M.C. Higgins, the Great 660, 805, 807
The Magical Adventures of Pretty Pearl 804, 806
The Mystery of Drear House 802
The People Could Fly 800, 801, 803, 807
The Planet of Junior Brown **805**, 1214, 1681
Sweet Whispers, Brother Rush **806**, 1243
A White Romance 859
Willie Bea and the Time the Martians Landed 714, 1243, 1881
Zeely 805, **807**

Hamley, Dennis
Hare's Choice **808**
Tigger and Friends 808

Hamm, Diane Johnston
Bunkhouse Journal **809**, 1553
Second Family 368, 898

Hammer, Charles
Wrong-Way Ragsdale 839, 883, 1353

Hamner, Earl
Spencer's Mountain 1251

Hamori, Laszlo
Dangerous Journey 1613

Hancock, Mary A.
The Thundering Prairie 201, 1874

Hancock, Sibyl
The Blazing Hills 810
Esteban and the Ghost 810
Freaky Francie 810
The Grizzly Bear 810
Old Blue **810**

Handford, Martin
Where's Waldo? 1974

Haney, Lynn
The Last Starfighter Storybook 1292

Hankey, Sally
A. Phillip Randolph 1245

Hanlon, Emily
Circle Home 811
It's Too Late for Sorry 648, 811
Love Is No Excuse 811
The Swing 47, 156, 480, **811**
The Wing and the Flame 614, 811

Hansen, Joyce
The Gift-Giver 57, **812**, 813
Home Boy 812, 813
Out From This Place 812, 813
Which Way Freedom? 812, **813**, 1602
Yellow Bird and Me 300, 785, 812, 813, 1202, 1379

Hansen, Ron
The Shadowmaker **814**, 1176

Hanson, Harvey
Game Time 756

Hanson, June Andrea
Summer of the Stallion 676, **815**
Winter of the Owl 815, 875

Hardcastle, Michael
Kickback 533, 588

Harding, William Harry
Alvin's Famous No-Horse 370, 536, 1317

Hare, Norma Q.
Who Is Root Beer? 1006

Hargreaves, Roger
Little Miss Chatterbox 778, 1198

Hargrove, Jim
Abraham Lincoln: 16th President 644
Daniel Boone: Pioneer Trailblazer 483

Harnett, Cynthia
The Cargo of the Madalena 1903

Harris, Dorothy Joan
The School Mouse and the Hamster 631

Harris, Jesse
Aidan's Fate 46, 445, 1177
The Obsession 548, 804
The Possession 1533
The Witness 213, 1928

Harris, Joel Chandler
Complete Tales of Uncle Remus 1084

Harris, Leona
Yvette 65

Harris, Marilyn
The Runaway's Diary 1185

Harris, Mark
The Doctor Who Technical Manual 1562

Harris, Mark Jonathan
Come the Morning **816**, 907
Confessions of a Prime Time Kid 816, 817
The Last Run 816, 817
Solay 816, 1938
With a Wave of the Wand 129, 816, **817**, 826

Harris, Robie H.
Rosie's Double Dare 425
Rosie's Razzle Dazzle Deal 1312

Harrison, David Lee
The Case of Og, the Missing Frog 1139

Harrison, Harry
The Men From P.I.G and R.O.B.O.T. 1442

Harshman, Terry Webb
Porcupine's Pajama Party 332, **818**

Hart, Carole
Delilah **819**
Now or Never 819

Hartley, Deborah
Up North in Winter 1116

Hartling, Peter
Crutches **820**, 821, 822
Old John 209, 820, **821**, 822
Oma 820, 821, **822**

Hartman, Evert
War Without Friends 1850

Hartman, Gail
For Sand Castles on Seashells 1797

Hartson, Eleanore
Maxie's Mystery Files: The Stalled Mall and Other Crazy Cases 631, 1080

Harvey, Brett
Cassie's Journey: Going West in the 1860's 1960
Growing Up on Eldridge Street 382
Immigrant Girl: Becky of Eldridge Street 1020
My Prairie Year 1909

Harvey, Dean
The Great Elephant of Harlan Kooter 295
The Secret Elephant of Harlan Kooter 21

Harvey, Jayne
Great-Uncle Dracula 526, 1107, 1521, 1688

Haseley, Dennis
The Cave of Snores 24, 823
The Old Banjo 823, 1925
Shadows 209, **823**, 1416, 1563, 1806
The Soap Bandit 823
The Thieves' Market 823

Haskins, Francine
I Remember "121" 367

Hass, E.A.
Incognito Mosquito, Private Insective 1055, 1313
Incognito Mosquito Takes to the Air 217, 968, 1313

Hass, Patricia Cecil
Swampfire 532

Hassler, Jon Francis
Four Miles to Pinecone 824
Jemmy **824**

Hatch, Mary Cottam
Thirteen Danish Tales 101

Hatchigan, Jessica
Dinosaurs Aren't Forever 171, 1607

Hathorn, Elizabeth
Freya's Fantastic Surprise 825, 1095
Thunderwith 159, 709, 751, 825
The Tram to Bondi Beach **825**

Hauff, Wilhelm
The Adventures of Little Mouk **826**
Cold Stone Heart 826

Haugaard, Erik Christian
The Boy and the Samurai **827**, 828
Leif the Unlucky 827
Little Fishes **828**
Orphans of the Wind 828
Prince Boghole 827, 828
Princess Horrid 827
The Rider and His Horse 1565
Samurai's Tale 827
The Untold Tale 163, 828, 1059

Haugen, Tormod
The Night Birds 46, 211, **829**

Author Index

Author Index

Author Index

S

Vansittart, Peter
The Dark Tower: Tales from the Past 1770

Vaughan, Marcia K.
The Sea-Breeze Hotel 1561
Wombat Stew 699

Vaura, Robert
Felipe, the Bullfighter 1535

Vautier, Ghislaine
Shining Stars: Greek Legends of the Zodiac 397

Vecere, Joel
A Story about Courage 16, 1038, 1515

Veglahn, Nancy
Follow the Golden Goose 1832

Velthuijs, Max
Crocodile's Masterpiece 415, 1842

Ventura, Piero
The Painter's Trick 732

Verne, Jules
20,000 Leagues Under the Sea 1852
Around the World in Eighty Days **1852**, 1853
From Earth to the Moon 1852
From the Earth to the Moon 1853
A Journey to the Center of the Earth 1852, 1853
The Mysterious Island 1852, 1853
Twenty Thousand Leagues Under the Sea **1853**

Verney, John
Seven Sunflower Seeds 1464

Very, Lydia
Little Red Riding Hood 1977

Vesey, Amanda
Hector's New Sneakers 1018

Vestly, Anne
Aurora and Socrates **1854**
Hello Aurora 1854

Viereck, Phillip
Sue's Secondhand Horse 1717, 1855
The Summer I Was Lost **1855**
Terror on the Mountains 1855

Vigna, Judith
Daddy's New Baby 537
Saying Goodbye to Daddy 1821

Vigor, John
Danger, Dolphins and Ginger Beer 1926

Vinge, Joan D.
Psion 324
Tarzan, King of the Apes 684
Willow: Based on the Motion Picture 1145

Vining, Elizabeth Gray
The Taken Girl 1354

Viorst, Judith
Alexander, Who Used to Be Rich Last Sunday **1856**
Earrings! 1856
The Good-Bye Book 840, 1856
I'll Fix Anthony 1856
Rosie and Michael 1856

Vivelo, Jackie
Beagle in Trouble: 12 Solve It Yourself Mysteries **1857**
Super Sleuth: 12 Solve It Yourself Mysteries 1857
Super Sleuth and the Bare Bones 1857
A Trick of the Light 614, 1857
We Wait in the Darkness 1857

Vogel, Ilse-Margret
Dodo Every Day 1858
Farewell, Aunt Isabell **1858**, 1859
My Summer Brother 1858, **1859**
My Twin Sister, Erika 1858, 1859
The Rainbow Dress and Other Tollush Tales 1859
Tikhon 447, 1357, 1858, 1859

Vogt, Esther Loewen
Harvest Gold 1773

Voight, Virginia Frances
Bobcat 1508
Red Blade and the Black Bear 811

Voigt, Cynthia
Building Blocks 776, 1382, **1860**, 1862, 1863
The Callender Papers 1496, 1860
Callender Papers **1861**
The Callender Papers 1862
The Callender Papers 1864
Come a Stranger 1566, **1862**, 1864, 1865
David and Jonathan 1860, 1861, 1864
Dicey's Song 360, 1860, 1861, 1862, **1863**, 1864
Homecoming 1860, 1861, 1863, **1864**
Izzy, Willy-Nilly 1826
Jackaroo 1861
On Fortune's Wheel 145, 1863
Orfe 1387
The Runner 1865
A Solitary Blue 1862, 1863, **1865**
Sons from Afar 1865
Tree by Leaf 1865
The Vandemark Mummy 111, 567, 959, 1337

Von Canon, Claudia
Inheritance 1535

Vos, Ida
Anna Is Still Here 1473, 1552
Hide and Seek 1153, 1499

Vozar, David
Yo, Hungry Wolf!: A Nursery Rap 1240, 1848, 1977

Vuong, Lynette Dyer
The Brocaded Slipper 1023, 1240

W

Waber, Bernard
Bernard 1866, 1867
Goodbye, Funny Dumpy-Lumpy 1504
I Was All Thumbs **1866**, 1867
Lyle Finds His Mother 1866, 1867
Mice on My Mind 1866, **1867**
The Snake, A Very Long Story 1866, 1867

Wachter, Oralee
No More Secrets for Me 1761

Waddell, Martin
Harriet and the Haunted School 12, 141, 1554
Harriet and the Robot 89, 1673, 1912, 1970
Let's Go Home, Little Bear 992
Little Obie and the Flood 819, 1100, 1585

Wade, Alan
I'm Flying 1063

Wade, Barrie
Little Monster 512

Wagener, Gerda
Leo the Lion 1161

Wagner, Jane
J.T. **1868**
The Search for Signs of Intelligent Life in the Universe 1868

Wagner, Jenny
John Brown, Rose, and the Midnight Cat 84

Wagner, Karen
Silly Fred 1369

Wahl, Jan
The Fisherman 1756
The Rabbit Club 1261
The Screeching Door: or, What Happened at the Elephant Hotel 1080
The Very Peculiar Tunnel 1841
Who Will Believe Tim Kitten? 1222

Waldorf, Mary
Jake McGee and His Feet 702

Waldron, Ann
Bluebury Collection 1869
The House on Pendleton Block 1488, 1869
The Integration of Mary-Larkin Thornhill 291
Integration of Mary-Larkin Thornhill 1534
The Integration of Mary-Larkin Thornhill **1869**
The Luckie Star 358, 1749, 1869
Scaredy Cat 690, 1809, 1869

Walker, Alice
Finding the Green Stone 366, 1870
Langston Hughes, American Poet **1870**, 1962
To Hell with Dying 1870

Walker, Barbara K.
A Treasury of Turkish Folktales 1022

Walker, David Harry
Big Ben 1235

Walker, Diana
The Hundred Thousand Dollar Farm 1278

Walker, Diane
Mother Wants a Horse 1810

Walker, Margaret
Jubilee 813

Walker, Marion Dane
Nell of Blue Harbor 450

Walker, Mary Alexander
The Scathach and Maeve's Daughters 1770
To Catch a Zombi 660

Walker, Paul Robert
The Slugger's Club 1112

Wallace, Barbara Brooks
Andrew, the Big Deal 1871, 1873
Argyle 1872
The Barrel in the Basement 1053, 1873
The Barrell in the Basement 1871
Claudia 1873
The Contest Kid and the Big Prize 1873
The Contest Kid Strikes Again 1872
The Farewell Kid 549
Hawkins 1872
The Interesting Thing That Happened at Perfect Acres, Inc. **1871**
Miss Switch to the Rescue 705, 1871
Palmer Patch **1872**

Peppermints in the Parlor 128, 265, 1871, **1873**
The Secret Summer of L.E.B. 1001, 1128, 1872

Wallace, Bill
Beauty **1874**, 1877
The Biggest Klutz in Fifth Grade 951, 1874, 1877
Biggest Klutz in Fifth Grade 1878
Buffalo Gal 1873, 1875
The Christmas Spurs 378, 1874, 1877
Danger in Quicksand Swamp 441, 1229, **1875**, 1878
Danger on Panther Peak 1875
A Dog Called Kitty 272, **1876**, 1878
Ferret in the Bedroom, Lizards in the Fridge 1876
Never Say Quit 499, 1193, 1875, 1878
Red Dog 707, 856, 1037, 1042, 1874, 1876, **1877**
Shadow in the Show 1877
Shadow on the Snow 1874
Snot Stew 639, 1876
Totally Disgusting 639, 1876
Trapped in Death Cave 222, 926, 1705, 1875, **1878**

Wallace, Daisy
Monster Poems 961, 1283

Wallace-Brodeur, Ruth
Callie's Way 1879
The Godmother Tree 611, 922
The Kenton Year 1859, **1879**
One April Vacation 1879
Steps in Time 1879
Stories From the Big Chair 1879

Wallin, Luke
Blue Wings 1415
Ceremony of the Panther 609, 685, 760, 1054, 1491

Wallin, Marie Louise
Tangles 1124

Walsh, Ellen Stoll
Mouse Paint 942
Theodore All Grown Up 888
You Silly Goose 1244

Walter, Mildred Pitts
Because We Are 1780, 1881
Brother to the Wind 768
The Girl on the Outside 1869, 1880, 1881
Have a Happy 224, 240
Justin and the Best Biscuits in the World **1880**, 1881
Lillie of Watts: A Birthday Discovery 1880
Lillie of Watts Takes a Giant Step 1880
Mariah Keeps Cool 805, 1880, 1881
Mariah Loves Rock **1881**
Trouble's Child 860
Two and Too Much 366, 601
Ty's One Man Band 141

Walton, Bryce
Hurricane Reef 53, 691, 1757

Wang, Mary Lewis
The Lion and the Mouse 896

Wang, Rosalind C.
Fourth Question 329

Wangerin, Walter
The Bible for Children 1882
The Book of Sorrows 1882, 1883

Title Index

This index alphabetically lists all titles featured in entries and those listed under "Other books by the author" and "Other books you might like." Each title is followed by the author's name and the number of the entry of that title. Bold numbers indicate featured main entries; other numbers refer to books recommended for further reading.

Boy in a Barn
Williams, Ursula Moray 820

A Boy in the Doghouse
Duffey, Betsy **543**, 963, 1739

Boy of Tache
Blades, Ann **147**, 1217

The Boy of the Bells
Simon, Carly 893

Boy of the Painted Cave
Denzel, Justin F. 85, 514

The Boy of the Three-Year Nap
Snyder, Dianne 1949

Boy on the Run
Bradley, Bianca 1045

Boy Tales of Childhood
Dahl, Roald 469

The Boy Who Could Fly
Newman, Robert 1329

The Boy Who Could Make Himself Disappear
Platt, Kin 1452

The Boy Who Didn't Believe in Spring
Clifton, Lucille 365, 367

The Boy Who Held Back the Sea
Locker, Thomas 1143

The Boy Who Lost His Face
Sachar, Louis 1569, 1570, 402, 1571, 1958

The Boy Who Made a Dragonfly
Hillerman, Tony 1057

The Boy Who Owned the School
Paulsen, Gary 1399

The Boy Who Remembered Everything
Abbott, Jennie 958

The Boy Who Reversed Himself
Sleator, William 1663

The Boy Who Sailed with Columbus
Foreman, Michael 54

The Boy Who Sang the Birds
Weston, John 563

The Boy Who Saved Earth
Slater, Jim 324, 335, 515

The Boy Who Stopped Time
Taber, Anthony 186

The Boy Who Walked on Air
Corbett, Scott 424

The Boy Who Wanted a Family
Gordon, Shirley **722**

The Boy Who Would Be a Hero
Lewis, Marjorie 1112

The Boy with the Helium Head
Naylor, Phyllis Reynolds 1063, 1312

Boy with Three Names
Gantz, Charlotte Orr 280

The Boy with Two Shadows
Mahy, Margaret 1181

Boy Without a Name
Lively, Penelope **1136**, 1138

The Boyhood of Grace Jones
Langton, Jane 1389

A Boy's Adventure
Twain, Mark 1834

Boys Are Yucko!
Hines, Anna Grosnickle 1426

Boys Here, Girls There
Levinson, Riki 993

Boys in the Gym
Levy, Elizabeth 1108

Boys' Life of Will Rogers
Keith, Harold 1004

The Boys Start the War
Naylor, Phyllis Reynolds 349, 1318

Brady
Fritz, Jean 124, 651, 813

The Bragging War
Haynes, Betsy 351

The Brain on Quartz Mountain
Anderson, Margaret Jean **43**, 1031

Brainstorm
Myers, Walter Dean 1303

Branded Runaway
Spencer, Zane 1775

Branigan's Dog: A Novel
Grace, Fran **727**, 1733

The Bratchets
Cooke, Edith Holden 1504

The Brats and Mr. Jack
Milton, Hilary H. 1216

Brave Buffalo Fighter
Fitzgerald, John D. 607

Brave Dog Blizzard
O'Toole, Sharon Salisbury 963

Brave Horse: The Story of Janus
Wellman, Manly Wade 853, 1618

Brave Irene
Steig, William **1732**

Brave Janet Reachfar
Duncan, Jane **547**

The Brave Little Tailor
Grimm, Jacob 101

The Bravest Dog Ever
Standiford, Natalie 668

Bravo, Burro!
Fante, John 52, 423

Bravo, Minski
Yorinks, Arthur 1974

Bread and Jam for Frances
Hoban, Russell 891, 892

The Bread Sister of Sinking Creek
Moore, Robin 1096, 1496, 1910

The Bread Winner
Whitmore, Arvella 42, 363, 1147, 1159, 1578

Breadsticks and Blessing Places
Boyd, Candy Dawson 1741

Break a Leg Betsy, Maybe
Kingman, Lee 1034

A Break with Charity: A Story about the Salem Witch Trails
Rinaldi, Ann 106

A Break with Charity: A Story about the Salem Witch Trials
Rinaldi, Ann 606

Breakaway
Hallman, Ruth 234

Breaker
Perez, Norah A. 996

Breaking Camp
Kroll, Steven 49

Breaking Loose
Halecroft, David 337, 340

Breaking Out
DeClements, Barthe 1304, 1512

Breaking the Ice
Mumma, Barbara J. 1849

Breaking the Ring
Englehart, Donna Walsh 572, 326

The Breat Mosquito, Bull and Coffin Caper
Lamb, Nancy 837

Brendan's Best-Timed Birthday
Gould, Deborah 725

Brian Foot-in-the-Mouth
Sullivan, Mary W. 1768

The Bridge to Nowhere
McDonald, Megan 680

Bridge to Terabithia
Paterson, Katherine **1386**, 1388, 1390

Bridge to Terebithia
Paterson, Katherine 1387, 1389

Bridger: The Story of a Mountain Man
Kherdian, David 88

The Bridges of Summer
Seabrooke, Brenda 1790

Bridget
LeRoy, Gen 1093

Bridle the Wind
Aiken, Joan 587

Brigham Young and Me, Clarissa
Williams, Barbara 1918

The Bright and Shining Breadboard
Hall, Rosalys Haskell 1851

Bright April
De Angeli, Marguerite 490, 492

Bright Candles: A Novel of the Danish Resistance
Benchley, Nathaniel 1982

Bright Days, Stupid Nights
Mazer, Harry 1215, 720

Bright Fawn and Me
Leech, Jay 712

Bright Shadow
Avi 70, 74, 121, 1477

Brighty of the Grand Canyon
Henry, Marguerite 853, 856

Brimhall Comes to Stay
Delton, Judy 512, 1772

Brimhall Turns Detective
Delton, Judy 183, 511

Brimhall Turns to Magic
Delton, Judy 1340

Bring to a Boil and Separate
Irwin, Hadley **966**, 1426

Bringing Nettie Back
Wilson, Nancy Hope 952, 1134, 1666

Bringing the Farmhouse Home
Whelan, Gloria 1897

British Folktales
Briggs, Katharine Mary 199

Broadway Chances
Hill, Elizabeth Starr 609, 882, 1502

The Brocaded Slipper
Vuong, Lynette Dyer 1023, 1240

The Broccoli Tapes
Slepian, Jan 639, 1666

Brogg's Brain
Platt, Kin 1451, 1452

The Broken Boy
Ackerman, Karen 581, 727, 829, 1383

The Broken Bridge: A Novel
Pullman, Philip 1479

Bronco Dogs
Cohen, Caron Lee 621, 699

The Bronze Bow
Speare, Elizabeth George 1566, **1708**, 1709, 1710

The Bronze King
Charnas, Suzy McKee **320**

Brooke and Her Rock Star Mom
Suzanne, Jamie 1385

Brother Dusty-Feet
Sutcliff, Rosemary 490

Brother Enemy
Mace, Elisabeth 1894

Brother in the Land
Swindells, Robert E. 1774

Brother Moose
Levin, Betty 245, 929, **1096**, 1098

Brother Night
Kelleher, Victor 1005

Brother of the Wolves
Thompson, Jean 1808

Brother to the Navajo
Gessner, Lynne 1448

Brother to the Wind
Walter, Mildred Pitts 768

The Brothers Lionheart
Lindgren, Astrid 1124, 1125

Brothers of the Heart
Blos, Joan W. 764

Brothers of the Wind
Yolen, Jane 1972

The Brothers Wrong and Wrong Again
Phillips, Louis 1783

Brown Bird Singing
Wosmek, Frances 1315

A Brown Bird Singing
Wosmek, Frances **1952**

The Good Luck Pencil
Stanley, Diane 1934

Good Master
Seredy, Kate 675

The Good Master
Seredy, Kate 1613

Good Morning Chick
Chukovsky, Kornei 341

The Good Morrow
Norris, Gunilla Brodde 1325

Good Night, Lewis
Ziefert, Harriet 1463

Good Night, Mr. Tom
Magorian, Michelle 592

Good-night Mr. Tom
Magorian, Michelle 789

Good Night, Mr. Tom
Magorian, Michelle **1177**, 1594

Good Night, Owl
Hutchins, Pat 1141

Good Night, Prof, Dear
Townsend, John Rowe 1819

Good, Says Jerome
Clifton, Lucille 367

The Good Stepmother
Rudolph, Marguerita 60, 1957

Good Stones
Epstein, Anne Merrick 1213, 1542, 1709

The Good, the Bad, and the Goofy
Scieszka, Jon 646, 1279, 1601

Good, the Bad, and the Rest of Us
Slaatten, Evelyn 1786

Good Work, Amelia Bedelia
Parish, Peggy 1374

Goodbye, Billy Radish
Skurzynski, Gloria 1466

Goodbye, Chicken Little
Byars, Betsy 114, 264, 1034, 1396

Goodbye, Dove Square
McNeill, Janet 1249

Goodbye, Funny Dumpy-Lumpy
Waber, Bernard 1504

Goodbye, My Island
Rogers, Jean 682, 767, **1539**, 1540, 1541

Goodbye, My Wishing Star
Grove, Vicki 115, **777**

Goodbye Pink Pig
Adler, Carole S. 6, 9

Goodbye, Ruby Red
Kaye, Geraldine 224, 1000

The Goodbye Summer
Bonsall, Crosby 174, 1040

Goodbye to the Trees
Shiefman, Vicky 993

Goodbye, Vietnam
Whelan, Gloria 1023

Goody Hall
Babbitt, Natalie 75, 78, 79

Goody Sherman's Pig
Christian, Mary Blount 1030, 1829

The Goof That Won the Pennant
Kalb, Jonah 425, **991**

Goose Dinner
Bunting, Eve 909

The Goose That Went to Hollywood
Bernsen, Paul S. 1069

Gooseberries to Oranges
Cohen, Barbara 381

Gopher, Tanker, and the Admiral
Climo, Shirley **368**, 1041, 1280

The Gorilla Did It
Hazen, Barbara Shook 839, 840

Gorilla Gorilla
Fenner, Carol 592

Gorilla Rescue
Bailey, Jill 90

Gorky Rises
Steig, William 1732, 1734

Gorp and the Space Pirates
Ross, Dave 1412

Gowie Corby Plays Chicken
Kemp, Gene 1011, 1431

Grace
Paton Walsh, Jill 1394, 1958

Grace Before Plowing
Masefield, John 1208

Grace in the Wilderness: After the Liberation, 1945-1948
Siegal, Aranka 1103, 1507, 1837

Grace in the Wilderness: After the Wilderness, 1945-1948
Siegal, Aranka 1641

Grady the Great
Strommen, Judith Bernie 346, 837

Gran at Coalgate
Cawley, Winifred **313**

The Grand Escape
Naylor, Phyllis Reynolds 784, 880, 1129

Grand Papa and Ellen Aroon
Monjo, F.N. **1275**

Grandaddy and Janetta
Griffith, Helen V. 773

Grandaddy's Place
Griffith, Helen V. 772, **773**, 1116

Grandfather
Baker, Jeannie 90

Grandfather's Day
Tomey, Ingrid 1821

Grandma Dragon's Birthday
Blocksma, Mary 149

The Grandma in the Apple Tree
Lobe, Mira 611

Grandma Remembers
Shecter, Ben 252, 725

Grandma Zoo
Gordon, Shirley 722

Grandmama's Joy
Greenfield, Eloise 754

Grandmas at Bat
McCully, Emily Arnold 562, 1222

Grandmas at the Lake
McCully, Emily Arnold 1222

Grandma's Latkes
Drucker, Malka 1026

Grandmother Cat and the Hermit
Coatsworth, Elizabeth 1551

A Grandmother for the Orphelines
Carlson, Natalie Savage 291, 294

A Grandmother's Story
Halak, Glenn 1073

Grandpa: A Young Man Grown Old
Sobol, Harriet Langsam 1704

Grandpa and Bo
Henkes, Kevin 772

Grandpa and Me
Tolan, Stephanie S. **1816**, 1817

Grandpa and My Sister Bee
Tate, Joan 1781

Grandpa Jake and the Grand Christmas
Amers, Mildred 1792, 800, 1147

Grandpa Putter and Granny Hoe
Fakih, Kimberly Olson 1955

Grandpa Ritz and Our Lucious Lovelies
Shyer, Marlene Fanta 1638

Grandpa Ritz and the Lucious Lovelies
Shyer, Marlene Fanta **1637**

Grandpa's Face
Greenfield, Eloise 755

Grandpa's Ghost Stories
Flora, James 629, 1116

Grandpa's Maria
Hellberg, Hans-Eric **848**

Grandpa's Mountain
Reeder, Carolyn 188, 1159, 1408, 1496

Grandpa's Slide Show
Gould, Deborah **725**

The Grange at High Force
Turner, Philip 603

Granny Is a Darling
Denton, Kady MacDonald 1412

The Granny Project
Fine, Anne 531

Granny Reardun
Garner, Alan 673

Granny was a Buffer Girl
Doherty, Berlie 1093

A Grass Green Gallop: Poems
Hubbell, Patricia 1015

Grass Songs
Turner, Ann Warren 1100, 1640, 1916

Grasshopper Summer
Turner, Ann Warren 1170, 1709, **1832**, 1833, 1909

Grave Doubts
Corbett, Scott 748

Graven Images
Fleischman, Paul **614**, 615, 617, 994

The Graveyard: And Other Not-So-Scary Stories
Warren, William E. **1886**

Gray Boy
Arnosky, Jim 1804

The Gray Ghosts of Taylor Ridge
Craig, M.S. 1519

The Gray Whales Are Missing
Thrush, Robin A. 1789

The Gray Wolf
MacDonald, George 1165

Great Advice From Lila Fenwick
McMullan, Kate 49, 1760

The Great Alexander the Great
Lasker, Joe 1071

The Great Bamboozelement
Flory, Jane 473

The Great Bamboozlement
Flory, Jane 630

The Great Bell of Peking
Greaves, Margaret 740

The Great Big Dummy
Schulman, Janet 1598, 1599

A Great Big Ugly Man Came Up and Tied His Horse to Me
Tripp, Wallace 1824

The Great Book Raid
Leach, Christopher 418, 1462

The Great Brain
Fitzgerald, John D. 607

The Great Brain at the Academy
Fitzgerald, John D. 607, 843, 1010, 1041, 1052, 1571

The Great Brain Does It Again
Fitzgerald, John D. 607

The Great Brain Reforms
Fitzgerald, John D. **607**

The Great Bullocky Race
Page, Michael F. 825, 1802

The Great Cadet
Alphin, Elaine Marie 937

The Great Cat Chase
Mayer, Mercer 1211

The Great Cheese Conspiracy
Van Leeuwen, Jean 779

The Great Christmas Kidnapping Caper
Van Leeuwen, Jean **1847**

The Great Computer Dating Caper
Bethancourt, T. Ernesto 144

The Great Condominium Rebellion
Snyder, Carol 1093, 1955

The Great Custard Pie Panic
Corbett, Scott 426

Great Dane Thor
Farley, Walter 589

Title Index

My Mother Is Not Married to My Father
Okimoto, Jean Davies　155, 817

My Mother Is the Smartest Woman in the World
Clymer, Eleanor　369, 370, 1293

My Mother Made Me!
Brain, Sharon　424

My Mother the Cat
Potter, Katherine　218

My Mother, the Witch
Blue, Rose　1727

My Mother's House, My Father's House
Christiansen, C.B.　849

My Name Is Brain Brian
Betancourt, Jeanne　300

My Name Is Maria Isabel
Ada, Alma Flor　1598, 1688

My Name Is Nobody
Wartski, Maureen Crane　279

My Name Is Not Angelica
O'Dell, Scott　1352, 1355, 1823

My Name Is San Ho
Pettit, Jayne　436, 510, 1670, 1944

My New Boy
Phillips, Joan　**1435**

My New Mom and Me
Wright, Betty Ren　537, **1957**

My Other Mother, My Other Father
Sobol, Harriet Langsam　**1704**

My Own Home
Hoopes, Lyn Littlefield　1141

My Own Private Sky
Beckman, Delores　**127**

My Pardner
Evans, Max　1874

My Parents Think I'm Sleeping: Poems
Prelutsky, Jack　1646

My Place
Wheatley, Nadia　125, 1802

My Prairie Christmas
Brett, Harvey　194

My Prairie Year
Brett, Harvey　194, 1909

My Puppy
Thaler, Mike　1798

My Robot Buddy
Slote, Alfred　237, **1673**

My Shalom, My Peace: Paintings and Poems by Jewish and Arab Children
Ofek, Uriel　1357

My Side of the Mountain
George, Jean Craighead　682, 685, 1855

My Sister Is Different
Wright, Betty Ren　1070, 1957

My Sister, My Science Report
Bechard, Margaret E.　898, 1562, 1919

My Sister Sif
Park, Ruth　178, 686, 1167, 1382, 1667

My Sister the Creep
Ransom, Candice　1484

My Sister the Meanie
Ransom, Candice　**1484**

My Sister, the Traitor
Ransom, Candice　1429, 1484

My Sister, the Vampire
Garden, Nancy　1359, 1410

My Sister's Keeper
Butler, Beverly　**253**, 1500, 1863

My Sister's Silent World
Arthur, Catherine　1941

My Song Is a Piece of Jade
De Gerez, Toni　1118

My Stars, It's Mrs. Gaddy
Gage, Wilson　1492

My Stepfather Shrank!
Dillon, Barbara　526, 1339, 1944

My Summer Brother
Vogel, Ilse-Margret　1858

My Teacher Glows in the Dark
Coville, Bruce　63

My Teacher Is an Alien
Coville, Bruce　580

My Trip to Alpha I
Slote, Alfred　1673, **1674**

My Twin Sister, Erika
Vogel, Ilse-Margret　1858, 1859

My Very Own Octopus
Most, Bernard　1866

My War with Goggle-Eyes
Fine, Anne　1273, 1372

My War with Mrs. Galloway
Orgel, Doris　730, 743, 1574, 1792

The Mysteries of Harris Burdick
Van Allsburg, Chris　1841, **1842**

The Mysterious Appearance of Agnes
Griffith, Helen　278, 769, 1629

The Mysterious Cases of Mr. Pin
Monsell, Mary Elise　64, **1277**

The Mysterious Disappearance of Leon (I Mean Noel)
Raskin, Ellen　1488, **1489**, 1490

The Mysterious Giant of Barletta
De Paola, Tomie　1750

The Mysterious Girl in the Garden
St. George, Judith　179, 442, 906, 1439

The Mysterious Image
Keene, Carolyn　1329

The Mysterious Island
Verne, Jules　1852, 1853

Mysterious Max
Stine, Megan　628

The Mysterious Mr. Ross
Alcock, Vivien　19, 20

Mysterious Powers of the Mind
Abrams, Laurence F.　1510

The Mysterious Tale of Gentle Jack and Lord Bumblebee
Sand, George　579

The Mysterious World of Marcus Leadbeater
Southall, Ivan　655

The Mysterious Zetabet
Corbett, Scott　**426**

Mysteriously Yours, Maggie Marmelstein
Sharmat, Marjorie Weinman　720, 1525

Mystery at Beach Bay
Van Steenwyk, Elizabeth　1849

Mystery at Camp Triumph
Christian, Mary Blount　669, 754, 1455, 1481

Mystery at Crane's Landing
Thum, Marcella　**1810**

Mystery at Fire Island
Campbell, Hope　260, 1630

The Mystery at Greystone Hall
Smaridge, Norah　1471

Mystery at Loon Lake
Cross, Gilbert B.　357

Mystery at MacAdoo Zoo
Heide, Florence Parry　671

Mystery at Moon Lake
Cross, Gilbert B.　448

The Mystery at Peacock Place
Craig, M.F.　**439**

Mystery at Sans Souci
Hausman, Jim　1451, 1488

Mystery at Snowshoe Mountain Lodge
Eisenberg, Lisa　932, 1302

Mystery at the Ball Game
McVey, R. Parker　412, 1669

The Mystery at the Ball Park
Cooper, John R.　1358

Mystery at the Doll Hospital
Honness, Elizabeth　911

Mystery at the Villa Caprice
Honness, Elizabeth　1488

The Mystery at Wolf River
Craig, M.S.　439, 1034, 1699, 623

The Mystery Beast of Ostergeest
Kellogg, Steven　1008

The Mystery Cup
Bothwell, Jean　1905, 1971

Mystery Day
Ziefert, Harriette　1649

Mystery Dolls From Planet Urd
Nixon, Joan Lowery　1649

Mystery Horse
Clark, Margaret Goff　532, 588

Mystery in the Ravine
Farley, Carol J.　585

Mystery Madness
Coontz, Otto　**416**

The Mystery Man
Corbett, Scott　427

Mystery of 22 East
Ware, Leon　**1885**

The Mystery of Animal Haven
Witter, Evelyn　1277

Mystery of Crocodile Island
Keene, Carolyn　1328

The Mystery of Drear House
Hamilton, Virginia　802

Mystery of Mordach Castle
MacKellar, William　282

The Mystery of Pony Hollow
Hall, Lynn　588, 1277

Mystery of the Bewitched Bookmobile
Heide, Florence Parry　844, **845**, 1778

Mystery of the Black Diamonds
Whitney, Phyllis A.　1903

The Mystery of the Boy Next Door
Montgomery, Elizabeth Rider　47, 1163

The Mystery of the Caramel Cat
Hall, Lynn　239, 437, 486

The Mystery of the Crimson Ghost
Whitney, Phyllis A.　73

Mystery of the Deadly Diamond
Howard, Elizabeth　918

The Mystery of the Deadly Diamond
Howard, Elizabeth　1451

The Mystery of the Diamond in the Wood
Kherdian, David　**1021**, 1022

The Mystery of the Dinosaur Graveyard
Adrain, Mary　14

The Mystery of the Disappearing Cars
Cheney, Cora　80

Mystery of the Disappearing Dogs
Brenner, Barbara　40, 1296

Mystery of the Eagle's Claw
Wosmek, Frances　1952

Mystery of the Fat Cat
Bonham, Frank　**172**, 879

The Mystery of the Fiery Message
Farley, Carol J.　1077

The Mystery of the Flooded Mine
Manus, Willard　125

Mystery of the Fog Man
Farley, Carol J.　585

The Mystery of the Galaxy Games
Carlson, Dale Bick　289

Mystery of the Gingerbread House
St. John, Wylly Folk　**1721**

The Mystery of the Greek Icon
Pickering, Mary Tyson　1904

The Mystery of the Gulls
Whitney, Phyllis A.　1903

Unfinished Portrait of Jessica
Peck, Richard 1865

The Unfrightened Dark:
Holland, Isabelle 144

The Unfrightened Dark
Holland, Isabelle 739, 900, 1481, 1699

Unicorn Alphabet
Mayer, Marianna 1210

The Unicorn and the Lake
Mayer, Marianna 741, **1210**

The Unicorn and the Plow
Moeri, Louise 1210, 1972

Unicorn Crossing
Luenn, Nancy 1210, 1972

Unicorn Moon
Cooper, Gale 1210

The Unicorn Treasury
Coville, Bruce 438, 741

Uninvited Ghosts and Other Stories
Lively, Penelope 411

Unleaving
Paton Walsh, Jill 1394, **1396**

Unmentionable! More Amazing Stories
Jennings, Paul 1220

Unmentionable! More Amazing Stories
Jennings, Paul 1223

The Unsinkable Molly Malone
Anderson, May 1447

Until the Celebration
Snyder, Zilpha Keatley 1695

The Untold Tale
Haugaard, Erik Christian 163, 828, 1059

The Unusual Jam Detective
Lampert, Emily 1967

Up a Road Slowly
Hunt, Irene 937

The Up and Down Spring
Hurwitz, Johanna 1132, 1776

Up Country
Carter, Alden R. 1754

Up from Jerico Tel
Konigsburg, E.L. 66, 112, 882, 1047, **1048**, 1182, 1329

Up Mountain One Time
Wilson, Willie **1926**

Up North in Winter
Hartley, Deborah 1116

Up Periscope
White, Robb 1902

Up the Chimney Down and Other Stories
Aiken, Joan 17, 1501

Up the Pier
Cresswell, Helen 442

Upchuck Summer's Revenge
Schwartz, Joel L. 49

Uphill All the Way
Hall, Lynn 109

Upon the Head of the Goat: A Childhood in Hungary, 1939-1944
Siegal, Aranka 1613, **1641**, 1767

The Ups and Downs of Carl Davis III
Guy, Rosa 636, 780, 1635

Ups and Downs of Jorie Jenkins
Bates, Betty 103

The Ups and Downs of Marvin
Hazen, Barbara Shook 839

Ups and Downs with Oink and Pearl
Chorao, Kay **328**

The Upside-Down Cat
Parsons, Elizabeth 95, 272, 784

Upside Down Man
Ellentuck, Shan 565

The Upstairs Room
Reiss, Johanna **1499**

Uptime, Downtime
Peel, John 1406

Urn Burial
Westall, Robert 1896

Us and Uncle Fraud
Lowry, Lois 1149, 1155, **1156**

Us, Inside a Teenage Gang
Green, Janet 238

The Useless Donkeys
Pender, Lydia 306, 1160

User Unfriendly
Vande Velde, Vivian 1558

V

Valda
Cotich, Felicia 1802

Valentine and Orson
Burkert, Nancy Ekholm **247**

Valentine Blues: An Aviva Granger Story
Betancourt, Jeanne 143

Valentine for a Dragon
Murphy, Shirley Rousseau 663

Valentine Frankenstein
Twohill, Maggie 1536

Valentine's Day
Guilfoile, Elizabeth 778

The Valentine's Day Mystery
Markham, Marion M. 1194

The Valley in Between
Donahue, Marilyn Cram 1877

The Valley of Deer
Dunlop, Eileen 551, 606, 1320, 1423, 1748

Valley of the Hawk
Loomis, Ruth 572

The Value of Fantasy
Johnson, Spencer 15

Vampire
Cusick, Richie Tankersley 45

The Vampire
Martin, Les 45

The Vampire Moves In
Sommer-Bodenburg, Angela 579, 923

The Vampire on the Farm
Sommer-Bodenburg, Angela 1031

The Vampire Tapestry
Charnas, Suzy McKee 320

Vampires: A Collection of Original Stories
Yolen, Jane 923

Vampires and Other Creatures of the Night
Gelman, Rita Golden 724, 1886

The Vandal
Schlee, Ann 1594

The Vandemark Mummy
Voigt, Cynthia 111, 567, 959, 1337

Vanishing Act
Morrison, Dorothy Nafus 571

The Vanishing People
Briggs, Katharine Mary 199

Varnell Roberts, Super Pigeon
Gray, Genevieve 736

Vasilissa the Beautiful
Winthrop, Elizabeth 1642

Vatsana's Lucky New Year
Gogol, Sara 1980

The Velvet Room
Snyder, Zilpha Keatley 1699

The Velveteen Rabbit
Williams, Margery 330, 1498, **1923**, 1270

The Vengence of the Witch-Finder
Bellairs, John 1319

Vengence of the Zulu King
Seed, Jenny 1127

Venus of Shadows
Sargent, Pamela 1586

Veronica Meets Her Match
Robinson, Nancy K. **1520**

Veronica, the Show-Off
Robinson, Nancy K. 1164, 1519, 1520

Veronica the Show-Off
Robinson, Nancy K. 1521

The Very Best of Friends
Wild, Margaret 1453

Very Brief Season
Girion, Barbara 708

Very Far Away From Anywhere Else
Le Guin, Ursula 1085

The Very Peculiar Tunnel
Wahl, Jan 1841

Very Private Performance
Grace, Fran 727

The Very Special Baby
Swindells, Robert E. 850

Vicki and the Black Horse
Savitt, Sam 1429

Victory Chimes
Waters, John Frederick 1399

The View Beyond My Father
Allan, Mabel Esther 38

The View From the Cherry Tree
Roberts, Willo Davis 136, 881, 1509, 1512, **1513**

The View From the Pighouse Roof
Olsen, Violet 1549

A Viking Settler
Caselli, Giovanni 134

Viking's Dawn
Treece, Henry 134, **1822**

The Village by the Sea
Fox, Paula 640, 641, **643**

Vinegar Pancakes and Vanishing Cream
Pryor, Bonnie 1173, 1315, 1474, 1476

Viola, Furgy, Bobbi and Me
Ethridge, Kenneth 1958

Viola Hates Music
Schick, Alice 1592

Violet's Finest Hour
Duggan, Alice 26

Violin
Allen, Robert Thomas 262

The Violin Case Case
Warfel, Diantha 542

Vision Quest
Service, Pamela F. 29, 373, 1614, **1615**, 1878

The Visionary
Sanders, Scott R. 1585

The Visionary Girls: Witchcraft in Salem Village
Starkey, Marion Lena 1727

The Visit
Degans, T. 1362, 1850, 679

A Visit to Grandma's
Carlson, Nancy L. 1222

A Visit to the Ocean
Simons, Barbara B. 1650

A Visit to William Blake's Inn
Willard, Nancy **1916**

Visiting Miss Pierce
Darby, Pat 102

Vixie, the Story of a Little Fox
Fox, Michael W. 264, 635

A Voice for Princess
Morressy, John 1292

The Voice from Mendelsohn's Maple
Ryan, Mary C. 821, 1562

The Voice of the Children
Jordan, June 755

The Voice of the Wood
Clement, Claude 85

Voices After Midnight
Peck, Richard 1367, 1404, 1405, **1406**, 1505

Title Index